FORMATION OF GOVERNMENT CONTRACTS

Fifth Edition

John Cibinic, Jr.

Ralph C. Nash, Jr.

Christopher R. Yukins

Nathaniel E. Castellano

Wolters Kluwer

This publication is designed to provide accurate and authoritative information in regard to the subject matter covered. It is sold with the understanding that the publisher and the author(s) are not engaged in rendering legal, accounting, or other professional services. If legal advice or other professional assistance is required, the services of a competent professional should be sought.

—From a *Declaration of Principles* jointly adopted by
a Committee of the American Bar Association and
a Committee of Publishers and Associations

Published by Wolters Kluwer in New York.

Wolters Kluwer Legal & Regulatory U.S. serves customers worldwide with CCH and Kluwer Law International products.

Printed in the United States of America

ISBN: 978-1-5438-8035-9

1 2 3 4 5 6 7 8 9 0

SUSTAINABLE FORESTRY INITIATIVE Certified Sourcing
www.sfiprogram.org
SFI-01051

About Wolters Kluwer Legal & Regulatory U.S.

Wolters Kluwer Legal & Regulatory U.S. delivers expert content and solutions in the areas of law, corporate compliance, health compliance, and reimbursement. Its practical solutions help customers successfully navigate the demands of a changing environment to drive their daily activities, enhance decision quality and inspire confident outcomes.

Serving customers worldwide, its legal and regulatory portfolio includes products under the CCH Incorporated, Kluwer Law International, ftwilliam.com and MediRegs names. They are regarded as exceptional and trusted resources for general legal and practice-specific knowledge, compliance and risk management, dynamic workflow solutions, and expert commentary.

ABOUT THE AUTHORS

JOHN CIBINIC, JR.

John Cibinic, Jr. was Professor Emeritus at The George Washington University Law School where he taught from 1963 to 1993. From 1966 to 1974, he was Director of the Government Contracts Program. A respected spokesman in the field of government contracts, Professor Cibinic conducted seminars and conferences on government contracts for professionals in government and corporations, and for lawyers. He also served as a consultant to government agencies, private corporations, and law firms. He was vice-chairman of the Cost and Pricing Committee of the Public Contract Section of the American Bar Association. Professor Cibinic coauthored several books, including *Formation of Government Contracts*, *Administration of Government Contracts*, *Competitive Negotiation: The Source Selection Process*, and *Construction Contracting*. He received an A.B. from the University of Pittsburgh and a J.D. from George Washington University. Together, with Professor Ralph Nash he coauthored the *Nash & Cibinic Report*, a monthly newsletter.

RALPH C. NASH, JR.

Ralph C. Nash, Jr., is Professor Emeritus of Law of The George Washington University, Washington, D.C., from which he retired in 1993. He founded the Government Contracts Program of the university's National Law Center in 1960 and was Director of the Program from 1960 to 1966 and from 1979 to 1984. He was Associate Dean for Graduate Studies, Research and Projects, of the Law Center from 1966 to 1972. Professor Nash has specialized in the area of Government Procurement Law. He worked for the Navy Department as a contract negotiator from 1953 to 1959, and for the American Machine and Foundry Company as Assistant Manager of Contracts and Counsel during 1959 and 1960. Professor Nash graduated *magna cum laude* with an A.B. degree from Princeton University in 1953, and earned his Juris Doctor degree from The George Washington University Law School in 1957. He is a member of Phi Beta Kappa, Phi Alpha Delta, and the Order of the Coif.

Professor Nash has been active as a consultant for government agencies, private corporations, and law firms on government contract matters. For a number of years, he has served widely as neutral advisor or mediator/arbitrator in alternate dispute resolution proceedings. He is a member of the Procurement

Round Table, and is a Fellow and serves on the Board of Advisors of the National Contract Management Association.

During the 1990s, Professor Nash was active in the field of acquisition reform. He served on the "Section 800 Panel" that recommended revisions to all laws affecting Department of Defense procurement, the Defense Science Board Task Force on Defense Acquisition Reform, and the Blue Ribbon Panel of the Federal Aviation Administration.

Professor Nash is the coauthor with John Cibinic, Jr. of a casebook, *Federal Procurement Law* (3d ed., Volume I, 1977, and Volume II, 1980). He and Professor Cibinic also coauthored five textbooks: *Formation of Government Contracts* (4th ed. 2011), *Administration of Government Contracts* (5th ed. 2016), *Cost Reimbursement Contracting* (3d ed. 2004), *Government Contract Claims* (1981), and *Competitive Negotiation: The Source Selection Process* (2d ed. 1999). He is coauthor with Leonard Rawicz of the textbook *Intellectual Property in Government Contracts* (6th ed. 2008), coauthor with seven other authors of the textbook *Construction Contracting* (1991), coauthor with Vernon Edwards, Steven L. Schooner and Karen O'Brien-DeBakey of *The Government Contracts Reference Book* (5th ed 2020), and coauthor with Steven Feldman of *Government Contract Changes* (3d ed. 2007). He has written several monographs for The George Washington University Government Contracts Program monograph series, and has published articles in various law reviews and journals. Since 1987, Professor Nash has been coauthor of a monthly analytical report on government contract issues, *The Nash & Cibinic Report.*

CHRISTOPHER R. YUKINS

Professor Christopher Yukins teaches on government contract formations and performance issues, anti-corruption measures, bid challenges, government contracts litigation, and comparative issues in public procurement law at The George Washington University Law School. He is an active member of the Public Contract Law Section of the American Bar Association, and is a member of the Procurement Roundtable, an organization of senior members of the U.S. procurement community. He is a faculty advisor to the *Public Contract Law Journal*, and has published on procurement reform in numerous journals, nationally and internationally. Professor Yukins regularly addresses audiences around the world on issues of procurement law and policy, anti-corruption, and international trade, and he lectures at the University of Paris-Nanterre, the University of Turin, Stockholm University, the International Anti-Corruption Academy (outside Vienna), and the United Nations ILO-ITC training facility (Turin). Together with his colleagues in the GW Law Government Procurement Law Program, he runs a colloquium series on procurement reform at The George Washington University Law School. In private practice, Professor Yukins has been an associate, partner and counsel at leading national firms; he is currently counsel to the firm of Arnold & Porter LLP. He previously served as an advisor to the U.S. delegation to the working group on reform of the UNCITRAL Model Procurement Law.

NATHANIEL E. CASTELLANO

Nathan Castellano is in private practice at Jenner & Block LLP, where he advises companies on all aspects of doing business with and litigating against the federal government. Mr. Castellano studied procurement law extensively at the George Washington University Law School, working as a research assistant to Professor Steven Schooner and graduating as a Murray Schooner Procurement Scholar. He served as a law clerk for the Honorable Jimmie V. Reyna at the U.S. Court of Appeals for the Federal Circuit and worked as a legal consultant in the World Bank Office of Suspension and Debarment. Mr. Castellano is a widely published author, with articles cited in leading treatises and used as course material.

CONTENTS

A complete table of contents for each chapter appears at the beginning of the chapter.

Chapter 14
COLLATERAL POLICIES

Chapter 15
CONTRACT AWARD CONTROVERSIES

Chapter 16
U.S. FEDERAL PROCUREMENT: AN INTERNATIONAL PERSPECTIVE

PREFACE

The first edition of *Formation of Government Contracts* was published in 1983, followed by editions in 1986, 1998 and 2011. The second and third editions were necessary to update the material based on the enactment of the Competition in Contracting Act in 1984 and the Federal Acquisition Streamlining Act in 1994. The third edition also encompassed the major rewrite of Part 15 of the Federal Acquisition in 1997. The fourth edition began to document all of these changes to determine how they impacted the process of entering into government contracts by reviewing all of the statutory and regulatory changes since that time as well as the decisions of the Government Accountability Office and the Court of Federal Claims. This fifth edition continues that process. The book is focused entirely on the *formation* of a contract—from the earliest planning until contract award. For our purposes, the award of a contract begins the process of contract administration and that is covered by Cibinic, Nash & Nagle, *Administration of Government Contracts*, 5th ed. 2016.

One of the major changes that has occurred in the last decade or two is the widespread use of indefinite delivery/indefinite quantity (IDIQ) contracts. For that reason, we have added a new Chapter 7 covering this procurement technique. This chapter covers not only the original formation of an IDIQ contract but also the issuance of task or delivery orders under these contracts. We have also added a new Chapter 8 covering simplified acquisition and a new Chapter 9 covering the procurement of commercial products and services. These topics have been given separate chapters because of their growing role the overall procurement process.

As with our earlier editions, our goal has been to make the reader aware of the statutes, regulations and decisions that establish the complex rule structure that is followed in the process of entering into government contracts. As all seasoned practitioners recognize, only when these elements of the process are synthesized can one truly know the rules of the game. This synthesis is carried out in each chapter of the book and we recommend that, to most effectively use the book, our readers become well versed in the detailed organization that is depicted in numerous topical subheads. We have also provided an index to assist in this process.

Having noted that the rule structure governing contract formation is complex, we hasten to add that federal contracting agencies are primarily responsible for the undue complexity of this field. Since the passage of the Competition in Contracting Act in 1984, making competitive negotiation the major contracting process, the agencies have adopted practices that make contract formation far too expensive and time-consuming. We address these practices in detail in Chapter 6 and have published a companion book, Nash, Cibinic & O'Brien-DeBakey, *Competitive Negotiation: The Source Selection Process*, 3d ed. 2011. While we are critical of these practices and have made numerous attempts to persuade agencies to streamline them, we confess that we have been less than successful. Contractors participating in the competitive negotiation process must reconcile themselves to the fact that they will be required to expend excessive amounts of time and money, frequently requiring the use of their most talented personnel, if they are to win a significant number of contracts.

The other major change that regularly occurs is in the selection of the proper type of contract—addressed in Chapter 12. For the last decade cost-reimbursement contracts have been in disrepute and DOD has discouraged the use of firm-fixed-price contracts. This has led to a renewed use of fixed-price incentive contracts with new guidance on their use. The current statutes and regulations continue to make the cost-plus-award-fee contract an undesirable arrangement. For many years we have observed a tradition for new people coming into the top positions in the Executive Branch to latch on to the theory that cost-reimbursement contracts are intrinsically bad and to attempt to move away from them. They neither know nor learn from past experience—which demonstrates conclusively that fixed-price contracts are only beneficial when, as FAR Part 16 clearly states, risks have been narrowed and rational prices can be arrived at.

A word about the currency of this edition. As to the citation of decisional law and the procurement regulations, it is current as of approximately the middle of 2021. As to statutory citations, it includes the new recodification of Title 10 which became effective on January 1, 2022. While the recodification made little substantive change, the title has been totally reorganized and incorporates some provisions that were previously designated as notes to sections of the title.

Finally, I want to acknowledge the work of Nathan Castellano, as he takes the place of John Cibinic as a coauthor. I am grateful for his work. Chris Yukins has also made a valuable contribution by adding Chapter 16 on comparative formation policies. I also want to thank Eve Lyon for the excellent work she did in revising Chapter 4—particularly, giving us the benefit of her extensive knowledge of organizational conflicts of interest. We have kept John's name on the book as an author because he is truly the author of much of the underlying logic of the book and was instrumental in working with me to lay out the fundamental principles of government contract formation. We worked together as a team for over 40 years and were both aware that we could not have written these books without our close collaboration.

Ralph C. Nash, Jr.
Washington, D.C.
May, 2023

CHAPTER 1

BASIC PRINCIPLES OF FEDERAL PROCUREMENT

§1.01 ABOUT THIS BOOK

This book covers contracts of *Executive Branch agencies* for the *procurement* of goods and services where the government is acting in the role of a buyer. While procurement is a major form of contracting activity of the federal government, it is only one of several types of contracting in which the government engages. Other types of contractual arrangements include sales of personal property, purchases and sales of real property, grants, cooperative agreements, "other transactions," and employment contracts. Many of the legal principles and general rules applicable to these nonprocurement transactions are the same as those applied to procurement. Thus, many statutes, regulations, and decisions involving these principles and general rules will apply to both procurement and nonprocurement transactions. However, this book does not cover the detailed rules that apply to these nonprocurement transactions.

Procurement of goods and services by the U.S. Government is a unique form of activity dominated by numerous specialized rules. These rules arise out of the nature of the government as a contracting party and the distinctive forms and procedures used in the procurement process. The rules governing this process are contained in statutes, regulations, informal guidance, and judicial and administrative decisions. Many are designed to protect the public's interest while assuring fair treatment to those who deal with the government. Most are of general application but some apply only to specific agencies. In addition, procurement is conducted under the general rules governing all contracts entered into by the federal government. This general rule structure is exemplified by the basic principles of contract law discussed in Chapter 2.

This chapter covers issues that are fundamental to the federal procurement process. The following section illustrates the role of procurement in the operation of the government by examining the variety of government organizations that procure goods and services and the statutes and regulations that cover this area. It also describes the different types of contractual transactions in which the government engages in order to show the relationship of procurement to other types of transactions. The next three sections consider how the special nature of the government as a contracting party is recognized by legal principles aimed at protecting the public from unauthorized or improper activity. This consideration starts with an examination of the statutes and regulations that control the procurement activities of government agencies and the methods of oversight used to assure compliance with these authorities. The next two sections analyze the special rules that apply to the authority of individual government personnel as well as the binding nature of the activities of contractor personnel. The chapter concludes with a survey of the standards of conduct required of those representing or dealing with the government.

§ 1.02 TRANSACTIONS AND AGENCIES

Procurement is an essential element of the operation of almost every organization within the executive branch. To achieve a full understanding of the procurement process, it is necessary to see the relationship of procurement to the other types of contractual transactions carried out by these agencies. To understand the full scope of the procurement process, one must be aware of the variety of agencies within the executive branch of the government and the statutes and regulations that govern the procurement activities of these agencies.

[A] Transactions

As noted earlier, procurement is only one of a number of contractual transactions in which the government regularly engages. Thus, procurement has a large number of special rules, and it also shares, in general, rules applicable to all contractual transactions of the federal government. These general rules of contract law are most frequently found in judicial decisions where fundamental contract law issues are raised. Similarly, statutes and regulations dealing with litigation against the federal government or with socioeconomic policies are often broadly applicable to contracts regardless of the nature of the transaction. In contrast, statutes and regulations dealing with contracting *procedures* are usually more specific in their application and may affect only particular types of transactions. However, here too there is a large degree of commonality in the rule structure. Many of the procedural rules developed for one type of activity have been adopted for others. Since procurement contracts have attracted the greatest degree of statutory and regulatory attention, the procurement rules are often used as models for rules in other types of contracting. Thus, while the discussion in this book is directed specifically to procurement contracts, some of the cases cited as precedent have involved other types of government contracts, and some of the procurement rules have application to other types of contracts.

The major categories of government transactions utilizing contractual agreements are:

- Procurement of goods and services
- Purchase of real property
- Sale of real or personal property
- Grants, cooperative agreements, cooperative research and development agreements, and "other transactions"
- Employment of personnel

Ordinarily, each of these transactions can be readily distinguished from the others. However, there can be a significant overlap between procurement transactions and other types of contractual arrangements. This section first discusses the types of transactions that are considered to be procurement of goods and services and the statutes and regulations applying to those contracts. It then considers the other types of government contracts and analyzes their relationship to procurement contracts.

[1] Procurement (Acquisition)

Government procurement, or "acquisition" as it is called in the Federal Acquisition Regulation (FAR), involves contracting for goods and services. The following guidance on the use of procurement contracts is provided at 31 U.S.C. § 6303:

> An executive agency shall use a procurement contract as the legal instrument reflecting a relationship between the United States Government and a State, a local government, or other recipient when—
>
> (1) the principal purpose of the instrument is to acquire (by purchase, lease, or barter) property or services for the direct benefit or use of the United States Government; or
>
> (2) the agency decides in a specific instance that the use of a procurement contract is appropriate.

Compare the definition of "acquisition" in FAR 2.101:

> Acquisition means the acquiring by contract with appropriated funds of supplies or services (including construction) by and for the use of the Federal Government through purchase or lease, whether the supplies or services are already in existence or must be created, developed, demonstrated and evaluated. . . .

See also the definition of "procurement" at 41 U.S.C. § 111: "'procurement' includes all stages of the process of acquiring property or services, beginning with the process for determining the need for property or services and ending with contract completion and closeout."

The Federal Circuit has relied on the statutory description of "procurement" at 31 U.S.C. § 6303 to confirm whether a given transaction is more properly classified as a procurement. See *Hymas v. United States*, 810 F.3d 1312 (Fed. Cir. 2016). The Federal Circuit also relies on the broad definition at 41 U.S.C. § 111 to determine the scope of the Court of Federal Claims protest jurisdiction. See *Distributed Sols., Inc. v. United States*, 539 F.3d 1340 (Fed. Cir. 2008). The provision in 31 U.S.C. § 6303 requiring that a procurement contract be for the direct benefit and use of the U.S. Government has not been applied literally by the Government Accountability Office (GAO). See, e.g., *Assisted Housing Servs. Corp.*, Comp. Gen. Dec. B-406738, 2012 CPD ¶ 236 (transaction for administration of housing assistance payment program should have been characterized as procurement, not cooperative agreement); *Civic Action Inst.*, 61 Comp. Gen. 637 (B-206372), 82-2 CPD ¶ 270 (if the instrument required performance, procurement was appropriate even though the performance was being acquired for others). There is also no requirement that the government pay for services in order to have a procurement contract. See Comp. Gen. Dec. B-257430, 1994 WL 612302, where a "memorandum of understanding" with an organization to assist it, at no cost, in conducting a study was found to be a procurement contract because the primary purpose of the agreement was to "obtain services in direct support of" the agency's statutory functions. However, a contract can only be a procurement contract if the agency obtains goods or services. See *Hymas*, 810 F.3d at 1328 (assisting private farmers to promote wildlife conservation where government did not directly benefit from farming service provided pursuant to the agreement); *Coastal Corp. v. United States*, 713 F.2d 728 (Fed. Cir. 1983) (implied contract to treat a bid honestly and fairly not a procurement contract because it calls for no goods and services). Neither will a contract be a procurement contract unless it is issued by "an executive agency." See *Agility Logistics Servs. Co. KSC v. Mattis*, 887 F.3d 1143 (Fed. Cir. 2018) (contracts formed with Iraqi Coalition Provisional Authority are not procurement contracts subject to Contract Disputes Act jurisdiction).

While the statutory definition of procurement mentions only property and services, other statutes may be more specific. In addition, the regulations contain a detailed description of the types of services included. The major categories of procurement are:

- supplies (products)
- construction
- services
- research and development
- rental of real property

Within each of these major categories are numerous specialized types of procurement. The classification of these types of procurement is extremely important for purposes of funding, types of contracts to be used, applicability of contract clauses, and coverage of socioeconomic provisions. See FAR 52.300 providing a matrix of solicitation provisions and contract clauses for specific types of procurement.

[a] Personal Property (Supplies)

FAR 2.101 defines "supplies" as follows:

> Supplies means all property except land or interest in land. It includes (but is not limited to) public works, buildings, and facilities; ships, floating

equipment, and vessels of every character, type, and description, together with parts and accessories; aircraft and aircraft parts, accessories, and equipment; machine tools; and the alteration or installation of any of the foregoing.

This definition of "supplies" is much more expansive than the meaning otherwise used in the FAR and is somewhat confusing. For example, contracts for the construction or repair of buildings and other permanent improvements to land are considered to be construction contracts, not supply contracts, FAR Part 36. However, contracts for the "construction" of ships are considered to be supply contracts, FAR 36.102. Nevertheless, some construction rules may be applied to contracts for work on ships. See, for example, *Southwest Marine, Inc.*, 64 Comp. Gen. 714 (B-218875.2), 85-2 CPD ¶ 104 (Miller Act performance and payment bonds applicable to ship conversion contract).

There are special rules and procedures governing the acquisition of certain types of supplies. For example, "major systems" are governed by OMB Circular A-109 and FAR Part 34. Detailed guidance on such procurements is contained in DoD Directives in the 5000 series.

For many years there were special rules governing the acquisition of automatic data processing equipment in the Brooks Act, 40 U.S.C. § 759. However, this Act was repealed by § 5101 of the Clinger-Cohen Act of 1996, and a new Information Technology Management Reform Act of 1996, Pub. L. No. 104-106, 40 U.S.C. § 11101 et seq. was substituted. This Act has been amended numerous times as Congress has attempted to force more effective procurement of information technology. This type of procurement is covered by FAR Part 39.

[b] Construction

FAR 2.101 contains the following definition of "construction:"

> Construction means construction, alteration, or repair (including dredging, excavating, and painting) of buildings, structures, or other real property. For purposes of this definition, the terms "buildings, structures, or other real property" include but are not limited to, improvements of all types, such as bridges, dams, plants, highways, parkways, streets, subways, tunnels, sewers, mains, power lines, cemeteries, pumping stations, railways, airport facilities, terminals, docks, piers, wharves, ways, lighthouses, buoys, jetties, breakwaters, levees, canals, and channels. Construction does not include the manufacture, production, furnishing, construction, alteration, repair, processing, or assembling of vessels, aircraft, or other kinds of personal property.

Construction contracts are unique because they generally involve improvements to government-owned property. Special rules governing these contracts are contained in FAR Part 36 and the matrix of contract clauses and solicitation provisions in FAR 52.301 covers construction as a separate category of procurement.

General authority for construction of buildings for the federal government is vested in the General Services Administration (GSA), 40 U.S.C. § 583. Regulations on the design and construction of buildings are in 41 C.F.R. Part 102-76. In addition to this general authority, many agencies have independent authority to construct various facilities for their own use.

The Clinger-Cohen Act of 1996 added 10 U.S.C. § 2305a (now 10 U.S.C. § 2341) and 41 U.S.C. § 253m (now 41 U.S.C. § 3309), permitting the acquisition of construction using a special two-phase design-build selection procedure. This procedure may be used when there will be significant costs in competing for the award. See FAR Subpart 36.3.

In order to provide protection for subcontractors, suppliers, and laborers, the Miller Act, 40 U.S.C. § 270a, requires that performance and payment bonds be obtained for construction contracts, 40 U.S.C. § 3131 et seq. FAR 28.102-1(a) applies this requirement to all domestic contracts over $150,000. The Act also requires that the FAR contain payment protection on smaller contracts. FAR 28.102-1(b) implements this requirement by mandating either a payment bond or an irrevocable letter of credit on contracts greater than $35,000 but less than $150,000. Bid guarantees are normally used when performance or payment bonds are required, FAR 28.101. See also *K-Con, Inc. v. United States*, 908 F.3d 719 (Fed. Cir. 2018) (discussing significance of Miller Act performance bonds).

[c] Services

FAR 37.101 defines a "service contract" as follows:

> "Service contract" means a contract that directly engages the time and effort of a contractor whose primary purpose is to perform an identifiable task rather than to furnish an end item of supply. A service contract may be either a nonpersonal or personal contract. It can also cover services performed by either professional or nonprofessional personnel whether on an individual or organizational basis. Some of the areas in which service contracts are found include the following:
>
> (1) Maintenance, overhaul, repair, servicing, rehabilitation, salvage, modernization, or modification of supplies, systems, or equipment.
>
> (2) Routine recurring maintenance of real property.
>
> (3) Housekeeping and base services.
>
> (4) Advisory and assistance services.
>
> (5) Operation of Government-owned equipment, facilities, and systems.
>
> (6) Communications services.
>
> (7) Architect-Engineering (see Subpart 36.6).
>
> (8) Transportation and related services (see Part 47).
>
> (9) Research and development (see Part 35).

Several types of services contracts are the subject of special statutory authorizations or procedures that supplement the general procurement statutes and regulations. One special type of services contract is architect-engineer (A-E) services. A-E services contracts are generally subject to the procurement statutes and regulations but are to be acquired under special negotiation procedures prescribed by the Brooks Architect-Engineering Act, 40 U.S.C. § 1101 et seq. See Chapter 10 for a discussion of these procedures. Other types of services contracts are discussed below.

[i] Transportation and Travel Services

Transportation and travel services may be acquired under procurement contracts subject to the procurement statutes and FAR Part 47, or under government bills of lading, travel requests, and other such documents under the provisions of the Transportation Act of 1940, 49 U.S.C. § 10721 and § 13712. Services procured under the Transportation Act are not subject to procurement statutes and regulations, FAR 47.000(a)(2). 40 U.S.C. § 602 makes the GSA responsible for prescribing policies and methods of procurement and supply for transportation and travel services and authorizes the Administrator of GSA to enter into contracts on behalf of executive agencies. These statutes are implemented in the Federal Property Management Regulations (FPMR). 41 C.F.R § 102-117 of this regulation deals with Transportation Management covering freight and household goods of government employees. 41 C.F.R. § 102-117.20 indicates that the Department of Defense (DoD) and uniformed members of civilian agencies are exempt from this regulation. DFARS Subparts 247.1 and 247.2 contain procedures applicable to DoD procurement of these transportation services.

Travel services are covered by separate regulations. 41 C.F.R. §§ 300-304 contain the Federal Travel Regulation which provides detailed rules on the permissible expenses for travel by employees of civilian agencies. GSA also enters into travel management services contracts for use by executive agencies. In addition, other agencies—primarily in DoD—issue travel service contracts. Structuring these contracts on a no-cost-no-fee basis has been held to be permissible under the procurement statutes and regulations, *T.V. Travel, Inc.*, 65 Comp. Gen. 109 (B-218198.6), 85-2 CPD ¶640; *N&N Travel & Tours, Inc.*, Comp. Gen. Dec. B-283731.2, 99-2 CPD ¶113. Payment under these contracts is frequently made by using travel cards issued to government employees under the authority of FAR 13.301.

[ii] Public Utility Services

The GSA Administrator is authorized under 40 U.S.C. § 501(a) to acquire "public utility services" for the use of executive agencies. However, DoD and the Department of Energy (DOE) have independent authority to procure utility services, and other agencies may obtain such authority by delegation from the

GSA, FAR 41.103(b). Contracts for utility services are subject to FAR Part 41 and may be made for periods not exceeding 10 years.

"Utility service" is not defined at 40 U.S.C. § 501(a), but FAR 41.101 contains the following definition:

> Utility service means a service such as furnishing electricity, natural or manufactured gas, water, sewage, thermal energy, chilled water, steam, hot water, or high temperature hot water. The application of part 41 to other services (e.g., rubbish removal, snow removal) may be appropriate when the acquisition is not subject to the Service Contract of 1965 (see 37.107).

Even though a service may fit the definition of a "public utility," FAR Part 41 procedures may not apply. See FAR 41.102(b) for utilities that are exempted from these procedures. See also DFARS Subpart 239.74.

[iii] Advisory and Assistance Services

Contracts for advisory and assistance services have been subject to special scrutiny and oversight because these services are closely related to inherently governmental functions. See Chapter 3 for a discussion of inherently governmental functions. These contracts are subject to FAR Subpart 37.2. FAR 2.101 contains a dense definition of advisory and assistance services.

FAR 37.203(a) permits the use of advisory and assistance services "to help managers achieve maximum effectiveness or economy in their operations." However, FAR 37.203(c) prohibits contracting for advisory and assistance services:

> (1) Used in performing work of a policy, decision-making, or managerial nature which is the direct responsibility of agency officials;
>
> (2) Used to bypass or undermine personnel ceilings, pay limitations, or competitive employment procedures;
>
> (3) Contracted for on a preferential basis to former Government employees;
>
> (4) Used under any circumstances specifically to aid in influencing or enacting legislation;
>
> (5) Used to obtain professional or technical advice which is readily available within the agency or another Federal agency.

Concern over the possible improper use of advisory and assistance services has resulted in the imposition of numerous management controls. 10 U.S.C. § 2304b (now 10 U.S.C. § 3405) and 41 U.S.C. § 4105 contain limitations on task order contracts for advisory and assistance services, including a five-year maximum length of such contracts. These statutes are implemented in FAR 37.2. In addition, OFPP Policy Letter 93-1, May 18, 1994 deals with management oversight of service contracting and incorporates many provisions of rescinded OMB Circular A-120 which dealt specifically with advisory and assistance services.

[iv] Concession Contracts

The government often obtains services under concession contracts. Under these contracts, the contractor is compensated for the services by fees charged to the public rather than payment by the government. If the contract merely allows the contractor to provide services to the public it will not be treated as a procurement contract. However, if the government receives a benefit from the transaction, the contract will be considered to be a procurement contract and the procurement statutes are applicable. The benefit may be one received by the government, or it may be the discharge of an obligation of the government.

For examples of concession contracts that are treated as procurement contracts because the contractor is required to perform work for the government, see *DNC Parks & Resorts at Yosemite, Inc.*, Comp. Gen. Dec. B-410998, 2015 CPD ¶ 127 (snow removal, litter removal, and maintenance, including paving and painting at facilities); *Recreation Res. Mgmt. of Am., Inc.*, Comp. Gen. Dec. B-406072, 2012 CPD ¶ 60 (maintenance of campgrounds, such as repairing and painting signs, benches, and fences; identifying and removing hazardous trees; and removing trash); and Great S. Bay Marina, Inc., Comp. Gen. Dec. B-293649, 2004 CPD ¶ 108 (reconstruction and rehabilitation services valued at over $3 million for government-owned facilities).

For examples of concession contracts that are treated as procurement contracts because the contractor is discharging a government obligation, see *Moboco, Inc.*, Comp. Gen. Dec. B-409186, 2014 CPD ¶ 46 (water transportation to National Park on island); *Public Commc's Servs., Inc.*, Comp. Gen. Dec. B-400058, 2009 CPD ¶ 154 (pro-bono telephone services for detainees which further the mission of the agency); *Total Med. Mgmt., Inc. v. United States*, 104 F.3d 1314 (Fed. Cir.), *cert. denied*, 522 U.S. 857 (1997) (medical services for dependents that the government is obligated to provide); *West Coast Copy, Inc.*, Comp. Gen. Dec. B-254044, 93-2 CPD ¶ 283 (copying services where government was obliged to provide copies to the public); and *Systems Planning Corp.*, Comp. Gen. Dec. B-244697.4, 92-1 CPD ¶ 516 (operation of Securities Exchange Commission Lost and Stolen Securities Program). Compare *Maritime Global Bank Grp.*, Comp. Gen. Dec. B-272552, 96-2 CPD ¶ 62 (on-base banking that agency was not obligated to provide).

The fact that the agency receives compensation from a concessionaire does not convert a concession contract into a procurement contract. See, e.g., *Good Food Serv., Inc.*, Comp. Gen. Dec. B-253161, 93-2 CPD ¶ 107 (cafeteria and vending service concession at federal office building); *YRT Servs. Corp. v. United States*, 28 Fed. Cl. 366 (1993) (concession awarded by the National Park Service executed under the National Park Systems Concessions Policy Act of 1965, 16 U.S.C. § 20 et seq.); and *Amfac Resorts, L.L.C. v. Dep't of Interior*, 282 F.3d 818 (D.C. Cir. 2002), *vacated & remanded*, 538 U.S. 803 (2003).

[d] Research and Development

Research and development is a specialized form of service contracting dealt with in FAR Part 35. The matrix of contract clauses and solicitation provisions in FAR 52.301 covers research and development as a separate category of procurement. Most agencies also have a separate appropriation for research and development contracts—requiring that this work be segregated from other types of work. FAR 35.001 contains definitions of applied research and development. FAR 35.002 contains the following statement of general principles applicable to contracting for research and development:

> The primary purpose of contracted R&D programs is to advance scientific and technical knowledge and apply that knowledge to the extent necessary to achieve agency and national goals. Unlike contracts for supplies and services, most R&D contracts are directed toward objectives for which the work or methods cannot be precisely described in advance. It is difficult to judge the probabilities of success or required effort for technical approaches, some of which offer little or no early assurance of full success. The contracting process shall be used to encourage the best sources from the scientific and industrial community to become involved in the program and must provide an environment in which the work can be pursued with reasonable flexibility and minimum administrative burden.

There are a number of techniques used to acquire research and development in addition to the standard negotiation technique. Basic research may be procured through broad agency announcements, 10 U.S.C. § 3012 (formerly § 2302) and 41 U.S.C. § 152. Contracts for research and development may also be awarded on the basis of unsolicited proposals. A number of agencies have the authority to use "other transactions" to perform research and development work. In addition, all major agencies must use a designated percentage of their research and development funds in awards of research contracts to small businesses, 15 U.S.C. § 638. See Chapter 10 for a discussion of procedures followed when broad agency announcements or other transactions are used to obtain research contracts.

In a very questionable decision, the Court of Federal Claims ruled that it did not have jurisdiction of a protest concerning a research and development contract because it was not a "procurement" contract, *R&D Dynamics Corp. v. United States*, 80 Fed. Cl. 715 (2007), *aff'd*, 309 Fed. Appx. 388 (Fed. Cir. 2009). The court apparently believed that the Small Business Innovative Research contract being protested was more in the nature of a grant and seems to have been influenced by the fact that R&D appropriations are separate from "procurement" appropriations. GAO has regularly taken jurisdiction of SBIR protests, understanding that they are procurements. See, for example, *Glatz Aeronautical Corp.*, Comp. Gen. Dec. B-416392, 2018 CPD ¶ 276, and *Made in Space, Inc.*, Comp. Gen. Dec. B-414490, 2017 CPD ¶ 195.

[e] Rental of Real Property

When the government seeks to lease property that the government owns, that transaction is not a procurement. See *Resource Conservation Grp., LLC v. United States*, 597 F.3d 1238 (Fed. Cir. 2010). However, when the government seeks to rent property owned by a private party, the procurement rules do apply. See *Forman v. United States*, 767 F.2d 875 (Fed. Cir. 1985), holding that the exclusion in the Office of Federal Procurement Policy Act (OFPP Act), 41 U.S.C. § 401 et seq. (now 41 U.S.C. § 1101 et seq.), of contracts for the acquisition of "real property in being" only applies to the acquisition of leases already in existence. Thus, the court held that acquiring a "new" lease (i.e., renting real property) was a procurement subject to the OFPP Act and the Contract Disputes Act. General authority for leasing real property for the federal government is vested in the GSA, 40 U.S.C. § 585. The GSA has, in turn, delegated authority for leasing of certain types of property and locations to other agencies, 41 C.F.R. § 102-72.30. Regulations on leasing real property are set forth in 41 C.F.R. Part 102-73. In addition, some agencies have independent authority to lease real property without regard to these regulations, 41 C.F.R. § 102-73.50.

In *Aerolease Long Beach & Satsuma Inv. Co. v. United States*, 31 Fed. Cl. 342, *aff'd*, 39 F.3d 1198 (Fed. Cir. 1994), the court dealt with a provision of the GSA regulations that conflicted with a FAR provision. The court held that, in the absence of an authorized deviation (none was present in this case), the GSA provision was invalid. This issue generated a Circuit split. Compare *60 Key Centre Inc. v. Admin. Of Gen. Servs. Admin.*, 47 F.3d 55 (2d Cir. 1995) (rejecting *Aerolease*), with *DeSciose v. Delbalzo*, 162 F.3d 1168 (9th Cir. 1998) (citing *Aerolease* for proposition that the FAR controls where the GSAR and FAR conflict).

[2] Other Contractual Arrangements

There are numerous other types of contractual relationships in which the federal government engages. The major nonprocurement transactions and their relationship to procurement are discussed in this section.

[a] Purchase of Real Property

The purchase of real property is not covered by the procurement statutes. See 10 U.S.C. § 3064 (formerly § 2303(a)), stating that the Armed Services Procurement Act (ASPA) applies to the procurement of "all property (other than land)," and 40 U.S.C. § 501(b)(1)(A), stating that GSA will procure and supply "personal property." In addition, the FAR system applies to the procurement of "property other than real property in being," 41 U.S.C. § 1121(c)(1)(A). 41 U.S.C. § 6301(c) provides that "Land may not be purchased by the Federal Government unless the purchase is authorized by law."

[b] Sale of Property

Article IV, Section 3, Clause 2 of the Constitution gives Congress the exclusive authority to dispose of federal government property. See, e.g., *Royal Indemn. Co. v. United States*, 313 U.S. 289 (1941). 40 U.S.C. § 541 et seq., grants the authority to "supervise and direct the disposition of surplus property" to the GSA Administrator, who may delegate this authority to other agencies. The statute is implemented by the Federal Management Regulations, 41 C.F.R. Part 102-38, and by subsidiary agency regulations such as the Defense Material Disposition Manual, DoD Manual 4160.21-M, Oct. 22, 2015, Change 2, Aug. 31, 2018. In addition to this general authority, specific statutory authority to dispose of property is granted to some agencies. See, for example, 16 U.S.C. § 472a granting the Secretary of Agriculture authority to sell timber from the national forests. The FAR does not apply to sales of property, *Sandia Die & Cartridge Co.*, Comp. Gen. Dec. B-218011, 85-1 CPD ¶ 308. See also *Monchamp Corp. v. United States*, 19 Cl. Ct. 797 (1990), holding that neither the procurement statutes nor the FAR apply to timber sales.

There can be considerable overlap between a property disposal contract and a procurement contract. In some cases, work that would ordinarily be accomplished under a procurement contract may be made a part of the property disposal contract. See, e.g., *Alamo Aircraft Supply, Inc.*, Comp. Gen. Dec. B-278215, 98-1 CPD ¶ 5 (contract to sell surplus property and give the government 80% of the proceeds of the sale was a contract to sell property subject to the Federal Property and Administrative Services Act not a procurement contract).

[c] Grants and Cooperative Agreements

Grants and cooperative agreements are used when the federal government intends to provide assistance or support to private organizations or to state and local governments. A grant without any contractual obligations on the part of the recipient may be characterized as a gift. See *Alabama v. Schmidt*, 232 U.S. 168 (1914) (Alabama had no contractual obligation to use land granted by Congress for public schools); *King County, Wash. v. Seattle School Dist. No. 1*, 263 U.S. 361 (1923) (congressional intent that grant money be used for public schools is not a requirement that grant money be used for public schools); *Madison County Bd. of Educ. v. Illinois Cent. R.R. Co.*, 939 F.2d 292 (1991) (grant of land for public schools was a gift and not an honorary trust arrangement).

However, most grants now require the recipient to use the funds or property only for specified purposes, 42 Comp. Gen. 289 (B-149441) (1962). Such grants are contractual agreements but are not procurement contracts, *Thermalon Indus., Ltd. v. United States*, 34 Fed. Cl. 411 (1995). See also *Westmoreland Human Opportunities, Inc. v. Walsh*, 246 F.3d 233 (3d Cir. 2001), treating a grant as a contract at a preliminary stage of the litigation, and *San Juan City College v.*

United States, 391 F.3d 1357 (Fed. Cir. 2004), treating a grant in the form of a "program participation agreement" as a contract.

Cooperative agreements have also been held to be contracts even though they are not procurement contracts, although the Federal Circuit has proven hesitant to find that the recipient of a cooperative agreement has any entitlement to money damages in the event of breach, which in some cases can result in dismissal for lack of jurisdiction. In *Trauma Serv. Grp., Ltd. v. United States*, 33 Fed. Cl. 426 (1995), *aff'd*, 104 F.3d 1321 (Fed. Cir. 1997), the Court of Federal Claims held that a cooperative agreement for shared health services, in which the government made no promise to compensate the recipient, was not a contract. The Federal Circuit affirmed the decision in Trauma based on the fact that the cooperative agreement did not call for the payment claimed by the plaintiff not on the basis that the agreement was not a contract, stating at 1326:

> [A]ny agreement can be a contract within the meaning of the Tucker Act, provided that it meets the requirements for a contract with the Government, specifically: mutual intent to contract including an offer and acceptance, consideration, and a Government representative who had actual authority to bind the Government. See *City of El Centro* [*v. United States*], 922 F.2d [816 (Fed. Cir. 1990)] at 820; Thermalon, 34 Fed. Cl. at 414. As such, contrary to the opinion of the trial court, a MOA can also be a contract—whether this one is, we do not decide.

In a subsequent line of decisions, the Federal Circuit has dismissed breach of cooperative agreement claims for lack of jurisdiction where it was not clear from the face of the agreement that the plaintiff was entitled to money damages in the event of breach. See *Rick's Mushroom Serv., Inc. v. United States*, 521 F.3d 1338 (Fed. Cir. 2008); *Higbie v. United States*, 778 F.3d 990 (Fed. Cir. 2015). This rule from *Rick's Mushroom* departs from the general rule that money damages are presumed to be an available and adequate remedy for breach of contract, and that therefore a plaintiff need not identify any additional money mandating source of law when alleging breach of contract under the Tucker Act. See, e.g., *LaBatte v. United States*, 899 F.3d 1373 (Fed. Cir. 2018) (compiling cases). Subsequent Federal Circuit decisions have rejected the government's attempts to apply *Rick's Mushroom* beyond the unique facts of that case, reaffirming the general presumption of money damages arising from a breach of contract, at least in the context of settlement agreements. In *Holmes v. United States*, 657 F.3d 1303, 1316 (Fed. Cir. 2011), the Federal Circuit found Tucker Act jurisdiction over two settlement agreements with expungement provisions, the purpose of which "clearly was to prevent Mr. Holmes from being denied future employment based on his record as the Navy maintained it prior to the agreements." On that basis, the Federal Circuit reasoned: "the agreements inherently relate to monetary compensation through relationship to Mr. Holmes's future employment." See also *LaBatte*, 899 F.3d at 1378-79 (finding jurisdiction over breach of settlement agreement); *Rocky Mountain Helium LLC v. United*

States, 841 F.3d 1320, 1326-27 (Fed. Cir. 2016) (finding jurisdiction over breach of settlement agreement). The Court of Federal Claims judges appear divided on the issue. Compare *San Antonio Housing Authority v. United States*, 143 Fed. Cl. 425 (2019), *with St. Bernard Parish Gov't v. United States*, 134 Fed. Cl. 730, 734-35 (2017), *aff'd on other grounds*, 916 F.3d 987 (Fed. Cir. 2019), *and Anchorage v. United States*, 119 Fed. Cl. 709, 712-13 (2015).

Unlike procurement contracts, which agencies have the inherent authority to use in carrying out authorized activities, assistance agreements require that an agency have specific statutory authority for their use, *Federal Facility Contributions to Capital Costs of Sewage Treatment Projects*, 59 Comp. Gen. 1 (B-194912) (1979). Many agencies have such statutory authority. See, for example, 6 U.S.C. § 112(b)(2) (DHS may "make contracts, grants, and cooperative agreements, and to enter into agreements with other executive agencies"); 10 U.S.C. § 4001 (formerly § 2358) (DoD may perform research and development by "contract, cooperative agreement, or grant"); 15 U.S.C. § 638(g) (agencies may award "funding agreements"—contracts, grants or cooperative agreements—to small businesses to carry out the SBIR program); 42 U.S.C. § 2473(c)(5) (NASA may enter into and perform such contracts, leases, cooperative agreements, or other transactions as may be necessary); 42 U.S.C. § 7256 (DOE may enter into and perform such contracts, leases, cooperative agreements, or other similar transactions). Although there is no overall grant procedural statute, individual statutes authorizing assistance programs often contain procedural and other requirements. See, for example, 7 U.S.C. § 3157(b) establishing the Department of Agriculture Research Grant Program (implemented in 7 C.F.R. Part 3400), and the National Science Foundation Act of 1950, 42 U.S.C. § 1862.

Neither grants nor cooperative agreements are governed by the procurement statutes or the FAR, *Trauma Serv. Grp., Ltd. v. United States*, 33 Fed. Cl. 426 (1995), *aff'd*, 104 F.3d 1321 (Fed. Cir. 1997). However, these assistance agreements are still governed by an array of statutes, regulations, and informal guidance. Previously, this guidance was scattered throughout multiple OMB "Circulars" addressing discreet issues. However, OMB updated and consolidated the circulars in December 2013 into omnibus grant guidance officially titled the "Uniform Administrative Requirements, Cost Principles, and Audit Requirements for Federal Awards." 78 Fed. Reg. 78590, Dec. 26, 2013 (adding 2 C.F.R. pt. 200). More common names include the "super circular," "uniform guidance," and "mega regulation." Agencies had until December 2014 to implement the guidance, with some adopting it in whole and others customizing the guidance to their unique needs.

Provisions concerning the disposition of patent rights in "funding agreements" (grants, cooperative agreements, and procurement contracts) with small businesses and nonprofit organizations are specified in 35 U.S.C. § 200 et seq. These provisions are implemented by the Department of Commerce in 37 C.F.R. Part 401. A few agencies have issued guidance on grants and cooperative agreements. See, for example, the DoD Grant and Agreement Regulations

(DoDGARs) at 32 C.F.R. Part 21 through Part 37 and the NASA Grant and Cooperative Agreement Handbook, 14 C.F.R. Part 1260.

Whether an assistance agreement takes the form of a grant or a cooperative agreement depends upon the government's degree of involvement in the activity being supported, *Xcavators, Inc.*, 59 Comp. Gen. 758 (B-198297), 80-2 CPD ¶ 229. The following guidance on the use of grants is provided at 31 U.S.C. § 6304:

> An executive agency shall use a grant agreement as the legal instrument reflecting a relationship between the United States Government and a State, a local government, or other recipient when—
>
> (1) the principal purpose of the relationship is to transfer a thing of value to the State or local government or other recipient to carry out a public purpose of support or stimulation authorized by a law of the United States instead of acquiring (by purchase, lease, or barter) property or services for the direct benefit or use of the United States Government; and
>
> (2) substantial involvement *is not expected* between the executive agency and the State, local government, or other recipient when carrying out the activity contemplated in the agreement (emphasis added).

The conditions for use of cooperative agreements are specified in 31 U.S.C. § 6305 as follows:

> An executive agency shall use a cooperative agreement as the legal instrument reflecting a relationship between the United States Government and a State, a local government, or other recipient when—
>
> (1) the principal purpose of the relationship is to transfer a thing of value to the State, local government, or other recipient to carry out a public purpose of support or stimulation authorized by a law of the United States instead of acquiring (by purchase, lease, or barter) property or services for the direct benefit or use of the United States Government; and
>
> (2) substantial involvement *is expected* between the executive agency and the State, local government, or other recipient when carrying out the activity contemplated in the agreement (emphasis added).

FAR 35.003(a) implements this statute by stating that "[g]rants or cooperative agreements should be used when the principal purpose of the transaction is to stimulate or support research and development for [a] public purpose [other than acquisition of supplies or services for the direct benefit or use of the federal government]." An agency may not avoid compliance with the procurement rules by using a cooperative agreement when a procurement contract is the proper vehicle. The distinction in these cases is between procuring services and providing assistance, with the cases holding that an arrangement to obtain services, even when other parties pay for them, will require the use of a procurement contract. See, e.g., *CMS Contract Mgmt. Servs. v. Mass. Housing Fin. Agency*, 745 F.3d 1379 (Fed. Cir. 2014) (acquisition of financing-relating services a procurement instrument, not cooperative agreement); *Assisted Housing Servs. Corp.*, Comp. Gen. Dec. B-406738, 2012 CPD ¶ 236 (HUD improperly used cooperative agreement instead of procurement when acquiring services to administer housing assistance payments); *Environmental Protection Agency-Inspector General—Cooperative Agreement—Procurement*, Comp. Gen. Dec. B-262110, 97-1 CPD ¶ 131 (support services to run a conference should be obtained under a procurement contract not a cooperative agreement). This distinction can become most obscure when an agency provides funds to support basic or applied research. In that situation, some agencies use grants while other agencies use procurement contracts. See *Energy Conversion Devices, Inc.*, Comp. Gen. Dec. B-260514, 95-2 CPD ¶ 121, holding that a cooperative agreement could properly be used when the primary purpose of the research was to "advance the state-of-the-art by supporting and stimulating research and development."

One of the purposes of the Federal Grant and Agreement Act was to "encourage competition in making grants and cooperative agreements," 31 U.S.C. § 6301. However, there is no overall statutory requirement for competition in such awards, *Burgos & Assocs.*, 58 Comp. Gen. 785 (B-194140), 79-2 CPD ¶ 194. In some cases, individual statutes require competition. See, for example, 7 U.S.C. § 450i(b). GAO will not consider protests that improper procedures have been used to award grants or cooperative agreements, *Sprint Commc'ns Co.*, Comp. Gen. Dec. B-256586, 94-1 CPD ¶ 300 (protest will only consider whether procurement contract should have been used and whether there was a conflict of interest). The Federal Circuit has confirmed that a similar rule applies to protests filed at the Court of Federal Claims under 28 U.S.C. § 1491(b). See *Hymas v. United States*, 810 F.3d 1312 (Fed. Cir. 2016) ("Our jurisprudence explains that the Claims Court's jurisdiction under 28 U.S.C. § 1491(b) 'exclusively' concerns 'procurement solicitations and contracts,' and that agencies escape the requirements of federal procurement law' under the CICA when using a cooperative agreement.")

[d] Other Transactions

Several major agencies have the authority to enter into "other transactions" that are neither procurement contracts, grants, nor cooperative agreements. For example, DoD has long had authority to use other transactions for basic, applied, and advanced research projects. See 10 U.S.C. § 4021 (formerly § 2371), stating:

> Additional Forms of Transactions Authorized—The Secretary of Defense and the Secretary of each military department may enter into transactions (other than contracts, cooperative agreements, and grants) under the authority of this subsection in carrying out basic, applied, and advanced

> research projects. The authority of this subsection is in addition to the authority provided in section 4001 of this title to use contracts, cooperative agreements, and grants in carrying out such projects.

DoD has also received broad authority to enter into other transactions for prototype projects. Section 845 of the National Defense Authorization Act for Fiscal Year 1994, Pub. L. No. 103-160, granted this authority on a temporary basis for "prototype projects that are directly relevant to weapons or weapon systems to be acquired or developed by the Department of Defense." This authority was periodically extended and broadened until the National Defense Authorization Act for FY 2016 made the authority permanent at 10 U.S.C. § 2371b, which has since been moved to 10 U.S.C. § 4022.

NASA has similar authority. See 42 U.S.C. § 2473, stating that the Administrator is authorized:

> to enter into and perform such contracts, leases, cooperative agreements, or other transactions as may be necessary in the conduct of its work and on such terms as it may deem appropriate, with any agency or instrumentality of the United States, or with any State, Territory, or possession, or with any political subdivision thereof, or with any person, firm, association, corporation, or educational institution.

Under this authority, NASA uses "Space Act Agreements" which are not procurement contracts. See *Rocketplane Kistler*, Comp. Gen. Dec. B-310741, 2008 CPD ¶ 22, and *Exploration Partners, LLC*, Comp. Gen. Dec. B-298804, 2006 CPD ¶ 201, holding that such an agreement to provide funding to encourage the development of a private space transportation system was not a procurement contract.

DOE also has this type of authority with regard to its nonnuclear research, development, demonstration, and commercial application program, 42 U.S.C. § 7256(g), while DHS has the same authority as DoD to use the authority for both research and prototype contracts, 6 U.S.C. § 391(a).

These agencies can use this "other transactions" authority for any type of work within the scope of the statutory delegation. GAO will not rule on the procedures used in awarding other transaction contracts but will consider whether a procurement contract should have been used. See *MD Helicopters, Inc.*, Comp. Gen. Dec. B-417379, 2019 CPD ¶ 120 (denying protest because protester did not allege a procurement contract should have been used); *MorphoTrust USA, LLC*, Comp. Gen. Dec. B-412711, 2016 CPD ¶ 133 (denying challenge to TSA use of other transaction authority because its statute permitted use for all work); *Energy Conversion Devices, Inc.*, Comp. Gen. Dec. B-260514, 95-2 CPD ¶ 121 (denying protest that a procurement contract should have been used because the principal purpose of the agreement was to stimulate and support the development of new manufacturing technology not to acquire services). GAO sustained a protest challenging DOD's issuance of a sole source follow-on production contract after entering into another transaction for a prototype project in *Oracle America, Inc.*, Comp. Gen. Dec. B-416061, 2018 CPD ¶ 180. GAO found that DoD did not comply with specific statutory requirements associated with the authority to award a sole source follow-on production contract in those circumstances. At least some protests challenging the procedures used in awarding other transactions may be heard in district courts, *MD Helicopters, Inc. v. United States*, 435 F. Supp. 3d 1003 (D. Ariz. 2020). In the first Court of Federal Claims decision addressing its protest jurisdiction over other transaction awards, the court declined to find that another transaction award was sufficiently "in connection with" a planned follow-on procurement to establish jurisdiction under 28 U.S.C. § 1491(b), notwithstanding that the Air Force had clearly and repeatedly explained that the protested other transaction award was intended to help offerors develop the launch systems that would be used to offer the launch services acquired through the upcoming FAR Part 12 procurement. See *Space Exploration Techs., Corp. v. United States*, 144 Fed. Cl. 433 (2019). The Court did, however, transfer the protest to district court, which ultimately denied the protest on the merits. *Space Exploration Techs. Corp. v. United States*, No. 2:19-cv-07927-ODW (GJSx), 2020 WL 7344615 (C.D. Cal. Sept. 24, 2020). For now, it appears that whether another transaction protest will be decided by the Court of Federal Claims or a district court depends on a judge's fact-specific finding of whether the other transaction is sufficiently "in connection" with a procurement.

When an agency uses its other transactions authority, it generally need not comply with the procurement statutes, the FAR, or the statutes and regulations applying to grants and cooperative agreements. However, it will be required to comply with any other statute of general applicability and may be subject to procurement-specific statutes to the extent they are incorporated into the statutory, regulatory, or contractual provisions governing the other transaction at issue. See, e.g., 10 U.S.C. § 4002 (formerly § 2371b(h)) (providing DoD other transactions for prototype projects "shall be treated as a Federal agency procurement for the purposes of [the Procurement Integrity Act]"). To make this determination, the terms of each statute must be analyzed closely. There is no uniform guidance as to which statutes apply to these other transactions. However, the DoDGARs contains substantial guidance in 32 C.F.R. Part 21 through Part 37, and DoD has issued various iterations of informal guidance for its other transactions authority. See Chapter 10 for a more complete discussion of other transactions.

[e] Cooperative Research and Development Agreements

Another form of contract is the cooperative research and development agreement (CRADA). The Federal Technology Transfer Act (FTTA), 15 U.S.C. § 3710a(d), defines a CRADA as follows:

> (1) [T]he term "cooperative research and development agreement" means any agreement between one or more Federal laboratories and one or more non-Federal parties under which the Government, through its laboratories, provides personnel, services, facilities, equipment, intellectual property, or other resources with or without reimbursement (but not funds to non-Federal parties) and the non-Federal parties provide funds, personnel, services, facilities, equipment, intellectual property, or other resources toward the conduct of specified research or development efforts which are consistent with the missions of the laboratory; except that such term does not include a procurement contract or cooperative agreement as those terms are used in sections 6303, 6304, and 6305 of title 31, United States Code;

15 U.S.C. § 3710a authorizes the directors of federal laboratories to enter into CRADAs. The purpose of these CRADAs is to "transfer federally owned or originated technology to State and local governments and to the private sector," 15 U.S.C. § 3710a(1). To accomplish this purpose, the Act permits federal laboratories to provide any resources *except federal funds* to the parties entering into CRADAs. The other parties can, and generally do, provide funding to support the work of the laboratory. Agencies with the authority to enter into other transactions could enter into an agreement similar to a CRADA and provide federal funds as part of the arrangement.

A CRADA cannot be awarded when a procurement contract is the proper instrument, *Chem Serv., Inc. v. Environmental Monitoring Sys. Lab.*, 12 F.3d 1256 (3d Cir. 1993). GAO will only consider protests to the award of CRADAs if there is an allegation that the agency is acting beyond is statutory authority, *Spire Corp.*, Comp. Gen. Dec. B-258267, 94-2 CPD ¶ 257.

CRADAs are not subject to the procurement statutes, the FAR, the statutes and regulations governing grants and cooperative agreements, or the statutes governing "other transactions." Furthermore, there is no governmentwide regulatory guidance and very little agency-wide guidance on the use of CRADAs. Thus, each agency is free to follow its own procedures. As with the case of "other transactions," other statutes pertaining to contracting by the federal government must be carefully analyzed to determine if they apply to CRADAs.

See Chapter 7 of Nash & Rawicz, *Intellectual Property in Government Contracts*, 6th ed. 2008, for a more complete discussion of CRADAs.

[f] Employment Contracts

The employment of individuals by the federal government is accomplished pursuant to civil service laws. See generally 5 U.S.C. § 2101 et seq. However, services may be acquired under a procurement contract, *either from an individual or an organization*, as long as an employer-employee relationship is not established between the government and the persons performing the services, *Sunbelt Props., Inc.*, Comp. Gen. Dec. B-249469, 92-2 CPD ¶ 353. As discussed above, the federal government enters into numerous contracts with different types of organizations for the performance of a wide variety of services. In addition, 5 U.S.C. § 3109 permits agencies to "procure by contract the temporary (not in excess of one year) or intermittent services of experts or consultants" when authorized by an appropriation or other statute.

In order to prevent agencies from circumventing the personnel laws, there are strict limitations on obtaining additional employees by contract. These limitations are implemented in the FAR 37.104(b) provision stating that "personal services contracts" are prohibited unless specifically authorized by statute. However, FAR 2.101 defines the term "personal services contract" as:

> a contract that, by its express terms or as administered, makes the contractor personnel appear to be, in effect, Government employees (see 37.104).

This definition does not appear to encompass contracts with individuals but only addresses contracts with organizations. However, the limitations on obtaining additional employees by contract applies to both types of contract. The only FAR guidance on contracts with individuals is the confusing statement in FAR 37.104(f) that the contracting officer must coordinate with the appropriate personnel office prior to entering into "personal services contracts" with individual experts or consultants.

There is no prohibition in the FAR of awarding contracts with individuals when they are treated as independent contractors. However, such contracts may not establish an employer-employee relationship. See, e.g., *Payment by Nat'l Mediation Bd. to A. Robert Lowry, Inc.*, Comp. Gen. Dec. B-217468, 1985 WL 52872 (contract for the services of a specific individual to act as an independent-contractor neutral arbitrator); *Lynn Francis Jones*, 63 Comp. Gen. 507 (B-214432) (1984) (employer-employee relationship found due to purely personal nature of services provided).

There is considerably more guidance on contracts with service contractors. There, it is clear that it is improper for the federal government to, in effect, hire employees through the creation of an employer-employee relationship between the government and a contractor's employees in a procurement contract, *United States Advisory Comm'n on Pub. Diplomacy*, 61 Comp. Gen. 69 (B-202159), 81-2 CPD ¶ 404. FAR 37.104(c) and (d) contain detailed guidance on this issue.

In *Lodge 1858, AFGE v. Webb*, 580 F.2d 496 (D.C. Cir.), *cert. denied*, 439 U.S. 927 (1978), the court held that *supervision* is the all-important factor in determining whether services are being performed under an employment arrangement or under an independent contractor relationship. The court recognized that either actual supervision or the contractual right to supervise could create an employer-employee relationship. Supervision was defined as "control of the individual workman's physical conduct." In this case, the service contracts were held not to violate the proscription because the government did not directly control the contractor's employees since all government orders were issued through the contractor's management. The court discussed all the FAR factors and held that it was not necessary for all the factors to be present; the critical item is supervision. See also *Information Ventures, Inc.*, Comp. Gen. Dec. B-290785, 2002 CPD ¶ 152 (requirement that government project officer monitor all work of contractor not the type of continuous supervision that creates a personal services contract); *Carr's Wild Horse Center*, Comp. Gen. Dec. B-285833, 2000 CPD ¶ 210 (performing work that is also to be done by government employees not an indication of a personal services contract); *Danoff & Donnelly*, Comp. Gen. Dec. B-243368, 91-2 CPD ¶ 95 (key personnel clause and required approval of personnel does not create personal services contract); *Minority Commc'ns, Inc.*, Comp. Gen. Dec. B-228230.2, 88-1 CPD ¶ 88 (fact that government approval is required for contractor to substitute employees for those identified in proposal does not constitute supervision even though contractor's traditional management prerogatives are infringed); *Work Sys. Design, Inc.*, Comp. Gen. Dec. B-213451, 84-2 CPD ¶ 226 (failure of contract to specify details of work direction does not create employer-employee relationship if written technical instructions are given to contractor's management); *Computer Sciences Corp.*, Comp. Gen. Dec. B-210800, 84-1 CPD ¶ 422 (criticizing excessive lower level management not an indication that agency will supervise contractor's employees); and *Cerberonics, Inc.*, Comp. Gen. Dec. B-192161, 78-2 CPD ¶ 354 (clause limiting contractor's replacement of key personnel not an indication that a personal services contract was created). In *Encore Mgmt., Inc.*, Comp. Gen. Dec. B-278903.2, 99-1 CPD ¶ 33, GAO concluded that the agency properly canceled a contract for clerical and administrative support services because the agency Inspector General had ruled that it was a personal services contract.

Despite the FAR's focus on supervision as the primary indicia of an employment relationship, several judicial decisions indicate that supervision is but one of several necessary elements needed to create and employment, suggesting that the FAR guidance is incomplete if not incorrect. See, e.g., *Costner v. United States*, 665 F.2d 1016 (Ct. Cl. 1981) (holding that supervision is only one of three elements that must be met to create an employment contract with the government—the other two being appointment as an employee and performance of a federal function); *Testan v. United States*, 424 U.S. 392, 402 (1976) ("one is not entitled to the benefit of a [Government] position until he has been duly appointed to it."); *Horner v. Acosta*, 803 F.2d 687, 692-93 (D.C. Cir. 1986) (appointment as a federal employee requires "a significant degree of formality" necessary to fulfill the appointment requirement of the civil services laws).

[B] Agencies Covered by Procurement Statutes

The terms "government" and "federal government" are used extensively in statutes, regulations, and in this book to refer to the United States in its contractual dealings. However, contracts are not made by the United States generally but are entered into by individual organizations in all three branches of the government. These numerous organizations are varied in nature, ranging from old-line departments to recently formed corporations. Some have very large procurement budgets and procurement organizations with thousands of employees while others perform a modest amount of contracting with a small number of personnel engaged in such activity. **Figure 1-1** contains the Organization Chart of the U.S. Government depicting the major governmental units.

While there is a small amount of procurement carried out by the legislative branch and the judicial branch, the vast majority of all procurement is done by the executive branch of the government.

[1] Statutes Governing Procurement

Congress has not adopted a single procurement statute for the entire government. Instead, there are two major statutes covering most government procurement—the Armed Services Procurement Act (ASPA), (formerly § 2302 et seq., reorganized across Title 10, Part V), and the Federal Property and Administrative Services Act (FPASA), 41 U.S.C. § 3101 et seq. The ASPA was passed in 1948, and the FPASA, which was modeled after the ASPA, was enacted in 1949. Through the years, the ASPA has been modified extensively, but the FPASA tends to be modified infrequently. In 1984, through the Competition in Contracting Act (CICA), Pub. L. No. 98-369, Congress made these two statutes almost identical. However, changes were subsequently made to both Acts with the result that over the next decade, the two statutes again diverged. The Federal Acquisition Streamlining Act of 1994 (FASA), Pub. L. No. 103-355, again brought the two statutes into closer conformity. The Clinger-Cohen Act of 1996, Pub. L. No. 104-106, retains this conformity by amending both statutes in most cases. Since that time, the ASPA has continued to be modified on a regular basis while the FPASA has not.

There are a few minor agencies not covered by either of these two statutes, most of which conduct their procurement under Revised Statutes 3709 and 3710, 41 U.S.C. § 5 and 41 U.S.C. § 8, respectively (pre-2011 codification). There are also several agencies, most notably the Postal Service and the Federal Aviation Administration, which have been specifically authorized to conduct their procurement without following the major procurement statutes. Finally, there is an overriding statute, the Office of Federal Procurement Policy Act (OFPPA), 41 U.S.C. § 1101 et seq., that contains a number of procurement rules covering almost all government agencies. The problems inherent in this unnecessarily complex and burdensome statutory scheme were recognized in the President's Blue Ribbon Commission on Defense Management, *A Quest for Excellence—Final Report to the President* (June 1986), which stated at 55, "[W]e recommend that Congress work with the Administration to recodify federal laws governing

THE GOVERNMENT OF THE UNITED STATES

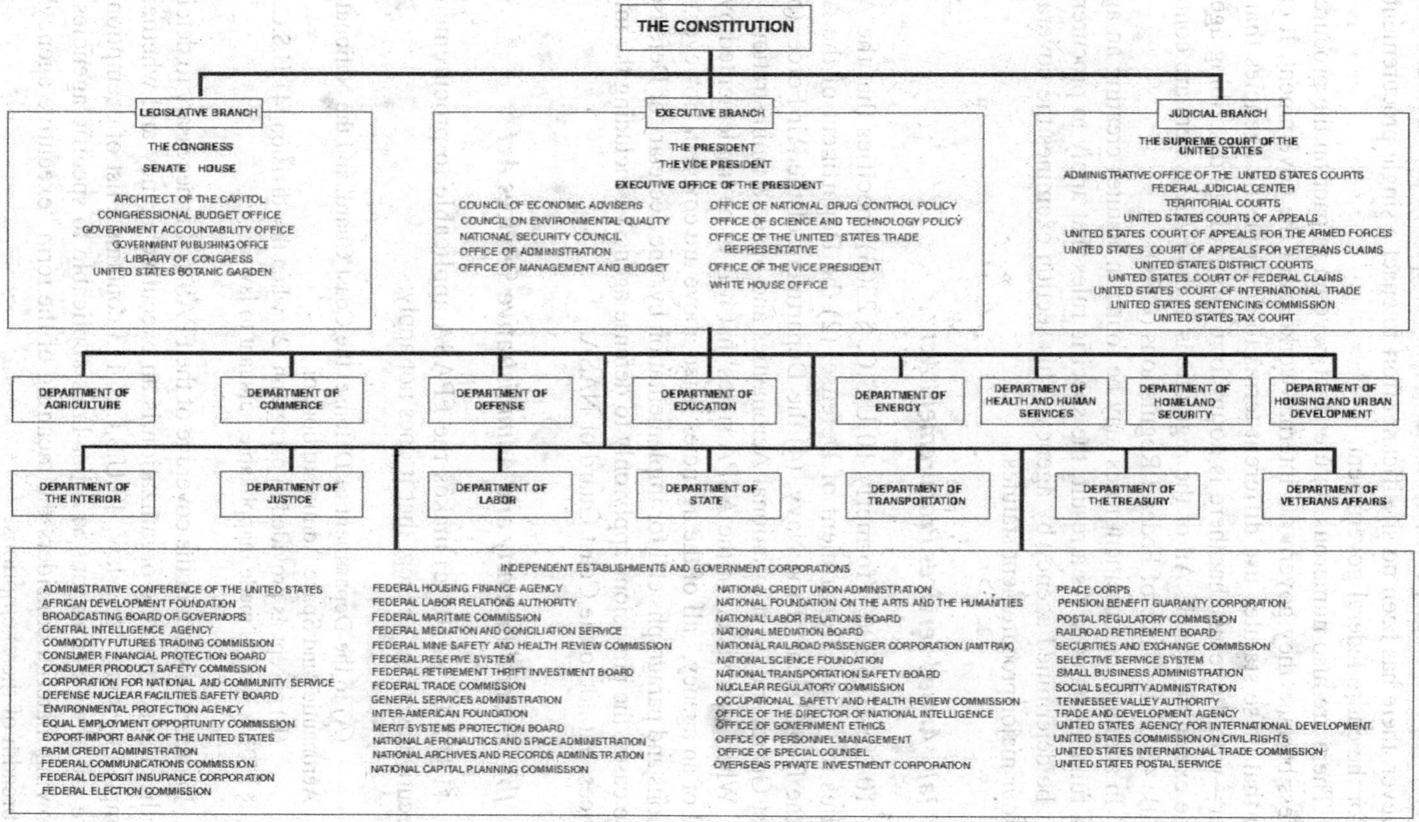

procurement in a single, consistent, and greatly simplified procurement statute." However, there has been no significant effort to enact a single procurement statute for the entire federal government.

There are also numerous statutes that have an impact on the procurement process because they govern the internal workings of the government. It can be seen that these statutes use different terms to describe the agencies that they cover—with the result that there is no uniform terminology describing agencies of the executive branch. All of the regulations in the FAR system are contained in Title 48 of the Code of Federal Regulations (CFR).

In addition, procurement rules may be found in statutes creating an agency or in funding statutes. As a result, the specific rules that apply to procurements must be determined agency by agency. This section examines the coverage of the four major procurement statutes.

[a] Armed Services Procurement Act

10 U.S.C. § 3063 (formerly 10 U.S.C. § 2303) specifies that the ASPA applies to (1) the Department of Defense, (2) the Department of the Army, (3) the Department of the Navy, (4) the Department of the Air Force, (5) the Coast Guard, and (6) the National Aeronautics and Space Administration.

When a provision in the ASPA states that it is to be implemented by "the head of an agency," all of the agencies listed above are covered. However, some sections and paragraphs call for implementation by "the Secretary of Defense." In those cases, the provisions apply only to defense agencies, including the military services, but not to the Coast Guard or NASA.

[b] Federal Property and Administrative Services Act

41 U.S.C. § 3101(c) makes the FPASA applicable to procurements of "executive agencies" except that it does not apply:

> (A) to the Department of Defense, the Coast Guard, and the National Aeronautics and Space Administration; or
>
> (B) except as provided in paragraph (2), when this division [41 U.S.C. § 3101 et seq.] is made inapplicable pursuant to law.

In order to ascertain the coverage of the FPASA, it is necessary to determine whether the contracting organization is an executive agency and whether it is exempted by some other law. 40 U.S.C. § 113 contains a list of exemptions and there are other exemptions in other laws applicable to specific agencies. The following material considers the meaning of the term "executive agency" and the breadth of the exemptions.

[i] Executive Agency

The term "executive agency" is defined in 40 U.S.C. § 102 as follows:

> (4) The term "executive agency" means—(A) an executive department or independent establishment in the executive branch of the Government; and (B) a wholly owned Government corporation.

Organizations other than the departments, establishments, and corporations listed in **Figure 1-1** can also be considered to be executive agencies if they perform procurement functions for the executive agencies. However, the mere fact that the government provides funding for the operation of an organization will not make that agency a federal instrumentality. See *United States v. Orleans*, 425 U.S. 807 (1976). The total factual circumstances surrounding the creation of the organization must be considered in determining whether it constitutes an executive agency under a particular statute, *Motor Coach Indus., Inc. v. Dole*, 725 F.2d 958, 964-65 (4th Cir. 1984) (trust formed by airlines at direction of FAA for purpose of receiving airport landing fees due to the United States and using those fees for the purchase of buses for passenger transportation to the airport deemed an executive agency subject to the FPASA). *Cf., Byers v. Intuit Inc.*, 564 F. Supp. 2d 385, 410 (E.D. Pa. 2008) (distinguishing *Motor Coach* where a public agency was not controlling the private party). An organization may be considered to be an executive agency for purposes of the procurement statutes but not a federal agency under other statutes. See *Flight Int'l Grp., Inc. v. Federal Reserve Bank of Chicago*, 583 F. Supp. 674, *vacated because of parties' settlement*, 597 F. Supp. 462 (N.D. Ga. 1984), where procurement by a Federal Reserve Bank was found to be governed by the FPASA. Even an Article I court may be considered an executive agency under the FPASA, despite its being listed within the judicial branch in **Figure 1-1**. Article I courts include the U.S. Court of Federal Claims, the U.S. Court of Military Appeals, the U.S. Court of Veterans Appeals, and the U.S. Tax Court.

[ii] 40 U.S.C. § 113 Exemptions

40 U.S.C. § 113 does not explicitly grant exemptions to the FPASA but provides that nothing "in this subtitle impairs or affects the authority" of 20 listed organizations whose transactions are totally or partially subject to its coverage. It is not clear whether this provision is intended to grant exemptions to the organizations listed or is merely supportive of exemption authority independently granted by some other statute. In addition, some of the exemptions have limited application.

[iii] Other Laws

41 U.S.C. § 113 has been interpreted to require that the statute relied upon for exemption contain "express terms" exempting the procurements from 41

U.S.C. § 3101 et seq. before the agency will be exempted. See *Andrus v. Glover Constr. Co.*, 446 U.S. 608 (1980), where the Court held that the Buy Indian Act, which authorizes the Secretary of the Interior to purchase "the products of Indian industry . . . in open market," does not authorize an exemption from the FPASA. The "express terms" exemption is apparently satisfied by 39 U.S.C. § 410(a), which states that "no Federal law dealing with public or Federal contracts . . . shall apply to the exercise of the powers of the Postal Service." The intent of Congress to exempt the Postal Service from the FPASA seems evident, even though the FPASA is not specifically mentioned. A clear exemption is contained at § 348 of Pub. L. No. 104-50, stating that after April 1, 1996, the Federal Aviation Administration will not be subject to a list of statutes including the FPASA, the OFPPA, 41 U.S.C. § 3101 et seq., and the Small Business Act, 15 U.S.C. § 631 et seq. See also the statutory language applicable to the Tennessee Valley Authority (TVA), 16 U.S.C. § 831h(b), and the Bonneville Power Administration (BPA), 16 U.S.C. § 832a(f). These statutes permit these organizations to enter into contracts "upon such terms and conditions and in such manner as [they] may deem necessary."

GAO has confirmed that the TVA, BPA, Postal Service, and others are indeed exempt from the FPASA. See, e.g., *NAC Int'l, Inc.*, Comp. Gen. Dec. B-310065, 2008 CPD ¶ 3; *International Line Bldrs.*, 67 Comp. Gen. 8 (B-227811), 87-2 CPD ¶ 345. But see *MFM Lamey Grp., LLC*, Comp. Gen. Dec. B-402377, 2010 CPD ¶ 81 (rejecting arguments that the Overseas Private Investment Corporation (OPIC) is immune from FPASA).

When a statute does contain the proper express terms exemption from the FPASA, courts will scrutinize the action taken under the statute to ensure that the statute is not being invoked in order to circumvent the FPASA provisions. See *Chem Serv., Inc. v. Environmental Monitoring Sys. Lab.*, 12 F.3d 1256 (3d Cir. 1993), where the court found that although the Federal Technology Transfer Act (FTTA) explicitly allowed research and development agreements without following the FPASA provisions, an agreement made under the FTTA that manifested the features of a traditional procurement contract had improperly bypassed the FPASA provisions.

[c] Revised Statutes 3709 and 3710

These basic procurement statutes originally applied to all government agencies. They were codified in 41 U.S.C. § 5 and § 8 prior to the 2011 codification of Title 41 and are now in 41 U.S.C. § 6101 and § 6103. They apply to procurement by the "Federal Government" when other statutes do not apply. Thus, unless otherwise excepted, they applied to procurement by all government organizations not within the executive branch. Exemptions from 41 U.S.C. § 5 did not necessarily exempt an agency from other procurement statutes. For example, the Buy American Act, 41 U.S.C. § 8302, provides that "[o]nly unmanufactured articles, materials, and supplies that have been mined or produced in the United States, and only manufactured articles, materials, and supplies that have been manufactured in the United States . . . shall be acquired for public use." (Prior to the 2011 codification, the Act included the phrase "notwithstanding any other provision of law".)

[d] Office of Federal Procurement Policy Act

The OFPPA, 41 U.S.C. § 1101 et seq., also applies to "executive agencies," which are defined in 41 U.S.C. § 133 as follows:

> [T]he term "executive agency" means—
>
> (A) an executive department specified in section 101 of title 5;
> (B) a military department specified in section 102 of title 5;
> (C) an independent establishment as defined in section 104(1) of title 5; and
> (D) a wholly owned Government corporation fully subject to chapter 91 of title 31.

The Act created the Office of Federal Procurement Policy (OFPP) in the Office of Management and Budget (OMB) and gives its Administrator broad powers to "provide overall direction of Governmentwide procurement policies, regulations, procedures, and forms for executive agencies," 41 U.S.C. § 1101(b)(1). It also contains a number of sections applicable to all "executive agencies," 41 U.S.C. § 1127 (limitations on compensation of contractor executives), § 1702 (requirement for "chief acquisition officers" in all but DoD), § 1704 (requirement to plan for and train the acquisition workforce), § 1705 (requirement for competition advocates), § 1708 (requirement for procurement notices), § 1709 (rules governing contracting out of agency work), § 1711 (value engineering requirement), § 1712 (requirement for record of procurements), §§ 1501-06 (establishment of cost accounting standards), §§ 1901-05 (simplified acquisition rules), § 1906 (laws inapplicable to commercial item procurements), § 1907 (laws inapplicable to commercial off-the-shelf item procurements), §§ 2101-07 (procurement integrity requirements), § 2301 (electronic commerce requirement), § 2308 (information technology procurement requirements), § 2309 (protection of constitutional rights of contractors), § 2310 (encouragement of performance-based service contracts), and § 2312 (establishing a Contingency Contracting Corps). These sections have been added to the statute periodically when Congress enacts a provision applicable to the entire executive branch without amending both the ASPA and the FPASA.

[2] Federal Acquisition Regulation System

Although Congress has not enacted a single statute covering all agencies, it has provided that a *single regulation* be promulgated in this area, 41 U.S.C. § 1121(b). This regulation is known as the Federal Acquisition Regulation

(FAR). It is written by the Defense Acquisition Regulations Council and the Civilian Agency Acquisition Council, FAR 1.201-1, and published under the auspices of the Secretary of Defense, the Administrator of National Aeronautics and Space, and the Administrator of General Services, 41 U.S.C. § 1303(a).

All of the major agencies with procurement functions issue supplementary regulations to implement the FAR. However, these FAR Supplements are required to be limited in scope in accordance with 41 U.S.C. § 1303(a)(2), as follows:

> Other regulations relating to procurement issued by an executive agency shall be limited to (A) regulations essential to implement Government-wide policies within the agency; and (B) additional policies and procedures required to satisfy the specific and unique needs of the agency.

The Administrator of the OFPP has the authority to rescind, revise, or deny promulgation of any regulation that does not meet these standards, 41 U.S.C. § 1303(a)(5). The Administrator also has the authority to issue regulations if the three designated agencies do not issue necessary regulations in a timely manner, 41 U.S.C. § 1121(d). However, these reserve powers have not been used, as the promulgation of the FAR has been achieved in a collegial manner.

The FAR and its many supplements are known as the "FAR system." These regulations are published in Title 48 of the Code of Federal Regulations and are updated periodically in the Federal Register.

§ 1.03 CONTRACTING POWERS

As a sovereign, the United States has inherent authority to contract. See *United States v. Tingey*, 30 U.S. 115 (1831), stating at 128:

> [W]e are of opinion that the United States have such a capacity to enter into contracts. It is in our opinion an incident to the general right of sovereignty; and the United States being a body politic, may, within the sphere of the constitutional powers confided to it, and through the instrumentality of the proper department to which those power are confided, enter into contracts not prohibited by law, and appropriate to the just exercise of those powers.

Statutes delegate power to the government agencies. In addition, they often contain requirements to be followed when contracts are used. Thus, statutes serve two purposes in the government contracting process. First, they are the principal means of authorizing and funding programs that are implemented, in whole or in part, by contracting with private parties. Second, they are used to place *limitations* on the way in which those contracting powers are exercised.

Statutes are supplemented by regulations that specify rules that must be followed in awarding contracts and that require the use of specified terms and conditions. When promulgated pursuant to statutory authority, regulations take on the status of law. Together, statutes and regulations are of supreme importance because the government can be contractually bound only through the proper exercise of validly conferred powers.

However, statutes and regulations are not self-enforcing. Control over the day-to-day activities of a government agency is usually vested in the head of the agency, who normally has great discretion in making contracts to carry out government programs. In most cases, these delegated powers are performed properly. However, differences of opinion often arise in interpreting statutes and regulations that may result in an improper use of power. In addition, whether by inadvertence or design, there are instances where an agency's contracting activity violates statutory or regulatory authority. Congress uses a number of oversight techniques to give reasonable assurance that the contracting powers are properly exercised.

This section discusses the statutory mechanisms that Congress uses to delegate powers and to provide funding to the government agencies; the degree of control that various statutes and regulations have over the contracting process; and the techniques used to oversee government agencies in the contracting process.

[A] Congressional Delegation of Power

The primary means that Congress uses to delegate power to the executive branch is the enactment of laws establishing new programs and the appropriation of funds to pay for these programs. This activity occurs each year in the "budget and appropriations" process of the federal government. This process is controlled by the Congressional Budget and Impoundment Control Act of 1974, 2 U.S.C. § 621 et seq., and various sections of Title 31. See also the Government Accountability Office, *Principles of Federal Appropriations Law*, also known as the "GAO Redbook." The third edition with annual updates and some chapters of the fourth edition are available at *https://www.gao.gov/legal/appropriations-law-decisions/red-book*.

This subsection first considers the legal requirements for congressional appropriations before contracts can be awarded. It then reviews the budget and appropriations process which is the primary means of conferring contracting power. Finally, it summarizes the manner that appropriations law impacts the contracting process.

[1] Need for Congressional Appropriation

Congress exerts authority over the contracting process through the use of its constitutional powers. Article 1, Section 9, Clause 7, of the Constitution provides that "[n]o money shall be drawn from the Treasury, but in Consequence of Appropriations made by Law." This provision of the Constitution prohibits any *payments* by agencies unless funds have been approved by Congress, *Cincinnati Soap Co v. United States*, 301 U.S. 308, 321 (1937) ("It means simply that no money can be paid out of the Treasury unless it has been appropriated by an act of Congress."). Congress has extended this control mechanism by restricting government agencies from *obligating funds* unless there is existing congressional authority. This proposition is embodied in the Anti-Deficiency Act, 31 U.S.C. § 1341(a), which states:

> (1) An officer or employee of the United States Government or of the District of Columbia government may not—
>
> (A) make or authorize an expenditure or obligation exceeding an amount available in an appropriation or fund for the expenditure or obligation; or
>
> (B) involve either government in a contract or obligation for the payment of money before an appropriation is made unless authorized by law.

In the contracting process the signing of a contract legally obligates the funds necessary to carry out the contract. Thus, government agencies cannot make *payments* under a contract or *enter into* a contract unless Congress has given them proper authority.

In order to obligate the government by contract, the agency must have received sufficient funds in an existing appropriations statute to cover the obligation, or there must be some other statute by which Congress specifically empowers an agency to make contracts without regard to the need for appropriations. The authority inherent in both types of statutes is called "budget authority." See 2 U.S.C. § 622(2).

The first, and most common, form of budget authority is an appropriation. Congress allows agencies to incur obligations and make payments for obligations through appropriations. They give agencies the power to enter into and pay for work under contracts. This type of budget authority will be discussed in more detail in subsequent sections.

"Borrowing authority," referred to at 2 U.S.C. § 622(2)(ii), can also apply to contracts. Borrowing authority allows government agencies to incur obligations and liquidate these obligations out of borrowed funds. Agencies with borrowing authority can enter into contracts and make payments with borrowed monies. See, for example, Comp. Gen. Dec. B-223857, 1987 WL 101593 (Feb. 27, 1987) (Commodity Credit Corporation violated the Anti-Deficiency Act because it had used all funds available from its borrowing authority but still had contractual obligations). Borrowing authority may consist of the authority to borrow from the Treasury, authority to borrow directly from the public, authority to borrow from the Federal Financing Bank, or a combination, *Principles of Federal Appropriations Law* 2-4 (4th ed. 2016). However, since direct appropriations provide more congressional control than borrowing authority, the Congressional Budget Act requires new borrowing authority to be limited to the extent or amounts provided in appropriations acts, 2 U.S.C. § 651(a).

"Contract authority," referred to at 2 U.S.C. § 622(2)(iii), is found in statutes authorizing contracts without regard to appropriations. See, for example, *People's Bank & Trust Co. v. United States*, 11 Cl. Ct. 554 (1987) (court found "contract authority" in applicable statutes and regulations governing FmHA); *New York Airways, Inc. v. United States*, 369 F.2d 743 (Ct. Cl. 1966) (although Congress did not grant appropriations, government was not relieved of contractual obligation because appropriations restrictions did not apply to 49 U.S.C. § 1376(c) giving contract authority). 31 U.S.C. § 1301(d) provides that for a law to be construed to authorize a contract for payment of money in excess of an appropriation, it must specifically state that such a contract may be made. Contract authority can be given in appropriations acts but is more frequently conferred in other legislation, *Principles of Federal Appropriations Law* 2-4 (4th ed. 2016). Like borrowing authority, 2 U.S.C. § 651(a) also restricts the use of new "contract authority" in future statutes by providing that it will be out of order for either house to consider any bill, resolution, conference report, or amendment that provides "new spending authority" beyond the amount of the appropriations for that fiscal year.

Another form of budget authority, which is characterized as "offsetting receipts and collections" in 2 U.S.C. § 622(2)(iv), is a revolving fund. Revolving funds allow government corporations and offices to generate income as well as expend money. Agencies are allowed to conduct public or intragovernmental transactions which generate income. Specific statutory authority allows these agencies to deposit the income in an appropriation or fund account. The agency is then permitted to make use of such income to finance continued operations. See *Principles of Federal Appropriations Law* 2-5 (4th ed. 2016) (calling them "offsetting collections"). For an example of a revolving fund, see 31 U.S.C. § 5142, which establishes such a fund for the Bureau of Engraving and Printing.

[2] Budget and Appropriations Process

The budget and appropriations process is the involved means that the federal government uses to arrive at the annual budget that supports its varied programs. The "budget and appropriations" process has three phases: the budget formulation phase, the authorization phase, and the appropriations phase. These phases are staggered to ensure that appropriation acts are passed before the beginning of the fiscal year on October 1, but Congress has infrequently adhered to this schedule.

[a] Budget Formulation Phase

The budgetary phase of the process begins with the administrative process of budget preparation and review. Agencies gather information through reviews of current operations, program objectives, and future plans. This, along with information from other federal departments, is used to prepare the President's budget, which must be submitted on or before the first Monday in February for the fiscal year starting the following October 1. See 2 U.S.C. § 631.

Upon receipt of the President's budget, the Budget Committees of the House of Representatives and the Senate begin work on a budget resolution which packages the entire federal budget for the following year. By February 15, the Congressional Budget Office must submit a budget report to the Budget Committees, and within 10 days of that date all other congressional committees with oversight over agency programs are required to submit their views and estimates to the Budget Committees. Then the Senate Budget Committee reports a concurrent resolution on the budget, and by April 15, Congress is required to complete action on the concurrent resolution. After the concurrent resolution is passed, annual authorization and appropriation bills can be considered, 2 U.S.C. § 631. The concurrent resolution establishes "target ceilings" for expenditures which are used to evaluate individual appropriations legislation, *Principles of Federal Appropriations Law* 2-14 (4th ed. 2016).

[b] Authorization of Appropriations

The next phase in the process is the authorization of appropriations. Before an appropriations statute is passed, there usually must be some separate statute authorizing the program or activity that is the subject of the appropriation. Although there is no general statutory provision to this effect, House of Representatives Rule XXI(2) prohibits the reporting out of general appropriations unless the proposed expenditures were "previously authorized by law." The Senate has similar rules, *Principles of Federal Appropriations Law* 2-19 (4th ed. 2016). In addition, Congress has required annual authorizations for some agencies. See, for example 42 U.S.C. § 7270 (DOE); 10 U.S.C. § 114 (DoD); and 42 U.S.C. § 2460 (NASA). GAO has described authorizations in *Principles of Federal Appropriations Law* (4th ed. 2016), starting at 2-56:

> Authorizations take many different forms, depending in part on whether they are contained in the organic legislation [of an agency] or are separate. Authorizations contained in organic legislation may be "definite" (setting dollar limitations either in the aggregate or for specific fiscal years) or "indefinite" (authorizing "such sums as may be necessary to carry out the provisions of this act"). An indefinite authorization serves little purpose other than to comply with House Rule XXI. Appropriation authorizations enacted as separate legislation resemble appropriations acts in structure, for example, the annual Department of Defense Authorization Acts.

Under this description, the authorization for an appropriation may be the organic act that established the agency, a separate statute establishing a particular program, or the annual authorization statutes required for some agencies. The purpose of these authorizations is to ensure that the legislative committees with oversight of specific agencies retain control over the programs that these agencies undertake.

Even if authorization statutes specify definite amounts that may not be exceeded, they are not binding on Congress in passing an appropriations act. Congress can appropriate a greater amount, 36 Comp. Gen. 240 (B-128902) (1956), or a lesser amount, 53 Comp. Gen. 695 (B-180517) (1974). When the amount appropriated is greater than that authorized, the intent to fund the program at the higher level must be clear, 64 Comp. Gen. 282 (B-214172) (1985) (table in appropriations conference report showing higher amounts than authorization not clear evidence that lump-sum appropriation exceeded authorization levels).

Although the Anti-Deficiency Act prohibits obligation of funds in excess of the amount "*available in an appropriation*," GAO has ruled that it is also a violation of the Act to obligate funds in excess of an authorization which has not clearly been increased by an appropriation, 64 Comp. Gen. 282 (B-214172) (1985) (relying on 60 Comp. Gen. 440 (B-201260) (1980)). This holding was based on the reasoning that funds exceeding the authorization were not "available" for obligation.

Annual authorization statutes usually contain a number of provisions governing the procurement process. See, for example, Title VIII of the various National Defense Authorization Acts.

[c] Appropriations Statutes

The final stage of the process is the passage of the annual appropriations statutes. In order to ensure that funds are available to operate the government in the fiscal year beginning on October 1, all appropriations acts should be enacted by September 30. There are a number of appropriation statutes, divided amongst the various departments and agencies. In most years, Congress has been unable to meet the statutory requirements for carrying out the appropriations process by the beginning of the fiscal year. In that case, appropriations called "continuing resolutions" are passed to permit agencies to continue their operations at the same level of funding as a previous fiscal year (frequently with explicit additional provisions).

Most agencies have separate appropriations for functions such as operation and maintenance, procurement, construction, and research and development. Such appropriations can be, and sometimes are, further divided so that specific amounts are allocated to particular programs, such as the construction of individual buildings, or to separate subcomponents of an agency, such as a bureau, command, or administration within a department.

Each of these statutes may contain numerous special sections, called "riders," directing certain contractual actions or limiting the use of the appropriation for specified purposes.

[3] Appropriations Law as It Affects the Contracting Process

The same means by which Congress delegates power to the executive branch—appropriations and authorizations—also enables Congress to limit that power. Thus, appropriations law is an important part of the contracting process. This subsection first reviews the rules determining the scope of each appropriation. It then considers the requirements that contracts be made only for purposes covered by an appropriation. Finally, it addresses the rule that contracts may be entered into only during the time that the appropriation is available for obligation.

[a] Scope of Appropriations

Appropriations are made for *designated purposes* during *specified fiscal years.* Thus, in entering into a contract, an agency must determine if an appropriation covers the activity being procured and if the appropriated funds may be used at the time the contract is formed. This determination is based on an analysis of the statute making funds available to the agency. For a law to be construed as an appropriation, 31 U.S.C. § 1301(d) requires that "the law specifically states that an appropriation is made." See *Principles of Federal Appropriations Law* (4th ed. 2016), stating at 2-23:

> Thus, the rule is that the making of an appropriation must be expressly stated. An appropriation cannot be inferred or made by implication. . . . Through the making of an appropriation must be expressly stated, a statute need not use the word "appropriation." If the statute contains a specific direction to pay and a designation of the funds to be used, such as a direction to make a specified payment or class of payments, "out of any money in the Treasury not otherwise appropriated," then this amounts to an appropriation.

Appropriations acts are not substantive law. Thus, the mere appropriation of money for a program does not mean that other laws applicable to the program may be ignored. In *Tennessee Valley Auth. v. Hill*, 437 U.S. 153 (1978), the Court ruled that the unspecified inclusion of funds to construct a dam did not constitute a repeal by implication of the Endangered Species Act, which had previously been held by the Supreme Court to prohibit construction of the dam. See *Mori Assocs., Inc. v. United States*, 102 Fed. Cl. 503 (2011) (discussing this "controversial" decision).

[b] Purpose of Appropriations

31 U.S.C. § 1301(a) states that "[a]ppropriations shall be applied only to the objects for which the appropriations were made except as otherwise provided by law." In other words, appropriations may be used only for the purpose for which they were appropriated. Thus, Congress has limited the government agencies'

expenditure of appropriated funds by denying the agencies the power to use funds for a purpose beyond that which the appropriations act allows. Agencies have considerable discretion in incurring all expenses reasonably necessary to carry out the purpose of the appropriation, 73 Comp. Gen. 171 (B-252467) (1994), but they are not authorized to use appropriated funds (1) for purposes that do not bear a logical relationship to the appropriation, (2) for purposes that are prohibited by law, or (3) from a general appropriation for an item that is specifically covered in another appropriation, Comp. Gen. Dec. B-230304, 1988 WL 227283. See also 73 Comp. Gen. 44 (B-254666) (1993); 67 Comp. Gen. 276 (B-226132) (1988).

The determination of the purposes covered by an appropriation is largely a question of determining the intent of Congress in making the appropriation. See *LTV Aerospace Corp.*, 55 Comp. Gen. 307 (B-183851), 75-2 CPD ¶ 203 (considering whether statements from the Congressional Conference Report on an appropriations act indicating that certain funds could only be used for a specified purpose imposed a legal restriction on the use of such funds); *Forest Serv.*, Comp. Gen. Dec. B-231711, 1989 WL 240615 (congressional committee's recommendation that a specific dollar amount be used for liquidating the debt of prior fiscal year was not binding because Congress did not impose the requirement in the appropriations act); and *Newport News Shipbuilding & Dry Dock Co.*, 55 Comp. Gen. 812 (B-184830), 76-1 CPD ¶ 136 (specific dollar amount for one ship in an appropriations committee report did not limit the amount the procuring agency could obligate for that ship out of an appropriation covering two ships).

Executive agencies have a measure of flexibility so that they can make adjustments for unforeseen developments or changed circumstances. Congress grants this flexibility by appropriating funds in lump-sum amounts. Such an appropriation is a *general purpose appropriation*—one appropriation made for a group of objects necessary for the performance of a broad function. The great majority of appropriations presently used for the procurement of supplies, services, research and development, ships, aircraft, and missiles are general purpose appropriations. Appropriations are also made for the accomplishment of a single object. Such appropriations are *specific purpose appropriations.*

Congress may stipulate, by statute, that certain types of appropriations only be authorized via specific purpose appropriations. For example, 41 U.S.C. § 6303, states:

> A contract to erect, repair, or furnish a public building, or to make any public improvement, shall not be made on terms requiring the Federal Government to pay more than the amount specifically appropriated for the activity covered by the contract.

This statute has been interpreted as imposing a special rule prohibiting the construction of public buildings or improvements unless appropriations specifically provide for the item, 38 Comp. Gen. 758 (B-138598) (1959) (appropriation for "necessary expenses" not broad enough to include the cost of construction for building alterations nor definite enough to comply with 41 U.S.C. § 6303 (previously § 12) requiring specific authorization for such work). In referring to this statute, GAO has stated that expenditures for such projects must "be authorized by specific appropriations," 42 Comp. Gen. 212 (B-146728) (1962). The use of the words "specific appropriations" is misleading, however, since the statute appears to require no more than a reference in an appropriations act or its legislative history that indicates that congressional authority for a project has, in fact, been granted. For example, in 38 Comp. Gen. 392 (B-137094) (1958), GAO denied a request to construct a special building for hydrostatic testing, painting, and maintaining helium tank cars under an appropriation designated for "acquiring and developing helium properties." In the absence of any legislative history establishing a congressional intent to attribute a broadened meaning to those general terms, GAO concluded that the necessary express statutory authority was lacking. With respect to the definitions of the terms "public building" and "public improvement," GAO has uniformly held that any structure in the form of a building not clearly of a temporary character qualifies as a public building or public improvement, 42 Comp. Gen. 212 (B-146728) (1962).

"Riders" on appropriations acts, whether for general or specific purpose, frequently impose explicit statutory restrictions that are binding on the agency. See Comp. Gen. Dec. B-300192, 2002 WL 31521299 (§ 117 of 2003 Continuing Resolution prohibits implementing the Office of Management and Budget Memorandum M-02-07calling for private sector printing, and no funds are available to pay for the printing of the President's Budget other than through the Government Printing Office). However, since annual appropriations acts are, by their nature, nonpermanent legislation, there is a presumption that legislative riders in annual appropriations are effective only for that fiscal year, *Building & Constr. Trades Dep't, AFL-CIO v. Martin*, 961 F.2d 269 (D.C. Cir.), *cert. denied*, 506 U.S. 915 (1992); 70 Comp. Gen. 351 (B-242142) (1991). A provision in an appropriations act may not be construed as permanent legislation unless the language or nature of the provision expresses a clear intent of Congress to make the provision permanent. See *United States v. Vulte*, 233 U.S. 509 (1914); *Atlantic Fish Spotters Ass'n v. Evans*, 321 F.3d 220 (1st Cir. 2003); Comp. Gen. Dec. B-230110, 1988 WL 227660, the principal means of establishing permanence is to include "words of futurity" in the provision of the appropriations act. Comp. Gen. Dec. B-323357, 2012 WL 2856820; *Cella v. United States*, 208 F.2d 783 (7th Cir. 1953) ("The use of the word 'hereafter' by Congress as a method of making legislation permanent is a well-known practice."). Other indications of permanence are if the provision is general in nature and bears no relation to the objects of the appropriations acts or if the provision would be meaningless if it were not interpreted to be a permanent legislation, 65 Comp. Gen. 588 (B-222097) (1986). See *Principles of Federal Appropriations Law*, Chapter 3 (4th ed. 2016) for extensive analysis of this issue.

31 U.S.C. § 1532 also ensures that appropriations are only used for the purposes covered by the appropriations act. This statute specifically prohibits transfer between appropriations unless specifically authorized by statute. See also 70 Comp. Gen. 592 (B-238024) (1991); 33 Comp. Gen. 216 (B-117393) (1953). However, the shifting of funds between objects in a lump-sum appropriation is not a transfer but a *reprogramming*. Reprogramming is a nonstatutory accommodation between government agencies and legislative committees. See *Principles of Federal Appropriations Law* 2-38 (4th ed. 2016). However, reprogramming agreements with Congress do not have the force and effect of law, *Blackhawk Heating & Plumbing Co. v. United States*, 622 F.2d 539 (Ct. Cl. 1980); *A.R.F. Prod., Inc.*, 56 Comp. Gen. 201 (B-186248), 76-2 CPD ¶ 541, and failure to follow reprogramming procedures will not justify cancellation of a contract entered into as a result of the shifting of funds, *LTV Aerospace Corp.*, 55 Comp. Gen. 307 (B-183851), 75-2 CPD ¶ 203. Furthermore, the denial of approval for reprogramming from one program element to another does not prohibit the agency from using other funds within the same program element, 65 Comp. Gen. 360 (B-220113) (1986).

[c] Obligation of Appropriations

Congress controls the expenditure of public funds by restricting the time in which appropriations may be used to incur *obligations*. For procurement transactions, 31 U.S.C. § 1501(a) provides that "[a]n amount shall be recorded as an obligation of the United States Government only when supported by documentary evidence." This would normally require a properly executed, written contractual document. However, the obligation arises when the government incurs a liability even though the documentary evidence is not yet available to support its recordation, 38 Comp. Gen. 81 (B-114876) (1958); Comp. Gen. Dec. B-317139, 2009 CPD ¶ 158. Thus, if the government acts in a way that legally binds it under contract law concepts, an obligation will have occurred.

In addition to the Anti-Deficiency Act preclusion of obligations not supported by appropriations or contract authority, 31 U.S.C. § 1517 requires an *apportionment* before an appropriation may be obligated. An apportionment is a distribution of appropriated funds made by the President through the OMB to executive agencies. Apportionments are made by time periods, usually quarters, and by activities to maintain control over the rate of obligation and expenditure of funds.

[i] Time for Obligation

The time when obligations may be made depends upon the type of appropriation. Basically, three types of appropriations are used. These are *annual appropriations*, *multiple-year appropriations*, and *no-year appropriations*. If an obligation is properly incurred during the period of availability of the appropriated funds, the appropriation will be available for *expenditure* to pay for the incurred obligation during the five subsequent fiscal years, 31 U.S.C. § 1552. Thereafter, the appropriation is canceled and the money is no longer available for expenditure—even if it was properly obligated before such cancellation, *United States Capitol Police—Advances to Volpe Center Working Capital Fund*, Comp. Gen. Dec. B-319349, 2010 WL 2310440. The result of this rule is that a contractor may not be paid from funds properly obligated to its contract after the five-year period has expired.

Annual appropriations may be obligated only in the specified fiscal year. Under an annual appropriation, if no obligation is made during the year for which the money was appropriated, the appropriation is said to "expire" and is no longer available for obligation. However, as discussed below, it will still be available to fund some additional contractual activities under contracts that were entered into during the fiscal year. Multiple-year appropriations are governed by the same principles except that they are available for obligation for a specified number of years rather than a single year. No-year appropriations are available for obligation until completely obligated and are not limited by time.

[ii] Bona Fide Needs Rule

Another limitation on obligation of annual appropriations is the "bona fide needs" rule, based on 31 U.S.C. § 1502(a), which states:

> The balance of an appropriation or fund limited for obligation to a definite period is available only for payment of expenses properly incurred during the period of availability or to complete contracts properly made within that period of availability and obligated consistent with section 1501 of this title. However, the appropriation or fund is not available for expenditure for a period beyond the period otherwise authorized by law.

Thus, annual funds, as well as multiple-year funds, may be used only to fulfill the *bona fide needs* of the fiscal year(s) for which the funds were appropriated. Agencies cannot obligate an annual appropriation for the needs of prior or subsequent years, Comp. Gen. Dec. B-229873, 1988 WL 228272; Comp. Gen. Dec. B-226801, 1988 WL 227859. Neither can they obligate multiple-year funds for the needs of subsequent fiscal years, Comp. Gen. Dec. B-235678, 1990 WL 278336; 68 Comp. Gen. 170 (B-232024) (1989); 55 Comp. Gen. 768 (B-132900) (1976).

A need may arise and be contracted for in one fiscal year but deliveries may not occur until the following or subsequent fiscal years because of necessary lead time. Thus, articles procured with annual funds do not have to be delivered or used in that fiscal year, so long as the need for the articles arose during the fiscal year, *U.S. Geological Survey*, Comp. Gen. Dec. B-226198, 1987 WL 102609. In addition, annual funds may be used to replenish stock for future use, 73 Comp. Gen. 259 (B-251706) (1994). However, if too long a period exists between contract award and delivery, especially for items that will be available on the open market at the time needed for use, the contract will not be considered as having fulfilled the needs of the fiscal year for which the funds were appropriated, 38 Comp. Gen. 628 (B-138574) (1959) (excessively long period to satisfy need where the units were ordered in April 1958 but would not be delivered until the later part of fiscal year 1960). But see 70 Comp. Gen. 296 (B-238940) (1991), where the agency was permitted to charge fiscal year 1989 appropriations for the cost of a training course scheduled to begin the first day of fiscal year 1990 because the two-week period between procurement and performance was not excessive.

It is also a violation of the bona fide needs rule to transfer funds (called "parking") to another agency for use in a subsequent fiscal year without a clear definition of the work to be obtained by the other agency, *Expired Funds and Interagency Agreements between GovWorks and the Dep't of Defense*, Comp. Gen. Dec. B-308944, 2007 CPD ¶ 157. See Chapter 11 for detailed coverage of the rules governing parking of funds.

Services that extend beyond the fiscal year may only be procured with annual funds to the extent they are nonseverable. GAO defined severable and nonseverable services in 73 Comp. Gen. 77 (B-240264), stating that services are severable if they can be divided into components that independently meet a separate need of the government. If the services constitute a specific, entire job with a defined end result that cannot be feasibly subdivided for separate performance, then they are nonseverable. See *Principles of Federal Appropriations Law* (3d ed. 2004) 5-23 through 5-28 for extensive analysis of the difference between severable and nonseverable services.

Services that are nonseverable should be charged to the year when the need for the services was identified.and the contract awarded, even though performance may extend beyond the fiscal year, 71 Comp. Gen. 428 (B-241415) (1992) (expert and consulting services contract may not be incrementally funded but must be funded from appropriation in year of contract award); 73 Comp. Gen. 77 (B-240264) (1994) (research work orders may not be incrementally funded but must be charged to appropriation for year of issuance of order). See also 60 Comp. Gen. 452 (B-174226) (1981); 50 Comp. Gen. 589 (B-171457) (1971). However, if the services are severable and continuous in nature, they must be charged to the appropriation current when the services are rendered, *Acumenics Research & Tech., Inc.*, Comp. Gen. Dec. B-224702, 87-2 CPD ¶ 128; 60 Comp. Gen. 219 (B-198574) (1981). When the agency has a multiple year appropriation, severable services can be procured for the years covered by that appropriation, *Severable Service Contracts*, Comp. Gen. Dec. B-317636, 2009 CPD ¶ 89.

If a bona fide need is identified in one year but the agency chooses not to satisfy the need in that year, it will be treated as a bona fide need of the year when the obligation was incurred. GAO has called this the "continuing need rule," Comp. Gen. Dec. B-207433, 83-2 CPD ¶ 401 (1983). See *Principles of Federal Appropriations Law* (3d ed. 2004) at 5-20.

The bona fide needs rule applies to all types of procurement in which Congress has limited the period of availability of funds. See 64 Comp. Gen. 163

(B-215825), where GAO applied it to prohibit procurement of sixth and seventh year needs on a multiyear program Congress had authorized for five years. However, it has been held not to apply to no-year appropriations, 43 Comp. Gen. 657 (B-152766), 1964 CPD ¶ 10. See 67 Comp. Gen. 553 (B-208637.2) (1988); and Comp. Gen. Dec. B-226922, 1987 WL 102387. In addition, to facilitate the procurement of severable services, Congress has created statutory exceptions to the bona fide needs rule that authorize contracts covering periods that do not correspond to the fiscal year. For example, DoD has authority to contract for certain types of services for 12-month periods beginning at any time during the fiscal year and to charge the appropriation current when the contract is made for the full 12 months of services, 10 U.S.C. § 3133 (formerly § 2410a). See *Funding of Maintenance Contract Extending Beyond Fiscal Year*, Comp. Gen. Dec. B-259274, 96-1 CPD ¶ 247.

[iii] Contract Modifications

When performance of contracts continues beyond the fiscal year of an annual or multiple-year appropriation, the question arises as to which fiscal year's appropriation is chargeable for changes and modifications. Generally, contract modifications that are found to be within the scope of the original contract are considered bona fide needs of the fiscal year when the original contract was made. Thus, the funds used on the original contract have been properly used to fund changes issued under the Changes clause, 23 Comp. Gen. 943 (B-41903) (1944), and price adjustments under an Economic Price Adjustment, Price Redetermination or Incentive Price Revision clause, 34 Comp. Gen. 418 (B-121982) (1955). This rule is premised on the theory that these clauses do not create new liabilities but simply make existing ones certain.

Modifications that are not within the scope of such clauses must use appropriations current at the time of the modification, Comp. Gen. Dec. B-257617, 1995 WL 231627 (funds available from downward price adjustment could not be used in subsequent fiscal year to buy additional quantities on indefinite-quantity contract); Comp. Gen. Dec. B-207433, 83-2 CPD ¶ 401 (funds available from downward price reduction could not be used in subsequent fiscal year to buy additional quantities even though their need had been identified in year contract was issued); 44 Comp. Gen. 399 (B-155876), 1965 CPD ¶ 4 (appropriation for year of contract award could not be used to fund change order to use better data to improve the quality of a completed study); 25 Comp. Gen. 332 (B-50425) (1945) (appropriation for year of contract award could not be used to fund change order issued after contract was completed because contractor was not required to perform such work).

In some cases, modifications arguably within the scope of the contract are not considered bona fide needs of the year in which the original agreement was made, and any price adjustments arising out of these modifications must be charged to a later year's appropriation, 59 Comp. Gen. 518 (B-195732) (1980). Letter contracts and contracts containing "limitation of cost" clauses are examples in which price adjustments must be charged to the later-year appropriations. See *Financial Crimes Enforcement Network—Obligations Under a Cost-Reimbursement, Nonseverable Services Contract*, Comp. Gen. Dec. B-317139, 2009 CPD ¶ 158 (discretionary cost increases in cost-reimbursement contracts that exceed contractually stipulated ceilings set forth in a Limitation of Cost clause must be treated as a bona fide need of the year when the overrun is funded); *Environmental Protection Agency*, 61 Comp. Gen. 609 (B-195732), 82-2 CPD ¶ 491 (allowing overruns to be funded from either the original appropriation or the current appropriation).

The same reasoning was used for letter contract conversions, *Obligating Letter Contracts*, Comp. Gen. Dec. B-197274, 84-1 CPD ¶ 90. Settlement of claims not related to contracts must be funded out of current year funds, *National Endowment of the Arts—Dep't of Justice—Appropriations Availability—Payment of Settlement*, Comp. Gen. Dec. B-255772, 1995 WL 500311. Similarly, settlement of contract claims at a board or court must be funded out of current year funds, on the basis that such claims give rise to a new liability, *Bureau of Land Management —Reimbursement of Contract Disputes Act Payments*, 63 Comp. Gen. 308 (B-211229) (1984). Compare *National Science Found.—Potential Antideficiency Act Violation by the National Science Board Office*, Comp. Gen. Dec. B-317413, 2009 CPD ¶ 94 (agreement by a contracting officer to give an equitable adjustment to cover an unauthorized commitment of an agency official was a new liability that had to be funded from current year funds). It is also improper to use current-year funds to finance a contract that has been awarded using prior year funds in violation of the Anti-Deficiency Act, 55 Comp. Gen. 768 (B-132900) (1976).

[iv] Reprocurement Contracts

If a contract is terminated for default, the amount of a reprocurement contract that is timely issued should be charged to the appropriation that was used for the original contract, 2 Comp. Gen. 130, 1922 WL 609; 34 Comp. Gen. 239 (B-121248) (1954). *Principles of Federal Appropriations Law* 5-28-32 (3d ed. 2004) calls such contracts "replacement contracts." This rule will not apply if the default termination is not issued in a timely manner, 32 Comp. Gen. 565 (B-114334) (1965) (contract not terminated until three and one-half years after award), or if the reprocurement is not conducted in a timely fashion, 60 Comp. Gen. 591 (B-198074), 81-2 CPD ¶ 33 (1981). In Comp. Gen. Dec. B-160834, 1967 WL 2019, GAO stated that this rule would not apply if the work on the reprocurement contract differed from the work on the original contract, but permitted use of the appropriations current at the time of the original contract where the reprocurement contract was for different vehicles but they served the same purpose and were the vehicles currently available in the open market.

The reprocurement contract rule has also been applied to contracts issued after a termination for convenience. See, for example, 34 Comp. Gen. 239 (B-121248) (1954) permitting use of the appropriation used for the original contract when that contract was terminated for default and subsequently converted to a termination for convenience by the agency. After ruling in 60 Comp. Gen. 591 (B-198074) (1981) that the reprocurement contract rule did not apply to convenience terminations, GAO reversed that position in *Funding of Replacement Contracts*, 68 Comp. Gen. 158 (B-232616), 88-2 CPD ¶ 602, and held that the rule did apply to contracts that were awarded after the original contract was terminated for convenience as the result of a successful protest. In *Navy, Replacement Contract*, 70 Comp. Gen. 230 (B-238548), 91-1 CPD ¶ 117, GAO extended the rule to terminations for convenience when the agency determined, on its own accord, that the original award had been improperly made. See *Herman Miller, Inc.*, 70 Comp. Gen. 287 (B-241582), 91-1 CPD ¶ 184, holding that this rule would only apply if the agency had made the original award "in good faith." See also 55 Comp. Gen. 1351 (B-185405) (1976) where the replacement contract rule was applied when an agency awarded a contract on the condition that the contractor was a small business and subsequently canceled the contract because the condition had not been fulfilled. This rule was extended to grant awards in *Dep't of Labor-Replacement Grants*, Comp. Gen. Dec. B-322628, 2012 WL 3143851.

[v] Contingent or Indefinite Liabilities

Where the government's liability is not definite in amount, there is a question as to the proper amount to be obligated. GAO has stated that when an agency signs a contract, it must obligate its "maximum potential liability" at that time, Comp. Gen. Dec. B-300480.2, June 6, 2003, *Unpub.* See, however, 34 Comp. Gen. 418 (B-121982) (1955) permitting a substantial amount of flexibility in determining the amount to be recorded as obligations for contracts involving liabilities that are indefinite in amount. In that decision, GAO agreed with a proposed DoD directive establishing the following policy with respect to obligations for various types of contracts that were subject to price redetermination or revision:

Type of Contract	Obligation Amount
Fixed-price contracts with economic price adjustment	Original fixed price
Price redeterminable contract	Original fixed price
Incentive contract	Target or billing price
Variations in quantity contracts	Price of quantity specified
Letter contracts	Specified maximum liability

GAO has stipulated, however, that to safeguard against the possibility of violating the Anti-Deficiency Act, the agency should administratively reserve sufficient funds to cover at least the excess of estimated increases over decreases of all such contracts. Thereafter, the amount recorded as the original obligation was required to be increased or decreased to reflect price revisions at the time such revisions were made. See also 55 Comp. Gen. 812 (B-184830) 76-1 CPD ¶ 136. In such cases, an administrative reserve, called a "commitment," may be made of the estimated amount of liability. See DoD 7000.14-R, *Dep't of Defense Financial Mgmt. Regulations*, Vol. 3, Chap. 8 (Feb. 2016). There are no uniform procedures governing the use of commitments. The decision to commit funds is made on a contract-by-contract basis depending on the likelihood of an under-obligation of funds, the amount of money available in the appropriation, and the need for flexibility in administering the appropriation.

When the government's liability under a contract is contingent on some future event that is not certain to occur, there is considerable controversy as to the proper treatment. In 37 Comp. Gen. 691 (B-114876) (1958), GAO ruled that claims made under the Changed Conditions clauses of several excavation contracts that were denied by the contracting officer did not require obligation of funds because they were contingent liabilities. At the same time GAO agreed with the agency that amounts to cover these contingent liabilities should be administratively reserved. However, GAO has stated that, absent specific statutory authority, indemnity provisions that subject the United States to contingent and undetermined liabilities and contain no limitations contravene the Anti-Deficiency Act, 62 Comp. Gen. 361 (B-201072), 83-1 CPD ¶ 501. In response to this decision the standard Insurance—Liability to Third Persons clause in FAR 52.228-7, which makes the government liable for claims of third parties not compensated by the contractor's insurance, was amended to include the following paragraph:

> (d) The Government's liability under paragraph (c) of this clause is subject to the availability of appropriated funds at the time a contingency occurs. Nothing in this contract shall be construed as implying that the Congress will, at a later date, appropriate funds sufficient to meet deficiencies.

The last sentence of this provision was included to overcome criticisms that indemnity provisions may create "coercive deficiencies." See *Project Stormfury*, 59 Comp. Gen. 369 (B-198206) (1980), stating that an agreement that is solely contingent on Congress passing an appropriation for its fulfillment may not violate the letter of the Act but violates its spirit; it could be considered a coercive deficiency in that Congress has little choice in such a situation.

GAO has continued to object to "open-ended indemnification agreements." See Comp. Gen Dec. B-321387, 2011 WL 1178327; Comp. Gen. Dec. B-303692, 2004 WL 3108400. See also *E.I. DuPont de Nemours & Co. v. United States*, 54 Fed. Cl. 361 (2002); and *Union Pacific Railroad Corp. v. United States*, 52 Fed. Cl. 730 (2002), refusing to enforce indemnification clauses because they violated the Anti-Deficiency Act. The decision in *DuPont* was reversed on the grounds that the Contract Settlement Act of 1944, 41 U.S.C. § 101 et seq., gave contract authority under the Anti-Deficiency Act to make agreements in excess of appropriations and the government had used that authority when it entered into a termination settlement at the end of the Second World War, *E.I. DuPont de Nemours & Co. v. United States*, 365 F.3d 1367 (Fed. Cir. 2004). See also *Shell Oil Co. v. United States*, 751 F.3d 1282 (Fed. Cir. 2014), discussing the same issue and agreeing with the basic proposition that indemnification clauses were subject to the Act. See also *Hercules, Inc. v. United States*, 516 U.S. 417 (1996), recognizing GAO's view on indemnification clauses.

Even if the amount is determinable, a clause subjecting the government to a contingent liability could violate the statute. See *Federal Data Corp.*, 60 Comp. Gen. 584 (B-194709), 81-2 CPD ¶28, where the agency was found to have violated the Anti-Deficiency Act by obligating only the rental payments but agreeing to be liable for the full price of the item in case of loss.

The government may possess statutory authority, which is the equivalent of contract authority, to include indemnification agreements in certain instances. For example, 10 U.S.C. § 3861 (formerly § 2354) permits indemnification for research and development activity, and the Price-Anderson Act, 42 U.S.C. § 2210, covers indemnification for nuclear risks. In addition, Exec. Order 11610, 36 Fed. Reg. 13755 (1971), uses Pub. L. No. 85-804 to permit heads of specified agencies to indemnify contractors from risks arising from unusually hazardous or nuclear activity.

[B] Control and Oversight of Procurement

Each of the three branches of the federal government—the Legislature, the Executive, and the Judiciary—plays an important role in controlling and overseeing the procurement system. Congress primarily acts by formal legislation, but also by informal means of influence. The Executive branch primarily governs procurement officials by promulgating formal regulations, but also contributes significant amounts of informal guidance. The Judiciary renders decisions to ensure that agencies comply with the statutes and regulations that bind them, and in doing so often plays the important role of interpreting those statutes and regulations. The legislative and executive branches have also developed means of overseeing agency compliance with procurement rules. The following material discusses the proper roles of the executive, legislative, and judicial branches with respect to procurement and considers the major techniques used to control and oversee the process.

[1] Executive Branch

The primary method of control of procurement in the executive branch is through the promulgation of regulations and informal guidance. The major executive branch oversight of procurement is conducted by Inspectors General.

[a] Regulations

Rules affecting contracting are promulgated in a number of different types of regulations. Executive Orders, issued by the President, OMB Circulars, and OFPP Policy Letters deal with matters having broad application throughout the executive branch. These regulations may be published to implement statutes or may be based upon executive branch policies. Another type of regulation affecting procurement is issued by an agency with oversight of a specific government program or policy. For example, the Department of Labor has issued regulations in Volume 29 of the Code of Federal Regulations under the Davis-Bacon Act, 40 U.S.C. § 276(a) (29 C.F.R. Part 5), and the Service Contract Act, 41 U.S.C. §§ 6701-07 (29 C.F.R. Part 4).

The most important regulations governing procurement are the regulations in the FAR system, discussed earlier. When these regulations use the term "must" or "shall," they are binding on contracting agencies, FAR 2.101. See, e.g., *Kingdomware Techs., Inc. v. United States*, 136 S. Ct. 1969 (2016) ("Unlike the word 'may', which implies discretion, the word 'shall' usually connotes a requirement."). The FAR also occasionally uses the term "should," meaning "an expected course of action or policy that is to be followed unless inappropriate for a particular circumstance," FAR 2.101; *Dell Federal Sys., L.P. v. United States*, 906 F.3d 982 (Fed. Cir. 2018). However, as reflected in the FAR "statement of guiding principles at FAR 1.102, if the regulations are less specific regarding an issue, an agency has the discretion to take the action:

> The role of each member of the Acquisition Team is to exercise personal initiative and sound business judgment in providing the best value product or service to meet the customer's needs. In exercising initiative, Government members of the Acquisition Team may assume if a specific strategy, practice, policy or procedure is in the best interests of the Government and is not addressed in the FAR nor prohibited by law (statute or case law), Executive order or other regulation, that the strategy, practice, policy or procedure is a permissible exercise of authority.

Many regulations regarding procurement are required to be posted for notice and an opportunity for comment before taking effect. 41 U.S.C. § 1707 requires notice and an opportunity for public comment prior to publication of procurement policies, regulations, procedures, or forms having a "significant effect beyond the internal operating procedures of the agency" or a "significant cost or administrative impact on contractors or offerors." Thus, final regulations in the FAR system may not take effect until 60 days after publication in the *Federal Register*. However, procurement policies, regulations, procedures, or forms may take effect earlier than 60 days after the publication date when there are compelling circumstances for the earlier effective date, but in no circumstances can the effective date be less than 30 days after the publication date. If the pre-promulgation notice is impracticable, the agency head may issue a temporary regulation with public comment invited before final promulgation.

Several agencies have moved significant parts of their procurement regulations to guidance documents which are not issued following the rules governing the issuance of formal regulations. See Procedures, Guidance and Information (PGI) of DoD, the Acquisition Guide of DOE, the Department of Homeland Security Acquisition Manual, the Transportation Acquisition Guide, and the GSA Acquisition Manual (GSAM). Such documents are unlikely to be given the legal status of formal regulations.

The legal status of a specific provision in a regulation is a subject of great uncertainty. The provision may be found to be an "interpretative" or "housekeeping" rule, which is intended as instructions to government personnel or to indicate the agency's interpretation of a statute. Other provisions may be found to be "substantive" or "legislative" rules that implement a statute. Either type of regulation may serve as notice of limitations on the authority of government employees or as an aid in determining the intention of the contracting parties. However, regulations will have the "force and effect of law" only if authorized by Congress, *Chrysler Corp. v. Brown*, 441 U.S. 281 (1979). There is not complete agreement as to the nature and extent of the required congressional authorization. *G.L. Christian & Assocs. v. United States*, 312 F.2d 418 (Ct. Cl.), *reh'g denied*, 320 F.2d 345 (Ct. Cl.), *cert. denied*, 375 U.S. 954 (1963), is the leading case for the proposition that provisions in procurement regulations that do not implement specific statutes may have the force and effect of law. In finding that an Armed Services Procurement Regulation (ASPR) provision mandating inclusion of a Termination for Convenience of the Government clause in defense contracts had the force and effect of law even though there was no specific statutory authority for such provision, the court looked to the general authority of the agency to issue procurement regulations and then considered the importance of the government policy. Considerable focus has been dedicated to finding a nexus between the regulatory provision and specific statutory authority rather than on the importance of the policy. See, e.g., *Liberty Mut. Ins. Co. v. Friedman*, 639 F.2d 164 (4th Cir. 1981); *United States v. New Orleans Pub. Serv., Inc.*, 553 F.2d 459 (5th Cir. 1977), *vacated & remanded on other grounds*, 436 U.S. 942 (1978); *Matter of Gary Aircraft Corp.*, 698 F.2d 775 (5th Cir.), *cert. denied*, 464 U.S. 820 (1983); *AFL-CIO v. Kahn*, 618 F.2d 784 (D.C. Cir.), *cert. denied*, 443 U.S. 915 (1979); *Chamber of Commerce v. Reich*, 74 F.3d 1322 (D.C. Cir. 1996); *UAW-Labor Employment & Training Corp. v. Chao*, 325 F.3d 360 (D.C. Cir. 2003).

In order for a regulation to affect legal relations, the contractor must have actual or constructive notice of the regulation. Constructive notice occurs when regulations have been published in the *Federal Register*, *Federal Crop Ins. Corp. v. Merrill*, 332 U.S. 380 (1947). The Freedom of Information Act, 5

U.S.C. § 552(a)(1), precludes constructive notice for matters "required to be published in the *Federal Register* and not so published," stating:

> Except to the extent that a person has actual and timely notice of the terms thereof, a person may not in any manner . . . be adversely affected by a matter required to be published in the *Federal Register* and not so published.

It also provides that "substantive rules" must be published in the *Federal Register*. Thus, for a regulation to have the force and effect of law, either it must be published in the *Federal Register* or the affected person must have actual notice. As provided at 5 U.S.C. § 552(a)(2)(C), "administrative staff manuals and instructions to staff that affect a member of the public" need only be made available for public inspection or copies offered for sale.

For decisions exploring when procurement rules qualify as substantive rules requiring notice and comment rather than interpretive guidance, see *Texas Instruments, Inc. v. United States*, 922 F.2d 810, 815 (Fed. Cir. 1990) ("The fact that the Defense Department has issued a non-public, internal directive that purports to add a limitation upon an ACO's authority to reach negotiated line item agreements, which limitation is not present in either statute or validly-issued regulation, cannot act to divest the ACO of the legal authority to make a decision that is final and conclusive."); *NI Indus., Inc. v. United States*, 841 F.2d 1104 (Fed. Cir. 1988) (CO abused discretion in relying on unpublished substantive rule); and *Timber Access Indus. Co. v. United States*, 553 F.2d 1250 (Ct. Cl. 1977) (plaintiff held to have had actual and timely notice of regulations contained in an unpublished Forest Service Manual and was therefore bound by the terms of the manual).

[b] Inspectors General

Established pursuant to the Inspector General Act of 1978, 5 U.S.C. App. 3 §§ 2-3, Inspectors General have broad investigative powers, and their investigations are required to be free of agency influence. They may make such investigations as they consider to be necessary or desirable. They have access to all records relating to any agency's programs and operations, 5 U.S.C. App. 3 § 6(a)(1), and may issue subpoenas for "all information, documents, reports, answers, records, accounts, papers, and other data and documentary evidence necessary in the performance" of their duties, 5 U.S.C. App. § 6(a)(4).

Inspector Generals have played a significant role in auditing and investigating the effectiveness of procurement by agencies in the executive branch. See, for example, DHS OIG Rep't OIG-19-44, *Audit of DHS' Issuance and Management of Other Transaction Agreements Involving Consortium Activities*; DoD IG Rep't DODIG-2019-114 (2019), *Audit of the Army Integrated Air and Missile Defense Programs*; and NASA IG Rep't IG-19-022, *Cybersecurity Management and Oversight at the Jet Propulsion Laboratory*.

[2] Legislative Branch

Congressional control over the procurement function is manifested in requirements and limitations included in procurement statutes, authorization acts, appropriations acts, and other statutes. Oversight of the procurement function by the legislative branch is conducted by Congress itself and by its agent, the Comptroller General of the United States, the head of the Government Accountability Office.

[a] Congressional Oversight

Among the principal means of congressional oversight are the investigations and hearings of its committees. Oversight of general procurement matters is largely carried out by the Homeland Security and Governmental Affairs Committee in the Senate, by the Government Reform Committee in the House of Representatives, and by the Small Business Committees of both houses of Congress. However, each legislative committee of Congress with authority over the programs of a procuring agency, such as the Armed Services Committees of the Senate and House, monitors the procurement practices of that agency, and the Appropriations Committees are quite active in reviewing selective procurement policies. Even when these congressional committees do not formally adopt statutory language establishing binding procurement rules, their views are normally given great respect by agencies in formulating contracting policies. Failure of the agencies to follow the "recommendations" of committees often leads to additional statutory requirements or limitations.

Historically, there have been a number of cases where Congress authorized a program and appropriated funds but the executive agency failed or refused to carry out the program or delayed or reduced the scope of the program. Such actions have been called *impoundments*. In litigation over impoundments, it was held that the executive branch had no inherent authority to refuse to allot funds where Congress had mandated their use. See, e.g., *Train v. City of N.Y.*, 420 U.S. 35 (1975), and *Train v. Campaign Clean Water, Inc.*, 420 U.S. 136 (1975), holding that there was a clear statutory interest and direction for the funds to be obligated in those cases. In response to increased litigation and political controversy over such impoundments, Congress passed the Congressional Budget and Impoundment Control Act of 1974, 2 U.S.C. § 681 et seq. The Act divides impoundments into *rescissions*, which cancel previously granted budget authority still unused and available for obligation, and *deferrals*, which delay the obligation or expenditure of budget authority. For a rescission to take place, the President must send a message to Congress requesting rescission of budget authority and must obtain a rescinding bill. If both houses of Congress do not pass a rescinding bill within 45 days of continuous session after the message is received, the funds must be made available for obligation. The President can defer funds by sending a special deferral message to Congress; if either house passes a simple resolution disapproving the deferral, funds must be made available for obligation. If there is no disapproval, the deferral remains in effect for the remainder of the fiscal year, at which time funds must be released or a new message sent. Although a number of separation of powers issues were raised by the Act, it stipulates that it shall not be construed as "asserting or conceding the constitutional powers or limitations of either Congress or the President," 2 U.S.C. § 681(1). The executive branch has, for the most part, complied with the Act. However, in *City of New Haven v. United States*, 634 F. Supp. 1449 (D.D.C. 1986), the court held that the one-House veto provision on deferrals violated the Constitution's separation of powers under the holding of *Immigration & Naturalization Serv. v. Chadha*, 462 U.S. 919 (1983). As a result, the court held that the deferral authority under the Act could not be used by the executive branch to defer the expenditure and issued an injunction ordering that the funds be made available. The court refused to decide the question of the President's authority to impound independently of the Act because the Act had been relied upon to defer the spending. After Congress passed legislation rejecting the deferrals, the D.C. Circuit dismissed an appeal of the decision as moot but agreed with the reasoning of the District Court, *City of New Haven v. United States*, 809 F.2d 900 (D.C. Cir. 1987). It has been held that the Act does not require the application of some part of the funds in a lump-sum appropriation to all of the objects for which it is appropriated so long as all of the funds in the appropriation are obligated, *International Union, United Automobile, Aerospace & Agricultural Implement Workers v. Donovan*, 746 F.2d 855 (D.C. Cir. 1984), *cert. denied*, 474 U.S. 825 (1985). The court reasoned that the only clear statutory intent and directive in a lump-sum appropriation is to obligate all of the funds.

Another example of congressional retention of power over implementation of statutes after they have been enacted into law was present in the statute creating the Cost Accounting Standards Board (CASB), 50 U.S.C. App. § 2168. The board was granted authority to promulgate regulations and cost accounting standards but was established as an agent of the Congress, independent of the executive branch. In addition, the Comptroller General was designated as the Chairman of the Board with the authority to appoint all of its members. The constitutionality of the CASB's rulemaking power was open to question in view of *Buckley v. Valeo*, 424 U.S. 1 (1976). In that case, dealing with the Federal Election Commission, the Court stated that rule-making is an administrative function and can be carried out only by persons appointed in compliance with Article II, Section 2, Clause 2 of the Constitution. The CASB did not meet this appointment criteria. See *Bowsher v. Synar*, 478 U.S. 714 (1986), holding that the Comptroller General was an agent of Congress. These constitutional issues were resolved when the CASB was reestablished by 41 U.S.C. § 422 (now §§ 1501-06) with membership composed entirely of members of the executive branch and members of the public.

In 1997, Congress attempted to decrease its Constitutional power by giving the President the power to veto parts of a bill in the Line Item Veto Act, 2 U.S.C.

§ 691 et seq. This Act was declared unconstitutional in *Byrd v. Raines*, 956 F. Supp. 25 (D.D.C. 1997), but that decision was vacated and reversed in *Raines v. Byrd*, 521 U.S. 811 (1997), on the grounds that the plaintiff Senators and Congressmen had no standing to bring the action. Subsequently, in *Clinton v. City of New York*, 524 U.S. 417 (1998), the Court held that the Act was unconstitutional because it violated the Presentment Clause of the Constitution, Art. I, § 7, cl. 2.

[b] Comptroller General

The Comptroller General of the United States and the Government Accountability Office (GAO), headed by the Comptroller General, have been given a prominent role in the oversight of government procurement and procurement-related functions. The office and the organization (called the General Accounting Office until 2004) were created by the Budget and Accounting Act of 1921, 42 Stat. 20, to provide Congress with a continuing review of the government's financial affairs. When originally established, GAO was given a number of responsibilities previously performed in the Treasury Department. The Act gave the office additional auditing functions, and from time to time, Congress has given new responsibilities to the Comptroller General. Currently, GAO audits government agencies and their contractors, decides contract award controversies and other procurement-related disputes, finally settles government financial accounts, and prescribes executive agency accounting principles.

In *Bowsher v. Synar*, 478 U.S. 714 (1986), the Court, in an opinion of five justices, held that since the Comptroller General is under the control of Congress, it violates the separation of powers doctrine of the Constitution for the Comptroller General to perform the executive functions of establishing a final estimate of expenditures and revenues. Thus, the Gramm-Rudman-Hollings Act, 2 U.S.C. § 901 et seq., was held unconstitutional. A concurring opinion agreed that the Comptroller General and GAO were part of the legislative branch but disagreed with the conclusion that the functions being performed by the Comptroller under the Act were executive functions. However, it held the Act to be unconstitutional under *Immigration & Naturalization Serv. v. Chadha*, 462 U.S. 919 (1983), because Congress could not delegate such a fundamental power to formulate national policy to an individual agent of Congress.

GAO procurement-related functions that are clearly legislative would be constitutional to the extent that they do not delegate to GAO powers that must be exercised by Congress itself. Clearly within this category of powers would be the broad investigative and audit powers of the Comptroller. These powers include the investigation of all matters relating to the receipt, disbursement, and use of public money, 31 U.S.C. § 712; the auditing of the financial transactions of each government agency, 31 U.S.C. § 3523; and the evaluation of programs and activities of government agencies, 31 U.S.C. § 717. In the performance of this audit function, GAO has access to all government records, and each agency is required to supply information GAO requires concerning audit 2 of the agency, 31 U.S.C. § 716. This statute also grants GAO subpoena power to compel the production of documents. In addition, GAO has the right to audit directly the pertinent books and records of contractors that are awarded negotiated contracts, 10 U.S.C. § 3841(d) (formerly § 2313) and 41 U.S.C. § 4706(d). Thus, these substantial oversight powers are preserved. In carrying out these powers, GAO regularly issues audit reports evaluating various agency's implementation of the procurement process and recommending improvements. See, for example, *F-35 Joint Strike Fighter: Action Needed to Improve Reliability to Prepare for Modernization Efforts*, GAO-19-341, Apr. 29, 2019; *Defense Acquisitions: Key Decisions to Be Made on Future Combat System*, GAO-07-376, Mar. 15, 2007; *Interagency Contracting: Franchise Funds Provide Convenience, But Value to DoD Is Not Demonstrated*, GAO-05-456, July 29, 2005; *Contract Management: Guidance Needed to Promote Competition for Defense Task Orders*, GAO-04-874, July 30, 2004; *Defense Acquisitions: Assessments of Major Weapon Programs*, GAO-04-248, Mar. 31, 2004; and *Contract Management: Restructuring GSA's Federal Supply Service and Federal Technology Service*, GAO-04-132T, Oct. 2, 2003.

For many years, GAO had several functions that were executive in nature and thus of questionable validity under *Bowsher*. Such functions included the power to settle all claims of or against the United States, 31 U.S.C. § 3702, the authority to collect or compromise claims due to the United States, 31 U.S.C. § 3711. These functions were transferred to agencies in the executive branch by The General Accounting Office Act of 1996, Pub. L. No. 104-316, § 202 and § 115. See also Pub. L. No. 105-85, § 1012.

GAO has been granted numerous powers dealing with the financial accounts to be maintained by executive agencies and the liability of government certifying and disbursing officers for losses or improper disbursement of funds. See, for example, 31 U.S.C. § 3511 (prescription of agency accounting principles); 31 U.S.C. § 3512(f) (review and approval of agency accounting systems); 31 U.S.C. § 3526(a) (settlement of financial accounts conclusive on executive agencies); and 31 U.S.C. § 3527 (relief of accountable officers for losses). These would appear to be executive powers.

One of the most effective control and oversight techniques used by GAO is the power to give advance decisions to certifying or disbursing officers involving payments or vouchers, 31 U.S.C. § 3529. Such decisions are almost always respected by agencies because they indicate how GAO will rule when reviewing financial accounts if payment is made. However, as a matter of law, these decisions are advisory only and are binding only upon GAO, 31 U.S.C. § 3526(b). See *Greene County Planning Bd. v. Federal Power Comm'n*, 559 F.2d 1227 (2d Cir. 1976), *cert. denied*, 434 U.S. 1086 (1978). Thus, this provision would not appear to be constitutionally offensive. However, it might lose its effectiveness if GAO's power to disallow accounts under 31 U.S.C. § 3526(a) were held to be an unconstitutional delegation of executive powers.

The most significant use of the 31 U.S.C. § 3529 advance-decision power in the past was in the area of contract award controversies. Although the statute mentions only decisions requested by certifying or disbursing officers, GAO agreed to give such advance decisions at the request of disappointed bidders and other parties who had an interest in a procurement. GAO's power in the contract award controversy area was formally authorized by the Competition in Contracting Act, Pub. L. No. 98-369, 31 U.S.C. § 3551 et seq., giving GAO the power to make recommendations on award controversies and requiring agencies to stay their procurements until a protest has been decided (with limited power for the agency to override the stay). In *Ameron, Inc. v. United States Army Corps of Eng'rs*, 809 F.2d 979 (3d Cir. 1986), this statute was held not to violate the Constitution because the protest procedure neither gives GAO executive power nor "interferes impermissibly with the executive's performance of its procurement duties." The Supreme Court granted certiorari, 485 U.S. 958 (1988), but subsequently dismissed the writ, 488 U.S. 915 (1988), without hearing argument. Accord, *Lear Siegler, Inc. v. Lehman*, 842 F.2d 1102, 1105 (9th Cir. 1988), *mod. on other grounds*, 893 F.2d 205 (9th Cir. 1989). The entire subject of contract award controversies is discussed in detail in Chapter 15.

GAO also has significant powers under the Congressional Budget and Impoundment Control Act of 1974, 2 U.S.C. § 681 et seq. The Act gives GAO a key role in impoundment. GAO:

- receives and reviews all deferral or rescission messages and informs Congress of the findings,
- reports any executive withholding of funds where the executive has not sent a message to Congress,
- reports to Congress if it is determined that a presidential deferral should be classed as a rescission, and
- has authority to bring suit to require that budget authority be made available

It would appear that these responsibilities are not executive branch functions.

[3] Judicial Branch

The role of the judiciary in disputes over the formation of government contracts has a complex history. The evolution of what is referred to as the "bid protest" process is described here. The mechanics of bid protest litigation is detailed in Chapter 15.

The prospect of judicial review of procurement contract award disputes appeared bleak at first. In a 1940 decision, *Perkins v. Lukens Steel Co.*, 310

U.S. 113 (1940), the Supreme Court held that a disappointed contractor lacked standing to obtain judicial review of an agency's award decision. Six years after *Perkins*, Congress enacted the Administrative Procedure Act (APA), which broadly waived the federal government's sovereign immunity as related to judicial review of administrative matters and created a baseline presumption that district courts could enjoin any final agency action that is arbitrary and capricious, an abuse of discretion, or otherwise not in accordance with law. 5 U.S.C. § 706. It is now well settled that "Congress rarely intends to prevent courts from enforcing its directive to federal agencies," and the Supreme Court "applies a 'strong presumption' favoring judicial review of administrative action," *Mach Mining, LLC v. EEOC*, 135 S. Ct. 1645, 1651 (2015). This is consistent with clear legislative pronouncements at the time of passing the APA. See, e.g., S. Rep. No. 752, 79th Cong., 1st Sess., 26 (1945); H.R. Rep. No. 1980, 79th Cong., 2d Sess., 41 (1946).

This APA administrative review process was applied to a bid protest in 1970. In *Scanwell Labs., Inc. v. Shaffer*, 424 F.2d 859 (D.C. Cir. 1970), the Court of Appeals for the District of Columbia Circuit held that Congress, in enacting the APA, had changed the premise underlying *Lukens Steel* and provided a disappointed offeror standing to challenge the award of a government contract. The D.C. Circuit recognized the strong public interest in allowing disappointed offerors to act as private attorneys-general to police the procurement process. Shortly after *Scanwell*, in *Keco Indus., Inc. v. United States*, 428 F.2d 1233 (Ct. Cl. 1970), the Court of Claims (predecessor to Court of Federal Claims and the Court of Appeals for the Federal Circuit) found that it also possessed jurisdiction over bid protests pursuant to the theory of an "implied contract to fairly and honestly consider and evaluate plaintiff's bid."

Congress found this fragmented and incomplete judicial review authority unsatisfactory. As a result, the Administrative Dispute Resolution Act of 1996 (ADRA), 5 U.S.C. § 571 et seq., granted jurisdiction to the Court of Federal Claims, with the authority to grant injunctive relief in both pre-award and post-award protests of procurement contracts. It also cancelled the district courts' *Scanwell* jurisdiction over procurement contracts but was silent on such jurisdiction over nonprocurement contracts. See Chapter 15 for a complete discussion of this jurisdiction.

[C] Contracts Varying from Statutory or Regulatory Requirements

Government agencies quite frequently use procedures or enter into contracts that, either intentionally or inadvertently, vary from the requirements of statutes or regulations. Some variations from the controls imposed by the applicable statutes and regulations are authorized since the need for flexibility is frequently recognized by provisions permitting *waiver* or *deviation*. However, without a waiver or deviation, the failure to follow precisely the prescribed procedures may result in an unauthorized transaction. Where no waiver or deviation is permitted, the failure to comply with the statute or regulation will also result in an unauthorized transaction. The following section discusses waiver and deviation procedures and the effect of noncompliance.

[1] Deviations and Waivers

The commonly used terminology describes departures from regulations as "deviations" and from statutes as "waivers." The procedures for deviating from regulations and waiving statutory requirements are generally strictly enforced.

[a] Deviations from Regulations

Authority and procedures for obtaining deviations from the regulations in the interest of providing some flexibility in the system are contained in FAR Subpart 1.4. Individual deviations, affecting only one "contract action," may be granted by agency heads, FAR 1.403. Class deviations, affecting more than one contract action, may be granted by agency heads, with the power delegated in some agencies, FAR 1.404. In addition, when an agency knows that it will require a class deviation on a permanent basis, it should propose a FAR revision. An individual deviation may not be granted for a procurement aimed at awarding a number of contracts for various geographic regions because such a procurement is not a single "contract action," *La Gloria Oil & Gas Co. v. United States*, 56 Fed. Cl. 211 (2003); *Tesoro Hawaii Corp. v. United States*, 58 Fed. Cl. 65 (2003), *rev'd on other grounds*, 405 F.3d 1339 (Fed. Cir. 2005). There is no similar deviation procedure for other executive branch regulations such as Executive Orders, OMB circulars, and OFPP policy letters.

When deviation authority is delegated, it is invariably given to a subordinate official in charge of the acquisition process. See, for example, DFARS Subpart 201.4. Thus, deviations by other officials will be ineffective. In *G.L. Christian & Assocs. v. United States*, 312 F.2d 418 (Ct. Cl.), *reh'g denied*, 320 F.2d 345 (Ct. Cl.), *cert. denied*, 375 U.S. 954 (1963), the court refused to find that a proper deviation had been obtained when an Assistant Secretary of Defense in charge of housing policy approved the omission of a required clause from a housing contract. See also *Johnson Mgmt. Grp. CFC, Inc. v. Martinez*, 308 F.3d 1245 (Fed. Cir. 2002); and *McDonnell Douglas Corp. v. United States*, 670 F.2d 156 (Ct. Cl. 1982) (deviation from the precise wording of a prescribed clause without obtaining approval pursuant to the regulations was beyond the authority of the contracting officer). In *Whittaker Corp.*, ASBCA 18422, 81-1 BCA ¶ 15,055, the board refused to find that a deviation was required when, after award of the contract, the contracting officer entered into a modification giving a board of contract appeals jurisdiction over a claim specifically excluded from jurisdiction by a mandatory contract clause. The board noted that the government received consideration for the modification and that the "granting of such a waiver was well within the ambit of the contracting officer's authority to administer the contract." The impact of the board's decision is that while the contracting officer had no authority to modify or exclude the clause without a deviation when the contract was formed, such authority existed during contract administration.

[b] Waiver of Statutory Requirements

In the absence of a specific statutory provision granting such authority, government officials do not have the authority to waive statutory requirements, *Centech Grp., Inc. v. United States*, 554 F.3d 1029 (Fed. Cir. 2009) (agency policy memorandum cannot waive the statutory requirement in 15 U.S.C. § 644(o)(1)(A) that a small business must perform 50% of the work with its own employees); *M-R-S Mfg. Co. v. United States*, 492 F.2d 835 (Ct. Cl. 1974) (requirements of the Truth in Negotiations Act not waivable by the contracting officer); *Harry L. Lowe & Assocs.*, 53 Comp. Gen. 620 (B-178307), 74-1 CPD ¶ 96 (requirement for a valid ICC operating authority for interstate motor transportation services cannot be waived by a government agency). However, Congress has provided such authority in a significant number of statutes. See, for example, 40 U.S.C. § 3131(d) (contracting officers may waive Miller Act bond requirements with respect to as much of the work as is to be performed in a foreign country if it is impracticable for the contractor to furnish such bonds); 40 U.S.C. § 3134(a) (department secretaries may waive the Miller Act bond requirements with respect to cost type contracts for construction of public buildings and procurement of certain material and supplies for the Army, Navy, Air Force, and Coast Guard); 40 U.S.C. § 501(a)(2) (Secretary of Defense may exempt the DoD from certain procurement methods and policies prescribed by the GSA unless the President directs otherwise); 41 U.S.C. § 40 (Secretary of Labor may provide exemptions from wage and hour requirements of the Walsh-Healey Act and the President may suspend certain sections of the Act upon judgment that such action would be in the public interest); 40 U.S.C. § 3706 (Secretary of Labor may provide "limitations, variations, tolerances, or exemptions" from the Contract Work Hours and Safety Standards Act); 41 U.S.C. § 6508 (Secretary of Labor may provide "limitations, variations, tolerances, or exemptions" from the Service Contract Act of 1965); 40 U.S.C. § 3147 (the President may suspend the provisions of the Davis-Bacon Act in the event of a national emergency); 46 U.S.C. § App. 1241(b) (the President or the Secretary of Defense may temporarily waive requirements of the Cargo Preference Act upon declaration that an emergency exists justifying such action); 10 U.S.C. § 3703(a)(3) (formerly § 2306a(b)(1)(B)) and 41 U.S.C. § 3503(a)(3) (head of procuring activity may waive requirement for cost or pricing data in exceptional cases).

A judicially forged exception to the requirement for specific statutory authority for a government official to waive a statute has been applied to the Assignment of Claims Act, 41 U.S.C. § 6305(b). This statute states that any prohibited assignment "shall cause the annulment of the contract." In *Tuftco Corp. v. United States*, 614 F.2d 740 (Ct. Cl. 1980), the court held that a contracting officer possessed the necessary authority to waive the statute. See also *D&H Distributing Co. v. United States*, 102 F.3d 542, 546 (Fed. Cir. 1996) ("It is well established, however, that the government can waive the statutory prohibitions against the assignment of contract rights if the contracting officer gives clear assent to the assignment."). This seemingly controverts not only conventional concepts of sources of authority, but also the specific policies inherent in the Act.

[2] Unauthorized Variations

When unauthorized procedures or terms and conditions are used, a variety of consequences may follow. In some cases, the government may be permitted to avoid the contract. In other instances, the contract may be rewritten to add a mandatory clause or exclude a prohibited clause. Finally, a contractor may be able to require the government to abide by mandatory procedures.

[a] Contract Avoidance

The most drastic consequence of a contract made in violation of a statute or a regulation with the force and effect of law is that the government has the right to avoid the contract. Such contracts have been variously described as "void ab initio," *Trilon Educ. Corp. v. United States*, 578 F.2d 1356 (Ct. Cl.), *aff'd*, 217 Ct. Cl. 284 (1978); "invalid," *Prestex Inc. v. United States*, 320 F.2d 367 (Ct. Cl. 1963); or "illegal," *Alabama Rural Fire Ins. Co. v. United States*, 572 F.2d 727 (Ct. Cl. 1978). Government avoidance is limited to clear-cut violations of statutes or regulations, *John Reiner & Co. v. United States*, 325 F.2d 438 (Ct. Cl. 1963), *cert. denied*, 377 U.S. 931 (1964). In *Reiner*, the court held that an improper "cancellation" should be treated as a termination for the convenience of the government, stating that the "binding stamp of nullity" should only be imposed when the illegality is "plain." In *United States v. Amdahl Corp.*, 786 F.2d 387 (Fed. Cir. 1986), the court stated that in determining whether an award is "plainly or palpably illegal," consideration should be given to whether a statute or regulation was violated because of some action or statement by the contractor or if the contractor was on direct notice that the procedures followed violated such rules. See *Total Med. Mgmt., Inc. v. United States*, 104 F.3d 1314 (Fed. Cir. 1997), where the court held the contract to be void because it was in direct conflict with governing regulations and the contractor knew that those regulations were controlling. Following avoidance, the contractor may not recover under the contract. Further, the contractor may be denied any compensation if fraud or other criminal conduct of the contractor was involved, *K & R Eng'g Co. v. United States*, 616 F.2d 469 (Ct. Cl.1980) (contractor not entitled to payments due for completed work on contracts involving a violation of the conflict of interest statute, 18 U.S.C. § 208, and government entitled to recover amounts already paid), or if the government received no benefit from the contractor's efforts, *Prestex Inc. v. United States*, 320 F.2d 367 (Ct. Cl. 1963) (government permitted to reject a shipment of supplies that conformed to the contract but not to the IFB).

However, where there has been no criminal conduct and the government has received a benefit from the contractor's performance, the contractor has been permitted to recover the value of the benefit conferred. See *Amdahl*, where the court stated at 393:

> [I]n many circumstances it would violate good conscience to impose upon the contractor all economic loss from having entered an illegal contract. Where a benefit has been conferred by the contractor on the government in the form of goods or services, which it accepted, a contractor may recover at least on a quantum valebant or quantum meruit basis for the value of the conforming goods or services received by the government prior to the rescission of the contract for invalidity. The contractor is not compensated under the contract, but rather under an implied-in-fact contract.
>
> * * *
>
> Even though a contract be unenforceable against the Government, because not properly advertised, not authorized, or for some other reason, it is only fair and just that the Government pay for goods delivered or services rendered and accepted under it. In certain limited fact situations, therefore, the courts will grant relief of a quasi-contractual nature when the Government elects to rescind an invalid contract. No one would deny that ordinary principles of equity and justice preclude the United States from retaining the services, materials, and benefits and at the same time refusing to pay for them on the ground that the contracting officer's promise was unauthorized, or unenforceable for some other reason. However, the basic fact of legal significance charging the Government with liability in these situations is its retention of benefits in the form of goods or services.

See also *New York Mail & Newspaper Transp. Co. v. United States*, 154 F. Supp. 271 (Ct. Cl.), *cert. denied*, 355 U.S. 904 (1957) (contract "null and void" for violating the advertising statute, but contractor entitled to recover for the value of services rendered to the date of avoidance not limited to quantum meruit); *Urban Data Sys., Inc. v. United States*, 699 F.2d 1147 (Fed. Cir. 1983) (contract invalid for violation of cost-plus-a-percentage-of-cost prohibition, but recovery permitted on quantum valebant basis); *Interagency Agreements*, Comp. Gen. Dec. B-309181, 2007 CPD ¶ 163 (leases violating the leasing statutes, 40 U.S.C. § 585 and 10 U.S.C. § 2661, were void ab initio but recovery might be possible on quantum meruit basis); and *Veridyne Corp. v. United States*, 83 Fed. Cl. 575 (2008) (interpreting *Amdahl* to require recovery of money paid for work performed only if the contractor has a conflict of interest or has bribed a government official).

Contractors have had great difficulty in proving that a contract that violated a statute was void. In a number of cases, the court has ruled that the intent of Congress was not to void a contract if it was violated. See *American Tel. & Tel. Co. v. United States*, 177 F.3d 1368 (Fed. Cir. 1999) (en banc), *reversing*, 124 F.3d 1471 (Fed. Cir. 1997), holding that a contract was not invalid because it did not comply with the requirements of § 8118 of the 1988 Fiscal Year Department of Defense Appropriations Act, Pub. L. No. 100-202 limiting the use of fixed-price type contracts. In a later opinion, the Federal Circuit also denied the contractor's appeal that the contract should be reformed from a fixed-price type contract to a cost-reimbursement contract, *American Tel. & Tel. Co. v. United States*, 307 F.3d 1374 (Fed. Cir. 2002), *cert. denied*, 540 U.S. 937 (2003). See also *United Pac. Ins. Co. v. United States*, 464 F.3d 1325 (Fed. Cir. 2006) (rejecting the argument that a contract was illegal because it violated statutory expenditure limitations on a military construction project); *Lee v. United States*, 895 F.3d 1363 (Fed. Cir. 2018) (rejecting argument that contract must be invalidated).

[b] Nonenforcement of Clause

Violation of a statute or a regulation with the force and effect of law can also lead to nonenforcement of a contract clause. If the clause benefits the contractor, this will result the contractor's inability to recover money in accordance with the provisions of that clause. For example, in *Johnson Mgmt. Grp. CFC, Inc. v. Martinez*, 308 F.3d 1245 (Fed. Cir. 2002), the court held that a special clause allowing subcontractor payments to constitute liquidation of advance payments should not be enforced because it conflicted with the statutory advance payments provisions. Similarly, in *E.I. DuPont de Nemours & Co. v. United States*, 54 Fed. Cl. 361 (2002), the court ruled that an Indemnification clause was "void and unenforceable" because it violated the Anti-Deficiency Act, 31 U.S.C. § 1341— with the result that the contractor was denied recovery under the clause. In 365 F.3d 1367 (Fed. Cir. 2004), the Federal Circuit agreed that the Act barred enforcement of an open-ended Indemnification clause but found that the Contract Settlement Act of 1944, 41 U.S.C. § 101 et seq. (pre-2011 codification), had granted contract authority to agree to the indemnification. Open-ended indemnification provisions have also been declared void by GAO, 7 Comp. Gen. 507 (A-21633) (1928); 35 Comp. Gen. 85 (B-117057) (1955); *Assumption by Government of Contractor Liability to Third Persons*, Comp. Gen. Dec. B-201072, 82-1 CPD ¶ 406, *recons. denied*, 62 Comp. Gen. 361, 83-1 CPD ¶ 501.

Nonenforcement of a clause can also result in the government's inability to enforce a clause against the contractor. For example, in *Mapco Alaska Petroleum, Inc. v. United States*, 27 Fed. Cl. 405 (1992), the court refused to enforce an Economic Price Adjustment clause that was not permitted by the FAR. The same result was reached in *Gold Line Refin., Ltd. v. United States*, 54 Fed. Cl. 285 (2002), and *La Gloria Oil & Gas Co. v. United States*, 56 Fed. Cl. 211 (2003). The opposite result was reached in *Williams Alaska Petroleum, Inc. v. United States*, 57 Fed. Cl. 789 (2003). In *Tesoro Haw. Corp. v. United States*, 405 F.3d 1339 (Fed. Cir. 2005), the court adopted the *Williams* view that the clause was in conformance with the FAR even though the great majority of the judges in the Court of Federal Claims had followed the *Mapco* reasoning. When an Economic Price Adjustment clause has been found unenforceable because it does not conform to the FAR, the court has fashioned different remedies. See *Barrett Refin. Corp. v. United States*, 242 F.3d 1055 (Fed. Cir. 2001), granting relief for an implied-in-fact contract promising to pay fair market value, and *Beta Sys., Inc. v. United States*, 838 F.2d 1179 (Fed. Cir. 1988), granting reformation to bring the clause into conformance.

[c] Inclusion or Exclusion of Mandatory Clause

A statute or a regulation with the force and effect of law may also impact the contract language to which the parties agreed. Thus, if a mandatory clause is required to be included in the contract, the contract will be read to include it even though it is not physically incorporated in the document, *G.L. Christian & Assocs. v. United States*, 312 F.2d 418 (Ct. Cl.), *reh'g denied*, 320 F.2d 345 (Ct. Cl.), *cert. denied*, 375 U.S. 954 (1963) (Termination for the Convenience of the Government clause); *Santa Fe—Andover Oil Co.*, ASBCA 35256, 88-2 BCA ¶ 20,607 (Disputes clause); *Bromley Contracting Co.*, DOTCAB 1284, 84-2 BCA ¶ 17,233 (Payment of Interest on Contractors' Claims clause); *Dayron Corp.*, ASBCA 24919, 84-1 BCA ¶ 17,213 (Government Property clause); *Benjamin P. Garcia*, ASBCA 18035, 73-2 BCA ¶ 10,196 (Equal Opportunity clause). Similarly, if a certain clause is prohibited, it will be read out of the contract even though it is physically present, *Johnson Mgmt. Grp. CFC, Inc. v. Martinez*, 308 F.3d 1245 (Fed. Cir. 2002) (special Liquidation of Advanced Payments clause); *Charles Beseler Co.*, ASBCA 22669, 78-2 BCA ¶ 13,483 (Value Engineering clause). The doctrine may also resolve disputes as to which version of clause applies. See *Call Henry, Inc. v. United States*, 855 F.3d 1348 (Fed. Cir. 2017).

In 1993, the Federal Circuit announced that the rule applied when the clause contained a significant procurement policy *or* when it was written to "benefit or protect the party seeking incorporation," *General Eng'g & Mach. Works v. O'Keefe*, 991 F.2d 775 (Fed. Cir. 1993) (correct Payments clause carries out significant procurement policy). Most decisions thereafter articulated one of these grounds when they incorporated a clause. See, e.g., *K-CON, Inc. v. Secretary of Army*, 908 F.3d 719 (Fed. Cir. 2018) (finding Miller act payment and performance bond requirements are deeply ingrained in procurement policy); *Dawkins General Contractors & Supply, Inc.*, ASBCA 48535, 03-2 BCA ¶ 32,305 (Time-and-Materials Payments clause "expresses a purpose sufficiently ingrained in public procurement policy" to require incorporation); *Labat-Anderson, Inc. v. United States*, 42 Fed. Cl. 806 (1999) (Protest After Award clause incorporated in contract "on either ground"); and *Amoroso Constr. Co. v. United States*, 12 F.3d 1072 (Fed. Cir. 1993) (Buy American Act clause incorporated because it carried out a significant procurement policy). Compare *Lambrecht & Sons, Inc.*, ASBCA 49515, 97-2 BCA ¶ 29,105, *recons. denied*, 98-1 BCA ¶ 29,389, refusing to incorporate a Variation in Estimated Quantities clause because it reflected "no significant or deeply ingrained public procurement policy."

There are cases subsequent to the *General Engineering* decision incorporating clauses into a contract without a discussion of whether they expressed significant policy. See, for example, *Gerald Cunningham*, AGBCA 98-155-2, 98-2 BCA ¶ 29,908 (Disputes clause 90-day appeal provision); *C&J Assocs. v. VA Med. Ctr.*, VABCA 3892, 95-2 BCA ¶ 27,834 (Termination for Convenience clause incorporated in a purchase order but Default clause not incorporated because it was not mandatory); *GAI Consultants, Inc.*, ENGBCA 6030, 95-2 BCA ¶ 27,620 (correct Changes clause incorporated in a contract for archeological investigation); *Alta Constr. Co.*, PSBCA 1463, 94-3 BCA ¶ 27,961 (regulatory language read into Termination for Convenience clause that was placed in the contract); and *Unit Data Servs. Corp. v. Dep't of Veterans Affairs*, GSBCA 10775-P-R, 93-3 BCA ¶ 25,964 (clause requiring small business set-aside contractor to perform at least 50% of the work with its own employees incorporated in contract). Compare *Boeing Defense & Space Grp.*, ASBCA 50048, 98-2 BCA ¶ 28,927 ("a tribunal properly may consider for guidance any pertinent authority which has the force and effect of law pursuant to *Christian*, including FAR 49.203(b). Clearly the contracting officer was obliged to adhere to FAR 49.203(b)"), with *Lockheed Martin Librascope Corp.*, ASBCA 50508, 99-1 BCA ¶ 30,635 (declining to apply incorporate Incentive Price Revision (Firm Target) clause because the parties had included another clause on that issue in the contract and the standard clause was not "of such importance as to reflect a deeply ingrained strand of, or a legislative intent for, public procurement policy, or a major government principle.")

If the statute or regulation is not mandatory with respect to the use of a clause, this rule will not apply. See *Professional Servs. Unified, Inc.*, ASBCA 48883, 96-1 BCA ¶ 28,073, where the board held that a contracting officer had correctly interpreted the FAR in using a Federal, State and Local Taxes clause which did not provide for price adjustments for subsequent tax increases. The board found that the clause giving price adjustments was to be used only in noncompetitive procurements and the procurement at issue was competitive. See also *Parcel 49C Ltd. p'ship v. General Servs. Admin.*, GSBCA 16377, 05-2 BCA ¶ 33,098 (GSA Equitable Adjustment clause in lease); *Mktg. & Mgmt. Info., Inc. v. United States*, 57 Fed. Cl. 665 (2003) (Termination for Convenience clause in commissary barter contract).

[3] Contractor Benefit

These rules involving statutes and regulations have been used primarily for the benefit of the government. Thus, courts have been prone to rule that, absent clear evidence of Congressional intent, statutes and regulations do not evidence an intent to benefit contractors. See *Cessna Aircraft Co. v. Dalton*, 126 F.3d 1442 (Fed. Cir. 1997), *cert. denied*, 525 U.S. 818 (1998); *American Tel. & Tel. Co. v. United States*, 307 F.3d 1374 (Fed. Cir. 2002), *cert. denied*, 540 U.S. 937 (2003). Notwithstanding that some statutes and regulations may primarily benefit the government, the Federal Circuit has recognized that "it is possible for a regulation or law to benefit both the government and private parties, *Todd Constr., L.P v. United States*, 656 F.3d 1306 (Fed. Cir. 2011); *BLR Grp. of America, Inc. v. United States*, 94 Fed. Cl. 354 (2010) (performance rating scheme in FAR Subpart 42.15 was intended to benefit both the contractor and the government, with the result that the court had jurisdiction to hear a challenge of the rating); *Magnum Opus Techs., Inc. v. United States*, 94 Fed. Cl. 512 (2010) (the requirement in FAR 17.207(f) that unevaluated options be competed was for the benefit of potential competitors). There are some earlier cases where contractors have obtained relief when statutes and regulations have been violated. In *Fletcher v. United States*, 392 F.2d 266 (Ct. Cl. 1968), the court held that regulations that are intended to define or state the rights of a class of persons are presumably intended for the benefit of those persons. Such regulations can be asserted for a contractor's benefit, *Moran Bros., Inc. v. United States*, 346 F.2d 590 (Ct. Cl. 1965) (Atomic Energy Commission procurement regulation that permitted appeals within 60 days had the effect of law, and appeal was timely even though it exceeded the 30-day limit included in the contract); 47 Comp. Gen. 457, B-162272, 1968 CPD ¶ 12 (mandatory government liability for insurance premiums read into the contract); *Bethlehem Steel Corp. v. United States*, 423 F.2d 300 (Ct. Cl. 1970) (regulation prescribing technique for determining the profit for defense contractors used for the benefit of contractors); *Chris Berg, Inc. v. United States*, 426 F.2d 314 (Ct. Cl. 1970) (ASPR provision giving contractors the right to correct clerical mistakes in bids binding on the government).

§ 1.04 AUTHORITY OF GOVERNMENT AND CONTRACTOR PERSONNEL

The formation or modification of a government contract may involve many government and contractor personnel with varying degrees of authority. Specialists representing both parties engage in activities such as cost and price analysis, technical review, preaward surveys, negotiation, and preparation of contract documents. Accountants, attorneys, auditors, engineers, and other specialists may represent both parties. The ultimate aim of their activity is the creation of a legally enforceable agreement. In the vast majority of the cases, this goal is achieved. However, legal problems concerning the authority of these personnel are frequently encountered—most often when the government refuses to recognize an alleged contractual agreement on the grounds that the contractor has dealt with an unauthorized person. Contractors occasionally raise the same defenses, but with much less success. This section first considers the legal principles relevant to determining the authority of government personnel, the consequences of dealing with unauthorized personnel, and the effect of notice of limitations on authority. It then examines a number of the same principles as applied to contractor personnel.

[A] Government Personnel

The fundamental rule regarding government personnel is that the government is not bound by unauthorized acts of its officers or agents, *Wilber Nat'l Bank v. United States*, 294 U.S. 120 (1935). The government has taken advantage of this rule by allocating the major grant of contractual authority to *a special and limited class of employees* called *contracting officers*. Contracting officers have the sole authority to legally bind the government to contracts and contract modifications, FAR 1.601(a). However, they are frequently not involved in the day-to-day activities that occur in the contract formation process. In some agencies, the designated contracting officer may be an active participant in the steps leading to signature of a contract, while in others, the contracting officer's role may be only to sign the document. Thus, during the formation process, a contractor may deal primarily with government personnel bearing titles such as contract specialist, contract negotiator, cost analyst, project manager, engineer, contracting officer's representative, auditor, and attorney. In many cases, those personnel who are not contracting officers may be delegated authority to perform specific functions even though the general grant of contractual authority is made only to contracting officers. Additionally, the authority of contracting officers may range from full authority, regardless of the nature and size of the transaction (plenary authority), to authority to perform only a limited class of contractual activities described by type and dollar amount. This fragmentation of authority in the contracting process has created difficult legal problems.

[1] Actual Authority Required

In private agency law, an employer will be bound by an employee under the legal theory of *apparent authority* if the employer has permitted the employee to assume authority or has held out the employee as possessing authority. See *Restatement, Second, Agency* § 8. Recognizing the importance of effective government control over the conduct of its agents, the courts and boards have rejected the apparent authority rule, holding that *actual authority* is required to bind the government. See *Federal Crop Ins. Corp. v. Merrill*, 332 U.S. 380 (1947), where the Court stated at 384:

> Whatever the form in which the Government functions, anyone entering into an arrangement with the Government takes the risk of having accurately ascertained that he who purports to act for the Government stays within the bounds of his authority. The scope of this authority may be explicitly defined by Congress or be limited by delegated legislation, properly exercised through the rule-making power. And this is so even though, as here, the agent himself may have been unaware of the limitations upon his authority. See, e.g., *Utah Power & Light Co. v. United States*, 243 U.S. 389, 409 (1917); *United States v. Stewart*, 311 U.S. 60 (1940).

For cases where government employees with apparent authority were found to have no actual authority, see *P.R. Burke Corp. v. United States*, 277 F.3d 1346 (Fed. Cir. 2002) (Assistant Plant Manager had no authority to permit deviation from specifications); *Starflight Boats v. United States*, 48 Fed. Cl. 592 (2001) (Deputy Chief of Procurement had no authority to order contractor to assist in investigation); *Total Procurement Serv., Inc.*, ASBCA 53258, 01-2 BCA ¶ 31,436 (Executive Director of Business Office had no authority to bind government to an electronic commerce agreement); *Healthcare Practice Enhancement Network, Inc.*, VABCA 5864, 01-1 BCA ¶ 31,383 (Chief Financial Officer of Veterans Administration medical center had no contracting officer authority); *Melrose Assocs., L.P. v. United States*, 43 Fed. Cl. 124 (1999) (Director of HUD State Field Office had no authority to waive regulations); *Jascourt v. United States*, 521 F.2d 1406 (Table) (Ct. Cl.), *cert. denied*, 423 U.S. 1032 (1975) (government not bound by the actions of the Deputy Assistant Secretary of Labor for Labor Relations, or the Director of the Division of Public Employees, since neither official had the authority to enter into a contract); *Housing Corp. v. United States*, 468 F.2d 922 (Ct. Cl. 1972) (HUD Secretary's unauthorized signature would not bind government as a third party responsible for costly changes); *Byrne Org., Inc. v. United States*, 287 F.2d 582 (Ct. Cl. 1961) ("letters of intent" issued by director and chief administrative officer of the National Capital Sesquicentennial Commission not binding on the government); and *Gordon Woodroffe Corp. v. United States*, 104 F. Supp. 984 (Ct. Cl. 1952) (special assistant to State Department coordinator for aid to Greece and Turkey had no authority to purchase equipment).

The fact that an official appears to be a superior of a contracting officer does not establish the authority of that official. See *Inter-Tribal Council of Nev., Inc.*, IBCA 1234-12-78, 83-1 BCA ¶ 16,433, stating at 81,745:

> The facts that the Assistant Area Director for Education was the "boss" for Area education matters, . . . that the CO sought his approval for a contract budget modification, . . . and that he was named as the "contact person" for

> negotiations for an upcoming contract . . . are irrelevant in this context. The best that can be said about them is that they are probative of the fact and conclusion that the Assistant Area Director had *apparent* authority here, which we have already noted is insufficient authority for [the contractor's] reliance under the *Federal Crop Insurance* rule.

See also *Henry Burge & Alvin White*, PSBCA 2431, 89-3 BCA ¶ 21,910, where a project manager was held to have no authority to relax the specifications. Compare *Zoubi v. United States*, 25 Cl. Ct. 581 (1992), where an "acting program director" was held to have authority to contract for services because he was responsible for obtaining such services and had obtained them in the past.

Within contracting offices, personnel with official-sounding titles such as contract specialist, contract negotiator, and contract administrator work for contracting officers and handle the day-to-day contracting activity of the government, but such personnel generally do not have authority to order additional work or to commit the government by virtue of their position. Contractors are expected to recognize this lack of authority. In *General Elec. Co.*, ASBCA 11990, 67-1 BCA ¶ 6377, *rev'd on other grounds*, 412 F.2d 1215 (Ct. Cl. 1969), the board stated at 29,525-26:

> [The contract specialist's] only function was to serve as contact point between the Government and [the contractor]. He can be considered little more than a messenger. There is no evidence that he was delegated any power to bind the Government; on the contrary the testimony establishes that he was delegated no authority to bind the Government. No authority to bind the Government for additional funds by demanding the report notwithstanding the funding situation can be implied from [his] position.

Thus, when a contractor negotiates a contract or a contract modification with a contract specialist, it must recognize that there will be no binding agreement until an actual contracting officer signs the contract or modification. See *First Crystal Park Assocs. Ltd. P'ship v. United States*, 130 Fed. Cl. 260 (2017) (government not bound by e-mail from contract specialist renewing lease); *JEM Transp., Inc. v. United States*, 120 Fed. Cl. 189 (2015) (government not bound by contract document forwarded by contract specialist but not signed by contracting officer); *Neenan v. United States*, 112 Fed. Cl. 325 (2013) (government not bound by statement of contract specialist: "it's a deal"); *Nascent Grp., J.V. v. United States*, 103 Fed. Cl. 338 (2012) (government project manager had no authority to exercise option); *Todd Pacific Shipyards Corp.*, ASBCA 55126, 08-2 BCA ¶ 33,891 (employee of contracting officer had no authority); *Total Procurement Serv., Inc.*, ASBCA 53258, 01-2 BCA ¶ 31,436 (Executive Director of program office had no authority to enter into contract); *Precision Standards, Inc.*, ASBCA 41375, 96-2 BCA ¶ 28,461 (contract administrator working for ACO had no authority to waive delivery schedule); *Anchor/Darling*

Valve Co., ASBCA 46109, 95-1 BCA ¶ 27,595 (procurement assistant had no authority to waive delivery schedule); and *Mil-Spec Contractors, Inc. v. United States*, 835 F.2d 865 (Fed. Cir. 1987) (government not bound by alleged oral agreement by contract negotiator). In *Kahaluu Constr. Co.*, ASBCA 33248, 90-2 BCA ¶ 22,663, the government argued that a binding agreement had been reached on a "Board on Changes Report" signed by a contractor's representative and government members of the board. However, the board found that neither the government members nor the contractor's representatives had authority to bind their respective parties.

[2] Delegation of Authority

The contracting authority in each agency flows from the head of the agency to contracting officers. See FAR 1.601(a), stating:

> [A]uthority and responsibility to contract for authorized supplies and services are vested in the agency head. The agency head may establish contracting activities and delegate broad authority to manage the agency's contracting functions to heads of such contracting activities. Contracts may be entered into and signed on behalf of the Government only by contracting officers. In some agencies, a relatively small number of high level officials are designated contracting officers solely by virtue of their positions. Contracting officers below the level of a head of a contracting activity shall be selected and appointed under 1.603.

This regulation recognizes two types of officials with contracting officer authority. At the upper level of the agency, in secretarial positions or as head of a contracting activity, officials have contracting authority "by virtue of their positions." These officials are not required to meet the qualification requirements for appointment and generally do not act as contracting officers except on special matters. Yet they have full authority to act as contracting officers. Below these officials are the *designated contracting officers*, appointed in accordance with the regulations discussed below.

Each agency is authorized to delegate contracting officer authority in accordance with its own procedures. See FAR 1.603-1, stating that the agency shall—

> establish and maintain a procurement career management program and a system for the selection, appointment, and termination of appointment of contracting officers. Agency heads or their designees may select and appoint contracting officers and terminate their appointments.

Thus, agency heads may appoint contracting officers or may delegate this authority. In some agencies authority has been delegated to appoint subsidiary contracting officers or other representatives. FAR 1.602-1(a) requires clear instructions in the appointment document, as follows:

> Contracting officers may bind the Government only to the extent of the authority delegated to them. Contracting officers shall receive from the appointing authority (see 1.603-1) clear instructions in writing regarding the limits of their authority. Information on the limits of contracting officers' authority shall be readily available to the public and agency personnel.

The term "contracting officer" is used to describe those individuals with the authority to execute contractual documents that bind the government and to sign determinations and findings and other internal documents. FAR 2.101 contains the following definition:

> Contracting Officer means a person with the authority to enter into, administer, and/or terminate contracts and make related determinations and findings. The term includes certain authorized representatives of the contracting officer acting within the limits of their authority as delegated by the contracting officer. "Administrative contracting officer (ACO)" refers to a contracting officer who is administering contracts. "Termination contracting officer (TCO)" refers to a contracting officer who is settling terminated contracts. A single contracting officer may be responsible for duties in any or all of these areas. Reference in this regulation to administrative contracting officer or termination contracting officer does not (a) require that a duty be performed at a particular office or activity or (b) restrict in any way a contracting officer in the performance of any duty properly assigned.

The first sentence of this FAR definition refers to the official who has been designated as a contracting officer. However, the second sentence creates confusion by stating that *the term includes* any "authorized representative" of the contracting officer. This broad definition of contracting officer is also included in the Definitions clause in FAR 52.202-1.

The inclusion of "authorized representatives" within the definition of contracting officer is very misleading, because formally designated contracting officers will normally have a much broader grant of authority than authorized representatives. In addition, not all representatives are appointed in the same manner or with the same degree of authority. The following discussion explores the method of appointment and stated scope of authority of three categories of government employees—designated contracting officers, contracting officer representatives, and other employees with contractual duties.

[a] Designated Contracting Officers

FAR 1.603-3 calls for the appointment of designated contracting officers *by name* using the Certificate of Appointment, Standard Form 1402. In addition, each agency is required to establish a system that ensures that each designated contracting officer is fully qualified by experience and training. The following guidance for selection criteria is given in FAR 1.603-2:

> In selecting contracting officers, the appointing official shall consider the complexity and dollar value of the acquisitions to be assigned and the candidate's experience, training, education, business acumen, judgment, character, and reputation. Examples of selection criteria include—
>
> (a) Experience in Government contracting and administration, commercial purchasing, or related fields;
>
> (b) Education or special training in business administration, law, accounting, engineering, or related fields;
>
> (c) Knowledge of acquisition policies and procedures, including this and other applicable regulations;
>
> (d) Specialized knowledge in the particular assigned field of contracting; and
>
> (e) Satisfactory completion of acquisition training courses.

More precise and demanding requirements have been called for in recent years. See, for example, Executive Order 12931, 59 Fed. Reg. 52387 (1994), requiring heads of agencies to:

> (h) Establish career education programs for procurement professionals, including requirements for successful completion of educational requirements or mandatory training for entry level positions and for promotion to higher level positions, in order to ensure a highly qualified procurement work force.

See also the Office of Personnel Management Standard for GS-1102 (the series for contracting professionals), which contains educational or experience requirements. A number of agencies have adopted higher standards for their contracting officers. See, for example, DFARS 201.603-2, imposing the following requirements on contracting officers in DoD:

> (1) In accordance with 10 U.S.C. 1724, in order to qualify to serve as a contracting officer with authority to award or administer contracts for amounts above the simplified acquisition, a person must
>
> (i) Have completed all contracting courses required for a contracting officer to serve in the grade in which the employee or member of the armed forces will serve;
>
> (ii) Have at least 2 years' experience in a contracting position;
>
> (iii) Have—
>
> (A) Received a baccalaureate degree from an accredited educational institution; and
>
> (B) Completed at least 24 semester credit hours, or equivalent, of study from an accredited institution of higher education in any of

the following disciplines: accounting, business finance, law, contracts, purchasing, economics, industrial management, marketing, quantitative methods, and organization and management; and

(iv) Meet such additional requirements, based on the dollar value and complexity of the contracts awarded or administered in the position, as may be established by the Secretary of Defense.

(2) The qualification requirements in paragraph (1)(iii) of this subsection do not apply to a DoD employee or member of the armed forces who

(i) On or before September 30, 2000, occupied

(A) A contracting officer position with authority to award or administer contracts above the simplified acquisition threshold; or

(B) A position either as an employee in the GS-1102 occupational series or a member of the armed forces in an occupational specialty similar to the GS-1102 series;

(ii) Is in a contingency contracting force; or

(iii) Is an individual appointed to a 3-year developmental position. Information on developmental opportunities is contained in DoD Instruction 5000.66, Defense Acquisition, Technology, and Logistics Workforce Education, Training and Career Development Program.

(3) Waivers to the requirements in paragraph (1) of this subsection may be authorized. Information on waivers is contained in DoD Instruction 5000.66.

[i] Internal Limitations on Authority

In each agency there are one or more contracting officers with plenary authority. Even these contracting officers, however, may be subject to internal regulations governing how that authority is exercised, and the contractor is responsible for being aware of any regulations made known to it through publication or otherwise, *Federal Crop Ins. Corp. v. Merrill*, 332 U.S. 380 (1947). In *Porter v. United States*, 496 F.2d 583 (Ct. Cl. 1974), *cert. denied*, 420 U.S. 1004 (1975), published regulations delegated authority to the high commissioner and the director of the Office of Territories to contract for shipping services "on behalf of the Trust Territory of the Pacific Islands." The contractor was deemed to have notice that these officials were acting for the Trust Territory government and had no authority to bind the United States. See also *Nascent Grp., J.V. v. United States*, 103 Fed. Cl. 338 (2012) (authority to issue task orders did not constitute authority to award new contract); *Gemini Elecs., Inc. v. United States*, 65 Fed. Cl. 55 (2005) (authority to contract for telephone services in one district did not allow such contracts outside of the district); *Johnson Mgmt. Grp., CFC, Inc. v. Martinez*, 308 F.3d 1245 (Fed. Cir. 2002) (contracting officer lacked authority to insert a clause in a contract that deviated from the FAR);

Harbert/Lummus Agrifuels Projects v. United States, 142 F.3d 1429 (Fed. Cir. 1998), *cert. denied*, 525 U.S. 1177 (1999) (contracting officer lacked authority to enter into an oral, unilateral contract to continue guaranteeing future borrowing requests until completion of a construction project because the delegation of authority required the preparation of a "separate prior written approval"); *Total Medical Mgmt. v. United States*, 104 F.3d 1314 (Fed. Cir. 1997) (person with contracting authority did not have authority to agree to provisions violating agency regulations); and *OAO Corp. v. United States*, 17 Cl. Ct. 91 (1989) (government not bound by handshake of contracting officer when approval of higher authority required; however, court did find an implied-in-fact contract).

Contractors are not bound by limitations in unpublished regulations, *Texas Instruments, Inc. v. United States*, 922 F.2d 810 (Fed. Cir. 1990) (government bound by ACO signature on agreement even though internal regulations required internal approvals). See also *Western Aviation Servs., Inc. v. General Servs. Admin.*, GSBCA 14165, 00-2 BCA ¶ 31,123 (contractor not bound by internal government manual); *NI Indus., Inc. v. United States*, 841 F.2d 1104 (Fed. Cir. 1988) (contractor not bound by limitations set forth in unpublished value engineering change proposal rule); *A-1 Garbage Disposal & Trash Serv.*, ASBCA 30623, 89-1 BCA ¶ 21,323 (contractor not bound by unpublished regulation of Small Business Administration); *New England Tank Indus. of N.H., Inc.*, ASBCA 26474, 88-1 BCA ¶ 20,395, *vacated & remanded on other grounds*, 861 F.2d 685 (Fed. Cir. 1988) (government bound to modification signed by contracting officer even though unpublished regulation prohibited agreement); and *Devil's Lake Sioux Tribe*, IBCA 1953, 88-1 BCA ¶ 20,320 (contractor not bound by a published regulation that was so vague and ambiguous that it could not be understood by a typical contractor). Compare *Trauma Serv. Grp. v. United States*, 104 F.3d 1321 (Fed. Cir. 1997), holding that a memorandum of agreement was not binding on the government even though it was signed by an official with proper authority because a DoD Instruction required approval of higher authority. The court did not discuss whether the instruction was available to the public.

If the contractor is aware of the unpublished regulation, it will be bound by the limitations contained therein. See *D.M. Summers, Inc.*, VABCA 2750, 89-3 BCA ¶ 22,123 (contractor could not recover for lost work because it had actual knowledge of changes in internal agency regulations that reduced the requirements of the contract). In *LDG Timber Enters., Inc. v. Glickman*, 114 F.3d 1140 (Fed. Cir. 1997), the court held that the government had the burden of proving that an internal regulation barred a contracting officer from taking normal action within his or her authority.

[ii] Functional Contracting Officers

In DoD, different types of contracting officers perform different functions. Contracting officers that award contracts are known as procuring contracting officers (PCOs); contracting officers that administer contracts are known as administrative contracting officers (ACOs); and contracting officers that handle contract terminations are known as terminating contracting officers (TCOs). In most other agencies, there is no such fragmentation of authority, with the result that the contracting officers who award contracts usually retain authority to administer or terminate them. There also may be additional specialized contracting officers with limited scopes of authority, such as corporate administrative contracting officers (CACOs).

FAR 1.603-3 requires that limitations on authority be included in the certificate of appointment of each contracting officer and that contractors be responsible for ascertaining the limits of authority of contracting officers. See, for example, *Strick Corp.*, ASBCA 15921, 73-2 BCA ¶ 10,077 (modification not binding because ACO had no authority to sign it); and *Atlantic, Gulf & Pac. Co.*, ASBCA 13533, 72-1 BCA ¶ 9415 (termination settlement not binding because TCO acted beyond authority). However, such limitations on authority will not control if they are neither published nor communicated to the contractor. See *Texas Instruments, Inc. v. United States*, 922 F.2d 810 (Fed. Cir. 1990) (government bound by ACO signature on agreement even though internal regulations required internal approvals).

FAR 42.302 contains a long list of functions that are normally delegated to contract administration offices (CAOs). When an agency has a separate ACO that person will generally be the head of a CAO and will generally have the functions listed in FAR 42.302(a)—some of which entail legally obligating the government. Note, however, that FAR 42.302(b) warns that the following functions are permitted only when specifically delegated:

> (1) Negotiate or negotiate and execute supplemental agreements incorporating contractor proposals resulting from change orders issued under the Changes clause. Before completing negotiations, coordinate any delivery schedule change with the contracting office.
>
> (2) Negotiate prices and execute priced exhibits for unpriced orders issued by the contracting officer under basic ordering agreements.
>
> (3) Negotiate or negotiate and execute supplemental agreements changing contract delivery schedules.
>
> * * *
>
> (7) Negotiate and definitize adjustments to contract prices resulting from exercise of an economic price adjustment clause (see subpart 16.2).
>
> (8) Issue change orders and negotiate and execute resulting supplemental agreements under contracts for ship construction, conversion, and repair.

[iii] Specific Designation by Contract

There is also a difference in the way contracting officer authority is distributed relative to supply versus construction contracts. In construction contracts, the contractor can generally expect to be informed of a single named individual who has authority to bind the government. There is usually no designation of ACOs; the field functions relating to the day-to-day administration of the contract are performed through contracting officer representatives (CORs). In supply and service contracts, there is usually no designation of a single person to serve as contracting officer. Thus, any employee of the agency who has been properly designated a contracting officer may act on any contract of the agency, provided that he or she is acting within the limits of this authority. This procedure gives the agency much greater internal operating flexibility, but it creates difficulties for contractors in ascertaining the authority of the person with whom they are dealing.

[iv] Dollar Limitations on Authority

There are frequently various tiers of contracting officers with decreasing amounts of authority given to each succeeding lower tier. This practice is particularly prevalent in supply and service contracting. At the top may be the contracting officer who signed the contract and has full ("plenary") authority within the agency. Below may be a contracting officer with authority to sign contracts, task or delivery orders and changes up to $500,000 in value, and another step down may be a contracting officer with authority to sign changes and task or delivery orders up to $25,000. The contractor must know this internal structure and be aware of the personnel and organizational changes that occur within the agency in order to determine whether a particular employee has authority at any given time. Since, as a general rule, no notice is given to contractors of such personnel or organizational changes, this task is a difficult one for the contractor that does not deal with the agency regularly.

Contractors must ascertain the monetary limitations on the authority of subsidiary contracting officers. See *General Constr. Servs., Inc.*, ASBCA 57187, 11-2 BCA ¶ 34,816 (employee with purchasing limit of $2,500 had no authority to agree to larger purchase); *Biofunction, LLC v. United States*, 92 Fed. Cl. 167 (2010) (pilot program costing $360,000 could not be procured by contracting officer with $10,000 limitation on authority); *Comspace Corp.*, DOTBCA 3095, 98-2 BCA ¶ 30,037 (delivery order not binding because it was in excess of $25,000 authority of contracting officer that signed it); *Edwards v. United States*, 22 Cl. Ct. 411 (1991) (government not bound when contracting officer agreed to modification above dollar limitation for agreements without approval of higher authority); and *Danac, Inc.*, ASBCA 30227, 90-3 BCA ¶ 23,246 (government would not have been bound by a settlement agreement above dollar limitation in contract, without approval of higher authority as provided for in contracting officer's warrant).

[b] Authorized Representatives

A considerable degree of confusion surrounds the term "authorized representative." One source of the confusion is the regulatory definition of contracting officer, discussed above, which defines the term to include "the authorized representatives of the contracting officer acting within the limits of their authority," FAR 2.101. However, authorized representatives traditionally have *a much narrower scope of authority* than those specifically appointed as contracting officers, and it should be clear that generally authorized representatives *do not have the authority to sign contracts or contract modifications*. See *Essen Mall Properties v. United States*, 21 Cl. Ct. 430 (1990), rejecting the argument that an authorized representative had the full authority of a contracting officer because of the regulatory definition.

Further confusion results from the varying methods used by contracting officers to appoint representatives—with some representatives being formally designated as contracting officer representatives and other representatives merely being assigned functions to be performed in the procurement process without specific use of the term "authorized representative" in their selection or appointment. For this reason, these two types of representatives are discussed separately.

[i] Formally Designated Representatives

There are a number of formally designated representatives who act on behalf of the government—primarily during contract administration. Depending upon the agency involved, these representatives may bear the title of contracting officer representative (COR), contracting officer technical representative (COTR), government technical representative (GTR), or government technical evaluator (GTE). See Cibinic, Nagle & Nash, *Administration of Government Contracts* (5th ed. 2016) for a detailed discussion of the appointment of such representatives and their major responsibilities.

These formally designated representatives frequently participate in modifications to contracts. However, limitations on authority of CORs or COTRs with regard to such modifications that have been communicated to the contractor are binding on the contractor. See *Winter v. Cath-dr/Balti Joint Venture*, 497 F.3d 1339 (Fed. Cir. 2007), holding pursuant to specific contract clauses that a COR had no authority to agree to contract modifications even though the contracting officer had informed the contractor that the COR had broad authority in administering the contract. The court stated that DFARS 201.602-2 *prohibited* the delegation of contracting officer authority to CORs. See also *Baistar Mech., Inc. v. United States*, 128 Fed. Cl. 504 (2016) (contractor should not have relied on COR's direction to perform work when it had no contract); *Dyno Grp. Inc.*, ASBCA 59074, 2014 BCA ¶ 35,575 (contractor should not have relied on COR's statement that additional work would be ordered); *ECC, Int'l*, ASBCA 55781, 2013 BCA ¶ 35,207 (neither project engineer nor COR had authority to make constructive changes to project); *Southwestern Security Servs., Inc. v. Dep't of Homeland Security*, CBCA 1264, 09-2 BCA ¶ 34,139 (COTR with authority to provide technical direction had no authority to order extra work); *S&M Mgmt., Inc. v. United States*, 82 Fed. Cl. 240 (2008) (government technical representative had no authority to approve specification deviations); *Catel, Inc.*, ASBCA 54627, 05-1 BCA ¶32,966 (COR had no authority to agree to pay for use of contractor property); *Elter S.A.*, ASBCA 52349, 01-2 BCA ¶31,547 & ASBCA 52791, 02-1 BCA ¶31,672 (government's construction representatives clearly had no authority to order changes); *California Consulting Eng'rs*, ASBCA 50355, 98-2 BCA ¶29,995 (COR had no authority to order extra work); *Niko Contracting Co. v. United States*, 39 Fed. Cl. 795 (1997) (COTR had no authority to promise that modification could be reopened); *Toloff Constr.*, AGBCA 95-227-3, 96-1 BCA ¶28,156 (COR had no authority to order extra work); *David W.E. Cabell*, VABCA 3402, 93-2 BCA ¶25,598 (COR has no authority to interpret an unambiguous contract in a manner that leads to additional compensation); *HTC Indus., Inc.*, ASBCA 40562, 93-1 BCA ¶25,560, *recons. denied*, 93-2 BCA ¶25,701, *aff'd*, 22 F.3d 1103 (Fed. Cir. 1994) (COTR had no authority to order contractor to continue performance while he sought additional funding in view of the specific language in the contract); *David W.E. Cabell*, VABCA 3402, 93-2 BCA ¶25,598 (COR had no authority to interpret an unambiguous contract in a manner that leads to additional compensation); *Construction Equip. Lease Co. v. United States*, 26 Cl. Ct. 341 (1992) (COR technical project officer had no authority to change contract in face of explicit language in appointment letter). The proper course of action when receiving an order for extra or changed work from such an employee is to demand that the order be issued by the contracting officer, *Adventure Grp., Inc.*, ASBCA 50188, 97-2 BCA ¶29,081 (contractor compensated for delay due to government refusal to resolve the need for extra work ordered by contract administrator).

Prior to *Winter v. Cath-dr/Balti*, there were numerous decisions holding the government bound by the actions of a COR or COTR acting within the scope of his or her authority, even if additional work was called for. See *Oliver Eng'g Servs.*, DOTBCA 2549, 94-3 BCA ¶27,203 (providing faulty technical information within scope of COTR's duties); *Hudson Contracting, Inc.*, ASBCA 41023, 94-1 BCA ¶26,466 (making government property available to contractor within authority of COR); *Diversified Marine Tech, Inc.*, DOTBCA 2455, 93-2 BCA ¶25,720 (granting permission to perform work within scope of COR's delegation when, as the government representative at the site, he was the most logical person to act); *MJW Enters., Inc.*, ENGBCA 5813, 93-1 BCA ¶25,405 (interpretation of vague specification within scope of COR's authority); and *Farr Bros., Inc.*, ASBCA 42658, 92-2 BCA ¶24,991 (COR had authority to order work suspension). In view of *Winter v. Cath-dr/Balti*, it is doubtful that the boards or courts will reach such a conclusion in the future—with a number of decisions holding that CORs have no authority, *Baistar Mech., Inc. v. United States*, 128 Fed. Cl. 504 (2016); *ECC Int'l*, ASBCA 55781, 13-1 BCA ¶35,207; *Sinil Co.*, ASBCA 55819, 09-2 BCA ¶34,213; and *States Roofing Corp.*, ASBCA 55500, 09-1 BCA ¶34,036. In *Circle, LLC*, ASBCA 58575, 15-1 BCA ¶36,025, engineers had no authority to direct the contractor to use a different method of performance.

[ii] Other Representatives

The vast majority of personnel involved in the contract formation process are designated neither as contracting officers nor authorized representatives. Some of these personnel, such as program managers, engineers and scientists, generate and fund the agency requirement which initiates the contracting process. Others are organizationally separate specialists, such as attorneys and auditors, from whom the contracting officer is required to request advice, FAR 1.602-2(c). All such personnel may receive information from contractors and may, in the course of their duties, participate in discussions or negotiations. Thus, their role may be seen as independent government representatives or as informally recognized representatives of the contracting officer. The regulations in this area do not clearly delineate the authority of these personnel and rarely require specific written designation as CORs.

In the past, the absence of formal delegation as a "representative" did not prevent the courts and boards of contract appeals from finding that these personnel were authorized representatives of the contracting officer. See, for example, *Cessna Aircraft Co.*, ASBCA 37726, 95-1 BCA ¶ 27,373 (government "evaluators" had authority to issue technical directions that changed contract because their direction was reportedly followed by COTR and contracting officer); *Zoubi v. United States*, 25 Cl. Ct. 581 (1992) (program director had authority to enter into a contract for interpreter services because his job carried with it an implied authorization to obtain all necessary personnel); *Walter Straga*, ASBCA 26134, 83-2 BCA ¶ 16,611 (project manager proper official to respond to technical inquiries and "was a representative of the contracting officer"); and *Contractors Equip. Rental Co.*, ASBCA 13052, 70-1 BCA ¶ 8183 (statement by contracting officer that official was "the man to satisfy" and deferral to him for equipment needs held "tantamount to a delegation de facto" as contracting officer's authorized representative). However, after the decision of the Federal Circuit in *Winter v. Cath-dr/Balti Joint Venture*, 497 F.3d 1339 (Fed. Cir. 2007), decisions refused to find such implied delegation of authority. See, for example, *Innoventor, Inc.*, ASBCA 55767, 17-1 BCA ¶ 36,798 (proposed modification sent by agency process engineer not an authorized change); *Circle, LLC*, ASBCA 58575, 15-1 BCA ¶ 36,025 (alleged rejection of work by agency engineers not a change); *P&K Contracting, Inc. v. United States*, 108 Fed. Cl. 380 (2012), *aff'd*, 534 Fed. Appx. 1000 (Fed. Cir. 2013) (agency technical official had no authority to promise contract modification); *Dubar v. Dep't of Agriculture*, CBCA 1895, 10-2 BCA ¶ 34,497 (agency "contact person" had no authority to contract for more work); *Hambone Constr., Inc. v. Dep't of Agriculture*, CBCA 1088, 09-2 BCA ¶ 34,258 (agency engineer had no authority to agree to pay for extra work); *Corners & Edges, Inc.*, ASBCA 55767, 09-1 BCA ¶ 34,019 (project officers had no authority to increase the work); *Corners & Edges, Inc. v. Dep't of Health & Human Servs.*, CBCA 648, 07-2 BCA ¶ 33,706 ("certified project officer" had no authority to extend performance period); and *California Business Tels. v. Dep't of Agriculture*, CBCA 135, 07-1 BCA ¶ 33,553 ("program analyst" that was the "point of contact" on the contract had no authority to order extra work).

When a contractor is expressly informed of limitations on the authority of these representatives, the contractor is generally unable to recover for unauthorized acts. Such notifications are often contained in letters to contractors or in contract clauses. See Cibinic, Nagle & Nash, *Administration of Government Contracts* (5th ed. 2016) for a detailed discussion of the impact of such communications.

[3] Dealing with Personnel Lacking Full Contractual Authority

As previously indicated, the vast majority of government personnel with whom a contractor deals do not possess full contractual authority; this does not mean, however, that dealings with such unauthorized personnel are without legal significance. This section considers several of the theories used to bind the government when the contractor has dealt with personnel possessing less than full authority to bind the government. The first of these theories is implied authority, where no authority has been specifically granted; the second is contracting officer ratification of the unauthorized act or statement; and the third is imputation of knowledge of unauthorized representatives to contracting officers.

[a] Implied Authority

As discussed above, it is highly unlikely that employees of contracting agencies with appointed contracting officers will be found to have implied authority. However, there are two unique situations where implied authority is likely to be found.

[i] Emergency Situations

The courts and boards have found that government employees with no authority to act in the contracting process have authority to bind the government in an emergency situation, *Philadelphia Suburban Corp. v. United States*, 217 Ct. Cl. 705 (1978) (firefighting foam to put out ship fire); *Halvorson v. United States*, 126 F. Supp. 898 (E.D. Wash. 1954) (equipment to deal with blizzard); *Sigma Constr. Co.*, ASBCA 37040, 91-2 BCA ¶ 23,926 (small alterations to ensure that concrete cured properly). See also *Baistar Mech., Inc. v. United States*, 128 Fed. Cl. 504 (2016), allowing a case to go to trial because the order of a COR might have been in response to an emergency. However, this means of overcoming the lack of authority has been construed narrowly. See *City of El Centro v. United States*, 922 F.2d 816 (Fed. Cir. 1990), *cert. denied*, 501 U.S. 1230 (1991), where the court found no emergency when border patrol agents had agreed to pay for hospital services for illegal aliens injured in a high-speed chase, and *Gardiner v. Virgin Islands Water & Power Authority*, 145 F.3d 635 (3d Cir.

1998), where the court refused to find an emergency where the contractor had provided services for 10 weeks following the occurrence of a hurricane.

[ii] Integral Part of Duty Theory

Authority to bind the government is generally implied when such authority is considered to be an integral part of the duties assigned to a government employee, *H. Landau & Co. v. United States*, 886 F.2d 322 (Fed. Cir. 1989). This theory was recognized in *Winter v. Cath-dr/Balti* but it has been followed in only a few cases. See *Rubio v. Agency for Int'l Development*, CBCA 2127, 11-1 BCA ¶ 34,717 (Deputy Mission Director had authority to direct the work); *Lubin Corp. v. United States*, 98 Fed. Cl. 53 (2011) (agency officials had authority to enter into confidentiality agreement with subcontractor); and *Stevens Van Lines, Inc. v. United States*, 80 Fed. Cl. 276 (2008) (upper level agency officials had authority to guarantee that the government would reimburse contractor for fees not included in the contract price). See also *First Fed. Lincoln Bank v. United States*, 54 Fed. Cl. 446 (2002), and *Commercial Fed. Corp. v. United States*, 55 Fed. Cl. 595 (2003) (making contractual agreements an integral part of promoting the acquisition of failing thrift organizations).

This rule appears to apply only with government offices that do not have a formalized contracting officer structure. See *Americopters, LLC v. United States*, 95 Fed. Cl. 224 (2010), stating at 231:

> Such authority will be implied only where it "is an essential or necessary part of the employee's occupation," and will not be implied "where an agency's regulations grant contracting authority to other agency employees." *BioFunction, LLC v. United States*, 92 Fed. Cl. 167, 172 (2010) (citing *SGS-92-X003 v. United States*, 74 Fed. Cl. 637, 652 (2007)).

Thus, in *BioFunction* the court rejected implied authority of a Postal Service district manager when the agency had contracting officers assigned to carry out its contracting functions. See also *Liberty Ammunition, Inc. v. United States*, 119 Fed. Cl. 368 (2014), *aff'd*, 835 F.3d 1388 (Fed. Cir. 2016) (Army officer in technical office had no implied authority to sign a nondisclosure agreement); and *P&K Contracting, Inc. v. United States*, 108 Fed. Cl. 380 (2012) (technical officer had no implied authority to authorize a change); *Gary v. United States*, 67 Fed. Cl. 202 (2005) (Assistant United States Attorneys and FBI Special Agents had no implied authority when Department of Justice had contracting officers assigned to deal with people that assist in criminal investigations). Compare *North American Landscaping, Constr. & Dredge Co.*, ASBCA 2127, 18-1 BCA ¶ 37,116, finding that the agency's project manager and project engineer had authority to direct extra work); and *Vargas v. United States*, 114 Fed. Cl. 226 (2014), finding it possible that employees of that department had made a contract with a "confidential informant."

Without discussion, the Federal Circuit in *Liberty Ammunition* stated that: "Authority is integral 'when the government employee could not perform his or her assigned tasks without such authority.'" *Liberty Ammunition*, 835 F.3d at 1402 (quoting *Flexfab, LLC v. United States*, 62 Fed. Cl. 139, 148 (2004), *aff'd*, 424 F.3d 1254 (Fed. Cir. 2005)). It is not clear whether this *Liberty Ammunition* test will foreclose the use of other formulations of the integral function test.

Several lower tribunals have attempted to define the integral function test. In *Cruz-Pagan v. United States*, 35 Fed. Cl. 59 (1996), the court framed the test as whether there was a "reasonably efficient alternative" to achieve the agency's objective. In holding that field agents of the Drug Enforcement Administration (DEA) had no implied authority to contract with informants, the court stated at 61:

> DEA could efficiently create . . . an expectation of compensation [by informants] without granting contracting authority to its field agents. For example, DEA could adopt internal procedures that grant contracting authority to supervisors of the field agents and oblige the field agents to secure approval from their supervisors before agreeing to provide compensation for assistance. Alternatively, DEA could establish procedures by which DEA would evaluate the value of the information or service provided and based on that evaluation grant compensation to informants on a fair and reasonable basis.

Leonardo v. United States, 63 Fed. Cl. 552 (2005), *aff'd*, 163 Fed. Appx. 180 (Fed. Cir. 2006), followed this analysis finding that a lower-level cultural affairs employee had no implied authority but that a Cultural Affairs Officer whose job was to "plan, coordinate and carry out cultural programs in support of public diplomacy objectives identified in the Country Plan" had implied authority (but that she did not ratify the arrangement of the lower-level employee). The court explained at 560:

> In contrast to the DEA field agents in *Cruz-Pagan*, who reported to field supervisors . . . Ms. Ignatius oversaw all programs and activities at the ACC and "reported directly to the Country Public Affairs Officer." The court sees no "reasonably efficient alternative," *Cruz-Pagan*, 35 Fed. Cl. at 61, to vesting Ms. Ignatius with authority to enter into contracts with artists that enables her effectively and efficiently to discharge her duties and fulfill the ACC's cultural mission. Nor has defendant presented any such alternatives. The court agrees with plaintiff that Ms. Ignatius' ability to enter into contracts was integral to the successful "planning, coordinating and carrying out [the United States Information Agency's] cultural programs," and to "managing the activities of the Cultural Center" efficiently.

Another explanation of this rule is found in *Aero-Abre, Inc. v. United States*, 39 Fed. Cl. 654 (1997), where the court stated at 657:

> In order to find implied actual authority, a court must conclude that the government intended to grant such authority but failed to do so explicitly due

> to some oversight or that such authority inheres in a particular position. See, e.g., *Cruz-Pagan v. United States*, 35 Fed. Cl. 59, 62-63 (1996) ("the doctrine of implied actual authority . . . serves to fill in the gap when an agency reasonably must have intended certain representatives to possess contracting authority but failed expressly to grant that authority"). Actual authority to bind the government has not been implied when a regulation, a contract, or a letter to the contractor expressly states that the employee does not have actual authority. See *Cruz-Pagan*, 35 Fed. Cl. at 62-63; *Construction Equip. Lease Co. v. United States*, 26 Cl. Ct. 341, 346-47 (1992); *Essen Mall Properties v. United States*, 21 Cl. Ct. 430, 444-45 (1990).

Another statement of the rule is that to find implied authority, there must have been some actual authority delegated. See *California Sand & Gravel, Inc. v. United States*, 22 Cl. Ct. 19 (1990), *aff'd*, 937 F.2d 624 (Fed. Cir. 1991), *cert. denied*, 502 U.S. 1057 (1992), where the Claims Court stated at 27:

> [A] person with some limited actual authority impliedly may have broader authority. However, a person with no actual authority may not gain actual authority through the court-made rule of implied actual authority. Specifically, the court may not substitute itself unconditionally for the executive agency in granting authority to an unauthorized person. The most the court can do is interpret the limited authority of an authorized person in a broader manner than ordinarily would be the case.

Other decisions following this reasoning include *Oasis Int'l Waters, Inc. v. United States*, 110 Fed. Cl. 87 (2013), and *Stout Rd. Assocs., Inc. v. United States*, 80 Fed. Cl. 754 (2008). However, the requirement was rejected as being too narrow in *Telenor Satellite Servs. v. United States*, 71 Fed. Cl. 114 (2006).

Whatever the formulation of the rule, it has been narrowly applied. See *Strickland v. United States*, 382 F. Supp. 2d 1334 (M.D. Fla. 2005) (agreeing that extra work was necessary on a ship repainting contract not integral part of the duties of port engineers); *Cornejo-Ortega v. United States*, 61 Fed. Cl. 371 (2004) (promising rewards to informants not integral part of the duties of field agents of the FBI); and *MTD Transcribing Serv.*, ASBCA 53104, 01-1 BCA ¶ 31,304 (arranging for transcription of a hearing not integral part of the job of an equal employment opportunity specialist).

[b] Ratification

Ratification is the adoption of an unauthorized act resulting in the act being given effect as if originally authorized, *Restatement, Second, Agency* § 82. In government contracting, representatives' unauthorized actions may subsequently be ratified by those with authority to bind the government. If the ratifying government official has actual or constructive knowledge of a representative's unauthorized act and expressly or impliedly adopts the act, ratification will be found, *Williams v. United States*, 127 F. Supp. 617 (Ct. Cl.), *cert. denied*, 349 U.S. 938 (1955). See also *Moran Bros. Co. v. United States*, 39 Ct. Cl. 486, 492 (1904) ("[I]f upon a full knowledge of the facts, the superior officer ratifies and confirms the action of his subordinate, is not that in law equivalent to an express authority in the subordinate at the time he ordered the performance of the labor?").

[i] Authority to Ratify

In general, the authority to ratify has been considered to be an integral part of an agent's authority without the need for specific statutory or regulatory coverage. For many years, the procurement regulations contained no specific ratification provisions. However, the government was held bound on the basis of ratifications without reference to regulatory authorities, *Michael Guth*, ASBCA 22663, 80-2 BCA ¶ 14,572; *Norwood Precision Prods.*, ASBCA 24083, 80-1 BCA ¶ 14,405.

In the 1970s and 1980s, agency regulations began to provide for ratification of unauthorized acts and to specify how such ratifications should be handled. Finally, in 1988, the following governmentwide guidance was added to FAR 1.602-3:

> (b) *Policy*. (1) Agencies should take positive action to preclude, to the maximum extent possible, the need for ratification actions. Although procedures are provided in this section for use in those cases where the ratification of an unauthorized commitment is necessary, these procedures may not be used in a manner that encourages such commitments being made by Government personnel.
>
> (2) Subject to the limitations in paragraph (c) of this subsection, the head of the contracting activity, unless a higher level official is designated by the agency, may ratify an unauthorized commitment.
>
> (3) The ratification authority in subparagraph (b)(2) of this subsection may be delegated in accordance with agency procedures, but in no case shall the authority be delegated below the level of chief of the contracting office.
>
> (4) Agencies should process unauthorized commitments using the ratification authority of this subsection instead of referring such actions to the General Accounting Office for resolution. (See 1.602-3(d).)
>
> (5) Unauthorized commitments that would involve claims subject to resolution under the Contract Disputes Act of 1978 should be processed in accordance with Subpart 33.2, Disputes and Appeals.
>
> (c) *Limitations*. The authority in subparagraph (b)(2) of this subsection may be exercised only when—
>
> (1) Supplies or services have been provided to and accepted by the Government, or the Government otherwise has obtained or will obtain a benefit resulting from performance of the unauthorized commitment;
>
> (2) The ratifying official has the authority to enter into a contractual commitment;

(3) The resulting contract would otherwise have been proper if made by an appropriate contracting officer;

(4) The contracting officer reviewing the unauthorized commitment determines the price to be fair and reasonable;

(5) The contracting officer recommends payment and legal counsel concurs in the recommendation, unless agency procedures expressly do not require such concurrence;

(6) Funds are available and were available at the time the unauthorized commitment was made; and

(7) The ratification is in accordance with any other limitations prescribed under agency procedures.

(d) *Nonratifiable commitments.* Cases that are not ratifiable under this subsection may be subject to resolution as recommended by the Government Accountability Office under its claim procedure (GAO Policy and Procedures Manual for Guidance of Federal Agencies, Title 4, Chapter 2), or as authorized by FAR Subpart 50.1. Legal advice should be obtained in these cases.

While these procedures are quite explicit, they have not prevented a finding of express ratification, *Tri-West Contractors, Inc.*, AGBCA 95-200-1, 97-1 BCA ¶ 28,662, or implied ratification, *Reliable Disposal Co.*, ASBCA 40100, 91-2 BCA ¶ 23,895. In the latter case, three contracting officers supported a request to pay the contractor for extra work but did not follow the FAR procedures. The board found that the failure to follow the FAR was not a bar to a finding of implied ratification. See also *BGT Holdings, LLC v. United States*, 984 F.3d 1003 (Fed. Cir. 2020) (knowledge of contracting officer that unauthorized officials had failed to furnish promised government property); *Guardian Safety & Supply LLC*, ASBCA 61932, 19-1 BCA ¶ 37,333 (giving assurances of payment and negotiating settlement with subcontractor); *American Gov't Servs., Inc. v. General Servs. Admin.*, CBCA 2294, 16-1 BCA ¶ 36,320 (continuing acceptance of performance after knowledge by employee in contracting office of payment without a contract); *Kumin Assocs., Inc.*, LBCA 94-BCA-3, 98-2 BCA ¶ 30,007 (contracting officer's review of changed drawings found to show implied ratification), and *Tripod, Inc.*, ASBCA 21305, 89-1 BCA ¶ 21,305 (contracting officer's knowledge of the contractor's complaints and review of inspection reports evidenced implied ratification). For a similar ruling under prior regulations, see *Driftwood of Ala.*, GSBCA 5429, 81-2 BCA ¶ 15,169. Compare *Stout Rd. Assocs. v. United States*, 80 Fed. Cl. 754 (2008); *Gary v. United States*, 67 Fed. Cl. 202 (2005); and *Kearfott Guidance & Navigation Corp.*, ASBCA 49271, 04-2 BCA ¶ 32,757, where the ratification regulation was invoked to deny ratification. In contrast in *Fish & Wildlife Serv.*, Comp. Gen. Dec. B-208730, 83-1 CPD ¶ 75, these ratification regulations were specifically invoked to support a finding of ratification.

Courts and boards do not possess the authority to ratify; they may only determine whether a ratification has occurred. They have recommended, however, that ratification authority be liberally exercised in cases where an injustice would result if the government did not become bound. See *Globe Indem. Co.*

v. United States, 102 Ct. Cl. 21 (1944), *cert. denied*, 324 U.S. 852 (1945), where the court stated at 38:

> The head of the department, or his duly authorized agent, of course, could have ratified these unauthorized acts, and in our opinion should have done so, since the work was necessary and for [the Government's] benefit, but he did not do so, and we are powerless to do it for him.
>
> From this case two lessons are to be drawn: (1) contracting officers and heads of departments should exercise the great powers conferred on them by these contracts to do equity; they should not feel under obligation to take advantage of technicalities, where to do so would defeat justice; (2) contractors must study their contracts and insist on compliance with their terms; before relying on any promise they should ascertain that it is made by a person having authority to make it.

[ii] Authority to Perform or Authorize Acts Being Ratified

The ratifying official must have the power to perform or authorize the unauthorized act, 22 Comp Gen. 1083 (B-33769) (1943). Thus, an official lacking the authority to enter into contracts cannot ratify an agreement, *Consortium Venture Corp. v. United States*, 5 Cl. Ct. 47 (1984); *Western Contract Furnishers*, PSBCA 317, 76-2 BCA ¶ 12,216. Similarly, illegal actions cannot be ratified because officials lack the authority to enter into illegal agreements. In *Trio Mach. Works, Inc.*, NASABCA 480-6, 82-1 BCA ¶ 15,465, *recons. denied*, 82-2 BCA ¶ 15,968, an alleged agreement between the contractor and a representative—whereby the contractor, for keeping a modification under a certain dollar amount, was to receive preferred treatment in future contract awards—was illegal and beyond the contracting officer's ratification authority. Similarly, where an agency purchased spark plugs on a sole source basis in violation of statutes requiring formal advertising, the Assistant Secretary of War could not subsequently ratify the transaction by classifying the spark plugs as an experimental item subject to negotiated procurement, 15 Comp. Gen. 618 (A-66806) (1936).

Proper authority to ratify was found in *California Human Dev. Corp. v. United States*, 87 Fed. Cl. 282 (2009), *aff'd*, 379 Fed. Appx. 979 (2010) (grants officer that ratified agreement had actual authority); and *Telenor Satellite Servs. v. United States*, 71 Fed. Cl. 114 (2006) (Deputy Assistant Secretary of State could ratify bailment contract). Compare *Kearfott Guidance & Navigation Corp.*, ASBCA 49271, 04-2 BCA ¶ 32,757, holding that an ACO had no authority to ratify because he was not the head of the contracting activity as required by the FAR. In contrast, in *American Gov't Servs., Inc. v. General Servs. Admin.*, CBCA 2294, 16-1 BCA ¶ 36,320, the board found that a contracting officer had ratified actions of an employee in the contracting office by continuing to accept performance after knowledge that there was no valid contract, and *B.V. Constr., Inc.*, ASBCA 47766, 04-1 BCA ¶ 32,604, the board found that a contracting officer had ratified actions allowing the contractor to perform work to correct defective specifications because a contract specialist who was required to report to the contracting officer had known of the action and accepted the benefits. Neither decision discusses the FAR requirement that ratification be given by the head of the contracting activity.

Under these rules, ratification normally requires action or inaction by a specific individual having the requisite authority to ratify the previously unauthorized act. However, some cases have found ratification without identifying such a specific individual (known as "institutional ratification"). In *Silverman v. United States*, 679 F.2d 865 (Ct. Cl. 1982), the court found that the agency ratified the agreement by accepting the benefits flowing from the unauthorized official's promise. See also *Rapp v. United States*, 2 Cl. Ct. 694 (1983), where the court found ratification where a government auctioneer's authority to extend the winning bidder's period of payment was in dispute: "[I]f any question remains as to the auctioneer's authority, it is rendered moot by the Customs Service's ratification of the announcement." Similarly institutional ratification was found in *Huntington Promotional & Supply, LLC v. United States*, 114 Fed. Cl. 760 (2014) (stating that there could be institutional ratification if the government agent who lacked contracting authority had "some similar type of authority"); and *Digicon Corp. v. United States*, 56 Fed. Cl. 425 (2003) (denying motion for summary judgment because facts indicated that institutional ratification had occurred). Compare *Hawkins & Powers Aviation, Inc. v. United States*, 46 Fed. Cl. 238 (2000), denying an institutional ratification claim because the government received no benefit; *City of El Centro v. United States*, 922 F.2d 816 (Fed. Cir. 1990), *cert. denied*, 501 U.S. 1230 (1991), where the Federal Circuit reversed a finding of institutional ratification by the Claims Court (16 Cl. Ct. 500 (1989)), and *Choe-Kelly, Inc.*, ASBCA 43481, 94-1 BCA ¶ 26,431, refusing to apply the institutional ratification logic. See, however, *Janowsky v. United States*, 133 F.3d 888 (Fed. Cir. 1998), remanding a case to the Court of Federal Claims to determine if institutional ratification occurred. In *Catel, Inc.*, ASBCA 54627, 05-1 BCA ¶ 32,966, the board found at 163,299 that *Janowsky* stood for the proposition that:

> Institutional ratification may occur giving rise to a contract where a government agency accepts benefits followed by a promise of payment by the agency or approval of payment by a senior agency official with authority to obtain reimbursement for the one providing those benefits.

See also *Digicon Corp. v. United States*, 56 Fed. Cl. 425, 426 (2003), stating that "it is well established that an agency can 'institutionally' ratify the contract, even in the absence of specific ratification by an authorized official" and finding such ratification when the agency accepted the benefits of the contested contract for 16 months. Similarly, in *Healthcare Practice Enhancement Network, Inc.*, VABCA 5864, 01-1 BCA ¶ 31,383, institutional ratification was found in where a committee including the contracting officer knew of an agreement made by the Chief Fiscal Officer of the agency and accepted the benefits of the agreement.

Compare *Gary v. United States*, 67 Fed. Cl. 202 (2005), concluding that institutional ratification cannot be found from the acts of "low-ranking Government employees" because that would subject the government to "wholly uncontrollable" expenditures. See also *Doe v. United States*, 58 Fed. Cl. 479 (2003), rejecting institutional ratification because there was no "active acceptance" of the plaintiff's performance.

[iii] Knowledge of Unauthorized Acts

A prerequisite to ratification is the ratifying official's knowledge, either actual or constructive, of the facts affecting the unauthorized action. In *United States v. Beebe*, 180 U.S. 343 (1901), the Court stated at 354:

> Where an agent has acted without authority and it is claimed that the principal has thereafter ratified his act, such ratification can only be based upon a full knowledge of all the facts upon which the unauthorized action was taken. This is as true in the case of the Government as in that of an individual. Knowledge is necessary in any event. Story on Agency, 9th ed. sec. 239, notes 1 and 2. If there be want of it, though such want arises from the neglect of the principal, no ratification can be based upon any act of his. Knowledge of the facts is the essential element of ratification, and must be shown or such facts proved that its existence is a necessary inference from them.

Lack of knowledge has also been found in *P&K Contracting, Inc. v. United States*, 108 Fed. Cl. 380 (2012) (no proof of contracting officer knowledge); *Corners & Edges, Inc.*, ASBCA 55767, 09-1 BCA ¶ 34,019 (no proof of contracting officer knowledge); *Dureiko v. United States*, 62 Fed. Cl. 340 (2004) (contracting officer testified that he had no knowledge of the alleged agreement); *California Sand & Gravel, Inc. v. United States*, 22 Cl. Ct. 19 (1990), *aff'd*, 937 F.2d 624 (Fed. Cir. 1991) (holding that there could be no ratification without "full knowledge of all facts" pertinent to the unauthorized commitment); and *Durocher Dock & Dredge, Inc.*, ENGBCA 5768, 91-3 BCA ¶ 24,145 (contracting officer, as the only official with authority to ratify, had no knowledge of the events).

The ratifying official may obtain actual knowledge from various sources, *Mick DeWall Constr.*, PSBCA 2580, 91-1 BCA ¶ 23,510 (contracting officer received notice within 10 days that COR had agreed to modification); *Brown Constr. Co.*, ASBCA 22648, 79-1 BCA ¶ 13,745 (contracting officer participated in a preconstruction conference where a representative stated that construction policy required a contract change); *Globe Constr. Co.*, GSBCA 2197, 67-2 BCA ¶ 6478 (contracting officer received notice of prior actions from his representative and through the contractor's formal claim for additional compensation).

A ratifying official may also gain knowledge constructively. Constructive notice was found in *Williams v. United States*, 127 F. Supp. 617 (Ct. Cl.), *cert. denied*, 349 U.S. 938 (1955), where an unauthorized Air Force officer and the contractor agreed that the contractor could use the Air Force's asphalt plant in return for seal coating the base's roads. The base contracting officer was held to have constructive knowledge of the agreement because the roads were wholly within the base where he was located.

Imputed knowledge from representatives may also serve as constructive knowledge of a ratifying official. See, for example, *W. Southard Jones, Inc.*, ASBCA 6321, 61-2 BCA ¶3182, where base technical personnel knew that the contractor's performance did not conform to contract drawings. This knowledge was imputed to the contracting officer, who frequently met with the base engineer and discussed projects at the base. When the relationship between two persons creates a presumption that one would have informed the other of certain events, the boards may impute the knowledge of one to the other. See *American Gov't Servs., Inc. v. General Servs. Admin.*, CBCA 2294, 16-1 BCA ¶36,320 (knowledge of employee in contracting office imputed to contracting officer); *B.V. Constr., Inc.*, ASBCA 47766, 04-1 BCA ¶32,604 (knowledge of a contract specialist imputed to contracting officer); and *Southwestern Sheet Metal Works, Inc.*, ASBCA 22748, 79-1 BCA ¶13,744, *recons. denied*, 79-2 BCA ¶13,949 (knowledge of inspectors functioning as contracting officer's "eyes and ears" imputed to contracting officer).

[iv] Adoption of Unauthorized Acts

The contractor must show that an authorized official has adopted the unauthorized action, either expressly, by conduct, or by silence. In *DBA Sys., Inc.*, NASABCA 481-5, 82-1 BCA ¶15,468, ratification did not occur because the contracting officer "consistently and expressly disavowed the purported funding agreement and likewise did nothing which, by implication, could be reasonably interpreted as his concurrence with [his representative's] belief that the overrun should be funded." See also *Prestex Inc. v. United States*, 320 F.2d 367 (Ct. Cl. 1963) (upon learning of deviations from specifications, the government repudiated the contract, never having accepted or used the product, so that no ratification of deviations existed).

An express adoption of an unauthorized act clearly establishes ratification, *Fish & Wildlife Serv.*, Comp. Gen. Dec. B-208730, 83-1 CPD ¶75 (authorized official signed a document expressing his intent to ratify the unauthorized act); *Globe Constr. Co.*, GSBCA 2197, 67-2 BCA ¶6478 (contracting officer stated that his subordinate's prior action had been done "within his authority").

An authorized official's adoption of an unauthorized act may result from conduct, *B.V. Constr., Inc.*, ASBCA 47766, 04-1 BCA ¶32,604 (sending a revised statement of work and an unpriced contract modification containing revised drawings); *Boeing Computer Servs.*, ASBCA 42674, 94-3 BCA ¶27,114 (acceptance of user manual containing procedure modifying the contract specifications); *T.W. Cole*, PSBCA 3076, 92-3 BCA ¶25,091 (acceptance of work with knowledge of order to modify it); *Henry Burge & Alvin White*, PSBCA 2431, 89-3 BCA ¶21,910 (acceptance of work with knowledge of modification); *Norwood Precision Prods.*, ASBCA 24083, 80-1 BCA ¶ 14,405 (payment for products accepted after a default termination indicated the official's adoption of the inspector's unauthorized acceptance); *Mil-Pak Co.*, GSBCA 5849, 83-1 BCA ¶ 16,482 (contracting officer ratified a "change order by unilaterally fixing the amount of the equitable adjustment"). But see *Leonardo v. United States*, 63 Fed. Cl. 552 (2005), finding inadequate proof of ratification when the plaintiff testified about relatively vague discussions with a government official with implied authority and the government did not call the official as a witness, and *Metcalf & Assocs.*, GSBCA 3190, 72-2 BCA ¶ 9516, where the board held that a contracting officer's award of compensation to a contractor for certain changes directed by unauthorized representatives did not constitute a ratification but was an attempt at settlement not binding upon the government.

Silence or inaction may also constitute adoption by an authorized official. See *KRW, Inc.*, DOTBCA 2572, 94-1 BCA ¶ 26,435 (contracting officer acquiesced in alteration of work product); *HFS, Inc.*, ASBCA 43748, 92-3 BCA ¶ 25,198 (contracting officer took no action on letter describing the order for extra work); *Gricoski Detective Agency*, GSBCA 8901, 90-3 BCA ¶ 23,131 (total inaction after letter was sent to contracting officer describing an order to change the method of performance); *Lox Equip. Co.*, ASBCA 8985, 1964 BCA ¶ 4463 (failure of contracting officer "to take effective action to correct the situation" adopted his inspector's directives); *Michael Guth*, ASBCA 22663, 80-2 BCA ¶ 14,572 (contracting officer affirmed by not questioning a manager's interpretation of liability provisions); *Brown Constr. Co.*, ASBCA 22648, 79-1 BCA ¶ 13,745 (contracting officer silent when unauthorized official prohibited the use of contract-designated plywood); and *Triangle Elec. Mfg. Co.*, ASBCA 15995, 74-2 BCA ¶ 10,783 (contracting officer's silence regarding representatives' interpretation "was conduct amounting to consent to the performance of such duties"). Compare *SAE Americon*, PSBCA 3866, 00-1 BCA ¶ 30,867, where no ratification by silence was found where the COR promptly notified the contractor that a construction technique was not required after finding out about the purported direction to use the technique. See also *Harbert/Lummus Agrifuels Projects v. United States*, 142 F.3d 1429 (Fed. Cir. 1998), *cert. denied*, 525 U.S. 1177 (1999), finding no ratification when a contracting officer was at a meeting where an unauthorized official made an oral promise to the contractor but did not object or warn the contractor. The court reasoned at 1433-34:

> In our case, the trial court merely found that the CO was present when the Deputy Director made the offer and was silent after the offer was made. There was no finding that the CO even heard the statement. This is not sufficient evidence to support a finding of actual knowledge by the CO of the offer. In addition, the facts as found by the trial court do not support imputing to the CO constructive knowledge of the unilateral contract. The mere fact that Harbert/Lummus continued performing its construction activities would not have put the CO on notice of the existence of a new, unilateral contract because Harbert/Lummus had been performing its construction activities

> before the offer by the Deputy Director in accordance with its construction contract with Agrifuels. In the absence of either actual or constructive knowledge of the unilateral contract, the CO's silence cannot be a ratification of the unilateral contract.

Acquiescence has been premised on the ratifying official's constructive notice coupled with silence. See *Williams v. United States*, 127 F. Supp. 617 (Ct. Cl.), *cert. denied*, 349 U.S. 938 (1955); *Southwestern Sheet Metal Works, Inc.*, ASBCA 22748, 79-1 BCA ¶ 13,744, *recons. denied*, 79-2 BCA ¶ 13,949; and *W. Southard Jones, Inc.*, ASBCA 6321, 61-2 BCA ¶ 3182.

[c] Knowledge Imputed to Authorized Personnel

In many cases it is important to determine whether the contracting officer or other authorized representative has knowledge of certain facts. Such knowledge may be important because the contract requires that information be furnished to the authorized person or that notice be given of events such as delays or constructive changes. In other situations, the legal significance of statements or acts of an authorized person depends upon whether the person was in possession of specific knowledge. Almost all instances of imputed knowledge arise in the contract administration process, but the legal principles are equally applicable to contract formation.

The authorized person is held to have knowledge under the common-law concept that a principal is charged with knowledge that an agent has a duty to deliver to the principal, *Restatement, Second, Agency* § 272. In applying this rule to government contracts, the courts and boards have imputed knowledge to contracting officers and other authorized persons when the nature of the relationship between the authorized person and the representative establishes a presumption that the authorized person would be informed. Thus, in *Sociometrics, Inc.*, ASBCA 51620, 00-1 BCA ¶ 30,620, the board imputed knowledge that the contractor was performing work even though an option had not been exercised because the COR was the "eyes and ears" of the contracting officer.

In most cases involving imputed knowledge, the unauthorized representative possesses actual knowledge obtained within the scope of his or her duties. However, two cases have held a contracting officer to have imputed knowledge although only constructive knowledge on the part of the representatives was demonstrated, *Inet Power*, NASABCA 566-23, 68-1 BCA ¶ 7020, and *W. Southard Jones, Inc.*, ASBCA 6321, 61-2 BCA ¶ 3182. Constructive notice to a representative has been expressly rejected in cases involving cost or pricing data. Because of the contractor's affirmative duty to submit such data, knowledge would not be imputed to the government if auditors lack actual knowledge. See *Libby Welding Co.*, ASBCA 15084, 73-1 BCA ¶ 9859 (contractor listed costs twice on bill that auditors overlooked and imputation held improper); and *Sylvania Elec. Prods., Inc.*, ASBCA 13622, 70-2 BCA ¶ 8387, *aff'd*, 479 F.2d

1342 (Ct. Cl. 1973) (auditors did not cross-check data and therefore failed to uncover a material cost error, but absent auditors' actual knowledge, the contracting officer was not charged with knowledge).

Knowledge of a wide variety of government officials has been imputed to the contracting officer. Thus, knowledge of technical personnel is frequently imputed, *Glenda R. Whitaker*, PSBCA 3443, 94-2 BCA ¶ 26,643 (knowledge of contractor's protests, having been communicated to those authorized by the contracting officer to administer the contract, may be imputed to the contracting officer); *Walter Straga*, ASBCA 26134, 83-2 BCA ¶ 16,611 (project manager's knowledge that the contractor's interpretation of the drawings differed from his own imputed to contracting officer); *Carl J. Bonidie, Inc.*, ASBCA 25769, 82-2 BCA ¶ 15,818 (Changes clause notice requirement was satisfied by knowledge of base civil engineer, whose recommendations apparently determined the contracting officer's contractual decisions). However, information possessed by a technical representative will not be imputed if the information is not the type that technical representatives would be presumed to convey to a contracting officer. See *Donat Gerg Haustechnik*, ASBCA 41197, 97-2 BCA ¶ 29,272, refusing to impute knowledge of technical person of nonconforming work, and *Franchi Realty Trust v. General Servs. Admin.*, GSBCA 11149, 92-3 BCA ¶ 25,180, not imputing a directive by a Drug Enforcement Administration representative concerning construction work.

Information obtained by inspectors that is pertinent to their duties has also been imputed to the contracting officer. See *Hudson Contracting, Inc.*, ASBCA 41023, 94-1 BCA ¶ 26,466, where the board upheld a government inspector's oral agreement for the furnishing of government property in return for the contractor providing equipment and an operator for unrelated government work. The board found that the government project manager, with authority to provide the government property involved, had imputed knowledge of the agreement "by virtue of [his] supervision of the inspector . . . [and his] extensive day-to-day involvement in the progress of the contract." However, not all relationships between contracting officers and inspectors are sufficiently close to raise the presumption that the contracting officer would be informed of relevant facts. See, for example, *Canadian Commercial Corp.*, ASBCA 17187, 76-2 BCA ¶ 12,145, *recons. denied*, 77-2 BCA ¶ 12,758, where an inspector's knowledge of design defects was not imputed to the contracting officer because "close contact between the resident Canadian inspector and the [government's] contract administration or technical personnel" was not established.

Knowledge of administrative and clerical personnel is far less likely to be imputed to the contracting officer. Compare *American Gov't Servs., Inc. v. General Servs. Admin.*, CBCA 2294, 16-1 BCA ¶ 36,320 (knowledge of employee in contracting office imputed to contracting officer); and *KRW, Inc.*, DOTBCA 2572, 94-1 BCA ¶ 26,435 (contract administrator's knowledge imputed to the contracting officer because the contractor had been directed to send reports to the contract administrator), with *JGB Enters. v. United States*, 63 Fed. Cl. 319 (2004) (small business specialist's knowledge of a subcontractor's difficulties in obtaining payment not imputed to the contracting officer), and *M.J. Newsom*, ASBCA 9799, 1964 BCA ¶ 4444 (airman's knowledge of the contractor's causes of delay not imputed because his relationship with the contracting officer was not sufficient to establish a presumption that the information would be reported).

Since auditors are expected to convey information to the contracting officer, information related to the audit function will be imputed. In *Chrysler Corp.*, ASBCA 17259, 75-1 BCA ¶ 11,236, *recons. denied*, 76-1 BCA ¶ 11,665, Army Audit Agency knowledge of the contractor's accrual account and the manner in which it operated was imputed to the contracting officer. Similarly, in *E-Sys., Inc.*, ASBCA 18877, 76-1 BCA ¶ 11,797, where the Defense Contract Audit Agency was aware of the contractor's pooling and allocation of material costs, this information was imputed to the contracting officer. See also *United States v. Hanna Nickel Smelting Co.*, 253 F. Supp. 784 (D. Or. 1966), *aff'd on other grounds*, 400 F.2d 944 (9th Cir. 1968) (contractor's accounting practices regarding allocation of capital items known by auditors); and *Western Elec. Co.*, ASBCA 21294, 79-1 BCA ¶ 13,550.

See Cibinic, Nagle & Nash, *Administration of Government Contracts* (5th ed. 2016) for a more complete discussion of imputed knowledge.

[B] Contractor Personnel

In contrast to the special rules pertaining to government representatives, general principles of agency law apply to contractor's representatives. There is considerably less litigation in this area.

[1] Delegation

Authority may be expressly or impliedly delegated to contractor's representatives. When a corporation is involved, the plenary authority to transact all the ordinary business of the corporation within its charter powers is vested in the board of directors. Express delegation of authority to others is normally contained in resolutions of the board of directors, which are often furnished to the government agencies with whom the corporate contractor does business.

FAR 4.102 requires the contracting officer to ascertain the authority of corporate officials as follows:

> (a) *Individuals*. A contract with an individual shall be signed by that individual. A contract with an individual doing business as a firm shall be signed by that individual, and the signature shall be followed by the individual's typed, stamped, or printed name and the words, "an individual doing business as ___" [insert name of firm].
>
> (b) *Partnerships*. A contract with a partnership shall be signed in the partnership name. Before signing for the Government, the contracting officer

shall obtain a list of all partners and ensure that the individual(s) signing for the partnership have authority to bind the partnership.

(c) *Corporations.* A contract with a corporation shall be signed in the corporate name, followed by the word "by" and the signature and title of the person authorized to sign. The contracting officer shall ensure that the person signing for the corporation has authority to bind the corporation.

(d) *Joint venturers.* A contract with joint venturers may involve any combination of individuals, partnerships, or corporations. The contract shall be signed by each participant in the joint venture in the manner prescribed in paragraphs (a) through (c) above for each type of participant. When a corporation is participating, the contracting officer shall verify that the corporation is authorized to participate in the joint venture.

(e) *Agents.* When an agent is to sign the contract, other than as stated in paragraphs (a) through (d) above, the agent's authorization to bind the principal must be established by evidence satisfactory to the contracting officer.

[2] Apparent Authority

The major difference between the legal rules applicable to government and contractor representatives is that a contractor may be bound by a representative possessing apparent authority. See *American Anchor & Chain Corp. v. United States*, 331 F.2d 860 (Ct. Cl. 1964), where the court stated at 862:

> Although the Federal Government still stands on the stricter requirements of actual authority for its own agents (see, e.g., *Federal Crop Ins. Corp. v. Merrill*, 332 U.S. 380 (1947)), the agents of Government contractors are governed by the usual rules.

See also *Kaco Contracting Co.*, ASBCA 44937, 01-2 BCA ¶ 31,584 9968 (government entitled to rely on apparent authority of contractor's agent to sign release of claims); and *Western Box-O-Matic Corp.*, GSBCA 3562, 73-1 BCA ¶ 9968 (government entitled to rely on apparent authority of contractor's plant manager to interpret contract language). Similarly, in *Deep Joint Venture v. General Servs. Admin.*, GSBCA 14511, 02-2 BCA ¶ 31,914, the person that negotiated and signed a lease for a joint venture was held to have apparent authority. In *Menches Tool & Die, Inc.*, ASBCA 21469, 78-1 BCA ¶ 13,167, the board rejected the contractor's arguments that it had never authorized its attorney to make certain statements, stating "[t]he Government has the right to assume an agent has actual or apparent authority to bind its principal."

However, if government employees know or should know that a contractor representative does not have contracting authority, that representative will not be found to have apparent authority. See *Peter Bauwens Bauunternehmung GmbH & Co. KG*, ASBCA 44679, 98-1 BCA ¶ 29,551 (contractor not bound by agreements of its project manager because government "knew or had reason to know" that he had no contracting authority); *Kahaluu Constr. Co.*, ASBCA 33248, 90-2

BCA ¶ 22,663 (proposed settlement agreement approved by an agent of a contractor and an agent of the government, both without authority, was not an offer to settle); *Piracci Corp.*, GSBCA 6007, 82-2 BCA ¶ 16,047 (contractor not bound by a settlement negotiated by attorney when government negotiator had no reason to believe that attorney had authority to settle a claim); *Colorado Security Agency, Inc.*, GSBCA 5650, 84-1 BCA ¶ 16,940 (contractor not bound because contracting officer knew contractor's employee had no authority); and *Ray Wilson Co.*, ASBCA 17084, 74-1 BCA ¶ 11,066 (government was not justified in inferring that a second-tier subcontractor's employees had authority to bind the contractor).

[3] Ratification and Estoppel

Even though the government deals with an unauthorized representative, the contractor will be bound if the action is ratified by an authorized official. In *Tectonics Asia Architects & Eng'rs, Inc.*, ASBCA 17067, 75-2 BCA ¶ 11,456, the contractor was held bound by an unauthorized amendment when it had continued performance for 2½ months with full knowledge of the terms of the amendment.

The principles of estoppel are also similarly applicable to the contractor. In *Ampex Corp.*, GSBCA 5913, 82-1 BCA ¶ 15,738, *recons. denied*, 82-2 BCA ¶ 15,858, the board held that the contractor was estopped to deny an agreement where a contractor's representative had informed the government that the contractor had agreed to accept the agreement. The board found that the representative did not have authority to make the agreement but did have the authority to convey information to the government, stating at 77,861:

> Granted, [the contractor's representative] was not an agent of the company authorized to bind it contractually. We have already indicated that we do not consider that to be the point in dispute. Rather, the issue is whether [the representative] had the authority to tell the Government that [the contractor] had agreed to be bound. If she had that authority, then [the contractor] is bound by her representation:
>
> > Except as to statements with relation to the agent's authority, in actions brought upon a contract or to rescind a contract, a disclosed or partially disclosed principal is responsible for unauthorized representations made incidental to it, if the contract is otherwise authorized and if true representations as to the same subject matter are within the authority or the apparent authority of the agent, unless the other party thereto has notice that the representations are untrue or unauthorized.
>
> > Restatement (Second), Agency (1958), § 162.

See also *E. Walters & Co. v. United States*, 576 F.2d 362 (Ct. Cl. 1978), where the contractor was estopped from seeking additional compensation for the performance of an allegedly improperly exercised option because it had performed the work without objection, and *Detroit Diesel Allison Div., Gen. Motors Corp.*, ASBCA 20199, 77-1 BCA ¶ 12,414, where the contractor was estopped to deny applicability of longstanding accounting practice. Contractors have also been held to be estopped from denying that they are subject to the standard disputes process after they have participated in that process to a significant extent, *H.R. Henderson & Co. v. United States*, 169 Ct. Cl. 228 (1965); *Norair Eng'g. Corp.*, ENGBCA 5244, 97-1 BCA ¶ 28,917. Compare *CRF v. United States*, 624 F.2d 1054 (Ct. Cl. 1980), stating that the contractor was not estopped to deny the validity of a contract awarded in a manner contrary to the regulations. In *E.L. Hamm & Assocs. v. England*, 26 Fed. Appx. 936 (Fed. Cir. 2002), the court held that a contractor was not estopped to assert a claim by a letter offering to perform at no cost because the government had not proved the authority of the person that sent the letter or that the government relied on the letter. Similarly, in *Piracci Corp.*, GSBCA 6007, 82-2 BCA ¶ 16,047, the board that held the contractor was not estopped on the basis, among others, that there was no justifiable reliance by the government.

§ 1.05 GOVERNMENT BOUND BY CONDUCT OF ITS AUTHORIZED AGENTS

Since the government can act only through its agents and employees, it is clear that it will be bound when authorized agents carry out their duties properly. However, government personnel cannot be expected to act only in ways favorable to the United States. Whether resulting from mistakes, negligence, or poor judgment, their statements, acts, or omissions are sometimes contrary to the government's best interests. This may become evident from later reflection or subsequent events, or it may be determined by the agents' advisers, superiors, or successors. In such cases, attempts may be made to avoid the consequences by repudiating or countermanding the agents' acts. There are two major concepts that are invoked to prevent the government from disowning authorized agents' acts or agreements, thereby making them binding on the government. The first concept is finality, the second is estoppel.

[A] Finality

The actions of a government employee acting within the scope of his or her employment are the actions of the government itself, and as with any contracting party, once the government has taken the final step toward committing a contractual act, it is bound by it. Once an authorized representative enters into a contract, not even Congress has the authority to abrogate it, *United States v. Winstar Corp.*, 518 U.S. 839 (1996).

[1] Sources of Finality

Finality of contractual acts may attach as a result of either the application of a legal rule or a provision of the contract that is interpreted as providing that finality attaches to a decision or action of a government agent. The clearest example of a legal rule creating finality occurs in the contract formation process where the normal binding effect of the acceptance of an offer is applied to the government. This rule of contract law states that at the time an offer is accepted, a binding contract is formed. See *United States v. Purcell Envelope Co.*, 249 U.S. 313 (1919), where the Court held that the government was bound when the Postmaster General accepted the offer of a company in a formally advertised procurement. Similarly, the government will be bound if an authorized official enters into a contract modification adjusting the price after a change has been ordered, *Liberty Coat Co.*, ASBCA 4119, 57-2 BCA ¶ 1576. See also *Airmotive Eng'g. Corp.*, ASBCA 15235, 71-2 BCA ¶ 8988, where the board held that the government was bound when a contracting officer entered into a contract amendment modifying the price to reflect the adoption of a value engineering proposal.

The most direct example of a contract clause providing for finality is the Disputes clause, which allows contracting officers to make final decisions when a dispute cannot be settled. The government was held bound by such decisions in *Bell Helicopter Co.*, ASBCA 17776, 74-1 BCA ¶ 10,411. Another such clause is the Inspection clause, which states that government acceptance of work will be final, with certain exceptions. In *C.H. McQuagge v. United States*, 197 F. Supp. 460 (W.D. La. 1961), the contracting officer had issued a certificate of final acceptance despite the knowledge of the government that the concrete used in airport taxiways did not measure up to the specifications. The court found the acceptance final and conclusive, stating at 468:

> In a case such as this, the government can only act through those to whom it has delegated authority to make decisions. It was within the discretion of the Contracting Officers to determine whether the work was acceptable to the government, and final acceptance by such officers was subject to being opened or questioned only upon evidence of collusion, fraud, or obvious error.

See also *Shea-Ball (JV)*, ENGBCA 5608, 99-1 BCA ¶ 30,277; *Mil-Spec Contractors, Inc. v. United States*, 835 F.2d 865 (Fed. Cir. 1987); *S.E.R., Jobs for Progress, Inc. v. United States*, 759 F.2d 1 (Fed. Cir. 1985); *Walsky Constr. Co.*, ASBCA 19875, 77-1 BCA ¶ 12,388; *Conrad Weihnacht Constr., Inc.*, ASBCA 20767, 76-2 BCA ¶ 11,963; and *Genuine Motor Parts of Pa., Inc.*, ASBCA 19063, 76-1 BCA ¶ 11,860.

Finality has also been found when the government acts under contract clauses that do not expressly state that the action is "final." One such clause that has been interpreted as creating finality is the Allowable Cost and Payment clause, FAR 52.216-7. See *Chrysler Corp.*, ASBCA 17259, 75-1 BCA

¶ 11,236, *recons. denied*, 76-1 BCA ¶ 11,665, holding that the predecessor Allowable Cost, Fixed Fee and Payment clause should be interpreted to bar the government from contesting the allowability of costs after final payment on the contract has been made. See also *MPR Assocs., Inc.*, ASBCA 54689, 05-2 BCA ¶ 33,115, holding the government bound to the agreements made in a final overhead rate negotiation even though the parties had not yet signed an "indirect cost rate agreement." In *Bell Aircraft Corp. v. United States*, 100 F. Supp. 661 (Ct. Cl. 1951), the court held that approval and payment of invoices under a cost-reimbursement contract was binding on the government at the time the payment was made. The same result was reached in *United States v. Mason & Hanger Co.*, 260 U.S. 323 (1922), and *Leeds & Northrup Co. v. United States*, 101 F. Supp. 999 (E.D. Pa. 1951). Finality was also found when a contracting officer made a decision to fund an overrun under the Limitation of Cost clause, *General Elec. Co. v. United States*, 412 F.2d 1215, *mot. for reh'g denied*, 416 F.2d 1320 (Ct. Cl. 1969), and where an award fee official determined the award fee under an Award Fee clause, *URS Consultants, Inc.*, IBCA 4285-2000, 02-1 BCA ¶ 31,812. Neither the Allowable Cost, Fixed Fee and Payment clause, the Limitation of Cost clause nor the Award Fee clause contains explicit language stating that decisions or actions of the contracting officer or award fee official will be final, yet the courts and boards have interpreted the clauses to have this effect. Compare *Litton Sys., Inc., Guidance & Control Sys. Div.*, ASBCA 45400, 94-2 BCA ¶ 26,895, holding that an administrative contracting officer's determination that the contractor was not in compliance with Cost Accounting Standards 405 and 410 was not entitled to finality because no contract clause provided that such decisions would be final. See also *JC&N Maint., Inc.*, ASBCA 51283, 02-1 BCA ¶ 31,799, finding no finality in pre-dispute representations of contracting officers which were not labeled final decisions and were part of an evolving course of negotiations between the contractor and the agency.

Finality has been found in a few instances where the act of the government was not communicated to the contractor at the time the act was taken. In *General Elec. Co. v. United States*, 412 F.2d 1215, *reh'g denied*, 416 F.2d 1320 (Ct. Cl. 1969), the court found a binding decision because the contracting officer had signed an internal memorandum stating that an overrun would be funded, even though this contracting officer's decision was not communicated to the contractor. The same result was reached in *Texas Instruments, Inc. v. United States*, 922 F.2d 810 (Fed. Cir. 1990), where an ACO had signed a price negotiation memorandum (PNM) agreeing to a negotiated settlement of a claim. The court found that this was a final decision, stating at 813-14:

> Under *General Electric*, the law presumes that when an ACO acquainted with the underlying facts signs an internal document, such as the PNM, that she has decided to express a definite opinion on the merits of the claim in the absence of contrary testimony or evidence. Such contrary evidence or testimony is lacking here.

These cases indicate that the government will be bound during contract administration by the doctrine of finality whenever an authorized employee signs a document or takes an action that is properly construed as resolving the issue at hand. See also *Boeing Co. v. United States*, 75 Fed. Cl. 34 (2007), holding that the award fee determination of the contractually designated Award Fee Determination Official was binding on the government even though internal agency procedures called for review of the decision at the Secretarial level (where it was disapproved).

A variety of other actions and determinations by government officials may also be final and binding on the government. For example, a determination by a contracting officer that the contractor's labor cost estimating technique was not defective was final and binding on the government and could not be revoked or overruled by his successor, *Bell Helicopter Co.*, ASBCA 17776, 74-1 BCA ¶ 10,411. In *Southern Waldrip & Harvick Co. v. United States*, 334 F.2d 245 (Ct. Cl. 1964), the court held that the chief of engineers could not overrule a finding of the contracting officer that a telegraphic bid modification had been timely received. The instructions to bidders had stated that a determination of timeliness of modifications would rest with the contracting officer. These instructions constituted an agreement between the government and the contractor and left the chief of engineers without authority to determine timeliness independently.

[2] Authority Required

For the action to be binding and final, the government employee must be acting within his or her authority. See *Trevco Eng'g & Sales*, VACAB 1021, 73-2 BCA ¶ 10,096, where the board found that an inspector had not been delegated the authority to make final acceptance. See also Comp. Gen. Dec. B-170360, 1971 WL 5837, stating that an award by a contracting officer to the second low bidder could be overruled by his superiors, because the contracting officer had no authority to make a valid award to anyone but the low responsible bidder; and 35 Comp. Gen. 63 (B-120714) (1955), stating that no finality attaches to payment contrary to the cost-plus-a-percentage-of-cost prohibition. Acts of unauthorized representatives that are ratified by an authorized official are also accorded finality, *Tucker & Assocs. Contracting, Inc.*, IBCA 1468-6-81, 83-1 BCA ¶ 16,140.

Since no government employee has the authority to violate the law, finality will not attach to a decision that violates public policy. See, for example, *ENCORP Int'l, Inc.*, ASBCA 49474, 99-1 BCA ¶ 30,254, finding an agreement of a contracting officer to release Miller Act payment bonds not entitled to finality because it was in violation of an important public policy.

[3] Government Bound by Prejudicial Decisions

The government is bound by the acts of its authorized representatives, even if their decisions are the result of poor judgment that is injurious to the government. In *Liberty Coat Co.*, ASBCA 4119, 57-2 BCA ¶ 1576, the contracting officer issued findings and determinations that certain changes reduced the contractor's costs and adjusted the contract price accordingly. A successor contracting officer issued new determinations and findings on the same changes and greatly increased the reductions in price. In ruling for the contractor that the original contracting officer's decision was binding, the board stated at 5671-72:

> The Government makes no allegation of mutual mistake and, while admitting that it has no other evidence of fraud or collusion, argues that we are required to draw such an inference from the gross disparity between the equitable adjustments agreed to by the original contracting officer and the "correct and equitable adjustment for the deviation[s]" as found by the successor contracting officer. Assuming for the purposes of decision on [the contractor's] motion, the validity of the successor contracting officer's determination of "correct and equitable" price adjustments, in the absence of even a scintilla of other evidence of fraud and collusion, we think the proper inference is that, relying on erroneous advice of his price analysts, the original contracting officer made a bad bargain. We are not aware of any authorities, nor has counsel invited our attention to any, holding that an agreement is vitiated by this fact alone.
>
> The Government seeks to distinguish these cases from our prior holdings on the ground that in their determination the Board did not consider its present argument that the original contracting officer acted "outside the bounds of his authority" in agreeing to allegedly grossly inadequate price adjustments. Under the terms of the standard "Changes" article of these contracts, and procurement regulations, the contracting officer had clear authority to make changes in the specifications of the contracts. Upon doing so he was specifically charged with the responsibility of determining whether the change caused "an increase or decrease in the cost of . . . this contract . . . ," and, upon such a determination, the clause continues, "an equitable adjustment shall be made in the contract price . . . and the contract shall be modified in writing accordingly." The Government's argument, reduced to its lowest common denominator, is that while the contracting officer had authority to make a good bargain, he had no authority to make a bad one. We are unable to accept such an argument. It confuses the contracting officer's authority to act with the judgment displayed by him in performing the act. It seeks to measure authority by the results obtained upon its exercise. Counsel has not cited, and we have been unable to find, any cases supporting this method of measuring authority.

While it cannot be said that the government "authorizes" its agents to make negligent decisions or to commit torts, it is liable for the agent's action if it is within the scope of his or her authority. See *Cooke v. United States*, 91 U.S. (1 Otto) 389 (1875), where the Court stated at 398:

> Laches is not imputable to the government, in its character as sovereign, by those subject to its dominion. Still a government may suffer loss through the negligence of its officers. If it comes down from its position of

> sovereignty, and enters the domain of commerce, it submits itself to the same laws that govern individuals there. Thus, if it becomes the holder of a bill of exchange, it must use the same diligence to charge the drawers and indorsers that is required of individuals; and, if it fails in this, its claim upon the parties is lost. Generally, in respect to all the commercial business of the government, if an officer specially charged with the performance of any duty, and authorized to represent the government in that behalf, neglects that duty, and loss ensues, the government must bear the consequences of his neglect. But this cannot happen until the officer specially charged with the duty, if there be one, has acted, or ought to have acted. As the government can only act through its officers, it may select for its work whomsoever it will; but it must have some representative authorized to act in all the emergencies of its commercial transactions. If it fails in this, it fails in the performance of its own duties, and must be charged with the consequences that follow such omissions in the commercial world.

See also *Rockwell Int'l Corp.*, EBCA C-9509187, 97-1 BCA ¶ 28,814 (government bound by provisions of settlement agreement entered into by Department of Justice and accepted by court); *Steward/Tampke, JV*, ASBCA 48929, 96-2 BCA ¶ 28,320 (government bound by settlement agreement to pay Contract Disputes Act interest); *Honeywell Fed. Sys., Inc.*, ASBCA 39974, 92-2 BCA ¶ 24,966 (government bound by contracting officer's determination that cost or pricing data not required because contractor met commercial item exemption); *Sterling Millwrights, Inc. v. United States*, 26 Cl. Ct. 49 (1992) (government bound where contracting officer made progress payments with full knowledge of costs included therein); and *Summit Contractors*, AGBCA 81-252-1, 86-1 BCA ¶ 18,632 (government bound by contract modification favorable to contractor).

It appears that the doctrine of finality will prevent recovery by the government when the government agent makes a unilateral mistake but not when the mistake is mutual. See *Chrysler Corp.*, ASBCA 17259, 75-1 BCA ¶ 11,236, *recons. denied*, 76-1 BCA ¶ 11,665, holding the government bound by incorrect determinations of an allowable cost but commenting that finality would not bar recovery on the theory of mutual mistake. See also *United States v. Hadden*, 192 F.2d 327 (6th Cir. 1951), holding that the government could not recover mistaken payments made to contractor's creditors because there was no "mistake of fact" and the "bankrupt had no knowledge of the mistake." Similarly, in *URS Consultants, Inc.*, IBCA 4285-2000, 02-1 BCA 31,812, *recons. denied*, 02-2 BCA ¶ 31,917, the government was held bound to allegedly mistaken award fee computations made by the award official and contracting officer in a CPAF contract. The board rejected the argument that the mistaken calculations were simple mathematical errors that might have been correctable. Compare *Institutional & Environmental Mgmt., Inc.*, ASBCA 32924, 90-3 BCA ¶ 23,118, holding that the government was not bound when the contracting officer mistakenly agreed to increase the contract price when state unemployment insurance taxes were increased. The board reasoned that this was a pure mistake because the contract placed the risk of higher state taxes on the contractor, stating at 116,073:

> Finality does not apply to this situation where the contracting officer was not exercising discretion or powers granted to her by virtue of the contract and her position. The contracting officer simply misinterpreted the contract to provide reimbursement to appellant of amounts which appellant was obligated by contract to include within its bid.

Of course, the government will not be bound by a bad decision of an employee who lacks authority, *Winn-Senter Constr. Co. v. United States*, 75 F. Supp. 255 (Ct. Cl. 1948) (absent special circumstances, government agent has no authority to order contractor to increase wages and agree to government reimbursement).

[B] Equitable Estoppel

Equitable estoppel is a concept that prohibits a party from escaping liability for statements, actions, or inactions if they have been relied on by the other party. It has traditionally been thought that two prerequisites exist for estopping the government: (1) the government's representative must have been acting within the scope of his or her authority, and (2) the government must be acting in its proprietary capacity rather than its sovereign capacity, *United States v. Georgia-Pacific Co.*, 421 F.2d 92 (9th Cir. 1970). The Supreme Court has altered the focus of the first prerequisite to the requirement that the act of the government must be one that is not barred by statute or published regulation, *OPM v. Richmond*, 496 U.S. 414, *reh'g denied*, 497 U.S. 1046 (1990). Once these threshold requirements are met, the normal common-law rules of estoppel apply. Thus, the government has been estopped based on its actions in the contracting process. See *Burnside-Ott Aviation Training Ctr., Inc. v. United States*, 985 F.2d 1574 (Fed. Cir. 1993), stating at 1581:

> The Claims Court improperly relied on *Richmond* to conclude that Burnside-Ott's equitable estoppel claim is barred as a matter of law. In particular, the Claims Court erred in concluding that *Richmond* stands for the proposition that equitable estoppel will not lie against the government for any monetary claim. The *Richmond* holding is not so broad. *Richmond* is limited to "claim(s) for the payment of money from the Public Treasury *contrary to a statutory appropriation*." 496 U.S. at 424 (emphasis added). Indeed, because the Supreme Court's analysis in *Richmond* is based entirely on the Appropriations Clause of the Constitution, Article 1, Section 9, Clause 7, which provides that "No Money shall be drawn from the Treasury, but in Consequence of Appropriations made by Law," its holding must be limited to claims of entitlement contrary to statutory appropriations.

> *Burnside-Ott's* assertion of a right to payment of money from the Public Treasury, however, is not based upon a statutory entitlement. Burnside-Ott's assertion is instead based upon its contract with the Navy. Nor does Burnside-Ott claim entitlement contrary to statutory eligibility criteria, as did Richmond. Thus, neither the holding nor analysis in *Richmond* is applicable in this case, and Burnside-Ott's equitable estoppel claim is not barred as a matter of law because of *Richmond*. Equitable estoppel may or may not apply in this case depending on facts yet to be established.

The elements of estoppel were detailed in *Mabus v. General Dynamics C4 Sys., Inc.*, 633 F.3d 1356, 1359 (Fed. Cir. 2011), where the court ruled that equitable estoppel, as a general matter, should be analyzed using a three-prong test: "(1) misleading conduct, which may include not only statements and actions but silence and inaction, leading another to reasonably infer that rights will not be asserted against it; (2) reliance upon this conduct; and (3) due to this reliance, material prejudice if the delayed assertion of such rights is permitted." For decisions following this reasoning, see *Allen Eng'g Contractor, Inc. v. United States*, 115 Fed. Cl. 457 (2014), and *P&K Contracting, Inc. v. United States*, 108 Fed. Cl. 380 (2012).

A significant limitation on estoppel against the government was the imposition of the additional requirement that the contractor show affirmative misconduct by the government. See *Zacharin v. United States*, 213 F.3d 1366 (Fed. Cir. 2000), stating at 1371:

> Although the Supreme Court has not adopted a per se rule prohibiting the application of equitable estoppel against the government under any circumstances, it has made it clear that "the government may not be estopped on the same terms as any other litigant." *Heckler v. Community Health Servs.*, 467 U.S. 51, 60, 81 L. Ed. 2d 42, 104 S. Ct. 2218 (1984). In particular, the Court has suggested that if equitable estoppel is available at all against the government some form of affirmative misconduct must be shown in addition to the traditional requirements of estoppel. See *Richmond*, 496 U.S. at 421; *INS v. Miranda*, 459 U.S. 14, 19, 74 L. Ed. 2d 12, 103 S. Ct. 281 (1982); *Schweiker v. Hansen*, 450 U.S. 785, 788, 67 L. Ed. 2d 685, 101 S. Ct. 1468 (1981). While the Supreme Court has not squarely held that affirmative misconduct is a prerequisite for invoking equitable estoppel against the government, this court has done so, see *Henry v. United States*, 870 F.2d 634, 637 (Fed. Cir. 1989); *Hanson v. Office of Personnel Management*, 833 F.2d 1568, 1569 (Fed. Cir. 1987), as has every other court of appeals, see *Tefel v. Reno*, 180 F.3d 1286, 1303 (11th Cir. 1999) (citing cases).

Since *Zacharin* the decisions have denied estoppel because of lack of proof of affirmative misconduct. See *MLJ Brookside, LLC v. General Servs. Admin.*, CBCA 3041, 15-1 BCA ¶ 35,935 (claim denied for failure to allege affirmative misconduct); *Lukos Vatc JV LLC v. United States*, 116 Fed. Cl. 108 (2014) (no affirmative misconduct in sending letter mistakenly informing contractor its mentor protégé agreement had been approved); *Northrop Grumman Corp.*, ASBCA 57625, 2014 BCA ¶35,501 (no evidence of affirmative misconduct in government contesting retirement benefit costs); *UniTech Servs. Grp., Inc.*, ASBCA 56482, 12-2 BCA ¶35,060 (discussing possible follow-on contract not affirmative misconduct); *SplashNote Sys., Inc.*, ASBCA 57403, 12-1 BCA ¶34,899 (challenging costs after approval of accounting system not affirmative misconduct); *United States v. Honeywell Int'l, Inc.*, 841 F. Supp. 2d 112 (D.D.C. 2012) (failure of the government to accept contractor offer to research an alleged false claim not affirmative misconduct); *Bernard Cap Co.*, ASBCA 56679, 10-1 BCA ¶34,387 (claim of equitable tolling of statute of limitations rejected for lack of proof of affirmative misconduct); *Data Computer Corp. of American v. United States*, 80 Fed. Cl. 606 (2008) (no affirmative misconduct in leading contractor to believe that overhead rates used to close out contract applied to all other contracts); *Alliant Techsys., Inc. v. United States*, 74 Fed. Cl. 566 (2007) (no affirmative misconduct when contracting officers led contractor to believe that they were agreeing to final overhead rates); (no affirmative misconduct estopping government from asserting that settlement agreement included claimed costs); *Kaeper Mach., Inc. v. United States*, 74 Fed. Cl. 1 (2006) (no affirmative misconduct when government allowed purchase order to lapse when contractor failed to deliver units); *Ervin & Assocs. v. United States*, 59 Fed. Cl. 267 (2004), *aff'd*, 120 Fed. Appx. 353 (Fed. Cir. 2005) (no affirmative misconduct found when agency gave contractor's data to competitors); *United Pacific Ins. Co.*, ASBCA 52419, 04-1 BCA ¶32,494, *aff'd*, 401 F.3d 1362 (Fed. Cir. 2005) (no affirmative misconduct when parties miscalculated contract balance at time of entering into takeover agreement and contracting officer did not inform surety when mistake was found); *Demarco Durzo Dev. Co. v. United States*, 60 Fed. Cl. 632 (2004) (no affirmative misconduct when contracting officer misstated date when lease would be terminated); and *Melrose Assocs., L.P. v. United States*, 45 Fed. Cl. 56 (1999) (no affirmative misconduct when government employee that executed two amendments failed to confirm her authority in advance, was ignorant as to the limitations on her authority and did not notify the contractor when she was made aware of the possible limitations on her authority). See also *Westinghouse Elec. Corp. v. United States*, 41 Fed. Cl. 229 (1998), discussing the need for affirmative misconduct but rejecting an estoppel argument on other grounds. In *Rumsfeld v. United Techs. Corp.*, 315 F.3d 1361 (Fed. Cir.), *cert. denied*, 540 U.S. 1012 (2003), the court remanded the case for trial on the estoppel issue, but the board denied the claim for lack of affirmative misconduct, *United Techs. Corp.*, ASBCA 47416, 06-1 BCA ¶33,289. The board decision contains a thorough discussion of the application of the affirmative misconduct requirement.

Prior to the Federal Circuit's ruling that affirmative misconduct was an essential element of an estoppel claim, when the official was acting within the scope of delegated authority and the actions were not prohibited by statute or regulation, estoppel would be found even though the action was based upon *a mistaken interpretation* of the government's obligations, *USA Petroleum Corp. v. United States*, 821 F.2d 622 (Fed. Cir. 1987); *Portmann v. United States*, 674 F.2d 1155 (7th Cir. 1982); *Broad Ave. Laundry & Tailoring v. United States*, 681 F.2d 746 (Ct. Cl. 1982). Note, however, that *Broad Avenue Laundry* was questionable precedent since the contracting officer's statement was contrary to a published regulation.

Because estoppel accomplishes the same result as finality, the two concepts are often confused. However, there are two important differences between finality and estoppel. Estoppel requires *detrimental reliance* by the party who seeks to invoke it, while reliance is not an element of finality. The other difference is that the statement or action leading to finality is by its very nature contractually binding upon the government through the operation of legal principles such as offer and acceptance, acceptance of goods, etc. The government is held bound by estoppel, however, because it would be *unfair* not to do so even though the statement, action, or inaction would not be contractually binding. Thus, the government has been estopped through its course of conduct as well as through its verbal representations. See *Dynamic Concepts, Inc.*, ASBCA 44738, 93-2 BCA ¶ 25,689 (government estopped when the contracting officer paid invoices exceeding the contract ceiling and the contractor continued performance in reliance on such conduct); *Peninsular ChemResearch, Inc.*, ASBCA 14384, 71-2 BCA ¶ 9066 (government required to accept results of accounting method it previously approved by implication); and *Litton Sys., Inc. v. United States*, 449 F.2d 392 (Ct. Cl. 1971) (government's knowledge of, acquiescence to, and approval of contractor's accounting system precluded retroactive disallowance of cost).

[1] Government Not Estopped by Unauthorized Actions

The government will not be estopped by the unauthorized actions of its representatives, *United States v. Georgia-Pacific Co.*, 421 F.2d 92 (9th Cir. 1970). Frequently, the lack of authority results from the action being contrary to statutory requirements. In such cases, courts will construe authority narrowly, *Schweiker v. Hansen*, 450 U.S. 785 (1981) (all courts have a duty to observe conditions defined by Congress for charging the public treasury); *OPM v. Richmond*, 496 U.S. 414, *reh'g denied*, 497 U.S. 1046 (1990) (government cannot be bound by payment contravening explicit statutory limitation). Similarly, in *Singer Co.*, ASBCA 17604, 75-2 BCA ¶ 11,401, *aff'd*, 576 F.2d 905 (Ct. Cl. 1978), the contractor submitted cost or pricing data that the government representative knew were not current. Since the government official had no authority to waive the requirements of the Truth in Negotiations Act, 10 U.S.C. § 3703 (formerly § 2306a), the government could not be estopped from obtaining a price reduction. The same rule applies when the employee is acting contrary to delegated authority, *Atlantic Gulf & Pac. Co. of Manila v. United States*, 207 Ct. Cl. 995 (1975) (no estoppel to disavow settlement agreement negotiated without required advance approval).

GAO has consistently ruled that the government cannot be estopped from rejecting bids that are nonresponsive or offers that do not meet the government's needs in a negotiated procurement. See *International Waste Indus.*, Comp. Gen. Dec. B-210500.2, 83-1 CPD ¶652, stating that "erroneous advice given by agency officials cannot estop the agency from rejecting a nonresponsive bid, since the agency is required to do so by law." The same result was reached in *Jensen Corp.*, 60 Comp. Gen. 543 (B-200277.2), 81-1 CPD ¶524; and *Trident Indus. Prod., Inc.*, 59 Comp. Gen. 742 (B-199138), 80-2 CPD ¶222. See also *International Med. Indus., Inc.*, 62 Comp. Gen. 31 (B-208235), 82-2 CPD ¶386, where no estoppel was found when a bidder was found nonresponsive in step two of a two-step sealed bidding procurement even though the nonconformity was present in the step one proposal which was accepted by the government. In *Eastern Marine, Inc.*, Comp. Gen. Dec. B-213945, 84-1 CPD ¶343, the same rule was applied to negotiated procurements by holding that the government cannot be estopped from rejecting a nonconforming proposal from the competitive range. In that case, GAO formulated the rule as a matter of legal authority by stating that "there exists no basis under the legal doctrine of estoppel for requiring the government to consider for award a proposal which does not meet the government's minimum needs." See also *Toyo Menka Kaisha, Ltd. v. United States*, 597 F.2d 1371 (Ct. Cl. 1979), where the court held that the government was not estopped to deny the validity of a contract since the contracting officer was not authorized to make an award on a nonresponsive bid.

Other cases finding no estoppel because of lack of authority include: *SUFI Network Servs., Inc. v. United* States, 108 Fed. Cl. 287 (2012) (government lawyer had no authority to sign settlement agreement); *United States v. Honeywell Int'l, Inc.*, 841 F. Supp. 2d 112 (D.D.C. 2012) (Department of Justice lawyers had no authority to waive the right to bring a false claims suit); *P&K Constr., Inc. v. United* States, 108 Fed. Cl. 380 (2012) (technical employees had no authority to agree to add work to contract); *AEY, Inc. v. United* States, 99 Fed. Cl. 300 (2011) (contracting officer had no authority to permit shipment of products made in communist country); *California Bus. Tels. v. Dep't of Agriculture*, CBCA 135, 07-1 BCA ¶33,553 (program analyst had no authority to expand scope of contract); *Conner Bros. Constr. Co. v. United States*, 65 Fed. Cl. 657 (2005) (contracting officer had limited authority); and *Healthcare Practice Enhancement Network, Inc.*, VABCA 5864, 01-1 BCA ¶31,383 (Chief Financial Officer of agency health center had no authority to enter into contract).

In *Urban Data Sys., Inc. v. United States*, 699 F.2d 1147 (Fed. Cir. 1983), a small business contract contained a cost-plus-percentage-of-cost pricing clause at the government's insistence. Because agents lack the authority to compensate contractors under such a clause, the government was not estopped to deny its validity. Urban was entitled to compensation, however, under quantum valebant.

[2] Sovereign Capacity Exception

It has been stated that the government will not be estopped from performing sovereign acts, *United States v. Georgia-Pacific Co.*, 421 F.2d 92 (9th Cir. 1970). In *United States v. Lazy FC Ranch*, 481 F.2d 985 (9th Cir. 1973), the court considered both the questions of lack of authority and actions within the government's sovereign capacity. Citing *Georgia-Pacific, Moser v. United States*, 341 U.S. 41 (1951), *Brandt v. Hickel*, 427 F.2d 53 (9th Cir. 1970), and *Schuster v. C.I.R.*, 312 F.2d 311 (9th Cir. 1962), the court stated at 989:

> The *Moser-Brandt-Schuster* line of cases establish the proposition that estoppel is available as a defense against the government if the government's wrongful conduct threatens to work a serious injustice and if the public's interest would not be unduly damaged by the imposition of estoppel. *Gestuvo v. District Dir. of I.N.S.*, 337 F. Supp. 1093 (C.D. Cal. 1971). This proposition is true even if the government is acting in a capacity that has traditionally been described as sovereign (as distinguished from proprietary) although we may be more reluctant to estop the government when it is acting in this capacity. See *Georgia-Pacific, supra.*

This case rejects the sovereign-capacity exception and also appears to reject the rule that the government is not estopped by unauthorized acts. However, the court found that "the agency's published regulations arguably permitted" the action taken by the government's representatives. The Supreme Court has not ruled on whether estoppel lies against the government when the government acted in its sovereign capacity. In *Schweiker v. Hansen*, 450 U.S. 785 (1981), the Court referred to *Lazy FC Ranch* in a footnote, stating, "We do not need to consider the correctness of these cases."

[3] Knowledge of Facts

When a claim of estoppel is based on the government not revealing facts, the contractor must prove that it did not know those facts. See *Henry H. Norman v. General Servs. Admin.*, GSBCA 15070, 02-2 BCA ¶ 32,042, denying recovery because, although the contractor did not know all of the detailed facts in the possession of the government with regard to the possibility of injury because of an insecure government building, it was aware of many of these facts. See also *Western Aviation Maint., Inc. v. General Servs. Admin.*, GSBCA 14165, 00-2 BCA ¶ 31,123 (parties had equal but incomplete knowledge of the facts); *Davis Grp., Inc.*, ASBCA 48431, 95-2 BCA ¶ 27,702 (contractor knew the contents of a contract clause).

[4] Reliance

Reasonable reliance by the contractor is an essential element of estoppel, *California-Pacific Utilities Co. v. United States*, 194 Ct. Cl. 703 (1971). In this case, the court held that the contractor could not claim reliance on an alleged agreement to include an indemnification clause in a permit when it had notice that the government official who allegedly agreed to include the clause did not have authority to do so. There are numerous decisions finding the contractor's alleged reliance to be unreasonable. See, for example, *Data Computer Corp. v. United States*, 80 Fed. Cl. 606 (2008) (unreasonable to rely on use of indirect cost rates to settle claims on one contract as final determination of rates for all contracts); *Melrose Assocs., L.P. v. United States*, 45 Fed. Cl. 56 (1999) (unreasonable to rely on government employees' signing contract amendments without checking to determine if they had authority); and *C Constr. Co.*, ASBCA 41706, 94-1 BCA ¶ 26,263 (unreasonable to rely on inadvertent specification deviation approved by architect/engineer).

Reliance on opinions or statements of future intention are frequently found to be unreasonable. See *Brenda R. Ronhaar*, AGBCA 98-147-1, 99-1 BCA ¶ 30,591 (reliance on opinion that options would be exercised unreasonable); *Robert Shaw Control Sys. Div. v. Dep't of the Army*, GSBCA 12714-P, 94-2 BCA ¶ 26,713 (reliance on government lawyer's opinion on legal rule unreasonable); *State Street Mgmt. Corp. v. General Servs. Admin.*, GSBCA 12374, 94-1 BCA ¶ 26,500 (unreasonable to rely on statement of future intention).

Reliance cannot occur when the contractor's action took place *before* the government act that is alleged to have created the estoppel. Thus, in *George G. Sharp, Inc.*, ASBCA 55385, 09-1 BCA ¶ 34,117, no reliance was found because a recommendation to fund overruns occurred after costs had been incurred. See *Rockwell Int'l Corp.*, ASBCA 20304, 76-2 BCA ¶ 12,131 (contractor changed its accounting system before the government acted); and *Codex Corp.*, ASBCA 17983, 75-2 BCA ¶ 11,554, *remanded on other grounds*, 226 Ct. Cl. 693 (1981) (costs were incurred before action by contracting officer). Estoppel was also denied in *Blount, Inc.*, VABCA 3719, 95-2 BCA ¶ 27,874, where the board found that although the subcontractor probably relied on the VA review finding that its system appeared to meet the specification requirements, there was no detrimental reliance by the prime contractor.

The contractor must prove that it actually relied on the government statement or act. See *General Elec. Co. v. United States*, 60 Fed. Cl. 782 (2004) (no proof that contractor relied on government position on costs in sale of division); *General Sec. Servs. Corp. v. General Servs. Admin.*, GSBCA 11381, 92-2 BCA ¶ 24,897 (no reliance on an alleged government waiver of the specification was found because the contractor did not indicate in negotiations that it was relying on the waiver); *Snowbird Indus., Inc.*, ASBCA 33027, 89-3 BCA ¶ 22,065 (no reliance where contractor did not know of government act alleged to create estoppel); and *Meridian Inc.*, PSBCA 2203, 89-2 BCA ¶ 21,648 (no evidence that contractor action occurred because of government act.

The Supreme Court's ruling in *Heckler v. Community Servs. of Crawford County, Inc.*, 467 U.S. 51 (1984), casts doubt as to the validity of reliance on oral advice as the basis for asserting estoppel against the government. The Court stated at 65:

> The appropriateness of respondent's reliance is further undermined because the advice it received from Travelers was oral. It is not merely the possibility of fraud that undermines our confidence in the reliability of official action that is not confirmed or evidenced by a written instrument. Written advice, like a written judicial opinion, requires its author to reflect about the nature of the advice that is given to the citizen, and subjects that advice to the possibility of review, criticism, and reexamination. The necessity for ensuring that governmental agents stay within the lawful scope of their authority, and that those who seek public funds act with scrupulous exactitude, argues strongly for the conclusion that an estoppel cannot be erected on the basis of the oral advice that underlay respondent's cost reports.

GAO has consistently held that, even with contractor's detrimental reliance in formulating its bid, a bidder relies "on any oral explanation at its own risk," *International Waste Indus.*, Comp. Gen. Dec. B-210500.2, 83-1 CPD ¶ 652. See also *Eastern Marine, Inc.*, Comp. Gen. Dec. B-213945, 84-1 CPD ¶ 343, rejecting a claim of estoppel against the government because it was based upon oral advice, allegedly received during telephone conversations, that was in direct conflict with the provisions in the RFP.

[5] Injury

Injury is essential to estoppel. The contractor must establish that its reliance has placed it in a worse position than it would have been in otherwise, *Chula Vista City School Dist. v. Bennett*, 824 F.2d 1573 (Fed. Cir. 1987), *cert. denied*, 484 U.S. 1042 (1988). See also *Grigor E. Atoian v. General Servs. Admin.*, GSBCA 12765, 95-1 BCA ¶ 27,444 (contractor's delay in filing claim in reliance on advice from government employee caused no loss or harm to contractor); *Okaw Indus., Inc.*, ASBCA 17863, 75-1 BCA ¶ 11,321, *recons. denied*, 75-2 BCA ¶ 11,571 (no injury to contractor from disallowance of settlement); *Simmonds Precision Prods., Inc.*, ASBCA 18110, 74-1 BCA ¶ 10,472 (government not estopped from assessing liquidated damages after two years absent proof of prejudice from delay); and *General Dynamics Corp.*, ASBCA 13868, 69-2 BCA ¶ 8044 (contractor not deprived of recovery of allocable costs by retroactive change of accounting system).

[6] Waiver

Closely related to and sometimes used interchangeably with estoppel is the concept of waiver—the relinquishment of a legal right. See *American Nat'l Bank & Trust Co. v. United States*, 23 Cl. Ct. 542 (1991); *Branch Banking & Trust Co. v. United States*, 98 F. Supp. 757, *cert. denied*, 342 U.S. 893 (Ct. Cl. 1951); and Comp. Gen. Dec. B-174410, June 30, 1972, *Unpub.* As with estoppel, the government will be bound by a waiver if the contractor relies upon it to its detriment, *De Vito v. United States*, 413 F.2d 1147 (Ct. Cl. 1969). However, a waiver may be retracted if it is not supported by consideration or if the contractor has not relied upon the waiver to its detriment, *Tri-West Contractors, Inc.*, AGBCA 95-200-1, 97-1 BCA ¶ 28,662; *Mark Dunning Indus.*, ASBCA 29599, 86-1 BCA ¶ 18,521.

The term "waiver" is frequently used in connection with the government's failure to promptly terminate a delinquent contractor when that contractor has relied on the government's failure to terminate by continuing performance or preparation for performance with the government's knowledge and express or implied consent. In such cases, the government will have waived its right to terminate the contractor for default by electing to allow the contractor to proceed rather than terminating. See *AEY, Inc.*, ASBCA 56470. 18-1 BCA ¶ 37,076 (government's failure to set a new delivery date with knowledge that shipments were in progress but would be late); *DODS, Inc.*, ASBCA 57667, 12-2 BCA ¶ 35,078, *recons. denied*, 13 BCA ¶ 35,203 (government's failure to set a new delivery date, coupled with its encouragement to continue work for 21 months); *Environmental Safety Consultants, Inc.*, ASBCA 51722, 11-2 BCA ¶ 34,848 (government's failure to set a new completion date, coupled with its encouragement to continue work for 11 months after the original completion date); *Divecon Servs., LP v. Dep't of Commerce*, GSBCA 15997, 04-2 BCA ¶ 32,656 (encouraging contractor to make expensive repairs and keep its personnel on stand-by); and *SIPCO Servs. & Marine, Inc. v. United States*, 41 Fed. Cl. 196 (1998) (government worked with the contractor for over seven months after the contract completion date). For a thorough discussion of this doctrine, see Chapter 10, Cibinic, Nash & Nagle, *Administration of Government Contracts* (5th ed. 2016).

The government's acceptance of nonspecification performance under a prior or current contract may give rise to a constructive waiver of specifications. The Court of Federal Claims explained the concept of constructive waiver of specifications in *Miller Elevator Co. v. United States*, 30 Fed. Cl. 662 (1994), at 687:

> While the constructive waiver of specifications incorporates estoppel theories into the legal doctrine of waiver, the theory finds basis in any certain interpretation given to a contract specification by the contracting parties. Once the parties continue performance under the interpretation, one party may not later seek to enforce a contrary interpretation, even if the former interpretation results in the constructive waiver of specifications.

The Court of Federal Claims has adopted a four-part test for constructive waiver. In *Hannon Elec. Co. v. United States*, 31 Fed. Cl. 135 (1994), the court stated at 147 that to establish a constructive waiver of specifications, the contractor must show that:

> (1) The [contracting officer] had notice that the work differed from the contract requirements. (2) Action or inaction of the [contracting officer] indicated that the non-specification performance was acceptable. (3) The contractor relied on the [contracting officer's] action or inaction. (4) It would be unfair to permit the Government to retract the waiver.

In *Gresham & Co. v. United States*, 470 F.2d 542 (Ct. Cl. 1972), waiver of the specifications was found when the government had accepted dishwashers without automatic dispensers in the previous 21 contracts. In *Hannon Elec.*, however, the contractor disregarded the contract's size requirements for load banks (electrical testing devices) and built larger, nonspecification load banks. Unbeknownst to the contractor, the government discovered that the load banks were too large before they were completed. Because the contractor was unaware of the government's knowledge of the deviation, no waiver was found because it could not have relied on the government's alleged acquiescence.

Acceptance of a small number of deviating performances will not constitute waiver, *Western States Constr. Co.*, ASBCA 37611, 92-1 BCA ¶ 24,418 (waiver on only two prior contracts—one with another contractor); *Kvaas Constr. Co.*, ASBCA 45965, 94-1 BCA ¶ 26,513 (waiver on four prior contracts). Waiver can, however, occur on a single contract. See *General Motors Corp.*, ASBCA 15807, 72-1 BCA ¶ 9405, where the government was held to have waived the reliability requirement by knowingly authorizing the contractor to proceed with production despite nonconformity with reliability criteria; and *Walsky Constr. Co.*, ASBCA 36940, 90-2 BCA ¶ 22,934, where waiver was found when the contracting officer permitted seal coating of a road at temperatures below the specified minimum.

Waiver of a required contract provision may require a higher standard of proof. See *Kearfott Guidance & Navigation Corp.*, ASBCA 49271, 04-2 BCA ¶ 32,757, *recons. denied*, 05-1 BCA ¶ 32,845, finding inadequate proof that the government had waived a paragraph of the Incentive Price Revision—Firm Target clause in FAR 52.216-16.

[7] Estoppel Improperly Used

In numerous cases involving finality of action, the boards and courts have unnecessarily used the term estoppel in holding that the government is bound. This, of course, has led to confusion because it has been the operation of the legal principle involved (acceptance of offer or goods, interpretation of contract, etc.) rather than the doctrine of equitable estoppel that has bound the government.

See, for example, *LDG Timber Enters., Inc.*, AGBCA 91-213-1, 95-2 BCA ¶27,906, where the board held the government was not estopped by a letter from the contracting officer granting a time extension. The board reasoned the contractor had not proved that it relied on the letter. In reversing this decision, the Federal Circuit held that the estoppel analysis was misused because the government was bound by the *promise* in the letter in accordance with "ordinary contract principles," *LDG Timber Enters., Inc. v. Glickman*, 114 F.3d 1140 (Fed. Cir. 1997). Similarly, in *McTeague Constr. Co. v. General Servs. Admin.*, GSBCA 14765, 01-1 BCA ¶31,203, the board rejected an estoppel claim and went on to analyze whether the government had entered into a contract to settle specified claims. See also *H & M Moving, Inc. v. United States*, 499 F.2d 660 (Ct. Cl. 1974) (ambiguous term construed in contractor's favor); *Emeco Indus. v. United States*, 485 F.2d 652 (Ct. Cl. 1973) (implied-in-fact contract existed based upon government's actions); *Dana Corp. v. United States*, 470 F.2d 1032 (Ct. Cl. 1972) (contractor's offer accepted); and *Gresham & Co. v. United States*, 470 F.2d 542 (Ct. Cl. 1972) (ambiguous term construed in contractor's favor based upon similar interpretation by government representative).

A good example of the confusion that exists in the use of the term "estoppel" is *Lockheed Shipbuilding & Constr. Co.*, ASBCA 18460, 75-1 BCA ¶11,246, *recons. denied*, 75-2 BCA ¶11,566. This controversial case involved broad multicontract, multiservice negotiations between Deputy Secretary of Defense Packard and the contractor whereby an overall settlement plan was negotiated. Pursuant to these negotiations, the contractor agreed to assume a fixed loss of $200 million under its C-5A contracts with the Air Force and to accept a $62 million settlement on its Navy contracts. The board held that Deputy Secretary Packard had impliedly assured the contractor that the $62 million settlement would be approved by "higher authorities" in the Navy, as required by regulations. Although the overall agreement between Deputy Secretary Packard and the contractor appeared to have all the elements of an enforceable contract, the board used the doctrine of estoppel to hold that the Navy higher authorities could not refuse to approve the $62 million settlement.

§1.06 SUITS AGAINST GOVERNMENT EMPLOYEES

Suits against government officers, employees, or agents are either of two types. First is the suit, almost always for monetary damages, that seeks to obtain relief directly from the officer, employee, or agent. The second seeks *relief from the government* by a suit against the employee, officer, or agent in his or her official capacity. Such suits were the normal means of seeking injunctive relief against the government prior to 1976.

Both types of litigation are generally subject to some form of "immunity" defense. Suits against the individual personally will invariably be challenged on the ground that the employee is entitled to the *personal immunity* that attaches to public employees. In suits against the officer or employee in his or her official capacity, the government may move for dismissal if it has not waived its *sovereign immunity* from such suits. Such suits are no longer necessary because 5 U.S.C. § 702, as amended in 1976, Pub. L. No. 94-574, 90 Stat. 2721, permits such suits to be filed directly against the "United States" in order to obtain injunctive relief against adverse agency action. Thus, the only necessity of naming the employee in such suits is to specify who should be enjoined in the event the plaintiff prevails. This section considers the first type of suit against government employees—those attempting to obtain monetary relief against the employees personally.

Traditionally, government employees were *immune from personal suit* when acting within the scope of their authority. The courts have recognized the necessity of protecting the freedom of federal officers and employees to exercise the discretion that is required for the proper execution of their duties by prohibiting suits against such employees in their personal capacity. In *Ove Gustavsson Contracting Co. v. Floete*, 299 F.2d 655 (2d Cir. 1962), *cert. denied*, 374 U.S. 827 (1963), a contractor brought suit against federal employees in their private capacities, seeking damages for alleged intentional and malicious falsification of progress reports filed with the government. Affirming the district court's grant of summary judgment for the government employees, the court stated at 658:

> [O]fficials of the federal Government are not personally liable for alleged torts based upon acts, done within the scope of their duties, which necessarily involved the exercise of a judgment or discretion which public policy requires be made without fear of personal liability.

This type of immunity has been referred to as *absolute immunity*.

When the government officer or employee is charged with violating a person's *constitutional rights*, a *qualified immunity* rather than an absolute immunity will be invoked. In *Scheuer v. Rhodes*, 416 U.S. 232 (1974), involving a suit under 42 U.S.C. § 1983 against the governor of Ohio and other high state officials for killing four demonstrators, the Court ruled that state officials could claim only a "qualified immunity." Thus, they would be immune only to the extent that the acts were within the scope of their duties, that they were done with a good-faith belief that they were correct, and that such belief was reasonable in light of the facts as they existed at the time of the acts. The Supreme Court extended this rule to federal government employees in *Butz v. Economou*, 438 U.S. 478 (1978), when violations of constitutional rights were alleged. Absolute immunity for constitutional violations was held to apply only to "those exceptional situations where it is demonstrated that absolute immunity is essential for the conduct of the public business." Subsequently, the Court has indicated that absolute immunity for constitutional violations is to be accorded to legislators and judges in their legislative and judicial capacities, respectively, to prosecutors and similar officials of executive agencies, and to executive officers engaged in adjudicative functions. Other federal officials who seek absolute exemption from personal liability for unconstitutional conduct must bear the burden of showing that public policy requires an exemption of that scope based on their functions, not merely their positions. See *Harlow v. Fitzgerald*, 457 U.S. 800 (1982).

In *Harlow*, senior presidential aides and advisers were charged with violating Fitzgerald's constitutional and statutory rights. The Court held that absolute immunity is not "an incident of the office of every presidential subordinate based in the White House." However, an official would be entitled to absolute immunity for constitutional violations by showing (1) "that the responsibilities of his office embraced a function so sensitive as to require a total shield from liability," and (2) "that he was discharging the protected function when performing the act for which liability is asserted." With respect to qualified immunity, the Court stated that it would not apply if the official "knew or reasonably should have known that the action he took within his sphere of official responsibility would violate the constitutional rights of the [plaintiff], or if he took the action with malicious intention to cause a deprivation of constitutional rights or other injury," further stating that "government officials performing discretionary functions generally are shielded from liability for civil damages insofar as their conduct does not violate clearly established statutory or constitutional rights of which a reasonable person would have known." The judge is to determine the threshold question of whether a clearly established law existed at the time of the action of which the government employee "knew or should have known."

The Supreme Court placed another limitation on absolute immunity in *Westfall v. Erwin*, 484 U.S. 292 (1988), ruling that absolute immunity would be granted only if the act was discretionary in nature. Thus, not all acts of high-level officials would necessarily be subject to absolute immunity. The Court also described at 295-96 the following policy reasons as supporting such immunity:

> The purpose of such official immunity is not to protect an erring official, but to insulate the decision making process from the harassment of prospective litigation. The provision of immunity rests on the view that the threat of liability will make federal officials unduly timid in carrying out their official duties, and that effective government will be promoted if officials are freed of the costs of vexatious and often frivolous damages suits.... This Court always has recognized, however, that official immunity comes at a great cost. An injured party with an otherwise meritorious tort claim is denied compensation simply because he had the misfortune to be injured by a federal official. Moreover, absolute immunity contravenes the basic tenet that individuals be held accountable for their wrongful conduct. We therefore have held that absolute immunity for federal officials is justified only when "the contributions of immunity to effective government in particular contexts outweighs the perhaps recurring harm to individual citizens." *Doe v. McMillan*, [412 U.S. 306, 320 (1973)].

In response to the Court's decision in *Westfall*, Congress enacted the Federal Employees Liability Reform and Tort Compensation Act of 1988, Pub. L. No. 100-694, which contained the following statement:

> It is the purpose of this Act to protect Federal employees from personal liability for common law torts committed within the scope of their employment, while providing persons injured by the common law torts with an appropriate remedy against the United States.

To achieve this purpose, the Act amended the Federal Torts Claims Act (FTCA), 28 U.S.C. § 1346(b) and § 2671 et seq., to restore the immunity that the Supreme Court had taken away in *Westfall*. The Act restored absolute immunity for suits for money damages when common-law torts are alleged and did not make the immunity dependent upon the discretionary nature of the employee's duties. In such cases, only the government may be sued. See 28 U.S.C. § 2679(b). This absolute immunity is broadly construed, *Hui v. Castaneda*, 559 U.S. 799 (2010). As a result, government employees have absolute immunity from suits for monetary compensation unless such suit is based on (1) an act totally outside of the scope of their employment, or (2) an act that deprives a person of his or her constitutional rights and the employee is not a member of the class of employees that has absolute immunity. The Supreme Court has held that this immunity applies even "when an FTCA exception precludes recovery against the government," *United States v. Smith*, 499 U.S. 160 (1991).

Under 28 U.S.C. § 2679(d), the Attorney General is to make a determination as to whether the act was accomplished within the scope of employment and may defend the employee and the United States if it is so determined. A certification that the employee was acting within the scope of employment has two effects: (1) the government is substituted as the defendant, and (2) the case is removed to federal district court if it has been filed in a state court. The certification or lack of certification is reviewable by the district court with regard to the substitution of the government as the proper party but a certification is conclusive as to removal from a state court, *Gutierrez de Martinez v. Lamagno*, 515 U.S. 417 (1995). This can lead to the anomalous result that, if a court finds the certification incorrect, the government employee becomes the defendant but the case remains in federal district court, *Garcia v. United States*, 88 F.3d 318 (5th Cir. 1996); *Ross v. Bryan*, 309 F.3d 830 (4th Cir. 2002). In *Osborn v. Haley*, 549 U.S. 225 (2007), the Court ruled that this review of the correctness of the certification applied in the situation where the defense was that the conduct never occurred as well as where the issue was whether the conduct was within the scope of employment. The Court also ruled that a district court rejection of the certification that the conduct was within the scope of employment could not be based on the pleadings but had to be based on the facts accepted by the judge in a trial. The Court recognized that this deprived the plaintiff of a jury trial but concluded that was the intent of 28 U.S.C. § 2679(d).

There is a further anomaly in this procedure. If the Attorney General refuses to certify, the defendant can appeal the lack of certification to a federal court. If that court finds that the conduct is not within the scope of employment, it will remand the case to state court under 28 U.S.C. § 2679(d)(3), and such remand is not appealable under 28 U.S.C. § 1447(d). The scope of this statute is discussed in *Powerex Corp. v. Reliant Energy Servs., Inc*, 551 U.S. 224 (2007). If the state court then concludes that the conduct was within the scope of employment, it will have to send the case back to the federal court. The unfairness of this procedure to the government employee accused of tortious conduct is discussed in *Foster v. Hill*, 497 F.3d 695 (7th Cir. 2007).

In *Aversa v. United States*, 99 F.3d 1200 (1st Cir. 1996), the court held that while federal law "does determine whether a person is a federal employee and the nature and contours of his or her federal responsibilities . . . state law governs whether the person was acting within the scope of that employment and those responsibilities." A good summary of the standards that are applied to determine whether actions are within the scope of employment is contained in *Davric Maine Corp. v. U.S. Postal Serv.*, 238 F.3d 58 (1st Cir. 2001), at 66:

> Under Maine law an employee's actions are within the scope of employment if they are of the kind that he is employed to perform, they occur within authorized time and space limits, and they are actuated by a purpose to serve the employee's master. See Restatement (Second) of Agency § 228, at 504 (1958), cited in *Bergeron [v. Henderson]*, 47 F. Supp. 2d [61 (D. Maine 1999)] at 65. Under the Restatement (Second), an action may be within the scope of employment although "forbidden, or done in a forbidden manner," see Restatement (Second) § 230, or even "consciously criminal or tortious," see *id.* § 231. Actions "relating to work" and "done in the workplace during working hours" are typically within the scope. See *id.* §§ 229, 233, 234. Whether the motivation of the employee is to serve the master's interest or his or her own private purposes is often an important element in this determination. See *id.* §§ 228, 235-236; see also *Lyons [v. Brown]*, 158 F.3d [650 (1st Cir. 1998)] at 609. Where seemingly work-related acts taken by the federal employee are done with a private purpose on the employee's part to retaliate or discriminate against the plaintiff, they may fall outside the scope of employment under Maine law; where the acts were done in good faith to serve the employer's interest, even if the federal employee's judgment was mistaken, then the conduct is likely within the scope of employment. See *Lyons*, 158 F.3d at 610.

Several situations have been held to be outside of the scope of employment, making the employee personally liable for his or her conduct. See *Johnson v. United States*, 534 F.3d 958 (8th Cir. 2008) (arrest by Bureau of Indian Affairs correctional officer); *Sullivan v. Shimp*, 324 F.3d 397 (6th Cir. 2003) (automobile accident returning from work site to home—Ohio law); *Ross v. Bryan* (an automobile accident while commuting to work—Virginia law); *Borneman v. United States*, 213 F.3d 819 (4th Cir. 2000) (intentional tort such as assault and battery during work frequently, but not always, outside of scope of employment—North Carolina law); *Mackey v. Milam*, 154 F.3d 648 (6th Cir. 1998) (sexual harassment outside scope of employment if done by employee with no control over plaintiff but within scope of employment if done by supervisor or other person with control over plaintiff—Ohio law). However, tortious conduct between employees in the workplace has been held to be within the scope of employment, *United States v. Tomscha*, 150 Fed. Appx. 18 (2d Cir. 2005) (circulating e-mail allegedly libeling union leader); *Taboas v. Mlynczak*, 149 F.3d 576 (7th Cir. 1998) (allegedly malicious and vindictive complaints lodged against a fellow employee within the scope of employment—Illinois law); *McLachlan v. Bell*, 261 F.3d 908 (9th Cir. 2001) (alleged circulation of false rumors and malicious gossip within scope of employment—California law). In addition, tortious conduct by a superior is held to be within the scope of employment, *Hendrix v. Snow*, 170 Fed. Appx. 68 (11th Cir. 2006), *cert. denied*, 549 U.S. 1208 (2007) (alleged discrimination and retaliation after filing complaints); *Singleton v. United States*, 277 F3d 864 (6th Cir. 2002) (alleged efforts of superior to have employee removed from his job, filing of false and degrading reports, punished him for pursuing his legal rights, and leaking confidential information about him within scope of employment—Ohio law); *Heuton v. Anderson*, 75 F.3d 357 (8th Cir. 1996) (posting pictures characterizing employees as pigs within scope of supervisor's employment—Iowa law). See also *Kashin v. Kent*, 457 F.3d 1033 (9th Cir. 2006), finding, under District of Columbia law, that a foreign service officer was acting within the scope of his employment when he had an automobile accident driving home from work in Russia. It is also held that individuals performing work for the government are not employees for these purposes if they qualify as independent contractors, *Creel v. United States*, 598 F.3d 210 (5th Cir. 2010); *Rodriguez v. Sarabyn*, 129 F.3d 760 (5th Cir. 1997).

§ 1.07 STANDARDS OF CONDUCT

In order to maintain public confidence in the federal procurement process, government and contractor employees must follow exemplary standards of conduct. As an overarching policy, FAR 3.101 admonishes that government business must be conducted in a manner above reproach, avoiding even the appearance of impropriety:

> Government business shall be conducted in a manner above reproach and, except as authorized by statute or regulation, with complete impartiality and with preferential treatment for none. Transactions relating to the expenditure of public funds require the highest degree of public trust and an impeccable standard of conduct. The general rule is to avoid strictly any conflict of interest or even the appearance of a conflict of interest in Government-contractor relationships. While many Federal laws and regulations place restrictions on the actions of Government personnel, their official conduct

must, in addition, be such that they would have no reluctance to make a full public disclosure of their actions.

Beyond this general policy, there are numerous statutory and regulatory provisions outlining the standards to be followed and the stringent penalties for noncompliance. This section discusses these standards in three broad categories—those dealing with *improper influence* on government decisions, those requiring *honesty and disclosure of relevant facts* in dealing with the government, and those barring *improperly disclosing or obtaining information*. A general discussion of the types of sanctions imposed for improper conduct is followed by a discussion of these three types of activities.

[A] Sanctions

Each statute prohibiting a certain type of conduct contains its own sanction or penalty. Since most of these sanctions involve straightforward criminal or civil fines or imprisonment, this section does not discuss the precise way that these penalties have been interpreted and enforced. In this regard, a government contractor or a government employee is treated the same as any other person guilty of a "white collar" crime. However, government contractors are also subject to additional sanctions that are considerably broader than the normal criminal and civil sanctions. In many if not most cases, these broader sanctions are a more serious threat to government contractors than the criminal or civil sanctions contained in the specific statutes covering the prohibited conduct. There are also additional sanctions applicable to government employees. This section considers those additional sanctions that provide drastic penalties for those engaged in improper conduct in the contracting process.

[1] Forfeiture and Cancellation

The first of these general sanctions against government contractors is *forfeiture* of all rights under the contract. The Supreme Court has held that the government can cancel a contract and need not pay for work done or benefit conferred if it is tainted with illegal conduct, *United States v. Mississippi Valley Generating Co.*, 364 U.S. 520 (1961) (conflict of interest); *Pan Am. Petroleum & Transp. Co. v. United States*, 273 U.S. 456 (1927). The Court of Claims went even further and held that the government can recover the full amount paid on a *completed contract* that is subsequently found to have been tainted with illegal conduct, *K & R Eng'g Co. v. United States*, 616 F.2d 469 (Ct. Cl. 1980) (bribery and conflict of interest). See also *Bureau of Land Mgmt.: Payment of Pocatello Field Office Photocopying Costs*, Comp. Gen. Dec. B-290901, 2003 CPD ¶ 2, holding that contract was void and unenforceable because it violated 44 U.S.C. § 501 requiring agencies to obtain all printing services through the Government Printing Office, and *Schuepferling GmbH & Co., KG*, ASBCA 45567, 98-2 BCA

¶ 29,828, holding that it was proper to refuse to pay for work on 22 fully performed delivery orders because the contractor had bribed the contracting specialist at the inception of the contract. While it has been held that a contract containing a contingent fee arrangement is also void and unenforceable, *Quinn v. Gulf & Western Corp.*, 644 F.2d 89 (2d Cir. 1981); *LeJohn Mfg. Co. v. Webb*, 222 F.2d 48 (D.C. Cir. 1955), the government may not cancel a contract for breach of the covenant where it knew of the arrangement during prolonged negotiations and the arrangement had many indicia of a bona fide covenant, *Companhia Atlantica De Desenvolvimento E Exploracao De Minas v. United States*, 180 F. Supp. 342 (Ct. Cl.), *cert. denied*, 364 U.S. 862 (1960). See also *Paradyne Corp. v. United States*, 647 F. Supp. 1228 (D.D.C. 1986), prohibiting the government from exercising a contract option at the same time it was charging the contractor with fraud pertaining to the option.

The fact that Congress may have specifically provided for other statutory or criminal sanctions does not deprive the United States of the right to cancel contracts "tainted with illegal conduct," *United States v. Acme Process Equip. Co.*, 385 U.S. 138 (1966) (statutory sanction for violation of Anti-Kickback Act, 41 U.S.C. § 51); *Horton J. Brown v. United States*, 524 F.2d 693 (Ct. Cl. 1975) (criminal sanction for violation of False Statement Act, 18 U.S.C. § 1001). However, the question has been raised concerning which officials in the government are authorized to cancel contracts and the nature of the activity that would entitle the government to cancel. In *Medico Indus., Inc.*, ASBCA 22141, 80-2 BCA ¶ 14,498, *recons. denied*, 80-2 BCA ¶ 14,665, *mot. to suspend hearings granted*, 81-1 BCA ¶ 14,983, it was held that the contracting officer was not authorized to cancel a contract because of improper conduct by a former government employee. The board distinguished *Mississippi Valley Generating Co.* on the grounds that it involved the more serious violation of action by a public official having simultaneous conflicting interests. The board also questioned whether improper conduct of a former government employee was a sufficiently serious violation to allow the government to cancel. Following the board's suspension of the hearing, the government sued in U.S. District Court for a declaratory judgment that the contract cancellation was authorized. The district court granted the contractor's motion to dismiss for lack of jurisdiction but in *United States v. Medico Indus., Inc.*, 685 F.2d 230 (7th Cir. 1982), the circuit court reversed, holding that the board of contract appeals did not have jurisdiction under the Disputes clause to determine whether 18 U.S.C. § 207(a) was violated and remanded the matter to the district court for disposition. Contrast *Four-Phase Sys., Inc.*, ASBCA 27487, 84-1 BCA ¶ 17,122, suggesting that the Contract Disputes Act gives jurisdiction to the appeals boards over a government affirmative defense of cancellation for a violation of 18 U.S.C. § 208. 18 U.S.C. § 218 provides for cancellation by the President or, under regulations prescribed by him, the head of any department or agency if there has been a final conviction for offenses involving bribery, gratuities, and conflicts of interest during and after government employment. Executive Order 12448, 48 Fed. Reg. 51281 (1983), delegates the authority to exercise this power to heads of executive agencies and provides that implementing regulations should contain specified procedural protections. FAR 3.705 sets forth the procedures for exercising this authority.

28 U.S.C. § 2514 also provides for the forfeiture of fraudulent claims, stating:

> A claim against the United States shall be forfeited to the United States by any person who corruptly practices or attempts to practice any fraud against the United States in the proof, statement, establishment, or allowance thereof.

See *Kellogg Brown & Root Servs., Inc. v. United States*, 728 F.3d 1348 (Fed. Cir. 2013), rejecting the argument that the statute covered fraud in the performance of a contract and denying forfeiture for receiving kickbacks because such conduct was not covered by the statute. Some earlier decisions had more broadly interpreted the statutes to cover such conduct relying on *Little v. United States*, 152 F. Supp. 84 (Ct. Cl. 1957). A full discussion of this conflict in the decisions is found in *AEY, Inc. v. United* States, 114 Fed. Cl. 619 (2014). For decisions forfeiting claims, see *Chapman Law Firm LPA v. United States*, 113 Fed. Cl. 555 (2013) (claim based on inaccurate inspection reports); *Railway Logistics Int'l v. United States*, 103 Fed. Cl. 252 (2012) (claim that contained overstated or imaginary costs); *Alcatec LLC v. United States*, 100 Fed. Cl. 502 (2011) (claim that was based on chaotic billing system to hide extent of inspections); *Daewoo Eng'g & Constr. Co. v. United States*, 73 Fed. Cl. 547 (2006), *aff'd*, 557 F.3d 1332 (Fed. Cir.), *cert. denied*, 558 U.S. 990 (2009) (forfeiture of potentially valid part of claim when major part was fraudulent); *Long Island Savings Bank, FSB v. United* States, 476 F.3d 917 (Fed. Cir. 2007) (entire claim forfeited because of fraud in the inducement); *Morse Diesel Int'l, Inc. v. United States*, 74 Fed. Cl. 601 (2007) (several claims that included unpaid bond costs); and *UMC Elecs. Co. v. United States*, 43 Fed. Cl. 776 (1999), *aff'd*, 249 F.3d 1337 (Fed. Cir. 2001) (claim subcontractor costs not claimed by subcontractor).

To obtain forfeiture under this statute, the government must prove its fraud claim by clear and convincing evidence, *Glendale Fed'l Bank, FSB v. United States*, 239 F.3d 1374 (Fed. Cir. 2001); *Commercial Contractors, Inc. v. United States*, 154 F.3d 1357 (Fed. Cir. 1998). See *Oasis Int'l Waters, Inc. v. United States*, 134 Fed. Cl. 405 (2017) (official certifying claim had honest belief they were valid); Horn & Assocs. v. United States, 123 Fed. Cl. 728 (2015) (statement claim was based on "actual costs incurred" not proof of fraud although costs were estimated); *Gulf Grp. Gen. Enters. Co. W.L.L. v. United States*, 114 Fed. Cl. 258 (2013) (lack of clear proof of intent to fraudulently inflate claims); *Hernandez Kroone & Assocs., Inc. v. United States*, 110 Fed. Cl. 496 (2013) (there was an arguable basis for estimated costs in claim); and *Liquidating Tr. Ester Duval of KI Liquidation, Inc. v. United States*, 89 Fed. Cl. 29 (2009) (lack of clear proof of intent to fraudulently bill for costs).

The boards of contract appeals cannot use 28 U.S.C. § 2514 to forfeit claims, *DEL Mfg. Co.*, ASBCA 43801, 94-3 BCA ¶ 27,239, and are precluded by 41 U.S.C. § 7103(c) from litigating the issue of fraud, *Simko Constr., Inc. v. United States*, 852 F.2d 540 (Fed. Cir. 1988). However, if a contractor has been found guilty of fraud during the performance of the contract, by decision or plea, the boards accept fraud as an affirmative defense and dismiss the case, *Laguna Constr. Co. v. Carter*, 828 F.3d 1364 (Fed. Cir. 2016); or deny jurisdiction because of the fraud, *Beech Gap, Inc.*, ENGBCA 5585, 95-2 BCA ¶ 27,879, *aff'd*, 86 F.3d 1177 (Fed. Cir. 1966). See also *Medica, S.A.*, ENGBCA PCC 142, 00-2 BCA ¶ 30,966, awarding the government the amount that has been paid to the contractor as a result of fraud. Furthermore, a board's granting of an appeal finding a claim valid is not binding if the government later obtains a court ruling of fraud, *J.E.T.S., Inc. v. United States*, 838 F.2d 1196 (Fed. Cir. 1988), *cert. denied*, 486 U.S. 1057 (1988). Thus, if there has been a finding of fraud in obtaining the contract, a board will deny a claim for payment for work already performed, *Dngbuk R&U Eng.g Co.*, ASBCA 58300, 13-1 BCA ¶ 35,389.

The Armed Services Board has ruled that it can assess whether a contract was void ab initio because of fraud in its inception without needing a prior determination that fraud had been committed, *International Oil Trading Co.*, ASBCA 57491, 18-1 BCA ¶ 36,985. In *Morse Diesel Int'l, Inc. v. United States*, 74 Fed. Cl. 601 (2007), claims for $53,534,679.16 were forfeited because the contractor had submitted false invoices and had paid illegal kickbacks. The claims were originally submitted to the GSBCA which had no jurisdiction under 28 U.S.C. § 2514 but were removed to the Court of Federal Claims under 41 U.S.C. § 609(d) (now § 7107(d)), permitting consolidation of claims on a contract, when the contractor filed claims on other contracts in that court, *Morse Diesel Int'l, Inc. v. United States*, 69 Fed. Cl. 558 (2006). This permitted the government to assert the fraud counterclaim. When the contractor asked for mandamus returning the original claims to the GSBCA because the claims were on different contracts, the Federal Circuit refused, *In re Morse Diesel Int'l, Inc.*, 163 Fed. Appx. 878 (Fed. Cir. 2006).

41 U.S.C. § 7103(c)(2) provides that if a contractor is unable to support any part of its claim because of misrepresentation of fact or fraud, the contractor will be liable to the government for the amount of such fraudulent claim. In *Daewoo Engineering* this led to a judgment for the government on a counterclaim under this statute for $50,629,855.88, the amount of the claim that was found to be fraudulent because it had been added "to get the attention of the contracting officer."

[2] Debarment

The second broad sanction is debarment of the contractor or its employees, that is, precluding participation in the government contracts process for a stated period of time. FAR 9.406-2 contains a long list of causes for debarment which are discussed in detail in Chapter 4.

Debarment precludes contracts with any agency of the federal government for a period of up to three years, FAR 9.406-4. However, some debarments last considerably longer. See, for example, *Roderick Nielson*, HUDBCA 99-C-107-D6, 99-2 BCA ¶ 30,569, where, over the opposition of the government, the board terminated a debarment that had been in effect for 10 years. Debarment of a company has been sustained for submitting false claims, *Dowling Group v. Williams*, No. 82-1775 (D.D.C. 1982), for bribery and collusive bidding, *Robinson v. Cheney*, 876 F.2d 152 (D.C. Cir. 1989); and for bribery, *Atlantic Chem. Co.*, GSBCA 5822-D, 80-2 BCA ¶ 14,801. Debarment of an officer of a company was also sustained when the company bribed government officials, *Taylor v. Marsh*, No. 81-2643 (D.D.C. 1982). For a rare case where the agency refused to debar a company and the court ordered the prior temporary action of suspension to be voided ab initio, see *Leon Sloan, Sr. & Jimmy Lee Furby v. Dep't of Housing & Urban Development*, 231 F.3d 10 (D.C. Cir. 2000). See also *Lion Raisins, Inc. v. United States*, 51 Fed. Cl. 238 (2001), where the court found a debarment to be an abuse of discretion because the agency had awarded five contracts between the time it found about the acts that allegedly indicated a lack of integrity and it issued the suspension order, and *Dantran, Inc., v. Dep't of Labor*, 171 F.3d 58 (1st Cir. 1999), where the court overturned a debarment for improper wage payments because there was substantial evidence that the contractor had complied with agency procedures. See Chapter 4 for a more complete discussion of debarment and suspension of contractors.

Debarment is a particularly harsh sanction because when an agency *proposes* to debar a contractor, it is immediately placed in the System for Award Management Exclusions, FAR 9.404(b)(1), and may not receive contract awards or solicitations thereafter, FAR 9.405(a), or consent to a subcontract award, FAR 9.405-2. See *IMCO, Inc. v. United States*, 97 F.3d 1422 (Fed. Cir. 1996), sustaining the dismissal of a protest where the agency deprived the Small Business Administration of the opportunity to issue a certificate of competency by proposing to debar the offeror. See also *FAS Support Servs., LLC*, Comp. Gen. Dec B-402464, 2010 CPD ¶ 105 (denying protest that agency failed to reinstate contractor after suspension was lifted); and *Aardvark Keith Moving, Inc.*, Comp. Gen. Dec. B-290565, 2002 CPD ¶ 134 (denying protest that the agency declared the protester ineligible because it was affiliated with a company that had been proposed for debarment five years earlier).

Even after a contractor is removed from the Exclusions List, its name remains on the GSA website containing the List as a firm that has been previously debarred. In *Hickey v. Chadick*, 649 F. Supp. 2d 770 (S.D. Ohio 2009), the court ruled that it had jurisdiction to hear a claim that this had injured the contractor because this aspect of the List could be used in making a future responsibility determination.

Debarment can be imposed simultaneously with civil or criminal penalties for the improper conduct. See *United States v. Glymph*, 96 F.3d 722 (4th Cir. 1996), holding that conviction for criminal fraud was proper because the prior debarment was not punitive but remedial—thus precluding any defense of double jeopardy. Accord, *United States v. Hatfield*, 108 F.3d 67 (4th Cir. 1997). See also *Hudson v. United States*, 522 U.S. 93 (1997), finding no double jeopardy in a criminal prosecution following a settlement that included a civil fine and an agreement to refrain from participation in government programs without written authorization from the agency.

[3] Suspension or Dismissal of Government Employees

A third broad sanction is suspension or dismissal of a government employee who has violated the standards of conduct. Such actions must be taken in accordance with 5 U.S.C. § 7513, which permits appeal by the employee to the Merit System Protection Board. See 5 C.F.R. Part 1200. Dismissal of employees was upheld in *Lachance v. Erickson*, 522 U.S. 262 (1998), where they gave false statements during investigations of misconduct. See also *Pollock v. Dep't of the Navy*, 369 Fed. Appx. 133 (Fed. Cir. 2010) (medical technician dismissed for failure to provide urine sample for random drug test); *Stevenson v. Dep't of Justice*, 189 Fed. Appx. 973 (Fed. Cir. 2006) (employee dismissed for failure to report arrest as required by agency standards of conduct); *Womer v. Hampton*, 496 F.2d 99 (5th Cir. 1974) (government inspector dismissed for taking payments from a contractor and not giving a satisfactory explanation for the payments); and *Polcover v. Secretary of Treasury*, 477 F.2d 1223 (D.C. Cir. 1973) (dismissal upheld when employee accepted a bribe even though he was later acquitted in a criminal prosecution—reasoning that the evidence was sufficient to meet a "preponderance of the evidence" test in the dismissal proceeding despite failing to meet the "beyond a reasonable doubt" test of the criminal action). The Court of Claims repeatedly held that agencies have broad discretion in selecting administrative sanctions for acceptances of bribes and gratuities. In *Jones v. United States*, 617 F.2d 233 (Ct. Cl. 1980), the court upheld a decision of the Civil Service Commission Appeals Review Board sustaining the dismissal of a Department of Agriculture meat inspector who had accepted a single bottle of whiskey from a meat packer. In *Parker v. United States*, 650 F.2d 287 (Ct. Cl. 1980), the court rejected the contention that dismissal of an employee who had accepted meals and entertainment valued at more than $3,000 from a contractor constituted an abuse of agency discretion. In *Lane v. United States*, 633 F.2d 1384 (Ct. Cl. 1980), the court upheld the dismissal of IRS auditors who had accepted a "whole series" of free meals from a firm being audited. See also *Baker v. Dep't of Health & Human Services*, 912 F.2d 1448 (Fed. Cir. 1990), sustaining dismissal of an employee that accepted a lunch during which he disclosed internal agency information; *Monahan v. United States*, 354 F.2d 306 (Ct. Cl. 1965), sustaining the dismissal of a procuring agency employee for permitting a contractor to pay for hotel rooms and accepting loans from three contractors; and *Miller v. United States Postal Serv.*, 712 F.2d 1006 (6th Cir. 1983), sustaining the dismissal of an employee for using inside information to benefit a company in which he had an interest.

Dismissal of an employee was also upheld for falsification of records which was a violation of 18 U.S.C. § 1001, *Santornino v. Dep't of Veterans Affairs*, 45 F.3d 442 (Fed. Cir. 1994) (affirming ruling of administrative law judge in unpublished opinion). See also *Pararas-Carayannis v. Dep't of Commerce*, 9 F.3d 955 (Fed. Cir. 1993) (upholding indefinite suspension without pay for laundering money for escort/prostitution operations, in violation of 18 U.S.C. § 1956(a)(3)); *Brook v. Corrado*, 999 F.2d 523 (Fed. Cir. 1993) (dismissal for possession of cocaine with intent to distribute it); *Stanek v. Dep't of Transportation*, 805 F.2d 1572 (Fed. Cir. 1986) (dismissal for solicitation of loan from company that might have benefited from employee's research); *Kumferman v. Dep't of Navy*, 785 F.2d 286 (Fed. Cir. 1986) (dismissal for theft of government property). *Brewer v. United States Postal Serv.*, 647 F.2d 1093 (Ct. Cl. 1981), *cert. denied*, 454 U.S. 1144 (1982) (dismissal of an employee with 27 years of service for falsifying time cards). Compare *Miguel v. Dep't of Army*, 727 F.2d 1081 (Fed. Cir. 1984), reversing an agency decision to dismiss an employee with 24 years of service for stealing two bars of soap.

[B] Codes of Conduct

For many years government employees have been subject to strict codes of conduct, Executive Order 11222, May 8, 1965. General rules governing such conduct are contained in the regulations of the Office of Personnel Management, 5 C.F.R. § 735. In addition, the Office of Government Ethics has promulgated detailed standards of conduct in 5 C.F.R. Part 2635. Agencies can supplement these regulations with the concurrence of the Officer of Government Ethics, 5 C.F.R. ¶ 2635.105. The following material elaborates on most of these ethical standards.

Government contractors are also expected to have codes of conduct governing their employees, 41 U.S.C. § 2303. See FAR 3.1002 stating:

> (b) Contractors should have a written code of business ethics and conduct. To promote compliance with such code of business ethics and conduct, contractors should have an employee business ethics and compliance training program and an internal control system that—
>
> (1) Are suitable to the size of the company and extent of its involvement in Government contracting;
>
> (2) Facilitate timely discovery and disclosure of improper conduct in connection with Government contracts; and
>
> (3) Ensure corrective measures are promptly instituted and carried out.

Mandatory codes of conduct are required for contracts of over $5.5 million that have a period of performance of over 120 days, FAR 3.1004(a). Such contracts must contain the Contractor Code of Business Ethics and Conduct clause at FAR 52.203-13 which requires contractors have such a code of conduct and to make *mandatory disclosures* to the agency inspector general and the contracting officer whenever it has *credible evidence* of—

> (A) A violation of Federal criminal law involving fraud, conflict of interest, bribery, or gratuity violations found in Title 18 of the United States Code; or
>
> (B) A violation of the civil False Claims Act (31 U.S.C. 3729-3733).

The clause also has detailed requirements for internal control systems and requires that these requirements be flowed down on subcontracts that are over the thresholds. In addition to the requirement for a code of conduct meeting the requirements of this clause, contractors subject to the clause must *disclose* unethical conduct to the government in a timely manner. This mandatory disclosure requirement was subject to considerable debate when the regulation was issued. See 73 Fed. Reg. 67064-090, Nov. 12, 2008, for a full discussion of the intent of this requirement.

Contractors with contracts under the thresholds for application of the clause are still subject to suspension or debarment for failure to meet these standards of conduct. See FAR 3.1003(a) stating:

> (2) Whether or not the clause at 52.203-13 is applicable, a contractor may be suspended and/or debarred for knowing failure by a principal to timely disclose to the Government, in connection with the award, performance, or closeout of a Government contract performed by the contractor or a subcontract awarded thereunder, credible evidence of a violation of Federal criminal law involving fraud, conflict of interest, bribery, or gratuity violations found in Title 18 of the United States Code or a violation of the civil False Claims Act. Knowing failure to timely disclose credible evidence of any of the above violations remains a cause for suspension and/or debarment until 3 years after final payment on a contract (see 9.406-2(b)(1)(vi) and 9.407-2(a)(8)).

Contractors are also subject to sanctions for failure to promptly remit an overpayment to the government. See FAR 3.1003(a) stating:

> (3) The Payment clauses at FAR 52.212-4(i)(5), 52.232-25(d), 52.232-26(c), and 52.232-27(l) require that, if the contractor becomes aware that the Government has overpaid on a contract financing or invoice payment, the contractor shall remit the overpayment amount to the Government. A contractor may be suspended and/or debarred for knowing failure by a principal to timely disclose credible evidence of a significant overpayment, other than overpayments resulting from contract financing payments as defined in 32.001 (see 9.406-2(b)(1)(vi) and 9.407-2(a)(8)).

[C] Improper Influence of Government Decisions

One of the most serious threats to the integrity of the procurement process is the possibility of conduct by contractors that will improperly influence the decisions of contracting officers and other government employees. To protect against this threat, there are a number of very strict criminal statutes, principally 18 U.S.C. § 201, which prohibits bribery and gratuities. While the elements of bribery and gratuity are addressed in turn below, the statutory definitions of "public official" and "official act" at § 201(a) are critical to the scope of both crimes, and are addressed at the outset.

"Public Official" is defined at § 201(a)(1) as follows:

> Member of Congress, Delegate, or Resident Commissioner, either before or after such official has qualified, or an officer or employee or person acting for or on behalf of the United States, or any department, agency or branch of Government thereof, including the District of Columbia, in any official function under or by authority of any such department, agency, or branch of Government, or a juror.

The class of "public officials" is an expansive one, consisting of federal prison administrators, *United States v. Alessio*, 528 F.2d 1079 (9th Cir.), *cert. denied*, 426 U.S. 948 (1976); IRS agents, *United States v. Johnson*, 647 F.2d 815 (8th Cir. 1981); congressional aides, *United States v. Carson*, 464 F.2d 424 (2d Cir. 1972), *cert. denied*, 409 U.S. 949 (1972); *United States v. Dixon*, 658 F.2d 181 (3d Cir. 1981); a privately employed grain inspector licensed by the Department of Agriculture, *United States v. Kirby*, 587 F.2d 876 (7th Cir. 1978); and a contracting officer's representative, *K & R Eng'g Co. v. United States*, 616 F.2d 469 (Ct. Cl. 1980).

Generally, persons that are in a position of public trust with regard to government funds are classified as public officials even though they are not directly employed by the federal government. See *United States v. Franco*, 632 F.3d 880 (5th Cir. 2011) (contractor running prison); *United States v. Kenney*, 185 F.3d 1217 (11th Cir. 1999) (government contractor); *United States v. Hang*, 75 F.3d 1275 (8th Cir. 1996) (employee of local housing authority); *United States v. Strissel*, 920 F.2d 1162 (4th Cir. 1990) (director of local housing authority); *United States v. Velazquez*, 847 F.2d 140 (4th Cir. 1988) (county jailer where jail housed federal as well as state prisoners, county jailers supervised federal inmates, and jail was subject to inspections by federal prison authorities); *United States v. Kirby*, 587 F.2d 876 (7th Cir. 1978) (privately employed grain inspector licensed by the Department of Agriculture); and *United States v. Griffin*, 401 F. Supp. 1222 (S.D. Ind. 1975), *aff'd without op.* 541 F.2d 284 (7th Cir. 1976) (privately employed broker under a HUD contract). Compare *United States v. Loschiavo*, 531 F.2d 659 (2d Cir. 1976) (Model Cities program administrator was not acting on behalf of federal government by suggesting leasing arrangement with one who bribed administrator).

"Official Act" is defined at § 201(a)(3) as follows:

> [A]ny decision or action on any question, matter, cause, suit, proceeding or controversy, which may at any time be pending, or which may by law be brought before any public official, in such official's official capacity, or in such official's place of trust or profit.

The Supreme Court adopted a narrow definition of "official act" in a case involving alleged bribery of former Virginia Governor McDonnell. See *McDonnell v. United States*, 136 S. Ct. 2355 (2016). The Court recognized that the statute requires a two-part test: "First, the Government must identify a 'question, matter, cause, suit, proceeding or controversy' that 'may at any time be pending' or 'may by law be brought' before a public official. Second, the Government must provide that the public official made a decision or took an action 'on' that question, matter, cause, suit, proceeding, or controversy, or agreed to." The question before the Court was whether arranging meetings, contacting other government officials, or hosting events, without more, could qualify as "official acts." The Court answered that question in the negative at 2371:

> Setting up a meeting, hosting an event, or calling an official (or agreeing to do so) merely to talk about a research study or to gather additional information, however, does not qualify as a decision or action on the pending question of whether to initiate the study. Simply expressing support for the research study at a meeting, event, or call—or sending a subordinate to such a meeting, event, or call—similarly does not qualify as a decision or action on the study, as long as the public official does not intend to exert pressure on another official or provide advice, knowing or intending such advice to form the basis for an "official act." Otherwise, if every action somehow related to the research study were an "official act," the requirement that the public official make a decision or take an action on that study, or agree to do so, would be meaningless.
>
> Of course, this is not to say that setting up a meeting, hosting an event, or making a phone call is always an innocent act, or is irrelevant, in cases like this one. If an official sets up a meeting, hosts an event, or makes a phone call on a question or matter that is or could be pending before another official, that could serve as evidence of an agreement to take an official act. A jury could conclude, for example, that the official was attempting to pressure or advise another official on a pending matter. And if the official agreed to exert that pressure or give that advice in exchange for a thing of value, that would be illegal.

[1] Bribery

18 U.S.C. § 201(b) makes it a criminal offense to *offer* or *give* a bribe to a government official or for a government official to *solicit* or *receive* a bribe. The crimes are defined as follows:

(b) Whoever—

(1) directly or indirectly, corruptly gives, offers or promises anything of value to any public official or person who has been selected to be a public official, or offers or promises any public official or any person who has been selected to be a public official to give anything of value to any other person or entity, with intent—

(A) to influence any official act; or

(B) to influence such public official or person who has been selected to be a public official to commit or aid in committing, or collude in, or allow, any fraud, or make opportunity for the commission of any fraud, on the United States; or

(C) to induce such public official or such person who has been selected to be a public official to do or omit to do any act in violation of the lawful duty of such official or person;

(2) being a public official or person selected to be a public official, directly or indirectly, corruptly demands, seeks, receives, accepts, or agrees to receive or accept anything of value personally or for any other person or entity, in return for:

(A) being influenced in the performance of any official act;

(B) being influenced to commit or aid in committing, or to collude in, or allow, any fraud, or make opportunity for the commission of any fraud, on the United States; or

(C) being induced to do or omit to do any act in violation of the official duty of such official or person.

[a] Thing of Value

To constitute bribery, the statute requires that something "of value" be given, offered, promised, solicited, or received. Courts have adopted an expansive reading of the value requirement for both bribery and gratuities. Most cases involving bribery under the statute understandably concern cash payments, *United States v. Huff*, 609 F.3d 1240 (11th Cir. 2010) (cash and merchandise to steer contracts to company); *United States v. Lianidis*, 599 F.3d 273 (3d Cir. 2010) (cash to steer contracts to company); *United States v. Peleti*, 576 F.3d 377 (7th Cir. 2009) (cash payment for assistance in obtaining contract); *United States v. Kinter*, 235 F.3d 192 (8th Cir. 2000), *cert. denied*, 532 U.S. 937 (2001) (cash payment to technical employee advising contracting officer during source selection); *United States v. Hollingshead*, 672 F.2d 751 (9th Cir. 1982) (cash payment to employee of Federal Reserve Bank); *United States v. Myers*, 635 F.2d 932 (2d Cir.), *cert. denied*, 449 U.S. 956 (1980) (cash paid by undercover agents to members of Congress); *United States v. Johnson*, 621 F.2d 1073 (10th Cir. 1980) (cash payment offered to FAA procurement official); *United States v. Strand*, 574 F.2d 993 (9th Cir. 1978) (cash payment by undercover agent to summer border guard); and *United States v. Arroyo*, 581 F.2d 649 (7th Cir. 1978), *cert. denied*, 439 U.S. 1069 (1979) (cash payments to Small Business Administration loan officers from loan applicant). However, a variety of other benefits have also been considered as "value" by courts in relation to bribery charges, *United States v. McDade*, 28 F.3d 283 (3d Cir. 1994), *cert. denied*, 514 U.S. 1003 (1995) (travel expenses); *United States v. Harary*, 457 F.2d 471 (2d Cir. 1972) (prostitutes and cameras); *United States v. Ellenbogen*, 365 F.2d 982 (2d Cir. 1966), *cert. denied*, 386 U.S. 923 (1967) (an automobile). It is not necessary for the government to establish the exact value of a bribe, since the express language of 18 U.S.C. § 201(b)(1) defines the offense as giving "anything of value" to a public official, *United States v. Rasco*, 853 F.2d 501 (7th Cir.), *post-conviction proceedings*, 697 F. Supp. 343 (N.D. Ill.), *cert. denied*, 488 U.S. 959 (1988).

[b] Corrupt Intent

To establish a violation of the provision, a specific "corrupt" intent on the part of the giver or receiver of the bribe must be proved. The requisite intent is proved by showing a quid pro quo—an expectation of a favorable official act in return for the bribe. In *United States v. Strand*, 574 F.2d 993 (9th Cir. 1978), where a U.S. Customs Service official was found to have violated this provision by soliciting and accepting an $800 payment in return for allowing drugs to be smuggled through a border checkpoint, the court discussed the intent required under 18 U.S.C. § 201(c) (now § 201(b)(2)(c)) at 995:

> To be guilty under § 201(c)(3), Strand must have "corruptly" accepted the $800 from the Customs agent for himself or some other person in return for knowingly violating his official duty. The requisite "corrupt" intent has been defined as "incorporating a concept of the bribe being the prime mover or producer of the official act." *United States v. Brewster*, 165 U.S. App. D.C. 1, 21, 506 F.2d 62, 82 (D.C. Cir. 1974). It is this element of quid pro quo that distinguishes the heightened criminal intent requisite under the bribery sections of the statute from the simple mens rea required for violation of the gratuity sections.

In proving the exchange or quid pro quo element, the accompanying intent to influence some identifiable public act must be shown. See *United States v. Abbey*, 560 F.3d 513 (6th Cir. 2009), holding that there need not be an explicit promise to perform a specific, identifiable act as long as there is an expectation of future acts to benefit the giver of the bribe. See also *United States v. Heard*, 709 F.3d 413 (5th Cir. 2013) (contractor gave airline ticket, lodgings and entrance to a golf tournament to an agency employee in exchange for a favorable recommendation on a pending contract award); *United States v. Jefferson*, 674 F.3d 332 (4th Cir.), *cert. denied*, 133 S. Ct. 648 (2012)

(Congressman accepted money in return for assisting a company in foreign business transactions); and *United States v. Heffler*, 402 F.2d 924 (3d Cir. 1968) (government technical employee solicited bribe in return for an offer to influence an award, even though he was not the awarding officer). Similarly, in *United States v. Arroyo*, 581 F.2d 649 (7th Cir. 1978), *cert. denied*, 439 U.S. 1069 (1979), an SBA loan officer was convicted of accepting a bribe even though the loan had already been consummated, because the loan officer had told the borrower that the loan had not yet been finalized. In *United States v. Pommerening*, 500 F.2d 92 (10th Cir.), *cert. denied*, 419 U.S. 1088 (1974), loan applicants were convicted of bribery for giving an SBA official a $5,000 automobile in exchange for expediting a $200,000 loan application to finance their car dealership. The number of reported cases involving government procurement officials and contractors is relatively small. The typical case involves payments made in the hope of influencing contract awards. In *United States v. Johnson*, 621 F.2d 1073 (10th Cir. 1980), the court found the requisite indicia of an expected quid pro quo where the contractor, who had given a $10,000 check to a government procurement agent, credited it on its books to government contracts it expected to win. *United States v. Iaconetti*, 540 F.2d 574 (2d Cir.), *cert. denied*, 429 U.S. 1041 (1976), involved a GSA inspector who was assigned to conduct a preaward survey of a contractor and was convicted of soliciting a bribe for offering to ensure the favorable treatment of the contractor by the "upper echelon" of GSA in exchange for 1% of the contract price.

Corrupt intent can be found even though some of the payments are for services rendered. For example, in *United States v. Biaggi*, 909 F.2d 662 (2d Cir. 1990), the court found corrupt intent in payments made by a contractor to a law firm that had rendered services because part of the payment was for "services" demanded by a Congressman who was "of counsel" to the firm.

[2] Gratuities

18 U.S.C. § 201(c) makes it a crime to offer or give a gratuity to a Government official or for a Government official to solicit or receive a gratuity. The crime is defined as follows:

> (c) Whoever—
>
> (1) otherwise than as provided by law for the proper discharge of official duty—
>
> (A) directly or indirectly gives, offers, or promises anything of value to any public official, former public official, or person selected to be a public official, for or because of any official act performed or to be performed by such public official, former public official, or person selected to be a public official; or

> (B) being a public official, former public official, or person selected to be a public official, otherwise than as provided by law for the proper discharge of official duty, directly or indirectly demands, seeks, receives, accepts, or agrees to receive or accept anything of value personally for or because of any official act performed or to be performed by such official or person.

This statute is implemented by Exec. Order No. 12674, 54 Fed. Reg. 15159 (1989), as modified by Exec. Order No. 12731, 55 Fed. Reg. 42547 (1990), and by the regulations at 5 C.F.R. § 2635 Subpart B, which provide a uniform set of rules for all executive branch employees.

[a] Thing of Value

A variety of benefits have been deemed to constitute "value" in relation to gratuities, including cash, meat, liquor, and clothing, *United States v. Romano*, 583 F.2d 1 (1st Cir. 1978); paid vacations, *United States v. Hartley*, 678 F.2d 961 (11th Cir. 1982); loans and promise of future employment, *United States v. Gorman*, 807 F.2d 1299 (6th Cir. 1986), *cert. denied*, 484 U.S. 815 (1987); and golf clubs, *United States v. Hoffmann*, 556 F.3d 871 (8th Cir. 2009). In *Gorman*, the court noted that the term "anything of value" should be broadly construed and not limited to gratuities as that word is commonly understood. In determining what constitutes a "thing of value," the court placed the focus on the subjective value the receiver of the gratuity attached to the items received. See *United States v. McDade*, 827 F. Supp. 1153 (E.D. Pa. 1993), *aff'd*, 28 F.3d 283 (3d Cir. 1994), where a U.S. congressman charged with accepting illegal gratuities argued that many of the gifts allegedly received, such as a golf jacket, a golf bag, and a golf umbrella, had only nominal value and were thus not "things of value" under the gratuities statute. The congressman cited *Gorman* to support the proposition that the term "anything of value" should be construed as meaning "substantial value." The court could find nothing in *Gorman* to support this argument and denied the congressman's motion to dismiss the indictment. The court noted that even the smallest of the items allegedly received was objectively valuable enough under the gratuities statute, and that the items may have also had additional subjective value to the congressman. As an example, the court noted that the golf jacket was a green jacket similar to the one awarded each year to the winner of the Masters Golf Tournament and, thus, presumably covetable by a golf lover.

The federal standards of conduct in 5 C.F.R. § 2635 contain extensive guidance on "gifts" to federal employees. 5 C.F.R. § 2635.203(b) provides the following definition of the term "gift:"

> *Gift* includes any gratuity, favor, discount, entertainment, hospitality, loan, forbearance, or other item having monetary value. It includes services

as well as gifts of training, transportation, local travel, lodgings, and meals, whether provided in-kind, by purchase of a ticket, payment in advance, or reimbursement after the expense has been incurred.

This regulation contains 10 exceptions to this definition as follows:

(1) Modest items of food and refreshments, such as soft drinks, coffee and donuts, offered other than as part of a meal;

(2) Greeting cards and items with little intrinsic value, such as plaques, certificates, and trophies, which are intended solely for presentation;

(3) Loans from banks and other financial institutions on terms generally available to the public;

(4) Opportunities and benefits, including favorable rates and commercial discounts, available to the public or to a class consisting of all Government employees or all uniformed military personnel, whether or not restricted on the basis of geographic considerations;

(5) Rewards and prizes given to competitors in contests or events, including random drawings, open to the public unless the employee's entry into the contest or event is required as part of his official duties;

(6) Pension and other benefits resulting from continued participation in an employee welfare and benefits plan maintained by a current or former employer;

(7) Anything which is paid for by the Government or secured by the Government under Government contract;

(8) Free attendance to an event provided by the sponsor of the event to:

(i) An employee who is assigned to present information on behalf of the agency at the event on any day when the employee is presenting;

(ii) An employee whose presence on any day of the event is deemed to be essential by the agency to the presenting employee's participation in the event, provided that the employee is accompanying the presenting employee; and

(iii) The spouse or one other guest of the presenting employee on any day when the employee is presenting, provided that others in attendance will generally be accompanied by a spouse or other guest, the offer of free attendance for the spouse or other guest is unsolicited, and the agency designee, orally or in writing, has authorized the presenting employee to accept;

(9) Any gift accepted by the Government under specific statutory authority, including:

(i) Travel, subsistence, and related expenses accepted by an agency under the authority of 31 U.S.C. 1353 in connection with an employee's attendance at a meeting or similar function relating to the employee's official duties which take place away from the employee's duty station, provided that the agency's acceptance is in accordance with the implementing regulations at 41 CFR chapter 304; and

(ii) Other gifts provided in-kind which have been accepted by an agency under its agency gift acceptance statute; and

(10) Anything for which market value is paid by the employee.

5 C.F.R. § 2635.204 contains detailed guidance on a number of additional exceptions that pertain to special situations. See, for example, the small value exception in 5 C.F.R. § 2635.204(a), which permits employees to accept unsolicited gifts with a value of $20 or less and an aggregate annual value of $50 per giver; 5 C.F.R. § 2635.204(b), which permits acceptance of gifts based on a personal relationship; 5 C.F.R. § 2635.204(d), which permits the acceptance of awards and honorary degrees with a value of no more than $200; 5 C.F.R. § 2635.204(e), which permits acceptance of gifts based on outside employment or business relationships; 5 C.F.R. § 2635.204(f), which permits acceptance of gifts in connection with political activities; 5 C.F.R. § 2635.204(g), which permits acceptance of free attendance for speakers and panelists in public meetings; and 5 C.F.R. § 2635.204(h), which permits acceptance of food and refreshments at social events where the invitation has been issued by other than a prohibited source. This regulation contains detailed guidance on these exceptions including numerous specific examples of their application.

Even though acceptance of a gift may be permitted by one of the described exceptions, the regulations note at 5 C.F.R. § 2635.204 that "it is never inappropriate and frequently prudent for an employee to decline a gift offered by a prohibited source if acceptance would cause a reasonable person to question the employee's integrity or impartiality." This would appear to make it inappropriate for a government employee to accept any gift from a contractor if the employee has official duties with regard to the contract. See 5 C.F.R. § 3601.103 for supplemental guidance provided for DoD employees.

[b] Purpose of Gratuity

The gratuity must be linked to a *specific* act that the official has performed or is expected to perform, *United States v. Sun-Diamond Growers of Cal.*, 526 U.S. 398 (1999). In reaching this conclusion, the Court held the statute did not intend to make it a crime to give gifts to employees merely because they held high positions in the government. Compare *United States v. Verrusio*, 762 F.3d 1, 15 (D.C. Cir. 2014) (finding sufficient connection), with *United States v. Arthur*, 544 F.2d 730 (4th Cir. 1976) (gift given to create goodwill was not a gratuity). In earlier cases, some circuits had construed the statute more broadly. See, for example, *United States v. Campbell*, 684 F.2d 141 (D.C. Cir. 1982), concluding that a gift offered or solicited merely to "generally influence" an official was sufficient to satisfy the "for or because of" element of the statute. See also *United States v. Evans*, 572 F.2d 455 (5th Cir.), *cert. denied*, 439 U.S. 870 (1978), stating at 480:

> The purpose of these statutes is to reach any situation in which the judgment of a government agent might be clouded because of payments or gifts made to him by reason of his position "otherwise than as provided by law for the proper discharge of official duty." Even if corruption is not intended by either the donor or the donee, there is still a tendency in such a situation to provide conscious or unconscious preferential treatment of the donor by the donee, or the inefficient management of public affairs. These statutes, like the predecessor legislation, are a congressional effort to eliminate the temptation inherent in such a situation.

In *United States v. Niederberger*, 580 F.2d 63 (3d Cir. 1978), where an IRS employee violated this statute by accepting five golfing trips, the court discussed the different degrees of intent required for establishing violations of the bribery and gratuity sections, at 68:

> It is clear, then, that § 201(c)(1) [now § 201(b)(1)] requires as one of its elements a quid pro quo. In fact, we find this to be the primary distinction between subsections (c)(1) and (g) [now § 201(c)]. Support for this view is found in *United States v. Brewster*, 165 U.S. App. D.C. 1, 506 F.2d 62 (1974), where the court, analyzing the differences between subsections (c)(1) and (g), held that "[t]he bribery section [(c)(1)] makes necessary an explicit quid pro quo which need not exist if only an illegal gratuity is involved." Id., at 11, 506 F.2d at 72.
>
> Thus, we find it unnecessary for the Government to allege in an indictment charging a § 201(g) offense that a gratuity received by a public official was, in any way, generated by some specific, identifiable act performed or to be performed by the official. A quid pro quo is simply foreign to the elements of a subsection (g) offense.

It is a violation of the statute to accept a gratuity for an act that has previously been performed for the giver. See *United States v. Ring*, 706 F.3d 460 (D.C. Cir.), *cert. denied*, 571 U.S. 827 (2013) (basketball tickets for prior help in expediting visa application); *United States v. Bishton*, 463 F.2d 887 (D.C. Cir. 1972) (supervisor's solicitation of $400 gift from employee for whom the supervisor had previously obtained a promotion); *United States v. Evans*, 572 F.2d 455 (5th Cir. 1978) (acceptance of $500 gratuity by an official who had previously accepted an offer of government employment but had not commenced work).

Since a gratuity need only be paid "for or because of any official act" (18 U.S.C. § 201(c)) and no quid pro quo need be proved, it may be difficult to discern whether the alleged payment was made out of friendship or other disinterested motive. While it is clear that *corrupt* intent need not be shown, the government must at least demonstrate *some* nexus between the giving or receiving of the thing of value and the employee's official position. In *United States v.*

Hoffman, 556 F.3d 871 (8th Cir. 2009), sufficient evidence of intent was found when golf clubs were given to a government employee that was responsible for giving a performance rating to the contractor (without proof that the rating was actually given). In *United States v. Standefer*, 610 F.2d 1076 (3d Cir. 1979), *aff'd*, 447 U.S. 10 (1980), sufficient evidence of intent was found despite a corporate officer's assertion that certain vacation trips to Florida given to an IRS employee were motivated by disinterested friendship, because no evidence was offered that similar gifts were given either prior or subsequent to the recipient's employment in the government, and a subordinate of the corporate officer characterized the relationship as a "business friendship." However, many of the reported cases actually involve facts reflecting an expectation of a quid pro quo, perhaps reflecting a prosecutorial reluctance to impose bribery sanctions in cases involving small payments. For example, in *United States v. Mosley*, 659 F.2d 812 (7th Cir. 1981), an Illinois state official, whose salary was entirely paid by the federal government under the CETA program, was convicted of violating 18 U.S.C. § 201(g) (now § 201(c)(1)(B)) for soliciting $50 payments from applicants for CETA jobs in exchange for favorable referral to CETA hiring agencies. In *United States v. Kirby*, 587 F.2d 876 (7th Cir. 1978), the defendants were convicted of conspiring to violate 18 U.S.C. § 201(f) (now § 201(c)(1)(A)) by making payments to grain inspectors in exchange for false certifications that inspected grain was of a higher quality than it actually was.

[c] Contract Termination

10 U.S.C. § 4651 (formerly § 2207) requires that all Department of Defense contracts over the simplified acquisition threshold contain a clause giving the government the right to terminate the contract if gratuities have been offered or paid. The standard clause used for this purpose the Gratuities clause in FAR 52.203-3. FAR 3.202 requires this clause to be used by all agencies. However, it is not applicable to contracts for personal services and contracts between the military departments or defense agencies and foreign governments that do not obligate Department of Defense funds, FAR 3.202. In addition to the right to terminate the contract, the clause gives agencies the right to damages for breach of contract and gives the Department of Defense the right to exemplary damages from three to ten times the "cost incurred by the contractor in giving [the] gratuities." See Cibinic, Nash & Nagle, *Administration of Government Contracts* (5th ed. 2016), for a discussion of the application of this clause.

[3] Conduct of Former Employees

The government has sought to prevent former government employees and military officers from making unfair use of their prior positions and affiliations. At the same time, the government recognizes the legitimate interest and rights of former employees to seek employment and to enter into business ventures. Thus, activity that seeks to influence government action or that would undermine confidence in the fairness of government activities is prohibited, but former government employees and military officers retain a great amount of freedom to pursue legally permissible activity.

[a] General Restrictions

18 U.S.C. § 207 restricts "officers and employees" in the following circumstances:

1. A former employee is prohibited for life from representing anyone else before the government on a particular matter the employee handled personally and substantially while a government official.
2. A former employee is prohibited for two years from representing a party on a particular matter that had been under the employee's official responsibility during the final year of the employee's government service.
3. A former employee is prohibited for one year from assisting others in trade or treaty negotiations in which the employee had been personally and substantially engaged during the employee's final year of government service.
4. A former senior level employee is prohibited for one year from making any communication or appearance before the employee's former agency regardless of prior involvement in the matter.
5. A former "very senior level" employee is prohibited for two years from contacting employees of the executive branch of the government.
6. A former senior level employee is prohibited for one year from representing any foreign entity before the government.

Criminal prosecutions under this statute are rare. However, alleged violations of this statute are frequently raised in contesting the validity of contracts. The most egregious conduct falling within this provision is hiring government employees before the award of a contract when they have worked on the procurement. A contracting officer's disqualification of an offeror for such conduct was sustained in *NKF Eng'g, Inc. v. United States*, 805 F.2d 372 (Fed. Cir. 1986). In that case, a former Navy civilian employee, who had participated substantially in the procurement process on a particular RFP, left federal employment to take a job with one of the offerors before the contract was awarded. That offeror subsequently submitted a price revision that was 33% lower than its earlier offer. The court upheld the disqualification of the offeror on the basis of an appearance of impropriety, even though the offeror claimed that it had carefully isolated the former government employee from its preparation of the final offer. The court agreed that the potential for an unfair competitive advantage so tainted the procurement process that the integrity of the process had been damaged. Similarly, in *Holmes & Narver Servs., Inc./Morrison-Knudson Servs., Inc. (JV)*, Comp. Gen. Dec. B-235906, 89-2 CPD ¶ 379, the GAO held that a company should be disqualified because it had hired three agency employees that had access to source selection information and wrote a proposal. Later decisions have refused to disqualify companies that hired agency employees to write proposals because there were no "hard facts" showing that this gave their employer a significant advantage, *VSE Corp.*, Comp. Gen. Dec. B-404833.4, 2011 CPD ¶ 268; *ITT Federal Servs. Corp.*, Comp. Gen. Dec. B-253740.2, 94-2 CPD ¶ 30. See *Oracle America, Inc. v. United States*, 144 Fed. Cl. 88 (2019), also refusing to disqualify a company that hired government employees because they did not play a significant role in structuring the procurement.

[i] Particular Matter

Violations of the first two restrictions require participation in a "particular matter" that was in the agency during the official's employment. 5 C.F.R. § 2641.201(h)(1) states that "[s]uch a matter typically involves a specific proceeding affecting the legal rights of the parties or an isolatable transaction . . . between identifiable parties." Excluded are formulation of general policy, rulemaking, and legislation, 5 C.F.R. § 2641.201(h)(2). For a violation to occur, the subsequent representation must concern the same matter in which the employee participated during employment, 5 C.F.R. § 2641.201(h)(3). These regulations contain numerous examples to illustrate the application of these rules.

There is little judicial interpretation of this term. See, however, *CACI, Inc.-Fed. v. United States*, 1 Cl. Ct. 352, *rev'd*, 719 F.2d 1567 (Fed. Cir. 1983), where the Justice Department issued an RFP for ADPE services for the Information Systems Support Group (ISSG) of the department. Before award was made, an offeror who had provided these services for some time alleged that a conflict existed in that a vice president of a competitor had previously served as chief of the ISSG. In issuing an injunction barring award, the Claims Court found that the employee was involved in the "same particular matter" while working for the government, a criterion that satisfies either § 207(a) or § 207(b). The Federal Circuit reversed, holding that a follow-on service contract did not cover the "same particular matter" as the prior contract because the nature of the services had evolved and were broader than those on the earlier contract. The court appears to have read the statute narrowly in arriving at this conclusion. Contrast the *CACI* decision with *United States v. Medico Indus., Inc.*, 784 F.2d 840 (7th Cir. 1986), holding that a contract amendment adding a large quantity of units to an existing contract was sufficiently related to the original contract to be the same particular matter. See also *United States v. Stadd*, 636 F.3d 630, 636-37 (D.C. Cir. 2011); *United States v. Nevers*, 7 F.3d 59, 63 (1993); *United States v. Walters*, No. 3:08-cr-148-WHB-JCS, 2009 U.S. Dist. LEXIS 58370 (S.D. Miss. July 2, 2009) (advice on how to obtain loans was a particular matter regarding the employee that then went to work for the company that he had advised); *United States ex rel. Wright v. Agip Petroleum Co.*, 2008 WL 11348433 (E.D. Tex. 2008).

[ii] Personal and Substantial Participation

Violation of the first restriction occurs only when there has been a personal and substantial participation in the matter during employment, as stated at 5 C.F.R. § 2641.201(h) stating:

> *Participate*. To "participate" means to take an action as an employee through decision, approval, disapproval, recommendation, the rendering of advice, investigation, or other such action, or to purposefully forbear in order to affect the outcome of a matter. An employee can participate in particular matters that are pending other than in his own agency. An employee does not participate in a matter merely because he had knowledge of its existence or because it was pending under his official responsibility. An employee does not participate in a matter within the meaning of this section unless he does so in his official capacity.
>
> *Personally*. To participate "personally" means to participate:
>
> (i) Directly, either individually or in combination with other persons; or
>
> (ii) Through direct and active supervision of the participation of any person he supervises, including a subordinate.
>
> *Substantially*. To participate "substantially" means that the employee's involvement is of significance to the matter. Participation may be substantial even though it is not determinative of the outcome of a particular matter. However, it requires more than official responsibility, knowledge, perfunctory involvement, or involvement on an administrative or peripheral issue. A finding of substantiality should be based not only on the effort devoted to a matter, but also on the importance of the effort. While a series of peripheral involvements may be insubstantial, the single act of approving or participating in a critical step may be substantial. Provided that an employee participates in the substantive merits of a matter, his participation may be substantial even though his role in the matter, or the aspect of the matter in which he is participating, may be minor in relation to the matter as a whole. Participation in peripheral aspects of a matter or in aspects not directly involving the substantive merits of a matter (such as reviewing budgetary procedures or scheduling meetings) is not substantial.

These regulations contain numerous examples to illustrate the application of these terms. Review of a proposed notice of income tax deficiency and recommendation for its issuance constituted personal and substantial participation, *United States v. Nasser*, 476 F.2d 1111 (7th Cir. 1973). Preparing a memorandum and answering a legal question were also held to be such participation. Review of a patent application was held to be sufficient involvement in *Kearney & Trecker Corp. v. Giddings & Lewis, Inc.*, 452 F.2d 579 (7th Cir. 1971), *cert. denied*, 405 U.S. 1066 (1972).

[iii] Representation

The basic prohibition in 18 U.S.C. § 207(a)(1) is on representational activities carried out "with the intent to influence." "Representation" may occur in the course of communications or appearances. 5 C.F.R. § 2641.201(d) states:

> (d) Communication or appearance—(1) Communication. A former employee makes a communication when he imparts or transmits information of any kind, including facts, opinions, ideas, questions or direction, to an employee of the United States, whether orally, in written correspondence, by electronic media, or by any other means. This includes only those communications with respect to which the former employee intends that the information conveyed will be attributed to himself, although it is not necessary that any employee of the United States actually recognize the former employee as the source of the information.
>
> (2) Appearance. A former employee makes an appearance when he is physically present before an employee of the United States, in either a formal or informal setting. Although an appearance also may be accompanied by certain communications, an appearance need not involve any communication by the former employee.
>
> (3) Behind-the-scenes assistance. Nothing in this section prohibits a former employee from providing assistance to another person, provided that the assistance does not involve a communication to or an appearance before an employee of the United States.

5 C.F.R. § 2641.201(e) provides the following guidance on the "intent to influence" element of this rule:

> (e) With the intent to influence—(1) Basic concept. The prohibition applies, only to communications or appearances made by a former Government employee with the intent to influence the United States. A communication or appearance is made with the intent to influence when made for the purpose of:
>
> (i) Seeking a Government ruling, benefit, approval, or other discretionary Government action; or
>
> (ii) Affecting Government action in connection with an issue or aspect of a matter which involves an appreciable element of actual or potential dispute or controversy.

5 C.F.R. § 2641.201(e)(2)(vi) makes it clear that there is no violation when a former employee makes a communication, at the initiation of the government, concerning work performed or to be performed under a government contract, during a routine government site visit to a contractor, "in the ordinary course of evaluation, administration, or performance of an actual or proposed contract." The regulation contains the following example:

> An agency official visits the premises of a prospective contractor to evaluate the testing procedure being proposed by the contractor for a research contract on which it has bid. A former employee of the agency, now employed by the contractor, is the person most familiar with the technical aspects of the proposed testing procedure. The agency official asks the former employee about certain technical features of the equipment used in connection with the testing procedure. The former employee may provide factual information that is responsive to the questions posed by the agency official, as such information is requested by the Government under circumstances for its convenience in reviewing the bid. However, the former employee may not argue for the appropriateness of the proposed testing procedure or otherwise advocate any position on behalf of the contractor.

See *Robert E. Derecktor of R.I., Inc. v. United States*, 762 F. Supp. 1019 (D.R.I. 1991), where the court, interpreting the predecessor to § 207(a), held that a former employee's delivery of a bid package to his former agency did not constitute an appearance within the meaning of this restriction and that the employee did not deliver the bid with the intent to influence. See, however, *United States v. Coleman*, 805 F.2d 474 (3d Cir. 1986), where a former employee's presence at a meeting related to tax cases, which had been within the employee's supervisory responsibility before retiring, was found to constitute representation within the meaning of this restriction.

18 U.S.C. § 207(j)(5) permits "communications solely for the purpose of furnishing scientific or technological information" to the agency. See *J. L. Assocs.*, Comp. Gen. Dec. B-201331.2, 82-1 CPD ¶ 99, where this exception was applied by the Air Force to a "briefing" by a retired military officer concerning the same activity that he had commanded. The briefing concerned the contractor's experience on similar work with other agencies and occurred before issuance of an RFP.

Under a predecessor statute, participation in the preparation of a claim for reimbursement was held not to violate the statute since it did not amount to "prosecution" of a claim, *Acme Process Equip. Co. v. United States*, 347 F.2d 509 (Ct. Cl. 1965), *rev'd on other grounds*, 385 U.S. 138 (1966).

[iv] Types of Employment or Contracting Permitted

Absent a violation of the specific provisions of 18 U.S.C. § 207, there is no general prohibition in this statute against *employment* of a former government employee by a contractor. 5 C.F.R. § 2641.101 provides:

> 18 U.S.C. § 207 prohibits certain acts by former employees (including current employees who formerly served in "senior" or "very senior" employee positions) which involve, or may appear to involve, the unfair use of prior Government employment. None of the restrictions of section 207 prohibits any former employee, regardless of Government rank or position, from accepting employment with any particular private or public employer.

> Rather, section 207 prohibits a former employee from providing certain services to or on behalf of non-Federal employers or other persons, whether or not done for compensation. These restrictions are personal to the employee and are not imputed to other.

For cases not applying this statute to mere employment, see *Perini/Jones, Joint Venture*, Comp. Gen. Dec. B-285906, 2002 CPD ¶ 68 (former employee that will serve as company's project manager who was in the procuring agency at time proposals were submitted and evaluated); *Medical Dev. Int'l*, Comp. Gen. Dec. B-281484.2, 99-1 CPD ¶ 68 (former employee that will serve as Associate Director of company and had policy position in agency); *Culp/Wesner/Culp*, Comp. Gen. Dec. B-212318, 84-1 CPD ¶ 17 (former agency employee in charge of preparing solicitation subsequently awarded subcontract); and *Bray Studios, Inc.*, Comp. Gen. Dec. B-207723, 82-2 CPD ¶ 373 (former agency employee now president of contractor and working in same area).

Neither is there any general prohibition against entering into contracts with former government employees, *Sterling Med. Assocs.*, 62 Comp. Gen. 230 (B-209493), 83-1 CPD ¶ 215 (former employee of Veterans Administration awarded contract by the Department of the Navy); *Edward R. Jereb*, 60 Comp. Gen. 298 (B-200092), 81-1 CPD ¶ 178 (restriction prohibiting award of services contract to former agency employees held invalid); *Western Eng'g & Sales Co.*, Comp. Gen. Dec. B-205464, 82-2 CPD ¶ 277 (former employee awarded contract by agency based on proposal submitted after employment terminated). See, however, *KAR Contracting, LLC*, Comp. Gen. Dec. B-310454, 2007 CPD ¶ 226, where the agency properly refused to contract with company whose founder had prepared the contract drawings; and *Aviation Enters., Inc. v. Orr*, 29 Cont. Cas. Fed. (CCF) ¶ 82,053 (D.D.C. 1981), *vacated*, 716 F.2d 1403 (D.C. Cir. 1983), where a contract award to a company owned by a former military officer was enjoined because of a "conflict of interest," without reference to the statute. In *KAR Contracting* GAO stated:

> In our view, the restrictions of 18 U.S.C. § 207 do not set the outer boundaries for a CO's reasonable exercise of discretion about whether the award of a contract will create the appearance of impropriety. Specifically, even if KAR can argue that the facts here would not support a criminal conviction for violation of the post-employment restrictions, that would not mean there was no reasonable basis for concluding that KAR was ineligible for award.

[b] Additional Statutory Restrictions

A broader post-employment restriction applicable to specific "former officials" is set forth in the Procurement Integrity Act at 41 U.S.C. § 2104, stating:

> (a) Prohibition. A former official of a Federal agency may not accept compensation from a contractor as an employee, officer, director, or consultant of the contractor within a period of one year after such former official—

(1) served, when the contractor was selected or awarded a contract, as the procuring contracting officer, the source selection authority, a member of the source selection evaluation board, or the chief of a financial or technical evaluation team in a procurement in which that contractor was selected for award of a contract in excess of $10,000,000;

(2) served as the program manager, deputy program manager, or administrative contracting officer for a contract in excess of $10,000,000 awarded to that contractor; or

(3) personally made for the Federal agency a decision to—

(A) award a contract, subcontract, modification of a contract or subcontract, or a task order or delivery order in excess of $10,000,000 to that contractor;

(B) establish overhead or other rates applicable to one or more contracts for that contractor that are valued in excess of $10,000,000;

(C) approve issuance of one or more contract payments in excess of $10,000,000 to that contractor; or

(D) pay or settle a claim in excess of $10,000,000 with that contractor.

(b) When compensation may be accepted. Subsection (a) does not prohibit a former official of a Federal agency from accepting compensation from a division or affiliate of a contractor that does not produce the same or similar products or services as the entity of the contractor that is responsible for the contract referred to in paragraph (1), (2), or (3) of subsection (a).

FAR 3.104-3(d)(2) provides detailed guidance on the calculation of the one-year period. FAR 3.104-3(d)(3) states that the statute does not prohibit employment by a division or affiliate of a contractor that does not produce the same or similar products or services as the division with which the official had previous contact. FAR 3.104-6 contains guidance on obtaining advice from agency ethics officials on the application of these rules. 41 U.S.C. § 2106 also provides that protests may no longer be filed based on an allegation that this statute has been violated unless the violation has been reported to the contracting agency within 14 days of learning of the violation. See *Honeywell Tech. Sols., Inc.*, Comp. Gen. Dec. B-400771, 2009 CPD ¶ 49 (protest denied because protester did not file within 14 days of learning that winning offeror had hired an agency official as a consultant). However, GAO has ruled on protests alleging that a contractor had obtained an unfair competitive advantage through revolving door violations, *Day & Zimmermann Pantex Corp.*, Comp. Gen. Dec. B-286016, 2001 CPD ¶ 96 (no indication that hired official impacted award decision); *PRC, Inc.*, Comp. Gen. Dec. B-274698.2, 97-1 CPD ¶ 115, *recons. denied*, 97-2 CPD ¶ 10 (no impropriety in the employment of the former Commanding Officer of the procuring agency who had obtained an opinion that he was not a procurement official under the statute although he had concurred in the acquisition plan and appointed the source selection official).

Prior to 1996, when the Procurement Integrity Act was revised, there were somewhat more stringent restrictions. There were also special purpose post-employment restrictions applicable to specifically identified personnel, 10 U.S.C. § 2397c, which were repealed by § 4304(b)(1) of the Clinger-Cohen Act of 1996.

[4] Conduct of Current Employees

There are numerous statutes and regulations circumscribing the activities of government employees. See, for example, 18 U.S.C. § 203 (limitation on receiving payment from others for official activity); 18 U.S.C. § 205 (prohibition against prosecuting claims); and 18 U.S.C. § 209 (prohibition against receiving compensation from other than United States for official duties). This section discusses the two major statutes applicable to government contracting. It also discusses administrative restrictions on contracting with organizations owned or controlled by government employees.

[a] General Restrictions

Officers and employees of the government with a financial interest in an organization are prohibited from participating personally and substantially in any matter concerning that organization and the government, 18 U.S.C. § 208. This provision was intended to expand the proscriptions against employee participation with the private sector beyond the prior § 434, which merely prohibited certain "transactions of business." The statute applies to acts of government employee outside of the United States, *United States v. Ayesh*, 702 F.3d 162 (4th Cir. 2012).

[i] Extent of Financial Interest

The Standards of Ethical Conduct contained in 5 C.F.R. § 2635 Subpart D provide detailed guidance implementing this statutory proscription. The following definition of "financial interest" is found at 5 C.F.R. § 2635.403(c):

> (1) Except as provided in paragraph (c)(2) of this section, the term financial interest is limited to financial interests that are owned by the employee or by the employee's spouse or minor children. However, the term is not limited to only those financial interests that would be disqualifying under 18 U.S.C. § 208(a) and § 2635.402. The term includes any current or contingent ownership, equity, or security interest in real or personal property or a business and may include an indebtedness or compensated employment relationship. It thus includes, for example, interests in the nature of stocks, bonds, partnership interests, fee and leasehold interests, mineral and other property rights, deeds of trust, and liens, and extends to any right to purchase or acquire any such interest, such as a stock option or commodity future. It does not include a future interest created by someone other than the employee, his spouse or dependent child or any right as a beneficiary of an estate that has not been settled.

> (2) The term financial interest includes service, with or without compensation, as an officer, director, trustee, general partner or employee of any person, including a nonprofit entity, whose financial interests are imputed to the employee under § 2635.402(b)(2)(iii) or (iv).

The Ethics in Government Act of 1978, 5 U.S.C. App. § 201 et seq., further requires the public disclosure of financial information by all political appointees and all civil service employees of GS-16 and above.

A financial interest is present if it is more than insubstantial, remote, or inconsequential. The Office of Government Ethics ruled in 83 OGE 1 (1983) that vested rights in a private corporation's pension plan constituted a financial interest. In another ruling dated August 17, 1979, the Office ruled that leaves of absence or reemployment rights with a former employer were financial interests in that company.

A statutory violation occurs when the employee has both a financial stake in the outcome of the transaction and a sufficient contact with the transaction. It seems clear that the threshold is quite low for both elements. In *United States v. Mississippi Valley Generating Co.*, 364 U.S. 520 (1961), the Court gave an expansive reading to the term "transacting business" in prior § 434 and found a violation of the statute where the employee's financial stake consisted of the potential business he had generated for another employer and where his contact with the transaction involved him in preliminary contract negotiations on behalf of both parties. In that case, a temporary employee of the Bureau of the Budget who served at the request of the bureau chief without pay also served as an officer of a bank. An offeror on an RFP for construction of a power plant negotiated the early stages of the contract with the temporary employee and also asked him to inquire into financing with bank officials. The temporary employee was not involved in the final contract negotiations but confidentially suggested revisions to the offeror's second proposal. Regarding the employee's financial stake, the Court held that positive corruption is not a prerequisite for violation of the conflicts statute and stated at 550, "[T]he statute is more concerned with what might have happened than with what actually happened." See also *Smith v. United States*, 305 F.2d 197 (9th Cir. 1962), where the court found a violation of § 434 even though the "transaction" consisted merely of an employee's failure to circumscribe the activities of subordinates who were involved in a conflict.

Although § 208 is much broader in scope than was § 434, the cases decided under this section do not appear to have given it as strict an interpretation as was given to the prior statute. See *Galen Medical Assocs., Inc. v. United States*, 369 F.3d 1324 (Fed. Cir. 2004) (no conflict when winning contractor's references were on evaluation panels because there was evidence of basis for low evaluations); *United States v. Ponnapula*, 246 F.3d 576 (6th Cir. 2001) (no conflict where a person acting for the Small Business Administration in the sale of foreclosed property took a $5,000 retainer for future employment from the buyer but had no substantial participation in the transaction because her actions with regard to the sale were only ministerial); *Cexec, Inc. v. Dep't of Energy*, GSBCA 12909-P, 95-1 BCA ¶ 27,380 (no conflict when an employee, whose wife had a financial interest in the winning contractor, had only peripheral contact with the procurement); and *United States v. Tierney*, 947 F.2d 854 (8th Cir. 1991) (no conflict because the fact that prosecutor's husband was representing defendant's insurance company was too remote a connection). See also *Grassetti v. Weinberger*, 408 F. Supp. 142 (N.D. Cal. 1976), where a grant applicant had been denied a grant by the National Cancer Institute, a division of the National Institutes of Health, whose evaluation team consisted of members also competing for research grants. Though the team had sufficient contact with the transaction, the court stated that although a conflict would arise where team members contributed to a decision as to whether to award themselves a grant, the allegation that a denial of a grant to another applicant would leave more money for the team was too remote to create a conflict.

The cases that have enforced § 208 have dealt with considerably greater financial interests and contact than that in *Mississippi Valley* or *Smith*. See, for example, *United States v. Stadd*, 636 F.3d 630 (D.C. Cir. 2011) (employee promoted the agency's allocation of funds to a research consortium that was employing his consulting firm); *United States v. Selby*, 557 F.3d 968 (9th Cir. 2009) (employee promoted the agency's use of software sold by husband's company); *United States v. Alfonzo-Reyes*, 384 F. Supp. 2d 523 (D.C.P.R. 2005) (employee participated in approving a loan where he would obtain part of the proceeds); *United States v. Bouchey*, 860 F. Supp. 890 (D.D.C. 1994) (alleged participation by government employee in conspiracy to pay inflated consulting fees); *United Tel. Co.*, GSBCA 10031-P, 89-3 BCA ¶ 22,108 (offeror disqualified because its subcontractor had used a government employee participating in the procurement as a consultant during the competition). *United States v. Irons*, 640 F.2d 872 (7th Cir. 1981) (program officer for HEW recommended to a contracting officer that an IFB be sent to a company he established for the purpose of receiving the IFB); *K & R Eng'g Co. v. United States*, 616 F.2d 469 (Ct. Cl. 1980) (chief of a branch of the Corps of Engineers took kickbacks and profits from contracts awarded by his office to a particular contractor after giving contractor advance notice of the IFB and of the maximum amount the Corps would pay); and *United States v. Conlon*, 628 F.2d 150 (D.C. Cir. 1980) (indictment under § 208 reinstated where it was shown that the director of the Bureau of Engraving, who was also president of the American Bank Note Development Corp. (ABNC), participated in decision-making regarding replacement of a Bureau signature system with one developed by ABNC).

[ii] Employment Discussions

Conducting employment negotiations has also been held to be a conflict of interest under 18 U.S.C. § 208. Employment discussions are considered a financial interest by the Standards of Ethical Conduct, 5 C.F.R. § 2635.603. The following definition of "seeking employment" is found at 5 C.F.R. § 2635.603(b):

> An employee is seeking employment once he has begun seeking employment within the meaning of paragraph (b)(1) of this section and until he is no longer seeking employment within the meaning of paragraph (b)(2) of this section.
>
> (1) An employee has begun seeking employment if he has directly or indirectly:
>
> (i) Engaged in negotiations for employment with any person. For these purposes, as for 18 U.S.C. § 208(a), the term negotiations means discussion or communication with another person, or such person's agent or intermediary, mutually conducted with a view toward reaching an agreement regarding possible employment with that person. The term is not limited to discussions of specific terms and conditions of employment in a specific position;
>
> (ii) Made an unsolicited communication to any person, or such person's agent or intermediary, regarding possible employment with that person. However, the employee has not begun seeking employment if that communication was:
>
> (A) For the sole purpose of requesting a job application; or
>
> (B) For the purpose of submitting a resume or other employment proposal to a person affected by the performance or nonperformance of the employee's duties only as part of an industry or other discrete class. The employee will be considered to have begun seeking employment upon receipt of any response indicating an interest in employment discussions; or
>
> (iii) Made a response other than rejection to an unsolicited communication from any person, or such person's agent or intermediary, regarding possible employment with that person.
>
> (2) An employee is no longer seeking employment when:
>
> (i) The employee or the prospective employer rejects the possibility of employment and all discussions of possible employment have terminated; or
>
> (ii) Two months have transpired after the employee's dispatch of an unsolicited resume or employment proposal, provided the employee has received no indication of interest in employment discussions from the prospective employer.
>
> (3) For purposes of this definition, a response that defers discussions until the foreseeable future does not constitute rejection of an unsolicited employment overture, proposal, or resume nor rejection of a prospective employment possibility.

Negotiations for employment were found in *United States v. Schaltenbrand*, 930 F.2d 1554 (11th Cir. 1991), *cert. denied*, 502 U.S. 1005 (1991), where an Air Force reserve officer approached a prospective employer, filled out an application, came for an interview, discussed his qualifications and indicated a willingness to meet company officials, even though neither side made any formal offer until after he was finished with the project; *United States v. Lord*, 710 F. Supp. 615 (E.D. Va. 1989), *aff'd*, 902 F.2d 1567 (4th Cir.1990), where a government program manager discussed employment with a contractor; and *United States v. Gorman*, 807 F.2d 1299 (6th Cir. 1986), *cert. denied*, 484 U.S. 815 (1987), where the government employee had an initial conversation with a company and gave them a list of conditions for employment. The Principal Deputy Assistant Secretary of the Air Force for Acquisition also pled guilty to a violation of § 208 when she met with an officer of a company to discuss future employment at the same time she was negotiating a major contract with that company. See *Lockheed Martin Aeronautics Co.*, Comp. Gen. Dec. B-295401, 2005 CPD ¶ 41, for a description of this plea agreement. Compare *Air Line Pilots Ass'n, Int'l v. Dep't of Transportation*, 899 F.2d 1230 (D.C. Cir. 1990), where no conflict was found when the Secretary of Transportation made a regulatory ruling at the time he was negotiating for employment with a law firm. The court based its conclusion of the fact that the law firm was not representing any of the parties to the regulatory ruling.

Once an employment discussion has commenced, it may be terminated by "rejection" of any possibility of employment. However, it is clear that terminating an immediate employment discussion will not result in "rejection" of an offer of employment if the discussion is only deferred. See *Express One Int'l, Inc. v. United States Postal Serv.*, 814 F. Supp. 93 (D.D.C. 1992), where the court enjoined award of a contract because the employee of a consultant of the procuring agency had told the winning offeror "he would not be available for a personal meeting or to discuss a position until after [award of the contract]."

Violations of § 208 are valid grounds for rejecting an offer. In *AT&T Commc'ns, Inc.*, GSBCA 9252-P, 88-2 BCA ¶ 20,805, an offeror was disqualified after receiving information from a government employee with whom it had discussed employment. Less stringent enforcement of this rule occurred in *Chemonics Int'l Consulting Div.*, 63 Comp. Gen. 14 (B-210426), 83-2 CPD ¶ 426, where GAO held that it was improper to withhold award from a firm that had offered employment to a government employee who had attended subsequent negotiations, and *CACI, Inc.-Fed. v. United States*, 1 Cl. Ct. 352, *rev'd*, 719 F.2d 1567 (Fed. Cir. 1983), where the court found no violation of § 208 when contract negotiations with a government employee occurred 16 months after an employment discussion had occurred. In *Four-Phase Sys., Inc.*, ASBCA 26794, 86-2 BCA ¶ 18,924, a violation of § 208 was found where employment negotiations occurred during the negotiation of a change order. As a result, the board held that the violation of § 208 was a valid defense to a breach of contract claim based on the change order.

[b] Procurement Integrity Restrictions

Additional restrictions on employment contacts or discussions are contained in 41 U.S.C. § 2103, stating:

> (a) Actions required. An agency official participating personally and substantially in a Federal agency procurement for a contract in excess of the simplified acquisition threshold who contacts or is contacted by a person that is a bidder or offeror in that Federal agency procurement regarding possible non-Federal employment for that official shall—
>
> (1) promptly report the contact in writing to the official's supervisor and to the designated agency ethics official (or designee) of the agency in which the official is employed; and
>
> (2) (A) reject the possibility of non-Federal employment; or
>
> (B) disqualify himself or herself from further personal and substantial participation in that Federal agency procurement until the agency authorizes the official to resume participation in the procurement, in accordance with the requirements of section 208 of title 18 and applicable agency regulations on the grounds that—
>
> (i) the person is no longer a bidder or offeror in that Federal agency procurement; or
>
> (ii) all discussions with the bidder or offeror regarding possible non-Federal employment have terminated without an agreement or arrangement for employment.

The Act is implemented in FAR 3.104-3(c)(2) which defines a "contact" as "any of the actions included as 'seeking employment' in 5 C.F.R. § 2635.603(b)" as well as "unsolicited communications from offerors regarding possible employment." FAR 3.104-5(a) also warns that contacts by "agents or other intermediaries" of an offeror may fall within these procedures. The first step in this procedure is an immediate reporting requirement when an agency official receives an employment contract, FAR 3.104-3(c)(1). This report must be submitted to the official's supervisor and the agency ethics official. The second step is for the official to either "reject the possibility of non-Federal employment" or disqualify himself or herself from further participation in the procurement. This disqualification decision appears to be in the sole discretion of the official. However, FAR 3.104-8(c) states that an official who "refuses to terminate employment discussions may be subject to agency administrative actions under 5 C.F.R. § 2635.604(d) if the official's disqualification from participation in a particular procurement interferes substantially with the individual's ability to perform assigned duties." Thus, an agency retains considerable control over this decision under the regulations.

FAR 3.104-5(b) contains the following additional reporting requirements:

> (b) *Disqualification notice.* In addition to submitting the contact report required by 3.104-3(c)(1), an agency official who must disqualify himself or herself pursuant to 3.104-3(c)(1)(ii) must promptly submit written notice of disqualification from further participation in the procurement to the contracting officer, the source selection authority if other than the contracting officer, and the agency official's immediate supervisor. As a minimum, the notice must —
>
> (1) Identify the procurement;
>
> (2) Describe the nature of the agency official's participation in the procurement and specify the approximate dates or time period of participation; and
>
> (3) Identify the offeror and describe its interest in the procurement.

After disqualification, FAR 3.104-5(c) places the decision on reinstatement of the official in the sole discretion of the agency as follows:

> (c) *Resumption of participation in a procurement.* (1) The official must remain disqualified until such time as the agency, at its sole and exclusive discretion, authorizes the official to resume participation in the procurement in accordance with 3.104-3(c)(1)(ii).
>
> (2) After the conditions of 3.104-3(c)(1)(ii)(A) or (B) have been met, the head of the contracting activity (HCA), after consultation with the agency ethics official, may authorize the disqualified official to resume participation in the procurement, or may determine that an additional disqualification period is necessary to protect the integrity of the procurement process. In determining the disqualification period, the HCA must consider any factors that create an appearance that the disqualified official acted without complete impartiality in the procurement. The HCA's reinstatement decision should be in writing.
>
> (3) Government officer or employee must also comply with the provisions of 18 U.S.C. 208 and 5 CFR part 2635 regarding any re-sumed participation in a procurement matter. Government officer or employee may not be reinstated to participate in a procurement matter affecting the financial interest of someone with whom the individual is seeking employment, unless the individual receives—
>
> (i) A waiver pursuant to 18 U.S.C. 208(b)(1) or (b)(3); or
>
> (ii) An authorization in accordance with the requirements of subpart F of 5 CFR part 2635.

The Act also narrows the scope of these restrictions. First, the rule only applies to contracts over the simplified acquisition threshold of $250,000. Second, the rule applies only to "Federal agency procurement"—which excludes sole source contracts and contract modifications. Note, however, that entertaining employment discussions or negotiations during such transactions would be a violation of 18 U.S.C. § 208 and 5 C.F.R. § 2635.603(b). A third narrowing is that the Act restricts only bidders and offerors making contacts to officials regarding future employment. However, FAR 3.104-5(a) warns that the disqualification may be required even where contacts are through an agent or intermediary of the bidder or offeror because that contact would be a violation of 18 U.S.C. § 208. See also 5 C.F.R. § 2635.603(c).

[c] Biased Decision-Making

One result of improper influence on government officials can be biased decision-making. This occurred in at least two instances when the Principal Deputy Assistant Secretary for Acquisition of the Air Force admitted favoring one company over others during the source selection process. As a result, two protests were granted several years after the award of the contracts calling for the agency to reopen a long-term contract to competition for the work that could be separated from the work that had already been accomplished. See *Lockheed Martin Aeronautics Co.*, Comp. Gen. Dec. B-295401, 2005 CPD ¶ 41, and *Lockheed Martin Corp.*, Comp. Gen. Dec. B-295402, 2005 CPD ¶ 24. These decisions contain a detailed analysis of the specific actions taken by the biased Air Force official to direct the award to the company that she favored.

[5] Conduct of Contractor Employees Performing Acquisition Functions

FAR Subpart 3.11 also restricts contractor employees performing acquisition functions from having a financial interest in or receiving gifts from contractors competing for contracts on which they work. FAR 3.1102 states the policy as followed:

> The Government's policy is to require contractors to—
>
> (a) Identify and prevent personal conflicts of interest of their covered employees; and
>
> (b) Prohibit covered employees who have access to non-public information by reason of performance on a Government contract from using such information for personal gain.

FAR 3.1103 requires contractors whose employees perform acquisition functions closely associated with inherently Government functions to—

> (1) Have procedures in place to screen covered employees for potential personal conflicts of interest by—
>
> (i) Obtaining and maintaining from each covered employee, when the employee is initially assigned to the task under the contract, a

disclosure of interests that might be affected by the task to which the employee has been assigned, as follows:

(A) Financial interests of the covered employee, of close family members, or of other members of the covered employee's household.

(B) Other employment or financial relationships of the covered employee (including seeking or negotiating for prospective employment or business).

(C) Gifts, including travel;

The employees that are covered by these procedures are defined in FAR 3.1101 as follows:

> Acquisition function closely associated with inherently governmental functions means supporting or providing advice or recommendations with regard to the following activities of a Federal agency:
>
> (1) Planning acquisitions.
>
> (2) Determining what supplies or services are to be acquired by the Government, including developing statements of work.
>
> (3) Developing or approving any contractual documents, to include documents defining requirements, incentive plans, and evaluation criteria.
>
> (4) Evaluating contract proposals.
>
> (5) Awarding Government contracts.
>
> (6) Administering contracts (including ordering changes or giving technical direction in contract performance or contract quantities, evaluating contractor performance, and accepting or rejecting contractor products or services).
>
> (7) Terminating contracts.
>
> (8) Determining whether contract costs are reasonable, allocable, and allowable.

See *BAE Sys. Tech. Sols. & Servs., Inc.*, Comp. Gen. Dec. B-411810.3, 2016 CPD ¶ 174, *recons. denied*, 2018 CPD ¶ 9, finding that a conflict had been mitigated when a contractor employee advising the agency had sold the stock in a competing company shortly after he realized he owned it.

[6] Contracting with Government Employees

Government employees who do not fall within the proscriptions of 18 U.S.C. § 208 because they are not involved in the procurement process are, nevertheless, restricted from entering into contracts with any agency of the government. FAR 3.601(a) states:

> Except as specified in 3.602, a contracting officer shall not knowingly award a contract to a Government employee or to a business concern or other

> organization owned or substantially owned or controlled by one or more Government employees. This policy is intended to avoid any conflict of interest that might arise between the employees' interests and their Government duties, and to avoid the appearance of favoritism or preferential treatment by the Government toward its employees.

Valiant Sec. Agency, Comp. Gen. Dec. B-205087, 81-2 CPD ¶ 367, *recons. denied*, 81-2 CPD ¶ 501, explains this policy as follows:

> Contracts between the Government and its employees are not expressly prohibited by statute except where the employee acts for both the Government and the contractor in a particular transaction or where the service to be rendered is such as could be required of the contractor in his capacity as a Government employee. 18 U.S.C. § 208 (1976); *Hugh Maher*, B-187841, March 31, 1977, 77-1 CPD ¶ 204. However, it has long been recognized that such contracts are undesirable because among other reasons they invite criticism as to alleged favoritism and possible fraud and that they should be authorized only in exceptional cases where the Government cannot reasonably be otherwise supplied. 27 Comp. Gen. 735 (1948); *Capital Aero, Inc.*, B-183833, September 30, 1975, 75-2 CPD ¶ 201; *Burgos & Associates, Inc.*, 59 Comp. Gen. 273 (1980), 80-1 CPD ¶ 155. The fact that a service would be more expensive if not obtained from an employee of the Government does not by itself provide support for a determination that the service cannot reasonably be obtained from other sources. 55 Comp. Gen. 681 (1976).

The sole exception to this prohibition is in FAR 3.602 which requires a determination by a high-level official that there is a "most compelling reason" to enter into a contract with a former government employee, such as when the government's needs cannot reasonably be otherwise met. The contracting officer has discretion in determining whether this exemption applies. Compare the *Valiant* case with *International Alliance of Sports Officials*, Comp. Gen. Dec. B-210172, 83-2 CPD ¶ 328, sustaining a contracting officer's decision to award a contract at approximately $223,000 in contrast to the next low offer of $275,000.

Substantial ownership or control is determined by the facts of each individual case. Mere employment by a government contractor is not prohibited by this restriction. See *National Serv. Corp.*, Comp. Gen. Dec. B-205629, 82-2 CPD ¶ 76 (no substantial ownership or control when government employee gave up partnership and became part-time bookkeeper); and *H H & K Bldrs., Inc.*, Comp. Gen. Dec. B-238095, 90-1 CPD ¶ 219 (sole owner's husband was government employee, but sufficient separation of ownership). Compare *Elecs. West, Inc.*, Comp. Gen. Dec. B-209720, 83-2 CPD ¶ 127 (change in title from President to Treasurer did not prevent disqualification). An agency does not have to establish with certainty that an employee has a substantially controlling interest but rather needs only to have a reason to believe that the government employee has such control, *Gurley's Inc.*, Comp. Gen. Dec. B-253852, 93-2 CPD ¶ 123. See *Elogene Thurman*, Comp. Gen. Dec. B-206325, 82-1 CPD

¶ 487 (award to wife of government employee improper when husband in fact ran the business); *American Truss & Mfg. Corp.*, Comp. Gen. Dec. B-205962, 82-1 CPD ¶ 477 (award improper where government employee owned 50% of stock and wife owned balance); *Marc Indus.*, Comp. Gen. Dec. B-246528, 92-1 CPD ¶ 273 (substantial control found where government employee represented the firm in prework conferences under prior contracts with the agency, served as the contact for any complaints about contract performance, and, based on his involvement with the firm, was disciplined for violating his agency's conflict of interest regulations); *KSR, Inc.*, Comp. Gen. Dec. B-250160, 93-1 CPD ¶ 37 (substantial control found where government employee was president and was one of five owners); and *Asia Resource Partners K.K.*, Comp. Gen. Dec. B-400552, 2008 CPD ¶ 201 (exclusion of company when husband of contracting officer was its president and majority owner). The restriction does not apply when a contractor employee has a similar conflict with a subcontractor, *Science Pump Corp.*, Comp. Gen. Dec. B-255737, 94-1 CPD ¶ 246. Furthermore, the rule does not apply if the employee has left government employment prior to award of the contract, *TransLogistics, LLC*, Comp. Gen. Dec. B-407215, 2012 CPD ¶ 334.

Some agencies have further restrictions on contracting with members of a former government employee's family. See, for example, *Joann Flora*, Comp. Gen. Dec. B-212776, 83-2 CPD ¶ 520 (regulations prohibiting contract with immediate member of the household of agency employee barred contract with unmarried party living as spouse); and *Heidi Holley*, Comp. Gen. Dec. B-211746, 83-2 CPD ¶ 241 (regulations stating that contracts should generally not be awarded to members of an agency employee's family and requiring close scrutiny barred award to spouse of agency employee required to supervise contract).

If the contracting officer inadvertently makes an award to a company owned or controlled by a government employee, GAO will not disturb the award absent an indication of favoritism or other impropriety, *Sterling Medical Assocs.*, 62 Comp. Gen. 230 (B-209493), 83-1 CPD ¶ 215; *Biosystems Analysis, Inc.*, Comp. Gen. Dec. B-198846, 80-2 CPD ¶ 149. In both cases, the employee worked for an agency other than the one awarding the contract. See also *Metro Offices, Inc.*, Comp. Gen. Dec. B-408477, 2013 CPD ¶ 239, denying a protest where the contracting officer did not know of the ownership at the time of award.

[7] Anti-Kickback Act

Contractors and subcontractors are prohibited from soliciting, accepting, or attempting to accept any kickbacks from their subcontractors by the Anti-Kickback Act of 1986, 41 U.S.C. §§ 8701-07. The Act contains a broad definition of the term "kickback," as follows:

> The term "kickback" means any money, fee, commission, credit, gift, gratuity, thing of value, or compensation of any kind that is provided to a

prime contractor, prime contractor employee, subcontractor, or subcontractor employee to improperly obtain or reward favorable treatment in connection with a prime contract or a subcontract relating to a prime contract.

The purpose of this statute is to prevent payments that impede the competitive process. The typical kickback is paid to a purchasing agent of a contractor or subcontractor to obtain the award of a subcontract without having to participate in a fair competition. The purchasing agent, in turn, takes some action that distorts the competition. The presumption is that the government eventually pays the amount of the kickback in higher prices, and the Act permits the procuring agency to reduce the price by the amount of the kickback, 41 U.S.C. § 8705(b). The Act also contains criminal and civil sanctions, 41 U.S.C. § 8706 and § 8707. Knowledge of the kickback by an employee is imputed to a contractor for the purpose of assessing the penalty in § 8706(a)(1), *Kellogg Brown & Root Servs., Inc. v. United States*, 728 F.3d 1348 (Fed. Cir. 2013); *United States ex rel. Vavra v. Kellogg Brown & Root Servs., Inc.*, 727 F.3d 343 (5th Cir. 2013).

The Act is implemented in FAR 3.502 and the Anti-Kickback Procedures clause at FAR 52.203-7. This clause requires the contractor to have internal procedures to detect and prevent kickbacks. It also requires the prompt reporting of kickbacks and cooperation with government agencies in the investigation of kickbacks. The clause is not required for contracts under $250,000 or contracts for the acquisition of commercial items, FAR 3.502-3. However, such procurements are still subject to the Act.

A contracting officer can offset the amount of a kickback from the contract price of the contract, 41 U.S.C. § 8705(b). However, this can only be done when a court has determined that a kickback has occurred. See *Turner Constr. Co. v. General Servs. Admin.*, GSBCA 16840, 06-2 BCA ¶ 33,391, for a thorough discussion of this procedure. In that decision, the board held that the contracting officer could determine the amount of the offset and that the board had jurisdiction over an appeal of this determination.

It is a violation of the Act to give a kickback to a government contractor without regard to whether there was an intent to obtain work on a government contract, *United States v. Purdy*, 144 F.3d 241 (2d Cir.), *cert. denied*, 525 U.S. 1020 (1998). A violation was also found in *Morse Diesel Int'l, Inc. v. United States*, 66 Fed. Cl. 788 (2005), 74 Fed. Cl. 601 (2007), when the contractor's surety bond broker paid 50% of its commissions to the contractor in exchange for the right to be its exclusive broker. See also *Aalco Forwarding, Inc.*, Comp. Gen. Dec. B-277241.8, 97-2 CPD ¶ 110 (payment of commissions or rebates from tariff rates from carriers to brokers under government contract were not per se violations), and *United States v. Guthrie*, 64 F.3d 1510 (10th Cir. 1995) (contractors can be required to pay restitution for violations).

[8] Covenant Against Contingent Fees

The government has a longstanding policy against the payment of contingent fees. This policy developed because of the government's concern that contingent fee arrangements expose government agencies to corrupting influences. It also reflects the government's recognition that such agreements could allow for the payment of exorbitant fees by contractors, leading to higher costs for the government, thereby resulting in an unnecessary waste of public funds. See *Quinn v. Gulf & Western Corp.*, 644 F.2d 89 (2d Cir. 1981). Thus, a clause is required in negotiated contracts by statute, 10 U.S.C. § 3321 (formerly § 2306) and 41 U.S.C. § 3901, and in sealed bid procurements by regulation, FAR 3.404. This clause is not required in contracts at or below the simplified acquisition threshold of $250,000 or in contracts for the acquisition of commercial items. The clause to be used is contained in FAR 52.203-5:

> COVENANT AGAINST CONTINGENT FEES (APR 1984)
>
> (a) The Contractor warrants that no person or agency has been employed or retained to solicit or obtain this contract upon an agreement or understanding for a contingent fee, except a bona fide employee or agency. For breach or violation of this warranty, the Government shall have the right to annul this contract without liability or, in its discretion, to deduct from the contract price or consideration, or otherwise recover, the full amount of the contingent fee.
>
> (b) "Bona fide agency," as used in this clause, means an established commercial or selling agency, maintained by a contractor for the purpose of securing business, that neither exerts nor proposes to exert improper influence to solicit or obtain Government contracts nor holds itself out as being able to obtain any Government contract or contracts through improper influence.
>
> "Bona fide employee," as used in this clause, means a person, employed by a contractor and subject to the contractor's supervision and control as to time, place, and manner of performance, who neither exerts nor proposes to exert improper influence to solicit or obtain Government contracts nor holds out as being able to obtain any Government contract or contracts though improper influence.
>
> "Contingent fee," as used in this clause, means any commission, percentage, brokerage, or other fee that is contingent upon the success that a person or concern has in securing a Government contract.
>
> "Improper influence," as used in this clause, means any influence that induces or tends to induce a Government employee or officer to give consideration or to act regarding a Government contract on any basis other than the merits of the matter.

A court will not enforce a contract for a contingent fee because it violates this statute, *LeJohn Mfg. Co. v. Webb*, 222 F.2d 48 (D.C. Cir. 1955); *Quinn v. Gulf & Western Corp.*, 644 F.2d 89 (2d Cir. 1981). However, it is improper to grant summary judgment refusing to enforce a contingent fee contract when there is a possibility that evidence could prove no violation, *Keefe Co. v. Americable*

Int'l, Inc., 169 F.3d 34 (D.C. Cir 1999) (letters from Congressmen supporting contractor's proposal not clear proof of violation).

The covenant does not prohibit the payment of all contingent fees—only those made for the purpose of obtaining a contract. In *Browne v. R & R Eng'g Co.*, 264 F.2d 219 (3d Cir. 1959), the court held that contingent fee services in connection with a proposed contract that did not involve any dealings with officials responsible for the award of contracts were not prohibited. GAO has followed this ruling. See *Holmes & Narver Servs., Inc.*, 70 Comp. Gen. 424 (B-242240), 91-1 CPD ¶ 373, where an incumbent contractor offered to sell access to its employees and competitively useful contract information to potential offerors who agreed to purchase inventory and equipment at set prices if they won the contract. GAO held that this was not a prohibited contingent fee arrangement because the payment would not be made for the purpose of soliciting or obtaining the contract at issue and the arrangement did not involve any dealings with government officials. See also *Kasler Elec. Co.*, DOTCAB 1425, 84-2 BCA ¶ 17,374, where a payment to a nonemployee estimator was contingent on award of the contract. The board held that the arrangement did not violate the covenant, since the estimator's function was to price out a bid and not to solicit a government contract. Compare *Howard Johnson Lodge*, Comp. Gen. Dec. B-244302.2, 92-1 CPD ¶ 305, finding a violation of the covenant because the sales agent was directly contacting government agencies about potential contracts.

In addition, the covenant does not apply to a "bona fide employee" or a "bona fide agency." See *Acme Process Equip. Co. v. United States*, 347 F.2d 538 (Ct. Cl. 1965), setting forth factors to be considered in determining whether the recipient of a contingent fee falls within this "bona fide" rule. The FAR contains no guidance on this issue. However, an earlier version of the FAR contained the following factors at FAR 3.408-2(c):

> (1) The fee should not be inequitable or exorbitant when compared to the services performed or to customary fees for similar services related to commercial business.
>
> (2) The agency should have adequate knowledge of the contractor's products and business, as well as other qualifications necessary to sell the products or services on their merits.
>
> (3) The contractor and the agency should have a continuing relationship or, in newly established relationships, should contemplate future continuity.
>
> (4) The agency should be an established concern that has existed for a considerable period, or be a newly established going concern likely to continue in the future. The business of the agency should be conducted in the agency name and characterized by the customary indicia of the conduct of regular business.
>
> (5) While an agency that confines its selling activities to Government contracts is not disqualified, the fact that an agency represents the contractor in Government and commercial sales should receive favorable consideration.

Established sales arrangements that are not confined to sales to the government do not violate the covenant, *Puma Indus. Consulting, Inc. v. Daal Assocs., Inc.*, 808 F.2d 982 (2d Cir. 1987). In *General Sales Agency*, Comp. Gen. Dec. B-247133.2, 92-1 CPD ¶ 544, a newly established arrangement with a sales organization for a 7½% contingent fee was held proper because the parties anticipated that the arrangement would be longstanding and no improper influence had been exerted to obtain the contract. See also *Howard Johnson Lodge*, Comp. Gen. Dec. B-244302.2, 92-1 CPD ¶ 305, where a 10% contingent fee was held proper because there was "no hint" of improper influence in the arrangement, Similarly, in *Convention Mktg. Servs.*, Comp. Gen. Dec. B-245660.3, 92-1 CPD ¶ 144, no violation was found where contractors had entered into contingent fee arrangements with sales agents to assist in the acquisition and preparation of contracts, but they had exerted no improper influence to solicit or obtain the contracts. GAO stated:

> The fact that an agent's fee is contingent upon the contractor receiving the contract award is insufficient to bring a fee arrangement under the contingent fee prohibition; rather, the regulation contemplates a specific demonstration that an agent is retained for the express purpose of contacting Government officials.

See *Wickes Indus., Inc.*, ASBCA 17376, 75-1 BCA ¶ 11,180, for a decision in which the government was not allowed to cancel a contract where a contingency arrangement was "bona fide" considering the factors set forth in the DAR.

[D] Honesty in Dealing

One of the most important requirements of the public contracting process is that contractors and subcontractors be honest in their dealings with governmental agencies and contractors. This section reviews this requirement by first discussing the applicable statutes and then considering the major types of conduct that have been found to violate this requirement.

[1] Statutory Requirements

In federal contracting, the requirement for honesty in dealing with the government is supported by a number of criminal and civil statutes imposing a variety of penalties on contractors and others who do not comply with the minimum standards of honesty.

[a] False Claims

The fundamental federal statute with the goal of promoting honesty in dealing is the False Claims Act. This Act was originally enacted in 1863 to prevent fraud in Civil War defense contracts and is now divided into a civil provision in 31 U.S.C. § 3729 and a criminal provision in 18 U.S.C. § 287.

[i] Civil Fraud

For many years this provision was set forth in 31 U.S.C. § 231. In 1982, it was codified in 31 U.S.C. § 3729, and then it was amended by the False Claims Amendments Act of 1986, Pub. L. No. 99-562, the Fraud Enforcement & Recovery Act of 2009, Pub. L. No. 111-21, and the Patient Protection & Affordable Care Act, Pub. L. No. 111-148, to read as follows:

> (a) Liability for certain acts.
>
> (1) In general. Subject to paragraph (2), any person who—
>
> (A) knowingly presents, or causes to be presented, a false or fraudulent claim for payment or approval;
>
> (B) knowingly makes, uses, or causes to be made or used, a false record or statement material to a false or fraudulent claim;
>
> (C) conspires to commit a violation of subparagraph (A), (B), (D), (E), (F), or (G);
>
> (D) has possession, custody, or control of property or money used, or to be used, by the Government and knowingly delivers, or causes to be delivered, less than all of that money or property;
>
> (E) is authorized to make or deliver a document certifying receipt of property used, or to be used, by the Government and, intending to defraud the Government, makes or delivers the receipt without completely knowing that the information on the receipt is true;
>
> (F) knowingly buys, or receives as a pledge of an obligation or debt, public property from an officer or employee of the Government, or a member of the Armed Forces, who lawfully may not sell or pledge property; or
>
> (G) knowingly makes, uses, or causes to be made or used, a false record or statement material to an obligation to pay or transmit money or property to the Government, or knowingly conceals or knowingly and improperly avoids or decreases an obligation to pay or transmit money or property to the Government,
>
> is liable to the United States Government for a civil penalty of not less than $5,000 and not more than $10,000, as adjusted by the Federal Civil Penalties Inflation Adjustment Act of 1990 (28 U.S.C. 2461 note; Public Law 104-410), plus 3 times the amount of damages which the Government sustains because of the act of that person.

(A) Intent

Under the False Claims Act, as amended in 1986, the government can establish liability without showing that the contractor had a specific intent to defraud as long as the act is committed "knowingly." Not defined in the original Act, "knowingly" is now defined in 31 U.S.C. § 3729(b) as (1) actual knowledge of the information, (2) acting in deliberate ignorance of the truth or falsity of the information, or (3) acting in reckless disregard of the truth or falsity of the information. Further, the Act specifically states that "no proof of specific intent to defraud is required."

Reckless disregard has been called the "loosest" of the three standards, and creates significant risk for government contractors, *United States ex rel. Siewick v. Jamieson Science & Eng'g., Inc.*, 214 F.3d 1372 (D.C. Cir. 2000). As the D.C. Circuit explained in *United States v. Science Applications Intern. Corp.*, 626 F.3d 1257, 1276 (D.C. Cir. 2010), "if a plaintiff can prove that a government contractor's structure prevented it from learning facts that made its claims for payment false, then the plaintiff may establish that the company acted in deliberate ignorance or reckless disregard of the truth of its claims." See also *United States ex rel. Wall v. Circle Constr., L.L.C.*, 697 F.3d 345 (6th Cir. 2012) (certifying Davis Bacon payrolls without including subcontractor labor); *United States v. Krizek*, 111 F.3d 934 (D.C. Cir. 1997) (failure to review Medicare claims prepared by others). Similarly, filing an equitable adjustment claim for "actual costs" when estimates are used is reckless disregard, *UMC Elecs. Co. v. United States*, 43 Fed. Cl. 776 (1999).

Failing to consult a lawyer prior to submitting a claim for payment is not reckless disregard, *United States ex rel. Quirk v. Madonna Towers, Inc.*, 278 F.3d 765 (8th Cir. 2002). Reckless disregard does not extend to simple negligence or mistakes, *United States v. Basin Elec. Power Coop.*, 248 F.3d 781 (8th Cir. 2001), *cert. denied*, 534 U.S. 1115 (2002) (no liability for misinterpretation of contract terms); *United States v. United Tech. Corp.*, 51 F. Supp. 2d 167 (D. Conn. 1999) (no liability for honest mistake); *Wang ex rel. United States v. FMC Corp.*, 975 F.2d 1412 (9th Cir. 1992) (engineering miscalculations and lack of engineering insight no more than innocent mistake); *First Interstate Bank v. United States*, 27 Fed. Cl. 348 (1992) (mere negligence by bank would not satisfy requirement of "knowing").

This risk created by the reckless disregard standard is compounded by the theory that a demand for payment can be false if the contractor submitting the invoice is not in compliance with contract requirements at the time of submission. Thus, the Supreme Court has held that there may be an "implied certification" of compliance in such situations if the contract requirement is "material," *Universal Health Servs., Inc. v. United States ex rel. Escobar*, 136 S. Ct. 1989 (2016). Under *Escobar*, there are two conditions to an implied certification theory: "First, the claim does not merely request payment, but also makes specific representations about the goods or services provided; and second, the defendant's failure to disclose noncompliance with material statutory, regulatory, or contractual requirements makes those representations misleading half-truths." 136 S. Ct. at 2001. See, e.g., *United States ex. Rel. Rose v. Stephens Institute*, 909 F.3d 1012 (9th Cir. 2018), amending and superseding 901 F.3d 1124 (9th Cir. 2018) (examining how *Escobar* impacted prior ruling on implied certification theory).

The analysis of intent and falsity often overlap, particularly where there is uncertainty as to whether or not a contractor has violated an ambiguous contract requirement or regulation. It is not sufficient to demonstrate that a claim is ultimately false; the intent standard must be satisfied as well. See, e.g., *United States ex rel. Gonzalez v. Planned Parenthood of L.A.*, 759 F.3d 1112 (9th Cir. 2014) (insufficient evidence of knowing falsity); *Horn & Assocs. v. United States*, 123 Fed. Cl. 728 (2015) (dismissing FCA claim where government failed to demonstrate knowledge of falsity). The reckless disregard standard is not satisfied when the law is unclear or when there is a legitimate good faith disagreement about the applicable law. As the Supreme Court explained in *Safeco Ins. Co. of Am. v. Burr*, 551 U.S. 47, 70 & n.20 (2007) "Where, as here, statutory text and relevant court and agency guidance allow for more than one reasonable interpretation, it would defy history and current thinking to treat a defendant who merely adopts one such interpretation as a knowing or reckless violator." See *United States ex re. Purcell v. MWI Corp.*, 807 F.3d 281 (D.C. Cir. 2015) (no FCA violation where: (1) the law or regulation is ambiguous; (2) defendant's interpretation is reasonable, and (3) no formal agency guidance indicated defendant's interpretation was wrong); *United States ex rel. K & R Ltd. P'ship v. Massachusetts Housing Finance Agency*, 530 F.3d 980 (D.C. Cir. 2008) (terms for calculating housing subsidy with HUD ambiguous); *United States ex rel. Ramadoss v. Caremark, Inc.*, 586 F. Supp.2d 668 (W.D. Tex. 2008) (Medicaid reimbursement rules subject to "good-faith disagreement"). However, if the submitter knows that the government interprets the regulation differently, a reasonable interpretation of an ambiguous regulation is a false claim, *United States ex rel. Minnesota Assoc. of Nurse Anesthetists v. Allina Health Sys. Corp.*, 276 F.3d 1032 (8th Cir. 2002).

(B) Submission of a Claim

The "submission of a false claim is the 'sine qua non' of a False Claims Act violation," *Urquilla-Diaz v. Kaplan Univ.*, 780 F.3d 1039 (11th Cir. 2015). The False Claims Act "at least requires the presence of a claim—a call upon the government fisc—for liability to attach," *Harrison v. Westinghouse Savannah River Co.*, 176 F.3d 776, 785 (4th Cir. 1999). See also *United States ex rel. Clausen v. Lab. Corp. of Am., Inc.*, 290 F.3d 1301, 1311 (11th Cir. 2002) ("Without the presentment of such a claim, while the practices of an entity that provides services to the Government may be unwise or improper, there is simply no actionable damage to the public fisc as required under the False Claims Act. The submission of a claim is thus not, . . . a 'ministerial act,' but the *sine qua non* of a False Claims Act violation."); *Crews v. NCS Healthcare of Ill., Inc.*, 460 F.3d 853 (7th Cir. 2006) (failure to demonstrate claim).

The 2009 amendments provided an express definition of "claim" at § 3729(b)(2):

> (A) any request or demand, whether under a contract or otherwise, for money or property and whether or not the United States has title to the money or property, that—
>
> (i) is presented to an officer, employee, or agent of the United States; or
>
> (ii) is made to a contractor, grantee, or other recipient, if the money or property is to be spent or used on the Government's behalf or to advance a Government program or interest, and if the United States Government—
>
> (I) provides or has provided any portion of the money or property requested or demanded; or
>
> (II) will reimburse such contractor, grantee, or other recipient for any portion of the money or property which is requested or demanded.
>
> (B) does not include requests or demands for money or property that the Government has paid to an individual as compensation for Federal employment or as an income subsidy with no restrictions on that individual's use of the money or property.

Prior to the 2009 amendments to the Act, a claim had to be "presented" to the government in order to constitute a false claim. Thus, a claim submitted to Amtrak, an organization receiving government funding, did not fall under the Act because Amtrak was not a government entity, *United States ex rel. Totten v. Bombardier Corp.*, 380 F.3d 488 (D.C. Cir. 2004). See also *Allison Engine Co. v. United States ex rel. Sanders*, 553 U.S. 662 (2008), holding that if the false claim was based on the submission of a false statement to a non-government entity, it only met the presentment requirement if it could be proved that the submitter of the statement intended that the government rely on it as a condition of payment. For example, in *United States v. Tieger*, 234 F.2d 589 (3d Cir.), *cert. denied*, 352 U.S. 941 (1956), the court found no claim, although the defendant had fraudulently induced the government to guarantee loans, because no demand for satisfaction of the guarantee had been made against the government. These holdings tended to relieve subcontractors and contractors with non-government entities from liability. The 2009 amendments to the Act were intended to bring these type situation under the Act. The express reference to money "spent or used on the Government's behalf or to advance a Government program or interest" effectively codifies the decision in *United States ex rel. DRC, Inc. v. Custer Battles LLC*, 562 F.3d 295 (4th Cir. 2009), holding the contractor liable for submitting a false claim to the Coalition Provisional Authority in Iraq because part of the funding for the authority came from the government.

False Claims Act liability also extends where a contractor has obtained the contract through fraudulent conduct and later submits valid claims for work performed. See *United States ex rel. Marcus v. Hess*, 317 U.S. 537 (1943), finding a claim because the contractor submitted a payment voucher on a contract obtained through collusive bidding. The Court held that the Act covered all claims "grounded in fraud." This is generally called "fraud in the inducement." See, e.g., *In re Baycol Prod. Litig.*, 732 F.3d 869 (8th Cir. 2013) ("claims for payment subsequently submitted under a contract initially induced by fraud do not have to be false or fraudulent in and of themselves in order to state a cause of action under the FCA"); *Veridyne Corp. v. United States*, 105 Fed. Cl. 769 (2012), *aff'd*, 758 F.3d 1371 (Fed. Cir. 2014) (false statements in proposal); *United States v. United Techs. Corp.*, 626 F.3d 313 (6th Cir. 2010) (false statements on how estimates were arrived at); *United States ex rel. Longhi v. Lithium Power Techs., Inc.*, 530 F. Supp.2d 888 (S.D. Tex. 2008), *aff'd*, 575 F.3d 458 (5th Cir. 2009) (false statements in proposals about past performance); *United States ex rel. Harrison v. Westinghouse Savannah River Co.*, 176 F.3d 776 (4th Cir. 1999) (false statements in supporting award of subcontract); *United States v. General Dynamics Corp.*, 19 F.3d 770 (2d Cir. 1994) (inflated cost estimates in subcontract submitted for approval by the government); *Hagood v. Sonoma County Water Agency*, 929 F.2d 1416 (9th Cir. 1991) (bid rigging). In a unique case, the court held that an intentionally low bid price could constitute fraud in the inducement, *Hooper v. Lockheed Martin Corp.*, 688 F.3d 1037 (9th Cir. 2012). Compare *United States ex rel. Laird v. Lockheed Martin Eng'g & Science Servs. Co.*, 491 F.3d 254 (5th Cir. 2007) (submitting low-cost estimate for cost-reimbursement contract not fraud in the inducement); *United States ex rel. Bettis v. Odebrecht Contractors of Cal., Inc.*, 393 F.3d 1321 (D.C. Cir. 2005) (submitting low bid for fixed-price contract not fraud in the inducement).

The demand for payment need not be one based on an existing contractual relationship since the Act encompasses all fraudulent attempts to cause the government to pay out a sum of money, *United States v. Neifert-White Co.*, 390 U.S. 228 (1968) (false application to Federal Commodity Credit Corp. for loan held to be claim). The Act has been held to apply to a subcontractor's failure to comply with specifications, *United States ex rel. Varljen v. Cleveland Gear Co.*, 250 F.3d 426 (6th Cir. 2001); a knowing misrepresentation about the need for and cost of using a subcontractor, *Harrison v. Westinghouse Savannah River Co.*, 176 F.3d 776 (4th Cir. 1999); endorsement and deposit of government checks known to have been issued by mistake, *United States v. McLeod*, 721 F.2d 282 (9th Cir. 1983); repeated inclusion of rejected items in shipments, *United States v. Milton Marks Corp.*, 240 F.2d 838 (3d Cir. 1957); fraudulently submitted Medicare health insurance claim forms by health care providers, *United States v. Lorenzo*, 768 F. Supp. 1127 (E.D. Pa. 1991); cashing fraudulently obtained social security checks, *United States v. Fowler*, 282 F. Supp. 1 (E.D.N.Y. 1968); and submission of false payroll reports, *United States v. Greenberg*, 237 F. Supp. 439 (S.D.N.Y. 1965).

"Reverse false claims" also fall under the Act. The reverse false claims provision specifies that: "any person who . . . knowingly makes, uses, or causes to be made or used, a false record or statement material to an obligation to pay or transmit money or property to the Government, or knowingly conceals or knowingly and improperly avoids or decreases an obligation to pay or transmit money or property to the Government . . . is liable to the United States Government," 31 U.S.C. § 3729(a)(1)(G). In other words, a "reverse false claim occurs when a defendant acts improperly to avoid paying an 'obligation' owed to the government," *United States ex rel. Petratos v. Genetech Inc.*, 855 F.3d 481 (3d Cir. 2017). For example, in *United States v. Pemco Aeroplex, Inc.*, 195 F.3d 1234 (11th Cir. 1999), a false claim was found where the contractor identified valuable and usable inventory as scrap and bought it at a very low price. See, e.g., *United States ex rel. Kasowitz Benson Torres LLP v. BASF Corp.*, 929 F.3d 721 (D.C. Cir. 2019) (finding no reverse false claim liability); *United States ex rel. Bahrani v. Conagra, Inc.*, 456 F.3d 1189 (10th Cir. 2006) (examining reverse false claim provision); *American Textile Mfrs. Inst., Inc. v. Limited, Inc.*, 190 F.3d 729 (6th Cir. 1999) (false statements made to avoid payment of fines were not reverse false claims because the obligation to the government must exist before the false statement is made); *United States v. Q Int'l Courier, Inc.*, 131 F.3d 770 (8th Cir. 1997) (no reverse false claim where no "existing, specific legal duty in the nature of a debt" was owed to the government).

(C) Materiality

Courts have long recognized materiality as a critical element of establishing False Claims Act liability under any theory, even before the notion of materiality was expressly incorporated into the Act by the 2009 amendments, Even where a claim might have contained a facial inaccuracy or error, courts nevertheless required some degree of materiality in the inaccuracy before imposing liability. See, e.g., *Harrison v. Westinghouse Savannah River Co.*, 176 F.3d 776, 785 (4th Cir. 1999) ("[L]iability under each of the provisions of the False Claims Act is subject to the further, judicially imposed requirement that the false statement or claim be material."). The 2009 amendments incorporated the word "materiality" directly into the Act, 31 U.S.C. § 3729(a)(1)(B), (G). "Materiality" is now defined in § 3729(b)(4) to mean "having a natural tendency to influence, or be capable of influencing, the payment or receipt of money or property."

The Supreme Court's *Escobar* decision elevated the importance of materiality, confirming that False Claims Act liability only attaches if the false claim is material. Thus, even where a claim may be inaccurate or wrong on its face, before imposing liability the court must determine that the inaccuracy was material to the government's decision to pay. See *Escobar*, stating at 136 S.Ct. 2003:

> The materiality standard is demanding. The False Claims Act is not "an all-purpose antifraud statute," or a vehicle for punishing garden-variety

> breaches of contract or regulatory violations. A misrepresentation cannot be deemed material merely because the Government designates compliance with a particular statutory, regulatory, or contractual requirement as a condition of payment. Nor is it sufficient for a finding of materiality that the Government would have the option to decline to pay if it knew of the defendant's noncompliance. Materiality, in addition, cannot be found where noncompliance is minor or insubstantial.
>
> In sum, when evaluating materiality under the False Claims Act, the Government's decision to expressly identify a provision as a condition of payment is relevant, but not automatically dispositive. Likewise, proof of materiality can include, but is not necessarily limited to, evidence that the defendant knows that the Government consistently refuses to pay claims in the mine run of cases based on noncompliance with the particular statutory, regulatory, or contractual requirement. Conversely, if the Government pays a particular claim in full despite its actual knowledge that certain requirements were violated, that is very strong evidence that those requirements are not material. Or, if the Government regularly pays a particular type of claim in full despite actual knowledge that certain requirements were violated, and has signaled no change in position, that is strong evidence that the requirements are not material. (internal quotations omitted)

Escobar confirms that, it is not enough to simply identify an inaccuracy or noncompliance in a claim or invoice to establish False Claims Act liability. Even where a claim is inaccurate on its face, it is always necessary to further determine that the inaccuracy is material. As phrased in *Escobar*, the False Claims Act does not create liability for "minor or insubstantial noncompliance," but rather for misrepresentations that are material, meaning they would have an impact on the government's decision to pay. See also *United States ex rel. Prather v. Brookdale Senior Living Cmtys., Inc.*, 892 F.3d 822 (6th Cir. 2018) (examining materiality criteria); *United States ex rel. Harman v. Trinity Indus. Inc.*, 872 F.3d 645 (5th Cir. 2017) (addressing significance to materiality analysis of government continuing to make payments after knowledge of allegedly false claims); *United States v. Luce*, 873 F.3d 999 (7th Cir. 2017) (same). Confirming that this materiality requirement has always been a prerequisite to False Claims Act liability, in *United States ex rel. Spay v. CVS Caremark Corp.*, 875 F.3d 746, 763 (3d Cir. 2017) the court concluded that the standards clarified in *Escobar* apply to conduct that occurred prior to the 2009 amendments to the False Claims Act.

Following *Escobar*, it is also clear that government continuation of the contract after knowledge of allegedly improper actions can be used to demonstrate that such actions were not material and therefore do not create liability. See, e.g., *United States ex. rel Kelley v. Serco, Inc.*, 846 F.3d 325 (9th Cir. 2017) (materiality lacking because government accepted progress reports despite their noncompliance with certain governing standards and continued to pay defendant for work performed after learning of relator's allegations); *United States ex rel. Petratos v. Genetech Inc.*, 855 F.3d 481 (3d Cir. 2017) (relator failed adequately to plead materiality where he failed to allege that government would not have reimbursed Medicare claims had it known about allegedly withheld information); *Abbott v. BP Exploration & Prod., Inc.*, 851 F.3d 384 (5th Cir. 2017) (government decision to allow operations to continue after investigation into alleged wrongdoing is strong evidence of non-materiality).

(D) *Qui Tam*

Any person may bring a civil action (termed "qui tam") under the Act "for the person and the United States," and the action is "brought in the name of the United States," 31 U.S.C. § 3730(b). The qui tam plaintiff (termed "the relator") files a civil complaint. The complaint is sealed while the government decides whether to take over the case. If the government intervenes, it bears primary responsibility for prosecuting the action, 31 U.S.C. § 3730(c)(1). If the government elects not to proceed with the action, the person who initiated the action has the right to conduct the action, 31 U.S.C. § 3730(c)(3). However, the government has the right to settle or dismiss the action, subject to a hearing to allow the relator to object, 31 U.S.C. § 3730(c)(2). Relators are entitled to a percentage of any award plus reasonable expenses and attorney fees, 31 U.S.C. § 3730(d).

Incentivizing relators and the private bar of attorneys often representing them on a contingency fee basis, relators are given a share of the government's monetary recovery and are granted whistleblower protection. The amount depends on whether the government elects to proceed with the action. 31 U.S.C. § 3730(d) provides that if the government proceeds with an action, the relator will receive at least 15% but not more than 25% of the proceeds, "depending upon the extent to which the person substantially contributed to the prosecution of the action." However, the relator is permitted to receive no more than 10% of the recovery if the action is based primarily on disclosures of specific information, allegations, or transactions in a criminal, civil, or administrative hearing; in a congressional, administrative, or GAO report, hearing, audit, or investigation; or from the news media. If the government does not take over the case, the relator receives not less than 25% nor more than 30% of the proceeds. In either case, the relator receives an amount for reasonable expenses plus reasonable attorneys' fees and costs.

Qui tam actions are barred if they are based upon a "public disclosure" in a federal hearing, audit or investigation or in the press of the fraudulent activity unless the relator is an "original source" of the information on which the fraud allegations are based, 31 U.S.C. § 3730(e)(4). This limitation on qui tam suits has generated a substantial amount of litigation which is peripheral to the actual proof of the fraud. Public disclosure has been found in a wide variety of circumstances. See *Schindler Elevator Corp. v. United States ex rel. Kirk*, 563 U.S. 401 (2011) (agency response to FOIA request); *United States ex rel. Paranich v. Sorgnard*, 396 F.3d 326 (3d Cir. 2005) (complaint in civil suit); *United States ex rel. Fine v. MK-Ferguson Co.*, 99 F.3d 1538 (10th Cir. 1996) (government audit report that had been sent to a state without any restriction on dissemination).

If public disclosure is found, the suit will not be barred unless it is based on the disclosed information. Most courts make this determination by analyzing whether the relator's allegations are substantially similar to information disclosed publicly, even if the relator learned the information from another source. See *United States ex rel. Zizic v. Q2Administrators, LLC*, 728 F.3d 228 (3d Cir. 2013) (claim "substantially similar" to information in public disclosure); *United States ex rel. Ondis v. City of Woonsocket*, 587 F.3d 49 (1st Cir. 2009) (claim substantially similar to newspaper accounts). If the relator is the original source of the information, public disclosure will not be a bar to the suit. Following the 2010 amendments, 31 U.S.C. § 3730(e)(4) now defines "original source" as—

> an individual who either (i) prior to a public disclosure under subsection (e)(4)(a), has voluntarily disclosed to the Government the information on which allegations or transactions in a claim are based, or (2) who has knowledge that is independent of and materially adds to the publicly disclosed allegations or transactions, and who has voluntarily provided the information to the Government before filing an action under this section.

A person who is obligated as part of his or her job to investigate and report fraud will not be considered an original source, *United States ex rel. Little v. Shell Exploration & Prod. Co.*, 690 F.3d 282 (5th Cir. 2012) (agency auditors).

Once a qui tam suit has been filed, no other person can file a "parasitic" suit based on the same facts. See 31 U.S.C. § 3730(b)(5), providing that "when a person brings a [qui tam action], no person other than the Government may intervene or bring a related action based on the facts underlying the pending action."

[ii] Criminal Fraud

As amended by the False Claims Amendments Act of 1986, 18 U.S.C. § 287 provides:

> Whoever makes or presents to any person or officer in the civil, military, or naval service of the United States, or to any department or agency thereof, any claim upon or against the United States, or any department or agency thereof, knowing such claim to be false, fictitious, or fraudulent, shall be imprisoned not more than five years and shall be subject to a fine in the amount provided in this title.

The same issues have arisen under this provision as those discussed with regard to civil fraud.

(A) Specific Intent

The courts have held that proof of specific intent to defraud the government is not necessary to prove criminal intent. Acting with "knowledge that the claim is false or fictitious is sufficient," *United States v. Maher*, 582 F.2d 842 (4th

Cir.), *cert. denied*, 439 U.S. 1115 (1978); *United States v. Precision Medical Labs., Inc.*, 593 F.2d 434 (2d Cir. 1978); *United States v. Milton*, 602 F.2d 231 (9th Cir. 1979). See also *United States v. Catton*, 89 F.3d 387 (7th Cir. 1996) (willfulness need not be charged); *Giuliano v. Everything Yogurt, Inc.*, 819 F. Supp. 240 (E.D.N.Y. 1993) (dishonesty, recklessness, deceptiveness, and deliberate disregard satisfied the intent requirement for fraud); and *United States v. Irwin*, 654 F.2d 671 (10th Cir. 1981) (comparing the language of the False Statements Act—which includes the term "willfully"—and concluding that the False Claims Act intentionally excludes the question of the state of mind of the claimant). Deliberate ignorance has been found sufficient to prove intent, *United States v. Wallace*, 40 F. Supp. 2d 131 (E.D.N.Y. 1999). However, no intent to defraud the government was found when a claim was submitted to the government of the Virgin Islands without knowledge that federal funds were involved, *United States v. Gumbs*, 283 F.3d 128 (3d Cir. 2002). In contrast, an intent to defraud has been found when the defendant presented a claim to a state knowing that a federal program was involved, *United States v. Beasley*, 550 F.2d 261 (5th Cir.), *cert. denied*, 434 U.S. 863 (1977). See also *United States v. Prigmore*, 243 F.3d 1 (1st Cir. 2001), holding that a defendant charged with violating regulation is entitled to an interpretation of that regulation that is "most congenial to their case theory and yet also objectively reasonable."

(B) Definition of Claim

The courts have followed the rule used in the Civil False Claims Act that a criminal false claim can occur only if there is a request for the payment of money or the transfer of property. However, a valid request for payment will be a false claim if it is made under a contract obtained by fraudulent means, *United States v. Winchester*, 407 F. Supp. 261 (D. Del. 1975). Presenting a voucher for payment knowing that the goods had not been properly inspected and accepted was also held to be a false claim, *United States v. U.S. Cartridge Co.*, 198 F.2d 456 (8th Cir. 1952), *cert. denied*, 345 U.S. 910 (1953).

The Act encompasses claims submitted indirectly to the government. For example, a claim submitted to a contractor processing Medicare claims for the government was held to be a false claim, *United States v. Precision Medical Labs., Inc.*, 593 F.2d 434 (2d Cir. 1978). Similarly, in *United States v. Beasley*, 550 F.2d 261 (5th Cir.), *cert. denied*, 434 U.S. 938 (1977), the court held that a claim submitted to the state of Louisiana for housing units never constructed was a claim against the federal government since federal funds were to be used for the payments.

(C) Materiality

There is general agreement among the circuits that a conviction is proper without proof of materiality of the claim, *United States v. Saybolt*, 577 F.3d 195 (3d Cir. 2009); *United States v. Lawrence*, 405 F.3d 888 (10th Cir. 2005), *cert.*

denied, 546 U.S. 955 (2006); *United States v. Logan*, 250 F.3d 350 (6th Cir.), *cert. denied*, 534 U.S. 895 (2001); *United States v. Upton*, 91 F.3d 677 (5th Cir. 1996); *United States v. Taylor*, 66 F.3d 254 (9th Cir. 1995); *United States v. Parsons*, 967 F.2d 452 (10th Cir. 1992); *United States v. Elkin*, 731 F.2d 1005 (2d Cir. 1984), *overruled on other grounds by United States v. Ali*, 68 F.3d 1468 (2d Cir. 1995). See, however, *Neder v. United States*, 527 U.S. 1 (1999), stating in a case not involving 18 U.S.C. § 287, "the common law could not have conceived of 'fraud' without proof of materiality" and requiring a jury instruction that it must find materiality.

[b] False Statements

The False Statements Act, 18 U.S.C. § 1001, as amended in 1996, Pub. L. No. 104-292, and in 2004, Pub. L. No. 108-458, provides:

> (a) Except as otherwise provided in this section, whoever, in any matter within the jurisdiction of the executive, legislative, or judicial branch of the Government of the United States knowingly and willfully—
>
> (1) falsifies, conceals or covers up by any trick, scheme, or device a material fact;
>
> (2) makes any materially false, fictitious or fraudulent statements or representation; or
>
> (3) makes or uses any false writing or document knowing the same to contain any materially false, fictitious or fraudulent statement or entry;
>
> shall be fined under this title, imprisoned not more than 5 years or, if the offense involves international or domestic terrorism (as defined in [18 USCS § 2331]), imprisoned not more than 8 years, or both.

The key elements of the conduct prohibited by this statute are "knowingly and willfully" making a false "statement."

[i] Definition of Statement

The scope of the False Statements Act is considerably broader than that of the False Claims Act. It has been held that the Act covers all false statements which might support fraudulent claims or which might pervert or corrupt the authorized functions of a government agency to which the statement was made, *United States v. Bedore*, 455 F.2d 1109 (9th Cir. 1972). The statement need not be on a government form if it affects the government, *United States v. Heuer*, 4 F.3d 723 (9th Cir.1993), *cert. denied*, 510 U.S. 1164 (1994) (bill of lading). The Act covers oral as well as written statements and unsworn as well as sworn statements, *United States v. Massey*, 550 F.2d 300 (5th Cir. 1977), as well as "private discussions" between members of the executive and legislative branches of the government, *United States v. Poindexter*, 951 F.2d 369 (D.C. Cir. 1991). It also covers the omission of information on a certified statement when the information should have been included, *United States v. Irwin*, 654 F.2d 671 (10th Cir. 1981). In *United States v. Johnson*, 937 F.2d 392 (8th Cir. 1991), the court stated at 395:

> It is generally recognized that section 1001 creates two distinct offenses with different elements: (1) concealing material facts from a federal agency by trick, scheme, or device; (2) making false or fraudulent statements of material facts to a federal agency. See *United States v. Mayberry*, 913 F.2d 719, 722 n.7 (9th Cir. 1990); *United States v. St. Michael's Credit Union*, 880 F.2d 579, 590 (1st Cir. 1989).

The transferring of acceptance stamps from goods that had been accepted to goods that had not been inspected was held to be a false statement, *United States v. Steiner Plastics Mfg. Co.*, 231 F.2d 149 (2d Cir. 1956). Statements made during settlement negotiations were also found to be false statements, *New York v. Sokol*, 113 F.3d 303 (2d Cir. 1997). Similarly, a padded estimate in a request for equitable adjustment was held to be a false statement, *United States v. White*, 765 F.2d 1469 (11th Cir. 1985). False statements were also found to be made by an employee of a contractor who included false information on a security questionnaire, *United States v. Dale*, 991 F.2d 819 (D.C. Cir. 1993); *Pitts v. United States*, 263 F.2d 353 (9th Cir.), *cert. denied*, 360 U.S. 935 (1959); and by an applicant for employment with a defense contractor who included false statements on the employment application, *United States v. Giarraputo*, 140 F. Supp. 831 (E.D.N.Y. 1956). False statements have also been found to have been made by government employees when stating that they have not disclosed bids, *United States v. Lupton*, 620 F.3d 790 (7th Cir. 2010), or they included false entries on documents during the transaction of government business, *United States v. Leviton*, 193 F.2d 848 (2d Cir. 1951), *cert. denied*, 343 U.S. 946 (1952); *United States v. Eisenmann*, 396 F.2d 565 (2d Cir. 1968). The question of the authority of the agency to seek or obtain the statement is not relevant if the false statement influences the agency, *United States v. Arcadipane*, 41 F.3d 1 (1st Cir. 1994).

In contrast, signing a contract with no intent to carry it out has been held not to constitute a false statement, *United States v. Blankenship*, 382 F.3d 1110 (11th Cir. 2004). The court reasoned at 1133-34:

> A contract is a document that serves only to establish a legal relationship between two parties; it gives each party nothing more than a legal expectancy in having the other party either perform or (generally) respond in damages. See, e.g., *Mississippi Valley Generating Co. v. United States*, 147 Ct. Cl. 1, 34, 175 F. Supp. 505 (1959) (Byran, J., concurring) ("A covenant of a contract is a pledge-something 'more than a promise and lesse [sic] than an Oath'-*to perform or respond in damages*.") (emphasis added), *rev'd on*

other grounds, *United States* v. *Mississippi Valley Generating Co.*, 364 U.S. 520, 81 S. Ct. 294, 5 L. Ed. 2d 268 (1961). It is not illegal for a party to breach a contract; a contract gives a party two equally viable options (perform or pay compensation), between which it is generally at liberty to choose. A "promise" contained in a contract is not a certification that the promisor will actually perform the specified acts, or presently intends to perform those acts, but is instead a grant of a legal right to the other party to either enjoy performance or receive damages. Indeed, the whole notion of "efficient breach" is that a party should abrogate its contractual responsibilities if a more profitable opportunity comes along. See *Thyssen, Inc.* v. *S.S. Fortune Star*, 777 F.2d 57, 63 (2d Cir. 1985) ("[B]reaches of contract that are in fact efficient and wealth-enhancing should be encouraged, and . . . such 'efficient breaches' occur when the breaching party will still profit after compensating the other party for its 'expectation interest.'").

Neither are literally true responses to ambiguous questions false statements, *United States* v. *Castro*, 704 F.3d 125 (3d Cir. 2013) (denial that money came from extortion victim literally true because money came from government agent in sting); *United States v. Good*, 326 F.3d 589 (4th Cir. 2003) (denial of conviction for burglary, theft, armed robbery, possession or distribution of stolen property, dishonesty, fraud, or misrepresentation, when defendant had pleaded guilty to embezzlement).

The Act applies to matters that involve a government agency's activity even though the false statement is not made to the government, *Ebeling v. United States*, 248 F.2d 429 (8th Cir.), *cert. denied sub nom. Emerling v. United States*, 355 U.S. 907 (1957) (false invoices submitted by subcontractor to contractor under price redeterminable contract); *United States v. Huber*, 603 F.2d 387 (2d Cir. 1979), *cert. denied*, 445 U.S. 927 (1980) (false statements made to hospitals receiving money under federal programs). See also *United States v. Popow*, 821 F.2d 483 (8th Cir. 1987) (false identification presented to custom inspector is a matter concerning INS); and *United States v. Herring*, 916 F.2d 1543 (11th Cir. 1990) (Georgia Department of Labor involves activity of U.S. Department of Labor).

[ii] Knowingly and Willfully

To fall within the scope of the Act, the statement must have been made with the intent to deceive, but the government need not prove an intent to defraud, *United States v. Lichenstein*, 610 F.2d 1272 (5th Cir. 1980); *United States v. Leo*, 941 F.2d 181 (3d Cir. 1991). In *United States v. Starnes*, 583 F.3d 196 (3d Cir. 2009), the court held that "specific intent" need not be proved and provided a thorough analysis of the term "knowingly and willfully." One court stated that the knowing and willful intent requirement was met when the government proved that the defendant knew that the false statement was necessary for the fraudulent scheme to succeed, *United States v. Beck*, 615 F.2d 441 (7th Cir. 1980). See also *United States v. Cutaia*, 511 F. Supp. 619 (E.D.N.Y. 1981), where criminal intent was found when the defendant was advised of the government's requirements and deliberately gave answers to avoid compliance. However, there can be no intent to deceive unless the statement is false at the time it is made, *United States v. McCarrick*, 294 F.3d 1286 (11th Cir. 2002) (alleged wrongdoing occurred after document was signed).

An honest misinterpretation on government forms precludes conviction under the Act, *United States v. Weatherspoon*, 581 F.2d 595 (7th Cir. 1978), but reckless disregard of the truthfulness of the statement and a conscious effort to avoid learning the truth will be deemed to be a knowing and willful false statement, *United States v. Evans*, 559 F.2d 244 (5th Cir. 1977), *cert. denied*, 434 U.S. 1015 (1978). See also *United States v. Puente*, 982 F.2d 156 (5th Cir.), *cert. denied*, 508 U.S. 962 (1993), holding that it was reckless disregard to sign a government form certifying that the offeror had never been convicted of a felony without reading it.

Generally proof that the contractor followed a reasonable interpretation of an ambiguous regulation or contract is sufficient to demonstrate that there was no intent to make a false statement. See *United States v. Whiteside*, 285 F.3d 1345 (11th Cir. 2002), holding that an ambiguous regulation prevented a finding of the requisite intent. The court stated at 1351-52:

> In a case where the truth or falsity of a statement centers on an interpretive question of law, the government bears the burden of proving beyond a reasonable doubt that the defendant's statement is not true under a reasonable interpretation of the law. *United States v. Migliaccio*, 34 F.3d 1517, 1525 (10th Cir. 1994) (holding that the government bears the burden to negate any reasonable interpretations that would make the defendant's statement correct); *United States v. Johnson*, 937 F.2d 392, 399 (8th Cir. 1991) (holding that one cannot be guilty of a false statement beyond a reasonable doubt when his statement is a reasonable construction); *United States v. Race*, 632 F.2d 1114, 1120 (4th Cir. 1980) (same); *United States v. Anderson*, 579 F.2d 455, 460 (8th Cir. 1978) (same); see also *United States v. Calhoon*, 97 F.3d 518, 526 (11th Cir. 1996) (noting that even though the Medicare regulations were clear regarding the royalty fees paid to a related party, the government failed to establish as a matter of *fact* that the fees claimed were actually in excess of what was clearly allowed under the regulations, and thus, had "failed to sustain its burden to prove the claim false by virtue of the nonreimbursable nature of the interest").

However, if the court finds the contractor's interpretation unreasonable, intent to defraud the government will be found, *United States v. White*, 765 F.2d 1469 (11th Cir. 1985) (statement that cost estimate reflected "actual hours" when time cards contained fewer hours); *United States v. Dale*, 991 F.2d 819 (D.C. Cir. 1993) (rule not applicable because defendant's interpretation "far too restrictive"). In addition, one circuit has held that the argument of ambiguity will not prevail if there is sufficient evidence that the contractor knew that the government had a contrary interpretation, *United States v. Carrier*, 654 F.2d 559 (9th Cir. 1981).

The maker of the false statement can be convicted even if he does not know that the federal government is involved in the transaction, *United States v. Baker*, 626 F.2d 512 (5th Cir. 1980); *United States v. Wright*, 988 F.2d 1036 (10th Cir. 1993).

[iii] Materiality

The Act did not originally mention materiality and the Supreme Court ruled that materiality was not an element of the offense, *United States v. Wells*, 519 U.S. 482 (1979). However, the Act was amended to require proof of materiality. The test of materiality is whether a statement has a natural tendency to influence, or is capable of influencing, the actions of a federal agency, *Kungys v. United States*, 485 U.S. 759 (1988); *United States v. Gaudin*, 515 U.S. 506 (1995); *United States v. McBane*, 433 F.3d 344 (3d Cir. 2005). There is no need to prove either reliance by the government, *United States v. Hicks*, 619 F.2d 752 (8th Cir. 1980), or actual pecuniary loss by the government, *United States v. Lichenstein*, 610 F.2d 1272 (5th Cir. 1980). Thus, a criminal false statement can occur even if the government employee hearing the statement knows that it is false at the time, *United States v. Goldfine*, 538 F.2d 815 (9th Cir. 1976) (statements made during administrative "compliance investigation"); *United States v. LeMaster*, 54 F.3d 1224 (6th Cir. 1995) (statements to FBI agents during investigation); *United States v. Turner*, 551 F.3d 657 (7th Cir. 2008) (statements to FBI agents during investigation). In *United States v. Safavian*, 644 F. Supp. 2d 1 (D.D.C. 2009), *aff'd*, 649 F.3d 688 (D.C. Cir. 2011), the court refused to overturn a jury verdict that held the defendant liable for making false statements to an agency ethics officer in the course of obtaining an advisory opinion. In *United States v. Coastal Contracting & Eng'g Co.*, 174 F. Supp. 474 (D. Md. 1959), a contractor knowingly submitted fictitious statements in connection with a change order proposal. They were not relied upon by the government negotiator because he thought the prices were entirely out of line. Nevertheless, the contractor violated the Act because the misstatements were material and were calculated to induce reliance and action.

Materiality in a false statement is a question of fact to be decided by the jury, *United States v. Gaudin*, 515 U.S. 506 (1995). Prior to *Gaudin* there were numerous decisions holding that materiality was a question of law.

[c] Truth in Negotiations

The Truth in Negotiations Act (TINA) (technically renamed as the Truthful Cost or Pricing Data Act) was added to the Armed Services Procurement Act in 1962 to improve the government's ability to negotiate contracts and contract modifications by ensuring that the government has the same factual data as the contractor at the time of price negotiations. The Act does this by requiring that offerors and contractors submit and certify "cost or pricing data" in circumstances where the government has no way, other than cost analysis, to determine that a price is reasonable. The requirement was added to the Federal Property and Administrative Services Act in 1985. The Federal Acquisition Streamlining Act of 1994, Pub. L. No. 103-355, amended these statutes to contain the same requirements in 10 U.S.C. § 2306a (subsequently moved to 10 U.S.C. §§ 3701-3708) and 41 U.S.C. §§ 3501-09. These statutes now require the submission of cost or pricing data on all negotiated contracts over $2,000,000 but prohibit obtaining such data when one of four exceptions applies. FAR Subpart 15.4 gives guidance on the procedures when obtaining data is mandatory. The application of these requirements is discussed in Chapter 13.

These statutes contain elaborate guidance on the contractual remedies available to the government if a contractor fails to comply with their requirements. See 10 U.S.C. § 3706 (formerly § 2306a). 41 U.S.C. § 3506(a) contains substantially the same requirement. The statutory provisions are implemented, with almost no additional guidance, in FAR 15.407-1 and two mandatory contract clauses: Price Reduction for Defective Cost or Pricing Data in FAR 52.215-10 and Price Reduction for Defective Cost or Pricing Data—Modifications in FAR 52.215-11.

[i] When the Government is Entitled to a Reduction

Although the statutes provide for price reduction only when the effect of the defective data is to increase the contract price by a "significant amount," the government has been permitted to recover any amount that the price has been increased by a defect. See, for example, *Conrac Corp. v. United States*, 558 F.2d 994 (Ct. Cl. 1977), where the court interpreted the statutory language as relieving agencies from having to pursue trivial claims but permitted claims in any amount that an agency considered to be meaningful. In that case, the claim was for an overpricing of $8,050 on a $548,100 contract. In *American Bosch Arma Corp.*, ASBCA 10305, 65-2 BCA ¶ 5280, the board held that a claim for $20,746 on a contract over $15 million was significant. In *Kaiser Aerospace & Elecs. Corp.*, ASBCA 32098, 90-1 BCA ¶ 22,489, *recons. denied*, 90-2 BCA ¶ 22,695, the board awarded a price reduction of $5,527.82 on orders under a basic ordering agreement of $2,754,581, holding that even if this might "appear to be insignificant," it was bound to award that amount by *Conrac*.

[ii] Government Reliance on Defective Data

In order to obtain a price reduction, the government must demonstrate that the contract price negotiated by the parties was increased because of government reliance on defective data. The government is aided in this task by the "natural and probable consequence" rule developed by the Armed Services Board in *Lambert Eng'g Co.*, ASBCA 13338, 69-1 BCA ¶ 7663; *McDonnell Douglas Corp.*, ASBCA 12786, 69-2 BCA ¶ 7897. This rule holds that the natural and probable consequence of the furnishing of defective data is a dollar-for-dollar increase in the negotiated price. This rule has been termed a "rebuttable presumption," *American Mach. & Foundry Co.*, ASBCA 15037, 74-1 BCA ¶ 10,409. However, it has the effect of requiring the contractor, in order to avoid a price reduction, to demonstrate that the price was not impacted by the defective data, *Sylvania Elec. Prods., Inc. v. United States*, 479 F.2d 1342 (Ct. Cl. 1973). See *EDO Corp.*, ASBCA 41448, 93-3 BCA ¶ 26,135, where the price was reduced by the full amount of a reduced price that a supplier gave a subcontractor, because the contractor could not furnish evidence to overcome the presumption that the contract price had been impacted by this amount.

The natural and probable consequence rule has led to a number of rulings that the contractor was responsible for a dollar-for-dollar price increase. See *Hughes Aircraft Co.*, ASBCA 46321, 97-1 BCA ¶ 28,972; *Limpiezas Corona S.A.*, ASBCA 45504, 96-1 BCA ¶ 28,137; *P.A.L. Sys. Co.*, GSBCA 10858, 91-3 BCA ¶ 24,259; *Millipore Corp.*, GSBCA 9453, 91-1 BCA ¶ 23,345; *Kaiser Aerospace & Elecs. Corp.*, ASBCA 32098, 90-1 BCA ¶ 22,489, *recons. denied*, 90-2 BCA ¶ 22,695; *Etowah Mfg. Co.*, ASBCA 27267, 88-3 BCA ¶ 21,054; *Boeing Military Airplane Co.*, ASBCA 33168, 87-2 BCA ¶ 19,714; *Sylvania Elec. Prods., Inc.*, ASBCA 13622, 70-2 BCA ¶ 8387, *aff'd*, 479 F.2d 1342 (Ct. Cl. 1973); and *Aerojet-General Corp.*, ASBCA 12264, 69-1 BCA ¶ 7664, *modified*, 70 BCA ¶ 8140.

Contractors have been successful in demonstrating lack of reliance in several cases. See, for example, *United Techs. Corp.*, ASBCA 51410, 05-1 BCA ¶ 32,860, *aff'd*, 463 F.3d 1261 (Fed. Cir. 2006), where the board held that the presumption of reliance was rebutted by proof that no government employees actually reviewed the defective data in preparing for the price negotiation. Similarly, in *Texas Instruments, Inc.*, ASBCA 30836, 89-1 BCA ¶ 21,489; and *Hughes Aircraft Co.*, ASBCA 30144, 90-2 BCA ¶ 22,847, the board found that the government would not have used current prices of materials because the contract price had been negotiated using average prices of materials based on accumulated costs after the materials went through the manufacturing process. Thus, the board concluded that no price reduction was called for because the government would not have used the data had it been disclosed. See also *Levinson Steel Co.*, ASBCA 16520, 73-2 BCA ¶ 10,116 (contracting officer testified he would not have used data); *Muncie Gear Works, Inc.*, ASBCA 18184, 75-2 BCA ¶ 11,380 (auditor would not have used data because he rejected similar data as inaccurate); and *Rose, Beaton & Rose*, PSBCA 459, 80-1 BCA ¶ 14,242 (government would not have reduced its offer because it contained far less overhead than indicated by undisclosed data).

Several defenses demonstrating that the government did not rely on defective data have been barred by the language in 10 U.S.C. § 3706 (formerly § 2306a) and 41 U.S.C. § 3506(c), which expressly precludes several defenses. Thus, it may no longer be possible to argue that there was no reliance because the contractor would not have accepted a lower price. This argument had been used successfully in *Universal Restoration, Inc. v. United States*, 798 F.2d 1400 (Fed. Cir. 1986). See also *Luzon Stevedoring Corp.*, ASBCA 14851, 71-1 BCA

¶ 8745 (contractor made take-it-or-leave-it offer); and *American Mach. & Foundry Co.*, ASBCA 15037, 74-1 BCA ¶ 10,409 (contractor in strong bargaining position). Similarly, in *J.S. Latsis Grp. of Cos.*, ENGBCA 4276, 86-2 BCA ¶ 18,853, the board denied any price reduction for nondisclosure of detailed information on overhead because the contracting officer had negotiated overhead rates on a gross basis without regard to the contents of the overhead pool.

[iii] Computing the Price Reduction

In computing the amount of a price reduction, the court or board must determine (1) the dollar amount that would have been included in the price had the data been disclosed and (2) the dollar amount that was included in the contract price because of the nondisclosure. The determination of the latter amount has led to significant controversy. In *Sperry Corp. Computer Sys.*, ASBCA 29525, 88-3 BCA ¶ 20,975, *aff'd sub nom., Unisys Corp. v. United States*, 888 F.2d 841 (Fed. Cir. 1989), the board used the labor dollars that the government's documents indicated had been included in the contract price. The board rejected the contractor's argument that a lower amount should be used because the parties had arrived at the price through a "bottom line" settlement. In *Grumman Aerospace Corp.*, ASBCA 35188, 90-2 BCA ¶ 22,842, the board used the labor rates agreed to by the parties in the negotiation of the contract price rather than the labor rate originally proposed by the contractor because "a contractor is not liable for overstated costs that were eliminated during the price negotiation process." In that case, the board rejected the government's argument that the labor hours in the contract price would have been derived from labor hours on a prior contract projected down a learning curve. The board found that the parties had concluded during the price negotiation that difficulties in performing the work would prevent learning and had therefore used the same number of hours for the new contract as had been incurred on the previous contract. In *McDonnell Douglas Helicopter Sys.*, ASBCA 50341, 99-2 BCA ¶ 30,546, the board stated that the correct amount was the amount the government should cost team used to establish the government's negotiating position. In *Etowah Mfg. Co.*, ASBCA 27267, 88-3 BCA ¶ 21,054, the board used the government estimate prior to the negotiation rather than the considerably higher amount included in the contract price. The board apparently concluded that the contractor's nondisclosure of relevant data was not the cause of the government's willingness to include a higher amount in the price and, therefore, that the contractor was not responsible for any amount greater than the difference between the government estimate and the amount derived from the undisclosed data.

The dollar amount that would have been included in the contract price had the data been disclosed has also created controversy. In *Sperry Corporation Computer System*, the board used the undisclosed labor dollars incurred in manufacturing the product 18 months before the negotiations even though there was evidence that the parties had agreed in the negotiations that a higher figure would be required for the instant contract because of decreases in volume. The precise amount in the undisclosed data was also used in *Etowah Manufacturing*. In earlier cases, the boards had been more willing to base the computation of this figure on the record of the actual negotiations. For example, in *Aerojet-General Corp.*, ASBCA 12873, 69-1 BCA ¶ 7585, the board noted that the parties had arrived at the contract price by splitting the difference in their final negotiation positions. The board therefore assumed that the defective data would have decreased the government's negotiation position by the amount of the defect and that the parties would have split the difference—resulting in a price reduction of one-half of the amount of the defective data. Similarly, in *Bell & Howell Co.*, ASBCA 11999, 68-1 BCA ¶ 6993, the board concluded that had the data been disclosed, the parties would not have been able to negotiate a firm-fixed-price contract. It therefore assumed that they would have negotiated an incentive contract with a 60/40 share and awarded a price reduction in the amount of 60 percent of the defect. For a later case using the negotiation history, see *Aerojet Ordnance Tenn.*, ASBCA 36089, 95-2 BCA ¶ 27,922, where the board concluded that the parties would not have arrived at a price reduced by the entire amount of the defects in submitting the data. The board reached a compromise reduction based on the figures generated by each party in a precontract technical analysis.

In order to make a full computation of the impact of the price reduction on the contract price, the price must be reconstructed using the pricing structure that the parties used in the original negotiation. Thus, the computation must also include all elements of the contractor's costs that would normally be added to the cost item that is adjusted because of the defective data. See, for example, *Grumman Aerospace Corp.*, ASBCA 35188, 90-2 BCA ¶ 22,842, where the board computed the price reduction for defective data on labor dollars by adding all categories of work that were estimated as percentages of labor dollars (manufacturing engineering, sustaining engineering, program management, and foreign sales) plus all applicable overheads, general and administrative expense, and profit. Similarly, in *Kaiser Aerospace & Elecs. Corp.*, ASBCA 32098, 90-1 BCA ¶ 22,489, *recons. denied*, 90-2 BCA ¶ 22,695, the price reduction for defective data on labor rates was computed by adding overhead, general and administrative expense, warranty, and profit.

[iv] Offset

Early in the litigation of price reductions for defective cost or pricing data, it was determined that a contractor was entitled, up to the amount of any price reduction, to offset any amount due to underpricing that had occurred because of defective data in the same pricing action, *Cutler-Hammer, Inc. v. United States*, 416 F.2d 1306 (Ct. Cl. 1969); *Lockheed Aircraft Corp. v. United States*, 432 F.2d 801 (Ct. Cl. 1970). This rule was incorporated in the statutes in 10 U.S.C. § 3706(d) (formerly § 2306a) and 41 U.S.C. § 3506(d).

Offsets are permitted only when the contractor proves that there was an understatement of "factual pricing data," *J.S. Latsis Grp. of Cos.*, ENGBCA 4276, 86-2 BCA ¶ 18,853. In that case, the board found that the evidence was very unclear, but if there were any errors to which a low price could be attributed, they were errors of judgment, not errors in cost or pricing data. Compare *Hughes Aircraft Co.*, ASBCA 46321, 97-1 BCA ¶ 28,972, where offsetting mistakes in the same packages of data as the nondisclosed reduced cost were permitted as offsets.

Offsets may not be made between different contracts, *Norris Indus., Inc.*, ASBCA 15442, 74-1 BCA ¶ 10,482; *Minnesota Mining & Mfg. Co.*, ASBCA 20266, 77-2 BCA ¶ 12,823, or between unrelated contract modifications, *Muncie Gear Works, Inc.*, ASBCA 18184, 75-2 BCA ¶ 11,380. Neither can offsets lead to a price increase by the contractor, *Baldwin Elecs., Inc.*, ASBCA 19683, 76-2 BCA ¶ 12,199 (offsets exceeding the claimed price reduction led to sustaining of contractor's appeal), or be used when the omitted costs have been recovered from the government through inclusion in an overhead account, *Aerojet Ordnance Tenn.*, ASBCA 36089, 95-2 BCA ¶ 27,922. However, offsets are proper even when the contractor has intentionally understated the dollar amounts in the data, *Rogerson Aircraft Controls*, ASBCA 27954, 85-1 BCA ¶ 17,725, *aff'd*, 785 F.2d 296 (Fed. Cir. 1986) (government knew of understatements and was not "hindered or deceived" by them). Offsets are also proper when a contractor is informed of an error and does not correct it when submitting its BAFO, *United Techs. Corp.*, ASBCA 51410, 04-1 BCA ¶ 32,556. A contractor has also been permitted to offset its omitted in-house costs of completing work from an overstated subcontract price for the same work, *TGS Int'l, Inc.*, ASBCA 31120, 87-2 BCA ¶ 19,683, *recons. denied*, 87-3 BCA ¶ 19,989.

[v] Defective Subcontractor Data

If subcontractor cost or pricing data have been submitted to the government before the negotiation of the contract price of a firm-fixed-price contract, the contractor is liable for defects in that data, *Lockheed Aircraft Corp. v. United States*, 432 F.2d 801 (Ct. Cl. 1970). In that case, the court held the contractor liable even though the subcontractor data had been submitted directly to the government, not to the contractor. The court reasoned that the contractor's liability was dictated by the contract clause requiring price reductions. See also *McDonnell Aircraft Co.*, ASBCA 44504, 97-1 BCA ¶ 28,977 (contractor liable for not furnishing updated subcontractor information when it had furnished original subcontractor data with its proposal). If subcontractor cost or pricing data are not submitted to the contractor until after the negotiation of the price of a firm-fixed-price contract, there is no contractor liability for a price reduction because there could be no government reliance on that data.

The contractor is expected to include price reduction clauses in all subcontracts under cost-reimbursement or fixed-price-incentive or redeterminable contracts, and price reductions obtained through such clauses are expected to be credited to the costs billed to the government, FAR 15.407-1(f)(2). This applies even though the subcontractor's cost or pricing data were never submitted to the government or used as the basis for the original contract price.

[vi] Interest and Penalties

The statutes require the addition of interest and penalties in certain cases where the government has overpaid the contractor as a result of defective cost or pricing data, as stated at 10 U.S.C. § 3706 (formerly § 2306a) and 41 U.S.C. § 3507.

[d] Contract Disputes Act of 1978

The Contract Disputes Act of 1978, 41 U.S.C. § 7103(b), provides that each claim over $100,000 must be certified with regard to four specific elements:

> For claims of more than $100,000 made by a contractor, the contractor shall certify that (A) the claim is made in good faith, (B) the supporting data are accurate and complete to the best of the contractor's knowledge and belief, (C) the amount requested accurately reflects the contract adjustment for which the contractor believes the Federal Government is liable, and (D) the certifier is authorized to certify the claim on behalf of the contractor.

Neither the statutes nor regulations specifically require the submission of supporting data. All that is expressly required is that the contractor certify that "supporting data" are accurate and complete. Although a certification that the data are "complete" could be interpreted as a requirement for submission, there has been disagreement over whether the contractor is affirmatively required to submit data. See *Joseph P. Mentor*, GSBCA 6757, 85-1 BCA ¶ 17,887, where the board held that the certification was not intended to force contractors to submit evidence in support of their claims, but was merely an "honesty" requirement designed to discourage inflated claims. However, the scope of the certification of data is broad. See *LaBarge Elecs.*, ASBCA 44401, 93-2 BCA ¶ 25,617, holding that supporting data for a claim cannot be limited to data concerning the amount but must also include data in support of entitlement. See also *Triasco Corp.*, ASBCA 42465, 91-2 BCA ¶ 23,969, stating that this certification covers "all supporting data." See Chapter 13 of Cibinic, Nash & Nagle, *Administration of Government Contracts* (4th ed. 2006) for an in-depth discussion of the certification requirements under the Contract Disputes Act.

The Contract Disputes Act contains drastic sanctions for the misrepresentation of facts when submitting a claim. 41 U.S.C. § 7103(c)(2) provides:

> If a contractor is unable to support any part of the contractor's claim and it is determined that such inability is attributable to misrepresentation of fact or fraud by the contractor, then the contractor is liable to the Federal

> Government for an amount equal to the unsupported part of the claim plus all of the Federal Government's costs attributable to the cost of reviewing the unsupported part of the claim. Liability under this paragraph shall be determined within 6 years of the commission of the misrepresentation of fact or fraud.

The Act contains no definition of fraud. However, 41 U.S.C. § 7101(9) defines "misrepresentation of fact" as follows:

> The term "misrepresentation of fact" means a false statement of substantive fact, or conduct that leads to a belief of a substantive fact material to proper understanding of the matter in hand, made with intent to deceive or mislead.

The boards of contract appeals have refused to rule on a counterclaim for the penalty prescribed in § 7103(c)(2) based on the statutory statement that contracting officers have no authority to rule on "a claim or dispute for penalties or forfeitures prescribed by statute or regulation which another Federal agency is specifically authorized to administer, settle or determine," § 7103(a)(5). See *Comada Corp.*, ASBCA 26613, 83-2 BCA ¶ 16,681 ("actions to enforce the Government's rights under [this provision] would be solely the responsibility of the Department of Justice and would be instituted by the United States in a court of competent jurisdiction"). Thus, the remedy in the boards of contract appeals for claims that have been found in another proceeding to be "tainted by fraud" is dismissal of the claim, *Laguna Constr. Co. v. Carter*, 828 F.3d 1364 (Fed. Cir. 2016); *Beech Gap, Inc.*, ENGBCA 5585, 95-2 BCA ¶ 27,879, *aff'd*, 86 F.3d 1177 (Fed. Cir. 1997); *P.H. Mech. Corp. v. General Servs. Admin.*, GSBCA 10567, 94-2 BCA ¶ 26,785. Following this view that the appeals boards have no jurisdiction over fraudulent claims, a board also refused to hear a contractor's claim that the contracting officer improperly assessed the penalty prescribed in that section, *Warren Beaves*, DOTCAB 1324, 83-1 BCA ¶ 16,232.

The result is that the statutory penalty has only been imposed by the Court of Federal Claims when the government asserts a counterclaim in a contractor suit. Such counterclaims can be asserted in the same manner that all fraud counterclaims are asserted in that court without a prior decision of the contracting officer, *Simko Constr., Inc. v. United States*, 852 F.2d 540 (Fed. Cir. 1988). This provision making the contractor liable to the government for the amount of the fraudulent claim is probably the most drastic sanction for submitting a false claim. See *Daewoo Eng'g & Constr. Co. v. United States*, 73 Fed. Cl. 547 (2006), *aff'd*, 557 F.3d 1332 (Fed. Cir. 2009), *cert. denied*, 558 U.S. 990 (2009), holding that the contractor was liable for $50,629,855.88—the amount it had added to a claim to get the government's attention.

Such counterclaims are generally asserted along with counterclaims under the False Claims Act and the False Statements Act, *UMC Elecs. Co. v. United States*, 43 Fed. Cl. 776 (1999); *Crane Helicopter Servs., Inc. v. United States*, 45 Fed. Cl. 410 (1999); *Commercial Contractors, Inc. v. United States*, 154 F.3d 1357 (Fed. Cir. 1998); *Chemray Coatings Corp. v. United States*, 29 Fed.

Cl. 278 (1993); *Tyger Constr. Co. v. United States*, 28 Fed. Cl. 35 (1993). See *JANA, Inc. v. United States*, 34 Fed. Cl. 447 (1995), where the court held that the government's counterclaim alleging fraud under the CDA was timely because the Act's six-year statute of limitations for fraud could begin to run no earlier than the submission of the contractor's certified claim, regardless of when the conduct rendering the contractor's false claim allegedly occurred.

[e] 10 U.S.C. § 3862 (formerly § 2410) Certification

Another statute dealing with certifying supporting data for requests for equitable adjustment and requests for relief under Pub. L. No. 85-804 on DoD contracts is 10 U.S.C. § 3862 (formerly § 2410). This statute was amended by the Federal Acquisition Streamlining Act of 1994, Pub. L. No. 103-355, to make it clear that the provision applies only to requests for equitable adjustment or for relief under Pub. L. No. 85-804. As amended, 10 U.S.C. § 2410 establishes the following certification requirement:

> (a) Certification Requirement.—A request for equitable adjustment to contract terms or request for relief under Public Law 85-804 (50 U.S.C. 1431 et seq.) that exceeds the simplified acquisition threshold may not be paid unless a person authorized to certify the request on behalf of the contractor certifies, at the time the request is submitted, that—
>
> (1) the request is made in good faith, and
>
> (2) the supporting data are accurate and complete to the best of that person's knowledge and belief.

This statute also does not contain a clear requirement for the submission of data. The Federal Acquisition Streamlining Act of 1994 also repealed the DoD-unique claim certification requirement formerly contained in 10 U.S.C. § 2410e, thus leaving the Contract Disputes Act claim certification as the single governmentwide standard.

[2] Types of Illegal Conduct

Since the 1980s government contractors have been heavily investigated and sued for failure to deal openly and honestly with the federal government. The major types of conduct that are subject to lawsuits are discussed below.

[a] Product Substitution

Product substitution generally refers to attempts by the contractor to deliver to the government a product that does not conform to the contract requirements. Such substitution can occur by mismarking products, deviating from specifications, and other types of conduct that may indicate an intention to deceive the government in the performance of the contract. Such conduct may subject contractors to criminal or civil sanctions under the False Claims Act. See, for example, *BMY-Combat Sys. Div. of Harsco Corp. v. United States*, 38 Fed. Cl. 109 (1997), finding false claims when the contractor knowingly failed to fully inspect military equipment. The court also voided final acceptance of the equipment and held the contractor liable for breach of contract. See also *Varljen v. Cleveland Gear Co.*, 250 F.3d 426 (6th Cir. 2001) (false claim when subcontractor changed manufacturing process without approval after qualifying item); *United States ex rel. Roby v. Boeing Co.*, 100 F. Supp. 2d 619 (S.D. Ohio 2000) (false claim to knowingly furnish helicopter transmission gears known to be defective); *United States v. Hangar One, Inc.*, 563 F.2d 1155 (5th Cir. 1977) (false claim to rig inspection system to omit required inspections and deliver rejected items); *Imperial Meat Co. v. United States*, 316 F.2d 435 (10th Cir.), *cert. denied*, 375 U.S. 820 (1963) (false claim when contractor substituted an inferior grade of meat on a DoD contract). In *United States v. National Wholesalers*, 236 F.2d 944 (9th Cir. 1956), *cert. denied*, 353 U.S. 930 (1957), the contractor indicated to the government that it would supply brand name regulators, but instead manufactured the regulators itself and attached false brand name labels before delivery. The court found the contractor liable for a false claim even though the regulators were in fact equal. See also *United States v. Aerodex, Inc.*, 469 F.2d 1003 (5th Cir. 1972), where the court found a false claim when the contractor knowingly substituted aircraft bearings which differed from the contract specifications, even though there was no proof that they were inferior. Other statutes used to prosecute product substitution include the False Statements Act, 18 U.S.C. § 1001, the conspiracy statutes, 18 U.S.C. § 286 and § 371, the mail and wire fraud statutes, 18 U.S.C. § 1341 and § 1343, and the Racketeer Influenced and Corrupt Organizations Act, 18 U.S.C. §§ 1961-1968.

Product substitution with an intent to defraud has also led to the loss of disputes cases in the boards of contract appeals. For example, in *D & H Constr. Co.*, ASBCA 37482, 89-3 BCA ¶ 22,070, the contractor's substitution of refrigerators with counterfeited certification labels rose to the level of fraud and voided final acceptance. Similarly, a default termination will be sustained if the contractor has fraudulently performed defective work, *Beech Gap, Inc.*, ENGBCA 5585, 95-2 BCA ¶ 27,879, *aff'd*, 86 F.3d 1177 (Fed. Cir. 1997).

When a contractor does not deliver goods that conform precisely to contract requirements there may not be an intent to defraud but the government still has contract remedies. Thus, it may obtain a price reduction equivalent to the amount of costs saved plus overhead and profit, *Santa Fe Eng'rs., Inc.*, ASBCA 44906, 93-1 BCA ¶ 25,298 (substitution of less expensive door); *Arnold M. Diamond, Inc.*, ASBCA 38974, 92-2 BCA ¶ 24,869 (use of fewer expansion joints than called for by specifications); *J.S. Alberici Constr. Co.*, GSBCA 10630, 92-1 BCA ¶ 24,392 (substitution of less expensive doors); *Bruce Andersen Co.*, ASBCA 29412, 89-2 BCA ¶ 21,872 (omission of work called for by contract). Even if the substitute is equal to that specified in the contract, acceptance may harm the procurement system, which is based on all competitors offering to furnish only the product called for in the contract. Allowing offerors to substitute products according to their own judgment would defeat the concept of bidding on an equal basis. See *Ideal Restaurant Supply Co.*, VACAB 570, 67-1 BCA ¶ 6237, where the board found that the government was justified in rejecting equivalent supplies that did not meet contract specifications and noted that allowing the contractor to substitute aluminum for nickel alloy and stainless steel in steam kettle parts could have a negative effect on the competitive bidding process. Similarly, in *J.L. Malone & Assocs.*, VABCA 2335, 88-3 BCA ¶ 20,894, *aff'd*, 879 F.2d 841 (Fed. Cir. 1989), the government rejected a contractor's substitution of a technically equivalent computer in the installation of a fire alarm system. The board stated that the preservation of the integrity of the competitive procurement system was more important than any benefits that could derive from replacing the specified computer with even a more advanced one at no extra cost to the government. See also *C.H. Hyperbarics, Inc.*, ASBCA 49375, 04-1 BCA ¶ 32,568, holding that the government properly rejected valves that were not of the same manufacture as other parts of the system, as required by the specifications.

[b] Mischarging/Accounting Fraud

Mischarging is the term used to describe a particular type of fraud involving the accounting treatment of costs by contractors. Mischarging is the false description and the improper charging of costs to a government contract. The contractual remedy for mischarging is the disallowance of the costs including all costs incurred because of the mischarging. See FAR 31.205-15 providing:

> (b) Costs incurred in connection with, or related to, the mischarging of costs on Government contracts are unallowable when the costs are caused by, or result from, alteration or destruction of records, or other false or improper charging or recording of costs. Such costs include those incurred to measure or otherwise determine the magnitude of the improper charging, and costs incurred to remedy or correct the mischarging, such as costs to rescreen and reconstruct records.

Mischarging can arise in several instances, including improper allocation of costs and charging of expressly unallowable costs to a contract. If a contractor includes an "expressly unallowable" cost in a proposal to settle indirect costs, the agency must assess a penalty against the contractor, in addition to disallowance of the cost, in the amount of the cost claimed plus interest on those costs, 10 U.S.C. § 3743 (formerly § 2324(b)); 41 U.S.C. § 4303(b). These sections also provide that the penalty will be double the amount of the claimed cost if it had been "determined to be unallowable in the case of such contractor before the submission of such proposal." These provisions are implemented in FAR

42.709. A cost is "expressly unallowable" only when there are no "reasonable differences of opinion" on allowability, *General Dynamics Corp.*, ASBCA 49372, 02-2 BCA ¶ 31,888. Penalties were assessed in *Inframat Corp.*, ASBCA 57741, 12-2 BCA ¶ 35,113 (undescribed costs); *Thomas Assocs., Inc.*, ASBCA 47126, 11-1 BCA ¶ 34,764 (life insurance premium not recorded as compensation); and *Fiber Materials, Inc.*, ASBCA 53616, 07-1 BCA ¶ 33,563 (patent costs and costs of cabin rented for employee use). See also *Raytheon Co.*, ASBCA 57743, 17-1 BCA ¶ 36,724, *recons.* denied, 18-1 BCA ¶ 37,129, *aff'd*, 940 F.3d 1310 (Fed. Cir. 2019), holding that the penalty applies only to costs made unallowable by the regulations not by an advanced agreement but that salaries of employees that were engaged in lobbying were expressly unallowable.

Mischarging is also subject to criminal and civil sanctions under the False Claims Act as well as other criminal sanctions. For example, in *United States v. McGunnigal*, 151 F.2d 162 (1st Cir.), *cert. denied*, 326 U.S. 776 (1945), a criminal conspiracy was found between welders and counters who manufactured and constructed ships under a cost-reimbursement contract resulted in inflated payroll costs. See *United States v. Maher*, 582 F.2d 842 (4th Cir. 1978), *cert. denied*, 439 U.S. 1115 (1979), where false claims requesting payments under a time-and-materials contract were submitted. The accountant involved was instructed to inflate labor hours on monthly billings, prepare new time sheets that conformed to the changes, trace over employees' signatures on the new time sheets, and destroy the originals. See also *KI Liquidation, Inc. v. United States*, 116 Fed. Cl. 338 (2014) (asserting supplier had been paid in order to receive contract payments); *Morse Diesel Int'l, Inc. v. United States*, 74 Fed. Cl. 601 (2007) (invoicing bond premiums before payment to surety); *United States v. Newport News Shipbuilding, Inc.*, 276 F. Supp. 2d 539 (E.D. Va. 2003) (charging costs of designing commercial ships to IR&D); *United States ex rel. Newsham v. Lockheed Missile & Space Co.*, 190 F.3d 963 (9th Cir. 1999) (allegedly billing costs of unproductive labor and time workers spent on personal projects); *Jana, Inc. v. United States*, 41 Fed. Cl. 735 (1998) (altering time cards); *United States ex rel. Mayman v. Martin Marietta Corp.*, 894 F. Supp. 218 (D.C. Md. 1995) (proposing low costs for work with intention of charging costs of performance to IR&D); *Young-Montenay, Inc. v. United States*, 15 F.3d 1040 (Fed. Cir. 1994) (altering subcontractor invoice in order to inflate progress payment); *United States v. TDC Mgmt. Corp.*, 24 F.3d 292 (D.C. Cir. 1994) (omission of information from cost reports); *United States v. Sperry Corp.*, Civ. 89-2472 (E.D.N.Y. 1991) (contractor employees falsely filled out time cards indicating work on one contract when the work was properly chargeable to other jobs); *United States v. Lagerbusch*, 361 F.2d 449 (3d Cir. 1966) (false representations in invoices submitted to cost-type contractor). See also *United States v. Richmond*, 700 F.2d 1183 (8th Cir. 1983). For an in-depth analysis of other mischarging cases, see Graham, *Mischarging: A Contract Dispute or a Criminal Fraud?*, 15 Pub. Cont. L.J. 208 (1985).

[c] Fraudulent Pricing

As discussed previously, the Truth in Negotiations Act requires that before price negotiations for negotiated contracts, government contractors must disclose the facts relevant to those negotiations and certify that the facts are accurate, complete, and current. However, the failure to submit complete, current, and accurate cost or pricing data has been treated as fraud in only a few cases. There are two types of defective pricing situations that are often treated as instances of fraud—the falsification of cost or pricing data, and the submission of inaccurate estimates.

[i] Fraudulent Data

For many years, *United States v. Foster Wheeler Corp.*, 447 F.2d 100 (2d Cir. 1971), which affirmed a district court decision that the contractor had committed civil fraud by submitting defective cost or pricing data, was the only reported decision in this area. More recently, in *UMC Elecs. Co. v. United States*, 43 Fed. Cl. 776 (1999), fraud was found when the contractor submitted full cost or pricing data to support its claim but listed its "actual costs" by summarizing its purchase order prices even though there were several instances where subcontractors and suppliers had not invoiced for work at those prices. The court found that the contractor knew full well the difference between actual costs and estimates because it had made the difference clear in prior submissions of cost or pricing data. The court therefore found that the inclusion by the contractor of uninvoiced costs in its statement of "actual costs" was a fraudulent statement. Fraud was also found in *United States v. Leo*, 941 F.2d 181 (3d Cir. 1991) (contractor's negotiator affirmatively stated that its estimate of subcontract prices would be difficult to attain when it had knowingly failed to provide the government with subcontract prices that had been substantially reduced); *United States v. Poarch*, 878 F.2d 1355 (11th Cir. 1989) (company's contracts administrator (1) told an employee to charge time to a wrong account in order to build up labor hours, and (2) omitted current labor-hour data from the submission of cost or pricing data that had been required by the contracting officer); and *United States v. Pimental & Duroyd Mfg. Co.*, 810 F.2d 366 (2d Cir. 1987) (contractor obtained quotations from eight vendors but submitted only the highest quote to the contracting officer while buying at the low price). A number of fraud cases in this area involve the creation and submission of false data by the contractor. See *United States v. Barnette*, 800 F.2d 1558 (11th Cir. 1986), *cert. denied*, 480 U.S. 935 (1987), where the contractor created false payroll records and false invoices from bogus vendors to inflate its proposed contract prices; and *United States v. Busher*, 817 F.2d 1409 (9th Cir. 1987), where the contractor falsified data relating to performance of work by subcontractors.

Cases litigating the issue of whether the government should obtain a price reduction for defective pricing appear to be easily distinguishable from those involving prosecution for civil or criminal fraud. Price reduction cases largely deal with technical interpretations of the submission requirement. In most instances, the contractor has made major submissions but has omitted some discrete data. The fraud cases generally involve either falsification of data or a scheme to obtain a higher price. Thus, if a contractor makes a serious effort to disclose the cost or pricing data used in preparing its proposal, it is probably not in jeopardy of being charged with fraud. However, a contractor that adopts practices that permit regular nondisclosure of such data is taking an unreasonable business risk. If the government concludes that higher prices are being obtained through the use of such practices, a charge of fraud is likely.

[ii] Inaccurate Estimates

In a few cases, contractors have been held liable for submitting egregiously inaccurate estimates. In the original case of this type, *United States ex rel. Taxpayers Against Fraud v. Singer Co.*, 889 F.2d 1327 (4th Cir. 1989), the fraud was found in not submitting the contractor's "best estimates" as certified on the Standard Form 1411 as follows:

> This proposal is submitted in response to the RFP, contract, modification, etc. in Item 1 and reflects our best estimates and/or actual costs as of this date and conforms with the instructions in FAR 15.804-6(b)(1). . . .

Similarly, in *United States v. Sperry Corp.*, Civ. 89-2472 (E.D.N.Y. 1991), the government alleged that the contractor submitted a low estimate on the original contract and after buying in submitted high estimates on the follow-on contracts where the contractor was the sole source. Subsequently, in *United States v. Bicoastal Corp.*, Cr. No. 92-CR-261 (N.D.N.Y. 1992), a contractor pleaded guilty to charges arising from the submission of inflated, fraudulent labor estimates on negotiated sole source contracts for flight simulators. The contractor had submitted cost estimates that included amounts allocated for fictitious jobs and personnel that purported to be necessary costs. The contractor certified that each cost estimate was its best estimate, while it routinely concealed a lower estimate. The Standard Form 1411 has been removed from the FAR but Table 15-2—Instructions for Submitting Cost/Price Proposals When Cost or Pricing Data Are Required, FAR 15.408, contains the following required statement (removing the word "best") on such proposals:

> This proposal reflects our estimates and/or actual costs as of this data and conforms with the instructions in FAR 15.403-5(b)(1) and Table 15-2. . . .

This removes the issue of whether the estimate submitted was the "best" estimate but does not affect the question of whether the estimate was fraudulently compiled.

Other fraud cases also involve the submission of estimates of a contract's cost of performance when the contractor is aware that the estimate does not reflect its anticipated allowable costs. See *United States v. White*, 765 F.2d 1469 (11th Cir. 1985), where the contractor submitted an estimate of the cost of fully performed work under change orders that was far higher than the actual costs that had been incurred and recorded in its accounting data. The court held that the contractor had represented to the government that its estimate reflected actual costs. See also *Railway Logistics Int'l v. United States*, 103 Fed. Cl. 252 (2012) (estimated costs not supported by any recorded costs); *Daewoo Eng'g & Constr. Co. v. United States*, 73 Fed. Cl. 547 (2006), *aff'd*, 557 F.3d 1332 (Fed. Cir. 2009), *cert. denied*, 558 U.S. 990 (2009) (false claim to add over $50 million to claim to get the attention of the contracting officer); *Harrison v. Westinghouse Savannah River Co.*, 176 F.3d 776 (4th Cir. 1999) (false claim to misstate the scope and length of work to be subcontracted in order to obtain government approval to subcontract); and *United States v. General Dynamics Corp.*, 19 F.3d 770 (2d Cir. 1994) (false claim to include kickbacks paid to subcontractor in cost estimates submitted to the government).

A slightly different situation arose in *United States v. United Techs. Corp.*, 626 F.3d 313 (6th Cir. 2010). There the court affirmed a holding that the contractor had made three false statements in how it had arrived at the price in its best and final offer on a competitive procurement but remanded on the assessment of damages. On remand, 950 F. Supp. 2d 949 (S.D. Ohio 2013), the court assessed almost $700 million in damages under the False Claims Act. This holding was reversed and remanded by *United States v. United Techs. Corp.*, 782 F.3d 718 (6th Cir. 2015). On remand the district court awarded $1,176,619 plus interest for excessive profits and $ 7 million for all of the invoices submitted on the contract, *United States v. United Techs. Corp.*, 190 F. Supp. 3d 752 (S.D. Ohio 2016).

[iii] Buying-In

Submitting a low price in order to obtain additional compensation during contract performance or through obtaining follow-on contracts is not per se fraudulent, *United States ex rel. Bettis v. Odebrecht Contractors of California, Inc.*, 297 F. Supp. 2d 272 (D.D.C. 2004), *aff'd*, 393 F.3d 1321 (D.C. Cir. 2005). After concluding that contracting at a low price could not be equated with falsely claiming money to which the contractor was not entitled, the district court reasoned at 281:

> The fact that a deflated bid alone cannot suffice to impose liability under the FCA is not, however, cured by merely adding a claim that defendant sought monies above and beyond the bid price. Such a proposition completely ignores the reality of government contracting where it is common for a contract that was bid at one price to ultimately cost far more. For instance, as previously noted, in a unit-price contract, such as [this] contract, the final price will necessarily be different if the actual quantities of materials turn

> out to be greater than the government's original quantity estimates. Further, as plaintiff concedes . . . , it is perfectly acceptable for the government to modify the scope of work or to change the design specifications. Alternatively, the final price can be increased if the government's representations about the nature of the project turn out to be inaccurate. Since there are a myriad of legitimate adjustments that can increase a contract price beyond the bid price, it necessarily follows that plaintiff cannot rest only on proof of a fraudulently induced contract by means of a low bid and an attempt by the bidder to obtain monies in excess of the bid price. Rather, there must be a claim "for money to which . . . [the contractor] is not legitimately entitled."

Compare *Hooper v. Lockheed Martin Corp.*, 688 F.3d 1037 (9th Cir. 2012), holding that there was a potential false claim if the contractor had intentionally submitted a low estimated cost in order to win a competition. See also Veridyne Corp. v. United States, 758 F.3d 1371 (Fed. Cir. 2014), finding a false claim when the company obtained a small business contract by grossly understating the estimated costs of the work.

[d] Equitable Adjustment Claims

Making false statements or allegations in equitable adjustment claims has also been found to be fraudulent. For example, in *United States ex rel. Wilkins v. North Am. Constr. Corp.*, 101 F. Supp. 2d 500 (S.D. Tex. 2000), the court found a proper allegation of fraud when the contractor based a differing site conditions claim on allegedly defective information that had been provided by the government when it had considerable information that the government information was accurate. In *Commercial Contractors, Inc. v. United States*, 154 F.3d 1357 (Fed. Cir. 1998), the court also found fraud in the substantive allegations in a differing site condition claim. Similarly, in *P.H. Mech. Corp. v. General Servs. Admin.*, GSBCA 10567, 94-2 BCA ¶ 26,785, fraud was found where a contractor falsified receipts, invoices and records supporting an equitable adjustment claim. See also *Shaw v. AAA Eng'g & Drafting, Inc.*, 213 F.3d 519 (10th Cir. 2000), where the contractor falsely inflated numbers on official work orders used to support an equitable adjustment claim. In *AAA Eng'g & Drafting, Inc.*, ASBCA 47940, 01-1 BCA ¶ 31,256, the board denied a subsequent equitable adjustment claim based on this court decision. Unsupported cost estimates for equitable adjustments have also been found to be fraudulent, *Railway Logistics Int'l v. United States*, 103 Fed. Cl. 252 (2012); *Daewoo Eng'g & Constr. Co. v. United States*, 557 F.3d 1332 (Fed. Cir.), *cert. denied*, 558 U.S. 990 (2009).

[E] Obtaining Information Improperly

There are several sanctions for improperly disclosing or obtaining information related to the procurement process. 18 U.S.C. § 1905 imposes criminal sanctions on any government employee that discloses trade secrets and other proprietary data obtained from any person or organization. The procurement integrity provisions in the Office of Procurement Policy Act, prohibit any person from disclosing "contractor bid or proposal information" or "source selection information" before contract award, 41 U.S.C. § 2102(a) or obtaining such information, 41 U.S.C. § 2102(b). There may also be improper conduct involved in obtaining information about a competitor. These various aspects of improperly obtaining information are discussed below. Improper access to information is also considered to be an organizational conflict of interest which is discussed in Chapter 4.

[1] Disclosure of Confidential Information by Government Employees

The GAO will hear protests from competitors claiming that the government has disclosed their proprietary information in the procurement process. However, it requires strong evidence to grant such a protest. See *Janico Bldg. Servs.*, Comp. Gen. Dec. B-290683, 2002 CPD ¶ 119, stating:

> We have recognized the right of a firm to protect its proprietary data from improper exposure in a solicitation in the context of a bid protest. *The Source*, B-266362, Feb. 7, 1996, 96-1 CPD ¶ 48 at 2; *Ingersoll-Rand Co.*, B-236391, Dec. 5, 1989, 89-1 CPD ¶ 517 at 2. Where a protester alleges that proprietary information was improperly disclosed, the record must establish that the protester was competitively prejudiced by the release before we will sustain a protest. *Rothe Dev., Inc.*, B-279839, July 27, 1998, 98-2 CPD ¶ 31 at 2-3; *Ursery Cos., Inc.*, B-258247, Dec. 29, 1994, 94-2 CPD ¶ 264 at 2. The possibility of competitive prejudice may not be established on the basis of speculation. *Rothe Dev., Inc., supra*, at 3; *JL Assocs., Inc.*, B-239790, Oct. 1, 1990, 90-2 CPD ¶ 261 at 4-5.

Most protests have denied relief under this standard. See *Congaree Grp., LLC*, Comp. Gen. Dec. B-415242, 2017 CPD ¶ 346 (location of parking lot not proprietary and no prejudice); *Centerra Grp., LLC*, Comp. Gen. Dec. B-412271.2, 2016 CPD ¶ 101 (staffing data not proprietary and no prejudice); *Coulson Aviation (USA), Inc.*, Comp. Gen. Dec. B-411525, 2015 CPD ¶ 272 (no proof that data in solicitation was not publicly available or general performance requirements logically developed by the agency); *Engineering Support Personnel, Inc.*, Comp. Gen. Dec. B-410448, 2015 CPD ¶ 89 (agency cost estimate using protester's performance data not proprietary); *Sentel Corp.*, Comp. Gen. Dec. B-244991, 91-2 CPD ¶ 519 (proprietary data was inadvertently disclosed to competitor). Compare *NEFF Instrument Corp.*, Comp. Gen. Dec. B-216236, 84-2 CPD ¶ 649, where GAO advised the agency to avoid disclosing proprietary data by either writing a performance specification or issuing a sole source contract to the owner of the data. See also *Chromalloy San Diego Corp.*,

Comp. Gen. Dec. B-416990.2, 2019 CPD ¶ 188, denying a protest asserting an unduly restrictive specification when the agency required competitors to have a license to use the original manufacturer's proprietary data.

Relief for disclosure of proprietary data during contract performance is granted as a breach of contract. See *Toyon Research Corp.*, Comp. Gen. Dec. B-409765, 2014 CPD ¶ 235, refusing to hear a protest that a contractor had disclosed proprietary data during performance because this was not a grounds for protest. In *Spectrum Sciences & Software, Inc. v. United States*, 98 Fed. Cl. 8 (2011), the court awarded substantial damages for disclosing proprietary data obtained during contract performance on a subsequent competitive procurement. Compare *CANVS Corp.*, ASBCA 57784, 18-1 BCA ¶ 37,156, denying relief after a careful analysis determining that the information disclosed was either publicly available or common knowledge.

18 U.S.C. § 1905 provides:

> Whoever, being an officer or employee of the United States or of any department or agency thereof, any person acting on behalf of the Office of Federal Housing Enterprise Oversight, or agent of the Department of Justice as defined in the Antitrust Civil Process Act (15 U.S.C. 1311-1314), or being an employee of a private sector organization who is or was assigned to an agency under Chapter 37 of title 5, publishes, divulges, discloses, or makes known in any manner or to any extent not authorized by law any information coming to him in the course of his employment or official duties or by reason of any examination or investigation made by, or return, report or record made to or filed with, such department or agency or officer or employee thereof, which information concerns or relates to the trade secrets, processes, operations, style of work, or apparatus, or to the identity, confidential statistical data, amount or source of any income, profits, losses, or expenditures of any person, firm, partnership, corporation, or association; or permits any income return or copy thereof or any book containing any abstract or particulars thereof to be seen or examined by any person except as provided by law; shall be fined under this title, or imprisoned not more than one year, or both; and shall be removed from office or employment.

The conviction of a government employee under 18 U.S.C. § 1905 for improper disclosure of information was affirmed in *United States v. Wallington*, 889 F.2d 573 (5th Cir. 1989). The court held that the Act was not overly broad to constitute a valid criminal statute.

[2] Disclosure of and Obtaining Bid or Proposal Information or Source Selection Information

The Clinger-Cohen Act of 1996 amended the Procurement Integrity Act, 41 U.S.C. § 2102, to streamline the provisions on disclosure of and obtaining information. The amended Act contains two provisions relating to such transmission of information. 41 U.S.C. § 2102(a), prohibits a "person" from knowingly disclosing "contractor bid or proposal information" or "source selection information" before award of a contract. The "person" covered is defined in 41 U.S.C. § 2102(a)(3) as anyone who:

> (A)(i) is a present or former official of the Federal Government, or
>
> (ii) is acting or has acted for or on behalf of, or who is advising or has advised the Federal Government with respect to, a Federal agency procurement; and
>
> (B) by virtue of that office, employment, or relationship has or had access to contractor bid or proposal information or source selection information.

The term "official" is defined in 41 U.S.C. § 2101(5) as (1) an officer as defined in 5 U.S.C. § 2104, (2) an employee as defined in 5 U.S.C. § 2105, and (3) a member of the uniformed forces as defined in 5 U.S.C. § 2101(3). FAR 3.104-3 adds to this the category of "special Government employees" as defined in 18 U.S.C. § 202. This statute gives a new test as to what persons are covered by this paragraph of the Act. They are persons who have either "acted" or "advised" regarding a federal agency procurement and have obtained information through that contact with the procurement. Neither the statute nor the implementation of this part of the Act in FAR 3.104-4 contain any guidance on the meaning of the terms "acted" or "advised," with the apparent effect that this rule applies to persons who have acted or advised no matter how small their contact with the procurement. This would seem to apply this part of the Act to virtually anyone who obtained information in the course of participating in the procurement, unless he or she was a total bystander that obtained information in the course of observing the procurement.

The second prohibition is in 41 U.S.C. § 2102(b), prohibiting a "person" from knowingly obtaining "contractor bid or proposal information" or "source selection information" before award of a contract to which the information pertains. The Act contains no definition of the "persons" covered by this paragraph with the result that it appears to apply to any contractor, other business entity, or individual that obtains information even if that person is not participating in the procurement. However, this prohibition applies only if the information is obtained from an "official;" *Geo Grp., Inc. v. United States*, 100 Fed. Cl. 223 (2011); *IBM Corp.*, Comp. Gen. Dec. B-425798.2, 2019 CPD ¶ 8. The only narrowing of the rule is that it is no longer a violation of the Act to solicit information if the information is not obtained.

The Act applies only to a "federal agency procurement," and this term is defined in 41 U.S.C. § 2101(f)(4) to mean only acquisitions using competitive procedures. This is an important reduction from the coverage of the prior Act because officials who have participated in sole source procurements or contract modifications are not covered by the current Act. However, the implementation of this provision of the Act in FAR 3.104-4 applies these rules without regard to this statutory limitation as follows:

> (a) Except as specifically provided for in this subsection, no person or other entity may disclose contractor bid or proposal information or source selection information to any person other than a person authorized, in accordance with applicable agency regulations or procedures, by the head of the agency or the contracting officer to receive such information.
>
> (b) Contractor bid or proposal information and source selection information must be protected from unauthorized disclosure in accordance with 14.401, 15.207, applicable law, and agency regulations.

This broadening of the prohibition beyond the scope of the Procurement Integrity Act reflects the fact that 18 U.S.C. § 1905 is a blanket prohibition of disclosure of proprietary information.

The two types of information protected from disclosure are defined in 41 U.S.C. § 2101 as follows:

> (2) The term "contractor bid or proposal information" means any of the following information submitted to a Federal agency as part of or in connection with a bid or proposal to enter into a Federal agency procurement contract, if that information has not been previously made available to the public or disclosed publicly:
>
> > (A) Cost or pricing data (as defined by section 2306a(h) of title 10 with respect to procurements subject to that section, and section 3501(a) of this title, with respect to procurements subject to that section).
> >
> > (B) Indirect costs and direct labor rates.
> >
> > (C) Proprietary information about manufacturing processes, operations, or techniques marked by the contractor in accordance with applicable law or regulation.
> >
> > (D) Information marked by the contractor as "contractor bid or proposal information", in accordance with applicable law or regulation.
>
> (7) The term "source selection information" means any of the following information prepared for use by a Federal agency to evaluate a bid or proposal to enter into a Federal agency procurement contract, if that information has not been previously made available to the public or disclosed publicly:
>
> > (A) Bid prices submitted in response to a Federal agency solicitation for sealed bids, or lists of those bid prices before public bid opening.
> >
> > (B) Proposed costs or prices submitted in response to a Federal agency solicitation, or lists of those proposed costs or prices.
> >
> > (C) Source selection plans.
> >
> > (D) Technical evaluation plans.
> >
> > (E) Technical evaluations of proposals.

(F) Cost or price evaluations of proposals.

(G) Competitive range determinations that identify proposals that have a reasonable chance of being selected for award of a contract.

(H) Rankings of bids, proposals, or competitors.

(I) The reports and evaluations of source selection panels, boards, or advisory councils.

(J) Other information marked as "source selection information" based on a case-by-case determination by the head of the agency, his designee, or the contracting officer that its disclosure would jeopardize the integrity or successful completion of the Federal agency procurement to which the information relates.

41 U.S.C. § 2107 contains a number of "savings provisions," as follows:

(h) *Savings Provisions.* This chapter does not—

(1) restrict the disclosure of information to, or its receipt by, any person or class of persons authorized, in accordance with applicable agency regulations or procedures, to receive that information;

(2) restrict a contractor from disclosing its own bid or proposal information or the recipient from receiving that information;

(3) restrict the disclosure or receipt of information relating to a Federal agency procurement after it has been canceled by the Federal agency before contract award unless the Federal agency plans to resume the procurement;

(4) prohibit individual meetings between a Federal agency official and an offeror or potential offeror for, or a recipient of, a contract or subcontract under a Federal agency procurement, provided that unauthorized disclosure or receipt of contractor bid or proposal information or source selection information does not occur;

(5) authorize the withholding of information from, nor restrict its receipt by, Congress, a committee or subcommittee of Congress, the Comptroller General, a Federal agency, or an inspector general of a Federal agency;

(6) authorize the withholding of information from, nor restrict its receipt by, the Comptroller General of the United States in the course of a protest against the award or proposed award of a Federal agency procurement contract; or

(7) limit the applicability of any requirements, sanctions, contract penalties, and remedies established under another law or regulation.

These provisions are implemented at FAR 3.104-4(e) and (f). It seems clear that these rules should not prevent open communication between contracting agencies and potential offerors regarding the work to be procured and the procurement strategy before solicitations are issued as long as specific finalized source selection plans and technical evaluation plans are not revealed. It also places no limitations on obtaining information during litigation. See *Pikes Peak Family Housing, LLC v. United States*, 40 Fed. Cl. 673 (1998), permitting normal discovery in an award protest citing ¶ (7) above providing for discovery in a court proceeding as a "remedy" covered by the saving provisions of the Act. However, they will permit disqualification of an offeror that has improperly obtained access to such information. See *Guardian Techs. Int'l*, Comp. Gen. Dec. B-270213, 96-1 CPD ¶ 104, where GAO agreed that it was proper to disqualify an offeror that had hired a government employee that had access to source selection information.

There are severe penalties for violating these provisions. See 41 U.S.C. § 2105 stating:

> (a) Criminal penalties. A person that violates section 2102 of this title to exchange information covered by section 2102 of this title for anything of value or to obtain or give a person a competitive advantage in the award of a Federal agency procurement contract shall be fined under title 18, imprisoned for not more than 5 years, or both.
>
> (b) Civil penalties. The Attorney General may bring a civil action in an appropriate district court of the United States against a person that engages in conduct that violates section 2102, 2103, or 2104 of this title. On proof of that conduct by a preponderance of the evidence—
>
> > (1) an individual is liable to the Federal Government for a civil penalty of not more than $50,000 for each violation plus twice the amount of compensation that the individual received or offered for the prohibited conduct; and
> >
> > (2) an organization is liable to the Federal Government for a civil penalty of not more than $500,000 for each violation plus twice the amount of compensation that the organization received or offered for the prohibited conduct.

[3] Information About Competitors

The techniques for gaining information about competitors are diverse and may or may not be proper. These techniques range from the benign, such as reading a competitor's sales brochure, to the potentially criminal, such as business espionage. In *Compliance Corp. v. United States*, 22 Cl. Ct. 193 (1990), *aff'd*, 960 F.2d 157 (Fed. Cir. 1992), the offeror approached employees of the incumbent contractor, who was competing for a follow-on services contract, to obtain detailed information on how the incumbent contractor was performing the work and to discover the contents of the incumbent's proposal for the follow-on work. Upon learning of this conduct, the contracting officer disqualified the offeror, and GAO sustained this action, *Compliance Corp.*, Comp. Gen. Dec. B-239252, 90-2

CPD ¶126, *recons. denied*, B-239252.3, 90-2 CPD ¶435. The Claims Court agreed with this decision, stating at 204:

> The court finds actual or attempted "industrial espionage" to be outside the realm of normal business practices, and the contracting officer is entitled to disqualify those who engage in such conduct, not only to protect the integrity of the contracting process, but also to deter others from similar conduct.

Similarly, in *Kellogg Brown & Root Servs., Inc.*, Comp. Gen. Dec. B-400787.2, 2009 CPD ¶54, GAO agreed that it was proper to disqualify a contractor from competing for task orders where it had been inadvertently sent information as to its competitors pricing strategy and had refused to isolate recipients of the information from performance of the task orders, and in *Computer Tech. Assocs., Inc.*, Comp. Gen. Dec. B-288622, 2001 CPD ¶187, GAO agreed that a competitor should be disqualified when it obtained and read e-mail transcripts of its competitors' oral presentations. The latter decision cites the Procurement Integrity Act provisions barring such conduct. See also *Huynh Serv. Co.*, Comp. Gen. Dec. B-242297.2, 91-1 CPD ¶562, where GAO concurred with an agency decision to terminate a contract for the convenience of the government after it learned that the low bidder might have obtained a competitor's pricing information before it submitted its bid, and *Litton Sys., Inc.*, 68 Comp. Gen. 422 (B-234060), 89-1 CPD ¶450, *recons. denied*, 68 Comp. Gen. 677 (B-234060.2), 89-2 CPD ¶228, where GAO disqualified an offeror that had obtained source selection information through a marketing consultant. Generally, however, GAO will not rule on protests that one competitor acted improperly with regard to another competitor—stating that this is a private dispute to be resolved in the courts, *Advanced Communications Sys., Inc.*, Comp. Gen. Dec. B-271040, 96-1 CPD ¶274 (allegation that competitor improperly obtained protester's proposal strategy and pricing information by hiring its employee); *Bildon, Inc.*, Comp. Gen. Dec. B-241375, 90-2 CPD ¶332 (allegation that company improperly obtained competitor's information by hiring employee who prepared proposal); *Garrett Corp.*, Comp. Gen. Dec. B-182991, 76-1 CPD ¶20 (allegation that competitor had obtained proprietary drawings by improper means); *York Indus., Inc.*, Comp. Gen. Dec. B-186958, 76-2 CPD ¶453 (allegation that competitor had used proprietary drawings in violation of license agreement).

A more appropriate course of action for a company that believes a competitor has improperly obtained its proprietary information may be to sue that company directly. See *GEO Grp. v. United States*, 100 Fed. Cl. 223 (2011), advising that it is only appropriate to sue the government when the data has been obtained while working on a government contract. The same result was reached in *GEO Grp., Inc.*, Comp. Gen. Dec. B-305012, 2011 CPD ¶153 (2011). GAO subsequently reaffirmed its position that it will only consider protest allegations involving a competitors misappropriation of proprietary information where the protest alleges wrongdoing on the part of the government, *IBM Corp.*, Comp. Gen. Dec. B-415798.2, 2019 CPD ¶ 82.

[4] Exchanging Information with Competitors

Offerors in fixed-price contracts are required by FAR 3.103-1 to certify that prices were arrived at independently without collusion between prospective contractors. This provision is implemented by the Certificate of Independent Price Determination solicitation provision in FAR 52.203-2. The contracting officer is directed to reject an offer if the certificate is altered, FAR 3.103-2(b).

Sanctions have been imposed on firms that entered into agreements on prices to be bid, *United States v. Portsmouth Paving Corp.*, 694 F.2d 312 (4th Cir. 1982) (criminal sanctions for bid rigging), as well as an agreement not to bid on a procurement, *Leitman v. McAusland*, 934 F.2d 46 (4th Cir. 1991) (debarment for collusive bidding). Collusive bidding will not be found unless there is proof of concerted action between two or more parties. In *Federal Trade Comm'n v. Lukens Steel Co.*, 454 F. Supp. 1182 (D.D.C. 1978), the court found no concerted action between Lukens and United States Steel Company in the pricing of steel plates for Navy ships when the two companies followed each other's published prices or prices obtained from the shipbuilder. The court stated at 1193 that: "The actions of each defendant appear to be based upon independent judgment, a consideration of the defendant's own business interest, and an assessment of the competition."

GAO usually will not rule on protests requesting that competing offerors be disqualified because of collusive bidding, *Shel-Ken Props., Inc.*, Comp. Gen. Dec. B-261443, 95-2 CPD ¶ 139 (1995); *Seyforth Roofing Co.*, Comp. Gen. Dec. B-241719.2, 91-1 CPD ¶ 268 (1991); *Automated Datatron, Inc.*, Comp. Gen. Dec. B-184022, 75-2 CPD ¶ 153. However, in denying such protests GAO has frequently stated that the alleged conduct was not improper. Thus, it has stated that it is not a violation of the independent pricing certificate for competitors to propose to use the same subcontractor, *McCombs Fleet Servs.*, Comp. Gen. Dec. B-278330, 98-1 CPD ¶ 24 (1998); for competitors to use a common subcontractor, *Ross Aviation, Inc.*, Comp. Gen. Dec. B-236952, 90-1 CPD ¶ 83 (1990); for affiliated firms to submit separate bids prepared by the same person, 51 Comp. Gen. 403 (B-174449), 1972 CPD ¶ 2 (1972); for a firm to bid as a joint venturer and also submit bids to competitors to perform work as a subcontractor, *Southern Maryland Gen. Contractors, Inc.*, 57 Comp. Gen. 277 (B-190270), 78-1 CPD ¶ 121 (1978); for partners sharing the same business address to submit separate bids, *Ace Reforestation, Inc.*, 65 Comp. Gen. 151 (B-220276), 85-2 CPD ¶ 704 (1985); or for a firm to mail letters to several potential competitors warning of possible legal action if they infringed patents, Comp. Gen. Dec. B-167152, 1969 WL 3728 (Aug. 14, 1969).

An agreement to fix prices in a government contract may also be illegal under the Sherman Act, 15 U.S.C. §§ 17. Agencies are required to report bids and proposals to the Attorney General if there is substantial evidence of a violation of antitrust laws, 10 U.S.C. § 3307 (formerly § 2305(b)(5)) and 41 U.S.C. § 3707. See FAR 3.303.

In many circumstances, however, information may legally be exchanged with competitors. Generally, if the prospective offeror legally obtains information directly from a competitor without any restriction on the ability to use that information, it is appropriate and legal to use that information in preparing proposals.

[F] Conspiracy

It is a crime for two or more persons to agree to (1) commit any offense against the United States, 18 U.S.C. § 371, or (2) defraud the United States, 18 U.S.C. § 286, if any of the persons perform an act to effect the conspiracy. The unlawful object of a conspiracy could be the violation of any civil or criminal statute, *United States v. Feola*, 420 U.S. 671 (1975). A conspiracy to commit bribery is clearly included, and conspiracies involving gratuities or conflicts of interest also fall within 18 U.S.C. § 371, *United States v. Razete*, 199 F.2d 44 (6th Cir.), *cert. denied*, 344 U.S. 904 (1952). However, it is not necessary for the agreed-upon action to be a violation of statute. An agreement to defraud the United States in any manner would qualify. It is not necessary that the government lose money or property as a result of the fraud. All that is required is that "[the government's] legitimate official action and purpose shall be defeated by misrepresentation, chicane or . . . overreaching," *Hammerschmidt v. United States*, 265 U.S. 182 (1924).

An agreement to give preferential treatment to an offeror for a government contract is prohibited, Executive Order 12674, § 101(h) as modified by Executive Order 12731; 5 C.F.R. § 2635.101(b)(8). In proving the existence of such an agreement, the government is not required to establish a formal express agreement but can show a tacit understanding between the parties, *United States v. Paramount Pictures, Inc.*, 334 U.S. 131 (1948). This understanding can be proved by circumstantial evidence, *Hamling v. United States*, 418 U.S. 87 (1974); *Glasser v. United States*, 315 U.S. 60 (1942).

CHAPTER 2

CONTRACT FORMATION PRINCIPLES

§ 2.01 INTRODUCTION

Although the federal government's purchasing procedures are governed extensively by statutes and regulations, the creation or modification of a contractual relationship between the government and the contractor is, for the most part, determined by common-law legal rules. See *Winstar v. United States,* 518 U.S. 839, 895 (1996) ("When the United States enters into contract relations, its rights and duties therein are governed generally by the law applicable to contracts between private individuals." (quoting *Lynch v. United States*, 292 U.S. 571 (1934))); *Priebe & Sons, Inc. v. United States*, 332 U.S. 407 (1947). As these rules have been applied to government contract cases, a body of federal law has developed as the primary source of law in this area. This federal law is generally consistent with the legal rules summarized in the *Restatement, Second, Contracts.* See, for, example, *Long Island Sav. Bank, FSB v. United States,* 503 F.3d 1234, 1245 (Fed. Cir. 2007). The *Uniform Commercial Code* (U.C.C.), although not binding upon the federal government, is also used to determine the rights and liabilities of the contracting parties when not inconsistent with federal law.

While as a general proposition the common law doctrines that apply to government contracts are similar to the state law that applies to contracts among private parties, the Supreme Court has also made clear that the government is not the same as a private contracting entity: "It is too late in the day to urge that the [g]overnment is just another private litigant, for purposes of charging it with liability, whenever it takes over a business theretofore conducted by private enterprise or engages in competition with private ventures." *Fed. Crop Ins. Corp. v. Merrill*, 332 U.S. 380 (1947). As the Claims Court explained in *Seaboard Lumber, Inc. v. United States*, this federal common law of contracts has developed primarily through decisions of the Federal Circuit, the Court of Federal Claims (and its predecessors), and the boards of contract appeals:

> It is undisputed that the law to be applied in cases related to federal contracts is federal and not state law. The federal law applied in breach of contract claims is not, however, created by statute but rather for the most part has been developed by the Court of Appeals for the Federal Circuit and the Court of Claims, with the Claims Court, or the Boards of Contract Appeals applying the law in the first instance. This federal contract law also reflects the various contract clauses developed over time for the benefit of both the sovereign and the contractor through the practice of agencies and the bargaining leverage of contractors. It has drawn as well upon traditional private contract law for analogies and concepts. However, it is a separate and distinct body of law.

15 Cl. Ct. 366 (1988), *aff'd* 903 F.2d 1560 (Fed. Cir. 1990).

As under the state law applicable to contracts among private parties, under the federal common law of contracts, enforceable promises are the essential requirements for a contract. See *Restatement, Second, Contracts* § 1, which defines "contract" as—

> a promise or a set of promises for the breach of which the law gives a remedy, or the performance of which the law in some way recognizes as a duty.

This chapter focuses on the legal principles used by the courts (primarily the U.S. Court of Appeals for the Federal Circuit and the U.S. Court of Federal Claims), the Government Accountability Office (GAO), and the boards of contract appeals to determine whether the government has entered into a relationship involving one or more enforceable promises. It first considers whether the parties have entered into a contractual relationship—whether they have manifested mutual assent. It then deals with whether their agreement is binding. Where applicable, the chapter includes a discussion of contract formation issues involving electronic transactions.

§ 2.02 MANIFESTATION OF MUTUAL ASSENT

In order to create a contractual relationship, the parties must each assent to the same terms and conditions, *American Bankers Ass'n v. United States*, 932 F.3d 1375 (Fed. Cir. 2019) ("there are four requirements to form a contract binding upon the government: (1) mutuality of intent to contract; (2) lack of ambiguity in offer and acceptance; (3) consideration; and (4) a government representative having actual authority to bind the United States in contract."). This mutual assent occurs when one party manifests an intent to be bound to a set of terms and conditions and the other party timely agrees to that relationship. Most often this process can be analyzed in terms of an offer and an acceptance. *See id.* ("To satisfy its burden to prove such a mutuality of intent, a plaintiff must show, by objective evidence, the existence of an offer and a reciprocal acceptance.") The party making the offer, referred to as the "offeror," communicates to the other party an intention to form a contract. To accept the offer forming a contract, the other party must assent in the manner invited or authorized. The manifestation of mutual assent may also occur absent an identifiable offer or acceptance. These concepts are stated in *Restatement, Second, Contracts* § 22, which provides:

> (1) The manifestation of mutual assent to an exchange ordinarily takes the form of an offer or proposal by one party followed by an acceptance by the other party or parties.
>
> (2) A manifestation of mutual assent may be made even though neither offer nor acceptance can be identified and even though the moment of formation cannot be determined.

See also U.C.C. § 2-204; *Silver State Land LLC v. United States*, 148 Fed. Cl. 217 (2020) (analyzing offer and acceptance); *Northeast Sav. v. United States*, 63 Fed. Cl. 507 (2005) (same).

This section first covers basic requirements, specifically capacity to contract and contractual intent and definiteness. It then analyzes the rules of offer and acceptance as they have been applied to the various types of contractual relationships entered into by the federal government. The section concludes with a discussion of the circumstances where the actions of the parties create an implied-in-fact contract.

[A] Basic Requirements

There are a number of basic requirements which must be satisfied in order for parties' communications to result in contractual obligations. Both parties must possess the legal capacity to contract, they must have contractual intent, and their agreement must be sufficiently definite to permit enforcement by a court or board of contract appeals.

[1] Capacity to Contract

Capacity to contract refers to the common law principle which provides that a person cannot be bound unless that person "has capacity to incur at least avoidable contractual duties," *Restatement, Second, Contracts* § 12. This rule is applicable to government contracts although its application is not common. There are also a number of special government contracts rules which deal with the same or analogous issues. For example, questions concerning the legal capacity of government agencies to contract are dealt with in Chapter 1, Section II under the topic "contracting powers." Similarly, those seeking to deal with the government are subject to rules concerning eligibility, suspension and debarment. See Chapter 4, Section II. In some cases, the term "capacity to contract" has been used, mistakenly, to refer to the question of whether a specific officer, employee or agent has the authority to bind an offeror. *See Video Eng'g Co.*, DOTCAB 72-5, 72-1 BCA ¶ 9432. Questions concerning such authority are dealt with in Chapter 1, Section III.

[a] Nature of Capacity to Contract

Determination of a party's capacity to contract depends on whether the party is a natural person, a partnership, a joint venture, or a corporation. For natural persons, *Restatement, Second, Contracts* § 12 states:

> A natural person who manifests assent to a transaction has the full legal capacity to incur contractual duties thereby unless he or she is:
>
> (a) under guardianship, or
> (b) an infant, or
> (c) mentally ill or defective, or
> (d) intoxicated.

However, this does not mean that such parties cannot enter into contracts. If a contracting party has no knowledge, or reason to know, that the other party is mentally ill or intoxicated, the lack of capacity will not prevent the formation of a contract. Further, a contract will be found if the party fails to disaffirm the transaction within a reasonable time after recovering from the mental illness or intoxication. With respect to infancy, the other party's notice or reason to know of the infancy is not required in order to permit the infant from rescinding the agreement. However, the failure to do so within a reasonable time after reaching the age of majority will permit the other party to enforce the contract, *Lonchyna v. Brown*, 491 F. Supp. 1352 (N.D. Ill. 1980) (armed services enlistment contract). These types of agreements are commonly referred to as "voidable."

Corporations are artificial persons and their contracting capacity is determined by their charters or articles of incorporation. Agreements which are not within the authority of such documents are called "ultra vires" and are considered to be *void ab initio*, meaning that a contract never came into being, *Rose Island Co. v. United States*, 105 Ct. Cl. 192 (1945). There, the court permitted the government to cancel an agreement for the purchase of stone on the grounds that the corporation it dealt with had no legal capacity to contract. The court found that the corporation's charter authorized it to conduct a public entertainment and amusement park but not to sell stone from a quarry which it owned. The laws of the state of incorporation will determine whether a corporation has the capacity to contract, Court of Federal Claims Rule 17(b); *Keeter Trading Co. v. United States*, 79 Fed. Cl. 243 (2007); *BLH, Inc. v. United States*, 2 Cl. Ct. 463 (1983); *Mather Constr. Co. v. United States*, 475 F.2d 1152 (Ct. Cl. 1973). Thus, if questions arise concerning capacity to contract, a certificate from the proper agency of the state of incorporation will be used to determine capacity, *Valley Constr. Co.*, Comp. Gen. Dec. B-184391, 75-2 CPD ¶ 393.

Most of the cases challenging corporate capacity involve situations where a corporation's charter has been suspended for failure to pay taxes or failure to file reports. State corporation laws contain elaborate provisions governing the conduct of a corporation whose charter has been suspended for such reasons. See *Easterbrook/Ramco*, ASBCA 42176, 94-2 BCA ¶ 26,658, where the board dismissed an appeal without prejudice because the company had entered into the contract during a period when its charter had been suspended but the applicable California law appeared to permit the company to sue for restitution of any benefits it had conferred on the party to the contract. Compare *Micro Tool Eng'g, Inc.*, ASBCA 31136, 86-1 BCA ¶ 18,680, where the board dismissed an appeal with prejudice because the company had entered into a contract at a time when it had been "involuntarily dissolved" for failure to file annual reports and the time for reinstatement under Florida law had expired. The same result was reached in *West Point Research, Inc.*, ASBCA 27185, 83-2 BCA ¶ 16,845 (applying Connecticut law); and *Services, Inc.*, ASBCA 42929, 93-1 BCA ¶ 25,514 (applying South Carolina law).

Loss of corporate capacity may also preclude a contractor from bringing a suit or appeal concerning a contract that was entered into when the company had capacity. In *USAC Aerospace Group, Inc.*, ASBCA No. 59114, 17-1 BCA ¶ 36,737, the board granted the government's motion to dismiss where the appellant failed to furnish credible evidence that the company was represented by a qualified corporate representative. See also *Computer Prods. Int'l, Inc. v. United States*, 26 Cl. Ct. 518 (1992), where a suit was dismissed because it was filed during a period when the company's charter had been suspended by the state of California and the Contract Disputes Act statute of limitations had run during the period of suspension. Compare *TPS, Inc.*, ASBCA 52421, 01-1 BCA ¶ 31,375 (board rejected motion to dismiss because according to Florida law, the facts giving rise to the claim occurred before dissolution and therefore was part of winding up the affairs of the corporation); *Ricmar Eng'g, Inc.*, ASBCA 44260, 97-2 BCA ¶ 29,084 (board rejected motion to dismiss because the company had been reinstated by the state of California and the board construed state law to require no prejudicial action to companies that had filed suits during suspension); *Teller Envtl. Sys., Inc.*, ASBCA 42092, 93-1 BCA ¶ 25,330 (board rejected motion to dismiss because the appeal had been filed within three years of dissolution, as permitted by Massachusetts law); *Allied Production Mgmt., Inc.*, DOTCAB 2466, 92-1 BCA ¶ 24,585 (board rejected motion to dismiss because California law permitted suits during suspension if company subsequently reinstated).

Questions concerning the contracting capacity of a partnership or a joint venture are determined by reference to the partnership or joint venture agreement. See GSAR 552.270-3(b) providing that for leases of real property, "a copy of either the partnership agreement or current Certificate of Limited Partnership" shall be furnished if required by the government. FAR 4.102(d) provides as follows with respect to joint ventures:

> A contract with joint venturers may involve any combination of individuals, partnerships, or corporations. The contract shall be signed by each participant in the joint venture in the manner prescribed in paragraphs (a) through (c) of this section for each type of participant. When a corporation is participating, the contracting officer shall verify that the corporation is authorized to participate in the joint venture.

As long as an organization possesses the capacity to contract, it is not necessary to spell out that capacity in the contract, *Pacific Far East Line, Inc.*, ASBCA 7629, 1963 BCA ¶ 3835.

[b] Time for Determining Capacity to Contract

A number of cases have involved the question of whether a corporation's capacity to contract is to be determined at time of bidding or time of award. In

West Point Research, Inc., ASBCA 27185, 83-2 BCA ¶ 16,845, no valid contract was found where the company had capacity at the time of bid opening but had lost capacity, through revocation of its corporate charter, at the time of award. See also *P.I.O. GmbH Bau und Ingenieurplanung*, GSBCA 15934-IBB, 04-1 BCA ¶ 32,592 (board, in general, will follow laws under which a legal entity was organized to determine what powers may have survived its dissolution); *Rosinka Joint Venture*, ASBCA 48143, 97-1 BCA ¶ 28,653 (same). Conversely, in *Casper Constr. Co.*, Comp. Gen. Dec. B-253887, 93-2 CPD ¶ 247, a corporation had been dissolved at the time of bid opening. It later became reinstated and under the laws of the state of incorporation, the reinstatement was made retroactive to the time of dissolution. Nevertheless, GAO held that the bid could not be accepted, reasoning:

> As a general rule, a sealed bid award may not be made to any entity different from that which submitted the bid, and where a bid represents that it was submitted by a corporation, it should be disregarded if no such corporation exists. *General Chem. Servs. Inc.*, B-241595, Jan. 30, 1991, 91-1 CPD ¶ 94. Otherwise, irresponsible parties could undermine sound competitive bidding procedures by submitting bids that could be avoided or backed up by real principals as their interests might dictate. *Id.* We believe Casper's bid was properly rejected. At the time of bid opening, on June 7, the corporation had been dissolved under the laws of Oregon since January 20, and was not reinstated until after award on June 15. Consequently, at the time of bid opening Casper was not a legally sufficient corporation for bidding purposes.

GAO reached the opposite result in a line of cases holding that bids may be accepted even though submitted in a corporate name prior to the date of incorporation. See *PHE/Master, Inc.*, 70 Comp. Gen. 689 (B-238367.5), 91-2 CPD ¶ 210, stating at 695:

> As PHE/Master pointed out to the Air Force in its letter dated May 22, 1990, there is ample legal authority permitting an entity, formed for the purpose of performing a particular government contract, to submit a proposal in the name of the corporation prior to formally incorporating. *See Telex Commc'ns, Inc., Mil-Tech Sys., Inc.*, B-212385; B-212385.2, [84-1 CPD ¶ 127, *recons. denied*, 84-1 CPD ¶ 440]; *see also Protectors, Inc.*, B-194446, Aug. 17, 1979, 79-2 CPD ¶ 128; *Oscar Holmes & Son, Inc.*; *Blue Ribbon Refuse Removal Inc.*, B-184099, Oct. 24, 1975, 75-2 CPD ¶ 251. At a minimum, these cases provided PHE/Master with a good faith basis for submitting its initial proposal under the corporate name. Accordingly, we find no reasonable basis for the Air Force to conclude that PHE/Master engaged in misrepresentation by submitting its proposal in the name of the corporation that was formally incorporated after proposal submission.

It is difficult to understand this distinction. It would seem that the offeror, by not going forward with the incorporation, would have the same ability to avoid any obligation as would the bidder in Casper. The bridge between the two lines of cases may lie in *Telex Commc'ns, Inc.*, Comp. Gen. Dec. B-212385, 84-1 CPD ¶ 127, *recons. denied*, 84-1 CPD ¶ 440, which held that, because the previously unincorporated bidder was bound under state law to fulfill its contractual obligations if the bid was accepted, protecting the government from the risk of nonperformance, the bid was properly considered by the government (citing *Protectors, Inc.*, Comp. Gen. Dec. B-194446, 79-2 CPD ¶ 128).

In *Tours, Lodging & Conferences, Inc.*, Comp. Gen. Dec. B-270478, 96-1 CPD ¶ 144, GAO held that an award to a joint venture was proper even though one of the venturers was a corporation which had been dissolved at time of submission of the offer but had been reinstated prior to award. The fact that the other joint venturer possessed the capacity to contract would appear to justify this result; because, again, the government was protected from the risk of nonperformance.

GAO has also dealt with the situation where an award was made to an offeror, which at the time of proposal submission and the time of award, had its corporate status automatically terminated for "an apparently inadvertent failure to pay an annual registration fee," *Triad Research, Inc.*, Comp. Gen. Dec. B-225793, 87-2 CPD ¶ 16. GAO held that the award was proper since the award was made to the "same entity" which submitted the offer. See also *Forbes Aviation, Inc.*, Comp. Gen. Dec. B-248056, 92-2 CPD ¶ 58. In these cases, GAO relied on state statutes which provided "that the corporation is responsible for any liabilities incurred during the period of termination, including 'contracts, acts, matters and things made, done or performed in its name and on its behalf by its officers and agents prior to its reinstatement, as if its articles of incorporation had remained at all times in full force and effect.'"

[2] Contractual Intent and Definiteness

In order for a contract to be formed, the parties must possess contractual intent and their agreement must be sufficiently definite to be enforced, *Modern Sys. Tech. Corp. v. United States*, 24 Cl. Ct. 360 (1991), *aff'd*, 979 F.2d 200 (Fed. Cir. 1992); see also *Total Med. Mgmt., Inc. v. United States*, 104 F.3d 1314 (Fed. Cir. 1997) (rejecting government argument that agreement was insufficiently definite). While the absence of definite terms may be evidence that the parties do not intend to enter into a contractual relationship, their existence does not necessarily require a finding that the parties had contractual intent.

[a] Contractual Intent

Whether the parties have indicated an intent to enter into a contractual relationship will be determined on a case-by-case basis, taking into consideration all the facts and circumstances surrounding the transaction. See *Texas Instruments*

Inc., v. United States, 922 F.2d 810 (Fed. Cir. 1991) ("Whether a legally enforceable contract has been formed by a meeting of the minds depends upon the totality of the factual circumstances."); *Mayfair Constr. Co.*, NASABCA 478-6, 80-2 BCA ¶ 14,772 ("entire context" of government granting of contractor's request for deviation was contractual).

[i] Preliminary Negotiations

One of the problems in determining contractual intent is whether the communications between the parties are merely preliminary negotiations contemplating future contractual agreements or whether they indicate an intent to presently enter into a contract.

Occasionally, the government announces publicly its desire to receive proposals for specified programs, services, or commodities. They may be included in statutes, regulations, circulars, or other media. Normally, these announcements are treated as preliminary inquiries or requests for offers, *Primary Metal & Mineral Corp. v. United States*, 556 F.2d 507 (Ct. Cl. 1977) (Department of Treasury regulation stating that all "requests" for silver bullion in exchange for silver certificates be directed to the fiscal assistant secretary held not to be an offer). If the statement merely reflects a future intent or a desire to begin negotiations, it will not be considered an offer. Such statements are invitations to begin negotiations or to submit offers and cannot be accepted to form a contract for goods and services. See *Elkhorn-Hazard Coal Co. v. Kentucky River Corp.*, 20 F.2d 67 (6th Cir. 1927).

However, they may constitute offers if they are sufficiently definite. In *Radium Mines, Inc. v. United States*, 153 F. Supp. 403 (Ct. Cl. 1957), the Atomic Energy Commission issued a circular expressing the Commission's desire to stimulate domestic production of uranium ore. The circular contained information as to the minimum price to be paid for ore, the time period in which the commission would purchase ore, grade specifications, and application instructions. The court held that the circular constituted an offer since it was sufficient to induce performance. Similarly, in *Griffin v. United States*, 215 Ct. Cl. 710 (1978), the service secretary published procedures and guidelines requesting meritorious suggestions relating to Minuteman Missile silos. Since the service secretary adopted suggestions that benefited the service, the court held that a valid contract was created. But see *Hayes v. United States*, 20 Cl. Ct. 150 (1990), which held that although a suggestion of a former Postal Service employee was implemented as part of the Employee Suggestion Program, a contractual relationship was not formed between the former employee and the government. The court found that the statutory and procedural requirements necessary to elevate such an agreement to the level of a contract had not been met. Similarly, in *Baker v. United States*, 50 Fed. Cl. 483, 495 (2001), the court noted that "[s]o long as it is reasonably apparent that some further act of the offeror is necessary, the offeree has no power to create contractual relations by an act of his own, and there is as yet no operative offer." Compare

Cutler-Hammer, Inc. v. United States, 441 F.2d 1179 (Ct. Cl. 1971), where a Treasury Department regulation regarding the sale of silver at a specific price was held not to be an offer because it was interpreted not to contain a promise by the government.

[ii] Non-Contractual Agreements

The government enters into several different types of agreements which it specifically indicates are not contracts. FAR 16.702 describes "basic agreements," which are instruments of "understanding" between agencies and contractors on contract clauses that will be used in future contracts between the parties. FAR 16.702(a) states that "[a] basic agreement is not a contract." "Basic ordering agreements," described in FAR 16.703, contain not only contract clauses, but a description of supplies or services to be provided and methods for "pricing, issuing, and delivering future orders" under the agreement. However, FAR 16.703(a) states that "[a] basic ordering agreement is not a contract." In addition, FAR 16.703(c) states:

> *Limitations*. A basic ordering agreement shall not state or imply any agreement by the Government to place future contracts or orders with the contractor or be used in any manner to restrict competition.

"Blanket purchase agreements," described in FAR 13.303, are agreements that agencies establish with contractors for placing repetitive orders in the future within the simplified acquisition threshold. FAR 13.303-3(a)(2) requires that such agreements contain a statement that the government "is obligated only to the extent of authorized purchases actually made." See *Production Packaging*, ASBCA 53662, 03-2 BCA ¶ 32,338, holding that the holder of the BPA had "no legal expectation to receive exclusive orders."

FAR 8.405-3 allows the use of blanket purchase agreements with General Services Administration (GSA) Federal Supply Schedules contracts, and purchases under BPAs entered into in conjunction with these GSA multiple award schedule contracts are not subject to the same dollar limitations that curb purchases under simplified acquisition BPAs in accordance with FAR 13.303-5(b)(1). While the FAR is silent on the contractual nature of these BPAs, it seems clear that they are not contracts but merely vehicles to allow agencies to place future orders. For a critique of these agreements see *Agencies Are Not Maximizing Opportunities for Competition or Savings Under Blanket Purchase Agreements Despite Significant Increase in Usage*, GAO-09-792, Sept. 9, 2009.

The line between "basic" agreements and enforceable contracts continues to shift, as the federal acquisition system evolves. *Modern Sys. Tech. Corp. v. United States*, 24 Cl. Ct. 360 (1991), *aff'd*, 979 F.2d 200 (Fed. Cir. 1992), dealt with a basic pricing agreement used by the Postal Service. The court concluded that the "plain language" of the agreement "appears to be contemplative of future contracts." It found "no language indicating any present intent that either party be bound," and concluded that the agreement was more like a basic ordering agreement.

The Federal Circuit held in *Crewzers Fire Crew Transport, Inc. v. United States*, 741 F.3d 1380 (Fed. Cir. 2014), that the BPA at issue in that case was not an enforceable contract. In doing so, the Federal Circuit analogized to the basic pricing agreements found unenforceable in *Modern Systems* and distinguished a schedule contract found enforceable in *Ace-Federal Reporters, Inc. v. Barram*, 226 F.3d 1329 (Fed. Cir. 2000), which included sufficient assurance of future government orders under specific terms to be deemed enforceable. The court's rationale in *Crewzers* is useful to distinguish which types of "basic" and "blanket" agreements may qualify as enforceable given their particular terms and conditions. It stated at 1383-84:

> In *Modern Systems,* this Court affirmed "on the basis" of the trial court's opinion, which concluded that the basic pricing agreement was not a binding contract because "the Postal Service is not obligated to place any orders, and . . . the contractor is not bound unless it accepts an order. The effect of this . . . is that the [basic pricing agreement] itself does not create any enforceable obligations between either party." *Modern Sys.*, 979 F.2d at 202. . . . [We] find persuasive, and particularly applicable here, the reasoning in *Modern Systems* given the structure of the agreements in question, which do not require the Government to order *any* work from the contractor even if the need for such work arises, and also do not require the contractor to accept the work if ordered.
>
> Crewzers argues that our decision in *Ace–Federal Reporters* mandates a finding that its BPAs are, in fact, binding contracts. We disagree. *Ace–Federal Reporters* concerned a multiple award schedule contract for transcription and court reporting services. Under this contract, "as consideration for the contractors' promises regarding price, availability, delivery, and quantity, the government promised that it would purchase only from the contractors on the schedule, with few exceptions" that allowed agencies to deviate from the schedule only by obtaining a waiver from the General Services Administration pursuant to 48 C.F.R. § 8.404–3 (1999). We held that the Government's promise provided sufficient consideration because of the "substantial business value" in limiting the competition pool to "between two and five authorized sources in each of the designated geographic regions," instead of the "18,000 other transcription services" available. *Id.* at 1332.
>
> In contrast, there is no language in the BPAs at issue here that requires the Forest Service to purchase resources only from the contractors on the BPAs' dispatch priority lists, much less to purchase under specific terms, *i.e.*, value and quantity. The BPAs explicitly provided that "the number of fire orders in process and actual fire conditions at the time of dispatch may require a deviation from normal procedures in order to respond effectively to such conditions." Furthermore, "[a]ny such deviation will be within the discretion of [the] Government, and *will not be deemed a violation of any term or condition of this Agreement.*" This nearly unfettered discretion to vary from normal procedures is much different from the defined, limited exceptions available to the Government in *Ace–Federal Reporters*.
>
> Nor is there any language that requires Crewzers to ensure the availability of the requested resources. Under the terms of the BPAs, Crewzers is

> required to respond to an order only if "willing and able[.]" The BPAs also do not impose any penalties on Crewzers for failing to maintain the availability of its resources. As provided in the BPAs, "If a Contractor cannot be reached or is not able to meet the time and date needed, the dispatcher may proceed with contacting the next resource on the dispatch priority list." Unlike the schedule contract in *Ace–Federal Reporters,* Crewzers's BPAs do not impose any binding obligations on the parties and cannot be used to invoke Tucker Act jurisdiction. We therefore affirm the decision of the Court of Federal Claims dismissing Crewzers's suits for lack of jurisdiction. (internal citations omitted)

See also *McLeod Group, LLC v. United States*, 142 Fed. Cl. 558 (2019), *aff'd* 2020 WL 7393229 (Fed. Cir. Dec. 17, 2020).

[b] Definiteness

The parties' agreement must be sufficiently complete and certain in its terms so that the promises and performances to be rendered can be reasonably determined. However, this does not mean that there be complete agreement on all terms. See *Penn-Ohio Steel Corp. v. United States*, 354 F.2d 254 (Ct. Cl. 1965), where the court found a contract because there had been agreement on "major matters in issue." Similarly, in *Town of North Bonneville, Wash. v. United States*, 5 Cl. Ct. 312 (1984), the court found a binding agreement in spite of the need for future agreements because the parties had indicated a present intent to be bound.

Restatement, Second, Contracts § 33 recognizes that:

> (1) Even though a manifestation of intention is intended to be understood as an offer, it cannot be accepted so as to form a contract unless the terms of the contract are reasonably certain.
>
> (2) The terms of a contract are reasonably certain if they provide a basis for determining the existence of a breach and for giving an appropriate remedy.
>
> (3) The fact that one or more terms of a proposed bargain are left open or uncertain may show that a manifestation of intention is not intended to be understood as an offer or as an acceptance.

See *Western States Constr. Co.*, ASBCA 16003, 72-2 BCA ¶ 9508 (contract found to exist even though price of contract was never agreed upon).

[i] Agreements to Agree

When the parties have agreed to negotiate some of the terms of the contract in the future, the lack of definiteness may not preclude the existence of a binding contract. Such arrangements are called "agreements to agree" and have been found binding if they are sufficiently definite to permit their enforcement. See

Folk Constr. Co., ENGBCA 5839, 93-3 BCA ¶ 26,094, finding that the parties mutually agreed to rescind the contract. The government argued that the condition that the unit prices would be determined through future negotiations made the bargain unenforceable. The board rejected this defense, stating at 129,726:

> Agreements in which certain terms are reserved for future negotiation ("agreements to agree"), while not favored traditionally, have been gaining approval where the criteria for resolution of the terms to be negotiated are sufficiently definite. The reservation of some terms for future agreement does not necessarily preclude a finding that a binding agreement has been made. However, this arrangement impliedly places an obligation on the parties to negotiate in good faith in an effort to resolve the outstanding issues. Courts then will evaluate the *bona fides* of the parties toward negotiation in order to ascertain when a breach has occurred if the remaining issues are not resolved.

The degree of definiteness necessary to form a binding contract has been decided on a case-by-case basis. In *Modern Sys. Tech. Corp. v. United States*, 24 Cl. Ct. 360 (1991), *aff'd*, 979 F.2d 200 (Fed. Cir. 1992), the court stated that, to be binding, a contract generally must be "sufficiently definite to permit determination of breach and remedies." In *Trauma Serv. Group, Ltd. v. United States*, 33 Fed. Cl. 426 (1995), *aff'd*, 104 F.3d 1321 (Fed. Cir. 1997), the court held that the CHAMPUS Memoranda of Understanding (MOU) at issue was unenforceable because it did not contain any indication of how to compute the salary of a person that was required to be furnished by the contractor. In contrast, in *Total Med. Mgmt., Inc. v. United States*, 104 F.3d 1314 (Fed. Cir. 1997), the court held that, in general, CHAMPUS MOUs were enforceable agreements because they called for the contractor to provide discounted medical services while the hospital was to provide free space and support staff and encourage military dependents to use the services, including payment details for most services. The court held that the determination of damages or specific performance would flow naturally from a breach of these duties. See also *Gardiner, Kamya & Assocs. v. United States*, 369 F.3d 1318 (Fed. Cir. 2004), holding that an agreement to negotiate the terms of a contract extension was sufficiently definite to form a binding contract.

Once an agreement to agree is found sufficiently definite, the question arises as to the extent of the duty concerning the undefined terms. The Federal Circuit has confirmed that "a provision which calls upon the parties to a contract to agree in the future on a specified point or contract term, often referred to as an 'agreement to agree,' imposes an obligation on the parties to negotiate in good faith." In *North Star Steel Co. v. United States*, 477 F.3d 1324 (Fed. Cir. 2007), the court held that failure to reveal information necessary to proceed with the contemplated negotiations would be a lack of good faith. See also *City of Tacoma v. United States*, 31 F.3d 1130 (Fed. Cir. 1994) (city had to agree to "reasonable" rates when they were subject to negotiation); *Aviation Contractor Employees, Inc. v. United States*, 945 F.2d 1568 (Fed. Cir. 1991) (refusal to negotiate would be lack of good faith); and *Calif. Human Dev. Corp. v. United States*,

87 Fed. Cl. 282 (2009) (plaintiff failed to establish bad faith negotiation); *Tennessee Valley Auth. v. United States*, 60 Fed. Cl. 665 (2004) (refusing to negotiate breached duty of good faith and fair dealing).

[ii] Letter Contracts

Federal procurement law recognizes a distinct class of agreements known as "letter contracts." A letter contract is a "written preliminary contractual instrument that authorizes the contractor to begin immediately manufacturing supplies or performing services," FAR 16.603-1. 10 U.S.C. §§ 3371-3377 (formerly § 2326) calls such contracts "undefinitized contractual actions" and restricts their use in various ways. See also FAR 16.603-2 permitting their use only when "(1) the Government's interests demand that the contractor be given a binding commitment so that work can start immediately and (2) negotiating a definitive contract is not possible in sufficient time to meet the requirement." See DFARS Subpart 217.74 for detailed guidance on the use of such contracts. A letter contract is typically followed by a more detailed agreement "definitizing" the parties' earlier agreement. See FAR 16.603-4 (required clauses).

The terms of a letter contract have been found sufficiently definite to bind the parties even though the parties failed to definitize the contract. In *Saul Bass & Assocs. v. United States*,505 F.2d 1386 (Ct. Cl. 1974), the government issued a letter of intent incorporating a contractor's design agreement, stating a monetary limitation and proposing the execution of a formal contract. The contractor performed, but no formal contract was agreed upon. The court found contractual agreement on the basis of the letters exchanged between the parties. For another case providing a remedy when the contractor completed performance but the parties failed to definitize the letter contract, see *Sanders Assocs. V. United States*, 423 F.2d 291 (Ct. Cl. 1970). See also *Wilco Floor Serv., Inc. v. United States*, 197 Ct. Cl. 902 (1972) (plaintiff entitled to costs from beginning of letter-contract term as opposed to date of definitized contract); *Kavourvas, Inc.*, Comp. Gen. Dec. B-226782, Oct. 20, 1987, *Unpub.* (even though expected definitized contract never came into existence, GAO ordered claimant be paid according to terms of letter contract). While some remedy may be available where the parties to a letter contract fail to definitize the terms, the Court of Federal Claims has dismissed such claims where not first presented to the contracting officer in accordance with the Contract Disputes Act. *J.Cooper & Assocs., Inc. v. United States*, 47 Fed. Cl. 280 (2000).

[B] Offer and Acceptance

Restatement, Second, Contracts § 24 defines "offer" as follows:

> An offer is the manifestation of willingness to enter into a bargain, so made as to justify another person in understanding that his assent to that bargain is invited and will conclude it.

Restatement, Second, Contracts § 50(1) defines "acceptance" as follows:

> Acceptance of an offer is a manifestation of assent to the terms thereof made by the offeree in a manner invited or required by the offer.

The time, manner, form, and any other conditions associated with the method of acceptance are generally within the control of the offeror and may be specified in the offer. When the offeror requests that the acceptance be in the form of a return promise the acceptance creates what is termed a "bilateral contract." The offeror may also request that the acceptance be in the performance of an act or forbearance; this being referred to as a "unilateral contract."

Except for simplified acquisitions, the government prefers to have the contractor make the offer, thereby obtaining the favored position of offeree. The government then has full control of when the contract is formed because it will not be bound to that contract until it manifests its acceptance. This is extremely important as it enables the contracting officer to determine which offer is most advantageous to the government and whether funds are available before deciding to accept. The government controls the terms of the offer by requiring that offerors agree to submit their offers in accordance with the terms provided in the solicitation.

[1] Solicitation and Submission of Offers or Quotations

[a] Sealed Bidding

In sealed bidding, the government solicits offers by issuing an Invitation for Bids (IFB) on Standard Form 33 (FAR 53.301-33). The IFB is not an offer by the government to purchase goods or services. The prospective contractor's bid is intended to be the offer and the government's award is the acceptance. See 42 Comp. Gen. 490 (B-150798) (1963), which noted that a bid submitted in response to a solicitation is an offer that may be accepted if sufficiently responsive. While the IFB is not an offer, it contains virtually all of the essential terms of the offer (standard and special clauses and the description of the work) except the price. This permits the government to ensure that all of the bidders compete on an equal basis, as discussed in Chapter 5. See *Lockheed Martin IR Imaging Sys., v. West*, 108 F.3d 319 (Fed. Cir. 1997); *Silver State Land LLC v. United States*, 148 Fed. Cl. 217 (2020).

[b] Negotiated Procurement

The process of negotiated procurement is more complex than that of sealed bidding. The opportunity to hold oral or written discussions in the procurement process raises the possibility that offerors may be requested to submit sequential offers. See *United States v. John McShain, Inc.*, 258 F.2d 422 (D.C. Cir. 1958), *cert. denied*, 358 U.S. 832 (1958), where the court stated at 424:

> Negotiation is a process of submission and consideration of offers until an acceptable offer is made, and accepted, or until it becomes apparent that no acceptable offer will be made.

The negotiation process is sufficiently flexible so that the government can also make an offer during the course of negotiations. The various forms of negotiated procurement are discussed below.

[i] Request for Proposals or Offers

The major form of solicitation in negotiated procurement is the Request for Proposals (RFP). This type of solicitation is generally accomplished using Optional Form 307 (FAR 53.302-307) or Standard Form 33. The RFP is not an offer but, like the IFB, requests the proposer to submit an offer, *Space Research Corp. v. United States*, 225 Ct. Cl. 721 (1980). See FAR 15.203(a). However, also like IFBs, when competition is solicited, the RFP will contain virtually all of the essential terms of the offer (standard and special clauses and the description of the work) except price and any enhancements that are being solicited. See Chapter 6 for a complete discussion of this process.

In competitive negotiation, if acceptance without discussions is not possible or desirable, the government conducts oral or written negotiations with all offerors within the competitive range. These offerors are then given the opportunity to submit another offer, which is called a "final proposal revision," FAR 15.307(b). Before FAR Part 15 was rewritten in 1997, see FAC 97-02, 62 Fed. Reg. 51225, Sept. 30, 1997, these offers were called "best and final offers" (BAFOs), FAR 15.611(a) (pre-1997 FAR). If the government is not satisfied with any such offer the process may be repeated and, in rare cases, the government may be the party making the ultimate offer.

[ii] Request for Quotations

When the government does not intend that offers be submitted in response to the initial solicitation in a negotiated procurement, it uses a Request for Quotations (RFQ) rather than an RFP. This procedure traditionally was used most commonly with sole source procurements, though the use of RFQs is now very common with multiple-award indefinite-delivery/indefinite-quantity contracts, including the General Services Administration's schedule contracts. RFQs are sometimes prepared on Standard Form 18 (FAR 53.301-18). Unlike bids or proposals following an IFB or RFP, quotations submitted in response to an RFQ are not considered to be offers that can be accepted, FAR 13.004(a); *Pricewaterhouse Coopers Public Sector, LLP*, Comp. Gen. Dec. B-415504, 2018 CPD ¶ 35 ("An RFQ, unlike an RFP or invitation for bids, does not seek offers that can be accepted by the government to form a contract. Rather, the government's purchase order represents the offer that the vendor may accept through performance or by a formal acceptance document."). Thus, as discussed further below, the government's order in response to the quotation does not form a contract; the agreement (offer and acceptance) arises only when the supplier accedes to the government's order (offer). Prior to FAC 97-02, the FAR permitted the use of RFQs in negotiated procurement. The FAR is now silent on this issue.

A variety of procedures may be used following the receipt of a quotation. In some cases, a quotation serves as the basis for beginning negotiations. Following the conclusion of these negotiations in major procurements, the government usually requests the prospective contractor to submit an offer that can be accepted by the government. This is often accomplished by the government sending a formal contract document to be signed by the contractor and presented to the government for acceptance. However, various other procedures may be followed, and in some instances the government becomes the offeror.

[c] Simplified Acquisition

FAR Part 13 sets forth procedures for simplified acquisitions. The standard procedure for simplified acquisitions is for the government to request quotations and to make offers through the issuance of purchase orders. The quoter is then free to reject or accept the offer. See *Computer Assocs. Int'l, Inc.*, Comp. Gen. Dec. B-292077.6, 2004 CPD ¶ 110 (in an RFQ situation, "it is the government that makes the offer . . . and no binding agreement is created until the vendor accepts the offer. . . . A vendor submitting a price quotation therefore could, the next moment, reject an offer from the government at its quoted price"). FAR 13.004(a) provides in part:

> Therefore, issuance by the Government of an order in response to a supplier's quotation does not establish a contract. The order is an offer by the Government to the supplier to buy certain supplies or services upon specified terms and conditions. A contract is established when the supplier accepts the offer.

See *Harney County Gypsum Co.*, AGBCA 93-190-1, 94-1 BCA ¶ 26,455, in which the firm's response to a request for price quotes and discussion of the firm's availability did not manifest an offer by the firm that could be accepted by the government. Once the purchase order has been issued, the supplier may then manifest acceptance through promise or performance, FAR 13.004(b). See *Sunshine Cordage Corp.*, ASBCA 38904, 90-1 BCA ¶ 22,382 (initial request for quotation on price of rope was not an offer, but purchase order by government in response to quotation by supplier was an offer). See Chapter 8 for a discussion of simplified acquisition procedures.

The purchase order, in simplified acquisitions, may be made on Optional Form 347 (FAR 53.302-347) or, for purchases not exceeding the micro-purchase threshold, Standard Form 44 (FAR 53.301-44). See FAR 53.213; FAR 13.306. Agencies also may use their own forms.

[d] Obligation to Consider Responses

Although the issuance of a solicitation may not be an offer by the government to contract for goods or services, the government may be obligated to fairly and honestly consider responses conforming to the solicitation. In determining whether such an obligation exists, the courts have used offer-and-acceptance analysis to find that the government entered into an implied-in-fact contract when the offer was submitted. This analysis served as the basis for giving the Court of Federal Claims jurisdiction to grant relief over award protests under the then-current version of 28 U.S.C. § 1491, *United States v. John C. Grimberg Co.*, 702 F.2d 1362 (Fed. Cir. 1983). See also *Aerolease Long Beach & Satsuma Inv. Co. v. United States*, 31 Fed. Cl. 342, *aff'd*, 39 F.3d 1198 (Fed. Cir. 1994), and *CACI, Inc.-Fed. v. United States*, 1 Cl. Ct. 352, *rev'd*, 719 F.2d 1567 (Fed. Cir. 1983), holding that issuance of a solicitation implied an offer to fairly and honestly consider all bids or proposals. When the Court of Federal Claims was given independent protest jurisdiction under 28 U.S.C. § 1491(b), there was a question as to whether the implied-in-fact jurisdiction under 28 U.S.C. § 1491(a) remained in effect. This issue was partially addressed in *Resource Conservation Group, LLC v. United States*, 597 F.3d 1238 (Fed. Cir. 2010), holding that the implied-in-fact contract jurisdiction under 28 U.S.C. § 1491(a)(1) remains in effect for nonprocurement contracts. *See also* Chapter 15 for further discussion of the continuing viability of implied-in-fact contract jurisdiction.

The government has also been held to have made an offer to give fair and impartial consideration to responses to a procurement notice published by the government, *Standard Mfg. Co. v. United States*, 7 Cl. Ct. 54 (1984); *Magnavox Elec. Sys. Co. v. United States*, 26 Cl. Ct. 1373 (1992). But see *Motorola, Inc. v. United States*, 988 F.2d 113 (Fed. Cir. 1993), which criticized the rationale of *Standard Manufacturing* and *Magnovox*, stating at 116:

> Government requests for information and responses from prospective bidders are not the equivalents of offer and acceptance. Such exchanges are not carried on with an expectation to presently affect legal relations. Rather, the parties are dealing . . . with an eye to the future, each being free, . . . to withdraw from the dialogue.

The court then differentiated this situation from the situation that arises when a bid actually has been submitted, finding at 116:

> In that circumstance there is a promise—the contractor's bid—which empowers the Government, upon acceptance, to bind the contractor to the terms

> of the solicitation. The essence of the contractor's engagement—the manifestation of an intention to be bound—warrants reading into the situation a reciprocal commitment from the Government, i.e., a promise to fairly and honestly consider the contractor's bid.

In *El Dorado Springs v. United States*, 28 Fed. Cl. 132 (1993), the court held that a Department of Housing and Urban Development invitation to submit an application for mortgage insurance did not imply a request for offers by the government. The court was therefore unwilling to find that an implied contract to fairly and honestly consider all offers existed. See also *Garchik v. United States*, 37 Fed. Cl. 52 (1996), where the court held that a *CBD* notice of procurement opportunity stating explicitly that it was not a request for offers did not create an implied contract to fairly and honestly consider the response. The court stated that the *Motorola* decision "implicitly" overruled *Standard Manufacturing* and *Magnovox*. Subsequently, in *Emery Worldwide Airlines, Inc. v. United States*, 264 F.3d 1071 (Fed. Cir. 2001), the Federal Circuit declined to decide whether the Court of Federal Claims had implied-in-fact jurisdiction in a case where the plaintiff had not submitted an offer but was contesting a sole source award, citing the fact that the *Motorola* court had "harshly criticized" *Standard Manufacturing*. See also *Pure Power!, Inc. v. United States*, 70 Fed. Cl. 739 (2006), holding that no implied-in-fact contract was created when a company submitted its products for testing to determine if they met the government's needs. But see *Comms. Constr. Servs. v. United States*, 116 Fed. Cl. 233 (2014) (acknowledging qualifying language in *Motorola* that undermines argument that "submission of a proposal is always required to establish the implied-in-fact contract").

[2] Requests for Information

When the government needs information on prices, delivery or other terms, it may use a Request for Information (RFI). Responses to RFIs are not offers that can be accepted, FAR 15.201(e). As a general rule GAO will dismiss as premature protest challenging the terms of pre-solicitation notices such as requests for information until the agency takes more concrete action such as issuing a solicitation. See *F-Star Zaragosa Port, LLC*, Comp. Gen. Dec. B-417414, 2019 CPD ¶ 148.

[3] Withdrawal or Modification of Offers

According to general contract-law principles, unless an offeror has made an enforceable agreement not to revoke an offer, the offer is freely revocable. See *Restatement, Second, Contracts* § 42:

> An offeree's power of acceptance is terminated when the offeree receives from the offeror a manifestation of an intention not to enter into the proposed contract.

Despite this general rule, there are a number of limitations on revocability. See *Restatement, Second, Contracts* § 87, which provides:

> (1) An offer is binding as an option contract if it
>
> (a) is in writing and signed by the offeror, recites a purported consideration for the making of the offer, and proposes an exchange on fair terms within a reasonable time; or
>
> (b) is made irrevocable by statute.
>
> (2) An offer which the offeror should reasonably expect to induce action or forbearance of a substantial character on the part of the offeree before acceptance and which does induce such action or forbearance is binding as an option contract to the extent necessary to avoid injustice.

These general limitations on revocability have been subsumed, to a degree, in the rules developed for government contracts. However, the term "option contract" has not been used in government contracts to describe all irrevocable offers.

In the procurement of goods and services, the revocability of an offer is dependent upon the type of procurement involved and the stage of the procurement. Revocation may occur through either modification or withdrawal of the offer. In sealed bidding, offers may be modified or withdrawn prior to the time set for bid opening, FAR 14.303. Another longstanding rule, however, is that bids may not be modified or withdrawn after the exact time for bid opening unless they are based on a mistake, *Refining Assocs. v. United States*, 109 F. Supp. 259 (Ct. Cl. 1953). However, the Late Submissions, Modifications, and Withdrawal solicitation provision in FAR 52.214-7(b)(2) states that a late modification of an otherwise successful bid that makes it terms more favorable to the government "will be considered at any time it is received and may be accepted."

In negotiated procurement, proposals (offers) may be withdrawn at any time prior to award, FAR 15.208(e). See ¶ (c)(8) of the Instructions to Offerors—Competitive Acquisition solicitation provision in FAR 52.215-1, which states:

> Proposals may be withdrawn at any time before award. Withdrawals are effective upon receipt of notice by the Contracting Officer.

See *United Elec. Motor Co.*, Comp. Gen. Dec. B-191996, 78-2 CPD ¶ 206.

"Modifications" and "revisions" of proposals are dealt with differently in FAR Part 15. With regard to modifications, ¶ (c)(6) of the Instructions to Offerors—Competitive Acquisition solicitation provision in FAR 52.215-1, states:

> Offerors may submit modifications to their proposals at any time before the solicitation closing date and time, and may submit modifications in response to an amendment, or to correct a mistake at any time before award.

This confusing provision presumably means that a modification to a proposal submitted after the closing date and time would be "late" and therefore not considered. However, FAR 15.208(b)(2) provides that a late modification of an otherwise successful proposal that would make its terms more favorable to the government "will be considered at any time it is received and may be accepted." In addition, the above provision appears to allow a modification submitted in response to an amendment to be considered if it is submitted by the time specified in the amendment. It also appears to permit an offeror to submit a modification to correct a mistake at any time prior to award, but GAO has not interpreted it in this manner. See Chapter 6 for a discussion of the late proposal and correction of mistake decisions.

The rule on proposal revisions is stated in ¶ (c)(7) of the Instructions to Offerors—Competitive Acquisition solicitation provision in FAR 52.215-1:

> Offerors may submit revised proposals only if requested or allowed by the Contracting Officer.

This provision is apparently a reference to FAR 15.307(b) which states that a contracting officer may request or allow proposal revisions "to clarify and document understandings reached during negotiations." That paragraph also discusses "final proposal revisions" that can be submitted by offerors after negotiations are concluded. All such revisions are, in effect, new offers which must also meet the strict timeliness rules. See, however, *NCR Gov't Sys. LLC*, Comp. Gen. Dec. B-297959, 2006 CPD ¶ 82, permitting acceptance of such a late proposal revision because it modified a proposal that was acceptable to the government. In contrast, in *Sunrise Med. HHG, Inc.*, Comp. Gen. Dec. B-310230, 2007 CPD ¶ 7, the agency properly refused to accept a late proposed price reduction because the offeror was not the "otherwise successful offeror." See Chapter 6 for a complete discussion of the rules regarding proposal revisions.

These rules would appear to indicate that offerors are not bound in any way when they submit a proposal. However, the standard form used as a cover sheet for solicitations, Standard Form 33, FAR 53.301-33, creates confusion here because it contemplates much less flexibility in the proposal process. The specific provision in Item 12 of this form requires the offeror to agree to be bound if its "offer is accepted within" a specified number of days "from the date of receipt of offers." This could be interpreted to be an adoption of the firm bid rule described in the above *Restatement*. However, it is likely that the issue will be governed by the more specific solicitation provisions discussed above.

The government also uses option clauses, giving it the right to order additional goods or services. Such options are offers by the contractor that are irrevocable for the stipulated period, *Contel Page Servs., Inc.*, ASBCA 32100, 87-1 BCA ¶ 19,540 (government timely exercised its option to extend contract when it sent the contractor written notice as well as an unsigned bilateral modification). See Chapter 12 for a complete discussion of the legal rules governing options.

The legal theories supporting the irrevocability of government contract offers have never been fully articulated. There is no government contract statute similar to U.C.C. § 2-205, which makes "firm" offers irrevocable. In dealing with sealed bids, the court in *Refining Assocs. v. United States*, 109 F. Supp. 259 (Ct. Cl. 1953), enforced the solicitation provision precluding withdrawal on the grounds that otherwise "innumerable frauds could be perpetrated against the United States." Irrevocability might also be supported on the theory that the offeror responding to solicitations receives consideration for agreeing not to revoke the offer in the form of the government's obligation to fairly and honestly consider all bids and proposals. As FAR 2.101 defines "option" as a "unilateral right" in an already existing contract, the consideration supporting the irrevocability of offers in option clauses is provided by the consideration present in the contract that contains the option clause, *Holly Corp.*, ASBCA 24975, 83-1 BCA ¶ 16,327.

While the theory of detrimental reliance in ¶ (2) of *Restatement, Second, Contracts* § 87 is potentially available to support the irrevocability of offers to contract with the government, it would appear to be applicable only to sealed bid contracting and to offers for amendments to existing contracts. In these situations, the government's expenditure of time and effort in evaluating the offers and preparing for acceptance could well be sufficient to bind offerors that agreed not to revoke. Although significantly more effort is expended by the government in negotiated procurements, the offeror's broad right of withdrawal makes this theory inapplicable.

Government offers in the form of purchase orders for simplified acquisitions may also be revoked at any time prior to acceptance, FAR 13.004(c). See *Harney County Gypsum Co.*, AGBCA 93-190-1, 94-1 BCA ¶ 26,455 (government's withdrawal of a purchase order for the rental of an excavator and operator did not constitute a breach of contract when the contractor had not yet accepted the offer in writing nor furnished an excavator and operator). The contracting officer may also modify purchase orders, without the contractor's written acceptance of the modification, FAR 13.302-3. See *University Sys., Inc. v. Dep't of Commerce*, GSBCA 10896-COM, 92-3 BCA ¶ 25,182 (insertion of a Termination for Default clause by unilateral modification to an already existing contract did not have to be accepted in writing by the contractor).

The procedures for withdrawing offers contain safeguards. Withdrawal is to be accomplished by written or telegraphic notice, facsimile, or in person if the identity of the person withdrawing the bid is established and such person signs a receipt, FAR 14.303. Guidance also may be found in the solicitation provision, FAR 52.214-7. Less detailed guidance for negotiated procurements is found in FAR 15.208(e). See also *John A. Maney*, GSBCA 6550, 83-2 BCA ¶ 16,744 (withdrawal of offers in government contracts regulated by provisions specific to the field and not necessarily by common law).

[4] Acceptance of Bids, Proposals (Offers), and Purchase Orders

To be binding, an acceptance must contain a manifestation of present intention to be bound. See *D&S Universal Mining, Inc.*, Comp. Gen. Dec. B-200815, 81-2 CPD ¶ 186, where GAO stated:

> In order for a binding contract to result, the contracting officer must unequivocally express an intent to accept an offer. Also, the acceptance of a contractor's offer by the Government must be clear and unconditional; it must appear that both parties intended to make a binding agreement at the time of the acceptance of the contractor's offer.

In *DeMatteo Constr. Co. v. United States*, 600 F.2d 1384 (Ct. Cl. 1979), mere notification to an offeror that its offer was "selected as the lowest responsive bid" did not constitute an acceptance. Similarly, in *Greenwood Co.*, ASBCA 12232, 67-2 BCA ¶ 6650, the contracting officer asked the bidder to come in and sign contract documents and to bring payment and performance bonds. The bidder complied. Subsequently, the contracting officer determined that it would be to the government's advantage to split the award as permitted by the IFB. The bidder contended that the entire contract had been awarded, but the board disagreed, finding that there had been no contract made for full performance because the contracting officer's request was not a "clear-cut expression of intention" to accept, stating at 30,829:

> Here, no clear-cut expression of intention to accept the bid and award a contract exists. [The bidder] was asked to bring in the payment and performance bonds undated, indicating that a contract date had not been established and the contract not yet awarded. In fact, the bonds were provisional, subject to annulment if a contract was not entered into. Nor did the contracting officer even sign the proposed contract on behalf of the Government, after [the bidder] had signed on its own behalf. In this light, that which transpired on 20 and 21 June 1966 must be considered as preparatory to the homologation of the contract. When the contracting officer failed to sign the proposed instrument signed by [the bidder], he did not, acting on behalf of [the Government], breach a contract, but preserved the STATUS QUO ANTE that no contract had yet come into existence.

In *Turping v. United States*, 913 F.3d 1060 (Fed. Cir. 2019), the Federal Circuit rejected the argument that the government was bound by the terms of a Multi-Employer Pension Plan (MEPP) that the government allegedly required a contractor to enter into with its employees because "nothing in the MEPP indicates intent by the Government to be in privity of contract with Lockheed's employees." See also *City of Klawock v. United States*, 2 Cl. Ct. 580 (1983), *aff'd*, 732 F.2d 168 (Fed. Cir. 1984), and *Edwards v. United States*, 22 Cl. Ct. 411 (1991), which appear to find no present intent to be bound because there were details remaining to be resolved. In both cases, the communications between the parties were susceptible to being read as conditional acceptances. In *Goldberger Foods, Inc. v. United States*, 23 Cl. Ct. 295 (1991), neither telephonic notice to a bidder that it was the lowest bidder nor public release of award information constituted a binding acceptance.

New modes of electronic commerce add interesting elements to these well-established rules regarding acceptance. FAR Subpart 4.5 allows government agencies to use electronic commerce in lieu of traditional paper-based contracting. The rules governing electronic commerce in government procurement continue to evolve. What is clear is that the generally accepted standard for an enforceable electronic signature—an electronic symbol that manifests an intention to sign under the Uniform Electronic Transactions Act § 2, or, pursuant to FAR 2.101, a "present intention to authenticate the writing"—should mean that the government and contractors may, under appropriate circumstances, be bound by "signatures" created and conveyed electronically.

[a] Time for Acceptance

Acceptance must occur within the time stated in the offer or a reasonable time if no time is stated. See *Restatement, Second, Contracts* § 41, which provides:

> (1) An offeree's power of acceptance is terminated at the time specified in the offer, or, if no time is specified, at the end of a reasonable time.
>
> (2) What is a reasonable time is a question of fact, depending on all the circumstances existing when the offer and attempted acceptance are made.

In IFBs and RFPs using Standard Form 33, the standard acceptance period is 60 days from opening of bids (in the case of IFBs) or from the date set for receipt of proposals (in the case of RFPs). Note that Item 12 of this form uses the term "date for receipt of offers" to imprecisely describe both situations. This clause also permits offerors to insert a longer or shorter acceptance period. But see *Imperial Maint., Inc.*, 71 Comp. Gen. 407 (B-247371), 92-1 CPD ¶ 464 (a 56-day bid guarantee period, made in the form of letters of credit, established the bid acceptance period even though the bidder did not insert that period in the bid form); *Dep't of the Army—Reconsideration*, B-251527.3, 93-2 CPD ¶ 178 (absent proof that contractor intended to hold earlier proposal open for possible acceptance, subsequent offers superseded earlier proposal).

The regulations also provide for the use of minimum acceptance periods. In construction IFBs and RFPs using Standard Form 1442 (FAR 53.301-1442), the contracting officer is required to insert a minimum acceptance period in Item 13D, and the offeror is permitted to offer a longer period in Item 17. FAR 52.214-16, applicable to contracts for other than construction, contains a solicitation provision for IFBs that is to be used when the contracting officer determines that a minimum acceptance period is necessary, FAR 14.201-6(j).

If acceptance does not occur during the specified period, no contract is formed. See 46 Comp. Gen. 371 (B-159639) (1966), stating at 372:

> [I]t is clear that expiration of the acceptance period operated to deprive the Government of any right to create a contract by acceptance action and to confer upon the bidder a right to refuse to perform any contract awarded to him thereafter.

This rule is applied strictly in the case of an attempted exercise of an option, *International Tel. & Tel. v. United States*, 453 F.2d 1283 (Ct. Cl. 1972).

Where no time for acceptance is specified by the offer, the government must accept within a reasonable time, *International Graphics, Div. of Moore Business Forms, Inc. v. United States*, 4 Cl. Ct. 515 (1984) (reasonable period held to be "obviously in excess of 14 days"). See *National Movers Co. v. United States*, 386 F.2d 999 (Ct. Cl. 1967), where acceptance at 3:00 p.m. on Friday, two days after bid opening, was held to be within a reasonable time even though work was required to begin on the following Monday morning. See also *Eagle Aviation, Inc. v. United States*, 9 Cl. Ct. 128 (1985), holding that a notice of award 32 days after submission of the proposal was a valid acceptance of the contractor's offer, and *One Way Constr., Inc.*, AGBCA 84-301-1, 85-1 BCA ¶ 17,839, holding that 23 days is not "an unduly long period of time from bid opening to award of contract."

The acceptance period may be extended in a number of different ways. The contracting officer may request offerors to extend the period if administrative difficulties prevent award before expiration of the bids, FAR 14.404-1(d), or if a protest prevents awarding the contract before expiration of the offers, FAR 33.103(f) (2) (agency-level protests); FAR 33.104(b)(3) (GAO protests). The acceptance period may also be extended on negotiated procurements without reopening discussions with offerors, *Science Info. Servs., Inc.*, Comp. Gen. Dec. B-207149.2, 82-2 CPD ¶ 477. While offerors are not required to extend their offers, such extensions are commonly granted because the offeror wishes to continue to be considered for award. However, it may be disadvantageous for a low bidder to extend in view of FAR 33.103(f)(2) and FAR 33.104(b)(3), which suggest that the contracting officer should consider award prior to resolution of a protest and expiration of a bid if the bidder refuses to extend the offer.

The acceptance period may also be extended through the submission of a bid protest. GAO has held that such an extension of the protester's acceptance period is automatic until the date of the decision and may be extended for a reasonable time thereafter, 52 Comp. Gen. 863 (B-177165) (1973). In *International Graphics v. United States*, 4 Cl. Ct. 515 (1984), the court ruled that an acceptance period may be extended through and beyond protest litigation if the "parties, through litigation or otherwise, have actually or constructively expressed their intent to accept the award." C.f. *Wit Assocs., Inc. v. United States*, 122 Fed. Cl. 1 (2015) (distinguishing *International Graphics* and finding offer expired where solicitation incorporated the thirty-day time period for acceptance of offers at FAR 51.212-1). See also *Ulstein Maritime, Ltd. v. United States*, 833 F.2d 1052 (1st Cir. 1987), explaining that the "expiration period on public contract solicitations is for the benefit of the bidders, who have the option of waiving this protection." In *Uffnor Textile Corp.*, Comp. Gen. Dec. B-205050, 81-2 CPD ¶ 443, GAO found another type of automatic extension when the bidder withdrew from the protest but agreed to accept the contracting officer's decision, reasoning that such expression of interest had the effect of extending the acceptance period.

Offerors submitting offers with acceptance periods equal to or greater than those requested by the solicitation have been permitted to revive their offers after the period has expired if doing so will not compromise the integrity of the competitive bidding system, *Consultants, Inc.*, Comp. Gen. Dec. B-286688.2, 2001 CPD ¶ 92; *Rubbermaid, Inc.*, Comp. Gen. Dec. B-238631, 90-1 CPD ¶ 444; *Strom Contracting Co.*, Comp. Gen. Dec. B-216115, 84-2 CPD ¶ 705. See also *Rentfrow, Inc.*, Comp. Gen. Dec. B-243215, 91-2 CPD ¶ 25, holding that where a firm proposed an adequate acceptance period in its original proposal, it could revive the offer once the original acceptance period had passed because doing so would not prejudice other offerors. Accord, *Shel-Ken Props., Inc.*, Comp. Gen. Dec. B-261443.3, 96-1 CPD ¶ 243. However, a bidder that offers a bid acceptance period shorter than that requested in an IFB may not extend that period or revive the bid in order to qualify for award because such an extension would be prejudicial to other bidders that offered the requested acceptance period. However, where the contract is awarded to another firm within the shorter acceptance period and the bidder that offered the shorter period protests the award, that bid may be accepted if the protest is sustained even though the acceptance period otherwise would have expired, *Phillips Cartner & Co.*, 69 Comp. Gen. 105 (B-236416), 89-2 CPD ¶ 492; *Professional Materials Handling Co.*, Comp. Gen. Dec. B-205969, 82-1 CPD ¶ 297, *recons. denied*, 82-1 CPD ¶ 501.

[b] Time When Acceptance Occurs

The time when acceptance occurs depends upon the type of acceptance requested by the offer and the mode of communication used. When the parties are face-to-face or communicating by telephone or teletype, the acceptance occurs as soon as the offeree has given assent to the transaction by statement or signature, *Restatement, Second, Contracts* § 64. There is little opportunity for controversy in such cases. Where the communication is by mail or telegraph, there are two views as to when acceptance occurs. The private common-law view holds that acceptance is effective when dispatched, *Adams v. Lindsell*, 106 Eng. Rep. 250 (K.B. 1818). This is commonly referred to as the "mailbox rule" and requires only that the offeree properly dispatch the notice of acceptance, *Restatement, Second, Contracts* § 63; *Republic of Sudan v. Harrison*, 139 S. Ct. 1048 (2019) ("As first-year law students learn in their course on contracts, there is a presumption that a mailed acceptance of an offer is deemed operated when 'dispatched' if it is 'properly addressed.'"). In government contracts, a contrary view was adopted by the Court of Claims, which ruled that an acceptance must be received by the offeror before a contract is created, *Rhode Island Tool Co. v. United States*, 128 F. Supp. 417 (Ct. Cl. 1955). That decision was premised on postal regulations that permitted reclaiming letters after deposit in the mail and on solicitation language that stated that a binding contract would be formed upon "receipt" of the notice of award.

Subsequently, the solicitation language was changed by the government to provide that a binding contract is formed when a notice of award is "mailed or otherwise furnished" to the offeror, FAR 52.214-10(d) and FAR 52.215-1(f)(10). Litigation involving solicitations containing this revised language has demonstrated that a potential conflict still remains. A concurring opinion in *G.C. Casebolt Co. v. United States*, 421 F.2d 710 (Ct. Cl. 1970), stated that "a valid contract is not formed until the acceptance is received by the offeror." The majority of the court disposed of the case on other grounds. In *Best Foam Fabricators, Inc. v. United States*, 38 Fed. Cl. 627 (1997), the court found that acceptance was communicated when the agency received the contractor's duly executed contracts. Similarly, in *Emeco Indus. v. United States*, 485 F.2d 652 (Ct. Cl. 1973), the court endorsed the requirement for an actual "communication" of the acceptance. See also *Romala Corp. v. United States*, 20 Cl. Ct. 435 (1990) (provisions included in letter sent by government after acceptance of original offer had been communicated were not part of contract). In contrast, the appeals boards have followed the reasoning of GAO in finding that the acceptance need only be mailed for a valid contract to come into being when specific language to that effect is used in the solicitation. See *Singleton Contracting Corp.*, IBCA 1770-1-84, 86-2 BCA ¶ 18,800 (relief from bid error was denied because board found mailed notice of award had already completed the contract as designated in solicitation); *Cisco Supply Co.*, GSBCA 5678, 81-1 BCA ¶ 15,103 (IFB required removal of purchased property within 15 days after award, and board found that time period began to run when notice of award was mailed as per solicitation language); and *Computer Wholesale Corp.*, GSBCA 4217, 76-1 BCA ¶ 11,859, *recons. denied*, 76-2 BCA ¶ 12,163 (board's reasoning was not necessarily inconsistent with the Court of Claims when solicitation specifically provided that once a written acceptance of award was mailed, contract was formed). In cases involving an acceptance not governed by this solicitation language, it has been held that the Court of Claims rule should be followed, *Titan Atlantic Constr. Corp.*, ASBCA 26007, 83-2 BCA ¶ 16,791.

The mailbox rule requires that the notice of award be placed in the United States mail, not delivered by a private overnight service, *G.E. Sales & Rentals*, GSBCA 13304, 1995 GSBCA LEXIS 409, nor placed in the agency mail system, *Albert H. Voight, Inc.*, GSBCA 4433, 76-1 BCA ¶ 11,789. The government, as offeree, carries the burden of proving timely and proper mailing of the award notice. See *C & L Petroleum Co.*, ASBCA 39844, 91-1 BCA ¶ 23,490, where the government failed to mail the notice of award by either registered or certified mail and thus could only submit evidence of usual practices to prove timely acceptance. The board found that type of evidence insufficient to carry the burden. But see *Hadi Zeghuzi*, ASBCA No. 53459, 02-1 BCA ¶ 31854, where the board found a binding contract despite "no evidence of mailing" where sale documents contemplated that "written award mailed (or otherwise furnished) . . . shall be deemed to result in a binding contract" and the contracting officer transmitted the notice of award by facsimile.

There is unanimity regarding the rule for exercise of options under existing contracts. Unless a contrary agreement is shown, all authorities hold that the acceptance is not effective until *received* by the offeror, *Dynamics Corp. of Am. v. United States*, 389 F.2d 424 (Ct. Cl. 1968); and *Restatement, Second, Contracts* § 63(b). FAR 17.207(a) requires that written notice of the exercise of the option be "provided" to the contractor within the time specified in the contract. And, "delivery of the written notice of option exercise must be to a person authorized to accept it on behalf of the contractor." *Griffin Servs., Inc.*, ASBCA No. 52280, 02-2 BCA 31943. While the *Restatement* uses the term "option contract" broadly to apply to all irrevocable offers—those in new contracts as well as those in existing contracts—the special acceptance rule for options has generally not been applied to firm offers for new government contracts. As discussed above, the *Rhode Island Tool* case reached the same conclusion. In *Cessna Aircraft Co.*, ASBCA 43196, 96-1 BCA ¶ 27,966, the board held that an option exercised by facsimile at 6:00 p.m. on a Saturday and received on the contractor's fax machine was effective even though the contractor did not become aware of the fax until the following Monday. The government had warned the contractor that it intended to exercise the option, which was due to expire at 12:00 midnight on Saturday, as soon as funds became available. It alerted the contractor to "stand by their fax machine."

When acceptance is to be accomplished by performance rather than promise, such as in simplified acquisitions, *Restatement, Second, Contracts* § 45 provides that *the beginning of performance* binds the offeror (the government) but not the offeree (the contractor). FAR 13.004(b) attempts nevertheless to permit later government withdrawal of its unilateral offer by defining acceptance as occurring when the supplier either furnishes the supplies or services or substantially performs the work. The FAR definition does not address, and should not alter, the *Restatement* rule that the contractor is not bound. The appeals boards have followed the FAR, to some degree, in determining when performance binds the government. See *OFF DODS, Inc.* ASBCA 57816, 12-2 BCA ¶ 35,082 ("If the contractor engages in 'substantial performance' in attempting to supply the item an option contract is created wherein the offer becomes irrevocable"); *Comtech Corp.*, ASBCA 55526, 08-2 BCA ¶ 33,982, finding that manufacturing noncompliant products was "substantial enough" to prevent the government from withdrawing its purchase order offer. See also *Harney County Gypsum Co.*, AGBCA 93-190-1, 94-1 BCA ¶ 26,455 (board found no acceptance, citing the substantial performance requirement in the FAR, but finding no significant performance); *Eastman Kodak Co.*, Comp. Gen. Dec. B-271009, 96-1 CPD ¶ 215 (an order for supplies or services in response to a seller's quotation does not establish a contract); *Federal Acquisition Mgmt. Training Serv.*, Comp. Gen. Dec. B-248871, 92-2 CPD ¶ 214 (agency may cancel purchase order prior to beginning of performance); *Sunshine Cordage Corp.*, ASBCA 38904, 90-1 BCA ¶ 22,382 (finding that the supplier/offeror is not bound to perform under a government offer for a unilateral contract).

When the government is bound to hold its purchase order offer open because the contractor has accepted by performance, the offer remains open only until the delivery date specified in the purchase order. Thus, if the contractor delivers no goods or defective goods on that date, there is no longer a contract, *Commwise, Inc.*, ASBCA 56580, 09-2 BCA ¶ 34,240 (defective goods); *TTF, L.L.C.*, ASBCA 58495, 13 BCA ¶ 35,403 ("The irrevocability of an offer partially performed lapses if an offeree fails to tender complete performance by the offer's specified date because, after not delivering timely, the offeree can no longer perform in accordance with the offer's terms"). See *Comtech Corp.*, ASBCA 55526, 08-2 BCA ¶ 33,982, containing a complete explanation of the rules governing "unilateral" contracts and treating the rule governing the expiration of the offer at 168,082:

> The "offer" presented by the POs is to buy certain supplies on specified terms and conditions if the offer is accepted by the act of delivering those goods on or before the date that the offer specifies. *Sunshine Cordage, supra,*90-1 BCA ¶ 22,382 at 112,471; *Amplitronics, Inc.*, ASBCA No. 33732, 87-2 BCA ¶ 19,906 at 100,703; *Ordnance Parts & Engineering Co.*, ASBCA No. 31166, 86-1 BCA ¶ 18,545 at 93,154; FAR 13.004(a). If complete performance in accordance with the offer's terms and conditions is not tendered, the "offer" lapses by its own terms. *E.g., Master Research & Manufacturing, Inc.*, ASBCA No. 46341, 94-2 BCA ¶ 26,747 at 133,071; *Ordnance Parts & Engineering Co.*, ASBCA No. 37985, 89-2 BCA ¶ 21,805 at 109,704; *Amplitronics, supra,*87-2 BCA ¶ 19,906 at 100,704. When an offer lapses by its own terms, the offeree (supplier) bears the costs of nonperformance. *Alsace Industrial, Inc.*, ASBCA No. 51709, 99-1 BCA ¶ 30,227 at 149,542, *recons. denied,* 1999 ASBCA LEXIS 47; *Western Mfg. Co.*, ASBCA No. 25089, 81-1 BCA ¶ 15,024 at 74,346.

[c] Conditional Acceptance

Under certain circumstances, the contracting officer wants to accept the offer but is unable or unwilling to obligate the government at that time. The most common situations occur when the contracting officer's acceptance is contingent upon either the availability of funding for the contract or the approval of higher authority. FAR 32.703-2 permits the contracting officer to initiate a contracting action properly chargeable to funds of the new fiscal year before these funds are available, provided that the solicitation and contract document include the following clause at FAR 52.232-18:

> AVAILABILITY OF FUNDS (APR 1984)
>
> Funds are not presently available for this contract. The Government's obligation under this contract is contingent upon the availability of appropriated funds from which payment for contract purposes can be made. No legal liability on the part of the Government for any payment may arise until funds are made available to the Contracting Officer for this contract and until the Contractor receives notice of such availability, to be confirmed in writing by the Contracting Officer.

The contracting officer may use this procedure for procurements involving operation and maintenance and continuing services necessary for normal operations, and for which Congress previously has consistently appropriated funds, unless statutory authority exists for use in other areas, FAR 32.703-2.

Another type of conditional acceptance is one subject to approval of higher authority. FAR 4.103 requires that the contracting officer use the following clause at FAR 52.204-1 in solicitations and contract documents if required by agency procedures:

> APPROVAL OF CONTRACT (DEC 1989)
>
> This contract is subject to the written approval of [*identify title of designated agency official here*] and shall not be binding until so approved.

If the condition occurs within a stated or reasonable time without attempted withdrawal by either party, both parties will be bound, *Thomson v. United States*, 357 F.2d 683 (Ct. Cl. 1966) (once condition of approval of contract by Attorney General's office was attained, parties to contract were bound); *Delco Elecs. Corp. v. United States*, 12 Cl. Ct. 367 (1987) (failure to issue required formal modification of contract prevented formation of a binding contract). Further, if the condition never occurs, neither party is bound unless one party has undertaken an obligation regarding the occurrence of the condition, *Monroe v. United States*, 184 U.S. 524 (1902) (lack of approval by chief of engineers as specified in contract prevented contract from being enforceable); *Municipal Leasing Corp. v. United States*, 1 Cl. Ct. 771 (1983) (government's motion for summary judgment denied due to its failure to use "best efforts" to secure the necessary funding that was condition of contract). See also *United States v. Newport News Shipbuilding & Dry Dock Co.*, 571 F.2d 1283 (4th Cir.), *cert. denied*, 439 U.S. 875 (1978) (negotiated settlement not binding on the government because condition of ultimate approval by Attorney General never received); and *Blackhawk Heating & Plumbing Co.*, VACAB 823, 81-2 BCA ¶ 15,400 (government not obligated to pay contractor full amount due under a settlement agreement because the agreement made the government's payment obligation contingent upon the availability of funds and Congress withdrew the appropriation of funds for the agreement before the final payment was due). But compare *Cherokee Nation v. Leavitt*, 543 U.S. 631 (2005) (Court rejected government's argument that government not bound to pay tribes because of "insufficient appropriations," notwithstanding qualifying statements in appropriations' legislative history), with *Maine Community Health Options v. United States*, 140 S. Ct. 1308 (2020) (finding government bound to statutory risk corridor payments where the relevant legislation did not utilize any available means for conditioning and limiting its obligations).

There is less certainty as to the degree to which either party is bound during the period prior to the occurrence of the condition or the passage of a reasonable or stated time for its occurrence. Since the offeror has usually invested considerable effort in the procurement, there is normally no desire to withdraw. Thus, most of the cases in this area have involved the government's refusal to proceed with the contractual action. One view of this legal issue is that either party is free to withdraw during this period. See *2 Williston on Contracts*, § 6:14 (4th ed. 1992), stating, in part, that an acceptance to take effect in the future is one that:

> adopts unequivocally the terms of the offer but states that it will not be effective until a certain contingency happens or fails to happen. . . . [T]here is, in effect, so to speak, an acceptance in escrow, which is not to take effect until the future. In the meanwhile, of course, neither party is bound and either may withdraw. Moreover, if the time at which the acceptance is to become effectual is unreasonably remote, the offer may lapse before the acceptance becomes effective. If neither party withdraws and the delay is not unreasonable, however, a contract will arise when the contingency happens or the stipulated event occurs.

The applicability of this reasoning should depend upon which party has control of the condition. If the condition is under the control of a third party, there would appear to be no sound reason for permitting either party to withdraw from such a conditional acceptance envisioned in the terms of the solicitation. In such an agreement, it could be argued that since neither party has control of the condition, both have agreed to be bound while awaiting its outcome. See, however, *City of Klawock v. United States*, 2 Cl. Ct. 580 (1983), *aff'd*, 732 F.2d 168 (Fed. Cir. 1984), and *American Gen. Leasing, Inc. v. United States*, 587 F.2d 54 (Ct. Cl. 1978), both supporting the proposition that if a contract is conditioned upon the action of a third party, no contract comes into existence until such action is completed. A better rule would be that a contract for the goods or services does not come into being but that the parties are contractually bound to await the occurrence of the condition for a reasonable period of time.

The more common conditions included in government contract solicitations are those within the control of the government. In such cases, typically some official above the contracting officer or outside the contracting agency must approve the transaction or provide funding. In *American Gen. Leasing, Inc. v. United States*, 587 F.2d 54 (Ct. Cl. 1978), it was held that the approving or funding official is under no obligation to the offeror. Similarly, in *Congress Constr. Corp. v. United States*, 314 F.2d 527 (Ct. Cl. 1963), *cert. denied*, 375 U.S. 817 (1963), the court assumed, *arguendo*, that the government was legally bound to use its "best efforts" to obtain the higher approval needed to complete negotiations, but that such efforts did not include "unreasonable and improper conduct," such as ignoring the orders of a superior officer. This would indicate that the government had a good faith obligation to attempt to obtain the required approval. See *Essen Mall Props. v. United States*, 21 Cl. Ct. 430 (1990), finding no "bad faith" in not approving contract because negotiations continued for four months after agency had decided not to go forward with deal. See also *Peninsula Group Capital Corp. v. United States*, 93 Fed. Cl. 720 (2010), where the court found no contract when the approval of the Secretary of the Army was blocked by legislation requiring competitive procedures to be used. Compare *Municipal Leasing Corp. v. United States*, 1 Cl. Ct. 771 (1983), where the contract provided that the Air Force would "use its best efforts to obtain appropriations." The court found that the Conditional Funding clause was modified by this provision. If the ultimate decision-maker within the government has no obligation, the government also is free of obligation as a practical matter.

If the government can freely avoid obligation in this manner, basic contract principles would give the offeror the same right unless there is an independent promise to be bound. For example, a conditional acceptance should not override a bidder's agreement not to withdraw a sealed bid. Once the period has expired, the bidder should be free to withdraw unless the government has assumed some obligation such as to use good faith in the decisional process. However, in one case, GAO held that a bidder could not withdraw following a conditional acceptance, 31 Comp. Gen. 477 (B-103842) (1952). There was no discussion of government obligation and no indication that the required approval was obtained within the bid acceptance period. The decision was supported by the questionable reasoning that a bid bond provided an independent basis for liability.

An offeror should not be bound to conditions not included in solicitations but unilaterally inserted by the offeree at the time of attempted acceptance. Since such an "acceptance" would not conform to the terms of the offer, no contract would be formed, *United States v. Braunstein*, 75 F. Supp. 137 (S.D.N.Y. 1947). This rule has been applied to the attempted exercise of an option where the board held that the contractor was not bound by an acceptance conditioned on the availability of funds; this clause was not present in the original contract which the contractor had satisfactorily performed, *Lear Siegler Inc.*, ASBCA 30224, 86-3 BCA ¶19,155. See also *Alutiiq Commercial Enters.*, LLC, ASBCA 61503, 20-1 BCA ¶37,506 ("Recognizing that the exercise of an option must be unconditional and set forth terms that are in accord with the option, any attempt by the government to alter the terms of the contractor's obligation under an option will render ineffective the purported exercise of the option."); *CTA Inc.*, ASBCA 47062, 00-2 BCA ¶ 30,946 (contractor had right to accept or reject the contracting officer's overture to "renegotiate" the contract's production option).

[d] Nonacceptance Responses to Offers

In some cases, offerees' communications are not intended to be acceptances; in others, attempted acceptances do not properly manifest an intent to accept. In such situations, the communication may be held to be a rejection of the offer, a counteroffer, or a request that the offeror alter the terms of the offer. Under traditional contract law, an acceptance must unequivocally conform to the terms of the offer in order to create a binding contractual agreement. See *First Commerce Corp. v. United States*, 335 F.3d 1373 (Fed. Cir. 2003) ("Under the traditional 'mirror image' rule of the common law, mismatch between offer and acceptance negates contractual liability."); *United States v. Braunstein*, 75 F. Supp. 137 (S.D.N.Y. 1947). *Restatement, Second, Contracts* § 58 provides:

> An acceptance must comply with the requirements of the offer as to the promise to be made or the performance to be rendered.

However, an acceptance is not invalid if it merely requests a change or addition to terms and is not made to depend on assent to the changed or added terms, *Restatement, Second, Contracts* § 61. See *Best Foam Fabricators, Inc. v. United States*, 38 Fed. Cl. 627 (1997), where the government argued that the contractor never accepted the offer because its letter accompanying the signed contract took exception to the inclusion of MIL-I-45208 and, therefore, constituted a counteroffer. The court disagreed, stating that the contractor's letter unequivocally requested that the contract be modified to remove MIL-I-45208. The court stated that neither this request nor any other portion of the letter even remotely suggested that the contractor's acceptance was dependent on the government's assent to the deletion. Thus, the court held that the request was not a counteroffer and did not invalidate the contractor's acceptance. See also *Walsh Constr. Co.*, ASBCA 52952, 02-2 BCA ¶ 32,024, *aff'd*, 80 Fed. Appx. 679 (Fed. Cir. 2003), holding that the government's correction of mathematical errors in the extension of unit prices at the time it accepted a bid was not a counteroffer but merely a proper interpretation of the bid.

Rejections and counteroffers terminate the offer unless a different intention is manifested. See *Restatement, Second, Contracts* § 38 and § 39:

> § 38. Rejection
>
> (1) An offeree's power of acceptance is terminated by his rejection of the offer, unless the offeror has manifested a contrary intention.

(2) A manifestation of intention not to accept an offer is a rejection unless the offeree manifests an intention to take it under further advisement.

§ 39. Counter-offers

(1) A counter-offer is an offer made by an offeree to his offeror relating to the same matter as the original offer and proposing a substituted bargain differing from that proposed by the original offer.

(2) An offeree's power of acceptance is terminated by his making of a counter-offer, unless the offeror has manifested a contrary intention or unless the counter-offer manifests a contrary intention of the offeree.

See also *First Commerce Corp. v. United States*, 335 F.3d 1373 (Fed. Cir. 2003) (quoting Restatement (Second) Contracts § 59: "A reply to an offer which purports to accept it but is conditional on the offeror's assent to terms additional to or different from those offered is not an acceptance but is a counter-offer.").

The *Restatement* further provides that a rejection or counteroffer does not necessarily terminate an offer where there is a binding promise by the offeror not to revoke the offer, *Restatement, Second, Contracts* § 37. In government contracts, this latter rule would prevent termination of offers in option clauses and in irrevocable offers in sealed bid procurements. In contrast, offers in negotiated contracts would be terminated by a rejection or counteroffer in view of the offeror's broad right to revoke the offer.

The most common type of counteroffer in government contracts occurs where the offeree attempts to conclude the transaction with different terms. Thus, an acceptance by the government that materially varies from the contractor's offer will be treated as a counteroffer, 26 Comp. Gen. 567 (B-63244) (1947) (government's insertion of level of permitted price increase in its acceptance made such acceptance a counteroffer); *Aero Corp.*, ASBCA 8178, 1963 BCA ¶ 3665 (purchase order by government containing terms "not previously set out, referred to or incorporated" turned purchase order into counteroffer); *Northpoint Investors*, Comp. Gen. Dec. B-209816, 83-1 CPD ¶ 523 (government's acceptance conditioned upon future actions by government was neither clear nor unconditional and thus constituted a counteroffer); *Ford Aerospace & Commc'ns Corp.*, ASBCA 34994, 91-3 BCA ¶ 24,108 (government's acceptance of offer only at lower sales rate found to be a counteroffer and not an acceptance); *Fedcar Co., Ltd.*, Comp. Gen. Dec. B-310980, 2008 CPD ¶ 70 (government acceptance of lease containing "material changes" to offer a counteroffer). The *Aero Corporation* case holds further that such a counteroffer may then be accepted by the original offeror. See also *First Commerce Corp. v. United States*, 60 Fed. Cl. 570 (2004), where a bank accepted the government's counteroffer by performing in accordance with its terms; and *Bloch Lumber Co.*, ASBCA 23512, 79-2 BCA ¶ 14,167, where the government accepted a counteroffer by accepting delivered items without objecting to the new terms. Compare, however, *Ford Aerospace & Commc'ns Corp.*, where before and during performance, the contractor maintained that a discrepancy had to be corrected by the government. The board refused to find acceptance by the contractor through performance because the government was unclear and ambiguous as to what course of action it would take. In *Dunrite Tool & Die Corp.*, ASBCA 16708, 73-1 BCA ¶ 9940, the board found that there were two counteroffers. The government was found to have made one counteroffer when it included different terms in its purported acceptance. The second counteroffer was found when the offeror's response incorporated different terms. Since the government subsequently rejected the offeror's counteroffer, the board concluded that no contract was ever formed. A government notice of award citing the RFP was held to be a counteroffer to an offer containing specifications different from those in the RFP, *Data Gen. Corp.*, ASBCA 21865, 79-2 BCA ¶ 14,185.

Generally, late acceptances have also been treated as counteroffers. See *Restatement, Second, Contracts* § 70, which states in part:

> A late or otherwise defective acceptance may be effective as an offer to the original offeror.

In order to prevent these types of acceptance communications from terminating the offer, the offeree must manifest an intention to keep the offer open. If such an intention is manifested, the offeree can make inquiries, suggest different terms, or propose a counteroffer while retaining the right to accept the original offer. See *Dudek & Bock Spring Mfg. Co.*, ASBCA 9753, 65-2 BCA ¶ 4931, where a government telegram requesting that a bidder confirm the unit price, provide an extended price, and confirm that it had received certain data was held not to terminate the government's power to accept the offer.

[C] Implied-in-Fact Contracts

An implied-in-fact contract occurs when the conduct of the parties indicates that they have actually manifested their mutual assent but an express offer or acceptance is absent. See *Restatement, Second, Contracts* § 4 and § 19, stating that promises may be inferred and that mutual assent may be determined from words or acts. Implied-in-fact contracts are also recognized in government contracts, *Baltimore & Ohio R.R. v. United States*, 261 U.S. 592 (1923). In *Kam-Almaz v. United States*, 682 F.3d 1364 (Fed. Cir. 2012), the Federal Circuit reiterated that an "implied-in-fact contract with the government requires proof of (1) mutuality of intent, (2) consideration, (3) an unambiguous offer and acceptance, and (4) actual authority on the part of the government's representative to bind the government in contract." As was noted above, and as was pointed out by the Federal Circuit in *Anderson v. United States*, 344 F.3d 1343, 1353 n.3 (Fed. Cir. 2003), these are the same elements that generally must be met to form a binding government contract, both express and implied-in-fact.

However, as in the case of express contracts, implied-in-fact contracts must be consistent with statutory and regulatory requirements, *Prestex Inc. v. United*

States, 320 F.2d 367 (Ct. Cl. 1963), and based on the conduct of authorized employees, *Yifrach v. United States*, 145 Fed. Cl. 691 (2019); *Peninsula Group Capital Corp. v. United States*, 93 Fed. Cl. 720 (2010); *D & F Marketing, Inc.*, ASBCA 56043, 09-1 BCA ¶34,108; *Humlen v. United States*, 49 Fed. Cl. 497 (2001); *Essen Mall Properties v. United States*, 21 Cl. Ct. 430 (1990); *Pacific Gas & Elec. Co. v. United States*, 3 Cl. Ct. 329 (1983), *aff'd*, 738 F.2d 452 (Fed. Cir. 1984); *Woodcraft Corp. v. United States*, 173 F. Supp. 613 (Ct. Cl. 1959). It has been very difficult for contractors to prove that they have met all of the elements of an implied-in-fact contract.

There have been a number of decisions involving "implied-in-fact" contracts as a result of litigation in the wake of the "savings and loan crisis" of the 1980s. See, e.g., *Home Sav. of Am. v. United States*, 399 F.3d 1341 (Fed. Cir. 2005) (discussing background to crisis). This line of cases is known generally as the *Winstar* cases, named after the Supreme Court's decision in *United States v. Winstar Corp.*, 518 U.S. 839 (1996). The Court's decision in *Winstar* confirmed that the owners of solvent savings and loan banks, that had originally negotiated favorable accounting agreements with the government when they purchased ailing savings and loan banks and then were damaged by a congressional change in banking reserve rules, could, under certain circumstances, recover damages from the government. These *Winstar* decisions, which have come primarily from the Court of Federal Claims (where over 100 *Winstar* cases were filed), and the Federal Circuit, obviously stem from nonprocurement contracts. Nevertheless, these decisions have helped clarify many areas of government contract law doctrine, including rules regarding implied-in-fact contracts.

[1] Course of Conduct

The implied-in-fact agreement may be established from a course of conduct followed by the parties. See *Forest Glen Props., LLC v. United States*, 79 Fed. Cl. 669 (2007), where a series of retroactive instruments confirmed implied-in-fact contracts, and *La Van v. United States*, 53 Fed. Cl. 290 (2002), *aff'd*, 382 F.3d 1340 (Fed. Cir. 2004), where extensive negotiations between the bank and officials of the FDIC indicated that they intended to enter into a binding contract. In the latter decision, the court cited *California Fed. Bank, FSB v. United States*, 245 F.3d 1342 (Fed. Cir. 2001), *cert. denied*, 534 U.S. 1113 (2002), where a binding contract was found based on the documents that were exchanged during extensive negotiations. The Federal Circuit did not identify whether it was finding an express contract or an implied-in-fact contract. In *Algonac Mfg. Co. v. United States*, 428 F.2d 1241 (Ct. Cl. 1970), a contract was awarded for the production of armor-plated gun carriage parts. By a contract modification, the government was to furnish the necessary armor plate and the contractor was to maintain, repair, protect, and preserve it so long as it was in its possession.

Following completion of performance, the contractor asked the government to remove the surplus armor plate from its plant. It was not removed. The contractor stored it for 11 years and later informed the government that it would assess a storage charge for that time. The court held that the government was liable for a reasonable charge on the basis of an implied-in-fact contract, stating at 676:

> In view of the duties, responsibilities, and obligations imposed on the [contractor] by the foregoing provisions to maintain, repair, protect, and preserve the armor plate as long as it was in its possession, it was reasonable for the [contractor] to conclude, after the contract was finished and it had requested the government several times in writing, as outlined above, to take possession of the property and the government failed to do so, that the government wished it to continue to care for, preserve, and store such property and that the government would pay it for doing so.

Similarly, in *Bruce-Andersen Co.*, ASBCA 28125, 83-2 BCA ¶ 16,892, a contractor made an agreement with the government to substitute five-eighth-inch plywood furring for the three-quarter-inch solid furring called for in the contract in order to correct a one-eighth-inch gap resulting from the government's contract drawings. At the time this agreement was reached, it was clear to both parties that each would benefit from the change. The contractor was silent as to the matter of potential net increased cost of the change. In addition, the contractor knew, or should have known, that the government agent with whom it dealt did not have the authority to approve changes involving additional costs to the government. Nevertheless, a year later, the contractor attempted to claim increased costs from the government for the change. The board held that, under the circumstances, there was an implied-in-fact agreement that the change was to be made on a no-cost basis, stating at 84,060:

> [The contractor] is in error in conceiving that express words that the change would be on a no-cost basis was [sic] the only mode for making an agreement to that effect. It is well settled that an agreement may be effected not only through the exchange of express verbal undertakings by the parties but also through conduct between them that, evaluated in the light of surrounding circumstances, manifests a mutual, albeit tacit, intent to be contractually bound. Such an agreement, implied in fact from such conduct is as actual as one reached verbally.

See also *OAO Corp. v. United States,* 17 Cl. Ct. 91 (1989), where the government encouraged the contractor to begin performance before the contract was awarded but later canceled the acquisition. The court granted relief for the contractor's costs based on an implied-in-fact contract. Compare *Northrop Grumman Corp. v. United States*, 63 Fed. Cl. 38 (2004), where the court could find no implied-in-fact contract based upon the parties' actions.

[2] Acceptance of Benefits

Implied-in-fact contracts may also be created through the acceptance of benefits with the knowledge that the contractor expects to be compensated, *Pacific Maritime Ass'n v. United States*, 108 F. Supp. 603 (Ct. Cl. 1952) (labor referral services by the contractor accepted with knowledge that compensation was expected); *Buffalo & Fort Erie Pub. Bridge Auth. v. United States*, 65 F. Supp. 476 (Ct. Cl. 1946) (premises used with knowledge that contractor expected compensation); *HFS, Inc.*, ASBCA 43750, 92-3 BCA ¶ 25,198 (plaintiff entitled to compensation under theory of "ratification by implication or inaction" where contracting officer knew or should have known contractor expected to receive compensation for software and services delivered); *Equitable Life Assurance Soc'y*, GSBCA 8909, 90-3 BCA ¶ 23,130 (directive to contractor/lessor to replace carpet in leased office space made with knowledge that contractor expected compensation); *Robert J. DiDomenico*, GSBCA 5539, 82-2 BCA ¶ 16,093 (building alterations not called for in the contract ordered with knowledge that contractor expected compensation).

Since implied-in-fact contracts require conduct of the parties manifesting assent, the mere conferring of a benefit on the government does not create a contractual relationship, *Mega Constr. Co. v. United States*, 29 Fed. Cl. 396 (1993). In private transactions, conferring a benefit may permit recovery under a restitutionary theory. In government contracts, however, sovereign immunity from suit has not been waived for restitutionary actions. Such claims have been called "quasi-contract" or "implied-in-law" contract claims, which are not actionable under the Tucker Act, 28 U.S.C. § 1491, or the Contract Disputes Act of 1978, 41 U.S.C. § 7101 et seq. These statutes waiving sovereign immunity for suits on express or implied contracts have been held to exclude suits on contracts implied in law. See *Trauma Serv. Group v. United States*, 104 F.3d 1321 (Fed. Cir. 1997); *Dureiko v. United States*, 62 Fed. Cl. 340 (2004). See *Merritt v. United States*, 267 U.S. 338 (1925), stating at 341:

> The Tucker Act does not give a right of action against the United States in those cases where, if the transaction were between private parties, recovery could be had upon a contract implied in law.

In *Russell Corp. v. United States*, 537 F.2d 474 (Ct. Cl. 1976), the court recognized this distinction and its inability to grant remedies on quasi-or implied-in-law contracts, stating at 609:

> Implied-in-fact contracts differ from contracts implied in law (quasi-contracts), where a duty is imposed by operation of law without regard to the intent of the parties. Such arrangements are treated as contracts for the purposes of remedy only. This court, of course, has no jurisdiction to render judgment against the United States based upon a contract implied in law.

See also *United States v. Mitchell,* 463 U.S. 206 (1983), confirming that the Tucker Act does not waive sovereign immunity for claims based on contracts implied in law. Therefore, the Court of Federal Claims and the boards of contract appeals lack jurisdiction in such cases.

[3] Incomplete Contract Formation

Implied-in-fact contracts have also been found to exist where the government and the contractor have unsuccessfully attempted to form an express contract, *Hughes Transp., Inc. v. United States*, 121 F. Supp. 212 (Ct. Cl. 1954). Similarly, such contracts have sometimes been found to exist where the government and a contractor enter into an incomplete agreement. If the parties have nonetheless exhibited contractual intent, a contract will be found to exist. See *Western States Constr. Co.*, ASBCA 16003, 72-2 BCA ¶ 9508, where the board commented on the failure of the parties to agree to a contract price at 44,302:

> In this case there was no manifestation of mutual assent or "meeting of the minds" as to the contract price. [The contractor] took the firm position that the legal contract price was $1,208,300, and the Government knew it. The Government took the equally firm position that the correct legal contract price was $1,098,300, and [the contractor] knew it. Each party clearly manifested to the other party its position as to the correct contract price, and each party manifested to the other party its disagreement with the other party's position as to the contract price. It does not follow, however, that the failure of the parties to arrive at a meeting of the minds on the contract price resulted in there being no contract. An agreed on contract price is not essential to the existence of a contract when there is agreement on all the other terms of contract and a manifestation of intent to make a contract, such as we have here.

See also *Howard Nettleton*, PSBCA 3454, 94-3 BCA ¶ 27,038, where the absence of an express agreement on price was insufficient to prevent recovery on a contract implied-in-fact.

An implied-in-fact contract may be found to exist on the basis of an implied acceptance of an express offer. In *Thomson v. United States*, 357 F.2d 683 (Ct. Cl. 1966), acceptance of a contractor's offer to perform surveying services was contingent upon approval of higher authority. The contracting office received notice of such approval but did not inform the contractor of that fact, and did not therefore expressly accept the offer. However, the court held that there was an implied acceptance by the actions and communications of the contracting officer that encouraged the contractor to perform. As a result, an implied-in-fact contract was held to have come into existence. In discussing the relationship between an implied acceptance and an implied-in-fact contract, the court stated at 791:

> It is fundamental, however, that acceptance of an offer may be manifested either expressly (as by words) or impliedly by conduct indicating assent

> to the proposed bargain. *Restatement 2d, Contracts* §§ 5, 21, 21A, 52 (Comment c) (Tent. ed. 1, 1964); I *Williston, Contracts* §§ 90, 91A (3d ed. 1957). The notion that assent to the terms of an agreement (i.e., acceptance) may be evinced by action or conduct underlies the rule, repeatedly recognized by the courts, that contracts may be "implied in fact."

See also *Padbloc Co. v. United States*, 161 Ct. Cl. 369 (1963), where because the contractor stipulated that the government could use its data only if the data were kept confidential, the government's use of the data constituted an implied promise of confidentiality.

§ 2.03 BINDING THE PARTIES

The manifestation of mutual assent is not in itself sufficient to bind a party to perform as promised. The law requires either that something be exchanged for the promise or that the promise be reasonably relied upon. The term given by the law to the former is "consideration," while the latter is called "promissory estoppel."

[A] Requirement for Signed Document

In private contract law, state Statutes of Frauds permit a party being charged in a contract suit who has not signed a document evidencing a contract to plead that failure—the lack of a signed document—as a defense. See generally *Restatement, Second, Contracts* § 110 and § 138; and U.C.C. § 2-201. There is no similar statute concerning government contracts, and it has been held that the absence of a signed written document does not preclude the enforceability of a government contract, *Escote Mfg. Co. v. United States*, 169 F. Supp. 483 (Ct. Cl. 1959) (valid contract existed despite the absence of the contracting officer's signature on the government's acceptance form because the form was sent with a letter indicating acceptance that was signed by the contracting officer).

[1] Written or Electronic Notice

Although there is no federal Statute of Frauds, there are a number of statutory and regulatory references indicating that contracts should be awarded in writing or by electronic means. See 10 U.S.C. § 3302 (formerly § 2305(b)); 41 U.S.C. § 3702(c) and § 3703(d), as well as FAR 14.408-1. Thus, the guidance which traditionally requires written notices of award for sealed bid and competitive negotiated procurement now contemplates electronic transmissions as well. See FAR Subpart 4.5 requiring the use of electronic commerce "whenever practicable or cost-effective."

The FAR 2.101 definition of "contracts" states that the term "includes all types of commitments that obligate the Government . . . and that, except as otherwise authorized, are in writing." "In writing," in turn, is defined by FAR 2.101 to include "any worded or numbered expression that can be read, reproduced, and later communicated, and includes electronically transmitted and stored information." The term "writing" is defined in 1 U.S.C. § 1 to include "printing and typewriting and reproductions of visual symbols by photographing, multigraphing, mimeographing, manifolding, or otherwise." The fiscal statutes also contain a provision relating to this issue. 31 U.S.C. § 1501(a)(1) states that one of the bases for recording an obligation of the United States is a "binding agreement . . . in writing . . . and executed." GAO has held that for purposes of the statute, electronic data interchanges constitute writings, *National Inst. of Standards & Tech.*, 71 Comp. Gen. 109 (B-245714), 96-2 CPD ¶ 225.

In *United States v. American Renaissance Lines, Inc.*, 494 F.2d 1059 (D.C. Cir.), *cert. denied*, 419 U.S. 1020 (1974), the court construed the appropriations recording statute to be a Statute of Frauds in refusing to hold a contractor to an oral agreement. The court rejected the government's argument that the statute was merely for purposes of recording obligations to facilitate auditing and that it was not applicable to government contracts. *Escote Mfg. Co. v. United States*, 169 F. Supp. 483 (Ct. Cl. 1959), and *Penn-Ohio Steel Corp. v. United States*, 354 F.2d 254 (Ct. Cl. 1965), earlier Court of Claims cases holding that government contracts need not be in writing to be binding, were dismissed in a statement that in neither case did a citation to the statute appear. The court's interpretation of the statute has not been followed by other courts. See *Narva Harris Constr. Corp. v. United States*, 574 F.2d 508 (Ct. Cl. 1978), where the Court of Claims recognized that an implied contract could exist even though some of the indicia of the agreement were oral statements concerning the transaction. In rejecting the government's claim that 31 U.S.C. § 1501 barred the contractor's recovery, the court stated at 244:

> In almost all such cases, there is some sort of oral representation on the part of some Government agent. Although the party seeking to recover from the Government may not rely on the oral representation, and may rely totally on other, independent facts to establish the presence of an implied in fact contract or to recover in quantum meruit, the Government now seeks to make the mere existence of the oral representation, characterized as an oral express contract not reduced to writing, sufficient to compel this court to close its eyes to all other surrounding facts. Clearly such an expansive interpretation of § 200 [1501] is unacceptable.

See also *Arakaki v. United States*, 62 Fed. Cl. 244 (2004) (refusing to dismiss, on bare jurisdictional grounds, claim based on alleged oral contract). In *Lublin Corp. v. United States*, 84 Fed. Cl. 678 (2008), the Court of Federal Claims rejected the government's argument that 31 U.S.C. § 1501 barred holding that an oral contract was binding, explaining at 688-89 (and compiling cases):

> [N]early a dozen decisions have chosen to follow [*Narva Harris*] in concluding that section 1501(a)(1) neither prohibits express oral nor implied-in-fact contracts. A number of other cases, among them several in the Court of Claims, conclude that unwritten contracts are enforceable under the Tucker Act.

The *American Renaissance Lines* holding is also inapplicable where the contracts involve the obligation of nonappropriated funds. See *Sam Won Dev. Co.*, ASBCA 16541, 74-2 BCA ¶ 10,730, recognizing a binding oral contract and distinguishing *American Renaissance Lines* on the ground that the statute has no application to agreements where nonappropriated funds are involved. See also *Robert P. Maier, Inc.*, GSBCA 4382, 76-1 BCA ¶ 11,873, and *Robert P. Maier, Inc.*, Comp. Gen. Dec. B-185177, 76-1 CPD ¶ 137, *recons. denied*, 76-2 CPD ¶ 163, holding that *American Renaissance Lines* is not applicable to sales of government property.

American Renaissance Lines was also distinguished where the government's bidding documents specify that acceptance will be oral, *Ross Indus.*, ASBCA 19563, 75-1 BCA ¶ 11,212, and where the parties acted with the mutual understanding that a contract had been formed, *Superior Asphalt & Concrete Co.*, AGBCA 75-142, 76-2 BCA ¶ 12,022, *recons. denied*, 77-2 BCA ¶ 12,851. In the latter case, the board stated at 62,559:

> We are persuaded that the weight of authority to the effect that there is no Federal Statute of Frauds applies in the case before us. Where the terms and conditions are fixed by the writing in the bid package which becomes the offer, oral acceptance with execution of the document intended by both parties in a routine manner results in an enforceable contract even though the parties fail to actually execute the document. The oral acceptance must, of course, be by a duly authorized contracting officer acting within the scope of his authority.

For a similar discussion, see the concurring opinion in *Eastern Salvage Assocs.*, ENGBCA 4046, 80-1 BCA ¶ 14,216. However, the Claims Court opinion in *Prestex Inc. v. United States*, 3 Cl. Ct. 373 (1983), contains *dicta* in note 5 stating that express oral contracts fail on the ground that they violate the recording statute.

The Claims Court has also noted that while 31 U.S.C. § 1501 "is rarely, if ever, the sole basis for invalidating an otherwise valid express oral agreement[,] . . . the provision manifests the general view that generally oral agreements provide a very shaky basis for granting relief by way of money judgments," *Edwards v. United States*, 22 Cl. Ct. 411 (1991).

[2] Signature

A handwritten signature is probably the most universally accepted evidence of an agreement to be bound by a contract's terms. As early as 1951, however,

GAO held that a signature does not have to be handwritten and that "any symbol adopted as one's signature when affixed with his knowledge and consent is a binding and legal signature," Comp. Gen. Dec. B-104590, Sept. 12, 1951, *Unpub.* 1 U.S.C. § 1 provides that "'signature' or 'subscription' includes a mark when the person making the same intended it as such." Under common law, it has been determined that audio tape recordings can be considered to constitute a "signed writing" and are sufficient to create a contract. See *Ellis Canning Co. v. Berstein*, 348 F. Supp. 1212 (D. Colo. 1972).

In the commercial sphere, the scope of recognizable "signatures" has expanded greatly with electronic commerce and with the federal and state laws to guide that commerce, the Electronic Signatures in Global and National Commerce (ESIGN) Act, 15 U.S.C. § 7001 et seq., and the Uniform Electronic Transactions Act (UETA). The ESIGN Act, for example, lends electronic signatures equal status with traditional signatures, and defines "electronic signatures" broadly to include any "electronic sound, symbol, or process, attached to or logically associated with a contract or other record and executed or adopted by a person with the intent to sign the record," 15 U.S.C. § 7006. UETA, for its part, contemplates an enormous range of signs and symbols of acquiescence as permissible electronic "signatures." The commentary to notes, for example:

> One's voice on an answering machine may suffice [as an electronic signature] if the requisite intention is present. Similarly, including one's name as part of an electronic mail communication also may suffice, as may the firm name on a facsimile. It also may be shown that the requisite intent was not present and accordingly the symbol, sound or process did not amount to a signature. . . . In any case the critical element is the intention to execute or adopt the sound or symbol or process for the purpose of signing the related record.

Although UETA is a uniform state statute, broadly adopted across the United States, it is not binding on federal procurement. Nor, in fact, is the ESIGN Act binding on federal agencies' procurement. See 15 U.S.C. § 7004. At the same time, however, the liberal approach taken by the two acts suggests that the boards and the courts are likely to take a similarly broad view of what qualifies as a permissible "signature" in electronic records used for federal contracting. See FAR 4.502 stating:

> (d) Agencies may accept electronic signatures and records in connection with Government contracts.

See also FAR 2.101 stating:

> *Signature* or *signed* means the discrete, verifiable symbol of an individual that, when affixed to a writing with the knowledge and consent of the individual, indicates a present intention to authenticate the writing. This includes electronic symbols.

The Court of Federal Claims decisions have cited the UETA as representative of "the commercial rules generally applied to electronic transmissions." *Insight Sys. Corp. v. United States*, 110 Fed. Cl. 564 (2013) (rejecting FAR interpretation that would be inconsistent with the UETA, asking: "Can it be that the drafters of the FAR intended a dramatically different rule to apply to contractors conducting electronic transactions in the Federal procurement sphere?"). In *Government Servs. Corp. v. United States*, 131 Fed. Cl. 409 (2017), the court noted that: "Although the UETA is not a federal law, the Government argues that it should determine the rights and liabilities of the parties."

The earlier cases laid the groundwork for the current broad understanding of "signatures" in an age of electronic contracting. In 1996, for example, GAO concluded that Electronic Data Interchange (EDI) technology, one of the earliest forms of electronic commerce, offered evidence of an intent to be bound that had the same attributes as a handwritten signature, *National Inst. of Standards & Tech.*, 71 Comp. Gen. 109 (B-245714), 96-2 CPD ¶ 225. In that case, GAO held that EDI systems using message authentication codes that follow the National Institute of Standards and Technology's (NIST) Computer Data Authentication Standard or digital signatures following NIST's Digital Standard, can produce a form of evidence of a signature.

Sending a signed document electronically may not be accepted as an electronic signature. *See General Dynamics C4 Sys.*, ASBCA 54988, 09-2 BCA ¶ 34,150, *rev'd on other grounds*, 633 F.3d 1356 (Fed. Cir. 2010), rejecting the argument that "electronic images" of delivery orders were signed documents because they did not contain a "digital signature" of the contracting officer. Similarly, GAO has rejected the acceptance of electronically submitted bid bonds on sealed bid procurements because there is no guarantee that such documents have not been altered from the actual original written bond, *TJ's Marine Constr. LLC*, Comp. Gen. Dec. B-402227, 2010 CPD ¶ 19; *Excel Bldg. & Dev. Corp.*, Comp. Gen. Dec. B-401955, 2009 CPD ¶ 262. See also *Teknocraft, Inc.*, ASBCA 55438, 08-1 BCA ¶ 33,846 (CDA claim sent by email with "//signed//" not valid because it contained no authenticated signature).

The requirement for authenticated signatures, transmitted using highly secure technologies, may prove out of step with evolving procurement law, which has traditionally accepted signatures in many forms, from faxes to photocopies. Where facsimile transmission is authorized, for example, GAO has held that a facsimile signature will be sufficient. In *American Eagle Indus., Inc.*, Comp. Gen. Dec. B-256907, 94-2 CPD ¶ 156, GAO held that a bidder's faxed modification did not render its bid nonresponsive merely because it instructed the agency to replace the original first page of its bid with a faxed page, thereby replacing the authorized agent's original signature with a faxed copy of the same agent's signature. Similarly, in *International Shelter Sys., Inc.*, 71 Comp. Gen. 142 (B-245466), 92-1 CPD ¶ 34, the protester argued that the facsimile and photocopy signatures did not equal an original signature and thus the bid was nonresponsive. GAO denied the protest and held that a photocopy of a signed bid document is binding as a duplicate of the original signed document because the signature still prevents the bidder from disavowing its obligations under the signed document.

An appeals board has followed GAO's reasoning that evidence of an intent to be bound has the same attributes as a handwritten signature. In *Regional Trucking, Inc.*, PSBCA 3918, 97-1 BCA ¶ 28,733, the board held that the hand-printed name and title of the contractor's president constituted acceptable evidence of the contractor's intent to be bound by the bid on which it was placed. The president had also hand-signed three other documents that were submitted as part of the bid and referred to the specific solicitation involved and the contractor subsequently completed, signed, and returned the preaward surveys. In reaching its decision, the board stated at 143,404:

> Courts, as well as the General Accounting Office, have long indicated a willingness to accept other than a handwritten signature on executory documents such as bid proposals. *See Ohl & Co. v. Smith Iron Works*, 288 U.S. 170, 176 (1932) (initials); *Benedict v. Lebowitz*, 346 F.2d 120 (2d Cir. 1965) (typed name); *Tabas v. Emergency Fleet Corporation*, 9 F.2d 648, 649 (E.D. Penn., 1926) (typed, printed or stamped signatures); *See also National Institute of Standards and Technology*, 71 Comp. Gen. 109 (1991) (use of electronic data interchange technology to create valid obligations). What is necessary is evidence of an intent to be bound. *Benedict v. Lebowitz, supra*; *see also*, *Peter J. O'Brien*, 96-2 CPD ¶ 91 (Aug. 29, 1996). In this case, Appellant hand printed the title of the corporation on the signature line, and hand printed "M.C. Johnson President" on the line calling for the name and title of the bidder. Mr. Johnson also hand signed three other documents which were submitted as a part of its bid, all of which either referred to the solicitation or highway route number. These actions constitute sufficient evidence of an intent to be bound by the bid documents. Furthermore, the fact that Appellant subsequently completed, signed and returned to Respondent the pre-award surveys, resolve any doubt of Appellant's intent to be bound by the bid it submitted.

[3] Superseding Requirement for Writing

Even though, as a general rule, oral agreements will bind the parties, a written document may be required by statutory or regulatory provisions or by limitations in a delegation of authority to a contracting officer. See, for example, *Harbert/Lummus Agrifuels Projects v. United States*, 142 F.3d 1429 (Fed. Cir. 1998), *cert. denied*, 525 U.S. 1177 (1999), holding that the government was not bound by an oral agreement of the contracting officer when his delegation of authority specifically required agreements to be in writing. See also *American Gen. Leasing, Inc. v. United States*, 587 F.2d 54 (Ct. Cl. 1978) (finding the government not bound by an oral agreement because both Standard Form 33 and the definition of "contract" in the Federal Procurement Regulation required contracts to be in writing); *Thomas Creek Lumber & Log Co. v. Kepthorne*, 250 Fed. Appx. 316 (Fed. Cir. 2007)_("Generally, a government contract must be in writing an signed by the parties before it binds them."); *Weeks v. United States*, 144 Fed. Cl. 34 (2019) (failure to reduce agreement to writing precluded contract formation); *NE Constr., Inc. v. United States*, 119 Fed. Cl. 596 (2015) (no contract formed where parties failed to reduce agreement to writing).

Most cases of this type of deal with contract modifications where the regulations have been interpreted as requiring a writing. See FAR 43.301(a)(1) requiring supplemental agreements (contract modifications) to be issued on Standard Form (SF) 30. In *SCM Corp. v. United States*, 595 F.2d 595 (Ct. Cl. 1979), the court held that the contractor and the contracting officer did not intend to be bound by their oral agreement settling a claim because of this requirement, stating at 598:

> Oral understandings which contemplate the finalization of the legal obligations in a written form are not contracts in themselves. When legal obligations between the parties *will be deferred* until the time when a written document is executed, there will not be a contract until that time. *See Restatement of Contracts* § 26 (1932). *See also Corbin on Contracts* § 30 (1963). Under the regulations, Government funds were not obligated until the execution of standard form 30. The parties were well aware of the fact that only the written contract modification could finalize their agreement. No commitments in the oral understanding to act in any way by either party were to be consummated until execution of the supplemental agreement. Whether the parties had reached a clear understanding of the terms of the settlement makes no difference and we specifically intimate no decision on that issue. We thus conclude that neither party was bound by its negotiations until standard form 30 was executed. This interpretation of the understanding and intent of the parties is supported by the actions of plaintiff in later seeking inclusion in the contract of an additional term for interest. Thus, we conclude that the representations made by telephone on January 6, 1976, did not constitute a contract.
>
> We note that this case does not squarely present the question of the enforceability of oral contracts with the Government. Instead, the case deals with the problem of what effect the parties' clear understanding of the procedures and regulations governing settlements had on their intent to consummate a binding contract. It should be kept in mind that oral understandings must first be contracts before they are enforceable. In this case, we simply hold that the understanding between the parties was not a contract and cannot sustain a breach of contract action in this court.

While the *SCM Corporation* decision was clearly based upon the conclusion that both parties did not intend to have a binding agreement until a SF 30 was signed, later decisions have focused on the need for a signed writing to modify an integrated contract. In *Mil-Spec Contractors, Inc. v. United States*, 835 F.2d 865 (Fed. Cir. 1987), the court cited the regulatory requirement for the use of a signed SF 30 in holding that an oral agreement was not a binding contract amendment. See also *Nat'l Sur. Corp. v. United States*, 118 F.3d 1542 (Fed. Cir. 1997) ("Although the contract requires that modifications be made by written change order (clause 3(a)), that oral modifications are ineffective unless confirmed in writing (clause 3(b)), and that under no other circumstances would the contracting officer's conduct be treated as modifying the contract (clause 3(c)), the government presented no evidence, either to the Court of Federal Claims or to this court, of the requisite procedures."); *Cooper Realty Co. v. United States*, 36 Fed. Cl. 284 (1996) ("Having failed to comply with the USPS rules and regulations, the oral agreement is not a valid contractual modification."). In *Daly Constr., Inc. v. Garrett*, 5 F.3d 520 (Fed. Cir. 1993), the court stated at 521:

> To recover on an express agreement with a government agency, the agreement must be in writing and signed by an authorized person. *Mil-Spec Contractors, Inc. v. United States*, 835 F.2d 865 (Fed. Cir. 1987). We need not here discuss whether any circumstances might warrant departure from that standard, for as to this particular contract modification Daly, although poorly used by the pattern of lengthy negotiation, apparent agreement, unwarranted delay, and broken promises, was not deceived. Daly knew the government was not bound in contract until a formal written modification was executed.

Board decisions have held that FAR 43.301 requires modifications to be in writing, *Kato Corp.*, ASBCA 51462, 06-2 BCA ¶33,293; *Johnson Mgmt. Group CFC, Inc.*, HUDBCA 96-C-132-C15, 00-2 BCA ¶31,116; *Marshall Associated Contractors, Inc., & Columbia Excavating, Inc. (J.V.)*, IBCA 1901, 98-1 BCA ¶29,965.

In contrast, the use of SF 30 was held to be a "mere formality" as long as the parties' agreement was in a signed writing, *Robinson Contracting Co. v. United States*, 16 Cl. Ct. 676 (1989), *aff'd*, 895 F.2d 1420 (Fed. Cir. 1989). See also *Adams Constr. Co.*, VABCA 4669, 97-1 BCA ¶28,801. While these decisions affect modifications to contracts, they do not deal with the initial formation of a contract.

[B] Consideration

Consideration can be described as the price bargained and paid for a promise. It may consist of an act, a forbearance, or a return promise. *Restatement, Second, Contracts* § 71 defines "consideration" as follows:

> (1) To constitute consideration, a performance or a return promise must be bargained for.
>
> (2) A performance or return promise is bargained for if it is sought by the promisor in exchange for his promise and is given by the promisee in exchange for that promise.

(3) The performance may consist of
(a) an act other than a promise, or
(b) a forbearance, or
(c) the creation, modification, or destruction of a legal relation.
(4) The performance or return promise may be given to the promisor or to some other person. It may be given by the promisee or by some other person.

The requirement for consideration flowing to the government is supported not only by the common-law rules but also by the rule that government officials generally do not have the authority to give up vested rights of the government without receiving consideration, *Simpson v. United States*, 172 U.S. 372 (1899). See also *Aviation Contractor Employees, Inc. v. United States*, 945 F.2d 1568 (Fed. Cir. 1991); *Metzger, Shadyac & Schwarz v. United States*, 12 Cl. Ct. 602 (1987); and *Joseph Pickard's Sons Co.*, ASBCA 13585, 73-1 BCA ¶ 10,026. The major exception to this rule is Pub. L. No. 85-804, 50 U.S.C. §§ 1431-35, which authorizes executive agencies to make or amend contracts without consideration when to do so would facilitate national defense. See FAR Part 50. In some circumstances particularly relevant to software transactions, an implied, revocable, nonexclusive copyright license may be found absent consideration. See *Bitmanagement Software GmBH v. United States*, 989 F.3d 938 (Fed. Cir. 2021).

[1] Form of Consideration

Generally, consideration in the typical sealed bid or negotiated government contract is found in the exchange of promises to perform positive duties. A bid or proposal is a promise to furnish supplies or services offered in exchange for the government's promise to pay for the work. The promise of compensation induces the offeror's promise of performance, and the offeror's promise to perform induces the award of the contract containing the government's promise to pay upon completion. Each party's promise serves as consideration for the other's. In unilateral contracts, as in some simplified acquisitions, consideration takes the form of an act, i.e., performance, induced by the government's promise to pay.

Consideration in contract modifications normally takes the form of promises by the contractor to perform work that is different from that originally required in exchange for the government's promise to pay a different price. See, for example, *Gardiner, Kamya & Assocs., P.C. v. Jackson*, 369 F.3d 1318 (Fed. Cir. 2004) (court, reversing board, found adequate consideration in agency's agreement to reprice earlier work in return for contractor's agreement in modification to perform certain work). In some cases, the consideration may be the agreement to forbear from exercising a right such as asserting a claim.

[a] Promises to Perform Duties

Cases in which consideration is not present may arise under different fact situations. In one type of case, the alleged promise or performance confers no benefit on the other party. In government contracts, this most often occurs when the government modifies a contract to benefit the contractor but receives no additional or different promise or performance in return. Under *Restatement, Second, Contracts* § 73, such modifications are without consideration because they involve performance of a preexisting duty that is neither doubtful nor the subject of honest dispute. See *Alpine Computers, Inc.*, ASBCA 54659, 05-2 BCA ¶ 32,997 (subcontractor delivery of equipment to agency when it was not paid by defaulted contractor); *National Micrographics Sys., Inc. v. United States*, 38 Fed. Cl. 46 (1997) (subcontractor delivery of computers to National Security Agency not valid consideration because insolvent contractor was already contractually obligated to deliver them); *AAA Eng'g & Drafting, Inc.*, ASBCA 36176, 91-2 BCA ¶ 23,812 (contract clause that provided for additional compensation as workload increased unenforceable where the government did not order the minimum amount of work specified in the contract); *Montefiore Hosp. v. United States*, 5 Cl. Ct. 471 (1984) (alleged agreement to modify contractual interest rate unenforceable because government received no benefit); *States Roofing & Metal Co.*, ASBCA 22091, 78-2 BCA ¶ 13,287 (change order that directed contractor to do work required under original contract for increased compensation not binding); and *A.O. Smith Corp.*, ASBCA 16788, 72-2 BCA ¶ 9688 (modification covering repair costs unenforceable since contractor was already obligated to make repairs). Furthermore, GAO has stated that a defaulted firm's bid on a reprocurement contract must be rejected if it is higher than the original contract price, on the grounds that acceptance of a higher bid would be tantamount to a contract modification increasing the price without any consideration for the government, *A.R.E. Mfg. Co.*, Comp. Gen. Dec. B-246161, 92-1 CPD ¶ 210; *Air, Inc.*, Comp. Gen. Dec. B-233501, 88-2 CPD ¶ 505. See, however, *Salsbury Indus. v. United States*, 17 Cl. Ct. 47 (1989), *aff'd*, 905 F.2d 1518 (Fed. Cir. 1990), indicating that the requirement to give notice would be sufficient to enforce the contract.

Another situation where no consideration exists is where one party has a right to avoid any contractual duties. See *Restatement, Second, Contracts* § 77. See also *3 Williston, Contracts* § 7:13 (4th ed., 1992), which states at 271, "An agreement wherein one party reserves the right to cancel at his pleasure cannot create a contract." This issue has been raised concerning the present Termination for the Convenience of the Government clause. An early government contracts case dealing with the question of lack of consideration and termination clause is *Sylvan Crest Sand & Gravel Co. v. United States*, 150 F.2d 642 (2d Cir. 1945), where the clause stated, "Cancellation by the Procurement Division may be effected at any time." The appellate court held that the contract was not illusory because it contained an implied promise by the government to give notice of cancellation within a reasonable time if it did not want to accept the goods. In *Torncello v. United States*, 681 F.2d 756 (Ct. Cl. 1982), the court extensively discussed the consideration issue and concluded that the scope of termination rights had to be limited to prevent the absence of consideration. The court also indicated that it disagreed with the reasoning in *Sylvan Crest* that the bare requirement to give notice constituted consideration. See also *Salsbury Indus. v. United States*, 17 Cl. Ct. 47 (1989), *aff'd*, 905 F.2d 1518 (Fed. Cir. 1990), where the court in a footnote reiterated that notice of impending termination might not constitute sufficient consideration in a contract with a Termination clause. In *Krygoski Constr. Co. v. United States*, 94 F.3d 1537 (Fed. Cir. 1996), the court interpreted *Torncello* to impose only the limitation of bad faith on such terminations without discussing whether this constituted consideration. See *Judiciary Plaza Limited Partnership v. Securities & Exchange Comm'n*, GSBCA 12920-SEC, 96-2 BCA ¶ 28,596, holding that a lease that granted the landlord broad termination rights was not invalid for lack of consideration. The board stated that upon signing the lease, the parties became subject to the obligations thereunder. The lease expressly described the parties' obligations in the event of a termination. See generally McConnell, *Note: Bad Faith as a Limitation on Terminations for Convenience: As Bad As They Say, Or Not So Bad?*, 32 Pub. Cont. L.J. 411 (2003).

In *Green Mgmt. Corp. v. United States*, 42 Fed. Cl. 411 (1998), the court held that the government's decision *not* to exercise its right to terminate for convenience was consideration for the contractor's agreement to a modification imposing restrictions on its method of performance. Since the government has very broad powers to terminate a contract for its convenience, this argument could be used to support modifications whenever a termination for convenience was in the interest of the government.

[b] Forbearance

Forbearance is a kind of consideration that does not involve the performance of any additional or modified duties. Perhaps the most common type of forbearance is involved in the settlement of claims. See *Restatement, Second, Contracts* § 74(1), which states:

> Forbearance to assert or the surrender of a claim or defense which proves to be invalid is not consideration unless
>
> (a) the claim or defense is in fact doubtful because of uncertainty as to the facts or the law, or
>
> (b) the forbearing or surrendering party believes that the claim or defense may be fairly determined to be valid.

See *Penn-Ohio Steel Corp. v. United States*, 354 F.2d 254 (Ct. Cl. 1965), where the government argued that a contractor's agreement to vacate a building was not consideration because a contract clause entitled the government to revoke the lease in case of a national emergency. The court found consideration because the contractor could have instituted a suit to enjoin the contractor's eviction from the plant under this legally questionable provision. Thus, the forbearance need not be on a claim that is legally correct. In *American Air Filter Co.*, ASBCA 14794, 72-1 BCA ¶ 9219, the government believed that a high-pressure cutout switch was a required item in a contract to furnish air conditioners. The contractor contended that the item was not required. The board held that the position of the contractor was incorrect, but because the claim was not completely unreasonable or in bad faith, the settlement of the claim by the government through contract modification was supported by consideration (the agreement by contractor to withdraw the claim). Compare *Institutional & Envtl. Mgmt.*, ASBCA 32924, 90-3 BCA ¶ 23,118, where a modification lacked consideration because the contractor's relinquished claim had "no color or claim of right." The board's reasoning is consistent with the general principle that consideration exists if one party is relinquishing a legal right or forbearing to exercise it in exchange for something from the other party, *Busby School Bd. of the N. Cheyenne Tribe*, IBCA 3007, 94-1 BCA ¶ 26,327; *ITT Gilfillan, Inc. v. United States*, 200 Ct. Cl. 367, 471 F.2d 1382 (1973). Several savings and loan cases have held that the government's forbearance in exercising its right to enforce regulatory requirements qualified as consideration for its contracts, *Hughes v. United States*, 498 F.3d 1334 (Fed. Cir. 2007), *cert. denied*, 552 U.S. 1309 (2008); *Franklin Fed. Sav. Bank v. United States*, 431 F.3d 1360 (Fed. Cir. 2005); *Admiral Financial Corp. v. United States*, 378 F.3d 1336 (Fed. Cir. 2004); *First Commerce Corp. v. United States*, 63 Fed. Cl. 627 (2005).

Another type of consideration through forbearance exists where the parties agree to release each other from a contract that has not been completely performed on either side. In *Savage Arms Corp. v. United States*, 266 U.S. 217 (1924), the Court stated at 220-21:

> A good deal is said by [the contractor] to the effect that this agreement was without consideration; but we need not stop to review the contention. It is enough to say that the parties to a contract may release themselves, in whole or in part, from its obligations so far as they remain executory, by mutual agreement without fresh consideration. The release of one is sufficient consideration for the release of the other. If authority for a rule so elementary be required, see, for example: *Hanson & Parker v. Wittenberg*, 205 Mass. 319, 326; *Collyer & Co. v. Moulton*, 9 R.I. 90, 92; *McCreery v. Day*, 119 N.Y. 1, 7; *Dreifus, Block & Co. v. Salvage Co.*, 194 Pa. St. 475, 486.

One example of such an agreement would be the no-cost termination authorized in FAR 49.402-4(c) (and set forth in FAR 49.603-6 and 49.603-7), through which a contractor, typically to avoid the threat of default termination, will agree to waive all claims in a "no cost" termination. In *Folk Constr. Co.*, ENGBCA 5839, 93-3 BCA ¶ 26,094, although not following the reasoning of

Savage Arms, the board found that the release of claims for additional compensation was valid consideration, stating at 129,728:

> [We] conclude that the release of claims element of the agreement satisfies the requirement for consideration. The claims were neither meritless on their face nor manufactured. Even if a tribunal subsequently determines that released or settled claims would have been resolved on their merits against the party advancing them, it will not *nunc pro tunc* divest the settlement of its consideration value.... Furthermore, withdrawal of even specious claims has been recognized as supplying consideration, where the defendant realizes the "nuisance value" of not defending against the allegations. See *Restatement, Second, Contracts* § 74(1).

Similarly, in *Aviation Contractor Employees, Inc. v. United States*, 945 F.2d 1568 (Fed. Cir. 1991), the claims were determined by the court to be meritless but were held to be the subject of an "honest dispute," with the result that their withdrawal was found to constitute consideration for a modification. See *Buesing v. United States,* 47 Fed. Cl. 621 (2000) ("A settlement agreement is a contract; mutual forbearance supplies the consideration.").

[2] Adequacy of Consideration

It is a well-established rule that the boards and courts will inquire only into whether there has been a bargained-for exchange and not into the adequacy of the consideration, *Silverman v. United States*, 679 F.2d. 865 (Ct. Cl. 1982); *Mills v. United States*, 410 F.2d 1255 (Ct. Cl. 1969). There is no requirement that the parties' obligations be relatively equal, *United States v. American Trading Co.*, 138 F. Supp. 536 (N.D. Cal. 1956); *Aywon Wire & Metal Corp.*, ASBCA 4966, 1963 BCA ¶3912. The Claims Court has stated that a contract does not lack mutuality merely because a particular promise is not offset by a similar promise or obligation. Rather, "the pertinent question is whether the agreement as a whole is supported by mutual consideration," *Florida Keys Aqueduct Auth. v. United States*, 7 Cl. Ct. 297 (1985), *aff'd*, 790 F.2d 95 (Fed. Cir. 1986). See also *Bailer v. United States*, 54 Fed. Cl. 459 (2002), *aff'd*, 94 Fed. Appx. 828 (Fed. Cir. 2004), where the court responded to the argument that the bank's bargain was so "bad" that it should not be enforced, stating at 499:

> The court, however, does not evaluate the adequacy of consideration, only the existence of consideration. Whether the arrangements were a "good deal" for one or the other or both parties is not a matter for the court. An implied-in-fact contract is a mutual endeavor, requiring a meeting of minds of both parties on all of the elements of a contract, including consideration. It is a long established rule that the court will inquire only into whether there has been a bargained for exchange, and not into the adequacy of consideration.

> The United States Court of Claims has stated: "As there is no indication of fraud or misrepresentation on the part of the plaintiff, the court is not concerned with the adequacy of the consideration furnished by the plaintiff" *Silverman v. United States,* 230 Ct. Cl. 701, 711, 679 F.2d 865, 871 (1982).

However, if the consideration furnished by a party is so inadequate as to cause the tribunal to determine that the agreement would be unconscionable, it will not be enforced. See *Hume v. United States,* 132 U.S. 406 (1889), stating at 410:

> That an agreement to pay $1200 a ton for shucks, actual worth not more than $35 a ton, is a grossly unconscionable bargain, defined in Bouvier's Law Dictionary to be "a contract which no man in his senses, not under delusion, would make, on the one hand, and which no fair and honest man would accept on the other," nobody can doubt. Such a contract, whether founded on fraud, accident, mistake, folly, or ignorance, is void at common law. It is not necessary to invoke the aid of a court of equity to reform it. Courts of law will always refuse to enforce such a bargain, as against the public policy of honesty, fair dealing, and good morals.

Similarly, GAO has indicated that it will not inquire into adequacy of the bargain when determining whether consideration exists. See, for example, 47 Comp. Gen. 170 (B-160886) (1967), stating at 173:

> However, it is well settled that the legal sufficiency of a promise or benefit is not dependent upon the adequacy of the bargain. In other words, an extravagant promise for an inadequate consideration will still be held to constitute legally sufficient consideration. See *Contracts,* 17 Am. Jur. 2d, sections 85, 92 and 102. Accordingly, we conclude that the portion of the amendment dealing with the culler-stacker is supported by consideration.

GAO has indicated that the reasoning behind the refusal to address the adequacy of the consideration lies in the belief that it is an issue of contract administration, better left to the individual agencies. See *Stancil-Hoffman Corp.*, Comp. Gen. Dec. B-193001.2, 80-2 CPD ¶ 226, stating:

> . The issue as to adequacy of the consideration received by the Air Force for relaxing the delivery schedule of VRC's contract pertains to a matter of contract administration since the reinstatement of the contract has been found to be proper. As such, it is not for resolution within our bid protest function. See *Acadian Airmotive Inc.*, B-196414, 80-1 CPD ¶ 270.

[3] Severability of Consideration

Government contracts involve a number of obligations of or benefits to each party. In general, such contracts are not divided into individual exchanges. Thus, the total benefit or detriment of one party is normally thought to be consideration for the total obligations of the other. Further, a single obligation or benefit can support a number of promises. See *Home Sav. of Am., F.S.B. v. United States*, 70 Fed. Cl. 303 (2006), finding that a single promise was adequate to constitute consideration for numerous promises by the other party, quoting 2 *Corbin on Contracts* § 5.12: "A single and undivided consideration may be bargained for and given as the agreed equivalent of one promise or of two promises or of many promises." However, these rules do not apply when the agreements are severable, for example, when a benefit or promise runs to only one portion of the contract. See *Telex Commc'ns, Inc. v. United States*, 40 Fed. Cl. 703 (1998), rejecting the contractor's argument that purchase orders based on a master contract were separate contracts, each subject to consideration requirement.

A few cases have found severable promises. In *Pennsylvania Exch. Bank v. United States*, 170 F. Supp. 629 (Ct. Cl. 1959), the contract called for work in four steps. Steps I, II, and III required the contractor to tool up and get ready to manufacture exchange tees. Step IV required the contractor to stand by and be prepared to manufacture the tees. The contractor claimed it was not bound since the government was not obligated to order any tees under Step IV. The court first found that the contract was not severable. It then held that consideration existed even though the contractor was reimbursed only for its costs in Steps I, II, and III. The contractor was benefited by obtaining, at government expense, the capacity to produce the tees. Similarly, in *Shipco Gen., Inc.*, ASBCA 29206, 86-2 BCA ¶ 18,973, the government granted an extension of the contract completion date in consideration of the contractor's release of a valid claim. The contract modification contained a separate provision applying liquidated damages to a more demanding delivery requirement. The board held that the parties did not intend that the time extension relate to the altered provisions regarding the delivery schedule. Therefore, the agreements were severable and the revised delivery schedule failed for lack of consideration by the government. See also 47 Comp. Gen. 170 (B-160886) (1967), where GAO divided a contract amendment into three separate agreements for the purpose of consideration and found one to lack sufficient consideration, and *Hemet Valley Flying Serv. Co. v. United States*, 7 Cl. Ct. 512 (1985), where the Forest Service paid the contractor to be available to fly. This payment was an indivisible part of the contract which furnished consideration for the contractor's obligation to satisfy all the Forest Service's flight order needs. Similarly, in *Enron Fed. Sys., Inc. v. United States*, 80 Fed. Cl. 382 (2008), the court rejected the contractor's argument that the amortization of capital improvements was divisible from balance of the contract, and in *Parcel 49C Limited Partnership v. General Servs. Admin.*, GSBCA 15222, 00-2 BCA ¶ 31,073, the board rejected the government's argument that a lease and its supplemental agreements were separate agreements. See also *Clear Creek Community Servs. Dist. v. United States*, 2017 WL 6520854 (2017) (discussing precedent).

Because a release of a claim must be supported by consideration, severability of consideration has been used to avoid general releases included in change orders. For example, compensation for the increased costs of change orders was held to be inadequate to support a general release of the contractor's subsequent claims arising from the defective government property that precipitated the change orders, *Dero Indus., Inc.*, ASBCA 16473, 72-1 BCA ¶ 9462. See also *Sam Won Dev. Co.*, ASBCA 16541, 74-2 BCA ¶ 10,730, where the board stated that such a release by the contractor would be gratuitous. Furthermore, when the parties do not intend a time extension to be the sole consideration for a change order, claims for additional compensation arising from the change order are not precluded, *Discon Corp.*, ASBCA 15981, 71-2 BCA ¶ 9069. Where, however, the amount agreed upon by the negotiating parties is not clearly related solely to the change order involved, or there is a good faith dispute concerning either the entitlement to the adjustment or its amount, the inclusion of a broader release or waiver will be supported by the compromise agreement, *Boston Shipyard Corp. v. United States Military Sealift Command*, 886 F.2d 451 (1st Cir. 1989); *Spellman Eng'g Inc.*, NASABCA 367-11, 69-2 BCA ¶ 7891. Of course, a release already called for by the contract upon completion of performance is not lacking consideration even though the contractor receives only amounts otherwise due, *IMS Engineers-Architects, P.C. v. United States*, 92 Fed. Cl. 52 (2010); *Optimum Designs, Inc.*, ASBCA 16986, 74-1 BCA ¶ 10,622; *Inland Empire Builders, Inc. v. United States*, 424 F.2d 1370 (Ct. Cl. 1970) (citing authorities). Such releases are based on the consideration contained in the government's promises in the original contract.

[4] Consideration in Variable Quantity Contracts

When the government wishes to obtain firm contractual commitments from contractors but is unable to forecast its precise needs, an indefinite-quantity contract is often used. There are three basic types of indefinite-quantity contracts. One of the most commonly used is the requirements contract, where the government agrees to purchase its "needs" or "requirements" from one contractor for a specified period of time. See FAR 16.503(a). There is no issue of consideration in this type of agreement because the contractor is bound to furnish items and the government agrees to purchase its requirements solely from the contractor, *United States v. Purcell Envelope Co.*, 249 U.S. 313 (1919); *Ceredo Mortuary Chapel, Inc. v. United States*, 29 Fed. Cl. 346 (1993); *Vehicle Maint. Servs. v. General Servs. Admin.*, GSBCA 11663, 94-2 BCA ¶ 26,893. In *Machlett Labs., Inc.*, ASBCA 16194, 73-1 BCA ¶ 9929, the board found an enforceable contract even though the government never placed a single order. Similarly, in 52 Comp. Gen. 732 (B-176901) (1973), it was held that the use of a clause providing that "no guarantee is given that any quantities will be purchased" did not render a requirements contract unenforceable for lack of consideration.

An unusual case where the court enforced a requirements contract is *Torncello v. United States*, 681 F.2d 756 (Ct. Cl. 1982). In that case, the contractor was awarded a requirements contract by the Navy for grounds maintenance and refuse removal. The contractor's bid itemization, accepted by the government, specified a per-call charge of $500 for any call under the pest control item. It turned out, however, that the Navy only needed gopher-control work which was customarily cheaper than $500 per call. Therefore, the Navy did not call the contractor for this work but instead requested such work from a competing bidder on the original solicitation. The contractor claimed that the Navy had breached its contract when it diverted work to a competing bidder. The court agreed and rejected the government's argument that the Termination for Convenience clause creates in the government an implicit right to refrain from giving a contractor work if it is not in the best interests of the government. The court stated at 772:

> In the case before us, the Navy had accepted Soledad's bid and had executed a contract knowing that another bid was lower. This contract bound the Navy to give to Soledad all of its pest control needs at the six housing projects covered. The Navy could not just walk away from this promise without making a mockery of the contract. It is nothing more than basic contract law that a power to terminate must be limited in some meaningful way, as measured by the requirement of consideration.... Therefore, we must read the termination for convenience clause in Soledad's contract to require some kind of change from the circumstances of the bargain or in the expectations of the parties.

A second type of indefinite-quantity contract requires the contractor to furnish all supplies or services ordered by the government but obligates the government to order only a stated minimum quantity. These are commonly referred to as "Indefinite-Delivery/Indefinite-Quantity" ("IDIQ") contracts. See FAR 16.504 and FAR 52.216-22. After the government has ordered the minimum quantity, it is free to order the remainder of its "needs" or "requirements" from either the same contractor or from any other source. However, the contractor continues to be bound to supply all that is ordered from it even after the minimum amount. Consideration to support this obligation of the contractor is found in the government's agreement to order the minimum quantity. See *J. Cooper & Assocs., Inc. v. United States*, 53 Fed. Cl. 8 (2002), *aff'd*, 65 Fed. Appx. 731 (Fed. Cir. 2003), stating at 17:

> Because the buyer is not obligated to purchase all requirements from the seller, unless the buyer contracts to purchase a minimum quantity, an IDIQ contract is "illusory and the contract unenforceable against the seller." *Mason v. United States*, 222 Ct. Cl. at 443 n.5, 615 F.2d at 1346, n. 5, (citing *Willard, Sutherland & Co. v. United States*, 262 U.S. at 493, 43 S. Ct. 592;

Corbin, *Contracts* § 157; *see also Coyle's Pest Control, Inc. v. Cuomo*, 154 F.3d 1302, 1304 (Fed. Cir.1998)).

The minimum order, however, must be for more than just a nominal amount in order for consideration to exist. See FAR 16.504(a)(2) stating:

> To ensure that the contract is binding, the minimum quantity must be more than a nominal quantity, but it should not exceed the amount that the Government is fairly certain to order.

See *Tennessee Soap Co. v. United States*, 126 F. Supp. 439 (Ct. Cl. 1954), holding that a $10 minimum amount was nominal. However, IDIQ contracts with very small minimums have been held to have sufficient consideration. See *Travel Centre v. Barram*, 236 F.3d 1316 (Fed. Cir. 2001) ($100 minimum revenue); *CW Gov't Travel, Inc.*, Comp. Gen. Dec. B-295530, 2005 CPD ¶ 59, *recons. denied*, 2005 CPD ¶ 205 ($2,500 minimum amount on a contract with the $15,000,000 maximum order amount); *ABF Freight Sys., Inc.*, Comp. Gen. Dec. B-291185, 2002 CPD ¶ 201 (minimum of a "few hundred dollars"); *TRS Research*, Comp. Gen. Dec. B-290644, 2002 CPD ¶ 159 ($10,000 minimum on contract with estimated value of $45 million). In *C.W. Over & Sons, Inc.*, Comp. Gen. Dec. B-274365, 96-2 CPD ¶ 223, GAO held that the requirement that the value of an IDIQ contract be more than nominal does not apply to individual task orders under a contract. In this case, GAO found it sufficient that there was a guarantee minimum value of $800,000 for the base contract period.

Another type of indefinite-quantity contract is one that does not bind the government either to purchase its requirements or to place a minimum order. Such contracts are often referred to as "wish, want or will" contracts and are unenforceable for lack of consideration where no order is placed, *Modern Sys. Tech. Corp.*, 24 Cl. Ct. 360 (1991); *Updike v. United States*, 69 Ct. Cl. 394 (1930). As discussed above, this issue arises in the case of blanket ordering agreements. See *Crewzers Fire Crew Transport, Inc. v. United States*, 741 F.3d 1380 (Fed. Cir. 2014). However, if the government places an order with the contractor, it will be treated as an offer that the contractor may accept to form a binding agreement as to that particular order. See, for example, *Bel Pre Health Care Ctr. v. United States*, 24 Cl. Ct. 495 (1991); *Ann Riley & Assocs.*, DOTBCA 2418, 93-3 BCA ¶ 25,963. In *Ralph Constr., Inc. v. United States*, 4 Cl. Ct. 727 (1984), the court found lack of consideration in an indefinite-quantity contract that contained no promised minimum quantity and no firm requirements promise because the government had reserved the right to assign work to its own workforce. However, rather than finding that the entire contract was unenforceable for lack of consideration, the court found that it was valid only to the extent it was performed. On this basis, the court held that the contractor was entitled to the reasonable value of the work completed but was not entitled to additional costs. See also *Satellite Servs., Inc.*, Comp. Gen. Dec. B-280945, 98-2 CPD

¶ 125, finding lack of consideration when the contract contained a government promise to allow awardees to enter into limited competition for future task orders, but the contracting officer could deny contractors the right to compete if it was "in the best interest of the government."

If a contract is susceptible to interpretation as either an indefinite-quantity contract without a specified minimum order or a requirements contract, the general rule is that the court should uphold it as a requirements type, *A-Transport Northwest Co. v. United States*, 27 Fed. Cl. 206 (1992).

[5] Consideration to Contractor

Although it is clear that the government must receive consideration for the execution of a contract modification, there is a split of authority on the need for the contractor to receive consideration. GAO has held that a contractor need not receive consideration to be bound by a contract modification, Comp. Gen. Dec. B-151383, Nov. 3, 1966, *Unpub.* See also *Mid-State Prods. Co. v. Commodity Credit Corp.*, 196 F.2d 416 (7th Cir. 1952); and *Equipment Corp. v. United States*, 98 Ct. Cl. 159 (1942).

It is doubtful if this rule will be followed at the current time. Several boards of contract appeals have held that a contractor must receive consideration. In one case, a $700 credit to the government for substitution of a conforming brand was held to be without consideration since the government was obligated to accept a conforming brand under the original contract, *Hunt Bldg. Marts*, DOTCAB 69-6, 69-2 BCA ¶ 8042. A second case involved the government's reduction of the contract price for a nonconforming item. Having determined that the item was acceptable, the board held that the agreement reducing the price was without consideration and, thus, not binding, *Airco Eng'rs*, AGBCA 245, 72-1 BCA ¶ 9215. In a third case, the government issued a unilateral contract modification adding a Liquidated Damages clause to the contract. The board held that because the amount of liquidated damages to be assessed in the event of delay is a vital condition affecting the price of a contract, the government's unilateral modification was not supported by consideration and, therefore, was not binding upon the contractor, *Jacqueline Howell, Ltd.*, ASBCA 27026, 82-2 BCA ¶ 16,086. See also *Yardney Tech. Prods., Inc.*, ASBCA 53866, 09-2 BCA ¶ 34,277, finding no consideration when the contractor agreed to correct a specification error for no increase in price.

In addition, at least one board of contract appeals has adopted the view in *Restatement, Second, Contracts* § 89 that allows modification of an executory agreement without consideration to the contractor—

> (a) if the modification is fair and equitable in view of circumstances not anticipated by the parties when the contract was made; or (b) to the extent provided by statute; or (c) to the extent that justice requires enforcement in view of a material change of position in reliance on the promise.

See *Florida East Coast Props., Inc.*, GSBCA 7538, 86-3 BCA ¶ 19,070; *Universal Bldg. Servs. Inc.*, GSBCA 7396, 85-1 BCA ¶ 17,732; *Zebra Corp.*, GSBCA 4723, 80-2 BCA ¶ 14,484.

[C] Promissory Estoppel

Promissory estoppel is a concept developed by the courts to enforce agreements on the basis of fairness and justice when consideration is not present but a person has reasonably relied on a promise. Whereas equitable estoppel is used to bar a party from raising a defense or objection, promissory estoppel is used to create a cause of action, *Knaub v. United States*, 22 Cl. Ct. 268 (1991). The necessary requirements for application of promissory estoppel are stated in *Restatement, Second, Contracts* § 90:

> (1) A promise which the promisor should reasonably expect to induce action or forbearance on the part of the promisee or a third person and which does induce such action or forbearance is binding if injustice can be avoided only by enforcement of the promise. The remedy granted for breach may be limited as justice requires.

Promissory estoppel has been infrequently used in government contracts, and it would appear that in some of the cases where is has been applied, it has been used unnecessarily. See, for example, *George H. Whike Constr. Co. v. United States*, 140 F. Supp. 560 (Ct. Cl. 1956), where the bidder entered into a written contract and performed it upon the assurance that the provision for reimbursement included in its bid would protect it from increased costs resulting from changes in labor regulations. It seems apparent that either the contractor's agreement or its subsequent performance should have been sufficient consideration. There was no need to resort to promissory estoppel since the "acts in reliance" were the very things bargained for by the government. See also *Lockheed Shipbuilding & Constr. Co.*, ASBCA 18460, 75-1 BCA ¶ 11,246, *recons. denied*, 75-2 BCA ¶ 11,566, and *Mercury Mach. & Mfg. Co.*, ASBCA 20068, 76-1 BCA ¶ 11,809, where all of the elements of consideration were present but the board held for the contractor based on "equitable or promissory estoppel." In *Louisiana Lamps & Shades*, ASBCA 45294, 95-1 BCA ¶ 27,577, the board held that the government did not establish promissory estoppel because the government did not prove that the terminating contracting officer relied on the contractor's promise to deliver the work by a certain date when deciding not to terminate the contractor for default.

There is a long line of decisions holding that the Court of Federal Claims has no jurisdiction over claims against the government on the theory of promissory estoppel because it is, in effect, a contract implied-in-law, over which the court has no jurisdiction. See *Landgraf v. United States*, 151 Fed. Cl. 326 (2020) ("the Court does not have jurisdiction over claims arising from promissory estoppel"); *Steinberg v. United States*, 90 Fed. Cl. 435, 443 (2009) ("Promissory estoppel . . . requires the court find an implied-in-law contract, [and therefore the court has no jurisdiction, because such] a claim [is one] for which the United States has not waived its sovereign immunity."); *LaMirage, Inc. v. United States*, 44 Fed. Cl. 192 (1999) (same); *Hubbs v. United States*, 20 Cl. Ct. 423, 427 (1990) ("[p]romissory estoppel is another name for an implied-in-law contract claim."). See *Craig-Buff Ltd. P'ship v. United States*, 69 Fed. Cl. 382 (2006), and *Sinclair v. United States*, 56 Fed. Cl. 270 (2003), reasoning that promissory estoppel is a theory used to "create" a contract "that would not otherwise exist" and such a contract must be an implied-in-law contract over which the court has no jurisdiction.

The Federal Circuit has not ruled on this issue in a precedential opinion. In a non-precedential decision, however, the Federal Circuit explained in a footnote that the *pro se* plaintiff raised claims of promissory estoppel, and then stated that "it is well established that the Court of Federal Claims does not have jurisdiction over such claims." *Piotrowski v. United States*, 722 Fed. Appx. 982 n.1 (Fed. Cir. 2018). And, in *Pacific Gas & Elec. Co. v. United States*, 3 Cl. Ct. 329 (1983), *aff'd*, 738 F.2d 452 (Fed. Cir. 1984), the court affirmed a decision denying a claim of promissory estoppel without a discussion of promissory estoppel.

This rationale does not recognize the distinction between promissory estoppel and implied-in-law contracts. Although both concepts are based upon considerations of justice and fairness, promissory estoppel requires that the person being charged make an actual promise, express or implied in fact. On the other hand, the "promises" referred to in contracts implied in law (alternatively referred to as "quasi contracts") are legal fictions. They are "implied" by courts to recognize that a person of good faith would want to pay compensation for a benefit that they received from another. They are based upon the legal and equitable rules of restitution, which, according to the Supreme Court, are not covered by the Tucker Act, *Merritt v. United States*, 267 U.S. 338 (1925).

The boards of contract appeals have also ruled that they have no jurisdiction over claims based on promissory estoppel. See *Relyant, LLC*, ASBCA 59809, 18-1 BCA ¶ 37,085; *P.J. Dick, Inc. v. General Servs. Admin.*, CBCA 461, 07-1 BCA ¶ 33,534; *RGW Commc'ns, Inc.*, ASBCA 54495, 05-2 BCA ¶ 32,972; *Embarcadero Center, Ltd.*, GSBCA 8526, 89-1 BCA ¶ 21,362. In *RGW Commc'ns* the board rejected the applicability of a prior case, *United Pacific Ins. Co.*, ASBCA 52419, 04-1 BCA ¶ 32,494, *aff'd*, 401 F.3d 1362 (Fed. Cir. 2005), which had discussed whether the elements of promissory estoppel existed because that discussion was in "a 'straw man' or 'even if' fashion." For other cases discussing whether the elements of promissory estoppel are present, see *Systems Mgmt. Am. Corp.*, ASBCA 45704, 97-1 BCA ¶ 28,820 (claim reinstated to determine whether contractor's reliance was based on assurances that option would be exercised); *State Street Mgmt. Corp. v. General Servs. Admin.*, GSBCA 12374, 94-1 BCA ¶ 26,500 (government statements not specific enough for reliance); and *Louisiana Lamps & Shades*, ASBCA 45294, 95-1 BCA

¶ 27,577 (government did not prove reliance in its claim based on promissory estoppel).

In *Law Mathematics & Tech., Inc. v. United States*, 779 F.2d 675 (Fed. Cir. 1985), on appeal from a board of contract appeals, the contractor argued that it took certain actions in reliance on the government's assurances that it would provide additional funds on the contract. The court held that even if the government had made such assurances and the contractor had relied upon them, the contractor still could not recover. The court held that the contractor's reliance would not have been reasonable, stating at 679:

> Finally, even if LMT had relied to its detriment on any promises or assertions, such reliance could not have been reasonable in this case. Dr. Sponsler is an attorney, with the ability to understand the specific limitations of the contract language. Moreover, Sponsler is also a former Navy employee, and should have been, if he was not, familiar with the uncertainty of relying on additional allocations to Navy research contracts.

In another appeal from a board of contract appeals, the government argued that promissory estoppel was not available against the government. In a decision not for precedent, the court did not address this argument, disposing of the appeal on the grounds that the contractor did not offer "any concrete evidence that it relied on a promise to change its position for the worse," *Delfour, Inc. v. Runyon*, 95 F.3d 1163 (Fed. Cir. 1996).

CHAPTER 3

ACQUISITION PLANNING

- [c] Functional Specifications
- [2] Sources of Specifications
  - [a] Government Specifications
    - [i] Military Specifications
    - [ii] Federal Specifications
  - [b] Nongovernment Standards
- [3] Improper Specifications
  - [a] Unduly Restrictive Specifications
  - [b] Unclear or Ambiguous Specifications
    - [i] Requirement for Clarity
    - [ii] Errors or Omissions in Specifications
    - [iii] Open or Indefinite Specifications
- [B] Consolidation/Bundling
  - [1] Consolidation
  - [2] Bundling
- [C] Draft Solicitations and Specifications

§ 3.06 Overall Cost to the Government
- [A] Acquisition Cost
- [B] Life-Cycle Cost
- [C] Design-to-Cost

§ 3.07 Procurement Notices
- [A] Presolicitation Notices and Conferences
  - [1] GPE Notice Requirements
  - [2] Presolicitation Exchanges with Industry
- [B] Solicitation of Bids or Proposals
  - [1] Alternate Means of Issuing Solicitations
    - [a] Paper or CD-ROM
    - [b] Facsimile
    - [c] Oral Solicitations
- [C] Notice Requirement
- [D] System for Award Management

§ 3.01 PLANNING PROCESS

"Acquisition planning" is an expansive term that includes actions aimed at stating the government's needs, identifying potential sources, and determining the techniques to be used to satisfy those needs. It is the first step in the procurement process. FAR 2.101 contains the following broad definition:

> "Acquisition planning" means the process by which the efforts of all personnel responsible for an acquisition are coordinated and integrated through a comprehensive plan for fulfilling the agency need in a timely manner and at a reasonable cost. It includes developing the overall strategy for managing the acquisition.

A well-planned procurement will be structured to comply with the numerous acquisition laws and regulations as well as to obtain, most effectively, the goods or services needed by the agency. A procurement that is not well planned can lead to numerous problems that waste the time and funds of both the procuring agency and the offerors.

This chapter reviews all elements of acquisition planning conducted by a procuring agency. The first section explains the planning process as mandated by law and implemented by regulation. The next two sections cover the requirement for competition and the selection of the contracting technique. The fourth section addresses identifying sources for obtaining goods or services. The fifth section deals with the preparation of the statement of work. The sixth section deals with the consideration of overall cost to the government in the acquisition planning process. The final section covers public announcements and solicitations.

The planning process brings all members of the acquisition team together to formulate the strategy that will be used to conduct a procurement.

[A] Requirement for Planning

As a result of deficiencies in the planning process, a number of agencies began to focus on the need for more formalized acquisition planning in the 1970s. Congress also identified this need during discussions on the Competition in Contracting Act of 1984 (CICA). As a result, the Armed Services Procurement Act and the Federal Property and Administrative Services Act now require that an executive agency "use advance procurement planning and market research" in preparing for the procurement of property or services, 10 U.S.C. § 3206(a)(1)(B) (formerly § 2305(a)(1)(A)(ii)); and 41 U.S.C. § 3306(a)(1)(B). FAR Part 7 implements this requirement.

FAR 7.102(b) states that "[t]he purpose of this planning is to ensure that the government meets its needs in the most effective, economical, and timely manner." The acquisition planning requirement in FAR 7.102 is pervasive:

> (a) Agencies shall perform acquisition planning and conduct market research (see part 10) for all acquisitions in order to promote and provide for—
>
> (1) Acquisition of commercial items or, to the extent that commercial items suitable to meet the agency's needs are not available, nondevelopmental items, to the maximum extent practicable; and
>
> (2) Full and open competition (see part 6), or, when full and open competition is not required in accordance with part 6, to obtain competition to the maximum extent practicable, with due regard to the nature of the supplies or services to be acquired . . .
>
> (3) Selection of appropriate contract type in accordance with part 16; and
>
> (4) Appropriate consideration of the use of pre-existing contracts, including interagency and intra-agency contracts, to fulfill the requirement, before awarding new contracts. (See 8.002 through 8.004 and subpart 17.5).

In some cases, the lack of adequate acquisition planning will place the agency in a position where it will attempt to acquire supplies and services without obtaining full and open competition. See *Freund Precision, Inc.*, 66 Comp. Gen. 90 (B-223613), 86-2 CPD ¶ 543 (failure to plan ahead precluded agency from evaluating protester's alternate product and resulted in sole source procurement); and *TeQcom, Inc.*, Comp. Gen. Dec. B-224664, 86-2 CPD ¶ 700 (failure to plan ahead effectively deprived offerors of any opportunity to qualify their products so that they could compete with the brand name manufacturer). In this regard, lack of advance planning does not justify noncompetitive procurement, as stated in 10 U.S.C. § 3204(e)(5)(A)(i) (formerly § 2304(f)(4)) and 41 U.S.C. § 3304(e)(5)(a)(i):

> In no case may the head of an agency—
>
> enter into a contract for property or services using procedures other than competitive procedures on the basis of the lack of advance planning . . .

See also FAR 6.301(c) prohibiting justification of contracting without full and open competition based on a lack of advance planning.

Cases finding a lack of advance planning include *Global Dynamics, LLC v. United States*, 137 Fed. Cl. 772 (2018) (lack of qualified employees and heavy workload not excuse for very slow corrective action); *XTec, Inc.*, Comp. Gen. Dec. B-410778.3, 2015 CPD ¶ 292 (issuance of solicitation with only "high-level" requirements led to cancellation of procurement with inadequate time for competition); *Cherokee Nation Techs., LLC v. United States*, 116 Fed. Cl. 636 (2014) (taking corrective action by cancelling award to protester and awarding bridge contract to incumbent contractor); *Innovation Dev. Enters. of Am., Inc. v. United States*, 108 Fed. Cl. 711 (2013) (failure to conduct market research or to include transition time in competing for follow-on services); *RBC Bearings*

Inc., Comp. Gen. Dec. B-401661, 2009 CPD ¶ 207 (failure to test product to provide competition for sole source); *eFedBudget Corp.*, Comp. Gen. Dec. B-298627, 2006 CPD ¶ 159 (no record of steps taken by agency to overcome proprietary software); *VSE Corp.*, Comp. Gen. Dec. B-290452.3, 2005 CPD ¶ 103 (no effort to plan for a competitive bridge contract when agency knew it would cancel solicitation for follow on contract); *Signals & Sys., Inc.*, Comp. Gen. Dec. B-288107, 2001 CPD ¶ 168 (agency took two years to draft performance specification permitting competition); *TLC Servs., Inc.*, Comp. Gen. Dec. B-252614, 93-1 CPD ¶ 481 (agency could not prepare work statement because of inadequate and inexperienced staff); and *K-Whit Tools, Inc.*, Comp. Gen. Dec. B-247081, 92-1 CPD ¶ 382 (agency took 10 months to determine requirements when it knew that the items were required by a fixed deadline).

Advance planning need not be entirely error-free or actually successful, *Infrastructure Def. Techs., LLC v. United States*, 81 Fed. Cl. 375 (2008); *Sprint Commc'ns Co.*, Comp. Gen. Dec. B-262003.2, 96-1 CPD ¶ 24. See also *Trailboss Enters., Inc.*, Comp. Gen. Dec. B-415812.2, 2018 CPD ¶ 171 (protest time necessitated a sole source bridge contract); *American Sys. Corp.*, Comp. Gen. Dec. B-412501.2, 2016 CPD ¶ 91 (corrective action necessitated a sole source bridge contract); *Filtration Dev. Co., LLC v. United States*, 60 Fed. Cl. 371 (2004) (agency made several unsuccessful attempts to address the problem before issuing the urgent procurement); *Bannum, Inc.*, Comp. Gen. Dec. B-289707, 2002 CPD ¶ 61 (while the agency's planning ultimately was unsuccessful, this was due to unanticipated events, not a lack of planning). However, the planning actions must be reasonable. In *New Breed Leasing Corp.*, Comp. Gen. Dec. B-274201, 96-2 CPD ¶ 202, GAO sustained a protest, finding that had the agency engaged in reasonable advance planning, it would not have taken more than a year after the solicitations were issued to realize that the solicitations were fundamentally flawed in failing to contain basic information. Similarly, in *Commercial Drapery Contractors, Inc.*, Comp. Gen. Dec. B-271222, 96-1 CPD ¶ 290, an agency sought to justify its issuance of purchase orders to a Multiple Award Federal Supply Schedule contractor at higher prices than offered by other Federal Supply Schedule contractors by arguing that it urgently needed the supplies and only the selected contractor could meet the delivery time. GAO sustained the protest, finding that the urgency resulted from delays caused by the agency's prior improper issuance of purchase orders to the same contractor for the same requirement and the subsequent cancellation of those orders in response to clearly meritorious protests. See, however, *Datacom, Inc.*, Comp. Gen. Dec. B-274175, 96-2 CPD ¶ 199, rejecting the protester's claim that the urgency necessitating a noncompetitive sole source award and contract modification resulted from the lack of advance planning. GAO found that the Air Force had failed to compete its procurement because a congressional report directed the agency to go no further in its effort to hold a competition of any kind. See also *Argon ST, Inc.*, Comp. Gen. Dec. B-402908, 2011 CPD ¶ 4 (planning adequate when agency took over a year to formulate plan for competition); *Diversified Tech. & Servs. of Virginia.*,

Inc., Comp. Gen. Dec. B-282497, 99-2 CPD ¶ 16 (refusing to fault agency where the procurement was delayed by the agency's efforts to implement a long-term acquisition plan).

Potential offerors' ability to assess and challenge agencies' acquisition planning is complicated by the mechanics of the protest process. Offerors generally have little real access to the agencies' internal planning documents, as those materials are generally not made public. See *Holmes & Narver Servs., Inc./Morrison-Knudsen Servs., Inc.,* Comp. Gen. Dec. B-235906, 89-2 CPD ¶ 379 (acquisition plan to be released to erase competitive imbalance). Moreover, even if a protest is brought, GAO has shown deference to agency planning processes, even if only minimal, *Warden Assocs., Inc.*, Comp. Gen. Dec. B-291440, 2002 CPD ¶ 223 (agency conducted sufficient planning under FAR Subpart 8.4 by simply contacting vendors); *Sales Res. Consultants, Inc.*, Comp. Gen. Dec. B-284943, 2000 CPD ¶ 102 (surveying schedule vendors adequate, so long as appropriately documented); *Wescam, Inc.*, Comp. Gen. Dec. B-285792, 2000 CPD ¶ 168 (agency produced written plan and e-mails reflecting internal planning); *N&N Travel & Tours, Inc.*, Comp. Gen. Dec. B-285164.2, 2000 CPD ¶ 146 (challenges to inadequate planning for IDIQ task order were outside GAO's limited jurisdiction). Furthermore, GAO has held that, if an agency does have a plan and deviates from that plan, that deviation is not a ground for protest, *Hubbell Elec. Heater Co.*, Comp. Gen. Dec. B-289098, 2000 CPD ¶ 15 ("Acquisition plans are internal agency instructions and as such do not give outside parties any rights."). Protesters at GAO must also show that they were prejudiced by a failure in the planning process, *Frasca Int'l, Inc.*, Comp. Gen. Dec. B-293299, 2004 CPD ¶ 38.

As a practical matter, therefore, sound acquisition planning is more likely to result from internal agency pressures than from external challenges by offerors. See FAR 7.104(d)(1) requiring that acquisition planning be coordinated with the agency small business specialist.

The fact that a procurement is noncompetitive does not necessarily establish that there was a lack of acquisition planning. See *Gichner Sys. Grp., Inc.*, Comp. Gen. Dec. B-414392, 2017 CPD ¶ 178 (limited number of items while planning a five-year competitive procurement); *Piedmont Propulsion Sys., LLC*, Comp. Gen. Dec. B-410914.2, 2015 CPD ¶ 119 (reasonable to determine that protester did not have necessary technical data); *Camden Shipping Corp.*, Comp. Gen. Dec. B-406171, 2012 CPD ¶ 76 (bridge contract justified after size protests made contract urgent); and *Starwin Indus.*, Comp. Gen. Dec. B-401576, 2009 CPD ¶ 199 (agency made a reasonable decision to limit competition to companies eligible for waiver of first article testing requirements). See also *Sprint Commc'ns Co., L.P.*, Comp. Gen. Dec. B-262003.2, 96-1 CPD ¶ 24, stating that there was no requirement that planning be successful. In *Rex Sys., Inc.*, Comp. Gen. Dec. B-239524, 90-2 CPD ¶ 185, the agency's continued negotiations with a failing contractor placed it in a position of urgency requiring a sole source award. Although GAO in "hindsight" indicated that it might disagree with how long the negotiations were allowed to continue, it was unable to say that such actions were unreasonable. GAO found that the efforts sought to establish the failing contractor as an alternate source and were therefore related to procurement planning and fostering competition. The fact that the efforts were unsuccessful did not constitute a lack of planning.

[B] Statement of Need

The acquisition plan should begin with a brief statement of need. The need for the acquisition is identified and documented by the program or technical personnel in the agency who prepare the budget justification. Generally, the need will have been fully justified during the budget process and can merely be restated in the acquisition plan. See OMB Circular A-11*: Preparation, Submission and Execution of the Budget* (2004), available at *www.omb.gov* (outlining steps to budget review process). If the acquisition planning is being done prior to preparing the budget, the agency will have to analyze its needs in a thorough manner as part of the acquisition plan.

The plan should "[s]pecify the required capabilities or performance characteristics of the supplies or the performance standards of the services being acquired and state how they are related to the need," FAR 7.105(a)(4). This requirement should assist the agency in identifying restrictive provisions in the statement of work that may preclude potential contractors from participating in the procurement. When such provisions are identified, an agency can address possible ways to eliminate them. The guidance on restrictive specifications is reviewed below in the discussion of specifications.

[C] Contents of Plan

The acquisition plan must identify all actions essential to the conduct of a successful procurement and establish milestones for their performance. See FAR 7.105, which provides the following general guidance regarding the elements of the acquisition plan:

> In order to facilitate attainment of the acquisition objectives, the plan must identify those milestones at which decisions should be made (see subparagraph (b)(18) below). The plan must address all the technical, business, management, and other significant considerations that will control the acquisition. The specific content of plans will vary, depending on the nature, circumstances, and stage of the acquisition.

FAR 7.105(a) contains a brief description of the elements of the acquisition plan under the category "Acquisition Background and Objectives," while FAR 7.105(b) describes additional elements under the category "Plan of Action." The Background and Objectives section considers what the government is buying, how it will evaluate price and other cost factors, where the work is to be performed, and the risks involved. The Plan of Action section describes the steps necessary to procure the identified articles or services. Although the elements are discussed separately, they are interrelated.

The contents of the acquisition plan also should include a summary of any contractual history, FAR 7.105(a). This summary, normally done by the contracting officer, should identify each previous procurement that impacts the current planning. This is a key element in the planning process because it identifies how the current procurement fits in the overall conduct of the agency's business. The contractual history also identifies those cases where the procurement is part of an ongoing program, such as the development of a new product. In such cases, the agency normally will have adopted an acquisition plan for the entire program, and the planning for each step in the program will merely verify that the overall plan is still valid. On the other hand, the contractual history may identify previous procurements that have been unsuccessful—indicating that a new approach is needed. Thus, the contractual history is a key starting point for the preparation of the plan.

The plan should contain a concise statement of the acquisition strategy to be followed. See, for example, DoD Instruction 5000.02, "Operation of the Defense Acquisition System" (Jan. 7, 2015, ch. 3, Aug. 10, 2017), which contained general guidance on arriving at a sound acquisition strategy within the Department of Defense. This regulation described the planning of an acquisition strategy for a new system as an iterative process that becomes increasingly more definitive as the system progresses from the initial stages of advanced research to production. Curiously, the FAR does not require agencies to include a summary of the acquisition strategy in the plan. Nonetheless, planners should strive to draft a clear and explicit statement of the agency's strategy to ensure that all agency personnel understand how the procurement goal is to be achieved.

In formulating the acquisition strategy, the entire planning team should review all acquisition alternatives that could be used to conduct the procurement. Any acquisition strategy that will enhance the procurement should be considered as an alternative, and all members of the team should be encouraged to propose ideas. This element of the plan calls for innovative thinking, especially if the acquisition techniques used in the past have not been fully successful.

The Plan of Action called for by FAR 7.105(b) also should include such considerations as the method for obtaining and using priorities, allocations, and allotments; consideration of make-or-buy programs; description of the test and evaluation program of the contractor and government; description of logistical support; applicable environmental issues associated with the acquisition; how security will be established, maintained, and monitored; what government property or information will be furnished to the contractor; what management system will be used by the government to monitor the contractor's effort; as well as any other consideration that might impact the procurement. For a discussion of these elements of the acquisition plan, see Chapter 1 of Nash, Cibinic & O'Brien-DeBakey, *Competitive Negotiation: The Source Selection Process* (3d ed. 2011).

[1] Acquisition Milestones

Each acquisition plan should contain a specific set of milestones for the procurement. The basic milestones are set forth in FAR 7.105(b)(21):

- Acquisition plan approval.
- Statement of work.
- Specifications.
- Data requirements.
- Completion of acquisition-package preparation.
- Purchase request.
- Justification and approval for other than full and open competition where applicable and/or any required D&F approval.
- Issuance of synopsis.
- Issuance of solicitation.
- Evaluation of proposals, audits, and field reports.
- Beginning and completion of negotiations.
- Contract preparation, review, and clearance.
- Contract award.

Any additional steps that are required to implement the acquisition plan should also be included in the milestone chart.

[2] Applicable Conditions

This part of the plan identifies the constraints that must be imposed on the end product of the procurement, as set forth in FAR 7.105(a)(2):

> *Applicable conditions.* State all significant conditions affecting the acquisition, such as
>
> (i) Requirements for compatibility with existing or future systems or programs and
>
> (ii) Any known cost, schedule, and capability or performance constraints.

Precise identification of significant conditions early in the procurement process enables the agency to explore steps that can be taken to reduce or eliminate constraints that could have a detrimental impact on the procurement being planned. For example, if a product to be procured must be fully compatible with items in the agency's inventory, the agency may have to provide detailed drawings in the procurement package or induce the original manufacturer to license other sources in order to obtain sufficient competition to ensure a reasonable price. In this case, identification of this constraint would lead to the adoption of a strategy that would make detailed drawings available to a number of competitors.

Of course, identification of a constraint does not guarantee that there is a strategy that will completely overcome it. Many constraints must be accepted as an inherent element of the procurement. However, early identification of such constraints is beneficial because it assists all members of the planning team in recognizing the limitations that must be accepted in the conduct of the procurement being planned.

[3] Justifications and Approvals

When the acquisition plan proposes a strategy that entails using a procurement procedure that is "other than competitive," 41 U.S.C. § 253(f)(2) and 10 U.S.C. § 3204(e) (formerly § 2304(e)) require the contracting officer to provide written justification for the use of such procedures, containing the following six elements:

> (A) a description of the agency's needs;
>
> (B) an identification of the statutory exception from the requirement to use competitive procedures and a demonstration, based on the proposed contractor's qualifications or the nature of the procurement, of the reasons for using that exception;
>
> (C) a determination that the anticipated cost will be fair and reasonable;
>
> (D) a description of the market survey conducted or a statement of the reasons a market survey was not conducted;
>
> (E) a listing of the sources, if any, that expressed in writing an interest in the procurement; and
>
> (F) a statement of the actions, if any, the agency may take to remove or overcome any barrier to competition before a subsequent procurement for such needs.

See FAR 6.303-2 for additional guidance on the contents of this justification.

This justification must be certified as accurate and complete by the contracting officer responsible for awarding the contract, 41 U.S.C. § 3304(e)(1)(A), 10 U.S.C. § 3204(e) (formerly § 2304(e)). It must then be reviewed and approved pursuant to 41 U.S.C. § 3304(e)(1)(B) and 10 U.S.C. § 3204(e) (formerly § 2304(e)), as implemented in FAR 6.304, as follows:

Contract Amount		**Approval Authority**
Over	**Not in Excess of**	
$700,000	$13,500,000	Competition advocate without delegation
$13,500,000	$68,000,000 $93,000,000 for DoD, NASA, or Coast Guard	Head of Procuring Activity or delegate (Flag Officer or GS-15 rank or above)
$68,000,000 $93,000,000 for DoD, NASA, or Coast Guard	———	Senior Procurement Executive of Agency without delegation

In addition, such Justifications and Approvals (J&As) must be published, 41 U.S.C. § 3304(f) and 10 U.S.C. § 3204(f) (formerly § 2304(f)). See FAR 6.305 calling for such publication on www.SAM.gov and providing guidance on the time and contents of this publication.

J&As should be prepared and approved during the acquisition planning process. However, they may be written subsequently and even after award if circumstances warrant, such as when preparation and approval prior to award would unreasonably delay the acquisition, FAR 6.303-1(c). While late preparation of a J&A may not represent good planning, the lateness will not affect the validity of an otherwise proper J&A, *Systems Integration & Mgmt., Inc.*, Comp. Gen. Dec. B-402785.2, 2010 CPD ¶ 207 (J&A written one week after protest was filed); *AUTOFLEX, Inc.*, Comp. Gen. Dec. B-240012, 90-2 CPD ¶ 294, *recons. denied*, 90-2 CPD ¶ 370 (J&A executed after the closing date for receipt of proposals but prior to award); and *Magnavox Elec. Sys. Co.*, Comp. Gen. Dec. B-258076.2, 94-2 CPD ¶ 266 (J&A not invalidated even though modified and signed by the approving authority after the lower-level officials had signed it and after a protest was filed). Similarly, if additional facts are learned after a J&A has been prepared, an amended J&A will satisfy the detailed requirements for information that must be included, *Minowitz Mfg. Co.*, Comp. Gen. Dec. B-228502, 88-1 CPD ¶ 1.

A procurement may be overturned if the J&A does not contain a reasonable explanation for the avoidance of full and open competition, *Career Sys. Dev. Corp.*, Comp. Gen. Dec. B-411346.11, 2018 CPD ¶ 176 (J&A did not consider protester's capability statement received in response to sole source announcement); *Sturm, Ruger & Co.*, Comp. Gen. Dec. B-235938, 89-2 CPD ¶ 375 (documentation not meeting the specific requirements applicable to J&As insufficient); *Racal Corp.*, Comp. Gen. Dec. B-233240, 89-1 CPD ¶ 169 (agency couldn't demonstrate its need to use a specific make and model specification); *NI Indus., Inc., Vernon Div.*, Comp. Gen. Dec. B-223941, 86-2 CPD ¶ 674 (elimination of one of two mobilization base contractors was not adequately justified where the J&A contained no statement of the particular facts and circumstances that would justify a sole source award); or if the J&A does not bear a reasonable relationship to the agency's actual requirements, *Sabreliner Corp.*, Comp. Gen. Dec. B-288030, 2001 CPD ¶ 170. See also *Google, Inc. v. United States*, 95 Fed. Cl. 661 (2011), where the court enjoined a sole source procurement because the justification was signed by an unauthorized official well after the procurement commenced and did not analyze the costs the agency would incur by dealing with only one contractor.

Class J&As are permitted if approved in writing in accordance with agency procedures, FAR 6.303-1(c). When class J&As are used, the approval level should be determined by the estimated total value of the class, FAR 6.304(c). Class J&As will not be sufficient if they do not relate to the particular facts and circumstances of the specific procurement being questioned, *NI Indus., Inc., Vernon Div.*, Comp. Gen. Dec. B-223941, 86-2 CPD ¶ 674.

[D] Preparation of Plan

An effective plan must be timely prepared and have the participation of all agency personnel whose input can affect its viability. In addition, attention should be given to program requirements as well as individual contracts.

[1] Time of Preparation

It is essential that acquisition planning be done early in the process to ensure that all actions necessary to carry out an effective procurement can be performed within the procurement cycle. FAR 7.104(a) provides that "[a]cquisition planning should begin as soon as the agency need is identified, preferably well in advance of the fiscal year in which contract award or order placement is necessary." This recognizes that a complex procurement may require up to several years from the time the requirement is identified until a contract is awarded. In such cases, acquisition planning must start at essentially the same time as the budget process and must be executed simultaneously. This, of course, means that if the requirement is ultimately not funded, some planning effort will be wasted. However, to ensure that the ultimate procurement is carried out effectively, such a risk may be unavoidable.

DoD Directive 5000.1, Mar. 15, 1996, identified that, in the acquisition of a new system, the acquisition process is concurrent with both the budgeting process and the requirements generation process. These three key management processes, then, are completely interactive, and acquisition planning must be done very early in the life of a new system. While this directive has been replaced with later instructions that do not include this guidance, this is still good guidance on the time that acquisition planning should commence.

The acquisition plan should be revised and changed whenever necessary. FAR 7.104(a) provides:

> At key dates specified in the plan or whenever significant changes occur, and no less often than annually, the planner shall review the plan and, if appropriate, revise it.

[2] Form of Plan

The FAR does not deal with the question of when written acquisition plans should be prepared but, rather, places this responsibility on agency heads, FAR 7.103(d). Some agencies, such as the DoD, require written plans only for large-dollar acquisitions (acquisitions for development when costs are $10 million or more and for production or services when costs are $50 million or more for all years) but permit the use of written plans for smaller procurements, DFARS 207.103(d)(C).

Civilian agencies tend to require written acquisition plans at lower-dollar thresholds. For example, the General Services Administration requires plans for almost all acquisitions, allowing "oral plans" in "unusual and compelling situations," GSA Acquisition Manual, ¶ 507.105(b).

[3] Responsibility for Preparing Plan

Although FAR 7.102 requires agencies to conduct acquisition planning, it does not require the contracting officer to manage the planning process—it merely permits each procuring agency to designate the person or office responsible for acquisition planning. The DoD provides that the program manager, or other official responsible for the program, has overall responsibility for acquisition planning, DFARS 207.103(g). GSA defines the "planner" as "the person residing in the requirements office" but then calls for the use of a broadly constituted "planning team," GSA Acquisition Manual, ¶ 507.104.

FAR 7.104(a) contemplates that acquisition planning be performed by a team:

> In developing the plan, the planner shall form a team consisting of all those who will be responsible for significant aspects of the acquisition, such as contracting, fiscal, legal, and technical personnel. The planner should review previous plans for similar acquisitions and discuss them with the key personnel involved in those acquisitions.

FAR 1.102(c) also states that the "Acquisition Team" should include the users of the supplies or services being procured. See also FAR 1.102-2(a)(7) stating:

> All members of the Team are required to employ planning as an integral part of the overall process of acquiring products or services. Although advance planning is required, each member of the Team must be flexible in order to accommodate changing or unforeseen mission needs. Planning is a tool for the accomplishment of tasks, and application of its discipline should be commensurate with the size and nature of a given task.

The members of the team should be identified in the acquisition plan, FAR 7.105(b)(10).

Although the FAR does not discuss the role of competition advocates in the planning process, their participation is essential in each executive agency and in each procuring activity within the agency. Appointed pursuant to 41 U.S.C. § 1705 and 10 U.S.C. § 3249 (formerly § 2318), competition advocates are responsible for challenging barriers to competition and promoting full and open competition. Agency-level advocates are given the additional duty of providing an annual report to the senior procurement executive on the agency's use of competition in contracting. They have been actively involved in acquisition planning in many procuring agencies. They generally work at a high level in the procuring agency with commensurate influence in determining the strategy that will be used by the agency in the prospective procurement. They also approve or review virtually all justifications for the use of other than competitive procedures. Thus, their agreement with the acquisition plan is essential to ensuring the success of the procurement.

[4] Scope of Plan

Acquisition planning has been performed by some agencies in a sporadic and fragmented manner. Requirements have often been identified and justified on a contract-by-contract basis without regard for long-term acquisition needs. There are, after all, relatively few regulations requiring plans to be made on a program-wide basis. DoD provides that written acquisition plans for large-dollar acquisitions should be prepared on a program basis, while other acquisition plans may be written on either a program or individual-contract basis, DFARS 207.103(e).

§ 3.02 COMPETITION REQUIREMENT

A major goal of acquisition planning is to use competition whenever feasible. In *HEROS, Inc.*, Comp. Gen. Dec. B-292043, 2003 CPD ¶ 111, GAO explained the link between acquisition planning and effective competition, and noted that, though there may be exceptions to competition, a lack of planning is no excuse for inadequate competition:

> [U]nder no circumstances may noncompetitive procedures be used due to a lack of advance planning by contracting officials. . . . Our Office has recognized that, while the requirement for advance planning does not mean that such planning must be completely error-free, . . . as with all procurement actions taken by an agency, the advance planning required under 10 U.S.C. § [3204] must be reasonable.
>
> In enacting CICA, Congress explained: "Effective competition is predicated on advance procurement planning and an understanding of the marketplace." S. Rep. No. 50, 98th Cong., 2d Sess. 18 (1984), *reprinted in* 1984 U.S.C.C.A.N. 2191. The Senate Report also quoted with approval the following testimony regarding the need for advance planning:
>
> > Opportunities for obtaining or improving competition have often been lost because of untimely, faulty, or the total lack of advance procurement planning. Noncompetitive procurement or inadequate competition also has resulted many times from the failure to develop specifications. . . . By requiring effective competition, Congress will serve notice on the agencies that they will need to do more than the minimum to comply with the statute. . . .
>
> Finally, in interpreting this statutory requirement, our Office has noted that contracting officials have a duty to promote and provide for competition and to obtain the most advantageous contract for the government. . . . In other words, contracting officials must act affirmatively to obtain and safeguard competition; they cannot take a passive approach and remain in a sole source situation when they could reasonably take steps to enhance competition.

The Competition in Contract Act of 1984 (CICA) specifically requires "full and open competition" to be attained by executive agencies in the conduct of sealed bid or competitive negotiation except as specifically permitted by statute. CICA also listed five other "competitive procedures," which are discussed in § 3.03. Full and open competition and other than full and open competition are discussed in this section.

[A] Full and Open Competition

The extent of competition required by the procurement statutes has been the subject of extensive debate and a number of statutory changes. Prior to passage of the CICA, the statutes provided that specifications and invitations for bids (IFBs) for formal advertising (now sealed bidding) "permit such free and full competition as is consistent with the procurement of property and services needed by the agency concerned," 10 U.S.C. § 2305(a) (pre-CICA version). See also the prior version of 41 U.S.C. § 253. For negotiated procurement, the Armed Services Procurement Act required that proposals be solicited from "the maximum number of qualified sources consistent with the nature and requirements of the supplies or services to be procured," 10 U.S.C. § 2304(g) (pre-CICA version). In 1984, the CICA required that "full and open competition" be used in sealed bid and competitive proposal procurements except when specifically exempted, 10 U.S.C. § 2304(a)(1)(A) (now 10 U.S.C. § 3201(a)(1)) and 41 U.S.C. § 253(a)(1)(A) (now 41 U.S.C. § 3301(a)(1)). The CICA defined the term "full and open competition" to mean that "all responsible sources are permitted to submit sealed bids or competitive proposals on the procurement," 41 U.S.C. § 403(6) (now 41 U.S.C. § 107).

Based upon claims that receipt in some cases of inordinately large numbers of proposals placed an undue and unnecessary burden on procurements, attempts were made to narrow the statutory definition. One draft of the Clinger-Cohen Act of 1996 provided for "efficient competition." However, the definition was not changed. Instead, § 4101 of the Act added a new provision to 10 U.S.C. § 2304(j) (now 10 U.S.C. § 3204) and 41 U.S.C. § 3301(c), as follows:

> The Federal Acquisition Regulation shall ensure that the requirement to obtain full and open competition is implemented in a manner that is consistent with the need to efficiently fulfill the Government's requirements.

Efficiency in competition was addressed in § 4103 of the Act, which provides that the contracting officer, in conducting a competitively negotiated procurement, may limit the number of proposals in the competitive range "to the greatest number that will permit an efficient competition among the offerors rated most highly," 10 U.S.C. § 3303(b) (formerly § 2305(b)(4)(B)) and 41 U.S.C. § 3703(b). This was a significant change from the earlier approach, which, under the prior regulation (FAR 15.609), was that the contracting officer was to include in the competitive range any "proposals that [had] 'a reasonable chance' of being selected for award, that is, those proposals which [were] technically acceptable as submitted or which [were] reasonably susceptible of being made acceptable through discussions." See *DBA Sys., Inc.*, Comp. Gen. Dec. B-241048, 91-1 CPD ¶ 36. This narrower approach to the "competitive range" meant, in effect, that normal competitive procedures could, in practice, be narrowed to accommodate agencies' efficiency concerns.

While these changes were made to the competitive negotiation procedures in 1996, Congress left in place the five other "competitive procedures" which are included in the definition of full and open competition in 10 U.S.C. § 3012 (formerly § 2302(2)) and 41 U.S.C. § 152.

GAO created an exception to the requirement that "all responsible sources" be allowed to compete by not requiring cancellation of a solicitation or an award merely because a prospective offeror was not furnished a copy of the solicitation, absent probative evidence of a conscious or deliberate effort to exclude the offeror. See *International Ass'n of Fire Fighters*, Comp. Gen. Dec. B-220757, 86-1 CPD ¶ 31. With solicitations now being posted on the

Internet, this rule places the responsibility on the potential competitors to make every reasonable effort to find the prospective procurement. The reasoning of GAO is stated in *Creative Mobility Grp., LLC*, Comp. Gen. Dec. B-410380.2, 2014 CPD ¶ 376, rejecting a protest because the protester failed to search the Internet, stating:

> [A] contracting agency must use reasonable methods to publicize its procurement needs and to timely disseminate solicitation documents to those entitled to receive them. *Kendall Healthcare Prods. Co.*, B-289381, Feb. 19, 2002, 2002 CPD ¶ 42 at 6. However, for a protest against an agency's solicitation dissemination to be sustained, a prospective contractor must demonstrate that it availed itself of every reasonable opportunity to obtain the solicitation documents. See *Allied Materials & Equip. Co., Inc.*, B-293231, Feb. 5, 2004, 2004 CPD ¶ 27 at 2-3.
>
> Here, the record confirms that the protester failed to avail itself of every reasonable opportunity to obtain the solicitation. As an initial matter, we note that the protester provides no reasonable basis for its delay in first contacting the contracting officer about the follow-on solicitation just 3 weeks prior to the scheduled expiration of its incumbent contract. Further, as explained by the agency above, the record reflects that the solicitation was easily obtainable from FBO using a variety of applicable search terms that reasonably should have been known to the protester. For example, a search by the applicable NAICS code (for home health care services), which code was known to the protester from its prior contract, would have returned the solicitation. Similarly, a search using the VA network to be served (i.e., VISN 11), or the use of other relevant search terms such as home medical equipment or HME, would have resulted in the user's prompt receipt of the published solicitation materials.

As long as an agency properly classifies a potential procurement on *SAM.gov*, this places the responsibility for learning about potential procurements on contractors.

[B] Other Than Full and Open Competition

"Other than competitive procedures" are not statutorily defined; the statutes merely list seven specific procurement situations where full and open competition is not required. Depending upon the circumstances, such procurements may be made on either a sole source basis or with limited competition. These exceptions, set forth in 41 U.S.C. § 3304(a) and 10 U.S.C. § 3204 (formerly § 2304(c)), state that other than competitive procedures may be used *only* in the following situations:

> (1) the property or services needed by the executive agency are available from only one responsible source (or, for the Defense Department, or

only from a limited number of responsible sources), and no other type of property or services will satisfy the needs of the executive agency;

(2) the agency's need for the property or services is of such an unusual and compelling urgency that the United States would be seriously injured unless the agency is permitted to limit the number of sources from which it solicits bids or proposals;

(3) it is necessary to award the contract to a particular source or sources in order—

(A) to maintain a facility, producer, manufacturer, or other supplier available for furnishing property or services in case of a national emergency or to achieve industrial mobilization;

(B) to establish or maintain an essential engineering, research, or development capability to be provided by an educational or other nonprofit institution or a federally funded research and development center;

(C) to procure the services of an expert for use, in any litigation or dispute (including any reasonably foreseeable litigation or dispute) involving the Federal Government, in any trial, hearing, or proceeding before any court, administrative tribunal, or agency, or to procure the services of an expert or neutral for use in any part of an alternative dispute resolution process, whether or not the expert is expected to testify;

(4) the terms of an international agreement or a treaty between the United States and a foreign government or international organization, or the written directions of a foreign government reimbursing the agency for the cost of the procurement of the property or services for such government, have the effect of requiring the use of procedures other than competitive procedures;

(5) subject to subsection 3201 of this title, a statute expressly authorizes or requires that the procurement be made through another executive agency or from a specified source, or the agency's need is for a brand-name commercial item for authorized resale;

(6) the disclosure of the agency's needs would compromise the national security unless the agency is permitted to limit the number of sources from which it solicits bids or proposals; or

(7) the head of the agency (who may not delegate the authority under this paragraph)—

(A) determines that it is necessary in the public interest to use procedures other than competitive procedures in the particular procurement concerned, and

(B) notifies the Congress in writing of such determination not less than 30 days before the award of the contract.

Where an agency had incorrectly relied upon one exception (the "expert" exception in ¶ (3)(C)), but the record supported the use of the ¶ (1) exception, GAO allowed the sole source procurement to stand, *SEMCOR, Inc.*, Comp. Gen. Dec. B-279794, 98-2 CPD ¶ 43. Similarly, in *PTC, Inc.*, Comp. Gen. Dec.

B-416863, 2019 CPD ¶ 48, GAO denied a protest when the agency had justified a sole source contract as a follow-on procurement when it should have used the ¶ (1) exception.

Justification for the use of other than competitive procedures on the basis of any exception other than ¶ (1) does not necessarily permit the use of sole source contracting. Competition is required from as many potential sources as is practicable. See 41 U.S.C. § 3304(d) and 10 U.S.C. § 3204(d) (formerly 10 U.S.C. § 2304(e)), which state:

> The head of an agency . . . using procedures other than competitive procedures to procure property or services by reason of the application of [¶ (2) or ¶ (6)] shall request offers from as many potential sources as is practicable under the circumstances.

The FAR requirement to solicit offers from as many sources as is practicable is not limited to ¶ (2) and ¶ (6) only. FAR 6.301(d), set forth below, is applicable to the statutory exceptions under ¶ (3), ¶ (4), ¶ (5), and ¶ (7) as well:

> When not providing for full and open competition, the contracting officer shall solicit offers from as many potential sources as is practicable under the circumstances.

Thus, procurements under all paragraphs except ¶ (1) (which generally applies when there is "only one responsible source") should be conducted with some degree of competition when circumstances permit.

Protests in this area have primarily been under ¶ (2) ("unusual and compelling urgency"), which is discussed further below. In *Total Indus. Packaging Corp.*, Comp. Gen. Dec. B-295434, 2005 CPD ¶ 38, GAO outlined its standard for deciding cases under ¶ (2):

> Although CICA requires that the agency request offers from as many potential sources as is practicable under the circumstances, 10 U.S.C. 2304(e); see Federal Acquisition Regulation (FAR) 6.302-5(c)(2), an agency may still limit the procurement to the only firm it reasonably believes can properly perform the work in the available time. *McGregor Mfg. Corp.*, B-285341, Aug. 18, 2000, 2000 CPD ¶ 151 at 6; *Hercules Aerospace Co.*, B-254677, Jan. 10, 1994, 94-1 CPD ¶ 7 at 3. We will object to the agency's determination only where the decision lacks a reasonable basis. *Signals & Sys., Inc.*, B-288107, Sept. 21, 2001, 2001 CPD ¶ 168 at 12.

A number of decisions have held that even though urgency permitted a procurement without full and open competition, the agency violated the statute by awarding a sole source contract. See *Innovation Dev. Enters. of Am., Inc. v. United States*, 108 Fed. Cl. 711 (2013) (agency failed to review its own files or issue a synopsis); *WorldWide Language Res., Inc.*, Comp. Gen. Dec. B-296984, 2005 CPD ¶ 206 (agency made no effort to find contractors other than the incumbent); *Kahn Indus., Inc.*, Comp. Gen. Dec. B-251777, 93-1 CPD ¶ 356 (agency failed to contact one of the potential sources because the firm's phone number was missing from the file and the agency opined that three quotes would be "good enough" in a situation of urgency); and *Ferranti Int'l Def. Sys., Inc.*, Comp. Gen. Dec. B-237760, 90-1 CPD ¶ 317 (agency could have negotiated with a third source that had expressed interest and had prior experience, without significantly delaying the ongoing procurement). GAO has also held that an agency violated the statute where it had conducted the procurement so inefficiently that a competitor did not have time to compete for the entire quantity, *Arrow Gear Co.*, 68 Comp. Gen. 612 (B-235081), 89-2 CPD ¶ 135.

[1] Only One Source Available

The first exception is the broadest and possibly most utilized exception to the requirement for full and open competition, FAR 6.302-1. It is intended to permit a sole source procurement "only when truly warranted," *Competition in Contracting Act: Report of Government Affairs Committee to Accompany S. 338*, S. Rep. No. 8-50, 98th Cong., 1st Sess. 21 (1983). GAO's standards for evaluating challenges under this exception were set forth in *Kearfott Guidance & Navigation Corp.*, Comp. Gen. Dec. B-292895.2, 2004 CPD ¶ 123:

> When an agency uses noncompetitive procedures under 10 U.S.C. § 2304(c)(1), it is required to execute a written J & A [Justification & Approval] with sufficient facts and rationale to support the use of the cited authority, and publish a notice to permit potential competitors an opportunity to challenge the agency's decision to procure without full and open competition. See 10 U.S.C. § 2304(f)(1)(A), (B); Federal Acquisition Regulation §§ 6.302-1(d)(1), 6.303, 6.304; *Marconi Dynamics, Inc.*, B-252318, June 21, 1993, 93-1 CPD ¶ 475 at 5. Our review of the agency's decision to conduct a sole source procurement focuses on the adequacy of the rationale and conclusions set forth in the J & A. When the J & A sets forth a reasonable justification for the agency's actions, we will not object to the award.

This section discusses the decisions contesting sole source procurements under both the prior statutes and the current statute to determine the meaning of this exception.

[a] Agency Discretion

An agency determination that a proposed contractor is the only source capable of meeting the technical needs of the agency is subject to close scrutiny but will not be overturned if the agency has properly justified its needs and there is a reasonable basis for its determination, *Mine Safety Appliances Co.*, Comp. Gen. Dec. B-233052, 89-1 CPD ¶ 127; *WSI Corp.*, Comp. Gen. Dec. B-220025,

85-2 CPD ¶ 626. The fact that the protester disagrees with the agency's technical evaluation does not in itself render the evaluation unreasonable, *International Sys. Mktg., Inc.*, Comp. Gen. Dec. B-215174, 85-2 CPD ¶ 166. However, when a responsible source has expressed interest in the procurement, the agency must make reasonable efforts to permit the source to compete, *Neil R. Gross & Co.*, 69 Comp. Gen. 292 (B-237434), 90-1 CPD ¶ 212. However, agency decisions that a protester cannot perform the work usually are sustained. See *CliniComp Int'l, Inc. v. United States*, 134 Fed. Cl. 736 (2017) (agency determined protester did not have sufficient experience); *Raytheon Co.*, Comp. Gen. Dec. B-414354, 2017 CPD ¶ 168 (agency determined protester's product did not meet the agency's requirements); and *Lyntronics, Inc.*, Comp. Gen. Dec. B-292204, 2003 CPD ¶ 140 (agency determined that "deliveries by a new source would be materially delayed").

GAO has, though, held that the availability of only one source has to be demonstrated "convincingly," *Daniel H. Wagner Assocs.*, 65 Comp. Gen. 305 (B-220633), 86-1 CPD ¶ 166. In most protests of sole source awards, agencies have been able to meet this test. See *Technology Advancement Grp., Inc.*, Comp. Gen. Dec. B-417609, 2019 CPD ¶ 290 (sole source award to install equipment justified because agency lacked proprietary technical data); *Trailboss Enters., Inc.*, Comp. Gen. Dec. B-415812.2, 2018 CPD ¶ 171 (bridge contract to incumbent justified because of costly transition required for other competitors); *Gichner Sys. Grp., Inc.*, Comp. Gen. Dec. B-414392, 2017 CPD ¶ 178 (only one company had completed first article testing of product urgently needed); *Raytheon Co. Integrated Def. Sys.*, Comp. Gen. Dec. B-400610, 2009 CPD ¶ 8 (sole source awards of follow-on contract are "unobjectionable" where agency determined that award to any other source would cause unacceptable delays); *EADS N. Am., Inc.*, Comp. Gen. Dec. B-291805, 2003 CPD ¶ 51 (sole source to Boeing proper when statute specifically authorized the lease of "Boeing 737 aircraft in commercial configuration"); *McKesson Automation Sys., Inc.*, Comp. Gen. Dec. B-290969, 2003 CPD ¶ 24 (agency computer security requirement not an unreasonable barrier, even though it left only one competitor); *Mnemonics, Inc.*, Comp. Gen. Dec. B-261476.3, 96-1 CPD ¶ 7 (agency reasonably determined that only one source could supply critically required items under an expedited delivery schedule); *Navistar Marine Instrument Corp.*, Comp. Gen. Dec. B-262221, 95-2 CPD ¶ 232 (sole source procurement proper where no other barometer had the ability to fit into a preexisting opening on the instrument control panel of the engine); *Nomura Enter., Inc.*, Comp. Gen. Dec. B-260977.2, 95-2 CPD ¶ 206 (sole source contract for engineering support services related to howitzer proper because agency reasonably concluded that unacceptable delays would occur if award was made to another source); and *Pilkington Aerospace, Inc.*, Comp. Gen. Dec. B-259173, 95-1 CPD ¶ 180 (agency reasonably awarded sole source contract for advanced design windshields for the F-15 aircraft).

Protests of sole source determinations have, however, been sustained if the facts indicate that other sources could satisfactorily meet the government's needs.

In *Sidereal Corp.*, Comp. Gen. Dec. B-210969, 83-2 CPD ¶ 92, GAO sustained a protest to a sole source award for automatic data processing equipment. The protester had recently won contracts for equipment similar to that which was procured, thus demonstrating that meaningful competition was possible. See also *Career Sys. Dev. Corp.*, Comp. Gen. Dec. B-411346.11, 2018 CPD ¶ 176 (agency failed to consider whether protester could perform bridge contract); *Global Dynamics, LLC v. United States*, 137 Fed. Cl. 772 (2018) (shortage of personnel to take corrective action not justification for award of fifth bridge contract); *Cherokee Nation Techs., LLC v. United States*, 116 Fed. Cl. 636 (2014) (bridge contract to incumbent after protester had won follow-on competition but agency took corrective action); McAfee, Inc. v. United States, 111 Fed. Cl. 696 (2013) (agency knew of several other sources); *eFedBudget Corp.*, Comp. Gen. Dec. B-298627, 2006 CPD ¶ 159 (agency never considered whether the costs associated with a purchase of additional license rights outweighed the benefits of competition); *Lockheed Martin Sys. Integration—Owego*, Comp. Gen. Dec. B-287190.2, 2001 CPD ¶ 110 (agency gave potential competitor incorrect information on requirements, and thus competitor could not fairly demonstrate its ability to meet agency's requirements); and *National Aerospace Grp., Inc.*, Comp. Gen. Dec. B-282,843, 99-2 CPD ¶ 43 (agency's documentation did not reasonably show that only named product would satisfy agency's needs, and did not show that agency's allegedly urgent need was not created by a lack of advance planning).

In making a determination that only one contractor is capable of meeting an agency's needs, it is improper for an agency to rely on the putative sole source contractor for technical advice and expertise. The agency should independently evaluate technical data and draw its own conclusions, *Aero Corp. v. Dep't of Navy*, 558 F. Supp. 404 (D.D.C. 1983). See also *National Aerospace Grp., Inc.*, Comp. Gen. Dec. B-282843, 99-2 CPD ¶ 43 (agency criticized for "unquestioning acceptance . . . of the [original equipment manufacturer's] apparent insistence that its product is unique in ways that are essential to its function but cannot be revealed").

[b] Privately Developed Products or Services

The determination to procure on a sole source basis may be justified under certain circumstances if the product or service being procured was developed at private expense. However, there are different rules depending on what proprietary rights are being asserted. For a complete discussion of the policies in this area see Chapter 8 of Nash & Rawicz, *Intellectual Property in Government Contracts* (6th ed. 2008).

[i] Patented Products or Services

The fact that a product or service is patented will *not* justify a sole source procurement. See FAR 27.102(b) ("Generally, the Government will not refuse to award a contract on the grounds that the prospective contractor may infringe a patent."). The statutory basis for this rule is 28 U.S.C. § 1498(a), which gives patent owners the right to reasonable compensation if an invention is used "by or for the United States without license," but does not permit patent owners to enjoin the use of patents in such cases. In 38 Comp. Gen. 276 (B-136916) (1958), GAO ruled that this statute requires the use of competitive procurement techniques when purchasing patented items, reasoning at 278:

> It is our view, however, that section 1498 appears clearly to constitute a modification of the patent law by limiting the rights of patentees insofar as procurement of supplies by the Government may be concerned, and by vesting in the Government a right to the use of any patents granted by it upon payment of reasonable compensation for such use. We believe that the statute is not consistent with any duty on the part of a contracting agency of the Government to protect the interests of patentees or licensees with respect to articles which it proposes to purchase, since the statute itself defines and provides an exclusive remedy for enforcement of the patentee's rights as to the Government. Any other interpretation would appear to us to impose an impossible burden upon Government procurement officials to determine the applicability and validity of any patents affecting any articles desired.

See also 53 Comp. Gen. 270 (B-177835) (1973), indicating that competitive negotiation could be used to obtain patented products if the circumstances for negotiation are present. It is proper to use a Patent Indemnity clause (transferring the risk of patent infringement to the contractor) in such cases, *Barrier-Wear*, Comp. Gen. Dec. B-240563, 90-2 CPD ¶ 421. Prior regulations explicitly permitted this technique but the current FAR is silent on this use of a Patent Indemnity clause to attempt to overcome the competitive advantage that this policy gives to the infringer.

[ii] Copyrighted Products or Services

Although 28 U.S.C. § 1498(b) contains substantially the same language relating to copyrights as 28 U.S.C. § 1498(a), the presence of a copyright has been held to be a valid reason for sole source procurement. See *ALK Assocs.*, Comp. Gen. Dec. B-237019, 90-1 CPD ¶ 113, upholding a sole source procurement of copyrighted software because the agency needed the identical software to meet its needs. GAO apparently reasoned that competitors could not re-create such software and/or that the agency or its contractors could not take the software through eminent domain procedures (as can occur with patents). See also *MFVega & Assocs., LLC*, Comp. Gen. Dec. B-291605.3, 2003 CPD ¶ 65 (agency properly sole-sourced to incumbent software provider, because agency "may properly take into account the existence of software data rights and licenses when determining whether only one responsible source exists"). The same logic probably explains the copyright provisions in ¶ (c)(2) of the Rights in Data—General clause in FAR 52.227-14 and ¶ (d) of the Rights in Technical Data—Noncommercial

Items clause in DFARS 252.227-7013, stating that a contractor may not use copyrighted material in the performance of the contract without the consent of the contracting officer unless it obtains a license from the owner of the copyright.

[iii] Products or Services Described by Proprietary Data

Since there is no statute comparable to 28 U.S.C. § 1498 covering proprietary data, it is the policy of the government to honor proprietary rights in technical data, FAR 27.402(b). This policy, now incorporated in 41 U.S.C. § 2302(a)(1) and 10 U.S.C. § 3771(a)(2) (formerly § 2320(a)(1)), states that procurement regulations may not impair "any other right in technical data otherwise established by law." The government's policy of honoring proprietary rights in technical data does not prevent the government from meeting its needs with an independent development project.

GAO has sustained sole source procurements where the product being procured could only be described by proprietary data, *Warmore, Inc.*, Comp. Gen. Dec. B-41740, 2019 CPD ¶ 253; *Coastal Seal Servs., LLC*, Comp. Gen. Dec. B-406219, 2012 CPD ¶ 111; *Aerospace Eng'g & Support, Inc.*, Comp. Gen. Dec. B-258546, 95-1 CPD ¶ 18; *TSI Microelectronics Corp.*, Comp. Gen. Dec. B-243889, 91-2 CPD ¶ 172; *Hydra Rig Cryogenics, Inc.*, Comp. Gen. Dec. B-234029, 89-1 CPD ¶ 442; *Turbo Mech., Inc.*, Comp. Gen. Dec. B-231807, 88-2 CPD ¶ 299; and *Quality Diesel Engines, Inc.*, Comp. Gen. Dec. B-210215, 83-2 CPD ¶ 1. See also *Piedmont Propulsion Sys., LLC*, Comp. Gen. Dec. B-410914.2, 2015 CPD ¶ 119, sustaining a sole source procurement for logistics support of a product based on proprietary rights to technical data. In such cases, GAO generally will not question an agency's legal determination that the sole source contractor has proprietary rights, *Fil-Coil Co.*, Comp. Gen. Dec. B-198105, 80-2 CPD ¶ 304. See *KSD, Inc. v. United States*, 72 Fed. Cl. 236 (2006), where the court upheld a sole source procurement because the contractor had created an entirely proprietary data package using IR&D funds in response to the agency's request for companies to devise solutions to a current problem.

Sole source procurements have also been justified where, "as a practical matter," it was not feasible to create a nonproprietary data package. See *Kessler Int'l Corp.*, Comp. Gen. Dec. B-230662, 88-2 CPD ¶ 27, holding that the agency reasonably determined that only one source could timely supply the needed part because it was a critical application part necessary for performing safety, mission, and readiness requirements. The government had no technical data package because the item had been developed at private expense. In *Rack Eng'g Co.*, Comp. Gen. Dec. B-194470, 79-2 CPD ¶ 385, GAO upheld the Navy's sole source procurement for interchangeable spare parts cabinets because the supplier had already supplied 87% of the Atlantic Fleet Carrier Force's needs, reasoning that the cost of redesigning and retooling to meet the interchangeability requirement would necessarily preclude any other offerors from competing. In *Worldwide Marine, Inc.*, Comp. Gen. Dec. B-212640, 84-1 CPD ¶ 152, GAO acknowledged there may have been some degree of agency negligence in failing to draft specifications, but nevertheless held that, faced with an urgent need for the purchase in question, the agency was justified in making a sole source award to the only company that possessed adequate data to produce the item. In *Masbe Corp.*, Comp. Gen. Dec. B-260253.2, 95-1 CPD ¶ 253, GAO upheld a sole source procurement for a critical military aircraft engine part because the agency did not have adequate data to establish qualification requirements for the part because this data was possessed by the original designer of the engine.

In some cases, GAO has held that agencies should prepare data packages or use performance specifications to facilitate competitive procurement. The fact that the agency would incur substantial cost in drafting a specification that could be used for competitive procurement was not adequate justification for sole source procurement in *Techniarts*, Comp. Gen. Dec. B-193263, 79-1 CPD ¶ 246. But see *Compressor Eng'g Corp.*, Comp. Gen. Dec. B-213032, 84-1 CPD ¶ 180, where GAO stated that it would be unreasonable for the agency to bear the cost of testing parts that would facilitate a competitive procurement. In *Command, Control & Commc'ns Corp.*, Comp. Gen. Dec. B-210100, 83-2 CPD ¶ 448, GAO rejected the agency's arguments that the urgency of its needs and the lack of proprietary data precluded a competitive award. While GAO recognized that the agency might have to satisfy its immediate needs on a sole source basis, urgency could not justify acquisition of computer systems over a five-year period where the systems were not complex technologically and the agency acknowledged that other vendors could duplicate the system "if given enough time." See also *Utech Prods. v. United States*, 148 Fed. Cl. 542 (2020), rejecting a sole source procurement based on the belief that only one company had a license to use necessary software when the agency did not consider whether other companies could obtain a license.

Agencies occasionally create nonproprietary technical data packages by reverse engineering proprietary products. Reverse engineering is the process of developing design specifications by inspection and analysis of a product. Although DFARS 217.7503 provides that reverse engineering by the government is the least desirable means of obtaining competition in the face of proprietary data, this practice has been found to be legal, *Westech Gear Corp. v. Dep't of Navy*, 907 F.2d 1225 (D.C. Cir. 1990); *American Hoist & Derrick, Inc. v. United States*, 3 Cl. Ct. 198 (1983). Sometimes nonproprietary technical data packages are created by awarding a contract to perform the reverse engineering, *EG&G Sealol*, Comp. Gen. Dec. B-232265, 88-2 CPD ¶ 558. When reverse engineering is too expensive to justify the effort to obtain competition, an agency can reasonably decide to continue the sole source procurement, *Gel Sys., Inc.*, Comp. Gen. Dec. B-231680, 88-2 CPD ¶ 316. See also *Kearfott Guidance & Navigation Corp.*, Comp. Gen. Dec. B-292895.2, 2004 CPD ¶ 123, agreeing that the product was too complicated to permit successful reverse engineering, and *AAI ACL Techs., Inc.*, Comp. Gen. Dec. B-258679.4, 95-2 CPD ¶ 243, finding a sole source award proper given the risk and cost associated with reverse engineering.

The most prevalent form of reverse engineering is for the government to suggest that companies reverse engineer a product in order to compete for a quantity of items to be procured. The major way that an agency initiates this type of reverse engineering is by providing proprietary items to competitors. With regard to spare parts, this procedure is encouraged by 10 U.S.C. § 3773 (formerly § 2320(d)), which states:

> The Secretary of Defense shall by regulation establish programs which provide domestic business concerns an opportunity to purchase or borrow replenishment parts from the United States for the purpose of design replication or modification, to be used by such concerns in the submission of subsequent offers to sell the same or like parts to the United States.

This technique is sometimes called "competitive copying."

Agencies also attempt to obtain competition in the face of proprietary data by having the contractor with the proprietary data license other contractors. In *Leigh Instruments, Ltd.*, Comp. Gen. Dec. B-233642, 89-1 CPD ¶ 149, the licensee complained that the contractor had failed to honor the license with the result that the licensee could not successfully compete on a procurement. GAO did not entertain the protest, characterizing such situations as disputes between two private parties.

10 U.S.C. § 3208 (formerly § 2305(d)) (the parallel provision for civilian agencies is at 41 U.S.C. § 3308(b)), requires agencies "to consider requiring offerors for development and production contracts for major systems to propose methods for obtaining competition."

10 U.S.C. § 3774(a) (formerly § 2320(e)) imposes a similar requirement on program managers to structure major weapon system procurements to obtain competition during sustainment.

[c] Unsolicited Proposals

Unsolicited proposals can provide the basis for a determination that the property or services are available from only one source. See 41 U.S.C. § 3304(b)(1), which states:

> [in the case of] a contract for property or services to be awarded on the basis of acceptance of an unsolicited research proposal, the property or services shall be considered to be available from only one source if the source has submitted an unsolicited research proposal that demonstrates a unique and innovative concept the substance of which is not otherwise available to the United States and does not resemble the substance of a pending competitive procurement.

10 U.S.C. § 3204(b) (formerly § 2304(d)(1)(A)) is substantively the same.

FAR Subpart 15.6 goes beyond these statutes and provides guidance on the handling of all unsolicited proposals for research work and other types of work. FAR 15.606-2(a) requires that each proposal be comprehensively evaluated, considering, at a minimum, the following factors:

> (1) Unique, innovative and meritorious methods, approaches, or concepts demonstrated by the proposal;
>
> (2) Overall scientific, technical, or socioeconomic merits of the proposal;
>
> (3) Potential contribution of the effort to the agency's specific mission;
>
> (4) The offeror's capabilities, related experience, facilities, techniques, or unique combinations of these that are integral factors for achieving the proposal objectives;
>
> (5) The qualifications, capabilities, and experience of the proposed principal investigator, team leader, or key personnel who are critical to achieving the proposal objectives; and
>
> (6) The realism of the proposed cost.

FAR 15.607 contains limitations on award of contracts based on unsolicited proposals:

> (a) A favorable comprehensive evaluation of an unsolicited proposal does not, in itself, justify awarding a contract without providing for full and open competition. The agency point of contact shall return an unsolicited proposal to the offeror, citing reasons, when its substance—
>
> > (1) Is available to the Government without restriction from another source;
> >
> > (2) Closely resembles a pending competitive acquisition requirement;
> >
> > (3) Does not relate to the activity's missions; or
> >
> > (4) Does not demonstrate an innovative and unique method, approach, or concept, or is otherwise not deemed a meritorious proposal.

FAR 15.607(b) goes on to state that if the unsolicited proposal has received a favorable comprehensive evaluation and is not subject to the above impediments, the agency can procure the work covered by the proposal. If it is for research work, such procurement can be on a sole source basis in accordance with FAR 6.302-1(a)(2)(i):

> Supplies or services may be considered to be available from only one source if the source has submitted an unsolicited research proposal that [meets the statutory requirements].

If the proposal is for other than research work, FAR 15.607(b) requires full and open competition unless one of the statutory exceptions is justified.

GAO has held that these provisions *do not* require award of a contract to a submitter of an unsolicited proposal—they merely *permit* award if the proposal is unique and innovative. Even when the proposal is unique and innovative, agencies have the discretion not to award a sole source contract. See *M3 Partners, LLC*, Comp. Gen. Dec. B-416685.6, 2020 CPD ¶ 154, stating that "an agency's determination not to make a sole-source award is one that is within the agency's discretion." See also *Rante Corp.*, Comp. Gen. Dec. B-411188, 2015 CPD ¶ 166; and *Digital Healthcare, Inc.*, Comp. Gen. Dec. B-296489, 2005 CPD ¶ 166. Challenges in court have been equally unsuccessful. See *Diaz v. United States*, 853 F.3d 1355 (Fed. Cir. 2017) (submitter not an interested party because proposal did not meet FAR requirements); *Scott v. United States*, 134 Fed. Cl. 755 (2017) (no proof that agency failed to properly evaluate proposal); and *Kimboko v. United States*, No. 99-5020, 2000 U.S. App. LEXIS 8959 (Fed. Cir. May 5, 2000) (no jurisdiction over claim that agency failed to follow FAR). Thus, it is very difficult to challenge an agency decision to reject an unsolicited proposal.

It is appropriate for an agency not to issue a sole source contract based on an unsolicited proposal where the data necessary for a competitive procurement are otherwise available to the government, *Saratoga Indus.*, Comp. Gen. Dec. B-219341, 85-2 CPD ¶ 247 (information in the unsolicited proposal was available from previous specifications or from publicly available information); *Georgetown Air & Hydro Sys.*, Comp. Gen. Dec. B-210806, 84-1 CPD ¶ 186 (unsolicited proposal incorporated information related to a forthcoming solicitation). In *LW Planning Grp.*, Comp. Gen. Dec. B-215539, 84-2 CPD ¶ 531, the government was found to have properly decided that the work in the unsolicited proposal required the work of an architect-engineer contractor and thus the work could not be done by the submitter.

It appears that a proposal could be "unique and innovative" even if it did not include proprietary information. FAR 15.609 permits unsolicited proposals to contain a legend prohibiting the disclosure, outside the government, of all information in the proposal or the use of such information for any purpose other than evaluation of the proposal. This regulation also establishes a procedure for government protection of the information even if the legends are not placed on the proposal. However, see *Xerxe Grp., Inc. v. United* States, 278 F.3d 1357 (Fed. Cir. 2002), ignoring this regulation and holding that the company had no rights because it failed to properly mark the data with proprietary legends. It has been held that the government does not violate a protectable trade secret by competitively soliciting for the item using data that were independently developed by the government, *Zodiac of N. Am., Inc.*, Comp. Gen. Dec. B-220012, 85-2 CPD ¶ 595; *Sellers, Connor & Cuneo*, 53 Comp. Gen. 161 (B-177436), *recons. denied*, 74-1 CPD ¶ 126. When the government makes such a claim, the protester must show with clear and convincing evidence that the specifications were derived from protester's proprietary data, *November Grp., Inc.*, Comp.

Gen. Dec. B-292483, 2003 CPD ¶ 165; *Ingersoll-Rand Co.*, Comp. Gen. Dec. B-236495, 89-2 CPD ¶ 542.

Many agencies now screen unsolicited research proposals to determine if they can be reviewed and considered under the broad agency announcement in effect at the time of receipt of the proposal. In most cases, the proposal will fall within one of the categories of research covered by this announcement and can be treated as a research proposal.

[d] Follow-On Contracts

Follow-on contracts are awards made to the contractor that has previously been awarded a design or manufacturing contract for the same item or that has previously performed the services being procured. CICA enacted two different provisions on this issue. Sole source contracting for follow-on contracts is permitted by 41 U.S.C. § 3304(b)(2) in the following circumstances:

> [in the case of] a follow-on contract for the continued development or production of a major system or highly specialized equipment, the property may be deemed to be available only from the original source and may be procured through procedures other than competitive procedures when it is likely that award to a source other than the original source would result in (i) substantial duplication of cost to the Government which is not expected to be recovered through competition, or (ii) unacceptable delay in fulfilling the executive agency's needs.

The same provision is contained in 10 U.S.C. § 3204(b) (formerly § 2304(d)(1)(B)) with additional language making it applicable to follow-on contracts for "highly specialized services." The Act requires the agency to determine and document that the cost of the initial capital investment made by the developer of new items cannot be offset by savings that would result from openly competing the item.

Most decisions on the scope of these statutes have sustained the sole source award. See *Harmonia Holdings Grp., LLC v. United States*, 145 Fed. Cl. 583 (2019) (completion of IT modernization effort); *DRS Sustainment Sys., Inc.*, Comp. Gen. Dec. B-417628, 2019 CPD ¶ 316 (continued development of complex weapon system); *Raytheon Co.*, Comp. Gen. Dec. B-409615, 2019 CPD ¶ 228 (completion of development effort of missile); *Humanetics Innovative Sols.*, Comp. Gen. Dec. B-416979.3, 2019 CPD ¶ 183 (highly specialized equipment); *PTC, Inc.*, Comp. Gen. Dec. B-406863, 2019 CPD ¶ 48 (reactivation of existing software licenses because it was far less expensive than buying new licenses); *AugustaWestland N. Am., Inc. v. United States*, 880 F.3d 1326 (Fed. Cir. 2018) (last quantity of helicopter fleet from original manufacturer); *FN America, LLC*, Comp. Gen. Dec. B-415261, 2017 CPD ¶ 380 (additional rifles to avoid substantial duplication of costs for competing rifle); *Unitron LP*,

Comp. Gen. Dec. B-406770, 2012 CPD ¶ 247 (additional quantity of product to avoid substantial duplication of costs and unacceptable delays); and *Raytheon Co.*, Comp. Gen. Dec. B-400610, 2009 CPD ¶ 8 (award to any other source would likely cause unacceptable delays).

Decisions overturning sole source contracts as follow-on procurements include *Innovation Dev. Enters. of Am., Inc. v. United States*, 108 Fed. Cl. 711 (2013) (numerous defects including lack of advanced planning, failure to conduct market research, failure to consider the protester's expressed interest in competing for the work, and failure to post sole source synopsis); and *Magnavox Elec. Sys. Co. v. United States*, 26 Cl. Ct. 1373 (1992) (agency had not adequately explored alternative sources).

Justifications for award of sole source procurements to the prior contractor have been most successfully challenged by the submission of proof that the competitor is equally capable of performing the work. See *Berkshire Computer Prods.*, Comp. Gen. Dec. B-240327, 91-1 CPD ¶ 464 (protester sold compatible equipment and software for a computer system); *Aerospace Research Assocs.*, Comp. Gen. Dec. B-201953, 81-2 CPD ¶ 36 (agency was aware of two other contractors that could possibly "satisfy the Government's minimum needs without undue technical risk . . . within the required time," yet failed to contact them about the solicitation); *Federal Data Corp.*, Comp. Gen. Dec. B-196221, 80-1 CPD ¶ 167 (after the agency's publication of intent to procure on a sole source basis, the agency received alternative responses indicating the likelihood that other concerns could meet the government's needs); and *Consolidated Elevator Co.*, 56 Comp. Gen. 434 (B-187624), 77-1 CPD ¶ 210 (companies other than the manufacturers of elevators could meet the government's maintenance needs).

[e] Small Business Contracts

Several of the small business programs permit the award of sole source contracts to meet the goals of those programs. These programs are discussed in Chapter 14.

[2] Unusual and Compelling Urgency

The second exception in the statute permits a procurement without full and open competition based on "unusual and compelling" urgency. This exception is narrowly construed because the acquisition planning process is intended to overcome all but the most compelling urgency situations. In *Filtration Dev. Co. v. United States*, 59 Fed. Cl. 658 (2004), the court outlined some of the substantive and temporal limitations on this CICA exception at 633:

> In keeping with its preference for "full and open competition," the statute indicates that "the head of an agency using procedures other than competitive procedures . . . by reason of the application of subsection (c)(2) . . . shall request

> offers from as many potential sources as practicable under the circumstances." 10 U.S.C. § 2304(e). The agency head's discretion to invoke the exception is also not unfettered; a justification is required and "[e]ach justification shall contain sufficient facts and rationale to justify the use of the specific authority cited." 48 C.F.R. § 6.303-2(a). In addition, the exception has been interpreted as containing an implicit limitation that "the agency take reasonable steps to accurately determine its needs and describe them." *Matter of Signals & Sys., Inc.*, B-288107, 2001 CPD ¶ 168, at 12, . . . (Sept. 21, 2001). The agency head's discretion is subject to this limitation because "the urgency justification cannot support the procurement of more than a minimum quantity needed to satisfy the immediate urgent requirement." *Id.*

Urgency has generally been found in circumstances where the agency has made reasonable efforts to obtain competition but has been unable to accomplish this goal because of insufficient time to fulfill critical agency requirements. For example, the need to continue weapon tests vital to the national security has met the urgency requirement, *Support Sys. Assocs.*, Comp. Gen. Dec. B-232473, 89-1 CPD ¶ 11. Urgency was also found to exist in *SSI Tech., Inc. v. United States*, 148 Fed. Cl. 147 (2020), and *SSI Tech., Inc.*, Comp. Gen. Dec. B-417917, 2019 CPD ¶ 418 (prior contractor defaulted and only one remaining qualified source); *T-L-C Sys.*, Comp. Gen. Dec. B-400369, 2008 CPD ¶ 195 (agency showed that immediate replacement of 51 failed fire alarms was necessary to prevent serious injury to property or loss of life); *McGregor Mfg. Corp.*, Comp. Gen Dec. B-285341, 2000 CPD ¶ 151 (exclusion of competitor was reasonable because the competitor's inability to provide usable parts caused the agency's urgency for procurement); *BlueStar Battery Sys. Corp.*, Comp. Gen. Dec. B-270111.2, 96-1 CPD ¶ 67 (procurement restricted to two manufacturers that had supplied batteries to the Army under previous contracts); *Alektronics, Inc.*, Comp. Gen. Dec. B-261431, 95-2 CPD ¶ 146 (sole source award of a critical military item reasonable where there was an inventory shortage and awardee was the only approved source); *All Points Int'l, Inc.*, Comp. Gen. Dec. B-260134, 95-1 CPD ¶ 252 (only one contractor was capable of meeting requirement relating to the growing Cuban and Haitian refugee population at the U.S. Naval Facility); *Purdy Corp.*, Comp. Gen. Dec. B-257432, 94-2 CPD ¶ 127 (no other source possessed or could reasonably access test stand that was needed quickly for examining discovered gearbox problem); and *Astron Inc.*, Comp. Gen. Dec. B-236922.2, 90-1 CPD ¶ 441 (insufficient time to test a nondevelopmental item). Compare *Al Ghanim Combined Grp. Co. Gen. Trad. & Cont. W.L.L. v. United States*, 56 Fed. Cl. 502 (2003) (defendant agency suggested basis for urgency exception may have eroded once President declared end of major hostilities in Iraq in May 2003); and *Honeycomb Co. of Am.*, Comp. Gen. Dec. B-227070, 87-2 CPD ¶ 209 (no urgency could be justified when the agency took eight months to award a contract for products to be delivered from 16 months to four years after award).

Unusual and compelling circumstances also will not be found when there is a lack of advance planning, *RBC Bearings Inc.*, Comp. Gen Dec. B-401661, 2009 CPD ¶ 207; *New Breed Leasing Corp.*, Comp. Gen. Dec. B-274201, 96-2 CPD ¶ 202; *TLC Servs., Inc.*, Comp. Gen. Dec. B-252614, 93-1 CPD ¶ 481. However, lack of advanced planning generally will not be found if the urgency is the result of corrective action responding to a protest, *American Sys. Corp.*, Comp. Gen. Dec. B-412501.2, 2016 CPD ¶ 91; *eAlliant, LLC*, Comp. Gen. Dec. B-407332.4, 2015 CPD ¶ 58; *Camden Shipping Corp.*, Comp. Gen. Dec. B-406171, 2012 CPD ¶ 76. See also *CWIS, LLC*, Comp. Gen. Dec. B-416530, 2018 CPD ¶ 321 (agency reasonably worked with contractor to cure problems until urgency occurred); *Bannum, Inc.*, Comp. Gen. Dec. B-289707, 2002 CPD ¶ 61 (while the agency's planning ultimately was unsuccessful, this was due to unanticipated events, not a lack of planning); and *Diversified Tech. & Servs. of Virginia, Inc.*, Comp. Gen. Dec. B-282497, 99-2 CPD ¶ 16 (refusing to fault the agency where procurement was delayed by the agency's efforts to implement a long-term acquisition plan).

Although urgency does not necessarily justify sole source procurement, an agency conducting a procurement under the urgency exception may limit competition to the only firm it reasonably believes can perform the work promptly and properly, *American Sys. Corp.*, Comp. Gen. Dec. B-412501.2, 2016 CPD ¶ 91; *eAlliant, LLC*, Comp. Gen. Dec. B-407332.4, 2015 CPD ¶ 58; *Camden Shipping Corp.*, Comp. Gen. Dec. B-406171, 2012 CPD ¶ 76. See also *CWIS, LLC*, Comp. Gen. Dec. B-416530, 2018 CPD ¶ 321 (agency reasonably determined that only one firm had staff and resources to quickly take over work); *Pegasus Global Strategic Sols., LLC*, Comp. Gen. Dec. B-400422.3, 2009 CPD ¶ 73 (agency reasonably determined from market research and testing that only the contract holder could meet its urgent requirements); *IMR Sys. Corp.*, Comp. Gen. Dec. B-222465, 86-2 CPD ¶ 36 (urgency justified a sole source procurement even though the protester had notified the agency that it could take over the work on three to five days' notice). Protests of sole source procurements were sustained in *Innovation Dev. Enters. of Am., Inc. v. United States*, 108 Fed. Cl. 711 (2013) (agency failed to do market research or determine if protester was capable), and *Earth Prop. Serv., Inc.*, Comp. Gen. Dec. B-237742, 90-1 CPD ¶ 273 (protester showed that it could begin performance "on short notice").

Although the statute does not indicate what type of "serious injury" must result to justify limiting competition, GAO has included possible financial injury within the scope of the term, *Arthur Young Co.*, Comp. Gen. Dec. B-221879, 86-1 CPD ¶ 536. In that case, the Navy was permitted to make a sole source award because it claimed that the incumbent was the only firm that could perform a management study in time and that the study was necessary to achieve an estimated $1.5 billion savings. Serious injury was also found in a potential failure of the agency's telephone system, *AT&T Info. Servs., Inc.*, 66 Comp. Gen. 58 (B-223914), 86-2 CPD ¶ 447, and potential poor operation of the agency's computer facility, *Data Transformation Corp.*, Comp. Gen. Dec. B-220581, 86-1 CPD ¶ 55. In addition, changed conditions, such as policy decisions to reduce budgets or reorder procurement priorities, do not generally indicate a lack of advance planning by an agency. See *Magnavox Elec. Corp.*, Comp. Gen. Dec. B-258076, 94-2 CPD ¶ 266, where problems in a data program created an unforeseen need for substantial additional quantities of its alternative.

Potential expiration of funds is not a justification under the urgency exception, FAR 6.301(c)(2); *AAI ACL Techs., Inc.*, Comp. Gen. Dec. B-258679.4, 95-2 CPD ¶ 243 (distinguishing the expiration of funds from the unavailability of funds). See *Computer Lines*, GSBCA 8206-P, 86-1 BCA ¶ 18,653, where the board stated at 93,805:

> We can first quickly dispel the notion that [the agency's] actions in this acquisition are somehow made legitimate by its concern that the period of availability for obligation of its funds was shortly to expire. *See* 31 U.S.C. § 1552(a)(2) (1982) (the unobligated balance of funds available for obligation for a definite period is withdrawn at the end of the period of availability for obligation, and it reverts to the Treasury). The procurement provisions of the CICA have put an end to the idea that the statutory duty to obtain maximum practicable competition is somehow suspended at the end of each fiscal year. The legislative history of the CICA clearly depicts Congressional disgust with unconscionable year-end spending abuses. *See*, H.R. Rep. No. 98-861, 98th Cong., 2d Sess. 1428 (1984), *reprinted in* 1984 U.S. Code Cong. & Ad. News 2116. We do not suggest that this acquisition was the sort of abusive spending that Congress had in mind when it prohibited agencies from entering into noncompetitive contracts "on the basis of the lack of advance planning or concerns related to the amount of funds available to the agency for procurement functions." [10 U.S.C. § 2304(f)(5)(A)] Nonetheless, we have previously held that concerns as to expiring funds have no place in protest proceedings before this Board, *Wordplex Corp.*, GSBCA No. 8193-P, 86-1 BCA ¶ 18,655 (Dec. 3, 1985), and we see no reason to depart from that holding here.

Frequently, the threat of appropriations expiring occurs because of a protest against the award. This problem has been ameliorated with regard to protests before the agency, GAO, or the courts by the provisions of 31 U.S.C. § 1558(a), which keep appropriations from expiring for 100 calendar days after the date of the final ruling on the protest.

When agencies use the urgency exception, they must limit the quantity of the supplies or services being procured to only the amount necessary to meet their needs prior to the time when competition can be obtained. See *SSI Tech., Inc.*, Comp. Gen. Dec. B-298212, 2006 CPD ¶ 183, where GAO analyzed the agency's computation of the number of units being procured under the urgency exception and found that it was greater than needed before a competitive procurement was completed. See also *Technica Corp.*, Comp. Gen. Dec. B-416542, 2018 CPD ¶ 348 (task order for one year with two six-month options reasonable to allow for competitive procurement of technical services); *Filtration Dev. Co., LLC v. United States*, 60 Fed. Cl. 371 (2004) (agency limited quantity to its minimum needs); *Signals & Sys., Inc.*, Comp. Gen. Dec. B-288107, 2001 CPD ¶ 168 (unreasonable to procure large quantity based on inadequate data on actual needs of agency). In *EOD Tech., Inc. v. United States*, 82 Fed. Cl. 12 (2008), the court denied a motion to enjoin the override of a stay that awarded a six-month bridge contract but enjoined the agency from proceeding on a sole source basis "absent exigent circumstances."

[3] Industrial Mobilization and Maintaining Critical Capability

The third exception permits a procurement under less than competitive procedures in order to achieve industrial mobilization or to establish or maintain critical engineering, research, or development capability provided by an educational or other nonprofit organization or federally funded research and development center, FAR 6.302-3(a)(2)(i) & (ii). An agency's decision under this exception will not be questioned as long as it can demonstrate that its determinations are related to its industrial mobilization needs. See *Ridgeline Indus. Inc.*, Comp. Gen. Dec. B-402105, 2010 CPD ¶ 22 (sole source contract to preserve the industrial base was reasonable where protester only had experience in producing tent components, not complete tents); *Right Away Foods/Shelf Stable Foods*, Comp. Gen. Dec. B-259859.3, 95-2 CPD ¶ 34 (award to third mobilization base producer proper where agency reasonably determined that the failure of either of the current producers would be catastrophic in the event of a military emergency); *Kilgore Corp.*, Comp. Gen. Dec. B-253672, 93-2 CPD ¶ 220 (sole source award to operate and maintain an ammunition plant based on mobilization need); *Lance Ordnance Co.*, Comp. Gen. Dec. B-246849, 92-2 CPD ¶ 29 (sole source award made to one of two mobilization base producers for smoke and illumination signals); *Greenbrier Indus., Inc.*, Comp. Gen. Dec. B-248177, 92-2 CPD ¶ 74 (agency divided its requirements for chemical suits among four active mobilization base producers to provide a continuation of each firm's minimum sustaining rate of production); and *Propper Int'l, Inc.*, Comp. Gen. Dec. B-229888, 88-1 CPD ¶ 296 (Navy hat considered an essential part of the enlisted person's uniform and designated industrial mobilization item).

A sole source contract for nine years to maintain a supplier of air tankers was rejected in *Coulson Aviation (USA) Inc.*, Comp. Gen. Dec. B-409356.2, 2014 CPD ¶ 106, where the agency had entered into the agreement to induce the company to withdraw a protest. GAO found that the contract was not required to keep the company as a supplier and that there were a number of other companies that met the requirement.

The exception under FAR 6.302-3(a)(2)(iii) extends as well to a sole source procurement to "acquire the services of an expert or neutral person for any current or anticipated litigation or dispute." In *SEMCOR, Inc.*, Comp. Gen. Dec. B-279794, 98-2 CPD ¶ 43, the Air Force had attempted to use this exception in acquiring, on a sole source basis, the services of a group of litigation support personnel who had long experience with certain Air Force litigation. GAO rejected that justification, finding that the litigation support personnel at issue hardly possessed true expertise, "special skill or knowledge of a particular subject, that may be combined with experience, which enables them to provide opinions, information, advice, or recommendations to those who call upon them."

[4] Terms of International Agreement or Treaty

This exception may be used when the terms of an international agreement or treaty or the request of a foreign government that will reimburse the agency designates a single source, FAR 6.302-4. See *L-3 Commc'ns Corp. v. United States*, 99 Fed. Cl. 283 (2011), holding that the exception applies even though the funds are U.S. aid funds given to the foreign government. See also *Hyperion, Inc. v. United States*, 120 Fed. Cl. 504 (2015) (agency properly honored foreign government request for sole source contract after successful protest of prior competitive procurement); *Goddard Indus., Inc.*, Comp. Gen. Dec. B-275643, 97-1 CPD ¶ 104 (agency's sole source purchase as part of foreign military sale at foreign government's request was permissible); *Pilkington Aerospace, Inc.*, Comp. Gen. Dec. B-260397, 95-2 CPD ¶ 122 (Israeli order for parts on sole source basis through U.S. agency).

There is no requirement that the foreign government initiate a sole source designation. Thus, in the absence of bad faith or an intention to circumvent competition, it is immaterial whether a United States agency recommends specific items or advises a foreign government as to what items might satisfy its needs. See *Bravura Information Tech. Sys., Inc.*, Comp. Gen. Dec. B-418755, 2020 CPD ¶ 277 (agency determined after market research that only one firm could perform work); and *Electro Design Mfg., Inc.*, Comp. Gen. Dec. B-280953, 98-2 CPD ¶ 142 (upholding agency's decision to combine system requirements into single procurement at foreign customer's request).

[5] Authorized by Another Statute

The use of other than competitive procedures is permitted when a statute expressly authorizes or requires that a procurement be made through another agency or from a specified source. See, for example, *National Telecommuting Inst., Inc. v. United States*, 123 Fed. Cl. 595 (2015) (agency followed procedures of Javits-Wagner-O'Day statute); and *Diversified Mgmt. Grp., A Joint Venture*, Comp. Gen. Dec. B-288443.2, 2001 CPD ¶ 175 (appropriate to sole-source per Javits-Wagner-O'Day statute). See also *Crosstown Courier Serv., Inc.*, Comp. Gen. Dec. B-405492, 2011 CPD ¶ 248 (appropriate to sole-source per Veterans First Contracting Program, 38 U.S.C § 8127); and although FAR 6.302-5 lists a number of statutory set-aside authorities that may make sole source procurement appropriate, in *HAP Constr., Inc.*, Comp. Gen. Dec. B-280044, 98-2 CPD ¶ 76,

GAO emphasized that FAR 6.302-5 does not mean that the procuring agency must use those statutory authorities.

Sole source awards under the Small Business Act's § 8(a) program are usually justified under this exception. See *Eagle Collaborative Computing Servs., Inc.*, Comp. Gen. Dec. B-401043.3, 2011 CPD ¶ 29, holding that full and open competition is not required for small procurements being conducted under the § 8(a) program in 15 U.S.C. § 637(a). See also *Professional Security Corp.*, Comp. Gen. Dec. B-410606, 2015 CPD ¶ 2, denying a protest of lack of an "adverse impact" review because the protester was not a small business entitled to such a review; and *SKC, LLC v. United States*, 136 Fed. Cl. 605 (2018), agreeing with agency's interpretation that no "adverse impact" statement was required.

10 U.S.C. § 3204(a)(5) (formerly § 2304(c)(5)) also authorizes the use of other than competitive procedures when "the agency's need is for a brand-name commercial item for authorized resale." See *Defense Commissary—Request for Advance Decision*, Comp. Gen. Dec. B-262047, 96-1 CPD ¶ 115, holding that under CICA, the Defense Commissary Agency could noncompetitively procure items bearing the USO Always Home brand name for resale in military stores.

[6] National Security

This exception permits an agency to limit the number of sources from which it solicits offers if the disclosure of the agency's needs would compromise the national security. See *Boeing Co.*, Comp. Gen. Dec. B-414706, 2017 CPD ¶ 274, sustaining a sole source award for "rehosting" electronics equipment to the only company with a top-secret clearance. See also *Root9B, LLC*, Comp. Gen. Dec. B-417801, 2020 CPD ¶ 4, ruling on a protest of a procurement where the agency used this exception to limit the competition for cybersecurity training to seven firms; and *Analytical Graphics, Inc. v. United* States, 135 Fed. Cl. 378 (2017), ruling on a protest of a procurement for space system awareness data where the agency used this exception and set the procurement aside for small business. See generally Clark, *Overcoming the Critical Challenges of Contingency Contracting: Understanding the Flexibility Permitted by CICA, Simplified Acquisition Procedures, and Small Purchases*, 28 Pub. Cont. L.J. 503, 512-13 (1999) (discussing CICA exceptions).

[7] Public Interest

This exception enables the head of the agency to make a determination that it is necessary in the public interest to use other than competitive procedures in a particular procurement. See *Sikorsky Aircraft Corp.*, Comp. Gen. Dec. B-403471, 2010 CPD ¶ 271, denying a protest that the Navy had improperly used this exception to buy Russian helicopters for the Afghanistan Air Force. GAO found that the Secretary of the Navy had properly determined that providing a helicopter with which the Afghans were familiar would assist the war effort. See also *CliniComp Int'l, Inc. v. United States*, 134 Fed. Cl. 736 (2017) (agreeing that it was in the public interest to issue a sole source contract to the company running the DOD health records system in order to have a single system for both DOD and the Department of Veterans Affairs); *Asiel Enters., Inc.*, Comp. Gen. Dec. B-408315.2, 2013 CPD ¶ 205 (holding that this exception could not be used to avoid competition by entering into a memorandum of agreement with a nonappropriated fund activity); *Spherix, Inc. v. United States*, 58 Fed. Cl. 514 (2003) (agreeing that it was in the public interest to issue a sole source modification to provide electronic modification services for national parks in order to bring all federal recreation sites into one reservation system); and *Zublin Del., Inc.*, Comp. Gen. Dec. B-227003.2, 87-2 CPD ¶ 149 (agreeing that it was in the public interest for the Navy to restrict competition to U.S. firms for construction of Navy housing in the Philippines because hiring foreign firms could jeopardize U.S. bases).

In late 2003, DoD cited this exception under FAR 6.302-7, to bar other nations which had joined the United States' coalition in Iraq from competing for certain Iraqi reconstruction contracts. See Deputy Secretary of Defense Paul Wolfowitz, December 5, 2003, Memorandum: Contracting in Iraq. The decision triggered an international uproar, and raised concerns as to whether that exercise of sole source authority violated the United States' obligations to allow equal access to U.S. procurement under the World Trade Organization's Government Procurement Agreement. See Pitchas, *World Trade Organisation/United States: Award of Prime Contracts for Infrastructure Reconstruction in Iraq—An Assessment Under the WTO Agreement*, 2004 Pub. Proc. L. Rev. NA85.

[8] Competition Excluding Particular Sources

41 U.S.C. § 3303(a)(1) provides that executive agencies are permitted to exclude particular sources in order to establish or maintain alternate sources if the agency head determines that to do so would—

> (A) increase or maintain competition and likely result in reduced overall costs for such procurement, or an anticipated procurement, of property or services;
>
> (B) be in the interest of national defense in having a facility (or a producer, manufacturer, or other supplier) available for furnishing the property or service in case of a national emergency or industrial mobilization;
>
> (C) be in the interest of national defense in establishing or maintaining an essential engineering, research, or development capability to be provided by an educational or other nonprofit institution or a Federally funded research and development center;
>
> (D) ensure the continuous availability of a reliable source of supply of the property or service;

(E) satisfy projected needs for the property or service determined on the basis of a history of high demand for the property or service; or

(F) satisfy a critical need for medical, safety, or emergency supplies.

Substantially the same provision is contained in 10 U.S.C. § 3203 (formerly § 2304(b)(1)).

The statutes are implemented in FAR 6.202(a). The second and fourth of these reasons are similar to the former 10 U.S.C. § 2304(a)(16), which permitted the use of negotiated procurement for mobilization purposes. The first reason gives statutory authority for developing a competitive second source by precluding an existing sole source contractor from participating in the second source competition or maintaining an alternate source by precluding the primary source from being awarded all of an agency's requirements. The third reason allows an agency to exclude profit-making organizations from research and development work. In *National Gov't Servs., Inc. v. United States*, 923 F.3d 977 (Fed. Cir. 2019), the court held that the Center for Medicare and Medicaid Services could use this authority to place an overall limitation on the percentage of work any one contractor could perform but ruled against the agency because it had not followed the procedures required by this authority. See also *Plasan North Am., Inc. v. United States*, 109 Fed. Cl. 561 (2013) (authority used to preclude a company with a portion of the work from winning another portion); *PWC Logistics Servs. Co.*, Comp. Gen. Dec. B-400660, 2009 CPD ¶ 67 (authority used to preclude a single company from winning contract in both zones of the country in order to maintain two sources); *Hawker Eternacell, Inc.*, Comp. Gen. Dec. B-283586, 99-2 CPD ¶ 96 (agency decision to exclude incumbent encompassed most reasons for exclusion under FAR).

FAR 6.202(b) provides that a determination and findings (D&F) by an agency head or designee must support the decision to exclude particular sources. Class D&Fs are not permitted; thus, a D&F must be made for each individual procurement action. After exclusion of particular sources, an agency is required to establish full and open competition using one of the competitive procedures, FAR 6.201.

[9] Reprocurement after Default Termination

FAR 49.402-6(b) provides that after a default termination, reprocurements of no more than the amount of work remaining to be performed are not subject to the statutory competition requirements, while reprocurements over the remaining quantity of work are to be treated as "new acquisitions." The FAR requires in the former case that the agency obtain competition "to the maximum extent practicable." GAO has held that in the case of a reprocurement after default, the statutes and regulations governing regular federal procurements are not strictly applicable, *AeroSage, LLC*, Comp. Gen. Dec. B-416200, 2018 CPD ¶ 233. Protests have been granted if an agency includes more work in the reprocurement, *Steel Point Sols., LLC*, Comp. Gen. Dec. B-418224, 2020 CPD ¶45 (more time added to service contract); *Master Sec., Inc.*, Comp. Gen. Dec. B-235711, 89-2 CPD ¶303 (inclusion of two one-year options in a sole source reprocurement contract). In addition, the government will be denied the excess costs of the reprocurement if it fails to act reasonably, *M.E.S, Inc. v. United States*, 104 Fed. Cl. 620 (2012) (four-year delay in conducting the reprocurement). However, contracting officers generally are vested with wide latitude to determine how needed supplies or services are to be reprocured after a default, *Vereinigte Geb Udereinigungsgesellschaft*, Comp. Gen. Dec. B-280805, 98-2 CPD ¶117. See *Maersk Line, Ltd.*, Comp. Gen. Dec. B-410445, 2015 CPD ¶16 (denying protest of award to second low price on original competition); *Bluff Springs Paper Co., Ltd./R.D. Thompson Paper Products Co. Joint Venture*, Comp. Gen. Dec. B-286797.3, 2001 CPD ¶160 (denying protest that the agency did not award to the second low bidder on the prior procurement); *Marvin Land Sys., Inc.*, Comp. Gen. Dec. B-276434, 97-2 CPD ¶4 (denying protest that the agency had issued a sole source contract); and *AT&T Corp.*, Comp. Gen. Dec. B-270344, 96-1 CPD ¶117 (denying protest of sole source award). Contracting officers may automatically exclude a defaulted contractor from the competition for the reprocurement, *Essan Metallix Corp.*, Comp. Gen. Dec. B-310357, 2008 CPD ¶5.

[C] Ordering Work Under Existing Contracts

Some sole source procurements can be justified because the contract terms permit buying from the contractor. However, this requires a careful analysis of the contract language and the conduct of the original procurement. Thus, merely because work is added to an existing contract by modification or change order does not justify the use of "other than competitive" procedures if the work is in reality a new procurement action.

Even if it has been determined that government action in modifying a contract has gone beyond the scope of the procurement, and therefore constitutes a de facto sole source procurement, GAO will deny the protest if a new sole source procurement could have been justified. *See Pegasus Global Strategic Sols., LLC*, Comp. Gen. Dec. B-400422.3, 2009 CPD ¶73, finding that the Army's sole source modification of a contract was reasonable based on market research and testing that only the contract holder could meet its urgent requirements. In *Tilden-Coil Constructors, Inc.*, Comp. Gen. Dec. B-211189.3, 83-2 CPD ¶236, the Army modified an ongoing contract, for the construction of eight buildings and a central energy plant, to authorize the incumbent to construct two additional buildings. GAO accepted the Army's explanation that additional costs and delayed completion dates would result from the overcrowding of the congested work site occasioned by the presence of another contractor. Similarly, in *Hercules Aerospace Co.*, Comp. Gen. Dec. B-254677, 94-1 CPD ¶7, the protester asserted that a contract modification for additional rocket motors and engineering services amounted to a de facto sole source procurement. Without deciding this issue, GAO held that the agency's decision to modify the contract of the only qualified contractor due to unusual and compelling circumstances was reasonable. Compare *Kent Watkins & Assocs.*, Comp. Gen. Dec. B-191078, 78-1 CPD ¶ 377, where the government apparently added another year's work by modification and later wrote a sole source justification for a new procurement after the protest had been lodged. The supporting reasons cited included that the incumbent contractor submitted the only response to the solicitation, the incumbent had gained special experience, and additional costs would be incurred in changing contractors. However, because the agency was aware of other companies interested in the solicitation, GAO found the sole source award improper.

[1] Change Orders

Change orders to existing contracts may be made on a sole source basis if they are within the general scope of the contract. Although GAO does not review contract administration matters, it will review an allegation that the government action should have been the subject of a new procurement. Similarly, the Court of Federal Claims will take jurisdiction of such allegations as protests not contract administration disputes.

GAO formulated a "scope of the competition" test to determine whether work has been improperly added to a contract. See *American Air Filter Co.*, 57 Comp. Gen. 567 (B-188408), 78-1 CPD ¶ 443, stating at 573:

> The impact of any modification is in our view to be determined by examining whether the alteration is within the scope of the competition which was initially conducted. Ordinarily, a modification falls within the scope of the procurement provided that it is of a nature which potential offerors would have reasonably anticipated under the changes clause.
>
> To determine what potential offerors would have reasonably expected, consideration should be given, in our view, to the procurement format used, the history of the present and related past procurements, and the nature of the supplies or services sought. A variety of factors may be pertinent, including: whether the requirement was appropriate initially for an advertised or negotiated procurement; whether a standard off-the-shelf or similar item is sought; or whether, *e.g.*, the contract is one for research and development, suggesting that broad changes might be expected because the Government's requirements are at best only indefinite.

This reasoning was adopted by the Federal Circuit in *AT&T Commc'ns, Inc. v. Wiltel, Inc.*, 1 F.3d 1201 (Fed. Cir. 1993).

Contract modifications have been found to be within the scope of the competition in *Vetterra, LLC*, Comp. Gen. Dec. B-417991, 2020 CPD ¶ 15 (changing forms for appraisal services in BPA); *Tetra Tech, Inc. v. United States*, 131 Fed. Cl. 653 (2017) (adding programs to support services contract);

Booz Allen Hamilton Eng'g Servs., Inc., Comp. Gen. Dec. B-411065, 2015 CPD ¶ 138 (changing task order to impose Service Contract Act requirements); Aircraft Charter Sols., Inc. v. United States, 109 Fed. Cl. 398 (2013) (adding requirement for secure transportation to contract for aviation support services); *American Apparel, Inc. v. United States*, 108 Fed. Cl. 11 (2012) (adding new work based on clause in contract stating agency had right to order more work); and *Ceradyne, Inc. v. United States*, 103 Fed. Cl. 1 (2012) (adding new work based on clause in contract stating agency could increase quantity if another contractor defaulted).

Contract modifications have been found to be outside of the scope of the competition in *Ian, Evan & Alexander Corp. v. United States*, 136 Fed. Cl. 390 (2018) (adding analytical work to contract calling for categorization of work); *Onix Networking Corp.*, Comp. Gen. Dec. B-411841, 2015 CPD ¶ 330 (adding cloud work to delivery order for software update services); *Poly-Pacific Techs., Inc.*, Comp. Gen. Dec. B-296029, 2005 CPD ¶ 105 (modification to solid waste disposal not anticipated by the underlying solicitation); *Cardinal Maint. Serv., Inc. v. United States*, 63 Fed. Cl. 98 (2004) (significant amount of work added and deleted); and *MCI Telecomms. Corp.*, Comp. Gen. Dec. B-276659.2, 97-2 CPD ¶ 90 (modification of network design and management services of the FTS 2000 contract under which AT&T supplied 60% of the federal government's intercity telecommunications services because it was not for additional services—distinguishing the case from *AT&T Commc'ns, Inc. v. Wiltel, Inc.*). See, however, *LDDS WorldCom*, Comp. Gen. Dec. B-266257, 96-1 CPD ¶ 50, finding the modification at issue there to be within the scope of the original contract because the added services could have been anticipated from the face of the contract and the added services were not materially different from the services currently produced under the contract.

[2] Extensions and Options

Contract extensions, exercise of contract options, and lease renewals can also constitute de facto sole source procurements. Extensions adding only time to permit the contractor to complete performance of the original work are almost always within the scope of the procurement. However, if the original contract is seen as a procurement of services for a specified period of time, extensions calling for additional time will frequently be held to be de facto sole source procurements. GAO has stated that "competition should be sought whenever it appears likely that the Government's position can be improved whether in terms of cost or performance," 51 Comp. Gen. 57 (B-165218) (1971). In *Washington Nat'l Arena Ltd P'ship*, 65 Comp. Gen. 25 (B-219136), 85-2 CPD ¶ 435, the government issued an amendment retroactively extending a contract that had expired four months earlier. GAO held that this action constituted an improper de facto sole source award. See also *Intermem Corp.*, Comp. Gen. Dec. B-187607, 77-1 CPD ¶ 263, where a mandatory requirements contract was modified twice to extend its expiration date. The agency issued a D&F (a written approval by an authorized official, clearly justifying the specific determination made), concluding that the extensions were in the best interests of the government because a lapse would disrupt a government-wide mandatory source of equipment and services, and user agencies would lose accumulated purchase credits. GAO found that the extensions became necessary only because the agency failed to timely solicit a follow-on contract, and the extensions were therefore not justified. In *Federal Data Corp.*, Comp. Gen. Dec. B-196221, 80-1 CPD ¶ 167, a short renewal of an ADPE lease pending replacement with government-owned equipment constituted an unjustified sole source procurement where responses to a CBD notice evidenced competitive interests in a solicitation. See also *Techno-Sciences, Inc.*, Comp. Gen. Dec. B-257686, 94-2 CPD ¶ 164, finding that the agency had improperly extended contracts on a sole source basis, stating that other responsible sources could have competed for the requirement had the agency engaged in adequate advance procurement planning. Compare *Navistar Def., LLC v. United States*, 146 Fed. Cl. 499 (2019), holding proper periodic extensions for five additional years on a five-year requirements contract which the protester agreed not to challenge.

Before an agency may exercise an option, in order to satisfy the requirement for full and open competition, "the option must have been evaluated as part of the initial competition," FAR 17.207(f). See also FAR 6.001, which contains the following statement of applicability of the competition requirements:

> This part applies to all acquisitions except—
>
> * * *
>
> (c) Contract modifications, including the exercise of priced options that were evaluated as part of the initial competition (see 17.207(f)), that are within the scope and under the terms of an existing contract.

If an option is not evaluated under the initial competition, FAR 17.207(f) prevents its exercise absent an appropriate justification and authorization that full and open competition is not required, *Major Contracting Servs., Inc.*, Comp. Gen. Dec. B-401472, 2009 CPD ¶ 170, *recons. denied*, 2009 CPD ¶ 250. Furthermore, an option may only be exercised at an amount that is "reasonably determinable from the terms of the basic contract," FAR 17.207(f). See *Magnum Opus Techs., Inc. v. United States*, 94 Fed. Cl. 512 (2010), rejecting exercise of options where the agency had agreed that the prices in the contract were unenforceable.

[3] Task and Delivery Orders

Task and delivery orders must also be within the scope of the original IDIQ contract. See Chapter 7 for a full discussion of this requirement.

§ 3.03 SELECTION OF PROCUREMENT STRATEGY

One of the initial decisions in the acquisition planning process is the selection of the procurement strategy. The initial decision is whether to issue a new contract or to acquire the needed products or services by issuing a task or delivery order against an existing contract. This is complex because, depending on the product or service being acquired, there may be several existing contracts with different terms and conditions available for use. Thus, if an agency concludes that it is necessary to have tailored terms and conditions, it may well decide to issue a new contract. Conversely, if the terms and conditions of an existing contract meet the agency's needs, the procurement can be implemented more expeditiously by issuing a task or delivery order against an existing contract. These various strategies are briefly described in this section and more fully dealt with later in the book.

[A] Issuing a New Contract

When the decision is made to issue a new contract, the procedures to be followed will depend on the size of the procurement, whether the work is a commercial product or service and whether FAR procedures will result in a satisfactory contract.

[1] Simplified Acquisition

Agencies are required to use simplified acquisition procedures "to the maximum extent practicable" for contracts for acquisition of property and services at amounts not greater than $250,000.00 (or $7 million or $13 million for certain commercial items discussed in FAR Subpart 13.5), FAR 13.003(a). This requirement does not apply if an agency can meet its requirement using—

(1) Required sources of supply under part 8 (e.g., Federal Prison Industries, Committee for Purchase from People Who are Blind or Severely Disabled, and Federal Supply Schedule contracts);
(2) Existing indefinite delivery/indefinite quantity contracts; or
(3) Other established contracts

FAR 13.003(g) provides considerable discretion to contracting agencies on the procedures that may be used for simplified acquisitions and states that contracting officers are required to use the "simplified manner that is most suitable, efficient, and economical in the circumstances of each acquisition." Agencies can make single purchases or issue Blanket Purchase Agreements for repetitive purchases, FAR 13.303. A major advantage in using these procedures is that a number of laws and regulations do not apply to simplified acquisitions, FAR 31.005 and 31.006.

Acquisitions below $10,000.00 are called "micro-purchases" and are generally conducted using Governmentwide commercial purchase cards, FAR 13.301.

The authority to make these purchases generally is widely delegated to agency employees that are not contracting officers. Guidance on this process is contained in FAR Subpart 13.3.

Acquisitions below the simplified acquisition threshold and above the micro-purchase threshold are set aside for small business. A detailed discussion of simplified acquisition procedures and micro-purchases is contained in Chapter 8.

[2] Commercial Products and Services

10 U.S.C. § 3453 (formerly § 2377) and 41 U.S.C. § 3307, state a preference for the acquisition of commercial products and services and require that procurements be structured to meet agency needs "to the maximum extent practicable" through the procurement of "commercial or nondevelopmental items." FAR 11.002(a)(2) implements this policy by stating that agencies are required to "define requirements in terms that enable and encourage offerors to supply commercial products and services," and offerors of commercial products and services are to be provided an opportunity to compete in such procurements.

FAR Part 12 carries out the statutory mandate to maximize the purchase of commercial products and services and provides procedures to be followed in these procurements. FAR 12.102 makes these procedures mandatory except for purchases—

(1) At or below the micro-purchase threshold;
(2) Using the Standard Form 44 (see 13.306);
(3) Using the imprest fund (see 13.305);
(4) Using the Governmentwide commercial purchase card as a method of purchase rather than only as a method of payment; or
(5) Directly from another Federal agency.

FAR 12.203 provides considerable discretion to contracting agencies on the procedures that may be used to procure commercial products and services, and the balance of FAR Subpart 12.2 contains guidance on key issues involving this type of procurement. When commercial products and services are procured, FAR 12.301 provides a special solicitation provision and gives guidance on limiting the statutes and clauses applicable to such procurements. Optional streamlined procedures are prescribed in FAR 12.603. A detailed discussion of the procurement of commercial products and services procedures is contained in Chapter 9.

[3] Standard Procurement Procedures

When buying products or services (including construction) that are not commercial and whose cost is anticipated to be above the simplified acquisition threshold, most new contract procurements are conducted under one of the two major procurement procedures—negotiation or sealed bidding. Agencies have almost total discretion in choosing which of these procedures is appropriate, 10 U.S.C. § 3206 (formerly § 2304(a)(1)(B)), 41 U.S.C. § 3301(a)(2). The only constraint in making this choice is 10 U.S.C. § 3201 (formerly § 2304(a)(2)) and 41 U.S.C. § 3301(b)(1) stating that sealed bidding must be used if the following four conditions are present:

1. time permits the solicitation, submission, and evaluation of sealed bids;

2. the award will be made on the basis of price and other price-related factors;

3. it is not necessary to conduct discussions with the responding sources about their bids; and

4. there is a reasonable expectation of receiving more than one sealed bid.

These requirements are implemented in FAR 6.401. There are only a few decisions holding that an agency was required to use sealed bidding. See *Defense Logistics Agency*, 67 Comp. Gen. 16 (B-227055.2), 87-2 CPD ¶ 365 (no need for discussions in procurement of commercial item); *Northeast Constr. Co.*, 68 Comp. Gen. 406 (B-234323), 89-1 CPD ¶ 402 (no need for discussions to ensure understanding of requirements when no technical proposals are required); *Racal Corp.*, 70 Comp. Gen. 127 (B-240579), 90-2 CPD ¶ 453 (no need for discussions to permit changes to the agency's requirements).

On the other hand, agency decisions to use negotiated procurement procedures are normally upheld. See *Weeks Marine, Inc. v. United States*, 575 F.3d 1352 (Fed. Cir. 2009), reversing a Court of Federal Claims decision finding that sealed bidding should have been used. The court reviewed the agency's decision to switch dredging contracts from sealed bidding to negotiated procurement and found that it met the rationality standard. See also *Ceres Env't Servs., Inc.*, Comp. Gen. Dec. B-310902, 2008 CPD ¶ 48 (need for accelerated schedule required non-price factors); *TLT Constr. Corp.*, Comp. Gen. Dec. B-286226, 2000 CPD ¶ 179 (discussions might be needed because of problems on prior procurements); *Enviroclean Sys., Inc.*, Comp. Gen. Dec. B-278261, 97-2 CPD ¶ 172 (discussions might be needed); *Comfort Inn South*, Comp. Gen. Dec. B-270819.2, 96-1 CPD ¶ 225 (need to consider past performance); and *Vantex Serv. Corp.*, Comp. Gen. Dec. B-266199, 96-1 CPD ¶ 29 (discussions needed because of problems on prior procurements).

[a] Negotiation Procedures

Negotiation procedures are used in most procurements that fall into this category in order to allow agencies to communicate with potential contractors during the procurement and negotiate for the best value. While negotiated contracts can be issued on a sole source or competitive basis, the procedures in FAR Part 15 deal mainly with competitive procedures.

The competitive procedures call for the issuance of a formal Request for Proposals, FAR 15.203, submission of written proposals by offerors, FAR 15.208, the evaluation of those proposals by the agency, FAR 15.305, award on the basis of the original proposals or establishing of a "competitive range," FAR 15.306(c), negotiation with the offerors in the competitive range, FAR 15.306(d), submission of "final proposal revisions," FAR 15.307, and award of one or more contracts. While FAR Part 15 describes this procedure, there is considerable discretion for agencies to vary the procedures to meet their needs on specific procurements. These procedures are discussed in detail in Chapter 6.

FAR Part 15 provides little guidance on sole source contracts except for the extensive guidance in FAR Subpart 15.4 aimed at ensuring that agencies negotiate fair and reasonable prices with sole source contractors. These procedures are discussed in detail in Chapter 13.

A high percentage of the contracts awarded through negotiated procedures are indefinite delivery/indefinite quantity (IDIQ) contracts. These contracts are used when an agency cannot establish firm quantities of products or services at the outset but needs to have the ability to place task or delivery orders when firm quantities are identified. Special procedures applicable to the issuance of IDIQ contracts are discussed in Chapter 7.

[b] Sealed Bidding Procedures

Sealed bidding procedures are used when an agency concludes that it is desirable to select the lowest priced bidder whose bid is responsive to the solicitation and who is determined to be a responsible firm. FAR Part 14 contains detailed guidance on conducting this highly formalized form of procurement. Invitations for Bids are issued, FAR 14.201, bids are submitted, FAR 14.302, bids are publicly opened, FAR 14.402, and one or more contracts are awarded, FAR 14.408.

An agency's decision to use sealed bidding procedures instead of competitive negotiation will be upheld unless it is clearly unreasonable. See *Eagle Fire, Inc.*, Comp. Gen. Dec. B-257951, 94-2 CPD ¶ 214 (no ambiguity in the specification requirements and agency could conduct a preaward survey to determine whether the low bidder was qualified and capable of performing the contract); *Tennessee Apparel Corp.*, Comp. Gen. Dec. B-253178.3, 94-1 CPD ¶ 104 (the specifications made price and price-related factors the only relevant evaluation criteria); *Machinewerks, Inc.*, Comp. Gen. Dec. B-258123, 94-2 CPD ¶ 238 (sealed bidding with bid samples an appropriate technique to ensure that the proposed product met the agency's needs); *Virginia Blood Servs.*, B-259717, 95-1 CPD ¶ 185 (no reason to conduct discussions or to consider factors other than price); *GlaxoSmithKline*, Comp. Gen. Dec. B-291822, 2003 CPD ¶ 77, and *Pfizer, Inc*., Comp. Gen. Dec. B-276362, 97-1 CPD ¶ 205 (price alone appropriate when competing drugs were technically equal). On the other hand, it is appropriate to cancel a sealed bid procurement and use negotiation procedures when sealed bid prices were substantially higher than the government estimate, *Perimeter Security Partners, LLC*, Comp. Gen. Dec. B-417591, 2019 CPD ¶ 305.

Sealed bidding was widely used prior to 1984 but is now used infrequently. The procedures applicable to sealed bidding are discussed in Chapter 5.

[B] Issuance of a Task or Delivery Order

When the decision is made to issue a task or delivery order, there may be more than one contract that can be used for that purpose. The choices are the Federal Supply Schedule, a multi-agency contract (MAC) or governmentwide acquisition contract (GWAC), or an IDIQ contract issued by the procuring agency.

[1] Federal Supply Schedule Contracts

The General Services Administration administers the Federal Supply Schedule (or Multiple Award Schedule) which lists a large number of pre-negotiated contracts for commercial products and services. Agencies can issue task or delivery orders or blanket purchase agreements against these contracts following the procedures in FAR Subpart 8.4. These procedures are "competitive procedures" which meet the statutory full and open competition requirements. See 10 U.S.C. § 3012 (formerly § 2302(2)(C)) and 41 U.S.C. § 152(3).

Agencies have considerable discretion in adopting streamlined procedures and orders can be placed using the electronic GSA Advantage website. The contracts contain fixed prices or fixed labor rates which have been negotiated by GSA, FAR 8.404(d), but agencies are expected to obtain competition for their task or delivery orders in order to obtain the most favorable price or rate, FAR 8.405-1(d)(3) and 8.405-2(c)(3). A detailed discussion of Federal Supply Schedule procedures is contained in Chapter 11

[2] GWACs and MACs

Agencies issue GWACs and MACs to be available for use by other agencies. These are IDIQ contracts for a category of products or services. Their terms and conditions are generally in accordance with FAR requirements. The rules governing use of these vehicles are discussed in Chapter 11. The procedures for the issuance of task and delivery orders against these contracts are discussed in Chapter 7.

[3] Agency IDIQ Contracts

Individual agencies also issue IDIQ contracts for the products or services that may be unique because of their specialized mission. These contracts have the advantage of limiting award to a relatively small number of contractors, facilitating subsequent competition. The procedures for the issuance of task and delivery orders against these contracts are discussed in Chapter 7.

[C] Research Contracting Procedures

There are several special procedures available when an agency is acquiring research work. Such work is generally acquired using broad agency announcements where agencies publish their areas of interest and evaluate proposals as they are submitted by research organizations. These procedures are "competitive procedures" which meet the statutory full and open competition requirements. They apply to standard research acquisitions and to small business innovative research contracts. 10 U.S.C. § 3012 (formerly § 2302) and 41 U.S.C. § 152(2). These procedures are discussed in detail in Chapter 11.

Some agencies have the authority to use "other transactions" to acquire research, prototypes or other work depending on the agency's statutory authority. Many such contracts are required to be on a cost-sharing basis. The broad purpose of this authority is to attract commercial firms to make advanced technology available to government agencies, but the authority is also used to award contracts to firms that deal primarily with the government. These procedures also are discussed in detail in Chapter 11.

[D] Other Competitive Procedures

10 U.S.C. § 3012 (formerly § 2302) and 41 U.S.C. § 152 specify two other special procedures that are "competitive procedures" meeting the statutory requirement for full and open competition. The first is the procurement of architectural or engineering services conducted in accordance with 40 U.S.C. § 1101 et seq. and FAR subpart 36.6. In this procedure contractors are selected on the basis of technical competence with price negotiated with the winning firm after it has been selected. This procedure also is discussed in detail in Chapter 11.

The second special procedure which is a "competitive procedure" meeting the statutory requirement for full and open competition is the small business set-aside procedure called for in 10 U.S.C. § 3012(4) (formerly § 2302(2)(D)) and 41 U.S.C. § 152(4). This procedure allows agencies to reserve contracts for selected classes of small businesses as discussed in detail in Chapter 14. Procurements using these set-asides are generally conducted as competitive negotiations following the procedures in Chapters 6.

§ 3.04 IDENTIFYING SOURCES

In planning a procurement, it is necessary to determine what sources, if any, exist to meet the government's needs. The number and nature of the sources will, in large part, determine the technique that can be used in the procurement. Other determinations that must be made in the planning stages deal with whether to satisfy the agency's needs from private or government sources. It is also essential to determine whether there are any mandatory sources.

The prospective sources of supplies and/or services that can meet the need must be stated in the acquisition plan, FAR 7.105(b)(1). In determining what sources can be used to fulfill their needs, the agencies may not be free to make a choice. Statutes, regulations, and existing contractual obligations often dictate what sources may or may not be used. One example is when purchases are required to be set aside for performance solely by small business concerns, 15 U.S.C. § 644(j). Indeed, one of the primary uses of market research is to determine whether there are small businesses available to fulfill particular requirements, on a set-aside basis. See *Information Ventures, Inc.*, Comp. Gen. Dec. B-294267, 2004 CPD ¶ 205 (market research inadequate because agency did not review known sources of information on small business sources); *SWR, Inc.*, Comp. Gen. Dec. B-294266, 2004 CPD ¶ 219; *Rochester Optical Mfg. Co.*, Comp. Gen. Dec. B-292247, 2003 CPD ¶ 138. Another example of a socioeconomic issue that must be addressed during market research is when products or services fall under the Buy American Act, 41 U.S.C. §§ 10a-10d. See Chapter 14 for an in-depth discussion of collateral policies, including important socioeconomic policies, that play a role in determining what sources are available to meet the government's procurement needs.

In most cases, the agency technical and program personnel and the contracting officer will know of potential sources that should be solicited. In addition, in most cases the contracting officer will be required to publicize the requirement as discussed in Section § 3.07. The contracting officer will also determine whether the procurement must be directed to a mandatory source or set aside for small or disadvantaged businesses.

[A] Market Research

The primary means for identifying sources is market research. The statutory requirements for market research are in 41 U.S.C. § 3306(a)(1), 41 U.S.C. § 3307, 10 U.S.C. § 3453 (formerly § 2377), and 6 U.S.C. § 796. Market research is defined in FAR 2.101:

> "Market research" means collecting and analyzing information about capabilities within the market to satisfy agency needs.

Market research is used not only to identify sources but to determine the best procurement strategy, focusing on identifying commercial products or services that will meet the government's needs, FAR 10.001(a)(3). Agencies are required to identify their needs and conduct market research *before* new specifications are prepared, FAR 10.001(a)(2)(i). The techniques that can be used to conduct market research are detailed in FAR 10.002(b)(2) as follows:

> (i) Contacting knowledgeable individuals in Government and industry regarding market capabilities to meet requirements.
>
> (ii) Reviewing the results of recent market research undertaken to meet similar or identical requirements.
>
> (iii) Publishing formal requests for information in appropriate technical or scientific journals or business publications.
>
> (iv) Querying the Governmentwide database of contracts and other procurement instruments intended for use by multiple agencies available at https://www.contractdirectory.gov/contractdirectory/ and other Government and commercial databases that provide information relevant to agency acquisitions.
>
> (v) Participating in interactive, on-line communication among industry, acquisition personnel, and customers.
>
> (vi) Obtaining source lists of similar items from other contracting activities or agencies, trade associations or other sources.
>
> (vii) Reviewing catalogs and other generally available product literature published by manufacturers, distributors, and dealers or available on-line.
>
> (viii) Conducting interchange meetings or holding presolicitation conferences to involve potential offerors early in the acquisition process.
>
> (ix) Reviewing systems such as the System for Award Management, the Federal Procurement Data System, and the Small Business Administration's Dynamic Small Business Search.

See *JRS Staffing Servs.*, Comp. Gen. Dec. B-414630, 2017 CPD ¶ 150, stating that "agencies need not use any particular methodology when conducting market research; measures such as prior procurement history, market surveys, and advice from the agency's small business specialist may all constitute adequate grounds for a contracting officer's decision."

When other than full and open competition procedures are used, FAR 6.303-2(a)(8) requires that justifications describe the market research conducted or the reasons why it was not conducted. GAO has held that an agency's reason for not conducting a market survey was adequate where it had supported the fact that a directed source was designated pursuant to an international agreement, *PacOrd*, Comp. Gen. Dec. B-238366, 90-1 CPD ¶ 466. GAO also upheld an agency's decision not to conduct a market survey where the agency stated that it had recently determined that there was only one domestic source for a product, *Lister Bolt & Chain, Ltd.*, Comp. Gen. Dec. B-224473, 86-2 CPD ¶ 305. The technique used for the market survey is in the discretion of the contracting officer, *AAA Eng'g & Drafting, Inc.*, Comp. Gen. Dec. B-236034.3, 93-1 CPD ¶ 295.

[1] Inadequate Market Research

Inadequate market research can be a fatal defect in the procurement process if there are sources available to meet the agency's needs that were not discovered or a procurement is based on improper information. In *K-Whit Tools, Inc.*, Comp. Gen. Dec. B-247081, 92-1 CPD ¶ 382, GAO held that the failure to conduct a market survey indicated that the need to contract sole source was due to a lack of advance planning and was unauthorized. See also *Palantir USG, Inc. v. United States*, 129 Fed. Cl. 218 (2016), *aff'd*, 904 F.3d 980 (Fed. Cir. 2018) (inadequate market research led to failure to identify commercial product that would meet agency needs); *Fire Risk Mgmt., Inc.*, Comp. Gen. Dec. B-411552, 2015 CPD ¶ 259 (failure to conduct adequate market survey led to failure to make small business set aside); *Triad Isotopes, Inc.*, Comp. Gen. Dec. B-411360, 2015 CPD ¶ 220 (failure to conduct adequate market survey led to improper small business set aside); *Innovation Development Enters. Of Am., Inc. v. United States*, 108 Fed. Cl. 711 (2013) (inadequate market research led to improper sole source decision); *DNO, Inc.*, Comp. Gen. Dec. B-406256, 2012 CPD ¶ 136 (inadequate market survey led to failure to make small business set aside); and *TMS Bldg. Maint.*, 65 Comp. Gen. 222 (B-220588), 86-1 CPD ¶ 68 (failure to contact other potential sources or to conduct a market survey evidenced a lack of advance planning and rendered the sole source award improper). In contrast, the results of a market survey may justify a sole source award, *DRS Sustainment Sys., Inc.*, Comp. Gen. Dec B-417628, 2019 CPD ¶ 316 (after market survey agency found award to protester would entail "unforeseen performance challenges"); *Interscience Sys., Inc.*, Comp. Gen. Dec B-201943, 82-2 CPD ¶ 187 (upholding determination to award contract on a sole source basis as a result of two market surveys). The results of a market survey have also been used to support the reasonableness of a bid price, *Eclipse Sys., Inc.*, Comp. Gen. Dec. B-216002, 85-1 CPD ¶ 267. Market research is also used to determine whether a procurement should be set aside for small business, *Analytical Graphics, Inc. v. United States*, 135 Fed. Cl. 378 (2017).

[2] Requests for Information

One technique for conducting market research is the use of solicitations for information or planning purposes. FAR 15.201(e) permits requests for information (RFIs) to be used in this manner as follows:

> RFIs may be used when the Government does not presently intend to award a contract, but wants to obtain price, delivery, other market information, or capabilities for planning purposes. Responses to these notices are not offers and cannot be accepted by the Government to form a binding contract. There is no required format for RFIs.

FAR 14.105-1 refers to this provision permitting its use on sealed bid procurements. RFIs are published on a website, *https:/SAM.gov*, the "Governmentwide Point of Entry" (GPE), the single point where government contracting opportunities greater than $25,000 can be accessed electronically by the public. FAR 5.204 requires that "presolicitation notices" be disseminated using the GPE. While FAR 5.205(c) does not address RFIs, it permits use of the GPE to transmit "special notices."

Contractors cannot rely on language in an RFI identifying the agency's requirements when a subsequent RFP contains different language ("should" vs. "shall"), *Raytheon Co.*, Comp. Gen. Dec. B-414354, 2017 CPD ¶168. However, agencies can rely on responses to RFIs to justify their chosen procurement strategy, *Major Contracting Servs., Inc.*, Comp. Gen. Dec. B-406980, 2012 CPD ¶288. Firms that do not respond to RFIs stand little chance of winning a protest of an agency's decision as to how to conduct a procurement, *MTU Maint. Canada, LTD*, Comp. Gen. Dec. B-411185, 2015 CPD ¶179.

GAO will not consider a protest concerning a procuring agency issuing an RFI in the GPE. See *CGI Fed., Inc.*, Comp. Gen. Dec. B-418807, 2020 CPD ¶276; and Onix Networking Corp., Comp. Gen. Dec. B-411841, 2015 CPD ¶330.

[3] Sources Sought Synopsis

Another technique for identifying potential sources is the issuance of a sources sought synopsis. Those synopses also are published on the *https://SAM.gov* website. FAR 5.205(a) states that contracting officers may publish in the GPE advance notices of their interest in potential research and development programs when market research does not produce a sufficient number of concerns to obtain adequate competition. These notices are called "Research and Development Sources Sought." Although the FAR appears to limit this technique for identifying potential sources to research and development contracts, it has been used widely for all types of procurement. See FAR 5.205(c) permitting use of the GPE to transmit "special notices."

> Contracting officers may transmit to the GPE special notices of procurement matters such as business fairs, long-range procurement estimates, prebid or preproposal conferences, meetings, and the availability of draft solicitations or draft specifications for review.

Firms that do not respond to sources sought synopses stand little chance of winning a protest of an agency's decision as to how to conduct a procurement, *MTU Maint. Canada, LTD*, Comp. Gen. Dec. B-411185, 2015 CPD ¶179. However, firms should not submit proposals or quotations to an agency in response to a sources sought synopsis because it is not a solicitation. See

AeroSage, LLC, Comp. Gen. Dec B-415893, 2018 CPD ¶ 142, denying a protest asserting that the agency should have awarded it a contract based on its response to a sources sought synopsis.

GAO has stated that agencies are "required to evaluate . . . responses in a reasonable manner," *Future Sols., Inc.*, Comp. Gen. Dec B-293194, 2004 CPD ¶ 39. Furthermore, if an agency uses a sources sought synopsis, it must make its essential requirements clear to potential offerors and allow them an opportunity to demonstrate their ability to comply before rejecting them as potential sources. In *Masstor Sys. Corp.*, 64 Comp. Gen. 118 (B-215046), 84-2 CPD ¶ 598, GAO sustained a protest where the agency rejected a potential source for failing to demonstrate compliance with a requirement that was neither set forth in the sources sought synopsis nor otherwise made known to the vendor. The government should not, however, include proprietary information in the sources sought synopsis. In *Research, Analysis & Dev., Inc. v. United States*, 8 Cl. Ct. 54 (1985), the plaintiff submitted an unsolicited proposal pertaining to a novel concept in state-of-the-art aircraft-sensor technology. The proposal included the proper restrictive proprietary legend. After having agreed to maintain the confidentiality of the information, the agency issued a sources sought synopsis requesting responses regarding the feasibility of a sensor system concept identical to that proposed by the plaintiff. The court held that the disclosure in the CBD of the proprietary information associated with the unsolicited proposal violated the government's implied-in-fact contractual obligation to protect the data and entitled the company to damages.

Sources sought synopses are a frequent means of determining whether there are two or more qualified small businesses allowing the agency to set aside the procurement for small businesses. See *Assessment & Training Sols. Consulting Corp. v. United States*, 92 Fed. Cl. 722 (2010), where the agency correctly concluded that a procurement should be placed under the 8(a) program (either as a set-aside or sole source) based on the responses to its sources-sought synopsis. In contrast, in *Metasoft, LLC*, Comp. Gen. Dec. B-402800, 2010 CPD ¶ 170, and *RhinoCorps Ltd. Co. v. United States*, 87 Fed. Cl. 261 (2009), the agency properly concluded from the responses to the synopsis that there were not two small businesses that could perform 50% of the work with their own forces. See also *Totolo/King v. United States*, 87 Fed. Cl. 680 (2009), where the agency was able to determine from the responses to the synopsis that there were not two small businesses with sufficient bonding capacity to perform the contract; *EMMES Corp.*, Comp. Gen. Dec. B-402245, 2009 CPD ¶ 53, where the agency was able to conclude, as a result of the responses to a sources sought synopsis that there were not two qualified small business firms; and *Information Ventures, Inc.*, Comp. Gen. Dec. B-400604, 2008 CPD ¶ 232, where none of the 26 small businesses that responded to the synopsis were found to be qualified.

GAO will not consider a protest against a procuring agency issuing a potential sources sought announcement in the GPE. See *Lockheed Martin Sys.*

Integration—Owego, Comp. Gen. Dec. B-287190.2, 2001 CPD ¶ 110. GAO considers only protests against solicitations already issued by agencies and awards made or proposed to be made under those solicitations, *Pancor Corp.*, Comp. Gen. Dec. B-234168, 89-1 CPD ¶ 328.

[B] Contractor Versus Government Performance

There are two policies that must be considered in determining whether work should be obtained through the procurement process. First, there is the policy governing whether work currently being performed by a government activity should be opened up to competition from private companies. The long-standing policy on this issue is stated in Office of Management and Budget (OMB) Circular No. A-76, *Performance of Commercial Activities* (May 2003) (Circular A-76), Second, there are the numerous policies calling for the use of mandatory sources. These two policies are addressed in this section.

[1] Reliance on Private Sources

As a result of concerns that government competition with the private sector is detrimental to the free enterprise system, the executive branch policy has been that, to the extent practicable, the government should rely on the private sector for commercially available goods and services. This policy was first enunciated in Bureau of the Budget Bulletin No. 55-4, Jan. 15, 1955. Subsequently it has been embodied in Circular A-76. By the 1990s this Circular called for a two-step acquisition process when an agency identified commercial work that was being performed by government personnel. The first step was a competition among contractors to determine which contractor was best able to compete for the work. The second step was a competition of this contractor with the government organization performing the work. This proved to be a cumbersome, time-consuming process that was judged to be ineffective. As a result OMB's Circular A-76 was completely rewritten in 2003, to maximize "competitive sourcing." See Office of Management & Budget, *The President's Management Agenda* 17 (2002). In the private sector, meanwhile, outsourcing (including "offshoring" abroad) was rapidly evolving into very sophisticated methods for "strategic sourcing." See Gottfredson, Puryear & Phillips, *Strategic Sourcing: From Periphery to the Core*, Harv. Bus. Rev., Feb. 1, 2005, *www.hbr.org*. Circular A-76 places less emphasis on moving more work to the private sector but is addressed, rather, at establishing firmer guidelines on what work should not be performed by the private sector because it is an "inherently governmental function." See OFPP Policy Letter 11-01, *Performance of Inherently Governmental and Critical Functions*, Sept. 12, 2011, 76 Fed. Reg. 56227. See also FAR Subpart 7.5. Legislative agencies are not subject to Circular A-76's requirements, *International Graphics v. United States*, 4 Cl. Ct. 186 (1983).

[a] The A-76 Moratorium

In 2008, the National Defense Authorization Act for FY 2008, Pub. L. No. 110-181, suspended DOD public-private competitions under OMB Circular A-76. A governmentwide moratorium on the conduct of Circular A-76 competitions was enacted by the Omnibus Appropriations Act for FY 2009, Pub. L. No. 111-8. These moratoriums have been extended through subsequent legislation—with the result that public-private competitions have not been conducted for over a decade.

[b] A-76 Procedures

Circular A-76 requires that each agency designate an official at the assistant secretary or equivalent level, the "Competitive Sourcing Official" (CSO), to be responsible for implementing its policies. Agencies must prepare annual inventories, as required by the Federal Activities Inventory Reform Act of 1998 (FAIR Act), Pub. L. No. 105-270, 31 U.S.C. § 501 note, of all their activities that are performed by federal employees but are not inherently governmental (i.e., are commercial). OMB is to review each agency's Commercial Activities Inventory and consult with the agency regarding its content. Upon the completion of this review and consultation, the agency must transmit a copy of the inventory to Congress and make it available to the public. The FAIR Act establishes an administrative appeals process under which an interested party may challenge the omission or the inclusion of a particular activity on the inventory. See Circular A-76, Attachment A, § D.

To compile these inventories each agency must evaluate its activities and functions and determine which are inherently governmental and which are commercial. All the commercial activities are listed on an inventory that includes known expansions and new requirements. Activities involving 10 full-time equivalent (FTE) personnel or fewer are listed separately from those with more than 10 FTEs. The inventory must, at a minimum, describe the number of FTEs involved, the nature and location of the activity, and the dates of last and next reviews. "Commercial" activities being performed by government personnel may be subject to competitive sourcing (the competitive outsourcing process described below); "inherently governmental" functions are not. While Circular A-76 includes guidance on what constitutes an "inherently governmental activity" at Attachment A, § B.1., agencies should rely on the guidance on inherently governmental functions in OFPP Policy Letter 11-01 and FAR Subpart 7.5.

When an agency determines that an activity is subject to competition, it is required to use the special competitive process, called an "A-76 competition," which is outlined in Attachment B to the revised Circular A-76. These competitions are to be between a "Most Efficient Organization" (MEO) made up, generally, of current government employees performing the function, which presents the "agency tender," versus offerors from the private sector.

The first step in this competition process under Circular A-76 is the naming of a Performance Work Statement team, to develop the statement of work against which the MEO and private offerors can compete. This team and the contracting officer and the source selection official are a separate team that runs the competition. Additionally, the agency must appoint an Agency Tender Official (ATO) to represent the MEO. This agency team that is competing for the work is required to be totally separated from the source selection team. The competition can be run as a sealed bid or as a negotiated procurement, and if negotiated procurement is selected the agency can use a "lowest price technically acceptable, phased evaluation, [or] tradeoff" process, Circular A-76, Attachment B, ¶ D.3.a.(3). Once the statement of work is completed, bids or proposals are solicited. Concurrently, an in-house estimate is prepared for submission to the contracting officer not later than the time established for receipt of proposals or bid opening, Circular A-76, Attachment B, ¶ D.3.a.(5). The evaluation procedure to be followed in the standard A-76 competition after the contracting officer receives the cost estimate from the ATO and the responses to the solicitation differs from conventional contracting procedures. Under what is termed the "conversion differential"—a price advantage given the MEO on the assumption that shifting the work from existing government employees will entail additional costs—10% or $10 million is added to the price or cost of the "incumbent source" (generally the best offer from a contractor). See Circular A-76, Attachment B, ¶ D.5.c.(4)(c).

Attachment B of Circular A-76 contains very detailed instructions on each step of this competition procedure, including use of the tradeoff process when the offers are evaluated on both price and non-price factors. However, the complexity of this process and the difficulty of applying such factors to MEOs has led most agencies to use a process where the selection is based on price alone. This policy decision is heavily influenced by the fact that the Circular requires that standard procedures be completed within one year of the time of the public announcement of the competition, Circular A-76, Attachment B, ¶ D.1.

The revised Circular A-76 explicitly contemplates "contests," or bid protests, brought through the agency-level bid protest process outlined in FAR 33.103, Circular A-76, Attachment B, ¶ F.1. These contests, to be brought only by "directly interested parties," may review any of the following actions taken in connection with a standard competition:

> (1) a solicitation;
>
> (2) the cancellation of a solicitation;
>
> (3) a determination to exclude a tender or offer from a standard competition;
>
> (4) a performance decision, including, but not limited to, compliance with the costing provisions of this circular and other elements in an agency's evaluation of offers and tenders; or
>
> (5) a termination or cancellation of a contract or letter of obligation if the challenge contains an allegation that the termination or cancellation is based in whole or in part on improprieties concerning the performance decision.

Pursuant to Ronald W. Reagan National Defense Authorization Act for Fiscal Year 2005, Pub. L. No. 108-375, and the National Defense Authorization Act for Fiscal Year 2008, Pub. L. No. 110-181, ATOs and "Designated Employee Agents" (DEAs) can protest A-76 competitions in the same way that contractors can protest. GAO's regulations state at 4 C.F.R. § 21.0(a):

> (2) In a public-private competition conducted under Office of Management and Budget Circular A-76 regarding performance of an activity or function of a Federal agency, or a decision to convert a function performed by Federal employees to private sector performance without a competition under OMB Circular A-76, interested party also means
>
> (A) The official responsible for submitting the Federal agency tender, and
>
> (B) Any one individual, designated as an agent by a majority of the employees performing that activity or function, who represents the affected employees.

In contrast, employees do not have standing to challenge these competitions in court, *National Federation of Federal Employees v. Cheney*, 883 F2d 1038 (D.C. Cir. 1989), *cert. denied*, 496 U.S. 936 (1990).

ATOs and DEAs have the authority to challenge any issue related to a competition that was started on or after January 28, 2008. With regard to competitions that were started prior to that date, they could only challenge the source selection decision. See *Gary Johnson—Designated Employee Agent*, Comp. Gen. Dec. B-310910.3, 2009 CPD ¶ 22; *Bruce Bancroft—Agency Tender Official*, Comp. Gen. Dec. B-400404.2, 2008 CPD ¶ 200. The strict timeliness rules apply to these officials, *Rhonda Podojil—Agency Tender Official*, Comp. Gen. Dec. B-311310, 2008 CPD ¶ 94. Protests of award to contractors were sustained in *Frank A. Bloomer—Agency Tender Official*, Comp. Gen. Dec. B-401482.2, 2009 CPD ¶ 203 (agency unreasonably accepted offeror's revised fringe benefit ratios in its cost realism analysis, its unsupported assumption that it could perform a significant portion of the workload 10% more efficiently, and its omission of labor cost associated with the material supply function from its cost proposal); and *Rosemary Livingston—Agency Tender Official*, Comp. Gen. Dec. B-401102.2, 2009 CPD ¶ 135, *recons. denied*, 2009 CPD ¶ 162 (record contains inconsistent statements by the agency in its contemporaneous evaluation and inadequate documentation of its findings regarding the tender's shortcomings).

GAO will not review the decision of whether to contract out because this is a matter of executive branch policy, *Desktop Alert, Inc.*, Comp. Gen. Dec. B-417170, 2019 CPD ¶ 29. However, GAO will review an agency decision to cancel the solicitation for an A-76 competition to determine whether there was a reasonable basis for the cancellation, *Zia Eng'g & Env't Consultants, LLC*, Comp. Gen. Dec. B-400127, 2008 CPD ¶ 156. Likewise, the courts have held that agency decisions under A-76 are internal managerial decisions that are not subject to judicial review, *International Graphics v. United States*, 4 Cl. Ct. 186 (1983).

A contractor protest was sustained in *New Dynamics Corp.*, Comp. Gen. Dec. B-401272, 2009 CPD ¶ 150, holding that the agency failed to reasonably consider whether the agency tender's material and supply costs were realistic. Compare *Phoenix Mgmt., Inc.*, Comp. Gen. Dec. B-299477, 2007 CPD ¶ 95, holding that the agency had properly found the protester's proposal unacceptable because it did not adequately explain its management approach.

[c] Statutory Limitations

Prior to the moratorium there were a number of statutory limitations on the procurement of services by contract.

[i] Department of Defense

Chapter 146 of Title 10 of the U.S. Code regulates the DoD's contracting-out process. 10 U.S.C. § 2461 prohibits direct conversion of work performed by civilian employees without first conducting a competition following the procedures of Circular A-76. 10 U.S.C. § 2463 requires the agency to issue guidelines and procedures "to ensure that consideration is given to using, on a regular basis . . . civilian employees to perform new functions and functions that are performed by contractors and could be performed by [such] civilian employees." These guidelines must give special consideration to using civilian employees to perform any function that

> (1) is performed by a contractor and—
>
> (A) has been performed by Department of Defense civilian employees at any time during the previous 10 years;
>
> (B) is a function closely associated with the performance of an inherently governmental function;
>
> (C) has been performed pursuant to a contract awarded on a non-competitive basis; or
>
> (D) has been performed poorly, as determined by a contracting officer during the 5-year period preceding the date of such determination, because of excessive costs or inferior quality; or
>
> (2) is a new requirement, with particular emphasis given to a new requirement that is similar to a function previously performed by Department of Defense civilian employees or is a function closely associated with the performance of an inherently governmental function.

This statutory provision also contains restrictions on using the A-76 procedures with such civilian functions.

10 U.S.C. § 2464 requires the agency to identify "core logistics capabilities" and the workload necessary to maintain these capabilities. This workload must be "sufficient . . . to ensure cost efficiency and technical competence in peacetime while preserving the surge capacity and reconstitution capabilities necessary to support fully the [agency's] strategic and contingency plans." This workload may not be contracted out pursuant to Circular A-76 unless the Secretary of Defense waives this requirement. These provisions do not apply to commercial items but the Act requires that Congress be notified when the agency determines that a military product is a commercial item. 10 U.S.C. § 2465 prohibits contracting out of firefighting or security-guard functions at any military installation or facility. This restriction does not apply to contracts outside of the United States and contracts for such work at contractor operated, government-owned facilities.

10 U.S.C. § 2466 prevents defense agencies and military departments from contracting out more than 50% of their respective depot maintenance workloads. Any funds that are not used for such a contract must be used for the performance of depot-level maintenance and repair workload by employees of the DoD.

[ii] National Park Service

The Volunteers in the Parks Act of 1969, amended by Pub. L. No. 98-540, 98 Stat. 2718 (1984), 43 U.S.C. § 1457a note, stated that Circular A-76 was not to apply to activities conducted by the National Park Service, United States Fish and Wildlife Service, and the Bureau of Land Management if those activities involve 10 FTEs or fewer. This was applicable for fiscal years 1985 through and including 1988. If the moratorium is lifted, this policy could be extended.

[2] Mandatory Sources

Various statutes and regulations require agencies to attempt to satisfy their needs for goods and services from specific sources prior to contracting with commercial sources. FAR Part 8 contains detailed guidance on mandatory sources. See also DFARS Part 208 for guidance on mandatory sources for defense procurement.

FAR 8.002 ranks mandatory sources in order of priority. Existing agency inventory is the first source considered. If the needed supply is not available from existing inventory, FAR 8.002 directs the agency to consider other sources in the following order: other agencies (excess supplies), Federal Prison Industries, the Committee for Purchase from People Who Are Blind or Severely Disabled, government, and wholesale supply sources that are maintained by DoD, GSA, or the Department of Veterans Affairs. If the agency's requirement is for services, agencies must consider the Committee for Purchase from People Who Are Blind or Severely Disabled. FAR 8.003 lists other mandatory sources as public utility services, printing services, leased motor vehicles, strategic and critical materials, and helium. The following discussion examines these mandatory sources of supply.

[a] Excess Personal Property

The Administrator of the GSA is authorized to prescribe policies and methods to promote utilization of excess personal property by the federal agencies pursuant to 40 U.S.C. § 521 et seq. This statute requires agencies to utilize excess personal property of other agencies to the fullest extent possible. The statute also charges agencies with the duty of monitoring excess property and either transferring or disposing of it as promptly as possible, 40 U.S.C. § 529. The GSA maintains catalogs of available excess property, issues bulletins, and provides other assistance to facilitate acquisition of excess personal property. FAR 8.102 requires procurement personnel to make "positive efforts" to utilize excess personal property before taking other procurement action.

[b] Government Printing Office

Virtually all printing, binding, and blank-book work for Congress, the Executive Office of the President, the judiciary (except the Supreme Court), and every executive department, independent office, and establishment of the government must be done by or through the Government Printing Office (GPO). Exceptions include those classes of work the Congressional Joint Committee on Printing considers sufficiently urgent or necessary to be done elsewhere, as well as work printed in field printing plants operated by an executive department, 44 U.S.C. § 501. FAR 8.802 mandates compliance with the regulations of the Congressional Joint Committee on Printing and vests responsibility for obtaining waivers and dealing with the Joint Committee in certain officials.

Printing is limited to "written graphic or published materials," *Veterans4You, LLC v. United States*, 985 F.3d 850 (Fed. Cir. 2021) (label and wallet card not printing). Prior decisions had defined printing broadly. See *Bureau of Land Mgmt.: Payment of Pocatello Field Office Photocopying Costs*, Comp. Gen. Dec. B-290901, 2003 CPD ¶ 2, holding that printing includes photocopying, and Comp. Gen. Dec. B-251481.4, Sept. 30, 1994, *Unpub.*, holding that printing includes duplicating processes using high-speed duplicating equipment. But see Comp. Gen. Dec. B-251481.3, Feb. 15, 1994, *Unpub.*, stating that a contract modification requiring a design system to have the capability of developing "reproducible masters" from the technical manual source data did not fall within the definition of printing. See also *Bureau of Land Mgmt.: Payment of Printing Costs by the Milwaukee Field Office*, Comp. Gen. Dec. B-290900, 2003 U.S. Comp. Gen. LEXIS 241, holding that sharing in the cost of printing a brochure under a cooperative agreement did not fall under this prohibition because the brochure was not "for the government" under 44 U.S.C. § 501.

Agencies implement these requirements by referring their printing requirement to the Government Printing Office. That office either performs the printing or contracts it out to its wide range of vendors throughout the United States. See *gpo.gov*.

[c] General Services Administration Stores Stock and Excess Property

The administrator of the GSA is authorized to operate supply centers and procure and supply personal property for executive agencies, 40 U.S.C. § 501. Pursuant to this authority, the GSA operates supply distribution facilities and maintains an inventory of stock items that constitute a mandatory source for executive agencies located within the United States. See 41 C.F.R. § 101-26.301. The GSA publishes a supply catalog that lists all items available from GSA stock.

GSA also has an electronic catalog, "GSAXcess," which tracks excess property and which is available through the GSA home page, "GSA Advantage!", which is an online ordering system that allows agencies to search through all GSA sources of supply and select the item that best meets their requirements. See FAR 8.103.

[d] General Services Administration Motorpools

The Federal Property and Administrative Services Act of 1949 authorizes GSA to provide motor vehicles to agencies of the federal government. See 40 U.S.C. § 602 directing GSA to—

> (1) take over from executive agencies and consolidate, or otherwise acquire, motor vehicles and related equipment and supplies;
> (2) provide for the establishment, maintenance, and operation (including servicing and storage) of motor vehicle pools or systems; and
> (3) furnish motor vehicles and related services to executive agencies for the transportation of property and passengers.

40 U.S.C. § 603 provides guidance on the implementation of this requirement and calls for the issuance of regulations on motor vehicles. See 41 C.F.R. Part 101-39. The Act authorizes the GSA to enter into rental or other arrangements and to utilize government-owned vehicles. The Act provides that requisitioning agencies should be charged for services rendered at prices calculated to recover all elements of cost. See FAR Subpart 8.11 for guidance on leasing motor vehicles.

[e] Federal Prison Industries

Federal Prison Industries, Inc. (FPI), also known as "UNICOR," is a wholly owned government corporation created by Congress in 1934 to administer industrial operations in federal penal and correctional institutions. FPI is authorized to produce commodities for consumption in penal institutions or for sale to the government, but is prohibited from selling to the public, 18 U.S.C. § 4122. For many years, all government agencies were required to purchase available quantities that met their needs from FPI.

The FPI's preference was modified by § 637 of the Consolidated Appropriations Act for 2005, Pub. L. No. 108-447, and the amendment of 10 U.S.C. 3905 (formerly § 2410n). FAR 8.602(a) implements these statutes.

If FPI has a "significant market share" (greater than 5%) of DOD procurements of a product, competition with industry is required, DFARS 208.602-70.

GAO does not consider protests of agency decisions that FPI supplies are not comparable because the statute calls for arbitration to determine this issue, *Federal Prison Indus., Inc.*, Comp. Gen. Dec. B-290546, 2002 CPD ¶ 112 (see FAR 8.602(d)). However, GAO will consider protests of agency evaluations in competitions between FPI and a competing contractor, *Federal Prison Indus., Inc.*, Comp. Gen. Dec. B-417100, 2019 CPD ¶ 71; and *Gentex Corp.*, Comp. Gen. Dec. B-400328, 2008 CPD ¶ 186. See also *Tennier Indus. Inc.*, Comp. Gen. Dec. B-403946.2, 2012 CPD ¶ 199, denying a protest asserting that FPI should not have been allowed to compete in a HUBZone set aside. GAO will also consider protests of procurements by FPI, *Patriot Sols., LLC*, Comp. Gen. Dec. B-413779, 2016 CPD ¶ 376.

[f] Surplus Strategic and Critical Materials

FAR 8.003 requires agencies to procure strategic and critical materials as follows:

> (d) Strategic and critical materials (e.g., metals and ores) from inventories exceeding Defense National Stockpile requirements (detailed information is available from the Defense National Stockpile Center, 8725 John J. Kingman Rd., Suite 3229, Fort Belvoir, VA 22060-6223).

[g] The Committee for Purchase from People Who Are Blind or Severely Disabled

Pursuant to the Javits-Wagner-O'Day Act (the JWOD Act), and the rules implementing the AbilityOne program, federal agencies are required to procure goods and services from a nonprofit agency serving people who are blind or a nonprofit agency serving people with other severe disabilities if those agencies can provide the needed commodities or services, 41 U.S.C. § 8501 et seq. This committee, appointed by the President, compiles a list of supplies and services that qualified agencies may provide (known as the Procurement List). Agencies must purchase these supplies or services if they are available within the period required, FAR 8.704. See *Goodwill Indus. of the Valleys*, Comp. Gen. Dec. B-415137, 2017 CPD ¶ 369, granting a protest when GSA included custodial services on the Procurement List in a lease of a building rather than procuring them from the AbilityOne agency.

FAR 8.703 notes that many items on the Procurement List are identified in the GSA Supply Catalogs or in catalogs issued by the Defense Supply Agency and the Department of Veterans Affairs. The procedures for ordering these supplies and services are set forth in FAR 8.705 and procedures for administering these orders are provided in FAR 8.706-716.

If a product is produced by both AbilityOne and Federal Prison Industries, FAR 8.602(c) states that FPI will grant a waiver for part of the requirement to be procured from AbilityOne without competition.

[h] Helium

FAR 8.502 requires agencies and their contractors and subcontractors to purchase "major helium requirements" from Federal helium suppliers, to the extent that supplies are available. FAR 8.503 excepts contractors and subcontractors that have purchased the helium prior to award. FAR 8.501 contains the following definition:

> Major helium requirement means an estimated refined helium requirement greater than 200,000 standard cubic feet (SCF) (measured at 14.7 pounds per square inch absolute pressure and 70 degrees Fahrenheit temperature) of gaseous helium or 7510 liters of liquid helium delivered to a helium use location per year.

FAR 8.504 requires periodic reports on helium purchased to the Bureau of Land Management.

§ 3.05 DESCRIBING THE WORK

The selection of the specification is a key element of the acquisition planning process because it is inherently related to the extent of competition and the procurement technique that can be used. Another critical decision is the amount of work that will be included in each solicitation. As discussed earlier, "new specifications" should not be prepared until market research has been conducted, 10 U.S.C. § 3453(c)(1)(A) (formerly § 2377(c)) and 41 U.S.C. § 3306(a).

[A] Specifications

The term "specifications" is used in this material to refer to work descriptions generally, including statements of work, drawings, and documents bearing the title "specifications."

With respect to specifications to be used in the procurement process, 10 U.S.C. § 3206(a)(2) (formerly § 2305(a)(1)(B)) provides:

> Each solicitation under this subchapter shall include specifications which—
>
> (A) consistent with the provisions of chapter 137 legacy provisions, permit full and open competition; and
>
> (B) include restrictive provisions or conditions only to the extent necessary to satisfy the needs of the agency or as authorized by law.

41 U.S.C. § 3306(a)(2) contains substantially the same requirements.

To meet the requirement for seeking "full and open competition," agencies should draft specifications "in terms that enable and encourage offerors to supply commercial products or commercial services" to the maximum extent possible. This requires that specifications be drafted only after there is full knowledge of what goods and services are commercially available. See FAR 11.002(a)(2)(ii).

[1] Generic Nature of Specifications

Once the market situation is known, agencies can choose among a number of types of specifications or combine types of specifications to explain their needs. 41 U.S.C. § 3306(a)(3) and 10 U.S.C. § 3206(a)(3) (formerly § 2305(a)(1)(C)) provide:

> [T]he type of specification included in a solicitation shall depend on the nature of the needs of the executive agency and the market available to satisfy such needs. Subject to such needs, specifications may be stated in terms of—
>
> (A) function, so that a variety of products or services may qualify;
>
> (B) performance, including specifications of the range of acceptable characteristics or of the minimum acceptable standards; or
>
> (C) design requirements.

FAR 11.002(a)(2)(i) sets forth the same concepts, albeit in slightly different language:

> State requirements with respect to an acquisition of supplies or services in terms of—
>
> (A) Functions to be performed;
>
> (B) Performance required; or
>
> (C) Essential physical characteristics.

These provisions state no preference regarding the type of specification to be used, giving the agency full discretion to prepare the type of specification best suited to satisfy its needs. See, however, FAR 11.101(a), which states a preference for "performance-oriented" specifications over "design-oriented" specifications. See also FAR 11.002(a)(2)(ii) requiring agencies to define their requirements in terms that allow offerors to provide commercial or nondevelopmental items. Regardless of the type of specification used, it must contain only those provisions necessary to meet the agency's needs.

Few specifications are composed solely of one type. The government must often combine specification types in order to describe its needs adequately and ensure full and open competition. See *Blake Constr. Co. v. United States*, 987 F.2d 743 (Fed. Cir. 1993), stating at 746:

> [T]he distinction between design and performance specifications is not absolute, and does not dictate the resolution of this case. Contracts may have both design and performance characteristics. *See, e.g., Utility Contractors, Inc. v. United States*, 8 Cl. Ct. 42, 50 n.7 (1985) ("Certainly one can find numerous government contracts exhibiting both performance and design specifications."), *aff'd mem.*, 790 F.2d 90 (Fed. Cir. 1986); *Aleutain Constructors v. United States*, 24 Cl. Ct. 372, 379 (1991) ("Government contracts not uncommonly contain both design and performance specifications."). It is not only possible, but likely that a contractor will be granted at least limited discretion to find the best way to achieve goals within the design parameters set by a contract. *See, e.g., Penguin Indus., Inc. v. United States*, 209 Ct. Cl. 121, 530 F.2d 934, 937 (Ct. Cl. 1976). "On occasion the labels 'design specification' and 'performance specification' have been used to connote the degree to which the government has prescribed certain details of performance on which the contractor could rely. However, those labels do not independently create, limit, or remove a contractor's obligations." *Zinger Constr. Co. v. United States*, 807 F.2d 979, 981 (Fed. Cir. 1986) (citations omitted). These labels merely help the court discuss the discretionary elements of a contract. It is the obligations imposed by the specification which determine the extent to which it is "performance" or "design," not the other way around.

See also *Purification Env't*, Comp. Gen. Dec. B-270762, 96-1 CPD ¶ 203, where the performance specification included a requirement that only a specified type of water treatment system be used. In such a case, GAO noted that—

> where the government does specify a certain design, it has long been established that the risk that the design is unsuited for the intended purpose is allocated to the government, based on a theory of implied warranty.

[a] Design Specifications

In *Blake Constr. Co. v. United States*, 987 F.2d 743 (Fed. Cir. 1993), the court described design specifications at 744:

> Design specifications . . . describe in precise detail the materials to be employed and the manner in which the work is to be performed. The contractor has no discretion to deviate from the specifications, but is "required to follow them as one would a road map." "Detailed design specifications

contain an implied warranty that if they are followed, an acceptable result will be produced." *Stuyvesant Dredging Co. v. United States*, 834 F.2d 1576, 1582 (Fed. Cir. 1987) (*citing United States v. Spearin*, 248 U.S. 132 (1918)).

When the government uses a design specification, it impliedly warrants that the specifications are suitable for their intended purposes. See *White v. Edsall Constr. Co.*, 296 F.3d 1081 (Fed. Cir. 2002), stating at 1084-85:

> When the Government provides a contractor with design specifications, such that the contractor is bound by contract to build according to the specifications, the contract carries an implied warranty that the specifications are free from design defects. *United States v. Spearin*, 248 U.S. 132, 136, 54 Ct. Cl. 187, 39 S. Ct. 59, 63 L. Ed. 166 (1918); *see also Essex Electro Eng'rs, Inc. v. Danzig*, 224 F.3d 1283, 1289 (Fed. Cir.2000); *USA Petroleum Corp. v. United States*, 821 F.2d 622, 624 (Fed. Cir.1987). This implied warranty attaches only to design specifications detailing the actual method of performance. It does not accompany performance specifications that merely set forth an objective without specifying the method of obtaining the objective. Because the implied warranty protects contractors who fully comply with the design specifications, the contractors are not responsible for the consequences of defects in the specified design. *Spearin*, 248 U.S. at 136.

See also *CEMS, Inc. v. United States*, 59 Fed. Cl. 168 (2003) ("It is established in government contract law that the government warrants the 'performability' of the design specifications it issues"). For complete coverage of the implied warranty of design specifications see Chapter 3 of Cibinic, Nash & Nagle, *Administration of Government Contracts* (5th ed. 2016).

[b] Performance Specifications

In *Blake Constr. Co. v. United States*, 987 F.2d 743 (Fed. Cir. 1993), the court discussed performance specifications at 744:

> Performance specifications "set forth an objective or standard to be achieved, and the successful bidder is expected to exercise his ingenuity in achieving that objective or standard of performance, selecting the means and assuming a corresponding responsibility for that selection." *J.L. Simmons Co. v. United States*, 188 Cl. Ct. 684, 412 F.2d 1360, 1362 (Ct. Cl. 1969).

In general, performance type specifications describe the government's requirements in terms of the end result that the agency desires rather than in terms of a precise description of the work to be done. In many cases, they promote more competition by giving contractors more flexibility. GAO denied a protest that the use of such specifications placed too much risk on the contractor by requiring substantial design effort, *McDermott Shipyards*, Comp. Gen. Dec. B-237049,

90-1 CPD ¶ 121. It cited *Pitney Bowes*, 68 Comp. Gen. 249 (B-233100), 89-1 CPD ¶ 157, for the view that such specifications are favored under CICA. See also *Flight Safety Int'l*, Comp. Gen. Dec. B-290595, 2002 CPD ¶ 138, where a separate contract line item number was not necessary when the agency provided enough information for offerors to use its business judgment to amortize pilot training costs; and *SouthEastern Techs., Inc.*, Comp. Gen. Dec. B-275636, 97-1 CPD ¶ 96, where the solicitation described the information with enough detail to enable all interested parties to prepare expressions of interest.

Performance specifications are much less likely than design specifications to be found to be unduly restrictive unless they contain a restrictive design feature. See, for example, *Sun Refining & Mktg. Co.*, Comp. Gen. Dec. B-239973, 90-2 CPD ¶ 305 (requirement for delivery of oil products by pipeline rather than by truck). Performance requirements, however, can be unduly restrictive in some instances, *Prime-Mover Co.*, Comp. Gen. Dec. B-201970, 81-2 CPD ¶ 325 (unnecessary speed and mechanical requirements for forklift vehicles); *Globe Air, Inc.*, Comp. Gen. Dec. B-180969.2, 75-1 CPD ¶ 57 (requirement that rotor blades on helicopter be no more than 37 feet in diameter). Compare *Glock, Inc.*, Comp. Gen. Dec. B-236614, 89-2 CPD ¶ 593 (requirement that handguns be double-action first shot, single-action subsequent shots reasonable for safety purposes); *Fluid Eng'g Assocs.*, 68 Comp. Gen. 447 (B-234540), 89-1 CPD ¶ 520 (requirement for independent roughing/backing pump system reasonable based on analysis of agency needs); and *Hallmark Packaging Prods., Inc.*, Comp. Gen. Dec. B-232218, 88-2 CPD ¶ 390 (requirement that trash bags pass tear-resistance test reasonable because it is a standard commercial test).

A DoD manual, Defense Standardization Program, DoD 4120.24-M, DSP Policies & Procedures (March 2000), at App. 1, ¶ AP1.66, defined a performance specification as one that "states requirements in terms of the required results with criteria for verifying compliance, but without stating the methods for achieving the required results. A performance specification defines the functional requirements for the item, the environment in which it must operate, and interface and interchangeability characteristics."

There are four types of performance-based specifications: commercial item descriptions (CIDs), guide specifications, standard performance specifications, and program-peculiar performance specifications. CIDs are only to describe requirements in terms of function, performance, and essential form and fit requirements. The guidance for CIDs is in the General Services Administration's *Federal Standardization Manual-2000*, and in DoD Manual 4120.24-M. Numerous military specifications are CID candidates.

Guide specifications standardize the function or performance requirements of common procurements like systems, subsystems, equipment, and assemblies. The guidance for guide specifications is also in the DoD Manual 4120.24-M.

[c] Functional Specifications

A functional specification describes the work to be performed in terms of end purpose or the government's ultimate objective, rather than how the work is to be performed. Functional specifications may be regarded as a particular type of performance specification—ones that describe the government's ultimate need or objective without specifying any particular approach or type of product that should be used to achieve the objectives. This should be contrasted with a so-called "product-oriented" performance type specification, which indicates the ultimate performance objectives of the government but also specifies a particular type of product or approach that must be used and the performance standards that must be met. Functional specifications have the advantage of permitting the widest possible competition. However, before functional specifications are introduced, the commercial market should be examined to guarantee that the needs of the government can and will be met through use of such specifications.

It has been very difficult to distinguish functional specifications from performance specifications when drafting a specification for procurement of equipment. See, for example, Federal Property Management Regulation Temporary Regulation E-69, 45 Fed. Reg. 9269, Feb. 12, 1980, which implemented a policy favoring purchase of commercially available products through so-called commercial item descriptions (CIDs) by providing the following definition of "functional specifications" at § 7(i):

> Functional specification. A description of a product in terms of its performance characteristics and intended use. It may include a statement of the qualitative nature of the product and, when necessary, will contain those minimum essential characteristics to which the product must conform.

Section 11(b) emphasized the use of functional specifications in both CIDs and any new or revised federal specifications:

> Stressing functional or performance requirements. Functional or performance requirements will be specified instead of design requirements. Design will be specified only to the extent that controls are necessary to achieve commonality and interchangeability or when it is clearly more efficient and effective to do so and is reflective of general industry practice. Design requirements such as dimensions, materials, composition, and formulation may be included only to the extent that these requirements are essential to the end use . . . and when the requirements are common practice.

Thus, functional specifications used on contracts for equipment are only slightly broader than performance specifications.

Functional specifications must be carefully prepared to ensure that competitors are not misled by overly general statements of the agency's requirements. In

CompuServe, Comp. Gen. Dec. B-188990, 77-2 CPD ¶ 182, GAO discussed the benefits and disadvantages of functional specifications:

> To use the approach advocated by the protester—functional specifications—in a procurement such as the present one can increase competition, which is desirable. However, using functional specifications is not free from complex, and potentially costly, difficulties. Initially, the Government must expend considerable effort in drafting the specifications. Offerors must then translate the specifications into their own individual equipment and software approaches. This can involve a considerable amount of detail, may result in a variety of solutions to the Government's requirements and may be quite costly. A substantial effort on the part of the Government is then required to evaluate the proposals. Whether an agency conducting a procurement like the present one should be required to take a functional approach, as opposed to specifying a DBMS package, is a question which cannot be answered in the abstract.

In *Project Software & Dev., Inc.*, GSBCA 8471-P, 86-3 BCA ¶ 19,082, the board held that the agency's failure to use a completely functional specification was not improper since major portions of the specification were stated in functional terms.

[2] Sources of Specifications

For many years, government specifications were required to be used when available. However, the FAR was revised in 1995 to drop this requirement and substitute the following broad guidance in FAR 11.101(a):

> Agencies may select from existing requirements documents, modify or combine existing requirements documents, or create new requirements documents to meet agency needs, consistent with the following order of precedence:
>
> (1) Documents mandated for use by law.
> (2) Performance-oriented documents.
> (3) Detailed design-oriented documents.
> (4) Standards, specifications and related publications issued by the Government outside the Defense or Federal series for the non-repetitive acquisition of items.

[a] Government Specifications

Federal and military specifications are generally detailed and include specific requirements on the characteristics of a product and the standards that it must meet. They provide for a clearly stated, mandatory level of quality that any contractor subject to them will be required to meet.

[i] Military Specifications

Traditionally, DoD had used thousands of military specifications and standards in its procurements. However, it became increasingly difficult to keep these specifications and standards attuned to normal commercial practices. In 1994, Defense Secretary William Perry issued a DoD policy mandating greater use of performance and commercial specifications in lieu of military specifications. The Memorandum for Secretaries of the Military Departments (June 29, 1994), stated in relevant part:

> Military Specifications and Standards: Performance specifications shall be used when purchasing new systems, major modifications, upgrades to current systems, and nondevelopmental and commercial items, for programs in any acquisition category. If it is not practicable to use a performance specification, a non-government standard shall be used. Since there will be cases when military specifications are needed to define an exact design solution because there is no acceptable non-government standard or because the use of a performance specification or non-government standard is not cost effective, the use of military specifications and standards is authorized as a last resort, with an appropriate waiver.

The intent of the policy was not to eliminate military specifications altogether, but to curtail the automatic development and imposition of unique military specifications as the cultural norm at DoD. When DoD was the leader in advanced technology, military specifications served a logical purpose. In recent years, however, industry has taken the lead in technological developments, and military specifications in lieu of industry standards are no longer optimal or cost-effective for either the government or the contractor. Thus, a modern DoD solicitation must describe the agency's needs with performance specifications or non-government standards. According to the policy of the Secretary Perry memorandum, military specifications are to be used only as a "last resort," and only after obtaining the proper waiver.

Although industry was generally pleased with the cancellation of overly burdensome "how to" military specifications, there was concern from some in industry, including, for example, the Aerospace Industry Association (AIA), regarding the effect of canceling specifications that define parts and materials used in aircraft manufacture worldwide. As DoD canceled specifications that constituted state of the art in actual commercial practices, the burden fell on industry to prepare new documents to replace those that were canceled. The AIA argued that where a military specification had in fact become a de facto commercial specification or international standard, its cancellation might well not result in cost savings to the government or its contractors.

In addition, the shift from military specifications to commercial specifications in principle required successful offerors to assume substantially greater levels of performance risk when the commercial specification was performance-oriented. In such cases, contractors encountering performance problems could no longer routinely assert that the contract requirements were met by showing that military specifications were precisely followed. The use of performance specifications also threatened the availability of the traditional government contractor defense to tort liability.

Approved specifications are listed in the DoD Index of Specifications and Standards (DODISS), online at the Defense Automated Printing Service (DAPS), eAccess database. A special section lists standard performance specifications that are used in multiple applications. The guidance for program-peculiar performance specifications is still being developed.

[ii] Federal Specifications

There are four basic categories of federal standardization documents that control the content of solicitations from the various federal agencies. First, federal specifications describe essential and technical requirements for items, materials, or services bought by the federal government. Federal specifications are coordinated with interested government agencies and industry during their development and are mandatory for use in procurement by government agencies.

Second, federal standards provide standard data for reference in federal specifications. There are two major categories of standards: federal test method standards, which are developed by the federal government when appropriate industry standards are not available; and packaging, marking, and material identification standards.

Third, Commercial Item Descriptions are simplified specifications intended to be used in the acquisition of products available in the commercial marketplace. Finally, Qualified Products Lists are lists of products, by plant, that have been tested for conformance with the appropriate specification requirements. A complete list of all federal standardization documents can be found in the *Index of Federal Specifications, Standards and Commercial Item Descriptions* (FPMR 101-29.1).

[b] Nongovernment Standards

Nongovernment standards are authored and published privately, usually with the help of and in conjunction with professional and technical societies or associations, such as the National Defense Industrial Association. Two common sources of nongovernment standards are the American Society for Testing and Materials and the American National Standards Institute.

[3] Improper Specifications

Specifications must promote full and open competition. Thus, specifications are improper if they unnecessarily require certain features or preclude certain products or services from being offered, or are unclear or ambiguous.

[a] Unduly Restrictive Specifications

The use of unduly restrictive specifications is prohibited by 41 U.S.C. § 3306(a)(2)(B) and 10 U.S.C. § 3206(a)(2)(B) (formerly § 2305(a)(1)(B)). An unduly restrictive specification is one that limits competition by including a requirement that exceeds the needs of the government, *Kohler Co.*, Comp. Gen. Dec. B-257162, 94-2 CPD ¶ 88. See *Booz Allen Hamilton, Inc.*, Comp. Gen. Dec. B-418449, 2020 CPD ¶ 178 (requiring contractor for audit services to be an independent public accountant); *Global Super Tanker Servs., LLC*, Comp. Gen. Dec. B-414987, 2017 CPD ¶ 345 (requiring air tankers with maximum capacity of 5000 gallons of retardant when agency could not show that it could not use larger tankers); *American Safety Council, Inc. v. United States*, 122 Fed. Cl. 426 (2015) (requiring broad intellectual property rights in contracts allowing vendors to provide online training services to companies); *Smith & Nephew, Inc.*, Comp. Gen. Dec. B-410453, 2015 CPD ¶ 90 (requiring bandages with a minimum fluid handling capacity of 20g/10cm2/24 hr when the agency could not identify an actual need); *NCS Techs., Inc.*, Comp. Gen. Dec. B-403435, 2010 CPD ¶ 281 (requiring all computer monitors to be made by same manufacturer); *SMARTnet, Inc.*, Comp. Gen. Dec. B-406512, 2009 CPD ¶ 34 (requirement that equipment be certified by agency at time of quotation). Compare *Analytical Sols.* by Kline, LLC, Comp. Gen. Dec. B-417161, 2019 CPD ¶ 105 (limit of three past performance references reasonable); *Plateau Software, Inc.*, Comp. Gen. Dec. B-416386, 2018 CPD ¶ 291 (requirement that meeting space be within 0.5 miles of Metro station reasonable); *Worldwide Language Res., LLC v. United States*, 127 Fed. Cl. 125 (2016) (defining relevant past performance at a dollar amount that only incumbent contractor could meet reasonable); *Vaden Indus., Inc.*, Comp. Gen. Dec. B-299338, 2007 CPD ¶ 48 (performance bond equal to 100% of the contract value and a payment bond equal to 10% of the contract value not unreasonable).

The Federal Circuit has held that a protester bears the burden of showing that a restrictive solicitation term "is so plainly unjustified as to lack a rational basis." Savantage Fin. Servs., Inc. v. United States, 595 F.3d 1282 (Fed. Cir. 2010). GAO has noted that, "[w]here a protester challenges a specification as unduly restrictive, that is, challenges both the restrictive nature of the specification and the agency's need for the restriction, the procuring agency has the responsibility of establishing that the specification is reasonably necessary to meet its legitimate needs," *APRO Int'l*, Comp. Gen. Dec. B-415149.2, 2017 CPD ¶ 368. GAO has also held that an agency's basis for using a restrictive specification will be held to be reasonable if it can "withstand logical scrutiny," *Glock, Inc.*, Comp. Gen. Dec. B-236614, 89-2 CPD ¶ 593. However, a stricter rule is applicable when the provision limits the competition to a single source. In that instance the agency must show convincingly that its needs cannot be met by firms possessing other than the exact experience stated, *Daniel H. Wagner, Assocs.*, 65 Comp. Gen. 305 (B-220633), 86-1 CPD ¶ 166.

GAO will not rule on protests that the specification was less restrictive than proper to meet the needs of an agency, *Al Baz 2000 Trading & Contracting Co., W.L.C.*, Comp. Gen. Dec. B-416622.2, 2018 CPD ¶ 422. See also *Hesco Bastion, Ltd.* v. United States, 136 Fed. Cl. 146 (2018), denying a protest arguing that the agency had improperly taken corrective action to remove restrictive salient characteristics from a brand name or equal procurement in order to obtain more competition.

Specifications written around a certain product are particularly susceptible to being found unduly restrictive. See, for example, *Racal Corp.*, Comp. Gen. Dec. B-233240, 89-1 CPD ¶ 169 (make and model specification). See, however, *Stavely Instruments, Inc.*, Comp. Gen. Dec. B-259548.3, 95-1 CPD ¶ 256, where GAO held that the specifications for X-ray units were not unduly restrictive even though only one company manufactured the product and the specifications were written around that product; Stavely did not challenge the technical specifications or otherwise assert that the specifications overstated or otherwise exceeded the Air Force's actual needs. Similarly, in *Messier-Bugatti Safran Grp.*, Comp. Gen. Dec. B-401064, 2009 CPD ¶ 109, a requirement that a product meet a specified design was held not unduly restrictive based on the agency's demonstration that the protester's design had a higher life-cycle cost.

A specification will not be held to be unduly restrictive if the agency can show that it has a legitimate need for the specified restrictive feature. See, for example, *T-Mobile USE, Inc.*, Comp. Gen. Dec. B-418394, 2020 CPD ¶ 142 (pre-emption communication requirement for parole and probation monitors); *Chromalloy San Diego Corp. v. United States*, 145 Fed. Cl. 708 (2019) (requirement that competitor for engine overhaul contract have access to engine manufacturer's manuals and used special tools of manufacturer); *Oracle Am., Inc. v. United States*, 144 Fed. Cl. 88 (2019), *aff'd*, 975 F.3d 1297 (Fed. Cir. 2020) (requirement that offeror have cloud security certification at time of proposal); *BHB Ltd. P'ship & Indiana Assocs. Ltd. P'ship*, Comp. Gen. Dec. B-417760, 2019 CPD ¶ 356 (single building requirement in lease competition to consolidate agencies); *Israel Aerospace Indus.*, Comp. Gen. Dec. B-417681, 2019 CPD ¶ 292 (requirement that repair contractor provide parts unobtainable from original manufacturer); *Cleveland Assets, LLC v. United States*, 132 Fed. Cl. 264 (2017) (rental cap in lease); *APRO Int'l*, Comp. Gen. Dec. B-415149.2, 2017 CPD ¶ 368 (requirement that program manager have a bachelor's degree (in any field) in contract to provide training services); *Vanguard Bldg., LP*, Comp. Gen. Dec. B-414207, 2017 CPD ¶ 98 (ceiling height and column spacing in leased building); and *Parcel 49C Ltd. P'ship v. United States*, 130 Fed. Cl. 109 (2016) (ceiling height and power requirements in leased building).

[b] Unclear or Ambiguous Specifications

If specifications are vague or ambiguous, they will not communicate the exact needs of the agency to the offerors. This will generally result in proposals that do not fully meet the agency's needs or do not give rise to the most satisfactory product or service that the offeror can provide. It may even result in some potential offerors deciding not to submit proposals because they assume the agency is not seeking their product or service. The outcome of such specifications is, thus, either reduced competition or the need for considerably greater clarification or discussion after the proposals have been submitted.

Specifications must provide a common basis for competition by allowing the competitors to price the same requirement. However, there is no requirement for absolute clarity; see *Repaintex Co.*, Comp. Gen. Dec. B-415390.4, 2018 CPD ¶ 227, stating:

> As a general rule, the contracting agency must give offerors sufficient detail in a solicitation to enable them to compete intelligently and on a relatively equal basis. *C3, Inc.*, B-241983.2, Mar. 13, 1991, 91-1 CPD ¶ 279 at 3. There is no legal requirement that a competition be based on specifications drafted in such detail as to completely eliminate all risk or remove every uncertainty from the mind of every prospective offeror. *Sunbelt Properties, Inc.*, B-249469 et al., Nov. 17, 1992, 92-2 CPD ¶ 353 at 4.

Most protests of ambiguous or vague specifications have occurred in sealed bid procurements where specification problems cannot be cleared up easily after bid opening. While there is more flexibility in negotiated procurements, agencies are still required to provide relatively clear and unambiguous specifications. The following discussion includes decisions on both sealed bid and competitively negotiated procurements where guidance is provided to ensure fair competition and obtain the best product or service to meet the agency's needs.

[i] Requirement for Clarity

Specifications and solicitations that are susceptible to more than one reasonable interpretation of what kind of performance is contemplated are ambiguous, often warranting amendment or cancellation of the solicitation, *Ashe Facility Servs. Inc.*, Comp. Gen. Dec. B-292218.3, 2004 CPD ¶ 80; *Arora Grp., Inc.*, Comp. Gen. Dec. B-288127, 2001 CPD ¶ 154. However, there is no requirement that a competition be based on specifications drafted in such detail as to eliminate completely any risk or remove every uncertainty from the mind of every prospective offeror, *ACME Endeavors, Inc.*, Comp. Gen. Dec. B-417455, 2019 CPD ¶ 224 (requirement to "thoroughly wash" vehicles sufficiently clear).

Unclear specifications are objectionable because they impede full and open competition by failing to ensure that offerors are competing on a "common" or "equal" basis. This rule is strictly enforced in sealed bid procurements and would appear to be equally applicable to competitively negotiated procurements using design specifications. See *Allied Signal, Inc.*, Comp. Gen. Dec. B-275032, 97-1 CPD ¶ 136 (solicitation ambiguous where two parties had reasonable interpretations as to backwards compatibility to two existing intelligence terminals);

MLC Fed., Inc., Comp. Gen. Dec. B-254696, 94-1 CPD ¶ 8 (RFP's system architecture requirement that equipment proposed be of the latest line could have referred only to the conceptual structure and functional behavior of the machine as distinct from the physical design); *Tektronix, Inc.*, Comp. Gen. Dec. B-225769, 87-1 CPD ¶ 580 (ambiguity when brand name product did not meet the salient characteristics).

An ambiguity will not be found if a protester submits a proposal that indicates that it agrees with the agency's interpretation of the specifications, *DocMagic, Inc.*, Comp. Gen. Dec. B-415702, 2018 CPD ¶ 96; *SunGard Data Sys., Inc.*, Comp. Gen. Dec. B-410025, 2014 CPD ¶ 304.

Specifications are not ambiguous when they contain clear performance requirements. Thus, an agency can properly elect to state its needs in terms of performance or functional requirements in order to encourage greater competition. See *University Research Corp.*, Comp. Gen. Dec. B-228895, 87-2 CPD ¶ 636, finding that a solicitation provided sufficient detail when most information had been given or was unnecessary for preparation of bid; and *Memorex Corp.*, Comp. Gen. Dec. B-212660, 84-1 CPD ¶ 153, finding that it was proper to define the requirement in terms of the "required capability and characteristics of the requested equipment" in order to invite innovative and independent approaches to meeting the agency's needs. In the latter case GAO relied to some extent on the fact that five proposals had been submitted in response to the RFP.

An agency may also impose risks on competitors when it does not have necessary information. See *Jones, Russotto & Walker*, Comp. Gen. Dec. B-283288, 99-2 CPD ¶ 111 (statement of work was detailed enough to permit prospective parties to apply their own cost data regarding tasks and responsibilities); *ANV Enters., Inc.*, Comp. Gen. Dec. B-270013, 96-1 CPD ¶ 40 (specification to test soil for the proper fertilizer requirements and to furnish and apply fertilizer did not impose undue risk where agency provided information on the types and quantities of fertilizer used historically); *Cobra Techs., Inc.*, Comp. Gen. Dec. B-254890, 94-1 CPD ¶ 35 (failure to include an estimate of the hours required to assist tenant moves not undue risk because there was no historical data to use and the IFB described what was to be required). See also *CWTSato Travel*, Comp. Gen. Dec. B-404479.2, 2011 CPD ¶ 87, finding no "undue risk" in a requirement that the offerors propose fixed prices over 15 years to include the requirement that they update their travel systems to meet federal changes in security requirements.

The apparent confusion of bidders evidenced by their varied responses to the solicitation can be indicative of ambiguity in the specification. See *Dynamic Corp.*, Comp. Gen. Dec. B-296366, 2005 CPD ¶ 125 (agency canceled solicitation when bidders submitted widely varying unit prices); *Brickwood Contractors, Inc.*, Comp. Gen. Dec. B-292171, 2003 CPD ¶ 120 (agency canceled solicitation when it found that a reasonable interpretation of specification would not meet its needs); *Neals Janitorial Serv.*, Comp. Gen. Dec. B-276625, 97-2 CPD ¶ 6 (agency canceled solicitation where specifications were so inadequate that bidders did not have a common basis on which to prepare bids); *Ferguson-Williams, Inc.*, Comp. Gen. Dec. B-258460, 95-1 CPD ¶ 39 (agency canceled solicitation where refuse collection and disposal requirements did not identify the agency's actual requirements and the three low bidders were misled).

[ii] Errors or Omissions in Specifications

Specifications may be improper due to errors or omissions even though they are definite and unambiguous, *Day & Zimmerman, Inc.*, Comp. Gen. Dec. B-212017, 84-1 CPD ¶ 377 (current operating data needed for competition for services); *Wood-Ivey Sys. Corp.*, 50 Comp. Gen. 50 (B-169977) (1970) (erroneous provision expressed fixed level of man hours required as opposed to estimated level); *Kleen-Rite Janitorial Servs., Inc.*, Comp. Gen. Dec. B-180345, 74-1 CPD ¶ 210 (bid sheet omitted blank space for an itemized price). The most common omission is the failure of a solicitation to list a brand name item's salient characteristics, *Mythics, Inc.*, Comp. Gen. Dec. B-418785, 2020 CPD ¶ 295; *Medfinity LLC*, Comp. Gen. Dec. B-413450, 2016 CPD ¶ 255; *Kingdomare Techs.*, Comp. Gen. Dec. B-407389, 2012 CPD ¶ 348; *California Indus. Facilities Res., Inc.*, Comp. Gen. Dec. B-403397.3, 2011 CPD ¶ 71.

Government construction contracts often attempt to overcome this problem of missing information by including an Omissions and Misdescriptions clause which requires the contractor to perform any omitted or misdescribed details of the work that are necessary to carry out the intent of the drawings or specifications. See ¶ (d) of the *Contract Drawings, Maps & Specifications* clause in DFARS 252.236-7001. However, this clause applies only to details, not to new sections of unspecified work. For example, in *Strauss Constr. Co.*, ASBCA 22791, 79-1 BCA ¶ 13,578, a contractor was not required to provide a particular fire extinguishing system whose description was omitted from the specifications because the particular system was not a "detail" under the clause. See *M.A. Mortenson Co.*, ASBCA 50716, 99-1 BCA ¶ 30,270, stating that the clause only covers the omission of work that is "manifestly" necessary to carry out the work.

Furthermore, the government may include contract clauses that require the contractor to assume the risk of specification or drawing errors or omissions. In 48 Comp. Gen. 750 (B-165953) (1968), GAO approved the use of such a clause, stating at 754:

> [W]e are not aware of any situations where [the] doctrine of implied warranty or representation as to the adequacy of Government specifications has been extended to cases where the Government discloses the inadequacies of such specifications and permits or requires the contractor to make necessary corrections.

See also *Rixon Elecs., Inc. v. United States*, 536 F.2d 1345 (Ct. Cl. 1976); *Varo, Inc.*, Comp. Gen. Dec. B-193789, 80-2 CPD ¶ 44.

[iii] Open or Indefinite Specifications

Provisions permitting offerors to select the applicable specification, like ambiguous specifications, may preclude competition on a common basis. In *Alpha Q, Inc.*, Comp. Gen. Dec. B-248706, 92-2 CPD ¶189, GAO ruled that a specification was improper because it required offerors to deliver parts for General Electric engines meeting "the latest revision of the General Electric drawing." GAO reasoned that FAR 10.008(b) required that the government furnish such information. That provision, now in FAR 11.201(a), states:

> Do not use general identification references, such as "the issue in effect on the date of the solicitation."

See also *Pulse Elecs., Inc.*, Comp. Gen. Dec. B-244764, 91-2 CPD ¶468, finding a specification improper because it required offerors to comply with military specifications and standards "in effect as of the date set for receipt of proposals."

[B] Consolidation/Bundling

One of the major decisions that must be made in the acquisition planning process is how much work to consolidate or package in a single procurement. The consolidation decision is usually a tradeoff between the type of competition that is obtained and the achievement of efficiencies in procuring the work. When different types of work are consolidated into a single procurement, there will inevitably be some companies that cannot compete because they are only capable of performing a segment of the work. On the other hand, other companies with broader capabilities will be attracted to the job and may be more vigorous competitors than if the work were fragmented into a number of procurements. Thus, the type of competition shifts when consolidation occurs. In addition, efficiencies are achieved through consolidation. One efficiency is a reduction of the administrative costs of awarding contracts by reducing the number of procurements that must be processed. Another efficiency is frequently achieved by having only one contractor responsible for coordinating the work. This ensures that the work is performed in a more coherent manner than if it were performed by multiple contractors. An additional efficiency is the reduction in the amount of contract administration that the procuring agency must perform. These efficiencies make consolidation an attractive alternative when planning procurements.

At the same time, however, consolidation raises serious policy concerns because it may, in practical effect, preclude at least some small businesses from competing. This concern was first addressed in the Small Business Reauthorization Act of 1997, Pub. L. No. 105-135, which initiated the effort to limit a specific type of consolidation called "bundling." Subsequent Congressional action has resulted in coverage of consolidation in 15 U.S.C.

§ 657q, and of bundling in 15 U.S.C. § 644(e). These statutes are implemented in 13 C.F.R. § 125.2(d) and FAR 7.107.

[1] Consolidation

Consolidation is defined in FAR 2.101 as follows:

> Consolidation or consolidated requirement—
>
> (1) Means a solicitation for a single contract, a multiple-award contract, a task order, or a delivery order to satisfy—
>
> (i) Two or more requirements of the Federal agency for supplies or services that have been provided to or performed for the Federal agency under two or more separate contracts, each of which was lower in cost than the total cost of the contract for which offers are solicited; or
>
> (ii) Requirements of the Federal agency for construction projects to be performed at two or more discrete sites.
>
> (2) Separate contract as used in this definition, means a contract that has been performed by any business, including small and other than small business concerns.

Pursuant to this definition, consolidation occurs when work is combined into a single procurement without regard to whether a small business had performed the prior work. If the estimated value of the contract exceeds $2 million, consolidation must be justified by a written determination of the senior procurement executive or chief acquisition officer of the agency that it will yield substantial benefits, FAR 7.107-2. This regulation contains the following guidance on the computation of benefits:

> (c) Such benefits may include cost savings or price reduction and, regardless of whether quantifiable in dollar amounts—
>
> (1) Quality improvements that will save time or improve or enhance performance or efficiency;
>
> (2) Reduction in acquisition cycle times;
>
> (3) Better terms and conditions; or
>
> (4) Any other benefit.
>
> (d) Benefits. (1) Benefits that are quantifiable in dollar amounts are substantial if individually, in combination, or in the aggregate the anticipated financial benefits are equivalent to—
>
> (i) Ten percent of the estimated contract or order value (including options) if the value is $94 million or less; or
>
> (ii) Five percent of the estimated contract or order value (including options) or $9.4 million, whichever is greater, if the value exceeds $94 million.

(2) Benefits that are not quantifiable in dollar amounts shall be specifically identified and otherwise quantified to the extent feasible.

(3) Reduction of administrative or personnel costs alone is not sufficient justification for consolidation unless the cost savings are expected to be at least 10 percent of the estimated contract or order value (including options) of the consolidated requirements, as determined by the senior procurement executive or chief acquisition officer (15 U.S.C. 657q(c)(2)(B)).

See FAR 7.107-2 for further guidance on implementing this restriction on consolidation.

In *Tyler Constr. Grp. v. United States*, 570 F.3d 1329 (Fed. Cir. 2009), the court held that the Corps of Engineers properly used an IDIQ contract to consolidate requirements for the design and construction of military facilities in an eight-state area.

[2] Bundling

Bundling is defined in FAR 2.101 as follows:

Bundling—(1) Means a subset of consolidation that combines two or more requirements for supplies or services, previously provided or performed under separate smaller contracts (see paragraph (2) of this definition), into a solicitation for a single contract, a multiple-award contract, or a task or delivery order that is likely to be unsuitable for award to a small business concern (even if it is suitable for award to a small business with a Small Business Teaming Arrangement) due to—

(i) The diversity, size, or specialized nature of the elements of the performance specified;

(ii) The aggregate dollar value of the anticipated award;

(iii) The geographical dispersion of the contract performance sites; or

(iv) Any combination of the factors described in paragraphs (1)(i), (ii), and (iii) of this definition.

(2) "Separate smaller contract" as used in this definition, means a contract that has been performed by one or more small business concerns or that was suitable for award to one or more small business concerns.

(3) This definition does not apply to a contract that will be awarded and performed entirely outside of the United States.

Pursuant to this definition, bundling occurs when work is combined into a single procurement and a small business had performed the prior work. FAR 7.107-3 requires the senior procurement executive of the agency to make a written determination that bundling will achieve substantial benefits. The regulation provides the following guidance on determining substantial benefits:

> (c) Such benefits may include, but are not limited to—
>
> (1) Cost savings;
> (2) Price reduction;
> (3) Quality improvements that will save time or improve or enhance performance or efficiency;
> (4) Reduction in acquisition cycle times, or
> (5) Better terms and conditions.
>
> (d) Benefits are measurably substantial if individually, in combination, or in the aggregate the anticipated financial benefits are equivalent to—
>
> (1) Ten percent of the estimated contract or order value (including options) if the value is $94 million or less; or
> (2) Five percent of the estimated contract or order value (including options) or $9.4 million, whichever is greater, if the value exceeds $94 million.
>
> (e) Reduction of administrative or personnel costs alone is not sufficient justification for bundling unless the cost savings are expected to be at least ten percent of the estimated contract or order value (including options) of the bundled requirements.
>
> * * *
>
> (g) In assessing whether cost savings and/or price reduction would be achieved through bundling, the agency and SBA shall—
>
> (1) Compare the price that has been charged by small businesses for the work that they have performed; or
> (2) Where previous prices are not available, compare the price, based on market research, that could have been or could be charged by small businesses for the work previously performed by other than a small business.

There are also special procedures that must be used when there is "substantial bundling," defined in FAR 7.107-4(a)(1) as follows:

> (i) $8 million or more for the Department of Defense; (ii) $6 million or more for the National Aeronautics and Space Administration, the General Services Administration, and the Department of Energy; or (iii) $2.5 million or more for all other agencies.

This regulation required agencies to take additional steps to ensure that small businesses are allowed to participate by teaming agreements or as subcontractors.

For decisions rejecting protests of bundling, see *InSap Servs., Inc.*, Comp. Gen. Dec. B-417596.2, 2019 CPD ¶ 343 (agency awarding support service contract bundling 10 prior contracts reasonably calculated benefits and concluded work could only be done by large business); *AeroSage, LLC*, Comp. Gen. Dec. B-416381, 2018 CPD ¶ 288 (protester did not prove that small businesses could not compete for bundled work); *Geo-Med, LLC v. United States*, 135 Fed. Cl. 742 (2017) (market research justified bundling); *Manus Medical, LLC*, Comp. Gen. Dec. B-412331, 2016 CPD ¶ 49 (protester did not prove that work was unsuitable for small businesses); *Edmunds Scientific Co.*, Comp. Gen. Dec. B-410179, 2014 CPD ¶ 336 (combining new requirements not bundling); *American Toner & Ink*, Comp. Gen. Dec. B-409528.7, 2014 CPD ¶ 161 (procurement for full range of office supply items that will be available for order by participating federal agencies properly bundled); *U.S. Electrodynamics, Inc.*, Comp. Gen. Dec. B-403516, 2010 CPD ¶ 275 (consolidation of requirements for global satellite services would result in improved performance, efficiency, and services, less redundancy, and significant cost savings); and *Nautical Eng'g, Inc.*, Comp. Gen. Dec. B-309955, 2007 CPD ¶ 204 (agency properly counted benefits other than cost savings in bundling decision). Bundling protests must be submitted before the submission of proposals, *Analytical Sols. by Kline, LLC*, Comp. Gen. Dec. B-417161, 2019 CPD ¶ 105, *recons. denied*, 2019 CPD ¶ 398.

If an agency bundles requirements but sets the procurement aside for small business, GAO will not consider a protest claiming that the agency violated the anti-bundling statute, *Health & Human Servs. Grp.*, Comp. Gen. Dec. B-294703, 2005 CPD ¶ 6. Thus, the only challenge available to a potential protester in such cases will be a claim that this is restrictive of competition. See *Frasca Int'l, Inc.*, Comp. Gen. Dec. B-293299, 2004 CPD ¶ 38 (consolidating requirements for pilot training with flight training devices not restrictive because protester did not show it could not compete).

[C] Draft Solicitations and Specifications

As noted above, FAR 15.201 explicitly recommends that agencies work aggressively to exchange information with industry, to improve the agencies' ultimate procurement decision-making. FAR 15.201 now specifically endorses the use draft RFPs. When draft solicitations or specifications are circulated for comment, they should be sent to all prospective offerors, and a *SAM.gov* announcement of their availability should be published. See FAR 5.205(c) permitting publication of federal business opportunities. Sufficient time should be given to potential bidders or offerors to submit meaningful comments, and the agency should take steps to assure all submitters that their comments have been given full consideration. Draft RFPs are very useful in identifying ambiguities or unclear language in a solicitation. See, for example, *BANC3, Inc.*, Comp. Gen. Dec. B-416386, 2018 CPD ¶ 316; and *Horizon Strategies*, Comp. Gen. Dec. B-415415, 2017 CPD ¶ 390, where questions in response to a draft RFP assisted the agency in clarifying its requirements. The use of a draft RFP led GAO to reject a protest that a procuring agency had given insufficient time to prepare proposals, *Coulson Aviation (USA), Inc.*, Comp. Gen. Dec. B-411306, 2015 CPD ¶ 214.

§ 3.06 OVERALL COST TO THE GOVERNMENT

One of the major considerations in acquisition planning is the overall cost to the government. Acquisition techniques should be chosen to induce contractors to provide products and services at the lowest possible cost commensurate with high quality and timely performance. The costs considered should be both the initial acquisition cost of the product or service and the operating or usage sustainment costs because the amount to be paid to a contractor may not be the only, or even the major, expenditure by the government in using the work obtained. Thus, it is important for the government to consider more than the contract price in determining what award is most advantageous to the government. FAR 7.105(a)(3) states:

> *Cost.* Set forth the established cost goals for the acquisition and the rationale supporting them, and discuss related cost concepts to be employed, including, as appropriate,
>
> (i) *Life-cycle cost.* Discuss how life-cycle cost will be considered. If it is not used, explain why. If appropriate, discuss the cost model used to develop life-cycle-cost estimates.
>
> (ii) *Design-to-cost.* Describe the design-to-cost objective(s) and underlying assumptions, including the rationale for quantity, learning-curve, and economic adjustment factors. Describe how objectives are to be applied, tracked, and enforced. Indicate specific related solicitation and contractual requirements to be imposed.
>
> (iii) *Application of should-cost.* Describe the application of should-cost analysis to the acquisition (see 15.407-4).

This part of the plan contains the agency's best analysis of the expected cost of the procurement and some of the techniques that will be used to ensure that this cost is reasonable and attainable.

[A] Acquisition Cost

The major element of the agency's "cost goals" will be the estimated cost of the products or services being procured. Ideally, this estimate of the acquisition cost will be made in conjunction with the budget process so that sufficient funds can be obtained to carry out the procurement. The cost estimate can be made using parametric data on the class of products or services being procured, data from past procurements of the same or similar products or services, or any other data that are relevant to arriving at the estimate. The higher the degree of accuracy of this cost estimate, the more smoothly the procurement will proceed because funds will be available as necessary to execute it. Thus, good acquisition planning demands that the agency devote sufficient effort to arriving at a valid cost estimate to ensure a satisfactory degree of accuracy.

The plan should also address measures that will be taken to ensure reasonable acquisition costs. When price competition is anticipated, it is generally assumed that the government will be able to contract at a reasonable price. Where price competition is not anticipated, the acquisition plan must address the efforts that will be made to ensure that reasonable prices can be negotiated. See Chapter 13 for a full discussion of this issue.

The acquisition plan should also address the type of contract that will be used to share the risks and motivate the contractor to control the costs of performance. While fixed-price type contracts are preferred, their use should be limited to situations where the performance risks can be predicted with a reasonable degree of accuracy. When this is not possible, a cost-reimbursement type contract is the preferred instrument. An intermediate form of contract, the incentive contract, is used in situations where the parties agree to share the risk that the work cannot be done within the originally estimated cost. Chapter 12 sets forth the guidance on selecting the contract type.

[B] Life-Cycle Cost

The plan must contain a discussion of how life-cycle cost logic will be used in the procurement. FAR 7.101 defines life-cycle cost to mean "the total cost to the Government of acquiring, operating, supporting, and (if applicable) disposing of the items being acquired," but contains no guidance on the application of this technique. See also DFARS 207.106(S-70), which requires, in planning for a major weapon system or subsystem, that a strategy be adopted to obtain sufficient proprietary rights and licenses to sustain the systems over their life cycle.

Essentially, assessing life-cycle costs attempts to identify products that are likely to impose the lowest costs on the agency over the total period that the product will be used and to plan for competition in procuring spare parts, as well as upgrade and overhaul of the product. To use the technique, acquisition officials must factor the prospective costs of using a product into the original source selection decision (which is frequently otherwise generally based made only on the basis of the initial acquisition costs). The best guidance available on the use of this technique is found in the Operating and Support Cost-Estimating Guide, March 2014 and DOD Instruction 5000.73, Cost Analysis Guidance and Procedures, March 13, 2020.

In instances where the cost of operating and maintaining the acquired product will be much greater than the initial acquisition cost, conducting a procurement without factoring in life-cycle costs can greatly increase the ultimate costs to the government. For example, it may be more expensive to purchase equipment with a low initial price that requires significantly more personnel or energy to operate than higher priced equipment. Similarly, low-priced equipment that will be expensive to maintain may not be the best buy for the agency.

Generally, these life-cycle costs are included in a procurement in one of two ways: (1) by including specific contract provisions establishing design goals or stating mandatory contract requirements for such factors as operating costs, maintainability, and reliability; or (2) by making life-cycle costs a part of the evaluation process in competitive source selections.

Factoring life-cycle costs into a procurement by using clauses containing mandatory contract requirements forces the contractor to consider the cost in computing the contract price. Thus, a warranty clause calling for the equipment to function over a specified period of time would induce the contractor to include in its price either the cost of repair of equipment that did not meet the warranty or the cost of designing and manufacturing equipment that had the required life. Similarly, a clause requiring the contractor to reimburse the government for all energy costs over a certain required amount would motivate the contractor to include such costs in the price if its equipment did not meet the requirement. Such clauses are the most direct way of factoring life-cycle costs into the procurement process because they ensure that the offered prices include each offeror's evaluation of the cost impact of the requirement. It is difficult, however, for agencies to formulate a complete set of contract clauses covering all life-cycle costs anticipated in the use of a product. Agencies must also consider that, while such warranties or other provisions as to excess costs will in effect shift risks to the contractor, such techniques may deter some companies from participating in the competition.

Another way to deal with life-cycle costs is to include contract clauses establishing goals, such as maintenance man-hours per aircraft flight hour or fuel consumption of vehicles. In order to ensure that such goals are effective, agencies frequently specify contractual penalties for missing the goal or incentives for making the goal. Alternatively, these goals can be taken into account in subjective award-fee determinations. Such clauses generally have a less direct impact on the contractor than a clause requiring full reimbursement of the government for failure to meet the life-cycle cost requirement.

The use of evaluation factors in the source selection process is the other way of addressing life-cycle costs. If sufficient information is available, the agency can, for example, make a reasonable estimate of the life-cycle costs of each competitor and add that estimate to the offered prices to determine whose which competitor's price is, in fact, lowest overall, *Columbia Inv. Grp.*, Comp. Gen. Dec. B-214324, 84-2 CPD ¶ 632, or the life-cycle cost estimate can be used indirectly to assist the source selection official in making a best value determination, *Storage Tech. Corp.*, Comp. Gen. Dec. B-215336, 84-2 CPD ¶ 190. See *Sikorsky Aircraft Co.*, Comp. Gen. Dec. B-299145, 2007 CPD ¶ 45, where the Air Force used a normalized calculation of "Most Probable Life-Cycle Cost" when it had obtained actual data from the offerors on prior usage of their helicopters. GAO granted the protest, reasoning that asking for the data obligated the agency to use the data. Subsequently, the Air Force amended the RFP to provide for a subjective evaluation of life-cycle costs without allowing the competitors to submit revised prices. GAO granted a protest of this procedure in *Sikorsky Aircraft Co.*, Comp. Gen. Dec. B-299145.5, 2007 CPD ¶ 155. See also *Lockheed Missile & Space Co. v. Dep't of the Treasury*, GSBCA 11776-P, 93-1 BCA ¶ 25,401, where the board found proper the agency's cost/technical tradeoff that resulted in an award to the highest technical, highest price offeror. The agency compared the differences in the value of technical features with the difference in overall cost to the government. Overall cost to the government included the offeror's prices for equipment, software, maintenance, support and any other solicited items, while the differences in value included the "productivity" of the proposed computer systems. Even though the agency paid hundreds of millions more in acquisition costs in order to obtain higher productivity, the Federal Circuit affirmed the decision of the board, *Lockheed Missiles & Space Co. v. Bentsen*, 4 F.3d 955 (Fed. Cir. 1993).

Another technique used by DoD in acquiring weapon systems is to obtain sufficient technical data and computer software with necessary license rights to obtain competition during sustainment of the system. See DFARS 207.106(S-70) setting forth these policies in the area of sustainment and DFARS 207.106(S-72) setting forth these policies in regard to maintaining competition through the life of a system. The techniques suggested include—

(i) Competitive prototyping.
(ii) Dual-sourcing.
(iii) Unbundling of contracts.
(iv) Funding of next-generation prototype systems or subsystems.
(v) Use of modular, open architectures to enable competition for upgrades.
(vi) Use of build-to-print approaches to enable production through multiple sources.
(vii) Acquisition of complete technical data packages.
(viii) Periodic competitions for subsystem upgrades.
(ix) Licensing of additional suppliers.
(x) Periodic system or program reviews to address long-term competitive effects of program decisions.

[C] Design-to-Cost

When the acquisition is for the development of a new product, the plan must also contain a discussion of the use of design-to-cost techniques. FAR 2.101 defines "design-to-cost" as

> a concept that establishes cost elements as management goals to achieve the best balance between life-cycle cost, acceptable performance, and schedule. Under this concept, cost is a design constraint during the design and development phases and a management discipline throughout the acquisition and operation of the system or equipment.

The purpose of this technique is to focus the contractor on the need to design an item that can be manufactured at an affordable cost. FAR 7.105(a)(3)(ii) describes the elements of this technique as follows:

> Describe the design-to-cost objective(s) and underlying assumptions, including the rationale for quantity, learning-curve, and economic adjustment factors. Describe how objectives are to be applied, tracked, and enforced. Indicate specific related solicitation and contractual requirements to be imposed.

In the 1990s, DoD addressed this issue in different terminology—adopting the practice of treating "cost as an independent variable." Paragraph 3.3.3.1 of DoD 5000.2-R, Mandatory Procedures for Major Defense Acquisition Programs and Major Automated Information System Acquisition Programs, March 15, 1996, called for continual cost/performance tradeoffs during system design and contemplated lowering performance requirements in order to achieve life-cycle goals. The current DoD guidance for weapon system procurement in the DoD Instruction 5000 publications does not discuss either design-to-cost or cost as an independent variable.

§ 3.07 PROCUREMENT NOTICES

Procurement notices are aimed at soliciting proposals or increasing meaningful competition by explaining the government's requirements. They are basic elements of a transparent public procurement system. There are several ways to disseminate information concerning the government's needs; in practical terms, the primary method today is *www.SAM.gov*, the website that is the government's "Governmentwide Point of Entry" (GPE) to federal business opportunities. There are also different techniques used to publicize solicitations, such as mailing lists and public posting of solicitations. This section covers the various notice requirements and concludes with a discussion on the use of publicizing procurements electronically through the use of the Internet, and e-mail.

[A] Presolicitation Notices and Conferences

Some procurement notices are designed primarily to give notice of present and planned procurements. The primary vehicle used is a synopsis of the proposed procurement posted at *SAM.gov*. Agencies may also use presolicitation notices and conferences or other techniques to develop competition well in advance of the prospective procurement.

[1] GPE Notice Requirements

The Small Business Act, 15 U.S.C. § 637(e), and 41 U.S.C. § 1708, establish *minimum standards* for the development of competition by requiring that contracting officers transmit a notice (synopsis) to the GPE for each covered contract action proposed procurement in excess of $25,000 and for proposed orders under basic agreements, basic ordering agreements, or similar agreements exceeding $25,000. FAR 5.101(b) suggests other methods of publicizing solicitations:

> (1) Preparing periodic handouts listing proposed contracts, and displaying them as in 5.101(a)(2).
>
> (2) Assisting local trade associations in disseminating information to their members.
>
> (3) Making brief announcements of proposed contracts to newspapers, trade journals, magazines, or other mass communication media for publication without cost to the Government.
>
> (4) Placing paid advertisements in newspapers or other communications media, subject to [restrictions].

The purposes served by this policy of publicizing proposed contract actions is stated as follows in FAR 5.002:

> Contracting officers must publicize contract actions in order to—
>
> (a) Increase competition;
>
> (b) Broaden industry participation in meeting Government requirements; and
>
> (c) Assist small business concerns, veteran-owned small business concerns, service-disabled veteran-owned small business concerns, HUBZone small business concerns, small disadvantaged business concerns, and women-owned small business concerns in obtaining contracts and subcontracts.

This publicizing policy gives potential competitors a short period to determine if they are capable of performing the proposed work. It provides that solicitations may not be issued earlier than 15 days after publication of the notice, and the closing date for the receipt of proposals may not be earlier than 30 days after issuance of the solicitation, FAR 5.203. FAR 5.203(d) calls for a "response time" of not less than 30 days from issuance of the notice for architect-engineer services and orders under basic ordering agreements. For research and development procurements, the required waiting period for the closing date for receipt of proposals is 45 days, FAR 5.203(e). For commercial items, FAR 12.603 permits the use of a combined synopsis/solicitation with a response time of not less than 15 days. These requirements set forth minimum periods only; many procuring agencies have found that extending the periods increases competition.

FAR 5.203(g) provides that contracting officers may, unless they have evidence to the contrary, presume that the notices are published one day after transmission to the GPE, but this presumption does not negate the statutory waiting periods. See *AUL Instruments, Inc.*, 64 Comp. Gen. 871 (B-216543),

85-2 CPD ¶ 324, reaching this same conclusion under earlier rules. Thus, FAR 5.203(g) requires contracting officers, upon learning that the notice was not published within the presumed one day period, to determine whether the date for receipt of proposals should be extended or the notice requirement waived for "unusual and compelling urgency" under FAR 5.202(a)(2). In *Shiloh Forestry, Inc.*, Comp. Gen. Dec. B-235449, 89-2 CPD ¶ 229, GAO upheld a decision to waive the requirement based on the urgency of the procurement even though the notice was never published. See also *Hercules Aerospace Co.*, Comp. Gen. Dec. B-254677, 94-1 CPD ¶ 7, where the contractor abandoned its argument that the Navy did not synopsize the solicitation after the Navy responded that there was an unusual and compelling urgency; *Electro-Methods, Inc.*, Comp. Gen. Dec. B-250931, 93-1 CPD ¶ 181, where the Air Force reasonably decided it had an "urgent need" for airplane engine duct supports and was therefore not required to synopsize the proposed acquisition. Similarly, in *JRW Mgmt. Co.*, Comp. Gen. Dec. B-260396.2, 95-1 CPD ¶ 276, GAO held that the agency's need for shuttle bus services had been classified as urgent, and the procurement was consequently exempt from the FAR's general synopsis and time period requirements.

According to 15 U.S.C. § 637(f) and 41 U.S.C. § 1708(c), the following information must be contained in GPE notices:

> (1) [An] accurate description of the property or services to be contracted for, which description (A) shall not be unnecessarily restrictive of competition, and (B) shall include, as appropriate, the agency nomenclature, National Stock Number or other part number, and a brief description of the item's form, fit, or function, physical dimensions, predominant material of manufacture, or similar information that will assist a prospective contractor to make an informed business judgment as to whether a copy of the solicitation should be requested;
>
> (2) provisions that—
>
> (A) state whether the technical data required to respond to the solicitation will not be furnished as part of such solicitation, and identify the source in the Government, if any, from which the technical data may be obtained; and
>
> (B) state whether an offeror, its product, or service must meet a qualification requirement in order to be eligible for award, and, if so, identify the office from which the qualification requirement may be obtained;
>
> (3) the name, business address, and telephone number of the contracting officer;
>
> (4) a statement that all responsible sources may submit a bid, proposal, or quotation (as appropriate) which shall be considered by the agency;
>
> (5) in the case of a procurement using procedures other than competitive procedures, a statement of the reason justifying the use of such procedures and the identity of the intended source; and

(6) in the case of a contract in an amount estimated to be greater than $25,000 but not greater than the simplified acquisition threshold or a contract for the procurement of commercial items using simplified procedures—

(A) a description of the procedures to be used in awarding the contract; and

(B) a statement specifying the periods for prospective offerors and the contracting officer to take the necessary preaward and award actions.

See FAR 5.207 calling for more specific information and implementing these requirements in different language.

A number of exemptions from the requirement for GPE notices are contained in 15 U.S.C. § 637(g) and 41 U.S.C. § 1708(b). These are summarized as follows in FAR 5.202:

1. procurements containing classified information,
2. urgent procurements,
3. procurement for foreign government,
4. 8(a) procurements and procurements from a specific source such as a workshop for the blind under the rules of the Committee for the Purchase from the Blind and Other Severely Handicapped,
5. procurement of utility services where there is only one source,
6. task or delivery orders,
7. SBIR procurements,
8. acceptance of an unsolicited proposal,
9. procurement of perishable substances,
10. procurement of brand name commercial items for authorized resale,
11. procurements under the terms of an existing contract that was previously synopsized,
12. DOD foreign procurements that are not covered by the World Trade Organization Government Procurement Agreement or a Free Trade Agreement,
13. simplified acquisition procurements with notice in the GPE permitting electronic responses,
14. procurement of experts in support of litigation, and
15. procurements waived by the head of an agency after consultation with SBA and OFPP.

It has also been held that the synopsis requirement is not directly applicable to reprocurements against defaulted contracts, *United States Pollution Control, Inc.*, Comp. Gen. Dec. B-225372, 87-1 CPD ¶ 96.

The government's failure to properly publish the required notice may invalidate a procurement. See *TMI Mgmt. Sys., Inc.*, Comp. Gen. Dec. B-401530, 2009 CPD ¶ 191, where GAO held that FEMA's misclassification for facilities support services on the GPE site under a "miscellaneous" product classification code improperly deprived vendors of an appropriate opportunity to respond to the solicitation. Similarly, in *Gourmet Distribs.*, Comp. Gen. Dec. B-259083, 95-1 CPD ¶ 130, GAO held that an agency did not use reasonable methods to obtain full and open competition when it improperly classified the announcement of a beverage vending services procurement under the classification category for leasing or renting equipment. See also *Information Ventures, Inc.*, Comp. Gen. Dec. B-293518, 2004 CPD ¶ 76 (synopsis lacked necessary information because it did not accurately describe the agency's requirements); *RII*, Comp. Gen. Dec. B-251436, 93-1 CPD ¶ 223 (cancellation and resolicitation proper where agency had misclassified a listing in the CBD as "research and development" instead of "professional, administrative, and management support services"); and *Frank Thatcher Assocs.*, 67 Comp. Gen. 77 (B-228744), 87-2 CPD ¶ 480 (misclassification of notice held to be a statutory violation requiring the award of protest costs (the contract had been performed)). Compare *Morris Guralnick Assocs.*, Comp. Gen. Dec. B-214751.2, 84-2 CPD ¶ 597, where the CBD notice appeared in the section for communications equipment rather than in the section on services where it properly belonged. GAO refused to recommend cancellation of the contract because the statute contains no expression of congressional intent to require agencies to cancel otherwise proper awards where the exact letter of the statute was not followed. GAO noted that the Navy complied with the spirit of the statute because notice was actually published and two firms were aware of the procurement. In *Pilkington Aerospace, Inc.*, Comp. Gen. Dec. B-259173, 95-1 CPD ¶ 180, where the Air Force failed to publish an amended CBD synopsis increasing the quantity of goods from 35 to 325, GAO agreed with the protester that the Air Force erred but denied the protest because the protester was not capable of meeting the increased needs. See also *Gott Corp.*, Comp. Gen. Dec. B-222586, 86-2 CPD ¶ 154, refusing to cancel the award for improper notice because the protester actually knew of the procurement in time to compete. Similarly, in *Space Vector Corp.*, Comp. Gen. Dec. B-253295.2, 93-2 CPD ¶ 273, GAO held that although the "GPS receiver integration" was a critical factor in the agency's sole source determination that should have been disclosed in the CBD synopsis, the protester was informed of this requirement during qualification discussions and was given the opportunity to demonstrate its capability.

One of the major functions of GPE notices is to alert potential competitors that an agency intends to conduct a procurement using other than competitive procedures. Thus, notices of procurements involving other than competitive procedures must contain a statement of the reason justifying such procedures and must identify the intended source, 41 U.S.C. § 1708(c)(5); FAR 5.207(c)(15). The failure to comply with this publication requirement was held not to require termination of the resulting sole source award in *AUL Instruments, Inc.*, 64 Comp. Gen. 871 (B-216543), 85-2 CPD ¶ 324, because there was no prejudice to the protester who did not appear able to meet the urgent requirements.

However, the publication of this notice is mandatory and when a potential contractor responds to such a notice, the agency must consider the response, 10

U.S.C. § 3204(e) (formerly § 2304(f)(1)(C)); 41 U.S.C. § 3304(e)(1)(C); FAR 6.302-1(d)(2). For decisions holding that a sole source award was unreasonable when the agency did not consider protester's capability statement received in response to the notice, see *Career Sys. Dev. Corp.*, Comp. Gen. Dec. B-411346.11, 2018 CPD ¶ 176; *Barnes Aerospace Grp.*, Comp. Gen. Dec. B-298864, 2006 CPD ¶ 204, and *Masstor Sys. Corp.*, 64 Comp. Gen. 118 (B-215046), 84-2 CPD ¶ 598. Prior to 1993 the Court of Federal Claims had followed this reasoning, holding that submission of a capability statement bound the government to an implied promise to fairly and honestly consider the response. This reasoning was rejected in *Motorola, Inc. v. United States*, 988 F.2d 113 (Fed. Cir. 1993), where the court stated that it is only the contractor's submission of a formal bid manifesting its intent to be bound by the solicitation's provision that justifies implying a reciprocal government commitment to fairly and honestly consider the bid. See *Pure Power!. Inc. v. United States*, 70 Fed. Cl. 739 (2006), and *Garchik v. United States*, 37 Fed. Cl. 52 (1996), holding that the court had no jurisdiction because the protester had responded to a request for information, which response was not a formal, responsive bid. See also *Communication Constr. Servs., Inc. v. United States*, 116 Fed. Cl. 233 (2014), holding that an offeror challenging an ambiguous solicitation provision (which must be done before submitting a proposal) can preserve its right plead the implied contract by submitting a proposal against the ambiguous solicitation.

Mere inclusion in the notice of the identity of the intended source and the reason justifying the lack of competition may be insufficient. In *Berkshire Computer Prods.*, Comp. Gen. Dec. B-240327, 91-1 CPD ¶ 464, GAO indicated that the notice should contain sufficient information to permit prospective offerors to respond in a meaningful way with alternative approaches. In *Racal-Milgo*, 66 Comp. Gen. 430 (B-225681), 87-1 CPD ¶ 472, GAO held that this did not require the inclusion of the agency's evaluation factors in the notice.

If a potential competitor fails to submit a timely expression of interest in response to a notice that other than competitive procedures will be used, it will be precluded from contesting the agency decision before GAO. Thus, when the agency specified in the CBD notice that there was a 45-day period for the submission of expressions of interest in competing on a procurement, GAO refused to rule on a protest from a firm that had not responded within that time, *Fraser-Volpe Corp.*, Comp. Gen. Dec. B-240499, 90-2 CPD ¶ 397. See also *Allerion, Inc.*, Comp. Gen. Dec. B-256986, 94-1 CPD ¶ 281 (protester must respond to CBD notices with a timely expression of interest in fulfilling the potential sole source requirement and must receive a negative agency response as a prerequisite to filing a protest challenging the agency's sole source decision). When a potential competitor submits a timely expression of interest that is subsequently rejected, a protest will be untimely if it is not filed within 10 days of the rejection, *Keco Indus., Inc.*, Comp. Gen. Dec. B-238301, 90-1 CPD ¶ 490.

[2] Presolicitation Exchanges with Industry

As noted above, FAR 15.201 encourages early exchanges with industry when competitive negotiations are employed. It states:

> (a) Exchanges of information among all interested parties, from the earliest identification of a requirement through receipt of proposals, are encouraged. Any exchange of information must be consistent with procurement integrity requirements (see 3.104). Interested parties include potential offerors, end users, Government acquisition and supporting personnel, and others involved in the conduct or outcome of the acquisition.
>
> (b) The purpose of exchanging information is to improve the understanding of Government requirements and industry capabilities, thereby allowing potential offerors to judge whether or how they can satisfy the Government's requirements, and enhancing the Government's ability to obtain quality supplies and services, including construction, at reasonable prices, and increase efficiency in proposal preparation, proposal evaluation, negotiation, and contract award.
>
> (c) Agencies are encouraged to promote early exchanges of information about future acquisitions. An early exchange of information among industry and the program manager, contracting officer, and other participants in the acquisition process can identify and resolve concerns regarding the acquisition strategy, including proposed contract type, terms and conditions, and acquisition planning schedules; the feasibility of the requirement, including performance requirements, statements of work, and data requirements; the suitability of the proposal instructions and evaluation criteria, including the approach for assessing past performance information; the availability of reference documents; and any other industry concerns or questions.

The techniques used to promote early exchanges of information are set forth in FAR 15.201(c), as follows:

> (1) Industry or small business conferences;
> (2) Public hearings;
> (3) Market research, as described in part 10;
> (4) One-on-one meetings with potential offerors (any that are substantially involved with potential contract terms and conditions should include the contracting officer; also see paragraph (f) of this section regarding restrictions on disclosure of information);
> (5) Presolicitation notices;
> (6) Draft RFPs;
> (7) RFIs;
> (8) Presolicitation or preproposal conferences; and
> (9) Site visits.

As stated in ¶ (a) it is important that any information exchanged with potential offerors be consistent with the Procurement Integrity Act. FAR 15.201 also provides guidance on the type of information that can be exchanged and the precautions that must be taken once a solicitation has been released, stating:

> (f) General information about agency mission needs and future requirements may be disclosed at any time. After release of the solicitation, the contracting officer shall be the focal point of any exchange with potential offerors. When specific information about a proposed acquisition that would be necessary for the preparation of proposals is disclosed to one or more potential offerors, that information shall be made available to the public as soon as practicable, but no later than the next general release of information, in order to avoid creating an unfair competitive advantage. Information provided to a particular offeror in response to that offeror's request shall not be disclosed if doing so would reveal the potential offeror's confidential business strategy. When a presolicitation or preproposal conference is conducted, materials distributed at the conference should be made available to all potential offerors, upon request.

Note that one-on-one exchanges with potential offerors meets the procurement integrity requirements, FAR 15.201(c)(4), but agency officials must exercise great care in treating potential offerors evenhandedly when one-on-one meetings are conducted. Thus, if such a meeting is held with one potential offeror, all other known companies that can meet the requirement should be offered a one-on-one meeting. Alternatively, the agency can post a notice of its willingness to hold one-on-one meetings on the GPE.

After a presolicitation conference has been held, attendees must be diligent in following up with the agency to ensure that they receive an RFP. See *Ketch Corp.*, Comp. Gen. Dec. B-240578, 90-2 CPD ¶ 447, where a protest was denied when the protester inadvertently did not receive a copy of the RFP. GAO held that no recourse was available because the protester made only one inquiry to the agency in the two months between the presolicitation conference and the mailing of the RFP. See also *O.J. Best Servs., Inc.*, Comp. Gen. Dec. B-276954, 97-1 CPD ¶ 23, holding that the protester bore the risk of nonreceipt where the record established that the RFP and the two subsequent amendments were mailed to the protester.

[B] Solicitation of Bids or Proposals

Traditionally each agency of the government maintained mailing lists of potential offerors and publicly posted solicitations. However, mailing lists were abolished in 2003, 68 Fed. Reg. 43855, July 24, 2003. During the same period electronic commerce became the primary means of distributing solicitations. See FAR 4.502 stating:

> (a) The Federal Government shall use electronic commerce whenever practicable or cost-effective. The use of terms commonly associated with paper transactions (e.g., *"copy," "document," "page," "printed," "sealed envelope," and "stamped"*) shall not be interpreted to restrict the use of electronic commerce. Contracting officers may supplement electronic transactions by using other media to meet the requirements of any contract action governed by the FAR (e.g., transmit hard copy of drawings).
>
> (b) Agencies may exercise broad discretion in selecting the hardware and software that will be used in conducting electronic commerce. However, as required by 41 U.S.C. 2301, the head of each agency, after consulting with the Administrator of OFPP, shall ensure that systems, technologies, procedures, and processes used by the agency to conduct electronic commerce—
>
> > (1) Are implemented uniformly throughout the agency, to the maximum extent practicable;
> >
> > (2) Are implemented only after considering the full or partial use of existing infrastructures;
> >
> > (3) Facilitate access to Government acquisition opportunities by small business concerns, small disadvantaged business concerns, women-owned, veteran-owned, HUBZone, and service-disabled veteran-owned small business concerns;
> >
> > (4) Include a single means of providing widespread public notice of acquisition opportunities through the Governmentwide point of entry and a means of responding to notices or solicitations electronically; and
> >
> > (5) Comply with nationally and internationally recognized standards that broaden interoperability and ease the electronic interchange of information, such as standards established by the National Institute of Standards and Technology.
>
> (c) Before using electronic commerce, the agency head shall ensure that the agency systems are capable of ensuring authentication and confidentiality commensurate with the risk and magnitude of the harm from loss, misuse, or unauthorized access to or modification of the information.
>
> (d) Agencies may accept electronic signatures and records in connection with Government contracts.

The electronic commerce technique that is used to disseminate solicitations is the GPE. See FAR 5.102(a) stating:

> (1) Except as provided in paragraph (a)(5) of this section, the contracting officer must make available through the GPE solicitations synopsized through the GPE, including specifications, technical data, and other pertinent information determined necessary by the contracting officer. Transmissions to the GPE must be in accordance with the interface description available via the Internet at *http://www.SAM.gov*.

(2) The contracting officer is encouraged, when practicable and cost-effective, to make accessible through the GPE additional information related to a solicitation.

(3) The contracting officer must ensure that solicitations transmitted using electronic commerce are forwarded to the GPE to satisfy the requirements of paragraph (a)(1) of this section.

(4) When an agency determines that a solicitation contains information that requires additional controls to monitor access and distribution (e.g., technical data, specifications, maps, building designs, schedules, etc.), the information shall be made available through the enhanced controls of the GPE, unless an exception in paragraph (a)(5) of this section applies. The GPE meets the synopsis and advertising requirements of this part.

(5) The contracting officer need not make a solicitation available through the GPE as required in paragraph (a)(4) of this section, when—

(i) Disclosure would compromise the national security (e.g., would result in disclosure of classified information, or information subject to export controls) or create other security risks. The fact that access to classified matter may be necessary to submit a proposal or perform the contract does not, in itself, justify use of this exception;

(ii) The nature of the file (e.g., size, format) does not make it cost-effective or practicable for contracting officers to provide access to the solicitation through the GPE; or

(iii) The agency's senior procurement executive makes a written determination that access through the GPE is not in the Government's interest.

In *NuWestern USA Constructors, Inc.*, Comp. Gen. Dec. B-275514, 97-1 CPD ¶ 90, GAO held that an agency's issuance of a solicitation only in electronic format (CD-ROM) was not unduly restrictive of competition or otherwise inconsistent with applicable law and regulation. The solicitation was sent to 63 firms. GAO found nothing in the procurement statutes or the Small Business Act that requires agencies to provide paper copies of solicitation documents upon request. Requiring firms to have access to computerized CD-ROM printing equipment or incur a charge to have another company do the printing was not considered unduly burdensome to prospective contractors. See also *Commonwealth Indus. Specialties, Inc.*, Comp. Gen. Dec. B-277833, 97-2 CPD ¶ 151, finding that requiring responses to a request for quotations be submitted though the agency's electronic bulletin board would promote efficiency and economy, and not be overly burdensome to prospective vendors.

[1] Alternate Means of Issuing Solicitations

In some cases, an agency may choose a means other than the GPE as the means of disseminating a solicitation.

[a] Paper or CD-ROM

FAR 5.102 contains the following guidance:

> (b) When the contracting officer does not make a solicitation available through the GPE pursuant to paragraph (a)(5) of this section, the contracting officer—
>
> (1) Should employ other electronic means (e.g., CD-ROM or electronic mail) whenever practicable and cost-effective. When solicitations are provided electronically on physical media (e.g., disks) or in paper form, the contracting officer must—
>
> (i) Maintain a reasonable number of copies of solicitations, including specifications and other pertinent information determined necessary by the contracting officer (upon request, potential sources not initially solicited should be mailed or provided copies of solicitations, if available);
>
> (ii) Provide copies on a "first-come-first-served" basis, for pickup at the contracting office, to publishers, trade associations, information services, and other members of the public having a legitimate interest (for construction, see 36.211); and
>
> (iii) Retain a copy of the solicitation and other documents for review by and duplication for those requesting copies after the initial number of copies is exhausted; and
>
> (2) May require payment of a fee, not exceeding the actual cost of duplication, for a copy of the solicitation document.

[b] Facsimile

FAR 15.203(d) permits the solicitation and receipt of proposals by facsimile, as follows:

> Contracting officers may issue RFPs and/or authorize receipt of proposals modifications, or revisions by facsimile.
>
> (1) In deciding whether or not to use facsimiles, the contracting officer should consider factors such as—
>
> (i) Anticipated proposal size and volume;
>
> (ii) Urgency of the requirement;
>
> (iii) Availability and suitability of electronic commerce methods; and
>
> (iv) Adequacy of administrative procedures and controls for receiving, identifying, recording, and safeguarding facsimile proposals, and ensuring their timely delivery to the designated proposal delivery location.

> (2) If facsimile proposals are authorized, contracting officers may request offeror(s) to provide the complete, original signed proposal at a later date.

Although the FAR is silent as to the use of facsimile for sealed bid procurements, this would appear to be permissible.

[c] Oral Solicitations

Oral solicitations may be used for any procurement falling within the simplified acquisition threshold, FAR 13.106-1(c). In addition, FAR 15.203(f) permits the use of oral solicitations for negotiated procurements, as follows:

> Oral RFPs are authorized when processing a written solicitation would delay the acquisition of supplies or services to the detriment of the Government and a notice is not required under 5.202 (*e.g.*, perishable items and support of contingency operations or other emergency situations). Use of an oral RFP does not relieve the contracting officer from complying with other FAR requirements.
>
> (1) The contract files supporting oral solicitations should include —
>
> (i) A description of the requirement;
>
> (ii) Rationale for use of an oral solicitation;
>
> (iii) Sources solicited, including the date, time, name of individuals contacted, and prices offered: and
>
> (iv) The solicitation number provided to the prospective offerors.
>
> (2) The information furnished to potential offerors under oral solicitations should include appropriate items from paragraph (e) of this section.

[C] Notice Requirement

Posting notice of a solicitation on the GPE meets the notice requirement without any further action. Protesters are charged with constructive notice of the contents of procurement actions published on the GPE. *DBI Waste Sys., Inc.*, Comp. Gen. Dec. B-400687, 2009 CPD ¶ 15. The doctrine of constructive notice creates a presumption of notice in law that cannot be rebutted. By definition the doctrine imputes knowledge to a party without regard to the party's actual knowledge of the matter at issue. See *Worldwide Language Res., Inc.*, Comp. Gen. Dec. B-296984, 2005 CPD ¶ 206, citing *Townsend v. Little*, 109 U.S. 504, 511 (1883) ("constructive notice is defined to be in its nature no more than evidence of notice, the presumption of which is so violent that the court will not even allow of its being controverted").

This rule applies to all potential offerors including incumbent contractors. See *DBI Waste Sys., Inc.*, Comp. Gen. Dec. B-400687, 2009 CPD ¶ 15 (status as incumbent contractor, former oral notice of acquisitions, or lack of

Internet access is not determinative for notice when solicitation posted on GPE); *PR Newswire Assoc., LLC*, Comp. Gen. Dec. B-400430, 2008 CPD ¶ 178 (agency not required to provide actual notice to incumbent even if provided actual notice to another offeror).

[D] System for Award Management

The System for Award Management (SAM) is envisioned as a method for the government to have one list of all entities wishing to contract with any agency of the government. The system serves the entire government, and it facilitates many aspects of the procurement process, including publicity, responsibility determinations, and payments. See FAR 2.101 stating:

> System for Award Management (SAM) means the primary Government repository for prospective Federal awardee and Federal awardee information and the centralized Government system for certain contracting, grants, and other assistance-related processes. It includes—
>
> (1) Data collected from prospective Federal awardees required for the conduct of business with the Government;
>
> (2) Prospective contractor-submitted annual representations and certifications in accordance with FAR subpart 4.12; and
>
> (3) Identification of those parties excluded from receiving Federal contracts, certain subcontracts, and certain types of Federal financial and non-financial assistance and benefits.

FAR 4.1102(a) requires all prospective contractors to be registered in the SAM database at the time of submission of an offer or quotation. See *Acon Traders, LLC*, Comp. Gen. Dec. B-417558, 2019 CPD ¶ 226, denying a protest that the protester's quotation had been rejected because of lack of registration.

FAR 4.1102(a) lists the following exceptions to this requirement:

> (1) Purchases under the micro-purchase threshold that use a Governmentwide commercial purchase card as both the purchasing and payment mechanism, as opposed to using the purchase card for payment only;
>
> (2) Classified contracts (see 2.101) when registration in SAM, or use of SAM data, could compromise the safeguarding of classified information or national security;
>
> (3) Contracts awarded by—
>
> (i) Deployed contracting officers in the course of military operations, including, but not limited to, contingency operations as defined in 10 U.S.C. 101(a)(13) or humanitarian or peacekeeping operations as defined in 10 U.S.C. 2302(8);
>
> (ii) Contracting officers located outside the United States and its outlying areas, as defined in 2.101, for work to be performed in support of diplomatic or developmental operations, including those performed

in support of foreign assistance programs overseas, in an area that has been designated by the Department of State as a danger pay post (see https://aoprals.state.gov/); or

(iii) Contracting officers in the conduct of emergency operations, such as responses to natural or environmental disasters or national or civil emergencies, e.g., Robert T. Stafford Disaster Relief and Emergency Assistance Act (42 U.S.C. 5121);

(4) Contracts with individuals for performance outside the United States and its outlying areas;

(5) Contracts awarded without providing for full and open competition due to unusual or compelling urgency (see 6.302-2);

(6) Contract actions at or below $30,000 awarded to foreign vendors for work performed outside the United States, if it is impractical to obtain SAM registration; and

(7) Micro-purchases that do not use the electronic funds transfer (EFT) method for payment and are not required to be reported (see subpart 4.6).

See FAR 4.1102 for further guidance on implementing the SAM registration requirements.

The System for Award Management provision at FAR 52.204-7 spells out the procedures for registration. DFARS 204.1103 contains additional guidance on registration procedures. Offerors are ineligible for award if they do not maintain their registration in SAM, *Dehler Mfg. Co.*, Comp. Gen. Dec. B-416601, 2018 CPD ¶ 368, *recons. denied*, 2019 CPD ¶ 92. However, if an offeror is registered at the time of award, it is proper to waive a solicitation requirement that it be registered at the time of submission of final proposal revisions, *C.L.R. Dev. Grp.*, Comp. Gen. Dec. B-409398, 2014 CPD ¶ 141.

FAR 4.1103 contains the following instructions to contracting officers on implementing the SAM requirements:

(a) Unless the acquisition is exempt under 4.1102(a), the contracting officer—

(1) Shall verify that the offeror or quoter is registered in SAM (see paragraph (b) of this section) at the time an offer or quotation is submitted;

(2) Should use the unique entity identifier to verify SAM registration—

(i) Via https://www.sam.gov; or

(ii) As otherwise provided by agency procedures; or

(3) Need not verify SAM registration before placing an order or call if the contract or agreement includes the provision at 52.204-7, System for Award Management, or the clause at 52.212-4, Contract Terms and Conditions—Commercial Items, or a similar agency clause, except when use of the Governmentwide commercial purchase card is contemplated as a method of payment. (See 32.1108(b)(2).)

> (b) If the contract action is being awarded in accordance with 4.1102(a)(5), the contractor is required to be registered in SAM within 30 days after contract award, or at least three days prior to submission of the first invoice, whichever occurs first.
>
> (c) Agencies shall protect against improper disclosure of information contained in SAM.
>
> (d) The contracting officer shall, on contractual documents transmitted to the payment office, provide the unique entity identifier, or, if applicable, the Electronic Funds Transfer indicator, in accordance with agency procedures.

Contracting officers are generally not required to verify the information in SAM except for checking whether the offeror is debarred or suspended, *DLF-CPC JV, LLC*, Comp. Gen. Dec. B-418581, 2020 CPD ¶ 218 (offeror had not updated SAM when it changed its address). Furthermore, contracting officers can waive minor defects in a registration. See *Cyber Protection Techs., LLC*, Comp. Gen. Dec. B-416297.2, 2018 CPD ¶ 270, stating:

> With respect to allegations that an offeror's SAM registration is inaccurate or incomplete, our Office has generally recognized that minor informalities related to SAM (or its predecessor systems) registration generally do not undermine the validity of the award and are waivable by the agency without prejudice to other offerors. See, e.g., High Plains Computing, Inc. d/b/a HPC Solutions, B-409736.2, Dec. 22, 2014, 2014 CPD ¶ 379; C.L.R. Dev. Grp., B-409398, Apr. 11, 2014, 2014 CPD ¶ 141 at 7. We have found no prejudicial error in these cases largely because an awardee's registration status does not implicate the terms of its proposal, and there is nothing to suggest that another offeror would have altered its proposal to its competitive advantage in response to a relaxed SAM registration requirement.

See also *Phoenix Env't Design, Inc.*, Comp. Gen. Dec. B-418473, 2020 CPD ¶ 173 (denying a protest that the agency waived allegedly inaccurate information); *Performance Sys., LLC*, Comp. Gen. Dec. B-416374, 2018 CPD ¶ 183 (denying a protest of waived inaccurate NAICS code); *CASS Pro. Servs. Corp.*, Comp. Gen. Dec. B-415941, 2018 CPD ¶ 163 (denying a protest of inaccurate information because the contracting officer checked to see that the address in SAM matched the address on the offer). Compare *United Valve Co.*, Comp. Gen. Dec. B-416277, 2018 CPD ¶ 268, requiring the agency to reconsider whether the winning offeror was eligible for award when there was confusion as to the CAGE code on the SAM.

CHAPTER 4

CONTRACTOR QUALIFICATION

§4.01 INTRODUCTION

A fundamental policy of the government is to award contracts only to qualified organizations. There are three separate techniques used to avoid awarding contracts to unqualified firms: (1) nonresponsibility determinations, (2) debarment and suspension actions, (3) disqualification because of an organizational conflict of interest (OCI). Critical differences exist between these types of disqualification techniques. Contracting officers make nonresponsibility determinations and make initial determinations on OCI disqualification as they award specific contracts. The Government Accountability Office and the Court of Federal Claims often review initial determinations on OCI disqualification. On the other hand, an agency official or agency board initiates debarment or suspension actions, actions which result in disqualification on an extended (or even permanent) basis. This chapter analyzes the important substantive and procedural aspects of each of these disqualification techniques.

§4.02 RESPONSIBILITY

Before awarding a contract, the contracting officer must determine whether a contractor is a "responsible" contractor. (While other procurement systems typically refer to contractors that are "qualified," the federal government system refers more specifically to "responsible" contractors in describing those eligible to contract.) The government has broad discretion in determining those firms with which it will enter into contractual agreements, *Perkins v. Lukens Steel Co.*, 319 U.S. 113 (1940).While government agencies had long followed the practice of refraining from awarding contracts to firms lacking qualifications to perform the specified work, the Armed Services Procurement Act (ASPA) first applied the concept of responsibility to advertised procurement, now codified at 10 U.S.C. § 3303 (formerly 10 U.S.C. § 2305). Similar language was included in the Federal Property and Administrative Services Act of 1949, 41 U.S.C. § 253(b). In 1962, the concept of responsibility was specifically applied to negotiation as well as to contracting by formal advertising (now sealed bidding) when 10 U.S.C. § 3302 (formerly § 2304) was added to the ASPA to provide negotiation procedures. The Competition in Contracting Act of 1984 (CICA), Pub. L. No. 98-369, provided fresh emphasis on the imperative of contractor responsibility. CICA reiterated earlier policy on providing for award in negotiated procurements only to a "responsible source," 10 U.S.C. § 2305(b)(4)(C) (now 10 U.S.C. § 3303); 41 U.S.C. § 253b(d)(2) (now 41 U.S.C. § 3702(b)), and for award in sealed bid procurements only to a "responsible bidder," 10 U.S.C. § 2305(b)(3) (now 10 U.S.C. § 3302); 41 U.S.C. § 253b(4) (now 41 U.S.C. § 3703(c)).

Subpart 9.1 of the FAR implements the statutory concept of responsibility. FAR 9.103 requires an *affirmative responsibility determination* as a prerequisite to award of a government contract. This requirement, as well as an expression of the policy on which it is based, is contained in FAR 9.103:

> (a) Purchases shall be made from, and contracts shall be awarded to, responsible prospective contractors only.
>
> (b) No purchase or award shall be made unless the contracting officer makes an affirmative determination of responsibility. In the absence of information clearly indicating that the prospective contractor is responsible, the contracting officer shall make a determination of nonresponsibility. If the prospective contractor is a small business concern, the contracting officer shall comply with subpart 19.6, Certificates of Competency and Determinations of Responsibility. (If Section 8(a) of the Small Business Act (15 U.S.C. 637) applies, see Subpart 19.8.)
>
> (c) The award of a contract to a supplier based on lowest evaluated price alone can be false economy if there is subsequent default, late deliveries, or other unsatisfactory performance resulting in additional contractual or administrative costs. While it is important that Government purchases be made at the lowest price, this does not require an award to a supplier solely because that supplier submits the lowest offer. A prospective contractor must affirmatively demonstrate its responsibility, including, when necessary, the responsibility of its proposed subcontractors.

Determination of contractor qualification requires consideration of whether the firm: (1) can be expected to complete the contract work on time and in a satisfactory manner; (2) is organized in such a way that doing business with it will promote various social and economic goals; and (3) satisfies other special standards of eligibility imposed by statutes and regulations.

As noted in ¶ (b) of this regulation, contracting officers make affirmative responsibility determinations for small businesses, but cannot make negative responsibility determinations for small businesses. Instead, contracting officers must refer all potential nonresponsibility determinations involving small businesses to the Small Business Administration which has exclusive authority to issue a Certification of Competency (COC) for small businesses, 15 U.S.C. § 637(b)(7), 13 C.F.R. § 125.5, and FAR 19.6. FAR 19.601 states:

> A Certificate of Competency (COC) is the certificate issued by the Small Business Administration (SBA) stating that the holder is responsible (with respect to all elements of responsibility, including, but not limited to, capability, competency, capacity, credit, integrity, perseverance, tenacity, and limitations on subcontracting) for the purpose of receiving and performing a specific Government contract.

See Chapter 14 for a complete discussion of this procedure.

Unlike the issue of "responsiveness" (discussed in Chapter 5), the responsibility of a prospective contractor is judged as of the time of award and not as of the time of submission of the offer, *A–B Computer Solutions, Inc.*, Comp. Gen.

Dec., B-415819, 2018 CPD ¶ 128; *CardioMetrix*, Comp. Gen. Dec. B-255748.2, 94-1 CPD ¶ 364. Thus, a firm that appears unqualified at the time bid or proposals are opened may nevertheless gain eligibility for award of the contract so long as it takes the steps necessary to become responsible by the time of award. In addition, information pertaining to how performance requirements will be met (rather than to the requirements themselves) relates to bidder responsibility and not to bid responsiveness; such information may be provided at any time prior to award, *FCi Fed., Inc.*, Comp. Gen. Dec. B-408558.7, 2015 CPD ¶ 245. The distinction between matters of responsiveness and responsibility is reviewed in detail in Chapter 5.

In most situations, this timing issue does not become a source of controversy because the prospective contractor's status will not vary significantly between the time of evaluation and the time of award. However, when there is a marked change of status, the rule can affect the outcome. For example, when a low bidder obtained adequate financing by forming a joint venture after bid opening, GAO held that the responsibility determination should be based on the resources of the joint venture, *Consortium HSG Technischer Service GmbH & GeBe Gebäude-und Betriebstechnik GmbH Südwest Co., Management KG* Comp. Gen. Dec. B-292699.6, 2004 CPD ¶ 134. Similarly, it has been held that a bidder is responsible if it obtains required licenses and permits after bid opening but before award, even though the invitation required the inclusion of the licenses with proposals, *Pond Security Group Italia, JV*, Comp. Gen. Dec. B-400149.3, 2008 CPD ¶ 233. See *United Seguranca, Ltda.*, Comp. Gen. Dec. B-294388, 2004 CPD ¶ 207, for a discussion of the impact of permits on responsibility. The principle of responsibility also is reflected in the timing of the submission of the FAR 52.222-25 certification of affirmative action program requirements that need not be submitted until immediately prior to award, *McCarthy Mfg. Co.*, 56 Comp. Gen. 369 (B-186550), 77-1 CPD ¶ 116; *Royal Indus.*, Comp. Gen. Dec. B-185571, 76-1 CPD ¶ 139. GAO modified its protest rules to situations when the contracting officer may have ignored information that would be expected to have a strong bearing on a responsibility determination. *GEO Group, Inc.*, Comp. Gen. Dec. B-405012, 2011 CPD ¶ 153; *Verestar Gov't Servs, Group*, Comp. Gen. Dec. B-291854, 2003 CPD ¶ 68. See also *Marinette Marine Corp.*, Comp. Gen. Dec. B-400697, 2009 CPD ¶ 16 where contrary to the protester's allegations, the contracting officer found the awardee responsible based on an updated responsibility determination.

Additionally, contracting officers are not required to perform a responsibility determination on task orders—relying instead on the responsibility determination made for the ID/IQ contract, *Alliant Enter. JV, LLC*, Comp. Gen. Dec. B-410352.5, 2015 CPD ¶ 209; *Booz Allen Hamilton, Inc.*, Comp. Gen. Dec. B-409272, 2014 CPD ¶ 84. Contracting officers, however, are required to consider any new information that generally pertains to very serious matters such as potential criminal activity before issuing a task order, *MicroTechs., LLC*, Comp. Gen. Dec. B-415214, 2018 CPD ¶ 48; *Enterprise Resource Planned Sys.*

Int'l, LLC, Comp. Gen. Dec. B-413805.5, 2017 CPD ¶ 215. This requirement to consider new information does not apply to task orders issued under the Federal Supply Schedule because the Federal Supply Schedule is a streamlined method of acquisition, *Advanced Tech. Sys., Inc.*, Comp. Gen. Dec. B-296493.6, 2006 CPD ¶ 151.

In addition, GAO's rules, revised as of 2003, make it clear that GAO will not review affirmative determinations of responsibility. See 4 C.F.R. § 21.5(c), stating:

> (c) *Affirmative determination of responsibility by the contracting officer*. Because the determination that a bidder or offeror is capable of performing a contract is largely committed to the contracting officer's discretion, GAO will generally not consider a protest challenging such a determination. The exceptions are protests that allege that definitive responsibility criteria in the solicitation were not met and those that identify evidence raising serious concerns that, in reaching a particular responsibility determination, the contracting officer unreasonably failed to consider available relevant information or otherwise violated statute or regulation.

Under the revised rules, GAO consistently holds it generally will not consider issues involving a contracting officer's affirmative responsibility determination except in circumstances identified in 4 C.F.R. 21.5(c), such as where protests allege the selected awardee does not meet a definitive responsibility criterion in the solicitation, or where protests identify evidence raising serious concerns the contracting officer unreasonably failed to consider in reaching a particular responsibility determination, *A–B Computer Solutions, Inc.*, Comp. Gen. Dec. B-415819, 2018 CPD ¶ 128; *Sum Co Eco-Contracting LLC*, Comp. Gen. Dec., B–409434, 2014 CPD ¶ 129. See also *FN Mfg., Inc.*, Comp. Gen. Dec. B-297172, 2005 CPD ¶ 212 (discussing history and purposes of revised GAO protest rule).

Generally, GAO limits its review of affirmative determinations of responsibility to very serious matters such as potential criminal activity. See, e.g., *FCi Fed., Inc.,* Comp. Gen. Dec. B-408558.7, 2015 CPD ¶ 245 (considering allegation that agency failed to consider an ongoing Justice Department investigation into whether the awardee's parent company defrauded the government when performing background investigations); *FN Mfg., Inc.*, Comp. Gen. Dec. B-297172, 2005 CPD ¶ 212 (considering allegation that agency failed to consider an ongoing investigation into whether the awardee defrauded the government on a prior contract for the same requirement). In contrast, GAO stated that an allegation that the selected awardee's "SAM registration does not include the NAICS code applicable to this procurement, or show any paving experience on its website, do not support the necessary threshold showing to trigger our Office's review of a challenge to an affirmative responsibility determination," *GEO Group, Inc.*, Comp. Gen. Dec. B-405012, 2011 CPD ¶ 153; *Hendry Corp.*, Comp. Gen. Dec. B-400224.2, 2008 CPD ¶ 164.

[A] Standards of Responsibility

Contracting officers address two basic issues when making responsibility determinations. The first is whether the prospective contractor will perform the contract. The second is whether the prospective contractor meets the eligibility requirements imposed by statute or regulation for the type of procurement. In the following material, the term "responsibility" is broadly used to encompass all matters relating to determination of contractor eligibility made on a contract-by-contract basis. However, statutes and regulations setting forth collateral social and economic standards of eligibility frequently do not use the term "responsibility."

[1] Performance-Related Standards of Responsibility

Performance-related standards are of two basic types: (1) general standards, which are mandated by the procurement regulations for application to all prospective contractors regardless of whether there is any mention of responsibility in the solicitation; and (2) special standards, or "definitive criteria," which are imposed in the solicitation at the discretion of the contracting officer. Special standards may be desirable when it is evident that unusual expertise or special facilities are needed for adequate contract performance, FAR 9.104-2.

[a] General Standards

General standards of responsibility address two distinct issues relating to whether the prospective contractor will perform in accordance with the contract terms. First, the general standards question whether the contractor possesses *the ability to render satisfactory performance*, that is, whether it can perform the work. Second, the general standards question whether the contractor has *the determination to use this ability* to complete the contract work in a satisfactory manner and whether the contractor has sufficient *integrity* to justify reliance on its agreement to perform.

[i] Ability to Perform

In determining whether a firm possesses the capability to satisfactorily perform the work, the contracting officer considers several distinct aspects of the prospective contractor's business structure.

(A) Financial Resources

A prospective contractor must, according to FAR 9.104-1(a):

> [h]ave adequate financial resources to perform the contract, or the ability to obtain them (see 9.104-3(a)).

Although the FAR does not contain specific guidance on techniques for determining financial responsibility, the criteria in practice are those traditionally used to gauge the financial health of any business organization. They include the ratio of assets to liabilities, working capital, cash flow projections, and credit ratings. Other factors, such as the firm's profitability and the liquidity of assets, are also frequently considered.

The contracting officer has broad discretion to use any current facts indicating financial weakness in making responsibility determinations, *Kompania e Sigurimeve Eurosig Sha,* Comp. Gen. Dec. B-414561.2, 2018 CPD ¶ 21. Thus, GAO has deferred to agency findings of nonresponsibility based on inadequate financial information, *Melbourne Commerce, LLC*, Comp. Gen. B-400049.2, 2009 CPD ¶ 14 (approved bank loan not proof of availability of funds); *Acquest Dev. LLC*, Comp. Gen. B-287439, 2001 CPD ¶ 101 (contradictory information); *West State, Inc.*, Comp. Gen. Dec. B-255693, 94-1 CPD ¶ 211 (contracting officer reasonably determined that the receipt of a judgment and the obtaining of a loan did not cure the negative net worth and negative working capital situation that had led to the prior SBA denial of a COC). Conversely, in *Schwendener/Riteway (J.V.)*, Comp. Gen. Dec. B-250865.2, 93-1 CPD ¶ 203, GAO reversed a finding of nonresponsibility when it concluded that the contracting officer had misinterpreted information concerning the protester's bonding capacity and schedule of values, and had also failed to seek relevant information regarding the true status of its current performance, thereby deciding unreasonably that the protester was financially and otherwise nonresponsible. Similarly, in *ESCO Marine, Inc.* Comp. Gen. Dec. B-401438, 2009 CPD ¶ 234, GAO reversed a finding of responsibility when it found that the contracting officer had miscalculated the amount of funds necessary to perform the contract. See also *CapRock Gov't Solutions, Inc.*, Comp. Gen. Dec. B-402490, 2010 CPD ¶ 124, denying a protest that the contracting officer should not have looked to the parent company's financial situation in finding that the offeror was responsible.

An offeror whose financial resources are questionable may obtain necessary assistance through association with another firm. The form of association may vary. However, if the entity submitting the bid or proposal ceases to exist as a legal entity, award may not be made to the firm that has succeeded to the interests of the offeror. Another limitation is that the transaction may not appear to be the mere transfer of a bid to a nonbidding entity. Contracting officers will consider the extent the assets of the parent company will be available to a joint venture, *Marine Terminals Corp.–East, Inc.*, Comp. Gen. Dec. B-410698.9, 2016 ¶ CPD 212; *FCi Fed., Inc.*, Comp. Gen. Dec., B-408558.7, 2015 CPD ¶ 245; *Ecompex, Inc.*, Comp. Gen. Dec., B-292865.4, 2004 CPD ¶ 149. Arrangements that have been found to be appropriate include the sale of all the offeror's stock to an organization with the necessary financial resources, *Telex Communications, Inc.*, Comp. Gen. Dec. B-212385, 84-1 CPD ¶ 127; and the sale of all the offeror's assets to an organization that has agreed to "assume" all open contracts and has guaranteed the performance of the transaction in question, *Gull Airborne*

Instruments, Inc., 57 Comp. Gen. 67 (B-188743), 77-2 CPD ¶344. In *Gull Airborne*, the transaction was approved on the grounds that the offeror did not cease to exist as a legal entity. GAO appears to have ignored the prohibition against transferring a bid to a nonbidding party. This prohibition will preclude any arrangement involving the acquisition of an offeror with insubstantial assets, *Mil-Tech Sys., Inc. v. United States*, 6 Cl. Ct. 26 (1984). A bidder may demonstrate financial capability by offering a performance bond, 33 Comp. Gen. 549 (B-119030) (1954). See also *G & C Enters., Inc.*, Comp. Gen. Dec. B-186748, 77-1 CPD ¶155, stating that additional resources may be obtained through a subcontractual or guaranteeship arrangement.

The fact that a contractor has filed a petition of bankruptcy does not, per se, require a finding of nonresponsibility, *Verestar Gov't Servs. Group*, Comp. Gen. Dec. B-291854, 2003 CPD ¶68; *Domar Indus. Co.*, Comp. Gen. Dec. B-202735, 81-2 CPD ¶199, but may be considered as a factor in such determination, *Rotech Healthcare, Inc.*, Comp. Gen. Dec. B-409020, 2014 CPD ¶28; *Harvard Interiors Mfg. Co.*, Comp. Gen. B-247400, 92-1 CPD ¶413. The appropriate question is whether the contractor has the necessary financial capability in spite of the bankruptcy.

(B) Ability to Comply with Delivery Schedule

According to FAR 9.104-1(b), a prospective contractor must:

> [b]e able to comply with the required or proposed delivery or performance schedule, taking into consideration all existing commercial and governmental business commitments.

A variety of factors may indicate inability to meet the schedule. See *Gray Graphics Corp.*, Comp. Gen. Dec. B-295421, 2005 CPD ¶37 (GAO deferred to agency's nonresponsibility determination based upon protester's late deliveries under recent contracts); *50 State Security Serv., Inc.*, Comp. Gen. Dec. B-272114, 96-2 CPD ¶123 (GAO upheld contracting officer's determination that the protester did not have the ability to have a sufficient number of guards in place when performance of the contract was to begin because there were only 18 days remaining prior to commencement of contract performance and the protester had not provided a list of names of prospective employees). Other decisions upholding negative responsibility determinations include *Colonial Press Int'l, Inc.*, Comp. Gen. Dec. B-408031, 2013 CPD ¶119 (offeror had made late deliveries in three of 18 orders and had not resolved its underlying performance problems); *Kilgore Flares Co.*, Comp. Gen. Gen. B-292944, 2004 CPD ¶8 (pre-award finding that the lowest priced offeror could not comply with the delivery schedule in the solicitation and also meet concurrent deliveries of the contracts already in place); *System Dev. Corp.*, Comp. Gen. Dec. B-212624, 83-2 CPD ¶644 (failure to present written confirmation of suppliers' and subcontractors' commitments to deliver items and equipment with long lead times); and

Computer Support Sys., Inc., Comp. Gen. Dec. B-261166, 95-2 CPD ¶ 30 (contracting officer observed and obtained information during a preaward survey that it lacked the resources and ability to comply with the IFB's short delivery schedule).

(C) Management and Technical Capability

According to FAR 9.104-1(e), a prospective contractor must:

> [h]ave the necessary organization, experience, accounting and operational controls, and technical skills, or the ability to obtain them (including, as appropriate, such elements as production control procedures, property control systems, quality assurance measures, and safety programs applicable to materials to be produced or services to be performed by the prospective contractor and subcontractors) (see 9.104-3(a)).

The best means of ascertaining whether the offeror has these capabilities is to appraise the offeror's present organization. See, for example, *IPI Graphics*, Comp. Gen. Dec. B-286830, 2001 CPD ¶ 12, 2001, where GAO held an offeror was nonresponsible because the offeror lacked adequate production controls and quality assurance methods to satisfy the quality requirements for printing and finishing. The preaward survey report showed that the offeror's quality control manager lacked knowledge of quality control procedures and test equipment. See also *Omneco, Inc.*, Comp. Gen. Dec. B-218343, 85-1 CPD ¶ 660 (protester's inability to implement an adequate quality assurance program plan in time to meet the performance schedule constituted a reasonable basis for a determination of nonresponsibility); *Products Research & Chem. Corp.*, Comp. Gen. Dec. B-214293, 84-2 CPD ¶ 122 (poor quality control system, production capacity, and purchasing ability); and *Data Integrators, Inc.*, Comp. Gen. Dec. B-410517, 2014 CPD ¶ 382 (offerors could not meet the security requirements of the solicitation.)

When the offeror is a joint venture, the capability of the new entity should be investigated. See *McKissack+Delcan JV II*, Comp. Gen. Dec. B-401973.2, 2010 CPD ¶ 28, holding that it was improper to find the joint venture nonresponsible based on its proposed accounting system when there was no apparent reason why the accounting system was inadequate for the cost-reimbursement contract that was to be awarded.

The determination of capability is often approached by investigating the prior experience of the prospective contractor. Nonresponsibility can be based on either experience demonstrating unsatisfactory performance, *Daisung Co.*, Comp. Gen. Dec. B-294142, 2004 CPD ¶ 196 (contracting officer's nonresponsibility determination reasonably based upon collateral investigations of vendor's poor performance on prior contracts); *Columbus Jack Corp.*, Comp. Gen. Dec. B-211829, 83-2 CPD ¶ 348 (poor quality assurance history), or lack of experience, Comp. Gen. Dec. B-169160, May 4, 1970, *Unpub.* (firm had no experience in type of work being procured). A responsibility finding was properly based on the individual experience of a firm's principal officers in *D.H. Kim Enters., Inc.*, Comp. Gen. Dec. B-255124, 94-1 CPD ¶ 86.

The past performance of a contractor can be used to determine that it does not have the capability to perform the current contract. For example, in *Pittman Mech. Contractors, Inc.*, Comp. Gen. Dec. B-242499, 91-1 CPD ¶ 439, GAO affirmed determinations of nonresponsibility based on a thorough evaluation of the performance records from eight prior contracts. The contracting officers had concluded that this performance record indicated that the contractor had problems with the quality of the work, the timeliness of performance, the effectiveness of management, and compliance with labor and safety standards. Similarly, in *Shepard Printing*, Comp. Gen. Dec. B-260362, 95-2 CPD ¶ 119, GAO agreed with a determination of nonresponsibility based on the contractor's performance record on several recent contracts for the same type of work.

The performance of a predecessor firm may be considered in determining the bidder's technical and management capability. For example, in *Sun Elec. Corp.*, Comp. Gen. Dec. B-202325, 81-2 CPD ¶ 112, although the prospective contractor was not established until 1980, it was the successor in interest to a prior corporation that had manufactured a similar product. The contracting officer properly considered this information in concluding that the prospective awardee had the requisite experience. Similarly, in *Oklahoma County Newspapers, Inc.*, Comp. Gen. Dec. B-270849, 96-1 CPD ¶ 213, the experience of the predecessor firm was relevant because the new firm had retained all of the key employees of the predecessor firm. GAO stated that the "key consideration is whether the experience evaluated reasonably can be considered predictive of the offeror's performance under the contract." See also *GM–Bulltrack, JV*, Comp. Gen. Dec. B-414591.6, 2018 CPD ¶ 378. It is also proper to evaluate the experience of key employees who have worked for another firm, *J.D. Miles & Sons, Inc.*, Comp. Gen. Dec. B-251533, 93-1 CPD ¶ 300; *Hawco Mfg. Co.*, Comp. Gen. Dec. B-265795, 95-2 CPD ¶ 191.

A contracting agency may also consider the experience of an offeror's parent firm in evaluating a proposal where the offeror has represented that all of the parent's resources would be committed to the project, *Tri-Star Indus., Inc.*, Comp. Gen. Dec. B-254767.2, 94-1 CPD ¶ 20; *Hardie-Tynes Mfg. Co.*, 69 Comp. Gen. 359 (B-237938), 90-1 CPD ¶ 347. Compare *FCi Fed., Inc.*, Comp. Gen. Dec. B-408558.7, 2015 CPD ¶ 245, where the contracting officer was required to consider the sale of a parent company as part of the responsibility determination. See *Medical Servs. Consultants, Inc.*, Comp. Gen. Dec. B-203998, 82-1 CPD ¶ 93, where GAO stated that in evaluating the experience of a newly formed subsidiary, an agency could use, but was not obligated to consider, the experience of a parent company.

In evaluating the management and technical capability of a corporation, it is proper to consider the experience of one or more of its principal officers. In *Hydromatics Int'l Corp.*, Comp. Gen. Dec. B-180669, 74-2 CPD ¶ 66, a newly formed company was declared nonresponsible for reasons of inadequate management because the firm's president and general manager had been instrumental in managing contracts awarded to other firms on which there was an unsatisfactory record of performance. Similarly, in *Normandeau Assocs., Inc.*, Comp. Gen. Dec. B- 417136, 2019 CPD ¶ 76, GAO held that an agency could consider the experience of the awardee's proposed personnel who performed similar work. See also *Harbor Servs., Inc.*, Comp. Gen. Dec. B-408325, 2013 CPD ¶ 214; and *Advant–EDGE Solutions, Inc.*, Comp. Gen. Dec. B- 400367.2, 2008 CPD ¶ 210.

(D) Facilities and Equipment

A prospective contractor must, according to FAR 9.104-1(f):

> [h]ave the necessary production, construction, and technical equipment and facilities, or the ability to obtain them (see 9.104-3(a)).

See *S.A.F.E. Export Corp.*, Comp. Gen. Dec. B-208744, 83-1 CPD ¶ 437, *recons. denied*, 83-2 CPD ¶ 90, upholding the contracting officer's determination of nonresponsibility based in part on the fact that S.A.F.E. apparently had no plant in either the United States or Europe, although the prospective contract required work in both places.

Contractors that do not have the necessary equipment and facilities at the time of evaluation for award can demonstrate responsibility by submitting "acceptable evidence" of ability to obtain the required resources, as stated at FAR 9.104-3(a):

> Acceptable evidence normally consists of a commitment or explicit arrangement, that will be in existence at the time of contract award, to rent, purchase, or otherwise acquire the needed facilities, equipment, other resources, or personnel.

In *McLaughlin Research Corp.*, Comp. Gen. Dec. B-247118, 92-1 CPD ¶ 422, GAO found the agency reasonably relied upon an "intent to leave" agreement as demonstrating the awardee's ability to use certain warehouse facilities during its performance; and in *Norfolk Shipbld'g & Drydock Corp.*, Comp. Gen. Dec. B-248549.2, 92-2 CPD ¶ 127, GAO decided a certification of drydocking availability related to a contractor's ability to perform and therefore was a matter of responsibility (not responsiveness) that need only be met prior to award. GAO stated that the solicitation cannot convert a matter of responsibility into one of responsiveness.

Plant and equipment are evaluated for safety as well as capacity to meet contract requirements, and the failure to correct prior safety deficiencies may be a basis for a finding of nonresponsibility, Comp. Gen. Dec. B-175545, Aug. 17, 1972, *Unpub.*

(E) Licenses and Permits

FAR 9.104-1(g) provides a prospective contractor must be "otherwise qualified to receive an award under applicable laws and regulations." The primary application of this provision is with regard to licenses and permits. These decisions, which have been somewhat confusing, focus on whether the licenses and permits are federal, state, or local and whether they are specifically required by the solicitation. Two rules, however, emerge from the decisions on licenses and permits.

First, contracting officers are able to make an affirmative determination of responsibility if the offeror has not obtained the license or permit before award, but can obtain the license or permit before the time of performance, *Impact Instrumentation, Inc.*, Comp. Gen. Dec. B-250968.2, 93-1 CPD ¶241 (premarketing approval by Food & Drug Administration); *Olson & Assocs. Eng'g, Inc.*, Comp. Gen. Dec. B-215742, 84-2 CPD ¶129 (state surveyor's license); *United Seguranca, Ltda.*, Comp. Gen. Dec. B-294388, 2004 CPD ¶207 (security guard licenses); *Solar Plexus, LLC*, Comp. Gen. Dec. B-402061, 2009 CPD ¶256 (state registration as construction contractor).

Second, contracting officers are not required to make negative determination of responsibility when they reasonably concludes that failure to obtain a required or necessary license or permit will not impair performance, *What-Mac Contractors, Inc.*, 58 Comp. Gen. 767 (B-192188), 79-2 CPD ¶179 (state license, not required by solicitation, which state intended to enforce); *U.S. Jet Aviation*, Comp. Gen. Dec. B-214093, 84-1 CPD ¶575 (FAA certificate required by solicitation). Thus, if the contracting officer determines that the work can be performed without the license, it is proper to hold the offeror responsible, *Transcontinental Enters., Inc.*, Comp. Gen. Dec. B-294765, 2004 CPD ¶240 (GAO would not disturb responsibility finding because most of work could be performed without missing permits).

Additionally, the cases discuss the degree of specificity of the solicitation requirement for licenses or permits and whether the contracting officer must consider the lack of a license or permit in making a responsibility determination. Where the solicitation merely includes a statement requiring offerors to "obtain any necessary licenses," as in the Permits and Responsibilities clause for construction contracts in FAR 52.236-7, the contracting officer is not required to consider state or local licenses or permits. The contracting officer can leave the matter of such licenses or permits to be resolved between the contractor and the state or local authorities, *P&R Water Taxi, Ltd.*, Comp. Gen. Dec. B-279014, 98-1 CPD ¶119; *Mercury Bus. Servs., Inc.*, Comp. Gen. Dec. B-237220, 89-2 CPD ¶443; *James C. Bateman Petroleum Servs., Inc.*, 67 Comp. Gen. 591 (B-232325), 88-2 CPD ¶170. But see *BDO USA, LLP*, Comp. Gen. Dec., B-416504.2, 2019 CPD ¶186 (challenge to determination of ineligibility sustained "where the agency failed to consider certain information provided by the protester to establish that it satisfied the facility clearance requirements set forth in the solicitation").

However, the contracting officer may consider lack of such license as bearing on responsibility where the contracting officer reasonably determines that enforcement attempts by state or local officials are likely and there is a reasonable possibility that such enforcement attempts could interrupt and delay performance if award is made to the unlicensed contractor, *Recyc Sys., Inc.*, Comp. Gen. Dec. B-216772, 85-2 CPD ¶ 216; *What-Mac Contractors, Inc.*, 58 Comp. Gen. 767 (B-192188), 79-2 CPD ¶ 179. If the contracting officer does not have reasonable grounds for determining that enforcement attempts by the state will impair performance, the absence of a license or permit cannot properly be considered, *Career Consultants, Inc.*, Comp. Gen. Dec. B-195913, 80-1 CPD ¶ 215. These same rules have been held to be applicable to federal licenses and permits, *Chipman Van & Storage, Inc.*, Comp. Gen. Dec. B-188917, 77-2 CPD ¶ 299. See, however, *What-Mac Contractors, Inc.*, 58 Comp. Gen. 767 (B-192188), 79-2 CPD ¶ 179, which indicates that the contracting officer must make a determination regarding federal licenses or permits in this situation. See also *Israel Aircraft Indus. Ltd.*, Comp. Gen. Dec. B-242552, 91-1 CPD ¶ 454, where denial of an Israeli import license was deemed sufficient to render an offeror nonresponsible; and *Cargo Transport Sys. Co.*, Comp. Gen. Dec. B- 411646.6, 2016 CPD ¶ 294, where the contractor had been evicted from all Kuwaiti port facilities.

License and permit requirement have also been interpreted to be a matter of contract administration rather than a matter of eligibility for award of a contract. See *Nilson Van & Storage, Inc.*, Comp. Gen. Dec. B-403009, 2010 CPD ¶ 198, holding that the IFB statement that "prospective contractors shall be approved and hold" federal and state licenses should be interpreted to allow award to a contractor before the licenses had been obtained. The same result was reached in *Advant–EDGE Solutions, Inc.*, Com. Gen. Dec. B- 400367.2, 2008 CPD ¶ 210, and *United Seguranca, Ltda.*, Comp. Gen. Dec. B-294388, 2004 CPD ¶ 207.

[ii] Will to Perform

This qualification standard is related to whether a prospective contractor has the will to perform, and is treated as an independent basis of responsibility by FAR 9.104-3(b), which states:

> *Satisfactory performance record.* A prospective contractor that is or recently has been seriously deficient in contract performance shall be presumed to be nonresponsible, unless the contracting officer determines that the circumstances were properly beyond the contractor's control, or that the contractor has taken appropriate corrective action. Past failure to apply sufficient tenacity and perseverance to perform acceptably is strong evidence of nonresponsibility. Failure to meet the quality requirements of the contract is a significant factor to consider in determining satisfactory performance. The contracting

> officer shall consider the number of contracts involved and the extent of deficient performance in each contract when making this determination. If the pending contract requires a subcontracting plan pursuant to Subpart 19.7, The Small Business Subcontracting Program, the contracting officer shall also consider the prospective contractor's compliance with subcontracting plans under recent contracts.

FAR 9.104-3(b) creates a strong presumption that a poor performance record indicates a lack of tenacity and perseverance. *See Information Res. Inc.*, Comp. Gen. Dec. B-271767, 96-2 CPD ¶ 38, where GAO upheld the agency's finding that the protester was nonresponsible based on poor past performance while contracts were awarded to other firms with poor records that recently had experienced serious performance deficiencies on similar contracts with the same agency, where the performance records of the other firms were substantially better than the protester's. See also *Mine Safety Appliances Co.*, Comp. Gen. Dec. B-266025, 96-1 CPD ¶ 86, upholding the contracting officer's determination of nonresponsibility based on a history of serious deficient contract performance; and, *Blocacor, LDA,* Comp. Gen. Dec. B-282122.3, 99-2 CPD ¶ 25, finding that the contracting officer reasonably concluded that the protester would have been found nonresponsible based upon dumped materials allegedly traceable to the protester. This presumption that poor performance reflects a lack of tenacity may be applied to the poor performance history of a subcontractor that is proposed for a major portion of the work, *L & M Mercadeo Int'l, S.A.*, Comp. Gen. Dec. B-250637, 93-1 CPD ¶ 124.

Tenacity and perseverance, by their nature, must be determined from past performance, *Ford Motor Co.*, Comp. Gen. Dec. B-207179, 83-1 CPD ¶ 72; *Particle Data, Inc.*, Comp. Gen. Dec. B-179144, 74-2 CPD ¶ 30. This may include performance on both private and government contracts, and such determination must be based on substantial evidence, 51 Comp. Gen. 288 (B-171729) (1971). The fact of poor performance or a default on one or several prior contracts is not per se a sufficient reason for a determination that the contractor lacks the requisite tenacity and perseverance—inquiry must be made into the nature and causes of the poor performance, *Marine Eng'rs Beneficial Ass'n*, Comp. Gen. Dec. B-181265, 74-2 CPD ¶ 298; 39 Comp. Gen. 705 (B-142055) (1960). If the offeror was delinquent in performance of numerous contracts while possessing the necessary equipment and production personnel, a finding of lack of tenacity and perseverance is justified, *Pittman Mech. Contractors, Inc.*, Comp. Gen. Dec. B-242499, 91-1 CPD ¶ 439. In *United Power & Control Sys., Inc.*, Comp. Gen. Dec. B-184662, 78-2 CPD ¶ 436, GAO affirmed the Navy's nonresponsibility determination where the bidder delivered nonconforming items under current government contracts that were similar to those called for in the procurement at hand even though it had the ability to perform.

A contractor may be found nonresponsible for lack of tenacity and perseverance based on prior failures to adhere to contract specifications, *Kennedy Van &*

Storage Co., Comp. Gen. Dec. B-180973, 74-1 CPD ¶ 334, even where the alleged deficiencies are still the subject of dispute between the contractor and the agency, *Halo Optical Prods., Inc.*, Comp. Gen. Dec. B-178573, 74-1 CPD ¶ 263; *Howard Elec. Co.*, 58 Comp. Gen. 303 (B-193899), 79-1 CPD ¶ 137; *Ford Motor Co.*, Comp. Gen. Dec. B-207179, 83-1 CPD ¶ 72. A lack of tenacity or perseverance has been found based on late deliveries caused by factors within the contractor's control, such as poor business practices, *Transport Tire Co.*, Comp. Gen. Dec. B-179098, 74-1 CPD ¶ 27; poor management and technical judgment, *Campbell Indus.*, Comp. Gen. Dec. B-238871, 90-2 CPD ¶ 5; a failure to diligently or aggressively take action to correct production problems, *Marine Eng'rs Beneficial Ass'n*, Comp. Gen. Dec. B-181265, 74-2 CPD ¶ 298; a failure to perform safely on a prior contract, *Air Unlimited*, Comp. Gen. Dec. B-189428, 77-2 CPD ¶ 294; and inadequate surveillance and supervision of subcontractors, *Bill Ward Painting & Decorating*, Comp. Gen. Dec. B-184612, 76-1 CPD ¶ 57. Even though a contractor has substantially performed its prior contracts on time, meeting minimum contract requirements, it may still be found to lack tenacity and perseverance based on the cumulative effect of a number of relatively minor deficiencies that, individually, would not warrant termination for default or finding unsatisfactory performance, 43 Comp. Gen. 257 (B-151121) (1963) (numerous minor deficiencies in performance of 11 of last 12 contracts); 49 Comp. Gen. 139 (B-166969) (1969) (almost 60% of recent contracts not completed on schedule); *Leslie & Elliott Co.*, Comp. Gen. Dec. B-237190, 90-1 CPD ¶ 100 (numerous deficiencies in five previous contracts). But see *Pulse Cos.*, Comp. Gen. Dec. B-184463, 76-1 CPD ¶ 376, where GAO objected to a nonresponsibility determination after the contractor had taken steps necessary to prevent recurrence of deficiencies.

The contracting officer has considerable discretion in determining what information will be used in appraising past performance. See *Standard Register Co.*, Comp. Gen. B-289579, 2002 CPD ¶ 54, where GAO deferred to the agency's decision to use performance at different contract facilities as a measure of nonresponsibility. In *Flameco Div. of Barnes Group, Inc.*, Comp. Gen. Dec. B-243872, 91-2 CPD ¶ 123, a finding of nonresponsibility was properly reached after consultation with the administrative contracting officer and consideration of inadequate performance under prior contracts for manufacture of the same part. See also *S.A.F.E. Export Corp.*, Comp. Gen. Dec. B-208744, 83-1 CPD ¶ 437, where a determination of nonresponsibility was found proper because it was based on default terminations of four previous contracts plus performance difficulties on two others. Even if there have been no default terminations, nonresponsibility can be properly determined based on delinquencies in performance, *Gray Graphics Corp.*, Comp. Gen. Dec. B-295421, 2005 CPD ¶ 37 (agency's nonresponsibility determination was reasonable based on information showing that protester had made late deliveries under recent contracts); *NJCT Corp.*, 64 Comp. Gen. 883 (B-219434), 85-2 CPD ¶ 342 (delinquencies on numerous contracts); *C.W. Girard, C.M.*, 64 Comp. Gen. 175 (B-216004), 84-2 CPD ¶ 704 (a number of delinquencies on one contract); *Pittman Mech. Contractors, Inc.*, Comp. Gen. Dec. B-242243.2, 91-1 CPD ¶ 525 (recent contract performance on similar work inadequate); *Marathon Watch Co., Ltd.*, Comp. Gen. Dec. B-247043, 92-1 CPD ¶ 384 (serious performance problems on four recent contracts). Conversely, the contracting officer may make an affirmative determination of responsibility despite unfavorable information concerning past performance, *REDM Corp.*, Comp. Gen. Dec. B-211197, 83-1 CPD ¶ 428.

Both the FAR and GAO decisions in this area indicate that circumstances surrounding nonperformance must be weighed to ascertain the seriousness of the delinquency in performance. Thus, GAO will not normally review protests of favorable determinations of responsibility even if the successful offeror had a previous contract terminated for default, *Pacific Fabrication*, Comp. Gen. Dec. B-219837.2, 85-2 CPD ¶ 263, or failed to meet obligations on prior contracts, *Norfolk Shipbuilding & Drydock Corp.*, Comp. Gen. Dec. B-218618, 85-1 CPD ¶ 604.

Information necessary to determine responsibility is generally obtained after bid opening or receipt of offer, FAR 9.105-1(b). However, FAR 9.104-6(a) requires the contracting officer to review the Federal Awardee Performance and Integrity Information System (FAPIIS) for adverse information "before award." A determination of nonresponsibility based on unsatisfactory performance is generally based on serious deficiencies in current or recent contracts, FAR 9.104-3(b). In *United Office Machs.*, 56 Comp. Gen. 411 (B-187193), 77-1 CPD ¶ 195, GAO held that the contracting officer's determination of nonresponsibility for lack of tenacity and perseverance may not be based on events that occurred more than three years prior to the determination when there is an adequate record of more recent experience. See *Universal Am. Enters., Inc.*, Comp. Gen. Dec. B-185430, 76-2 CPD ¶ 373, and *Consolidated Airborne Sys., Inc.*, 55 Comp. Gen. 571 (B-183293), 75-2 CPD ¶ 395, indicating that contracts completed within one year of the responsibility determination are "recent" contracts. Compare *Maywood Cab Co.*, Comp. Gen. Dec. B-187550, 77-1 CPD ¶ 288, finding improper a determination of nonresponsibility based on termination for default of similar contracts nine months earlier, where no preaward survey had been conducted in the interim and the deficiencies were readily correctable.

[B] Integrity and Business Ethics

FAR 9.104-1(d) states that a prospective contractor must have "a satisfactory record of integrity and business ethics." FAR 9.104-1(d) does not define the term "integrity"; however, the term generally means probity, honesty, and uprightness. Many of the cases with nonresponsibility determinations based on lack of integrity involve criminal violations—the indictment of an officer and the conviction of an employee of the company for criminal offenses, income tax evasion, and fraud. See also *Traffic Moving Sys., Inc.*, Comp. Gen. Dec.

B-248572, 92-2 CPD ¶ 152, affirming a nonresponsibility determination based upon a prior criminal conviction of the protester's president; and *Myers Investigative & Sec. Servs., Inc.*, Comp. Gen. Dec. B-288468, 2001 CPD ¶ 189, broadly deferring to agency's reasonable determination that awardee was responsible, despite conflicting submissions asserting that awardee may have attempted to mislead agency regarding necessary permits.

Assessments of an offeror's integrity is more complex because contracting officers have more information. The FAPIIS, launched in 2010, has integrated much of the information that a contracting officer is to review in making a responsibility determination with regard to a contractor's past performance and integrity. See FAR 9.104-6. FAPIIS was established under § 872 of the Duncan Hunter National Defense Authorization Act of 2009, Pub. L. No. 110-417. In addition to providing contracting officers with ready access to contractor suspension and debarment information, and to contractor past performance information, FAPIIS also includes nonresponsibility determinations, default terminations, defective pricing determinations, administrative agreements entered into to resolve suspension or debarment proceedings, and information (self-reported by contractors) on criminal convictions, civil judgments, and adverse administrative actions related to past federal contracts or grants. The legislation, and the implementing regulations, give contractors procedural mechanisms in place to challenge adverse information in FAPIIS. See also *Todd Constr., L.P. v. United States*, 94 Fed. Cl. 100 (2010) (Court of Federal Claims had jurisdiction to hear challenges to adverse past performance evaluations, under Contract Disputes Act). Contracting officers must use care in assessing this information because some of it will be based on preliminary determinations of contracting agencies (such as default terminations) that have not yet been finally resolved. However, contracting officers have considerable discretion in this regard. See, for example, *Commissioning Solutions Global, LLC*, Comp. Gen. Dec. B-403542, 2010 CPD ¶ 272, denying a protest that a contracting officer had considered a default termination in evaluating past performance even though it had been converted to a termination for convenience.

Congress amended the statute to require a publicly available website which would contain information in FAPIIS, excluding past performance information. See § 3010 of Pub. L. No. 111-212. While previously much (if not all) of this information had, at least in principle, been available to contracting officials on inquiry, FAPIIS marked a significant step forward in consolidating this adverse information on contractor responsibility as well as making much of the information publicly available on the Internet. FAPIIS marked a high-water mark in a longstanding debate over how much transparency to bring to federal contracting; notably, at roughly the same time, regulators abandoned a parallel initiative to make federal contracts publicly available on the Internet, in part because of concerns over the costs and risks of posting sensitive contractor information in a public forum, 76 Fed. Reg. 7522, Feb. 10, 2011.

Therefore, contracting officers must review the information available in FAPIIS (*www.ppirs.gov*) and other past performance information. Then contracting officers must document how they considered the FAPIIS information before awarding a contract in excess of the simplified acquisition threshold, FAR 9.104-6. FAR Subpart 42.15, which is relevant to the responsibility determination, broadly defines past performance information as information regarding a contractor's actions under previously awarded contracts. Past performance information can include a contractor's record of conforming to contract requirements and standards of good workmanship, the contractor's record of cost control, of meeting contract schedules, the contractor's history of "reasonable and cooperative behavior and commitment to customer satisfaction," certain large contractor's diligence in reporting executive compensation (per FAR Subpart 4.14), the contractor's record of integrity and business ethics, and "the contractor's business-like concern for the interest of the customer."

FAR 3.1002 states that all contractors should have a written code of business ethics and conduct and FAR 3.100a(a) requires that the Contractor Code of Business Ethics and Conduct clause at FAR 52.203-13 be inserted in all contracts over $5.5 million with a performance period of more than 120 days. This clause requires the contractor to make a mandatory report, to the contracting officer and the cognizant inspector general, if the contractor has substantial evidence that the contractor has engaged in certain crimes (such as bribes or gratuities), has received significant overpayments, or has committed a civil fraud in violation of the False Claims Act. See American Bar Association, *Guide to the Mandatory Disclosure Rule* (Huffman & Levy, eds., 2010). This information, as well as administrative settlements regarding such matters must appear in the FAPIIS system. While FAR 3.1003(a)(2) treats these disclosures as causes for suspension or debarment, GAO has held that they also may be used to determine a bidder's integrity, *Drexel Indus., Inc.*, Comp. Gen. Dec. B-189344, 77-2 CPD ¶ 433.

Additionally, findings of lack of integrity have been upheld based on an allegedly false certification submitted under requirements of prior government contracts, *Mayfair Constr. Co.*, Comp. Gen. Dec. B-192023, 78-2 CPD ¶ 187; repeated violations of state environmental laws, *Standard Tank Cleaning Corp.*, Comp. Gen. Dec. B-245364, 92-1 CPD ¶ 3; an indictment that had been dismissed because of procedural deficiencies, *P.T. & L. Constr. Co.*, 55 Comp. Gen. 343 (B-183966), 75-2 CPD ¶ 208; a pending debarment for violations of the Service Contract Act, *Greenwoods's Transfer & Storage Co.*, Comp. Gen. Dec. B-186438, 76-2 CPD ¶ 167; and a plea of nolo contendere in an antitrust case, *Colonial Baking Co.*, Comp. Gen. Dec. B-185305, 76-2 CPD ¶ 59. See also *Garten-und Landschaftsbau GmbH Frank Mohr*, Comp. Gen. Dec. B-237276, 90-1 CPD ¶ 186, and *Frank Cain & Sons, Inc.*, Comp. Gen. Dec. B-236893, 90-1 CPD ¶ 44 (reasonable determination that protester was nonresponsible based upon a criminal investigation report that called into question the protester's integrity under recent procurements); *Becker & Schwindenhammer, GmbH*,

Comp. Gen. Dec. B-225396, 87-1 CPD ¶ 235 (contracting officer properly relied on an Army CID report of improper substitution of materials to support nonresponsibility determination); *Americana de Comestibles S.A.*, Comp. Gen. Dec. B-210390, 84-1 CPD ¶ 289 (proper nonresponsibility determination based on confidential information contained in a discontinued Army CID investigative file

Contracting officers can also exercise discretion in concluding that the evidence is not sufficient to call for a nonresonsibility determination. See *ANHAM FZCO,* Comp. Gen. Dec. B-415969, 2018 CPD ¶ 184 (allegations relating to the chairman and his relationship with parent company were considered as part of the affirmative responsibility determination); *DynCorp Int'l LLC*, Comp. Gen. Dec. B-411465, 2015 CPD ¶ 228 (proper affirmative responsibility determination because the contracting officer reasonably considered the pending False Claims Act litigation within the broader context of the awardee's present responsibility); *Universal Techs. Inc.*, Comp. Gen. Dec. B-248808.2, 92-2 CPD ¶ 212 (failure to identify criminal convictions did not influence an affirmative responsibility determination because it was not made in bad faith); and *Tutor-Saliba Corp.*, Comp. Gen. Dec. B-255756, 94-1 CPD ¶ 223 (allegations of involvement in Brazilian government scandals found to be insubstantial).

Determinations of nonresponsibility may be based on the lack of integrity of those having close relationships with the offeror. In *Bilfinger Berger AG Sede Secondaria Italiana*, Comp. Gen. Dec. B-402496, 2010 CPD ¶ 125, GAO upheld a nonresponsibility determination based on the fact that a related company had been debarred and the two companies had shared resources. See also *Speco Corp.*, Comp. Gen. Dec. B-211353, 83-1 CPD ¶ 458 (lack of integrity of a bidder's key employee properly constituted grounds for finding bidder nonresponsible when it appeared that significant influence might be exercised by the key employee in performance of the contract); *Americana de Comestibles S.A.*, Comp. Gen. Dec. B-210390, 84-1 CPD ¶ 289 (unsatisfactory record of integrity of company's president deemed sufficient in itself to justify the contracting officer's finding that the firm was not responsible). *Compare Najlaa Int'l Catering Servs.*, Comp. Gen. Dec. B-402434, 2010 CPD ¶ 107, holding that the contracting officer had properly found a company responsible even though a former director had bribed an agency to obtain a contract because the director had acted independently and the company had dismissed him when it learned of this conduct.

Similarly, the integrity of a predecessor firm may be considered in determining the responsibility of a bidder. In *R.H. Ritchey*, Comp. Gen. Dec. B-205602, 82-2 CPD ¶ 28, GAO based its nonresponsibility determination on the fact that the managing partner of the predecessor firm had been convicted of false pretenses in connection with a previous contract. A low bidder's relationship with another contractor that, it was conceded, lacked integrity, may also support a finding of nonresponsibility, *John Carlo, Inc.*, Comp. Gen. Dec. B-204928, 82-1 CPD ¶ 184. In that case, although the protester argued there was no substantial relationship between it and the disreputable contractor, GAO found that there were both past and present dealings between the two contractors in which the protester allowed the other to both bid and perform work in the protester's name.

Determinations of nonresponsibility based upon lack of integrity involve special considerations because of the rule requiring "due process" if such a determination "stigmatizes" the offeror, *Old Dominion Dairy Prods., Inc. v. Secretary of Def.*, 631 F.2d 953 (D.C. Cir. 1980); *Related Indus., Inc. v. United States*, 2 Cl. Ct. 517 (1983). See *Omneco, Inc.*, Comp. Gen. Dec. B-218343, 85-1 CPD ¶ 660, stating that this rule does not apply to an initial determination of nonresponsibility. The elements of such "due process" are discussed below. See also *Afghan Am. Army Servs. Corp. v. United States*, 106 Fed. Cl. 714 (2012) (finding an abuse of discretion when the contracting officer declared the protester nonresponsible because it had been proposed for debarment but had been given no opportunity to respond to the charges that it had forged documents); *NEIE, Inc. v. United States*, No. 13-164 C, 2013 WL 6406992, 2013 U.S. Claims LEXIS 1909 (Nov. 26, 2013) (finding an abuse of discretion when the protester had been given no opportunity to respond to charges of misrepresentation).

[1] Special Standards

Contracting officers are permitted to define more specific responsibility criteria by including special standards of responsibility, sometimes called "definitive performance criteria," in the solicitation. Such definitive responsibility criteria "concern the capability of the offeror, not a specific product, and they are objective standards established by the agency as a precondition to award," *Vador Ventures, Inc.*, Comp. Gen. Dec. B-296394, 2005 CPD ¶ 155. Definitive responsibility criteria are specific and objective standards established by an agency for use in a particular procurement to measure an offeror's ability to perform the contract, *Great Lakes Dredge & Dock Co., LLC*, Comp. Gen. Dec. B-416073, 2018 CPD ¶ 194. Discussing such definitive responsibility criteria, FAR 9.104-2(a) states:

> When it is necessary for a particular acquisition or class of acquisitions, the contracting officer shall develop, with the assistance of appropriate specialists, special standards of responsibility. Special standards may be particularly desirable when experience has demonstrated that unusual expertise or specialized facilities are needed for adequate contract performance. The special standards shall be set forth in the solicitation (and so identified) and shall apply to all offerors.

As noted above, although GAO generally bars protests involving affirmative responsibility determinations, GAO left the door open to protests "that allege that definitive responsibility criteria in the solicitation were not met," 4 C.F.R. § 21.5(c). Thus, despite GAO's general reluctance to review agencies' determinations that contractors *are* responsible, GAO will still allow protests that challenge an agency's failure to enforce such definitive responsibility criteria. See *Public Facility Consortium I, LLC*, Comp. Gen. B-295911, 2005 CPD ¶ 170 (discussing exception).

As GAO noted in *Charter Envtl., Inc.*, Comp. Gen. Dec. B-297219, 2005 CPD ¶ 213, definitive responsibility criteria, "limit the class of contractors to those meeting specified qualitative and quantitative qualifications necessary for adequate performance, e.g., unusual expertise or specialized facilities" because definitive responsibility criteria are a precondition to award. Special standards must be thoughtfully drawn since they limit competition. However, when special standards are based on essential government needs, the special standard effectively narrows the field of eligible firms warning unqualified firms not to expend needless effort in preparing offers. In *Great Lakes Dredge & Dock Co., LLC*, Comp. Gen. Dec. B-416073, 2018 CPD ¶ 194, GAO stated that special standards of responsibility limit the class of bidders to those meeting specified qualitative and quantitative qualifications necessary for adequate contract performance.

Contracting officers may not waive special standards of responsibility, *Mary Kathleen Collins Trust*, Comp. Gen. Dec. B-261019.2, 96-1 CPD ¶ 164. Thus, GAO will overrule an affirmative determination of responsibility when the contracting officer does not have a reasonable basis to conclude that the bidder satisfies a special responsibility standard, *George Hyman Constr. Co.*, Comp. Gen. Dec. B-265798, 95-2 CPD ¶ 173 (there was a "reasonable possibility of prejudice" in the waiver of a "very restrictive" key personnel experience requirement). But see *Great Lakes Dredge & Dock Co., LLC*, Comp. Gen. Dec. B-416073, 2018 CPD ¶ 194, stating that a contracting agency has broad discretion to determine whether a bidder meets definitive responsibility criteria, since the agency bears the brunt of any difficulties experienced in obtaining the required performance. Nevertheless, the contracting officer must obtain evidence that an offeror meets the criteria since compliance is a prerequisite to award. Therefore, GAO will review the record to determine whether evidence of compliance reasonably demonstrates the criterion has been met. See also *Firma Hermann Leis,* Comp. Gen. Dec. B- 295956, 2005 CPD ¶ 102 ("In determining compliance with a definitive responsibility criterion, in the absence of RFP language to the contrary, an agency may consider the experience of the corporation's principal officers, the experience of the firm's employees, and the experience of a predecessor company acquired by the 'bidding entity.'"); *Evans, Inc.*, Comp. Gen. Dec. B-216260.2, 85-1 CPD ¶ 535 (regular dealer permitted to certify as manufacturer). See also *Aero Sys., Inc.*, Comp. Gen. Dec. B-215892, 84-2 CPD ¶ 374, where GAO determined that despite the offeror's failure to meet the precise definitive criteria, it could still be found responsible because it had clearly demonstrated that it had equivalent capability (possession of Canadian license instead of FAR 13.5 certificate), and *Stocker & Yale, Inc.*, Comp. Gen. Dec. B-238251, 90-1 CPD ¶ 475, where the agency's right to determine if an awardee's licenses were the equivalent of the IFB requirements was acknowledged. This discretion is not granted, however, if the definitive criteria are stated with specificity, *Power Sys.*, Comp. Gen. Dec. B-210032, 83-2 CPD ¶232. In that case, the solicitation required experience on the same product offered in the bid, and GAO ruled that experience on no other product would suffice.

Additionally, definitive criteria must be necessary to assure satisfaction of the government's needs. See *Software City*, Comp. Gen. Dec. B-217542, 85-1 CPD ¶475, concurring with an agency requirement that offerors present a letter from the source of the goods guaranteeing the supply of the product because the agency needed a continuous supply. Compare *Keeson, Inc.*, Comp. Gen. Dec. B-245625, 92-1 CPD ¶108, finding the provisions on regulatory violations and prior defaults unreasonably broad and the provision requiring that the organization have five years' experience unduly restrictive in that it did not recognize experience of the personnel working for the organization. See also *Haughton Elevator Div., Reliance Elec. Co.*, 55 Comp. Gen. 1051 (B-184865), 76-1 CPD ¶294, where GAO found that an experience requirement was unduly restrictive because the awardee, while not meeting the requirement, was successfully performing the contract. In *International Computaprint Corp.*, 55 Comp. Gen. 1043 (B-185403), 76-1 CPD ¶289, and *Topley Realty Co.*, 65 Comp. Gen. 510 (B-221459), 86-1 CPD ¶398, GAO found definitive responsibility criteria unduly restrictive because the agency had ignored the requirement in making the award. To the extent that a special standard requires the offeror to complete a "testing or other quality assurance demonstration" before award, it must be justified in writing pursuant to 10 U.S.C. §3243 (formerly §2319) or 41 U.S.C. §3311. See FAR Subpart 9.2. In *Altex Enters., Inc.*, 67 Comp. Gen. 184 (B-228200), 88-1 CPD ¶7, GAO overturned a blanket requirement that all individual sureties provide a first deed of trust on the unencumbered value of real estate because no unusual circumstances justified the blanket requirement.

In addition, solicitation provisions must be specific, objective, and mandatory to qualify as definitive responsibility criteria, *John C. Grimberg Co. v. United States*, 185 F.3d 1297 (Fed. Cir. 1999). See *Eggs & Bacon, Inc.*, Comp. Gen. Dec. B-402591.2, 2010 CPD ¶193 ("in order to be a definitive responsibility criterion, the solicitation provision must reasonably inform offerors that they must demonstrate compliance with the standard as a precondition to receiving the award"). In *Weldtest, Inc.*, Comp. Gen. Dec. B-216747.2, 84-2 CPD ¶612, a requirement that "offerors may be required to prove that they have experience in comparable work" was held to be neither "specific and objective" nor "mandatory." Similarly, a solicitation provision enumerating the requirements in FAR 9.104 did not create definitive responsibility criteria, *MPC Containment Sys., LLC*, Comp. Gen. Dec. B-416188.2, 2018 CPD ¶251. In *AT&T Corp.*, Comp. Gen. Dec. B-260447.4, 96-1 CPD ¶200, GAO found a lack of specificity when the solicitation stated that the "facilities and services under the contract shall be in accordance with all applicable tariffs, rates, charges, rules, regulations or requirements of the FCC." Similarly, a provision "reserving the right" to consider performance in the last two years was held not to meet these requirements, *Old Dominion Sec.*, Comp. Gen. Dec. B-216534, 85-1 CPD ¶78, and a requirement for "corporate experience" was held not to be sufficiently specific or objective, *Alliance Props. Inc.*, Comp. Gen. Dec. B-214769, 84-2 CPD ¶ 14. Compare *J. Baranello & Sons*, 58 Comp. Gen. 509 (B-192221), 79-1 CPD ¶ 322, where the standards were met by a solicitation requiring three years' experience and installation of comparable equipment on two prior projects.

Additionally, it is important to distinguish definitive responsibility criteria from specification requirements. In *ARI Phoenix, Inc.*, Comp. Gen. Dec. B-416878, 2018 CPD ¶ 363, a requirement that the awardee actually perform with employees possessing the appropriate certification required by the RFQ was a matter of contract administration because it was not as part of the evaluation criteria and the RFQ contained no language requiring offerors to establish their qualifications before award. Similarly, in *Power Testing Inc.*, Comp. Gen. Dec. B-197190, 80-2 CPD ¶ 72, GAO characterized a statement in the solicitation requiring the contractor to use a foreperson with at least five years' experience as a statement of how the work was to be performed rather than an aspect of responsibility that had to be satisfied at the time of award. See also *Thames Towboat Co.*, Comp. Gen. Dec. B-282982, 99-2 CPD ¶ 100 ("Specifications of minimum technical requirements do not establish standards relating to an offeror's ability to perform the contract," and thus do not reflect responsibility; "rather, they describe the item offerors are to furnish if they are awarded the contract."). Compare *J2A2 JV, LLC*, Comp. Gen. Dec. B-401663.4, 2010 CPD ¶ 102 ("requirements that a prospective contractor have a specified number of years of experience in a particular area and a designated number of projects completed within a specified time period are definitive responsibility criteria; that is, they are specific and objective standards designed to measure a prospective contractor's ability to perform the contract"). Specification statements rather than definitive responsibility criteria were also found in *Markhurd Aerial Surveys, Inc.*, Comp. Gen. Dec. B-210108, 83-1 CPD ¶ 51 (solicitation requirement stated that the contractor was required to use personnel with minimum crew experience); *Data Gen. Corp.*, Comp. Gen. Dec. B-252239, 93-1 CPD ¶ 457 (solicitation stated that "all personnel performing under the resulting contract must have a minimum of one year experience" in similar work); and *Satellite Servs., Inc.*, Comp. Gen. Dec. B-219679, 85-2 CPD ¶ 224 (solicitation stated that all personnel must be fully qualified to perform).

Moreover, in order to properly find that an awardee meets the criteria, an agency must base its determination upon adequate and objective evidence, *T. Warehouse Corp.*, Comp. Gen. Dec. B-248951, 92-2 CPD ¶ 235. In that case, GAO reviewed the facts and determined that they did not support the agency's determination that the criteria had been met. Similarly, in *Prime Mortgage Corp.*, 69 Comp. Gen. 618 (B-238680.2), 90-2 CPD ¶ 48, GAO reversed a finding of responsibility when the contracting officer had no objective evidence that the offeror had $100,000 working capital as required by the solicitation. Compare *Coastal Elecs., Inc.*, Comp. Gen. Dec. B-250718, 93-1 CPD ¶ 144, where GAO reviewed certificates of training and determined that they met the criteria. See also *Reyna–Capital Joint Venture*, Comp. Gen. Dec. B-408541, 2013 CPD ¶ 253 (record showed the awardee met the IFB's licensing requirements submitting copies of a Texas electrical contractor license and Texas master electrician licenses for four personnel with its bid); and *US21, Inc.*, Comp. Gen. Dec. B-411561, 2015 CPD ¶ 264, (contracting officer could rely on the awardee's submission of a Certificates of Analysis (CoA) to determine the awardee meet the definitive responsibility requirement to have a CoA from all suppliers listed on the offeror's Fuel Source Data Sheet).

A contract requirement that a commercial product be furnished is not a definitive responsibility criterion, *PTR-Precision Techs., Inc.*, Comp. Gen. Dec. B-243439, 91-2 CPD ¶ 110; *Blue Tee Corp.*, Comp. Gen. Dec B-246623, 92-1 CPD ¶ 289. See also *Symtron Sys., Inc.*, Comp. Gen. Dec. B-242244, 91-1 CPD ¶ 282, holding that a commercial product requirement involves an affirmative determination of responsibility and generally is not reviewable.

One of the most common types of special standards deals with experience requirements. GAO has recognized the propriety of limiting contract awards to those bidders that have had a minimum amount of experience doing work comparable to that required by the contract, 35 Comp. Gen. 161 (B-124614) (1955) (service contract); *American Sterilizer Co.*, Comp. Gen. Dec. B-207518, 82-2 CPD ¶ 453 (supply contract for biohazardous use); *Karl Doll GmbH*, Comp. Gen. Dec. B-213556, 84-1 CPD ¶ 604 (boiler firing services); *Urban Masonry Corp.*, Comp. Gen. Dec. B-213196, 84-1 CPD ¶ 48 (erection of precast concrete); *R.R. Mongeau Eng'rs, Inc.*, Comp. Gen. Dec. B-213330, 84-1 CPD ¶ 333 (installation of cathodic protection equipment). GAO has accepted the use of such provisions where the interests of the government would thereby be served, provided that the special standards are included in the invitation, 37 Comp. Gen. 196 (B-133707) (1957); 45 Comp. Gen. 4 (B-156520) (1965).

Requirements for special facilities have also been expressed as definitive responsibility criteria, *Aero Corp.*, Comp. Gen. Dec. B-201581, 81-1 CPD ¶ 338. See *Auto Discount Rent-N-Drive Sys., Inc.*, Comp. Gen. Dec. B-197236, 80-2 CPD ¶ 73, finding that a requirement that the awardee demonstrate that its dispatching facility was located in a certain geographical area was a definitive criterion. Other decisions upholding definitive responsibility criteria include *Ampex Corp.*, Comp. Gen. Dec. B-212356, 83-2 CPD ¶ 565 (business reference requirements); *United States Crane Certification Bureau, Inc.*, Comp. Gen. Dec. B-197433, 80-1 CPD ¶ 247 (accreditation requirements); *School for Educ. Enrichment*, Comp. Gen. Dec. B-199003, 80-2 CPD ¶ 286; *E.J. Nachtwey*, Comp. Gen. Dec. B-209562, 83-1 CPD ¶ 104 (music degree from a special music school); and *Townsco Contracting Co.*, Comp. Gen. Dec. B-240289, 90-2 CPD ¶ 313 (requirement for bidders that have been regularly engaged "in airfield paving for the three years immediately preceding").

Definitive responsibility criteria can be demonstrated by showing that affiliates or subcontractors meet the criteria, *Tutor-Saliba Corp.*, Comp. Gen. Dec. B-255756, 94-1 CPD ¶ 223. In that case, GAO stated:

> As a general rule, the experience of a technically qualified subcontractor or third party—such as an affiliate or consultant—may be used to satisfy definitive responsibility criteria relating to experience for a prospective prime contractor. *Gelco Servs., Inc.*, B-253376, Sept. 14, 1993, 93-2 CPD ¶ 163, *recon. denied*, B-253376.2, Oct. 27, 1993, 93-2 CPD ¶ 261; *Tama Kensetsu Co., Ltd, and Nippon Hodo*, B-233118, Feb. 8, 1989, 89-1 CPD ¶ 128. However, where a solicitation contains a criterion which by its express language prohibits satisfying a particular experience requirement through the experience of a prospective subcontractor, such a provision limits the prime contractor from relying on a subcontractor to comply with the experience criterion. See *Allen-Sherman-Hoff Co.*, B-231552, Aug. 4, 1988, 88-2 CPD ¶ 116.

GAO has also held that a joint venture meets a definitive criteria requirement if only one of the venturers satisfies the requirement, *Hellenic Technodomiki, S.A.*, Comp. Gen. Dec. B-265931, 96-1 CPD ¶ 91. Experience of employees working for other companies can also be used to demonstrate that the offeror meets an experience requirement, *Tucson Mobilephone, Inc.*, Comp. Gen. Dec. B-258408.3, 95-1 CPD ¶ 267. In the same vein, GAO found that the explicit requirement to include a copy of an actual Saudi business license created a definitive responsibility; however, an offeror could satisfy the licensing requirement by maintaining a sponsorship or teaming effort with a Saudi Arabian company, *Dalma Tech2 Co.*, Comp. Gen. Dec. B-411015, 2015 CPD ¶ 135.

While GAO generally will not review the SBA's refusal or decision to issue a COC because SBA has conclusive authority to determine a small business firm's responsibility, GAO will consider whether the solicitation contains definitive responsibility criteria and compliance with those criteria, *MPC Containment Sys., LLC*, Comp. Gen. Dec. B-416188.2, 2018 CPD ¶ 251.

[2] Collateral Requirements

Offerors that do not meet specific requirements imposed by statute or regulation may be excluded from contracting even though they appear otherwise fully able and willing to perform the work specified in the solicitation. These requirements are termed "collateral" because they are not involved with the performance of the work called for by the contract. In some cases, they are closely related to the responsibility issue, while in others they are separate eligibility considerations. See, however, FAR 9.104-1(g) (to be determined responsible, prospective contractor must be "otherwise qualified and eligible to receive an award under applicable laws and regulations"), which apparently makes all such issues matters of responsibility.

[a] Equal Employment Opportunity

The equal employment opportunity policies of the federal government are covered in Chapter 14. A major element of these policies is the development of affirmative action plans and programs. FAR 22.802(b) prohibits award of a contract to a person "who has been found ineligible" by the Office of Federal Contract Compliance Programs (OFCCP) of the Department of Labor. In addition, 41 C.F.R. § 60-2.2(b) requires a nonresponsibility determination if a contracting officer finds that a contractor does not have an affirmative action program that complies with the government's standards. See 51 Comp. Gen. 551 (B-174816) (1972), where GAO, citing 41 C.F.R. § 60-2.2, stated that the contracting officer was correct in finding the prospective contractor nonresponsible because the contractor was not in compliance with the equal employment opportunity requirements at one of its establishments.

For awards of contracts of $10 million or more, excluding construction, the contracting officer must request a clearance from the OFCCP before award of the contract, FAR 22.805(a).

[b] Small Business Subcontracting

In 1978, Pub. L. No. 95-507 amended 15 U.S.C. § 637 to require that solicitations for certain contracts that offer subcontracting possibilities contain a clause requiring any bidder who is selected for award to submit a detailed small business subcontracting plan to the procuring agency. FAR 19.702(a) applies this to solicitations for over $700,000 ($1.5 million for construction). 15 U.S.C. § 637(d)(5)(B) indicates that failure to comply with these requirements will result in a nonresponsibility determination:

> If, within the time limit prescribed in regulations of the Federal agency concerned, the bidder selected to be awarded the contract fails to submit the subcontracting plan required by this paragraph, such bidder shall become ineligible to be awarded the contract. Prior compliance of the bidder with other subcontracting plans shall be considered by the Federal agency in determining the responsibility of such bidder for the award of the contract. The subcontracting plan of the bidder awarded the contract shall be included in and made a material part of the contract.

See *Devcon Sys. Corp.*, Comp. Gen. Dec. B-197935, 80-2 CPD ¶ 46, affirming the contracting officer's holding that submission of a small business subcontracting plan is a matter of responsibility rather than responsiveness, and permitting the firm, until the time of award, to submit an acceptable plan. Accord *A.B. Dick Co.*, Comp. Gen. Dec. B-233142, 89-1 CPD ¶ 106. Thus, because the negotiation and ultimate approval of a subcontracting plan involved a question of the successful offeror's responsibility, those negotiations do not involve evaluation and discussion of the successful offeror's proposal, and do not trigger the obligation to open discussions with all offerors, *General Dynamics—Ordnance & Tactical Sys.*, Comp. Gen. Dec. B-295987, 2005 CPD ¶ 114; *AmClyde Engineered Prods. Co.*, Comp. Gen. Dec. B-282,271, 99-2 CPD ¶ 5; *Kahn Instruments, Inc.*, Comp. Gen. Dec. B-277973, 98-1 CPD ¶ 11. See also *Columbia Research Corp.*, 61 Comp. Gen. 194 (B-202762), 82-1 CPD ¶ 8, finding a 16-page plan adequate although the offeror proposed no small business subcontracts for the procurement under consideration.

[c] Government Employees

An agency's decision to contract with a firm directly or indirectly controlled by a government employee raises unique, and potentially serious, issues of responsibility because of potential conflicts of interest. See generally Luci, Jr., *Contracting with Government Employees: An Overly Restrictive Rule, A Comparison, and a Compromise,* 27 Pub. Cont. L.J. 37 (1997). FAR 3.601(a) provides explicit policy guidance on contracting with employees of the federal government:

> Except as specified in 3.602, a contracting officer shall not knowingly award a contract to a Government employee or to a business concern or other organization owned or substantially owned or controlled by one or more Government employees. This policy is intended to avoid any conflict of interest that might arise between the employees' interests and their Government duties, and to avoid the appearance of favoritism or preferential treatment by the Government toward its employees.

GAO's decision in *Valiant Sec. Agency*, Comp. Gen. Dec. B-205087, 81-2 CPD ¶ 367, *recons. denied*, 81-2 CPD ¶ 501, explained:

> Contracts between the Government and its employees are not expressly prohibited by statute except where the employee acts for both the Government and the contractor in a particular transaction or where the service to be rendered is such as could be required of the contractor in his capacity as a Government employee. 18 U.S.C. § 208 (1976); *Hugh Maher*, B-187841, March 31, 1977, 77-1 CPD ¶ 204. However, it has long been recognized that such contracts are undesirable because among other reasons they invite criticism as to alleged favoritism and possible fraud and that they should be authorized only in exceptional cases where the Government cannot reasonably be otherwise supplied. 27 Comp. Gen. 735 (1948); *Capital Aero, Inc.*, B-183833, September 30, 1975, 75-2 CPD ¶ 201; *Burgos & Associates, Inc.*, 59 Comp. Gen. 273 (1980), 80-1 CPD ¶ 55. The fact that a service would be more expensive if not obtained from an employee of the Government does not by itself provide support for a determination that the service cannot reasonably be obtained from other sources. 55 Comp. Gen. 681 [B-184716] (1976).

The sole exception to the prohibition in FAR 3.601 is in FAR 3.602, which requires a determination by a high-level official that there is a "most compelling reason to [enter into a contract], such as when the Government's needs cannot reasonably be otherwise met." The contracting officer has discretion in determining whether this exemption applies. Compare the *Valiant* case with *International Alliance of Sports Officials*, Comp. Gen. Dec. B-210172, 83-2 CPD ¶ 328, sustaining a contracting officer's decision to award a contract to an employee-owned company at approximately $223,000 in contrast to the next low offer of $275,000.

Substantial ownership or control is determined by the facts of each individual case. Mere employment by a government contractor is not prohibited by this restriction. See *National Serv. Corp.*, Comp. Gen. Dec. B-205629, 82-2 CPD ¶ 76 (no substantial ownership or control when government employee gave up partnership and became part-time bookkeeper); *HH & K Bldrs., Inc.*, Comp. Gen. Dec. B-238095, 90-1 CPD ¶ 219 (sole owner's husband was government employee, but sufficient separation of ownership). Compare *Electronics W., Inc.*, Comp. Gen. Dec. B-209720, 83-2 CPD ¶ 127 (change in title from president to treasurer did not prevent disqualification). An agency does not have to establish with certainty that an employee has a substantially controlling interest but rather need only have "a reason to believe" that the government employee has such control, *Gurley's, Inc.*, Comp. Gen. Dec. B-253852, 93-2 CPD ¶ 123. See *Elogene Thurman*, Comp. Gen. Dec. B-206325, 82-1 CPD ¶ 487 (award to wife of government employee improper when husband in fact ran the business); *Applied Res. Corp.*, Comp. Gen. Dec. B-249258, 92-2 CPD ¶ 272 (disqualification proper where spouse of firm's president was the contracting officer's supervisor and relationship was not disclosed on financial disclosure form); *American Truss & Mfg. Corp.*, Comp. Gen. Dec. B-205962, 82-1 CPD ¶ 477 (award improper where government employee owned 50% of stock and wife owned balance); *Marc Indus.*, Comp. Gen. Dec. B-246528, 92-1 CPD ¶ 273 (substantial control found where government employee represented the firm in prework conferences under prior contracts with the agency, served as the contact for any complaints about contract performance, and, based on his involvement with the firm, was disciplined for violating his agency's conflict of interest regulations); and *KSR, Inc.*, Comp. Gen. Dec. B-250160, 93-1 CPD ¶ 37 (substantial control found where government employee was president and was one of five owners).

Some agencies have restrictions on dealing with close relatives of employees. See *Joann Flora*, Comp. Gen. Dec. B-212776, 83-2 CPD ¶ 520 (regulation prohibiting contract with "immediate member of the household" of agency employee barred contract with unmarried party living as spouse); and *Heidi Holley*, Comp. Gen. Dec. B-211746, 83-2 CPD ¶ 241 (regulations stating that contracts should generally not be awarded to members of an agency employee's family and requiring close scrutiny barred award to spouse of agency employee required to supervise contract). However, see *J. Allen Grafton*, Comp. Gen. Dec. B-212986, 84-1 CPD ¶ 263, in which GAO found that an agency unreasonably rejected a quotation from the son of an agency employee, when there was no showing that the employee had responsibility for the resulting contract and no indication that the father had disclosed any confidential agency information or otherwise influenced the procurement.

If the contracting officer inadvertently makes an award to a company owned or controlled by a government employee, GAO will not disturb the award absent an indication of favoritism or other impropriety, *Sterling Med. Assocs.*, Comp. Gen. Dec. B-209493, 83-1 CPD ¶ 215; *Biosystems Analysis, Inc.*, Comp. Gen. Dec. B-198846, 80-2 CPD ¶ 149. In both cases, the employee worked for an agency other than the one awarding the contract.

[d] Guard and Security Service

The Anti-Pinkerton Act of 1893, a very dated statutory bar against contracting for armed guards, is set forth at 5 U.S.C. § 3108, and states:

> An individual employed by the Pinkerton Detective Agency, or similar organization, may not be employed by the Government of the United States or the government of the District of Columbia.

This Act has been narrowly construed by FAR 37.109, to bar only the hiring of "quasi-military armed forces," by stating:

> Contracts with "Pinkerton Detective Agencies or similar organizations" are prohibited by 5 U.S.C. § 3108. This prohibition applies only to contracts with organizations that offer quasi-military armed forces for hire, or with their employees, regardless of the contract's character. An organization providing guard or protective services does not thereby become a "quasi-military armed force," even though the guards are armed or the organization provides general investigative or detective services.

This guidance limiting the application of the Act to "quasi-military" forces is derived from *United States ex rel. Weinberger v. Equifax, Inc.*, 557 F.2d 456 (5th Cir. 1977), *cert. denied*, 434 U.S. 1035 (1978). It was adopted by GAO in 57 Comp. Gen. 524 (B-139965) (1978). In *Old Dominion Security*, Comp. Gen. Dec. B-216534, 85-1 CPD ¶ 78, it was held that the low bidder was not precluded by the Anti-Pinkerton Act from receiving a contract for security guard services since all personnel assigned to the project were licensed and employed solely as uniformed security guards. Whether a prospective contractor must be precluded from government contracting due to the Anti-Pinkerton Act is a matter for contracting officer determination subject to GAO review, *Inter-Con Sec. Sys., Inc.*, Comp. Gen. Dec. B-192188, 79-1 CPD ¶ 86. Notably, GAO in 1978 itself questioned the continuing relevance of the Anti-Pinkerton Act, 57 Comp. Gen. 524 (B-139965), and others have noted that the Act may not be viable, given the vast increase in the use of private armed guards by the government, including the use of private guards to defend highly sensitive missions abroad. See Davidson, *Ruck Up: An Introduction to the Legal Issues Associated with Civilian Contractors on the Battlefield,* 29 Pub. Cont. L.J. 233, 253-54 (2000).

§4.03 ORGANIZATIONAL CONFLICTS OF INTEREST

Organizational conflicts of interest (OCIs) may arise when the award of a government contract creates bias or provides an unfair competitive advantage. The policy on OCIs started with a 1963 memorandum from the Department of Defense directing contracting officers to ensure the award of a contract was conflict free. The 1963 policy memorandum became an appendix in the Armed Services Procurement Regulation, which then became subpart 9.5 of the FAR.

Although subpart 9.5 has not changed significantly since 1963, OCIs have evolved into a dynamic area of government contracting. Methods to resolve OCIs became less effective and the conflicts became more complex. Three reasons explain this phenomenon: consolidation within the industries serving the federal government; an increased reliance on contractor services, requiring the use of subjective judgment to perform functions once done by government employees; and a greater use of IDIQ contracts, which have broad and less specific statements of work. See Gordon, *Organizational Conflicts of Interest: A Growing Integrity Challenge,* 35 Pub. Cont. L.J. 25 (2005).

Litigation on OCIs began in the late 1980's challenging the discretionary application of FAR subpart 9.5. These protests at GAO and the Court of Federal Claims show that it is difficult to identify and resolve conflicts and that the factually intense nature of OCIs requires tailored resolutions based on the particular facts of each conflict.

FAR subpart 9.5 contains competing obligations for contracting officers. FAR 9.506(d)(3) requires that they resolve conflicts before award, but FAR 9.504 also requires that they provide reasonable opportunities to avoid disqualification. In addition, FAR subpart 9.5 gives contracting officers two primary duties: "identify" whether a conflict exists and "resolve" the conflict before award, *Epoch Eng'g Inc.*, Comp. Gen. Dec. B-276634, 97-2 CPD ¶72. Exploring these two duties provides a means of understanding OCIs and requires knowing both the regulations and the protest decisions. Just as importantly, the discussion at the end of this section on solicitation "provisions" and contract "clauses" explains how advanced planning and communications can reduce litigation currently frustrating the procurement process.

[A] Identification

FAR subpart 9.5 provides examples of situations that create an actual or potential OCI, but then warns conflicts may occur in situations not covered in the FAR. (A potential conflict becomes an actual conflict with the award of a second government contract.) *Aetna Gov't Health Plans, Inc.* Comp. Gen. Dec. B-254397.15, 95-2 CPD ¶ 129, augments the FAR examples with three categories of conflicts:

(1) unequal access to information,
(2) impaired objectivity, and
(3) biased ground rules.

Later decisions develop tests for conflicts based on unequal access to information and conflicts based on impaired objectivity.

Identifying conflicts goes beyond examining the interests of the awardee and its subcontractors. OCI examinations include other business relationships of the awardee, e.g., joint ventures, partnerships, subsidiaries, and affiliates. There may be no basis to distinguish between a firm and its affiliate(s) in cases involving impaired objectivity or biased ground rules, *Aetna*; *Filtration Dev. Co. v. United States*, 60 Fed. Cl. 371 (2004). Although *Aetna* states some affiliations may be too remote to create a conflict, the concept of remoteness is subjective. The concept of remoteness is so vague some view *Aetna* and its progeny as a per se rule with regard to affiliation.

[1] Requirement for "Hard Facts"

Although the Supreme Court in *United States v. Mississippi Valley Generating Co.*, 364 U.S. 520 (1961), held that an *appearance* of a personal conflict of interest that violated a statutory prohibition was sufficient to invalidate a contract, the Federal Circuit held in *Turner Constr. Co. v. United States*, 645 F.3d 1377 (Fed. Cir. 2011), that hard facts were necessary to disqualify a contractor for an OCI. The facts of this case illustrate how challenging it is to apply the OCI rules. *Turner* involved a phased acquisition to redesign a hospital. Due to the complexity of the project, the agency sought support from the joint venture of Hayes, Seay, Mattern & Mattern (HSMM) and Hellmuth, Obata & Kassbaum (HOK). The agency selected Turner Construction to build the hospital on August 24, 2009. Ellerbe Becket (EB), a subcontractor to Turner Construction, was to coordinate the project design—an effort constituting about 1.5% of Turner's price.

Separately, the Board of Directors of EB began to consider diversifying. Five firms expressed interest; AECOM, which owned HSMM was one of the interested firms. EB management opened its data room to the interested firms and required the interested firms to sign confidentiality agreements. Shareholders announced the merger between EB and AECOM on October 26, 2009. The result of the merger meant that EB, the subcontractor of Turner Construction, also was affiliated with a member of the joint venture team supporting the agency on the hospital redesign. The disappointed offerors filed a protest with the GAO, alleging the merger between EB and AECOM created three OCIs. GAO found unequal access to information and biased ground rule

OCIs, *McCarthy/Hunt*, JV, Comp. Gen. Dec. B-402229.2, 2010 CPD ¶68; *B.L. Harbert-Brasfield & Gorrie, JV*, Comp. Gen. Dec. B-402229, 2010 CPD ¶69.

Subsequently, in *Turner Constr. v. United States*, 94 Fed. Cl. 561 (2010), the Court of Federal Claims reached the opposite conclusion. It found that no member of AECOM who accessed EB's data room, supported the agency on the acquisition of the hospital redesign. Additionally, only one member of HSSM supporting the agency on the redesign knew about the potential merger. This individual recused himself from supporting the redesign, notifying the contracting officer about the conflict. The agency agreed this recusal sufficiently prevented a possible conflict of interest. Affirming the lower court's decision, the Federal Circuit created the need for hard facts, at 1387, drawing:

> [A] distinction between circumstances where "hard facts" indicate the existence or potential existence of impropriety and circumstances such as these where the finding of an OCI relies on inferences based upon "suspicion and innuendo."

By eliminating "appearance" from the OCI calculus, *Turner* places the onus on the protester to prove an actual or potential OCI exists. Likewise, *Turner* affects the rigor by which the government examines OCIs, requiring investigations with hard facts that support the government's conclusions on OCIs. Although these investigations usually result in written reports, contracting officers must only document significant conflicts, FAR 9.504(d); *PAI Corp. v. United States*, 614 F.3d 1347 (Fed. Cir. 2010); *McVey Co. v. United States*, 111 Fed. Cl. 38 (2013).

GAO will not substitute its judgment absent clear evidence that the agency's conclusion is unreasonable, *LOGC2, Inc.*, Comp. Gen. Dec. B-416075, 2018 CPD ¶204; *Visual Connections, LLC*, Comp. Gen. Dec. B-416759, 2018 CPD ¶413; *Trandes Corp.*, Comp. Gen. Dec. B-411742, 2015 CPD ¶317; and *Health Innovation & Tech. Venture*, Comp. Gen. Dec. B-411608.2, 2015 CPD ¶298. The Court of Federal Claims applies a similar standard, *McVey Co. v. United States*, 111 Fed. Cl. 38 (2013). GAO will sustain a protest when GAO finds the agency's investigation ignores relevant facts, *C2C Innovative Solutions, Inc.*, Comp Gen. Dec. B-416289, 2018 CPD ¶269 (protest sustained because the contracting officer failed to evaluate whether a potential OCI was created by a corporate structure that allowed a wholly-owned subsidiary to review decisions on appeal from the parent company's own claims process).

[2] Types of Conflicts

Since the GAO decision in *Aetna*, the decisions analyzing OCIs have dealt with them in the three categories identified in that decision rather than in the categories discussed in the FAR.

[a] Unequal Access to Information

An OCI due to unequal access to information is created when a contractor has access to nonpublic information which may provide the firm with an unfair competitive advantage in a later competition for a government contract. Unequal access to information invokes the principle of an unfair competitive advantage, but does not involve the principle of bias. Conflicts involving unequal access to information are commonplace given the number of support service contracts that require the use of proprietary data belonging to another contractor.

Conflicts based on unequal access to information best correlate to FAR 9.505-4 on access to proprietary information. FAR 9.505-4 states an unfair competitive advantage exists when a contractor competing for award for any Federal contract possesses—

> (1) Proprietary information that was obtained from a Government official without proper authorization; or
>
> (2) Source selection information (as defined in [FAR] 2.101) that is relevant to the contract but is not available to all competitors, and such information would assist that contractor in obtaining the contract.

FAR 9.505-4 explains that a contractor does not gain an unfair competitive advantage when restrictions are imposed because "restrictions protect the information and encourage companies to provide it when necessary for contract performance." In addition, no conflict on unequal access to information occurs when data is voluntarily provided without limitations on use or is available from other sources without restrictions, FAR 9.505-4(a)(1) and (2). FAR 9.505-4(b) also requires an interrelated third-party agreement between the contractor gaining access to the data and the contractor owning the proprietary information.

ARINC Eng'g Servs., LLC v. United States, 77 Fed. 196 (2007), provides a test to determine when access to data creates an unfair competitive advantage. There, the court asked:

- Whether the information was unavailable to potential offerors;
- Whether the nonpublic information would have been useful responding to a solicitation; and
- Whether the contractor would be afforded an unfair competitive advantage by having access to the nonpublic information.

Hard facts are required to support each element of the test. Use is presumed when hard facts exist proving the test, but the presumption of use may be rebutted by other hard facts. The lack of evidence regarding use does not constitute hard facts sufficient to rebut the presumption, *AT&T Research*, Comp. Gen. Dec. B-413012, 2016 CPD ¶ 237. Mitigation efforts to screen or to wall off certain individuals to prevent an improper disclosure of information, however, constitute hard facts rebutting the presumption of use, *BAE Sys. Tech. Solutions & Servs., Inc.*, Comp. Gen. Dec. B-411810.3, 2016 CPD ¶ 168. *BAE Systems* states signed Nondisclosure Agreements (NDAs) are adequate mitigation in the absence of facts showing NDAs failed to prevent an unfair competitive advantage. See also *LOGZONE, Inc.*, Comp. Gen. Dec. B-416029, 2018 CPD ¶ 190, which discusses the elements necessary to prove an OCI on unequal access to information and explains the role of NDAs.

Unequal access to information can encompass more than access to proprietary information or source selection information, *Dell Servs. Fed. Gov't*, Comp. Gen. Dec. B-414461.3, 2018 CPD ¶ 213. In *Johnson Controls World Servs., Inc.*, Comp. Gen. Dec. B-286714.2, 2001 CPD ¶ 20, a conflict of unequal access occurred when the awardee's proposed subcontractor had nonpublic information about the agency's maintenance activities since the awardee's subcontractor also maintained the agency's Executive Management Information System database under another contract. *Johnson Controls World* reasoned that FAR 9.505(b) recognizes "conflicts may arise in situations not expressly covered in this section 9.505." Other decisions where GAO found potential OCIs due to unequal access to "nonpublic information" include: *C2C Innovative Solutions, Inc.*, Comp. Gen. Dec. B-416289, 2018 CPD ¶ 269 (agency did not reasonably evaluate whether its awardee's subsidiary had access to non-public, competitively useful information held in the Medicare appeals system as a result of performing another government contract); *Dell Servs. Fed. Gov't, Inc.*, Comp. Gen, Dec. B-414461, 2017 CPD ¶ 192 (offeror had copies of the proposals the protester submitted for other efforts); *AT & T Gov't Solutions, Inc.*, Comp. Gen. Dec. B-413012, 2016 CPD ¶ 237 (awardee's subcontractor provided acquisition support to the competition); and *Ktech Corp.*, Comp. Gen. Dec. B-285330, 2002 CPD ¶ 77 (subcontractor had access to protester's technical information through its work in assisting the agency in monitoring the protester's performance on prior contract).

However, many protests are denied because hard facts fail to prove the awardee has specific information that created an unfair competitive advantage. See *VSolvit, LLC v. United States*, 151 Fed. Cl. 678 (2020) (no proof of specific facts known by incumbent contractor that would create competitive advantage); *Technology Automation & Mgmt., Inc.*, Comp. Gen. Dec. B-418063.3, 2020 CPD ¶ 343 (most of the information publicly available); *Mortgage Contracting Servs., LLC*, Comp. Gen. Dec. B-418483.2, 2020 CPD ¶ 340 (extracting information about protester from mass of information would have been too costly to be useful); *LOGZONE, Inc.*, Comp. Gen. Dec. B-416029, 2018 CPD ¶ 190 (both the awardee and disappointed offeror proposed to use subcontractors from the incumbent and the subcontractor possessed similar information); *Superlative Techs., Inc.*, Comp. Gen. Dec. B-416711, 2018 CPD ¶ 410 (protester failed to present hard facts how the information provided the awardee an unfair competitive advantage); *Atlantic Sys. Group, Inc.*, Comp. Gen. Dec. B-415405, 2018 CPD ¶ 19 (protest denied where prior work did not grant the awardee or the awardee's subcontractor access to non-public information that would provide an unfair competitive advantage); *BAE Sys. Tech. Solutions & Servs., Inc.*, Comp. Gen. Dec. B-411810.3 2016 CPD ¶ 174 (Leidos did not receive a competitive advantage because the old SAIC provided the acquisition support); *ITT Corp.-Elec. Sys.*, Comp. Gen. Dec. B-202808, 2010 CPD ¶ 178 (agency had contractual right to provide the information); *Alabama Aircraft Indus., Inc. v. United States*, 83 Fed. Cl. 666 (2008), *aff'd*, 586 F.3d 1372 (Fed. Cir. 2009) (work on prior engineering services contract provided no specific information giving competitive advantage on aircraft maintenance contract); *ARINC Eng'g Servs., LLC v. United States*, 77 Fed. Cl. 196 (2007) (work on prior contract was different and unrelated to work on the new contract); *Integrated Concepts & Research Corp.*, Comp. Gen. Dec. B-309803, 2008 CPD ¶ 117 (no unequal access existed because the awardee was not a subcontractor under another contract); and *Enterprise Info. Servs., Inc.*, Comp. Gen. Dec. B-405152, 2011 CPD ¶ 174 (no conflict because nondisclosure agreements protected confidential and proprietary information).

In addition, no conflict due to unequal access to information exists when the information is voluntarily furnished to an agency without proprietary legends, *Snell Enters. Inc.*, Comp. Gen. Dec. B-290113, 2002 CPD ¶ 115. Additionally, no conflict exists when the source of the information is a private person. See *Ellwood Nat'l Forge Co.*, Comp. Gen. Dec. B-402089.3, 2010 CPD ¶ 250 (no conflict when information was obtained by a former employee and consultant of protester notwithstanding that the former employee may have had subsequent opportunity to obtain the same information through performance of a government contract); *GEO Group, Inc.*, Comp. Gen. Dec., B-405012, 2011 CPD ¶ 153 (no conflict where the protester's business manager voluntarily provided the protester's confidential information to the awardee's CEO); and *Mgmt. Sciences for Health*, Comp. Gen. Dec. B-416041, 2018 CPD ¶ 197 (no conflict where record shows the protester voluntarily disclosed the information to the awardee's subcontractor pursuant to a previous arm's length agreement between firms).

Additionally, no conflict due to unequal access to information exists when the knowledge is due to a natural competitive advantage. FAR 9.505-2(a)(3) recognizes a natural competitive advantage as part of the exception for development work and states this advantage is not unfair and does not create an OCI. Decisions on natural competitive advantage include: *Optimum Tech., Inc.*, Comp. Gen. Dec. B-266339.2, 96-1 CPD ¶ 188 (prior performance of similar requirements by awardee's subcontractor does not provide an unfair competitive advantage and "any advantage accruing is merely that of an incumbent contractor"); *Harmonia Holdings, LLC*, Comp. Gen. Dec. B-407186.2, 2013 CPD ¶ 66 (incumbency did not create an OCI unless there were hard facts the incumbent "prepared the RFP or set its ground rules, had unequal access to non-public information of the nature that gives rise to an OCI, or otherwise had impaired objectivity"); and *H P Enterprise Serv., LLC*, Comp. Gen Dec. B-409169.3, 2014 CPD ¶ 179, where GAO held:

> [A]n offeror may possess unique information, advantages, and capabilities due to its prior experience under a government contract-either as an incumbent contractor or otherwise; further, the government is not necessarily required to equalize competition to compensate for such an advantage, unless there is evidence of preferential treatment or other improper action. . . . *CACI, Inc.-Fed.*, B-403064.2, Jan. 28, 2011, 2011 CPD ¶ 31 at 10; *MASAI Techs. Corp.*, B-298880.3, Sept. 10, 2007, 2007 CPD ¶ 179 at 8.

Other cases on natural competitive advantage include: *Snell Enters., Inc.*, Comp. Gen. Dec. B-290113, 2002 CPD ¶ 115; *ARINC Eng'g Serv., LLC*, 77 Fed. Cl. 196 (2007); *Philadelphia Produce Mkt. Wholesalers, LLC*, Comp. Gen. Dec. B-298751.5, 2007 CPD ¶ 87; *Alabama Aircraft Indus., Inc.–Birmingham v. United States*, 83 Fed. Cl. 666 (2008); and *Millennium Corp., Inc.*, Comp. Gen. Dec. B-412866, 2016 CPD ¶ 168.

[b] Impaired Objectivity

An OCI due to impaired objectivity occurs when a contractor's other interests may impair judgment and objectivity in the performance of work under the prospective contract, *Alion Sci. & Tech. Corp.*, B-297342, 2006 CPD ¶ 1. The classic example of impaired objectivity is when a firm is in a position to evaluate its own work under another government contract. Impaired objectivity best correlates to FAR 9.505-3 on providing evaluation services; however, the decisions define impaired objectivity more broadly. According to *Pragmatics Inc.*, Comp. Gen. Dec. B-407320.2, 2013 CPD ¶ 83; and *PURVIS Sys., Inc.*, Comp. Gen. Dec. B-293807.3, 2004 CPD ¶ 177, the test for a conflict on impaired objectivity is:

> (i.) Whether the statement of work requires the use of subjective judgment, and
>
> (ii.) Whether a contractor has a financial interest in the outcome of its performance.

Alion states an OCI based on impaired objectivity involves bias since the conflicting roles have the potential to influence the contractor's judgment. However, some support contracts do not involve the contractor's judgment and do not give contractors the same amount of discretion regarding performance, e.g., training, painting, maintaining hardware, and performing facilities services.

Examples of impaired objectivity include: *AT&T Corp.*, Comp. Gen. Dec. B-417107.4, 2020 CPD ¶ 283 (awardee would be evaluating its work under another contract); *Safal Partners, Inc.*, Comp. Gen. Dec. B-416937, 2019 CPD ¶ 20 (awardee could financially benefit by recommending grantees for technical assistance under one contract and providing assistance to grantees under a second contract); *C2C Innovative Solutions, Inc.*, Comp. Gen. Dec. B-416289, 2018 CPD ¶ 269 (awardee's wholly-owned subsidiary would review decisions on appeal from the parent company's own claims process); *NCI Info. Sys., Inc.*, Comp. Gen. Dec. B-412870.2, 2016 CPD ¶ 310 (awardee would be in a position to recommend systems manufactured by its parent company); *The Analysis Group LLC*, Comp. Gen. Dec. B-401726, 2009 CPD ¶ 237 (the winning offeror would perform technical analysis on the same type products it was selling); *L–3 Serv., Inc.*, Comp. Gen. Dec. B-400134.11, 2009 CPD ¶ 171 (awardee would be evaluating own work under another contract); and *Nortel Gov't Solutions, Inc.*, Comp. Gen. Dec. B-299522.5, 2009 CPD ¶ 10 (awardee would be required to review and provide input on designs it furnished under a separate contract). Compare *TDS, Inc.*, Comp. Gen. Dec. B-292674, 2003 CPD ¶ 204 (no OCI was found when a subcontractor with an existing contract with the agency for "monitoring" work on new contracts did not have the task of "evaluating" the performance of the prospective contractor on the new contract).

Hard facts are needed to establish the two elements of impaired objectivity: whether the contract requires the use of judgment and whether the contractor has a conflicting interest. The first prong asks whether the statement of work requires the use of subjective judgment. Two indicia of subjective judgment are: the presence of contract clauses for Key Personnel and educational requirements. A Key Personnel clause suggests the government will be relying on the judgment of the contractor. Likewise, detailed qualifications for personnel suggests the government intends to rely on the contractor's judgment. But the language in the statement of work is the most important indicator of subjective judgment. Requirements containing words and phrases such as analyze, study, develop recommendations, develop programs, develop strategies, and provide advice involve the use of subjective judgment. And these words and phrases are commonly found in support service contracts. For example, in *PURVIS Sys., Inc.*, Comp. Gen. Dec. B-293807.3, 2004 CPD ¶ 177, GAO found a conflict based on impaired objectivity in part because the statement of work required "analysis, evaluation and judgment."

Not all support service contracts involve the use of subjective judgment. *Computers Universal, Inc.*, Comp. Gen. Dec. B-292794, 2003 CPD ¶ 20, states a contractor uses subjective judgment when deciding what maintenance is required or how well the maintenance is to be performed. However, a contractor does not use subjective judgment when implementing a maintenance schedule. Other support contracts that do not involve subjective judgment include: *Overlook Sys. Techs., Inc.*, Comp. Gen. Dec. B-298099.4, 2006 CPD ¶ 185 (answering telephone inquiries about the operation of a piece of equipment should not raise any significant concern about an OCI because the task involves objective answers to straightforward inquiries that are quickly resolved during the course of a telephone call); *Serco, Inc.*, Comp. Gen. Dec. B 404033, 2011 CPD ¶ 302 (no OCI because the contractor was not required to make recommendations); and *Software Eng'g Servs., Inc.*, Comp. Gen. Dec. B-401645, 2010 CPD ¶ 150 (no OCI where an alleged conflict of interest involved a subcontractor, who was also the prime contractor in another phase of the program, because the solicitation specifically did not preclude the subcontractor's involvement in both phases of the program).

Having a competing interest is the second prong needed to establish impaired objectivity. The potential for bias arises when the contractor has some type of competing interest that may influence how the contractor exercises its judgment, *Greenleaf Co.*, Comp. Gen. Dec. B-293105.18, 2006 CPD ¶ 79. Cases finding a competing interest include: *Alion Sci. & Tech. Corp.*, Comp. Gen. Dec. B-297342, 2006 CPD ¶ 1 (financial interest found where awardee, a manufacturer of spectrum-dependent products, would perform analysis, evaluate and formulate policies and regulations that could affect the sale of spectrum-dependent products manufactured by the awardee or the awardee's competitors); *Leboeuf v. Abraham*, 347 F.3d 315 (D.C. Cir. 2003) (financial interest involved the awardee reviewing its prior work); *Greenleaf Constr. Co.*, Comp. Gen. Dec. B-293105.18, 2006 CPD ¶ 19 (financial interest existed even though the awardee sold its conflicting interest since the awardee would be overseeing the closing firm and had accepted compensation over a period covered by the contract—GAO found the potential existed that awardee might make biased recommendations to keep that closing firm viable until the debt was paid); *J&E Assocs., Inc.*, Comp. Gen. Dec. B-278771, 98-1 CPD ¶ 77 (financial interest where educational institution would provide training and also would counsel government employees on the appropriate educational institution and verify its own billing statements); *Washington Util. Group*, Comp. Gen. Dec. B-266333, 96-1 CPD ¶ 27 (a proposed contractor and its major subcontractor were unable to provide unbiased contracting and technical advice to the agency because they had numerous contacts with the industry being solicited); *KPMG Peat Marwick*, Comp. Gen. Dec. B-255224, 94-1 CPD ¶ 111 (financial interests found where awardee would have been reviewing its own audits performed for the agency's predecessor); and *ICF Inc.*, Comp. Gen. Dec. B-241372, 91-1 CPD ¶ 124, (disqualification upheld because contractor would evaluate the efficiency of sister corporation that had "response action" contracts with the Environmental Protection Agency).

In contrast, see *Marinette Marine Corp.* Comp. Gen. Dec. B-400697, 2009 CPD ¶ 16 (no impaired objectivity where a consultant advised both the agency and the winning offeror because the consultant had no financial interest in the outcome of the competition); *N.D. Lea & Assocs.* Comp. Gen. Dec. B-208445, 83-2 CPD ¶ 21 (no OCI when a company that had served as a subcontractor on one prior contract was not sufficiently involved in the rail standardization program to justify barring it from reviewing new awards in the program); *Visual Connections, LLC*, Comp. Gen. Dec. B-416759, 2018 CPD ¶ 413 (no conflict when the awardee's subcontractor also was the systems integrator because the systems integrator would not be responsible for oversight and would not be judging its own performance); *Teledyne-Commodore, LLC*, Comp. Gen. Dec. B-278408.5, 99-1 CPD ¶ 60 (no impaired objectivity where an agency used a company to assist in evaluating proposals, but the company had no financial interest in the outcome of the competition); and *CH2M Hill, Ltd.*, Comp. Gen. Dec. B-259511, 95-1 CPD ¶ 203 (no conflict where the president of a subcontractor chaired a community commission that was the focal point for relocation efforts caused by government downsizing because the commission had no control over the agency's efforts that would be facilitated by the contract).

[c] Biased Ground Rules

An OCI due to biased ground rules is created when a firm, as part of its performance of a government contract, has in some sense set the ground rules for another government contract, e.g., writing the statement of work or the specifications, evaluating proposals, or advising on the acquisition strategy. In biased ground rules, the concern is that the firm could skew the future competition, whether intentionally or not, in favor of itself, *Aetna Gov't Health Plans, Inc.* Comp. Gen. Dec. B-254397.15, 95-2 CPD ¶ 129. Biased ground rules involve both bias and unfair competitive advantage, *The Pragma Corp.*, Comp. Gen. Dec. B-255236, 94-1 CPD ¶ 124; FAR 9.505-5(a)(2).

Biased ground rules can be unintentional where a contractor is naturally biased to view things a certain way. In *Celadon Labs., Inc.*, Comp. Gen. Dec. B-298533, 2006 CPD ¶ 158, GAO sustained a protest regarding the use of outside evaluators to a broad agency announcement when the potential research involved two different, competing technologies. The protester alleged bias because all of the panel members were associated with one technology; no one on the panel was involved with the competing technology the protester used. Although *Celadon* is not a classic biased ground rules case, it demonstrates how bias can exist for other than financial reasons and how bias can be unintentional.

Conflicts based on biased ground rules best correlate to FAR 9.505-2 regarding the preparation of specifications or work statements. FAR 9.505-2 addresses situations where a contractor prepares and furnishes complete specifications covering nondevelopmental items, which will be used in a competitive acquisition. Biased ground rules also include any effort that in some sense establishes the basis for a future competition. See, for example, *Aetna,* and *Systems Made Simple, Inc.*, Comp. Gen. Dec. B-412948.2, 2016 CPD ¶ 207. No precise test for biased ground rules exists except that the contractor 1) set ground rules or otherwise uses subjective judgment to support a future competition and 2) has a financial interest in the second competition.

Cases where hard facts failed to establish biased ground rûles include: *Pillar Sys. Corp.*, Comp. Gen. Dec. B-408221, 2013 CPD ¶ 172 (GAO denied an allegation that the former project manager, now an employee of the awardee, prepared the statement of work (SOW) when the agency said it prepared the SOW); *Systems Made Simple, Inc.*, Comp. Gen. Dec. B-412948.2, 2016 CPD

¶ 207 (GAO denied an allegation that agency used a study prepared by the awardee's parent company when hard facts showed the agency relied on a study prepared by another contractor); *Trailboss Enters., Inc.*, Comp. Gen. Dec. B-415970, 2018 CPD ¶ 171 (an allegation that certain solicitation provisions favored the incumbent, and that the agency failed to disclose the composition of the incumbent contractor's workforce were not hard facts sufficient to establish biased ground rules); *Superlative Techs., Inc.*, Comp. Gen. Dec. B-415405, 2018 CPD ¶ 19 (the protester alleged that the awardee and its subcontractor worked on earlier task orders that helped shape the competition, but facts showed earlier task orders did not involve acquisition planning); and *Valor Co. Mgmt., LLC*, Comp. Gen. Dec. B- 405306, 2011 CPD ¶ 221 (the record confirmed that awardee's subcontractor did not prepare the report the agency used to draft the statement of work).

In contrast, hard facts established biased ground rules in: *L–3 Serv., Inc.*, Comp. Gen. Dec. B-400134.11, 2009 CPD ¶ 171 (contractor played a major, but not sole role drafting a work statement); *Lucent Techs. World Servs., Inc.*, Comp. Gen. Dec. B-295462, 2005 CPD ¶ 55 (awardee participated in the preparation of the specifications even though agency commented and altered the specifications); *Basile, Baumann, Prost & Assocs., Inc.*, Comp. Gen. Dec. B-274870, 97-1 CPD ¶ 15 (offeror prepared statement of work and agency cost estimate); *Ressler Assocs., Inc.*, Comp. Gen. Dec. B-244110, 91-2 CPD ¶ 230 (protester had prepared portions of the statement of work without contracting officer's knowledge); *Int'l Business Machines Corp.*, Comp. Gen. Dec. B-410639, 2015 CPD ¶ 41 (employee of the team member of the awardee assisted in the development of the solicitation, the performance work statement, and other acquisition documents for the procurement); and *HBI–GF, JV*, Comp. Gen. Dec. B-415036, 2017 CPD ¶ 331 (contractor reviewed specifications and agency included most of the contractor's comments in the solicitation).

Biased ground rules exist even if the company assisting in the preparation of the specification believes that there will be no competition. See *Energy Sys. Group*, Comp. Gen. Dec. B-402324, 2010 CPD ¶ 73 where the company participated as a subcontractor in preparing a feasibility study for an energy-saving contract believing that the utility contractor would be awarded the contract on a sole source basis. When the agency later decided to use a competitive procurement, GAO ruled that the subcontractor had an OCI and could not participate in the competition.

Additionally, biased ground rules require the contractor/offeror have a significant interest in the outcome of the competition. See *American Mgmt. Sys., Inc.*, Comp. Gen. Dec. B-285645, 2000 CPD ¶ 163 (no OCI where a firm performing work for the agency had a "marketing alliance" with several of the competitors, but had no relationship with regard to the procurement); *Professional Gunsmithing Inc.*, B-279048.2, 98-2 CPD ¶ 49 (entitlement of consultant employed by the agency to help evaluate proposals to trademark royalties from awardee on products other than those to be provided under the contract was speculative and too remote to create a significant conflict of interest); *Int'l Mgmt. & Communications Corp.*, Comp. Gen. Dec. B-272456, 96-2 CPD ¶ 156 (awardee's interest in receiving repayment of debt owed to its affiliate organization by the awardee was not significant because the relationship between the awardee/contract and the repayment of the debt was indirect); *Valdez Int'l Corp.*, Comp. Gen. Dec. B-402256.3, 2011 CPD ¶ 13 (an ordinary purchaser/supplier relationship is not a financial interest creating an OCI); and *Gov't Scrap*, Comp. Gen. Dec. B-295585, 2005 CPD ¶ 60 (the theoretical possibility that the awardee will act in bad faith under its contract does not establish an OCI).

[i] Basic Exceptions

Subpart 9.5 describes exceptions to FAR 9.505-2 which do not constitute conflicts. The first group of exceptions involves:

> (i) Contractors that furnish at Government request specifications or data regarding a product they provide, even though the specifications or data may have been paid for separately or in the price of the product; or
>
> (ii) Situations in which contractors, acting as industry representatives, help Government agencies prepare, refine, or coordinate specifications, regardless of source, provided this assistance is supervised and controlled by Government representatives.

The first group of exceptions includes use of a data package from the original designer/manufacturer and paid for by the government, which the government will use as part of future competitions. The original manufacturer may participate in the subsequent competition. The second group of exceptions also includes contractors acting as industry representatives to help the government prepare a statement of work or specifications. In this situation, typically the government obtains input through an open information call, like a Request for Information, rather than a task under an existing contract. The twin evils associated with biased ground rules are attenuated by the fact that the government receives input from multiple contractors.

FAR 9.505-2(b)(1) contains another group of exceptions that allow a contractor that assisted or prepared the work statement to participate in the follow-on competition when:

1. It is the sole source;
2. It has participated in the development and design work; or
3. More than one contractor has been involved in preparing the work statement.

The exception in FAR 9.505-2(b)(1)(i) for sole source situations recognizes the lack of financial interest necessary to create a conflict. OCI concerns cannot prevent a sole source contractor from preparing the statement of work or specification of a contract when agency intends to have the contractor perform the future production contract on a sole source basis. In this case, any concern with bias or unfair competitive advantage is offset by the fact the requirement will be awarded without competition. However, contracting officers still need to be concerned about conflicts in sole source situation when the effort involves a future competition, and in the potential for bias or conflicts to influence the underlying decision to proceed on a sole source basis.

The exception in FAR 9.505-2(b)(1)(iii) applies when more than one contractor helped prepare the statement of work and has been recognized by earlier decisions, *SRI Int'l*, Comp. Gen. Dec. B-224424, 86-2 CPD ¶ 404 (denied a conflict of interest exists when the awardee proposed to utilize 3 members of 10–member advisory panel); *American Rocket Co.*, Comp. Gen. Dec. B-232391, 89-1 CPD ¶ 6 (use of phased development approach for the development of a propulsion system did not result in a potential conflict of interest requiring exclusion from the subsequent work phases of any one of multiple awardees under initial work effort); and *American Artisan Prods., Inc.*, Comp. Gen. Dec. B-292559, 2003 CPD ¶ 176 (GAO denied a protest where the awardee's subcontractor was one of many contractors working on the specifications). But *L–3 Serv., Inc.*, Comp. Gen. Dec. B-400134.11, 2009 CPD ¶ 171, distinguishes *American Artisan Prods., Inc.*, stating the decision in *American Artisan* relied on the fact "the firm alleged to have the biased ground rules organizational conflict of interest did not 'perform the type of work solicited." Additionally, GAO does not automatically apply the exception in FAR 9.505-2(b)(1)(iii) as shown in *Systems Made Simple, Inc.*, Comp. Gen. Dec. B-412948.2, 2016 CPD ¶ 207. *Systems Made Simple* examined which study the agency used to prepare the specification and found the agency ordered a second study because the awardee's study was "so generic in nature" that the agency did not rely on it. A question remains how decisions will apply the exception in FAR 9.505-2(b)(1)(iii). This question is particularly relevant when an agency primarily relies on one contractor or when two contractors are advising on different parts of the statement of work.

[ii] Research and Development Exception

Subpart 9.5 excludes development and design work from the policies on organizational conflicts of interest. FAR 9.505(b)(1)(ii) provides an exception for development and design, but FAR 9.505-2(a)(3) gives more guidance, stating:

> In development work, it is normal to select firms that have done the most advanced work in the field. These firms can be expected to design and develop around their own prior knowledge. Development contractors can frequently start production earlier and more knowledgeably than firms that did not participate in the development, and this can affect the time and quality of production, both of which are important to the Government. In many instances the

> Government may have financed the development. Thus, while the development contractor has a competitive advantage, it is an unavoidable one that is not considered unfair; hence no prohibition should be imposed.

Decisions help distinguish biased ground rules from situations where the development exception applies. *Alliant Techsys., Inc.*, Comp. Gen. Dec. B-410036, 2014 CPD ¶ 324, involved a limited competition between Alliant and Raytheon for HARM missiles. Alliant alleged Raytheon had an OCI because the defense sector of Texas Instruments, which subsequently became part of Raytheon, developed the original AGM–88 HARM system. Alliant asserted that the Air Force failed to conduct a meaningful OCI analysis by failing to consider whether (1) Raytheon had an undue influence on the specifications and (2) whether Raytheon enjoyed unequal access to certain proprietary information. Although GAO agreed that Raytheon designed and developed the HARM missile and had access to certain information as a result of its design and development work, Raytheon had a competitive advantage enjoyed by developers, an advantage not prohibited under the OCI rules. GAO stated "the mere existence of a prior or current contractual relationship between a contracting agency and a contractor does not create an unfair competitive advantage unless the alleged advantage was created by an improper preference or unfair action by the procuring agency." In addition, GAO stated while the offeror had access to certain proprietary information as a result of its development work, "such a competitive advantage enjoyed by a developer is not considered an unfair one prohibited under the OCI rules." See also AA*R Mfg., Inc.*, Comp. Gen. Dec. B-418339, 2020 CPD ¶ 106, and AA*R Mfg., Inc. v. United States*, 149 Fed. Cl. 525 (2020), applying the development contractor exception to a subcontractor that had participated in the design of a new pallet.

Additionally, in *American Rocket Co.*, Comp. Gen. Dec. B-232391, 89-1 CPD ¶ 6, GAO found an agency's use of a phased development approach did not create an OCI requiring the exclusion of awardees in subsequent phases of development. In *Analytic Sciences Corp.*, Comp. Gen. Dec. B-218074, 85-1 CPD ¶ 464, the protester challenged its disqualification that its participation in an earlier phase of the program created a conflict. GAO questioned whether performance of the first-phase contract gave the firm an unfair advantage competing for the second-phase procurement and recommended the agency determine whether the exception for developer and design applied. GAO believed "the possible development and design nature of the contract to analyze the Center's requirements and write the work statement may exempt the firm from any competitive restriction in accordance with the FAR."

It appears GAO is more likely to apply the exception in FAR 9.505-2(a)(3) to the development of systems. GAO did not apply the exception for development in *SSR Eng'rs, Inc.*, Comp. Gen. Dec. B-282244, 99-2 CPD ¶ 27 (upheld the agency's disqualification, rejecting the protester's argument that Part 36 does not preclude the firm that developed the scope of work from being part of a design-build team); *LW Planning Group*, Comp. Gen. Dec. B-215539, 84-2 CPD ¶ 531 (conflict when a contractor that had prepared a work statement was awarded a subsequent contract to revise a master plan); *Basile, Baumann, Prost & Assocs., Inc.*, Comp. Gen. Dec. B-274870, 97-1 CPD ¶ 15 (conflict when the contractor that prepared a work statement received follow-on work to evaluate government land for its suitability for recreational uses); and *Ressler Assocs., Inc.*, Comp. Gen. Dec. B-244110, 91-2 CPD ¶ 230 (conflict barring competing for a follow-on contract for more design and development work because the contractor surreptitiously prepared a work statement for that contract—GAO reasoned the exception for development only applied if the follow-on work called for the production of units).

[d] Systems Engineering and Technical Direction

The three OCIs defined by decisional law track with FAR 9.505, but they do not define a conflict which corresponds to FAR 9.505-1 on systems engineering and technical direction (SETA). Systems engineering can involve all three types of conflicts: unequal access to information, impaired objectivity, and biased ground rules. *Filtration Dev. Co. v. United States*, 60 Fed. Cl. 371 (2004), states that contractors, subcontractors, and their affiliates that provide systems engineering are categorically precluded from providing their own products in later stages of the program unless the agency obtains a waiver.

FAR 9.505-1 restricts contractors that provide systems engineering and technical direction, stating:

> (a) A contractor that provides systems engineering and technical direction for a system but does not have overall contractual responsibility for its development, its integration, assembly, and checkout, or its production shall not—
>
> (1) Be awarded a contract to supply the system or any of its major components; or
>
> (2) Be a subcontractor or consultant to a supplier of the system or any of its major components.

FAR 9.505-1(b) recognizes systems engineering and technical direction encompasses a combination of activities that have the potential to create an OCI. Systems engineering may involve: determining specifications (biased ground rules), identifying and resolving interface problems (impaired objectivity), developing test requirements (impaired objectivity), evaluating test data (impaired objectivity), and supervising design (impaired objectivity). Technical direction may involve: developing work statements (biased ground rules), determining parameters (impaired objectivity), directing other contractors' operations (impaired objectivity), and resolving technical controversies (impaired objectivity). Systems engineering and technical direction usually require that contractors have access to information that would provide an unfair competitive advantage. Consequently, the FAR cautions that systems engineering and technical direction give the contractor "a highly influential and responsible position in determining a system's basic concepts and supervising their execution by other contractors," FAR 9.505-1(b).

Nortel Gov't Solutions, Inc., Comp. Gen. Dec. B-299522.5, 2009 CPD ¶ 10, describes the type of conflict systems engineering creates where the awardee for the enterprise management services would review and offer input on systems engineering solutions to a system the awardee proposed on a second contract. *PURVIS Sys. Inc.*, Comp. Gen. Dec. B-293807.3, 2004 CPD ¶ 177, involves impaired objectivity where a contract to evaluate undersea warfare systems created a conflict because awardee manufactured 12 of these 59 systems. *Filtration Dev. Co., LLC v. United States*, 60 Fed. Cl. 371 (2004), found a conflict where the contractor performed SETA tasks for procurement also was responsible for designing, developing and manufacturing the UH–60 Blackhawk helicopter. *Epoch Eng'g, Inc.* B-276634, 97-2 CPD ¶ 72, discusses a conflict created when the awardee of a contract to provide engineering and technical support service had a subcontractor that was a shipbuilder.

As discussed in the section on conflicts based on statute, Congress passed statutes restricting the activities SETA contractors can perform.

[B] Resolution

A contracting officer's second duty is to explore ways to prevent the conflict from disqualifying a contractor, the duty known as resolution. An inadequate effort can lead to remand by the Court of Federal Claims requiring the contracting officer to fully investigate the alleged OCI, *American K-9 Detection Servs., LLC v. United States*, 155 Fed. Cl. 248 (2021).

Resolution involves four methods—avoid, neutralize, mitigate, and waive. Decisions explore how these methods of resolution address significant OCIs before award. The contracting officer must allow the offeror to respond before the contracting officer determines a conflict cannot be mitigated, *Informatics Corp. v. United States*, 40 Fed. Cl. 508 (2004).

Although FAR subpart 9.5 mentions the methods of resolution, the guidance on resolution mostly comes from the GAO and court decisions. FAR 9.503 provides the authority to waive. FAR 9.507-2 describes the clause to limit future contracting. But FAR subpart 9.5 fails to provide examples of avoidance or mitigation. Subpart 9.5 does not explain that resolution requires actions by the contractor, by the government, or both. Subpart 9.5 does not explain a resolution may involve a combination of methods and techniques to adequately address a conflict.

GAO examines the facts of each resolution to determine whether clear evidence in a contemporaneous record supports how the agency decided to resolve a conflict, examinations that are detailed given the fact-specific nature of OCIs. In *Social Impact, Inc.* Comp. Gen. Dec. B-412941, 2016 CPD ¶ 203, for example, GAO applied a fact-specific inquiry into the identification and resolution of conflicts before determining there was no "clear evidence that the agency's conclusion" was unreasonable. See also *A-P-T Research, Inc.* Comp. Gen. Dec. B-43731.2, 2017 CPD ¶ 112.

[1] Avoid

Avoidance prevents an OCI from happening and, therefore, is the cleanest way to address OCIs. Avoidance normally requires actions on the part of the government and typically occurs early in the acquisition process. The need for early action is obvious since avoidance usually involves modifying requirements, which are written at the beginning of the acquisition process. The government's ability to avoid OCIs, however, has been limited by the increased use of support service contractors and by consolidations within industry. Below are some of the more common techniques to avoid conflicts.

[a] Eliminating subjective judgment from the statement of work

Subjective judgment gives the contractor significant discretion and involves words such as advise, analyze, evaluate, or recommend. A conflict is created when the exercise of judgment could have an effect on other financial interests of the company. Eliminating subjective judgment from the statement of work may avoid impaired objectivity. For example, monitoring a required schedule does not involve subjective judgment; the contractor is not making decisions about what maintenance is required. See *Strategic Mgmt. Solutions, LLC*, Comp. Gen. Dec. B-416598.3, 2019 CPD ¶ 426, where the agency changed "shall" to "may" in the work statement to allow the contractor to avoid making a judgment where it had a potential conflict.

[b] Eliminating a contractor or a group of contractors

GAO allows a contracting officer to exclude an offeror or a class of offerors from a competition in order to remedy a conflict. Agencies may exclude an offeror from a competition even when no actual impropriety can be found, so long as the agency's decision is based upon fact rather than mere innuendo or suspicion of a potential OCI. Although contracting officers are granted wide latitude in their business judgment, GAO requires the contracting officer to ensure impartial, fair, and equitable treatment of all contractors, *Lucent Techs. World Serv., Inc.*, Comp. Gen. Dec. B-295462, 2005 CPD ¶ 55; *VRC, Inc.*, Comp. Gen. Dec. B-310100, 2007 CPD ¶ 208; and *KAR Contracting, LLC*, Comp. Gen. Dec. B-310454, 2007 CPD ¶ 226. However, these decisions predate *Turner* and its requirement for hard facts. See *Archimedes Global, Inc.*, Comp.

Gen. Dec. B-415886.2, 2018 CPD ¶ 179 (disqualification overturned where record showed the exclusion "was not based on facts, but rather on innuendo and supposition").

The measures NASA took during its competition for the operation and maintenance of the Michoud Assembly Facility (MAF) provide an example of excluding a class of contractors. MAF housed several aerospace contractors which NASA excluded from competition to operate and manage MAF. NASA did not want the prospective operator of MAF also to be a user/tenant since the operator would be in a position to make decisions regarding resource allocations, decisions that could favor one aerospace manufacturer over another. NASA received six proposals after its exclusion, an exclusion announced early in the procurement process and reflected in the solicitation.

[c] Divestiture

The contractor may elect to divest itself of conflicting interests; however, a contracting officer cannot insist upon divestiture. *TrailBlazer Health Enters., LLC*, Comp. Gen. Dec. B-406175, 2012 CPD ¶ 78, discusses divestiture as an option the awardee proposed. Nevertheless, contractors have questioned divestiture. *BAE Sys. Tech. Solutions & Serv., Inc.*, Comp. Gen. Dec. B-411810.3, 2016 CPD ¶ 174, demonstrates GAO relied on divestiture plus passage of time as a way to avoid a conflict. SAIC reorganized into two separate firms, one called SAIC and the other called Leidos, Inc. GAO held the divestiture avoided a conflict with the awardee, Leidos, even though the old Science Applications International Corp (SAIC) helped prepare the solicitation. Other decisions indicate GAO requires divestiture plans be specific before divestiture can resolve an OCI, *TriCenturion, Inc.*, Comp. Gen. Dec. B-406032, 2012 CPD ¶ 52; *C2C Solutions, Inc.*, Comp. Gen. Dec. B-401106.5, 2010 CPD ¶ 38; *Cahaba Safeguard Adm'rs, LLC*, Comp. Gen. Dec. B-401842.2, 2010 CPD ¶ 39. But see *Greenleaf Constr. Co.*, Comp. Gen. Dec. B-293105.18, 2006 CPD ¶ 19, where conflict existed even though the awardee sold its conflicting interest in the closing firm, but the contract required the awardee oversee how the firm, which purchased the closing firm, performed. GAO found the awardee's judgment and objectivity "could be impaired if its performance could potentially affect the ability of the owner of the closing agent contractor to make the payments owed." See also *Wisconsin Serv. Ins. Corp. v. United States*, 151 Fed. Cl. 22 (2020), where divestiture was a major part of an acceptable mitigation plan.

[2] Neutralize

Neutralizing counteracts the effects of a potential or actual OCI, through a limitation on future contracting. The conflict remains, but the effect of the conflict is negated. Although the elements comprising a conflict due to impaired objectivity and/or biased ground rules still exist, a limitation on future competition prevents a potential conflict from becoming an actual conflict since the limitation prevents the contractor from exploiting its financial interest. FAR subpart 9.5 seems to favor limitations on future competition, but industry tries to evade this method. The section on clauses discusses FAR guidance on the clause needed to implement a limitation on future contracting.

Not many decisions deal with limitations on future contracting. But see *BCMC, LLC*, Comp. Gen. Dec. B-413988.2, 2017 CPD ¶ 74 (GAO rejected challenges to how an agency implemented a limitation on future contracting as a matter of contract administration outside of GAO's jurisdiction); *L-3 Serv.*, Comp. Gen. Dec., B-400134.11, 2009 CPD ¶ 171 (illustrates the wisdom of waiving a limitation on future contracting over claiming new facts do not support the initial limitation); *Axiom Resource Mgmt., Inc.*, Comp. Gen. Dec. B-298870.3, 2007 CPD ¶ 117 (future OCIs resolved by barring the awardee from competing as a prime contractor or subcontractor on future support contracts to provide healthcare benefits directly to TRICARE benefit recipients); and *CACI, Inc.-Fed.*, Comp. Gen Dec. B-413860.4, 2018 CPD ¶ 17 (FAR 9.503 allows agencies to waive existing limitations on future contracting).

Although limitations on future contracting effectively resolve conflicts, changes in the marketplace make it difficult to obtain restrictions on future contracting. Consolidations reduce the number of contractors capable of performing the effort; engineering contractors have merged with or are affiliated with production contractors. Fewer contractors are willing to perform the smaller, up-front effort if they must forego the opportunity to propose on the larger follow-on effort due to the restriction required by a limitation on future contracting. The refusal to accept limitations on future contracting forces the government to find other methods of resolution.

[3] Mitigate

Mitigation does not remove the conflict; mitigation involves actions that reduce the harm caused by a conflict to an acceptable level. The concept of "acceptable" makes mitigation the most challenged method of resolution. Both the government and the contractor may be involved in mitigation actions. A mitigation plan captures the actions a contractor will take to address the conflict. A mitigation plan should usually be incorporated in the contract to make compliance with the plan a contract requirement. Although the awardee and the contracting officer negotiate the mitigation plan, the contracting officer determines what constitutes acceptable mitigation.

Decisions discuss the following techniques the parties used to mitigate an OCI, but this is not an exclusive listing; other techniques may also be appropriate in any given case.

[a] Firewalls

The FAR discusses firewalls when describing conflicts involving unfair access to information. FAR 9.505-4 states a contractor does not gain an unfair competitive advantage when *restrictions* are imposed. Restrictions typically involve firewalls that isolate information about a project and the personnel with access to protected information to one part of a company, preventing other parts of the company from having knowledge or influence over the project. A firewall should prevent personnel with access to the sensitive information from using that information on another project where the protected data may be useful. Firewalls do not address the requirements in FAR 9.505-4(b) that contractors gaining access to information obtain an agreement with the contractor that owns the proprietary information.

Firewalls may require Nondisclosure Agreements (NDAs) requiring individuals sign commitments to protect information. An individual NDA can be used to obtain an individual commitment to protect information as condition to use of the information. A corporate NDA, signed by the corporate official with contractual authority, can be used to obtain a corporate commitment to protect information. See *Solers, Inc.*, Comp. Gen. Dec. B-418500.2, 2020 CPD ¶ 261, and *BAE Sys. Tech. Solutions & Servs., Inc.*, Comp. Gen. Dec. B-411810.3, 2016 CPD ¶ 168, finding signed NDAs adequately mitigated unequal access to information in the absence of hard facts showing NDAs failed to prevent an unfair competitive advantage.

Restrictions on personnel take firewalls and NDAs a step further, preventing individuals with nonpublic information from positions where the knowledge of the information creates an unfair competitive advantage. Restrictions on personnel limit a contractor from allowing an employee to participate in proposal activities where knowing source selection information would create an unfair competitive advantage. Restricting the movement of personnel is not common, yet is useful to protect source selection information in situations where the contractor is otherwise free from an OCI, e.g., having access to source selection information and the support service does not require subjective judgment.

The restriction or firewall should be in the contract that provides the access to the information to prevent a conflict in the second contract. *Netstar–1 Gov't Consulting, Inc. v. United States*, 98 Fed. Cl. 729 (2011), discusses how an after-the-fact mitigation plan which included declarations, NDAs, and firewalls, failed to protect protester's proprietary information. The section on clauses discusses two agency clauses that create contractual restrictions to prevent conflicts based on unequal access to information.

Finally, GAO has held that firewalls, in and of themselves, only resolve conflicts due to unequal access to information. Decisions holding that firewalls alone do not adequately mitigate impaired objectivity include: *Aetna; Johnson Controls World Serv., Inc.*, B-286714.2, 2001 CPD 20; *PURVIS Sys. Inc.*, B-293807.3, 2004 CPD ¶ 96; *LEADS Corp.*, Comp. Gen. Dec. B-292465, 2003

CPD ¶ 197; *Nortel Gov't Solutions, Inc.*, Comp. Gen. Dec. B-299522.5, 2009 CPD ¶ 10; *First Coast Serv. Options, Inc.*, Comp. Gen. Dec. B-401429, 2010 CPD ¶ 6; and *Leidos, Inc.*, Comp. Gen. Dec. B-417994, 2019 CPD ¶ 425.

[b] Use of Another Contractor

Conflicts based on impaired objectivity can be resolved by having another contractor that has no conflict perform the portion of the SOW creating the conflict. The mitigation plan must document how use of a nonconflicted party will mitigate the conflict. Additionally, the mitigation plan must firewall the party with the conflict from the party that is conflict free. The firewall avoids the improper flow of information, thereby preventing the contractor with the conflict from applying improper influence on the contractor that is conflict free. This technique, however, is best used to mitigate conflicts of a subcontractor.

Limiting this technique to conflicts at the subcontractor level addresses two of GAO's concerns. In *Alion Sci. & Tech. Corp.*, Comp. Gen. Dec. B-297342, 2006 CPD ¶ 1, GAO observed the firewall between the prime and the subcontractor reduces the prime's ability to oversee work performed by the subcontractor. GAO also questioned the wisdom of this technique when the conflict involved a large percentage of the SOW. In *Epoch Eng'g, Inc.*, Comp. Gen. Dec. B-276634, 97-2 CPD ¶ 72, GAO asked whether the contractor performing the work had enough qualified personnel to perform the particular task without being dependent upon the personnel from the firm with the conflict.

Even with these concerns, GAO recognizes a firewall between a contractor and a subcontractor free from conflict as an effective technique to mitigate conflicts. See *Business Consulting Assocs., LLC*, Comp. Gen. Dec. B-299758.2, 2007 CPD ¶ 134 (contractor would perform work when subcontractor had an OCI); *Alion Sci. & Tech. Corp.*, Comp. Gen. Dec. B-297022.4, 2006 CPD ¶ 146 (contractor with OCI agreed to transfer the one-third of work impacted by the OCI to a firewalled subcontractor); *Deutsche Bank*, Comp. Gen. Dec. B-289111, 2001 CPD ¶ 210 (contractor with OCI agreed to transfer work impacted by the conflict to firewalled subcontractor that would report directly to agency).

If a subcontractor has a conflict, a contractor can mitigate it by demonstrating that it has sufficient resources to ensure that no conflicted work will be assigned to that subcontractor, *URS Fed. Servs., Inc.*, Comp. Gen. Dec. B-417643.2, 2020 CPD ¶ 75. See also *Epoch Eng'g, Inc.*, Comp. Gen. Dec. B-276634, 97-2 CPD ¶ 72 (the awardee's proposed conflict mitigation plan included a number of safeguards designed to detect potential conflicts and to assign work under those task orders to itself and/or another subcontractor); *SC&A, Inc.*, Comp. Gen. Dec. B-270160.2, 96-1 CPD ¶ 197 (awardee successfully avoided a potential conflict one of its subcontractors had by performing the conflicted task without using the subcontractor's personnel); and *Overlook Sys. Techs., Inc.*, Comp. Gen. Dec. B-298099.4, 2006 CPD ¶ 185 (reassigning work to a firewalled subcontractor resolved bias which the firewall itself could not mitigate).

[c] Release of Information

Another technique to mitigate a conflict involves the release of nonpublic information. Releasing information reduces an unfair competition, but does not address bias associated impaired objectivity or biased ground rules. More importantly, this technique cannot be used with proprietary information. In an early OCI decision, *GIC Agricultural Group*, 72 Comp. Gen. 14 (B-249065), 92-2 CPD ¶ 263, GAO found that an agency unwittingly based the statement of work in a solicitation on a study prepared by a contractor and then the agency did not disqualify contractor from the competition. In sustaining the protest, GAO said that, at a minimum, the agency should provide a copy of the study to the protester. Although it is questionable whether GAO would propose this corrective action now, the decision shows that releasing information can mitigate OCIs. Examples of the technique include: *Harmonia Holdings, LLC*, Comp. Gen Dec. B-407186.2, 2013 CPD ¶ 66 (GAO recognized the release of information about the hardware and software configuration mitigated any possible unfair competitive advantage the incumbent contractor enjoyed); *Superlative Techs., Inc.*, Comp. Gen. Dec. B-415405, 2018 CPD ¶ 19 (the contracting officer released the government's staffing plan estimate to all offerors to mitigate an allegation that incumbency gave one offeror an unfair competitive advantage); *Thomas Solutions, Inc*., Comp. Gen. Dec. B-415311.7, 2018 CPD ¶ 418 (the contracting officer disclosed the names of the evaluation members after an investigation showed the evaluator's names became common knowledge); and *CACI, Inc.-Fed.*, Comp. Gen. Dec. B-413860.4, 2018 CPD ¶ 17 (the agency released the Independent Government Cost Estimate to offerors in response to an inadvertent disclosure of certain proprietary cost information).

[d] Monitoring

Monitoring is a useful technique to mitigate conflicts and is a particularly effective way to address the unique issues associated with IDIQ contracts. FAR subpart 9.5 requires contracting officers resolve all OCIs prior to award; however, the government issues orders after award of the IDIQ contract. See, for example, *Alion Sci. & Tech. Corp.*, Comp. Gen. Dec. B-297342, 2006 CPD ¶ 1, and *Overlook Sys. Techs., Inc.*, Comp. Gen. Dec. B-298099.4, 2006 CPD ¶ 185, two decisions involving IDIQ contracts with broad statements of work which required the contacting officer resolve all possible conflicts associated with future orders before awarding the IDIQ contract.

Daniel I. Gordon in his article entitled, *Organizational Conflicts of Interest: A Growing Integrity Challenge*, 35 Pub. Cont. L.J. 25 (2005), states that the greater use of IDIQ contracts with broad and less specific statements of work has contributed to a growing number of OCIs. Additionally, work under an earlier order may create a conflict with regard to eligibility for work in future orders. See, for example, *C2C Innovative Solutions, Inc.*, Comp. Gen. Dec., B-416289, 2018 CPD ¶ 269 (the protester alleged the awardee had an impaired objectivity OCI between a task order issued under another IDIQ contract and the current task order); and *LOGC2, Inc.*, Comp. Gen. Dec. B-416075, 2018 CPD ¶ 204 (GAO did not find task orders held by awardee's subcontractor created conflicts based on impaired objectivity and unequal access to information).

Monitoring usually is part of an acceptable resolution of conflicts in future orders; it is almost impossible to resolve unknown conflicts at award. But self-monitoring alone does not adequately mitigate a conflict. See *Analysis Group*, Comp. Gen. Dec. B-401726, 2009 CPD ¶ 404, and *J&E Assoc., Inc.*, Comp. Gen. Dec. B-278771, 98-1 CPD ¶ 77, where GAO held that mere oversight only identified conflicts of interest as they arise, but "would do nothing to avoid, mitigate, or neutralize such conflicts." Nevertheless, monitoring can be a *key* part of mitigating potential conflicts associated with future task orders if the mitigation plan also lists the types of resolution the contractor will accept. This type of mitigation plan describes possible conflicts, requires the contractor to review each task order for a conflict, and requires the contractor to notify the contracting officer when a conflict is identified. This type of mitigation plan also lists the types of resolution the contractor will accept, resolutions listed like a "waterfall" beginning with firewalls (the least onerous) and ending with a limitation on future contracting (the most onerous). The contracting officer decides whether the order creates a conflict and then selects the appropriate technique to resolve the conflict.

In *Social Impact, Inc.*, Comp. Gen. Dec. B-412941, 2016 CPD ¶ 203, which involves the type of mitigation plan discussed above, GAO upheld the mitigation plan, finding the mitigation plan set forth "specific procedures for identifying potential OCIs" and charged the contractor "with implementing and adhering to those procedures." The plan required the contractor to report on a number of specific areas and involved the agency with assessment of potential future OCIs when new requirements were assigned.

Additionally, monitoring can be an effective technique to address conflicts involving impaired objectivity. Decisions upholding monitoring as a way to resolve impaired objectivity include: *Inquiries, Inc.*, Comp. Gen. Dec. B-418486, 2020 CPD ¶ 182 (no OCI where contractor could schedule work to favor its company but agency had a system to monitor this activity); *SafalPartners, Inc.*, Comp. Gen. Dec. B-416937, 2019 CPD ¶ 20 (although a contractor can offer its input to the agency as part of monitoring, the government must retain the ultimate decision-making authority for monitoring to reasonably mitigate impaired objectivity); *Visual Connections, LLC*, Comp. Gen. Dec. B-416759, 2018 CPD ¶ 413 (no impaired objectivity because the government had ultimate responsibility for the program); *Wyle Labs., Inc.*, Comp. Gen. Dec.

B-288892, 2002 CPD ¶ 12 (no OCI where a contractor operated a top-level laboratory and several lower level laboratories but GAO accepted the agency's argument that government personnel would do the actual monitoring of performance of all of the laboratories); *LEADS* 292465, 2003 CPD ¶ 197 (mitigation plan included a provision requiring the contractor to notify the contracting officer of any task order for which it desired to compete so that the agency could avoid using the contractor's personnel on that task order). But compare *ASM Research*, Comp. Gen. Dec. B-412187, 2016 CPD ¶ 38 (impaired objectivity exists "even where the agency asserts that it is not relying solely on the contractor's input, and where the government retains the ultimate decision-making authority").

[4] Waivers

Waivers do not resolve the conflict; waivers allow the agency head or a designee to disregard FAR subpart 9.5. FAR 9.503 states:

> The agency head or a designee may waive any general rule or procedure of this subpart by determining that its application in a particular situation would not be in the Government's interest. Any request for waiver must be in writing, shall set forth the extent of the conflict, and requires approval by the agency head or a designee. Agency heads shall not delegate waiver authority below the level of head of a contracting activity.

Historically, agencies were reluctant to waive OCI and, instead, relied on other methods to address conflicts. But this reluctance to use waivers seems to have waned and protesters have attempted to challenge the validity of waivers. In *AT&T Gov't Solutions, Inc.*, B-407720, 2013 CPD ¶ 45, the agency argued a waiver made issues about OCI academic. GAO agreed, stating "the FAR authority here permits waiver of any general rule or procedure within FAR Subpart 9.5." However, GAO also noted that a protester may separately challenge the agency's waiver. *AT&T* shifts the litigation from whether an agency properly identified and resolved a conflict to whether an agency correctly waived a conflict. In *Concurrent Techs. Corp.*, Comp. Gen. Dec. B-412795.2, 2017 CPD ¶ 25, GAO denied an allegation that the waiver was incomplete, and therefore, not effective. The protester alleged the waiver was incomplete because the official failed to adequately consider the full record. GAO found that the agency acted reasonably because the waiver complied with the requirements of FAR 9.503.

The decisions in *AT&T* and *Concurrent* laid the foundation for the decision in *CACI, Inc.-Fed.*, Comp. Gen Dec. B-413860.4, 2018 CPD ¶ 17, which addresses multiple allegations regarding a waiver. Like *Concurrent*, the protesters argued the waiver was ineffective because the agency's investigation was incomplete and unreasonable. GAO examined the waiver against the record to ensure the agency understood the nature of the conflict. Both *CACI* and *Concurrent* demonstrate the advantage of having an OCI investigation before the agency waives a conflict. The OCI investigation helps the agency demonstrate it knew the risks associated with the waiver. The protesters then argued the OCI waiver was unreasonable because the waiver relied on allegations in the protest and not the facts in the record. GAO disagreed, holding that the waiver showed the agency did not rely on its conclusions in its OCI investigation of the protest allegation, which found no conflict existed and, instead, the agency considered whether the waiver was in the best interests of the government.

The protesters continued challenging the waiver, arguing agencies could not waive an OCI after the competitive harm occurred. The agency waived an alleged conflict involving unequal access of information when the alleged harm occurred before the agency released the solicitation. GAO dismissed this challenge, stating:

> FAR 9.503 provides agencies the authority to waive "any general rule or procedure" of FAR subpart 9.5. This provision does not set forth a time at which the waiver must take place, nor does the provision prohibit waiver after a particular point in time.

Finally, the protesters questioned whether the waiver was in the "best interest of the government," a challenge that may be the most effective way to overturn future waivers. After reviewing the actions of the agency in *CACI*, GAO said disagreements with the agency were not sufficient "to conclude that the agency exceeded its authority or abused its discretion in waiving the OCIs here."

Although GAO denied the final challenge, this challenge may reveal limitations on the use of waivers. Waivers cannot be arbitrary or capricious; agencies cannot exceed their authority. Waivers require balancing the interests of the government against the protections of FAR subpart 9.5. The agency in *CACI* easily demonstrated government interests outweighed the protections of subpart 9.5. First, the agency did not believe an OCI existed, which indicated the conflict was not significant. Second, the agency waived residual conflicts after taking remedial action by releasing the Independent Government Cost Estimate to address an advertent disclosure of proprietary information.

Taking remedial action and then waiving residual conflicts helps agencies justify why the government's interest outweigh the protections in FAR subpart 9.5. See, for example, *Enterprise Servs., LLC*, Comp. Gen. Dec. B-417329, 2019 CPD ¶ 205. Although a waiver does nothing to resolve the conflict, the agency has taken remedial measures to lessen the conflict before waiving the residual conflict. Remedial measures demonstrate the agency did not completely ignore the conflict. The classic remedial action involves establishing a firewall before waiving the residual bias associated with impaired objectivity. In addition, government interests may involve the amount of available competition, e.g., granting a waiver to create effective competition, and the type of conflict being waived, e.g., bias affects government's interest while unfair competitive advantage affects both government's interest and industry's interests.

Issuing a waiver is also a way for an agency to overcome questionable OCI allegations when it is important to allow the awardee to proceed to performance, *Perspecta Enter. Solutions, LLC*, Comp. Gen. Dec. B-418533.2, 2020 CPD ¶ 213.

[C] Procedures: Solicitation Provisions and Contract Clauses

The procedures in FAR subpart 9.5 can reduce the amount of OCI litigation. The most important procedure requires contracting officers to identify and evaluate potential OCIs *as early in the acquisition process as possible*, FAR 9.504(a)(1)(i). At the same time, contracting officers are to "avoid creating unnecessary delays, burdensome information requirements, and excessive documentation" and only need to formally document their judgment "when a substantive issue concerning potential organizational conflict of interest exists," FAR9.504 (d). A solicitation provision documents the contracting officer's judgment and allows contracting officers to control the dialogue on OCIs.

Clauses on OCI are equally as important as solicitation provisions; clauses implement the resolution methods selected to address the OCI. Clauses create the limitation on future contracting; clauses help implement mitigation plans; and clauses restrict the use of nonpublic information.

Also, the presence of OCI provisions and clauses prompts offerors to ask questions about conflicts during the source selection process. It is better to address OCI concerns before proposals are submitted instead of litigating OCI allegations after award.

Yet contracting officers often do not use solicitation provisions or contract clauses because the concept of "significant" only requires a solicitation provision and contract clauses when an acquisition involves a significant, potential conflict. In addition, while FAR 9.506 states contracting officers may avoid, neutralize, or mitigate a conflict, FAR 9.507 only provides guidance on limitations on future contracting.

[1] Procedures for Solicitation Provisions

FAR 9.506 entitled "Procedures" describes the procedures that govern use of solicitation provisions to address OCI issues.

FAR 9.506(a) requires contracting officers first to seek information on an offeror's financial interest from within the government or from other readily available sources. GAO has held contracting officers cannot solely rely on representations of financial interests provided by offerors, *Diversified Collection Serv., Inc.*, Comp. Gen. Dec. B-406958.3, 2013 CPD ¶ 23; *Analysis Group, LLC*, Comp. Gen. Dec. B-401726, 2009 CPD ¶ 237. Notwithstanding GAO's interpretation of FAR 9.506(a), contractors best know their financial interests and the government best knows whether the requirement has the potential to create a conflict. A solicitation provision can require offerors identify all conflicting interests. Industry, however, objected to certifying their representations on conflicting interests, requesting these representations be limited to an offeror's "best knowledge and belief." Contractors do not necessarily know all of the interests of their affiliates and team members.

FAR 9.506(b) requires contracting officers to decide when "a particular acquisition involves a significant potential organizational conflict of interest," a requirement that applies to all competitions. If a significant, potential OCI exists, the procedures require the contracting officer to prepare a recommended course of action, draft a solicitation provision and, if necessary, draft a contract clause. The procedures envision communications with industry since contracting officers are to "consider additional information provided by prospective contractors in response to the solicitation or during negotiations." Finally, the contracting officer must resolve the conflict prior to award "consistent with the approval or other direction by the head of the contracting activity." The need to involve the head of the contracting activity suggests significant conflicts were unusual when FAR subpart 9.5 was written in the 1960's.

FAR 9.507-1, provides that solicitations which have a significant potential OCI, shall contain a provision that—

> (a) Invites offerors' attention to this subpart;
>
> (b) States the nature of the potential conflict as seen by the contracting officer;
>
> (c) States the nature of the proposed restraint upon future contractor activities; and
>
> (d) Depending on the nature of the acquisition, states whether or not the terms of any proposed clause and the application of this subpart to the contract are subject to negotiation.

The obligation to state "the nature of the potential conflict as seen by the contracting officer" verifies that the government is in the best position to know how the statement of work may create a conflict. However, not all offerors will have a conflict or will have the same conflict because each offeror has different financial interests. Also, these different financial interests may create conflicts a contracting officer cannot identify easily.

Additionally, a solicitation provision starts a dialogue between the agency and the offerors about OCIs. A solicitation provision tells offerors how the contracting officer views the potential conflict; OCI clauses in the solicitation outline potential resolutions. This information triggers questions and opinions offerors have on potential conflicts. And the procedures in FAR 9.506 require contracting officers to "consider additional information provided by prospective contractors in response to the solicitation or during negotiations."

While not expressly citing FAR subpart 9.5, GAO expects agencies to respond to questions offerors raise about OCIs. GAO presumes harm when an agency fails to respond to OCI allegations raised during the source selection process. See *Celadon Labs., Inc.*, Comp. Gen. Dec. B-298533, 2006 CPD ¶ 158, and *Satellite Tracking of People, LLC*, Comp. Gen. Dec. B-411845, 2015 CPD ¶ 347. Assuming the contracting officer cannot find credible evidence supporting the allegation, the contracting officer should explain in writing why the facts do not constitute an OCI in order to rebut this presumption. If the contracting officer believes the allegation is credible, then the contracting officer should take steps to resolve the conflict.

In addition, a solicitation provision allows a contracting officer to set rules or restrictions. FAR 9.507-1 gives the contracting officer the authority to propose restraints upon future contracting and then to decide whether the restraints are subject to negotiations. The ability to establish rules regarding limitations to future contracting suggests the contracting officer has the authority to set other rules on OCIs. These other rules could involve other methods of resolution and agency decisions on OCI matters.

Protests typically do not involve solicitations with an OCI provision. Two reasons explain why these solicitation provisions are missing. First, FAR 9.506(b) requires a solicitation provision when "the contracting officer decides that a particular acquisition involves a *significant* potential organizational conflict of interest." But the word "significant" is subjective. Protesters see a significant conflict; contracting officers see a remote conflict. Decisions, therefore, focus on whether a significant conflict exits and not whether the solicitation should have included a provision on OCI.

Second, the lack of a model solicitation provision also explains why few solicitations contain provisions on OCIs. Contracting officers are accustomed to the provisions in Part 52 of the FAR which are "plug and play," but the factually intense nature of OCI prevents "plug and play" provisions. The contracting officer must tailor each solicitation provision to reflect the actual or potential conflict created by the requirement. Consequently, contracting officers do not handcraft a solicitation provision unless the conflict is glaring.

But contracting officers should not look for reasons to avoid including provisions on OCI in solicitations; solicitation provisions are key to minimizing OCIs. FAR 9.506 requires contracting officers to analyze requirements to determine whether a conflict or potential conflict exists. Sharing this OCI analysis in a solicitation provision relays the agency's position on conflicts. An agency's position on a conflict may influence whether a contractor will expend bid and proposal costs. Therefore, contracting officers should include a solicitation provision when the facts suggest questions about a whether conflict may exist and the solicitation is likely to be protested. Concerns about conflicts arise when:

- Contractors supported the solicitation effort,
- The program has a contractor providing systems engineering or technical support,

- An existing contract will interface with the work being solicited e.g., existing contract for quality assurance (QA) and a solicitation for effort the QA contractor will oversee.

Although these circumstances do not necessarily require disqualification, these circumstances raise concerns about the possibility of a conflict.

Just as importantly, a solicitation provision can establish "rules" in the solicitation. Following Federal Circuit precedent, the Court of Federal Claims requires that offerors challenge rules of the competition no later than receipt of proposals when a party believes a solicitation contains a patent error, *Blue & Gold, Fleet, L.P. v. United States*, 492 F.3d 1308 (Fed. Cir. 2007); and *COMINT Sys. Corp. v. United States*, 700 F.3d 1377 (Fed. Cir. 2012). *Blue & Gold* states that this requirement prevents a contractor with knowledge of a defect from "taking advantage of the government and other bidders, and avoids costly after-the-fact litigation." The court in *RMGS, Inc. v. United States*, 140 Fed. Cl. 728 (2018), found a disappointed bidder gave up its ability to allege that an OCI clause was too broad because it filed its protest after contract award. A solicitation provision is an excellent place to announce this rule.

GAO follows a different rule on timeliness of protests challenging OCI issues. Typically, GAO treats most OCI allegations as matters that must be raised after award and will generally dismiss as premature pre-award OCI allegation, *Liquidity Servs., Inc.* Comp. Gen. Dec. B-409718, 2014 CPD ¶ 221; *North Wind, Inc.*, Comp. Gen. Dec. B-404880.7, 2012 CPD ¶ 314; and *REEP, Inc.*, Comp. Gen. Dec. B-290688, 2002 CPD ¶ 158. However, GAO's timeliness rules require that disappointed offerors file protests before the closing time for the receipt of proposals when the protester is aware of the facts giving rise to the potential OCI, and the agency has communicated whether the conflict requires disqualification. See *Abt Assocs., Inc.*, Comp. Gen. Dec. B-294130, 2004 CPD ¶ 174. In *Honeywell Tech. Solutions, Inc.*, Comp. Gen. Dec. B-400771, 2009 CPD ¶ 49, GAO dismissed an OCI allegation as untimely where the agency explained why an OCI did not preclude the awardee from competing in written answers to questions about the solicitation. Compare *Systems Made Simple, Inc.*, Comp. Gen. Dec. B-412948.2, 2016 CPD ¶ 207 (protest was not untimely because the agency's questions and answers did not advise vendors whether the agency had considered and resolved OCI concerns); and *Deque Sys., Inc.*, Comp. Gen. Dec. B-415965.4, 2018 CPD ¶ 226 (GAO dismissed a protest challenging agency's corrective action as premature "where the protester merely anticipates improper prejudicial agency action").

Accordingly, there may be advantages available for contracting officers that are willing and able to prepare a solicitation provision which contains their initial OCI determinations. These determinations need to explain whether and why FAR subpart 9.5 disqualifies certain contractors from the competition. The solicitation provision also should summarize any actions the government took to reduce a conflict to an acceptable level. This information should prevent contractors from spending bid and proposal costs needlessly and should reduce the number of post-award protests on OCIs to the extent the issues are clearly covered in the ground rules of the solicitation.

Finally, decisions illustrate how subjective the word "significant" is and how risky it is to rely on this word. Instead, contracting officers should include a provision on OCIs in the solicitation even when the contracting officer believes the conflict is remote or has been reasonably resolved. A solicitation provision notifies offerors about conclusions made on conflicts, information that can act as rules of the competition. A solicitation provision moves conversations about conflicts from protests filed after award to dialogues held before the submission of proposals. An effective solicitation provision mitigates the risk that OCIs will surface as disruptive post award protest issues.

[2] OCI Clauses

Clauses are essential to execute the resolution methods selected to address conflicts. OCI clauses implement limitations on future contracting, help implement mitigation plans, and create restrictions to protect information. Like solicitation provisions, few decision exist on OCI clauses because of the lack of standardized clauses and the resistance to accept a clause limiting future contracting.

FAR 9.507-2 gives guidance on a clause to limit future contracting, stating:

> (a) If, as a condition of award, the contractor's eligibility for future prime contract or subcontract awards will be restricted or the contractor must agree to some other restraint, the solicitation shall contain a proposed clause that specifies both the nature and duration of the proposed restraint. The contracting officer shall include the clause in the contract, first negotiating the clause's final terms with the successful offeror, if it is appropriate to do so (see 9.506(d)).
>
> (b) The restraint imposed by a clause shall be limited to a fixed term of reasonable duration, sufficient to avoid the circumstance of unfair competitive advantage or potential bias. This period varies. It might end, for example, when the first production contract using the contractor's specifications or work statement is awarded, or it might extend through the entire life of a system for which the contractor has performed systems engineering and technical direction. In every case, the restriction shall specify termination by a specific date or upon the occurrence of an identifiable event.

FAR 9.507-2 requires parties to negotiate the terms of the clause before award since the limitation on future contracting resolves the conflict. The restriction on future contracting "shall be limited to a fixed term of reasonable duration, sufficient to avoid the circumstance of unfair competitive advantage or potential bias," FAR 9.507-2. FAR 9.507-1, however, gives the contracting officer the ability to propose a clause in the solicitation and to state whether the clause is subject to negotiation. In addition to establishing the length of the restriction, the restriction should be limited to the effort creating the conflict. Failure to limit the effort could restrict the contractor from performing any future work.

Subpart 9.5 does not contain a standard clause to limit future contracting and, instead, the contracting officers must draft a new clause for each solicitation and contract. The NASA FAR Supplement, however, contains a clause to restrict competition—the Limitation of Future Contracting clause at NFS 1852.209-710.

While not essential, clauses also help implement mitigation plans. A clause incorporates the mitigation plan in the contract, making compliance with the plan a requirement of the contract. Such a clause addresses how changes to the statement of work will affect the mitigation plan and requires the contractor to report any changes that may create new conflicts, e.g., new business or mergers.

In addition, as discussed previously in relation to firewalls, clauses can prevent conflicts based on unequal access to information by restricting information about the project and the personnel with access to protected information. Such clauses that restrict nonpublic information should become contractual obligations. Two agencies have clauses restricting the use of nonpublic information accessed in the first contract: Access to Sensitive Information at NFS 1852.237-72, and Limitations on the Use or Disclosure of Government-Furnished Information Marked with Restrictive Legends at DFARS 252.227-7025.

DFARS 209.505-4 states that support contractors may be required to enter into nondisclosure agreements directly with the third-party asserting restrictions on limited rights to technical data, commercial technical data, or restricted rights to computer software. On the other hand, NFS 1809.505-4 provides that contractors and subcontractors do not need "to enter into separate, interrelated third party agreements" when the contract contains the Release of Sensitive Information clause at NFS 1852.237-73. This clause requires offerors and contractors to agree "NASA may release their sensitive information when requested by service providers" subject to the safeguards and protections delineated in the Access to Sensitive Information clause at 1852.237-72. See NFS 1837.203-71 on the release of contractors' sensitive information.

Not surprisingly, the acquisition community recognizes that the lack of a solicitation provision and clauses in FAR subpart 9.5 creates unnecessary litigation. The proposed rewrite of this subpart attempted to cure this issue by providing a solicitation provision and clauses contracting officers can use to resolve OCI concerns. See 76 Fed. Reg. 23236 (Apr. 26, 2011). The rewrite was controversial and never finalized. But the proposed clauses and solicitation provision in the rewrite provide a starting point for contracting officers to tailor provisions and clauses unique to each conflict.

The NASA OCI Guide also contains useful model contract clauses and a model solicitation provision on OCIs. These model clauses and solicitation provision were not subject to rulemaking and, therefore, act only as templates to handcraft clauses and provisions. The NASA OCI Guide also explains other issues contracting officers should address during the source selection process.

[D] Ancillary Matters

[1] Statutory Restrictions

Although the guidance in FAR subpart 9.5 is based on policy, Congress passed various statutes that create a separate framework for conflicts, frameworks unique to the Department of Energy (DOE), DoD, and NASA. These statutes explain why FAR 9.502(d) states "acquisitions subject to unique agency organizational conflict of interest statutes are excluded from the requirements of this subpart."

DOE has three statutes on conflicts affecting DOE procurements. The Federal Energy Administration Act of 1974, Pub. L. No. 93-275, authorizes certain research and development efforts subject to organizational conflicts of interest concerns. Public Law 95-39 establishes statutory requirements for avoiding organizational conflicts of interest for functions of the Department derived from the Energy Research and Development Administration. Public Law 95-70 establishes statutory requirements for avoiding organizational conflicts of interest for functions of the Department derived from the Federal Energy Administration. DOE implemented these statutory restrictions in subpart 909.5 of the Department of Energy Acquisition Regulation (DEAR). The DEAR requires that the provision Organizational Conflicts of Interest Disclosure-Advisory and Assistance Services at DEAR 952.209-8, be included in solicitations for advisory and assistance services expected to exceed the simplified acquisition threshold. The DEAR also requires the Organizational Conflicts of Interest clause at 952.209-72, in solicitations and contracts for advisory and assistance services expected to exceed the simplified acquisition threshold.

Likewise, 10 U.S.C. § 4292 (formerly § 2410p) prohibits DoD from using lead systems integrators beyond low-rate initial production. In addition, § 207 of the Weapons System Acquisition Reform Act of 2009, Pub. L. No. 111-23, places restrictions on DoD's use of systems engineering and technical assistance contractors in major defense acquisitions. DFARS 209.570 contains restrictions on lead systems integrators and DFARS 209.717 contains restrictions on systems engineering and technical assistance contractors.

Both DFARS 209.705 and DFARS 209.715 prescribe solicitation provisions and clauses. DFARS 209.705-4 requires the Limitations on Contractors Acting as Lead System Integrators provision at 252.209-7006, in solicitations when the acquisition strategy envisions the use of a lead system integrator for a major defense program. DFARS 209.705-4 requires the Prohibited Financial Interests for Lead System Integrators clause at 252.209-7007, in contracts when the contractor will fill the role of a lead system integrator for the acquisition of a major system. DFARS 209.715-8 requires the Notice of Prohibition Relating to Organizational Conflict of Interest—Major Defense Acquisition Program provision at 252.209-7008, in solicitations for systems engineering and technical assistance for major defense acquisition programs or pre-major defense acquisition programs. This provision notifies offerors of the statutory prohibitions in § 207 in Public Law 111-23. DFARS 209.715-8 also requires the Organizational Conflict of Interest—Major Defense Acquisition Program clause at 252.209-7009, implementing the prohibitions in Public Law 111-23.

Similarly, § 830 of the NASA Transition Authorization Act of 2017, Pub. L. No. 115-10, places limitations on NASA regarding major acquisition programs. These limitations focus on systems engineering and technical assistance, professional services, management support services, and technical evaluation. Both NASA's and DoD's statutory restrictions highlight Congressional concerns about the conflicts created by systems engineering and technical direction.

[2] Conflicts Created By Use of Government Employees

The use of former government employees that have been involved in the acquisition process is not treated as an OCI under FAR subpart 9.5. However, FAR 3.101-1 states general standards for procurement, one of which is "to avoid strictly any conflict of interest or even the appearance of a conflict of interest in Government-contractor relationships." *Health Net Fed. Servs., LLC*, Comp. Gen. Dec. B-401652.3, 2009 CPD ¶ 220, examines an awardee who hired a former government employee to help prepare the winning proposal. The record showed this employee, when working for the government, identified problems and weaknesses in the current TRICARE managed contractor system, discussed particular approaches and options for resolving the concerns, and debated the pros and cons and impacts of particular approaches. The record also showed, at a minimum, the former government employee, had access to information on the protester's performance on the predecessor contract, information which was both "non-public propriety" data and relevant to the current solicitation.

GAO concluded in *Health Net* that there was no OCI based on unequal access to information because that only occurs when the performance of a government contract gives the contractor access to information that provides an unfair competitive advantage. However, GAO held that FAR 3.101-1 required the contracting officer to ascertain whether this use of a former government employee created the appearance of impropriety which gave the offeror an unfair competitive advantage. GAO, though, acknowledged the standard under FAR subpart 3.1 was virtually indistinguishable from the standard to determine whether an offeror gained an unfair competitive advantage due to unequal access to information under subpart 9.5.

Not surprisingly, the agency and the intervenor argued there was no conflict because the former government employee complied with the Procurement Integrity Act (PIA) and had letters from the agency ethics attorney addressing his work to prepare the proposal for the awardee. But Health Net did not allege a PIA violation. GAO held that a firm can be "disqualified from a competition based upon the appearance of impropriety which is created by this situation—even if no actual impropriety can be shown—so long as the determination of an unfair competitive advantage is based on hard facts and not on mere innuendo or suspicion."

Later decisions analyze *Health Net* differently. *Northrop Grumman Sys. Corp.*, Comp. Gen. Dec. B-412278.7, 2017 CPD ¶ 299, discusses how GAO examines these decisions under both FAR 3.101-1 and subpart 9.5. In *Northrop Grumman*, GAO restated that challenges regarding hiring former government employees with access to nonpublic, competitively useful information are more accurately categorized as unfair competitive advantages under FAR subpart 3.1. However, GAO acknowledged that it had issued decisions treating allegations concerning former government employees as OCIs based on unequal access to information. See *Liquidity Servs., Inc.*, Comp. Gen. Dec. B-409718, 2014 CPD ¶ 221, and *Science Applications Int'l Corp.*, Comp. Gen. Dec. B-406921, 2012 CPD ¶ 267. In addition, *Northrop Grumman* identifies one significant difference between section 3.101 and subpart 9.5—"FAR subpart 3.1 does not permit the agency to waive concerns arising under that subpart."

As expected, the decisions following *Health Net* build upon the original decision. In *International Resources Group*, Comp. Gen. Dec. B-409346.2, 2014 CPD ¶ 369, GAO clarified *Health Net*, holding that prejudice will be presumed without the need for an inquiry whether that information was actually used when an awardee hired a former government employee who possesses competitively useful nonpublic information. *Jacobs Tech. Inc. v. United States*, 100 Fed. Cl. 198 (2011), explains that a violation of the PIA "requires an affirmative act by the offeror to obtain source selection information" and simply having knowledge due to government service is not enough to support a possible PIA violation. *Dell Serv. Fed. Gov't, Inc.*, Comp. Gen. Dec. B-414461, 2017 CPD ¶ 192, involves a competing contractor that possessed two earlier proposals from the incumbent contractor, but the PIA investigation concluded no competitive harm occurred because the current procurement was dissimilar to the proposals. The PIA investigation also excluded disclosure from the government and, instead, found an employee of a subcontractor likely disclosed the proposals. However, *Dell* found competitive harm because the disclosure created an OCI based on unequal access. Other post *Health Net* decisions include: *Perspecta Enter. Solutions, LLC*, Comp. Gen. Dec. B-418533.2, 2020 CPD ¶ 213 (no conflict because former employee had no access to competitively useful information); *Booz Allen Hamilton, Inc.*, Comp. Gen. Dec. B-418125, 2020 CPD ¶ 28 (no conflict because former employee had not participated in procurement); *Harmonia Holdings Group, LLC v. United States*, 144 Fed. Cl. 726 (2019) (no conflict because no hard facts showing that former employees had access to sensitive information); *ORBIS Sibro, Inc.*, Comp. Gen. Dec. B-417406.2, 2019 CPD ¶ 404 (no conflict because no hard facts showing that former employee had access to procurement sensitive information); *Interactive Info. Solutions, Inc.* Comp. Gen. Dec. B-415126.2, 2018 CPD ¶ 115 (no violation or conflict because the former government employee hired by the awardee did not have access to competitively useful information and did not help prepare the proposal);

Arctic Slope Mission Serv., LLC, Comp. Gen. Dec. B-412851, 2016 CPD ¶ 169 (no conflict found because proposed program manager, a current employee of the agency, was not involved in preparing the proposal); and *Threat Mgmt. Group*, Comp. Gen. Dec. B-407766.6, 2013 CPD ¶ 167 (no violation of 3.101 or subpart 9.5 when the awardee proposed a government employee to be its program manager and the individual was "a government employee at all times relevant to this procurement"). In *Obsidian Solutions Group, LLC,* Comp. Gen. Dec. B-417134, 2019 CPD ¶ 156, GAO held that the protester had been improperly excluded from the competition because its subcontractor had hired a former government employee, reasoning that there could be no unfair competitive advantage because the agency was going to award multiple contracts to all qualified offerors.

More interestingly, the decisions following *Health Net* spawned a new avenue to challenge awards with some challenges going beyond former government employees preparing proposals. Many GAO decisions refused to extend *Health Net* when the alleged competitive advantage comes from one firm receiving information from another firm. GAO stated this situation essentially amounts to a private dispute between private parties, *GEO Group*, Comp. Gen. Dec. B-405012, 2011 CPD ¶ 153; *Ellwood Nat'l Forge Co.*, Comp. Gen. Dec. B-402089.3, 2010 CPD ¶ 250; *Mgmt. Sciences for Health*, Comp. Gen. Dec. B-416041, 2018 CPD ¶ 197. But see *North Wind, Inc.* Comp. Gen. Dec. B-404880.7, 2012 CPD ¶ 314 where GAO did not deny the allegation as a dispute between two private parties, but, instead, denied the allegation because the information did not provide a competitive advantage.

The Office of Government Ethics adds to this complexity by declining to view *Health Net* as a post-employment restriction. Instead, the Office of Government Ethics views *Health Net* as a restriction on the type of work contractors may allow former government employees to perform. Then, *Health Net* correctly states "a person's familiarity with the type of work required resulting from the person's prior position in the government is not, by itself, evidence of an unfair competitive advantage." When a contractor hires a former government employee possessing valuable source selection information, the contractor should restrict that employee from all proposal activities where the former government employee's knowledge could give the contractor an unfair competitive advantage.

§ 4.04 DEBARMENT AND SUSPENSION

Debarment and suspension are drastic sanctions, precluding a company or individual from contracting with executive agencies. Debarments are defined as actions which "exclude a contractor from Government contracting and Government-approved subcontracting for a reasonable, specified period," FAR 2.101. Suspensions are temporary exclusions "pending the completion of investigation or legal proceedings, when it has been determined that immediate action is necessary to protect the Government's interest," FAR 9.407-1(b)(1). Contractors "proposed for debarment" are also excluded temporarily, FAR 9.404(b)(1). While this exclusion appears to relate only to contractors proposed for debarment for procurement violations, it has also been permitted in the case of a contractor proposed for debarment under the Davis-Bacon Act, *Salazar Constr. Co.*, 67 Comp. Gen. 115 (B-228071), 87-2 CPD ¶ 542.

There are two types of debarments: *procurement* and *inducement*. Procurement debarments and suspensions are carried out following the procedures in FAR Subpart 9.4, with the purpose of avoiding certain business risks associated with engaging in a contractual relationship with a firm. These risks relate directly to the procurement involved and include delivery of unacceptable products or services, waste of public funds, and contractor fraud. Thus, procurement debarment and suspension are the "appropriate means to effectuate" an express regulatory policy of ensuring "the Government's protection" by allowing contracting "with responsible contractors only," FAR 9.402(a)-(b). This basis for debarment and suspension involves behavior "of so serious or compelling a nature that it affects the present responsibility" of the contractor, FAR 9.406-2(c) and FAR 9.407-2(c). This type of sanction, referred to as "procurement," "nonresponsibility," or "administrative" debarment or suspension, is used by procuring agency officials as an integral part of the procurement process.

Inducement debarments have a different purpose—to induce contractors to perform government contracts in ways that will further fundamental social and economic goals, such as equal employment opportunity, the payment of prescribed minimum wages, and environmental protection. Debarments based upon a contractor's failure to participate effectively in furtherance of these goals have been referred to as "inducement" or "statutory" debarments because they are generally based upon statutory provisions. The grounds and procedures for these debarments are set forth in a variety of regulations issued by agencies outside of the procurement process such as the Department of Labor (DOL) and the Environmental Protection Agency (EPA). While the statutes, executive orders, and regulations creating and implementing these debarments are often imprecise in their terminology (using either "listing" or "ineligible," for example, apparently to mean the same thing) all sanctions that preclude contract awards for a specific period of time are encompassed in the discussion of debarment in this section (suspension is not used to induce contractors to carry out these goals). FAR 9.400(b) describes inducement debarments as declarations of "ineligibility" and states that it does not prescribe the policies or procedures applicable to them. However, they have the same effect as debarments issued by the procuring agencies.

All contractors that are "debarred, suspended, proposed for debarment or declared ineligible" are listed in the System for Award Management (SAM) exclusions list, FAR 9.404(a). This list also includes all entities excluded from nonprocurement transactions, making debarments of such entities applicable to procurement contracts, FAR 9.404(b)(1). Guidance on the broad scope of nonprocurement transactions is contained in, 2 C.F.R. Part 180. This list is compiled by GSA, and is posted on the Internet at *https://www.sam.gov*, FAR 9.404(d). Contracting officers use the SAM exclusions list to carry out the policies regarding debarred and suspended contractors.

Procurement debarment or suspension decisions are made by agency heads or designees rather than contracting officers. FAR 9.403 defines these designees as the "debarring official" and the "suspending official"; typically, authority over the suspension and debarment functions is lodged in one official. Debarment or suspension actions preclude contracting officers from awarding contracts to debarred or suspended contractors, FAR 9.405(a). Thus, debarment and suspension override the responsibility determination process including the SBA COC procedure.

Procurement and inducement debarments are treated differently when contracts are awarded to debarred firms through government inadvertence. Contracts awarded to firms debarred under statutes may be void ab initio, *Paisner v. United States*, 150 F. Supp. 835 (Ct. Cl. 1957), *cert. denied*, 355 U.S. 941 (1958), while contracts awarded to firms debarred pursuant to agency regulation are often voidable at the option of the government, *P.E.C. Corp.*, ASBCA 14241, 69-2 BCA ¶ 8056.

This section discusses the bases for debarment and suspension, the impact of these actions, and the procedures used to impose these sanctions.

[A] Exercise of Discretion

Even though the purposes of procurement and inducement debarments are different, both require the exercise of discretion in making the debarment or suspension decision. Thus, even though a cause for debarment has been clearly demonstrated, the debarring official must consider such factors as the seriousness of the improper conduct, mitigating circumstances, and remedial actions that have been taken.

[1] Procurement Debarments or Suspensions

Procurement debarments or suspensions are generally considered actions to be taken to protect the government from future misconduct, as FAR 9.402(b) states:

> The serious nature of debarment and suspension requires that these sanctions be imposed only in the public interest for the Government's protection and not for purposes of punishment. Agencies shall impose debarment or suspension to protect the Government's interest and only for the causes and in accordance with the procedures set forth in this subpart.

Under this policy, the primary consideration in imposing these sanctions should be the offeror's "present and likely future responsibility" rather than the mere fact that a past offense has been committed, *Roemer v. Hoffman*, 419 F. Supp. 130 (D.D.C. 1976). Courts have rejected the contention that debarment is punitive and that debarment violates double jeopardy, *Schorr v. Roberson*, Civ. Action No. 15-1290, (D.D.C. 2018); *Hudson v. United States*, 522 U.S. 93 (1997); *Bae v. Shalala*, 44 F.3d 489 (7th. Cir. 1995); *United States v. Bizzell*, 921 F.2d 263 (10th Cir. 1990), or that debarment is a form of criminal punishment, *United States v. Hatfield*, 108 F.3d 67 (4th Cir. 1997). However, one circuit court has stated that every debarment "is a form of punishment," *Fischer v. RTC*, 59 F.3d 1344 (D.C. Cir. 1995).

Conduct constituting grounds for debarment is sufficient to raise doubts concerning present responsibility. However, debarment officials must consider the seriousness of the contractor's conduct and any mitigating circumstances in deciding whether to impose debarment. FAR 9.406-1(a) provides:

> The existence of a cause for debarment, however, does not necessarily require that the contractor be debarred; the seriousness of the contractor's acts or omissions and any remedial measures or mitigating factors should be considered in making any debarment decision.

This regulatory policy establishes two key points. First, debarment is not to be an automatic consequence of a cause for debarment; rather, the debarment official is to exercise discretion. Second, it is appropriate not to debar in circumstances where the contractor's acts or omissions are not serious or where mitigating factors are strong. For example, the Housing and Urban Development (HUD) Board of Contract Appeals did not impose debarment where the contractor had rectified the misdeeds (making false statements to HUD) and produced letters indicating its present responsibility, *Lawrence C. Shank*, HUDBCA 82-724-D43, 83-1 BCA ¶ 16,439. In *Roemer*, the court remanded the debarment of a contractor based upon a conviction for accepting monies from a manufacturer's representative because the agency had not given a "hard look" to factors affecting the question of the firm's "present responsibility." The court discussed the kind of mitigating factors it considered relevant at 132:

> [T]he plaintiff has suggested a number of factors which appear to diminish the force of that conviction as an indication of Roemer's present responsibility. These factors touch on Roemer's character before the offense occurred, the circumstances surrounding the offense, the deterrent effect of the prior 29-month suspension, of the conviction, and of the payment to the government of $3,600 in restitution, the length of time which has passed since the offense and since the conviction, and Roemer's character since the offense and conviction.

In *Silverman v. Defense Logistics Agency*, 817 F. Supp. 846 (S.D. Cal. 1993), the court terminated a debarment based on a plea of guilty to a misdemeanor (with a fine of $250), because the debarring official had failed to consider the mitigating circumstance that the plea had been made to avoid an indictment for an offense of which the plaintiff did not believe he was guilty. The court also doubted if the agency was correct in finding the plaintiff not presently responsible when it had continued to contract with his company for six years after the alleged offense. In *C. & J. Harmon*, AGBCA 77-198, 79-1 BCA ¶13,705, the Agriculture board overturned a debarment based upon a firm's failure to satisfy contract requirements where the agency "mechanically" applied the debarment sanction without giving consideration to "surrounding" circumstances. In *Friedler v. GSA*, 271 F. Supp. 3d 40 (D.D.C. 2017), the court affirmed that agencies must consider the entire record when making a debarment decision as required by FAR 9.406–3(d). The court explained an agency would not have the entire record "unless the contractor has an opportunity to respond to the alleged bases for debarment."

Compare *Puma Co.*, GSBCA 6934-D, 83-1 BCA ¶16,349, and *Atlantic Chem. Co.*, GSBCA 5822-D, 80-2 BCA ¶14,801, where the board agreed that mitigating factors should be considered but deferred to the discretionary decision of the debarring official. See *David K. Alberta*, AGBCA 93-189-7, 94-2 BCA ¶26,923, where the board reduced the length of a contractor's debarment because its conviction for previous illegal activities did not demonstrate that it lacked present responsibility justifying continuation of the debarment. In *United States Testing Co.*, EPADEBAR 89-0021-00, Apr. 23, 1991, *Unpub.*, the board analogized the standard of "adequate evidence" in support of suspension to that of "probable cause" in support of a warrant. It noted that an adequate evidence showing need not rise to the level of that necessary for a successful criminal prosecution or a formal debarment. Similarly, in *Kirkpatrick v. White*, 351 F. Supp. 2d 1261, 1282 (N.D. Ala. 2004), the district court described the "adequate evidence" standard as "an extremely low standard of proof."

DFARS 209.406-1(a) has placed certain limitations on the debarring official's discretion to forgo debarment, stating:

> (ii) Before the debarring official decides not to suspend or debar in the case of an indictment or conviction for a felony, the debarring official must determine that the contractor has addressed adequately the circumstances that gave rise to the misconduct, and that appropriate standards of ethics and integrity are in place and are working.

This reflects a broader reliance upon compliance systems by enforcement officials to ensure the integrity of the contracting process. DFARS 209.406-1 provides:

> (a)(i) When the debarring official decides that debarment is not necessary, the official may require the contractor to enter into a written agreement which includes—

> (A) A requirement for the contractor to establish, if not already established, and to maintain the standards of conduct and internal control systems prescribed by Subpart 203.70; and
>
> (B) Other requirements the debarring official considers appropriate.

See Zucker & Fratarcangeli, *Administrative Compliance Agreements: An Effective Tool In The Suspension And Debarment Process*, 15 Clause 4 (Board of Contract Appeals Bar Ass'n Winter 2004); Seymour, Note, *Refining the Source of the Risk: Suspension and Debarment in the Post-Andersen Era*, 34 Pub. Cont. L.J. 357 (2005). Ultimately, however, suspension or debarment is a matter for the reviewing official's discretion, and it is the contractor's burden to show that suspension or debarment is not warranted, for example because adequate controls have been put in place, FAR 9.406-1(a). See Thomas, Annotation, *Judicial Review of Administrative Order Debarring Defense Contractor from Contracting with Federal Government*, 91 A.L.R. Fed. 868.

[2] Inducement Debarments

Statutes and other regulations providing for inducement debarments do not contain the clear statement of purpose included in FAR 9.402(b), but similar principles have been applied. These debarments are now subject to the government-wide Nonprocurement Common Rule (NCR) which sets forth the common policies and procedures that federal agencies must use in taking suspension or debarment actions. See 2 C.F.R. Part 180.

Nonetheless, these agencies have broad discretion in determining to debar a firm or person. Thus, under the Service Contract Act of 1965, 41 U.S.C. § 6706, the Secretary of Labor is given discretion to refrain from debarring violators upon a finding of "unusual circumstances." See *White Glove Bldg. Maint., Inc. v. Hodgson*, 459 F.2d 175 (9th Cir. 1972), affirming the discretion of the Secretary not to debar violators under the pre-1972 version of the Act, which simply stated that contracts should not be awarded to violators "unless the Secretary otherwise recommends." In *Washington Moving & Storage Co.*, SCA-168, Mar. 12, 1974, the Secretary of Labor identified the factors to be considered in deciding whether "unusual circumstances" are present:

> Whether "unusual circumstances" are present in a case within the meaning of the Act must be determined on the basis of the facts and circumstances of the particular case. Some of the principal factors which must be considered in making this determination are whether there is a history of repeated violations of the Act; the nature, extent, and seriousness of past or present violations; whether the violations were willful, or the circumstances show there was culpable neglect to ascertain whether certain practices were in compliance, or culpable disregard of whether they were or not, or other culpable conduct

> (such as deliberate falsification of records); whether the respondent's liability turned on bona fide legal issues of doubtful certainty; whether the respondent has demonstrated good faith, cooperation in the resolution of issues, and a desire and intention to comply with the requirements of the Act; and the promptness with which employees were paid the sums determined to be due them. It is clear that the mere payment of sums found due employees after an administrative proceeding, coupled with an assurance of future compliance, is not in itself sufficient to constitute "unusual circumstances" warranting relief from the ineligible list sanction. It is also clear that a history of recurrent violations of identical nature, such as repeated violations of identical minimum wage or recordkeeping provisions, does not permit a finding of "unusual circumstances."

See also *Federal Food Serv., Inc. v. Donovan*, 658 F.2d 830 (D.C. Cir. 1981), where the court reversed a decision of the Secretary of Labor debarring a contractor for "de minimis" underpayments under the Service Contract Act, concluding that the Secretary's failure to consider whether the facts warranted a finding of "unusual circumstances" constituted an "arbitrary" act. The court held that "use of debarment against innocent and petty violations was not intended." But see the Department of Labor Administrative Review Board's decision in *Coast Indus., Inc.*, DOL ARB No. 04-004, ALJ No. 2002-SCA-003 (Feb. 28, 2005), which pointed out that the SCA's debarment provision "is a particularly unforgiving provision of a demanding statute," and that a "contractor seeking an 'unusual circumstances' exemption from debarment must, therefore, run a narrow gauntlet." The board there noted, per *Vigilantes v. Administrator of Wage & Hour Div.*, 968 F.2d 1412, 1418 (1st Cir. 1992), that the "legislative history of the SCA makes clear that debarment of a contractor who violated the SCA should be the norm, not the exception, and only the most compelling of justifications should relieve a violating contractor from that sanction." See also *Dantran, Inc. v. Dep't of Labor*, 246 F.3d 36, 41 (1st Cir. 2001) (discussing violator's burden in establishing "unusual circumstances").

The Davis-Bacon Act, 40 U.S.C. § 276a, authorizes GAO to debar firms that have "disregarded their obligations" under the Act. GAO acts on recommendations of the Secretary of Labor, and has held that it will exercise limited discretion—debarring firms for "substantial violations" but not for "technical violations," *Bryant Paint Contracting, Inc.*, 64 Comp. Gen. 549 (B-217337) (1985). Thus, in *Rams-Head Constr., Inc.*, Comp. Gen. Dec. B-222063, Aug. 13, 1986, *Unpub.*, GAO refused to follow the debarment recommendation of the Secretary of Labor because there was insufficient evidence of "willful" violation of the Act; the contractor's not paying workers was based on either inadvertence or a justified concern that they had improperly reported hours worked. Compare *Phoenix Paint Co.*, Comp. Gen. Dec. B-242728, Jan. 2, 1992, *Unpub.*, debarring a contractor that had falsified payroll records even though it claimed that the violation was inadvertent (based on bad advice), had cooperated in the investigation, and had made restitution to the workers. See also *Mashburn Elec. Co.*, Comp. Gen. Dec. B-189471, 78-1 CPD ¶ 277, holding that such mitigating circumstances will not preclude debarment when there have been substantial violations of the Act. The Secretary of Labor also exercises discretion in determining whether to recommend debarment of a firm to GAO per the standards set forth at 29 C.F.R. § 5.12. See also *Thomas & Sons Bldg. Contractors, Inc.*, ARB No. 98-164, ALJ No. 96-DBA-33, at n.3 (June 8, 2001) (comparing Davis-Bacon and SCA debarment procedures).

Executive Order 11246, as amended, gives the Secretary of Labor the power to refrain from debarring firms not in compliance with contractual equal employment obligations, because § 209 of the executive order states that the Secretary "may" provide for debarment of noncomplying firms. See also the implementing regulations, at 41 C.F.R. § 60-1.24(c)(2), indicating that the director of the DOL's Office of Federal Contract Compliance Programs (OFCCP) should seek to resolve instances of violations through "informal means," such as conciliation agreements, before invoking sanctions. See Hordell, McWilliams III, Hoffman & Persico, *Employment Law for Contractors: A Primer*, 39 Proc. Lawyer 3 (ABA Winter 2004).

Clean Air Act and Federal Water Pollution Control Act regulations provide for the debarment of companies that violate the Acts, 40 C.F.R. § 32.110(d). See *Burke v. Environmental Protection Agency*, 127 F. Supp. 2d 235 (D.D.C. 2001) (five-year debarment not arbitrary because debarring official had considered potential mitigating factors); *Brent Stromberg*, EPA No. 07-0226-03, 2008 EPADEBAR LEXIS 4 (one year debarment based on conviction of perjury, with a thorough review of mitigating circumstances). However, an agency or the EPA debarring official may grant an exception to the regulations and permit a contractor to be eligible for a contract, 40 C.F.R. § 32.120.

The Buy American Act also provides for debarment, 41 U.S.C. § 8303(c). See *Glazer Constr. Co. v. United States*, 50 F. Supp. 2d 85 (D. Mass. 1999), holding that debarment was mandatory under the Act but, if not, there was no abuse of discretion.

[B] Causes for Debarment

Statutes and regulations list a number of causes that, in the absence of mitigating or other circumstances, will support debarment.

[1] Procurement Debarments

FAR 9.406-2 contains a list of acts that are sufficiently serious to warrant debarment proceedings—*conviction* of or *civil judgment* for offenses showing lack of business integrity, *serious* violation of contract terms, and other causes showing a lack of present responsibility.

[a] Lack of Business Integrity

FAR 9.406-2(a) permit debarment if there has been a conviction of or as civil judgment for the following types of conduct that indicate a lack of business integrity:

> (1) Commission of fraud or a criminal offense in connection with (i) obtaining, (ii) attempting to obtain, or (iii) performing a public contract or subcontract;
>
> (2) Violation of Federal or State antitrust statutes relating to the submission of offers;
>
> (3) Commission of embezzlement, theft, forgery, bribery, falsification or destruction of records, making false statements, tax evasion, violating Federal criminal tax laws, or receiving stolen property;
>
> (4) Intentionally affixing a label bearing a "Made in America" inscription (or any inscription having the same meaning) to a product sold in or shipped to the United States or its outlying areas, when the product was not made in the United States or its outlying areas (see Section 202 of the Defense Production Act (Pub. L. 102-558)); or
>
> (5) Commission of any other offense indicating a lack of business integrity or business honesty that seriously and directly affects the present responsibility of a Government contractor or subcontractor.

Most business integrity debarments have been based upon conviction of criminal offenses in dealing with the federal government. Included are such acts as bid rigging and mail fraud in violation of 18 U.S.C. § 1341, *John F. Azzarelli*, HUDBCA 82-671-D12, 82-1 BCA ¶ 15,677; bribing public officials in violation of 18 U.S.C. § 201, *Thomas P. Prickett*, GSBCA 6311-D, 82-1 BCA ¶ 15,736; perjury before a grand jury in connection with investigation of another government contractor, *William A. Fuhrman*, HUDBCA 79-431-D46, Oct. 14, 1980, *Unpub.*; presenting fraudulent claims in violation of 18 U.S.C. § 287, *Ira F. Gassman*, GSBCA D-3, 79-1 BCA ¶ 13,771; submitting false income tax information in violation of 18 U.S.C. § 1001, *Clarence L. White*, HUDBCA 79-382-D32, July 12, 1979, *Unpub.* (later reinstated); failing to file a federal income tax return in violation of 26 U.S.C. § 7203, *Nathan A. Hicks*, HUDBCA 79-438-D51, Jan. 7, 1980, *Unpub.*; taking kickbacks in violation of 18 U.S.C. § 874, *Thomas M. Zakucia*, HUDBCA 79-348-D7, Dec. 3, 1979, *Unpub.*; failing to immediately notify the appropriate agency of an unlawful release of a hazardous substance as required by 42 U.S.C. § 9603(b), *John R. Fields*, EPADEBAR 93-0289-00, Nov. 13, 1995, *Unpub.*; and knowingly failing to dispose of asbestos contaminated material in accordance with the Clean Air Act, 42 U.S.C. § 7412, *Ellis "Ray" Kiser*, EPADEBAR 93-0253-01, Nov. 2, 1995, *Unpub.*

Occasionally, a debarment will be based upon convictions of criminal acts in connection with other governmental dealings. See, for example, *Lundin Constr. Co.*, DOT Fin. Asst. Pgm. Dkt. No. 2, Mar. 11, 1985, 43 Fed. Cont.

Rep. 657 (bid rigging conviction in state court). The FAR gives no guidance as to what other offenses might indicate a lack of business integrity or honesty. See generally Seymour, Note, *Refining the Source of the Risk: Suspension and Debarment in the Post-Andersen Era,* 34 Pub. Cont. L.J. 357 (2005) (discussing cases where debarments arose based on bad acts outside federal contracting, and arguing that there should be a nexus between bad act and government contracting). It is not clear, for example, whether conviction for commission of a crime of violence might fall within this category.

FAR 2.101 contains the following broad definition of "conviction":

> "Conviction" means a judgment or conviction of a criminal offense by any court of competent jurisdiction, whether entered upon a verdict or a plea, and includes a conviction entered upon a plea of nolo contendere.

Generally, convictions establish the facts necessary to support a debarment without the submission of additional evidence to the debarring official. However, there is some disagreement on this rule in the case of a conviction based on a plea of nolo contendere. Despite the clearly stated intention of the government in the above definition, the HUD Board of Contract Appeals held that independent evidence must be introduced in a debarment proceeding to prove the alleged criminal acts when a conviction is based upon a plea of nolo contendere, *Milton H. Girard*, HUDBCA 82-730-D47, 83-1 BCA ¶ 16,544; *Willie J. Hope*, HUDBCA 80-521-D52, 81-1 BCA ¶ 15,045. See also *Sam Ligon*, HUDBCA 83-798-D29, Jan. 4, 1984, *Unpub.*, where independent evidence of the facts was used to prove the commission of the criminal act in lieu of the plea of nolo contendere. The EPA board has reached a similar conclusion. In *Mark P. Young*, EPADEBAR 93-00-25-03, Jan. 6, 1994, *Unpub.*, the board stated that "fundamental fairness requires that the respondents be provided an opportunity to complete their submission of information and arguments."

[b] Serious Violation of Contract Terms

FAR 9.406-2 contains the following description of this category of debarment, for failure to comply with a contract's terms:

> The debarring official may debar—
>
> * * *
>
> (b)(1) A contractor, based upon a preponderance of the evidence, for any of the following—
>
> > (i) Violation of the terms of a Government contract or subcontract so serious as to justify debarment, such as—
> >
> > > (A) Willful failure to perform in accordance with the terms of one or more contracts; or

(B) A history of failure to perform, or of unsatisfactory performance of, one or more contracts.

This provision appears to give considerable discretion to debarring officials—both as to the conduct that will justify debarment and the amount of evidence necessary to prove the conduct. Thus, failure to perform repairs within the time specified in the contract and failure to obtain a timely extension of the period of performance provided grounds for debarment in *Wilbert T. Alexander & Alexander Realty Co.*, HUDBCA 81-648-D47, 82-1 BCA ¶ 15,649. See also *WEDJ/Three C's, Inc. v. Dep't of Def.*, No. 4:CV-05-2427, 2006 U.S. Dist. LEXIS 50363 (M.D. Pa. July 24, 2006) (alteration of test reports to hide product deficiencies); *Andrew Calhoun*, HUDBCA 82-676-D14, 82-2 BCA ¶ 15,921 (unexcused failure to perform 17 contracts for purchase and repair of rental property); *Mayer Co.*, HUDBCA 81-544-D1, 82-1 BCA ¶ 15,473 (serious inadequacies in supervision and control by corporate managers of a property management firm, including the failure to make mortgage payments and obtain liability insurance); *Donald Schutte*, AGBCA 77-189, 79-2 BCA ¶ 13,902 (three-year debarment for installing a well within a building foundation in violation of state requirements the contractor knew or should have known); *Howard Bigelow*, HUDBCA 80-467-D15, 82-2 BCA ¶ 15,798 (three-year debarment for persistent failure to supervise employees and poor business practices leading to noncompliance with HUD regulations). However, in *Rudy Barnes & Rudy Barnes Co.*, HUDBCA 81-588-D15, 82-2 BCA ¶ 16,001, the contractor's failure to complete two HUD contracts was held insufficient where the contractor's difficulties arose in part from an excessive agency delay in awarding one of the contracts, and a history of failure on a large number of contracts was not involved.

FAR 9.406-2(b)(1) also permits debarment, based on a preponderance of the evidence, for violations of the Drug-Free Workplace Act, intentionally mislabeling a product "Made in America," or commission of an unfair practice relating to foreign trade, and federal tax delinquency.

In a major shift in federal procurement law, in late 2008 the rule was broadened, to call for "mandatory disclosure" of certain wrongful acts, so that a contractor may be subject to debarment under FAR 9.406-2(b)(1) upon:

(vi) Knowing failure by a principal, until 3 years after final payment on any Government contract awarded to the contractor, to timely disclose to the Government, in connection with the award, performance, or closeout of the contract or a subcontract thereunder, credible evidence of—

(A) Violation of Federal criminal law involving fraud, conflict of interest, bribery, or gratuity violations found in Title 18 of the United States Code;

(B) Violation of the civil False Claims Act (31 U.S.C. 3729-3733); or

> (C) Significant overpayment(s) on the contract, other than overpayments resulting from contract financing payments as defined in 32.001.

The implementing clause, Contractor Code of Business Ethics and Conduct in FAR 52.203-13, also calls for comprehensive contractor compliance systems, to support those disclosure obligations by identifying and addressing violations of law. See generally American Bar Association, Public Contract Law Section, *Guide to the Mandatory Disclosure Rule: Issues, Guidelines, and Best Practices* (2010).

Another cause for debarment was added to FAR 9.406-2(b)(2) covering the employment of undocumented immigrants:

> A contractor [may be debarred] based on a determination by the Secretary of Homeland Security or the Attorney General of the United States, that the contractor is not in compliance with Immigration and Nationality Act employment provisions (see Executive Order 12989, as amended by Executive Order 13286). Such determination is not reviewable in the debarment proceedings.

[c] Other Causes Showing Lack of Present Responsibility

FAR 9.406-2(c) contains the following omnibus category of causes for debarment:

> any other cause of so serious or compelling a nature that it affects the present responsibility of a Government contractor or subcontractor.

This provision, which gives extremely broad discretion to the debarring official, can relate either to performance or integrity issues. See, for example, *Robert Walker, Mark Walker, Alto Leasing Corp.*, GSBCA 7585-D, Mar. 11, 1985, *Unpub.*, where the board found that the contractor's misrepresentation to third parties of its contractual relationship with the GSA demonstrated absence of integrity and lack of present responsibility, and *Kiesel Co.*, EPADEBAR 94-0091-00, Aug. 28, 1995, *Unpub.*, where the charge was improper storage of one drum of hazardous waste (PCB) without required markings. In *Robinson v. Cheney*, 876 F.2d 152 (D.C. Cir. 1989), the court affirmed the debarment of a military clothing supplier that had been indicted for bribing a government official and collusive bidding. The court found no abuse of discretion in finding that the contractor did not have present responsibility based on uncontroverted evidence supplied by one witness that had been granted immunity from criminal prosecution.

[2] Inducement Debarments

Causes for inducement debarments are specifically enunciated in each statute or regulation covering the public policy at issue.

[a] Equal Employment Opportunity

Section 209(a)(6) of Executive. Order No. 11246 empowers the Secretary of Labor to debar any firm that fails to comply with the terms of the Equal Employment clause in FAR 52.222-26. Paragraph (c)(9) of this clause incorporates this policy, specifically stating that "the Contractor may be declared ineligible for further Government contracts" as a possible sanction for violation of these requirements. See *BFI Waste Servs.*, 68 Fed. Reg. 7394 (2003) (consent decree because of inadequate compliance); *Goya de Puerto Rico, Inc.*, 67 Fed. Reg. 53028 (2002) (same).

This debarment sanction has been invoked against firms failing to submit acceptable affirmative action plans, *Ingersoll Milling Mfg. Co.*, 42 Fed. Reg. 41330 (1977); *Loffland Bros. Co.*, 44 Fed. Reg. 22835 (1979). In the latter debarment action, the director of OFCCP rejected the contractor's contention that its failure to submit an acceptable affirmative action plan should not be grounds for debarment since it had successfully completed performance of the specified contract work. Failure to meet the minority utilization goals in an affirmative action plan has also been used as the basis for debarment, *Anastasia Bros. Corp.*, 42 Fed. Reg. 42932 (1977). See also *Painting Corp. of Detroit, Inc.*, 43 Fed. Reg. 30919 (1978), where a debarment action was based in part upon a contractor's failure to make a good faith effort to meet minority utilization goals.

The debarment authority under Executive Order No. 11246 has also been invoked for certain procedural violations. In *Uniroyal, Inc. v. Marshall*, 482 F. Supp. 364 (D.D.C. 1979), the court upheld an OFCCP debarment order based upon the contractor's failure to comply with regulations giving the government access to employment records needed to conduct a discrimination investigation. In *First Alabama Bank of Montgomery v. Donovan*, 692 F.2d 714 (11th Cir. 1982), the court upheld a debarment based upon a refusal to cooperate in a compliance review under Executive. Order No. 11246. See also *OFCCP v. Prudential Ins. Co.*, 23 F.E.P. Cases 492 (DOL 1980), where debarment resulted from a contractor's failure to give OFCCP computer tapes containing detailed personnel, salary, and organizational material, and *Painting Corp. of Detroit, Inc.*, 43 Fed. Reg. 22836 (1978), where a debarment order was based in part upon a firm's refusal to supply workforce data.

[b] Labor Statutes

While only the Davis-Bacon Act, 40 U.S.C. § 276a-2(a), the Walsh-Healey Act, 41 U.S.C. § 6504, and the Service Contract Act, 41 U.S.C. § 6706, specifically provide for debarment, the Secretary of Labor has adopted a rule authorizing debarment for violations of labor-related statutes that do not, in themselves, specifically authorize debarment, 29 C.F.R. § 5.1. The Contract Work Hours and Safety Standards Act, 40 U.S.C. § 3701 et seq., is perhaps the most important among these. See *Copper Plumbing & Heating Co. v. Campbell*, 290 F.2d 368

(D.C. Cir. 1961), and *Janik Paving & Constr., Inc. v. Brock*, 828 F.2d 84 (2d Cir. 1987), sustaining the right of the Secretary of Labor to debar in the absence of statutory provisions. See also *Foundation for Fair Contracting, Ltd. v. G & M Eastern Contracting & Double E, LLC*, 259 F. Supp. 2d 329 (D.N.J. 2003) (reviewing regulatory scheme for enforcement, and holding administrative proceedings for potential debarment foreclosed False Claims Act action by qui tam relator). The standard for debarment under the Davis-Bacon Act is a showing of disregard of obligations to employees and subcontractors. The standard in the other labor statutes is aggravated or willful violation of the statutory requirements, 29 C.F.R. § 5.12(a)(1).

The DOL has also adopted the debarment sanction for violations of the Vietnam-Era Veterans Readjustment Assistance Act of 1974, 41 C.F.R. § 60-250.28(e), and the Rehabilitation Act of 1973, 41 C.F.R. § 60-741.28(e). See *Commonwealth Aluminum Corp.*, 59 Fed. Reg. 22178 (1994); *Blaine Constr. Co.*, 59 Fed. Reg. 17120 (1994); and *Layton Constr. Co.*, 58 Fed. Reg. 61922 (1993).

[c] Buy American

41 U.S.C. § 8303(c) authorizes the head of a contracting agency to debar a contractor from receiving future construction contracts for violations of the Buy American Act in performing construction contracts. See FAR 25.206(c)(4) implementing this statute.

Although Buy American Act requirements also apply to supply contracts, neither the statute nor the FAR explicitly provides for debarment for violations. However, it would appear that debarment in this area could be accomplished as a serious violation of contract terms under FAR 9.406-2(b).

[d] Environmental Statutes

The EPA is authorized to declare facilities (not contractors) ineligible to receive contracts if they are convicted of violations of the Clean Water Act, 33 U.S.C. § 1368, and the Clean Air Act, 42 U.S.C. § 7606. These statutes are implemented by Executive Order 11738, 38 Fed. Reg. 25161 (1973), which was initially addressed in the governmentwide nonprocurement common rule (NCR), 68 Fed. Reg. 66534 (2003); the statutory requirements are now addressed in the EPA provisions under OMB's governmentwide nonprocurement debarment guidance, at 2 C.F.R. Part 1532. Part 1532 adopts the OMB governmentwide guidance, 2 C.F.R. Part 180, as the EPA policies and procedures for nonprocurement debarments and suspensions under the governing environmental statutes. The EPA rules, which supplement the general OMB guidance, explain how persons and firms will be debarred or suspended for certain criminal violations of the Clean Water Act and the Clean Air Act. EPA specifically reserves the right to suspend or debar other facilities of firms that might not fall under the mandatory suspension and debarment provisions, 2 C.F.R. § 1532.1115.

The EPA regulations 2 C.F.R. § 1532.1130 -.1135 warn contractors that they are immediately placed on the SAM list when they are convicted of a violation of the Clean Water Act and the Clean Air Act and that they will stay on the list until they have demonstrated to the debarring official "certifies that the condition giving rise to your conviction has been corrected." The prior EPA rule contained broader grounds for debarment which were upheld in *United States v. Del Monte de Puerto Rico, Inc.*, 9 E.R.C. 1495 (D.P.R. 1976); *United States v. Interlake, Inc.*, 432 F. Supp. 987 (N.D. Ill. 1977); and *United States v. United States Steel*, 10 E.R.C. 1751 (N.D. Ill. 1977). In *ITT Rayonier Inc. v. United States*, 651 F.2d 343 (5th Cir. 1981), the plaintiff contended that these opinions did not examine the legislative history of the Federal Water Pollution Control Act, which would show that EPA was denied this authority. The court deemed the issue moot and did not rule on it.

[C] Causes for Suspension

The causes for suspension are somewhat narrower than those for debarment. There are no inducement-type causes, and the procurement causes are limited to integrity issues and "serious and compelling" causes that affect the present responsibility of the contractor. However, there is considerable discretion because the test is "*suspected, upon adequate evidence*" rather than conviction or civil judgment.

FAR 9.407-2 specifies the following causes for suspension:

> (a) The suspending official may suspend a contractor suspected, upon adequate evidence, of—
>
> (1) Commission of fraud or a criminal offense in connection with (i) obtaining, (ii) attempting to obtain, or (iii) performing a public contract or subcontract;
>
> (2) Violation of Federal or State antitrust statutes relating to the submission of offers;
>
> (3) Commission of embezzlement, theft, forgery, bribery, falsification or destruction of records, making false statements, tax evasion, violating Federal criminal tax laws, or receiving stolen property; or
>
> (4) Violations of the Drug-Free Workplace Act of 1988 (Public Law 100-690), as indicated by—
>
> (i) Failure to comply with the requirements of the clause at 52.223-6, Drug-Free Workplace; or
>
> (ii) Such a number of contractor employees convicted of violations of criminal drug statutes occurring in the workplace as to indicate that the contractor has failed to make a good faith effort to provide a drug-free workplace (see 23.504);

(5) Intentionally affixing a label bearing a "Made in America" inscription (or any inscription having the same meaning) to a product sold in or shipped to the United States or its outlying areas, when the product was not made in the United States or its outlying areas (see section 202 of the Defense Production Act (Public Law 102-558));

(6) Commission of an unfair trade practice as defined in 9.403 (see section 201 of the Defense Production Act (Pub. L. 102-558)); or

(7) Delinquent Federal taxes in an amount that exceeds $3,000. See the criteria at 9.406-2(b)(1)(v) for determination of when taxes are delinquent; or

(8) Knowing failure by a principal until 3 years after final payment on any Government contract awarded to the contractor, to timely disclose to the Government, in connection with the award, performance, or closeout of the contract or a subcontract thereunder, credible evidence of—

(i) Violation of Federal criminal law involving fraud, conflict of interest, bribery, or gratuity violations found in Title 18 of the United States Code;

(ii) Violation of the civil False Claims Act (31 U.S.C. 3729-3733); or

(iii) Significant overpayment(s) on the contract, other than overpayments resulting from contract financing payments as defined in 32.001; or

(9) Commission of any other offense indicating a lack of business integrity or business honesty that seriously and directly affects the present responsibility of a Government contractor or subcontractor.

(b) Indictment for any of the causes in paragraph (a) above constitutes adequate evidence for suspension.

(c) The suspending official may upon adequate evidence also suspend a contractor for any other cause of so serious or compelling a nature that it affects the present responsibility of a Government contractor or subcontractor.

Because suspensions may be ordered before conviction or judgment, the FAR requires that a suspension action be based upon "adequate evidence." *See Lion Raisins, Inc. v. United States*, 51 Fed. Cl. 238 (2001) (applying test to find suspension arbitrary and capricious when agency continued to award contracts to contractor *after* learning of alleged bad acts but *before* suspension). FAR 9.407-1(b)(1) provides:

> Suspension is a serious action to be imposed on the basis of adequate evidence, pending the completion of investigation or legal proceedings, when it has been determined that immediate action is necessary to protect the Government's interest. In assessing the adequacy of the evidence, agencies should consider how much information is available, how credible it is given the circumstances, whether or not important allegations are corroborated,

> and what inferences can reasonably be drawn as a result. This assessment should include an examination of basic documents such as contracts, inspection reports, and correspondence.

FAR 9.407-2(b) indicates that an outstanding indictment for criminal conduct of the type identified in the regulations as grounds for debarment by itself constitutes "adequate evidence" of criminal conduct upon which a suspension may be based. See *James A. Merritt & Sons v. Marsh*, 791 F.2d 328 (4th Cir. 1986), and *Alexander & Alexander, Ltd.*, HUDBCA 82-727-D46, 83-1 BCA ¶ 16,229. However, the Department of Transportation has held an indictment to be a rebuttable presumption of adequate evidence, thereby shifting the burden of rebutting the adequacy of the evidence to the contractor, *Mainelli, DOT Fin. Asst. Prog.*, Dkt. No. 12, July 22, 1985. Adequate evidence has been likened to the probable cause necessary for an arrest, a search warrant, or a preliminary hearing, *Horne Bros., Inc. v. Laird*, 463 F.2d 1268 (D.C. Cir. 1972); *Kirkpatrick v. White*, 351 F. Supp. 2d 1261 (N.D. Ala. 2004); *McCoy's Super Tread, Inc.*, GSBCA 7039-S, 83-2 BCA ¶ 16,751. In *Bio-Tech Research Labs., Inc.*, HUDBCA 94-C-154-D21, Sept. 28, 1995, *Unpub.*, the HUD board defined the "adequate evidence" needed to support a suspension as a "minimal standard of proof" and as "information sufficient to support the reasonable belief that a particular act or omission has occurred." See also *United States Testing Co.*, EPADEBAR 89-0021-00, Apr. 23, 1991, *Unpub.*

Historically, GAO reviewed suspensions for arbitrary or capricious action. In *TS Generalbau GmbH*, Comp. Gen. Dec. B-246034, 92-1 CPD ¶ 189, GAO approved a suspension that was based upon "an ongoing investigation of the alleged bribery of Government employees." In *SDA Inc.*, Comp. Gen. Dec. B-253355, 93-2 CPD ¶ 132, approval was given to a suspension based upon "unrebutted, detailed allegations" of misconduct involving fraudulent real estate transactions and substantial sums of money that were contained in a civil complaint filed by the Resolution Trust Corporation (a government entity). See also *BASIX, Inc.*, Comp. Gen. Dec. B-255613, 94-1 CPD ¶ 194, where GAO approved exclusion of a company from a competition because of its suspension based upon an indictment alleging conspiracy to commit securities fraud, bank fraud, and mail fraud. In *Shinwha Elecs.*, Comp. Gen. Dec. B-290603, 2002 CPD ¶ 154, however, GAO announced that it would no longer hear challenges to agency suspension and debarment decisions:

> [O]ur Office will no longer review, even under a limited standard, protests that an agency improperly suspended or debarred a contractor from receiving government contracts. Because the FAR sets forth specific procedures for both imposing and challenging a suspension or debarment action, see FAR §§ 9.406-3(b), 9.407-3(b), we conclude that the appropriate forum for resolving such disputes is with the contracting agency.

[D] Scope and Duration

Because debarments and suspensions are for the protection of the government, debarring officials have considerable discretion in tailoring their scope and duration. In certain areas, however, the regulations limit this discretion but provide for waivers or exemptions. This section discusses the government agencies that must respect debarment or suspension orders, the entities to which such orders apply, the duration of such orders, their effect during the procurement process, and the permissible activities of debarred or suspended entities.

[1] Agencies Affected

FAR 9.406-1(c) and FAR 9.407-1(d) provide that debarments and suspensions are "effective throughout the executive branch" unless waived by the procuring agency. It is clear that these provisions make debarments and suspensions by any executive branch agency binding on all other executive branch agencies. FAR 9.404 requires the GSA to administer the internet-based SAM, which contains the names of all contractors that are debarred, suspended, proposed for debarment, or ineligible for contracts, as well as all entities excluded from participation in nonprocurement transactions under the "Nonprocurement Common Rule" (NCR), 2 C.F.R. Part 180. FAR 9.403 defines the NCR, giving examples of these nonprocurement transactions as "grants, cooperative agreements, scholarships, fellowships, contracts of assistance, loans, loan guarantees, subsidies, insurance, payments for specified use and donation agreements." Since FAR 9.405 precludes contracting officers from awarding contracts to any entity on this list, this "common rule" bars contracting with a broad spectrum of entities that have been excluded from participation in federal programs.

It is clear from the statutes that most inducement-type debarments are binding throughout the federal government. Debarments ordered by the Secretary of Labor under the Walsh-Healey Act, 41 U.S.C. § 6504, the Service Contract Act, 41 U.S.C. § 6706, and debarments ordered by GAO for violations of the Davis-Bacon Act, 40 U.S.C. § 276a-2(a), are mandatory for all government agencies. Listing of a facility by the EPA for violations of the Clean Air Act and the Clean Water Act generally precludes all government agencies from making award of any contract to be performed at the listed facility. The construction provisions of the Buy American Act, 41 U.S.C. § 8303(c), also apply to all agencies of the government. In contrast, equal employment debarments under Executive Order 11246 apply only to executive branch agencies. All of these inducement debarments are included on the GSA consolidated list.

Procuring agencies generally are not permitted to contract with debarred or suspended firms or individuals. However, FAR 9.406-1(c) and FAR 9.407-1(d) provide that thia requirement can be waived by the agency head or the agency head's designee and must be based on "compelling reasons." The NCR similarly contemplates exceptions allowed, for example, by the head of the agency involved. See 2 C.F.R. § 180.135. While these provisions appear to permit contracting in the face of all debarments, the only statutory provisions that explicitly grant such discretion to procuring activities are the Clean Air Act and the Clean Water Act. DFARS 209.405(a) contains the following guidance on the "compelling reasons" that may warrant granting an exception:

> Examples of compelling reasons are—
>
> (i) Only a debarred or suspended contractor can provide the supplies or services;
>
> (ii) Urgency requires contracting with a debarred or suspended contractor;
>
> (iii) The contractor and a department or agency have an agreement covering the same events that resulted in the debarment or suspension and the agreement includes the department or agency decision not to debar or suspend the contractor; or
>
> (iv) The national defense requires continued business dealings with the debarred or suspended contractor.

[2] Entities Covered

Debarment and suspension orders may apply to those entities sufficiently connected with the misconduct to make dealing with them detrimental to the interest of the government. Under FAR 9.406-1(a) and FAR 9.407-1(a), "contractors" are debarred or suspended. FAR 9.403 contains the following definition:

> *Contractor* means any individual or other legal entity that—
>
> (1) Directly or indirectly (e.g., through an affiliate), submits offers for or is awarded, or reasonably may be expected to submit offers for or be awarded, a Government contract, including a contract for carriage under Government or commercial bills of lading, or a subcontract under a Government contract; or
>
> (2) Conducts business, or reasonably may be expected to conduct business, with the Government as an agent or representative of another contractor.

This definition includes affiliates of a company as well as its officers and employees. It also reaches companies for which tainted officers or employees perform work. The following discussion treats business entities separately from officers and employees.

[a] Business Entities

The government deals with a variety of types of business entities. An entity may be debarred or suspended based on the acts of its own employees or based upon its association with entities or individuals that have committed improper acts. An entity may also escape debarment or suspension if it purges itself by severing its relationship with offending individuals or entities.

FAR 9.406-1(b) deals with the breadth of the debarment with respect to business entities and permits the debarring official to include "affiliates" within the scope of the debarment:

> Debarment constitutes debarment of all divisions or other organizational elements of the contractor, unless the debarment decision is limited by its terms to specific divisions, organizational elements, or commodities. The debarring official may extend the debarment decision to include any affiliates of the contractor if they are—
>
> (1) Specifically named; and
>
> (2) Given written notice of the proposed debarment and an opportunity to respond (see 9.406-3(c)).

FAR 9.403 contains the following definition of "affiliates":

> Business concerns, organizations, or individuals are affiliates of each other if, directly or indirectly, (1) either one controls or has the power to control the other, or (2) a third-party controls or has the power to control both. Indicia of control include, but are not limited to, interlocking management or ownership, identity of interests among family members, shared facilities and equipment, common use of employees, or a business entity organized following the debarment, suspension, or proposed debarment of a contractor which has the same or similar management, ownership, or principal employees as the contractor that was debarred, suspended, or proposed for debarment.

One of the issues raised by these provisions is whether an entire entity should be debarred or suspended. Although FAR 9.406-1 gives broad discretion, it has been very rare for a debarment or suspension to cover less than the entire business entity. See GSA Press Release, *GSA Suspends Enron and Arthur Andersen and Former Officials*, Press Release No. 9930 (Mar. 15, 2002) (available at *www.gsa.gov*) (entire corporations suspended). Compare Air Force Press Release, *Air Force Lifts Boeing Suspension,* Press Release No. 020305 (Mar. 4, 2005) (suspension of only three business units related to bad acts).

For a case narrowing the scope of a procurement debarment, see *Peter Kiewit & Sons' Co. v. U.S. Army Corps of Eng'rs*, 534 F. Supp. 1139 (D.D.C. 1982), *rev'd on other grounds*, 714 F.2d 163 (D.C. Cir. 1983), where the district court held that the contractor "should not be prevented from doing business with the United States." The court reasoned that criminal acts that had been committed by two small subsidiaries and one small division were not sufficient to exclude the balance of the organization from being awarded contracts for different types of work, given that the contractor had discharged the employees responsible for the illegal acts. The circuit did not rule on this issue but reversed on the grounds that the district court should not have taken the case until the administrative process had been completed. Compare *Dowling Group v. Williams*, Civ. Action No. 82-1775 (D.D.C. 1982), permitting debarment of all entities of a small company and agreeing with the debarring official's distinction of the *Kiewit* case on the ground that *Kiewit* was "a large corporation with over 11,000 employees."

FAR 9.406-1(b) also gives broad discretion to include affiliates in a debarment order if notice is given. Debarment of affiliates is proper to prevent circumvention of the sanctions by operating through separate entities. Normally, however, an affiliate generally would not be debarred if it was not connected in any way to the entity that committed the improper act. See 51 Comp. Gen. 65 (B-173016) (1971), affirming an agency decision not to debar an affiliate because there could have been valid reasons for the creation of the affiliate other than avoidance of the debarment. See also *Roy C. Markey*, HUDBCA 82-712-D33, 83-2 BCA ¶ 16,688, affirming the decision to debar two companies as long as they were controlled by an individual who had committed improper acts in his capacity as a sole proprietor. Even though there was no proof that they had participated in the improper acts, it was clear that these affiliates could be used to circumvent the debarment were they not included within the scope of it. See also Zucker, *The Boeing Suspension: Has Increased Consolidation Tied the United States Department of Defense's Hands*, 2004 Pub. Proc. L. Rev. 260, 271 (discussing Air Force strategy in suspending only three Boeing units); Madsen, *The Government's Debarment Process: Out-of-Step with Current Ethical Standards,* 2004 Pub. Proc. L. Rev. 252 (arguing that a "debarment system that is overly focused on individuals or narrowly drawn operational segments within a company and which too freely permits waivers for contractors with questionable business ethics contrasts sharply, and is out-of-step, with other government efforts to reform and re-emphasize responsibility and accountability in corporate governance").

Affiliation depends on control, and control is a question of fact to be determined by the debarment official. For example, in *Alexandria Printing & Photo Servs.*, EBCA 285-3-83(D), 83-2 BCA ¶ 16,570, the appellant company argued that it was not an affiliate because it was a sole proprietorship under the control of Mary P., who was legally separated from Earl P. and who had filed for divorce. However, in looking at all the facts, including the facts that the wife was employed as a full-time cashier at another store, was not an experienced printer, and was subsidized in her business operations by the husband, the board found a factual basis for debarment of the appellant company on the ground of affiliation. See also *Robinson v. Cheney,* 876 F.2d 152 (D.C. Cir. 1989) (founder and owner of equitable interest was "affiliate" for purposes of debarment); *Michael C. Kantrow*, HUDBCA 95-A-109-D7, Aug. 2, 1995, *Unpub.* (affiliation where an individual who pleaded guilty to causing submission of a false change order was part owner of and exercised management authority over the affiliated company); *Detek, Inc.*, Comp. Gen. Dec. B-261678, 95-2 CPD ¶ 177 (affiliation where one entity was purchased by a key employer of the other, both shared several key management employees, and they planned to engage in a prime/subcontractor relationship); and *ABL Indus., Inc.*, Comp. Gen. Dec. B-207335, 82-2 CPD ¶ 119 (affiliation when the owner of a suspended firm transferred ownership of another firm to his wife, and that second firm used the key employees and facilities of the suspended firm). Compare *Provident Maint. Servs., Inc.*, GSBCA 7640-D, Apr. 23, 1985, *Unpub.*, where no affiliation was found even though there was friendship, joint use of office space, and previous business relationships. GAO has also upheld an agency determination that a debarred company's wholly owned subsidiary was ineligible for award where the debarred company created the affiliate after the agency debarred the parent company, *Solid Waste Servs., Inc.*, Comp. Gen. Dec. B-218445, 85-1 CPD ¶ 703.

FAR 9.406-5(c) provides that entities participating in a joint venture may be debarred for acts of the venture:

> The fraudulent, criminal, or other seriously improper conduct of one contractor participating in a joint venture or similar arrangement may be imputed to other participating contractors if the conduct occurred for or on behalf of the joint venture or similar arrangement, or with the knowledge, approval, or acquiescence of these contractors. Acceptance of the benefits derived from the conduct shall be evidence of such knowledge, approval, or acquiescence.

Generally, misconduct of an officer or employee of a business entity may result in the debarment or suspension of the entity. FAR 9.406-5(a) recognizes this fact but implicitly recognizes that there may be circumstances when such acts should not be imputed to the business entity:

> The fraudulent, criminal, or other seriously improper conduct of any officer, director, shareholder, partner, employee or other individual associated with a contractor may be imputed to the contractor when the conduct occurred in connection with the individual's performance of duties for or on behalf of the contractor, or with the contractor's knowledge, approval, or acquiescence. The contractor's acceptance of the benefits derived from the conduct shall be evidence of such knowledge, approval, or acquiescence.

Thus, a debarment probably would be improper if an employee's misconduct was totally outside the knowledge or control of the business entity.

Where the employee is an officer of the entity or exercises significant control over the entity, the acts are generally imputed to the entity. See, for example, *Robinson v. Cheney*, 876 F.2d 152 (D.C. Cir. 1989), where a company was debarred for acts of its president even though the other employees knew nothing of the acts. See also *Mikulec v. Dep't of the Air Force*, Civ. Action No. 84-2248 (D.D.C. 1985) (president at time of misconduct and "corporate official" at time of suspension); *Park Poly Bag Corp.*, GSBCA 5744-S, 80-2 BCA ¶ 14,600 (president, vice president, and sole shareholders); *Arun Gaind, & Gaind Assocs., Inc.*, EPADEBAR 92-0007-01, Mar. 3, 1995, *Unpub.* (president at all times); and

Hy-Tex Mktg., Inc., EPADEBAR 93-0217-04, Nov. 22, 1994, *Unpub.* (president, principal stockholder, and sole managerial employee). In *Joseph E. Berrigan & Berrigan, Daniel, Litchfield & Olsen*, HUDBCA 84-894-D46, July 12, 1985, *Unpub.*, a lawyer was debarred but his law firm was not because there was no evidence that the law firm was aware of the lawyer's culpable conduct or that the lawyer controlled the firm. Business entities have also been debarred because they have associated with persons who were debarred or guilty of prior misconduct. In such cases, the entity is described as an affiliate and control is required. See, for example, *Thomas P. Prickett,* GSBCA 6311-D, 82-1 BCA ¶ 15,736, where a company was debarred based on the previous debarment of its sole shareholder. Compare *Canales v. Paulson*, 2006 U.S. Dist. LEXIS 61915 (D.D.C. 2006), temporarily barring a debarment of a company based on a misdemeanor of the person forming the company. The court was persuaded that the debarment might have been improper because the conduct occurred prior to the formation of the company when its founder was a government employee. After the agency withdrew the debarment of the company, the individual's debarment was held improper because of failure of the debarring official to consider mitigating factors, *Canales v. Paulson*, No. 06-1330 (GK), 2007 U.S. Dist. LEXIS 50924 (D.D.C. July 16, 2007).

The issue of control may be mitigated by a compliance agreement between the agency and the contractor corporation facing potential suspension or debarment, if the contractor can show that the employee(s) engaged in bad acts have been removed from any control of the corporation. In *Jerry A. Costacos*, GSBCA 7547-D, Apr. 9, 1985, *Unpub.*, a company escaped debarment by showing that its debarred vice president for operations did not "control" the company because he was "walled off" from involvement in government contracts. Compare *Robinson*, where the court sustained debarment of a company where the president and sole stockholder placed the company in trust after being indicted for alleged criminal conduct. The court agreed that, in such a situation, there was not a sufficient divesting of interest.

[b] Individuals

The FAR does not directly discuss the debarment of individuals, but FAR 9.403 includes within the definition of "contractor" "any individual" who "[c]onducts business, or reasonably may be expected to conduct business, with the Government as an agent or representative of another contractor." In addition, FAR 9.406-5(b) permits imputation of acts of a contractor to any employee or other person connected to the misconduct:

> The fraudulent, criminal, or other seriously improper conduct of a contractor may be imputed to any officer, director, shareholder, partner, employee, or other individual associated with the contractor who participated in, knew of, or had reason to know of the contractor's conduct.

It can be seen that the scope of this provision is very broad. Thus, not being a contractor employee does not shield an individual from being debarred from future government contracts.

The debarment of an individual operating as a sole proprietorship was accomplished under the Federal Procurement Regulation (predecessor to the FAR) pursuant to regulations that permitted debarment of individuals. See *Dimitrious A. Mavrophilipos*, GSBCA D-5, 80-1 BCA ¶ 14,446. Under HUD regulations, individuals operating as a sole proprietorship were debarred as contractors, *Robert C. Gennaro*, HUDBCA 81-632-D37, 83-1 BCA ¶ 16,141. This result also could be proper under the current FAR. The confusion of terminology in this area is illustrated in *Charles Kirkland*, HUDBCA 80-541-D60, 82-1 BCA ¶ 15,743, where an individual was debarred for improper conduct, and a sole proprietorship and a company through which he dealt were also debarred as affiliates. See also *Edward M. Alba*, HUDBCA 83-820-D39, 84-2 BCA ¶ 17,242. In *Harold Estes*, HUDBCA 83-793-D24, 84-2 BCA ¶ 17,241, an individual was debarred for illegal acts as a subcontractor and his sole proprietorship was debarred as an affiliate.

When an individual has not been operating as a sole proprietorship but is an employee of a business entity, debarment has been based on several different theories. Under the prior HUD regulations, at former 24 C.F.R. § 24.105, employees were debarred under a broad definition of "contractor." See *Marvin B. Awaya*, HUDBCA 84-834-D6, 84-2 BCA ¶ 17,3200, where a housing program analyst came within the definition of contractor because he administered funds; *Nathaniel H. Armstrong, John A. Breland & Bo-rite Co.*, HUDBCA 82-687-D20, 84-3 BCA ¶ 17,634, where officers, directors, and part owners of a subcontractor came within the definition of contractor because they were indirect recipients of HUD funds; and *John F. Azzarelli*, HUDBCA 82-671-D12, 82-1 BCA ¶ 15,677, where a vice president of a company was debarred for illegal acts because he was a "contractor." See also *Facchiano Constr. Co. v. Dep't of Labor*, 987 F.2d 206 (3d Cir. 1993), where the court concluded that the DOL had the authority to debar "responsible officers" of a contractor but not officers who did not know of the conduct; *Janik Paving & Constr., Inc. v. Brock*, 828 F.2d 84 (2d Cir. 1987), where the court affirmed the debarment of a company's president without discussing his connection to the misconduct; and *TS Generalbau GmbH*, Comp. Gen. Dec. B-246034, 92-1 CPD ¶ 189, where GAO approved a DOD suspension of "an individual authorized to sign contracts" by imputing the contractor's misconduct (bribery) to the individual. Compare *John R. Morris*, HUDBCA 84-836-D8, 84-2 BCA ¶ 17,245, where the government did not prove that a maintenance man was a contractor. Under the predecessor regulation, the FPR, which provided for debarment of individuals, the corporation's president and vice president who participated in the illegal conduct were suspended, *Park Poly Bag Corp.*, GSBCA 5744-S, 80-2 BCA ¶ 14,600.

Under the FAR standard, individuals can be debarred if they "participated in, knew of or had reason to know" of the contractor's misconduct, FAR 9.406-5(b).

See *American Floor Consultants & Installations, Inc. v. United States,* 70 Fed. Cl. 235 (2006) (controlling individuals and affiliates reached by debarment order); *WEDJ/Three C's, Inc. v. Dep't of Def.*, No. 4:CV-05-2427, 2006 U.S. Dist. LEXIS 50363 (M.D. Pa. July 24, 2006) (violation of contractor imputed to president and owner, contract administrator and project engineer); *Glazer Constr. Co. v. United States,* 52 Fed. Cl. 513 (2002) (violations of contractor imputed to senior employee with knowledge); *Kisser v. Cisneros,* 14 F.3d 615 (D.C. Cir. 1994) (debarment of executive vice president who had participated in the alleged misconduct sustained, rejecting the argument that the debarring agency was required to explain why all officers and employees who participated in the conduct were not similarly debarred). Compare *Alf v. Donley*, 666 F. Supp. 2d 60 (D.D.C. 2009) (debarment of CEO of company enjoined because debarring official did not consider all evidence in the record and imputing knowledge of offenses merely because official was CEO was improper (relying on *Novicki*)); *Impresa Construzioni Geom. Domenico Garufi v. United States*, 238 F.3d 1324 (Fed. Cir. 2001) ("past criminal activities by a corporate officer do not automatically establish that the bidder fails the responsibility requirement"); *Novicki v. Cook*, 946 F.2d 938 (D.C. Cir. 1991) (debarment of the president and CEO of a contractor vacated because there was inadequate proof of "reason to know" of the misconduct, and the agency may have erroneously applied a strict liability or "should have known" standard to the individual's conduct); *Caiola v. Carroll*, 851 F.2d 395 (D.C. Cir. 1988) (debarment of two company officers that was based on the "reason to know" standard overturned when the agency could not explain why it had terminated debarment proceedings against a third officer, seemingly in similar circumstances). See also *Taylor v. Marsh*, Civ. Action No. 81-2643 (D.D.C. 1982), where an officer and 50% shareholder was debarred under the DAR based upon her own negligence, and *Mikulec v. Dep't of the Air Force*, Civ. Action No. 84-2248 (D.D.C. 1985), where the president of a company was suspended following an indictment.

[3] Duration of Orders

Debarment orders are normally for a specified fixed period of time, while suspension orders are for an indefinite but limited period.

[a] Debarment Orders

FAR 9.406-4 contains the following provision concerning the duration of procurement debarment:

> (a)(1) Debarment shall be for a period commensurate with the seriousness of the cause(s). Generally, debarment should not exceed 3 years, except that—

(i) Debarment for violation of the provisions of the Drug-Free Workplace Act of 1988 (see 23.506) may be for a period not to exceed 5 years; and

(ii) Debarments under 9.406-2(b)(2) shall be for one year unless extended pursuant to paragraph (b) of this subsection.

(2) If suspension precedes a debarment, the suspension period shall be considered in determining the debarment period.

(b) The debarring official may extend the debarment for an additional period, if that official determines that an extension is necessary to protect the Government's interest. However, a debarment may not be extended solely on the basis of the facts and circumstances upon which the initial debarment action was based. Debarments under 9.406-2(b)(2) may be extended for additional periods of one year if the Secretary of Homeland Security or the Attorney General determines that the contractor continues to be in violation of the employment provisions of the Immigration and Nationality Act. If debarment for an additional period is determined to be necessary, the procedures of 9.406-3 shall be followed to extend the debarment.

(c) The debarring official may reduce the period or extent of debarment, upon the contractor's request, supported by documentation, for reasons such as—

(1) Newly discovered material evidence;

(2) Reversal of the conviction or civil judgment upon which the debarment was based;

(3) Bona fide change in ownership or management;

(4) Elimination of other causes for which the debarment was imposed; or

(5) Other reasons the debarring official deems appropriate.

FAR 9.406-1(a) requires the debarring official to consider "the seriousness of the contractor's acts or omissions and any remedial measures or mitigating factors" in making the debarment decision. See *Glazer Constr. Co. v. United States*, 50 F. Supp. 2d 85 (D. Mass. 1999), questioning the finding that a contractor had "willfully" violated the Buy American Act but sustaining the debarment based on the fact of the violation. Compare *Watts-Healy Tibbitts A JV v. United States*, 84 Fed. Cl. 253 (2008), agreeing that a contracting officer properly considered corrective measures and mitigating factors in declaring responsible a contractor that had been guilty of bid-rigging.

These issues are also considered in determining the period of a debarment. See *Thomas M. Zakucia*, HUDBCA 79-348-D7, Dec. 3, 1979, *Unpub.*, where a proposed debarment of five years for taking illegal kickbacks was reduced to 30 months where there was no evidence that the individual had acted improperly in the intervening six years since the conviction, and he was remorseful for his criminal activities. Similarly, in *Normal D. Wilhelm*, HUDBCA 82-679-D15, 82-2 BCA ¶ 16,002, the board reduced a debarment period based on a corporate president's conviction for bid rigging because it was convinced he had partially reformed. A "nominal period of debarment" was still necessary, however, because the president did not seem to understand why collusive bidding was illegal, because he did not sufficiently alter the operations of the firm, and because he retained individuals formerly involved in the crime. In *Bruce E. Betterton*, EPADEBAR 93-0217-02, Apr. 25, 1995, *Unpub.*, mitigating circumstances, including lesser culpability for the offenses and cooperation with investigating officials, persuaded the board to reduce the debarment to a two-year period including the suspension period. In *Ellis "Ray" Kiser*, EPADEBAR 93-0253-01, Nov. 2, 1995, *Unpub.*, a three-year debarment of the CEO and owner of a contractor that had improperly disposed of asbestos was reduced to two years after considering the owner's one-year preliminary exclusion under the FAR, the seriousness of the misconduct, the fact that the present facility contained no asbestos, and information presented as mitigating factors and remedial measures. See also *James J. Wannamacher*, HUDBCA 81-585-D14, 82-1 BCA ¶ 15,474, where the board stated that the contractor's conviction for submission of a false certification, based on a plea of nolo contendere, along with extensive evidence showing the violation to be of a continuing pattern and practice, would normally warrant the imposition of a substantial period of debarment. However, only a one-year debarment was imposed because the term was all the agency had sought. In *Shane Meat Co. v. Dep't of Def.*, 800 F.2d 334 (3d Cir. 1986), the court affirmed a three-year debarment based on the failure of the contractor to ensure that delivery of defective products would not be repeated by changing its senior officers. The court held that the debarring official was reasonable in reaching this conclusion even though the contractor had a record of satisfactory performance for the five years subsequent to the illegal conduct. In *Sidney Spiegal*, HUDBCA 91-5908, 93-1 BCA ¶ 25,294, the board held that the fact that bid rigging was a regular practice in public real estate auctions in the District of Columbia did not excuse or mitigate the practice and should not be used to reduce an individual's three-year debarment.

Debarments for periods longer than three years have been affirmed when the causes for the actions have been egregious. See *Coccia v. Defense Logistics Agency*, Civ. Action No. 89-6544 (E.D. Pa. 1992), where the court affirmed the DLA's debarment of an individual for 15 years because, acting as a procurement official, he had seriously corrupted the procurement system by taking bribes in exchange for procurement information. The court agreed with the judgment of the debarring official that the evidence did not demonstrate that the individual could deal honestly with the government within the 15-year period. See also *Martin Dale Jeffus*, 2003 EPADEBAR 4, Aug. 14, 2003, debarring an official of a company for 10 years. It appears, however, that long debarments will be carefully scrutinized. See, for example, *Lake Doctors, Inc.*, EPADEBAR 93-0133-00, Aug. 8, 1995, *Unpub.*, where a five-year debarment for using pesticides in a manner inconsistent with their labeling was reduced to a four-year period with full credit for the period of suspension, due to the presence of mitigating and remedial measures. See also *William R. Absalom*, HUDBCA 82-746-D45,

83-1 BCA ¶ 16,390, where, even though the appellant's mitigating factors were unpersuasive, the board reduced the period of debarment from five to three years because the government's evidence did not support the longer period for the contractor's false statements made to HUD.

The FAR does not specifically address the permissibility of debarments for indefinite periods. However, under the prior HUD regulations, a few such debarments were ordered in exceptional cases. In *Don L. Blankenship*, HUDBCA 81-547-D3, Mar. 27, 1981, *Unpub.*, the board imposed debarment for an indefinite period of time because the firm willfully violated the terms of a prior debarment settlement agreement; in 1993, the board declined to reinstate Blankenship because his conduct "remains unexplained, uncorrected and unrepented," *Don Louis Blankenship*, HUDBCA 93-C-D15, June 29, 1993, *Unpub.* In *Charles Kirkland*, HUDBCA 80-541-D60, 82-1 BCA ¶ 15,743, an individual who procured two false certifications, breached his fiduciary obligations as a broker to the parties in a HUD-assisted transaction, and willfully violated HUD regulations and procedures displayed a course of conduct "so fraught with improprieties" that debarment "for an indefinite period of not less than five years" was imposed. Some years later, in *Charles Kirkland*, HUDBCA 90-5285-D57, Jan. 14, 1991, *Unpub.*, the HUD board, after comparing Kirkland's sanctions to those imposed for similar violations, granted his request for reinstatement and ordered the debarment terminated immediately. See also *Charles Howell*, HUDBCA 85-933-D17, Sept. 13, 1985, *Unpub.*, where the board reversed an indefinite debarment imposed five-and-one-half years earlier, on the basis of newly discovered material evidence that the conduct that gave rise to the debarment was neither egregious nor willful. In *Joseph A. Strauss, The Phoenix Assocs., Ltd.*, HUDBCA 95-G-113-D11, May 19, 1995, *Unpub.*, the board considered an imposing list of mitigating factors and changed an indefinite debarment to a five-year debarment with credit given for the period of suspension; in *Philip D. Winn*, HUDBCA 95-G-108-D6, June 9, 1995, *Unpub.*, an indefinite debarment was changed to a four-year debarment.

FAR 9.406-4(b) and (c) provide guidance on extending the period of debarment. See *Lasmer Indus., Inc. v. Defense Supply Ctr. Columbus*, No. 2:08-cv-0286, 2008 U.S. Dist. LEXIS 51460 (S.D. Ohio June 13, 2008), where the court took limited jurisdiction of a request to enjoin such an extension. The agency had given notice of an extended debarment because the contractor continued to accept contracts during the period it was debarred. In *S.A.F.E. Export Corp.*, 65 Comp. Gen. 530 (B-222308), 86-1 CPD ¶ 413, GAO permitted the extension of an earlier debarment based on continued lack of integrity by the company in subsequent business dealings.

FAR 9.406-4(a)(2) provides that debarring officials shall give consideration to a preceding period of suspension in determining the period of debarment. Under prior regulations, the board, in *Park Poly Bag Corp.*, GSBCA 5826-D, Mar. 9, 1981, *Unpub.*, held that setting a debarment period without considering a preceding period of suspension was arbitrary and capricious. See *Thomas*

P. Prickett, GSBCA 6311-D, 82-1 BCA ¶ 15,736, remanding a case to the debarring official to consider adjusting the debarment period. Although the HUD regulations did not contain such a provision, the HUD Board of Contract Appeals followed this practice, *Curtis Jerome Kennedy*, HUDBCA 78-319-D49, 79-2 BCA ¶ 13,896; *Thomas M. Zakucia*, HUDBCA 79-348-D7, Dec. 3, 1979, *Unpub.* See also *Bradley Shane Hartman*, HUDBCA 93-0133-10, Oct. 11, 1995, *Unpub.*, where the board, after considering the record, agreed to a two-and-one-half-year debarment "with full credit for the period of suspension." Compare, however, *Andrew Nuccitelli*, HUDBCA 78-321-D51, July 17, 1979, *Unpub.*, where the board refused to reduce the debarment period by the period of suspension because of the particularly egregious nature of the contractor's activities and the absence of mitigating factors. In *Arun Gaind, & Gaind Assocs., Inc.*, EPADEBAR 92-0007-01, Mar. 3, 1995, *Unpub.*, the board, after considering limited mitigating factors and finding that the original violations were egregious, sustained the refusal to "give credit" for Gaind's 33-month suspension in imposing a three-year debarment.

The duration of inducement debarments is controlled primarily by the statute or regulations establishing the debarment. For example, the Davis-Bacon Act specifies a three-year period of debarment for firms found to be in violation of the statute, 40 U.S.C. § 276a-2(a). While the Walsh-Healey Act, 41 U.S.C. § 6504, and the Service Contract Act of 1965, 41 U.S.C. § 6706, also specify a three-year debarment period, the Secretary of Labor has discretion to impose a shorter-term or no debarment. The Buy American Act, 41 U.S.C. § 8303(c), also specifies a three-year period. In *J.B. Kies Constr. Co.*, Comp. Gen. Dec. B-250797, 93-1 CPD ¶ 127, the company was debarred for five and one-half years because the debarment was effective for three years after date of publication of the list of ineligible firms, and the company's name was not included on the list until two and one-half years after it was debarred.

In contrast, facilities listed for noncompliance with the Clean Water Act and the Clean Air Act will remain on the list until compliance is demonstrated. EPA regulations at 2 C.F.R. § 1532.1205 state that a written petition to reinstate the eligibility of a facility may be submitted to the EPA debarring official. The petitioner bears the burden of providing sufficient information and documentation to establish, by a preponderance of the evidence, that the condition giving rise to the ineligibility finding has been corrected.

Section 209(a)(6) of Executive Order 11246 also provides that the Secretary of Labor may debar a firm "until such contractor has satisfied the Secretary of Labor that such contractor has established and will carry out personnel and employment policies in compliance with the provisions of this order." Thus, 41 C.F.R. § 60-1.27 permits debarments for an indefinite period. Firms declared ineligible may be entitled to reinstatement upon submitting proof that "they have established and will carry out employment policies and practices in compliance with the Order and implementing regulations (the equal opportunity clause)," 41 C.F.R. § 60-1.31.

Debarring officials may not have as much discretion to reduce the duration of all inducement debarments. See *Mashburn Elec. Co.*, Comp. Gen. Dec. B-189471, 78-1 CPD ¶ 277, where GAO stated that while the duration of debarments under the Walsh-Healey Act and Service Contract Act could be reduced, there was no similar authority to reduce the duration of a debarment under the Davis-Bacon Act. See 29 C.F.R. § 5.12(c), stating that firms shall be removed from the ineligible bidders list upon demonstrating current responsibility to comply with the labor standards of the applicable statutes.

[b] Suspension Orders

FAR 9.407-4 gives specific guidance on the duration of suspension orders:

> (a) Suspension shall be for a temporary period pending the completion of investigation and any ensuing legal proceedings, unless sooner terminated by the suspending official or as provided in this subsection.
>
> (b) If legal proceedings are not initiated within 12 months after the date of the suspension notice, the suspension shall be terminated unless an Assistant Attorney General requests its extension, in which case it may be extended for an additional 6 months. In no event may a suspension extend beyond 18 months, unless legal proceedings have been initiated within that period.
>
> (c) The suspending official shall notify the Department of Justice of the proposed termination of the suspension, at least 30 days before the 12-month period expires, to give that Department an opportunity to request an extension.

The regulation was promulgated in response to *Horne Bros., Inc. v. Laird*, 463 F.2d 1268 (D.C. Cir. 1972), where the court criticized an indefinite suspension. The regulation, however, provides for suspension as long as a criminal proceeding is actively being conducted without regard to the total length of the suspension. For instance, in *BASIX, Inc.*, Comp. Gen. Dec. B-255613, 94-1 CPD ¶ 194, the suspension remained in effect "pending resolution of the indictment" of the contractor's CEO. Similarly, in *MetaTRACE, Inc.*, EPADEBAR 90-0001-00, Aug 30, 1990, *Unpub.*, the suspension remained in effect "pending completion of investigation or ensuing proceedings, including debarment action." There is some question as to whether this complies with the spirit of the *Horne Brothers* decision. In *U.S. Testing Co.*, EPADEBAR 89-0021-00, Apr. 23, 1991, *Unpub.*, the board, after concluding that additional information evidenced "an altered corporate culture as well as organizational and procedural changes," ordered the company's suspension terminated.

[4] Effect of Listing

FAR 9.405(a) precludes the award of contracts or the solicitation of offers from contractors that are debarred, suspended, or proposed for debarment. FAR

9.405(b) refers contracting officers to the SAM exclusions list, issued by the GSA, to determine which contractors are subject to this requirement. However, contractors on the list might submit bids or proposals, even if listed. Thus, FAR 9.405(d) contains the following procedures to ensure that the government does not deal with listed contractors:

> (1) After the opening of bids or receipt of proposals, the contracting officer shall review the exclusion records in SAM.
>
> (2) Bids received from any listed contractor in response to an invitation for bids shall be entered on the abstract of bids, and rejected unless the agency head determines in writing that there is a compelling reason to consider the bid.
>
> (3) Proposals, quotations, or offers received from any listed contractor shall not be evaluated for award or included in the competitive range, nor shall discussions be conducted with a listed offeror during a period of ineligibility, unless the agency head determines, in writing, that there is a compelling reason to do so. If the period of ineligibility expires or is terminated prior to award, the contracting officer may, but is not required to, consider such proposals, quotations, or offers.
>
> (4) Immediately prior to award, the contracting officer shall again review the exclusion records in SAM to ensure that no award is made to a listed contractor.

Contracting officers have been permitted to refuse to deal with companies that are closely related to companies on the SAM exclusions list. For example, in *Bilfinger Berger AG Sede Secondaria Italiana*, Comp. Gen. Dec. B-402496, 2010 CPD ¶ 125, the protester was properly declared nonresponsible because the contracting officer believed that a debarred firm to which it was closely related would perform part of the work. GAO concluded that the contracting officer had properly rejected the firm's representation that it would not use the debarred firm. The Court of Federal Claims reached the opposite conclusion in *Bilfinger Berger AG Sede Secondaria Italiana v. United States*, 389 Fed. Cl. 94 (2010). See also *Aardvark Keith Moving, Inc.*, Comp. Gen. Dec. B-290565, 2002 CPD ¶ 134, where a contracting officer properly rejected the proposal of a firm because it was affiliated with a firm that was proposed for debarment. The contracting officer had reached this conclusion from information submitted with the proposal and a Dun & Bradstreet report—which GAO found sound evidence even though the protester submitted evidence in the protest that there was no affiliation.

This regulation gives the contracting officer considerable discretion in deciding whether to reinstate an offeror if a debarment or suspension is lifted during the competition. See *FAS Support Servs., LLC*, 93 Fed. Cl. 687 (2010), and *FAS Support Servs., LLC*, Comp. Gen. Dec. B-402464, 2010 CPD ¶ 105, finding no abuse of discretion when a contracting officer did not reinstate such an offeror because he determined that there was little likelihood that it could win the competition and reinstatement would have delayed the procurement. Under prior similar regulations, it was held that a contracting officer could properly refuse to award a contract to a bidder that had been proposed for debarment at the time of bid opening but had settled the issues (ending the debarment proceedings) at the time of award, *Instruments by Precision Ltd.*, Comp. Gen. Dec. B-235339, 89-2 CPD ¶ 138. Compare *Tracor Applied Sci., Inc.*, Comp. Gen. Dec. B-221230.2, 86-1 CPD ¶ 189, holding that a contracting officer had discretion to award to a firm that was suspended or debarred at the time the offer was submitted, so long as it was not ineligible at the time of award, or to deny award even if the suspension or debarment was being reconsidered at the time of evaluation.

The FAR gives the contracting officer discretion to award to an offeror on the SAM exclusion list when there is a "compelling reason," but it appears that agencies may be reluctant to find such compelling reasons. See *J.B. Kies Constr. Co.*, Comp. Gen. Dec. B-250797, 93-1 CPD ¶ 127, affirming a finding of no compelling reason where the bids were opened two days before the debarment ended and the debarment had been delayed for over two years because of "administrative oversight." In *TS Generalbau GmbH*, Comp. Gen. Dec. B-246034, 92-1 CPD ¶ 189, GAO rejected the argument that the contractor had been arbitrarily suspended "just days before the bid opening and contract award," and in *Baxter Healthcare Corp.*, Comp. Gen. Dec. B-253455.3, 94-1 CPD ¶ 301, the protester was found ineligible for award where its suspension was not lifted until the afternoon after award and the contracting officer did not know that the suspension was about to end.

Contracting officers must be diligent in determining the status of offerors. See *R.J. Crowley, Inc.*, Comp. Gen. Dec. B-253783, 93-2 CPD ¶ 257, where GAO sustained a protest when the contracting officer had checked the latest monthly list but had not reviewed the electronic update, and the "monthly" list was several months out of date.

One contractor was found to have standing to bring a suit to have its name removed for the debarred list archive, *Hickey v. Chadick*, 649 F. Supp. 2d 770 (S.D. Ohio 2009). The court concluded that contracting officers might use the archive to determine that the contractor was nonresponsible. For a description of the multiple efforts of this contractor to overcome the impact of a debarment, see *Lasmer Indus., Inc v. AM Gen., LLC*, 741 F. Supp. 2d 829 (S.D. Ohio 2010) (statute of limitations barred suit against competitor that allegedly gave agency false information leading to the debarment).

[5] Permissible Activities

While debarment and suspension are government-wide, they do not bar entities from all activities related to government contracting. Some inducement debarments are limited to a certain type of activity. Further, debarments and suspensions do not necessarily affect existing contracts or subcontracting activities.

[a] Limited Debarments

Some inducement debarments are limited in nature. For example, a Buy American Act debarment under 41 U.S.C. § 8303(c) extends to contracts for construction, alterations, or repairs of public buildings or public works. The statute is silent as to other types of work. In debarments under the Clean Air Act and the Clean Water Act, debarments apply only to a "facility."

[b] Existing Contracts

FAR 9.405-1 provides guidance on whether current contracts are to be continued:

> (a) Notwithstanding the debarment, suspension, or proposed debarment of a contractor, agencies may continue contracts or subcontracts in existence at the time the contractor was debarred, suspended, or proposed for debarment unless the agency head directs otherwise. A decision as to the type of termination action, if any, to be taken should be made only after review by agency contracting and technical personnel and by counsel to ensure the propriety of the proposed action.
>
> (b) For contractors debarred, suspended, or proposed for debarment, unless the agency head makes a written determination of the compelling reasons for doing so, ordering activities shall not—
>
> > (1) Place orders exceeding the guaranteed minimum under indefinite quantity contracts;
> >
> > (2) Place orders under optional use Federal Supply Schedule contracts, blanket purchase agreements, or basic ordering agreements; or
> >
> > (3) Add new work, exercise options, or otherwise extend the duration of current contracts or orders.

General Services Administration regulations provide that termination for default is appropriate if the circumstances giving rise to the debarment or suspension also constitute a default in performance under the contract. If the debarment is based on reasons unrelated to performance, default termination is inappropriate. However, termination for convenience or cancellation is authorized if "the contractor presents a significant risk to the Government in completing a current contract," GSAR 509.405-1(a). See *Integrated Sys. Group, Inc. v. Dep't of the Army*, GSBCA 12613-P, 94-2 BCA ¶ 26,618, where the board approved the convenience termination of a contractor that had been proposed for debarment. There is no special DoD regulatory provision on the effect of debarment on termination of current contracts, although DFARS 209.405-1, as with FAR 9.405-1, warns against placing orders in excess of the minimum amount on an indefinite quantity contract, or against Federal Supply Schedule contracts. This regulation also states that "[t]his includes the exercise of options."

[c] Subcontracts

FAR 9.405-2(a) provides that contracting officers may not consent to subcontracts "subject to consent" under FAR Subpart 44.2. FAR 9.409 requires the inclusion of the Protecting the Government's Interests When Subcontracting with Contractors Debarred, Suspended or Proposed for Debarment clause at FAR 52.209-6 in all contracts with a value exceeding $30,000. Paragraph (b) of this clause provides:

> Other than a subcontract for a commercially available off-the-shelf item, the Contractor shall not enter into any subcontract, in excess of $30,000 with a Contractor that is debarred, suspended, or proposed for debarment by any executive agency unless there is a compelling reason to do so.

Paragraph (d) of this clause requires notification of the contracting officer prior to the award of any subcontract to a listed subcontractor.

However, subpart 9.4 was amended to more fully limit subcontracting with ineligible contractors. FAR 9-402(b) states:

> The Government suspends or debars contractors to protect the Government's interests. By operation of the clause at 52.209-6, Protecting the Government's Interests When Subcontracting with Contractors Debarred, Suspended or Proposed for Debarment, contractors shall not enter into any subcontract in excess of $35,000, other than a subcontract for a commercially available off-the-shelf item, with a contractor that has been debarred, suspended, or proposed for debarment unless there is a compelling reason to do so. If a contractor intends to enter into a subcontract in excess of $35,000, other than a subcontract for a commercially available off-the-shelf item, with a party that is debarred, suspended, or proposed for debarment as evidenced by the party's having an active exclusion record in SAM (see 9.404), a corporate officer or designee of the contractor is required by operation of the clause at 52.209-6, Protecting the Government's Interests when Subcontracting with Contractors Debarred, Suspended, or Proposed for Debarment, to notify the contracting officer, in writing, before entering into such subcontract. For contracts for the acquisition of commercial items, the notification requirement applies only for first-tier subcontracts. For all other contracts, the notification requirement applies to subcontracts at any tier. The notice must provide the following:
>
> (1) The name of the subcontractor;
>
> (2) The contractor's knowledge of the reasons for the subcontractor having an active exclusion record in SAM;
>
> (3) The compelling reason(s) for doing business with the subcontractor notwithstanding its having an active exclusion record in SAM; and,
>
> (4) The systems and procedures the contractor has established to ensure that it is fully protecting the Government's interests when

> dealing with such subcontractor in view of the specific basis for the party's debarment, suspension, or proposed debarment.
>
> Therefore, FAR 9-402(b) precludes subcontracts with an ineligible contractor when the dollar amount is more than $35,000 or the subcontract is not for a commercially available off-the-shelf item. Additionally, FAR 52.209-6 requires contractors to notify the contracting officer before entering into such subcontracts with ineligible contractors. Contractors could receive adverse past performance if they fail to follow the notification requirements in FAR 52.209-6.

In contrast, some inducement debarments have always covered subcontractors. It seems clear under EPA regulations that agencies may not award contracts where part of the performance would take place in a subcontractor facility that has been listed for violation of the Clean Air Act or the Clean Water Act. See 2 C.F.R. § 1532.220.

[E] Debarment and Suspension Procedures

This section considers the debarment and suspension procedures employed by the various contracting agencies and discusses the procedural due process requirements in debarment and suspension actions. Because suspension and debarment of a firm is quite serious and may even be fatal, the courts have recognized that certain due process protections must be afforded before these measures are invoked. See FAR 9.406-3(b) and FAR 9.407-3(b), stating that agencies shall establish procedures governing the debarment and suspension decision-making process that are "as informal as is practicable, consistent with principles of fundamental fairness." Executive Order 12549 created a set of procedural "Common Rules" that retained the due process structure outlined in FAR 9.406-3(b) and FAR 9.407-3(b). The final guidelines were accepted, with certain modifications, by 28 administrative agencies, including the EPA, HUD, and the DOE, 53 Fed. Reg. 19161 (1988). The governmentwide Nonprocurement Common Rule (NCR), was updated by the member agencies in 2003, 68 Fed. Reg. 66534. On May 11, 2004, 69 Fed. Reg. 26,276, OMB established a new title 2 of the Code of Federal Regulations, which is comprised of two subtitles. Subtitle A, entitled "Government-wide Grants and Agreements," contains OMB policy guidance to Federal agencies on grants and agreements. Part 180 of that Subtitle sets forth the OMB Guidelines to agencies (the NCR) on governmentwide debarment and suspension, regarding nonprocurement actions. Subtitle B, entitled "Federal Agency Regulations for Grants and Agreements," contains the regulations of Federal agencies implementing the OMB guidance, as those regulations apply to grants and other financial assistance agreements and nonprocurement transactions. The FAR procedures and the NCR procedures are, by design, closely parallel.

[1] Notice

An agency is not required to provide notice that it is contemplating the suspension of a contractor. Many small contractors receive the notice that they have been proposed for debarment or are suspended after they have been included on the SAM exclusions list. Large contractors generally overcome the lack of a notice requirement by tracking investigative actions so that they can present their arguments before they are place on the exclusions list.

[a] Referral and Investigation

FAR 9.406-3(a) requires agencies to establish "procedures for the prompt reporting, investigation, and referral to the debarring official of matters appropriate for that official's consideration." Usually, suspension and debarment actions are initiated upon receipt by the agency of information of an indictment or conviction. Suspension and debarring officials receive indictment and conviction notice from U.S. Attorneys' offices, Inspector General offices, and other government investigative organizations, as well as such sources as newspaper articles, competitors, and qui tam relators. However, any employee of an agency can refer a matter to the debarring official.

[b] Elective Communications

No notice of contemplated proceedings is required before a contractor is suspended or proposed for debarment. In *Shermco Indus., Inc. v. Secretary of the Air Force*, 584 F. Supp. 76 (N.D. Tex. 1984), the court observed at 88:

> Whether notice given a suspended contractor is sufficient depends on several considerations. The first is whether timing of the notice allowed meaningful opportunity to rebut the charges. Two recent Court of Appeals decisions seem to impose different due process requirements for the timing of notice of a suspension. In *Transco [Security, Inc. v. Freeman*, 639 F.2d 318, 323 (6th Cir.), *cert. denied*, 454 U.S. 820 (1981)], the contractor received no notice until after the suspension. Although the Sixth Circuit discussed whether the notice there involved was constitutionally infirm due to vagueness and the inconsistent explanations given by the agency for its decision to suspend, the court gave no indication that notice, to be constitutionally sufficient, had to be given before suspension.
>
> On the other hand, in *Old Dominion Dairy Products, Inc. v. Secretary of Defense*, 631 F.2d 953 (D.C. Cir. 1980), the D.C. Circuit held that a contractor was denied due process when it was not told, before two non-responsibility determinations, that it was under investigation and, after the determinations, was told only that they were based on the lack of a "satisfactory record of integrity."

* * *

> Under the circumstances of this case, the constructive notice provided to Shermco, by way of a draft of the proposed indictment against it, was constitutionally sufficient. This draft indictment was delivered to Shermco several months before suspension proceedings were instituted; it sufficiently informed Shermco of the existence of an investigation and the substance of the charges against it.

This same issue arises with the listing of contractors that are proposed for debarment—the notice is received after they are included on the list.

Over time, agencies adopted the practice of sending an informal notice, commonly known as a "Show Cause" letter or a "Request for Information." Agencies use these informal methods of communication when there are questions about a contractor's present responsibility. A "Request for Information" asks the contractor for information with supporting documentation. A "Show Cause" contains the agency's concerns about the contractor's present responsibility, requests the contractor explain why it is still responsible, and asks the contractor to provide supporting documentation why it should not be excluded.

A "Show Cause" letter and a "Request for Information" help agencies determine whether a contractor should be suspended or debarred. These communications do not result in a contractor being listed on SAM as an ineligible contractor unlike a proposed notice of debarment. Agencies usually send a "Show Cause" or a "Request for Information" when an agency has concerns about a contractor's responsibility, but exclusion is not appropriate without further information. A "Show Cause" letter gives the contractor the ability to respond before being listed on the EPLS; however, a "Show Cause" also allows agencies to expand the reasons for debarments beyond indictments and convictions.

Procedures for such preventive communications vary with each agency. For example, the DoD has incorporated a particular avenue of communication into its acquisition regulations, stating at DFARS 209.402, App. H-103:

> A contractor who becomes aware of a pending indictment or allegations of wrongdoing that the contractor believes may lead to a suspension or debarment action may contact that debarring and suspending official or designee to provide information as to the contractor's present responsibility.

Preventative communications may appeal to the agency's pragmatism. For instance, the contractor may argue to the agency that it would be against its interest to begin debarment procedures because debarment or listing will disrupt the flow of a product that is indispensable to the government or will affect future procurements that have few competitors. A contractor also could propose settlement or compliance agreement as an alternative to debarment.

If the contractor is successful in proving its responsibility to the agency's satisfaction, the result is usually described in a settlement or compliance agreement. This document sets forth the findings of the informal communications between the parties and the terms upon which the finding of responsibility has been conditioned. Such administrative agreements are made public by posting on the online Federal Awardee Performance and Integrity Information System (FAPIIS), FAR 9.406-3(f)(1) (debarment); FAR 9.407-3(e)(1) (suspension). In the event that this exchange does not prevent a debarment, early recognition of the problem will accelerate the fact-finding and hearing process and result in the removal of the contractor's name from the proposed debarment list with as little damage as possible (assuming, of course, that the proposed debarment is unsuccessful).

[c] Notice of Suspension or Notice of Proposed Debarment

Contractors must be given notice of the grounds upon which suspension and debarment actions are based, FAR 9.406-3(c) (proposed debarment); FAR 9.407-3(c) (suspension); NCR § 180.615. However, as stated above, once a contractor receives notice that it has been proposed for debarment or suspension, it is already included on the SAM exclusions list, FAR 9.404. In *Horne Bros., Inc. v. Laird*, 463 F.2d 1268 (D.C. Cir. 1972), the court concluded that a contractor could not be subjected to a "protracted suspension" without being given "some specific notice" of the charges upon which the suspension was based. In *Transco Sec., Inc. v. Freeman*, 639 F.2d 318 (6th Cir. 1981), the court overturned the suspension of a contractor suspected of fraud in obtaining a government contract since the agency had failed to give adequate notice of the charges, stating at 323:

> The general notice which appellants received did not permit adequate preparation for participation in a meaningful way in any forthcoming hearing or equivalent proceeding. Appellants were suspended for, among other things, "billing irregularities." At the time this information was received, appellants had performed a number of contracts for the GSA over several years at various locations. Appellants were not told to which of these contracts the "billing irregularities" referred. Without further identifying information of at least the contract involved, and approximate date of misbillings, it would be at best onerous and at worst virtually impossible to effectively gather and present relevant information refuting this general charge.

See also *ATL, Inc. v. United States*, 736 F.2d 677 (Fed. Cir. 1984), requiring notice "sufficiently specific to permit the suspended contractor to collect and present relevant evidence refuting the charges," and *Electro-Methods, Inc. v. United States*, 728 F.2d 1471 (Fed. Cir. 1984), finding adequate notice where the contractor had been provided and in fact rebutted all the evidence considered by the suspension authority. In *SDA Inc.*, Comp. Gen. Dec. B-253355, 93-2 CPD ¶ 132, GAO found sufficient notice where a contractor had been suspended on the basis of detailed, unrebutted allegations of misconduct contained in a civil complaint filed by the federal government. See also *Reeve Aleutian Airways,*

Inc. v. United States, 982 F.2d 594 (D.C. Cir. 1993), where the court found sufficient notice in a letter referring to an adverse report on the contractor's performance. But see *Friedler v. GSA*, 271 F. Supp. 3d 40 (D.D.C. 2017) where a debarment was overturned because the debarment notice failed to notify the affected contractor about two new causes for debarment in the debarment notice, causes the agency relied upon when debarring the contractor.

FAR 9.406-3(c) requires that contractors and "specifically named affiliates" be given advance notification of proposed debarment actions as well as at least a general statement of the reasons for the proposed debarment. See *S.A.F.E. Export Corp.*, Comp. Gen. Dec. B-222308.2, 86-2 CPD ¶44, where GAO found adequate notice to an unnamed affiliate because the principal officer of the affiliate and the principal company received actual notice. With respect to suspension actions, the regulations provide for notice *immediately after* the suspension has been invoked, FAR 9.407-3(c).

[d] Designation of Lead Agency

Because contractors often do business with various government agencies, more than one agency may have an interest in suspension or debarment of an entity. FAR 9.402(d) provides for the designation of a lead agency as follows:

> When more than one agency has an interest in the debarment or suspension of a contractor, the Interagency Committee on Debarment and Suspension, established under Executive Order 12549, and authorized by Section 873 of the National Defense Authorization Act for Fiscal year 2009 (Pub. L. 110-417), shall resolve the lead agency issue and coordinate such resolution among all interested agencies prior to the initiation of any suspension, debarment, or related administrative action by any agency.

NCR § 180.620 also has informal procedures to designate the lead agency. Where a contractor is known to have involvement with more than one agency, the agencies consult with one another to determine which agency will handle the matter. Often, the agency with which the contractor does the most business (based on dollar value of contracts and subcontracts) is designated the lead agency. However, there may be extenuating circumstances where there is an overriding interest in another agency being the lead agency. For example, the EPA may take the lead for cases involving violations of the environmental laws.

[2] Presentation of Matters in Opposition

Basic fairness in debarment proceedings requires that a party be given an "opportunity to present evidence," *Gonzales v. Freeman*, 118 U.S. App. D.C. 180, 334 F.2d 570 (D.C. Cir. 1964). Moreover, after a reasonable period of time following imposition of a suspension, the firm may be entitled to a "hearing" involving at least an opportunity to refute the basis for the suspension, unless a hearing would be inappropriate for reasons of national security or would prejudice a pending or imminent criminal prosecution of the firm, *Horne Bros., Inc. v. Laird*, 463 F.2d 1268 (D.C. Cir. 1972).

[a] Opportunity to Be Heard in Opposition

FAR 9.406-3(b)(1) and FAR 9.407-3(b)(1) contain the minimal guidance that debarment and suspension proceedings "shall afford the contractor (and any specifically named affiliates) an opportunity to submit, in person, in writing, or through a representative, information and argument in opposition to the proposed" action. FAR 9.406-3(b)(2) and FAR 9.407-3(b)(2) then state that in debarment actions not based on conviction or civil judgment and in suspension actions not based on an indictment, if it is found that the contractor's submission *raises a genuine dispute over facts material to the proposed action*, the agency must:

> (i) Afford the contractor an opportunity to appear with counsel, submit documentary evidence, present witnesses, and confront any person the agency presents; and
>
> (ii) Make a transcribed record of the proceedings and make it available at cost to the contractor upon request, unless the contractor and the agency, by mutual agreement, waive the requirement for a transcript.

Agencies have been granted considerable discretion in following this two-step procedure in deciding whether there is a genuine dispute of fact to justify such an actual hearing. See *Robinson v. Cheney*, 876 F.2d 152 (D.C. Cir. 1989), affirming the agency's denial of a hearing on the grounds that the alleged factual disputes were minor in nature and did not go to the central issues in the case. See also *IMCO, Inc. v. United States*, 33 Fed. Cl. 312 (1995), affirming the debarring official's denial of a hearing on the basis that there were no seriously contested facts. This limited-hearing approach was also upheld in *Transco Sec., Inc. v. Freeman*, 639 F.2d 318 (6th Cir. 1981), where the court stated at 322-23:

> Under the present regulations, promulgated following *Horne Brothers*, suspended contractors denied a hearing are provided the opportunity to present information or argument, in person, in writing, or through representation in opposition to the suspension. Thus under the current regulations, suspended contractors will not "dangle in suspension for a period of one year or more" before being given an opportunity to rebut charges. 463 F.2d at 1271. Under most circumstances, this opportunity coupled with proper notice will timely cure such errors as suspending the wrong contractor or suspending a contractor based on mere suspicion, unfounded allegation, or error.

Thus, when an agency follows this two-step procedure, a contractor that is proposed for debarment or is suspended must, in order to obtain a hearing, demonstrate in its initial written submission that there are significant factual disputes. On the other hand, there is nothing in the FAR precluding an agency from granting hearings in less restrictive circumstances.

FAR 9.406-3(d) and FAR 9.407-3(d)(2) call for written findings of fact when an actual hearing is conducted. They also permit the debarring official to delegate the conduct of such a hearing by stating that "matters involving disputed material facts" may be referred to another official. Some agencies have established a separate hearing officer as a matter of course. For example, GSA provides that if there is a genuine dispute of material fact, the suspending official must refer the matter to the fact-finding official, GSAR 509.406-3(d)(3). See also DFARS Appendix H-104 stating:

> (a) . . . If the debarring and suspending official has determined a genuine dispute of material fact(s) exists, a designated fact-finder will conduct the fact-finding proceeding. The proceeding before the fact-finder will be limited to a finding of the facts in dispute as determined by the debarring and suspending official.
>
> (b) The designated fact-finder will establish the date for a fact-finding proceeding, normally to be held within 45 working days of the contractor's presentation of matters in opposition. An official record will be made of the fact-finding proceeding.
>
> (c) The Government's representative and the contractor will have an opportunity to present evidence relevant to the facts at issues. The contractor may appear in person or through a representative in the fact-finding proceeding.
>
> (d) Neither the Federal Rules of Evidence nor the Federal Rules of Civil Procedure govern fact-finding. Hearsay evidence may be presented and will be given appropriate weight by the fact-finder.
>
> (e) Witnesses may testify in person. Witnesses will be reminded of the official nature of the proceeding and that any false testimony given is subject to criminal prosecution. Witnesses are subject to cross-examination.

Obtaining a hearing does not necessarily give the contractor the same due process rights it would have in civil litigation. For example, in *Electro-Methods, Inc. v. United States*, 728 F.2d 1471 (Fed. Cir. 1984), the court, commenting on a suspension, held that the "concept of due process cannot be extended so far, in the circumstances of this case, as to mandate that a 'meaningful' hearing include permitting the contractor to subpoena and examine FBI agents involved in an on-going criminal investigation, as well as other government and industry officials, to prove its case." However, some minimal evidentiary standards may apply. See *James J. Burnett*, HUDBCA 80-501-D42, 82-1 BCA ¶15,716, where the board held that hearsay evidence alone would not normally be sufficient to support a debarment.

During fact finding the contractor is not be permitted to challenge facts that were the basis of a conviction or civil judgment, NCR § 180.830.

[b] Right of Confrontation

Although the court in *Horne Bros., Inc. v. Laird*, 463 F.2d 1268 (D.C. Cir. 1972), suggested that there may be a right to confront adverse witnesses if a suspension is protracted, FAR 9.406-3(b)(2)(i) and FAR 9.407-3(b)(2)(i) provide for an opportunity to confront agency witnesses *only* when there is a dispute as to material facts. *Robinson v. Cheney*, 876 F.2d 152 (D.C. Cir. 1989), significantly limits this right by analogizing the situation to that of courts deciding motions for summary judgment without a hearing. See also *Reeve Aleutian Airways, Inc. v. United States*, 982 F.2d 594 (D.C. Cir. 1993), commenting that a hearing where no government witnesses were present was sufficient because the contractor could have called them.

Cross-examination of adverse witnesses is generally permitted during fact finding. See the DFARS above, GSAR 509.406-3(d)(3)(viii), and NCR § 180.840. However, confrontation and cross-examination of adverse witnesses have not been required where material facts are not in dispute, *Titan Constr. Co. v. Weinberger*, Civ. Action No. 85-5533 (D.N.J. 1986); *Taylor v. Marsh*, Civ. Action No. 81-2643 (D.D.C. 1982); *Commonwealth Labs., Inc.*, AGBCA 94-0059-01, Apr. 17, 1995, *Unpub.*

[3] Timing Requirements

FAR 9.406-3(c) and NCR § 180.820, provide that within 30 days of receipt of notice of proposed debarment or suspension, the respondent may present information or argument in opposition. In actions based upon "a conviction or judgment, or in which there is no genuine dispute over material facts," the debarring official will make a decision based upon the administrative record. No time is specified for this decision. If no suspension is in effect, the decision must be made within 30 working days after receipt of "any information and argument submitted by the contractor, unless the debarring official extends this period for good cause," FAR 9.406-3(d).

[F] De Facto Debarment and Suspension

There have been a number of decisions finding actions of the government that exclude contractors from the opportunity to receive award to be de facto debarments. The reasoning in such cases is that since the effect of the action was the same as a suspension or debarment, it was improper, because the agency did not observe due process requirements. The FAR contains no guidance on the type of actions that constitute de facto debarments. The decisions giving such guidance are covered in this section.

[1] Multiple Nonresponsibility Determinations

Multiple determinations of nonresponsibility may be tantamount to a debarment. See 43 Comp. Gen. 140 (B-151269) (1963), holding it improper to make successive nonresponsibility determinations for the same criminal offense without initiating debarment proceedings. See also Comp. Gen. Dec. B-175845, Mar. 9, 1973, *Unpub.*, where GAO upheld a nonresponsibility determination for alleged labor violations without the agency having undertaken formal debarment proceedings, but stated that "continued refusal to award contracts. . . . as a result of a nonresponsibility determination based upon the same alleged labor violations as involved here without invoking and following the applicable debarment procedures would be of doubtful validity." In *Myers & Myers, Inc. v. United States Postal Serv.*, 527 F.2d 1252 (2d Cir. 1975), the court found de facto debarment where the Postal Service refused to renew six delivery contracts because of suspected criminal conduct. See *Dynamic Aviation v. Department of the Interior*, 898 F. Supp. 11 (D.D.C. 1995), where the court recognized a possibility of a de facto debarment in the government's one-year revocation of a contractor's pilot's credentials coupled with a refusal to test and inspect until a federal bureau specifically requested the contractor's services, which would not occur until a card has been issued; and *Leslie & Elliott Co. v. Garrett*, 732 F. Supp. 191 (D.D.C. 1990), where a de facto debarment was found because the Navy attacked the contractor's integrity and developed a policy to declare the contractor nonresponsible on all contracts. In *Shermco Indus. v. Secretary of the Air Force*, 584 F. Supp. 76 (N.D. Tex. 1984), involving integrity issues, the court stated, "a procuring agency cannot make successive determinations of nonresponsibility on the same basis; rather it must initiate suspension or debarment procedures at the earliest practicable date following the first determination of nonresponsibility."

GAO has refused to find de facto debarments when the finding of nonresponsibility can be referred to the SBA for the granting of a Certificate of Competency, *Sermor, Inc.*, Comp. Gen. Dec. B-219132.2, 85-2 CPD ¶ 444 (five consecutive nonresponsibility determinations based on financial capability); *Pittman Mech. Contractors, Inc.*, Comp. Gen. Dec. B-242499, 91-1 CPD ¶ 439 (four contemporaneous nonresponsibility determinations). GAO has also refused to find de facto debarments when a number of nonresponsibility determinations have been made contemporaneously, *Mexican Intermodal Equip., S.A. de C.V.*, Comp. Gen. Dec. B-270144, 96-1 CPD ¶ 31 (two nonresponsibility determinations did "not demonstrate that they were part of a long-term disqualification attempt . . . [but were] . . . merely a reflection of the fact that the determinations were based on the same current information"); *Shepard Printing*, Comp. Gen. Dec. B-260362, 95-2 CPD ¶ 119 (seven nonresponsibility determinations within three-month period based on same information as to deficient quality); *Government Contract Advisory Servs., Inc.*, Comp. Gen. Dec. B-255918, 94-1 CPD ¶ 181 (three concurrent nonresponsibility determinations by different contracting officers based on same information); *Garten-und Landschaftsbau GmbH Frank Mohr*, Comp. Gen. Dec. B-237276, 90-1 CPD ¶ 186 (two nonresponsibility determinations based on integrity issues). It seems clear that a single nonresponsibility determination will not be considered to be a de facto debarment, *Redondo-Borges v. United States HUD*, 421 F.3d 1 (1st Cir. 2005).

GAO has cautioned that in order for an agency's nonresponsibility determinations to qualify as a de facto suspension or debarment, the agency must have had an intent to exclude. In *Quality Trust, Inc.*, Comp. Gen. Dec. B-289445, 2002 CPD ¶ 41, for example, GAO noted that "de facto debarment occurs when the government uses nonresponsibility determinations as a means of excluding a firm from government contracting or subcontracting, rather than following the debarment regulations and procedures set forth at FAR Subpart 9.4." A necessary element of a de facto debarment, GAO noted, "is that an agency intends not to do business with the firm in the future."

[2] Blacklists, Holdups, and Passovers

Actions or communications indicating a refusal to deal with a contractor in the future have been held to be de facto debarments or suspension. In *Airco, Inc. v. Cecil D. Andrus*, 26 Cont. Cas. Fed. (CCF) ¶ 83,636 (D.D.C. 1979), the contractor was threatened with placement of an "informal blacklist" by the Department of the Interior (DOI). Specifically, the agency threatened to notify its customers and contractors that Airco was in violation of an agency regulation that would prevent such customers from doing business with Airco. The court found that while the DOI had not canceled or terminated any contract with Airco and had not put Airco on an "ineligible" list, the effect on Airco was the same as a formal debarment but without the protective procedures to which Airco would have been entitled by a formal debarment action. Similarly, in *Peter Kiewit & Sons' Co. v. U.S. Army Corps of Eng'rs*, 534 F. Supp. 1139 (D.D.C. 1982), *rev'd on other grounds*, 714 F.2d 163 (D.C. Cir. 1983), the court found a de facto debarment by the Army when it held Kiewit in abeyance under a "temporary declaration of ineligibility" and denied it a contract award without providing notice and an opportunity to be heard. See also *Highview Eng'g, Inc. v. Corps of Engineers*, No. 3:08-CV-647-S, 2010 U.S. Dist. LEXIS 75102 (W.D. Ky. July 23, 2010) (agency employees statements that they did not want a subcontractor included in proposals demonstrated de facto debarment); *Art-Metal USA, Inc. v. Solomon*, 473 F. Supp. 1 (D.D.C. 1978) (de facto debarment where the GSA terminated contract for convenience and then held in abeyance four other contract awards pending the completion of a GSA investigation into possible contract abuses).

Informal statements of the contracting officer may be sufficient to indicate an intention not to award future contracts. For example, in *Related Indus., Inc. v. United States*, 2 Cl. Ct. 517 (1983), the court found de facto debarment where the contracting officer proposed to find Related nonresponsible on one award but also declared that he would not award any future contract to plaintiff or to any company with which plaintiff was associated. Compare *Community Econ. Dev. Corp. v. United States*, 577 F. Supp. 425 (D.D.C. 1983), where there was a justifiable basis for a single nonresponsibility determination. Although the contractor contended that the contracting officer told him he was debarred, the subsequent deposition of the contracting officer stating that the contractor was welcome to bid on future procurements and regularly would be sent future solicitations led the court to conclude that the alleged statement, if true, was made in the heat of the moment. In *Bannum, Inc.*, Comp. Gen. Dec. B-249758, 92-2 CPD ¶373, while an agency official's remark that she and her supervisors "were tired of Bannum's rhetoric," a remark made over two years earlier, may have reflected a lack of judgment, the facts did not support the contractor's contention that it had been de facto debarred.

It has also been held that the "passover" procedure under Executive Order 11246, where contractors are found not in compliance with equal employment obligations, constitutes a de facto debarment, *Pan Am. World Airways, Inc. v. Marshall*, 439 F. Supp. 487 (S.D.N.Y. 1977); *Sundstrand Corp. v. Marshall*, 17 FEP Cases 432 (N.D. Ill. 1978).

Although not decided under the de facto debarment rubric, two cases have found that stigmatizing communications that inhibit the award of future contracts constitute a deprivation of a contractor's "liberty interest," *Old Dominion Dairy Prods., Inc. v. Secretary of Defense*, 631 F.2d 953 (D.C. Cir. 1980); *Conset Corp. v. Community Servs. Admin.*, 655 F.2d 1291 (D.C. Cir. 1981). In both cases, the stigmatizing communications related to the integrity of the contractor, and there is some question as to whether this logic would apply to other grounds of nonresponsibility. See *John Carlo, Inc. v. Corps of Eng'rs of the U.S. Army*, 539 F. Supp. 1075 (N.D. Tex. 1982), listing four factors to consider when deciding if a finding of nonresponsibility amounts to a de facto debarment:

> (1) were other persons or government agencies apprised of the contracting officer's finding of nonresponsibility; (2) was the information circulated for the purpose of preventing [contractor] from securing future contracts with the government; (3) did circulation of the information in fact stigmatize [contractor]; and (4) has [contractor] suffered any losses in government business attributable to the contracting officer's determination of nonresponsibility.

In *Frank Cain & Sons, Inc.*, Comp. Gen. Dec. B-236893, 90-1 CPD ¶44, GAO found proper the contracting agency's determination that the bidder was nonresponsible based on information in a criminal investigation report that called into question the bidder's integrity.

CHAPTER 5
SEALED BIDDING

§5.01 INTRODUCTION

Sealed bidding, previously known as formal advertising and often called "tendering" internationally, has long been used by the federal government to select contractors on the basis of price competition with publicly opened bids. Congress passed the first statute dealing with advertising in 1809, requiring that "all purchases and contracts for supplies or services . . . shall be made either by open purchase, or by previously advertising for proposals," 2 Stat. 536. The Attorney General stated that the purpose of this statute was to prevent favoritism, 2 Ops. Att'y Gen. 257 (1829), and to prevent the notorious mischief of making contracts privately, 6 Ops. Att'y Gen. 99 (1853). From time to time, additional formalities were adopted. See, e.g., 5 Stat. 522, 526 (1842), 5 Stat. 614, 617 (1843), 5 Stat. 790, 795 (1845). In 1861, the statutory requirements for advertising were reaffirmed, 12 Stat. 220. This statute was subsequently incorporated into Revised Statute 3709, the forerunner of 41 U.S.C. §6101 (formerly 41 U.S.C. §5). In the years that followed, numerous Comptroller of the Treasury, Comptroller General, and court decisions implemented the statute by further defining the procedures to be followed in formal advertising. Following World War II, these procedures were adopted by Congress in the Armed Services Procurement Act of 1947, and the Federal Property and Administrative Services Act. These statutes were further modified by the Competition in Contracting Act of 1984 (CICA), Pub. L. No. 98-369, and the Federal Acquisition Streamlining Act of 1994 (FASA), Pub. L. No. 103-355.

Sealed bidding was the predominant technique used in government contracting until World War II. During the war its use was suspended in order to efficiently award contracts to obtain necessary war materials. After the war the statutes reinstated it as the preferred technique, but negotiation was permitted under specified statutory exceptions. Thereafter, sealed bidding was used for the majority of federal procurement actions, but the more significant dollar expenditures were made using negotiation procedures. As discussed in Chapter 3, the CICA ended the practice of "favoring" the use of sealed bidding when it made sealed bidding and competitive negotiation parallel procedures for meeting the statutory competition requirements. At the present time, less than 10% of federal procurement dollars are spent in sealed bid procurements. The statutory procedures for sealed bidding are now contained in 10 U.S.C. §3302 (formerly §2305) and 41 U.S.C. §3702. The key provisions describing the unique features of sealed bidding are in 10 U.S.C. §3302. Substantially the same language is in 41 U.S.C. §3702. The statutory requirements for sealed bidding are implemented in FAR Part 14.

This chapter first considers the procedures applicable to the submission and public opening of sealed bids. It then deals with the concept of responsiveness—whether the bid conforms in all material respects to the invitation. The evaluation of bids and the award of the contract is next discussed. The last two sections cover mistakes in bids and two-step sealed bidding. The other key aspect of sealed bidding—determining whether the prospective contractor is responsible—is covered in Chapter 4.

§ 5.02 BIDDING AND OPENING PROCEDURE

The fundamental concept of sealed bidding is that the public interest is best served when the government describes its needs with precision, conducts an open competition to obtain the best price, opens the bids publicly, and awards to the responsible bidder that submits the lowest price and agrees without qualification to meet all the material contract requirements. In this system, discretion of government employees is reduced to a minimum, and public opening ensures that the award decision is subject to public scrutiny. Thus, it has been stated that sealed bidding is aimed at securing the most advantageous contract for the government by maximizing free and open competition; preventing favoritism, collusion, or fraud; and giving all interested parties an opportunity to compete, *United States v. Brookridge Farm, Inc.*, 111 F.2d 461 (10th Cir. 1940). Bidders must prepare their bids independently without the knowledge of whether other bidders are competing for award or of the contents of other bids. Public opening ensures all parties that the award is being made in conformance with the solicitation. Bids are "firm" for a specified period of time—with the result that withdrawal or modification of a bid after opening is permitted only in the limited circumstances of mistake.

Sealed bidding does not afford the government the option of evaluating the merits of technical proposals and paying somewhat more to obtain a higher quality product or service. It *requires* that if award is made, it must be made to the responsive bidder with the lowest price even if the product or service offered is only minimally acceptable. Thus, its successful use is almost completely dependent on the government's ability to describe its needs in a way that ensures that the winning contractor will be *contractually bound* to perform satisfactory work.

[A] Solicitation of Bids

The solicitation of sealed bids is accomplished through a written document called an Invitation for Bids (IFB). The government makes copies of IFBs available to prospective bidders, typically electronically using the federal central posting site, *www.SAM.gov*, and may give further notice of the solicitation through advertising or posting notices of the solicitation in public places. See Chapter 3, Section IV for a discussion of public announcements and solicitations.

[1] Invitations for Bids

In order to ensure that all bidders compete on an equal basis, IFBs must contain all of the essential terms of the contract so that bidders may submit offers by merely filling in the price and schedule, if required, completing the necessary certifications, and signing the offer, FAR 14.101(a). Solicitations are issued on multipurpose standard forms used for both sealed bid and negotiated procurements. The contracting officer may use Standard Form 33 (Solicitation, Offer and Award) or Standard Form 1447 (Solicitation/Contract) or may issue the solicitation on a special form, FAR 14.201-2(a); FAR 53.214. Standard Form 1442 (Solicitation, Offer, and Award) is prescribed for use on construction contracts, FAR 36.701(b); FAR 53.236-1(e). One of these standard forms is used in most cases because they contain blanks with the essential information that must be filled in by both the contracting officer and the bidder. This entire package is designed so that all bidders can make legally sufficient and comparable offers under the same terms and conditions by furnishing the required information and inserting their price and delivery schedule.

FAR 14.201-1 requires, with certain exceptions such as construction contracts, that solicitations and resulting contracts be prepared using the Uniform Contract Format "to the maximum practicable extent." Standard Form 33 is the most commonly used standard form because it is structured to use this format. However, the contracting officer is permitted to use a "simplified contract format," FAR 14.201-9, and should use Standard Form 1447 when this format is used, FAR 53.214(d).

The Uniform Contract Format consists of the following Parts and Subparts:

Section	Title
Part I—The Schedule	
A	Solicitation/contract form
B	Supplies or services and prices
C	Description/specifications
D	Packaging and marking
E	Inspection and acceptance
F	Deliveries or performance
G	Contract administration data
H	Special contract requirements
Part II—Contract Clauses	
I	Contract clauses

(continues)

Part III—List of Documents, Exhibits, and Other Attachments	
J	List of documents, exhibits, and other attachments
Part IV—Representations and Instructions	
K	Representations, certifications, and other statements of bidders
L	Instructions, conditions, and notices to bidders
M	Evaluation factors for award

This format is structured so that Parts I, II, and III become the contract, when awarded, while Part IV is retained in the contract file, FAR 14.201-1(c). Part I of the format contains the unique provisions pertaining to the procurement, including, as Section A, Standard Form 33, FAR 14.201-2. Section B requires the bidders to fill in the bid prices, while the other sections in Part I contain the contract terms provided by the government. Part II, Section I, contains the clauses for the proposed contract, FAR 14.201-3, including standard contract clauses contained in FAR Part 52 and special clauses used by the agency and not included in Part I. FAR 52.3 contains a matrix giving guidance on the required and optional clauses to be incorporated into the various types of contracts. FAR 52.102-1 encourages incorporation of clauses by reference, "to the maximum extent practicable," if permitted by FAR 52.3 or if they are contained in agency-wide procurement regulations such as the Department of Defense Federal Acquisition Regulation Supplement (DFARS).

Part III, Section J, contains a list of all attachments to the contract, providing the title, date, and number of pages for each document, FAR 14.201-4. Part IV, Section K, contains all representations and certifications as well as any other provision that must be filled in by the bidders, FAR 14.201-5(a). This section, by clustering all of these requirements in a single section, reduces the possibility of bidders failing to fill out a necessary form. Many of those certifications are required to be provided annually online, through *https://www.SAM.gov*, see FAR 4.120(a). Section L contains all of the instructions to bidders on procedures that will be followed in evaluating bids and selecting the bidders—commonly known as "solicitation provisions." See FAR 52.101, which defines a solicitation provision as "a term or condition used only in solicitations and applying only before contract award." FAR 14.201-6 contains a long list of the standard solicitation provisions used in sealed bid procurements. Section M contains all of the "price-related factors" other than bid price that will be evaluated in selecting the low bidder, FAR 14.201-5(c).

Once a solicitation is issued, communication between the procuring agency and prospective bidders is discouraged except through the procurement official named in the solicitation for that purpose. Routine questions that do not require an amendment to the solicitation or do not involve the clarification of ambiguous provisions may be answered orally or by letter. If the procurement is complex or numerous questions have been raised, the procuring agency may convene a pre-bid conference for all interested parties. See FAR 14.208, 14.211. A pre-bid conference, however, is "never [to] be used as a substitute for amending a defective or ambiguous invitation," FAR 14.207.

The solicitation therefore serves a number of functions in the procurement process. It must: (1) lay out the ground rules of the competition, including the information to be supplied by bidders and the bid opening time; (2) contain the specifications or incorporate them by reference when permitted; and (3) contain all the terms and conditions of the proposed contract except the bid prices. Both the substantive requirements of the solicitation and the procedures by which it is publicized can influence the degree of competition that is obtained.

[2] Amendment of IFBs

A contracting officer may—because of revised needs, or errors or deficiencies in the solicitation—find it necessary to change the solicitation by issuing an amendment. FAR 14.208 outlines the procedures for the issuance of amendments to IFBs:

> (a) If it becomes necessary to make changes in quantity, specifications, delivery schedules, opening dates, etc., or to correct a defective or ambiguous invitation, such changes shall be accomplished by amendment of the invitation for bids using Standard Form 30, Amendment of Solicitation/ Modification of Contract. The fact that a change was mentioned at a pre-bid conference does not relieve the necessity for issuing an amendment. Amendments shall be sent, before the time for bid opening, to everyone to whom invitations have been furnished and shall be displayed in the bid room.
>
> (b) Before amending an invitation for bids, the contracting officer shall consider the period of time remaining until bid opening and the need to extend this period.
>
> (c) Any information given to a prospective bidder concerning an invitation for bids shall be furnished promptly to all other prospective bidders as an amendment to the invitation—
>
> > (1) if such information is necessary for bidders to submit bids or
> >
> > (2) if the lack of such information would be prejudicial to uninformed bidders. The information shall be furnished even though a pre-bid conference is held. No award shall be made on the invitation unless such amendment has been issued in sufficient time to permit all prospective bidders to consider such information in submitting or modifying their bids.

Only information that would cause prejudice to uninformed bidders needs to be distributed per FAR 14.208, *Hunt Constr. Grp., Inc. v. United States*, 281 F.3d 1369 (Fed. Cir. 2002).

Even though the regulations provide that an amendment shall be sent to each concern to whom the IFB has been furnished, GAO has consistently held that a bidder bears the risk of not receiving an amendment, assuming that such failure is not the result of a failure to follow the regulations governing distribution of solicitation materials, *Navistar Marine Instrument Corp.*, Comp. Gen. Dec. B-277143, 98-1 CPD ¶ 53, or the product of a conscious and deliberate effort by the agency to exclude the bidder from participating in the competition, *Monterey Advanced Imaging Ctr.*, Comp. Gen. Dec. B-253152, 93-2 CPD ¶ 118; *Southwestern Enters., Inc.*, Comp. Gen. Dec. B-245491.2, 92-1 CPD ¶ 88; *GSX Gov't Servs., Inc.*, Comp. Gen. Dec. B-239549.2, 91-1 CPD ¶ 12.

The underlying theory is that the agency discharges its legal responsibility when it issues and dispatches an amendment in sufficient time to permit all bidders to consider the amendment in formulating their bids, *Southern Techs., Inc.*, 67 Comp. Gen. 204 (B-228516), 88-1 CPD ¶ 57; *Maintenance Pace Setters, Inc.*, Comp. Gen. Dec. B-212757, 84-1 CPD ¶ 98; *Eugene Ricciardelli, Inc.*, Comp. Gen. Dec. B-212871, 83-2 CPD ¶ 640. Hence, in *Electro-Mechanical Indus., Inc.*, 52 Comp. Gen. 281 (B-176839) (1972), an amendment issued to the bidder, but addressed incorrectly, provided no basis for cancellation. GAO stated that "the propriety of a particular procurement must be determined from the government's point of view upon the basis of whether adequate competition and reasonable prices were obtained, not upon whether every possible prospective bidder was afforded an opportunity to bid." Thus, late receipt of an amendment will require cancellation and resolicitation if adequate competition is not received as a result of the transmission defect. For example, in *Andero Constr., Inc.*, 61 Comp. Gen. 253 (B-203898), 82-1 CPD ¶ 133, GAO ignored the general rule that the bidder bears the risk of non-delivery of an amendment to the solicitation, because the agency failed to affirmatively establish that it complied with DAR 2-208 (similar to FAR 14.208), and three of four bidders appeared not to have received the amendment in the mail. The agency never affirmatively stated that the amendments were mailed, and thus GAO recommended that the agency cancel the IFB and resolicit its requirements. See also *Gadsden Moving & Storage Co.*, Comp. Gen. Dec. B-250658, 93-1 CPD ¶ 134, where GAO found that the agency had deprived the protester of the opportunity to compete by not providing the protester with a copy of the amendment in a timely manner. GAO stated that the agency conceded that it used an incorrect mailing address, the protester took reasonable steps to obtain the amendment, and the agency had received only one bid. In *Phillip Sitz Constr.*, Comp. Gen. Dec. B-245941, 92-1 CPD ¶ 101, GAO found that because the agency had sent the IFB to the protester, it was required to place the protester on the mailing list and to send it any solicitation amendments. The agency conceded that the protester was not included on the mailing list and that it did not send the amendment. Further, GAO stated that as a result of the agency's actions, only one responsive bid was received, thereby undermining the CICA mandate for full and open competition.

[3] Time for Submission of Bids

Bidders must be given sufficient time to submit bids. See FAR 14.202-1, stating:

> (a) Policy. A reasonable time for prospective bidders to prepare and submit bids shall be allowed in all invitations, consistent with the needs of the Government. (For construction contracts, see 36.303(a).) A bidding time (i.e., the time between issuance of the solicitation and opening of bids) of at least 30 calendar days shall be provided when synopsis is required by Subpart 5.2.
>
> (b) Factors to be considered. Because of unduly limited bidding time, some potential sources may be precluded from bidding and others may be forced to include amounts for contingencies that, with additional time, could be eliminated. To avoid unduly restricting competition or paying higher-than-necessary prices, consideration shall be given to such factors as the following in establishing a reasonable bidding time: (1) degree of urgency; (2) complexity of requirement; (3) anticipated extent of subcontracting; (4) whether use was made of pre-invitation notices; (5) geographic distribution of bidders; and (6) normal transmittal time for both initiations and bids.

Contracting officers may extend (or postpone) the bidding time in order to increase competition, *Warrior Serv. Co.*, Comp. Gen. Dec. B-417491, 2019 CPD ¶ 178; *Combustion Equip. Co.*, Comp. Gen. Dec. B-228291, 87-2 CPD ¶ 627.

FAR 14.208(b) provides that no award should be made on an invitation unless an amendment has been issued in sufficient time to permit all prospective bidders to consider such information in submitting or modifying their bids. However, the amount of time necessary will be determined by the complexity of the amendment. In *Pacific Contractors, Inc.*, Comp. Gen. Dec. B-190568, 78-2 CPD ¶ 97, GAO found that the contracting officer acted reasonably in affording four of five bidders less than one day and a fifth bidder less than one hour to consider the effect of an amendment, where the amendment was simple in nature and none of the bidders (including the protester) objected prior to bid opening. In *Tom Walsh & Assocs.*, Comp. Gen. Dec. B-212750, 84-1 CPD ¶ 78, GAO again determined that the protester had been given sufficient time (six days) to consider the amendment. Conversely, 45 Comp. Gen. 651 (B-158766) (1966) held that no award should be made where amendments to the IFB were furnished to prospective bidders only two days before bid opening. GAO rejected the government's argument that since six bidders were able to respond, sufficient time was available; the six bidders were all located nearer to the bidding site than the protester.

It is within the contracting officer's discretion to extend the bidding time when it appears that there was insufficient time to consider an amendment to a solicitation. See *Tolina Constr. Co.*, Comp. Gen. Dec. B-213028, 84-1 CPD

¶ 244, where it was determined that the contracting officer had not abused his discretion when he extended bid opening by one week in order to allow potential bidders additional time to consider a material amendment to the IFB. The contracting officer made this decision on the day prior to bid opening because no bids had been received and he feared that competition had been restricted by the issuance of the amendment. Compare *T & A Painting, Inc.*, Comp. Gen. Dec. B-229655, 88-1 CPD ¶ 435 (contracting officer appropriately refused to extend time for response).

[B] Submission of Bids

Bids that are submitted in accordance with the IFB bind the bidder once they are opened. However, the regulations permit their withdrawal before bid opening.

[1] Method of Submission

As discussed in Chapter 2, bids are *offers* submitted in the precise form specified by the government in the IFB. The method of submission of sealed bids is covered by a standard solicitation provision set forth in FAR 52.214-5:

> SUBMISSION OF BIDS (DEC 2016)
>
> (a) Bids and bid modifications shall be submitted in sealed envelopes or packages (unless submitted by electronic means)—
>
> (1) Addressed to the office specified in the solicitation, and
>
> (2) Showing the time and date specified for receipt, the solicitation number, and the name and address of the bidder.
>
> (b) Bidders using commercial carrier services shall ensure that the bid is addressed and marked on the outermost envelope or wrapper as prescribed in subparagraphs (a)(1) and (2) of this provision when delivered to the office specified in the solicitation.
>
> (c) Facsimile bids, modifications, or withdrawals, will not be considered unless authorized by the solicitation.
>
> (d) Bids submitted by electronic commerce shall be considered only if the electronic commerce method was specifically stipulated or permitted by the solicitation.

Bids may be submitted through the United States Postal Service, any other delivery service, or may be hand delivered. Bids should be submitted in a sealed envelope or package on the forms provided in the IFB. However, such submission is not required if the bidder is careful to comply fully with the IFB. Failure to seal a bid envelope is a minor informality that will not prevent the consideration of the bid, *Rhoads Constr. Co.*, Comp. Gen. Dec. B-242992, 91-1 CPD ¶ 561. Upon receipt of an unsealed bid the government should place the bid in a sealed envelope. Last-minute changes on the packaging may well prove ineffective: unsigned or uninitialed bid modifications noted on the outside of the bid envelopes may not be accepted by the receiving agency unless the bid or modification is otherwise accompanied by evidence of the bidder's intent to be bound by the modification, *R.F. Lusa & Sons Sheetmetal, Inc.*, Comp. Gen. Dec. B-281180.2, 98-2 CPD ¶157.

Bids must be submitted prior to bid opening. Paragraph (c) of the Late Submissions, Modifications, and Withdrawals of Bids solicitation provision in FAR 52.214-7 states:

> Acceptable evidence to establish the time of receipt at the Government installation includes the time/date stamp of that installation on the bid wrapper, other documentary evidence of receipt maintained by the installation, or oral testimony or statements of Government personnel.

This provision has been strictly enforced, *Brian X. Scott*, Comp. Gen. Dec. B-410195, 2014 CPD ¶335; *Pershield, Inc.*, Comp. Gen. Dec. B-256827, 94-2 CPD ¶46.

[a] Bids Submitted By Other Means

The Submission of Bid solicitation provision allows submission of bids electronically or by facsimile *only* if there is another solicitation provision permitting submission using that method. The FAR contains standard solicitation provisions for the submission of a facsimile bid (Facsimile Bids, FAR 52.214-31). However, there is no standard provision for the submission of electronic bids. If there is no separate solicitation provision allowing submission using one of these methods, such a bid must be rejected, *Heath Constr., Inc.*, Comp. Gen. Dec. B-403417, 2010 CPD ¶202 (facsimile bid); *H. Bendzulla Contracting*, Comp. Gen. Dec. B-246112, 91-2 CPD ¶441 (facsimile bid). See also *Recreonics Corp.*, Comp. Gen. Dec. B-246339, 92-1 CPD ¶249 (bid nonresponsive where bidder acknowledged a material amendment by facsimile transmission, which was not permitted by the solicitation); and *Michelin Aircraft Tire Corp.*, Comp. Gen. Dec. B-248498, 92-2 CPD ¶142 (agency properly rejected a bid modification sent by facsimile when the bidder had been orally advised by an agency contract specialist that the modification should be sent in that manner because the agency's equipment had become inoperative).

If the IFB contains the Facsimile Bids solicitation provision, the bidder may submit the bid in the form permitted, but care must be exercised to ensure that the bid precisely complies with the technical requirements of the applicable provision. For example, the clause requires that all required representations and information be submitted just as if the bid had been mailed, *Triple D Orchards, Inc.*, Comp. Gen. Dec. B-219648, 85-2 CPD ¶525. The Facsimile Bids provision requires that a proper signature be included and makes the offeror responsible for all defects in the bid due to faulty transmission or reception. This provision has been strictly enforced against the offeror even in cases where the offeror had proof of transmission of the facsimile, *International Garment Processors*, Comp. Gen. Dec. B-299674, 2007 CPD ¶ 130; *Groh Gmbh*, Comp. Gen. Dec. B-291980, 2003 CPD ¶ 53; *S.W. Elecs. & Mfg. Corp.*, Comp. Gen. Dec. B-249308, 92-2 CPD ¶ 320. Bids transmitted by facsimile must be received in the office designated for the receipt of bids before the time set for bid opening. The controlling time is the time the *last page* of the bid is received by the agency (not when the transmission begins), *Amigo-JT Joint Venture*, Comp. Gen. Dec. B-292830, 2003 CPD ¶ 224; *Radar Devices, Inc.*, Comp. Gen. Dec. B-249118, 92-2 CPD ¶ 287. However, if the bid is late due to mishandling on the part of the government, the bid will be considered timely.

Although there is no standard clause for the submission of electronic bids, as discussed in Chapter 3, electronic commerce is the preferred method. This is recognized by FAR 14.202-8 authorizing contracting officers to call for the submission of electronic bids and stating that "if electronic bids are authorized, the solicitation shall specify the electronic commerce method(s) that bidders may use." While the normal method of submitting an electronic bid would be through *www.SAM.gov*, agencies have used different strategies for using electronic commerce, only some of which have proven successful. See, e.g., *USA Info. Sys., Inc.*, Comp. Gen. Dec. B-291488, 2002 CPD ¶ 205 (vendor bore burden of triggering electronic updates); *Jack Faucett Assocs., Inc.*, Comp. Gen. Dec. B-279347, 98-1 CPD ¶ 155 (procurement under the Federal Acquisition Computer Network (FACNET), a failed experiment in federal electronic commerce); *Comspace Corp.*, Comp. Gen. Dec. B-274037, 96-2 CPD ¶ 186 (electronic quotations forwarded by private intermediary).

[b] Notice of Nonsubmission of Bid

Traditionally, as part of the formal, paper-based exchange between vendor and agency, the vendor was to advise the agency if the vendor, although declining to bid, wanted to receive future solicitation materials. That clause (FAR 52.214-9) was dropped from the FAR as agencies moved to electronic systems for distributing notices of bidding opportunities. See 68 Fed. Reg. 43854, July 24, 2003.

[2] Firm Bid Rule

As discussed in Chapter 2, sealed bids are subject to the "firm bid rule," which prohibits modification or withdrawal of bids after bid opening. The rationale for this rule is that it would be detrimental to the competitive bidding system if bidders were allowed to withdraw their bids after they have had an opportunity to discover what other bidders have offered. The only major exceptions to the firm bid rule are for mistakes in bid, discussed below, and for reverse auctions, which though not specifically addressed in the FAR, are increasingly common in federal procurement. See "Reverse Auctions," GAO-18-446, July 18, 2018 (reporting extensive use of technique); *Wyse Tech., Inc.*, Comp. Gen. Dec. B-297454, 2006 CPD ¶23 (challenge regarding use of reverse auction mechanism); Volk, Note, *A Principles-Oriented Approach to Regulating Reverse Auctions*, 37 Pub. Cont. L.J. 127 (2007); Yukins, *A Case Study in Comparative Procurement Law: Assessing UNICTRAL's Lessons for U.S. Procurement,* 35 Pub. Cont. L.J. 457 (2006). In a reverse auction, unlike a traditional sealed bid procurement, bidders are allowed to lower their bids in response to their competitors' bids, in an extended competition to win the award.

Under traditional sealed bidding, in contrast, bidders are expected to submit and remain committed to a firm bid. The firm bid rule is incorporated in both Standard Form 33 and Standard Form 1447. Block 12 of Standard Form 33 provides:

> [T]he undersigned agrees, if this offer is accepted within calendar days (60 calendar days unless a different period is inserted by the offeror) from the date for receipt of offers specified above, to furnish any or all items upon which prices are offered at the price set opposite each item, delivered at the designated point(s), within the time specified in the schedule.

Block 11 of Standard Form 1447 provides:

> If offer is accepted by the government within calendar days (60 calendar days unless offeror inserts a different period) from the date set forth in blk 9 above, the contractor agrees to hold its offered prices firm for the items solicited herein and to accept any resulting contract subject to the terms and conditions stated herein.

In *W.A. Scott v. United States*, 44 Ct. Cl. 524 (1909), the Court of Claims recognized the distinction between private and government contracts and would not allow the withdrawal of a bid deposit, and explained why concerns about corruption played such an important part in the government's relatively inflexible rules for bidding. The court stated at 527:

> The agents of the Government stand upon a different footing from private individuals in the matter of advertising for the letting of contracts in behalf of the United States. They have no discretion. They must accept the lowest or the highest responsible bid, or reject all and readvertise. Private individuals are not required thus to act. Hence it is apparent that Government agents should be allowed a reasonable time after the opening of bids before they are allowed to be withdrawn so they can be afforded opportunities to ascertain whether collusion or fraud had been perpetrated against the United States by the parties engaged in the bidding. It is also apparent that if the rule of allowing immediate withdrawals after the results of the bidding are made

> known, frauds innumerable could be perpetrated against the United States and thus public justice would be greatly hampered.

In *Refining Assocs. Inc. v. United States*, 109 F. Supp. 259 (Ct. Cl. 1953), the court reiterated that bids were irrevocable for the time stated in the invitation. In that case, the invitation for bids stipulated that after the opening of bids no bid could be withdrawn. In holding the bid to be irrevocable, the court stated at 262:

> [The bidder] submitted its bid subject to these provisions, and agreed that [the Government] should have 15 days from the date of opening to consider the bids. In so doing, [the bidder] was accorded the right of having its bid considered on the merits, and this right was conditioned on the premise that the bid would remain open during the time specified.

See *Nation-Wide Reporting & Convention Coverage*, GSBCA 8309, 88-2 BCA ¶ 20,521, where the IFB specifically required that the bidder keep its offer open for 90 days from the opening of bids. The board held that the bidder could not revoke its bid during this period and that, once the bids were opened, the government's "acceptance after an attempted withdrawal . . . create[d] a valid contract" and failure to perform after this acceptance justified default termination. See also *Western Adhesives*, GSBCA 7449, 85-2 BCA ¶ 17,961 (acceptance of bid during an extended acceptance period created a valid contract even though bidder attempted to withdraw bid). Compare *Granco Indus., Inc.*, GSBCA 14900, 01-1 BCA ¶ 31,173 (contractor not bound by firm bid rule as to line items that were withdrawn when contractor agreed to extend bid pending government review).

[3] Modification or Withdrawal of Bids Prior to Bid Opening

Bids may be freely modified or withdrawn as long as this is accomplished no later than *the exact time set for bid opening*. Such modification or withdrawal is effective if it is in accordance with the procedures set forth in the Late Submissions, Modifications, and Withdrawal of Bids solicitation provision in FAR 52.214-7. These procedures are summarized in FAR 14.303 as follows:

> (a) Bids may be modified or withdrawn by any method authorized by the solicitation, if notice is received in the office designated in the solicitation not later than the exact time set for opening of bids. If the solicitation authorizes facsimile bids, bids may be modified or withdrawn via facsimile received at any time before the exact time set for receipt of bids, subject to the conditions specified in the provision prescribed in 14.201-6(v). Modifications received by facsimile shall be sealed in an envelope by a proper official.
>
> (1) The official shall—
>
> (i) Write on the envelope—(A) The date and time of receipt and by whom; and (B) The number of invitation for bids; and

> (ii) Sign the envelope. (2) No information contained in the envelope shall be disclosed before the time set for bid opening.
>
> (b) A bid may be withdrawn in person by a bidder or its authorized representative if, before the exact time set for opening of bids, the identity of the persons requesting withdrawal is established and that person signs a receipt for the bid.
>
> (c) Upon withdrawal of an electronically transmitted bid, the data received shall not be viewed and shall be purged from primary and backup data storage systems.

Paragraph (c) of FAR 14.303 was added in 1995 as part of a broader initiative to address the use of electronic commerce in federal government contracting. The provision reflects the concern with protecting the confidentiality of withdrawn bids, in an era when a paper-based bid can no longer be simply withdrawn and destroyed. Under the new ¶ (c), the electronically submitted bid is not to be viewed and electronic records of the withdrawn bid are to be purged, as well.

These procedures have been held to preclude a bidder from withdrawing a bid by telephone, *Ruggiero v. United States*, 420 F.2d 709 (Ct. Cl. 1970); *John A. Maney*, GSBCA 6550, 83-2 BCA ¶ 16,744. See *Satellite Servs.*, Comp. Gen. Dec. B-207631.2, 83-1 CPD ¶ 357, where a bidder telephonically requested that the agency return its bid. When the agency failed in its attempt to comply with the request, the bidder continued to participate in the procurement and was eventually awarded the contract. GAO denied a protest of a competitor, holding that a telephone request for withdrawal from other than a telegraph company will not be honored. It appears that a valid withdrawal would have occurred if the agency had returned the bid. Withdrawal in person is permitted, but failure to return the bid has been considered sufficient evidence that such withdrawal did not occur, *Tomahawk Constr. Co.*, Comp. Gen. Dec. B-243582, 91-2 CPD ¶ 137.

[C] Cancellation of Procurement Before Opening

Agencies have considerable discretion in cancelling a procurement before the time of bid opening. FAR 14.209 states:

> (a) The cancellation of an invitation for bids usually involves a loss of time, effort, and money spent by the Government and bidders. Invitations should not be cancelled unless cancellation is clearly in the public interest; e.g., (1) where there is no longer a requirement for the supplies or services or (2) where amendments to the invitation would be of such magnitude that a new invitation is desirable.

Determining whether cancellation is "in the public interest" is a highly discretionary decision. See *Diversified Mgmt. Grp., A Joint Venture*, Comp. Gen. Dec. B-288443.2, 2001 CPD ¶ 175 (cancellation appropriate where failed to determine whether procurement should be set aside); *Lynch Machinery Co.*,

Comp. Gen. Dec. B-256279.2, 94-2 CPD ¶ 15 (cancellation appropriate to amend restrictive specification).

[D] Public Opening

Public opening of bids is one of the key elements of sealed bidding, and public bid opening is recognized internationally as an important protection against corruption. The importance of public opening was recognized by GAO in *Computer Network Corp.*, 55 Comp. Gen. 445 (B-183639), 75-2 CPD ¶ 297, stating at 451:

> The public advertising statute, 41 U.S. Code § 253(b) (1970), requires that: "All bids shall be publicly opened at the time and place stated in the advertisement." We have interpreted this requirement for a public opening to mean that the bid must publicly disclose the essential nature and type of the products offered and those elements of the bid which relate to price, quantity and delivery terms. 53 Comp. Gen. 24 (1973). The purpose of public opening of bids for public contracts is to protect both the public interest and bidders against any form of fraud, favoritism or partiality and such openings should be conducted to leave no room for any suspicion of irregularity. *Page Airways, Inc., et al.*, 54 Comp. Gen. 120 (1974), 74-2 CPD ¶ 99; 48 Comp. Gen. 413 (1968).

Bids must be closely guarded prior to opening to ensure that no bidder has access to the bids of competitors. FAR 14.401 provides the following guidance on the safeguarding of bids received prior to the time for bid opening:

> (a) All bids (including modifications) received before the time set for the opening of bids shall be kept secure. Except as provided in paragraph (b) of this section, the bids shall not be opened or viewed, and shall remain in a locked bid box, a safe, or in a secured, restricted-access electronic bid box. If an invitation for bids is cancelled, bids shall be returned to the bidders. Necessary precautions shall be taken to ensure the security of the bid box or safe. Before bid opening, information concerning the identity and number of bids received shall be made available only to Government employees. Such disclosure shall be only on a "need to know" basis. When bid samples are submitted, they shall be handled with sufficient care to prevent disclosure of characteristics before bid opening.
>
> (b) Envelopes marked as bids but not identifying the bidder or the solicitation may be opened solely for the purpose of identification, and then only by an official designated for this purpose. If a sealed bid is opened by mistake (e.g., because it is not marked as being a bid), the envelope shall be signed by the opener, whose position shall also be written thereon, and delivered to the designated official. This official shall immediately write on the envelope (1) an explanation of the opening, (2) the date and time opened, and (3) the invitation for bids number, and shall sign the envelope. The official shall then immediately reseal the envelope.

If a bid is returned unopened to the bidder, it may not be considered even if the basis for return was improper, *Leggett & Platt, Inc.*, Comp. Gen. Dec. B-246733, 92-1 CPD ¶ 314 (Federal Express envelope contained two bids, and agency returned envelope to bidder unopened because of action taken with respect to the other procurement); *Dima Contracting Corp.*, Comp. Gen. Dec. B-186487, 76-2 CPD ¶ 208 (bid was returned unopened because of reference on envelope to another IFB).

The procedures for public opening of unclassified bids are contained in FAR 14.402-1:

> (a) The bid opening officer shall decide when the time set for opening bids has arrived and shall inform those present of that decision. The officer shall then (1) personally and publicly open all bids received before that time, (2) if practical, read the bids aloud to the persons present, and (3) have the bids recorded. The original of each bid shall be carefully safeguarded, particularly until the abstract of bids required by 14.403 has been made and its accuracy verified.
>
> (b) Performance of the procedure in paragraph (a) above may be delegated to an assistant, but the bid opening officer remains fully responsible for the actions of the assistant.
>
> (c) Examination of bids by interested persons shall be permitted if it does not interfere unduly with the conduct of Government business. Original bids shall not be allowed to pass out of the hands of a Government official unless a duplicate bid is not available for public inspection. The original bid may be examined by the public only under the immediate supervision of a Government official and under conditions that preclude possibility of a substitution, addition, deletion, or alteration in the bid.

Under these procedures, bids "are publicly opened . . . and the bid prices are generally announced and available for examination by interested persons," *Neals Janitorial Serv.*, Comp. Gen. Dec. B-279633, 98-1 CPD ¶ 156. For national security reasons, a different bid opening procedure must be used for classified bids. See FAR 14.402-2 stating:

> The opening of classified bids shall not be accessible to the general public. Openings may be witnessed and the results recorded by those bidder representatives (a) who have been previously cleared from a security standpoint and (b) who represent bidders who were invited to bid. Bids shall be made available to those persons authorized to attend the opening of bids. No public record shall be made of bids or bid prices received in response to classified invitations for bids.

Public opening is required even if only one bid is received and the contracting officer knows before reading the bid that it will be rejected, *Wessel Co.*, Comp. Gen. Dec. B-189629, 77-2 CPD ¶ 152.

Inherent in the public opening procedure is the availability of the bid and its accompanying documents for public inspection. Typically the bid prices are recorded on an Abstract of Offers form (Standard Form 1409), which is also made available for public inspection per FAR 14.403(b). See *Neals Janitorial Serv.*, Comp. Gen. Dec. B-279633, 98-1 CPD ¶ 156. Thus, it is improper to fail to read an unclassified bid publicly and to make it available for public inspection, Comp. Gen. Dec. B-170049, Aug. 2, 1970, *Unpub*. However, the failure to publicly read a bid is a deviation of form, not substance, which does not affect the validity of an otherwise proper award. If the bidders have an opportunity to examine the awardee's bid, there is no prejudice in failing to publicly read it, *A. A. Beiro Constr. Co.*, Comp. Gen. Dec. B-192664, 78-2 CPD ¶ 425. See also *George C. Martin, Inc.*, 55 Comp. Gen. 110 (B-182175), 75-2 CPD ¶ 55; and *Moir Ranch & Constr. Co.*, Comp. Gen. Dec. B-191616, 78-1 CPD ¶ 423. However, bids that may not be publicly read because they contain information that the bidder considers "proprietary" must be rejected as nonresponsive, *Spotless Janitorial Servs., Inc.*, Comp. Gen. Dec. B-295620, 2005 CPD ¶ 36, even if the bidder authorizes disclosure after bids are opened, *Sperry-Univac*, Comp. Gen. Dec. B-200378, 81-1 CPD ¶ 38; *Computer Network Corp.*, 55 Comp. Gen. 445 (B-183639), 75-2 CPD ¶ 297. See also *Industrial Acoustics Co.*, Comp. Gen. Dec. B-255123.2, 94-1 CPD ¶ 220 (prohibition against disclosing required test data); *Prestex, Inc.*, Comp. Gen. Dec. B-195251.2, 79-2 CPD ¶ 411 (prohibition against revealing place of performance in a small business set-aside); *Warner Labs., Inc.*, Comp. Gen. Dec. B-189502, 77-2 CPD ¶ 314 (prohibition against disclosure of unit prices); and 53 Comp. Gen. 24 (B-178140) (1973) (prohibition against disclosure of descriptive data relating to responsiveness of bid). However, a prohibition on disclosure of information that deals only with a bidder's responsibility will not require rejection, *Ace-Federal Reporters, Inc.*, 54 Comp. Gen. 340 (B-181451), 74-2 CPD ¶ 239.

The premature opening of bids raises a serious question regarding the propriety of the procurement. Ordinarily such a circumstance requires that all bids be rejected and the matter resolicited unless later bidders did not obtain an unfair advantage, 34 Comp. Gen. 395 (B-122707) (1955). In *Chemical Compounding Corp.*, Comp. Gen. Dec. B-210317, 83-1 CPD ¶ 499, GAO held that it was not unreasonable to cancel a solicitation where the premature opening coincided with inadequate and ambiguous specifications. In determining whether the solicitation should be canceled when bids are prematurely opened through error or inadvertence, GAO considers the impact on both the bidders who submitted the prematurely opened bids and the other bidders. An alternate remedy is to give the bidder whose bid has been prematurely opened sufficient time to revise its bid, even if that requires extending the period for bidding, *Bartomeli Co.*, 71 Comp. Gen. 237 (B-246060), 92-1 CPD ¶ 170. See *Leach Corp.*, Comp. Gen. Dec. B-212534, 83-2 CPD ¶ 623, and *Boyd Lumber Co.*, Comp. Gen. Dec. B-189641, 77-2 CPD ¶ 315, holding that giving the bidders of the prematurely opened bids the opportunity to confirm, modify, or withdraw the bids was sufficient protection. It is not clear how the opportunity to modify a bid assists the bidder whose bid has been prematurely opened when there is evidence that other bidders have learned of the amount of the bid. However, there is no adequate means of correcting this error once it has been made, and to restrict the procurement to the bidders whose bids have been opened prematurely would be prejudicial to other bidders, *Air, Inc.*, 69 Comp. Gen. 504 (B-238468), 90-1 CPD ¶ 533.

[E] Bid Opening Time

To be considered for award, bids must be "submitted so that they will be received in the office designated in the Invitation for Bids . . . not later than the exact time set for opening of bids," FAR 14.302(a). The regulations provide that the contracting officer should announce to those present when the time for bid opening has arrived, FAR 14.402-1(a). A bid may be submitted up to, or simultaneously with, the time the bid opening officer announces that the time for bid opening has arrived, *Carothers Constr., Inc. v. United States*, 18 Cl. Ct. 745 (1989); *Amfel Constr., Inc.*, Comp. Gen. Dec. B-233493.2, 89-1 CPD ¶ 477.

The determination of the bid opening officer of when the opening time has arrived is binding unless it is clearly unreasonable. See *W.W. Asphalt*, Comp. Gen. Dec. B-235560, 89-2 CPD ¶ 106, upholding a determination that a bid was untimely when late by the opening officer's clock even though it was one minute early by the Federal Express courier's hand-held computer. See also *Swinerton & Walberg Co.*, Comp. Gen. Dec. B-242077.3, 91-1 CPD ¶ 318, and *Chattanooga Office Supply Co.*, Comp. Gen. Dec. B-228062, 87-2 CPD ¶ 221 (bid untimely when late by bid opening office clock even though timely by telephonic report); *Lambert Constr. Co.*, Comp. Gen. Dec. B-181794, 74-2 CPD ¶ 131 (bid modification found to be late based on agency time stamp even though modification was timely according to Western Union); and 51 Comp. Gen. 173 (B-173392) (1971) (bid found to be late based on the time shown on the clock in the bid opening room even though bid was timely according to the clock in the hall). See also *General Eng'g Corp.*, Comp. Gen. Dec. B-245476, 92-1 CPD ¶ 45, upholding a determination that a bid was late based on the bid opening room clock even though the watch of an Army civil engineering technician, who was in the bid room when the protester first appeared with its bid, stated that the time was 10:59 and 45 seconds a.m., and the bid opening room clock was shown, after bid opening, to be about three minutes fast.

Occasionally, a bid opening officer's declaration of bid opening time has been shown to be unreasonable. See *William F. Wilke, Inc. v. Dep't of the Army*, 485 F.2d 180 (4th Cir. 1973), where a bid that was hand delivered four minutes after the scheduled bid opening could not be considered even though no other bids had been opened, and the bid opening officer announced after receipt of the late bid: "It is now 3:00 p.m." Similarly, contracting officers cannot arbitrarily use the time on their own watch as evidence of the bid opening time when the clock in the bid opening room shows another time, 41 Comp. Gen. 807 (B-148972) (1962). However, opening officers may reasonably rely on the time shown by their watch if the bid opening room is not equipped with a clock, and only "persuasive independent evidence" will rebut the reasonableness of this reliance, *Tate Architectural Prods., Inc.*, Comp. Gen. Dec. B-191361, 78-1 CPD ¶ 389. This rule is based on GAO's view that the bid opening officer's declaration is prima facie evidence of the time for bid opening. Unless there is a clear record to contradict this evidence, the authorized declaration serves as the criterion of lateness, *MACETO, Inc.*, Comp. Gen. Dec. B-207878, 82-2 CPD ¶ 300; *Peter Kiewit & Sons' Co.*, Comp. Gen. Dec. B-189022, 77-2 CPD ¶ 41; *Hyster Co.*, 55 Comp. Gen. 267 (B-182995), 75-2 CPD ¶ 176. See *Nueva Constr. Co.*, Comp. Gen. B-270009, 96-1 CPD ¶ 84, where the agency properly rejected bid as late when the protester submitted its bid seconds after the bid opening officer reasonably declared that the set time for bid opening had arrived even though the bid opening clock continued to display the same minute in time.

If the government admits that its time determination was incorrect, it may accept a bid that was determined to be late but was actually submitted on time. In *Washington Mech. Contractors, Inc. v. United States*, 612 F. Supp. 1243 (N.D. Cal. 1984), bids were due by 2:30 p.m., and the bidder's agent had been standing at a wall phone until 2:29 p.m. waiting for a final figure. The agent had previously synchronized his watch with the phone company's time service. The agent received the final figure and inserted it into the bid forms, walked to the bid opening room (which took less than 30 seconds), and tried to submit its bid. The bid opening officer said the bid was late and would not stamp it. An assistant who was present in the room said that the bid opening officer should at least stamp the envelope as received. By this time 30 seconds had passed, and the stamp read 2:31 p.m. Subsequent testing by the government indicated that the clock was one to three minutes fast and the bid was held to have been properly accepted.

The relevant time for determining whether a bid is timely received by the government is that time when the bidder relinquishes possession of its bid. If a bidder does not relinquish control of a bid prior to the bid opening officer's announcement of bid opening, it will be considered late even if the bid is time/date stamped before bid opening. In *J. C. Kimberly Co.*, Comp. Gen. Dec. B-255018.2, 94-1 CPD ¶ 79, although the bid was time/date stamped 2:29 p.m., the bid was late because it was not tendered to the bid opening officer until after the 2:30 p.m. announcement that the time for receipt of bids has passed. In contrast, in *Reliable Bldrs., Inc.*, Comp. Gen. Dec. B-249908.2, 93-1 CPD ¶ 116, a bid that was time/date stamped at 2:01 p.m. was not considered late because the record showed that the bidder relinquished control of the bid by 2:00 p.m., the exact time called for in the solicitation, and prior to the bid opening officer's declaration of the time for bid opening. A bid handed to and returned by the agency receptionist outside the designated bid opening room does not constitute submission of the bid, *J.C.N. Constr. Co.*, Comp. Gen. Dec. B-250815, 93-1

CPD ¶ 166. Even if the bidder is in the bid opening room, a bid received an instant late must be rejected. In *Lucero*, Comp. Gen. Dec. B-228425, 87-2 CPD ¶ 566, GAO rejected a bid as late under the following circumstances:

> Bids were due by 2:00 p.m. September 25, 1987 in the conference room of the District Ranger's Office. At approximately 1:50 or 1:55 p.m. of that day, Lucero entered the conference room after returning from an unsuccessful attempt to locate and inspect the timber sale area. When Lucero arrived, the bid receiving agent introduced himself, inquired as to whether Lucero had an updated form, advised him to complete the appropriate forms "right away," and answered Lucero's questions. Another Forest Service agent then assisted Lucero in completing the forms and at 1:59 p.m. advised him that he had one minute remaining in which to submit the bid. At 1:59 p.m. and 55 seconds, Lucero placed the unsealed envelope in front of him, but did not submit it. At 2:00 the bid receiving agent announced that the time for receiving sealed bids had expired. Lucero attempted then to submit his bid but was advised that it could not be accepted since it was after 2:00 p.m.

A bid that is relinquished simultaneously with the announcement of closing will be considered timely, *Carothers Constr., Inc. v. United States*, 18 Cl. Ct. 745 (1989).

The timeliness requirement is not satisfied merely because the bid is in the government's possession. The bid must be delivered to the exact location specified in the solicitation or it will be considered late, unless the failure to arrive on time is a result of government mishandling, *Alpha Tech. Servs., Inc.*, Comp. Gen. Dec. B-243715, 91-2 CPD ¶ 56 (bid delivered to government installation approximately two hours before bid opening but not received in bid opening room until next day was late); *Larry J. Robinson & Co.*, Comp. Gen. Dec. B-234991, 89-1 CPD ¶ 559 (delivery to central switchboard area insufficient).

FAR 14.402-3 permits bid opening officers to postpone the time scheduled for bid opening. Generally, this occurs when the contracting officer has reason to believe that an "important segment" of bidders have been delayed for causes beyond their control and without their fault or negligence (*i.e.*, flood, fire, weather conditions), or when an emergency or unanticipated event interrupts the normal government process, making the scheduled bid opening impractical. See *B.L.I. Constr. Co.*, Comp. Gen. Dec. B-239246.2, 90-2 CPD ¶ 85, in which an extension was permitted so that bidders could get to the designated room on time. Note, however, that postponing the date set for bid opening is strictly within the contracting officer's discretion, *Educational Planning & Advice, Inc.*, Comp. Gen. Dec. B-274513, 96-2 CPD ¶ 173 (determination to proceed with bid opening despite hurricane not an abuse of discretion). When a postponement occurs due to an interruption in the normal government process and urgent government requirements prevent amendment of the solicitation under FAR 14.208, bid opening is extended to "the first work day on which normal government processes resume," at the same time of day as originally specified in the solicitation.

[F] Late Bids

The government has adopted very strict requirements precluding the consideration of late bids unless precisely defined exceptions are met. See FAR 14.304, which was revised in 1999 as part of an effort to provide a single standard for late offers under commercial, sealed bid, and negotiated acquisitions. The FAR provision states:

> (b)(1) Any bid, modification, or withdrawal of a bid received at the Government office designated in the IFB after the exact time specified for receipt of bids is "late" and will not be considered unless it is received before award is made, the contracting officer determines that accepting the late bid would not unduly delay the acquisition; and—
>
> (i) If it was transmitted through an electronic commerce method authorized by the IFB, it was received at the initial point of entry to the Government infrastructure not later than 5:00 p.m. one working day prior to the date specified for receipt of bids; or
>
> (ii) There is acceptable evidence to establish that it was received at the Government installation designated for receipt of bids and was under the Government's control prior to the time set for receipt of bids.
>
> (2) However, a late modification of an otherwise successful bid, that makes its terms more favorable to the Government, will be considered at any time it is received and may be accepted.
>
> * * *
>
> (f) The contracting officer must promptly notify any bidder if its bid, modification, or withdrawal was received late, and must inform the bidder whether its bid will be considered, unless contract award is imminent and the notices prescribed in 14.409 would suffice.

[1] Bids in Paper Form

A bid in paper form that is under the control of the government at the specified time is not late. However, the bidder must have proof that it had relinquished control to an official at the government office when the bid is not delivered to the specified office on time. See *Stephen Lucas Constr., LLC*, Comp. Gen. Dec. B-402654, 2010 CPD ¶ 138 (Federal Express tracking sheet showing that agency employee signed for bid before specified time adequate evidence that bid was under control of agency). If there is any fault on the part of the bidder, the bid will be considered late, *Aquaterra Contracting, Inc.*, Comp. Gen. Dec. B-400065, 2008 CPD ¶ 138 (protest denied because protester failed to take reasonable steps to ensure proper delivery, and failure to take available steps to ensure timely delivery was paramount cause of bid's late receipt); *InfoGroup, Inc.*, Comp. Gen. Dec. B-294610, 2004 CPD ¶ 190 (lateness due to contractor fault in not providing correct room number to Federal Express). On the other hand, if the lateness is due to government fault, the bid can be accepted. See *Weeks Marine, Inc.*, Comp. Gen. Dec. B-292758, 2003 CPD ¶183, holding that the contracting officer properly accepted a bid delivered to the opening room one minute late because the IFB specified the wrong room.

Under the late bid rule in effect prior to 1999, bids were not late if the failure to receive them at the specified office was due to government mishandling. The decisions on this old rule may be instructive in deciding whether a bid is in the control of the agency (under the new rule). Under the mishandling rule, GAO assessed the reasonableness of agency determinations that late receipt of a hand-carried bid was due primarily to government mishandling, *Dep't of Housing & Urban Dev.—Reconsideration*, Comp. Gen. Dec. B-279575.2, 98-2 CPD ¶105.

In *Watson Agency, Inc.*, Comp. Gen. Dec. B-241072, 90-2 CPD ¶506, GAO found government mishandling where a guard placed the bid in the wrong safe, and the agency subsequently failed to remove the bid from the guardhouse and deliver it to the Center's Classified Mails and Files Branch for distribution, in accordance with agency procedures. Government mishandling was found in *John J. Kirlin, Inc.*, Comp. Gen. Dec. B-250244, 92-2 CPD ¶419, where a contractor representative delivered a hand-carried bid to the wrong bid opening officer, relying upon a sign on the entrance door to the building that the bid opening room for an IFB for "Compilation of 13 Construction Jobs" had been changed. The representative interpreted the sign to mean that the IFB for his construction project had been combined with other solicitations and that the room had been changed. Compounding the confusion, the bid opening officer for the combined construction jobs accepted the bid and clocked it at 1:46 p.m. without noticing that the envelope listed a different solicitation number. Mishandling was also found in *AABLE Tank Servs., Inc.*, Comp. Gen. Dec. B-273010, 96-2 CPD ¶180 (contract specialist identified in the solicitation as contact person for further information misdirected bid); *Gair's Med. Transcription Servs.*, Comp. Gen. Dec. B-257426, 94-2 CPD ¶115 (contracting officer failed to remove bid from safe prior to bid opening); *Victoria Inn Ltd.*, Comp. Gen. Dec. B-256724, 94-2 CPD ¶37 (bid package misfiled in bid cabinet); and *Data Gen. Corp.*, Comp. Gen. Dec. B-252239, 93-1 CPD ¶457 (installation postal authorities received bid two days prior to bid opening but did not deliver bid to contracting office due to the absence of a driver with a security clearance). No mishandling was found in *PDP Analytical Servs.*, Comp. Gen. Dec. B-251776.2, 93-1 CPD ¶294 (due to accumulation of mail over the Christmas holidays, the mail took longer to sort and was not distributed until after bid opening); *Environmental Control Techs.*, Comp. Gen. Dec. B-250859, 93-1 CPD ¶172 (bid received at the installation post office 40 minutes prior to bid opening but, as a result of the installation's normal mail delivery, did not arrive at the place for receipt of bids until after bid opening).

If the bidder significantly contributed to late receipt of a bid, any subsequent government mishandling is not the paramount reason for the bid's late receipt. See *Adirondack Constr. Corp.*, Comp. Gen. Dec. B-280015, 98-2 CPD ¶ 55 (while the agency changed the bid opening room less than one hour before bid opening, the bidder's actions significantly contributed to the late receipt of the bid); *Aquaterra Contracting, Inc.*, Comp. Gen. Dec. B-400065, 2008 CPD ¶ 138 (bidder's erroneous labeling was paramount cause of delayed delivery); *Bill Strong Enters., Inc.*, Comp. Gen. Dec. B-260721, 95-2 CPD ¶ 10 (Federal Express, contributed significantly to the late receipt of the bid by not including the correct label on the bid).

Although the prior rule referred to government mishandling only at the government installation after receipt, GAO avoided strict application of the rule where government mishandling in the process of receipt caused the lateness. See, for example, *Microflect*, 66 Comp. Gen. 269 (B-225118), 87-1 CPD ¶ 173 (bid mailed by express mail was delivered to the post office four and one-half hours before bid opening but was not picked up by the agency in time for bid opening); *Howard Mgmt. Grp.*, Comp. Gen. Dec. B-221889, 86-2 CPD ¶ 28 (agency misinformed bidder that it had a telex machine); *Standard Prods. Co.*, Comp. Gen. Dec. B-215832, 85-1 CPD ¶ 86 (agency failed to pay for telex service); *Sun Int'l*, Comp. Gen. Dec. B-208146, 83-1 CPD ¶ 78 (government failure to follow established procedures for receiving express mail on the weekends was the paramount cause of the bid's late receipt; the bid was therefore acceptable despite never being in the government's possession); *Kings Point Mfg. Co.*, Comp. Gen. Dec. B-199992, 81-1 CPD ¶ 293 (government cancellation of authorized Western Union terminal without notice); and *I & E Constr. Co.*, 55 Comp. Gen. 1340 (B-186766), 76-2 CPD ¶ 139 (locking the building designated for receipt of bids constituted government mishandling under the "intent and the spirit" of the late bid regulations).

As required by the current rule, government mishandling could not be found until the bidder established, with documented evidence, that the bid was actually received at the government facility prior to bid opening, *Power Connector, Inc.*, Comp. Gen. Dec. B-256362, 94-1 CPD ¶ 369. See *Pacific Tank Cleaning Servs., Inc.*, Comp. Gen. Dec. B-279111, 98-2 CPD ¶ 2 (evidence did not establish that bid was timely received and remained under the government's control until it was first discovered six days after bid opening); *J.C.N. Constr. Co.*, Comp. Gen. Dec. B-270068, 96-1 CPD ¶ 42 (record of a commercial carrier insufficient evidence to support the contention that the bid was timely delivered). However, commercial carrier records could be considered if the record contained corroborating relevant evidence, including statements by government personnel, *Stephen Lucas Constr., LLC*, Comp. Gen. Dec. B-402654, 2010 CPD ¶ 138. In *Eliscu & Co.*, Comp. Gen. Dec. B-211617, 84-1 CPD ¶ 75, GAO refused to consider the issue of government mishandling because the only proof available for bid receipt was the government stamp that recorded the delivery as being late.

[2] Electronically Submitted Bids

FAR 14.304(b)(1)(i) contains separate language covering bids that are submitted electronically requiring that, if they are not received on time at the designated office, they will be accepted if they were received in the agency one day ahead of the bid opening date. In *Sea Box, Inc.*, Comp. Gen. Dec. B-291056, 2002 CPD ¶ 181, GAO ruled that the parallel provision pertaining to the submission of competitive proposals established an exclusive rule that barred the assertion that the proposal was late due to government mishandling. In that case, the electronic proposal was received on time at the agency server but not transmitted to the designated agency office on time. See also *PMTech, Inc.*, Comp. Gen. Dec. B-291082, 2002 CPD ¶ 172, strictly interpreting this electronic submission rule. Compare *Watterson Constr. Co. v. United States*, 98 Fed. Cl. 84 (2011), reaching the opposite conclusion from *Sea Box*.

Prior to the 1999 revision of the rule, the government mishandling rule was applied to bids submitted by facsimile or electronically. See *Brazos Roofing, Inc.*, Comp. Gen. Dec. B-275113, 97-1 CPD ¶ 43 (where the agency amended a solicitation so close to the deadline for submitting bids that submission by facsimile was the only practicable alternative to bidders, a bid received late due to an inoperable facsimile machine considered government mishandling); *Butt Constr. Co.*, Comp. Gen. Dec. B-258507, 95-1 CPD ¶ 45 (government mishandling the paramount cause of late receipt of a facsimile bid modification received at least seven minutes prior to bid opening time where the facsimile machine was only a short distance from the opening room). However, the rule was strictly applied. See *Roy McGinnis & Co.*, Comp. Gen. Dec. B-275988, 97-1 CPD ¶ 156 (bidder did not allow sufficient time for facsimile bid to be brought to bid room); *Stack-On Prods. Co.*, Comp. Gen. Dec. B-181862, 74-2 CPD ¶ 220 (late bid modification could not be considered even though it was received on the telex machine on time but was not transcribed for 50 minutes because the operator was busy). In an unusual case, *Scherr Constr. Co. v. United States*, 5 Cl. Ct. 249 (1984), the failure of the government to inform a bidder of the flex-time schedule during which the government office operated was found to be the primary cause of the nonreceipt of the contractor's telegraphic modification on the day before bid opening. The late bid rule, however, remained intact since the court ultimately determined that Western Union's lack of diligence in delivering the modification the following day when the government office was open was the primary cause for nonreceipt.

[3] Hand-Carried Bids

The regulations have never provided exceptions for late bids that are hand carried. See *Williams Bldg. Co.*, Comp. Gen. Dec. B-415317.3, 2018 CPD ¶ 159 (bid delivered on time but given back to bidder and returned after bid opening time was late); *Nueva Constr. Co.*, Comp. Gen. Dec. B-270009, 96-1 CPD ¶ 84 (bid delivered seconds after bid opening officer declared that the time for bid opening stated in the solicitation had arrived was late); *J. C. Kimberly Co.*, Comp. Gen. Dec. B-255018.2, 94-1 CPD ¶ 79 (hand-carried bid received after bid opening officer declared that the time for bid opening had arrived was late); and *GS Edwards*, Comp. Gen. Dec. B-255202, 94-1 CPD ¶ 54 (hand-carried bid delivered three minutes late could not be considered); and *George W. Kane, Inc.*, Comp. Gen. Dec. B-245382.2, 92-1 CPD ¶ 143 (bid late although hand carried and placed on desk in bid opening room because IFB called for delivery to bid depository location and control was not relinquished in bid opening room on time). See also *Boulder Constr., Inc.*, Comp. Gen. Dec. B-250671, 93-1 CPD ¶ 122; *Wyoming Sawmills, Inc.*, Comp. Gen. Dec. B-248331, 92-2 CPD ¶ 45; and *General Eng'g Corp.*, Comp. Gen. Dec. B-245476, 92-1 CPD ¶ 45.

A bid that is delivered by commercial carrier is considered to be "hand carried" and is considered late if it does not arrive timely at the location designated in the solicitation, *Barnes Elec. Co.*, Comp. Gen. Dec. B-241391.2, 91-1 CPD ¶ 10; *Hans Olsen Egg Co.*, Comp. Gen. Dec. B-235085, 89-2 CPD ¶ 75.

Late hand-carried bids have been properly accepted where the government was responsible for the lateness. See *Weeks Marine, Inc.*, Comp. Gen. Dec. B-292758, 2003 CPD ¶ 183 (incorrect address specified in the solicitation for the delivery of bids); *Palomar Grading & Paving, Inc.*, Comp. Gen. Dec. B-274885, 97-1 CPD ¶ 16 (incorrect address specified in the solicitation for the delivery of bids); *Ed Kocharian & Co.*, Comp. Gen. Dec. B-271186, 96-1 CPD ¶ 170 (office designated for bid opening was locked); *Kelton Contracting, Inc.*, Comp. Gen. Dec. B-262255, 95-2 CPD ¶ 254 (agency properly accepted a late hand-carried bid where agency clerk placed the bid package in the wrong mail slot); *Power Connector, Inc.*, Comp. Gen. Dec. B-256362, 94-1 CPD ¶ 369 (agency personnel misdirected delivery of bid package to the wrong floor); *Pearl Props.*, Comp. Gen. Dec. B-249519, 92-2 CPD ¶ 333 (bid received three-and-one-half hours prior to bid opening but placed in the bottom of a mail tote); *Ranco Constr., Inc.*, Comp. Gen. Dec. B-246345, 92-1 CPD ¶ 234 (employee failed to expedite delivery of package as instructed and instead placed bid in normal delivery); *Richards Painting Co.*, Comp. Gen. Dec. B-232678, 89-1 CPD ¶ 76 (hand-carried bid delivered three minutes after bid opening because the front door of the government building was locked, and the bid opening room was different from the unstaffed room designated for the receipt of hand-carried bids); *Baeten Constr., Co.*, Comp. Gen. Dec. B-210681, 83-2 CPD ¶ 203 (government official misdirected the delivery person); and *Dale Woods*, Comp. Gen. Dec. B-209459, 83-1 CPD ¶ 396 (government changed the room for bid delivery without informing all bidders).

If the government is not the cause of the lateness of the hand-carried bid, generally no other excuse will assist the bidder in having its bid considered. See *Great Plains Asbestos Control, Inc.*, Comp. Gen. Dec. B-271841, 96-2 CPD ¶ 19 (commercial carrier leaving bid at military installation's freight terminal no excuse); *Ironhorse, Ltd.*, Comp. Gen. Dec. B-256582, 94-1 CPD ¶ 176, and *B.E.C. Med. Prods.*, Comp. Gen. Dec. B-256483, 94-1 CPD ¶ 159 (severe weather no excuse); *Braceland Bros., Inc.*, Comp. Gen. Dec. B-248234, 92-2

CPD ¶ 69 (messenger delivering bids to wrong address no excuse); *John Holtman & Sons, Inc.*, Comp. Gen. Dec. B-246062, 92-1 CPD ¶ 187 (bid delivered to warehouse rather than the office specified in the solicitation was late); *High Vacuum Equip. Corp.*, Comp. Gen. Dec. B-224511, 86-2 CPD ¶ 189 (flight delays no excuse); *National Minority Research Dev. Corp.*, Comp. Gen. Dec. B-220057, 85-2 CPD ¶ 303 (automobile accident no excuse); *Key Airlines*, Comp. Gen. Dec. B-214122, 84-1 CPD ¶ 242 (late bid properly rejected despite bidder never receiving an official copy of the IFB); *Northwest Instrument*, Comp. Gen. Dec. B-200873, 80-2 CPD ¶ 373 (traffic delays and business necessity do not excuse late bid); and *Unitron Eng'g Co.*, 58 Comp. Gen. 748 (B-194707), 79-2 CPD ¶ 155 (closing of a common carrier's offices due to the Three Mile Island nuclear emergency did not serve as an excuse for late delivery of hand-carried bid).

Similarly, a bidder's failure to follow solicitation procedures will generally be considered the primary reason for the late delivery rather than improper government action, *Sencland CDC Enters.*, Comp. Gen. Dec. B-252796, 93-2 CPD ¶ 36 (bid rejected as late where commercial carrier delivered bids to the mail room rather than to the bid depository for hand-carried bids in accordance with the solicitation instructions); *Gould Metal Specialists Inc.*, Comp. Gen. Dec. B-246686, 92-1 CPD ¶ 311 (bid was delivered to the mailing address rather than the address for hand-carried bids).

§ 5.03 RESPONSIVENESS

A key element of the sealed bidding system is that nonresponsive bids may not be considered by contracting officers and must be rejected. This *responsiveness* requirement is derived from the statutory provision providing that award be made to the bidder "whose bid conforms to the solicitation," 10 U.S.C. § 3302 (formerly § 2305(b)(3)); 41 U.S.C. § 3702(b). The purpose of this requirement is to promote fairness and objectivity, and to encourage wide competition by requiring all bidders to bid on exactly the same work and to the same terms and conditions—permitting the selection of the winning bidder solely on the basis of price. Thus, the responsiveness requirement ensures that a bidder will not receive an award by offering to perform the work perhaps less expensively but in a manner that represents a material deviation from the terms of the IFB. This promotes the integrity of the procurement process by protecting other bidders that might also have proposed such a method had they known that the government was willing to accept it. At the same time, however, the strict responsiveness requirement may result in the government's loss of the benefit of diverse and innovative solutions—explaining, in part, why over time federal agencies have shifted away from the use of sealed bidding for more complex requirements.

The mandatory rejection rule also prevents bidders with ambiguous bids from having "two bites at the apple" by contending, after seeing the competing bids, that their bids conformed to the solicitation (or did not conform), depending on the interpretation that is most beneficial to them.

The requirement for mandatory rejection has made responsiveness a focal point for award controversies. If the low bidder can be disqualified as nonresponsive, the next bidder in line becomes eligible to receive the award at a higher price. Thus, both the government and the bidder could be "losers" if a bid is found to be nonresponsive. This section first examines the criteria used in determining whether a nonconformity is sufficient to require the bid being classified as nonresponsive. It next considers the disposition of nonconforming bids and the limited circumstances under which an award may be made on the basis of a nonresponsive bid. The section concludes with an analysis of the types of nonconforming bids and the factors that determine whether such bids are nonresponsive.

[A] Criteria for Determining Responsiveness

A bid is nonconforming if it fails to comply exactly with the literal requirements of the IFB. However, not all nonconforming bids are nonresponsive. In determining whether a nonconforming bid is nonresponsive, the focus may be either on the nature of the nonconformity or on the effect of the nonconformity on the competition. This section first considers whether the nonconformity is *sufficiently material* to warrant rejection of the bid or is merely an *immaterial deviation* that may be waived. It then examines the extent to which *prejudice to other bidders* resulting from a nonconformity determines responsiveness. The section concludes with a discussion of the distinction between responsiveness of bids and responsibility of bidders.

[1] Materiality of Nonconformity

The FAR defines responsiveness in terms of materiality of the nonconformity. See FAR 14.301(a), stating:

> To be considered for award, a bid must comply in all material respects with the invitation for bids. Such compliance enables bidders to stand on an equal footing and maintain the integrity of the sealed bidding system.

Thus, a bid that contains an immaterial nonconformity is not considered to be a nonresponsive bid. Such nonconformities are called *minor informalities*. FAR 14.405 defines a "minor informality." The clearest example of a minor informality is the failure to meet IFB requirements that deal with the form rather than the substance of the bid. For example, minor informalities have been found when a bidder failed to initiate an erasure correction on the bid form as required by the IFB, *Werres Corp.*, Comp. Gen. Dec. B-211870, 83-2 CPD ¶ 243, and when a bidder failed to initial changes to a bid as required by the IFB, *Stone Forest Indus., Inc.*, Comp. Gen. Dec. B-246123, 92-1 CPD ¶ 161. In *E-Systems, Inc.*, Comp. Gen. Dec. B-190693, 78-1 CPD ¶ 236, GAO upheld the contracting officer's determination that the bidder's use of "n/c" instead of "n" to indicate items for which the government would not be charged was a minor informality. See also *Image Contracting*, Comp. Gen. Dec. B-253038, 93-2 CPD ¶ 95 (failure to indicate to which of two locations bidder intended to deliver the items); *Storage Tech. Corp. v. Dep't of the Army*, GSBCA 12626-P, 94-1 BCA ¶ 26,548 (use of dashes instead of "none" in procurement integrity certificate); *Boardsen Assocs.*, Comp. Gen. Dec. B-245876, 92-1 CPD ¶ 115 (failure to insert "none" in procurement integrity certificate to indicate no previous violations); *Grumman Aerospace Corp.*, 64 Comp. Gen. 553 (B-216068), 85-1 CPD ¶ 596 (failure to include positive dollar amount for separate line item contrary to procuring agency's requirements); and *Dyneteria, Inc.*, 54 Comp. Gen. 345 (B-181470) (1975) (dashes inserted in lieu of price).

Nonconformities that have a trivial or de minimis effect on price will also be considered immaterial. What constitutes "de minimis" will be determined on a case-by-case basis. For example, in *Brutoco Eng'g & Constr., Inc.*, 62 Comp. Gen. 111 (B-209098), 83-1 CPD ¶ 9, GAO held the agency should have waived as a minor informality a bidder's failure to acknowledge a wage rate amendment that increased bid price by only 0.8% of the $95,213 difference between the low bidder and the second low bidder, concluding at 112:

> [I]nsofar as the effect on the competitive bid system is concerned, Brutoco's failure to acknowledge the amendment cannot reasonably be construed to affect the competition such that the competitive bid system will be adversely affected if the firm is permitted now to cure the defect by acknowledging the amendment.

See also *Marine Power & Equip. Co.*, 62 Comp. Gen. 75 (B-208393), 82-2 CPD ¶ 514 ($100 deficiency in required bid deposit of 20% of $75,522 properly waived as minor deviation); and *Roan Corp.*, Comp. Gen. Dec. B-211228, 84-1 CPD ¶ 116, *recons. denied*, 84-1 CPD ¶ 211 (heavily front-loaded bid with option periods presented waivable minor informality because of project's high startup costs).

Failure to submit mandatory information has been held to be an immaterial deviation when the agency does not intend to use the information to determine which bid is in line for award. Thus, a bid not furnishing required price lists was held to be responsive because the agency did not intend to use the lists to determine the bid prices, *American Spare Parts, Inc.*, Comp. Gen. Dec. B-224745, 87-1 CPD ¶ 4. See also *W.M. Schlosser Co.*, Comp. Gen. Dec. B-258284, 94-2 CPD ¶ 234, where a bid was found responsive, in spite of the fact that it did not contain required descriptive literature, because the agency had no intention of using the literature to determine if the proposed work complied with the contract requirements.

The minor informality rule has also been applied to technically nonresponsive bids where the bid otherwise leaves no doubt as to the intention of the bidder to offer an acceptable bid. In *AABCO, Inc. v. United States*, 3 Cl. Ct. 109 (1983), the failure of a bidder to code each of the prices on a magnetic tape exactly as required by the solicitation was properly waived as a minor informality. The Claims Court held that there was no doubt whatsoever as to the intended bids, stating at 119:

> A mere glance at the printout that accompanied the submitted tape would confirm the exact dollars and cents that the [contractor] intended to bid.

See also *Sere Constr. Corp.*, Comp. Gen. Dec. B-205098, 82-1 CPD ¶ 453 (failure to provide unit prices waivable because single unit price provided sufficient bidding pattern to allow accurate pricing of any contract modification); *MKB Constructors (J.V.)*, Comp. Gen. Dec. B-250413, 93-1 CPD ¶ 50 (failure to submit a price for 1 of 60 line items was a minor informality where the intended price of the missing line item could be determined from the bid itself); *Mike Johnson, Inc.*, Comp. Gen. Dec. B-271943, 96-2 CPD ¶ 66 (failure to break the contract work into three line items of work per revised bid schedule was a minor informality because the revised schedule did not add any additional work beyond that encompassed in the original bid schedule). However, when the bid fails to provide sufficient information to allow the contracting officer to determine the details of the intended bid, it must be rejected. See *Croman Corp.*, Comp. Gen. Dec. B-409496, 2014 CPD ¶ 137 (lack of line item prices for an option year); and *Norris Paint & Varnish Co.*, Comp. Gen. Dec. B-206079, 82-1 CPD ¶ 425 (no information in bid to determine whether bidder had a valid Qualified Products List test number as required by IFB).

Statements in invitations as to the automatic effect of noncompliance with certain provisions on responsiveness are not controlling where noncompliance involves a minor deviation, *Mid-South Metals, Inc.*, Comp. Gen. Dec. B-257056, 94-2 CPD ¶ 78 (submission of multiple credit card accounts as bid guarantee was responsive, even though solicitation prohibited the use of multiple credit card accounts); *Isometrics, Inc.*, Comp. Gen. Dec. B-212434, 83-2 CPD ¶ 618 (failure to supply shipping information as required by the IFB does not render bid nonresponsive when agency was able to derive the information from other bids). In *D.N. Owens Co.*, 57 Comp. Gen. 231 (B-190749), 78-1 CPD ¶ 66, even though the solicitation required rejection of bids for nonresponsiveness if bidders failed to submit bid samples, GAO held that the failure to submit the sample was a minor irregularity since the extent of detail in the specifications made the sample unnecessary.

The decision as to whether a particular nonconformity constitutes a minor deviation has sometimes been characterized as a discretionary one for the contracting officer, Comp. Gen. Dec. B-172227, May 13, 1971, *Unpub.* Cases where proper waiver was found include *Consolidated Contracting Eng'g*, Comp. Gen. Dec. B-274319, 96-2 CPD ¶ 174 (failure to acknowledge amendment properly waived where the amendment results in less stringent obligations on the bidder);

Elliott Co., Comp. Gen. Dec. B-212897, 84-1 CPD ¶130 (failure to include Qualified Price List information was properly waived when the information could be obtained from other facts within the bid); *Massee Bldrs., Inc.*, 61 Comp. Gen. 227 (B-204450), 82-1 CPD ¶72 (failure to utilize additive method in bid construction as stated in IFB properly waived); *Gillette Indus., Inc.*, Comp. Gen. Dec. B-194552, 79-2 CPD ¶59 (failure to acknowledge "trivial amendment" properly waived).

GAO has required waiver in several cases and has suggested award to the protester, even though the contracting officer "in his discretion" had previously refused to waive the nonconformity, *Fort Mojave/Hummel, J.V.*, Comp. Gen. Dec. B-296961, 2005 CPD ¶181 (low bidder's failure to acknowledge amendment that merely clarified requirements already contained in the solicitation and otherwise had a negligible effect on the quality and price of the project); *Jackson Enters.*, Comp. Gen. Dec. B-286688, 2001 CPD ¶25 (failure to acknowledge amendment setting forth agency answers to bidders' questions that did not contain material information and did not alter bidders' legal obligations); *Schuster Eng'g, Inc.*, Comp. Gen. Dec. B-275044, 97-1 CPD ¶29 (failure to acknowledge amendment because the amendment only relaxed performance requirements); *Legare Constr. Co.*, Comp. Gen. Dec. B-257735, 94-2 CPD ¶173 (failure to meet price limitation); *Shipco Gen., Inc.*, Comp. Gen. Dec. B-204259, 81-2 CPD ¶161 (failure to complete size status certifications); *National Radio Co.*, Comp. Gen. Dec. B-198240, 80-2 CPD ¶67, *recons. denied*, 80-2 CPD ¶165 (failure to list separate price for first article testing, regardless of IFB warnings, because the bid indicated that such cost was included in the price of the basic item); *MB Assocs.*, Comp. Gen. Dec. B-197566, 80-1 CPD ¶383 (failure to acknowledge amendment that decreased performance costs). In an unusual case, *Champion Road Mach. Int'l Corp.*, Comp. Gen. Dec. B-200678, 81-2 CPD ¶27, GAO reversed the contracting officer by ruling that a two horsepower difference between the item offered and the performance required constituted a minor deviation. Another example of a liberal interpretation of the minor deviation rule is *Albano Cleaners, Inc. v. United States*, 455 F.2d 556 (Ct. Cl. 1972), where the contractor had qualified the bid by refusing delivery services for orders of less than $50. The court held that the contracting officer should have waived the deviation because the qualification was not a substantial deviation from the solicitation.

[2] Prejudice to Other Bidders

A number of cases have focused on the prejudice to other bidders rather than on the degree of nonconformity in determining whether a bid is nonresponsive. Thus, a material nonconformity that gives the bidder no advantage or that operates only to the disadvantage of the bidder will not require rejection. See *Gibraltar Indus., Inc.*, Comp. Gen. Dec. B-218537.3, 85-2 CPD ¶24 (failure to acknowledge amendment that reduced quantity of items required under the contract properly waived); and *Action Mfg. Co.*, Comp. Gen. Dec. B-208205.2, 82-2 CPD ¶ 526 (failure to indicate which of two equally acceptable designs would be used, as required by the IFB, waived and bid properly accepted). In *Davidson-Kelson, Inc.*, Comp. Gen. Dec. B-212551, 83-2 CPD ¶ 589, where an amendment reduced the cost of performance, and no competitive advantage accrued to the bidder as a result of its failure to acknowledge, the error was waived. GAO stated:

> [T]he bidder's failure to acknowledge an amendment containing a lessened requirement could only be prejudicial to the bidder's own competitive position and even possibly beneficial to the position of the other bidders.

See also *Conrad Indus., Inc.*, Comp. Gen. Dec. B-213974.2, 84-2 CPD ¶ 156 (failure to acknowledge amendment changing delivery terms from "f.o.b. destination" to "f.o.b. origin" properly waived); and *Patterson Enters. Ltd.*, Comp. Gen. Dec. B-207105, 82-2 CPD ¶ 133 (failure to acknowledge amendment extending completion deadline for construction project properly waived). However, a different result is obtained when, in addition to reducing performance cost, the amendment imposes additional work, *Hutto Appliance & Refrigeration Serv.*, Comp. Gen. Dec. B-201585, 81-1 CPD ¶ 495. See also *Childrey Contract Servs., Inc.*, Comp. Gen. Dec. B-258653, 95-1 CPD ¶ 60 (failure to clearly demonstrate that bid price includes work added by amendment renders bid nonresponsive).

For other cases involving application of the "no prejudice" rule, see *Keco Indus., Inc.*, 64 Comp. Gen. 48 (B-216396.2), 84-2 CPD ¶ 491 (second low bidder could not conceivably become low even if permitted the same nonconformity); *Leslie & Elliott Co.*, 64 Comp. Gen. 279 (B-216676), 85-1 CPD ¶ 212 (failure to provide a price for a bid item waived); and *Energy Maint. Corp.*, 64 Comp. Gen. 425 (B-215281.3), 85-1 CPD ¶ 341 (ambiguity as to low bidder's price waived where bid would be low by a significant margin under least favorable interpretation). Thus, GAO has, under limited circumstances, required waiver of an otherwise significant deviation where no competitive advantage would result.

[3] Responsiveness versus Responsibility

It is critical to determine whether a nonconformity deals with the responsiveness of a bid or the responsibility of the bidder. Responsiveness, an area in which the contracting officer has limited discretion, deals with the question of whether the contractor *has promised to do exactly what the government has requested*. Responsibility, on the other hand, involves the question of whether the contractor *can or will perform as it has promised*, and the contracting officer is accorded a great deal of discretion in reaching this conclusion. Questions of responsiveness are determined only on the basis of information submitted with the bid and on the facts available at the time of bid opening. Conversely, responsibility determinations are made on the basis of all information that may be submitted or available up to the time of award. These concepts are often confused, particularly when the IFB contains specific requirements concerning bidders' responsibility characteristics—such as the requirement for submission of information relating to responsibility. As a general rule, matters that deal with bidder responsibility cannot be converted into matters of responsiveness merely by inserting a provision into the IFB requiring rejection of bids that do not comply, *SourceLink Ohio, LLC*, Comp. Gen. Dec. B-299258, 2007 CPD ¶ 50 (requirement that bidders submit data use agreement describing how health data would be protected related to responsibility, not responsiveness); *Joint Venture Conscoop-Meyerinck*, Comp. Gen. Dec. B-278243, 98-1 CPD ¶ 83 (agency properly took corrective action in treating information required with bid regarding systems integrator to perform work as a matter of responsibility, not responsiveness); *LORS Med. Corp.*, Comp. Gen. Dec. B-259829, 95-1 CPD ¶ 222 (requirement for submission of information regarding company's policies and procedures relates to responsibility even though IFB required information to be submitted with bid); *Employers Sec. Co.*, GSBCA 6917, 85-1 BCA ¶ 17,885 (requirement that bidder possess an operating license properly relates to responsibility, notwithstanding solicitation language stating that it affects responsiveness); *Lithographic Pubs. Inc.*, Comp. Gen. Dec. B-217263, 85-1 CPD ¶ 357 (solicitation provision stating that bids would be considered nonresponsive if the bidder had defaulted on prior government contract could not convert a matter of responsibility into one of responsiveness); *Marine Power & Equip. Co.*, Comp. Gen. Dec. B-208393, 82-2 CPD ¶ 514 (specific solicitation provisions could not convert the issue of an agent's authority into a matter of bid responsiveness). However, some matters, such as those discussed below, although dealing with the likelihood of obtaining promised performance, have been permitted to be treated as matters of responsiveness.

[a] Quantity in Use Provisions

The requirement that a product have a "quantity in use" for a stated period of time may be considered to deal with responsiveness, even though the requirement deals more with a bidder's ability to satisfy the government's needs than with the bidder's agreement to do so. See Comp. Gen. Dec. B-175493.1, Apr. 20, 1972, *Unpub.*, where GAO discussed quantity in use requirements in a responsiveness context. In *Sunsav, Inc.*, Comp. Gen. Dec. B-205004.2, 82-2 CPD ¶ 476, GAO held that if the requirement relates to the performance history and reliability of the contract *product* and the solicitation requires that the information be furnished, the requirement relates to bid responsiveness and evidence of compliance must be submitted prior to bid opening. The same result was reached by the General Services Administration Board of Contract Appeals in *Micro Star Co.*, GSBCA 8717-P, 87-1 BCA ¶ 19,474.

The key is whether the solicitation clearly establishes that the agency is seeking to assure itself of the reliability of the equipment rather than the capability of the offeror, *National Energy Res., Inc.*, Comp. Gen. Dec. B-206275, 83-1 CPD ¶ 108 (requirement of coal analysis reports related to the suitability of the product and not to the producer's qualifications). However, the distinction between quantity in use requirements and "experience" requirements is often obscure. For example, in *Cubic Western Data, Inc.*, 57 Comp. Gen. 17 (B-189578), 77-2 CPD ¶ 279, GAO found the statement that "each bidder, in order to demonstrate his qualifications . . . shall . . . show that he has successfully executed a contract for the design . . . of equipment of the complexity of this contract within . . . two years" related to the bidder's responsibility. Thus, if a quantity in use requirement does not pertain exclusively to the item procured, but includes generally similar equipment previously produced by the offeror, the quantity in use requirement is a matter of responsibility, *Carco Elecs.*, Comp. Gen. Dec. B-186747, 77-1 CPD ¶ 172; *United Power & Control Sys., Inc.*, Comp. Gen. Dec. B-184662, 76-1 CPD ¶ 340; 52 Comp. Gen. 647 (B-175254.2) (1973). Similarly, if information regarding use of the product is requested, but the agency has established no standards for measuring the level of successful use, it will be a matter of responsibility and not responsiveness, *W.M. Schlosser Co.*, Comp. Gen. Dec. B-258284, 94-2 CPD ¶ 234.

[b] Bid Guarantees

Another area where the concepts of responsiveness and responsibility are confused is that of bid guarantees. Such bid guarantees, commonly in the form of bid bonds, are necessary when a performance bond is required from the winning bidder, FAR 28.101-1(a). Despite the fact that the bid guarantee relates to whether the contractor will perform (responsibility), it is considered such a material requirement that it has been made a matter of bid responsiveness. Thus, ¶ (a) of the Bid Guarantee solicitation provision in FAR 52.228-1 states that failure to furnish a required bid guarantee by the time of bid opening "may be cause for rejection of the bid." FAR 28.101-4(a) *requires* rejection of bids not including required bid guarantees, but FAR 28.101-4(c) gives the contracting officer discretion to waive noncompliance as follows:

> Noncompliance with a solicitation requirement for a bid guarantee shall be waived in the following circumstances unless the contracting officer determines in writing that acceptance of the bid would be detrimental to the Government's interest when—
>
> (1) Only one offer is received. In this case, the contracting officer may require the furnishing of the bid guarantee before award;
>
> (2) The amount of the bid guarantee submitted is less than required, but is equal to or greater than the difference between the offer price and the next higher acceptable offer;

(3) The amount of the bid guarantee submitted, although less than that required by the solicitation for the maximum quantity offered, is sufficient for a quantity for which the offeror is otherwise eligible for award. Any award to the offeror shall not exceed the quantity covered by the bid guarantee;

(4) The bid guarantee is received late, and late receipt is waived under 14.304;

(5) A bid guarantee becomes inadequate as a result of the correction of a mistake under 14.407 (but only if the bidder will increase the bid guarantee to the level required for the corrected bid);

(6) A telegraphic offer modification is received without corresponding modification of the bid guarantee, if the modification expressly refers to the previous offer and the offeror corrects any deficiency in bid guarantee;

(7) An otherwise acceptable bid bond was submitted with a signed offer, but the bid bond was not signed by the offeror;

(8) An otherwise acceptable bid bond is erroneously dated or bears no date at all; or

(9) A bid bond does not list the United States as obligee, but correctly identifies the offeror, the solicitation number, and the name and location of the project involved, so long as it is acceptable in all other respects.

GAO acceded to this policy in 38 Comp. Gen. 532 (B-137319) (1958) on the grounds that permitting bidders to submit bid bonds after bids had been opened gave them "two bites at the apple." This damaged the integrity of the procurement process by providing the low bidder that had not furnished a bond with the option of winning the competition by furnishing the bond or dropping out by not furnishing it. Since that time, rejection of bids as nonresponsive because of the lack of a proper bid guarantee has been sustained, *IMR Dev. Corp.*, Comp. Gen. Dec. B-408585, 2013 CPD ¶ 266; *Morrison Constr. Servs.*, Comp. Gen. Dec. B-266233, 96-1 CPD ¶ 26; *Johnston Eng'g, Inc.*, Comp. Gen. Dec. B-258180, 94-2 CPD ¶ 246; *Secur-Data Sys., Inc.*, Comp. Gen. Dec. B-255090, 94-1 CPD ¶ 68. For a circuit court case agreeing with this reasoning, see *Professional Bldg. Concepts, Inc. v. City of Central Falls*, 974 F.2d 1 (1st Cir. 1992). This issue must be determined based on the documents submitted with the bid. Thus, it is improper to reject a bid with a facially proper bid guarantee because of knowledge that the surety will not provide the performance bond if the bidder is awarded the contract, *Aeroplate Corp. v. United States*, 67 Fed. Cl. 4 (2005).

Contracting officers' decisions to waive the requirement that bid security be submitted with the bid have been sustained when one of the FAR situations applies or where there is another valid reason for waiver, *R.P. Richards Constr. Co.*, Comp. Gen. Dec. B-260965, 95-2 CPD ¶ 128 (bid bond with incorrect solicitation number but with other indicia tying it to the IFB); *Centex-Great Southwest*

Corp., Comp. Gen. Dec. B-258578, 95-1 CPD ¶ 19 (bid bond less than 20% of bid price but greater than difference between low and next low bid); *S.J. Amoroso Constr. Co.*, Comp. Gen. Dec. B-240687, 90-2 CPD ¶ 432 (bid bond not listing United States as obligee but containing other indicia that it was for the bid). In a few cases, GAO has also sustained protests that the contracting officer failed to waive this requirement, *Hostetter, Keach & Cassada Constr., LLC*, Comp. Gen. Dec. B-403329, 2010 CPD ¶ 246 (discrepancy between name of bidder and name of bid bond principal but record showed they were the same entity); *Castle Floor Covering*, 70 Comp. Gen. 530 (B-242718), 91-1 CPD ¶ 510 (cashier's check made out to "Farmers Home Bureau, U.S. Government" in lieu of "Farmers Home Administration" is minor error); *Haag Elec. & Constr., Inc.*, 70 Comp. Gen. 180 (B-240974), 91-1 CPD ¶ 29 (bid bond for less than amount required but more than difference between bid and next low bid). See also *Tip Top Constr., Inc. v. United States*, 563 F.3d 1338 (Fed. Cir. 2009), holding that a contracting officer properly rejected a bid guarantee that pledged mined coal which was not an acceptable form of security.

[c] Ability to Perform

The argument that a bidder's inability to perform should be taken to mean that it does not intend to perform and that the bid is therefore nonresponsive is usually rejected, *Tessa Structures, LLC*, Comp. Gen. Dec. B-298835, 2006 CPD ¶ 199 (agency determination that inability to meet contract schedule was matter of responsiveness); *Peterson Accounting*, Comp. Gen. Dec. B-257411, Sept. 24, 1994, *Unpub.* (agency allegation that bidder failed to submit information to demonstrate ability to perform work); *Luhr Bros., Inc.*, Comp. Gen. Dec. B-248423, 92-2 CPD ¶ 88 (allegation that "bidder-generated production rate" used to determine low bidder on IFB calling for payment based on bid unit prices "is so much a part of the price structure that it has been elevated to a matter of responsiveness"); *American KAL Enters., Inc.*, Comp. Gen. Dec. B-211938, 84-1 CPD ¶ 66 (protest that bidder was unable to meet domestic products requirement); *Grace Indus., Inc.*, Comp. Gen. Dec. B-212263.3, 84-1 CPD ¶ 212 (allegation that bidder was unable to comply with IFB requirement).

For a unique case where a bid valid on its face was held nonresponsive, see 46 Comp. Gen. 275 (B-159560), Oct. 7, 1966, where it was found that the bidder did not intend to comply with the IFB although the bid conformed to the IFB. GAO found that contacts between the bidder and government personnel prior to bidding indicated that the bidder was unable and did not intend to perform in accordance with the IFB. Compare *Radio TV Reports, Inc.*, Comp. Gen. Dec. B-192958, 79-2 CPD ¶ 27, reaching the opposite conclusion where the agency learned that a bidder would not conform strictly with the IFB but that it had a satisfactory means of performance.

[d] Certification Requirements

Bidders are frequently required to submit certifications and representations with their bids. This practice often led to confusion on the part of the bidders when these requirements were scattered throughout the IFB. However, under the Uniform Contract Format required by FAR 14.201-1, all certifications and representations must be included in Section K of the IFB, if they have not been submitted annually to *www.SAM.gov* as required by FAR 4.1201. If certifications and representations are omitted or are furnished with signatures or other information missing, this raises a question of whether a bid must be rejected, as being nonresponsive. As a general rule, if the information in the certification deals with the bidder's responsibility, the bid should not be rejected and the missing information may properly be submitted after bid opening, *J. Morris & Assocs.*, Comp. Gen. Dec. B-259767, 95-1 CPD ¶213 (certification that bidder is or is not a small, disadvantaged business is not a matter of responsiveness); *Norfolk Shipbld'g. & Drydock Corp.*, Comp. Gen. Dec. B-248549, 92-2 CPD ¶127 (although a solicitation required certification of drydocking availability to be submitted with bid, certification concerns bidder's capability to perform and is a matter of responsibility); *PacifiCorp Capital, Inc.*, GSBCA 10884-P, 91-1 BCA ¶23,598 (requirement that reconditioned equipment be "certified as new" not a matter of responsiveness); *Grifco*, Comp. Gen. Dec. B-240549, 90-2 CPD ¶143 (certificate disclosing whether any facilities are on the EPA list of facilities violating the Clean Air Act or the Clean Water Act is a matter of bidder responsibility); *Intermountain Elec., Inc.*, Comp. Gen. Dec. B-236953.2, 90-1 CPD ¶143 (certificate regarding status as debarred or suspended bidder a matter of responsibility); *Jersey Maid Distribs., Inc.*, Comp. Gen. Dec. B-217307, 85-1 CPD ¶307 (bid certifications were not necessary to determine whether the bid meets specifications requirements since they relate to responsibility); *Deterline Corp.*, Comp. Gen. Dec. B-208986, 83-1 CPD ¶427 (certification that bidder is a regular dealer or manufacturer of product may be submitted up to time of award); *C.R. Hipp, Inc.*, Comp. Gen. Dec. B-212093, 83-2 CPD ¶418 (failure to complete Standard Form 19-B, "Representations and Certifications," relates to bidder's responsibility); *Fisher Berkeley Corp.*, Comp. Gen. Dec. B-196432, 80-1 CPD ¶26 (failure to include testing certification may be waived if bid indicates equipment has been tested and meets the specifications); *Jets, Inc.*, Comp. Gen. Dec. B-194017, 79-1 CPD ¶269 (failure to accurately complete affidavit regarding surety net worth is a matter of responsibility).

Bidders are now required to submit their certifications and representations annually by submitting the Online Representations and Certifications Application, FAR Subpart 4.12. This policy is implemented by the inclusion of the Annual Representations and Certifications clause in FAR 52.204-8 in IFBs. The expiration of this registration does not make a bid nonresponsive because it can be updated prior to award, *Veterans Constr. of South Carolina, LLC*, Comp. Gen. Dec. B-401723.2, 2010 CPD ¶36.

However, if a missing or defective certificate raises doubt over whether the bidder has agreed to perform in accordance with the IFB or whether the product offered meets the contract requirements, the bid must be rejected, *New Zealand Fence Sys.*, Comp. Gen. Dec. B-257460, 94-2 CPD ¶ 101 (failure to certify that bidder under a total small business set-aside for supply items would provide end items manufactured or produced by small business concerns); *Camar Corp.*, Comp. Gen. Dec. B-248485, 92-2 CPD ¶ 140 (failure to submit certified test report that product had been tested under specified conditions); *Koch Corp.*, Comp. Gen. Dec. B-212304.4, 84-2 CPD ¶ 132 (failure to certify product's performance history relates to product quality); *Phaostron Instrument & Elec. Co.*, Comp. Gen. Dec. B-214169, 84-1 CPD ¶ 474 (failure to certify that bidder would supply previously approved, identified components); *B.K. Instrument Inc.*, Comp. Gen. Dec. B-212162.2, 84-1 CPD ¶ 189 (failure to meet source control certification requirements); *Fraser-Volpe Corp.*, Comp. Gen. Dec. B-213910, 84-1 CPD ¶ 35 (failure to certify that component parts would be purchased from a designated group).

On occasion, the government has treated certifications that serve an important public policy as matters of responsiveness even though they relate more directly to issues of responsibility. See *Northeast Constr. Co. v. Romney*, 485 F.2d 752 (D.C. Cir. 1973); *Rossetti Contracting Co. v. Brennan*, 508 F.2d 1039 (7th Cir. 1974); and *Astro Pak Corp.*, Comp. Gen. Dec. B-183556, 75-2 CPD ¶ 97, which deal with affirmative action plans for equal employment opportunity that were required to be submitted along with the bids. In *Northeast Construction*, the bidder failed to fill in its affirmative action goals in the space provided but did sign the document agreeing to comply with the plan included in the IFB, which specified the minimum acceptable goals. Nevertheless, the bid was considered nonresponsive because the omissions created doubts regarding enforceability of the bidder's commitment because its bid was inconsistent with the instructions of the plan. These decisions have been mooted with respect to EEO certificates because of changes in the procedures making the certificate a matter of responsibility, FAR 14.405(f).

In *Worcester Elec. Assocs.*, Comp. Gen. Dec. B-193064, 79-1 CPD ¶ 236, a specification requirement that bidders submit Underwriter Laboratories (UL) listing cards was held to be a matter of responsiveness, because the purpose of the cards was to provide evidence that the equipment being offered conformed to certain standards of safety and performance. But see *Fisher Berkeley Corp.*, Comp. Gen. Dec. B-196432, 80-1 CPD ¶ 26, where the UL certification itself was considered a matter of responsibility as long as the bidder promised that its product would be and was UL certified.

[e] Information or Data to Be Submitted

When data or information is required to be submitted with the bid, the purpose for which the data or information is to be used will determine whether it is a matter of responsiveness or responsibility. Thus, if descriptive data are to be used to determine a bidder's *ability or capacity to perform*, the matter will be one of *responsibility*, and failure to submit the information with the bid will not cause its rejection. For decisions finding lack of information a matter of responsibility, see *Savin Business Machs. Corp.*, Comp. Gen. Dec. B-191163, 78-1 CPD ¶ 447 (preventive maintenance plan, key operator instruction plan, and samples of paper to be used with photocopying equipment); *Science Applications, Inc.*, Comp. Gen. Dec. B-193479, 79-1 CPD ¶ 167 (personnel resumes); *Career Consultants, Inc.*, Comp. Gen. Dec. B-198727, 80-2 CPD ¶ 285 (IFB requirement for statement of licensing status); *Seacoast Trucking & Moving Co.*, Comp. Gen. Dec. B-200315, 80-2 CPD ¶ 235 (description of equipment to be used in performing refuse services); *Career Consultants, Inc.*, Comp. Gen. Dec. B-200506.2, 81-1 CPD ¶ 414 (requirement for security clearances); *Skyline Credit Corp.*, Comp. Gen. Dec. B-209193, 83-1 CPD ¶ 257 (written performance procedures); *Siska Constr. Co.*, 64 Comp. Gen. 384 (B-218208.2), 85-1 CPD ¶ 331 (affiliation and parent company data as well as certificate of independent pricing); *Master Power, Inc.*, Comp. Gen. Dec. B-238468.2, 90-2 CPD ¶ 434 (furnishing incorrect qualification test number for qualified product); *RKR, Inc.*, Comp. Gen. Dec. B-247619.2, 92-2 CPD ¶ 289 (equate evidence of compliance with zoning laws); *CardioMetrix*, Comp. Gen. Dec. B-255748.2, 94-1 CPD ¶ 364 (designation of place of performance). See also *Commercial Window & Door Co.*, Comp. Gen. Dec. B-211280, 83-2 CPD ¶ 582 (bid that failed to include test results concerning product performance held responsive because IFB failed to warn bidders that submission requirement involved responsiveness and the information was not necessary to determine conformance with specifications).

On the other hand, information or data may be required to be submitted with the bid for purposes of more precisely determining *the nature of the work that the bidder is agreeing to accomplish* is considered to go to the *responsiveness* of the bid. Requiring the submission of such data can protect the government from bids that are responsive on their face, because they take no exception to the IFB but are based on performing in a manner that does not conform to the solicitation. The two major techniques used by the government for this purpose are requirements for *descriptive literature* and *bid samples.*

Neither of these techniques should be used indiscriminately because they may unduly increase the cost of bidding. FAR 14.202-4(b) gives the following guidance regarding the use of bid samples:

> The use of bid samples would be appropriate for products that must be suitable from the standpoint of balance, facility of use, general "feel," color, pattern, or other characteristics that cannot be described adequately in the specification. However, when more than a minor portion of the characteristics of the product cannot be adequately described in the specification, products should be acquired by two-step sealed bidding or negotiation, as appropriate.

FAR 14.202-5(a) provides the following guidance with respect to descriptive literature:

> Contracting officers must not require bidders to furnish descriptive literature unless it is needed before award to determine whether the products offered meet the specification and to establish exactly what the bidder proposes to furnish.

Where the purpose of the data is to enable the procuring agency to determine precisely what the bidder intends to supply, the matter will be considered to deal with responsiveness. This is the only purpose for which bid samples may be submitted, FAR 14.202-4(a)(2). For example, in *Western Waterproofing Co.*, Comp. Gen. Dec. B-183155, 75-1 CPD ¶ 306, the bidder was required to furnish data demonstrating that the stone proposed for use met the IFB criteria. GAO reasoned that this provision did not deal with the bidder's ability to perform but was aimed at describing the articles to be supplied. See also *National Energy Res., Inc.*, Comp. Gen. Dec. B-206275, 83-1 CPD ¶ 108 (failure to include data regarding the suitability of the coal to be provided was a matter of responsiveness).

[B] Consequences of Nonconforming Bids

The consequences of submitting a nonconforming bid depend on the nature of the nonconformity and the time it is discovered.

[1] Minor Informalities

Once a defect is found to be minor, award must be made, if at all, to the low bidder who is otherwise responsible. The contracting officer has the choice of either giving the bidder an opportunity to cure the deficiency or waiving it, whichever is in the best interest of the government, FAR 14.405; *Champion Road Mach. Int'l Corp.*, Comp. Gen. Dec. B-200678, 81-2 CPD ¶ 27; *Astrophysics Research Corp.*, 66 Comp. Gen. 211 (B-224532), 87-1 CPD ¶ 65. If the bidder refuses to cure the deficiency, then award may be made on the basis of the bid as submitted.

If a sealed bid procurement is canceled because the agency determines that the only bid at a reasonable price is nonresponsive, and the agency subsequently determines that the defect in the bid was a minor informality, the agency may reinstate the IFB and award to that bidder, *Bilt-Rite Contractors, Inc.*, Comp. Gen. Dec. B-259106.2, 95-1 CPD ¶ 220.

[2] Material Nonconformities

This section discusses the requirement for rejection of nonresponsive bids, the legal effect of an award on the basis of a nonresponsive bid, and the limited cases in which such awards are sanctioned by GAO.

[a] Rejection Required

FAR 14.404-2(a) states that "any bid that fails to conform to the essential requirements of the solicitation shall be rejected." In commenting on the rationale for this rule, the court, in *Toyo Menka Kaisha, Ltd. v. United States*, 597 F.2d 1371 (Ct. Cl. 1979), stated at 1377:

> These principles rest upon and effectuate important public policies. "Rejection of irresponsive bids is necessary if the purposes of formal advertising are to be attained, that is, to give everyone an equal right to compete for Government business, to secure fair prices, and to prevent fraud." *Prestex Inc. v. United States, supra*, 162 Ct. Cl. at 626, 320 F.2d at 372 (footnote omitted). The requirement that a bid be responsive is designed to avoid unfairness to other contractors who submitted a sealed bid on the understanding that they must comply with all of the specifications and conditions in the invitation for bids, and who could have made a better proposal if they imposed conditions upon or variances from the contractual terms the government had specified. The rule also avoids placing the contracting officer in the difficult position of having to balance the more favorable offer of the deviating bidder against the disadvantages to the government from the qualifications and conditions the bidder has added. In short, the requirement of responsiveness is designed to avoid a method of awarding government contracts that would be similar to negotiating agreements but which would lack the safeguards present in either that system or in true competitive bidding. See R. Nash & J. Cibinic, *Federal Procurement Law*, 260 (3d ed. 1977).
>
> Responsiveness is determined by reference to the bids when they are opened and not by reference to subsequent changes in a bid. *Id.* at 261. Allowing a bidder to modify a nonresponsive bid when, upon opening the bids, it appears that the variations will preclude an award, would permit the very kind of bid manipulation and negotiation that the rule is designed to prevent. Otherwise bidders would be encouraged to submit nonresponsive bids on terms favorable to the government but subject to certain conditions, in the hope that if their bids were the top ones, they could then negotiate about and retain some of their proposed changes. In this way they could obtain a contract that they could not have received had they complied with the specification in the invitation for bids.

It is immaterial whether the nonconformity is deliberate or occurs by mistake, or whether the bidder is willing to correct or modify the bid to conform to the terms of the invitation, *Legeay, Inc.*, Comp. Gen. Dec. B-218307, 85-1 CPD ¶ 338 (fact that bidder alleged mistake and offered to correct an insufficient acceptance period held irrelevant); *AVS Inc.*, Comp. Gen. Dec. B-218205, 85-1 CPD ¶ 328 (irrelevant that bid guarantee deficiency may have resulted from innocent error on the part of the surety); *Public Entity Underwriters, Ltd.*, Comp. Gen. Dec. B-213745, 84-2 CPD ¶ 326 (clerical error may not be corrected after opening to make bid responsive). In *Amendola Constr. Co.*, Comp. Gen. Dec. B-214258, 84-1 CPD ¶255, GAO stated:

> The fact that [the protester] has subsequently explained that the 15-day period it offered was a mistake and that it is willing to waive its restriction is irrelevant. A bid which is nonresponsive on its face may not be changed, corrected or explained by the bidder after bid opening since to permit this would give the firm the option of accepting or rejecting a contract after bids are exposed.

See also *Parco, A Div. of Blue Mountain Prods., Inc.*, Comp. Gen. Dec. B-211016, 83-1 CPD ¶318, refusing to allow a nonresponsive bid to be considered for correction after bid opening because to permit a change after bid opening would be tantamount to permitting the submission of a new bid after the competitors' bids have been revealed.

[b] Validity of Award

Award to a bidder whose bid contains a material nonconformity has been held to be void *ab initio*, *Prestex Inc. v. United States*, 320 F.2d 367 (Ct. Cl. 1963). See also *Albano Cleaners, Inc. v. United States*, 455 F.2d 556 (Ct. Cl. 1972), where the court stated at 559:

> [The Government] may disclaim a contract on the ground of voidness *ab initio* because of the nonresponsiveness of the bid. Where a public contract is to be let pursuant to formal advertising, the strictures upon [the Government's] contracting agent are such "that the contract awarded must be the contract advertised and *** if it is not, the Government is not bound, since [the Government's] contracting agent could not bind the Government beyond his actual authority." *Prestex Inc. v. United States*, 162 Ct. Cl. 620, 625, 320 F.2d 367, 371 (1963).

Thus, a bidder who receives such an award runs a great risk if the government decides to cancel the award. If the contract is declared void *ab initio*, the contractor will generally be entitled to payment only for benefits conferred on the government, *United States v. Amdahl Corp.*, 786 F.2d 387 (Fed. Cir. 1986). However, to the extent that any expenditures made in performance do not confer a benefit upon the government, they may not be recovered, *Toyo Menka Kaisha, Ltd. v. United States*, 597 F.2d 1371 (Ct. Cl. 1979).

GAO has recommended termination for convenience rather than cancellation when there has been an award to a nonresponsive bidder, *Fischer-White-Rankin Contractors, Inc.*, Comp. Gen. Dec. B-213401, 84-1 CPD ¶471, *withdrawn because much work done*, 84-1 CPD ¶640; *Harris Constr. Co.*, 64 Comp. Gen. 628 (B-218387), 85-1 CPD ¶710. This result follows the reasoning that cancellation is only proper when the illegality of the contract is "plain," *John Reiner &*

Co. v. United States, 325 F.2d 438 (Ct. Cl. 1963), *cert. denied*, 377 U.S. 931 (1964), or "palpable," *Warren Bros. Roads Co. v. United States*, 355 F.2d 612 (Ct. Cl. 1965). This reasoning was also followed by the General Services Board of Contract Appeals, *International Bus. Machs. Corp.*, GSBCA 9703-P, 89-1 BCA ¶ 21,389, *rev'd on other grounds*, 892 F.2d 1006 (Fed. Cir. 1989).

[c] Award

On a number of occasions GAO has sanctioned awards on the basis of nonresponsive bids. This is generally done only if all the bids submitted are nonresponsive, the bid in question satisfies the government's requirements, and no competing bidder would be prejudiced as a result of the award. In *K. B. Constr.*, Comp. Gen. Dec. B-214192, 84-1 CPD ¶ 223, the failure of all bidders to submit required test manufacturer's data permitted award to the low bidder.

A crucial element in the decisions sanctioning award to a nonresponsive bidder is GAO's finding that, under the circumstances, acceptance of the nonresponsive bid would not prejudice other bidders, *Singleton Contracting Corp.*, Comp. Gen. Dec. B-211259, 83-2 CPD ¶ 270 (award proper where both bids were nonresponsive for same material nonconformity, and acceptance resulted in a contract that satisfied government needs). In *E.F. Matelich Constr. Co.*, Comp. Gen. Dec. B-207600, 82-2 CPD ¶ 291, GAO stated that "[t]he test of prejudice . . . is whether it is reasonably clear that another bidder, given the benefit of a similarly relaxed requirement . . . would have bid in such a manner that it would have been in line for award." See *Esko & Young, Inc.*, 61 Comp. Gen. 192 (B-204053), 82-1 CPD ¶ 5, where the failure of the sole bidder to include a conforming bid acceptance period did not require rejection since "no bidding advantage accrues to the single bidder . . . because there were no competitors who . . . subjected themselves to the risks of maintaining their bid process for the longer period." See also *Fluid Sys, Inc.*, Comp. Gen. Dec. B-225880, 87-1 CPD ¶ 20, where an award was upheld where the IFB required a two-inch-diameter drain for feed pump lube oil modification kits, but the low bidder could supply only a one-and-three-quarter-inch-diameter model because it was the only model available. GAO reasoned that the substituted product met the government's needs and no other bidders were prejudiced.

In a number of these cases, award is sanctioned because cancellation of the procurement after bids have been exposed is seen as a greater evil. In *Big State Enters.*, 64 Comp. Gen. 482 (B-218055), 85-1 CPD ¶ 459, GAO stated at 484:

> [W]e believe that in spite of the specification deficiency, the determination to make an award was reasonable and less of a compromise to the competitive bidding system than resolicitation after exposure of all prices would have been. See *GAF Corp. et al.*, 53 Comp. Gen. 586 (1974), 74-1 CPD ¶ 68.

These GAO decisions sanctioning award on the basis of the most advantageous nonresponsive bid are based on pragmatism. The standard alternatives would be for the contracting officer to reject all bids and resolicit sealed bids, *Gulf & Western Healthcare, Inc.*, Comp. Gen. Dec. B-209684, 83-2 CPD ¶ 248, competitive proposals, or two-step sealed bids, 34 Comp. Gen. 364 (B-121831) (1965). In case of urgency, it might also be possible to negotiate with all bidders if less than full and open competition could be justified. See *Bus Indus. of Am., Inc.*, Comp. Gen. Dec. B-208366, 83-1 CPD ¶ 222, approving this technique in a case that arose prior to the Competition in Contracting Act. Since these alternatives would all involve the expenditure of additional time and effort, it is clearly more expedient to make the award to the bidder submitting the most advantageous, albeit nonresponsive, bid.

This pragmatism, however, may be shortsighted. It ignores the possibility that the requirement that was not met may have deterred other potential bidders from entering the competition at all. These decisions also ignore decisions such as *Prestex Inc. v. United States*, 320 F.2d 367 (Ct. Cl. 1963), holding that award to a nonresponsive bidder constitutes a prohibited waiver of responsiveness criteria and does not obligate the government. The courts focus more on the prejudice to potential bidders, while GAO addresses the issue of prejudice only in terms of actual bidders.

[C] Types of Nonconforming Bids

The determination of whether a nonconformity is material depends upon the facts of the case and the nature of the nonconformity. This section examines some of the common types of nonconforming bids.

[1] Differing Products or Services

Any bid that fails to conform to the essential requirements or applicable specifications of an invitation must be rejected. FAR 14.404-2(b) states that bids offering materially differing products or services from those solicited must be rejected as nonresponsive. See, for example, *Kincaid Equip. Mfg.*, Comp. Gen. Dec. B-246079, 92-1 CPD ¶ 140 (bid offering a belt-driven threshing cylinder where IFB required a hydrostatically driven threshing cylinder); *Mobile Drilling Co.*, Comp. Gen. Dec. B-216989, 85-1 CPD ¶ 199 (offer to furnish a drill with a torque capacity of 6,000 ft.-lbs. at 27 R.P.M. instead of the required capacity of 5,800 ft.-lbs. at 50 R.P.M.); *Jensen Corp.*, Comp. Gen. Dec. B-213677, 84-1 CPD ¶ 544 (bid offering a two-roll flatwork commercial ironer when the IFB called for a four-roll ironer); and *Sheffield Bldg. Co.*, Comp. Gen. Dec. B-181242, 74-2 CPD ¶ 108 (bidder's failure to include spud engines when the specifications called for derrickboats equipped with spud engines).

When the government solicits products on a "brand name or equal" basis, a bidder offering an "equal" product must establish that it conforms to all the salient characteristics of the brand-name product listed in the IFB. A failure to do so will result in bid rejection, *RCP Shelters, Inc.*, Comp. Gen. Dec. B-256258, 94-1 CPD ¶ 336 (descriptive literature submitted with bid failed to show compliance with the salient characteristics); *Alternate Power & Energy Corp.*, Comp. Gen. Dec. B-228746, 87-2 CPD ¶ 440 (although offered product possessed required features, bid rejected where literature submitted with bid did not clearly show conformance with IFB requirements). Any information used to show conformance to the salient characteristics must have been commercially available prior to bid opening and must not have been developed afterward, *Elastomeric Roofing Assocs.*, 68 Comp. Gen. 426 (B-234125), 89-1 CPD ¶ 451. To allow bidders to submit other than preexisting, commercially available material would give the bidder control over the responsiveness of its bid, *Monitronics*, Comp. Gen. Dec. B-228219, 87-2 CPD ¶ 527. However, bidders have been permitted to submit such information after bid opening. See *Lappen Auto Supply Co.*, Comp. Gen. Dec. B-261475, 95-2 CPD ¶ 68.

Bids that fail to meet salient characteristics of the solicitation must be rejected as nonresponsive even if the offered items function as well as the brand-name units and satisfy the intent of the specifications, *SDV Furniture & Servs., LLC*, Comp. Gen. Dec. B-401221, 2009 CPD ¶ 108 (bid offering acoustic panels with "better" internal sound baffling" rejected because dimensions did not match salient characteristics); *Advanced Med. Sys., Inc.*, Comp. Gen. Dec. B-258945, 95-1 CPD ¶ 67 (bid rejected as nonresponsive where proposed "equal" product could digitally display one fetal heart rate, but IFB for fetal heart monitor required digital display of two fetal heart rates); *T & T Prods., Inc.*, Comp. Gen. Dec. B-243898, 91-2 CPD ¶ 139 (bid stating "equal" product had cable diameter of "0.75 inches nominal" rejected as nonresponsive where IFB required a cable diameter between 0.8 and 0.875 inches); *United Mach.*, Comp. Gen. Dec. B-227923, 87-2 CPD ¶ 54 (bid rejected as nonresponsive where, although the offered "equal" washer extractor may have functioned as well as the brand name, the protester conceded that the offered product did not meet all the specifications of the IFB); *Paul F. Pugh & Associated Prof'l Eng'rs*, Comp. Gen. Dec. B-199920, 80-2 CPD ¶ 358 (although aluminum conductors offered may function as well as brand-name units, bid was properly rejected as nonresponsive because IFB for power cables listed copper as a salient characteristic). Even a brand-name product listed in the IFB may not be accepted as responsive if it fails to meet listed salient characteristics and, in effect, constitutes a "differing" product, *Vista Scientific Corp.*, Comp. Gen. Dec. B-185170, 76-1 CPD ¶ 212. But see *Central Power Eng'g Corp.*, Comp. Gen. Dec. B-215658.2, 85-1 CPD ¶ 85, where the bid listed a brand-name model number that represented an upgraded version of the brand-name model solicited. GAO upheld the agency's determination that although designated somewhat differently, the model offered met all the salient characteristics of the solicitation and was in essence the same brand-name item called for in the IFB. See also *GAF Corp.*, 53 Comp. Gen. 586 (B-179744), 74-1 CPD ¶ 68, reinstating a canceled IFB and permitted award to a brand-name product that did not conform to all listed salient characteristics.

Nonconformities of bids that are merely a matter of form and not substance or that are immaterial or inconsequential variations from the exact requirements of an IFB may not be rejected as nonresponsive. FAR 14.405 requires minor informalities or irregularities to be corrected or waived if no prejudice will result to other bidders, or where the deviation has only a negligible effect on price, quality, quantity, or delivery when compared with the total cost or scope of supplies or work to be furnished. See, for example, *W.M. Schlosser Co.*, Comp. Gen. Dec. B-258284, 94-2 CPD ¶ 234 (bidder's failure to submit requested equipment history with bid that would not be used to evaluate bid waived as an immaterial deviation); *Universal Applicators, Inc.*, Comp. Gen. Dec. B-232670, 88-2 CPD ¶ 591 (failure to certify that bid price was not based on "spray painting" when IFB required a liquid roof sealant held to be an immaterial deviation); *Astrophysics Research Corp.*, 66 Comp. Gen. 211 (B-224532), 87-1 CPD ¶ 65 (10-pound discrepancy between 410-pound X-ray screening machine bid and 400-pound machine specified in IFB; IFB requirement waived as a minor informality where item met government need and there was no prejudice to other bidders); *Evans, Inc.*, Comp. Gen. Dec. B-216260.2, 85-1 CPD ¶ 535 (118.5-inch dryer minor deviation from 120-inch specification requirement); *Magnaflux Corp.*, Comp. Gen. Dec. B-211914, 84-1 CPD ¶ 4 (29.5-inch bath tank minor deviation to specification requiring 30-inch tank); and *Champion Road Mach. Int'l Corp.*, Comp. Gen. Dec. B-200678, 81-2 CPD ¶ 27 (bid offering 168-horsepower road grader where solicitation specified 170 horsepower held responsive where deviation had no effect on price, quality, quantity, or delivery).

There are a few seemingly inconsistent decisions. See *Yale Materials Handling Corp.*, Comp. Gen. Dec. B-250208, 92-2 CPD ¶ 360 (bid offering forklift exceeding specified dimensions in the IFB by about one-half inch was a material deviation affecting the quality of the forklift and was rejected as nonresponsive); *Taylor-Forge Engineered Sys., Inc.*, 69 Comp. Gen. 54 (B-236408), 89-2 CPD ¶ 421 (bid offering delivery f.o.b. origin where IFB required f.o.b. destination constituted a material deviation); and 43 Comp. Gen. 209 (B-151968) (1963) (award of contract canceled where bid offered paper cutter that materially deviated from the IFB specifications by affecting price and quality, even though the product would better serve the agency's needs).

[2] Failure to Agree to IFB Delivery Schedule

An IFB's delivery schedule is a material requirement of the solicitation, and any bid that fails to conform to the delivery schedule is nonresponsive and must be rejected, FAR 14.404-2(c). Thus, a bid offering a delivery period greater than the maximum delivery period permitted under the terms of the solicitation will be rejected as nonresponsive, *Chrysler Corp.*, Comp. Gen. Dec. B-249492, 92-2

CPD ¶253 (bid offering "shipments" within 90 days rejected as nonresponsive where IFB required "delivery" within 90 days); *Rhimco Indus., Inc.*, Comp. Gen. Dec. B-247600, 92-1 CPD ¶499 (IFB required delivery of all items within 120 days after award, but protester's bid offered delivery of one half of the requirements); *Delta Scientific Corp.*, Comp. Gen. Dec. B-233485, 88-2 CPD ¶516 (bid's delivery schedule of 120 days was rejected where IFB stated bidders could offer delivery schedule longer than the desired 60 days but within the required 90 days); *Meyer Tool & Mfg.*, Comp. Gen. Dec. B-222595, 86-1 CPD ¶537 (bid rejected as nonresponsive where numbers in proposed delivery period were transposed, due to a clerical error, from 120 days to 210 days, which exceeded the 180 days required by the IFB); *Mar-Mac Precision Corp.*, Comp. Gen. Dec. B-214604, 84-2 CPD ¶164 (failure to acknowledge an amendment that doubled the delivery requirements for the first 180 days of the contract rendered bid nonresponsive). Even a bid footnote objecting to and qualifying a required delivery schedule has rendered a bid nonresponsive, *Sunoptic, Inc.*, Comp. Gen. Dec. B-194722, 79-1 CPD ¶351. But see *TEREX Corp.*, Comp. Gen. Dec. B-212441, 84-1 CPD ¶330, where a bid that failed to offer delivery within 30 days was improperly rejected as nonresponsive because the IFB merely called for a "desired" delivery date of 30 days, and the offered delivery date was "reasonable."

The bid must indicate that the bidder is agreeing to meet the required date. In Comp. Gen. Dec. B-170287, Aug. 18, 1970, *Unpub.*, *recons. denied*, 50 Comp. Gen. 379 (1970), the invitation required delivery in 150 days and had a desired delivery date of 120 days. The bidder offered delivery in "approximately 120 days (as requested)." This deviation was found to be material and rendered the bid nonresponsive since no firm date was bid. But see Comp. Gen. Dec. B-175342, Mar. 27, 1972, *Unpub.*, where an approximate delivery date of 30 days did not render a bid nonresponsive when the required date was 90 days. GAO distinguished the earlier case by noting that the "approximate period of offered delivery is significantly greater in the instant case than in the earlier case both in terms of the absolute number of days between the approximate date and the deadline and the relative period involved."

When the IFB requires delivery within a certain time from date of contract award, bidders may specify delivery times starting from receipt of contract award documents. In such cases, FAR 11.403(e) requires that five calendar days (normal mail delivery time) be added to the bidder's date (one day if the notice of award is transmitted electronically), and if this date is later than the IFB required date, the bid is considered nonresponsive. See, for example, *AMP Inc.*, Comp. Gen. Dec. B-230120, 88-1 CPD ¶163 (bid offering a delivery schedule of 150 days after receipt of an order rejected as nonresponsive because it effectively added five days to the IFB required schedule as an allowance for delivery through ordinary mails); and *Discount Mach. & Equip.*, Comp. Gen. Dec. B-223048.2, 86-2 CPD ¶5 (bid offering a delivery period of 90 days after receipt of contract, where

IFB required 90 days from contract award, in effect added five days for delivery of award documents through the mail and was rejected as nonresponsive).

A bid will also be nonresponsive if it indicates that the proposed schedule will result in unsatisfactory performance. See *Red John's Stone, Inc.*, Comp. Gen. Dec. B-280974, 98-2 CPD ¶ 135 (bidder's performance schedule required planting outside of growing season).

[3] Conditions Altering the Invitation

Bids that impose conditions altering the requirements of the invitation or limiting the rights of the government must be rejected. FAR 14.404-2(d) states:

> A bid shall be rejected when the bidder imposes conditions that would modify requirements of the invitation or limit the bidder's liability to the Government, since to allow the bidder to impose such conditions would be prejudicial to other bidders. For example, bids shall be rejected in which the bidder—
>
> (1) Protects against future changes in conditions, such as increased costs, if total possible costs to the Government cannot be determined;
>
> (2) Fails to state a price and indicates that price shall be "price in effect at time of delivery";
>
> (3) States a price but qualifies it as being subject to "price in effect at time of delivery";
>
> (4) When not authorized by the invitation, conditions or qualifies a bid by stipulating that it is to be considered only if, before date of award, the bidder receives (or does not receive) award under a separate solicitation;
>
> (5) Requires that the Government is to determine that the bidder's product meets applicable Government specifications; or
>
> (6) Limits rights of the Government under any contract clause.

[a] Modifying Material Requirements of the IFB

Any bid that imposes conditions that would modify the material requirements of the solicitation will be rejected as nonresponsive, *Fire-Trol Holdings, LLC v. United States*, 68 Fed. Cl. 281 (2005) (bid nonresponsive when it stated that government would be required to acquire material that bidder was required to furnish); *Antennas for Commc'ns*, Comp. Gen. Dec. B-253950, 93-2 CPD ¶ 48 (bid nonresponsive when it stated that government damages for delay "shall be billed at a rate of $1,000 per day"); *NR Vessel Corp.*, Comp. Gen. Dec. B-250925, 93-1 CPD ¶ 128 (bid conditioned on the government disposing of hazardous waste was rejected as nonresponsive where the IFB placed responsibility for disposal on the contractor); *Lathan Constr. Corp.*, Comp. Gen. Dec. B-250487, 93-1 CPD ¶ 107 (bid nonresponsive where document captioned "Contractor's Qualifications and Exclusions" excluded permit and engineering fees required by the IFB); *General Elec. Co.*, Comp. Gen. Dec. B-228191, 87-2 CPD ¶ 585 (bid rejected for taking exception to two parts of the IFB's warranty provision). See also *Garney Cos.*, Comp. Gen. Dec. 196075.2, 81-1 CPD ¶ 62 (bidder reserved right to use unacceptable pipe installation technique); *State Mut. Book & Periodical Serv., Ltd.*, Comp. Gen. Dec. B-191008.2, 78-1 CPD ¶ 264 (exception to specified delivery method); *National Ambulance Co.*, 55 Comp. Gen. 597 (B-184439), 75-2 CPD ¶ 413 (bid conditioned on receipt of local license); *Joy Mfg. Co.*, 54 Comp. Gen. 237 (B-181136), 74-2 CPD ¶ 183 (bid reserved the right to change prices if costs increase even though the IFB required a firm-fixed-price); and 43 Comp. Gen. 382 (B-152470) (1963) (bid stated that alignment of turbine and generator shafts would be accomplished at contractor's plant in Japan rather than in the United States as specified in the IFB).

If there is no prohibition in the IFB against conditions limiting the size of the award, the imposition of such a condition will not render the bid nonresponsive. In *Orvedahl Constr., Inc.*, 63 Comp. Gen. 288 (B-213408), 84-1 CPD ¶ 405, bids were entered on two line items at $781,000 and $622,000, respectively, along with a condition stipulating that no award over $1,000,000 would be accepted. The rejection of Orvedahl's bid was held improper because the bidder's obligation to perform according to the terms and conditions of the IFB was not affected in any way. See also FAR 14.404-5, which allows bidders to condition acceptance upon award of all or a specified group of items, unless the IFB expressly prohibits "all or none" or similarly restricted bids. See *Mansfield Assocs.*, Comp. Gen. Dec. B-242270, 91-1 CPD ¶ 284 (agency's failure to incorporate a provision expressly permitting "all or none" bids did not constitute an express prohibition of such bidding); and *Phillips Cartner & Co.*, 69 Comp. Gen. 105 (B-236416.2), 89-2 CPD ¶ 492 ("all or none" qualification did not render bid nonresponsive since the IFB did not expressly prohibit such bid qualifications).

A bid may be responsive in spite of a qualifying legend contained in the bid literature where it is reasonably clear from the bid that a "subject to change" legend is not intended to reserve the right to the bidder to change the offered product or to deviate from the material requirements of the invitation, *Syntrex Inc.*, 63 Comp. Gen. 360 (B-212781.2), 84-1 CPD ¶ 522. See also *Yale Materials Handling Corp.*, Comp. Gen. Dec. B-228974.2, 87-2 CPD ¶ 550, where, although the bid was held nonresponsive on other grounds, GAO stated that a handwritten statement, which immediately followed the "subject to change" clause, that all requirements will be met, effectively deleted the conditional language. Similarly, where a bid statement merely clarifies the bidder's understanding of the IFB without limiting any material provisions, the bid is responsive, *Westinghouse Elec. Corp.*, Comp. Gen. Dec. B-187487, 76-2 CPD ¶ 455.

[b] Limiting Rights of the Government

If a bid attempts to limit the rights of the government under any contract clause, the bid will be rejected as nonresponsive, *New Dimension Masonry,*

Inc., Comp. Gen. Dec. B-258876, 95-1 CPD ¶ 102 (bid rejected as nonresponsive where cover letter conditioned bid upon the use of a government storage area); *Municipal Leasing Sys., Inc.*, Comp. Gen. Dec. B-242648.2, 91-1 CPD ¶ 495 (bid language "after 12 months" limited the agency's right to exercise a purchase option within the first 12 months of the contract); *F.J. Dahill Co.*, Comp. Gen. Dec. B-235272, 89-2 CPD ¶ 103 (bid nonresponsive because it contained statement that bidder would not work on hazardous substances and would leave site if any were found); *Gelco Payment Sys., Inc.*, Comp. Gen. Dec. B-234957, 89-2 CPD ¶ 27 (bid stating that either party may cancel upon 30 days' notice attempted to limit the government's rights under the "termination for convenience" clause and was rejected as nonresponsive); *Integrated Research & Info. Sys.*, Comp. Gen. Dec. B-196456, 80-1 CPD ¶ 130 (bid specified that procuring agency rather than the bidder would pay shipping costs); *Kari-Vac, Inc.*, Comp. Gen. Dec. B-194202, 79-2 CPD ¶ 4 (bid conditioned upon payment by the government of 1% interest charge for payments made after 30 days). But see 48 Comp. Gen. 306 (B-164639) (1968), holding that a statement on one competitor's own bid form that "no withholding will be allowed without the prior written consent of the seller" did not affect the responsiveness of the bid, even though that it appeared to limit the government's rights. GAO stated at 310-11:

> In this instance we do not believe that the acceptance of the MSA bid, including the wording "no withholding will be allowed without the prior written consent of the seller," resulted in any diminution of the rights which the Government would have without that language. If the Government does withhold any or all of the contract price by reason of a claim against the contractor, we are not aware of any remedy available to the contractor except an action for the amount withheld, and in the event of such an action it is our opinion the Government could assert its claim either as a cross-claim or as a separate action.

[c] Limiting Liability to the Government

A bid that attempts to limit the bidder's liability to the government as proposed in the invitation will be rejected as nonresponsive, *AAA Roofing Co.*, Comp. Gen. Dec. B-240852, 90-2 CPD ¶ 485 (form submitted with bid imposing limitations on bidder's future liability to the government); *Contech Constr. Co.*, Comp. Gen. Dec. B-241185, 90-2 CPD ¶ 264 (bid included notation "impossible" next to two interim schedule requirements; argument that these were only estimator's notes rejected); *Roche Biomedical Labs., Inc.*, Comp. Gen. Dec. B-233123, 88-2 CPD ¶ 368 (bid claiming the right and privilege of terminating contract upon certain conditions); *Southwest Marine of San Francisco, Inc.*, 66 Comp. Gen. 22 (B-224508), 86-2 CPD ¶ 388 (bid stating contractor "shall take every precaution to contain contaminate" from abrasive ship blasting since statement attempted to limit its liability to the government for any environmental violations); *Dr. Beurt R. Servaas*, HUDBCA 83-780-B1, 83-2 BCA ¶ 16,690 (bid request for waiver of first 12 months' interest and principal payment); *Dubie-Clark Co.*, Comp. Gen. Dec. B-186918, 76-2 CPD ¶ 194 (exception to liquidated damages).

[d] Barring Public Disclosure

Bids containing restrictions that prevent public disclosure are nonresponsive if they effectively keep competing bidders from knowing the essential nature and type of products offered or those elements of the bid that relate to quantity, price, and delivery terms, *Industrial Acoustics Co.*, Comp. Gen. Dec. B-255123.2, 94-1 CPD ¶ 220 (bid properly rejected as nonresponsive where bid restricted disclosure of required test data necessary to determine responsiveness of bid); *VACAR Battery Mfg. Co.*, Comp. Gen. Dec. B-223244.2, 86-2 CPD ¶ 21 (bid restricting public disclosure rejected as nonresponsive despite disclosure of the restricted bid price at bid opening); *Sperry-Univac*, Comp. Gen. Dec. B-200378, 81-1 CPD ¶ 38 (bid stamped "proprietary" properly rejected as nonresponsive because disclosure of price at bid opening was limited). But where the limitations on disclosure of a company's information relate solely to its ability to perform and not to price, quantity, or delivery, rejection is not required, *Tennessee Apparel Corp.*, Comp. Gen. Dec. B-253178.3, 94-1 CPD ¶ 104.

[4] Indefinite, Uncertain, or Ambiguous Bids

Bids that are indefinite, uncertain, or ambiguous are normally rejected as nonresponsive. The test is whether "the face of the bid indicates the bidder's intent to be bound" by the government's acceptance of the bid, *Orvedahl Constr., Inc.*, 63 Comp. Gen. 288 (B-213408), 84-1 CPD ¶ 405. See *Entwistle Co.*, Comp. Gen. Dec. B-192990, 79-1 CPD ¶ 112, stating:

> When determining the responsiveness of a bid, the controlling factor is not whether the bidder intends to be bound, but whether this intention is apparent from the bid as submitted. 42 Comp. Gen. 502 (1963). Thus, if [the low bidder's] bid is ambiguous, as Entwistle seems to contend, then the intent to be bound is not apparent from the bid submitted and [the low bidder's] bid must be found nonresponsive. See *James W. Boyer Company*, B-187539, November 17, 1976, 76-2 CPD ¶ 433. In 48 Comp. Gen. 757 at 760 (1969), we stated:
>
> > The mere allegation that something is ambiguous does not make it so. Similarly, some factor in a written instrument may be somewhat confusing and puzzling without constituting an ambiguity, provided that an application of reason would serve to remove the doubt. In other words, an ambiguity exists only if two or more *reasonable* interpretations are possible.

Thus, where a bid is subject to two reasonable interpretations, one of which would make it responsive and the other nonresponsive, the bid must be rejected as ambiguous, *Reid & Gary Strickland Co.*, Comp. Gen. Dec. B-239700, 90-2 CPD ¶ 222 (notation on bid schedule stating that bidder had "allowed" $500,000 for doors ambiguous because it could be interpreted as indicating an intent to offer something other than a firm-fixed-price contract); *Banks Ship Rigging Corp.*, Comp. Gen. Dec. B-239853, 90-2 CPD ¶ 181 (two reasonable interpretations concerning bidder's proposed delivery date); *Wasteco Container Servs., Inc.*, Comp. Gen. Dec. B-240309, 90-2 CPD ¶ 372 (bid notation that "prices are based on dumping fees of $26 per ton" created an ambiguity as to intended price under an IFB for a firm-fixed-price contract). The consideration of ambiguous bids for award would give the bidder an unfair competitive advantage by giving it the opportunity to withdraw or affirm the bid after seeing the bids of competitors. In this regard GAO, in *Fire & Tech. Equip. Corp.*, Comp. Gen. Dec. B-192408, 78-2 CPD ¶ 91, stated:

> Only material available at bid opening may be considered by the contracting officer when determining the responsiveness of the bid. To permit explanations after bid opening to render responsive a bid which is nonresponsive on its face would be tantamount to granting an opportunity to submit a new bid. 52 Comp. Gen. 602 (1973). Thus, a nonresponsive bid may not be corrected and it does not matter whether the failure to comply with the requirements of the IFB was due to inadvertence, mistake or otherwise. 45 Comp. Gen. 433 (1966).

In *Don's Wheelchair & Ambulance Serv., Inc.*, Comp. Gen. Dec. B-216790, 85-1 CPD ¶ 82, a bid was found to be nonresponsive because it permitted the bidder to elect one of two prices, only one of which would result in award to the bidder. However, in *Hughes & Hughes*, 68 Comp. Gen. 194 (B-233624), 89-1 CPD ¶ 61, GAO found no ambiguity where the bidder submitted two conflicting bid sheets, reasoning that it was clear that the bid sheet with the later notations was the one that would be binding on the bidder.

[a] Conditioning the Offer

Bids that are ambiguous regarding whether they represent an unconditional offer to comply with the specifications are nonresponsive, *B&C Indus., Inc.*, Comp. Gen. Dec. B-244471.4, 91-2 CPD ¶ 314 (shipping information included with bid created an ambiguity as to whether bid would conform to the IFB's packaging requirement); *G.S. Link & Assocs.*, Comp. Gen. Dec. B-238600, 90-1 CPD ¶ 479 (statement that bid would comply with EPA guidelines rendered bid ambiguous with respect to whether the offered paper products would comply with the required waste paper content); *John C. Grimberg, Inc.*, Comp. Gen. Dec. B-218231, 85-1 CPD ¶ 305 (bidder's failure to unconditionally acknowledge referenced sketch created uncertainty concerning whether the bid was an unequivocal offer to meet material requirements of the solicitation). Bids also have been rejected when required descriptive literature submitted with them stated that specifications were "subject to change," *Air & Hydraulic Equip., Inc.*, Comp. Gen. Dec. B-250332, 93-1 CPD ¶ 54. However, if other language negates the "subject to change" provision, the bid has been held to be responsive. See *Yale Materials Handling Corp.*, Comp. Gen. Dec. B-228974.2, 87-2 CPD ¶ 550 (bid need not be rejected as nonresponsive where handwritten statement that all required specifications will be met immediately following the "subject to change" provision effectively deleted such language from bid); and *Waukesha Motor Co.*, Comp. Gen. Dec. B-178494, 74-1 CPD ¶ 329 (cover letter, stating that all equipment would meet specifications, negated the "subject to change" clause and did not render the bid nonresponsive).

If required bid literature—submitted to establish conformance to the specifications—does not clearly indicate such conformance, the bid is considered ambiguous and rejection will result, *AMSCO Scientific*, Comp. Gen. Dec. B-255313, 94-1 CPD ¶ 112. Similarly, where a bidder submits unsolicited bid literature that either takes exception to the specifications or renders the bid ambiguous as to whether or not the item offered will comply with the specifications, the bid will be rejected, *Nu-Lite Elec. Wholesalers, Inc.*, Comp. Gen. Dec. B-248383, 92-2 CPD ¶ 104.

The insertion of unsolicited part or model numbers in a bid, even where included only for a bidder's internal control purposes, creates an ambiguity regarding whether the bidder is offering to comply completely with the specifications, *IFR, Sys., Inc.*, Comp. Gen. Dec. B-222533, 86-2 CPD ¶ 224, *recons. denied*, 86-2 CPD ¶ 601. Thus, a bid containing unsolicited part numbers must be rejected as nonresponsive unless either the bid contains an express statement that the designated parts conform to the specifications or the contracting officer determines, from data available before bid opening, that the parts conform, *Infab Corp.*, Comp. Gen. Dec. B-238423, 90-1 CPD ¶ 506. In *Buckingham Mfg. Co.*, Comp. Gen. Dec. B-239999, 90-2 CPD ¶ 224, a bid ambiguity created by the unsolicited insertion of a part number resulted in rejection because the ambiguity could not be resolved by reference to the bid itself, commercial literature, or other data available at the time of bid opening. See also *Wright Tool Co.*, Comp. Gen. Dec. B-212343, 83-2 CPD ¶ 457; *Abbott Labs.*, Comp. Gen. Dec. B-183799, 75-2 CPD ¶ 171; *Lift Power, Inc.*, Comp. Gen. Dec. B-182604, 75-1 CPD ¶ 13; and 50 Comp. Gen. 8 (B-169813) (1970). However, ambiguities created by unsolicited insertions of model numbers can be resolved by an express bid statement that the designated model numbers comply with the IFB specification, *Millipore Corp.*, Comp. Gen. Dec. B-234979, 89-2 CPD ¶ 31; *Carco Elecs.*, Comp. Gen. Dec. B-186747, 77-1 CPD ¶ 172; *Huey Paper & Material, Stacor Corp.*, Comp. Gen. Dec. B-185762, 76-1 CPD ¶ 382.

Although reference to commercially available literature or to documents that are submitted with the bid may clarify an otherwise ambiguous bid, this literature is to be used only to "fill in the gaps" and may not negate what is in the bid itself, *IFR, Inc.*, Comp. Gen. Dec. B-203391.4, 82-1 CPD ¶ 292. Note, also, that where the contracting agency obtained literature that detracted from the second low bidder's bid, the agency's refusal to consider contemporaneously available literature that showed the bid was in compliance was irrational, *Essex Electro Eng'rs, Inc. v. United States*, 3 Cl. Ct. 277 (1983).

[b] Requests That Vary from the IFB

Bidders can also create uncertainty regarding their bids when they "request" additions to or variations from the IFB, because it is then not clear how such a request should be interpreted. In *National Oil & Supply Co.*, Comp. Gen. Dec. B-198321, 80-1 CPD ¶ 437, one bidder included the following provision:

> Please be advised that National Oil would like to be relieved against freight increases. Due to the unsteady trend of increasing freight rates by the common carriers, we are unable to predict an adequate freight rate. . . . We would wish to escalate our freight rates with verification along with those imposed upon us by carriers.

GAO upheld the agency's determination of nonresponsiveness, explaining:

> With regard to National's contention that the wording in its cover letter was merely precatory in nature, i.e., the expression of a request rather than taking exception to the terms of the invitation, the meaning of those words must be determined within the context of existing circumstances. Here, we do not find it unreasonable to view National's "request" as something more than a mere wish or desire, for if National's bid were accepted it could be argued that DLA would be legally bound, contrary to the IFB's cited clauses, to absorb unanticipated increases in freight costs above and beyond those which might be included in increases in posted prices.
>
> * * *
>
> At best, National's bid, including its cover letter, is subject to two possible interpretations, under one of which it would be responsive and under the other nonresponsive. We have consistently held that the rejection of such a bid is required and that it would be prejudicial to other bidders to permit the bidder creating the ambiguity to select, after bid opening, the interpretation to be adopted.

See also *A & Z Eng'g Co.*, Comp. Gen. Dec. B-222806, 86-1 CPD ¶ 388 (bid containing a request to use a different type of alloy than required in the IFB was properly rejected as nonresponsive since the request indicated that without the deviation the bidder could not manufacture the item as specified in the invitation).

GAO has allowed bidders to "confirm" bids to a contracting officer who finds them ambiguous, stating that, in such situations, the low bidder is not given any advantage in being permitted to confirm its intended bid price because the confirmation is not inconsistent with the only reasonable interpretation of the bid, *Wismer & Becker Contracting Eng'rs*, Comp. Gen. Dec. B-198674, 80-2 CPD ¶ 170. See also 39 Comp. Gen. 653 (B-141591) (1960).

FAR 52.232-15 prescribes a standard solicitation clause for use when no progress payments are intended:

> PROGRESS PAYMENTS NOT INCLUDED (APR 1984)
>
> A progress payments clause is not included in this solicitation, and will not be added to the resulting contract at the time of award. Bids conditioned upon inclusion of a progress payment clause in the resulting contract will be rejected as nonresponsive.

In contrast, FAR 32.405(b) does not prohibit the request for advance payments:

> Bidders may request advance payments before or after award, even if the invitation for bids does not contain an advance payment provision. However, the contracting officer shall reject any bid requiring that advance payments be provided as a basis for acceptance.

Prior to the GAO decision in *Canadian Commercial Corp.*, 62 Comp. Gen. 113 (B-207777), 83-1 CPD ¶ 16, *recons. denied*, 83-1 CPD ¶ 275, bids containing requests for advance payments were held responsive while bids requesting progress payments were held as conditions that rendered the bid nonresponsive. Compare *Potomac Iron Works, Inc.*, Comp. Gen. Dec. B-200075, 81-1 CPD ¶ 15 (bid "requesting" advance payments was not a condition or qualification, and rejection was improper) with 45 Comp. Gen. 809 (B-158915) (1966) (bid stating "Progress Payments are Requested" under an IFB that did not provide for progress payments renders bid nonresponsive, even though the word "request" is, in the ordinary sense, precatory in nature).

In *Canadian Commercial Corp.*, the distinction between progress payments and advance payments was held irrelevant. GAO stated that the issue is not whether a bidder requests advance or progress payments, but whether the request is a condition or a mere wish or desire. Whether a "request" is a condition or a mere wish or desire must be determined from the meaning of the words under the circumstances. GAO, relying primarily on the reasoning in *Potomac Iron Works, Inc.*, Comp. Gen. Dec. B-200075, 81-1 CPD ¶ 15, determined that the statement, "Progress payments, in accordance with governing U.S. procurement regulations, are requested" was a precatory request that did not affect the responsiveness of the bid. See also *GMI, Inc.*, 69 Comp. Gen. 557 (B-239064), 90-2 CPD ¶ 8, where a request for progress payments did not render a bid nonresponsive in the absence of circumstances showing that the request was more than a mere wish or desire.

[c] Uncertainties as to Price

If a total bid price is uncertain, the bid is not responsive, *Associated Mech., Inc.*, Comp. Gen. Dec. B-243892, 91-2 CPD ¶ 192 (telegram submitted prior to bid opening created uncertainty as to whether bidder proposed to deduct $311.00 from bid or $311,000 because it was unclear whether a comma or period preceded the zeros); *Harris Constr. Co.*, 64 Comp. Gen. 702 (B-218387.2), 85-2 CPD ¶ 92 (garbled telegraphic modification increasing bid price to an uncertain amount received prior to bid opening required rejection of bid). Similarly, a bid is nonresponsive if its intended price cannot be determined from all the bid documents submitted at the time of bid opening, *Massillon Constr. & Supply, Inc.*, Comp. Gen. Dec. B-407931, 2013 CPD ¶ 85 (bid contained no rice for optional work); *United States Coast Guard—Advance Decision*, Comp. Gen. Dec. B-252396, 93-1 CPD ¶ 286 (cover letter submitted with bid requesting additional charge of $1,000 per hour for government preacceptance tests when the IFB provided no means of estimating the amount of testing and, thus, the bid price could not be calculated with any certainty). However, an ambiguity as to a low bidder's intended price does not render a bid nonresponsive if the bid would be low by a significant margin under all possible interpretations, *Ryan Co.*, Comp. Gen. Dec. B-238932, 90-1 CPD ¶ 557. GAO holds that these ambiguities can be resolved without prejudice to other bidders, *Energy Maint. Corp.*, 64 Comp. Gen. 425 (B-215281.3), 85-1 CPD ¶ 341. Similarly, GAO has stated that when it is clear from the bid itself what price was intended, or where on the basis of logic and experience it can be determined that only one price makes sense, correction of a bid and displacement of another bidder is allowed, *J&J Maint., Inc.*, Comp. Gen. Dec. B-251355, 93-1 CPD ¶ 187. See also *R.R. Gregory Corp.*, Comp. Gen. Dec. B-217251, 85-1 CPD ¶ 449, holding that award to the bidder was proper even though the bid contained a price discrepancy because only one price could reasonably be regarded as the intended bid.

[d] Offers to Comply

Bidders often attempt to resolve ambiguities in their bids by including statements to the effect that they are offering to comply with all terms of the invitation. Overall offers to comply will cure bid discrepancies only if they are specific, resolve all doubts as to the bidder's intention, and remove any option to deviate from the invitation, Comp. Gen. Dec. B-179024, Oct. 30, 1973, *Unpub.* Successful offers to comply were present in *Millipore Corp.*, Comp. Gen. Dec. B-234979, 89-2 CPD ¶ 31 (insertion of a model number did not render bid ambiguous since the bid contained an express statement that the product identified conformed to the technical requirements of the IFB); *Syntrex Inc.*, Comp. Gen. Dec. B-212781.2, 84-1 CPD ¶ 522 (bidder's cover letter offering to comply with all material specifications overcame "subject to change" clause contained in bid literature); *Calma Co.*, Comp. Gen. Dec. B-209260.2, 83-2 CPD ¶ 31 (statement in bidder's descriptive literature indicating that it intends to supply processors with the 500,000 bytes of memory required by the IFB clarifies preprinted literature indicating that the processors have only 440,000 bytes of memory).

However, a "blanket" promise of compliance with the specifications of an IFB is not sufficient to establish the responsiveness of a bid that does not demonstrate compliance apart from that promise, *Electrophysics Corp.*, Comp. Gen. Dec. B-258674, 95-1 CPD ¶ 63 (bid rejected as nonresponsive where descriptive literature submitted with bid failed to demonstrate that the offered product would satisfy a salient characteristic in the IFB, despite a blanket statement of compliance); *Amjay Chems.*, Comp. Gen. Dec. B-252502, 93-1 CPD ¶ 426 (blanket offer in bid cover letter to comply with all IFB specifications was properly rejected as nonresponsive where unsolicited descriptive literature established noncompliance); *IRT Corp.*, Comp. Gen. Dec. B-233134, 89-1 CPD ¶ 216 (blanket statement in cover letter that bidder will meet specification requirements did not cure bid's failure to provide required descriptive literature); *JoaQuin Mfg. Corp.*, Comp. Gen. Dec. B-228515, 88-1 CPD ¶ 15 (bid rejected as nonresponsive where required descriptive literature demonstrated nonconformance with IFB requirement, despite blanket statement of compliance); *Eclipse Sys., Inc.*, Comp. Gen. Dec. B-216002, 85-1 CPD ¶ 267 (bidder's general reference to supplying item in accordance with military specification did not overcome ambiguity raised in cover letter). See also *Zero Mfg., Co.*, Comp. Gen. Dec. B-210123.2, 83-1 CPD ¶ 416 (bid that did not conform was not cured by statement that item would be equal to or better than that specified).

[5] Failure to Furnish Required Items or Information

Failure to furnish items or information required to be submitted with the bid can render a bid nonresponsive. However, if sufficient information is otherwise contained in the bid documents to determine the missing information, the bid will be responsive, *Inland Assocs.*, Comp. Gen. Dec. B-213579, 84-1 CPD ¶ 398 (registration status of modem is matter of FCC public record); *Abbot Power Corp.*, Comp. Gen. Dec. B-192792, 79-1 CPD ¶ 295 (failure to submit dimensions on drawing was a minor deviation since the information could be obtained from other information in the bid).

[a] Descriptive Literature and Bid Samples

When descriptive literature or bid samples are necessary to determine if the items being offered meet the specifications, standard solicitation provisions are used to alert the bidders to this requirement. See the Bid Samples provision in FAR 52.214-20 and the Descriptive Literature provision in FAR 52.214-21. These provisions state that failure to furnish the literature or samples will require rejection of the bid. They are operative only when the IFB specifies the precise descriptive literature or bid samples that are required. Alternate provisions are to be used if there is a possibility that the requirement will be waived for some of the bidders. FAR 14.202-5(d) provides that an agency may waive the descriptive literature requirements for specific bidders. It states that:

> (1) The contracting officer may the requirement for descriptive literature if—
>
> (i) The bidder states in the bid that the product being offered is the same as a product previously or currently being furnished to the contracting activity; and
>
> (ii) The contracting officer determines that the product offered by the bidder complies with the specification requirements of the current invitation for bids. When the contracting officer waives the requirement, see 14.201-6(p)(2).
>
> (2) When descriptive literature is not necessary and a waiver of literature requirements of a specification has been authorized, the contracting officer must include a statement in the invitation that, despite the requirements of the specifications, descriptive literature will not be required.
>
> (3) If the solicitation provides for a waiver, a bidder may submit a bid on the basis of either the descriptive literature furnished with the bid or a previously furnished product. If the bid is submitted on one basis, the bidder may not have it considered on the other basis after bids are opened.

FAR 14.202-4(e) contains a similar provision permitting the waiver of the requirement for bid samples. See *Entwistle Co.*, Comp. Gen. Dec. B-192990, 79-1 CPD ¶ 112, permitting waiver of a descriptive literature requirement where the bidder instead provided the contract number of a contract where it had supplied equipment that met the contract specifications. GAO affirmed the contracting officer's determination that this was an expression of intent to supply that equipment on the current contract.

Failure to furnish the descriptive literature called for by the IFB will result in a bid's rejection as nonresponsive, *American Material Handling, Inc.*, Comp. Gen. Dec. B-278107, 97-2 CPD ¶ 177 (reservation of right in descriptive literature to make specification changes without notice); *FFR-Bauelemente + Bausanierung GmbH*, Comp. Gen. Dec. B-274828, 97-1 CPD ¶ 7 (failure to include descriptive literature to ascertain whether item met salient characteristics of brand-name product); *RMTC Sys., Inc. v. Dep't of the Army*, GSBCA 12637-P, 94-2 BCA ¶ 26,614 (failure to submit descriptive literature to demonstrate that product was "equal" to the specified brand name); *AMSCO Scientific*, Comp. Gen. Dec. B-255313, 94-1 CPD ¶ 112 (ambiguous descriptive literature);

TIMCO Elec. Power & Controls, Inc., Comp. Gen. Dec. B-248308, 92-2 CPD ¶ 84 (bid did not contain specific descriptive literature required by IFB); and *BSC Indus., Inc.*, Comp. Gen. Dec. B-237299, 90-1 CPD ¶ 152 (agency received only partial descriptive literature; bidder contention that far more literature had been provided with bid was unproven). Even where the descriptive literature requirement is imprecise, a bid may be rejected for failure to include any of the required literature or if what was furnished evidences nonconformance with the specifications, *Baker Co.*, Comp. Gen. Dec. B-216220, 85-1 CPD ¶ 254; *Clackamas Commc'ns, Inc.*, Comp. Gen. Dec. B-209387, 83-1 CPD ¶ 549.

Imprecise requirements for descriptive data will be less likely to lead to a determination that a noncompliant submission is nonresponsive. For example, failure to furnish "drawings . . . showing overall dimensions of reactors" as required by the IFB did not render a bid nonresponsive in *Abbot Power Corp.*, Comp. Gen. Dec. B-192792, 79-1 CPD ¶ 295. In that case, GAO found that the agency reasonably determined that the purpose of the clause was "substantially met" by the material furnished, though the bidder did not state that the offered product was a previously furnished one. See also *Tri-Servs., Inc.*, Comp. Gen. Dec. B-245698, 92-1 CPD ¶ 75, stating that a bidder's failure to include required information regarding overhead and costs did not render the bid nonresponsive since the information was not material to bid evaluation or the bidder's obligation to perform.

Failure to provide bid samples as required by an invitation will also render a bid nonresponsive, *B.E.C. Med. Prods.*, Comp. Gen. Dec. B-256483, 94-1 CPD ¶ 159 (late submission of bid sample); *EEV, Inc.*, Comp. Gen. Dec. B-253061, 93-2 CPD ¶ 52; *Canon U.S.A., Inc.*, Comp. Gen. Dec. B-249521, 92-2 CPD ¶ 388, *recons. denied*, 93-1 CPD ¶ 219. Where an invitation requires that bid samples strictly comply with listed specifications, a sample that fails to demonstrate conformance renders a bid nonresponsive, *Aqua-Trol Corp.*, Comp. Gen. Dec. B-246473.2, 92-1 CPD ¶ 420; *ATD-American Co.*, Comp. Gen. Dec. B-227134, 87-2 CPD ¶ 58. However, bid samples need not meet every specification requirement that the items to be furnished under the contract must meet, but rather may be evaluated solely for the characteristics specified in the solicitation's bid sample provision, *LSL Indus., Inc.*, Comp. Gen. Dec. B-239486, Sept. 10, 1990, *Unpub.*; *Sherwood Med. Co.*, Comp. Gen. Dec. B-231184, 88-2 CPD ¶ 171; FAR 14.202-4(b)(3) and (d)(1)(ii). In addition, a bid is not necessarily nonresponsive for failing to include a bid sample "as part of the bid" as long as the sample is submitted to the agency in a responsive manner that identifies it with the procurement before bid opening, *Alan Scott Indus.*, Comp. Gen. Dec. B-200391.2, 81-1 CPD ¶ 525; *Unique Packaging, Inc.*, 54 Comp. Gen. 157 (B-181940), 74-2 CPD ¶ 125.

Submission of bid samples or descriptive literature not required by the IFB will generally not be considered as qualifying the bid and will be disregarded, FAR 14.202-4(f) and FAR 14.202-5(e). However, if the literature or sample indicates that the bidder is conditioning its bid, it will be rejected as nonresponsive, *Products for Indus.*, Comp. Gen. Dec. B-257463, 94-2 CPD ¶ 128.

[b] Bid Guarantees

FAR 14.404-2(j) states that when a bid bond or guarantee is required and a bidder fails to furnish it in accordance with the IFB, the bid shall be rejected as nonresponsive unless one of the stated exceptions in FAR 28.101-4, as discussed in A.3.b. of this section, is otherwise applicable, *Secur-Data Sys., Inc.*, Comp. Gen. Dec. B-255090, 94-1 CPD ¶ 68 (bid that did not include required bid guarantee was properly rejected despite the bidder's assertion that the guarantee was included in its bid package).

Submission of a defective bid bond or bid guarantee is as fatal to a bid as the total failure to submit a bid bond or guarantee. The determinative question as to the acceptability of bonds and guarantees containing defects is whether the bid documents submitted with the bid establish that the bond or guarantee is enforceable by the government should the bidder fail to meet its obligations, *A.W. & Assocs.*, 69 Comp. Gen. 737 (B-239740), 90-2 CPD ¶ 254; *F&F Pizano*, 64 Comp. Gen. 805 (B-219591.2), 85-2 CPD ¶ 234. For example, in *BCI Constr. USA, Inc.*, Comp. Gen. Dec. B-407451, 2012 CPD ¶ 349, a bid bond that referenced an incorrect solicitation number was deemed defective, and in *BW JV1, LLC*, Comp. Gen. Dec. B-401841, 2009 CPD ¶ 249, a bid bond executed by only one member of a joint venture was defective when the joint venture agreement required the signature of both companies. Similarly, in *Interstate Rock Prods., Inc. v. United States*, 50 Fed. Cl. 349 (2001), a bid bond that omitted the penal sum was defective.

Copies of bid guarantees (rather than the original document) have not been accepted as proof that the signatory is bound. See *TJ's Marine Constr. LLC*, Comp. Gen. Dec. B-402227, 2010 CPD ¶ 19, stating:

> For the bid guarantee to be viewed as enforceable, the surety must appear to be clearly bound based on the information in the possession of the contracting officer at the time of bid opening. *Frank & Son Paving, Inc.*, B-272179, Sept. 5, 1996, 96-2 CPD ¶ 106 at 1. Copies of bid guarantee documents, whether transmitted electronically or hand-delivered, generally do not satisfy the requirement for a bid guarantee since there is no way, other than by referring to the original documents after bid opening, for the contracting agency to be certain that there had not been alterations to which the surety had not consented and could use as a basis to disclaim liability. *Excel Bldg. & Dev. Corp.*, B-401955, Dec. 23, 2009, 2009 CPD ¶ at 3. See *Jay-Brant Gen. Contractors*, B-274986, Jan. 10, 1997, 97-1 CPD ¶ 17 at 3; *G&A Gen. Contractors*, B-236181, Oct. 4, 1989, 89-2 CPD ¶ 308 at 1.

When the bid guarantee is signed by a person with a power of attorney, the bidder must submit proof of the authenticity of the power of attorney. There has been considerable controversy as to the extent of proof required. Compare *Hawaiian Dredging Constr. Co. v. United States*, 59 Fed. Cl. 305 (2004) (computer-generated powers of attorney and certificates with mechanically applied signatures proof of authenticity), with *All Seasons Constr., Inc.*, Comp. Gen. Dec. B-291166.2, 2002 CPD ¶ 212, and *All Seasons Constr., Inc. v. United States*, 55 Fed. Cl. 175 (2003) (signatures generated as part of the power of attorney, as opposed to being affixed to the document after its generation, do not serve to validate the document). See also *Hydro-Dredge Corp.*, Comp. Gen. Dec. B-214408, 84-1 CPD ¶ 400 (although penal amount listed on the bid bond was sufficient, the attorney-in-fact who signed the bond had the authority to bind the surety for only a fraction of the amount required by the IFB); *H.W. Houston Constr. Co.*, Comp. Gen. Dec. B-258581, 95-1 CPD ¶ 47 (bid properly rejected where the solicitation number on the bid bond was "whited out" and retyped without evidence of the surety's consent, and there was another ongoing procurement to which the altered number could refer); and *Pioneer Constr. Co.*, Comp. Gen. Dec. B-227948, 87-2 CPD ¶ 279 (bid properly rejected where the penal amount was typed over "white out," and there was no evidence that the surety had consented to an alteration).

Failure to include a penal sum on a bond also results in a nonresponsive bid, *Allen County Bldrs. Supply*, 64 Comp. Gen. 505 (B-216647), 85-1 CPD ¶ 507. Failure to provide a bid bond or guarantee that is effective for the entire bid acceptance period also renders a bid nonresponsive, *J.C. & N. Maint., Inc.*, Comp. Gen. Dec. B-229556, 87-2 CPD ¶ 567; *McNamara–Lunz Warehouses, Inc.*, Comp. Gen. Dec. B-188100, 77-1 CPD ¶ 448, *recons. denied*, 77-2 CPD ¶ 149. However, where the government extends the bid acceptance period but fails to require extension of the bid bond, expiration of the bid bond prior to award does not render a bid nonresponsive, *Holk Dev., Inc.*, Comp. Gen. Dec. B-230830.2, 88-2 CPD ¶ 543; *Engle Acoustic & Tile, Inc.*, Comp. Gen. Dec. B-190467, 78-1 CPD ¶ 72.

FAR 28.101-2(b) requires bid guarantees to be for a minimum of 20% of the bid price but not to exceed $3 million. However, FAR 28.101-4(c)(2) requires waiver of the deficiency in the amount of the bid guarantee if the guarantee amount submitted is "equal to or greater than the difference between the offer price and the next higher acceptable offer." Such waiver has been accepted by GAO, *Centex-Great Sw. Corp.*, Comp. Gen. Dec. B-258578, 95-1 CPD ¶ 19, and waiver was required in one case, *Haag Elec. & Constr., Inc.*, 70 Comp. Gen. 180 (B-240974), 91-1 CPD ¶ 29. However, GAO has affirmed the exercise of discretion by a contracting officer that determined that the bid guarantee was not sufficient to equal the difference in bids in an indefinite-delivery, indefinite-quantity contract where the bids were stated in terms of multipliers, not dollar amounts, *Apex Servs., Inc.*, Comp. Gen. Dec. B-255118, 94-1 CPD ¶ 95. See also *P.B. Eng'g Co.*, Comp. Gen. Dec. B-244640, 91-2 CPD ¶ 80 (bid nonresponsive when bid guarantee 24% lower than required amount); and *Drill Constr. Co.*,

Comp. Gen. Dec. B-239783, 90-1 CPD ¶ 538 (submission of bid bond for half the required penal amount rendered bid nonresponsive).

FAR 28.202 provides guidance on the use of corporate sureties for bid bonds and requires that only sureties listed in Department of Treasury Circular 570 will be acceptable. Thus, bids submitting bonds by other corporate sureties are nonresponsive, *Envirotox Techs., Inc.*, Comp. Gen. Dec. B-250091, 92-2 CPD ¶ 186. See also *Siska Constr. Co.*, Comp. Gen. Dec. B-218428, 85-1 CPD ¶ 669, *recons. denied*, 85-2 CPD ¶ 102 (lack of notice in solicitation that unlisted surety was unacceptable is not an excuse for using unlisted surety, because the requirement for listed surety is in regulations and instructions to bond form).

Bid bonds may be furnished by individual sureties if the surety pledges assets equal to the amount of the bond, FAR 28.203. See *C. E. Wylie Constr. Co.*, Comp. Gen. Dec. B-234225, 89-1 CPD ¶ 427 (bid responsive where individual sureties demonstrated sufficient net worth to cover the penal amounts of the bonds); and *O.V. Campbell & Sons Indus., Inc.*, Comp. Gen. Dec. B-229555, 88-1 CPD ¶ 259 (completed SF 24 is proper "on its face" when executed by two individual sureties whose affidavits indicate that, subject to further investigation, they both have a net worth at least equal to the penal amount of the bond). A bid containing bid bonds furnished by individual sureties is responsive even if the sureties fail to file a pledge of assets, *Burtch Constr.*, Comp. Gen. Dec. B-240695, 90-2 CPD ¶ 423; *R.C. Benson & Sons, Inc.*, Comp. Gen. Dec. B-240251.2, 90-2 CPD ¶ 92. This is because a pledge of assets assists the contracting officer in determining the financial acceptability of individual sureties, which is a matter of responsibility, not responsiveness.

FAR 28.203-1 provides that funds pledged by individual sureties can be provided by either an escrow account or a lien on real property. The requirements for an escrow account are very demanding. See *K.C. Elec. Constr.*, Comp. Gen. Dec. B-411591, 2015 CPD ¶ 277, finding that the agency properly rejected a bid guarantee because the escrow account did not (1) contain the contracting agency's name; (2) provide the CO with the sole and unrestricted right to draw upon any or all funds deposited in the account; and (3) provide that the terms of the escrow account could not be amended without the CO's consent. FAR 28.203-2 provides that only cash, readily marketable assets or irrevocable letters of credit are acceptable assets. In *Tip Top Constr. Corp.*, Comp. Gen. Dec. B-311305, 2008 CPD ¶ 91, GAO agreed that coal was not a readily marketable asset.

Where the bidder named on the bid form differs from the principal name on the bid bond, the bid must be rejected unless it can be established that the bidder is "the same legal entity as the principal," *Gem Eng'g Co.*, Comp. Gen. Dec. B-251644, 93-1 CPD ¶ 303; *Scotsman Grp., Inc.*, Comp. Gen. Dec. B-245634, 92-1 CPD ¶ 57 (bid properly rejected where publicly available information submitted after bid opening did not demonstrate that the principal named on the bid bond and the named bidder were the same legal entity); *New Solid, Ltd.*,

Comp. Gen. Dec. B-246357, 92-1 CPD ¶ 163 (bid properly rejected where bid bond identified "Eugene E. and Ingride Harmon" as principals, and the bidder identified in the bid form was "Eugene E. Harmon, owner"). See also *Tower Elevator Corp.*, Comp. Gen. Dec. B-192064, 78-2 CPD ¶ 188, stating that wholly owned subsidiaries and parent corporations are not "identical legal entities." Compare *Castle Floor Covering*, 70 Comp. Gen. 530 (B-242718), 91-1 CPD ¶ 510, where waiver of the defect was required because a cashier's check made out to "Farmers Home Bureau, U.S. Government" would be binding even though the procurement was by the "Farmers Home Administration."

The form of the bid guarantee may vary so long as the requisite monetary obligation by the surety is certain, *Niles Janitor Serv. & Supply, Inc.*, Comp. Gen. Dec. B-246575.3, 92-1 CPD ¶ 256 (bid properly rejected as nonresponsive where irrevocable letter of credit incorporated a force majeure provision of the Uniform Customs and Practices for Documentary Credits Act, which created uncertainty as to the liability of the issuing bank); *Central Mech., Inc.*, 61 Comp. Gen. 566 (B-206555), 82-2 CPD ¶ 150 (bidder's offer to assign funds allegedly due the bidder from the government was rejected because the amount actually owed was undetermined); *Colorado Elevator Serv., Inc.*, Comp. Gen. Dec. B-206950.2, 82-1 CPD ¶ 434 (letter of credit from a bank stating that it is subject to the bank's standard review process is not a firm commitment and renders bid nonresponsive). Where a bid guarantee does not list the United States as the obligee, an agency may waive the noncompliance since the guarantee correctly identified the offeror, the solicitation number, and the name of the location of the project involved, *S.J. Amoroso Constr. Co.*, Comp. Gen. Dec. B-240687, 90-2 CPD ¶ 432; *Nationwide Roofing & Sheet Metal, Inc.*, 64 Comp. Gen. 474 (B-216845), 85-1 CPD ¶ 454 (use of United States Postal Service bond form for a GSA procurement did not render bid nonresponsive where the intent of the surety and the principal to be bound to the government was clearly shown).

[c] List of Subcontractors

Generally, a requirement to list subcontractors or suppliers in bids involves a matter of responsibility, because an agency utilizes these lists to evaluate subcontractor qualifications or the bidder's ability to meet equal employment opportunity requirements, *CDM Fed. Programs Corp.*, Comp. Gen. Dec. B-249022, June 23, 1992, *Unpub.*; *Norfolk Dredging Co.*, Comp. Gen. Dec. B-229572.2, 88-1 CPD ¶ 62; *A. Metz, Inc.*, Comp. Gen. Dec. B-213518, 84-1 CPD ¶ 386. However, if the requirement for bidders to list their proposed subcontractors is intended to prevent "bid shopping," the failure to furnish required subcontractor lists requires rejection of a bid as nonresponsive, *Industrial Structures, Inc.*, 64 Comp. Gen. 768 (B-219500), 85-2 CPD ¶ 165; *Lazos Constr. Co.*, Comp. Gen. Dec. B-211966, 83-2 CPD ¶ 201; *McCrory Constr. Co.*, Comp. Gen. Dec. B-192913, 79-1 CPD ¶ 64. A contractor who plans to do categories of work with its own employees must so indicate if required by the

IFB, or the bid will be found nonresponsive for failure to list subcontractors, *Brisk Waterproofing Co. v. GSA*, Civ. Action No. 77-0659 (D.D.C. 1977). The listing of alternate subcontractors also renders a bid nonresponsive, *Burn Constr. Co.*, Comp. Gen. Dec. B-192196, 78-2 CPD ¶ 139. See also *Dawson Constr. Co.*, Comp. Gen. Dec. B-208547, 82-2 CPD ¶ 551, finding the rejection of a bid for failing to list all subcontractors improper because the IFB called only for a listing of those doing on-site work.

[6] Accurate Completion of Bids and Documents

Bids and accompanying documents must be accurately completed if they are to be considered responsive. FAR 14.301(d) states:

> Bids should be filled out, executed, and submitted in accordance with the instructions in the invitation. If a bidder uses its own bid form or a letter to submit a bid, the bid may be considered only if
>
> (1) The bidder accepts all the terms and conditions of the invitation; and
>
> (2) Award on the bid would result in a binding contract with terms and conditions that do not vary from the terms and conditions of the invitation.

This rule was applied in *J.C. Adams, Inc.*, Comp. Gen. Dec. B-252132, 93-1 CPD ¶ 394, where a bid was held nonresponsive because the bidder submitted a bid schedule that it had prepared itself, which varied from the material requirements of the solicitation's bid schedule. Similarly, in *Weber Constr.*, Comp. Gen. Dec. B-233848, 89-1 CPD ¶ 309, a bidder's omission of SF 1442, which contained material provisions of the solicitation, rendered the bid nonresponsive, because it was unclear whether the bidder would be unequivocally committed to all the material requirements of the invitation. See also *ATR Logistics Co. LLC*, Comp. Gen. Dec. B-402606, 2010 CPD ¶ 140 (bid nonresponsive when it failed to follow bidding schedule in amendment which it acknowledged); *Dillingham Ship Repair*, Comp. Gen. Dec. B-218653, 85-2 CPD ¶ 167 (bid nonresponsive for failure to include unit prices as required by the solicitation, even though the bid contained a lump sum for the total amount). In addition, a bid that contains uncertainties as to the identity of the bidder must be rejected as nonresponsive because, upon award, the bidder could avoid its obligations under the contract, *Sunrise Int'l Grp., Inc.*, Comp. Gen. Dec. B-252735.2, 93-2 CPD ¶ 58 (award was improper where contracting officer concluded that the bid was submitted by T.B.F. Enterprises using Budget Inns of America (BIA) as a trade name without contemporaneous, publicly available evidence demonstrating that "BIA" was in fact "T.B.F. Enterprises"); *Martin Co.*, Comp. Gen. Dec. B-178540, 74-1 CPD ¶ 234 (bid in the name of "Martin Co., Inc." was properly rejected as nonresponsive because the company bidding was in fact "Martin Co.," a sole proprietorship, and award to anyone other than the bidder named in the bid would be an improper substitution of entities).

Bids may be accepted despite a failure to complete the bid accurately if the deficiency is not material and the obligations of the parties are not altered, *J & K Plumbing & Heating Co.*, 71 Comp. Gen. 241 (B-246000), 92-1 CPD ¶174 (bidder's failure to return bid schedule was waived as a minor informality where bidder signed and submitted SF 1442, which incorporated the specifications of the IFB and therefore obligated the bidder to perform in accordance with the material requirements of the IFB); *Walker Constr.*, Comp. Gen. Dec. B-246759, 92-1 CPD ¶319 (failure to submit a bid for an alternate item does not render a bid nonresponsive where the alternate item was not awarded); *S.J. Amoroso Constr. Co.*, Comp. Gen. Dec. B-240687, 90-2 CPD ¶432 (bid guarantee that did not list the United States as the obligee was waived as a minor defect because the guarantee correctly identified the bidder, the solicitation number, and the name of the location of the project involved); *Hild Floor Mach. Co.*, Comp. Gen. Dec. B-217213, 85-1 CPD ¶456 (failure to furnish spare parts price list is waivable because bidders were not required to commit to specific prices).

Unsigned bids are generally nonresponsive, *FCC Constr., Inc.*, Comp. Gen. Dec. B-250304, 93-1 CPD ¶28; *Stafford Grading & Paving Co.*, Comp. Gen. Dec. B-245907, 92-1 CPD ¶66; *Loop to Loop Messenger Serv.*, Comp. Gen. Dec. B-241068, 90-2 CPD ¶519. Unsigned bids, even though accompanied by bid samples, must be considered nonresponsive, *Jonard Indus. Corp.*, Comp. Gen. Dec. B-192979, 79-1 CPD ¶5. See also Comp. Gen. Dec. B-148235, Mar. 23, 1962, *Unpub.*, stating that the presence of a bidder's representative at bid opening was not sufficient to overcome the lack of a signature on the bid or to indicate an intention to be bound to the material requirements of the solicitation.

If it can independently be established that the bidder submitting an unauthorized bid intended to be bound, the bid should be accepted. See FAR 14.405(c), which allows a bidder's failure to sign a bid to be waived as a minor informality only if:

> (1) The unsigned bid is accompanied by other material indicating the bidder's intention to be bound by the unsigned bid (such as the submission of a bid guarantee or a letter signed by the bidder, with the bid, referring to and clearly identifying the bid itself); or
>
> (2) The firm submitting a bid has formally adopted or authorized, before the date set for opening of bids, the execution of documents by typewritten, printed, or stamped signature and submits evidence of such authorization and the bid carries such a signature[.]

See *Micon Corp.*, Comp. Gen. Dec. B-249231, 92-2 CPD ¶293 (bidder's failure to sign SF 1442 waived where bid bond accompanying the bid was properly signed and referenced the solicitation); *Tomahawk Constr. Co.*, Comp. Gen. Dec. B-243582, 91-2 CPD ¶137 (failure to submit an originally signed bid held a minor informality because accompanying amendments, bid bond, and letter contained original signature of bidder); and *Wilton Corp.*, 64 Comp. Gen. 233 (B-218064), 85-1 CPD ¶ 128 (bidder's failure to sign bid waived as a minor informality where bid was accompanied by a signed amendment acknowledgment). However, an irrevocable letter of credit does not negate a bidder's failure to sign its bid in the same fashion as a properly executed bid bond, because it does not require the bidder's signature as a party to the instrument, *Cable Consultants, Inc.*, Comp. Gen. Dec. B-215138, 84-2 CPD ¶ 127.

The evidence of intent to be bound must be submitted prior to bid opening. To permit submission of this evidence after bid opening would give the bidder an improper advantage, *A & E Indus., Inc.*, Comp. Gen. Dec. B-239846, 90-1 CPD ¶ 527 (bid signed with a rubber stamp signature was properly rejected because there was no evidence that prior to bid opening, the use of a rubber stamp signature had been authorized); *Power Master Elec. Co.*, Comp. Gen. Dec. B-223995, 86-2 CPD ¶ 615 (bid that included typewritten signature does not evidence intent to be bound when typewritten signature was not authorized). In this regard, GAO stated in Comp. Gen. Dec. B-160856, Mar. 16, 1967, *Unpub.*:

> The reasoning behind this rule is that when a bid lacks a proper signature, and there is no other clear indication in the bid submission that the purported bidder intended to submit the bid, the contracting officer has no assurance that the bid was submitted by someone with authority to bind the bidder. For that reason, acceptance of such a bid would not have automatically obligated the named bidder to perform the contract advertised. The test in cases where bids are not manually signed is whether the bid as submitted will result in a binding contract upon acceptance of the bid by the Government without confirmation of the bidder's intention.

Bids must also be signed by authorized employees of the bidder. GAO has held that the level of evidence required to establish the authority of a particular person to sign and thus bind a corporation is for the contracting officer to determine, and that the burden of proof rests with the bidder, *Alpha Q, Inc.*, Comp. Gen. Dec. B-234403.2, 89-2 CPD ¶ 401; *Central Mech. Constr., Inc.*, Comp. Gen. Dec. B-220594, 85-2 CPD ¶ 730; *Dragon Servs., Inc.*, Comp. Gen. Dec. B-208081, 82-2 CPD ¶ 86. The evidence required to establish the authority of the signer to bind a corporation may be presented at any time prior to award. Failure to furnish such information at bid opening will not render a bid nonresponsive, *Southwest Maint. Serv.*, Comp. Gen. Dec. B-258178, 94-2 CPD ¶ 243; *Goss Fire Protection, Inc.*, Comp. Gen. Dec. B-253036, 93-2 CPD ¶ 97.

For other irregularities in the completion of the bid form that may be waived as minor informalities, see *Corbin Superior Composites, Inc.*, Comp. Gen. Dec. B-236777.2, 90-1 CPD ¶ 2 (bidder's failure to complete "contingent fee representation" clause); *Alpha Q, Inc.*, Comp. Gen. Dec. B-234403.2, 89-2 CPD ¶ 401 (failure to return SF 33, the cover sheet used in most government procurements, with signature); *O.V. Campbell & Sons Indus., Inc.*, Comp. Gen. Dec. B-229555, 88-1 CPD ¶ 259 (failure of surety to properly complete bid bonds);

All Star Maint., Inc., Comp. Gen. Dec. B-231618, 88-2 CPD ¶ 181 (bidder's failure to submit the required certifications and representations with bid at bid opening); *TCI, Ltd.*, 65 Comp. Gen. 23 (B-220578), 85-2 CPD ¶ 433 (failure to return the number of copies required by the invitation); *Bond Transfer & Storage Co.*, Comp. Gen. Dec. B-210251, 83-1 CPD ¶ 87 (failure to mark the solicitation number, date, and time of opening on the bid envelope); *Patterson Pump Co.*, Comp. Gen. Dec. B-200165, 80-2 CPD ¶ 453 (failure to return all specification pages where SF 33 was properly executed); *Johnson Auto Parts*, Comp. Gen. Dec. B-182102, 74-2 CPD ¶ 157 (submission of the bid on the addendum rather than on the IFB forms). See also *Excavation Constr., Inc. v. United States*, 494 F.2d 1289 (Ct. Cl. 1974), which held that reference to an incorrect date for an addendum and the use of a superseded job number in the bid were waivable informalities.

[7] Accompanying Letter, Literature, and Other Material

Letters, preprinted forms, descriptive literature, or other material submitted with a bid are considered part of the bid and can affect its responsiveness. Thus, if they condition the bid, they may render it nonresponsive. For example, bids accompanied by cover letters that conditioned the bid were found nonresponsive in *Air Prep Tech., Inc.*, Comp. Gen. Dec. B-252833, 93-1 CPD ¶ 459 (cover letter stating bidder's proposed conveyor system will be powered by a hydraulic motor where IFB required a compressed air motor); *Perkin-Elmer Corp.*, 63 Comp. Gen. 27 (B-236175.2), 89-2 CPD ¶ 352 (cover letter offered a shorter bid acceptance period than required by the IFB); *Taylor-Forge Engineered Sys., Inc.*, 69 Comp. Gen. 54 (B-236408), 89-2 CPD ¶ 421 (cover letter and bid form contained conflicting delivery terms, thus rendering the bid ambiguous); *Northwest Ground Covers & Nursery*, Comp. Gen. Dec. B-201609, 81-1 CPD ¶ 81 (cover letter requested that bidder be allowed to withdraw bid if it was a successful bidder on another government contract).

FAR 14.202-5(e) provides that unsolicited descriptive literature will be treated under the same procedures set forth in FAR 14.202-4(f) for unsolicited bid samples:

> Bid samples furnished with a bid that are not required by the invitation generally will not be considered as qualifying the bid and will be disregarded. However, the bid sample will not be disregarded if it is clear from the bid or accompanying papers that the bidder's intention was to qualify the bid. (See 14.404-2(d) if the qualification does not conform to the solicitation.)

Thus, unsolicited descriptive literature will not be considered as qualifying a bid unless it is clear from the bid as a whole that it is intended as a qualification. In *Balantine's South Bay Caterers, Inc.*, Comp. Gen. Dec. B-250223, 93-1 CPD ¶ 39, GAO stated that unsolicited descriptive literature, which reasonably raised a question regarding whether the offered services complied with the material requirements of the IFB, could not be disregarded, because the cover letter referenced the solicitation number and described the literature as "pertinent information." See also *Delta Chem. Corp.*, Comp. Gen. Dec. B-255543, 94-1 CPD ¶ 175 (bid was properly rejected where unsolicited literature rendered uncertain the bidder's obligation to furnish the exact product called for under the IFB). However, unsolicited descriptive literature that takes exception to the IFB requirements to an immaterial extent only will not render the bid nonresponsive, *Brown Boveri Elec., Inc.*, Comp. Gen. Dec. B-209338, 83-1 CPD ¶ 342.

When descriptive literature is required for bid evaluation, any statements reserving the right to alter or change the specifications generally will render the bid nonresponsive, *Air & Hydraulic Equip., Inc.*, Comp. Gen. Dec. B-250332, 93-1 CPD ¶ 54; *Erincraft, Inc.*, Comp. Gen. Dec. B-235829, 89-2 CPD ¶ 332 (uncontradicted legend on descriptive literature submitted with bid stating that "all specifications are subject to change"); *Galaxy Distrib., Inc.*, Comp. Gen. Dec. B-220535, 85-2 CPD ¶ 441 ("subject to change" legend in required descriptive literature rendered bid nonresponsive because nothing else in the bid indicated that the legend was not intended to reserve the right to change or deviate from the material requirements of the IFB). However, when a bid contains sufficient assurances that the bidder intends to meet all contract requirements, despite the subject to change disclaimer, it may properly be held responsive, *Yale Materials Handling Corp.*, Comp. Gen. Dec. B-228974.2, 87-2 CPD ¶ 550; *Tektronix, Inc.*, 66 Comp. Gen. 704 (B-227800.2), 87-2 CPD ¶ 315 (bid otherwise indicates the bidder's intent to conform to the specifications); *Syntrex Inc.*, 63 Comp. Gen. 360 (B-212781.2), 84-1 CPD ¶ 522 (sufficient indication in the bid that the bidder intended to meet all the contract requirements); *Waukesha Motor Co.*, Comp. Gen. Dec. B-178494, 74-1 CPD ¶ 329 (cover letter stated that "all equipment and tests will be completed to specifications").

Other materials have resulted in findings of nonresponsiveness, even though the bid forms conformed exactly to the IFB. See *Star Brite Constr. Co.*, Comp. Gen. Dec. B-255206, 94-1 CPD ¶ 89 (notation in bid bond that stated bond was null and void if the "contract includes the removal of asbestos"); *Northwestern Motor Co.*, Comp. Gen. Dec. B-244334, 91-2 CPD ¶ 249 (handwritten note on bid created an ambiguity regarding a material requirement of the IFB); and *Contech Constr. Co.*, Comp. Gen. Dec. B-241185, 90-2 CPD ¶ 264 (notations in bid that the required performance schedule was "impossible" created uncertainty as to whether bidder agreed to the required performance terms).

[8] Failure to Acknowledge Amendments

The failure of a bidder to acknowledge receipt of an amendment containing a material requirement prior to bid opening renders a bid nonresponsive. In assessing whether a failure to acknowledge an amendment should have been waived, the issue is whether "something about the change . . . reflect[s] a legitimate need of the agency such that its requirements will not be met if the contractor performs to the unamended specifications," *Stanger Indus., Inc.*, Comp. Gen. Dec. B-279380, 98-1 CPD ¶ 157. See *T&S Maint. Servs.*, Comp. Gen. Dec. B-278598, 98-1 CPD ¶ 54 (an amendment is material, "even if it has only a trivial price impact, if it changes the legal relationship between the parties, such as by increasing or decreasing the contractor's obligation in a material manner"); *Overstreet Elec. Co.*, Comp. Gen. Dec. B-283830, 2000 CPD ¶ 8 ("An amendment is generally not material under this regulation where it has the effect of decreasing the price, quantity, quality, delivery, or the bidder's legal obligations, without materially increasing any of these matters."). There are many examples of nonresponsive bids because of failure to acknowledge a material amendment. See *MG Mako, Inc.*, Comp. Gen. Dec. B-404758, 2011 CPD ¶ 88 (amendment contained material terms affecting legal relationship of the parties); *Skyline ULTD, Inc.*, Comp. Gen. Dec. B-297800.3, 2009 CPD ¶ 128 (amendment added work to original requirement); *Hackney Grp.*, Comp. Gen. Dec. B-261241, 95-2 CPD ¶ 100 (amendment eliminated inconsistency in amount of work to be performed); *Farrar Aerospace*, Comp. Gen. Dec. B-259364, 95-1 CPD ¶ 165 (amendment required the manufacturing of parts stated in the specifications); *G.R. Spanaugle & Sons, Inc.*, Comp. Gen. Dec. B-257784, 94-2 CPD ¶ 178 (amendment limited the hours after regular work hours during which certain construction work could be performed); and *Mike Vanebo*, 64 Comp. Gen. 780 (B-219019), 85-2 CPD ¶ 184 (amendment required upward wage rate revision). This is because, absent acknowledgment of a material amendment, a bidder would not be obligated to the terms of the IFB as amended, *Jenness Woodkuts*, Comp. Gen. Dec. B-257345, 94-2 CPD ¶ 112. Even if the amendment was not acknowledged because it was never received, a bid must be rejected as nonresponsive unless the failure was the result of a deliberate and conscious effort to exclude the bidder from competing for the contract, *Southeastern Enters., Inc.*, Comp. Gen. Dec. B-245491.2, 92-1 CPD ¶ 88; *Shemya Constructors*, 68 Comp. Gen. 213 (B-232928.2), 89-1 CPD ¶ 108; or unless the record indicates that the agency did not make a reasonable effort to mail the amendment in accordance with regulatory requirements, *Andero Constr., Inc.*, 63 Comp. Gen. 253 (B-203898), 82-1 CPD ¶ 133 (agency compliance with a regulation is not established where three of four bidders appear not to have received the amendment in the mail).

FAR 14.405(d)(1) allows a bidder's failure to acknowledge receipt of an amendment to be waived as a minor informality if the bid demonstrates that the bidder received the amendment. For examples of constructive acknowledgment of amendments, see *Mark Dunning Indus., Inc. v. United States*, 142 Fed. Cl. 734 (2019), and *Mark Dunning Indus., Inc.*, Comp. Gen. Dec. B-415890.2, 2018 CPD ¶ 382 (bid included a substantive change required by amendment); *Bonded Maint. Co.*, Comp. Gen. Dec. B-235207, 89-2 CPD ¶ 51 (bid included a new pricing schedule established by an amendment); and *Professional Aviation Maint. & Mgmt. Servs., Inc.*, Comp. Gen. Dec. B-232078, 88-2 CPD

¶ 350 (cover letter stated it would comply with requirement in amendment). But see *C Constr. Co.*, 67 Comp. Gen. 107 (B-228038), 87-2 CPD ¶ 534, holding that award to the bidder was improper because submission of the bid on the amended bid opening date is not sufficient to show that the bidder constructively acknowledged an amendment extending the bid opening date.

FAR 14.405(d)(2) also permits a bidder's failure to acknowledge an amendment to be waived if the amendment is trivial in nature. Thus, in *Pro Alarm Co.*, 69 Comp. Gen. 727 (B-240137), 90-2 CPD ¶ 242, GAO stated that a bidder's failure to acknowledge an amendment could be waived since the amendment had no effect or a negligible effect on quantity, quality, delivery, or price. See also *DBI Waste Sys., Inc.*, Comp. Gen. Dec. B-400687, 2009 CPD ¶ 15 (failure to acknowledge amendment substituting an item that cost the same as the originally specified item); *Lumus Constr., Inc.*, Comp. Gen. Dec. B-287480, 2001 CPD ¶ 108 (failure to acknowledge amendment that merely clarified specification requirements); *Wirco, Inc.*, 65 Comp. Gen. 255 (B-220327), 86-1 CPD ¶ 103 (failure to acknowledge amendment that added two containers to the previously scheduled deliveries because the bidder was obligated to provide the correct number of containers, and the effect on price, if any, was negligible).

In determining whether an amendment has a trivial impact, the increase in the cost of performance and the relative difference between the bid prices will be considered, *Marino Constr. Co.*, 61 Comp. Gen. 269 (B-204970), 82-1 CPD ¶ 167. Thus, a minimal cost increase will not be considered trivial if it represents a material difference between the two lowest bidders, *Gulf Elec. Constr. Co.*, 68 Comp. Gen. 719 (B-235635), 89-2 CPD ¶ 272 (failure to acknowledge amendment with an estimated cost impact of $650 rendered bid nonresponsive because that increase in price was double the difference between the low and second low bid, and 30% of the difference between the lowest bid and the protester's third lowest responsive bid); *Power Sys. Diesel Inc.*, Comp. Gen. Dec. B-224635, 86-2 CPD ¶ 599 (bidder's failure to acknowledge amendment rendered bid nonresponsive because the estimated increase in costs was 9.5% of the difference between the two lowest bids); *M. C. Hodom Constr. Co.*, Comp. Gen. Dec. B-209241, 83-1 CPD ¶ 440 (bidder's failure to acknowledge amendment that increased bid price only 0.25% rendered bid nonresponsive because that increase constituted 11.25% of the difference between the two low bidders); *Navaho Corp.*, Comp. Gen. Dec. B-192620, 79-1 CPD ¶ 24 (bid rejected as nonresponsive because bidder failed to acknowledge amendment that increased bid price by only 0.25% of low bid but was 13.34% of the difference between two lowest bidders).

However, in *K Servs.*, Comp. Gen. Dec. B-238744, 90-1 CPD ¶ 556, the procuring agency properly waived the failure to acknowledge an amendment with an estimated cost impact of $502.50, which was only 0.1% of the bidder's bid and 6.6% of the difference between the low and second low bid. Similarly in *G.C. Smith Constr. Co.*, Comp. Gen. Dec. B-213525, 84-2 CPD ¶ 100, the low bidder's failure to acknowledge an amendment with an estimated increase in contractor costs of $2,390 should not have been rejected, because this was 0.262% of the bidder's bid and 4.92% of the difference between the two low bids. The determination regarding the price impact of an amendment to an IFB may not be based on the value placed on it by the bidder seeking a waiver, but rather on the government's estimate, *Ira Gelber Food Servs., Inc.*, 55 Comp. Gen. 599 (B-184308), 75-2 CPD ¶ 415; 53 Comp. Gen. 64 (B-178640) (1973).

Generally, a bidder's failure to acknowledge an amendment that merely restates or clarifies the original solicitation and does not change the legal obligations it imposed may be waived as a minor informality, *Cedar Elec., Inc.*, Comp. Gen. B-402284.2, 2010 CPD ¶ 79 (waiver proper when amendment made prior requirement more specific); *Futura Sys. Inc.*, 70 Comp. Gen. 365 (B-242060), 91-1 CPD ¶ 327 (rejection was improper where amendment made no substantial changes to the original warranty provision, and, by signing its bid, the bidder was bound to the original IFB); *Adak Commc'ns Sys., Inc.*, 67 Comp. Gen. 208 (B-228341), 88-1 CPD ¶ 74 (although bidder failed to acknowledge an amendment that changed line items for costs and required the use of manufacturer-approved parts and equipment, rejection of the bid was improper because the amendment merely clarified the bidder's obligations to provide parts for maintenance and repair work under the IFB). Compare *John D. Lucas Printing Co.*, Comp. Gen. B-285730, 2000 CPD ¶ 154 (agency should not have waived bidder's failure to acknowledge amendment which clarified patent ambiguity).

However, amendments that have more than a negligible effect on price, quantity, quality, or delivery are material, and the failure to acknowledge them may not be waived, *Specialty Contractors, Inc.*, Comp. Gen. Dec. B-258451, 95-1 CPD ¶ 38 (amendment that changed required color of roofing panels from "dark bronze" to "medium bronze" under circumstances indicating that color was a material requirement); *MIBO Constr. Co.*, Comp. Gen. Dec. B-224744, 86-2 CPD ¶ 678 (amendment deleting the optional use of asbestos roofing materials significantly affected the quality of performance); *Belfort Instrument Co.*, Comp. Gen. Dec. B-218561, 85-2 CPD ¶ 135 (amendment issued to correct defective and ambiguous technical specifications which affected the quality of the services solicited).

Failure to acknowledge an amendment revising wage rates generally cannot be waived because this would give the bidder the opportunity to become ineligible for award by not curing the defect, *Grade-Way Constr. v. United States*, 7 Cl. Ct. 263 (1985). See *Tri-Tech Int'l, Inc.*, Comp. Gen. Dec. B-246701, 92-1 CPD ¶ 304, where failure to acknowledge an amendment increasing wage rates made the bid nonresponsive even though the fringe benefit rate decreased more than the wages increased, and *Promethean Constr., Co.*, Comp. Gen. Dec. B-255222, 94-1 CPD ¶ 78, where failure to acknowledge an amendment increasing wage rates made the bid nonresponsive even though the rate increase impacted a class of workers that the bidder did not intend to use. Thus, failure to acknowledge a wage rate amendment can only be waived if the bidder can demonstrate that it was already obligated to pay the wages in the amendment, *ABC Project Mgmt.*,

Inc., Comp. Gen. Dec. B-274796.2, 97-1 CPD ¶ 74. For example, if the bidder's employees are already covered by a collective bargaining agreement calling for wages as high as those in the revised wage determination, the failure to acknowledge an amendment containing that determination may be waived, *ABC Paving Co.*, 66 Comp. Gen. 47 (B-224408), 86-2 CPD ¶ 436; *Brutoco Eng'g & Constr., Inc.*, 62 Comp. Gen. 111 (B-209098), 83-1 CPD ¶ 9.

Oral rather than written acknowledgment of a material amendment is unacceptable and renders a bid nonresponsive, *Alcon, Inc.*, Comp. Gen. Dec. B-228409, 88-1 CPD ¶ 114; *Protex Sys., Inc.*, Comp. Gen. Dec. B-201146, 84-1 CPD ¶ 265. In *MET Elec. Testing, Inc.*, 60 Comp. Gen. 321 (B-201146), 81-1 CPD ¶ 202, GAO stated at 322-23:

> Permitting oral acknowledgment of a material amendment is detrimental to the competitive bidding process in two ways. First, it allows a bidder "two bites at the apple," by giving it the sole discretion to accept or reject the contract after bid opening, by affirming or denying that it intended to be bound by the amendment and, hence, the agreement. See *National Investigation Bureau, Inc.*, B-191759, July 18, 1978, 78-2 CPD ¶ 44. Second, because of the bidder's failure to timely acknowledge the amendment in writing, the terms of the resulting contract are not clear since the written bid acknowledges the terms of the solicitation, but not relevant amendments.

In *Construction Catering, Inc.*, Comp. Gen. Dec. B-207987, 82-2 CPD ¶ 49, GAO stated, referring to 33 Comp. Gen. 508 (B-119732) (1954), that oral acknowledgment of an immaterial amendment is permissible.

§ 5.04 EVALUATION AND AWARD

10 U.S.C. 3302 (formerly § 2305(b)(3)) states the following requirements with respect to evaluation and award of sealed bids:

> (a) **Opening of bids.**—Sealed bids shall be opened publicly at the time and place stated in the solicitation.
>
> (b) **Criteria for awarding contract.**—The head of the agency shall evaluate the bids in accordance with section 3301(a) of this title without discussions with the bidders and, except as provided in section 3301(b) of this title, shall award a contract with reasonable promptness to the responsible bidder whose bid conforms to the solicitation and is most advantageous to the United States, considering only price and the other price-related factors included in the solicitation.
>
> (c) **Notice of award.**—The award of a contract shall be made by transmitting, in writing or by electronic means, notice of the award to the successful bidder. Within three days after the date of contract award, the head of the agency shall notify, in writing or by electronic means, each bidder not awarded the contract that the contract has been awarded.

10 U.S.C. § 3301, in turn, provides:

> (a) Award.—The head of an agency shall evaluate sealed bids and competitive proposals and make an award based solely on the factors specified in the solicitation.
>
> (b) Rejection.—All sealed bids or competitive proposals received in response to a solicitation may be rejected if the head of the agency determines that such action is in the public interest.

Essentially the same requirements are in 41 U.S.C. § 3702. This language expresses the fundamental goal of sealed bid procurement—to base the award solely on objectively determined lowest cost to the government, 47 Comp. Gen. 658 (B-163890) (1968). A bid price that is inordinately low may only be rejected if the bidder is determined to be nonresponsible, *JCMCS*, Comp. Gen. Dec. B-409407, 2014 CPD ¶ 125. However, such low prices raise the issue of whether the bidder has made a mistake as discussed in Section IV.

The evaluation process necessary to determine which bidder is offering the lowest cost to the government can vary from the simple to the complex, depending on the circumstances of the procurement. For procurements involving the purchase of multiple items, indefinite quantities, or for an extended performance period, the evaluation process becomes more complicated, and evaluation criteria must be stated in the IFB. Price adjustment provisions such as discounts or economic price adjustment clauses can also become part of the evaluation process. The greatest complexity sometimes occurs when "other price-related factors" are introduced into the evaluation formula. All of these issues are addressed in this section.

The section also considers the procedures followed in awarding sealed bid contracts. Difficulties can arise when multiple awards are contemplated or when the contracting agency cannot make the award decision by the time the bids expire. Award based upon bids at below cost (so-called buy-ins) are also considered.

The section concludes with a discussion of cancellation of the procurement after bid opening. 10 U.S.C. § 3301 (formerly § 2305(b)(2)) and 41 U.S.C. § 3701(b) give broad discretion in the area, stating:

> All sealed bids or competitive proposals received in response to a solicitation may be rejected if the head of the agency determines that such action is in the public interest.

However, cancellation is a serious matter because of the time and expense involved in preparing a bid and because bidders can be prejudiced if the competition is reopened after bids have been exposed. Thus, cogent and compelling reasons are usually required to support this course of action.

[A] Evaluation Process

The fundamental rule is that the bid evaluation process must be performed on the basis of the factors set forth in the IFB so that bidders are able to compete on a fair and equal basis, 36 Comp. Gen. 380 (B-127801) (1956).

[1] Evaluation of Bid Prices

The solicitation must set forth the price evaluation method that will be used and the contracting officer must adhere to it. See *Jacobs Transfer, Inc.*, 53 Comp. Gen. 797 (B-180195), 74-1 CPD ¶ 213, where the invitation stated the evaluation would be on the basis of prices under Schedules A and B combined. However, just before bid opening the contracting officer orally stated that only the price of Schedule A would be evaluated. This was held improper because the contracting officer did not adhere to the price evaluation criteria set forth in the invitation. In *Southeastern Servs., Inc.*, 56 Comp. Gen. 668 (B-187872), 77-1 CPD ¶ 390, GAO stated the basic principle at 670:

> Revised evaluation criteria may not be used after bid opening to justify award, because bidders have not competed on that basis.

However, if the protester cannot show harm from the alteration of the price evaluation scheme, the IFB is not required to be cancelled. See *Williams Elevator Co.*, Comp. Gen. Dec. B-210049, 83-2 CPD ¶ 327, where the solicitation called for the evaluation of contract prices for a one-year period, but the contracting officer changed the evaluation method by tripling the prices to reflect the total cost to the government for the full three-year contract. The alteration was upheld because the disappointed bidder failed to show that its price would have been low had the IFB evaluation scheme been followed. Thus, it was not prejudiced by the different evaluation method.

[a] *Accurate Reflection of Lowest Cost*

The IFB evaluation criteria must reflect the lowest cost to the government based on the total work to be performed. If the evaluation scheme does not assure that award will be made to the bidder offering the lowest overall cost to the government during actual performance, cancellation of the IFB is required, *Maintenance Inc.*, Comp. Gen. Dec. B-208036, 83-1 CPD ¶ 631.

Agencies sometimes use evaluation criteria that preclude them from determining which bidder offers the lowest cost to the government. The most common error is overestimating the agency's needs. In *Southeastern Servs., Inc.*, 56 Comp. Gen. 668 (B-187872), 77-1 CPD ¶ 390, *recons. denied, Dyneteria, Inc.*, Comp. Gen. Dec. B-187872, 77-2 CPD ¶ 134, the solicitation for a food service contract calling for the evaluation of meal prices outside the contract range was held improper because it bore no relation to the agency's actual requirements. GAO stated at 670:

> Our office has held that the lowest bidder must be measured by the total and actual work to be awarded. Any measure which incorporates more or less than the work to be contracted in selecting the lowest bidder does not obtain the benefits of full and free competition required by the procurement statutes.

In this case, the IFB evaluation method was based on more meals than the Air Force needed; it did not ensure, therefore, that award would be made to the bidder offering the most favorable cost to the government. See also *Heritage Reporting Corp.*, Comp. Gen. Dec. B-248860.2, 92-2 CPD ¶ 276 (IFB for the base period of an option contract grossly overestimated quantities of transcripts needed by the government); and *W.H. Smith Hardware Co.*, Comp. Gen. Dec. B-228127, 87-2 CPD ¶ 556 (IFB listed a unit as four casters instead of one, which was an overstatement of the agency's needs).

Sometimes the statement of estimated quantities for evaluation purposes is unclear, making it difficult to ascertain the lowest bidder. See *Duramed Homecare, Inc.*, Comp. Gen. Dec. B-260047, 95-1 CPD ¶ 257 (IFB failed to provide estimated quantities for some of the items); *Ferguson-Williams, Inc.*, Comp. Gen. Dec. B-258460, 95-1 CPD ¶ 39 (after bid opening, the agency determined that the three lowest bidders had misunderstood the estimated quantities); *MTL Sys., Inc.*, Comp. Gen. Dec. B-245363, 91-2 CPD ¶ 569 (IFB failed to include a price adjustment for accelerated delivery or the number of items that required the accelerated delivery); and *Robinson Mills & Williams*, Comp. Gen. Dec. B-236956.3, 90-1 CPD ¶ 156 (IFB failed to provide estimates for any of the specific services to be performed).

In some cases, the lowest bidder cannot be ascertained because the line items in the IFB do not include all factors that need to be considered in the evaluation equation. See, for example, *S.W. Monroe Constr. Co.*, Comp. Gen. Dec. B-256382, 94-1 CPD ¶ 362 (IFB failed to include a complete line item for a service that the government wanted performed and the quantity required on a different line item) *Bayfone of Tampa*, Comp. Gen. Dec. B-242925, 91-1 CPD ¶ 535 (the line item for telephone usage did not account for the number of telephones that would be using each type of service); and *Temps & Co.*, 65 Comp. Gen. 640 (B-221846), 86-1 CPD ¶ 535 (IFB calling for an assortment of personnel, but hourly wages excluded the amount of time that each temporary employee would work). In *Exclusive Temporaries of Ga.*, Comp. Gen. Dec. B-220331.2, 86-1 CPD ¶ 232, the line items included both full- and part-time work. It was unclear whether one or both line items should be filled out and what would be used to evaluate the bids. Thus, the IFB resulted in bids that "could not be evaluated on an equal basis" and would not necessarily render the lowest cost.

In some instances, an agency has used a mathematical method in the evaluation scheme that does not result in arriving at the actual lowest bid. In *Chemical*

Tech., Inc., Comp. Gen. Dec. B-187940, 77-1 CPD ¶ 126, the price evaluation entailed the averaging of five prices for varying quantities of monthly meals. However, historical data revealed that 50% of the time the meal service fell under only two of the five meal quantities. Since the method of evaluation gave no assurance that award would be made to the bidder offering the lowest cost to the government, GAO decided that the evaluation scheme was faulty. For another case where averaging was found not to discern the lowest bidder, see *Temps & Co.*, 65 Comp. Gen. 640 (B-221846), 86-1 CPD ¶ 535, where the IFB requested an assortment of personnel at different wage prices, and the agency attempted to average the wages to come up with a low bidder.

A defect in the evaluation scheme caused by a mistake by the agency may also make the lowest bidder difficult to determine. In *Earthworks of Sumter, Inc.*, Comp. Gen. Dec. B-232067.2, 89-1 CPD ¶ 9, bids were to be evaluated on a base period of four months. However, the Air Force mistakenly sent Earthworks a seven-month schedule, on which it consequently bid. The contracting officer tried to rectify the mistake by calculating a four-month bid out of Earthworks' estimate, but after protest, this method was deemed faulty. See also *Balva Financial Corp.*, Comp. Gen. Dec. B-235872, 89-2 CPD ¶ 263 (IFB called for evaluation of the price of one item two times, and therefore the lowest overall price to the government could not be calculated); and *R.P. Densen Contractors, Inc.*, 66 Comp. Gen. 31 (B-222627), 86-2 CPD ¶ 401 (evaluation clause used an algebraic sum of all adjustments applied to the base bid, which did not accurately measure the cost to the government).

As noted earlier, a defective evaluation scheme, such as those mentioned above, does not alone preclude award. Where award of the contract to the current lowest bidder under the defective IFB would serve the best interests of the government and the other bidders would not be prejudiced, award to the lowest bidder is permitted. In *Square Deal Trucking Co.*, Comp. Gen. Dec. B-183695, 75-2 CPD ¶ 206, *recons. denied*, 75-2 CPD ¶ 303, the invitation specified evaluation based on unit prices. One bidder's prices were low for monthly unit charges, but the price for the entire year of the contract was not low. GAO recommended award of the contract on the basis of the lowest overall price rather than on the basis of unit prices.

In cases where the award was unavoidably delayed for administrative reasons or due to protests, resulting in a shortened contract period, award is permitted to a bidder who was evaluated as low under the IFB performance period, even though that bidder's price was not low for the actual, shorter performance period, *Maintenance Pace Setters, Inc.*, Comp. Gen. Dec. B-208768.3, 83-2 CPD ¶ 514; *International Tech. Servs. Corp.*, Comp. Gen. Dec. B-198314, 81-1 CPD ¶ 18. Even though the evaluation of bid prices did not reflect the actual work to be performed, award was sanctioned because bid prices had been exposed, and to resolicit would cost the government as much or more than it would cost to make the award to the current low bidder.

[b] Unbalanced Bids

There are two aspects to unbalanced bidding—"mathematical" unbalancing and "material" unbalancing. A bid is not subject to rejection because of unbalancing unless it is found to be *both* mathematically and materially unbalanced. The first involves a mathematical evaluation to determine whether a bid is based upon inflated prices for some work and perhaps understated prices for other work. See *Wescott Elec. Co.*, Comp. Gen. Dec. B-417448, 2019 CPD ¶ 174, stating that unbalanced bidding cannot occur unless some of the prices are overstated. The second aspect—material unbalancing—involves an assessment of the cost impact of a mathematically unbalanced bid. A bid is materially unbalanced if there is a reasonable doubt that the acceptance of a mathematically unbalanced bid will result in the lowest ultimate cost to the government, *Continental Collection & Disposal, Inc.*, Comp. Gen. Dec. B-238842.2, 90-1 CPD ¶ 591. Unbalanced bidding is used for several reasons: (a) it may help a bidder to conceal its pricing strategy from its competitors; (b) it may permit a bidder to recover larger sums for earlier performed work, giving it both an advance payment as well as shifting some of the risk of the contract to the government; (c) it may enable a bidder to become the lowest evaluated bidder through speculation on the accuracy of the government's quantity estimates in the invitation for bids; and (d) it may be used by bidders as a hedge against losses in cases where a program does not run to completion.

The "materially unbalanced" test is set forth in the Contract Award—Sealed Bidding solicitation provision in FAR 52.214-10(e), which provides:

> The Government may reject a bid as nonresponsive if the prices bid are materially unbalanced between line items or subline items. A bid is materially unbalanced when it is based on prices significantly less than cost for some work and prices which are significantly overstated in relation to cost for other work, and if there is a reasonable doubt that the bid will result in the lowest overall cost to the Government even though it may be the low evaluated bid, or if it is so unbalanced as to be tantamount to allowing an advanced payment.

Another provision at FAR 9.306(j) requires contracting officers to warn offerors not to submit unbalanced offers for contracts that involve separately priced first articles. See also FAR 14.404-2. A bid can be found to be materially unbalanced if it creates a reasonable doubt as to whether award will be made to the lowest cost bid. GAO's view of what constitutes "reasonable doubt" has evolved over the years. In *Lear Siegler, Inc.*, Comp. Gen. Dec. B-205594.2, 82-1 CPD ¶ 632, GAO recognized that when a bid is front-loaded, so that it only becomes low "late" in the contracting period, and the program does not run to completion, the government will not be able to take advantage of the low prices, and therefore will pay more than would be the case if prices had been balanced over the total contracting period. In *Lear Siegler*, the IFB called for the operation of a transportation motor pool with one base period and three option periods. The contracting officer awarded the contract to SAE, and Lear Siegler protested, claiming that the bid was mathematically and materially unbalanced. GAO found that, "in view of SAE's front-loaded bid structure and the fact that it is not until well after the exercise of the third and final option year that SAE's total cost becomes low, there is reasonable doubt that award to SAE will result in the lowest ultimate cost to the Government."

GAO has sometimes determined that an agency's intent to exercise all options suffices to overcome an unbalancing situation. See *Ronsons SDVOSB P&L JV-1*, Comp. Gen. Dec. B-410605, 2015 CPD ¶ 1, finding that the option work for construction was needed and had been budgeted in future years, and *Rust Int'l Corp.*, Comp. Gen. Dec. B-256886.2, 94-2 CPD ¶ 84, finding that there was no doubt that the agency intended to have construction work completed over the option period of two years. However, other cases have made contractor reliance upon this logic dangerous. See, e.g., *Residential Refuse Removal, Inc.*, Comp. Gen. Dec. B-247198.6, 92-2 CPD ¶ 444, observing that despite "a contracting agency's intent to exercise all options, there is sufficient reason to doubt the low ultimate cost anticipated from a mathematically unbalanced bid where it does not become low until very late in a contract term."

Another theory previously advanced by GAO for rejecting a materially unbalanced bid was that a grossly front-loaded bid is "tantamount to an advance payment," which is prohibited by 31 U.S.C. § 3324, except when otherwise expressly authorized by law, *Riverport Indus., Inc.*, 64 Comp. Gen. 441 (B-216707), 85-1 CPD ¶ 364. The rationale for rejection on this basis was that such an advance payment was analogous to an interest-free loan, thereby giving the bidder a competitive advantage, *Barnard-Slurry Walls*, Comp. Gen. Dec. B-274973, 97-1 CPD ¶ 23; *ACC Constr. Co.*, Comp. Gen. Dec. B-250688, 93-1 CPD ¶ 142. GAO no longer applies the advance payment reasoning because FAR 14.408-1(b) calls for price analysis considering unbalanced bids to determine whether they are materially unbalanced using the risk analysis procedures in FAR 15.404-1(g). See *Ultimate Concrete, L.L.C.*, Comp. Gen. Dec. B-412255, 2016 CPD ¶ 201; and *W.B. Constr. & Sons, Inc.*, Comp. Gen. Dec. B-405818, 2012 CPD ¶ 17. Compare *Fire-Trol Holdings, LLC v. United States*, 68 Fed. Cl. 281 (2005), agreeing with this procedure, with *Ultimate Concrete, LLC v. United States*, 127 Fed. Cl. 77 (2016), assessing whether a front-end loaded bid constituted an advanced payment. Note, however, that the Contract Award—Sealed Bidding solicitation provision still embodies the advance payment concept. See *Enco Dredging*, Comp. Gen. Dec. B-284107, 2000 CPD ¶ 44, noting this discrepancy in the FAR but denying a protest where the contracting officer accepted a significantly unbalanced bid because they risk of overpayment was not perceived to be great—based on a payment provision that restricted payment of some costs until the end of the project.

[i] Front-Loaded Construction Contracts

Front-loading of a construction contract follows the same general pattern found in all unbalancing situations, that is, a bidder will usually structure its bid to recover progress payments for early work in amounts significantly in excess of the cost of that work. For an example of a front-loaded construction bid, see *Dement Constr. Co.*, Comp. Gen. Dec. B-192794, 78-2 CPD ¶ 399, where the two low bidders for the construction job submitted the following figures for the first two items of work to be performed:

Item	Universal	Dement	Government's Estimated Cost
1. Mobilization	$2,749,318	$30,000	$22,600
2. Clearing & Grubbing	$120,505	$1,192,000	$202,860

Based on the government's estimated cost, GAO held that the bids must be rejected since "both bidders unbalanced their bids for these early items of work in an effort to recover the sums that must be expended for mobilization and preparation prior to actual commencement of construction." See also *L. W. Matteson, Inc.*, Comp. Gen. Dec. B-290224, 2002 CPD ¶ 89; and *Industrial Bldrs., Inc.*, Comp. Gen. Dec. B-283749, 99-2 CPD ¶ 114, finding rejection of grossly front-loaded bids proper.

To justify a front-loaded bid, the bidder will sometimes state that it included start-up costs in the progress payment schedule, *Jasper Painting Serv., Inc.*, Comp. Gen. Dec. B-251092, 93-1 CPD ¶ 204. In that case, GAO stated:

> Because start-up costs properly may be factored into an offer, a relatively front-loaded price does not automatically establish that an offer is unbalanced. However, the start-up costs may not carry a disproportionate share of the total contract price.

When start-up costs have been factored into the front end of a bid, award is generally not allowed, *ACC Constr. Co.*, Comp. Gen. Dec. B-250688, 93-1 CPD ¶ 142, unless the front-loading is so minor that it represents no more than a proportionate share of the contract work, *Cottrell Eng'g Corp.*, Comp. Gen. Dec. B-252891, 93-2 CPD ¶ 66 (bidder had unique mobilization costs because it was located far away, and prices were not deemed to be inflated). Another situation where some unbalancing has been found unobjectionable is in cases where a bidder intends to acquire unique equipment for which it will have no other use. See *Roan Corp.*, Comp. Gen. Dec. B-211228, 84-1 CPD ¶ 116. See also *Ultimate Concrete, L.L.C.*, Comp. Gen. Dec. B-412255, 2016 CPD ¶ 20, and *Ultimate Concrete, LLC v. United States*, 127 Fed. Cl. 77 (2016) (permitting award to a bidder with a high price for optional work because it was unlikely that such work would be required at the outset of the contract); and *Ken Leahy Constr., Inc.*, Comp. Gen. Dec. B-290186, 2002 CPD ¶ 93 (permitting the inclusion of mobilization costs of option work in the cost of the base work because the costs were not "significantly overstated.").

[ii] Quantity Estimates

Unbalancing can also occur in multiple item requirements and indefinite-quantity contracts. In these contracts, bids are evaluated on the basis of estimated quantities, and unbalancing can occur when a bidder believes that the actual quantities ordered by the government will vary from the estimates. In such cases, the bidder submits an unbalanced bid, with higher prices on items believed to have underestimated quantities and lower prices on items believed to have been overestimated.

For an example of such unbalanced bidding, see *Michael O'Connor, Inc.*, Comp. Gen. Dec. B-183381, 76-2 CPD ¶ 8, involving the installation of partitions in certain government buildings where the bidder submitted the following bids:

IFB Item	IFB Estimated Quantities	Actual Prior Year Requirements	Bld
5	16,000	0	0 (N/C)
31	10	426	$249 per unit

The government based its estimates on an average of the previous years' requirements. The bidder based its bid on only the prior year's actual requirements. For Item 5, the IFB estimate significantly overstated the quantity, and the bidder took advantage of this by bidding "no charge." For Item 31, the bidder increased its unit bid price because the government had underestimated its needs. As a result, the bidder was evaluated low but would not have represented the actual lowest cost to the government. See also *Burney & Burney Constr. Co.*, Comp. Gen. Dec. B-292458.2, 2004 CPD ¶ 49; *Alice Roofing & Sheet Metal Works, Inc.*, Comp. Gen. Dec. B-275477, 97-1 CPD ¶ 86; and *Copy Graphics*, Comp. Gen. Dec. B-273028, 96-2 CPD ¶ 185.

GAO stated in *Robertson & Penn, Inc.*, Comp. Gen. Dec. B-234082, 89-1 CPD ¶ 365, that "a low bid for a requirements type contract is not materially unbalanced unless it can be shown that the Government's estimates are so unreliable that award to the low bidder will not result in the lowest cost to the Government." See *Belton Roofing & Remodeling Co.*, Comp. Gen. Dec. B-277651, 97-2 CPD ¶ 131; and *Ostrom Painting & Sandblasting, Inc.*, Comp.

Gen. Dec. B-250827.2, 93-1 CPD ¶ 390, recommending that the IFB be canceled due to inaccurate government estimates. Thus, to determine that a mathematically unbalanced bid is not materially unbalanced, the government estimate must be sufficiently accurate to ensure that the mathematically unbalanced bid does not create a reasonable doubt that the government will be awarding to the lowest bidder. See *South Atlantic Constr. Co., LLC*, Comp. Gen. Dec. B-286592.2, 2001 CPD ¶ 63 (accuracy of estimates not in question and only few of many items unbalanced); *Beldon Roofing Co.*, Comp. Gen. Dec. B-283970, 2000 CPD ¶ 21 (accuracy of estimates not in question and work to be done at almost same time); *Adam II, Ltd.*, Comp. Gen. Dec. B-209194, 83-2 CPD ¶ 102 (Air Force estimates based on historical experience were sufficiently accurate). If the estimates in the IFB are not sufficiently accurate, the bids will be found unbalanced and the IFB will be canceled, *Edward B. Friel, Inc.*, 55 Comp. Gen. 231 (B-183381), 75-2 CPD ¶ 164. However, there is no requirement that the government's estimates be absolutely correct; they need only come from the best information available, thereby providing a reasonably accurate representation of the agency's needs, *Custom Envtl. Serv., Inc.*, 70 Comp. Gen. 184 (B-241052), 91-1 CPD ¶ 38.

[iii] Option Contracts

Unbalanced bidding occurs in option contracts when prices submitted for the base period are higher than the option year prices. As in other types of contracts, a two-step analysis is followed. First, it must be determined if a bid is mathematically unbalanced. If so, it must then be determined if the bid is materially unbalanced.

GAO has altered the analysis of mathematical unbalancing of option contracts in recent years. Originally, a bid with high base-year prices was found to be balanced if the base year contained only those costs chargeable to that year through normal accounting practices. Thus, a bid would be found to be mathematically balanced if it allocated all start-up costs to the base year or included a high base-year price because it used generally accepted accelerated techniques for allocating equipment costs, *M & M Servs., Inc.*, Comp. Gen. Dec. B-228717, 87-2 CPD ¶ 382; *Fidelity Moving & Storage Co.*, Comp. Gen. Dec. B-222109.2, 86-1 CPD ¶ 476; and *Professional Reprographic Servs.*, Comp. Gen. Dec. B-210608, 83-1 CPD ¶ 653.

GAO has now rejected this reasoning and has held that a bid will be found to be mathematically unbalanced if the government pays more than "reasonable value" for the work even though the "high" prices are based upon the contractor's projected costs, *Eastex Maritime, Inc.*, Comp. Gen. Dec. B-256164, 94-1 CPD ¶ 340 (bid found unbalanced when it allocated all start-up costs to base bid). This rule has been applied to both start-up costs and equipment depreciation costs. See *Residential Refuse Removal*, 72 Comp. Gen. 68 (B-247198.6), 92-2 CPD ¶ 444, stating:

> An individual bidder's business decisions for front-loading costs, e.g., the bidder's use of a particular depreciation method, are not generally material to the issue of mathematical unbalancing. *Mitco Water Labs., Inc.*, B-249269, Nov. 2, 1992, 92-2 CPD ¶ (reasons for front-loading bid to cover equipment renovation costs are irrelevant); *Government Leasing Corp.*, [B-245939, 92-1 CPD ¶ 117] (accelerated depreciation method not considered for determination of mathematical unbalancing); *Westbrook Indus., Inc.*, Comp. Gen. 139, 92-1 CPD ¶ 30 (reason for front-loading of equipment costs not considered for determination of mathematical unbalancing); *Professional Waste Sys., Inc.; Tri-State Servs. of Tex.*, [67 Comp. Gen. 68, 87-2 CPD ¶ 477] (method of financing a bidder's equipment costs not considered for determination of mathematical unbalancing). It is only where, because of the unique nature of the contract or of the equipment required to perform the contract, the equipment will have little or no value to the ordinary bidder in the event of early contract termination that we will consider a bidder's reasons for front-loading. See e.g., *Roan Corp.*, B-211228, Jan. 25, 1984, 84-1 CPD ¶ 116 (front-loading costs in the base year of a bid for a contract to lease a fleet of law enforcement vehicles did not mathematically unbalance the bid where, in the event of early termination, there was no market for leasing fleets of used law enforcement vehicles.) *Id.*

See also *Inventory Accounting Serv.*, Comp. Gen. Dec. B-245906, 92-1 CPD ¶ 116 (even though business reasons existed for front-loading, the fact that it would result in advance payment and possibly a windfall to the bidder made bid mathematically unbalanced); *DGS Contract Servs., Inc.*, Comp. Gen. Dec. B-245400, 92-1 CPD ¶ 16 (offeror expected to "apportion" cost of generic equipment over entire contract period to avoid mathematical unbalancing); and *Omega One Co.*, Comp. Gen. Dec. B-251316.2, 93-1 CPD ¶ 254 (mathematically unbalanced when base was 31 to 46% higher than option prices, and work required no "unique or specialized" equipment). The rule has also been applied to unique performance techniques where an offeror justifies the high front-end costs by the cost of initiating "sophisticated" techniques, *McConico Inv. Mgmt. Corp.*, Comp. Gen. Dec. B-251895, 93-1 CPD ¶ 346. These decisions demonstrate that in order to escape the onus of mathematically unbalancing, option prices must be essentially the same as base year prices. This has been characterized as "value-based analysis"—meaning that GAO is insisting that the analysis be based upon "value" to the government not the costs to be incurred by the contractor.

As already noted, the determination of whether a mathematically unbalanced bid containing options is materially unbalanced has also changed. In early cases, if the government expected to exercise an option and there was a reasonable expectation that funds would be available, GAO held that a mathematically unbalanced bid was not materially unbalanced, *K.P. Food Servs., Inc.*, 60 Comp. Gen. 1 (B-198427.2), 82-1 CPD ¶ 289. However, in *Lear Siegler, Inc.*, Comp. Gen. Dec.

B-205594.2, 82-1 CPD ¶ 632, and subsequent cases, GAO found that even if the government agency expected to exercise the options and funds were available, a bid would be found to be materially unbalanced if the government would not actually realize the cost advantage associated with the mathematically unbalanced bid until late in the contract term. GAO reasoned that there was a risk that the government would not realize such cost advantage if intervening events occurred, such as termination by default or failure to exercise an option, and the contractor would experience a windfall. See, for example, *Williams Elec. Co.*, Comp. Gen. Dec. B-275019, 97-1 CPD ¶ 25 (bid was materially unbalanced because the agency was unsure if it would exercise any of the options, and the protester's bid was low only if all three options were exercised); *Crown Laundry & Dry Cleaners, Inc.*, Comp. Gen. Dec. B-208795.2, 83-1 CPD ¶ 438 (bid was not low until fourth month of second option period, so despite the agency's intent to exercise all options, intervening events could cause a windfall); and *Westbrook Indus., Inc.*, 71 Comp. Gen. 139 (B-245019.2), 92-1 CPD ¶ 30 (when bid is not low until the 35th month, there is reason to believe intervening events could occur). GAO has held that a bid that does not become low until the final contract year is materially unbalanced on its face, *Fidelity Moving & Storage Co.*, Comp. Gen. Dec. B-222109.2, 86-1 CPD ¶ 476; *Inventory Accounting Serv.*, Comp. Gen. Dec. B-245906, 92-1 CPD ¶ 116. In other situations, GAO has determined that when the agency intends to use all of the option periods and there is no evidence to the contrary, there is no reasonable doubt, *MCI Constructors, Inc.*, Comp. Gen. Dec. B-274347, 96-2 CPD ¶ 210. This is more apt to occur when the bid will become low relatively early in the contract, *Grunley Schlosser*, Comp. Gen. Dec. B-274012, 96-2 CPD ¶ 158 (bid became low with the exercise of the first option); *Tri-Ark Indus.*, Comp. Gen. Dec. B-270756, 96-1 CPD ¶ 194 (bid became low in the second month of the first option period); *Integrated Protection Sys., Inc.*, Comp. Gen. Dec. B-254457.2, 94-1 CPD ¶ 24 (bid became low in first six months of first option year); *Omega One Co.*, Comp. Gen. Dec. B-251316.2, 93-1 CPD ¶ 254 (bid became low in second month of second option year, so no reasonable doubt existed); *Aquasis Servs., Inc.*, Comp. Gen. Dec. B-228044, 87-2 CPD ¶ 426 (bid became low in eighth month of first option year, so no reasonable doubt existed). But see *Storage Tech. Corp.*, GSBCA 9345-P, 88-2 BCA ¶ 20,667, where, although the bid did not become low until its fourth option year, the board held that because the contract was for maintenance, the Army would reasonably exercise all options since it intended to keep the equipment.

[iv] First Article Contracts

Unbalanced bidding may also occur in contracts requiring the delivery of first articles. In this situation, a contractor charges a large amount for the first article and lower amounts for production articles. GAO has followed the same reasoning as that used in contracts containing options, holding that, even if special equipment and tooling are needed for those first articles, it is improper not to amortize these costs over all of the articles when that tooling will be needed throughout the period of the contract, *Nebraska Aluminum Castings, Inc.*, Comp. Gen. Dec. B-222476, 86-1 CPD ¶ 582, *recons. denied*, 86-2 CPD ¶ 335, *recons. denied*, 86-2 CPD ¶ 515. Thus, if costs other than the unique costs of manufacturing and testing first articles are allocated to the first article, a mathematically unbalanced bid is likely to be found, *Star Dynamic Corp.*, Comp. Gen. Dec. B-248919.3, 93-1 CPD ¶ 63; *LBCO, Inc.*, Comp. Gen. Dec. B-254995, 94-1 CPD ¶ 57. When a first article price that is mathematically unbalanced is grossly front-loaded it cannot be accepted because that would be tantamount to allowing an advance payment. See *Riverport Indus., Inc.*, 64 Comp. Gen. 441 (B-218626), 85-1 CPD ¶ 364, *recons. denied*, 85-2 CPD ¶ 108 (first article unit prices were $185,000 and the production unit prices were $250); *Islip Transformer & Metal Co.*, Comp. Gen. Dec. B-225257, 87-1 CPD ¶ 327 (first article unit prices were $15,000 and the production unit prices were $408.90); *Nebraska Aluminum Castings*, Comp. Gen. Dec. B-222476, 86-1 CPD ¶ 582, *recons. denied*, 86-2 CPD ¶ 335, and 86-2 CPD ¶ 515 (first article unit prices were $22,510 and the production unit prices were $19.17); *Edgewater Mach. & Fabricators, Inc.*, Comp. Gen. Dec. B-219828, 85-2 CPD ¶ 630 (first article unit prices were $125,000 and the production unit prices were $301).

[v] Alternative to Cancellation

GAO has suggested a number of alternatives to cancelling the invitation in the case of unbalanced bids. In *TWI Inc.*, 61 Comp. Gen. 99 (B-202966), 81-2 CPD ¶ 424, GAO ruled that the Navy's estimate was not sufficiently accurate to assure that a mathematically unbalanced bid would represent the actual lowest cost to the government. It therefore recommended award to the next lowest mathematically balanced bid. In *Dement Constr. Co.*, Comp. Gen. Dec. B-192794, 78-2 CPD ¶ 399, GAO condoned negotiation with an unbalanced bidder to reduce the effect of the unbalancing. The Army originally canceled the IFB because award on the basis of the front-loaded bid would result in an advance payment of funds for work not yet performed. However, after "an understanding" was reached that payment for the item would be "over the life of the contract," the IFB was reinstated.

[c] Time Value of Money

In order to determine which bid represents the actual lowest cost to the government, the time value of money should be considered. See, for an explanation of this basic concept, *Linolex Sys., Inc.*, 53 Comp. Gen. 895 (B-179047), 74-1 CPD ¶ 296, stating at 901:

> A dollar received today is worth more than a dollar received next year, and conversely, to postpone spending a dollar until next year gives one the

> opportunity to earn interest on that dollar or otherwise productively use it for the 1-year period.

For procurements involving a considerable length of time, such as option contracts where base and several option years must be evaluated, good procurement practice would consider the time value of money to ensure that award is made to the bidder representing the "actual" lowest cost to the government. In order for the contracting agency to be able to consider the time value of money in the evaluation of bids, it must be itemized in the IFB as an evaluation factor, *General Tel. Co.*, 57 Comp. Gen. 89 (B-187793), 77-2 CPD ¶ 376 (not appropriate to consider present value in deciding whether to purchase or lease equipment in absence of IFB provision). Neither the FAR nor most agency implementing regulations contain provisions for such consideration.

The government has included IFB provisions for the present value of money in the evaluation process in some procurements. See *Linolex Sys., Inc.*, 53 Comp. Gen. 895 (B-179047), 74-1 CPD ¶ 296, where the following paragraph was used in an ADPE procurement:

> A present value method will be used in calculation of all costs. The discount rate will be applied annually. The rate used will be current average market yield, rounded to the nearest one-eighth of one percent, on outstanding treasury marketable obligations with approximately five years remaining to maturity at the time proposals are received. As an example, if the rate were six percent, the factors would be:

Year from Contract Award	Discount Factor
1	.943
2	.890
3	.840
4	.792
5	.747

This evaluation method could be used in the evaluation process for procurements where front-loading is expected to occur. However, it does not preclude other types of unbalancing. In future solicitations, the government might consider using the rate of interest established by the Secretary of the Treasury. For another example of a bid that took present value into consideration, see *Centurial Prods.*, 64 Comp. Gen. 858 (B-216517), 85-2 CPD ¶ 305 (guidelines established by the Water Resources Council required that agencies determine the present value of future expenditures before converting them to an annual equivalent cost).

Factoring in the time value of money in an evaluation removes much of the advantage that bidders attempt to gain through unbalanced bids, and it is proper to structure an IFB calling for such an evaluation, *Solon Automated Servs., Inc.*, Comp. Gen. Dec. B-206449.2, 82-2 CPD ¶ 548. However, absent a clause requiring consideration of the cost of money, GAO will not consider the additional cost to the government in interest expense that would result from award to a bidder that front-loaded its prices for earlier items, *Farrell Constr. Co.*, 57 Comp. Gen. 597 (B-191786), 78-2 CPD ¶ 45.

One means of quantifying the time value of money is the prompt payment discount. However, FAR 14.408-3 prohibits the consideration of prompt payment discounts for evaluation purposes. See *Alco Envtl. Servs., Inc.*, Comp. Gen. Dec. B-251053.6, 93-2 CPD ¶ 192; *IFR Sys., Inc.*, Comp. Gen. Dec. B-222533, 86-2 CPD ¶ 224; *Hayes Int'l Assocs.*, Comp. Gen. Dec. B-220471, 86-1 CPD ¶ 8; and *O.K. Tool & Die Co.*, Comp. Gen. Dec. B-219806, 85-2 CPD ¶ 398.

As a legislative agency, the Government Printing Office (GPO) is not subject to FAR 14.408-3, and the GPO may therefore consider prompt payment discounts in the evaluation of its bids, *Capitol Hill Blueprint Co.*, Comp. Gen. Dec. B-220354, 85-2 CPD ¶ 550. The IFB must provide that the discount will be used in evaluation, *Advanced Design Fabrication Corp.*, Comp. Gen. Dec. B-246341, 92-1 CPD ¶ 250; *Western Pub. Co.*, Comp. Gen. Dec. B-224376, 86-2 CPD ¶ 249.

[d] Bids Including Price Adjustments

Since only contracts with fixed prices or fixed prices subject to economic adjustment can be used in sealed bid procurements, a bid stating that a price adjustment could be made if the cost of petroleum increased was required to be rejected as nonresponsive, *Re Con Paving, Inc.*, Comp. Gen. Dec. B-198294, 80-1 CPD ¶ 297. See also *Margaret Greenidge*, Comp. Gen. Dec. B-265979, 96-1 CPD ¶ 80, finding that an agency properly rejected a bid as nonresponsive when the protester included a handwritten notation on the bid schedule stating that "yearly increases is based on 3% or COLA, whichever is greater." Bids containing ceilings on such adjustments have been permitted but such bids must be evaluated at the ceiling. In the absence of a stated ceiling, practical considerations may permit consideration of the bid. See *Copes-Vulcan Div., Blaw-Knox Co.*, 36 Comp. Gen. 259 (B-127372) (1956), where the low bidder stated that if more than three X-rays per valve were required, the price would be increased by $2.50 per X-ray. The IFB had stated that bids were to include the cost of all X-rays required but did not specify the number of X-rays. GAO held that rejection of the low bid was improper since 35 extra X-rays per unit would be necessary before the low bidder's price would be greater than the next low bid. There was no real possibility that such a large number would be required.

Bids based on economic price adjustment (EPA) provisions may be considered for award. FAR 14.408-4 gives the following guidance on the evaluation of EPA provisions:

> (a) Bidder proposes economic price adjustment.
>
> (1) When a solicitation does not contain an economic price adjustment clause but a bidder proposes one with a ceiling that the price will not exceed, the bid shall be evaluated on the basis of the maximum possible economic price adjustment of the quoted base price.
>
> (2) If the bid is eligible for award, the contracting officer shall request the bidder to agree to the inclusion in the award of an approved economic price adjustment clause (see 16.203) that is subject to the same ceiling. If the bidder will not agree to an approved clause, the award may be made on the basis of the bid as originally submitted.
>
> (3) Bids that contain economic price adjustments with no ceiling shall be rejected unless a clear basis for evaluation exists.
>
> (b) Government proposes economic price adjustment.
>
> (1) When an invitation contains an economic price adjustment clause and no bidder takes exception to the provisions, bids shall be evaluated on the basis of the quoted prices without the allowable economic price adjustment being added.
>
> (2) When a bidder increases the maximum percentage of economic price adjustment stipulated in the invitation or limits the downward economic price adjustment provisions of the invitation, the bid shall be rejected as nonresponsive.
>
> (3) When a bid indicates deletion of the economic price adjustment clause, the bid shall be rejected as nonresponsive since the downward economic price adjustment provisions are thereby limited.
>
> (4) When a bidder decreases the maximum percentage of economic price adjustment stipulated in the invitation, the bid shall be evaluated at the base price on an equal basis with bids that do not reduce the stipulated ceiling. However, after evaluation, if the bidder offering the lower ceiling is in a position to receive the award, the award shall reflect the lower ceiling.

This evaluation procedure gives a bid including an EPA clause no advantage, because the bid must be evaluated at the ceiling price. Most EPA clauses contain the required price ceiling since such ceilings are included in the standard clauses in FAR 52.216. For an example of a solicitation that contained a 15% ceiling on option-year prices, see *Echelon Serv. Co.*, 62 Comp. Gen. 542 (B-208720.2), 83-2 CPD ¶ 86. In *Phipps Products Corp.*, Comp. Gen. Dec. B-194840, 79-2 CPD ¶ 200, the solicitation included a 20% ceiling, but the bidder inserted an escalation clause without a price ceiling. GAO held that where a price ceiling cannot be determined with certainty, the bid must be rejected as nonresponsive.

A bid that fails to provide a base rate to which the economic price adjustment clause applies is nonresponsive, *Galaxy Custodial Servs., Inc.*, 64 Comp. Gen. 593 (B-215738), 85-1 CPD ¶ 658. Similarly, if the IFB requires that prices be the same for all years, subject to an economic price adjustment clause, a bid that offers a fixed rate for price increases for later years is nonresponsive, *First Am. Engineered Solutions*, Comp. Gen. Dec. B-289051, 2001 CPD ¶ 207.

To allow for fair evaluation of bids, EPA clauses must reflect some objective standard, other than the bidder's own prices upon which price adjustments will be made, *Roarda, Inc.*, Comp. Gen. Dec. B-204524.5, 82-1 CPD ¶ 438 (IFB defective because it allowed the contractor to adjust prices for petroleum products based on its own price changes). Similarly, in *Hampton Metro. Oil Co.*, Comp. Gen. Dec. B-186509, 76-2 CPD ¶ 471, the solicitation for petroleum products allowed bidders to use their own posted prices in conjunction with the EPA provision. GAO concluded that the IFB was properly canceled because it was impossible to ensure that bidders would not indiscriminately raise their posted prices after contract award. It was therefore impossible for the government to determine which bids ultimately would result in the lowest cost to the government. For an example of the type of objective factor that can be used to determine price adjustments, see *American Transparents Plastics Corp.*, Comp. Gen. Dec. B-210898, 83-2 CPD ¶ 539 (Department of Labor's Producer Price Index for the market price of resin used to make plastic bags was upheld as a valid method for price adjustment).

The analysis used for EPA clauses also extends to other types of price adjustments. In *H. Edward Chozick*, 50 Comp. Gen. 733 (B-171938) (1971), the bid provided for 1½% interest per month on past due invoices, and GAO stated at 735:

> So far as concerns your position that the inclusion of the demand for interest on past due invoices should be treated as a reverse prompt payment, in addition to the fact that its consideration would be contrary to 5 Comp. Gen. 649, the solicitation form has no provision for reverse prompt payment discounts and to consider such discounts could well add a substantial conjectural factor to the evaluation process to the detriment of the competitive bid system's integrity.

GAO would not allow this clause in a bid because it obligated the government to pay interest on unpaid invoices, and the contracting officer did not have the authority—at that time—to obligate the government for such payments.

[2] Evaluation of "Other Price-Related Factors"

FAR 14.101(e) allows award on the basis of "price and other price-related factors." While the contracting officer has considerable discretion in selecting which price-related factors will be evaluated, any factors chosen must be identified in the solicitation so that all bidders may prepare their bids on an equal and well-informed basis, *Hunot Fire Retardant Co.*, Comp. Gen. Dec. B-286679.2, 2001 CPD ¶ 94 (agency could not have evaluated clean-up costs after contract work because IFB did not specify such costs); *Respiratory & Convalescent Specialties Inc.*, Comp. Gen. Dec. B-255176, 94-1 CPD ¶ 101 (IFB failed to include oxygen rental charges as a price-related factor, failed to advise bidders how these rental charges would be evaluated, and gave no quantity estimate); *E & T Elecs., Inc.*, Comp. Gen. Dec. B-238099.2, 90-2 CPD ¶ 24 (evaluation factors including cost to government of shipping equipment, cost savings from using a local contractor, and a discount offered for certain repairs could not be utilized because they were not specified in the IFB). See also *Old Dominion Sec.*, Comp. Gen. Dec. B-216534, 85-1 CPD ¶ 78, where the incumbent contractor argued that its bid ($52,560) was lower than a competing bid ($52,122) if the agency considered the cost of changing contractors. Such costs could not be considered because the IFB did not include transition costs as a factor in evaluating bids.

A price-related factor must allow the government to arrive at a reasonable estimate of the actual cost impact on the government. See *Todd Pacific Shipyards Corp.*, Comp. Gen. Dec. B-281383, 99-1 CPD ¶ 28, sustaining a protest that the cost of moving a ship was grossly understated with the result that bidders at different locations could not be fairly evaluated.

FAR 14.201-8 lists some of the price-related factors that may be considered in bid evaluation:

> (a) Foreseeable costs or delays to the Government resulting from such factors as differences in inspection, locations of supplies, and transportation. If bids are on a f.o.b. origin basis (see 47.303 and 47.305), transportation costs to the designated points shall be considered in determining the lowest cost to the Government.
>
> (b) Changes made, or requested by the bidder, in any of the provisions of the invitation for bids, if the change does not constitute a ground for rejection under 14.404.
>
> (c) Advantages or disadvantages to the Government that might result from making more than one award (see 14.201-6(q)). The contracting officer shall assume, for the purpose of making multiple awards, that $500 would be the administrative cost to the Government for issuing and administering each contract awarded under a solicitation. Individual awards shall be for the items or combinations of items that result in the lowest aggregate cost to the Government, including the assumed administrative costs.
>
> (d) Federal, State, and local taxes (see Part 29).
>
> (e) Origin of supplies, and, if foreign, the application of the Buy American Act or any other prohibition on foreign purchases (see Part 25).

With regard to ¶ (c), see *Weather Experts, Inc.*, Comp. Gen. Dec. B-255103, 94-1 CPD ¶ 93 (agency accepted the low aggregate bid, but should have accepted multiple bids, because even with the $500 administrative costs, the multiple bid option was lower); and *Patrick Loman*, B-254527, 93-2 CPD ¶ 340 (protest against aggregate award provision denied where IFB provided a reasonable method of assuring the lowest cost to the government).

With regard to ¶ (e), see *Gardner Zemke Co.*, Comp. Gen. Dec. B-234857, 89-2 CPD ¶ 66, and *Dictaphone Corp.*, 58 Comp. Gen. 234 (B-192318), 79-1 CPD ¶ 49, where, for evaluation purposes, a 6% Buy American factor was added to the price bid to furnish a foreign product. GAO has also stated that an agency may not consider the Buy American Act differential if it is not included in the IFB. See Chapter 14.

FAR 14.201-8 is not an inclusive list of price-related factors. In *Tek-Lite, Inc.*, Comp. Gen. Dec. B-230298, 88-1 CPD ¶ 241, GAO found an evaluation factor set forth in the solicitation for a value engineering royalty to be a proper evaluation factor even though it is not listed in FAR 14.201-8.

[a] Transportation

The most common price-related factor is the cost of transportation. If the IFB provides that bids are to be made on an f.o.b. destination basis, the costs of transportation are included in the bid price and separate evaluation is not required. When bids are on an f.o.b. origin basis, FAR 14.201-8(a) requires consideration of transportation costs to the designated place of delivery. See *Marten C. Robb & Son*, B-256516, 94-1 CPD ¶ 392 (a reasonable estimate of the cost per mile was included in evaluating the bids to ensure that the government would obtain the lowest actual cost). If the exact destination is unknown at the time of the solicitation and the procuring agency is unable to predict even the general destination, transportation costs cannot be a factor in bid evaluation, *Wachtel, Wiener & Ross*, 52 Comp. Gen. 679 (B-177763) (1973). FAR 47.305-3 provides guidance on f.o.b. origin solicitations and requires the use of the Evaluation—F.O.B. Origin solicitation clause in FAR 52.247-47 to inform bidders that costs of transportation will be evaluated. If the exact destination is unknown at the time of solicitation but the general geographic locations can be reasonably established, the solicitation should include a tentative destination for the purposes of evaluation only, FAR 47.305-5(b). See *Entron, Inc.*, Comp. Gen. Dec. B-189362, 77-2 CPD ¶ 414, upholding the contracting agency's use of hypothetical delivery points for evaluation purposes since the actual destinations were unknown at the time of solicitation.

In order to evaluate transportation costs accurately, the procuring agency must require bidders to provide certain information with their bids such as minimum size of shipments, guaranteed shipping weights, and information regarding packing and crating, FAR 47.305-1. Part 52 of the FAR contains a number of standard solicitation provisions used to obtain this information. The most commonly used provision of this type is the Guaranteed Shipping Characteristics solicitation provision in FAR 52.247-60. This provision provides that if the specified information is not included in a particular bid, the government may include either the highest bidder's information or a government estimate to evaluate the bid. In *F&H Mfg. Corp.*, Comp. Gen. Dec. B-212254, 83-2 CPD ¶ 676, GAO affirmed the validity of using government estimates to evaluate bids where the bidders did not submit guaranteed maximum shipping weights and dimensions for shipments of Army vehicle parts. The clause in this IFB also provides for a price adjustment as follows:

> If the item shipping costs, based on the actual shipping characteristics, exceed the item shipping costs used for evaluation purposes, the Contractor agrees that the contract price shall be reduced by an amount equal to the difference between the transportation costs actually incurred, and the costs which would have been incurred if the evaluated shipping characteristics had been accurate.

In *Kalyn Inc.*, Comp. Gen. Dec. B-237909, 90-1 CPD ¶ 331, GAO denied a protest contending that this solicitation provision permitted bidders to provide false information that reduced their evaluated transportation costs, thereby giving them an unfair competitive advantage, reasoning that the provision compensated for this problem by providing for a downward adjustment in price if the actual shipping costs were higher than those estimated because the bid's shipping weights or dimensions were exceeded. Similarly, in *Capital Indus., Inc.*, Comp. Gen. Dec. B-190818, 78-2 CPD ¶ 17, GAO recognized the practice of bidders' intentionally understating shipping dimensions as an alternative to reducing the bid price. The only limit on this practice appears to be that bidders may not understate the guaranteed weight or dimensions in a manner that creates doubt as to their intent to comply with the solicitation's specifications, *Survival Products, Inc.*, Comp. Gen. Dec. B-235431.3, 89-2 CPD ¶ 464, *modified*, 90-1 CPD ¶ 118 (GAO recommended cancellation of the procurement because of shipping information indicating bidder's intent not to comply with one possible interpretation of ambiguous specification). See, for example, *Canadian Commercial Corp.*, Comp. Gen. Dec. B-236850, 90-1 CPD ¶ 3 (dimensions in bid that exceeded the IFB's dimensions did not render the bid nonresponsive); *Trojan Indus. Inc.*, Comp. Gen. Dec. B-220620, 86-1 CPD ¶ 143 (assertion that the transportation costs of the machine were based on incorrect dimensions had no bearing because a bidder may understate the guaranteed dimensions to effectuate a price reduction); and *Drexel Contract Furniture*, Comp. Gen. Dec. B-180598, 74-1 CPD ¶ 324 (in procurement of household furniture for use abroad, bidders were allowed to guarantee less weight than actual in order to meet competition).

Once the agency has the information from the bids, it is required to evaluate transportation costs on the basis of the most economical means of transportation available at bid opening. Thus, lower rates secured by the bidder after bid opening cannot be considered, *Williams & Jensen*, 52 Comp. Gen. 614 (B-176346)

(1973). GAO has held that an evaluation of bids that was not based upon freight rates available to the government at bid opening was improper because permitting bidders to shop for attractive shipping rates after opening is inconsistent with the sealed bidding system, *Isometrics, Inc.*, Comp. Gen. Dec. B-219057.3, 86-1 CPD ¶ 2. The method of shipment used for evaluation must not vary from that required in the IFB. See *Ellinor Corp.*, 54 Comp. Gen. 901 (B-182384), 75-1 CPD ¶ 254, recommending cancellation of an award to the low evaluated bidder because transportation costs had been evaluated on the basis of uneconomical, albeit realistic, partial truck loads rather than full truck loads as required by the invitation. The government need not use commercial methods of transportation in its evaluation of its potential costs; it can transport the products itself if this would be most economical, since the government is not limited to commercial methods of transportation, *Capital Indus., Inc.*, Comp. Gen. Dec. B-190818, 78-2 CPD ¶ 17.

[b] Life-Cycle Costs

The procuring agency can provide for evaluation of life-cycle costs such as the cost of operation, maintenance, and other costs of ownership when the basis for determining these costs is identified in the IFB. See *Mor-Flo Indus., Inc.*, Comp. Gen. Dec. B-192687, 79-1 CPD ¶ 390, where life-cycle cost estimates for gas and electric water heaters were used in bid evaluation. See also *Swintec Corp.*, Comp. Gen. Dec. B-225657, 87-1 CPD ¶ 378, where life-cycle costs such as the cost of downtime, repairs, parts, supplies, etc., were evaluated in the procurement of electric typewriters. An agency need not include all possible life-cycle costs in the IFB, *Staber Indus., Inc.*, Comp. Gen. Dec. B-276077, 97-1 CPD ¶ 174 (agency used energy costs but not costs or water and detergent in procuring washers). Neither must its computation of life-cycle costs be completely accurate as long as it follows rational procedures stated in the IFB, *Olympia USA, Inc. v. United States*, 6 Cl. Ct. 550 (1984).

To evaluate life-cycle costs, the IFB need not spell out the evaluation methodology with mathematical precision. It is sufficient if the bidders can arrive at a reasonable estimate of the costs that will be used by the government to make the evaluation. For example, in 36 Comp. Gen. 380 (B-127801) (1956), the IFB for the construction of a radio communications system provided for evaluation of maintenance costs over 15 years of service. After bid opening the contracting officer fixed these costs at $3,000 per repeater station. GAO held that the evaluation factors were stated with sufficient clarity in the invitation to enable a bidder, on the basis of available data and past expenses, to make an estimate of the effect of the evaluation factor on its bid; and an award under the IFB was, therefore, proper.

While FAR 7-105(a)(3)(i) requires the consideration of life-cycle costs in acquisition planning decisions, and there are obvious benefits from including such factors in the evaluation of bids, there has been relatively little use of such factors. GAO has recommended that the procuring agencies make greater use of life-cycle costing, Comp. Gen. Dec. B-178214, May 21, 1973, *Unpub.* See also Office of Management and Budget Memorandum for Agency Senior Procurement Executives, Sept. 9, 1991, where the Administrator noted that the application of life-cycle costing has been inadequate and needs to be expanded, and OFPP Policy Letter 92-4, which requested that agencies implement life-cycle costing whenever feasible and appropriate in order for the government to save money in the long run.

[c] Miscellaneous

Other evaluation factors that may be used if mentioned in the IFB include storage and time-related costs, *Borg Warner Corp.*, 57 Comp. Gen. 103 (B-189275), 77-2 CPD ¶ 420; the cost of potential delays and changes in the course of contract performance, *ACS Constr. Co.*, B-250372.2, 93-1 CPD ¶ 106; the cost of first article testing to the extent that such cost can be realistically estimated, FAR 9.306(i); and the cost that results from varying locations of performance, *Cascade Gen., Inc.*, Comp. Gen. Dec. B-272271, 96-2 CPD ¶ 52. See *Homexx Int'l Corp.*, Comp. Gen. Dec. B-192034, 78-2 CPD ¶ 219, where $70,000, the estimated cost of first article testing, was added to the bid price of any bidder that had not previously produced the items. See also *Flexfab, Inc.*, Comp. Gen. Dec. B-221186, 86-1 CPD ¶ 188, where GAO determined that the agency properly considered the protester's price for first article testing when the IFB specifically required that bidders include a price for it, which would be evaluated. Government inspection costs may also be added to the bids for evaluation purposes, but in 52 Comp. Gen. 997 (B-177887) (1973), GAO stated that it was inappropriate to add such costs for evaluation purposes when there was already an inspector in residence in the contractor's plant. The reasoning is that "no actual cost to the Government is incurred nor can it be said at the time of evaluation of bids that any costs would, in fact, be incurred if the award were made to a prospective contractor with an inspector already in residence."

[3] Evaluation of Equal Low Bids

FAR 14.408-6 outlines the procedures that must be followed when two or more equal low bids are received:

> (a) Contracts shall be awarded in the following order of priority when two or more low bids are equal in all respects:
>
> (1) Small business concerns that are also labor surplus area concerns.
>
> (2) Other small business concerns.
>
> (3) Other business concerns.

(b) If two or more bidders still remain equally eligible after application of paragraph (a) above, award shall be made by a drawing by lot limited to those bidders. If time permits, the bidders involved shall be given an opportunity to attend the drawing. The drawing shall be witnessed by at least three persons, and the contract file shall contain the names and addresses of the witnesses and the person supervising the drawing.

(c) When an award is to be made by using the priorities under this 14.408-6, the contracting officer shall include a written agreement in the contract that the contractor will perform, or cause to be performed, the contract in accordance with the circumstances justifying the priority used to break the tie or select bids for a drawing by lot.

In *Randy Int'l, Ltd.*, 53 Comp. Gen. 466 (B-179880), 74-1 CPD ¶ 11, GAO stated that once a tie has occurred between two low evaluated bids, no other evaluation factors should be considered if not delineated in the IFB. Thus, additional factors, such as past performance record, experience of a bidder's personnel, and shipment security may not be considered. Similarly, in *Richard A. Schwartz Assocs.*, Comp. Gen. Dec. B-214979, 84-1 CPD ¶ 695, the protester's greater technical competence was held an extraneous factor that could not be used to break the tie. Thus, lots must be drawn to determine the winner when there are tie bids, *Van Ben Indus., Inc.*, Comp. Gen. Dec. B-234875, 89-2 CPD ¶ 52; *Berklay Air Servs. Corp.*, Comp. Gen. Dec. B-179880, 74-1 CPD ¶ 115.

The tied bidders should be given the opportunity to attend the drawing to avoid raising doubts concerning its fairness. See *Alderson Reporting Co.*, Comp. Gen. Dec. B-205552.2, 82-1 CPD ¶ 128, criticizing the procuring agencies for performing the drawing by lot without inviting the tied bidders. Compare *Vetcorp, Inc.*, Comp. Gen. Dec. B-402519, 2010 CPD ¶ 114, accepting the drawing of lots without the offerors being present in a commercial item procurement that did not follow sealed bidding procedures. Note that since equal low bids may indicate price fixing, identical bids may be reported to the Department of Justice for investigation of possible collusive bidding practices. FAR 3.303(d).

[B] Award

The major issues involved in awarding a sealed bid contract are the procedures to be followed, the determination of whether to make a single award or multiple awards, and the treatment of below-cost bids (also referred to as "buy-ins").

[1] Procedures

FAR 14.408-1 outlines the award procedures in sealed bid procurements, discussed further below.

[a] Notice of Award

Award can be made by using the award portion of Standard Form 33, Solicitation, Offer and Award. FAR 14.408-1(d) provides that if "an offer leads to further changes," the resulting contract shall be prepared as a bilateral document on SF 26, Award/Contract. This regulation further provides that use of the award portion of SF 33 or SF 26 does not preclude the additional use of informal documents, including telegrams and notices of awards.

Notice of award must be in writing. Oral notice is not sufficient since the government's acceptance of an offer must be clear and unconditional, *James M. Smith, Inc.*, Comp. Gen. Dec. B-233877, 89-1 CPD ¶ 390 (low bidder sought and received assurances that it would be awarded the contract, but GAO held that retraction of the oral award was proper); *Phillip C. Clarke Elec. Constr. Inc.*, Comp. Gen. Dec. B-226594, 87-1 CPD ¶ 629 (low bidder was notified by telephone, but IFB was subsequently canceled and GAO held the oral notice ineffective). See also *R.J. Crowley, Inc.*, ASBCA 28730, 86-1 BCA ¶ 18,739, where oral notification without a follow-up ratification was held insufficient to establish award.

The award must be made on the basis of the IFB and the responsive bid. The contracting officer may not unilaterally impose different terms on the low bidder, *CRF v. United States*, 624 F.2d 1054 (Ct. Cl. 1980). See Chapter 2 for further discussion of government acceptance issues.

[b] Determining the Acceptance Period

As discussed earlier, bidders are subject to the firm bid rule if they include a promise in their bids to hold them open for a specified period of time. The standard cover sheets for sealed bid procurements, Standard Forms 33 and 1447, call for an acceptance period of 60 days but permit the bidder to insert a different period. In instances where neither of these forms is used, FAR 14.201-6(i) provides a Period for Acceptance of Bids solicitation provision in FAR 52.214-15 containing the same provisions. These provisions permit bidders to specify less than 60-day acceptance periods. See *Perkin-Elmer Corp.*, 69 Comp. Gen. 27 (B-236175.2), 89-2 CPD ¶ 352, holding that, even though the bidder had filled in "30 days" in another part of the bid, the bid's inclusion of the FAR 52.214-15 clause superseded that number because the bidder did not include its own 30-day period in the clause.

When the contracting officer determines that a minimum acceptance period "must be specified," FAR 14.201-6(j) provides a Minimum Bid Acceptance Period solicitation provision in FAR 52.214-16 to be used in all contracts except those for construction. The use of this provision is at the sole discretion of the contracting officer because the FAR contains no guidance as to its use. The provision allows the agency to designate a number of calendar days as the minimum acceptance period and permits bidders to enter a longer acceptance period, but warns that a bid with a shorter period will be rejected. See *Paragon Inv. Corp.*, Comp. Gen. Dec. B-241715, 91-1 CPD ¶ 95, where a provision required a minimum acceptance period of 90 days, but the bidder entered 30 days. Although Paragon claimed that the insertion of "30 days" was a clerical error because it meant 30 days longer than the specified 60 days in Block 12 of SF 33, GAO held that the "error" was not a minor informality and the bid was nonresponsive. See also *Winsar Corp.*, Comp. Gen. Dec. B-226507, 87-1 CPD ¶ 585, where the bidder sent with the bid a standard letter containing a shorter acceptance period, and GAO held the bid nonresponsive. Similarly, in *Sundt Corp.*, Comp. Gen. Dec. B-274203, 96-2 CPD ¶ 171, GAO found a bid nonresponsive where the bidder acknowledged the solicitation amendment changing the minimum acceptance period from 90 to 120 calendar days, but inserted 90 in the bid form blank for proposing an acceptance period. In *Kim's Gen. Maint., Inc.*, Comp. Gen. Dec. B-275823, 97-1 CPD ¶ 128, GAO reasoned that because the protester failed to include SF 1447 with its bid, there was no way for the agency to verify whether the protester took exception to the 120-day minimum acceptance period and thus found the bid to be nonresponsive.

The FAR 52.214-16 provision provides that it supersedes any other provisions in the IFB dealing with the minimum acceptance period. However, care must be taken not to insert acceptance periods in these other provisions. See, for example, *Siems Rental & Sales Co.*, Comp. Gen. Dec. B-257773, 95-1 CPD ¶ 51, where the FAR 52.214-16 provision required an acceptance period of 60 days, but the bidder inserted "30 days" in Block 12 of SF 33. The bidder asserted that its insertion of "30 days" was of no consequence because SF 33 contained a note stating: "Item 12 does not apply if the solicitation includes the provisions at 52.214-16, Minimum Bid Acceptance Period." GAO rejected this argument holding that, at best, the bid was ambiguous and therefore nonresponsive. See also *Perkin-Elmer Corp.*, 69 Comp. Gen. 27 (B-236175.2), 89-2 CPD ¶ 352, where the IFB incorrectly contained both the FAR 52.214-15 and the FAR 52.214-16 provisions, calling for a 60-day bid acceptance period. GAO held that the insertion of "30 days" in the FAR 52.214-15 clause rendered the bid ambiguous and therefore nonresponsive.

[c] Extensions from Bidders

The contracting officer frequently finds that award cannot be made within the time that the bids are firm. When this occurs, bidders are usually requested to extend the time for acceptance. FAR 14.404-1(d) provides:

> Should administrative difficulties be encountered after bid opening that may delay award beyond bidders' acceptance periods, the several lowest bidders whose bids have not expired (irrespective of the acceptance period specified in the bid) should be requested, before expiration of their bids, to extend

> in writing the bid acceptance period (with consent of sureties, if any) in order to avoid the need for resoliciting.

This practice gives bidders the opportunity to choose to remain in the competition or to withdraw. Since the low bidders make this decision with knowledge of how their bids compare to the other bids, they can assess the likely profitability of the contract and make a decision based on this assessment.

To remain in the competition, a bidder's extension must be unqualified and unconditional. In *Klein Constr. Co.*, Comp. Gen. Dec. B-201599, 81-1 CPD ¶ 158, an extension was rejected when the bidder also reserved the right to request additional time or money, even though that qualification was subsequently withdrawn. See *S.J. Groves & Sons Co.*, Comp. Gen. Dec. B-207172, 82-2 CPD ¶ 423, where, when the bidder conditioned an extension on an increase in its bid price, GAO interpreted this as a refusal to extend the bid "as originally submitted." See also *Dawson Constr. Co.*, Comp. Gen. Dec. B-244204, 91-1 CPD ¶ 523; and *GTA Containers, Inc.*, Comp. Gen. Dec. B-234395.3, 89-2 CPD ¶ 37 (bidder conditioned extension of bid acceptance period upon an increase in price and thus was ineligible for award).

Although the regulations only permit extension of bids before they expire, GAO has held that the government may accept *an expired bid* that has subsequently been revived through a bidder's actual or constructive waiver, provided that such waiver is not done with the intention of taking advantage of the other bidders. See *Mission Van & Storage Co.*, 53 Comp. Gen. 775 (B-180112), 74-1 CPD ¶ 195, stating at 778-79:

> In 46 Comp. Gen. 371 (1966), the low bidder extended its bid acceptance period when requested to do so 3 days after the original 60 day period had lapsed. We held that the bid properly could be accepted because the integrity of the competitive bidding system would not be compromised thereby and because there would be no prejudice to another bidder whose 60 day acceptance period had also expired. We distinguished that situation from the one in 42 Comp. Gen. 604, *supra*, in which the low bidder offered an acceptance period of only 20 days while the second low bidder offered the more customary 60 days. There we held that the low bid, which was not extended until more than 2 weeks after expiration of the original 20 day period, should not be accepted because the low bidder "sought and gained an advantage after bid opening in the nature of an option not sought by other bidders, of renewing its bid in short increments or allowing it to lapse as dictated by market conditions," and that "the integrity of the competitive bidding system would best be served by making an award to the second low bidder." 46 Comp. Gen. 371, 373.
>
> * * *
>
> We do not think that acceptance of DeWitt's bid would compromise the competitive bidding system. Unlike the bidders in 42 Comp. Gen. 604 and 48 *id.* 19, DeWitt did not seek any advantage over other bidders. It offered the standard 60 day acceptance period rather than an unusually short one. Furthermore, it is reasonably clear that DeWitt intended and considered its

> bid to be viable at least during the pendency of this protest. We have taken the position that a protest to this Office during a bidder's acceptance period could be viewed as tolling the bid acceptance period pending resolution of the protest, 50 Comp. Gen. 357 (1970). . . . Accordingly, we would not object to an award to DeWitt.

For cases involving prejudice to other bidders, see *MKB Mfg. Corp.*, Comp. Gen. Dec. B-208451, 83-1 CPD ¶ 204, where, when other bidders extended their bids before expiration of their 60-day acceptance period, it was held improper to allow MKB to revive its bid more than 15 days after expiration of its 60-day acceptance period because it would give MKB an unfair advantage over the other bidders; and *Esprit Int'l Corp.*, Comp. Gen. Dec. B-276294, 97-1 CPD ¶ 106, where allowing the protester to revive its bid after the expiration of its 14-day acceptance period would afford the protester an unfair advantage since its initial exposure to the risk of the marketplace was for a shorter period.

A waiver will be deemed to have occurred if, following expiration of the acceptance period, the bidder is still willing to accept award on the basis of the bid as submitted, *Cecile Indus., Inc.*, Comp. Gen. Dec. B-207277.3, 82-2 CPD ¶ 299. For an unusual case, see *Input Data, Inc.*, GSBCA 4937-R, 80-2 BCA ¶ 14,711, where the board found that the contractor was bound to perform a contract awarded after bid expiration, even though it had failed to execute a bid extension mailed to the contracting officer. Its failure to disavow a notice of award and the request for a modification delaying performance were "consistent with ratification of his bid and acceptance of the signed contract." The board distinguished *A.C. Ball Co.*, ASBCA 19375, 75-1 BCA ¶ 11,298, where a contractor fulfilled only the minimum quantity on an indefinite-quantity contract awarded after bid expiration. The board found that the contractor had accepted only a "counter-offer," the terms of which were limited to performance of the minimum quantity order, reasoning that the transaction lacked the strong evidence of communications and meetings between the parties which were consistent only with contract recognition.

GAO has also held that filing a protest tolls the acceptance period, *Phillips Cartner & Co.*, 69 Comp. Gen. 105 (B-236416.2), 89-2 CPD ¶ 492. Thus, where the award is made to another firm within the protester's shorter acceptance period, the protester's bid may be accepted if the protest is sustained, even though the acceptance period otherwise would have expired, *Professional Materials Handling Co.*, Comp. Gen. Dec. B-205969, 82-1 CPD ¶ 297. Similarly, award to the initial awardee after the protest is denied is proper without regard to the expiration of the awardee's bid, if the awardee actively participated in the protest, *Native Res. Dev., Inc.*, Comp. Gen. Dec. B-246597.2, 92-2 CPD ¶ 15; *Werres Corp.*, Comp. Gen. Dec. B-211870, 83-2 CPD ¶ 243. In effect, this prevents a protester from excluding the awardee by filing a protest by allowing tolling of the expiration period by participation in the protest. In *International Graphics v. United States*, 4 Cl. Ct. 515 (1984), the court extended the tolling concept by holding that "the bid acceptance period should remain open as long as the parties, through litigation or otherwise, have actually or constructively expressed their intent to accept the award."

Bids that have expired due to cancellation of a solicitation may generally be revived upon reinstatement of the solicitation, unless the bids have been returned and reinstatement would compromise the integrity of the competitive bidding system, *Baker Mfg. Co.*, 59 Comp. Gen. 573 (B-197016), 80-2 CPD ¶ 1. Even though the government has requested multiple extensions, it is not required to make an award, *Maceto Inc.*, Comp. Gen. Dec. B-216166, 84-2 CPD ¶ 277 (although Navy requested four extensions of the original bid acceptance period, Maceto had no legal right to require the Navy to award the contract).

[2] Multiple versus Aggregate Awards

Considerable confusion has surrounded the award of contracts for multiple items. Part of the problem stems from the number of alternatives available to both the government and bidders when dealing with multiple items. The Contract Award—Sealed Bidding solicitation provision in FAR 52.214-10, used for all procurements except construction contracts, states:

> (c) The Government may accept any item or group of items of a bid, unless the bidder qualifies the bid by specific limitations. Unless otherwise provided in the Schedule, bids may be submitted for quantities less than those specified. The Government reserves the right to make an award on any item for a quantity less than the quantity offered, at the unit prices offered, unless the bidder specifies otherwise in the bid.

The Contract Award—Sealed Bidding—Construction solicitation provision in FAR 52.214-19 contains a slightly different provision:

> (c) The Government may accept any item or combination of items, unless doing so is precluded by a restrictive limitation in the solicitation or the bid.

Under these provisions, awards may be made to one or more bidders for one or more items or to one bidder for all items, whichever is in the best interests of the government, Comp. Gen. Dec. B-149085, Aug. 28, 1962, *Unpub.*; 47 Comp. Gen. 233 (B-162092) (1967). See *Staab Constr. Corp.*, Comp. Gen. Dec. B-298454, 2006 CPD ¶ 136, agreeing that it was proper to award a contract for only one item of work where there were no bids within the funding limit for the other item of work and the IFB contained the FAR 52.214-19 provision.

Absent solicitation language requiring an aggregate award, the government must make multiple awards if different bidders offer the low evaluated price on each item to be awarded, *Action Mobile Transp., Inc.*, Comp. Gen. Dec. B-275427.2, 97-1 CPD ¶ 132; *TAAS Israel Military Indus. Ltd.*, Comp. Gen.

Dec. B-258039.3, 95-1 CPD ¶ 32; *Weather Experts, Inc.*, Comp. Gen. Dec. B-255103, 94-1 CPD ¶ 93; *HFS Inc.*, Comp. Gen. Dec. B-246018, 92-1 CPD ¶ 160. In this respect, GAO has required that in order to make an aggregate award, it must result in the lowest cost to the government, *S.J. Groves & Sons Co.*, 55 Comp. Gen. 936 (B-184260), 76-1 CPD ¶ 205; 47 Comp. Gen. 233 (B-162092) (1967) (aggregate award improper when based on considerations of centralized management and administration, when multiple awards would have resulted in a lower cost to the government). But if a bidder offers a low aggregate bid that is less than the sum of its bids on individual items, award should be made to the low aggregate bid. See 47 Comp. Gen. 658 (B-163890) (1968), upholding the agency's consideration of a combination bid for tractors and loaders that resulted in a lower overall cost to the government than on an item-by-item basis. In *Moir Ranch & Constr. Co.*, Comp. Gen. Dec. B-191616, 78-1 CPD ¶ 423, a bidder, offering an additional 10% discount if all eight of its bid items were accepted, was properly awarded the contract even though other bidders offered lower prices on individual items and without the discount, the total cost would have been lower under multiple awards.

If the solicitation notifies bidders that award will be made to the low aggregate bidder, then an aggregate award must be made even though such an award may be more costly to the government, *Northeast Constr. Co.*, 61 Comp. Gen. 317 (B-205246), 82-1 CPD ¶ 293. In *Northeast*, GAO sustained a protest because the agency split the base bid requirement between two bidders instead of making one aggregate award to the low bidder. However, it is proper to make a partial award if funds to make an aggregate award are not available. In *FBF Indus., Inc.*, Comp. Gen. Dec. B-252574, 93-1 CPD ¶ 477, the protester asserted that the agency should have evaluated bids on an item-by-item basis and made partial award. GAO denied the protest, stating that the solicitation provided that bids would be evaluated on an "all or none" basis for all items and did not contain a multiple awards clause. If the solicitation requires an aggregate award but multiple awards would serve the government's needs and there is no reasonable basis for an aggregate award, the solicitation must be canceled and the work reprocured, *Hawthorne Uniform Mfg. Co.*, Comp. Gen. Dec. B-200363, 81-1 CPD ¶ 68 (resolicitation recommended since there was no reason for the aggregate award restriction in the solicitation, and the contracting officer could have made multiple awards at a lower total cost to the government); *Roy's Rabbitry*, Comp. Gen. Dec. B-193628, 79-1 CPD ¶ 305 (resolicitation recommended because aggregate award restricted the competition unnecessarily to large producers, and multiple awards could meet the government's needs). See also *Com-Tran of Michigan, Inc.*, Comp. Gen. Dec. B-200845, 80-2 CPD ¶ 407. But see *Alcon Div. of Boyles Bros. Drilling Co.*, Comp. Gen. Dec. B-241058, 91-1 CPD ¶ 46, where a partial award was sustained where the only bidder submitting an aggregate bid within the agency funding limitation had bid some of the items at amounts exceeding the statutory funding limitations. GAO held that the aggregate award language did not preclude the agency from making an award to that bidder for all of the items that were within the statutory limitation.

In construction contracts, the agency frequently obtains bids on additive and deductive elements of the work and reserves the right to award to the lowest aggregate bidder on the combination of items that fall within the agency's funding limitation. See DFARS PGI 236.213 for guidance on the use of this technique. The Additive or Deductive Items solicitation provision is at DFARS 252.236-7007. Under this clause the low bidder is determined by the low bid for the best combination of items within the funding limitation applicable *at the time of bid opening*, even if this amount varies from the funding limitation set forth in the solicitation, *Rodriguez & Del Valle, Inc.*, Comp. Gen. Dec. B-239224, 90-2 CPD ¶ 29 (award to bidder not low on base bid but low on base bid plus all additives sustained because agency budget officer certified prior to bid opening that sufficient funds were available); *Martz Constr. Corp.*, Comp. Gen. Dec. B-213320, 84-1 CPD ¶ 29 (award to bidder not low on base bid and all additives but low on base bid plus two additives sustained because that was all that could be awarded within the funding limitation); *Applicators, Inc.*, Comp. Gen. Dec. B-270162, 96-1 CPD ¶ 32 (award to bidder not low on base bid and additives but low on base bid sustained because that was all that could be awarded within the funding limitation); *Atherton Constr., Inc.*, Comp. Gen. Dec. B-266345, 96-1 CPD ¶ 51 (award made to low base bidder, without including additives, because funds available prior to bid opening were insufficient to cover even the lowest base bid). Once this low bidder has been determined, award can be made for more items if more funds become available thereafter—even if such award would not be to the low bidder for those items, *Sammy Garrison Constr. Co.*, Comp. Gen. Dec. B-215453, 84-2 CPD ¶ 545. In this case, the award was sustained even though the protester had submitted the low bid on the items included in the award—because the awardee was the low bidder on the items that could be included within the funding limitation. In one unusual case, there were no funds available at the time of bid opening, but GAO ruled that it was proper to award subsequently to the low bidder on the base bid minus all deductive items when funds became available for that amount of work, *Gartrell Constr., Inc.*, Comp. Gen. Dec. B-237032, 90-1 CPD ¶ 46. GAO rejected the protester's contention that it should have received the award because it was the low bidder on the base bid. An earlier solicitation provision gave the agency the flexibility to select the additive or deductive items after bid opening, but the funds available at the time of bid opening still controlled the determination of the low bidder, *Delta Indus. Contractors, Inc.*, Comp. Gen. Dec. B-226949, 87-1 CPD ¶ 569 (award to bidder not low on base bid but low on base bid plus additives sustained where such items were within the funding limitation); *Huntington Constr., Inc.*, 67 Comp. Gen. 499 (B-230604), 88-1 CPD ¶ 619 (protest sustained when agency determined low bidder based on lower figure than the funding limitation at the time of bid opening). It has been held improper to treat options the same as additive items when the solicitation does not call for the evaluation of options, *N-K Constr. Co.*, Comp. Gen. Dec. B-224534, 87-1 CPD ¶ 188.

When an agency uses an additive clause with somewhat ambiguous language, it will be interpreted to require award to the low bidder on the base price plus the additive items that are actually included in the award. For example, in *John C. Grimberg Co.*, Comp. Gen. B-284013, 2000 CPD ¶ 11, the IFB stated:

> The Government reserves the right to select all, none or any combination thereof of the Add Alternates listed above. A single award will be made to the lowest priced responsive and responsible bidder inclusive of the Base Bid and sum total of the Add Alternates.
>
> A single award will be made to the lowest priced responsive and responsible bidder.

GAO rejected the argument that this required award to the low bidder on the base bid plus all of the additives, ruling that it should be interpreted to require award to the low bidder on the base bid plus the additive work that was actually included in the award. See also *National Servs., Inc.*, Comp. Gen. B-400836.2, 2009 CPD ¶ 58, interpreting similarly ambiguous language to require award to the low bidder on the base bid plus the additives that were included in the award.

Prices may generally be submitted for individual items, for combinations of items, or on an "all or none" basis. An "all or none" bid precludes award to that bidder for less than the total number of items. FAR 14.404-5 provides:

> Unless the solicitation provides otherwise, a bid may be responsive notwithstanding that the bidder specifies that award will be accepted only on all, or a specified group, of the items. Bidders shall not be permitted to withdraw or modify "all or none" qualifications after bid opening since such qualifications are substantive and affect the rights of other bidders.

See *Steel King Indus., Inc.*, Comp. Gen. Dec. B-209239, 83-1 CPD ¶ 473, recommending award to an all or none bidder that submitted the lowest overall price for the items bid. In *Canova Moving & Storage Co.*, Comp. Gen. Dec. B-207168, 83-1 CPD ¶ 59, GAO stated that an "all or none" bidder does not have the option to decide after bid opening whether it will accept an award on less than the total number of items.

The Contract Award—Sealed Bidding solicitation provision in FAR 52.214-10 gives the government the right to make an award for less than the quantity advertised unless the bidder has restricted the government's right to do so by an "all or none" bid or by a provision limiting award for less than a stated quantity of any item. Awards for a lesser quantity of an item than that advertised could have a serious impact on the bidder's pricing. Thus, the government is only permitted to make such awards when the contracting officer learns of a reduced need after bid opening or has accepted a lower bid on a portion of the quantity, Comp. Gen. Dec. B-173666, Oct. 1, 1971, *Unpub.* If the contracting officer learns of a reduced need before award, FAR 14.208(a) requires an amendment to the IFB reflecting the reduction. Failure to follow this procedure would make it unconscionable to hold the bidder to the bid price, Comp. Gen. Dec. B-170808, May 14, 1971, *Unpub.* The government is not required to award for lesser quantities and may award the total quantity of an item or the entire group of items advertised even though a partial award would result in a lower cost to the government for the items awarded. See *General Fire Extinguisher Corp.*, 54 Comp. Gen. 416 (B-181796), 74-2 CPD ¶ 278, stating that "an all or none bid, lower in the aggregate than any combination of individual bids available, may be accepted by the Government even though a partial award could be made at a lower unit cost." See also *George C. Martin, Inc.*, 55 Comp. Gen. 100 (B-182175), 75-2 CPD ¶ 55, where the IFB called for separate bid prices for two facilities on Schedules A and B, respectively. X submitted the low total bid for both schedules and bid on an "all or none" basis, which was not precluded by the IFB. Y bid low on Schedule B. Had the government desired to award only on Schedule B (a partial award), it would have awarded that item to Y. However, since both schedules were being awarded, it was proper to make the award to X.

If a solicitation prohibits "all or none" offers, such offers are allowed as long as the offeror submits separate offers for each of the items called for, *Amerisource-Bergen Drug Corp. v. United States*, 60 Fed. Cl. 30 (2004). In this case, the court ruled that award at prices for all regions covered was proper because the offeror had also submitted offers for separate prices for several regions.

[3] Award to Below-Cost Bidders

Receipt of a below-cost bid requires the contracting officer to exercise special care in the evaluation and award process. Such bids cannot be summarily rejected, because they offer the government a low price for obtaining the work. Yet they may pose the risk of default or poor contract performance such as deviating from the specifications to reduce costs. The actions the government should take depend on the circumstances underlying the bid.

There are several reasons a bidder may submit a below-cost bid: (1) by mistake, *Darwin Constr. Co.*, Comp. Gen. Dec. B-213314, 84-1 CPD ¶ 154; (2) through incompetence; (3) to eliminate competitors, *National Reporting Co.*, Comp. Gen. Dec. B-199497, 80-2 CPD ¶ 142; (4) to retain a team of employees within its organization; (5) to break into a new government market, *Flexible Metal Hose Mfg. Co. v. United States*, 4 Cl. Ct. 522 (1984); (6) to cover a portion of its fixed costs in a period of slow sales; or (7) to obtain work with the intention of recouping losses through future changes or contracts (known as "buying-in"); *Diemaster Tool, Inc.*, Comp. Gen. Dec. B-238877, 90-1 CPD ¶ 375.

The FAR does not contain comprehensive guidance on dealing with below-cost bids. However, the FAR coverage of improper business practices does address "buying-in," which FAR 3.501-1 defines as:

> submitting an offer below anticipated costs, expecting to—
> (1) Increase the contract amount after award (e.g., through unnecessary or excessively priced change orders); or
> (2) Receive follow-on contracts at artificially high prices to recover losses incurred on the buy-in contract.

The regulations do not require that contracting officers reject such bids. FAR 3.501-2 cautions the contracting officer to be certain that possible losses are not recouped during performance or on follow-on contracts, stating:

> (a) Buying-in may decrease competition or result in poor contract performance. The contracting officer must take appropriate action to ensure buying-in losses are not recovered by the contractor through the pricing of (1) change orders or (2) follow-on contracts subject to cost analysis.
>
> (b) The Government should minimize the opportunity for buying-in by seeking a price commitment covering as much of the entire program concerned as is practical by using—
>
> (1) Multiyear contracting, with a requirement in the solicitation that a price be submitted only for the total multiyear quantity; or
>
> (2) Priced options for additional quantities that, together with the firm contract quantity, equal the program requirements (see Subpart 17.2).
>
> (c) Other safeguards are available to the contracting officer to preclude recovery of buying-in losses (e.g., amortization of nonrecurring costs (see 15.408, Table 15-2, paragraph A, Column (2)) under "Formats for Submission of Line Item Summaries") and treatment of unreasonable price quotations (see 15.405).

Although not likely, if the below-cost bid violates antitrust laws, such as predatory pricing, the procuring agency must report this practice to the Department of Justice, 41 U.S.C. § 3707; 10 U.S.C. § 3307 (formerly § 2305(b)(5)); and FAR 3.303(a).

The other major issues raised by below-cost bids are mistakes and nonresponsibility, which are more fully discussed in § 5.05 of this chapter. An unusually low bid must be verified to assure that no mistake has been made, but upon such verification, award is proper. See *Associated Contractors & Renovators, Inc.*, HUDBCA 83-809-B4, 83-2 BCA ¶ 16,755, stating at 83,308:

> There is no requirement that a contractor must submit a bid that provides for any profit, let alone a substantial profit. In fact, a bidder can even submit a negative profit "buy-in" so long as that bid is submitted with full knowledge of its cost implications and is not based on a mistake.

The contracting officer must also assure that the prospective contractor is responsible. See *TECOM Inc.*, Comp. Gen. Dec. B-215291, 84-1 CPD ¶ 644, stating:

> The submission of a below-cost bid is not illegal and provides no basis for challenging the award of a government contract to a responsible prospective contractor. Whether the low bidder can perform the contract at the price bid is a matter of responsibility. Our office does not review protests concerning affirmative determinations of responsibility absent a showing that the contracting officer acted fraudulently or in bad faith or that definitive responsibility criteria in the solicitation have not been met.

See also *Seaton Van Lines, Inc.*, Comp. Gen. Dec. B-217298, 85-1 CPD ¶ 26.

[C] Cancellation after Bid Opening

While, as discussed earlier, agencies have considerable discretion to cancel a procurement prior to bid opening, cancellation after bid opening is a serious matter because it can give bidders an unfair advantage if they are later permitted to recompete with knowledge of the prior bids. FAR 14.404-1(a) permits such cancellation only for compelling reasons:

> (1) Preservation of the integrity of the competitive bid system dictates that, after bids have been opened, award must be made to that responsible bidder who submitted the lowest responsive bid, unless there is a compelling reason to reject all bids and cancel the invitation.
>
> (2) Every effort shall be made to anticipate changes in a requirement before the date of opening and to notify all prospective bidders of any resulting modification or cancellation. This will permit bidders to change their bids and prevent unnecessary exposure of bid prices.
>
> (3) As a general rule, after the opening of bids, an invitation should not be cancelled and resolicited due solely to increased requirements for the items being acquired. Award should be made on the initial invitation for bids and the additional quantity should be treated as a new acquisition.

GAO has stated that the determination of whether a sufficiently compelling reason exists for bid cancellation is "primarily within the discretion of the administrative agency and will not be disturbed absent proof that the decision was clearly arbitrary, capricious, or not supported by substantial evidence," *Ace-Federal Reporters, Inc.*, Comp. Gen. Dec. B-237414, 90-1 CPD ¶ 144. In some cases, GAO has sustained a cancellation because there was no showing of bad faith or fraud on the part of the agency, *J. Morris & Assocs.*, Comp. Gen. Dec. B-256840, 94-2 CPD ¶ 47 (cancellation was proper where the agency determined that prices were unreasonable and there was no showing of bad faith or fraud);

Moore's Cafeteria Servs., Inc., Comp. Gen. Dec. B-234063.4, 89-2 CPD ¶ 11 (cancellation of an IFB in order to initiate a solicitation under § 8(a) of the Small Business Administration Act was upheld because there was no showing of bad faith or fraud on the part of the agency). In cases where the agency erroneously cancels the solicitation after bid opening, reinstatement of the IFB may be proper if it would not prejudice other bidders and if the award under the original solicitation would serve the actual needs of the government, *Bilt-Rite Contractors, Inc.*, Comp. Gen. Dec. B-259106.2, 95-1 CPD ¶ 220.

When an agency cancels a solicitation after opening, all facts and circumstances will be considered in determining whether appropriate grounds for cancellation existed, *International Graphics, Div. of Moore Bus. Forms, Inc. v. United States*, 5 Cl. Ct. 100 (1984) (A-76 cost comparison was conducted after cancellation of a solicitation and was used to prove that the government had a compelling reason to cancel the solicitation); *McGhee Constr., Inc.*, Comp. Gen. Dec. B-250073.3, 93-1 CPD ¶ 379 (all relevant information was considered to determine that cancellation was appropriate); *I.T.S. Corp.*, Comp. Gen. Dec. B-242725, 91-1 CPD ¶ 518 (when agency's initial reason was inadequate, other information justified cancellation).

In most cases where an IFB is defective, GAO will recommend cancellation of the entire IFB. However, there may be certain situations where only partial cancellation of the solicitation is appropriate. In such a case, the government may cancel the defective portion of the IFB and award a contract for the remainder of the solicitation items to the bidder submitting the lowest bid for those items, *Adrian Supply Co.*, Comp. Gen. Dec. B-240871, 90-2 CPD ¶ 515.

The FAR offers guidance to determine when cancellation is proper. FAR 14.404-1(b) requires cancellation in only one circumstance—when the agency finds that it has not properly disclosed the identity or availability of the necessary specifications. In all other situations, cancellation is discretionary provided that there is a compelling reason. FAR 14.404-1(c) lists some compelling reasons:

> Invitations may be canceled and all bids rejected before award but after opening when . . . the agency head determines in writing that—
>
> (1) Inadequate or ambiguous specifications were cited in the invitation;
>
> (2) Specifications have been revised;
>
> (3) The supplies or services being contracted for are no longer required;
>
> (4) The invitation did not provide for consideration of all factors of cost to the Government, such as cost of transporting Government-furnished property to bidders' plants;
>
> (5) Bids received indicate that the needs of the Government can be satisfied by a less expensive article differing from that for which the bids were invited;

(6) All otherwise acceptable bids received are at unreasonable prices, or only one bid received and the contracting officer cannot determine the reasonableness of the bid price;

(7) The bids were not independently arrived at in open competition, were collusive, or were submitted in bad faith . . . ;

(8) No responsive bid has been received from a responsible bidder;

(9) A cost comparison as prescribed in the OMB Circular A-76 and Subpart 7.3 shows that performance by the Government is more economical; or

(10) For other reasons, cancellation is clearly in the public's interest.

[1] Compelling Reasons for Cancellation

Cancellation is only proper if the interests of the government in canceling outweigh the expense and time of resolicitation and the impact on the competitive system resulting from disclosure of bidders and bid prices. This section discusses the major compelling reasons.

[a] Solicitation Defects

Failure to state proper evaluation criteria in the solicitation is a compelling reason to cancel, *Armco, Inc.*, Comp. Gen. Dec. B-210018, 83-1 CPD ¶ 553 (evaluation criteria inconsistent with other provisions of the solicitation). Where there is no assurance that compliance with a bid evaluation formula would result in the lowest cost to the government, the solicitation is materially defective, and cancellation is proper, *Veterans Elec., LLC*, Comp. Gen. Dec. B-415064.2, 2018 CPD ¶ 42 (specifications did not adequately describe the requirements, making price estimate difficult); *Great Lakes Dredge & Dock Co.*, Comp. Gen. Dec. B-407502.2, 2013 CPD ¶ 48 (there was ambiguity regarding the price to be paid for a particular CLIN); *Dynamic Corp.*, Comp. Gen. Dec. B-296366, 2005 CPD ¶ 125 (IFB provisions on how to propose prices so ambiguous that bidders submitted different pricing information); *Paragon Van Lines, Inc.*, Comp. Gen. Dec. B-291820.2, 2003 CPD ¶ 79 (IFB contained inconsistent performance period and outdated Service Contract Act wage determination); *S.W. Monroe Constr. Co.*, Comp. Gen. Dec. B-256382, 94-1 CPD ¶ 362 (evaluation scheme did not set forth a common basis for evaluating offers); *Bayfone of Tampa*, Comp. Gen. Dec. B-242925, 91-1 CPD ¶ 535 (line item prices were based on defective criteria); *Earthworks of Sumter, Inc.*, Comp. Gen. Dec. B-232067.2, 89-1 CPD ¶ 9 (no basis for determining low bidder because IFB ambiguities permitted bids on different bases); *Reliable Reproductions, Inc.*, Comp. Gen. Dec. B-201137, 81-1 CPD ¶ 100 (defective evaluation method permitted bidders to submit materially unbalanced bids).

Solicitations have been properly canceled when it was apparent that a majority of bidders were misled by the solicitation, *Neals Janitorial Serv.*, Comp. Gen. Dec. B-276625, 97-2 CPD ¶ 6 (information in solicitation and ascertainable from site visit were inadequate for bidders to establish the actual work load requirements); *Ferguson-Williams, Inc.*, Comp. Gen. Dec. B-258460, 95-1 CPD ¶ 39 (three lowest bidders misunderstood the estimated quantities in the IFB); *P.J. Dick, Inc.*, Comp. Gen. Dec. B-259166, 95-1 CPD ¶ 131 (bidders were misled where conflicting terms in IFB caused some bidders to include sales taxes in price while others did not); *Hughes & Smith, Inc.*, Comp. Gen. Dec. B-245969, 91-2 CPD ¶ 530 (bidders were misled because Certification of Procurement Integrity in IFB contained no signature line); *A&P Surgical Co.*, 62 Comp. Gen. 256 (B-206111.2), 83-1 CPD ¶ 263 (IFB misled five out of six bidders to offer foreign melted specialty metals when the government required specialty metals melted in the United States).

Estimated quantities that are found to differ significantly from actual anticipated quantities provide a proper basis for cancellation, *C-Cubed Corp.*, Comp. Gen. Dec. B-289867, 2002 CPD ¶ 72; *Ferguson-Williams, Inc.*, Comp. Gen. Dec. B-258460, 95-1 CPD ¶ 39. See *Heritage Reporting Corp.*, Comp. Gen. Dec. B-248860.2, 92-2 CPD ¶ 276 (estimates for base period were exaggerated by 68%). Cancellation is also proper where award is based on estimated quantities, but the solicitation failed to include estimated quantities for all items, *MTL Sys., Inc.*, Comp. Gen. Dec. B-245363, 91-2 CPD ¶ 569.

[b] Specification Defects

FAR 14.404-1(c)(1) states that "inadequate or ambiguous specifications" can be compelling reasons for cancellation. Use of specifications that do not adequately describe the government's actual needs generally provide a compelling reason for cancellation, *Continuum Eng'g*, Comp. Gen. Dec. B-409723, 2014 CPD ¶ 215 (agency did not fully state training requirements); *Brickwood Contractors, Inc.*, Comp. Gen. Dec. B-292171, 2003 CPD ¶ 120 (specification ambiguous and permitted bid that did not meet agency needs); *Cycad Corp.*, Comp. Gen. Dec. B-255870, 94-1 CPD ¶ 253 (IFB did not reflect the agency's needs where a requirement for commercial, off-the-shelf products was omitted); *Renic Gov't Sys.*, Comp. Gen. Dec. B-249484, Nov. 9, 1992, *Unpub.* (IFB failed to include the agency's requirement that work be done by a lawyer licensed in Texas); *United States Elevator Corp.*, Comp. Gen. Dec. B-225625, 87-1 CPD ¶ 401 (agency did not include specifications for major repairs and replacement parts); *Intercomp Co.*, Comp. Gen. Dec. B-213059, 84-1 CPD ¶ 540 (without revised weight and testing requirements for aircraft scales, specifications did not reflect the Navy's needs); *Heart of Am. Police Supply*, Comp. Gen. Dec. B-210911, 84-1 CPD ¶ 423 (specification failed to describe all required features of a brand-name product adequately which resulted in unacceptable bids).

Vague and ambiguous specifications are another compelling reason for cancellation, *Meds Mktg., Inc.*, Comp. Gen. Dec. B-213352, 84-1 CPD ¶318 (specification was so vague that it was not clear what Meds' legal obligation would be if awarded the contract); *Commercial Envelope Mfg. Co.*, Comp. Gen. Dec. B-213272, 84-1 CPD ¶206 (specification was not specific enough to procure center-seam envelopes needed by the IRS). Preservation of the integrity of the competitive bidding system requires that an agency not award a contract if it intends to negotiate specifications after award. See *W.M. Grace, Inc.*, Comp. Gen. Dec. B-202842, 81-2 CPD ¶121, stating:

> An attempt by the contracting officer to negotiate changes with the low bidder which amount to a substantial deviation from the original specifications would be prejudicial to the other bidders because the contract after negotiation would not be the same as that offered the other bidders under the invitation.

See also *Source AV, Inc.*, Comp. Gen. Dec. B-238017, 90-1 CPD ¶336, upholding cancellation of an IFB and denied the protester's argument that modification after award was appropriate, because an agency cannot award a contract with the intention of significantly modifying the terms of the solicitation.

A compelling reason for cancellation exists when an agency concludes that the government's needs can be satisfied by a less expensive design differing from that called for by the IFB, *Jarrett S. Blankenship Co.*, Comp. Gen. Dec. B-211582, 83-2 CPD ¶516 (specification of air-conditioning units with copper coils and fins properly canceled where aluminum coils could meet agency needs at a lesser cost); *Sunrise Int'l Grp.*, Comp. Gen. Dec. B-256912, 94-2 CPD ¶31 (cancellation of IFB for short-order meals was reasonable when full-course meals would meet government's needs at lesser cost); *Uffner Textile Corp.*, Comp. Gen. Dec. B-204358, 82-1 CPD ¶106 (specifications overstated minimum needs when smaller zipper and less restrictive batting specifications would be more cost effective and satisfy the needs of the government).

Cancellation is also appropriate if the agency determines that its specification is unduly restrictive, *Cummins Power Sys., LLC*, Comp. Gen. Dec. B-402079.2, 2010 CPD ¶20 (requirement that bidder be a certified distributor of product); *Hroma Corp.*, Comp. Gen. Dec. B-285053, 2000 CPD ¶88 (requirement that bidder perform 60% of work with own forces); *Siemens Power Corp.*, Comp. Gen. Dec. B-257167, 94-2 CPD ¶160 (specifications overstated type of equipment needed).

[c] Alternate Performance by Government

When the services covered by the invitation could be performed by in-house personnel at a cost savings to the government, cancellation is proper, *Currents Constr., Inc.*, Comp. Gen. Dec. B-236735.2, 90-1 CPD ¶236. See also *Ameriko Maint. Co.*, Comp. Gen. Dec. B-243728, 91-2 CPD ¶191 (GSA determined that it could save nearly $3 million by maintaining in-house performance of the services required by the solicitation). In *Powertronic Sys., Inc.*, Comp. Gen. Dec. B-210283, 83-2 CPD ¶ 346, GAO stated that when the government can build an urgently needed item faster in-house than by contracting out, cancellation of an IFB that would not meet the urgency of the need is proper. See also *Bush-Herrick, Inc.*, Comp. Gen. Dec. B-209683, 83-1 CPD ¶ 669. Cancellation is also appropriate where a solicited item is available within the government at a lower cost, and the available item meets the agency's needs, *Nedlog Co.*, Comp. Gen. Dec. B-212665, 84-1 CPD ¶ 215 (Army's needs met by substituting in-house dry mix beverages for the solicited liquid beverages); *Essex Electro Eng'rs, Inc.*, Comp. Gen. Dec. B-206012.3, 82-2 CPD ¶ 307 (adequate decommissioned generator sets were available within the government).

[d] Lack of Fair Competition

Cancellation is appropriate when competition on an equal basis has been thwarted, *Honeywell, Inc.*, Comp. Gen. Dec. B-210000, 83-1 CPD ¶ 445 (because Air Force did not make historical data or estimates of number of required service calls available, nonincumbent contractors lacked necessary information for intelligent bid preparation). See also *GS Elektro-Schewe GmbH*, Comp. Gen. Dec. B-259103.2, 95-1 CPD ¶ 196 (because agency sent a document to at least one bidder which required a specification that was not included in the IFB, competition on an equal basis was not assured); *HDL Research Lab, Inc.*, Comp. Gen. Dec. B-254863.3, 94-1 CPD ¶ 298 (specifications were biased in favor of the awardee and may have restricted competition when only three of the 66 bidders that were solicited submitted a bid); *Werres Corp.*, Comp. Gen. Dec. B-255379, 94-1 CPD ¶ 153 (solicitation was ambiguous and misled bidders because of an inconsistency between the pricing schedule and the specifications); *Air Inc.*, 69 Comp. Gen. 504 (B-238468), 90-1 CPD ¶ 533 (potential bidders had an unfair advantage where four bids were opened prematurely); *Jackson Marine Cos.*, Comp. Gen. Dec. B-212882, 84-1 CPD ¶ 402 (payment provision put undue economic risk on contractor and discouraged potential bidders from participating in the procurement); and *Downtown Copy Ctr.*, 62 Comp. Gen. 65 (B-206999.6), 82-2 CPD ¶ 503 (inaccurate estimated quantities gave incumbent contractor an unfair advantage). In *Mott Haven Truck Parts, Inc.*, Comp. Gen. Dec. B-210775, 83-2 CPD ¶ 189, untimely dispatch of a material IFB amendment (one day prior to bid opening) was a compelling reason for cancellation due to lack of adequate competition.

[e] Insufficient Funds

The contracting agency's determination that funds are not available for the contract is a compelling reason for cancellation, *Welch Constr., Inc.*, Comp.

Gen. Dec. B-411879, 2015 CPD ¶ 351; *Vinculum Sols., Inc.*, Comp. Gen. Dec. B-408337, 2013 CPD ¶ 191; *Sea Box, Inc.*, Comp. Gen. Dec. B-400198, 2008 CPD ¶ 163; *First Enter.*, Comp. Gen. Dec. B-292967, 2004 CPD ¶ 11. See *First Enter. v. United States*, 61 Fed. Cl. 109 (2004), for a detailed analysis of the discretion afforded an agency in cancelling an IFB when the bids exceed its estimate. Where Congress passes legislation that prohibits obligating funds, cancellation is proper, *Consolidated Maint. Co.*, Comp. Gen. Dec. B-209766, 83-1 CPD ¶ 225 (Joint Continuing Resolution of Dec. 21, 1982, prohibited the agency from obligating funds for the custodial services involved in the solicitation). See also *Satellite Servs., Inc.*, Comp. Gen. Dec. B-225624, 87-1 CPD ¶ 314, finding that cancellation was proper where a congressional appropriations restriction created uncertainties concerning funding.

[f] Inaccurate Statement of Government Needs

FAR 14.404-1(c)(2) states that cancellation may be appropriate where specifications require revision. See, for example, *Corcel Corp.*, Comp. Gen. Dec. B-311332, 2008 CPD ¶ 125, where cancellation was permitted when the agency found that the specification permitted delivery of a valve that did not meet the agency's technical requirements. A compelling reason for cancellation exists where the other parts of the original IFB are inaccurate and must be revised to reflect the needs of the government, *Days Inn Marina*, Comp. Gen. Dec. B-254913, 94-1 CPD ¶ 23 (preaward surveys showed that the stated geographic restriction was insufficient to satisfy government's requirements); *McGhee Constr., Inc.*, Comp. Gen. Dec. B-250073.3, 93-1 CPD ¶ 379 (solicitation failed to reflect agency's need where additional construction services were required); *I.T.S Corp.*, Comp. Gen. Dec. B-242725, 91-1 CPD ¶ 518 (IFB for mail and message services omitting material duties and functions did not reflect agency's requirements); *News Printing, Inc.*, Comp. Gen. Dec. B-274773.2, 97-1 CPD ¶ 68 (significant decrease in estimated quantity provided compelling reason to cancel the IFB).

Changing the specifications of a procurement after bid opening to express the government's new needs constitutes sufficient reason for cancellation, *I.T.S. Corp.*, Comp. Gen. Dec. B-243223, 91-2 CPD ¶ 55 (deployment of troops to hostile area created a need for additional counseling services); *Holk Dev., Inc.*, Comp. Gen. Dec. B-236765.2, 90-1 CPD ¶ 65 (additional work required when asbestos was discovered); *Dyneteria, Inc.*, Comp. Gen. Dec. B-211525.2, 84-2 CPD ¶ 484 (Air Guard conversion from F-4 to F-16 fighters and C-130 to C-5A transports would significantly change manning requirements, aircraft servicing, and fuel consumption); *Tecom, Inc.*, Comp. Gen. Dec. B-213815.2, 84-2 CPD ¶ 152 (material workload changes caused IFB to fail to represent the government's needs); *Electric Maint. & Installation Co.*, Comp. Gen. Dec. B-213005, 84-1 CPD ¶ 292 (Army Corps of Engineers advised that change in river water level would require use of two motors involved in IFB earlier than the expected delivery time).

FAR 14.404-1(c)(3) states that cancellation is proper where supplies or services are no longer required. See *Orange Personnel Servs., Inc.—Recons.*, Comp. Gen. Dec. B-256164.2, 95-1 CPD ¶ 26 (cancellation of solicitation of berthing services for two Ready Reserve Force ships proper where the ships were being repositioned and services were no longer needed); *International Typewriter Exch.*, Comp. Gen. Dec. B-205989.3, 82-2 CPD ¶ 279 (cancellation of solicitation for manual typewriters was proper where conversion to electric typewriters negated the requirement for solicited item).

[g] Unreasonable Prices

Solicitations may properly be canceled if bid prices are unreasonable. FAR 14.404-1(c)(6) permits cancellation if the contracting officer determines in writing that "[a]ll otherwise acceptable bids received are at unreasonable prices." A determination of price unreasonableness may be based upon a comparison of bid prices with such factors as government estimates, past procurement history, current market conditions, or any other relevant factors, *Bay Cities Refuse Serv., Inc.*, Comp. Gen. Dec. B-250807, 93-1 CPD ¶ 151 (all bids were unreasonably high compared with the independent government estimate); *Omega Container, Inc.*, Comp. Gen. Dec. B-206858.2, 82-2 CPD ¶ 475 (agency properly compared Omega's small business bid prices with government estimates, the bid prices of an ineligible bidder, and past procurement prices of the item). Similarly, in *Logistics Int'l, Inc.*, Comp. Gen. Dec. B-254810, 94-1 CPD ¶ 28, a contracting officer properly compared an incumbent large business contractor's price for similar contracts with small business bids and found that the small business bids were unreasonable.

Cancellation is a proper exercise of agency discretion where bids exceed government estimates, even where the low responsible bid was as little as 7.2% greater than the government estimate, *Building Maint. Specialists, Inc.*, Comp. Gen. Dec. B-186441, 76-2 CPD ¶ 233. See *Perimeter Sec. Partners, LLC*, Comp. Gen. Dec. B-417591, 2019 CPD ¶ 305 (23.5% greater); *Norfolk Dredging Co.*, Comp. Gen. Dec. B-417213, 2019 CPD ¶ 127 (more than 24% greater); *Overstreet Elec. Co.*, Comp. Gen. Dec. B-284691, 2000 CPD ¶ 79 (32% greater); *J. Morris & Assocs.*, Comp. Gen. Dec. B-256840, 94-2 CPD ¶ 47 (23% greater); and *Kinetic Structures Corp. v. United States*, 6 Cl. Ct. 387 (1984) (27% greater).

A bid submitted by a commercial concern may be unreasonably high if the marketplace, which includes nonprofit associations, can satisfy the government's needs for substantially less, *International Alliance of Sports Officials*, 63 Comp. Gen. 162 (B-210491), 84-1 CPD ¶ 63 (nonprofit organization could perform for 30% less).

A determination of unreasonable price will be sustained barring bad faith or fraud, *California Shorthand Reporting*, Comp. Gen. Dec. B-250302.2, 93-1 CPD ¶202. In *Stewart-Thomas Indus., Inc.*, Comp. Gen. Dec. B-196295, 80-1 CPD ¶175, the contracting officer asked a prior supplier to explain its failure to bid. The supplier responded by offering a price 40% lower than the lowest bidder. In discussing the propriety of the contracting officer's cancellation of the invitation, GAO stated:

> Stewart-Thomas [low bidder] believes that any award to other than itself at its bid price would be improper because the actions of the contracting activity constituted an impermissible auction. After bids were opened and prices disclosed, the activity, in essence, allegedly attempted to find firms which could offer better prices, notwithstanding the fact that 80 firms had already been solicited on the original solicitation and only seven cared to bid. *Stewart-Thomas*, citing *Interscience Systems, Inc.*, 59 Comp. Gen. 68 (B-194497), 79-2 CPD ¶306, states the activity not only improperly permitted a potential bidder to possibly adjust its price knowing the prices offered by other parties, but it also gave a bidder who had not bothered to bid originally a second bite at the procurement.
>
> * * *
>
> The contracting activity's purpose in contacting the prior contractor was not to require a bid from it, but only to ascertain the validity of the former prices in the current market. In the circumstances, we consider the action proper. Although any cancellation for unreasonable prices may result in nonbidders having another chance to bid (and with the knowledge of the prior bid prices), the competition the second time also provides those bidders who bid unreasonable prices the first time another opportunity to bid as well and this time at reasonable prices.

In some instances, rejected bids are used as the standard of reasonableness. See *Sigma West Corp.*, Comp. Gen. Dec. B-247916, 92-2 CPD ¶31 (nonresponsive bid was 12.5% lower and the defect of the nonresponsive bid had a negligible impact on price); *Dutra/AmClyde (J.V.)*, Comp. Gen. Dec. B-249364.2, 92-2 CPD ¶453 (government estimate and nonresponsive bid were used to determine that bid prices were unreasonable); *Colonial Ford Truck Sales, Inc.*, Comp. Gen. Dec. B-179926, 74-1 CPD ¶80 (nonresponsive bid was 13% lower even though the government had paid higher prices in three of five previous procurements); and *Hercules Demolition Corp.*, Comp. Gen. Dec. B-186411, 76-2 CPD ¶173 (even though the only responsive bid was within the government estimate, it was 36% higher than an "unacceptable" bid).

[h] Impossible to Perform Work Within Schedule

Cancellation is proper when the agency determines that it is not possible to perform the work as called for by the schedule in the IFB, *Chenega Mgmt., LLC*,

Comp. Gen. Dec. B-290598, 2002 CPD ¶ 143. See also *Gaffny Plumbing & Heating Corp.*, Comp. Gen. Dec. B-209815, 83-1 CPD ¶ 648 (delays in completing another construction project made installation of fire sprinkler system impractical); *Champion Structure Co.*, Comp. Gen. Dec. B-198863, 80-2 CPD ¶ 291 (inconsistent provisions rendered performance impossible); and 53 Comp. Gen. 92 (B-178106) (1973) (because of delay in award, the work could not be completed within the government preferred time).

[i] Miscellaneous

Compelling reasons to cancel the IFB have been found where the agency discovered after bid opening that a similar item was on the Federal Supply Schedule from which the agency was required to make its purchases, *Raymond Corp.*, Comp. Gen. Dec. B-246410, 92-1 CPD ¶ 252; *Security Mgmt. Assocs.*, Comp. Gen. Dec. B-214186, 84-2 CPD ¶ 83; where the agency failed to include required wage determination provision in the solicitation, *Dismantlement & Envtl. Mgmt. Co.*, Comp. Gen. Dec. B-257632, 94-2 CPD ¶ 151 (Service Contract Act); *Sunspot Garden Ctr. & Country Craft Gift Shop*, Comp. Gen. Dec. B-237065.2, 90-1 CPD ¶ 224 (Davis-Bacon Act); *Logistical Support, Inc.*, Comp. Gen. Dec. B-212689.3, 84-1 CPD ¶ 191 (Service Contract Act); where the solicitation violates a statute, *Pavel Enters., Inc.*, Comp. Gen. Dec. B-249332, 92-2 CPD ¶ 330; where improper set-aside provisions were included in the IFB, *Midland Transp., Co.*, Comp. Gen. Dec. B-201319, 81-2 CPD ¶ 89; where the agency, although required to do so, did not set the procurement aside, *Baker Support Servs., Inc.*, Comp. Gen. Dec. B-256192.3, 95-1 CPD ¶ 75; *Ryon, Inc.*, Comp. Gen. Dec. B-256752.2, 94-2 CPD ¶ 163; where the completion of another construction project would allow the Air Force to continue its missions without disruption, *S. Sys. Corp.*, Comp. Gen. Dec. B-259827, 95-1 CPD ¶ 221; where the government was unable to timely furnish required government-furnished material and equipment, *Aul Instruments, Inc.*, Comp. Gen. Dec. B-195887, 80-1 CPD ¶ 98; *Monarch Enters., Inc.*, Comp. Gen. Dec. B-201688, 81-1 CPD ¶ 483; and where an "or equal" component of a "brand name or equal" clause was inadvertently omitted, *Seaward Int'l, Inc.*, Comp. Gen. Dec. B-199040, 81-1 CPD ¶ 23.

Occasionally bidders protest an agency's decision to go forward with the solicitation. If GAO agrees that a compelling reason exists and disagrees with the agency's decision not to cancel, it will recommend cancellation, *Gourmet Distribs.*, Comp. Gen. Dec. B-259083, 95-1 CPD ¶ 130 (agency misclassified the invitation in the *Commerce Business Daily*); *Respiratory & Convalescent Specialties, Inc.*, Comp. Gen. Dec. B-255176, 94-1 CPD ¶ 101 (IFB failed to identify an evaluation factor and failed to provide estimates for an item); *Duramed Homecare*, 71 Comp. Gen. 193 (B-245766), 92-1 CPD ¶ 126 (requirements in the IFB were 12 times the amount of the agency's actual past use); *Bartomeli Co.*, 71 Comp. Gen. 237 (B-246060), 92-1 CPD ¶ 170 (protester's bid was prematurely opened and disclosed); *Elrich Constr. Co.*, Comp. Gen.

Dec. B-187726, 77-1 CPD ¶ 105 (no quantity estimates were specified in a requirement-type IFB).

[2] Reasons for Cancellation—Not Compelling

Even though competition is somewhat flawed, the defects may not be sufficiently compelling to call for cancellation. The Court of Federal Claims has emphasized the unfairness of cancellation after the bids have been exposed and has closely scrutinized the agency's basis for cancellation. See *Kiewit Infrastructure West Co. v. United States*, 147 Fed. Cl. 700 (2020), rejecting the cancellation based on the price being significantly higher than the government estimate because the contracting officer did not analyze whether the government estimate was accurate. See also *Great Lakes Dredge & Dry Docks Co. v. United States*, 60 Fed. Cl. 350 (2004) (agency's determination that the specifications were restrictive did not withstand analysis); *Overstreet Elec. Co. v. United States*, 47 Fed. Cl. 728 (2000) (cancellation based on high bid price compared to government estimate based on irrational assumptions); *California Marine Cleaning, Inc. v. United States*, 42 Fed. Cl. 281 (1998) (cancellation based on a potential defect in the way bids were delivered to the agency but there was no evidence of an actual problem); *Vanguard Sec., Inc. v. United States*, 20 Cl. Ct. 90 (1990) (cancellation based on allegedly ambiguous IFB provisions improper when court found provisions clear).

[a] No Prejudice and Low Bidder Meets Agency's Needs

Cancellation after bid opening is generally inappropriate where an IFB or specification defect did not cause any competitive prejudice and an award under the solicitation would serve the actual needs of the government, *Massaro Co.*, Comp. Gen. Dec. B-280772.2, 98-2 CPD ¶ 123 (IFB pricing requirements subject to only one reasonable interpretation); *Canadian Commercial Corp.*, Comp. Gen. Dec. B-255642, 94-1 CPD ¶ 202 (no bidder prejudiced where an allegedly ambiguous provision only had one reasonable interpretation); *Sierra Forest Prods.*, Comp. Gen. Dec. B-245393, 92-1 CPD ¶ 4 (failure to send required form to prospective bidders did not prejudice bidders when they were on notice of the requirement and could have obtained a copy of the missing form); *Richard Hoffman Corp.*, Comp. Gen. Dec. B-212775.2, 83-2 CPD ¶ 656 (solicitation was ambiguous regarding pricing of informational items but no bidder was misled); *American Mut. Protective Bureau*, 62 Comp. Gen. 354 (B-209192), 83-1 CPD ¶ 469 (IFB ambiguous but no prejudice where all six bidders correctly computed their bids); *Tennessee Valley Serv. Co.—Recons.*, Comp. Gen. Dec. B-188771, 77-2 CPD ¶ 241 (no bidder prejudiced by having the contracting officer multiply the unit prices by the applicable estimated quantities to determine the low bidder).

A solicitation was improperly canceled on the grounds of a purported ambiguity where evidence available from the offeror's cost proposals that tended to disprove the ambiguity was ignored, *Apex Int'l Mgmt. Servs., Inc.*, 60 Comp. Gen. 172 (B-200008), 81-1 CPD ¶ 24.

[b] Potential Competitor Not Solicited

Failure to solicit a potential competitor is not a compelling reason for cancellation if competition is otherwise adequate, prices are reasonable, the agency does not deliberately exclude a bidder, and it complies with all regulations governing the distribution and advertisement of a solicitation, *Eagle Creek Archaeological Servs., Inc.*, Comp. Gen. Dec. B-258480, 95-1 CPD ¶ 43 (agency did not deliberately exclude bidder, and the record showed there was adequate competition and reasonable prices); *Energy Mgmt. Sys.*, Comp. Gen. Dec. B-258391, 94-2 CPD ¶ 208 (no showing that agency deliberately excluded a bidder from competition where bidder failed to review the CBD and to apply for inclusion on the mailing list); *Cinema Color Grp.*, Comp. Gen. Dec. B-210666, 83-2 CPD ¶ 257 (advertising procurement under heading of "photographic equipment" not shown to be a deliberate attempt to preclude protester from bidding).

However, where an agency fails to comply with the statutory and regulatory requirements regarding distribution of solicitations, cancellation is appropriate, *Goodway Graphics of Virginia, Inc.*, Comp. Gen. Dec. B-297789, 2006 CPD ¶ 54 (agency failed to solicit two incumbents and failed to post procurement on *fedbizopps.gov*); *Kertzman Contracting, Inc.*, Comp. Gen. Dec. B-259461.2, 95-1 CPD ¶ 226 (agency failed to send amendment to a bidder on the mailing list); *Telos Field Eng'g*, Comp. Gen. Dec. B-257747, 94-2 CPD ¶ 172 (agency failed to obtain "full and open" competition when it only provided copies of the solicitation to four firms considered to be industry leaders). In addition, an agency's failure to solicit an incumbent contractor may not satisfy the "full and open" competition requirement, *Pratt & Lambert, Inc.*, Comp. Gen. Dec. B-245537, 92-1 CPD ¶ 48; *Kimber Guard & Patrol, Inc.*, Comp. Gen. Dec. B-248920, 92-2 CPD ¶ 220.

[c] Increases in Quantity Only

Where the government determines that additional quantities of the same item are needed after bid opening, cancellation is not generally deemed compelling. FAR 14.404-1(a)(3) provides:

> As a general rule, after the opening of bids, an invitation should not be canceled and resolicited due solely to increased requirements for the items being acquired. Award should be made on the initial invitation for bids and the additional quantity should be treated as a new acquisition.

FAR 14.404-1(a)(3) only applies in cases where an agency is procuring products and not where the agency is procuring services, *Bangar Contractors Corp.*, Comp. Gen. Dec. B-240071, 90-2 CPD ¶ 295; *Bill McCann*, Comp. Gen. Dec. B-234199.2, 89-1 CPD ¶ 554. GAO has discussed this regulation on several occasions but has not decided any case where increases in quantity alone were at issue, *Dyneteria, Inc.*, Comp. Gen. Dec. B-211525.2, 84-2 CPD ¶ 484 (closely interrelated aspects of fuel management operations made the above provision inapplicable); *Genco Tool & Eng'g Co.*, 61 Comp. Gen. 281 (B-204582), 82-1 CPD ¶ 175 (insufficient funds were also at issue); and *ABC Demolition Corp.*, Comp. Gen. Dec. B-192111, 78-2 CPD ¶ 339 (change in agency needs involved additional performance of a different nature than that required under the solicitation).

[3] Partial Cancellation

There are situations after bid opening where partial cancellation of the solicitation is justified. See *Hampton Metropolitan Oil Co.*, Comp. Gen. Dec. B-186030, 76-2 CPD ¶ 471, stating:

> [W]e believe the provisions of ASPR 2-404.1(b) [now FAR 14.404-1(b)], which merely refer to cancellation of an IFB, must be read as permitting cancellation of either all or a portion of the IFB, as may be required by the circumstances, and not as requiring cancellation of the IFB in toto or not at all.

Where the solicitation includes, but is not limited to, work for an item that the agency does not need, or where there is a solicitation defect that directly affects only a portion of the invitation's bid items, and the government has the right under the solicitation to accept any item or groups of items, the contracting officer should cancel only the affected portion of the IFB, *Telemarc, Inc.*, Comp. Gen. Dec. B-242339, 91-1 CPD ¶ 375 (ambiguous specification for a line item of the solicitation justified cancellation of that one item); *Hartridge Equip. Corp.*, Comp. Gen. Dec. B-230039, 88-1 CPD ¶ 284 (cancellation proper for line item where specification for line item was defective); *Kan-Du Tool & Instrument Corp.*, Comp. Gen. Dec. B-210819, 83-2 CPD ¶ 12 (proper for Army to cancel 8,699 items and award 1,549 items to responsive bidders). See also *Adrian Supply Co.*, Comp. Gen. Dec. B-240871, 90-2 CPD ¶ 515 (partial cancellation appropriate where bid prices for line item exceeded government estimate by more than 100%); *Duracell, Inc.*, Comp. Gen. Dec. B-229538, 88-1 CPD ¶ 145 (partial cancellation proper where agency could not legally award 40% of the solicitation to bidder); and *McGregor Printing Corp.*, Comp. Gen. Dec. B-207084, 82-2 CPD ¶ 240 (proper for GSA to cancel portions of two solicitations because of decreased demand and amount of space available in certain depots).

[4] Reinstatement of the Solicitation

Although the FAR does not directly address reinstatement of a procurement after cancellation, FAR 14.404-1 does contain the following guidance on "completion of the acquisition after cancellation":

> (e) Under some circumstances, completion of the acquisition after cancellation of the invitation for bids may be appropriate.
>
> > (1) If the invitation for bids has been canceled for the reasons specified in subparagraphs (c) (6), (7), or (8) of this subsection, and the agency head has authorized, in the determination in paragraph (c) of this subsection, the completion of the acquisition through negotiation, the contracting officer shall proceed in accordance with 15.103.
> >
> > (2) If the invitation for bids has been canceled for the reasons specified in subparagraphs (c)(1), (2), (4), (5), or (10) of this subsection, or for the reasons in subparagraphs (c)(6), (7), or (8) of this subsection and completion through negotiation is not authorized under subparagraph (e)(1) of this subsection, the contracting officer shall proceed with a new acquisition.

GAO has stated that this provision only prohibits reinstatement of a procurement that was properly canceled. See *KAL Maint., Inc.*, Comp. Gen. Dec. B-225429, 87-1 CPD ¶ 207, stating:

> Although, as the protester points out, the FAR, 48 C.F.R. § 14.404-1(e)(2), does not expressly state that it applies only to IFB's which have been canceled properly, we think it logical to apply it only in that context, because the provision's purpose is to prescribe a second competition where the results of the first have been invalidated by some defect. It permits the government to set things right—through revising the specifications, for example—and obtain competition based upon an accurate statement of the government's needs. Here, the original IFB in fact was not defective (although for some time after bid opening the Air Force erroneously thought that it was) and it did result in competition from 17 bidders, including the protester. Since an award under the original IFB would serve the government's needs, a second competition would only prejudice those bidders whose prices have been exposed and afford the protester, the eighth low bidder, an opportunity to improve its competitive position. *See ADAK* [*Communications Sys., Inc.*, B-222546, July 24, 1986, 86-2 CPD ¶ 103]; *Woodson Construction Co.—Reconsideration*, B-221530.2, May 23, 1986, 86-1 CPD ¶ 483; *Suburban Industrial Maintenance Co.*, B-188179, June 28, 1977, 77-1 CPD ¶ 459. Reinstatement therefore is necessary to protect the integrity of the competitive procurement system by avoiding an unfair bidding situation after the bids were made public. *See ADAK, supra; Lanier Business Products, Inc.*, B-203977, Feb. 23, 1982, 82-1 CPD ¶ 159.

Thus, reinstatement is appropriate as a means of promoting the integrity of the bidding system when the cancellation was improper, *Bilt-Rite Contractors, Inc.*, Comp. Gen. Dec. B-259106.2, 95-1 CPD ¶ 220 (reinstatement was proper where IFB was erroneously canceled because agency incorrectly believed that low bid was nonresponsive); *U.S. Rentals*, 69 Comp. Gen. 395 (B-238090), 90-1 CPD ¶ 367 (IFB reinstated where apparent inconsistency in solicitation did not prejudice any bidder). However, where the agency's actual needs have changed since the issuance of the original solicitation, GAO will recommend resolicitation, rather than reinstatement, *TWI Inc.*, Comp. Gen. Dec. B-202966.4, 82-2 CPD ¶ 487.

Upon reinstatement of the solicitation, bids may generally be revived, *U.S. Rentals*, 69 Comp. Gen. 395 (B-238090), 90-1 CPD ¶ 367; *Sac & Fox Indus., Ltd.*, Comp. Gen. Dec. B-231873, 88-2 CPD ¶ 250. This is appropriate even where bids have been returned to all offerors, if a record of the contents of the bids has been made. In *Baker Mfg. Co.*, 59 Comp. Gen. 573 (B-197016), 80-2 CPD ¶ 1, an abstract of bids provided suitable evidence of original bid prices and responsiveness. However, bids could not be revived in *L.V. Anderson & Sons, Inc.*, Comp. Gen. Dec. B-189835, 77-2 CPD ¶ 249, where no record of the contents of the bids was made prior to their return.

§ 5.05 MISTAKES

Mistakes are a major exception to the firm bid rule used in sealed bidding, *Refining Assocs. v. United States*, 109 F. Supp. 259 (Ct. Cl. 1953). The process of bid preparation and submission is frequently hectic. Specifications and drawings must be analyzed, subcontractors' and vendors' bids coordinated, and costs estimated—usually in a short period of time. In such an environment, mistakes are common. It has long been recognized that it would not be fair for the government to take advantage of a bid containing a mistake when the government knew or should have known of the mistake, *Chernick v. United States*, 372 F.2d 492 (Ct. Cl. 1967). See also *Pavco, Inc.*, ASBCA 23783, 80-1 BCA ¶ 14,407; *Black Diamond Energies, Inc.*, Comp. Gen. Dec. B-241370, 91-1 CPD ¶ 119.

This exception has been exceedingly difficult to administer. Once bids are opened and announced, low bidders may be tempted to assert that mistakes have been made in order to increase their price or to avoid award. Bidders that are not low may identify mistakes that, if corrected, would make them low. In all such cases, the integrity of the bidding process may be threatened if correction of mistakes is too liberally permitted. Hence, a sophisticated set of rules has evolved to deal with mistakes in bids.

The first section analyzes the types of mistakes that are covered by these rules. The second section discusses the responsibility of the contracting officer when mistakes are suspected. Finally, the third section reviews the actions that can be taken after it has been ascertained that a mistake in bid has occurred.

[A] Defining Mistake

Relief is only provided for certain types of mistakes. Although the FAR is silent on this issue, the courts, boards, and GAO make a distinction between *ministerial errors* and *judgmental errors* in granting relief for mistakes in bids. In *Ruggiero v. United States*, 420 F.2d 709 (Ct. Cl. 1970), the court stated at 713:

> The mistake . . . must be . . . a clear cut clerical or arithmetical error, or misreading of specifications, and the authorities cited do not extend to mistakes of judgment.

The court also ruled that negligence by the bidder was not a bar to relief since in most cases where relief had been granted the bidders had been "guilty of egregious blunders." See *BCM Corp. v. United States*, 2 Cl. Ct. 602 (1983), pointing out that "the reasonableness of the mistake is not relevant" to the rules relating to mistakes in bid.

[1] Business Judgment

Bidders make numerous business judgments in the process of submitting bids. They must assess the complexity of the task, determine the amount of effort required to perform the work, and decide whether to perform the work with their own forces or by subcontract. If their judgments in these areas prove to be in error, relief will not be granted. Thus, when a bidder makes a business judgment, it assumes the responsibility that the judgment may be faulty and is "taking a conscious gamble with known risks," *Liebherr Crane Corp. v. United States*, 810 F.2d 1153 (Fed. Cir. 1987). See also *Giesler v. United States*, 232 F.3d 864 (Fed. Cir. 2000) (failure to read specification); *RQ Constr., Inc.*, ASBCA 52376, 01-2 BCA ¶ 31,627 (failing to determine the effort needed to use an arguably specified material); *Aydin Corp. v. United States*, 669 F.2d 681 (Ct. Cl. 1982) (errors concerning the nature and costs of materials necessary to perform the work); *American Ship Bldg. Co. v. United States*, 654 F.2d 75 (Ct. Cl. 1981) (not fully assessing the difficulty of the work); *National Line Co. v. United States*, 607 F.2d 978 (Ct. Cl. 1979) (determinations of the adequacy of plant, equipment, personnel, and the attainable rate of production); *Wyodak Enters., Inc.*, VABCA 3678, 95-1 BCA ¶ 27,493 (underestimation of effort required to comply with contract requirements); *Franklin Pavkov Constr. Co.*, HUDBCA 93-C-C13, 94-3 BCA ¶ 27,078 (underestimation of square footage due to bidder's lack of site inspection); *Fan, Inc.*, GSBCA 7836, 91-1 BCA ¶ 23,364 (using past experience to estimate the number of ventilation units needing adjustment); *EDC/MTI (J.V.)*, ENGBCA 5631, 90-2 BCA ¶ 22,669 (inaccurate assessments of the availability and cost of insurance); *Overhead Elec. Co.*, ASBCA 25656, 85-2 BCA ¶ 18,026 (neglecting to obtain prices from a supplier); *SCM Corp.*, ASBCA 26544, 85-1 BCA ¶ 17,783 (knowingly using a low overhead rate); and *Superior Servs.*, ASBCA 28300, 84-3 BCA ¶ 17,547 (failing to consider the costs of providing supplies and equipment).

A mistake that is neither a mistake in business judgment nor a misreading of the specifications but was inadvertent was held to be the type of mistake that is correctable, *Will H. Hall & Son, Inc. v. United States*, 54 Fed. Cl. 436 (2002). There, the bidder had failed to read a caveat in a subcontractor's bid excluding required work. However, relief was denied because of lack of clear and convincing evidence of the intended bid.

[2] Clerical or Arithmetical Errors

Clerical or arithmetical errors are the most common types of mistakes for which relief is granted. See, for example, *Paragon Energy Corp. v. United States*, 645 F.2d 966 (Ct. Cl. 1981), *recons. denied*, 230 Ct. Cl. 884 (1982) (omission of one element of cost estimates); *McCarty Corp. v. United States*, 499 F.2d 633 (Ct. Cl. 1974) (numbers transposed on bid document); *Government Micro Res., Inc. v. Dep't of the Treasury*, GSBCA 12364-TD, 94-2 BCA ¶ 26,680 (reversal of discount and cost rates in offer preparation); *Michaels Constr. Co.*, Comp. Gen. Dec. B-257764, 94-2 CPD ¶ 176 (using incorrect number of square feet to calculate the unit price); *Pipeline Constr., Inc.*, Comp. Gen. Dec. B-256799, 94-2 CPD ¶ 21 (omitting a zero when transcribing from worksheet to final bid); *C Constr. Co.*, Comp. Gen. Dec. B-253198.2, 93-2 CPD ¶ 198 (mistaken use of macro computer command resulted in a misleading screen); *Columbia Pac. Constr. Co.*, Comp. Gen. Dec. B-207313, 82-1 CPD ¶ 436 (dividing rather than multiplying in making metric conversion); and *PK Contractors, Inc.*, Comp. Gen. Dec. B-205482, 82-1 CPD ¶ 368 (error in pagination resulted in failure to include estimated costs on one page of estimating sheets).

Relief has also been given for clerical or arithmetical errors made by suppliers and subcontractors. See *R.P. Richards Constr. Co.*, Comp. Gen. Dec. B-258923, 95-1 CPD ¶ 103, granting relief for a subcontractor's typographical error, stating that the error "precludes the bidder from making a knowing judgment about its actual intended bid." See also *Chemtronics, Inc.*, ASBCA 30883, 88-2 BCA ¶ 20,534, granting relief when the bidder relied on erroneous quotation from the only supplier of a particular commodity. But see *Triax Pac., Inc.*, ASBCA 41891, 94-1 BCA ¶ 26,380, denying relief because the subcontractor's price misquotation was obviously lower than any other quote received. The board reasoned that the bidder "assumed the risk of [the subcontractor's] mistaken ... quote because it failed to investigate thoroughly the 'dramatically higher' ... quote it received."

In some cases, determining whether there is a clerical or arithmetical error or a mistake in judgment is very difficult. See, for example, *Ruggiero v. United States*, 420 F.2d 709 (Ct. Cl. 1970), where the court concluded that failure to include an "all or none" stipulation in a multiple-item contract was a clerical mistake because the price of one item made no commercial sense without the other items; and *JAL Constr., Inc.*, AGBCA 80-117-3, 81-1 BCA ¶ 14,850, where an omission of work in a subcontractor's estimate due to a misunderstanding between the bidder and the subcontractor was held to be a clerical error. In *Rockwell Int'l Corp.*, ASBCA 41095, 95-1 BCA ¶ 27,459, the board found it unnecessary to determine whether the selection of the wrong algorithm was a clear-cut clerical or mathematical error or an error in judgment. Rather, it denied relief on the grounds that the "error" occurred in the use of a complex algorithm which was not "clear cut" and, therefore, did not meet the test for an arithmetical mistake.

[3] Misreading Specifications

Misreading of specifications is not considered to be an error in business judgment when it involves the quantity or nature of the work rather than the effort required to perform the work. See *Walter Straga*, ASBCA 26134, 83-2 BCA ¶ 16,611, where the contractor's estimate was based upon an unreasonable but mistaken interpretation of the specifications. The board granted relief, finding the misreading of the specifications as to the quantity of items covered was not an error in business judgment. See also *Faulkner Corp.*, VABCA 2998, 90-1 BCA ¶ 22,507, where relief was granted when the contractor misread ambiguous plan headings and mistakenly substituted one for the other; and *BDF Tesa Corp.*, GSBCA 8307, 89-3 BCA ¶ 21,925, where relief was granted when the contractor mistakenly believed its masking tape would meet the military's strict specifications. Similarly, in *BCM Corp. v. United States*, 2 Cl. Ct. 602 (1983), a contractor who unreasonably misinterpreted the contract specification obtained relief because a mistake in judgment had not occurred. When determining its bid price the bidder failed to include a particular, identifiable portion of work and had not underestimated the work it thought was included. See *Derek & Dana Contracting, Inc. v. United States*, 7 Cl. Ct. 627 (1985) (mistakenly believing that one part of the specified work would be included only when an addendum was issued); *WICO, Inc.*, EBCA 125-6-80, 80-2 BCA ¶ 14,790 (basing bid on obsolete drawings); and *Ralph Larsen & Son, Inc. v. United States*, 17 Cl. Ct. 39 (1989) ("unilateral mistake" when subcontractors misinterpreted specifications). For a case finding no mistake when the contractor's subcontractor misinterpreted the specifications, see *H. Fair Assocs.*, ASBCA 26950, 82-2 BCA ¶ 16,112. There, the board concluded that the contractor had made a judgmental error in relying on the subcontractor and the subcontractor had made a judgmental error in "not examining all of the specifications and drawings"—apparently reasoning that they were so clear that the subcontractor would not have arrived at its interpretation if it had conducted a thorough examination.

No misreading of the specifications is found where the contractor makes a judgment as to the amount of effort or the cost that is required to perform the work. See *Aquila Fitness Consulting Sys., Ltd.*, Comp. Gen. Dec. B-286488,

2001 CPD ¶ 4 (decision to use part-time employees when specification required full-time employees); *Northern NEF, Inc.*, ASBCA 44996, 94-3 BCA ¶ 27,094 (decision to use an employee at a lower wage than permitted by Service Contract Act wage determination); *Boeing Computer Servs.*, ASBCA 42674, 94-3 BCA ¶ 27,114 (decision to use fewer employees than required to perform work); *Klinger Constructors, Inc.*, ASBCA 41006, 91-3 BCA ¶ 24,218 (failure to include state tax in price); *Dick & Kirkman, Inc.*, VABCA 1545, 84-3 BCA ¶ 17,662 (assumption, on advice of a supplier, that a portion of the specifications could be ignored); *Technology Chem., Inc.*, ASBCA 26304, 82-2 BCA ¶ 15,927 (deliberate choice to use a cheaper, nonconforming material).

Lack of information in the specifications is not a misreading of the specifications. See *Zafer Constr. Co.*, ASBCA 56769, 17-1 BCA ¶ 17,776, stating at 179,230:

> Where there are gaps, inconsistencies, or insufficient information in the solicitation documents, and the contractor's failure to inquire with the government results in an erroneous proposal, the contractor assumes the risk of its failure to inquire. See, e.g., *Giesler v. United States*, 232 F.3d 864, 870-71 (Fed. Cir. 2000) (appellant's bid without having verified the specifications cannot be construed as a "misreading"); *DynCorp*, 2017-1 BCA ¶ 36,653 (appellant's decision to submit a proposal without having first inquired into "gaps" in the solicitation data was a business judgment).

Failure to read and consider the contract specifications does not constitute a "misreading," *Liebherr Crane Corp. v. United States*, 810 F.2d 1153 (Fed. Cir. 1987) (failure to read 94 of 98 specifications was a "conscious gamble with known risks" and treated as an error in business judgment). See also *Minority Enters., Inc.*, ASBCA 45549, 95-1 BCA ¶ 27,461 (contractor correctly read three golf course drawings but did not read fourth); *Electrical Sys. Eng'g Co.*, ASBCA 37147, 90-2 BCA ¶ 22,715 (reprocurement contractor used bill of materials of terminated contractor but did not read contract specifications); and *Universal Constr. Co.*, NASABCA 83-1092, 93-3 BCA ¶ 26,173 (contractor failed to read drawings along with specifications as contract stipulated). But see *Minnesota Well Drillers*, ASBCA 26097, 82-1 BCA ¶ 15,539, where the board found a mistake where the contractor failed to read revised specifications describing harder material to be drilled than that called out in the original IFB. The board stated at 77,045:

> [The contractor's] stupidity in bidding without reading the revised specifications does not forfeit relief because such foolishness or a variation thereof is common to most bidders who err in bidding and such conduct is of diminished importance in deciding whether to reform a contract. *Chris Berg v. United States*, 192 Ct. Cl. 176, 426 F.2d 314 (1970).

The board reached this decision partially on the theory that there had not been a mistake in business judgment because most contractors in this area did not read specification revisions.

[B] Knowledge of Error and Verification

Although some mistakes are identified by the bidder, most of the controversy over mistakes revolves around the question of whether the government should have identified the mistake. The rationale underlying relief in this situation is that it would be unfair for the government to hold a bidder to a bargain when the government knew of or should have discerned the mistake and called it to the attention of the bidder. If the government appropriately notifies the bidder of a possible mistake or the bidder alleges a mistake, the bidder can request withdrawal or modification of the bid or can elect to stand by the bid as originally submitted.

If the government fails to notify the bidder of a suspected mistake, it may subsequently be subject to a claim for price adjustment, or the contractor may use a claimed mistake as a basis for avoiding performance obligations. To eliminate these problems the regulations impose verification requirements on the contracting officer. FAR 14.407-1 provides the following guidance:

> After the opening of bids, contracting officers shall examine all bids for mistakes. In cases of apparent mistakes and in cases where the contracting officer has reason to believe that a mistake may have been made, the contracting officer shall request from the bidder a verification of the bid, calling attention to the suspected mistake. If the bidder alleges a mistake, the matter shall be processed in accordance with this section 14.407. Such actions shall be taken before award.

The verification process must be followed precisely in order to assure the bidder fair treatment. This section first discusses the circumstances under which the government obtains actual knowledge of a mistake or is held to have reason to know of it. It then deals with the adequacy of the verification process.

[1] Knowledge or Reason to Know

There are relatively few litigated cases where the government actually knows of an error and awards without adequate verification. One example is *Walter Straga*, ASBCA 26134, 83-2 BCA ¶ 16,611, where the government project manager's actual knowledge of the contractor's error was imputed to the contracting officer. See also *Derek & Dana Contracting, Inc. v. United States*, 7 Cl. Ct. 627 (1985), where the bidder orally advised the bid opening official that certain costs were not included in the bid.

In determining whether the government *should have known* of the mistake, the general test is whether a reasonable person, knowing all the facts and circumstances, would have suspected a mistake. See *Chernick v. United States*, 372 F.2d 492 (Ct. Cl. 1967), where the court stated at 496:

> The test of what an official in charge of accepting bids "should" have known must be that of reasonableness, *i.e.*, whether under the facts and circumstances of the case there were any factors which reasonably should have raised the presumption of error in the mind of the contracting officer; among such factors are obvious wide range of bids, and gross disparity between the price bid and the value of the article which was the subject of the bid.

The circumstances that can put the contracting officer on notice are more specifically detailed in *BCM Corp. v. United States*, 2 Cl. Ct. 602 (1983), at 610:

> An oft-cited article, Doke, *Mistakes in Government Contracts—Error Detection Duty of Contracting Officer*, 18 S.W.L.J. I (1964) ("Doke"), delineates these general categories: (1) facially apparent errors, such as multiplication errors made when computing unit prices into total price; (2) disparity in prices among the bids; (3) disparity between the bid and the private government estimate; (4) disparity between the bid and the cost of prior procurements of the same item; (5) disparity between the bid price and, if the contracting officer knows it, the market value for the goods.

These rules are not applied mechanically, and no single rule is either necessary or sufficient to impute knowledge of error. Thus, the government will properly be charged with knowledge only after a full consideration of all the circumstances, *Darwin Constr. Co.*, GSBCA 6590, 84-1 BCA ¶ 17,230, *recons. denied*, 84-2 BCA ¶ 17,356. See *Troise v. United States*, 21 Cl. Ct. 48 (1990), where the contractor purposely deviated from the contract specifications to arrive at its bid as it had done in a previous contract. The court held that since the bid was not out of line with the government estimate and the other bids, the contracting officer did not have to "speculate as to the basis of the contractor's bid" because to hold thus "would make the United States an insurer of its contractor's mistakes."

The most common situation putting the contracting officer on constructive notice of a possible error is a disparity between a favorable bid and the other bids or the government's estimate. In *Government Micro Res., Inc. v. Dep't of the Treasury*, GSBCA 12364-TD, 94-2 BCA ¶ 26,680, constructive notice was imputed when the bidder's price of $864,482 was 62% less than the government's lowest estimate, 31% less than the supplier's schedule price, and 33% less than the other vendor's quote. The board rejected the government argument that, based upon an audit report on a proposed contract of $130 million, it could expect large discounts on the supplier's list price. Constructive notice was also imputed in *L & D Indus., Inc.*, ASBCA 38239, 91-2 BCA ¶ 23,718, where there was an "obvious and substantial" disparity among the bidder's bid of $50.45, bids of $132.00 and $145.70 by the other low vendors, and a previous solicitation price of $15740 received for the same item; *George A. Harris Enters., Inc.*, GSBCA 9888, 90-1 BCA ¶ 22,405, where the bid was over 24% lower than the next lowest bid and "the contract was not large or particularly complex" so should not have produced the disparity that it did; *Figgie Int'l, Inc.*, ASBCA 27541, 83-1 BCA ¶ 16,421, where the bidder's failure to include costs for packaging should have been noted by the contracting officer because all other responsive bids were from 43% to 82% higher than the bid, and the bidder had not significantly increased its price from that of a prior contract with significantly less costly packaging requirements. GAO has found constructive notice when there was a disparity between the mistaken bid, the only other bid, and the prior year's contract price, *Ace Window Cleaning Co.*, Comp. Gen. Dec. B-183380, 75-1 CPD ¶ 379; a significant variation from the average of all other bids (127% higher) and from the next low bidder (59% higher), *American Food Serv. Equip., Inc.*, Comp. Gen. Dec. B-181878, 74-2 CPD ¶ 83; a variation from the bidder's general pattern of prior bids and the market prices for that item, *Calumet Y Farm Store*, Comp. Gen. Dec. B-181284, 74-2 CPD ¶ 11; and when the only bid received varied 21% over the government estimate, *Murphy Elevator Co.*, Comp. Gen. Dec. B-180607, 74-1 CPD ¶ 164.

Other factors in the bid may also place the contracting officer on notice that a mistake may have been made. See *Franklin Pavkov Constr. Co.*, HUDBCA 93-C-C13, 94-3 BCA ¶ 27,078 (bidder's estimate was based on 200 square feet of work and the contracting officer knew the need far exceeded that figure and the only other bid estimated 2,000 square feet); and *Carter Chevrolet Agency*, GSBCA 10142, 90-2 BCA ¶ 22,804 (bidder inconsistently priced vehicles with extra options the same or less than vehicles without options). Another example can be seen in *Connelly Containers, Inc. v. United States*, 7 Cl. Ct. 423 (1985), where, while a bid was only 5% lower than the other lowest bid, the disparity of individual bid prices should have alerted the contracting officer to the possibility of mistake. In that instance, the prices for shipping identical containers were higher for shorter distances than for longer distances.

Constructive knowledge will not be found if the disparity is insufficiently wide and there are no other indications that a mistake has been made. Insufficient disparity has been found where the bid is far below the government estimate but is close to other bids, *Beyley Constr. Grp. Corp.*, ASBCA 55692, 08-2 BCA ¶ 33,999, *aff'd*, 351 Fed. Appx. 446 (Fed. Cir. 2009) (bid 20.69% below government estimate but next low bid only 2.52% higher than contractor's bid); *Conner Bros. Constr. Co. v. United States*, 65 Fed. Cl. 657 (2005) (bid 90.3% of government estimate and approximately 12% under next low bidder); *R.J. Sanders, Inc. v. United States*, 24 Cl. Ct. 288 (1991) (bid 32% less than Navy's estimate but only 18% less than next low bid); *Electrical Sys. Eng'g Co.*, ASBCA 37147, 90-2 BCA ¶ 22,715 (bid 18.4% lower than government estimate and 6.7% away from next low bid). Insufficient disparity has also been found where the bid is far below all other bids but is close to the government estimate, *T.R. Orr, Inc.*, IBCA 3143, 94-2 BCA ¶26,865 (bid of $37,750 was much less than only other bid of $59,711, but government estimate was $41,100); *Triax Pac., Inc.*, ASBCA 41891, 94-1 BCA ¶26,380 (bid was 1.63% higher than government estimate, 13.78% lower than second low bid, and 14.94% lower than third low bid); *AQA Sys., Inc.*, ASBCA 45051, 93-3 BCA ¶25,996 (bid of $154,000 was close to government estimate of $167,450 even though the only other two bids were much higher at $274,700 and $600,000); *Edsall Constr. Co.*, IBCA 2450, 89-3 BCA ¶22,177 (disparity of $1,540,000, $1,678,010, and $1,712,000 in bids); and *C.E. Wylie Constr. Co.*, ASBCA 25587, 81-2 BCA ¶15,427 ($10,000 error on a $6 million procurement).

Even in instances where the disparity may be sufficiently wide, if the government can successfully explain the reasoning that led to a decision not to request verification, constructive notice will not be found. In *Hankins Constr. Co. v. United States*, 838 F.2d 1194 (Fed. Cir. 1988), a cluster of higher bids was explained with the theory of "high balling" from offerors that were not interested in receiving the job unless they would make a large profit. See also *Walsh Constr. Co. of Illinois*, ASBCA 52952, 02-1 BCA ¶32,024 (bid on one line item was quite low but total bid appeared close to other bids and government estimate); *Packard Constr. Corp.*, ASBCA 45996, 94-1 BCA ¶26,512 (bid was 13% less than government estimate but contracting officer knew that in a similar previous situation the same bidder had bid below the government estimate, had made no complaint of error, and had performed the contract); *Triax Pac., Inc.*, ASBCA 41891, 94-1 BCA ¶26,380 (government explained that it believed the bidder had bid low to "buy in" or because it did not make a site visit); *Wheeled Coach Indus. v. General Servs. Admin.*, GSBCA 10314, 93-1 BCA ¶25,245 (government's two-part price analysis search for errors was accepted even though a line item search would have discerned error); *Folgore Mobile Welding, Inc.*, ASBCA 33250, 88-3 BCA ¶21,172 (low bid partially explained because contracting officer knew the bidder was experienced, with excellent references, and that there had been a business slump in the oil industry); and *Singleton Contracting Co.*, ASBCA 26862, 82-2 BCA ¶15,994, *aff'd*, 723 F.2d 68 (Fed. Cir. 1983) (allegedly mistaken bid, only other bid, and government estimate were $123,460, $247,000, and $98,000, respectively, but variations did not place the contracting officer on notice of a mistake because (a) the contracting officer reasonably believed the high bid contained errors, (b) the bidder "enjoyed a reputation of skill, integrity and competency in bidding and contracting," and (c) there was reason to believe that the government estimate was adequate, although low, while the bidder's bid was "exactly on target.").

[2] Adequacy of Verification Request

A contracting officer on notice of a possible mistake must not only request verification of the bid, but also disclose the particular reasons that led to the suspicion, FAR 14.407-3(g)(1). In *Klinger Constructors, Inc.*, ASBCA 41006, 91-3 BCA ¶ 24,218, the board summarized this concept, stating at 121,125:

> [T]he bid verification request should aim at informing the bidder of all the pertinent factors that indicate to the contracting officer that an error might have been made. The adequacy of verification will turn on an assessment of the reasonableness of the contracting officer's disclosure.

Absent such a disclosure, the request is inadequate, *United States v. Metro Novelty Mfg. Co.*, 125 F. Supp. 713 (S.D.N.Y. 1954). See *Caddell Constr. Co. v. United States*, 125 Fed. Cl. 30 (2016) (bidder told its price was higher than the government estimate when it was 16.6% lower); *United States v. Hamilton Enters., Inc.*, 711 F.2d 1038 (Fed. Cir. 1983) (bidder not informed of large variation in manhours between its bid and government estimate, 1,941 versus 6,402 hours, respectively); *BCM Corp. v. United States*, 2 Cl. Ct. 602 (1983) (the third low bidder was told neither of the 18% variation between its bid price and the government estimate nor that the contracting officer was on notice of a possible misinterpretation of the solicitation); *BDF Tesa Corp.*, GSBCA 8307, 89-3 BCA ¶ 21,925 (verification request only stated that bid was too low without disclosing 70.7% to 79.3% disparity with other bids and a 10.3% to 36.3% disparity between bid and previous purchase prices for similar item); *Chemtronics, Inc.*, ASBCA 30883, 88-2 BCA ¶ 20,534 (form letter did not inform contractor of the gross disparity between its offer and that of the next lowest bidder or the government's funding estimate); *Ardmore Constr. Co.*, VABCA 2026, 85-1 BCA ¶ 17,743 (request for cost breakdown without advising bidder of suspected error); *Manistique Tool & Mfg. Co.*, ASBCA 29164, 84-3 BCA ¶ 17,599 (verification request did not state a mistake was suspected and did not disclose wide difference in bid prices); and *Walter Straga*, ASBCA 26134, 83-2 BCA ¶ 16,611 (verification request identifying price disparity where government knew exact nature of error).

A verification request was found to be adequate in *Solar Foam Insulation*, ASBCA 46921, 94-2 BCA ¶ 26,901, where the contracting officer alerted the bidder to a disparity between its bid, the next two low bids, and the government estimate. The board found the verification request adequate even though the contracting officer failed to note that the error was found in a particular column of the bid and mistakenly said that the difference between the bid and the next lowest was $32,699, where it was really $113,669. See also *McClure Elec. Constructors, Inc. v. Dalton*, 132 F.3d 709 (Fed. Cir. 1997) (bidder not told of error suspected but asked to verify its bid and given abstract showing that next low bid was almost 20% higher); *Fields Roof Serv., Inc.*, VABCA 3147, 90-3 BCA ¶ 23,232 (bidder told of difference between its bid of $417,545 and next lowest bid of $460,000); *Tri-States Serv. Co.*, ASBCA 31139, 90-3 BCA ¶ 23,059 (bidder told that its bid of $694,000 was less than the government's estimate of $779,983 for direct labor, and much less than the government's total estimate of $911,187); *W.B. & A., Inc.*, ASBCA 32524, 89-2 BCA ¶21,736 (bidder informed that its overall bid was low and attention called to five specific areas: edging, storm drainage, grass cutting, trash pickup, and tree removal); and *Central Mech., Inc.*, ASBCA 26543, 85-1 BCA ¶17,711 (bidder advised of disparity between its bid and the government estimate and that the bid was 10.2% under second low bid).

If verification is obtained but the contracting officer still has reason to believe a mistake has been made, a second verification request is required if the government has not revealed all of the information to the bidder, *United States v. Hamilton Enters., Inc.*, 711 F.2d 1038 (Fed. Cir. 1983). In *Hamilton*, the verification request pointed out a disparity with the other bids and asked for a manning chart. After verification, a contract was awarded. The court held that a second verification request was required because the government had not revealed that the bidder's estimate of man-hours was significantly lower than the government's estimate.

[C] Bidder's Action after Mistake Identification

When a mistake in bid has been identified, the bidder must determine what course of action to follow. The easiest course is to request withdrawal of the bid. However, in many cases the bidder may attempt to persuade the agency to correct the mistake. If correction will maintain the status of a low bidder at a higher bid price, this is generally the bidder's most desirable course of action. However, it raises questions as to the integrity of the competitive bidding process. If correction results in the bid no longer being low, it is tantamount to withdrawal. In some cases, a low bidder may request correction but also be willing to accept award at the mistaken price if correction is denied. Finally, bidders that are not low may attempt to correct mistakes in order to become low. This course of action is the most controversial in terms of its effect on the integrity of the competitive bidding process. All of these courses of action are discussed below.

[1] Withdrawal of Bid

The power to allow a bidder to withdraw its bid is vested in "an official above the contracting officer," FAR 14.407-3(c)(2). For many years, the regulations permitted withdrawal of a bid after bid opening if the bidder could prove the existence of a mistake by "clear and convincing" evidence, FPR 1-2.406-3(a)(3); DAR 2-406.3(a)(1). However, GAO followed a considerably more lenient policy concerning withdrawal after bid opening, generally permitting withdrawal even though there had been little more than a bare allegation of error by the bidder. For example, in 52 Comp. Gen. 258 (B-176111) (1972), GAO allowed withdrawal of the bid where the only evidence to support a mistake consisted of admittedly self-serving employee affidavits and unverified worksheets. This lenient withdrawal policy was apparently based on the rule that acceptance of a bid with knowledge of error does not consummate a valid and binding contract, *Alta Elec. & Mech. Co. v. United States*, 90 Ct. Cl. 466 (1940). See also 36 Comp. Gen. 441 (B-129736) (1956), stating at 444:

> In undertaking to bind a bidder by acceptance of a bid after notice of a claim of error by the bidder, the Government virtually undertakes the burden of proving either that there was no error or that the bidder's claim was not made in good faith.

In *Texas Turbo Jet, Inc.*, Comp. Gen. Dec. B-195303, 79-2 CPD ¶ 117, GAO stated that withdrawal would be permitted if the bidder is able to make a "prima facie" case in support of the alleged mistake. See also *Murphy Bros., Inc.*, 58 Comp. Gen. 185 (B-189756), 78-2 CPD ¶ 440.

FAR 14.407-3(c)(2) moved toward GAO's practice by permitting withdrawal of bids even if the evidence of mistake is less than clear and convincing but still "reasonably supports the existence of a mistake."

Subsequent GAO decisions continued to follow this lenient withdrawal policy. See *H.A. Lewis, Inc.*, Comp. Gen. Dec. B-249368, 92-2 CPD ¶ 351 (withdrawal permitted where agency finds calculations used to allege mistake "make no sense under the circumstances"); *Weather Data Servs., Inc.*, Comp. Gen. Dec. B-241621, 91-1 CPD ¶ 185 (withdrawal allowed where bidder alleges mistake without any documentation showing how mistake was made); *McGeary Co.*, Comp. Gen. Dec. B-230713, 88-1 CPD ¶ 586 (withdrawal permitted even though Navy's allegation that "mistaken" price was a conscious choice to bid low is found reasonable); *Southwest Marine, Inc.*, Comp. Gen. Dec. B-225686, 87-1 CPD ¶ 510 (withdrawal granted even where the credibility of worksheet used to establish mistake is in doubt and the only testimony was from interested parties); and *C.T. Lighting, Inc.*, Comp. Gen. Dec. B-214462, 84-2 CPD ¶ 102 (withdrawal permitted despite contracting officer's contention that evidence of mistake was fabricated).

FAR 14.407-3(c)(1) also permits withdrawal of a bid if the evidence of the existence of a mistake is clear and convincing but the evidence of the intended bid is not. This is the typical case when withdrawal is the only possible course of action other than contract award. See, for example, *American Block Co.*, Comp. Gen. Dec. B-235053, 89-2 CPD ¶ 90, where evidence of a mistake was clear and convincing because the bidder clearly based its bid price on the wrong type of item, but a discrepancy in a worksheet prevented the establishment of the intended bid. See also *Northwest Builders*, 67 Comp. Gen. 278 (B-228555), 88-1 CPD ¶ 200, where discrepancies in computer-generated estimates and printouts established a mistake, but because of wide range of possibilities, the intended bid could not be established.

[2] Rejection of Bid

Although the FAR does not deal directly with rejection of mistaken bids, where it is clear that a mistake in bid has been made, rejection of the bid is proper unless it is apparent that the bid both as submitted and intended will remain low. FAR 14.407-3(g)(4) indirectly recognizes the possibility of rejection of bids containing serious mistakes in providing the following guidance regarding when to evaluate a bid as submitted:

> Where the bidder fails or refuses to furnish evidence in support of a suspected or alleged mistake, the contracting officer shall consider the bid as submitted unless (i) the amount of the bid is so far out of line with the amounts of other bids received, or with the amount estimated by the agency or determined by the contracting officer to be reasonable, or (ii) there are other indications of error so clear, as to reasonably justify the conclusion that acceptance of the bid would be unfair to the bidder or to other bona fide bidders. Attempts made to obtain the information required and the action taken with respect to the bid shall be fully documented.

GAO has recognized that this provision provides authority for the rejection of bids containing mistakes. See *Orbas & Assocs.*, Comp. Gen. Dec. B-255276, 94-1 CPD ¶ 139, stating:

> A contracting officer's decision to reject an apparently mistaken bid under the authority of FAR 14.406-3(g)(5) [now (4)] is subject to question only where it is shown to be unreasonable. See Pamfilis Painting, Inc., B-237968, Apr. 3, 1990, 90-1 CPD ¶ 355; TLC Fin. Group, [Comp. Gen. Dec.; B-237384, 90-1 CPD ¶ 116]. Where it is clear that a mistake has been made, the bid cannot be accepted, even if the bidder verifies the bid price, denies the existence of a mistake, or seeks to waive an admitted mistake, unless it is clear that the bid, both as submitted and intended, would remain low. Trataros Constr., Inc., B-254600, Jan. 4, 1994, 94-1 CPD ¶ 1; Atlantic Serv., Inc., B-245763, Jan. 30, 1992, 92-1 CPD ¶ 125. Acceptance of such clearly erroneous bids would be unfair to other bidders. See 51 Comp. Gen. 498 (1972); Atlantic Serv., Inc., supra; Panoramic Studios, B-200664, Aug. 17, 1981, 81-2 CPD ¶ 144; FAR § 14.406-3(g)(5). Clearly erroneous bids subject to rejection include those based upon a misinterpretation of solicitation requirements. See, e.g., Atlantic Servs., Inc., supra; Innovative Refrigeration Concepts, B-242515, Mar. 27, 1991, 91-1 CPD ¶ 332; Martin Contracting, B-241229.2, Feb. 6, 1991, 91-1 CPD ¶ 121.

In *Odyssey Int'l, Inc.*, Comp. Gen. Dec. B-296855.2, 2006 CPD ¶ 49, rejection was found improper because the low bidder had provided clear evidence of a mistake which increased its bid but kept it low.

However, rejection of mistaken low bids has been found proper in some circumstances even if the bidder verifies the bid price. See *Trataros Constr., Inc.*,

Comp. Gen. Dec. B-254600, 94-1 CPD ¶ 1 (bid verified where bid price on item would not even cover the cost to produce that item); *Suffield Serv. Co.*, Comp. Gen. Dec. B-245579, 92-1 CPD ¶ 54 (bid verified where a group of percentage markups were obviously miscalculated); and *Prince Constr. Co.*, Comp. Gen. Dec. B-213496, 84-1 CPD ¶ 159 (bidder orally stated that an error had been made but refused to furnish evidence and later verified bid).

Rejection is also proper when the bidder denies the existence of a mistake. See *DGS Contract Servs., Inc.*, Comp. Gen. Dec. B-237157.2, 90-1 CPD ¶ 162 (bidder first claimed mistake based on subcontractor error and then claimed that there was no mistake); and *MTR, Inc.*, Comp. Gen. Dec. B-216685, 84-2 CPD ¶ 457, *recons. denied*, 84-2 CPD ¶ 624 (bidder refused to acknowledge mistake but contracting officer concluded, on convincing evidence, that bid was grossly low).

Rejection is proper even when the bidder seeks to waive an admitted mistake. See *Atlantic Servs. Inc.*, Comp. Gen. Dec. B-245763, 92-1 CPD ¶ 125, where the erroneous bid was rejected even though the bidder tried to "stand by" the bid and accept award. This decision was reached because award would be prejudicial to the other bidders if the bidder's mistaken bid would not have remained low after correction. See also *H. Martin Constr. Co.*, Comp. Gen. Dec. B-201352, 81-1 CPD ¶ 268, where GAO stated that the contracting officer "must reject" a clearly mistaken bid even though there had been no allegation of mistake.

The last basis for rejection would permit the contracting officer to reject the bid in those cases where award might result in an unfair contract. See *Southern Cal. Eng'g Co.*, Comp. Gen. Dec. B-255945, 94-1 CPD ¶ 271 (bid was much lower than all other bids and did not conform to specifications); and *Zeta Constr. Co.*, Comp. Gen. Dec. B-244672, 91-2 CPD ¶ 428 (bid based on major misinterpretation of the specifications).

An unstated reason for rejection of bids containing serious mistakes, even where there has been a proper verification, is to avoid the risk of a subsequent claim for reformation based on unconscionability. See, for example, *White Abstract Co.*, Comp. Gen. Dec. B-183643, 75-2 CPD ¶ 98 (would have cost $5,500 to perform item priced at $100); *Yankee Eng'g Co.*, Comp. Gen. Dec. B-180573, 74-1 CPD ¶ 333 ($106,000 mistake on $199,669 contract not discovered through verification); and 53 Comp. Gen. 187 (B-178795) (1973) (bid 74% below next low bid and only 1/12 of next low bid for first article unit).

[3] Correction of Mistake

The most frequent request of a contractor after discovery of a mistake is that the mistake be corrected. The precise facts of the procurement determine the rules that apply to such requests. Unless the mistake is an apparent clerical error (discussed below), the power to allow a bidder to correct a mistake in its bid is vested in the agency head, FAR 14.407-3(a), and is subject to the following guidelines.

[a] Correction of Low Bid Upward

Where the low bidder seeks to correct the bid upward—but the corrected bid remains the low bid—both the existence of the mistake and the bid actually intended must be established by "clear and convincing evidence," FAR 14.407-3(a). The clear and convincing standard has been strictly adhered to. See 53 Comp. Gen. 232 (B-179084) (1973), stating that correction will be permitted if the bidder establishes by clear and convincing evidence:

1. That an error has occurred;
2. The manner in which the error occurred; and
3. The amount of the intended bid price.

This three-part standard has been used regularly by GAO. See, for example, *Pipeline Constr. Inc.*, Comp. Gen. Dec. B-256799, 94-2 CPD ¶ 21; *J. Schouten Constr., Inc.*, Comp. Gen. Dec. B-256710, 94-1 CPD ¶ 353; and *L.F. Leiker Constr. Co.*, Comp. Gen. Dec. B-238496, 90-1 CPD ¶ 453. FAR 14.407-3(g)(2) provides the following similar guidance:

> The request [of the contractor] must be supported by statements (sworn statements, if possible) and shall include all pertinent evidence such as the bidder's file copy of the bid, the original worksheets and other data used in preparing the bid, subcontractors' quotations, if any, published price lists, and any other evidence that establishes the existence of the error, the manner in which it occurred, and the bid actually intended.

Despite the skepticism evidenced by some contracting officers as to the accuracy of worksheets offered by bidders to prove the amount of a mistake, an agency cannot refuse a bidder an opportunity to demonstrate the amount of the intended bid by clear and convincing evidence, *Chris Berg, Inc. v. United States*, 426 F.2d 314 (Ct. Cl. 1970); Comp. Gen. Dec. B-163284, Apr. 1, 1968, *Unpub*.

[i] Types of Evidence

Since the bidder must prove the amount of the intended bid price as well as the mistake, documentary evidence of the details of the original estimate almost always must be submitted. Such evidence is usually in the form of worksheets and other materials used during bid preparation. GAO has been quite liberal in accepting the validity of such materials. For example, a bidder was allowed to correct its bid despite erasures on the worksheets where the worksheet figures were corroborated by subcontractor bids and internal estimates for work intended to be done in-house, 51 Comp. Gen. 503 (B-174608) (1972). See also *IAP-Leopardo Constr., Inc.*, Comp. Gen. Dec. B-401923 2009 CPD ¶ 248 and *IAP-Leopardo Constr., Inc. v. United States*, No. 09-856C, 2010 WL 307881 (Fed. Cl. Jan. 14, 2010) (worksheets showing misplaced decimals, subcontractor bids and affidavits stating authenticity of documents); *Cooper Constr., Inc.*, Comp. Gen. Dec. B-285880, 2000 CPD ¶ 153 (handwritten worksheets, although somewhat sloppy, clearly showed the mistake and the intended bid); *H.A. Sack Co.*, Comp. Gen. Dec. B-278359, 98-1 CPD ¶ 27 (computer diskette containing a spreadsheet file dated on the date of bid opening and a statement that these were the original documents used in preparing bid were sufficient evidence); *Black Diamond Energies, Inc.*, Comp. Gen. Dec. B-241370, 91-1 CPD ¶ 119 (worksheet confirmed the costs of omitted installation work and total corrected price for item (delivered and installed) was still less than government estimate and in line with other bids); *BAL/BOA Servs., Inc.*, Comp. Gen. Dec. B-233157, 89-1 CPD ¶ 138 (entry of one subcontractor quote for landscaping was erased and substituted by another lower quote when this price was omitted from final bid and it was very unlikely that this cost was included in any other cost); and *Vrooman Constructors, Inc.*, Comp. Gen. Dec. B-226965.2, 87-1 CPD ¶ 606 (numerous crossouts on the worksheet allowed because they were corrections of obvious arithmetic errors or erroneously repeated figures, and the worksheet was otherwise in good order).

When the prebid materials do not contain erasures or other evidence of modification, correction has been even more readily allowed. See *Huber, Hunt & Nichols, Inc.*, Comp. Gen. Dec. B-271112, 96-1 CPD ¶ 246 (worksheets and affidavits established clear and convincing evidence of the mistake and the intended bid); *Severino Trucking Co.*, Comp. Gen. Dec. B-259080.2, 95-1 CPD ¶ 160 (comparison between three worksheets revealed that two were calculated by adding a 25% profit/overhead factor but the third omitted this factor); *R.P. Richards Constr. Co.*, Comp. Gen. Dec. B-258923, 95-1 CPD ¶ 103 (bidder offered $48,200 instead of $148,200 because the worksheet was not made to accommodate six-digit numbers); *ACS Constr. Co.*, Comp. Gen. Dec. B-257775, 94-2 CPD ¶ 179 (worksheets and subcontractor quotes showed that bidder failed to include in final bid the price for steel hooks that were essential to contract requirements); *Southern Techs. Inc.*, Comp. Gen. Dec. B-256190, 94-1 CPD ¶ 321 (subcontractor facsimile demonstrated that bidder omitted costs for certain equipment by overlooking the relevant number on the facsimile); *Shoemaker & Alexander, Inc.*, Comp. Gen. Dec. B-241066, 91-1 CPD ¶ 41 (examination of worksheet and adding machine tape showed the bidder dropped a zero when transferring electrical work price from worksheet to final bid and bid $200,000 rather than $2,000,000); *Continental Heller Corp.*, Comp. Gen. Dec. B-230559, 88-1 CPD ¶ 571 (worksheets, project fee analysis, and adding machine tapes established transcription error of $450,000); *Riverport Indus., Inc.*, 64 Comp. Gen. 441 (B-216707), 85-1 CPD ¶ 364, *recons. denied*, 85-2 CPD ¶ 108 (worksheet showed that material costs had been calculated but not added to the bid price); and *Hughes & Smith, Inc.*, Comp. Gen. Dec. B-181140, 74-2 CPD ¶ 68 (presence of a mathematical error was plain on the worksheets).

In *Schoutten Constr. Co.*, Comp. Gen. Dec. B-215663, 84-2 CPD ¶ 318, a protester questioned the validity of worksheets supporting the correction of a mistake placing the low bid within 1.9% of the second low bidder. In finding that the criminal statutes partially protected the competitive bidding system from fraudulent evidence, GAO stated:

> Finally, Schoutten has, in essence, questioned the bona fides of the worksheets and has pointed out in this regard that they are not accompanied by a sworn statement as required under FAR 14.406.3(g)(2), 48 Fed. Reg. 42181 (1983). This section of the FAR provides that correction requests "must be supported by statements (sworn statements if possible) and shall include all pertinent evidence such as . . . original worksheets." First, we point out that we have found that the penalties prescribed by 18 U.S.C. § 1001 (1982) could apply to false statements or representations by a bidder. *D.L. Draper Associates*, B-213177, Dec. 9, 1983, 83-2 CPD ¶ 662. In part because of this statutory protection, we have sanctioned the use of handwritten and computer printout worksheets which are readily susceptible to tampering. *D.L. Draper*, B-213177, *supra*. Moreover, we have explicitly accepted the agency consideration of handwritten worksheets which contained numerous erasures. 51 Comp. Gen. 503, 505 (1972). Schoutten's misgivings about the bona fide nature of the alleged mistake and the worksheets were not shared by the contracting officer. Nor do we find that they are supported by the record which appears to reflect only a rather elementary error in mathematics. Accordingly, we find that the protestor has failed to meet its burden of affirmatively proving its case in this respect. *Grandville Electric, Inc.*, B-213406, Feb. 22, 1984, 84-1 CPD ¶ 222.

See also *Ogden Allied E. States Maint.*, Comp. Gen. Dec. B-239550, 90-2 CPD ¶ 166, where the bidder did not use affidavits to prove mistake. GAO accepted this partially because the criminal code provided statutory protection against false statements or representations made by a bidder. But see *American Block Co.*, Comp. Gen. Dec. B-235053, 89-2 CPD ¶ 90, where correction was denied because the credibility of the bidder's evidence was in doubt. In that case, the bidder claimed the subcontractor gave a quote for the wrong item, the subcontractor claimed the bidder solicited quotes for the wrong item, and there were unexplained discrepancies between the original and corrected worksheets.

Even if the credibility of the evidence submitted is not directly questioned, if the documents are found insufficient, correction will not be permitted. See *Herman Constr. Grp., Inc.*, Comp. Gen. Dec. B-415408, 2018 CPD ¶ 18 (no clear evidence of mistake or of intended bid); *Bighorn Lumber Co.*, Comp. Gen. Dec. B-299906, 2007 CPD ¶ 173 (clear evidence of mistake but no clear evidence of intended bid); *Miramar Constr., Inc.*, Comp. Gen. Dec. B-298609, 2006 CPD ¶ 169 (explanation that person compiling bid "overrode" electronic spreadsheet illogical based on documents submitted); *Will H. Hall & Son, Inc. v. United States*, 54 Fed. Cl. 436 (2002) (uncorroborated affidavit not supported by worksheets that do not prove intended bid); *Si-Nor, Inc.*, Comp. Gen. Dec. B-288990, 2001 CPD ¶ 204 (worksheets undated and contained ambiguities); *CRK-JVC/Shockley*, Comp. Gen. Dec. B-265937, 96-1 CPD ¶ 85 (varying explanations for the mistake but two different base bid worksheets did not reflect the actual base bid); *Special Sys. Servs., Inc.*, Comp. Gen. Dec. B-259865.2, 95-1 CPD ¶ 241 (no explanation of how bid was prepared or how mistake occurred and the worksheets were not "in good order"); *U.S. Gen., Inc.*, Comp. Gen. Dec. B-245452, 92-1 CPD ¶ 8 (only evidence provided was an undated worksheet containing a series of previously unsubmitted line item prices and no backup documents to support the source of the numbers); *Imprints From the Past*, Comp. Gen. Dec. B-240447, 90-2 CPD ¶ 413 (uncertainty between two conflicting groups of worksheets); *Gunco, Inc.*, Comp. Gen. Dec. B-238910, 90-2 CPD ¶ 46 ("unexplained inconsistencies" between two worksheets that confirmed the bid price and a third worksheet that seemed to establish a $100,000 larger bid under the vague heading "Additional Costs"); and *Edmonds Elec. Co.*, Comp. Gen. Dec. B-214063, 84-1 CPD ¶ 615 ("worksheet" was prepared after bid opening to show the mistake that had been made).

GAO has treated computer evidence in the same manner as worksheets. In *Applied Constr. Tech. Inc.*, Comp. Gen. Dec. B-258426, 95-1 CPD ¶ 22, correction was allowed when the mistake was due to a computer spreadsheet program that had not been updated to account for an IFB amendment. See *Construction Tech. Grp., Inc.*, Comp. Gen. Dec. B-283857, 2000 CPD ¶ 15 (mistake in formula in spreadsheet but mistake clear); *PLC Constructors Canada, Inc.*, Comp. Gen. Dec. B-274697, 96-2 CPD ¶ 239 (computer spreadsheet showed how bidder made a mistake when it attempted to substitute one subcontractor's quote for its own estimate); *Interstate Constr., Inc.*, Comp. Gen. Dec. B-248355, 92-2 CPD ¶ 86 (computer spreadsheet showed bid of $800 for electrical work instead of an intended $600,000); and *Price/CIRI Constr.*, Comp. Gen. Dec. B-230603, 88-1 CPD ¶ 500 (computer spreadsheet, including handwritten notations, demonstrated how bidder broke down the cost for 13 items and then failed to submit a price for one of them). However, when computer spreadsheets become very complicated, they can raise questions as to the sufficiency of the evidence to prove a mistake. See *Metric Constructors, Inc.*, Comp. Gen. Dec. B-285854, 2000 CPD ¶ 195, where the agency properly rejected correction because the spreadsheets made it impossible to determine exactly how an omitted subcontract price would have been added to the bid. Compare *D.L. Draper Assocs.*, Comp. Gen. Dec. B-213177, 83-2 CPD ¶ 662, following the same logic as in *Schoutten*, finding that the criminal statutes were applicable to computer-generated information and adequately protected the government from deception.

The most common failure in meeting the clear and convincing evidence standard occurs in proving the intended amount of the bid. For example, a bidder was not allowed to correct a bid where it could not substantiate the additional overhead and profit claimed as a result of having omitted several subcontract prices from the bid price, Comp. Gen. Dec. B-176357, Aug. 29, 1972, *Unpub.* The bidder omitted $488,065 in subcontract items from the bid and substantiated that figure. It then added $20,000 for additional overhead and $30,000 for additional profit on the omitted figures. The bidder, however, did not normally use a fixed percentage rate in bidding overhead and profit, but rather derived those figures "after considering all of the other variable factors." Accordingly, the figures for overhead and profit were held to be arbitrary and not substantiated by the bidder's worksheets or records. A bid that indicated the bidder mistakenly bid on a quantity 24 times greater than that called for in the IFB could not be corrected by taking 1/24 of it because the bidder might well have included price reductions in its bid for the larger quantities, 49 Comp. Gen. 48 (B-165852) (1969). In *Three O Constr., S.E.*, Comp. Gen. Dec. B-255749, 94-1 CPD ¶ 216, correction was denied because the bidder gave inconsistent explanations of its intended bid price without supplying conclusive evidence to show which explanation was accurate. First, the bidder claimed a mistaken portion of the bid had to be increased by 40% for payroll tax; then the bidder claimed that the payroll tax had been accounted for, but that the mistaken portion needed to be marked up by 15% for workers' compensation. See also *4-S Constr., Inc.*, Comp. Gen. Dec. B-248090, 92-1 CPD ¶ 523 (worksheet indicates the price for mechanical work was omitted but presence of subcontractor quote for that item is not enough to establish intended bid because the bidder used different subcontractors for the job and might have done so again); and *L.F. Leiker Constr. Co.*, Comp. Gen. Dec. B-238496, 90-1 CPD ¶ 453 (blank line on worksheet for concrete work is evidence of mistake, but bidder's use of one cost analysis for concrete work at one site does not mean that the bidder would use same analysis to compute omitted price).

If there is a factor that prevents the intended bid from being established conclusively, but the bid would remain low even if that factor were included, the bid can be corrected. Where a bidder requests only the addition of direct costs and does not request the addition of overhead, profit, or other markups the bid may be so corrected, provided that the bid would have been low even if overhead, profit and other markups had been included, *IAP-Leopardo Constr., Inc.*, Comp. Gen. Dec. B-401923 2009 CPD ¶ 248 (subcontract amounts); 49 Comp. Gen. 480 (B-167068) (1970) (material cost); 51 Comp. Gen. 503 (B-174608) (1972) (subcontract addition). If the addition of overhead or profit might make the bid as corrected no longer low, then such correction (without overhead and profit) will not be allowed, *Camp Lewis Tent & Awning Co.*, Comp. Gen. Dec. B-182047, 74-2 CPD ¶ 174. In *Western Alaska Contractors*, Comp. Gen. Dec. B-220067, 86-1 CPD ¶ 66, correction was allowed to include a missing subcontractor quote because work papers showed that it was on the spreadsheet but not carried over to the final bid. However, markup on this omitted quote was not allowed because a formula for calculating this percentage was not on the worksheet and a pattern for calculating this percentage could not be derived from examining other subcontractor quotes. See also *Severino Trucking Co.*, Comp. Gen. Dec. B-259080.2, 95-1 CPD ¶ 160 (correction allowed where bidder rounded up final number in original bid, but did not attempt to do so in corrected bid when even rounded bid remained low); and *Avanti Constr. Corp.*, Comp. Gen. Dec. B-229839, 88-1 CPD ¶ 262 (correction allowed for error in transcription between worksheets, but overhead and profits were not allowed to be added because the bidder originally used an estimate rather than the final bid to calculate these numbers).

The clear and convincing test does not require absolute precision in ascertaining the amount the bidder could have bid. In *Chris Berg, Inc. v. United States*, 426 F.2d 314 (Ct. Cl. 1970), the court stated that an "uncertainty within a relatively narrow range is not inconsistent with 'clear and convincing evidence' of what the bid would have been." In that case, the low bidder sought correction, but the government would not agree because the "rounding off" of numbers in the worksheets made it impossible to precisely ascertain the intended bid. The Court of Claims stated that the bidder had successfully established the intended bid price and that the "rounding off" was de minimis. GAO expanded this reasoning in *P.K. Painting Co.*, Comp. Gen. Dec. B-247357, 92-1 CPD ¶ 424, where the bidder was required to round down its corrected bid because it had done so with all numbers before correction, stating, "In [these] circumstances, correction is limited to increasing the contracting price only to the bottom end of the range of uncertainty." See *Roy Anderson Corp.*, Comp. Gen. Dec. B-292555, 2003 CPD ¶ 179 ("narrow" range of uncertainty ($86,000 in price of $39,498,340) not of concern); *Hampton Rds. Mech. Contractors, Inc.*, Comp. Gen. Dec. B-257908, 94-2 CPD ¶ 201 (range of $35 in $350,000 procurement inconsequential); *Precon Constr. Co.*, Comp. Gen. Dec. B-255294.1, 94-1 CPD ¶ 239 (despite several discrepancies between the worksheet and bid price and despite an admitted mistake that bidder does not attempt to correct, correction was allowed because highest in range was still $80,000 low in $1 million procurement); and *Red Samm Constr., Inc.*, Comp. Gen. Dec. B-250891.2, 93-1 CPD ¶ 178 (rounding up and down in bid calculation prevented determination of exact number of intended bid, but correction was allowed when bid would remain low even if always rounded up). See also *Bromley Contracting Co. v. United States*, 596 F.2d 448 (Ct. Cl. 1979), where a mistake of failing to add overhead and profit to a bid was remedied by assuming that these factors would have been computed at the same rates used on previous bids.

GAO has held that when an agency allows correction of bid based on evidence that is not totally clear and convincing, it will not override the decision unless it is unreasonable, *Gulf-Atlantic Constructors, Inc.*, Comp. Gen. Dec. B-289032, 2002 CPD ¶ 2. There, the decision was found reasonable even though there were "inconsistencies and gaps" in the evidence presented.

[ii] When Corrected Bid Comes Very Close to Next Bid

Sometimes the corrected bid price is extremely close to the next low bid. In this situation, there is a balancing required between the clarity of the evidence and the closeness of the bids. The closer the correction brings the bid to the next low bid, the greater the need for clear evidence, and the stricter the examination of that evidence, *Vrooman Constructors, Inc.*, Comp. Gen. Dec. B-226965.2, 87-1 CPD ¶ 606. This policy serves as a safeguard against bidders knowingly bidding low, declaring mistake, and fraudulently increasing their bid to an amount just under the second low bid by showing how the "error" was made, *R.H. Whelan Co.*, Comp. Gen. Dec. B-203248, 81-2 CPD ¶ 123. There is no specific percentage or dollar amount at which bids automatically become too close to be corrected, *International Serv. Corp.*, Comp. Gen. Dec. B-246159, 92-1 CPD ¶ 191.

If the evidence presented is sufficient, correction will be allowed even to the smallest of margins. In *J. Schouten Constr., Inc.*, Comp. Gen. Dec. B-256710, 94-1 CPD ¶ 353, correction was permitted to bring the bid within $700 of the next low bid in a $338,000 procurement because there was an obvious addition error on a worksheet, there was an affidavit from the worksheet compiler, and the worksheet was provided within 24 hours of the opening of bids. See also *Prudent Techs., Inc.*, Comp. Gen. Dec. B-401736.3, 2009 CPD ¶ 254 (correction allowed within 1% when arithmetic mistakes were clear on face of bid); *Odyssey Int'l, Inc.*, Comp. Gen. Dec. B-296855.2, 2006 CPD ¶ 49 (correction allowed within $2,584 of second low bid of $7,319,800 when spreadsheets clearly showed the mistake); *B&M Cillessen Constr. Co.*, Comp. Gen. Dec. B-287449.2, 2001 CPD ¶ 100 (correction allowed within $12,707 of second low bid of $4,855,000 when worksheets showed omission of state tax); *Pacific Components, Inc.*, Comp. Gen. Dec. B-252585, 93-1 CPD ¶ 478 (correction allowed to within 1% when mistake was obvious from review of erroneous quote from only subcontractor); *International Serv. Corp.*, Comp. Gen. Dec. B-246159, 92-1 CPD ¶ 191 (correction allowed to within 0.0235% when the worksheets showed that the bidder neglected to multiply unit price by quantity); *Vrooman Constructors, Inc.*, Comp. Gen. Dec. B-226965.2, 87-1 CPD ¶ 606 (correction allowed to 0.6% where 15 of 16 divisions were carried from a worksheet to the final bid, but one was not); and *Guardian Constr.*, Comp. Gen. Dec. B-220982, 86-1 CPD ¶ 224 (correction permitted to bring bid within 1% where misplaced decimal is obvious from adding machine tape).

Even though correction would place the bid very close to the next bid, correction will almost always be permitted if the mistake is apparent on the face of the bid. See *Ogden Allied E. States Maint.*, Comp. Gen. Dec. B-239550, 90-2 CPD ¶ 166, where correction was allowed to within 1% where transcription error was apparent on the face of the bid. But see 48 Comp. Gen. 748 (B-166748) (1969), denying relief where correction would be within $613 in a $272,000 procurement.

When correction would bring the bid close to the next low bid and the evidence of the mistake and the intended bid is not clear, correction will be denied. In *RJS Constructors*, Comp. Gen. Dec. B-257457, 94-2 CPD ¶ 130, correction was denied to within 0.13% of the next low bid even though the worksheet showed that if it had been added correctly the bid total should have been $375,960 rather than $276,379. Correction was denied because the credibility of the worksheet was in question, it did not contain entries for overhead and profit, and there were many inconsistencies between subcontractor quotes and the bid submitted. See also *Metric Constr. Co.*, Comp. Gen. Dec. B-259573, 95-1 CPD ¶ 197 (numerous discrepancies in addition and percentage calculation prevent correction to within 0.28%); *Northwest Bldrs.*, 67 Comp. Gen. 278 (B-228555), 88-1 CPD ¶ 200 (correction to within 1% not allowed because changes were undocumented and unexplained); and *Conner Bros. Constr. Co.*, Comp. Gen. Dec. B-228232.2, 88-1 CPD ¶ 103 (no correction to within 1% where worksheets and affidavits do not explain why certain costs were added and deducted from one subcontractor total, but not from two others). Similarly, correction was denied when the evidence was not clear in *Sam Gonzales, Inc.*, Comp. Gen. Dec. B-216728, 85-1 CPD ¶ 125 (amount of overhead not clear); and *D.L. Draper Assocs.*, Comp. Gen. Dec. B-213177, 83-2 CPD ¶ 662 (computer printout and unsworn statement not sufficiently strong evidence).

[b] Displacement of Otherwise Low Bid

A stricter standard than the clear and convincing evidence standard applies if correction would reduce the bid price and displace the otherwise low bid. FAR 14.407-3(a) provides that mistakes cannot be corrected in such circumstances unless both the mistake and the bid actually intended are ascertainable substantially from the invitation and the bid itself. This requirement makes it very difficult to displace a low bidder through bid correction. See *Armstrong & Armstrong, Inc. v. United States*, 356 F. Supp. 514 (E.D. Wash. 1973), *aff'd*, 514 F.2d 402 (9th Cir. 1975), where a discrepancy between the sum of unit prices and the total bid price was found to be insufficient evidence to support a downward correction of the final price displacing the low bidder.

For cases were GAO denied correction, see *Nabholz Bldg. & Mgmt. Corp.*, Comp. Gen. Dec. B-274930, 96-2 CPD ¶ 196 (bidder claimed an ambiguity that let it to mistakenly include its bond costs under both a base bid line item and a bond costs line item); *Mallory Elec. Co.*, Comp. Gen. Dec. B-244699, 91-2 CPD ¶ 394 (clerical error apparent on the face of the bid was subject to two interpretations as to the intended bid, only one of which made the bid low); *Bullrun Mountain Honey Co.*, Comp. Gen. Dec. B-243325, 91-1 CPD ¶ 344 (bidder claimed a waiver of a 10% small business preference was an obvious mistake on the face of the bid); *R.C. Constr. Co.*, Comp. Gen. Dec. B-241176.2, 91-1 CPD ¶ 118 (bidder obviously overbid for an item, but it could not be determined whether the unit should be one square foot or 100 square feet); *Christos Painting*

& Contracting Corp., Comp. Gen. Dec. B-225647, 87-1 CPD ¶ 361 (bidder claimed line item entered in units of 100 as "19(19)" should be read as zero instead of $1,900); *Crystal Contracting Corp.*, Comp. Gen. Dec. B-223531, 86-2 CPD ¶ 433 (bid not corrected because "error" occurred in a schedule of deductions not appearing on the bid itself); and *Mayrant Constructors, Inc.*, Comp. Gen. Dec. B-215274, 84-1 CPD ¶ 617 (bidder claimed it was obvious that an entry of "449,668" was intended to be 49,668). GAO has used the same reasoning to refuse correction to break a tie bid, *W.G. James, Inc.*, 64 Comp. Gen. 561 (B-218230), 85-1 CPD ¶ 623.

GAO has permitted the use of rationales based upon past experience and other information in applying this high evidentiary standard. For example, in *Frontier Contracting Co.*, Comp. Gen. Dec. B-214260.2, 84-2 CPD ¶ 40, the bidder submitted an amendment to a bid as follows:

Base Bid			
Item 1	Add	Deduct	$133,752
Item 2	Add	Deduct	$60,000
Total Base Bid	Add	Deduct	$193,752
Additive			
Item 3	Add	Deduct	$84,000
Total	Add	Deduct	$277,752

GAO permitted the deduction of the figures, reasoning that the contracting officer had correctly concluded, based on the other bids and past experience with this contractor, that the only logical interpretation was that the figures were to be deducted rather than added. In *Allied Signal Avionics Inc.*, Comp. Gen. Dec. B-258457, 95-1 CPD ¶ 192, GAO permitted a line item for a two-year warranty to be changed from $50,268 to "no charge." This was allowed because the bidder had inserted "no charge" in four of five line items for the same warranty, had inserted "no charge" in five of five line items for the same warranty on an alternate bid, and the amount bid for that line item was the same as an item directly above on the bid sheet. See also *Wright & Morrissey*, Comp. Gen. Dec. B-417105, 2019 CPD ¶ 84 (bidder's notation on CLINS 2 and 3, "Included in our Base Bid; We assume this is a breakout" showed that these prices had mistakenly been included in CLIN 1); *Concorde Battery Corp.*, 68 Comp. Gen. 523 (B-235119), 89-2 CPD ¶ 17 (correction allowed where bidder put total for line items 1 through 3 in line item 4 when line item 4 should have been an "inconsequential expense," and five out of seven bidders made this mistake); *George E. Failing Co.*, Comp. Gen. Dec. B-233207, 89-1 CPD ¶ 203 (bidder's entire bid package used to determine that bidder bid twice for three line items); and *Technical Support Servs., Inc.*, Comp. Gen. Dec. B-232488, 88-2 CPD ¶ 464 (correction allowed where bidder included a line item that was not supposed to be added to the total when five other bidders made this same error). But see *Electronic Space Sys. Corp.*, Comp. Gen. Dec. B-236006, 89-2 CPD ¶ 381, where correction was denied when the bidder offered two different prices on a basic and optional requirements schedule for the same item. Through prior dealings with contracts of this nature, the contracting officer determined that the higher price for the basic schedule was an often-used bidding strategy.

The most difficult application of this rule is in cases of a mistake in the extension of unit prices or the addition of subtotals. In most of these cases, it is not clear from the face of the bid whether the mistake is in the total price or in the subtotal or unit price. In *OTKM Constr., Inc.*, 64 Comp. Gen. 830 (B-219619), 85-2 CPD ¶ 273, *recons. denied*, 65 Comp. Gen. 202, 86-1 CPD ¶ 53, GAO permitted correction based on the internal consistency of the elements of the bid price, but stated the following general principles at 833-34:

> We have previously considered whether a bid may be corrected so as to displace an otherwise low bidder where there is a discrepancy between the correct mathematical total of lump sum and extended price items and the stated total of such items. In *DeRalco, Inc.*, B-205120, May 6, 1982, 82-1 CPD ¶ 430, we sustained a protest against the agency's determination to correct such a discrepancy as an apparent clerical error where neither the nature of the alleged mistake nor the bid actually intended could be determined without benefit of advice from the bidder. We noted that there was no one obvious or apparent explanation for the discrepancy. The difference did not suggest where the mistake might have been made and the stated total was not so grossly out of line with the other bid or with the government's estimate as to be patently erroneous. We found that the discrepancy could reasonably be attributed either to a mistake in totaling the items or to an incorrectly stated item.

See *Patterson Pump Co.*, Comp. Gen. Dec. B-200165, 80-2 CPD ¶ 453, permitting correction in such circumstances. Compare *Wilkinson & Jenkins Constr. Co.*, Comp. Gen. Dec. B-182687, 75-1 CPD ¶ 77, where the protesting bidder inadvertently entered a bid on the original bidding schedule rather than the amended bidding schedule, which had reduced the estimated quantity for one item. The bidder entered a unit price for the item and an extended price based on the larger estimated quantity. The IFB contained a statement that when there was a conflict between the unit price and the extension, the unit price would be considered to be the bid. Nevertheless, GAO did not permit correction of the extended price to reflect the smaller quantity of work because to do so would displace the low bidder, reasoning that the intended bid was not ascertainable from the bid documents since it was not clear that the bidder would not have bid a higher unit price for the lower quantity. See also *Argee Corp.*, 67 Comp.

Gen. 421 (B-230165.3), 88-1 CPD ¶ 482, where correction was not allowed when a discrepancy existed between the unit prices and the extended prices because neither the unit prices nor the extended total was out of line with the other bids or the government estimate and there was no indication as to where the mistake occurred. Accord *Seabee Constr., LLC*, Comp. Gen. Dec. B-416436, 2018 CPD ¶ 244; *Roy McGinnis & Co.*, Comp. Gen. Dec. B-239710, 90-2 CPD ¶ 251; and *Virginia Beach Air Conditioning Corp.*, 69 Comp. Gen. 132 (B-237172), 90-1 CPD ¶ 78. But see *J&J Maint., Inc.*, Comp. Gen. Dec. B-251355, 93-1 CPD ¶ 187, where correction of a unit price to reflect an extended price was allowed because the unit price total was clearly out of line with the government estimate and all other bids and the extended price was not. Further, dropping a zero from the unit price and multiplying by the stipulated 12-month period would result in the extended price See also *Marann Inventories, Inc.*, Comp. Gen. Dec. B-237467, 90-1 CPD ¶ 89, where correction was allowed where the uncorrected unit price, if extended, would result in a figure of $1.6 million above the next highest bid.

[c] Correction of Nonresponsive Bids

FAR 14.407-3 prohibits the use of mistake correction techniques to make nonresponsive bids responsive. However, GAO has permitted limited correction of nonresponsive bids if the same standards used to correct bids which displace low bids are satisfied, *United Food Servs.*, 65 Comp. Gen. 167 (B-218228.3), 85-2 CPD ¶ 727; and *Fujitsu Imaging Sys. of Am., Inc.*, Comp. Gen. Dec. B-241733.2, 91-1 CPD ¶ 243. See also *Ultimate Concrete, L.L.C.*, Comp. Gen. Dec. B-412255, 2016 CPD ¶ 20, and *Ultimate Concrete, LLC v. United States*, 127 Fed. Cl. 77 (2016), allowing correction of an unbalanced bid where the correction merely balanced the line items without changing the total price.

Most cases involving successful correction of nonresponsive bids have involved invitations containing a number of bid items where bidders have incorrectly entered or omitted prices for one or more of the items. In *Slater Elec. Co.*, Comp. Gen. Dec. B-183654, 75-2 CPD ¶ 126, GAO dealt with this kind of situation, stating:

> Basically, even though a bidder fails to submit a price for an item in a bid, that omission can be corrected if the bid, as submitted, indicates not only the probability of error but also the exact nature of the error and the amount intended. B-151332, June 27, 1963. The rationale for this exception is that where the consistency of the pricing pattern in the bidding documents establishes both the existence of the error and the bid actually intended, to hold that the bid is nonresponsive would be to convert what appears to be an obvious clerical error of omission to a matter of nonresponsiveness. B-157429, August 19, 1965.

See also *MKB Constructors (J.V.)*, Comp. Gen. Dec. B-250413, 93-1 CPD ¶ 50; *Werres Corp.*, Comp. Gen. Dec. B-211870, 83-2 CPD ¶ 243; and *Lyon Shipyard, Inc.*, Comp. Gen. Dec. B-208978, 82-2 CPD ¶ 287, where a bid was considered to be responsive and the omitted item treated as a mistake when it was shown that the cost of the omitted bid item had been included in the contractor's total bid price. Compare *Automated Marketing Sys., Inc.*, Comp. Gen. Dec. B-230014, 88-1 CPD ¶ 289, denying a protest that contended that the contracting officer should have permitted correction when the protester included no bid prices in its bid.

In *Wellco Enters., Inc.*, Comp. Gen. Dec. B-237512, 90-1 CPD ¶ 196, the low bidder neglected to include option prices for two of its block bidding quantities. Correction was permitted because the bid included consistent percentage increases from base to option prices. Correction was allowed in *Burnside-Ott Aviation Training Ctr., Inc.*, Comp. Gen. Dec. B-228937, 87-2 CPD ¶ 461, even though the low bidder had not bid the same price for the omitted device everywhere on the bid. This was allowed because the bidder had bid "NC" (no charge) for all other subitems under which this device was grouped and for all work to be done in the transitional period when this work was to be done. Correction was also permitted on similar facts in *Slater Elec. Co.*, Comp. Gen. Dec. B-183654, 75-2 CPD ¶ 126, even though the bidder had not bid exactly the same price for the item everywhere in the bid. The price of the item wherever found in the bid had only varied by $.02, and GAO reasoned this was a de minimis variation. This case may be an unwarranted extension of the exception permitting correction of nonresponsive bids. As long as the exception is limited to situations where the mistake and the bid intended are plain on the face of the bid, the opportunities for abuse are small. Once the exception is enlarged to include situations where the intended bid is plainly within a de minimis range, abuses could increase. Bidders would be given the opportunity to press for correction of the bid if award would be advantageous or plead nonresponsiveness if they did not want the award.

[d] Clerical Errors

Clerical errors not apparent on the face of the bid are correctable to the same extent as other errors as examined in this section. However, for many years, the regulations have treated apparent clerical errors as a separate class of mistake that can be corrected with less formal procedures than other types of mistakes. Apparent clerical errors are the only type of mistake that the contracting officer can correct without deferring to the agency head or any other higher officer. FAR 14.407-2 provides the following guidance:

> (a) Any clerical mistake, apparent on its face in the bid, may be corrected by the contracting officer before award. The contracting officer first

shall obtain from the bidder a verification of the bid intended. Examples of apparent mistakes are—

(1) Obvious misplacement of a decimal point;

(2) Obviously incorrect discounts (for example, 1 percent 10 days, 2 percent 20 days, 5 percent 30 days);

(3) Obvious reversal of the price f.o.b. destination and price f.o.b. origin; and

(4) Obvious mistake in designation of unit.

The difficulty with this guidance is that what is an obvious error to some may not be obvious to everyone. *McCarty Corp. v. United States*, 499 F.2d 633 (Ct. Cl. 1974), illustrates the problem. The IFB called for itemized bids on three separate items of work and for a total bid. Bidders were instructed that they must bid on all three items. McCarty's president instructed his subordinate to bid $140,000 for item 1, $434,000 for item 2, $100,000 for item 3, and $674,000 for the total bid. However, the subordinate transposed two numbers on item 2 recording $443,000 rather than $434,000. All other figures, including the total, were recorded as instructed. Morris, another bidder, included $155,000 for item 1, $389,000 for item 2, $137,000 for item 3, and $690,000 for the total bid. The actual total of the bid prices for items 1, 2, and 3 was $681,000 rather than the $690,000 listed. In reviewing the bids, the government officials discovered the discrepancies in the bid totals and, without verifying the intended bid, treated these as apparent clerical errors, correcting the totals to reflect the sum of the individual items. This made the other bid total $681,000 and McCarty's bid $683,000. McCarty requested permission to correct its bid to show $434,000 as the amount quoted for item 2 and to leave the total at $674,000. This was denied, and the contract was awarded to Morris. McCarty protested to GAO and sought damages in the Court of Claims. The Court of Claims held that it was wrong to treat the mistakes in the McCarty and Morris bids as clerical mistakes apparent on the face of the bid. Instead, the mistakes involved a difference between the arithmetical sum of the amounts quoted on the three items comprising the bid and the amount listed as the total bid. It was impossible to tell from the face of the bid whether the bidder had made a mistake in entering one of the three item prices or in calculating the total. Correction of the Morris bid was not appropriate since the correction would have resulted in displacing the low bidder, and the "existence of the mistake and the bid actually intended" were not "ascertainable substantially from the invitation and the bid itself." On the other hand, the McCarty bid could have been corrected since the correction would not change its total price nor result in the displacement of the low bidder since the other bid would not be low without correction. See also *Armstrong & Armstrong, Inc. v. United States*, 356 F. Supp. 514 (E.D. Wash. 1973), *aff'd*, 514 F.2d 402 (9th Cir. 1975), reaching a similar result.

Even though the Court of Claims in the McCarty case stated that the mistake in that case was not an "apparent clerical error," GAO has continued to so label similar errors. See, for example, *Ace-Federal Reporters, Inc.*, 54 Comp. Gen. 340 (B-181451), 74-2 CPD ¶ 239, where one item of the bid was supposed to equal the difference between two other items but did not. The procuring agency and GAO treated this as an apparent clerical error and stated as a proposition that when one item is a function of arithmetic between two other items, the initial entries will be considered correct and the error will be in the arithmetic. This decision is inconsistent with both the letter and the spirit of the *McCarty* case. But see *North Landing Line Constr. Co.*, Comp. Gen. Dec. B-239662, 90-2 CPD ¶ 60, where correction in this situation was allowed to conform to the total price of two items. The intended bid for the mistaken item was ascertained by subtracting the price of the other item from the total price bid.

In *DeRalco, Inc.*, Comp. Gen. Dec. B-205120, 82-1 CPD ¶ 430, GAO sustained a protest against correction by a contracting officer and provided the following guidance:

> Prior decisions of our Office have stressed that, before the authority to correct a mistake under DAR § 2-406.2 may be invoked, the contracting officer must be able to ascertain the intended bid without the benefit of advice from the bidder. *See, e.g.*, 46 Comp. Gen. 77, 82 (1966) (only logical conclusion was that bidder had stated prices in reverse); 45 Comp. Gen. 682 (1966) (written words indicating a price 1,000 times the cost reflected in other bids and in prior contracts were patently in error; bid could be corrected based upon bidder's written figures); *Engle Acoustic & Tile, Inc.*, B-190467, January 27, 1978, 78-1 CPD 72 (obvious misplaced decimal point); *Edward E. Davis, Contracting, Inc.*, B-187132, November 17, 1976, 76-2 CPD 429 (obvious error in designation of unit). By contrast, we have held that, where the intended bid could not be determined from the bid alone, a mistake was not correctable as a clerical error under DAR § 2-406.2. *See, e.g., Western Equipment of Oregon*, B-204125, December 8, 1981, 81-2 CPD 447 (intended bid could not be determined from the bid alone where neither the unit price nor the extended price was grossly out of line); *Sundance Construction, Inc.*, B-182485, February 28, 1975, 75-1 CPD 123 (intended bid could not be determined by multiplying the quoted unit prices by the correct unit).

A good example of a true apparent clerical error is found in 52 Comp. Gen. 604 (B-177368) (1973), where the IFB required bidders to enter prices for an initial quantity of oscilloscopes and four follow-on order quantities, and bidders were required to enter prices for each quantity. The low bidder entered one price for the initial quantity and three of the four follow-on order quantities. However, the bidder failed to enter a price for follow-on order No. 3. Since the bidder had followed a consistent price pattern, bidding the same price for smaller as well as larger numbers of oscilloscopes, it was held that the mistake could be treated as an apparent clerical error and corrected. See *Action Serv. Corp.*, Comp. Gen. Dec. B-254861, 94-1 CPD ¶ 33, where an entry of "$5,0005" was allowed to be corrected to "$5,005" when $5,005 multiplied by 12 months equaled the submitted extended total; the extended total of $60,060, when added with the other extended totals, equaled the total bid; and $5,005 was in line with other bids for this item and $50,005 was not. See also *Cashman Dredging & Marine Contracting Co.*, Comp. Gen. Dec. B-401547, 2009 CPD ¶ 179 (correction of unit price of $425,000 to match extended price of $1,425,000 when the fact that the extended price was added to the total price demonstrated a clerical error); *SDV Constr. Grp., LLC*, Comp. Gen. Dec. B-400703, 2009 CPD ¶ 11 (award at base price minus amount entered for deductive item or work proper even though IFB required deductive items to be bid at net amount); *Mid Eastern Bldrs., Inc.*, Comp. Gen. Dec. B-290717, 2002 CPD ¶ 164 (disregarding of price of $2,178,689 when other document showed that the 2 should be 7 and all other bids in range of $7 to $10 million); *Northwest Piping, Inc.*, Comp. Gen. Dec. B-233796, 89-1 CPD ¶ 333 (correction of discrepancy between unit and extended prices is allowed where only the unit price was logical in light of the government estimate and the other bids); *Military Waste Mgmt., Inc.*, Comp. Gen. Dec. B-228862, 87-2 CPD ¶ 424 (correction permitted where bidder inserted its unit price on a per-housing-unit basis instead of the proper per-month basis); and *S.C. Jones Servs., Inc.*, Comp. Gen. Dec. B-226972, 87-1 CPD ¶ 583 (bidder failed to add a certain portion of the work into the final bid).

The Preparation of Bids solicitation clause in FAR 52.214-12 contains the following curious statement in ¶ (c):

> In case of discrepancy between a unit price and an extended price, the unit price will be presumed to be correct, subject, however, to correction to the same extent and in the same manner as any other mistake.

No protest has been found where a contracting officer relied on this statement in determining that a clerical error should be corrected. However, this provision would not appear to give any stronger weight to the unit prices than would be obtained by a thorough analysis of the bid documents.

[4] Award After Unsuccessful Request for Correction

One of the parties may desire award at the original bid price after a mistake has been alleged or suspected. The government may want to take advantage of the low bid, or the bidder may want to take the risk of performing the work at the original bid price.

[a] Award Required

The FAR is not clear on whether award is required on the basis of the bids as submitted when evidence does not establish that a mistake has been made. FAR 14.407-3(d) states that the agency head "*may* make a determination that the bid be neither withdrawn nor corrected" when the evidence does not establish the existence of a mistake or an intended bid. On the other hand, FAR 14.407-3(g)(2) states that the contracting officer *"shall* consider the bid as originally submitted" if the bidder verifies that there is no mistake. Similarly, FAR 14.407-3(g)(5) states that the "contracting officer *shall* consider the bid as submitted" if the bidder fails or refuses to submit evidence of the mistake. Gross errors are excepted from this requirement. While it is common practice to award the contract on the original bid after the bidder has verified the bid, it is much less common for the contracting officer to award the contract if the contractor requests withdrawal of the bid. Award in such cases conflicts with the liberal withdrawal policy of GAO. GAO has stated, however, that when the low responsible bidder submitting a responsive bid alleges error and seeks to withdraw its bid but is unable to make at least a prima facie showing of the existence of error, the firm bid rule prohibits the bidder from revoking the original bid, *Texas Turbo Jet, Inc.*, Comp. Gen. Dec. B-195303, 79-2 CPD ¶ 117. See also *Duro Paper Bag Mfg. Co.*, 65 Comp. Gen. 186 (B-217227), 86-1 CPD ¶ 6. See also *Herman Constr. Grp., Inc.*, Comp. Gen. Dec. B-415480, 2018 CPD ¶ 18, stating that after a bidder failed to prove its alleged mistake the agency could either "award the contract . . . at the original bid price or consider whether withdrawal of [the] bid is appropriate under the circumstances."

[b] Award Permitted

In some cases, bidders desire to obtain the award even though a mistake has been established. The first section discusses the situation where the bidder seeks award of the contract at the original bid price if correction of an alleged mistake is denied. The second section discusses those cases where the bidder seeks award at the original bid price but reserves the right to assert a claim for reformation of the contract after award.

[i] Waiver

If a bidder seeks correction but is unable to prove the intended bid, it is ordinarily not permitted to then waive the mistake and be awarded the contract at the actual bid price. The rationale for this policy is that it would give such a bidder a competitive advantage if it could decide whether to accept the award after opening had exposed the other bids, 37 Comp. Gen. 579 (B-135272) (1958); 52 Comp. Gen. 706 (B-177482) (1973). Nevertheless, limited exceptions to the rule have developed. In early decisions, GAO ruled that if the bidder agreed to accept the award at the bid price notwithstanding that a mistake was established by clear and convincing evidence, the contract could be awarded at the bid price provided that the bid would remain low even if the correction were allowed, Comp. Gen. Dec. B-168673, Apr. 7, 1970, *Unpub.* However, the bidder had to request award at its original bid price if correction was not granted and the bid had to be clearly low before and after correction, 52 Comp. Gen. 706 (B-177482) (1973); *Teledyne*

McCormick Selph, Comp. Gen. Dec. B-182026, 75-1 CPD ¶ 136. GAO reasoned in such cases that award of the contract to the bidder at the mistaken bid price would not result in prejudice to another bidder, *Arkay Prods. Corp.*, Comp. Gen. Dec. B-181596, 74-2 CPD ¶ 219. These cases did not make clear when the contractor was required to indicate its willingness to accept award at the original bid price if correction of the mistake was denied. However, it was clear that the contracting officer had no obligation to offer award at the original price if the bidder had remained silent on the issue. In a subsequent decision, GAO clarified this area by stating that when the bidder does not include with the request for correction a statement of willingness to accept the award at the original bid price, the contracting officer may either make award to another bidder or request the protesting bidder to accept award at the original bid price, *Guy F. Atkinson Co.*, 55 Comp. Gen. 546 (B-183842), 75-2 CPD ¶ 378. This policy permits the bidder to wait to see if the bid is corrected before deciding whether or not to accept the award at the bid price if it is willing to take the risk that the contracting officer will not offer award at the original price. See *Edmonds Elec. Co.*, Comp. Gen. Dec. B-214063, 84-1 CPD ¶ 615.

Clear evidence that the bid would remain low was found in *National Heat & Power Corp.*, Comp. Gen. Dec. B-212923, 84-1 CPD ¶ 125, where the requested correction, while not sufficiently clear to support correction, would have had to be tripled for the bid to cease being low. Waiver of a mistake was denied in *William G. Tadlock Constr.*, Comp. Gen. Dec. B-251996, 93-1 CPD ¶ 382 (bidder's worksheets did not demonstrate the intended bid price and comparison of the allegedly mistaken item with the government estimate indicated that the bid as corrected might not have remained the low bid); *C Constr. Co.*, Comp. Gen. Dec. B-242717, 91-1 CPD ¶ 540 (the requested correction would have brought the bid within 1.2% of the next low bidder); *LABCO Constr., Inc.*, Comp. Gen. Dec. B-219437, 85-2 CPD ¶ 240 (the correction requested did not contain all potential costs of alleged mistake and inclusion of such costs would have raised bid above next low bidder); *DSG Corp.*, Comp. Gen. Dec. B-210818.3, 84-1 CPD ¶ 476 (two conflicting sets of worksheets made it unclear that the bid would have remained low); and *Hanauer Mach. Works*, Comp. Gen. Dec. B-196369, 80-1 CPD ¶ 178 (the addition of all potential costs of the alleged mistake brought the bidder very close to or even over the next low bid).

If a bidder decides not to request correction of a mistake after clear statements from the contracting officer that it has a right to pursue relief, it will be held to the ensuing contract, *Roy Case Constr. Co.*, ASBCA 52898, 02-1 BCA ¶ 31,665. There, the bidder had misinterpreted the specification but did not investigate the rights that it had under the regulations.

[ii] Accepting Award with a Reservation of Right

Award without correction following an allegation of mistake may be permitted where the contractor agrees to accept award at the original price while reserving a right to seek reformation of the resulting contract. In *JAL Constr., Inc.*, AGBCA 80-117-3, 81-1 BCA ¶ 14,850, the board took jurisdiction of a contractor's claim for reformation under a contract that had been awarded at the original bid price with an understanding that the awardee would be permitted to present evidence in support of a claim for an increase in contract price attributable to an alleged mistake in bid. The board denied the claim for reformation, however, holding that the contractor had failed to establish the intended bid by clear and convincing evidence. See also *Fortec Constructors*, Comp. Gen. Dec. B-179204, 74-1 CPD ¶ 285, agreeing that this was a proper procedure.

§ 5.06 TWO-STEP SEALED BIDDING

Two-step sealed bidding is a procurement method that combines elements of sealed bidding and negotiation. The first step is flexible and resembles negotiation. In this step, the government agency initiates the procedure by publishing a Request for Technical Proposals (RFTP), which outlines the government's requirements. Bidders then submit one or more unpriced technical proposals to satisfy these requirements, and discussions may be held with the offerors. Only those offerors who have submitted acceptable technical proposals are invited to submit step-two sealed bids on price. Offerors bid only on their own proposals, under rules similar to sealed bidding. Award is made to the low responsible bidder submitting a responsive bid.

Two-step formal advertising was suggested in 1957 during the course of the investigation of the Armed Services Procurement Act of 1947 by the House Armed Services Subcommittee for Special Investigations. The subcommittee recommended that the Air Force attempt a two-step procurement procedure in an effort to obtain more competition in military procurements. The Air Force agreed to test the procedure, and in 1959 the procedure was officially adopted by the Armed Services. In a series of decisions published in 1960, GAO concurred with the Armed Services Procurement Regulation (ASPR) on two-step formal advertising, 40 Comp. Gen. 35 (B-143277) (1960) and 40 Comp. Gen. 40 (B-143277) (1960). In 1963, similar provisions were incorporated in the Federal Procurement Regulations (FPR).

This procedure was adopted at a time when sealed bidding was the statutorily preferred method of procurement but negotiated procurement was more commonly used for major procurements, and there was some congressional dissatisfaction with this situation. Thus, two-step sealed bidding was seen as a means of satisfying the need for flexibility obtained through the use of negotiation while still selecting the winner through sealed bid procedures. The Competition in Contracting Act did away with much of the need for two-step sealed bidding by elevating negotiated procurement to the same status as sealed bidding procurement. However, the CICA still authorized the use of two-step sealed bidding by providing that the agencies "shall use the competitive procedure or combination of competitive procedures that is best suited under the circumstances of the procurement," 10 U.S.C. § 3201(a)(2) (formerly § 2304(a)(1)(B)) and 41 U.S.C. § 253(a)(1)(B) (now 41 U.S.C. § 3301(a)(2)). The current regulations concerning two-step sealed bidding are set forth at FAR Subpart 14.5.

Two-step sealed bidding procedures offer certain advantages. First, it encourages competition for government contracts. Contractors that might not have competed under the more structured sealed bidding process may participate in the first step of this process because alternative approaches in the design specifications are encouraged. Second, the price competition of step two makes the award decision public and easily defendable because the decision is based on price alone. Third, the FAR provisions for two-step sealed bidding are the only regulations that explicitly authorize a procedure for the submission of multiple bids by an offeror, FAR 14.503-1(a)(10). Fourth, step one allows the government to take full advantage of industry's expertise and experience without the costly use of development or research contracts. In addition, the government hopes to develop adequate technical data packages through the two-step procedure to allow subsequent acquisitions to be made by conventional sealed bidding, FAR 14.501.

Two-step sealed bidding also has disadvantages. The process is generally time-consuming and costly for the government and for bidders who must draw up detailed technical proposals to meet the government's specifications. The two-step procedure also may result in the procurement of a product that is not the best or most cost-effective overall because, in contrast to competitive negotiation, there are no trade-offs between technical performance and cost in either step. Thus, in step one the government might deem a less desirable proposal unacceptable because it is unable to evaluate how a cost savings would counterbalance the proposal's comparatively diminished performance or quality. Similarly, in step two an offeror will generally quote on its least costly design in order to maximize the chance of success even though a better value would be obtained if the government obtained the more expensive design. Since the government must accept the least costly proposal in step two, it may be compelled to turn down proposals that, though slightly higher priced, are markedly superior technically to the lowest-cost proposal. Finally, the system allows a bidder to forbid competitors from examining its technical proposal by including a restrictive legend on the proposal. This raises serious questions concerning the public nature of the procurement. Despite the disadvantages, two-step sealed bidding can be an effective procurement technique.

[A] Decision to Use Two-Step Sealed Bidding

The factors to be considered by an agency in selecting two-step sealed bidding are set forth in FAR 14.502:

> (a) Unless other factors require the use of sealed bidding, two-step sealed bidding may be used in preference to negotiation when all of the following conditions are present:

(1) Available specifications or purchase descriptions are not definite or complete or may be too restrictive without technical evaluation, and any necessary discussion, of the technical aspects of the requirement to ensure mutual understanding between each source and the Government.

(2) Definite criteria exist for evaluating technical proposals.

(3) More than one technically qualified source is expected to be available.

(4) Sufficient time will be available for use of the two-step method.

(5) A firm-fixed-price contract or a fixed-price contract with economic price adjustment will be used.

(b) None of the following precludes the use of two-step sealed bidding:

(1) Multi-year contracting.

(2) Government property to be made available to the successful bidder.

(3) A total small business set-aside (see 19.502-2).

(4) The use of a set-aside or price evaluation preference for HUBZone small business concerns (see subpart 19.13).

(5) The use of a set-aside for service-disabled veteran-owned small business concerns (see subpart 19.14).

(6) The use of a set-aside for economically disadvantaged women-owned small business concerns and women-owned small business concerns eligible under the Women-Owned Small Business Program (see subpart 19.15).

(7) A first or subsequent production quantity is being acquired under a performance specification.

[1] Sufficient Technical Data and Appropriate Specifications

The regulations, written before the passage of the CICA, provide that the nature of the available specifications is a major factor in determining whether to use two-step sealed bidding. The regulations permit its use when performance specifications ("criteria . . . for evaluating technical proposals") are available, FAR 14.502(a)(2), but the agency does not have detailed specifications or only has detailed specifications that are "too restrictive," FAR 14.502(a)(1). Thus, two-step procurement was devised for the situation where an agency sees a need for evaluating the detailed specifications before awarding a contract and wants to induce contractors to develop detailed specifications.

There are no objective guidelines for deciding whether the available specifications are too indefinite, incomplete, or restrictive to permit two-step procurement. Thus, the fulfillment of the prerequisite that detailed specifications are lacking has been granted wide agency discretion. See 52 Comp. Gen. 854

(B-177206) (1973) (two-step sealed bidding appropriate where the Air Force had detailed specifications for all aspects of a procurement of management services, except with respect to data processing and software operations); Comp. Gen. Dec. B-170135, Feb. 5, 1971, *Unpub.* (Navy's statement accepted that the required antenna coupler groups lacked detailed specifications although similar items were already used by Navy); 40 Comp. Gen. 514 (B-144432) (1961) (contracting officers found to be best qualified to review and evaluate the sufficiency of available technical data for procurement of diesel engine generators). Compare *ALS Elecs. Corp.*, Comp. Gen. Dec. B-181731, 74-2 CPD ¶ 214 (lack of experience of an agency in procuring a technical item was not a sufficient justification for using two-step procurement if the specification was sufficiently detailed to permit sealed bidding).

Although lack of detailed specifications may require the use of two-step sealed bidding, the contracting officer must have definite performance specifications providing criteria for the evaluation of the technical proposals, FAR 14.502(a)(2). Again, there are no objective guidelines for determining the adequacy of the available performance specifications, and fulfillment of the prerequisite of definite performance specifications has also been granted wide agency discretion, 50 Comp. Gen. 346 (B-170268) (1970) (determination of how to best satisfy Navy's requirement of ship hull blast cleaner is left to the discretion of contracting officer).

[2] Availability of Competition

The availability of competition is the other major factor to be considered in deciding whether to use two-step sealed bidding, FAR 14.502(a)(3). If there is likely not to be any competition for the contract, GAO recommends using negotiation rather than two-step procurement, *Allen Osborne Assocs.*, Comp. Gen. Dec. B-235568.3, 89-2 CPD ¶ 279. The competition requirement is met if there is more than one technically qualified source at the end of the step-one competition, even if only one responsive bid is submitted in step two, *Exide Power Sys. Div. of ESB, Inc.*, Comp. Gen. Dec. B-186793, 76-2 CPD ¶ 140. However, if there is only one qualified source at the end of step one, two-step sealed bidding should be discontinued, and negotiated procurement should be used, *Exide Power Sys. Div., ESB, Inc.*, 57 Comp. Gen. 653 (B-191159), 78-2 CPD ¶ 106. It is proper to cancel a negotiated procurement and use two-step sealed bidding when the agency learns of the availability of competition through the submission of an unsolicited proposal, Comp. Gen. Dec. B-154070, June 24, 1964, *Unpub.* See also *Radionics, Inc.*, ASBCA 22727, 81-1 BCA ¶ 15,011, where two-step sealed bidding was used to develop a second source for an item that had been previously procured through sole source negotiation.

[3] Agency Discretion

To date, no agency decision to use two-step procurement has been overturned—based on the reasoning that agencies have broad discretion in deciding whether to use this technique, 50 Comp. Gen. 346 (B-170268) (1970); 40 Comp. Gen. 514 (B-144432) (1961). The few cases concerning the selection of two-step sealed bidding that have found their way to the courts have been resolved in favor of the procuring agency. For example, in *Wheelabrator Corp. v. Chafee*, 455 F.2d 1306 (D.C. Cir. 1971), the court stated that the decision to use two-step formal advertising rather than negotiation was "an exercise of discretion which Congress committed solely to the discretion of the head of the agency, and which is not reviewable in court." For surprising instances where two-step sealed bidding was used on procurements soliciting fixed labor rates for IDIQ contracts, see *AllWorld Language Consultants, Inc.*, Comp. Gen. Dec. B-298831, 2006 CPD ¶ 198; and *SOS Int'l, Ltd.*, Comp. Gen. Dec. B-295533.2, 2005 CPD ¶ 128. The protesters did not raise the argument that sealed bidding can be used only for firm-fixed-price contracts and GAO did not comment on this unusual use of the technique.

[B] Step One

FAR 14.501(a) contains the following description of step one:

> Step one consists of the request for, submission, evaluation, and (if necessary) discussion of a technical proposal. No pricing is involved. The objective is to determine the acceptability of the supplies or services offered. As used in this context, the word "technical" has a broad connotation and includes, among other things, the engineering approach, special manufacturing processes, and special testing techniques. It is the proper step for clarification of questions relating to technical requirements. Conformity to the technical requirements is resolved in this step, but not responsibility as defined in 9.1.

The focus in this step is on the preparation of the RFTPs, the evaluation of proposals, and discussions with offerors.

[1] Request for Technical Proposals

FAR 14.503-1(a) identifies the information that must be included in an RFTP. The RFTP may include delivery or "performance requirements," but these requirements are not considered evaluation factors under step one and are not binding on the government, FAR 14.503-1(b). In this context, the term "performance requirements" should be construed as factors unrelated to the technical competency of a proposal. For example, in *Diversified Contract Servs., Inc.*, Comp. Gen. Dec. B-234660, 89-1 CPD ¶ 590, GAO held that the government was not required to announce a bonding requirement in its RFTP because the bond was a performance requirement that did not affect the technical focus of step one. Additionally, quantities specified in the RFTP are not binding on the government, Comp. Gen. Dec. B-163050, Mar. 27, 1968, *Unpub.*

However, performance requirements (also known as "performance specifications") are considered evaluation factors under step one when the performance requirements state the needs of the government that must be met by the step-one proposal. For example, in *Aerostat Servs. P'ship*, Comp. Gen. Dec. B-244939.2, 92-1 CPD ¶ 71, GAO upheld the Air Force's rejection of a technical proposal because the manning levels for the operation of a radar system did not fulfill the Air Force's performance requirements. See also *Halter Marine, Inc.*, Comp. Gen. Dec. B-239119, 90-2 CPD ¶ 95 (performance requirement of a patrol boat's speed a technical evaluation factor); and *HSQ Tech.*, Comp. Gen. Dec. B-227054, 87-2 CPD ¶ 77 (performance requirement of computer communications rate at 9600 baud a technical evaluation factor). While performance specifications in the RFTP should be relatively flexible in order to encourage varying proposals, the requirements must be sufficiently definite to state the government's needs accurately and to provide offerors with equal opportunities for submitting proposals. When the step-one evaluation is based upon requirements not set forth in the RFTP or ambiguously set forth, GAO has generally found that an unequal basis for competition has arisen. See *Federal Computer Corp.*, 66 Comp. Gen. 139 (B-223932), 86-2 CPD ¶ 665 (improper rejection of step-one proposal for failure to meet Navy's unstated requirements for automatic data processing system); *Tenavision, Inc.*, Comp. Gen. Dec. B-216274, 85-1 CPD ¶ 427 (rejection improper when based on GSA contract number listing requirement that was ambiguously set forth in RFTP); *Masstor Sys. Corp.*, Comp. Gen. Dec. B-206091, 82-2 CPD ¶ 262 (where solicitation provision has two reasonable interpretations and the ambiguity is not so obvious as to impose a duty on the offeror to seek clarification, it is improper for the agency to reject the offeror's proposal for failure to comply with the agency's interpretation); and *RCA Corp.*, 57 Comp. Gen. 809 (B-190247), 78-2 CPD ¶ 213 (camera sample not required by RFTP could not be used as evaluation factor).

GAO may also find an unequal basis for competition if the government significantly changes its requirements from the RFTP specifications, but does not issue an amendment to all bidders. For example, in 53 Comp. Gen. 47 (B-178192) (1973), the government was obligated to amend its RFTP before accepting a technical proposal with a ladder incorporated in the antenna rather than separate from the antenna as originally contemplated in the RFTP. See also *Helmets Ltd.*, 71 Comp. Gen. 281 (B-246301), 92-1 CPD ¶ 241 (proposal that represents a basic change in RFTP helmet design can only be accepted if Navy gives other offerors an opportunity to submit revised proposals); and *Irvin Indus. Canada, Ltd. v. Department of the Air Force*, 924 F.2d 1068 (D.C. Cir. 1990) (when no acceptable technical proposals were submitted, agency was not allowed to disregard material changes of its RFTP for only one offeror, but must negotiate with all offerors).

The determinative question regarding the adequacy of the specifications is whether the bidders are competing on a common basis, *Simulaser Corp.*, Comp. Gen. Dec. B-233850, 89-1 CPD ¶ 236, *recons. denied*, 89-2 CPD ¶ 65. However, absent a showing of prejudice to the protesting offeror, the mere existence of an improper evaluation of technical requirements does not provide a compelling reason to cancel or redo step one of the procurement.

Early GAO decisions treated late technical proposals with some leniency, 45 Comp. Gen. 24 (B-156466) (1965); Comp. Gen. Dec. B-160324, Feb. 16, 1967, *Unpub.* However, in 1973, GAO advised the General Services Administration "that in our view late proposals under step one should be treated in strict accordance with the terms of the solicitations" and heralded a shift toward more rigid adherence to deadlines, 52 Comp. Gen. 726 (B-177284) (1973). Currently, FAR 14.201-6(r) requires that the RFTP include the solicitation provision set forth at FAR 52.214-23. This provision provides that a late technical proposal will not be considered unless (1) the contracting officer determines that accepting it would not unduly delay the acquisition, and (2) any of the three following conditions is present:

> (i) If it was transmitted through an electronic commerce method authorized by the request for technical proposals, it was received at the initial point of entry to the Government infrastructure not later than 5:00 p.m. one working day prior to the date specified for receipt of proposals; or
>
> (ii) There is acceptable evidence to establish that it was received at the Government installation designated for receipt of offers and was under the Government's control prior to the time set for receipt; or
>
> (iii) It is the only proposal received and it is negotiated under part 15 of the Federal Acquisition Regulation.

This provision parallels the provision for late bids in sealed bidding, discussed earlier, where the late-is-late rule is strictly enforced. Accordingly, late technical proposals submitted under two-step procurement will be rejected unless they fall within one of the exceptions defined in the late proposal clause, *Baron & Assocs.*, Comp. Gen. Dec. B-213898, 84-1 CPD ¶ 80. Under the provision in effect until 1999, once a timely proposal was submitted that was acceptable or reasonably susceptible to being made acceptable, late responses to amendments of the RFTP or to agency requests for revisions could be accepted if further negotiations under step one were to be conducted. See *Control Central Corp.*, Comp. Gen. Dec. B-214466.2, 84-2 CPD ¶ 28 (failure to submit a timely revised proposal did not exclude bidder from further competition when negotiations are reopened by subsequent amendment); and *Angstrom, Inc.*, 59 Comp. Gen. 588 (B-193261), 80-2 CPD ¶ 20 (late response to amendment of RFTP allowed because subsequent amendments continued negotiations under step one). Additionally, there is no regulatory requirement for a common cutoff date for receipt of revised proposals after discussions, *J&J Maint., Inc.*, Comp. Gen. Dec. B-240802, 90-2 CPD ¶504, *recons. denied*, 91-1 CPD ¶396.

[2] Evaluation of First-Step Proposals

FAR 14.503-1(e)(1) states that after proposals have been received, they are to be categorized as acceptable, unacceptable, or reasonably susceptible to being made acceptable. Offerors who submit unacceptable proposals are to be notified of that determination promptly and are to be advised that revisions will not be considered, FAR 14.503-1(g). However, failure to give prompt notice is a mere procedural irregularity and, therefore, does not invalidate the procurement, *Shughart & Assocs.*, Comp. Gen. Dec. B-226970, 87-2 CPD ¶56; 48 Comp. Gen. 349 (B-165050) (1968).

Contracting officers are given wide latitude in the evaluation of technical proposals, *Hughes Missile Sys. Co.*, Comp. Gen. Dec. B-257627.2, 94-2 CPD ¶256. Nevertheless, there have been a number of disputes between the offeror and the government regarding whether a proposal was properly evaluated—leading to delays in completing the two-step sealed bidding procurement. For example, in *Angstrom, Inc.*, 59 Comp. Gen. 588 (B-193261), 80-2 CPD ¶20, bidding disputes extended the procurement time of a commercial, off-the-shelf item to 33 months.

[a] Acceptable Proposals

To be acceptable, a technical proposal must conform to the basic or essential requirements of the specifications, FAR 14.503-1(e)(2). However, variations from less significant details of the specifications are permissible in an acceptable proposal. See *Angstrom, Inc.*, 59 Comp. Gen. 588 (B-193261), 80-2 CPD ¶20, holding that a proposal need comply only with basic or essential requirements, not all details of specifications. The difficulty is that it is not always readily ascertainable which of the RFTP requirements are "basic" and, therefore, must be complied with and which are minor details that may be waived. Because there are few objective standards by which basic requirements of specifications may be differentiated from specification details, the contracting officer is given wide discretion in making this determination. See *Ricoh America's Corp.*, Comp. Gen. Dec. B-402239, 2010 CPD ¶55, finding no errors in concluding that all four proposals were acceptable, and *Hughes Missile Sys. Co.*, Comp. Gen. Dec. B-257627.2, 94-2 CPD ¶256, denying a protest of an agency's evaluation of a proposal as acceptable, even though one agency evaluator disagreed with the decision.

Once a proposal is classified as acceptable, it is permitted to compete in step two. There are no degrees of qualification within the acceptable category. Thus, superior and more costly proposals may compete with those that are minimally adequate and less costly, Comp. Gen. Dec. B-159469, Mar. 22, 1967, *Unpub.*

[b] Proposals That Are Reasonably Susceptible to Being Made Acceptable

FAR 14.503-1(f) provides the following guidance on dealing with proposals that are reasonably susceptible to being made acceptable:

> (1) The contracting officer may proceed directly with step two if there are sufficient acceptable proposals to ensure adequate price competition under step two, and if further time, effort and delay to make additional proposals acceptable and thereby increase competition would not be in the Government's interest. If this is not the case, the contracting officer shall request bidders whose proposals may be made acceptable to submit additional clarifying or supplementing information. The contracting officer shall identify the nature of the deficiencies in the proposal or the nature of the additional information required. The contracting officer may also arrange discussions for this purpose. No proposal shall be discussed with any offeror other than the submitter.

Despite this guidance, GAO has stated that the first step of two-step sealed bidding contemplates the qualification of as many proposals as possible, *Hughes Missile Sys. Co.*, Comp. Gen. Dec. B-257627.2, 94-2 CPD ¶ 256. However, this goal of maximization of competition does not mean that an agency is required to classify a proposal as reasonably susceptible of being made acceptable if it fails to meet the basic requirements of the RFTP or can only be made acceptable through extensive revisions. See *Technology Research Int'l*, Comp. Gen. Dec. B-245174, 91-2 CPD ¶ 470 (agency is not required to afford an offeror an opportunity to revise its proposal if major rewrite is necessary); and *Infotec Dev., Inc.*, Comp. Gen. B-235568, 89-2 CPD ¶ 215 (although only one acceptable proposal was left after step one, agency was not required to consider other proposals that required major revisions). Although GAO will commonly defer to the government's decision to reject a proposal where substantial revision is necessary, *Network Sys. Solutions, Inc.*, Comp. Gen. Dec. B-249733, 92-2 CPD ¶ 410, GAO may overturn the decision if there is evidence that the government's evaluation was unreasonable and the proposal was susceptible to being made acceptable. See *Coastal Gov't Servs., Inc.*, Comp. Gen. Dec. B-250820, 93-1 CPD ¶ 167 (agency unreasonably determined that proposal was technically unacceptable based on minor informational deficiencies and proposal ambiguities); and *A.R.E. Mfg. Co.*, Comp. Gen. Dec. B-224086, 86-2 CPD ¶ 395 (decision unreasonable where Navy cannot explain how or why conclusion of unacceptability was reached).

The amount of discussion or clarification that is appropriate and which proposals are reasonably susceptible to being made acceptable are matters of agency discretion, *Ronnoc, Inc.*, Comp. Gen. Dec. B-243729, 91-2 CPD ¶ 163. Although the step-one process is stated to be similar to negotiated procurement, when the government decides that a step-one proposal is reasonably susceptible to being made acceptable, there is no requirement that the government hold "meaningful discussions" with the offeror, *Datron Sys., Inc.*, Comp. Gen. Dec. B-220423.2, 86-1 CPD ¶ 264. It is sufficient if the offeror is notified of deficiencies and afforded the opportunity to address them, *Lockheed Cal. Co.*, Comp. Gen. Dec. B-218143, 85-1 CPD ¶ 676. See also FAR 14.503-1(f)(1).

Discussions resulting in revised proposals that are classified as acceptable are regularly upheld as proper, Comp. Gen. Dec. B-179587, Sept. 27, 1973, *Unpub.* (modification effected in step-one discussions substituted hydraulic actuators for mechanical ones); and *Guardian Elec. Mfg. Co.*, Comp. Gen. Dec. B-191871, 79-1 CPD ¶ 321 (extensive discussions needed to qualify proposal upheld). Additionally, protests alleging that a deficiency in discussions resulted in a proposal's rejection are generally denied. See *Applied Research Tech.*, Comp. Gen. Dec. B-240230, 90-2 CPD ¶ 358 (agency not required to conduct successive rounds of discussions and revisions of proposals); and *Anchor Conveyors, Inc.*, Comp. Gen. Dec. B-215624, 84-2 CPD ¶ 451 (FAA's effort to qualify proposal upheld as reasonable where agency identified deficient areas and afforded bidder an opportunity to correct those deficiencies in revised proposal).

Agencies can limit step-one discussions if there is a possibility of technical transfusion (revealing a competitor's proprietary information). The FAR addresses this technique only with regard to negotiated procurement but it is illegal as a general matter under 18 U.S.C. § 1905. For examples of cases involving technical transfusion in two-step procurement, see *Aerial Image Corp.*, Comp. Gen. Dec. B-219174, 85-2 CPD ¶ 319, upholding an agency's decision not to hold discussions because of the danger of disclosing another offeror's innovative approach to an audio-video slide show, and *General Elec. Can., Inc.*, Comp. Gen. Dec. B-230584, 88-1 CPD ¶ 512, denying a protest alleging technical transfusion as being based on mere speculation by the protester.

The FAR does not explicitly ban technical leveling during step-one discussions and, as discussed in Chapter 6, this prohibition has been removed from the guidance on competitive negotiations. However, GAO applied the general prohibition on technical leveling during discussions found in FAR 15.610(d) (pre FAC 97-02, September 30, 1997 version). In *Applied Research Tech.*, Comp. Gen. Dec. B-240230, 90-2 CPD ¶ 358, GAO stated that successive rounds of discussion during step one are precluded because of the FAR 15.610(d) ban on technical leveling. See also *Essex Electro Eng'rs, Inc.*, Comp. Gen. Dec. B-210366, 83-1 CPD ¶ 650, holding that an agency is not required to engage in technical leveling to bring a proposal up to the level of other proposals.

Even when technical leveling was prohibited, GAO addressed the technical transfusion claim, which was easier to establish, and ignored the difficult technical leveling claim. See *J&J Maint., Inc.*, Comp. Gen. Dec. B-240802, 90-2 CPD ¶ 504, approving acceptance of revised proposal following discussions after finding no evidence of technical transfusion, but disregarded claims of technical leveling.

The amount of time to be allotted to discussion is also a discretionary matter. For example, in Comp. Gen. Dec. B-178071, May 22, 1973, *Unpub.*, GAO upheld the contracting officer's decision to allow 60 additional days to make a proposal acceptable after the date on which two other proposals qualified as acceptable.

[c] Unacceptable Proposals

FAR 14.503-1(e)(2) states:

> Any proposal which modifies, or fails to conform to the essential requirements or specifications of, the request for technical proposals shall be considered nonresponsive and categorized as unacceptable.

A proposal may also be unacceptable because it contains insufficient information to permit a determination that the offeror possesses sufficient technical understanding of the work, *Radiation Sys., Inc.*, Comp. Gen. Dec. B-211732, 83-2 CPD ¶ 434. The cases uniformly follow the principle established in FAR 14.503-1(g) that the government does not have a duty to initiate or continue discussions with the offeror in order to clarify a clearly unacceptable proposal, that would require considerable time and effort to be made acceptable, *Network Sys. Solutions, Inc.*, Comp. Gen. Dec. B-249733, 92-2 CPD ¶ 410 (offeror should not have assumed that it would be afforded opportunity to make further clarifications); *Gichner Iron Works, Inc.*, Comp. Gen. B-230009, 88-1 CPD ¶ 459 (upholding rejection of proposal that would require substantial revisions); and *Colbar, Inc.*, Comp. Gen. Dec. B-227555.4, 88-1 CPD ¶ 168 (upholding evaluation team consensus that proposal for food service would require total rewrite).

[d] Erroneous Evaluations

In reviewing protests of allegedly improper evaluations, GAO will not substitute its judgment for that of the agency that retains wide discretion, but will examine the record to determine whether the evaluation was reasonable and in accord with listed criteria, and whether there were any violations of procurement statutes or regulations, *Anchor Conveyors, Inc.*, Comp. Gen. Dec. B-215624.2, 84-2 CPD ¶ 451. GAO lacks technical expertise to oversee the judgments of the procuring agencies and, therefore, is reluctant to review the step-one evaluation process. Thus, the technical judgment of the agency is accepted unless it is shown to be erroneous, arbitrary, or not in good faith, *Kay & Assocs.*, Comp. Gen. Dec. B-234509, 89-1 CPD ¶ 567.

In contrast, GAO exercises judgment in matters considered to be legal in nature. See, e.g., Comp. Gen. Dec. B-170825.2, Mar. 12, 1971, *Unpub.*, where the meaning and effect of a specification as opposed to whether a product met the specification was declared to be a matter of law within the province of GAO to decide. See also *Federal Computer Corp.*, 66 Comp. Gen. 139 (B-223932), 86-2 CPD ¶ 665 (protest that evaluation factor was not set forth in RFTP); and *E.C. Campbell, Inc.*, Comp. Gen. Dec. B-205533, 82-2 CPD ¶ 34 (award overturned because agency improperly failed to consider awardee's noncompliance with material specification requirement).

Offerors that can demonstrate that a determination of unacceptability is improper are not foreclosed from further participation in the procurement. In 43 Comp. Gen. 255 (B-152261) (1963), a contractor revised a proposal and submitted a second-step bid based on the revised proposal within three days of learning that the proposal had been rejected. GAO permitted the contractor to participate in the second step, stating that the speed with which the proposal was made acceptable showed it had been erroneously rejected as unacceptable in the first instance. See also *Tenavision, Inc.*, Comp. Gen. Dec. B-218794, 85-2 CPD ¶ 62, awarding a protester bid preparation costs incurred in step one of a two-step sealed bid procurement because the offeror's proposal was improperly rejected in step one. However, if the unacceptable proposal is not corrected prior to the submission of the step-two bids, it may not be considered for award. Such proposals are still nonresponsive, and the strict rules of formal advertising applicable to the second step do not permit correction of the proposal at that stage. See 45 Comp. Gen. 487 (B-157084) (1966), holding improper the revision of a proposal during step two. Compare Comp. Gen. Dec. B-160324, Apr. 5, 1967, *Unpub.*, allowing a step-two bid on a proposal initially deemed unacceptable but made competitive before step two.

[C] Step Two

Generally, the second step of two-step sealed bidding is conducted in accordance with the procedures applicable to sealed bidding. See FAR 14.501(b), which states:

> Step two involves the submission of sealed priced bids by those who submitted acceptable technical proposals in step one. Bids submitted in step two are evaluated and the awards made in accordance with Subparts 14.3 and 14.4.

However, there are a number of unique aspects of the sealed bidding procedures used in step two.

Upon completion of step one, invitations for bids are issued to offerors whose technical proposals have been determined acceptable under step one. Limiting competition in step two to acceptable proposals is an exception to the normal sealed bid procedures but is an essential element of two-step sealed bidding. This limitation has been strictly enforced. See Comp. Gen. Dec. B-170175, Apr. 21, 1971, *Unpub.*, where a successful participant in the first step, unable to obtain the required bond, was prohibited from bidding in the second step under the name of a different company that could be bonded. But see *G&C Enters., Inc.*, Comp. Gen. Dec. B-186748, 76-2 CPD ¶ 367, *recons. denied*, 77-1 CPD ¶ 155, where an acceptable step-one proposer was permitted to bid in a joint venture with an outside party in step two.

While participants in step two are limited to those submitting acceptable proposals in step one, step-one participants are not legally bound to participate in step two. The application of this rule could lead to the situation where only one bid is submitted in step two. However, this should not cause cancellation of the procurement unless the bidder was aware that the other successful step-one offerors did not intend to bid.

The regulations provide that the step-two invitation for bids shall "prominently state that the bidder shall comply with the specifications and the bidder's technical proposal," FAR 14.503-2(a)(3). This requirement has been strictly enforced. Products that vary from the RFTP and the accepted technical proposals in step one cannot be accepted in step two, *Qualimetrics, Inc.*, Comp. Gen. Dec. B-227044.3, 87-2 CPD ¶ 100. However, when the bidder deviates from the solicitation in the technical proposal, but would still be the lowest bidder, absent such deviation, the award is proper, *Lusardi Constr. Co.*, Comp. Gen. Dec. B-210276, 83-2 CPD ¶ 297 (price benefit of deviations from specifications did not affect relative standing of bidders); *Essex Electro Eng'rs, Inc.*, Comp. Gen. Dec. B-213892, 84-1 CPD ¶ 434 (relaxation of requirements found not to result in price advantage).

FAR 14.503-2(a)(4) states that it is unnecessary to publish and synopsize second-step IFBs. However, "names of firms which have submitted acceptable proposals in step one are required to be listed in the GPE for the benefit of prospective subcontractors," FAR 14.503-2(b). Negligent failure to list the names of acceptable proposals before the second step has not been fatal to the procurement, *Bailey Controls Co.*, Comp. Gen. Dec. B-256189, 94-1 CPD ¶ 320. However, a failure to publish that is done in bad faith could require readvertisement if the government's interest in full competition has been affected or if the omitted bidder can establish prejudice, Comp. Gen. Dec. B-166315, Aug. 15, 1969, *Unpub.*

[1] Responsiveness

There are two unique aspects of responsiveness in two-step sealed bidding. First, the bid must conform to all of the significant procurement documents. Second, GAO has sometimes stated that there is a presumption of responsiveness.

[a] Nonconforming Bids

In order to be eligible for award in two-step sealed bidding, bids must conform to the RFTP, to the technical proposal as approved by the procuring agency in step one, and to any additional requirements in the step-two invitation for bids. However, it is not necessary for the bidder to physically incorporate the technical proposal in the second-step bid. The bid is considered responsive if it summarizes the technical proposal, as long as the summary is consistent with the acceptable technical proposal. Incorporation by reference or acknowledgment that the bid is in accordance with the accepted proposal is also sufficient, 52 Comp. Gen. 821 (B-177423) (1973).

An invitation to submit a second-step bid does not eliminate the possibility that the offeror will be found nonresponsive after receipt of second-step bids based on a nonconformity included in the step-one proposal. In *International Med. Indus., Inc.*, 62 Comp. Gen. 31 (B-208235), 82-2 CPD ¶ 386, an offeror's step-one proposal included a 30-day bid acceptance period rather than the 45-day period included in the RFTP and this was not altered in the step-two bid. Based upon this nonconformity the company was found nonresponsive in step two. See also *American Tel. & Tel. Co.*, Comp. Gen. Dec. B-193454, 79-1 CPD ¶ 365 and 52 Comp. Gen. 783 (B-177220) (1973). When GAO states that when such a bid is nonresponsive, it is tantamount to a finding that the procuring agency has made an erroneous determination of acceptability in step one.

Bidders can also be found nonresponsive by failing to comply with or taking exception to the requirements of the IFB. See *Tel-Instrument Elecs. Corp.*, Comp. Gen. Dec. B-291309, 2002 CPD ¶ 203 (cover letter required agency to provide equipment not called for in RFTP); *Metric Sys. Corp.*, Comp. Gen. Dec. B-256343, 94-1 CPD ¶ 360 (exception to indemnification clause); *Parsons Precision Prods., Inc.*, Comp. Gen. Dec. B-249940, 92-2 CPD ¶ 431 (cover letter to bid changing payment terms); *KW Control Sys., Inc.*, Comp. Gen. Dec. B-246963, 91-2 CPD ¶ 543 (total payment obligation inconsistent with IFB requirements); *American Monorail, Inc.*, Comp. Gen. Dec. B-181226, 74-2 CPD ¶ 69 (bid with exception to required delivery schedule); and 52 Comp. Gen. 223 (B-176138) (1972). Compare *SOS Int'l, Ltd.*, Comp. Gen. Dec. B-295533.2, 2005 CPD ¶ 128, finding a step-two bid responsive when it contained tiered prices (based on the quantity of work ordered) which were not called for in the IFB—because all of the prices were low.

Similarly, if a price for a certain item is not necessary for the agency's determination of the low bidder, failure to include the price in the step-two bid does not make the bidder nonresponsive, *Educational Computer Corp.*, Comp. Gen. Dec. B-227078, 87-2 CPD ¶ 156.

[b] Presumption of Responsiveness

GAO has sometimes stated that bidders in the second step are entitled to a presumption of responsiveness. See *Spectrolab, Inc.*, Comp. Gen. Dec. B-180008, 74-1 CPD ¶ 321 (bid was ambiguous but GAO presumed offeror meant to be responsive); *Federal Aviation Admin.*, Comp. Gen. Dec. B-193238, 79-1 CPD ¶ 136 (offeror specifically addressed in step one an item that was omitted in step two). The rationale for this rule is that the time, effort, and money a bidder expends in participating in two-step sealed bidding would make it unlikely that the bidder would disqualify the bid by varying from the accepted proposal or the requirements of the specifications, 45 Comp. Gen. 221 (B-157454) (1965). Using this presumption of responsiveness, GAO has approved awards to firms despite deviations that would lead to determinations of nonresponsiveness in a regular sealed bid procurement. For example, in 45 Comp. Gen. 221 (B-157454), the bidder placed "N/A," indicating "not applicable," in the amount column of the item covering the furnishing of certain data related to the end item of the procurement. This created an ambiguity as to whether the bidder was refusing to provide the item or was offering to provide it at no cost. In similar situations in standard sealed bid procurements, such bids are routinely found nonresponsive. However, in this case GAO held that the bidder was responsive based on the asserted presumption of responsiveness. Similarly, in 50 Comp. Gen. 337 (B-169874) (1970), GAO found a bid responsive even though the bidder submitted descriptive literature that was not consistent with the government's requirements. See also *Spectrolab, Inc.*, Comp. Gen. Dec. B-180008, 74-1 CPD ¶ 321; and Comp. Gen. Dec. B-178764, June 27, 1973, *Unpub.*

The presumption of responsiveness is not applicable when the step-two bid takes specific exception to a material requirement that has a significant effect on price, *Universal Comm. Sys., Inc.*, Comp. Gen. Dec. B-205032, 82-2 CPD ¶ 236. See also *Parsons Precision Prod., Inc.*, Comp. Gen. Dec. B-249940, 92-2 CPD ¶ 431 (conflict in payment terms); *Southwestern Bell Corp.*, GSBCA 10321-P, 90-1 BCA ¶ 22,545 (omission of cost of growth requirement); and *Abar Ipsen Indus.*, Comp. Gen. Dec. B-219499.2, 86-1 CPD ¶ 7 (delivery schedule and price terms in conflict).

While the Court of Federal Claims has not stated that there is a presumption of responsiveness, it has found a step-two bid responsive when the bidder submitted a signed "back side" of the SF 1442 but did not submit the front side, *ECDC Envtl., L.C. v. United States*, 40 Fed. Cl. 236 (1998). The court concluded that the terms on the front side could be "inferred" from the fact that the bidder signed the back side.

[2] Data Protection

The two-step regulations require the contracting officer to safeguard step-one proposals against disclosure to unauthorized persons. See FAR 14.503-1, which states:

> (c) Upon receipt, the contracting officer shall—
>
> (1) Safeguard proposals against disclosure to unauthorized persons;

(2) Accept and handle data marked in accordance with 15.609 as provided in that section; and

(3) Remove any reference to price or cost.

Thus, competitors have no way of determining whether the step-one proposal, as accepted by the government, varies from the RFTP. This conflicts with the public opening concept of sealed bidding. See FAR 14.404-4, which states that if a bidder restricts the disclosure of sufficient information to permit competing bidders to know the essential nature of the offer, the bid is nonresponsive. This special procedure has been accepted by GAO as a necessary part of two-step sealed bidding, 46 Comp. Gen. 34 (B-158865) (1966); Comp. Gen. Dec. B-164106, Nov. 8, 1968, *Unpub*. See also *Powers Regulator Co.*, Comp. Gen. Dec. B-181251, 74-2 CPD ¶ 98, rejecting a protester's contention that only a competitor's review of step-one proposals could protect the integrity of the competitive bidding system. GAO indicated that review by GAO was sufficient.

This rule does not apply to elements of the bid that are not included in the step-one proposal. Thus, the prices bid in step two must be disclosed. Therefore, a bid that restricts release of a price in a two-step sealed bid procurement must be found nonresponsive and be rejected, *Northern Telecom, Inc.*, Comp. Gen. Dec. B-209412, 83-1 CPD ¶ 382. Additionally, an agency may disclose prices for a similar prior contract so that potential bidders on the current contract have the same opportunity to bid competitively, *B.C. Cleaning & Maint. Corp.*, Comp. Gen. Dec. B-225909, 87-1 CPD ¶ 56.

[3] Discontinuing Step Two

FAR 14.404-1 lists the circumstances under which cancellation of two-step sealed bid procurement is permitted after the step-two bids are opened. Cancellation at this stage most often results because the government has not obtained sufficient price competition, evidenced by the fact that the bid prices are too high. See *Perimeter Sec. Partners, LLC*, Comp. Gen. Dec. B-417591, 2019 CPD ¶ 305 (cancellation appropriate when prices were well over government estimate); and *Aero Innovations, Ltd.*, Comp. Gen. Dec. B-227677, 87-2 CPD ¶ 332 (cancellation and resolicitation appropriate when restrictive specifications resulted in limited competition). The contracting officer has substantial discretion in concluding that lack of price competition justifies cancellation and may use the bid of a nonresponsive bidder in this determination of price unreasonableness, *McCarthy Mfg. Co.*, 56 Comp. Gen. 369 (B-186550), 77-1 CPD ¶ 116; Comp. Gen. Dec. B-168972, Apr. 14, 1970, *Unpub*. The procurement may also be canceled because the specifications failed to state or overstated the needs of the government. However, the presence of ambiguous specifications is a justification for cancellation only if there is a compelling reason, for instance, where an award would not meet the government's needs or a bidder would be prejudiced. See *Diversified Energy Sys.*, Comp. Gen. Dec. B-245593.3, 92-1

CPD ¶ 293, where cancellation was held to be appropriate because ambiguous specifications led to an overstatement of the agency's needs. Compare *Hydro Power Equip. Co.*, Comp. Gen. Dec. B-205263, 82-1 CPD ¶ 466, finding no compelling reason to cancel despite ambiguous specifications. Additionally, the procurement may be canceled if the agency determines from a cost comparison that it would be more advantageous to perform the services with agency personnel, *United Media Corp.*, Comp. Gen. Dec. B-259425.2, 95-1 CPD ¶ 289.

If the procurement is canceled in step two, the contracting agency may readvertise step two, initiate a new sealed bid procurement, or negotiate the contract. If negotiation is selected as the best means of obtaining the work, the competition may not be limited to the companies that submitted acceptable technical proposals, 46 Comp. Gen. 360 (B-159665) (1966). In one interesting case, GAO ruled that it was proper for an agency to obtain the item by negotiating a lease/purchase arrangement after cancellation of the two-step sealed bid procurement because the bids exceeded the funds available to the agency, 48 Comp. Gen. 471 (B-165013) (1968). Although GAO suggests cancellation of step two and initiation of negotiations when step one results in only one acceptable proposal, the contracting officer has the discretion to proceed to step two, *Allen Osborne Assocs.*, Comp. Gen. Dec. B-235568.2, 89-2 CPD ¶ 279.

CHAPTER 6

BASIC NEGOTIATION PROCEDURES

§ 6.01 NEGOTIATED PROCUREMENT

The term "negotiation" has been broadly used to refer to any procurement technique other than sealed bidding (previously known as "formal advertising"). In use since World War II, it was initially introduced into the procurement statutes by the Armed Services Procurement Act (ASPA) in 1948 and the Federal Property and Administrative Services Act (FPASA) in 1949 as an "exception" to procurement by formal advertising. Its use was authorized only if formal advertising was determined not to be "feasible and practicable" and one of a number of enumerated "exceptions" was present. Both of these acts were amended by the Competition in Contracting Act (CICA) of 1984 to make competition the norm in federal procurement, placing competitive negotiation on an equal footing with sealed bidding. See *Weeks Marine, Inc. v. United States*, 575 F.3d 1352 (Fed. Cir. 2009), *rev'ng*, 79 Fed. Cl. 22 (2007) (court not permitted to substitute its judgment as to the need for negotiation); *Ceres Envtl. Servs., Inc.*, Comp. Gen. Dec. B-310902, 2008 CPD ¶ 48 ("The determination as to whether circumstances support the use of negotiated procedures is largely a discretionary matter within the purview of the contracting officer. . . . However, an agency must reasonably conclude that the conditions requiring use of sealed bidding are not present.").

The original ASPA and FPASA did not specify any procedures to be used in negotiating contracts and did not distinguish between sole source contracts and contracts arrived at competitively. However, subsequent statutes have incorporated various requirements aimed at ensuring fair treatment when competition is used to select the contractor, while remaining silent on the procedures to be followed in sole source procurements (except for the truth in negotiation requirements discussed in Chapter 13).

The result is that agencies have wide discretion as to the procedures to be used for sole source procurements. FAR 15.002(a) appears to assume that agencies will issue an RFP to the selected contractor to initiate the negotiation process, but this is not mandatory. Hence, when the parties have a firm understanding of the contract requirements, such as with a follow-on contract, they can go directly into negotiations, or the agency can issue an RFQ directing the contractor to submit a price proposal (the FAR is silent on this use of an RFQ). When the agency has not previously acquired the product or service but has determined through market research that only one source is available, the use of an RFP would be a sound way to inform the contractor of the agency's requirements on which a price proposal could be based. In neither instance is there any need for capability information, evaluation factors, or the other elements of a competitive negotiation. See FAR 15.300 stating that FAR Subpart 15.3 is only applicable to competitive negotiations. The key element in such procurements is the detailed negotiation of the price or cost and fee and reaching agreement on the specifications and terms and conditions. Once the parties have concluded this negotiation, the contracting officer will normally prepare an integrated contract document, obtain the contractor's signature, and then formalize the contract by signing the document.

In contrast, there are several mandatory procedures that apply to competitively negotiated procurements. The first Congressional effort to address these procedures occurred in 1962. Following complaints that noncompetitive practices were used by the Department of Defense (DoD) in negotiating contracts, the ASPA was amended by Pub. L. No. 87-653, to require "oral or written discussions" with all offerors submitting proposals within a "competitive range." Award without discussions was permitted only if the reasonableness of price could be determined through adequate competition or prior cost experience. These requirements were subsequently imposed on civilian agencies by the Federal Procurement Regulations. CICA restated and supplemented these requirements and made them statutorily applicable to civilian agency contracts. In addition, it introduced the term "competitive proposals" for negotiated contracts. Subsequent statutory changes, including the Federal Acquisition Streamlining Act of 1994 (FASA), Pub. L. No. 103-355, and the Clinger-Cohen Act of 1996, Pub. L. No. 104-106, required increased detail in stating evaluation factors and subfactors, removed restrictions on making awards without discussions, permitted limitation of the competitive range for purposes of efficiency, and required extensive debriefing of offerors. However, rather than specifying any single technique, the present statutes provide a framework within which procuring agencies have flexibility to devise varying strategies.

The purpose of competitive negotiation is to permit agencies to use more discretionary procedures than permitted in the sealed bidding process. As a result, proposals are not available for public inspection prior to award. The concept of responsiveness does not apply and proposals which vary from the RFP are not required to be rejected. Discussions and bargaining are permitted which can result in modifications of proposals by offerors to correct deficiencies or to enhance their offers. In selecting the contractor, the agency need not award to the low-priced offeror but can make tradeoffs between cost or price and other factors. The flexibility of negotiation is reflected in FAR 15.306(d), stating:

> Negotiation are exchanges . . . between the Government and offerors, that are undertaken with the intent of allowing the offeror to revise its proposal. These negotiations may include bargaining. Bargaining includes persuasion, alteration of assumptions and positions, give-and-take, and may apply to price, schedule, technical requirements, type of contract, or other terms of a proposed contract.

The negotiation process gives contracting officials the option to seek proposal modifications, but they are not required to do so if acceptance of the most favorable initial proposal(s) is in the best interests of the government. We call this the "standard" procedure to indicate that, while it is commonly followed, it is not mandatory.

Through the years much of the flexibility available in negotiated procurements became lost due to overly complex solicitations including unnecessarily large numbers of evaluation factors and subfactors. In an attempt to reverse this trend, FAR 15.002 establishes a policy aimed at minimizing the complexity of negotiated procurements as follows:

> (a) *Sole-source acquisitions*. When contracting in a sole source environment, the request for proposals (RFP) should be tailored to remove unnecessary information and requirements, e.g., evaluation criteria and voluminous proposal preparation instructions.
>
> (b) *Competitive acquisitions*. When contracting in a competitive environment, the procedures of this part are intended to minimize the complexity of the solicitation, the evaluation, and the source selection decision, while maintaining a process designed to foster an impartial and comprehensive evaluation of offerors' proposals, leading to selection of the proposal representing the best value to the Government (see 2.101).

This chapter focuses on the competitive negotiation procedures covered by FAR Part 15. Special negotiation procedures involved in specific types of procurements are dealt with in Chapters 7 through 10. The pricing of all types of negotiated contracts, both competitive and noncompetitive, is covered in Chapter 13.

§ 6.02 COMPETITIVE PROCUREMENT STRATEGIES

The procurement statutes give agencies a great degree of discretion in devising competitive strategies designed to fulfill the government's needs. This permits the source selection decision to be made by balancing other factors against costs to the government. Thus, a starting point in the process is for the agency to determine the fundamental basis that will be used to make the source selection decision. In this chapter, we describe this statement of the basis for making the source selection decision as the "decisional rule." 41 U.S.C. § 3306(c)(1)(C) and 10 U.S.C. § 3206(c) (formerly § 2305(a)(3)(A)(iii)) contain the following minimal requirements to be observed in stating the decisional rule for a procurement:

> (1) In general. In prescribing the evaluation factors to be included in each solicitation for competitive proposals, the head of an agency—
>
> > (A) shall (except as provided in paragraph (3)) clearly establish the relative importance assigned to the evaluation factors and subfactors, including the quality of the product or services to be provided (including technical capability, management capability, prior experience, and past performance of the offeror);

(B) shall (except as provided in paragraph (3)) include cost or price to the Federal Government as an evaluation factor that must be considered in the evaluation of proposals; and

(C) shall disclose to offerors whether all evaluation factors other than cost or price, when combined, are—

(i) significantly more important than cost or price;
(ii) approximately equal in importance to cost or price; or
(iii) significantly less important than cost or price.

(2) Restriction on implementing regulations. The regulations implementing paragraph (1)(C) may not define the terms "significantly more important" and "significantly less important" as specific numeric weights that would be applied uniformly to all solicitations or a class of solicitations.

Although previous versions of FAR Part 15 did not use the term, procurements in which the selection was based on a tradeoff between price and other factors came to be known as "best value" procurements. However, the "Rewrite" of FAR Part 15, contained in FAC 97-02, 62 Fed. Reg. 51224, Sept. 30, 1997, uses the term "best value" more broadly. It encompasses all procurement strategies, whether or not based on tradeoffs. FAR 15.302 states: "The objective of source selection is to select the proposal that represents the best value." The term is now defined in FAR 2.101 as follows:

> "Best value" means the expected outcome of an acquisition that, in the Government's estimation, provides the greatest overall benefit in response to the requirement.

FAR 15.101, entitled "Best value continuum," elaborates on this concept as follows:

> An agency can obtain best value in negotiated acquisitions by using any one or a combination of source selection approaches. In different types of acquisitions, the relative importance of cost or price may vary. For example, in acquisitions where the requirement is clearly definable and the risk of unsuccessful contract performance is minimal, cost or price may play a dominant role in source selection. The less definitive the requirement, the more development work required, or the greater the performance risk, the more technical or past performance considerations may play a dominant role in source selection.

Under this concept, procurement officials determine, in advance of soliciting proposals, what type of selection process will be best for the government. Where differences in non-cost factors will not materially impact the agency's needs, award on the basis of the lowest evaluated price would be appropriate. Where differences in non-cost factors will be material and the agency is willing to pay a higher price, a tradeoff process would be called for. Where differences in non-cost factors are the major consideration and variable prices are acceptable, award to the most acceptable non-cost factors would be appropriate. The following material discusses the two processes described in the FAR plus other potential strategies that are permissible under the ASPA and the FPASA.

[A] Tradeoff Process

As previously indicated, this strategy had previously been known as the best value technique. The hallmark of the system is that it permits the determination of best value to be made *after the receipt of proposals*. It is described in FAR 15.101-1 as follows:

> (a) A tradeoff process is appropriate when it may be in the best interest of the Government to consider award to other than the lowest priced offeror or other than the highest technically rated offeror.
>
> (b) When using the tradeoff process, the following apply:
>
> (1) All evaluation factors and significant subfactors that will affect contract award and their relative importance shall be clearly stated in the solicitation; and
>
> (2) The solicitation shall state whether all evaluation factors other than cost or price, when combined, are significantly more important than, approximately equal to, or significantly less important than cost or price.
>
> (c) This process permits tradeoffs among cost or price and non-cost factors and allows the Government to accept other than the lowest priced proposal. The perceived benefits of the higher-priced proposal shall merit the additional cost, and the rationale for tradeoffs must be documented in the file in accordance with 15.406.

This process gives the source selection official very broad discretion when the offeror with the lowest cost to the government has not been evaluated best on the non-cost factors. There, the ultimate decision is made on a subjective judgment as to whether a higher cost to the government is worth the added value of the non-cost factors. See *TRW, Inc., v. Widnall*, 98 F.3d 1325 (Fed. Cir. 1996); *Environmental Chemical Corp.*, Comp. Gen. Dec. B-275819, 97-1 CPD ¶ 154. It is clear that this judgment as to the value of the non-cost factors need not be quantified, FAR 15.308. See *Widnall v. B3H Corp.*, 75 F.3d 1577 (Fed. Cir. 1996), stating that these tradeoff decisions must be based on a "reasoned explanation" of the decision but need not be based on quantification of the non-cost factors. The same result was reached by GAO in *Systems Mgmt., Inc.*, Comp. Gen. Dec. B-287032.5, 2002 CPD ¶ 29; *Kay & Assoc., Inc.*, Comp. Gen. Dec. B-258243.7, 96-1 CPD ¶ 266, and *EG&G Team*, Comp. Gen. Dec. B-259917.3, 95-2 CPD ¶ 175. If the agency does quantify some of the non-cost evaluation factors, GAO will not scrutinize the quantification for accuracy but will focus on the overall rationality of the best value decision, *DDD Co.*, Comp. Gen. Dec. B-276708, 97-2 CPD ¶ 44.

In the past, some agencies have attempted to devise numerical formulas to make this tradeoff appear to be *objective*. Some of these formulas have used a total point system by assigning points to the price, others have assigned dollar values to the non-price factors and a third have divided the price by the points assigned to non-price factors to come up with a dollars per point figure. Such techniques have been accepted as tools to be used in evaluating the relative merits of proposals. However, GAO has indicated that these are only evaluation techniques and that the source selection official should still exercise judgment in determining whether the merits of the highest scored proposal are worth paying a higher price. See *C&B Constr., Inc.*, Comp. Gen. Dec. B-401988.2, 2010 CPD ¶ 1, stating "a selection decision may not be made on point scores alone where the agency selection official has inadequate documentation on which to base a reasoned decision." See also *Harrison Sys., Ltd.*, 63 Comp. Gen. 244 (B-212675), 84-1 CPD ¶ 572 (recommending that a total point system not be used in combination with a statement that award will be made to the offeror receiving the highest number of points); *Storage Tech. Corp.*, Comp. Gen. Dec. B-215336, 84-2 CPD ¶ 190 (dollar values assigned to non-price factors only to be used as a *guide* to the selection official); and *Moran Assocs.*, Comp. Gen. Dec. B-240564.2, 91-2 CPD ¶ 495 (cost/technical ratio formula only one tool to assure that the government was getting the best buy). In addition, a number of agencies have prohibited or strongly discouraged the use of such formulas.

A tradeoff process allowing an agency to award two contracts to the most advantageous pair of offerors, potentially excluding the second highest rated offeror, was held to be impermissible in *Blue Origin Florida, LLC*, Comp. Gen. Dec. B-417839, 2019 CPD ¶ 388. GAO concluded that the problem with this technique was that the evaluation criteria in the RFP might not be the actual basis for award and the offerors had no way of knowing whether their proposals contained similar weaknesses or strengths with other proposals (which would allow selection of a lower rated proposal).

The tradeoff process with subjective judgments as to best value has been the most widely used process with the result that it has generated most of the protests. The issues in these protests are covered in detail in the balance of this chapter.

[B] Lowest Price Technically Acceptable Source Selection Process

The FAR now describes this Lowest Price Technically Acceptable (LPTA) strategy as a "best value" procedure but the best value determination is made by the agency at the time the strategy is chosen, before receipt or analysis of proposals. Thus, when an agency has decided to use this strategy, it has decided that the best value will be obtained by paying the lowest price offered by any offeror that submits an acceptable "technical proposal" and has stated in the RFP that the decision will be made in this manner. A procurement is *not* a lowest price technically acceptable procurement if the RFP states that a tradeoff will be made but the source selection official concludes that the competitors are essentially equal on the non-price factors and awards to the offeror with the lowest price, *Apptis, Inc.*, Comp. Gen. Dec. B-403249, 2010 CPD ¶ 237.

FAR 15.101-2 describes this process as follows:

> (a) The lowest price technically acceptable source selection process is appropriate when best value is expected to result from selection of the technically acceptable proposal with the lowest evaluated price.
>
> (b) When using the lowest price technically acceptable process, the following apply:
>
> (1) The evaluation factors and significant subfactors that establish the requirements of acceptability shall be set forth in the solicitation. Solicitations shall specify that award will be made on the basis of the lowest evaluated price of proposals meeting or exceeding the acceptability standards for non-cost factors. If the contracting officer documents the file pursuant to 15.304(c)(3)(iii), past performance need not be an evaluation factor in lowest price technically acceptable source selections. If the contracting officer elects to consider past performance as an evaluation factor, it shall be evaluated in accordance with 15.305. However, the comparative assessment in 15.305(a)(2)(i) does not apply. If the contracting officer determines that a small business' past performance is not acceptable, the matter shall be referred to the Small Business Administration for a Certificate of Competency determination, in accordance with the procedures contained in subpart 19.6 and 15 U.S.C. § 637(b)(7).
>
> (2) Tradeoffs are not permitted.
>
> (3) Proposals are evaluated for acceptability but not ranked using the non-cost/price factors.
>
> (4) Exchanges may occur (see 15.306).

Note that the term "technical" means all non-cost factors.

Extensive use of the process has led to restrictions on its use in § 813 of the National Defense Authorization Act for FY 2017, Pub. L. No. 114-328, as amended by § 822 of the National Defense Authorization Act for FY 2018, Pub. L. No. 115-91, and § 880 of the National Defense Authorization Act for FY 2019, Pub. L. No. 115-232. These restrictions are slightly different for DOD and the other agencies. FAR 15.101-2 provides the following restrictions for non-DOD agencies:

> (c) Except for DoD, in accordance with section 880 of the John S. McCain National Defense Authorization Act for Fiscal Year 2019 (Pub. L. 115–232, 41 U.S.C. 701 Note), the lowest price technically acceptable source selection process shall only be used when—

(1) The agency can comprehensively and clearly describe the minimum requirements in terms of performance objectives, measures, and standards that will be used to determine the acceptability of offers;

(2) The agency would realize no, or minimal, value from a proposal that exceeds the minimum technical or performance requirements;

(3) The agency believes the technical proposals will require no, or minimal, subjective judgment by the source selection authority as to the desirability of one offeror's proposal versus a competing proposal;

(4) The agency has a high degree of confidence that reviewing the technical proposals of all offerors would not result in the identification of characteristics that could provide value or benefit to the agency;

(5) The agency determined that the lowest price reflects the total cost, including operation and support, of the product(s) or service(s) being acquired; and

(6) The contracting officer documents the contract file describing the circumstances that justify the use of the lowest price technically acceptable source selection process.

(d) Except for DoD, in accordance with section 880 of the John S. McCain National Defense Authorization Act for Fiscal Year 2019 (Pub. L. 115–232, 41 U.S.C. 3701 Note), contracting officers shall avoid, to the maximum extent practicable, using the lowest price technically acceptable source selection process in the case of a procurement that is predominantly for the acquisition of—

(1) Information technology services, cybersecurity services, systems engineering and technical assistance services, advanced electronic testing, audit or audit readiness services, health care services and records, telecommunications devices and services, or other knowledge-based professional services;

(2) Personal protective equipment; or

(3) Knowledge-based training or logistics services in contingency operations or other operations outside the United States, including in Afghanistan or Iraq.

DFARS 215.101-2-70 provides for the following restrictions for DOD:

(a) Limitations.

(1) In accordance with section 813 of the National Defense Authorization Act for Fiscal Year 2017 (Pub. L. 114-328) as amended by section 822 of the National Defense Authorization Act for Fiscal Year 2018 (Pub. L. 115-91) (see 10 U.S.C. 2305 note), the lowest price technically acceptable source selection process shall only be used when—

(i) Minimum requirements can be described clearly and comprehensively and expressed in terms of performance objectives, measures, and standards that will be used to determine the acceptability of offers;

(ii) No, or minimal, value will be realized from a proposal that exceeds the minimum technical or performance requirements;

(iii) The proposed technical approaches will require no, or minimal, subjective judgment by the source selection authority as to the desirability of one offeror's proposal versus a competing proposal;

(iv) The source selection authority has a high degree of confidence that reviewing the technical proposals of all offerors would not result in the identification of characteristics that could provide value or benefit;

(v) No, or minimal, additional innovation or future technological advantage will be realized by using a different source selection process;

(vi) Goods to be procured are predominantly expendable in nature, are nontechnical, or have a short life expectancy or short shelf life (See PGI 215.101-2-70(a)(1)(vi) for assistance with evaluating whether a requirement satisfies this limitation);

(vii) The contract file contains a determination that the lowest price reflects full life-cycle costs (as defined at FAR 7.101) of the product(s) or service(s) being acquired (see PGI 215.101-2-70(a)(1)(vii) for information on obtaining this determination); and

(viii) The contracting officer documents the contract file describing the circumstances justifying the use of the lowest price technically acceptable source selection process.

(2) In accordance with section 813 of the National Defense Authorization Act for Fiscal Year 2017, as amended by section 822 of the National Defense Authorization Act for Fiscal Year 2018 (Pub. L. 115-91) (see 10 U.S.C. 2305 note), contracting officers shall avoid, to the maximum extent practicable, using the lowest price technically acceptable source selection process in the case of a procurement that is predominately for the acquisition of—

(i) Information technology services, cybersecurity services, systems engineering and technical assistance services, advanced electronic testing, or other knowledge-based professional services;

(ii) Items designated by the requiring activity as personal protective equipment (except see paragraph (b)(1) of this section); or

(iii) Services designated by the requiring activity as knowledge-based training or logistics services in contingency operations or other operations outside the United States, including in Afghanistan or Iraq.

(b) Prohibitions.

(1) In accordance with section 814 of the National Defense Authorization Act for Fiscal Year 2017 as amended by section 882 of

> the National Defense Authorization Act for Fiscal Year 2018 (see 10 U.S.C. 2302 note), contracting officers shall not use the lowest price technically acceptable source selection process to procure items designated by the requiring activity as personal protective equipment or an aviation critical safety item, when the requiring activity advises the contracting officer that the level of quality or failure of the equipment or item could result in combat casualties. See 252.209-7010 for the definition and identification of critical safety items.
>
> (2) In accordance with section 832 of the National Defense Authorization Act for Fiscal Year 2018 (see 10 U.S.C. 2442 note), contracting officers shall not use the lowest price technically acceptable source selection process to acquire engineering and manufacturing development for a major defense acquisition program for which budgetary authority is requested beginning in fiscal year 2019.
>
> (3) Contracting officers shall make award decisions based on best value factors and criteria, as determined by the resource sponsor (in accordance with agency procedures), for an auditing contract. The use of the lowest price technically acceptable source selection process is prohibited (10 U.S.C. 254b).

Prior to the passage of these statutes, both the Court of Federal Claims and GAO had ruled that agencies had broad discretion to use the LPTA process. See, for example, *Phoenix Mgmt. Inc. v. United States*, 127 Fed. Cl. 358 (2016) (base support services); *Wittenberg Weiner Consulting, LLC*, Comp. Gen. Dec. B-413457, 2016 CPD ¶ 320 (Navy procurement for program management and future requirements planning services); and *Technica Corp.*, Comp. Gen. Dec. B-413339, 2016 CPD ¶ 264 (Defense Information Systems Agency procurement for solution engineering and implementation support services). Since the statutes have been implemented, agencies have continued to receive considerable discretion in selecting the LPTA process. See *Verizon Bus. Network Servs., Inc.*, Comp. Gen. Dec. B-418331.3, 2020 CPD ¶ 235 (installation and support of basic Internet, wi-fi, and voice services and hardware does not violate restriction because agency was not willing to pay more for anything exceeding its specified requirements).

A procurement calling for a price/past performance tradeoff among the highest rated technical quotations was not an LPTA process, *Inserso Corp.*, Comp. Gen. Dec. B-417791, 2019 CPD ¶ 370. GAO rejected the protester's argument that the statutory restrictions barred the use of LPTA *criteria.*

Agencies have used the LPTA technique for cost-reimbursement contracts as well as fixed price contracts. See *Abacus Tech. Corp.*, Comp. Gen. Dec. B-412375, 2016 CPD ¶ 50, using the LPTA technique for a multiple-award IDIQ services contract calling for the issuance of cost-plus-fixed-fee task orders, with a firm-fixed-price contract line item for a transition period, and cost-reimbursement CLINs for travel. The agency performed a cost realism analysis to determine the probable cost to be included in the "price." A similar use of the technique occurred in *General Dynamics Advanced Info. Sys., Inc.*, Comp. Gen. Dec. B-411771, 2015 CPD ¶ 322, where the GAO sustained the protest because of an improper cost realism analysis. Fixed labor rates have also been treated as prices. See *Starry Assocs., Inc.*, Comp. Gen. Dec. B-410968.2, 2015 CPD ¶ 253, and Comp. Gen. Dec. B-410968.3, 2015 CPD ¶ 401, where the agency conducted an LPTA competition under the Federal Supply Schedule for a labor-hour task order with a one-year base period and four one-year options.

One important aspect of this technique is that the non-cost evaluation factors are all of equal importance. Thus, the failure of a proposal to meet any *one* of the factors will preclude award to the offeror submitting the proposal and allow the agency to drop that offeror from the competition. See, for example, *Consummate Comput. Consultants Sys., LLC*, Comp. Gen. Dec. B-410566.2, 2015 CPD ¶ 176 (lack of sufficient information to show qualification of proposed project manager); *Jungang Auto. Co.*, Comp. Gen. Dec. B-402623.2, 2010 CPD ¶ 144 (protester failed to meet the experience requirement in the RFP); *Building Restoration Corp.*, Comp. Gen. Dec. B-402000, 2010 CPD ¶ 15 (protester had inadequate construction schedule and its safety officer also was to act as the quality control officer); and *Dubinsky v. United States*, 44 Fed. Cl. 509 (1999) (agency precluded from awarding to an offer that had material failures to meet mandatory requirements). In *Level 3 Commc'ns, LLC*, Comp. Gen. Dec. B-412854, 2016 CPD ¶ 171, the GAO denied a protest that the company had been dropped from the competition for failure to meet three mandatory information submission requirements. The Court of Federal Claims reached the opposite conclusion in *Level 3 Commc'ns, LLC v. United States*, 129 Fed. Cl. 487 (2016), ruling that it was arbitrary and capricious to declare a non-cost quotation unacceptable when the incumbent contractor offered to perform for $60,128,000 compared to a price of $98,664,800 for the awardee. The court reasoned that in such circumstances the agency was required to conduct discussions allowing the company to correct the defective information, citing *BCPeabody Constr. Servs., Inc. v. United States*, 112 Fed. Cl. 502 (2013). See also DFARS 215.306(d) stating that for procurements over $100 million discussions "should" be conducted.

The fact that agency can reject a proposal that does not meet a non-cost evaluation factor does not preclude establishing a competitive range and giving an offeror the opportunity to cure the noncompliance. See *NCS/EML JV, LLC*, Comp. Gen. Dec. B-412277, 2016 CPD ¶ 21, where discussions properly were held with a number of offerors to clear up problems in their proposals. However, it is improper to conduct discussions to obtain more than an acceptable rating on a non-cost factor, *Rosemary Livingston*, Comp. Gen. Dec. B-401102.2, 2009 CPD ¶ 135. Discussions can also be held to obtain lower prices, *TransAtlantic Lines, LLC*, Comp. Gen. Dec. B-411242, 2015 CPD ¶ 204. See, however, *Excelsior Ambulance Serv., Inc. v. United States*, 124 Fed. Cl. 581 (2015), where the agency conducted discussions to obtain lower prices and dealt with a protest after award by allowing the awardee to "clarify" its technical proposal. The court granted the ensuing protest because this was an improper clarification although the matter could have been dealt with in the discussions. In establishing a competitive range, it is proper to exclude a competitor that has no realistic prospect of winning the competition, *Regency Enters. Servs., LLC*, Comp. Gen. Dec. B-418448, 2020 CPD ¶ 165.

One major benefit of this strategy is that the agency can greatly shorten the evaluation process because, once the low-price proposal has been found to be technically acceptable, there is no need to evaluate the acceptability of any of the other proposals. This streamlined process can be used as long as the agency has used the Instruction to Offerors—Competitive Acquisition solicitation provision in FAR 52.215-1 which states in ¶ (f)(4) that the agency intends to award without discussions. This technique was used in *U.S. Security Assocs., Inc. v. United States*, 123 Fed. Cl. 663 (2015). See also in *T.W. LaQuay Marine, LLC v. United States*, 127 Fed. Cl. 748 (2016), where the agency evaluated only one of the non-cost factors for all of the offerors and then evaluated the acceptability of only the low-price offeror on the other non-cost factors.

Since the term "technically acceptable proposals" in the FAR refers to all non-cost factors, it includes factors dealing with the capability of the offerors as well as the technical details of the performance which is offered in the proposal. While FAR 15.101-2(b) refers only to "past performance" as requiring reference to Small Business Administration (SBA), the same rule would apply to other "capability" factors. See, e.g., *Vantex Serv. Corp.*, Comp. Gen. Dec. B-266199, 96-1 CPD ¶ 29, holding that when "traditional" responsibility factors such as "experience" are evaluated on a "go/no-go" basis, the matter must be referred to the SBA if the proposal is determined unacceptable because of such factors. See also *Dynamic Aviation—Helicopters*, Comp. Gen. Dec. B-274122, 96-2 CPD ¶ 166; and *Environsol, Inc.*, Comp. Gen. Dec. B-254223, 93-2 CPD ¶ 295. One way to deal with this issue is to state in the RFP that a small business offeror with no relevant past performance or no information on past performance will be rated "acceptable." This technique has been found reasonable in *Phoenix Mgmt., Inc. v. United States*, 127 Fed. Cl. 358 (2016), and *Y&K Maint., Inc.*, Comp. Gen. Dec. B-405310.2, 2011 CPD ¶ 239.

It has been held that "no narrative justifications" are required to support the assessment that an element of a technical proposal is unacceptable, *Al Ghanim Combined Grp. Co. Gen. Trad. & Cont. W.L.L. v. United States*, 56 Fed. Cl. 502 (2003) (evaluators merely circled "pass" or "fail" on an evaluation sheet). The court derived this rule from FAR 15.305(a)(3) stating that an "assessment of each offeror's ability to accomplish the technical requirements" was required only in tradeoff procurements. The court did not consider FAR 15.305(a) calling for documentation of "relative strengths, significant weaknesses, and risks."

Although the LPTA technique is similar to sealed bidding, protests that sealed bidding should have been used have been denied. See *Saxon Corp.*, Comp. Gen. Dec. B-216148, 85-1 CPD ¶ 87 (impossible to draft sufficiently precise specifications for a sealed bid procurement); *Essex Electro Eng'rs, Inc.*,

65 Comp. Gen. 242 (B-221114), 86-1 CPD ¶ 92 (agency needed to be able to conduct discussions); and *Vantex Serv. Corp.*, Comp. Gen. Dec. B-266199, 96-1 CPD ¶ 29 (agency needed to be able to conduct discussions).

[C] Combination of Tradeoff and LPTA Processes

Although FAR Part 15 does not directly address the combination of these two processes, FAR 15.101 indicates that a "combination of source selection approaches" may be used. Thus, an agency could subject some of the evaluation factors to a "go/no-go" test (acceptable/unacceptable), while providing that others are to be evaluated on the relative strengths, weaknesses, and risks. This technique would enable tradeoffs to be made for those factors subject to evaluation on their relative strengths, weaknesses, and risks while requiring rejection of the proposals not meeting the minimum requirements for those subject to the "go/no-go" test. Another strategy might be to subject all factors to a "go/no-go" test for the proposal to receive further consideration and then to evaluate the relative strengths, weaknesses, and risks of those determined to be acceptable. These types of strategies were discussed in Chapter 2 of the GSA Handbook, Source Selection Procedures, APD P 2800.2, July 21, 1987, which provided the following guidance:

> [A] go, no-go approach can be applied to some or all of the major evaluation factors or subfactors identified in the solicitation. When all factors are go, no-go the process is equivalent to the lowest-priced acceptable proposal approach discussed above. When the "greatest value concept" is used, some evaluation factors may be used as discriminators and be evaluated on a go, no-go basis. An evaluation factor such as "management" may be used as a discriminator for evaluation on a go, no-go basis. If the "management" factor is scored adequate, it may, or may not, have further relevance in the evaluation process. . . . The evaluation process may be structured so that the factor has no further relevance . . . if it is scored adequate. On the other hand, the evaluation process may be structured so that the factor is scored and the merits of the proposal considered in the ultimate award decision. An adequate score in such an area is therefore a minimum requirement for selection. . . . This approach is frequently used in situations in which the product is subject to testing to establish whether it meets certain requirements outlined in the solicitation.

This method has been used in a number of situations and has not been questioned by either GAO or the Court of Federal Claims. See *Coast to Coast Computer Prods., Inc.*, Comp. Gen. Dec. B-409528.33, 2014 CPD ¶ 346 (tradeoff between socio-economic status and price among offerors that had submitted acceptable technical proposals); *Linc Gov't Servs., LLC v. United States*, 95 Fed. Cl. 155 (2010) (tradeoff between past performance and price among offerors that had submitted acceptable technical proposals); *Integrated Concepts & Research Corp.*, Comp. Gen. Dec. B-309803, 2008 CPD ¶ 117 (tradeoff of proposal risk, past performance and price among the acceptable technical proposals); *Utility Tool & Trailer, Inc.*, Comp. Gen. Dec. B-310535, 2008 CPD ¶ 1 (tradeoff of delivery, small business participation and price among the acceptable technical proposals); *Brewbaker White Sands JV*, Comp. Gen. Dec. B-295582.4, 2005 CPD ¶ 176 (tradeoff between past performance and price among offerors that had submitted acceptable technical proposals); *Sterling Servs., Inc.*, Comp. Gen. Dec. B-286326, 2000 CPD ¶ 208 (evaluation of past performance in a "Technically Acceptable—Performance/Price Tradeoff" procurement); and *ECI Telecom, Inc.*, 64 Comp. Gen. 688 (B-218533), 85-2 CPD ¶ 73 (go, no-go evaluation of all technical subfactors). See also *FMB Laundry, Inc.*, Comp. Gen. Dec. B-261837.2, 95-2 CPD ¶ 274, where the protester argued that the RFP was deficient because it failed to specify what weight would be accorded to the technical factors in relation to price. GAO stated that the fact that relative weight of acceptability verses price was not spelled out was irrelevant because the solicitation did not contemplate gradations in acceptability rankings as it was essentially a go/no-go determination. This procedure has been upheld in a procurement containing a "5000 round service life" requirement, *Smith & Wesson Div., Bangor Punta Corp. v. United States*, 782 F.2d 1074 (1st Cir. 1986), *reh'g and reh'g en banc denied, Unpub.* (1986), where a product was excluded from further consideration based on tests of samples which cracked before firing 5000 rounds. GAO has approved similar procedures where offerors had an opportunity to correct deficiencies found in initial testing, *Centennial Computer Prods., Inc.*, Comp. Gen. Dec. B-212979, 84-2 CPD ¶ 295.

[E] Highest Technically Rated with Fair and Reasonable Price

Because of the lack of a price to evaluate when awarding an IDIQ contract, GSA created the "highest technically rated with fair and reasonable price" technique. This technique ranks the competitors based on their scores for experience, past performance and certifications, selects a designated number of firms and assesses their loaded labor rates to ensure that they are fair and reasonable. Any firms without fair and reasonable rates are dropped from the competition and another firm is added until the designated number of firms is achieved. The technique was approved by GAO in *Sevatec, Inc.*, Comp. Gen. Dec. B-413559.3, 2017 CPD ¶ 3. The technique is described in more detail in Chapter 7.

The GAO decision in *Sevatec* approved of the use of the "highest technically rated with fair and reasonable price" technique to select a pool of IDIQ contractors, but in *Noble Supply & Logistics, Inc.*, Comp. Gen. Dec. B-418141, 2020 CPD ¶ 32, GAO ruled that this technique cannot be used when awarding a single award BPA under the Federal Supply Schedule. GAO reached this conclusion based on the reasoning that the award of BPAs and task or delivery orders under the Federal Supply Schedule must be based on a tradeoff between price and the non-price factors. Subsequently, GAO ruled that the technique was properly used to award a task order under an IDIQ contract, *Sumaria Sys., Inc.*, Comp. Gen.

Dec. B-418796, 2020 CPD ¶ 296. This decision would appear to indicate that this technique can be used for single award FAR Part 15 competitions.

[F] Negotiations After Source Selection

Two "alternative source selection procedures" that had been identified in the earlier FAR 15.613 were the NASA "source evaluation board" and the DoD "Four-Step" procedures for use in contracting for research and development. The essential distinguishing element of these procedures was the selection of the winning offeror before the conduct of negotiations. Their fundamental premise was that the most competent contractor was the one submitting the best original proposal. These procedures are no longer alluded to in the FAR, but they appear to be acceptable procedures in contracting for technically complex work. This is explained in a comment by DoD in its promulgation of proposed revisions to the DFARS to implement the FAR Part 15 Rewrite, stating at 62 Fed. Reg. 63050 (Nov. 26, 1997):

> DFARS guidance on the four-step source selection process and the alternate source selection process have been removed, as the new guidance at FAR 15.101, best value continuum, clearly allows such source selection processes.

For an example of the current use of this procedure, see *Veterans Tech., LLC*, Comp. Gen. Dec. B-310303.2, 2008 CPD ¶ 31.

The original guidance on the procedure was contained in the 1970 NASA Procurement Directive 70-15, which stated in part:

> In cost-reimbursement type contracts and all research and development contracts, ambiguities and uncertainties in the proposals of such firms shall be pointed out during discussions by the contracting officer, but not deficiencies.

Although GAO refused to rule that this original NASA procedure was in violation of the statutory requirement for discussions, it did find that it needed clarification, stating in 51 Comp. Gen. 621 (B-173677) (1972) at 622-23:

> We think the propriety of the prohibition in NASA Procurement Directive 70-15 against discussing "deficiencies" must be considered in the light of these problems. We think certain weaknesses, inadequacies, or deficiencies in proposals can be discussed without being unfair to other proposers. There well may be instances where it becomes apparent during the course of negotiations that one or more proposers have reasonably placed emphasis on some aspect of the procurement different from that intended by the solicitation. Unless this difference in the meaning given the solicitation is removed, the proposers are not competing on the same basis. Similarly, if a proposal is deemed weak because it fails to include substantiation for a proposed approach or solution, in the circumstance where the inadequacy appears to

> have arisen because of a reasonable misunderstanding of the amount of data called for, we believe the proposer should be given the opportunity, time permitting, to furnish such substantiation. Thus, it seems to us that the prohibition in NASA Procurement Directive 70-15 against discussing "deficiencies" needs clarification.

Subsequently, NASA made minor modifications to the policy. The complete regulatory statement was in NFS 18-15.613-71(b)(5):

> (ii) Cost-reimbursement contracts and all contracts for research and development.
>
> (A) The contracting officer, in concert with or on behalf of the SEB, will conduct written and/or oral discussions of the effort to be accomplished and the cost of the effort with all offerors determined to be within the competitive range. The discussions are intended to assist the SEB or other evaluators (1) in understanding fully each offeror's proposal and its strengths and weaknesses based upon the individual efforts of each offeror; (2) in assuring that the meanings and the points of emphasis of RFP provisions have been adequately conveyed to the offerors so that all are competing equally on the basis intended by the Government; (3) in evaluating the personnel proposed by each firm; and (4) in presenting a report to the Source Selection Official that makes the discriminations among proposals clear and visible. In this process, prior to contractor selection, the Government's interests are not served by its assuming the role of an information exchange or clearinghouse.
>
> (B) In cost-reimbursement type contracts and all research and development contracts, the contracting officer shall point out instances in which the meaning of some aspect of a proposal is not clear and instances in which some aspects of the proposal failed to include substantiation for a proposed approach, solution, or cost estimate.
>
> (C) However, where the meaning of a proposal is clear and the Board has sufficient information to assess its validity and the proposal contains a weakness which is inherent in an offeror's management, engineering, or scientific judgment, or which is the result of its own lack of competence or inventiveness in preparing its proposal, the contracting officer shall not point out the weaknesses. Discussions are useful in ascertaining the presence or absence of strengths and weaknesses. The possibility that such discussions may lead an offeror to discover that it has a weakness is not a reason for failing to inquire into a matter where the meaning is not clear or where insufficient information is available, since understanding of the meaning and validity of the proposed approaches, solutions, and cost estimates is essential to a sound selection. Offerors should not be informed of the relative strengths or weaknesses of their proposals in relation to those of other offerors.

This guidance was deleted from the regulation in 63 Fed. Reg. 44,408 (Aug. 19, 1998).

GAO commented on the revised procedure in *Sperry Rand Corp.*, 54 Comp. Gen. 408 (B-181460), 74-2 CPD ¶ 276:

> The NASA procedure represents one approach to meeting the statutory requirement for written and oral discussions, 10 U.S.C. § 2304(g) [now 10 U.S.C. § 2304(a)]. In part, at least, the underlying rationale is that to point out deficiencies during the discussions would compromise the competition, because weaker proposals would be improved, and a leveling effect would occur. To avoid this, discussions are limited to clarification of proposals; after selection, the agency then negotiates the best possible contract on terms most advantageous to the Government. Considered in the abstract, potential conflicts between the procedure and the statutory requirement can be envisioned; for instance, as appears to be contemplated by [the protester], a situation where the discussions are so limited in scope and content that they amount to little more than a ceremonial exercise, with the meaningful discussions transposed almost entirely into the final negotiations stage.

NASA decisions to defer discussions until after selection of the source based on this policy were affirmed in *Program Res., Inc.*, Comp. Gen. Dec. B-192964, 79-1 CPD ¶ 281; *Pioneer Contract Servs., Inc.*, Comp. Gen. Dec. B-197245, 81-1 CPD ¶ 107; and *Taft Broad. Corp.*, Comp. Gen. Dec. B-222818, 86-2 CPD ¶ 125. However, discussions were not meaningful where NASA waived a regulation concerning interest rates for one offeror yet failed to inform the other offeror of the waiver during discussions, *Union Carbide Corp.*, 55 Comp. Gen. 802 (B-184495), 76-1 CPD ¶ 134. GAO held that discussions were required because this was not a question of technical transfusion.

DoD adopted a similar procedure for R&D procurements when it developed its Four-Step negotiation process, DFARS 215.613 (pre-Rewrite). Step one called for very limited discussions prior to source selection. DFARS 215.613-70(f) provided:

> (2) In conducting step one—(i) Limit discussions to only what is necessary to ensure that both parties understand each other; (ii) Do not tell offerors about deficiencies in their proposals; and (iii) Provide written clarifications to all offerors when it appears the Government's requirements have been misinterpreted.

Following the completion of step one, the agency solicited restricted best and final offers and then selected the source. In order to ensure that the government ultimately got the best possible procurement, the technique then permitted full negotiation after source selection where the government agency had the opportunity to press for changes in the winner's proposal as long as they did not alter the basis for the source selection. The DoD Four-Step procedure was challenged in *GTE Sylvania, Inc.*, 57 Comp. Gen. 715 (B-188272), 77-2 CPD

¶ 422, where GAO made an extensive analysis of the procedure and concluded that the limited discussions actually conducted met the statutory requirement. For a full evaluation of the Four-Step procedure, questioning whether it meets the statutory requirement for discussions, see Smith, *The New "Four Step" Source Selection Procedure: Is the Solution Worse Than the Problem?*, 11 Pub. Ct. L. Rev. 322 (1980).

EPA's version of the Four-Step procedure, PIN 77-15, was challenged in *Roy F. Weston, Inc.*, Comp. Gen. Dec. B-197949, 80-1 CPD ¶ 340. Although the protester contended that the items not brought up in discussion were deficiencies, GAO disagreed, stating:

> [W]e think a more accurate description would be that they were the differences in the relative merits of the proposals, as viewed by the [technical evaluation panel]. If they were truly weaknesses or deficiencies, then there would have been an obligation on the part of EPA to discuss the areas with Weston, assuming no danger of technical transfusion, notwithstanding PIN 77-15.

This would appear to indicate that the limitation on discussions in this type of procurement procedure will not be permitted in some circumstances.

§ 6.03 EVALUATION FACTORS AND SUBFACTORS

Evaluation factors and subfactors (often called "evaluation criteria") describe the matters which are to be considered in determining which proposal will be most advantageous to the government. A major cause of extended and costly source selections is the use of a large number of evaluation factors. Thus, the best way to streamline the source selection process is to use a small number of evaluation factors. This reduces the cost of preparing proposals and the time and cost of evaluating the proposals.

FAR 15.304 contains the following general guidance on the selection of evaluation factors:

> (a) The award decision is based on evaluation factors and significant subfactors that are tailored to the acquisition.
>
> (b) Evaluation factors and significant subfactors must—
>
> > (1) Represent the key areas of importance and emphasis to be considered in the source selection decision; and
> >
> > (2) Support meaningful comparison and discrimination between and among competing proposals.

While this general guidance is imprecise, it does provide a degree of assistance in selecting an appropriate number of evaluation factors. First, it indicates that evaluation factors should be chosen based on the characteristics of each acquisition. Thus, ¶ (a) calls for "tailoring" the factors to the acquisition. This precludes merely using the same factors that have been used in the past on similar acquisitions and suggests a new analysis for each new source selection. Second, ¶ (b)(1) calls for factors that focus on "key areas of importance"—with the implication that only major areas of importance should be evaluated. In following this guidance, contracting officers must point out to the other members of the acquisition team that, as a general proposition, *all* key areas of importance will be included in the specifications as mandatory requirements. Thus, when the contract is awarded, the contractor will be obligated to meet these requirements. Since this is the case, there is no necessity to evaluate all of the key areas of importance—only the major areas need be evaluated. This proposition is reinforced by ¶ (b)(2) requiring evaluation factors to "support meaningful comparison and discrimination." This requires the acquisition team to review past acquisitions of the same or similar products or services to ascertain which evaluation factors have actually discriminated among the competitors. When it is found that a factor has not served this purpose—with the competitors having had similar strengths, weaknesses, and risks—that factor should not be used in the new procurement. Following this analytical process, the acquisition team should strive to minimize the number of evaluation factors using only those that will ensure award to the offeror that will provide the best value to the government.

The specific number and types of evaluation factors and subfactors depend upon the nature of the procurement and the needs of the government. Procuring officials have broad discretion in selecting the factors and in determining their relative importance. See *Government & Military Certification Sys., Inc.*, Comp. Gen. Dec. B-411261, 2015 CPD ¶ 192, where GAO stated:

> The determination of a contracting agency's needs, including the selection of evaluation criteria, is primarily within the agency's discretion and we will not object to the use of particular evaluation criteria so long as they reasonably relate to the agency's needs in choosing a contractor that will best serve the government's interests. SML Innovations, B-402667.2, Oct. 28, 2010, 2010 CPD ¶ 254 at 2.

Within this broad authority, Congress has required that, as a minimum, the evaluation factors must include cost to the government and "quality of the products or services" and that all factors and significant subfactors and their relative importance must be disclosed in the solicitation, 10 U.S.C. § 3206 (formerly § 2305(a)(3)) and 41 U.S.C. § 3306(c)(1). FAR 15.304 implements these requirements, with additional factors, as follows:

> (c) The evaluation factors and significant subfactors that apply to an acquisition and their relative importance are within the broad discretion of agency acquisition officials, subject to the following requirements:

(1) Price or cost to the Government shall be evaluated in every source selection (10 U.S.C. 2305(a)(3)(A)(ii) and 41 U.S.C. 3306(c)(1)(B)) (also see part 36 for architect-engineer contracts);

(2) The quality of the product or service shall be addressed in every source selection through consideration of one or more non-cost evaluation factors such as past performance, compliance with solicitation requirements, technical excellence, management capability, personnel qualifications, and prior experience (10 U.S.C. 2305(a)(3)(A)(i) and 41 U.S.C. 3306(c)(1)(A)); and

(3)(i) Except as set forth in paragraph (c)(3)(iii) of this section, past performance shall be evaluated in all source selections for negotiated competitive acquisitions expected to exceed the simplified acquisition threshold.

(ii) For solicitations that are not set aside for small business concerns, involving consolidation or bundling, that offer a significant opportunity for subcontracting, the contracting officer shall include a factor to evaluate past performance indicating the extent to which the offeror attained applicable goals for small business participation under contracts that required subcontracting plans (15 U.S.C. 637(d)(4)(G)(ii)).

(iii) Past performance need not be evaluated if the contracting officer documents the reason past performance is not an appropriate evaluation factor for the acquisition.

(4) For solicitations that are not set aside for small business concerns, involving consolidation or bundling that offer a significant opportunity for subcontracting, the contracting officer shall include proposed small business subcontracting participation in the subcontracting plan as an evaluation factor (15 U.S.C. 637(d)(4)(G)(i)).

(5) If telecommuting is not prohibited, agencies shall not unfavorably evaluate an offer that includes telecommuting unless the contracting officer executes a written determination in accordance with FAR 7.108(b).

DFARS 215.304 also contains mandatory factors for major weapon systems and information technology procurements.

The evaluation factors specified in a solicitation not only notify the offerors of what will be evaluated, they also state either the promises which must be included in each proposal or the issues that will be evaluated to assess the capability of the offeror. In this book we refer to these two types of evaluation factors as "offer factors" and "capability factors." Offer factors, which should be incorporated into the contract as binding requirements, include price or estimated cost and fee and any other features that will become part of the offeror's contractual undertaking, such as the precise product or service to be furnished, an offered delivery schedule, a specific warranty, or any other promise made by the offeror that will become part of the contract. Capability factors typically include past performance, experience, key personnel, and understanding of the work. Some capability factors, such as key personnel, can be treated as offer factors if the agency decides to incorporate the information submitted by the offeror into the contract. As far as evaluation and source selection is concerned, this classification is not relevant, but the solicitation should inform the offerors which factors will be made contractual promises, and which will be used solely for evaluation purposes. This matter will be discussed in § 6.05, below. The following section deals with the types of evaluation factors and subfactors which might be used by an agency, the requirements for their disclosure, and the indication of their relative importance.

[A] Commonly Used Evaluation Factors

Neither the statutes nor the FAR deal coherently with the classification of evaluation factors. Both statutes combine non-cost factors dealing with the capability of the offeror with those describing offers solicited by the RFP under the broad category "quality." See 10 U.S.C. § 3306 (formerly § 2305(a)(3)(A)(i)) and 41 U.S.C. § 3306(c)(1)(A) specifying evaluation of the "quality of the product or services to be provided (including technical capability, management capability, prior experience, and past performance of the offeror)." FAR 15.304(c)(2) contains this same classification with the addition of "compliance with solicitation requirements" and "personnel qualifications."

Rather than combining non-cost factors under this general heading of quality, the following material distinguishes between factors dealing with the capability of the offeror and those which relate to offers solicited by the RFP.

[1] Offer Factors

Offer factors are those factors that will result in contractual promises made by the contractor to the government beyond the promises embodied in the RFP. In the normal competitive procurement, the government spells out the greater portion of the offer it is soliciting in the RFP—including the contract specifications and the terms and conditions. If an offeror signs the proposal without taking exception to any mandatory element of the RFP, it has agreed to make the offer solicited by the government and those promises play no further role in the evaluation process. If an offeror takes exception to a mandatory element of the RFP, award to that offeror is precluded until the matter has been cleared up by amending the RFP or having the offeror withdraw the exception.

Thus, in this discussion, offer factors are additional promises that are solicited by the RFP and incorporated into the resulting contract, either by reference or, preferably, by specific contract terms that are agreed to by both parties.

[a] *Cost to the Government*

The one offer evaluation factor that is present in almost all negotiated procurements is cost to the government. Offerors submit this offer by filling out Section B of the Uniform Contract Format when they submit their proposals. This discussion of cost to the government includes the amount to be paid to the contractor and other costs which the government might incur in procuring and using products or services.

[i] Amount to Be Paid to the Contractor

In almost all cases cost to the government is evaluated by comparing the amounts proposed by each offeror. However, it is proper to normalize the cost directing all offerors to propose a budget that makes the best use of a stated funding level, *ICF Inc.*, Comp. Gen. Dec. B-414247, 2017 CPD ¶ 118.

The amount to be paid to the contractor depends on the pricing arrangement to be used in the contract. When a firm-fixed-price contract is involved, the offeror's proposed price, not a mere estimate of the "realistic" cost, is the criterion which must be used in evaluating the proposal, *IBM Corp.*, Comp. Gen. Dec. B-299504, 2008 CPD ¶ 64; *Verestar Gov't Servs. Grp.*, Comp. Gen. Dec. B-291854, 2003 CPD ¶ 68; *Litton Sys., Inc.*, 63 Comp. Gen. 585 (B-215106), 84-2 CPD ¶ 317. This rule is followed because the contractor bears the risk of costs exceeding the price of a firm-fixed-price contract. Thus, an agency has broad discretion in awarding to a contractor with a low price, *U.S. Security Assocs., Inc. v. United States*, 123 Fed. Cl. 663 (2015); *Sierra Nevada Corp.*, Comp. Gen. Dec. B-410485, 2015 CPD ¶ 23; *ABSG Consulting, Inc.*, Comp. Gen. Dec. B-404863.7, 2013 CPD ¶ 185. If the agency wants to assess the impact of a low price, it can only do that by stating in the RFP that it will conduct a price realism analysis or assess understanding of the work, *General Dynamics, American Overseas Marine*, Comp. Gen. Dec. B-401874.14, 2012 CPD ¶ 85. If the price realism analysis raises doubts as to the offeror's ability to perform at the offered price, the problem should be treated in the evaluation of non-price factors, such as performance risk, or as a matter of responsibility, *Pemco Aeroplex, Inc.*, Comp. Gen. Dec. B-310372.3, 2008 CPD ¶ 126 (risk of low price properly evaluated because RFP called for evaluation of "proposal risk" by assessing "price realism"); *Alabama Aircraft Indus., Inc.—Birmingham v. United States*, 83 Fed. Cl. 666 (2008) (risk of low price in *Pemco Aeroplex* procurement not properly assessed because of flaws in agency reasoning); *Guam Shipyard*, Comp. Gen. Dec. B-311321, 2008 CPD ¶ 124 (low price properly assessed as "very high" risk when it was 23% under government estimate); *CSE Constr.*, Comp. Gen. Dec. B-291268.2, 2002 CPD ¶ 207 (where the RFP contains no relevant evaluation factor pertaining to price realism or understanding, a determination that an offeror's price on a fixed-price contract is a responsibility issue). Similarly, if the agency believes that the offeror's price indicates a lack of understanding of the work to be performed, this should be taken into consideration in the evaluation of capability or the determination of responsibility. See *Wackenhut Servs., Inc.*, Comp. Gen. Dec. B-286037, 2001 CPD ¶ 114 (low price of two offerors properly led to assessment of lack of understanding of the work but no requirement to make detailed assessment of elements of price of offeror with total price in line with other offerors); *Centech Grp., Inc.*, Comp. Gen. Dec. B-278715, 98-1 CPD ¶ 108 (low option year prices indicated "an inherent lack of technical competence"). Furthermore, an agency may eliminate an offeror from the competitive range if it fails to submit information demonstrating that its low price is reasonable, *International Outsourcing Servs., LLC v. United States*, 69 Fed. Cl. 40 (2005). GAO has taken note of the fact that there is no regulatory requirement for a price realism analysis—FAR 15.305(a)(1) merely provides that cost realism analyses may be used "in exceptional cases, on other competitive fixed-price-type contracts (see 15.404-1(d)(3))," *Team BOS/Naples—Gemmo S.p.A./DelJen*, Comp. Gen. Dec. B-298865.3, 2008 CPD ¶ 11. However, a price realism analysis will be required when the RFP states that the agency "may" make such an analysis, *B&B Medical Servs., Inc.*, Comp. Gen. Dec. B-409705.4, 2015 CPD ¶ 198; *Al Qabandi United Co.*, Comp. Gen. Dec. B-310600.3, 2008 CPD ¶ 112; *Computer Sciences Corp.*, Comp. Gen. Dec. B-298494.2, 2007 CPD ¶ 103.

The FAR does not address the evaluation of fixed-price incentive contracts. In the past, GAO stated that target cost should be used to evaluate the proposed prices, *Televiso Elecs.*, 46 Comp. Gen. 631 (B-159922) (1967). In *Serv-Air, Inc.*, 58 Comp. Gen. 362, 79-1 CPD ¶ 212, GAO held that the target price of one offeror could be contrasted with the ceiling price of another offeror in a "best case/worst case" comparison. In *Motorola, Inc.*, Comp. Gen. Dec. B-236294, 89-2 CPD ¶ 484, GAO condoned the use of the ceiling price to evaluate cost to the government. The use of target prices alone might be logical if all offerors are proposing to use the same fixed-price incentive formula with the same ceiling. However, if the RFP permits the offerors to propose different formulas, it is better practice to use the ceiling price as the evaluation factor because this is the only element of the formula that is common to all offerors. With respect to realism of target cost proposals, FAR 15.305(a)(1) states that "Cost realism analyses may also be used on fixed-price incentive contracts"—apparently permitting use of probable target cost as an evaluation factor. GAO reached this conclusion in *Eurest Support Servs.*, Comp. Gen. Dec. B-285813.3, 2003 CPD ¶ 139, holding that an agency must assess the realism of proposed target costs and adjust them for evaluation purposes if they are unrealistic. See also *Allied-Signal Aerospace Co.*, Comp. Gen. Dec. B-250822, 93-1 CPD ¶ 201, finding an agency decision to adjust target cost to reflect unrealistically low estimate "a prudent exercise of agency discretion"; and *Universal Techs., Inc.*, Comp. Gen. Dec. B-241157, 91-1 CPD ¶ 63, finding that the agency properly compared a realistic proposed target cost of one offeror with the proposed ceiling price of a competitor in making the source selection tradeoff decision. If target price is used as the evaluation factor, the target profit should be adjusted if a cost realism analysis indicates an adjustment of the target cost. However, GAO has held that it is improper to adjust the ceiling price upward in connection with increasing the target cost based on a cost realism analysis, *Raytheon Co.*, Comp. Gen. Dec. B-242484.2, 91-2 CPD ¶ 131.

In cost-reimbursement contracts, both the realistic expected cost of performance and the proposed fee should be used as evaluation factors. FAR 15.305(a)(1) requires that a cost realism analysis be conducted "to determine what the Government should realistically expect to pay for the proposed effort," and FAR 15.404-1(d)(2)(i) states that the probable cost "shall be used for purposes of evaluation to determine the best value." This is consistent with GAO decisions, *Space Systems/Loral LLC.*, Comp. Gen. Dec. B-413131, 2016 CPD ¶ 242; *Boeing Sikorsky Aircraft Support*, Comp. Gen. Dec. B-277263.2, 97-2 CPD ¶ 91. If circumstances prevent an agency from determining the probable cost of performance, it is proper to refuse to award the contract to that offeror, *Lockheed Martin Integrated Sys., Inc.*, Comp. Gen. Dec. B-410189.5, 2016 CPD ¶ 273, *recons. denied*, 2017 CPD ¶ 258 (sale of division after submission of proposal). GAO has held that where the RFP is amended to call for a cost-reimbursement rather than a fixed-price contract, the agency should also amend the RFP to explicitly include cost realism as an evaluation factor and notify offerors that proposed costs may be adjusted accordingly, *Varian Assocs., Inc.*, Comp. Gen. Dec. B-209658, 83-1 CPD ¶ 658. In that case, the initial RFP had listed "Lowest Evaluated Cost to the Government" as a factor, but, although the protest was denied, GAO stated that the better practice was to amend the solicitation. See Chapter 13 for a detailed discussion of cost realism analysis.

It is improper to use a "cost risk" evaluation factor as the sole means of evaluating differences in probable cost, *DKW Communications, Inc.*, Comp. Gen. Dec. B-411182, 2015 CPD ¶ 178. This factor was the difference between the proposed cost and the probable cost of each offeror but did not reflect the difference between the probable costs of the competitors.

In a cost-plus-incentive-fee contract, agencies normally evaluate the realism of the proposed target cost, but a low target cost can be assessed as a risk because it precludes the full impact of the incentive formula (providing no incentive to reduce costs below the minimum cost), *Prism Maritime, LLC*, Comp. Gen. Dec. B-409267.2, 2014 CPD ¶ 124; *Bechtel Hanford, Inc.*, Comp. Gen. Dec. B-292288, 2003 CPD ¶ 199.

The evaluation of fee depends on what type of cost-reimbursement contract is used. In a cost-plus-fixed-fee contract, the proposed fixed-fee should be used as the evaluation factor, rather than a "realistic" estimate of the fee, since the former reflects a more reliable judgment, *Booz, Allen & Hamilton*, 63 Comp. Gen. 599 (B-213665), 84-2 CPD ¶ 329. In a cost-plus-award-fee contract, it is proper to specify the amount of the award fee in the RFP, *General Dynamics One Source, LLC*, Comp. Gen. Dec. B-400340.5, 2010 CPD ¶ 45 (in effect precluding its use as an evaluation factor). Conversely, it is also proper to use the offeror's proposed fee structure as the evaluation factor, *Management Servs., Inc.*, Comp. Gen. Dec. B-206364, 82-2 CPD ¶ 164. Thus, in this situation, it is permissible to give a higher evaluation to an offeror that proposes a lower base fee,

Wisconsin Physicians Serv. Ins. Corp., Comp. Gen. Dec. B-401068.14, 2013 CPD ¶ 34, a larger award fee pool, *Savannah River Tech. & Remediation, LLC*, Comp. Gen. Dec. B-415637, 2018 CPD ¶ 70, a higher maximum fee, *Boeing Sikorsky Aircraft Support*, Comp. Gen. Dec. B-277263.2, 97-2 CPD ¶ 91, or to an offeror that proposes to share its award fees with its employees on the theory that this will motivate them to perform better, *Cleveland Telecomm. Corp.*, 73 Comp. Gen. 303 (B-257294), 94-2 CPD ¶ 105. Compare *Research Triangle Inst.*, Comp. Gen. Dec. B-278254, 98-1 CPD ¶ 22, where an offeror was given a higher evaluation for proposing a low award fee.

[ii] Other Costs to the Government

Products or services purchased by the government, on either a fixed-price or cost-reimbursement basis, may result in the government incurring costs of acquisition or ownership that are not included in the contract price or cost. There is little clear guidance on the consideration of such costs as evaluation factors. The procurement statutes might be interpreted to require that other costs to the government be specified as evaluation factors. They state that solicitations "shall at a minimum include" evaluation factors, "including cost or price, cost-related or price-related factors and subfactors," 10 U.S.C. § 3206(b) (formerly 10 U.S.C. § 2305(a)(2)(A)(i)) and 41 U.S.C. § 3306(b)(1)(A). However, the FAR does not repeat this language, with FAR 15.304(c)(1) merely stating that "[p]rice or cost to the Government shall be evaluated in every source selection." GAO has not interpreted the statutes or the regulations as requiring the consideration of such costs in evaluating proposals, *Kastle Sys., Inc.*, Comp. Gen. Dec. B-231990, 88-2 CPD ¶ 415. See also *Sensis Corp.*, Comp. Gen. Dec. B-265790.2, 96-1 CPD ¶ 77 (life-cycle costs are not required to be evaluated as part of the cost/price evaluation). However, the failure to consider other costs to the government could lead to poor procurement decisions. As a matter of practice, other costs to the government are frequently used as evaluation factors or subfactors whether objectively quantified or subjectively determined.

The most common cost of acquisition used as an evaluation criterion is transportation costs. This is one of the few areas in which evaluation of costs incurred by the government is mandated. FAR 47.305-2 provides that a solicitation for supplies will specify that offers may be f.o.b. origin, f.o.b. destination, or both, and that they will be evaluated based on the lowest overall cost to the government. In such cases, a solicitation calling for f.o.b. origin must require the offeror to furnish the government with applicable data necessary to compute transportation costs which the government will pay and the government must use the lowest available rates, *Gold Line Ref., Ltd.*, Comp. Gen. Dec. B-248600, 92-2 CPD ¶ 153 (proper to use informational quotes from transportation carriers).

Costs incurred as a result of owning an item are part of what is known as "life cycle" costs, and should be considered during acquisition planning, FAR 7.105(a)(3)(i). FAR 7.101 defines life cycle costs as "the total cost to the

Government of acquiring, operating, supporting, and (if applicable) disposing of the items being acquired." The magnitude of the costs beyond the original acquisition costs can greatly exceed the item's purchase price or production cost. See, for example, *Lockheed Missiles & Space Co. v. Dep't of the Treasury*, GSBCA 11776-P, 93-1 BCA ¶ 25,401, *aff'd*, 4 F.3d 955 (Fed. Cir. 1993), in which such costs resulted in awarding the contract to an offeror whose price totaled $1.4 billion over others whose prices were $900 and $700 million. Extensive agency analysis, quantified in dollar figures, illustrated the differences between the technical proposals and justified paying the price premium.

Agencies are given broad discretion in selecting the life cycle costs that will be evaluated. See *NCS Techs., Inc.*, Comp. Gen. Dec. B-405192.2, 2011 CPD ¶ 230, denying a protest that the agency had included life cycle costs as an evaluation factor. In *ViON Corp.*, Comp. Gen. Dec. B-256363, 94-1 CPD ¶ 373, where the RFP contained a clear description of the factors that would be considered in determining life cycle costs, GAO denied the protest that environmental costs, such as cooling, electricity, and space should have been included. GAO concluded that the agency properly decided not to consider these factors because its prior experience indicated that they were not useful discriminators between technical solutions. On the other hand, if an agency predetermines that a specified technique will be used to reduce life-cycle costs, an offeror must show that the technique is ineffective if it chooses not to use the technique, *Carothers Constr., Inc.*, Comp. Gen. Dec. B-405241.4, 2012 CPD ¶ 225 (RFP required solar panels unless not life-cycle cost effective).

Quantification of life-cycle costs in dollar amounts in not required, *Advanced Turbine Engine Co.*, Comp. Gen. Dec. B-417324, 2019 CPD ¶ 204 (adjectival rating of engine operating and support costs and offered rights in technical data); *Raytheon.Co.*, Comp. Gen. Dec. B-298626.2, 2007 CPD ¶ 185 (adjectival rating of life cycle costs permissible when RFP stated that such costs would not be a "driver" in the source selection process); *L-3 Communications Corp.*, Comp. Gen. Dec. B-299014, 2007 CPD ¶ 26 (technical proposal downgraded because of higher life-cycle costs); *Ingalls Shipbldg., Inc.*, Comp. Gen. Dec. B-275830, 97-1 CPD ¶ 180 (price premium justified because awardee's proposed life-cycle cost reduction *approach* provided the greatest probability of achieving the greatest life cycle cost savings). However, if an agency changes its evaluation from an objective to a subjective technique, that must be clearly stated in an amendment to the RFP, *Lockheed Martin Sys. Integration-Owego*, Comp. Gen. Dec. B-299145.5, 2007 CPD ¶ 155.

If the RFP requires the submission of specific life-cycle cost information, that information must be used in evaluating such costs, *Sikorsky Aircraft Co.*, Comp. Gen. Dec. B-299145, 2007 CPD ¶ 45. See also *Boeing Co.*, Comp. Gen. Dec. B-311344, 2008 CPD ¶ 114, sustaining a protest because the agency did not correctly use the data submitted by the protester to calculate the life cycle costs of proposed air tankers. Quantified life-cycle costs have been the critical element in several source selections. See, for example, *Sundstrand Corp.*,

Comp. Gen. Dec. B-227038, 87-2 CPD ¶ 83 (approving award to offeror with substantially higher unit price on turbine engines due to superior life cycle cost savings); and *American Airlines Training Corp.*, Comp. Gen. Dec. B-217421, 85-2 CPD ¶ 365 (finding that future flight training costs more than made up for the large price differential).

If life-cycle costs are evaluated in a cost-reimbursement contract, it is proper to adjust the proposed costs to a realistic amount, *Jacobs COGEMA, LLC*, Comp. Gen. Dec. B-290125.2, 2016 CPD ¶ 16.

Pursuant to 10 U.S.C. § 2377 (now § 3454), Enclosure 6 of DOD Instruction 5000.02, "Operation of the Defense Acquisition System," Jan. 26, 2017, required program managers of major weapon systems to prepare as Life-Cycle Sustainment Plan early in the process. DFARS PGI 207.105(b)(13)(i) states that the acquisition plan should describe "the extent of integrated logistics support planning, including total life cycle system management and performance-based logistics." However, these requirements apparently do not require the use of life cycle costs as an evaluation factor, as more definitive language was contained in DAR 1-335 and that regulation was not interpreted as imposing such a requirement, *Big Bud Tractors, Inc. v. United States*, 2 Cl. Ct. 188, *aff'd*, 727 F.2d 1118 (Fed. Cir. 1983); *Big Bud Tractors, Inc.*, Comp. Gen. Dec. B-209858, 83-1 CPD ¶ 127. GAO found that although the regulation "requires" that life cycle costs be considered as a factor during the procurement cycle, "we do not read the regulation as requiring that [life cycle costs] be an evaluation factor for each award." Accord *Prudential-Maryland Joint Venture Co. v. Lehman*, 590 F. Supp. 1390 (D.D.C. 1984). Use of life-cycle costs as evaluation factors in defense procurements is thus left to the discretion of the contracting officer. Other decisions affirming an agency decision not to evaluate life-cycle costs include *Sikorsky Aircraft Co.*, Comp. Gen. Dec. B-403471, 2010 CPD ¶ 271 (no requirement to evaluate life-cycle costs in sole source procurement based on public interest exception to CICA); *Spectrum Sys., Inc.*, Comp. Gen. Dec. B-401130, 2009 CPD ¶ 110 (protest of omission of life-cycle costs must be submitted before proposal); *General Elec. Aerospace Sys.*, Comp. Gen. Dec. B-250514, 93-1 CPD ¶ 101 (no requirement to evaluate cost of limited rights in technical data); *Hawaiian Tel. Co.*, Comp. Gen. Dec. B-187871, 77-1 CPD ¶ 298 (evaluation of possible termination costs would be too speculative).

If life cycle costs are not identified as an evaluation factor, they may not be evaluated, *Marquette Medical Sys., Inc.*, Comp. Gen. Dec. B-277827.5, 99-1 CPD ¶ 90 (agency improperly evaluated the savings from receiving new equipment versus the costs of receiving upgraded equipment). See *Interspiro, Inc. v. United States*, 72 Fed. Cl. 672 (2006), where the agency properly did not evaluate life cycle costs because the RFP contained no statement they would be evaluated. Compare *Engineered Air Sys., Inc.*, Comp. Gen. Dec. B-283011, 99-2 CPD ¶ 63, where GAO found that the agency properly evaluated extended warranties when the RFP merely stated that the agency would "give evaluation credit for proposed features that met or exceeded the stated objectives."

When life cycle costs are an evaluation factor, it is unclear whether a general statement in the solicitation informing offerors that such costs are to be evaluated is adequate, or whether it is necessary to specify the particular costs to be evaluated. In *Lanier Bus. Prods., Inc.*, 60 Comp. Gen. 306 (B-200695), 81-1 CPD ¶ 188, *recons. denied ex rel., Dictaphone Corp.*, Comp. Gen. Dec. B-200695.2, 81-2 CPD ¶ 511, resolicitation was recommended where the RFQ merely stated that life cycle costing would be employed and did not adequately inform offerors of the specific evaluation factors to be used. However, in *Southwestern Bell Tel. Co.*, Comp. Gen. Dec. B-200523.3, 82-1 CPD ¶ 203, GAO stated:

> Where an agency makes it clear that its evaluation will be based on an analysis of expected system life-cycle costs without qualification, offerors may reasonably expect that all determinable elements of cost will be taken into account.

These cases illustrate the difficulties created by vague language describing the life cycle costs that will be evaluated. The offerors clearly had difficulty ascertaining what costs would be evaluated, with the result that the ground rules of the competition were not clearly disclosed in the RFP. See also *AM Int'l*, Comp. Gen. Dec. B-200200 81-1 CPD ¶ 258, stating that "[w]hen life-cycle costs are to be evaluated, we believe that the solicitation should not only indicate the fact, but also the useful life period that will be utilized in the evaluation."

When the RFP states that life cycle costs are to be evaluated and requests data as to the costs that a proposed item will produce, the agency must use the data to assess the amount of life cycle costs to be attributed to each proposal, *Sikorsky Aircraft Co.*, Comp. Gen. Dec. B-299145, 2007 CPD ¶ 45. In that case, GAO sustained a protest because the agency had obtained maintenance data for each proposed helicopter but had used a normalized number attributing the same maintenance costs to different helicopters.

[b] Non-Cost Offer Factors

Where the contractor is merely required to comply with specifications furnished by the government and the terms and conditions in the RFP, there will be no non-cost offer evaluation factors and no need for technical or management proposals. However, in some procurements the government solicits or permits offerors to propose alterations to the specifications or terms and conditions and treats these offers as evaluation factors. When such alterations are used as evaluation factors, the agency is indicating to offerors that they are of value to the agency and that the agency will therefore consider paying a higher price to obtain that value. When this is done, the general practice is to subsequently amend the specifications and terms and conditions so that the awarded contract makes these offers contractually binding. However, agencies can treat these factors as capability factors and not incorporate them into the contract if they do not want to be contractually bound to them. See *DGR Assocs., Inc.*, Comp. Gen. Dec. B-285428, 2000 CPD ¶ 145, denying a protest asserting that the agency should not have assessed enhancements proposed by an offeror because they were not incorporated into the contract as promises.

The use of non-cost offer factors greatly complicates the task of offerors because they must attempt to anticipate the value that the agency will give to different amounts of enhanced performance or alteration of terms and conditions. To ease this problem, the best practice is for agencies to use such factors only when they cannot specify their precise requirements in the RFP.

[i] Enhancements

Probably the most common type of non-cost offer factor is enhancements to the work or results called for by the specifications. In such cases the specification generally will call for a minimum level of performance and the RFP will indicate that the agency will evaluate greater performance. In such cases, the best practice is for the agency to clearly delineate the range of enhancements it is willing to consider so that offerors do not propose enhancements that are of no benefit to the agency. It is also good practice to obtain price proposals for different levels of enhancements to enable the agency to compare proposals at each level of performance. However, the use of general language stating that enhancements will be evaluated has been approved even when the offerors had to speculate as to the value of specific enhancements. See *Lexis-Nexis*, Comp. Gen. Dec. B-260023, 95-1 CPD ¶ 14, where GAO held that the RFP was sufficiently specific as to enhancements when it listed the areas where enhancements would be evaluated and gave some examples of features that were of value to the agency. When agencies state in the RFP that they are seeking enhancements, they must evaluate them. See *Northrop Grumman Info. Tech., Inc.*, Comp. Gen. Dec. B-400134.10, 2009 CPD ¶ 167 (agency required to consider enhancement when RFP stated that offerors would be evaluated on "extent to which" they exceeded a requirement); *Boeing Co.*, Comp. Gen. Dec. B-311344, 2008 CPD ¶ 114 (statement requesting offerors to satisfy as many technical requirements as possible); *Humana Military Healthcare Servs.*, Comp. Gen. Dec. B-401652.2, 2009 CPD ¶ 219 (general requirement that offerors proposing enhancements "should describe and demonstrate its benefit, monetary or otherwise, to the Government").

General statements in the RFP indicating that the agency was seeking superior performance have also been found to be sufficient to alert offerors that the agency was going to evaluate enhancements. See, for example, *Innovative Test Asset Solutions, LLC*, Comp. Gen. Dec. B-411687, 2016 CPD ¶ 68 (inclusion in RFP of "innovations and efficiencies" subfactor); *IPlus, Inc.*, Comp. Gen. Dec. B-298020, 2006 CPD ¶ 90 (statement that award would be made to the "offeror whose proposal represented the best value" sufficient to alert offerors that agency would evaluate "innovations and creative approached"); *SGT, Inc.*,

Comp. Gen. Dec. B-294722.4, 2005 CPD ¶ 151 (dedicated person to perform required job an enhancement when RFP evaluation factor was "comprehensiveness of the proposed approach, and likelihood of successfully meeting the solicitation requirements"); *Rome Research Corp.*, Comp. Gen. Dec. B-291162, 2002 CPD ¶ 209 (RFP sought "enhancements of value" in management proposals); *Moreland Corp.*, Comp. Gen. Dec. B-283685, 2002 CPD ¶ 4 (RFP statement that agency would evaluate "the quality of the building and the design concept" in a competition for a clinic); *Medical Dev. Int'l*, Comp. Gen. Dec. B-281484.2, 99-1 CPD ¶ 68 (RFP requirement for technical proposals indicated that enhancements would be evaluated); and *Engineering & Prof'l Servs., Inc.*, Comp. Gen. Dec. B-262179, 95-2 CPD ¶ 266 (RFP requirement that each offeror submit a matrix detailing where their systems met or exceeded the RFP requirements and desirable features). A protest of improper evaluation of enhancements must be specific as to which enhancements were not evaluated, *Aero Simulation, Inc.*, Comp. Gen. Dec. B-411373, 2015 CPD ¶ 233.

Agencies have also sought a "monetized value" of proposed enhancements. Appendix B of the DoD "Source Selection Procedures," August 20, 2022, recommends considering the use of the "Value Adjusted Total Evaluated Price Tradeoff" procedure. This procedure identifies a monetary value of evaluation factors in the RFP and incorporates these amounts in the ultimate source selection decision. See *DynCorp Int'l LLC*, Comp. Gen. Dec. B-415349, 2018 CPD ¶ 12, denying a protest that the monetized value of more flight hours for training aircraft in an aircraft maintenance competition was not an accurate computation on the grounds that the computation was not a cost/price factor but rather a means of assessing technical merit. In *L-3 Army Sustainment, LLC*, Comp. Gen. Dec. B-415349.2, 2018 CPD ¶ 13, concerning the same procurement, GAO refused to consider whether the enhancements were beyond the needs of the agency, stating that this was an issue that it did not review unless it was clearly unreasonable. In both of these protests the GAO stated that an agency could properly monetize the value of enhancements even though this was not called for in the RFP.

If the RFP does not call for evaluation of enhanced performance, an agency is free to disregard proposed enhancements that it concludes do not benefit the agency, *Team BOS/Naples-Gemmo S.p.A/DelJen*, Comp. Gen. Dec. B-298865.3, 2008 CPD ¶ 11; *U-Tech Servs. Corp.*, Comp. Gen. Dec. B-284183.3, 2002 CPD ¶ 78.

[ii] Technical Solutions

It has been common practice to request technical proposals providing solutions to meet a government requirement. This originated in competitions for development contracts where an agency wanted to evaluate proposed designs of a new system to assess which was most likely to meet its needs. The technique has been carried over into service contracts where competing solutions to a need are sought. These solutions can be an offer factor if the technical proposal is incorporated into the contract as a promise to perform in accordance with the proposal. More often they are a capability factor where the contract does not make the solution mandatory but uses it to assess the capability of the offeror.

Making technical proposals contractually binding has the effect of making them the baseline against which to measure the contractor's performance. This will arguably benefit the government if the proposal contains performance requirements that are more demanding than the original government specification. In that case, the government will be able to hold the contractor bound to perform in accordance with its proposal (assuming that it contains promissory language), but it will have deprived the contractor of some of the flexibility that it would have had if it was performing to a government performance requirement. Conversely, making the proposal contractually binding will harm the government if the proposal contains performance requirements that are less demanding than the original government specification. In that case, effort demanded by the government to meet its original performance requirements may well be construed as a contractual change for which the government will be required to give an equitable adjustment. See, for example, *Northrop Grumman Corp. v. United States*, 47 Fed. Cl. 20 (2000), holding that the contractor was not entitled to equitable adjustments for work not required by its technical proposal because the proposal was not incorporated into the contract.

Agencies vary widely in their practice of incorporating these technical proposals into their contracts and the practice usually cannot be discerned from protests involving this type of evaluation factor. However, there are many examples of protests involving competing technical solutions. See, for example, *General Dynamics Land Sys.*, Comp. Gen. Dec. B-412525, 2016 CPD ¶ 89 (evaluation of competing designs of amphibious combat vehicles); *Raytheon Co.*, Comp. Gen. Dec. B-408906.4, 2015 CPD ¶ 120 (evaluation of night vision goggles with developmental rifle-mounted thermal sights); *Southwind Constr.* Servs., *LLC*, Comp. Gen. Dec. B-410333.2, 2015 CPD ¶ 64 (evaluation of design of HVAC system); *Northrop Grumman Sys. Corp.*, Comp. Gen. Dec. B-298954, 2007 CPD ¶ 63 (evaluation of proposed radars in response to a government statement of objectives); *ViaSat, Inc.*, Comp. Gen. Dec. B-291152, 2002 CPD ¶ 211 (evaluation of proposed communication satellite terminals to meet stated performance requirements); and *DRS Sys., Inc.*, Comp. Gen. Dec. B-289928.3, 2002 CPD ¶ 192 (evaluation of proposed thermal imaging systems against an agency purchase description).

The best way to evaluate technical solutions is to conduct the procurement in two phases, selecting two or more contractors in the first phase to build sample products, testing the competing products, and awarding the second phase contract to the contractor with the best product. See, for example, *Northrop Grumman Space & Missile Sys. Corp.*, Comp. Gen. Dec. B-400837, 2009 CPD ¶ 52, where this technique was used to procure vehicles for the Army and Marine Corps, and *Textron, Inc. v. United States*, 74 Fed. Cl. 277 (2006), where this technique was used to procure ships for the Coast Guard. The advantage of this technique is that it allows the agency to evaluate the actual technical solution rather than the described technical solution (which may not actually be achieved during contract performance).

An intermediate technique is to award contracts to demonstrate some elements of a new system and then conduct a competition for full scale design of a system. See *Sierra Nevada Corp.*, Comp. Gen. Dec. B-410485, 2015 CPD ¶ 23, where NASA awarded three demonstration contracts followed by two development contracts to provide crew transportation to the International Space Station.

[iii] Specific Products or Services

In some cases, an agency will use a performance specification and evaluate specific products or services that will meet that specification. This technique is most practicable when there are a variety of products or services in the marketplace that will meet the agency's performance requirements and the agency will benefit by obtaining competitive prices for each product or service in order to identify the best value at the time of contract award. See, for example, *CSRA, LLC*, Comp. Gen. Dec. B-417635, 2018 CPD ¶ 341 (demonstration of a product during an oral presentation); *PatriotVetIT, LLC*, Comp. Gen. Dec. B-412188.2, 2016 CPD ¶ 96 (evaluation of mobile MRI equipment to perform specified services); *Omega Apparel, Inc.*, Comp. Gen. Dec. B-409715, 2015 CPD ¶ 3 (agency testing of sample products); *Swets Info. Servs.*, Comp. Gen. Dec. B-410078, 2014 CPD ¶ 311 (demonstration of on-line database); *Raytheon Co.*, Comp. Gen. Dec. B-409651, 2014 CPD ¶ 207 (evaluation of previous tests of the proposed products); *MD Helicopters, Inc.*, Comp. Gen. Dec. B-298502, 2006 CPD ¶ 164 (commercially available helicopters); and *Integrated Sys. Grp.*, Comp. Gen. Dec. B-272336, 96-2 CPD ¶ 144 (central processing units). This technique cannot be used when the offered product or service is not available. Another technique is to perform a risk analysis in an attempt to ensure that the best value decision is based not only on the quality of the offered product or service but also on the risk that the offeror may not be able to perform as promised. See, for example, *Alliant Techs., Inc.*, Comp. Gen. Dec. B-276162, 97-1 CPD ¶ 141, where GAO denied a protest challenging the risk assessment of the technical feasibility of manufacturing the proposed product at the offered price. See also *Martin Marietta Corp.*, Comp. Gen. Dec. B-259823.4, 96-1 CPD ¶ 265, denying a protest that the agency had found that the protester's technical approach to meeting the specification was "unsatisfactory," and had awarded the contract to an offeror whose approach was rated "good."

[iv] Process or Techniques to Be Used

Another non-cost offer factor is the process or technique that the offeror intends to use to meet the government's performance requirements. This factor can be used in two ways. If it is used to evaluate the offeror's understanding of the work or capability to perform the work, it is a capability factor. However, if the agency intends to incorporate the technique or process into the contract, making it contractually binding, it will be an offer factor. In most instances, the best practice is to treat this as a capability factor—giving the contractor the freedom to meet the performance requirements using some other technique or process —but there are some instances where an agency has determined that the specific technique or process has an identified value that will not be achieved by the use of any other technique or process. In such cases, this should be treated as an offer factor.

When a proposed process or technique is used as an evaluation factor, it is good practice to evaluate the comparative risk of using different techniques. See, for example, *IndraSoft, Inc.*, Comp. Gen. Dec. B-414026, 2017 CPD ¶ 30 (denying protest that the agency had evaluated a proposal for improved supply chain management software by integrating two existing programs as higher risk than a proposal for using legacy software); *Robbins-Gioia, Inc.*, Comp. Gen. Dec. B-274318, 96-2 CPD ¶ 222 (denying protest that the agency had evaluated a proposal for the use of "state-of-the-art software architecture" as having moderate risk as compared to a proposal to use off-the-shelf software). In such cases, the agency is conducting a form of design competition requiring the evaluation of the potential effectiveness of the offered designs. See, for example, *AT&T Corp.*, Comp. Gen. Dec. B-261154.4, 96-1 CPD ¶ 232, where GAO agreed that the agency's evaluation of competing designs was performed effectively.

[v] Terms and Conditions

A fifth type of non-cost offer factor is an enhanced or specific term or condition. Enhanced terms and conditions should be treated in the same manner as other enhancements—the agency should state a minimum acceptable level and the range of enhanced performance which it considers to be of potential value. Specific terms and conditions that the agency requires to be filled out with explicit information should be clearly stated so that the offerors clearly understand the information that will be incorporated in the contract.

A common enhanced term or condition is a warranty clause where the agency solicits better warranty coverage than the minimum specified in the RFP. See *Integrated Sys. Grp.*, Comp. Gen. Dec. B-272336, 96-2 CPD ¶ 144, where offers were obtained for "extended warranties" of one and two years. A warranty evaluation factor can also be stated as an open-ended factor, allowing each offeror to propose the warranty offered. See *American Material Handling, Inc.*, Comp. Gen. Dec. B-410899, 2015 CPD ¶ 106 (protester's quotation unacceptable for not offering extended warranty); *DRS Laurel Techs.*, Comp. Gen. Dec. B-410330, 2014 CPD ¶ 365 (protester's offered two-year workmanship warranty not sufficiently explained); *Eomax Corp.*, Comp. Gen. Dec. B-311391, 2008 CPD ¶ 130 (protester properly downgraded for proposing only a one year warranty on a high price product); *Scot, Inc.*, Comp. Gen. Dec.

B-295569, 2005 CPD ¶ 66 (proposed extended warranty properly evaluated as providing only a small advantage when equipment was going to be stored for long periods); *Landoll Corp.*, Comp. Gen. Dec. B-291381, 2003 CPD ¶ 40 (longer warranty properly evaluated as a strength).

Another common example of a specific term or condition is the Key Personnel clause that is used in many service procurements. As discussed below, key personnel are a frequently used capability factor but when the names of the key personnel are incorporated into a Key Personnel clause, this factor becomes an offer factor because the contractor promises to use the specified personnel unless they become unavailable. While the evaluation of key personnel can be a strong predictor of performance, it is only completely valid if the personnel proposed by the offer actually work on the contract. See, for example, *American Sys. Corp.*, Comp. Gen. Dec. B-413952.3, 2017 CPD ¶ 204, where the protester was properly downgraded because it did not agree that its key personnel would be available for the entire task order. This is not the effect of most Key Personnel clauses which generally call for the use of key personnel listed in the clause or equally qualified personnel approved by the contracting officer. This is, of course, a necessary part of the process because the contractor cannot guarantee that employees will stay with the company or be willing to work on the contract.

Agencies follow different procedures to ensure that offerors have commitments from proposed key personnel. GAO has approved strict enforcement of a requirement for letters of intent for all key personnel, *DataSource, Inc.*, Comp. Gen. Dec. B-412468, 2016 CPD ¶ 59. See also *KPMG Peat Marwick, LLP*, Comp. Gen. Dec. B-259479.2, 95-2 CPD ¶ 13, *recons. denied*, 95-2 CPD ¶ 26, where GAO sustained a protest where the agency had ordered the winning contractor to substitute personnel less qualified than that required by the RFP. Similarly, an agency may not downgrade an offeror for an inadequate key person if that position is not called for in the RFP, *General Revenue Corp.*, Comp. Gen. Dec. B-414220.2, 2017 CPD ¶ 106. On the other hand, GAO will deny a protest for lack of such commitments if the solicitation does not require such letters, *Salient Federal Solutions, Inc.*, Comp. Gen. Dec. B-410174.3, 2016 CPD ¶ 104. Thus, agencies must follow the solicitation procedures with regard to key personnel.

[vi] Delivery or Completion Schedule

In some instances, the agency will use the delivery or completion schedule as an offer factor. In such cases, the RFP will state a required time of performance and will permit offerors to propose shorter times of performance. If award is made on the basis of earlier performance, that earlier time must be made a contractually binding requirement, *A&D Fire Protection Inc.*, Comp. Gen. Dec. B-288852.2, 2002 CPD ¶ 74. This technique should never be used unless the agency has determined that it will benefit from earlier performance, and, in such cases, the RFP should clearly state the amount of earlier performance that will be of value. See *Rotair Indus., Inc.*, Comp. Gen. Dec. B-276435.2, 97-2 CPD ¶ 17, finding that the agency's selection of a higher-priced vendor with a shorter delivery schedule was reasonable because the agency determined that a longer delivery schedule would have a detrimental impact on the continuing back-order status of the critical application item being procured. Like other enhancements, it is also good practice to obtain price proposals on a step ladder basis so that offers can be rationally compared. When earlier performance is stated to be as an evaluation factor, offerors should understand that the agency will favorably evaluate earlier delivery. However, they generally will not know the weight that will be given to the evaluation. See, for example, *Utility Tool & Trailer, Inc.*, Comp. Gen. Dec. B-310535, 2008 CPD ¶ 1 (proper to not pay significantly higher price for small delivery advantage); *Charles Kendall & Partners, Ltd.*, Comp. Gen. Dec. B-310093, 2007 CPD ¶ 210 (proper to pay significantly higher price for substantial delivery advantage); *American Material Handling, Inc.*, Comp. Gen. Dec. B-297536, 2006 CPD ¶ 28 (proper to pay somewhat higher price for delivery advantage).

[2] Capability Factors

"Capability factors" are those factors that will be used to evaluate the relative ability of the competing offerors to perform the contract. These factors are never made part of the contract because they do not constitute contractual promises made by the offeror. However, as discussed above, they frequently include enhancements, technical solutions, or descriptions of a process or technique to be used that are included in technical or management proposals that are required to be submitted by each offeror. Whether such evaluation factors are offer factors or capability factors depends entirely on whether the agency intends to incorporate them into the contract as promises or merely use them to evaluate capability. When they are treated as capability factors, they will be discussed below as part of the "understanding the work" factor.

The evaluation of capability is essentially an assessment of the risk that an offeror will not successfully perform the proposed contract. The DoD "Source Selection Procedures," August 20, 2022, applicable to all procurements over $10 million, calls for the assessment of technical risk either as a separate evaluation factor or as part of the evaluation of the technical merits of competing proposals. These procedures call for the separate evaluation of past performance in terms of "performance confidence assessments." This method of describing a risk assessment has been accepted as rational, *CCITE/SC*, Comp. Gen. Dec. B-400782, 2008 CPD ¶ 216 (unknown confidence rating justified because of lack of relevant past performance); *United Paradyne Corp.*, Comp. Gen. Dec. B-297758, 2006 CPD ¶ 47 (technique acceptable but not used rationally). Other agencies follow similar risk evaluation techniques. See, for example, *Noblis, Inc.*, Comp. Gen. Dec. B-414055, 2017 CPD ¶ 33 describing a General Services

Administration "likelihood of successfully performing" the work assessment including the risk of a low cost estimate, and *Consolidated Eng'g Servs., Inc.*, Comp. Gen. Dec. B-311313, 2008 CPD ¶146, describing a Social Security Administration "confidence/performance risk" assessment covering both past performance and experience, and granting the protest because different assessments were given to the two final competitors even though they were both highly rated.

Performance risk is an inherent evaluation factor even though it is not disclosed in the RFP, *AHNTECH, Inc.*, Comp. Gen. Dec. B-299806, 2007 CPD ¶213; *AIA Todini-Lotos*, Comp. Gen. Dec. B-294337, 2004 CPD ¶211. Performance risk is most frequently assessed with regard to past performance. See *Lockheed Martin MS2 Tactical Sys.*, Comp. Gen. Dec. B-400135, 2008 CPD ¶157 (high performance risk proper based on poor past performance of major subcontractor); *Midwest Metals*, Comp. Gen. Dec. B-299805, 2007 CPD ¶131 (risk determined from past performance data system); *Boersma Travel Servs.*, Comp. Gen. Dec. B-297986.2, 2006 CPD ¶175 (moderate risk because agency could not understand information submitted by protester); *TPL, Inc.*, Comp. Gen. Dec. B-297136.10, 2006 CPD ¶104 (moderately low risk because of "fair" past performance ratings on most comparable contracts). However, it can be used with regard to any evaluation factor. See, for example, *Northrop Grumman Sys. Corp.*, Comp. Gen. Dec. B-414312, 2017 CPD ¶128 (risk of incomplete status of offeror's software, firmware, and hardware development effort); *PricewaterhouseCoopers Public Sector, LLP*, Comp. Gen. Dec. B-413316.2, 2017 CPD ¶12 (risk of low labor rates); *MCT JV*, Comp. Gen. Dec. B-311245.2, 2008 CPD ¶121, *recons. denied*, 2008 CPD ¶167 (significant risk from unrealistically capped overhead rates); *Fintrac, Inc.*, Comp. Gen. Dec. B-311462.2, 2008 CPD ¶191 (no perceived risk from lack of fixed fee in proposal); *Commercial Window Shield*, Comp. Gen. Dec. B-400154, 2008 CPD ¶134 (risk of vague staffing plan); *Global Solutions Network, Inc.*, Comp. Gen. Dec. B-298682.3, 2008 CPD ¶131 (risk of single person staffing two key positions); *Guam Shipyard*, Comp. Gen. Dec. B-311321, 2008 CPD ¶124 (high risk of unrealistically low price and mediocre past performance); *AT&T Corp.*, Comp. Gen. Dec. B-299542.3, 2008 CPD ¶65 (staffing plan created performance risk); *Raytheon Co.*, Comp. Gen. Dec. B-298626.2, 2007 CPD ¶185 (lack of data on product created high performance risk); *Savantage Fin. Servs., Inc.*, Comp. Gen. Dec. B-299798, 2007 CPD ¶214 (high performance risk based on evaluation of technical proposal submitted to demonstrate understanding of the work).

[a] Responsibility Determinations Distinguished

Since capability factors deal with the same matters that are considered in making responsibility determinations, it is important to distinguish between these two processes. Agencies commonly evaluate factors and subfactors related to responsibility, notwithstanding the fact that a formal responsibility determination must ultimately be made before award of the contract. Such factors and subfactors frequently include experience, staffing, and past performance. This process does not officially constitute a responsibility determination as long as these factors are evaluated on a variable basis. Therefore, it does not conflict with the Small Business Administration's (SBA) authority to resolve questions concerning the responsibility of small businesses. In *Electrospace Sys., Inc.*, 58 Comp. Gen. 415 (B-192574), 79-1 CPD ¶ 264, GAO stated at 425:

> Since neither 10 U.S.C. § 2304(g) nor applicable regulations in any way restrict the "other factors" that may be used by agencies in selecting the proposal having the greatest value to the Government, we have not prohibited procuring agencies from using responsibility-related factors in making *relative* assessments of the merits of competing proposals. There is no indication on the face of Public Law 95-89 or in the legislative history of the law that Congress intended to eliminate this long-standing practice as far as the evaluation of small business proposals are concerned. Thus, neither the cited precedent (40 Comp. Gen., *supra*) of advertised procurements nor the 1977 Public Law prevents the relative-assessment evaluation of responsibility-related information contained in small business proposals.

See also *Nomura Enters., Inc.*, Comp. Gen. Dec. B-277768, 97-2 CPD ¶ 148, where the small business protester asserted that the evaluation of its past performance concerned a matter of its responsibility and was thus subject to SBA's Certificate of Competency (COC) procedures. GAO disagreed, stating:

> An agency may use traditional responsibility factors, such as experience or past performance, as technical evaluation factors, where, as here, a comparative evaluation of those areas is to be made. *Dynamic Aviation—Helicopters*, B-274122, Nov. 1, 1996, 96-2 ¶ 166 at 3. A comparative evaluation means that competing proposals will be rated on a scale relative to each other, as opposed to a pass/fail basis. *Id.* The record shows that the award here clearly was based on a comparative assessment of Nomura's and Defense's past performance records. Where a proposal is downgraded or found deficient pursuant to such an evaluation, the matter is one of relative technical merit, not nonresponsibility which would require a referral to the SBA.

In *T. Head & Co.*, Comp. Gen. Dec. B-275783, 97-1 CPD ¶ 169, GAO held that an evaluation of capability factors that resulted in the conclusion that the offeror's proposal was "unacceptable" was not a determination of nonresponsibility because the evaluation had been arrived at in the course of a best value procurement where past performance was being evaluated on a variable basis and "unacceptable" was merely the lowest adjectival rating available. Compare *Phil Howry Co.*, Comp. Gen. Dec. B-291402.3, 2003 CPD ¶ 33, where GAO ruled that refusing to award to the only company that had submitted a proposal because its past performance was rated "marginal/little confidence" was a nonresponsibility determination because there had been no comparative assessment (no other offeror to compare with). This indicates that an agency will be required to allow a small business offeror to apply for a COC when it refuses to award to that offeror because of poor past performance when it is the only offer received.

It is improper to use responsibility-related factors or subfactors if the evaluation is merely to determine acceptability of a proposal, *Sanford & Sons Co.*, 67 Comp. Gen. 612 (B-231607), 88-2 CPD ¶ 266; *Angelo Warehouses Co.*, Comp. Gen. Dec. B-196780, 80-1 CPD ¶ 228. In *Sanford*, the agency determined that the small business offeror's past performance did not meet the minimum acceptable standard of performance. GAO ruled that since this was tantamount to a determination that the protester was not responsible, the company was entitled to request a Certificate of Competency from the SBA. For other decisions finding that an agency had improperly used responsibility factors to determine technical acceptability on a go/no go basis, see *Competitive Range Solutions, LLC*, Comp. Gen. Dec. B-413104.10, 2017 CPD ¶ 124 (examples in proposal did not demonstrate capability to perform); *AeroSage, LLC*, Comp. Gen. Dec. B-409627, 2014 CPD ¶ 192 (lack of proof of ability to meet delivery requirement); *ECC Renewables, LLC*, Comp. Gen. Dec. B-408907.3, 2014 CPD ¶ 60 (lack of proof of financial capability); *Federal Support Corp.*, 71 Comp. Gen. 152 (B-245573), 92-1 CPD ¶ 81 (lack of experience), and *Clegg Indus., Inc.*, 70 Comp. Gen. 679 (B-242204.3), 91-2 CPD ¶ 145 (lack of company and personnel experience). See also *FitNet Purchasing Alliance*, Comp. Gen. Dec. B-410263, 2014 CPD ¶ 344 holding that a finding in a reverse auction that the small business protester had poor past performance was tantamount to a nonresponsibility determination. Compare *MicroTechs., LLC*, Comp. Gen. Dec. B-414670, 2017 CPD ¶ 236 (ruling proposal unacceptable for lack of information not a finding of lack of capability); *DA Defense Logistics HQ*, Comp. Gen. Dec. B-411153.3, 2015 CPD ¶ 358 (past performance rating of satisfactory confidence not a finding of nonresponsibility even though RFP called for award to offerors with substantial confidence); *Jay Shapiro & Assocs., Inc.*, Comp. Gen. Dec. B-411174, 2015 CPD ¶ 174 (other offerors had higher technical ratings); *Tyonek Worldwide Servs., Inc.*, Comp. Gen. Dec. B-409326, 2014 CPD ¶ 97 (ruling technical approach unacceptable not a finding of lack of capability).

This rule is of paramount importance in lowest priced technically acceptable procurements because any negative evaluation of an offeror's capability could only be used to disqualify the offeror. See *W.P. Tax & Acct. Grp.*, Comp. Gen. Dec. B-411899, 2015 CPD ¶ 331 granting a protest because the agency's determination of technical unacceptability due to too few labor hours for the work was a finding of lack of responsibility entitling the company to seek a COC.

This rule does not apply to proposals submitted by large businesses. Thus, responsibility-type factors may be used to determine lack of acceptability of proposals from large businesses. See *Oak Ridge Associated Univ.*, Comp. Gen. Dec. B-245694, 92-1 CPD ¶ 86 (lack of experience required by RFP); *Aerostat Servs. P'ship*, Comp. Gen. Dec. B-244939.2, 92-1 CPD ¶ 71 (failure to propose manning adequate to meet specifications); *Color Ad Signs & Displays*, Comp. Gen. Dec. B-241544, 91-1 CPD ¶ 154 (lack of required experience); *Sach Sinha & Assocs., Inc.*, 69 Comp. Gen. 108 (B-236911), 90-1 CPD ¶ 50 (personnel did not meet education and experience requirement of RFP).

[b] Past Performance

10 U.S.C. § 3206 (formerly § 2305(a)(3)(A)) and 41 U.S.C. § 3306(c)(1)(A) do not include past performance as one of the potential evaluation factors in source selection. However, 41 U.S.C. § 1126) requires the adoption of procedures "that encourage the consideration of the offerors' past performance in the selection of contractors." FAR 15.304(c)(3) makes past performance a mandatory factor as follows:

> (3)(i) Past performance, except as set forth in paragraph (c)(3)(iii) of this section, shall be evaluated in all source selections for negotiated competitive acquisitions expected to exceed the simplified acquisition threshold.
>
> (ii) For solicitations that are not set aside for small business concerns, involving consolidation or bundling, that offer a significant opportunity for subcontracting, the contracting officer shall include a factor to evaluate past performance indicating the extent to which the offeror attained applicable goals for small business participation under contracts that required subcontracting plans (15 U.S.C. 637(d)(4)(G)(ii)).
>
> (iii) Past performance need not be evaluated if the contracting officer documents the reason past performance is not an appropriate evaluation factor for the acquisition.

See also the OFPP publication, Best Practices for Collecting and Using Current and Past Performance Information, May 2000, OFPP Memorandum, Making Better Use of Contractor Performance Information, July 10, 2014: and DoD publication, A Guide to Collection and Use of Past Performance Information, May 2003.

The evaluation of past performance reduces the emphasis on merely writing good proposals in favor of focusing on actual performance on prior contracts. Past performance can be evaluated as a separate evaluation factor or as a subfactor. Even before the FAR requirement, there was no question that this was a proper factor in the evaluation process, *Ferranti Int'l Def. Sys., Inc.*, Comp. Gen. Dec. B-237555, 90-1 CPD ¶ 239, even though it may give the incumbent contractor with a good performance record an advantage in the competition, *Bendix Field Eng'g Corp.*, Comp. Gen. Dec. B-241156, 91-1 CPD ¶ 44; *Engineering & Computation, Inc.*, Comp. Gen. Dec. B-275180.2, 97-1 CPD ¶ 47.

While past performance can be used as either a factor or a subfactor, it is good practice to avoid using it in both situations simultaneously. For example, in *Center for Educ. & Manpower Res.*, Comp. Gen. Dec. B-191453, 78-2 CPD ¶ 21, it was held impermissible to evaluate past performance as a factor and also use past performance in the evaluation of technical and management factors. GAO reasoned that this gave a higher weight to past performance than was indicated in the RFP. A similar result was reached in *Metric Sys. Corp.*, Comp. Gen. Dec. B-210218.2, 83-2 CPD ¶ 394. Compare *Global Assocs., Ltd.*, Comp. Gen. Dec. B-275534, 97-1 CPD ¶ 129, rejecting a protest that undue weight had been given to past performance, and *United Ammunition Container, Inc.*, Comp. Gen. Dec. B-275213, 97-1 CPD ¶ 58, rejecting a protest asserting that past performance should have been evaluated separately and also in evaluating technical approach and management. See also *Halter Marine, Inc.*, B-255429, 94-1 CPD ¶ 161, finding the evaluation to be unreasonable because the agency gave overwhelming emphasis to past performance by repeated consideration of that factor in both the technical merit and quality control capability factors.

The FAR guidance on past performance contains several references to the importance of the relevance of past performance, including the following statements in FAR 15.305(a)(2):

> (i) . . . The currency and relevance of the information, source of the information, context of the data, and general trends in contractor's performance shall be considered
>
> (ii) . . . The source selection authority shall determine the relevance of similar past performance information.

GAO has interpreted these provisions are imposing a mandatory requirement on agencies to assess the relevance of past performance, *DRS C3 Sys., LLC*, Comp. Gen. Dec. B-310825, 2008 CPD ¶ 103; *Clean Harbors Envtl. Servs., Inc.*, Comp. Gen. Dec. B-296176.2, 2005 CPD ¶ 222.

While the regulation contains no explanation of the term "relevance of past performance information," it would appear to mean that an agency should give more weight to past performance on work that is like the work being procured (and conversely little or no weight to past performance of work that is dissimilar to the work being procured). See the Department of Defense "Source Selection Procedures," August 20, 2022, stating:

> With respect to relevancy, more relevant past performance will typically be a stronger predictor of future success and have more influence on the past performance confidence assessment than past performance of lesser relevance.

Thus, the RFP should be clear that the offerors should refer their most relevant projects for consideration of past performance. This is particularly important because there are numerous instances where GAO has ruled that agencies properly downgraded an offeror because of lack of relevant past performance even though it had very good past performance on dissimilar projects. See *Commissioning Solutions Global, LLC*, Comp. Gen. Dec. B-403542, 2010 CPD ¶ 272, stating:

> [T]he RFQ provided for a qualitative assessment of vendors' past performance, and instructed vendors to identify "at least" two relevant contracts in the past 3 years. To the extent that [the protester] is complaining that the RFQ did not specifically state that the agency might credit a vendor for having a number of relevant contracts, we think such a consideration would be logically encompassed by or related to considering the quality of the vendor's past performance. *Birdwell Bros. Painting & Refinishing*, B-285035, July 5, 2000, 2000 CPD ¶ 129 at 6.

In effect, such reasoning allows an agency to consider lack of comparable experience in the evaluation of past performance. For example, NASA uses an evaluation scheme that rates offerors' past performance in accordance with the relevance of their experience. Thus, to receive an "excellent" past performance rating, an offeror must have experience that is "highly relevant." GAO has accepted this scheme without comment in many protests including *Alpha-Omega Change Eng'g, Inc.*, Comp. Gen. Dec. B-413478.3, 2016 CPD ¶ 331 (giving higher past performance rating because of more relevant experience); *FN Mfg., LLC*, Comp. Gen. Dec. B-402059.4, 2010 CPD ¶ 104 (downgrading past performance proper when RFP stated relevance would be evaluated based on whether experience was comparable in complexity, size or value" of proposed effort); *ASRC Research & Tech. Solutions, LLC*, Comp. Gen. Dec. B-400217, 2008 CPD ¶ 202 (protest granted because scheme not followed); *Wackenhut Servs., Inc.*, Comp. Gen. Dec. B-400240, 2008 CPD ¶ 184 (protest denied because scheme followed). See also *Gonzales-McCaulley Inv. Grp., Inc.*, Comp. Gen. Dec. B-402544, 2010 CPD ¶ 127 (agency reasonably downgraded past performance because protester lacked experience on agency work); *AT&T Corp.*, Comp. Gen. Dec. B-299542.3, 2008 CPD ¶ 65 (to obtain "excellent" past performance rating, offeror had to have "highly relevant" experience); *Sherrick Aerospace*, Comp. Gen. Dec. B-310359.2, 2008 CPD ¶ 17 (agency determination that winning offeror had relevant experience justified low risk past performance evaluation); *JWK Int'l Corp.*, Comp. Gen. Dec. B-297758.3, 2006 CPD ¶ 142 (agency rating of little confidence justified when offeror had very good past performance on contract that was "somewhat relevant").

When an agency has called for the submission of references of the most relevant past performance, it must evaluate such past work, *General Revenue Corp.*, Comp. Gen. Dec. B-414220.2, 2017 CPD ¶ 106; *Shaw-Parsons Infrastructure Recovery Consultants, LLC*, Comp. Gen. Dec. B-401679.4, 2010 CPD ¶ 77.

Agencies must use care in stating in the RFP what projects are relevant to the current project because GAO has granted protests when an agency did not follow its own relevance guidelines. See, for example, *XPO Logistics Worldwide Gov't Servs., LLC*, Comp. Gen. Dec. B-412628.6, 2017 CPD ¶ 88 (somewhat relevant rating improper when past performance did not meet the RFP "scope and magnitude" requirement); *Martin Elecs., Inc.*, Comp. Gen.

Dec. B-290846.3, 2003 CPD ¶ 6 (improper to fail to consider late deliveries on incomplete contract when RFP called for consideration of performance "occurring within the past three years to the date of the solicitation closing"). Compare *All Phase Envtl., Inc.*, Comp. Gen. Dec. B-292919.2, 2004 CPD ¶ 62, agreeing that pest control work was relevant to ground maintenance when the RFP called for relevant performance on "contracts of a similar size, scope, dynamic environment, and complexity." GAO has also agreed that an agency is not bound by an experience relevance standard if the past performance relevance standard is stated in very general terms, *KIC Dev., LLC*, Comp. Gen. Dec. B-309869, 2007 CPD ¶ 184. In an unusual case, both GAO and the Court of Federal Claims agreed that an agency properly considered large contracts not relevant to a procurement where most of the work would be on projects in the range of $15,000 to $1.7 million, *J.C.N. Constr. Co. v. United States*, 60 Fed. Cl. 400 (2004); *J.C.N. Constr. Co.*, Comp. Gen. Dec. B-293063, 2004 CPD ¶ 12.

In using past performance as an evaluation factor, the agency should state the scope of the factor in the RFP. See FAR 15.305(a)(2), which states:

> (iii) The evaluation should take into account past performance information regarding predecessor companies, key personnel who have relevant experience, or subcontractors that will perform major or critical aspects of the requirement when such information is relevant to the instant acquisition.

Notwithstanding this guidance suggesting the evaluation of the performance of key personnel, GAO has ruled that it is proper to exclude key personnel from the evaluation of past performance, *JWK Int'l Corp.*, Comp. Gen. Dec. B-297758.3, 2006 CPD ¶ 142 (accepting explanation that information on skills of key personnel does not assist in evaluation of past performance of offeror). When an agency sees that two companies have the same key person (the operations manager), it can reasonably attribute the past performance of one company to the other, *Daylight Tree Serv. & Equip., LLC*, Comp. Gen. Dec. B-310808, 2008 CPD ¶ 22. In addition, an agency may reasonably determine that prior experience of key personnel does not overcome lack of corporate experience, *Blue Rock Structures, Inc.*, Comp. Gen. Dec. B-287960, 2001 CPD ¶ 184.

With regard to subcontractors to be used by the offeror, agencies can evaluate their past performance even though the RFP does not explicitly call for such evaluation, *ACME Indus., Inc.*, Comp. Gen. Dec. B-414023, 2017 CPD ¶ 22; *AC Techs., Inc.*, Comp. Gen. Dec. B-293013, 2008 CPD ¶ 26; *Singleton Enters.*, Comp. Gen. Dec. B-298576, 2006 CPD ¶ 157. Thus, subcontractor performance is a frequent element of the past performance evaluation. See *K2 Solutions, Inc.*, Comp. Gen. Dec. B-417689, 2019 CPD ¶ 330 (proper to give less weight to subcontractor past performance than to that of joint venture partner); *Advanced C4 Solutions, Inc.*, Comp. Gen. Dec. B-416259.2, 2018 CPD ¶ 344 (proper to evaluate "non-significant" subcontractor when RFP is silent on issue); *Kevco T/A All Star Disposal & Recycling Corp.*, Comp. Gen. Dec. B-405553.3, 2017 CPD ¶ 5 (proper to balance positive subcontractor past performance against no relevant contractor work); *Lockheed Martin MS2 Tactical Sys.*, Comp. Gen. Dec. B-400135, 2008 CPD ¶ 157 (high risk rating justified when 50% subcontractor had poor past performance); *STG, Inc.*, Comp. Gen. Dec. B-298543, 2006 CPD ¶ 166 (proper to limit subcontractor evaluations to work with government agencies); *Arora Grp., Inc.*, Comp. Gen. Dec. B-297838.3, 2006 CPD ¶ 143 (proper to reduce performance rating because of mediocre subcontractor past performance). Compare *USATREX Int'l, Inc.*, Comp. Gen. Dec. B-275592, 98-1 CPD ¶ 99, limiting past performance/experience to the offeror only. However, major subcontractors must be evaluated if the RFP calls for such evaluation, *Verdi Consulting, Inc.*, Comp. Gen. Dec. B-414103.2, 2017 CPD ¶ 136. Agencies can properly assign a medium rating when a proposed subcontractor has excellent past performance/experience but the offeror has no relevant past performance/experience, *Iplus, Inc.*, Comp. Gen. Dec. B-298020, 2006 CPD ¶ 90.

The evaluation of past performance is essentially an evaluation of the likelihood that the offeror will successfully perform the contract. The Department of Defense "Source Selection Procedures," August 20, 2022, applicable to all procurements over $10 million, call for the separate evaluation of past performance in terms of "performance confidence assessments." This form of evaluating past performance has been sustained in *Engility Corp.*, Comp. Gen. Dec. B-413120.3, 2017 CPD ¶ 70 (limited confidence rating supported by past performance problems); *K-MAR Indus., Inc.*, Comp. Gen. Dec. B-411262, 2015 CPD ¶ 189 (correct substantial confidence rating allowed award to low price without evaluating other offerors' past performance); *Veterans Elite, Inc.*, Comp. Gen. Dec. B-409233, 2014 CPD ¶ 64 (substantial confidence more valuable than satisfactory confidence); *CMJR, LLC*, Comp. Gen. Dec. B-405170, 2011 CPD ¶ 175 (limited confidence proper). Compare *Computer Sciences Corp.*, Comp. Gen. Dec. B-408694.7, 2014 CPD ¶ 331, granting a protest because the agency gave undue weight to recent performance when the RFP called for "an integrated analysis of recency, relevancy, and the quality of "work performed," "focusing on the quality of the work performed and the relevancy to the acquisition."

[c] Experience

In most procurements the capability of an offeror cannot be determined accurately without considering the type and extent of its experience. FAR 15.304(c)(2) suggests that agencies evaluate "prior experience." It appears to be a common belief that an evaluation of relevant past performance entails an evaluation of experience, but this is only an indirect way of assessing experience. In fact, while past performance and experience are both components of a contractor's capability that involve enquires into the past, their evaluation entails asking entirely different questions. To determine a contractor's experience the questions are: What have you done? and How many times or for how long have you done it? The question for past performance is: How well have you done it? To further complicate this issue, the protest decisions contain conflicting statements on the relationship of experience and past performance. See, for example, *Telcom Sys. Servs., Inc. v. Dep't of Justice*, GSBCA 13272-P, 95-2 BCA ¶ 27,849, where the board stated that experience must be considered when evaluating past performance. In that case, the board stated that "[i]t is unreasonable to suggest that past performance does not encompass experience." In contrast, in *Hughes Georgia, Inc.*, Comp. Gen. Dec. B-272526, 96-2 CPD ¶ 151, GAO indicated that experience was not included in the evaluation of past performance. Other cases appear to indicate that there is a good deal of confusion on this issue. For example, many GAO decisions have allowed an agency to evaluate experience in the course of evaluating "relevant" past performance, *TPL, Inc.*, Comp. Gen. Dec. B-297136.10, 2006 CPD ¶ 104, while in *Ameriko, Inc.*, Comp. Gen. Dec. B-272989, 96-2 CPD ¶ 167, GAO did not object to the consideration of past performance although the evaluation factor in the RFP was "experience." It has also been acceptable to treat corporate experience as a subfactor to past performance and "client satisfaction," *McGoldrick Constr. Servs. Corp.*, Comp. Gen. Dec. B-310340.3, 2008 CPD ¶ 120. See, however, *United Paradyne Corp.*, Comp. Gen. Dec. B-297758, 2006 CPD ¶ 47, where GAO disapproved factoring an average of an offeror's experience into its past performance rating (in effect reducing the past performance rating for experience on work that was not similar to the work to be performed on the proposed contract).

In order to reduce such confusion, it is highly desirable to evaluate past performance and experience separately. See *Executive Court Reporters, Inc.*, Comp. Gen. Dec. B-272981, 96-2 CPD ¶ 227, stating that past performance and experience should be separate factors and evaluated separately. See also *Smart Innovative Solutions*, Comp. Gen. Dec. B-400323.3, 2008 CPD ¶ 220 (lack of "relevant experience" properly considered); *Engineering Constr. Servs., Inc.*, Comp. Gen. Dec. B-310311.2, 2008 CPD ¶ 6 ("relevant experience" properly evaluated as separate subfactor); *Alpha Genesis, Inc.*, Comp. Gen. Dec. B-299859, 2007 CPD ¶ 167 (corporate experience and past performance evaluated properly); and *JAVIS Automation & Eng'g, Inc.*, Comp. Gen. Dec. B-290434, 2002 CPD ¶ 140 (past performance and experience evaluated together).

The RFP should state whether the agency intends to evaluate corporate experience, experience of key personnel, or both. There is a great deal of discretion in making this determination and GAO has held that the experience of key personnel can be evaluated under a "corporate experience" factor unless the RFP precludes such evaluation, *Data Mgmt. Servs. Joint Venture*, Comp. Gen. Dec. B-299702, 2007 CPD ¶ 139; *Dix Corp.*, Comp. Gen. Dec. B-293964, 2004 CPD ¶ 143. Nonetheless, it is better practice to state in the RFP precisely what experience is to be evaluated. See *Johnson Controls Sec. Sys., LLC*, Comp. Gen. Dec. B-296490.3, 2007 CPD ¶ 100 (corporate experience and experience of proposed staff); *Leader Commc'ns Inc.*, Comp. Gen. Dec. B-298734, 2006 CPD ¶ 192 (experience of key personnel and corporate experience); *KIC Dev., LLC*, Comp. Gen. Dec. B-297425.2, 2006 CPD ¶ 27 (RFP stated that experience requirement could be met by experience of key personnel or subcontractors); *Sigmatech, Inc.*, Comp. Gen. Dec. B-271821, 96-2 CPD ¶ 101 (corporate experience plus "sufficient personnel with ample qualifications"). It has also been held to be proper to evaluate corporate experience and key personnel experience separately, giving a low rating on corporate experience even though the key personnel have good experience, *Population Health Servs., Inc.*, Comp. Gen. Dec. B-292858, 2003 CPD ¶ 217.

Once it has been determined that experience is to be evaluated, the types of experience relevant to the procurement must be determined. Often, RFPs merely indicate that experience on "similar" projects will be considered, *Planning Sys., Inc.*, Comp. Gen. Dec. B-292312, 2004 CPD ¶ 83 ("similar or directly related work experience within the past five years of similar scope, magnitude or complexity to that detailed in the SOW"); *Telestar Corp.*, Comp. Gen. Dec. B-275855, 97-1 CPD ¶ 150 (experience required on projects "of similar size and scope related to this effort"). However, there are many factors to be considered in determining similarity, including dollar value, complexity, and nature of the work. Some RFPs go into great detail specifying the types of experience considered important and, in some cases, their relative importance, *Government Contract Solutions, LLC*, Comp. Gen. Dec. B-414000, 2017 CPD ¶ 41 (five years' experience with specified software program); *Cooperative Muratori & Cementisti, G.M.C.*, Comp. Gen. Dec. B-413308, 2016 CPD ¶ 281 (construction of new facility of at least 800 square meters and initial contract value of at least $6 million completed with the last seven years); *Vox Optima, LLC*, Comp. Gen. Dec. B-400451, 2008 CPD ¶ 212 ("40,000 annual billable hours in public affairs work"); *Burns and Roe Servs. Corp.*, Comp. Gen. Dec. B-296355, 2005 CPD ¶ 150 ("similar in complexity (*i.e.*, type of work, size (contracts in excess of $5,000,000 per year).

Furthermore, agencies have been permitted to specify very limited types of relevant experience. See, for example, *Amaze Techs., LLC*, Comp. Gen. Dec. B-418949, 2020 CPD ¶ 347, where GAO described the experience requirement as follows:

> An experience example was recent if it was performed within 5 years before the date the RFP was issued, and was performed for at least one year. An experience example was relevant if it demonstrated experience in all of the following areas: (1) providing and maintaining a staff of 14 people or more, all of whom have at least a bachelor's degree and 5 or more years of experience, and holding a minimum security clearance level of secret or equivalent; (2) [development, security, operations (DevSecOps)], [Scaled Agile Framework (SAFe)], and Agile software development activities; and (3) a total contract/task value of approximately $3 million or more per year.

See also *SKE Int'l, Inc.*, Comp. Gen. Dec. B-311383, 2008 CPD ¶ 111 (construction of multiple vertical construction multi-discipline projects simultaneously); *Zolon Tech, Inc.*, Comp. Gen. Dec. B-299904.2, 2007 CPD ¶ 183 (experience in specific technology to be used in design of information system—consultant's experience properly downgraded because he was not a subcontractor); *MELE Assocs., Inc.*, Comp. Gen. Dec. B-299229.4, 2007 CPD ¶ 140 (experience in four tasks to be performed); *Systems Application & Techs., Inc.*, Comp. Gen. Dec. B-270672, 96-1 CPD ¶ 182 (experience with contracting agency); *CAN Indus. Eng'g, Inc.*, Comp. Gen. Dec. B-271034, 96-1 CPD ¶ 279 (experience with the agency's system that was to be tested under the contract). For a very detailed enumeration of experience requirements see the ALLIANT 2 GWAC procurement that was approved in *Sevatec, Inc.*, Comp. Gen. Dec. B-413559.3, 2017 CPD ¶ 17.

Even where solicitations use terms such as "similar" or "relevant" in describing the nature of the experience, the cases have been quite liberal in permitting the government to use specific discriminators that are not stated in the solicitation. See *EastCo Bldg. Servs., Inc.*, Comp. Gen. Dec. B-275334.2, 97-1 CPD ¶ 83, holding that the totality of the RFP will be considered in determining whether offerors were given appropriate notice of the factors to be considered. GAO concluded that offerors should have known what projects were "similar" from the fact that the RFP required each offeror to specify the "the type of facility, gross square footage, services performed, and duration" of its prior projects. See also *Aviate L.L.C.*, Comp. Gen. Dec. B-275058.6, 97-1 CPD ¶ 162 (a factor used was the awardee's experience on "performance based contracting" although the RFP did not specifically call for that type of experience). Compare *Omniplex World Servs. Corp.*, Comp. Gen. Dec. B-290996.2, 2003 CPD ¶ 7, where GAO held that it was improper to eliminate an offeror from the competition for not having experience running a detention facility when the RFP called for the evaluation of "'guard/custody officer' experience similar in size, scope and complexity to the RFP work requirements."

Experience of major subcontractors is usually an indication of an offeror's experience, *Kellogg Brown & Root Servs., Inc.*, Comp. Gen. Dec. B-298694.7, 2007 CPD ¶ 124, even if the subcontractor has performed a large amount of the work, *ITT Corp.*, Comp. Gen. Dec. B-310102.6, 2010 CPD ¶ 12. If the RFP includes a statement to this effect, the experience of proposed subcontractors must be included in the evaluation, *KC Dev., LLC*, Comp. Gen. Dec. B-297425.2, 2006 CPD ¶ 27.

The critical question then is whether the agency can make a valid assessment of capability from past performance and experience alone or whether additional capability factors should be used. The answer depends on the specific procurement. For example, in some manufacturing contracts, the agency may believe that it is essential to evaluate the facilities of each offeror. In service contracts, some agencies believe it is crucial to evaluate key personnel. Most agencies believe it is advantageous in research and development contracts to evaluate understanding of the work. It is important to select an array of factors that provide a balanced assessment of the capability of each offeror to perform the work called for by the contract but to limit the number of capability factors as much as practicable.

[d] Key Personnel

One of the most commonly used evaluation factors is the key personnel that the offeror intends to use to perform the contract. It is an especially useful means of assessing the capability of offerors in research and development and service contracts where the quality of the people will likely be a major determinant of the quality of the performance. However, this is only so if the contractor that wins the competition actually uses the key personnel that have been proposed. Many agencies attempt to make key personnel an offer factor by using Key Personnel clauses in solicitations requiring the offeror to use the personnel designated in the proposal (or equal personnel).

Key personnel can be a useful evaluation factor if an agency obtains sufficient information to make a meaningful assessment of the qualifications of the people that are proposed. This generally requires obtaining more than resumes that merely list academic and job experience. See, for example, *Anders Constr., Inc.*, Comp. Gen. Dec. B-414261, 2017 CPD ¶ 121 (RFP required detailed experience, training and certification requirements for proposed divers); *Deloitte Consulting, LLP*, Comp. Gen. Dec. B-412125.2, 2016 CPD ¶ 119 (RFP required a minimum of 5+ years of experience leading Information Architecture teams for a large federal health system/organization); *CIGNA Gov't Servs., LLC*, Comp. Gen. Dec. B-401068.4, 2010 CPD ¶ 230 (RFP contained generally stated education and experience requirements); *Resource Title Agency, Inc.*, Comp. Gen. Dec. B-402484.2, 2010 CPD ¶ 118 (detailed information on role of key personnel and whether they were committed to any other work); *Savannah River Alliance, LLC*, Comp. Gen. Dec. B-311126, 2008 CPD ¶ 88 (RFP required resumes, references, letters of commitment and participation in oral presentation); *Systems Res. & Applications Corp.*, Comp. Gen. Dec. B-299818, 2008 CPD ¶ 28 (RFP required evidence that personnel had experience with type of work being procured); *Maden Techs.*, Comp. Gen. Dec. B-298543.2, 2006 CPD ¶ 167 (RFP required degree requirements and related experience for stated number of years); and *Advanced Tech. Sys., Inc.*, Comp. Gen. Dec. B-296493.5, 2006 CPD ¶ 147 (resumes had to identify when key personnel were also being proposed for another contract being competed at the same time). Nonetheless, agencies have been permitted to depend entirely on sketchy resumes. See *Powersolv, Inc.*, Comp. Gen. Dec. B-402534, 2010 CPD ¶ 206 (protest granted when agency evaluated qualifications of key person not called for by RFP); *D&J Enters., Inc.*, Comp. Gen. Dec. B-310442, 2008 CPD ¶ 8 (protester properly excluded from competition range when it submitted experience of key personnel in lieu of required resumes); *Operational Res. Consultants, Inc.*, Comp. Gen. Dec. B-299131.1, 2007 CPD ¶ 38 (protester properly downgraded because resume of proposed project manager did not clearly show required type of experience);

Critical Incident Solutions, LLC, Comp. Gen. Dec. B-298077, 2006 CPD ¶ 88 (quotation unacceptable because resume did not show required experience and agency not required to review other material which allegedly showed experience); *Tessada & Assocs., Inc.*, Comp. Gen. Dec. B-293942, 2004 CPD ¶ 170 (proposal properly downgraded because resume did not clearly show that person met experience requirement); and *Aerotek Scientific LLC*, Comp. Gen. Dec. B-293089, 2004 CPD ¶ 21 (resume improperly evaluated with regard to experience requirement). In one instance, the agency was permitted to rely on resumes that were required to omit any reference to the name of the person or his or her work on the incumbent contract (depriving the agency of the ability to evaluate the most critical experience of the person), *SNAP, Inc.*, Comp. Gen. Dec. B-402746, 2010 CPD ¶ 165.

If the solicitation does not call for the evaluation of a key position, it is improper to perform such an evaluation, *General Revenue Corp.*, Comp. Gen. Dec. B-414220.2, 2017 CPD ¶ 106. However, it is proper to evaluate elements of a key person's experience that are not specifically listed in the solicitation but are related to the specified requirements, *URS Fed. Servs., Inc.*, Comp. Gen. Dec. B-413333, 2016 CPD ¶ 286 (proper to rate person unacceptable for not meeting requirements in sample description of work requirement even though he met the requisite experience requirements). In *DV United, LLC*, Comp. Gen. Dec. B-411620, 2015 CPD ¶ 300 the protester was properly downgraded for not proposing key personnel when the solicitation made this optional.

[e] Facility to Be Used

Another evaluation factor that may be used in best value procurements is the evaluation of an offeror's proposed facility. See *Conrex, Inc.*, Comp. Gen. Dec. B-266060.2, 96-1 CPD ¶ 46 (proposal reasonably downgraded because offeror failed to adequately describe its facility); and *Bannum, Inc.*, Comp. Gen. Dec. B-270640, 96-1 CPD ¶ 167 (agency reasonably excluded protester from competitive range because the facility that the protester proposed would require major renovations which could not be completed within the 60-day commencement time period). An offeror's facility may also be evaluated as a subfactor, *Schleicher Community Corrs., Inc.*, Comp. Gen. Dec. B-270499.3, 97-1 CPD ¶ 33.

[f] Financial Capability

Earlier, there was considerable controversy over whether the financial ability of offerors should be used as an evaluation factor or subfactor. In *Delta Data Sys. Corp. v. Webster*, 744 F.2d 197 (D.C. Cir. 1984), the court followed the general rule that factors related to responsibility could be used for comparative purposes and applied this rule to permit the comparative evaluation of the financial condition of the offerors in a long-term contract. In arriving at this result, the court reversed a contrary conclusion of GAO on the same case, *Delta Data Sys. Corp.*, Comp. Gen. Dec. B-213396, 84-1 CPD ¶ 430. GAO continued to adhere to the premise that financial condition should be used as an evaluation factor only when there is some special justification for doing so. See *Flight Int'l Grp., Inc.*, 69 Comp. Gen. 741 (B-238953.4), 90-2 CPD ¶ 257, ruling that downgrading an offeror' management capabilities on the basis of financial weakness was actually a finding of nonresponsibility. See also *Velos, Inc.*, Comp. Gen. Dec. B-400500.8, 2010 CPD ¶ 13, holding that it is improper to find a performance risk because the protester did not submit a current Dun & Bradstreet report. However, there are cases where GAO has permitted the use of financial condition as a specific evaluation factor, *Greyback Concession*, Comp. Gen. Dec. B-239913, 90-2 CPD ¶ 278 (no discussion of special justification used to justify evaluation of financial condition); *E.H. White & Co.*, Comp. Gen. Dec. B-227122.3, 88-2 CPD ¶ 41 (competition between small businesses). In the normal procurement situation, there is little justification for making a comparative evaluation of financial condition and generally this should be left to the responsibility determination.

[g] Live Demonstrations/Sample Tasks

An effective way to evaluate capability is to require the offerors to show the agency how they will deal with a hypothetical or real task that represents the work that will be called for by the contract. Written responses to sample tasks have been used as evaluation factors for many years while live demonstrations are a recent approach.

In using sample tasks, the competitors are usually required to submit their explanation of how they will carry out the task in their proposals, but they can also be given the task during an oral presentation, FAR 15.102(c)). GAO regards this technique as a form of test with the result that agencies need not discuss deficient answers if they establish a competitive range, *Technology Applications, Inc.*, Comp. Gen. Dec. B-238259, 90-1 CPD ¶ 451.

Sample tasks are a way to focus the technical proposal on one or more specific parts of the work called for by the contract. As such, agencies are afforded broad discretion in evaluating the responses to the sample task, *Synaptek Corp.*, Comp. Gen. Dec. B-410698.6.10, 2016 CPD ¶ 78. See, for example, *AMEC-Gilbane, JV*, Comp. Gen. Dec. B-413778, 2017 CPD ¶ 11, where GAO ruled that the protester was properly excluded from the competitive range because of a poor response to a sample task order. Compare *Mevacon-NASCO JV*, Comp. Gen. Dec. B-414329, 2017 CPD ¶ 144, where the GAO granted as protest because the agency gave undue weight to a defective answer to a sample problem.

In 2016 the Department of Homeland Security conducted a competition to write software using agile techniques (called "FLASH") by substituting live demonstrations for technical proposals. Each competitor spent a half day having a team write software under the surveillance of DHS personnel who assessed their performance and the end product. The agency concluded that this was a valuable way to assess capability but that they could not regularize the process in the face of 111 competitors. The agency therefore canceled the procurement after nine companies protested. See *EDC Consulting, LLC*, Comp. Gen. Dec. B-414175.10, 2017 CPD ¶ 185, where GAO dismissed the protests. It seems clear that failing to limit the number of competitors as was planned fatally flawed the implementation of this technique. Nonetheless, for procurement with a single major task that can be evaluated by observation, this appears to be a superior way to evaluate capability.

[h] Written Proposals to Demonstrate Understanding the Work or Soundness of Approach

A common means of evaluating capability of the offerors is to require the submission of technical and management proposals to assess each offeror's understanding of the work or the soundness of the approach of the offerors. As discussed above, such proposals can also be used to solicit non-cost elements of the offer such as enhancements, technical solutions, or processes or techniques to be used to perform the work. Some agencies make it mandatory to include such an evaluation factor. Thus, Air Force Mandatory Procedure 5315.304.4.4.1.1 requires the factor "Mission Capability" on all procurements of $1 million or more (to assess "the offeror's capability to satisfy the government's requirements"), and NASA Source Selection Guide 1815.304-70 requires the factor "Mission Suitability" on all procurements of $50 million or more (optional on smaller procurements).

The DoD Source Selection Procedures, August 20, 2022, identify this factor as the "technical" factor which includes all non-cost factors except past performance. Thus, in this context the term "technical" appears to include management issues. See the following statement when "technical" proposals are solicited:

> 2.3.2.5. Technical. The purpose of the technical factor(s) is to assess the offeror's proposed approach, as detailed in its proposal, to satisfy the Government's requirements. There are many aspects which may affect an offeror's ability to meet the solicitation requirements. Examples include technical approach, risk, management approach, personnel qualifications, facilities, and others. The evaluation of risk is related to technical assessment. Consistent with and dependent on the best value method selected, coordinate with the [Requirements Owner] to provide offerors the monetary value of performance or capabilities above threshold whenever possible when deemed to be in the best interest of the Government.

This factor assumes that an offeror's capability can be evaluated by requiring it to submit a preliminary design or a technical/management plan that describes, at some specified level of detail, how the contract will be performed. To the extent that these written submissions are created by the personnel that will ultimately perform the contract, it is conceivable that this is a valid assumption. Thus, in research and development procurements, as well as in design-build competitions, where preliminary designs prepared by the offerors' own personnel are commonly used as a means of evaluating the capabilities of the competitors, the requirement for such designs may be a valid means of assessing the capability of the offerors. However, while such designs provide an agency with a considerable amount of information concerning the preliminary view of the offeror as to how the needs of the government can be best satisfied, they add a great amount of cost and time to the source selection process. In particular, the costs of the offerors are greatly increased because they are forced to create the preliminary design in order to participate in the competition, and the time required for the competition is greatly increased because the competitors must be given time to create the designs and the agency must allocate a significant period to evaluate the designs. Nonetheless, such design competitions have been accepted as a valid way of ascertaining the competence of the competitors. See, for example, *ITT Indus. Space Sys., LLC*, Comp. Gen. Dec. B-309964, 2007 CPD ¶ 217 (mission suitability properly evaluated in procurement of new land imaging instrument to be included in satellite); *Sikorsky Aircraft Co.*, Comp. Gen. Dec. B-299145, 2007 CPD ¶ 45 (mission capability properly evaluated but life-cycle cost improperly evaluated in procurement of new helicopter); *Compunetix, Inc.*, Comp. Gen. Dec. B-298489.4, 2007 CPD ¶ 12 (mission suitability properly evaluated in procurement of new mission voice systems). Unfortunately, procurements of this type frequently also call for technical and management plans to achieve other contract goals such as reliability and maintainability of the produce being designed. Such requirements add significantly to the cost and time required for the procurement with questionable added value.

In service contracting, this design-competition technique has been emulated by calling for the submission of technical and management plans to assess the offerors' understanding of the work. Here there is far greater doubt as to the validity of the process because it is far less likely that the plans will be written by the personnel that will ultimately perform the work. In fact, it is well understood that many technical/management plans are prepared by specialized proposal-writing personnel. Furthermore, it is doubtful if such plans are a valid means of assessing capability, since there are numerous instances where fully capable offerors were downgraded because of badly written plans. For examples of incumbent contractors losing competitions because of inadequate proposals, see *ManTech Int'l Corp.*, Comp. Gen. Dec. B-311074, 2008 CPD ¶ 87 (contractor whose performance had been rated excellent had not written good responses to sample problems); *HealthStar VA, PLLC*, Comp. Gen. Dec. B-299737, 2007 CPD ¶ 114 (contractor left information out of its proposal); *Executive Sec. & Eng'g Techs., Inc.*, Comp. Gen. Dec. B-270518, 96-1 CPD ¶ 156 (contractor failed to provide information on its corporate experience); and *Management*

Tech. Servs., Comp. Gen. Dec. B-251612.3, 93-1 CPD ¶ 432 (contractor failed to include required information on how it intended to obtain and train its workforce). Successful incumbent contractors have also been excluded from the competitive range for poorly written technical/management plans, *PTSI Managed Servs., Inc.*, Comp. Gen. Dec. B-411412, 2015 CPD ¶ 236 (contractor's transition plan lacked detail); *Pedus Bldg. Servs., Inc.*, Comp. Gen. Dec. B-257271.3, 95-1 CPD ¶ 135 (sloppy technical proposal); *Premier Cleaning Sys., Inc.*, Comp. Gen. Dec. B-255815, 94-1 CPD ¶ 241 (omission of required documentation on capabilities of project manager currently managing the contract). See also *McAllister & Assocs., Inc.*, Comp. Gen. Dec. B-277029, 98-1 CPD ¶ 85, where an experienced contractor was dropped from the competitive range because it had submitted a poorly written technical proposal.

This type of assessment of understanding of the services to be performed through the use of technical/management plans is particularly questionable when the services being procured are routine, non-technical services. In these instances, even the most competent offerors are not likely to have personnel that can write good technical and management proposals and the ability to write such proposals gives little indication that they will be good performers. Nonetheless, there are numerous instances of offerors losing competitions for such services based on the evaluation of such plans. See, for example, *AHNTECH, Inc.*, Comp. Gen. Dec. B-299806, 2007 CPD ¶ 213 (food services); *Financial & Realty Servs., LLC*, Comp. Gen. Dec. B-299605.2, 2007 CPD ¶ 161 (warehouse operations and labor services); *Meeks Disposal Corp.*, Comp. Gen. Dec. B-299576, 2007 CPD ¶ 127 (refuse collection and recycling services set aside for small businesses); *Philadelphia Produce Mkt. Wholesalers, LLC*, Comp. Gen. Dec. B-298751, 2006 CPD ¶ 193 (fresh fruit and vegetable set aside for small businesses); *Leader Commc'ns Inc.*, Comp. Gen. Dec. B-298734, 2006 CPD ¶ 192 (business support services); *Advanced Fed. Servs. Corp.*, Comp. Gen. Dec. B-298662, 2006 CPD ¶ 174 (administrative support for government facility set aside for 8(a) businesses); *Kola Nut Travel, Inc.*, Comp. Gen. Dec. B-296090.4, 2005 CPD ¶ 184 (travel services set aside for small businesses); and *Cortez, Inc.*, Comp. Gen. Dec. B-292178, 2003 CPD ¶ 184 (facility logistics services).

It is proper to call for a risk assessment of the probability that a proposed management or technical plan will create performance problems. See DoD Source Selection Procedures calling for the assessment of technical risk:

> 3.1.2.1.2. Technical Risk Rating. Assessment of technical risk, which is manifested by the identification of weakness/weaknesses, considers potential for disruption of schedule, increased costs, degradation of performance, the need for increased Government oversight, and/or the likelihood of unsuccessful contract performance.

This technique has been upheld in *Northrop Grumman Sys. Corp.*, Comp. Gen. Dec. B-414312, 2017 CPD ¶ 128 (denying a protest that the agency had assessed a technical solution as having "moderate risk" because of undeveloped software and firmware); *Trend Western Tech. Corp.*, Comp. Gen. Dec. B-275395.2, 97-1 CPD ¶ 201 (denying a protest that the agency had assessed a plan as having "moderate risk" because the staffing level was low); *Sensis Corp.*, Comp. Gen. Dec. B-265790.2, 96-1 CPD ¶ 77 (agency properly found moderate risk because the protester did not have a mature software development process); and *Hydro Eng'g, Inc. v. United States*, 37 Fed. Cl. 448 (1997) (agency properly found specific elements of a technical and management proposal created a risk of timely performance and technical compliance).

[B] Unlisted Factors or Subfactors

FAR 15.304(d) required that the RFP state clearly "all factors and significant subfactors that will affect contract award." The best practice is to list in the RFP all evaluation factors and subfactors that the agency intends to evaluate. However, failure of the agency to specifically identify an evaluation factor will be excused if the solicitation fairly advises offerors that the factor will be considered. See *SupplyCore, Inc.*, Comp. Gen. Dec. B-411548.2, 2017 CPD ¶ 72, stating:

> An agency may properly apply evaluation considerations that are not expressly identified in the RFP if those considerations are reasonably and logically encompassed within the stated evaluation criteria, so long as there is a clear nexus linking them.

For an example of this broad interpretation, see *Canadian Commercial Corp.*, Comp. Gen. Dec. B-276945, 97-2 CPD ¶ 48, where the solicitation requested proposals for a commercial off-the-shelf boat with proven marine performance. The fact that the agency considered the failure of the protester to provide performance data or that the protester had not previously built the boat did not constitute the evaluation of unstated factors. These factors were held to be reasonably understood as related to and relevant to the agency's assessment of risk of whether the protester would successfully deliver a product conforming to the solicitation requirements. See also *ERP Servs. Inc.*, Comp. Gen. Dec. B-419315, 2021 CPD ¶ 85 (use of orange "confirm" button (rather than green) related to "user-centered design and human factors" factor); *Northrop Grumman Sys. Corp.*, Comp. Gen. Dec. B-414312, 2017 CPD ¶ 128 (power consumption reasonably related to aircraft integration subfactor); *MILVETS Sys. Tech., Inc.*, Comp. Gen. Dec. B-411721.2, 2016 CPD ¶ 42 (experience of personnel logically encompassed in evaluation of staffing plan); *USGC, Inc.*, Comp. Gen. Dec. B-400184.2, 2009 CPD ¶ 9 ("disincentive plan" forgoing profit for tasks not meeting performance work statement requirements fell within technical approach factor); *AT&T Corp.*, Comp. Gen. Dec. B-299542.3, 2008 CPD ¶ 65 (being manufacturer of equipment related to factor assessing ability to provide equipment); *Apptis, Inc.*, Comp. Gen. Dec. B-299457, 2008 CPD ¶ 49 (proof of concept demonstration factor encompassed observations that company personnel were inefficient even though the demonstration was successful); *C. Young Constr., Inc.*, Comp. Gen. Dec. B-309740, 2007 CPD ¶ 198 (multiple-position personnel related to technical qualifications of key personnel factor); *Client Network Servs.*, Inc., Comp. Gen. Dec. B-297994, 2006 CPD ¶ 79 (knowledge of labor market related to staffing factor); *Ridoc Enter., Inc.*, Comp. Gen. Dec. B-292962.4, 2004 CPD ¶ 169 (management of subcontractors related to management plan factor); *Israel Aircraft Indus.*, Comp. Gen. Dec. B-274389, 97-1 CPD ¶ 41 (enhanced safety intrinsic to technical evaluation of equipment); *Myers Investigative & Security Servs., Inc.*, Comp. Gen. Dec. B-272947.2, 96-2 CPD ¶ 114 (solicitation clearly put offerors on notice that relevant experience would be evaluated under the past performance factor); and *Science & Tech., Inc.*, Comp. Gen. Dec. B-272748, 97-1 CPD ¶ 121 (offerors could not reasonably ignore factor left off the list of subfactors in section M but which was discussed in section L).

Innovations and creative approaches are an integral element of technical evaluation in a best value procurement even if there is no evaluation factor so stating, *Tetra Tech, Inc. v. United States*, 137 Fed. Cl. 367 (2017); *ViroMed Labs., Inc.*, Comp. Gen. Dec. B-310747.4, 2009 CPD ¶ 32; *IAP World Servs., Inc.*, Comp. Gen. Dec. B-297084, 2005 CPD ¶ 199. Quantification of the factor is also within the scope of an evaluation factor, *DynCorp Int'l LLC*, Comp. Gen. Dec. B-415349, 2018 CPD ¶ 12.

This broad interpretation is not unbounded. See, for example, *Crawford RealStreet Joint Venture*, Comp. Gen. Dec. B-415193.2, 2018 CPD ¶ 121 (evaluation of price reasonableness without any page limitation did not show that offeror was required to submit data justifying price); *Pinnacle Solutions, Inc.*, Comp. Gen. Dec. B-414360, 2017 CPD ¶ 172 (evaluation of whether general manager had full hiring authority not encompassed in requirement that general manager have full authority to act for contractor); *General Revenue Corp.*, Comp. Gen. Dec. B-414220.2, 2017 CPD ¶ 106 (evaluation of credentials of person not listed as key person); *Phoenix Air Grp., Inc.*, Comp. Gen. Dec. B-412796.2, 2016 CPD ¶ 308 (evaluation of whether proposal met 100 mandatory performance requirements not logically foreseeable from the information requested in the offeror capability form); *Sterling Medical Corp.*, Comp. Gen. Dec. B-412407, 2016 CPD ¶ 73 (evaluation of length of management experience not related to contingency plans for unforeseen events); *Metis Solutions, LLC*, Comp. Gen. Dec. B-411173.2, 2015 CPD ¶ 221 (submission of quality control plan not required by evaluation factor calling for description of quality control approach).

The requirement to list "significant subfactors" has been liberally interpreted to permit the nondisclosure of subfactors which are logically and reasonably related to the stated evaluation factors, *Buffalo Organization for Social & Tech. Innovation, Inc.*, Comp. Gen. Dec. B-196279, 80-1 CPD ¶ 107 See also

Hydro Eng'g, Inc. v. United States, 37 Fed. Cl. 448 (1997). In spite of this liberal interpretation, it is not good practice to omit subfactors. The best practice is to give the offerors as full an explanation of the factors that will be considered as is practicable. In addition, there are cases granting protests when a subfactor that is not logically related to the stated factor is used. See, for example, *Global Analytic Info. Tech. Servs., Inc.*, Comp. Gen. Dec. B-298840.2, 2007 CPD ¶ 57, finding that the incumbent contractors' methods of improving their performance was not related to the "management approach" factor because it was an "incumbent-specific factor" that could not have been foreseen by the incumbents. See also *American K-9 Detection Servs., Inc.*, Comp. Gen. Dec. B-400464.6, 2009 CPD ¶ 107 (GAO suggested that, in a corrective reopening of the competition, the agency should list the 10 subfactor "categories" to its evaluation of technical capability that had not been listed in the original competition); *PWC Logistics Servs. Co.*, Comp. Gen. Dec. B-400660, 2009 CPD ¶ 67 (agency required to include subfactor stating criteria for dividing work when two contracts were to be awarded).

There have been numerous protests where unlisted subfactors have been held to be logically related to a factor. For example, the requirement that the project director be available at the outset of the procurement was held to be logically related to the "Personnel Qualifications" evaluation factor, *Health Mgmt. Sys.*, Comp. Gen. Dec. B-200775, 81-1 CPD ¶ 255. See also *Building Restoration Corp.*, Comp. Gen. Dec. B-402000, 2010 CPD ¶ 15 (experience with work listed in specification sufficiently related to technical excellence subfactor); *RCL Components, Inc.*, Comp. Gen. Dec. B-400175, 2009 CPD ¶ 98 (relative amount of government contracting experience sufficiently related to "programmatic and logistical considerations" and "type of contract" factors); *Smart Innovative Solutions*, Comp. Gen. Dec. B-400323.3, 2008 CPD ¶ 220 (method of communication with offices sufficiently related to coordination with offices factor); *International Bus. & Tech. Consultants, Inc.*, Comp. Gen. Dec. B-310424.2, 2008 CPD ¶ 185 ("long-term, on-the-ground experience" sufficiently related to professional experience factor); *Cornell Cos.*, Comp. Gen. Dec. B-310548, 2007 CPD ¶ 212 (distance and remoteness of site of housing prisoners sufficiently related to site location factor); *SCS Refrigerated Servs., LLC*, Comp. Gen. Dec. B-298790, 2006 CPD ¶ 186 (location and evidence of firm contractual agreement with back-up sources sufficiently related to identification of back-up sources factor); *Client Network Servs., Inc.*, Comp. Gen. Dec. B-297994, 2006 CPD ¶ 79 (knowledge of job market in area sufficiently related to approach to managing staff and staffing fluctuations" factor); *Nicholson/Soletanche Joint Venture*, Comp. Gen. Dec. B-297011.3, 2006 CPD ¶ 70 (record of performing directional drilling sufficiently related to past performance factor); *Management Sys. Designers, Inc.*, Comp. Gen. Dec. B-244383.4, 91-2 CPD ¶ 518 ("Compliance with Stated Minimum Requirements," "Additional Experience/Qualifications of Key Personnel," and "Experience in the Topical Area" sufficiently related to the "Personnel Qualifications" factor).

Subfactors need not be included on a separate list if they are described in a narrative form in the description of the factor, *Moran Assocs.*, Comp. Gen. Dec. B-240564.2, 91-2 CPD ¶ 495. In that case, GAO apparently believed that a diligent offeror would identify the subfactors from the narrative description. See also *ITT Electron Tech. Div.*, Comp. Gen. Dec. B-242289, 91-1 CPD ¶ 383, holding that there was no need to disclose an evaluation "checklist" when the items on the list were reasonably related to the evaluation factors. In *Stone Webster Eng'g Corp.*, Comp. Gen. Dec. B-255286.2, 94-2 CPD ¶ 306, the protester contended that the evaluation was improper because the agency evaluated proposals on a basis of an evaluation factor, "general strategy," that was not listed as an evaluation factor in the RFP. The agency stated that general strategy was not a separate evaluation criterion but was, however, considered as part of the evaluation of several factors that were set forth in the RFP. GAO agreed, finding that the RFP did state that strategy formulation and selection of appropriate tactics would be a significant subfactor under the understanding the anticipated work evaluation factor.

If a subfactor will have an inordinate impact on the evaluation of a factor, it will be found to be a "significant" subfactor which must be identified in the RFP as having such impact. See *Lloyd H. Kessler, Inc.*, Comp. Gen. Dec. B-284693, 2000 CPD ¶ 96, requiring the listing of a very specific type of experience when that was the most important subfactor. See also *Devres, Inc.*, 66 Comp. Gen. 121 (B-224017), 86-2 CPD ¶ 652, where GAO required listing of a subfactor for specific experience even though it was related to the "general experience" that had been listed. The specific experience subfactor was 60% of the general experience factor and 25% of the total scoring (it was larger than any other factor). Compare *Noble Supply & Logistics*, Comp. Gen. Dec. B-411229.3, 2015 CPD ¶ 232, holding that annual revenue was not a significant subfactor in assessing the relevance of past performances.

Listed subfactors must include only elements that bear a relationship to the subfactor. Thus, GAO has held that the financial condition of an offeror was not properly included in the subfactor "ability to meet the published schedule requirements of the Government at an acceptable level of risk," *Flight Int'l Grp., Inc.*, 69 Comp. Gen. 741 (B-238953.4), 90-2 CPD ¶ 257.

[C] Relative Importance

There are two aspects of the statutory requirement to provide a statement of relative importance in the RFP. At the highest level, there must be a statement of the procurement strategy described in Section I, above. This is the relationship of cost/price to the non-cost/price factors required by 10 U.S.C. § 3206 (formerly § 2305(a)(3)(A)(iii)) and 41 U.S.C. § 3306(c)(1)(C). Below that level, there must be some indication of the relative importance of the factors and subfactors within the non-cost or price areas, 10 U.S.C. § 3206 (formerly § 2305(a)(2)(A)(ii)) and 41 U.S.C. § 3306(c)(1)(A).

[1] Relationship of Cost/Price to Other Factors

At a minimum, the RFP must indicate the decisional logic that the agency intends to use to make the selection decision. See *Signatron, Inc.*, 54 Comp. Gen. 530 (B-181782), 74-2 CPD ¶ 386, where GAO stated at 535:

> We believe that each offeror has a right to know whether the procurement is intended to achieve a minimum standard at the lowest cost or whether cost is secondary to quality. Competition is not served if offerors are not given any idea of the relative values of technical excellence and price.

Thus, the solicitation must describe the procurement strategy that will be used to make the award.

If an agency has decided to use the lowest price, technically acceptable proposal decisional rule, the RFP should include a statement to that effect, FAR 15.101-2(b)(1). If the agency has decided to use a tradeoff decisional rule, it has a variety of ways to state that rule in the RFP. The following is provided, by way of illustration, as language that may be included in an RFP to convey essential information to the offerors:

> Award will be made to that offeror whose proposal contains the combination of those criteria offering the best overall value to the Government. This will be determined by comparing differences in the value of the non-cost criteria with differences in cost to the Government. In making this comparison . . . (select the applicable alternative)
>
> No. 1 (Non-cost criteria most important)—non-cost criteria are significantly more important than cost to the Government because the Government is more concerned with obtaining superior performance than with making an award at the lowest overall cost to the Government. However, the Government will not make an award at a significantly higher overall cost to the Government to achieve slightly superior performance.
>
> No. 2 (Non-cost criteria and cost to the Government of equal importance)—non-cost criteria and cost to the Government are of equal importance because the Government is concerned with striking the most advantageous balance between the non-cost criteria and cost to the Government.
>
> No. 3 (Cost to the Government most important)—cost to the Government is significantly more important than non-cost criteria because the Government is more concerned with making an award at the lowest overall cost to the Government than with obtaining superior performance. However, the Government will not make an award based on a proposal with significantly inferior performance in order to achieve a small savings in cost to the Government.

This language attempts to tell offerors that the best value decision would ultimately be made on the basis of marginal differences between the competitors and that the agency would pay more for marginal differences in non-cost features but not a lot more for a small difference. This, of course, describes the essence of a tradeoff selection.

The shorter version of this rule in 10 U.S.C. § 3206 (formerly § 2305(a)(3)(A)(iii)) and 41 U.S.C. § 3306(c)(1)(C) is implemented in FAR 15.304(e) as follows:

> The solicitation shall also state, at a minimum, whether all evaluation factors other than cost or price, when combined, are—
>
> (1) Significantly more important than cost or price;
> (2) Approximately equal to cost or price; or
> (3) Significantly less important than cost or price.

It is proper to state in the RFP that past performance is "more important" than price (rather than "significantly more important" than price) when that is a correct statement, *Braswell Servs., Grp. Inc.*, Comp. Gen. Dec. B-276694, 97-2 CPD ¶ 18. However, when an agency uses the "more important" statement, it is improper to then treat the non-cost factors as significantly more important, *Johnson Controls Sec. Sys., LLC*, Comp. Gen. Dec. B-296490.3, 2007 CPD ¶ 100.

Failure to include any statement of relative importance of cost to the government versus non-cost factors is an issue apparent on the fact of the RFP which must be protested before the submission of proposals, *Cherokee Info. Servs., Inc.*, Comp. Gen. Dec. B-291718, 2003 CPD ¶ 49.

Since the ultimate source selection decisions is based on marginal differences between the offerors, the relationship of cost to the government and non-cost factors is actually variable. Agencies have included different types of statements in the RFP describing this fact. See, for example, *DLM&A, Inc. v. United States*, 6 Cl. Ct. 329 (1984), providing the following RFP statement at 330:

> [C]ost is not expected to be the controlling factor in the selection of a Contractor for this solicitation. The degree of importance of cost as a factor could become greater depending upon the equality of the proposals for other factors evaluated; where competing proposals are determined to be substantially equal, total cost and other cost factors would become the controlling factor.

Another example can be found in *EG&G Ortec*, Comp. Gen. Dec. B-213347, 84-1 CPD ¶ 182, *recons. denied*, 84-1 CPD ¶ 372, where the RFP contained the full point scoring system plus the following statement:

> You are advised that paramount consideration shall be given to the evaluation of technical proposals rather than cost or price. It is pointed out,

> however, that should technical competence between offerors be considered approximately the same, then cost or price could become paramount.

In some cases, GAO has held that this type of statement does not meet the requirement to state relative importance. See *Ogden Support Servs., Inc.*, Comp. Gen. Dec. B-270354, 96-1 CPD ¶ 175, where the RFP only stated that "cost would become more important as the difference in technical evaluation scores decreases and that cost 'may become' determinative when proposals are technically equal." GAO stated that this scheme failed to state the relative importance of the cost factor.

Some agencies have used the term "relative weight" to describe "relative importance," and in some cases they have used percentage weights to assign points in a numerical scoring system. Stating relative weights meets the requirement to state relative importance. See, for example, *GC Servs. Ltd. P'ship*, Comp. Gen. Dec. B-298102, 2006 CPD ¶ 96 (past performance and experience weighted at 45%, technical approach weighted at 30%, and management approach weighted at 25% of non-cost score); *Joint Mgmt. & Tech. Servs.*, Comp. Gen. Dec. B-294229, 2004 CPD ¶ 208 (technical approach—35%, key/critical personnel—25%, management approach—20%, experience—10%, past performance—10%).

Failing to state relative "weights," when that term is used, will be found to be a failure to meet the requirement to state relative importance. See *ENCORP Int'l, Inc.*, Comp. Gen. Dec. B-258829, 95-1 CPD ¶ 100, where the agency had explicitly refrained from stating the relative weights of the "more important" technical factors listed in the RFP. Instead, the RFP stated:

> When making tradeoff decisions during proposal preparation, offerors should remember that the Government prefers to obtain better offeror experience, past performance, and better savings. However, the *relative influence* that any of these factors will have on the source selection decision will ultimately depend on the marginal differences among the competing offerors, which will not be known until the proposals have been analyzed and compared to one another. Therefore, the Government has not assigned *weights* to these factors. (emphasis added)

In a footnote GAO stated that this scheme failed to comply with the Competition in Contracting Act, which required, at a minimum, all evaluation factors and significant subfactors and their relative importance. See also *Bio-Rad Labs., Inc.*, Comp. Gen. Dec. B-297553, 2007 CPD ¶ 58 (no disclosure of relative weights of technical subfactors); and *SOS Interpreting, Ltd.*, Comp. Gen. Dec. B-293026, 2005 CPD ¶ 26 (no disclosure of relative weight of past performance or of technical subfactors).

[2] Relative Importance of Other Factors

There are a number of different methods of specifying the relative importance of the factors other than cost or price.

[a] Listing Factors

A questionable technique for disclosing the relative importance of non-cost factors is merely to list the factors that will be evaluated in the RFP with no statement of relative importance. In such cases the offerors are expected to assume that all evaluation criteria are of approximately equal importance. See, for example, *Recogniti, LLP*, Comp. Gen. Dec. B-410658, 2015 CPD ¶ 49; and *Carol Solomon & Assocs.*, Comp. Gen. Dec. B-271713, 96-2 CPD ¶ 28, where GAO applied the presumption of equality in the absence of a contrary indication of relative importance in the RFP. This rule also applies to subfactors with no statement of relative importance, *CBE Grp., Inc.*, Comp. Gen. Dec. B-414220.51, 2017 CPD ¶ 129

[b] Descending Order of Importance

Another inferior method of indicating relative order of importance is to list the non-cost factors and state that they are listed in descending order of importance. GAO has upheld use of this method where the evaluation scheme "reflects a reasonable downward progression of evaluation weights," *Optimum Tech., Inc.*, Comp. Gen. Dec. B-266339.2, 96-1 CPD ¶ 188. See also *Puglia Eng'g of California, Inc.*, Comp. Gen. Dec. B-297413, 2006 CPD ¶ 33; *A&W Maint. Servs., Inc.*, Comp. Gen. Dec. B-255711.2, 95-1 CPD ¶ 24; and *North-East Imaging, Inc.*, Comp. Gen. Dec. B-256281, 94-1 CPD ¶ 332. Thus, a mere statement that the evaluation factors are listed in the order of their relative importance, without specifically assigning a weight to each, is satisfactory so long as the difference between the importance assigned to any one factor and that assigned to the factor either immediately preceding or immediately following it is small. See *Sperry Rand Corp.*, Comp. Gen. Dec. B-179875, 74-2 CPD ¶ 158, stating that where one factor is to have predominant consideration over the other factors, this should be disclosed. See also *Finlen Complex, Inc.*, Comp. Gen. Dec. B-288280, 2001 CPD ¶ 167, holding that the 5% weight of past performance was required to be disclosed because offerors could have expected this subfactor to have a higher weight.

Where a solicitation lists evaluation factors and subfactors in descending order of importance, such an evaluation scheme does not indicate that the subfactors of lower-weighted factors are necessarily of less individual weight than subfactors of higher-weighted factors, *Brown & Root, Inc.*, Comp. Gen. Dec. B-270505.2, 96-2 CPD ¶ 143. However, when technical factors are listed in descending order, it is improper to evaluate one of them on a pass/fail basis, *Helicopter Transport Servs. LLC*, Comp. Gen. Dec. B-400295, 2008 CPD ¶ 180.

[c] Adjectival Descriptions of Importance

Another technique for disclosing relative importance of the non-cost factors is to provide an adjectival description of the relationship of the factors. It has been common practice to use such descriptions when the agency actually has firm weights for the non-cost factors. See, for example, *ITT Federal Servs. Int'l Corp.*, Comp. Gen. Dec. B-296783, 2007 CPD ¶ 43, where the RFP stated:

> The RFP advised that the price/cost and business/management/technical approach factors were equal in importance, and that each was significantly more important than past performance, and further, that the past performance and business/management/technical approach factors together were more important than price/cost.

These adjectival statements are also commonly used to describe complex source selection schemes. See, for example, *MD Helicopters, Inc.*, Comp. Gen. Dec. B-298502, 2006 CPD ¶ 178, where GAO described the relationship of the factors as follows:

> The RFP provided for a "best value" evaluation of [Federal Aviation Administration] certification (which was evaluated as a "go/no go" criteria) and five other evaluation factors: price, technical, producibility/management (P/M), logistics, and past performance. Price was stated to be more important than technical, technical more important than P/M, and price and technical combined were significantly more important than P/M, logistics, and past performance. P/M and logistics were stated to be of equal importance and each was more important than past performance.

While these types of statements are difficult to decipher, they have been found to convey sufficient information to the offerors as to the relative importance of the factors.

[d] Numerical Systems

The relative importance of factors and subfactors may also be indicated by disclosing the numerical point score or percentage for each evaluation criterion in the RFP. An agency's RFP disclosures of its numerical systems must be sufficient to inform prospective offerors of how the rating system will apply to their proposals. In *National Capital Med. Found. Inc.*, Comp. Gen. Dec. B-215303.5, 85-1 CPD ¶ 637, the RFP failed to inform offerors that proposals would receive zero points out of a possible 110 allocated to "admission objectives" and 200 allocated to "quality objectives" if any one of the subcriteria under these objectives was rated less than acceptable regardless of the merits of the others. GAO found that application of such an undisclosed scoring scheme was arbitrary and inconsistent with the RFP requirements.

[e] Subfactors

As with primary areas of the evaluation, an offeror may assume that all subfactors are of substantially equal importance in the absence of advice to the contrary, *North Am. Tel. Assoc.*, Comp. Gen. Dec. B-187239, 76-2 CPD ¶ 495; *Tracor, Inc.*, 56 Comp. Gen. 62 (B-186315), 76-2 CPD ¶ 386. However, if a subfactor is to play an important role in the source selection decision, that must be stated in the RFP. See, for example, *H. J. Grp. Ventures, Inc.*, Comp. Gen. Dec. B-246139, 92-1 CPD ¶ 203, where GAO found improper heavy reliance on past performance when that criterion had been listed as a "general consideration" but not included in the list of other criteria which were stated in relative order of importance. See also *J.A. Jones Mgmt. Servs., Inc.*, Comp. Gen. Dec. B-254941.2, 94-1 CPD ¶ 244, where the agency improperly had greatly exaggerated the weight the RFP assigned to the key personnel evaluation factor; and *University of Michigan*, 66 Comp. Gen. 538 (B-225756), 87-1 CPD ¶ 643, where it was improper to place heavy reliance on one criterion when the RFP appeared to indicate that four technical criteria were of relatively equal weight.

[3] Minimum Requirements

If an RFP provides that offerors must meet specified minimum requirements, award may not be made to an offeror that fails to meet the minimum requirements. Conversely, if the RFP does not clearly state a minimum requirement, the government may not reject a proposal which does not meet that requirement, *RJO Enters., Inc.*, Comp. Gen. Dec. B-260126.2, 95-2 CPD ¶ 93, nor drop a proposal from the competitive range for not meeting the requirement, *Omniplex World Servs. Corp.*, Comp. Gen. Dec. B-290996.2, 2003 CPD ¶ 7. Similarly if an agency uses a performance specification allowing an offeror to devise a solution, the agency is not required to inform other offerors that it intends to select an offeror with a desirable solution, *Cerner Corp.*, Comp. Gen. Dec. B-293093, 2004 CPD ¶ 34. In *ACS Sys. & Eng'g, Inc.*, Comp. Gen. Dec. B-275439.3, 97-1 CPD ¶ 126, GAO upheld an agency's corrective action allowing resubmission of BAFOs after its requirements had changed, stating that "[i]t is fundamental that offerors must be advised of a procuring agency's actual minimum requirements." See also *Lobar, Inc.*, Comp. Gen. Dec. B-247843.3, 92-2 CPD ¶ 139, where GAO required the agency to reopen the procurement and amend the RFP to state the minimum requirements that the agency was actually using in the evaluation of proposals. In *CNA Indus. Eng'g, Inc.*, Comp. Gen. Dec. B-271034, 96-1 CPD ¶ 279, the agency awarded a contract to an offeror who had similar experience with a similar software system. GAO held that the award was based on an improper relaxation of the agency's minimum requirement that offerors demonstrate expertise and experience with the agency's own software system. However, there is no need for an agency to formulate minimum requirements for each evaluation factor in order to satisfy minimum requirements disclosures, if objective measures are not relevant to the source selection, *W.B. Jolley*, 68 Comp. Gen. 443 (B-234490), 89-1 CPD ¶ 512.

Similarly, minimum requirements need not be stated if the agency is open to consideration of varying levels of performance, *Dismas Charities*, Comp. Gen. Dec. B-298390, 2006 CPD ¶ 131 (no minimum number of parking spaces although only a few spaces was considered a weakness); *National Beef Packing Co.*, Comp. Gen. Dec. B-296534, 2005 CPD ¶ 168 (no minimum delivery requirement stated when RFP permitted offerors to propose alternate delivery schedules); *Carson & Assocs., Inc.*, GSBCA 9411-P, 88-2 BCA ¶ 20,778 (no need to state minimum staffing levels when agency considered staffing levels variable depending on proposed method of performing the work). Thus, an agency must only disclose in the RFP any minimum requirements that it intends to actually use in the evaluation.

If a minimum requirement is stated clearly in the RFP, there is no need to state additionally that it will be evaluated on a pass/fail basis, *OfficeMax, Inc.*, Comp. Gen. Dec. B-299340.2, 2007 CPD ¶ 158. Conversely, if the RFP states that a requirement will be evaluated on a pass/fail basis, offerors should assume that it is a minimum requirement, *National Shower Express, Inc.*, Comp. Gen. Dec. B-293970, 2004 CPD ¶ 140. However, some agencies include both statements in the RFP. See, for example, *Nu-Way, Inc.*, Comp. Gen. Dec. B-296435.5, 2005 CPD ¶ 195.

§ 6.04 REQUESTS FOR PROPOSALS

Once specifications have been adopted, a procurement strategy has been selected and evaluation factors and subfactors and their relative importance have been determined, the government must provide this information to potential offerors. In addition, offerors must be advised of the type of contract that will be used and the terms and conditions which it will contain. Finally, offerors must be given instructions on what must be submitted. The Request for Proposals (RFP) is the means by which these matters are communicated. See FAR 15.203(a):

> Requests for proposals (RFPs) are used in negotiated acquisitions to communicate Government requirements to prospective contractors and to solicit proposals. RFPs for competitive acquisitions shall, at a minimum, describe the—
>
> (1) Government's requirement;

(2) Anticipated terms and conditions that will apply to the contract. The solicitation may authorize offerors to propose alternative terms and conditions. If the solicitation permits offerors to submit one or more additional proposals with alternative line items (see 52.204-22 or 52.212-1(e)), the evaluation approach should consider the potential impact of the alternative line items on other terms and conditions or the requirement (e.g., place of performance or payment and funding requirements) (see 15.206);

(i) The solicitation may authorize offerors to propose alternative terms and conditions, including the contract line item number (CLIN) structure; and

(ii) When alternative CLIN structures are permitted, the evaluation approach should consider the potential impact on other terms and conditions or the requirement (e.g., place of performance or payment and funding requirements) (see 15.206);

(3) Information required to be in the offeror's proposal; and

(4) Factors and significant subfactors that will be used to evaluate the proposal and their relative importance.

Thus, it can be seen that the RFP serves a number of functions and that a well-organized and well-drafted RFP is essential to achieving an effective and efficient procurement.

[A] Organization of the RFP

FAR 15.204 requires that RFPs be prepared using the Uniform Contract Format—specified in FAR 15.204-1(b) as follows:

UNIFORM CONTRACT FORMAT

Part I—The Schedule	
SECTION	TITLE
A	Solicitation/contract form
B	Supplies or services and prices/costs
C	Description/specifications/statement of work
D	Packaging and marking
E	Inspection and acceptance
F	Deliveries or performance

(continues)

G	Contract administration data
H	Special contract requirements
Part II—Contract Clauses	
I	Contract clauses
Part III—List of Documents, Exhibits, and Other Attachments	
J	List of attachments
Part IV—Representations and Instructions	
K	Representations, certifications, and other statements of offerors or respondents
L	Instructions, conditions, and notices to offerors or respondents
M	Evaluation factors for award

Parts I, II and III become part of the contract and Section K is to be incorporated into the contract by reference.

FAR 15.204 provides that the Uniform Contract Format "need not be used" for:

> (a) Construction and architect-engineer contracts (see part 36).
> (b) Subsistence contracts.
> (c) Supplies or services contracts requiring special contract formats prescribed elsewhere in this part that are inconsistent with the uniform format.
> (d) Letter requests for proposal (see 15.203(e)).
> (e) Contracts exempted by the agency head or designee.

[B] Contract Provisions

The contract provisions in Parts I, II, and III of the Uniform Contract Format constitute a complete contract except for the prices or costs and fee in Part B, which the offeror must fill out when the proposal is submitted. Thus, as in the case of sealed bidding, the government normally writes an entire contract in the course of preparing the RFP. However, in negotiated procurement, the RFP may solicit additive or alternate offers which will vary the terms of the RFP and require rewriting of the contract after negotiation has occurred.

FAR 15.204-2(a) provides that Standard Form 33 (Solicitation, Offer and Award), or Optional Form 308 (Solicitation and Offer—Negotiated Acquisition) may be used as the cover sheet for the RFP and will constitute Section A of the contract. These forms contain a significant amount of key information, as well as blocks for the signatures of the prospective contractor. In addition, the SF 33 contains a block for the signature of the contracting officer, which permits it to be used as an award form. The most important information is the time by which the proposal must be submitted and the requirement for signature of the proposal by an authorized representative of the contractor. The information contained on these forms must be included in the RFP if these forms are not used. See FAR 15.204-2(a)(2).

FAR 15.204-2(b) contains the following guidance on the information to be included in Section B of the RFP:

> Include a brief description of the supplies or services; e.g., item number, national stock number/part number if applicable, nouns, nomenclature, and quantities. (This includes incidental deliverables such as manuals and reports.)

The purpose of this section is to give offerors a summary description of the contract requirements and provide a place for offerors to submit their proposed prices. Thus, the descriptions of the work in this section are very brief—with details left to Section C.

The number of line items or subline items is discretionary with the procuring agency subject to the rules in FAR Subpart 4.10. DFARS PGI Subpart 204.71 contains detailed requirements for line item numbering in DOD contracts.

Section C contains the detailed description of the work to be performed under the contract. The contract specification is usually a detailed document that has evolved in an agency over a number of procurements or a new document written specifically for the procurement. In either case, the RFP must provide specific information to prospective offerors on the applicable specifications. However, the RFP generally will incorporate the specifications by reference except in certain situations. See FAR Subpart 11.2.

FAR 15.204-2(d) provides that Section D should contain packaging, packing, preservation, and marking provisions. Detailed guidance on this issue is left to agency regulations.

Section E should contain the special clauses that the agency will use in inspecting and accepting the work. In most cases, the procuring agency will include the appropriate standard inspection clause from FAR 52.246. FAR Subpart 46.2 contains detailed guidance on the selection of standard inspection clauses or other inspection clauses to minimize the costs to the government and utilize the contractor's inspection capabilities to the maximum extent consistent with obtaining the necessary quality of work.

Section F contains guidance on the time and place of contract performance in accordance with FAR Subpart 11.4. FAR 52.211-9 contains a number of alternate clauses to be used in specifying the time of delivery as either a firm contract requirement or a desired time. When the time is specified as a firm contract requirement, an offer may be rejected if it fails to comply with the requirement. Note, however, that offerors whose initial proposals do not comply with the required delivery schedules should still be considered for the competitive range. Unlike sealed bid procurements, negotiated procurements permit giving offerors the opportunity to satisfy government requirements through discussions. Therefore, an offeror in negotiated procurements that fails to comply with delivery times in its proposal should not be automatically labeled nonresponsive and rejected since this error could easily be corrected during discussions. See *Hollingsead Int'l*, Comp. Gen. Dec. B-227853, 87-2 CPD ¶ 372; *Xtek, Inc.*, Comp. Gen. Dec. B-213166, 84-1 CPD ¶ 264; *DPF Inc.*, Comp. Gen. Dec. B-180292, 74-1 CPD ¶ 303. These decisions seem to contradict ¶ (b) of the Time of Delivery clause in FAR 52.211-8, which states that if the proposed delivery date is "later than the required delivery date, the offer will be considered nonresponsive and rejected." This language only applies to sealed bid procurements and should be deleted from the clause when it is used in negotiated procurements. Alternates I and II of the Time of Delivery clause in FAR 52.211-9 do not need to be altered in this way because they contain a ¶ (b) which omits such language.

In some cases, agencies use special time of performance clauses which make the time of performance, within a range, an evaluation factor. GAO has sanctioned the use of time of performance as an evaluation factor, especially when the procurement is urgent. See *Shirley Constr. Corp.*, 70 Comp. Gen. 62 (B-240357), 90-2 CPD ¶ 380 (total time of performance one of four evaluation criteria); and *Hydroscience*, Comp. Gen. Dec. B-227989, 87-2 CPD ¶ 501 (offeror's proposal properly devalued due to uncertainty as to time of performance when swift performance was crucial).

FAR 15.204-2(g) requires that Section G include accounting and appropriation data as well as contract administration information or instructions other than those pertaining to the solicitation. DFARS PGI 204.7107 requires contracting offices to use accounting classification reference numbers (ACRNs) in order to process certain contract data through the Military Standard Contract Administration Procedures (MILSCAP). MILSCAP utilizes the ACRNs to relate contract administration records to the long-line accounting classification used to obligate funds on the contract.

FAR 15.204-2(h) provides that Section H may contain any special contract requirements that are not contained in Section I. While this gives procuring agencies almost total discretion on how to use this section, many agencies include clauses which are specially written for the procurement.

Section I contains most of the standard clauses for the proposed contract. Standard contract clauses are contained in FAR Part 52. The matrix in FAR Subpart 52.3 gives guidance on the clauses to be incorporated into the various types of contracts. Clauses are either (1) required, (2) required when applicable, or (3) optional. FAR 52.102(a) requires incorporation of clauses by reference to the "maximum practical extent" even if they—

(1) Are used with one or more alternates or on an optional basis;

(2) Are prescribed on a "substantially as follows" or "substantially the same as" basis, provided they are used verbatim;

(3) Require modification or the insertion by the Government of fill-in material (see 52.104); or

(4) Require completion by the offeror or prospective contractor. This instruction also applies to provisions completed as annual representations and certifications.

FAR 52.103 provides that when clauses are incorporated by reference they are to be identified by FAR number, title, and date or agency regulation number, title, and date.

The requirement to incorporate by reference clauses that must be filled in by one of the parties can result in an incomplete contract. See, for example, Alternate I of the Rights in Data—General clause in FAR 52.227-14 which specifies a blank space for the uses that a government agency can make of limited rights technical data which is frequently incorporated in contracts without filling in the uses. FAR 52.104 contains the following guidance on filling in such clauses:

> (d) When completing blanks in provisions or clauses incorporated by reference, insert the fill-in information directly below the title of the provision or clause identifying to the lowest level necessary to clearly indicate the blanks being filled in.

If a clause that is incorporated by reference requires an offeror to fill in blanks, the offeror should print out the clause, fill in the blanks and submit the clause with its proposal. The only guidance on this procedure is the partial guidance in FAR 52.102(c) which requires contracting officers to identify, in special situations, such clauses in order to alert offerors that they must be filled in.

When an agency deviates from a standard clause, FAR 52.107(f) requires it to alert offerors to such deviation by including the following Authorized Deviation in Clauses clause from FAR 52.252-6 in the RFP:

> (a) The use in this solicitation or contract of any Federal Acquisition Regulation (48 CFR chapter 1) clause with an authorized deviation is indicated by the addition of (DEVIATION) after the date of the clause.
>
> (b) The use in this solicitation or contract of any [insert regulation name] (48 CFR) clause with an authorized deviation is indicated by the addition of (DEVIATION) after the name of the regulation.

Deviations are only effective if they are approved by an official with the authority to take such actions. See Chapter 1.

Section J contains all attachments and exhibits to the contract. FAR 15.204-4 requires that the title, date, and number of pages be listed for each of these documents. There is no provision dealing with the incorporation of these items by reference.

The requirements for certifications or representations by the offeror are contained in Section K. The government uses these provisions to determine the status of the offeror and to ensure that the offeror will be in compliance with the socioeconomic requirements of the procurement. Thus, these provisions create a self-monitoring mechanism permitting offerors to establish their compliance by certification rather than by proving that certain requirements are met. In order to reduce the administrative burden on offerors, the government has adopted a policy of annual online representations and certifications using the System for Award Management (SAM). All prospective contractors are required to participate in this system, FAR 4.1201. Offerors are alerted to this requirement be the inclusion in the RFP of the Annual Representations and Certifications solicitation provision in FAR 52.204-8 and the System for Award Management clause in FAR 52.204-7. When this is done, FAR 4.1202 calls for the omission from the RFP of the separate clauses requiring certifications and representations—which are listed in that regulation.

[C] Solicitation Provisions

The solicitation provisions specify the ground rules under which proposals are to be submitted and evaluated and award is to be made. FAR 2.101 contains the following definition:

> Solicitation provision or provision means a term or condition used only in solicitations and applying only before contract award.

These provisions will consist of standard terms or conditions dealing with the submission of proposals, specialized instructions relating to the specific procurement and a statement of the evaluation factors and subfactors and their relative importance. The RFP may be transmitted by electronic commerce or facsimile and may authorize the submission of proposals using electronic commerce or facsimiles, FAR 203(c) and (d).

[1] Standard Provisions

FAR 15.209 requires the inclusion of a number of standard provisions in the RFP. FAR 15.209(a) requires that the FAR 52.215-1, Instructions to Offerors—Competitive Acquisition be included in all competitive solicitations where the government intends to award a contract without discussions. This provision does not prohibit conducting discussions if award without discussions is not feasible. Alternate I is to be used if the government has determined, in advance, that it will conduct discussions. When Alternate I is included, award without discussions is not permitted. This provision incorporates definitions and rules involving a number of matters, including modification and withdrawal of proposals, consideration of late proposals, acceptable restrictions on disclosure of information, and award. FAR 15.209(a)(2) also calls for the use of Alternate II to this solicitation provision when the government would be willing to accept alternate proposals. The use of this alternate allows the government to award a contract to an offeror submitting an alternate proposal without having to amend the RFP and provide all offerors the opportunity to compete on that alternate, *Litton Sys., Inc. v. Dep't of Transp.*, GSBCA 12911-P, 94-3 BCA ¶ 27,263. However, Alternate II "reserves the right" of the government to amend the RFP if the agency chooses to obtain competition on the alternate requirements.

FAR 15.209 also provides guidance on a number of additional provisions that are commonly used in RFPs. FAR 15.209(b) requires the use of the FAR 52.215-2, Audit and Records—Negotiation provision or one of its alternate provisions in all negotiated procurements except for simplified acquisitions, acquisition of utility services at established rates or acquisition of commercial items. FAR 15.209(e) requires the use of the FAR 52.215-5, Facsimile Proposals provision in all RFPs permitting the use of such proposals. FAR 15.209(f) requires use of the FAR 52.215-6, Place of Performance provision in all RFPs where the place of performance is not specified by the government. FAR 15.209(h) requires the use of the FAR 52.215-8, Order of Precedence—Uniform Contract Format provision in all RFPs using the uniform contract format.

[2] Specific Instructions—Section L

These instructions are the key to obtaining quality proposals. In the past, the failure to give clear and well-organized guidance in Section L has been one of the most common defects in the competitive negotiation process. FAR 15.204-5(b) contains only the following brief discussion of this area, stating:

> Insert in this section solicitation provisions and other information and instructions not required elsewhere to guide offerors or respondents in preparing proposals or responses to requests for information. Prospective offerors or respondents may be instructed to submit proposals or information in a specific format or severable parts to facilitate evaluation. The instructions may specify further organization of proposal or response parts, such as—
>
> (1) Administrative;
> (2) Management;
> (3) Technical;
> (4) Past performance; and
> (5) Certified cost or pricing data (see Table 15-2 of 15.408) or data other than certified cost or pricing data.

Instructions for the submission of certified cost or pricing data should not call for certification at the time of submission of the data. Certification is only required when the parties have reached agreement on the price, FAR 15.406-2.

This generalized coverage gives little advice to contracting officers as to the purpose of these specific instructions and the nature of the information which is to be furnished by offerors. It also does not deal with identification of the strategy which the agency has decided to use.

[a] Procurement Strategy

Either Section M or the instructions in Section L should identify the procurement strategy that will be used in making the award. This entails the inclusion of a clear statement of whether the agency is using the tradeoff process, the lowest price, technically acceptable proposal process, some combination of these two, or any other strategy that the agency has selected. See § 6.02, above.

The instructions should also describe the type of contract that is to be used and the objectives that the agency has in the procurement. It is also helpful to include a description of the time that the agency intends to take to evaluate proposals and the intended date of award of the contract. Guidance of this nature is very beneficial to offerors in assisting them to allocate resources to the competition.

It is also very helpful to offerors if the instructions include specific information on the evaluation process that will be followed. In particular, evaluation standards should be disclosed. See *Omniplex World Servs. Corp.*, Comp. Gen. Dec. B-290996.2, 2003 CPD ¶ 7; *RJO Enters., Inc.*, Comp. Gen. Dec. B-260126.2, 95-2 CPD ¶ 93; and *Sarasota Measurements & Controls, Inc.*, Comp. Gen. Dec. B-252406, 93-1 CPD ¶ 494, requiring the inclusion of evaluation standards in RFPs when they constituted government requirements. While GAO has not required the disclosure of evaluation standards that merely give guidance to evaluators in assessing the relative value of factors or subfactors, *A-P-T Research, Inc.*, Comp. Gen. Dec. B-414825, 2017 CPD ¶ 337 (past performance relevance rating system); *Open Sys. Science of Virginia, Inc.*, Comp. Gen. Dec. B-410572, 2015 CPD ¶ 37 (use of point scoring system); *Computer Assocs. Int'l, Inc.*, Comp. Gen. Dec. B-292077.3, 2004 CPD ¶ 163 (revised point rating system), the inclusion of such standards in the RFP is good practice because it provides fuller information on the agency's acquisition strategy.

[b] Required Submissions

In the past, offerors have been requested to submit much information pertaining to their capability to perform in detailed technical and management "proposals." As discussed above, much of this type of information comes under the category of "capability factors" to be used solely for evaluation purposes as opposed to "offer factors" to be incorporated into the contract. The RFP should make a clear distinction between these matters and should specify what information is to be furnished. "Technical proposals" should only be required where offerors are permitted to offer differing supplies or services than those specified in the RFP or where the government is requesting offerors to provide solutions to its needs.

Offerors should be provided detailed guidance on the information to be furnished for evaluation purposes. A well written RFP will contain a precise correlation between the information to be furnished and the evaluation factors and subfactors identified in Section M. Where different evaluation factors are to be evaluated by different personnel, the agency may wish to have the relevant information packaged in separate sections of the proposals.

Data on past performance and experience will have to be obtained from each offeror in most procurements. This will normally entail obtaining information on a specified number of recent contracts where the offeror has performed similar types of work. Generally, agencies request the names of key people that can be called as references and data as to the work done on the contract and problems encountered in its performance. FAR 15.305(a)(2)(ii) contains guidance on obtaining information on past performance. It requires RFPs to "authorize offerors to provide information on problems encountered on the identified contracts and the offeror's corrective actions." This is most readily done by requiring that each offeror submit a short self-assessment of its performance on each of the referenced contracts.

The RFP should also specifically identify the cost or pricing information needed by the contracting officer to evaluate the cost/price proposal of the offeror. Since there are no standard solicitation provisions in the FAR for requesting such information, the contracting officer must draft a provision for each procurement detailing the information required. See Chapter 13 for a discussion of the types of information that should be requested.

[c] Oral Presentations

In recent years agencies have used oral presentations in lieu of written proposals to assess the relative capability of the offerors to perform the work required by the prospective contract. Such presentations have proved to be a superior means of assessing capability because they permit the agency to communicate directly with the offeror's personnel that will perform the work rather than reading technical proposals that may have been written by professional proposal writers. FAR 15.102 provides the following guidance on the use of oral presentations:

> (a) Oral presentations by offerors as requested by the Government may substitute for, or augment, written information. Use of oral presentations as a substitute for portions of a proposal can be effective in streamlining the source selection process. Oral presentations may occur at any time in the acquisition process and are subject to the same restrictions as written information, regarding timing (see 15.208) and content (see 15.306). Oral presentations provide

an opportunity for dialogue among the parties. Pre-recorded videotaped presentations that lack real-time interactive dialogue are not considered oral presentations for the purposes of this section, although they may be included in offeror submissions, when appropriate.

(b) The solicitation may require each offeror to submit part of its proposal through oral presentations. However, certifications, representations, and a signed offer sheet (including any exceptions to the Government's terms and conditions) shall be submitted in writing.

Although FAR 15.102(b) provides that offerors may be required to submit "part of its proposal" through oral presentations, FAR 15.102(f) precludes incorporation of oral statements in the contract by reference and provides that any information from an oral presentation that is to be incorporated in the contract must be put in writing.

FAR 15.102(c) indicates that such presentations are suitable for obtaining information, as follows:

> Information pertaining to areas such as an offeror's capability, past performance, work plans or approaches, staffing resources, transition plans, or sample tasks (or other types of tests) may be suitable for oral presentations. In deciding what information to obtain through an oral presentation, consider the following:
>
> (1) The Government's ability to adequately evaluate the information;
>
> (2) The need to incorporate any information into the resultant contract;
>
> (3) The impact on the efficiency of the acquisition; and
>
> (4) The impact (including cost) on small businesses. In considering the costs of oral presentations, contracting officers should also consider alternatives to on-site oral presentations (e.g., teleconferencing, video teleconferencing).

FAR 15.102(d) requires that RFPs provide offerors with sufficient information to understand what is sought in the oral presentation. It suggests a description of the following issues:

> (1) The types of information to be presented orally and the associated evaluation factors that will be used;
>
> (2) The qualifications for personnel that will be required to provide the oral presentation(s);
>
> (3) The requirements for, and any limitations and/or prohibitions on, the use of written material or other media to supplement the oral presentations;
>
> (4) The location, date, and time for the oral presentations;
>
> (5) The restrictions governing the time permitted for each oral presentation; and

(6) The scope and content of exchanges that may occur between the Government's participants and the offeror's representatives as part of the oral presentations, including whether or not discussions (see 15.306(d)) will be permitted during oral presentations.

There are several important issues that should be addressed in the RFP. First, it should state that the presentation is intended to address the key issues that are expected to arise during performance of the contract rather than the general qualifications of the offeror. These key issues can be specifically identified in the RFP or chosen by each offeror, at the discretion of the agency. The RFP should also state that the offeror's personnel attending the oral presentation should be the people that will be managing the performance of the key issue areas—whether they be employees of the offeror or of a prospective subcontractor. The RFP should then state the time allocated to an initial presentation by the offeror and the time allocated to dialog between the parties—in the form of a question-and-answer session, an interview, or the solution of a sample task. As a general proposition, it is good practice to devote more time to this dialog than to the initial presentation. It is implicit that when the RFP calls for an oral presentation, the subjects covered will be part of the evaluation process, *Brooks Range Contract Servs., Inc.*, Comp. Gen. Dec. B-401231, 2009 CPD ¶ 129.

The FAR makes it clear that agency officials may ask questions and seek further detail during the oral presentation, and this is consistent with prior decisions, *NAHB Research Found., Inc.*, Comp. Gen. Dec. B-219344, 85-2 CPD ¶ 248 (aggressive questioning permissible). However, both the Court of Federal Claims and GAO have rejected protests that the agency did not use the oral presentation to obtain full information on the capability of an offeror. See *Bean Stuyvesant, L.L.C. v. United States*, 48 Fed. Cl. 303 (2000) (offeror properly downgraded for not discussing an issue—with no agency effort to raise the issue in the dialog); *Oceaneering Int'l, Inc.*, Comp. Gen. Dec. B-287325, 2001 CPD ¶ 95 (agency didn't raise omitted issue with offeror). Agencies that conduct oral presentations in this manner lose the full benefit of the technique. While this is legally acceptable, it is not good practice to fail to explore areas where the offeror has omitted information that is necessary to determine its full capability to perform the work.

Agencies may adopt reasonable rules governing the nature of the presentations, including limitations on the length and nature of the presentations, *American Sys. Corp.*, 68 Comp. Gen. 475 (B-234449), 89-1 CPD ¶ 537. They may also require that offerors meet mandatory requirements in an RFP before being eligible to make an oral presentation, *Inte-Great Corp.*, Comp. Gen. Dec. B-272780, 96-2 CPD ¶ 159.

Agencies have specified two procedural requirements for oral presentations that have not enhanced the process. The first is the requirement that slides to be used must be submitted with the original proposal. While this requirement has been strictly enforced, *KSEND v. United States*, 69 Fed. Cl. 103 (2005), it is difficult to perceive how it reduces any advantage that might accrue to offerors that make their presentation later than other offerors. The second is the requirement restricting the nature of the media used in the presentation, such as requiring only black and white slides. Such a requirement merely precludes the use of media that is most effective in demonstrating the offeror's ability to deal with a potential area of difficulty—such as a color slide of a pie chart. Requirements of these types should not be called for in the RFP.

Agencies may either preclude or permit discussions during the oral presentation, FAR 15.102(d)(6). However, if discussions occur, the agency must comply with the rules governing negotiations with all offerors in the competitive range, FAR 15.102(g). In *Sierra Military Health Servs., Inc.*, Comp. Gen. Dec. B-292780, 2004 CPD ¶ 55, GAO stated the rule as follows:

> The FAR generally anticipates "dialogue among the parties" in the course of an oral presentation, FAR § 15.102(a), and we see nothing improper in agency personnel expressing their view about vendors' quotations or proposals, in addition to listening to the vendors' presentations, during those sessions. Once the agency personnel begin speaking, rather than merely listening, in those sessions, however, that dialogue may constitute discussions. As we have long held, the acid test for deciding whether an agency has engaged in discussions is whether the agency has provided an opportunity for quotations or proposals to be revised or modified. See, e.g., *TDS, Inc.*, B-292674, Nov. 12, 2003, 2003 CPD ¶ 204 at 6; *Priority One Servs., Inc.*, B-288836, B-288836.2, Dec. 17, 2001, 2002 CPD ¶ 79 at 5. Accordingly, where agency personnel comment on, or raise substantive questions or concerns about, vendors' quotations or proposals in the course of an oral presentation, and either simultaneously or subsequently afford the vendors an opportunity to make revisions in light of the agency personnel's comments and concerns, discussions have occurred. *TDS, Inc., supra*, at 6; see FAR § 15.102(g).

Compare *Development Alternatives, Inc.*, Comp. Gen. Dec. B-279920, 98-2 CPD ¶ 54, holding that requesting additional details concerning information in a proposal during an oral presentation did not constitute discussions, with *Global Analytic Info. Tech. Servs., Inc.*, Comp. Gen. Dec. B-298840.2, 2007 CPD ¶ 57, holding that allowing an offeror to submit revised pricing *after* an oral presentation was a discussion. See also *Sapient Gov't Servs., Inc.*, Comp. Gen. Dec. B-412163.2, 2016 CPD ¶ 11, finding no discussion in an oral presentation because the exchange of information did not alter anything in the prior written proposal and the winning contractor was not allowed to revise anything said during the oral presentation.

[3] Evaluation Factors and Subfactors—Section M

The evaluation factors and subfactors to be used must be identified in Section M. FAR 15.204-5(c) provides minimal guidance, merely directing that the agency:

> Identify all significant factors and any significant subfactors that will be considered in awarding the contract and their relative importance (see 15.304(d)).

This provision also requires that the contracting officer insert one of the statements of relative importance in FAR 15.304(e) in the RFP (stating that non-price factors are "significantly more important," "approximately equal to," or "significantly less important" than the price factors). However, GAO has ruled that this requirement was met when the RFP contained an accurate statement that the non-price factor was "more important" than price, rather than "significantly more important," *Braswell Servs., Grp.*, Comp. Gen. Dec. B-276694, 97-2 CPD ¶ 18. As discussed in Section II., the relative importance of the non-price evaluation factors and subfactors should also be stated in this section.

[D] Method of Submission of Offers and Information

Traditionally, the offer and information were submitted together in paper media in a sealed envelope. However, there are a growing number of procurements where facsimile or electronic submission is permitted or required. In addition, part of or all the required information may be submitted in an oral presentation discussed above.

[1] Paper Media

Paragraph (c) of the Instructions to Offerors—Competitive Acquisition solicitation provision in FAR 52.215-1(c) provides guidance on the basic procedure to be followed in submitting offers and information:

> (1) Unless other methods (e.g., electronic commerce or facsimile) are permitted in the solicitation, proposals and modifications to proposals shall be submitted in paper media in sealed envelopes or packages (i) addressed to the office specified in the solicitation, and (ii) showing the time and date specified for receipt, the solicitation number, and the name and address of the offeror. Offerors using commercial carriers should ensure that the proposal is marked on the outermost wrapper with the information in paragraphs (c)(1)(i) and (c)(1)(ii) of this provision.
>
> (2) The first page of the proposal must show—
>
> (i) The solicitation number;

(ii) The name, address, and telephone and facsimile numbers of the offeror (and electronic address if available);

(iii) A statement specifying the extent of agreement with all terms, conditions, and provisions included in the solicitation and agreement to furnish any or all items upon which prices are offered at the price set opposite each item;

(iv) Names, titles, and telephone and facsimile numbers (and electronic addresses if available) of persons authorized to negotiate on the offeror's behalf with the Government in connection with this solicitation; and

(v) Name, title, and signature of person authorized to sign the proposal. Proposals signed by an agent shall be accompanied by evidence of that agent's authority, unless that evidence has been previously furnished to the issuing office.

[2] Facsimile or Electronic Submission

FAR 4.502(a) encourages the use of electronic commerce "whenever practicable or cost-effective." FAR 15.203(c) provides that when electronic commerce is an authorized means of submission, the RFP must "specify the electronic commerce method(s) that offerors may use (see Subpart (d))." There is no standard FAR solicitation provision specifying the method to be used—with the result that agencies are permitted to adopt different methods. FAR 4.502(b) contains general guidance on the use of electronic commerce.

FAR 15.203(d) provides that proposals may be submitted by facsimile, depending on the following considerations:

(i) Anticipated proposal size and volume;
(ii) Urgency of the requirement;
(iii) Availability and suitability of electronic commerce methods; and
(iv) Adequacy of administrative procedures and controls for receiving, identifying, recording, and safeguarding facsimile proposals, and ensuring their timely delivery to the designated proposal delivery location.

FAR 15.209(e) requires the use of the FAR 52.215-5 Facsimile Proposals provision in an RFP when submission by facsimile is authorized. The instructions for handling unreadable portions of facsimile or electronic submissions contained in this provision are set forth in FAR 15.207(c).

Offerors assume the risk of nonreceipt of their facsimile transmissions, *S.W. Elecs. & Mfg. Corp.*, Comp. Gen. Dec. B-249308, 92-2 CPD ¶ 320; *Microscope Co.*, Comp. Gen. Dec. B-257015, 94-2 CPD ¶ 157; *International Garment Processors*, Comp. Gen. Dec. B-299674, 2007 CPD ¶ 130. Offerors also assume the risk of nonreceipt of electronic transmissions, *Blue Glacier Mgm't Grp., Inc.*, Comp. Gen. Dec. B-412897, 2016 CPD ¶ 177 (e-mail blocked when attachments triggered the agency anti-phishing system); *Advanced Decisions Vectors, Inc.*,

Comp. Gen. Dec. B-412307, 2016 CPD ¶ 18 (e-mail blocked by agency spam system); *Federal Acquisition Servs. Team, LLC,* Comp. Gen. Dec. B-410466, 2015 CPD ¶ 20 (e-mail blocked for being too long); *Joint Venture Penauillie Italia S.p.A.; Cofathec S.p.A.; SEB.CO S.a.s.; CO.PEL.S.a.s.,* Comp. Gen. Dec. B-298865, 2007 CPD ¶ 7 (e-mail received by agency lacked required data); *Sea Box, Inc.,* Comp. Gen. Dec. B-291056, 2002 CPD ¶ 181 (e-mail proposal late when received at agency initial point of entry on time but not received by contracting office until after required time). Protests have been granted if non-receipt is due to a systemic failure of the agency's electronic commerce system, *S.D.M. Supply, Inc.,* Comp. Gen. Dec. B-271492, 96-1 CPD ¶ 288.

[E] Amendment and Cancellation of the RFP

When needs or circumstances change or when adding new information or correcting defects is necessary, the agency may be required to amend or cancel the RFP. Cancellations are permitted when the government no longer has a need for the work or lacks funds. However, where the government still intends to proceed with the procurement, the RFP should be amended. See FAR 15.206(a), which states:

> When, either before or after receipt of proposals, the Government changes its requirements or terms and conditions, the contracting officer shall amend the solicitation.

Amendments can either require or permit cancellation and resolicitation or allow the procurement to proceed depends upon the nature and timing of the changes. An amendment without cancellation has the advantage of permitting the government to continue on with the procurement. Thus, it may be more attractive to procurement officials since it saves both time and administrative effort. Conversely, cancellation and resolicitation may expand the field of competition and result in a more advantageous deal for the government.

[1] Cancellation and Resolicitation

The only FAR provision dealing with cancellation and resolicitation is FAR 15.206(e), stating:

> If, in the judgment of the contracting officer, based on market research or otherwise, an amendment proposed for issuance after offers have been received is so substantial as to exceed what prospective offerors reasonably could have anticipated, so that additional sources likely would have submitted offers had the substance of the amendment been known to them, the contracting officer shall cancel the original solicitation and issue a new one, regardless of the stage of the acquisition.

The pre-FAR 15 Rewrite version of this regulation had an additional provision which directed that the new solicitation be furnished to all firms originally solicited and any added to the original mailing list. Under current procedures, a new solicitation on the government-wide point of entry would be expected to alert all potential competitors to the procurement, but it would also seem appropriate for the agency to explicitly resolicit those companies that had responded to the original solicitation.

[a] Required Cancellation

Cancellation of an RFP after offerors have expended the effort to prepare proposals is not a desirable course of action. In *Loral Fairchild Corp.*, Comp. Gen. Dec. B-242957.2, 91-2 CPD ¶ 218, GAO stated that the changes would have to "significantly alter the purpose or nature of the contract" or change the "field of competition" in order to require a cancellation. See *Denwood Props. Corp.*, Comp. Gen. Dec. B-251347.2, 93-1 CPD ¶ 380, where the changes involved a reduction in the amount of space to be leased and the agency's desire to open the competition to consider build-to-suit facilities. GAO stated that "it would not have been proper" to simply amend the specifications because the changes were substantial and would likely increase the field of competition.

GAO has stated that generally cancellation is appropriate where changes to the solicitation are expected to result in increased competition or lower prices. See *Blue Rock Structures, Inc.*, Comp. Gen. Dec. B-400811, 2009 CPD ¶ 26 (rewriting specifications to obtain better prices through increased competition); *North Shore Medical Labs, Inc.*, Comp. Gen. Dec. B-311070, 2008 CPD ¶ 144 (original RFP did not promote effective competition); *SEI Grp., Inc.*, Comp. Gen. Dec. B-299108, 2007 CPD ¶ 35 (agency decided to revise procurement strategy to reduce costs); *Glen/Mar Constr., Inc.*, Comp. Gen. Dec. B-298355, 2006 CPD ¶ 117 (proposed prices were much higher than agency budget); *Goode Constr., Inc.*, Comp. Gen. Dec. B-288655.4, 2002 CPD ¶ 25 (adopting a different construction schedule); *Noelke GmbH*, Comp. Gen. Dec. B-278324.2, 98-1 CPD ¶ 46 (updating requirements and improving evaluation scheme to obtain increased competition); and *Robertson Leasing Corp.*, Comp. Gen. Dec. B-275152, 97-1 CPD ¶ 49 (relaxing the specifications). Compare *Pro-Fab*, Comp. Gen. Dec. B-243607, 91-2 CPD ¶ 128, refusing to allow the contracting officer to cancel the solicitation because there was no reason to believe that any added competition would result from a resolicitation, nor was there any real prospect for additional cost savings.

Whether the field of competition would be increased by competition depends upon the facts and circumstances of each individual case. Thus, a number of cases have held that cancellation and resolicitation was not required even though significant changes were made. For example, in *Claude E. Atkins Enters., Inc*, Comp. Gen. Dec. B-241047, 91-1 CPD ¶ 42, a change from a 690-day, eight-phase construction schedule to one of 630 days with two phases was found not to be an appreciable change. See also *Defense Grp., Inc.*, Comp. Gen. Dec. B-253795, 94-1 CPD ¶ 196, where a 12.3% increase in overall contract effort was not considered a substantial change to the basic nature of the contemplated contract. For other cases finding that cancellation of a solicitation was not required because the change was not substantial, see *Government Contract Servs. Co.*, Comp. Gen. Dec. B-294367, 2004 CPD ¶ 215 (amendment clarifying that alternate methods of performance were acceptable); *New Jersey & H St. Ltd. P'ship*, Comp. Gen. Dec. B-288026, 2001 CPD ¶ 125 (changing 15 year lease term to 14 years); *Cape Fear Paging Co.*, Comp. Gen. Dec. B-252160.2, 93-1 CPD ¶ 347 (elimination of separate line item and combining prices into remaining item); and *SMS Data Prods. Grp v. Austin*, 940 F.2d 1514 (Fed. Cir. 1991) (changing the solicitation by advancing the commercial availability date of laptop computers).

[b] Discretionary Cancellation and Resolicitation

Although cancellation and resolicitation after the receipt of proposals subjects the competitors that responded to the solicitation to added cost and effort, because of the possibility of increased competition procurement officials have considerable discretion in making this decision. In this regard, the FAR 14.404-1(a) "compelling reason" basis for cancellation of an IFB after bid opening is not applicable. In *CFM Equip. Co.*, Comp. Gen. Dec. B-251344, 93-1 CPD ¶ 280, GAO held that an agency needs only a "reasonable basis" to cancel an RFP. In discussing the difference between the standards for canceling an RFP or IFB, GAO stated:

> Under FAR 15.608 (b)(4), a procuring agency may reject all proposals received in response to an RFP if cancellation is clearly in the government's interest. Thus, as a general rule, in a negotiated procurement the contracting agency need only demonstrate a reasonable basis to cancel a solicitation after receipt of proposals, as opposed to the "cogent and compelling" reason required to cancel an IFB where sealed bids have been opened. *Xactex Corp.*, B-241739, May 5, 1992, 92-1 CPD ¶ 423. The standards differ because in procurements using sealed bids, competitive positions are exposed as a result of the public opening of bids, while in negotiated procurements there is no public opening. *ACR Elecs., Inc.*, B-232130.2; B-232130.3, Dec. 9, 1988, 88-2 CPD ¶ 577. The question presented by this protest is whether the agency's second thoughts about its procurement strategy have a reasonable basis.

GAO has held that cancellation with the intent to resolicit is also proper if the agency finds that it had not done a good job in stating its requirements. See *Applied Res, Inc.*, Comp. Gen. Dec. B-400144.7, 2009 CPD ¶ 161 (prolonged protests led to reassessment of requirements); *Optimum Servs., Inc.*, Comp. Gen. Dec. B-401051, 2009 CPD ¶ 85 (program funding reduced after protest of original procurement); *Knight's Armament Co.*, Comp. Gen. Dec. B-299469, 2007 CPD ¶ 85 (offered products did not meet agency needs requiring revision of specifications); *ELEIT Tech., Inc.*, Comp. Gen. Dec. B-294193.2, 2004 CPD ¶ 203 (agency decided to bundle work into larger package); *Surgi-Textile*, Comp. Gen. Dec. B-289370, 2002 CPD ¶ 38 (specifications found to be inadequate); *Robertson Leasing Corp.*, Comp. Gen. Dec. B-275152, 97-1 CPD ¶ 49 (cancellation to recompete under relaxed specifications in order to increase competition and reduce costs to the government); *Nidek, Inc.*, Comp. Gen. Dec. B-272255, 96-2 CPD ¶ 112 (medical staff needed time to develop an accurate statement of its needs so that all firms could submit an offer); *Chant Eng'g Co.*, Comp. Gen. Dec. B-270149.2, 96-1 CPD ¶ 96 (government needs were overstated and the agency determined that enhanced competition would result from a relaxation of the requirements); and *JRW Mgmt. Co.*, Comp. Gen. Dec. B-260396.2, 95-1 CPD ¶ 276 (cancellation because agency received only one response and recognized that it could meet its needs with an alternate approach that presented an opportunity for increased competition).

Cancellation and resolicitation is also appropriate where necessary to ensure fair competition, *IT Corp.*, Comp. Gen. Dec. B-289517.3, 2002 CPD ¶ 123. In an unusual situation, cancellation was appropriate in order to avoid protests based on a disagreement between GAO and the Executive Branch over the priority that should be given the HUBZone contractors, *All Seasons Apparel, Inc.*, Comp. Gen. Dec. B-401805, 2009 CPD ¶ 221. See also *Kenco Assocs., Inc.*, Comp. Gen. Dec. B-297503, 2006 CPD ¶ 24, where cancellation was found a proper response to congressional criticism of the procurement.

Cancellation and resolicitation may also be proper if an agency finds a better procurement strategy. See *Starlight Corp.*, Comp. Gen. Dec. B-297904.2, 2006 CPD ¶ 65 (RFP needed to be rewritten to clarify experience requirement); *Logistics Solutions Grp., Inc.*, Comp. Gen. Dec. B-294604.7, 2005 CPD ¶ 141 (RFP no longer reflected agency needs); *VSE Corp.*, Comp. Gen. Dec. B-290452.2, 2005 CPD ¶ 111 (almost five years had passed since original proposals); *Best Foam Fabricators, Inc.*, Comp. Gen. Dec. B-259905.3, 95-1 CPD ¶ 275 (cancellation to obtain the items from the organization designated by the Committee for Purchase from the Blind and Other Severely Handicapped rather than another offeror under the solicitation); *General Projection Sys.*, 70 Comp. Gen. 345 (B-241418.2), 91-1 CPD ¶ 308 (cancellation because item was solicited in the RFP on a "brand name" rather than on a "brand name or equal" basis and an acceptable equal item was proposed). However, cancellation was found unreasonable when the agency had no cogent explanation of why it exercised a FAR 52.217-8 option after receiving a successful offer, *Walker Dev. & Trading Grp., Inc.*, Comp. Gen. Dec. B-413924, 2017 CPD ¶ 21, and when the RFP had called for a price-only competition and the agency intended to reopen the competition on a sealed bidding basis, *Rand & Jones Enters. Co.*, Comp. Gen. Dec. B-296483, 2005 CPD ¶ 142.

Compared to GAO, some Court of Federal Claims judges have imposed greater scrutiny to an agency's authority and decision to cancel a solicitation. Compare *Seventh Dimension, LLC v. United States*, 160 Fed. Cl. 1 (2022), with *Madison Servs., Inc. v. United States*, 92 Fed. Cl. 120 (2010).

[2] Amendment Without Cancellation

Even if the agency decides not to cancel the RFP, an amendment is required if changes would have a significant impact on competition, See *CGI Fed., Inc.*, Comp. Gen. Dec. B-410330.2, 2014 CPD ¶ 366 (significant change in ordering strategy); *Global Computer Enters., Inc.*, Comp. Gen. Dec. B-404597, 2011 CPD ¶ 69 (materially different schedule for issuance of task orders); *Symetrics Indus., Inc.*, Comp. Gen. D'c. B-274246.3, 97-2 CPD ¶ 59 (agency's estimate for the amount of work to be ordered under an ID/IQ contract changed significantly). This requirement is enforced even after the receipt of final proposal revisions, *Northrop Grumman Info. Tech., Inc.*, Comp. Gen. Dec. B-295526, 2005 CPD ¶ 45 (amendment required when agency requirements changed the day before award to the selected source); *Digital Techs., Inc.*, Comp. Gen. Dec. B-291657.3, 2004 CPD ¶ 235 (amendment proper when agency added quantities prior to award). Protesters must show that they are prejudiced by failure to amend the RFP. *In Management Sys. Designers, Inc.*, Comp. Gen. Dec. B-244383.8, 92-1 CPD ¶ 496, prejudice was found where an offeror showed that it might have revised its proposal. *Compare NV Servs.*, Comp. Gen. Dec. B-284119.2, 2000 CPD ¶ 64, where no prejudice was found when the agency added somewhat less than ten percent more work after award but the protester did not prove that its costs would have materially changed.

For decisions discussing the relationship between an agency's obligation to amend the solicitation and the protester's obligation to demonstrate prejudice, see *Blue Origin Fed'n, LLC v. United States*, 157 Fed. Cl. 74 (2021); *Medline Indus., Inc. v. United States*, 155 Fed. Cl. 522 (2021); *Blue Origin Fed'n, LLC, Dynetics, Inc.*, Comp. Gen. Dec. B-419783, 2021 CPD ¶ 265.

FAR 15.206(d) requires an amendment to take advantage of an offer that deviates from the RFP as follows:

> If a proposal of interest to the Government involves a departure from the stated requirements, the contracting officer shall amend the solicitation, provided this can be done without revealing to the other offerors the alternate solution proposed or any other information that is entitled to protection (see 15.207(b) and 15.306(e)).

See *Beta Analytics Int'l, Inc. v. United States*, 44 Fed. Cl. 131 (1999) (reduced labor hours from mandatory hours in RFP); *Loral Terracom*, 66 Comp. Gen. 272 (B-224908), 87-1 CPD ¶ 182 (different technical approach suggested by an offeror). Amendments are not required if a claimed deviation is from a provision that is not mandatory or material, *Howard Cooper Corp. v. United States*, 763 F. Supp. 829 (E.D. Va. 1991). See *AEL Defense Corp.*, Comp. Gen. Dec. B-251376, 93-1 CPD ¶ 256, where GAO denied a protest that award had been made to an offeror that did not comply with a design requirement, stating that the design was not mandatory under the hierarchy established in the specification. Similarly, a contracting officer was not required to issue an amendment to an RFP after changing specified computer systems where the government provided all equipment necessary for performance of the contract and the change brought about no cost savings to offerors, *Optimum Says., Inc.*, Comp. Gen. Dec. B-194984, 80-2 CPD ¶ 32. See also *WaveLink, Inc. v. United States*, 154 Fed. Cl. 245 (2022).

An amendment is also called for where the relative importance of the evaluation factors is altered, *Hyperbaric Techs., Inc.*, Comp. Gen. Dec. B-293047.2, 2004 CPD ¶ 87 (adding the relative importance of factors when original RFP contained no such guidance); *Unisys Corp.*, 67 Comp. Gen. 512 (B-230019.2), 88-2 CPD ¶ 35 (clarifying the importance of cost), the standards for evaluating past performance have changed, *Cooperativa Muratori Riuniti*, Comp. Gen. Dec. B-294980.5, 2005 CPD ¶ 144, or the overall evaluation scheme is changed, *Ripple Effect Comms., Inc.*, Comp. Gen. Dec. B-413722.2, 2017 CPD ¶ 27 (deleting the requirement for a price realism analysis); *CGI Federal Inc.*, Comp. Gen. Dec. B-410330.2, 2014 CPD ¶ 388 (greatly reducing the projected number of units per delivery order); *Omniplex World Servs. Corp.*, Comp. Gen. Dec. B-290996.2, 2003 CPD ¶ 7 (adding an experience requirement); *Galler Assocs., Inc.*, Comp. Gen. Dec. B-210204, 83-1 CPD ¶ 515 (changing from low cost acceptable offer scheme to best value scheme). See also *Lockheed Martin Sys. Integration-Owego*, Comp. Gen. Dec. B-299145.5, 2007 CPD ¶ 155, granting a protest because the agency did not allow the offerors to submit completely new proposals when the amendment made a major change in how support costs would be evaluation.

[a] Issuance of Amendments

FAR 15.210(b) provides that Standard Form 30, Amendment of Solicitation/Modification of Contract or Optional Form 309, Amendment of Solicitation "may be used to amend solicitations." Prior to the FAR 15 Rewrite, the use of Standard Form 30 was mandatory. Whether issued on these forms or otherwise in writing or electronically, the amendment must provide offerors sufficient information to determine the changed requirements. FAR 15.206(g) states that, "At a minimum, the following information should be included in each amendment":

> (1) Name and address of issuing activity.
> (2) Solicitation number and date.
> (3) Amendment number and date.

(4) Number of pages.
(5) Description of the change being made.
(6) Government point of contact and phone number (and electronic or facsimile address, if appropriate).
(7) Revision to solicitation closing date, if applicable.

As is the case of solicitations, amendments must normally be sent on the government-wide point of entry website, FAR 5.102, *Latvian Connection, LL*, Comp. Gen. Dec. B-411489, 2015 CPD ¶ 251. However, FAR 15.206(f) permits oral notice of the amendment when "time is of the essence." It states that, in such a case, "The contracting officer shall document the contract file and formalize the notice with an amendment." The importance of formalizing the notice in writing is illustrated in cases where the protester contends that it did not receive the notice that the agency claimed had been issued orally. In *Lockheed, IMS*, Comp. Gen. Dec. B-248686, 92-2 CPD ¶ 180, a protest was successful when the offeror denied that it received oral notice of the amendment, and the government did not follow up with an RFP amendment or other written confirmation. See also *CoMont, Inc.*, 65 Comp. Gen. 66 (B-219730), 85-2 CPD ¶ 555 (stressing that amendments must be made in writing); and *I.E. Levick & Assocs.*, Comp. Gen. Dec. B-214648, 84-2 CPD ¶ 695 (failure to issue a written amendment is a procedural defect whenever an offeror effectively denies having been advised orally). However, oral amendments were given full effect in *AVL Books.Com, Inc.*, Comp. Gen. Dec. B-295780, 2005 CPD ¶ 46 (other competitors understood the addition of an evaluation factor); *Family Stress Clinics of Am.*, Comp. Gen. Dec. B-270993, 96-1 CPD ¶ 223 (extending the closing date for submission of proposals indefinitely because of shutdown of the contracting agency).

In *Labat-Anderson Inc.*, 71 Comp. Gen. 252 (B-246071), 92-1 CPD ¶ 193, GAO suggested that notification of changes might be accomplished by either raising the issue in discussions with all offerors within the competitive range or issuing an amendment to the RFP. It would appear that the discussion method would only be appropriate for relatively simple changes.

[b] Actual Notice or No Prejudice

The failure to issue an amendment has been excused where the protesting offeror had actual notice of the change. See *General Offshore Corp.*, Comp. Gen. Dec. B-249601, 92-2 CPD ¶ 391, holding that the protester had received adequate notice of changed requirements through negotiations; and *Collins & Aikman Corp.*, Comp. Gen. Dec. B-247961, 92-2 CPD ¶ 41, stating in a footnote that an amendment was not required since the protester had knowledge of the change.

Failure to amend an RFP has also been excused where the protester was unable to demonstrate that it was prejudiced by the lack of notice. In *Saratoga Dev. Corp. v. United States*, 777 F. Supp. 29 (D.D.C. 1991), the court held that the test for prejudice is whether the protester would have altered its proposal to its competitive advantage, and further that the protester has the burden of showing how it would have responded to notice of the change. No prejudice was found in *Canberra Indus.*, Comp. Gen. Dec. B-271016, 96-1 CPD ¶ 269 (protester did not present any evidence that it would have altered its proposal had it known of relaxed specifications); *Environmental Tectonics Corp.*, Comp. Gen. Dec. B-209423, 83-1 CPD ¶ 81 (protester admitted that it could not have bettered its own proposed delivery time). GAO will not overturn an award in which the agency has changed the evaluation criteria without notifying the offerors if the losers are not prejudiced by the change, *Akal Security, Inc.*, Comp. Gen. Dec. B-261996, 95-2 CPD ¶ 216; *Delta Dental Plan*, Comp. Gen. Dec. B-260461, 95-1 CPD ¶ 293.

[c] Firms to Be Notified

FAR 15.206 specifies that amendments must be furnished as follows:

> (b) Amendments issued before the established time and date for receipt of proposals shall be issued to all parties receiving the solicitation.
>
> (c) Amendments issued after the established time and date for receipt of proposals shall be issued to all offerors that have not been eliminated from the competition.

Once a competitive range has been established, agencies are not required to issue amendments to offerors outside the competitive range so long as the amendment is not directly related to the reason for the excluded offeror's rejection, *Amperif Corp.*, Comp. Gen. Dec. B-211992, 84-1 CPD ¶ 409. This is the case even where the change is significant, *Labat-Anderson Inc.*, Comp. Gen. Dec. B-246071, 92-1 CPD ¶ 193. For instance, a company dropped from the competitive range was not required to be notified that the agency had negotiated a fixed-price contract in lieu of a cost-type contract, *Westinghouse Elec. Corp.*, Comp. Gen. Dec. B-197768, 80-1 CPD ¶ 378. See also *Loral Terracom, Marconi Italiana*, Comp. Gen. Dec. B-224908, 87-1 CPD ¶ 182, where an amendment recognizing alternative methods of satisfying the agency's requirements was properly limited to offerors within the competitive range. Similarly, an amendment need not be sent to an offeror that has been eliminated during the first phase of a two-phase procurement, *Golden Mfg. Co. v. United States*, 107 Fed. Cl. 264 (2012). Compare *AirTrak Travel*, Comp. Gen. Dec. B-292101, 2003 CPD ¶ 117 (amendment significantly altering the risks imposed on the contractor required to be sent to all competitors); *Information Ventures, Inc.*, Comp. Gen. Dec. B-232094, 88-2 CPD ¶ 443 (amendment relaxing specifications required to be sent to an excluded offeror because it directly related to the reasons for exclusion). See also *Hamilton Tool Co.*, Comp. Gen. Dec. B-218260.1, 85-1 CPD ¶ 566, where resolicitation of all offerors was required when different requirements were arrived at with the only offeror in the competitive range. *In Lobar Inc.*, Comp. Gen. Dec. B-247843.3, 92-2 CPD ¶ 139, GAO found that the agency had acted properly when, after determining that the specifications exceeded the government's minimum needs, it amended the RFP and reopened with all offerors, both those within and outside the competitive range.

Even though the regulations provide that the amendment shall be sent to each prospective offeror, GAO has consistently held that the offeror bears the risk of not receiving an amendment, assuming that full and open competition has been found and it has not been shown that there was a conscious and deliberate effort by the agency to exclude the offeror from participating in the competition, *CardioMetrix*, Comp. Gen. Dec. B-270701, 96-1 CPD ¶ 149; *CDA Inc.*, Comp. Gen. Dec. B-224971, 87-1 CPD ¶ 163; *Maryland Computer Servs., Inc.*, Comp. Gen. Dec. B-216990, 85-1 CPD ¶ 187. The underlying theory is that the agency discharges its legal responsibility when it issues and dispatches an amendment in sufficient time to permit all offerors to consider the amendment in formulating their offers. In *LexisNexis, Inc.*, Comp. Gen. Dec. B-299381, 2007 CPD ¶ 73, an amendment posted on the FedBizOpps website hyperlinked to the agency website did not excuse the protester's failure to find it. In *CompuServe*, Comp. Gen. Dec. B-192905, 79-1 CPD ¶ 63, an amendment issued to the offeror, but addressed incorrectly, provided no basis for extending the closing date for initial proposals even though the offeror's late acknowledgment was prompted by late receipt of the amendment. However, in *Andero Constr., Inc.*, 61 Comp. Gen. 253 (B-203898), 82-1 CPD ¶ 133, GAO ignored the general rule that the offeror bears the risk of non-delivery of an amendment where three of four offerors appeared not to have received the amendment in the mail.

§ 6.05 PREPARATION AND SUBMISSION OF PROPOSALS

The term "proposal" is generally used broadly to refer to an offeror's entire submission in response to an RFP, consisting of both an offer which can be accepted by the government and information to be considered by the government in evaluating the offeror's capability or elements of its offer. The term has also been used to describe separate parts of the submission. Thus, RFPs often request that offerors organize submissions into separate portions called "Technical Proposals," "Management Proposals," and "Cost Proposals." Because FAR Part 15 does not recognize the distinction between the offer and information, it is necessary to determine whether its use of the term "proposal" in a particular provision is intended to refer to the offer or both the offer and the required information. Some contracting officers have recognized the distinction between these two portions of the submission and have drafted their RFPs so that the offer and information in the offeror's submission can be readily distinguished. The following discussion uses the term "proposal" to refer to the total submission in response to an RFP and the terms "offer" and "information" to distinguish between the two components of the submission.

[A] The Offer

The offer describes what the contractor is willing to agree to and its terms becomes part of the contract when accepted by the government. See FAR 2.101 which contains the following definition of the term "offer":

> "Offer" means a response to a solicitation that, if accepted, would bind the offeror to perform the resultant contract.

In the typical negotiated contract, the offer consists of the terms specified in the RFP (specifications, clauses, etc. contained in Parts I, II and III of the Uniform Contract Format) and the cost/price specified by the offeror. FAR 15.204-2(a)(1) provides for the use of Optional Form (OF) 308, Solicitation and Offer—Negotiated Acquisition, or Standard Form (SF) 33, Solicitation, Offer and Award to prepare RFPs. These forms refer to the various sections of the RFP which will become part of the contract, refer to the prices "which are offered," and provide spaces for a signature and for the "offer date." FAR 15.204-2(a)(2)(ix) requires that the solicitation include the "offer expiration date" when the forms are not used.

[1] Intention to Be Bound

To be considered for award, the offer must evidence an intent to be bound to the terms and conditions in the RFP and any amendments. This is evidenced by the signature on SF 33 and OF 308, which bind the offeror to the terms and conditions of the RFP. In addition, the offeror must acknowledge receipt of any amendments to the RFP.

[a] Signature

Paragraph (c) of the Instructions to Offerors—Competitive Acquisition solicitation provision in FAR 52.215-1 contains the following guidance making signature of the proposal mandatory:

> (2) The first page of the proposal must show—
>
> * * *
>
> (v) Name, title, and signature of person authorized to sign the proposal. Proposals signed by an agent shall be accompanied by evidence of that agent's authority, unless that evidence has been previously furnished to the issuing office.

FAR 2.101 defines "signature" as follows:

> Signature or signed means the discrete, verifiable symbol of an individual that, when affixed to a writing with the knowledge and consent of the individual, indicates a present intention to authenticate the writing. This includes electronic symbols.

See also FAR 4.502(d) permitting the use of electronic signatures when a proposal is to be submitted electronically. In *Tishman Constr. Corp.*, Comp. Gen. Dec. B-292097, 2003 CPD ¶ 94, the agency was required to honor a timely signed electronic proposal even though the required paper proposal was not submitted on time. GAO concluded that the late submission of the paper proposal was a "minor, immaterial deviation from the solicitation requirements." However, in *Distributed Solutions, Inc.,* Comp. Gen. Dec. B-416394, 2018 CPD ¶ 279, GAO agreed that an agency could properly reject a proposal including only a typewritten name. In commenting of this issue in the following footnote, GAO cast doubt on whether an agency was required to accept electronic signatures:

> [W]e do not agree with the protester that the Electronic Signatures in Global and National Commerce ('E–SIGN' Act mandates that SPAWAR accept DSI's CEO's typewritten name as an official signature. See Protest at 6, citing E-SIGN Act, 15 U.S.C. § 7001 et seq. As an initial matter, the Act is not applicable to the Department of Defense. See COS/MOL at 16, citing 41 U.S.C. § 2301(f). Moreover, the E-SIGN Act expressly provides that a governmental agency need not accept electronic signatures with respect to a contract. See 15 U.S.C. § 7001(b)(2); see also *Excel Building & Dev. Corp.*, B-401955, Dec. 23, 2009, 2009 CPD ¶ 262 at 4 n.4 (discussing Office of Management and Budget (OMB) guidance regarding government discretion to use or accept electronic signatures). Indeed, the FAR provides that agencies may accept electronic signatures and records in connection with government contracts; it does not provide a regulatory obligation that an electronic signature be accepted without reservation. See FAR § 4.502(d).

GAO has also held that it is proper to reject a proposal which does not contain a signature if the RFP contemplates award on the basis of initial proposals, *SWR, Inc.*, Comp. Gen. Dec. B-278415, 97-2 CPD ¶ 166; *Valencia Tech. Servs., Inc.*, Comp. Gen. Dec. B-223288, 86-2 CPD ¶ 40. It would appear that unsigned offers could be considered if the RFP included Alternate I to the Instructions to Offerors—Competitive Acquisition provision in FAR 52.215-1, precluding the agency from making an award on the basis of the initial proposals.

GAO has followed sealed bidding cases when competitive proposals are signed by agents. Thus, evidence of an agent's authority may be submitted after opening of proposals but proof that an offeror submitting a proposal in its own name was acting as an agent may not be submitted after opening. See *Hay-Holland Co.*, Comp. Gen. Dec. B-233002, 89-1 CPD ¶ 102, where the agency properly rejected an offer which was signed and subscribed by an agent without mention of the agent-principal relationship. GAO rejected the protester's contention that the incorrect signature was a clerical error which should have been corrected through discussions. In *WorldWide Parts, Inc.*, Comp. Gen. Dec. B-244793, 91-2 CPD ¶ 156, GAO held that an agent who submits a proposal listing itself as the offeror may not submit evidence after the closing date for receipt of proposals to show the agent-principal relationship because to do so would constitute an improper transfer of a proposal. See also *American Material Handling, Inc.*, Comp. Gen. Dec. B-253818, 93-2 CPD ¶ 246 (award to an entity other than that named in original offer is improper).

A proposal which is properly signed by one offeror may be transferred or assigned to another firm only if such a transfer is affected by operation of law, which is interpreted to include a merger, a corporate reorganization, a sale of an entire business or that portion of a business embraced by a proposal, or other means not barred by anti-assignment statutes, *Numax Elecs., Inc.*, 54 Comp. Gen. 580 (B-181670), 75-1 CPD ¶ 21. See *Telex Communications, Inc.*, Comp. Gen. Dec. B-212385, 84-1 CPD ¶ 127, permitting award to a company that had sold all of its stock to another company. However, if the bid or proposal is the only asset transferred, award may not be made to the new company. *Premier Security*, Comp. Gen. Dec. B-275908.2, 97-2 CPD ¶ 15.

[b] Cover Letters

It is not good practice to include a cover letter with a proposal because any statements in the cover letter may be found to have conditioned the offer being made by the offeror. In this regard, GAO has followed the sealed bidding rule making conditioned bids nonresponsive. See, for example, *New Dimension Masonry, Inc.*, Comp. Gen. Dec. B-258876, 95-1 CPD ¶ 102. Thus, a contracting officer was found entitled to reject a proposal where a cover letter stating that its product was a "fit, form and function replacement" of the product described in the RFP, *Potomac Elec. Corp.*, Comp. Gen. Dec. B-311060, 2008 CPD ¶ 63. GAO concluded that the contracting officer had properly concluded that this statement could indicate that the product did not meet all of the salient characteristics that were included in the RFP. A similar result was reached in *INDUS Tech., Inc.*, Comp. Gen. Dec. B-297800.13, 2007 CPD ¶ 116, where cover letters accompanying the proposals provided for an acceptance period of 180 days, and the solicitation required a minimum acceptance period of 350 days and specifically stated that proposals providing less than the minimum acceptance period would be rejected.

[c] Acknowledging Receipt of Amendments

Offerors are required to acknowledge the receipt of amendments to the solicitation either upon receipt or on the cover sheet of the proposal. The

Instructions to Offerors—Competitive Acquisition solicitation provision in FAR 52.215-1(b) provides:

> If this solicitation is amended, all terms and conditions that are not amended remain unchanged. Offerors shall acknowledge receipt of any amendment to this solicitation by the date and time specified in the amendment(s).

If a contracting officer posts a set of questions and answers to a solicitation on its website but does not designate them as an amendment, they will be treated as an amendment because they have a significant impact on the terms of the procurement, *Linguistic Sys., Inc.*, Comp. Gen. Dec. B-296221, 2005 CPD ¶ 104.

The failure to acknowledge receipt of a material amendment precludes award to that offeror on the basis of the initial proposal, *Nomura Enter., Inc.*, Comp. Gen. Dec. B-277768, 97-2 CPD ¶ 148. Agencies are also permitted to reject an offer where a material amendment has not been acknowledged, *TTCC, Inc.*, Comp. Gen. Dec. B-412874, 2016 CPD ¶ 137; *ECI Def. Grp.*, Comp. Gen. Dec. B-400177, 2008 CPD ¶ 141; *Skyline ULTD, Inc.*, Comp. Gen. Dec. B-297800.3, 2006 CPD ¶ 128; *Integrated Bus. Solutions, Inc.* Comp. Gen. Dec. B-292239, 2003 CPD ¶ 122. However, a contracting officer may establish a competitive range and permit the offeror to acknowledge the amendment in negotiations, *Grove Res. Solutions, Inc.*, Comp. Gen. Dec. B-296228, 2005 CPD ¶ 133; *International Filter Mfg. Corp.*, Comp. Gen. Dec. B-235049, 89-1 CPD ¶ 586; *Galaxy Aircraft Instruments Co.*, Comp. Gen. Dec. B-194356, 80-1 CPD ¶ 364. The choice of which alternative to follow will depend upon the degree of competition and the value of the offer in relation to the other offers.

If the offeror shows that it has received the amendment by reflecting its terms in its offer, it will be found to have constructively acknowledged receipt of the amendment, *Language Servs. Assocs., Inc.*, Comp. Gen. Dec. B-297392, 2006 CPD ¶ 20 (quotation); *Pitney* Bowes, *Inc.*, Comp. Gen. Dec. B-294868, 2005 CPD ¶ 10 (quotation). Thus, the failure to acknowledge an amendment does not preclude award where "the offeror is otherwise obligated to perform in accordance with the terms of the solicitation," *E. Frye Enters., Inc.*, Comp. Gen. Dec. B-258699.2, 95-1 CPD ¶ 64.

If an amendment does not contain material provisions, failure to acknowledge it should be waived as a minor informality, *International Data Sys., Inc.*, Comp. Gen. Dec. B-277385, 97-2 CPD ¶ 96.

The mere fact that an offeror does not receive an amendment is no excuse for failure to acknowledge the amendment where full and open competition and reasonable prices are obtained and the agency did not deliberately exclude the offeror from competition, *CDA, Inc.*, Comp. Gen. Dec. B-224971, 87-1 CPD ¶ 163, and *O.J. Best Servs., Inc.*, Comp. Gen. Dec. B-276954, 97-1 CPD ¶ 231 (of 21 offers received, 19 acknowledged receipt of the amendments)

[2] Offer Strategy

There are a number of strategies which may be available to an offeror. These include deciding on the pricing and other aspects of the offer, whether to make an offer on all the items covered by the RFP, and whethto submit alternate or multiple offers.

[a] Best Terms

One of the most difficult decisions to make is whether to submit an offer containing the best possible offer the firm can make or one reserving some improvements for the later stages of the process. The problem is that, in a competitive environment, the offeror may not get an opportunity to make concessions and improve the offer. See *Advanced American Diving Serv.*, Comp. Gen. Dec. B-274766, 97-1 CPD ¶ 1, denying a protest that the agency should have established a competitive range to obtain better terms. In this regard, ¶ (f)(4) of the FAR 52.215-1 Instructions to Offerors—Competitive Acquisition provision warns offerors that:

> The Government intends to evaluate proposals and award a contract without discussions with offerors (except clarifications described in FAR 15.306 (a)). *Therefore, the offeror's initial proposal should contain the offeror's best terms from a cost or price and technical standpoint.* [Emphasis supplied.]

Even where the solicitation indicates that the government plans to undertake discussions with offerors within the competitive range, an offer at less than the best possible terms runs the risk of being found to be outside the competitive range. This leads to the conclusion that in many, if not most, acquisitions the best strategy is to submit the best offer initially.

[b] Items Offered

Where the RFP calls for a number of severable items and the solicitation does not specifically require that offers be made on all the items, the offeror must decide whether to submit an offer on all the items or only some of them. The only FAR provision dealing with this issue is contained in ¶ (c)(4) of the FAR 52.215-1 Instructions to Offerors—Competitive Acquisition solicitation provision, stating, "Unless otherwise specified in the solicitation, the offeror may propose to provide any item or combination of items." If it decided to submit an offer covering all the items, the offeror should also consider whether to condition its offer on award of all the items. This condition, termed an "all or none" offer, would insure that the offeror would not receive partial awards. In such a case, the all-or-none prices will be compared with the price combinations for all the items offered by other offerors without an all-or-none condition, *Banknote Corp. of Am., Inc.*, Comp. Gen. Dec. B-245528.2, 92-1 CPD ¶ 53. If no such condition is contained in the offer, ¶¶ (f)(5) and (f)(6) of the FAR 52.215-1 Instructions to Offerors—Competitive Acquisition solicitation provision permit the government to award multiple contracts for all or a part of any contract line items. See Chapter 5, Section III for a further discussion of the rules for evaluating multiple item solicitations.

[c] Alternate or Multiple Offers

Offerors may want to consider submitting more than one offer. This may be particularly desirable when the specifications permit the offeror to determine the way that the work will be performed such as in a performance or functional specification. See also FAR 11.002(e) permitting agencies to identify performance levels as targets rather than as fixed or minimum requirements. In other cases, an offeror may conclude that a non-specification offer will have sufficient advantages for the government that it might be persuaded to consider amending the specifications to permit its consideration. The term "alternate proposal" has sometimes been used to refer to these two different situations. It has been used to describe the case where an offeror submits two or more offers each meeting the RFP requirements. It has also been used to describe the case where the offeror submits one offer meeting the requirements and another which does not, or merely submits one offer which does not conform to the RFP.

> FAR 15.209(a)(2) states that if an agency is willing to accept alternate proposals, it should include a paragraph substantially the same as the following Alternate II paragraph in the Instruction to Offerors—Competitive Acquisition solicitation provision in FAR 52.215-1: Offerors may submit proposals that depart from stated requirements. Such proposals shall clearly identify why the acceptance of the proposal would be advantageous to the Government. Any deviations from the terms and conditions of the solicitation, as well as the comparative advantage to the Government, shall be clearly identified and explicitly defined. The Government reserves the right to amend the solicitation to allow all offerors an opportunity to submit revised proposals based on the revised requirements.

This alternate is also to be used in cost-reimbursement contracts with State and local governments, educational institutions and other nonprofit organizations.

When it buys commercial items, the government encourages the submission of multiple offers. See the Instruction to Offerors—Commercial Items solicitation provision in FAR 52l.212-1 stating:

> (e) Multiple offers. Offerors are encouraged to submit multiple offers presenting alternative terms and conditions, including alternative line items (provided that the alternative line items are consistent with subpart 4.10 of

the Federal Acquisition Regulation), or alternative commercial items for satisfying the requirements of this solicitation. Each offer submitted will be evaluated separately.

[i] Nonconforming Offers

If an offeror submits an alternate offer that materially deviates from the requirements of the RFP, the government may not award to that offeror but must revise the RFP to permit other offerors to propose to the deviation, FAR 15.206(d). See *Labat-Anderson, Inc.*, 71 Comp. Gen. 252 (B-246071.5), 92-1 CPD ¶ 193, holding that it was improper to accept an offer which deviated from a staffing level required by the RFP. In *Citrus College*, Comp. Gen. Dec. B-293543, 2004 CPD ¶ 104, it was held that it was proper for an agency to amend the RFP to permit alternate proposals after one offeror had done so. The proper course was followed in *Simmonds Precision Prods., Inc.*, Comp. Gen. Dec. B-244559.3, 93-1 CPD ¶ 483, where, upon the agency's receipt of a deviating offer containing terms that were more attractive than those required by the RFP, other offerors were given the opportunity to submit revised offers.

An offer is not nonconforming, however, if the RFP states that the agency reserves the right to award to a proposal that does not meet all of the mandatory requirements of the solicitation, *Litton Sys., Inc. v. Dep't of Transp.*, GSBCA 12911-P, 94-3 BCA ¶ 27,263. In that case, the board held that the agency was not required to amend the RFP to permit award to an alternate offer that did not conform to the mandatory requirements because all of the offerors had been informed that the agency might follow that procedure.

Both GAO and the Court of Federal Claims have ruled that an agency need not evaluate an alternate pricing proposal because the RFP contained no provision allowing such a proposal, *Geiler/Schrudde & Zimmerman*, Comp. Gen. Dec. B-412219, 2016 CPD ¶ 16; *Geiler/Schrudde & Zimmerman v. United States*, 133 Fed. Cl. 578 (2017), *affd*, 743 Fed. Appx. 974 (Fed. Cir. 2018). In contrast, both GAO and the Court of Federal Claims have discussed evaluations of alternate proposals without any indication that the RFP permitted such proposals, *Dell Fed. Sys., L.P.*, Comp. Gen. Dec. B-404996, 2011 CPD ¶ 151 (agreeing with the agency's decision to find an alternate proposal responding to a delivery order technically unacceptable); *Metropolitan Van & Storage, Inc. v. United States*, 92 Fed. Cl. 232 (2010) (holding awardee's technical proposal unacceptable compared to protester's alternate proposals); *Manufacturing Eng'g Sys., Inc.*, Comp. Gen. Dec. B-293299.3, 2004 CPD ¶ 194 (assessing the agency's decision not to award to a multiple alternate proposal). This would appear to indicate that agencies have the option whether to evaluate alternate proposals in the absence of RFP language. Where the RFP prohibits alternative proposals, the Court of Federal Claims has held that an offeror submitting multiple proposals was nonconforming and ineligible for award. *Elevated Techs., Inc., v.*

United States, 160 Fed. Cl. 257 (2022). To be safe, offerors desiring to submit alternate proposals should request that the RFP be amended to permit this action.

Agencies are free to reject alternate proposals that do not meet the contract requirements. See *Baltimore Gas & Elec. Co.*, Comp. Gen. Dec. B-406057, 2012 CPD ¶ 34, stating:

> [W]hile alternate offers that took exceptions to the RFP requirements were permitted, nothing in the RFP prevented the agency from evaluating the exceptions offered and rejecting them as unacceptable. In fact, agencies have a duty to evaluate alternate offers and exceptions to determine whether such exceptions would be advantageous to the government. See *Dell Fed. Sys., L.P.*, B-404996, B-404996.2, July 22, 2011, 2011 CPD ¶ 151 at 3-5; *Northern Light Prods.*, B-401182, June 1, 2009, 2009 CPD ¶ 117 at 3-4.

The same result was reached in *Velos, Inc.*, Comp. Gen. Dec. B-400500.8, 2010 CPD ¶ 13, *Tin Mills Props., LLC v. United States*, 82 Fed. Cl. 584 (2008), and *Aeroflex Text Sols.*, Comp. Gen. Dec. B-295380, 2005 CPD ¶ 51. GAO has also held that an offeror must protest patently ambiguous provisions in an RFP allowing alternate proposals prior to submitting the proposal, *Navistar Def., LLC*, Comp. Gen. Dec. B-401865, 2009 CPD ¶ 258.

The absence of RFP language allowing an alternate proposal does not necessarily mean that offers which deviate from the RFP must be rejected. The sealed bid concept of "responsiveness," does not apply to negotiated procurements, *Gardiner, Kamya & Assocs., P.C.*, Comp. Gen. Dec. B-258400, 95-1 CPD ¶ 191. Thus, the contracting officer has the discretion to include such an offer in the competitive range and seek to have a nonconformity cured through discussions or to amend the solicitation as required by FAR 15.206(g). However, the offeror takes the risk that the offer will be rejected and the offeror excluded from the competitive range. See *Bencor-Petrifond*, Comp. Gen. Dec. B-254205, 93-2 CPD ¶ 208 (proposal departed from RFP's construction schedule); and *Discount Mach. & Equip., Inc.*, Comp. Gen. Dec. B-241444, 90-2 CPD ¶ 474 (offeror unable to meet technical provisions). Which course of action will be taken by the contracting officer will depend upon the number and nature of conforming offers received and the benefits offered by the nonconforming offer. However, an offer that is totally out of compliance with the RFP may not be considered, *Best W. Quantico Inn/Conference Ctr.*, Comp. Gen. Dec. B-209500, 83-1 CPD ¶ 164. In that case, the offeror responded to an RFP with only a "contract pricing proposal" when the RFP required a "technical proposal."

It is not improper to submit a noncompliant alternate offer to ensure that an agency does use ambiguous RFP language to award on a seemingly improper basis. See *Power Connector, Inc.*, Comp. Gen. Dec. B-285395, 2000 CPD ¶ 152, rejecting the contention that an alternate offer of a foreign product was "gaming the system" when the RFP called for a domestic product but contained a description of how foreign products would be evaluated.

[ii] Multiple Conforming Offers

The present FAR Part 15 does not deal with the submission of multiple conforming offers. Nevertheless, GAO has held that there is no need for the solicitation to contain a provision authorizing multiple offers for them to be considered, *Educational Media, Inc.*, Comp. Gen. Dec. B-225457.2, 87-1 CPD ¶ 498, and *Federal Computer Corp.*, 66 Comp. Gen. 139 (B-223932), 81-2 CPD ¶ 665. See also 33 Comp. Gen. 499 (B-119646) (1954); and 39 Comp. Gen. 892 (B-142957) (1960), holding that the submission of multiple offers are appropriate competitive techniques. For an instance where an alternate offer was selected for contract award, see *OK Produce*, Comp. Gen. Dec. B-299058, 2007 CPD ¶ 31.

To be valid, such alternate offers must conform to the terms of the solicitation. See *Aeroflex Test Solutions*, Comp. Gen. Dec. B-295380, 2005 CPD ¶ 51, holding that the contracting officer properly did not consider an alternate offer that did not contain fixed prices as required by the RFP. See also *P.G. Elecs., Ltd.*, Comp. Gen. Dec. B-261883, 95-2 CPD ¶ 202, where the agency could not evaluate an alternate offer of an extended warranty because its terms were unclear, and *Head, Inc.*, Comp. Gen. Dec. B-299523, 2007 CPD ¶ 109, where an alternate offer was not dealt with because of lack of supporting documentation. Compare *Citrus Coll.*, Comp. Gen. Dec. B-293543, 2004 CPD ¶ 104, where GAO rejected the contention that the agency accepted an alternate proposal that did not comply with the RFP requirements because the protester did not prove prejudice.

Agencies are accorded broad discretion in evaluating alternative offers. See *Phoenix Air Grp., Inc.*, Comp. Gen. Dec. B-412796.2, 2016 CPD ¶ 308 (assessing the agency's decision to award to a multiple alternate proposal); *Beretta USA Corp.*, Comp. Gen. Dec. B-406376.2, 2013 CPD ¶ 186 (agreeing that agency was not required to find missing information in alternate proposal); and *Avue Techs. Corp.*, Comp. Gen. Dec. B-298380.4, 2008 CPD ¶ 182 (assessing the agency's decision to exclude alternate proposals from the competitive range).

While the receipt of multiple offers can be of value to the government, they do require additional evaluation. This could be unduly burdensome in cases where substantial evaluation effort is required such as where a large number of different approaches are proposed or there are a large number of multiple proposals. See, for example, *Moreland Corp.*, Comp. Gen. Dec. B-291086, 2002 CPD ¶ 197, where five offerors submitted 14 offers and alternate offers, and *Banknote Corp. of Am., Inc.*, Comp. Gen. Dec. B-245528.2, 92-1 CPD ¶ 53, where the evaluation was complicated and delayed by the fact that one offeror submitted four separate price offers and another submitted ten. Thus, agencies can properly preclude multiple offers by including a provision in the solicitation prohibiting more than one offer, *ACS State Healthcare, LLC*, Comp. Gen. Dec. B-292981, 2004 CPD ¶ 57; *Dale Stevens Constr.*, Comp. Gen. Dec. B-242234, 91-1 CPD ¶ 354. However, such a provision will not necessarily prevent separate offers from being submitted by separate, but affiliated, firms. In *Robbins-Gioia,*

Inc., Comp. Gen. Dec. B-274318, 96-2 CPD ¶ 222, the RFP stated that (1) "an offeror may submit a maximum of one fully compliant proposal," (2) "no alternate proposals will be accepted," and (3) "if an offeror submits more than one proposal, all proposals will be returned without evaluation." GAO denied the protest against consideration of both offers, holding that the general rule is that contracting agencies may accept bids and offers from affiliated firms unless doing so would prejudice the government's interests or give the affiliated offerors an unfair advantage over other offerors.

[d] Unbalanced Offers

Where the solicitation contains multiple items or multiple option years, offerors may seek to obtain a competitive advantage by unbalancing the prices. Paragraph (f)(8) of the FAR 52.215-1 Instructions to Offerors—Competitive Acquisition provision warns offerors that their offers may be rejected if the prices are materially unbalanced, stating:

> The Government may determine that a proposal is unacceptable if the prices proposed are materially unbalanced between line items or subline items. Unbalanced pricing exists when, despite an acceptable total evaluated price, the price of one or more contract line items is significantly overstated or understated as indicated by the application of cost or price analysis techniques. A proposal may be rejected if the Contracting Officer determines that the lack of balance poses an unacceptable risk to the Government.

FAR 15.404-1(g)(3) contains a discretionary rule stating that an unbalanced offer may be rejected if the contracting officer determines that the lack of balance "poses an unacceptable risk to the Government." GAO has reasoned that this entails an evaluation of the risk of overstated prices not understated prices, *First Fin. Assocs., Inc.*, Comp. Gen. Dec. B-415713, 2018 CPD ¶ 76. See *Green Tech. Grp., LLC*, Comp. Gen. Dec. B-417368, 2019 CPD ¶ 219, and *Crown Point Sys.*, Comp. Gen. Dec. B-413940, 2017 CPD ¶ 19, concluding that the risk of understated prices is a matter of price realism not unbalanced pricing. In *Green Tech. Grp., LLC v. United States*, 147 Fed. Cl. 231 (2020), the court disagreed, holding that the FAR required a risk assessment of understated prices because they could pose a performance risk.

GAO has ruled that an agency cannot reject an offer merely because it contains overstated prices but must assess the risk of such prices, *Omnicell, Inc.*, Comp. Gen. Dec. B-414021, 2017 CPD ¶ 42; *Triumvirate Env't, Inc.*, Comp. Gen. Dec. B-406809, 2012 CPD ¶ 244. If the risk of unbalanced pricing is inherent in inaccurate estimated quantities, that must be protested before the submission of a proposal, *XPO Logistics Worldwide Gov't Servs., LLC*, Comp. Gen. Dec. B-412628.6, 2017 CPD ¶ 88.

For cases affirming the contracting officer's acceptance of unbalanced prices because of no unacceptable risk, see *L-3 Brashear*, Comp. Gen. Dec. B-413138.4, 2017 CPD ¶ 65 (discussions led contracting officer to conclude risk was acceptable); *Crowley Tech. Mgmt., Inc.*, Comp. Gen. Dec. B-412690.2, 2016 CPD ¶ 130 (agency analysis indicated that it was unlikely that it would order quantities with high prices); *Academy Facilities Mgmt. v. United States*, 87 Fed. Cl. 441 (2008) (detailed analysis indicated final prices not significantly unbalanced); *Scot, Inc.*, Comp. Gen. Dec. B-295569, 2005 CPD ¶ 66 (price of most likely quantity to be purchased lower than competitors); and *Semont Travel, Inc.*, Comp. Gen. Dec. B-291179, 2002 CPD ¶ 200 (price of high-price base year was not out of line even if lower-priced option years were not exercised). See also *Cherokee Painting LLC*, Comp. Gen. Dec. B-311020.3, 2009 CPD ¶ 18, where no unacceptable risk was found by analyzing past prices which had not resulted in undue costs to the government, and *Citywide Managing Servs. of Port Washington, Inc.*, Comp. Gen. Dec. B-281287.12, 2001 CPD ¶ 6, rejecting a protest even though the agency had not analyzed the risk of unbalanced prices because the protester did not submit evidence that the government would pay higher prices. For cases agreeing that an offer should be rejected because of undue risk, see *U.S. Electrodynamics, Inc.*, Comp. Gen. Dec. B-414678, 2017 CPD ¶ 252; *L. W. Matteson, Inc.*, Comp. Gen. Dec. B-290224, 2002 CPD ¶ 89.

[3] Modification, Revision and Withdrawal

The RFP forms specify the time within which the government may accept offers. Block 12 of SF 33 provides that the offeror agrees to perform the work "if this offer is accepted within *60 calendar days unless a different date is inserted by the offeror*." Block 4 of OF 308, in turn, states, "Offers valid for 60 days unless a different period is entered here." Neither of these provisions prohibits the offeror from modifying, revising or withdrawing the offer prior to its acceptance. While the relevant FAR sections cited below speak in terms of modification, revision and withdrawal of "proposals," it is evident from the context that they are referring to "offers" and not "information." See, for example, FAR 15.208 which is titled, "Submission, modification, revision, and withdrawal of *proposal*" but which states in ¶ (a), "Offerors are responsible for submitting *ofs*, and any revisions and modifications to them."

[a] Modification

FAR 15.001 defines a modification as follows:

> Proposal modification is a change made to a proposal before the solicitation closing date and time, or made in response to an amendment, or made to correct a mistake at any time before award.

This definition indicates that the term "proposal modification" is intended to cover the narrow situation where the offeror desires to modify its offer before it is contacted by the agency. By its terms, the definition precludes such modifications after the solicitation closing date and time unless the modification is made in response to an amendment to the solicitation. However, the definition also includes the situation where the offeror desires to correct a mistake in its offer after the closing date of the solicitation. This issue of mistake correction will be discussed in the following section dealing with Exchanges and Communications. FAR 15.508 provides that mistakes discovered after award are to be processed substantially in accordance with the mistake in bid procedures set forth in FAR 14.407-4.

[b] Revision

FAR 15.001 uses the term "revision" to cover the situation where an offeror changes the terms of its offer after the solicitation closing date and time. It defines a revision as follows:

> Proposal revision is a change to a proposal made after the solicitation closing date, at the request of or as allowed by a contracting officer, as the result of negotiations.

This definition permits offers to be "revised" only as a result of negotiations and negotiations will take place only after a competitive range has been established. See FAR 15.307. The subject of offer revisions will be covered in the discussion of competitive range below.

[c] Withdrawal

Offers may be withdrawn by an offeror at any time prior to acceptance. See ¶ (c) of the Instructions to Offerors—Competitive Acquisition solicitation provision at FAR 52.215-1, which states:

> (3)(v) Proposals may be withdrawn by written notice received at any time before award. Oral proposals in response to oral solicitations may be withdrawn orally. If the solicitation authorizes facsimile proposals, proposals may be withdrawn via facsimile received at any time before award, subject to the conditions specified in the provision at 52.215-5, Facsimile Proposals. Proposals may be withdrawn in person by an offeror or an authorized representative, if the identity of the person requesting withdrawal is established and the person signs a receipt for the proposal before award.
>
> * * *
>
> (8) Proposals may be withdrawn at any time before award. Withdrawals are effective upon receipt of notice by the Contracting Officer.

A similar provision is contained in FAR 15.208(e), which also contains the internal government procedures for disposing of withdrawn proposals, including electronically submitted proposals. Although this FAR 52.215-1 provision contains no guidance on the withdrawal of electronically submitted proposals, it can be assumed that they can be withdrawn electronically as long as the electronic transmission is received by the agency before acceptance of the proposal.

The broad right of withdrawal before award in the present FAR is consistent with previous FAR provisions and GAO has consistently accepted the FAR provision as governing and has held that a signed offer is revocable before acceptance and, therefore, is not a firm offer, *Pedestrian Bus Stop Shelters, Ltd.*, 63 Comp. Gen. 265 (B-212570), 84-1 CPD ¶ 331. The Armed Services Board of Contract Appeals has described an offeror's right to withdraw its offer prior to award as a "fundamental protection," *Toyad Corp.*, ASBCA 26785, 85-3 BCA ¶ 18,354.

[4] Timely Submission Required

Although earlier drafts had proposed liberalizing the rule concerning late proposals, the final FAR Part 15 Rewrite reestablished the "late is late" rule. Thus, offerors must use great care to ensure the timely submission of offers, modifications or revisions. This strict rule, with very limited exceptions, is contained in ¶ (c)(3) of the FAR 52.215-1 Instructions to Offerors—Competitive Acquisition solicitation provision as follows:

> (i) Offerors are responsible for submitting proposals, and any modifications or revisions, so as to reach the Government office designated in the solicitation by the time specified in the solicitation. If no time is specified in the solicitation, the time for receipt is 4:30 p.m., local time, for the designated Government office on the date that proposal or revision is due.
>
> (ii)(A) Any proposal, modification, or revision received at the Government office designated in the solicitation after the exact time specified for receipt of proposals is "late" and will not be considered unless it is received before award is made, the Contracting Officer determines that accepting the late proposal would not unduly delay the acquisition; and—
>
> > (1) If it was transmitted through an electronic commerce method authorized by the solicitation, it was received at the initial point of entry to the Government infrastructure not later than 5:00 p.m. one working day prior to the date specified for receipt of proposals; or
> >
> > (2) There is acceptable evidence to establish that it was received at the Government installation designated for receipt of proposals and was under the Government's control prior to the time set for receipt of proposals; or
> >
> > (3) It is the only proposal received.

(B) However, a late modification of an otherwise successful proposal that makes its terms more favorable to the Government, will be considered at any time it is received and may be accepted.

(iii) Acceptable evidence to establish the time of receipt at the Government installation includes the time/date stamp of that installation on the proposal wrapper, other documentary evidence of receipt maintained by the installation, or oral testimony or statements of Government personnel.

(iv) If an emergency or unanticipated event interrupts normal Government processes so that proposals cannot be received at the office designated for receipt of proposals by the exact time specified in the solicitation, and urgent Government requirements preclude amendment of the solicitation, the time specified for receipt of proposals will be deemed to be extended to the same time of day specified in the solicitation on the first work day on which normal Government processes resume.

Essentially the same language is contained in FAR 15.208.

The government's determination of the time of receipt is binding unless it is clearly unreasonable. Thus, a contracting official's reliance on the time/date clock in the government office generally will be found to be reasonable, *Haskell Co.*, Comp. Gen. Dec. B-292756, 2003 CPD ¶ 202 (reasonable reliance on time/date clock that turned to 14:01 shortly after proposal received); *States Roofing Corp.*, Comp. Gen. Dec. B-286052, 2000 CPD ¶ 182 (reasonable reliance on time/date clock rather than wall clock in same room); *Pat Mathis Constr. Co.*, Comp. Gen. Dec. B-248979, 92-2 CPD ¶ 236 (reasonable reliance on time/date clock which showed offer's proposal to be one minute late rather than clock in conference room adjoining the proposal delivery point). If the agency does not record the time of receipt of proposals, a Federal Express receipt signed by an agency employee may be used to establish that a proposal was timely received, *M.J.S., Inc.*, Comp. Gen. Dec. B-244410, 91-2 CPD ¶ 344.

The late-is-late rule has been enforced strictly and the offer must be received by the government exactly on time and at the place specified in the RFP. See, for example, *Airrus Mgmt. Sys., LLC*, Comp. Gen. Dec. B-218275, 2018 CPD ¶ 275 (6 minutes late). See also *Koba Assocs., Inc.*, Comp. Gen. Dec. B-265854, 95-2 CPD ¶ 212 (hand-carried proposal delivered to the depository office three minutes after time specified for receipt of proposals late); *Hallcrest Sys., Inc.*, Comp. Gen. Dec. B-215328, 84-2 CPD ¶ 334 (hand-carried proposal received one minute late rejected); and *Priest & Fine, Inc.*, Comp. Gen. Dec. B-213603, 84-1 CPD ¶ 358 (hand-delivered proposal received two minutes late not considered).

When submission of offers by facsimile is authorized by inclusion in the RFP of the Facsimile Proposals solicitation provision in FAR 52.215-5, the offeror must prove that the complete proposal was received by the closing time. See *GROH GmbH*, Comp. Gen. Dec. B-291980, 2003 CPD ¶ 53, holding that a proposal was late when the agency claimed it had not received the fax transmission and the RFP included the agency fax number but not the clause. Even if the fax is transmitted before opening, it must get to the place designated in the solicitation on time, *Instrument Assocs.*, Comp. Gen. Dec. B-256814, 94-2 CPD ¶ 52 (bid was rejected where both sender's and agency's fax activity reports showed fax was transmitted on time but did not get to opening on time); and *Microscope Co.*, Comp. Gen. Dec. B-257015, 94-2 CPD ¶ 157 (proposal was rejected even though offeror's telephone records showed timely transmission where agency provided sworn statement by contract specialist responsible for checking fax machine that proposal was not received on time). Further, the entire message must be received before the time for submission, *Cyber Digital, Inc.*, Comp. Gen. Dec. B-270107, 96-1 CPD ¶ 20; *Radar Devices, Inc.*, Comp. Gen. Dec. B-249118, 92-2 CPD ¶ 287 (where transmission began before closing but completed after closing, contracting officer could only consider preclosing transmission). However, the date/time notation on a facsimile has been used as evidence that a BAFO was timely received when the agency did not apply its own date/time stamp upon actual receipt, *Essex Electro Eng'rs, Inc.*, Comp. Gen. Dec. B-238207, 90-1 CPD ¶ 438. The fact that the government's fax machine is out of order, out of paper, or busy will not excuse the failure to meet the required time, *Brookfield Dev., Inc.*, Comp. Gen. Dec. B-255944, 94-1 CPD ¶ 273 (BAFO due at 4 p.m. rejected where transmission began at 3:50 but was not completed until 4:16 because the government's fax machine was busy).

When the RFP required submission of both paper and electronic proposals, failure of the paper version to arrive on time after timely receipt of the electronic version was a minor informality that should have been waived by the contracting officer, *Tishman Constr. Corp.*, Comp. Gen. Dec. B-292097, 2003 CPD ¶ 94.

[5] Circumstances Permitting Acceptance of Late Offers

GAO ruled for a number of years that contracting officers could avoid the late-is-late rule by extending the closing time for proposals or final proposal revisions when they found out that a late proposal or revision was about to be submitted or had been submitted. See *Ivy Mech. Co.*, Comp. Gen. Dec. B-272764, 96-2 CPD ¶ 83; *Geo-Seis Helicopters, Inc.*, Comp. Gen. Dec. B-299175, 2007 CPD ¶ 135. However, in *Geo-Seis Helicopters, Inc. v. United States*, 77 Fed. Cl. 633 (2007), the Court of Federal Claims ruled that the FAR late-is-late provision pertaining to both proposals and final proposal revisions is binding on the contracting officer and prohibits extending the closing time after the time has passed. However, this does not preclude extending the closing time before it has occurred, *Allied Materials & Equip. Co. v. United States*, 81 Fed. Cl. 448 (2008), and such an extension can be made by e-mail, *Guardian Moving & Storage Co. v. United States*, 122 Fed. Cl. 117 (2015), but it is improper to give an extension to only one of the competitors, *Progressive Indus., Inc. v. United States*, 129 Fed. Cl. 457 (2016). Thus, it appears that the only grounds for accepting a late proposal are the exceptions discussed below.

[a] Electronic Submission

The FAR has adopted a special rule for a late electronically submitted proposals, stating that they will only be acceptable if they are "received at the initial point of entry to the Government infrastructure not later than 5:00 p.m. one working day prior to the date specified for receipt of proposals." There is no explanation for this unusually strict rule but GAO has held that the correct reading of the FAR is that this rule is the exclusive rule for electronically submitted proposals, *Sea Box, Inc.*, Comp. Gen. Dec. B-251056, 2002 CPD ¶ 181. Thus, it held in that case that the rule on government control of proposals and revisions did not apply when they were submitted electronically. The Court of Federal Claims has reached the opposite conclusion, holding that the government control rule applies to electronically submitted proposals, *Watterson Constr. Co. v. United States*, 98 Fed. Cl. 84 (2011) (agency server sent proposal to contracting office four minutes late); *Insight Sys. Corp. v. United States*, 110 Fed. Cl. 564 (2013) (agency server could not acquire quotes from Google server). Notwithstanding these court decisions, GAO has continued to adhere to the *Sea Box* rule, *Spanish Sols. Language Servs., LLC*, Comp. Gen. Dec. B-418191, 2020 CPD ¶ 20 (proposal transmitted six minutes before deadline but received eight minutes after deadline); *Peers Health*, Comp. Gen. Dec. B-413557.3, 2017 CPD ¶ 93 (quotation reached government server one minute before deadline but did not reach contracting office until three hours later). GAO and the Court of Federal Claims also disagree on whether receipt by a government server constitutes receipt on time. In *Peers Health* GAO held that timely receipt by the server did not meet the solicitation requirement for receipt in the contracting office. In contrast, in *Insight Systems* the court held that timely receipt by a Google cloud server being used by the agency met the requirement of being in possession of the government. Similarly, in *Federal Acquisition Servs. Team, LLC v. United States*, 124 Fed. Cl. 690 (2016), the court held that timely receipt by the first server in a sequence of servers met the government control requirement. However, if the offeror is responsible for the late submission, the court will strictly enforce the late-is-late rule, *Naval Sys., Inc. v. United States*, 153 Fed. Cl. 166 (2021) (government proof of nonreceipt far stronger than protester proof of transmission); *Criterion Sys., Inc. v. United States*, 144 Fed. Cl. 409 (2019) (90 second late).

Government security requirements have imposed severe difficulties on the submission of electronic proposals. See, for example, *Advanced Decisions Vectors, Inc.*, Comp. Gen. Dec. B-412307, 2016 CPD ¶ 18, denying a protest where it appears that the quotation was blocked by the agency's anti-virus, spam and spyware interdiction system. The agency had taken the precaution of stating in the RFQ that the agency would acknowledge receipt of quotations, but the protester took no action when it received no acknowledgement. This situation indicates that both the government and offerors must exercise special care to ensure that proposals are received on time. See also *SigNet Techs., Inc.*, Comp. Gen. Dec. B-417435, 2019 CPD ¶ 247 (server would not accept zip files);

Airrus Mgmt. Sys., LLC, Comp. Gen. Dec. B-416358, 2018 CPD ¶ 275 (three attempted transmissions blocked by agency server for being too long); *Washingtonian Coach Corp.*, Comp. Gen. Dec. B-413809, 2016 CPD ¶ 378 (proposal rejected by server because it exceeded agency size limit even though size limit was not disclosed in solicitation); *Blue Glacier Mgmt. Grp., Inc.*, Comp. Gen. Dec. B-412897, 2016 CPD ¶ 177 (quotation apparently rejected by agency anti-phishing filter).

Numerous decisions illustrate the GAO's strict enforcement of the late-is-late rule with regard to electronic proposals or final proposal revisions. See *Symetrics Indus., LLC*, Comp. Gen. Dec. B-298759, 2006 CPD ¶ 154, where proposals were due by 3:00 p.m., Symetrics' electronically submitted final proposal revision was received by the agency's server at 2:57:41 p.m. but did not reach the contracting office until 3:01 p.m. Because the contracting office was the designated place for submission of proposals, GAO ruled that the late-is-late rule applied and the contracting officer was correct in rejecting the proposal. Further, GAO ruled that the exception for government control of proposals did not apply. See also *GSI Constr. Corp.*, Comp. Gen. Dec. B-418967, 2020 CPD ¶ 336 (e-mail proposal delivered on time but e-mail was not a designated mode of transmission); *Western Star Hospital Auth., Inc.*, Comp. Gen. Dec. B-414216.2, 2017 CPD ¶ 152 (electronic proposal late when offeror's e-mail provider delayed transmission); *Tele-Consultants, Inc.*, Comp. Gen. Dec. B-414135, 2017 CPD ¶ 132 (electronic proposal late because offeror did not click the signature button); *Team Housing Solutions*, Comp. Gen. Dec. B-414105, 2017 CPD ¶ 55 (electronic proposal late because it was sent to wrong electronic site); *Johnson Controls Gov't Sys., LLC*, Comp. Gen. Dec. B-411862.2, 2015 CPD ¶ 357 (electronic proposal late because protester failed to click "submit response" button on website); *C2G Ltd. Co.*, Comp. Gen. Dec. B-411131, 2015 CPD ¶ 157 (reverse auction bid sent one second before closing late because it took 5 to 15 seconds to record bid); *Federal Acquisition Servs. Team, LLC*, Comp. Gen. Dec. B-410466, 2015 CPD ¶ 20 (electronic proposal late because it was too large and offeror did not respond to "undeliverable" bounce back message); *Urban Title, LLC*, Comp. Gen. Dec. B-311437.3, 2009 CPD ¶ 31 (electronic final proposal revision late even though it was transmitted 12 minutes before closing time because it arrived at agency five weeks later); *PMTech, Inc.*, Comp. Gen. Dec. B-291082, 2002 CPD ¶ 172 (electronic proposal late even though it was transmitted 13 minutes before closing time). In *Integrated Bus. Solutions, Inc.*, Comp. Gen. Dec. B-292239, 2003 CPD ¶ 122, an electronic proposal was late when it was received two minutes late and the RFP did not permit the submission of proposals electronically. The same strict result was reached in *Conscoop—Consorzia Fra Coop. Di Prod. E Lavoro v. United States*, 62 Fed. Cl. 219 (2004) (electronic proposal late even though it was transmitted two minutes before the closing time because it arrived at agency over an hour later); and *Integrated Bus. Solutions, Inc. v. United States*, 58 Fed. Cl. 420 (2003). In *Labatt Food Serv., Inc. v. United States*, 84 Fed. Cl. 50 (2008), the court overlooked the late electronic submission of a final proposal revision and ruled that the procurement should be redone because the RFP required proposals to be submitted by fax and all business had been conducted electronically. GAO had reached the opposite result in *Labatt Food Serv., Inc.*, Comp. Gen. Dec. B-310939.6, 2008 CPD ¶ 162.

In one decision, GAO ruled that it was improper to reject a timely proposal sent to the wrong website because the agency contract specialist saw the proposal, *AECOM Tech. Servs., Inc.*, Comp. Gen. Dec. B-411862, 2015 CPD ¶ 353. Compare *Onsite OHS*, Comp. Gen. Dec. B-406449, 2012 CPD ¶ 178, where a proposal sent to the same wrong site was properly rejected because no agency official saw it.

Once electronic commerce is adopted as the means for publicizing RFPs and submitting proposals, offerors are responsible for monitoring the website for RFPs and amendments. Thus, failure to see an RFP when it is posted is not an excuse for late submission of a proposal, *Optelec U.S., Inc.*, Comp. Gen. Dec. B-400349, 2008 CPD ¶ 192. In that case, the protester had registered on the FedBizOpps website and applied for automatic notification of proposals but had failed to notice that the website had discontinued this practice, resulting in late receipt of the RFP and late submission of the proposal.

[b] Offers That Are "Under the Control" of the Government

The second exception to the late-is-late rule is that offers, revisions, and modifications can be accepted if they are "received at the Government installation designated for receipt" and "under the Government's control" by the closing time. This appears to be a less stringent test than under the prior regulation which provided that offers, revisions and modifications submitted by regular mail, by facsimile, or hand carried that did not arrive at the designated office by the closing time could be considered only if the lateness was due primarily to government mishandling. However, in order to avail itself of the current rule an offeror must show that the proposal was both "received" and "under the control." Thus, a proposal delivered to the agency at the wrong address would be "under the control" of the agency but would not have been "received" because it was not delivered to the "designated" office, *Shirlington Limousine & Transp., Inc.*, Comp. Gen. Dec. B-299241.2, 2007 CPD ¶ 68. Several decisions have found proposals to be not under the control of the government, *National Beef Packing Co.*, Comp. Gen. Dec. B-415754, 2018 CPD ¶ 77 (UPS truck arrived at base gate but no delivery to designated office); *U.S. Aerospace, Inc.*, Comp. Gen. Dec. B-403464, 2010 CPD ¶ 225 (wandering messenger did not relinquish physical custody of the proposal until after the closing time); *Immediate Sys. Res., Inc.*, Comp. Gen. Dec. B-292856, 2003 CPD ¶ 227 (proposal that was time-stamped by a security guard and then taken to the contracting office after the closing time).

The Court of Federal Claims has arrived at a more lenient interpretation of these requirements. See *Electronic On-Ramp, Inc. v. United States*, 104 Fed. Cl. 151 (2012), holding that these tests were met when a courier arrived at the base gate on time but, through a miscommunication with the contracting officer, did not get the proposal to the contracting office on time and a slightly different electronic proposal was received on time. The court found government control when "the offeror relinquishes control over the proposal such that the offeror no longer can modify the proposal." In *Johnson Controls Gov't Sys., LLC v. United States*, 125 Fed. Cl. 289 (2016), the court found that this test was not met when the contractor did not follow the delivery instructions in the solicitation.

Under the prior rule, mishandling by the U.S. Postal Service did not constitute "Government mishandling," *California State Univ., Fullerton*, Comp. Gen. Dec. B-243020.2, 91-1 CPD ¶ 452. See also *Northwest Heritage Consultants*, Comp. Gen. Dec. B-299547, 2007 CPD ¶ 93, where, under the current rule, GAO found that a Postal Service tracking record was found to be insufficient proof of delivery.

An offeror cannot meet the requirement that the government has "received" the proposal on time if it is at fault for the late delivery. See, for example, *Sector One Security Solution*, Comp. Gen. Dec. B-400728, 2008 CPD ¶ 224, where the agency refused delivery of a proposal sent by UPS messenger. GAO denied the protest because the offeror had not made special arrangements for hand-carried proposals as required by the RFP. See also *GGear*, Comp. Gen. Dec. B-413216, 2016 CPD ¶ 223 (offeror did not deliver proposal to correct office); *Castle Grp.*, Comp. Gen. Dec. B-297853, 2006 CPD ¶ 55 (offeror did not use the full address required by the RFP); *Info Grp. Inc.*, Comp. Gen. Dec. B-294610, 2004 CPD ¶ 190 (offeror failed to use room number provided in RFP); *Environmental, Inc.*, Comp. Gen. Dec. B-294057, 2004 CPD ¶ 138 (offerors delivered courier-delivered proposals to address for mailed proposals).

[c] Modifications to "Otherwise Successful" Proposals

Under FAR 15.208(b)(2), the contracting officer can accept a modification to an "otherwise successful" proposal if it makes the terms of the offer more favorable to the government. However, this rule deals only with modifications to offers that have already been determined to be winning offers. Thus, the rule cannot be used to accept a final proposal revision that is late, *Philips Healthcare Informatics*, Comp. Gen. Dec. B-405382.2, 2012 CPD ¶ 220. See *LATG, Inc.*, Comp. Gen. Dec. B-409679.2, 2014 CPD ¶ 226, and *Sunrise Medical HHG, Inc.*, Comp. Gen. Dec. B-310230, 2008 CPD ¶ 7, precluding an offeror from making itself the "otherwise successful offeror" by submitting a late proposal modification. See also *Northstar Location Servs., LLC*, Comp. Gen. Dec. B-409722.10, 2015 CPD ¶ 153 (second phase proposal not a modification because first phase had been cancelled); *Team Sys. Int'l, LLC*, Comp. Gen. Dec. B-410420, 2014 CPD ¶ 378 (original proposal unacceptable); and *Masai Techs.*

Corp. v. United States, 79 Fed. Cl. 433 (2007) (late proposal modifications properly rejected because protester had been told previously that its proposal was unacceptable); and *Omega Sys., Inc.*, Comp. Gen. Dec. B-298767, 2006 CPD ¶ 170 (late proposal revisions properly rejected because offeror had been told in discussions that it was not in line for award). Compare *NCR Govt. Sys. LLC*, Comp. Gen. Dec. B-297959, 2006 CPD ¶ 82, holding that it was proper to accept a late addition to the winning offeror's final proposal revisions because the addition was not instrumental in the award decision.

[d] Emergencies or Unanticipated Events

The "emergency or unanticipated event" exception in ¶ (3)(iv) applies only if the event impacts the operations of the government agency. See *Conscoop—Consorzia Fra Coop. Di Prod. E Lavoro v. United States*, 62 Fed. Cl. 219 (200 (government electronic mail system fully functional and five proposals received in spite of regional power failure); *Educational Planning & Advice, Inc.*, Comp. Gen. Dec. B-274513, 96-2 CPD ¶ 173 (four bidders submitted timely bids and agency proceeded to bid opening in spite of hurricane emergency); and *Unitron Eng'g Co.*, 58 Comp. Gen. 748 (B-194707), 79-2 CPD ¶ 155 (Mail deliveries were normal and five bids received in spite of blizzard).

To show that there was an unanticipated event, a protester must submit clear proof that "normal government processes were interrupted," *National Beef Packing Co., LLC*, Comp. Gen. Dec. B-415754, 2018 CPD ¶ 77. See *CFS-INC, JV*, Comp. Gen. Dec. B-401809.2, 2010 CPD ¶ 85, holding that a severe snowstorm met this standard for one day but that the proposal was late when it was not delivered the next day when the government office was partially open.

[e] Government Fault

Although not addressed expressly in the FAR, GAO has ruled that when government actions are the "sole or paramount" cause of the lateness, the offer should be considered. See *CCSC, Inc.*, Comp. Gen. Dec. B-404802.3, 2011 CPD ¶ 187, stating:

> [A late proposal] can be considered if it is shown that some government impropriety during or after receipt at the government installation was the sole or paramount cause of the late arrival at the designated place. *Chappy Corp.*, B-252757, July 20, 1993, 93-2 CPD ¶ 44 at 3. Improper government action in this context is affirmative action that makes it impossible for the offeror to deliver the proposal on time. *Lani Eko & Co., CPAs, PLLC*, B-404863, June 6, 2011, 2011 CPD ¶ 118 at 3.

Even when government action was partially the fault of the lateness, it has been difficult to prove that it was the sole or paramount cause. See *Vizocom*,

Comp. Gen. Dec. B-418246.2, 2020 CPD ¶ 72 (offeror only left courier 30 minutes to clear security at facility); *National Beef Packing Co. LLC*, Comp. Gen. Dec. B-415754, 2018 CPD ¶ 77 (conflicting evidence of whether there was a security delay at gate); *ERC, Inc.*, Comp. Gen. Dec. B-405563, 2011 CPD ¶ 254 (driver chose not to wait in line at gate); *U.S. Aerospace, Inc.*, Comp. Gen. Dec. B-403464 2010 CPD ¶ 225 (messenger went to wrong gate); *Kesser Int'l*, Comp. Gen. Dec. B-296294, 2005 CPD ¶ 127 (20 minute security delay on a military base should have been foreseen by the offeror); *O.S. Sys., Inc.*, Comp. Gen. Dec. B-292827, 2003 CPD ¶ 211 (contractor should have left time to deal with difficult base security). However, a few decisions have found for the contractor. See, for example, *Latvian Connection, LLC*, Comp. Gen. Dec. B-411489, 2015 CPD ¶ 251 (offerors given less than two days to respond to substantial amendment to the RFP); and *Hospital Klean of Texas, Inc.*, Comp. Gen. Dec. B-295836, 2005 CPD ¶ 185 (designated building was locked).

In *Gunter Constr., Inc.*, Comp. Gen. Dec. B-412039, 2015 CPD ¶ 375, GAO found government fault in providing the e-mail address of the wrong contracting officer for the submission of final proposal revisions (which that contracting officer did not open or forward) but denied the protest because the agency had destroyed the e-mail. GAO cited *Project Resources, Inc.*, Comp. Gen. Dec. B-297968, 2006 CPD ¶ 58, for the proposition that even negligent destruction of a proposal does not entitle a protester to relief.

[f] Waiver

Paragraph (f)(3) of the FAR 52.215-1 Instructions to Offerors—Competitive Acquisition solicitation provision states—"The Government may waive informalities and minor irregularities in proposals received." The Court of Federal Claims has issued two decisions holding that this provision applies to late proposals. In *Electronic-On-Ramp, Inc. v. United States*, 104 Fed. Cl. 151 (2012), the court held that waiver was required because an electronic proposal was submitted on time, but the paper copy was late due to miscommunication between the courier and the contract specialist. The contracting officer had ruled that the proposal was late because the RFP stated that the paper copy controlled, and the electronic copy had been edited to correct minor errors. In *T Square Logistics Servs. Corp. v. United States*, 134 Fed. Cl. 550 (2017), when the Federal Express driver encountered bad weather, the protester called the contract specialist to report the problem and was told that it was not a problem because the FedEx receipt showed that the company had shipped the proposal on time. The count ruled that this was not a waiver but enjoined performance by a competitor to allow the agency to consider whether it should waive this minor informality.

[B] Information

The typical RFP will require the offeror to furnish a considerable amount of information. Much of the information will deal with the offeror's capability to perform, including such subjects as past performance, experience, facilities and equipment, financial capacity and key personnel. Requests for information dealing with how the offeror intends to perform the work and what techniques it will use in managing the work often call for the offeror to include this information in what have been called "technical proposals" and "management proposals." Such requests for information have been criticized as creating "essay contests" and some agencies have stopped requiring them. They should be distinguished from RFP provisions which require the offeror to include in the offer details of the work or explanations of the offer which may or may not be incorporated into the contract. When such technical information is to be incorporated into the contract, it should be accomplished through negotiations and included in a revised offer or in the final contract document.

Offerors must use great care in including required information in the designated part of the proposal because agencies are not required to seek or use information in the wrong part of the proposal. See *BANC3, Inc.*, Comp. Gen. Dec. B-416486, 2018 CPD ¶ 316 (agency not required to "piece together disparate parts of proposal"); *Serka Taahhut Insaat, A.S.*, Comp. Gen. Dec. B-416391.2, 2018 CPD ¶ 284 (agency not required to look in other parts of proposal to find information missing from organization chart); *KSC BOSS Alliance, LLC*, Comp. Gen. Dec. B-416334, 2018 CPD ¶ 267 (agency not required to seek information in price proposal when RFP called for basis of estimate in technical proposal); and *MES Simulation & Training Corp.*, Comp. Gen. Dec. B-416210, 2018 CPD ¶ 261 (agency not required to consider past performance information when technical proposal did not contain detailed description of how protester would meet maintenance requirement). In *MicroTechs., LLC*, Comp. Gen. Dec. B-415214, 2018 CPD ¶ 48, the agency properly refused to consider cross referenced information because it would have violated the RFPs page limitations.

[1] Technical Information

Offerors may be required to furnish technical information which will be used in assessing the offeror's "know how" or the degree of risk involved in the way the offeror intends to perform. When such information is required, offerors should devote full attention to ensuring that their information describes sound technical solutions and contains thorough documentation. Proposals with significant informational deficiencies are excluded as a matter of course, *MicroTechs., LLC*, Comp. Gen. Dec. B-418700, 2020 CPD ¶ 260; *Reagent World, Inc.*, Comp. Gen. Dec. B-415489, 2018 CPD ¶ 51; *AHNTECH, Inc.*, Comp. Gen. Dec. B-299806, 2007 CPD ¶ 213; and submissions that are not supported with sufficient technical information may be excluded from the competitive range, *Hamilton Sundstrand Power Sys. v. United*

States, 75 Fed. Cl. 512 (2007); *Hamilton Sundstrand Power Sys.*, Comp. Gen. Dec. B-298757, 2006 CPD ¶ 209; *LaBarge Prods., Inc.*, Comp. Gen. Dec. B-287841, 2001 CPD ¶ 177. Page limitations on the length of technical proposals are not accepted as an excuse for insufficient technical information, *Professional Performance. Dev. Grp., Inc.*, Comp. Gen. Dec. B-311273, 2008 CPD ¶ 101 (35-page limitation).

If the RFP calls for a specific description of how the work will be performed, the offeror can be downgraded for not supplying such information, *People, Tech. & Processes, LLC*, Comp. Gen. Dec. B-413104.19, 2018 CPD ¶ 314 (explanation of experience and expertise not adequate to meet requirement to provide description of technical approach); *Navarre Corp.*, Comp. Gen. Dec. B-414505.6, 2018 CPD ¶ 242 (fact that company was incumbent does not meet requirement for describing approach); *Armedia, LLC*, Comp. Gen. Dec. B-415525, 2018 CPD ¶ 26 (lack of explanation of techniques to be used). Merely repeating portions of the RFP (termed "parroting" the RFP) is a poor strategy. See *Government Telecommc'ns, Inc.*, Comp. Gen. Dec. B-299542.2, 2007 CPD ¶ 136; and *Bannum, Inc.*, Comp. Gen. Dec. B-271075, 96-1 CPD ¶ 248, where offerors were eliminated from the competitive range because they repeated back portions of the specification without affirmatively demonstrating the merits of their technical approach. Parroting solicitation language almost always leads to downgrading of the technical proposal, *DEI Consulting*, Comp. Gen. Dec. B-401258, 2009 CPD ¶ 151. Similarly, merely promising to meet the requirements in the RFP will almost invariably lead to a poor evaluation, *TSC Enters., LLC*, Comp. Gen. Dec. B-415731, 2018 CPD ¶ 71 (blanket statement of compliance insufficient); *IVI Corp.*, Comp. Gen. Dec. B-310766, 2008 CPD ¶ 21 (blanket offer to submit an "equal" product not sufficient to show that it would meet salient characteristics); *Hubbell Elec. Heater Co.*, Comp. Gen. Dec. B-289098, 2002 CPD ¶ 15 (blanket promise to conform to ISO 9000 insufficient to demonstrate ability to do so).

If the RFP requires the submission of test data to show that an offered product meets the specifications, an offer can be rejected for failing to submit compete test data, *General Dynamics C4 Sys., Inc.*, Comp. Gen. Dec. B-299675.2, 2008 CPD ¶ 122. Technical information may also be necessary to instruct an agency on how to conduct the test of a sample. See *L-3 Commc'ns EOTech, Inc.*, Comp. Gen. Dec. B-311453, 2008 CPD ¶ 139, denying a protest where an agency did not properly use a sample because of lack of information on how to tighten a locking nut.

If an RFP calls for the submission of a sample task response, care must be used to submit a full description of the offeror's approach to performing the task. See *Veterans Tech., LLC*, Comp. Gen. Dec. B-310303.2, 2008 CPD ¶ 31 (response failed to include technical approach or demonstration of competence of personnel).

A misrepresentation as to the technical capabilities of a proposed product can be construed as a false statement under 31 U.S.C. § 1001, subjecting the offeror to civil liability under the False Claims Act, 31 U.S.C. § 3729, *United States ex rel. Westrick v. Second Chance Body Armor, Inc.*, No 04-280 (RWR) (D.D.C. 2010). See *Harrison v. Westinghouse Savannah River Co.*, 176 F.3d 776 (4th Cir. 1999), holding that false statements about how a contract will be performed could be false claims.

[2] Management Information

The offeror may be called upon to explain how it plans to manage the work to attain the promised technical solution. While technical information focuses on how the work will be performed, management information focuses on whether the offeror's organization will manage its resources to achieve those results. The offeror will be required to show the government what personnel and material resources it will use and how it will organize and control those resources to bring the contract work to a successful conclusion. As is the case with technical proposals, lack of detail in management proposals will generally result in lower scores and general statements will not suffice, *Dewberry Crawford Grp.*, Comp. Gen. Dec. B-415940, 2018 CPD ¶ 297 (table with bullet points not adequate explanation of management approach); *Credence Mgmt. Solutions, LLC*, Comp. Gen. Dec. B-415960, 2018 CPD ¶ 294 (lack of identification of tools, templates or processes to be used); *Skyline Ultd., Inc.*, Comp. Gen. Dec. B-416101, 2018 CPD ¶ 259 (lack of detailed quality control plan and methodology for hiring employees); *Innovative Pathways, LLC*, Comp. Gen. Dec. B-416100.2, 2018 CPD ¶ 212 (lack of detailed plan for "phase-out"); *Onsite OHS, Inc.*, Comp. Gen. Dec. B-415987, 2018 CPD ¶ 164 (lack of statement that offeror had contractual relationship with organizations proposal stated it would work with); *MVL-SAGA JV LLC*, Comp. Gen. Dec. B-415610, 2018 CPD ¶ 91 (no explanation of roles of joint venture partners); *IBM Corp.*, Comp. Gen. Dec. B-415575, 2018 CPD ¶ 61 (no detailed explanation of low staffing); *Dexis Consulting Grp.*, Comp. Gen. Dec. B-415483, 2018 CPD ¶ 10 (no "Evidence of specific methods and techniques for completing each discrete task, to include such items as quality assurance, and customer-service" as called for in RFP); *Kuhana-Spectrum*, Comp. Gen. Dec. B-401270, 2010 CPD ¶ 61 (no discussion of how the responsibilities, experience and qualifications of major officials would contribute to successful contract performance); *SPAAN Tech, Inc.*, Comp. Gen. Dec. B-400406, 2009 CPD ¶ 46 (little rationale for proposed organizational structure); *DIY, Inc.*, Comp. Gen. Dec. B-293105.13, 2005 CPD ¶ 50 (insufficient description of methods of conducting management and marketing services for homes); In *Avue Techs. Corp.*, Comp. Gen. Dec. B-298380.4, 2008 CPD ¶ 182, a proposal was rejected for failing to demonstrate that the offeror was agreeing to the agency's requirements regarding proprietary information.

[3] Representations and Certifications

Section K of the RFP will contain a number of representations and certifications that must be filled out by the offeror. Offerors are properly excluded from the competition if they submit a false representation or certification, *Southwestern Bell Tel. Co.*, Comp. Gen. Dec. B-292476, 2003 CPD ¶ 177; *Hedgecock Elec., Inc.*, Comp. Gen. Dec. B-274776.2, 97-1 CPD ¶ 51. See *Universal Techs. Inc.*, Comp. Gen. Dec. B-248808.2, 92-2 CPD ¶ 212, holding that a firm need not be disqualified if the agency determines that the false certification was not made in bad faith. Compare *Tiger Enters., Inc.*, Comp. Gen. Dec. B-292815.3, 2004 CPD ¶ 19, recommending immediate termination of a contract that was awarded based on a false certification that the offeror met the small business size standard. However, the contracting agency is not required to investigate a certification to determine if it is false unless it has information so indicating, *E.D.I., Inc.*, Comp. Gen. Dec. B-251750, 93-1 CPD ¶ 364.

[4] Capability Information

Most RFPs call for the submission of information showing the offeror's capabilities as part of the technical or management proposal or as separate information. The most important types of capability information deal with experience, past performance, and the personnel who will perform the contract. As a general rule, submission of specific information is far more effective than the mere inclusion of general statements on the abilities of the organization, *Honolulu Marine, Inc.*, Comp. Gen. Dec. B-245329, 91-2 CPD ¶ 586; *EAP Consultants*, Comp. Gen. Dec. B-238103, 90-1 CPD ¶ 358. See *Capitol Drywall Supply, Inc.*, Comp. Gen. Dec. B-400721, 2009 CPD ¶ 17, where a proposal was downgraded because it did not include specific information showing experience and relevant past performance, *Prudent Techs., Inc.*, Comp. Gen. Dec. B-297425, 2006 CPD ¶ 16, where a proposal was rated unacceptable because the protester did not furnish specific capability information in the form required by the RFP, and *MIL Corp.*, Comp. Gen. Dec. B-297508, 2006 CPD ¶ 34, and *Carpetmaster*, Comp. Gen. Dec. B-294767, 2004 CPD ¶ 226, where proposals were downgraded for failure to submit specific information as requested by the solicitation.

Offerors should exercise care in the assertions that they make concerning their capability. See *United States ex rel. Longhi v. Lithium Power Techs., Inc.*, 530 F. Supp.2d 888 (S.D. Tex. 2008), *aff'd*, 575 F.3d 458 (5th Cir. 2009), *cert. denied*, 559 U.S. 1067 (2010), assessing triple the contract price as damages because the contractor misrepresented its prior experience, its arrangements with another firm and the extent of its facilities in its proposal. See also *Dual, Inc.*, Comp. Gen. Dec. B-280719, 98-2 CPD ¶ 133, sustaining a protest for misrepresentation because the winning offeror had stated that it would perform the work at a particular division when, in fact, it was negotiating the sale of that division to another company while the procurement was being conducted. For other sustained protests see *FCi Fed., Inc.*, Comp. Gen. Dec. B-408558.7, 2015 CPD ¶ 245 (winning offeror did not disclose that it had been sold and prior parent company's resources were to be used to perform contract); *Wyle Labs., Inc.*, Comp. Gen. Dec. B-408112.2, 2014 CPD ¶ 16 (winning offeror did not disclose that it was planning to divide the company into two entities); and *Greenleaf Constr. Co.*, Comp. Gen. Dec. B-293105.18, 2006 CPD ¶ 19 (winning offeror had not informed the agency that two of the designated key personnel had stated they would not work on contract). Compare *Dell Servs. Fed. Gov't, Inc.*, Comp. Gen. Dec. B-412340, 2016 CPD ¶ 43, denying a protest claiming nondisclosure because the impending corporate restructuring of the awardee's parent would not have any effect on the awardee's performance and there was no indication that the awardee planned to rely on the resources of its corporate parent.

[a] Experience and Past Performance

Information concerning an offeror's experience and past performance record will be required to be furnished in almost all procurements. Experience deals with the types of work which the offeror or its employees have performed and past performance deals with how well the work has been performed. While the request may not clearly distinguish between the two, both types of information will be important.

In addition to complying with the RFP's specific requests for past performance information, offerors should include additional information which would explain or supplement the information furnished. Thus, the offeror should provide a detailed analysis of its past performance on contracts that are similar to the procurement in question and should demonstrate that those contracts are relevant to the evaluation of its performance for the current effort, *OneSource PCS, LLC*, Comp. Gen. Dec. B-419222, 2021 CPD ¶ 17. If the RFP requires offerors to obtain questionnaires from references, it is the offeror's responsibility to ensure that the questionnaires are submitted, *Capitol Drywall Supply, Inc.*, Comp. Gen. Dec. B-400721, 2009 CPD ¶ 17; *American Floor Consultants, Inc.*, Comp. Gen. Dec. B-294530.7, 2006 CPD ¶ 97, and that they are submitted by an independent source, *Metro Mach. Corp.*, Comp. Gen. Dec. B-295744, 2005 CPD ¶ 112 (evaluation by offeror of subcontractors did not meet RFP requirement for independent evaluation). Where there have been instances of poor or unsuccessful past performance, the offeror should provide any factual information which would establish extenuating circumstances. In addition, factual information on steps taken to correct or avoid such occurrences should be included. See *West Sound Servs. Grp., LLC*, Comp. Gen. Dec. B-406583.4, 2014 CPD ¶ 208 (protest denied when protester failed to include information on upward trend in performance); *Del-Jen Int'l Corp.*, Comp. Gen. Dec. B-297960, 2006 CPD ¶ 81 (protest denied when protester did not demonstrate that it had corrected past deficiencies in performing as incumbent contractor); *Hanley Indus., Inc.*, Comp. Gen. Dec. B-295318, 2005 CPD ¶ 20 (low rating of past performance justified when protester did not take opportunity to submit evidence of corrective action); *Si-Nor, Inc.*, Comp. Gen. Dec. B-292748.2, 2004 CPD ¶ 10 (low rating of past performance justified when agency was given only partial evidence of corrective action). The past performance of a parent company may be used if the offeror can show that the parent will participate in performing the prospective contract, *Frontier Sys. Integrators, LLC*, Comp. Gen. Dec. B-298872.3, 2007 CPD ¶ 46.

When information on experience is requested, a detailed description of past efforts should be provided, *M. Erdal Kamisli, Ltd.*, Comp. Gen. Dec. B-291522, 2003 CPD ¶ 19, and lack of detailed information may lead to downgrading the proposal, *Office Design Grp.*, Comp. Gen. Dec. B-415853.3, 2018 CPD ¶ 265 (lack of explanation of how employees met experience requirements); *Ampous, Inc.*, Comp. Gen. Dec. B-415708, 2018 CPD ¶ 113 (resumes did not show required experience). If the RFP specifically calls for proof of experience by submitting a signed contract, this requirement may be strictly enforced, *ABSG Consulting, Inc.*, Comp. Gen. Dec. B-413155.14, 2016 CPD ¶ 287. In some cases, the RFP may require information on the experience of both the offeror and its personnel. Where an offeror has not had the specific experience required, the lack of corporate experience may be overcome by the experience of employees or subcontractors, *ACME Indus, Inc.*, Comp. Gen. Dec. B-414023, 2017 CPD ¶ 22 (evaluating experience of employees or subcontractors a useful way to predict success in performing contract); and *EBA Eng'g, Inc.*, Comp. Gen. Dec. B-275818, 97-1 CPD ¶ 127 (a competitor for a service contract was entitled to use the experience of the incumbent employees). If a parent or affiliate company's resources will be used to perform the contract, information on their experience may be provided but an agency is not required to consider this information, *Eagle Eye Elec., LLC*, Comp. Gen. Dec. B-415562, 2018 CPD ¶ 33.

[b] Key Personnel

The personnel that the offeror intends to use in performing the contract are often of prime importance. Thus, resumes of key personnel are frequently required in some cases are submitted even when they have not been requested. The importance of complying with resume requirements is demonstrated by *Verizon Fed., Inc.*, Comp. Gen. Dec. B-293527, 2004 CPD ¶ 186, where an offeror was rated unacceptable because of missing and incomplete resumes even though it was rated outstanding in past performance. See also *SOC, LLC*, Comp. Gen. Dec. B-415460.2, 2018 CPD ¶ 20 (protester rated unacceptable because of vague description of work of key person); *DEI Consulting*, Comp. Gen. Dec. B-401258. 2009 CPD ¶ 151 (protester properly downgraded because it did not specify which of its offered engineers would be the senior engineer); *Client Network Servs., Inc.*, Comp. Gen. Dec. B-297994, 2006 CPD ¶ 79 (protester properly downgraded because the resumes it submitted did not meet the page limitations or format requirements in the RFP). In *Earth Resources Tech.*,

Inc., Comp. Gen. Dec. B-416415, 2018 CPD ¶ 312, GAO rejected the argument that the agency should have rated the communication skills of its employees highly because its personnel had seen them make presentations at conferences, stating that technical evaluations are "dependent on the information furnished "not agency knowledge. Compare *Global Solutions Network, Inc.*, Comp. Gen. Dec. B-298682.3, 2008 CPD ¶ 131, denying a protest that the agency allowed the winning offeror to submit resumes exceeding the RFP page limitation—because the protester was not prejudiced. GAO used similar reasoning in granting a protest where the agency had improperly downgraded a proposal because the resumes did not include information that it had learned during discussions, *Arora Grp.*, Comp. Gen. Dec. B-293102, 2004 CPD ¶ 61.

Offerors have also been disqualified from the competition because of inaccuracies in listing key personnel, *Electronic Data Sys. Fed. Corp.*, GSBCA 9869-P, 89-2 BCA ¶ 21,655, *recons. denied*, 89-2 BCA ¶ 21,778, *aff'd in part, vacated in part sub. nom. Planning Research Corp. v. United States*, 971 F.2d 736 (Fed. Cir. 1992) (submission of 101 resumes with no intention to use the personnel); *Ultra Tech. Corp.*, Comp. Gen. Dec. B-230309.6, 89-1 CPD ¶ 42 (proposing person as "lead technician" without obtaining his permission); *ManTech Advanced Sys. Int'l., Inc.*, Comp. Gen. Dec. B-255719.2, 94-1 CPD ¶ 326 (misrepresenting availability of incumbent personnel); *Patricio Enters., Inc.*, Comp. Gen. Dec. B-412738, 2016 CPD ¶ 145 (misrepresenting commitment of proposed personnel). Compare *Patriot Contract Servs., LLC v. United States*, 388 F. Supp. 2d 1010 (N.D. Cal. 2005), holding that the winning offeror had not clearly known that most of the key personnel would not be available when the contract was awarded a year after their names had been submitted, and *Orion Int'l Techs. v. United States*, 66 Fed. Cl. 569 (2005), holding that there was no misrepresentation when an employee of the incumbent contractor had signed a noncompete agreement but appeared willing to work for the offeror. In *CBIS Fed., Inc.*, 71 Comp. Gen. 319 (B-245844.2), 92-1 CPD ¶ 308, and *Greenleaf Constr. Co.*, Comp. Gen. Dec. B-293105.18, 2006 CPD ¶ 19, GAO stated that when an offeror finds that proposed personnel are no longer available, the offeror should withdraw the names and propose substitutes in the best and final offer. However, *Chenega Healthcare Servs., LLC*, Comp. Gen. Dec. B-416158, 2018 CPD ¶ 200, and *Chenega Healthcare Servs., LLC v. United States*, 138 Fed. Cl. 644 (2018), hold that an agency may reject the submission of a substitute person and reject the offeror for inability to provide the required key person.

In many cases, the offeror will be required to furnish evidence that the listed key personnel will be available for performance if the offeror receives the award. In such cases, GAO has ruled that award would be improper if the offeror does not supply information ensuring that key personnel would be available to perform the contract, *ManTech Field Eng'g Corp.*, Comp. Gen. Dec. B-245886.4, 92-1 CPD ¶ 309. Thus, failure to do so will result in the submission being held to be unacceptable or downgraded, *Native American Indus. Distribs., Inc.*, Comp.

Gen. Dec. B-310737.3, 2008 CPD ¶76 (signed nondisclosure agreements not substitutes for required letters of commitment); *Xeta Int'l Corp.*, Comp. Gen. Dec. B-255182, 94-1 CPD ¶109 (failure to provide required letters of commitment for proposed key personnel). Compare *Science Applications Int'l Corp.*, Comp. Gen. Dec. B-290971, 2002 CPD ¶184, holding that a commitment statement on signed resumes met the requirement for a letter of commitment.

[C] Rules Governing Submission

The RFP will specify the method of submitting offers and information and the format that must be observed. The failure to follow these instructions may result in the submission being rejected. See *Environmental Control Div., Inc.*, Comp. Gen. Dec. B-255181, 94-1 CPD ¶115, where GAO found that the agency properly rejected a protester's BAFO which was transmitted by facsimile in response to the agency's facsimile transmitted request for BAFOs because the solicitation did not allow for offers or modifications to be transmitted by facsimile.

[1] Method of Submission

The basic method of submission of offers and information is in paper media in a sealed envelope. However, there are a growing number of procurements where facsimile or electronic submission is permitted or required. In addition, part or all of the required information may be submitted in an oral presentation.

[a] Paper Media

Paragraph (c) of the Instructions to Offerors—Competitive Acquisition solicitation provision in FAR 52.215-1 provides guidance on the basic procedure to be followed in submitting offers and information:

> (1) Unless other methods (e.g., electronic commerce or facsimile) are permitted in the solicitation, proposals and modifications to proposals shall be submitted in paper media in sealed envelopes or packages (i) addressed to the office specified in the solicitation, and (ii) showing the time and date specified for receipt, the solicitation number, and the name and address of the offeror. Offerors using commercial carriers should ensure that the proposal is marked on the outermost wrapper with the information in paragraphs (c)(1)(i) and (c)(1)(ii) of this provision.
>
> (2) The first page of the proposal must show—
>
> (i) The solicitation number;
>
> (ii) The name, address, and telephone and facsimile numbers of the offeror (and electronic address if available);

(iii) A statement specifying the extent of agreement with all terms, conditions, and provisions included in the solicitation and agreement to furnish any or all items upon which prices are offered at the price set opposite each item;

(iv) Names, titles, and telephone and facsimile numbers (and electronic addresses if available) of persons authorized to negotiate on the offeror's behalf with the Government in connection with this solicitation; and

(v) Name, title, and signature of person authorized to sign the proposal. Proposals signed by an agent shall be accompanied by evidence of that agent's authority, unless that evidence has been previously furnished to the issuing office.

[b] Facsimile or Electronic Submission

FAR 15.203(c) provides that when electronic commerce is an authorized means of submission, the RFP must "specify the electronic commerce method(s) that offerors may use (see Subpart 4.5)." FAR 15.209(e) requires the contracting officer to include the Facsimile Proposals solicitation provision in FAR 52.215-5 in an RFP when submission by facsimiles is authorized. The instructions for handling unreadable portions of facsimile or electronic submissions contained in this provision are set forth in FAR 15.207(c).

Offerors assume the risk of having their facsimile or electronic transmissions considered, *S.W. Elecs. & Mfg. Corp.*, Comp. Gen. Dec. B-249308, 92-2 CPD ¶ 320. Thus, evidence of transmission will not be considered evidence of receipt by the agency, *Advanced Decisions Vectors, Inc.*, Comp. Gen. Dec. B-412307, 2016 CPD ¶ 18 (e-mail); *International Garment Processors*, Comp. Gen. Dec. B-299674, 2007 CPD ¶ 130 (facsimile).

[c] Oral Presentations

Oral presentations, as discussed earlier, have been used for some time to enable procurement officials to obtain information leading to additional understanding of the offerors' capability and features of their offers. However, it was not until the FAR Part 15 Rewrite that comprehensive coverage was adopted for these procedures. FAR 15.102 provides detailed guidance on obtaining information, but not offers, through this process. The RFP should identify the process that the agency will require offerors to follow in making the oral presentation. See FAR 15.102(d). If there is any ambiguity in the RFP as to the precise process to be followed, an offeror should request more detail from the contracting officer. Agencies may require that offerors meet mandatory requirements in an RFP before being eligible to make an oral presentation, *Inte-Great Corp.*, Comp. Gen. Dec. B-272780, 96-2 CPD ¶ 159, and it is very common practice to conduct oral presentations with only those offerors in the competitive range.

The offeror should use the oral presentation to demonstrate that it is fully capable of performing the critical tasks on the proposed contract. This is usually best done by discussing these tasks and identifying key problems that are anticipated and proposed methods of dealing with those problems. Lengthy discussion of the general capabilities of the offeror is generally not as effective as specific identification of the capability to perform key tasks. See *Client Network Servs., Inc.*, Comp. Gen. Dec. B-297994, 2006 CPD ¶ 79, where an offeror was downgraded because it covered general capability in the oral presentation rather than addressing the issues involved in the procurement for which it was competing. It is also important that all of the designated tasks be addressed adequately during the oral presentation. See *Leidos Innovations Corp.*, Comp. Gen. Dec. B-415514, 2018 CPD ¶ 88 (proper downgrading for lack of detail on specific issues); *Dev Tech. Grp.*, Comp. Gen. Dec. B-412163, 2016 CPD ¶ 10 (proper downgrading for weak response to problem posed during presentation); *Astro Sys., Inc*, Comp. Gen. Dec. B-411881.2, 2015 CPD ¶ 371 (proper downgrading for weak response to questions asked during presentation); *Square Logistics Servs. Corp.*, Comp. Gen. Dec. B-291851, 2003 CPD ¶ 160 (downgrading required when presentation did not address some of the specified sub-elements of the work).

Offerors should consider whether the key personnel that they propose to use will be available to attend the oral presentation. See *Sandi Grp., Inc.*, Comp. Gen. Dec. B-401218, 2009 CPD ¶ 123, holding that the protester was properly denied the opportunity to make an oral presentation (or to compete for the work) when its project manager left the company after the proposal had been submitted and the agency refused to permit substitution of another person because that would constitute a late proposal revision.

Offerors should exercise care in the assertions that they make in their oral presentations. See *Johnson Controls Sec. Sys.*, Comp. Gen. Dec. B-296490, 2007 CPD ¶ 102, where an offeror was faced with potential disqualification because it misrepresented in its oral presentation that it was taking required actions to qualify its personnel. Compare *EBA Eng'g, Inc.*, Comp. Gen. Dec. B-275818, 97-1 CPD ¶ 127, where the protester argued that the winning offeror had been guilty of misrepresentation by stating that it would hire all necessary incumbent employees to perform the service contract that was the subject of the competition. GAO held that this was not a defect in the procurement because the offeror had inserted a statement in its BAFO correcting this overly broad statement.

The offeror's oral presentation team will often be composed of key personnel who will perform or personally direct the work if awarded the contract, such as project managers, task leaders, and other in-house staff. If a significant amount of the work will be subcontracted, it may be appropriate for members of the subcontractor staff to make the relevant presentation. The offeror's team should demonstrate that it has the expertise to satisfy the requirement. Compare *ARTEL, Inc.*, Comp. Gen. Dec. B-248478, 92-2 CPD ¶ 120, where the agency concluded from an oral presentation that there were serious doubts as to the quality and availability of the offeror's key personnel, and *Planning & Dev. Collaborative Int'l*, Comp. Gen. Dec. B-299041, 2007 CPD ¶ 28, where an offeror was downgraded because its team did not work well together during an oral presentation, with *Savannah River Alliance, LLC*, Comp. Gen. Dec. B-311126, 2008 CPD ¶ 88, where the agency selected a contractor based, to large measure, on the fact that its team functioned very well in solving problems during the oral presentation,. It can be seen that one of the most important aspects of an oral presentation is the ability of the offeror's participants to function well as a team. See *Gulf Coast Petroleum Reserve Operations, LLC*, Comp. Gen. Dec. B-409004.2, 2014 CPD ¶ 41, where the protester was downgraded because its team did not function well in answering questions.

The present regulations make it clear that agency officials may ask questions and seek further detail. This is consistent with prior decisions, *NAHB Research Found., Inc.*, Comp. Gen. Dec. B-219344, 85-2 CPD ¶ 248 (aggressive questioning permissible). Offerors have been properly downgraded because they did not give convincing responses to questions during an oral presentation. See *Zolon Tech, Inc.*, Comp. Gen. Dec. B-299904.2, 2007 CPD ¶ 183 (no member of offeror's team could answer a question about a critical aspect of the proposed work); *Advanced Tech. Sys., Inc.*, Comp. Gen. Dec. B-296493.5, 2006 CPD ¶ 147, (team responded that it had not yet decided on what management tool to use). See also *Systems Research & Applications Corp.*, Comp. Gen. Dec. B-299818, 2008 CPD ¶ 28, where a protest was granted, in part, because the agency failed to ask the protester to explain a term used in the oral presentation and then downgraded the protester because it did not understand the term.

Agencies may also adopt reasonable rules governing the nature of the presentations, including limitations on the length and nature of the presentations, *American Sys. Corp.*, 68 Comp. Gen. 475 (B-234449), 89-1 CPD ¶ 537.

Agencies may either preclude or permit discussions during the oral presentation, FAR 15.102(d)(6). However, if discussions occur, the agency must comply with the rules governing negotiations with all offerors in the competitive range, FAR 15.102(g). See *Global Analytic Info. Tech. Servs., Inc.*, Comp. Gen. Dec. B-298840.2, 2007 CPD ¶ 57, holding that a discussion had occurred when an agency asked for more detailed pricing information during the oral presentation and the offeror subsequently submitted the information using revised pricing logic. Most protests on this issue have found that no discussions occurred during the oral presentation, *Sapient Gov't Servs., Inc.*, Comp. Gen. Dec. B-412163.2, 2016 CPD ¶ 11 (follow-up questions not a discussion): *Sierra Military Health Servs., Inc.*, Comp. Gen. Dec. B-292780, 2004 CPD ¶ 55 (probing staffing information in original presentation not discussion); *Development Alternatives, Inc.*, Comp. Gen. Dec. B-279920, 98-2 CPD ¶ 54 (question and answer session not discussions).

It has been common practice for agencies to require the submission of slides to be used in the oral presentation at the time the original proposal is submitted. This requirement has been strictly enforced, *KSEND v. United States*, 69 Fed.

Cl. 103 (2005) (proposal properly rejected when transparencies were not submitted with offer). See also *Innovative Mgmt., Inc.*, Comp. Gen. Dec. B-291375, 2003 CPD ¶ 11, finding no basis for a protest when the agency lost the transparencies with the result that the protester had to use copies during the presentation.

[2] Format and Style

The format and style of a submission are intangible considerations in winning competitions. A good submission is organized and written so that it can be read by government evaluators of many different functional and technical disciplines such as management, contracting, engineering, legal, accounting, and others. Some features the offeror will want to consider in developing its proposal are:

Inclusion of an *executive summary* to highlight the salient aspects. A good summary may be read by the source selection official and other agency officials too busy to read the entire document.

An *index* which cross-references the statement of work to the information and the offer. This can be valuable in showing the government exactly how the offer matches the evaluation factors expressed in the RFP.

The *organization* of the submission should indicate that the offeror is orderly, thorough, and effective. It should be made easy to break out into component parts (frequently separate volumes) for evaluation by technical, business, and pricing personnel.

The way in which a submission is presented can have a significant effect on its evaluation. See *Epsilon, Inc.*, Comp. Gen. Dec. B-419278, 2021 CPD ¶ 71, and *Orbis, Inc.*, Comp. Gen. Dec. B-408033.2, 2013 CPD ¶ 148 (proposals downgraded for typographical errors); *Fintrac, Inc.*, Comp. Gen. Dec. B-311462.2, 2008 CPD ¶ 191 (agency not required to correct for typographical error); and *Engineering & Envt., Inc.*, Comp. Gen. Dec. B-271868.3, 96-2 CPD ¶ 182 ("many typographical errors and misspelling" and "inattention to detail").

Proposals are also routinely downgraded for very minor misstatements. See *Performance Sys., LLC*, Comp. Gen. Dec. B-416374, 2018 CPD ¶ 283 (description of security status as "Top Secret, SCI eligible" led agency reasonably to conclude that this left ambiguous whether the person had an active top secret clearance); and *EMTA Insaat Taahhut Ve Ticaret, A.S.*, Comp. Gen. Dec. B-416391, 2018 CPD ¶ 280 (offeror labeled its person in charge of the project the "managing director" when the RFP required it to identify the"program manager").

Solicitations frequently require information to be submitted in specified formats and these requirements must be followed. See *Safeguard Base Operations, LLC v. United States*, 144 Fed. Cl. 304 (2019), and *Safeguard Base Operations, LLC*, Comp. Gen. Dec. B-415588.6, 2018 CPD ¶ 426 ("plug numbers" omitted from price list); *Serka Taahhut Insaat, A.S.*, Comp. Gen. Dec. B-416391.2, 2018 CPD ¶ 284 (required "lines of authority" not on organization chart but in other parts of proposal); *Sallyport Global Holdings, Inc.*, Comp. Gen. Dec. B-415460, 2018 CPD ¶ 23 (pricing information not on Microsoft Excel); *Enterprise Servs., LLC*, Comp. Gen. Dec. B-414513.2, 2017 CPD ¶ 241 (labor hours omitted from required basis of estimate formats); *Arbinger Co.*, Comp. Gen. Dec. B-413156.21, 2017 CPD ¶ 100 (required attachment not included); *Technatomy Corp.*, Comp. Gen. Dec. B-411583, 2015 CPD ¶ 282 (no updated version of pricing template); *SBSI, Inc.*, Comp. Gen. Dec. B-410923, 2015 CPD ¶ 112 (identification of offeror and subcontractors not hidden as required by RFP).

Proposals are routinely rejected for failure to supply required information. See, for example, *Distributed Sols., Inc.*, Comp. Gen. Dec. B-416394, 2018 CPD ¶ 279 (cover letter lacked affirmative statements required by RFP); *ZemiTek, LLC*, Comp. Gen. Dec. B-415313, 2018 CPD ¶ 181 (lack of resumes for lower-level employees not clearly required by RFP); *Software Eng'g Servs. Corp.*, Comp. Gen. Dec. B-415694.2, 2018 CPD ¶ 97 (lack of proper document to demonstrate experience); *Strategic Resources, Inc.*, Comp. Gen. Dec. B-411024.3, 2015 CPD ¶ 200 (lack of plug number furnished in RFP); *Bethel-Webcor JV*, Comp. Gen. Dec. B-410772, 2015 CPD ¶ 96 (lack of copy of mentor-protégé agreement); *PCMG*, Comp. Gen. Dec. B-410797, 2015 CPD ¶ 73 (Internet site instead of technical literature). Information in the wrong part of a proposal is also a frequent grounds for rejection, *Enterprise Servs., LLC*, Comp. Gen. Dec. B-414513.2, 2017 CPD ¶ 241 (labor hours per labor category in price volume but not in technical volume); *Graybar*, Comp. Gen. Dec. B-410886, 2015 CPD ¶ 102 (past performance information in wrong volume). *Science Applications Int'l Corp. v. United States*, 108 Fed. Cl. 235 (2012) (management information in wrong volume).

It is the offeror's responsibility to ensure its submission is, in all respects, a complete document, *Westvold & Assocs.*, Comp. Gen. Dec. B-201032, 81-1 CPD ¶ 354. It should also be a coherent document—both within each section and among sections. One of the most common failings is the inclusion of conflicting data and information in the technical, management, and cost sections. See, for example, *Earle Palmer Brown Cos.*, 70 Comp. Gen. 667 (B-243544) 91-2 CPD ¶ 134, where the agency properly adjusted the contractor's price upward upon determining that the contractor could not pay the salary of required personnel for the cost offered in its proposal; and *AmerInd, Inc.*, Comp. Gen. Dec. B-248324, 92-2 CPD ¶ 85, where the agency properly determined that the costs offered by the protester bore no relation to the cost of personnel for whom the protester submitted resumes.

Where data can be summarized in graphic form, it is often good practice to include such charts and graphs. They are particularly valuable when page limitations make it necessary to present information in the most concise form. However, such charts and graphs should be simple and direct. Although the FAR Part 15 Rewrite eliminated the Unnecessarily Elaborate Proposals or Quotations solicitation provision, it is still sound advice not to submit unnecessarily elaborate brochures or other presentations beyond those sufficient to present a complete and effective response to a solicitation. In *Professional Data Servs., Inc.*, Comp. Gen. Dec. B-220002, 33 Cont. Cases Fed. (CCF) ¶ 74,331, Dec. 13, 1985, the GAO upheld the agency's rejection of the protester's offer because it was overly elaborate. Conversely, when a proposal has been rejected because it lacks detail or specifics, GAO routinely rejected the argument that the proposal could not be more detailed without violating the unnecessarily elaborate proposal prohibition, *TLC Sys.*, Comp. Gen. Dec. B-243220, 91-2 CPD ¶ 37; *Global Valuation Serv.*, Comp. Gen. Dec. B-230753, 88-1 CPD ¶ 604.

Another formal requirement in many solicitations is a page limitation for some or all of the sections of the proposal. Page limitations are strictly enforced, *Benaka, Inc.*, Comp. Gen. Dec. B-418639, 2020 CPD ¶ 371 (cover page included when RFP stated page limitation included "all pages"); *DKW Communications, Inc.*, Comp. Gen. Dec. B-412652.3, 2016 CPD ¶ 143 (agency improperly permitted offeror to compress line spacing); *Tetra Tech AMT*, Comp. Gen. Dec. B-411934.2, 2016 CPD ¶ 136 (proposal unacceptable because excess pages were not given to evaluators); *Client Network Servs., Inc.*, Comp. Gen. Dec. B-297994, 2006 CPD ¶ 79 (proposal properly downgraded for excess pages and using smaller font); *Electronic Design, Inc.*, Comp. Gen. Dec. B-279662.2, 98-2 CPD ¶ 69 (agency improperly permitted offeror to include material greatly exceeding page limitations in BAFO without informing other offerors). However, an agency can waive the page limitations if they are violated by all of the offerors and there is no competitive advantage given to the selected offeror, *Vencore, Inc.*, Comp. Gen. Dec. B-416994.2, 2019 CPD ¶ 221. In *Macfadden & Assocs., Inc.*, Comp. Gen. Dec. B-275502, 97-1 CPD ¶ 88, GAO reasoned that an agency can automatically reject an entire proposal that exceeds a page limit rather than evaluate only the proposal pages within the limit when the language of the solicitation explicitly states that this course of action will be followed. In *HSQ Tech.*, Comp. Gen. Dec. B-277048, 97-2 CPD ¶ 57, the RFP stated that noncompliance with the stated page limitation "could result in elimination of the offer from the proposal process." GAO followed the logic in *Macfadden* stating that "could" meant that such a proposal could not automatically be rejected but rather may properly be rejected only if there was a reasonable basis for the rejection. GAO found that the agency reasonably concluded that the proposal without the excess pages was unacceptable since it lacked material sections of the technical proposal and the entire price proposal.

Clever offerors have found ways to maximize their submitted information by closely reading the page limitations and using their exclusions. See *Technology Innovation Alliance LLC v. United States*, 149 Fed. Cl. 105 (2020), where the winning contractor used "text boxes" to include information in permitted small type size; *Solers Inc.*, Comp. Gen. Dec. B-418500.2, 2020 CPD ¶ 261, where the winning contractor avoided the page limitations on technical proposals—by including detailed experience information in its executive summary; *CACI, Inc.-Federal*, Comp. Gen. Dec. B-418110.3, 2020 CPD ¶ 181, where the winning contractor included detailed text in permitted "figures"; and *Lockheed Martin Corp.*, Comp. Gen. Dec. B-411365.2, 2015 CPD ¶ 294, where both competitors avoided the page limitations on technical proposals by including information in their basis of estimate in their cost proposals that had no page limitations.

Paragraph (c)(iv) of the Instructions to Offerors—Competitive Acquisition solicitation provision in FAR 52.215-1 contains a further formal requirement—that offerors must provide the names, titles, and telephone and facsimile numbers of persons authorized to negotiate on the offeror's behalf. While there is no indication that a proposal can be rejected for failure to comply with this requirement, the information should be furnished as a matter of course in each proposal.

[3] Proprietary Data

FAR 15.207(b) provides that proposals must be "safeguarded from unauthorized disclosure throughout the source selection process." This provision merely instructs the contracting officer on the protections that are required to be used in handling the data. Offerors are permitted to place proprietary markings on their proposals to ensure that such protection is given. The following ¶ (e) in FAR 52.215-1 implements this regulation:

> Offerors that include in their proposals data that they do not want disclosed to the public for any purpose, or used by the Government except for evaluation purposes, shall—
>
> (1) Mark the title page with the following legend:
>
>> This proposal includes data that shall not be disclosed outside the Government and shall not be duplicated, used, or disclosed—in whole or in part—for any purpose other than to evaluate this proposal. If, however, a contract is awarded to this offeror as a result of—or in connection with—the submission of this data, the Government shall have the right to duplicate, use, or disclose the data to the extent provided in the resulting contract. This restriction does not limit the Government's right to use information contained in this data if it is obtained from another source without restriction. The data subject to this restriction are contained in sheets *[insert numbers or other identification of sheets]*; and
>
> (2) Mark each sheet of data it wishes to restrict with the following legend:
>
>> Use or disclosure of data contained on this sheet is subject to the restriction on the title page of this proposal.

This provision permits offerors to mark all data in the proposal—whether technical, management, or financial data—with the prescribed legend, and requires government agencies to protect such data during the source selection process, and thereafter for the losing offerors. However, if the contract is awarded, this provision states that the government's obligation to protect the data of the winning offeror ceases, and, thereafter, the government's right to disclose the information is governed by the clauses of the contract. FAR 27.407 permits civilian agencies to use the following Rights in Proposal Data clause in FAR 52.227-23:

> Except for data contained on pages ___, it is agreed that as a condition of award of this contract, and notwithstanding the conditions of any notice appearing thereon, the Government shall have unlimited rights (as defined in the Rights in Data—General clause contained in this contract) in and to the technical data contained in the proposal dated ___, upon which this contract is based.

When this clause is included in the contract, the offeror should be careful to fill in the pages where there is proprietary data. See *General Atronics Corp.*, ASBCA 49196, 02-1 BCA ¶ 31,798, where the contractor was held to have given the government unlimited rights to software submitted without proprietary legends even though it had inserted "all" in the clause. With regard to properly marked technical data submitted to civilian agencies, protection would be determined by the terms of the Rights in Data—General clause in FAR 52.227-14 when it is included in the resulting contract. If this clause is not included in the contract, there may well be no government promise to protect proprietary technical data. Even if the clause is included in the contract, it contains no government promise to protect management and financial data. Thus, offerors dealing with civilian agencies desiring to protect such data should request that a clause be included in the contract for that purpose.

With regard to proposal data submitted to the Department of Defense, DFARS 227.7103-6(e)(1) and DFARS 227.7203-6(b) require the inclusion of the Rights in Bid or Proposal Information clause in DFARS 252.227-7016 in all contracts for noncommercial items. This clause provides:

> (c) Government rights subsequent to contract award—The Contractor agrees—
>
> > (1) Except as provided in paragraphs (c)((2), (d), and (e) of this clause, the Government shall have the rights to use, modify, reproduce, release, perform, display, or disclose information contained in the Contractor's bid or proposal within the Government. The Government shall not release, perform, display, or disclose such information outside the Government without the Contractor's written permission.
> >
> > (2) The Government's right to use, modify, reproduce, release, perform, display, or disclose information that is technical data or computer software required to be delivered under this contract are determined by the Rights in Technical Data-Noncommercial Items, Rights in Noncommercial Computer Software and Noncommercial Computer

> Software Documentation, or Rights in Noncommercial Technical Data and Computer Software-Small Business Innovative Research (SBIR) Program clause(s) of this contract.

The clauses specified in ¶ (2) give protection to all technical data pertaining to items, components, or processes developed at private expense and all computer software developed at private expense as well as to all such data developed with mixed funding if such data contains the legends specified in the clauses. In *Boeing Co. v. Sec'y of the Air Force*, 983 F.3d 1321 (Fed. Cir. 2020), the court held that an offeror may also mark data developed at government expense with a legend stating that it owned the rights to the data and did not permit third parties to use the data without a license. The clause does not cover management and financial data. Thus, such data that is submitted with the prescribed proprietary legends would appear to be protected.

Both 10 U.S.C. § 3309 (formerly § 2305(g)) and 41 U.S.C. § 4702(b) prohibits disclosure of proposal data pursuant to requests under the Freedom of Information Act, 5 U.S.C. § 552, unless it is incorporated in the contract by reference. These statutes would appear to override the above contract language limiting the protection for the winning contractor.

FAR 15.309 provides additional instructions concerning the protection of data in unsolicited proposals. This procedure directs contracting officers to protect data in proposals even though legends are omitted and advises contracting officers to attempt to persuade offerors to delete legends that are different from the prescribed legend. This procedure also authorizes contracting officers to reject proposals with deviating legends. See, however, *Xerxe Grp., Inc. v. United States*, 278 F.3d 1357 (Fed. Cir. 2002), where the court ignored the FAR language calling for the protection of unmarked data and held that the offeror gave up all rights by not marking the data. This decision requires companies submitting unsolicited proposals to carefully follow the FAR marking instructions. See also FAR 15.609(e), noting that the provisions of the Freedom of Information Act override this government promise to protect information—as was established in *Petkas v. Staats*, 501 F.2d 887, 163 U.S. App. D.C. 327 (D.C. Cir. 1974).

§ 6.06 COMMUNICATIONS TO FACILITATE EVALUATION

Following the submission of offers, there are many occasions when communications between the government and one or more of the offerors would facilitate the evaluation process. After the receipt of initial offers, such communications can assist the government in determining whether to make an award on initial proposals or in deciding which offerors should be included in the competitive range. Communications can also be helpful if questions arise after the submission of final revised offers. In these situations, communications may also be necessary when mistakes are suspected or alleged. However, if any of these communications become "discussions," the government loses the right to award without conducting discussions with all offerors in the competitive range.

This limitation on the ability of an agency to communicate with offerors during proposal evaluation places contracting officials in a dilemma. To maximize efficiency, they want to award contracts on the basis of the initial proposals as frequently as possible, and if they establish a competitive range and conduct discussions, they want to award a contract based on the final proposal revisions that are received thereafter. Yet, in both of these situations, they do not want to award a contract without fully understanding the proposals of the competitors. Thus, they may need to communicate with one or more offerors during evaluation of the proposals or final proposal revisions. Limited communications, called "clarifications," are permissible, but contracting officials must always be conscious of the need to avoid conducting discussions. Unfortunately, the statutes, regulations and decisions in this area have not been very helpful in assisting them in deciding what communications with one or more offerors would preclude award without discussions or would require reopening discussion with all other offerors within the competitive range.

An attempt to permit more robust communications was made in the FAR Part 15 Rewrite effort in 1996-97. However, there was criticism of the initial rule, relaxing the rules on communications, because of its perceived potential for unfair treatment of the competitors. This concern was addressed in the comments explaining the final rule, which backed off of the initial rule, at 62 Fed. Reg. 51226 (1997):

> Some respondents expressed concerns that the increased exchanges between the Government and industry throughout the acquisition process increased the risk of unfair practices. The final rule encourages earlier and more meaningful exchanges of information between the Government and potential contractors to achieve a better understanding of the Government's requirements and the offerors' proposals. This rule contains limits on exchanges that preclude favoring one offeror over another, revealing offerors' technical solutions, revealing prices without the offerors' permission, and knowingly furnishing source selection information.

The result has been that the current rule in FAR 15.306 has not encouraged "more meaningful exchanges" but has left contracting officials in the same dilemma that they faced before the FAR Rewrite.

[A] Development of Statutory and Regulatory Language

At the center of the confusion over the effect of communications are the statutory terms "discussions" and "clarification," neither of which are defined in the statutes. The term "discussions" was originally incorporated into Title 10 by Pub. L. No. 87-653 on Sept. 10, 1962, providing for oral or written discussions with all offerors within the competitive range and award on initial proposals without discussions. GAO interpreted these provisions as requiring "discussions" with all offerors in the competitive range "if negotiations (*i.e.*, discussions) be conducted with one of the offerors," 46 Comp. Gen. 191 (B-158686), 1966 CPD ¶ 76. The regulations did not attempt to define "discussions" until the FAR was published in April 1984. At that time the term "clarification" was also defined as a communication distinct from a "discussion." Shortly thereafter, the Competition in Contracting Act, Pub. L. No. 98-369, provided that "discussions conducted for the purpose of minor clarification" would not prohibit award without discussions. The same terminology is now contained in 10 U.S.C. § 3303 (formerly § 2305(b)(4)(A)), as follows:

> The head of an agency shall evaluate competitive proposals in accordance with section 3301(a) of this title and may award a contract—
>
> (1) after discussions with the offerors, provided that written or oral discussions have been conducted with all responsible offerors who submit proposals within the competitive range; or
>
> (2) based on the proposals received, without discussions with the offerors (other than discussions conducted for the purpose of minor clarification) provided that the solicitation included a statement that proposals are intended to be evaluated, and award made, without discussions, unless discussions are determined to be necessary.

Essentially the same language is contained in 41 U.S.C. § 3703(a).

The following definitions of "clarification" and "discussion" remained in FAR 15.601 until they were removed by the FAR Part 15 Rewrite:

> "Clarification," as used in this subpart, means communication with an offeror for the sole purpose of eliminating minor irregularities, informalities, or apparent clerical mistakes in the proposal. It is achieved by explanation or substantiation, either in response to Government inquiry or as initiated by the offeror. Unlike discussion (see definition below), clarification does not give the offeror an opportunity to revise or modify its proposal, except to the extent that correction of apparent clerical mistakes results in a revision.
>
> "Discussion," as used in this subpart, means any oral or written communication between the Government and an offeror (other than communications conducted for the purpose of minor clarification), whether or not initiated by the Government, that (a) involves information essential for determining the acceptability of a proposal, or (b) provides the offeror an opportunity to revise or modify its proposal.

In addition, FAR 15.607 contained detailed provisions dealing with mistakes disclosed before award. That entire section was also removed in the Par 15 Rewrite.

Post-submission communications are now addressed under FAR 15.306 titled, "Exchanges with offerors after receipt of proposals." Three types of exchanges are covered: (1) clarifications and award without discussion, (2) communications prior to establishing the competitive range, and (3) negotiations with offerors within the competitive range. This section discusses the first two types of communications. It also discusses the treatment of mistakes alleged before award. Negotiations with offerors within the competitive range will be discussed in a later section.

[B] Clarifications and Award Without Discussions

FAR 15.306(a) contains the following coverage of "clarifications" prior to award without discussions:

> (a) *Clarifications and award without discussions.* (1) Clarifications are limited exchanges, between the Government and offerors, that may occur when award without discussions is contemplated.
>
> (2) If award will be made without conducting discussions, offerors may be given the opportunity to clarify certain aspects of proposals (e.g., the relevance of an offeror's past performance information and adverse past performance information to which the offeror has not previously had an opportunity to respond) or to resolve minor or clerical errors.

The comments accompanying its publication indicate that the deletion of the previous definitions and the adoption of the above language were intended to permit increased exchanges of information while still complying with the statutory requirements for award without discussions. See 62 Fed. Reg. 51228-29 (1997), stating:

> (1) *Clarifications.* We drafted the rule to allow as much free exchange of information between offerors and the Government as possible, while still permitting award without discussions and complying with applicable statutes. The proposed rule did not differentiate between exchanges of information when award without discussions was contemplated versus when a competitive range would be established. Public comment pointed out that the proposed rule language may allow exchanges beyond what is permitted by applicable statute when making award without discussions. In drafting the second proposed rule, we limited these exchanges. The resulting language still permits more exchange of information between offerors and the Government than the current FAR. This policy is expected to help offerors, especially small entities that may not be familiar with proposal preparation, by permitting easy clarification of limited aspects of their proposals.

An earlier draft would have enabled the government to obtain "relevant information (in addition to that submitted in the offeror's proposal) needed to understand and evaluate the offeror's proposal." It further provided that "[t]he nature and extent of communications between the Government and offerors is a matter of contracting officer judgment."

The statutory term "minor clarification" and the FAR term "limited exchanges" are not in themselves meaningful. Relatively small alterations can result in an offer being revised. Thus, in determining the extent to which the final Rewrite "permits more exchange of information" than the prior FAR rules, it is necessary to consider the purpose of the exchange. If the exchange is intended to obtain a revision to the offer, oral or written discussions and final revised offers will be required. Conversely, it would appear that information exchanges which are conducted with all offerors that are similarly situated and do not vary the terms of their offers should not preclude award without discussions. Some decisions of GAO and the Court of Federal Claims have looked outside of FAR 15.306(a) to arrive at this interpretation of the permissible scope of clarifications. See *Antarctic Support Assocs. v. United States*, 46 Fed. Cl. 145 (2000); *Cubic Def. Sys., Inc. v. United States*, 45 Fed. Cl. 450 (1999); and *MG Indus.*, Comp. Gen. Dec. B-283010.3, 2000 CPD ¶ 17, looking to the FAR 15.306(d) rule on "discussions" and reasoning that if a discussion pursuant to that definition did not occur, the agency must have been conducting clarifications. Using different reasoning, the court in *Information Tech. & Applications Corp. v. United States*, 51 Fed. Cl. 340 (2001), affirmed in a 2 to 1 decision, 316 F. 3d 1312 (Fed. Cir. 2003), held that the additional information sought by the contracting officer was better described by the rule in FAR 15.306(b) (communications "to enhance understanding of proposals; allow reasonable interpretation of proposals; or facilitate the Government's evaluation process") but that, since it did not fall within the discussion rule in FAR 15.306(d), it was a permissible clarification. Conversely, GAO has cited other language in FAR 15.306(b) (such communications "shall not be used to cure proposal deficiencies or material omissions, materially alter the technical or cost elements of the proposal, and/or otherwise revise the proposal") to conclude that an exchange was not a clarification, *Alltech Eng'g. Corp.*, Comp. Gen. Dec. B-414002.2, 2017 CPD ¶ 49. This reasoning can be explained by the fact that exchanges that occur during the initial evaluation of proposals are simultaneously covered by the rules in both FAR 15.306(a) and (b). However, GAO decisions discussed below follow various reasoning in distinguishing between "clarifications" and "discussions."

[1] Clarifications Concerning Offer Revisions

A major problem with the statutory and regulatory coverage of discussions and clarifications has been the ambiguous use of the word "proposal"—sometimes referring to the entire submission of each offeror (the offer plus information solicited by the RFP) and other times referring only to the offer. While any changes or additions to information will result in a revision to the information that was included in the proposal, such changes or additions should be distinguished from offer revisions. Revisions are defined in FAR 15.001, as follows:

> "Proposal revision" is a change to a proposal made after the solicitation closing date, at the request of or as allowed by a contracting officer, as the result of negotiations.

While the word "proposal" is used in this definition, a reasonable interpretation is that it refers to offers only without including the information that has been submitted in response to the RFP. This interpretation makes the most sense because the definition indicates that these revisions result from "negotiations" and it is not likely that the contracting officer would negotiate over information. Generally, negotiations are conducted over the terms of the offer, which will be incorporated into the contract. Such revisions would result from changes in the price, time for performance, description of the work or other terms of the contract.

However, the word "proposal" is interpreted, material changes to the terms of the offer made in a proposal likely exceed the scope of clarifications. See, for example, *Safeguard Base Operations, LLC v. United States*, 989 F.3d 1326 (Fed. Cir. 2021) (allowing submission of omitted line item prices not possible withing scope of clarifications); *Dell Fed. Sys., L.P. v. United States*, 906 F.3d 982 (Fed. Cir. 2018) (allowing correction of proposed equipment due to ambiguous RFP provision reasonably determined to require discussions); *Global Language Center*, Comp. Gen. Dec. B-413503.8, 2017 CPD ¶ 238 (calling for submission of required travel rates); *General Dynamics One Source LLC*, Comp. Gen. Dec. B-400340.5, 2010 CPD ¶ 45 (correcting mandatory percentage of costs at which award fee had to be proposed); *Manthos Eng'g., LLC*, Comp. Gen. Dec. B-401751, 2009 CPD ¶ 216 (obtaining mandatory option prices); *Kellogg Brown & Root Servs., Inc.*, Comp. Gen. Dec. B-400614.3, 2009 CPD ¶ 50 (clearing up offeror's "assumption" attached to its cost proposal that raised question whether it would comply with mandatory technical specification); *Tiger Truck, LLC*, Comp. Gen. Dec. B-400685, 2009 CPD ¶ 19 (obtaining revised prices); *C. Young Constr., Inc.*, Comp. Gen. Dec. B-309740, 2007 CPD ¶ 198 (clearing up offeror's proposal to staff job that did not comply with mandatory specification); *Nu-Way, Inc.*, Comp. Gen. Dec. B-296435.5, 2005 CPD ¶ 195 (resolving ambiguity in offeror's proposal as to whether its equipment met mandatory requirement); *Cooperativa Maratori Riuniti-Anese*, B-294747, 2004 CPD ¶ 210 (allowing offeror to revise offer to meet required completion data); *DynCorp Int'l LLC*, Comp. Gen. Dec. B-294232, 2004 CPD ¶ 187 (allowing offeror to explain inadequacies in mandatory staffing plan); *Priority One Servs., Inc.*, Comp. Gen. Dec. B-288836, 2002 CPD ¶ 79 (changes to cost proposal); *International Res. Grp.*, Comp. Gen. Dec. B-286663, 2001 CPD ¶ 35 (e-mail containing a list of "technical and cost comments"); and *Dubinsky v. United States*, 43 Fed. Cl. 243 (1999) (telephone call to "clear up" specification compliance and warranties). Compare *S4, Inc.*, Comp. Gen. Dec. B-299817, 2007 CPD ¶ 164, holding that a request that the offeror confirm that it would comply with contract requirement was not a discussion because it did not allow the offeror to alter the offer.

In *Language Servs. Assocs., Inc.*, Comp. Gen. Dec. B-297392, 2006 CPD ¶ 20, however, GAO held that a "clarification" of the quoted prices stating that the offeror "would like to reserve the right to negotiate with the [agency] an adjustment in pricing" if the agency's estimated quantities were incorrect was not a discussion.

[2] Clarifications Concerning Information

While clarifications involving revisions to material terms of an offer are not permitted, information exchanges which do not concern changes to offers may be appropriate in the clarification process. However, it is useful to distinguish between information concerning the capability of the offeror and information relating to the features of the offer. While the former may be thought to clearly fall under the FAR 15.206(a) "minor clarification" category, past decisions dealing with information relating to the offer make inclusion of this type of clarification more problematic.

As noted above, the distinction between clarifications and discussions is particularly difficult because the decisions use the ambiguous word "proposal" in ruling on this issue. GAO summarized its view of the clarification rule in *SigNet Techs., Inc.*, Comp. Gen. Dec. B-418677, 2020 CPD ¶ 244 as follows:

> Discussions occur when an agency communicates with an offeror for the purpose of obtaining information essential to determine the acceptability of a proposal, or provides [the offeror with an opportunity to revise or modify its proposal in some material respect. *IR Techs.*, B-414430 et al., June 16, 2017, 2017 CPD ¶ 162 at 12. Clarifications, on the other hand, are limited exchanges between the agency and offerors that may occur when contract award without discussions is contemplated; an agency may, but is not required to, engage in clarifications that give offerors an opportunity to clarify certain aspects of proposals or to resolve minor or clerical errors. FAR 15.306(a); *CJW-Desbuild JV, LLC*, B-414219, Mar. 17, 2017, 2017 CPD ¶ 94 at 3. Agencies have broad discretion as to whether to seek clarifications from offerors, and offerors have no automatic right to clarifications regarding proposals. *Valkyrie Enterprises, LLC*, B-414516, June 30, 2017, 2017 CPD ¶ 212 at 5. Clarifications cannot be used to cure proposal deficiencies or material omissions, materially alter the technical or cost elements of the proposal, or otherwise revise the proposal. *Alltech Eng'g Corp.*, B-414002.2, Feb. 6, 2017, 2017 CPD ¶ 49 at 6.

As discussed below, the question of whether the clarification gave the offeror an opportunity to submit information to make its proposal "acceptable" or to "materially alter" its proposal is decided on a case-by-case basis.

[a] Capability Information

Capability information deals with the offeror's ability to perform as promised, as opposed to information pertaining to what has been promised. FAR 15.306(a)(2) recognizes that this is an appropriate area of communication, identifying past performance information as an example of the class of information which should be subject to "clarification."

If the determination of capability is made through a determination that the offeror is a "responsible" contractor, the typical actions during such determinations have not been found to be discussions, *Octo Consulting Group, Inc. v. United States*, 2018 U.S. Claims LEXIS 626 (2018) (permitting revision of subcontracting plans); *McKissacki + Delcan JV II*, Comp. Gen. Dec. B-401973.2, 2010 CPD ¶ 28 (determining whether offeror had compliant accounting system); *Dynamic Res., Inc.*, Comp. Gen. Dec. B-277213, 97-2 CPD ¶ 100 (preaward survey); and *Unicco Gov't Servs.*, Inc., Comp. Gen. Dec. B-277658, 97-2 CPD ¶ 134 (site visit to offeror's facility and inspection of equipment).

The same rule is followed with regard to exchanges that determine whether an offeror's plan to mitigate an organizational conflict of interest is satisfactory, *Cahaba Safeguard Administrators, LLC*, Comp. Gen. Dec. B-401844.2, 2010 CPD ¶ 39 ("such exchanges are more closely related to matters concerning the offeror's responsibility"). The same result was reached in *DRS Federal Servs., Inc.*, Comp. Gen. Dec. B-417643.2, 2020 CPD ¶ 75; and *C2C Solutions, Inc.*, Comp. Gen. Dec. B-401106.6, 2010 CPD ¶ 145.

The rule in FAR 15.306(a) is not as clear when the determination of capability is made as part of a tradeoff procurement. The Federal Circuit appears to have concluded that relatively broad reasoning should be followed in ascertaining the scope of FAR 15.306(a). See *Information Tech. & Applications Corp. v. United States*, 316 F.3d 1312 (Fed. Cir. 2003), holding that requests for information about the qualifications of subcontractors and the amount of work they would perform were clarifications not discussions because the information did not "change the terms of its proposal to make it more appealing to the government." This decision indicates that weight should be given to the intent of the agency in communication with the offerors. See also *Davis Boat Works, Inc. v. United States*, 111 Fed. Cl. 342 (2013) (seeking detailed information on the "proven processes" offeror had stated proved its capability was a clarification); *G4S Tech. CW LLC v. United States*, 109 Fed. Cl. 708 (2013) (asking whether proposed key person had required certifications). When an agency intends to probe capability information in the clarification process, this should be clearly stated in the RFP. Furthermore, all offerors should be treated in the same manner when this type of clarification is conducted. This will ensure that no offeror is given a preference prior to award without discussions by being given the opportunity to supplement or explain its capability while a competitor is not given the same opportunity.

GAO had reached the same result as the court in *Information Tech. & Applications Corp.*, B-288510, 2002 CPD ¶ 28, reasoning that this subcontractor information pertained to the relevance of the offeror's past performance. Several court decisions have also followed similar reasoning. See *Antarctic Support Assocs. v. United States*, 46 Fed. Cl. 145 (2000) (the names of references to vouch for the fact that a proposed subcontractor would continue to operate in the face of a declaration of bankruptcy); and *Forestry Surveys & Data v. United States*, 44 Fed. Cl. 493 (1999) (several offerors queried about aspects of their performance on prior contracts). See also *Griffy's Landscape Maint., LLC v. United States*, 46 Fed. Cl. 257 (2000), holding that an agency was *obligated* to verify a lack of required information relating to an offeror's insurance coverage in its proposal. The court reasoned that not including such information was a mistake that was apparent to the contracting officer and, therefore, should have led to a verification request. The court held that such a verification request was in the nature of a clarification not a discussion.

Subsequent GAO decisions have not followed the broad reasoning of the court in *Information Technology*. See, for example, *Computer Scis. Corp.*, Comp. Gen. Dec. B-298494.2, 2007 CPD ¶ 103, where GAO explicitly rejected the argument that subcontracting plans could be made acceptable through the clarification process. In reaching this conclusion, it stated that its prior decisions holding that improvement of a subcontracting plan during an assessment of responsibility of the offeror was not a discussion did not apply when capability of the offerors was to be determined on a comparative basis. However, GAO has sometimes found that capability information can be obtained through the clarification process. See, for example, *Dawson Solutions, LLC*, Comp. Gen. Dec. B-418587, 2020 CPD ¶ 216 (asking whether key personnel certifications would be current at time of award (but not obtaining missing certifications)); *SOS Int'l, Ltd.*, Comp. Gen. Dec. B-402558.3, 2010 CPD ¶ 131 (determining whether joint venturer would be used on contract); *Kuhana-Spectrum Joint Venture, LLC*, Comp. Gen. Dec. B-400803, 2009 CPD ¶ 36 (missing certifications and representations can be corrected during clarification); *USGC, Inc.*, Comp. Gen. Dec. B-400184.2, 2009 CPD ¶ 9 (explanations of composition of labor in acceptable technical proposals properly obtained through clarifications); *United Med. Sys.-DE, Inc.*, Comp. Gen. Dec. B-298438, 2006 CPD ¶ 148 (obtaining information showing that offeror had necessary equipment to perform work promised by the offer was proper clarification); *Park Tower Mgmt. Ltd.*, Comp. Gen. Dec. B-295589, 2005 CPD ¶ 77, and *Park Tower Mgmt. Ltd. v. United States*, 67 Fed. Cl. 548 (2005) (checking with offeror to determine whether it still intended to hire incumbent contractor's personnel was proper clarification); *AHNTECH, Inc.*, Comp. Gen. Dec. B-293582, 2004 CPD ¶ 113 (52 "clarification requests" seeking more information on how offeror would perform the work were proper clarifications); and *Citrus Coll.*, Comp. Gen. Dec.

B-293543, 2004 CPD ¶ 104 (obtaining explanation of manning chart a proper clarification).

Other GAO decisions reach the opposite conclusion holding that capability information can only be obtained through discussions when the information is obtained to determine the "acceptability" of a proposal. See *SOC LLC*, Comp. Gen. Dec. B-415460.2, 2018 CPD ¶ 20 (obtaining more information on required license and experience of key person); *Arbinger Co.*, Comp. Gen. Dec. B-413156.21, 2018 CPD ¶ 100 (permitting submission of revised attachments related to the experience scores earned by the offeror); *Cascadian American Enters.*, Comp. Gen. Dec. B-412208.3, 2016 CPD ¶ 29 (obtaining additional information on key personnel); *DataSource, Inc.*, Comp. Gen. Dec. B-412468, 2016 CPD ¶ 59 (obtaining missing letter of intent from one of 29 key personnel); *General Injectables & Vaccines, Inc.*, Comp. Gen. Dec. B-298590, 2006 CPD ¶ 173 (clearing up inadequate responses to a significant number of the system security plan questions); *T.J. Lambrecht Constr., Inc.*, Comp. Gen. Dec. B-294425, 2004 CPD ¶ 198 (obtaining experience information that offeror had omitted from proposal); *Verizon Fed., Inc.*, Comp. Gen. Dec. B-293527, 2004 CPD ¶ 186 (obtaining resumes required to be submitted with proposal); *ACS State Healthcare, LLC*, Comp. Gen. Dec. B-292981, 2004 CPD ¶ 57 (amplifying poorly written aspects of technical proposal); *Ballast Ham Dredging BV*, Comp. Gen. Dec. B-291848, 2003 CPD ¶ 76 (obtaining required information on capability to schedule work); *Priority One Servs., Inc.*, Comp. Gen. Dec. B-288836, 2002 CPD ¶ 79 (allowing offeror to substitute key personnel for those that were unavailable or unacceptable); and *J.A.Jones/IBC J.V.*, Comp. Gen. Dec. B-285627, 2000 CPD ¶ 161 (obtaining additional information about the qualifications of offeror's design team).

Allowing an offeror to provide required representations and certifications that have been omitted from a proposal has been deemed a clarification by GAO, *Kuhana-Spectrum Joint Venture, LLC*, Comp. Gen. Dec. B-400803, 2009 CPD ¶ 36; *Doty Bros. Equip. Co.*, Comp. Gen. Dec. B-274634 96-2 CPD ¶ 234. GAO reasoned that such an omission is a "minor irregularity" which can be corrected through the clarification process.

[b] Offer Information

Early decisions dealing with offer information made a distinction between obtaining information explaining the features of an offer and revisions to the offer which would preclude award without discussions. *See Amram Nowak Assocs., Inc.*, Comp. Gen. Dec. B-187253, 76-2 CPD ¶ 454; and *Keco Indus., Inc.*, Comp. Gen. Dec. B-170990, Nov. 17, 1971, Unpub. However, following the adoption of the definition of "discussion" in the former FAR 15.601, communications were found to be discussions even though the terms of the offer were not changed. Those holdings were based on the language in the definition stating that discussion "involves information essential for determining the acceptability of a proposal." See *Integration Tech. Grp., Inc.*, Comp. Gen. Dec. B-274288.5, 97-1 CPD ¶ 214 (identification of components to be furnished); *Integration Tech. Grp.*, Comp. Gen. Dec. B-274288, 97-1 CPD ¶ 214 (identification of components to be furnished); and *Strategic Analysis, Inc.*, Comp. Gen. Dec. B-270075.4, 96-1 CPD ¶ 41 (inquiry of employment status of designated key employee where RFP required letters of intent for proposed key personnel not current employees). Compare *Houston Air, Inc.*, Comp. Gen. Dec. 292382, 2003 CPD ¶ 144, finding no discussions where agency sought corrections to weight and balance information; *WECO Cleaning Specialists, Inc.*, Comp. Gen. Dec. B-279305, 98-1 CPD ¶ 154, finding no discussions where the agency obtained cost or pricing data to ensure that the offeror's price was realistic; and *Robotic Sys. Tech.*, Comp. Gen. Dec. B-278195.2, 98-1 CPD ¶ 20, finding no discussions where the offeror explained its cost proposal but did not add any information that was not included in the original proposal.

There continues to be a variety of decisions under the current FAR 15.306(a). In general, obtaining information to explain an offeror's proposed costs or prices has been held to be a proper clarification as long as the offeror does not alter the proposed cost or price. See *Qwest Gov't Servs., Inc.*, Comp. Gen. Dec. B-418649, 2020 CPD ¶ 237 (determining meaning of terms in pricing workbook" supporting offered prices); *Strategic Resources, Inc.*, Comp. Gen. Dec. B-419151, 2020 CPD ¶ 399 (seeking additional detail supporting prices from all offerors); *Enterprise Servs., LLC*, Comp. Gen. Dec. B-415368.2, 2018 CPD ¶ 44 (obtaining verification that pricing was not changed by corporate spin-off); *SRA Int'l, Inc.*, Comp. Gen. Dec. B-413220.4, 2017 CPD ¶ 173 (confirming that proposed G&A rates were blended rates as concluded by agency evaluator); *PricewaterhouseCoopers Public Sector, LLP*, Comp. Gen. Dec. B-413316.2, 2017 CPD ¶ 12 (asking offeror to confirm that technical proposal was based on labor rates in price table); *Mil-Mar Century Corp. v. United States*, 111 Fed. Cl. 508 (2013) (more information on cost of component and proof that labor hours are adequate); *Environmental Quality Mgmt., Inc.*, Comp. Gen. Dec. B-402247.2, 2010 CPD ¶ 75 (request to show that "fringe rate" had been applied to labor rates when rate was "hidden" in spreadsheet); *Allied Tech. Grp., Inc.*, Comp. Gen. Dec. B-402135, 2010 CPD ¶ 152 (explanation that offeror would be bound by pricing of a line item that it had denoted as "n/a" in its proposal and that costs excluded by terms of proposal would not be required to perform work); *VMD Sys. Integrators, Inc.*, Comp. Gen. Dec. B-401037.4, 2009 CPD ¶ 252 (question whether proposed rates had been audited by DCAA); *Career Training Concepts, Inc. v. United States*, 83 Fed. Cl. 215 (2008), and *Career Training Concepts, Inc.*, Comp. Gen. Dec. B-311429, 2009 CPD ¶ 97 (request for the elements of the offeror's price and an explanation of the escalation rate used to determine the price); *Colson Servs. Corp.*, Comp. Gen. Dec. B-310971, 2008 CPD ¶ 85 (request as to whether offered rebates were on a monthly or annual basis a proper clarification because it did not represent "a meaningful opportunity to revise pricing"); *NCR Gov't Sys. LLC*, Comp. Gen. Dec.

B-297959, 2006 CPD ¶ 82 (request for a revised catalog of prices when the offer contained all of the required prices with the catalog being merely a backup document); *SecureNet Co. v. United States*, 72 Fed. Cl. 800 (2006) (obtaining price realism analysis from DCAA); *SRS Techs.*, Comp. Gen. Dec. B-291618.2, 2003 CPD ¶ 70 (request for information on how accounting system dealt with uncompensated overtime); *Northeast MEP Servs., Inc.*, Comp. Gen. Dec. B-285963.9, 2001 CPD ¶ 66 (obtaining assurance that estimated costs covered all required services when some government evaluators thought the technical proposal might have indicated otherwise); and *MG Indus.*, Comp. Gen. Dec. B-283010.3, 2000 CPD ¶ 17 (obtaining assurance that proposed price covered solicitation requirements). These decisions frequently stated that the exchange is a clarification because the information was not required to determine the acceptability of the proposal.

The decisions vary with regard to obtaining information as to other elements of an offer. Several GAO decisions hold that obtaining explanations about an offered product or service is a discussion. See *DataSource, Inc.*, Comp. Gen. Dec. B-412468, 2016 CPD ¶ 59 (obtaining missing letter of intent from one of 29 key personnel); *Cascadian Amer. Enters.*, Comp. Gen. Dec. B-412208.3, 2016 CPD ¶ 29 (obtaining additional information on key personnel); *4D Security Solutions, Inc.*, Comp. Gen. Dec. B-400351.2, 2009 CPD ¶ 5 (explanation of characteristics of offered product could not be obtained during clarifications because this would allow the company to "materially alter or explain its quotation by having the agency consider information not contained within the four corners of its initial quotation"); *Government Telecomms., Inc.*, Comp. Gen. Dec. B-299542.2, 2007 CPD ¶ 136 (obtaining information to determine whether offered products were available on the market could not be done through clarifications because this "would have involved material changes to the offeror's proposal"); *Gemmo-CCC*, Comp. Gen. Dec. B-297447.2, 2006 CPD ¶ 182 (obtaining required information describing the offered product would constitute discussions because it "would involve submission of information necessary to make the proposal acceptable"); *Southern California Eng'g, Inc.*, Comp. Gen. Dec. B-296244, 2005 CPD ¶ 134 (obtaining missing pump specifications needed to determine acceptability of product could only be done through discussions); *QuickHire, LLC*, Comp. Gen. Dec. B-293098, 2004 CPD ¶ 33 (clearing up vague or incomplete technical description of product offered would have required discussions); *ProMar*, Comp. Gen. Dec. B-292409, 2003 CPD ¶ 187 (obtaining missing product literature showing compliance with specifications would have required discussions); and *eMind*, Comp. Gen. Dec. B-289902, 2002 CPD ¶ 82 (obtaining required course descriptions nor permissible through clarifications).

In contrast, other decisions have found proper clarifications. See *Level 3 Communications, LLC v. United States*, 129 Fed. Cl. 487 (2016) (obtaining maps that conform to RFP requirements when nonconforming maps had been submitted with proposal with a statement that it would comply with the requirements); *i4 Now Solutions, Inc.*, Comp. Gen. Dec. B-412369, 2016 CPD ¶ 47 (determining whether offeror would use government program rather than its own as proposed); *Houston Air, Inc.*, Comp. Gen. Dec. B-292382, 2003 CPD ¶ 144 (obtaining updated information on product when offeror had already submitted acceptable information); *Firearms Training Sys., Inc. v. United States*, 41 Fed. Cl. 743 (1998) (demonstration of offered computer-operated simulator).

Confirming an agency's understanding of a proposal generally been held to be a proper clarification. See *Red River Computer Co.*, Comp. Gen. Dec. B-414183.8, 2018 CPD ¶ 7 (obtaining confirmation that vendor would meet terms and conditions when no such confirmation was required by solicitation); *Pontiac Flying LLC*, Comp. Gen. Dec. B-414433, 2017 CPD ¶ 188 (confirming that agency could order work from either of the offered pricing schedules); *Tetra Tech, Inc.*, Comp. Gen. Dec. B-409095, 2014 CPD ¶ 108 (confirming that offeror had same interpretation of specification as agency); *IAP-Leopardo Constr., Inc.*, Comp. Gen. Dec. B-408890, 2014 CPD ¶ 11 (confirming that offeror accepted liability for government property as required by RFP).

GAO has also held that obtaining information to clear up a "material proposal deficiency" cannot be done through the clarification process, *URS Grp., Inc.*, Comp. Gen. Dec. B-402820, 2010 CPD ¶ 175. In that case, the "deficiency" was naming the parent company, without the required security clearance, as the offeror while stating in the technical proposal that the work would be performed by a part of the company that had the required clearance. Similarly, in *Professional Performance Dev. Grp., Inc.*, Comp. Gen. Dec. B-311273, 2008 CPD ¶ 101, GAO held that clarifications could not be used to clear up "informational deficiencies [that] would have required major revisions to the . . . proposal." See also *Pontiac Flying LLC*, Comp. Gen. Dec. B-414433, 2017 CPD ¶ 188; *Lovelace Sci. & Tech. Servs.*, Comp. Gen. Dec. B-412345, 2016 CPD ¶ 23; *Sletten Cos./Sletten Constr. Co.*, Comp. Gen. Dec. B-402422, 2010 CPD ¶ 97; *Superior Gunite*, Comp. Gen. Dec. B-402392.2, 2010 CPD ¶ 83; *JWK Int'l Corp. v. United States*, 52 Fed. Cl. 650 (2002), *aff'd*, 56 Fed. Appx. 474 (Fed. Cir. 2003); and *eMind*, Comp. Gen. Dec. B-289902, 2002 CPD ¶ 82, stating that clarifications may not be used "to cure proposal deficiencies or material omissions, materially alter the technical or cost elements of the proposal, or otherwise revise the proposal." The quoted language is from the rule on communications prior to establishing a competitive range in FAR 15.306(b)—indicating that these decisions are applying this test to determine when a clarification is precluded under FAR 15.306(a).

It can be seen that there is a lack of clarity in the decisions regarding the distinction between clarifications and discussions when the government obtains additional information regarding offers. With the deletion of the FAR 15.601 definitions of discussions and clarification, and the stated intent of the drafters of the FAR Part 15 Rewrite, it is arguable that agencies should be permitted to seek explanations of offers before award without discussions. This would be in accord with earlier holdings of GAO prior to the adoption of the FAR.

If an agency adopts this interpretation of the FAR Part 15 Rewrite, it should clearly state in the RFP that it reserves the right to seek information clarifying any element of an offer prior to award without discussions. Thereafter, in following this procedure, it should exercise great care to ensure that all offerors are treated evenhandedly. Thus, if any offeror is permitted to clarify its offer, all other offerors whose offers are not fully understood should also be given an opportunity to clarify or explain their offers.

[3] The Permissive Nature of Clarifications

Because FAR 15.306(a) is permissive rather than mandatory, most decisions hold that contracting officers have a great deal of discretion in determining whether to ask for clarification of some element of a proposal. See *Gulf Grp., Inc. v. United States*, 61 Fed. Cl. 338 (2004), where the agency evaluation team stated that clarification of the protester's experience was necessary, but the source selection official proceeded to award to a competitor without obtaining the clarification. The court denied the protest, stating at 360:

> In support of its argument that the Corps's failure to exercise its discretionary authority was itself an abuse of discretion, Gulf Group notes the announced goal of the clarifications policy: "This policy is expected to help offerors, especially small entities that may not be familiar with proposal preparation, by permitting easy clarification of limited aspects of their proposals." Gulf Group argues that it is exactly the sort of business this regulation was intended to benefit. But the benefit that was created, if it could even be characterized as such, was not the *right* to clarify information in proposals. The benefit, instead, is that whenever the contracting officials think a clarification of certain aspects of a proposal would be helpful, *they* have the discretion to seek such a clarification, even when discussions with all bidders would not occur. The FAR allows, but does not require, such exchanges to take place. As this Court has found, "an agency representative has broad discretion to decide whether to communicate with a firm concerning its performance history." *JWK International Corp v United States*, 52 Fed. Cl. 650, 661 (2002).

See also *Valkyrie Enters., LLC*, Comp. Gen. Dec. B-414516, 2017 CPD ¶ 212; *Alltech Eng'g. Corp.*, Comp. Gen. Dec. B-414002.2, 2017 CPD ¶ 49; and *Hi-Tec Sys., Inc.*, Comp. Gen. Dec. B-402590, 2010 CPD ¶ 156, holding that agencies have "broad discretion as to whether to seek clarification from offerors."

In spite of the discretionary clarification rule, the Court of Federal Claims has held that clarifications were required when an agency knew that an offeror had mistakenly failed to submit information. See *RX Joint Venture, LLC v. United States*, 140 Fed. Cl. 13 (2018), stating at 17-18:

> The permissive nature of clarifications does not insulate from judicial review a CO's decision to not seek clarification. BCPeabody [Constr. Servs., Inc. v. United States], 112 Fed. Cl. [433 (2009)] at 512 ("[The court] cannot accept the implication that there are never situations in which a contracting officer's discretion would be abused by a failure to seek clarification."). A critical component of evaluating a CO's decision to not seek clarification is whether the CO should have discerned that the protestor made an error rather than a deliberate decision. See Dell Fed. Sys. v. United States, 133 Fed. Cl. 92, 106 (2017) (deeming relevant the fact that the government "had notice that a clerical error had likely occurred"), appealed docketed, No. 17-2554 (Fed. Cir. Sept. 15, 2017); Level 3 Commc'ns, LLC v. United States, 129 Fed. Cl. 487, 505 (2016) (giving weight to the fact that the offeror made representations in the proposal concerning the substance of the missing information); BCPeabody, 112 Fed. Cl. at 512 (considering that the offeror submitted a duplicate page and that the CO knew the substance of the missing information); Griffy's Landscape Maint. LLC v. United States, 46 Fed. Cl. 257, 259-60 (2000) (requiring clarification when the missing information "clearly indicate[d] a clerical mistake").

In contrast, in *JBlanco Enters., Inc.*, Comp. Gen. Dec. B-402905, 2010 CPD ¶ 186, a protest that a "minor" error in completing a demonstration project should have been clarified was denied on the grounds that allowing correction of the error would have defeated the purpose of the demonstration (to prove capability).

The discretionary clarification rule has resulted in a number of decisions holding that an agency is not required to permit an offeror to submit information explaining or rebutting adverse past performance information on which it has had no previous opportunity to comment. See *SKE Int'l, Inc.*, Comp. Gen. Dec. B-311383, 2008 CPD ¶ 111; *JWK Int'l Corp. v. United States*, 52 Fed. Cl. 650 (2002); *NMS Mgmt., Inc.*, Comp. Gen. Dec. B-286335, 2000 CPD ¶ 197. In *General Dynamics—Ordnance & Tactical Sys.*, Comp. Gen. Dec. B-295987, 2005 CPD ¶ 114, GAO indicated that giving an offeror such an opportunity would be required "where there clearly is a reason to question the validity of the past performance information" being used by the agency. See *A. G. Cullen Constr., Inc.*, Comp. Gen. Dec. B-284049.2, 2000 CPD ¶ 45, holding that clarifications would be required in this situation if there was a clear abuse of discretion such as where there were obvious inconsistencies between a reference's narrative comments and the actual ratings the reference gives the offeror. Compare *United Coatings*, Comp. Gen. Dec. B-291978.2, 2003 CPD ¶ 146, applying this standard but finding no abuse of discretion because the agency had no reason to question the validity of the adverse information; *General Dynamics-Ordnance & Tactical Sys.*, Comp. Gen. Dec. B-295987, 2005 CPD ¶ 114, finding no abuse of discretion because agency had firsthand knowledge of the adverse information; and *Bannum, Inc.*, Comp. Gen. Dec. B-298281.2, 2006 CPD ¶ 163, finding no prejudice in failing to discuss adverse past performance information because protester had received high rating in spite of adverse information.

The discretionary clarification rule has also resulted in a number of decisions holding that clarifications can be conducted with only one offeror, *DynCorp Int'l LLC v. United States*, 76 Fed. Cl. 528, 540 (2007). See also *General Dynamics—Ordinance & Tactical Sys.*, Comp. Gen. Dec. B-295987, 2005 CPD ¶ 114, stating:

> [C]larifications, in contrast to discussions, do not trigger a requirement that the agency seek clarifications from other offerors. See *Landoll Corp.*, B-291381 et al., Dec. 23, 2002, 2003 CPD ¶ 40 at 8; *Priority One Servs., Inc.*, B-288836, B-288836.2, Dec. 17, 2001, 2002 CPD ¶ 79 at 5; *Global Assocs. Ltd.*, B-271693, B-271693.2, Aug. 2, 1996, 96-2 CPD ¶ 100 at 4. While we recognize that there may be a rare situation where it would be unfair to request clarification from one offeror but not from another, the mere fact that an agency requests clarification from one offeror and not another, does not constitute unfair treatment.

Similarly, in *INDUS Tech., Inc.*, Comp. Gen. Dec. B-297800.13, 2007 CPD ¶ 116, it was proper to not clarify whether a cover letter statement was intended to indicate that the offeror would not comply with a mandatory requirement even though the agency had clarified issues in other proposals, and in *Landoll Corp.*, Comp. Gen. Dec. B-291381, 2003 CPD ¶ 40, it was proper not to clarify issues because such action would not have changed the protester's competitive position. Thus, only when clarification with only one offeror is perceived as resulting in unfair treatment to another offeror, will such action be held to be improper.

[C] Communications Prior to Establishing the Competitive Range

The previous FAR did not deal with the subject of communications with parties prior to the establishment of the competitive range. The following detailed provisions were incorporated into FAR 15.306(b) by the FAR Part 15 Rewrite:

> (b) *Communications with offerors before establishment of the competitive range.* Communications are exchanges, between the Government and offerors, after receipt of proposals, leading to establishment of the competitive range. If a competitive range is to be established, these communications—
>
> (1) Shall be limited to the offerors described in paragraphs (b)(1)(i) and (b)(1)(ii) of this section and—
>
> (i) Shall be held with offerors whose past performance information is the determining factor preventing them from being placed within the competitive range. Such communications shall address adverse past performance information to which an offeror has not had a prior opportunity to respond; and
>
> (ii) May only be held with those offerors (other than offerors under paragraph (b)(1)(i) of this section) whose exclusion from, or inclusion in, the competitive range is uncertain;

> (2) May be conducted to enhance Government understanding of proposals; allow reasonable interpretation of the proposal; or facilitate the Government's evaluation process. Such communications shall not be used to cure proposal deficiencies or material omissions, materially alter the technical or cost elements of the proposal, and/or otherwise revise the proposal. Such communications may be considered in rating proposals for the purpose of establishing the competitive range;
>
> (3) Are for the purpose of addressing issues that must be explored to determine whether a proposal should be placed in the competitive range. Such communications shall not provide an opportunity for the offeror to revise its proposal, but may address—
>
> (i) Ambiguities in the proposal or other concerns (e.g., perceived deficiencies, weaknesses, errors, omissions, or mistakes (see 14.407)); and
>
> (ii) Information relating to relevant past performance; and
>
> (4) Shall address adverse past performance information to which the offeror has not previously had an opportunity to comment.

The promulgation comments indicate that these provisions were adopted to assuage the concerns of small business commenters. See 62 Fed. Reg. 51229 (1997):

> Public comments indicated that the second proposed rule did not establish a "bright line" distinction between when communications conducted in order to establish a competitive range end, and when discussions begin. Small businesses were concerned that the Government may conduct inappropriate communications with selected offerors prior to the establishment of the competitive range to the detriment of small businesses. We revised the final rule to accommodate this concern by clearly defining when discussions begin. We adopted this alternative to preclude the occurrence of the inappropriate communications that concerned small businesses.

While these provisions seem unnecessary, they appear to give the contracting officer considerable discretion in seeking both offer and capability information on offers when their inclusion in the competitive range is uncertain. Seeking such information permits the agency to make the competitive range determination based on a full understanding of the proposal—furthering the goal of establishing a competitive range consisting of only those offerors that are most highly rated. The only limitation on such communications is that the offers may not be revised, FAR 15.306(b)(2) and (3). The only way to carry out the intent of this provision of facilitating the competitive range determination is to interpret the term "proposal" to mean "offer."

Where the evaluation indicates, with certainty, that an offer is outside the competitive range, communication is required for adverse past performance information which the offeror has not had an opportunity to address, FAR

15.306(b)(1)(i); *Presidio Networked Solutions, Inc.*, Comp. Gen. Dec. B-408128.33, 2014 CPD ¶ 316. However, communications concerning other issues with the proposal are discretionary with the agency. See *People, Tech. & Processes, LLC*, Comp. Gen. Dec. B-417208, 2019 CPD ¶ 113 (no requirement that agency seek missing information regarding key personnel); *L-3 Commc'ns EOTech, Inc.*, Comp. Gen. Dec. B-311453, 2008 CPD ¶ 139 (no requirement that agency ask offeror whether its test procedure was correctly written when the offered product had failed the procedure); *Professional Performance Dev. Grp., Inc.*, Comp. Gen. Dec. B-311273, 2008 CPD ¶ 101 (no requirement that agency give protester the opportunity to correct significant informational deficiencies); *Government Telecomms., Inc.*, Comp. Gen. Dec. B-299542.2, 2007 CPD ¶ 136 (no requirement that agency allow offeror to cure "proposal deficiencies or material omissions"); and *The Cmty. P'ship LLC*, Comp. Gen. Dec. B-286844, 2001 CPD ¶ 38 (protester properly excluded from competitive range without communication because decision not uncertain and past performance not determining factor). With respect to offers that are clearly within the competitive range, there is no need for communications prior to the conduct of negotiations.

The 2022 DOD "Source Selection Procedures" calls for all communications with offerors to be conducted by the issuance of Evaluation Notices (ENs) with the designation of whether they are "clarification," "communications," or "discussion." However, in major procurements with limited competition, where it is clear that all of the competitors will be included in the competitive range, ENs of all types are frequently sent to the competitors during the evaluation process to speed up the flow of information. This process is described in *Leidos, Inc.*, Comp. Gen. Dec. B-409214.4, 2015 CPD ¶ 63, *Pinnacle Solutions, Inc.*, Comp. Gen. Dec. B-406998, 2012 CPD ¶ 338, and *Boeing Co.*, Comp. Gen. Dec. B-311344, 2008 CPD ¶ 114.

[D] Oral Presentations

As discussed earlier, oral presentations were incorporated into FAR 15.102 by the 1997 Rewrite. FAR 15.102(a) states that oral presentations can occur at any time during the acquisition process. It appears that most oral presentations occur shortly after the submission of written proposals but they can also occur following the establishment of a competitive range.

FAR 15.102 appears to indicate that oral presentations conducted prior to award without discussions or establishing a competitive range can encompass both capability information and information explaining offers but may not be used to permit an offeror to alter its offer. It is clear that this regulation authorizes broadened exchange of information when oral presentations are conducted. FAR 15.102 does not use the term "clarification" and the FAR 15.102(c) suggested subjects for presentations consist of both capability and offer information. FAR 15.102(a) indicates that such presentations may "substitute for, or augment, written information," and that they are "subject to the same restrictions as written information." Thus, is appears that oral presentations should be subject to the same rules as written information. See also FAR 15.102(g) stating:

> If, during an oral presentation, the Government conducts discussions (see 15.306(d)), the Government must comply with 15.306 and 15.307.

This provision, by its reference to FAR 15.306(d), indicates that award on initial offers would be precluded only where the communications are the negotiations described in FAR 15.306(d).

The very nature of oral presentations involves obtaining additional information as to the capability of each offeror making a presentation. See FAR 15.102(a) and (b) describing oral presentations as a means for each offeror to submit "portions" or "part" of its proposal through such presentations. In such circumstances, the entire oral presentation process can be regarded as the initial obtaining of information to be used for evaluation of each offeror's capability and there can be no issue of proposal revision since all information submitted would be initial proposal information. This interpretation will be effective as long as the agency does not elicit information during the oral presentation that significantly varies information contained in the written proposal. The dialog during an oral presentation also inevitably involves the exchange of information. Thus, it should be expected that a broader range of communications would be permitted. See *Sapient Gov't Servs., Inc.*, Comp. Gen. Dec. B-112163.2, 2016 CPD ¶ 11, where the oral presentation consisted of a problem-solving session followed by clarification questions. The GAO held that no discussion had occurred because the question/answer process was "simply a component of the oral presentation itself." See also *Rivada Mercury, LLC v. United States*, 131 Fed. Cl. 663 (2017) (seeking technical information about ambiguities and gaps in proposal during in oral presentation not a discussion); *Sierra Military Health Servs., Inc.*, Comp. Gen. Dec. B-292780, 2004 CPD ¶ 55 (information provided in an oral presentation before the agency personnel had asked any questions "could not have been the result of discussions"); *Synoptic Sys. Corp.*, Comp. Gen. Dec. B-290789.4, 2003 CPD ¶ 42 (obtaining information about the lines of communication within the offeror's organization not a discussion); *Aliron Int'l, Inc.*, Comp. Gen. Dec. B-285048.2, 2000 CPD ¶ 125 (seeking amplification of parts of proposal not a discussion); and *General Physics Fed. Sys., Inc.*, Comp. Gen. Dec. B-275934, 97-1 CPD ¶ 171 (oral presentations, including a question and answer session, not a discussion because no unfair treatment). On the other hand, allowing an offeror to change its offer as a result of the exchange during an oral presentation has been held to be a discussion, *Global Analysis Info. Tech. Servs., Inc.*, Comp. Gen. Dec. B-298840.2, 2007 CPD ¶ 57 (offeror changed option prices); *TDS, Inc.*, Comp. Gen. Dec. B-2988402, 2003 CPD ¶ 204 (offeror changed price and technical proposal). In any event, it is clear that agencies will be required to follow the procedure for an oral presentation described in the RFP and will also be required to treat all offerors evenhandedly in conducting oral presentations.

If an agency anticipates a large number of offerors, it generally will conduct oral presentations only with the remaining offerors after the competitive range has been established or after a down-select. If the oral presentations are conducted after a competitive range, it would not matter if discussions occurred during the oral presentation or later in the process. See, for example, *L&M Techs., Inc.*, Comp. Gen. Dec. B-278044.5, 98-1 CPD ¶ 131, finding that the agency had followed proper procedures in conducting an oral presentation with offerors in the competitive range, conducting discussions immediately thereafter, obtaining and evaluating best and final offers, and obtaining another set of best and final offers without conducting additional oral presentations. See also *RTF/TCI/EAI J.V.*, Comp. Gen. Dec. B-280422.3, 98-2 CPD ¶ 162, where oral presentations were conducted only with offerors in the competitive range. If oral presentations were conducted in order to determine which offerors should be placed in the competitive range, the rules in FAR 15.306(b) would apply, but there would appear to be little or no harm if discussions occurred at this time since the offerors would be requested to submit final proposal revisions after the conclusion of discussions. See, e.g., *Dynamic Res., Inc.*, Comp. Gen. Dec. B-277213.2, 97-2 CPD ¶ 100.

FAR 15.102 contains the following additional guidance on the procedures to be followed when oral presentations are required:

> (e) The contracting officer shall maintain a record of oral presentations to document what the Government relied upon in making the source selection decision. The method and level of detail of the record (e.g., videotaping, audio tape recording, written record, Government notes, copies of offeror briefing slides or presentation notes) shall be at the discretion of the source selection authority. A copy of the record placed in the file may be provided to the offeror.
>
> (f) When an oral presentation includes information that the parties intend to include in the contract as material terms or conditions, the information shall be put in writing. Incorporation by reference of oral statements is not permitted.

While this regulation gives the contracting officer the choice of the method of documentation, GAO has granted protests when the documentation did not indicate the content of the presentation that led to a reduced score for the protester, *Checchi & Co. Consulting, Inc.*, Comp. Gen. Dec. B-285777, 2001 CPD ¶ 132. In that case there was conflicting evidence as to what subjects the protester had covered in its presentation and no "contemporaneous record" of the presentation. See also *HomeSafe Alliance, LLC*, Comp. Gen. Dec. B-418266.5, 2020 CPD ¶ 350 (inadequate record of questions and answers); *Connected Global Solutions, LLC*, Comp. Gen. Dec. B-418266.4, 2020 CPD ¶ 349 (sparse, unsigned notes inadequate documentation); *Johnson Controls Sec. Sys.*, Comp. Gen. Dec. B-296490, 2007 CPD ¶ 102 (agency criticized for lack of any documentation of presentation); *e-LYNXX Corp.*, Comp. Gen. Dec.

B-292761, 2003 CPD ¶ 219 (lack of documentation required hearing that produced conflicting testimony which did not resolve protest); *J & J Maint., Inc.*, Comp. Gen. Dec. B-284708.2, 2000 CPD ¶ 106 (evaluators' notes on the presentation insufficient because they did not summarize the presentation), and *Future-Tec Mgmt. Sys., Inc.*, Comp. Gen. Dec. B-283793.5, 2000 CPD ¶ 59 (lack of any documentation led to granting of protest). These cases indicate that some recording of the presentation should be made in order to create the type of evidence required by GAO. See *Resource Dimensions, LLC*, Comp. Gen. Dec. B-404536, 2011 CPD ¶ 50, granting a protest when the agency's notes on a question and answer session conflicted with the technical evaluation. The agency had videotaped the initial presentation of the protester but had not recorded the question-and-answer session with the result that the agency prepared notes and allowed the protester to edit the notes to reflect its answers to the agency's questions. In *Leidos Innovations Corp.*, Comp. Gen. Dec. B-415504, 2018 CPD ¶ 88, GAO held that the agency evaluator's assessment of weaknesses were confirmed by a detailed review of the oral presentation. In *Strategic Resources, Inc.*, Comp. Gen. Dec. B-419151, 2020 CPD ¶ 399, GAO held that detailed slides and evaluators notes were sufficient documentation.

[E] Mistakes

The statutes do not deal with the subject of mistakes discovered or alleged prior to award. Prior to the FAR Rewrite, FAR 15.607 contained detailed procedures directing contracting officers to examine proposals for mistakes. Where communications were considered to prejudice "the interest of other offerors" or where correction of a mistake would require reference "to documents, worksheets, or other data outside the solicitation and proposal," the mistake could be corrected only through oral or written discussions with all offerors within the competitive range. These provisions were removed in the final Rewrite and the FAR now contains only fragmentary procedures for correction of mistakes.

Under the FAR Rewrite as was the case under the prior regulations, allegations of error and requests for *verification* and subsequent verifications that mistakes have not been made are not discussions but may be conducted as necessary to clarify whether a mistake has been made, *U.S. Facilities, Inc.*, Comp. Gen. Dec. B-293029, 2004 CPD ¶ 17; *R&B Rubber & Eng'g, Inc.*, Comp. Gen. Dec. B-214299, 84-1 CPD ¶ 595. Similarly, since a proposal may be *withdrawn* freely, communications resulting in withdrawal do not require discussions with all offerors. However, the FAR contains no explicit requirement that a contracting officer request verification when a mistake is suspected (as is the case in sealed bidding under FAR 14.407-1) and it is doubtful that GAO will impose such a requirement. Compare *CSE Constr.*, Comp. Gen. Dec. B-291268.2, 2002 CPD ¶ 207, holding that verification that a low price was not mistaken was required before rejecting the offer, with *FedSys, Inc.*, Comp. Gen. Dec. B-401453, 2009 CPD ¶ 181, holding that the agency was not permitted to verify whether seemingly irrational labor rates were mistaken because that would have been a discussion. Some decisions of the Court of Federal Claims have also required verification. See *Caddell Constr. Co. v. United States*, 125 Fed. Cl. 30 (2016) stating at 48:

> The duty to verify price is set forth in Part 14 of the FAR that governs sealed biding, not in Part 15 that governs negotiated procurements. 48 C.F.R. § 14.407-3(g). However, the Court has repeatedly applied the price verification requirement to negotiated procurements. See, e.g., *PHT Supply Corp. v. United States*, 71 Fed. Cl. 1, 21 (2006) ("Although the duty to raise mistakes in an offeror's proposal is no longer set forth explicitly in the regulations governing negotiated procurements, that duty undoubtedly still exists."); *Griffy's Landscape Maint. LLC v. United States*, 46 Fed. Cl. 257, 259 (2000) (holding that the duty to verify price extends to negotiated procurements).

See also *BCPeabody Constr. Servs. v. United States*, 112 Fed. Cl. 502 (2013), requiring clarification of a clerical error when the contracting officer knew of the error.

The deletion of the pre-Rewrite FAR 15.607 and its requirements for *correction* of mistakes through the discussion process raises the question of what types of mistakes may be corrected without requiring discussions with all offerors in the competitive range. It appears that the authors of the FAR Part 15 Rewrite intended to adopt the rule applicable to sealed bidding when they indicated in FAR 15.001 that a "Proposal modification" is a change made to a proposal "to correct a mistake at any time before award." This would allow correction of mistakes prior to award without discussions as is done in sealed bidding procurements. See FAR 14.407 and the discussion in Chapter 5. Application of these rules would require that the contracting officer request verification of an offer whenever a mistake was suspected and would permit correction of a mistake at any time that it met the requirements of the regulation. This would permit the contracting officer to deal with mistakes as they were identified or disclosed without losing the right to award the contract without discussions. See *U.S. Facilities, Inc.*, Comp. Gen. Dec. B-293029, 2004 CPD ¶ 17, holding that asking the offeror to verify its price or request correction of a mistake did not constitute discussions. Thus, logically correction of a mistake to an *offer* should not be treated as a clarification but as a distinct process that should routinely occur as an agency is evaluating a proposal. Stated differently, correction of a mistake in an offer should be considered to be the only alteration to an offer that can properly occur prior to award without discussions—as occurs regularly in the sealed bidding process.

However, FAR 15.306(a) includes communications to "resolve minor or clerical errors" as an element of "clarifications" with the result that decisions have focused on whether a mistake was a "minor or clerical error." Thus, "material" errors cannot be corrected in clarifications, *Dell Fed. Sys., L.P. v. United States*, 906 F.3d 982 (Fed. Cir. 2018); *ManTech Advanced Sys. Int'l, Inc. v.*

United States, 141 Fed. Cl. 493 (2019). Some court decisions have been willing to give the term "minor or clerical error" a relatively broad construction. See *Octo Consulting Grp., Inc. v. United States*, 2018 U.S. Claims LEXIS 626 (Fed. Cl. 2018) (correcting mistaken data entry to conform to other date in the proposal); *Galen Med. Assocs., Inc. v. United States*, 369 F.3d 1324 (Fed. Cir. 2004) (raising price to correct an "obvious" mathematical error), and *International Res. Recovery, Inc. v. United States*, 64 Fed. Cl. 150 (2005) (correcting a tonnage capacity when the contracting officer concluded from the proposal that it had stated a monthly capacity when it meant to state an annual capacity).

Other decisions hold that a mistake cannot be a minor or clerical error, correctable in the clarification process, unless it is apparent on the face of the proposal. See *Nuclear Diagnostic Prods.*, Comp. Gen. Dec. B-416227, 2018 CPD ¶ 239 (complex mathematical error not readily seen); *Abacus Tech. Corp.*, Comp. Gen. Dec. B-413421, 2016 CPD ¶ 317 (detailed evaluation of proposal indicated no clerical error but just sloppy proposal); *Wyle Labs., Inc.*, Comp. Gen. Dec. B-412964, 2016 CPD ¶ 144 (agency not required to "surmise" the protester had submitted the wrong resume for a key person); *Constellation W., Inc. v. United States*, 125 Fed. Cl. 505 (2015) (missing prices correctable only through discussions); *DynCorp Int'l LLC v. United States*, 76 Fed. Cl. 528 (2007) (obvious mathematical error detected by contracting officer meets this requirement); *Environmental Quality Mgmt., Inc.*, Comp. Gen. Dec. B-402247.2, 2010 CPD ¶ 75 (transposition of percentage of work to be done by team members not reasonably identifiable in proposal); *Joint Venture Penauillie Italia S.p.A.; Cofathec S.p.A.; SEB.CO S.a.s.; CO.PEL.S.a.s.*, Comp. Gen. Dec. B-298865, 2007 CPD ¶ 7 (omission of option year pricing not a correctable mistake during the clarification process, because the existence of the mistake and the amount intended by the offeror was not clear from the face of the proposal); *Paraclete Contracts*, Comp. Gen. Dec. B-299883, 2007 CPD ¶ 153 (improper to obtain clarification of ambiguous prices by using mistake correction procedures because the prices were not "apparent on the face of its offer"); *Battelle Mem'l Inst.*, Comp. Gen. Dec. B-299533, 2007 CPD ¶ 94 (decision not to obtain clarification of omitted option prices by using mistake correction procedures proper because the prices "were not apparent on the face of the proposal"); and *CIGNA Gov't Servs., LLC*, Comp. Gen. Dec. B-297915.2, 2006 CPD ¶ 74 (improper to obtain clarification of level of effort in final proposal revision when correct level was not apparent on revision's face). However, where an agency seeks confirmation that it has correctly identified an error in a proposal, and the agency has also surmised, on its own, the correct answer, that exchange is a clarifications, *Safal Partners*, Comp. Gen. Dec. B-416937, 2019 CPD ¶ 20; *Barbaricum LLC*, Comp. Gen. Dec. B-416728, 2019 CPD ¶ 153.

Some decision have found errors to not constitute minor or clerical because discussions would have been required, *Defense Base Servs., Inc*, Comp. Gen. Dec. B-414591, 2017 CPD ¶ 243 (obtaining omitted legally binding teaming agreement); *NOVA Corp.*, Comp. Gen. Dec. B-411851, 2015 CPD ¶ 345 (obtaining omitted DD Form 254); *ADNET Sys., Inc.*, Comp. Gen. Dec. B-408685.3, 2014 CPD ¶ 173 (correction of NAICS code discrepancies would have entailed seeking additional information); and *Omega World Travel, Inc.*, Comp. Gen. Dec. B-283218, 2002 CPD ¶ 5 (correcting erroneous application of discount rate). In a few cases, errors have been found to be correctable because they were minor or clerical, *New Directions Techs., Inc.*, Comp. Gen. Dec. B-412703.2, 2016 CPD ¶ 214 (transposed numbers in cost volume of proposal); *EMS Ice, Inc.*, Comp. Gen. Dec. B-401688.3, 2009 CPD ¶ 211 (line item prices had not been carried forward correctly to "Net" amount for each line item); *IPlus, Inc.*, Comp. Gen. Dec. B-298020, 2006 CPD ¶ 90 (contract line item prices corrected to match sub line item prices and to delete the price from a contract line item that called for no price); *National Beef Packing Co.*, Comp. Gen. Dec. B-296534, 2005 CPD ¶ 168 (labeling of a product (changing "case ready ground beef" to "coarse ground beef") corrected because the specifications clearly called for coarse ground beef).

FAR 15.306(b)(3)(i) includes "errors, omissions, or mistakes (see 14.407)" as items which might be addressed prior to the establishment of the competitive range. This appears to indicate that there is more discretion to correct mistakes prior to establishing the competitive range—permitting an agency to correct a mistake that kept an offeror out of the competitive range. However, there are several decisions holding that agencies have the discretion to refuse to allow an offeror to correct mistakes at this stage of the process. See *CJW-Desbuild JV, LLC*, Comp. Gen. Dec. B-414219, 2017 CPD ¶ 94 (provision applies only when agency is establishing a competitive range); *Battelle Mem'l Inst.*, Comp. Gen. Dec. B-299533, 2007 CPD ¶ 94 (alleged mistake held to be a "proposal deficiency" which should not be cleared up under this rule); *Aeronautical Instrument & Radio Co.*, Comp. Gen. Dec. B-298582.2, 2007 CPD ¶ 10 (protester did not furnish required evidence of mistake); and *U.S. Reconstruction & Dev. Corp.*, Comp. Gen. Dec. B-296195, 2005 CPD ¶ 126 (proposing nonconforming work not type of mistake that fell within rule).

§ 6.07 EVALUATION OF PROPOSALS

Evaluation is an ongoing process that starts upon the receipt of proposals, continues during communications and negotiations, and concludes with the evaluation of final proposal revisions. The purpose of evaluation is to assess the quality of each offer and to determine the capability of each offeror. However, this may be done only by evaluating proposals in terms of the evaluation factors set forth in the RFP. The results of proposal evaluation are explained in narrative comments of the evaluators and are generally summarized in some type of scoring system. FAR 15.305(a) states the basic rules for proposal evaluation as follows:

Proposal evaluation is an assessment of the proposal and the offeror's ability to perform the prospective contract successfully. An agency shall evaluate competitive proposals and then assess their relative qualities solely on the factors and subfactors specified in the solicitation. Evaluations may be conducted using any rating method or combination of methods, including color or adjectival ratings, numerical weights, and ordinary rankings. The relative strengths, deficiencies, significant weaknesses, and risks supporting proposal evaluation shall be documented in the contract file.

[A] The Evaluation Process

Because there is no guidance in the FAR on the methodology used by agencies to evaluate proposals, they are free to perform the evaluation in any reasonable manner that ensures fairness and objectivity. See FAR 1.102-2(c)(3) stating that "[a]ll . . . prospective contractors shall be treated fairly and impartially but need not be treated the same." This requires that, after receipt, all proposals must be evaluated, FAR 15.306(c)(1), and such evaluation should be done with the same degree of care. Thereafter, agencies may drop excessively deficient proposals from the evaluation process if that procedure is called for in the RFP. See *McCann-Erickson USA, Inc.*, Comp. Gen. Dec. B-414787, 2017 CPD ¶ 300, holding that the agency had improperly dropped the protester from the competition when a cursory preliminary review of its proposal revealed minor correctable informational issues and there was no RFP provision warning of such a procedure.

NFS 1816.305-70 contains the following shortened procedure:

> (a) The contracting officer shall not complete the initial evaluation of any proposal when it is determined that the proposal is unacceptable because:
>
> (1) It does not represent a reasonable initial effort to address the essential requirements of the RFP or clearly demonstrates that the offeror does not understand the requirements;
>
> (2) In research and development acquisitions, a substantial design drawback is evident in the proposal, and sufficient correction or improvement to consider the proposal acceptable would require virtually an entirely new technical proposal; or
>
> (3) It contains major deficiencies or omissions or out-of-line costs which discussions with the offeror could not reasonably be expected to cure.

When an agency intends to separate the cost and technical evaluations, this procedure is usually facilitated by requiring the offerors to submit their cost and technical proposals in separate packages. In this situation, it has been common practice to withhold the cost information from technical personnel with the result that the technical package describes the work to be done but may not include a description of the resources (labor hours of the contractor and its major subcontractors) proposed to perform the various tasks on the contract. Without such resource information, the technical evaluation will be imprecise at best. The FAR Part 15 Rewrite addresses this problem by providing in FAR 15.305(a)(4) that "[c]ost information may be provided to members of the technical evaluation team." A well-written RFP requires that resource information (labor hours but not labor or indirect cost rates) be included in the technical package. If the RFP does not contain this requirement, the agency should extract this resource information from the cost proposal and provide it to the technical evaluators. This will permit them to arrive at an accurate assessment of the offerors' technical understanding of the requirements as well as their ability to perform the work described in the RFP. See *AmerInd, Inc.*, Comp. Gen. Dec. B-248324, 92-2 CPD ¶ 85, where GAO affirmed the contracting officer's adjustment of an offeror's cost proposal to reflect the salaries of personnel discussed in the technical proposal. See also *Satellite Servs., Inc.*, Comp. Gen. Dec. B-286508, 2001 CPD ¶ 30, where a protest was sustained because the winning offeror's low estimate of resources in its price proposal was not used by the technical evaluators to assess its understanding of the work. Compare *Arcadia U.S., Inc.*, Comp. Gen. Dec. B-412828, 2016 CPD ¶ 198, holding that it was improper to assess the impact of a low price on the technical proposal because the agency found no problems with the technical proposal.

Objectivity is generally sought by having the same evaluators review each proposal or portion of a proposal. However, if it is impractical to do so, proposals can be evaluated by different personnel. See *Design Concepts, Inc.*, Comp. Gen. Dec. B-186125, 76-2 CPD ¶ 365 (30 proposals divided among the evaluators); *T.V. Travel, Inc.*, 65 Comp. Gen. 109 (B-218198), 85-2 CPD ¶ 640 (37 proposals evaluated in six groups); and *Innovative Logistics Techniques, Inc.*, Comp. Gen. Dec. B-275786.2, 97-1 CPD ¶ 144 (one evaluator reviewed both proposals and two evaluators each reviewed one proposal). Oral presentations can also be evaluated by different personnel, *Quality Elevator Co.*, Comp. Gen. Dec. B-276750, 97-2 CPD ¶ 28. The key question is whether the evaluation fairly reflects the strengths and weaknesses of each proposal. See *EDC Consulting, LLC*, Comp. Gen. Dec. B-414175.10, 2017 CPD ¶ 185, where the agency dropped a procurement evaluating live demonstrations when it concluded that multiple evaluators had not reached consistent results.

Agencies may change evaluators during the course of a procurement. For example, initial proposals may be evaluated by one set of evaluators, and final proposal revisions by another, *Data Flow Corp.*, 62 Comp. Gen. 506 (B-209499), 83-2 CPD ¶ 57. Similarly, an agency may re-evaluate proposals using a more experienced group of evaluators, *WR Sys., Ltd*, Comp. Gen. Dec. B-287477, 2001 CPD ¶ 118; *SOS Interpreting, Ltd.*, Comp. Gen. Dec. B-287505, 2001 CPD ¶ 104; *Pro-Mark, Inc.*, Comp. Gen. B-247248, 92-2 CPD ¶ 124. New evaluators may also be used after the agency has lost a protest, *LIS, Inc.*, Comp. Gen. B-400646.4, 2010 CPD ¶ 18; *Burchick Constr. Co.*, Comp.

Gen. B-400342.3, 2009 CPD ¶ 102; *PRC, Inc.*, Comp. Gen. Dec. B-233561.8, 92-2 CPD ¶ 215, or has decided to take corrective action to forestall a protest, *Domain Name Alliance Registry*, Comp. Gen. B-310803.2, 2008 CPD ¶ 168. Occasionally, the agency will be ordered to create a new evaluation team, *Wackenhut Servs., Inc. v. United States*, 85 Fed. Cl. 273 (2008). See *Matrix Int'l Logistics, Inc.*, Comp. Gen. Dec. B-277208, 97-2 CPD ¶ 94, for a case where GAO did not object to the fact that a different team of evaluators arrived at significantly different evaluations. However, most agencies attempt to use the same evaluation personnel throughout the procurement.

[1] Disparate Evaluations

Frequently, the same factors are evaluated by a number of evaluators who arrive at a different assessment of the merits of the proposals and different scores. GAO has stated that it is not unusual for individual evaluators to reach differing conclusions when judging competing proposals since both objective and subjective judgments are involved, *Henry Schein, Inc.*, Comp. Gen. Dec. B-405319, 2011 CPD ¶ 264. Similarly, in *Alexander & Tom, Inc.*, Comp. Gen. Dec. B-412358, 2016 CPD ¶ 46, it was proper for the technical evaluation chairman to reach a different conclusion from the evaluators. In *Group GPS Multimedia*, Comp. Gen. Dec. B-310716, 2008 CPD ¶ 34, it was proper for the source selection official to make the final evaluation when two technical evaluators could not agree, and in *EBA Ernest Bland Assocs.*, Comp. Gen. Dec. B-270496, 96-1 CPD ¶ 148, GAO found nothing unusual or improper in the fact that two individual agency evaluators gave widely divergent scores to the same proposal. Therefore, disparities in evaluator scores alone do not suffice to show improper or irrational evaluation schemes, even if the final scores are averaged. See *Cube-All Star Servs. (J.V.)*, Comp. Gen. Dec. B-291903, 2003 CPD ¶ 145 (all evaluators did not identify same technical deficiencies). See *Inlingua Sch. of Language*, Comp. Gen. Dec. B-229784, 88-1 CPD ¶ 340, finding unfairness in a point adding system which scored questions answered as "not applicable" with zeros, thereby penalizing the protester for meaningless data. Similarly, consensus evaluations must be supported by rational conclusions, *Magnum Med. Personnel, A Joint Venture*, Comp. Gen. Dec. B-297687.2, 2006 CPD ¶ 99.

There is no requirement that agencies develop consensus scores in order to reconcile disparate evaluations, *Smart Innovative Solutions*, Comp. Gen. Dec. B-400323.3, 2008 CPD ¶ 220. Nonetheless, whenever possible the agency should attempt to reconcile disparate scores to ensure that the evaluators have not made obvious mistakes in their evaluation. GAO has recognized that there can be disparities between individual evaluators and the consensus that is finally arrived at. See *Concurrent Techs. Corp.*, Comp. Gen. Dec. B-412795.2, 2017 CPD ¶ 25, stating:

> [I]t is not unusual for individual evaluator ratings to differ significantly from one another, or from the consensus ratings eventually assigned; indeed, the reconciling of such differences among evaluators' viewpoints is the ultimate purpose of a consensus evaluation. *J5 Sys., Inc.*, B-406800, Aug. 31, 2012, 2012 CPD ¶ 252 at 13. The overriding concern for our purposes is not whether an agency's final evaluation conclusions are consistent with earlier evaluation conclusions (individual or group), but whether they are reasonable and consistent with the stated evaluation criteria, and reasonably reflect the relative merits of the proposals. Id.; see, e.g., *URS Fed. Tech. Servs., Inc.*, B-405922.2, B-405922.3, May 9, 2012, 2012 CPD ¶ 155 at 9

See *Jacobs Tech., Inc.*, Comp. Gen. Dec. B-413389, 2016 CPD ¶ 312 (consensus evaluation need not track changes in individual evaluators' conclusions); *James Constr.*, Comp. Gen. Dec. B-402429, 2010 CPD ¶ 98 (proper consensus of "acceptable" when evaluators had ratings of "good," "good," and "good/acceptable"); *Robbind-Gioia, LLC*, Comp. Gen. Dec. B-402199, 2010 CPD ¶ 67 (proper for consensus report to reflect views of only one evaluator); *Bering Straits Tech. Servs., LLC*, Comp. Gen. Dec. B-401560.3, 2009 CPD ¶ 201 (proper consensus of "good" when three evaluators rated proposal "excellent" and one rated it "good"); *Systems Research & Applications Corp.*, Comp. Gen. Dec. B-299818, 2008 CPD ¶ 28 (not unusual for individual evaluator ratings to differ from one another, or to differ from the consensus ratings eventually assigned); *Domain Name Alliance Registry*, Comp. Gen. Dec. B-310803.2, 2008 CPD ¶ 168 (proper consensus of "minor weakness" when two evaluators found no weakness and one found major weakness); *Systalex Corp.*, Comp. Gen. Dec. B-400109, 2008 CPD ¶ 148 (strength found by one evaluator need not be reflected in consensus score); *Veterans Tech., LLC*, Comp. Gen. Dec. B-310303.2, 2008 CPD ¶ 31 (consensus evaluation can vary from evaluation of all evaluators); and *General Injectables & Vaccines, Inc.*, Comp. Gen. Dec. B-298590, 2006 CPD ¶ 173 ("pressure" on evaluators to reach consensus did not demonstrate irrational evaluation).

Consensus evaluations have been held to be rational and reliable even when the agency has destroyed the evaluation records of individual evaluators, *Government Acquisitions, Inc.*, Comp. Gen. Dec. B-401048, 2009 CPD ¶ 137; *Alliance Tech. Servs., Inc.*, Comp. Gen. Dec. B-311329, 2008 CPD ¶ 108; *Joint Mgmt. & Tech. Servs.*, Comp. Gen. Dec. B-294229, 2004 CPD ¶ 208, merely averaged the individual scores, *Trusted Base, LLC*, Comp. Gen. Dec. B-401670, 2009 CPD ¶ 218; or permitted the individual evaluators to not record their evaluations, *Dellew Corp.*, Comp. Gen. Dec. B-298233.2, 2006 CPD ¶ 144.

In *United Int'l Investigative Servs., Inc. v. United States*, 41 Fed. Cl. 312 (1998), the court held that the agency had acted improperly in failing to permit the evaluators to discuss their evaluations in an effort to arrive at a consensus when the source selection plan called for such a "group discussion." This decision is unusual because it has generally been held that agencies are not bound by their internal source selection plans.

[2] Retention of Evaluation Documents

Agencies should retain all of the evaluation documents created during the evaluation process. FAR 4.801(a) requires agencies to establish contract files "containing the records of all contractual transactions." FAR 4.801(b) requires that these files "constitute a complete history of the transaction for the purpose of—(4) Furnishing essential facts in the event of litigation or congressional inquiries." In *Pitney Bowes Gov't Solutions, Inc. v. United States*, 93 Fed. Cl. 327 (2010), the court held that destruction of evaluators' worksheets violated this requirement and ruled that the contracting officer responsible for destroying the worksheets might be subject to sanctions for spoilation of evidence. No sanctions were imposed because the worksheets were later recovered, *Pitney Bowes Gov't Solutions, Inc. v. United States*, 94 Fed. Cl. 1 (2010)

GAO has reached the opposite conclusion, holding in numerous decisions that it does not object to the destruction of the worksheets of individual evaluators as long as a consensus evaluation supports the source selection decision. See *MSI-Tetra Tech*, Comp. Gen. Dec. B-414517, 2017 CPD ¶ 194, stating:

> The destruction of individual evaluator documents, however, does not render an agency's evaluation unreasonable per se; rather, we will consider the record adequate if the consensus documents and source selection decision sufficiently document the agency's rationale for the evaluations. Joint Mgmt. and Tech. Servs., B-294229, B-294229.2, Sept. 22, 2004, 2004 CPD ¶ 208 at 3-4.

Nonetheless, on occasion GAO has held a hearing in order to determine the substantive conclusions reached by each individual evaluator. See *Dynalantic Corp.*, Comp. Gen. Dec. B-274944.2, 97-1 CPD ¶ 101, where such a hearing was held and the agency was directed to pay the protester for the cost of the hearing when the protest was granted on other grounds.

[B] Agency Discretion

Just as the procuring agency has great discretion in selecting evaluation factors, its evaluation will not be disturbed unless it is arbitrary or in violation of procurement statutes or regulations, and GAO is especially deferential in dealing with technical evaluations. See *Sierra Nevada Corp.*, Comp. Gen. Dec. B-415233, 2018 CPD ¶ 50, stating:

> The evaluation of an offeror's proposal is a matter within the agency's discretion. B-409941, B-409941.2, Sept. 18, 2014, 2014 CPD ¶ 290 at 6. In reviewing a protester's challenge to the agency's evaluation of proposals, our role is to determine whether the evaluation was reasonable and in accordance with applicable statutes and regulations and the solicitation. *Id.* A protester's disagreement with the evaluation does not make that evaluation

> unreasonable. *VT Griffin Servs., Inc.*, B-299869.2, Nov. 10, 2008, 2008 CPD ¶ 219 at 4. Our Office affords particular deference to the technical expertise of agency personnel where, as here, the judgments concern matters of human life and safety. *Inter-Con Security Systems, Inc.*, B-403538.8, B-403538.9, Jan 10, 2012, 2012 CPD ¶ 245 at 6.

The Court of Federal Claims also gives considerable deference to agency evaluations. See *Advanced Mgmt. Strategies Grp., Inc. v. United States*, 139 Fed. Cl. 404 (2018), finding an arbitrary evaluation but stating at 410:

> We review such agency action pursuant to the standards set forth in the Administrative Procedures Act ("APA"), 5 U.S.C. § 706 (2012). 28 U.S.C. § 1491(b)(4) (setting the standard of review for bid protests to those proscribed in the APA. Thus, to prevail the protester must establish that the agency acted arbitrarily or capriciously or acted in a manner that was not in accordance with law. 5 U.S.C. § 706. This means that the protestor must demonstrate that the agency lacked a rational basis or violated applicable law or regulation. See *Impresa Construzioni Geom. Domenico Garufi v. United States*, 238 F.3d 1324, 1332-33 (Fed. Cir. 2001). If the agency "examines the relevant data and articulates a satisfactory explanation," the decision will not be second-guessed by the court. *Gulf Grp. Inc. v. United States*, 61 Fed. Cl. 338, 351 (2004). But, "where the agency fails to undertake a review or fails to documents such review, we must conclude that it acted irrationally." *Starry Assocs., Inc. v. United States*, 127 Fed. Cl. 539, 549 (2016) (citing *AshBritt, Inc. v. United States*, 87 Fed. Cl. 344, 370 (2009)).

Thus, agencies have broad discretion in the evaluation process. Notwithstanding this broad discretion, however, evaluations must be able to withstand scrutiny as to their reasonableness and must be made in accordance with the evaluation scheme described in the RFP. Thus, agency evaluations have been overturned if they are irrational, not in compliance with the RFP, arbitrary, or not based on evidence in the record.

[1] Irrational Evaluations

Irrational evaluations involve evaluation decisions which are inherently erroneous and could not be used even if specifically outlined in the RFP. For example, in *Dynalantic v. United States*, 945 F.2d 416 (Fed. Cir. 1991), the offeror's significantly less expensive offer was rejected based on an unreasonable assumption that Dynalantic was ignorant of industry standards. Expert testimony illustrated that the Air Force itself lacked such knowledge. See also *Savannah River Tech. & Remediation, LLC*, Comp. Gen. Dec. B-415637, 2018 CPD ¶ 70 (finding awardee's technical approach viable when only study of technique found it was dangerous); *SURVICE Eng'g Co.*, Comp. Gen. Dec. B-414519, 2017 CPD ¶ 237 (giving strength for hiring incumbent workforce while not giving incumbent strength for keeping its workforce); *MLU Servs., Inc.*, Comp. Gen. Dec. B-414555.3, 2017 CPD ¶ 225 (evaluating experience of firm that was not proposed to do any work); *XPO Logistics Worldwide Gov't Servs., LLC*, Comp. Gen. Dec. B-412828.6, 2017 CPD ¶ 88 (finding past performance "somewhat relevant" when all projects were small in comparison with contract requirements); *Jacobs Tech., Inc.*, Comp. Gen. Dec. B-413389, 2016 CPD ¶ 312 (unreasonable assessment of response to hypothetical scenario); *Veterans Evaluation Servs., Inc.*, Comp. Gen. Dec. B-412940, 2016 CPD ¶ 185 (computing price by averaging unit prices for work with different quantities); *Patricio Enters., Inc.*, Comp. Gen. Dec. B-412740, 2016 CPD ¶ 152 (using past performance evaluation scheme that downgraded exceptional performance of relevant contracts); *PMO P'ship Joint Venture*, Comp. Gen. Dec. B-401973.3, 2010 CPD ¶ 29 (joint venture's proposed overhead rate structure rejected based on CAS criteria when offeror was not subject to CAS); *Humana Military Healthcare Servs.*, Comp. Gen. Dec. B-401652.2, 2009 CPD ¶ 219 (protester's prior practice of obtaining discounts not rejected in evaluation of cost proposal); *Engineering Mgmt. & Integration, Inc.*, Comp. Gen. Dec. B-400356.4, 2009 CPD ¶ 114 (offeror downgraded for not providing required percentage of certified employees when it provided the raw number of such employees); *Honeywell Tech. Solutions, Inc.*, Comp. Gen. Dec. B-400771, 2009 CPD ¶ 49 (past performance on a very small contract was relevant to work called for by contract being competed); *Serco Inc. v. United States*, 81 Fed. Cl. 463 (2008) (past performance ratings based on survey that did not match contract requirements); *Sikorsky Aircraft Co.*, Comp. Gen. Dec. B-299145, 2007 CPD ¶ 45 (life-cycle cost evaluation normalized when RFP called for data from each offeror on past costs); *Systronics, Inc.*, Comp. Gen. Dec. B-293102, 2006 CPD ¶ 15 (noncomplying quotation given a high score); *Arora Grp.*, Comp. Gen. Dec. B-297346, 2004 CPD ¶ 61 (offeror downgraded because required certifications were not listed on resume when they were included in response to discussion question); *T Square Logistics Servs.* Corp., Comp. Gen. Dec. B-291851, 2003 CPD ¶ 160 (high scores given to areas not covered in oral presentation); *Eurest Support Servs.*, Comp. Gen. Dec. B-285813.3, 2003 CPD ¶ 139 (unreasonable evaluation of realism of quantity of labor needed to perform fixed price incentive contract); *Dismas Charities, Inc.*, Comp. Gen. Dec. B-292091, 2003 CPD ¶ 125 (failure to consider all information submitted in proposal); *M&S Farms, Inc.*, Comp. Gen. Dec. B-290599, 2002 CPD ¶ 174 (high past performance score based on receipt of more questionnaires); *PADCO, Inc.—Costs*, Comp. Gen. Dec. B-289096.3, 2002 CPD ¶ 135 (acceptance, without analysis, of proposed indirect cost rates far below incurred rates); *Perini/Jones, (J.V.)*, Comp. Gen. Dec. B-285906, 2002 CPD ¶ 68 (giving company credit for experience for affiliated company that would not perform work on contract); *OSI Collection Servs.*, Inc., Comp. Gen. Dec. B-286597, 2001 CPD ¶ 18 (past performance evaluation based on numerical scores detailing number of failures where offerors had disparate amount of work); *Summit Research Corp.*, Comp. Gen. Dec. B-287523, 2001 CPD ¶ 176 (exclusion of small business offeror from evaluation of small business participation); *Green Valley Transp., Inc.*, Comp. Gen. Dec. B-285283, 2000 CPD ¶ 133 (assessing number of performance problems when offerors had disparate amounts of work); and *AIU N. Am., Inc.*, Comp. Gen. Dec. B-283743.2, 2000 CPD ¶ 39 (failing to consider resources of corporation that acquired offeror when evaluating such resources). ad personal knowledge of the information).

[2] Evaluations Not in Compliance with the RFP

Evaluations will be found to be improper if the evaluators do not comply with the evaluation scheme set forth in the RFP. This generally requires that the evaluation process be completed during the source selection—issues cannot be left for resolution after contract award, *Sabreliner Corp.*, Comp. Gen. Dec. B-290515, 2003 CPD ¶ 4.

In most trade off procurements, the RFP will call for a comparative assessment of various aspects of the proposals and this requires the agency evaluators to identify and assess the relative merits of the proposals. Thus, merely finding that disparate proposals are satisfactory or acceptable will be found to fail to comply with the RFP requirements because that amounts to conducting a LPTA procurement, *Patriot Solutions, LLC*, Comp. Gen. Dec. B-413779, 2016 CPD ¶ 376; *FirstLine Transp. Sec., Inc. v. United States*, 100 Fed. Cl. 359 (2011). See, for example, *Systems Research & Applications Corp.*, Comp. Gen. Dec. B-299818, 2008 CPD ¶ 28, where GAO stated:

> Where, as here, the RFP states a best value evaluation plan—as opposed to selection of the lowest priced, technically acceptable offer—evaluation of proposals is not limited to determining whether a proposal is merely technically acceptable; rather, proposals should be further differentiated to distinguish their relative quality under each stated evaluation factor by considering the degree to which technically acceptable proposals exceed the stated minimum requirements or will better satisfy the agency's needs. See *The MIL Corp.*, B-294836, Dec. 30, 2004, 2005 CPD ¶ 29 at 8; *Johnson Controls World Servs., Inc., Meridian Mgmt. Corp.*, B-281287.5 et al., June 21, 1999, 2001 CPD ¶ 3 at 8.

Agencies must also perform the evaluation in accordance with the procedures in the RFP. See *Ernst & Young, LLP v. United States*, 136 Fed. Cl. 475 (2018) (evaluating past performance of company that was not a "major subcontractor" as required by RFP); *ANHAM FZCO*, Comp. Gen. Dec. B-415969, 2018 CPD ¶ 184 (evaluating affiliate contracts when RFP stated only two teaming members' contracts would be considered); *East Coast Util. Constructors, Ltd.*, Comp. Gen. Dec. B-415493, 2018 CPD ¶ 30 (not evaluating past performance of managers when RFP called for evaluation of management team); *Red River Computer Co.*, Comp. Gen. Dec. B-414183.4, 2017 CPD ¶ 157 (allowing winning offeror to propose pricing technique not permitted by

RFP); *Verdi Consulting, Inc.*, Comp. Gen. Dec. B-414103.2, 2017 CPD ¶ 136 (not evaluating option year prices as required by RFP); *General Revenue Corp.*, Comp. Gen. Dec. B-414220.2, 2017 CPD ¶ 106 (ignoring much past performance information not in CPARs); *Walden Sec.*, Comp. Gen. Dec. B-413523.6, 2017 CPD ¶ 105 (not permitting comments on adverse past performance as required by RFP); *Phoenix Air Grp., Inc.*, Comp. Gen. Dec. B-412796.2, 2016 CPD ¶ 308 (accepting offer of aircraft not complying with RFP); *Professional Serv. Indus., Inc.*, Comp. Gen. Dec. B-412721.2, 2016 CPD ¶ 234 (giving credit for program manager that did not meet RFP requirements); *Deloitte Consulting, LLP*, Comp. Gen. Dec. B-412125.2, 2016 CPD ¶ 119 (giving credit for key personnel that did not meet RFP requirements); *Milani Constr., LLC*, Comp. Gen. Dec. B-401942, 2010 CPD ¶ 87 (improperly determining that the protester's price was unreasonably low when there was no indication in the RFP that price realism would be considered). *PMO P'ship Joint Venture*, Comp. Gen. Dec. B-403214, 2010 CPD ¶ 256 (requiring cost data in accordance with Table 15-2 of FAR 15.408 when no such requirement in RFP); *General Dynamics One Source, LLC*, Comp. Gen. Dec. B-400340.5, 2010 CPD ¶ 45 (accepting incentive fee lower than fee specified in RFP); *Ashbury Int'l Grp., Inc.*, Comp. Gen. Dec. B-401123, 2009 CPD ¶ 140 (not testing product sample of selected offeror as required by the RFP); *General Dynamics Info. Tech.*, Comp. Gen. Dec. B-299873, 2007 CPD ¶ 194 (using labor rates proposed by an offeror in one table when the RFP stated that the rates in another table would be used if there was an inconsistency); *KIC Dev., LLC*, Comp. Gen. Dec. B-297425.2, 2006 CPD ¶ 27 (determining offeror did not meet experience requirement when RFP allowed subcontractor experience to meet requirement); *Clean Harbors Envt'l Servs., Inc.*, Comp. Gen. Dec. B-296176.2, 2005 CPD ¶ 222 (treating all past performance as equally relevant when RFP called for assessing varying degrees of relevance); *Lockheed Martin Corp.*, Comp. Gen. Dec. B-293679, 2004 CPD ¶ 115 (determining that proposal met RFP requirement to fully describe design features of product based on evaluator's knowledge of subcontractor's competence); *Computer Info. Specialist, Inc.*, Comp. Gen. Dec. B-293049, 2004 CPD ¶ 1 (relying on blanket statements of compliance when RFP called for submission of specific information showing compliance); *Johnson Controls World Servs., Inc.*, Comp. Gen. Dec. B-281287.5, 2001 CPD ¶ 3 (giving no credit for proposals with greater technical merit); and *Saco Defense Corp.*, Comp. Gen. Dec. B-283885, 2000 CPD ¶ 34 (rating proposal low risk when offeror did not provide detailed information required by RFP to make the assessment).

Evaluations have been found not to comply with the RFP even when the agency had no knowledge of the noncompliance. See, for example, *CBIS Fed., Inc.*, 71 Comp. Gen. 319 (B-245844.2), 92-1 CPD ¶ 308, where the agency gave high scores to proposed personnel to perform the work and later found that the contractor had no "letters of commitment" with two of the key personnel. GAO granted the protest because the evaluation was not in accord with the RFP requirement that each offeror furnish the names of key personnel that would actually be used to perform the contract.

[3] Arbitrary Evaluations

Evaluations are found to be arbitrary when offerors are not treated equally in the evaluation process. To demonstrate unequal treatment, the Federal Circuit recently explained that a protester must show that it was given a disparate rating for something in its proposal that was "substantively indistinguishable" from or nearly identical to that thing in other proposals, *Office Design Grp. v. United States*, 951 F.3d 1366 (Fed. Cir. 2020). Prior to the Federal Circuit's statement of this standard, the GAO and Court of Federal Claims had decided a number of decisions discussing equal treatment. In *BAE Sys. Tech. Sols. & Servs., Inc.*, Comp. Gen. Dec. B-414931.2, 2018 CPD ¶ 54, the protester was downgraded but the winning offeror was not downgraded for the same lack of information. See also *American Corr. Healthcare, Inc. v. United States*, 137 Fed. Cl. 395 (2018) (downgrading protester for not offering a service when there was doubt whether winning offeror would provide the same service); *360 IT Integrated Solutions*, Comp. Gen. Dec. B-414650.7, 2018 CPD ¶ 188 (giving strengths to winning offeror but not the protester for same features in management and technical proposals); *Tribalco, LLC*, Comp. Gen. Dec. B-414120, 2017 CPD ¶ 73 (finding proposal unacceptable for lack of detail when winning offeror's proposal also lacked detail); *CSR, Inc.*, Comp. Gen. Dec. B-413973, 2017 CPD ¶ 64 (considering unlisted CPARs of winning offeror but not of protester); *Halbert Constr. Co.*, Comp. Gen. Dec. B-413213, 2016 CPD ¶ 254 (downgrading protester for adverse relevant past performance of but not winning offeror); *Arctic Slope Mission Servs., LLC*, Comp. Gen. Dec. B-410992.5, 2016 CPD ¶ 39 (holding non-incumbent offerors to higher standard than incumbents); *BayFirst Solutions, LLC v. United States*, 102 Fed. Cl. 677 (2012) (disparate rating of subcontractors); *Brican, Inc.*, Comp. Gen. Dec. B-400760.4, 2010 CPD ¶ 32 (crediting one offeror with experience of subcontractor when protester given no credit in spite of proposing same subcontractor); *AINS, Inc.*, Comp. Gen. Dec. B-402602, 2010 CPD ¶ 141 (giving negative evaluation to product capability when same evaluation not given to winning offeror's product that also did not meet the requirement); *Ahtna Support & Training Servs., LLC*, Comp. Gen. Dec. B-400947.2, 2009 CPD ¶ 119 (crediting only one offeror with experience of subcontractor); *ITT Fed. Servs. Int'l Corp.*, Comp. Gen. Dec. B-296783, 2007 CPD ¶ 43 (using one competitor's staffing approach to adjust the costs of protester an unfair practice); *Magnum Med. Personnel, A Joint Venture*, Comp. Gen. Dec. B-297687.2, 2006 CPD ¶ 99 (disparate evaluations of capability); *BAE Tech. Servs., Inc.*, Comp. Gen. Dec. B-296699, 2006 CPD ¶ 91 (using different standard to evaluate offerors' proposed initiatives to reduce staffing); *PGBA, LLC v. United States*, 60 Fed. Cl. 196 (2004) (downgrading one offeror for lack of specificity without applying same standard to other offerors); *Ashe*

Facility Servs., Inc., Comp. Gen. Dec. B-292218.3, 2004 CPD ¶ 80 (giving credit for experience of key personnel in evaluating corporate experience only to awardee); and *Southwestern Bell Tel. Co.*, Comp. Gen. Dec. B-292476, 2003 CPD ¶ 177 (equal evaluations when awardee had ethical problems).

An extreme form of arbitrary evaluation is evident in situations where the procuring agency purposely favors one offeror over another. For example, in *Xerox Corp. v. United States*, 21 Cl. Ct. 278 (1990), the agency displayed an unethical and even criminal bias toward the awardee. It changed the RFP to omit a requirement that the awardee could not satisfy. It also met secretly with the awardee to allow it to improve its evaluation by correcting a mistake in its proposal, after BAFOs had been submitted, without allowing other offerors to change their proposals. The entire procurement was eventually voided, and Xerox obtained reimbursement for all costs. See also *Lockheed Martin Corp.*, Comp. Gen. Dec. B-295402, 2005 CPD ¶ 24, where the source selection official changed the RFP technical requirements to favor a contractor with which she was negotiating future employment. Similarly, in *Lockheed Martin Corp.*, Comp. Gen. Dec. B-295401, 2005 CPD ¶ 41, the source selection official pressured the evaluators into changing their evaluations and then awarded the contract to the contractor with which she was negotiating future employment.

[4] Evaluation Not Based on Evidence

Evaluation decisions must be based on evidence to support an agency's decision; they must have a rational basis. In *Radiation Oncology Grp. of WNY, PC*, Comp. Gen. Dec. B-310354.2, 2009 CPD ¶ 136, GAO sustained a protest because the agency concluded two proposals were technically equal but had no evidence demonstrating that their unequal evaluations were incorrect. See also *Trident Vantage Sys., LLC*, Comp. Gen. Dec. B-415944, 2018 CPD ¶ 166 (no evidence supporting agency relevancy of past performance determinations); *Next Tier Concepts, Inc.*, Comp. Gen. Dec. B-414337, 2017 CPD ¶ 161 (technical evaluators not informed of very low price); *AdvanceMed Corp.*, Comp. Gen. Dec. B-414373, 2017 CPD ¶ 160 (faulty cost realism analysis when cost proposal conflicted with technical proposal); *NCI Information Sys., Inc.*, Comp. Gen. Dec. B-412870.2, 2016 CPD ¶ 310 (no evidence in price realism analysis that price was not unrealistically low); *MicroTechs., LLC*, Comp. Gen. Dec. B-413091, 2016 CPD ¶ 219 (evaluation of employee compensation based on incorrect salary survey); *CliniComp Int'l, Inc. v. United States*, 117 Fed. Cl. 722 (2014) (no evidence showing winning offeror met specification requirement); *Irving Burton Assocs., Inc.*, Comp. Gen. Dec. B-401983.3, 2010 CPD ¶ 92 (evaluation of transition plan not supported by proposal after surplus pages were removed); *Cahaba Safeguard Admins., LLC*, Comp. Gen. Dec. B-401842.2, 2010 CPD ¶ 39 (agency accepted OCI mitigation plan containing no detailed implementation information); *AshBritt, Inc. v. United States*, 87 Fed. Cl. 344 (2009) (no evidence supporting protester's lower score); *Spherix, Inc.*, Comp. Gen. Dec. B-2945723, 2005 CPD ¶ 3 (agency "projected" offeror's staffing level with no evidence to support projection); *National City Bank of Indiana*, Comp. Gen. Dec. B-287608.3, 2002 CPD ¶ 190 (no evidence to support conclusion low staffing was adequate); *DynCorp Int'l, LLC*, Comp. Gen. Dec. B-289863, 2002 CPD ¶ 83 (no evidence to support rejection of technical evaluators' concern of inadequate staffing); *Meredian Mgmt.*, Comp. Gen. Dec. B-281287.10, 2001 CPD ¶ 5 (inadequate staffing not factored into evaluation); *SWR, Inc.*, Comp. Gen. Dec. B-286161.2, 2001 CPD ¶ 32 (lack of experience not demonstrated by information provided by protester); *OneSource Energy Servs., Inc.*, Comp. Gen. Dec. B-283445, 2000 CPD ¶ 109 (report of telephone conversation with references not a fair reflection of conversation); *Maritime Berthing, Inc.*, Comp. Gen. Dec. B-284123.3, 2000 CPD ¶ 89 (evaluation that offeror met specification requirement when evidence in proposal and known to agency proved otherwise); and *Future-Tec Mgmt. Sys., Inc.*, Comp. Gen. Dec. B-283793.5, 2000 CPD ¶ 59 (cost realism adjustment based on misunderstanding of the cost proposal).

GAO has deemed evaluations improper where the agency ignores evidence. See, for example, *Intercon Assocs., Inc.*, Comp. Gen. Dec. B-298282, 2006 CPD ¶ 121, where GAO sustained a protest because the "evaluation judgments are, in many instances, either factually incorrect, internally contradictory, or so cryptic that we are unable to discern the basis for the evaluators' concerns." See also *Contrack Int'l, Inc.*, Comp. Gen. Dec. B-401871.5, 2010 CPD ¶ 126 (evaluation of "excellent" past performance ignoring adverse information); *Velos, Inc.*, Comp. Gen. Dec. B-400500.8, 2010 CPD ¶ 13 (source selection decision based on consultant's report that ignored technical panel report); *MMI Fed. Mktg. Serv. Corp.*, Comp. Gen. Dec. B-297537, 2006 CPD ¶ 38 (evaluation that offeror met Berry Amendment requirement when evidence indicated it did not); *Cogent Sys., Inc.*, Comp. Gen. Dec. B-295990.4, 2006 CPD ¶ 179 (evaluators ignored different product offered in final proposal revision); and *Locus Tech., Inc.*, Comp. Gen. Dec. B-293012, 2004 CPD ¶ 16 (evaluators ignored significant portion of final proposal revision).

Although it is generally an offeror's responsibility to present a well-written proposal, GAO has also rejected evaluation results in some cases when it becomes apparent that the evaluators do not understand the data available to them. For example, in *Mine Safety Appliance Co.*, 69 Comp. Gen. 562 (B-238597.2), 90-2 CPD ¶ 11, the evaluation was overturned when the evaluators "extrapolated" successful performance after the offeror had failed the required tests. GAO concluded that the agency should not have proceeded with the procurement without determining why the item did not perform properly. See also *Haworth, Inc.*, Comp. Gen. Dec. B-297077, 2005 CPD ¶ 215 (evaluators did not see that descriptive literature concerning product indicated that it did not meet specifications).

[C] Using Factors Contained in the RFP

FAR 15.305(a) follows the language in 10 U.S.C. § 3206 (formerly § 2305(b)(1)) and 41 U.S.C. § 3701(a), stating that evaluation shall be based solely on the factors and subfactors specified in the RFP. Thus, GAO has stated that it is generally improper to add or substitute evaluation criteria after proposals have been submitted and reviewed by government evaluators. See *Grey Advertising, Inc.*, 55 Comp. Gen. 1111 (B-184825), 76-1 CPD ¶ 325, stating that "once offerors are informed of the criteria against which proposals will be evaluated, it is incumbent upon the procuring activity to adhere to those criteria." Thus, unless the solicitation has been amended, the entire evaluation must be based on the stated factors throughout the competitive negotiation process.

[1] Scope of Evaluation

Notwithstanding the requirement that only stated factors may be evaluated, agencies have been permitted to broaden the scope of the evaluation by considering all issues that are related to a factor and to narrow the scope of the evaluation by only considering those issues that are perceived to be relevant to the factor.

[a] Broadening the Scope

Agencies may evaluate any issue that is logically related to a stated evaluation factor. See *Bank St. Coll. of Educ.*, 63 Comp. Gen. 393 (B-213209), 84-1 CPD ¶ 607, where GAO stated at 400:

> As far as consistency with the evaluation criteria is concerned, while the source selection official may not judge the merits of the proposals based on criteria that offerors were not advised would be considered, the official may properly take into account specific, albeit not expressly identified, matters that are logically encompassed by or related to the stated criteria.

This relationship will be found if a consideration is not listed in Section M but is discussed in Section L of the RFP, *J.A. Jones Grupo de Servicios, SA*, Comp. Gen. Dec. B-283234, 99-2 CPD ¶ 80; *Science & Tech., Inc.*, Comp. Gen. Dec. B-272748, 97-1 CPD ¶ 121. See also *NEQ, LLC v. United States*, 88 Fed. Cl. 38 (2009), where it was found proper to evaluate the presence of the offerors' personnel in listed cities when they were required to submit charts and maps showing the location of their personnel, and *Forestry, Surveys & Data*, Comp. Gen. Dec. B-276802.3, 97-2 CPD ¶ 46, where experience was properly evaluated when it was not listed as a factor in the solicitation but experience questionnaires were required to be submitted.

Agency evaluation personnel are given considerable discretion in determining which considerations are within the scope of an evaluation factor. This discretion has been very broad when factors involving the capability of the offerors are being evaluated. For example, in *Homequity, Inc.*, Comp. Gen. Dec. B-223997, 86-2 CPD ¶ 685, it was held proper for evaluators to consider the cumulative experience of the offerors' key personnel in evaluating the "organization and experience" factor, and in *Cygnus Corp.*, Comp. Gen. Dec. B-275957, 97-1 CPD ¶ 202, evaluation of the experience of key personnel was proper when the evaluation factor was "corporate experience." See also *NEQ, LLC v. United States*, 88 Fed. Cl. 38 (2009) (metropolitan presence of offerors' offices properly considered in evaluating quick response time requirement); *Professional Perf. Dev. Grp., Inc.*, Comp. Gen. Dec. B-311273, 2008 CPD ¶ 101 ("tested relationships" with required personnel properly considered under RFP calling for evaluation of how offeror would respond to "temporary staffing surges"); *Savannah River Alliance, LLC*, Comp. Gen. Dec. B-311126, 2008 CPD ¶ 88 (diverse experience of key personnel properly considered in evaluating innovative approaches and broad experience); *Matthews Mfg., Inc.*, Comp. Gen. Dec. B-299518, 2007 CPD ¶ 110 (producing the identical product properly considered in evaluating "existing manufacturing capabilities"); *Base Techs., Inc.*, Comp. Gen. Dec. B-293061.2, 2004 CPD ¶ 31 (length of relevant experience of key personnel properly considered in evaluating "qualifications" of key personnel); *Network Eng'g, Inc.*, Comp. Gen. Dec. B-292996, 2004 CPD ¶ 23 (use of incumbent personnel properly considered in evaluating "relevant staff experience"); *Gentex Corp.—Western Ops.*, Comp. Gen. Dec. B-291793, 2003 CPD ¶ 66 (funding profile properly considered in evaluating offeror's ability to meet program objectives including development effort "within cost and schedule constraints"); *IBP, Inc.*, Comp. Gen. Dec. B-289296, 2002 CPD ¶ 39 (special consideration for performance as incumbent contractor considered under "experience" factor); *NCLN20, Inc.*, Comp. Gen. Dec. B-287692, 2001 CPD ¶ 136 (organizational structure and transaction plan considered under staffing plan); and *Oceaneering Int'l, Inc.*, Comp. Gen. Dec. B-287325, 2001 CPD ¶ 95 (contingency of lack of availability of mobilization port considered under mobilization factor). An evaluation issue has also been found to be within the scope of the RFP because it was raised during discussions with the offerors, *Intermagnetics Gen. Corp.*, Comp. Gen. Dec. B-286596, 2001 CPD ¶ 10. See also *Interstate Elec. Corp.*, Comp. Gen. Dec. B-286466, 2001 CPD ¶ 29, where an unlisted evaluation factor was found proper because it was identified in an oral presentation as well as in Section L of the RFP.

Considerable discretion has also been granted to agencies in determining which considerations are related to offers. For example, in *International Bus. Machs. Corp. v. Dep't of Treasury*, GSBCA 11777-P, 92-3 BCA ¶ 25,401, *aff'd*, *Lockheed Missiles & Space Co. v. Bentsen*, 4 F.3d 955 (Fed. Cir. 1993), the board held that the agency properly evaluated the productivity of the proposed computer systems in the technical and cost evaluation even though productivity was not mentioned in the list of factors. The board stated that the protesters should not have been surprised that the agency would be concerned about productivity because it was inherent in the evaluation of computer systems for use by government agencies. In this regard, agencies can evaluate the extent that an offeror proposes to exceed the agency's requirement when it evaluates the offer. See *IAP World Servs., Inc.*, Comp. Gen. Dec. B-297084, 2005 CPD ¶ 199, stating:

> [In a best value procurement,] the agency is not limited to determining whether a proposal is merely technically acceptable; rather, proposals may be evaluated to distinguish their relative quality by considering the degree to which they exceed the minimum requirements or will better satisfy the agency's needs. *Israel Aircraft Indus., Ltd., MATA Helicopters Div.*, B-274389 et al., Dec. 6, 1996, 97-1 CPD ¶ 41 at 5-6; *Meridian Corp.*, B-246330.3, July 19, 1993, 93-2 CPD ¶ 29 at 6-7.

See also *Tri-Starr Mgmt. Servs., Inc.*, Comp. Gen. Dec. B-408827.2, 2015 CPD ¶ 43 (intent to use automation to deliver services); *USGC, Inc.*, Comp. Gen. Dec. B-400184.2, 2009 CPD ¶ 9 (innovative disincentive plan offered agency a way to reduce risk); *Cerner Corp.*, Comp. Gen. Dec. B-293093, 2004 CPD ¶ 34 (selection of approach that agency evaluated as best meeting RFP's performance goals); *Israel Aircraft Indus., Ltd.*, Comp. Gen. Dec. B-274389, 97-1 CPD ¶ 41 (enhanced safety of aircraft subsystem intrinsic to stated evaluation factors covering performance and usability of subsystem); *Hydro Eng'g, Inc. v. United States*, 37 Fed. Cl. 448 (1997) (efficiency, reliability and maintainability of equipment properly considered in evaluating design of equipment); and *JoaQuin Mfg. Corp.*, Comp. Gen. Dec. B-275185, 97-1 CPD ¶ 48 (weight, number of footings, and visibility properly related to the suitability of design evaluation factor).

Also inherent in the evaluation of technical and management factors is the *risk* involved in successfully carrying out the proposed management or technical approach to be performed under the prospective contract. Thus, the scoring can account for such risks even though the RFP does not describe this aspect of the evaluation process. See, for example, *Lockheed Martin Integrated Sys., Inc.*, Comp. Gen. Dec. B-410189.5, 2016 CPD ¶ 273 (spin-off of part of company created potential risk of employee retention); *ManTech Sys. Eng'g Corp.*, Comp. Gen. Dec. B-412132, 2016 CPD ¶ 37 (agency accepted risk of lack of experience for lower price); *Preferred Sys. Solutions*, Comp. Gen. Dec. B-291750, 2003 CPD ¶ 56 (transition plan and resumes of key personnel demonstrated that management plan offered lower risk even though such information was not required by RFP); *S-Tron*, Comp. Gen. Dec. B-244767.2, 92-1 CPD ¶ 409 (possibility that protester could not meet expedited delivery schedule was a proper reason to deduct points from the proposal); *Honeywell, Inc.*, Comp. Gen. Dec. B-238184, 90-1 CPD ¶ 435 (proposed reverse engineering of software created the risk of a failure to meet required schedules and costs); and *AT&T Techs., Inc.*, Comp. Gen. Dec. B-237069, 90-1 CPD ¶ 114 (inability to test computerized system until in actual use created great technical and scheduling risks). It is also common practice to make risk a stated evaluation factor, See, for example, *Northrop Grumman Sys. Corp.*, Comp. Gen. Dec. B-414312, 2017 CPD ¶ 128, where the SSA made a different risk determination that the SSAC.

In spite of the breadth of the rules permitting significant leeway in interpreting the scope of the listed evaluation factors, an agency may not evaluate an issue that has no relationship to the factors contained in the RFP. GAO has stated that there must be a "clear nexus between the stated and unstated criteria," *Sterling Medical Corp.*, Comp. Gen. Dec. B-412407, 2016 CPD ¶ 73; *Global Analytic Info. Tech. Servs., Inc.*, Comp. Gen. Dec. B-298840.2, 2007 CPD ¶ 57. See *EFS Ebrex SARL*, Comp. Gen. Dec. B-416076, 2018 CPD ¶ 201 (improper to use experience benchmarks in source selection plan but not in RFP); *Conley & Assocs., Inc.*, Comp. Gen. Dec. B-415458.3, 2018 CPD ¶ 161 (improper to credit offeror with meeting criteria in fixed price CLIN with personnel charged to cost-reimbursement CLIN); *Pinnacle Solutions, Inc.*, Comp. Gen. Dec. B-414360, 2017 CPD ¶ 172 (improper imposition of detailed requirements of management proposal); *General Revenue Corp.*, Comp. Gen. Dec. B-414220.2, 2017 CPD ¶ 106 (improper use of detailed requirements for quality control manager when RFP silent on issue); *Innovative Test Asset Solutions, LLC*, Comp. Gen. Dec. B-411687, 2016 CPD ¶ 68 (lack of realistic cost savings not part of evaluating technical risk); *360Training.com, Inc. v. United States*, 106 Fed. Cl. 177 (2012) (improper to consider probation of organization in evaluating of status of individual trainers); *T-C Transcription*, Comp. Gen. Dec. B-401470, 2009 CPD ¶ 172 (improper to downgrade proposal for lack of resumes when RFP did not call for their submission); *Consolidated Eng'g Servs., Inc.*, Comp. Gen. Dec. B-311313, 2008 CPD ¶ 146 (improper to evaluate whether offeror had performed all services in a single past contract when factor was experience of "size, scope and complexity" of proposed work); and *Meridian Mgmt. Corp.*, Comp. Gen. Dec. B-285127, 2000 CPD ¶ 121 (maintenance and repair of specialized laboratory equipment not within scope of services for laboratories when offerors were not permitted to see laboratories before proposing and no specialized equipment mentioned in RFP).

Agencies may not evaluate price realism if it is not explicitly or implicitly listed as a factor, *NVE, Inc. v. United States*, 121 Fed. Cl. 169 (2015); *NJVC, LLC*, Comp. Gen. Dec. B-410035, 2014 CPD ¶ 307. However, implicit references to price realism have been found in a number of cases. See *Science Applications Int'l Corp.*, Comp. Gen. Dec. B-407105, 2012 CPD ¶ 310 (determining whether proposed prices were compatible with the scope of effort, were not unbalanced, and were neither excessive nor insufficient); *ViON Corp. v. United States*, 122 Fed. Cl. 559, 564 (2015) (determining whether proposal reflects an inherent lack of competence or failure to comprehend the complexity and risks of the program); *FCN, Inc. v. United States*, 115 Fed. Cl. 335 (2014) (unreasonably low offers may be rejected); *SEEMA, Inc.*, Comp. Gen. Dec. B-277988, 98-1 CPD ¶ 12 (management factor because it included the evaluation of understanding of the work); *Centech Grp., Inc.*, Comp. Gen. Dec. B-278715,

98-1 CPD ¶ 108 (technical competence factor); and *Arora Grp., Inc.*, Comp. Gen. Dec. B-277674, 98-1 CPD ¶ 64 (proposal risk factor).

Other cases have found lack of an implicit reference. See *UnitedHealth Military & Veterans Servs., LLC v. United States*, 132 Fed. Cl. 529 (2017) (only program commitments and contract terms and conditions factors); *Earth Res. Tech., Inc.*, Comp. Gen. Dec. B-416415, 2018 CPD ¶ 312 (only price reasonableness); *PricewaterhouseCoopers Pub. Sector LLP*, Comp. Gen. Dec. B-415129.3, 2018 CPD ¶ 272 (only the level of effort, amount of labor, and other costs to determine "whether the total price is reasonable"); *Possehn Consulting*, Comp. Gen. Dec. B-278579, 98-1 CPD ¶ 10 (only past performance, experience, or key personnel factors). In *Systems Plus, Inc.*, Comp. Gen. Dec. B-415559, 2018 CPD ¶ 27, GAO held that the following statement did not indicate that the agency would perform a price realism analysis:

> The Government will evaluate the reasonableness of the total price which will reflect the proposed labor mix as a result of the offeror's understanding of the Government's requirements. The total price analysis is a reflection of the offeror's understanding of the Government's requirements . . .

[b] Narrowing the Scope

Agencies have also been permitted to evaluate only those considerations that they perceive to be relevant to an evaluation factor. See, for example, *Plasan North. Am., Inc. v. United States*, 109 Fed. Cl. 561 (2013), holding that it was proper not to consider past performance on vehicle armor contracts in a procurement of body armor. See also *EastCo Bldg. Servs., Inc.*, Comp. Gen. Dec. B-275334, 97-1 CPD ¶ 83 (evaluation of past performance of only contracts of similar size proper even though RFP did not mention this limitation); *AVIATE L.L.C.*, Comp. Gen. Dec. B-275058.6, 97-1 CPD ¶ 162 (evaluation of awardee's experience on performance-based contracting proper although RFP did not specifically call for that type of experience); *AWD Techs., Inc.*, Comp. Gen. Dec. B-250081.2, 93-1 CPD ¶ 83 (experience in the specific work called for by the contract properly given heavy weight when the evaluation factor was denominated "past project experience").

[2] Failure to Evaluate a Stated Factor

Once an evaluation factor has been included in the RFP, the agency may not ignore that factor. In *Cardkey Sys., Inc.*, Comp. Gen. Dec. B-239433, 90-2 CPD ¶ 159, an evaluation was found improper because it did not consider a feature of the system being procured that had been designated as "desirable" in the RFP. GAO found that the protester had increased its price to provide the feature and was prejudiced by the fact that the feature was not considered during the evaluation. See also *General Dynamics Info. Tech.*, Comp. Gen. Dec. B-299873, 2007 CPD ¶ 194 (agency used labor rates proposed by an offeror in one table when the RFP stated that the rates in another table would be used if there was an inconsistency); *Advanced Sys. Dev., Inc.*, Comp. Gen. Dec. B-298411, 2006 CPD ¶ 137 (agency did not evaluate price proposals for "completeness" of supporting data when RFP stated it would be evaluated); *Lowe & Assocs., Inc.*, Comp. Gen. Dec. B-297444.2, 2006 CPD ¶ 76 (RFP on-site performance requirement ignored in evaluation); *KIC Dev., LLC*, Comp. Gen. Dec. B-297425.2, 2006 CPD ¶ 27 (agency determined offeror did not meet experience requirement when RFP allowed subcontractor experience to meet requirement); *EPW Closure Servs., LLC*, Comp. Gen. Dec. B-294910, 2006 CPD ¶ 3 (agency failed to assess stated factor in evaluation); *Lockheed Martin Corp.*, Comp. Gen. Dec. B-293679, 2004 CPD ¶ 115 (agency determined that proposal met RFP requirement to fully describe design features of product based on evaluator's knowledge of subcontractor's competence); *Computer Info. Specialist, Inc.*, Comp. Gen. Dec. B-293049, 2004 CPD ¶ 1 (agency relied on blanket statements of compliance when RFP called for submission of specific information showing compliance); *CSE Constr.*, Comp. Gen. Dec. B-291268.2, 2002 CPD ¶ 207 (evaluation of understanding of work when that was not a stated factor); *Priority One Servs., Inc.*, Comp. Gen. Dec. B-288836, 2002 CPD ¶ 79 (no determination of probable cost of offers in cost reimbursement contract); *Wackenhut Int'l, Inc.*, Comp. Gen. Dec. B-286193, 2001 CPD ¶ 8 (failure to make "comprehensive review of compensation plans" as called for by RFP); and *Saco Def. Corp.*, Comp. Gen. Dec. B-283885, 2000 CPD ¶ 34 (rating proposal low risk when offeror did not provide detailed information required by RFP to make the assessment).

The same rule applies to past performance. When it is designated as an evaluation factor, a source selection official may not ignore information regarding poor past performance of an offeror, *G. Marine Diesel*, 68 Comp. Gen. 577 (B-236622), 89-2 CPD ¶ 101 (agency failed to use data within agency regarding poor performance of ongoing contract), or good past performance, *Univox California, Inc.*, Comp. Gen. Dec. B-210941, 83-2 CPD ¶ 395 (agency failed to use data furnished by offeror); *Inlingua Schs. of Languages*, Comp. Gen. Dec. B-229784, 88-1 CPD ¶ 340 (agency failed to use data within agency relating to performance as incumbent contractor). Neither may it treat all past performance as equally relevant when the RFP called for assessing varying degrees of relevance, *Clean Harbors Envt'l Servs., Inc.*, Comp. Gen. Dec. B-296176.2, 2005 CPD ¶ 222.

[3] Subfactors

When a subfactor is specified in the RFP, it is subject to the same rule applying to factors—it may not be ignored in the evaluation. Thus, it was improper for an agency to fail to consider six of twelve specified evaluation subfactors where the effect was to increase the relative importance of price from 30% to 50%, *Dynalectron Corp.*, Comp. Gen. Dec. B-187057, 77-1 CPD ¶ 95. If subfactors are listed without any indication of relative importance, they will be treated as equally important. Thus, giving such a subfactor "predominant" importance is improper, *Isratex, Inc. v. United States*, 25 Cl. Ct. 223 (1992). See also *Bio-Rad Labs., Inc.*, Comp. Gen. Dec. B-297553, 2007 CPD ¶ 58 (improper to rate subfactors in descending order of importance when the RFP contained no statement of relative importance); *Lloyd H. Kessler, Inc.*, Comp. Gen. Dec. B-284693, 2000 CPD ¶ 96 (improper to give a subfactor very heavy importance without notice in the RFP). Contrast *Apptis Inc.—Costs*, Comp. Gen. Dec. B-402146.3, 2010 CPD ¶ 123, holding that it was proper to give a marginal rating on a factor based on a weakness in one of four subfactors, with *Mevacon-NASCO JV*, Comp. Gen. Dec. B-414329, 2017 CPD ¶ 144, holding that it was improper to give a marginal rating on a factor based on a weakness in one of three subfactors when the strengths in the other subfactors outweighed the weaknesses. See also *New Directions Techs., Inc.*, Comp. Gen. Dec. B-412703.2, 2016 CPD ¶ 241, stating that the fact that subfactors are equally weighted does not preclude an agency from finding that one is a discriminator between offerors.

When a subfactor is not specified in the RFP, it may be used in the evaluation of offers if it meets the relationship rule discussed above. GAO has been liberal in applying this rule. See, for example, *Bendix Field Eng'g Corp.*, Comp. Gen. Dec. B-241156, 91-1 CPD ¶ 44, where the past performance factor listed two subfactors, "technical performance" and "schedule performance," yet GAO ruled that it was proper to downgrade past performance because of a cost overrun on a prior contract. See also *Barnes & Reinecke, Inc.*, Comp. Gen. Dec. B-236622, 89-2 CPD ¶ 572, where past efforts in designing tracked vehicles were found to be reasonably related to a subfactor covering "knowledge of Tracked Armored Vehicles." In *Stewart-Warner Elecs. Corp.*, Comp. Gen. Dec. B-235774.3, 89-2 CPD ¶ 598, GAO permitted the evaluation of 31 technical subfactors where the RFP called for "paying appropriate premiums for measured increments of quality."

Subfactors need not be included on a separate list if they are described in a narrative form in the description of the factor, *Moran Assocs.*, Comp. Gen. Dec. B-240564.2, 91-2 CPD ¶ 495. In that case GAO apparently believed that a diligent offeror would identify the subfactors from the narrative description. See also *ITT Electron Tech. Div.*, Comp. Gen. Dec. B-242289, 91-1 CPD ¶ 383, holding that there was no need to disclose an evaluation checklist when the items on the list were reasonably related to the evaluation factors. In *Stone Webster Eng'g Corp.*, Comp. Gen. Dec. B-255286.2, 94-2 CPD ¶ 306, the protester contended that the evaluation was improper because the agency evaluated proposals on a basis of "general strategy," which was not listed as an evaluation factor in the RFP. The agency stated that general strategy was not a separate evaluation criterion but was, however, considered as part of the evaluation of several factors that were set forth in the RFP. GAO agreed, finding that the RFP did state that strategy formulation and selection of appropriate tactics would be a significant subfactor under the understanding the anticipated work evaluation factor.

[4] Changing Factors or Subfactors

As discussed earlier, FAR 15.206 provides specific guidance governing changes to government requirements. These rules also apply to changes to the evaluation factors. Thus, if an agency determines during the evaluation process that different evaluation factors will yield a more sound source selection decision, it may amend the RFP to ensure that the offerors have an opportunity to respond to the new evaluation factors. Thus, GAO has held that changes in evaluation factors are ordinarily permitted during the course of a negotiated procurement so long as the offerors are given the opportunity to respond to them, *Consulting & Program Mgmt.*, 66 Comp. Gen. 229 (B-225369), 87-1 CPD ¶ 229. Similarly, in *H.J. Grp. Ventures, Inc.*, Comp. Gen. Dec. B-246139.3, 92-2 CPD ¶ 116, it was found proper to add an evaluation factor for performance risk and permit new proposals.

One result of this rule is that a material relaxation of requirements for the winning offeror without informing the other competitors is improper, *Innovation Assocs., Inc.*, Comp. Gen. Dec. B-414408, 2017 CPD ¶ 181 (award to offeror that failed to meet several minimum specification requirements); *Intelsat General Corp.*, Comp. Gen. Dec. B-412097, 2016 CPD ¶ 30 (award to offeror that proposed satellite that did not provide coverage called for by specification); *Courtland Mem'l Hosp.*, Comp. Gen. Dec. B-286890, 2001 CPD ¶ 48 (disregard of "preferences" in RFP); *ACS Gov't Solutions Grp., Inc.*, Comp. Gen. Dec. B-282098, 99-1 CPD ¶ 106 (relaxation of specification guidance on use of in-house system); and *Barents Grp., L.L.C.*, Comp. Gen. Dec. B-276082, 97-1 CPD ¶ 164 (relaxation of requirement to submit resumes in specific labor category).

The requirement that offerors be advised of changes in evaluation factors does not apply to changes in subfactors that are reasonably related to stated evaluation factors but which are not themselves listed in the RFP, *Dynalectron Corp.*, Comp. Gen. Dec. B-199741, 81-2 CPD ¶ 70. In that case, GAO reasoned that the unlisted subcriterion which was changed "was devised in order to assist the technical evaluators in their internal deliberations."

The same procedures must be used when an agency changes the evaluation scheme. Thus, it is not improper for an agency to issue an amended solicitation altering the relative importance of the evaluation factors, *Unisys Corp.*, 67 Comp. Gen. 512 (B-230019.2), 88-2 CPD ¶ 35 (clarifying the importance of cost), or the overall evaluation scheme, *Galler Assocs., Inc.*, Comp. Gen. Dec. B-210204, 83-1 CPD ¶ 515 (changing from low cost acceptable offer scheme to trade off scheme), *American Lawn Serv., Inc.*, Comp. Gen. Dec. B-267715, 95-2 CPD ¶ 278 (changing from trade off scheme to lowest priced, technically acceptable basis). It is also proper to amend the evaluation scheme in the solicitation to accommodate a method of performance suggested by an offeror, *Loral Terracom*, 66 Comp. Gen. 272 (B-224908), 87-1 CPD ¶ 182 (different technical approach). Of course, such changes are only permissible if all offerors still under consideration are informed of the change, *Labat-Anderson Inc.*, 71 Comp. Gen. 252 (B-246071), 92-1 CPD ¶ 193 (change required by issuance of amendment to RFP or by raising issue in discussions).

GAO will not overturn an award in which the agency has changed the evaluation criteria without notifying the offerors if the losers are not prejudiced by the change, *FKW Inc. Sys.*, Comp. Gen. Dec. B-235989, 89-2 CPD ¶ 370; *Akal Security, Inc.*, Comp. Gen. Dec. B-261996, 96-1 CPD ¶ 33; *Mc Rae Indus., Inc.*, Comp. Gen. Dec. B-287609.2, 2001 CPD ¶ 127.

[D] Disqualification of an Offeror

A body of decisions have held an offeror may be disqualified from the procurement if the agency learns during the evaluation that the offeror has violated a criminal statute or committed some other serious impropriety. Such disqualification is not a determination of lack of responsibility and thus need not be referred to the Small Business Administration if the offeror is a small business, *NKF Eng'g, Inc. v. United States*, 805 F.2d 372 (Fed. Cir. 1986); *Compliance Corp. v. United States*, 22 Cl. Ct. 193 (1990), *aff'd*, 960 F.2d 157 (Fed. Cir. 1992). The result of this rule is that an offeror may be immediately dropped from the evaluation when the agency learns of the impropriety.

One type of violation that has led to such disqualification is material misrepresentation. See *American Sys. Corp.*, Comp. Gen. Dec. B-417387, 2019 CPD ¶ 238, stating:

> In order to establish an impermissible bait and switch, a protester must show that: (1) the awardee either knowingly or negligently represented that it would rely on specific personnel that it did not have a reasonable basis to expect to furnish during contract performance, (2) the misrepresentation was relied on by the agency, and (3) the agency's reliance on the misrepresentation had a material effect on the evaluation results. *DKW Commc'ns, Inc.*, B-414476, B-414476.2, June 23, 2017, 2017 CPD ¶ 206 at 9.

Similarly, in *Alaska Structures, Inc. v. United States*, 144 Fed. Cl. 80 (2019), the court held that intent to misrepresent was required to support a mandatory disqualification. Compare *NetCentrics Corp. v. United States*, 145 Fed. Cl. 158 (2019), and *NetCentrics Corp.*, Comp. Gen. Dec. B-417285.3, 2019 CPD ¶ 211, holding that an agency had the discretion to disqualify a company for an inadvertent misrepresentation, with *Bannum, Inc. v. United States*, 119 Fed. Cl. 291 (2014), *aff'd*, 616 Fed. Appx. 420 (Fed. Cir. 2015). holding that an agency had the discretion not to disqualify a company for an inadvertent misrepresentation.

Other cases disqualifying offerors for material misrepresentation include *T3I Solutions, LLC*, Comp. Gen. Dec. B-418034, 2019 CPD ¶ 428 (proposing to use an employee of the incumbent contractor without any communication with the employee); *Sev1Tech, Inc.*, Comp. Gen. Dec. B-416811, 2018 CPD ¶ 429 (falsely stating it had negotiated contingent offers with incumbent staff when they had not given consent); *Patricio Enters., Inc.*, Comp. Gen. Dec. B-412738, 2016 CPD ¶ 145 (stating offeror had signed letters from prospective employees when there were none); *GTA Containers, Inc. v. United States*, 103 Fed. Cl. 194 (2012) (using alleged subcontractor's past performance when it had no intention of using that subcontractor); *Patriot Contract Servs.—Advisory Opinion*, Comp. Gen. Dec. B-294777.3, 2005 CPD ¶ 97 (submission of resumes without discussing salary as required by RFP and misstatements as to reasons why they subsequently rejected employment); *ACS Gov't Servs., Inc.*, Comp. Gen. Dec. B-293014, 2004 CPD ¶ 18 (falsely representing that three key personnel had agreed to work for the firm); *S.C. Myers & Assocs., Inc.*, Comp. Gen. Dec. B-286297, 2001 CPD ¶ 16 (submission of name of key person with knowledge that that person would only remain on job during initial phase of contract); and *Electronic Data Sys. Fed. Corp.*, GSBCA 9869-P, 89-2 BCA ¶ 21,655, *recons. denied*, 89-2 BCA ¶ 21,778, *aff'd sub. nom. Planning Research Corp. v. United States*, 971 F.2d 736 (Fed. Cir. 1992) (submission of resumes of 101 personnel to be employed on contract with no intent to use those workers). See also *Biospherics, Inc.*, Comp. Gen. Dec. B-253891.2, 93-2 CPD ¶ 333, where GAO agreed that an offeror should be disqualified when it failed to comply with an RFP requirement that it disclose any personnel proposed for the contract had also been proposed for another contract being competed at the same time.

One way to deal with the use of incumbent personnel is to state that the company will consider replacing listed key personnel with incumbent personnel if it wins the competition, *Knight Point Sys., LLC*, Comp. Gen. Dec. B-416602, 2018 CPD ¶ 371; *Systems Plus, Inc.*, Comp. Gen. Dec. B-415559, 2018 CPD ¶ 27. Compare *Insight Tech. Solutions, Inc.*, Comp. Gen. Dec. B-417388, 2019 CPD ¶ 239, finding it proper to list the incumbent employees and state that they will be replaced if not available as long as the solicitation does not require letters of commitment.

Disqualification is generally not proper when the misrepresentation is inadvertent rather than intentional, *Johnson Controls Sec, Sys.*, Comp. Gen. Dec. B-296490, 2007 CPD ¶ 102 (no recommendation to disqualify offeror when agency recorded false statement but record of oral presentation did not clearly indicate that statement had been made); *Integration Techs. Grp., Inc.*, Comp. Gen. Dec. B-291657, 2003 CPD ¶ 55 (no recommendation to disqualify offeror that had misrepresented the role of important subcontractor); *Tucson Mobilephone, Inc.*, Comp. Gen. Dec. B-258408.3, 95-1 CPD ¶ 267 (record did not support a finding that offeror intentionally misrepresented that it had lead technician's permission to use his credentials); and *Universal Techs., Inc.*, Comp. Gen. Dec. B-248808.2, 92-2 CPD ¶ 212 (false certification not made in bad faith). In *Mantech Field Eng'g Corp.*, Comp. Gen. Dec. B-245886.4, 92-1 CPD ¶ 309, *recons. denied*, 92-2 CPD ¶ 89, although the offeror made no attempt to determine whether personnel were available prior to submitting its BAFO, GAO did not find an intentional misrepresentation and recommended that discussions be reopened.

GAO has held that the degree of misrepresentation will establish whether an offeror must be barred from the procurement. See *Aerospace Design & Fabrication, Inc.*, Comp. Gen. Dec. B-278896.2, 98-1 CPD ¶ 139, holding that the agency was not required to disqualify an offeror that had falsely stated that it had commitments from three of its five key personnel because the misrepresentation was not "pervasive."

It is unlikely that a misrepresentation will be found when an offeror makes statements about events that will occur in the future. For example, no misrepresentation was found when an offeror stated that its product was a nondevelopmental item but numerous changes were required to meet requirements, *Northrop Grumman Corp. v. United States*, 50 Fed. Cl. 443 (2001). See also *Crown Point Sys.*, Comp. Gen. Dec. B-413940, 2017 CPD ¶ 19 (fact that proposed procedures are unlikely to be met a matter of contract administration); *R&D Maint. Servs., Inc.*, Comp. Gen. Dec. B-292342, 2003 CPD ¶ 162 (disqualification not required when company subcontracted work that was proposed to be performed in-house); *Ann Riley & Assocs., Ltd*, Comp. Gen. Dec. B-271741.3, 97-1 CPD ¶ 122 (violation of subcontracting limitation due to events during performance).

The Court of Federal Claims has held that there is no misrepresentation if the offeror learns after submission of its final proposal revisions that its key personnel will not be available but does not inform the government, *OAO Corp. v. United States*, 49 Fed. Cl. 478 (2001); *Golden IT, LLC v. United States*, 157 Fed. Cl. 680 (2022). The court reasoned that it was not clear that there was a legal duty to update a proposal in this manner. GAO reached the opposite result in *General Revenue Corp.*, Comp. Gen. Dec. B-414220.2, 2017 CPD ¶ 106, and *Greenleaf Constr. Co.*, Comp. Gen. Dec. B-293105.18, 2006 CPD ¶ 19, holding that an offeror had the duty to inform the government of changes in personnel and technical approach. This rule creates a dilemma because the agency can then reject the proposal because of lack of the key person, *Chenega Healthcare Servs., LLC*, Comp. Gen. Dec. B-416158, 2018 CPD ¶ 200. See also *Wyle Labs., Inc.*, Comp. Gen. Dec. B-408112.2, 2014 CPD ¶ 16, holding that award could not be made to a company that had significantly changed its corporate status, and *Dual, Inc.*, Comp. Gen. Dec. B-280179, 98-2 CPD ¶ 133, holding that there had been a misrepresentation when an offeror sold a division employing the listed personnel after submitting its proposal but did not inform the agency of the sale.

Offerors have also been disqualified for violating or appearing to violate the conflict of interest laws barring retired government employees from participating in certain government procurements, 18 U.S.C. § 207 (representation of contractor in matter where there has been substantial prior involvement). See, for example, *NKF Eng'g, Inc. v. United States*, 805 F.2d 372 (Fed. Cir. 1986) (offeror properly disqualified when it hired a member of the Navy source selection board after the initial evaluation and prior to the submission of the best and final offer); *International Resources Grp.*, Comp. Gen. Dec. B-409346.2, 2014 CPD ¶ 369 (sustaining protest of award to company that hired former director of agency office conducting procurement); *Guardian Techs. Int'l*, Comp. Gen. Dec. B-270213, 96-1 CPD ¶ 104 (recommending disqualification of company whose president had access to inside information because he was former employee of procuring agency); and *Naddaf Int'l Trading Co.*, Comp. Gen. Dec. B-238768.2, 90-2 CPD ¶ 316 (ruling that the contracting officer had properly disqualified an offeror that employed a retired military officer who had contacted the Small Business Administration to argue for the issuance of a Certificate of Competency). Compare *Dewberry Crawford Grp.*, Comp. Gen. Dec. B-415940.11, 2018 CPD ¶ 298 (company not disqualified because former employee had not helped draft work statement and had no proprietary information); *CNA Corp. v. United States*, 81 Fed. Cl. 722 (2008) (company not disqualified because its principal investigator had not participated "substantially" in the program before he left the agency). The outcome of these cases is dependent on a detailed analysis of the role of the former employee and the impact to the procurement. See *VSE Corp.*, Comp. Gen. Dec. B-404833.4, 2011 CPD ¶ 268, where GAO questioned whether the contracting officer's decision to terminate a contract for convenience because the agency deputy program manager had been employed by the contractor was based on "hard facts."

Offerors have also been disqualified for conducting employment discussions with a current government employee, 18 U.S.C. § 208 (engaging in discussion of future employment with government official); 41 U.S.C. § 423 (engaging in any discussion of future employment with a procurement officer). See *Lockheed Martin Corp.*, Comp. Gen. Dec. B-295402, 2005 CPD ¶ 24, granting a protest asserting that a government official that had been convicted of violating 18 U.S.C. § 208 had steered a contract to a competitor.

Conflicts of interest involving current government employees with a financial interest in a company may also disqualify offerors from the procurement, 18 U.S.C. § 208 (participation in procurement involving offeror in which employee had financial interest); FAR Subpart 3.6 (award of contract to company owned or controlled by government employee). For example, in *Revnet Env't & Analytical Lab., Inc.*, Comp. Gen. Dec. B-221002.2, 86-2 CPD ¶ 102, the contracting officer disqualified an offeror that had submitted an offer developed by a government employee who had attempted to disassociate himself from his company by turning it over to his wife.

The responsibility for determining whether an offeror should be disqualified due to a conflict of interest rests with the agency and will be upheld by GAO so long as the decision is reasonable. See *Cygnus Corp.*, Comp. Gen. Dec. B-275957, 97-1 CPD ¶ 202, where the protester asserted that the offeror should have been disqualified from the competition because the offeror's spouse was a government employee. The protester argued that by virtue of having vested marital property rights, the government employee possessed substantial ownership or control of the offeror such that the matter constituted a conflict of interest. GAO denied the protest finding no evidence of substantial control or interest such as to warrant disqualification.

Offerors are also properly disqualified because of an organizational conflict of interest, *DSD Lab., Inc. v. United States*, 46 Fed. Cl. 467 (2000). There the court sustained a disqualification because the company had given advice to the agency on structuring the procurement and participated in writing the work statement. Other cases where offerors have been properly disqualified include *HBI-GF, JV*, Comp. Gen. Dec. B-415036, 2017 CPD ¶ 331 (company prepared specification); *International Bus. Mach. Corp.*, Comp. Gen. Dec. B-410639, 2015 CPD ¶ 41 (employee of team member worked with agency during acquisition planning and drafting performance work statement); *Noonan & Assocs.*, Comp. Gen. Dec. B-409103, 2014 CPD ¶ 29 (company's performance of curriculum development contract barred it from competing for training course); *Lucent Techs. World Servs. Inc.*, Comp. Gen. Dec. B-295462, 2005 CPD ¶ 55 (company prepared specification for commercial-type item); *Aetna Gov't Health Plans, Inc.*, Comp. Gen. Dec. B-254397.15, 96-2 CPD ¶ 129 (impaired objectivity); *QualMED, Inc. v. Office of Civilian Health & Med. Program of the Uniformed Servs.*, 934 F. Supp. 1227 (D. Col. 1996) (agreeing that GAO had power to make recommendation in *Aetna)*. In *L-3 Servs., Inc.*, Comp. Gen. Dec. B-400134.11, 2009 CPD ¶ 171, GAO recommended that a subcontractor with an OCI be excluded from the competition but that the agency could reopen the competition allowing the contractor to obtain a new subcontractor. Protests of organizational conflict of interest will generally be sustained if the agency does not investigate a potential violation, *C2C Innovative Solutions, Inc.*, Comp. Gen. Dec. B-416289, 2018 CPD ¶ 269; *A-P-T Research, Inc.*, Comp. Gen. Dec. B-413731.2, 2017 CPD ¶ 112; *DRS Tech. Servs., Inc.*, Comp. Gen. Dec. B-411573.2, 2015 CPD ¶ 363.

Improperly obtaining information during the procurement process may also serve as a grounds for disqualify offerors. For example, in *Kellogg Brown & Root Servs., Inc.*, Comp. Gen. Dec. B-400787.2, 2009 CPD ¶ 54, the protester was properly disqualified from competing for two task orders when its employee had received an e-mail from the contracting officer containing proprietary information and had not immediately deleted it from his computers. GAO held that the contracting officer had cause to disqualify the protester because of an appearance of impropriety even though the employee stated that he had not read the document. See also *Computer Tech. Assocs., Inc.*, Comp. Gen. Dec. B-288622, 2001 CPD ¶ 187 (reasonable to disqualify protester whose employees had seen transcripts of competitors' oral presentations); *Litton Sys., Inc.*, 68 Comp. Gen. 422 (B-234060), 89-1 CPD ¶ 450, *recons. denied*, 68 Comp. Gen. 677 (B-234060.2) 89-2 CPD ¶ 228 (contractor disqualified for obtaining government information through a marketing consultant); *AT&T Commc'ns, Inc.*,

GSBCA 9252-P, 88-2 BCA ¶ 20,805 (offeror disqualified when it had been given the range of its competitor's prices by a government employee with whom it had conducted employment discussions and to whom it had given gratuities). Similarly, in *Compliance Corp.*, Comp. Gen. Dec. B-239252, 90-2 CPD ¶ 126, *recons. denied*, Comp. Gen. Dec. 239252.3, 90-2 CPD ¶ 435, the contracting officer properly disqualified an offeror who had obtained government information from an incumbent service contractor through the use of "industrial espionage." The Federal Circuit agreed with this decision in *Compliance Corp. v. United States*, 22 Cl. Ct. 193 (1990), *aff'd*, 960 F.2d 157 (Fed. Cir. 1992), holding that industrial espionage was a valid ground for disqualification (even though no government personnel were involved) because such activity puts the integrity of the procurement system at risk.

Offerors that give bribes or gratuities to government employees will also be disqualified. See *Litton Sys., Inc.*, 68 Comp. Gen. 422 (B-234060), 89-1 CPD ¶ 450, *recons. denied*, 68 Comp. Gen. 677 (B-234060.2), 89-2 CPD ¶ 228, ordering termination of a major contract due to bribery of a high-ranking government employee by the awardee. See also *Howema Bau-GmbH*, Comp. Gen. Dec. B-245356, 91-2 CPD ¶ 214 (excluding protester from contract consideration due to suspected bribery of government officials); and *National Roofing & Painting Corp.*, ASBCA 36,551, 90-2 BCA ¶ 22,936 (voiding contract because it was "tainted with fraud from its inception as well as during performance").

[E] Assessment of Strengths, Weaknesses and Risks

One of the most significant parts of the evaluation process is the assessment of the strengths, deficiencies, significant weaknesses and risks of each proposal and the assessment of their relative qualities, FAR 15.305(a). This is the critical information that is used to make the source selection decision and serves as the documentation supporting that decision. The FAR contains no guidance on the timing of these assessments but it has been common practice to direct the evaluators to make their initial evaluation by only assessing each proposal's quality in meeting the requirements of the RFP and its evaluation factors and then to have the evaluators or some other group make the assessment of the relative merits of the competing proposals. In a case where the Air Force regulation required this two-step procedure, the Court of Federal Claims held that permitting the evaluators to make the comparative assessment was a "harmless regulatory violation," *Aero Corp. v. United States*, 38 Fed. Cl. 237 (1997). See also *Food Servs. of Am.*, Comp. Gen. Dec. B-276860, 97-2 CPD ¶ 55, and *ASR Mgmt. & Tech. Servs.*, Comp. Gen. Dec. B-244862.3, 92-1 CPD ¶ 383, where GAO noted that comparative assessments were made by technical evaluators but did not comment on the use of the procedure. Thus, it appears that agencies can use a two-step evaluation process or evaluate the proposals by making a comparative assessment in the initial evaluation. Whatever system is used, it should be clear that the end result of the evaluation process is a comparative assessment of the relative merits of the proposals because that must be the basis for the ultimate source selection decision, FAR 15.308.

[1] Documenting the Assessment

FAR 15.305(a) requires documentation as follows:

> The relative strengths, deficiencies, significant weaknesses, and risks supporting proposal evaluation shall be documented in the contract file.

This documentation is generally prepared in narrative form simultaneously with some notation of a rating or scoring and describes the reasons that the evaluators have assigned the scores to each proposal. Thus, these narratives identify the "strengths, weaknesses, and risks" of each proposal that have led to the score that has been assigned. A fully documented evaluation will contain such narratives for each score—generally at the lowest level of scoring in the evaluation scheme. It is very helpful if these narratives contain a reference to the specific pages of the proposal that contain the information on which the evaluation is based.

These narrative statements can be prepared by each individual evaluator or as a summary evaluation by all of the evaluators that have assessed the element of the proposals being evaluated. Preparation of these narratives at the same time the proposals are scored provides an excellent discipline for the evaluators because it forces them to justify their scores. If the narratives are prepared by the entire evaluation team, this will also force evaluators to reconcile disparate scores or at least to focus on the reason for the disparities. Thus, such narratives can improve the scoring as well as flow valuable information to the source selection official. When a consensus evaluation document is prepared, it is important that it include sufficient explanation of the assessment so that it can be reviewed in the event of a protest, *DGR Assocs., Inc.*, Comp. Gen. Dec. B-285428, 2000 CPD ¶ 145.

Although the FAR gives no guidance on the extent of documentation required, it is clear that GAO demands sufficient documentation to permit consideration of a protest asserting that the agency has not followed the evaluation scheme in the RFP. See *Satellite Servs., Inc.*, Comp. Gen. Dec. B-415458.3, 2018 CPD ¶ 161, stating:

> In reviewing protests of an agency's evaluation and source selection decision, our Office will not reevaluate proposals; rather, we review the record to determine whether the evaluation and source selection decision are reasonable and consistent with the solicitation's evaluation criteria, and applicable procurement laws and regulations. *Velos, Inc.*, B-400500.8, B-400500.9, Dec. 14, 2009, 2010 CPD ¶ 13 at 11; *Keeton Corrections, Inc.*, B-293348, Mar. 4, 2004, 2005 CPD ¶ 44 at 6. While we will not substitute our judgement for that of the agency, we will sustain a protest where the agency's

> conclusions are inconsistent with the solicitation's evaluation criteria, undocumented, or not reasonably based. *DRS ICAS, LLC*, B-401852.4, B-401852.5, Sept. 8, 2010, 2010 CPD ¶ 261 at 4-5. In addition, contracting agencies are required to adequately document their evaluation results, and sufficiently support the findings on which award determinations are made. *Savvee Consulting, Inc.*, B-408416, B-408416.2, Sept. 18, 2013, 2013 CPD ¶ 231 at 7.

See also *ManTech Advanced Sys. Int'l, Inc.*, Comp. Gen. Dec. B-415497, 2018 CPD ¶ 60, criticizing an agency's "overly aggressive efforts to limit document production."

This appears to be a flexible requirement based on the complexity of each source selection. In *Champion-Alliance, Inc.*, Comp. Gen. Dec. B-249504, 92-2 CPD ¶ 386, GAO held that relatively little documentation was required from the agency because the requirements under the RFP were fairly unambiguous and the proposals were very similar. See also *Quality Elevator Co.*, Comp. Gen. Dec. B-276750, 97-2 CPD ¶ 28, where inadequate documentation was overlooked because the proposals were very similar. In *Worldwide Information Network Sys., Inc.*, Comp. Gen. Dec. B-408548, 2013 CPD ¶ 254, GAO stated that there was "no absolute requirement that evaluation records must include narrative explanations for every score assigned." It has also been held that there is no need for narrative statements when the proposal was acceptable with no notable advantages or disadvantages, *PRC, Inc.*, Comp. Gen. Dec. B-274698.2, 97-1 CPD ¶ 115.

There are numerous protests that have been sustained because of insufficient documentation. See *360 IT Integrated Solutions*, Comp. Gen. Dec. B-414650.7, 2018 CPD ¶ 188 (no documentation supporting past performance rating based on subcontractor performance); *Savannah River Tech. & Remediation, LLC*, Comp. Gen. Dec. B-415637, 2018 CPD ¶ 70 (no contemporaneous evidence supporting agency determination that proposed technical approach was feasible); *TOTE Servs., Inc.*, Comp. Gen. Dec. B-414295, 2017 CPD ¶ 158 (no documentation supporting relevancy of past performance determinations); *CSR, Inc.*, Comp. Gen. Dec. B-413973, 2017 CPD ¶ 64 (no documentation supporting differences in evaluation of corporate experience); *Glacier Tech. Solutions, LLC*, Comp. Gen. Dec. B-412990.2, 2016 CPD ¶ 311 (no explanation of good rating when proposed approach was rejected); *Radiation Oncology Grp. of WNY, PC*, Comp. Gen. Dec. B-310354.2, 2009 CPD ¶ 136 (agency record contained no "comprehensive assessment or listing of the proposals' strengths and weaknesses"); *Panacea Consulting, Inc.*, Comp. Gen. Dec. B-299307.4, 2007 CPD ¶ 141 (no statement of strengths or weaknesses supporting numerical scores); *Pemco Aeroplex, Inc.*, Comp. Gen. Dec. B-310372, 2007 CPD ¶ 2, *recons. denied*, 2008 CPD ¶ 24 (no documentation supporting element of price realism analysis); *Systems Research & Applications Corp.*, Comp. Gen. Dec. B-299818, 2008 CPD ¶ 28 (evaluators' worksheets contained no explanation of scoring); *Intercon Assocs., Inc.*, Comp. Gen. Dec. B-298282, 2006 CPD ¶ 121 (evaluator documents "factually incorrect, internally contradictory," or "cryptic"); *Keeton Corrs., Inc.*, Comp. Gen. Dec. B-293348, 2005 CPD ¶ 44 (no evidence that source selection official was presented with details of evaluation); *National City Bank of Indiana*, Comp. Gen. Dec. B-287608.3, 2002 CPD ¶ 190 (no documentation explaining why staffing reductions would allow offeror to meet technical requirements); *Bank of Am.*, Comp. Gen. Dec. B-287608, 2001 CPD ¶ 137 ("virtually no evaluator worksheets" showing the basis for cost realism calculations and adjustments); *BAE Sys.*, Comp. Gen. Dec. B-287189, 2001 CPD ¶ 86 (no indication that a "potential strength" included in the protester's technical proposal was considered by the agency evaluators); *J & J Maint., Inc.*, Comp. Gen. Dec. B-284708.2, 2000 CPD ¶ 106 (no narratives showing how numerical scores were reconciled); and *Future-Tec Mgmt., Sys., Inc.*, Comp. Gen. Dec. B-283793.5, 2000 CPD ¶ 59 (insufficient documentation of evaluation to understand source selection decision). In a rare case, *Helicopter Transport Servs. LLC*, Comp. Gen. Dec. B-400295, 2008 CPD ¶ 180, where the agency arrived at an evaluation of an offeror's past performance by a discussion by a group of evaluators providing their experience working with the offerors, GAO granted the protest because of lack of documentation, stating:

> In an evaluation that takes into account the agency's own knowledge of offerors' performance, the fundamental requirement that evaluation judgments be documented in sufficient detail to show that they are reasonable and not arbitrary must still be met. *Omega World Travel, Inc.*, B-271262.2, July 25, 1996, 96-2 CPD ¶ 44 at 4.

It appears to be relatively common practice for agencies to destroy evaluators' worksheets when consensus evaluations are arrived at. However, this practice was held improper in *Pitney-Bowes Gov't Solutions, Inc. v. United States*, 93 Fed. Cl. 327 (2010), based on the record retention requirements in FAR Subpart 4.8. No sanctions were imposed on the agency for spoilation of evidence because backup copies of the documents were recovered and supplied to the protester, *Pitney-Bowes Gov't Solutions, Inc. v. United States*, 94 Fed. Cl. 1 (2010).

GAO had not sanctioned agencies for destroying evaluator worksheets, *Government Acquisitions, Inc.*, Comp. Gen. Dec. B-401048, 2009 CPD ¶ 137; *Joint Mgmt. & Tech. Servs.*, Comp. Gen. Dec. B-294229, 2004 CPD ¶ 208; *Community P'ship LLC*, Comp. Gen. Dec. B-286844, 2001 CPD ¶ 38; *Structural Pres. Sys., Inc.*, Comp. Gen. Dec. B-285085, 2000 CPD ¶ 131. See, however, *Dynalantic Corp.*, Comp. Gen. Dec. B-274944.2, 97-1 CPD ¶ 101, where GAO permitted the agency to attempt to justify the evaluation of the protester in a hearing after it had destroyed the evaluators' work papers. In sustaining the protest because of the lack of rationale supporting the decision,

GAO granted protest costs and noted that they were higher because of the need for a hearing. It was also noted that the agency had decided to discontinue the practice of destroying work papers.

[2] Comparison of Proposals

The other part of the narratives is the statement of the "relative qualities of the proposals." As noted above, this comparison of the proposals has generally been done as a second step in the evaluation process and is frequently done by the evaluation board or the evaluation team leaders. The 2016 DoD "Source Selection Procedures," applicable to all procurements over $10 million, calls for tis to be done by the Source Selection Advisory Council. In many ways, this is the most important part of the narratives because it summarizes the information needed by the source selection official to make the selection decision.

This comparison of proposals should be prepared in sufficient detail to identify each area where there is a significant difference between proposals. Ideally, the narrative will contain a concise description of the difference and an assessment of the *value of the difference* or the *impact* that the difference will have on the procuring agency. This value/impact statement in the areas of technical and management provides the key information needed by the source selection official in making the tradeoff with the cost/price differences among offerors. Thus, such narratives provide the source selection official clear information concerning the relative advantages or disadvantages of proposals in a way that scores, such as numbers, colors, or adjectives obviously cannot.

Agencies are permitted considerable discretion in identifying the values and impacts of competing proposals during this comparative assessment. See *DynCorp Int'l LLC*, Comp. Gen. Dec. B-415349, 2018 CPD ¶ 12, stating:

> It is well-established that a procuring agency is in the best position to determine its own needs and the best method for accommodating them, and our Office will not question that determination absent clear evidence that it is unreasonable. See, e.g., *Canaveral Maritime, Inc.*, B-238356.2, July 17, 1990, 90-2 CPD ¶ 41 at 5; *New York Wire Co.*, B-235821, Sept. 19, 1989, 89-2 CPD ¶ 246 at 1. Further an agency may properly apply a particular evaluation methodology that is not specifically identified in a solicitation where the methodology is rational and consistent with the solicitation's stated evaluation criteria. See, e.g., *Mission Essential Personnel, LLC*, B-410431.9, B-410431.10, Mar. 18, 2015, 2015 CPD ¶ 109 at 9; *Bonner Analytical Testing Co.*, B-409586.2, Aug. 7, 2014, 2014 CPD ¶ 258 at 4.

There are numerous decisions deferring to an agency's assessment that one proposal is technically superior to another. See, for example, *DynCorp Int'l, LLC*, Comp. Gen. Dec. B-415873, 2018 CPD ¶ 157 (past performance superior); *Kiewit Infrastructure West Co.*, Comp. Gen. Dec. B-415421, 2018 CPD ¶ 55 (technical approach superior); *Sev1Tech, Inc.*, Comp. Gen. Dec. B-413758.6,

2017 CPD ¶ 145 (superior technical approach); *Alphaport, Inc.*, Comp. Gen. Dec. B-414086, 2017 CPD ¶ 69 (superior technical capability). On the other hand, protests will be sustained if an agency has not performed a rational assessment. See, for example, *Immersion Consulting, LLC*, Comp. Gen. Dec. B-415155.4, 2018 CPD ¶ 187 (conflicting agency assessment of effect of staffing plan); *Savannah River Tech. & Remediation, LLC*, Comp. Gen. Dec. B-415637, 2018 CPD ¶ 70 (inadequate assessment of unproven technical approach); *Global Language Center*, Comp. Gen. Dec. B-413503.8, 2017 CPD ¶ 238 (disparate treatment of past performance); *EFW, Inc.*, Comp. Gen. Dec. B-412608, 2016 CPD ¶ 304 (no comparative assessment of past performance ratings); *Trailboss Enters., Inc.*, Comp. Gen. Dec. B-407093, 2013 CPD ¶ 232 (no assessment of relative merits of proposals); *LIS, Inc.*, Comp. Gen. Dec. B-400646.2, 2010 CPD ¶ 5 (no discussion of "relative proposal strengths, deficiencies, significant weaknesses, and risks").

[F] Rating

After assessment of proposals, agencies generally rate some or all of the evaluation factors as a means of summarizing the evaluations to assist the source selection official in making the tradeoff decision between the competing proposals. Thus, rating systems are notational devices which provide a rough means of measuring differences between proposals. However, it is clear that, in almost all cases, the ratings alone will not support a source selection decision. See *Noble Supply & Logistics*, Comp. Gen. Dec. B-414511.6, 2018 CPD ¶ 46, stating:

> It is well-established that ratings, be they numerical, adjectival, or color, are merely guides for intelligent decision making in the procurement process. See *Environmental Restoration, LLC*, B-406917, Sept. 28, 2012, 2012 CPD ¶ 266 at 5. The relevant considerations are the agency's qualitative assessments of proposals. See *Archer Western Contractors, Ltd.*, B-403227, B-403227.2, Oct. 1, 2010, 2010 CPD ¶ 262 at 5.

For decisions sustaining protests because of a mechanical comparison of ratings, see *Technatomy Corp.*, Comp. Gen. Dec. B-414672.5, 2018 CPD ¶ 353; *Mission1st Grp., Inc.*, Comp. Gen. Dec. B-413028.4, 2017 CPD ¶ 364; *West Coast Gen. Corp.*, Comp. Gen. Dec. B-411916.2, 2015 CPD ¶ 392; *Celta Servs., Inc.*, Comp. Gen. Dec. B-411835, 2015 CPD ¶ 362; *Clay Grp., LLC*, B-406647, 2012 CPD ¶ 214; *One Largo Metro LLC*, B-404896, 2011 CPD ¶ 128.

In general, an agency's deviation from the RFP rating system cannot be challenged, *MINACT, Inc.*, Comp. Gen. Dec. B-400951, 2009 CPD ¶ 76 (adjectival rating permissible when RFP called for numerical scoring); *Trajen, Inc.*, Comp. Gen. Dec. B-296334, 2005 CPD ¶ 153 (use of three adjective system instead of five called for by RFP not grounds for protest); *BRC Assocs., Inc.*,

Comp. Gen. Dec. B-237156, 90-1 CPD ¶ 145 (numerical scoring of subfactors permitted even though the RFP stated that subfactors did not have assigned points).

Thus, when source selection decisions are based on the strengths, weakness, and risks in the proposals, protests of incorrect ratings are routinely denied. See, for example, *Blackwater Lodge & Training Ctr., Inc. v. United States*, 86 Fed. Cl. 488 (2009) ("Courts should look beyond the adjectival ratings because proposals awarded the same adjectival ratings are not necessarily equal in quality."); *Karrar Sys. Corp.*, Comp. Gen. Dec. B-310661.3, 2008 CPD ¶ 55 ("focus on the adjectival ratings . . . misplaced"); *GAP Solutions, Inc.*, Comp. Gen. Dec. B-310564, 2008 CPD ¶ 26 ("Where the evaluators and source selection official reasonably consider the underlying bases for the ratings . . . a protester's disagreement over the actual adjectival or numeric ratings assigned essentially is inconsequential"); *Pemco Aeroplex, Inc.*, Comp. Gen. Dec. B-310372, 2008 CPD ¶ 2 (proposals with same adjectival rating "not necessarily of equal quality"); *Raymond Assocs., LLC*, Comp. Gen. Dec. B-299496, 2007 CPD ¶ 107 (purportedly irrational averaging of subfactor ratings not relevant when decision considered strengths and weaknesses); *Mechanical Equip. Co.*, Comp. Gen. Dec. B-292789.2, 2004 CPD ¶ 192 ("the protesters' disagreement over the actual adjectival ratings is essentially inconsequential"). This reasoning has been followed by GAO even when the protester had alleged that the scoring system called for by the RFP misled the protester in deciding what effort to propose, *Northrop Grumman Tech. Servs., Inc.*, Comp. Gen. Dec. B-291506, 2003 CPD ¶ 25. There the agency had used a computerized system that gave the same point score to "good" and "excellent" but had not actually relied on the system in making the final source selection decision.

Most rating systems do not rate all of the factors and subfactors. Technical factors appear to be the most frequently rated while price or cost is the least frequently rated. This is logical because the marginal difference in price or cost between the proposals, which will be used to make the source selection decision, is clearly apparent in dollar amounts and rating tends to obscure rather than illuminate this difference. However, GAO has held that it is proper to give adjectival ratings to life cycle costs, *Raytheon Co.*, Comp. Gen. Dec. B-298626.2, 2007 CPD ¶ 185.

Rating systems are particularly useful when there are a large number of evaluation factors and subfactors. However, as the number of factors decreases, there is less need for ratings. For example, there have been a number of procurements were the only factors were past performance and price. In that case, there would appear to be no need to assign rating to the proposals.

Any system can be used as long as it provides meaningful differentiation among proposals of various merit. The most frequently used systems are adjectival rating systems, color coding, numerical scoring, and ranking. These are the systems identified in FAR 15.305(a).

[1] Adjectival Ratings

Adjectival rating systems are widely used and generally call for the use of four or five ratings such as excellent, good, fair and poor or outstanding, highly acceptable, acceptable, marginally acceptable and unacceptable. They have the disadvantage of providing very few gradations to distinguish between proposals—making the scoring somewhat imprecise as a tool to measure the marginal differences between proposals. However, GAO has accepted the use of these systems—finding that they can give the source selection official a clear understanding of the relative merit of the proposals, *Dynamics Research Corp.*, Comp. Gen. Dec. B-240809, 90-2 CPD ¶ 471. The acceptance of such systems is justified because they do not form the basis for the ultimate source selection decisions. See *PricewaterhouseCoopers Public Sector, LLP*, Comp. Gen. Dec. B-415504, 2018 CPD ¶ 35, stating:

> [T]he essence of an agency's evaluation is reflected in the evaluation record itself, not the adjectival ratings, and the relevant question is whether the record shows that the agency fully considered the actual qualitative differences in vendors' quotations. See *Stateside Assocs., Inc.*, B-400670.2, B-400670.3, May 28, 2009, 2009 CPD ¶ 120 at 8; *InfoZen, Inc.*, B-408234 et al., July 23, 2013, 2013 CPD ¶ 211 at 8.

See also *Lockheed Martin Corp. v. United States*, 124 Fed. Cl. 709 (2016), stating at 728:

> The rating itself is less important than the rationale behind it. Thus "[c]ourts should look beyond the adjectival ratings because proposals awarded the same adjectival ratings are not necessarily equal in quality." *Blackwater Lodge & Training Ctr., Inc. v. United States*, 86 Fed. Cl. 488, 514 (2009).

Nonetheless, there are numerous protests asserting that the adjectival rating are incorrect and such protests are sustained if it appears that the ratings have impacted the source selection decision. See, for example, *EFS Ebrex SARL*, Comp. Gen. Dec. B-416076, 2018 CPD ¶ 201 ("marginal" experience rating not proper based on RFP experience requirements); *General Revenue Corp.*, Comp. Gen. Dec. B-414220.2, 2017 CPD ¶ 106 (past performance ratings irrational); *M7 Aerospace LLC*, Comp. Gen. Dec. B-411986, 2016 CPD ¶ 100 (no evidence that all proposals rated "acceptable" were technically equivalent); Standard *Commc'ns, Inc. v. United States*, 101 Fed. Cl. 723 (2011) (no explanation of why award to lower priced "acceptable" proposal was of more value that protester's "good" proposal); *Redstone Tech. Servs.*, Comp. Gen. Dec. B-259222, 95-1 CPD ¶ 181 (the contracting officer had mechanically applied the adjectival scoring system without documenting whether the relative differences represented any meaningful qualitative differences); and *Deployable Hosp. Sys., Inc.*, Comp. Gen. Dec. B-260778, 95-2 CPD ¶ 65 (two offerors with significantly different levels of experience were scored as "acceptable"). Compare *Wackenhut Servs., Inc.*, Comp. Gen. Dec. B-400240, 2008 CPD ¶ 184, denying a protest that the agency had not given it a higher rating because it had more good adjectival scores, stating that such scores "should not be mechanically derived or applied." The opposite result was reached in *Wackenhut Servs., Inc. v. United States*, 85 Fed. Cl. 273 (2009), where the court enjoined the procurement, in part because the agency had been arbitrary and capricious in scoring the proposals without adequate documentation of how the scores were arrived at. Compare *Femme Comp Inc. v. United States*, 83 Fed. Cl. 704 (2008), where the court found that the agency's scoring was flawed but that the flaw amounted to "harmless error," to *Information Scis. Corp. v. United States*, 80 Fed. Cl. 759 (2008), where the court granted a protest, in part because of inaccurate scoring.

[2] Color Coding

Most color rating systems are very similar to adjectival rating in the fact that they have very few ratings. Thus, the notational system, in itself, does not provide very clear gradations between proposals. See, for example, the Air Force system discussed earlier which distinguishes categories only as blue, green, yellow, and red. The DoD "Source Selection Procedures" requires all defense agencies to use a color-coding system consisting of blue, purple, green yellow and red when rating the "technical" evaluation factor.

In spite of the minimal gradation in color coding systems, GAO has agreed with the use of color coding, holding that such a system does not produce "an artificial equality in the ratings," *Ferguson-Williams, Inc.*, 68 Comp. Gen. 25 (B-231827), 88-2 CPD ¶ 344. GAO has also held that a color rating system does not prevent the agency from gaining a clear understanding of the relative merits of the proposals, *Gracon Corp.*, Comp. Gen. Dec. B-293009, 2004 CPD ¶ 58, and *Bendix Field Eng'g Corp.*, Comp. Gen. Dec. B-241156, 91-1 CPD ¶ 44. See also *Hogar Crea, Inc.*, Comp. Gen. Dec. B-311265, 2008 CPD ¶ 107, denying a protest that since the offerors were given the same color scores, they should have been treated as equal.

These decisions are based on the view that the color coding will not be the basis of the source selection decision, but that the source selection official will be provided with an analysis of the relative strengths and weaknesses of the proposals. See *Precision Mold & Tool*, Comp. Gen. Dec. B-400452.4, 2009 CPD ¶ 84, stating that, when strengths and weaknesses are used to make the source selection decision, "the color rating assigned is inconsequential in the analysis." See also *Cherry Road Techs.*, Comp. Gen. Dec. B-296915, 2005 CPD ¶ 197, rejecting the argument that the color rating scheme "lacked coherent standards" and that the assigned colors were inconsistent with the evaluation. Thus, when such scoring does not differentiate between proposals of unequal merit, great care should be exercised to ensure that the differences between the proposals are documented. See *Innovative Mgmt. & Tech. Approaches, Inc.*, Comp. Gen. Dec.

B-413084, 2016 CPD ¶ 217, finding it irrational to assign a "green" to the incumbent's transition plan but denying the protest because lack of prejudice).

[3] Numerical Systems

Numerical systems have typically assigned 100 or 1000 points to the factors being scored numerically. Most agencies that have used numerical scoring have scored only the technical and management factors. However, a few agencies have used total numerical systems—scoring price or cost as well as the other factors. There is no requirement that numerical scoring be used, *HGS Eng'g, Inc.*, Comp. Gen. Dec. B-412042, 2015 CPD ¶ 390. The DoD "Source Selection Procedures" prohibits the use of numerical ratings.

[a] Partial Systems

The advantage of numerical scoring systems is that they generally contain a large number of gradations which permits greater differentiation between proposals. However, GAO has approved systems which reduce the number of gradations by prohibiting the use of certain scores. See *Hoffman Mgmt., Inc.*, 69 Comp. Gen. 579 (B-238752), 90-2 CPD ¶ 15 (10-5-0 scoring system with 0 points given for meeting minimum requirements); *American Sys. Corp.*, Comp. Gen. Dec. B-247923.3, 92-2 CPD ¶ 158 (10-4-2-0 system); and *Fox & Co.*, Comp. Gen. Dec. B-197272, 80-2 CPD ¶ 340 (10-8-5-2-0 system). These systems tend to distort the differences between proposals but GAO has not seen the distortion as a serious problem—probably because the scores are not used as the basis of the source selection decision.

The apparent accuracy of numerical scoring can mislead source selection officials into believing that the total scores provide a precise overall assessment of the relative strengths and weaknesses of the proposals. See, for example, *Serco Inc. v. United States*, 81 Fed. Cl. 463 (2008), where the court granted a protest because the agency had used a point scoring system that resulted in "false statistical precision." The flaw detected by the court was that the agency had scored subfactors adjectivally, converted these scores into whole numbers, averaged the whole number to arrive at a numerical value for each offeror that went to three decimal places, and then used this data to make the source selection decision. See also *Castro & Co.*, Comp. Gen. Dec. B-412398, 2016 CPD ¶ 53 (protest sustained because award was made to the higher point score without analyzing basis for score); *Celta Servs., Inc.*, Comp. Gen. Dec. B-411835, 2015 CPD ¶ 362 (protest sustained because source selection decision based primarily on point scores); *Midland Supply, Inc.*, Comp. Gen. Dec. B-298720, 2007 CPD ¶ 2 (protest sustained because the source selection decision was based on "a mechanical comparison of the offerors' total point scores"). Compare *GAP Solutions, Inc.*, Comp. Gen. Dec. B-310564, 2008 CPD ¶ 26, where the source selection official properly ignored minor differences in numerical scores, determined that the offerors were "technically equal," and awarded to the low price offeror.

Protests have been granted when numerical scoring does not provide similar scores for similar proposals. See, for example, *Century Envtl. Hygiene, Inc.*, Comp. Gen. Dec. B-279378, 98-1 CPD ¶ 164, granting a protest because the agency identified weaknesses in proposals but gave different scores to the competitors without any explanation of the differences. See also *Ogden Servs., Inc.*, Comp. Gen. Dec. B-270012.2, 96-1 CPD ¶ 177 (no explanation of why awardee received a near perfect score under past performance factor when proposal did not demonstrate mail/service or similar experience as required by RFP); and *Engineering & Computation,* Inc., Comp. Gen. Dec. B-261658, 95-2 CPD ¶ 176 (no documentation explaining protester's low scores where it appeared to have addressed a perceived weakness in its BAFO). Similarly, in *SDA, Inc.*, Comp. Gen. Dec. B-248528.2, 93-1 CPD ¶ 320, a protest was granted because the numerical scores given for experience were irrational. The agency had used a system where an offeror was given a zero score if over half of the prior projects it listed were under an undisclosed size—even if many of the projects indicated substantial experience.

[b] Totally Numerical Systems

Some agencies have used totally numerical systems to select sources. There are three systems of this nature that have been commonly used.

[i] Total Point Scoring

This system assigns point scores to each evaluation factor and makes the source selection decision based on the total point scores. In such a system all criteria, including price or cost, are numerically scored. Generally, price is scored by giving the lowest price proposal the total points assigned to the criteria and computing the number of points for the other proposals in accordance with their relationship to the lowest price. Although this evaluation technique totally obscures the tradeoff between price and the other evaluation factors, GAO has ruled that an evaluation that one offeror has achieved the highest number of points will validly support the selection of that offeror for award. See *Barnard Constr. Co.*, Comp. Gen. Dec. B-271644, 96-2 CPD ¶ 18, stating:

> Our Office has specifically recognized the propriety of using such a formula in selecting an offeror. See *Stone & Webster Eng'g Corp.*, B-255286.2, Apr. 12, 1994, 94-1 CPD ¶ 306; *Management Sys. Designers, Inc.*, B-244383.3, Sept. 30, 1991, 91-2 CPD ¶ 310. Because the awardee's proposal earned the highest combined price/technical score under the specified formula, the agency was not required to perform price/technical tradeoff analysis to justify the selection decision.

The same result was reached in *Tulane Univ.*, Comp. Gen. B-259912, 95-1 CPD ¶ 210, and *Securigard, Inc.*, Comp. Gen. Dec. B-248584, 92-2 CPD ¶ 156.

An illustration of the difficulties created by this system is found in *Harrison Sys., Ltd.*, 63 Comp. Gen. 379 (B-212675), 84-1 CPD ¶ 572, where price was assigned 30 points and the proposals were:

A $1,150,782
B $1,392,293

Offeror A was given 30 points and Offeror B was given 24.79 points derived from the following formula:

$$\frac{\$1,150,782}{\$1,392,293} \times 30 = 24.79 \text{ points}$$

After completing the technical evaluation, the agency computed the results of the total evaluation as follows:

Proposal	Cost	Technical	Total
A	30 points	59.88 points	89.88 points
B	24.79 points	70 points	94.79 points

However, the source selection official was unwilling to blindly follow the RFP and award to Offeror B on the basis of the highest point score. The source selection official made an independent analysis and determined that the technical proposals were of equal merit. The contract was therefore awarded to Offeror A based on its low price. GAO upheld this decision but stated that it would have granted the protest if the source selection official had independently analyzed whether the difference in technical merit was worth the difference in price. This example demonstrates the pitfalls inherent in the total point evaluation system. The simple summation of points to obtain a total score gives the appearance of mathematical exactitude but there is no assurance that points assigned to one set of criteria have the same value to the government as points assigned to another set of criteria. Thus, award on the sole basis of the total points may not provide the government with the best value.

Some agencies have used the total point evaluation system but have not stated in the RFP that award would be made to the offeror earning the most points. In that situation, it is proper to make a normal tradeoff analysis and award to the offeror with the best value, *DATEX, Inc.*, Comp. Gen. Dec. B-270268.2, 96-1 CPD ¶ 240; *Paxson Elec. Co. v. United States*, 14 Cl. Ct. 634 (1988). See *Midland Supply, Inc.*, Comp. Gen. Dec. B-298720, 2007 CPD ¶ 2, holding that the use of a normal tradeoff is required in this situation. Thus, it is not clear what is added to the evaluation process by giving point scores to price when a full tradeoff analysis is going to be made.

The use of numerical scoring methods which produce "distorted" scores has been discouraged. In *Custom Janitorial Serv.*, Comp. Gen. Dec. B-205023, 82-2 CPD ¶ 163, GAO criticized the use of "spread scoring," in which the proposal with the lowest realistic cost received the maximum number of points and that with the highest cost received zero, concluding that this system produced distorted results when applied to the two offerors in the competitive range. See also *Tennessee Wholesale Drug Co.*, Comp. Gen. Dec. B-243018, 91-2 CPD ¶ 9, holding that a system which improperly reduced the importance of price as an evaluation factor unfairly distorted the scores. In *Lingtec, Inc.*, Comp. Gen. Dec. B-208777, 83-2 CPD ¶ 279, a form of mathematical analysis in which prices closest to the government estimate received maximum points and deviations from the estimate were penalized was held improper, as it penalized lower prices more than higher ones. It can be argued that any system which assigns scores by formula will potentially produce distorted results and thus should not be used.

[ii] Conversion to Dollar Values

Another completely numerical system determines the relative value of all evaluation factors according to their expected impact on the life cycle cost of the item being procured. An example of this method is found in *Storage Tech. Corp.*, Comp. Gen. Dec. B-215336, 84-2 CPD ¶ 190, in which GAO described the method as follows:

> Section IV.3 of the RFP, "Evaluation of Proposals" . . . states that award will be "made to that responsible offeror whose proposal is in the best interests of the VA, cost and other factors considered." Section H.1.3 of the RFP lists the additional factors that the VA would consider. These factors were ranked in order of importance based on their maximum dollar impact on ESLC and listed in descending order of importance. . . . For each of these factors, the VA assigned a dollar credit or assessment commensurate with the cost savings/avoidance or added cost to be incurred by the VA with each proposal system. The VA indicates that the technical evaluation "dollars" are not intended to be precise indicators of actual value, but, rather, like a point score, will serve as a guide to the selecting official. The VA states that the dollar figures arrived at for these additional factors will be compared to the ESLC to determine which proposal is in the VA's best interests and award will be made on that basis.

See also *C.M.P., Inc.*, Comp. Gen. Dec. B-216508, 85-1 CPD ¶ 156, where the agency made the entire evaluation in dollars by assigning dollar amounts for the value of three years of previous performance, guarantee of performance, and remedial and preventive maintenance services.

Assigning dollar values to all evaluation factors is an extremely rare form of proposal evaluation. However, it is not uncommon to assign dollar values to some of the evaluation factors and this is recommended by the DoD "Source Selection Procedures." See, for example, *Cessna Aircraft Co.*, Comp. Gen. Dec. B-261953.5, 96-1 CPD ¶ 132, where this occurred. GAO indicated that it would accept the judgment of the agency in such cases stating that life-cycle cost analysis "involves the exercise of informed judgment and . . . [its use] will not [be] question[ed] . . . unless it clearly lacks a reasonable basis." See also *Global Assocs., Ltd.*, Comp. Gen. Dec. B-275534, 97-1 CPD ¶ 129 (quantified values of non-price factors properly used to determine best value); *Continental Airlines, Inc.*, Comp. Gen. Dec. B-258271.4, 97-1 CPD ¶ 81 (adjusted prices based on monetary benefits of non-price factors properly used in making selection decision).

[iii] Dollars Per Point

The third numerical system is the dollars per point system. In this system all of the criteria other than cost are scored numerically and the prices proposed are used to compute a mathematical relationship. An earlier version of DARCOM Pamphlet 1715-3 described this system as follows:

> (3) *Evaluation of lowest dollar per technical quality point ($/q.p.)*. The concept of selecting the best technical proposal for the dollar is supportable by the dollar/technical point relationships. This factor can be determined by dividing the cost of the proposal by the total unweighted raw score developed for "technical." With the knowledge contained in the RFP that this relationship will be given consideration and will force offerors to tradeoff between cost and technical factors in order to prepare the best possible proposal at a fair and reasonable price, $/q.p. relationship by itself is not justification for selection; but is only considered an additional factor to offer to the SSA in making the decision. An example area is below:

In some instances, a dollar per quality point system has been used as the sole basis for source selection. GAO has approved this method even when a losing competitor submitted a lower priced proposal that was technically acceptable, *Shapell Gov. Hous., Inc.*, 55 Comp. Gen. 839 (B-183830), 76-1 CPD ¶ 161. See *Management Sys. Designers, Inc.*, Comp. Gen. Dec. B-244383.3, 91-2 CPD ¶ 310, where GAO accepted the use of this technique as the sole basis for the source selection even though the RFP reserved the right to make an independent cost/technical tradeoff decision. See also *Frank E. Basil, Inc.*, Comp. Gen. Dec. B-208133, 83-1 CPD ¶ 91, allowing such an award even though the protester's price was significantly lower.

This technique gives an appearance of greater precision than is justified by the point scores assigned because point scoring inherently is less precise than price, yet the use of a ratio between the scores assumes that they are of equal precision. Thus, it is better to use this technique as one method of evaluating the merits of the proposals. See *Moran Assocs.*, Comp. Gen. Dec. B-240564.2, 91-2 CPD ¶ 495, where the agency did this and GAO stated:

> We have recognized that such a cost/technical ratio formula can be a proper tool for the government to utilize in determining which proposal is the most advantageous to the government. See *Morrison-Knudsen Co., Inc.*, B-237800.2, 90-1 CPD ¶ 443. Here, the ratio was only one tool utilized to assure that the government was getting the best buys, given relative technical rankings and costs. The record shows that awards were not made to the offerors with the best ratios.

[4] Ranking

The direct ranking of proposals, without the aid of scores, has also been upheld, as numerical scoring does not "transform the technical evaluation into a more objective process," *Development Assocs., Inc.*, Comp. Gen. Dec. B-205380, 82-2 CPD ¶ 37. GAO has even stated that "ranking proposals may be a more direct and meaningful method" than numerical scoring, *Maximus*, Comp. Gen. Dec. B-195806, 81-1 CPD ¶ 285. However, ranking is infrequently used because it bypasses the scoring of proposals in terms of how well they meet the RFP requirements. To overcome this potential difficulty, an agency can use initial scoring but then provide overall ranking to the source selection official to aid in the decision, *Cerner Corp.*, Comp. Gen. Dec. B-293093, 2004 CPD ¶ 34. However, ranking is done, it does not overcome the necessity of identifying the strengths, weaknesses and risks in the proposals.

[G] Evaluation of Specific Factors

A number of evaluation factors are commonly used in most competitively negotiated procurements. These factors have been subject to such numerous protests that there is extensive guidance on the pitfalls that can be encountered in their evaluation.

[1] Price or Cost to the Government

Unless there is a statutory exclusion, price or cost to the government is a mandatory evaluation factor. In fixed-price contracts, the agency must make a price reasonableness determination and may make a price realism determination as part of the evaluation process. In cost-reimbursement contracts, the evaluation factor must be probable cost to the government which must be determined by making a cost realism analysis. This critical part of the evaluation process is discussed in detail in Chapter 13.

[2] Past Performance

Past performance has become a major evaluation factor, and it has become common to see agencies using only two evaluation factors—price and past performance. See *USA Elecs.*, Comp. Gen. Dec. B-275389, 97-1 CPD ¶ 75, where GAO agreed that it was rational to award to an offeror with a good past performance but a higher price. Thus, protests are sustained if an agency does not make a fair and even-handed assessment of the past performance of each offeror, *CSR, Inc.*, Comp. Gen. Dec. B-413973, 2017 CPD ¶ 64 (using CPARS data for unlisted projects for the winning offeror but not the protester); *Halbert Constr. Co.*, Comp. Gen. Dec. B-413213, 2016 CPD ¶ 254 (downgrading protester but not winning offeror for poor performance on somewhat relevant projects); *Myers Investigative & Sec. Servs., Inc.*, Comp. Gen. Dec. B-288468, 2001 CPD ¶ 189 (similar data on two offerors treated differently); *Beneco Enters., Inc.*, Comp. Gen. Dec. B-283512, 2000 CPD ¶ 175, B-283512.3, 2000 CPD ¶ 176 (ratings did not correspond to information in the contract file).

In the numerous protests of past performance evaluations GAO has accorded agencies considerable discretion. See *Onsite OHS, Inc.*, Comp. Gen. Dec. B-415987, 2018 CPD ¶ 164, stating:

> An agency's evaluation of past performance, which includes its consideration of the relevance, scope, and significance of an offeror's performance history, is a matter of discretion which we will not disturb unless the assessment is unreasonable or inconsistent with the solicitation criteria. *WingGate Travel, Inc.*, B-412921, July 1, 2016, 2016 CPD ¶ 179 at 4; *Metropolitan Life Ins. Co.*, B-412717, B-412717.2, May 13, 2016, 2016 CPD ¶ 132 at 14. Where a protester challenges an agency's past performance evaluation, we will review the evaluation to determine if it was reasonable and consistent with the solicitation's evaluation criteria and procurement statutes and regulations, and to ensure that the agency's rationale is adequately documented. *DynCorp Int'l, LLC*, B-412451, B-412451.2, Feb. 16, 2016, 2016 CPD ¶ 75 at 14; *Falcon Envtl. Servs., Inc.*, B-402670, B-402670.2, July 6, 2010, 2010 CPD ¶ 160 at 7. A protester's disagreement with the agency's judgment, without more, is insufficient to establish that an evaluation was improper. *WingGate Travel, Inc., supra*; *Beretta USA Corp.*, B-406376.2, B-406376.3, July 12, 2013, 2013 CPD ¶ 186 at 10.

This broad discretion permits agencies to refuse to accept an offeror's explanation for an adverse past performance rating, *DynCorp Int'l LLC*, Comp. Gen. Dec. B-415349, 2018 CPD ¶ 12; and *Engility Corp.*, Comp. Gen. Dec. B-513120.3, 2017 CPD ¶ 70. In *Veteran Nat'l Trans., LLC*, Comp. Gen. Dec. B-415011, 2018 CPD ¶ 81, GAO found that the agency had properly concluded that alleged labor law violations supported a marginal rating even though the protester was challenging the holding in a DOL proceeding. See also *Master Lock Co., LLC*, Comp. Gen. Dec. B-309982.2, 2009 CPD ¶ 2 (denying protest that contractor with highly satisfactory past performance had only been rated "good"); *ITT Indus. Space Sys., LLC*, Comp. Gen. Dec. B-309964, 2007 CPD ¶ 217 (denying protest that agency had not properly considered a variety of performance information); *S3 Ltd.*, Comp. Gen. Dec. B-288195, 2001 CPD ¶ 164 (agency acted properly in finding some performance risk after evaluating somewhat conflicting assessments of several people that had worked on a contract where the protester had encountered problems); *KELO, Inc.*, Comp. Gen. Dec. B-284601.2, 2000 CPD ¶ 110 (agency rejected explanations of performance problems); and *MAC's General Contractor*, Comp. Gen. Dec. B-276755, 97-2 CPD ¶ 29 (agency could give a poor evaluation based on a default termination that was still in litigation—stating that such an evaluation may be based on a "reasonable perception of inadequate prior performance"). Agencies may also exercise their discretion to downgrade an offeror that does not submit the past performance information called for by the RFP, *Al Andalus Gen. Contracts Co. v. United States*, 86 Fed. Cl. 252 (2009). However, this broad discretion does not permit use of an irrational evaluation system. See *Shaw-Parsons Infrastructure Recovery Consultants, LLC*, Comp. Gen. Dec. B-401679.8, 2010 CPD ¶ 211 (agency used numerical scoring system that penalized protester for references on less relevant contracts); *Green Valley Trans, Inc.*, Comp. Gen. Dec. B-285283, 2000 CPD ¶ 133 (agency used the total number of instances of defective performance without regard to the volume of work of the competitors). Neither is an agency permitted to deviate from the RFP description of the evaluation process, *General Revenue Corp.*, Comp. Gen. Dec. B-414220.2, 2017 CPD ¶ 106 (agency disregarded past performance of team members when RFP allowed such information).

A similar degree of discretion is accorded by the Court of Federal Claims, *Akal Sec.y, Inc. v. United States*, 87 Fed. Cl. 311 (2009); *Gulf Grp. Inc. v. United States*, 61 Fed. Cl. 338 (2004); *Maintenance Eng'rs v. United States*, 50 Fed. Cl. 399 (2001).

One of the major tasks in evaluating contractor past performance information is to distinguish between a few inconsequential problems and a significant record of inferior performance. See, for example, *Mark Dunning Indus., Inc.*, Comp. Gen. Dec. B-413321.4, 2017 CPD ¶ 248 (agency concluded that final CPARS rating overcame interim reports of problematic performance); *Federal Maint. Log. Solutions, LLC*, Comp. Gen. Dec. B-412270.6, 2016 CPD ¶ 351 (source selection official concluded that several "safety incidents" did not mar an overall excellent performance record); *Metropolitan Life Ins. Co.*, Comp. Gen. Dec. B-412717, 2016 CPD ¶ 132 (agency concluded that final CPARS rating overcame problems encountered during performance); *Marinette Marine Corp.*, Comp. Gen. Dec. B-400697, 2009 CPD ¶ 16 (agency closely reviewed a single case of inferior performance and concluded that it would not impact the work on the contract to be awarded); *MCT JV*, Comp. Gen. Dec. B-311245.2, 2008 CPD ¶ 121 (agency reasonably found "outstanding" past performance even though offeror had encountered some problems in the past); and *BFI Waste Sys.*

of Nebraska, Inc., Comp. Gen. Dec. B-278223, 98-1 CPD ¶ 8 (contracting officer reasonably found that awardee's performance overall during the past five to six years overcame alleged deficiencies its performance under the incumbent contract).

In contrast, when contracting officers received a significant number of negative comments on an offeror's past performance, they have properly been given lower ratings. See, for example, *Vectrus Sys. Corp.*, Comp. Gen. Dec. B-412581.3, 2017 CPD ¶ 10 (numerous instances of poor performance merited a rating of only "satisfactory confidence"); *Ultra Elecs. - 3 Phoenix, Inc.*, Comp. Gen. Dec. B-412998, 2016 CPD ¶ 305 (poor performance on three out of four contracts should be given an "unsatisfactory" rating); *Torres-Advanced Enters. Solutions, LLC*, Comp. Gen. Dec. B-412755.2, 2016 CPD ¶ 167 (poor performance at five locations deserved a "no confidence" rating); and *Excel Mfg., LLC*, Comp. Gen. Dec. B-412332.2, 2016 CPD ¶ 200 (delivery of numerous defective products led to a rating of only "good" performance).

Care must also be exercised in determining responsibility for past performance problems. See *Pemco Aeroplex, Inc.*, Comp. Gen. Dec. B-310372, 2008 CPD ¶ 2, where the agency properly gave an offeror a rating of "satisfactory confidence" after carefully assessing the cause of prior performance difficulties, and *Sumaria Sys., Inc.*, Comp. Gen. Dec. B-299517, 2007 CPD ¶ 122, where the agency properly rechecked with the personnel on a referenced contract to obtain more current information on the cause of the problem. Compare *Sikorsky Aircraft Co.*, Comp. Gen. Dec. B-299145.4, 2007 CPD ¶ 78, where the protester was downgraded based on a negative report from the program manager on an ongoing contract where significant problems had been encountered. Although GAO ruled that this was proper, there was little indication that the agency had investigated to determine whether the problems were caused by the government, or the contractor and four other customers of the protester reported very good past performance. It is also proper to defer the assessment of responsibility for a prior problem when an agency investigation is still underway, *Metson Marine Servs., Inc.*, Comp. Gen. Dec. B-299705, 2007 CPD ¶ 159.

[a] Sources and Reliability of Past Performance Information

Past performance information is obtained in several ways. Most agencies have obtained the information from offerors and from references submitted by the offerors or other organizations that have dealt with the offeror. FAR 15.305(a)(2)(ii) requires that offerors be permitted to identify all such organizations to whom they have sold similar goods or services. While there may be some question as to the reliability of such information, the practice of calling references and other organizations for whom the offeror has worked has not been challenged. However, care must be exercised to ensure that offerors are given the same opportunity to submit reference information. See *Aerospace Design & Fabrication, Inc.*, Comp. Gen. Dec. B-278896.2, 98-1 CPD ¶ 139, sustaining a protest because one offeror had been permitted to submit more reference information than was permitted by the RFP. In *Serco, Inc. v. United States*, 81 Fed. Cl. 463 (2008), the court held that this method of data collection was unreliable because the surveys were taken using a set of questions that did not correspond to the evaluation considerations used in the selection process. See also *Cooperativa Muratori Riuiniti*, Comp. Gen. Dec. B-294980.5, 2005 CPD ¶ 21 (survey that was not geared to the evaluation criteria held to be arbitrary and capricious); *Dismas Charities, Inc.*, Comp. Gen. Dec. B-292091 2003 CPD ¶ 125 (questionnaires were "materially flawed" and contrary to the FAR when the agency did not provide references with instructions on how to score offeror's past performance).

In using references, random sampling has been permitted, *MilTech, Inc.*, Comp. Gen. Dec. B-275078, 97-1 CPD ¶ 208, and there is no requirement that strenuous efforts be made to contact references, *Richen Mgmt., LLC*, Comp. Gen. Dec. B-409697, 2014 CPD ¶ 211; *Guam Shipyard*, Comp. Gen. Dec. B-311321, 2008 CPD ¶ 124, or that all references given by the offeror be contacted, *Sunrise Med. HHG, Inc.*, Comp. Gen. Dec. B-310230, 2008 CPD ¶ 7; *U.S. Tech. Corp.*, Comp. Gen. Dec. B-278584, 98-1 CPD ¶ 78. Thus, an agency is not required to make multiple attempts to contact references, *Halbert Constr. Co.*, Comp. Gen. Dec. B-413213, 2016 CPD ¶ 254; *Dictyon LLC*, Comp. Gen. Dec. B-405504, 2011 CPD ¶ 253. Neither is an agency required to seek corrections to incorrectly submitted reference information, *Green Earthworks Constr., Inc.*, Comp. Gen. Dec. B-410724, 2015 CPD ¶ 68. Furthermore, agencies may contact a different number of sources for different offerors, *IGIT, Inc.*, Comp. Gen. Dec. B-275299.2, 97-2 CPD ¶ 7. Although contacting only a single reference would not appear to yield an adequate sample, this questionable practice has also been permitted, *Neal R. Gross & Co.*, Comp. Gen. Dec. B-275066, 97-1 CPD ¶ 30; *HLC Indus., Inc.*, Comp. Gen. Dec. B-274374, 96-2 CPD ¶ 214. Thus, adverse past performance assessments have been considered to be reliable when they were based on a single contract, *Compania De Asesoria Y Comercio, S.A.*, Comp. Gen. Dec. B-278358, 98-1 CPD ¶ 26 (seven deficiency reports on prior contract); *ECC Int'l Corp.*, Comp. Gen. Dec. B-277422, 98-1 CPD ¶ 45 (significant difficulties on prior production contract). If the references cannot be contacted with reasonable efforts, an agency may give an offeror a poor past performance rating, *Consolidated Eng'g Servs., Inc.*, Comp. Gen. Dec. B-277273, 97-2 CPD ¶ 86.

Some agencies have used questionnaires to obtain past performance information and this practice has been approved by GAO, *Continental Serv.*, Co., Comp. Gen. Dec. B-274531, 97-1 CPD ¶ 9; *SWR, Inc.*, Comp. Gen. Dec. B-276878, 97-2 CPD ¶ 34. Although this is a questionable practice, use of scores on questionnaires without supporting information or commentary has also been approved, *Pacific Ship Repair & Fabrication, Inc.*, Comp. Gen. Dec. B-279793, 98-2 CPD ¶ 29; *Boeing Sikorsky Aircraft Support*, Comp. Gen. Dec. B-277263.2, 97-2 CPD ¶ 91.

It is proper to use the ratings on cost-plus-award-fee contracts in the assessment of past performance, *Oceaneering Int'l, Inc.*, Comp. Gen. Dec. B-278126, 98-1 CPD ¶ 133.

Another way to obtain past performance information is through data collection systems. FAR 42.1502 requires the preparation of CPARS performance evaluation reports on all contracts and orders over the simplified acquisition threshold except for task and delivery orders under agency IDIQ contracts. FAR 42.1503(g) limits the retention and use of the information to three years after the completion of contract performance. Under this regulation, contractors are given 14 calendar days to submit comments, rebuttal statements, or provide additional information. The completed evaluated information cannot be released to other than government personnel and the contractor whose performance is being evaluated during the period the information is being used for source selection purposes, FAR 42.1503(d). Detailed guidance on preparing the CPARS evaluations is contained in FAR 42.1503(b). FAR 36.201 also requires the collection of performance information on all construction contracts over $700,000, while FAR 36.604 requires the collection of performance information on all architect-engineer contracts over $35,000.

Additional information is collected in the Federal Awardee Performance and Integrity Information System (FAPIIS). See FAR 42.1503 stating:

> (h) Other contractor performance information. (1) Agencies shall ensure information is accurately reported in the FAPIIS module of CPARS within 3 calendar days after a contracting officer—
>
> (i) Issues a final determination that a contractor has submitted defective cost or pricing data;
>
> (ii) Makes a subsequent change to the final determination concerning defective cost or pricing data pursuant to 15.407-1(d);
>
> (iii) Issues a final termination for cause or default notice;
>
> (iv) Makes a subsequent withdrawal or a conversion of a termination for default to a termination for convenience;
>
> (v) Receives a final determination after an administrative proceeding, in accordance with 22.1704(d)(1), that substantiates an allegation of a violation of the trafficking in persons prohibitions in 22.1703(a) and 52.222-50(b); or
>
> (vi) Determines that a contractor has a history of three or more unjustified reduced or untimely payments to small business subcontractors under a single contract within a 12-month period (see 42.1502(g)(2))

FAR 9.104-7(c) also required that contracts over $550,000 contain the "Information Regarding Responsibility Matters" clause in FAR 52.209-7 which requires any contractor with "active" contracts and grants with a value over $10 million to submit the following information to FAPIIS:

(1) Whether the offeror, and/or any of its principals, has or has not, within the last five years, in connection with the award to or performance by the offeror of a Federal contract or grant, been the subject of a proceeding, at the Federal or State level that resulted in any of the following dispositions:

(i) In a criminal proceeding, a conviction.

(ii) In a civil proceeding, a finding of fault and liability that results in the payment of a monetary fine, penalty, reimbursement, restitution, or damages of $5,000 or more.

(iii) In an administrative proceeding, a finding of fault and liability that results in—

(A) The payment of a monetary fine or penalty of $5,000 or more; or

(B) The payment of a reimbursement, restitution, or damages in excess of $100,000.

(iv) In a criminal, civil, or administrative proceeding, a disposition of the matter by consent or compromise with an acknowledgment of fault by the Contractor if the proceeding could have led to any of the outcomes specified in paragraphs (c)(1)(i), (c)(1)(ii), or (c)(1)(iii) of this provision.

(2) If the offeror has been involved in the last five years in any of the occurrences listed in (c)(1) of this provision, whether the offeror has provided the requested information with regard to each occurrence

These contracts must also contain the "Updates of Publicly Available Information Regarding Responsibility Matters" clause in FAR 52.209-9. This clause requires the above information to be updated every six months.

Failure to accurately report the required information may be grounds for rejection of a proposal. See *FEI Sys.*, Comp. Gen. Dec. B-414852.2, 2017 CPD ¶ 349 (proper to reject a quotation from a company that did not comply with the FAR 9.104-7(c) clause). Compare *Government Acquisitions, Inc.*, Comp. Gen. Dec. B-408426, 2013 CPD ¶ 277, rejecting a protest that an awardee had failed to report an administrative settlement to FAPIIS because the settlement stated there was no admission of fault. See also *Language Select LLP*, Comp. Gen. Dec. B-415097, 2017 CPD ¶ 359 (granting a protest because the agency did not support its determination that FAPIIS data showing a termination for cause was a "minor issue" creating a "small risk"); and *iGov*, Comp. Gen. Dec. B-408128.24, 2014 CPD ¶ 329 (denying a protest because negative CPARS data confirmed marginal past performance rating even if FAPIIS data on termination was misused).

Another source of past performance information is agency personnel that have dealt with the offeror in the past. FAR 15.305(a)(2)(ii) states that the agency "shall consider . . . information obtained from any other sources, when evaluating past performance." In *Paragon Sys., Inc.*, Comp. Gen. Dec. B-299548.2, 2007 CPD ¶ 178, GAO rejected the contention that such information should not be used, finding it proper to contact personnel on a referenced contract that was not included in the offeror's information. Thus, agencies can seek information from a variety of sources in order to assess the past performance of an offeror. It is proper to use information within the government as well as the information obtained from references, *PHT Supply Corp. v. United States*, 71 Fed. Cl. 1 (2006), as well as a past default termination of the offeror, *Precision Prosthetics, Inc.*, Comp. Gen. Dec. B-401023, 2009 CPD ¶ 83. In rating past performance with the same agency, it is proper for the evaluators to use their personal knowledge of an offeror's performance of contracts with the agency. See *TEAM Support Servs., Inc.*, Comp. Gen. Dec. B-279379.2, 98-1 CPD ¶ 167; *Omega World Travel, Inc.*, Comp. Gen. Dec. B-271262.2, 96-2 CPD ¶ 44; and *HLC Indus., Inc.*, Comp. Gen. Dec. B-274374, 96-2 CPD ¶ 214. In these cases, GAO commented that the agency was, in effect, using itself as a reference.

The subjectivity of some past performance information has led to questions about its reliability. FAR 42.1501 defines "past performance information" as follows:

> Past performance information is relevant information, for future source selection purposes, regarding a contractor's action under previously awarded contracts. It includes, for example, the contractor's record of—
>
> (1) Conforming to contract requirements and to standards of good workmanship;
>
> (2) Forecasting and controlling costs;
>
> (3) Adherence to schedules, including the administrative aspects of performance;
>
> (4) Reasonable and cooperative behavior and commitment to customer satisfaction;
>
> (5) Reporting into databases (see subpart 4.14, and reporting requirements in the solicitation provisions and clauses referenced in 9.104-7);
>
> (6) Integrity and business ethics; and
>
> (7) Business-like concern for the interest of the customer.

Although the elements of this definition dealing with "reasonable and cooperative behavior" and "customer satisfaction" allow a great deal of subjectivity in the evaluations, GAO has denied a protest that these elements permit contracting officers to rely on "gossip and innuendo," *RMS Indus.*, Comp. Gen. Dec. B-247229, 92-1 CPD ¶ 451.

[b] Relevance of the Data

FAR 15.305(a)(2)(i) requires agencies to consider the relevance of past performance information. Thus, it is improper to give performance on less relevant work the same weight as performance on highly relevant work. See *United Paradyne Corp.*, Comp. Gen. Dec. B-297758, 2006 CPD ¶ 47, granting a protest because the agency had averaged the past performance evaluations for highly relevant work and far less relevant work. See also *360 IT Integrated Solutions*, Comp. Gen. Dec. B-414650.7, 2018 CPD ¶ 188 (protester improperly downgraded for poor subcontractor performance when subcontractor would do little of the work); *Patricio Enters., Inc.*, Comp. Gen. Dec. B-412740, 2016 CPD ¶ 152 (protester improperly downgraded by using a mechanical system that arbitrarily assessed relevance); *Ne. Military Sales, Inc.*, Comp. Gen. Dec. B-404153, 2011 CPD ¶ 2 (failure to consider adverse information on same type work); *Shaw-Parsons Infrastructure Recovery Consultants, LLC; Vanguard Recovery Assistance, Joint Venture*, Comp. Gen. Dec. B-401679.8, 2010 CPD ¶ 211 (agency improperly reduced the score of past performance that was less relevant thereby penalizing an offeror for submitting such references); *ASRC Res. & Tech. Solutions, LLC*, Comp. Gen. Dec. B-400217, 2008 CPD ¶ 202 (failure to consider the substantial difference in size between the awardee's past performance references and the size of the contemplated contract, as required by the solicitation); *DRS C3 Sys., LLC*, Comp. Gen. Dec. B-310825, 2008 CPD ¶ 103 (ignoring assessment of poor performance on highly relevant contract); *Harbors Envtl. Servs., Inc.*, Comp. Gen. Dec. B-296176.2, 2005 CPD ¶ 222 (giving incumbent contractor and awardee identical ratings, although awardee's references were for services smaller and less complex than service being procured); and *KMR, LLC*, Comp. Gen. Dec. B-292860, 2003 CPD ¶ 233 (using references for different work when solicitation stated evaluation would be based on performance of "same or similar" work).

Agencies have considerable discretion in determining what prior work will yield a meaningful assessment of the competence of the offeror to perform the contract being awarded. See, for example, *Enterprise Servs., LLC*, Comp. Gen. Dec. B-415368.2, 2018 CPD ¶ 44 (agency not required to consider congressional hearings, GAO reports and newspaper articles covering on a failed contract); *BillSmart Solutions, LLC*, Comp. Gen. Dec. B-413272.4, 2017 CPD ¶ 325 (agency not required to review information other than CPARS and responses from references); *Orbital Sciences Corp.*, Comp. Gen. Dec. B-414603, 2017 CPD ¶ 249 (agency not required to review an IG report giving general comments on the winning contractor's performance); *J.E. McAmis, Inc.*, Comp. Gen. Dec. B-412321, 2016 CPD ¶ 40 (proper to assess older projects for similar work); *ManTech Int'l Corp.*, Comp. Gen. Dec. B-311074, 2008 CPD ¶ 87 (proper to give same relevance to similar work as to exact work called for by contract). Similarly, a protest was denied when the agency considered the quality of prior work more relevant than the small size of the contracts on which the work was done, *SP Sys., Inc. v. United States*, 86 Fed. Cl. 1 (2009). However, agencies have lost protests when they have disregarded relevant information. See, for example, *Best Value Tech., Inc.*, Comp. Gen. Dec. B-412624.3, 2017 CPD ¶ 50 (agency disregarded most recent CPARs); *DKW Communs., Inc.*, Comp. Gen. Dec.

B-411182, 2015 CPD ¶ 178 at 8 (agency ignored relevant positive past performance information and instead relied exclusively upon adverse information); *Exelis Sys. Corp.*, Comp. Gen. Dec. B-407111, 2012 CPD ¶ 340 (agency ignored relevant information when evaluating protester's proposal); and *DRS C3 Sys., LLC*, Comp. Gen. Dec. B-310825, 2008 CPD ¶ 103 (ignoring assessment of poor performance on highly relevant contract). In one unusual situation, an agency properly determined that work on smaller projects was more relevant than work on larger projects because the contract to be awarded would require work on small projects, *J.C.N. Constr. Co. v. United States*, 60 Fed. Cl. 400 (2004); *J.C.N. Constr. Co.*, Comp. Gen. Dec. B-293063, 2004 CPD ¶ 12.

GAO has required that agencies consider past performance on work that is "too close at hand" to the current procurement. This requires an agency to obtain information on a contract with the agency for the same services, *International Bus. Sys., Inc.*, Comp. Gen. Dec. B-275554, 97-1 CPD ¶ 114. GAO granted the protest in part because of the fact that the contracting officer had also been the contracting officer on the prior contract and had recently written a letter stating that the offeror's performance on the prior contract had been "exemplary." GAO stated the rule that "some information is simply too close at hand to require offerors to shoulder the inequities that spring from an agency's failure to obtain, and consider, the information." The same result was reached in *East-West Indus., Inc.*, Comp. Gen. Dec. B-297391.2, 2006 CPD ¶ 161 (prior contract with agency); *International Res. Recovery, Inc. v. United States*, 64 Fed. Cl. 150 (2005) (settlement agreement with agency replacing a default termination); *Seattle Sec. Servs., Inc. v. United States*, 45 Fed. Cl. 560 (2000), and *SCIENTECH, Inc.*, Comp. Gen. Dec. B-277805.2, 98-1 CPD ¶ 33. This rule was also applied to reference information on past contracts that the agency had required but did not use, *Shaw-Parsons Infrastructure Recovery Consultants, LLC*, Comp. Gen. Dec. B-401679.4, 2010 CPD ¶ 77.

In recent decisions, the "too close at hand" rule has been narrowly applied. See *Leidos Innovations Corp.*, Comp. Gen. Dec. B-415514, 2018 CPD ¶ 88, stating:

> We have generally limited application of this principle to situations where the alleged "close at hand" information relates to contracts for the same services with the same procuring activity, or information personally known to the evaluators. *Veterans Elite, Inc.*, B-409233, Feb. 10, 2014, 2014 CPD ¶ 64 at 4.

See also *Chenega Healthcare Servs., LLC*, Comp. Gen. Dec. B-416158, 2018 CPD ¶ 200, stating that the rule does not apply to any matter other than past performance, and *McConnell Jones Lanier & Murphy, LLP*, Comp. Gen. Dec. B-409681.3, 2015 CPD ¶ 341, stating that the rule does not override explicit RFP language on what information will be considered. Other decisions refusing to apply the rule include *Orbital Sciences Corp.*, Comp. Gen. Dec. B-414603,

2017 CPD ¶ 249 (rule doesn't cover Inspector General report on prior contract); *Shaw-Parsons Infrastructure Recovery Consultants, LLC; Vanguard Recovery Assistance, Joint Venture*, Comp. Gen. Dec. B-401679.4, 2010 CPD ¶ 77 (rule was not violated when the evaluators did not know about incumbent's performance, even though the COTR for the incumbent contract was an advisor to the evaluation board); *Firestorm Wildfire Suppression, Inc.*, Comp. Gen. Dec. B-3120136, 2007 CPD ¶ 218 (rule did not apply when evidence did not show evaluators knew of report prepared by different agency, even though the report was provided to official of their own agency); and *Paragon Sys., Inc.*, Comp. Gen. Dec. B-299548.2, 2007 CPD ¶ 178 (rule did not apply where comments written by agency inspectors critical of selectee's performance under previous task order had been lost, were not referred to in evaluation file, and were unknown to source selection authority, although known to the evaluators).

It is common practice to describe what work is relevant in the RFP and agencies are required to follow that description in the evaluation process. In numerous procurements, the RFP states that references should be provided for "the same or similar work" as that being procured with guidance on the size of contracts that were performed. When such a description is included in the RFP, the agency will be required to apply it in the evaluation process. See *Honeywell Tech. Solutions, Inc.*, Comp. Gen. Dec. B-400771, 2009 CPD ¶ 49 (evaluation unreasonable when agency gave "excellent" rating when prior contracts were much smaller than proposed contract and RFP called for evaluation of "similar" work); *Continental RPVs*, Comp. Gen. Dec. B-292768.2, 2004 CPD ¶ 56 (evaluation unreasonable when agency gave the awardee the same low risk rating for past performance as it gave the incumbent, even though it appeared that the awardee had not done as much of the "same or similar" work as the incumbent); *Southwestern Bell Tel. Co.*, Comp. Gen. Dec. B-292476, 2003 CPD ¶ 177 (evaluation unreasonable when agency failed to consider awardee's record of integrity and business ethics, as required by RFP, and the awardee's record was problematical); *Martin Elecs., Inc.*, Comp. Gen. Dec. B-290846.3, 2003 CPD ¶ 6 (evaluation unreasonable when agency failed to consider negative past performance information with respect to contracts that were "recent" as defined by RFP); *Sonetronics, Inc.*, Comp. Gen. Dec. B-289459.2, 2002 CPD ¶ 48 (evaluation unreasonable when RFP contemplated evaluation on basis of "at least" three completed contracts for similar work and agency gave awardee perfect score for past performance based on only one completed contract for similar work); *Finlen Complex, Inc.*, Comp. Gen. Dec. B-288280, 2001 CPD ¶ 167 (agency gave past performance far less weight than indicated in solicitation); and *Meridian Mgmt. Corp.*, Comp. Gen. Dec. B-285127, 2000 CPD ¶ 121 (agency downgraded offeror for failure to submit references that were not required by RFP). However, "same or similar" description does not require agency to review only identical work, *Tiger Truck LLC*, Comp. Gen. Dec. B-310759, 2008 CPD ¶ 44; *DGR Assocs., Inc.*, Comp. Gen. Dec. B-285428, 2000 CPD ¶ 145.

It is proper to give heavier weight to work for the same agency than work for private buyers, *Court Copies & Images, Inc.*, Comp. Gen. Dec. B-277268, 97-2 CPD ¶ 85. In *Systems Integration & Dev., Inc.*, Comp. Gen. Dec. B-271050, 96-1 CPD ¶ 273, GAO also denied a protest that using the past performance of an incumbent gave the incumbent an unfair competitive advantage.

FAR 15.305(a)(2)(iii) states that agencies "should take into account . . . predecessor companies, key personnel . . . or subcontractors" when assessment of their performance is relevant. When an agency intends to evaluate these elements, the RFP may benefit from language seeking appropriate information. See *Alphaport, Inc.*, Comp. Gen. Dec. B-414086, 2017 CPD ¶ 69 (evaluation of minor subcontractors' past performance proper because RFP "reserved the right" to evaluate such subcontractors); *MILVETS Sys. Tech., Inc*, Comp. Gen. Dec. B-409051.7, 2016 CPD ¶ 53 (evaluation of past performance of subcontractors and key personnel proper because solicitation contained clear language permitting submission of such information). This FAR provision's use of "should," is not mandatory with the result that GAO has permitted agencies to limit the scope of their evaluation of past performance to only the contractor submitting the proposal. See *Caduceus Healthcare, Inc.*, Comp. Gen. Dec. B-414965, 2017 CPD ¶ 329 (limit appropriate for high visibility project); *Valor Constr. Mgmt., LLC*, Comp. Gen. Dec. B-405365, 2011 CPD ¶ 226 (limit appropriate for complex project). Compare *Iyabak Constr., LLC*, Comp. Gen. Dec. B-409196, 2014 CPD ¶ 62, holding that precluding past performance information on key personnel and "parent, affiliate or {separate} division was improper because it was restrictive of competition. In contrast, GAO held in *Logistics Mgmt. Int'l, Inc.*, Comp. Gen. Dec. B-412837, 2016 CPD ¶ 159, that not assessing the key person in a newly formed company was not restrictive of competition.

With regard to key personnel, it is proper to evaluate a new company solely on the basis of the past performance of its key personnel, *JSW Maint., Inc.*, Comp. Gen. Dec. B-400581.5, 2009 CPD ¶ 182; *DRA Software Training*, Comp. Gen. Dec. B-289128, 2002 CPD ¶ 11. See also *SDS Int'l v. United States*, 48 Fed. Cl. 742 (2001) (proper to evaluate past performance of supervisor of training); *Lynwood Mach. & Eng'g, Inc.*, Comp. Gen. Dec. B-287652, 2001 CPD ¶ 138 (proper to evaluate past performance of "special project manager"); *General Atomics*, Comp. Gen. Dec. B-287348, 2001 CPD ¶ 169 (proper to evaluate past performance of a *Grp.* of key personnel that had worked on project when the contract was held by another company); *SDS Int'l*, Comp. Gen. Dec. B-285822, 2000 CPD ¶ 167 (proper to evaluate past performance of one key person of newly formed company). On the other hand, it is also proper not to evaluate key personnel separately, *KIRA, Inc.*, Comp. Gen. Dec. B-287573, 2001 CPD ¶ 152; *Urban-Meridian Joint Venture*, Comp. Gen. Dec. B-287168, 2001 CPD ¶ 91; *SWR, Inc.*, Comp. Gen. Dec. B-286044.2, 2000 CPD ¶ 174.

It has also been held proper to evaluate past performance of subcontractors in evaluating a contractor, *DynCorp Int'l, LLC*, Comp. Gen. Dec. B-415873, 2018 CPD ¶ 157 (proper to downgrade contractor for poor subcontractor performance); *Triad Logistics Servs. Corp.*, Comp. Gen. Dec. B-296511.3, 2005 CPD ¶ 189 (proper to rate contractor with no past performance record "very good" when major subcontractor had excellent ratings); *Information Tech. & Applications Corp. v. United States*, 51 Fed. Cl. 340 (2001) (even subcontractors performing minor elements of work may be evaluated); and *Neal R. Gross & Co.*, Comp. Gen. Dec. B-275066, 97-1 CPD ¶ 30 (adverse performance rating proper even though poor performance was attributable to some extent to subcontractors, because the prime contractor always bears responsibility for the work of subcontractors).

Although the FAR is silent on the issue, agencies have also been permitted to evaluate the performance of parent companies and affiliates when their resources will be used to perform the contract, *Humana Military Healthcare Servs.*, Comp. Gen. Dec. B-401652.2, 2009 CPD ¶ 219; *Ecompex, Inc.*, Comp. Gen. Dec. B-292865.4, 2004 CPD ¶ 149. See also *Daylight Tree Serv. & Equip., LLC*, Comp. Gen. Dec. B-310808, 2008 CPD ¶ 23 (information on affiliated company at same address as offeror is relevant). Compare *Health Net Fed. Servs., LLC*, Comp. Gen. Dec. B-401652.3, 2009 CPD ¶ 220, granting a protest because the agency gave credit for past performance of a parent company and affiliates without proof of what prior contracts they had performed or what work they would do on current contract. If the agency finds no evidence that the resources of the parent or affiliate organization will be used and there is no other relevant past performance, it is proper to assign a neutral rating to the offeror, *Bering Straits Tech. Servs. LLC*, Comp. Gen. Dec. B-401560.3, 2009 CPD ¶ 201.

A number of agencies have used the questionable logic of treating the relevance of past performance as an assessment of the offeror's experience by giving offerors without much relevant work lower scores on their past performance evaluation, and this has been accepted by GAO. See *STG, Inc.*, Comp. Gen. Dec. B-415580.3, 2018 CPD ¶ 221 (rating of "satisfactory" based on references rating relevance as "superior," "satisfactory' and "neutral'); *Gonzales-McCaulley Inv. Grp.. Inc.*, Comp. Gen. Dec. B-402544, 2010 CPD ¶ 127 ("weakness" given for less relevant work); *ACS State Healthcare, LLC*, Comp. Gen. Dec. B-292981, 2004 CPD ¶ 57 (lower past performance rating justified by less relevant experience); *Five-R Co.*, Comp. Gen. Dec. B-288190, 2001 CPD ¶ 163 (proper to give only "satisfactory/confidence" score to protester because its past projects were not like work being procured); *Gulf Grp., Inc.*, Comp. Gen. Dec. B-287697, 2001 CPD ¶ 135 (score lowered because relevance of past work was "limited"); *J.A. Jones Mgmt. Servs., Inc.*, Comp. Gen. Dec. B-284909.5, 2001 CPD ¶ 64 (assessment reduced because of less relevant past performance); *Birdwell Bros. Painting & Refinishing*, Comp. Gen. Dec. B-285035, 2000 CPD ¶ 129 (score lowered because no past work of the size and complexity of the instant contract); *Marathon Constr. Corp.*, Comp. Gen. Dec. B-284816, 2000 CPD ¶ 94 (score lowered because no work of the type called for by the instant contract); *Molina Eng'g, Ltd./Tri-J Indus., Inc. Joint Venture*, Comp. Gen. Dec. B-284895, 2000 CPD ¶ 86 (score of "amber/high risk" based on lack of contracts of similar size and scope as instant contract); *Dellew Corp.*, Comp. Gen. Dec. B-284227, 2000 CPD ¶ 52 (assessment of higher performance risk than winning offeror because of lack of relevant work); *Clean Venture, Inc.*, Comp. Gen. Dec. B-284176, 2000 CPD ¶ 47 (score of "fair" for very good performance on contracts of less complexity than instant contract); *Champion Serv. Corp.*, Comp. Gen. Dec. B-284116, 2000 CPD ¶ 28 (higher performance risk because of less relevant work than winning contractor). See also *CPS Professional Servs., LLC*, Comp. Gen. Dec. B-409811, 2014 CPD ¶ 260, where GAO granted a protest because the agency had considered two offerors to have low risk when one had more relevant contracts than the other. Compare *Airwork Limited-Vinnell Corp. (a Joint Venture)*, Comp. Gen. Dec. B-285247, 2000 CPD ¶ 150, where GAO agreed with the agency that it was not required to give the protester a higher past performance rating because it had more relevant work experience. A clearer way to evaluate the amount of experience of an offeror is to treat "experience" as a separate evaluation factor.

[c] Corrective Action and Explanations

FAR 15.305(a)(2)(ii) requires that offerors be permitted to submit information on corrective action that has been taken to overcome past performance problems, and agencies have lost protests for failure to tell an offeror that corrective action is necessary to cure a past performance problem, *Alliant Techsystems, Inc.*, Comp. Gen. Dec. B-260215.4, 95-2 CPD ¶ 79.

Agencies have been given broad discretion in assessing whether corrective action will overcome prior performance problems. See, for example, *Lockheed Martin MS2 Tactical Sys.*, Comp. Gen. Dec. B-400135, 2008 CPD ¶ 157, and *Parmatic Filter Corp.*, Comp. Gen. Dec. B-285288.3, 2001 CPD ¶ 71, where the agency determined that the corrective action of one offeror was more effective than the corrective action of the protester. There are numerous instances where the refusal to adjust past performance ratings to reflect corrective action has been upheld. See *Walden Security*, Comp. Gen. Dec. B-413523.10, 2017 CPD ¶ 278 (agency properly concluded that corrective action only rated a "very good" rating); *PAE Aviation & Tech. Servs., LLC*, Comp. Gen. Dec. B-413338, 2016 CPD ¶ 283 (agency properly concluded that corrective action only rated a "satisfactory" rating); *ProActive Techs., Inc.*, Comp. Gen. Dec. B-412757.5, 2016 CPD ¶ 244 (agency properly concluded that corrective action did not overcome poor performance); *Day & Zimmermann Pantex Corp.*, Comp. Gen. Dec. B-286016, 2001 CPD ¶ 96 (agency discounted protester's claim that it had rectified poor prior performance); and *GEC-Marconi Elec. Sys. Corp.*, Comp. Gen. Dec. B-276186, 97-2 CPD ¶ 23 (evaluators not convinced that on-time delivery on recent contracts demonstrated that offeror had corrected problems that led to late delivery on earlier contracts).

GAO and the Court of Federal Claims have also affirmed agency decisions to accept the corrective action taken by an offeror as curing the performance problems. See *Blackwater Lodge & Training Ctr., Inc. v. United States*, 86 Fed. Cl. 488 (2009), where the agency had assessed the performance risk as "low" after considering the offeror's new procedures to correct safety problems on past contracts. See also *Pemco Aeroplex, Inc.*, Comp. Gen. Dec. B-310372, 2008 CPD ¶ 2 (agency properly gave an offeror a rating of "satisfactory confidence" after carefully assessing the cause of prior performance difficulties); and *CWIS, LLC*, Comp. Gen. Dec. B-287521, 2001 CPD ¶ 119 (winning offeror's score was reasonably increased based on corrective action). Compare *PAE Aviation & Tech. Servs., LLC*, Comp. Gen. Dec. B-413338, 2016 CPD ¶ 283 (agency properly concluded that corrective action only rated a "satisfactory" rating); *ProActive Techs., Inc.*, Comp. Gen. Dec. B-412757.5, 2016 CPD ¶ 244 (agency properly concluded that corrective action did not overcome poor performance).

Agencies should also carefully evaluate explanations for inferior performance. See *Pemco Aeroplex, Inc.*, Comp. Gen. Dec. B-310372, 2008 CPD ¶ 2 (agency properly gave an offeror a rating of "satisfactory confidence" after carefully assessing the cause of prior performance difficulties); and *Sumaria Sys., Inc.*, Comp. Gen. Dec. B-299517, 2007 CPD ¶ 122 (agency properly rechecked with the personnel on a referenced contract to obtain more current information on the cause of the problem). However, an agency is not required to seek explanations which the offeror has not brought to its attention, *Advanced Computer Concepts*, Comp. Gen. Dec. B-408084, 2013 CPD ¶ 126.

[d] Offerors With No Past Performance

41 U.S.C. § 1126(b) states the following rule with regard to evaluating offerors where the agency has no past performance information:

> If there is no information on past contract performance of an offeror or the information on past contract performance is not available, the offeror may not be evaluated favorably or unfavorably on the factor of past contract performance

After originally requiring a "neutral" rating in these circumstances, FAR 15.305(a)(2)(iv) now contains essentially the same language as the statute. The DOD "Source Selection Procedures" calls for a "neutral confidence" rating in these circumstances and states that ratings of "substantial confidence" or "satisfactory confidence" can be determined to be "worth more" than "neutral confidence." An offeror cannot be excluded from the competitive range "solely" on the basis of a "neutral" rating, *Xtreme Concepts, Inc.*, Comp. Gen. Dec. B-413711, 2016 CPD ¶ 372, or an "unknown confidence" rating, *Ryan P. Slaughter*, Comp. Gen. Dec. B-411168, 2016 CPD ¶ 344. In a LPTA procurement "neutral" should be considered to be "acceptable," *NEIE Med. Waste Servs., LLC*, Comp. Gen. Dec. B-412793.2, 2016 CPD ¶ 213. In *Precision Asset Mgmt. Corp. v. United States*, 135 Fed. Cl. 342 (2017), the court held that the agency was required to inform the protester of a neutral rating in conducting discussions so that it could submit more information.

There are numerous cases affirming an agency's assigning a "neutral" rating because the offeror has no contracts or similar size or complexity. See, for example, *Wolf Creek Fed. Servs., Inc.*, Comp. Gen. Dec. B-409187, 2014 CPD ¶ 61 (subsidiaries' performance not counted because they would not play meaningful role in contract performance); *Commissioning Solutions Global, LLC*, Comp. Gen. Dec. B-401553, 2009 CPD ¶ 210 (all three referenced contracts much smaller than instant procurement); *CMC & Maint., Inc.*, Comp. Gen. Dec. B-292081, 2003 CPD ¶ 107 (referenced contracts smaller and dissimilar from instant procurement); *Kalman & Co.*, Comp. Gen. Dec. B-287442.2, 2002 CPD ¶ 63 (no contracts of similar size or similarity with instant procurement); *MCS of Tampa, Inc.*, Comp. Gen. Dec. B-288271.5, 2002 CPD ¶ 52 (two referenced contracts were smaller and no information could be obtained on only similar contract). Similarly, GAO has affirmed "neutral" ratings when an offeror has no contracts that have been completed within a reasonable time of the competition. See *Futurecom, Inc.*, Comp. Gen. Dec. B-400730.2, 2009 CPD ¶ 42 ("neutral" rating appropriate when offeror has no relevant contracts that have been completed in last three years).

A "neutral" rating is improper when there is data meeting the RFP requirements. See *East Coast Utility Contractors, Ltd.*, Comp. Gen. Dec. B-415493, 2018 CPD ¶ 30 (agency failed to consider past performance of executives as called for in RFP); *GBTI Solutions, Inc.*, Comp. Gen. Dec. B-409114.3, 2014 CPD ¶ 45 (agency failed to contact references as called for in RFP).

This rule covers not only offerors with no relevant past performance but also offerors where the agency is unable to obtain data. See *Halbert Constr. Co.*, Comp. Gen. Dec. B-413213, 2016 CPD ¶ 254 (agency made reasonable attempt to contact references); *Batelco Tel. Co.*, Comp. Gen. Dec. B-412783, 2016 CPD ¶ 155 (no information in PPIRS database); *WKG & Assocs., LLC*, Comp. Gen. Dec. B-409835, 2014 CPD ¶ 250 (no references responded to questionnaires); *Bering Straits Tech. Servs., LLC*, Comp. Gen. Dec. B-401560.3, 2009 CPD ¶ 201 (protester did not show that affiliated companies would perform any part of the work and proposed a project manager that had only worked on a small contract that required similar work); *Herley Indus., Inc.*, Comp. Gen. Dec. B-400736.2, 2009 CPD ¶ 48 (offeror had not furnished past performance information on two of the three elements of the work); *Advanced Data Concepts, Inc.*, Comp. Gen. Dec. B-277801.4, 98-1 CPD ¶ 145 (offices in the same agency failed to complete reference questionnaires). However, a neutral rating should not be assigned if an offeror intentionally fails to submit required past performance information, *Forest Regeneration Servs. LLC*, Comp. Gen. Dec. B-290998, 2002 CPD ¶ 187.

GAO has accorded agencies wide discretion in implementing this rule. Thus, GAO has agreed that a neutral rating can be assessed as a lower rating than higher ratings. See *SITEC Consulting, LLC*, Comp. Gen. Dec. B-413526.4, 2017

CPD ¶ 164 ("confidence" superior to "neutral"); *General Revenue Corp.*, Comp. Gen. Dec. B-414220.2, 2017 CPD ¶ 106 ("marginal" lower than "neutral"); *Asset Mgmt. Real Estate*, Comp. Gen. Dec. B-407214.5, 2014 CPD ¶ 57 ("good" superior to "neutral"); *American Floor Consultants, Inc.*, Comp. Gen. Dec. B-294530.7, 2006 CPD ¶ 9 ("high confidence" superior to "neutral"). GAO has also affirmed giving an offeror with no performance record a "good" rating when that rating connoted "adequately sufficient," *Oceaneering Int'l, Inc.*, Comp. Gen. Dec. B-278126, 98-1 CPD ¶ 133. GAO explained that "good" in the rating scheme was not substantively different from "neutral" when it meant merely adequate. However, it is clearly improper to give an offeror with no performance record a "red" rating, *MIL Corp.*, Comp. Gen. Dec. B-294836, 2005 CPD ¶ 29. Furthermore, GAO has rejected the contention that a contract should not be awarded to an offeror with a neutral rating based on no relevant past performance, *M&M Ret. Enters., LLC*, Comp. Gen. Dec. B-297282, 2005 CPD ¶ 224.

When agencies evaluate past performance in terms of performance risk, there is some question as to how an offeror with no record of past performance should be scored. See *Phillips Indus., Inc.*, Comp. Gen. Dec. B-280645, 98-2 CPD ¶ 74, where the protester questioned the legality of a finding that such an offeror posed a performance risk but GAO denied the protest because the contract had been awarded to a slightly higher-priced offeror with excellent past performance.

[3] Experience

As noted above, the experience of the offerors is evaluated either as part of the evaluation of past performance or as a separate evaluation factor. The latter practice is superior because it allows the agency to make a separate assessment of whether the offerors have performed work that is similar to the work being procured and to use the fact that they have such experience in determining the risk that they will not successfully accomplish the work. In the Alliant 2 GWAC procurement discussed earlier in the chapter, experience was the major non-price evaluation factor.

Proposals must be treated equally under the experience evaluation factor. Unequal treatment was found in *Will Tech., Inc.*, Comp. Gen. Dec. B-413139.4, 2018 CPD ¶ 209 (agency gave "enhanced scrutiny" to protester's program manager but not to winner); *Ahtna Support & Training Servs., LLC*, Comp. Gen. Dec. B-400947.2, 2009 CPD ¶ 119 (agency assessed the experience of subcontractor of one offeror but not of protester); *Ashe Facility Servs., Inc.*, Comp. Gen. Dec. B-292218.3, 2004 CPD ¶ 80 (agency assessed the experience of key personnel of one offeror, but not the protester); and *U.S. Prop. Mgmt. Serv. Corp.*, Comp. Gen. Dec. B-278727, 98-1 CPD ¶ 88 (agency unequally evaluated the experience of the protester and the awardee where both firms were newly formed corporations).

As in the case of past performance, agencies are accorded considerable discretion in assessing the relevance of past work to the work to be performed on the contract, *K-Mar Indus., Inc.*, Comp. Gen. Dec. B-400487, 2009 CPD ¶ 159. See *Zolon Tech, Inc.*, Comp. Gen. Dec. B-299904.2, 2007 CPD ¶ 183, where GAO denied a protest when the agency surprisingly downgraded the protester on experience because it intended to use a consultant with experience rather than having employees with the requisite experience. See also *IBM Corp.*, Comp. Gen. Dec. B-415798, 2018 CPD ¶ 130 (no requirement to evaluate information known to agency personnel); *ICF, Inc.*, Comp. Gen. Dec. B-414247, 2017 CPD ¶ 118 (agency properly rated staff with limited experience as satisfactory not excellent); *ActioNet, Inc.*, Comp. Gen. Dec. B-409050.2, 2014 CPD ¶ 37 (agency properly downgraded protester for lack of required details explaining experience); *Alpha Genesis, Inc.*, Comp. Gen. Dec. B-299859, 2007 CPD ¶ 167 (agency was free to evaluate only the amount of experience not the quality of the experience when the RFP narrowly stated the evaluation factor); *Financial & Realty Services, LLC*, Comp. Gen. Dec. B-299605.2, 2007 CPD ¶ 161 (agency properly downgraded protester because it did not comply with RFP requirement to match its experience with each contract task); *MarLaw-Arco MFPD Mgmt.*, Comp. Gen. Dec. B-291875, 2003 CPD ¶ 85 (agency properly did not give experience with agency work higher value that experience with other comparable work); *M. Erdal Kamisli, Ltd.*, Comp. Gen. Dec. B-291522, 2003 CPD ¶ 19 (agency permitted to give higher experience rating to offeror that listed the most projects on which it had comparable experience). However, GAO will grant a protest if the evaluation is irrational. See, for example, *Cooperativa Muratori Riuniti*, Comp. Gen. Dec. B-294980, 2005 CPD ¶ 21, where GAO granted a protest when the agency downgraded the protester because no single referenced contract was of the magnitude of the current procurement but that procurement called for multiple items of work and the protester had numerous prior contracts whose work cumulated to the magnitude being procured. Similarly, in *Olympus Bldg. Servs., Inc.*, Comp. Gen. Dec. B-285351, 2000 CPD ¶ 178, a protest was granted when the agency gave experience ratings on the basis of the size of buildings that had been managed and averaged the ratings, but did not inform the offerors of this scoring method, with the result that the protester submitted more projects than required, yielding a lower experience assessment.

When experience is stated as a separate factor, the agency must demonstrate that it actually evaluated this factor, *Bio-Rad Labs., Inc.*, Comp. Gen. Dec. B-297553, 2007 CPD ¶ 58. However, if an offeror fails to provide the information on experience requested by the RFP, the agency can drop the offeror from the competition, *Prudent Techs., Inc.*, Comp. Gen. Dec. B-297425, 2006 CPD ¶ 16. See also *Sam Facility Mgmt., Inc.*, Comp. Gen. Dec. B-292237, 2003 CPD ¶ 147, where the agency properly downgraded the protester because it had not provided the required details on past contracts in the experience section of its proposal—even though the details were in the past performance section. GAO commented that "agencies evaluating one section of a proposal are not obligated to go in search of needed information." See also *JAVIS Automation & Eng'g, Inc.*, Comp. Gen. Dec. B-290434, 2002 CPD ¶ 140 (offeror downgraded for lack of details required by RFP).

When experience is to be evaluated, the standard to be used is normally stated in the RFP and agencies must adhere to this description. See *Consolidated Eng'g Servs., Inc.*, Comp. Gen. Dec. B-311313, 2008 CPD ¶ 146, sustaining a protest where the agency downgraded the protester because it had not obtained its experience on a single contract when the RFP contained a "no one contract" standard. Protests have also been sustained in *EFS Ebrex SARL*, Comp. Gen. Dec. B-416076, 2018 CPD ¶ 201 (agency used undisclosed benchmarks); *Doyon-Am. Mech., JV; NAJV, LLC*, Comp. Gen. Dec. B-310003, 2008 CPD ¶ 50 (agency evaluated experience of parent/affiliated companies when RFP stated only projects on which offeror served as prime contractor or teaming partner would be considered); *GlassLock, Inc.*, Comp. Gen. Dec. B-299931, 2007 CPD ¶ 216 (agency gave double credit for good experience by including it in the evaluation of a proposed project plan factor as well as the experience factor); *Data Mgmt. Servs. Joint Venture*, Comp. Gen. Dec. B-299702, 2007 CPD ¶ 139 (agency improperly considered experience on smaller projects when RFP required experience of projects of "similar" magnitude but protest denied for lack of prejudice; Court of Federal Claims held agency interpreted RFP properly in *Data Mgmt. Servs. Joint Venture v. United States*, 78 Fed. Cl. 366 (2007)); *L-3 Commc'ns Titan Corp.*, Comp. Gen. Dec. B-299317, 2007 CPD ¶ 66, *recons. denied*, 2007 CPD ¶ 121 (agency concluded offerors had equal experience when one had more and the RFP stated that more credit would be given "the greater the extent" of experience); *KIC Dev., LLC*, B-297425.2, 2006 CPD ¶ 27 (agency did not evaluate the experience of subcontractors and key personnel as permitted by RFP); *Myers Investigative & Sec. Servs., Inc.*, Comp. Gen. Dec. B-288468, 2001 CPD ¶ 189 (agency evaluated only experience with agency when there was no such RFP statement); *Mechanical Contractors, S.A.*, Comp. Gen. Dec. B-277916, 97-2 CPD ¶ 121 (agency gave no weight to industry certifications as demonstrating experience although the RFP required information as to such certifications). This requirement to follow the RFP description is enforced loosely by reading the description broadly. See *LCLC Inc/CfMRF*, Comp. Gen. Dec. B-414357, 2017 CPD ¶ 153 (agency properly evaluated corporate and key personnel experience that was recent and relevant); *RCL Components, Inc.*, Comp. Gen. Dec. B-400175, 2009 CPD ¶ 98 (agency properly evaluated experience because the RFP description of the past performance evaluation included a statement that relevancy would be determined by the "magnitude of effort and complexities").

Agencies frequently evaluate the experience of prospective subcontractors and this is proper when there is some indication in the RFP that it will be done, *Archer Western Fed. JV*, Comp. Gen. Dec. B-410168.2, 2014 CPD ¶ 351; *PAI Corp. v. United States*, 2009 U.S. Claims LEXIS 320 (2009). GAO has gone further and held that subcontractor experience can be evaluated even when the

RFP does not provide for such evaluation as long as the RFP permits the use of subcontractors, *Kellogg Brown & Root Servs., Inc.*, Comp. Gen. Dec. B-298694.7, 2007 CPD ¶ 124. This reasoning has also been applied to the evaluation of the experience of key personnel when the RFP does not specifically state that such information would be considered in the evaluation of the offeror's experience, *Dix Corp.*, Comp. Gen. Dec. B-293964, 2004 CPD ¶ 143. However, there is no requirement that an agency evaluate key personnel as part of the evaluation of corporate experience, *Blue Rock Structures, Inc.*, Comp. Gen. Dec. B-287960.2, 2001 CPD ¶ 184.

When an offeror has no experience but intends to use subcontractors with good experience, an agency can reach a balanced evaluation of the overall experience, *IPlus, Inc.*, Comp. Gen. Dec. B-298020, 2006 CPD ¶ 90. This same reasoning applies when an agency is evaluating the experience of key personnel that is gained working for another contractor. See *STEM Int'l, Inc.*, Comp. Gen. Dec. B-295471, 2005 CPD ¶ 19, where GAO concurred with the agency's balancing of good experience of key personnel with no experience of the protester.

Where a solicitation indicates that experience will be evaluated, the agency may evaluate the extent to which an offeror's specific experience is directly related to the work required by the contract even when there is no statement in the RFP to that effect. See *International Bus. & Tech. Consultants, Inc.*, Comp. Gen. Dec. B-310424.2, 2008 CPD ¶ 185, where the agency properly considered whether the offerors had experience performing the precise work called for by the contract. See also *American Artisan Prods., Inc.*, B-293801.2, 2004 CPD ¶ 127 (proper to evaluate whether offerors had experience in setting up specific types of exhibits called for by RFP); *High Country Contracting*, Comp. Gen. Dec. B-278649, 98-1 CPD ¶ 39 (contracting officer reasonably determined that the protester's proposal posed a moderate risk because it had limited relevant construction experience).

[4] Key Personnel

When an agency decides to evaluate key personnel as a separate factor, it should assess the experience of the personnel rather than merely reviewing resumes. See, for example, *Savannah River Alliance, LLC*, Comp. Gen. Dec. B-311126, 2008 CPD ¶ 88, where the agency evaluated resumes, made reference checks, reviewed letters of commitment and then required the key personnel to attend an oral presentation where they worked sample tasks. GAO rejected the protester's contention that the evaluation was not correctly done when the agency concluded that the protester's personnel were not as experienced as the winning offeror. See also *PAI Corp.*, Comp. Gen. Dec. B-298349, 2006 CPD ¶ 124 (proper to determine that certain experience of a key person did not qualify as the type of experience required by the RFP); and *Base Techs., Inc.*, Comp. Gen. Dec. B-293061.2, 2004 CPD ¶ 31 (proper to consider experience of key personnel even though it was not explicitly stated in the RFP). The disadvantage of only reviewing resumes is seen in *S2 Analytical Solutions, LLC*, Comp. Gen. Dec. B-416513, 2018 CPD ¶ 331 (agency downgraded protester because experienced person's academic credentials did not meet RFP requirement), and *DEI Consulting*, Comp. Gen. Dec. B-401258, 2009 CPD ¶ 151 (agency downgraded protester because of lack of full information in the resume). GAO denied these protests but it appears that the agency acted without adequate information as to the qualifications of the key person in arriving at this result. Compare *Trammell Crow Co.*, Comp. Gen. Dec. B-311314.2, 2008 CPD ¶ 129, holding that the agency was required to disclose the downgrading of key personnel in discussions because they were significant weaknesses.

It is proper to evaluate a key person even if the agency knows that he will not be assigned to the contract for its full duration, *U.S. Facilities, Inc.*, Comp. Gen. Dec. B-293029, 2004 CPD ¶ 17 (project manager had been promoted but was committed to stay with project until a suitable replacement was found). Conversely, an agency has discretion to drop a competitor when an agency finds that the project manager will leave the company after the contract work has commenced successfully, *S. C. Myers & Assocs., Inc.*, Comp. Gen. Dec. B-286297, 2001 CPD ¶ 16. See also *MCR Eng'g Co.*, Comp. Gen. Dec. B-287164, 2001 CPD ¶ 82, where it was found proper to ignore the fact that former key employees had assisted the offeror in achieving good past performance because it had continued to perform well after they left the company.

An offer can be rejected for failure to disclose that a key person has become unavailable after submission of the proposal, *Greenleaf Constr. Co.*, Comp. Gen. Dec. B-293105.18, 2006 CPD ¶ 19. However, if this unavailability is disclosed, the agency can refuse to accept the substitution of another person and drop the offeror from the competition, *Chenega Healthcare Servs., LLC v. United States*, 138 Fed. Cl. 644 (2018); *Chenega Healthcare Servs., LLC*, Comp. Gen. Dec. B-416158, 2018 CPD ¶ 200. As noted above, the Court of Federal Claims judges have issued decisions departing from GAO's precedent on key personnel issues.

[5] Technical and Management Plans

Agencies have very broad discretion in evaluating technical and management plans. See *Hernandez Eng'g, Inc.*, Comp. Gen. Dec. B-286336, 2001 CPD ¶ 89, stating:

> The evaluation of technical proposals is primarily the responsibility of the contracting agency. Our Office will not make an independent determination of the merits of technical proposals; rather, we will examine the record to ensure that the agency's evaluation was reasonable and consistent with the stated evaluation criteria. *Litton Sys., Inc.*, B-237596.3, Aug. 8, 1990, 90-2 CPD ¶ 115 at 8. A protester's mere disagreement with the agency's

evaluation does not render the evaluation unreasonable. *SWR Inc.*, B-286044.2, B-286044.3, Nov. 1, 2000, 2000 CPD ¶ 174 at 3.

As discussed earlier, there are two types of technical and management plans that are used as evaluation factors. The first type is the description of the work that is being proposed to meet the agency's needs. This can be treated as an *offer* that will be included in the contract but, more frequently, it is a means of evaluating *capability*. The second type is the description of the processes that will be used that demonstrates that the offeror has the capability to perform the work. When these plans are used to evaluate capability, they are generally submitted under an evaluation factor described as "understanding the work" or "soundness of approach." NASA calls such plans "mission suitability" and the Army and the Air Force calls them "mission capability."

Agencies frequently include experience of the offeror or of its key personnel, as discussed above, in the evaluation of these plans.

[a] Description of Work

The evaluation of the work that an offeror proposes to do to meet the requirements of the RFP is primarily within the province of the technical staff of the agency. Thus, neither GAO nor the Court of Federal Claims will overturn such a technical evaluation unless it is clearly irrational. For decisions denying protests of technical evaluations, see *Jacobs Tech., Inc.*, Comp. Gen. Dec. B-410441.15, 2018 CPD ¶ 338 (inadequate explanation of methods to reduce staffing); *Jacobs Tech., Inc.*, Comp. Gen. Dec. B-411784, 2015 CPD ¶ 342 (failure to describe how protester would use unoccupied facility); *Straughan Envtl, Inc.*, Comp. Gen. Dec. B-411650, 2015 CPD ¶ 287 (unclear approach to meeting surge requirement); *Research Analysis & Maint., Inc.*, Comp. Gen. Dec. B-410570.6, 2015 CPD ¶ 239 (lack of data to support low staffing); *Walsh Constr. Co.*, Comp. Gen. Dec. B-410015, 2014 CPD ¶ 291 (failure to demonstrate a capable and flexible approach to project execution); *Robbins-Gioia, LLC*, Comp. Gen. Dec. B-402199, 2010 CPD ¶ 67 (lack of detailed explanation of how contract goal would be achieved); *Savannah River Tank Closure, LLC*, Comp. Gen. Dec. B-400953, 2009 CPD ¶ 78 (winner proposed superior technical approach); *Savannah River Alliance, LLC*, Comp. Gen. Dec. B-311126, 2008 CPD ¶ 88 (winner offered superior key personnel); *Wackenhut Int'l, Inc.*, Comp. Gen. Dec. B-299022, 2007 CPD ¶ 44 (excessively long workweek); *Smiths Detection, Inc.*, Comp. Gen. Dec. B-298838, 2007 CPD ¶ 5 (inferior software design); *Gemma-CCC*, Comp. Gen. Dec. B-297447.2, 2006 CPD ¶ 182 (failure to submit required data showing that proposed product met agency requirements); *Integrate, Inc.*, Comp. Gen. Dec. B-296526, 2005 CPD ¶ 154 (failure to show that proposed software met RFP requirements); *TDF Corp.*, Comp. Gen. Dec. B-288392, 2001 CPD ¶ 178 (inadequate staffing); *SOS Interpreting, Ltd.*, Comp. Gen. Dec. B-287505, 2001 CPD ¶ 104 (inadequate system for handling sensitive information); *United Def. LP*, Comp. Gen. Dec. B-286925.3, 2001 CPD ¶ 75 (offered product inferior); *ABIC, Ltd.*, Comp. Gen. Dec. B-286460, 2001 CPD ¶ 46 (insufficient staffing and inadequate staff coverage of key work); and *Coastal Drilling, Inc.*, Comp. Gen. Dec. B-285085.3, 2000 CPD ¶ 130 (offered product did not meet a mandatory requirement).

In contrast, protests were sustained in *A-P-T Research, Inc.*, Comp. Gen. Dec. B-413731.2, 2017 CPD ¶ 112 (agency assumed offeror could retain incumbent's staff at low salaries); *Glacial Tech. Solutions, LLC*, Comp. Gen. Dec. B-412990.2, 2016 CPD ¶ 311 (agency accepted without explanation staffing methodologies that evaluators had rejected); *Meridian Mgmt. Corp.*, Comp. Gen. Dec. B-281287.10, 2001 CPD ¶ 5 (agency gave high rating to technical proposal that did not contain employees with skills necessary for the job); and *OneSource Energy Servs., Inc.*, Comp. Gen. Dec. B-283445, 2000 CPD ¶ 109 (low rating for inadequate staffing was based on the agency's estimate of staffing needs without analysis of the proposal to determine if it was based on a "unique approach" or skilled staff).

It is proper to make a risk assessment of the probability that a proposed management or technical approach will create performance problems. See, for example, *IBM Corp.*, Comp. Gen. Dec. B-415575, 2018 CPD ¶ 61 (risk of low staffing); *CACI Enter. Solutions, Inc.*, Comp. Gen. Dec. B-412648, 2016 CPD ¶ 111 (risk of low staffing); *Ultra Elecs. Ocean Sys., Inc.*, Comp. Gen. Dec. B-400219, 2008 CPD ¶ 183 (proposed revisions to the design of product created potential performance risk); *Compunetix, Inc.*, Comp. Gen. Dec. B-298489.4, 2007 CPD ¶ 12 (significant modification needed for product posed a technical risk); and *Hydro Eng'g, Inc. v. United States*, 37 Fed. Cl. 448 (1997) (specific elements of a technical and management proposal created a risk of timely performance and technical compliance).

When an agency evaluates the actual product to be delivered, it is highly unlikely that a protest will be successful. See, for example, *MD Helicopters, Inc.*, Comp. Gen. Dec. B-298502, 2006 CPD ¶ 164, denying a protest where the agency based its technical evaluation on four hours of flight testing of competitive helicopters. See also *Beechcraft Defense Co.*, Comp. Gen. Dec. B-406170.2, 2013 CPD ¶ 147, where the agency assigned a risk because the proposed aircraft had not completed testing requirements.

[b] Understanding the Work

A less rational, but common, type of evaluation of technical and management plans assesses whether the offeror has proven that it has the requisite capability by demonstrating an understanding of the work in the way the plan is written. Agencies also have wide latitude in making this subjective type of evaluation. See, for example, *KSC BOSS Alliance, LLC*, Comp. Gen. Dec. B-416334, 2018 CPD ¶ 267 (failure to provide detailed explanation of management approach); *Battelle Mem. Inst.*, Comp. Gen. Dec. B-413570.3, 2017 CPD ¶ 174 (failure to provide detailed explanation of processes to achieve called for performance); *Alion Sci. & Tech. Corp.*, Comp. Gen. Dec. B-410666, 2015 CPD ¶ 91 (lack of detail in management approach); *Dellew Corp.*, Comp. Gen. Dec. B-410216, 2014 CPD ¶ 339 (inadequate staffing/labor mix); *Cylab, Inc.*, Comp. Gen. Dec. B-402716, 2010 CPD ¶ 163 (program management approach did not address specific program requirements); *Government Acquisitions, Inc.*, Comp. Gen. Dec. B-401048, 2009 CPD ¶ 137 (offeror failed to submit resumes required in management plan); *Kuhana-Spectrum Joint Venture, LLC*, Comp. Gen. Dec. B-400803, 2009 CPD ¶ 36 (management plan misdescribed mentor/protégé program and omitted key personnel); *LOGMET, LLC*, Comp. Gen. Dec. B-400355.2, 2008 CPD ¶ 175 (proposed staffing plan showed lack of understanding of requirements); *Professional Performance Dev. Grp., Inc.*, Comp. Gen. Dec. B-311273, 2008 CPD ¶ 101 (numerous informational deficiencies in plans); Comp. Gen. Dec. B-309964, 2007 CPD ¶ 217 (inadequate coverage of required technical maturation plans); *Operational Res. Consultants, Inc.*, Comp. Gen. Dec. B-299131.1, 2007 CPD ¶ 38 (technical proposal failed to discuss some required areas); *Bernard Cap Co.*, Comp. Gen. Dec. B-297168, 2005 CPD ¶ 204 (manufacturing approach not as sound as winning offeror); *TekStar, Inc.*, Comp. Gen. Dec. B-295444, 2005 CPD ¶ 53 (technical and management proposals did not demonstrate capability); *LifeCare, Inc.*, Comp. Gen. Dec. B-291672, 2003 CPD ¶ 95 (poorly written and incomplete technical proposal); *Chart Indus., Inc.*, Comp. Gen. Dec. B-288248, 2001 CPD ¶ 174 (technical plan very general, lacking sufficient detail); *Strategic Res., Inc.*, Comp. Gen. Dec. B-287398, 2001 CPD ¶ 131 (management plan lacked detail in dealing with staffing issues); *Fisherman's Boat Shop, Inc.*, Comp. Gen. Dec. B-287592, 2001 CPD ¶ 123 (required network schedule omitted option items and merely added start and finish dates to items listed in RFP); *Evolving Res., Inc.*, Comp. Gen. Dec. B-287178, 2001 CPD ¶ 83 (management plan failed to adequately describe its process for managing task orders); *ITT Fed. Sys. Int'l Corp.*, Comp. Gen. Dec. B-285176.4, 2001 CPD ¶ 45 (lack of sufficient detail in technical proposal); and *Calian Tech. (US), Ltd.*, Comp. Gen. Dec. B-284814, 2000 CPD ¶ 85 (technical plan showed lack of understanding of work to be performed).

In contrast, protests were sustained in *ARES Tech. Servs. Corp.*, Comp. Gen. Dec. B-415081.2, 2018 CPD ¶ 153 (failure to consider impact of OCI mitigation plan on proposed technical approach); *ENSCO, Inc.*, Comp. Gen. Dec. B-414844, 2017 CPD ¶ 357 (multiple errors in evaluating management approach plus not enforcing page limitations); and *Pinnacle Solutions, Inc.*, Comp. Gen. Dec. B-414360, 2017 CPD ¶ 172 (unreasonable evaluation of management approach).

The great latitude accorded to the agency in this area is demonstrated by the cases that deny protests even though the agency has awarded the contract to a company that did not submit a plan with the detail required by the RFP. See, for example, *GTE Hawaiian Tel. Co.*, Comp. Gen. Dec. B-276487.2, 97-2 CPD ¶ 21, where the agency had required each offeror to address compliance with more than 1,300 technical requirements but had imposed an 800-page limit on technical proposals. GAO denied a protest that the winning offeror had not addressed all the requirements. See also *JW Assocs., Inc.*, Comp. Gen. Dec. B-275209, 97-1 CPD ¶ 57, where GAO initially granted a protest, in part because the agency had not documented its evaluation of a technical plan, but subsequently denied the protest when the agency reevaluated the technical plan of the winning offeror and determined that it was adequate even though it contained far less detail than the plan of the protester, and *SDS Int'l, Inc.*, Comp. Gen. Dec. B-279361, 98-2 CPD ¶ 7, affirming an agency's evaluation of a technical proposal as acceptable even though it did not describe the technical approach to be used as called for in the RFP, reasoning that the offeror had complied with the RFP by stating that it was capable of performing and that the contract specification was so detailed that there was little room for describing a technical approach different from that specification. Compare *ITT Fed. Servs. Int'l Corp.*, Comp. Gen. Dec. B-29783, 2007 CPD ¶ 43 (protest granted where staffing plan was downgraded because it had less staff than irrational government estimate); *Engineering Mgmt. & Integration, Inc.*, Comp. Gen. Dec. B-291672, 2003 CPD ¶ 95 (protest granted where offeror was rejected for not furnishing required staffing information but had actually furnished more complete information in a different form).

In some cases, this type of evaluation drops offerors that are known to be capable from the competition. See, for example, *Raloid Corp.*, Comp. Gen. Dec. B-297176, 2005 CPD ¶ 205, denying a protest by a company that had successfully manufactured a product in the past but was downgraded because it did not state precisely how the product would be manufactured as required by the RFP. Similarly, in *Ideamatics, Inc.*, Comp. Gen. Dec. B-297791.2, 2006 CPD ¶ 87, the company that had created a computerized system was determined to have only had a fair understanding of that system and a fair ability to maintain and enhance the system because of its inadequate description of these functions in its technical proposal. Successful incumbents (where the agency has explicit knowledge of their capabilities) frequently lose competitions for failure to write good technical or management proposals. See *ManTech Int'l Corp.*, Comp. Gen. Dec. B-311074, 2008 CPD ¶ 87 (poor response to sample task); *HealthStar VA, PLLC*, Comp. Gen. Dec. B-299737, 2007 CPD ¶ 114 (incomplete information because of page limitations); *BAE Sys. Norfolk Ship Repair, Inc.*, Comp. Gen. Dec. B-297879, 2006 CPD ¶ 75 (downgrading of management approach satisfactory even though offeror had successfully managed prior projects); and *International Res. Recovery, Inc. v. United States*, 60 Fed. Cl. 1 (2004) (failure to submit mobilization plan for work it was currently performing).

Protests have been granted when the agency does not evenhandedly evaluate such proposals. See, for example, *Will Tech., Inc.*, Comp. Gen. Dec. B-413139.4, 2018 CPD ¶ 209 (agency had used higher level of scrutiny of protester's experience); *Northrop Grumman Info. Tech., Inc.*, Comp. Gen. Dec. B-400134.10, 2009 CPD ¶ 167 (agency had given the same evaluation to proposals offering different levels of subcontracting). *Electronic Design, Inc.*, Comp.

Gen. Dec. B-279662.2, 98-2 CPD ¶ 69 (agency conducted the competition on an unequal basis by permitting the awardee to include in its BAFO a 1,700-page appendix that had been rejected initially because it exceeded the page limitation); and *Tidewater Homes Realty, Inc.*, Comp. Gen. Dec. B-274689, 96-2 CPD ¶ 241 (agency had given the protester low scores for lack of detail but had given the winning offeror high scores for a proposal containing a similar level of detail).

§ 6.08 DECISION TO AWARD

Upon the completion of the evaluation of offers, the agency must decide whether to make an award without negotiations or to establish a competitive range and conduct negotiations with all the offerors within the competitive range. Whether award without negotiations is permissible depends upon a number of factors, including the provisions included in the solicitation, the offers received, and the nature of communications between the agency and the offerors. Within these parameters, the agency has broad discretion in deciding whether to award or to negotiate. It also has broad discretion in establishing the competitive range. The statutory and regulatory requirements concerning the exercise of these discretionary determinations have evolved over the years.

Although the statutes use the phrase "award without discussions," the phrase "award without negotiations" is more descriptive of the concept and avoids use of the same term to describe two different types of communications. The statutory provisions authorizing award "based on the proposals received," give two different meanings to the word "discussions." It is used to describe both the communications which are permitted prior to award on the basis of proposals received and the communications which are to occur after the competitive range is established. See 10 U.S.C. § 3206(b)(2)(B) (formerly § 2305(b)(4)(A)(ii)) and 41 U.S.C. § 3703(a)(2) stating that award can be made on the basis of proposals received "without discussions with the offerors (other than discussions conducted for the purpose of minor clarifications)." The same different meanings of "discussions" are contained in 10 U.S.C. § 3303(a) (formerly § 2305(a)(2)(B)(ii)(I) and 41 U.S.C. § 3306(b)(2)(B)(i). In addition, the FAR Part 15 Rewrite removed the definition of "discussions" which had previously appeared in the FAR. It envisions that the exchanges between the agency and the offerors after establishment of the competitive range will constitute "negotiations" which "may include bargaining," FAR 15.306(d).

[A] Background

The government policy concerning whether to award without negotiations or to establish a competitive range and conduct discussions has changed several times over the years. The original statutory standard permitted award on an "initial proposal . . . where it can be clearly demonstrated from the existence of adequate competition or accurate prior cost experience that acceptance of an initial proposal without discussion would result in fair and reasonable prices," 10 U.S.C. § 2304(g) (1964). However, CICA changed the standard substituting "full and open competition" for "adequate competition" and "lowest overall cost to the Government" for "fair and reasonable prices." These changes were interpreted by GAO to mean that award would have to be made on the basis of the lowest evaluated price unless the proposal was technically unacceptable and that price/quality/capability tradeoffs where not permitted. See, e.g., *Information Spectrum, Inc.*, Comp. Gen. Dec. B-233208, 89-1 CPD ¶ 187. In 1990, recognizing that the "lowest overall cost" standard was too restrictive, causing unnecessary competitive range determinations thereby increasing the cost and time of procurements, Congress removed the "lowest overall cost" language and made related changes for defense contracts, § 802 of the National Defense Authorization Act for 1991, Pub. L. No. 101-510. Four years later, the same changes were adopted for non-defense agencies by the Federal Acquisition Streamlining Act of 1994, Pub. L. No. 103-355.

[B] Solicitation Provisions

While recognizing that award without negotiations would be preferable in many situations, Congress was concerned that competitors would not submit their best offers if they believed that the agency would likely conduct negotiations. Thus, 10 U.S.C. § 3206(b)(2)(B) (formerly § 2305(a)(2)(B)(ii)(I)) and 41 U.S.C. § 3306(b)(2)(B)(i) require that the solicitation indicate whether the agency intends to award without negotiations or intends to conduct negotiations, stating that the solicitation shall include:

> [E]ither a statement that the proposals are intended to be evaluated with, and award made after, discussions with the offerors, or a statement that the proposals are intended to be evaluated, and award made, without discussions with the offerors (other than discussions conducted for the purpose of minor clarification) unless discussions are determined to be necessary.

Neither the statute nor the regulations provide any directions related to selecting the appropriate provision. FAR 15.209(a) merely requires that once this determination is made, the appropriate solicitation provision is to be adopted.

[1] Award Without Negotiations Intended

Paragraph (f)(4) of the standard FAR 52.215-1 Instructions to Offerors—Competitive Acquisition solicitation provision permits award without negotiations as follows:

> The Government intends to evaluate proposals and award a contract without discussions with offerors (except clarifications as described in FAR 15.306 (a)). Therefore, the offeror's initial proposal should contain the offeror's best terms from a cost or price and technical standpoint. The Government reserves the right to conduct discussions if the Contracting Officer later determines them to be necessary. If the Contracting Officer determines that the number of proposals that would otherwise be in the competitive range exceeds the number at which an efficient competition can be conducted, the Contracting Officer may limit the number of proposals in the competitive range to the greatest number that will permit an efficient competition among the most highly rated proposals.

While indicating that award without negotiation is intended, this provision gives the agency the option to conduct negotiations when they are determined to be "necessary." However, FAR 15.306(a)(2) requires that when such a determination is made, "the rationale for doing so shall be documented in the contract file." This provision apparently reflects the congressional concern that offerors might not make their best offers in their original submission if they expect negotiations to take place. Thus, the government should not avail itself of this option as a matter of course.

Incorporation of the substance of this notice into solicitations has been held to put offerors on notice that they should not expect to have an opportunity to revise their offers. See, e.g., *Robotic Sys. Tech.*, Comp. Gen. Dec. B-278195.2, 98-1 CPD ¶ 20, stating:

> [S]ince the RFP advised offerors that the agency intended to make award without discussions, RST could not reasonably presume that it would have a chance to improve its proposal through discussions. *Scientific-Atlanta, Inc.*, B-255343.2, B-255343.4, Mar. 14, 1994, 94-1 CPD ¶ 325 at 8-9.

An offeror does not have a *right* to award on the basis of an initial proposal, *ViroMed Labs., Inc.*, Comp. Gen. Dec. B-310747.4, 2009 CPD ¶ 32; *Kisco Co.*, Comp. Gen. Dec. B-216953, 85-1 CPD ¶ 334.

[2] Negotiations Intended

When the agency has determined that it intends to conduct negotiations, the following Alternate I to the FAR 52.215-1 ¶ (f)(4) solicitation provision is to be used:

> The Government intends to evaluate proposals and award a contract after conducting discussions with offerors whose proposals have been determined to be within the competitive range. If the Contracting Officer determines that the number of proposals that would otherwise be in the competitive range exceeds the number at which an efficient competition can be conducted, the Contracting Officer may limit the number of proposals in

> the competitive range to the greatest number that will permit an efficient competition among the most highly rated proposals. Therefore, the offeror's initial proposal should contain the offeror's best terms from a price and technical standpoint.

When this provision is used, the government may not make award without negotiations, *American Native Med, Transp., LLC*, Comp. Gen. Dec. B-276873, 97-2 CPD ¶ 73.

[C] Deciding Whether or Not to Negotiate

Neither the statutes nor the FAR specify criteria for determining whether or not to hold negotiations. 10 U.S.C. § 3303 (formerly § 2305(b)(4)(A)) merely states:

> The head of an agency shall evaluate competitive proposals in accordance with section 3301(a) of this title and may award a contract—
>
> (1) after discussions with the offerors, provided that written or oral discussions have been conducted with the responsible offerors who submit proposals within the competitive range; or
>
> (2) based on the proposals received, without discussions with the offerors (other than discussions conducted for the purpose of minor clarification) provided that the solicitation included a statement that proposals are intended to be evaluated, and award made, without discussions, unless discussions are determined necessary.

Substantially the same language is contained in 41 U.S.C. § 3703(a)(2).

Under the CICA standard, negotiations appeared to have been the favored procedure. However, the statutory changes have served to make award without negotiations at least an equally appropriate procedure. House Report 101-665, 101st Cong., 2d Sess. (accompanying Pub. L. No. 101-510) discussed some of the factors to consider in making the selection. However, it did not go so far as indicating a preference for either procedure, stating, "The committee does not recommend a preference for conducting discussions or not conducting discussions, believing that this is more appropriately dealt with in regulation." The FAR has not adopted any guidance implementing these statutes. Thus, the lack of statutory or regulatory direction leaves the agency with broad discretion in determining whether or not negotiations should be conducted either in advance or after offers are received. See, however, DFARS 215.306(c)(1) stating: "For acquisitions with an estimated value of $100 million or more, contracting officers should conduct discussions." This appears to state a policy for major procurements that award without negotiations should be used infrequently. This DFARS presumption in favor of discussions for large procurements has generated significant protest litigation and another divide between the standards applied at

GAO and the Court of Federal Claims. See *Oak Grove Techs., LLC v. United States*, 155 Fed. Cl. 84 (2021).

[1] Award Without Negotiations

Award without negotiations is one of the most important techniques that agencies have adopted to streamline their procurements. House Report 101-665 recognized the advantages of this process by noting the following benefits of making awards without negotiations:

- Significant reduction of acquisition lead-time
- Permitting award on technical superiority when discussions are not needed
- Lessening the chances of wrongful disclosure of source selection information
- Reduction of the government's overall acquisition costs by reducing the amount a contractor is spending on bid and proposal costs

An additional benefit is the avoidance of final proposal revisions which include arbitrary price reductions. Such reductions have resulted in excessively low prices which can create serious difficulties during contract performance.

[a] Agency Discretion

There are numerous protest decisions recognizing the broad discretion given to agencies to make the decision to award without negotiations. See, e.g., *Armedia, LLC*, Comp. Gen. Dec. B-415525, 2018 CPD ¶ 26 (no requirement to discuss apparent OCI with offeror not selected without discussions); *Synectic Solutions, Inc.*, Comp. Gen. Dec. B-299086, 2007 CPD ¶ 36 (agency reasonably selected higher priced, higher technically rated proposal based on initial proposals); *Colmek Sys. Eng'g*, Comp. Gen. Dec. B-291931.2, 2003 CPD ¶ 123 (reasonable to award without discussions to higher priced proposal and not let protester correct weaknesses in its proposal).

GAO has generally held that the mere possibility that lower prices or better technical solutions might result from negotiations is not sufficient to overcome the agency's determination to forego negotiations. *See Tribalco, LLC*, Comp. Gen. Dec. B-414120, 2017 CPD ¶ 73, stating:

> In general, an agency is under no obligation to conduct discussions where a solicitation includes [a statement that award without discussions is intended]. See FAR § 15.306(a)(3); *Colmek Sys. Eng'g*, B-291931.2, July 9, 2003, 2003 CPD ¶ 123 at 7. Further, a contracting officer has broad discretion in deciding whether to hold discussions, *Integration Techs. Group, Inc.*,

B-274288.5, June 13, 1997, 97-1 CPD ¶ 214 at 6, and an agency's decision not to initiate discussions is a matter our Office generally will not review, *Kiewit La. Co.*, B-403736, Oct. 14, 2010, 2010 CPD ¶ 243 at 3.

A striking example of this broad discretion is *Level 3 Communications, LLC*, Comp. Gen. Dec. B-412854, 2016 CPD ¶ 171, where the agency had awarded a contract for $98 million rather than negotiate to clear up deficiencies in the protester's quotation for $60 million. GAO denied the protest following its standard reasoning. The Court of Federal Claims reached the opposite result in *Level 3 Commc'ns, LLC v. United States*, 129 Fed. Cl. 487 (2016), concluding that not conducting negotiations to obtain a lower price was "arbitrary and capricious and an abuse of discretion."

Award without negotiations has been held to be improper if the agency cannot make a clear determination as to which offeror has proposed the best value without discussions. See, for example, *Jonathan Corp.*, Comp. Gen. Dec. B-251698.3, 93-2 CPD ¶ 174, *recons. denied*, 93-2 CPD ¶ 233, where the agency had determined that competing technical proposals were essentially equal and had awarded without negotiations to the offeror with the lowest probable cost. GAO found that the agency's cost realism analysis was flawed, with the result that it was unclear which proposal represented the best value to the government. Where negotiations were necessary to ascertain the probable costs of the competing offerors, GAO held that award without negotiations was improper. This reasoning was followed by the Court of Federal Claims in *Day & Zimmermann Servs. v. United States*, 38 Fed. Cl. 591 (1997), where the agency had conducted a flawed cost realism analysis in a procurement where the competing offerors had been evaluated as being very close on the other evaluation factors. The court held that it was improper to award without negotiations when discussions were needed to determine an accurate probable cost in order to make a rational tradeoff decision. Award without negotiations was also held to be improper if neither proposal was acceptable, *Tribalco, LLC*, Comp. Gen. Dec. B-414120, 2017 CPD ¶ 73.

[b] Lack of Discussions

The rule was established many years ago that once a discussion was held with one offeror, the agency could no longer award on the basis of initial proposals but was required to establish a competitive range and conduct discussions with all offerors within the range, 50 Comp. Gen. 202 (B-170751) (1970). However, as discussed earlier, communications in the form of clarifications have always been permissible prior to award on the basis of the initial proposals.

An exception to this rule was created in *Environmental Chemical Corp.*, Comp. Gen. Dec. B-416166.3, 2019 CPD ¶ 217, holding that it was permissible to reopen discussions with only one offeror in the competitive range in order to allow it to correct a weakness that had not be disclosed in the original discussions.

[2] Decision to Negotiate

The nature of the specifications and the extent to which technical merit is to be considered in a tradeoff procurement will be critical in determining whether to indicate in the solicitation that negotiations are intended. This was noted in H.R. Rep. 101-665, which stated:

> The committee believes that when technical characteristics that cannot be quantified in cost terms are so critical that they are weighed more than lowest overall cost, the government may need discussions to ensure a clear understanding by both the government and the contractor of what the government truly needs and can get.

Where the solicitation indicates that award without negotiations is anticipated, the decision to negotiate will depend on the facts and circumstances of the procurement. Even though the criteria for such an award are present, negotiations would be called for if circumstances indicate that the government could obtain a significantly better bargain. This would be the case where one or more otherwise favorable offers contain defects. This is particularly so where the defects are readily correctable. See *Day & Zimmermann Servs. v. United States*, 38 Fed. Cl. 591 (1997), where the court questioned the decision to award without discussions when the competitors were very close and the agency made a speculative cost realism determination that could have been verified through discussions. In *Veda Inc. v. United States*, Civ. Action No. 93-0518-LFO (D.D.C. 1993), the court found that the decision to conduct discussions was reasonable because the contracting officer had serious problems with Veda's Small Business and Small Business Subcontracting Plan and deemed it unacceptable. Negotiations may also be called for when offers vary substantially from government estimates, *Jonathan Corp.*, Comp. Gen. Dec. B-251698.3, 93-2 CPD ¶ 174. In deciding whether to negotiate in such situations, the agency should balance the delay and expense involved in conducting negotiations with the potential benefits which might be obtained. It should also consider the effect on competitors, such as unduly increasing bid and proposal expense.

[D] Determining the Competitive Range

Prior to 1996, many agencies had included a large number of companies in the competitive range—resulting in unduly high bid and proposal costs and excessively long evaluation periods. In one case, this resulted in the recovery of the costs of remaining in the competition because the protester was placed in the competitive range without any real chance for award, *SMS Data Prods., Grp., Inc.*, GSBCA 8589-P, 87-1 BCA ¶ 19,496. These negative effects of broad inclusion of offerors in the competitive range were recognized as detrimental to the competitive negotiation process; and, in 1995, Congress was requested to amend the procurement statutes to permit more limited competitive range determinations.

[1] Standards for Inclusion

The current standard for inclusion in the competitive range and for determining its size were established by the Clinger-Cohen Act of 1996, Pub. L. No. 104-106, and the promulgation of the FAR Part 15 Rewrite.

[a] Statutory Changes

In passing the Clinger-Cohen Act, Congress recognized that the inclusion of large numbers of offers in the range can unnecessarily increase the time and cost of procurements and considered a number of ways in which the size of the range could be limited. Alternatives aimed at replacing the requirement for "full and open competition" were rejected because of concerns that they would lead to noncompetitive practices. However, two provisions were adopted which the FAR Council has relied upon to change the standards for determining inclusion in the competitive range. First, 10 U.S.C. § 3103 (formerly 2304(j)) and 41 U.S.C. § 3301(c) require that "full and open competition" be conducted "efficiently" as follows:

> The Federal Acquisition Regulation shall ensure that the requirement to obtain full and open competition is implemented in a manner that is consistent with the need to efficiently fulfill the Government's requirements.

More specifically, 10 U.S.C. § 3303(b) (formerly § 2305(b)(4)(B)) and 41 U.S.C. § 3703(b) permit the contracting officer to limit the competitive range:

> If the contracting officer determines that the number of offerors that would otherwise be included in the competitive range . . . exceeds the number at which an efficient competition can be conducted, the contracting officer may limit the number of proposals in the competitive range, in accordance with the criteria specified in the solicitation, to the greatest number that will permit an efficient competition among the offerors rated most highly in accordance with the criteria.

[b] FAR Part 15 Rewrite

The FAR implementation of these statutes appears to call for a two-step process. First, the agency is required to establish a competitive range which is to include, "all of the most highly rated proposals," FAR 15.306(c)(1). Then, the agency must decide if the number of such proposals is too large for an "efficient competition." If so, FAR 15.306(c)(2) permits the number to be limited as follows:

> After evaluating all proposals in accordance with 15.305(a) and paragraph (c)(1) of this section, the contracting officer may determine that the number of most highly rated proposals that might otherwise be included in the competitive range exceeds the number at which an efficient competition can be conducted. Provided the solicitation notifies offerors that the competitive range can be limited for purposes of efficiency (see 52.215-1(f)(4)), the contracting officer may limit the number of proposals in the competitive range to the greatest number that will permit an efficient competition among the most highly rated proposals (10 U.S.C. § 2305(b)(4) and 41 U.S.C. § 253b(d)).

[c] Most Highly Rated Offers and Efficient Competition

Neither the statutes nor the FAR attempt to define these terms. Draft versions of the FAR Part 15 Rewrite had listed factors to be considered in limiting the competitive range but these were deleted from the final Rewrite to permit "the facts of the instant acquisition to guide the contracting officer" in limiting the competitive range, 62 Fed. Reg. 51228 (1997). Similarly, the Rewrite does not contain a definition of "efficiency." However, the promulgation comments make it clear that the cost and time involved in conducting negotiations were the primary factors in rejecting the prior "when in doubt leave them in" rule.

The determination of which offers are the "most highly rated" will depend upon the facts and circumstances of each procurement. Under the current FAR, as under the prior regulations, the determination will be based on a comparison of the proposals. Thus, a break or gap in the evaluation scores might be the basis for determining the most highly rated offerors. See *Community P'ship LLC*, Comp. Gen. Dec. B-286844, 2001 CPD ¶ 38, and *Arsenault Acquisition Corp.*, Comp. Gen. Dec. B-276959, 97-2 CPD ¶ 74, affirming the use of this technique. For other protests denying claims of improper exclusion from the competitive range, *see Loc Performance Prods., Inc. v. United States*, 145 Fed. Cl. 57 (2019) (five proposals with acceptable technical rating included); *Cylab, Inc.*, Comp. Gen. Dec. B-402716, 2010 CPD ¶ 163 (three technically weak proposals excluded, four proposals included); *Orion Mgmt., LLC*, Comp. Gen. Dec. B-400680.2, 2009 CPD ¶ 21 (lowest rated of three proposals excluded); *Computer & Hi-Tech Mgmt., Inc.*, Comp. Gen. Dec. B-293235.4, 2004 CPD ¶ 45 (agency has discretion to determine which proposals are most highly rated); *Aliron Int'l, Inc.*, Comp. Gen. Dec. B-285048.2, 2000 CPD ¶ 125 (lowest rated of four proposals excluded); *Northwest Procurement Inst., Inc.*, Comp. Gen. Dec. B-286345, 2000 CPD ¶ 192 (two highly rated proposals included—protester's lower-rated proposal excluded); and *Wilson 5 Servs. Co.*, Comp. Gen. Dec. B-285343.2, 2000 CPD ¶ 157 (top two offerors included based on break in scores even though excluded protester had lower price). Compare *ABIC Ltd.*, Comp.

Gen. Dec. B-286460, 2001 CPD ¶ 46, where an agency included six offerors in the range even though there was a clear gap after the third offeror.

The comparative approach to determining the competitive range generally precludes the use of a predetermined cut-off score as a means of determining the range, *DOT Sys., Inc.*, Comp. Gen. Dec. B-186192, 76-2 CPD ¶ 3. In 50 Comp. Gen. 59 (B-169645) (1970), the RFP contained a minimum score, 75, below which proposals would be deemed outside the competitive range. As a result of this cut-off score, five proposals with point scores between 71.4 and 74.8 were excluded. GAO held that these five proposals could not be excluded from the competitive range solely because of failure to meet the cut-off score. In *National Veterans Law Ctr.*, 60 Comp. Gen. 223 (B-198738), 81-1 CPD ¶ 58, the contracting agency established an evaluation score of 80 points, arguing that the score was only a "qualifying score" meant to inform the offerors of the relative importance of each area of evaluation. GAO found no difference between this "qualifying score" and a "predetermined cut-off score . . . used to establish the competitive range" and reiterated the impropriety of its use. Nevertheless, GAO has upheld the exclusion of an offeror based on a predetermined cut-off score when the score of the excluded proposal was so low in comparison with scores on other proposals that no prejudicial effect could be said to exist, *Monarch Enters., Inc.*, Comp. Gen. Dec. B-233303, 89-1 CPD ¶ 222.

Reduction of the competitive range on the basis of efficiency is more problematic. The FAR Councils appear to have concluded that, as a general rule, no more than three offerors should be included in the competitive range. See 62 Fed. Reg. 51226 stating that "award is nearly always made to one of the three most highly rated offerors." Nonetheless, the FAR contains no such guidance. See, however, NFS 1815.306, which contains the following statement:

> (c)(2) A total of no more than three proposals shall be a working goal in establishing the competitive range. Field installations may establish procedures for approval of competitive range determinations commensurate with the complexity or dollar value of an acquisition.

It seems clear that elimination of proposals that have been determined to be among those most highly rated would be likely to subject an agency to protests of unfair treatment. Thus, elimination of such proposals should be done very cautiously. Where negotiations are not anticipated to be complex or time consuming, a relatively large number of offerors might not result in inefficiency. In contrast, where the nature of the procurement and the offers require substantial negotiations and complex offer revisions, limiting the competitive range would be desirable. In such cases the agency should carefully document the differences between the proposals and endeavor to eliminate those proposals that do not have a good chance of winning the competition. If, as the FAR seems to indicate, reduction requires the elimination of "most highly rated" offers, it is difficult to see what rationale would support the elimination of offerors from the competitive range when other offerors that had similar evaluations were included in the range. It would be sounder practice to include all of the most highly rated offerors in the range. See, however, *COGAR Grp., Ltd.*, Comp. Gen. Dec. B-413004, 2016 CPD ¶ 189, denying a protest where efficiency was achieved by putting eight proposals in the competitive range on the basis of price alone, even though there was very little differentiation with the excluded proposals, and *Kathpal Techs., Inc.*, Comp. Gen. Dec. B-283137.3, 2000 CPD ¶ 6, where GAO suggested that using this technique might have been a way to limit the number of competitors in a situation where the agency had received over 200 proposals. Compare *Meridian Mgmt. Corp.*, Comp. Gen. Dec. B-285127, 2000 CPD ¶ 121, granting a protest where the agency achieved an efficient number of competitors by dropping all proposals with low scores or high prices. GAO reasoned that the agency had not considered the protester's low prices in dropping it because of a questionable poor evaluation of its non-price factors.

[2] Discretion to Include or Exclude

Under the current FAR, as under the prior regulations, the agencies continue to have broad discretion in determining whether to include or exclude an offer within the competitive range. Thus, it can be anticipated that their decisions will not be disturbed unless they are clearly shown to be arbitrary or unreasonable. See, for example, *Loc Performance Prods., Inc. v. United States*, 145 Fed. Cl. 57 (2019), where the court stated that it would not overrule a competitive range decision unless it was "clearly unreasonable," and *DynaLantic Corp.*, Comp. Gen. Dec. B-416855, 2019 CPD ¶ 11, stating that the determination of whether a proposal is in the competitive range is a matter "within the discretion of the contracting agency." Accord, *Impresa Construzioni Geom. Domenico Garufi v. United States*, 44 Fed. Cl. 540 (1999), *aff'd*, 238 F.3d 1324 (Fed. Cir. 2001). See also *NAE-TECH Remediation Servs.*, Comp. Gen. Dec. B-402158, 2010 CPD ¶ 89, where GAO emphasized the great discretion in this area and summarily rejected the protester's contention that it should not have been excluded from the competitive range because it had intended to correct its defects during discussions. Compare *Progressive Indus., Inc.*, 129 Fed. Cl. 457 (2016), finding an abuse of discretion when the contracting officer allowed the technical evaluators to determine the competitive range without informing them that one of the offerors had been allowed to enhance its proposal prior to their evaluation.

Nonetheless, contracting officers must treat all offerors fairly. Thus, they are not free to treat similarly situated offerors differently. See *Isometrics, Inc. v. United States*, 5 Cl. Ct. 420 (1984), where the exclusion of a proposal that might legitimately have been excluded due to a failure to comply with RFP requirements was held to be improper because a similarly situated offeror was included in the competitive range and given an opportunity to cure the problems. See also *Columbia Research Corp.*, Comp. Gen. Dec. B-284157, 2000 CPD ¶ 158, holding that an offeror was improperly excluded when comparison of its technical proposal to the higher scored proposals revealed no material differences in either the quantity or magnitude of the weaknesses and its cost proposal was the lowest. Compare *Outdoor Venture Corp.*, Comp. Gen. Dec. B-401351.2, 2009 CPD ¶ 194, finding no unequal treatment when one offeror with deficiencies in its technical proposal was included and the protester with deficiencies in its technical proposal was excluded because its deficiencies were "of greater significance."

The discretion to include or exclude offerors from the competitive range permits agencies to include marginal proposals in the competitive range in order to broaden the competition. See, for example, *440 E. 62d St. Co.*, Comp. Gen. Dec. B-276058.2, 98-1 CPD ¶ 73, denying a protest asserting that it should have been excluded from the competitive range because it was weak on several evaluation factors.

[a] Factors to be Considered

The statutes require that the competitive range be established "solely on the factors specified in the solicitation," 10 U.S.C. § 3301(a) (formerly § 2305(b)(1) and (4)(A)) or "considering only cost or price and the other factors included in the solicitation," 41 U.S.C. § 3703(c). This requirement is repeated in FAR 15.306(c)(1) and FAR 15.305(a). However, in some instances a complete evaluation of each element of each offer would not appear to be necessary prior to determining the competitive range. If one or more aspects of an offer is so inferior to other offers as to make it unlikely that it could be improved through negotiations, it would not be reasonable to invest more time and effort into evaluating other aspects of the offer. See NFS 1815.305-70, Identification of Unacceptable Proposals, stating:

> (a) The contracting officer shall not complete the initial evaluation of any proposal when it is determined that the proposal is unacceptable because:
>
> (1) It does not represent a reasonable initial effort to address the essential requirements of the RFP or clearly demonstrates that the offeror does not understand the requirements;
>
> (2) In research and development acquisitions, a substantial design drawback is evident in the proposal, and sufficient correction or improvement to consider the proposal acceptable would require virtually an entirely new technical proposal; or
>
> (3) It contains major technical or business deficiencies or omissions or out-of-line costs which discussions with the offeror could not reasonably be expected to cure.
>
> (b) The contracting officer shall document the rationale for discontinuing the initial evaluation of a proposal in accordance with this section.

While an offeror has a right to have its offer fairly evaluated, the government should not be required to perform expensive and useless exercises.

There is support for this interpretation in recent decisions. See *Priority One Servs., Inc.*, Comp. Gen. Dec. B-415201.2, 2018 CPD ¶ 182; and *AMEX-Gilbane, JV*, Comp. Gen. Dec. B-413778, 2017 CPD ¶ 11.

However, technically inferior but acceptable proposals may not be rejected without considering cost or price, *Arc-Tech, Inc.*, Comp. Gen. Dec. B-400325.3, 2009 CPD ¶ 53; *Femme Comp, Inc. v. United States*, 83 Fed. Cl. 704 (2008); *Information Scis. Corp. v. United* States, 73 Fed. Cl. 70 (2006); *Global, A 1" Flagship Co.*, Comp. Gen. Dec. B-297235, 2006 CPD ¶ 14; *Columbia Research Corp.*, Comp. Gen. Dec. B-284157, 2000 CPD ¶ 158; *Kathpal Techs., Inc.*, Comp. Gen. Dec. B-283137.3, 2000 CPD ¶ 6. Neither can a proposal with a neutral rating on past performance be excluded without considering price, *Xtreme Concepts, Inc.*, Comp. Gen. Dec. B-413711, 2016 CPD ¶ 372; *Ryan P. Slaughter*, Comp. Gen. Dec. B-411168, 2016 CPD ¶ 344. See, however, *Loc Performance Prods., Inc. v. United States*, 145 Fed. Cl. 57 (2019), where the court held that it was proper to "winnow" the proposals to establish an efficient competitive range by using only the technical factor.

It is improper to exclude a proposal from the competitive range based on only the scores without assessing the basis for the scoring, *Pinnacle Solutions, Inc.*, Comp. Gen. Dec. B-414360, 2017 CPD ¶ 172. Compare *Adino, Inc.*, Comp. Gen. Dec. B-412144, 2016 CPD ¶ 7, denying a protest where the competitive range was determined by including the two offerors with point scores above 30 points.

[b] Inclusion of Defective or Unacceptable Proposals

Because negotiations are conducted for the purpose of giving offerors the opportunity to cure weaknesses or deficiencies or to modify other aspects of their proposals, an offer need not be excluded from the competitive range solely because it fails to conform to the RFP. In this respect, the competitive range decision is very different from the "nonresponsiveness" determination in sealed bid contracting. See *Carahsoft Tech. Corp. v. United States*, 86 Fed. Cl. 325 (2009), where the court stated "a technically unacceptable proposal may be considered for award if the proposal would otherwise be competitive and if its technically unacceptable terms can be cured by the offeror in a revised proposal," and *Construcciones Aeronauticas, S.A.*, Comp. Gen. Dec. B-244717, 91-2 CPD ¶ 461, where GAO stated that "the concept of competitive range—whether the proposal is or can be readily made acceptable—is incompatible with responsiveness." See also *Grove Res. Solutions, Inc.*, Comp. Gen. Dec. B-296228, 2005 CPD ¶ 133; and *SWR, Inc.*, Comp. Gen. Dec. B-286229, 2000 CPD ¶ 196, noting that the purpose of establishing a competitive range is to cure deficiencies.

In an LPTA procurement, it is permissible to establish a competitive range based on the proposed prices even if all of the proposals are technically unacceptable, *Regency Enters. Servs., LLC*, Comp. Gen. Dec. B-418448, 2020 CPD ¶ 165. Thus, an agency could include only the two lowest price proposals in the competitive range when they had only minor issues that were easily correctable and the third lowest proposal was considerably higher, *Environmental Restoration, LLC*, Comp. Gen. Dec. B-413781, 2017 CPD ¶ 15.

[c] Exclusion for Deficiencies

While proposals with significant deficiencies may be included in the competitive range, they may also be excluded. Contracting officers have been given broad discretion in making this determination. Thus, exclusion has been found proper in *Advanced Software Sys., Inc.*, Comp. Gen. Dec. B-414892.2, 2019 CPD ¶ 51 (proposal did not address stated requirement); *DynaLantic Corp.*, Comp. Gen. Dec. B-416855, 2019 CPD ¶ 11 (proposal had major informational deficiencies); *All Computer Consulting, Inc.*, Comp. Gen. Dec. B-401204, 2009 CPD ¶ 132 (proposal did not demonstrate that proposed product met specification requirements); *L-3 Commc'ns. EOTech, Inc.*, Comp. Gen. Dec. B-311453, 2008 CPD ¶ 130 (bid sample failed tests—Court of Federal Claims reached opposite result in *L-3 Commc'ns. EOTech, Inc. v. United States*, 83 Fed. Cl. 643 (2008)); *Pacific Lock Co.*, Comp. Gen. Dec. B-309982, 2007 CPD ¶ 191 (proposal did not clearly prove that product was "U.S. made"); *Kolob Canyons Air Serv.*, Comp. Gen. Dec. B-398240.2, 2006 CPD ¶ 106 (proposal did not demonstrate that aircraft contained required avionics); *Integration Techs. Grp., Inc.*, Comp. Gen. Dec. B-295958, 2005 CPD ¶ 99 (offered product did not meet specifications); *CliniComp, Int'l*, Comp. Gen. Dec. B-294059, 2004 CPD ¶ 209 (product not commercially available as required by RFP); *Wahkontah Servs., Inc.*, Comp. Gen. Dec. B-292768, 2003 CPD ¶ 214 (proposal merely parroted back RFP requirements); *Americom Gov't Servs., Inc.*, Comp. Gen. Dec. B-292242, 2003 CPD ¶ 163 (proposal included conditions on contract requirements); *B.E. Meyers & Co.*, Comp. Gen. Dec. B-283796, 2000 CPD ¶ 9 (proposal was very short and incomplete); and *Novavax, Inc.*, Comp. Gen. Dec. B-286167, 2000 CPD ¶ 202 (offeror took exception to important requirement of RFP). A proposal was also properly excluded where the offeror informed the agency that it needed more time to resolve a zoning deficiency with the local authorities, *Dismas Charities, Inc.*, Comp. Gen. Dec. B-284754, 2000 CPD ¶ 84.

A technically acceptable proposal may be properly determined to be outside the competitive range because the contracting officer believes that the prospective costs of performance are too high and cannot be reduced sufficiently without detracting from the proposal's technical acceptability, *Tracor Marine, Inc.*, Comp. Gen. Dec. B-222484, 86-2 CPD ¶ 150 (denying protest even though protester's technical score was highest). See also *Radio Sys., Inc.*, Comp. Gen. Dec. B-255080, 94-1 CPD ¶ 9 (price 350% higher than the low offeror); *Everpure, Inc.*, Comp. Gen. Dec. B-226395.2, 88-2 CPD ¶ 264 (sustaining exclusion of higher priced proposal even though that left only one offeror in the competitive range); *Systems Integrated*, Comp. Gen. Dec. B-225055, 87-1 CPD

¶ 114 (30% higher proposed costs); and *Jack Faucett Assocs.*, Comp. Gen. Dec. B-224414, 86-2 CPD ¶ 310 (35% higher costs).

A technically acceptable proposal may also be properly determined to be outside the competitive range because the contracting officer believes that the proposed price is unrealistically low, *International Outsourcing Servs., LLC*, Comp. Gen. Dec. B-295959, 2006 CPD ¶ 6. See also *DS, Inc.*, Comp. Gen. Dec. B-289676, 2002 CPD ¶ 58 (proposal contained insufficient costs to perform the work); *Molina Eng'g, Ltd./Tri-J Indus., Inc. J.V.*, Comp. Gen. Dec. B-284895, 2000 CPD ¶ 86 (proposal with unrealistically low price); and *McDonald Constr. Servs., Inc.*, Comp. Gen. Dec. B-285980, 2000 CPD ¶ 183 (proposal was approximately 10% lower in price but was much lower rated on technical factors).

[d] Exclusion for Informational Deficiencies

Information related to the capability of the offeror is frequently called for and the failure to furnish such information has been held to be a valid reason for exclusion from the competitive range. Thus, informational deficiencies in technical or management proposals used to assess the offerors' understanding of the work constitute valid reasons for exclusion of an offeror from the competitive range. *See KSC BOSS Alliance, LLC*, Comp. Gen. Dec. B-416334, 2018 CPD ¶ 267 (multiple information weaknesses and high price); *Pinnacle Solutions, Inc.*, Comp. Gen. Dec. B-414380.2, 2018 CPD ¶ 154 (lack of detailed information on labor relations plan); *D&J Enters., Inc.*, Comp. Gen. Dec. B-310442, 2008 CPD ¶ 8 (insufficient information on key personnel and organizational structure); *Professional Performance Dev. Grp.. Inc.*, Comp. Gen. Dec. B-311273, 2008 CPD ¶ 101 (information provided either parroted back RFP's requirements or stated intent to comply with RFP); *Femme Comp, Inc. v. United States*, 83 Fed. Cl. 704 (2008) (information was in wrong volume of proposal as delineated in RFP); C. *Martin Co.*, Comp. Gen. Dec. B-299382, 2007 CPD ¶ 74 (proposal appeared to use old information not responding to current requirements); *B&S Transp., Inc.*, Comp. Gen. Dec. B-299144, 2007 CPD ¶ 16 (insufficient information on management and operational approach); *Sigma One Corp.*, Comp. Gen. Dec. B-294719, 2005 CPD ¶ 49 ("overly general" treatment of required information); *Wahkontah Servs., Inc.*, Comp. Gen. Dec. B-292768, 2003 CPD ¶ 214 (information provided either parroted back in whole or part RFP's requirements or lacked sufficient information and detail to determine that offeror understood work required); *DSC Cleaning, Inc.*, Comp. Gen. Dec. B-292125, 2003 CPD ¶ 118 (no references provided); *LaBarge Prod., Inc.*, Comp. Gen. Dec. B-287841, 2001 CPD ¶ 177 (insufficient information on experience and qualifications as well as insufficient technical information); and *EAA Capital Co., L.C.C.*, Comp. Gen. Dec. B-287460, 2001 CPD ¶ 107 (insufficient information on management capability, technical plan and prior experience).

Where the information that is not submitted is for the purpose of verifying whether the offered products or services conform to specifications, exclusion from the competitive range has been held to be justified. See *Hamilton Sundstrand Power Sys. v. United States*, 75 Fed. Cl. 512 (2007) (lack of narrative description as to how product complies with purchase description); *TMC Design Corp.*, Comp. Gen. Dec. B-296194.3, 2005 CPD ¶ 158 (lack of details about product's capabilities—exclusion proper even though testing of product was to be conducted prior to award decision); *Consultants in Continual Improvement*, Comp. Gen. Dec. B-289351, 2002 CPD ¶ 40 (proposal did not give details of the offeror's proprietary method of performing the work); and *Speegle Constr., Inc.*, Comp. Gen. Dec. B-286063, 2000 CPD ¶ 190 (offeror that had not provided the technical solutions required by the RFP).

Proposal page limitations are not excuses for failing to provide required information. In *Infotec Dev., Inc.*, Comp. Gen. Dec. B-238980, 90-2 CPD ¶ 58, a proposal was properly excluded for lack of information after the agency rejected 49 pages of the proposal which exceeded the page limitations in the RFP. Similarly, in *Management & Indus. Techs. Assocs.*, Comp. Gen. Dec. B-257656, 94-2 CPD ¶ 134, the RFP had a 20-page limit and the protester submitted over 200 pages of material. The agency removed the pages which exceeded the page limit and found the remaining pages deficient and excluded the protester from the competitive range. See also *HSQ Tech.*, Comp. Gen. Dec. B-277048, 97-2 CPD ¶ 57, finding it proper to exclude a proposal that exceeded the overall 300-page limitation with the result that none of its price proposal was included in the evaluation; and *Integrated Tech. Works, Inc.—Telara, Inc.*, Comp. Gen. Dec. B-286769.5, 2001 CPD ¶ 141, where the refusal to evaluate pages exceeding the 30-page limitation made an offeror technically unacceptable.

Offerors have been properly excluded from the competitive range for informational deficiencies demonstrating their understanding of the work even when the agency knows that they are fully capable of performing, *HealthStar VA, PLLC*, Comp. Gen. Dec. B-299737, 2007 CPD ¶ 114. Thus, incumbent contractors have been excluded from the competitive range for informational deficiencies, *SPAAN Tech, Inc.*, Comp. Gen. Dec. B-400406, 2009 CPD ¶ 46 (failure to provide information on quality assurance plan); *International Res. Recovery, Inc. v. United States*, 60 Fed. Cl. 1 (2004) (failure to submit mobilization plan for work currently being performed); *Interactive Communication Tech., Inc.*, Comp. Gen. Dec. B-271051, 96-1 CPD ¶ 260 (incumbent's technical proposal lacked detailed information on technical approach and staffing); *Pedus Bldg. Servs., Inc.*, Comp. Gen. Dec. B-257271.3, 95-1 CPD ¶ 135 (sloppy technical proposal did not demonstrate that incumbent contractor understood how to perform the work). An incumbent contractor has also been excluded from the competitive range for failing to meet an RFP requirement as to how the work is to be performed even though they have successfully performed the work a different way, *Saftey-Kleen (Pecatonica), Inc.*, Comp. Gen. Dec. B-290838, 2002 CPD ¶ 176.

[e] Competitive Range of One

Prior to the new rules on establishing the competitive range, an agency's decision to include only one offeror in the competitive range was subject to close scrutiny due to the elimination of competition, *Birch & Davis Int'l, Inc. v. Christopher*, 4 F.3d 970 (Fed. Cir. 1993); and *Besserman Corp.*, Comp. Gen. Dec. B-237327, 90-1 CPD ¶ 191. A competitive range of one was overturned in a number of cases. See *Dynalantic Corp.*, Comp. Gen. Dec. B-274944.2, 97-1 CPD ¶ 101 (deficiencies of eliminated proposal were minor and easily correctable and price was lower); *Coastal Gov't Servs., Inc.*, Comp. Gen. Dec. B-250820, 93-1 CPD ¶ 167 (inadequacies were minor and could have been easily resolved during discussions); *Stay, Inc.*, Comp. Gen. Dec. B-247606, 92-1 CPD ¶ 481 (reasons for exclusion of protester were minor and some deficiencies were also found in awardee's proposal); *Corporate Strategies, Inc.*, Comp. Gen. Dec. B-239219, 90-2 CPD ¶ 99 (lower priced proposals that were eliminated were rated excellent or good and had weaknesses that could have been resolved by discussions).

Based on the new competitive range rules, GAO no longer follows this rule. Thus, since the FAR now uses the term "most highly rated proposals," an agency is permitted to include only one proposal in the competitive range if no other proposal has a reasonable chance of being selected for award, *Enterprise Servs., LLC*, Comp. Gen. Dec. B-414513.2, 2017 CPD ¶ 241; *TekStar, Inc.*, Comp. Gen. Dec. B-295444, 2005 CPD ¶ 53; *Information Sys. Tech. Corp.*, Comp. Gen. Dec. B-291747, 2003 CPD ¶ 72; *SDS Petroleum Prods., Inc.*, Comp. Gen. Dec. B-280430, 98-2 CPD ¶ 59, or if all other proposals have deficiencies, *General Atomics Aeronautical Sys., Inc.*, Gen. Dec. B-311004, 2008 CPD ¶ 105 (protester's proposal would have required major revisions); *M&M Investigations, Inc.*, Gen. Dec. B-299369.2, 2007 CPD ¶ 200 (protester's proposal was 30% higher in price and not rated best technically); and *SOS Interpreting, Ltd.*, Comp. Gen. Dec. B-287505, 2001 CPD ¶ 104 (TEP rated proposal conditionally acceptable overall, which meant proposal did not meet all requirements). In the *SDS* decision, GAO rejected the argument that the agency was required to keep the top rated proposals in the competition because of the new language in the FAR and the deletion of the prior language stating that the competitive range should include "all proposals with a reasonable chance for award." See also *Firearms Training Sys., Inc. v. United States*, 41 Fed. Cl. 743 (1998), where the court held that the new FAR language permitted a competitive range of one. In that case, the court also held that the new FAR gave the agency broad discretion in determining when to establish the competitive range—allowing the agency to conduct a demonstration of proposed products before establishing the competitive range. Compare *Bean Stuyvesant, L.L.C. v. United States*, 48 Fed. Cl. 303 (2000), upholding a determination that only one offeror was in the competitive range but stating that "strict scrutiny" should continue to be given to such determinations under the new FAR.

[3] Changes in the Competitive Range

The competitive range is dynamic rather than static. Thus, as an agency learns more about an offer, through communications, negotiations or reevaluation, the competitive range may be altered to reflect the current status of the offerors.

[a] Removal from the Competitive Range

Procuring agencies are not bound by initial determinations to include offers within the competitive range, *Intown Properties, Inc.*, Comp. Gen. Dec. B-250232, 93-1 CPD ¶ 43. In this regard, FAR 15.306 provides that an offer originally included in the competitive range may be removed, as follows:

> (c)(3) If the contracting officer, after complying with paragraph (d)(3) of this section, decides that an offeror's proposal should no longer be included in the competitive range, the proposal shall be eliminated from consideration for award. Written notice of this decision shall be provided to unsuccessful offerors in accordance with 15.503.
>
> * * *
>
> (d)(5) If, after discussions have begun, an offeror originally in the competitive range is no longer considered to be among the most highly rated offerors being considered for award, that offeror may be eliminated from the competitive range whether or not all material aspects of the proposal have been discussed, or whether or not the offeror has been afforded an opportunity to submit a proposal revision (see 15.307(a) and 15.503(a)(1)).

Thus, if during or after discussions it becomes clear that a proposal should not have been included in the competitive range or no longer belongs in that range, the offeror may be precluded from further discussions and/or from submitting final proposal revisions. In *iAccess Techs., Inc. v. United States*, 143 Fed. Cl. 521 (2019); *Priority One Servs., Inc.*, Comp. Gen. Dec. B-415201.2, 2018 CPD ¶ 182; *Cedge Software Consultants, LLC v. United States*, 117 Fed. Cl. 419 (2014), and *Hamilton Sundstrand Power Sys.*, Comp. Gen. Dec. B-298757, 2006 CPD ¶ 194, proposals with significant deficiencies were included in the competitive range but dropped when discussions did not clear up the deficiencies. See also *Impresa Construzioni Geom. Domenico Garufi v. United States*, 44 Fed. Cl. 540 (1999), *aff'd*, 238 F.3d 1324 (Fed. Cir. 2001) (proper to exclude offeror from competitive range when answers to discussion questions show lack of understanding of work); *Dismas Charities, Inc.*, Comp. Gen. Dec. B-284754, 2000 CPD ¶ 84 (proper to drop an offeror when necessary information was not included in BAFO); and *Labat-Anderson, Inc. v. United States*, 42 Fed. Cl. 806 (1999) (proper exclusion when BAFO was technically unacceptable). Compare *Symtech Corp.*, Comp. Gen. Dec. B-289332, 2002 CPD ¶ 43 (agency had no reasonable basis for dropping a proposal from the competitive range because of its response to discussion questions); and *Voith Hydro, Inc.*, Comp. Gen. Dec. B-277051, 97-2 CPD ¶ 68 (offeror improperly dropped from the competitive range based on deficiencies in its BAFO when the deficiencies had been apparent in a question and answer session during oral presentations but had not been identified by the agency during negotiations).

[b] Addition or Reinstatement to the Competitive Range

Offerors excluded or removed from the competitive range are required to be given prompt "preaward" notice of exclusion, FAR 15.503 (a)(1) and may request a "preaward debriefing," FAR 15.505. Following notice or debriefing the agency may discover that the offer was mistakenly excluded. Under such circumstances, it would be appropriate for the agency to include or reinstate the offer in the range. However, the inclusion would have to be based on the offer as originally submitted. FAR 15.307(a) prohibits the agency from accepting or considering revisions to offers once they are excluded:

> If an offeror's proposal is eliminated or otherwise removed from the competitive range, no further revisions to that offeror's proposal shall be accepted or considered.

In *Cambridge Sys., Inc.*, Comp. Gen. Dec. B-400680, 2009 CPD ¶ 12, GAO denied a protest that the agency had reopened the procurement and added two companies to the competitive range after the sole company in the original competitive range was found to be ineligible for award.

§ 6.09 NEGOTIATIONS

The procurement statutes require written or oral discussions with all offerors in the competitive range, but do not indicate the purpose of the discussion process, the matters to be discussed, or the procedures to be followed in conducting negotiations. The FAR Rewrite made a number of substantial changes in the rules for discussions and recognized that discussions means negotiation which includes bargaining with the view to "allowing the offeror to revise its proposal," 62 Fed. Reg. 51229 (1997). FAR 15.306(d) states:

> *Exchanges with offerors after establishment of the competitive range.* Negotiations are exchanges, in either a competitive or sole source environment, between the Government and offerors, that are undertaken with the intent of allowing the offeror to revise its proposal. These negotiations may include bargaining. Bargaining includes persuasion, alteration of assumptions and positions, give-and-take, and may apply to price, schedule, technical requirements, type of contract, or other terms of a proposed contract. When negotiations are conducted in a competitive acquisition, they take place after establishment of the competitive range and are called discussions.

This new description of the process of discussions with offerors in the competitive range encourages contracting officers to conduct in-depth negotiations with each offeror. However, if such negotiations alter the contract requirements or terms and conditions included in the RFP, all offerors still in the competition must be informed of the alteration by an amendment to the RFP, FAR 15.206(a) and (c). Protests for not doing this have been sustained in *DZSP 21, LLC v. United States*, 139 Fed. Cl. 110 (2018) (material changes in requirements after five years of protested awards); *CGI Fed., Inc.*, Comp. Gen. Dec. B-410330.2, 2014 CPD ¶ 366 (agency changed methodology for evaluating prices); *Red River Holdings, LLC v. United States*, 87 Fed. Cl. 768 (2009) (agency relaxed mandatory specification requirements); *Trammell Crow Co.*, Comp. Gen. Dec. B-311314.2, 2008 CPD ¶ 129 (agency altered key evaluation factor); *OTI Am., Inc. v. United States*, 68 Fed. Cl. 646 (2005) (agency used internal evaluation criteria inconsistently without amending RFP to inform offerors of criteria); *Northrop Grumman Info. Tech., Inc.*, Comp. Gen. Dec. B-295526, 2005 CPD ¶ 45 (agency significantly changed its approach to exercising options after receipt of final proposal revisions); *Systems Mgmt., Inc.*, Comp. Gen. Dec. B-287032, 2001 CPD ¶ 85 (agency relaxed mandatory solicitation requirement); and *Mangi Env't Grp., Inc. v. United States*, 47 Fed. Cl. 10 (2000) (agency relaxed mandatory requirements). Compare *CG Servs. Ltd P'ship*, Comp. Gen. Dec. B-416443, 2018 CPD ¶ 313 (no need to change general statement of needs in first phase of procurement); *Northrop Grumman Sys. Corp.*, Comp. Gen. Dec. B-412278.7, 2017 CPD ¶ 312 (no need to change broad statement of work even though added work identified by technical personnel); *Guardian Moving & Storage Co. v. United States*, 122 Fed. Cl. 117 (2015) (requirement for amendment does not apply to extension of final proposal revision deadline); and *Leidos, Inc.*, Comp. Gen. Dec. B-409214.4, 2015 CPD ¶ 63 (no need to change broad performance work statement even though procurement had been delayed two years).

Furthermore, if the alteration is "so substantial as to exceed what prospective offerors reasonably could have anticipated," the contracting officer must cancel the solicitation and issue a new one, FAR 15.206(e). See *AirTrak Travel*, Comp. Gen. Dec. B-292101, 2003 CPD ¶ 117, recommending reopening the competition to all vendors when the agency had issued an amendment to the RFP that significantly altered the risk imposed on contractors by the original RFP. Immaterial alterations to the RFP do not require such reopening. See *Companion Data Servs., LLC*, Comp. Gen. Dec. B-410022, 2014 CPD ¶ 300 (modifying list of hardware and software to be maintained not material); *Golden Mfg. Co. v. United States*, 107 Fed. Cl. 264 (2012) (updating process specification and changing material for clothing not a cardinal change); and *Government Contract Servs. Co.*, Comp. Gen. Dec. B-294367, 2004 CPD ¶ 215 (offeror that had not competed not entitled to cancellation of the solicitation because the amendment to the RFP did not substantially alter it).

[A] Purpose of Negotiations

Among the stated purposes of the FAR Rewrite were to increase the "scope of discussions," 62 Fed. Reg. 51225 (1997), and to "require a more robust exchange of information during discussions," 62 Fed. Reg. 51229 (1997). Implementing the policy favoring enhanced discussions, FAR 15.306(d)(2) states that the primary purpose of negotiations is to obtain best value for the government:

> The primary objective of discussions is to maximize the Government's ability to obtain best value, based on the requirement and the evaluation factors set forth in the solicitation.

See DoD Source Selection Procedures repeating this statement at 3.4.1.and adding: "Discussions are highly recommended for source selections."

This is consistent with the view expressed by GAO that discussions should be conducted "to the end that competition is maximized and the Government is assured of receiving the most favorable contract," 51 Comp. Gen. 621 (B-173677) (1972). Although there is no express statement requiring the agencies to "assist" an offeror to improve its offer, other changes in the FAR support the propriety of appropriately assisting an offeror to improve its offer. See FAR 15.306(d) stating:

> (3) . . . The contracting officer . . . is encouraged to discuss other aspects of the offeror's proposal that could, in the opinion of the contracting officer, be altered or explained to enhance materially the proposal's potential for award.
>
> (4) In discussing other aspects of the proposal, the Government may, in situations where the solicitation stated that evaluation credit would be given for technical solutions exceeding any mandatory minimums, negotiate with offerors for increased performance beyond any mandatory minimums, and the Government may suggest to offerors that have exceeded any mandatory minimums (in ways that are not integral to the design), that their proposals would be more competitive if the excesses were removed and the offered price decreased.

Furthermore, the earlier prohibition of "technical leveling" (former FAR 15.610(d)) was removed in the FAR Rewrite. Thus, it would appear that assistance would be appropriate if all offerors are treated fairly, the rules against improper disclosure of source selection information are observed, and the assistance is not a response to an offeror's incompetence. See *First Preston Hous. Initiatives, LP*, Comp. Gen. Dec. B-293105.2, 2004 CPD ¶ 221, recognizing that helping offerors improve their proposals is proper because "such improvement is precisely what the discussion process envisions."

A careful reading of the above FAR provisions indicates that they *do not* state a mandatory rule requiring contracting officers to engage in robust negotiations with offerors in the competitive range. Rather, they are *permissive*—presumably to keep them from being grounds for protest. This is clear from the additional language in FAR 15.306(d)(3):

> However, the contracting officer is not required to discuss every area where the proposal could be improved. The scope and extent of discussions are a matter of contracting officer judgment.

The result is that the *mandatory* requirement for discussion is narrowly stated in FAR 15.306(d)(3) as follows:

> At a minimum, the contracting officer must, subject to paragraphs (d)(5) and (e) of this section and 15.307(a), indicate to, or discuss with, each offeror still being considered for award, deficiencies, significant weaknesses, and adverse past performance information to which the offeror has not yet had an opportunity to respond.

In spite of this narrow description of the mandatory discussion rule, conducting limited discussions is not sound policy. Particularly, attempting to draw distinctions between "deficiencies" and "weaknesses" and to determine when a "weakness" is "significant," would be difficult, at best, and of questionable benefit. Furthermore, GAO and court decisions in this area are somewhat unpredictable. Thus, contracting officers should fully explore the offers that are in the competitive range and conduct meaningful negotiations on all elements of the proposal which could be altered to improve the chance of the offeror winning the competition.

[B] Negotiating to Obtain Best Value

Negotiations are not an end in themselves. The purpose of the policy favoring robust negotiations is to obtain the most favorable contract for the government. Obtaining best value does not necessarily mean negotiating the lowest possible price and imposing the greatest possible risk on the contractor. While the contracting officer is required to ensure that the government does not pay a higher price than is necessary, it is also incumbent on the contracting officer to make certain that the price is not so low as to impede performance. See FAR 9.103(c) which indicates the various problems that can result from a price which is too low:

> The award of a contract to a supplier based on lowest evaluated price alone can be false economy if there is subsequent default, late deliveries, or other unsatisfactory performance resulting in additional contractual or administrative costs. While it is important that Government purchases be made at the lowest price, this does not require an award to a supplier solely because that supplier submits the lowest offer.

It is also important that the appropriate contract type be selected so that too great a risk is not imposed on the contractor. See FAR 16.103(a):

> Selecting the contract type is generally a matter for negotiation and requires the exercise of sound judgment. Negotiating the contract type and negotiating prices are closely related and should be considered together. The objective is to negotiate a contract type and price (or estimated cost and fee) that will result in reasonable contractor risk and provide the contractor with the greatest incentive for efficient and economical performance.

The following material contains a detailed analysis of the legal rules distinguishing between mandatory and permissive negotiations, which are identified in GAO and Court of Federal Claims decisions as the requirement for "meaningful discussions." Contracting officers must be aware of these rules but should recognize that they do not identify a clear line of demarcation. The inexact nature of this line is illustrated by the following standard statement in *Integrated Medical Solutions, LLC,* Comp. Gen. Dec. B-418754, 2020 CPD ¶ 287:

> Meaningful discussions must be sufficiently detailed so as to lead an offeror into the areas of its proposal requiring amplification or revision in a manner to materially enhance the offeror's potential for receiving the award; however, that does not obligate an agency to spoon-feed an offeror or to discuss every area where the proposal could be improved. FAR 15.306(d)(3); *Management Scis. for Health*, B-416041, B-416041.2, May 25, 2018, 2018 CPD ¶ 197 at 9. Moreover, although discussions may not be conducted in a manner that favors one offeror over another, discussions are not required to be identical among offerors and need only be tailored to each offeror's proposal. FAR 15.306(d)(1), (e)(1); *HP Enter. Servs., LLC*; *Aon Nat'l Flood Servs.*, B-413967 et al., Jan. 17, 2017, 2017 CPD ¶ 26 at 9.

In the face of this lack of clarity, it is not good business practice to attempt to limit the issues raised during negotiations to the smallest number that will satisfy the legal rules. Rather, contracting officers should err on the side of robust negotiations where all elements of a proposal that have been downgraded are identified and explained to each offeror in the competitive range.

[1] Deficiencies and Weaknesses

The terms "deficiency" and "weakness" have been at the center of much confusion in the discussion process. Prior to the FAR Part 15 Rewrite, when the only mandatory discussion requirement was that the agency address deficiencies, GAO had found inadequate discussions where the contracting officer failed to discuss "weaknesses" in an offeror's technical and management proposals where it had received low scores because of lack of detail in the proposal, *Eldyne, Inc.*, Comp. Gen. Dec. B-250158, 93-1 CPD ¶ 430. GAO explained this ruling in

Dep't of the Navy—Recons., Comp. Gen. Dec. B-250158.4, 93-1 CD ¶ 422, stating that to have "meaningful discussions an agency must point out "weaknesses, deficiencies or excesses in proposals necessary for an offeror to have a reasonable chance of being selected for award."

When the Rewrite was issued, this rule appeared to have been adopted in FAR 15.306(d)(3), requiring the disclosure in negotiations of not only "deficiencies" but also "significant weaknesses" and "other aspects of its proposal that could . . . be altered or explained to enhance materially the proposal's potential for award." However, in *MCR Fed., Inc.*, Comp. Gen. Dec. B-280969, 99-1 CPD ¶ 8, a protest was denied where the agency had failed to discuss the fact that a technical evaluation was scored as "acceptable" because it met all of the solicitation requirements. GAO stated, "We do not read the revised Part 15 language to change the legal standard so as to require discussion of all proposal areas where ratings could be improved." Similarly, in *Du & Assocs., Inc.*, Comp. Gen. Dec. B-280283.3, 98-2 CPD ¶ 156, GAO stated that it did not view the Rewrite "as having changed the prior legal requirements governing discussions." Subsequently, in 2001 the language "other aspects of its proposal that could . . . be altered or explained to enhance materially the proposal's potential for award" was removed from the mandatory rule, FAC 2001-02, 66 Fed. Reg. 65347 (Dec. 18, 2001).

The result is that the current rule requires the discussion of "deficiencies" and "significant weaknesses." These terms are defined in FAR 15.001:

> *Deficiency*, as used in this subpart, is a material failure of a proposal to meet a Government requirement or a combination of significant weaknesses in a proposal that increases the risk of unsuccessful contract performance to an unacceptable level.
>
> *Weakness*, as used in this subpart, is a flaw in the proposal that increases the risk of unsuccessful contract performance. A "significant weakness" in the proposal is a flaw that appreciably increases the risk of unsuccessful contract performance.

Subsequent decisions provide little confidence that deficiencies and significant weaknesses can be distinguished from other matters that must be discussed. For example, some cases have held that only "material" problems need be discussed. See *Q Integrated Cos., LLC v. United States*, 126 Fed. Cl. 124 (2016), stating at 144:

> Many decisions emphasize that deficiencies and weaknesses must be "material," granting protests where the matter in question precluded the offeror from receiving the award, and denying protests where disclosing the matter would not have improved the offeror's chance for award. [John Cibinic, Jr., et al., *Formation of Government Contracts*, 894-95 (4th ed. 2011)] (citing numerous cases, including *Cube Corp. v. United States*, 46 Fed. Cl. 368, 384 (2000) ("Plaintiff has not demonstrated how [disclosure of

the evaluation information] would have improved materially Cube's chance for award."), and *CRAssociates, Inc.*, B-282075.2, 2000 CPD ¶ 63 ("Had the agency pointed out these matters, CRA could have added additional information. . . . Discussions cannot be meaningful where, as here, the agency fails to advise the offerors, in some way, of material proposal deficiencies.").

Compare this reasoning with the statement in FAR 15.306(d)(3) that contracting officers "are *encouraged* to discuss other aspects" of a proposal that could "be altered or explained to enhance *materially* the proposal's potential for award." This discretionary provision has been cited as the rule to be followed in considering a protest in several decisions. See *Honeywell Tech. Solutions, Inc.*, Comp. Gen. Dec. B-414329, 2017 CPD ¶ 144; *InfoPro, Inc.*, Comp. Gen. Dec. B-408642.2, 2015 CPD ¶ 59.

Lack of discussion of material issues has been found in a few instances. See *Dismas Charities, Inc.*, Comp. Gen. Dec. B-284754, 2000 CPD ¶ 84, where lack of proof of zoning for a building was identified as a material deficiency but the protest was denied because of lack of proof of prejudice.

Some decisions rely on the FAR definition of "significant weakness" as a flaw that increases the risk of unsuccessful performance. See *Mevacon-NASCO JV*, Comp. Gen. Dec. B-414329, 2017 CPD ¶ 144 (proposal did not demonstrate an adequate approach or an understanding of the work); *Raytheon Co.*, Comp. Gen. Dec. B-404998, 2011 CPD ¶ 232 (experience ratings stating that "program success could be jeopardized"). However, GAO has held that a weakness that is "the determinative factor in the award" is not necessarily a significant weakness, *Management Sci. for Health*, Comp. Gen. Dec. B-416041, 2018 CPD ¶ 197.

The determination of what constitutes a significant weakness appears to be highly subjective. See *ANHAM FZCO*, Comp. Gen. Dec. B-415969, 2018 CPD ¶ 184 (factor rated "good" not a significant weakness); *ExecuTech Strategic Consulting, LLC*, Comp. Gen. Dec. B-410893, 2015 CPD ¶ 103 (lack of experience of some personnel rated "moderate risk" not significant weakness); *Nuclear Production Partners LLC*, Comp. Gen. Dec. B-407948.10, 2014 CPD ¶ 86 (cost savings found infeasible not significant weakness); *DMS-All Star Joint Venture*, Comp. Gen. Dec. B-310932.6, 2009 CPD ¶ 212 (concerns about labor rates and other costs not significant weaknesses).

A number of protests have been denied because the issue was minor or it did not appear that it would change the outcome of the competition. See *Ryder Move Mgmt., Inc. v. United States*, 48 Fed. Cl. 380 (2001) (interpretation of data that could not be altered in another proposal); *J.A. Jones/Bell, J.V.*, Comp. Gen. Dec. B-286458, 2001 CPD ¶ 17 (one area of concern that protester did not show how it could have improved its proposal). GAO has frequently stated that an agency "is under no obligation to discuss every aspect of the proposal which received less than the maximum score," *ManTech Sec. Techs. Corp.*, Comp. Gen. Dec. B-297133.3, 2006 CPD ¶ 77. The Court of Federal Claims is in accord with this view, *Structural Assocs., Inc./Comfort Sys. USA (Syracuse) Joint*

Venture v. United States, 89 Fed. Cl. 735 (2009); *WorldTravelServ. v. United States*, 49 Fed. Cl. 431 (2001); *Dynacs Eng'g Co. v. United States*, 48 Fed. Cl. 124 (2000). See also *SEAIR Transport Servs.*, Inc., Comp. Gen. Dec. B-274436, 96-2 CPD ¶ 224, holding that the protester was not entitled to discussions which would essentially have been conducted solely to permit it to achieve a perfect score in all areas. Minor weaknesses were also found in *International Bus. & Tech. Consultants, Inc.*, Comp. Gen. Dec. B-310424.2, 2008 CPD ¶ 185 (weakness that agency itself considered minor in the evaluation); *Cornell Cos.*, Comp. Gen. Dec. B-310548, 2007 CPD ¶ 212 (weakness that did not prevent protester from having a reasonable chance to win); *PWC Logistics Servs., Inc.*, Comp. Gen. Dec. B-299820, 2007 CPD ¶ 162 (criticisms of risk management plan when it was rated "at the low end" of "highly acceptable"); *IAP World Servs., Inc.*, Comp. Gen. Dec. B-297084, 2005 CPD ¶ 199 (agency not required to discuss all areas where protester did not receive "highest possible rating"); *American Ordnance, LLC*, Comp. Gen. Dec. B-292847, 2004 CPD ¶ 3 (only minor weaknesses when proposal was rated "good"); *4-D Neuroimaging*, Comp. Gen. Dec. B-286155.2, 2001 CPD ¶ 183 (relative disadvantages in comparison to competitor); *KIRA, Inc.*, Comp. Gen. Dec. B-287573, 2001 CPD ¶ 152 (lack of experience of subcontractor that was not considered material); *SDOS Interpreting, Ltd.*, Comp. Gen. Dec. B-287477.2, 2001 CPD ¶ 84 (higher price that was considered reasonable); *Digital Sys. Grp., Inc.*, Comp. Gen. Dec. B-286931, 2001 CPD ¶ 50 (two marginal past performance ratings that were not considered significant weaknesses).

It can be seen that the distinction between "deficiencies" and "weaknesses" is problematic. Attempting to draw distinctions between these terms and to determine when a "weakness" is "significant," would be difficult, at best, and of questionable benefit. Thus, contracting officers should fully explore the offers which are in the competitive range and conduct meaningful negotiations on all elements of the proposal which could be altered to improve the chance of the offeror winning the competition.

[2] Offer Information

In many cases, there is uncertainty as to exactly what performance is being offered. This may result from an offeror's failure to provide required information or from questions as to the meaning of terms in the offer. To the extent that these matters have not been cleared up in pre-competitive range communications and the offeror is included in the competitive range, they should be addressed in the negotiation. When an agency finds that it needs information to evaluate the proposal but that information was not explicitly called for by the RFP, it must request that information, *Ashbury Int'l Grp., Inc.*, Comp. Gen. Dec. B-401123, 2009 CPD ¶ 140. See also *Bank of Am.*, Comp. Gen. Dec. B-287608, 2001 CPD ¶ 137 (agency required to discuss numerous instances of lack of detail where protester could have improved proposal); *CRAssociates, Inc.*, Comp.

Gen. Dec. B-282075.2, 2000 CPD ¶ 263 (agency required to identify missing information and information it did not understand); and *Mechanical Contractors, S.A.*, Comp. Gen. Dec. B-277916.2, 98-1 CPD ¶ 68 (perceived informational gaps in proposal). Since it is frequently difficult to determine whether an informational deficiency is due to lack of clear guidance in the RFP, contracting officers should normally point out such deficiencies during discussions.

Inadequate discussions have also been found when the agency needs additional information to fully evaluate an offeror's proposal. See *Tiger Truck, LLC*, Comp. Gen. Dec. B-400685, 2009 CPD ¶ 19 (agency failed to obtain sufficient information to determine whether offered product complied with the Trade Agreements Act); *Cogent Sys., Inc.*, Comp. Gen. Dec. B-295990.4, 2005 CPD ¶ 179 (agency failed to seek information on whether product met requirements); and *Cotton & Co. LLP*, Comp. Gen. Dec. B-282808, 99-2 CPD ¶ 48 (agency did not clear up issues where it was clear protester misunderstood solicitation).

When the solicitation contains a clear requirement for information, the agency has a very low disclosure requirement in the negotiation process. See, for example, *Wade Perrow Constr.*, Comp. Gen. Dec. B-255332.2, 94-1 CPD ¶ 266, finding no requirement to identify missing information when Section L of the RFP contained a clear requirement for the information. See also *Trajen, Inc.*, Comp. Gen. Dec. B-296334, 2005 CPD ¶ 153, finding adequate discussions when the agency requested the submission of information already required by the RFP. Compare *Burchick Constr. Co.*, Comp. Gen. Dec. B-400342, 2008 CPD ¶ 203, sustaining a protest where the agency did not discuss weaknesses in a technical proposal that were based on inadequate information that was required by the RFP. GAO reasoned that the informational deficiencies were significant weaknesses that could have been corrected if the protester had been informed of them.

Agencies have also been required to conduct discussions in order to ascertain whether an offeror is submitting an alternate proposal, *Peirce-Phelps, Inc.*, Comp. Gen. Dec. B-238520.2, 91-1 CPD ¶ 385.

[3] Capability Information

Prior to the December 2001 revision, FAR 15.306(d)(3) required discussion of adverse past performance information only if it was a "significant weakness" or a "deficiency." This led to GAO denying protests of lack of discussion of such information, *Digital Sys. Grp., Inc.*, Comp. Gen. Dec. B-286931, 2001 CPD ¶ 50 ("marginal" ratings); *ITT Fed. Servs. Int'l Corp.*, Comp. Gen. Dec. B-283307, 99-2 CPD ¶ 76 ("good" rating). The Court of Federal Claims followed this reasoning and permitted very limited discussions of past performance issues, *JWK Int'l Corp. v. United States*, 49 Fed. Cl. 371 (2001), *aff'd*, 279 F.3d 985 (2002) (sufficient discussion when contracting officer identified an "unsatisfactory" rating in a "discussion letter").

In contrast, the current FAR requires that, to the extent that past performance information has not been discussed with an offeror prior to establishing the competitive range, negotiations must address adverse past performance information to which the offeror has not previously had an opportunity to comment, FAR 15.306(b)(3). Once such a discussion occurs, the agency must follow the requirement that meaningful discussions be held with all offerors in the competitive range, *Gulf Copper Ship Repair, Inc.*, Comp. Gen. Dec. B-293706.5, 2005 CPD ¶ 108. However, some decisions have still held that past performance need not be discussed if it is not considered a deficiency or significant weakness, *REO Sol., LLC v. United States*, 125 Fed. Cl. 659 (2016) (fair/some confidence rating); *Wolf Creek Fed. Servs., Inc.*, Comp. Gen. Dec. B-409187, 2014 CPD ¶ 61 (neutral rating).

Discussions have been found inadequate where the agency did not inform the offeror of adverse past performance information, *Precision Asset Mgmt. Corp. v. United States*, 135 Fed. Cl. 342 (2017) (neutral rating that impacted selection decision); *Q Integrated Cos., LLC v. United States*, 126 Fed. Cl. 124 (2016) (rating that work was not relevant); and *DynCorp Int'l, LLC*, Comp. Gen. Dec. B-409874.2, 2016 CPD ¶ 348 (rejecting argument that an agency need not discuss past performance information known to agency personnel). Compare *JWK Int'l Corp. v. United States*, 49 Fed. Cl. 371 (2001), *aff'd*, 279 F.3d 985 (2002) (an "unsatisfactory" rating was identified in a discussion letter); and *Davies Rail & Mech. Works, Inc.*, Comp. Gen. Dec. B-283911.2, 2000 CPD ¶ 48 (past problems were listed in a discussion letter).

When a contractor has had an opportunity to address past performance issues, no additional discussion of adverse past performance information is necessary. Thus, if the past performance has been dealt with in a CPARS report, it need not be addressed during discussions, *L-3 Army Sustainment LLC*, Comp. Gen. Dec. B-415349.2, 2018 CPD ¶ 13; *Erickson Helicopters, Inc.*, Comp. Gen. Dec. B-409903, 2014 CPD ¶ 288. See also *Stateside Assocs., Inc.*, Comp. Gen. Dec. B-400670.2, 2009 CPD ¶ 120 (adverse performance had been addressed during performance of task orders); *Del-Jen Int'l Corp.*, Comp. Gen. Dec. B-297960, 2006 CPD ¶ 81 (adverse performance had been addressed during contract administration); *PharmChem, Inc.*, Comp. Gen. Dec. B-292408.2, 2004 CPD ¶ 60 (adverse performance had been addressed during contract administration). Neither is there a requirement to discuss such information when it was not material in deciding not to award to the company. See *Standard Commc'ns, Inc.*, Comp. Gen. Dec. B-296972, 2005 CPD ¶ 200 (no requirement to discuss relevance of information when it is clear to the agency); *Maytag Aircraft Corp.*, Comp. Gen. Dec. B-287589, 2001 CPD ¶ 121 (discussions would not have changed the facts); *Digital Sys. Grp., Inc.*, Comp. Gen. Dec. B-286931, 2001 CPD ¶ 50 (marginal ratings would not have enhanced potential for award); *ABIC, Ltd.*, Comp. Gen. Dec. B-286460, 2001 CPD ¶ 46 (low ratings were not the determinative factor in eliminating protester from competitive range); *ITT*

Fed. Servs. Int'l Corp., Comp. Gen. Dec. B-283307, 99-2 CPD ¶ 76 ("good" ratings were not significant weaknesses).

When the offeror is told of adverse past performance information, the agency may not reveal the names of individuals providing the adverse information, FAR 15.306(e)(4). This prohibition does not appear to preclude revealing the name of the contractor or government agency from whom the information was obtained or the contract or project that the information relates to, and indeed, such information would be necessary in order to permit the offeror to provide its comments rebutting the information or explaining the steps that it had taken to ensure that the problem would not recur.

When capability is being assessed by requiring a technical proposal to demonstrate understanding of the work required to meet the agency's needs, the requirement for identification of a deficiency is reduced. See *ITT Fed. Sys. Int'l Corp.*, Comp. Gen. Dec. B-285176.4, 2001 CPD ¶ 45, stating:

> [T]he requirement for meaningful discussions does not require [giving] the offeror the opportunity to learn each and every weakness associated with its proposal during discussions, particularly whereas here one aspect of the evaluation was to test the offerors' technical understanding.

[4] Cost and Price Negotiations

Under the pre-Rewrite FAR, there was a hesitancy on the part of some agencies to conduct meaningful cost or price negotiations. This was caused partly by the admonition in pre-Rewrite FAR 15.610(e)(2) that the contracting officer not use "auction techniques," which were broadly defined.

The Rewrite replaced the prohibition of auction techniques with the following language in FAR 15.306(e):

> Government personnel engaged in the acquisition shall not engage in conduct that—
>
> (3) Reveals an offeror's price without that offeror's permission. However, the contracting officer may inform an offeror that its price is considered by the Government to be too high, or too low, and reveal the results of the analysis supporting that conclusion. It is also permissible, at the Government's discretion, to indicate to all offerors the cost or price that the Government's price analysis, market research, and other reviews have identified as reasonable (41 U.S.C. 423(h)(1)(2)).

In addition, FAR 15.306(d)(3) includes cost and price among examples of "other aspects of [a] proposal" which might be enhanced through negotiations. Thus, the FAR now permits full price negotiation with each offeror in the competitive range. The best guidance has been issued by NASA in NFS 1815.306, stating:

> (d)(3)(A) The contracting officer shall identify any cost/price elements that do not appear to be justified and encourage offerors to submit their most favorable and realistic cost/price proposals, but shall not discuss, disclose, or compare cost/price elements of any other offeror. The contracting officer shall question inadequate, conflicting, unrealistic, or unsupported cost information; differences between the offeror's proposal and most probable cost assessments; cost realism concerns; differences between audit findings and proposed costs; proposed rates that are too high/low; and labor mixes that do not appear responsive to the requirements. No agreement on cost/price elements or a "bottom line" is necessary.

See *MCT JV*, Comp. Gen. Dec. B-311245.2, 2008 CPD ¶ 121, holding that the agency was required to indicate to the protester that there was a significant disparity between the allocation of the labor hours in its cost and technical proposals. Compare *Metro Mach. Corp.*, Comp. Gen. Dec. B-295744, 2005 CPD ¶ 112, where an adequate discussion occurred when the agency asked for an explanation of the proposed labor rates without telling the protester that it concluded they were unrealistically low, and *Engineering Servs. Unlimited, Inc.*, Comp. Gen. Dec. B-291275, 2003 CPD ¶ 15, where no violation of the FAR was found when the agency told the protester that its labor rates were significantly lower than incumbent rates.

Agencies must disclose unreasonably high prices in discussions, *Veterans Evaluation Servs., Inc.*, Comp. Gen. Dec. B-412940, 2016 CPD ¶ 185; *Gas Turbine Engines, Inc.*, Comp. Gen. Dec. B-401868.2, 2009 CPD ¶ 257; *Tiger Truck, LLC*, Comp. Gen. Dec. B-400685, 2009 CPD ¶ 19; *Creative Info. Tech.*, Inc., Comp. Gen. Dec. B-293073.10, 2005 CPD ¶ 110. However, GAO has not required agencies to discuss price with offerors whose prices are not "unreasonably" high (even though they are considerably higher than other prices or government estimate). See *Mainstream Engr' g Corp.*, Comp. Gen. Dec. B-415524, 2018 CPD ¶ 90 (price approximately 22% higher than government estimate); *Southeastern Kidney Council*, Comp. Gen. Dec. B-412538, 2016 CPD ¶ 90 (price approximately 32% higher than winning offeror); *DB Consulting Grp.. Inc.*, Comp. Gen. Dec. B-401543.2, 2010 CPD ¶ 109 (price approximately 40% higher than winning offeror); *Integrated Concepts & Research Corp.*, Comp. Gen. Dec. B-309803, 2008 CPD ¶ 117 (estimated cost of sample task triple that of competitor due to different solution); *DeTekion Sec. Sys., Inc.*, Comp. Gen. Dec. B-298235, 2006 CPD ¶ 130 (price 22% higher than winning offeror); *MarLaw-Arco MFPD Mgmt.*, Comp. Gen. Dec. B-291875, 2003 CPD ¶ 85 (although price was "significantly" higher than awardee, it was "reasonable" and only somewhat higher than government estimate); *Hydraulics Int'l, Inc.*, Comp. Gen. Dec. B-284684, 2000 CPD ¶ 149 (although price was 70% higher than winning offeror, it was not "inherently unreasonable" when the technical proposal was considered). In other cases, very limited discussion of a high price have been held to be sufficient, *WorldTravelService*, Comp. Gen. Dec. B-284155.3, 2001 CPD ¶ 68 (protester told that is should "take a look" at its prices because they were "way too high"); *Wackenhut Int'l, Inc.*, Comp. Gen. Dec. B-286193, 2001 CPD ¶ 8 (suggestion that protester "revise its price to make it more favorable"); *WinStar Fed. Servs.*, Comp. Gen. Dec. B-284617, 2000 CPD ¶ 92 (protester told to "review sharpening [its] pencil" and that numerous prices "significantly exceed" the government's estimate).

The Court of Federal Claims has followed GAO reasoning on this issue. See *Tech Sys., Inc.*, 98 Fed. Cl. 228 (2011), holding that there was no requirement to discuss a high price that was not unreasonably high even though it was the sole basis for the award decision. See also *Lyon Shipyard, Inc. v. United States*, 113 Fed. Cl. 347 (2013), reaching the same conclusion but stating that an agency was required to discuss a price that would preclude award to the firm. Compare *WorldTravelService v. United States*, 49 Fed. Cl. 431 (2001), holding that an agency must disclose during discussions that it has concluded that a price is "too high." The court made it clear, however, that there was no requirement to tell the offeror how much it was too high.

In spite of the failure to make discussion of a high price mandatory, agencies are permitted to attempt to get lower prices by telling an offeror that its price is high compared to other prices, *Bannum, Inc.*, Comp. Gen. Dec. B-298235, 2014 CPD ¶ 232; *DeTekion Sec. Sys., Inc.*, Comp. Gen. Dec. B-298235, 2006 CPD ¶ 130.

Neither has GAO required that offerors be specifically told that their price was unrealistically low as long as they were informed that the agency was looking at this issue. See *SEEMA, Inc.*, Comp. Gen. Dec. B-277988, 98-1 CPD ¶ 12, denying a protest where the agency did not tell the protester that its price was considered unrealistic but told it that its price was significantly below the government estimate and not supported by the cost-savings data included in its proposal. Compare *Robinson's Lawn Servs., Inc.*, Comp. Gen. Dec. B-299551.5, 2009 CPD ¶ 45, denying a protest that the price discussions had induced the protester to raise its prices resulting in loss of the competition where the agency told both offerors that their prices were unrealistically low. In contrast, in *Advanced Sys. Dev., Inc.*, Comp. Gen. Dec. B-298411, 2006 CPD ¶ 137, GAO held that an unfair discussion had occurred when the agency induced a competitor to lower its price by not disclosing that it corrected an error to raise the price and telling the competitor that its price violated a price target—resulting in award to the competitor.

[5] Sample Tasks

An agency may limit discussions of a deficiency when the deficient score relates to the offeror's general understanding of the technical aspects of the work as demonstrated by its submission of a solution to a sample task, *Veteran Tech. Partners III, LLC*, Comp. Gen. Dec. B-418461.13, 2021 CPD ¶ 145. In *Technology Applications, Inc.*, Comp. Gen. Dec. B-238259, 90-1 CPD ¶ 451, GAO stated:

> Where an offeror's responses to sample tasks are used to test its understanding of the technical requirements of a contemplated contract, as opposed to being used to evaluate the adequacy of its technical approach to the contract work, an agency need not specify during discussions all identified deficiencies in the offeror's approach to the tasks.

GAO reasoned that if the purpose of the task is to determine whether the offeror has the background and understanding to identify and resolve the technical issues that would arise during contract performance, to require the agency to discuss weak sample task results would defeat the purpose of using the response to a sample task to determine the offeror's understanding of the work. See also *Mevacon-NASCO JV*, Comp. Gen. Dec. B-414329, 2017 CPD ¶ 144 (no need to discuss detailed errors in sample problem); *Fluor Daniel, Inc.*, Comp. Gen. Dec. B-262051, 95-2 CPD ¶ 241 (no need to discuss weakness in "limited scenario"); *Delany, Siegel, Zorn & Assocs., Inc.*, Comp. Gen. Dec. B-258221.2, 95-2 CPD ¶ 7 (no need to discuss "sample report"); and *NDI Eng'g Co.*, Comp. Gen. Dec. B-245796, 92-1 CPD ¶ 113 (no need to discuss low scores on responses to a sample task). In *MCR Fed., Inc.*, Comp. Gen. Dec. B-280969, 99-1 CPD ¶ 8, GAO found no requirement to discuss an "acceptable" sample task rating when the agency had discussed a "marginal" sample task rating with the winning offeror.

Although discussions of sample task responses are not generally required, an agency may open discussions in order to better understand the response. However, if that occurs, the discussions must be meaningful. See *Integrated Concepts & Research Corp.*, Comp. Gen. Dec. B-309803, 2008 CPD ¶ 117 (informing offeror that amount of labor in sample task appeared high sufficient to alert protester that its price was high); *Serco, Inc.*, Comp. Gen. Dec. B-298266, 2006 CPD ¶ 120 (discussions elicited more information from offerors but agency misused information in evaluation process); *Delphinus Eng'g, Inc.*, Comp. Gen. Dec. B-298266, 2006 CPD ¶ 7 (discussions requested explanation of low price but protester provided in explanation in final proposal revision); *American Sys. Corp.*, Comp. Gen. Dec. B-292755, 2003 CPD ¶ 225 (evaluation notice sufficient to alert protester to issues even though it was misunderstood).

[6] Product Demonstrations

When the agency requires offerors to demonstrate their product as part of the evaluation and then conducts discussions with the offerors still in the competitive range, it must discuss any perceived weaknesses revealed in the demonstration. In *Apptis, Inc.*, Comp. Gen. Dec. B-299457, 2008 CPD ¶ 49, the agency claimed that there was no such requirement because the demonstration revealed difficulty in using the product which could not be corrected (arguing that the sample task reasoning applied). GAO rejected this argument, stating:

> [E]ven though Apptis could not change the events that transpired at its . . . demonstration, the agency was nevertheless required to point out the weaknesses it observed and provide the firm with an opportunity to address them. Thus, for example, Apptis's discussion responses and/or FPR could have refuted the agency's purported observations, provided explanations as to why the events occurred, or proposed methods by which to address the agency's associated concerns.

Compare *Cerner Corp.*, Comp. Gen. Dec. B-293093, 2004 CPD ¶ 34, holding that there was no requirement that a contractor be advised that its product used an approach that was considered to be less effective than a competing product, and *SeaArk Marine, Inc.*, Comp. Gen. Dec. B-292195, 2003 CPD ¶ 108, holding that there was no requirement for discussions after a product demonstration when the RFP precluded such discussions.

[7] Correction of Mistakes

Prior to the FAR Rewrite, most mistakes in proposals were corrected during oral or written discussions. See pre-Rewrite FAR 15.607(c). The Rewrite deleted this guidance and covers mistakes in a very cursory way, mentioning only that minor or clerical errors may be resolved through clarifications and discussions may be held prior to establishing a competitive range with offerors whose exclusion or inclusion in the competitive range is uncertain. The FAR is silent on correction of mistakes during negotiations, but it seems apparent that the contracting officer should notify offerors of suspected mistakes if they have not been identified previously.

Correcting a mistake is often a discussion "unless the mistake is minor and both the existence of the mistake and what was actually intended are clearly apparent from the face of the proposal, *Pioneering Evolution, LLC*, Comp. Gen. Dec. B-412016, 2015 CPD ¶ 385; *ManTech Advanced Sys. Int'l v. United States*, 141 Fed. Cl. 493 (2019); *DynCorp Int'l LLC v. United States*, 76 Fed. Cl. 528 (2007). However, if the contracting officer perceives a clear mistake, where what was actually intended is clearly apparent in a final proposal revision, it is proper to allow its correction without reopening discussions, *EMS Ice, Inc.*, Comp. Gen. Dec. B-401688.3, 2009 CPD ¶ 211.

If a contracting officer perceives a possible mistake in a proposal, it is proper to include that offeror in the competitive range in order to correct the mistake through discussions, *KSC BOSS Alliance, LLC*, Comp. Gen. Dec. B-416334, 2018 CPD ¶ 267. However, no GAO decisions indicate that an offeror must be included in the competitive range for the purpose of dealing with a perceived mistake. In contrast, the Court of Federal Claims held in *Level 3 Commc'ns, LLC v. United States*, 129 Fed. Cl. 487 (2016), that it was an abuse of discretion not to hold a discussion to clear up a minor error when the protester's price was substantially lower than that of the awardee.

If an offeror is included in the competitive range, good practice would require that all mistakes be identified. A few pre-FAR Rewrite decisions required this practice, *Analytical & Research Tech., Inc. v. United States*, 39 Fed. Cl. 34 (1997). See also *Fidelity Techs. Corp.*, Comp. Gen. Dec. B-276425, 97-1 CPD ¶ 197, sustaining a protest where the protester's proposal included an apparently erroneous, small, disadvantaged business (SDB) certification and the contracting officer failed to provide the protester an opportunity to correct it. See also *American Mgmt. Sys., Inc.*, Comp. Gen. Dec. B-215283, 84-2 CPD ¶ 199, sustaining a protest where the offeror's proposal indicated a unit charge for tape storage of $2.50 per tape per day in one area and $2.50 per tape per year in another and the contracting officer failed to resolve the discrepancy during discussions. Similarly, in *Dep't of the Air Force*, 67 Comp. Gen. 372 (B-229059.2), 88-1 CPD ¶ 357, GAO modified its recommendation of an earlier opinion, admitting that it had overlooked the fact that a contracting officer had failed to clarify or correct a significant price error in one offeror's BAFO that increased the offered price significantly. In the earlier opinion, *Centel Bus. Sys.*, 67 Comp. Gen. 156 (B-229059), 87-2 CPD ¶ 629, GAO sustained the protest and recommended that the offer be reevaluated as if the protester had not made the error. Compare *Contel Info. Sys., Inc.*, Comp. Gen. Dec. B-220215, 86-1 CPD ¶ 44, finding that an agency had no obligation to correct a mistake that was the fault of the offeror and could not be easily detected by the contracting officer.

[C] Conduct of Negotiations

Contracting agencies have broad discretion in conducting negotiations. See FAR 15.306(d)(3) stating that "the scope and extent of discussions are a matter of contracting officer judgment." However, within this discretion, negotiations must be meaningful and must be conducted in a way that offerors are treated fairly. See *International Dev. Grp. Advisory Servs., LLC*, Comp. Gen. Dec. B-416551, 2018 CPD ¶ 358, stating that "discussions must be meaningful, equitable, and not misleading." GAO has also stated that discussions must fairly and reasonably lead an offeror into areas of its offer "requiring amplification or revision, *L-3 Army Sustainment, LLC*, Comp. Gen. Dec. B-415349.2, 2018 CPD ¶ 13. Compare *LOGC2, Inc.*, Comp. Gen. Dec. B-416075, 2018 CPD ¶ 204, stating:

> All-encompassing discussions are not required, nor is the agency obligated to "spoon-feed" an offeror as to each and every item that could be revised to improve its proposal; an agency is not required to advise an offeror of a minor weakness that is not considered significant, even where the weakness subsequently becomes a determinative factor in choosing between two closely ranked proposals. See *Vizada Inc.*, B-405251 et al., Oct. 5, 2011, 2011 CPD ¶ 235 at 11.

Thus, if an agency discusses a deficiency in one aspect of a proposal, it is not required to identify that same deficiency in another part of the proposal, *Olgoonik Logistics, LLC*, Comp. Gen. Dec. B-415569, 2018 CPD ¶ 36; *AdvanceMed Corp.*, Comp. Gen. Dec. B-415360, 2018 CPD ¶ 4.

The rules regarding discussions apply throughout the negotiation process. Thus, if a reevaluation of a proposal after submission of proposal revisions identified a deficiency that was not found in the initial evaluation, that deficiency must be identified in additional discussions, *Innovative Pathways, LLC*, Comp. Gen. Dec. B-416100.2, 2018 CPD ¶ 212; *Veterans Evaluation Servs., Inc.*, Comp. Gen. Dec. B-412940, 2016 CPD ¶ 185.

However, agencies are not required to reopen discussions with regard to deficiencies and weaknesses that first appear in a proposal revision, *iAccess Techs., Inc. v. United States*, 143 Fed. Cl. 521 (2019); *Leader Communications, Inc.*, Comp. Gen. Dec. B-417152.2, 2019 CPD ¶ 241; *Tele-Consultants, Inc. v. United States*, 142 Fed. Cl. 686 (2019); *LOGC2, Inc.*, Comp. Gen. Dec. B-416075, 2018 CPD ¶ 204; *Iron Bow Techs., LLC v. United States*, 133 Fed. Cl. 764 (2017).

[1] Form of Negotiations

The descriptions in FAR 15.306(d) of negotiation as including bargaining and in FAR 15.307(b) of negotiating until the parties reach understanding make it clear that the FAR Councils believed that discussions would include more exchanges where the contracting officer and the offeror conduct negotiations until they reach an understanding of the best offer that each offeror can make. However, it does not appear from the description in protest decisions that this has occurred. Rather, there continue to be numerous instances of pro forma discussions where the agency merely sends offerors a list of deficiencies and significant weaknesses. While it is doubtful whether this type of negotiation is a satisfactory communication device, it has not been questioned by either GAO or the Court of Federal Claims. See, for example, *Fort Carson Support Servs. v. United States*, 71 Fed. Cl. 571 (2006), finding a list of discussion questions designated either "weaknesses" or "deficiencies" adequate to inform protester of areas to be addressed in its final proposal revisions. See also *Kerr Contractors, Inc. v. United States*, 89 Fed. Cl. 312 (2009) (discussion letters sent to all offerors); *DRS C3 Sys., LLC*, Comp. Gen. Dec. B-310825, 2008 CPD ¶ 103 (letter listing "discussion questions" and calling for written response); *Korrect Optical, Inc.*, Comp. Gen. Dec. B-288128, 2001 CPD ¶ 171 (letter with list of "significant deficiencies"); *Interstate Elec. Corp.*, Comp. Gen. Dec. B-286466, 2001 CPD ¶ 29 (telecopied "evaluation notices" identifying specific concerns); and *Davies Rail & Mech. Works, Inc.*, Comp. Gen. Dec. B-283911.2, 2000 CPD ¶ 48 (letter with list of "deficiencies and weaknesses"). See also *KPMG Peat Marwick*, Comp. Gen. Dec. B-258990, 95-1 CPD ¶ 116, holding that there was no requirement that the agency conduct face-to-face discussions in addition to, or in lieu of, written discussions; and *Austin Elecs.*, 54 Comp. Gen. 60 (B-180690), 74-2 CPD ¶ 61, rejecting the protester's assertion that the agency was required to conduct give-and-take oral discussions.

The DoD Source Selection Procedures describes the discussion process at 3.4.3:

> This is accomplished through the release of Evaluation Notices (ENs). ENs are prepared by the SSEB and reviewed by the PCO and Legal Council. All ENs shall clearly indicate the type of exchange being conducted (*e.g.* clarification, communication, etc.). Any EN addressing a proposal deficiency or weakness shall clearly indicate that a deficiency/weakness exists.

In spite of the numerous decisions permitting written discussions, it is doubtful that this procedure is an adequate form of communication when there are significant deficiencies or weaknesses. See *Logistic Sys., Inc.*, 59 Comp. Gen. 548 (B-196254), 80-1 CPD ¶ 442, finding that there had been inadequate communication of the deficiencies when the agency sent the offeror an elaborate list of deficiencies and conducted no oral discussions. See also *Hughes STX Corp.*, Comp. Gen. Dec. B-278466, 98-1 CPD ¶ 52, where very brief written discussion questions were held to have misled the offeror as to the level of concern the agency had as to the realism of the proposed labor costs, and *Gas Turbine Engines, Inc.*, Comp. Gen. Dec. B-401868.2, 2009 CPD ¶ 257, criticizing the agency for sending the same form letter to each offeror in the competitive range.

Oral discussions can be held over the telephone, Comp. Gen. Dec. B-157156, Nov. 8, 1965, *Unpub.*, by teleconference, *ITT Corp., Sys. Div.*, Comp. Gen. Dec. B-310102.6, 2010 CPD ¶ 12, or in a face-to-face meeting. However, meetings are appropriate in major procurements where there are significant deficiencies or weaknesses. The information conveyed orally should be carefully documented to ensure that the offeror fully understands the issue. See *New Jersey & H St., LLC*, Comp. Gen. Dec. B-311314.3, 2008 CPD ¶ 133, sustaining a protest when the protester asserted that it had never been told of a weakness that the agency claimed it had disclosed. When meetings are held, there is no requirement that agreement be reached on each issue, 52 Comp. Gen. 161 (B-176223) (1972).

[2] Meaningful Negotiations

The FAR Rewrite emphasizes that negotiations with each offeror in the competitive range includes bargaining to obtain the best offer. Thus, FAR 15.306(d)(4) permits bargaining about the optimum technical solution that can be offered by each offeror as well as price and the terms and conditions of the contract. Furthermore, FAR 15.307(b) implies that negotiations will be conducted to reach "understandings." The goal is clearly to encourage agencies to conduct in-depth negotiations to fulfill the obligation to conduct meaningful negotiations.

Prior to the FAR Rewrite the emphasis was on *the minimum standards* that a contracting officer had to meet to conduct meaningful negotiations. In *Boeing Sikorsky Aircraft Support*, Comp. Gen. Dec. B-277263.3, 97-2 CPD ¶ 91, GAO made the following observations concerning meaningful negotiations:

> Discussions cannot be meaningful unless they lead an offeror into those aspects of its proposal that must be addressed in order for it to have a reasonable chance of being selected for award, and afford an offeror an opportunity to revise its proposal to satisfy the government's requirements. *Global Indus., Inc.*, B-270592.2 et al, Mar. 29, 1996, 96-2 CPD ¶ 85 at 4-5; *Stone & Webster Eng'g Corp.*, B-255286.2, Apr. 12, 1994, 94-1 CPD ¶ 306 at 10-11. An agency may not consciously coerce or mislead an offeror during discussions (see *Eagle Tech., Inc.*, B-236255, Nov. 16, 1989, 89-2 CPD ¶ 468 at 3-4), nor may it inadvertently mislead an offeror through the framing of discussion questions into responding in a manner that does not address the agency's concerns. *Peckham Vocational Indus., Inc.*, B-257100, Aug. 26, 1994, 94-2 CPD ¶ 81 at 6.

[a] Specific Identification

When an agency decides to negotiate with the offerors in the competitive range, it is good practice to specifically identify any issue that could be addressed to improve a competitor's chance for award. However, that does not require an agency to "identify each and every flaw" in a proposal, *Active Network, LLC v. United States*, 130 Fed. Cl. 421 (2017).

Nonetheless, vague statements that do not identify a specific issue have been held to be inadequate discussions. See *AMEC Earth & Envtl., Inc.*, Comp. Gen. Dec. B-401961, 2010 CPD ¶ 151 (asking questions about functions of software did not indicate that agency had determined software was inadequate for job); *AINS, Inc.*, Comp. Gen. Dec. B-400760.4, 2010 CPD ¶ 32 (request for new schedule did not convey agency concern that proposed schedule was too aggressive); *New Jersey & H St., LLC*, Comp. Gen. Dec. B-311314.3, 2008 CPD ¶ 133 (general statement to all competitors that evaluation factor was important but no indication to protester of specific issues with its compliance); *AT&T Corp.*, Comp. Gen. Dec. B-299542.3, 2008 CPD ¶ 65 (reference to lack of information on staffing plan but no indication that agency believed it contained too few personnel); *Creative Info. Tech., Inc.*, Comp. Gen. Dec. B-293073.10, 2005 CPD ¶ 110 (agency's statement that price was "overstated" did not inform protester that it had grossly overestimated the level of effort anticipated by the agency); *Lockheed Martin Simulation, Training & Support*, Comp. Gen. Dec. B-292836.8, 2005 CPD ¶ 27 (statement that protester was responsible for making proposal "responsive, clear and accurate" and that responses should be "strategic, not just tactical" insufficient to alert protester to specific weaknesses). In *Advanced Sys. Dev., Inc.*, Comp. Gen. Dec. B-298411, 2006 CPD ¶137, the agency's statement that the offeror had violated the RFP's price target led the protested to reduce its price when the agency's concern was that the price was too low. GAO sustained the protest after the protester had been awarded the contract at the low price.

GAO has also stated that, in general, once discussions are opened, the agency is required to point out all deficiencies in the offeror's proposal, not merely selected areas. See *Multimax, Inc.*, Comp. Gen. Dec. B-298249.6, 2006 CPD ¶165, where offerors were misled when the agency identified some labor rates as high but did not identify other labor rates that were also high.

When a competitive range offeror's proposal indicates that it does not understand the evaluation scheme, the agency must raise this issue, *Lockheed Martin Corp.*, Comp. Gen. Dec. B-293679, 2004 CPD ¶115. There the agency did not inform the protester that it had rejected proposed manufacturing cost savings if a product the protester was proposing to design was manufactured in its facilities because it planned to compete the production work.

[b] Lack of Identification Excused

In a number of cases, factors surrounding a procurement have been found to excuse the agency from specifically identifying areas where offers should be amplified or changed. However, it is better practice for agencies to err on the side of greater communication rather than relying on these rulings to win a protest.

A lack of specific identification will not be fatal if the offeror has been given sufficient information to provide notice of the deficiency. See *Greenland Contrs. v. United States*, 131 Fed. Cl. 216 (2017) (discussion of one high priced CLIN sufficient when other CLIN prices were high but reasonable); *Cedge Software Consultants, LLC v. United States*, 117 Fed. Cl. 419 (2014) (tailored discussion sufficient when issue was complex); *Kerr Contractors, Inc. v. United States*, 89 Fed. Cl. 312 (2009) (asking protester to address "risk" of work at proposed level sufficient to indicate that agency considered level too low); *Academy Facilities Mgmt. v. United States*, 87 Fed. Cl. 441 (2009) (use of term "overstated" when price appeared high and "significantly overstated" when price appeared both high and unbalanced was sufficient indication of government concerns); *SelectTech Bering Straits Solutions JV*, Comp. Gen. Dec. B-400964, 2009 CPD ¶100 (statement that staffing levels were low sufficient without identifying that only some were low and others were high); *New Breed, Inc.*, Comp. Gen. Dec. B-400554, 2009 CPD ¶4 (no requirement to identify specific weaknesses when protester told that its risk management and quality control plans were weak); *Karrar Sys. Corp.*, Comp. Gen. Dec. B-310661, 2008 CPD ¶51 (request to confirm that prices were based on RFP data sufficient to indicate that prices were considered high); *Mechanical Equip. Co.*, Comp. Gen. Dec. B-292789.2, 2004 CPD ¶192 (statement that manning was "inadequate" sufficient without indicating how low the estimate was); *Hanford Envtl. Health Found.*, Comp. Gen. Dec. B-292858.2, 2004 CPD ¶ 164 (no need to tell protester staffing was considered high when agency told it to more effectively describe staffing); *T-L-C Sys.*, Comp. Gen. Dec. B-287452, 2001 CPD ¶ 106 (general warning that proposal did not meet RFP requirement for full documentation sufficient to alert protester to lack of clarity of product literature); *J.A. Jones/Bell, J.V.*, Comp. Gen. Dec. B-286458, 2001 CPS ¶ 17 (request for reasoning to support use of technique sufficient to indicate that agency was critical of technique); and *Information Network Sys., Inc.*, Comp. Gen. Dec. B-284854, 2000 CPD ¶ 104 (question as to adequacy of labor rates sufficient to indicate concern with workforce retention risk).

[3] Reaching Agreement on Final Proposals

In adopting the term "negotiations" to describe the discussion process, the FAR Rewrite appears to have embraced the concept that negotiations should result in agreement between the parties as to the final proposal that will be submitted by the offeror. Thus, FAR 15.307(b) calls for proposal revisions to "document understandings reached during negotiations." FAR 15.001 amplifies this concept with the following definition:

> Proposal revision is a change to a proposal made after the solicitation closing date, at the request of or as allowed by a contracting officer, as the result of negotiations.

This concept was adopted by the Army in *Contracting for Best Value: A Best Practices Guide to Source Selection*, AMC-P 715-3 (Jan. 1, 1998), which stated:

> During discussions, our objective should be to reach complete agreement between and understanding by the Government and the offeror regarding all of the basic requirements in the solicitation. In essence, obtaining a contract that demonstrates the greatest promise of meeting the solicitation's requirements and no surprises after award is the goal of both the Government and the offeror.

Similar guidance was contained in NFS 1815.306(d)(3) (pre-2004 version):

> (B) The contracting officer shall discuss contract terms and conditions so that a "model" contract can be sent to each offeror with the request for final proposal revisions. If the solicitation allows, any proposed technical performance capabilities above those specified in the RFP that have value to the Government and are considered proposal strengths should be discussed with the offeror and proposed for inclusion in that offeror's "model" contract. These items are not to be discussed with, or proposed to, other offerors. If

the offeror declines to include these strengths in its "model" contract, the Government evaluators should reconsider their characterization as strengths.

The goal of reaching agreement with each competing offeror during the negotiation places a significant burden on the contracting officer because such "agreements" cannot guarantee to any offeror that it will win the competition. During negotiations of this type, the agency personnel must work with each offeror to assist it to make the best offer it is capable of but, at the same time, must alert each offeror to the fact that the ultimate selection decision will be based on analysis of the relative merits of the competing offers. Throughout such negotiations, the offerors must be treated in an evenhanded fashion with regard to the information revealed. Furthermore, agency personnel must exercise great care not to reveal elements of one offer to any other offeror.

Care must be exercised to ensure that interim revisions to offers are documented in writing and are understood to supersede the original offer. See *CCL, Inc.*, Comp. Gen. Dec. B-251527, 93-1 CPD ¶ 354, *recons. denied*, 93-2 CPD ¶ 178, ruling that although revised prices submitted by an offeror during negotiations revoked the original offer, they were not new offers that served the purpose of keeping the offer open for 60 days as called for by the Standard Form 33 cover sheet of the original offer. GAO reached this conclusion because the letter submitting the revised prices contained no indication that the offeror intended to keep them open for 60 additional days.

[4] Fair Treatment of Offerors

Fair treatment of offerors is a cornerstone of effective competition. Thus, assuring that all offerors are treated fairly is a major concern when conducting negotiations. See FAR 1.102-2 stating:

> (1) An essential consideration in every aspect of the [Federal Acquisition] System is maintaining the public's trust. Not only must the System have integrity, but the actions of each member of the Team must reflect integrity, fairness, and openness. The foundation of integrity within the System is a competent, experienced, and well-trained, professional workforce. Accordingly, each member of the Team is responsible and accountable for the wise use of public resources as well as acting in a manner which maintains the public's trust. Fairness and openness require open communication among team members, internal and external customers, and the public.

GAO identified fairness during the discussion process as a fundamental requirement in 51 Comp. Gen. 621 (B-173677) (1972), stating at 622:

> [T]he statute [now 10 U.S.C. § 2305(b)(4)(A)] should not be interpreted in a manner which discriminates against or gives preferential treatment to any

competitor. Any discussion with competing offerors raises the question as to how to avoid unfairness and unequal treatment.

The Court of Federal Claims identified the fact that fairness continues to be an integral part of the negotiation/discussion process in *Dynacs Eng'g Co. v. United States*, 48 Fed. Cl. 124 (2000), where it found unfair discussions when, during reopened discussions, the agency identified "weaknesses" that had been identified in the first round of discussions, but not addressed, with one offeror but not with the protester.

[a] Even-handed Treatment

Fairness requires the agency to ensure that offerors compete on an equal basis. Thus, offerors must be treated even-handedly. One of the most common examples of lack of even-handed treatment is where the agency gives information to one or more offerors but fails to provide the same information to other offerors who might be able to use it to their advantage. See *Raytheon Co. v. United States*, 809 F.3d 590 (Fed. Cir. 2015) agreeing that an agency properly reopened a competition after it had advised only one of the offerors of its new interpretation of IR&D rules. See also *Kerr Contractors, Inc. v. United States*, 89 Fed. Cl. 312 (2009), noting that "agencies are not required to conduct identical discussions with each offeror" but rather they "should tailor discussions to each offeror's proposal."

Lack of fairness was found in *ManTech Advanced Sys. Int'l, Inc.*, Comp. Gen. Dec. B-416734, 2018 CPD ¶ 408 (agency assessed a weakness to protester but not awardee for same problem); *Progressive Indus., Inc.*, 129 Fed. Cl. 457 (2016) (agency allowed one offeror to improve its proposal before technical evaluations began); *Heritage Reporting Corp.*, Comp. Gen. Dec. B-409331.2, 2014 CPD ¶ 112 (agency discussed all weaknesses with other offerors but not protester); *Ashbury Int'l Group, Inc.*, Comp. Gen. Dec. B-401123, 2009 CPD ¶ 140 (improper to tell only one offeror that management plan should be submitted); *American K-9 Detection Servs., Inc.*, Comp. Gen. Dec. B-400464.6, 2009 CPD ¶ 107 (agency allowed one offeror to correct deficiency making proposal technically acceptable without telling protester that its option prices created a "performance risk"); *Boeing Co.*, Comp. Gen. Dec. B-311344, 2008 CPD ¶ 114 (in continuing discussions, agency told protester it had met requirement and did not reveal that it had altered this conclusion while continuing to work with competitor to ensure that it met the requirement); *Advanced Sys. Dev., Inc.*, Comp. Gen. Dec. B-298411, 2006 CPD ¶ 137 (agency induced competitor to lower its price by misleading discussions and then selected competitor based on low price); *Martin Elecs., Inc.*, Comp. Gen. Dec. B-290846.3, 2003 CPD ¶ 6 (agency discussed delivery deficiencies with only one offeror); and *TDS, Inc.*, Comp. Gen. Dec. B-292674, 2003 CPD ¶ 204 (agency gave two competitors far more detailed questions than those given protester).

The fairness requirement also applies when an agency takes corrective action after losing a protest. See *Centerra Grp., LLC v. United States*, 138 Fed. Cl. 407 (2018) (agency allowed the previously wining contractor to correct its proposal errors without giving the protester an opportunity to submit a revised proposal); *Excelsior Ambulance Serv., Inc. v. United States*, 124 Fed. Cl. 581 (2015) (agency allowed one offeror to rewrite its proposal which exceeded the scope of the corrective action).

While fairness requires even-handed treatment of offerors with similar deficiencies, it does not require the agency to spend an equal amount of time with all offerors, or to discuss the same areas. See FAR 15.306(d)(1) stating that discussions "are tailored to each offeror's proposal." The Court of Federal Claims has recognized that the content and extent of negotiations with each offeror will be determined by the extent of the issues raised by each proposal, *Lockheed Martin Corp. v. United States*, 124 Fed. Cl. 709 (2016). See *Lockheed Martin Corp.*, Comp. Gen. Dec. B-293679, 2004 CPD ¶ 115, where GAO responded to an agency evaluator's statement that he was told that, to be fair, he had to ask the same questions of each offeror by stating:

> This advice is directly contrary to the FAR, which provides that discussions should be "tailored to each offeror's proposal." FAR § 15.306(d)(1).

Thus, an agency may properly conduct "extensive discussions with offerors whose initial proposals contain technical deficiencies while conducting more limited discussions with offerors whose proposals contain fewer weaknesses or deficiencies," *Pacific Architects & Eng'rs, Inc.*, Comp. Gen. Dec. B-236432, 89-2 CPD ¶ 494, or afford those with technically acceptable proposals only an opportunity to submit a final proposal, *Weinschel Eng'g Co.*, 64 Comp. Gen. 524 (B-217202), 85-1 CPD ¶ 574. The agency may also reveal the government's cost estimate to an offeror proposing a cost considered too high without disclosing the estimate to an offeror submitting an acceptable proposed cost, *HP Enter. Servs., LLC*, Comp. Gen. Dec. B-413967, 2017 CPD ¶ 26. See also *Biospherics, Inc.*, Comp. Gen. Dec. B-285065, 2000 CPD ¶ 118, finding no unequal discussions where the agency discussed low price with one offeror but did not discuss high price with the protester, and *Ralph G. Moore & Assocs.*, Comp. Gen. Dec. B-270686, 96-1 CPD ¶ 118, holding that an agency did not conduct unequal discussions when it discussed the awardee's unreasonably low price and did not discuss the protester's reasonable price. See also *CSC Gov't Sols. LLC v. United States*, 129 Fed. Cl. 416 (2016) (continued discussion with protester not unfair when agency accepted competitor's adjusted hourly estimates); *PharmChem, Inc.*, Comp. Gen. Dec. B-291725.3, 2003 CPD ¶ 148 (clearing up role of one required employee proper when no such discussion was necessary with incumbent protester); and *WorldTravelService*, Comp. Gen. Dec. B-284155.3, 2001 CPD ¶ 68 (proper to identify technical deficiencies with one offeror only when the other offerors have no such deficiencies).

When the procurement is conducted on a low-price, technically acceptable basis, there is no requirement for discussion with an offeror that has submitted a technically acceptable proposal, *Commercial Design Grp., Inc.*, Comp. Gen. Dec. B-400923.4, 2009 CPD ¶ 157. GAO reasoned that there was no value in helping such an offeror improve its proposal.

Under the FAR Part 15 Rewrite the rules regarding fairness were somewhat altered. Thus, in *Synetics, Inc. v. United States*, 45 Fed. Cl. 1 (1999), the court ruled that it was fair to tell an offeror a precise way to improve its proposal, citing the removal of the prohibition of technical leveling in FAR 15.306(e) as well as the encouragement to "enhance materially the proposal's potential for award," in FAR 15.306(d)(3). See also *Mantech Telecomms. & Info. Sys. Corp. v. United States*, 49 Fed. Cl. 57 (2001), where the court held that it was fair to conduct multiple rounds of discussions, noting that the FAR Part 15 Rewrite had eliminated the limitations on multiple rounds as well as the prohibition of technical leveling.

[b] Misleading Negotiations

In addition to treating offerors even-handedly, an agency may not mislead an offeror during negotiations, *Raytheon Co.*, Comp. Gen. Dec. B-416211, 2018 CPD ¶ 262. In that case the discussions suggested Raytheon's approach to one issue was unsatisfactory inducing it to propose another approach which the agency downgraded. Other decision finding misleading discussions include *Shearwater Mission Support, LLC*, Comp. Gen. Dec. B-416717, 2018 CPD ¶ 402 (agency told protester some of its prices were unreasonably low without price realism statement in RFP); *Caddell Constr. Co. v. United States*, 125 Fed. Cl. 30 (2016) (agency told protester its price was higher than government estimate when it was lower); *EFW, Inc.*, Comp. Gen. Dec. B-412608, 2016 CPD ¶ 304 (agency addressed one element of work when it considered overall costs unrealistic); *Paragon Tech. Grp., Inc.*, Comp. Gen. Dec. B-412636, 2016 CPD ¶ 113 (agency told protester to remove "assumptions" about future pricing when it was concerned about low prices); *Delfasco, LLC*, Comp. Gen. Dec. B-409514.3, 2016 CPD ¶ 192 (agency failed to inform protester of six "outstanding weaknesses" in its final proposal revision); *Velos, Inc.*, Comp. Gen. Dec. B-400500, 2010 CPD ¶ 3 (agency agreed to terms in software license and then rejected revised proposal including those terms); *Multimax, Inc.*, Comp. Gen. Dec. B-298249.6, 2006 CPD ¶ 165 (agency identified only some labor rates that were higher than government estimate); *Spherix, Inc.*, Comp. Gen. Dec. B-294572.3, 2005 CPD ¶ 183 (agency implied that RFP requirements were firm while accepting an alternate solution from a competitor); and *Cygnus Corp.*, Comp. Gen. Dec. B-292649.3, 2004 CPD ¶ 162 (agency stated that the discussions "resulted in agreement of all technical and cost issues raised during negotiations" when it had identified a number of undiscussed weaknesses). Compare *American Med. Prof'ls, Inc.*, Comp. Gen. Dec. B-275784, 97-1 CPD ¶ 134 (not misleading to ask offeror to verify that it could perform at the quoted prices); *Analytical & Research Tech., Inc.*, Comp. Gen. Dec. B-276064, 97-1 CPD ¶ 200 (protester unreasonably interpreted agency's explanation regarding staffing requirements as permitting an approach that was inconsistent with the solicitation requirements); *Ideal Elec. Sec. Co.*, Comp. Gen. Dec. B-298221, 98-2 CPD ¶ 14 (agency had not misled the protester into offering only a small price reduction by stating that its price was competitive and its escalation ratios appeared reasonable); and *DMS All-Star Joint Venture v. United States*, 90 Fed. Cl. 653 (2010) (not misleading to point out only one of several pricing issues when protester given opportunity to revise prices).

[c] Prohibited Conduct

The FAR Part 15 Rewrite made significant changes in specifying the conduct which is improper. FAR 15.306(e) provides the following limitations on communications:

> Government personnel involved in the acquisition shall not engage in conduct that—
>
> (1) Favors one offeror over another;
>
> (2) Reveals an offeror's technical solution, including unique technology, innovative and unique uses of commercial items, or any information that would compromise an offeror's intellectual property to another offeror;
>
> (3) Reveals an offeror's price without that offeror's permission. However, the contracting officer may inform an offeror that its price is considered by the Government to be too high, or to low, and reveal the results of the analysis supporting that conclusion. It is also permissible, at the Government's discretion, to indicate to all offerors the cost or price that the Government's price analysis, market research, and other reviews have identified as reasonable (41 U.S.C. 423(h)(1)(2));
>
> (4) Reveals the names of individuals providing reference information about an offeror's past performance; or
>
> (5) Knowingly furnishes source selection information in violation of 3.104 and 41 U.S.C. 423(h)(1)(2).

The first three prohibitions were substantially rewritten in the FAR Part 15 Rewrite to reduce their scope. Thus, as discussed earlier, the "technical leveling" prohibition was eliminated and the "auction" prohibition was narrowed. The second prohibition of revealing another offeror's technical solution, previously described as "technical transfusion," was not significantly altered from the prior FAR. The fourth prohibition was added by the Rewrite. The fifth prohibition refers to a portion of the Procurement Integrity Act.

In addition to these prohibitions, there are criminal statutes broadly prohibiting disclosure of certain types of information, such as.18 U.S.C. § 1905.

Thus, violation of these statutory provisions could result in criminal liability. See *Panafax Corp.*, Comp. Gen. Dec. B-201176, 81-1 CPD ¶ 515, *recons. denied*, 81-2 CPD ¶ 220, where a disclosure to another offeror of Panafax's identity as an offeror and the fact that Panafax was offering a newly developed machine enabled the offeror to lower its price 27%, $1 below Panafax's price. A referral was made to the Department of Justice and GAO sustained the protest, stating that the disclosure of information enabled the other offeror to determine what equipment its competitor was offering and at approximately what price. See Chapter 1, Section VII for a discussion of these statutory provisions.

[i] Favoring One Offeror

The first prohibition covered "technical leveling" in the pre-Rewrite FAR. Thus, prior to the Rewrite, agencies were prohibited from coaching offerors to bring them up to the level of a competitor. However, there were no protests finding that such coaching had actually occurred. As discussed earlier, such coaching is now encouraged as long as it does not involve providing information from a competitor's proposal. The protest decisions now frequently cite the first prohibition barring favoring one offeror in holding that agencies have engaged in unfair treatment, *HomeSafe Alliance, LLC*, Comp. Gen. Dec. B-418266.5, 2020 CPD ¶ 350 (agency told protester its relatively low price was high); *Global Language Center*, Comp. Gen. Dec. B-413503.8, 2017 CPD ¶ 238 (agency allowed only one offeror to correct its final proposal revision); *Caddell Constr. Co. v. United States*, 125 Fed. Cl. 30 (2016) (misleading an offeror into lowering its price); *Deloitte Consulting, LLP*, Comp. Gen. Dec. B-412125.2, 2016 CPD ¶ 119 (agency advised only one offeror that references were "somewhat relevant"); *Hyperion, Inc. v. United States*, 115 Fed. Cl. 541 (2014) (award to company whose proposal indicated on its face that it would not meet the subcontracting limitation); *Marathon Medical Corp.*, Comp. Gen. Dec. B-408052, 2014 CPD ¶ 162 (agency allowed only one offeror to demonstrate that its proposal was acceptable); *Boeing Co.*, Comp. Gen. Dec. B-311344, 2008 CPD ¶ 114 (agency misled protester into believing that it had met performance objective); *Sytronics, Inc.*, Comp. Gen. Dec. B-297346, 2006 CPD ¶ 15 (winning offeror was told its price was "excessive" while protester with similar price was told that its price was "high"); *Martin Elecs., Inc.*, Comp. Gen. Dec. B-290846.3, 2003 CPD ¶ 6 (winning offeror was "favored" because its poor past performance was probed while the protester's was not) and *Chemonics Int'l, Inc.*, Comp. Gen. Dec. B-282555, 99-2 CPD ¶ 61 (personnel which the agency believed were unsuitable were probed in one offer but not the other.

[ii] Technical Transfusion

Helping an offeror to improve its proposal through the use of information gained from another offer was described in the pre-FAR Rewrite as "technical transfusion." It is now described in the second prohibition as revealing information that is "unique" or "intellectual property." In addition to being illegal, there is a procurement policy reason for refraining from such conduct. In 51 Comp. Gen. 621 (B-173677) (1972), GAO enunciated this reason for avoidance of this practice, stating that if the government disclosed technical innovations to other offerors, offerors would tend to hold back technical innovation from the negotiation process. Thus, the government would lose the benefits accruing from contractor innovation during negotiation.

It has been very difficult for a protester to establish that technical transfusion has taken place because GAO requires proof "that the contracting agency either directly or indirectly disclosed one offeror's technical approach to another offeror," *Northwest Reg'l Educ. Lab.*, Comp. Gen. Dec. B-222591.3, 87-1 CPD ¶ 4. Thus, even if the protester can prove similarities to its technical approach in a competitor's BAFO, the lack of actual evidence of disclosure will lead to a denial of the protest, *Le Don Computer Servs., Inc.*, Comp. Gen. Dec. B-225451.2, 87-1 CPD ¶ 441. Similarly, speculative protests of possible technical transfusion are summarily denied, *Sparta, Inc.*, Comp. Gen. Dec. B-228216, 88-1 CPD ¶ 37. A lack of technical transfusion has been found in *Ashe Facility Servs., Inc.*, Comp. Gen. Dec. B-292218.3, 2004 CPD ¶ 80 (asking about equipment to be used for ground maintenance work); *WorldTravelServ.*, Comp. Gen. Dec. B-284155.3, 2001 CPD ¶ 68 (asking about use of interpreters where RFP required special treatment for patients speaking different languages); *Voith Hydro, Inc.*, Comp. Gen. Dec. B-277051, 97-2 CPD ¶ 68 (advising offeror to use proven manufacturing facility); and *Creative Mgmt. Tech., Inc.*, Comp. Gen. Dec. B-266299, 96-1 CPD ¶ 61 (asking offeror to provide specific documents showing capability when such documents were not called for by RFP but had been provided by competitor). In *Gentex Corp.—Western Operations*, Comp. Gen. Dec. B-291793, 2003 CPD ¶ 66, the protester contended that since its initial proposal contained variation in quantity and warranty clauses and its competitor's did not, transfusion occurred when the clauses appeared in the competitor's revised proposal. The protester argued that the transfusion resulted when the agency asked the competitor whether it would "consider putting a variation clause in the contract" and what were its "[t]houghts on warranty." GAO ruled that "technical transfusion" had not occurred since there was not a "disclosure of a unique or ingenious technical solution from a competitor's proposal." It also ruled that the questions were not improper because they were "neutral."

If one offeror proposes a technical approach not permitted by the RFP but which the agency would like to consider, it is not improper to disclose to other offerors that the agency is willing to consider alternative approaches (as long as the specific technical approach proposed is not disclosed), *Rix Indus., Inc.*, Comp. Gen. Dec. B-241498, 91-1 CPD ¶ 165; *Loral Terracom*, 66 Comp. Gen. 272 (B-224908), 87-1 CPD ¶ 182. In addition, if the procuring agency is aware of a technical concept prior to the submission of a proposal incorporating that concept, conveying the concept to another offeror is not technical transfusion,

Dynalectron Corp., Comp. Gen. Dec. B-216201, 85-1 CPD ¶ 525. See also *Litton Sys., Inc.*, Comp. Gen. Dec. B-239123, 90-2 CPD ¶ 114, finding no technical transfusion when the procuring agency discussed with all offerors the need for testing which was first identified by the protester. GAO accepted the procuring agency's explanation that all the offerors had identified the need to verify that the various proposed techniques met the contract requirement and the discussions of specific testing flowed from this mutual identification of a gap in the RFP. It is also not improper to permit an offeror for a follow-on service contract to visit the government site where the incumbent contractor is performing the work, *Contact Int'l Corp.*, 70 Comp. Gen. 115 (B-237122.3), 90-2 CPD ¶ 442.

[iii] Revealing Prices

Prior to the FAR Rewrite, the third prohibition banned "auctions." However, it was narrowed considerably in the Rewrite so that it now prohibits only the disclosure of prices without consent. See *Strand Hunt Constr., Inc.*, Comp. Gen. Dec. B-292415, 2003 CPD ¶ 167, noting that the auction prohibition was removed from the FAR. In addition, this provision permits disclosure of government estimates of reasonable costs or prices. This rewritten language has been interpreted to allow agencies to reveal a considerable amount of pricing information to offerors. There is general agreement that it allows an agency to tell an offeror that its price is considered to be "high," *Dynacs Eng'g Co. v. United States*, 48 Fed. Cl. 124 (2000). Other decisions permitting disclosure of information include *KTS Solutions, Inc.*, Comp. Gen. Dec. B-418665.2, 2020 CPD ¶ 271 (no impropriety when prices had been released in debriefings and "not as a result of preferential treatment or other improper action on the part of the agency"); *Chenega Fed. Sys., LLC*, Comp. Gen. Dec. B-299310.2, 2007 CPD ¶ 196 (revealing detailed government analysis of offeror's probable costs); *Kaneohe Gen. Servs., Inc.*, Comp. Gen. Dec. B-293097.2, 2004 Comp. Gen. ¶ 50 (disclosing government estimate to all offerors in second round of discussions); *Engineering Servs. Unlimited, Inc.*, Comp. Gen. Dec. B-291275, 2003 CPD ¶ 15 (questioning the low level of labor rates in proposal); *Korrect Optical, Inc.*, Comp. Gen. Dec. B-288128, 2001 CPD ¶ 171 (revealing average prices of five offerors in competitive range); and *OMV Med., Inc. v. United States*, 219 F.3d 1337 (Fed. Cir. 2000) (stating that proposed salaries were below "current average annual salaries"). Compare *DynCorp Int'l, LLC v. United States*, 148 Fed. Cl. 568 (2020), holding that this prohibition precludes an agency from revealing that an offeror's prices are higher than other offeror's prices without the latter's permission.

It might be argued that this provision precludes the use of reverse auction procedures where prices are electronically posted without disclosing the company submitting the price. There is no decision on whether FAR 15.306(e)(3) bears on this issue, but GAO ruled in *MTB Grp., Inc.*, Comp. Gen. Dec. B-295463, 2005

Comp. Gen. ¶ 40, that reverse auctions do not violate the procurement statutes when used in simplified acquisitions, stating:

> Regarding MTB's specific objection—that the reverse auction here is impermissible because it will result in disclosure of its price—we find no basis for objecting to the agency's approach. MTB is correct that the Act prohibits government officials and those acting on behalf of the government from knowingly disclosing contractor quotation or proposal information before award. 41 U.S.C. § 423(a). However, that prohibition is not absolute. Rather, the Act specifically provides that it does not "restrict the disclosure of information to, or its receipt by, any person or class of persons authorized in accordance with applicable agency regulations or procedures, to receive the information," 41 U.S.C. § 423(h)(1), and does not "restrict a contractor from disclosing its own quote or proposal information or the recipient from receiving that information." 41 U.S.C. § 423(h)(2). We think the price disclosure under HUD's reverse auction procedures falls within the exception language, although we are aware of no judicial or other authoritative interpretation of these provisions. First, under the procedure the agency has established, vendors actually will disclose their own prices—albeit, as a condition of competing—by entering the prices on the auction website; as noted, a vendor's disclosing its own price is not prohibited under the Act. Moreover, even if the price disclosure were considered to be by government officials due to its nature as a precondition to a vendor's competing, the disclosure is pursuant, and integral, to the reverse auction procurement procedures established by the agency; we thus would view the disclosure as being to persons authorized by agency procedures to receive the information, consistent with the exception language. See generally *DGS Contract Serv., Inc. v. United States*, 43 Ct. Cl. 227, 236 (1999); *Ocean Servs., LLC.*, B-292511.2, Nov. 6, 2003, 2003 CPD ¶ 206 at 5 (neither the Act nor the FAR establishes an absolute prohibition against disclosure of price information, and both make clear that prices can be disclosed under certain circumstances) [FN omitted].

The same result was reached in *MTB Grp., Inc. v. United States*, 65 Fed. Cl. 516 (2005). That decision contains a long discussion of the applicability of the Freedom of Information Act to this issue.

[iv] Names of Reference Individuals

While it is clear that offerors will know the references that they provide to an agency to ascertain their past performance and experience, the FAR prohibits revealing the names of the individuals working for the referenced agency or company that have provided the information. See *Kapthal Techs., Inc.*, Comp. Gen. Dec. B-291637.2, 2003 Comp. Gen. ¶ 69, denying a protest arguing that failure to provide this information kept the protester from responding adequately to adverse past performance information. The intent of this prohibition is not clear and there is no indication of the harm that is done by revealing these names.

Perhaps the goal is to obtain a more forthright appraisal of the performance of the offeror providing the reference.

[v] Procurement Integrity

The reference to the Procurement Integrity Act (implemented in FAR 3.104) only prohibits the release of source selection information. However, the Act also prohibits the release of contractor bid or proposal information—which should have been included in this segment of the regulation. See Chapter 1 for a discussion of the scope of this Act.

[d] Procedure Following Improper Disclosure

There are very few reported instances of agencies violating the rules prohibiting conduct discussed above. However, there are numerous situations where an agency has lost a protest after awarding the contract with the result that the price of the winning contractor (and perhaps other prices) have been revealed. In that situation, the agency must balance its corrective action of reopening the competition against the unfairness to the offerors whose prices have been disclosed to its competitors. *LaBarge Prods., Inc. v. West*, 46 F.3d 1547 (Fed. Cir. 1995) describes this balance at 1555:

> [In making this decision] several competing concerns come into play. First, is "the bastion of federal procurement policy that all offerors must possess equal knowledge of the same information in order to have a valid procurement." [Logicon, Inc. v. United States, 22 Cl. Ct. 776 (1991)] at 788. All offerors cannot have equal knowledge if one knows the previous bid of another. Secondly, the government has a strong interest in ensuring that the procurement meets its needs. Thirdly, in a negotiated procurement, the contracting officer is entrusted with a relatively high degree of discretion. *Burroughs Corp. v. United States*, 617 F.2d 590, 597-98, 223 Ct. Cl. 53, 65 (1980). The contracting officer's discretion extends to the application of procurement regulations, which includes reopening discussions and requesting a best and final offer. *Logicon, Inc.*, 22 Cl. Ct. at 782; *DLM & A, Inc. v. United States*, 6 Cl. Ct. 329, 331 (1984); FAR § 15.600 (1984) (the FAR "prescribes policies and procedures for selection of a source or sources in competitive negotiated acquisitions"). A rule that prevents the government from requesting further offers after one potential contractor's bid has been revealed protects the first of these concerns but can impinge upon the second and third.

In considering the facts, the court concluded that reopening the competition was a rational course of conduct. See *Dell Fed. Sys., L.P. v. United States*, 906 F.3d 982 (Fed. Cir. 2018), holding that the test in reviewing the agency's action is its rationality not whether it was "narrowly tailored." In that case, the decision to reveal all of the prices and conduct a new competition was held to be rational because the original procurement had significant defects.

The general rule stated by GAO is that the requirement for full and open competition overrides the prohibitions against improper disclosure—with the result that the proper course of action is frequently to reopen the competition permitting all offerors to compete with only the awardees price being known to the competitors. See *Pan Am Support Servs., Inc.*, 66 Comp. Gen. 457 (B-225964.2), 87-1 CPD ¶ 512, stating at 460:

> [C]oncerns as to technical leveling or technical transfusion do not necessarily overcome the need to remedy a procurement which has failed to satisfy the statutory requirement for full and open competition. See *Roy F. Weston, Inc.—Request for Reconsideration*, B-221863.3, Sept. 29, 1986, 86-2 CPD ¶ 324. Similarly, the risk of an auction is generally viewed as secondary to the preservation of the integrity of the competitive procurement system through the taking of appropriate corrective action. *Environmental Tectonics Corp.—Reconsideration*, B-225474.2 et al., Apr. 9, 1987, 87-1 CPD ¶ [96].

This appears to be the most common course of action when a price has been revealed but corrective action must be taken. This occurred in *ManTech Telecomms. & Info. Sys. Corp. v. United States*, 49 Fed. Cl. 57 (2001), *aff'd*, 30 Fed. Appx. 995 (Fed. Cir. 2002), where the court agreed that totally new final proposal revisions were justified, carefully reviewed the competitor's pricing information that had been revealed to the protester, and enjoined the agency from undertaking the corrective action of revealing the protester's price. The court held that the information that was proposed to be revealed was broader and that a fair round of final proposal revisions could be conducted without revealing any more pricing information. Several decisions have approved reopening the competition even though the original winner's prices have been disclosed. See, for example, *Jackson Tech., Inc.*, Comp. Gen. Dec. B-416314, 2018 CPD ¶ 271; *IDEAL Indus., Inc.*, Comp. Gen. Dec. B-416416, 2018 CPD ¶ 253; *Jackson Contractor Grp., Inc.*, Comp. Gen. Dec. B-402348.2, 2010 CPD ¶ 154; *IMS Servs., Inc. v. United States*, 33 Fed. Cl. 167 (1995). See also *SYMVIONICS, Inc.*, Comp. Gen. Dec. B-293824.2, 2004 CPD ¶ 204, and *Alatech Healthcare, LLC*, Comp. Gen. Dec. B-289134.3, 2002 CPD ¶ 73, where the protesters argued that they should be provided with a competitor's unit prices since their unit prices had been disclosed in a debriefing. GAO noted that while such a technique might be acceptable where prices have been improperly disclosed, it was not required in these cases because disclosure of prices in a debriefing is not improper. GAO also frequently recommends that a competition be reopened after the winning offeror's prices have been revealed, *Harper Constr. Co.*, Comp. Gen. Dec. B-415042, 2018 CPD ¶ 47; *Mevacon-NASCO JV*, Comp. Gen. Dec. B-414329, 2017 CPD ¶ 144; *Verdi Consulting, Inc.*, Comp. Gen. Dec. B-414103.2, 2017 CPD ¶ 136; *Tribalco, LLC*, Comp. Gen. Dec. B-414120, 2017 CPD ¶ 73; *SRA*

Int'l, Inc., Comp. Gen. Dec. B-410973, 2016 CPD ¶ 32. See also *Chapman Law Firm Co. v. United States*, 71 Fed. Cl. 124 (2006), prohibiting an agency from reopening discussion with only one offeror when the agency would benefit from competition.

A similar technique that disadvantages the winning offeror is to cancel the procurement and issue a new RFP after one or more prices have been revealed. See *American Warehouse Sys., LLC*, Comp. Gen. Dec. B-412543, 2016 CPD ¶ 66 (changed requirements justified cancellation and reprocurement); *Sealift, Inc.*, Comp. Gen. Dec. B-412041.2, 2016 CPD ¶ 99 (ambiguous solicitation justified cancellation and reprocurement); and *BayFirst Sols., LLC v. United States*, 104 Fed. Cl. 493 (2012) (procurement errors justified cancellation, obtaining interim services by issuance of task order and reprocurement of future services). Compare *Superlastive Techs., Inc.*, Comp. Gen. Dec. B-310489, 2008 CPD ¶ 12, finding it improper for the agency to have cancelled a solicitation because of disclosure of internal agency information to one offeror and then award a sole source contract to a company using that offeror as a subcontractor.

In contrast to the rule on pricing information, an agency is required to disclose to all competitors detailed information on solicitation requirements that has been disclosed to one offeror in the debriefing process, *Raytheon Tech. Servs. Co.*, Comp. Gen. Dec. B-404655.4, 2011 CPD ¶ 236; *SYMVIONICS, Inc.*, Comp. Gen. Dec. B-293824.2, 2004 CPD ¶ 204. See also *American K-9 Detection Servs., Inc.*, Comp. Gen. Dec. B-400464.6, 2009 CPD ¶ 107, granting a protest because the agency conducted another round of discussions and final proposal revisions but did not disclose all of the protester's deficiencies and significant weaknesses.

Some agencies have attempted to avert the unfairness to the winning offeror by limiting reopened discussions and revised proposal revisions to only those issues dealt with in the original protest. See *Deloitte Consulting, LLP*, Comp. Gen. Dec. B-412125.6, 2016 CPD ¶ 355, stating:

> Where the corrective action does not also include amending the solicitation, we will not question an agency's decision to restrict proposal revisions when taking corrective action so long as it is reasonable in nature and remedies the established or suspected procurement impropriety. See, *Consolidated Eng'g Servs., Inc.*, B-293864.2, Oct. 25, 2004, 2004 CPD ¶ 214 at 3-4; *Computer Assocs. Int'l*, [B-292077.2, 2003 CPD ¶ 157]. In reviewing the reasonableess of an agency's restrictions on proposal revisions in the context of discussions to implement corrective action, we will consider whether the discussions, and permitted revisions in response to discussions, are expected to have a material impact on other areas of the offeror's proposal. *Evergreen Helicopters of Alaska, Inc.*, B-409327.3, Apr. 14, 2014, 2014 CPD ¶ 128 at 8; *Honeywell Technology Solutions, Inc.*, B-400771.6, Nov. 23, 2009, 2009 CPD ¶ 240 at 4.

In *Deloitte* GAO found the limitation to only the key personnel issue improper because that impacted other parts of the original proposal. However, it has frequently been found proper to limit proposal revisions to the non-price aspects of the competing proposals but to deny the opportunity to revise prices. See *Leidos, Inc.*, Comp. Gen. Dec. B-409214.4, 2015 CPD ¶ 63 (amplifying information on "basis of estimates"); *Evergreen Helicopters of Alaska, Inc.*, Comp. Gen. Dec. B-409327.3, 2014 CPD ¶ 128 (requiring submission of additional data on offered aircraft); *Alliant Techsys., Inc.*, Comp. Gen. Dec. B-405129.3, 2012 CPD ¶ 50 (correcting "assumptions" of one offeror); *ST Aerospace Engines Pte., Ltd.*, Comp. Gen. Dec. B-275725.3, 97-2 CPD ¶ 106 (correcting past performance evaluation); *Krueger Int'l, Inc.*, Comp. Gen. Dec. B-260953.4, 96-1 CPD ¶ 235 (curing informational deficiencies).

Another technique to avert the unfairness to the winning offeror is to conduct another round of final proposal revisions releasing all of the previous prices. This was approved in *Systems Plus, Inc.*, Comp. Gen. Dec. B-413703.8, 2017 CPD ¶ 141; See also *Veterans Evaluation Servs., Inc.*, Comp. Gen. Dec. B-412940, 2016 CPD ¶ 185, where the GAO recommended reopening the competition when its decision contained all of the prices.

[D] Proposal Revisions

Under the pre-Rewrite FAR, changes to offers following negotiations were termed "best and final offers" (BAFOs). The Rewrite changed this terminology to deal with both "proposal revisions" and "final proposal revisions." FAR 15.001 defines "proposal revision" as a revision that occurs "as a result of negotiations:"

> "Proposal revision" is a change to a proposal made after the solicitation closing date, at the request of or as allowed by a contracting officer, as the result of negotiations.

FAR 15.307(b) contains the following coverage of such proposal revisions and also addresses "final proposal revisions:"

> The contracting officer may request or allow proposal revisions to clarify and document understandings reached during negotiations. At the conclusion of discussions, each offeror still in the competitive range shall be given an opportunity to submit a final proposal revision. The contracting officer is required to establish a common cut-off date only for receipt of final proposal revisions. Requests for final proposal revisions shall advise offerors that the final proposal revisions shall be in writing and that the Government intends to make award without obtaining further revisions.

Thus, this guidance deals with two types of proposal revisions: "proposal revisions" and "final proposal revisions."

The first type of proposal revision is made to "clarify and document understandings reached during negotiations." This language appears to deal with alterations to the original *offer* made by the offeror since it is unlikely that the contracting officer would reach an "understanding" regarding information submitted by the offeror to demonstrate its capability or to support its offer. Thus, this new FAR appears to permit contracting agencies to request an offeror to put revisions to its offer in writing in order to ensure that the parties have reached a clear understanding on the terms of the potential contract they have negotiated. This practice has been followed by some contracting agencies in the past—especially on relatively complex procurements. See NFS 1815.306(d)(3)(C) (pre-2004), which called for reaching agreement on a "model contract" with each offeror during negotiations. Under the FAR Rewrite, contracting agencies may adopt this procedure if they believe that it will enhance the competitive negotiation process.

The second type of proposal revision is the "final proposal revision." Obtaining such revisions is mandatory, and all offerors remaining in the competitive range must be permitted to submit their proposal revisions on a common cutoff date. See *Piquette & Howard Elec. Serv., Inc.*, Comp. Gen. Dec. B-408435.3, 2014 CPD ¶ 8, granting a protest because the agency had not called for final proposal revisions after conducting discussions with one offeror. In the initial draft of the FAR Rewrite, obtaining such revisions was permissive and no common cutoff date was required. However, there were major objections to this change to the process, with the result that the FAR Councils withdrew the proposal and adopted a final rule essentially the same as the prior BAFO rule. Because the protest decisions in this area had focused on this mandatory BAFO process, they are equally applicable to the new rule.

Final proposal revisions can include alterations to the original offer as well as revisions to any part of the original proposal. Thus, offerors can submit additional information to enhance their capability assessment or to support their offers. For example, it has been common practice to propose different personnel or to revise a technical proposal that is being used to assess the offeror's understanding of the work. They can also include additional information supporting offered prices or technical performance. The amount of information submitted will depend on the number of weaknesses and deficiencies identified in the negotiations, but agencies should use care to ensure that the offeror has the full opportunity to address all such weaknesses and deficiencies in its proposal revision.

[1] Requesting Final Proposal Revisions

If the negotiations with the offerors in the competitive range have not been carried to the point of agreement between the parties, all that the request for final proposal revisions requires is that the offeror be clearly informed of the common cutoff date for submission of the final proposal. There is no need for a statement that negotiations are concluded or for a statement that award may be made without further discussions, *OMNIPLEX World Servs. Corp.*, Comp. Gen. Dec. B-406251, 2012 CPD ¶ 113. However, a request for final proposal revisions should contain clear language as to its nature and that a common cutoff date has been established. See *Omniplex World Servs. Corp. v. United States*, 105 Fed. Cl. 706 (2012), disagreeing with GAO and granting a protest because of unclear language in a letter asking for proposal revisions. It is good practice to warn offerors that significant changes in their proposals that have not been discussed may lead to a rescoring of the proposal to their detriment and will not generally require additional negotiations. See *Jacobs Serv. Co.*, Comp. Gen. Dec. B-262088.3, 97-1 CPD ¶ 220, finding that the agency had not misled an offeror when it warned that changes to the staffing allocations could result in a finding that the proposal was unacceptable.

Oral requests may be necessary on some procurements and are not prohibited by the FAR. However, they should be followed up in writing, to ensure that there is no misunderstanding. See *Woodward Assocs., Inc.*, Comp. Gen. Dec. B-216714, 85-1 CPD ¶ 274, where, under prior regulations, the protester misinterpreted an ambiguous oral request for a second round of BAFOs as a request for reconfirmation of its price. GAO ruled that another round of discussions should be held to correct the confusion that had occurred as a result of the unclear nature of the oral request and the lack of a written confirmation. When oral requests for BAFOs were followed up by a written confirmation, no relief was granted if the offeror misconstrued the request, *KMS Fusion, Inc.*, Comp. Gen. Dec. B-242529, 91-1 CPD ¶ 447; *Israel Aircraft Indus., Ltd.*, Comp. Gen. Dec. B-239211, 90-2 CPD ¶ 84. In *SSI*, Comp. Gen. Dec. B-413486, 2016 CPD ¶ 322, GAO found no unfairness in a task order procurement when the agency based its source selection decision on information orally exchanged during discussions without obtaining written final proposal revisions. GAO distinguished this from a FAR Part 15 procurement.

If the negotiations have been carried to the point of agreement with each offeror in the competitive range, the agency may expect the final proposal revisions to reflect that agreement. However, under FAR 15.307(b), offerors can submit a final offer that varies from such agreement in any way that they desire. Final offers that vary substantially from the prior agreement can lead to difficulties in the procurement process because they require the agency to expend resources in evaluating the new offer and create the risk of misunderstandings between the parties. In some cases they have led to the need for additional negotiations and a new set of final proposals. Thus, some agencies have attempted to reduce the number of unforeseen changes to the offers by including specific guidance in the request for final revisions, including the agreement that has been reached.

For a case agreeing that it is proper to require offerors to substantiate changes to their proposals that alter prices, see *Cessna Aircraft Co.*, Comp. Gen. Dec. B-261953.5, 96-1 CPD ¶ 132. See also *Sutron Corp.*, Comp. Gen. Dec. B-270456, 96-1 CPD ¶ 143, agreeing with an agency's evaluation that an unexplained BAFO price reduction posed a high performance risk that rendered the protester's proposal unacceptable.

In any case, the aim should be to receive a proposal from each competitor that the agency fully understands and can accept if it is determined to be most advantageous to the government. This is achievable under the FAR Rewrite because full communication is permitted in the negotiation process.

Generally, the request for proposal revisions is open-ended in permitting alterations to the original proposals, *Quest Diagnostics, Inc. v. United States*, 110 Fed. Cl. 716 (2013). However, in limited circumstances it is permissible to limit the scope of such revisions. Thus, GAO will review the record to see if the agency has a "reasonable basis for restricting the scope of revisions," *Computer Assocs. Int'l, Inc.*, Comp. Gen. Dec. B-292077.2, 2003 CPD ¶ 157. See *Honeywell Tech. Solutions, Inc.*, Comp. Gen. Dec. B-400771.6, 2009 CPD ¶ 240 (limiting revisions to past performance information needed to overcome prior protest); *Rel-Tek Sys. & Design, Inc.*, Comp. Gen. Dec. B-280463.7, 99-2 CPD ¶ 1 (limiting revisions to areas that had been identified in prior protest as being ambiguous); *Krueger Int'l, Inc.*, Comp. Gen. Dec. B-260953.4, 96-1 CPD ¶ 235 (limiting revisions to the submission of samples and additional technical information but prohibited new prices); and *Metron Corp.*, Comp. Gen. Dec. B-227014, 87-1 CPD ¶ 642 (limiting revisions to only costs and prices). Compare *Castro & Co.*, Comp. Gen. Dec. B-415508.4, 2018 CPD ¶ 74, granting a protest because the limitations were narrower than the scope of an amendment to the RFP. When a request for final proposals contains restrictions on the permissible alterations, the agency must abide by those restrictions and not consider additional alterations submitted by offerors, *DynaLantic Corp.*, 68 Comp. Gen. 413 (B-234035), 89-1 CPD ¶ 421 (technical alterations should not have been considered when agency had called for "best and final price and delivery schedule" and had stated "negotiations have been concluded").

[a] Reasonable Time

To foster fair competition, the established common cut-off date should allow sufficient time for all offerors in the competitive range to submit their final offer revisions. When discussions are conducted sequentially, this means that the closing date should give adequate time to the last offeror with whom discussions were conducted. However, the amount of time is highly dependent on the circumstances. See *Morris Guralnick Assocs., Inc.*, Comp. Gen. Dec. B-218353, 85-2 CPD ¶ 50 (allowing one day for submission of BAFOs reasonable when both competitors were able to submit proposals within that time period); *Evergreen Landscaping, Inc.*, Comp. Gen. Dec. B-239241, 90-2 CPD ¶ 36 (six days reasonable for submission of BAFOs where both offerors were given the same amount of time and both offerors were located in the same city); *FRC Int'l, Inc.*, Comp. Gen. Dec. B-255345, 94-1 CPD ¶ 125 (two hours and fifteen minutes reasonable for submission of BAFOs where there was decreasing availability and increasing price of the item needed and the offerors' proposals were scheduled to expire within two days).

When negotiations have been carried to the point of agreement with each of the competitors, it would appear that less time is required for the preparation of final proposal revisions. In that case each offeror might need to do no more than verify that its negotiated agreement is still valid. However, additional time should be allowed if it is clear that offerors will submit proposal revisions dealing with informational deficiencies or weaknesses.

[b] Common Cut-off Date

The FAR 15.307(b) requirement for a common cut-off date for the receipt of final revisions has been justified as necessary to preserve the integrity of the competition in order to minimize the possibility of information in one proposal "leaking" to another offeror with a later closing date. See *Federal Data Corp.*, Comp. Gen. Dec. B-236265.4, 90-1 CPD ¶ 504; and *Kleen-Rite Corp.*, Comp. Gen. Dec. B-209474, 83-1 CPD ¶ 512, stressing the need for such a common cutoff date as an essential part of the competitive negotiation process. The purpose of establishing a common cutoff date is to prevent offerors from being treated unfairly or being prejudiced. See *Comprehensive Health Servs., Inc. v. United States*, 70 Fed. Cl. 700 (2006), stating at 730-31:

> Had NASA considered new information supplied after the cut-off date, as a revision to the offeror's proposal, the agency would have violated FAR 15.307(b) and such conduct reasonably could have been viewed as according CHS with preferential treatment. *See Integrated Bus. Solutions v. United States*, 58 Fed. Cl. 420, 428 (Fed. Cl. 2003) ("Here, as GAO recognized, it would have been unfair to require the other offerors to submit FRPs by the March 13 deadline but permit IBS to confirm its initial proposal days later."); *Dubinsky v. United States*, 43 Fed. Cl. 243, 263-64 (Fed. Cl. 1999) ("[B]y providing a common cut-off date, it sets a level playing field on which [the offerors] may compete for the contract.") . . . .

However, prejudice does not necessarily occur because there is no common cutoff date. See *Sotera Def. Solutions, Inc.*, Comp. Gen. Dec. B-414056, 2017 CPD ¶ 46 (no prejudice when offeror allowed back into competitive range was given same amount of time as other offerors); *PAE Gov't Servs., Inc.*, Comp. Gen. Dec. B-407886, 2013 CPD ¶ 92 (no prejudice because offeror with later date was not awarded a contract); *Metropolitan Interpreters & Translators, Inc.*, Comp. Gen. Dec. B-403912.4, 2012 CPD ¶ 130 (no prejudice because winning offeror was given same amount of time to submit final proposal revisions); *Special Operations Grp., Inc.*, Comp. Gen. Dec. B-287013, 2001 CPD ¶ 73 (noting lack of common date but not citing it as basis for sustaining protest); *Gas Turbine Corp.*, Comp. Gen. Dec. B-251265, 93-1 CPD ¶ 400 (no prejudice in allowing one competitor "an additional few days"). Compare *Raytheon*

Tech. Servs. Co., Comp. Gen. Dec. B-404655.4, 2011 CPD ¶ 236, finding prejudice when an offeror allowed back into the competitive range had three more months to take advantage of changes in the labor market.

The contracting officer may extend the closing date for receipt of final proposal revisions if such extension will enhance competition, *Guardian Moving & Storage Co. v. United States*, 122 Fed. Cl. 117 (2015). The court commented that such an extension was proper even if it only benefitted the offeror that had requested it because there was no prejudice to the other offerors. See also *Fort Biscuit Co.*, Comp. Gen. Dec. B-247319, 92-1 CPD ¶ 440, where extension of the closing date was proper to permit a competitor to submit a proposal that would not have otherwise been submitted, and *TRS Design & Consulting Servs.*, Comp. Gen. Dec. B-218668.2, 85-2 CPD ¶ 370, where the agency properly extended the closing date after it misinformed one of two offerors, causing it to miss the original closing date.

[c] Late Final Revisions

The Instructions to Offerors—Competitive Acquisition solicitation provision at FAR 52.215-1 defines "late" proposals, modifications, or final revisions as those received after the designated time for receipt. Thus, late final proposal revisions are normally rejected unless they meet one of the exceptions to these rules—discussed earlier. Once the time for submission has passed, the agency cannot extend the time to accept a proposal that has not met the deadline, *Geo-Seis Helicopters, Inc. v. United States*, 77 Fed. Cl. 633 (2007).

As discussed earlier, GAO and the Court of Federal Claims disagree on the rule applicable to electronically submitted proposals. GAO has held that the FAR rule allowing consideration of late proposals only if they were submitted 24 hours early is the exclusive rule for electronically submitted proposals, *Sea Box, Inc.*, Comp. Gen. Dec. B-251056, 2002 CPD ¶ 181. See *Symetrics Indus., LLC*, Comp. Gen. Dec. B-298759, 2006 CPD ¶ 154, applying that rule to final proposal revisions. On the other hand, the court has held that the rule on government control of proposals applies to electronically submitted proposals, *Watterson Constr. Co. v. United States*, 98 Fed. Cl. 84 (2011) (agency server sent proposal to contracting office four minutes late); *Insight Sys. Corp. v. United States*, 110 Fed. Cl. 564 (2013) (agency server could not acquire quotes from Google server). In spite of these court decisions, GAO has continued to adhere to the *Sea Box* rule, *Peers Health*, Comp. Gen. Dec. B-413557.3, 2017 CPD ¶ 93. However, in *ICI Servs., Inc.*, Comp. Gen. Dec. B-409231.2, 2014 CPD ¶ 132, a final proposal revision was found to be submitted timely when it was sent by e-mail to a contract specialist even though the RFP called for submission to the agency's electronic portal. GAO reasoned that the proposal revision was timely because it was received by the agency installation designated for receipt before the due date.

GAO has also applied the late proposal revision rule to a situation where the agency called for the submission of responses to "items for negotiation" by a specified date even though the request did not use the term "final proposal revision," *Seven Seas Eng'g & Land Surveying*, Comp. Gen. Dec. B-294424.2, 2004 CPD ¶ 236.

Although a late final offer generally may not be considered for award, it has been held to be a revocation of the original offer precluding award on the basis of the original offer, *Integrated Bus. Sols., Inc. v. United States*, 58 Fed. Cl. 420 (2003); *Integrated Bus. Sols., Inc.*, Comp. Gen. Dec. B-292239, 2003 CPD ¶ 122.

[2] Procedure Following Receipt of Final Revisions

After receipt of final proposal revisions, the agency must reevaluate the proposals as quickly as possible. It is then in a position to proceed to source selection and award of a contract. However, under some circumstances, it may be necessary to reopen negotiations. An agency can obtain clarification of final proposal revisions, *VMD Sys. Integrators, Inc.*, Comp. Gen. Dec. B-401037.4, 2009 CPD ¶ 252; *IPlus, Inc.*, Comp. Gen. Dec. B-298020, 2006 CPD ¶ 90; *Antarctic Support Assocs. v. United States*, 46 Fed. Cl. 145 (2000), or correct a mistake in a final proposal revision, *Joint Threat Servs.*, Comp. Gen. Dec. B-178168, 98-1 CPD ¶ 18, but, if it enters into negotiations/discussions with one offeror, it must reopen discussions with all offerors in the competitive range, *Global Language Center*, Comp. Gen. Dec. B-413503.8, 2017 CPD ¶ 238; *Rotech Healthcare, Inc.*, Comp. Gen. Dec. B-413024, 2016 CPD ¶ 225; *International Res. Grp.*, Comp. Gen. Dec. B-286663, 2001 CPD ¶ 35, unless there has been no prejudice to the protester, *USATREX Int'l, Inc.*, Comp. Gen. Dec. B-275592, 98-1 CPD ¶ 99.

[a] Reevaluation

The first step after receipt of final proposal revisions is the reevaluation of each proposal to determine its current status in the competition. The failure to correctly assess the changes an offeror made in a proposal can lead to the granting of a protest. See, for example, *Celta Servs., Inc.*, Comp. Gen. Dec. B-411835, 2015 CPD ¶ 362 (agency based source selection decision on weaknesses that were corrected in final proposal revision); *Ashbury Int'l Grp., Inc.*, Comp. Gen. Dec. B-401123, 2009 CPD ¶ 140 (agency failed to test article submitted with final proposal revisions); *Contingency Mgmt. Grp., LLC*, Comp. Gen. Dec. B-309752, 2008 CPD ¶ 83 (agency's acceptance of nonconforming assumption of requirements in offeror's final proposal revision gave it unfair advantage over others); *Johnson Controls Sec. Sys.*, Comp. Gen. Dec. B-296490, 2007 CPD ¶ 102 (agency based award on material misrepresentation in final proposal revisions); *ITT Fed. Servs. Int'l Corp.*, Comp. Gen. Dec.

B-296783, 2007 CPD ¶ 43 (agency ignored requirement that offeror explain basis for reduced labor hours); *Advanced Sys. Dev., Inc.*, Comp. Gen. Dec. B-298411, 2006 CPD ¶ 137 (agency lack of understanding of awardee's revised prices led to irrational decision); *YORK Bldg. Servs., Inc.*, Comp. Gen. Dec. B-296948.2, 2005 CPD ¶ 202 (agency only evaluated final proposal revisions for acceptability); *Spherix, Inc.*, Comp. Gen. Dec. B-294572.3, 2005 CPD ¶ 183 (unfair evaluation of final proposal revisions); *Lockheed Martin Info. Sys.*, Comp. Gen. Dec. B-292836, 2003 CPD ¶ 230 (significant evaluation errors). If the offeror changes an aspect of its original proposal in the final proposal revisions, it is improper to evaluate the omitted element in making the final decision, *ANHAM FZCO*, Comp. Gen. Dec. B-415969, 2018 CPD ¶ 184.

Agency evaluators have the same discretion in evaluating final proposal revisions that they have in evaluating original proposals. Thus, an agency may use information in a cost proposal to downgrade a technical proposal, *Cygna Project Mgmt.*, Comp. Gen. Dec. B-236839, 90-1 CPD ¶ 21. Similarly, BAFOs were permitted to be downgraded for failing to specifically elaborate on how the work will be performed, *Northwestern Travel Agency, Inc.*, Comp. Gen. Dec. B-244592, 91-2 CPD ¶ 363, or how its costs have been estimated, *Labat-Anderson, Inc.*, Comp. Gen. Dec. B-287091, 2001 CPD ¶ 79. In *Fintrac, Inc.*, Comp. Gen. Dec. B-311462.2, 2008 CPD ¶ 191, GAO found that the agency had properly altered the weights of evaluation subfactors to correct an error in the original evaluation. Final proposal revision changes may also be disregarded if the agency concludes that they do not affect the initial evaluation, *Cobra Techs., Inc.*, Comp. Gen. Dec. B-280475, 98-2 CPD ¶ 98. In *SelectTech Bering Straits Solutions JV*, Comp. Gen. Dec. B-400964, 2009 CPD ¶ 100, the agency properly downgraded an offeror when it did not include initially proposed enhancements in the model contract submitted with its final proposal revisions, the agency correctly reasoning that the enhancement would not be contractually binding.

In assessing the impact of final proposal revisions, the agency can totally reevaluate the proposals, *Information Sys. Tech. Corp.*, Comp. Gen. Dec. B-288490.2, 2002 CPD ¶ 120, or reevaluate only the changes from the original proposal, *Ecology & Env't, Inc.*, Comp. Gen. Dec. B-277061.2, 97-2 CPD ¶ 65. It has been found proper for agency evaluators to assess the changes that revisions have made to the original proposal and report them to the source selection official, *Northwest Reg'l Educ. Lab.*, Comp. Gen. Dec. B-222591.3, 87-1 CPD ¶ 74; *VSE Corp.*, Comp. Gen. Dec. B-224397, 86-2 CPD ¶ 392, or to take the changes into consideration when making the source selection decision, *Marinette Marine Corp.*, Comp. Gen. Dec. B-400697, 2009 CPD ¶ 16; *Palmetto GBA, LLC*, Comp. Gen. Dec. B-298962, 2007 CPD ¶ 25. See also *Aircraft Porous Media, Inc.*, Comp. Gen. Dec. B-241665.2, 91-1 CPD ¶ 356, *recons. denied*, 91-1 CPD ¶ 613 (proper for agency not to bother rescoring because the changes in the BAFO could not have altered the original determination that two proposals were technically equal); *Cygnus Corp.*, Comp. Gen.

Dec. B-275957, 97-1 CPD ¶ 202 (agency acted properly in deciding that no technical rescoring was necessary when the competitors had made only minor changes to proposals that had been evaluated as excellent in the original scoring); and *Health Mgmt. Res., Inc.*, Comp. Gen. Dec. B-270185, 96-1 CPD ¶ 23 (rescoring not required because the agency found that each offeror "had improved to the same degree"). However, a lack of documentation showing that BAFOs have been evaluated will lead to a sustained protest, *Biospherics, Inc.*, Comp. Gen. Dec. B-278508.4, 98-2 CPD ¶ 96.

There is no requirement that the final proposals be evaluated by the same evaluators that scored the original proposals, *Data Flow Corp.*, 62 Comp. Gen. 506 (B-209499), 83-2 CPD ¶ 57. GAO has stated that there is nothing unreasonable about the fact that new evaluators reached different conclusions than the original evaluators, *Domain Name Alliance Registry*, Comp. Gen. Dec. B-310803.2, 2008 CPD ¶ 168. However, in limited circumstances GAO has held that agencies must provide a reasonable explanation for different evaluations of essentially the same final proposal as the original proposal, particularly where the same source selection official is responsible for both source selections, *eAlliant, LLC*, Comp. Gen. Dec. B-407332.6, 2015 CPD ¶ 229.

[b] Reopening Negotiations

Reopening negotiations is not a desirable course of action. It adds time and expense to the procurement and extends the time when information may be improperly disclosed. See *Mine Safety Appliances Co.*, Comp. Gen. Dec. B-242379.5, 92-2 CPD ¶ 76, holding that the conduct of another round of negotiations in the absence of a valid reason tends to undermine the integrity of the competitive negotiation process. Pre-Rewrite FAR 15.611(c) stated that negotiations should not be reopened "unless it is clearly in the Government's best interests to do so." In addition, DFARS 215.611 prohibited contracting officers from reopening negotiations unless higher-level approval was obtained. However, the FAR Part 15 Rewrite removed this coverage, leaving the matter to the contracting officer's discretion under the circumstances surrounding each procurement. In *Dynacs Eng'g Co.,* Comp. Gen. Dec. B-284234, 2000 CPD ¶ 50, GAO noted this change in holding that the agencies use of multiple rounds of discussions was not improper. Similarly, DoD requirement for higher level approval has been deleted from the DFARS.

Agencies are required to reopen discussions if the evaluation of the offeror's final proposal identifies significant weaknesses or deficiencies that were not identified in the original evaluation and hence not discussed in the original discussion, *Veterans Evaluation Servs., Inc.*, Comp. Gen. Dec. B-412940, 2016 CPD ¶ 185; *Al Long Ford*, Comp. Gen. Dec. B-297807, 2006 CPD ¶ 68; *Consolidated Eng'g Servs., Inc. v. United States*, 64 Fed. Cl. 617 (2005); *DevTech Sys., Inc.*, Comp. Gen. Dec. B-284860.2, 2001 CPD ¶ 11. See *Carahsoft Tech. Corp. v. United States*, 86 Fed. Cl. 325 (2009), holding that it is proper to reopen discussions in such circumstances even if the deficiency makes the proposal unacceptable. Furthermore, if discussions are reopened with one offeror in the competitive range, they must be reopened with all other offerors still in the range, *Global Language Center*, Comp. Gen. Dec. B-413503.8, 2017 CPD ¶ 238; *Cigna Gov't Servs., LLC*, Comp. Gen. Dec. B-297915.2, 2006 CPD ¶ 74; *Lockheed Martin Aeronautics Co.*, Comp. Gen. Dec. B-295401, 2005 CPD ¶ 41.

It is proper to reopen discussions if questions are not resolved in one offeror's proposal revisions, *General Dynamics—Ordnance & Tactical Sys.*, Comp. Gen. Dec. B-401658, 2009 CPD ¶ 217; substantial questions requiring discussions are raised by one of the BAFOs, *Ocean Tech., Inc.*, Comp. Gen. Dec. B-183749, 75-2 CPD ¶ 262; previously existing ambiguities are not discovered until after submission of BAFOs, 52 Comp. Gen. 409 (B-176913) (1973); *Swedlow, Inc.*, 53 Comp. Gen. 564 (B-178212), 74-1 CPD ¶ 55; additional technical information is needed to evaluate the proposals, *Introl Corp.*, Comp. Gen. Dec. B-194570, 80-1 CPD ¶ 41; government estimates are discovered to be in error, *Dyneteria, Inc.*, Comp. Gen. Dec. B-181707, 75-1 CPD ¶ 86; government requirements change, *ACS Sys. & Eng'g, Inc.*, Comp. Gen. Dec. B-275439.2, 97-1 CPD ¶ 126; incorrect information was provided to one offeror during discussions, *Computer Related Servs., Inc.*, Comp. Gen. Dec. B-244638, 91-2 CPD ¶ 420; specifications were not clear, *ES, Inc.*, Comp. Gen. Dec. B-258911.2, 95-1 CPD ¶ 168; or deficiencies in initial BAFO prevented offeror's acceptance, *Dube Travel Agency & Tours, Inc.*, Comp. Gen. Dec. B-270438, 96-1 CPD ¶ 141. Also upheld was a decision to reopen discussions and request a second round of BAFOs after the recommended awardee's place of performance had become unavailable and the quality of materials required by the government had changed, *Hayes Int'l Corp. v. United States*, 7 Cl. Ct. 681 (1985).

If discussions are reopened, it is proper to raise issues that were brought to an offeror's attention in the initial discussions, *Dynacs Eng'g Co.*, Comp. Gen. Dec. B-284234, 2000 CPD ¶ 50. GAO stated that this was an acceptable means of "maximizing the Government's ability to obtain best value" as called for by FAR 15.306(d)(2).

While the agency has the discretion to call for another round of proposals, it also has the discretion to refuse to do so. See *Textron, Inc. v. United States*, 74 Fed. Cl. 277 (2006), where the agency was not required to reopen negotiations when it asked for additional test data during the original discussions and concluded that the new data indicated a deficiency in the proposed ship without giving the protester the opportunity to explain the data. Thus, the agency is not obligated to bring up deficiencies remaining from the initial proposal when the offeror has already been informed of the deficiency, *LIS, Inc.*, Comp. Gen. Dec. B-400646.4, 2010 CPD ¶ 18; *ITT Indus. Space Sys., LLC*, Comp. Gen. Dec. B-309964, 2007 CPD ¶ 217; *Ideamatics, Inc.*, Comp. Gen. Dec. B-297791.2, 2006 CPD ¶ 87; *Si-Nor, Inc.*, Comp. Gen. Dec. B-290150.4, 2003 CPD ¶ 45.

It is also proper not to conduct further negotiations to clarify or amplify newly introduced aspects of its final proposal revision. See *SMS Data Prods.*

Grp., Inc., Comp. Gen. Dec. B-414548, 2017 CPD ¶ 222 (proposing new but unsatisfactory solution); *URS Fed. Servs., Inc.*, Comp. Gen. Dec. B-408678.5, 2014 CPD ¶ 186 (proposing less experienced employees a weakness); *Sabre Sys., Inc.*, Comp. Gen. Dec. B-402040.2, 2010 CPD ¶ 128 (incomplete data in response to weakness in original proposal); *Akal Sec., Inc.*, Comp. Gen. Dec. B-401469, 2009 CPD ¶ 183 (reduced staffing was a weakness); *Honeywell Tech. Solutions, Inc.*, Comp. Gen. Dec. B-400771, 2009 CPD ¶ 49 (protester demonstrated lack of understanding of requirement in responding to prior discussed weaknesses); *DRS C3 Sys., LLC*, Comp. Gen. Dec. B-310825, 2008 CPD ¶ 103 (design submitted in response to discussions inferior); *L-3 Commc'ns Corp.*, Comp. Gen. Dec. B-299227, 2007 CPD ¶ 83 (substitution of another product indicated a lack of technical competence); *MD Helicopters, Inc.*, Comp. Gen. Dec. B-298502, 2006 CPD ¶ 164 (level pricing over long contract posed a risk); *Air Prods. Healthcare*, Comp. Gen. Dec. B-298293, 2006 CPD ¶ 123 (new information on sufficiency of services did not to meet agency requirements); *Mechanical Equip. Co.*, Comp. Gen. Dec. B-292789.2, 2004 CPD ¶ 192 (lack of supporting data in final proposal revisions); *Cube-All Star Servs., Joint Venture*, Comp. Gen. Dec. B-291903, 2003 CPD ¶ 145 (proposal revision made proposal unacceptable); and *NLX Corp.*, Comp. Gen. Dec. B-288785, 2001 CPD ¶ 198 (significantly reduced price imposed a risk). Thus, an offeror takes the risk that aspects of its proposal included in the final proposal revisions for the first time will be found unacceptable by the agency, *Beachcraft Def. Co.*, Comp. Gen. Dec. B-406170.2, 2013 CPD ¶ 147 ("white paper" submitted to refute agency concerns led to finding of high risk); and *Global Solutions Network, Inc.*, Comp. Gen. Dec. B-298682.3, 2008 CPD ¶ 131 (single employee filling two key positions);

It is also proper not to conduct further negotiations if an offeror's situation changes after submission of its final proposal revisions, *Pioneering Evolution, LLC*, Comp. Gen. Dec. B-412016, 2015 CPD ¶ 385 (key person became unavailable).

This rule has been carried to the extreme in holding that an agency need not reopen discussions to permit correction of a mistake in the BAFO, *Standard Mfg. Co.*, 65 Comp. Gen. 451 (B-220455), 86-1 CPD ¶ 304; *American Elec. Lab., Inc.*, 65 Comp. Gen. 62 (B-219582), 85-2 CPD ¶ 545. Compare *FCC.O&M, Inc.*, Comp. Gen. Dec. B-238610.2, 91-1 CPD ¶ 26, where it was found proper to conduct another round of discussions in order to correct a mistake in the winning offeror's proposal.

§ 6.10 SOURCE SELECTION

Upon completion of the evaluation of the proposals, the agency is prepared to select the winning contractor(s). FAR 15.302 states: "The objective of source selection is to select the proposal that represents the best value." When the FAR 15.101-2 lowest-price technically acceptable source selection process is used, the selection decision can be made quite quickly because it does not involve tradeoffs. The only matters for determination are whether the lowest priced offer is technically acceptable and whether that offeror is responsible. Thus, there is not even a need to evaluate the technical acceptability of higher priced offerors. In FAR 15.101-2 tradeoff procurements, offers other than the lowest priced or other than the highest technically rated may be selected. Depending upon the evaluation factors and the evaluation scheme, this can be a more difficult decision requiring a significant degree of judgment to be exercised in selecting the source.

[A] Source Selection Authority

While the procurement statutes provide that the "agency," 41 U.S.C. § 253b(d)(3), or the "executive agency," 10 U.S.C. § 3303 (formerly § 3703(c)), shall award the contract, the FAR provisions focus on the individual who will make the selection and award decisions. This individual is called the source selection authority (SSA). FAR 15.303(a) provides that the contracting officer is the SSA "unless the agency head appoints another individual for a particular acquisition or group of acquisitions." In many agencies, particularly in large dollar value procurements, the SSA is a high-level agency official.

[1] Responsibilities

The source selection responsibilities of the SSA are set out in FAR 15.303(b), as follows:

> (4) Ensure that proposals are evaluated based solely on the factors and subfactors contained in the solicitation (10 U.S.C. 2305(b)(1) and 41 U.S.C. 3703(c));
>
> (5) Consider the recommendations of advisory boards or panels (if any);
>
> and
>
> (6) Select the source or sources whose proposal is the best value to the Government (10 U.S.C. 2305(b)(4)(B) and 41 U.S.C. 3703(d)).

In addition, the SSA must make a determination of whether to award without negotiation, award after receiving final proposal revisions, or call for further revisions.

Another responsibility of the SSA is to determine whether to cancel the solicitation. Under some circumstances, it would not be appropriate to continue a procurement and make an award. In this regard, the procurement statutes provide that "all . . . proposals . . . may be rejected if the head of the agency determines that such action is in the public interest," 10 U.S.C. § 3301(b) (formerly § 2305(b)(2)) and 41 U.S.C. § 3701(b). FAR 15.305(b) vests the authority to make this determination in the SSA. Pre-Rewrite FAR 15.608(b) dealt with this subject and contained a number of examples where rejection of all offers would be justified. It also required a determination, in writing, that one of the identified factors was present. However, this provision was deleted in the Rewrite which merely authorizes rejection if the SSA determines rejection to be in the "best interest of the Government." The SSA has broad discretion in making such determinations. Hence, cancellations have been found appropriate in *Open Spirit, LLC v. United States*, 131 Fed. Cl. 756 (2017) (agency encountered more stringent environmental regulations impacting procurement of leased building); *FFTF Restoration Co., LLC v. United States*, 86 Fed. Cl. 226 (2009) (agency encountered delays in awarding the contract, faced budget limitations and concluded that the remaining work could be more effectively performed by the incumbent contractor); *Advancing Tech. Sys. II*, Comp. Gen. Dec. B-415464.4, 2018 CPD ¶ 416 (agency found a better procurement vehicle); and *Lasmer Indus., Inc.*, Comp. Gen. Dec. B-400866.2, 2009 CPD ¶ 77 (it was more advantageous to procure the part from an existing contract). Cancellation is proper if the original procurement does not generate effective competition, *North Shore Med. Labs, Inc.*, Comp. Gen. Dec. B-311070, 2008 CPD ¶ 144 (no acceptable proposals and stringent RFP requirement limited competitors); *DCMS-ISA, Inc. v. United States*, 84 Fed. Cl. 501 (2008) (small business set aside cancelled because none of the competitors had sufficient experience); *Knight's Armament Co.*, Comp. Gen. Dec. B-299469, 2007 CPD ¶ 85 (none of the offered products met agency needs); *Glen/Mar Constr., Inc.*, Comp. Gen. Dec. B-298355, 2006 CPD ¶ 117 (all offered prices much higher than agency budget); *Sunshine Kids Serv. Supply Co.*, Comp. Gen. Dec. B-292141, 2003 CPD ¶ 119 (only HUBZone competitor submitted unacceptable proposal); *Nutech Laundry & Textiles, Inc.*, B-291739, 2003 CPD ¶ 34 (small business price was much higher than government estimate). Cancellation and resolicitation is also proper where the lowest price cannot be determined to be reasonable, *Razorcom Teleph & Net, LLC v. United States*, 56 Fed. Cl. 140 (2003); *Process Control Techs. v. United States*, 53 Fed. Cl. 71 (2002), and *Interstate Rock Prods., Inc. v. United States*, 50 Fed. Cl. 349 (2001). Another proper basis for cancellation is when the agency determines that there is another source for the product or service. See *Klinge Corp. v. United States*, 83 Fed. Cl. 773 (2008) (agency used Federal Supply Schedule after mistakenly concluding that protester's offer was noncompliant with the Trade Agreements Act); *Borenstein Grp., Inc.*, Comp. Gen. Dec. B-309751, 2007 CPD ¶ 174 (agency found that existing contract could be used); *Management Solutions, L.C.*, Comp. Gen. Dec. B-298883, 2006 CPD ¶ 197 (agency found item was required to be procured from Federal Prison Industries); and *CAT Flight Servs., Inc.*, Comp. Gen. Dec. B-294186, 2004 CPD ¶ 178 (agency found existing contract).

However, rejection of all offers and requiring resubmission or cancellation of the solicitation is a serious matter, particularly where substantial effort is required in the submission and evaluation of offers. Thus, rejection and cancellation would not be appropriate where concerns with the procurement could be addressed through negotiations, *A&W Flamar GmbH*, Comp. Gen. Dec.

B-278486, 98-1 CPD ¶ 40. Cancellation was held to be improper where the agency did not submit evidence to show that it intended to change its policy underlying the procurement, *FMS Inv. Corp. v. United States*, 139 Fed. Cl. 221 (2018), where agency officials could not support their reason for cancellation and there was an appearance of bias against the protester, *Starry Assocs., Inc. v. United States*, 127 Fed. Cl. 539 (2016), where prices had been disclosed and the agency intended to move to a sealed bid procurement, *Rand & Jones Enters. Co.*, Comp. Gen. Dec. B-296483, 2005 CPD ¶ 142, where the winning small business was found nonresponsible without referring the matter to the Small Business Administration, *Phil Howry Co.*, Comp. Gen. Dec. B-291402.3, 2003 CPD ¶ 33, where a determination of excessive price was not warranted, *Nutech Laundry & Textile, Inc. v. United States*, 56 Fed. Cl. 588 (2003), and where the sole reasons were to avoid contracting with an offeror, *Parcel 49C Ltd. P'ship v. United States*, 31 F.3d 1147 (Fed. Cir. 1994), and *126 Northpoint Plaza Ltd. P'ship v. United States*, 34 Fed. Cl. 105 (1995).

[2] Independent Judgment

FAR 15.308 requires that, while the SSA may use the analyses of other participants in the process, the source selection decision must represent the SSA's independent judgment. The information furnished to the SSA can vary in nature and detail. It may consist only of evaluation results or may also contain further analyses and recommendations for award. The SSA must make an assessment of the information and determine whether it conforms to the evaluation factors specified in the solicitation and whether it is sufficient to make a rational selection for award. Thus, merely reiterating the SSEB's findings was held not to demonstrate that the SSA had exercised independent judgment, *2M Research Servs., LLC v. United States*, 139 Fed. Cl. 471 (2018). Compare *ATSC Aviation, LLC v. United States*, 141 Fed. Cl. 670 (2019), stating at 701:

> The Selection Authority "may use reports and analyses prepared by others" when exercising independent judgment regarding selection decisions. FAR § 15.308. The Selection Authority does not need to duplicate the extensive analysis performed by the Evaluation Board, nor document every detail that forms the basis of the selection decision. Evidence of review of the relevant assessments and of a decision consistent with such findings suffices to find the Selection Authority's decision to be coherent and reasonable.

See also *Dewberry Crawford Grp.*, Comp. Gen. Dec. B-415940.10, 2018 CPD ¶ 297, holding that an SSA properly adopted a source selection document prepared by the SSEB when he stated that the document gave him a detailed understanding of the relative merits of the proposals with which he concurred.

In fulfilling his or her obligations, the SSA can become deeply involved in all aspects of the procurement. See *Digital Sys. Grp., Inc.*, Comp. Gen. Dec.

B-286931, 2001 CPD ¶ 50, rejecting a protest that the contracting officer, acting as the SSA, had approved the source selection plan, conducted discussions, served as a member of the evaluation board and the cost team. The decision states that "While it is conceivable that a CO's active participation in multiple stages of the evaluation process could compromise that process, that clearly is not the case here." See also *JW Holding Grp. & Assocs., Inc.*, Comp. Gen. Dec. B-285882.3, 2003 CPD ¶ 126, denying a protest that the SSA served as the head of the price evaluation team. Compare *Wackenhut Servs., Inc. v. United States*, 85 Fed. Cl. 273 (2008), suggesting that it may have been improper for the SSA to influence the evaluators during the evaluation process.

A suggestion from the contracting officer that the SSA "beef up" the explanations for arriving at the source selection decision did not indicate that the SSA had not exercised independent judgment, *Microdyne Outsourcing, Inc. v. United States*, 72 Fed. Cl. 694 (2006). Similarly, the SEB's updating of past performance information after source selection did not indicate that the SEB had "usurped" the SSA's function when the contracting officer stated that he had briefed the SSA of the new information, *Hanford Integrated Infrastructure Servs., Contractor, LLC*, Comp. Gen. Dec. B-418411, 2020 CPD ¶ 159.

[a] Evaluations or Recommendations

In smaller procurements the SSA (generally the contracting officer) may participate in the entire evaluation process with the result that there is no need to communicate the results of the evaluation to the SSA. However, in larger procurements there will be such a need because the SSA has not participated in the evaluation. In that situation agencies generally require the preparation of written documentation summarizing the results of the evaluation and often require briefings of the SSA. See DoD Source Selection Procedures containing extensive guidance at 1.4 on the roles of the various participants (SSA, SSAC, SSEB, PCO) in this process. Procedures that communicate summaries of the evaluations to the SSA have been sustained as fully adequate to ensure rational source selection decisions. See, for example, *Sabreliner Corp.*, Comp. Gen. Dec. B-242023, 91-1 CPD ¶ 326, where GAO stated:

> The SSA is not required to personally review the proposals or the complete evaluation documentation, but can rely upon a briefing that presents the results of the proposal evaluation. See *Systems & Processes Eng'g Corp.*, B-234142, May 10, 1989, 89-1 CPD ¶ 441. Here, the SSA, in addition to receiving a technical evaluation briefing, reviewed the proposal analysis report, which set forth, among other things, a description of the evaluation standards and criteria; a description of the competing proposals; a comparative evaluation analysis of the proposal; the offerors' proposed prices/costs; and the performance risk assessment.

In most cases the SSA can rely on the assessments of the evaluators and the evaluation board's conclusions. See *PiperCoughlin, LLC*, Comp. Gen. Dec. B-414352.2, 2018 CPD ¶ 143 (SSA based decision on SSAC's changes to SSEB report); *Oasis Sys., LLC*, Comp. Gen. Dec. B-407273,54, 2014 CPD ¶ 199 (SSA based decision on SSEB's report); *Wyle Labs., Inc.*, Comp. Gen. Dec. B-311123, 2009 CPD ¶ 96 (SSA based decision on SSEB's overriding of evaluators judgment of risk); *MD Helicopters, Inc.*, Comp. Gen. Dec. B-298502, 2006 CPD ¶ 164 (SSA based decision detailed discussions with SSEB, SSAC and users or product being procured); *Metro Mach. Corp.*, Comp. Gen. Dec. B-295744, 2005 CPD ¶ 112 (SSA accepted evaluation assessments of three evaluation committees); and *Computer Scis. Corp. v. United States*, 51 Fed. Cl. 297 (2001) (SSA based decision on evaluators comparative assessment of offerors' past performance). However, merely reiterating the findings of the SSEB was held inadequate, *2M Research Servs., LLC v. United States*, 139 Fed. Cl. 471 (2018). Compare *Dewberry Crawford Grp.*, Comp. Gen. Dec. B-415940.11, 2018 CPD ¶ 298, denying a protest when the SSA relied on a draft "source selection decision document" prepared by the SSEB.

When there is disagreement among the evaluators or within an evaluation board, the SSA may have a heightened responsibility to explain his or her reliance on the evaluation report. See *Information Scis. Corp. v. United States*, 73 Fed. Cl. 70 (2006), *amended*, 75 Fed. Cl. 406 (2007), sustaining a protest where the SSA adopted a minority report almost verbatim in the source selection decision. The court held that this did not demonstrate the exercise of independent judgment—apparently because the SSA did not explain why the minority view was correct. Compare *PAE-Parsons Global Logistics Servs., LLC v. United States*, 147 Fed. Cl. 294 (2020), denying a protest where the SSA rejected the SSAC's recommended source selection decision.

[b] Reliance Not Justified

The SSA is not entitled to rely upon faulty evaluations. Thus, the SSA is ultimately responsible for any mistakes made in the evaluation process. In *J.A. Jones Mgmt. Servs., Inc.*, Comp. Gen. Dec. B-276864, 97-2 CPD ¶ 47, GAO observed:

> While an agency's initial review of proposals may be done independently, it is necessary for the agency at some point to make a rational comparison of the relative merits of directly competing proposals. The agency's SSA cannot make a rational comparison where the evaluators' point scores do not accurately reflect the relative strengths and weaknesses of the competing proposals and the record lacks adequate documentation in support of such technical point scores. Here, the dearth of evaluation narratives or other explanations in this evaluation record and the SSA's summary reliance on the point scores, which have been sufficiently shown by the protester to be

> inaccurate in numerous areas, lead us to the conclusion that the SSA could not and did not make a reasonable selection decision. See *Adelaide Blomfield Management Co.*, [Comp. Gen. Dec. B-253128.2, 93-2 CPD ¶ 197], at 4-6. In sum, on the evaluation record furnished to our Office—consisting of point scores and cursory narratives—we find the absence of a consistent, reasonable and accurate evaluation scoring as well as the absence of supporting narrative documentation; moreover, the agency has offered no substantive response to the protester's concerns in response to the protest, and our review shows none. Here, we simply are unable to assess the reasonableness of the agency's selection decision. Accordingly, we sustain the protest.

Thus, protests have been granted when the SSA made the selection decision based on the conclusions of the evaluators but it was later determined that the conclusions were unsupported. See *HomeSafe Alliance, LLC*, Comp. Gen. Dec. B-418266,5, 2020 CPD ¶ 350 (SSA relied on undocumented evaluation of oral presentation and mistakes in determining responsibility); *Harmonia Holdings Grp., LLC*, Comp. Gen. Dec. B-417475.3, 2019 CPD ¶ 333 (SSA relied on erroneous evaluations that were without documentary support); *2M Research Servs., LLC v. United States*, 139 Fed. Cl. 471 (2018) (SSA relied on SSEB mistaken inclusion of winning offeror in competitive range); *American Corr. Healthcare, Inc. v. United States*, 137 Fed. Cl. 395 (2018) (SSA relied on evaluators' failure to determine whether offered services were available); *Immersion Consulting, LLC*, Comp. Gen. Dec. B-415155.4, 2018 CPD ¶ 187 (SSA relied on erroneous evaluation by SSEB); *EFW, Inc.*, Comp. Gen. Dec. B-412608, 2016 CPD ¶ 34 (SSA relied on SSEB's conclusion of high risk when protester offered as 100% share above target cost in an FPI contract); *BAE Syst. Information & Electronic Sys. Integration, Inc.*, Comp. Gen. Dec. B-408565, 2013 CPD ¶ 278 (SSA relied on evaluation that had removed weaknesses without any explanation); *Health Net Fed. Servs., LLC*, Comp. Gen. Dec. B-401652.3, 2009 CPD ¶ 220 (SSA relied on evaluator's conclusion that corporate parent of offeror met experience requirement when neither had investigated role of parent); *Contingency Mgmt. Grp., LLC*, Comp. Gen. Dec. B-309752, 2008 CPD ¶ 83 (decision based on responses to scenario in RFP where evaluators did not consider impact of proposals that altered the assumptions in the scenario with the result that they were able to propose lower prices); *Apptis, Inc.*, Comp. Gen. Dec. B-299457, 2008 CPD ¶ 49 (SSA relied on SSEB's improper use of past performance to evaluate risk of technical solution); *Keeton Corrs., Inc.*, Comp. Gen. Dec. B-293348, 2005 CPD ¶ 44 (SSA relied on misleading narrative supporting contracting officer's evaluation of past performance); *SDS Int'l, Inc.*, Comp. Gen. Dec. B-291183, 2003 CPD ¶ 137 (SSA based decision on evaluators' misreading of technical proposal); *Ashland Sales & Serv. Co.*, Comp. Gen. Dec. B-291206, 2003 CPD ¶ 36 (SSA relied on contracting officer document that contained factual errors); *Shumaker Trucking & Excavating Contractors, Inc.*, Comp. Gen. Dec. B-290732, 2002 CPD ¶ 169 (SSA endorsed contracting officer's conclusion that was based on higher point score with no consideration of strengths and weaknesses); *Green Valley Trans., Inc.*, Comp. Gen. Dec. B-285283, 2000 CPD ¶ 133 (SSA followed the evaluators' theory that past performance should be rated on the basis of the number of late deliveries without considering the volume of shipments); *CRAssociates, Inc.*, Comp. Gen. Dec. B-282075.2, 2000 CPD ¶ 63 (SSA relied on faulty technical evaluation and mathematical scoring mistakes); and *Saco Def. Corp.*, Comp. Gen. Dec. B-283885, 2000 CPD ¶ 34 (SSA relied on an evaluation that the prospective winning offeror had furnished sufficient information to demonstrate that its quality system was adequate). Compare *WellPoint Military Care Corp. v. United States*, 953 F.3d 1373 (Fed. Cir. 2020), where the source selection decision was upheld because the mistakes in the initial evaluation were not carried forward to the source selection decision.

[c] Ordering Reevaluation

The SSA can order a complete reevaluation if there are doubts about the validity of the initial evaluation. See *Team BOS/Naples—Gemmo S.p.A./DelJen*, Comp. Gen. Dec. B-298865.3, 2008 CPD ¶ 11 (not questioning reevaluation when SSA found errors in initial evaluation); *East/West Indus., Inc.*, Comp. Gen. Dec. B-278734.4, 98-1 CPD ¶ 143 (not questioning reconvening the evaluators to perform a more detailed evaluation of the proposals); and *EBA Eng'g, Inc.*, Comp. Gen. Dec. B-275818, 97-1 CPD ¶ 127 (finding proper agency's decision to replace panel members in order to avoid the appearance of impropriety).

[d] Rescore or Conduct Own Evaluation

The SSA is not bound by the rankings, scores, or recommendations of either the evaluators, boards or other intermediate groups, as long as the official has a rational basis for the differing evaluation. See *IBM Corp.*, Comp. Gen. Dec. B-415798, 2018 CPD ¶ 130, stating that SSAs "have inherent authority to independently evaluate proposals." In some cases, source selection officials merely ignore the ratings and make the source selection decision based on the narratives. However, in most instances, an attempt is made to make the ratings an accurate reflection of the merits of the proposals.

There have been numerous protest decisions upholding rescoring by source selection officials, either explicitly or implicitly. See *SOC, LLC*, Comp. Gen. Dec. B-418487.2, 2021 CPD ¶ 75 (SSA reassessed past performance evaluation); *BEAT, LLC*, Comp. Gen. Dec. B-418235, 2020 CPD ¶ 64 (SSA agreed with cost analyst's new evaluation of protester's G&A rate accounting); *East Coast Utility Contractors, Ltd.*, Comp. Gen. Dec. B-415463, 2018 CPD ¶ 30 (SSA agreed with CO's upgrading of two subfactors); *Advanced Tech. Sys., Inc.*, Comp. Gen. Dec. B-413291, 2016 CPD ¶ 309 (SSA changed marginal rating to unacceptable rating based on "material deficiency"); *CyQuest Business Solutions, Inc.*, Comp. Gen. Dec. B-410366, 2015 CPD ¶ 13 (SSA downgraded past performance rating);

TPL, Inc., Comp. Gen. Dec. B-297136.10, 2006 CPD ¶ 104 (SSA disagreed with evaluators' assessment of program management subfactor); *University Research Co.*, Comp. Gen. Dec. B-294358.6, 2005 CPD ¶ 83 (contracting officer disregarded assessments of evaluator and found technical proposals equal); *Synoptic Sys. Corp.*, Comp. Gen. Dec. B-290789.4, 2003 CPD ¶ 42 (SSA reevaluated proposals after outcome prediction by GAO); and *Sayed Hamid Behbehani & Sons, WLL*, Comp. Gen. Dec. B-288818.6, 2002 CPD ¶ 163 (SSA reevaluated proposals without reference to original evaluations).

When an SSA makes an independent assessment, it will be subject to scrutiny for reasonableness. See *Prism Maritime, LLC*, Comp. Gen. Dec. B-409267.2, 2014 CPD ¶ 124 (SSA unreasonably reversed all negative findings of evaluators); *Consolidated Eng'g Servs.Inc.*, Comp. Gen. Dec. B-311313, 2008 CPD ¶ 146 (SSA changed experience evaluation based on issues not in RFP); *AT&T Corp.*, Comp. Gen. Dec. B-299542.3, 2008 CPD ¶ 65 (no explanation of how SSA arrived at different conclusion than evaluators regarding the impact of overstaffing); *IDEA Int'l, Inc. v. United States*, 74 Fed. Cl. 129 (2006) (SSA awarded to low price without considering evaluators' conclusion that protester had "slightly stronger proposal"); *DynCorp Int'l LLC*, Comp. Gen. Dec. B-289863, 2002 CPD ¶ 83 (SSA discounted weaknesses in awardee's proposal without explaining rationale for decision); and*AIU North Am., Inc.*, Comp. Gen. Dec. B-283743.2, 2000 CPD ¶ 39 (SSA's determination that technical proposals were equal was neither supported by contemporaneous documentation nor satisfactorily explained during the protest).

In a number of cases, a source selection decision has been upheld on the basis that the SSA implicitly rescored some aspect of the evaluation. For example, in *PRC Kentron, Inc.*, Comp. Gen. Dec. B-230212, 88-1 CPD ¶ 537, rescoring was permitted to overcome the over reliance on incumbency by the evaluators, but "no formal rescoring was performed." See also *GTE Hawaiian Tel. Co.*, Comp. Gen. Dec. B-276487.2, 97-2 CPD ¶ 21 (SSA acted rationally in ignoring a significant difference in technical scores that seemed to greatly overstate the actual difference between the offerors); *NKF Eng'g, Inc.*, Comp. Gen. Dec. B-232143, 88-2 CPD ¶ 497 (contracting officer properly considered the protester's score an exaggeration of its technical superiority because the evaluation committee did not consider relevant factors in management and employee transition when giving the scores); and *CRC Sys., Inc.*, Comp. Gen. Dec. B-207847, 83-1 CPD ¶ 462 (contracting officer implicitly lowered the protester's high score because its offer did not satisfy all the RFP requirements). In an unusual case, *Bank St. Coll. of Educ.*, 63 Comp. Gen. 393 (B-213209), 84-1 CPD ¶ 607, *recons. denied*, 84-2 CPD ¶ 445, the agency director overturned a finding of technical superiority made by a technical evaluation panel without actually altering the technical scores. GAO approved this intervention into the selection process finding that the director properly concluded that the awardee's proposal was actually technically superior because the level of effort in the protester's proposal deviated significantly from the RFP's estimated level of effort.

Implicit rescoring is not sound practice and should be avoided. When the source selection official concludes that rescoring is necessary, the contract file should contain a clear indication of the rescoring that has occurred and the justification for that rescoring.

The SSA is also permitted to conduct a completely independent evaluation if the original evaluation is not acceptable. See *Benchmark Sec., Inc.*, Comp. Gen. Dec. B-247655.2, 93-1 CPD ¶ 133, where GAO affirmed the decision of the SSA after he completely altered the evaluation of the offerors, determined that the two best proposals were technically equal and that costs of performance would be equivalent, and selected the incumbent contractor—commenting that the evaluation and source selection were well reasoned and thoroughly documented. See also *Murphy Co.*, Comp. Gen. Dec. B-415589, 2018 CPD ¶ 39 (upholding SSA's reassessment of protester's technical proposal); *Fort Carson Support Servs. v. United States*, 71 Fed. Cl. 571 (2006) (upholding SSA's reassessment of past performance of protester); *Jason Assocs. Corp.*, Comp. Gen. Dec. B-278689, 98-1 CPD ¶ 67 (upholding SSA's reevaluation of sample writings when it became known that they had been previously accepted by the agency); *EBA Eng'g, Inc.*, Comp. Gen. Dec. B-275818, 97-1 CPD ¶ 127 (upholding SSA's independent assessment when the evaluation panel was severely divided); *LTR Training Sys., Inc.*, Comp. Gen. Dec. B-274996, 97-1 CPD ¶ 71 (upholding SSA's decision to bypass the evaluations and make a completely independent assessment of the proposals determining that they were technically equal in merit); and *Ryan Assocs., Inc.*, Comp. Gen. Dec. B-274194, 97-1 CPD ¶ 2 (upholding SSA's independent cost/technical tradeoff differing from the technical evaluators' tradeoff analysis based on criticism of the contracting officer).

The SSA is permitted to use information in one of the segments of a proposal to alter an evaluation of another segment. For example, in a procurement which precluded the technical evaluators from seeing the pricing proposal, the source selection evaluation board made substantial adjustments to the technical evaluation based on information in the pricing proposal. GAO denied a protest—ruling that this procedure was entirely proper, *Cygna Project Mgmt.*, Comp. Gen. Dec. B-236839, 90-1 CPD ¶ 21. Failure to correlate the information in the segments of an offeror's proposal can lead to an irrational evaluation or at least to a poor selection of the source. Hence, SSAs should ensure that such correlation is made, with commensurate adjustments to the scores, before the source selection decision is made.

[3] Allegations of Bias

Offerors are entitled to fair and impartial treatment in the source selection process and have a right to an unbiased determination of which source should receive the award. In a number of cases, charges have been made that the selection was based upon favoritism. However, it has been very difficult to overcome a decision through the allegation of bias of the SSA. In *Avtel Servs., Inc. v.*

United States, 70 Fed. Cl. 173 (2005), the court held that a protester must overcome the presumption that government officials act in good faith in order to prove bias. In *Conax Fla. Corp. v. United States*, 641 F. Supp. 408 (D.D.C. 1986), *aff'd*, 824 F.2d 1124 (D.C. Cir. 1987), the court held that even if a protester establishes some degree of bias, it cannot win unless it can show that the source selection decision was unreasonable. In addition, in *Howard Cooper Corp. v. United States*, 763 F. Supp. 829, 841 (E.D. Va. 1991), the court, quoting *Arrowhead Metals, Ltd. v. United States*, 8 Cl. Ct. 703, 712 (1985), stated that claims of bias must be established by "well-nigh irrefragable proof." In *GE Gov't Servs., Inc. v. United States*, 788 F. Supp. 581 (D.D.C. 1992), a protester attempted to establish bias by providing statements about the SSA that demonstrated he was prejudiced against the protester. The protester also submitted evidence of sexual improprieties with a contractor employee. The court denied any relief because there was no proof that the source selection decision was affected by any alleged bias. It based its decision, to a large extent, on the fact that other agency officials that had participated in the procurement had also arrived at the decision that the selected contractor had offered the "best value" to the government.

GAO also requires very clear evidence of bias, *enrGies, Inc.*, Comp. Gen. Dec. B-408609.9, 2014 CPD ¶ 158. For example, in *Centra Tech., Inc.*, Comp. Gen. Dec. B-274744, 97-1 CPD ¶ 35, GAO found no evidence that the personal relationship between the director of the Johnson Space Center and the president of the awardee firm improperly influenced the SSA's decision because the SSA was in a subordinate position to the director. GAO pointed out that although the director appointed the SSA, the director was not involved in the evaluation nor was there any evidence that the director had any contact with the source selection team during the course of the procurement. See also *TruLogic, Inc.*, Comp. Gen. Dec. B-297252.3, 2006 CPD ¶ 29 (failure to follow recommendation of evaluation panel not evidence of bias); *Millar Elevator Serv. Co.*, Comp. Gen. Dec. B-284870.5, 2001 CPD ¶ 34 (no proof of bias in letter written to a competitor by the project manager on a previous project, who was serving as an evaluator, suggesting that it could win this procurement by performing well on that project); and *J.A. Jones Grupo d Servicios, SA*, Comp. Gen. Dec. B-283234, 99-2 CPD ¶ 80 (no bias when contracting officer advised the incumbent contractor to make its oral presentation as if it were a new contractor and not rely on fact that it was the incumbent).

In several instances GAO has dealt with source selection decision effected by bias when the SSA admitted bias toward the Boeing Co. See *Lockheed Martin Aeronautics Co.*, Comp. Gen. Dec. B-295401, 2005 CPD ¶ 41 (protest sustained when biased SSA required technical ratings be changed and discussions to be reopened to favor Boeing); *Lockheed Martin Corp.*, Comp. Gen. Dec. B-295402, 2005 CPD ¶ 24 (protest sustained when biased senior procurement official deleted a requirement and its evaluation factor to favor Boeing). See also *Ball Aerospace & Techs. Corp.*, Comp. Gen. Dec. B-298522, 2006 CPD ¶ 113, rejecting a protest because it was not timely filed after the public admission of bias.

Although GAO normally rejects allegations of bias, it has recommended, in the face of protests of unfair treatment of an offeror, that the agency appoint a new source selection team to reevaluate the proposals. See, for example, *Meridian Mgmt. Corp.*, Comp. Gen. Dec. B-281287.10, 2001 CPD ¶ 5 (unequal treatment of offerors "makes it advisable to convene a new source selection team"). Agencies have also appointed new personnel as a means of overcoming allegations of bias. See *U-Tech Servs. Corp.*, Comp. Gen. Dec. B-284183.3, 2002 CPD ¶ 78 (entirely new team); *RTF/TCI/EAI J.V.*, Comp. Gen. Dec. B-280422.3, 98-2 CPD ¶ 162 (new evaluators); and *EBA Eng'g, Inc.*, Comp. Gen. Dec. B-275818, 97-1 CPD ¶ 127 (chairman of evaluation panel).

[B] Selection Decision

Neither the procurement statutes nor the FAR specify detailed standards for the source selection decision. The statutes merely require that the award is to be made "to the responsible source whose proposal is most advantageous to the United States, considering only cost or price and the other factors included in the solicitation," 10 U.S.C. § 3303(c) (formerly § 2305(b)(4)(C)) or "based solely on the factors specified in the solicitation," 41 U.S.C. § 3701(a). The FAR adds little, simply stating that the selection decision "shall be based upon a comparative assessment of proposals against all source selection criteria in the solicitation," FAR 15.308. Thus, the rules governing the source selection decision have been derived from decisions in contract award controversies.

The elements of the source selection decision are the comparative assessment of the proposals against the evaluation criteria and the ultimate tradeoff decision if the lowest price proposal is not rated most highly on the non-price factors, *Arrowpoint Corp.*, Comp. Gen. Dec. B-417375.2, 2019 CPD ¶ 367. The SSA has broad discretion in making the tradeoff decision but must make the decision consistent with the description of the evaluation factors and evaluation scheme in the solicitation.

[1] Broad Discretion in Tradeoff Decision

If the selection decision is based on the evaluation factors enumerated in the RFP, the selection official has broad discretion in determining which offer is most advantageous to the government. See *Lockheed Missiles & Space Co. v. Bentsen*, 4 F.3d 955 (Fed. Cir. 1993), stating that "effective contracting demands broad discretion." Thus, the selection will be upheld so long as there is a coherent and reasonable explanation for the selection, *Latecoere Int'l, Inc. v. Dep't of the Navy*, 19 F.3d 1342 (11th Cir. 1994). To be successful, a protester must show the selection to be "irrational or unreasonable," *Analytical & Research Tech.*,

Inc. v. United States, 39 Fed. Cl. 34 (1997). In *Advanced C4 Solutions, Inc.*, Comp. Gen. Dec. B-416250.2, 2018 CPD ¶ 344, GAO stated:

> Source selection officials in negotiated best-value tradeoff procurements have broad discretion in making price/technical tradeoffs, and the extent to which one may be sacrificed for the other is governed only by the tests of rationality and consistency with the solicitation's evaluation criteria. *Democracy Int'l, Inc.*, B-415243, B-415243.2, Dec. 13, 2017, 2018 CPD ¶ 293 at 4.

[2] Consistency with the Solicitation

Despite having a great deal of discretion in making the ultimate tradeoff decision, the SSA must follow the guidance in the RFP as to the way the selection decision will be made. However, GAO holds that there is no requirement that the SSA comply with the source selection plan adopted by the agency in formulating the procurement, *Delta Dental of Cal.*, Comp. Gen. Dec. B-296307, 2005 CPD ¶ 152. See *SaxmanOne, LLC*, Comp. Gen. Dec. B-414748, 2017 CPD ¶ 264, stating: "It is the RFP, not internal evaluation materials, that forms the compact between the agency and offerors about how proposals will be evaluated." In contrast, some decisions of the Court of Federal Claims have assessed the impact of the agency's failure to follow the source selection plan. See *Fort Carson Support Servs. v. United States*, 71 Fed. Cl. 571 (2006) (agency's failure to adhere to its source selection plan made its source selection decision arbitrary), *USfalcon, Inc. v. United States*, 92 Fed. Cl. 436 (2010) (failure to follow the source selection plan without the approval of the SSA could be evidence of an erroneous evaluation); *Progressive Indus., Inc. v. United States*, 129 Fed. Cl. 457 (2016) (deviation from procedures in source selection plan part of analysis leading to conclusion that corrective action was not rational). Other decisions of the court have held that internal documents confer no right on offerors, *Manson Constr. Co. v. United States*, 79 Fed. Cl. 16 (2007); *Allied Tech. Grp., Inc. v. United States*, 94 Fed. Cl. 16 (2010), *aff'd*, 649 F.3d 1320 (Fed. Cir. 2011); *Atlantic Diving Supply, Co. v. United States*, 107 Fed. Cl. 244 (2012).

[a] Consideration of All Factors

The SSA must consider all evaluation factors as called for by the RFP and may not introduce new factors or subfactors into the process. See *DRS Tech. Servs., Inc.*, Comp. Gen. Dec. B-411573.2, 2015 CPD ¶ 363 (improper to fail to require narrative explanation of low labor hours as required by RFP); *Navistar Def., LLC*, Comp. Gen. Dec. B-401865, 2009 CPD ¶ 258 (improper to fail to consider risk of lack of key tooling when RFP stated that existing production capability would be evaluated for risk); *Apptis, Inc.*, Comp. Gen. Dec. B-299457, 2008 CPD ¶ 49 (past performance improperly used to evaluate risk of technical solution); *ProTech Corp.*, Comp. Gen. Dec. B-294818, 2005 CPD ¶ 73 ("betterments" not given consideration called for by RFP); *KIRA, Inc.*, Comp. Gen. Dec. B-287573, 2001 CPD ¶ 152 (improper to consider possible bankruptcy of subcontractor because financial ability was not a factor); *Courtland Mem'l Hosp.*, Comp. Gen. Dec. B-286890, 2001 CPD ¶ 48 (one factor not given the importance stated in the RFP and another factor ignored); *Wackenhut Int'l, Inc.*, Comp. Gen. Dec. B-286193, 2001 CPD ¶ 8 (improper to not consider full compensation plan when RFP called for comprehensive review of plans); *Meridian Mgmt. Corp*, Comp. Gen. Dec. B-285127, 2000 CPD ¶ 121 (improper to consider experience in performing specialized work when RFP gave no indication that such work was required); *Lloyd H. Kessler, Inc.*, Comp. Gen. Dec. B-284693, 2000 CPD ¶ 96 (improper to consider undesignated special experience that was treated as 40% of total non-price evaluation); and *AIU North Am., Inc.*, Comp. Gen. Dec. B-283743.2, 2000 CPD ¶ 39 (agency did not consider the "availability of corporate resources" factor).

The evaluation criteria in the RFP must be followed even if this produces an irrational result. See *Unified Indus., Inc.*, Comp. Gen. Dec. B-237868, 90-1 CPD ¶ 346, *recons. denied*, 90-2 CPD ¶ 120, where the agency was required to follow the RFP statement that all offerors would be evaluated using "the same number of hours" even though this meant evaluating the incumbent contractor on labor hours that it would not incur in performing the proposed contract. GAO dismissed the Navy's argument that this would be "irrational and unrealistic" holding that the rule requiring evaluation in accordance with the RFP was firm. Clearly, in this case, the agency should have amended the evaluation criteria in the RFP when it found that the stated criteria produced an irrational result.

As discussed in § 6.03, this rule does not prevent evaluation using any matters within the scope of the factors and subfactors set forth in the RFP, and there are numerous cases giving a broad interpretation of scope.

[b] Follow Selection Scheme

The SSA must follow the decisional scheme described in the RFP. For example, if the RFP states that award will be made to the proposal with the best value based on a tradeoff analysis, the agency may not select the lowest-priced offer among those proposals that are technically acceptable, *Patriot Solutions, LLC*, Comp. Gen. Dec. B-413779, 2016 CPD ¶ 376; and *Special Operations Grp., Inc.*, Comp. Gen. Dec. B-287013, 2001 CPD ¶ 73. Neither may an agency evaluate one of the non-price factors on a pass/fail basis when the RFP lists it as a factor to be used in making a tradeoff decision, *Helicopter Transport Servs., LLC*, Comp. Gen. Dec. B-400295, 2008 CPD ¶ 180. GAO concluded that no tradeoff had been made in these circumstances even though the source selection decision stated that the winning offeror's proposal was "considered the best value to the government based on past performance and technical capability." Furthermore, the agency must use the RFP evaluation factors in their order of importance, *BayFirst Sols., LLC v. United States*, 102 Fed. Cl. 677 (2012), and may not use an unstated factor, *Laboratory Corp. of Am. Holdings v. United States*, 116 Fed. Cl. 643 (2014).

In a tradeoff procurement, an SSA may not select the offerors with the highest rated technical proposals as long as they have fair and reasonable prices. See *Technatomy Corp.*, Comp. Gen. Dec. B-414672.5, 2018 CPD ¶ 353, reasoning that there was no tradeoff between technical and price. See also. *Beacon Auto Parts*, Comp. Gen. Dec. B-287483, 2001 CPD ¶ 116 (agency improperly awarded to the offeror with the best technical score after determining that it had proposed a "fair and reasonable" price); *Electronic Design, Inc.*, Comp. Gen. Dec. B-279662.2, 98-2 CPD ¶ 69 (agency improperly chose the best technical offer from those that were priced within the agency budget).

An agency must include in its tradeoff analysis any lower-priced offeror that submits an acceptable proposal, *Finlen Complex, Inc.*, Comp. Gen. Dec. B-288280, 2001 CPD ¶ 167. See also *Coastal Env'ts, Inc.*, Comp. Gen. Dec. B-401889, 2009 CPD ¶ 261 (improper tradeoff between the two offerors that had been rated "good" on the non-price factors, omitting consideration of lower offerors that had been rated "acceptable"); *T-C Transcription, Inc.*, Comp. Gen. Dec. B-401470, 2009 CPD ¶ 172 (improper tradeoff between offeror rated "excellent" on non-price factors and lowest priced offeror rated "good"—omitting other offerors rated "good"); *Universal Bldg. Maint., Inc.*, Comp. Gen. Dec. B-282456, 99-2 CPD ¶ 32 (improper consideration of only the four highest ranked technical proposals with the result that no tradeoff analysis was made of the protester's lowest price proposal).

Award may not be made to an offeror that fails to meet a "material solicitation requirement." See *Wyle Labs., Inc.*, Comp. Gen. Dec. B-412964, 2016 CPD ¶ 14 (confusing information as to a proposed key person); *Trandes Corp.*, Comp. Gen. Dec. B-411742, 2015 CPD ¶ 317 (key person did not meet RFP education and experience requirement); *Paradigm Techs., Inc.*, Comp. Gen. Dec. B-409221.2, 2014 CPD ¶ 257 (unavailable key person required by RFP to be listed in proposal); In this situation the agency could have dealt with the situation by conducting discussions but properly chose not to.

When making multiple awards, an agency must perform a tradeoff analysis between all of the offerors with acceptable offers. Thus, it is improper to drop the highest rated technical proposal because it contains such a high price that it does not win against the lowest price proposal, *Beneco Enters., Inc.*, Comp. Gen. Dec. B-283154, 2000 CPD ¶ 69. GAO reasoned that the protester might have won against the two other awardees that had higher prices even though they had higher technical evaluations than the lowest price proposal. See also *Boeing Sikorsky Aircraft Support*, Comp. Gen. Dec. B-277263.2, 97-2 CPD ¶ 91, ruling that probable cost was a mandatory element of the source selection decision in a procurement involving a cost-reimbursement contract, and *Geo-Centers, Inc.*, Comp. Gen. Dec. B-276033, 97-1 CPD ¶ 182, holding that the offerors' costs to perform sample tasks had to be considered in making a source selection decision on a cost-reimbursement contract. In *MIS Farms, Inc.*, Comp. Gen. Dec. B-290599, 2002 CPD ¶ 174, GAO held that it was improper to deduct points when an offeror met a mandatory minimum requirement.

[c] Evenhanded Treatment

The SSA must treat all of the offerors evenhandedly. See *SURVICE Eng'g Co.*, Comp. Gen. Dec. B-414519, 2017 CPD ¶ 237, granting a protest because the source selection decision was based on a high rating for the winning offeror for planning to hire the incumbent workforce while the incumbent did not get a high rating for retaining its own workforce. See also *IBM Corp.*, Comp. Gen. Dec. B-406934, 2013 CPD ¶ 89 (source selection decision was based on features in the winning offeror's proposed system that the evaluators did not perceive were included in the lower priced system of the protester); and *BayFirst Sols., LLC v. United States*, 102 Fed. Cl. 677 (2012) (source selection decision was based on disparate past performance evaluations).

[d] Use of Ratings

In tradeoff procurements, the SSA is required to make the source selection decision by comparing the differences in non-price factors with the differences in prices. See FAR 15.308 calling for a "comparative assessment of proposals against all source selection criteria in the solicitation." In almost all cases this means that the ratings assigned to the proposals should not be used, by themselves, to make the source selection decision. See *Tantara Corp.*, Comp. Gen. Dec. B-416003.2, 2018 CPD ¶ 193, stating:

> As our office has consistently recognized, ratings, be they numerical, adjectival, or color, are merely guides to intelligent decision-making in the procurement process. *One Largo Metro LLC et al.*, B-404896 *et al.*, June 20, 2011, 2011 CPD ¶ 128 at 14. Thus, where the evaluation and source selection decision reasonably consider *the underlying basis for the ratings*, the protester's disagreement over the actual adjectival ratings is essentially inconsequential in that it does not affect the reasonableness of the judgments made in the source selection decision. (Italics added).

See *Enhanced Veterans Sols., Inc. v. United States*, 131 Fed. Cl. 565 (2017), denying a protest because the agency assessed the cause of the weakness not the fact that it was scored as a weakness, and *Allied Signal, Inc.*, Comp. Gen. Dec. B-272290, 96-2 CPD ¶ 121, stating that "a selection should reflect the procuring agency's considered judgment of whether significant technical differences exist in the proposals that identify a particular proposal as technically superior regardless of close scores or ratings among proposals." See also *Arctic Slope Tech. Servs., Inc.*, Comp. Gen. Dec. B-411778, 2017 CPD ¶ 6 (use of adjectival ratings without considering substantive differences in factors); *Wackenhut Servs., Inc. v. United States*, 85 Fed. Cl. 273 (2008) (no tradeoff between price and nonprice factors); *Shumaker Trucking & Excavating Contractors, Inc.*, Comp. Gen. Dec. B-290732, 2002 CPD ¶ 169 (higher point score on technical not justification for selection of higher price offer); *DevTech Sys., Inc.*, Comp. Gen. Dec. B-284879, 2000 CPD ¶ 200 (based on detailed analysis, 6% higher technical score does not indicate superior technical proposal). In *Computer Tech. Servs., Inc.*, Comp. Gen. Dec. B-271435, 96-1 CPD ¶ 283, GAO approved the SSA's probing of the evaluation team to determine the significance of differences in point scores, stating:

> Selection officials must decide whether the point scores show technical superiority and what that difference may mean in terms of contract performance. *See Grey Advertising, Inc.*, 55 Comp. Gen. 1111 (1976) 76-1 CPD ¶ 325.
>
> * * *
>
> Source selection officials in appropriate circumstances properly may conclude that a numerical scoring advantage based primarily on incumbency does not indicate an actual technical superiority that would warrant paying a higher price, *Sparta, Inc.*, B-228216, Jan. 15, 1988, 88-1 CPD ¶ 37; see also *Northern Virginia Serv. Corp.*, B-258036.2; B-258036.3, Jan. 23, 1995, 95-1 CPD ¶ 36, n. 5 (citing *NUS Corp.; The Austin Co.*, B-221863; B-221863.2, June 20, 1986, 86-1 CPD ¶ 574), and we see nothing unreasonable about the SSA's conclusion here. Accordingly, we think that the SSA's conclusion that [the protester's] numerical rating advantage did not reflect an actual technical superiority that would warrant paying its higher price also was a reasonable exercise of the SSA's discretion.

This logic was approved by the Federal Circuit in *Lockheed Missiles & Space Co. v. Bentsen*, 4 F.3d 955 (Fed. Cir. 1993), where the court stated at 960:

> Neither the FAR nor the broad language of the RFP requires that evaluation points be proportional to cost. Accordingly, a proposal which is one point better than another but costs millions of dollars more may be selected if the agency can demonstrate within a reasonable certainty that the added value of the proposal is worth the higher price. Here, as we have already noted, the [agency] tradeoff analysis revealed that the dollar value of the two technical subfactors together with the value of the nonquantified discriminators justified the additional price to the [winning offeror's] proposal.

Accord, *Grumman Data Sys. v. Dalton*, 88 F. 3d 990 (Fed. Cir. 1996). Thus, the selection will be upheld so long as there is a coherent and reasonable explanation for the selection, *Latecoere Int'l, Inc. v. Dep't of Navy*, 19 F.3d 1342 (11th Cir. 1994).

[i] Improper Reliance on Scores

Since the tradeoff decision must be made on the basis of the relative strengths, weaknesses and risks of the proposals, a bare comparison of point scores will not demonstrate that the agency has made a rational source selection decision. See *West Coast General Corp.*, Comp. Gen. Dec. B-411916.2, 2015 CPD ¶ 392, stating:

> [W]hile the source selection document contained summaries of the strengths and weaknesses of the proposals, and the source selection decision states that it compared the proposals by considering strengths and weaknesses, nothing in the record reflects such a comparison. Rather, the record shows that the selection decision relied entirely on a mechanical comparison of the total technical scores (which were calculated based on a mechanical application of the maximum available point score and weights assigned for each factor) and prices, the majority of which were unsubstantiated. We do not find this selection decision to be reasonable. We sustain this basis for protest.

This requirement does not apply if the agency uses a highest technically rated proposals with fair and reasonable price source selection scheme. See *Sevatec, Inc.*, Comp. Gen. Dec. B-413559.3, 2017 CPD ¶ 3, stating:

> Here, the agency has structured its solicitation such that there are no underlying "strengths" or "weaknesses" to be evaluated. Indeed, the RFP has provided for an "objective" point scoring system, where there will be no trade-off of proposal benefits relative to the proposed price. In those scenarios where our Office has found the mechanical application of point scores to be unreasonable, this is because the agency was required to conduct a qualitative assessment (i.e., consideration of strengths and weaknesses) of the proposals. As the solicitation here expressly does not envision a qualitative assessment beyond the review and verification of the point scores, we find no basis to sustain the protesters' challenge to the agency's source selection process.

There are several GAO decisions finding a tradeoff source selection unreasonable because it was based on a "mechanical comparison" of scores. See *Qbase, LLC*, Comp. Gen. Dec. B-416377.9, 2020 CPD ¶ 367 (decision based solely on adjective ratings); *Celta Servs., Inc.*, Comp. Gen. Dec. B-411835, 2015 CPD ¶ 362 (decision based on point score of technical evaluation panel); *Midland Supply, Inc.*, Comp. Gen. Dec. B-298720, 2007 CPD ¶ 2 (decision based on total points without any tradeoff analysis); *Johnson Controls World Servs., Inc.*, Comp. Gen. Dec. B-289942, 2002 CPD ¶ 88 (decision based solely on number of "outstanding" and "highly satisfactory" ratings); *Opti-Lite Optical*, Comp. Gen. Dec. B-281693, 99-1 CPD ¶ 61 (decision based solely on point scores for technical and price when RFP did not state award would be made to offeror with most points); and *Teltara Inc.*, Comp. Gen. Dec. B-280922, 98-2 CPD ¶ 124 (decision based on percentage differences in price and technical scores). In *Wackenhut Servs., Inc.*, Comp. Gen. Dec. B-400240, 2008 CPD ¶ 184, the protester argued that its proposal was superior because it received more "strengths" than the winning offeror. GAO denied the protest concluding that the protester was asking for a "mathematical or mechanical consideration" of the scores which was not the correct way to make the source selection decision. The Court of Federal Claims reached the opposite conclusion in *Wackenhut Servs., Inc. v. United States*, 85 Fed. Cl. 273 (2008), concluding that the source evaluation board's increase of point scores was arbitrary because it was not adequately justified. This may indicate that the court is more willing to grant relief when there are disparities in scoring—even though the scores are not the ultimate basis for the source selection decision.

[ii] General Statements

General statements as to the merits of the various proposals are also insufficient to demonstrate that a satisfactory tradeoff analysis has been made. See *Serco, Inc. v. United States*, 81 Fed. Cl. 463 (2008), stating at 496-97:

> [FAR 15.308] requires the agency to make a business judgment as to whether the higher price of an offer is worth the technical benefits its acceptance will afford. *See, e.g., TRW, Inc.*, 98 F.3d at 1327; *Dismas Charities, Inc.*, 61 Fed. Cl. at 203. Doing this, the decisional law demonstrates, obliges the agency to do more than simply parrot back the strengths and weaknesses of the competing proposals—rather, the agency must dig deeper and determine whether the relative strengths and weaknesses of the competing proposals are such that it is worth paying a higher price. Second, in performing the tradeoff analysis, the agency need neither assign an exact dollar value to the worth associated with the technical benefits of a contract nor otherwise quantify the non-cost factors. FAR § 15.308 ("the documentation need not quantify the tradeoffs that led to the decision"); *Widnall v. B3H Corp.*, 75 F.3d 1577, 1580 (Fed. Cir. 1996). But, this is not to say that the magnitude of the price differential between the two offers is irrelevant—logic suggests that as that magnitude increases, the relative benefits yielded by the higher-priced offer must also increase. *See Beneco Enters., Inc.*, 2000 CPD ¶ 69 at 5 (1999). To conclude otherwise, threatens to "minimize[] the potential impact of price" and, in particular, to make "a nominal technical advantage essentially determinative, irrespective of an overwhelming price premium." *Coastal Sci. and Eng'g, Inc.*, 89-2 CPD ¶ 436 at 2 (1989); *see also Lockheed Missiles & Space Co.*, 4 F.3d at 959-60. Finally—and many cases turn on this point—the agency is compelled by the FAR to document its reasons for choosing the higher-priced offer. Conclusory statements, devoid of any substantive content, have been held to fall short of this requirement, threatening to turn the tradeoff process into an empty exercise. Indeed, apart from the regulations, generalized statements that fail to reveal the agency's tradeoff calculus deprive this court of any basis upon which to review the award decisions.

See Johnson Controls World Servs., 2002 CPD ¶ 88 at 6; *Satellite Servs., Inc.*, 2001 CPD ¶ 30 at 9-11; *Si-Nor, Inc.*, 2000 CPD ¶ 159 at 3 (1999).

See *Blue Rock Structures, Inc.*, Comp. Gen. Dec. B-293134, 2004 CPD ¶ 63, sustaining a protest where the source selection decision merely concluded that the protester's higher rated proposal was essentially equal to the winning proposals without any discussion or analysis of the differences in the proposals. See also *Standard Commc'ns, Inc. v. United States*, 101 Fed. Cl. 723 (2011) (mere statement that "higher-priced proposal does not exhibit sufficient superiority in the non-Price factors to warrant an award."); *FirstLine Transp. Sec., Inc. v. United States*, 100 Fed. Cl. 359 (2011) (statement that technical superiority not worth price premium); *LIS, Inc.*, Comp. Gen. Dec. B-400646.2, 2010 CPD ¶ 5 (general statement that selected offeror addressed all agency concerns without any analysis of strength, weaknesses or risks in proposals); *Systems Research & Applications Corp.*, Comp. Gen. Dec. B-299818, 2008 CPD ¶ 28 (no qualitative assessment of strengths of competing proposals to satisfy agency requirements using different approaches); *Preferred Sys. Solutions, Inc.*, Comp. Gen. Dec. B-292322, 2003 CPD ¶ 166 (general statement that the proposals had "nearly equivalent ratings in non-cost areas" inadequate explanation of why protester's highly rated proposal was not worth its higher costs and prices); *Johnson Controls World Servs., Inc.*, Comp. Gen. Dec. B-289942, 2002 CPD ¶ 88 (general statement that higher scored proposal contained "no discernible benefits" inadequate demonstration of tradeoff analysis); *Si-Nor, Inc.*, Comp. Gen. Dec. B-282064, 2000 CPD ¶ 159 (bare statement that better past performance was worth over 10% more); *Lloyd H. Kessler, Inc.*, Comp. Gen. Dec. B-284693, 2000 CPD ¶ 96 (mere statement that "concerns arising from reports of adverse past performance" justified paying a higher cost); *Beneco Enters., Inc.*, Comp. Gen. Dec. B-283154, 2000 CPD ¶ 69 (statement that "the benefits and advantages" of the protester's higher-rated technical proposal did not justify "payment of the significant additional price" and is not "in the best interest of the Government" insufficient proof of rational tradeoff analysis); and *TRW, Inc.*, 68 Comp. Gen. 511 (B-234558), 89-1 CPD ¶ 584 ("Monte Carlo" risk analysis, computing potential costs of improving proposal with low ratings not a demonstration that tradeoff analysis considered differences in evaluations).

[iii] Determinations of Equality

There are a large number of cases where the SSA properly exercises discretion by comparing differences in technical ratings by evaluators and determining that the technical merit of competing offers is relatively equal, thus allowing contracts to be awarded to the lower-cost offeror. For example, in *AM Pierce & Assocs., Inc.*, Comp. Gen. Dec. B-413128, 2016 CPD ¶ 270, the SSA compared the "strengths" in two competing proposals and found that they were essentially equal, with the result that the single remaining strength of the higher cost proposal was found not to be worth the difference in cost.

In most cases such determinations of equality are made without explicitly rescoring the proposals. For example, in *Engility Servs., LLC*, Comp. Gen. Dec. B-416588.3, 2020 CPD ¶ 110, the SSA properly awarded the contract to the low-priced offeror after concluding that the technical proposals were substantially equal even though the protester's proposal had been rated higher by the evaluators. See also *CyberData Techs., Inc.*, Comp. Gen. Dec. B-417084.3, 2019 CPD ¶ 212 (SSA considered the "qualitative value" of the quotations and found them equal); *Oracle America, Inc.*, Comp. Gen. Dec. B-417046, 2019 CPD ¶ 74 (SSA recognized that neither proposal received any strengths, weaknesses, significant weaknesses, deficiencies, nor uncertainties to potentially distinguish them from one another); *Lynxnet, LLC*, Comp. Gen. Dec. B-409791, 2014 CPD ¶ 233 (SSA carefully reviewed evaluations and found both proposals superior but equal); and *RONCO Consulting Corp.*, Comp. Gen. Dec. B-280113, 98-2 CPD ¶ 41 (technical evaluation committee advised the contracting officer that it had no preference among three offerors with different technical scores).

Such a determination of equality has also been supported in a case where the RFP called for precise numerical scores for technical and cost factors and stated that award would be made to the offeror with the highest number of points. GAO stated that the source selection official would not have been permitted to alter the cost/technical tradeoff announced in the RFP but was entitled to rescore the proposals by determining that the technical proposals were equal, *Harrison Sys., Ltd.*, 63 Comp. Gen. 379 (B-212675), 84-1 CPD ¶ 572. See also *Crowley Maritime Salvage*, Comp. Gen. Dec. B-234555, 89-1 CPD ¶ 555 (award to lower point total permissible where contracting officer determined that a 14.4% difference in technical score was not significant).

Determinations of equality will be overturned if they are not supported by reasoned analysis. See, for example, *Arctic Slope Tech. Servs., Inc.*, Comp. Gen. Dec. B-411776, 2017 CPD ¶ 6 (equality determination based solely of equal scores); *Radiation Oncology Grp. of WNY, PC*, Comp. Gen. Dec. B-310354.2, 2009 CPD ¶ 136 (no support for contracting officer's conclusion that offerors with different point scores were equal); *DynCorp*, Comp. Gen. Dec. B-232999, 89-1 CPD ¶ 152 (no rational explanation for ignoring evaluators' concerns).

The selection official is not required to find the proposals equal when the point differential is small. See *Super Teams Operating Co.*, Comp. Gen. Dec. B-260100, 95-1 CPD ¶ 246, where the protester received a technical score of 83.3, the awardee received a score of 86.7, and a third (high-cost) offeror received a technical score of 91.1. The source selection official considered the 86.7 and 91.1 scores to be technically equal. The protester argued that if difference of 4.4 points makes two proposals technically equal, the smaller difference of 2.9 points must make its proposal equal to the awardee's technical proposal. GAO denied the protest, stating that "closeness of point scores does not necessarily indicate that proposals are essentially equal." The source selection official determined that there were significant differences in the technical merit between the proposals and this difference was reflected in the narrative summaries.

[e] Impact of Statement of Relative Importance

In tradeoff procurements, the statement of relative importance in the RFP does not play a significant rule in the source selection decision. This is because the tradeoff between price/cost and non-price/cost factors made by the selection official must still be based on the established criteria and the ultimate decision will be based on an assessment of whether the difference in the non-price/cost factors is worth the difference in price/cost. For example, if the RFP states that non-price factors are significantly more important than price/cost, award would rationally be made to the low price/cost offer when the difference in the non-price factors was small. Conversely, if the RFP states that price/cost is significantly more important than the non-price/cost factors, award would rationally be made to a higher priced/cost offer when there was a significant difference in the non-price/cost factors. Thus, whatever the statement of relative importance, a reasonable tradeoff between price/cost and the other factors cannot be challenged.

Most RFPs have stated that the non-price/cost factors are more important than price/cost. Nonetheless, selection of a lower priced proposal is justified if the SSA determines that the benefits in the non-price/cost factors offered by the high priced offeror are not worth the higher cost. See, for example, *Bahrain Maritime & Mercantile Int'l BSC*, Comp. Gen. Dec. B-407575.6, 2014 CPD ¶ 320, agreeing with a decision that a price premium of 9.32% was too high to justify award to a competitor that had submitted a clearly superior proposal or the non-price factors. See also *Epic Sys., Inc.*, Comp. Gen. Dec. B-418104, 2020 CPD ¶ 1 (slightly better technical evaluation not worth over 50% price premium); *Centerra Grp., LLC*, Comp. Gen. Dec. B-414800, 2017 CPD ¶ 307 (better past performance and small business rating not worth $52 million premium); *Smartronix, Inc.*, Comp. Gen. Dec. B-411970.9, 2016 CPD ¶ 362 (technical superiority not worth almost $16 million higher price); *i4 Now Solutions, Inc.*, Comp. Gen. Dec. B-412369, 2016 CPD ¶ 47 (better past performance not worth 25% higher price); *DRS Tech. Servs., Inc.*, Comp. Gen. Dec. B-407575.6, 2015 CPD ¶ 377 (better technical/management rating not worth over $20 million premium); *Pricewaterhouse Coopers, LLP*, Comp. Gen. Dec. B-409885, 2014 CPD ¶ 289 (significantly better sample task response not worth over $30 million premium); *HP Enter. Servs., LLC*, Comp. Gen. Dec. B-409169.3, 2014 CPD ¶ 179 (better technical approach not worth $1.4 million annual premium).

In these circumstances, the SSA is also permitted to select an offeror that has proposed a significantly higher price if the benefits in the non-price/cost factors can be identified. See, for example, *NextStep Tech., Inc.*, Comp. Gen. Dec.

B-416877, 2019 CPD ¶ 16 (considerably higher technical and management rating justified over 60% higher price); *Pacific-Gulf Marine, Inc.*, Comp. Gen. Dec. B-415375, 2018 CPD ¶ 124 (strong past performance justified over $4 million (5.7%) higher price); *Enterprise Servs., LLC*, Comp. Gen. Dec. B-415517, 2018 CPD ¶ 83 (superior technical solution justified $757 million higher price); *Chemonics Int'l, Inc.*, Comp. Gen. Dec. B-409346.3, 2014 CPD ¶ 368 (higher rated technical proposals justified paying almost 50% higher price); *Comprehensive Health Servs., Inc.*, Comp. Gen. Dec. B-310553, 2008 CPD ¶ 9 (technically superior proposal justified paying almost 10% higher price); *Textron, Inc. v. United States*, 74 Fed. Cl. 277 (2006) (technical superiority of design justified paying $43 million (12%) higher price); *Remington Arms Co.*, Comp. Gen. Dec. B-297374, 2006 CPD ¶ 32 (superior sample rifle justified over $5 million higher price); and *Standard Commc's, Inc.*, Comp. Gen. Dec. B-296972, 2005 CPD ¶ 200 (program management and staffing risk justified over 20% higher price).

In numerous cases, the higher priced proposal is selected at a minimally higher price/cost. See, for example, *Lukos, LLC*, Comp. Gen. Dec. B-416343.2, 2018 CPD ¶ 282 (overall lower risk justified 1.8% higher price); *Raytheon Co.*, Comp. Gen. Dec. B-414062.3, 2017 CPD ¶ 71 (outstanding technical maturity justified 6% higher price); *DynCorp Int'l, LLC*, Comp. Gen. Dec. B-414647.2, 2017 CPD ¶ 342 (better past performance ratings justified 2% higher price); *Raytheon Co.*, Comp. Gen. Dec. B-408906.4, 2015 CPD ¶ 120 (lower risk design justified 2.9% higher price);

In contrast, award to the higher-priced offeror has been overturned in a few cases where the benefits could not be demonstrated. See *Sturm, Ruger & Co.*, Comp. Gen. Dec. B-250193, 93-1 CPD ¶ 42, overturning a $1,366,550 award to an offeror receiving a technical score of 94 points when the protester had received a score of 89 points and had proposed a price of $768,012. GAO rejected the agency's contention that price should only be considered when the technical scores were equal and held that, in such a best value procurement, award to the higher-priced offer "should be supported by a specific, documented determination that the technical superiority of the higher-priced offer warrants the additional cost involved, even where, as here, cost is stated to be the least important factor." See also *ITT Fed. Servs. Int'l Corp.*, Comp. Gen. Dec. B-296783, 2007 CPD ¶ 43 (unreasonable evaluation made decision to pay higher price questionable); *YORK Bldg. Servs., Inc.*, Comp. Gen. Dec. B-296948.2, 2005 CPD ¶ 202 (flawed evaluation made decision to pay higher price questionable); *Spherix, Inc.*, Comp. Gen. Dec. B-294572.3, 2005 CPD ¶ 183 (failure to consider relative similarities and differences in the two proposals made decision to pay higher price questionable); *Beautify Prof'l Servs. Corp.*, Comp. Gen. Dec. B-291954.3, 2003 CPD ¶ 178 (award to highest rated past performance without considering that it was 25% higher in price not proper); and *CRAssocs., Inc.*, Comp. Gen. Dec. B-282075.2, 2000 CPD ¶ 63 (inadequate documentation and potential evaluation errors made decision to pay significantly higher costs questionable).

When the RFP states that price is more important than the other factors, the SSA can award the contract to the offeror with a higher price if the differences in the non-price/cost factors are worth paying the higher costs. Thus, in *Frequency Eng'g Lab. Corp.*, Comp. Gen. Dec. B-225606, 87-1 CPD ¶ 393, award at a price of $57.6 million was permitted when the protester had offered a price of $51.2 million but had proposed to use less qualified personnel whom the agency evaluated as posing a much higher risk that performance would not be successfully accomplished. See also *Centex Constr. Co.*, Comp. Gen. Dec. B-238777, 90-1 CPD ¶ 566 (award to offeror with slightly higher price justified by strong technical rating); *Oklahoma Aerotronics, Inc.*, Comp. Gen. Dec. B-237705.2, 90-1 CPD ¶ 337 (award to an offeror with 2% higher price justified by the lower technical risk obtained); and *F.A.S. Sys. Corp.*, Comp. Gen. Dec. B-236344, 89-2 CPD ¶ 512 (award to offeror with $1,100,000 higher price justified when detailed agency evaluation indicated significantly stronger technical ability).

When the price/cost factor and the non-price/cost factors are stated to be equal, the source selection official has the greatest discretion to make a "best value" source selection decision. In, *Dextera Corp.*, Comp. Gen. Dec. B-415516.2, 2018 CPD ¶ 66, selection of a higher priced, higher technically rated offeror was affirmed because the lower priced offeror's limited experience posed a risk. See also *GM-Bulltrack, JV*, Comp. Gen. Dec. B-414591.6, 2018 CPD ¶ 378 (award to lower priced offerors because protester's highly rated proposal was very high priced); *HGS Eng'g, Inc.*, Comp. Gen. Dec. B-412042, 2015 CPD ¶ 390 (award to lower priced offerors because somewhat better non-price factor ratings not worth $1.5 million price differential); *J.C.N. Constr. Co.*, Comp. Gen. Dec. B-293063, 2004 CPD ¶ 12 (award at higher price because of higher technical rating); *Kay & Assocs., Inc.*, Comp. Gen. Dec. B-291269, 2003 CPD ¶ 12 (award at higher price because of better past performance). However, the tradeoff that is made between cost and non-price/cost must still be justified as being rational. See, for example, *Kempter-Rossman Int'l*, Comp. Gen. Dec. B-220772, 86-1 CPD ¶ 127, finding it unreasonable to award to a 2% lower-priced offer when the competitive offer had a 25% technical superiority and the RFP gave equal weight to the price and technical factors.

[3] Documentation

Agencies must prepare documentation demonstrating that the source selection decision was reasonable and consistent with the solicitation. Prior to the FAR Rewrite, the FAR was somewhat unclear as to the documentation required to support selection decisions. However, GAO required agencies to submit documentation when awards were protested. See *Quality Elevator Co.*, Comp. Gen. Dec. B-276750, 97-2 CPD ¶ 28, stating:

> While judgments concerning the evaluation of proposals are by their nature subjective, they must be reasonable; such judgments must bear a rational relationship to the announced criteria upon which proposals were to be evaluated. *Management Technology, Inc.*, B-257269.2, Nov. 8, 1994, 95-1 CPD ¶ 248 at 6-7. Implicit in the foregoing is that the rationale for these judgments must be documented in sufficient detail to show that they are not arbitrary and that there was a reasonable basis for the selection decision. . . . Where there is inadequate supporting documentation for an award decision, we cannot conclude that the agency had a reasonable basis for the decision. *Hattal & Assocs.*, 70 Comp. Gen. 632, 637 (1991), 91-2 CPD ¶ 90 at 7.

The FAR Rewrite adopted a more rigorous documentation requirement following the guidance established by GAO. See FAR 15.308 stating the following requirement:

> The source selection decision shall be documented, and the documentation shall include the rationale for any business judgments and tradeoffs made or relied on by the SSA, including benefits associated with additional costs. Although the rationale for the selection decision must be documented, that documentation need not quantify the tradeoffs that led to the decision.

See also FAR 15.305(a) requiring documentation of the evaluations:

> (3) *Technical evaluation.* When tradeoffs are performed (see 15.101-1), the source selection records shall include—
>
> (i) An assessment of each offeror's ability to accomplish the technical requirements; and
>
> (ii) A summary, matrix, or quantitative ranking, along with appropriate supporting narrative, of each technical proposal using the evaluation factors.

The documentation need not be contained in the ultimate award decision, but it must be present in the record. See *Connected Global Solutions. LLC*, Comp. Gen. Dec. B-418266.4, 2020 CPD ¶ 349 (SSA concurred with the findings of the SSEB and the SSAC and accepted the tradeoff recommendation of the SSAC); *All Star-Cabaco Enter. (JV)*, Comp. Gen. Dec. B-290133, 2002 CPD ¶ 127 (SSA accepted the recommendation of the SSEB which contained qualitative tradeoff documentation). However, merely accepting evaluators' recommendations that do not contain such tradeoff analyses is insufficient, *Universal Bld'g Maint., Inc.*, Comp. Gen. Dec. B-282456, 99-2 CPD ¶ 32.

[a] Rationale for Business Judgment

If an agency's documentation does not demonstrate that the source selection decision is rational, a protest will be granted. See *Matrix Int'l Logistics, Inc.*,

Comp. Gen. Dec. B-272388.2, 97-2 CPD ¶ 89, where the determination of the SSA that two technical proposals were "essentially equal" was not supported in the documentation submitted by the agency. GAO sustained the protest, stating:

> An agency which fails to adequately document its evaluation of proposals or [the] source selection decision bears the risk that its determinations will be considered unsupported, and absent such support, our Office may be unable to determine whether the agency had a reasonable basis for its determinations.

See also *HomeSafe Alliance, LLC*, Comp. Gen. Dec. B-418266,5, 2020 CPD ¶ 350 (inadequate documentation of oral presentation); *Trident Vantage Sys., LLC*, Comp. Gen. Dec. B-415944, 2018 CPD ¶ 166 (inadequate documentation of relevance of past performance); *M7 Aerospace, LLC*, Comp. Gen. Dec. B-411986, 2016 CPD ¶ 100 (no evidence of a qualitative assessment of the merits of the offerors' differing approaches); *Navistar Def., LLC*, Comp. Gen. Dec. B-401865, 2009 CPD ¶ 258 (no documentation to support rating of "good" past performance (rather than "excellent") which agency stated was based on negative comments that had been inadvertently destroyed); *Radiation Oncology Grp. of WNY, PC*, Comp. Gen. Dec. B-310354.2, 2009 CPD ¶ 136 (no documentation showing that contracting officer considered strengths and weaknesses of competing proposals—merely a statement that offerors with different point scores were equal); *ACCESS Sys., Inc.*, Comp. Gen. Dec. B-400623.3, 2009 CPD ¶ 56 (no documentation showing that agency made meaningful tradeoff analysis); *AT&T Corp.*, Comp. Gen. Dec. B-299542.3, 2008 CPD ¶ 65 (no documentation showing how SSA arrived at different conclusion than evaluators regarding the impact of overstaffing); *Apptis, Inc.*, Comp. Gen. Dec. B-299457, 2008 CPD ¶ 49 (no documentation to support findings regarding demonstration of proposed solution); *Systems Research & Applications Corp.*, Comp. Gen. Dec. B-299818, 2008 CPD ¶ 28 (no documentation showing that SSA made a qualitative assessment of strengths of competing proposals to satisfy agency requirements using different approaches); *Panacea Consulting, Inc.*, Comp. Gen. Dec. B-299307.4, 2007 CPD ¶ 141 (no documentation showing that agency made meaningful tradeoff analysis—only numerical scores); *Bank of Am.*, Comp. Gen. Dec. B-287608, 2001 CPD ¶ 137 (documents contained multiple errors and reflected various mistakes and/or omissions); *Beacon Auto Parts*, Comp. Gen. Dec. B-287483, 2001 CPD ¶ 116 (documentation contained no indication that a cost/technical tradeoff had been made); *Cortland Mem'l Hosp.*, Comp. Gen. Dec. B-286890, 2001 CPD ¶ 48 (documentation did not show that agency followed evaluation criteria); and *J&J Maint., Inc.*, Comp. Gen. Dec. B-284708.2, 2000 CPD ¶ 106 (no adequate documentation of oral presentation or strengths, weaknesses or risks of proposals).

GAO has not demanded that the documentation cover every element of the selection decision as long as it supports the overall rationale used by the SSA. See

Octo Consulting Grp., Inc., Comp. Gen. Dec. B-413116.53, 2017 CPD ¶ 139, stating:

> Where a price/technical tradeoff is to be made, the source selection decision must be documented, and the documentation must include the rationale for any tradeoffs, including the benefits associated with additional costs. Federal Acquisition Regulation (FAR) § 15.308; *The MIL Corp.*, B-297508, B-297508.2, Jan. 26, 2006, 2006 CPD ¶ 34 at 13. However, there is no need for extensive documentation of every consideration factored into a tradeoff decision, nor is there a requirement to quantify the specific cost or price value difference when selecting a higher-priced, higher-rated proposal for award. FAR § 15.308; *Advanced Fed. Servs. Corp.*, B-298662, Nov. 15, 2006, 2006 CPD ¶ 174 at 5.

The documentation need not comply literally with the requirement of the FAR that it contain a statement of the "strengths, weaknesses and risks" as long as it explains the selection decision. See *Nirvana Enter., Inc.*, Comp. Gen. Dec. B-414951.2, 2018 CPD ¶ 5, stating:

> With regard to documentation, it need only be sufficient to establish that the agency was aware of the relative merits and costs of the competing proposals and that the source selection be reasonably based. See *General Dynamics, American Overseas Marine*, B-401874.14, B-401874.15, Nov. 1, 2011, 2012 CPD ¶ 85 at 16.

See also *PRC, Inc.*, Comp. Gen. Dec. B-274698.2, 97-1 CPD ¶ 115, where the documentation was found adequate because it identified all of the "significant discriminators" between the proposals even though it did not record strengths and weaknesses of the individual proposals.

[b] Post-Protest Documentation

While documentation compiled contemporaneously with the evaluation and the source selection decision is required by the FAR, the lack of contemporaneous documentation will not be fatal in a protest if the evaluation and selection can be shown to be reasonable and in conformance with the evaluation criteria. Thus, documentation supporting the source selection decision may be created by the agency after the filing of a protest. See *Remington Arms Co.*, Comp. Gen. Dec. B-297374, 2006 CPD ¶ 32, stating:

> While we generally give little weight to reevaluations prepared in the heat of the adversarial process, post-protest explanations that provide a detailed rationale for contemporaneous conclusions, as is the case here, simply fill in previously unrecorded details, and will generally be considered in our review of the rationality of selection decisions, so long as those explanations are credible and consistent with the contemporaneous record. *NWT*,

Inc.: PharmChem Labs., Inc., B-280988, B-280988.2, Dec. 17, 1998, 98-2 CPD ¶ 158 at 16.

Thus, documentation supporting the source selection decision may be provided by the agency after the filing of a protest as long as that documentation is consistent with the rationale used in making the original decision, *Ideal Elec. Sec. Co.*, Comp. Gen. Dec. B-283398, 99-2 CPD ¶ 87; *MCR Fed., Inc.*, Comp. Gen. Dec. B-280969, 99-1 CPD ¶ 8. See also *TLT Constr. Corp.*, Comp. Gen. Dec. B-286226, 2000 CPD ¶ 179 (agency's post-protest explanation of its determination to use negotiated procedures held to be consistent with the evaluation plan); *Pickering Firm, Inc.*, Comp. Gen. Dec. B-277396, 97-2 CPD ¶ 99 (source selection decision affirmed based on evaluator worksheets and consensus ratings created after protest to support a "sparse" memorandum prepared at time of selection decision), *Environmental Affairs Mgmt., Inc.*, Comp. Gen. Dec. B-277270, 97-2 CPD ¶ 93 (source selection decision affirmed based on "legal brief, a contracting officer's statement, and declarations made by the SSA and the chairman of the [source evaluation committee]," all prepared after the protest was filed); *AT&T Corp.*, Comp. Gen. Dec. B-260447.4, 96-1 CPD ¶ 200 (source selection decision affirmed based on the agency protest report, which presented extensive and detailed narratives concerning the strengths of the awardee's technical and management proposals when this information was consistent with the less detailed contemporaneous documentation); and *Sociometrics, Inc.*, Comp. Gen. Dec. B-261367.2, 95-2 CPD ¶ 201 (although the details of the cost realism analysis were not spelled out in a contemporaneous document, the contracting officer adequately explained the details of the analysis in an agency protest report).

GAO has refused to rely on post-protest explanations of the source selection decision that have been prepared by the agency's legal counsel, *Radiation Oncology Grp. of WNY, PC*, Comp. Gen. Dec. B-310354.2, 2009 CPD ¶ 136. In that case the SSA had only stated that she determined the offerors were "essentially technically equal" with no further explanation.

The Court of Federal Claims has also admitted documentation filed after the plaintiff has lost a GAO protest, *Wackenhut Servs., Inc. v. United States*, 85 Fed. Cl. 273 (2008).

A common technique for remedying insufficient documentation has been for GAO to hold a hearing where agency officials can explain the evaluation and source selection decision. A number of protests have been denied on the basis of such information. See *Noble Supply & Logistics*, Comp. Gen. Dec. B-410788.4, 2015 CPD ¶ 243 (testimony of SSA explained how the decision had been arrived at); *Manassas Travel, Inc.*, Comp. Gen. Dec. B-294867.3, 2005 CPD ¶ 113 (testimony providing more details regarding strengths of winning offeror); *SOS Interpreting, Ltd.*, Comp. Gen. Dec. B-287505, 2001 CPD ¶ 104 (testimony providing detailed rationale for selection decision held to be credible and consistent with contemporaneous record); *Northeast MEP Servs., Inc.*, Comp. Gen. Dec. B-285963.5, 2001 CPD ¶ 28 (chairman of evaluation board explained the basis for determining that protester had weaknesses); *Draeger Safety, Inc.*, Comp. Gen. Dec. B-285366, 2000 CPD ¶ 139 (testimony of evaluator after evaluation documentation was destroyed accepted as providing acceptable contemporaneous documentation supporting selection decision); *Simborg Dev., Inc.*, Comp. Gen. Dec. B-283538, 2000 CPD ¶ 12 (testimony gave credible explanation of selection decision); *NWT, Inc.*, Comp. Gen. Dec. B-280988.2, 98-2 CPD ¶ 158 (based on transcript and hearing, GAO concluded that "while not recorded at the time, the agency did compare performance levels"); *Pacifica Servs., Inc.*, Comp. Gen. Dec. B-280921, 98-2 CPD ¶ 137 (detailed rationale given in declaration and hearing was held to "simply fill in unrecorded details") and *Jason Assocs. Corp.*, Comp. Gen. Dec. B-278689, 98-1 CPD ¶ 67 (source selection affirmed based on testimony). GAO has even permitted such later explanations in the extreme case where the agency has destroyed the original documentation, *Southwest Marine, Inc.*, Comp. Gen. Dec. B-265865.4, 96-1 CPD ¶ 56. In contrast, the hearing may confirm that the agency has made a flawed source selection decision, *Keeton Corrs., Inc.*, Comp. Gen. Dec. B-293348, 2005 CPD ¶ 44 (hearing showed SSA had been given faulty information on past performance); *Preferred Sys. Solutions, Inc.*, Comp. Gen. Dec. B-292322, 2003 CPD ¶ 166 (hearing showed that SSA did not make independent decision); *Sabreliner Corp.*, Comp. Gen. Dec. B-288030, 2001 CPD ¶ 170 (testimony repeated "errors" and "inconsistencies" in documentation supporting sole source procurement).

There is some disagreement on the weight to be accorded to documentation that is created after a protest has been filed. One judge in the Court of Federal Claims has stated that it should be accorded the "same deference" given to documentation created at the time the selection decision was made, *Tech Sys., Inc. v. United States*, 50 Fed. Cl. 216 (2001). Another judge treated such documentation as mere "argument," *Cubic Applications, Inc. v. United States*, 37 Fed. Cl. 339 (1997). GAO accords "greater weight to contemporaneous source selection materials rather than documents . . . prepared in response to protest contentions," *DynCorp*, 71 Comp. Gen. 129 (B-245289), 91-2 CPD ¶ 575. Thus, documentation that offers new justifications for the selection decision rather than amplifying the original justification will be highly suspect. See *Boeing Sikorsky Aircraft Support,* Comp. Gen. Dec. B-277263.2, 97-2 CPD ¶ 91, refusing to rely on the agency's mock source selection decision based on the assumption that all the protester's complaints were valid, stating:

> While we consider the entire record, including statements and arguments made in response to a protest in determining whether an agency's selection decision is supportable, we accord greater weight to contemporaneous source selection materials rather than judgments, such as the selection officials' reevaluation here, made in response to protest contentions. *Dyncorp*, 71 Comp. Gen. 129, 134 n.12 (1991), 91-2 CPD ¶ 575 at 7 n.13; *Southwest Marine, Inc.; American Sys. Eng'g Corp.*, B-265865.3, B-265865.4, Jan. 23,

> 1996, 96-1 CPD ¶ 56 at 10. As pointed out above, the agency does not acknowledge that it erred. Rather, we are faced with an agency's efforts to defend, in the face of a bid protest, its prior source selection through submission of new analyses, which the agency itself views as merely hypothetical and which are based on information that the agency continues to argue is not accurate. The lesser weight that we accord these post-protest documents reflects the concern that, because they constitute reevaluations and redeterminations prepared in the heat of an adversarial process, they may not represent the fair and considered judgment of the agency, which is a prerequisite of a rational evaluation and source selection process.

See also *Deloitte Consulting, LLP*, Comp. Gen. Dec. B-412125.2, 2016 CPD ¶ 119 (granting protest because post-protest explanation of past performance contacts were not in accord with record); *Celta Servs., Inc.*, Comp. Gen. Dec. B-411835, 2015 CPD ¶ 362 (granting protest because post-protest rationale conflicted with contemporaneous statements); *Systems Research & Applications Corp.*, Comp. Gen. Dec. B-299818, 2008 CPD ¶ 28 (granting protest because agency officials showed at hearing that they did not qualitatively assess the merits of the proposals); *Si-Nor, Inc.*, Comp. Gen. Dec. B-292748.2, 2004 CPD ¶ 10 (rejecting argument that dissimilar prior contract was not used to evaluate experience); *ManTech Envt'l Research Servs. Corp.*, Comp. Gen. Dec. B-292602, 2003 CPD ¶ 221 (rejecting post-protest reevaluation because it was performed by the same personnel defending the protest); *Dismas Charities, Inc.*, Comp. Gen. Dec. B-292091, 2003 CPD ¶ 125 (rejecting post-protest reevaluation of past performance); *Johnson Controls World Servs., Inc.*, Comp. Gen. Dec. B-289942, 2002 CPD ¶ 88 (rejecting sufficiency of post-protest addendum that still did not contain comparative assessment of strength of protester's technical proposal); *Wackenhut Servs., Inc.*, Comp. Gen. Dec. B-286037, 2001 CPD ¶ 114 (rejecting justification for selection decision that was not reflected in contemporaneous record); *BAE Sys.*, Comp. Gen. Dec. B-287189, 2001 CPD ¶ 86 (rejecting explanation of evaluation that was inconsistent with record); *Farmland Nat'l Beef*, Comp. Gen. Dec. B-286607, 2001 CPD ¶ 31 (rejecting undocumented testimony that telephone call occurred); *CRAssociates, Inc.*, Comp. Gen. Dec. B-282075.2, 2000 CPD ¶ 63 (post-protest documentation does not overcome contemporaneous record showing improper evaluation); *Maritime Berthing, Inc.*, Comp. Gen. Dec. B-284123.3, 2000 CPD ¶ 89 (rejecting documentation using new date from offeror not contained in original proposal).

[c] Quantification of Non-Price Factors

Quantification of technical ratings is not required when a tradeoff decision is made, FAR 15.308. This rule was established by the Court of Appeals for the Federal Circuit in *Lockheed Missiles & Space Co. v. Bentsen*, 4 F.3d 955 (Fed. Cir. 1993). See also *EG&G Team*, Comp. Gen. Dec. B-259917, 95-2 CPD ¶ 175, stating that "the source selection authority has discretion to determine how to balance cost and technical advantages in making an award decision in a best value procurement." Quantification was not required in *Enterprise Servs., LLC*, Comp. Gen. Dec. B-415517, 2018 CPD ¶ 83; *MD Helicopters, Inc.*, Comp. Gen. Dec. B-298502, 2006 CPD ¶ 164; *Basic Contracting Servs., Inc.*, Comp. Gen. Dec. B-284649, 2000 CPD ¶ 120; and *A.G. Cullen Constr., Inc.*, Comp. Gen. Dec. B-284049.2, 2000 CPD ¶ 45.

When quantification of the benefit of making an award to a higher-priced offer is practical, the tradeoff should be justified in terms of dollars. See, for example, *Continental Airlines, Inc.*, Comp. Gen. Dec. B-258271.4, 97-1 CPD ¶ 81, holding that the agency had made a valid tradeoff decision by quantifying most of the non-price evaluation factors; and *Global Assocs., Ltd.*, Comp. Gen. Dec. B-275534, 97-1 CPD ¶ 129, where quantification of many of the non-price factors was found to be proper. See *Satellite Servs., Inc.*, Comp. Gen. Dec. B-286508, 2001 CPD ¶ 30, stating:

> While quantification of the value of technical differences is not required, a source selection official may quantify the value of technical differences in dollar terms as part of a cost/technical tradeoff; the quantification, however, must be rationally based and consistent with the RFP. *University of Kansas Med. Ctr.*, B-278400, Jan. 26, 1998, 98-1 CPD ¶ 120 at 6.

See *Olin Corp.*, Comp. Gen. Dec. B-283401, 99-2 CPD ¶ 88, finding that the SSA properly rejected the quantification of one offeror's litigious record of past performance because there was no way to accurately predict its future behavior.

It is also proper to quantify in-house costs necessitated by an offeror's proposed method of performance in order to determine the full cost of award to that offeror, *Cerner Corp.*, Comp. Gen. Dec. B-293093, 2004 CPD ¶ 34 (additional costs in using protester's software and following protester's deployment schedule).

[C] Post Selection Communication

Neither the procurement statutes nor the FAR deal with the subject of communications between the agency and the selected offeror after selection has been made and before award. However, in many cases, it is necessary to clear up uncertainties or to resolve remaining issues before award can be made. In other cases, the agency may wish to negotiate more favorable terms or prices with the selected source. Thus, it is essential to determine whether such communications constitute negotiations which would require the agency to negotiate with all those who submitted offers (if award was being made on the basis of initial proposals) or with all those remaining in the competitive range if final offer revisions have been requested.

[1] Negotiations Not Permitted

The general rule is that negotiation with only one offeror is prohibited. Such negotiations would occur if an offeror were given the opportunity to revise its offer to establish that the offer is acceptable. See *SmitKline Beecham Pharms., N.A.*, Comp. Gen. Dec. B-252226.2, 93-2 CPD ¶ 79, stating:

> It is a fundamental principle of federal procurement that all offerors must be treated equally. *Loral Terracom*; *Marconi Italiana*, 66 Comp. Gen. 272 (1987), 87-1 CPD ¶ 182. Thus, the conduct of discussions with one offeror generally requires that discussions be conducted with all offerors whose offers are within the competitive range and that offerors have an opportunity to submit revised offers. *Microlog Corp.*, B-237486, Feb. 26, 1990, 90-1 CPD ¶ 227. This rule applies even to post-selection negotiations that do not directly affect the offerors' relative standing, because all offerors are entitled to an equal opportunity to revise their proposals. *PRC Information Sciences Co.*, 56 Comp. Gen. 768 (1977), 77-2 CPD ¶ 11.

See also *Priority One Servs., Inc.*, Comp. Gen. Dec. B-288836, 2002 CPD ¶ 79 (offeror required to replace personnel not found to be acceptable and raising salary levels for some personnel); *The Futures Grp. Int'l*, Comp. Gen. Dec. B-281274.5, 2000 CPD ¶ 148 (agreeing to cap on indirect cost rates during a protest a material change in offer requiring discussions with all competitors in competitive range); and *Global Assocs., Ltd.*, Comp. Gen. Dec. B-271693.2, 96-2 CPD ¶ 100 (offer as received could not have been accepted). *In Matrix Int'l Logistics, Inc.*, Comp. Gen. Dec. B-272388.2, 97-2 CPD ¶ 89, GAO held that correction of a mistake in awardee's price after receipt of best and final offers required "discussions" with all offerors where the intended price was not ascertainable from the offer and the solicitation. In assessing the post selection communication cases, GAO focuses on whether there is a "reasonable possibility of prejudice" to the other offerors, *Labat-Anderson Inc.*, 71 Comp. Gen. 252 (B-246071.2), 92-1 CPD ¶ 193.

[2] Clarifications and Nonmaterial Changes

Communications in the nature of clarifications that would be permissible under FAR 15.306(a) do not require communications with other offerors. See above for a discussion of this type of communications. Thus, "touch up negotiations" have been permitted, *Medical Care Dev., Inc.*, Comp. Gen. Dec. B-227848.3, 87-2 CPD ¶ 371. In addition, discussing or requiring changes in nonmaterial aspects of an offer would not require negotiations with other offerors. See *Acepex Mgmt. Corp.*, Comp. Gen. Dec. B-283080, 99-2 CPD ¶ 77 (obtaining comments on the validity of a protest not a change to the offer); *Assets Recovery Sys., Inc.*, Comp. Gen. Dec. B-275332, 97-1 CPD ¶ 67 (change in payment provision did not increase or decrease overall value of offer);

Optimum Sys., Inc., Comp. Gen. Dec. B-194984, 80-2 CPD ¶ 32 (substitution of computer would have had same effect on all offerors); and *Information Sys. & Networks Corp.*, Comp. Gen. Dec. B-220661, 86-1 CPD ¶ 30 (negotiations to obtain a small reduction in price). See also *L.G. Lefler v. United States*, 6 Cl. Ct. 514 (1984), where the offer would have been lowest even without the negotiated price change.

It appears that communications of this type are contemplated by the guidance in FAR 15.504, which states:

> The contracting officer shall award a contract to the successful offeror by furnishing the executed contract or other notice of the award to that offeror.
>
> (a) If the award document includes information that is different than the latest signed proposal, as amended by the offeror's written correspondence, both the offeror and the contracting officer shall sign the contract award.

This provision apparently permits the contracting officer to include information in the final contract that is different from the prior documentation in the proposal and proposal revisions. Such information would be the likely result of post-selection communications to clear up minor problems.

[3] Negotiations Permitted

There are several situations in which negotiations with only the selected source will be permitted.

[a] Alternate Source Selection Procedures

As discussed in § 6.02, prior to 1997, pre-Rewrite, FAR 15.613 permitted agencies to adopt alternate source selection procedures. Several agencies, including DoD and NASA adopted a procedure which permitted a degree of negotiation with only the selected offeror. Under the NASA procedure and the DoD "Four-Step" procedure set forth in pre-Rewrite DFARS 215.613-70, the agency conducted limited communications with all offerors within the competitive range and then negotiated the final contract price, terms, and conditions with the selected offeror. However, the negotiations could not permit any changes in the government's requirements or the offer which would affect the source selection decision. GAO recognized that such procedures met the statutory requirements for conducting oral or written discussions with all offerors within the competitive range.

To adopt this procedures, it must be spelled out clearly in the solicitation so that offerors will be able to compete on a common basis. In addition, negotiations must not (1) change the government's requirements, (2) make an unacceptable offer acceptable, (3) change the basis for selection or (4) otherwise prejudice other offerors. See *SAMS El Segundo, LLC*, Comp. Gen. Dec. B-291620.3, 2003 CPD ¶ 48, where the agency adopted a phased selection procedure calling for negotiations with the selected offeror. See also *Northrop Grumman Tech. Servs., Inc.*, Comp. Gen. Dec. B-291506, 2003 CPD ¶ 25, where the agency added an item of government-furnished property before award—following a procedure specified in the RFP.

[b] Competitive Range of One

Post selection negotiations have been held to be appropriate where only one offeror was found to be in the competitive range. Prior to the EAR Part 15 rewrite, GAO had made it clear that a decision to have a competitive ranges of one would be carefully scrutinized in the interest of achieving full and open competition. The statutory and regulatory changes in describing the competitive range have made competitive ranges of one more acceptable. See *Clean Serv. Co.*, Comp. Gen. Dec. B-281141.3, 99-1 CPD ¶ 36, stating:

> [T]he FAR Part 15 rewrite provides that "based on the ratings of each proposal against all evaluation criteria, the contracting officer shall establish a competitive range comprised of all of the most highly rated proposals." FAR 15.306(c)(1); see *SDS Petroleum Prods., Inc.*, [B-280430, Sept. 1, 1998, 98-2 CPD ¶ 59]. We have concluded that the Part 15 rewrite does not require that agencies retain a proposal in the competitive range simply to avoid a competitive range of one; conducting discussions and requesting best and final offers from offerors with no reasonable chance of award would benefit neither the offerors nor the government. *Id.* at 6; see also 62 Fed. Reg. 51,224, 51,226 (1997) (retaining marginal offers in competitive range imposes additional and largely futile effort and cost on government and industry).

The judges at the Court of Federal Claims have reached different conclusions as to whether close scrutiny should be given to competitive ranges of one. See *Rivada Mercury, LLC v. United States*, 131 Fed. Cl. 663 (2017), discussing this issue and reviewing the varied decisions. See *System Dynamics Int'l, Inc. v. United States*, 130 Fed. Cl. 499 (2017), concluding that the proper standard to be applied to challenges of a competitive range of one is whether the exclusion of the protester's proposal was arbitrary or capricious.

Most decisions after the FAR Rewrite have affirmed the competitive range of one. See *Progress for Bakersfield Veterans LLC v. United States*, 151 Fed. Cl. 622 (2020) (only one offeror most highly rated); *Enterprise Servs., LLC*, Comp. Gen. Dec. B-414513.2, 2017 CPD ¶ 241 (only one offeror most highly rated); *Straughan Envt'l., Inc.*, Comp. Gen. Dec. B-411650, 2015 CPD ¶ 287 (protester with low cost estimate eliminated when agency concluded fixing weaknesses would raise estimate); *Bannum, Inc. v. United States*, 118 Fed. Cl. 139 (2014) (protester eliminated for failing to submit required information); *L-3 Commc'ns EOTech, Inc.*, Comp. Gen. Dec. B-311453, 2008 CPD ¶ 139 (protester eliminated for failing to meet essential requirement); *General Atomics Aeronautical Sys., Inc.*, Comp. Gen. Dec. B-311004, 2008 CPD ¶105 (protester eliminated based on significant deficiencies); *M&M Investigations, Inc.*, Comp. Gen. Dec. B-299369.2, 2007 CPD ¶200 (protester did not have reasonable chance for award); *Brian X. Scott*, Comp. Gen. Dec. B-298568, 2006 CPD ¶156 (protester required change in contract terms); *TekStar, Inc.*, Comp. Gen. Dec. B-295444, 2005 CPD ¶53 (protester eliminated based on materially deficient proposal); *National Shower Express, Inc.*, Comp. Gen. Dec. B-293970, 2004 CPD ¶140 (protester's proposal stated only that it would comply with requirements); and *Information Sys. Tech. Corp.*, Comp. Gen. Dec. B-291747, 2003 CPD ¶72 (protester did not have reasonable chance for award). In *Outdoor Venture Corp.*, Comp. Gen. Dec. B-401351.2, 2010 CPD ¶194, GAO concurred with the agency decision to put one unacceptable offeror in the competitive range while excluding another unacceptable offeror that had more deficiencies. For decisions finding an improper competitive range of one, see *Addx Corp.*, Comp. Gen. Dec. B-417804, 2020 CPD ¶118 (agency did not include assessment of low cost in excluding protester); and *Global, A 1st Flagship Co.*, Comp. Gen. Dec. B-297235, 2006 CPD ¶14 (agency included awardee's technically unacceptable proposal and excluded protester's "highly acceptable" technical proposal, on the basis that protester's evaluated cost/price was 15% higher than the awardee's). These cases indicate that a competitive range of one is appropriate when one offeror is clearly superior.

§6.11 AWARD

Once a source selection decision has been made, the contracting officer is to make the award with "reasonable promptness" by transmitting the notice of award "in writing or by electronic means," 10 U.S.C. § 3303(c) (formerly § 2305(b)(4)(C)) and 41 U.S.C. § 3703(d). Additional procedures for making awards are outlined in FAR 15.504:

> The contracting officer shall award a contract to the successful offeror by furnishing the executed contract or other notice of the award to that offeror.
>
> (a) If the award document includes information that is different than the latest signed proposal, as amended by the offeror's written correspondence, both the offeror and the contracting officer shall sign the contract award.
>
> (b) When an award is made to an offeror for less than all of the items that may be awarded and additional items are being withheld for subsequent award, each notice shall state that the Government may make subsequent awards on those additional items within the proposal acceptance period.

In some cases, the notice of award might constitute an acceptance by the government of an offer contained in a final proposal revision or initial proposal. This would occur, for example, in a situation where the government was fully in agreement with all the terms of that offer and merely desired to enter into a binding contract immediately. However, in many cases the contracting officer will want to prepare an integrated contractual document and obtain the signature of both parties to that document, as described in FAR 15.504(a) above. In such cases the notice of award may merely notify the offeror that it has been selected for award and that the integrated document will be forwarded in due course. Offerors should be aware that there are varying procedures used in this area and should ensure that they have a legally binding document before beginning work.

Statutory and regulatory requirements for a notice of award to be "in writing or by electronic means" raise the question of whether the contracting officer can form a contract by giving an oral notice of award. There is sparse litigation dealing with this subject, but the cases that do exist suggest strongly that an oral notice would not be effective. See, for example, *R.J. Crowley, Inc.*, ASBCA 28730, 86-1 BCA ¶ 18,739. In addition, GAO has enforced the FAR requirement that award of the contract be in written form. See *Litton Sys., Inc.*, Comp. Gen. Dec. B-229921, 88-1 CPD ¶ 448, holding that the protester's argument that partial award had been made orally over the phone was irrelevant in light of an actual written award made to another offeror, as was required. In *G. McMillan & Co.*, Comp. Gen. Dec. B-239805, 90-2 CPD ¶ 214, GAO stated, in reference to an argument that a protester was due expenses it incurred in anticipation of receiving a contract award, that "[s]ince the law and regulations require written notice of award, we think it unlikely that the protester could establish that a contract resulted from the alleged oral advice." GAO generally will not consider protests as to the "adequacy" of the award because that is a "procedural matter," *Al Hamra Kuwait Co.*, Comp. Gen. Dec. B-288970, 2001 CPD ¶ 208.

When award is made by obtaining the signature of both of the parties, it is usually made on one of the standard forms prescribed by the government. If the government is merely accepting an offer without alteration by awarding on the basis of the initial proposals or final proposal revisions that have not changed the original offer, it can accomplish this by signing Standard Form (SF) 33, FAR 53.301-33, or SF 1442, FAR 53.301-1442, if these have been used as the cover page for the solicitation.

If Optional Form (OF) 308, FAR 53.302-308, has been used in transmitting the solicitation, this is not possible because that form has no place for signature by the contracting officer. If there have been alterations to the RFP during the procurement process, the agency can use either SF 26, FAR 53.301-26, or OF 307, FAR 53.302-307, as the cover page to the integrated contract. Alternatively, an agency can create its own award cover page as long as it complies with FAR 15.504 as follows:

> (c) If the Optional Form (OF) 307, Contract Award, Standard Form (SF) 26, Award/Contract, or SF 33, Solicitation, Offer and Award, is not used to award the contract, the first page of the award document shall contain the Government's acceptance statement from Block 15 of that form, exclusive

> of the Item 3 reference language, and shall contain the contracting officer's name, signature, and date. In addition, if the award document includes information that is different than the signed proposal, as amended by the offeror's written correspondence, the first page shall include the contractor's agreement statement from Block 14 of the OF 307 and the signature of the contractor's authorized representative.

Merely signing the cover page to an RFP can lead to confusion if there have been alterations to the RFP during the procurement process. See *F & F Lab., Inc.*, ASBCA 33007, 89-1 BCA ¶ 21,207, where the contracting officer signed SF 26 after the contractor had stated in its offer that it would supply a candy bar at variance with that called for by the specifications. The board held the government bound on the theory that the offer was incorporated by reference into the contract by the terms of the standard form. The listing of provisions on the standard form can also have consequences when these forms are used for acceptance. For example, in *Codex Corp.*, GSBCA 8186-P, 86-1 BCA ¶ 18,590, the contracting officer and the awardee signed the cover page of SF 26, where the table of contents indicated which sections of the contract were to be incorporated. In actuality, one of the sections was missing from the contract due to a clerical error. The board found that the parties had entered into a binding contract and that, despite its absence from the actual contract, the section in question was incorporated into the contract by reference on the cover page.

As a general rule, when written or oral discussions have been held and new offers requested, award is made by acceptance of the new offer (in one of the forms described above). However, award has been permitted on the basis of an original offer where the offeror did not submit a BAFO in response to the request for BAFOs, *MR&S/AME*, Comp. Gen. Dec. B-250313.2, 93-1 CPD ¶ 245. In this case, GAO reasoned that the offeror had agreed to an extension that kept its original offer open beyond the award date and the submission of a BAFO was permissible, not mandatory. GAO also ruled that contacting the offeror to find out why no BAFO had been submitted was not a post-BAFO discussion. Award has not been permitted on the basis of the initial offer where the offeror submitted its BAFO late, *Touchstone Textiles, Inc.*, Comp. Gen. Dec. B-272230.4, 96-2 CPD ¶ 107. In that case GAO reasoned that the agency could not ignore the intent conveyed by the submission of a modified proposal and, thus, the late BAFO constituted a revocation of the initial offer. Revocation of the original offer was also found when an offeror submitted its final proposal revisions in unauthorized electronic form that arrived late, *Integrated Bus. Solutions, Inc.*, Comp. Gen. Dec. B-292239, 2003 CPD ¶ 122; *Integrated Bus. Solutions, Inc. v. United States*, 58 Fed. Cl. 203 (2003).

[A] Contents of Contract

The contracting parties should ensure that the award document is clear as to the contents of the contract. If award is made by signing SF 33 or SF 1442, the parties will have agreed that the contract consists of the documents referred to on those forms plus any amendments to the solicitation. This would appear to exclude any parts of the offeror's proposal that were submitted in separate documents, including any cover letter to the proposal. However, if the contractor includes contract language conflicting with the RFP, it may create an ambiguity which should be cleared up. See, for example, *Catel, Inc.*, ASBCA 52224, 02-1 BCA ¶ 31,731, holding the contractor bound when it attempted to exclude work that was required by the specifications but was held bound to the specifications because its language was vague. See also *Ferguson-Williams, Inc.*, ENGBCA 6482, 99-1 BCA ¶ 30,731, where the contractor's statement in Part B that home office overhead was included in its price conflicted with a special contract clause in Part I. The board ruled that the contractor was not entitled to be reimbursed its home office overhead because a solicitation provision stated that "financial data submitted with an offer . . . will [not] form a part of the resulting contract." Apparently, in neither case did either party recognize their lack of agreement on the terms of the contract—with the contractor being penalized for not clearly up the problem.

When SF 33 or SF 1442 are used and an offeror conditions the offer by altering the solicitation requirements in a material way, the award would not be binding on the offeror because the government's acceptance would not match the offer. Thus, the issue must be addressed before award. When the agency wants to incorporate material in the contract that is not part of the solicitation, then SF 26, OF 307, or an agency form should be used. In such cases the contracting officer should clearly indicate what documents are part of the contract. When SF 26 is used, the contracting officer can rewrite the contract documents, check block 17 on the form, and send the new contract to the offeror for signature. The offeror's proposal will not be part of the contract unless it is specifically listed, *Loral Aerospace Corp.*, ASBCA 46373, 97-2 BCA ¶ 29,128, but, if it is listed, it will be part of the contract, *Ervin & Assocs., Inc. v. United States*, 59 Fed. Cl. 267 (2004), *aff'd*, 120 Fed. Appx. 353 (Fed. Cir. 2005). Alternatively, the contracting officer can incorporate the offeror's proposal in the contract, sign the form, and check block 18. In either case the form should clearly identify what is part of the contract in order to avoid confusion on this issue. See the discussion of *F & F Lab., Inc.* and *Codex Corp.*, above.

OF 307 ameliorates the problem of potential confusion in using SF 26 by omitting blocks 17 and 18 and providing in block 14 that the contract will consist of "this document and any documents attached or incorporated by reference." However, the clarity of the document is still dependent on a clear statement of the contents of the contract.

The most troublesome issue in determining what is part of the contract is the question of whether proposals are part of the contract. Because the typical proposal contains considerable material that is in the nature of information or other non-promissory type material, it is generally not good practice to incorporate the entire proposal in the contract. Furthermore, the proposal may contain detailed data that conflicts with the contract specifications. The lack of clarity as to the contents of the contract can easily lead to litigation. See *Singer-General Precision, Inc.*, ASBCA 13241, 73-2 BCA ¶ 10,258, where the board had to resolve the question of whether the specifications or the conflicting technical proposal embodied the agreement of the parties. It gave no general rule but stated:

> [The contractor] was not free to ignore clearly stated contractual requirements merely because the Government found the technical proposal acceptable and incorporated it into the contract. On the other hand, the Government could not with immunity require [the contractor] to perform work which was contrary to stated details, design and concepts in the proposal. When consideration is given to the specific claims, we will if applicable and necessary to decide a particular claim give further consideration to the contentions of the parties as presented in this general issue.

The board then analyzed each claim of the contractor for an equitable adjustment to determine what the parties had agreed to. See also *TRW, Inc.*, ASBCA 27299, 87-3 BCA ¶ 19,964, where the contracting officer incorporated the proposal into the contract to the extent it did not deviate from the government specifications. The board held that one aspect of the proposal was binding because it was promissory and another aspect was not binding because it was not promissory. Compare *Omni Corp. v. United States*, 41 Fed. Cl. 585 (1998), holding that a contractor was not bound to perform work in accordance with a technique described in its technical proposal which was not incorporated (the agency had unsuccessfully attempted to bind the contractor to perform such work by vague language in Section M of the RFP).

Silence on the status of proposals has also led to difficulties. See, for example, *Johnson Controls, Inc.*, ASBCA 25714, 82-1 BCA ¶ 15,779, holding the government bound to the terms of a technical proposal that was not clearly incorporated into the contract because it clearly stated that the contractor was offering to perform the work in a way that deviated with a detailed specification statement. In contrast, in *Northrop Grumman Corp. v. United States*, 47 Fed. Cl. 20 (2000), the court held that the contractor's proposal was not the baseline for determining whether constructive changes had occurred because the proposal was not incorporated into the contract. See also *Consolidated Sec. Servs. Corp.*, GSBCA 7714, 86-1 BCA ¶ 18,597, holding that the details of a pricing proposal were not part of a contract. This result conformed with the Contract Award solicitation provision in FAR 52.215-16, which stated that neither financial data nor representations concerning facilities or financing would "form part of the resulting contract." This helpful language was removed from the FAR by the FAR Part 15 Rewrite.

There have also been problems with contractual statements that do not contain clear promissory language. See, for example, *Hamilton Secs. Advisory Servs., Inc. v. United States*, 60 Fed. Cl. 144 (2004), denying a government claim that the contractor breached the contract because it could find no clear promise, stating at 158-59:

> The United States Court of Appeals for the Federal Circuit has advised that the "requirement of certainty in contracts serves two purposes. One is the need to determine whether the parties in fact intended to contract at all, and the other relates to the ability of a court to determine when a breach has occurred and to formulate any appropriate remedy." *Aviation Contractor Employees, Inc. v. United States*, 945 F.2d 1568, 1572 (Fed. Cir. 1991) (citing RESTATEMENT § 33) ("The terms of a contract are reasonably certain if they provide a basis for determining the existence of a breach and for giving an appropriate remedy.") and *Neeley v. Bankers Trust Co.*, 757 F.2d 621 (5th Cir. 1985), wherein the United States Court of the Fifth Circuit held that:
>
> > the entire contract falls with the failure of indefinite promises . . . . Like most questions of contract law, whether a promise or other term forms an essential part of an agreement depends primarily upon the intent of the parties. Thus, an *"essential" promise denotes one that the parties reasonably regarded, at the time of contracting,* as a vitally important ingredient in their bargain. Failure to fulfill such a promise, in other words, would seriously frustrate the expectations of one or more of the parties as to what would constitute sufficient performance of the contract as a whole. *Courts refuse to enforce agreements that contain indefinite promises or terms they deem essential precisely because judicial clarification of the uncertainty entails great danger of creating intentions and expectations that the parties themselves never entertained.*
>
> *Id.* at 628 (emphasis added); *see also Ace-Federal Reporters, Inc. v. Barram*, 226 F.3d 1329, 1332 (Fed. Cir. 2002); *Modern Sys. Tech. Corp. v. United States*, 979 F.2d 200, 202 (Fed. Cir. 1992); *Brookhaven Hous. Coalition v. Solomon*, 583 F.2d 584, 593 (2d Cir. 1978) (holding that "a court cannot decree performance of an agreement unless it can discern with reasonable certainty and particularity what the terms of the agreement are. *To consummate an enforceable agreement, the parties must not only believe that they have made a contract, they must also have expressed their intent in a manner that is susceptible of judicial interpretation.*") (emphasis added).

In *United Techs. Corp.*, ASBCA 46880, 97-1 BCA ¶ 28,818, the board interpreted nonpromissory language as promissory because the Secretary of the Navy had made a firm promise to the contractor but the contracting officer had used nonpromissory language in the contract (using the terms "intends to permit the Contractor to compete" for future work when the Secretary had guaranteed the right to compete). The board based its decision to a large degree on the fact that the contractor had sought to obtain promissory language and had been told by a number of officials that "intends" would be interpreted to mean "agrees."

[B] Time for Acceptance

Once an offer expires the government loses the power to form a contract by acceptance. The Instructions to Offerors—Competitive Acquisition solicitation provision in FAR 52.215-1 specifies the time that an offeror holds its offer open:

> (d) *Offer expiration date*. Proposals in response to this solicitation will be valid for the number of days specified in the solicitation cover sheet (unless a different period is proposed by the offeror).

Block 4 of OF 308 follows this provision by stating that offers will be valid for 60 days unless a different period is entered in the block. The standard solicitation forms, SF 33 and SF 1442, used to solicit both sealed bids and competitive proposals, contain statements that offerors agree to be bound by their offers if they are accepted within a stated number of days. While these provisions were written to require bidders on sealed bid procurements to submit firm bids, they also appear to limit the time in which a competitive proposal can be accepted. GAO has ruled, however, that, although these provisions contain dates when the offers expire, the agency can accept an expired offer after all offers have expired if the offeror waives the expiration date. See *Fletcher Constr. Co.*, Comp. Gen. Dec. B-248977, 92-2 CPD ¶ 246, reasoning:

> Even assuming that protester's interpretation of the acceptance period clause on the SF 1442 on which BAFOs were submitted is correct, and that all offers including the protester's had expired by the time of award, it is not improper for an agency to accept an expired offer for a proposed award without reopening negotiations. *Protective Materials Co., Inc.*, B-225495, Mar. 18, 1987, 87-1 CPD ¶ 303. Where the acceptance period has expired on all offers, the contracting officer may allow the successful offeror to waive the expiration of its proposal acceptance period without reopening negotiations to make an award on the basis of the offer as submitted, since waiver under these circumstances is not prejudicial to the competitive system. *Sublette Elec., Inc.*, B-232586, Nov. 30, 1988, 88-2 CPD ¶ 540.

This rule has been followed in *Scot, Inc.*, Comp. Gen. Dec. B-295569, 2005 CPD ¶ 66 (procurement with expiration date in RFP); *Pride Mobility Prod. Corp.*, Comp. Gen. Dec. B-292822.5, 2005 CPD ¶ 72 (procurement with expiration date in RFP amendment); and *CDA Investment Techs., Inc.*, Comp. Gen. Dec. B-272093.3, 97-1 CPD ¶ 102, *recons. denied*, 97-1 CPD ¶ 103 (procurement using SF 33). In *Krug Life Scis., Inc.*, Comp. Gen. Dec. B-258669.2, 95-1 CPD ¶ 111, GAO permitted waiver of the expiration date when the protester had kept its acceptance period open by sending in unsolicited extensions but the winning offeror had permitted its offer to expire. See also *BioGenesis Pacific, Inc.*, Comp. Gen. Dec. B-283738, 99-2 CPD ¶ 109, rejecting a contention that the agency improperly issued an amendment to the RFP extending the expiration date after it expired.

If an offeror submits an offer with an expiration date shorter than that required by the RFP, it will not be permitted to waive the expiration date after its offer has expired because that is prejudicial to the competitive system. See *Camden Shipping Corp. v. United States*, 89 Fed. Cl. 433 (2009), stating at 440:

> Permitting revival of an offer would compromise the integrity of the competitive process if the offeror designated a shorter acceptance period than that requested by the solicitation, and other offerors specified the longer period. *Espirit Int'l Corp.,* [Comp. Gen. Dec. B-276294, 97-1 CPD ¶ 106], at 1; *The Vemo Co.,* [Comp. Gen. Dec. B-243390, 91-2 CPD ¶ 443], at 2; *Fred Rutledge,* [63 Comp. Gen. 253 (B-213474),] 84-1 CPD ¶ 297, at 1; . . . If an offeror shortens the length of time its offer is open, it faces less exposure to the market risk of price fluctuation than other offerors. *Postmaster Gen.,* at 4; *see also Espirit Int'l Corp.,* at 1. Permitting an offeror to revive its offer after the shorter acceptance period has expired would be unfair, because it would allow the offeror to take its risk in increments, assessing after its offer expired whether the market situation had changed, while other offerors have no such opportunity.

The same result was reached in *Data Express*, Comp. Gen. Dec. B-234468, 89-1 CPD ¶ 507, where the protester had allowed its offer to expire by not acknowledging an amendment to the RFP that extended the expiration date of offers. See also *NECCO Inc.*, Comp. Gen. Dec. B-258131, 94-2 CPD ¶ 218, following the same reasoning in a case where the bidder on a sealed bid procurement responded to a request for an extension of the expiration date of a bid with an agreement to extend the date for a shorter length of time and then had its bid expire.

If neither the RFP nor the offer contain an expiration date, to be valid an award must be made within a reasonable time after receipt of a proposal or final proposal revisions. However, once a reasonable time has expired, the offer will no longer be open for award. See *Western Roofing Serv.*, 70 Comp. Gen. 323 (B-232666.4), 91-1 CPD ¶ 242, *recons. denied*, 91-1 CPD ¶ 566, where the agency had delayed action on a procurement for over a year and then reopened the procurement by requesting another round of BAFOs. When one of the original offerors protested because it had never received the request for a BAFO, GAO denied the protest holding that the agency was correct in assuming that the earlier BAFO had expired and, hence, award could be made only to an offeror that had submitted a new BAFO. GAO reasoned that the offer had expired in view of the statutory mandate for agencies to award promptly, 41 U.S.C. § 253b(d)(4), and the *Uniform Commercial Code* rule that offers without expiration dates remain open only for a reasonable time, U.C.C. § 2-205. GAO found that the 13 months that had passed between the submission of the BAFO and the award was too long a period to constitute a reasonable time. See *M.J.S., Inc.*, Comp. Gen. Dec. B-244410, 91-2 CPD ¶ 344, holding that a BAFO with no expiration date could clearly be accepted one month after submission.

Generally, contracting officers obtain proposal extensions from offerors when they find that there will be substantial delays in awarding the contract. GAO has found this to be proper when the agency has valid reasons for extending the time of award, *Saco Def., Inc.*, Comp. Gen. Dec. B-240603, 90-2 CPD ¶ 462 (11-month delay to permit a small business reasonable time to cure a responsibility problem and to conduct discussions); *Trim-Flite, Inc.*, 67 Comp. Gen. 550 (B-229926.4), 88-2 CPD ¶ 124 (eight-month delay to correct agency errors); *American Identification Prods., Inc.*, Comp. Gen. Dec. B-227599, 87-2 CPD ¶ 42 (six-month delay to evaluate samples). In *Ocean Tech., Inc.*, Comp. Gen. Dec. B-236470, 89-2 CPD ¶ 189, GAO denied a protest claiming that the proposal extension had been signed by an unauthorized employee of the offeror because the award could have been made even if the offer expired.

If an offeror agrees to hold its offer open and is later awarded the contract, it takes the risk of cost increases that may have occurred in the intervening period. See *Magna Enters., Inc.*, ASBCA 51188, 02-1 BCA ¶ 31660, stating at 156,419-20:

> Magna voluntarily extended its offer repeatedly, and used that time to resolve the Government's serious concerns over Magna's ability to perform. Although the offer remained open for a protracted period, that time was not shown to be unreasonable under the circumstances. Magna assumed the risk in this fixed-price supply contract that potential subcontractors or suppliers might become unavailable, or that prices could increase. *Consolidated Airborne Systems, Inc. v. United States*, 348 F.2d 941 (Ct. Cl. 1965); *D.W. Clark, Inc.*, ASBCA No. 45562, 94-3 BCA ¶ 27,132. A contractor is properly terminated for default when it fails to perform due to price increases during an extended offer period.

See also *Ordnance Parts & Eng'g Co.*, ASBCA 44327, 93-2 BCA ¶ 25,690, where the contractor was properly terminated for default when it failed to perform because of significant price increases that had occurred in the year that it held its offer open.

[C] Delay of Award By Protest

When a preaward protest is filed, the award is generally delayed until the protest is resolved. This imposes the burden on the winning offeror if such delayed award increases its costs of performance or otherwise makes it more difficult to perform the work. However, a winning offeror is not required to remain available for award in the face of a protest.

If an agency decides to withhold award pending the outcome of a protest, the selected offeror, as well as other offerors that might be in line for award, will normally be requested to keep their offers open. In addition, the protester's offer will be held to have remained open by virtue of the protest, 50 Comp. Gen. 357 (B-170178) (1970). Thus, upon conclusion of the protest, the agency will normally be able to make award in accordance with the original procurement if that is the proper course of action. GAO has permitted this outcome by holding that expiration dates may be waived and offers revived by the offeror in negotiated procurements because the only right conferred by expiration dates is upon the offeror, *Riggins & Williamson Mach. Co.*, 54 Comp. Gen. 783 (B-182801), 75-1 CPD ¶ 168. GAO has specified that revival of offers or waiver of expiration dates for the purpose of awarding the contract must be done "on the basis of the offer as submitted," *Donald N. Humphries & Assocs.*, 55 Comp. Gen. 432 (B-183292), 75-2 CPD ¶ 275. Under these circumstances, GAO has repeatedly held that, because the offer was not altered, no reopening of negotiations was necessary as it was not prejudicial to the competitive system. See *Sublette Elec., Inc.*, Comp. Gen. Dec. B-232586, 88-2 CPD ¶ 540; *Protective Materials Co.*, Comp. Gen. Dec. B-225495, 87-1 CPD ¶ 303; and *Medical Coaches, Inc.*, Comp. Gen. Dec. B-196339.2, 79-2 CPD ¶ 308, where the offers were not altered and, therefore, no further discussions were found to have been held by the agency. In *Ocean Tech., Inc.*, Comp. Gen. Dec. B-236470, 89-2 CPD ¶ 189; and *Data Tech. Indus., Inc.*, Comp. Gen. Dec. B-197858, 80-2 CPD ¶ 2, GAO specifically noted that the actual request that an offeror waive the expiration date of its offer did not constitute discussions requiring the reopening of negotiations with all offerors. See also *Rentfrow, Inc.*, Comp. Gen. Dec. B-243215, 91-2 CPD ¶ 25, holding that it was proper to request a waiver of the expiration date only from the winning offeror.

Offerors that elect to keep their offers open during the protest period and are subsequently awarded the contract have no recourse thereafter. GAO has refused to grant delay damages in such circumstances. See *Trim-Flite, Inc.*, 67 Comp. Gen. 550 (B-229926.4), 88-2 CPD ¶ 124, stating at 550:

> A delay in meeting procurement milestones generally is a procedural deficiency which does not provide a basis of protest because it has no effect on the validity of the procurement. *American Identification Products, Inc.*, B-227599, July 13, 1987, 87-2 CPD ¶ 42. While an agency is required to award a contract with reasonable promptness, the 8-month period here from closing date to award is not unreasonable per se given the attempts by the agency to correct the matters raised in offerors' complaints and protests through reevaluations. See *Id.* The fact that the delays may have been the result of initial agency errors in the procurement is irrelevant; once the errors occurred . . . the [agency's] proper course of action was to take steps to correct the errors. The award delay was merely an unfortunate, but necessary, by-product of the [agency's] proper action.

Subsequently, GAO ruled that delay in award of a contract is not a protestable issue, *Federal Sales Serv., Inc.*, Comp. Gen. Dec. B-237978, 90-1 CPD ¶ 249. See also *M.A. Mortenson Co. v. United States*, 843 F.2d 1360 (Fed. Cir. 1988), where the court denied a price adjustment when the contractor had extended its bid expiration date by 77 days and later claimed additional compensation to reflect the fact that this time extension had forced it to perform in winter weather. Similarly, in *DeMatteo Constr. Co. v. United States*, 600 F.2d 1384 (Ct. Cl. 1979), the contractor was denied compensation for a suspension of work when it extended its expiration date pending the outcome of a protest. On the other hand, if performance is stayed after award, the contractor is entitled to compensation under the Protest After Award clause in FAR 52.233-3.

[D] Date of Award

There has been controversy on the date that an award through government acceptance of a firm's offer creates a binding contract. This issue can be important when a firm attempts to withdraw its offer before it has received the government's acceptance but finds that the acceptance was placed in the mail before the withdrawal. The traditional common-law rule was that the contract was binding when acceptance of the offer is dispatched (the "mailbox" rule). However, this rule was rejected by the Court of Claims in *Emeco Indus., Inc. v. United States*, 485 F.2d 652 (Ct. Cl. 1973), and *Rhode Island Tool Co. v. United States*, 128 F. Supp. 417 (Ct. Cl. 1955), where the court, relying on postal regulations allowing the retrieval of mailed documents from the mail by the sender, reasoned that award does not occur until the offeror receives the mailed document. See also *Titan Atlantic Constr. Corp./The Gallegos Corp., a Joint Venture*, ASBCA 26007, 83-2 BCA ¶ 16,791, following this rule in determining that acceptance of a government offer by the contractor was not binding until the government received the acceptance. This decision contains a complete history of the evolution of this rule. Following the *Emeco* decision, some of the government forms stated that acceptance was effective when placed in the mail (adopting the old "mailbox" rule), and several appeals boards held that these forms governed. See *Adaptive Concepts, Inc.*, ASBCA 73123, 96-1 BCA ¶ 28,248; *G.E. Sales & Rentals v. General Servs. Admin.*, GSBCA 13304, 1995 GSBCA LEXIS 409; *Singleton Contracting Corp.*, IBCA-1770-1-84, 86-2 BCA ¶ 18,800; *Computer Wholesale Corp.*, GSBCA 4217, 76-1 BCA ¶ 11,859; and *IMCO Precision Prods., Inc.*, ASBCA 17572, 73-2 BCA ¶ 10,250. GAO also concluded that the language in these forms was controlling in making the "mailbox" rule applicable, *Wolverine Diesel Power Co.*, 57 Comp. Gen. 468 (B-189789), 78-1 CPD ¶ 375 (telegraphic acceptance effective when dispatched). Although no decisions have been found on this issue, since the Instruction to Offerors—Competitive Acquisition solicitation provision in FAR 52.215-1 contains language essentially the same as that construed by the board and GAO decisions, it would appear that acceptance will be effective when the government mails the signed SF 33, SF 1442 or OF 307. The solicitation provision states in ¶ (f):

> (10) A written award or acceptance of proposal mailed or otherwise furnished to the successful offeror within the time specified in the proposal shall result in a binding contract without further action by either party.

The parties may agree to an effective date of the contract other than the date of execution of the contract document. In *Northrop Worldwide Aircraft Servs., Inc.*, ASBCA 45216, 96-2 BCA ¶ 28,574, the agency amended Standard Form 26 to read "conditional/award," whereby the parties agreed that the contract effective date would be the date on which it received approval from the secretary of the agency. The approval occurred subsequent to the date the form was executed, and it was this later date that the board recognized as the effective date of the contract.

§ 6.12 NOTICES AND DEBRIEFINGS

Agencies are required to notify offerors when they are eliminated from the competition and to provide debriefings when requested. Section 1014 of FASA, amending 10 U.S.C. § 2305(b), and § 1064 of FASA, amending 41 U.S.C. § 253b, added new guidance on postaward debriefings. Section 4104 of the Clinger-Cohen Act of 1996, further amended 10 U.S.C. § 2305(b) and 41 U.S.C. § 253b (now 41 U.S.C. § 3704 and § 3705) to add a new provision on preaward debriefings. The pre- and post-award debriefing provisions of title 10 are now codified at § 3304 and § 3305, respectively. These statutes are implemented in FAR 15.605 and FAR 15.606.

[A] Preaward Notices and Debriefings

Preaward notices and debriefings serve a number of purposes. Early notice of exclusion from the competition will permit excluded offerors to turn their attention to other contracting opportunities. It will also conserve resources since offerors will be on notice that investing further expense on the procurement would not be productive. These purposes were noted in the promulgation comments of the FAR Part 15 Rewrite at 62 Fed. Reg. 51226 (1997):

> This final rule insures that offerors with little probability of success are advised early on that their competitive position does not merit additional expense in a largely futile attempt to secure the contract.
>
> This knowledge will benefit both large and small entities, but will be especially beneficial to small entities that have constrained budgets. These entities will be able to conserve scarce bid and proposal funds and employ their resources on more productive business opportunities.

Another function of the preaward notice is that it provides an offeror an opportunity to challenge its elimination from the competition by requesting a preaward debriefing and determining whether to file a preaward protest or request alternative dispute resolution of its objection to the exclusion. While additional effort may be required of procurement personnel and delays in the procurement result if protests are filed, early resolution will be to the public's advantage if the exclusion was not appropriate. Corrective action is less time consuming and expensive to all parties if undertaken while the procurement is in process than after award.

[1] Preaward Notices

Although the procurement statutes do not specifically state that preaward notice of exclusion from competition is to be given, the requirement for such notice is implicit in the offeror's right to request a preaward debriefing. Thus, FAR 15.503(a) requires preaward notices of exclusion as follows:

> Preaward notices—(1) Preaward notices of exclusion from competitive range. The contracting officer shall notify offerors promptly in writing when their proposals are excluded from the competitive range or otherwise eliminated from the competition. The notice shall state the basis for the determination

The term "or otherwise eliminated from the competition" is not defined. It apparently is meant to implement the statutory phrase "or otherwise excludes such an offeror from further consideration prior to the final source selection decision" providing for preaward debriefing, 10 U.S.C. § 3305 (formerly § 2305(b)(6)(A)) and 41 U.S.C. § 3705(a). Determinations of exclusion which would qualify for such notice would include determinations that an offeror is not responsible or otherwise not eligible for award or that an offer is inexcusably late (FAR 15.208(c)) or is unacceptable. It might also be argued that an offeror is "eliminated from the competition" when another offeror is selected for award. Contradicting such an interpretation is the statutory language providing for preaward debriefing for an excluded offeror "prior to the final source selection decision." While the FAR would be free to go beyond the statutory mandate, it is doubtful if this is the correct interpretation because FAR 15.503(a)(2) specifically provides for post-selection, preaward notice for small business setasides, as follows:

> Preaward notices for small business set-asides. In addition to the notice in paragraph (a)(1) of this section, when using a small business set-aside (see Subpart 19.5), upon completion of negotiations and determinations of responsibility, but prior to award, the contracting officer shall notify each offeror in writing of the name and location of the apparent successful offeror. The notice shall also state that

(i) The Government will not consider subsequent revisions of the offeror's proposal; and

(ii) No response is required unless a basis exists to challenge the small business size status of the apparent successful offeror. The notice is not required when the contracting officer determines in writing that the urgency of the requirement necessitates award without delay or when the contract is entered into under the 8(a) program (see 19.805-2).

[2] Preaward Debriefings

The statutory provisions for preaward debriefings at 10 U.S.C. § 3304 (formerly § 2305(b)(6)(A)) and 41 U.S.C. § 3705(a) are implemented in FAR 15.505, as follows:

> Offerors excluded from the competitive range or otherwise excluded from the competition before award may request a debriefing before award (10 U.S.C. 2305(b)(6)(A) and 41 U.S.C. 253b(f)-(h)).
>
> (a)(1) The offeror may request a preaward debriefing by submitting a written request for debriefing to the contracting officer within 3 days after receipt of the notice of exclusion from the competition.
>
> (2) At the offeror's request, this debriefing may be delayed until after award. If the debriefing is delayed until after award, it shall include all information normally provided in a postaward debriefing (see 15.506(d)). Debriefings delayed pursuant to this paragraph could affect the timeliness of any protest filed subsequent to the debriefing.
>
> (3) If the offeror does not submit a timely request, the offeror need not be given either a preaward or a postaward debriefing. Offerors are entitled to no more than one debriefing for each proposal.
>
> (b) The contracting officer shall make every effort to debrief the unsuccessful offeror as soon as practicable, but may refuse the request for a debriefing if, for compelling reasons, it is not in the best interests of the Government to conduct a debriefing at that time. The rationale for delaying the debriefing shall be documented in the contract file. If the contracting officer delays the debriefing, it shall be provided no later than the time postaward debriefings are provided under 15.506. In that event, the contracting officer shall include the information at 15.506(d) in the debriefing.
>
> (c) Debriefings may be done orally, in writing, or by any other method acceptable to the contracting officer.
>
> (d) The contracting officer should normally chair any debriefing session held. Individuals who conducted the evaluations shall provide support.
>
> (e) At a minimum, preaward debriefings shall include—
>
> (1) The agency's evaluation of significant elements in the offeror's proposal;
>
> (2) A summary of the rationale for eliminating the offeror from the competition; and

(3) Reasonable responses to relevant questions about whether source selection procedures contained in the solicitation, applicable regulations, and other applicable authorities were followed in the process of eliminating the offeror from the competition.

(f) Preaward debriefings shall not disclose—

(1) The number of offerors;
(2) The identity of other offerors;
(3) The content of other offerors' proposals;
(4) The ranking of other offerors;
(5) The evaluation of other offerors; or
(6) Any of the information prohibited in 15.506(e).

(g) An official summary of the debriefing shall be included in the contract file.

Because ¶ (a)(3) limits offerors to a single debriefing and ¶ (a)(2) permits offerors to request a postaward debriefing in lieu of a preaward debriefing, they must exercise care in deciding the type of debriefing to request when they have been excluded from the competition prior to the award decision. If they believe that they have been unfairly eliminated from the competition, they will undoubtedly elect a preaward debriefing to determine the basis for the agency's action. However, because the procurement is ongoing, ¶ (f) severely limits the amount of information that can be given to the offeror in this type of debriefing. Thus, in cases where the offeror does not intend to challenge its exclusion from the competition but desires to learn how to improve its competitive position in future procurements, a postaward debriefing is a sensible election because far more information can be obtained in a postaward debriefing. This election also benefits the procuring agency because it permits debriefing at a time when the workload of the source selection team is likely to be smaller than it would be prior to award. The safe procedure to follow in requesting a postaward debriefing is to request a preaward debriefing, including a request that it be deferred until postaward. See 10 U.S.C. § 3305 (10 U.S.C. § 2305(b)(6)(B)), and 41 U.S.C. § 3705(c) stating that postaward debriefings are required in this situation *only* if a preaward debriefing has been requested and refused.

Great care should be exercised by offerors in this regard because if they learn in a postaward debriefing that they were excluded from the competitive range because of deficiencies in their proposal, a protest of faulty evaluation may be held to be untimely. This occurred in *United Int'l Investigative Servs., Inc.*, Comp. Gen. Dec. B-286327, 2000 CPD ¶ 173, where GAO rejected the protest as being untimely, stating that, since postaward debriefings were only "required" if the agency refused the preaward debriefing, the protester's free choice to delay the debriefing made the protest untimely. See *Loc Performance Prods., Inc.*, Comp. Gen. Dec. B-417431, 2019 CPD ¶ 149, applying this rule and noting that the protester would have learned of the grounds of protest had it received the offered preaward debriefing.

GAO will not review an agency's decision to delay the debriefing until after award, *Global Eng'g & Constr.*, Comp. Gen. Dec. B-275999.3, 97-1 CPD ¶ 77. In that case, Global requested a preaward debriefing after the agency excluded its proposal from the competitive range. The agency denied Global's request on the ground that preaward debriefings in the procurement would not be in the government's best interest. The agency also stated that a preaward debriefing would require redirecting the agency's resources "which would not best serve our customers' needs or be a wise expenditure of U.S. tax dollars." GAO stated that the offeror would not be prejudiced by the denial of the preaward debriefing because it would be entitled to receive a postaward debriefing and, if it filed a protest after award, work on the procurement would be stayed. In GAO's view, an agency postponing the debriefing "may find it difficult to marshal the resources to defend its earlier decision" and that "simply may prejudice the agency in defending the protest." Although GAO found that Global presented several valid reasons why preaward debriefings should be encouraged, it still denied the protest.

GAO has strictly enforced the requirement that a preaward debriefing be requested within three days of receipt of the notice of exclusion from the competitive range. See *Information Unlimited, Inc.*, Comp. Gen. Dec. B-415716.40, 2019 CPD ¶ 352, where the protester did not promptly respond when it could not open a debriefing attached to an e-mail. See also *International Res. Grp.*, Comp. Gen. Dec. B-286663, 2001 CPD ¶ 35, holding that when the notice of exclusion is sent by the agency electronically after business hours, the first day for the computation should be the first business day after the day that the notice was sent.

[B] Postaward Notices and Debriefings

Postaward notices and debriefings serve a number of functions in addition to those served by preaward notices and debriefings. In addition to advising offerors that their offers are no longer under consideration and providing them with information to challenge the selection, postaward debriefings can provide offerors with "an indication of how those offerors can improve their chances for success in future procurements," Sen. Rep. 103-258 accompanying FASA, Pub. L. No. 103-355. By identifying the source selected, postaward notices also provide information which other offerors may use for subcontracting opportunities.

[1] Postaward Notices

The procurement statutes require notice of contract award to be given to "all other offerors within 3 days after date of contract award in writing or by electronic means of the rejection of their proposals," 10 U.S.C. § 3304 (formerly § 2305(b)(4)(C)) and 41 U.S.C. § 3704(a). This requirement is implemented in FAR 15.503(b) as follows:

> *Postaward notices.* (1) Within 3 days after the date of contract award, the contracting officer shall provide written notification to each offeror whose proposal was in the competitive range but was not selected for award (10 U.S.C. 2305(b)(5) and 41 U.S.C. 253b(c)) or had not been previously notified under paragraph (a) of this section. The notice shall
>
> (i) The number of offerors solicited;
> (ii) The number of proposals received;
> (iii) The name and address of each offeror receiving an award;
> (iv) The items, quantities, and any stated unit prices of each award. If the number of items or other factors makes listing any stated unit prices impracticable at that time, only the total contract price need be furnished in the notice. However, the items, quantities, and any stated unit prices of each award shall be made publicly available, upon request; and
> (v) In general terms, the reason(s) the offeror's proposal was not accepted, unless the price information in paragraph (b)(1)(iv) of this section readily reveals the reason. In no event shall an offeror's cost breakdown, profit, overhead rates, trade secrets, manufacturing processes and techniques, or other confidential business information be disclosed to any other offeror.
>
> (2) Upon request, the contracting officer shall furnish the information described in paragraph (b)(1) of this section to unsuccessful offerors in solicitations using simplified acquisition procedures in Part 13.
>
> (3) Upon request, the contracting officer shall provide the information in paragraph (b)(1) of this section to unsuccessful offerors that received a preaward notice of exclusion from the competitive range.

[2] Postaward Debriefings

The statutory requirements for postaward debriefings, 10 U.S.C. § 3304 (formerly § 2305(b)(5)) and 41 U.S.C. § 3704, are implemented in FAR 15.506 which provides:

> (a)(1) An offeror, upon its written request received by the agency within 3 days after the date on which that offeror has received notification of contract award in accordance with 15.503(b), shall be debriefed and furnished the basis for the selection decision and contract award.
>
> (2) To the maximum extent practicable, the debriefing should occur within 5 days after receipt of the written request. Offerors that

requested a postaward debriefing in lieu of a preaward debriefing, or whose debriefing was delayed for compelling reasons beyond contract award, also should be debriefed within this time period.

(3) An offeror that was notified of exclusion from the competition (see 15.505(a)), but failed to submit a timely request, is not entitled to a debriefing.

(4)(i) Untimely debriefing requests may be accommodated.

(ii) Government accommodation of a request for delayed debriefing pursuant to 15.505(a)(2), or any untimely debriefing request, does not automatically extend the deadlines for filing protests. Debriefings delayed pursuant to 15.505(a)(2) could affect the timeliness of any protest filed subsequent to the debriefing.

(b) Debriefings of successful and unsuccessful offerors may be done orally, in writing, or by any other method acceptable to the contracting officer.

(c) The contracting officer should normally chair any debriefing session held. Individuals who conducted the evaluations shall provide support.

(d) At a minimum, the debriefing information shall include—

(1) The Government's evaluation of the significant weaknesses or deficiencies in the offeror's proposal, if applicable;

(2) The overall evaluated cost or price (including unit prices) and technical rating, if applicable, of the successful offeror and the debriefed offeror, and past performance information on the debriefed offeror;

(3) The overall ranking of all offerors, when any ranking was developed by the agency during the source selection;

(4) A summary of the rationale for award;

(5) For acquisitions of commercial items, the make and model of the item to be delivered by the successful offeror; and

(6) Reasonable responses to relevant questions about whether source selection procedures contained in the solicitation, applicable regulations, and other applicable authorities were followed.

(e) The debriefing shall not include point-by-point comparisons of the debriefed offeror's proposal with those of other offerors. Moreover, the debriefing shall not reveal any information prohibited from disclosure by 24.202 or exempt from release under the Freedom of Information Act (5 U.S.C. 552) including—

(1) Trade secrets;

(2) Privileged or confidential manufacturing processes and techniques;

(3) Commercial and financial information that is privileged or confidential, including cost breakdowns, profit, indirect cost rates, and similar information; and

(4) The names of individuals providing reference information about an offeror's past performance.

(f) An official summary of the debriefing shall be included in the contract file.

In addition, 10 U.S.C. § 3304(c) (formerly § 2305(b)(5)(B)(vii)) requires DOD, NASA and the Coast Guard to give a protester "an opportunity . . . to submit, within two business days after receiving a postaward debriefing, additional questions related to the debriefing." This Act then states;

(C) The agency shall respond in writing to any additional question submitted under subparagraph (B)(vii) within five business days after receipt of the question. The agency shall not consider the debriefing to be concluded until the agency delivers its written responses to the disappointed offeror.

This gives an offeror five days after the questions have been answered to file a protest at GAO and activate the statutory stay (discussed below) but also precludes a protest until the questions have been answered, *Celeris Sys., Inc.*, Comp. Gen. Dec. B-416890, 2018 CPD ¶ 354. If no questions are submitted, this two-day period does not extend the five-day time for filing the protest, *NIKA Techs., Inc. v. United States*, 987 F.3d 1025 (Fed. Cir. 2021).

31 U.S.C. § 3553(d)(4)(A)(ii) makes the stay from proceeding with performance of an awarded contract in the event of a protest dependent on the debriefing. Under this provision, the stay will go into effect if a protest is received within five days after a postaward debriefing. This provision penalizes agencies that do not conduct their postaward debriefings in a timely fashion. Although agencies can wait, by doing so they lengthen the time that a protester has to evaluate the merits of any projected protest.

A debriefing must be timely requested and acted upon in order to preserve the offeror's rights. First, the right to the statutory stay from proceeding with performance after award will be lost if the protest is not filed within five days after a debriefing date *offered* by the agency, FAR 33.103(f)(3), not the actual date of the debriefing. Second, the right to protest to GAO will be lost entirely if the protest is not filed within 10 days of the date a debriefing is *offered* by the agency. See *Pentec Envtl., Inc.*, Comp. Gen. Dec. B-276874.2, 97-1 CPD ¶ 199, where a protest was found untimely because the protester delayed the debriefing one month after the date offered by the agency in order to obtain information through a Freedom of Information Act request. See also *Professional Rehabilitation Consultants, Inc.*, Comp. Gen. Dec. B-275871, 97-1 CPD ¶ 94, dismissing a postaward debriefing protest because the protester waited two months to request a debriefing after it was informed that it had not received the award.

GAO will not consider a protest of an inadequate debriefing, *CAMRIS Int'l, Inc*, Comp. Gen. Dec. B-416561, 2018 CPD ¶ 285. However, an inadequate debriefing can extend the time that an offeror has to protest even if the time to stay the performance of the contract has passed. For example, in *Geo-Centers, Inc.*, Comp. Gen. Dec. B-276033, 97-1 CPD ¶ 182, GAO sustained a protest that was filed three months after contract award and two months after a debriefing that did not contain sufficient details to disclose the basis for the protest, ruling that the protest was timely because it was filed within 10 days after the protester learned of the grounds for protest in a response to a request for the information pursuant to the Freedom of Information Act. Similarly, in *Biospherics, Inc.*, Comp. Gen. Dec. B-278278, 98-1 CPD ¶ 161, the protester asserted that the agency failed to inform it of adverse past performance information during discussions. The agency countered that this argument was not timely because it had informed the protester during debriefing that the protester had been ranked lower than the awardee under the past performance factor and it did not receive a perfect score on this factor. GAO held that the protest filed more than 10 days of the debriefing was timely because the protester was not informed during the debriefing of the degree to which its proposal was downgraded under this factor and did not know the specific adverse past performance information being considered by the agency.

A losing firm may obtain more relief in the Court of Federal Claims, where the protest timeliness requirements are not as strict. See, for example, *Tin Mills Props., LLC v. United States*, 82 Fed. Cl. 584 (2008), where the court ordered the contracting officer to inform the protester of the precise reasons for its exclusion from the competitive range when the debriefing had been extremely cursory, even after repeated requests by the protester for detailed information.

CHAPTER 7

INDEFINITE DELIVERY/INDEFINITE QUANTITY CONTRACTS

Chapter 7

INDEFINITE DELIVERY/INDEFINITE QUANTITY CONTRACTS

§7.01 INTRODUCTION

One of the major changes that has come about as a result of the acquisition reform effort in the 1990s is the widespread use of indefinite delivery/indefinite quantity (IDIQ) contracts. A major advantage of IDIQ contracts is that one or more contractors are immediately available to provide quotations for a task or delivery order for needed services or products. If agencies limit the scope of these quotations, they can then award the order in a short period of time.

In 1994, the Federal Acquisition Streamlining Act, Pub. L. No. 103-355, adopted statutory provisions on "task and delivery order" contracts which the FAR applies to IDIQ contracts. These provisions have been amended several times and are now codified in 10 U.S.C. §§ 3401-3406 (formerly §§ 2304a-d) and 41 U.S.C. § 4101-06 and implemented in FAR 16.504-505. The following definitions are contained in 10 U.S.C. § 3401 and 41 U.S.C. § 4101:

> (1) The term "delivery order contract" means a contract for property that—
>
> A. does not procure or specify a firm quantity of property (other than a minimum or maximum quantity); and
>
> B. provides for the issuance of orders for the delivery of property during the period of the contract.
>
> (2) The term "task order contract" means a contract for services that—
>
> A. does not procure or specify a firm quantity of services (other than a minimum or maximum quantity); and
>
> B. provides for the issuance of orders for the performance of tasks during the period of the contract.

One major purpose of these statutes is to ensure that these types of contracts will be sufficiently precise to enable offerors to ascertain the scope of the work to be ordered so that they can submit meaningful offers. See 10 U.S.C. § 3403 and 41 U.S.C. § 4103(b), stating:

> (b) *Solicitation*. The solicitation for a task or delivery order contract shall include the following:
>
> (1) The period of the contract, including the number of options to extend the contract and the period for which the contract may be extended under each option, if any.
>
> (2) The maximum quantity or dollar value of the services or property to be procured under the contract.
>
> (3) A statement of work, specifications, or other description that reasonably describes the general scope, nature, complexity, and purposes of the services or property to be procured under the contract.

See *Valenzuela Eng'g, Inc.*, Comp. Gen. Dec. B-277979, 98-1 CPD ¶ 51, containing letters from GAO to the Secretaries of the Air Force and the Army criticizing their services for using and issuing a contract with a statement of work that was so broad that it did not comply with this statute. GAO described the overly broad work statement as follows:

> [The] request for proposals (RFP) [called for] "Operation and Maintenance (O&M) and incidental repair and replacement services for Government facilities." The RFP's work statement identifies no specific facilities or locations at which these services are to be performed. It provided that the services being acquired "will include operation, preventive maintenance, commissioning, management, and incidental repair and replacement of all systems, equipment, and components inherent in Government facilities such as but not limited to medical, non-medical, training, administrative, plants, labs and storage facilities." These facilities were initially limited by location "in the continental United States, Hawaii and Alaska," but this was subsequently modified to add the words "and outside the continental United States."

Compare *CW Gov't Travel, Inc.*, Comp. Gen. Dec. B-295530.2, 2005 CPD ¶ 139 (procurement of worldwide military transportation services not too broad); *Phoenix Scientific Corp.*, Comp. Gen. Dec. B-286817, 2001 CPD ¶ 24 (IDIQ contract to provide unplanned maintenance services for all Air Force-managed weapons systems not too broad where Air Force placed concrete reviewable limits on availability of contract). In *Computers Universal, Inc.*, Comp. Gen. Dec. B-293548, 2004 CPD ¶ 78, GAO did not object to a very broad "statement of objectives" as the basis for a procurement, noting, however, its "concern about whether the use of such broad long-term IDIQ contracts undermines the efficiencies that full and open competition would produce."

IDIQ contracts can be awarded to a single concern or to multiple concerns. FAR 2.101 describes a multiple-award contract as a single contract although a separate contractual document would be issued to each awardee. The extensive use of these contracts and the prevalence of single award contracts are reported by the Government Accountability Office. See *Agencies Widely Used Indefinite Contracts to Provide Flexibility to Meet Mission Needs*, GAO-17-329 (Apr. 2017), indicating that approximately one third of government contract obligations from fiscal years 2011 through 2015 were placed on IDIQ contracts. Additionally, GAO reported that approximately 60% of these amounts were for single award (not multiple award) contracts and approximately 70% of these amounts were for services with the balance for products. See also *Defense Contracting: Use by the Department of Defense of Indefinite-Delivery Contracts from Fiscal Years 2015 through 2017* (May 10, 2018), GAO-18-412R, reporting that approximately 40% of DOD obligations from fiscal years 2015 through 2017 were placed on IDIQ contracts. Of these amounts, approximately 75% were for single award contracts. These GAO reports also indicate that the amount of IDIQ contracting has increased each year of the study.

A significant number of governmentwide acquisition contracts (GWACs) and multiagency contracts are also awarded as IDIQ contracts. These contracts, open to all agencies, all have multiple awardees permitting intense competition for task and delivery orders. They are discussed further in Chapter 11.

IDIQ contracts can be awarded for any type of work because delivery orders relate to contracts for supplies and task orders relate to contracts for services. See *Tyler Constr. Grp. v. United States*, 570 F.3d 1329 (Fed. Cir. 2009), holding that construction work could be treated as a service under an IDIQ contract because there was no statute or regulation prohibiting this practice—citing FAR 1.102(d).

10 U.S.C. § 3405 and 41 U.S.C. § 4105 contain special limitations on task order contracts for "advisory and assistance services" if the contract period exceeds three years and the estimated contract amount is over $10 million (FAR 16.505(c)(2) has adjusted this amount to $13.5 million). In such cases, a single contract can be awarded only if the head of the executive agency determines that because the services required under the contract are unique or highly specialized, it is not practicable to award more than one contract. "Advisory and assistance services" are defined in 31 U.S.C. § 1105(g)(2)(A) as follows:

> [T]he term "advisory and assistance services" means the following services when provided by nongovernmental sources:
>
> (i) Management and professional support services.
> (ii) Studies, analyses, and evaluations.
> (iii) Engineering and technical services.

A more complete definition of advisory and assistance services is included in FAR 2.101. See *Nations, Inc.*, Comp. Gen. Dec. B-272455, 96-2 CPD ¶ 170, holding that, pursuant to this expansive FAR definition, training services were included in management and professional support services. See also *Cubic Applications, Inc. v. United States*, 37 Fed. Cl. 345 (1997), holding that a procurement to conduct "computer driven battle simulation exercises" was a procurement of advisory and assistance services.

The following Indefinite Quantity clause in FAR 52.216-22 is used in all IDIQ contracts:

> INDEFINITE QUANTITY (OCT 1995)
>
> (a) This is an indefinite-quantity contract for the supplies or service specified, and effective for the period stated, in the Schedule. The quantities of supplies and services specified in the Schedule are estimates only and are not purchased by this contract.
>
> (b) Delivery or performance shall be made only as authorized by orders issued in accordance with the Ordering clause. The Contractor shall furnish to the Government, when and if ordered, the supplies or services specified in the Schedule up to and including the quantity designated in the Schedule as the

"maximum." The Government shall order at least the quantity of supplies or services designated in the Schedule as the "minimum."

(c) Except for any limitations on quantities in the Order Limitations clause or in the Schedule, there is no limit on the number of orders that may be issued. The Government may issue orders requiring delivery to multiple destinations or performance at multiple locations.

(d) Any order issued during the effective period of this contract and not completed within that period shall be completed by the Contractor within the time specified in the order. The contract shall govern the Contractor's and Government's rights and obligations with respect to that order to the same extent as if the order were completed during the contract's effective period; *provided*, that the Contractor shall not be required to make any deliveries under this contact after [*insert date*].

This chapter will cover both the statutory and regulatory requirements for entering into IDIQ contracts and the issuance of task or delivery orders under these contracts.

§ 7.02 AWARDING THE BASE IDIQ CONTRACT

The base IDIQ contract has always been awarded following the competitive negotiation procedures discussed in Chapter 6. However, there are a number of issues in this award process that are distinct from the general rules governing competitively awarded contracts for a defined scope of work (i.e., for definite quantities).

[A] Adequate Minimum Quantity

As discussed in Chapter 2, to be binding on the contractor, an IDIQ contract must contain a minimum quantity that is more than "nominal," FAR 16.504(a)(2). In *Tennessee Soap Co. v. United States*, 126 F. Supp. 439 (Ct. Cl. 1954), a $10 minimum order was held to be nominal. See also *Goldwasser v. United States*, 325 F.2d 722 (Ct. Cl. 1963), where the court found that a contract with a minimum quantity of $100 compared to an estimated price of $40,000 "would have been a one-sided bargain, bordering upon lack of mutuality." The court did not decide this issue since it held the contract to be a requirements contract. GAO has stated that the analysis of whether a minimum is nominal should be based on "the nature of the acquisition as a whole," *CW Gov't Travel, Inc.*, Comp. Gen. Dec. B-295530, 2005 CPD ¶ 59. In that case, a minimum of $2,500 in transaction fees was not nominal although the contract permitted orders up to $150,000,000. GAO reasoned that since each transaction fee would approximate $5, the minimum represented a significant number of transactions. See also *Library of Congress—Obligation of Guaranteed Minimums for Indefinite-Delivery, Indefinite-Quantity Contracts Under the FEDLINK*

Program, Comp. Gen. Dec. B-318046, 2009 Comp. Gen. LEXIS 126 (minimum of $500 not nominal when purchases could be as high as $15 million but no reliable data available to judge amount of orders); *Information Ventures, Inc.*, Comp. Gen. Dec. B-299255, 2007 CPD ¶ 80 ($1,000.00 minimum quantity not nominal); *ABF Freight Sys., Inc.*, Comp. Gen. Dec. B-291185, 2002 CPD ¶ 201, and *ABF Freight Sys., Inc. v. United States*, 55 Fed. Cl. 392 (2003) (minimums of approximately 5% of work not nominal); *Carr's Wild Horse Center*, Comp. Gen. Dec. B-285833, 2000 CPD ¶ 210 (minimum of 100 animals not nominal in contract to handle up to 100,000 animals); *Aalco Forwarding, Inc.*, Comp. Gen. Dec. B-277241.15, 98-1 CPD ¶ 87 ($25,000 minimum per contract in multiple award contracts for moving goods not nominal even though $75,000,000 work anticipated). A nominal minimum amount for each task will not invalidate an IDIQ contract if it contains a non-nominal minimum for the entire contract, *C.W. Over & Sons, Inc.*, Comp. Gen. Dec. B-274365, 96-2 CPD ¶ 223.

The minimum quantity need not be ordered at the time the contract is issued as long as the government promises to buy a meaningful minimum amount of goods or services, *Federal Elec. Corp.*, ASBCA 11726, 68-1 BCA ¶ 6834; Comp. Gen. Dec. B-160063, Feb. 10, 1967, Unpub. In *Federal Elec. Corp. v. United States*, 486 F.2d 1377 (Ct. Cl. 1973), *cert. denied*, 419 U.S. 874 (1974), the court upheld the board decision but stated that the contractor was bound to the contract because the minimum quantity had been ordered at the same time the parties entered into the contract. Since the minimum was a substantial quantity, the time the first order was placed would appear to be irrelevant to the issue of whether the contractor was bound to perform the contract. However, the minimum quantity must be for a bona fide need of the agency in the year of the appropriation cited, *Small Business Administration-Indefinite-Delivery Indefinite-Quantity Contract Guaranteed Minimum*, Comp. Gen. Dec. B-321640, 2011 CPD ¶ 184 (agency improperly raised minimum quantity at end of fiscal year in order to obligate funds).

When an IDIQ contract contains options for additional items or years of services, there is no requirement that there be a minimum quantity supporting each option, *Varilease Tech. Grp., Inc. v. United States*, 289 F.3d 795 (Fed. Cir. 2002). This is based on the reasoning that the minimum for the base year is consideration for the options. See also *RJO Enters., Inc.*, ASBCA 50981, 03-1 BCA ¶ 32,137; *EFG Assocs., Inc.*, ASBCA 50342, 99-2 BCA ¶ 30,525.

If an IDIQ contract contains no specified minimum quantities, the court or board may find a means of furnishing a minimum in order to prevent the contract from failing for lack of consideration. For example, in *Howell v. United States*, 51 Fed. Cl. 516 (2002), the court found that the parties intended to enter into a binding contract and concluded that it could furnish a reasonable minimum of $1,000 per contract using its power to supply a "missing essential term" under Restatement (Second) of Contracts § 204. In another case where an IDIQ contract contained no minimum, the contractor was held to be entitled to assume that the estimated quantities were the minimum quantities that would be ordered, *Apex*

Int'l Mgmt. Servs., Inc., ASBCA 38087, 94-2 BCA ¶ 26,842. The Indefinite Quantity clause calls for the inclusion in the contract schedule of both minimum quantities and estimated quantities, but the board held that the absence of minimum quantities was an ambiguity for which the government was responsible as the drafter of the contract. Compare *Carrington Grp., Inc. v. Dep't of Veterans Affairs*, CBCA 2091, 12-1 BCA ¶ 34,993, holding that an IDIQ contract with no minimum failed for lack of consideration, with the contractor entitled only to payments already made. See also *Delfour, Inc.*, PSBCA 3333, 95-1 BCA ¶ 27,524, *recons. denied*, 95-2 BCA ¶ 27,908, *aff'd*, 95 F.3d 1163 (Fed. Cir. 1996), where a contract stating that it was an IDIQ contract and containing a minimum quantity of $10,000 was held to constitute an IDIQ contract even though it also stated that it had an "initial contract value" of $1 million.

IDIQ contracts contain a Termination for the Convenience of the Government clause which permits the government to terminate the contract before ordering the minimum quantity. In *Southwest Lab. of Oklahoma, Inc.*, Comp. Gen. Dec. B-251778, 93-1 CPD ¶ 368, GAO held that a special clause stating this proposition did not destroy the consideration supporting the contract because the promise of the government to pay termination costs and profit was sufficient consideration. GAO ruled, however, that a further provision of the clause making a failure to order the minimum an automatic termination for convenience was improper because it was an attempt to convert a government breach into a termination for convenience—in conflict with the holding in *Maxima Corp. v. United States*, 847 F.2d 1549 (Fed. Cir. 1988).

When a contract calling for some work at a fixed-price and additional work on an IDIQ basis specifies that the fixed-price component is to be used as the guaranteed minimum, the government is not obligated to guarantee an additional minimum amount of work under the indefinite-quantity component, *Mac's Cleaning & Repair Serv.*, ASBCA 49652, 97-1 BCA ¶ 28,748, *aff'd*, 132 F.3d 51 (Fed. Cir. 1997). Similarly, in a contract with some indicia of an IDIQ contract calling for reimbursement of costs, the initial funding of costs was held to meet the requirement for a non-nominal minimum, *Sociotechnical Research Applications, Inc.*, IBCA 3969-98, 01-1 BCA ¶ 31,235.

[B] Structuring the Contract

10 U.S.C. § 3403 and 41 U.S.C. § 4103 contain the requirements on the structure of an IDIQ contract as follows:

> (b) *Solicitation.* The solicitation for a task or delivery order contract shall include—
>
> > (1) the period of the contract, including the number of options to extend the contract and the period for which the contract may be extended under each option;

(2) the maximum quantity or dollar value of the services or property to be procured under the contract; and

(3) a statement of work, specifications, or other description that reasonably describes the general scope, nature, complexity, and purposes of the services or property to be procured under the contract.

The major elements of the IDIQ contract are the minimum quantities, the maximum quantities, the period of performance, the types or permissible orders, and the statement of work. The minimums and maximums can be stated in dollars or units of work, FAR 16.504(a).

[1] Minimum Quantities

As discussed above, the minimum quantity must be more than a nominal quantity to ensure that the contract is legally binding. The only other guidance contained in FAR 16.504(a)(2) is that the minimum quantity should not exceed the amount "that the Government is fairly certain to order." All other information on minimum quantities must be included in the contract schedule. A minimum order limitation is to be included in ¶(a) of the mandatory Order Limitations clause in FAR 52.216-19; this does not serve as a minimum quantity but rather as a protection against very small orders.

There appears to be a tendency for contracting officers to specify very low contract minimums in order to limit the government's liability in the event its requirements change during the life of the contract and to avoid obligating significant amounts of funds at the inception of the contract. However, better prices may be obtained if higher minimum quantities are specified. When multiple contracts are awarded and orders will be placed competitively, the ordering process should control the prices, and there will be little need for concern about the impact of low minimum quantities.

In multiple item IDIQ contracts, minimum quantities can also be stated for each item or type of services. This gives the offerors assurance that the government intends to order each item and may provide some inducement for the offerors to avoid unbalanced pricing. However, it is proper to use only a single contract minimum, *C.W. Over & Sons, Inc.*, Comp. Gen. Dec. B-274365, 96-2 CPD ¶223; *Sunbelt Props., Inc.*, Comp. Gen. Dec. B-249307, 92-2 CPD ¶309.

In IDIQ contracts containing options, there is no need for a minimum quantity for each option because the minimum quantity for the base contract provides consideration for the entire contract, *Varilease Tech. Grp., Inc. v. United States*, 289 F.3d 795 (Fed. Cir. 2002); *Five Star Elec., Inc.*, ASBCA 44984, 96-2 BCA ¶28,421.

When an agency awards an IDIQ contract, it must immediately obligate an amount of funds that corresponds to the minimum quantity, *Bureau of Customs and Border Protection—Automated Commercial Environment Contract*, Comp. Gen. Dec. B-302358, 2004 Comp. Gen. LEXIS 271; *Interagency Agreements—*

Obligation of Funds Under an Indefinite Delivery, Indefinite Quantity Contract, Comp. Gen. Dec. B-308969, 2007 CPD ¶ 120.

[2] Maximum Quantities

FAR 16.504(a)(1) provides that the contract should contain a maximum quantity that should be "reasonable" and "based on market research, trends on recent contracts for similar supplies or services, survey of potential users, or any other rational basis." The maximum "may be stated as number of units or as dollar values." When multiple awards are made, the contract should clearly state that the maximum applies to all orders not any individual contract.

While care should be used in ensuring that maximum quantities are not overstated, there is no government liability for such overstatement, *C.F.S. Air Cargo, Inc.*, ASBCA 40694, 91-2 BCA ¶ 23,985, *aff'd*, 972 F.2d 1353 (Fed. Cir. 1992). See also *Supreme Foodservice GmbH*, Comp. Gen. Dec. B-405400.1, 2011 CPD ¶ 244, denying a protest that the maximum quantity was overstated when the President had ordered a troop withdrawal but the agency did not have firm information as to the impact of the withdrawal. Compare *Chronos Sols., LLC*, Comp. Gen. Dec. B-417870.2, 2020 CPD ¶ 306, sustaining a protest when the maximum quantity appeared to be overstated as a result of the coronavirus pandemic.

FAR 16.504(a)(3) also permits maximum quantities for any single task or delivery order and maximum quantities that may be ordered during any specified period of time. The Order Limitations clause in FAR 52.216-19 contains the following paragraph, which is to be filled in by the contracting officer to specify such maximums:

> (b) *Maximum order*. The Contractor is not obligated to honor—
>
> (1) Any order for a single item in excess of [*insert dollar figure or quantity*];
>
> (2) Any order for a combination of items in excess of [*insert dollar figure or quantity*]; or
>
> (3) A series of orders from the same ordering office within . . . days that together call for quantities exceeding the limitation in subparagraph (1) or (2) above.

This paragraph should be carefully tailored to fit the circumstances of each procurement. In addition, the contract maximum quantity should be stated in the contract schedule.

Paragraph (d) of the Order Limitations clause requires the contractor to honor an order above the maximums stated in the clause if timely notice is not given of its intention not to fill the order. Failure to give notice that it will not fill the order is the contractor's sole remedy when such an order is issued, *NMS*

Mgmt., Inc., ASBCA 53444, 03-2 BCA ¶ 32,340. In *General Cutlery v. General Servs. Admin.*, GSBCA 13154, 96-1 BCA ¶ 27,957, the board affirmed the default termination of a contractor that had not filled an order above the maximum quantity but had not given notice of its intention not to fill the order. If the contractor elects to fill an order above the maximum quantity, it is entitled to no compensation above the contract price for the added work, *WIT Assocs., Inc.*, ASBCA 61547, 19-1 BCA ¶ 37,322.

Where the IDIQ contract fails to set maximum amounts for a portion of the work to be performed, the government may not order unlimited quantities of work, and the amount ordered will be measured by the standard of reasonableness under the circumstances, *Computer Scis. Corp.*, ASBCA 24035, 82-2 BCA ¶ 15,923.

[3] Mandatory Participation

Although there is no guidance on this issue, some agencies have used a provision requiring holders of multiple award IDIQ contracts to compete for each task or delivery order issued by the agency. See, for example, *OMNIPLEX World Servs. Corp.*, Comp. Gen. Dec. B-295698, 2005 CPD ¶ 43, denying a protest that a provision requiring participation and allowing the agency to issue task orders to contract holders that do not submit a quotation at agency estimates based on ceiling labor rates. GAO found such a provision proper, stating:

> Contrary to the protester's arguments, the fact that all of the ID/IQ contractors can be considered for performance for all of the task orders to be issued under the ID/IQ contracts, including those which the contractor is not interested in performing and/or is not submitting a proposal, is not inconsistent with the FAR provisions governing ID/IQ contracts. These provisions require that an ID/IQ contract holder "must furnish any additional quantities [over and above the minimum stated quantity] not to exceed the stated maximum." FAR § 16.504(a)(1). Thus, so long as the orders do not exceed the maximum quantity, ID/IQ contract holders can be potentially required to perform on all task orders where it is found to be the best value.

[4] Provisions Allowing Changing the Pool of Contractors

When an agency intends to award multiple IDIQ contracts that extend over a number of years, it is not uncommon for one or more of the contract holders to be unsuccessful in competing for task or delivery orders. It is therefore good practice to provide in such contracts that either party can terminate their participation by giving notice to the other party. Such provisions can also provide that the government can add a contractor to the pool of contractors.

For an example of a provision allowing the addition of contractor to the original pool of awardees, see *National Air Cargo Grp., Inc. v. United States*, 126 Fed. Cl. 281 (2016), where the contract stated:

> 1. Recompetition
>
> 1.1 The Government will initially establish the awardee pool by competitively awarding multiple-award IDIQ contracts. *As future task order requirements within the program ceiling totals materialize, over the life cycle of this program, the Government will compete those requirements amongst all existing IDIQ contract holders to determine if the contract holders can adequately fulfill the needed capability. The Government reserves the right to reopen the competition under this solicitation if there is [a] shortfall in meeting the requirements among the existing IDIQ contract holders or if it is in the Government's best interest to add new contractors to the original pool of IDIQ contract holders.* When/if the Government decides to reopen the solicitation, an announcement will be posted via FedBizOps allowing new . . . offerors the opportunity to compete in a full and open competition for an IDIQ contract and task orders to meet the new requirements. Any existing IDIQ contract holder will not re-compete for an IDIQ contract. The competitions will use the same evaluation methodology and documentation (updated to reflect changes in regulatory provisions, requirements and certifications) as the original competition. (Emphasis added.)

In this case, the court rejected the protester's argument that the agency had improperly added a competitor to the pool after award but before meeting the conditions of the italicized sentences. See also *ADVENTureOne, LLC*, Comp. Gen. Dec. B-408685.23, 2019 CPD ¶ 329, denying a protest of unduly restrictive evaluation criteria in a procurement to add small businesses to the OASIS GWAC.

[5] Length of the Contract

Paragraph (f) of 10 U.S.C. § 3403 allows a base period of five years and options for five additional years, with a period of no longer than 10 years without the approval of the head of the agency. There is no similar provision in 41 U.S.C. § 4101 et seq. FAR 16.504(a)(4)(i) merely states that IDIQ contracts must specify the period of performance including options. FAR 17.204(e) also contains a general five-year limitation on all contracts. 10 U.S.C. § 3204(c)(1)(B) (formerly § 2304(d)(3)) and 41 U.S.C. § 3304(c)(1)(B) contain a one-year limitation on contracts over the simplified acquisition threshold that are awarded without full and open competition based on urgency, unless the head of the agency determines that exceptional circumstances apply. 10 U.S.C. § 3405(c) and 41 U.S.C. § 4105(c) limit task or delivery order contracts for advisory and assistance services to five years, unless a specific statute permits a longer period.

Some agencies have interpreted this guidance as calling for IDIQ contracts to have a base period of one or two years with one or more option years. However, the same result can be achieved by writing the contract for a five-year period, with or without option years. This would minimize the need to follow the regulatory rules on the exercise of options. In either case, orders cannot be issued until appropriations are available and the order is for a bona fide need of the agency in the year ordered.

If the IDIQ contract is written for a period longer than one year by the inclusion of options, the contracting officer has the choice of several standard clauses—the Option for Increased Quantities clause in FAR 52.217-6, the Option to Extend Services clause in FAR 52.217-8, or the Option to Extend the Term of the Contract clause in FAR 52.217-9. If this last clause is used, exercise of the option does not procure additional work but merely extends the period when work can be ordered, *Five Star Elecs., Inc.*, ASBCA 44984, 96-2 BCA ¶28,421. Contracting officers must exercise care in including these clauses because they confer different rights on the government, as discussed in Chapter 12.

If the contract is for a period of longer than one year without options, ¶(a) of the mandatory Ordering clause in FAR 52.216-18 will include an end date for ordering that corresponds to the final day of the last year covered by the contract. If such a contract contains firm prices, the contracting officer should ensure that the prices are still in line with current prices that are available from other vendors. This would not be of concern if multiple contracts have been awarded and the prices of each task or delivery order are to be established by competition among the contractors.

The Indefinite Quantity clause also provides for the insertion in ¶(d) of a date after which no "deliveries" are to be made. When this clause is used for services, this is presumably the final date that services may be performed.

[6] Types of Permissible Orders

FAR 16.501-2(c) states that indefinite-delivery contracts "may provide for any appropriate cost or pricing arrangement under Part 16." It has been common practice to allow for fixed-price, time and materials or cost-reimbursement orders depending on the nature of the work being ordered. See *URS Fed. Support Servs., Inc.*, Comp. Gen. Dec. B-407573, 2013 CPD ¶31, ruling that agencies have broad discretion in stating the types of orders that can be placed and denying a protest that an IDIQ contract was too broad because it allowed the issuance of fixed-price, time and materials or cost-reimbursement orders. If time-and-materials orders are permitted, the required determinations and findings supporting their use, discussed in Chapter 12, should be prepared—either at the time of issuance of the base IDIQ contract or at the time issuance of a time-and-materials task order.

When the IDIQ contract allows the issuance of multiple type of orders, the based contract should contain the required terms and conditions for each type of order allowed. FAR Subpart 52.3 contains a matrix that provides detailed guidance on the selection of FAR clauses. Agencies should also include agency-specific clauses that are applicable to these different types of orders. There is no guidance on whether these terms and conditions can be omitted from the base IDIQ contract but later included in each task order.

[7] Statement of Work

The statement of work can describe a broad scope of work, but it should be sufficiently precise to allow competing offerors to understand the range of task or delivery orders that the agency intends to order under the contract. See *Chronos Sols., LLC*, Comp. Gen. Dec. B-417870.2, 2020 CPD ¶ 395, granting a protest because the estimated amounts of work had not been updated to reflect legislative changes that occurred after the issuance of the RFP.

There is a general preference for performance-oriented statements of work instead of precise specifications and statements of work that encourage furnishing commercial products and services, FAR 11.002(a)(2). See also FAR 37.102 stating with regard to service contracts:

> (e) Agency program officials are responsible for accurately describing the need to be filled, or problem to be resolved, through service contracting in a manner that ensures full understanding and responsive performance by contractors and, in so doing, should obtain assistance from contracting officials, as needed. To the maximum extent practicable, the program officials shall describe the need to be filled using performance-based acquisition methods.

[8] Ordering Procedures

FAR 16.504(a)(4) requires that a solicitation for an IDIQ contract state the procedures that will be used to place the task or delivery orders under the contract, stating:

> (iv) State the procedures that the Government will use in issuing orders, including the ordering media, and, if multiple awards may be made, state the procedures and selection criteria that the Government will use to provide awardees a fair opportunity to be considered for each order (see 16.505(b)(1));

Thus, the contract schedule should contain a detailed description of the procedures that will be followed in issuing task or delivery orders under the contract. In particular, agencies that intend to issue orders electronically or by facsimile must explicitly include this procedure in the schedule. See *General Dynamics*

C4 Sys., Inc., ASBCA 54988, 09-2 BCA ¶ 34,150, finding electronic orders invalid in accordance with ¶ (c) of the clause because there was no schedule language calling for the use of this technique. This decision was reversed in *Mabus v. General Dynamics C4 Sys., Inc.*, 633 F.3d 1356 (Fed. Cir. 2011), on the grounds that the contractor was estopped from asserting its rights under the clause because it had accepted electronic orders for over four years.

In *Information Ventures, Inc.*, Comp. Gen. Dec. B-299255, 2007 CPD ¶ 80, GAO denied a protest asserting that the RFP should have stated the precise evaluation factors that would be used in task order competitions. GAO described the statement of procedures that it found sufficient as follows:

> The solicitation here explains that to provide all contractors a fair opportunity to be considered for each order, the agency will issue an RFTOP for each requirement to each contractor. The RFTOP is to contain information comparable to a competitive solicitation, including a statement of work, instructions to the contractors for responding to the RFTOP, and evaluation and award factors. Each proposal received in response to an RFTOP is to be evaluated on both technical and cost, and, at the agency's discretion, on the basis of past performance and cost control on previous projects. The evaluation criteria will be specified in the RFTOP and may vary depending on the emphasis of the project. The government is to issue the order to the contractor whose proposal it determines to represent the best value.

[9] Terms and Conditions

Each IDIQ contract must contain terms and conditions that are appropriate for the type of work being procured. If commercial items are called for, the contract should contain the terms and conditions prescribed by FAR Part 12. If noncommercial work is called for, the contract should contain all of the clauses prescribed in FAR 52.301. When the IDIQ contract allows the issuance of fixed-price, time and materials and cost-reimbursement task or delivery orders, the contract will have to include all of the terms and conditions appropriate for these varying types of contracts.

The Ordering clause in FAR 52.216-18 states that the terms and conditions in the basic IDIQ contract override any terms and conditions in a task or delivery order. See *Relyant, LLC*, ASBCA 59809, 18-1 BCA ¶ 37,085 (denying claim of changed work because specifications in IDIQ contract were never altered); *Financial & Realty Servs., LLC v. General Servs. Admin.*, CBCA 5354, 16-1 BCA ¶ 36,472 (deciding payment dispute using payment paragraph of Contract Terms and Conditions—Commercial Items clause in FAR 52.212-4 contained in IDIQ contract); *Fortis Networks, Inc. v. Dep't of Interior*, CBCA 4176, 15-1 BCA ¶ 36,066 (interpreting provision of IDIQ contract requiring negotiation of fuel price before issuance of task orders); *Alliance Roofing & Sheet Metal, Inc.*, ASBCA 59663, 15-1 BCA ¶ 35,981 (upholding task order warranties because no warranty provision in IDIQ contract); *Southern Def. Sys., Inc.*, ASBCA 54045, 12-1 BCA ¶ 34,949 (interpreting provisions of IDIQ contract to allow modification of initial "pass-through rate" in delivery orders); *George G. Sharp, Inc.*, ASBCA 55385, 09-1 BCA ¶ 34,117 (excusing failure to give notice of delivery order overruns required by Limitation of Cost clause in cost-reimbursement IDIQ contract because of unforeseen events); and *Analysas Corp.*, ASBCA 54183, 04-1 BCA ¶ 32,629 (interpreting Limitation of Cost clause in cost-reimbursement IDIQ contract to apply to each delivery order).

[C] Multiple Award Preference

The statutory multiple award preference for task order and delivery order contracts in 10 U.S.C. § 3403(d) and 41 U.S.C. § 4103(d) contains detailed requirements intended to make it difficult to award an IDIQ contract to a single source. However, FAR 16.504(c) gives agencies considerable discretion in making the decision as to when to award multiple contracts, stating:

> Multiple award preference—
>
> (1) *Planning the acquisition.* (i) Except for indefinite-quantity contracts for advisory and assistance services as provided in paragraph (c)(2) of this section, the contracting officer must, to the maximum extent practicable, give preference to making multiple awards of indefinite-quantity contracts under a single solicitation for the same or similar supplies or services to two or more sources.
>
> (ii) (A) The contracting officer must determine whether multiple awards are appropriate as part of acquisition planning. The contracting officer must avoid situations in which awardees specialize exclusively in one or a few areas within the statement of work, thus creating the likelihood that orders in those areas will be awarded on a sole-source basis; however, each awardee need not be capable of performing every requirement as well as any other awardee under the contracts. The contracting officer should consider the following when determining the number of contracts to be awarded:
>
> (*1*) The scope and complexity of the contract requirement.
>
> (*2*) The expected duration and frequency of task or delivery orders.
>
> (*3*) The mix of resources a contractor must have to perform expected task or delivery order requirements.
>
> (*4*) The ability to maintain competition among the awardees throughout the contracts' period of performance.
>
> * * *
>
> (C) The contracting officer must document the decision whether or not to use multiple awards in the acquisition plan or

contract file. The contracting officer may determine that a class of acquisitions is not appropriate for multiple awards (see subpart 1.7)

* * *

(2) *Contracts for advisory and assistance services.* (i) Except as provided in paragraph (c)(2)(ii) of this section, if an indefinite-quantity contract for advisory and assistance services exceeds 3 years and $13.5 million, including all options, a contracting officer must make multiple awards unless—

(A) The contracting officer or other official designated by the head of the agency determines in writing, as part of acquisition planning, that multiple awards are not practicable. The contracting officer or other official must determine that only one contractor can reasonably perform the work because either the scope of work is unique or highly specialized or the tasks so integrally related;

(B) The contracting officer or other official designated by the head of the agency determines in writing, after the evaluation of offers, that only one offeror is capable of providing the services required at the level of quality required; or

(C) Only one offer is received.

(ii) The requirements of paragraph (c)(2)(i) of this section do not apply if the contracting officer or other official designated by the head of the agency determines that the advisory and assistance services are incidental and not a significant component of the contract.

When an agency is obtaining a significant amount of supplies or services over long periods of time through the use of IDIQ contracts, there are sometimes substantial benefits to be obtained through the issuance of more than one contract. The major benefits of the continuous competition that can be achieved under multiple contracts are the ability to control the prices of individual task and delivery orders and the ability to award such orders based on the past performance of the contractors. Multiple contracts also permit the agency to award IDIQ contracts to contractors with varying skills—giving the government access to a broader range of competence than would be possible with only a single contract. It has been held permissible to restrict multiple awards to affiliates when there was a risk that failure of performance of affiliated contractors would jeopardize the agency's program, *District Moving & Storage, Inc.*, Comp. Gen. Dec. B-272070, 96-2 CPD ¶ 60. Such a restriction does not preclude a contractor from competing as both a contractor and a subcontractor, *Point Blank Enterprises, Inc.*, Comp. Gen. Dec. B-411839, 2015 CPD ¶ 345.

Agencies also have considerable discretion to decide how many IDIQ contracts to award in order to ensure sufficient competition at the task or delivery order level. See *Sevatec, Inc.*, Comp. Gen. Dec. B-413559.3, 2017 CPD ¶ 3, stating:

> [T]he agency explains that it has taken a number of steps in structuring the Alliant 2 program to ensure competition at the task order level. First, the agency explains that its initial draft RFP only provided for 40 awards, but that the agency ultimately concluded that 60 awards would "most effectively serve the needs of its federal agency customers by providing a pool of 'best-in-class' contractors." Also, Alliant 2 includes "participation" standards, which require that every Alliant 2 awardee submit a minimum number of proposals annually. Finally, Alliant 2 awardees are required to meet certain "production" standards, which require that every Alliant 2 awardee receive a certain value of task orders over the life of the contract. The agency explains that this will help ensure high quality competition in order for awardees to meet their participation and production standards. Given that GSA intends to make 60 awards, requires the successful awardees to compete for a certain number of task orders each year, and requires awardees to have performed a certain amount of work each year, we do not find any basis for concluding that the agency's decision to limit the number of awardees to 60 is inconsistent with its stated goal of maintaining competition at the task order level throughout the period of performance.

See also *Cybermedia Techs., Inc.*, Comp. Gen. Dec. B-405511.3, 2011 CPD ¶ 180 (eight awards at significant break in pricing reasonable); *R.C.O. Reforesting*, Comp. Gen. Dec. B-280774.2, 98-2 CPD ¶ 119 (two awards because the agency had insufficient administrative personnel).

When the agency intends to award multiple contracts, the following Single or Multiple Awards solicitation provision in FAR 52.216-27 is used to alert offerors of this intention:

> SINGLE OR MULTIPLE AWARDS (OCT 1995)
>
> The Government may elect to award a single delivery order contract or task order contract or to award multiple delivery order contracts or task order contracts for the same or similar supplies or services to two or more sources under this solicitation.

[D] Single Award Decision

10 U.S.C. § 3403(d) grants authority to make single awards, stating:

> (3)(A) No task or delivery order contract in an amount estimated to exceed $100,000,000 (including all options) may be awarded to a single source unless the head of the agency determines in writing that—
>
> > (i) the task or delivery orders expected under the contract are so integrally related that only a single source can reasonably perform the work;

(ii) the contract provides only for firm, fixed price task orders or delivery orders for—

(I) products for which unit prices are established in the contract; or

(II) services for which prices are established in the contract for the specific tasks to be performed;

(iii) only one source is qualified and capable of performing the work at a reasonable price to the government; or

(iv) because of exceptional circumstances, it is necessary in the public interest to award the contract to a single source.

(B) The head of the agency shall notify the congressional defense committees within 30 days after any determination under clause (i), (ii), (iii), or (iv) of subparagraph (A).

(4) The regulations implementing this subsection shall—

(A) establish a preference for awarding, to the maximum extent practicable, multiple task or delivery order contracts for the same or similar services or property under the authority of paragraph (1)(B); and

(B) establish criteria for determining when award of multiple task or delivery order contracts would not be in the best interest of the Federal Government.

41 U.S.C. § 4103(d)(3) contains substantially the same language except that the congressional notification requirement is only applicable when the ¶ (A)(iv) justification for a single source is used. This multiple award preference is implemented in FAR 16.504(c) with regard only to IDIQ contracts. See *Harris IT Servs. Corp.*, Comp. Gen. Dec. B-411699, 2015 CPD ¶ 293, holding that a single source delivery order not specifying definitive quantities of work but calling for the issuance of subsequent delivery orders violated this multiple award preference.

FAR 16.504(c)(1)(B) states the circumstances requiring contracting officers to use a single award contract as follows:

(B) The contracting officer must not use the multiple award approach if—

(1) Only one contractor is capable of providing performance at the level of quality required because the supplies or services are unique or highly specialized;

(2) Based on the contracting officer's knowledge of the market, more favorable terms and conditions, including pricing, will be provided if a single award is made;

(3) The expected cost of administration of multiple contracts may outweighs the expected benefits of making multiple awards;

(4) The projected orders are so integrally related that only a single contractor can reasonably perform the work;

(5) The total estimated value of the contract is less than the simplified acquisition threshold; or

(6) Multiple awards would not be in the best interests of the Government.

This gives a contracting officer considerable discretion in determining that a single award contract will be of greatest benefit to the government. However, this decision must be supported by documentation in the contract file, FAR 16.504(c)(1)(C).

If the contract will exceed $100 million, including all options, the head of the agency must address more stringent criteria. See FAR 16.504(c)(1)(D), stating:

> (D)(1) No task or delivery order contract in an amount estimated to exceed $100 million (including all options) may be awarded to a single source unless the head of the agency determines in writing that—
>
> (i) The task or delivery orders expected under the contract are so integrally related that only a single source can reasonably perform the work;
>
> (ii) The contract provides only for firm-fixed price (see 16.202) task or delivery orders for —
>
> (A) Products for which unit prices are established in the contract; or
>
> (B) Services for which prices are established in the contract for the specific tasks to be performed;
>
> (iii) Only one source is qualified and capable of performing the work at a reasonable price to the Government; or
>
> (iv) It is necessary in the public interest to award the contract to a single source due to exceptional circumstances.
>
> (2) The head of the agency must notify Congress within 30 days after any determination under paragraph (c)(1)(ii)(D)(1)(iv) of this section.
>
> (3) The requirement for a determination for a single-award contract greater than $112 million:
>
> (i) Is in addition to any applicable requirements of Subpart 6.3.
>
> (ii) Is not applicable for architect-engineer services awarded pursuant to Subpart 36.6.

With DOD procurements, the above Congressional notification requirement is not applicable if a J&A has been prepared justifying the use of other than competitive procedures, DFARS 216.504(c)(3)(i).

Determinations to make a single award occasionally have been held not to be properly based on the factors set forth in the FAR. See *CW Gov't Travel, Inc. v. United States*, 110 Fed. Cl. 462 (2013) (fact that protester's proposal was "marginal" with correctable issues did not justify denying it award and selecting only one awardee); *Information Ventures, Inc.*, Comp. Gen. Dec. B-403321, 2010 CPD ¶ 223 (fact that when multiple contracts were issued, some contractors did not provide acceptable products not a justification for single award); *One Source Mech. Servs., Inc.*, Comp. Gen. Dec. B-293692, 2004 CPD ¶ 112 (administrative cost and time required to conduct competitions between multiple awardees not a justification for single award); *WinStar Commc'ns, Inc. v. United States*, 41 Fed. Cl. 748 (1998) (failure to consider the benefits of multiple awards); and *Nations, Inc.*, Comp. Gen. Dec. B-272455, 96-2 CPD ¶ 170 (single requirements contract not proper for advisory and assistance services over dollar threshold requiring multiple awards). In *IBM U.S. Federal*, Comp. Gen. Dec. B-407073.3, 2013 CPD ¶ 142, GAO recommended corrective action because a single award contract had been improperly competed. The Court of Federal Claims held that the GAO decision was irrational and effectively reinstated the original award, *Amazon Web Servs., Inc. v. United States*, 113 Fed. Cl. 102 (2013).

In the highly publicized "JEDI" procurement, where the Department of Defense sought a single award IDIQ contract for up to $10 billion in cloud computing services over 10 years, the GAO initially upheld the single award determination, deferring to the contracting officer's findings regarding the complexity of managing multiple cloud environments. *Oracle America, Inc.*, Comp. Gen. Dec. B-416657, 2018 CPD ¶ 391. The Court of Federal Claims and the Federal Circuit found that the single award determination was not supported by the statutorily required determination and finding, but nevertheless denied the pre-award solicitation challenge for lack of prejudice. See *Oracle America, Inc. v. United States*, 144 Fed. Cl. 88 (2019), *aff'd*, 975 F.3d 1279 (Fed. Cir. 2020). The JEDI procurement was subsequently caught in a postaward protest quagmire, cancelled, and ultimately replaced by a multiple award IDIQ acquisition strategy.

Single awards have been affirmed in a number of other cases. See *Delta Risk, LLC*, Comp. Gen. Dec. B-416420, 2018 CPD ¶ 305 (single contract justified because of only one compliant proposal); *CWTSatoTravel*, Comp. Gen. Dec. B-404479.3, 2012 CPD ¶ 281 (single award justified when protester could not be ready to perform upon award); *KSD, Inc. v. United States*, 72 Fed. Cl. 236 (2006) (single award for proprietary products justified); *Outdoor Venture Corp.*, Comp. Gen. Dec. B-288894.2, 2002 CPD ¶ 13 (single award justified when only one acceptable proposal received); *SmithKline Beecham Pharms.*, Comp. Gen. Dec. B-277253.4, 97-2 CPD ¶ 78 (single award justified by belief of contracting officer that more favorable terms will be achieved by a single requirements contract); *Cubic Applications, Inc. v. United States*, 37 Fed. Cl. 345 (1997) (single award justified because advisory and assistance services being procured are so integrally related that they could not be performed by more than one contractor).

In *Palantir USG, Inc.*, Comp. Gen. Dec. B-412746, 2016 CPD ¶ 138, GAO agreed that a single IDIQ contract was justified because the agency needed to design a new system. The Court of Federal Claims and the Federal Circuit subsequently rejected the acquisition strategy and agreed with Palantir that the Army's market research had failed against the statutory obligation to prioritize commercially available solutions rather than develop a new solution from scratch in *Palantir Techs. Inc. v. United States*, 128 Fed. Cl. 21 (2016), *aff'd*, 904 F.3d 960 (Fed. Cir. 2018).

There appears to be three types of work being selected for single award contracts. The first type is sequential work on a single overriding project where tasks are ordered to reach a technological end result. This use of a single award contract can be very advantageous to an agency because it allows the parties to work together to define succeeding requirements as the technological work progresses. Procurements of this nature, including *Rivada Mercury, LLC v. United States*, 131 Fed. Cl. 663 (2019) (multi-year contract to build-out, deploy, and operate a nationwide public safety broadband network that will transform the nation's emergency response system by consolidating public safety use of the radio spectrum, which will permit emergency responders across the country to use devices that are compatible with one another); *American Sys. Corp.*, Comp. Gen. Dec. B-415361, 2018 U. S. Comp. Gen. LEXIS 320 (a five-year contract for over $110 million for "integrally related" test and evaluation services, including support for test and evaluation planning, test conduct, data collection and analysis, and results reporting that are provided to federal and state agencies, coalition partners, and commercial entities to aid in the design, development, acquisition, integration, deployment, operational use, and sustainment of new and enhanced information technology/national security system capabilities); and *Palantir USG*, Inc., Comp. Gen. Dec. B-412746, 2016 CPD ¶ 138 (a six-year multi-million dollar contract to develop a system for the processing and dissemination of multi-sensor intelligence and weather information "to the warfighter").

The second type of work being procured under single award IDIQ contracts is services supporting a government activity where continuity of the workforce is necessary. Procurements of this nature include *Tyonek Global Servs., LLC*, Comp. Gen. Dec. B-417188.2, 2019 CPD ¶ 354 (a four-year contract for support services for aircraft, aircraft engines, and associated components and materials undergoing depot-level maintenance at several Naval Air Stations); *IT Concepts, Inc. v. United States*, No. 18-542C, 2019 U.S. Claims LEXIS 225 (Fed. Cl. Feb. 15, 2019) (a five-year contract for human resource information system division support services in the Patent Office); *Telos Identity Mgmt. Sols., LLC v. United States*, 143 Fed. Cl 687 (2019) (a 10-year contract for "enrollment services for programs, populations, initiatives or functions required, authorized, serviced by, or partnered with TSA"); *General Dynamics Information Tech., Inc.*, Comp. Gen. Dec. B-415568, 2018 CPD ¶ 63 (a five-year contract for "IT services that NGA users will need to perform their daily activities at their desks, offices, conference rooms and classrooms"); *PacArctic, LLC*,

Comp. Gen. Dec. B-413914.3, 2017 CPD ¶ 177 (a four-year contract for support services for advisory and assistance services to support the Office of the Deputy Chief Management Officer in managing and improving business analytic operations); *ASRC Commc'ns, Ltd.*, Comp. Gen. Dec. B-414319.2, 2017 CPD ¶ 167 (a five-year contract for system engineering and technical assistance for the Army Contracting Command-Orlando's Program Executive Office for Simulation, Training, and Instrumentation); *Rollout Sys., LLC*, Comp. Gen. Dec. B-414145, 2017 CPD ¶ 104 (a four-year contract for technical and management support services for the Research, Development, Test and Evaluation Infrastructure Division of the Naval Air Warfare Center Aircraft Division); and *Al Raha Grp. for Tech. Servs.*, Comp. Gen. Dec. B-412963.3, 2016 CPD ¶ 262 (a five-year contract for supply services in support of the Royal Saudi Air Force, including logistics support personnel, supply chain management related to consumable items, and print plant operations).

The other type of work where a single award contract is chosen appears to be work calling for the performance of a variety of relatively straightforward tasks. This is a questionable use of a single award contract but that issue was not protested in these decisions. Procurements of this nature include *Tope Tech., LLC*, Comp. Gen. Dec. B-416663.6, 2019 CPD ¶ 362 (a four-year contract for a broad variety of minor construction projects at the U.S. Army Dugway Proving Ground, Utah); *NCS/EML Joint Venture II, LLC*, Comp. Gen. Dec. B-417686, 2019 CPD ¶ 345 (an eight-year contract for services, including force protection, facility management, and grounds maintenance/landscaping at the Marine Corps Base, Quantico, Virginia); *PiperCoughlin, LLC*, Comp. Gen. Dec. B-414352.2, 2018 CPD ¶ 143 (a five-year contract for training support services for civil-service employees who deploy throughout the world as part of their civilian employment); *Glacier Tech. Sols., LLC*, Comp. Gen. Dec. B-412990.3, 2017 CPD ¶ 91 (a five-year contract for services, including administrative support, data management, data collection, instrumentation, information technology services, and logistics support for various Army test centers and directorates); and *CACI-ISS, Inc.*, Comp. Gen. Dec. B-412074, 2016 CPD ¶ 35 (a three-year contract for security and surveillance services for secure construction projects throughout South Korea).

In an unusual protest, the court rejected the argument that the language in the RFP bound the agency to award a single IDIQ contract for all of the work, *Glenn Def. Marine (Asia) PTE, Ltd. v. United States*, 97 Fed. Cl. 311 (2011).

When an agency decides to make a single award, this should be clearly stated in the RFP and the Single or Multiple Awards solicitation provision should not be included in the RFP. See *American Sys. Corp.*, Comp. Gen. Dec. B-415361, 2018 U.S. Comp. Gen. LEXIS 320, denying a protest of a single award where the RFP contained that provision but also contained a clear statements of the intention to make a single award. GAO concluded that this was an ambiguity that should have been protested before submitting a proposal.

[E] Evaluation and Award

The FAR gives very little guidance on the evaluation and award of IDIQ contracts. However, normal negotiation and tradeoff techniques, as discussed in Chapter 6, have been used in most cases. This entails the evaluation of cost or price and an array of potential evaluation factors—usually including past performance, experience, and understanding of the work (demonstrated by technical and management proposals). See Chapter 6 for a discussion of the benefits of reducing the number of evaluation factors to simplify and speed up the source selection process.

The evaluation of prices presents special challenges because the nature of the IDIQ contract is that there is no total price at the outset yet the statutes make price a mandatory evaluation factor. Thus, agencies have used different techniques to approximate prices for evaluation purposes, usually involving the evaluation of unit prices or fixed labor rates multiplied by estimated quantities contained in the RFP, or the proposed prices of sample tasks. GAO has ruled that the mere evaluation of unit prices or fixed labor rates without multiplying these rates by estimated quantities to arrive at an estimated "price" is improper, *KISS Eng'g Corp.*, 65 Comp. Gen. 549 (B-221356), 86-1 CPD ¶ 425 (rejecting the use of an average labor rate, including indirect costs, profit, and material, because there was "no necessary relationship between this rate and the likely actual cost of the contract"); *West Coast Copy, Inc.*, Comp. Gen. Dec. B-254044, 93-2 CPD ¶ 283 (rejecting the comparison of unit prices for various types of copying without factoring in the quantities of labor that would be used to perform the work); *SCIENTECH, Inc.*, Comp. Gen. Dec. B-277805.2, 98-1 CPD ¶ 33 (rejecting comparison of fixed labor rates and fee ceilings); *S.J. Thomas Co.*, Comp. Gen. Dec. B-283192, 99-2 CPD ¶ 73 (rejecting the comparison of "mark-up rates," excluding labor rates and material, for construction work); *AirTrak Travel*, Comp. Gen. Dec. B-292101, 2003 CPD ¶ 117 (rejecting the averaging of travel service area "transaction fees" when usage will vary between areas); *R&G Food Serv., Inc.*, Comp. Gen. Dec. B-296435.4, 2005 CPD ¶ 194 (rejecting comparison of unit prices for meals, mileage and hand washing because they were not multiplied by estimated quantities); *6K Sys., Inc.*, Comp. Gen. Dec. B-408124.3, 2014 CPD ¶ 347 (rejecting selection of unit labor rates to compare prices); and *Veterans Evaluation Servs., Inc.*, Comp. Gen. Dec. B-412940, 2016 CPD ¶ 185 (rejecting addition of unit prices for medical procedures to arrive at "prices"). The Court of Federal Claims disagreed with this reasoning in *Linc Gov't Servs., LLC v. United States*, 95 Fed. Cl. 155 (2010), where the court denied a protest that the agency had compared unit prices without multiplying them by estimated quantities. In that procurement the agency had provided estimated quantities in the RFP and had used them to check the proposed unit prices to ensure that they were not unbalanced. See also *Bristol-Myers Squibb Co.*, Comp. Gen. Dec. B-294944.2, 2005 CPD ¶ 16, and *SmithKline Beecham Corp.*, Comp. Gen. Dec. B-283939, 2000 CPD ¶ 19, where comparing unit prices of drug dosages was proper because the expected dosage per day was the major use of the drug and the agency had no way to estimate other uses.

In most procurements using the tradeoff technique, this leaves agencies with two possible ways to evaluate price—using estimated quantities stated in the RFP multiplied by proposed unit prices or fixed labor rates to arrive at a total "price" or obtaining prices for sample tasks. GAO has endorsed the use of estimated quantities, *LexisNexis*, Comp. Gen. Dec. B-402114, 2010 CPD ¶ 17; *Bering Straits Tech./Servs., LLC*, Comp. Gen. Dec. B-401560.3, 2009 CPD ¶ 201; *Health Servs. Int'l, Inc.*, Comp. Gen. Dec. B-247433, 92-1 CPD ¶ 493. However, the estimated quantities must be a reasonably accurate estimate of the agency's requirements. Compare *Chronos Sols., LLC*, Comp. Gen. Dec. B-417870.2, 2020 CPD ¶ 306 (agency required to review its estimated quantities when coronavirus pandemic occurred prior to award).

GAO has also endorsed the use of sample tasks where offerors are required to propose "binding" fixed unit prices or labor rates and to use such prices or rates in arriving at their price for the sample task(s) that are proposed, *CW Gov't Travel, Inc.*, Comp. Gen. Dec. B-295530.2, 2005 CPD ¶ 139. However, the sample tasks must be representative of the type of work that is expected to be performed on the contract, *MAR*, Comp. Gen. Dec. B-414810.5, 2018 CPD ¶ 266 (sample task covered almost half of the work); *U.S. Electrodynamics, Inc.*, Comp. Gen. Dec. B-414678, 2017 CPD ¶ 252 (two sample tasks were for designated work even though offerors were to propose innovative methods); *Dayton T. Brown, Inc.*, Comp. Gen. Dec. B-402256, 2010 CPD ¶ 72 (sample task encompassed many of the anticipated labor categories); *Information Ventures, Inc.*, Comp. Gen. Dec. B-299255, 2007 CPD ¶ 80 ("Although the sample task here is not reflective of the full range of services that the agency may order under the contracts to be awarded, we are not persuaded that it is not sufficiently typical of the work to be performed"); *Metro Mach. Corp.*, Comp. Gen. Dec. B-297879.2, 2006 CPD ¶ 80 (cost realism analysis flawed because "notational" tasks were not sufficiently representative of work). Furthermore, when an agency has no reasonable method to prepare a representative sample task, a hypothetical sample task has been approved when the protester could not show that its use led to an unreasonable evaluation of the actual costs of performance, *High Point Schaer*, 70 Comp. Gen. 524 (B-242616), 91-1 CPD ¶ 509; *Aalco Forwarding, Inc.*, Comp. Gen. Dec. B-277241.15, 98-1 CPD ¶ 87. The use of sample tasks will be rejected if the agency does not ensure that the labor rates used to price the sample tasks are realistic, *I.M. Sys. Group*, Comp. Gen. Dec. B-404583, 2011 CPD ¶ 64. If a sample task is ambiguous, it must be protested before the submission of proposals, *Mevacon/NASCO JV*, Comp. Gen. Dec. B-414329, 2017 CPD ¶ 144.

Some agencies have used a combination of unit labor rates and sample tasks. See *General Dynamics Information Tech., Inc.*, Comp. Gen. Dec. B-415568, 2018 CPD ¶ 63 (a sample task, the first actual task and proposed fixed labor rates multiplied by undisclosed estimated labor hours); *Computer Sciences Corp.*, Comp. Gen. Dec. B-408694.7, 2014 CPD ¶ 331 (a fixed-price sample task, a cost-reimbursement sample task and evaluation of fixed labor rates); and *Intelligent Decisions, Inc.*, Comp. Gen. Dec. B-409686, 2014 CPD ¶ 213 (two sample tasks and proposed maximum labor rates times estimated quantities).

The General Services Administration has used an innovative technique to select the pool of contractors for its IDIQ GWACs called the "highest technically rated with fair and reasonable price" technique. Under this technique the government does not compare prices in a tradeoff selection but merely evaluates whether the highest technically rated offerors have proposed fair and reasonable prices. Its use on the OASIS GWAC was approved in *Octo Consulting Grp., Inc. v. United States*, 117 Fed. Cl. 334 (2014). Its use on the ALLIANT 2 GWAC was approved in *Sevatec, Inc.*, Comp. Gen. Dec. B-413559.3, 2017 CPD ¶ 17. In that decision, the GAO explained the technique as follows:

> The RFP provides that the agency will select approximately 60 awardees using a "highest technically rated [] with a fair and reasonable price" evaluation scheme. Under this source selection process, offerors are to assign themselves points in the following categories: relevant experience; past performance; systems, certifications, and clearances; and organizational risk assessment. The RFP provides a total of 83,100 possible points under these categories, and further provides a detailed explanation of the point scheme, including the elements that make up the categories and explanations as to what documents are to be provided to support an offeror's scores.
>
> Under the RFP's point-based evaluation, the agency established a point scheme that "maximizes objectivity." For example, approximately half of the total available points relate to an offeror's experience in information technology (IT). Offerors are to submit evidence of relevant contractual experience in established IT-related categories, and experience in "leading-edge" IT-related categories. The agency's point scoring system provides that, if an offeror has met the requirement and provided supporting documentation, then an offeror is awarded all points under that element or sub-element.
>
> As relevant to these protests, the RFP provides 7,500 possible points under the organizational risk assessment (ORA) category. According to the RFP, these points are "only available for demonstrating that the offeror has previously performed in the proposed business arrangement."
>
> * * *
>
> The RFP's source selection process provides that the agency will first rank all offerors by highest point score to lowest point score using the offeror's document verification and self-scoring. The agency will then identify the offerors with the top 60 technical scores, and verify that the scores are accurate. After the top 60 firms are identified and their scores are verified, the evaluation team will analyze the pricing of these 60 offerors for fairness and reasonableness. With regard to prices, offerors are to submit a narrative explaining their basis of estimate, addressing direct labor rates, indirect costs, and profit, among other things. Offerors are also to submit a complete pricing

> spreadsheet which contains the cost elements (direct labor, fringe benefits, overhead, general and administrative (G&A), and profit) of its pricing proposal. The rates in the pricing spreadsheet will be used as the ceiling rates for year 1 of the master contract for time and material and labor hour contracts, and are to be based on the rate for the highest qualified employee within each labor category. In evaluating prices, the agency will determine whether the proposed rates (direct, indirect, and profit) are fair and reasonable.
>
> If any of the top 60 offerors' prices are found to be fair and reasonable, those firms will be awarded a contract. If any of the top 60 offerors' prices are found not to be fair and reasonable, those firms will be excluded from the competition. The process will continue until 60 awardees have been identified. The RFP provides that, at the end of the evaluation process, the agency will have awarded approximately 60 contracts to the firms with the highest technical scores that have fair and reasonable pricing.

This technique has several unique features. First, it confines the "technical proposals" to experience, past performance, certifications/clearances and organizational risk assessment. Thus, it omits any requirement for a written proposal stating how an offeror proposes to perform or manage the prospective work called for by the contract. Second, it contains detailed guidance on the scoring of each evaluation factor, with each offeror to self-score itself and document the score—subject to verification by the agency. Third, it evaluates price by assessing the reasonableness of each offeror's cost elements and profit without any comparison among offerors. Thus, an offeror's price is to be assessed as fair and reasonable if its cost and profit rates comport with the rates that it charges to other customers. In effect, this provides the agency with a pool of contractors with the most experience and qualifications to perform the information technology work called for by the GWAC.

In finding that this new technique was appropriate, the GAO in *Sevatec* stated:

> [T]he Federal Acquisition Regulation (FAR) does not expressly identify a "highest technically rated with a fair and reasonable price" type evaluation scheme as reflected in the agency's solicitation. In this regard, FAR subpart 15.1, Source Selection Processes and Techniques, specifically provides for a "lowest price technically acceptable" (LPTA) source selection process, and a "tradeoff" process. FAR §§ 15.101-1, 15.101-2. Nevertheless, the FAR explicitly recognizes that these two processes are not the only source selection processes available to the agency, as FAR § 15.100 provides that the two processes are only "some" of the processes available. Further, FAR § 1.102(d) states that the agency:
>
> > may assume if a specific strategy, practice, policy, or procedure is in the best interests of the Government and is not addressed in the FAR, nor prohibited by law (statute or case law), Executive order, or other regulation, that the strategy, practice, policy or procedure is a permissible exercise of authority.

> The FAR also specifies a "best value continuum" in FAR § 15.101, which provides that the "less definitive the requirement . . . the more technical or past performance considerations may play a dominant role in the selection." Section § 15.101-1(a) of the FAR also states, with regard to the tradeoff selection process, that a tradeoff "is appropriate when it may be in the best interests of the Government to consider award to other than the lowest priced offeror or other than the highest technically rated offeror." Under this FAR provision, the FAR envisions at least two other source selection processes other than a tradeoff: a process that results in award to the "lowest priced offeror," and a process that results in award to "the highest technically rated offeror." We thus find no basis in the FAR to object to a proposed source selection process that contemplates award to the highest technically rated offerors without using a tradeoff process.

Protests arguing that this technique was too strictly followed on the ALLIANT 2 Small Business GWAC were denied in *Dynanet Corp. v. United States*, 139 Fed. Cl. 579 (2018); *Technical & Mgmt. Res., Inc., LLC v. United States*, 139 Fed. Cl. 589 (2018); *Criterion Sys., Inc. v. United States*, 140 Fed. Cl. 29 (2018); and *RX Joint Venture, LLC v. United States*, 140 Fed. Cl. 13 (2018). In *Citizant, Inc. v. United States*, 142 Fed. Cl. 260 (2019), the court granted a protest on the ALLIANT 2 Small Business GWAC because the contracting officer had made errors in adjusting the score of Citizant and had been inconsistent in determining whether the offerors had fair and reasonable prices. This decision led to the agency withdrawing all of the prior awards that had been made and cancelling the procurement.

GAO has stated clearly that this technique cannot be used if the RFP states that the winners will be selected by making a tradeoff between prices and the other evaluation factors, *Millennium Corp.*, Comp. Gen. Dec. B-416485.2, 2018 CPD ¶ 329.

DOD, NASA and the Coast Guard have also been authorized to compete IDIQ contracts without evaluating price in defined circumstances. Section 825 of the National Defense Authorization Act for FY 2017, Pub. L. No. 114-328, added the following provision to 10 USC § 3206(c)(3) (formerly § 2305(a)(3)):

> (3) Exceptions for certain multiple task or delivery order contracts.—If the head of an agency issues a solicitation for multiple task or delivery order contracts under section 3403(d)(1)(B) of this title for the same or similar services and intends to make a contract award to each qualifying offeror—
>
> (A) cost or price to the Federal Government need not, at the Government's discretion, be considered under paragraph (1)(B) as an evaluation factor for the contract award; and
>
> (B) if, pursuant to subparagraph (A), cost or price to the Federal Government is not considered as an evaluation factor for the contract award—
>
> (i) the disclosure requirement of paragraph (1)(C) shall not apply; and

(ii) cost or price to the Federal Government shall be considered in conjunction with the issuance pursuant to section 3406(c) of this title of a task or delivery order under any contract resulting from the solicitation.

(4) Definition.—In paragraph (3), the term "qualifying offeror" means an offeror that—

(A) is determined to be a responsible source;

(B) submits a proposal that conforms to the requirements of the solicitation; and

(C) the contracting officer has no reason to believe would likely offer other than fair and reasonable pricing.

This provision is implemented in FAR 16.304(c)(1)(ii) giving contracting officers the discretion to use the technique in all multiple award IDIQ procurements above the simplified acquisition threshold. The FAR adopts a different definition of "qualifying offeror" than the statute, providing in FAR 2.101:

> *Qualifying offeror*, as used in 13.106-1 and 15.304, means an offeror that is determined to be a responsible source, submits a *technically acceptable* proposal that conforms to the requirements of the solicitation, and the contracting officer has no reason to believe would be likely to offer other than fair and reasonable pricing (10 U.S.C. 2305(a)(3)(D)). (Italics added.)

There is no guidance on the technique that should or could be used to determine that a proposal is "technically acceptable." However, the FAR Council included the following explanation in 85 Fed. Reg. 40069, July 2, 2020:

> The section 825 definition of a "qualifying offeror" includes language that the offeror "submits a proposal that conforms to the requirements of the solicitation." The rule refers to a "qualifying offeror" as an offeror that "submits a technically acceptable proposal that conforms to the solicitation." The terms "technically acceptable" and "conforms" have different meanings to Government contracting personnel. A proposal can conform to the requirements for the solicitation (e.g., meeting a required page limit or proposal format), but not demonstrate that the offeror can meet the stated technical requirements (e.g., having necessary certifications or offering the requisite services) of the Government. This clarification ensures contracting officers, when using the authorities in section 825, also evaluate whether a proposal meets the minimum technical requirements stated in the solicitation.

Note that this explanation does not require a technical proposal per se but only that the contracting officer structure the solicitation so that the agency can evaluate whether each proposal meets the "minimum technical requirements" in the solicitation. Presumably, this could be determined by evaluating past performance and experience rather than by requiring technical proposals. See *SigNet Techs., Inc.*, Comp. Gen. Dec. B-418677, 2020 CPD ¶ 244, where the agency used a technical evaluation factor based on the proposed solution to a sample problem to determine whether the offeror had sufficient knowledge to be qualified to perform the contract. Based on the evaluation of the initial offers without conducting either clarifications or discussions, the agency awarded 17 contracts out of the 31 offerors. GAO denied the protest that the agency should have requested clarifications to the sample task solutions.

These contracts must also be for "the same or similar services." That is an opaque reference to the possibility that an agency might make multiple awards to a group of contractors, each of which was uniquely qualified to perform one type of service. This, of course, would be opposed to the basic premise of the statute which is that cost or price can be omitted from the initial evaluation because it will be evaluated when task orders are competed. The FAR Council explained this interpretation of the rule in the Federal Register as follows:

> When price or cost is not evaluated during contract award, the contracting officer shall consider price or cost as a factor for the award of each order under the contract. In accordance with statute, the rule specifies that, when using the authority of section 825, the solicitation must be for the "same or similar services." This language aligns with the guidance at FAR 16.504(c)(1)(i), which requires contracting officers, to the maximum extent practicable, to give preference to making multiple awards of indefinite-quantity contracts under a single solicitation for the same or similar supplies or services to two or more sources. By ensuring that a solicitation using the authority of section 825 is for the "same or similar services," the contracting officer will avoid situations in which awardees specialize exclusively in one or a few areas within the statement of work, thus creating the likelihood that orders in those areas will be awarded on a sole-source basis (FAR 16.504(c)(1)(ii)(A)) and, in turn, negating the purpose of the statute to obtain price competition at the task order level-where service requirements are apt to be more definite and offers more meaningfully comparable.

The technique applies to *all* IDIQ contracts and defers the consideration of price to the task or delivery orders issued under these contracts. The requirement that contracts be awarded to all "qualifying offerors," makes the statute significantly different from the GSA technique because GSA designates a specific number of awardees no matter how many proposals are submitted while the statute requires award of a potentially far greater number of contracts. This statute is also very different from the GSA technique because it leaves the determination of the non-price evaluation factors up to each agency that uses the technique. Thus, while GSA focuses on experience and past performance, an agency using this statute could call for technical and management proposals and exclude offerors that did not fully comply with the requirements for these proposals. This would make the competition far more elaborate than the GSA technique and would probably lead to many more protests that the proposal evaluation was not conducted fairly.

[F] Government Liability for Inaccurate Estimated Quantities

As discussed above, in order to evaluate prices or costs in IDIQ contracts, the government frequently includes estimated quantities of work. The price or cost evaluation is then performed by multiplying the quoted unit prices or costs times the estimated quantities to arrive at the total price or cost. Paragraph (a) of the Indefinite Quantities clause warns offerors that these estimates are not ordered quantities but merely estimates.

In contrast to the rule governing requirements contracts discussed in Chapter 12, the estimates in IDIQ contracts impose no liability on the government if they are negligently arrived at, *Travel Centre v. Barram*, 236 F.3d 1316 (Fed. Cir. 2001). The court reached this conclusion following the questionable reasoning that the contractor could not reasonably rely on these estimates because the only legal obligation of the government was to order the minimum quantity of work. The court stated at 1319:

> Regardless of the accuracy of the estimates delineated in the solicitation, based on the language of the solicitation for the IDIQ contract, Travel Centre could not have had a reasonable expectation that any of the government's needs beyond the minimum contract price would necessarily be satisfied under this contract.

This reasoning ignores the fact that the contractor had to rely on the estimates because it was well aware of the fact that they would be used to evaluate its proposed prices. Nonetheless, the rule that the government is not liable for negligent or misleading estimates in IDIQ contracts has been followed in *Commissioning Sols. Global, LLC*, ASBCA 59254, 14-1 BCA ¶ 35,695 (fact that minimum was $3,000.00 and contract should have been for agency's requirements irrelevant); *Thefaf Al-Rafidain Contracting Co.*, ASBCA 59014, 14-1 BCA ¶ 35,573 (fact that minimum amount was $10,000.00 and maximum amount was $30 million not relevant); *Transtar Metals, Inc.*, ASBCA 55039, 07-1 BCA ¶ 33,482 (fact that contractor incurred large start-up costs not relevant); *White Sands Constr., Inc.*, ASBCA 51875, 02-2 BCA ¶ 31,858 (the board stated "how the estimates were determined is simply not relevant"); and *Abatement Constr. Corp. v. United States*, 58 Fed. Cl. 594 (2003) (no government liability for negligent estimate prepared when agency intended to issue a requirements contract but subsequently issued an IDIQ contract). If an IDIQ contract contains a fixed price line item, the government will be liable for negligent estimates of the volume of work on which the fixed price was based, *Ravens Grp., Inc. v. United States*, 112 Fed. Cl. 39 (2013).

If the agency explicitly directs offerors to rely on government estimates in arriving at their prices, the agency will be liable for inaccurate estimates without regard to whether they have been negligently prepared, *Admiral Elevator v. Social Sec. Admin.*, CBCA C-470, 07-2 BCA ¶ 33,676. In that case the offerors were required to provide two on-site personnel at all times but had to allocate their costs to unit priced maintenance work which was estimated to be sufficient to permit recovery of those costs. The board reasoned at 166,730:

> [The agency's] response [to inquiries from potential offerors] makes clear that SSA intended that offerors use the agency's estimates as a basis for their contract pricing and additionally expected offerors to construct their pricing on the assumption that the costs of the mandated on-site personnel would be recovered, under the per-unit, per-month pricing structure, no matter how many elevators were to be maintained in any particular month. Internal communications among SSA employees involved in the procurement and the deposition testimony of an SSA contracting officer confirm the agency's expectations as to use of the estimates by offerors. This case is consequently like several others in which the Court of Appeals for the Federal Circuit and its predecessor Court of Claims found an agency responsible for the losses which a contractor suffered because, in pricing the contract, it reasonably relied on material, incorrect agency representations in solicitations. Among these cases are *Brown [Constructors, Inc. v. Pena]*, 132 F.3d [724 (Fed. Cir. 1997)] at 729 (erroneous representation as to soil content, due to incorrect washed sieve analysis); *Summit Timber Co. v. United States*, 677 F.2d 852 (Ct. Cl. 1982) (erroneous representation as to boundaries within which timber could be cut, due to incorrect markings); *Everett Plywood & Door Corp. v. United States*, 419 F.2d 425 (Ct. Cl. 1969) (erroneous representation as to volume of timber available for cutting in oddly-shaped area, due to incorrect estimates by inexperienced personnel); and *United Contractors v. United States*, 368 F.2d 585 (Ct. Cl. 1966) (erroneous representation as to subsurface conditions, due to incorrect soil borings). Indeed, the contractor's position is even stronger in this case than it was in those, because here the contractor not only was expected to rely on the key information, but also was told to rely on that information.

This reasoning was followed in *IAP World Servs., Inc.*, CBCA 2709, 13-1 BCA ¶ 35,335.

§ 7.03 ISSUING TASK OR DELIVERY ORDERS

The ordering of work under IDIQ contracts is subject to different rules than those applicable to the award of contracts. The general procedures for ordering are contained in the following mandatory Ordering clause in FAR 52.216-18:

> ORDERING (AUG 2020)
>
> (a) Any supplies and services to be furnished under this contract shall be ordered by issuance of delivery orders or task orders by the individuals or activities designated in the Schedule. Such orders may be issued from _____ through _____ [insert dates].

(b) All delivery orders or task orders are subject to the terms and conditions of this contract. In the event of conflict between a delivery order or task order and this contract, the contract shall control.

(c) A delivery order or task order is considered "issued" when—

(1) If sent by mail (includes transmittal by U.S. mail or private delivery service), the Government deposits the order in the mail;

(2) If sent by fax, the Government transmits the order to the Contractor's fax number; or

(3) If sent electronically, the Government either—

(i) Posts a copy of the delivery order or task order to a Government document access system, and notice is sent to the Contractor; or

(ii) Distributes the delivery order or task order via email to the Contractor's email address.

(d) Orders may be issued by methods other than those enumerated in this clause only if authorized in the contract.

Some agencies use ordering clauses that contain more detailed guidance on the ordering process. See, for example, the Ordering (May 2011) clause in DFARS 252.216-7006, the Task Ordering Procedures clause in NFS 1816.515-80, and the Placement of Orders (Jan. 2016) clause in GSAR 552.216-72.

[A] Within the Scope of the Contract

A task or delivery order may not "increase the scope, period or maximum value" of the contract. Such increases may only be accomplished "by modification of the contract," 10 U.S.C. § 3406(f) and 41 U.S.C. § 4103(e). Although not specifically stated in these sections, procurement notices and competition would be required for such actions unless a noncompetitive award could be justified since the exemption from competition is only applicable to task or delivery orders within the scope of the contract. In contrast, contract modifications of task orders for advisory and assistance services are explicitly stated to be subject to competition requirements, 10 U.S.C. § 3405(g) and 41 U.S.C. § 4105(g)(2). Under limited circumstances, a one-time extension not exceeding six months may be made on a "sole source basis," 10 U.S.C. § 3405(h) and 41 U.S.C. § 4105(h).

FASA permits the award of task and delivery order contracts using "a statement of work that clearly specifies all tasks to be performed or property to be delivered under the order," 10 U.S.C. § 3406(e) and 41 U.S.C. § 4103(b)(3). Thus, task and delivery orders can potentially cover a broad spectrum, depending upon the nature of the work statement in the base IDIQ contract.

In *Western Pilot Serv.*, Comp. Gen. Dec. B-415732, 2018 CPD ¶ 104, GAO elaborated on the criteria for determining whether an order is outside the scope, including the fundamental issue of whether potential offerors on the IDIQ contract would have considered that such an order might be issued:

> When a protester alleges that the issuance of a task or delivery order under an IDIQ contract is beyond the scope of the underlying contract, and thus falls within CICA's competition requirement, our Office examines whether the order is materially different from the original contract, as reasonably interpreted. *DynCorp Int'l LLC*, [B-402349, Mar. 15, 2010, 2010 CPD ¶ 59 at 6]; *Floro & Assocs.*, B-285451.3, B-285451.4, Oct. 25, 2000, 2000 CPD ¶ 172 at 6. Evidence of a material difference is found by reviewing the circumstances attending the original procurement; any changes in the type of work, performance period, and costs between the contract as awarded and the order as issued; and whether the original solicitation effectively advised offerors of the potential for the type of orders issued. *Symetrics Indus.*, Inc., B-289606, Apr. 8, 2002, 2002 CPD ¶ 65 at 5. Additionally, we consider whether the agency itself has historically procured the task order services under a separate contract, such that it appears that the agency itself has viewed the task order services as separable and essentially different in nature. *Data Transformation Corp.*, B-274629, Dec. 19, 1996, 97-1 CPD ¶ 10 at 6. The overall inquiry is whether the order is of a nature which potential offerors reasonably would have anticipated. *DynCorp Int'l, LLC, supra*, at 7-8 (sustaining protest of out-of-scope task order where services required under a TORP were not reasonably contemplated when the IDIQ contracts were awarded, even though there was some overlap in the services requested in the TORP and those required under the IDIQ contracts).

Task orders were found to be within the scope of the contract in *C3.ai, Inc.*, Comp. Gen. Dec. B-418676, 2020 CPD ¶ 256 (rejecting argument that calling for the use of new technologies was outside scope because contract was written with broad language to allow just such work); *Global Dynamics, LLC*, Comp. Gen. Dec. B-417776, 2019 CPD ¶ 366 (rejecting argument that agency improperly limited competition to contractors having two IDIQ contracts for different types of personnel); *People, Tech. & Processes, LLC*, Comp. Gen. Dec. B-417273, 2019 CPD ¶ 173 (rejecting argument that examples in statement of work limited types of training because the statement also contained a general description of covered work); *American Sys. Grp.*, Comp. Gen. Dec. B-415381, 2018 CPD ¶ 86 (rejecting argument that position descriptions in task order differed from base IDIQ contract because the contract had a "wide range" of professional services); and *Lockheed Martin Fairchild Sys.*, Comp. Gen. Dec. B-275034, 97-1 CPD ¶ 28 (modernization of computer-based training within scope of contract for automatic data processing systems integration and support services). In *Draeger, Inc.*, Comp. Gen. Dec. B-414938, 2017 CPD ¶ 308, a scope protest was denied as untimely because the protester had inquired as to the scope of the contract when it was originally competed and had not protested the agency's broad interpretation at that time.

The background and circumstances surrounding the award of a contract may indicate that an order under an otherwise broad work statement is not within the scope of the contract. See *Alliant Sols., LLC*, Comp. Gen. Dec. B-415994, 2018 CPD ¶ 173 (task order for migrating to and operating a cloud facility outside the scope of IDIQ contract for research and analysis involving cloud systems); *Western Pilot Serv.*, Comp. Gen. Dec. B-415732, 2018 CPD ¶ 104 (task order for flight services materially different from on-call services called for by IDIQ contract); *DynCorp Int'l LLC*, Comp. Gen. Dec. B-402349, 2010 CPD ¶ 59 (task orders for the mentoring and training Afghani troops outside the scope of IDIQ contracts for the DoD Counter Narcoterrorism Technology Program Office); *Anteon Corp.*, Comp. Gen. Dec. B-293523, 2004 CPD ¶ 51 (task order request for cloth cover sheets for electronic passport covers outside the scope of a contract for credit card-sized plastic cards); and *Data Transformation Corp.*, Comp. Gen. Dec. B-274629, 97-1 CPD ¶ 10 (operation of nationwide debt collection system outside the scope of a litigation support contract). In *Comdisco, Inc.*, Comp. Gen. Dec. B-277340, 97-2 CPD ¶ 105, GAO sustained a protest where an agency exceeded the scope of its task orders for computer equipment and related services by permitting computer hardware/software to constitute more than its allotted share of a contract.

Modifications of IDIQ contracts must also be within the scope of the original contract. See *Ian, Evan & Alexander Corp. v. United States*, 136 Fed. Cl. 390 (2018), applying the same reasoning that is used for task or delivery orders to a modification and finding it outside of the scope of the original contract.

The issue of "out-of-scope" task orders exploded in importance in the summer of 2004, when it emerged that the Army had purchased interrogation services for Baghdad's Abu Ghraib prison through an information technology services contract. See Fay, *AR 15-6 Investigation of the Abu Ghraib Detention Facility and 205th Military Intelligence Brigade*, 47-52, 116-17, available at *http://news.findlaw.com/nytimes/docs/dod/fay82504rpt.pdf*. The Interior Department's Inspector General (it was an Interior unit that coordinated the interrogator task orders) also articulated, step by step, how the customer agencies abused the flexible task-order contracts to obtain these services. See Devaney, Inspector General, U.S. Department of the Interior, *Review of 12 Procurements Placed Under General Services Administration Federal Supply Schedules 70 and 871 by the National Business Center (Assignment No. W-EV-OSS-0075-2004) (July 16, 2004)*. See generally McCullough & Edmonds, *Contractors on the Battlefield Revisited: The War in Iraq and Its Aftermath*, 04-06 Briefing Papers 1, 11-12 (May 2004). A high point in the controversy came in mid-December 2004, when the GSA Inspector General released a compendium of audits, collectively over 400 pages long, on procurement practices at various GSA regional centers. GSA IG, *Compendium of Audits of the Federal Technology Service Regional Client Support Centers (Dec. 14, 2004)*. See Hardy, *FTS Pledges Improvement*, Fed. Computer Week. These audits presented a sweeping critique of task-order contracting practices across many GSA regional centers, and identified failures in competition and contracting practices in literally hundreds of GSA task orders.

At the same time, IDIQ contracting (known more commonly as "framework" contracting abroad) gained broader acceptance in other nations, and became an accepted method of procurement internationally. See Yukins, *Are IDIQs Inefficient? Sharing Lessons with European Framework Contracting*, 37 Pub. Cont. L.J. 545 (2008).

[B] Verification of Prices

FAR 16.505(b)(3) requires the contracting officer to follow the procedures in FAR subpart 15.4 when the base IDIQ contract does not contain prices for the work ordered. This would require a separate cost or price analysis for such a task or delivery order, as discussed in Chapter 13, and a determination that the price is fair and reasonable. This determination will be relatively straightforward when multiple award contracts are being used and competitive prices are obtained on each task or delivery order. See *ACADEMI Training Center*, Comp. Gen. Dec. B-415416, 2018 CPD ¶ 3, holding that GAO would not review the need to conduct discussions to ensure price reasonableness when there were only two competitors for a task order. In the case of single award contract, the determination will become more difficult as market conditions change. Certainly, if market research revealed that better prices were available, the continued use of an IDIQ contract would be questionable. See FAR 10.001(a)(2)(v) requiring agencies to conduct market research before issuing a task or delivery order for other than a commercial product or commercial service in excess of the simplified acquisition threshold. However, orders under IDIQ contracts are not subject to the synopsis requirement, FAR 5.202(a)(6).

[C] Ordering Under Multiple Award Contracts

The basic requirement for issuing orders under multiple award contracts, originally introduced in FASA, is that holders of such contracts be given a "fair opportunity" to compete for awards, FAR 16.505. However, substantial criticism of the effectiveness of this rule led to the congressional imposition of more stringent requirements on agencies. The first statute of this nature was § 803 of the National Defense Authorization Act for FY 2002, applicable only to the Department of Defense and implemented in DFARS 216.505-70. This was followed by § 843 of the National Defense Authorization Act for FY 2008, Pub. L. No. 110-181, and § 863 of the National Defense Authorization Act for FY 2009, Pub. L. No. 110-417, adding more stringent requirements for larger orders of all agencies to 10 U.S.C. § 3406 and 41 U.S.C. § 4106(d).

[1] Fair Opportunity—Notice Requirement

The fair opportunity requirement is implemented in FAR 16.505(b)(1) as follows:

> (i) The contracting officer must provide each awardee a fair opportunity to be considered for each order exceeding the micro-purchase threshold issued under multiple delivery-order contracts or multiple task-order contracts, except as provided for in paragraph (b)(2) of this section.

The exceptions are listed in this FAR provision as follows:

> (A) The agency need for the supplies or services is so urgent that providing a fair opportunity would result in unacceptable delays.
>
> (B) Only one awardee is capable of providing the supplies or services required at the level of quality required because the supplies or services ordered are unique or highly specialized.
>
> (C) The order must be issued on a sole-source basis in the interest of economy and efficiency because it is a logical follow-on to an order already issued under the contract, provided that all awardees were given a fair opportunity to be considered for the original order.
>
> (D) It is necessary to place an order to satisfy a minimum guarantee.
>
> (E) For orders exceeding the simplified acquisition threshold, a statute expressly authorizes or requires that the purchase be made from a specified source.
>
> (F) In accordance with section 1331 of Public Law 111-240 (15 U.S.C. 644(r)), contracting officers may, at their discretion, set aside orders for any of the small business concerns identified in 19.000(a)(3). When setting aside orders for small business concerns, the specific small business program eligibility requirements identified in part 19 apply.
>
> (G) For DoD, NASA, and the Coast Guard, the order satisfies one of the exceptions permitting the use of other than full and open competition listed in 6.302 (10 U.S.C. 2304c(b)(5)). The public interest exception shall not be used unless Congress is notified in accordance with 10 U.S.C. 2304(c)(7).

When these exceptions are used, the agency must prepare a written justification as described in FAR 16.505(b)(2)(ii). These justifications can be certified by the contracting officer on orders not exceeding $750,000, but above that amount they must be approved by the competition advocate (up to $15 million), the head of the procuring activity (up to $75 million (or $100 million for DOD, NASA and the Coast Guard)) or the senior procurement executive (for higher amounts), FAR 16.505(b)(2)(ii)(C). Justifications for orders above the simplified acquisition threshold must be made publicly available on *SAM.gov* within 14 days of issuing an order, FAR 16.505(b)(2)(ii)(D).

After the task and delivery order statute had been implemented and numerous IDIQ contracts had been awarded, Congress concluded that a mandatory fair opportunity requirement was not sufficient, in itself, to ensure sufficient competition. As a result, the statutory changes discussed above required the issuance of regulations calling for notification of all contractors with task or delivery order contracts of potential task or delivery orders. This, of course, allows any holder of a contract to tell the agency that it is capable of performing the proposed order. In addition, Congress enacted enhanced competition requirements for large orders (currently $6 million). FAR 16.505(b)(1) implements these requirements by stating:

> (iii) *Orders exceeding the simplified acquisition threshold.* (A) Each order exceeding the simplified acquisition threshold shall be placed on a competitive basis in accordance with paragraph (b)(1)(iii)(B) of this section, unless supported by a written determination that one of the circumstances described at 16.505(b)(2)(i) applies to the order and the requirement is waived on the basis of a justification that is prepared in accordance with 16.505(b)(2)(ii)(B);
>
> (B) The contracting officer shall—
>
> (1) Provide a fair notice of the intent to make a purchase, including a clear description of the supplies to be delivered or the services to be performed and the basis upon which the selection will be made to all contractors offering the required supplies or services under the multiple-award contract; and
>
> (2) Afford all contractors responding to the notice a fair opportunity to submit an offer and have that offer fairly considered.
>
> (iv) *Orders exceeding $6 million.* For task or delivery orders in excess of $6 million, the requirement to provide all awardees a fair opportunity to be considered for each order shall include, at a minimum—
>
> (A) A notice of the task or delivery order that includes a clear statement of the agency's requirements;
>
> (B) A reasonable response period;
>
> (C) Disclosure of the significant factors and subfactors, including cost or price, that the agency expects to consider in evaluating proposals, and their relative importance;
>
> (D) Where award is made on a best value basis, a written statement documenting the basis for award and the relative importance of quality and price or cost factors; and
>
> (E) An opportunity for a postaward debriefing in accordance with paragraph (b)(6) of this section.

Contractors can submit complaints about the lack of as fair opportunity to an agency task and delivery order ombudsman. See the Task-Order and Delivery-Order Ombudsman clause in FAR 52.216-32 which is included in all multiple award IDIQ contracts. This clause contains the name of the ombudsman but suggests that complaints be submitted initially to the contracting officer of the ordering activity. It also notes that these complaints are subject to the strict GAO timeliness rules. See *UXB KEMRON Remediation Servs., LLC*, Comp. Gen. Dec. B-401017.4, 2010 CPD ¶ 251, holding that an appeal to the agency ombudsman was not an agency protest which stayed the time allowed for a GAO protest.

On almost all of the protests asserting that an agency has not afforded a contractor a fair opportunity, GAO has ruled in favor of the agency. See *Credence Mgm't Sols., LLC*, Comp. Gen. Dec. B-417389.2, 2019 CPD ¶ 283 (reliance on past performance evaluations reasonable); *Boswell & Dunlop, LLP*, Comp. Gen. Dec. B-416623, 2018 CPD ¶ 351 (fair opportunity rule satisfied by posting solicitation on fedbizops); *Technica Corp.*, Comp. Gen. Dec. B-416542, 2018 CPD ¶ 348 (issuance of sole source task order based on urgency reasonable because agency had expended planning time attempting to resolve problems with protester that had an option for the work); *NTD DATA Servs., Fed. Gov't, Inc.*, Comp. Gen. Dec. B-416123, 2018 CPD ¶ 215 (protester participated in procurement until it was excluded from competitive range); *PricewaterhouseCoopers Public Sector, LLP*, Comp. Gen. Dec. B-415504, 2018 CPD ¶ 35 (fair opportunity rule does not require agency to adopt a strict late quotation rule); *Ocean Sols., Inc.*, Comp. Gen. Dec. B-415422, 2018 CPD ¶ 22 (protester opted out in phase one of procurement and was not prejudiced by a subsequent amendment making an immaterial change to the RFQ); *Aegis Defense Servs., LLC*, Comp. Gen. Dec. B-412755, 2016 CPD ¶ 98 (fair opportunity rule does not permit contractor to challenge task order on the ground that it will preclude a fair opportunity to compete for future task orders); *Enterprise Information Servs., Inc.*, Comp. Gen. Dec. B-403028, 2010 CPD ¶ 213 (fair opportunity rule does not preclude agencies from requiring recertification of size status); and *Doug Boyd Enters., LLC*, Comp. Gen. Dec. B-298237.2, 2007 CPD ¶ 147 (fair opportunity rule does not guarantee that holder of IDIQ contract will be given enough business to remain a viable business entity). See, however, *Inquires, Inc.*, Comp. Gen. Dec. B-417415.2, 2020 CPD ¶ 54, sustaining a protest where the agency added work to a task order on a sole source basis citing an exception to the fair opportunity rule but the GAO found that the added work created an organizational conflict of interest. GAO has also stated that the advanced planning requirement, discussed in Chapter 3, does not apply to orders issued under IDIQ contracts, *Technica Corp.*, Comp. Gen. Dec. B-416542, 2018 CPD ¶ 348.

Appeals of the lack of a fair opportunity have been heard by the Court of Federal Claims on the ground that these are Contract Disputes Act claims that the agency breached the basic IDIQ contract, *Vanquish Worldwide, LLC v. United States*, 147 Fed. Cl. 390 (2020); *Digital Techs., Inc. v. United States*, 89 Fed. Cl. 711 (2009). Compare *Orbis Sibro, Inc. v. United States*, 117 Fed. Cl. 446 (2014), where the court concluded that it did not have Contract Disputes Act jurisdiction over a claim of lack of fair opportunity because the claim solely concerned issues dealing with the evaluation of a task order.

There is a split between the GAO and the Court of Federal Claims as to whether the fair opportunity rule permits a contractor holding an IDIQ contract to protest the award of another IDIQ contract. See *National Air Cargo Grp., Inc.*, Comp. Gen. Dec. B-411830.2, 2016 CPD ¶ 85; and *Aegis Defense Services, LLC*, Comp. Gen. Dec. B-412755, 2016 CPD ¶ 98 (holding it does not), and *National Air Cargo Grp., Inc. v. United States*, 127 Fed. Cl. 707 (2016) (holding it does). See also *Al Qabandi United Co.*, Comp. Gen. Dec. B-415353.8, 2018 CPD ¶ 419, rejecting a protest against adding a blanket purchase agreement to a multiple award contract.

Appeals of the lack of a fair opportunity have been heard by the boards of contract appeals as contract disputes regarding compliance with the IDIQ contract, not protests concerning the issuance of task or delivery orders. See *Smart Way Transportation Servs.*, ASBCA 60315, 16-1 BCA ¶ 36,569 (no breach of the fair opportunity rule because the agency had conducted no competitive procurements of task orders when the contract was in effect); *SIA Constr., Inc.*, ASBCA 57693, 14-1 BCA ¶ 35,762 (alleged improper government conduct in competing delivery orders); *PAW & Assocs., LLC*, ASBCA 58534, 13-1 BCA ¶ 35,462, 15-1 BCA ¶ 36,078 (alleged breach of IDIQ contract by disclosing proprietary information in task order competition); *L-3 Communications. Corp.*, ASBCA 54920, 08-1 BCA ¶ 33,857 (breach of IDIQ contract by improper evaluation of cost/price factor in delivery order competition—damages are cost of preparing quotation); and *Community Consulting Int'l*, ASBCA 53489, 02-2 BCA ¶ 31,940 (alleged breach of statement in IDIQ contract that competition would be limited to the four awardees of contracts). See also *A-Son's Constr., Inc. v. Dep't of Housing & Urban Development*, CBCA 3491, 15-1 BCA ¶ 36,184, taking jurisdiction of a dispute concerning the interpretation of the provisions of an IDIQ contract.

[2] Source Selection Procedures

Agencies have broad authority to use streamlined and effective procedures in conducting the competition among contractors holding task and delivery order contracts. Thus, they can structure the solicitation to allow free communication between agency personnel and offerors throughout the competitive process as long as they ensure that they are treating all offerors fairly and evenhandedly. FAR 16.505(b)(1) contains the following guidance.

> (ii) The contracting officer may exercise broad discretion in developing appropriate order placement procedures. The contracting officer should keep submission requirements to a minimum. Contracting officers may use streamlined procedures, including oral presentations. If the order does not exceed the simplified acquisition threshold, the contracting officer need not contact each of the multiple awardees under the contract before selecting an order awardee if the contracting officer has information available to ensure that each awardee is provided a fair opportunity to be considered for each order. The competition requirements in part 6 and the policies in subpart 15.3 do not apply to the ordering process. However, the contracting officer must—

(A) Develop placement procedures that will provide each awardee a fair opportunity to be considered for each order and that reflect the requirement and other aspects of the contracting environment;

(B) Not use any method (such as allocation or designation of any preferred awardee) that would not result in fair consideration being given to all awardees prior to placing each order;

(C) Tailor the procedures to each acquisition;

(D) Include the procedures in the solicitation and the contract;

(E) Consider price or cost under each order as one of the factors in the selection decision.

(F) Except for DoD, ensure the criteria at 15.101-2(c)(1)-(5) are met when using the lowest price technically acceptable source selection process; and;

(G) Except for DoD, avoid using the lowest price technically acceptable source selection process to acquire certain supplies and services in accordance with 15.101-2(d).

The above FAR guidance gives agencies broad discretion to use simplified procedures to award orders and it is good practice to use streamlined procedures on smaller orders. On large orders most agencies have chosen to use procedures mirroring the FAR Part 15 procedures, using a more formal source selection process. GAO has also sanctioned the use of the highest technically rated proposal with a fair and reasonable price procedure in *Sumaria Sys., Inc.*, Comp. Gen. Dec. B-418796, 2020 CPD ¶ 296. See the earlier discussion on the use of this technique in awarding the original IDIQ contract.

When agencies adopt FAR Part 15 procedures, they are subject to the rules followed by the GAO and the Court of Federal Claims in protests of FAR Part 15 procurements. For decisions applying the FAR Part 15 rules, see *Sigmatech, Inc.*, Comp. Gen. Dec. B-419565, 2021 CPD ¶ 241 (reasonable to drop protester from competitive range); *MCR Federal, LLC*, Comp. Gen. Dec. B-416654.2, 2019 CPD ¶ 335 (eight days insufficient time to submit final proposal revisions requiring extensive staffing changes); *Cyberdata Techs., Inc.*, Comp. Gen. Dec. B-417084, 2019 CPD ¶ 34 (selection decision in tradeoff procurement must look behind ratings of vendors); Tatitlek Techs., Inc., Comp. Gen. Dec. B-416111, 2018 CPD ¶ 410 (proper application of cost realism analysis); *Enterprise Servs., LLC*, Comp. Gen. Dec. B-414230.3, 2018 CPD ¶ 323 (no requirement to discuss significant weakness in responding to amended RFQ); *Jacobs Tech., Inc.*, Comp. Gen. Dec. B-416314, 2018 CPD ¶ 271 (proper to comply with meaningful discussion requirement by reopening competition after award to clear up ambiguity); *Skyline Ultd, Inc.*, Comp. Gen. Dec. B-416028, 2018 CPD ¶ 192 (meaningful discussions conducted but agency not required to allow final proposal revisions); *Vector Planning & Servs., Inc.*, Comp. Gen. Dec. B-415005, 2017 CPD ¶ 360 (agency can select higher priced offeror with better value when using tradeoff technique); *FEI Sys.*, Comp. Gen. Dec. B-414852.2, 2017 CPD ¶ 349 (agency not required to ask for clarifications); *SMS Data*

Prods. Group, Inc., Comp. Gen. Dec. B-414548, 2017 CPD ¶ 222 (meaningful discussions conducted); *Smartronix, Inc.*, Comp. Gen. Dec. B-413721.2, 2017 CPD ¶ 59 (proper application of cost realism analysis on cost-reimbursement LPTA task order); *Leader Communications, Inc.*, Comp. Gen. Dec. B-412819, 2016 CPD ¶ 197 (GAO evaluation of technical proposals is limited); *DLT Sols., Inc.*, Comp. Gen. Dec. B-412237, 2016 CPD ¶ 19 (agency not required to ask for clarifications); *Sapient Gov't—Servs., Inc.*, Comp. Gen. Dec. B-412163.2, 2016 CPD ¶ 11 (oral presentation not a discussion); and *Advanced Alliant Sols. Team, LLC*, Comp. Gen. Dec. B-410207, 2014 CPD ¶ 4 (price realism analysis satisfactory). In *NTD DATA Servs. Fed. Gov't, Inc.*, Comp. Gen. Dec. B-416123, 2018 CPD ¶ 215, GAO stated that FAR 15.306 was not applicable but then determined that the agency had fairly narrowed the competitive range. In *SSI*, Comp. Gen. Dec. B-413486, 2016 CPD ¶ 322, GAO explicitly stated that the FAR Part 15 rules do not apply and held that it was proper to accept written information following oral discussions and allow no final proposal revisions.

[3] Debriefing

There is no general requirement for debriefing competitors for task or delivery orders. However, when the competition is for an order exceeding $6 million, agencies are required by FAR 16.505(b)(1)(iv) to provide notice of the award and a postaward debriefing to unsuccessful offerors following the procedures in FAR 15.503(b)(i) and FAR 15.506. Protests at GAO based on information learned at a debriefing must be filed within 10 days of the debriefing, *CDO Techs., Inc.*, Comp. Gen. Dec. B-416989, 2018 CPD ¶ 370.

[D] Ordering Procedures

In addition to the procedures discussed above that are applicable to multiple award IDIQ contracts, there are a number of procedures and rules that are applicable to all IDIQ contracts.

[1] Synopsis Requirement

There is no requirement to synopsize solicitations for task or delivery orders, FAR 5.202(a)(6), 16.505(a)(1), except when ordering items "peculiar to one manufacturer," FAR 16.505(a)(4). In such brand name or equal procurements, the contracting officer must prepare a justification demonstrating that the item is urgently needed, unique or a logical follow-on to an earlier order. Such justifications for orders over $30,000 must be posted on the agency website and provided, along with the solicitation to all contractors with the task or delivery order contract. These justifications are not required if the order is placed on a single award IDIQ contract that was awarded based on full and open competition.

[2] Structuring the Solicitation

Solicitations for task and delivery orders are generally prepared in the form of Requests for Quotations, Task Order Requests for Proposals, or Requests for Proposals. FAR 16.505(a) contains the following rules regarding these solicitations:

> (2) Individual orders shall clearly describe all services to be performed or supplies to be delivered so the full cost or price for the performance of the work can be established when the order is placed. Orders shall be within the scope, issued within the period of performance, and be within the maximum value of the contract.
>
> (3) Performance-based acquisition methods must be used to the maximum extent practicable, if the contract or order is for services (see 37.102(a) and Subpart 37.6).
>
> * * *
>
> (7) Orders placed under indefinite-delivery contracts must contain the following information:
>
> (i) Date of order.
>
> (ii) Contract number and order number.
>
> (iii) For supplies and services, line item number, subline item number (if applicable), description, quantity, and unit price or estimated cost and fee (as applicable). The corresponding line item number and subline item number from the base contract shall also be included.
>
> (iv) Delivery or performance schedule.
>
> (v) Place of delivery or performance (including consignee).
>
> (vi) Any packaging, packing, and shipping instructions.
>
> (vii) Accounting and appropriation data.
>
> (viii) Method of payment and payment office, if not specified in the contract (see 32.1110(e)).
>
> (ix) North American Industry Classification System code (see 19.102(b)(3)).

GAO has ruled that this regulation, along with the fair opportunity rule, prohibits an agency from issuing a single order that calls for the subsequent issuance of orders as the work is defined, *Harris IT Servs. Corp.*, Comp. Gen. Dec. B-411699, 2015 CPD ¶ 293 (calling the prohibited order a "single, second-tier IDIQ instrument"). See also *DLT Sols., Inc.*, Comp. Gen. Dec. B-412237, 2016 CPD ¶ 19, confirming GAO's view that such task orders are improper. Compare *Sek Sols., LLC v. United States*, 117 Fed. Cl. 43 (2014), finding an IDIQ contract to establish a catalog of products proper.

If the base IDIQ contract permits a variety of type of orders, such as fixed price, cost-reimbursement or time-and-materials, the task or delivery order should specify which type will be applicable in order to have equal competition among the competitors. NFS 1816.505-70(c)(2) contains a mandatory requirement that task orders contain "the same pricing structure from all offerors."

[3] Late Quotations

The late-is-late rule discussed in Chapter 6 does not apply to quotations submitted to an agency for a task or delivery order unless the solicitation specifically states that quotations will not be considered unless they are submitted by a specified date. See *PricewaterhouseCoopers Pub. Sector, LLP*, Comp. Gen. Dec. B-415504, 2018 CPD ¶ 35, explaining:

> An RFQ, unlike an RFP or invitation for bids, does not seek offers that can be accepted by the government to form a contract. Rather, the government's purchase order represents the offer that the vendor may accept through performance or by a formal acceptance document. *DataVault Corp.*, B-248664, Sept. 10, 1992, 92-2 CPD ¶ 166 at 2. It follows that language in an RFQ (or, in this case, the contracting officer's request for FRQs) requesting quotations by a certain date cannot be construed as establishing a firm closing date for receipt of quotations, absent a late quotation provision expressly providing that quotations must be received by that date to be considered. *Instruments & Controls Serv. Co.*, B-222122, June 30, 1986, 86-2 CPD ¶ 16 at 3. Agencies should thus consider any quotations received prior to source selection if no substantial activity has transpired in evaluating quotations and other vendors would not be prejudiced.

[4] Time of Effectiveness

The Ordering clause in FAR 52.216-18 requires the government to state a specific period during which orders can be issued. In addition, paragraph (d) of the Indefinite Quantity clause in FAR 52.216-22 states:

> (d) Any order issued during the effective period of this contract and not completed within that period shall be completed by the Contractor within the time specified in the order. The contract shall govern the Contractor's and Government's rights and obligations with respect to that order to the same extent as if the order were completed during the contract's effective period; provided, that the Contractor shall not be required to make any deliveries under this contract after [insert date].

Thus, the ordering period does not govern the time of performance of orders which can extend beyond the issuance date, *DayDanyon Corp.*, ASBCA 57611,

14-1 BCA ¶35,507, *clarified on recons.*, 14-1 BCA ¶35,616, *aff'd*, 600 Fed. Appx. 739 (Fed. Cir. 2015) (IDIQ contract stating that orders could be issued "from date of contract award through two years" allows orders to be issued for full two years in spite of other ambiguous language).

The Ordering clause also states that mailed orders will be effective when deposited in the mail, fax orders will be effective when "transmitted," and electronic orders will be effective when either "posted" or "distributed." This, in effect, adopts the "mailbox rule," discussed in Chapter 2, making orders effective when mailed, transmitted, posted or distributed not when they are received.

[5] Failure to Order Minimum Quantity

If the government terminates the IDIQ contract before the end date for ordering, it will be excused from its promise to order a minimum quantity, leaving the contractor with only the right to collect termination costs and profit, *DayDanyon Corp.*, ASBCA 57611, 14-1 BCA ¶35,507, *clarified on recons.*, 14-1 BCA ¶35,616, *aff'd*, 600 Fed. Appx. 739 (Fed. Cir. 2015). Computation of termination costs and profit are discussed below.

If the government fails to terminate the minimum quantity before the end of the ordering period, its failure to order the minimum quantity will constitute a breach of contract with compensation based on appropriate damages reflecting the injury to the contractor. In *Maxima Corp. v. United States*, 847 F.2d 1549 (Fed. Cir. 1988), the court held that the government was not permitted to recoup its payment of the minimum dollar amount of the contract by retroactively terminating for convenience. This appeared to entitle the contractor to the entire minimum amount of the contract even though it had not incurred the costs of the unordered work—which some commentators interpreted as a holding that the correct calculation of damages for the unordered elements of the minimum quantity was the entire minimum price on the theory that this minimum dollar amount had been promised in return for the contractor's maintenance of the capability to perform the minimum quantity. See, for example, *Mid-Eastern Indus., Inc.*, ASBCA 53016, 02-1 BCA ¶31,657. However, in *PHP Healthcare Corp.*, ASBCA 39207, 91-1 BCA ¶23,647, the board refused to award the entire price for the unordered work, holding that the contract was not for the maintenance of a capability. Thus, it required the contractor to prove damages—the amount of costs incurred plus anticipated profits on the minimum quantity. See also *Apex Int'l Mgmt. Servs., Inc.*, ASBCA 38087, 94-2 BCA ¶26,842; and *Golden West Bldrs.*, PSBCA 3378, 93-3 BCA ¶26,195, following the same reasoning.

In contrast, in *Merrimac Mgmt. Inst., Inc.*, ASBCA 45291, 94-3 BCA ¶27,251, the board stated that damages should be computed by deducting the costs that would have been incurred from the price of the minimum quantity. This was confirmed as the correct method of calculating damages in

White v. Delta Constr. Int'l, Inc., 285 F.3d 1040 (Fed. Cir. 2002), stating at 1044-45:

> All that the court held in *Maxima* was that the government could not retroactively terminate the contract for convenience after the contract had been fully performed. *Cf. Krygoski Constr. Co. v. United States*, 94 F.3d 1537, 1542 n.2 (Fed. Cir. 1996) ("*Maxima* stands for the proposition the Government cannot retroactively create a breach in order to change the Government's obligations under a completed contract."). The court did not purport to and did not decide any question concerning the proper measure of damages in that situation. The court discussed and rejected the various theories upon which the government sought to justify its retroactive termination and to uphold the Board's direction that the contractor refund to the government the balance of the contractual minimum. The court did so, however, only in connection with its conclusion that the retroactive termination was improper.
>
> To be sure, the result of the court's decision in *Maxima* was that the contractor would retain the amount the government had paid it, representing the difference between the guaranteed minimum and the amount of work the government had ordered. That resulted, however, not because the court approved the basis of payment (it did not address that issue), but because the court found improper the method the government used to recapture the payment (retroactive termination for convenience). *Maxima* did not decide anything about the propriety of the basis of calculating damages that the Board used in this case. Fairly and carefully read, *Maxima* cannot properly be understood to hold that where there is an indefinite-quantity contract with a guaranteed minimum and the contractor is obligated to be ready to perform a certain amount of work, the contractor is entitled to receive the amount by which the government falls short of the guaranteed minimum.

Thus, the correct measure of damages would be the minimum dollar amount minus the costs that would have been incurred had the minimum amount been ordered. See, however, *National Housing Group, Inc. v. Dep't of Housing & Urban Development*, CBCA 340, 11-1 BCA ¶ 34,644, *recons. denied*, 12-1 BCA ¶ 35,033 (damages could be calculated using either expectancy theory (lost management fees) or reliance theory (cost incurred waiting for work)); *Admiral Elevator v. Social Sec. Admin.*, CBCA 470, 07-2 BCA ¶ 33,676 (board would accept "any workable, sensible approach" which calculates damages that put the contractor in the same position it would have been in had the minimum quantity been ordered); *Greenlee Constr. Co. v. General Servs. Admin.*, CBCA 415, 07-2 BCA ¶ 33,619 ("Any costs the contractor might have incurred from performing work valued at the guaranteed minimum amount must be subtracted from that amount to reach the correct figure for damages"); and *Jim Phillips Contracting, Inc.* IBCA 4319, 04-1 BCA ¶ 32,416 (awarding profits that the contractor would have earned when the government ordered no work (determined on the basis of a "jury verdict" based on conflicting evidence)). See *Admiral Elevator v. Social*

Sec. Admin., CBCA 470, 08-2 BCA ¶ 33,884, where the board awarded damages on a unique IDIQ contract by reducing the price for work not done by the cost of materials required for that work and the price for work that it should have anticipated would not be ordered (under a contract clause warning that some work would not be needed).

[6] Termination for Convenience

Once the government has ordered the minimum quantity, it is not required to order additional quantities and no further action is required to end the contract. However, since all IDIQ contracts contain a Termination for Convenience clause, the government can also terminate the contract under that clause. In *International Data Prods. Corp. v. United States*, 492 F.3d 1317 (Fed. Cir. 2007), the court held that the government was not obligated to pay either termination costs or warranty and upgrade costs after termination because the clause limited the government's obligation to the contract price. The court reasoned that the contract price was the $35 million that the agency had paid for the ordered equipment, and, since the contractor had been paid that amount in full, it had no further rights under the Termination for Convenience clause (or under any other legal theory).

However, if the termination occurs before the orders have reached the minimum quantity, the compensation should include repricing of unit prices necessary to recover fixed costs that were spread over the minimum quantity, *SteelCare, Inc.*, GSBCA 5491, 81-1 BCA ¶ 15,143. In *Montana Refining Co.*, ASBCA 44250, 94-2 BCA ¶ 26,656, the board remanded the case to the parties to compute "damages" even though the contracting officer had issued a termination for convenience for most of the unordered minimum quantity 18 days before the end of the contract period. The board did not discuss whether such "damages" should include anticipated profit. In contrast, in *Montana Refining Co.*, ASBCA 50515, 00-1 BCA ¶ 30,694, the board found a valid partial termination for convenience when the termination order was issued four months before the end of the contract period.

GAO has ruled, as a general matter, that it will not review terminations because they are matters of contract administration. However, GAO will review terminations of task orders under its protest authority if the termination is "based in whole or in part on alleged improprieties concerning the award of the order," *AMAR Health IT, LLC*, Comp. Gen. Dec. B-414384.3, 2018 CPD ¶ 111; *Bay Area Travel, Inc.*, Comp. Gen. Dec. B-400442, 2009 CPD ¶ 65.

[7] Protests

Protests of task and delivery orders are addressed in Chapter 15.

Protests asserting that a task or delivery order was outside of the scope of the contract have always been accepted by the GAO and the Court of Federal

Claims. See, for example, *Alliant Sols., LLC*, Comp. Gen. Dec. B-415994, 2018 CPD ¶ 173 (task order for migrating to and operating a cloud facility outside the scope of IDIQ contract for research and analysis involving cloud systems); *Western Pilot Serv.*, Comp. Gen. Dec. B-415732, 2018 CPD ¶ 104 (task order for flight services materially different from on-call services called for by IDIQ contract); *BayFirst Sols., LLC v. United States*, 104 Fed. Cl. 493 (2012) (task order for different work within scope because broad language in IDIQ contract stated that task order holders could be required to provide different types of employees to different offices of the agency).

The original task and delivery order statutes as enacted in FASA precluded any protests of task or delivery orders other than on grounds of scope. However, 10 U.S.C. § 3406(f) and (g) and 41 U.S.C. § 4106(e) and (f) now require agencies to have a task and delivery order ombudsman and allow protests to GAO for large orders—orders in excess of $25 million for DOD, NASA and the Coast Guard and in excess of $10 million for other agencies. GAO receives in excess of 300 protests per year under this authority. Some agencies take the position that GAO's exclusive jurisdiction over such protests also precludes agency protests.

The Court of Federal Claims is not empowered to hear task or delivery order protests other than scope protests. However, where an agency issued a task order simultaneously with the award of the original IDIQ contract, the court took jurisdiction of the protest because failure to receive the task order was intrinsically connected with the protester's evaluation leading to the award of the IDIQ contract to its competitor, *PAE-Parsons Global Logistics Servs. v. United States*, 145 Fed. Cl. 194 (2019); 147 Fed. Cl. 294 (2020). This reasoning was followed in *Fluor Intercontinental, Inc. v. United States*, 147 Fed. Cl. 309 (2020).

GAO applies these thresholds to the order that is being protested, *Goldbelt Glacier Health Servs., LLC*, Comp. Gen. Dec. B-410378, 2014 CPD ¶ 281 (actual dollar amount of order issued is appropriate measure of task order value). In *EA Eng'g, Sci., & Tech., Inc.*, Comp. Gen. Dec. B-411967.2, 2016 CPD ¶ 106, GAO took jurisdiction of a protest asserting that its task order had been terminated because it was over the threshold, even though the subsequently awarded task order was under the threshold. GAO reasoned that the protester could not challenge the new task order but could challenge the termination. However, in *AMAR Health IT, LLC*, Comp. Gen. Dec. B-414384.3, 2018 CPD ¶ 111, GAO refused to follow this ruling because the original task order had "lapsed" rather than being terminated.

As is the case with protests for base contracts, protests of solicitation defects in task or delivery orders must be submitted prior to the closing date for the receipt of quotations, *MicroTechs., LLC*, Comp. Gen. Dec. B-417442, 2019 CPD ¶ 201; *Antico Cantiere Del Legno Giovanni Aprea Di Cataldo S.R.L.*, Comp. Gen. Dec. B-414112, 2017 CPD ¶ 58.

CHAPTER 8
SIMPLIFIED ACQUISITION

§ 8.01 INTRODUCTION

Known for many years as "small purchases," simplified acquisition now encompasses three different classes of procurement—micro-purchases, simplified acquisition, and purchases of commercial items over the simplified acquisition threshold for contingency operations as discussed below. The rules governing these procurements are promulgated in the FAR under authority granted by the Federal Acquisition Streamlining Act of 1994 (FASA), Pub. L. No. 103-355, and the Clinger-Cohen Act of 1996, Pub. L. No. 104-106. Neither the statutes nor the regulations provide any detailed procedures for these purchases. Rather, they relieve contracting officers from most of the procedures required for sealed bidding and conventional negotiated procurement.

The statutory provisions mandating the use of simplified acquisition procedures are contained in 41 U.S.C. §§ 1901-05. Directions for agencies to use them are provided in 10 U.S.C. § 3572 (formerly § 2302b) and 41 U.S.C. § 3305(a). The major thrust of these statutes is to allow the government efficiently to issue contracts for smaller acquisitions with simpler terms and conditions. The government's policy is that simplified acquisition procedures are to be used to the "maximum extent practicable," FAR 13.003(a). Purchases over the micro-purchase threshold but not more than the simplified acquisition threshold must be set aside exclusively for small business concerns in accordance with FAR Subpart 19.5, FAR 13.003(b)(1). The authority to use simplified acquisition procedures does not relieve agencies of their obligation to use the required sources of supply specified in Part 8 of the FAR.

FAR 13.002 specifies the following purposes of simplified acquisition procedures:

> (a) Reduce administrative costs;
>
> (b) Improve opportunities for small, small disadvantaged, women-owned, veteran-owned, HUBZone, and service-disabled veteran-owned small business concerns to obtain a fair proportion of Government contracts;
>
> (c) Promote efficiency and economy in contracting; and
>
> (d) Avoid unnecessary burdens for agencies and contractors.

§ 8.02 THRESHOLDS

The original thresholds for simplified acquisitions and micro-purchases in FASA have been modified by the adoption of 41 U.S.C. § 1993 to grant greater authority in times of emergency. The threshold applies to the entire price of the procurement including options. See FAR 13.106-1(e) stating:

> (e) *Use of options*. Options may be included in solicitations, provided the requirements of subpart 17.2 are met and the aggregate value of the acquisition and all options does not exceed the dollar threshold for use of simplified acquisition procedures.

FAR Subpart 17.2 requires that a solicitation state whether an option will be evaluated in awarding a contract, *Seaborn Health Care, Inc. v. United States*, 55 Fed. Cl. 520 (2003). See also *SMS Sys. Maint. Servs., Inc.*, Comp. Gen. Dec. B-284550.2, 2000 CPD ¶ 127 (options must be included in determining whether micro-purchase threshold is exceeded).

[A] Simplified Acquisition

The original upper threshold for simplified acquisition in 1995 was $100,000, 41 U.S.C. § 403(11). However, the statutes have been amended several times to increase that threshold in specific circumstances. In addition, the threshold has been raised, pursuant to 41 U.S.C. § 1908, to account for escalation. The current thresholds are prescribed in FAR 2.101 as follows:

> *Simplified acquisition threshold* means $ 250,000, except for—
>
> (1) Acquisitions of supplies or services that, as determined by the head of the agency, are to be used to support a contingency operation or to facilitate defense against or recovery from nuclear, biological, chemical, or radiological attack (41 U.S.C. 428a), the term means—
>
> (i) $ 800,000 for any contract to be awarded and performed, or purchase to be made, inside the United States; and
>
> (ii) $ 1.5 million for any contract to be awarded and performed, or purchase to be made, outside the United States.
>
> (2) Acquisitions of supplies or services that, as determined by the head of the agency, are to be used to support a humanitarian or peacekeeping operation (10 U.S.C. 2302), the term means $500,000 for any contract to be awarded and performed, or purchase to be made, outside the United States.

The threshold for simplified acquisitions for commercial items is $7,500,000 or $15,000,000 if the contract is to support a contingency operation or to facilitate defense against or recovery from nuclear, biological, chemical, or radiological attack, FAR 13.500.

[B] Micro-Purchases

The original threshold for micro-purchases in 1995 was $2,500. However, this amount has been adjusted for inflation and the statutes have been amended several times to increase that threshold in specific circumstances. FAR 2.101 implements these statutes by prescribing the following thresholds:

> *Micro-purchase threshold* means $ 10,000, except it means—
>
> (1) For construction subject to 40 U.S.C. chapter 31, subchapter IV, Wage Rate Requirements (Construction), $ 2,000;

(2) For acquisitions of services subject to 41 U.S.C. chapter 67, Service Contract Labor Standards, $ 2,500; and

(3) For acquisitions of supplies or services that, as determined by the head of the agency, are to be used to support a contingency operation or to facilitate defense against or recovery from nuclear, biological, chemical, or radiological attack, as described in 13.201(g)(1), except for construction subject to 40 U.S.C. chapter 31, subchapter IV, Wage Rate Requirements (Construction) (41 U.S.C. 1903)—

(i) $ 20,000 in the case of any contract to be awarded and performed, or purchase to be made, inside the United States; and

(ii) $ 35,000 in the case of any contract to be awarded and performed, or purchase to be made, outside the United States.

(4) For acquisitions of supplies or services from institutions of higher education (20 U.S.C. 1001(a)) or related or affiliated nonprofit entities, or from nonprofit research organizations or independent research institutes—

(i) $10,000; or

(ii) A higher threshold, as determined appropriate by the head of the agency and consistent with clean audit findings under 31 U.S.C. chapter 75, Requirements for Single Audits; an internal institutional risk assessment; or State law.

[C] Breaking Down Purchases to Fit Within Thresholds Prohibited

Agencies are prohibited from "breaking down" procurements that aggregate more than the thresholds to permit use of the procedures within the applicable threshold, 41 U.S.C. § 1901(b) and FAR 13.003(c)(2). Thus, a $300,000 procurement could not be properly acquired using three $100,000 purchase orders. Similarly, if an agency has an identified recurring need for supplies or services, it is improper to enter into a series of small purchases to fulfill this need. In *L.A. Sys. v. Dep't of the Army*, GSBCA 13472-P, 96-1 BCA ¶ 28,220, the board held that the determination of whether a "fragmentation" or breaking down of a quantity occurs depends upon the knowledge of the user, not the contracting officer. The board stated at 140,915-16:

> That the contracting officer had no "advance knowledge of the megacenter's total requirements" is not dispositive of the issue. The prohibition in FAR 13.103(c) against breaking down requirements into several purchases that are less than the simplified acquisition threshold does not excuse fragmentation merely because the contracting officer is unaware that a series of orders is actually one requirement. To read the regulation as respondent suggests would allow a contracting officer to receive orders for a fragmented requirement and circumvent the regulation as long as the contracting officer is not told of the true nature of the requirement by individuals who had such knowledge.

See also *Critical Process Filtration, Inc.*, Comp. Gen. Dec. B-400746, 2009 CPD ¶ 25, holding it improper to issue a purchase order for an indefinite quantity with a limitation on orders to the amount of the simplified acquisition threshold when the estimated quantity was greater than the threshold.

Fragmentation was permitted when an agency issued monthly purchase orders to the incumbent contractor for services during the resolution of a protest, *Keeton Corr., Inc. v. United States*, 59 Fed. Cl. 753 (2004). The court reasoned that such fragmentation was a proper balancing of the requirement for full and open competition above the simplified acquisition threshold with the beneficial purpose of the stay of the award of a new contract during a protest. Similarly, fragmentation was permitted while an agency is establishing the grounds for full and open competition above the simplified acquisition threshold, *Petchem, Inc. v. United States*, 99 F. Supp. 2d 50 (D.D.C. 2000) (permissible to make spot purchases of tugboat services after a competitively negotiated procurement did not yield offers at prices comparable to local market prices); *Master Security, Inc.*, Comp. Gen. Dec. B-274990, 97-1 CPD ¶ 21 (permissible to use small purchase procedures to make month-to-month procurements of critically needed services until a "a fully competitive award is possible"); *Mas-Hamilton Grp., Inc.*, 72 Comp. Gen. 6 (B-249049), 92-1 CPD ¶ 259 (permissible to use small purchase procedures to make "short-term, filler buys" of urgently needed product until a fully competitive award could be completed).

FAR 13.003(c)(2) states that requirements should not be broken down "merely" to take advantage of the threshold. While that language is not contained in 41 U.S.C. § 1901(b), it appears that fragmentation would be appropriate if there were a valid reason to do so. One reason might be to permit small businesses to take advantage of the procurement. Another possible reason might be lack of funding. In *L.A. Systems*, the government argued that it could not "consolidate" the procurement because of a lack of available funding and that to allow funds to accumulate would result in a loss of funding. However, the board found that sufficient funds were available for the total requirement before the first order was placed.

[D] Thresholds Applicable to Both Solicitation Estimates and Award Values

The dollar values apply to *both* the amount estimated for the procurement and resulting contract values. Thus, if a procurement is begun using other than simplified procedures based on an estimate that exceeds the applicable threshold, simplified procedures may not be used even though the price of the source selected is lower than the threshold, *Global Communications Solutions, Inc.*, Comp. Gen. Dec. B-299044, 2007 CPD ¶ 30 (commercial item test program threshold). Conversely, even though a solicitation was issued under simplified procedures, award may not be made above the applicable threshold. However, award on the basis of simplified procedures would be proper if the selected source reduced its price to come within the threshold. Protests that a procurement exceeds the threshold must be submitted before responding to a solicitation if the violation is obvious, *Baldt, Inc.*, Comp. Gen. Dec. B-402596.3, 2010 CPD ¶ 139.

Once an award is properly made using simplified acquisition procedures, there is no requirement that the actual amount paid under the contract be below the threshold. The contract may be modified to an amount above the threshold to cover unforeseen circumstances such as a change order or an unexpected overrun in the quantity of work, *Jones Seeding & Sprigging Co.*, 63 Comp. Gen. 497 (B-215260), 84-2 CPD ¶ 87.

§ 8.03 MICRO-PURCHASES

Purchases under the micro-purchase threshold may be conducted using any of the simplified acquisition procedures in FAR Subpart 13.3. Micro-purchases do not require the incorporation of provisions or clauses.

The authority to make micro-purchases is frequently delegated to nonprocurement personnel. See FAR 1.603-3, stating:

> (b) Agency heads are encouraged to delegate micro-purchase authority to individuals who are employees of an executive agency or members of the Armed Forces of the United States who will be using the supplies or services being purchased. Individuals delegated this authority are not required to be appointed on an SF 1402, but shall be appointed in writing in accordance with agency procedures.

A contractor must exercise care to ensure that government employees without contracting officer authority do not exceed their delegated authority to make micro-purchases. See, however, *Healthcare Practice Enhancement Network, Inc.*, VABCA 5864, 01-1 BCA ¶ 31,383, holding that a purchase above the micro-purchase threshold was ratified by a contracting officer that did not take action after learning of the unauthorized use of micro-purchase authority.

These purchases are generally made using the governmentwide commercial purchase card. See FAR 13.201(b) stating that these cards are "the preferred method to purchase and to pay for micro-purchases." Sparse guidance on the use of purchase cards is contained in FAR 13.301. Additional guidance is contained in DFARS 213.301.

[A] Sources

Micro-purchases are not reserved exclusively for small businesses, and the Buy American Act is not applicable. However, the requirements in FAR Part 8, Required Sources of Supplies and Services, apply to purchases within the micro-purchase threshold, FAR 13.201(e).

[B] Procedures

Based on the authority granted in 41 U.S.C. § 1902, the following purchase guidelines are set forth in FAR 13.203:

(a) *Solicitation, evaluation of quotations, and award.* (1) To the extent practicable, micro-purchases shall be distributed equitably among qualified suppliers.

(2) Micro-purchases may be awarded without soliciting competitive quotations if the contracting officer or individual appointed in accordance with 1.603-3(b) considers the price to be reasonable.

(3) The administrative cost of verifying the reasonableness of the price for purchases may more than offset potential savings from detecting instances of overpricing. Therefore, action to verify price reasonableness need only be taken if—

(i) The contracting officer or individual appointed in accordance with 1.603-3(b) suspects or has information to indicate that the price may not be reasonable (e.g., comparison to the previous price paid or personal knowledge of the supply or service); or

(ii) Purchasing a supply or service for which no comparable pricing information is readily available (e.g., a supply or service that is not the same as, or is not similar to, other supplies or services that have recently been purchased on a competitive basis).

(b) *Documentation.* If competitive quotations were solicited and award was made to other than the low quoter, documentation to support the purchase may be limited to identification of the solicited concerns and an explanation for the award decision.

See *Michael Ritschard*, Comp. Gen. Dec. B-276820, 97-2 CPD ¶ 32 (protest that agency improperly refused to solicit a potential source denied where agency conducted the acquisition in accordance with micro-purchase procedures), and *Navistar Marine Instrument Corp.*, Comp. Gen. Dec. B-278075, 97-2 CPD ¶ 168 (acquisition was micro-purchase not subject to competition requirements and therefore unpriced purchase order was properly awarded on a sole source basis).

A vendor cannot appeal a directive from a contracting officer to agency personnel with micro-purchase authority to reduce their use of a single vendor in order to distribute such purchases "equitably among qualified suppliers," *Tom & Tony's Auto Wrecker Serv. v. General Servs. Admin.*, GSBCA 15698, 03-1 BCA ¶ 32,161. The board concluded that it had no jurisdiction to hear such an appeal because the vendor had no contract covering more than the numerous single orders that it had received.

[C] Terms and Conditions

There are very few required or specified terms and conditions for micro-purchases. See FAR 13.201(d) stating:

> (d) Micro-purchases do not require provisions or clauses, except as provided at 13.202 and 32.1110. This paragraph takes precedence over any other FAR requirement to the contrary, but does not prohibit the use of any clause.

FAR 13.202 does not require the insertion of a clause in a micro-purchase but states that the Unenforceability of Unauthorized Obligations clause in FAR 52.232-39 "automatically applies" to all micro-purchases. This clause voids any indemnification provision in a license agreement in order to comply with the Anti-Deficiency Act, 31 U.S.C. § 1341.

FAR 32.1110 deals with payment by electronic funds transfer. The provision applicable to micro-purchases states:

> (d) If payment under a written contract will be made by a charge to a Government account with a third party such as a Governmentwide commercial purchase card, then the contracting officer shall insert the clause at 52.232-36, Payment by Third Party, in solicitations and contracts. Payment by a purchase card may also be made under a contract that does not contain the clause at 52.232-36, to the extent the contractor agrees to accept that method of payment. When the clause at 52.232-36 is included in a solicitation or contract, the contracting officer shall also insert the clause at 52.232-33, Payment by Electronic Funds Transfer—System for Award Management, or 52.232-34, Payment by Electronic Funds Transfer—Other Than System for Award Management, as appropriate.

§ 8.04 SIMPLIFIED ACQUISITION PROCEDURES

The rules in FAR Part 13 for conducting simplified acquisitions apply to procurements over the micro-purchase threshold. These rules are intended to give contracting agencies an expeditious way to enter into contracts that do not involve the expenditure of major amounts of government funds, FAR 13.002. While not stated as a purpose, one of the Congressional goals in adopting higher thresholds for simplified acquisitions was to reduce the number of terms and conditions in these contracts in order to attract companies that were neither familiar with nor equipped to deal with the complex terms and conditions required to be included in higher priced contracts.

FAR 13.003(a) requires that the procedures prescribed in FAR Part 13 be used "to the maximum extent practicable." See *Southeast Tech. Servs.*, Comp. Gen. Dec. B-272374.2, 97-1 CPD ¶ 107, where GAO informed an agency that simplified procedures were applicable to a procurement. These procedures are not required to be followed in the circumstances enumerated in FAR 13.003(a):

> This policy does not apply if an agency can meet its requirement using—
>
> (1) Required sources of supply under part 8 (e.g., Federal Prison Industries, Committee for Purchase from People Who are Blind or Severely Disabled, and Federal Supply Schedule contracts);
>
> (2) Existing indefinite delivery/indefinite quantity contracts; or
>
> (3) Other established contracts.

[A] Competition Requirements

In contrast to micro-purchases, agencies are expected to obtain competition on simplified acquisitions.

[1] Degree of Competition

41 U.S.C. § 1901(c) requires that competition be promoted "to the maximum extent practicable." See FAR 13.104 providing the following guidance on meeting this requirement:

> The contracting officer must promote competition to the maximum extent practicable to obtain supplies and services from the source whose offer is the most advantageous to the Government, considering the administrative cost of the purchase.
>
> (a) The contracting officer must not—
>
> (1) Solicit quotations based on personal preference; or
>
> (2) Restrict solicitation to suppliers of well-known and widely distributed makes or brands.
>
> (b) If using simplified acquisition procedures and not providing access to the notice of proposed contract action and solicitation information through the Governmentwide point of entry (GPE), maximum practicable competition ordinarily can be obtained by soliciting quotations or offers from sources within the local trade area. Unless the contract action requires synopsis pursuant to 5.101 and an exception under 5.202 is not applicable, consider solicitation of at least three sources to promote competition to the maximum extent practicable. Whenever practicable, request quotations or offers from two sources not included in the previous solicitation.

As long as the agency makes a reasonable effort to obtain competition and does not intentionally and improperly exclude an interested source from competing, it will be found to have met this standard. In *S.D.M. Supply, Inc.*, Comp.

Gen. Dec. B-271492, 96-1 CPD ¶ 288, *recons. denied*, 96-2 CPD ¶ 203, the GAO indicated that this encompasses both the obtaining and consideration of quotations, stating:

> In meeting this requirement, agencies must make reasonable efforts, consistent with efficiency and economy, to afford all eligible and interested vendors an opportunity to compete. *RMS Indus.*, B-247074, Mar. 18, 1992, 92-1 CPD ¶ 290. Agencies have a fundamental obligation to have procedures in place not only to receive quotations, but also to reasonably safeguard quotations actually received and to give them fair consideration. *East West Research, Inc.*, B-239565, B-239566, Aug. 21, 1990, 90-2 CPD ¶ 147, *aff'd, Defense Logistics Agency—Recons.*, B-239565.2, B-239566.2, Mar. 19, 1991, 91-1 CPD ¶ 298.

The GAO found that the agency failed to meet this standard when it lost quotations due to a previously identified "systemic" failure of its computer system. In doing so, the GAO distinguished those cases where "the occasional negligent loss of a quotation by an agency does not entitle the supplier to any relief." For example, in *Shubhada, Inc.*, Comp. Gen. Dec. B-292437, 2003 CPD ¶ 161, a protest was denied when the protester claimed that the agency had lost a part of its quotation but there was no systemic failure in the agency's procedures. See also *B&S Transport, Inc.*, Comp. Gen. Dec. B-407589, 2012 CPD ¶ 354 (agency did not receive e-mail sent by vendor verifying low price); *American Material Handling, Inc.*, Comp. Gen. Dec. B-281556, 99-1 CPD ¶ 46 (agency did not receive an electronically submitted quotation because its computer malfunctioned).

FAR 13.104(b) provides that when electronic solicitation procedures are not used, maximum practicable competition ordinarily can be obtained by soliciting quotations or offers from at least three sources within the local trade area. However, if the contracting officer is aware of additional sources that wish to participate in the competition, they should be accorded an opportunity to submit offers or quotations. See *Military Agency Servs. Pty., Ltd.*, Comp. Gen. Dec. B-290414, 2002 CPD ¶ 130, stating:

> We have recognized that while the solicitation of three vendors may be sufficient to satisfy the statutory requirement to promote competition to maximum extent practicable where there is no synopsis requirement, see *SF & Wellness*, B-272313, Sept. 23, 1996, 96-2 CPD ¶ 122 at 2; *Omni Elevator Co.*, B-246393, Mar. 6, 1992, 92-1 CPD ¶ 264 at 2, an agency may not, consistent with this requirement, deliberately fail to solicit a responsible source which expressed interest in competing. *Bosco Contracting, Inc.*, B-270366, Mar. 4, 1996, 96-1 CPD ¶ 140 at 3; *Kahn Indus., Inc.; Midwest Dynamometer & Eng'g Co.*, B-251777, B-251777.2, May 3, 1993, 93-1 CPD ¶ 356 at 4-5.

It is difficult to demonstrate that an agency "deliberately excluded" a prospective vendor. See *Phoenix Envt'l Design, Inc.*, Comp. Gen. Dec. B-418304, 2020 CPD ¶ 91 (agency orally solicited three vendors but did not solicit protester because it had submitted high prices on prior procurement); *Bluehorse Corp.*, Comp. Gen. Dec. B-415641, 2018 CPD ¶ 93 (agency orally solicited three vendors and was unaware of protester); *Desktop Alert, Inc.*, Comp. Gen. Dec. B-408707, 2014 CPD ¶ 48 (agency limited vendors to authorized resellers of brand name equipment); *GMA Cover Corp.*, Comp. Gen. Dec. B-288018, 2001 CPD ¶ 144 (vendor was not in local database); and *The Source*, Comp. Gen. Dec. B-266362, 96-1 CPD ¶ 48 (agency supply officer failed to advise contracting officer of the protester's interest in the procurement). In contrast, improper exclusion was found in *Solutions Lucid Grp., LLC*, Comp. Gen. Dec. B-400967, 2009 CPD ¶ 198 (agency knew protester was interested in competing); and *Bosco Contracting, Inc.*, Comp. Gen. Dec. B-270366, 96-1 CPD ¶ 140 (exclusion based on an alleged record of poor past performance which was not supported by the record).

[2] Finding Sources

Contracting officers are not required to perform extensive market research in conducting a simplified acquisition. However, they need to be aware of potential small businesses that have the competence to successfully provide the required products or services. FAR 13.102 contains the following guidance:

> (a) Contracting officers should use the System for Award Management (see subpart 4.11) via https://www.sam.gov as their primary sources of vendor information. Offices maintaining additional vendor source files or listings should identify the status of each source (when the status is made known to the contracting office) in the following categories:
>
> (1) Small business.
>
> (2) Small disadvantaged business.
>
> (3) Women-owned small business concern, including economically disadvantaged women-owned small business concerns and women-owned small business concerns eligible under the Women-owned Small Business (WOSB) Program.
>
> (4) HUBZone small business.
>
> (5) Service-disabled veteran-owned small business.
>
> (6) Veteran-owned small business.
>
> (b) The status information may be used as the basis to ensure that small business concerns are provided the maximum practicable opportunities to respond to solicitations issued using simplified acquisition procedures.

[3] Sole Source

Sole source procurement is authorized if the contracting officer makes a determination that "only one source is reasonably available," FAR 13.106-1(b)(1). The decision will be supported if the contracting officer makes a reasonable decision to limit the competition. See *Medfinity, LLC*, Comp. Gen. Dec. B-412068, 2015 CPD ¶ 378 (procuring brand name medical equipment required to allow transfer of patient data to existing equipment); *Information Ventures, Inc.*, Comp. Gen. Dec. B-290785, 2002 CPD ¶ 152 (access to proprietary membership list needed to carry out contract work); *Midwest Dynamometer & Eng'g Co.*, Comp. Gen. Dec. B-252168, 93-1 CPD ¶ 408 (contracting officer contacted three sources and found that only one would meet the government's needs). However, it is improper to issue sole source purchase orders to selected companies holding blanket purchase agreements, *Envirosolve LLC*, Comp. Gen. Dec. B-294974.4, 2005 CPD ¶ 106.

Sole source procurement can also be justified on the basis of urgency. See *Summit Techs., Inc.*, Comp. Gen. Dec. B-419126, 2020 CPD ¶ 384 (short bridge contract to winning offeror after award blocked by protest); *AeroSage LLC*, Comp. Gen. Dec. B-410648.2, 2015 CPD ¶ 111 (emergency procurement after protest); *Flowlogic*, Comp. Gen. Dec. B-289173, 2002 CPD ¶ 22 (after failed competitive procurement, contracting officer contacted known source of urgently needed software); and *Aleman & Assocs., Inc.*, Comp. Gen. Dec. B-287275, 2001 CPD ¶ 93 (three-month contract issued to incumbent contractor during the resolution of a protest). However, urgency is not a proper justification if the agency is not diligent in conducting market research to identify sources, *Europe Displays, Inc.*, Comp. Gen. Dec. B-297099, 2005 CPD ¶ 214.

[B] Solicitation and Procurement Notices

Agencies are given broad discretion in determining whether to solicit quotes or offers and in choosing techniques to use for the solicitation.

[1] Quote or Offer

The traditional method of solicitation for small purchases has been the Request for Quotations (RFQ), and this method is preserved in the simplified acquisition regulations. This technique places the government in the position of being the offeror with the quoter having the right either to accept or reject the offer. FAR 13.004(a) states:

> A quotation is not an offer and, consequently, cannot be accepted by the Government to form a binding contract. Therefore, issuance by the Government of an order in response to a supplier's quotation does not establish a contract. The order is an offer by the Government to the supplier to buy certain supplies or services upon specified terms and conditions. A contract is established when the supplier accepts the offer.

Using an RFQ presents a substantially lower risk for the supplier than that which would be incurred if the supplier were making an offer. If the quote contains judgmental errors or costs go up, the supplier can escape a loss contract by simply refusing to accept the government's offer or by making a counteroffer, *Bloch Lumber Co.*, ASBCA 23512, 79-2 BCA ¶ 14,167. This reduced risk could reduce contingencies and result in lower quoted prices. Alternatively, a company could agree to perform only part of the quoted work. See *Howell It Is*, AGBCA 2003-137-2, 03-1 BCA ¶ 32,244, where the quoter rejected the award of the full quantity but stated that it would perform a portion of the work. When the contracting officer agreed to this, the board held that the contract was for only that portion of the work.

Using an RFQ also gives the agency more flexibility in conducting a procurement. See, for example, *AeroSage, LLC*, Comp. Gen. Dec. B-417289, 2019 CPD ¶ 151, finding it was reasonable for the contracting officer to require a written acceptance of the government's offer within three hours. See also *Computer Assocs. Int'l, Inc.*, Comp. Gen. Dec. B-292077.3, 2004 CPD ¶ 163, *recons. denied*, 2004 CPD ¶ 110, where the GAO held that it was proper to award a contract to a quoter whose quotation had "expired," reasoning:

> A quotation . . . is not a submission for acceptance by the government to form a binding contract; rather, vendor quotations are purely informational, *Zarc Int'l, Inc.*, B-292708, Oct. 3, 2003, 2003 CPD ¶ 172 at 2. In the RFQ context, it is the government that makes the offer, albeit generally based on the information provided by the vendor in its quotation, and no binding agreement is created until the vendor accepts the offer. Federal Acquisition Regulation (FAR) § 13.004(a). A vendor submitting a price quotation therefore could, the next moment, reject an offer from the government at its quoted price. Because vendors in the RFQ context hold the power of acceptance and their submissions are purely informational, there is nothing for vendors to hold open; thus, it simply does not make sense to apply the acceptance period concept or the attendant rules regarding expiration of bids or offers to RFQs. As a consequence, notwithstanding the statement in Serena's revised price quotation that "this offer is valid through June 31 [sic], 2003," Serena's discounted price was "valid," or not, at Serena's option, both before and after the date mentioned in the quotation—on whatever date the agency might present an offer to the firm.

Under the broad discretion afforded by FAR Part 13, an agency could request offers (either proposals or bids) rather than quotations. However, the regulations give no suggestions as to when it would be advantageous to do so. One reason might be that timing is critical and it is essential to have the contract formed at the time the government makes the award decision. In *Seaborn Health Care, Inc. v United States*, 55 Fed. Cl. 520 (2003), the contracting officer's mistaken "acceptance" of a quotation was found not to be a determinative indication that the agency intended to use competitive negotiation procedures in FAR Part 15 in conducting the procurement.

[2] Method of Solicitation

Solicitations may be made orally, on paper, or electronically. FAR 13.106-1(c) calls for the use of oral solicitations "to the maximum extent practicable" when the procurement does not exceed the simplified acquisition threshold. However, it warns that oral solicitation may not be practicable for procurements over $25,000 (because of the notice requirements). In that case, FAR 13.003(e) and (f) favor the use of electronic commerce. FAR 13.106-1(d) then states:

> *Written solicitations.* If obtaining electronic or oral quotations is uneconomical or impracticable, the contracting officer should issue paper solicitations for contract actions likely to exceed $ 25,000. The contracting officer shall issue a written solicitation for construction requirements exceeding $ 2,000.

It is not clear when obtaining electronic quotations would be impracticable or why that would call for a written solicitation. However, a written solicitation would be appropriate if the contracting officer knows that some local firms do not monitor the governmentwide point of entry. See *Latvian Connection General Trading & Constr., LLC*, Comp. Gen. Dec. B-409442, 2014 CPD ¶ 135 (written solicitation without electronic posting proper for foreign procurement).

When electronic commerce is used, the agency may make the material available only on the Internet and post amendments to the solicitation on the website, allowing potential competitors to register for e-mail notification of such amendments, *USA Information Sys., Inc.*, Comp. Gen. Dec. B-291488, 2002 CPD ¶ 205. Such electronic amendments are adequate to inform offerors of changes to the solicitation, *Linguistic Sys., Inc.*, Comp. Gen. Dec. B-296221, 2005 CPD ¶ 104. However, posting an amendment on an agency website is not constructive notice of receipt (as it would be if posted on the governmentwide point of entry), *Latvian Connection, LLC*, Comp. Gen. Dec. B-411489, 2015 CPD ¶ 251.

Although agencies are required to make Internet postings accessible, they need not be posted on regional listings as long as potential offerors can find the solicitation by a reasonable search, *Jess Bruner Fire Suppression*, Comp. Gen. Dec. B-296533, 2005 CPD ¶ 163. When the solicitation is posted on the governmentwide point of entry, potential vendors should search multiple terms to ensure that they have been diligent, *Creative Mobility Grp., LLC*, Comp. Gen. Dec. B-410380.2, 2014 CPD ¶ 376 (protester failed to search NAICS code).

[3] Procurement Notices

The requirements for public notice of procurements depends upon their estimated dollar value. The regulations do not prescribe any public notice requirements for procurements not in excess of $15,000. For procurements expected to exceed $15,000 but not exceed $25,000, a notice must be publicly displayed or posted electronically, FAR 5.101(a)(2). For procurements in excess of $25,000, a notice must be published in the governmentwide point of entry (*http://www.SAM.gov*) at least 15 days before issuance of a solicitation, FAR 5.203(a). However, solicitation for commercial products or services can be combined with the notice, thus eliminating the 15-day waiting period, FAR 12.603. Exceptions to this notice requirement are contained in FAR 5.202. Detailed guidance on the preparation of notices is contained in FAR 5.207(a).

Notices must contain a "clear and concise description" of the supplies or services being acquired, FAR 5.207(c). See *TMI Mgmt. Sys., Inc.*, Comp. Gen. Dec. B-401530, 2009 CPD ¶ 191 (notice insufficient when it misclassified a procurement for facilities support services under a "miscellaneous" product classification code); *M.D. Thompson Consulting, LLC*, Comp. Gen. Dec. B-297616, 2006 CPD ¶ 41 (notice of sole source contract extension insufficient when it did not describe precise services required); *Information Ventures, Inc.*, Comp. Gen. Dec. B-293518, 2004 CPD ¶ 76 (notice insufficient when it did not match the requisition for the services sent to the contracting office). Agencies are generally expected to notify potential quoters of changes in their requirements. However, if a quoter is aware that the agency is willing to consider alternate products, no formal notice is required, *Aqua-Flo, Inc.*, Comp. Gen. Dec. B-283944, 99-2 CPD ¶ 116.

[4] Time of Submission of Quotes or Offers

Contracting officers are given broad discretion to determine the time and manner for the submission of responses. Deadlines for responses to solicitations are required to be set to afford suppliers a reasonable opportunity to respond, FAR 13.003(h)(2). See FAR 5.203(b) stating:

> The contracting officer should consider the circumstances of the individual acquisition, such as the complexity, commerciality, availability, and urgency, when establishing the solicitation response time.

Short response times have been held to be inadequate, *Information Ventures, Inc.*, Comp. Gen. Dec. B-293541, 2004 CPD ¶ 81 (less than two days); *Sabreliner Corp.*, Comp. Gen. Dec. B-288030, 2001 CPD ¶ 170 (three hours); *Jack Faucett Assocs., Inc.*, Comp. Gen. Dec. B-279347, 98-1 CPD ¶ 155 (one day). However, when price is the only evaluation factor and the need is urgent, short response times have been permitted, *Military Agency Servs. Pty., Ltd.*, Comp. Gen. Dec. B-290414, 2002 CPD ¶ 130.

Responses may be required to be oral, on paper, or submitted by electronic means. The needs of the agency will be considered in determining whether the time and method selected is reasonable. For an early decision affirming the use of electronic means, see *Arcy Mfg. Co.*, Comp. Gen. Dec. B-261538, 95-2 CPD ¶ 283, where the agency stated that it would consider quotations only if submitted on its electronic bulletin board (EBB). The protester claimed that this placed an undue burden on small businesses. GAO denied the protest, stating:

> With regard to the burden imposed on the protesters by the requirement that quotes be electronically transmitted, the essential difference between the electronic method of responding to RFQs and the paper method is that under the electronic method the protester is required to have access to a personal computer, certain telecommunications software, and a modem. These items are readily available for purchase in the commercial marketplace, or, as the record demonstrates, should a vendor not desire to purchase such equipment, access to the EBB can be obtained by contacting an EDI service provider. As such, we fail to see how requiring access to the EBB can be considered overly burdensome to a prospective DISC supplier.
>
> In our view, the record establishes that the agency has a reasonable basis for requiring that quotes be submitted electronically and that this requirement is not overly burdensome on the vendor community. In this regard, we note that no potential vendor is precluded from submitting quotes; only the format of quotes is being restricted. *See Essex Electro Eng'rs, Inc.*, B-252288.2, 93-2 CPD ¶ 47 (protest that proposal format instructions were overly burdensome because they required an unnecessary amount of desktop publishing capabilities was denied where the formatting requirements were determined reasonable and could easily be met using a personal computer). In sum, under the circumstances here, DISC's requirement that quotes be submitted electronically is reasonable and consistent with the mandate that it promote competition to the maximum extent practicable for small purchase acquisitions.

Commonwealth Indus. Specialties, Inc., Comp. Gen. Dec. B-277833, 97-2 CPD ¶ 151, reached the same result.

[5] Standing Quotations

FAR 13.103 permits the use of "standing price quotations" in lieu of the solicitation of specific quotations as follows:

> Authorized individuals do not have to obtain individual quotations for each purchase. Standing price quotations may be used if—
>
> (a) The pricing information is current; and
>
> (b) The Government obtains the benefit of maximum discounts before award.

This procedure is used extensively by the Department of Veterans Affairs.

There is no definition in the FAR of a standing price quotation but generally an agency would call for vendors to submit prices that remain open for a designated period of time—against which orders can be placed without further solicitation. However, in *Southeast Tech. Servs.*, Comp. Gen. Dec. B-289065, 2001 CPD ¶ 206, the agency awarded a contract to a company that had submitted a quotation in response to the agency's contact during market research after it concluded that the responses to its RFQ were unsatisfactory. The GAO held that this was a proper use of the standing price quotation procedure, stating:

> Southeast asserts that MGC's quotation should not have been considered because it was not submitted in response to the RFQ. However, there is no requirement that agencies consider only quotations in response to an RFQ; under FAR § 13.103, a standing quotation properly may be considered in a simplified acquisition if it is current. As noted above, MGC's quotation, received in connection with the agency's earlier attempt to have the laboratory furniture installed, was current, with an acceptance period of 45 days after September 5. Southeast claims that MGC gained an unfair competitive advantage by submitting its quotation before the solicitation was advertised. However, both MGC's and Southeast's quotations were evaluated on the same basis, and the award decision had nothing to do with the times at which the quotations were submitted. There thus is no basis for finding that MGC enjoyed an unfair advantage.

[C] Procedures

FAR 13.003(g) gives wide latitude in the procedures that can be used for simplified acquisitions by allowing "any appropriate combination" of the procedures in other parts of the FAR and encouraging the use of "innovative approaches, to the maximum extent practicable." This has been held to permit the use of reverse auction procedures where the participants are required to allow the agency to reveal their prices (but not their names), *MTB Grp., Inc.*, Comp. Gen. Dec. B-295463, 2005 CPD ¶ 40; *MTB Grp., Inc. v. United States*, 65 Fed. Cl. 516 (2005).

The absence of statutory or regulatory procedures does not permit agencies to use arbitrary or unfair selection procedures. See *General Metals, Inc.*, 72 Comp. Gen. 54 (B-249259), 92-2 CPD ¶ 319, stating that simplified acquisition procedures must be conducted "consistent with the concern for fair and equitable treatment that is inherent in any federal procurement."

[1] Source Selection Procedure

FAR 13.106-1(a)(2) states:

> (i) When soliciting quotations or offers, the contracting officer shall notify potential quoters or offerors of the basis on which award will be made (price alone or price and other factors, e.g., past performance and quality).
>
> (ii) Contracting officers are encouraged to use best value.
>
> * * *

(v) Except for DoD, contracting officers shall ensure the criteria at 15.101-2(c)(1)–(5) are met when using the lowest price technically acceptable source selection process.

(vi) Except for DoD, avoid using the lowest price technically acceptable source selection process to acquire certain supplies and services in accordance with 15.101-2(d).

While this guidance permits the selection decision to be based solely on price, ¶ (ii) appears to encourage the trading off of price with past performance and/or "quality." Quality could be determined by product literature, experience in performing required services or some other means. Use of the lowest price technically acceptable procedure is permitted but significantly restricted by the guidance in ¶ (v) and ¶ (vi). For similar guidance pertaining to DOD, see DFARS 213.106-1(a)(2)(ii).

The use of options is permitted by FAR 13.106-1(e):

(e)Use of options. Options may be included in solicitations, provided the requirements of subpart 17.2 are met and the aggregate value of the acquisition and all options does not exceed the dollar threshold for use of simplified acquisition procedures.

In effect, the threshold requirement practically limits the use of options to acquisitions that are within the special threshold requirements above the standard $250,000 threshold.

[2] Evaluation Factors

When evaluation factors in addition to price are used, their relative importance need not be stated in the solicitation and subfactors need not be included, FAR 13.106-1(a)(2). See, however, *Finlen Complex, Inc.*, Comp. Gen. Dec. B-288280, 2001 CPD ¶ 167, holding that relative importance must be disclosed when the agency requires the submission of "detailed proposals addressing unique government requirements." The GAO has indicated that where relative importance is not indicated, it will be presumed that the factors will be given "approximately equal weight," *Bio-Rad Labs., Inc.*, Comp. Gen. Dec. B-297553, 2007 CPD ¶ 58 (protest granted when agency used subfactors in descending order of importance); *Carol Soloman & Assocs.*, Comp. Gen. Dec. B-271713, 96-2 CPD ¶ 28. However, the FAR does not contain such a statement.

There appears to be considerable flexibility in the amount of information on the evaluation process that must be disclosed in the solicitation. See, for example, *General Metals, Inc.*, 72 Comp. Gen. 54 (B-249259), 92-2 CPD ¶ 319, and *Essner Metal Works, Inc.*, Comp. Gen. Dec. B-251599, 93-1 CPD ¶ 285, holding that the fact that the agency would add or deduct an amount from quoted prices when quoters deviated from the suggested delivery schedule need not be disclosed when the solicitation called for "earliest possible delivery." See also

Vocational Resources, Inc., Comp. Gen. Dec. B-242396, 91-1 CPD ¶ 414, holding that items required to be addressed in the technical proposal were properly evaluated even though "not designated as evaluation factors." The GAO found that "quoters could reasonably expect that their technical proposals would be evaluated in these four areas." Similarly, in *Maryland Office Relocators*, Comp. Gen. Dec. B-291092, 2002 CPD ¶ 198, the agency properly evaluated the amount of packing material in a transportation contract even though this was not stated as an evaluation factor because the RFQ required offerors to specify the number of crates that were included in the offered price. See, however, *Forestry, Surveys & Data*, Comp. Gen. Dec. B-276802.3, 97-2 CPD ¶ 46, which indicates that requiring a quoter to submit an experience questionnaire but not specifically identifying experience as an evaluation factor was improper.

[3] Evaluation

FAR 13.106-2(b) encourages agencies to simplify their evaluation procedures, stating:

> (1) The contracting officer has broad discretion in fashioning suitable evaluation procedures. The procedures prescribed in parts 14 and 15 are not mandatory. At the contracting officer's discretion, one or more, but not necessarily all, of the evaluation procedures in part 14 or 15 may be used.
>
> * * *
>
> (3) If using price and other factors, ensure that quotations or offers can be evaluated in an efficient and minimally burdensome fashion. Formal evaluation plans and establishing a competitive range, conducting discussions, and scoring quotations or offers are not required. Contracting offices may conduct comparative evaluations of offers. Evaluation of other factors, such as past performance—
>
> (i) Does not require the creation or existence of a formal data base; and
>
> (ii) May be based on information such as the contracting officer's knowledge of and previous experience with the supply or service being acquired, customer surveys, or other reasonable basis.

Quotes or offers must be evaluated using the evaluation factors established in the solicitation, FAR 13.106-2(a)(2). The evaluation must also meet a standard of fairness. See *Wellspring Worldwide, Inc.*, Comp. Gen. Dec. B-417282.2, 2020 CPD ¶ 10, stating:

> When using [simplified acquisition] procedures, an agency must conduct the procurement consistent with a concern for fair and equitable competition and must evaluate quotations in accordance with the terms of the solicitation. *McLaurin Gen. Maint., Inc.*, B-411443.2, B-411443.3, Jan. 14, 2016, 2016 CPD ¶ 41 at 3; *ERIE Strayer Co.*, B-406131,

> Feb. 21, 2012, 2012 CPD ¶ 101 at 4. In reviewing protests of an allegedly improper simplified acquisition evaluation, our Office examines the record to determine whether the agency met this standard and exercised its discretion reasonably. *Computers Universal, Inc.*, B-297552, Feb. 14, 2006, 2006 CPD ¶ 42 at 4-5.

In applying this standard, GAO held that the agency had been reasonable in assigning weaknesses to the protester's technical approach and in awarding to a vendor with a lower price even though the protester was rated better in past performance, experience, and technical approach. See also *Kardex Remstar, LLC*, Comp. Gen. Dec. B-418157, 2020 CPD ¶ 56 (agency found quotation unacceptable based on reasonable interpretation of specification requirement); *Far North Forestry, LLC*, Comp. Gen. Dec. B-417502.2, 2019 CPD ¶ 331 (reasonable to award to seemingly unrealistically low price because solicitation did not call for price realism analysis); *LCLC Inc/CfMRF*, Comp. Gen. Dec. B-414357, 2017 CPD ¶ 153 (reasonable to evaluate similar experience as meeting relevant experience requirement); *McLaurin Gen, Maint., Inc.*, Comp. Gen. Dec. B-411443.2, 2016 CPD ¶ 41 (reasonable to count "FY 2014-2015" as two years necessary to meet experience requirement); and *Recogniti, LLP*, Comp. Gen. Dec. B-410658, 2015 CPD ¶ 49 (reasonable to evaluate the past performance of vendor's founder and to award to higher priced, more highly rated vendor). *Compare Marquis Solutions, LLC*, Comp. Gen. Dec. B-419891, 2021 CPD ¶ 316 (agency did not treat quoters evenhandedly and did not adequately document evaluation); *TekSynap Corp.*, Comp. Gen. Dec. B-419464, 2021 CPD ¶ 130 (unreasonable evaluation of technical proposals).

It is proper to quantify a nonprice evaluation factor, *Multi-Spec Prods. Corp.*, Comp. Gen. Dec. B-287135, 2001 CPD ¶ 72 (amount added to price for each day promised delivery exceeded desired delivery time). Agencies may also determine that a quotation is "technically unacceptable" because of insufficient detail in the quotation to demonstrate compliance with the statement of work requirements, *DeVal Corp.*, Comp. Gen. Dec. B-402182, 2009 CPD ¶ 260; or because of poor past performance, *Court Copies & Images, Inc.*, Comp. Gen. Dec. B-277268, 97-2 CPD ¶ 85.

Failure to consider an evaluation factor will result in the award being improper. See, for example, *Ann Riley & Assocs., Ltd.*, Comp. Gen. Dec. B-241309.2, 91-1 CPD ¶ 142, where the Federal Energy Regulatory Commission solicited quotations for stenographic services to be awarded to the firm proposing the most favorable "cost to the public." GAO held that it was improper to award on the basis of a quote that proposed to make bonus payments to the government because they did not constitute a cost to the public. See also *New Brunswick Scientific Co.*, Comp. Gen. Dec. B-246291, 92-1 CPD ¶ 141 (company may not be selected based on technical criteria not included in solicitation). In *Vocational Resources, Inc.*, Comp. Gen. Dec. B-242396, 91-1 CPD ¶ 414, it was held improper for the agency not to use all of the factors that quoters could reasonably expect to be considered.

[4] Communications After Receipt of Quotations

There is no requirement for an agency to communicate with vendors after quotations have been submitted. However, if an agency does seek additional information from a vendor, it appears that GAO will apply the FAR Part 15 clarification/discussion dichotomy. See *Innovative Quality Solutions, LLC*, Comp. Gen. Dec. B-419009.2, 2020 CPD ¶ 407, stating:

> [A]lthough an agency is not required to conduct discussions under simplified acquisition procedures, any exchanges that do occur with vendors in FAR part 13 procurements, like all other aspects of such procurements, must be fair and equitable. *Northstate Heavy Equipment Rental*, B-416821, Dec. 19, 2018, 2018 CPD ¶ 430 at 5. Our Office has looked to FAR part 15 as guidance in making this determination.

See also *American Material Handling, Inc.*, Comp. Gen. Dec. B-410899, 2015 CPD ¶ 106, where a contract specialist sought additional information from two vendors in an attempt to make their quotations technically acceptable but the agency then disqualified the protester on the grounds that the process was a clarification which precluded the use of some of the information because it was a "material modification" to the quotation. GAO agreed with this conclusion, reasoning:

> Where, in response to clarification requests, an agency receives information that seeks to materially modify a proposal or quotation, we will not consider the communications to be discussions where the agency does not rely on the modification in its evaluation. *S4, Inc.*, B-299817, B-299817.2, Aug. 23, 2007, 2007 CPD ¶ 164 at 7.

Similarly, in *International Waste Indus.*, Comp. Gen. Dec. B-411338, 2015 CPD ¶ 196, an agency communicated with a vendor to induce it to agree to the payment terms of the RFQ. GAO rejected the agency's argument that this was a clarification and granted the protest because the agency had not had a discussion with the protester, stating:

> The agency's communications with the awardee invited a response from Mahto [the awardee] that was necessary to determine the acceptability of Mahto's quotation and, in fact, resulted in Mahto being permitted to supplement or alter its quotation. This is quintessentially the nature of discussions, not clarifications. *Kardex Remstar, LLC*, B-409030, Jan. 17, 2014, 2014 CPD ¶ 1 at 4. Accordingly, we conclude that the Air Force, having conducted discussions with Mahto, was required to also conduct discussions with all other vendors in the competition . . .

Compare *Ranger American of the Virgin Islands, Inc.*, Comp. Gen. Dec. B-418539, 2020 CPD ¶ 194, finding that a communication was a clarification not a discussion.

On the other hand, the contracting officer also has considerable discretion in working with quoters to bring their quotations into compliance with the solicitation requirements as long as all quoters are treated evenhandedly. Thus, the contracting officer is free to work with quoters that deviate from the solicitation. See *Williams-Trane Co.*, Comp. Gen. Dec. B-283522, 99-2 CPD ¶ 91, permitting several contacts with noncompliant quoters, and *United Marine Int'l, LLC*, Comp. Gen. Dec. B-281512, 99-1 CPD ¶ 44, permitting negotiation with the only quoter that submitted an acceptable quotation to obtain minor additional work. See also *DataVault Corp.*, Comp. Gen. Dec. B-248664, 92-2 CPD ¶ 166, where the GAO stated:

> [T]he government may seek and consider revisions to a quotation under small purchase procedures any time prior to the government's issuance of a purchase order. *See Instruments & Controls Serv. Co.*, 65 Comp. Gen. 685 [B-222122] (1986), 86-2 CPD ¶ 16; *Oregon Innovative Prods.*, B-231767, Aug. 2, 1988, 88-2 CPD ¶ 110.

It is also proper to require a data package demonstrating that a product meets the specifications if the agency cannot determine that it has been previously accepted, *Viking, Inc.–USA*, Comp. Gen. Dec. B-401528, 2009 CPD ¶ 176. Compare *SKJ & Assocs., Inc.*, Comp. Gen. Dec. B-291533, 2003 CPD ¶ 3, holding that it was improper to reject a proposal for an inadequate technical proposal when the solicitation gave no guidance on the contents of the proposal.

If the contracting officer establishes a competitive range, quoters with substantially similar quotations must be included in the range and the discussions, *Kathryn Huddleston & Assocs., Ltd.*, Comp. Gen. Dec. B-289453, 2002 CPD ¶ 57. When an agency conducts discussions, it will be held to the "meaningful discussion" standard which the GAO has imposed on FAR Part 15 procurements, *Wellspring Worldwide, Inc.*, Comp. Gen. Dec. B-417282.2, 2020 CPD ¶ 10 (no requirement to inform vendor of high price unless it is unreasonably high); *ERIE Strayer Co.*, Comp. Gen. Dec. B-406131, 2012 CPD ¶ 101 (agency improperly conducted discussions only with the awardee).

The lack of a requirement to conduct discussions allows a contracting officer to find a quotation unacceptable without communicating with the quoter, *i4 Grp. Consulting, LLC*, Comp. Gen. Dec. B-418842, 2020 CPD ¶ 270; *Trade Links Logistics Gen. Trading Co.*, Comp. Gen. Dec. B-416571, 2018 CPD ¶ 326, to use negative past performance information without verifying it with the quoter, *John Blood*, Comp. Gen. Dec. B-290593, 2002 CPD ¶ 151; *Lynwood Mach. & Eng'g, Inc.*, Comp. Gen. Dec. B-285696, 2001 CPD ¶ 113, or to use a clearly mistaken price in the evaluation without asking for verification of the price, *Paraclete Contracts*, Comp. Gen. Dec. B-299883, 2007 CPD ¶ 153. Neither is the contracting officer required to resolve ambiguities in quotations, *Liberty Test Equip.*, Comp. Gen. Dec. B-409916, 2014 CPD ¶ 246.

[5] Source Selection Decision

When the agency is trading off price against non-price factors, the contracting officer has broad discretion in selecting the winning quoter. Thus, the contracting officer can decide not to award to a higher-rated, higher-priced proposal because it was not worth paying the associated price premium, *LCLC Inc/CfMRF*, Comp. Gen. Dec. B-414357, 2017 CPD ¶ 153. Such a decision can be made even when the RFQ states that technical factors were significantly more important than price, *Wellspring Worldwide, Inc.*, Comp. Gen. Dec. B-417282.2, 2020 CPD ¶ 10. Conversely, the contracting officer can award to higher priced, more highly rated vendor, *Recogniti, LLP*, Comp. Gen. Dec. B-410658, 2015 CPD ¶ 49.

Award can be made only if the price is determined to be fair and reasonable. See FAR 13.106-3 giving the following guidance:

> (a) Basis for award. Before making award, the contracting officer must determine that the proposed price is fair and reasonable.
>
> (1) Whenever possible, base price reasonableness on competitive quotations or offers.
>
> (2) If only one response is received, include a statement of price reasonableness in the contract file. The contracting officer may base the statement on—
>
> (i) Market research;
>
> (ii) Comparison of the proposed price with prices found reasonable on previous purchases;
>
> (iii) Current price lists, catalogs, or advertisements. However, inclusion of a price in a price list, catalog, or advertisement does not, in and of itself, establish fairness and reasonableness of the price;
>
> (iv) A comparison with similar items in a related industry;
>
> (v) The contracting officer's personal knowledge of the item being purchased;
>
> (vi) Comparison to an independent Government estimate; or
>
> (vii) Any other reasonable basis.
>
> (3) Occasionally an item can be obtained only from a supplier that quotes a minimum order price or quantity that either unreasonably exceeds stated quantity requirements or results in an unreasonable price for the quantity required. In these instances, the contracting officer should inform the requiring activity of all facts regarding the quotation or offer and ask it to confirm or alter its requirement. The file shall be documented to support the final action taken.

FAR 13.106-3 also contains guidance on documentation, stressing that it should be minimalized unless there has been a trade-off decision:

> (b) File documentation and retention. Keep documentation to a minimum. Purchasing offices shall retain data supporting purchases (paper or electronic) to the minimum extent and duration necessary for management review purposes (see subpart 4.8). The following illustrate the extent to which quotation or offer information should be recorded:
>
> (1) Oral solicitations. The contracting office should establish and maintain records of oral price quotations in order to reflect clearly the propriety of placing the order at the price paid with the supplier concerned. In most cases, this will consist merely of showing the names of the suppliers contacted and the prices and other terms and conditions quoted by each.
>
> (2) Written solicitations (see 2.101). For acquisitions not exceeding the simplified acquisition threshold, limit written records of solicitations or offers to notes or abstracts to show prices, delivery, references to printed price lists used, the supplier or suppliers contacted, and other pertinent data.
>
> (3) Special situations. Include additional statements—
>
> (i) Explaining the absence of competition (see 13.106-1 for brand name purchases) if only one source is solicited and the acquisition does not exceed the simplified acquisition threshold (does not apply to an acquisition of utility services available from only one source); or
>
> (ii) Supporting the award decision if other than price-related factors were considered in selecting the supplier.

However, GAO requires sufficient documentation to allow review of the evaluation and source selection decision if a protest is filed, *Marquis Solutions, LLC*, Comp. Gen. Dec. B-419891, 2021 CPD ¶ 316; *TekSynap Corp.*, Comp. Gen. Dec. B-419464, 2021 CPD ¶ 130.

[6] Late Quotations

Late quotations must be considered unless the solicitation contains a late quotations clause, other bidders would be prejudiced, or the agency has begun the award process. See *John Blood*, Comp. Gen. Dec. B-274624, 96-2 CPD ¶ 233, stating:

> Under simplified acquisition procedures, agencies generally may seek and consider revisions to a quotation any time prior to award. *See DataVault Corp.*, B-248664, Sept. 10, 1992, 92-2 CPD ¶ 166. Where, as here, an RFQ does not contain a late quotations provision—but merely requests quotations by a certain date—that date is not considered to be a

firm closing deadline; consequently, so long as the award process has not begun, an agency is not precluded from considering a quotation received after that date. *AFT Constr. Co., Inc.*, B-260829, July 18, 1995, 95-2 CPD ¶ 29.

In *Instruments & Controls Serv. Co.*, 65 Comp. Gen. 685 (B-222122), 86-2 CPD ¶ 16, the GAO stated that the "failure to do so would be inconsistent with the statutory requirement for competition to the maximum extent practicable." See also *Payne Constr.*, Comp. Gen. Dec. B-291629, 2003 CPD ¶ 46; *G.E.G. Sugar Blues & Noe's Colors*, Comp. Gen. Dec. B-284117, 2000 CPD ¶ 29, granting a protest because the agency did not consider a late quotation. Two exceptions to this requirement were noted in *Compspace Corp.*, Comp. Gen. Dec. B-274037, 96-2 CPD ¶ 186. Late quotations would not have to be considered if substantial activity had transpired in evaluating quotations or if other firms would be prejudiced. The GAO explained:

> When, as here, the RFQ does not contain a late quotations clause, but merely requests quotations by a certain date, that date is not considered a firm date for purposes of determining whether a quotation may form the basis for an award. *A&B Trash Serv.*, B-250322, Jan. 22, 1993, 93-1 CPD ¶ 53. Rather, the agency is not precluded from considering a quotation received after the announced due date provided that no substantial activity has transpired in evaluating quotations, and the other firms submitting quotations would not be prejudiced. *Id.* Activity is deemed substantial where the agency has begun the award process prior to receiving the late quotation. *Adrian Supply Co.*, 68 Comp. Gen. 575 (1989), 89-2 CPD ¶ 99.

See also *Joint Sys., Inc.*, Comp. Gen. Dec. B-298573, 2006 CPD ¶ 150 (proper to reject information submitted after evaluation had been completed); *RMG Indus. Sales*, Comp. Gen. Dec. B-281632, 99-1 CPD ¶ 58 (proper to reject late amended final quotation after "substantial activity" in evaluating quotations had occurred).

Although a late quotations clause is not prescribed by the regulations, purchasing agents and contracting officers may include such a clause in a solicitation. The GAO decisions indicate that a late quotations provision must expressly provide that quotations must be received by the specified date to be considered. See, for example, *Instruments & Controls Serv. Co.*, 65 Comp. Gen. 685 (B-222122), 86-2 CPD ¶ 16. Thus, language that "merely suggests" the submission of quotes by a specified date would not qualify. Neither would language that advises quoters that failure to submit a quote by a specified date "may result in your quotation not being considered for award," *Adrian Supply Co.*, 68 Comp. Gen. 575 (B-235352), 89-2 CPD ¶ 99.

If a late quotations clause is included, it will be strictly enforced, *Data Integrators, Inc.*, Comp. Gen. Dec. B-310928, 2008 CPD ¶ 27; *Zebra Techs. Int'l, LLC*, Comp. Gen. Dec. B-296158, 2005 CPD ¶ 122. See also *Alpha*

Executive Servs., Inc., Comp. Gen. Dec. B-246173, 92-1 CPD ¶ 197, holding that the agency "acted reasonably" in declining to consider a late proposal when the solicitation had included a late quotations clause. *Compare Williams-Trane Co.*, Comp. Gen. Dec. B-283522, 99-2 CPD ¶ 91, denying a protest of acceptance of late information from the winning vendor when the clause was included because the agency had allowed all of the quoters to submit information after the quotation date.

Some simplified acquisitions use the standard clauses for commercial items. In that case, the Instructions to Offerors—Commercial Items clause at FAR 52.212-1 states:

> (f) *Late submissions, modifications, revisions, and withdrawals of offers.* (1) Offerors are responsible for submitting offers, and any modifications, revisions, or withdrawals, so as to reach the Government office designated in the solicitation by the time specified in the solicitation. If no time is specified in the solicitation, the time for receipt is 4:30 p.m., local time, for the designated Government office on the date that offers or revisions are due.
>
> (2)(i) Any offer, modification, revision, or withdrawal of an offer received at the Government office designated in the solicitation after the exact time specified for receipt of offers is "late" and will not be considered unless it is received before award is made, the Contracting Officer determines that accepting the late offer would not unduly delay the acquisition; and—
>
> > (A) If it was transmitted through an electronic commerce method authorized by the solicitation, it was received at the initial point of entry to the Government infrastructure not later than 5:00 p.m. one working day prior to the date specified for receipt of offers; or
> >
> > (B) There is acceptable evidence to establish that it was received at the Government installation designated for receipt of offers and was under the Government's control prior to the time set for receipt of offers; or
> >
> > (C) If this solicitation is a request for proposals, it was the only proposal received.

This is a confusing provision when it is incorporated into an RFQ because it refers to "offers" which are not submitted in response to an RFQ. Nonetheless, it was strictly enforced to bar the award based on a late quotation in *M. Braun, Inc.*, Comp. Gen. Dec. B-298935.2, 2007 CPD ¶ 96. The GAO "assumed" the clause applied to quotations because the agency had cited the clause in defending the protest.

When electronic quotations are submitted, the quote is considered received on the date it is received by the agency, not the date the quoter submits it to a Value Added Network, *Comspace Corp.*, Comp. Gen. Dec. B-274037, 96-2 CPD ¶ 186. There, the only evidence of government receipt showed that the quote was received by the government after award, too late to be considered.

[a] Disclosure of Prices

There are no rules in FAR Part 13 prohibiting the disclosure of prices during a competition. However, the Procurement Integrity Act, 41 U.S.C. §§ 2101-07, prohibits the disclosure of vendor prices, with certain exceptions. See *MTB Grp., Inc.*, Comp. Gen. Dec. B-295463, 2005 CPD ¶ 40, ruling that disclosure of prices in a reverse auction was permissible, stating:

> [T]he Act prohibits government officials and those acting on behalf of the government from knowingly disclosing contractor quotation or proposal information before award. 41 U.S.C. § 423(a) [now § 2102]. However, that prohibition is not absolute. Rather, the Act specifically provides that it does not "restrict the disclosure of information to, or its receipt by, any person or class of persons authorized in accordance with applicable agency regulations or procedures, to receive the information," 41 U.S.C. § 423(h)(1) [now § 2107(1)], and does not "restrict a contractor from disclosing its own quote or proposal information or the recipient from receiving that information." 41 U.S.C. § 423(h)(2) [now § 2107(2)]. We think the price disclosure under HUD's reverse auction procedures falls within the exception language, although we are aware of no judicial or other authoritative interpretation of these provisions. First, under the procedure the agency has established, vendors actually will disclose their own prices—albeit, as a condition of competing—by entering the prices on the auction website; as noted, a vendor's disclosing its own price is not prohibited under the Act. Moreover, even if the price disclosure were considered to be by government officials due to its nature as a precondition to a vendor's competing, the disclosure is pursuant, and integral, to the reverse auction procurement procedures established by the agency; we thus would view the disclosure as being to persons authorized by agency procedures to receive the information, consistent with the exception language. *See generally DGS Contract Serv., Inc. v. United States*, 43 Ct. Cl. 227, 236 (1999); *Ocean Servs., LLC.*, B-292511.2, Nov. 6, 2003, 2003 CPD ¶ 206 at 5 (neither the Act nor the FAR establishes an absolute prohibition against disclosure of price information, and both make clear that prices can be disclosed under certain circumstances).

See also *MTB Grp., Inc. v. United States*, 65 Fed. Cl. 516 (2005), reaching the same conclusion.

[b] Award

Although the FAR contains no provision on failure to meet mandatory requirements, award cannot be made to a quoter that does not agree to meet such requirements. See *CAMS, Inc.*, Comp. Gen. Dec. B-292546, 2003 CPD ¶ 191, stating:

> A quote that fails to conform to material terms and conditions of the solicitation should be considered unacceptable and may not form the basis

> for an award. *United Coatings*, B-291978.2, July 7, 2003, 2003 CPD ¶ 146; *see Rel-Tek Sys., & Design, Inc.*, B-280463.3, Nov. 25, 1998, 99-1 CPD ¶ 2 at 3. The terms in a solicitation governing inspection and acceptance are material requirements that must be met without qualification—regardless of whether the solicitation sets them out as minimum requirements—because they affect the government's rights under the resulting contract.

See also *Multi-Spec Products Corp.*, Comp. Gen. Dec. B-287135, 2001 CPD ¶ 72, denying a protest that the selected contractor did not meet a mandatory delivery date because the RFQ allowed later dates. Had the delivery date been mandatory, award would have been improper. See *Muddy Creek Oil & Gas, Inc.*, Comp. Gen. Dec. B-296836, 2005 CPD ¶ 143 (agency properly rejected quotation that altered terms in the statement of work); *American Floor Consultants & Installations, Inc.*, Comp. Gen. Dec. B-294934, 2004 CPD ¶ 248 (agency properly rejected quotation that did not contain descriptive literature to support the offered "equal" item); *Elementar Americas, Inc.*, Comp. Gen. Dec. B-282698, 99-2 CPD ¶ 17 (proper to reject quotation that did not furnish required descriptive literature to show that the technical requirements were met); and *CDS Network Sys., Inc.*, Comp. Gen. Dec. B-281200, 98-2 CPD ¶ 154 (proper to reject a quotation that did not provide required documentation).

Award need not be made to the firm submitting the lowest quotation if the contracting officer makes a good faith finding that award to a different firm is in the best interests of the government and that the price is reasonable, *Environmental Tectonics Corp.*, Comp. Gen. Dec. B-280573, 98-2 CPD ¶ 140 (superior past performance justified paying higher price); *University of Kansas Med. Center*, Comp. Gen. Dec. B-278400, 98-1 CPD ¶ 120 (technical superiority justified paying higher price); *Creative Elecs., Inc.*, Comp. Gen. Dec. B-206684, 83-2 CPD ¶ 95 (assumed better warranty service justified paying higher price). However, the decision to award to a higher priced quoter in order to obtain best value must be rational, *e-LYNXX Corp.*, Comp. Gen. Dec. B-292761, 2003 CPD ¶ 219. See *National Aerospace Grp., Inc.*, Comp. Gen. Dec. B-281958, 99-1 CPD ¶ 82, holding that it was not reasonable to pay a significantly higher price merely because the low quoter had no prior performance record. In that case the contracting officer had made no comparative assessment of the risk involved in dealing with a new vendor. Compare *Northwest Mgmt., Inc.*, Comp. Gen. Dec. B-277503, 97-2 CPD ¶ 108, finding an award to a slightly higher priced quoter to be rational when the contracting officer assessed the lower priced quoter as posing more risk.

Agencies may make either a single ("all-or-none") award or multiple award if vendors are so advised in the solicitation, FAR 13.101(b)(1). If the solicitation is silent, multiple awards must be made if that yields the lowest total price to the government after considering administrative cost savings, *Para Scientific Co.*, Comp. Gen. Dec. B-299046.2, 2007 CPD ¶ 37.

Where price was identified as the only evaluation factor, it was improper not to award to the quoter that took no exception to the RFQ and submitted the lowest price, *Cromartie Constr. Co.*, Comp. Gen. Dec. B-271788, 96-2 CPD ¶ 48. The GAO also indicated that where price is the only evaluation factor, the quote of a small business may not be rejected because the agency believes that it is too low. In such a situation, the matter is one of responsibility, requiring reference to the Small Business Administration. The same result was reached in *Possehn Consulting*, Comp. Gen. Dec. B-278579, 98-1 CPD ¶ 10.

If an agency has solicited offers, award will be made by accepting the offer in the same way that this is accomplished in standard negotiated procurement. If an agency has solicited quotations, award will be made by issuance of a purchase order. In such cases, the contracting officer must determine whether the contractor will be required to provide a written acceptance of the purchase order—forming a bilateral contract, FAR 13.302-3(a). Alternatively, FAR 13.004(b) states:

> [T]he supplier may indicate acceptance by furnishing the supplies or services ordered or by proceeding with the work to the point where substantial performance has occurred.

If the latter procedure is adopted, the government is not contractually bound until substantial performance has occurred. Thereafter, it may terminate or cancel the order, FAR 13.004(c), but it will be subject to compensate the contractor in accordance with FAR 13.302-4. However, if the contractor does not deliver the products at the time specified in the RFQ, the government's offer will be considered to have lapsed with the result that the government is not liable to compensate the contractor for costs incurred to that time, *Smart Bus. Machines v. United States*, 72 Fed. Cl. 706 (2006); *Rex Sys., Inc.*, ASBCA 45,301, 93-3 BCA ¶ 26,065.

[c] Documentation and Retention

FAR 13.106-3 contains the following requirement for very minimal documentation:

> (b) *File documentation and retention*. Keep documentation to a minimum. Purchasing offices shall retain data supporting purchases (paper or electronic) to the minimum extent and duration necessary for management review purposes (see subpart 4.8). The following illustrate the extent to which quotation or offer information should be recorded:
>
> > (1) Oral solicitations. The contracting office should establish and maintain records of oral price quotations in order to reflect clearly the propriety of placing the order at the price paid with the supplier concerned. In most cases, this will consist merely of showing the names of the suppliers contacted and the prices and other terms and conditions quoted by each.

(2) Written solicitations (see 2.101). For acquisitions not exceeding the simplified acquisition threshold, limit written records of solicitations or offers to notes or abstracts to show prices, delivery, references to printed price lists used, the supplier or suppliers contacted, and other pertinent data.

(3) Special situations. Include additional statements—

(i) Explaining the absence of competition (see 13.106-1 for brand name purchases) if only one source is solicited and the acquisition does not exceed the simplified acquisition threshold (does not apply to an acquisition of utility services available from only one source); or

(ii) Supporting the award decision if other than price-related factors were considered in selecting the supplier.

In *Universal Bldg. Maint., Inc.*, Comp. Gen. Dec. B-282456, 99-2 CPD ¶ 32, the GAO granted a protest because the agency provided no documentation to support a price/technical trade-off. This would indicate that agencies should include a short description of the basis for determining the winning quoter in the contract file.

[d] Notice and Debriefing

FAR 13.106-3(c) states that notice to "unsuccessful suppliers shall be given only if requested or required." However, this would not appear to preclude the agency from giving notice as a courtesy. Furthermore, a notice of award is required to be published electronically if the award is over $25,000 and "if there is likely to be any subcontract," 41 U.S.C. § 1708(a)(3); FAR 5.301(a). Once notification is requested, an agency's failure to respond in a timely fashion is improper, *Professional Data Sys.*, GSBCA 8475-P, 86-3 BCA ¶ 19,083.

If a supplier requests information on an award that was based on factors other than price alone, FAR 13.106-3(d) provides that a brief explanation of the basis for the contract award decision must be provided.

[D] Use for Commercial Products and Services

FAR 13.500(a) authorizes contracting agencies to use the simplified procedures of Part 13 if the contracting officer "reasonably expects, based on the nature of the supplies or services sought, and on market research, that offers will include only commercial products or commercial services." Such procedures may be used for procurements not exceeding $7,500,000, or $15,000,000 if the procurement is "in support of a contingency operation or to facilitate the defense against or recovery from cyber, nuclear, biological, chemical, or radiological attack," FAR 13.500(e). The simplified procedures are to be used to the "maximum extent practicable," FAR 13.500(b).

FAR 13.501 requires special documentation when sole source contracts are awarded under this authority. This documentation must meet the requirements of FAR 6.303-2 in justifying the solicitation of only one source, FAR 13.501(a)(1)(ii). For proposed contracts over $250,000, but not exceeding $750,000, the contracting officer must certify that the justification for sole source procurement is accurate and complete, FAR 13.501(a)(2)(i). For proposed contracts in excess of $750,000, but not exceeding $15,000,000, the approval must be by the competition advocate of the procuring activity on a non-delegable basis, FAR 13.501(a)(2)(ii). For proposed contracts in excess of $15,000,000, but not exceeding $75,000,000 (for DOD, NASA, and the Coast Guard $100,000,000), the approval must be by the head of the procuring activity on a non-delegable basis, FAR 13.501(a)(2)(iii). For proposed contracts in excess of $75,000,000 (for DOD, NASA, and the Coast Guard $100,000,000), the approval must be by the senior procurement executive head of the agency on a non-delegable basis (except for DOD), FAR 13.501(a)(2)(iv).

For all such procurements, the contract file is to include a brief description of the procedures used, the number of offers received, the basis for the award, and any justification required for a sole source procurement, FAR 13.501(b).

[E] Blanket Purchase Agreements

Blanket purchase agreements (BPAs) are a "simplified method of filling anticipated repetitive needs for supplies or services by establishing 'charge accounts' with qualified sources of supply," FAR 13.303-1(a). In entering into a BPA, the parties agree to a set of terms and conditions that will be applicable to future purchases but do not agree to any specific purchase.

BPAs are recommended for use by FAR 13.303-2(a) in implementing the simplified acquisition procedures in the following circumstances:

> (1) There is a wide variety of items in a broad class of supplies or services that are generally purchased, but the exact items, quantities, and delivery requirements are not known in advance and may vary considerably.
>
> (2) There is a need to provide commercial sources of supply for one or more offices or projects in a given area that do not have or need authority to purchase otherwise.
>
> (3) The use of this procedure would avoid the writing of numerous purchase orders.
>
> (4) There is no existing requirements contract for the same supply or service that the contracting activity is required to use.

The major advantage of BPAs is that they permit a vendor to respond to a number of orders and to submit consolidated invoices on a regular basis. FAR 13.303-3(a)(6) provides guidance on the invoicing provisions that can be included in BPAs. A BPA is also a convenient way for a contracting officer to negotiate an across-the-board discount for all of the supplies or services furnished by a single supplier, FAR 13.303-2(d).

BPAs are established by contracting officers when they find that repetitive purchases are being made from a supplier. There is no need for a requisition for any specific supplies or services to initiate a BPA, FAR 13.303-2(d).

[1] Number and Effect of BPAs

BPAs may be established with a single supplier or with multiple suppliers depending on the needs of the agency, FAR 13.303-2(c). However, the existence of a BPA does not justify purchasing from the holder of a single BPA on a sole source basis or avoiding any required small business set-aside, FAR 13.303-5(c). FAR 13.303-5(d) contains the following guidance:

> (d) If, for a particular purchase greater than the micro-purchase threshold, there is an insufficient number of BPAs to ensure maximum practicable competition, the contracting officer shall—
>
> (1) Solicit quotations from other sources (see 13.105) and make the purchase as appropriate; and
>
> (2) Establish additional BPAs to facilitate future purchases if—
>
> (i) Recurring requirements for the same or similar supplies or services seem likely;
> (ii) Qualified sources are willing to accept BPAs; and
> (iii) It is otherwise practical to do so.

In *Envirosolve LLC*, Comp. Gen. Dec. B-294974.4, 2005 CPD ¶ 106, GAO held that it was improper to award BPAs without competition and then issue orders against them on a noncompetitive basis, interpreting this competition requirement as follows:

> Agencies are not required to request proposals or to conduct a competition before establishing BPAs. *Information Sys. Tech. Corp.*, B-280013.2, Aug. 6, 1998, 98-2 CPD ¶ 36 at 3. After a BPA is established, however, otherwise applicable competition requirements still apply to all procurements under the BPA. FAR § 13.303-5(a) (BPA to be used only for purchases that are otherwise authorized by law or regulation); *Information Sys. Tech. Corp., supra.* Moreover, the existence of a BPA does not justify purchasing from only one source. FAR § 13.303-5(c). If, for a procurement in excess of $2,500 there is an insufficient number of established BPAs to ensure maximum practicable competition, the contracting officer must solicit quotations from other sources. FAR § 13.303-5(d)(1).

GAO subsequently ruled that there is no requirement for competition among holders of multiple BPAs because the agency conducted competition in selecting these BPA contractors, *Logan, LLC*, Comp. Gen. Dec. B-294974.6, 2006 CPD

¶ 188 (agency rotated awards and excluded protester from award during investigation of improprieties). In contrast, it is proper under this FAR guidance to compete non-BPA holders against BPA holders. See *AudioCARE Sys.*, Comp. Gen. Dec. B-283985, 2000 CPD ¶ 24, discussing a procurement where this occurred.

When an agency conducts a competition among BPA holders, its award decision will be subject to protest, *C&B Constr., Inc.*, Comp. Gen. Dec. B-401988.2, 2010 CPD ¶ 1. In that case, the protest was sustained because the agency did not document its trade-off decision sufficiently to demonstrate that the higher priced quotation was the best value.

The late quotation rules, discussed earlier, apply to quotations for BPAs, *Zebra Techs. Int'l, LLC*, Comp. Gen. Dec. B-296158, 2005 CPD ¶ 122.

A BPA is not a contract because the government is not obligated to issue any orders. See *Production Packaging*, ASBCA 53662, 03-2 BCA ¶ 32,338, holding that a supplier with a BPA has "no legal expectation to receive exclusive orders" and stating at 159,972:

> It is well established that a BPA is not a contract. Rather, a BPA is nothing more than an agreement of terms by which the Government could purchase. *See, e.g., Mid-America Officials Ass'n*, ASBCA No. 38678, 89-3 BCA ¶ 22,231 at 111,775-76. Until the Government places an order under a BPA, no contract is formed for lack of consideration. Julian Freeman, ASBCA No. 46675, 94-3 BCA ¶ 27,280 at 135,906.

Even if an order is issued under a BPA, that order can still be terminated if the BPA includes a Termination for the Convenience of the Government clause, *Dehdari General Trading & Contracting EST.*, ASBCA 53987, 03-1 BCA ¶ 32,249. In that case, the order for a one-year lease was terminated after one month with no liability for the government to pay the rental for the remaining 11 months. See also *Zhengxing v. United States*, 71 Fed. Cl. 732, *aff'd*, 204 Fed. Appx. 885 (2006), where failure to issue orders was held not to be an improper termination, and *Janice L. Cox*, ASBCA 50587, 03-1 BCA ¶ 32,205, where reassigning the work to another supplier after work had commenced was treated as a termination for convenience not a breach of the order.

[2] Terms and Conditions

FAR 13.303-3(a) requires that BPAs contain, at a minimum, terms and conditions covering the following matters:

> (1) *Description of agreement*. A statement that the supplier shall furnish supplies or services, described in general terms, if and when requested by the contracting officer (or the authorized representative of the contracting officer) during a specified period and within a stipulated aggregate amount, if any.

(2) *Extent of obligation.* A statement that the Government is obligated only to the extent of authorized purchases actually made under the BPA.

(3) *Purchase limitation.* A statement that specifies the dollar limitation for each individual purchase under the BPA (see 13.303-5(b)).

(4) *Individuals authorized to purchase under the BPA.* A statement that a list of individuals authorized to purchase under the BPA, identified either by title of position or by name of individual, organizational component, and the dollar limitation per purchase for each position title or individual shall be furnished to the supplier by the contracting officer.

(5) *Delivery tickets.* A requirement that all shipments under the agreement, except those for newspapers, magazines, or other periodicals, shall be accompanied by delivery tickets or sales slips that shall contain [prescribed] minimum information.

* * *

(6) *Invoices.* One of the following statements shall be included [prescribing the use of either summary invoices or itemized invoices submitted at least monthly].

BPAs must also contain the applicable clauses for simplified acquisitions that are discussed below, FAR 13.303-4. They can also include the optional Terms and Conditions—Simplified Acquisitions (Other Than Commercial Items) clause in FAR 52.213-4 when appropriate, FAR 13.303-8.

[F] Laws and Clauses Not Applicable

In carrying out the objective of reducing the number of contract clauses applicable to simplified acquisitions, 41 U.S.C. § 1905 makes certain laws inapplicable to these procurements. These laws are listed in FAR 13.005. FAR 13.006 lists additional provisions and clauses that are inapplicable to contracts and subcontracts at or below the simplified acquisition threshold even though the provision or clause is merely for the purpose of informing contractors that they are subject to a statute. Contractors performing simplified acquisitions must be independently aware that they are subject to these statutes.

The Terms and Conditions—Simplified Acquisitions (Other Than Commercial Products and Commercial Services) clause at FAR 52.213-4 may be used in simplified acquisitions over the micro-purchase threshold that are not for commercial products or services, FAR 13.302-5(d). This clause lists the statutory and regulatory provisions that are applicable to simplified acquisitions as well some of the standard provisions covering inspection/acceptance, excusable delays, termination for convenience, termination for cause and warranty. It may be tailored to fit the needs of the procuring agency, FAR 13.302-5(d)(2)(ii), pursuant to the following guidance:

Modifications (i.e., additions, deletions, or substitutions) must not create a void or internal contradiction in the clause. For example, do not add

> an inspection and acceptance or termination for convenience requirement unless the existing requirement is deleted. Also, do not delete a paragraph without providing for an appropriate substitute.

While this clause is not mandatory, a clause of this nature is necessary to inform the contracting parties of the basic terms of their contract.

When the simplified acquisition is for commercial products or services, the clauses applicable to such procurement, as discussed in Chapter 9, should be used.

[G] Forms

There are a number of forms that are available, but not mandatory, when using simplified acquisition procedures. FAR 13.307(a) calls for the use of the SF 1449, Solicitation/Contract/Order for Commercial Products or Commercial Services, in most instances where commercial products or services are being procured. For noncommercial products or services, FAR 13.307(b) provides:

> (1) Except when quotations are solicited electronically or orally, the SF 1449; SF 18, Request for Quotations; or an agency form/automated format may be used. Each agency request for quotations form/automated format should conform with the SF 18 or SF 1449 to the maximum extent practicable.
>
> (2) Both SF 1449 and OF 347, Order for Supplies or Services, are multipurpose forms used for negotiated purchases of supplies or services, delivery or task orders, inspection and receiving reports, and invoices. An agency form/automated format also may be used.

FAR 13.307(c) provides that three forms can be used for both commercial and noncommercial products or services: the OF 336, Continuation Sheet, the OF 348, Order for Supplies or Services Schedule—Continuation, and the SF 30, Amendment of Solicitation/Modification of Contract. Alternatively, agency regulations may prescribe their own forms or an automated format.

FAR 13.306 prescribes the use of the SF 44, Purchase Order—Invoice—Voucher, which is a multipurpose pocket-size purchase order form designated primarily for on-the-spot, over-the-counter micro-purchases.

FAR 13.307(e) prescribes the use of the SF 1165, Receipt for Cash—Subvoucher, for purchases using imprest funds or third-party drafts.

For military departments, DD Form 1155, Orders for Supplies or Services, must be used for purchases made using the simplified acquisition procedures of FAR Part 13, DOD PGI 213.307-1(b). This guidance prohibits the use of Optional Forms 347 and 348. Civilian agencies may also use special forms when using simplified acquisition procedures. For example, the General Services Administration uses GSA Form 300, Order for Supplies or Services; GSA Form 3186, Order for Supplies or Services; or GSA Form 3186B, Order for Supplies or Services (EDI) when making simplified acquisitions, GSA Acquisition Manual 513.302-70(c). The Department of Agriculture uses Form AD-838, Purchase Order, in lieu of Optional Forms 347 and 348, AGAR 453.213. The Environmental Protection Agency permits the use of Form 1900-8, Procurement Request/Order, in lieu of Optional Forms 347 and 348 for simplified acquisitions, EPAAR 1513.505. DOE provides that Optional Forms 347 and 348 or DOE F 4250.3, Order for Supplies or Services, may be used for purchase orders using simplified acquisition procedures, DEAR 913.307(b).

CHAPTER 9

COMMERCIAL PRODUCTS AND SERVICES

§ 9.01 INTRODUCTION

In recent years, there have been a number of initiatives in government procurement designed to take advantage of products and services available in the commercial marketplace. These initiatives have focused on the use of commercial product or service descriptions rather than government-unique specifications. They have also been aimed at using commercial buying practices and eliminating statutory and regulatory provisions that either discourage commercial firms from competing for government business or unnecessarily increase the costs of performance. As a result, a number of provisions were adopted by the Federal Acquisition Streamlining Act of 1994 (FASA), Pub. L. No. 103-355, and the Clinger-Cohen Act of 1996, Pub. L. No. 104-106, to promote the acquisition of "commercial items." The term "commercial items" was used from 1994 until 2021 when the FAR was revised to substitute the terms "commercial products" and "commercial services." This change was made by the National Defense Authorization Act for Fiscal Year 2018, Pub. L. No. 115-232, to more clearly state that the policies calling for maximum use of commercial buying practices apply to both services and products.

The statutory provisions, designed to promote and facilitate the procurement of commercial products and services, include 10 U.S.C. § 3453 (formerly § 2377(b)) which requires that:

> The head of an agency shall ensure that procurement officials in that agency, to the maximum extent practicable—
>
> (1) acquire commercial services, commercial products, or nondevelopmental items other than commercial products to meet the needs of the agency;
>
> (2) require prime contractors and subcontractors at all levels under the agency contracts to incorporate commercial services, commercial products, or nondevelopmental items other than commercial products as components of items supplied to the agency;
>
> (3) modify requirements in appropriate cases to ensure that the requirements can be met by commercial services or commercial products or, to the extent that commercial products suitable to meet the agency's needs are not available, nondevelopmental items other than commercial products;
>
> (4) state specifications in terms that enable and encourage bidders and offerors to supply commercial services or commercial products or, to the extent that commercial products suitable to meet the agency's needs are not available, nondevelopmental items other than commercial products in response to the agency solicitations;
>
> (5) revise the agency's procurement policies, practices, and procedures not required by law to reduce any impediments in those policies, practices, and procedures to the acquisition of commercial products and commercial services; and

(6) require training of appropriate personnel in the acquisition of commercial products and commercial services.

Substantially the same requirements are included in 41 U.S.C. § 3307(c). Congress has also granted special authority to use commercial services and commercial products procurement procedures in 41 U.S.C. § 1903(c). In addition, agency competition advocates are responsible for "promoting the acquisition of commercial services and commercial products," 41 U.S.C. § 1705(c). Other provisions dealing with the procurement of commercial products and services are scattered throughout various statutes that are discussed in the following material.

FAR Part 12 is the primary regulation implementing the commercial products and services statutes, while FAR Subpart 13.5 covers the procurement of commercial products and services using the simplified acquisition procedures discussed in Chapter 8. In addition, a number of different FAR Parts deal with commercial products and services. For example, requirements for market research, the drafting of specifications, and the solicitation of offers are covered in FAR Parts 10, 11, and 5, respectively. The rules applicable to pricing commercial products and services are contained in FAR Part 15. See Chapter 13. This chapter deals with the special rules applicable to contracts for commercial products and services excluding procurements using simplified acquisition procedures in FAR Subpart 13.5.

Although commercial products and services procedures permit agencies to adopt commercial practices to the greatest possible extent, they do not alter the basic rules of contracting as discussed in Chapters 2 and 3. See *Altos Fed. Grp.*, ASBCA 53523, 07-2 BCA ¶ 33,657, rejecting the government's argument that the commercial item procedures in effect at that time precluded a contractor's claim for a mistake in its offer that should have been seen by the contracting officer, and stating at 166,673:

> The Board considered a similar argument in *Orion Technology, Inc.*, ASBCA No. 54608, 06-1 BCA ¶ 33,266, wherein appellant sought contract reformation based upon a unilateral mistake discovered after award. The government defended against the claim by asserting that FAR 14.407 Mistakes in Bids did not apply to awards made under FAR subpart 13.5 Test Program for Certain Commercial Items, and argued that simplified acquisition procedures imposed only the duty of reasonableness upon the contracting officer. The Board disagreed, and distinguished facilitating the procurement process by avoiding unnecessarily constrictive procedures from precluding contractors from obtaining relief due to government error, and held that "While [FAR 13.106-2 Evaluation of Quotations or Offers ¶ (b)(1)] gives the contracting officer flexibility as to evaluation procedures, it does not affect the principles applicable to remedies for mistakes disclosed after award," *Orion*, 06-1 BCA at 164,853. *Accord, Finlen Complex, Inc.*, [Comp. Gen. Dec.] B-288280, [2001 CPD ¶ 167] at 7 ("the labeling of a procurement as 'simplified' does not absolve the agency from its obligation to treat vendors fairly").

§ 9.02 DEFINITIONS

The term "commercial item," as originally defined in 41 U.S.C. § 103(12) and FAR 2.101, included both commercial supplies and commercial services. However, supplies and services were given disparate treatment, with the definition of commercial supplies being much broader than the definition of commercial services. The terminology was further complicated by the fact that when used alone, the term "item" most often referred to supplies only. In addition, nondevelopmental items and commercial off-the-shelf items were distinct subcategories of commercial supplies. As discussed above, these terminology problems were dealt with by adopting slightly revised definitions for commercial services and commercial products. The following material deals with these definitions.

The definition of supplies or services as a "commercial item" cannot be successfully protested unless the protester can show that it has been prejudiced by that classification, *Johnson Controls World Servs., Inc.*, Comp. Gen. Dec. B-285144, 2000 CPD ¶ 108; *Global Solutions Network, Inc.*, Comp. Gen. Dec. B-298682, 2006 CPD ¶ 179.

[A] Supplies (Products)

The statutes and the FAR contained a general definition of commercial supplies (called "items") and special definitions of nondevelopmental items and commercial off-the-shelf items.

[1] General Definition

The following general definition of commercial supplies was contained in FAR 2.101, which was identical to the definition contained in 41 U.S.C. § 103 except that additional language was added to ¶ (3)(ii) of the FAR definition:

> Commercial item means—
>
> (1) Any item, other than real property, that is of a type customarily used by the general public or by nongovernmental entitles for purposes other than governmental purposes, and—
>
> (i) Has been sold, leased, or licensed to the general public; or
>
> (ii) Has been offered for sale, lease, or license to the general public;
>
> (2) Any item that evolved from an item described in paragraph (1) of this definition through advances in technology or performance and that is not yet available in the commercial marketplace, but will be available in the commercial marketplace in time to satisfy the delivery requirements under a Government solicitation;

(3) Any item that would satisfy a criterion expressed in paragraphs (1) or (2) of this definition, but for—

(i) Modifications of a type customarily available in the commercial marketplace; or

(ii) Minor modifications of a type not customarily available in the commercial marketplace made to meet Federal Government requirements. Minor modifications means modifications that do not significantly alter the nongovernmental function or essential physical characteristics of an item or component, or change the purpose of a process. Factors to be considered in determining whether a modification is minor include the value and size of the modification and the comparative value and size of the final product. Dollar values and percentages may be used as guideposts, but are not conclusive evidence that a modification is minor;

The new definition of commercial products is slightly restructured but effectively the same as the previous definition:

Commercial product means—

(1) A product, other than real property, that is of a type customarily used by the general public or by nongovernmental entities for purposes other than governmental purposes; and

(i) has been sold, leased, or licensed, or offered for sale, lease, or license, to the general public; or

(ii) Has been offered for sale, lease, or licensed to the general public;

(2) A product that has evolved from a product described in paragraph (1) of this definition through advances in technology or performance; and that is not yet available in the commercial marketplace but will be available in the commercial marketplace in time to satisfy the delivery requirements under a Government solicitation.

(3) A product that would satisfy a criterion expressed in paragraph (1) or (2) except for—

(i) modifications of a type customarily available in the commercial marketplace; or

(ii) minor modifications of a type not customarily available in the commercial marketplace made to meet Federal Government requirements. "Minor modifications" means modifications that do not significantly alter the nongovernmental function or essential physical characteristics of an item or component, or change the purpose of a process. Factors to be considered in determining whether a modification is minor include the value and size of the modification and the comparative value and size of the final product. Dollar values and percentages may be used as guideposts, but are not conclusive evidence that a modification is minor;

(4) Any combination of products meeting the requirements of paragraph (1), (2), or (3) of this definition that are of a type customarily combined and sold in combination to the general public.

(5) A product, or combination of products, referred to in paragraphs (1) through (4) of this definition, even though the product, or combination of products, is transferred between or among separate divisions, subsidiaries, or affiliates of a contractor; or

(6) A nondevelopmental item, if the procuring agency determines the product was developed exclusively at private expense and sold in substantial quantities, on a competitive basis, to multiple State and local governments or to multiple foreign governments.

This broad definition includes a large number of products, as long as they meet the key test of being of a type customarily used for nongovernmental purposes. Thus, the government can be the first purchaser of such a product even though it is not being sold commercially at the time of the procurement. The definition also includes modified products as long as they are of the type customarily available in the marketplace or the modifications are minor. Under prior DoD policy, certifications from offerors that their products met the definition were sufficient to justify award using the commercial item procedures, *Coherent, Inc.*, Comp. Gen. Dec. B-270998, 96-1 CPD ¶ 214 (product had been offered for sale); *Canberra Indus., Inc.*, Comp. Gen. Dec. B-271016, 96-1 CPD ¶ 269 (modifications in offered product were minor). GAO has held that the determination that a product meets the commercial item definition "is largely within the discretion of the contracting agency," *NLB Corp.*, Comp. Gen. Dec. B-286846, 2001 CPD ¶ 67. The determination that a product meets the commercial product definition is usually made by evaluating literature obtained during market research, *Gichner Sys. Grp., Inc.*, Comp. Gen. Dec. B-414287, 2017 CPD ¶ 129 (shelter modified to be transported on military aircraft commercial because it was offered for sale on company's website); *GIBBCO LLC*, Comp. Gen. Dec. B-401890, 2009 CPD ¶ 255 (housing units were commercial even though they were required to meet two special government requirements); *Firearms Training Sys., Inc.*, Comp. Gen. Dec. B-292819.2, 2004 CPD ¶ 107 (weapon simulators, as an entire system, were commercial); *NABCO, Inc.*, Comp. Gen. Dec. B-293027, 2004 CPD ¶ 15 (modifications were both of a type customarily offered in the commercial marketplace and minor), or by evaluating samples of the product, *Premier Eng'g & Mfg., Inc.*, Comp. Gen. Dec. B-283028, 99-2 CPD ¶ 65 (modifications were both of a type customarily offered in the commercial marketplace and minor).

[2] Nondevelopmental Items (Products)

Nondevelopmental items were covered by the statutes and regulations in two different ways. However, these were codified into a single definition in 41

U.S.C. § 110. FAR 2.101 breaks this definition into two segments. First, a nondevelopmental item was considered to be a commercial item if it met the following requirements contained in the definition of "commercial item:"

> (8) A nondevelopmental item, if the procuring agency determines that the item was developed exclusively at private expense and sold in substantial quantities, on a competitive basis, to multiple State and local governments.

This definition was changed to include sales to foreign governments in the above new definition of "commercial product."

The second definition of nondevelopmental items applied when it was treated as a separate category of item subject to the congressional policies encouraging the purchase of commercial items *or* nondevelopmental items discussed earlier. For this purpose, the term "nondevelopmental item" is given a narrower definition in FAR 2.101 as follows:

> (a) Any previously developed item of supply *used exclusively for governmental purposes* by a Federal agency, a State or local government, or a foreign government with which the United States has a mutual defense cooperation agreement;
>
> (b) Any item of supply described in paragraph (a) of this definition that requires only minor modification or modifications of a type customarily available in the commercial marketplace in order to meet the requirements of the procuring department or agency; or
>
> (c) Any item of supply being produced that does not meet the requirements of paragraph (a) or (b) solely because the item is not yet in use. (Italics added)

Under the first definition, an item will qualify even if it has also been sold commercially. However, under the second definition, it can only have been sold to governmental entities. See *Lucent Techs. World Servs., Inc.*, Comp. Gen. Dec. B-295462, 2005 CPD ¶ 55, discussing these definitions.

Care must be exercised in using these two definitions because some of the policies discussed in this section apply only to commercial products, while other policies apply as well to nondevelopmental items (as defined in the narrower sense). If a solicitation permits proposals for either commercial products or nondevelopmental items, the second definition will be used and minor modifications will be acceptable, *Trimble Navigation, Ltd.*, Comp. Gen. Dec. B-271882, 96-2 CPD ¶ 102 (award on the basis of a proposed nondevelopmental item improper because modifications were major). When an agency called for a "NDI commercial item," GAO agreed with the agency that either a commercial item or an NDI item would meet the requirements of the solicitation, *Avtron Mfg., Inc.*, Comp. Gen. Dec. B-280758, 98-2 CPD ¶ 148. If the solicitation calls for the use of COTS/NDI components "to the maximum extent practicable," it will not be subject to the NDI procurement procedures, *Recon-Optical, Inc.*, Comp. Gen. Dec. B-286529, 2001 CPD ¶ 14.

[3] Commercially Available Off-the-Shelf Items (Products)

These products were defined in 41 U.S.C. § 104 which was amended to change the word "item" to "product." The FAR 2.101 definition is:

> Commercially available off-the-shelf (COTS) item—(1) Means any item of supply (including construction material) that is—
>
> (i) A commercial product (as defined in paragraph (1) of the definition of commercial product);
>
> (ii) Sold in substantial quantities in the commercial marketplace; and
>
> (iii) Offered to the Government, under a contract or subcontract at any tier, without modification, in the same form in which it is sold in the commercial marketplace; and
>
> (2) Does not include bulk cargo, as defined in 46 U.S.C. 40102(4), such as agricultural products and petroleum products.

Although this definition requires that a COTS item be "without modification," GAO has permitted an agency to use its discretion in determining that software met the definition even though it would require "minimal configuration," *Cerner Corp.*, Comp. Gen. Dec. B-293093, 2004 CPD ¶ 34. See also *SAP Public Servs., Inc.*, Comp. Gen. Dec. B-297535.2, 2006 CPD ¶ 39, denying a protest that the COTS requirement was not met when interfaces between COTS software modules did not meet the COTS requirement. Compare *Chant Eng'g Co.*, Comp. Gen. Dec. B-281521, 99-1 CPD ¶ 45, holding that a product did not meet the COTS definition when the offeror stated that it would use COTS components "to the fullest extent possible;" and *CliniComp, Int'l*, Comp. Gen. Dec. B-294059, 2004 CPD ¶ 209, holding that software "still in testing" did not meet the COTS definition. In *Dynamic Access Sys.*, Comp. Gen. Dec. B-295356, 2005 CPD ¶ 34, GAO denied a protest of a procurement calling for COTS software even though it excluded the protester's software that had been written for a government agency but had not been sold commercially.

[B] Services

The statute and the FAR included two types of services within the definition of commercial items. In the 2018 revision, 41 U.S.C. § 103a was added to cover these commercial services. The definitions in that section are essentially the same as the previous definitions except for editorial changes.

[1] Services in Support of Commercial Products

FAR 2.101 contains the following definition, which conforms to the new definition 41 U.S.C. § 103a:

> (5) Installation services, maintenance services, repair services, training services, and other services if—
>
> (i) Such services are procured for support of a commercial product as defined in this section, regardless of whether such services are provided by the same source or at the same time as the commercial product; and
>
> (ii) The source of such services provides similar services contemporaneously to the general public under terms and conditions similar to those offered to the Federal Government;

[2] Stand-alone Services

The stand-alone services that constitute commercial services were defined in FAR 2.101 as follows:

> (6) Services of a type offered and sold competitively in substantial quantities in the commercial marketplace based on established catalog or market prices for specific tasks performed and under standard commercial terms and conditions. This does not include services that are sold based on hourly rates without an established catalog or market price for a specific service performed. For purposes of these services—
>
> (i) Catalog price means a price included in a catalog, price list, schedule, or other form that is regularly maintained by the manufacturer or vendor, is either published or otherwise available for inspection by customers, and states prices at which sales are currently, or were last, made to a significant number of buyers constituting the general public; and
>
> (ii) Market prices means current prices that are established in the course of ordinary trade between buyers and sellers free to bargain and that can be substantiated through competition or from sources independent of the offerors.

The first sentence of this definition substantially adopted the definition contained in 41 U.S.C. § 103 except that it added the term "of a type." The second sentence was not contained in the statute but was derived from the legislative history, House Conf. Rep. 103-712. The third sentence, including the definitions, was added by Federal Acquisition Circular 2001-01, 66 Fed. Reg. 53483 (Oct. 22, 2001). This definition has been very difficult to understand because of the ambiguity of some of its language. However, it seems clear that to fall within this category of services, the precise services need not have been specifically sold but merely must be "*of a type* offered and sold competitively . . . in the commercial marketplace." In addition, such sales must have been based on "prices for *specific tasks*." There is no guidance on the breadth of a specific task under this definition, but some agencies have interpreted it to include all the work called for under a contract, such as performing janitorial services on a building. Nor is there any guidance as to whether fixed hourly rates can constitute "prices" if the services are sold commercially on that basis and the rates can be established through catalogs, market research or competition.

With regard to services being "of a type" sold commercially, see *Aalco Forwarding, Inc.*, Comp. Gen. Dec. B-277241.8, 97-2 CPD ¶ 110, where GAO held that an agency properly determined that moving household goods for military personnel could be acquired under commercial item procedures because such services were a "type" offered and sold in the commercial marketplace. See also *SHABA Contracting*, Comp. Gen. Dec. B-287430, 2001 CPD ¶ 105, holding that tree thinning services were commercial because they were widely sold in the commercial marketplace; and *Crescent Helicopters*, Comp. Gen. Dec. B-284706, 2000 CPD ¶ 90, holding that helicopter flight services were commercial even though they were custom tailored for the government. Other GAO decisions, not challenging that the services were commercial but dealing with the procedures used, provide an indication of the variety of types of services that have been treated as commercial, *Global Solutions Network, Inc.*, Comp. Gen. Dec. B-298682.3, 2008 CPD ¶ 131 (task order management and financial support); *ABF Freight Sys., Inc.*, Comp. Gen. Dec. B-291185, 2002 CPD ¶ 201 (motor-carrier freight services); *Daly Assocs.*, Comp. Gen. Dec. B-287908, 2001 CPD ¶ 139 (training of Army spouses in facilitating, leadership, and group skills); *Lynwood Mach. & Eng'g, Inc.*, Comp. Gen. Dec. B-285696, 2001 CPD ¶ 113 & Comp. Gen. Dec. B-287652, 2001 CPD ¶ 138 (weighing, banding, crimping, and relocation of lead); *Rockwell Elec. Commerce Corp.*, Comp. Gen. Dec. B-286201, 2001 CPD ¶ 65 (telephone call answering service); *Cortland Mem. Hosp.*, Comp. Gen. Dec. B-286890, 2001 CPD ¶ 48 (community-based outpatient medical clinic); *Symtech Corp.*, Comp. Gen. Dec. B-285358, 2000 CPD ¶ 143 (technical and administrative support of offices dealing with administration, resources management, financial management, acquisition, and technical publications as well as the research library and the reproduction center); and *Birdwell Bros. Painting & Refinishing*, Comp. Gen. Dec. B-285035, 2000 CPD ¶ 129 (maintenance of military housing). Compare *Carr's Wild Horse Ctr.*, Comp. Gen. Dec. B-285833, 2000 CPD ¶ 210, where the contracting officer determined that support of a program promoting the adoption of animals was not a commercial service; and *C.W. Gov't Travel, Inc.*, Comp. Gen. Dec. B-283408, 99-2 CPD ¶ 89, where the contracting officer determined that travel services were not commercial because several of the tasks being required were not sold commercially.

The most difficult interpretative problem with this definition was determining when a market price is "substantiated through competition or from sources independent of the offeror." The terminology seems to recognize that many market prices are obtained through competition for a specific project, such as constructing or cleaning a building. But the requirement that such commercial market prices be "substantiated" can be interpreted to require the contracting officer to ascertain what prices were obtained. A more sensible reading is that what must be substantiated is that competition is the normal way to obtain market prices for the specific type of commercial service being procured.

The 2018 statutory definition adopted parts but not all of the FAR definition and added some new provisions. This was implemented by the following definition in FAR 2.101:

> (2) Services of a type offered and sold competitively in substantial quantities in the commercial marketplace based on established catalog or market prices for specific tasks performed or specific outcomes to be achieved and under standard commercial terms and conditions. For purposes of these services—
>
> (i) Catalog price means a price included in a catalog, price list, schedule, or other form that is regularly maintained by the manufacturer or vendor, is either published or otherwise available for inspection by customers, and states prices at which sales are currently, or were last, made to a significant number of buyers constituting the general public; and
>
> (ii) Market prices means current prices that are established in the course of ordinary trade between buyers and sellers free to bargain and that can be substantiated through competition or from sources independent of the offerors;
>
> (3) A service referred to in paragraphs (1) or (2) of this definition, even though the service is transferred between or among separate divisions, subsidiaries, or affiliates of a contractor.

[C] Key Terms

The statutory and regulatory definitions of commercial products and services use a number of key terms that are not defined. The following definitions of these terms and related terms were previously incorporated into FAR 15.804-3, but were removed from the FAR by Federal Acquisition Circular 90-32, Sept. 18, 1995.

[1] General Public

The term "general public" is used in the definition of commercial products and services supporting such products. Earlier versions of DFARS 202.101 defined it as follows:

> *General public and non-governmental entities*, as used in the definition of *commercial item* at FAR 2.101, do not include the Federal Government or a State, local, or foreign government (Pub. L. 110-181, section 815(b)).

A previous FAR definition stated:

(5) The "general public" is a significant number of buyers other than the Government or affiliates of the offeror; the item involved must not be for Government end use. For the purpose of this subsection 15.804-3, items acquired for "Government end use" include items acquired for foreign military sales.

[2] Substantial Quantities

The phrase "sold in substantial quantities" is applicable only to stand-alone services and commercially available off-the-shelf products. The previous FAR definition stated:

(4) An item is "sold in substantial quantities" only when the quantities regularly sold are sufficient to constitute a real commercial market. Nominal quantities, such as models, samples, prototypes, or experimental units, do not meet this requirement. For services to be sold in substantial quantities, they must be customarily provided by the offeror, using personnel regularly employed and equipment (if any is necessary) regularly maintained solely or principally to provide the services.

[D] Making the Commerciality Determination

In most agencies, the contracting officer is responsible for making the determination that the product or service to be acquired is commercial. FAR 12.202 describes market research as the essential element in making this determination as follows:

(a) Market research (see 10.001) is an essential element of building an effective strategy for the acquisition of commercial items and establishes the foundation for the agency description of need (see part 11), the solicitation, and resulting contract.

(b) The description of agency need must contain sufficient detail for potential offerors of commercial items to know which commercial products or services may be suitable. Generally, for acquisitions in excess of the simplified acquisition threshold, an agency's statement of need for a commercial item will describe the type of product or service to be acquired and explain how the agency intends to use the product or service in terms of function to be performed, performance requirement or essential physical characteristics. Describing the agency's needs in these terms allows offerors to propose methods that will best meet the needs of the Government.

There is no requirement that the commerciality determination by formally documented. See *Zodiac of North Am.*, Comp. Gen. Dec. B-409084, 2014 CPD ¶ 79, stating:

> [T]here is no requirement that an agency formally evaluate or document whether an offered item is a commercial item, absent a solicitation provision requiring a separate commerciality determination or some indication that the proposed items are not commercial.

Furthermore, GAO will not decide a commerciality protest unless the protester shows that it will be prejudiced by the use of commercial procedures, *Pilot Xpress, LLC*, Comp. Gen. Dec. B-417292, 2019 CPD ¶ 182.

In order to regularize this determination and streamline the process, DOD has adopted special procedures. The Defense Contract Management Agency has a Commercial Item Group that is available to contracting officers to assist in making the commerciality determination. See DOD PGI 212.102(1)(a). The Group also maintains a database of all prior determinations which contracting officers can consult. DFARS 212.102(a)(ii) allows contracting officers to rely on prior determinations and limits their ability reach a noncommerciality determination to as follows:

> (A) The contracting officer may presume that a prior commercial item determination made by a military department, a defense agency, or another component of DoD shall serve as a determination for subsequent procurements of such item. See PGI 212.102(a)(ii) for information about items that the Department has historically acquired as military unique, noncommercial items.
>
> (B) If the contracting officer does not make the presumption that a prior commercial item determination is valid, and instead chooses to proceed with a procurement of an item previously determined to be a commercial item using procedures other than the procedures authorized for the procurement of a commercial item, the contracting officer shall request a review of the commercial item determination by the head of the contracting activity that will conduct the procurement. Not later than 30 days after receiving a request for review of a commercial item determination, the head of a contracting activity shall—
>
> > (1) Confirm that the prior determination was appropriate and still applicable; or
> >
> > (2) Issue a determination that the prior use of FAR part 12 procedures was improper or that it is no longer appropriate to acquire the item using FAR part 12 procedures, with a written explanation of the basis for the determination (see 212.70).

DFARS 212.102(a)(iii) also allows contracting officers to treat products and services provided by nontraditional defense contractors as commercial items. DFARS 212.001 contains the following definition:

> Nontraditional defense contractor means an entity that is not currently performing and has not performed any contract or subcontract for DoD that is subject to full coverage under the cost accounting standards prescribed pursuant to 41 U.S.C. 1502 and the regulations implementing such section, for at

least the 1-year period preceding the solicitation of sources by DoD for the procurement (10 U.S.C. 2302(9)).

§ 9.03 SOLICITATION, EVALUATION, AND AWARD

The statutory goal is to use procurement procedures that "reduce any impediments . . . to the acquisition of commercial products and commercial services," 10 U.S.C. § 3453(b)(5) (formerly § 2377(b)(5)) and 41 U.S.C. § 3307(c)(5). Such impediments should be identified by the contracting officer in the course of performing the required market research to determine the availability of commercial products or services as discussed in Chapter 3. See FAR 12.202. In general, it can be expected that the major impediments will be excessive requirements for proposal information and data during contract performance. See, for example, *Worldwide Primates, Inc.*, Comp. Gen. Dec. B-294481, 2004 CPD ¶ 206, where the agency required detailed technical proposals and found only two of the nine proposals received were satisfactory, and *Phantom Prods., Inc.*, Comp. Gen. Dec. B-283882, 2000 CPD ¶ 7, denying a protest that the agency had not sufficiently specified the detailed information needed for the evaluation of technical and management proposals. Based on an understanding of the impact of such requirements on the government's ability to attract offers from commercial sellers, the procurement should be structured to minimize the effect of such impediments by streamlining the source selection process. The procedural guidance discussed in this section contains sufficient flexibility to permit contracting with commercial sources in most situations.

[A] Type of Contract

Section 8002 of the Federal Acquisition Streamlining Act, Pub. L. No. 103-355, contained the following provision on the appropriate type of contract for the procurement of commercial items:

> (d) Use of firm, fixed price contracts. The Federal Acquisition Regulation shall include, for acquisitions of commercial items—
>
> (1) a requirement that firm, fixed price contracts or fixed price with economic price adjustment contracts be used to the maximum extent practicable; and
>
> (2) a prohibition on use of cost type contracts.

This statute was implemented in FAR 12.207 requiring that contracts for commercial items be either firm-fixed-price or fixed-price with economic price adjustment and prohibiting the use of any other type of contract. This provision also provided that indefinite-delivery contracts could be used if they call for the establishment of prices on one of these two bases. The effect of this implementation was that time-and-materials and labor-hour contracts could not be used to procure commercial items even though they would have been permissible under the statute. Congress clarified the guidance on this issue in § 1432 of the National Defense Authorization Act for Fiscal Year 2004, Pub. L. No. 108-136. That section amended § 8002 to expressly authorize the use of time-and-materials and labor-hour contracts for the procurement of commercial services. See 41 U.S.C. § 3307(e)(4)(B). As a result, FAR 12.207 was amended to permit limited use of such contracts:

> (b)(1) A time-and-materials contract or labor-hour contract (see Subpart 16.6) may be used for the acquisition of commercial services when—
>
> (i) The service is acquired under a contract awarded using—
>
> (A) Competitive procedures (e.g., the procedures in 6.102, the set-aside procedures in Subpart 19.5, or competition conducted in accordance with Part 13);
>
> (B) The procedures for other than full and open competition in 6.3 provided the agency receives offers that satisfy the Government's expressed requirement from two or more responsible offerors; or
>
> (C) The fair opportunity procedures in 16.505 (including discretionary small business set-asides under 16.505(b)(2)(i)(F)), if placing an order under a multiple award delivery-order contract; and
>
> (ii) The contracting officer—
>
> (A) Executes a determination and findings (D&F) for the contract, in accordance with paragraph (b)(2) of this section (but see paragraph (c) of this section for indefinite-delivery contracts), that no other contract type authorized by this subpart is suitable;
>
> (B) Includes a ceiling price in the contract or order that the contractor exceeds at its own risk; and
>
> (C) Prior to increasing the ceiling price [follow detailed procedures prescribed in the regulation].
>
> (2) Each D&F required by paragraph (b)(1)(ii)(A) of this section shall contain sufficient facts and rationale to justify that no other contract type authorized by this subpart is suitable. At a minimum, the D&F shall—
>
> (i) Include a description of the market research conducted (see 10.002(e));
>
> (ii) Establish that it is not possible at the time of placing the contract or order to accurately estimate the extent or duration of the work or to anticipate costs with any reasonable degree of confidence;
>
> (iii) Establish that the requirement has been structured to maximize the use of firm-fixed-price or fixed-price with economic price adjustment contracts (e.g., by limiting the value or length of the time-and-material/labor-hour contract or order; establishing fixed prices for portions of the requirement) on future acquisitions for the same or similar requirements; and

> (iv) Describe actions planned to maximize the use of firm-fixed-price or fixed-price with economic price adjustment contracts on future acquisitions for the same requirements.
>
> (3) See 16.601(d)(1) for additional approval required for contracts expected to extend beyond three years.

When an agency decides that a time-and-materials or labor-hour contract is appropriate, the solicitation should include the Time-and-Materials/ Labor-Hour Proposal Requirements—Commercial Acquisition provision in FAR 52.216-31.

Several other provisions can be added to these basic contract types. For example, FAR 12.301(e)(2) permits the use of options in procurements of commercial products and services. In addition, FAR 12.207(d) was added by FAC 2001-13, 68 Fed. Reg. 13201 (Mar. 18, 2003), to permit the use of award fees and incentives based on factors other than cost.

A more restrictive provision on the use of time-and-materials and labor-hour contracts is contained in DFARS 212.207 as follows:

> (b) In accordance with section 805 of the National Defense Authorization Act for Fiscal Year 2008 (Pub. L. 110-181), use of time-and-materials and labor-hour contracts for the acquisition of commercial services is authorized only for the following:
>
> (i) Services acquired for support of a commercial [product] . . .
>
> (ii) Emergency repair services.
>
> (iii) Any other commercial services only to the extent that the head of the agency concerned approves a written determination by the contracting officer that—
>
> (A) The services to be acquired are commercial services as defined in [the definition of commercial services at FAR 2.101] (41 U.S.C. 403(12)(F));
>
> (B) If the services to be acquired are subject to FAR 15.403-1(c)(3)(ii), the offeror of the services has submitted sufficient information in accordance with that subsection;
>
> (C) Such services are commonly sold to the general public through use of time-and-materials or labor-hour contracts; and
>
> (D) The use of a time-and-materials or labor-hour contract type is in the best interest of the Government.

[B] Specifications

FAR 12.202(b) provides the following guidance on specifications for procurements of commercial products and services:

> (b) The description of agency need must contain sufficient detail for potential offerors of commercial products or commercial services to know

which commercial products or commercial services may be suitable. Generally, for acquisitions in excess of the simplified acquisition threshold, an agency's statement of need for a commercial product or commercial service will describe the type of commercial product or commercial service to be acquired and explain how the agency intends to use the product or service in terms of function to be performed, performance requirement or essential physical characteristics. Describing the agency's needs in these terms allows offerors to propose methods that will best meet the needs of the Government.

The preference for the acquisition of commercial products and services may significantly weaken the general rule that specifications may not be unduly restrictive. Thus, when an agency decides to use a commercial product or service, it will be difficult for a competitor to argue that it should have opened up the competition to noncommercial products or services. See, for example, *Dynamic Access Sys.*, Comp. Gen. Dec. B-295356, 2005 CPD ¶ 34, finding that requiring a COTS product was not unduly restrictive when the agency had determined that use of such a product would reduce its life-cycle costs.

In the case of products, the description can be a brand name but the agency must follow the requirement in FAR 11.104 that the salient characteristics of the product be provided, *Elementar Americas, Inc.*, Comp. Gen. Dec. B-289115, 2002 CPD ¶ 20. However, the agency is not required to provide the brand name of a product that meets its requirements if it provides all of its functional requirements, *Omega World Travel, Inc.*, Comp. Gen. Dec. B-280456.2, 98-2 CPD ¶ 73. If salient characteristics are not specified, the agency must accept an offer of a purportedly equal product unless the offered product is significantly different from the brand name product, *Veterans Healthcare Supply Solutions, Inc.*, Comp. Gen. Dec. B-407223.2, 2013 CPD ¶ 3. See also *Access Logic, Inc.*, Comp. Gen. Dec. B-274748, 97-1 CPD ¶ 36, *recons. & mod.*, 97-1 CPD ¶ 159, holding that, while the use of functional or performance specifications is appropriate, the agency must advise offerors of its "specific ideas" of what features would satisfy its needs. See also *Candle Corp. v. United States*, 40 Fed. Cl. 658 (1998), holding that when an agency relaxes a specification requirement for a commercial item, the solicitation must be amended to permit all competitors an equal opportunity to compete for the relaxed requirement.

[1] Solicitation

The FAR contains general guidance on the solicitation procedures to be followed in acquiring commercial products and services, as well as a "streamlined" solicitation procedure. The contracting officer has complete discretion as to the procedure to be used.

[a] General Guidance

The initial guidance states in FAR 12.203 that the contracting officer "shall use" the policies in FAR Part 12 "in conjunction with the policies and procedures" in FAR Parts 13, 14, and 15 "as appropriate for the particular acquisition." This appears to give the contracting officer complete freedom in selecting the solicitation procedure—including the use of sealed bidding or competitive negotiation procedures. See *Johnson Controls World Servs., Inc.*, Comp. Gen. Dec. B-285144, 2000 CPD ¶ 108 (sealed bidding appropriate procedure for base operations and maintenance services). However, the balance of the guidance makes it clear that simplification is desirable. Thus, sealed bidding or standard negotiation procedures should be used very rarely in the procurement of commercial items. However, as discussed below, the protests to GAO indicate that agencies frequently structure their commercial products and services acquisitions like competitively negotiated procurements with multiple evaluation factors.

Unless the streamlined procedure is used, the contracting officer must use Standard Form 1449, Solicitation/Contract/Order for Commercial Products and Commercial Services, when issuing written solicitations and awarding contracts and placing orders for commercial products and services. This form may also be used for documenting receipt, inspection, and acceptance of commercial products and services, FAR 12.204. FAR 12.205 provides the following guidance for solicitations for commercial products and services:

> (a) Where technical information is necessary for evaluation of offers, agencies should, as part of market research, review existing literature generally available in the industry to determine its adequacy for purposes of evaluation. If adequate, contracting officers shall request existing product or service literature from offerors of commercial products or commercial services in lieu of unique technical proposals.
>
> (b) Contracting officers should allow offerors to propose multiple offers that will meet a Government need in response to solicitations for commercial products or commercial services. The contracting officer shall evaluate each offer separately.
>
> (c) Consistent with the requirements at 5.203(b), the contracting officers may allow fewer than 30 days response time for receipt of offers for commercial products or commercial services, unless the acquisition is subject to NAFTA or the Trade Agreements Act (see 5.203(h)).

FAR 12.301(b) provides two standard solicitation provisions, described as follows:

> (1) The provision at 52.212-1, Instructions to Offerors—Commercial Products and Commercial Services. This provision provides a single, streamlined set of instructions to be used when soliciting offers for commercial products and commercial services and is incorporated in the solicitation by reference (see Block 27a, SF 1449). The contracting officer may tailor these

> instructions or provide additional instructions tailored to the specific acquisition in accordance with 12.302.
>
> (2) The provision at 52.212-3, Offeror Representations and Certifications—Commercial Products and Commercial Services. This provision provides a single, consolidated list of representations and certifications for the acquisition of commercial products and commercial services and is attached to the solicitation for offerors to complete. This provision may not be tailored except in accordance with Subpart 1.4. Use the provision with its Alternate I in solicitations issued by DoD, NASA, or the Coast Guard.

FAR 12.302 provides the following guidance on the permissible tailoring of the FAR 52.212-1 solicitation provision:

> The provision and clauses established in this subpart are intended to address, to the maximum extent practicable, commercial market practices for a wide range of potential Government acquisitions of commercial products and commercial services. However, because of the broad range of commercial products and commercial services acquired by the Government, variations in commercial practices, and the relative volume of the Government's acquisitions in the specific market, contracting officers may, within the limitations of this subpart, and after conducting appropriate market research, tailor the provision at 52.212-1, Instructions to Offerors—Commercial Products and Commercial Services, . . .

DFARS 212.301(f) requires the use of additional solicitation provisions in Department of Defense procurements.

[b] Streamlined Procedures

The FAR also permits the use of simplified acquisition procedures for procurements of commercial products and services in amounts not exceeding \$7,500,000. A higher threshold is applicable to procurements not exceeding \$15,000,000 as prescribed by FAR 13.500(c) as follows:

> (1) The acquisition is for commercial products or commercial services that, as determined by the head of the agency, are to be used in support of a contingency operation or to facilitate the defense against or recovery from cyber, nuclear, biological, chemical, or radiological attack; or
>
> (2) The acquisition will be treated as an acquisition of commercial products or commercial services in accordance with 12.102(f)(1).

If an agency conducts a procurement under this provision when it has no reasonable evidence that the threshold will not be exceeded, the procurement will be held to be improper, *Global Communications Solutions, Inc.*, Comp. Gen. Dec. B-299044, 2007 CPD ¶ 30.

The major advantage of this streamlined procedure is described in FAR Subpart 12.6. This permits the combining of the synopsis and solicitation into a single document with a response time no longer than is necessary to give potential offerors a reasonable opportunity to respond to the solicitation. This allows greatly shortening the statutory requirements for standard procurements that require a 15-day synopsis period and a 30-day offer period. The guidance on the use of this fast procedure is set forth in FAR 12.603, as follows:

> (a) When a written solicitation will be issued, the contracting officer may use the following procedure to reduce the time required to solicit and award contracts for the acquisition of commercial products or commercial services. This procedure combines the synopsis required by 5.203 and the issuance of the solicitation into a single document.
>
> (b) When using the combined synopsis/solicitation procedure, the SF 1449 is not used for issuing the solicitation.
>
> (c) To use these procedures, the contracting officer shall—
>
> (1) Prepare the synopsis as described at 5.207.
>
> (2) In the Description, include the following additional information:
>
> (i) The following statement:
>
> This is a combined synopsis/solicitation for commercial products or commercial services prepared in accordance with the format in FAR subpart 12.6, as supplemented with additional information included in this notice. This announcement constitutes the only solicitation; proposals are being requested and a written solicitation will not be issued.
>
> (ii) The solicitation number and a statement that the solicitation is issued as an invitation to bid (IFB), request for quotation (RFQ) or request for proposal (RFP).
>
> (iii) A statement that the solicitation document and incorporated provisions and clauses are those in effect through Federal Acquisition Circular ________.
>
> (iv) A notice regarding any set-aside and the associated NAICS code and small business size standard.
>
> (v) A list of contract line item number(s) and items, quantities and units of measure, (including option(s), if applicable).
>
> (vi) Description of requirements for the items to be acquired.
>
> (vii) Date(s) and place(s) of delivery and acceptance and FOB point.
>
> (viii) A statement that the provision at 52.212-1, Instructions to Offerors—Commercial Products and Commercial Services, applies to this acquisition and a statement regarding any addenda to the provision.
>
> (ix) A statement regarding the applicability of the provision at 52.212-2, Evaluation—Commercial Products and Commercial Services, if used, and the specific evaluation criteria to be included

in paragraph (a) of that provision. If this provision is not used, describe the evaluation procedures to be used.

(x) A statement advising offerors to include a completed copy of the provision at 52.212-3, Offeror Representations and Certifications—Commercial Products and Commercial Services, with its offer.

(xi) A statement that the clause at 52.212-4, Contract Terms and Conditions—Commercial Products and Commercial Services, applies to this acquisition and a statement regarding any addenda to the clause.

(xii) A statement that the clause at 52.212-5, Contract Terms and Conditions Required To Implement Statutes Or Executive Orders—Commercial Products and Commercial Services, applies to this acquisition and a statement regarding which, if any, of the additional FAR clauses cited in the clause are applicable to the acquisition.

(xiii) A statement regarding any additional contract requirement(s) or terms and conditions (such as contract financing arrangements or warranty requirements) determined by the contracting officer to be necessary for this acquisition and consistent with customary commercial practices.

(xiv) A statement regarding the Defense Priorities and Allocations System (DPAS) and assigned rating, if applicable.

(xv) The date, time and place offers are due.

(xvi) The name and telephone number of the individual to contact for information regarding the solicitation.

(3) Allow response time for receipt of offers as follows:

(i) Because the synopsis and solicitation are contained in a single document, it is not necessary to publish a separate synopsis 15 days before the issuance of the solicitation.

(ii) When using the combined synopsis and solicitation, contracting offerors shall establish a response time in accordance with 5.203(b) (but see 5.203(h)).

(4) Publicize amendments to solicitations in the same manner as the initial synopsis and solicitation.

This procedure permits a 15 day combined synopsis and response time. See *GIBBCO LLC*, Comp. Gen. Dec. B-401890, 2009 CPD ¶ 255, denying a protest that a 22-day response time was unreasonable, and *American Artisans Prods., Inc.*, Comp. Gen. Dec. B-281409, 98-2 CPD ¶ 155, denying a protest that 15 days was too short when five offers were received within that time.

[c] Commercial Solutions Openings

A special acquisition technique is available to some agencies. Section 879 of the National Defense Authorization Act for FY 2017, Pub. L. No. 114-328, authorized DOD to carry out a pilot program to "acquire innovative commercial items, technologies, and services through a competitive selection of proposals resulting from a general solicitation and the peer review of such proposals." This process is essentially the same as the broad agency announcement process described in FAR 35.016 (discussed in Chapter 10) and is a "competitive procedure" which satisfies the statutory requirement for full and open competition. Section 880 of the Act gives the same authority to the Department of Homeland Security and the General Services Administration.

Section 879(c) of the Act contains the following "limitations:"

> (1) IN GENERAL.—The Secretary may not enter into a contract or agreement under the pilot program for an amount in excess of $100,000,000 without a written determination from the Under Secretary for Acquisition, Logistics, and Technology or the relevant service acquisition executive of the efficacy of the effort to meet mission needs of the Department of Defense or the relevant military department.
>
> (2) FIXED-PRICE REQUIREMENT.—Contracts or agreements entered into under the program shall be fixed-price, including fixed-price incentive fee contracts.
>
> (3) TREATMENT AS COMMERCIAL ITEMS.—Notwithstanding section 2376(1) of title 10, United States Code, items, technologies, and services acquired under the pilot program shall be treated as commercial items.

As indicated above, this procedure is to be used to obtain "innovative" products and services. The Act contains the following definition:

> [T]he term "innovative" means—
>
> (1) any technology, process, or method, including research and development, that is new as of the date of submission of a proposal; or
>
> (2) any application that is new as of the date of submission of a proposal of a technology, process, or method existing as of such date.

DOD implemented this statute by a memorandum "Class Deviation–Defense Commercial Solutions Opening Pilot Program," June 26, 2018. The memorandum requires Contracting Officers to ensure that the CSO—

- Describes the agency's interest, either for an individual program requirement or for broadly defined areas of interest covering the full range of the agency's requirements;
- Describes the criteria for selecting proposals, their relative importance, and the method of evaluation, including, where applicable, the potential type of data rights that may be determined necessary to meet DoD's minimum needs;

- Specifies the period of time during which proposals submitted in response to the CSO will be accepted;
- Contains instructions for the preparation and submission of proposals;

Notice of the availability of the CSO is to be published on the Government-wide point of entry (SAM.gov) and in scientific, technical and engineering periodicals. More detailed guidance on the use of CSOs is contained in the General Services Administration "Commercial Solutions Opening (CSO) Guide," June 1, 2018. See also the Department of Homeland Security "Commercial Solutions Opening Pilot Program Guide," July 17, 2019.

As with broad agency announcements, this is a rolling evaluation process with awards made when the peer reviewers in an agency identify a promising technical proposal. However. it covers a broader span of work than the broad agency announcement which is limited to research work. This allows an agency to publicize a problem area seeking white papers or proposals for commercial solutions to the problem. When it identifies a promising solution, it can immediately negotiate a FAR contract for a commercial product or service or an other transaction research or prototype agreement. This greatly shortens the time between identification of a requirement and award. See *Oracle America, Inc.*, Comp. Gen. Dec. B-416061, 2018 CPD ¶ 180, where the agency selected REAN Cloud, LLC to perform a prototype other transaction after reviewing its white paper submitted in response to a CSO.

While this can be a very quick and efficient process, it depends on the ability of the parties to reach agreement on the terms of the contract. There are two major issues that must be negotiated—the price and the technical data terms. The contracting officer or the Agreements Officer is required to ensure that the price is fair and reasonable. The DOD memorandum indicates that price should be a minor evaluation issue, stating:

> The primary evaluation factors for selecting proposals for award shall be technical, importance to agency programs, and funds availability. Price shall be considered to the extent appropriate, but at a minimum, to determine that the price is fair and reasonable.

In negotiating the data to be delivered and the rights to use that data, the needs of the government should be balanced with the contractor's need to protect its proprietary position in the commercial marketplace. This would indicate the government should insist on no more than Government-purpose rights. The DOD memorandum contains no guidance on this important issue. However, the GSA Guide contains the following instructions:

> The contracting officer shall assess the impact of intellectual property rights on the Government's total life cycle cost (e.g. installation, operating, and maintenance costs) of the product or service. For example, where the

Government overestimates the intellectual property rights it will need, the Government might pay for unused rights and dissuade new businesses from entering into a contract. If the intellectual property rights are underestimated, the Government may not acquire sufficient rights for use during the item's life cycle (e.g. operations, maintenance, follow-on procurements). As a result, the contracting officer must carefully assess the intellectual property needs of the Government. When appropriate, consider providing the contractor the IP rights for new adaptations of existing commercial products.

[d] Pricing Information

Contracting officers are prohibited from requiring certified cost or pricing data when they acquire commercial products or services, FAR 15.403-1(c)(3)(i). However, this prohibition applies only if the contracting officer determines in writing "that the offeror has submitted sufficient information to evaluate, through price analysis, the reasonableness of the price of such services," FAR 15.403-1(c)(3)(ii)(A). FAR 15.403-1(c)(3)(ii) provides the following guidance on the information that would be sufficient:

> (B) In order to make this determination, the contracting officer may request the offeror to submit prices paid for the same or similar commercial services under comparable terms and conditions by both Government and commercial customers; and
>
> (C) If the contracting officer determines that the information described in paragraph (c)(3)(ii)(B) of this section is not sufficient to determine the reasonableness of price, other relevant information regarding the basis for price or cost, including information on labor costs, material costs and overhead rates may be requested.

See Chapter 13 for a more detailed discussion of pricing contracts for commercial products and services.

[e] Late Proposals

Paragraph (f) of the FAR 52.212-1 solicitation provision contains the same strict late offer provision that is included in sealed bid and negotiated procurements. This requirement is strictly enforced, *CCSC, Inc.*, Comp. Gen. Dec. B-404802.3, 2011 CPD ¶ 187 (no government mishandling of proposal when protester did not allow sufficient time for government screening of proposal); *Labatt Food Serv., Inc.*, Comp. Gen. Dec. B-310939.6, 2008 CPD ¶ 162 (time specified in solicitation governs over default time in the provision); *Kesser Int'l*, Comp. Gen. Dec. B-296294, 2005 CPD ¶ 127 (proposal rejected because it was two minutes late). Obtaining additional information to support an offeror's technical proposal was held to violate the late proposal rule, *Radiation Oncology Grp. of WNY, PC*, Comp. Gen. Dec. B-310354.2, 2009 CPD ¶ 136. In *Labatt*

GAO denied an additional grounds of protest asserting that none of the proposal revisions should have been accepted because they were sent by e-mail which was not allowed by the solicitation. GAO reasoned that there was no prejudice when all offerors followed the same procedure. The Court of Federal Claims disagreed, enjoining the award of the contract in *Labatt Food Serv., Inc. v. United States*, 84 Fed. Cl. 50 (2008).

Although this provision permits acceptance of late offers from an "otherwise successful offeror," GAO agreed that it was proper to reject a late modification lowering the price from an offeror that had not yet been determined to be the successful offeror. See *Sunrise Med. HHG, Inc.*, Comp. Gen. Dec. B-310230, 2008 CPD ¶ 7, stating:

> [A]n offeror cannot make itself the "otherwise successful offeror" by submitting a late proposal modification; instead the offeror must already be the offeror in line for award prior to the time the late proposal modification is submitted. *Phyllis M. Chestang*, B-298394.3, Nov. 20, 2006, 2006 CPD ¶ 176 at 5 n.3. In this regard, an offeror cannot avail itself of the late proposal submission provision where the agency has not already identified an "otherwise successful offeror." *Global Analytic Info. Tech. Servs., Inc.*, B-298840.2, Feb. 6, 2007, 2007 CPD ¶ 57 at 5-6.

In *M. Braun, Inc.*, Comp. Gen. Dec. B-298935.2, 2007 CPD ¶ 96, GAO assumed that this provision also applied to late quotations (even though it used the term "proposal") because the agency had made that assumption.

[2] Evaluation Scheme

The general guidance on the evaluation scheme to be used in the acquisition of commercial products and services indicates that the contracting officer has broad latitude in selecting the evaluation factors and may conduct commercial products or services procurement without evaluation factors. This would entail the procurement of commercial products or services on the basis of price alone. However, FAR 12.206 states that past performance "should be an important element in every evaluation." The balance of the guidance on evaluation factors is directed to supply contracts where agencies are urged not to solicit technical proposals. See FAR 12.205 stating:

> (a) Where technical information is necessary for evaluation of offers, agencies should, as part of market research, review existing literature generally available in the industry to determine its adequacy for purposes of evaluation. If adequate, contracting officers shall request existing product or service literature from offerors of commercial products or commercial services in lieu of unique technical proposals.

See also FAR 12.602(b) providing as follows for streamlined procurements:

> For many commercial products or commercial services, the criteria need not be more detailed than technical (capability of the item offered to meet the agency need), price, and past performance. Technical capability may be evaluated by how well the proposed products or services meet the Government requirement instead of predetermined subfactors. Solicitations for commercial products or commercial services do not have to contain subfactors for technical capability when the solicitation adequately describes the intended use of the commercial product or commercial service. A technical evaluation would normally include examination of such things as product or service literature, product samples (if requested), technical features, and warranty provisions. Past performance shall be evaluated in accordance with the procedures in section 13.106 or subpart 15.3, as applicable. The contracting officer shall ensure the instructions provided in the provision at 52.212-1, Instructions to Offerors—Commercial Products and Commercial Services, and the evaluation criteria provided in the provision at 52.212-2, Evaluation—Commercial Products and Commercial Services, are in agreement.

In spite of this sound guidance, agencies tend to ignore the FAR and call for technical proposals in commercial products or services procurements for relatively straightforward supplies and services. See, for example, *ERP Servs., Inc.*, Comp. Gen. Dec. B-419315, 2021 CPD ¶ 85 (DNS resolver services, as well as a system to store and analyze various information logged by the DNS resolver); *DeWitt & Co.*, Comp. Gen. Dec. B-417194, 2019 CPD ¶ 126 (grounds maintenance); *Command Mgmt. Servs., Inc.*, Comp. Gen. Dec. B-310261, 2008 CPD ¶ 29 (lodging, meal and transportation services); *OK Produce*, Comp. Gen. Dec. B-299058, 2007 CPD ¶ 31 (fresh fruit and vegetables); *Philadelphia Produce Market Wholesalers, LLC*, Comp. Gen. Dec. B-298751, 2006 CPD ¶ 193 (fresh fruit and vegetables); *NCR Gov't Sys. LLC*, Comp. Gen. Dec. B-297959, 2006 CPD ¶ 82 (computer system for retail stores); *Cogent Sys., Inc.*, Comp. Gen. Dec. B-295990.4, 2005 CPD ¶ 179 (fingerprint identification system). Such practices, of course, deprive the agency of the benefit of streamlining that the FAR suggests.

An agency is not required to state how a product will be tested and may use any rational test procedure, *IMLCORP LLC*, Comp. Gen. Dec. B-310582, 2008 CPD ¶ 15 (subjective test of acoustical properties of device by Navy personnel satisfactory). It is also proper to evaluate a product by using the results of studies of the product and field reports from users even though the offer has submitted samples of a modified product. See *Silynx Commc'ns, Inc.*, Comp. Gen. Dec. B-310667, 2008 CPD ¶ 36, stating:

> We find that the agency's determination was reasonable. First, nothing in the solicitation contemplated or required the agency to conduct product inspection or testing, or to permit product demonstrations; in fact, the RFP's instructions called for submission of product samples only where such

> samples were otherwise required under the terms of the solicitation, and there was no such requirement for product samples in the RFP. Rather, the RFP contemplated that offerors would include product literature or other information—for example, test data or feedback from prior or current users of their product—to demonstrate compliance with the RFP's requirements, and that, after award, the contractor would conduct first article testing and field user evaluation demonstrations to verify compliance of its product with the performance characteristics proposed in the firm's offer. Thus, there was nothing improper in the agency's declining to conduct an inspection or to perform testing of the Silynx product, or to permit demonstrations as part of the evaluation process.
>
> Second, we find no basis to object to the agency's reliance on the informal inquiry of operational force members and the audiologist's opinion. While the inquiry of the operational forces was informal in nature, there is no indication in the record that it did not accurately reflect the users' opinions. Silynx has submitted no information—for example, its own user feedback information or test data for either of its proposed earpieces—showing different results from the information obtained by the agency.

When evaluation factors are used, FAR 12.301(c) provides a standard solicitation provision in FAR 52.212-2. This provision calls for the insertion of the evaluation factors and their relative importance. Agencies are also permitted to use a different solicitation provision if they are using the procedures of FAR Parts 13, 14 or 15, FAR 12.301(c)(2). If the agency chooses to use simplified acquisition procedures, no statement of relative importance is required, FAR 12.602. However, the agency may not mislead competitors as to the relative importance of a factor. See *Finlen Complex, Inc.*, Comp. Gen. Dec. B-288280, 2001 CPD ¶ 167, granting a protest in a procurement of commercial services using simplified procedures contained multiple evaluation factors because past performance was given very little importance. If an agency conducts the procurement using FAR Part 15 procedures, GAO will disregard the FAR requirement for a statement of relative importance and apply the normal rule giving equal weight to evaluation factors and subfactors where no relative importance statement is included in the solicitation, *Bio-Rad Labs., Inc.*, Comp. Gen. Dec. B-297553, 2007 CPD ¶ 58.

As with all other types of procurement, evaluation must be based on the factors stated in the solicitation, FAR 12.602(b). The basic standard is that "an agency must conduct the procurement consistent with a concern for fair and equitable competition and must evaluate quotations [or offers] in accordance with the terms of the solicitation," *DOER Marine*, Comp. Gen. Dec. B-295087, 2004 CPD ¶ 252. See also *General Revenue Corp.*, Comp. Gen. Dec. B-414220.2, 2017 CPD ¶ 106 (agency unreasonably either ignored or discounted relevant past performance information); *Access Logic, Inc.*, Comp. Gen. Dec. B-274748, 97-1 CPD ¶ 36, *recons. & mod.*, 97-1 CPD ¶ 159 (proposed commercial product may not be rejected on the basis of technical requirements not set forth in the solicitation). Compare *InterOcean Sys., Inc.*, Comp. Gen. Dec. B-290916, 2002 CPD ¶ 178, agreeing that an agency properly evaluated proposals in accordance with unspecified subfactors as permitted by the FAR. It is permissible to cancel the procurement after receipt of proposals if the evaluation factors are inadvertently omitted from the solicitation, *Nidek, Inc.*, Comp. Gen. Dec. B-272255, 96-2 CPD ¶ 112.

[3] Communications After Receipt of Quotations or Offers

FAR Part 12 contains no guidance on communications with competitors after the receipt of quotations or offers. However, ¶ (g) of the Instructions to Offerors – Commercial Products and Commercial Services solicitation provision states that, except for procurements using sealed bidding procedures, the agency intends to award without discussions but reserves the right to hold discussions. This gives the agency the right to award without discussions, *Liberty Test Equipment*, Comp. Gen. Dec. B-409916, 2014 CPD ¶ 246, or to conduct discussions, *American Recycling Sys., Inc.*, Comp. Gen. Dec. B-292500, 2003 CPD ¶ 143 (extensive communication with the potential vendor and the manufacturer of the quoted product permitted). See also *United Marine Int'l LLC*, Comp. Gen. Dec. B-281512, 99-1 CPD ¶ 44 (negotiation with only company with best quotation permitted). With regard to procurements using competitive negotiation procedures, it would be expected that the rules pertaining to clarifications and discussions, discussed in Chapter 6, would be followed. Exchanges have been found to be clarifications not discussions in *MG Indus.*, Comp. Gen. Dec. B-283010.3, 2000 CPD ¶ 17 (request for explanation of the pricing terms of the quotation); and *National Beef Packing Co.*, Comp. Gen. Dec. B-296534, 2005 CPD ¶ 168 (description of product). However, the controlling factor will probably be the way the procurement is actually conducted. See, for example, *Kathryn Huddleston & Assocs., Ltd.*, Comp. Gen. Dec. B-289453, 2002 CPD ¶ 57, where the agency solicited quotations but then conducted the procurement as if it were a competitive negotiation. GAO held that rules governing the establishment of a competitive range and discussions were applicable, stating:

> Although an agency is not required to establish a competitive range or conduct discussions under simplified acquisition procedures, we think that where an agency avails itself of these negotiated procurement procedures, the agency should fairly and reasonably treat quoters in establishing the competitive range and conducting discussions. See *Finlen Complex, Inc.*, B-288280, Oct. 10, 2001, 2001 CPD ¶ 167 at 8-10.
>
> * * *
>
> Under [FAR Part 15] rules, the determination of whether a proposal is in the competitive range is principally a matter within the discretion of the procuring agency. *Dismas Charities, Inc.*, B-284754, May 22, 2000, 2000 CPD ¶ 84 at 3. FAR § 15.306(c) allows an agency to establish a competitive

range consisting of only the most highly-rated proposals. Under the regulation, agencies properly may eliminate proposals that are deemed to have no realistic prospect for award. *SDS Petroleum Prods., Inc.*, B-280430, Sept. 1, 1998, 98-2 CPD ¶ 59 at 5-6. Judgments regarding which proposals are included in the competitive range must be made in a relatively equal manner. An agency cannot reasonably exclude a proposal from the competitive range where the strengths and weaknesses found in that proposal are similar to those found in proposals included in the competitive range. *Columbia Research Corp.*, B-284157, Feb. 28, 2000, 2000 CPD ¶ 158 at 4; *Nations, Inc.*, B-280048, Aug. 24, 1998, 99-2 CPD ¶ 94 at 6-10.

Following this reasoning, in *American Material Handling, Inc.*, Comp. Gen. Dec. B-410899, 2015 CPD ¶ 106, GAO held that the contracting officer properly had refused to accept a material modification to an offer that had been submitted in response to a clarification request. See also *Dubinsky v. United States*, 43 Fed. Cl. 243 (1999), where the court found that FAR Part 15 procedures had been used and ruled that the agency had not complied with those procedures when it conducted discussions with only the awardee. Similarly, in *ERIE Strayer Co.*, Comp. Gen. Dec. B-406131, 2012 CPD ¶ 101, GAO sustained a protest when an agency conducted discussions with only the awardee. Compare *Paraclete Contracts*, Comp. Gen. Dec. B-299883, 2007 CPD ¶ 153, holding that no clarification of a mistake was required when the agency used simplified procedures.

If an agency establishes a competitive range, it is improper to exclude a company based solely on its "neutral" past performance rating, *Xtreme Concepts Inc.*, Comp. Gen. Dec. B-413711, 2016 CPD ¶ 372.

[4] Source Selection and Award

The only guidance on source selection and the award of contracts for commercial items is found in FAR 12.602(c), dealing with streamlined procedures, as follows:

> Select the offer that is most advantageous to the Government based on the factors contained in the solicitation. Fully document the rationale for selection of the successful offeror including discussion of any tradeoffs considered.

Award on the basis of the initial proposals is permissible when there is a reasonable basis for distinguishing between the proposals because ¶ (g) of the FAR 52.212-1 solicitation provision calls for such award, *Chem-Spray-South, Inc.*, Comp. Gen. Dec. B-400928.2, 2009 CPD ¶ 144 (significant price differential led agency to conclude that there was a clear winner); *Silynx Commc'ns, Inc.*, B-310667, 2008 CPD ¶ 36 (awardee was only offeror with acceptable technical proposal).

As in other types of procurement, award to an offeror that does not comply with the solicitation is improper, *Wyse Tech., Inc.*, Comp. Gen. Dec. B-297454, 2006 CPD ¶ 23 (failure to submit required Trade Agreements Act certificate).

When evaluation factors other than price are used, the source selection must be based on a reasoned trade-off analysis. See *General Dynamics C4 Sys., Inc.*, Comp. Gen. Dec. B-299675.2, 2008 CPD ¶ 122, agreeing that award to a higher priced offeror was proper when the protester did not meet the mandatory requirements of the solicitation; and *BTC Contract Servs., Inc.*, Comp. Gen. Dec. B-295877, 2005 CPD ¶ 96, confirming an award to a higher priced offeror based on better past performance. Compare *American Auto Logistics LP*, Comp. Gen. Dec. B-409207, 2014 CPD ¶ 319, denying a protest arguing that the agency should have awarded the contract to a higher rated offeror even though it had proposed a significantly higher price. See also *Midland Supply, Inc.*, Comp. Gen. Dec. B-298720, 2007 CPD ¶ 2, granting a protest because the agency used a point scoring system (including point scoring price) and, without further analysis, selected the offeror with the highest number of points. GAO stated:

> While this is a commercial-item procurement, it was conducted using negotiated procedures, at least in terms of the substance of the agency's actions. n5 Specifically, the solicitation provided that the combination of technical evaluation factors—past performance and delivery—would be considered significantly more important than price in determining the proposals that were most advantageous to the government. Under this type of evaluation scheme, an agency has the discretion to determine whether the technical advantage associated with an offeror's proposal is worth its higher price. The propriety of a price/technical tradeoff turns not on the difference in the technical scores or ratings per se, but on whether the agency's judgment concerning the significance of the difference is reasonable and adequately justified in light of the evaluation scheme. *Opti-Lite Optical*, B-281693, Mar. 22, 1999, 99-1 CPD ¶ 61 at 4.
>
> In order for our Office to perform a meaningful review of an agency's award determination, the agency is required to have adequate documentation to support its evaluation of proposals and its award decision. *Century Envtl. Hygiene, Inc.*, B-279378, June 5, 1998, 98-1 CPD ¶ 164 at 4; *Biospherics, Inc.*, B-278508.4 et al., Oct. 6, 1998, 98-2 CPD ¶ 96 at 4; *Arco Mgmt. of Wash., D.C., Inc.*, B-248653, Sept. 11, 1992, 92-2 CPD ¶ 173 at 3. An award decision is not reasonable where there is no documentation or explanation to support the price/technical tradeoff and where the agency makes its award decision based strictly on a mechanical comparison of the offerors' total point scores. *Universal Bldg. Maint., Inc.*, B-282456, July 15, 1999, 99-2 CPD ¶ 32 at 4; see also FAR §§ 12.602(c), 15.308.

[C] Special Authority

In 41 U.S.C. § 428a and § 437 (now 41 U.S.C. § 1903(c)), Congress granted special authority to use commercial item procurement procedures for certain classes of procurement. When this authority is exercised, a few special procedures are applicable. This authority and the special procedures are described in FAR 12.102 as follows:

> (f)(1) Contracting officers may treat any acquisition of supplies or services that, as determined by the head of the agency, are to be used to facilitate defense against or recovery from cyber, nuclear, biological, chemical, or radiological attack, as an acquisition of commercial products or commercial services.
>
> (2) A contract in an amount greater than $20 million that is awarded on a sole source basis for a product or service treated as a commercial product or commercial service under paragraph (f)(1) of this section but does not meet the definition of a commercial product or commercial service as defined at FAR 2.101 shall not be exempt from—
>
> (i) Cost accounting standards (see subpart 30.2); or
>
> (ii) Cost or pricing data requirements (see 15.403).

[D] Terms and Conditions

One of the major elements of the policy favoring the procurement of commercial products or services was the elimination of as many contract clauses as was practicable. The FASA amended a number of laws to state that they did not apply to the procurement of commercial items and added 41 U.S.C. § 430 (now 41 U.S.C. § 1906) requiring the FAR to include a list of laws that were not applicable to contracts and subcontracts for commercial items. Subsequently, § 4203 of the Clinger-Cohen Act of 1996 enacted 41 U.S.C. § 431 (now 41 U.S.C. § 1907) requiring that the FAR list laws that are not applicable to the procurement of commercial off-the-shelf items.

[1] Standard Commercial Products and Services

There are two standard clauses for commercial products and services procurements. The first contains the operating clauses for contract performance while the second covers the statutory and executive order provisions applicable to government procurement in general.

[a] Operating Provisions

FAR 52.212-4 provides a standard contract clause, Contract Terms and Conditions—Commercial Products and Commercial Services, which contains 22 specific provisions to be used in contracts for commercial products and services. Many of these provisions are greatly shortened versions of the standard clauses used in the procurement of supplies such as the termination clauses, the inspection clauses, the changes clause, and the disputes clause. An Alternate I clause is provided for use in time-and-materials and labor-hour contracts. This clause includes a different Inspection/Acceptance provision (¶ a), some additional definitions (¶ e), and an elaborate Payments provision (¶ (i)).

The contracting officer is authorized to "tailor" certain of these provisions, but only to reflect commercial practices, FAR 12.302(a). However, FAR 12.302(b) provides that the following clauses, which implement statutory requirements, may not be tailored:

> (1) Assignments;
> (2) Disputes;
> (3) Payment (except as provided in subpart 32.11);
> (4) Invoice;
> (5) Other compliances; and
> (6) Compliance with laws unique to government contracts.

FAR 12.213 contains the following guidance to contracting officers on the subject of tailoring:

> It is a common practice in the commercial marketplace for both the buyer and seller to propose terms and conditions written from their particular perspectives. The terms and conditions prescribed in this Part 12 seek to balance the interests of both the buyer and seller. These terms and conditions are generally appropriate for use in a wide range of acquisitions. However, market research may indicate other commercial practices that are appropriate for the acquisition of the particular item. These practices should be considered for incorporation into the solicitation and contract if the contracting officer determines them appropriate in concluding a business arrangement satisfactory to both parties and not otherwise precluded by law or Executive order.

FAR 12.302 prohibits tailoring or use of clauses that do not follow customary commercial practice unless a waiver is obtained:

> (c) *Tailoring inconsistent with customary commercial practice*. The contracting officer shall not tailor any clause or otherwise include any additional terms or conditions in a solicitation or contract for commercial products or commercial services in a manner that is inconsistent with customary commercial practice for the commercial products or commercial services being acquired unless a waiver is approved in accordance with agency procedures. The request for waiver must describe the customary commercial practice found in the marketplace, support the need to include a term or condition that is inconsistent with that practice and include a determination that use of the customary commercial practice is inconsistent with the needs of the Government. A waiver may be requested for an individual or class of contracts for that specific item.

Inclusion of a clause not in accordance with commercial practice is improper if no waiver is obtained, *Red River Waste Solutions, LP*, Comp. Gen. Dec. B-411760.2, 2016 CPD ¶ 45, *recons. denied*, 2016 CPD ¶ 162 (refuse collection on a per ton basis); *Verizon Wireless*, Comp. Gen. Dec. B-406854, 2012 CPD ¶ 260 (several terms in wireless telecommunications procurement); *Smelkinson Sysco Food Servs.*, Comp. Gen. Dec. B-281631, 99-1 CPD ¶ 57 (clause requiring disclosure of internal profit data). Compare *JRS Staffing Servs.*, Comp. Gen. Dec. B-410098, 2014 CPD ¶ 312, denying a protest where the agency required advance notice of substitution of personnel because of security clearance needs); *Northrop Grumman Tech. Servs., Inc.*, Comp. Gen. Dec. B-406523, 2012 CPD ¶ 197, denying a protest where the agency had industry input supporting a fixed-price rate for flight hours for five years, and *American Coll. of Physicians Servs., Inc.*, Comp. Gen. Dec. B-294881, 2005 CPD ¶ 1, denying a protest where the protester could not identify a specific clause that had been tailored. These tailoring restrictions are not applicable to Federal Supply Schedule procurements, *HealthDataInsights, Inc.*, Comp. Gen. Dec. B-409409, 2014 CPD ¶ 134.

Adequately justified waivers will withstand a protest of inconsistent terms, *U.S. Foodservice, Inc.*, Comp. Gen. Dec. B-404786, 2011 CPD ¶ 102.

Since the FAR 52.212-4 clause contains provisions reflecting supply contracting practices, tailoring may be required when it is used for other types of contracts such as procurements of services and construction. See the July 3, 2003 memorandum from the Administrator of the Officer of Federal Procurement Policy noting that FAR Part 12 is not equipped to handle "differing site conditions, change orders, and suspension of work" that are likely to arise during new construction or non-routine alteration and repair services. Instead of recommending tailoring, the memorandum states that Part 12 procedures should not be used for this type of work.

There have been a number of contract appeals requiring the board to interpret the FAR 52.212-4 clause and the decisions indicate that they will generally apply the same legal principles to this clause as have been applied to the standard contract clauses. However, following commercial practice, this clause gives the government greater rights than the standard inspection clause with regard to post-acceptance rights. See the following provisions:

> (a) *Inspection/Acceptance*. The Contractor shall only tender for acceptance those products or services that conform to the requirements of this contract. The Government reserves the right to inspect or test any supplies or services that have been tendered for acceptance. The Government may require repair or replacement of nonconforming supplies or reperformance of nonconforming services at no increase in contract price. If repair/replacement or reperformance will not correct the defects or is not possible, the Government may seek an equitable price reduction or adequate consideration for acceptance of nonconforming supplies or services. The Government must exercise its postacceptance rights (1) within a reasonable time after the defect was

discovered or should have been discovered; and (2) before any substantial change occurs in the condition of the item, unless the change is due to the defect in the item.

* * *

(o) Warranty. The Contractor warrants and implies that the products delivered hereunder are merchantable and fit for use for the particular purpose described in this contract.

See *John Snow, Inc. v. United States*, 78 Fed. Cl. 763 (2007), discussing these differences in a dispute involving a contract that contained both the FAR 52.212-4 clause and standard clauses. Decisions applying the inspection provision include *Earthstar Constr. & Logistics Co.*, ASBCA 58086, 13-1 BCA ¶ 35,461 (government rejection of products was timely); *Fischer Imaging Corp.*, VABCA 6125-6127, 02-2 BCA ¶ 32,003, and VABCA 6343, 02-2 BCA ¶ 32,048 (government final inspection within a reasonable time after delivery and use of the commercial product required in order to preserve the clause's post-acceptance rights). In *Professional Mgmt. Consulting Servs., LLC*, ASBCA 61861, 20-1 BCA ¶ 37,638, the board held that a deviation to the clause deprived the government of the right to claim an equitable adjustment for defective work. In *Bay Shipbuilding Co.*, DOTBCA 4153, 03-1 BCA ¶ 32,256, the board held that this provision required the contractor to bear the cost of reinspecting government property that might have been damaged by defectively performed services.

The changes paragraph in the FAR 52.212-4 clause (¶ (c)) is unique in the fact that it does not permit the government to issue unilateral changes—with the result that it is questionable whether there can be constructive changes. See *Tkacz Eng'g, LCC*, ASBCA 60358, 18-1 BCA ¶ 36,940, ruling that there can be no constructive changes under the clause. Compare *SAWADI Corp.*, ASBCA 53073, 01-1 BCA ¶ 31,357, where the board, without citing the contract clause, decided four constructive changes claims for extra work, two constructive suspension of work claims, and one constructive acceleration claim. The boards have ruled on constructive changes claims without citing the clause in *Stobil Enter.*, ASBCA 61688, 19-1 BCA ¶ 37,242 (claim for extra work denied because government interpretation of specification was correct); *Keller Mech. Servs., Inc.*, ASBCA 56318, 09-1 BCA ¶ 34,111 (claim for extra work granted based on ambiguous specifications); *Service Rodriguez Barragan, S.L.*, ASBCA 54622, 08-1 BCA ¶ 33,812 (claim for extra work denied because of patent ambiguity); *Arcadis U.S., Inc. v. Dep't of Interior*, CBCA 918, 08-1 BCA ¶ 33,807 (claim for extra work denied based on interpretation of unilateral modification); *California Bus Tels. v. Dep't of Agriculture*, CBCA 135, 07-1 BCA ¶ 33,553 (claim for extra work denied because no contracting officer ordered it); *Range Tech.* Corp., ASBCA 51943, 06-2 BCA ¶ 33,371 (claim for extra work denied because contractor voluntarily performed extra work); *Bradford E. Englander, Liquidating Trustee for Dulles Networking Assocs., Inc.*, VABCA 6473, 01-2

BCA ¶ 31,466 (claim for extra work granted). These cases may be instances where the board found jurisdiction in the Disputes paragraph of the clause. See also *Madison Lawrence, Inc.*, ASBCA 56551, 09-2 BCA ¶ 34,235, where the board found that the contractor had filed a proper Disputes clause claim for reformation based on alleged government misstatements of the amount of work to be performed. In contrast, in *Hawaii CyberSpace*, ASBCA 54065, 04-2 BCA ¶ 32,744, the board noted the difference in the changes language but ruled that the contractor should be compensated for extra work because it had been directed by the contracting officer. Compare *Bridget Allen*, ASBCA 54696, 05-1 BCA ¶ 32,871, *aff'd*, 177 Fed. Appx. 977 (Fed. Cir.), *cert. denied*, 549 U.S. 903 (2006), where the board denied a constructive changes claim but the contract contained a standard Changes clause as well as the FAR 52.212-4 clause.

A number of appeals have sustained terminations for cause (¶ (m)). In *Double B Enter., Inc.*, ASBCA 52010, 01-1 BCA ¶ 31,396, the board rejected a claim of excusable delay and held that a termination for cause was valid even though it occurred the day after delivery was required. See also *John's Tile & Carpet Serv.*, ASBCA 61479, 20-1 BCA ¶ 37,573 (defective work); *SCS Bld'g Maint., Inc. v. General Servs. Admin.*, CBCA 5766, 20-1 BCA ¶ 37992 (defective work); *Axxon Int'l, LLC*, ASBCA 61549, 20-1 BCA ¶ 37,564 (contractor failed to pay small business subcontractor in accordance with the FAR 52.232-40 clause); *Walker Dev. & Trading Grp., Inc. v. Dep't of Veterans Affairs*, CBCA 5907, 19-1 BCA ¶ 37,376 (contractor failed to perform services on required date); *LKJ Crabbe, Inc.*, ASBCA 60331, 18-1 BCA ¶ 37,193 (contractor statement it was financially unable to complete contract an anticipatory repudiation); *United Healthcare Partners, Inc.*, ASBCA 58123, 16-1 BCA ¶ 36,374 (contractor anticipatorily repudiated by stating it intended to stop work unless the government paid its invoices); *Earthstar Constr. & Logistics Co.*, ASBCA 58086, 13-1 BCA ¶ 35,461 (contractor delivered used rather than new products); *ZIOS Corp.*, ASBCA 56626, 2010 BCA ¶ 34,344 (contractor failed to perform on time); *Thomson & Pratt Ins. Assocs., Inc. v. Dep't of State*, GSBCA 15979-ST, 05-1 BCA ¶ 32,944 (contractor refused to provide disputed insurance coverage); *Falls Mfg., Inc.*, DOTBCA 4149, 04-2 BCA ¶ 32,632 (less than 50% of the commercial products had been delivered by the delivery date); *Sigma Tech Enter., Inc.*, ASBCA 52774, 04-1 BCA ¶ 32,484 (product did not meet specification requirements); *Specialty Trans., Inc. v. United States*, 57 Fed. Cl. 1 (2003) (contractor refused to continue performance); *Aerobotics Corp.*, ASBCA 52134, 02-2 BCA ¶ 31,974 (nonperformance of a purchase order for the design, fabrication, and demonstration of three models of an unmanned aircraft proper when contractor had assumed the risk of commercial impracticability by accepting a performance specification); *Ultimate Labs., Inc.*, VABCA 6641, 02-1 BCA ¶ 31,663 (non-delivery a valid grounds for termination—rejecting contractor's argument that it properly refused to deliver eyeglasses because it believed that they were going to be prescribed improperly); *Integrated Sys. Grp., Inc. v. Social Security Admin.*, GSBCA 14054-SSA, 98-2

BCA ¶29,848 (contractor refused to deliver a domestic product as required by the contract's Buy American clause). When a contract is terminated for cause, the government can recover any amounts paid for work not performed, *Ucensys Research Corp. v, Nuclear Regulatory Comm.*, CBCA 4241, 19-1 BCA ¶37,402.

Decisions finding terminations for cause improper include *AEY, Inc.*, ASBCA 56470, 18-1 BCA ¶37,076 (government waived delivery schedule and failed to issue cure notice and contractor encountered excusable delays); *Free & Ben, Inc.*, ASBCA 56129 09-1 BCA ¶34,127 (denying government motion for summary judgment because there was evidence that its failure to cooperate with the contractor caused the contractor's failure to perform the contract); *ALKAI Consultants, LLC*, ASBCA 55581, 09-1 BCA ¶34,058 (contractor was excusably delayed when the government failed to cooperate and the contractor encountered unforeseen conditions during performance); and *Trinity Installers, Inc.*, AGBCA 2004-139-1, 05-1 BCA ¶32,868 (contractor had substantially completed performance of the construction work). It has also been held that the agency need not permit the terminated contractor to compete for the reprocurement contract, *Essan Metallix Corp.*, Comp. Gen. Dec. B-310357, 2008 CPD ¶5.

The termination for cause paragraph does not contain the requirement for a cure notice prior to terminations for causes other than late delivery. However, FAR 12.403(c)(1) requires a cure notice in such cases and the boards have held that this requirement applies, *Bulova Techs. Ordnance Sys., LLC*, ASBCA 59089, 18-1 BCA ¶37,183; *Brent Packer & Myrna Palasi v. Social Security Admin.*, CBCA 5038, 16-1 BCA ¶36,260. See also *KSC-TRI Sys., USA, Inc.*, ASBCA 54638, 06-1 BCA ¶33,145, holding that the procedures in FAR Part 49 do not apply when this clause is used and that cure notices need not allow ten days to cure, and *Geo-Marine, Inc. v. General Servs. Admin.*, GSBCA 16247, 05-2 BCA ¶33,048, holding that no cure notice is required if the contractor repudiated the contract. If a cure notice is issued, the contract can be terminated if the contractor does not provide adequate assurances that it will meet the new date, *Grow Life General Trading, LLC*, ASBCA 60398, 19-1 BCA ¶37,361.

Although the excusable delays provision (¶(f)) is much shorter than the standard provision and does not mention subcontractor delays, it has been held that a contractor is responsible for delays that are the fault of subcontractors, *General Injectables & Vaccines, Inc. v. Gates*, 527 F.3d 1375 (Fed. Cir. 2008); *Wellington House v. General Servs. Admin.*, GSBCA 14665, 99-1 BCA ¶30,279. In contrast, in *The NTC Grp., Inc.*, ASBCA 53720, 04-2 BCA ¶32,706, the board found an excusable delay when a service contractor could not hire the critical incumbent employees because their employers (the incumbent contractors) conspired to prevent their employment.

The termination for convenience paragraph ¶(l) gives the government the right to terminate the contract at will, *ACLR, LLC v. United States*, 147 Fed. Cl. 548 (2020). It provides that the contractor will be paid a percentage of the contract price which reflects "the percentage of the work performed" and the "reasonable charges [it] can demonstrate . . . have resulted from the termination." The percentage of work is calculated as a percentage of the contract price attributable to the work done before the termination. See *ESCgov, Inc.*, ASBCA 58852, 17-1 BCA ¶ 36,772 (contractor compensated for 10 days of use of software licenses rather than full monthly payment); *Corners & Edges, Inc. v. Dep't of Health & Human Servs.*, CBCA 762, 08-2 BCA ¶ 33,961 (contractor had been paid on a percentage of work basis for services when the government had paid the monthly amount for services rendered up to the time of the termination).

The "reasonable charges" provision was interpreted narrowly until *SWR, Inc.*, ASBCA 56708, 15-1 BCA ¶ 35,832, holding that it included "the recovery of those charges incurred that 'do not relate to work completed' but should be reimbursed to fairly compensate the contractor whose contract has been terminated." This includes the amounts recovered in non-commercial contract terminations such as preparatory expenses not recovered because of the termination plus settlement expenses. See *Microtechnologies, LLC v. Dep't of Justice*, CBCA 6772, 21-1 BCA ¶ 37830, *aff'd* (denying recovery of cost of software maintenance purchased before exercise of option for additional year); *Globe Trailer Mfg., Inc.*, ASBCA 60979, 19-1 BCA ¶ 37,392 (denying recovery of cost of design work, specialized tooling, or constructive changes to the design that were allocated to terminated work but were contractually required to be charged to first article CLIN); *First Division Design, LLC*, ASBCA 60049, 18-1 BCA ¶ 37,201 (compensation denied because of lack of proof of costs incurred); *American Boys Constr. Co.*, ASBCA 60515, 17-1 BCA ¶ 36,856 (denying recovery of material costs incurred before issuance of notice to proceed); *First Division Design, LLC*, ASBCA 60951, 17-1 BCA ¶ 36,736 (denying recovery of home office overhead). See also *Corners & Edges, Inc. v. Dep't of Health & Human Servs.*, CBCA 762, 08-2 BCA ¶ 33,961, where the board accepted a broad interpretation of the "reasonable charges" provision, including unamortized costs and settlement expenses, although it found that the contractor had incurred no such charges.

The termination for convenience paragraph gives the government the right to terminate all or any part of the contract but contains no provision granting an equitable adjustment to reprice the unterminated work when there is a partial termination. Thus, such an equitable adjustment was denied in *Individual Dev. Assocs., Inc.*, ASBCA 53910, 04-2 BCA ¶ 32,740, *recons. denied*, ASBCA 55174, 06-2 BCA ¶ 33,349. In *Individual Dev. Assocs., Inc.*, ASBCA 55174, 08-1 BCA ¶ 33,754, the board held that a contract line item terminated after it had commenced was properly treated as a partial termination. The right to partially terminate a commercial item contract was also upheld in *Dehdari General Trading & Contracting EST*, ASBCA 53987, 03-1 BCA ¶ 32,249, and *Hermes Consolidated, Inc.*, ASBCA 52308, 02-1 BCA ¶ 31,767. In *Hermes* the agency significantly reduced the guaranteed minimum quantity of an indefinite delivery/indefinite quantity contract eight days before the end of the one-year ordering period but the board rejected the contractor's argument that it was entitled to be paid the price of the unordered quantity in accordance with *Maxima Corp. v. United States*, 847 F.2d 1549 (Fed. Cir. 1988), citing *Montana Refining Co.*, ASBCA 50515, 00-1 BCA ¶ 30,694, for the proposition that "the expiration of the basic performance period is the demarcation line for retroactive terminations." A constructive termination for convenience was found in *Praecomm, Inc. v. United States*, 78 Fed. Cl. 5, *aff'd*, 296 Fed. Appx. 929 (Fed. Cir. 2008), where the agency accepted delivery of radios but modified the provision requiring the contractor to install them. The court rejected the contractor's argument that this action was a constructive change or a breach of contract (thus denying compensation). See also *JKB Sols. & Servs., LLC v. United States*, 150 Fed. Cl. 252 (2020) (constructive partial termination limited government liability to work performed).

[b] Statutory and Executive Order Provisions

FAR 52.212-5 provides a standard clause, Contract Terms and Conditions Required to Implement Statutes or Executive Orders—Commercial Products and Commercial Services, that sets forth the mandatory clauses that must be included in these procurements. An additional clause is prescribed for use on Department of Defense procurements in DFARS 252.212-7001. The contracting officer must check the appropriate provisions in these clauses in accordance with the instructions in the various parts of the FAR or DFARS prescribing the use of these clauses. FAR 12.503 and DFARS 212.503, respectively, list the statutes that do not apply. The FAR 52.212-5 clause also contains a list of the 24 statutes and executive orders that must be passed down to subcontractors when required by the clause. See the guidance in FAR 12.504 which includes a list of the statutes that are not applicable to subcontractors. DFARS 212.504 contains a list of additional statutes that are not applicable to subcontractors.

Contractors should be aware that there are other statutes that are of general applicability in the United States that are also not listed in this clause. See ¶ (r) of the FAR 52.212-4 clause, stating:

> (r) Compliance with laws unique to Government contracts. The Contractor agrees to comply with 31 U.S.C. 1352 relating to limitations on the use of appropriated funds to influence certain Federal contracts; 18 U.S.C. 431 relating to officials not to benefit; 40 U.S.C. 327, et seq., Contract Work Hours and Safety Standards Act; 41 U.S.C. 5158, Anti-Kickback Act of 1986; 41 U.S.C. 265 and 10 U.S.C. 2409 relating to whistle-blower protections; 49 U.S.C. 40118, Fly American; and 41 U.S.C. 423 relating to procurement integrity.

[2] Commercial Off-the-Shelf Items

The Clinger-Cohen Act of 1996 also required a FAR list of provisions not applicable to commercial off-the-shelf items. See 41 U.S.C. § 1907:

(a) Inclusion in Federal Acquisition Regulation.

(1) In general. The Federal Acquisition Regulation shall include a list of provisions of law that are inapplicable to contracts for the procurement of commercially available off-the-shelf items. A provision of law properly included on the list pursuant to paragraph (2) does not apply to contracts for the procurement of commercially available off-the-shelf items. This section does not render a provision of law not included on the list inapplicable to contracts for the procurement of commercially available off-the-shelf items.

(2) Laws to be included. A provision of law described in subsection (b) shall be included on the list of inapplicable provisions of law required by paragraph (1) unless the Administrator makes a written determination that it would not be in the best interest of the Federal Government to exempt contracts for the procurement of commercially available off-the-shelf items from the applicability of the provision.

(3) Other authorities or responsibilities not affected. This section does not modify, supersede, impair, or restrict authorities or responsibilities under—

(A) section 15 of the Small Business Act (15 U.S.C. 644); or

(B) bid protest procedures developed under the authority of—

(i) [31 U.S.C. §§ 3551 et seq.];

(ii) section 2305(e) and (f) of title 10; or

(iii) [41 U.S.C. §§ 3706 and 3707].

(b) Covered law. Except as provided in subsection (a)(3), a provision of law referred to in subsection (a)(1) is a provision of law that the Administrator determines imposes Federal Government-unique policies, procedures, requirements, or restrictions for the procurement of property or services on persons whom the Federal Government has awarded contracts for the procurement of commercially available off-the-shelf items, except for a provision of law that—

(1) provides for criminal or civil penalties; or

(2) specifically refers to this section and provides that, notwithstanding this section, it shall be applicable to contracts for the procurement of commercially available off-the-shelf items.

This provision is implemented in FAR 12.505, stating:

COTS items are a subset of commercial items. Therefore, any laws listed in sections 12.503 and 12.504 are also inapplicable or modified in their applicability to contracts or subcontracts for the acquisition of COTS items. In addition, the following laws are not applicable to contracts for the acquisition of COTS items:

(a)(1) 41 U.S.C. 10a, portion of first sentence that reads "substantially all from articles, materials, or supplies mined, produced, or manufactured, as the case may be, in the United States," Buy American Act—Supplies, component test (see 52.225-1 and 52.225-3).

(2) 41 U.S.C. 10b, portion of first sentence that reads "substantially all from articles, materials, or supplies mined, produced, or manufactured, as the case may be, in the United States," Buy American Act—Construction Materials, component test (see 52.225-9 and 52.225-11).

(b) 42 U.S.C. 6962(c)(3)(A), Certification and Estimate of Percentage of Recovered Material.

[3] Commercial Computer Software

FAR 12.212 states that commercial computer software and commercial computer software documentation must be acquired "under licenses customarily provided to the public to the extent such licenses are consistent with Federal law." There is no mandatory FAR clause for such procurements but an optional clause is provided in FAR 52.227-19. When an agency agrees to use the supplier's commercial clause, it must specify which terms are inconsistent with federal law, FAR 27.405-3(b). Several agencies have issued standard clauses meeting this requirement. See the General Services Administration's Commercial Supplier Agreements—Unenforceable Clauses clause at 1552.232-75; and the Environmental Protection Agency's Commercial Supplier Agreements—Unenforceable Clauses clause at EPAR 1552.232-75.

For DoD procurements of commercial computer software and commercial computer software documentation DFARS 227.7202-4 states that there is no standard clause, and DFARS 227.7202-3 calls for the use of the supplier's commercial license unless the agency has needs not covered by the license. This regulation contains no guidance on dealing with provisions in the commercial license that conflict with federal law.

§ 9.04 GSA ONLINE MARKETPLACES

Section 846 of the National Defense Authorization Act for Fiscal Year 2018, Pub. L. No. 115-91, directed the General Services Administration and the Office of Management and Budget to establish and implement an ecommerce program for agencies to purchase commercially available off the-shelf products through online marketplaces. The legislation stated that the purpose of the program is to enhance competition, expedite procurement, and ensure reasonable pricing of commercial products.

In 2020, GSA began implementing the commercial platforms program as a proof of concept for three years. During this phase, government purchase card holders within 13 selected federal agencies can access the online marketplaces to purchase products at prices below the micro-purchase threshold. GSA awarded three contracts to Amazon Business, Fisher Scientific Co. L.L.C., and Overstock Government. The ordering procedures for the program provide that all micro-purchase policies and procedures apply, including requirements for use of mandatory government sources and environmentally sustainable products, and that agency users should review the pricing and terms of similar items from at least two suppliers to promote competition. See *GSA ONLINE MARKETPLACES: Plans to Measure Progress and Monitor Data Protection Efforts Need Further Development*, GAO-1-104572 (Sept. 2021), for a description of the program.

CHAPTER 10

OTHER NEGOTIATION PROCEDURES

§ 10.01 INTRODUCTION

In addition to the standard negotiation procedure discussed in Chapter 6, the special procedures for IDIQ contracts discussed in Chapter 7, the simplified procedures discussed in Chapter 8 and the commercial item procedures discussed in Chapter 9, a number of special procedures are used in various classes of negotiated procurements. The procurement statutes contain provisions permitting the use of these special procedures in order to simplify the procurement process or adapt it to the unique conditions that are encountered in specific markets. This chapter covers the following procedures:

- The "other transactions" procedures used by many agencies for research, prototypes and other specified requirements.
- The broad agency announcement procedures used to procure research work in general and under the small business innovative research program.
- The small business innovative research procedure.
- The architect-engineer services procedure.
- The two-step design-build procedure for the procurement of construction work.
- The procedures for the procurement of information technology.
- The major special procedures that have been adopted by specific agencies to enhance their ability to carry out their procurement missions.

§ 10.02 OTHER TRANSACTIONS

The term "other transactions" signifies a contract that pursuant to specific statutory authority can be awarded without following the procurement statutes or the Federal Acquisition Regulations. This authority was given to NASA at the time the agency was created in 1958 by Pub. L. No. 85-568, § 203(c). It was subsequently given to DOD in 1989 to procure research work, previously codified at 10 U.S.C. § 2371, now at 10 U.S.C. § 4021. The extent of the authority varies between agencies, depending on the statutory grant of authority. A 2016 GAO report, *Federal Acquisitions: Use of "Other Transaction" Agreements Limited and Mostly for Research and Development Activities*, GAO-16-209, identified the agencies and the uses made of this authority. The following eleven agencies have OT authority:

Agency	Statute	Activities
Department of Defense	10 U.S.C. § 4021 10 U.S.C. § 4022	Basic, applied & advanced research Prototypes
Department of Energy	42 U.S.C. § 7256	Research, development & demonstration projects
Advanced Research Projects Agency—Energy	42 U.S.C. § 16538	Research, development & demonstration projects
Department of Health and Human Services	42 U.S.C. § 247d-7e	Advanced research & development
Department of Homeland Security	6 U.S.C. § 391	Basic, applied & advanced research & development and prototypes
Department of Transportation	49 U.S.C. § 5312	Research, development, demonstration & deployment projects
Transportation Security Administration	49 U.S.C. § 114(m)	All functions of agency
Federal Aviation Administration	49 U.S.C. § 106(l)	All functions of agency
National Aeronautics and Space Administration	51 U.S.C. § 20113(e)	All functions of agency
Domestic Nuclear Detection Office	6 U.S.C. § 596	All functions of agency
National Institutes of Health	42 U.S.C. §§ 282(n), 284n(b), 285b-3, & 287a	Research & demonstrations

Other transaction agreements (OTAs) are intended to give agencies a high degree of flexibility in order to permit them to contract with organizations that otherwise would not be willing to enter into government contracts. The basic goal of OTAs is to induce commercial organizations to participate with government agencies in using leading-edge commercial technology to solve to problems that an agency is charged with solving. However, they are also being used as a method of speeding up the procurement process and avoiding the stringent competition requirements discussed in Chapter 3. Section 876 of the National Defense

Authorization Act for Fiscal Year 2016, Pub. L. No. 114-92, even states a preference for the use of OTAs in procuring research and prototypes.

[A] Definition of Types of OTAs

The major types of OTAs are research and prototypes and in both cases the definitions of these types of work tend to be expansive. It should also be noted that there are some variations between the agencies.

[1] Research

10 U.S.C. § 4021 allows for the use of OTAs on "basic, applied or advanced" research projects. While the FAR does not implement this statutory authority, it does provide definitions for these terms that give some context for their meaning. FAR 2.101 defines basic research as follows:

> Basic research means that research directed toward increasing knowledge in science. The primary aim of basic research is a fuller knowledge or understanding of the subject under study, rather than any practical application of that knowledge.

FAR 35.001 defines applied research as follows:

> Applied research means the effort that (a) normally follows basic research, but may not be severable from the related basic research; (b) attempts to determine and exploit the potential of scientific discoveries or improvements in technology, materials, processes, methods, devices, or techniques; and (c) attempts to advance the state of the art. When being used by contractors in cost principle applications, this term does not include efforts whose principal aim is the design, development, or testing of specific items or services to be considered for sale; these efforts are within the definition of development, given below.

There is no FAR definition of advanced research. The DOD *Other Transactions Guide*, November 2018 (DOD Guide) refers to these OTAs as "science and technology" OTAs.

[2] Prototypes

There is no definition of "prototype" in the statutory grant of this authority. 10 U.S.C. § 4022(e)(5) contains a definition of "prototype project" which is implemented in the DOD Guide as follows:

> *Prototype project*. The definition of a "prototype project" in the context of an OT is as follows: a prototype project addresses a proof of concept,

model, reverse engineering to address obsolescence, pilot, novel application of commercial technologies for defense purposes, agile development activity, creation, design, development, demonstration of technical or operational utility, or combinations of the foregoing. A process, including a business process, may be the subject of a prototype project.

Although assistance terms are generally not appropriate in OT agreements, ancillary work efforts that are necessary for completion of the prototype project, such as test site training or limited logistics support, may be included in prototype projects. A prototype may be physical, virtual, or conceptual in nature.

The Department of Homeland Security Management Directive 0771.1 contains a much shorter definition:

> *Prototype*: With regard to OTs for Prototype Projects, a "prototype" generally can be described as a physical or virtual model used to evaluate the technical or manufacturing feasibility or utility, to the DHS mission, of a particular technology, process, concept, end item, or system.

The scope of the definition of a "prototype" has been litigated in GAO protests. See *Oracle America, Inc.*, Comp. Gen. Dec. B-416061, 2018 CPD ¶ 180, holding that the following definition was compliant:

> Seeking the prototyping of a robust and scalable software development environment to enable the modernization of Department of Defense (DoD) command and control systems in a cloud infrastructure. Environment must include a scalable software development and production platform to enable continuous integration, continuous delivery, and operation of new applications, as well as the containerization, rehosting, and refactoring of existing DoD applications. Additionally, ideal solutions will consist of an ecosystem of software and platforms to rapidly deploy advanced commercial capabilities, to include, but not limited to[:] workflow, geospatial services, data analytics and visualization, and data management.

See also *ACI Techs., Inc.*, Comp. Gen. Dec. B-417011, 2019 CPD ¶ 24, holding that the following two technology areas were properly found to be prototypes:

> 8. *Outreach and Standards*—Develop standards and practices to foster commercial development of secure, trusted and assured parts. Document and promulgate security-enhancing design practices across government, industry, and academia in the areas of standard program outreach material; standard training material; Government and industry standards and best practices; and self-service libraries of standards and best practices.
>
> * * * *
>
> 18. *Microelectronics and Electronic Warfare focused*—Workforce Development—Develop access to training and skill development for

> university, DoD, and small businesses. This includes SOTA processes for test articles and training; promoting design challenges and hacks around hardware [intellectual property (IP)] development/assurance.

[B] Limitations on Use of OTAs

While agencies are given broad discretion in selecting an OTA as the appropriate contracting technique, there are two limitations that have arisen in making this decision. The first relates to OTAs for research work and the second relates to OTAs for prototypes.

[1] Research

A number of the statutes permitting the use of OTAs for research contain provision that require specific determinations before the agency chooses to use an OTA. For example, 10 U.S.C. § 4021(e) states that before using an OTA, the agency must determine that the effort does not duplicate research being conducted under existing DOD programs. The DOD Guide advises that the "project team" must "ensure" that the first requirement is met and must make a statement that it is not feasible to use another instrument. Several of the statutes authorizing the use of OTAs contain similar requirements but they are not uniform in this respect. Hence, when dealing with an agency, its statute must be consulted to determine the limitations on its authority.

GAO has denied several protests arguing that the agency had misused its OT authority, *Rocketplane Kistler*, Comp. Gen. Dec. B-310741, 2008 CPD ¶ 22 (use of procurement contract or grant by NASA not feasible because project was to stimulate commercial enterprise); *MorphoTrust USA, LLC*, Comp. Gen. Dec. B-412711, 2016 CPD ¶ 133 (TSA statute gave it broad authority to use OTAs); *ACI Techs., Inc.*, Comp. Gen. Dec. B-417011, 2019 CPD ¶ 24 (protester failed to provide facts showing duplicative research).

[2] Prototypes

The limitation regarding prototypes concerns the unique DOD authority to procure production of the product if the prototype proves to be successful. The original DOD prototype authority did not permit production work to be included in a prototype OTA. However, 10 U.S.C. § 4022(f) (formerly § 2371b(f)) now permits inclusion of production work in a prototype OTA (allowing the production work to be obtained without competition) if (1) the prototype OTA was awarded using competitive procedures and (2) the prototype work was successfully completed. See DFARS 206.001-70 stating:

(a) Also excepted from the competition requirements of FAR part 6 are follow-on production contracts for products developed pursuant to the "other transactions" authority of 10 U.S.C. 4022 for prototype projects when—

(1) The other transaction agreement includes provisions for a follow-on production contract;

(2) The contracting officer receives sufficient documentation from the agreements officer of the other transaction agreement for the prototype project that the requirements of 10 U.S.C. 4022 sections (f)(2)(A) and (B) and, when applicable, section (a)(2) have been met.

(3) See PGI 206.001-70(b) for additional guidance;

(4) The participants in the transaction successfully completes the prototype or sub-prototype project provided for in the transaction; and

(5)(i) There is a written determination that—

(A) The requirements of 10 U.S.C. 2371b(d) are met; and

(B) The use of the authority of 10 U.S.C. 2371b is essential to promoting the success of the prototype project; and

(ii)(A) For actions in excess of $100 million, but not in excess of $500 million including all options, the determination is executed by the senior procurement executive; and

(B) For actions in excess of $500 million including all options, the determination is—

(1) Executed by the Under Secretary of Defense for Research and Engineering or the Under Secretary of Defense for Acquisition and Sustainment; and

(2) Provided to the congressional defense committees at least 30 days prior to contract award.

In *Oracle America, Inc.*, Comp. Gen. Dec. B-416061, 2018 CPD ¶ 180, GAO sustained a protest that these conditions had not been met when the agency awarded a production contract. The DOD Guide contains the following guidance with regard to "follow-on production:"

> During the planning of the acquisition, the Government team should identify any potential follow-on prototyping and/or production activities. At a minimum, potential follow-on activities, to include follow-on production *shall* be identified in the solicitation and any resulting OT Agreements. The level of fidelity for production follow-on efforts is naturally limited by the nature of prototyping efforts. Therefore, the level of detail required as to follow-on activities needs to be sufficient for prospective technology providers within the technology sector to make an informed decision whether to bid on the prototyping effort, with the understanding that size, scope and value of potential follow-on activities may vary.

The DOD Guide also requires that the OTA contain a provision defining "successful completion."

[C] Cost Sharing

One of the distinctive features of OTAs is that many of call for cost sharing by the contractor. Since most of these cost-sharing requirements follow the DOD provisions, those requirements will be addressed below.

[1] Research

For research OTs, to the extent DoD determines practicable, government resource contributions should not exceed contributions from other parties. 10 U.S.C. § 4021(e)(2). Relevant here, the DOD Guide states:

> While the default position in the statute is generally a 50/50 resource share, the final amount of the share should be based on full consideration of factors such as the partner's resources, prior investment in the technology, commercial vs. military relevance, unusual performance risk, and precompetitive nature of the project.

[2] Prototypes

For prototype OTs, cost sharing is one of four independent justifications an agency may rely on to use the authority, pursuant to 10 U.S.C. § 4022(d)(1). Other justifications include significant participation of at least one nontraditional contractor or non-traditional research institution, significant small business participation, and a determination by the senior procurement executive.

[3] Calculation of Contractor Share

The DOD Guide addresses the resources that a contractor may count as part of its share of the costs as follows:

> Contributions can be in cash or non-cash form, and costs can be either direct or indirect, so long as contributions are allowable, allocable, reasonable, and consistently accounted for by the awardee. This may include labor, materials, equipment, usage rights in Intellectual Property, and facilities costs, as well as independent R&D costs that may be reimbursed later by DoD through overhead rates on other awarded efforts. Forfeiture of fee, profit, or cost of money would not be consistent with general cost principles and should not be included in any resource-shared arrangement.
>
> If resource-sharing is used, then the non-Federal amounts counted as provided, or to be provided, by parties other than the Federal Government may not include costs that were incurred before the date on which the OT agreement becomes effective. Costs offered as a resource-share that were incurred for a project after the beginning of negotiations, but prior to the date the OT agreement becomes effective, may be counted as non-Federal amounts

> if and to the extent that the Agreements Officer determines in writing that: (1) the party other than the Federal Government incurred the costs in anticipation of the OT agreement; and (2) it was appropriate for the entity to incur the costs before the OT agreement became effective in order to ensure the successful implementation of the OT agreement.

[D] Consortia

One of the unique aspects of OTAs is their use of consortia to address technical issues that are of interest to an agency. A number of consortia have been formed in specific areas of technology—consisting of nonprofits, academic institutions, and/or contractors. Agencies refer a statement of its needs to the lead member of the consortium and that organization alerts its members to the problem. One or more single members can then submit solution papers to the government agency or the consortium can form a team of members that will work together on an OTA. The following is a partial list of the many active consortia:

- Consortium for Command, Control and Communications in Cyberspace
- System of Systems Enterprise Consortium
- Consortium for Energy, Environment and Demilitarization
- Defense Mobility Enterprise/National Advanced Mobility Consortium
- DoD Ordnance Technology Consortium/National Armaments Consortium
- Vertical Lift Consortium
- National Spectrum Consortium
- Medical Technology Enterprise Consortium
- Medical CBRN Defense Consortium
- Countering Weapons of Mass Destruction Consortium
- Sensors, Communications, Electronics Consortium
- Aviation and Missile Technology Consortium
- Space Enterprise Consortium
- Air Force Consortium Initiative
- Underseas Technology Innovation Consortium

The use of consortia can facilitate the contracting process because it provides a means of communication of an agency need to a pre-established group of organizations that are working in an area of technology. It is also beneficial in that it allows the members of the consortium to work together to address a problem. However, there is a disadvantage to this process because if the problem is referred only to the consortium, organizations that are not members are excluded from proposing solutions. There is no requirement that agencies deal exclusively with consortia, but it appears that a number of agencies have followed this practice. For an example of an OTA acquisition seeking an organization to create a consortium, see *ACI Techs., Inc.*, Comp. Gen. Dec. B-417011, 2019 CPD ¶ 24. For a critique of the use of consortia see *COVID-19 CONTRACTING: Actions Needed to Enhance Transparency and Oversight of Selected Awards*, GAO-21-501 (July 2021).

[E] Contracting Procedures

Agencies have great flexibility in devising the procedures that are used to award OTAs. As discussed in Chapter 1, there is significant uncertainty as to where and how agency use of OTAs may be protested. However, given the absence of objective statutory or regulatory restrictions, agencies will enjoy broad discretion to establish a contracting process that is reasonable under the circumstances.

[1] Competition Requirement

The statutory requirement that FAR contracts must be awarded by obtaining "full and open competition" does not apply to OTAs. Furthermore, the statutes allowing for the use of research OTAs generally do not contain a competition requirement. In contrast, the DOD prototype statute, 10 U.S.C. § 4022(b)(2), states that "competitive procedures" should be used "to the maximum extent practicable." In either case, since a major goal of OTAs is to gain access to commercial technology, agencies should reach out to determine the technology that is available. The DOD Guide deals with this process as the dual step of "market intelligence" and "publicizing for solutions."

"Market intelligence" is described in part as follows:

> Gaining market intelligence is an integral part of the development of the acquisition approach and is an ongoing process. To understand industry norms, the current state of technology across multiple sectors, and identify the innovative leaders in industry, the team must conduct research and outreach activities within the relevant technology sectors. Research and outreach activities can include, but are not limited to: researching trade publications; attending technology demonstrations, conferences, conventions, seminars, and trade shows; compiling a capabilities database; conducting reverse industry days; and participating in standards committees and communities of interest. In some cases, the team may find the following efforts beneficial: conducting crowdsourcing events; publishing surveys; participating in technology focused social media groups; conducting industry events; leveraging

> chambers of commerce, Procurement Technical Assistance Centers, technology consortia, and trade associations; and/or leveraging DoD Tech scouting activities. When the team publishes surveys or requests for capabilities through the Government Point of Entry (www.FedBizOpps.gov) or other open forum, it should strive to find innovative ways to attract the right performers and encourage them to participate. Comprehensive market intelligence should identify the industry leaders and the state-of-the-art in a given technology area.

The DOD guide suggests that after the agency has thoroughly explored the market, it should define the problem it is seeking assistance in solving and publicize that problem statement. The Guide makes the following suggestions on the means of publication:

> [T]here is a . . . wide range of methods by which to solicit solutions and the Government team need not be confined to using a Request for Proposals (RFP) process. Overarching calls for solutions similar to a Broad Agency Announcement (BAA), Annual Plan Call for White Papers, or a Commercial Solutions Openings are just a few examples of possible solicitation methods to make calls for solutions across a wide array of problem sets. Requests for white paper, oral presentations, panel pitches are also common methods for effectively soliciting OT solutions. Additionally, agencies are encouraged to leverage other events, activities, or even authorities to provide for the collection of potential solutions. Some examples where acquisition teams have been creative in performing solicitation outreach include: Tech Demonstrations, Design Sprints, Hackathons, Innovation Workshops, Rodeos, Shark Tank-like presentations, Prize Contests and other similar events that can be leveraged to solicit for solutions.

The broad agency announcement procedure is discussed in a subsequent section of this chapter. Note that it meets the statutory requirement for using "competitive procedures."

[2] Selecting the Source(s)

After obtaining proposed solutions from various organizations, the agency will generally select one or more sources with which to negotiate an OTA. Agencies that sponsor research aimed at solving national problems, such as NIH, frequently use a peer review process to select the best proposal. Agencies that are seeking solutions to their own problems, such as DOD, generally select the sources using their own employees. However, there is great flexibility in involving the most knowledgeable participants in this process.

The selection decision is not necessarily made by trading off price and nonprice evaluation factors but is often based on ascertaining the best technical solution to the problem. In this regard, it is not uncommon to select more than one organization for award of an OTA.

[3] Types of OTAs

There is no restriction on structuring OTAs as cost-reimbursement, fixed-price, or a combination thereof The DOD Guide speaks in terms of "expenditure-based agreements" and "fixed amount agreements." The DoD Guide suggests that expenditure-based agreements are not suitable unless the contractor has an accounting system that allows for the identification and allocation of costs to the OTA:

> *Accounting Systems*—When structuring the OT agreement for an expenditure-based or resource-sharing type project, the Government team should consider the capability of the awardee's accounting system. Agreements that impose requirements that will cause an awardee to revise or alter its existing accounting system are discouraged. The Government team should not enter into an OT agreement that provides for payment based on amounts generated from the awardee's financial or cost records if the awardee does not have an accounting system capable of identifying the amounts/costs to individual agreements/contracts.

When an expenditure-based agreement is used, the parties will likely have to agree on the cost principles that are applicable to the OTA and the extent of audit that is afforded the government. These agreements may allow for the regular reimbursement of costs including indirect costs at a negotiated rate.

The parties can negotiate milestone payments to align payment with performance objectives. The DOD Guide states:

> Well-structured, payable milestones can serve the dual purpose of meeting cash flow needs of the performer and as a management tool to verify observable achievements on the critical path to project success. Failure to achieve milestone/technical goals forces a management analysis and decision. There is not one uniform clause or set of procedures for payable milestones. Payable milestone procedures vary, depending on the inherent nature of the agreement and as such, may be non-consecutive; conditional; contingency based; incrementally funded; included as priced options within the prototype project; or designed in any other manner, or combination of manners, that are appropriate under the circumstances of the individual effort. It is important to note that optional milestones do not become part of the project agreement terms unless exercised and funded by the Government.

[4] Negotiating the Terms and Conditions

There is considerable flexibility in negotiating the terms and conditions of an OTA. However, the parties should use care in identifying the issues that may arise during performance and including clauses in the OTA that define the rights of the parties. The DOD Guide contains guidance on the following issues that should be addressed:

- Intellectual property—see below
- Title to property—the government generally does not take title
- Payment procedures—electronic invoicing preferred
- Changes—choose between unilateral or bilateral
- Disputes—alternate dispute resolution preferred
- Termination—possibly by either party
- Remedies—consider possibility of recoupment by government
- Recovery of funds—possibility of contractor buying a prototype
- Comptroller General access—mandatory only for prototype OTAs over $ 5 million
- Flow down provisions—consider audit and intellectual property issues

[5] Intellectual Property

Frequently the most difficult issue that the parties to an OTA must address is their respective rights to intellectual property. Contractors need to consider what rights they will give to the government with regard to the existing intellectual property that they are going to use the carry out the OTA. The government needs to consider what intellectual property it will need if the results of the OTA is a product that will be introduced into its inventory or if the OTA develops technology that should be made available to the public. It is good practice for both parties to use specialists in intellectual property matters in negotiating these rights. Appendix F of the DOD Guide makes it clear that the FAR-based clauses are not mandatory and gives the following guidance on negotiating special provisions governing intellectual property:

> It is important that the [Agreements Officer] be familiar with IP rights under the Bayh-Dole Act (35 U.S.C. § 201-204) for patents and 10 U.S.C. § 2320-21 for technical data; however, these statutes do not apply to OTs and *negotiation of rights of a different scope is permissible and encouraged.* At a minimum, the AO should ensure that the agreement addresses the following:
>
> a. *Disputes*: Disputes clauses included in the agreement can accommodate specialized disputes arising under the IP clauses, such as the exercise of IP marchin rights or the validation of restrictions on technical data or computer software.
>
> b. *Flow-down*: Determine whether it is necessary that the IP clauses applicable to the awardee flow down to subawardees, including whether to allow other subawardees to submit any applicable IP license directly to the Government.

c. *Licensing*: Consider restricting awardees from licensing technology developed under the OT to domestic or foreign firms under circumstances that would hinder potential domestic manufacture or use of the technology.

d. *Export*: Be aware that export restrictions prohibit awardees from disclosing or licensing certain technology to foreign firms.

e. *Additional rights*: Consider including in the IP clauses any additional rights available to the Government in the case of inability or refusal of the private party or team to continue to perform.

f. *Time based*: It may also be appropriate to consider negotiating time periods after which the Government will automatically obtain greater rights (for example, if the original negotiated rights limited Government's rights for a specified period of time to permit commercialization of the technology).

g. *Patents*: Negotiate a patents rights clause necessary to accomplish program objectives and foster the Government's interest while balancing the needs of the performer. In determining what represents a reasonable arrangement under the circumstances, the AO should consider the Government's needs for patents and patent rights to use the developed technology, or what other IP rights will be needed should the agreement provide for trade secret protection instead of patent protection.

h. *Trade Secret Protection*: Consider allowing subject inventions to remain trade secrets as long as the Government's interest in the continued use of the technology is protected. In making this evaluation, the AO should consider whether allowing the technology to remain a trade secret creates an unacceptable risk of a third party patenting the same technology, the Government's right to utilize this technology with third parties, and whether there are available means to mitigate these risks outside of requiring patent protection.

i. *Software data rights*: Refers to a combined copyright, know-how, and/or trade secret license that defines the Government's ability to use, reproduce, modify, release, and disclose technical data and computer software. The focus of license negotiations often centers on the Government's ability to release or disclose outside the Government. In addition, computer software licenses require additional consideration because restrictions may impact the Government's use, maintenance, and upgrade of computer software used as an operational element of the prototype technology. The OT should typically address definitions, allocation of rights, delivery requirements, and restrictive legends. The OT should account for certain emergency or special circumstances in which the Government may need additional rights, such as the need to disclose technical data or computer software for emergency repair or overhaul.

j. *Commercial data*: The AO should consider commercial technical data and commercial computer software. The government typically does not need extensive rights in commercial technical data and software. However, depending on the project scope and goals, the Government may need to negotiate for greater rights in order to utilize the developed technology.

k. *Cyber Incident Reporting*: Ensure the company is properly protecting data and compliant with specific Government reporting procedures in the event Government data is compromised.

l. *Authorization and Consent*: Authorization and consent policies provide that work by an awardee under an agreement may not be enjoined by reason of patent infringement and shifts liability for such infringement to the government (see 28 U.S.C. 1498). The Government's liability for damages in any such suit may, however, ultimately be borne by the awardee in accordance with the terms of a patent indemnity clause. The agreement should not include an authorization and consent clause when both complete performance and delivery are outside the United States, its possessions, and Puerto Rico.

m. *Notice and Assistance:* Notice policy requires the awardee to notify the AO of all claims of infringement that come to the awardee's attention in connection with performing the agreement. Assistance policy requires the Awardee, when requested, to assist the Government with any evidence and information in its possession in connection with any suit against the government, or any claims against the Government made before suit has been instituted that alleges patent or copyright infringement arising out of performance under the agreement.

n. *Indemnity*: Indemnity clauses mitigate the Government's risk of cost increases caused by infringement of a third-party owned patent. Such a clause may be appropriate if the supplies or services used in the prototype technology developed under the agreement normally are or have been sold or offered for sale to the public in the commercial open market, either with or without modifications. In addition, where trade secret protection is allowed in lieu of patent protection for patentable subject inventions, a perpetual patent indemnity clause might be considered as a mechanism for mitigating risks. The agreement should not include a clause whereby the Government expressly agrees to indemnify the awardee against liability for infringement.

[F] Applicable Statutes

While the procurement statutes are not applicable to OTAs, the transactions (and the parties performing them) are subject to statutes of general applicability. The parties should be careful to independently determine which statutes apply. The following statutes likely fall into this category of general applicability:

- False Claims Acts, 18 U.S.C. § 287 (criminal) and 31 U.S.C. § 3729 et seq. (civil)
- Anti-Deficiency Act, 31 U.S.C. § 1341

- Civil Rights Act, 42 U.S.C. § 2000d et seq.
- Trade Secrets Act, 18 U.S.C. § 1905
- Freedom of Information Act, 5 U.S.C. § 552 (see the exception in 10 U.S.C. § 4021(i))
- Judgment Fund Act, 31 U.S.C. § 1304
- Bribery and Gratuities Act, 18 U.S.C. § 201
- Economic Espionage Act, 18 U.S.C. § 1831-39
- Tucker Act, 28 U.S.C. § 1491(a)

The following statutes should also be analyzed on a case-by-case basis to assess their applicability:

- Anti-Kickback Act, 41 U.S.C. § 8701 et seq.
- Covenant Against Contingent Fees, 10 U.S.C. § 2306(b) (now § 3321(b)), 41 U.S.C. § 3901(b)
- Procurement Integrity Act, 41 U.S.C. § 2101 et seq.
- Service Contract Act, 41 U.S.C. § 6701 et seq.
- Walsh-Healy Act, 41 U.S.C. § 6501 et seq.
- Buy American Act, 41 U.S.C. § 8301 et seq.
- Trade Agreements Act, 19 U.S.C. § 2511 et seq.

§ 10.03 BROAD AGENCY ANNOUNCEMENT PROCEDURE

Research contracts or grants can be awarded through a "broad agency announcement" (BAA) procedure that meets the requirement for full and open competition. See 10 U.S.C. § 3012(2) (formerly § 2302(2)(B)) and 41 U.S.C. § 152(2) which recognize that this procedure is a "competitive procedure," described as follows:

> the competitive selection for award of basic research proposals resulting from a general solicitation and the peer review or scientific review (as appropriate) of such proposals.

See the following definition in FAR 2.101:

> Broad agency announcement means a general announcement of an agency's research interest including criteria for selecting proposals and soliciting the participation of all offerors capable of satisfying the Government's needs (see 6.102(d)(2)).

This competitive procedure differs significantly from sealed bid or competitive proposal procedures. Here research organizations propose to undertake different research tasks in response to periodic announcements of broad areas of research interest by the various contracting agencies. The agencies then sequentially review these proposals and award contracts until funds run out in a particular area.

The nomenclature for BAAs varies from agency to agency. One common term is the Program Research and Development Announcement (PRDA) used by the Department of Energy and the Department of the Air Force. NASA uses the terms "Announcement of Opportunity," "NASA Research Announcements" and "NASA Acquisition of Investigations."

Agencies have considerable discretion in fashioning the specific procedure to the used in this form of procurement. However, basic rules are set forth in FAR 35.016. Some agencies have issued guides on proposal preparation. See NFS 1852.235-72 and the NASA *NRA Proposers Guidebook*; and the Department of the Air Force *BAA and PRDA: A Guide for Industry* and *BAA and PRDA Proposal Preparation Instructions.*

[A] Nature of Work

Although the statutes permit the use of this procedure for "basic research," the FAR implementation of the statute permits the use of this procedure for a broader classification of work by including "applied research" and "development not related to the development of a specific system or hardware procurement" within the description of this "competitive procedure," FAR 6.102(d)(2). The legislative history of this provision, H. Rep. 861, 98th Cong., 2d Sess. 7517, *reprinted in* 1984 U.S.C.C.A.N. 1445, 2111, indicates that the drafters of the statute considered basic research as research "directed toward increasing knowledge of a subject apart from any clear or necessary practical application of that knowledge." It is questionable whether "applied research" and "development," as defined in FAR 31.205-18 and FAR 35.001, fall within the scope described in the legislative history. Nevertheless, in response to a request from the FAR Secretariat, GAO indicated that it had no objection to the inclusion of "applied research" in the proposed FAR implementation, Comp. Gen. Dec. B-227314, Aug. 6, 1987. However, there was no mention of "development" by GAO.

FAR 35.016(a) contains the following guidance on the type of work than can be procured using the BAA procedure:

> This paragraph prescribes procedures for the use of the broad agency announcement (BAA) with Peer or Scientific Review (see 6.102(d)(2)) for the acquisition of basic and applied research and that part of development not related to the development of a specific system or hardware procurement. BAA's may be used by agencies to fulfill their requirements for scientific study and experimentation directed toward advancing the state-of-the-art or

increasing knowledge or understanding rather than focusing on a specific system or hardware solution. The BAA technique shall only be used when meaningful proposals with varying technical/scientific approaches can be reasonably anticipated.

The Department of Energy has more specific guidance on when PRDAs should be used. See DEAR 917.7301-1 stating:

(b) The PRDA should not replace existing acquisition procedures where a requirement can be sufficiently defined for solicitation under standard advertised or negotiated acquisition procedures. Similarly, it should not inhibit or curtail the submission of unsolicited proposals. However, a proposal which is submitted as though it were unsolicited but is in fact germane to an existing PRDA shall be treated as though submitted in response to the announcement or returned without action to the proposer, at the proposer's option. Further, the PRDA is not to be used in a competitive situation where it is appropriate to negotiate a study contract to obtain analysis and recommendations to be incorporated in the subsequent request for proposals.

The NASA guidance in NFS 1835.016-71 states:

An NRA [NASA Research Announcement] is used to announce research interests in support of NASA's programs, and, after peer or scientific review using factors in the NRA, select proposals for funding. Unlike an RFP containing a statement of work or specification to which offerors are to respond, an NRA provides for the submission of competitive project ideas, conceived by the offerors, in one or more program areas of interest. An NRA shall not be used when the requirement is sufficiently defined to specify an end product or service.

DoD has special authority to broaden the scope of its BAA contracts. See 10 U.S.C. § 4004 (formerly § 2302e) stating:

(a) Authority.—A contract initially awarded from the competitive selection of a proposal resulting from a general solicitation referred to in section 3012(2) of this title may contain a contract line item or contract option for—

(1) the development and demonstration or initial production of technology developed under the contract; or

(2) the delivery of initial or additional items if the item or a prototype thereof is created as the result of work performed under the contract.

(b) Limitations.—

(1) Minimal amount.—A contract line item or contract option described in subsection (a)(2) shall require the delivery of the minimal amount of initial or additional items to allow for the timely competitive

> solicitation and award of a follow-on development or production contract for those items.
>
> (2) **Term.**—A contract line item or contract option described in subsection (a) shall be for a term of not more than 2 years.
>
> (3) **Dollar value of work.**—The dollar value of the work to be performed pursuant to a contract line item or contract option described in subsection (a) may not exceed $100,000,000, in fiscal year 2017 constant dollars.
>
> . . . .

Agencies have used these procedures for a wide variety of efforts, including the procurement of new products. See, for example, *Land O'Frost*, ASBCA 52012, 03-2 BCA ¶ 32,395 (production of chicken breast fillets as part of the Meals Ready to Eat program); *Gamut Elec., LLC*, Comp. Gen. Dec. B-292347, 2003 CPD ¶ 150 (state-of-the-art counterdrug equipment); *Energy Conversion Devices, Inc.*, Comp. Gen. Dec. B-260514, 95-2 CPD ¶ 121 (improvements in manufacturing technology); *TRW, Inc.*, Comp. Gen. Dec. B-258347, 95-1 CPD ¶ 15 (development and flight test of a gel propellant divert and attitude control system); *Golden Mfg. Co.*, Comp. Gen. Dec. B-255347, 94-1 CPD ¶ 183, *recons. denied*, 94-2 CPD ¶ 28 (manufacturer field coats using commercial processes).

[B] Announcements

In this form of procurement, an agency publishes its areas of interest and private organizations submit proposals for specific projects within a specified area. Awards are made to proposals that are judged to be promising until the funds have been utilized. Thus, the competition is for funding within an area of interest rather than to perform a task that has been specified by the agency. However, the area of interest may be very narrowly defined, making the procedure much like a normal competitive procurement. See *TRW, Inc.*, Comp. Gen. Dec. B-258347, 95-1 CPD ¶ 15, sustaining a best value type award decision in a narrowly defined area.

The FAR treats broad agency announcements (BAAs) as another type of solicitation. Thus, FAR 35.016(c) states:

> The availability of the BAA must be publicized through the Governmentwide point of entry (GPE) and, if authorized pursuant to subpart 5.5, may also be published in noted scientific, technical, or engineering periodicals. The notice shall be published no less frequently than annually.

Following this guidance, many agencies publish a list of areas of interest semi-annually or annually. In such cases, many awards for different subjects of research within the general area may be made under a single BAA—doing away with the need for the issuance of a large number of individual RFPs. In contrast, some agencies also issue narrowly focused BAAs calling for proposals to perform a specific type of project. These BAAs are almost indistinguishable from RFPs that are issued in the competitive negotiation process. A challenge to the use of a BAA in lieu of an RFP must be submitted to GAO before the closing time for receipt of proposals, *Gamut Elec., LLC*, Comp. Gen. Dec. B-292347, 2003 CPD ¶ 150.

FAR 35.016(f) provides that BAAs need not be synopsized pursuant to FAR Subpart 5.2. In effect, this makes the BAA a combined synopsis/solicitation with no mandatory waiting period between the two.

There is no mandatory late proposal rule associated with BAAs. See NFS 1852.235-72 covering proposals submitted in response to NASA Research Announcements:

> (g) *Late Proposals*. Proposals or proposal modifications received after the latest date specified for receipt may be considered if a significant reduction in cost to the Government is probable or if there are significant technical advantages, as compared with proposals previously received.

[1] Contracts or Other Instruments

Not all BAAs result in the award of contracts. Agencies issuing BAAs usually retain the option of funding the research under a contract or using a grant, cooperative agreement, or other form of assistance agreement. The requirements of the procurement statutes and the FAR apply only if a contract is used. As discussed in Chapter 1, when the agency decides to use another funding instrument, different statutory or regulatory requirements may be prescribed. See *Energy Conversion Devices, Inc.*, Comp. Gen. Dec. B-260514, 95-2 CPD ¶ 121, concluding that the principal purpose of the contract was not the acquisition of supplies or services and, therefore, use of an "other transaction" in lieu of a procurement contract was justified.

In the case of the Air Force, NASA, and DOE, the general policy is to use contracts for profit-making organizations and grants for nonprofit organizations and universities. However, contracts may be used for nonprofit organizations and universities to obtain tighter control over research projects involving substantial acquisition of equipment or considerable subcontracting. Classified research is also usually done under a contract.

[2] Requirement for Competition

The legislative history, H. Rep. 861, 98th Cong., 2d Sess. 7517, *reprinted in* 1984 U.S.C.C.A.N. 1445, 2111, makes it clear that the authority of 10 U.S.C. § 2302(2)(B) (now § 4004) and 41 U.S.C. § 152(2) may not be used if the general solicitation precludes the participation of capable individuals or firms:

> By recognizing such procurement of basic research as competitive, the conferees intend to promote the participation of all individuals or companies capable of supporting the government's needs in this important area. Any agency procurement which cannot meet this standard and, in fact, restricts participation, must be justified and approved under the requirements in this substitute for other than competitive procurement procedures.

Thus, if a BAA limits the submission of proposals to certain firms or individuals, procurement on the basis of other than full and open competition must be justified. See, for example, *Right Away Foods/Shelf Stable Foods*, Comp. Gen. Dec. B-259859.3, 95-2 CPD ¶ 34 (limitation of competition justified on the need to maintain the mobilization base). See DFARS 235.016 encouraging agencies to reserve "discrete or severable areas of research interest" in BAAs for "exclusive competition among historically black colleges and universities and minority institutions."

[3] Content

FAR 35.016 specifies the following requirements for BAAs:

> (b) The BAA, together with any supporting documents, shall—
>
> (1) Describe the agency's research interest, either for an individual program requirement or for broadly defined areas of interest covering the full range of the agency's requirements;
>
> (2) Describe the criteria for selecting the proposals, their relative importance, and the method of evaluation;
>
> (3) Specify the period of time during which proposals submitted in response to the BAA will be accepted; and
>
> (4) Contain instructions for the preparation and submission of proposals.

Agencies are free to add other requirements as necessary. See, for example, *HMX, Inc.*, Comp. Gen. Dec. B-291102, 2003 CPD ¶ 52, where the agency added a requirement for the submission of "certifiable" cost or pricing data in all proposals over $550,000. GAO denied the protest that HMX's proposal had not been selected for negotiations because it refused to submit the data—ruling that this protest was not timely because the problem was apparent when the BAA was posted, and therefore the protest was required prior to the submission of proposals. See also *Spaltudaq Corp.*, Comp. Gen. Dec. B-400650, 2009 CPD ¶ 1, where the agency required cost proposals that were "auditable" by the Defense Contract Audit Agency.

[C] Discussions with Proposers

Agency discussions with proposers occur in several stages. Prior to submitting a proposal the researcher is encouraged to talk informally with agency scientists in order to ascertain the degree of interest in the proposed research. Some agencies will also consider a preliminary proposal or a brief outline of a proposal. These contacts must be initiated by the proposer. The appropriate scientist is usually identified in the BAA. After a proposal has been submitted, the agency may contact a representative of the proposing institution, usually the principal investigator, for any necessary clarification.

The contacts between the agency and proposer differ considerably from the type of contacts allowed in the standard procedures. There is no guidance on the type or extent of assistance that should be provided during this process. Such guidance is less necessary in this context, as proposers are generally proposing to do different tasks, and it is proper to make the selection based on the original proposals with no discussion with the proposers, *Energy & Envtl. Research Corp.*, Comp. Gen. Dec. B-261422, 95-2 CPD ¶ 81. However, when proposals are being compared, the basic rule of fair treatment of all offerors in FAR 1.102-2(c) applies even though it is not mentioned in FAR 35.016. In addition, when the agency uses the BAA procedure to obtain head-to-head competition against a specific requirement, GAO has imposed the "meaningful discussion" rule that is used in competitively negotiated procurements, *Interstate Elecs. Corp.*, Comp. Gen. Dec. B-286466, 2001 CPD ¶ 29.

When a proposal has been selected based on its technical merit, the agency may have to negotiate the terms and conditions before award of a contract. In such cases, the agency has considerable discretion in deciding that it cannot reach agreement on the terms and conditions. See *Spaltudaq Corp.*, Comp. Gen. Dec. B-400650, 2009 CPD ¶ 1, stating:

> Although we find that [the agency] had no obligation to follow the specific requirements for discussions set forth in FAR Part 15, agencies may not conduct themselves in an arbitrary manner, and they must negotiate in good faith and in a manner consistent with the BAA. See *Health Servs. Mktg. & Dev. Corp.*, B-241830, Mar. 5, 1991, 91-1 CPD ¶ 247 at 7.
>
> * * *
>
> [T]he BAA provided for post-selection negotiations with firms that were selected for award. The BAA permitted the agency to discontinue discussions if an offeror failed to provide necessary information in a timely manner, or if the parties failed to reach agreement on contract terms within a reasonable time. Here, the record shows that over a 4-month period, the parties engaged in good faith negotiations in an attempt to reach agreement over the parties' rights to intellectual property, but that no agreement could be reached. The record shows that Spaltudaq proposed a number of approaches that limited or restricted the government's rights, and the agency repeatedly objected to these approaches. The agency articulated its "final negotiation position" regarding intellectual

> property in its August 7, 2008 letter and unambiguously stated that "the Government is unwilling to consider" recent proposal changes that would limit or restrict the government's rights to data or inventions. Despite this admonition, Spaltudaq responded with a revised statement of work that included previously submitted proposal revisions to restrict the intellectual property rights granted to the agency. In our view, the agency reasonably determined that the parties had failed to reach agreement within a reasonable time, and the agency could discontinue negotiations on this basis alone.

If an agency decides that it is in its best interest to award only a single contract, it may negotiate more favorable terms with that contractor without any requirement to conduct discussions with other offerors, as least where the solicitation provides for such a procedures. *Blue Origin Federation, LLC*, Comp. Gen. Dec. B-419783, 2021 CPD ¶ 265; *Blue Origin Fed'n, LLC v. United States*, 157 Fed. Cl. 74 (2021).

[D] Evaluation of Proposals

FAR 35.016(d) specifies the following requirements for evaluating BAA proposals:

> Proposals received as a result of the BAA shall be evaluated in accordance with evaluation criteria specified therein through a peer or scientific review process. Written evaluation reports on individual proposals will be necessary but proposals need not be evaluated against each other since they are not submitted in accordance with a common work statement.

This is generally consistent with the rule applicable to conventional negotiated procurement. The following discussion focuses on some of the unique aspects of this type of contracting, including the requirement for peer or scientific review.

[1] Evaluation Factors

FAR 35.016(e) prescribes the following factors and states the primary basis for the evaluation of proposals:

> The primary basis for selecting proposals for acceptance shall be technical, importance to agency programs, and fund availability. Cost realism and reasonableness shall also be considered to the extent appropriate.

The use of unstated criteria is not permitted in evaluating proposals, but criteria that are reasonably related to stated criteria may be used, *Avogadro Energy Sys.*, Comp. Gen. Dec. B-244106, 91-2 CPD ¶ 229. There, GAO reviewed and approved the evaluation criteria in a BAA for basic research, finding that, to the extent that unstated criteria were present, they were reasonably related to stated criteria and so caused no prejudice to the selection process. See also *Interstate Elec. Corp.*, Comp. Gen. Dec. B-286466, 2001 CPD ¶ 29 (proper to evaluate whether proposal met a "minimum" requirement in PRDA); *ABB Lummus Crest, Inc.*, Comp. Gen. Dec. B-244440, 91-2 CPD ¶ 252 (allegation of evaluation based upon an unstated criterion—access to rights in proprietary data—not proved).

Although a formal responsibility determination is not made, responsibility-related factors are taken into account. Particularly important in contracting for basic research are the qualifications of the principal investigator and other key personnel, as the success of the endeavor is likely to depend more on these individuals than on the characteristics of the sponsoring institution.

[2] Peer or Scientific Review

Peer or scientific review is a process of proposal review that utilizes a group of experts in the field represented by the proposal to evaluate the proposal merit. Peer or scientific review can be done by government or outside scientists and can take a number of forms. The evaluation can be done by assembling panels of scientists, by receiving evaluations by mail, or by hiring a contractor to evaluate all proposals.

The use of outside evaluators is probably the most controversial element of this process. When this is done, there are two major issues that must be addressed. First, steps must be taken to ensure that outside evaluators do not disclose proprietary information that they have received in the review process. DEAR 915.207-70 contains the most complete coverage of this issue. It permits marking of all proposals with a prescribed proprietary legend and requires outside evaluators to sign the following nondisclosure agreement prior to receipt of the proposal:

> Nondisclosure Agreement
>
> Whenever DOE furnishes a proposal for evaluation, I, the recipient, agree to use the information contained in the proposal only for DOE evaluation purposes and to treat the information obtained in confidence. This requirement for confidential treatment does not apply to information obtained from any source, including the proposer, without restriction. Any notice or restriction placed on the proposal by either DOE or the originator of the proposal shall be conspicuously affixed to any reproduction or abstract thereof and its provisions strictly complied with. Upon completion of the evaluation, it is agreed all copies of the proposal and abstracts, if any, shall be returned to the DOE office which initially furnished the proposal for evaluation. Unless authorized by the Contracting Officer, I agree that I shall not contact the originator of the proposal concerning any aspect of its elements.
>
> Recipient: ____________________
> Date: ____________________

The second issue is the potential conflict of interest of outside reviewers. Such reviewers should not be permitted to participate in the review of proposals submitted in response to an area covered by the BAA in which they have some other interest.

The most complete guidance on this issue is in the regulations of the Public Health Service at 42 C.F.R. § 52h.5 as follows:

> (b) A reviewer with a real conflict of interest must recuse him/herself from the review of the application or proposal, except as otherwise provided in this section.
>
> > (1) A reviewer who is a salaried employee, whether full-time or part-time, of the applicant institution, offeror, or principal investigator, or is negotiating for employment, shall be considered to have a real conflict of interest with regard to an application/proposal from that organization or principal investigator, except that the Director may determine there is no real conflict of interest or an appearance of a conflict of interest where the components of a large or multicomponent organization are sufficiently independent to constitute, in effect, separate organizations, provided that the reviewer has no responsibilities at the institution that would significantly affect the other component.
> >
> > (2) Where a reviewer's real conflict of interest is based upon the financial or other interest of a close relative or professional associate of the reviewer, that reviewer must recuse him/herself, unless the Director provides a waiver in accordance with paragraph (b)(4) of this section.
> >
> > (3) For contract proposal reviews, an individual with a real conflict of interest in a particular proposal(s) is generally not permitted to participate in the review of any proposals responding to the same request for proposals. However, if there is no other qualified reviewer available having that individual's expertise and that expertise is essential to ensure a competent and fair review, a waiver may be granted by the Director to permit that individual to serve as a reviewer of those proposals with which the reviewer has no conflict, while recusing him/herself from the review of any particular proposal(s) in which there is a conflict of interest.
> >
> > (4) The Director may waive any of the requirements in paragraph (b) of this section relating to a real conflict of interest if the Director determines that there are no other practical means for securing appropriate expert advice on a particular grant or cooperative agreement application, contract project, or contract proposal, and that the real conflict of interest is not so substantial as to be likely to affect the integrity of the advice to be provided by the reviewer.
>
> (c) Any appearance of a conflict of interest will result in recusal of the reviewer, unless the Director provides a waiver, determining that it would be difficult or impractical to carry out the review otherwise, and the integrity of the review process would not be impaired by the reviewer's participation.

See *Herdon Sci. & Software, Inc.*, Comp. Gen. Dec. B-245505, 92-1 CPD ¶ 46 (allegation of conflict of interest unfounded where evaluators were excluded from review or discussion of any proposal which they submitted as a principal or collaborator or which was supported by an institutional affiliate).

[E] Award

After the technical and cost evaluations are completed, a designated agency official reviews the information and decides whether to accept the proposal for negotiation. The award decision is discretionary. See, for example *AEC-ABLE Eng'g Co.*, Comp. Gen. Dec. B-257798.2, 95-1 CPD ¶ 37, reviewing a number of allegations that the agency had improperly selected two other proposals but holding that the agency was justified in awarding to those companies. See also *INRAD, Inc.*, Comp. Gen. Dec. B-284021, 2000 U.S. Comp. Gen. LEXIS 39, finding that the agency's decision not to fund a proposal was consistent with the terms of the PRDA. Challenges to technical evaluations are almost always denied because GAO defers to the agency's technical assessment of the merits of a proposal. See *Tamper Proof Container Sys. Corp.*, Comp. Gen. Dec. B-402191, 2010 CPD ¶ 46, stating:

> In reviewing a protest of an agency's proposal evaluation, it is not our role to reevaluate proposals. Rather, we will consider only whether the evaluation was reasonable and consistent with the terms of the solicitation and applicable procurement statutes and regulations. *Gamut Elecs., LLC*, B-292347, B-292347.2, Aug. 7, 2003, 2003 CPD ¶ 150 at 4; *HMX, Inc.*, B-291102, Nov. 4, 2002, 2003 CPD ¶ 52 at 7. An offeror's mere disagreement with an agency's judgment is not sufficient to establish that the agency acted unreasonably. *HMX, Inc., supra.*

See also *Microcosm, Inc.*, Comp. Gen. Dec. B-277326, 97-2 CPD ¶ 133.

FAR 35.016(d) provides that in making awards, there is no need to evaluate proposals against each other. However, this may not be the case when proposals are required to be submitted on a common date. NASA provides the following guidance on selecting proposals submitted in response to its Research Announcements in NFS 1852.235-72:

> (j) Evaluation Techniques. Selection decisions will be made following peer and/or scientific review of the proposals. Several evaluation techniques are regularly used within NASA. In all cases proposals are subject to scientific review by discipline specialists in the area of the proposal. Some proposals are reviewed entirely in-house, others are evaluated by a combination of in-house and selected external reviewers, while yet others are subject to the full external peer review technique (with due regard for conflict-of-interest and protection of proposal information), such as by mail or through assembled panels. The final decisions are made by a NASA selecting official. A proposal which

is scientifically and programmatically meritorious, but not selected for award during its initial review, may be included in subsequent reviews unless the proposer requests otherwise.

(k) Selection for Award.

(1) When a proposal is not selected for award, the proposer will be notified. NASA will explain generally why the proposal was not selected. Proposers desiring additional information may contact the selecting official who will arrange a debriefing.

(2) When a proposal is selected for award, negotiation and award will be handled by the procurement office in the funding installation. The proposal is used as the basis for negotiation. The contracting officer may request certain business data and may forward a model award instrument and other information pertinent to negotiation.

§ 10.04 SMALL BUSINESS INNOVATIVE RESEARCH PROGRAM

Another special procedure permitted by 10 U.S.C. § 3012(5) (formerly § 2302(2)(E)) and 41 U.S.C. § 152(5) is competitive selection of research proposals resulting from a general solicitation and peer or scientific review solicited pursuant to the Small Business Act, 15 U.S.C. § 638. This section of the Small Business Act, known as the Small Business Innovation Development Act, Pub. L. No. 97-219, became effective in October 1982 and created the Small Business Innovation Research (SBIR) program. This section of the Act was substantially amended in 2000 by the Small Business Reauthorization Act of 2000, Pub. L. No. 106-554. A small program administered along with the SBIR program is the Small Business Technology Transfer Program (STTR) created by Pub. L. No. 102-564 in 1992. The Act was substantially amended again in 2011 by Title LI of Pub. L. No. 112-81. The purposes of these programs are to increase participation in government-funded research and development by small innovative firms and to provide incentives for the conversion of research into commercial applications. Firms owned or controlled by United States entities with 500 or fewer employees are eligible for participation in the program, 13 C.F.R. § 121.702. These statutes are not permanent legislation but extensions have been passed on a regular basis. See § 854 of Pub. L. No. 115-232, extending the programs through September 30, 2022.

The statute is implemented by the Small Business Administration in the *Small Business Innovation Research Program and Small Business Technology Transfer Program Policy Directive*, 84 Fed. Reg. 12794, Apr. 2, 2019. Because there is no FAR implementation of the directive, this directive constitutes the main source of guidance in this area. GAO has held that in the absence of an express statutory provision, the policy directive's terms (in this case, providing for payment of a profit) will take precedence over an agency's regulations, *Appropriations/Financial Mgmt.*, 71 Comp. Gen. 310 (B-245032) (1992). The

SBA maintains a website providing full information on the program at http://www.sba.gov/sbir/.

SBIR-STTR contracts have significant benefit to small businesses because they allow the contractor to maintain proprietary rights in technical data developed in the course of performing the contract. 15 U.S.C. § 638(j)(2)(A) requires that small businesses under this program be permitted to "retain rights to data generated by the concern in the performance of an SBIR award for a period of not less than 4 years." This requirement is implemented by the use of two clauses—the FAR Rights in Data—SBIR Program (DEC 2007) clause in FAR 52.227-20 (maintaining proprietary rights for four years "after acceptance of all items to be delivered under this contract") and the DFARS Rights in Noncommercial Technical Data and Computer Software—Small Business Innovative Research (SBIR) Program (June 1995) clause in DFARS 252.227-7018 (maintaining proprietary rights for five years "after completion of the project from which such data were generated"). The Policy Directive changes the SBIR/STTR data rights period to 20 years from the date of execution of the first SBIR/STTR contract but this requirement has not yet been implemented in the procurement regulations. See *CANVS Corp.*, ASBCA 57784, 18-1 BCA ¶ 37,156, denying a contractor's claim for breach of contract by disclosing SBIR data. The board concluded that the disclosure did not reveal proprietary data and that the contractor had, itself, publicly disclosed the data.

[A] Description of SBIR Program

Section 638(f) of the Small Business Act requires each agency with an "extramural budget" for research and development of over $100 million to expend 3.2% of its R&D funds on SBIR contracts, grants or cooperative agreements with small businesses. Section 638(n) requires each agency with an "extramural budget" for research and development of over $1 billion to expend 0.45% of its R&D funds on STTR contracts, grants or cooperative agreements with small businesses. Statutory requirements for this program are contained in 15 U.S.C. § 638(o). This program provides for the awarding of contracts to small business concerns for the purpose of conducting cooperative research and development with a nonprofit research institution, such as a university. The agencies with this mandate run the two programs as joint programs with SBIR/STTR regulations and websites.

The program consists of three phases that are designed to take an idea through the stages of research, development and demonstration, and commercial application. Phase I solicits research proposals by the issuance of broad agency announcements (or equivalent documents) describing agency requirements or areas of interest. Section 9 of the Policy Directive calls for giving priority to "manufacturing-related research and development" and "energy efficiency or renewable energy system research and development." There is also an emphasis on selecting proposals that exhibit a "commercialization" potential. Phase I awards are generally limited to $150,000 and expected to be completed in six months for SBIR and one year for STTR.

Phase II is a follow-on phase to further develop work that has be identified as fruitful in Phase I, with additional emphasis on the "commercial potential" of the technology. This is a sole source phase which is initiated by an application submitted during the Phase I work. Agencies are permitted to issue a second Phase II contract or grant and, under specified conditions in a pilot program, a third Phase II contract or grant. Phase II awards are generally limited to $1,000,000 (with agencies permitted to add 50%) and expected to be completed in two years.

Phase III is the final follow-on phase that can be privately funded to develop a commercial application or government funded with other than SBIR/STTR funds to develop a product or service or continue development efforts for government applications. This work "may be for products, production, services, R/R&D, or any such combination." This is another sole source phase with strict limits on giving such work to a contractor other than the organization that performed the prior work in Phases I and II. There are no dollar or time limits on the scope of these Phase III contracts or grants.

The program is designed to assist small businesses by establishing simplified and fairly uniform procedures, while also allowing sufficient flexibility to the participating agencies. Thus, the SBA's Office of Innovation establishes certain guidelines, primarily concerning the timing and content of SBIR solicitations. The individual procuring agencies unilaterally determine the categories of research to be included in the SBIR/STTR program, issue solicitations, evaluate and select projects, and administer the resulting agreements. Agencies are free to choose the SBIR/STTR funding instrument, consistent with the Grants and Cooperative Agreements Act.

[B] Phase I Solicitation and Proposals

Section 4 of the Policy Directive describes the Phase I solicitation as follows:

> (a) *Phase I.* Phase I involves a solicitation of contract proposals or grant applications (hereinafter referred to as proposals) to conduct feasibility-related experimental or theoretical R/R&D related to described agency requirements. These requirements, as defined by agency topics contained in a solicitation, may be general or narrow in scope, depending on the needs of the agency. The object of this phase is to determine the scientific and technical merit and feasibility of the proposed effort and the quality of performance of the [Small Business Concern] with a relatively small agency investment before consideration of further Federal support in Phase II.
>
> (1) Several different proposed solutions to a given problem may be funded.

(2) Proposals will be evaluated on a competitive basis. Agency criteria used to evaluate SBIR proposals must give consideration to the scientific and technical merit and feasibility of the proposal along with its potential for Commercialization. Considerations may also include program balance with respect to market or technological risk or critical agency requirements.

(3) Agency benchmarks for progress towards Commercialization must be met to be eligible to participate in Phase I of the program. *See* § 6(a) of this Policy Directive for a description of this Phase I eligibility requirement.

(4) Agencies may require the submission of a Phase II proposal as a deliverable item under Phase I.

The solicitation process used in this phase is essentially the same as that used for broad agency announcements. Each procuring agency is required to issue a "program solicitation" at least once a year setting forth the categories of research in which Phase I proposals are to be solicited. These solicitations are incorporated into an SBA "Master Schedule" which spaces the solicitations throughout the year in order to permit small businesses to participate to the maximum practicable extent. Section 5 of the Policy Directive describes this coordination process as follows:

(b) *Master Schedule*. The Act requires issuance of SBIR/STTR Phase I Program Solicitations in accordance with a Master Schedule coordinated between SBA and the SBIR/STTR Participating Agency. The SBA office responsible for coordination is: Office of Innovation, U.S. Small Business Administration, 409 Third Street SW, Washington, DC 20416. Phone: (202) 205-6450. Fax: (202) 205-7754. Email: *technology@sba.gov*. Website: *www.SBIR.gov*.

Appendix I of the Policy Directive requires program solicitations to be prepared "in a simple, standardized, easy-to-read, and easy-to-understand format," including "a cover sheet, a table of contents, and the following sections in the order listed."

1. Program Description
2. Certifications
3. Proposal Preparation Instructions and Requirements
4. Method of Selection and Evaluation Criteria
5. Considerations
6. Submission of Proposals
7. Scientific and Technical Information Sources
8. Submission Forms

9. Research Topics

Appendix I of the Policy Directive contains detailed guidance on the information to be included in each of these areas and all the information and forms a firm needs in order to submit a proposal. The solicitation must indicate if external review is to be used as part of the evaluation process. The main body of the solicitation is the description of research topics for which proposals are being solicited. Section 8 of the Policy Directive also contains guidance on the terms and conditions that should be included in the solicitation.

A research topic can be canceled at any time, *Pike Creek Computer Co.*, Comp. Gen. Dec. B-290329, 2002 CPD ¶ 106 (irrelevant that company had expended proposal funds prior to cancellation).

A firm can protect proprietary information in its proposal by following the marking instructions in Appendix 1 of the Policy Directive:

> (1) *Proprietary Information in Proposals.* The following statement must be included in all SBIR/STTR Program Solicitations:
>
> Information contained in unsuccessful proposals will remain the property of the Applicant. The Federal Government may, however, retain copies of all proposals. Public release of information in any proposal submitted will be subject to existing statutory and regulatory requirements. If proprietary information is provided by an Applicant in a proposal, which constitutes a trade secret, commercial or financial information, it will be treated in confidence, to the extent permitted by law, provided that the proposal is clearly marked by the Applicant as follows:
>
> > (A) The following legend must appear on the title page of the proposal:
> >
> > This proposal contains information that shall not be disclosed outside the Federal Government and shall not be duplicated, used, or disclosed in whole or in part for any purpose other than evaluation of this proposal, unless authorized by law The Government shall have the right to duplicate, use, or disclose the data to the extent provided in the resulting contract if award is made as a result of the submission of this proposal . . . The information subject to these restrictions are contained on all pages of the proposal except for pages [insert page numbers or other identification of pages that contain no restricted information.]
> >
> > (End of Legend); and
> >
> > (B) The following legend must appear on each page of the proposal that contains information the Applicant wishes to protect:
> >
> > Use or disclosure of information contained on this sheet is subject to the restriction on the title page of this proposal.

Firms submitting proposals must be careful to provide accurate information about their capabilities and resources. See *United States ex rel. Longhi v. Lithium Power Techs, Inc.*, 575 F.3d 458 (5th Cir. 2009), *cert. denied*, 559 U.S. 1067 (2010), holding a recipient of an SBIR contract liable under the Civil False

Claims Act, 31 U.S.C. § 3729. The firm had misrepresented the extent of its facilities and the relationships it had with other organizations and had failed to disclose its prior work on SBIR grants.

[C] Evaluation and Selection of Phase I Proposals

Appendix 1 of the Policy Directive contains the following requirements for the evaluation criteria:

> (1) The SBIR/STTR Participating Agency must develop a standardized method in its evaluation process that will consider, at a minimum, the following factors:
>
> (i) The technical approach and the anticipated agency and commercial benefits that may be derived from the research.
>
> (ii) The adequacy of the proposed effort, and its relationship to the fulfillment of requirements of the research topic or subtopics.
>
> (iii) The soundness and technical merit of the proposed approach and its incremental progress toward topic or subtopic solution.
>
> (iv) Qualifications of the proposed Principal Investigators/Project Managers, supporting staff, and consultants.
>
> (v) Evaluations of proposals require, among other things, consideration of a proposal's commercial potential as evidenced by:
>
> (A) The SBC's record of commercializing SBIR or other research,
>
> (B) the existence of Phase II funding commitments from private sector or non-SBIR funding sources,
>
> (C) the existence of Phase III follow-on commitments for the subject of the research, and,
>
> (D) the presence of other indicators of the commercial potential of the idea.
>
> (2) The factors in (b)(1) above and other appropriate evaluation criteria, if any, must be specified in the "Method of Selection" section of SBIR Program Solicitations.

Section 8 of the Policy Directive cautions that there may be a conflict of interest if awards are made to small businesses that are owned by or employ current or previous government employees. See *R&D Dynamics Corp.*, Comp. Gen. Dec. B-285979.2, 2000 CPD ¶ 193, finding no conflict when agency evaluators had dealt with a winning contractor on earlier projects.

Some agencies limit contact with proposers during the proposal preparation and evaluation stage, but these limitations are not directly required by the Policy Directive.

The selection of proposals for award of Phase I contracts is a highly discretionary process. In *Systems Research Co.*, Comp. Gen. Dec. B-260280.2, 95-2

CPD ¶ 62, GAO confirmed that, in conducting an SBIR procurement, agencies have wide discretion and, absent a violation of applicable regulations or solicitation provisions or a finding of fraud or bad faith, the agency's decision of which proposals it will fund will not be disturbed. Winning a protest of a Phase I selection is particularly difficult because there are frequently a large number of proposals submitted against each research topic. See *Glatz Aeronautical Corp.*, Comp. Gen. Dec. B-416392, 2018 CPD ¶ 276 (product ready for commercialization not appropriate for a Phase I award); *KR3Tech, Inc.*, Comp. Gen. Dec. B-413692, 2016 CPD ¶ 364 (agency assessment of technical weaknesses in proposal reasonable); *Mercury Data Sys., Inc.*, Comp. Gen. Dec. B-413217, 2016 CPD ¶ 256 (agency reasonably evaluated technical proposal); *Science, Math, & Eng'g, Inc.*, Comp. Gen. Dec. B-410509, 2015 CPD ¶ 31 (proposal reasonably downgraded for lack of specificity); *Advanced Photon Applications, LLC*, Comp. Gen. Dec. B-409860, 2014 CPD ¶ 249 (no evidence of potential for commercialization explained low ranking); *Glatz Aeronautical Corp.*, Comp. Gen. Dec. B-405851, 2012 CPD ¶ 19 (proposal properly ranked 18th out of 20 proposals); *GEA Eng'g, P.C.*, Comp. Gen. Dec. B-405318, 2011 CPD ¶ 219 (proposal rejected for exceeding page limitation); *NW Sys.*, Comp. Gen. Dec. B-401352, 2009 CPD ¶ 152 (omitted information led to failure to award contract); *Nautical Control Sols., LP*, Comp. Gen. Dec. B-299918, 2007 CPD ¶ 215 (evaluation based on inadequate data reasonable); *Fantastic Data*, Comp. Gen. Dec. B-299076, 2007 CPD ¶ 32 (bias of evaluators not demonstrated); *Quimba Software*, Comp. Gen. Dec. B-299000, 2007 CPD ¶ 14 (agency evaluation of proposal reasonable); *Glatz Aeronautical Corp.*, Comp. Gen. Dec. B-293968.2, 2004 CPD ¶ 160 (selection of more innovative proposals reasonable); *Noble Sols.*, Comp. Gen. Dec. B-294393, 2004 CPD ¶ 197 (proposal technically unacceptable); and *Bostan Research, Inc.*, Comp. Gen. Dec. B-274331, 96-2 CPD ¶ 209 (page limitation not an excuse for failure to submit required information). See also *Right Direction Tech. Sols., LLC*, Comp. Gen. Dec. B-414366.2, 2017 CPD ¶ 202, holding that a protester cannot challenge the evaluation of the winning offeror's proposal when it was not next in line for award. Compare *Celadon Labs., Inc.*, Comp. Gen. Dec. B-298533, 2006 ¶ CPD 158, granting a protest because the agency had used outside evaluators that had a conflict of interest with the protester because they worked for firms that were promoting competitive technology.

[D] Phase II Selection Procedures

Small businesses that have received Phase I contracts can request continuation of the project through the award of a Phase II contract. In addition, the National Institutes of Health, the Department of Defense, and the Department of Education can award a Phase II SBIR contract or grant to a small business that did not receive a Phase I SBIR or STTR award. Other agencies cannot award Phase II contracts to small businesses that did not receive a Phase I award and such small businesses cannot protest the lack of an award to the GAO, *Made in*

Space, Inc., Comp. Gen. Dec. B-414490, 2017 CPD ¶ 195. Sequential Phase II awards are also permitted.

Section 4 of the Policy Directive describes the Phase II procedure as follows:

> (2) Funding must be based upon the results of work performed under a Phase I award and the scientific and technical merit, feasibility and commercial potential of the Phase II proposal. Phase II awards may not necessarily complete the total research and development that may be required to satisfy commercial or Federal needs beyond the SBIR/STTR Program. The Phase II Funding Agreement with the awardee may, at the discretion of the awarding agency, establish the procedures applicable to Phase III agreements. The Government is not obligated to fund any specific Phase II proposal.
>
> (3) The SBIR Phase II award decision process requires, among other things, consideration of a proposal's commercial potential. Commercial potential includes the potential to transition the technology to private sector applications, Government applications, or Government contractor applications. Commercial potential in a Phase II proposal may be evidenced by:
>
> (i) the SBC's record of successfully commercializing SBIR/STTR or other research;
>
> (ii) the existence of Phase II funding commitments from private sector or other non-SBIR/STTR funding sources;
>
> (iii) the existence of Phase III, follow-on commitments for the subject of the research; and
>
> (iv) other indicators of commercial potential of the idea.

Agencies have substantial discretion in deciding whether a project should be continued by the award of a Phase II contract. The decision is made on a case-by-case basis and can be dependent on the amount of funds available to the agency for SBIR work. Thus, protests of such awards are unlikely to succeed. See *Vehicle Data Science, Inc.*, Comp. Gen. Dec. B-413205, 2016 CPD ¶ 224 (weaknesses in consensus report accurately reflected evaluators' conclusions); *Pacific Blue Innovations*, Comp. Gen. Dec. B-405397, 2012 CPD ¶ 301 (proposal reasonably found to have technical weaknesses); *R&D Dynamics Corp.*, Comp. Gen. Dec. B-298766, 2006 CPD ¶ 195 (reasonable to award to only those 19 contractors evaluated highest when that used up available funds); *RDAS Corp.*, Comp. Gen. Dec. B-294848, 2004 CPD ¶ 253 (no support for protester's contention that agency decision not to fund work was based on erroneous technical conclusion); *U S Positioning Grp., LLC*, Comp. Gen. Dec. B-294027, 2004 CPD ¶ 133 (not unreasonable to consider deliverables when agency only has sufficient funds to award one Phase II contract); *R&D Dynamics Corp.*, Comp. Gen. Dec. B-285979.3, 2000 CPD ¶ 201 (not unreasonable to award to highest evaluated proposal when funds were only available to award one Phase II contract); and *I.S. Grupe, Inc.*, Comp. Gen. Dec. B-278839, 98-1 CPD ¶ 86 (technical evaluation of outside evaluator reasonable). See also

InkiTiki Corp., Comp. Gen. Dec. B-291823.4, 2003 CPD ¶ 104, where GAO denied a protest that the Phase I contractor had not been invited to submit a Phase II proposal. GAO held that the agency had properly based its decision not to invite a proposal on the review of the work during Phase I.

There are a few decisions granting protests of improper selection procedures. See *Global Aerospace Corp.*, Comp. Gen. Dec. B-414514, 2017 CPD ¶ 198 (agency documentation indicated that evaluators misunderstood protester's Phase II proposal); *Intellectual Properties, Inc.*, Comp. Gen. Dec. B-280803.2, 99-1 CPD ¶ 83 (failure to award Phase II contract based on reasons that were not supported by the comments of the evaluators that had reviewed the Phase II proposal in detail); and *Intellectual Props., Inc.*, Comp. Gen. Dec. B-280803, 98-2 CPD ¶ 115 (failure to award Phase II contract was based on lack of private sector funding—a factor not specified in the solicitation). See also *R&D Dynamics Corp. v. United States*, 80 Fed. Cl. 715 (2007), *aff'd*, 309 Fed. Appx. 388 (Fed. Cir. 2009), where the Court of Federal Claims inexplicably ruled that it had no jurisdiction to hear this type of protest because SBIR procurements were not procurement contracts. Compare *Sperient Corp.*, 113 Fed. Cl. 1 (2013), holding that Phase II contracts were procurement contracts requiring claims to be filed using Contract Disputes Act procedures.

If the negotiations for a Phase II contract require effort beyond the funding of the Phase I effort, the contractor bears the risk that such costs will not be recoverable from the government, *RADCON Radar Control Sys.*, ASBCA 50022, 99-2 BCA ¶ 30,571. In that case, the board also ruled that it had no jurisdiction over a claim that the government had prevented obtaining private financing for a continuation of the project by misrepresenting the level of success of the Phase II work. See also *California Consulting Eng'rs*, ASBCA 50355, 98-2 BCA ¶ 29,995, denying a claim for additional money spent to build a prototype to support its Phase II proposal (which did not lead to the award of a contract).

A contractor performing a fixed-price Phase II contract can be assessed an equitable price reduction under the Inspection of Research and Development—Fixed Price clause in FAR 52.246-7 in its contract, *M.L. Energia, Inc.*, ASBCA 55947, 12-2 BCA ¶ 35,110, See *M.L. Energia, Inc.*, ASBCA 58975, 19-1 BCA ¶ 37,298, deciding the amount of the price reduction. Similarly, a contractor performing a cost-reimbursement SBIR contract is subject to the FAR Cost Principles, *Quimba Software, Inc. v. United States*, 132 Fed. Cl. 676 (2017) (deferred compensation allowable); *Accurate Automation Corp.*, ASBCA 59727, 15-1 BCA ¶ 35,954 (unpaid executive compensation unallowable); *Metron, Inc.*, ASBCA 56624, 12-2 BCA ¶ 35,066 (executive compensation reasonable). Cost-reimbursement SBIR contracts also contain the Limitation of Cost clause in FAR 52.232-20 which allows denial of compensation for costs above the estimated costs if the contractor fails to give notice of the overrun as required by the clause, *PHI Applied Physical Sciences, Inc.*, ASBCA 56581, 13-1 BCA ¶ 35,308. Compare *Applied Tech. Assocs., Inc.*, ASBCA 49200, 98-1

BCA ¶29,633, holding that the government was obligated to pay an amount exceeding the funds provided for a fixed-price Phase II contract because the unique Limitation of Government Obligation clause in the contract did not contain a statement that the contractor could cease working when it had expended all of the funds allotted to the contract.

Appendix 1 of the Policy Directive allows cost sharing in SBIR contracts but states that cost sharing may not be an evaluation factor. Nonetheless, the Department of Defense has experimented with a "fast track" procedure that permits Phase I contractors to submit proposals for Phase II contracts for consideration on an expedited basis—based on the agreement of an outside investor to provide 50% of the funding of the Phase II project. In *R&D Dynamics Corp.*, Comp. Gen. Dec. B-285979.2, 2000 CPD ¶193, GAO denied a protest that agency officials had discouraged the protester from submitting a fast-track proposal based on lack of evidence plus the clear statement in the regulations that fast track proposals were encouraged and that they had a far greater chance of obtaining funding.

[E] Phase III Selection Procedures

Phase III contracts are awarded when the agency decides to use non-SBIR/STTR funds to continue the project. They are unique in the fact that they can be awarded to a contractor that is not a small business. Section 4 of the Policy Directive describes the Phase III procedure as follows:

> (c) *Phase III*. Phase III refers to work that derives from, extends, or completes an effort made under prior SBIR/STTR Funding Agreements, but is funded by sources other than the SBIR/STTR programs. Phase III work is typically oriented towards Commercialization of SBIR/STTR research or technology, including through further R/R&D work.
>
> (1) *Phase III work*. Each of the following types of activity constitutes SBIR/STTR Phase III work:
>
> (i) Commercial application (including R/R&D, testing and evaluation of products, services or technologies for use in technical or weapons systems) of SBIR/STTR-funded R/R&D that is financed by non-Federal sources of capital. (Note: The guidance in this Policy Directive regarding SBIR/STTR Phase III pertains to the non-SBIR/STTR federally funded work described in (ii) and (iii) below. It does not address private agreements an SBIR/STTR firm may make in the Commercialization of its technology, except for a subcontract to a Federal contract that may be a Phase III.).
>
> (ii) SBIR/STTR-derived products or services intended for use by the Federal Government, funded by non-SBIR/STTR sources of Federal funding.

(iii) Continuation of SBIR/STTR work, funded by non-SBIR/STTR sources of Federal funding including R/R&D.

(2) *Data rights.* A Phase III award is, by its nature, an SBIR/STTR award, has SBIR/STTR status, and must be accorded SBIR/STTR data rights. If an SBIR/STTR Awardee receives a Funding Agreement (whether competed, direct award, sole sourced or a subcontract) for work that derives from, extends, or completes efforts made under prior SBIR/STTR Funding Agreements, then the Funding Agreement for the new work must have all SBIR/STTR Phase III status and SBIR/STTR Data Rights.

(3) *Competition Requirement.* The competitions for SBIR/STTR Phase I and Phase II awards satisfies any competition requirement of the Armed Services Procurement Act, the Federal Property and Administrative Services Act, and the Competition in Contracting Act. An agency that wishes to fund an SBIR/STTR Phase III award, which is an extension of prior Phase I and/or Phase II awards, is not required to conduct another competition for the Phase III award in order to satisfy those statutory provisions. As a result, in conducting actions relative to a Phase III SBIR/STTR award, it is sufficient to state for purposes of a Justification and Approval, if it is deemed required by the agency, that the project is a SBIR/STTR Phase III award that is derived from, extends, or completes efforts performed under prior SBIR/STTR Funding Agreements and is authorized pursuant to 15 U.S.C. 638(r)(4). Further justification is not needed.

(4) Phase III work may be for products, production, services, R/R&D, or any such combination.

(5) There is no limit on the number, duration, type, or dollar value of Phase III awards made to a business concern. There is no limit on the time that may elapse between a Phase I or Phase II award and Phase III award, or between a Phase III award and any subsequent Phase III award. A Federal Agency may enter into a Phase III SBIR/STTR agreement at any time with a Phase II Awardee. Similarly, a Federal Agency may enter into a Phase III SBIR/STTR agreement at any time with a Phase I Awardee. A subcontract to a federally funded prime contract may be a Phase III award.

If an agency is going to pursue the technology that has been developed under an SBIR/STTR contract, there is a strong preference that a contract be awarded to the SBIR/STTR contractor. The Policy Directive requires agencies to "make a good faith effort to negotiate with such Awardees" and to award them the Phase III contract to the "greatest extent practicable." If award is made to another organization, notice must be given to the SBA and the SBA may appeal such decision to the head of the contracting activity. Upon receipt of an appeal, the head of the contracting activity must issue a written decision within 30 days and the agency must suspend the award pending the decision. The SBA also notifies Congress of any such awards.

In spite of this strong preference for award of a Phase III contract to the SBIR contractor, award to a subcontractor on the Phase II work was upheld in *Night Vision Corp. v. United States*, 469 F.3d 1369 (Fed. Cir. 2006), *cert. denied*, 550 U.S. 934 (2007). In that instance, the agency conducted a competitive procurement for the Phase III work, giving potential offerors access to the prototype delivered on the Phase II contract but not disclosing the data delivered by the Phase II contractor. The court held that the statutory preference conferred no rights on the Phase II contractor, stating at 1373-74:

> The only specific requirement that § 638(j)(2)(C) imposes is that the Administrator "modify the policy directives issued pursuant to this subsection to provide for . . . (C) procedures to ensure, to the extent practicable, that an agency which intends to pursue . . . a technology developed by a small business concern under an SBIR program enters into follow-on, non-SBIR funding agreements with the small business concern for such research, development or production." The Administrator has done so. *See SBIR Research Program Policy Directive*, 67 Fed. Reg. 60,072, 60,075-076 (Sept. 24, 2002) (noting that the special acquisition preference given to SBIR awardees is "a preference and is not mandatory" and that "[i]t is clear that Congress intends, to the greatest extent practicable, that agencies issue Phase III awards to the SBIR awardees that developed the technology"); *SBIR Research Program Policy Directive*, 58 Fed. Reg. 42,607, 42,612 (Aug. 10, 1993) ("A Federal agency may enter into a third phase agreement with a small business concern for additional work to be performed during or after the second phase period. . . . Agencies which intend to pursue research, research and development or production of a technology developed by a small business concern under the STTR [Small Business Technology Transfer] Program will give special acquisition preference . . . to the STTR company which developed the technology").
>
> * * *
>
> Nothing in § 638(j), however, bars the government from [choosing to use competitive procedures to select the follow-on contractor] or requires it to (1) select a Phase III procurement and (2) award the contract therefor to the small business concern that performed the Phase I and II contracts. We decline to read into those contracts such a requirement for, and commitment by, the government. Whatever may be the policy favoring small business in the present situation, there is simply no valid basis for reading such a requirement into the contract.

See also *Complere, Inc.*, Comp. Gen. Dec. B-406553, 2012 CPD ¶ 189, rejecting jurisdiction over a protest that an agency refused to award a Phase III contract and potentially was going to violate the Phase II protester's data rights by performing further work in-house. Compare *Toyon Research Corp.*, Comp. Gen. Dec. B-409765, 2014 CPD ¶ 235, taking jurisdiction of a protest that the agency solicited proposals that should have been found to constitute Phase III work but denying the protest because the new solicitation did not clearly call for work that "derived from" the protester's Phase II work.

Companies that are successors in interest and have obtained novations of Phase I and II contracts are eligible for Phase III awards. See *ASRC Fed. Data Network Techs., LLC*, Comp. Gen. Dec. B-409765, 2014 CPD ¶ 235, sustaining a protest where the agency had awarded a Phase III contract to a successor in interest of the company that had performed the Phases I and II work but had not obtained novations of those prior contracts. This ruling was based on a strict reading of the SBA Policy Directive.

§ 10.05 ARCHITECT-ENGINEER CONTRACTS

Architectural or engineering services must be procured in accordance with the procedures set forth in the Brooks Act. This statute was originally enacted as 40 U.S.C. §§ 541-44 and codified in Pub. L. No. 107-217, Aug. 21, 2002, as 40 U.S.C. §§ 1102-04. It is implemented in FAR Subpart 36.6. These procedures meet the Competition in Contracting Act mandate to use "competitive procedures," 10 U.S.C. § 3012 (formerly § 2302(2)(A)); 41 U.S.C. § 152(1). The Brooks Act was passed in 1972 after GAO notified Congress in 46 Comp. Gen. 556 (B-152306), 1966 CPD ¶ 110, that the existing practices in awarding architect-engineer (A-E) contracts "represent a deviation from the statutory requirements expressed in 10 U.S.C. § 2304(g) that proposals from a maximum number of qualified sources shall be solicited and that written or oral discussions be conducted with all responsible offerors who submit proposals within a competitive range, price and other factors considered." The Act amended the Federal Property and Administrative Services Act by ratifying the longstanding practice of procuring A-E services without price competition. The Act states that the government's policy is to "negotiate a contract for architectural and engineering services at compensation which the agency head determines is fair and reasonable," 40 U.S.C. § 1104(a).

The Act only applies if the prospective contract is primarily for A-E services. See FAR 36.601-3 stating:

> (c) When the contract statement of work includes both architect-engineer services and other services, the contracting officer shall follow the procedures in this subpart if the statement of work, substantially or to a dominant extent, specifies performance or approval by a registered or licensed architect or engineer. If the statement of work does not specify such performance or approval, the contracting officer shall follow the procedures in Parts 13, 14, or 15.
>
> These procedures must be used for task orders as well as for new procurements, § 1427 of the Services Acquisition Reform Act of 2003, Pub. L. No. 108-136. See FAR 8.403(c) stating:
>
> > (8) In accordance with section 1427(b) of Public Law 108-136, for requirements that substantially or to a dominant extent specify performance of architect-engineer services (as defined in 2.101), agencies—
> >
> > (i) Shall use the procedures at Subpart 36.6; and

(ii) Shall not place orders for such requirements under a Federal Supply Schedule.

Although A-E services are an integral part of a design-build contract, it does not appear that these procedures are required to be used on such contracts. FAR Subpart 36.3 is silent on this issue. See *Fluor Enters., Inc. v. United States*, 64 Fed. Cl. 461 (2005), concluding that the Brooks Act does not apply to design-build contracts. See also *Neeser Constr., Inc./Allied Bldrs. Sys., A Joint Venture*, Comp. Gen. Dec. B-285903, 2000 CPD ¶ 207, where Brooks Act procedures were not followed on a design-build procurement without protest, and *Tyler Constr. Grp. v. United States*, 83 Fed. Cl. 94 (2008), *aff'd*, 570 F.3d 1329 (Fed. Cir. 2009), rejecting the argument that indefinite delivery/indefinite quantity contracts could not be used for design-build projects without discussing the applicability of the Brooks Act.

[A] Definition of Architect-Engineer Services

In 1988, Pub. L. No. 100-656 and Pub. L. No. 100-679 amended the Brooks Act definition of A-E services to establish three independent categories of A-E services. See 40 U.S.C. § 1102(2). This definition is implemented in FAR 2.101 as follows:

> Architect-engineer services, as defined in 40 U.S.C. 1102, means—
>
> (1) Professional services of an architectural or engineering nature, as defined by State law, if applicable, that are required to be performed or approved by a person licensed, registered, or certified to provide those services;
>
> (2) Professional services of an architectural or engineering nature performed by contract that are associated with research, planning, development, design, construction, alteration, or repair of real property; and
>
> (3) Those other professional services of an architectural or engineering nature, or incidental services, that members of the architectural and engineering professions (and individuals in their employ) may logically or justifiably perform, including studies, investigations, surveying and mapping, tests, evaluations, consultations, comprehensive planning, program management, conceptual designs, plans and specifications, value engineering, construction phase services, soils engineering, drawing reviews, preparation of operating and maintenance manuals, and other related services.

In *Forest Serv., Dep't of Agriculture*, 68 Comp. Gen. 555 (B-233987), 89-2 CPD ¶ 47, GAO discussed the reason for the amendment to the A-E services definition, as follows:

> The legislative history of Pub. L. No. 100-656, § 42, 102 Stat. 3853 (1988), indicates that the amendment is intended to clarify the definition of A-E services in response to the General Accounting Office decisions issued

since the enactment of the Brooks Act, "which have had the effect of narrowing the application of the law, particularly in the field of surveying and mapping." 134 Cong. Rec. H10058 (daily ed. Oct. 12, 1988) (statement of Mr. Myers).

GAO stated that the amendment required a modification of the two-prong test enunciated in prior decisions, stating:

> Clause (C) of the 1988 amendment includes in the definition "other professional services of an architectural or engineering nature, or incidental services, which members of the architectural and engineering professions (and individuals in their employ) may logically or justifiably perform. . . ." The statute then lists services such as surveying and mapping which fall into this category. Thus, the revised definition now makes it clear that "incidental services" means types of services which are incidental to (part of) A-E services, and not, as we previously have held, incidental to an A-E project. The test to be applied in making this determination, then, is not whether the service is incidental to a traditional A-E project; rather, it is first, whether the service is the type which is incidental to professional services of an architectural or engineering nature, and if so, whether the service is one which members of the architectural and engineering profession may logically or justifiably perform.

Thus, even though services are not connected with the design of a structure, they will be defined as A-E services if they are the type normally performed by A-E firms. See *White Shield, Inc.*, 68 Comp. Gen. 696 (B-235522), 89-2 CPD ¶ 257 (cadastral surveying and mapping services); *Fodrea Land Surveys*, Comp. Gen. Dec. B-236413, 89-2 CPD ¶ 364 (traditional surveying and mapping of land). See, however, FAR 36.601-4(a)(4) stating:

> [M]apping services that are not connected to traditionally understood or accepted architectural and engineering activities, are not incidental to such architectural and engineering activities or have not in themselves been considered architectural and engineering services shall be procured pursuant to Parts 13, 14, and 15.

See *Management Ass'n for Private Photogrammetric Surveyors v. United States*, 492 F. Supp. 2d 540 (E.D. Va. 2007), rejecting a challenge to this interpretation of the statute.

Other types of A-E services include computer-assisted design and drafting services, *EBA Ernest Bland Assocs.*, Comp. Gen. Dec. B-270496, 96-1 CPD ¶ 148; conducting flood studies, *Northwest Hydraulic Consultants, Inc.*, Comp. Gen. Dec. B-266211, 95-2 CPD ¶ 229; inspection and maintenance of work on towers and an antenna, *Fantozzi Co.*, Comp. Gen. Dec. B-265631, 95-2 CPD ¶ 255; and comprehensive long-term environmental services, *ABB Envtl. Servs., Inc.*, Comp. Gen. Dec. B-258258.2, 95-1 CPD ¶ 126. Compare *Photo Science,*

Inc., Comp. Gen. Dec. B-296391, 2005 CPD ¶ 140 (services to identify, measure and analyze natural resource habitats and cultural resource sites, using Global Positioning System services and Geographic Information Systems data management services not A-E services); and *Terra Surveys*, Comp. Gen. Dec. B-294015, 2004 CPD ¶ 155 (services requiring installation of equipment to monitor water levels not A-E services).

In a departure from the general conclusion that A-E services relate to land or buildings, GAO held in *Tridentis, LLC*, Comp. Gen. Dec. B-412539, 2016 CPD ¶ 92, that naval architectural and marine engineering services fell within the definition of A-E services, concluding that "nothing on the face of the statute" precludes the use of A-E procedures to procure such services.

[B] Gathering Qualification Data

Each agency that procures A-E services is required to maintain files containing current data on the qualifications of A-E firms that desire contracts with the agency. FAR 36.603 contains the following guidance:

> (a) *Establishing offices*. Agencies shall maintain offices or permanent evaluation boards, or arrange to use the offices or boards of other agencies, to receive and maintain data on firms wishing to be considered for Government contracts. Each office or board shall be assigned a jurisdiction by its parent agency, making it responsible for a geographical region or area, or a specialized type of construction.
>
> (b) *Qualifications data*. To be considered for architect-engineer contracts, a firm must file with the appropriate office or board the Standard Form 330, "Architect-Engineer Qualifications," Part II, and when applicable, SF 330, Part I.
>
> (c) *Data files and the classification of firms*. Under the direction of the parent agency, offices or permanent evaluation boards shall maintain an architect-engineer qualifications data file. These offices or boards shall review the SF 330 filed, and shall classify each firm with respect to:
>
> (1) Location;
> (2) Specialized experience;
> (3) Professional capabilities; and
> (4) Capacity, with respect to the scope of work that can be undertaken. A firm's ability and experience in computer-assisted design should be considered, when appropriate.

The Standard Form 330 contains two parts. Part II lists the general qualifications of a firm, consisting of a list of the key personnel and projects performed in the last five years. Part I lists the team that will be used to perform a specific prospective project with information on their experience on prior projects, with the result that this part of the form can only be submitted when a specific project is identified. A-Es and agencies should update Part II of the form on a regular basis, FAR 36.603(d). See *Dhillon Eng'rs, Inc.*, Comp. Gen. Dec. B-209687, 83-1 CPD ¶ 268, criticizing a six-month lag in recording information on prior contract awards and recommending that the agency update the information before the selection board's final recommendation.

Agencies are also required to prepare performance reports at the conclusion of each A-E project with a value of $35,000 or more, FAR 36.604 and 42.1502(f). These reports are submitted electronically to the CPARS and are required to be used in making the decision as to the qualification of specific A-E firms, FAR 42.1503(e). DFARS 236.604 requires Department of Defense activities to make this report using DD Form 2631.

[C] Announcement of Requirements

The Brooks Act originally provided that the agency was required to "publicly announce all requirements for architectural and engineering services," 40 U.S.C. § 542. When the Act was codified in 2002, this requirement was revised in 40 U.S.C. § 1103(d) to state that the selection of an A-E firm "shall be based on criteria established and published by the agency head." FAR 36.601-1 implements this requirement by calling for a public announcement of all requirements for A-E services. This policy is implemented in FAR 5.205(d)(1) which requires posting a synopsis on the governmentwide point of entry for any proposed A-E contract expected to exceed $25,000. FAR 5.207(c)(13) states that the synopsis should contain the following information:

> For Architect-Engineer projects and other projects for which the supply or service codes are insufficient, provide brief details with respect to: location, scope of services required, cost range and limitations, type of contract, estimated starting and completion dates, and any significant evaluation factors.

This synopsis serves as a solicitation—alerting firms that want to compete for a project that they should submit a SF 330 to the agency. See *Wadell Eng'g Corp.*, 60 Comp. Gen. 11 (B-199171), 80-2 CPD ¶ 269, noting that no other solicitation is used in this form of procurement. Therefore, after publishing the synopsis, agencies must allow a 30-day response time from the date of publication before taking further action if the procurement exceeds the simplified acquisition threshold, FAR 5.203(d). A firm that does not respond to this notice is not necessarily excluded from consideration, as A-E firms are selected based on forms on file with the agency. However, the synopsis allows interested firms that have not done so to file the proper forms or to update data already on file. The synopsis also alerts firms which might wish to protest some aspect of the procurement. An agency may refuse to consider a firm that has not submitted the information by the time required by the synopsis, *Northwest Heritage Consultants*, Comp. Gen. Dec. B-299547, 2007 CPD ¶ 93.

If the agency prepares a preliminary conceptual design, it is not required to release it to the A-E firms. See *Hack v. Dep't of Energy*, 538 F. Supp. 1098 (D.D.C. 1982), rejecting a request for such a design pursuant to the Freedom of Information Act. 5 U.S.C. § 552.

[D] Evaluation Criteria

The policy of the Brooks Act is to award A-E contracts on the basis of competence and qualifications. This involves a two-step process: (1) selection based upon demonstrated competence and qualifications, and (2) post-selection negotiation of a fair and reasonable price.

Each contractor is evaluated in terms of professional qualifications, specialized experience in the type of work required, capacity to perform on time, past performance, location in the area of the project (provided this criterion leaves an appropriate number of qualified firms), and acceptability under other appropriate evaluation criteria, FAR 36.602-1(a). This latter broad category allows agencies to add criteria appropriate to a specific project. See *Design Eng'g, Inc.*, Comp. Gen. Dec. B-408336.3, 2014 CPD ¶ 144 ("knowledge of locality").

Firms also may be evaluated on the basis of the project design. FAR 36.602-1(b) provides that design competitions may be used, with the approval of the agency head or a designee, when unique situations exist involving prestige projects, sufficient time is available for the production and evaluation of designs, and the design competition will benefit the project after considering its costs. See *Archimania*, Comp. Gen. Dec. B-414653, 2017 CPD ¶ 254, where the agency did not call for a design but evaluated the firms based on (1) past performance on design; (2) philosophy and design intent; (3) lead designer profile; and (4) lead designer portfolio.

There is no FAR requirement that A-E work be equitably distributed among competing firms, *Fantozzi Co.*, Comp. Gen. Dec. B-265631, 95-2 CPD ¶ 255, *recons. denied*, 96-1 CPD ¶ 220. However, DOD PGI 236.602-1(a)(6) calls for the consideration of "equitable distribution of work" as a "secondary factor" that should not have greater significance than qualifications and past performance. See *Coffman Eng'rs, Inc.*, Comp. Gen. Dec. B-416724, 2018 CPD ¶ 409, denying a protest where the agency made an error in evaluating this factor but found the winning offeror had stronger ratings on the other factors, and *Liberty Assocs., Inc.*, Comp. Gen. Dec. B-232650, 89-1 CPD ¶ 29, denying a protest where the agency found that equitable distribution of work was outweighed by other performance- and qualification-based factors. However, GAO sustained a protest when the Navy failed to consider this factor, *Randolph Eng'g, Inc.*, Comp. Gen. Dec. B-192375, 79-1 CPD ¶ 465. In *ABB Envtl. Servs., Inc.*, Comp. Gen. Dec. B-258258.2, 95-1 CPD ¶ 126, the fact that equitable distribution of work was not a listed evaluation factor but was nonetheless used to resolve a tie, was deemed not to have prejudiced the protester because (1) it was applied equally to all offerors and (2) it was implausible to believe that the protester would not have competed had it known that this factor would be used.

These criteria are applied at two stages. The information submitted or on file with the agency is reviewed and not less than three firms are chosen for discussions "regarding concepts and the relative utility of alternative methods of furnishing the required services," FAR 36.602-3(c). After these discussions, the top three firms are ranked according to the evaluation criteria as well as the merit of each firm's concepts. In reaching the decision as to the ranking, the board "may take into account considerations, even if unstated, that are reasonably related to or encompassed by the stated evaluation criteria," *Reid Planning, Inc.*, Comp. Gen. Dec. B-412942, 2016 CPD ¶ 202. See, however, *Risk Analysis & Mitigation Partners*, Comp. Gen. Dec. B-409687, 2014 CPD ¶ 214, sustaining a protest because the agency used criteria that were "so removed" from the stated criteria that the protester could not have reasonably understood that those issues should be addressed in its proposal. In some cases, firms have been called upon to make oral presentations and it is proper to require their submitted materials to match their presentations, *Metcalf & Eddy Servs., Inc.*, Comp. Gen. Dec. B-298421.2, 2007 CPD ¶ 61.

When a source selection official is unable to choose between offerors on the basis of the established factors, other "rationally related" factors may be considered, *Group Hosp. Serv., Inc.*, 58 Comp. Gen. 263 (B-190401), 79-1 CPD ¶ 245. However, under no circumstances is cost or price to be considered. In *Mounts Eng'g; Dep't of the Interior—Request for Advance Decision*, 64 Comp. Gen. 772 (B-218489), 85-2 CPD ¶ 181, because the agency found two A-E firms "equally preferred," it requested cost proposals prior to selection. GAO sustained the protest, stating at 777:

> [G]iven the legislative mandate to rank A-E firms without reference to compensation, we believe that the fee proposed by a firm is not a factor rationally related to deciding which A-E firm is most highly qualified. . . .

Since most factors considered in the Brooks Act evaluation process are responsibility-related, determinations of no responsibility are rare in this type of procurement. In *Richard Sanchez Assocs.*, 64 Comp. Gen. 603 (B-218404.2), 85-1 CPD ¶ 661, after the firm had been tentatively selected, negotiations were terminated due to the firm having fewer employees than the agency had believed. GAO held that since A-E selection procedures concern a firm's capabilities and qualifications relative to other firms rather than minimal responsibility, no referral to SBA for a Certificate of Competency was required when assessing relative capability. See also *Nomura Enters., Inc.*, Comp. Gen. Dec. B-236217, 89-2 CPD ¶ 437, holding that, although certain evaluation criteria encompassed traditional elements of responsibility, this did not convert a technical finding that the protester was less qualified and experienced than other firms into a finding of nonresponsibility.

Although neither the Brooks Act nor the FAR contain a requirement for a statement of relative importance of the evaluation criteria, such a statement is frequently included in the synopsis. A statement of relative importance is required to be included in the synopsis by DFARS 236.602-1. See *Mounts Eng'g*, 65 Comp. Gen. 476 (B-218489.4), 86-1 CPD ¶ 358, rejecting a protest challenging the importance given to the distance of the offerors' offices from the project site.

[E] Use of IDIQ Contracts

Although FAR Subpart 36.6 does not address the issuance of IDIQ contracts for A-E services, this has become common practice. In that case, an agency normally would award one or more contracts in accordance with the procedures discussed in Chapter 7, as modified to meet the requirements of FAR Subpart 36.6. When the agency intends to make multiple awards, it generally would select more than three contractors for negotiations. See, for example, *SCST Eng'g*, Comp. Gen. Dec. B-414601, 2017 CPD ¶ 247, where the agency held preliminary discussions with seven highly qualified firms and two qualified firms, but, based on these discussions, conducted negotiations with only the highly qualified firms. GAO denied the protest finding that the agency had properly determined that the protester was not highly qualified. See also *Design Eng'g, Inc.*, Comp. Gen. Dec. B-408336.3, 2014 CPD ¶ 144, where the agency interviewed eight firms, ranked the top four firms and negotiated and awarded IDIQ contracts to the two top firms, and *Vanguard Recovery Assistance v. United States*, 99 Fed. Cl. 81 (2011), where the agency ranked seven firms and awarded IDIQ contracts to the four top firms.

[F] Source Selection Personnel

Evaluation boards are made up of professional personnel, from the government or A-E firms, who are capable of appraising the qualifications of the prospective A-Es. FAR 36.602-2 provides:

> (a) When acquiring architect-engineer services, an agency shall provide for one or more permanent or ad hoc architect-engineer evaluation boards (which may include preselection boards when authorized by agency regulations) to be composed of members who, collectively, have experience in architecture, engineering, construction, and Government and related acquisition matters. Members shall be appointed from among highly qualified professional employees of the agency or other agencies, and if authorized by agency procedure, private practitioners of architecture, engineering, or related professions. One Government member of each board shall be designated as the chairperson.
>
> (b) No firm shall be eligible for award of an architect-engineer contract during the period in which any of its principals or associates are participating as members of the awarding agency's evaluation board.

GAO will not grant a protest that board members were not qualified unless the protester can show "possible fraud, bad faith, or a conflict of interest," *Geographic Res. Solutions*, Comp. Gen. Dec. B-260402, 95-1 CPD ¶ 278; *IDG Architects*, 68 Comp. Gen. 683 (B-235487), 89-2 CPD ¶ 236. In *Shah & Assocs.*, Comp. Gen. Dec. B-257405, 94-2 CPD ¶ 123, GAO rejected the argument that this regulation requires that one member of the board be an architect and another be a construction manager.

[G] Appraising Firms' Qualifications

The first step in the selection process is to appraise each firm's qualifications using SF 330 and the reports in the CPARS. In deciding which firms to hold discussions with, agencies are permitted but not required to use information not included in these data systems. See *FACE Assocs., Inc.*, Comp. Gen. Dec. B-211877, 83-2 CPD ¶ 643, finding that the Brooks Act, which provides that firms should be encouraged to submit statements of qualifications and performance data annually, evidenced a legislative intent to avoid burdensome investigations into the firms' qualifications for each procurement.

Some agencies also gather past performance information from recent clients of the A-E firms. See *Shaw-Parsons Infrastructure Recovery Consultants, LLC*, Comp. Gen. Dec. B-401679.4, 2010 CPD ¶ 77, holding that when an agency requires the submission of questionnaires from recent clients, it must include that information in the evaluation of a firm's past performance because it is too close at hand to ignore. See also *SEI Group, Inc.*, Comp. Gen. Dec. B-400829, 2009 CPD ¶ 51, where an agency properly sought and relied on questionnaires from recent clients when it found that one potential A-E firm had no data in the PPIRS.

It is proper to include in the appraisal the qualifications of subcontractors and consultants that will be used on the project, *Foundation Eng'g Sci., Inc.*, Comp. Gen. Dec. B-292834, 2003 CPD ¶ 229.

When an agency learns that information on the standard forms is misleading or inaccurate, it may terminate negotiations with a firm that has been tentatively selected, *Veterans Design Assocs.*, Comp. Gen. Dec. B-242080, 91-1 CPD ¶ 265; and *Richard Sanchez Assocs.*, 64 Comp. Gen. 603 (B-218404.2), 85-1 CPD ¶ 661. The evaluation board is also free to change its ranking upon receipt of new information, *SCST Eng'g*, Comp. Gen. Dec. B-441601, 2017 CPD ¶ 247 (updated evaluation as a result of discussions); *Henderson Design Grp.*, Comp. Gen. Dec. B-248973.3, 92-2 CPD ¶ 406 (misleading information discovered); *Harding Lawson Assocs., Inc.*, Comp. Gen. Dec. B-230219, 88-1 CPD ¶ 483 (award of another contract led to reevaluation of ability to timely perform).

GAO and the Court of Federal Claims give considerable deference to agency evaluators and will only review evaluations to determine if they are reasonable and in accordance with the stated evaluation criteria, *Great Southern Eng'g, Inc. v. United States*, 128 Fed. Cl. 739 (2016); *AMEL Techs., Inc.*, Comp. Gen. Dec.

B-412587.2, 2016 CPD ¶ 163; *OLBN Architectural Serv., Inc.*, Comp. Gen. Dec. B-402444.4, 2011 CPD ¶ 55.

[H] Discussions

FAR 36.602-3(c) requires that the evaluation board conduct discussions with at least three firms as follows:

> (c) Hold discussions with at least three of the most highly qualified firms regarding concepts and the relative utility of alternative methods of furnishing the required services.

There is no requirement to point out deficiencies and significant weaknesses during these discussions because the procedures of FAR Part 15 do not apply to A-E procurements, *HydroGeoLogic, Inc.*, Comp. Gen. Dec. B-311263, 2008 CPD ¶ 218; *Metcalf & Eddy Servs., Inc.*, Comp. Gen. Dec. B-298421.2, 2007 CPD ¶ 61. Thus, there is no requirement to raise the issue of adverse past performance information in these discussions, *SEI Group, Inc.*, Comp. Gen. Dec. B-400829, 2009 CPD ¶ 51. Neither is there any requirement that the full board participate in the discussions with the selected firms. See *Pickering Firm, Inc.*, Comp. Gen. Dec. B-277396, 97-2 CPD ¶ 99, finding it proper to have subordinates attend the discussions as long as one board member was present.

Some agencies have conducted oral presentations as part of these discussions. See *McKissack-URS Partners, JV*, Comp. Gen. Dec. B-406489.2, 2012 CPD ¶ 162 (protester could not reasonably believe that the oral presentation board was different from the main evaluation board); *HydroGeoLogic, Inc.*, Comp. Gen. Dec. B-311263, 2008 CPD ¶ 218 (oral presentation adequately dealt with "concepts and the relative utility of alternate methods").

[I] Selection and Ranking of Firms

After discussions the evaluation board prepares a selection report recommending the top three firms in order of preference, FAR 36.602-3(d). The selection report must include a narrative of the board's discussions and evaluation in order to allow the selection authority to review the recommendation. GAO sustained a protest where no documentation of the board's reasoning was created, rejecting the contention that because architects and engineers "are called upon to exercise their professional judgment . . . the process is necessarily a highly subjective one which does not lend itself to reasoned statements of the basis on which the selection is made," *Wadell Eng'g Corp.*, 60 Comp. Gen. 11 (B-199171), 80-2 CPD ¶ 269. See also *Weston Sols., Inc. v. United*, 95 Fed. Cl. 311 (2010), *aff'd*, 44 Fed. Appx. 926 (Fed. Cir. 2011), remanding a case to clarify inadequate documentation as to the rankings. However, in *ABB Envtl. Servs., Inc.*, Comp. Gen. Dec. B-258258.2, 95-1 CPD ¶ 126, the fact that the evaluation board was orally advised that its report was inadequate and was instructed to revise it (rather than rejecting the report outright and stating the reasons therefor in writing) was deemed to be a deficiency of form that did not affect the validity of the selection decision. See also *Pickering Firm, Inc.*, Comp. Gen. Dec. B-277396, 97-2 CPD ¶ 99, where supplemental documentation was accepted to bolster "sparse" original documentation.

The final ranking is made by the agency head or another designated selection authority. The selection official reviews the board's recommendations with the advice of staff and technical representatives and selects the most qualified firms in order of preference. The selection official may select from only those firms on the board's list, FAR 36.602-4, but exercises an independent evaluation function, *SRG Partnership, PC*, 56 Comp. Gen. 721 (B-188444), 77-1 CPD ¶ 438. However, if the highest-ranked firm is not the firm most highly rated by the evaluation board, a written explanation must be provided, FAR 36.602-4(b).

GAO has consistently held that it will not upset the A-E selection decision as long as the record shows that the agency reasonably evaluated the protester's qualifications in accordance with the stated evaluation criteria. See *AMEL Techs., Inc.*, Comp. Gen. Dec. B-412587.2, 2016 CPD ¶ 163; *URS Consultants*, Comp. Gen. Dec. B-27506, 97-1 CPD ¶ 100; *Geographic Res. Sols.*, Comp. Gen. Dec. B-260402, 95-1 CPD ¶ 278; and *CH2M Hill, Ltd.*, Comp. Gen. Dec. B-259511, 95-1 CPD ¶ 203. GAO has also denied a protest that the agency materially altered the project requirements without permitting new conceptual designs to be submitted, *Kerry Lindale*, Comp. Gen. Dec. B-276057, 97-1 CPD ¶ 165.

FAR 36.602-5 allows two "short selection processes," consisting of selection by the board or by the chairperson of the board, when the contract is not expected to exceed the simplified acquisition threshold. The agency may also use a longer process including "reselection boards" if it desires.

In other cases, agencies may use more elaborate procedures. In *URS Consultants*, Comp. Gen. Dec. B-275068, 97-1 CPD ¶ 100, the agency followed a two-stage procedure to make its selection. The process was described as follows:

> The CBD synopsis indicated that GSA would select a contractor through a two-stage process. Stage I would establish the architectural, mechanical and electrical engineering, and industrial hygienist design capabilities of interested A/E firms and their key designers. During Stage I, interested firms were to submit standard forms (SF) 254 and 255 for the A/E design firm only and additional information including: 8 X 10 graphics and written descriptions of relevant prior completed projects; a statement from their key designers regarding the firm's design philosophy and the parameters that apply specifically to the modernization of buildings; their key designers' portfolios; and biographical profiles of their key designers. After the qualifications statements and related materials were evaluated, a short list of at least three firms would be selected for participation in Stage II. The synopsis stated that, during Stage II, each short-list offeror's entire project team—including the A/E design

> firm, its key designers, and all the consultants that will work on the project—would be evaluated. This evaluation was to be based upon submission of SFs 254 and 255 which reflected the entire project team and would include a face-to-face interview with each project team.

See also *SCST Eng'g*, Comp. Gen. Dec. B-441601, 2017 CPD ¶ 247, where the agency conducted discussions to gain a fuller understanding of the competitors' qualifications to receive one of seven IDIQ contracts, and *Gene Corp.*, Comp. Gen. Dec. B-274390-2, 97-1 CPD ¶ 225, where the selection procedure involved site visits, live-test demonstrations, and oral presentations. The solicitation contained 18 evaluation criteria and 38 sub criteria.

[J] Price Negotiations

Final ranking by the selection official authorizes the contracting officer to begin negotiations with the most highly rated firm, FAR 36.606(a). The contracting officer should ordinarily request a proposal from the firm "ensuring that the solicitation does not inadvertently preclude the firm from proposing the use of modern design methods," FAR 36.606(b). Such methods, such as computer-assisted design, should be discussed in negotiations if not covered in the firm's proposal, FAR 36.606(d).

The negotiation process differs significantly from discussions in standard competitive procurement. This is primarily because 40 U.S.C. § 1104(a) requires the agency to negotiate a contract at a "fair and reasonable" price although the statute does not permit the agency to consider price in selecting the contractor. FAR 36.606(a) states that these negotiations "shall be conducted in accordance with Part 15" without explaining the meaning of this statement.

If the contracting officer is unable to negotiate a reasonable price or is otherwise unable to negotiate a satisfactory contract, negotiations should be formally terminated and negotiations should begin with the second-ranked firm, 40 U.S.C. § 1104(b); FAR 36.606(f). In *Drowsy Assocs.*, Comp. Gen. Dec. B-248216, 92-1 CPD ¶ 533, the contracting officer's decision to terminate negotiations when, after 10 months, the parties could not come to a mutually acceptable agreement was not arbitrary or unreasonable. FAR 36.606(f) provides that the contracting officer should request a written final proposal revision from a firm prior to terminating negotiations. This procedure continues until a satisfactory contract is negotiated. See *Inca Eng'rs, Inc.*, 69 Comp. Gen. 34 (B-236406), 89-2 CPD ¶ 371.

Negotiation may involve matters other than price. See FAR 36.606(e) calling for the negotiation of subcontractors that will be used on the project because the standard clause Subcontractors and Outside Consultants (Architect-Engineer Services) at FAR 52.244-4 requires that only such subcontractors be used on the project. In contrast, when a design competition is held as a basis for selection, the government will not be bound to the design proposed by the selected firm unless the solicitation so provides, *Kerry Lindale*, Comp. Gen. Dec. B-276057, 97-1 CPD ¶ 165.

[K] Debriefings

FAR 36.607(b) calls for debriefing of successful and unsuccessful firms after the final selection of the source—with the debriefing following the procedures of FAR Part 15. However, an unsuccessful firm cannot wait until a debriefing to file a protest to GAO because the timeliness exception in 4 CFR 21.2(a)(2) does not apply to A-E procurements, *McKissack-URS Partners, JV*, Comp. Gen. Dec. B-406489.2, 2012 CPD ¶ 162. Furthermore, GAO will not consider protests of misleading or inaccurate debriefings, *AMEL Techs., Inc.*, Comp. Gen. Dec. B-412611, 2016 CPD ¶ 103.

[L] Fee Limitations

There are a number of statutory provisions requiring A-E contracts to contain limitations on the amount that can be paid for A-E services. The statute applicable to most civilian agencies, 41 U.S.C. § 254(b), contained the following provisions applicable to A-E contracts:

> [I]n the case of a cost-plus-a-fixed-fee contract the fee shall not exceed 10 percent of the estimated cost of the contract, exclusive of the fee, as determined by the agency head at the time of entering into such contract (except . . . that a fee inclusive of the contractor's costs and not in excess of 6 percent of the estimated cost, exclusive of fees, as determined by the agency head at the time of entering into the contract, of the project to which such fee is applicable is authorized in contracts for architectural or engineering services relating to any public works or utility project).

In the 2011 codification, Pub. L. No. 111-350, the meaning of this provision was changed to state in 41 U.S.C. § 3905(b):

> (3) Architectural or engineering services. The fee in a cost-plus-a-fixed-fee contract for architectural or engineering services relating to any public works or utility project may include the contractor's costs and shall not exceed 6 percent of the estimated cost, not including the fee, as determined by the agency head at the time of entering into the contract, of the project to which the fee applies.

This codification would apply the fee restriction only to cost-plus-fixed-fee contracts whereas the prior statute was applicable to all types of A-E contracts. Since codification are not intended to substantively alter the law, it is not obvious whether this language should be read to preclude application of the fee restriction to other types of A-E contracts.

The statute applicable to DoD, NASA, and the Coast Guard, 10 U.S.C. § 3322(b) (formerly § 2306(d)), contains different language, stating:

> The fee for performing a cost-plus-a-fixed-fee contract for architectural or engineering services for a public work or utility plus the cost of those services to the contractor may not be more than 6 percent of the estimated cost of that work or project, not including fees. The fee for performing any other cost-plus-a-fixed-fee contract may not be more than 10 percent of the estimated cost of the contract, not including the fee.

In addition, each of the military services has fee limitation provisions in 10 U.S.C. § 7540(b) (Army), 10 U.S.C. § 8612(b) (Navy & Marine Corps), and 10 U.S.C. § 9540(b) (Air Force). These provisions state:

> The fee for any service under this section may not be more than 6 percent of the estimated cost, as determined by the Secretary, of the project to which it applies.

As implemented in the FAR, the 6% limitation applies to all A-E contracts, whether they are fixed-price or cost-reimbursement. See FAR 15.404-4(c) stating:

> (4)(i) The contracting officer shall not negotiate a price or fee that exceeds the following statutory limitations, imposed by 10 U.S.C. 2306(d) and 41 U.S.C. 3905:
>
> * * *
>
> (B) For architect-engineer services for public works or utilities, the contract price or the estimated cost and fee for production and delivery of designs, plans, drawings, and specifications shall not exceed 6 percent of the estimated cost of construction of the public work or utility, excluding fees.

This 6% limitation is computed as a percentage of the estimated cost of the project being designed. In order to comply with this requirement, the agency must have a sufficient definition of the work to be designed to permit it to arrive at a reasonable estimate of this cost of the construction. See FAR 36.605(a) requiring the agency to prepare an independent cost estimate for contracts exceeding the simplified acquisition threshold based on a detailed analysis of the work, "as though the Government were submitting a proposal," and provide it to the contracting officer prior to negotiations. See also *Fluor Enters., Inc. v. United States*, 64 Fed. Cl. 461 (2005), holding that, since under the civilian agency fee limitation statute an agency had no authority to issue a contract calling for A-E services without a project estimate, such a contract was unenforceable. The court rejected the government's argument that the 6% limitation should be imposed on the actual costs of construction and remanded to the agency to determine and pay, under a quantum meruit theory, the reasonable value of the A-E services based on its best judgment of what the estimated cost of the construction would have been when the A-E contract was issued (even though the court accepted the fact that the work had not been defined at that time because part of the work of the A-E was to define the construction that was needed).

In *Fluor* the court held that these statutory limitations apply to any portion of a contract that calls for A-E work. The court reasoned at 479:

> § 254(b) [now § 3905] indicates that a fee not in excess of 6% of the estimated cost is "authorized in *contracts for architectural or engineering services* related to any public works." § 254(b) (emphasis added). At least facially, there is nothing ambiguous about this language that might suggest that its applicability should only extend to contracts *primarily* or *substantially* for A&E services or, alternatively, that A&E services to be rendered as part of a broad professional services contract like Fluor's might somehow be exempt from the statute's purview.

The court supported its interpretation as follows at 481:

> That interpretation of the fee limitation—that it only applies to a limited range of services despite the variety of services called for in the contract—is consistent with opinions from administrative bodies that have interpreted the statute. The Comptroller General has expressed the opinion that "the codifications of the 1939 statutes *apply to all types of contracts* and that costs which do not relate to the preparation of designs, plans, drawings, and specifications may be regarded as not subject to the 6-percent limitation imposed by those statutes." 46 Comp. Gen. 556, 560 (Dec. 12, 1966) (emphasis added). "In light of the legislative history of the Brooks Act, we have held that the Act applies to the procurement of services which uniquely or to a substantial or dominant extent logically requires performance by a professionally licensed and qualified A-E firm." *In re Assoc. of Soil & Foundation Eng'rs*, 61 Comp. Gen. 377, 378 (May 6, 1982). Logically, if services that do not properly fall within the Brooks Act's circumspection of "architectural or engineering services" or, even more apparent, are not architectural or engineering services at all, then the fees for those services are not rightly subject to the § 254(b) fee limitation. However, the presence of such services—even if they represent a substantial or predominant portion of the contract—does not exempt from the fee limitation the fees for those services that are properly within the scope of the Brooks Act provisions.

This rule is stated in DFARS 236.606-70 as follows:

> (c) The six percent limit applies only to that portion of the contract (or modification) price attributable to the preparation of designs, plans, drawings, and specifications. If a contract or modification also includes other services, the part of the price attributable to the other services is not subject to the six percent limit.

The reference to "other services" should be construed to mean services that are not within the broad scope of A-E work as discussed above.

The 6% limitation also applies to contract modifications. DFARS 236.6-6-70 gives the following guidance:

> (b) The six percent limit also applies to contract modifications, including modifications involving—
>
> (1) *Work not initially included in the contract.* Apply the six percent limit to the revised total estimated construction cost.
>
> (2) *Redesign.* Apply the six percent limit as follows—
>
> (i) Add the estimated construction cost of the redesign features to the original estimated construction cost;
>
> (ii) Add the contract cost for the original design to the contract cost for redesign; and
>
> (iii) Divide the total contract design cost by the total estimated construction cost. The resulting percentage may not exceed the six percent statutory limitation.

In *Fluor* the court also held that 41 U.S.C. § 254(b) (now § 3905(b)(3)) calls for a dual limitation when an agency procures A-E services using a cost-reimbursement contract. In that case, the 6% limitation applies to the total of the estimated cost and the fixed fee of the contract and the 10% limitation applies to the fixed fee as a percentage of the estimated costs. The court illustrated this rule as follows at 473-74:

> To illustrate these concepts, a hypothetical construction project is helpful. If the government were to procure A&E services for a building whose estimated total cost was $2 million . . . , then the 6% fee limitation applicable to A&E services under § 254(b) would limit the A&E contractor's allowable costs and fixed fee to no more than $120,000 (6% of $2 million is $120,000). However, if the estimated costs of the A&E contractor's services—those actual costs for which the contractor would be reimbursed under the cost-plus-fixed-fee scenario—were only $80,000, then the fixed fee that the contractor would receive could be no more than $8,000 because the 10% fee limitation applicable to all cost-plus-fixed-fee contracts under § 254(b) would apply (10% of $80,000 is $8,000).

Under that scenario, the A&E contractor's total fee, including both his reimbursable costs and his fixed fee, would be no more than $88,000. This total fee would not run afoul of the 6% fee limitation because it is less than $120,000. On the other hand, if the same A&E contractor's estimated costs were not $80,000, but instead were $115,000, the maximum fixed fee that the A&E contractor could receive would be $5,000. Even though 10% of $115,000 (the reimbursable costs) is $11,500, the 6% fee limitation would restrict the A&E contractor to no more than $120,000 for both reimbursable costs and fixed fees.

This makes the use of a cost-reimbursement contract for A-E services a risky venture because once the A-E contractor reaches the estimated cost, the contractor is no longer required to perform—with the result that the agency would have no way to require the A-E to complete the design and would be unable to provide additional funding above the 6% limitation. It is questionable whether 10 U.S.C. § 3322(b) (formerly § 2306(d)) leads to the same result because that statute appears to apply the 10% fee limitation to contracts other than A-E contracts. However, these statutes are so poorly written that it is difficult to predict how they will be interpreted.

[M] Contract Clauses

There are three mandatory clauses for A-E contracts, FAR 36.609. The first, the Responsibility of the Architect-Engineer Contractor clause at FAR 52.236-23 requires the A-E contractor to "correct or revise any errors or deficiencies in its designs, drawings, specifications and other services" without additional compensation. This clause also states that this remedy is "in addition to any other rights and remedies provided by law." In *Parsons Main, Inc.*, ASBCA 51355, 02-2 BCA ¶ 31,886 the board enumerated the elements that the government must prove to require the contractor to redesign under this clause at 157,537:

> To prevail in a defective design claim under the FAR 52.236-23 Responsibility of the Architect-Engineer Contractor clause, the Government has the burden of establishing three elements of proof: (1) Did the construction contractor substantially comply with the A-E's design in the manner intended by the A-E? (2) Did the A-E exercise its skill, ability and judgment negligently, instead of with reasonable care, with respect to the design? (3) Was the A-E's defective design the proximate cause of damage to the Government? *See Brunson Associates, Inc.*, ASBCA No. 41201, 94-2 BCA ¶ 26,936 at 134,152; *Ralph M. Parsons Co.*, ASBCA No. 24347, 85-1 BCA ¶ 17,787 at 88,901-02, *recon. denied.* 85-2 BCA ¶ 18,112; *Benjamin S. Notkin & Associates,* ASBCA No. 29336,86-1 BCA ¶ 18,535 at 93,123 (Gov't has burden of proof of negligent A-E design claim).

In *BPLW Architects & Eng'rs, Inc. v. United States*, 106 Fed. Cl. 521 (2012), the A-E was held liable for faulty design when it provided negligent underfloor piping and civil site grading designs that did not comply with the contract requirements and the applicable standard of care. In *Gee & Jenson Eng'rs, Architects & Planners v. United States*, 2008 WL 4997488, 2008 U.S. Claims LEXIS 504 (Fed. Cl. 2008), the A-E was held liable for faulty design when it did not provide for roof flashing that was clearly required by the specifications. In *Brunson Assocs., Inc.*, ASBCA 41201, 94-2 BCA ¶ 26,936, the A-E was held to have negligently designed a building that did not survive snow loads that could have been anticipated. In that case, the board also rejected the defense that the government had been negligent in accepting the design. Compare *C.*

H. Guernsey & Co. v. United States, 65 Fed. Cl. 582 (2005) (no negligence when A-E demonstrated that its design could be complied with).

The Work Oversight in Architect-Engineer Contracts clause at FAR 52.236-24 provides that the work is subject to the "general oversight, supervision, direction, control and approval" of the contracting officer.

The Requirements for Registration of Designers clause at FAR 52.236-25 requires that the preparation, review and approval of the design be performed by architects and engineers registered to practice in a state, the District of Columbia or an "outlying area of the United States."

There is also a standard clause provided when the agency decides to impose funding limitations on the project costs. This clause, Design Within Funding Limitations at FAR 52.236-22, requires the A-E firm to redesign the project without an increase in price if the construction cost exceeds the funding limitation in the contract. The requirement is not applicable to increases in price outside of the control of the A-E firm. FAR 36.609-1(c) requires the use of this clause except when—

> (1) the head of the contracting activity or a designee determines in writing that cost limitations are secondary to performance considerations and additional project funding can be expected, if necessary,
>
> (2) the design is for a standard structure and is not intended for a specific location, or
>
> (3) there is little or no design effort involved.

This clause does not require the A-E to prepare a design that results in an ultimate project cost within the budget, only to permit contract award within the budget, *Parsons Main, Inc.*, ASBCA 51355, 02-2 BCA ¶ 32,051. The clause was strictly enforced in *Anlauf Ingenieur-Consulting*, ASBCA 37361, 90-1 BCA ¶ 22,352. In *Moshe Safdie & Assocs., Inc. v. General Servs. Admin.*, CBCA 1849, 14-1 BCA ¶ 35,564, the contractor was denied recovery of the cost of redesign except for costs caused by changes in the work directed by the government.

A-E contracts also generally include the Changes clause provided in FAR 52.243-1, Alternate III. See *Michael Roth & Assocs. v. United States*, 133 Fed. Cl. 279 (2017), rejecting the contractor's contention that work after it informed the government that the funding limitation could not be met was a change. See also *Taylor & Partners, Inc.*, VABCA 4898, 97-1 BCA ¶ 28,970, holding that alterations called for in the 75% design review were not changes but rather were normal alterations in the course of project design. Similarly, no changes were found because of additional work required in design reviews in *DMJM H&N, Inc.*, ASBCA 56557, 09-2 BCA ¶ 34,173, and *Planned Envtl. Design Corp.*, ASBCA 47599, 96-1 BCA ¶ 28,001. See also *GBQC Architects v. Gen. Servs. Admin.*, GSBCA 15578, 02-1 BCA ¶ 31,846, finding no changes when an A-E allegedly accelerated its performance of construction phase services but could not prove that the government ordered such acceleration. However, if the government requires work that is clearly not called for in the original contract, compensation will be granted, *Moshe Safdie & Assocs.*(added blast and LEED requirements); *Wyatt/Rhodes Architects, Inc.*, ASBCA 38938, 90-1 BCA ¶ 22,476 (attending an extra meeting); and *Lenz GmbH Architect-Engineer*, ASBCA 36819, 90-3 BCA ¶ 23,220 (government failed to cooperate during the design process). For a case discussing the interrelationship of the Changes clause and the Design Within Funding Limitations clause, see *Fanning, Phillips & Molnar*, VABCA 3856, 96-1 BCA ¶ 28,214.

§ 10.06 TWO-PHASE DESIGN-BUILD SELECTION PROCEDURES

Traditionally, the federal government has obtained new buildings and other civil works by contracting with an architect-engineering firm (A-E) for design of the project, soliciting competitive bids or proposals for the construction of the project, and awarding a contract to the successful offeror. This is known as the design-bid-build delivery system. Although this system has worked satisfactorily in many instances, it is relatively slow and it has the disadvantage of separating design responsibility from construction responsibility. Thus, the system has been criticized for not bringing sufficient consideration of constructibility into the design process and for subjecting the government to claims of the construction contractor for design defects. This has imposed considerable liability on the government because, in using detailed construction drawings, the government is liable to the contractor on a standard that approaches strict liability yet its claims against the A-E for defective design are generally judged by a standard of negligence.

Private owners, finding themselves in this same situation, have increasingly turned to a delivery system known as design-build. Under this system, the owner contracts initially with a single entity for both the design and the construction of the project. This entity is selected by a careful interview process, and the owner then proceeds to work with the design-build contractor for the remainder of the project. Usually, after the full scope of the project is determined (but before the detailed design is developed), the design-build contractor will agree to deliver the entire project within a guaranteed maximum price. The design-build contractor is not a construction contractor. It is a team composed of A-Es and constructors that work together from the beginning of design to the completion of construction to ensure that the owner receives the most cost-effective project that the team is capable of producing.

Federal agencies such as the Postal Service, the General Services Administration, and the Army Corps of Engineers began using the design-build system in the 1980s but they concluded that the contractor should be selected using a competitive negotiation process. See the General Services Administration publication "Design Excellence Policies and Procedures, Chapter 9 Design-Build" (Feb. 1, 2016) and the Corps of Engineers publication

"Design-Build Contracting," Corps of Engineers Regulation 1180-1-9 (Mar. 31, 2012). The Navy Facilities Engineering Command also has master RFP templates for different types of design-build projects. This procedure placed a heavy burden on offerors because these agencies generally required extensive design work as a part of the second phase of the competition and, even if the agency pays a stipend to the losing offerors, this frequently will not cover the cost of the design effort.

Section 4105 of the Clinger-Cohen Act of 1996 amended 10 U.S.C. § 2305a (now § 3241) and 41 U.S.C. § 253m (now § 3309) to include new "design-build selection procedures." This section of the Act establishes a series of new acquisition rules—known as two-phase selection procedures—that must be followed when an agency decides to use the design-build delivery system and concludes that extensive design proposals will be required. The regulatory implementation added a new FAR Subpart 36.3.

[A] Authorization and Criteria for Use

The following statement on when the new procedure should be used is set forth in 10 U.S.C. § 2305a (now § 3241):

> *Authorization*—Unless the traditional acquisition approach of design-bid build established under the Brooks Architect-Engineers Act (41 U.S.C. § 541 et seq.) is used or another acquisition procedure authorized by law is used, the head of an agency shall use the two-phase selection procedures for entering into a contract for the design and construction of a public building, facility, or work when a determination is made that the procedures are appropriate for use.

Substantially the same language is used in 41 U.S.C. § 3309(a). FAR 36.104 uses virtually the same language but also includes the following sentence:

> Other acquisition procedures authorized by law include the procedures established in this part and other parts of this chapter and, for DoD, the design-build process described in 10 U.S.C. 2862.

The "chapter" referred to is the entire Federal Acquisition Regulation, including Part 15 covering competitive negotiation procedures. Thus, there are essentially two delivery systems for construction projects—design-bid-build and design-build. If design-bid-build is chosen, the design effort must be done using the Brooks Act procedures discussed above. Thereafter, the construction can be procured using sealed bidding, negotiation, or construction management. If design-build is chosen, either a one-step or two-step procedure may be used. The one-step procedure would follow normal competitive negotiation procedures. The two-step procedure would follow this new statutory two-phase procedure. The Corps of Engineers guidance recognizes the one-step process while the GSA guidance does not. For a case where the Corps used a combination of the A-E selection procedure and the design-build procedure to award an unpriced contract to design and construct border fences and roads, see *Fisher Sand & Gravel Co.*, Comp. Gen. Dec. B-417496, 2019 CPD ¶ 280, and *Fisher Sand & Gravel Co. v. United States*, 143 Fed. Cl. 247 (2019) (refusing to reject the override of a stay of the procurement pending the outcome of the GAO protest based on the declaration of as national emergency).

Contracting officers must consider the following criteria set forth in 10 U.S.C. § 2305a (now § 3241) to determine whether the two-phase procedure is appropriate:

> (b) *Criteria for use.*—A contracting officer shall make a determination whether two-phase selection procedures are appropriate for use for entering into a contract for the design and construction of a public building, facility, or work when the contracting officer anticipates that three or more offers will be received for such contract, design work must be performed before an offeror can develop a price or cost proposal for such contract, the offeror will incur a substantial amount of expense in preparing the offer, and the contracting officer has considered information such as the following:
>
> (1) The extent to which the project requirements have been adequately defined.
>
> (2) The time constraints for delivery of the project.
>
> (3) The capability and experience of potential contractors.
>
> (4) The suitability of the project for use of the two-phase selection procedures.
>
> (5) The capability of the agency to manage the two-phase selection process.
>
> (6) Other criteria established by the agency.

Substantially the same guidance is in 41 U.S.C. § 3309(b). These criteria are repeated in FAR 6.301(b). The key criteria are the requirement for design work and the resulting incurrence of cost by offerors. If extensive design work will be required with commensurate high proposal costs, the two-phase design-build procedure should be used. If little design work or proposal costs will be required, the normal competitive negotiation procedure will likely be the most efficient procedure.

Neither the FAR nor the statutes contain any guidance on when the design-build delivery system should be used in preference to the design-bid-build delivery system. Thus, this decision is left entirely to the discretion of each contracting agency. However, if the agency is considering the use of a design-build procedure, the criteria set forth above must be considered.

[B] Procedures

The agency develops, either in-house or by contract, a scope of work statement for inclusion in the solicitation that defines the project and provides prospective offerors with sufficient information regarding the government's requirements (which may include criteria and preliminary design, budget parameters, and schedule or delivery requirements) to enable the offerors to submit proposals that meet the government's needs. If the agency contracts for development of this work statement, it must contract for A-E services in accordance with the Brooks Architect-Engineers Act, 40 U.S.C. § 1102 et seq. In that case, as discussed on Chapter 4, the A-E that drafts the work statement will be disqualified from the competition because of an organizational conflict of interest, *Energy Sys. Grp.*, Comp. Gen. Dec. B-402324, 2010 CPD ¶ 73 (protester drafted report that was used to create work statement); *B.L. Harbert-Brasfield & Gorrie, JV*, Comp. Gen. Dec. B-402229, 2010 CPD ¶ 69 (protester assisted in preparation of agency design concept and in evaluating technical proposals). The GAO decision in the latter case was reversed because of lack of "hard facts" that an OCI existed, *Turner Constr. Co. v. United States*, 645 F.3d 1377 (Fed. Cir. 2011). An organization that performs a peer-review function in the early stages of the procurement may also be disqualified for an OCI, *HBI-GF JV*, Comp. Gen. Dec. B-415036, 2017 CPD ¶ 331.

A two-phase procurement can utilize a single solicitation covering both phases or sequential solicitations, FAR 36.303. In either case, FAR 36.303-1 provides the following guidance on the solicitation instructions covering phase one:

> (a) Phase One of the solicitation(s) shall include—
>
> (1) The scope of work;
>
> (2) The phase-one evaluation factors, including—
>
> (i) Technical approach (but not detailed design or technical information);
>
> (ii) Technical qualifications, such as—
>
> (A) Specialized experience and technical competence;
>
> (B) Capability to perform;
>
> (C) Past performance of the offeror's team (including the architect-engineer and construction members); and
>
> (iii) Other appropriate factors (excluding cost or price related factors, which are not permitted in Phase One);
>
> (3) Phase-two evaluation factors (see 36.303-2); and
>
> (4) A statement of the maximum number of offerors that will be selected to submit phase-two proposals. The maximum number specified shall not exceed five unless the contracting officer determines, for that particular solicitation, that a number greater than five is in the Government's interest and is consistent with the purposes and objectives of two-phase design-build selection procedures.

The intent of this guidance is to ensure that the phase one competition will not be unduly expensive. Thus, detailed design work and cost or price proposals are *prohibited.* The result is that the phase one competition is primarily based on the evaluation of the capabilities of the competing teams. This is appropriate because success of the entire technique depends on selecting a highly competent team. Two things must be evaluated here—the competence of the individual members of the team (as well as their key employees) and the ability of the team members to work together. The key data that should be used to perform this evaluation are information on the experience and past performance records of both the members of the team and the team itself. An agency may evaluate the amount of experience each offeror has in performing design-build contracts, *J.C.N. Constr. Co.*, Comp. Gen. Dec. B-293063, 2004 CPD ¶ 12, in designing projects similar to the proposed project, *Neeser Constr., Inc./Allied Bldrs. Sys., A Joint Venture*, Comp. Gen. Dec. B-285903, 2000 CPD ¶ 207; or in constructing similar projects, *CTI-NAN JV, LLC*, Comp. Gen. Dec. B-400979, 2009 CPD ¶ 118.

The rules regarding exchanges in FAR 15.306 do not apply to Phase 1 competitions. Thus, there is no requirement to communicate with the offerors before selecting the firms that will be admitted to Phase 2, *Engineering Design Techs., Inc.*, Comp. Gen. Dec. B-404783.2, 2012 CPD ¶ 128. See *Intercontinental Constr. Contracting, Inc.*, Comp. Gen. Dec. B-415040, 2018 CPD ¶ 82 (proper to consider adverse past performance information not submitted by the protester without discussing it); *Defense Base Servs., Inc.*, Comp. Gen. Dec. B-414591, 2017 CPD ¶ 243 (proper to seek clarifications from only one firm). However, agencies can conduct discussions if desired, *Linc Gov't Servs., LLC*, Comp. Gen. Dec. B-404783.2, 2012 CPD ¶ 128 (discussions properly held only with nine firms ranked most qualified).

Evaluation of Phase 1 proposals is highly discretionary with the result that successful protests are unlikely. See, for example, *Herman Constr. Grp., Inc.*, Comp. Gen. Dec. B-416778.2, 2019 CPD ¶ 9 (protester failed to include information in proposal); *Constructure-Trison JV, LLC*, Comp. Gen. Dec. B-416741.2, 2018 CPD ¶ 397 (protester failed to include required document in proposal); *Dawson Enters., LLC*, Comp. Gen. Dec. B-414591.2, 2017 CPD ¶ 301 (protester rated weak on experience even though subcontractors had extensive experience); *Williams Bldg. Co.*, Comp. Gen. Dec. B-413262.2, 2017 CPD ¶ 103 (protester's lower ratings correct); *Trade Eastern, Inc.*, Comp. Gen. Dec. B-411857, 2015 CPD ¶ 350 (protester rated "unknown confidence" on past performance because it omitted required information); *RORE, Inc.*, Comp. Gen. Dec. B-410759, 2015 CPD ¶ 94 (protester rated weak on architectural design experience); *Bryan Constr., Inc.*, Comp. Gen. Dec. B-409135, 2014 CPD ¶ 51 (protester lacked relevant experience and past performance); However, a protest will be sustained if the agency has not treated the firms equally, *Halbert Constr. Co.*, Comp. Gen. Dec. B-413213, 2016 CPD ¶ 254, or if it has used an unstated evaluation factor, *McGoldrick Constr. Servs. Corp.*, Comp. Gen. Dec. B-409252.2, 2014 CPD ¶ 114.

The second phase of this procedure is conducted with the most highly qualified offerors in phase one, FAR 36.303-1(b). In order to carry out the intent of the statute, the number of offerors should be limited to three in most cases (the guidance is no more than five). In this phase, standard competitive negotiation procedures are used. See FAR 36.303-2, which states:

> (a) Phase Two of the solicitation(s) shall be prepared in accordance with Part 15, and include phase-two evaluation factors, developed in accordance with 15.304. Examples of potential phase-two technical evaluation factors include design concepts, management approach, key personnel, and proposed technical solutions.
>
> (b) Phase Two of the solicitation(s) shall require submission of technical and price proposals, which shall be evaluated separately, in accordance with part 15.

The key evaluation factors in this phase will be the proposed design, the capability of the offerors, and the price. In accordance with FAR Part 15, the solicitation is required to identify all significant subfactors and the relative importance of the factors. The agency has considerable discretion in deciding to award to an offeror with a higher price in order to obtain desirable design features, *TMG Servs., Inc.*, Comp. Gen. Dec. B-410929, 2015 CPD ¶ 121; *Nippo Corp.*, Comp. Gen. Dec. B-402363.2, 2010 CPD ¶ 112; *JVSCC*, Comp. Gen. Dec. B-311303.2, 2009 CPD ¶ 138. Conversely, an agency can award to an offeror with a lower price even though its proposed design is not rated highest, *Walton Constr.*, Comp. Gen. Dec. B-407621, 2013 CPD ¶ 29. While the proposed designs will almost always be a significant evaluation factor, the agency need not evaluate whether the design proposal demonstrates compliance with every element of the specification, *Medlin Constr. Group*, Comp. Gen. Dec. B-286166, 2000 CPD ¶ 199.

While the price will normally be an important factor, the solicitation should make it clear that the agency will not give a high value to a price that is too low to permit the contractor to give the agency the level of quality that it needs. Thus, the RFP should state that the agency is looking for a reasonable price and will perform a price realism analysis to ensure that no award will be made at a price that is unrealistically low. Price realism must be explicitly stated as an evaluation factor in order to make such assessment. See *CSE Constr.*, Comp. Gen. Dec. B-291268.2, 2002 CPD ¶ 207 (improper to assess price realism when the evaluation factor in the RFP was price reasonableness); *SAMS El Segundo, LLC*, Comp. Gen. Dec. B-291620.3, 2003 CPD ¶ 48 (price realism also used to assess understanding of the work). An agency may want to include its estimate of the price range of the project in the RFP in order to avoid this problem.

A unique technique is to call for a build-to-budget proposal specifying the agency's budget for the project. In such cases, the agency must make it clear whether it will evaluate offers under the budget. See *PCCP Constructors, LLC*, Comp. Gen. Dec. B-405036, 2011 CPD ¶ 156, sustaining a protest where this was not clear and the only offeror proposing a lower price was awarded the contract.

In the past, offerors have been required to include detailed information on all aspects of the proposed project, including conceptual designs, and agencies have then evaluated and scored the numerous elements of each proposal. This has resulted in a lengthy evaluation process. The process can be conducted more efficiently if the design information called for in the phase-two RFP is limited to the amount of design effort necessary to arrive at a guaranteed maximum price. There is no need to evaluate the details of the proposed design if the performance specification is adequately written and the capability of the offerors is an important evaluation factor.

Following evaluation of the proposals, the agency can select a contractor without discussions or conduct discussions to enable offerors to enhance their proposals. The agency has considerable discretion in proceeding directly to award when there is a clear superior proposal, *Sletten Cos./Sletten Constr. Co.*, Comp. Gen. Dec. B-402422, 2010 CPD ¶ 97.

[C] Multiple Awards

Some agencies have procured design-build work on smaller projects by awarding IDIQ contracts to multiple contractors. This enables the agency to enter into contracts with two or more companies and then obtain the design-build work by individual task orders which are issued after a competition between those companies. For protests involving this technique, see *GM-Bulltrack, JV*, Comp. Gen. Dec. B-414591.6, 2018 CPD ¶ 378 (29 proposals, 11 selected for Phase 2, 5 awards); *Tri-Technic, Inc.*, Comp. Gen. Dec. B-412037, 2016 CPD ¶ 5 (24 proposals, 5 selected for Phase 2, 3 potential awards); *KWR Constr., Inc. v. United States*, 124 Fed. Cl. 345 (2015) (25 proposals, 13 selected for Phase 2, 4 awards); *Engineering Design Techs., Inc.*, Comp. Gen. Dec. B-408811.2, 2014 CPD ¶ 182 (83 proposals, 17 selected for Phase 2, 10 awards); *Nan, Inc.*, Comp. Gen. Dec. B-407718, 2013 CPD ¶ 72 (9 proposals, 6 selected for Phase 2, 3 awards); *Linc Gov't Servs., LLC*, Comp. Gen. Dec. B-404783.2, 2012 CPD ¶ 128 (27 proposals, 9 selected for Phase 2, 6 awards). For a procurement where the agency required all of the initial offerors to submit a priced demonstration project in their Phase 1 proposal even though these prices would only be reviewed if the offeror was place in Phase 2, see *Equa Solutions, Inc.*, Comp. Gen. Dec. B-409848.2, 2014 CPD ¶ 354. This technique places an inordinate burden on the offerors.

Task orders under these IDIQ contracts are normally conducted following the task order procedures discussed in Chapter 7. See, for example, *United Excel Corp.*, Comp. Gen. Dec. B-415442, 2018 CPD ¶ 16 (agency conducted meaningful discussions); *M.A. Mortenson Co.*, Comp. Gen. Dec. B-413714, 2016 CPD ¶ 361 (agency's discussions were adequate); *Tabcon, Inc.*, Comp. Gen. Dec. B-411554, 2015 CPD ¶ 257 (agency properly assessed the non-price evaluation factors in selecting a higher priced offeror); and *Carothers Constr., Inc.*, Comp. Gen. Dec. B-405241.4, 2012 CPD ¶ 225 (agency did not conduct unequal discussions).

[D] Single Phase Procurements

When an agency requirement can be met by furnishing a simple structure or a factory-built product, a single-phase procurement is likely the most effective technique. In such cases, there will not be a requirement for extensive design or pricing effort. See, for example, *EMTA Insaat Taahhut Ve Ticaret, A.S.*, Comp. Gen. Dec. B-416391, 2018 CPD ¶ 2880 (inadequate non-price factors proposal on procurement of fire station); *Armstrong Elevator Co.*, Comp. Gen. Dec. B-415809, 2018 CPD ¶ 120 (stringent experience requirement not unduly restrictive in procurement of modernization of elevators and escalators); *West Constr., Inc.*, Comp. Gen. Dec. B-406511, 2012 CPD ¶ 184 (selection of lower priced, lower rated proposal for parking garage proper even though price was less important factor); *Cornerstone Constr. Co.* Comp. Gen. Dec. B-402747, 2011 CPD ¶ 54 (selection of lower priced proposal with design improvements for health clinic). See *K-Con Bldg. Sys. v. United States*, 131 Fed. Cl. 275 (2017), where the single-phase project was issued as a Federal Supply Schedule order, and *Macro-Z Tech.*, ASBCA 56711, 12-1 BCA ¶ 35,000, where the single-phase project was issued as an initial task order to a single award IDIQ contract. In *West Coast Gen. Corp.*, Comp. Gen. Dec. B-411916.2, 2015 CPD ¶ 392, GAO sustained a protest because the source selection decision was based on a mechanically derived point scores for the technical factor and unsubstantiated pricing data.

[E] Type of Contract

The most difficult problem in using the two-phase design-build procedure is determining the type of contract that will be used. Most government agencies have been unwilling to use the commercial technique of awarding the contract and establishing a guaranteed maximum price after the contractor has performed sufficient design work to obtain reasonable estimates of the actual construction costs that will be incurred. As a result, in order to award a fixed-price type contract, they have adopted techniques that require a significant amount of design effort prior to the award of the contract resulting from the phase-two competition. When this is done as part of the phase-two competition, it places a significant financial burden on the competitors unless the agency compensates them for all or a part of this effort. Some agencies have reduced this burden by employing another A-E to undertake preliminary design effort and included these preliminary drawings and specifications in the design-build RFP. When this is done, that A-E will not be permitted to compete for the design-build contract because it will have an organizational conflict of interest, *SSR Eng'rs, Inc.*, Comp. Gen. Dec. B-282244, 99-2 CPD ¶ 27.

Providing detailed requirements, of course, partially negates one of the advantages of the design-build technique—the transferring of full liability for defective design to the contractor. See *CDM Constructors, Inc.*, ASBCA 60454,

18-1 BCA ¶ 37,190, *recons. denied*, 19-1 BCA ¶ 37,332, (government liable for defective concept drawings); *KOO Constr., Inc.*, ASBCA 61389, 18-1 BCA ¶ 37,119 (government can be liable for delay in addressing conflicting specification language); *Donohue Elec., Inc.*, VABCA 6618, 03-1 BCA ¶ 32,129 (government liable for contract change when it required equipment not called for in 50% design furnished to design-build offerors "for information"); *M.A. Mortenson Co.*, ASBCA 39978, 93-3 BCA ¶ 26,189 (government liable for incorrect information in 35% design provided to contractor). Compare *Parsons Evergreene, LLC*, ASBCA 58634, 18-1 BCA ¶ 37,137 (35% design provided by government "irrelevant" after contractor's design was approved by government); *United Excel Corp.*, VABCA 6937, 04-1 BCA ¶ 32,485 (contractor denied recovery for ambiguous preliminary specification because it knew of the ambiguity at the time it submitted its phase-two price); *Fire Sec. Sys., Inc.*, VABCA 5559-63, 02-2 BCA ¶ 31,977 (government not liable for accuracy of drawings furnished "for information only" when specification required contractor to make its own measurements of the spaces being renovated). The inclusion of design details in the design-build RFP also imposes detailed requirements on the contractor which can be enforced by the government. See *PBS&J Constructors, Inc.*, ASBCA 57814, 14-1 BCA ¶ 35,680 (enforcing a specification requirement covering footings for building); *BYA Int'l, LLC*, ASBCA 58031, 13-1 BCA ¶ 35,424 (enforcing a specification requirement covering building walls); *WPC, Inc.*, ASBCA 53964, 04-1 BCA ¶ 32,476 (enforcing a specification requirement covering a method of performance of the work), and *FSEC, Inc.*, ASBCA 49509, 99-2 BCA ¶ 30,512 (enforcing "prescriptive" specification requirement). Furthermore, if the work performed is necessary to meet the performance requirements of the design-build specification, the contractor is not entitled to additional compensation when the government insists on such work, *Fluor Intercontinental, Inc. v. Dep't of State*, CBCA 490, 12-1 BCA ¶ 34,989; *Wade Perrow Constr., Inc.*, ASBCA 53021, 03-1 BCA ¶ 32,476.

Another alternative is to use a cost-reimbursement contract for the design-build effort. FAR Subpart 36.3 contains no guidance on this possibility but it is clearly appropriate under FAR Part 16. When this type of contract is chosen, the agency is required to evaluate cost realism and to use probable cost of performance (not estimated cost) as an evaluation factor, FAR 15.404-1(d)(2). See *Pueblo Envtl. Sols, LLC*, Comp. Gen. Dec. B-291487, 2003 CPD ¶ 14, holding that the contracting officer properly adjusted the protester's cost estimate upward to reflect too few manhours to perform the work.

[F] Source Selection and Contract Award

Selection of the contractor on the basis of the proposal with the best value to the government and award of the contract is done following the procedures for standard competitive negotiations. See Chapter 6 for a full discussion of these procedures.

In a number of instances, the agency has incorporated the winning offeror's design proposal in the contract by reference. This, in effect, freezes the design to the extent that such a proposal includes detailed materials or performance techniques. This reduces the flexibility of the contractor to provide the best value project to the government and makes the elements of the design proposal mandatory performance requirements to the extent that they constitute firm promises. See *Metcalf Constr. Co. v. United States*, 102 Fed. Cl. 334 (2011), *rev'd on other grounds*. 742 F.3d 984 (Fed. Cir. 2014), enforcing contract provision requiring contractor to construct in accordance with approved design unless a variance was obtained, and *Sherman R. Smoot Corp.*, ASBCA 52150, 03-1 BCA ¶ 32,073, rejecting the contractor's argument that it was entitled to provide an "equal" product when it included a specific type of lighting fixture in its design proposal without including salient characteristics of the fixture in its design proposal. See also *Elam Woods Constr. Co.*, ASBCA 52448, 01-1 BCA ¶ 31,305, holding the contractor bound to perform the work included in its technical proposal even though its price did not appear to include that work. The board reasoned that the work described in the proposal was a contemporaneous interpretation of the RFP requirements. In that procurement, the contracting officer had attempted to deal with the potential problem of a conflict between the performance specifications and the contractor's proposed design by including the following provision in the RFP:

> The criteria specified in this RFP are binding contract criteria and in cases of any conflict, subsequent to award, between RFP criteria and Contractor's proposal, design, and submittals, the RFP criteria shall govern unless there is a written agreement between the Contracting Officer and the Contractor waiving the specific requirement or accepting a specific condition pertaining to the offer.

This provision was not relied on by the board in deciding the dispute. Compare *Medlin Constr. Group*, Comp. Gen. Dec. B-286166, 2000 CPD ¶ 199, where the RFP made it clear that the contract specifications controlled by stating:

> Final design submissions found to be not in compliance with the requirements of the RFP will be returned to the Contractor for correction and resubmission. The Contractor shall make such modifications as may be necessary to bring the design into compliance at no change in contract price and schedule. . . .

See also *Swinerton Bldrs. Northwest*, ASBCA 57329, 17-1 BCA ¶ 36,738, and *PGDC/Teng Joint Venture*, ASBCA 56573, 10-1 BCA ¶ 34,423, holding that the RFP specification superseded a conflicting provision in the contractor's proposal even though the proposal was part of the contract. Compare *MARCON Eng'g, Inc.*, ASBCA 57471, 15-1 BCA ¶ 35,974, holding that the contractor's design superseded the RFP specifications—allowing recovery of the costs of complying with the specifications, and *ADT Constr. Group, Inc.*, ASBCA 55307, 09-2 BCA ¶ 34,200, holding that the contractor's proposal clarified the RFP's ambiguous language on whether the project would be performed on a fast-track basis.

[G] Performance Issues

Although the contractor assumes much of the risk during the design phase of the contract, the government has the normal risks during construction because it includes the standard construction contract clauses in design-build contracts. See, for example, *GSC Constr., Inc.*, ASBCA 59046, 19-1 BCA ¶ 37,393 (government liable for constructive changes); *John C. Grimberg Co.*, ASBCA 58791, 18-1 BCA ¶ 37,191, *recons. denied*, 19-1 BCA ¶ 37,227 (government liable for site conditions differing from those depicted in the specifications pursuant to the Differing Site Conditions clause in FAR 52.236-2); *Turner Constr. Co. v. Smithsonian Inst.*, CBCA 2862, 17-1 BCA ¶ 38,739 (government liable for loss of productivity due to unforeseen conditions in building during renovation); *Yalte-Desbuild Joint Venture v. Dep't of State*, CBCA 3350, 17-1 BCA ¶ 36,870 (government liable for nondisclosure of vital information); *Nova Grp./Tutor-Saliba v. United States*, 125 Fed. Cl. 469 (2016) (government liable for constructive changes); *Tetra Tech Facilities Constr., LLC*, ASBCA 58568, 16-1 BCA ¶ 36,562 (government liable for differing site conditions); *Fluor Intercontinental, Inc. v. Dep't of State*, CBCA 1559, 13-1 BCA ¶ 35,334 (government liable for acceleration); *Strand Hunt Constr., Inc.*, ASBCA 55905, 13-1 BCA ¶ 35,287 (government liable for government-caused delays pursuant to the Suspension of Work clause in FAR 52.242-14). Compare *Kiewit Infrastructure W., Co. v. United States*, 972 F.3d 1322 (Fed. Cir. 2020) (contractor not liable for environmental conditions at site where solicitation indicates no further environmental analysis necessary); *Bell/Heery, A Joint Venture v. United States*, 739 F.3d 1324 (Fed. Cir. 2014) (government not liable for actions of state government impeding contract performance).

§ 10.07 INFORMATION TECHNOLOGY

Another new acquisition procedure established by the Clinger-Cohen Act of 1996, Pub. L. No. 104-106, 40 U.S.C. § 11302, relates to information technology. The Act repealed the Brooks Act, 40 U.S.C. § 759, giving the General Services Administration (GSA) central authority over the purchase of information technology for the federal government, and gave each agency the authority to procure information technology to meet its needs, 40 U.S.C. § 11314. This effectively abolished the Federal Information Resources Management Regulation (FIRMR), which was the primary regulation on the acquisition of information technology. This type of procurement is now done using normal procurement procedures following a few special rules in FAR Part 39.

The Director of the Office of Management and Budget (OMB) has major responsibilities with regard to the government's information technology investments. See 44 U.S.C. § 3504(h) stating:

> (h) With respect to Federal information technology, the Director shall—
>
> (1) in consultation with the Director of the National Institute of Standards and Technology and the Administrator of General Services—
>
> (A) develop and oversee the implementation of policies, principles, standards, and guidelines for information technology functions and activities of the Federal Government, including periodic evaluations of major information systems; and
>
> (B) oversee the development and implementation of standards under section 11331 of title 40;
>
> (2) monitor the effectiveness of, and compliance with, directives issued under subtitle III of title 40 [40 USC § 11101 et seq.] and directives issued under section 322 of title 40;
>
> (3) coordinate the development and review by the Office of Information and Regulatory Affairs of policy associated with Federal procurement and acquisition of information technology with the Office of Federal Procurement Policy;
>
> (4) ensure, through the review of agency budget proposals, information resources management plans and other means—
>
> (A) agency integration of information resources management plans, program plans and budgets for acquisition and use of information technology; and
>
> (B) the efficiency and effectiveness of inter-agency information technology initiatives to improve agency performance and the accomplishment of agency missions; and
>
> (5) promote the use of information technology by the Federal Government to improve the productivity, efficiency, and effectiveness of Federal programs, including through dissemination of public information and the reduction of information collection burdens on the public.

See also 40 U.S.C. § 11302(b) stating:

> *Use of information technology in Federal programs.* The Director shall promote and improve the acquisition, use, security, and disposal of information technology by the Federal Government to improve the productivity, efficiency, and effectiveness of Federal programs, including through dissemination of public information and the reduction of information collection burdens on the public.

This authority has been implemented by the issuance of OMB Circular A-130. This circular was last updated in July 2016.

FAR 2.101 defines information technology as follows:

> Information technology means any equipment, or interconnected system(s) or subsystem(s) of equipment, that is used in the automatic acquisition, storage, manipulation, management, movement, control, display, switching, interchange, transmission, or reception of data or information by the agency.
>
> (1) For purposes of this definition, equipment is used by an agency if the equipment is used by the agency directly or is used by a contractor under a contract with the agency that requires—
>
> (i) Its use; or
>
> (ii) To a significant extent, its use in the performance of a service or the furnishing of a product.
>
> (2) The term "information technology" includes computers, ancillary equipment, software, firmware and similar procedures, services (including support services), and related resources.
>
> (3) The term "information technology" does not include any equipment that—
>
> (i) Is acquired by a contractor incidental to a contract; or
>
> (ii) Contains imbedded information technology that is used as an integral part of the product, but the principal function of which is not the acquisition, storage, manipulation, management, movement, control, display, switching, interchange, transmission, or reception of data or information. For example, HVAC (heating, ventilation, and air conditioning) equipment, such as thermostats or temperature control devices, and medical equipment where information technology is integral to its operation, are not information technology.

Each agency is required to have a Chief Information Officer to oversee the entire information technology program of the agency, 40 U.S.C. § 11315.

[A] Planning Information Technology Procurements

Because of the large amount that the government invests in information technology, there are special requirements that must be met in planning such procurements. 40 U.S.C. § 11312(b) requires that each agency implement a process for acquiring information technology that:

> (1) provide[s] for the selection of investments in information technology (including information security needs) to be made by the executive agency, the management of those investments, and the evaluation of the results of those investments;
>
> (2) [is] integrated with the processes for making budget, financial, and program management decisions in the executive agency;

(3) include[s] minimum criteria to be applied in considering whether to undertake a particular investment in information systems, including criteria related to the quantitatively expressed projected net, risk-adjusted return on investment and specific quantitative and qualitative criteria for comparing and prioritizing alternative information systems investment projects;

(4) identif[ies] information systems investments that would result in shared benefits or costs for other federal agencies or state or local governments;

(5) identif[ies] quantifiable measurements for determining the net benefits and risks of a proposed investment; and

(6) provide[s] the means for senior management personnel of the executive agency to obtain timely information regarding the progress of an investment in an information system, including a system of milestones for measuring progress, on an independently verifiable basis, in terms of cost, capability of the system to meet specified requirements, timeliness, and quality.

Paragraph 8.d.1 of OMB Circular A-130 implements these requirements with regard to acquisition policies as follows:

Agencies shall:

a) Make use of adequate competition, analyze risks (including supply chain risks) associated with potential contractors and the products and services they provide, and allocate risk responsibility between Government and contractor when acquiring IT;

b) Conduct definitive technical, cost, and risk analyses of alternative design implementations, including consideration of the full life cycle costs of IT products and services, including but not limited to, planning, analysis, design, implementation, sustainment, maintenance, re-competition, and retraining costs, scaled to the size and complexity of individual requirements;

c) Consider existing Federal contract solutions or shared services when developing planned information systems, available within the same agency, from other agencies, or from the private sector to meet agency needs to avoid duplicative IT investments;

d) Acquire IT products and services in accordance with Government-wide requirements;

e) Ensure that decisions to improve existing information systems with custom developed solutions or develop new information systems are initiated only when no existing alternative private sector or governmental source can efficiently meet the need, taking into account long-term sustainment and maintenance;

f) Structure acquisitions for major IT investments into useful segments, with a narrow scope and brief duration, in order to reduce risk, promote flexibility and interoperability, increase accountability, and better match mission need with current technology and market conditions;

g) To the extent practicable, modular contracts for IT, including orders for increments or useful segments of work, should be awarded within 180 days after the solicitation is issued. If award cannot be made within 180 days, agencies shall consider cancelling the solicitation. The IT acquired should be delivered within 18 months after the solicitation resulting in award of the contract was issued;

h) Align IT procurement requirements with larger agency strategic goals;

i) Promote innovation in IT procurements, including conducting market research in order to maximize utilization of innovative ideas; and

j) Include security, privacy, accessibility, records management, and other relevant requirements in solicitations.

FAR 39.102 provides further guidance as follows:

(a) Prior to entering into a contract for information technology, an agency should analyze risks, benefits, and costs. (See part 7 for additional information regarding requirements definition.) Reasonable risk taking is appropriate as long as risks are controlled and mitigated. Contracting and program office officials are jointly responsible for assessing, monitoring and controlling risk when selecting projects for investment and during program implementation.

(b) Types of risk may include schedule risk, risk of technical obsolescence, cost risk, risk implicit in a particular contract type, technical feasibility, dependencies between a new project and other projects or systems, the number of simultaneous high risk projects to be monitored, funding availability, and program management risk.

(c) Appropriate techniques should be applied to manage and mitigate risk during the acquisition of information technology. Techniques include, but are not limited to: prudent project management; use of modular contracting; thorough acquisition planning tied to budget planning by the program, finance and contracting offices; continuous collection and evaluation of risk-based assessment data; prototyping prior to implementation; post implementation reviews to determine actual project cost, benefits and returns; and focusing on risks and returns using quantifiable measures.

[B] Performance-Based and Results-Based Management

40 U.S.C. § 11303 provides that the Director of OMB is required to encourage performance-based and results-based management for agency information technology programs, and 40 U.S.C. § 11302(b) requires the Director to promote the efficient acquisition and use of information technology through the capital planning process. The Director is required to review an agency's management practices based on the performance and results of its information technology programs and investments, and to issue clear and concise directions to ensure that agencies have effective and efficient capital planning processes that are used to select, control, and evaluate the results of major information systems investments

and to ensure that agency information security is adequate. Agencies are required to follow these procedures by 40 U.S.C. §§ 11312 and 11313.

These requirements are implemented in OMB Circular A-130. Paragraph 5.a.

[C] Modular Contracting

41 U.S.C. § 2308 requires agencies to use modular contracting to the maximum extent practicable for acquisition of information technology major systems. Under modular contracting, an agency's need for a system is satisfied by successive acquisitions of interoperable increments. Each increment complies with common or commercially accepted standards applicable to information technology so that the increments are compatible with other increments of information technology comprising the system.

This statute is implemented in FAR 39.103 as follows:

> (a) . . . . Modular contracting is intended to reduce program risk and to incentivize contractor performance while meeting the Governments need for timely access to rapidly changing technology. Consistent with the agency's information technology architecture, agencies should, to the maximum extent practicable, use modular contracting to acquire major systems (see 2.101) of information technology. Agencies may also use modular contracting to acquire non-major systems of information technology.
>
> (b) When using modular contracting, an acquisition of a system of information technology may be divided into several smaller acquisition increments that—
>
> (1) Are easier to manage individually than would be possible in one comprehensive acquisition;
>
> (2) Address complex information technology objectives incrementally in order to enhance the likelihood of achieving workable systems or solutions for attainment of those objectives;
>
> (3) Provide for delivery, implementation, and testing of workable systems or solutions in discrete increments, each of which comprises a system or solution that is not dependent on any subsequent increment in order to perform its principal functions;
>
> (4) Provide an opportunity for subsequent increments to take advantage of any evolution in technology or needs that occur during implementation and use of the earlier increments; and
>
> (5) Reduce risk of potential adverse consequences on the overall project by isolating and avoiding custom-designed components of the system.
>
> (c) The characteristics of an increment may vary depending upon the type of information technology being acquired and the nature of the system being developed. The following factors may be considered:

(1) To promote compatibility, the information technology acquired through modular contracting for each increment should comply with common or commercially acceptable information technology standards when available and appropriate, and shall conform to the agency's master information technology architecture.

(2) The performance requirements of each increment should be consistent with the performance requirements of the completed, overall system within which the information technology will function and should address interface requirements with succeeding increments.

(d) For each increment, contracting officers shall choose an appropriate contracting technique that facilitates the acquisition of subsequent increments. Pursuant to Parts 16 and 17 of the Federal Acquisition Regulations, contracting officers shall select the contract type and method appropriate to the circumstances (e.g., indefinite delivery, indefinite quantity contracts, single contract with options, successive contracts, multiple awards, task order contracts). Contract(s) shall be structured to ensure that the Government is not required to procure additional increments.

(e) To avoid obsolescence, a modular contract for information technology should, to the maximum extent practicable, be awarded within 180 days after the date on which the solicitation is issued. If award cannot be made within 180 days, agencies should consider cancellation of the solicitation in accordance with 14.209 or 15.206(e). To the maximum extent practicable, deliveries under the contract should be scheduled to occur within 18 months after issuance of the solicitation.

GSA issued an *Acquisition White Paper on Modular Contracting*, July 25, 1997 giving additional guidance on this type of contracting. This paper warns that there are risks in using modular contracting because the modules may not be fully compatible. To overcome this problem, the paper recommends that prior to undertaking modular contracting the agency should formulate agencywide information technology architecture based on common and commercial standards.

Section 804 of the National Defense Authorization Act for Fiscal Year 2010, Pub. L. No. 111-84, contains the following additional requirements for DoD acquisitions of information technology:

(a) NEW ACQUISITION PROCESS REQUIRED.—The Secretary of Defense shall develop and implement a new acquisition process for information technology systems. The acquisition process developed and implemented pursuant to this subsection shall, to the extent determined appropriate by the Secretary—

(1) be based on the recommendations in chapter 6 of the March 2009 report of the Defense Science Board Task Force on Department of Defense Policies and Procedures for the Acquisition of Information Technology; and

(2) be designed to include—

(A) early and continual involvement of the user;

(B) multiple, rapidly executed increments or releases of capability;

(C) early, successive prototyping to support an evolutionary approach; and

(D) a modular, open-systems approach.

[D] Share-in-Savings Contracts

There was temporary authority for agencies to enter into share-in-savings contracts for information technology in 41 U.S.C. § 266a. This statute was never implemented nor used. See *Federal Contracting: Share-In-Savings Initiative Not Yet Tested*, GAO-05-736, July 26, 2005. This statute was allowed to expire in 2005.

[E] Governmentwide Acquisition Contracts

The Clinger-Cohen Act required the Director of OMB to designate one or more agencies as "executive agent" for governmentwide acquisitions of information technology, 40 U.S.C. § 11302(e). When so designated, heads of agencies are authorized to award such contracts, 40 U.S.C. § 11314(a)(2). These governmentwide acquisition contracts (GWACs) are indefinite delivery/indefinite quantity contracts that permit any agency to issue task orders for information technology without complying with the requirements of the Economy Act, 31 U.S.C. § 1535. See FAR 17.500(b)(2). See Chapter 11 for a discussion of these contracts.

[F] Federal Supply Schedule Orders

A large number of information technology procurements were accomplished using contractors on Schedule 70 of the GSA multiple award schedules issued as part of the Federal Supply Schedule. This schedule contained over 5000 contracts covering a wide span of information technology supplies and services. This schedule has now been consolidated with "special item numbers" (SINs) for information technology products. The procedures used to issue task orders against these contracts are covered in Chapter 11.

§ 10.08 OTHER AGENCY PROCEDURES

In addition to the "other procedures" specified in 10 U.S.C. § 2302(2) (now § 3012) and 41 U.S.C. § 152, some agencies have statutory authority to use special procurement procedures in an effort to streamline the acquisition process. The procedures described below provide the affected agencies with considerably greater latitude to conduct their procurements following more business-like practices.

[A] Federal Aviation Administration

Pub. L. No. 104-50 exempted the Federal Aviation Administration (FAA) from the Federal Property and Administrative Services Act, the Federal Acquisition Regulation and a number of other designated statutes, 49 U.S.C. § 40110(d)(2). As a result, on April 1, 1996, the FAA issued a separate procurement regulation entitled the Federal Aviation Administration Acquisition Management System (AMS). The AMS was issued in June 1997 and has been revised several times. It is not published in the Federal Register but is available at http://fast.faa.gov/.

The AMS differs from the FAR in that it is a combined contracting and program management system. It also differs in that it confers considerably greater discretion on contracting personnel—with fewer prescriptive rules than the FAR. For a critique of the system, see *Air Traffic Control: FAA's Acquisition Management Has Improved, but Policies and Oversight Need Strengthening to Help Ensure Results*, GAO-05-23, Dec. 2004.

Under the AMS, there are two competitive procurement methods available for obtaining products and services through the FAA contracting process. The first method is described under "Complex and Noncommercial Source Selection" and is used for complex, large-dollar, developmental, and noncommercial items and services. The second method is described under "Commercial and Simplified Purchase Method" and is typically used for commercial items that are less complex, small in dollar value, and shorter term.

[1] Complex and Noncommercial Source Selection

AMS 3.2.2.3 provides that there are five phases in complex and noncommercial source selection:

- Planning
- Screening
- Selection
- Debriefing (as requested)
- Lessons Learned

Procurement planning is required for all FAA procurements except for those procurements using the commercial and simplified purchasing methods and those for real property and utilities, AMS 3.2.1.1. The planning can be accomplished by the preparation of a formal written procurement plan, AMS 3.2.1.2.2, or by a procurement strategy meeting, AMS 3.2.1.2.3. Independent government cost estimates are required for all procurements over $100,000, with a few exceptions, AMS 3.2.1.2.4.

The screening process is the fundamental method used by the FAA to select a contractor that will provide the best value to the FAA. It consists of one to three steps in limiting the competition depending on the complexity of the procurement. The document issued to potential competitors to carry out this process is called a screening information request (SIR). AMS 3.2.2.3.1.2.1 describes this process as follows:

> The purpose of the SIR is to obtain information, which will ultimately allow the FAA to identify the offeror that provides the best value, make a selection decision, and award the contract to conclude the competitive process. A SIR is a request by the FAA for documentation, information, presentations, proposals, or binding offers. Three categories of SIRs (see below) may be used according to the procurement strategy adopted by the service organization. Once the public announcement has been released, the SIR may be released to start the competitive process. The service organization will determine the type(s) of SIR(s) that are appropriate for each procurement.

For a given procurement, the FAA may make a selection decision after one SIR, or the FAA may have a series of SIRs (with a screening decision after each one) to arrive at the selection decision. This will depend on the types of products and services to be acquired and the specific source selection approach chosen by the service organization. When it is desired to make a selection decision after one SIR, that SIR should be a request for offer (see below). In general when multiple SIRs are contemplated, the initial SIR should request general information, and future SIRs should request successively more specific information.

AMS 3.2.2.3.1.2.1 describes three potential categories of SIRs. The first category is a request for only "qualification information" in order to screen out those companies that do not meet the FAA's minimum qualification requirements. The end result of this step is the establishment of a qualified vendor list (QVL). When this is done, only qualified vendors may compete for future procurements of the product or service with the result that no other companies are notified of the procurement.

The second category of SIR requests "screening information" from potential contractors. This information is essentially the same information that is included in the normal RFP—consisting of all information that the agency determines to be necessary to select the source. Thus, it should focus on information that directly relates to the key discriminators for the procurement. Types of information that may form the basis of a screening request include equipment/products for FAA testing, capability statements, draft/model contracts, technical proposals (including oral presentations, if appropriate), commercial pricing information, financial information, cost or price information, and cost or price proposals.

Each SIR requesting screening information must include some cost or pricing information appropriate to the specific SIR level of detail.

The last category of SIR is the "request for offer," which is a request for an offeror to commit formally to provide the products or services required by the acquisition. The request for offer may take the form of an SIR, a proposed contract, or a purchase order. The response to the request for offer is a binding offer and will become a binding contract if signed by the contracting officer. If this type of SIR is used, the agency can request an offer from only the offeror that has been selected as a result of the evaluation of the second category SIR.

The AMS encourages open communication with the potential contractors without imposing the formalized clarification/discussion logic of the FAR. See AMS 3.2.2.3.1.2.2 stating:

> Communications with all potential offerors should take place throughout the source selection process. During the screening, selection, and debriefing phases of source selection, communications are coordinated with the CO. Communications may start in the planning phase and continue through contract award. All SIRs should clearly inform offerors how communications will be handled during the initial screening phase.

The purpose of communications is to ensure there are mutual understandings between the FAA and the offerors about all aspects of the procurement, including the offerors' submittals/ proposals. Information disclosed as a result of oral or written communication with an offeror may be considered in the evaluation of an offeror's submittal(s).

AMS 3.2.2.3.1.2.3 encourages the use of a flexible evaluation methodology as follows:

> The evaluation methodology should be set up to allow for maximum flexibility in selecting the offeror(s) providing the best value. To facilitate such flexibility, the following should be considered in setting up evaluations:
>
> Relative importance between criteria is not required (when relative importance is used, the relative order of importance between criteria should be disclosed).
>
> Each SIR may incorporate separate and/or distinct criteria that relate to the specific SIR discriminators.
>
> The use of either adjectival or numerical ratings is acceptable.
>
> Comparative evaluations between offerors' proposals/products are acceptable.
>
> The service organization should be selective/inventive concerning the screening requirements for document submissions (e.g., oral presentations, sample tests, plant visits, etc.).
>
> Communications with offerors during the evaluation may help clarify submittals, allow a fuller understanding of the offeror submittals, and provide a more comprehensive evaluation.

> Testing of products is encouraged to the maximum extent practical ("try before you buy").
>
> Award based on initial offers to other than the low cost or price offer is allowed.

The selection decision is based on the stated evaluation criteria, including cost or price considerations, and the source selection official must document the selection decision in a decision memorandum including the rational basis supporting the screening or selection decision, AMS 3.2.2.3.1.3. The contracting officer then transmits a proposed contract to the selected offeror, AMS 3.2.2.3.1.3.

All offerors that participated in the competitive process are notified of the award and given three working days from receipt of the notification to request a debriefing, AMS 3.2.2.3.1.4.

The last phase in this method is the preparation of a lessons learned memorandum, AMS 3.2.2.3.1.5. The purpose of this memorandum is to relay the agency's procurement experiences to other FAA personnel. The memorandum should highlight those issues that had a significant impact on their procurement.

[2] Commercial and Simplified Purchase Method

This method permits the FAA to acquire commercial products and services from the marketplace using a simplified purchase method and best commercial practices. AMS 3.2.2.5.1 calls for procurement planning to—

- determine whether commercial items meet the FAA's needs;
- identify potential commercial sources; and
- publicly announce requirements in excess of $100,000.

Under this method, the contracting officer "should solicit an appropriate number of vendors to ensure quality products and services are delivered in a timely manner at a fair and reasonable price," and should state requirements in commercial terms, AMS 3.2.2.5.2.

AMS 3.2.2.5.3 gives maximum flexibility in selecting an efficient procurement process, as follows:

> The CO should determine the appropriate screening approach and format for vendor's responses (e.g., electronic, written, oral, use of standard commercial or FAA forms). The CO may also conduct communications with individual offerors, as appropriate, to address offeror understanding of the requirement, performance capability, prices, and other terms and conditions. For commercially available products, the CO is encouraged to use "commercial competition techniques" such as continuing market research throughout

the process by using vendor proposals as the source of prices and commercially available capabilities and sharing that information with other vendors.

The contracting officer's selection decision is to be based on the FAA's stated evaluation criteria, AMS 3.2.2.5.4. The selection criteria should include such factors as price, functional specifications, delivery capability, warranty, and payment terms, AMS 3.2.2.5.4. The method of selection and rationale for awards should be documented, as well as a determination that the price is fair and reasonable, AMS 3.2.2.5.4.1.

[3] Protests

Protests of FAA procurements may not be taken to GAO, 49 U.S.C. § 40110(d)(2)(F). Rather, they are handled by the FAA Office of Dispute Resolution for Acquisition (ODRA), 14 C.F.R. § 17.5. Procedures for such protests are published at 14 C.F.R. Part 17, Subparts A and B. See also AMS 3.9. These procedures are similar to those followed by GAO except that they contain greater emphasis on using the alternative disputes resolution procedures prescribed in Subpart D. Decisions of the ODRA can be appealed to the Court of Appeals for the District of Columbia Circuit or any other circuit having jurisdiction over the protester, 49 U.S.C. § 46110(d)(4). See also *J.A. Jones Mgmt. Servs. v. FAA*, 225 F.3d 761 (D.C. Cir. 2000); and *Multimax, Inc. v. FAA*, 231 F.3d 882 (D.C. Cir. 2000).

[B] Postal Service

The Postal Reorganization Act of 1970, Pub. L. No. 91-375, codified at 39 U.S.C. § 101 et seq., abolished the old Post Office Department and in its place created the U.S. Postal Service as an independent establishment of the executive branch. Under the Act, Congress exempted the Postal Service from most statutes and regulations relating to government procurement, 39 U.S.C. § 410(a). The Postal Service follows special procedures that were set forth in the *U.S. Postal Service Procurement Manual* until 1997. That was followed by the *U.S. Postal Service Purchasing Manual* that was issued in several editions between 1997 and 2005. These manuals were canceled with the issuance of very general policies in 39 C.F.R. Part 601 in May 2005, with revisions in October 2007. Pending the issuance of new detailed procedures, interim procedures were set forth in the *U.S. Postal Service Interim Internal Purchasing Guidelines*, May 19, 2005. Subsequently, on May 1, 2006 the agency published *Postal Service Supplying Principles and Practices* (SPs and Ps). These SPs and Ps are not published in the Federal Register but are available online. Since they are not referenced in 39 C.F.R. Part 601, it is likely that they do not have the force and effect of law and therefore are not binding on the agency. See *Asia Pacific Airlines v. United States*, 68 Fed. Cl. 8 (2005), *appeal dismissed*, 171 Fed.

Appx. 837 (Fed. Cir. 2006), holding that the Purchasing Manual had the force and effect of law because it was referenced in 39 C.F.R. Part 601 and granting injunctive relief because the agency did not follow the procedures in the manual.

The basic policy set forth in 39 C.F.R. § 601.105(b) is that the Postal Service "may decline to accept or consider proposals when a person or organization exhibits unacceptable conduct or business practices that do not meet reasonable business expectations or does not provide a high level of confidence about the entity's current or future business relations." The regulation contains illustrations of the kinds of conduct that will be sanctioned and provides guidance on how such decisions can be contested.

The Postal Service SPs and Ps contain detailed discussion of procurement policies and procedures which are stated to be "advisory and illustrative" and "for internal use only." Thus, they confer broad discretion on procurement officials to adopt procedures that will attain "best value." They are in the nature of a purchasing manual, containing far more guidance on the conduct of the acquisition process than is contained in the Federal Acquisition Regulation. They place a heavy emphasis on thoroughly planning procurements by conducting market research, communications with industry, risk analysis, and preparation of requirement documents.

The Postal Service SPs and Ps do not require full and open competition, but rather require only "adequate competition," stating:

> Competitive purchases should be made on the basis of adequate competition whenever feasible. Adequate competition means the solicitation of a sufficient number of the best qualified suppliers to ensure that the required quality and quantity of goods and services are obtained when needed and that the price that is fair and reasonable.

The guidance emphasizes, much like the FAA, that it is highly beneficial to prequalify suppliers before a competition is actually conducted.

Publicizing procurements is done on the governmentwide point of entry but such publication is discretionary. Offers are solicited using Requests for Proposal and contracting officers are encouraged to make RFPs available to any company that requests one. The competitive negotiation process used is much like FAR Part 15 except that it gives contracting officers far more freedom to use commercial practices. Thus, there is no firm rule on the time allowed for submission of proposals, late proposals may be accepted, evaluators are permitted to make comparative evaluations of proposals, and communications are encouraged at any time during the procurement process to obtain a better value from the competitors. All communications are called "discussions" and the following broad guidance is given:

> During the evaluation process, including during oral presentations, discussions may be held with any supplier to clear up misunderstandings or uncertainties or to gain a better understanding of the supplier's proposal

> (including price) in order to obtain a more informed comparison of the relative value of individual proposals.
>
> After proposal comparisons have been made, further discussions may be held to address any outstanding matters. Suppliers whose offers are the subject of discussion at any stage must be given sufficient time to revise their proposals in light of those discussions.
>
> The guidance distinguishes between "discussions" and "negotiations," and recommends negotiations as the final step in the process of selecting the winning offeror:
>
> Discussions and negotiations are not the same. . . . Generally, negotiations are held with one or more suppliers after [the team] has determined that . . . [their] proposal has the best chance of providing the Postal Service the best value. The goal of negotiations is to come to final agreement on contract terms and conditions, including contract type and price.
>
> * * *
>
> Before opening negotiations, [the team] must clearly categorize negotiation objectives that are either *must* points (terms and conditions that are essential to desired contract performance that the Postal Service must obtain), or *give* points (terms and conditions that are not central to the Postal Service obtaining best value). . . . In order to avoid deadlock, the Contracting Officer will have to properly balance what is given and what is taken, especially as final agreement becomes more imminent, while focusing on obtaining the *must* points.

This provision is significantly different from the FAR Part 15 process in that there is no competitive range determination, no mandatory discussions with offerors in the competitive range, no final proposal revisions, and the contracting officer is permitted to negotiate with the winning offeror after selection of the source.

The Postal Service also has special procedures for purchasing architect-engineer services, construction, design-build contracting, construction management services, mail transportation, professional/technical and consultant services, and information technology.

Protests may not be taken to GAO, *Falcon Sys., Inc.*, 65 Comp. Gen. 584 (B-222549), 86-1 CPD ¶ 462, *recons. denied*, 86-1 CPD ¶ 526, but they may be taken to the Court of Federal Claims, *Hewlett-Packard Co. v. United States*, 41 Fed. Cl. 99 (1998); *Emery Worldwide Airlines, Inc. v. United States*, 49 Fed. Cl. 211, *aff'd*, 264 F.3d 1071 (Fed. Cir. 2001). 39 C.F.R. § 601.107(b) also provides for internal procedures to consider protests as follows:

> (b) *Policy*. It is the policy of the Postal Service and in the interest of suppliers to resolve disagreements by mutual agreement between the supplier and the responsible contracting officer. All disagreements arising in connection with the purchasing process must be lodged with the responsible contracting officer in writing via facsimile, e-mail, hand delivery, or U.S. Mail, within ten days of the date the supplier received notification of award or ten days

from the date the supplier received a debriefing. During the supplier-contracting officer ten-day resolution period, the responsible contracting officer's management may help to resolve the disagreement. At the conclusion of the ten-day resolution period, the contracting officer must communicate, in writing, to the supplier his or her resolution of the disagreement.

(c) *Alternative dispute resolution*. Alternative dispute resolution (ADR) procedures may be used, if agreed to by all interested parties. The use of ADR to resolve the disagreement must be considered, regardless of the nature of the disagreement or when it occurred during the purchasing process. If the use of ADR is agreed upon, the ten-day limitation is suspended; if the parties cannot reach an agreement under ADR, the supplier has ten days to lodge its disagreement with the [Supplier Disagreement Resolution] Official.

39 C.F.R. § 601.108 attempts to narrow the extent of judicial resolution of these protests by the following provisions relating to resolution of protests by the Supplier Disagreement Resolution (SDR) Official:

(b) Scope and applicability. This procedure is established as the sole and exclusive means to resolve disagreements under § 601.107 and contests of decisions under § 601.105. This procedure is intended to expeditiously resolve disagreements that are not resolved at the responsible contracting officer level; to reduce litigation expenses, inconvenience, and other costs for all parties; to facilitate successful business relationships with Postal Service suppliers, the supplier community, and other persons; and to develop further the basis for the Postal Service's purchasing decisions and the administrative records concerning those decisions. All disagreements under § 601.107 and contests of decisions under § 601.105 will be lodged with and resolved, with finality, by the SDR Official under and in accordance with the sole and exclusive procedure established in this section.

* * *

(f) *Guidance*. In considering and in resolving a disagreement, the SDR Official will be guided by the regulations contained in this part and all applicable public laws enacted by Congress. Non-Postal Service procurement rules or regulations and revoked Postal Service regulations will not apply or be taken into account in resolving disagreements. Failure of any party to provide requested information may be taken into account by the SDR Official in the decision.

(g) *Final resolution by the SDR Official and final contract award of the Postal Service*. A resolution by the SDR Official will be final and binding. If the SDR Official's final resolution affirms the original contract award of the contracting officer, the contracting officer's original contract award becomes the Postal Service's final contract award, and may be subject to judicial review as described in paragraph (h) of this section. If the SDR Official's final resolution directs that the Postal Service terminate the contract award and issue a new solicitation, recompete the requirement, or reevaluate the current award, the contracting officer shall implement promptly the SDR Official's final resolution. However, any contract award made by the contracting officer after a resolicitation, recompetition, or reevaluation directed by the SDR Official is not a final contract award of the Postal Service that may be subject to judicial review unless and until disagreements concerning that contract award have been lodged and resolved with finality by the SDR Official.

(h) *Judicial review*. The Postal Service's final contract award, as described in paragraph § 601.108(g), may be appealed to a Federal court with jurisdiction based only upon an alleged violation of the regulations contained in this part or an applicable public law enacted by Congress. The party lodging the disagreement may seek review of the Postal Service's final contract award only after the mandatory administrative remedies provided under § 601.107 and § 601.108 have been exhausted.

These procedures were adopted in 70 Fed. Reg. 20,292, Apr. 19, 2005, and amended slightly in 72 Fed. Reg. 58,251, Oct. 15, 2007; 75 Fed. Reg. 1541, Jan. 12, 2010; and 79 Fed. Reg. 65,342, Nov. 4, 2014. No reported judicial decision has been found challenging their validity.

Chapter 11

INTERAGENCY ACQUISITIONS

§11.01 USE OF INTERAGENCY ACQUISITION

Interagency acquisition is a process in which one agency acquires supplies or services by placing an order against a contract awarded by another agency or by asking another agency to award a contract or place an order on its behalf. It permits agencies to benefit from the efficiencies achievable through the use of contracts already in existence and from the specialized expertise of other agencies with respect to certain types of purchases. Rules and guidance for the conduct of interagency acquisitions are in the FAR and agency FAR supplements, publications of the Office of Federal Procurement Policy and in publications and at websites of the agencies that provide interagency acquisition services.

Interagency acquisitions are conducted mainly through the use of three types of "vehicles"—contracts established under various statutes:

- General Services Administration (GSA) schedule contracts under 40 U.S.C. § 501 and 41 U.S.C. § 153(3) and schedule contracts awarded by other agencies;
- Governmentwide Acquisition Contracts (GWACs) for information technology under 40 U.S.C. § 11302(e); and
- Multiagency Contracts (MACs) under the Economy Act, 31 U.S.C. § 1535.

These vehicles are indefinite-delivery indefinite-quantity (IDIQ) contracts that contain (a) lists of available items of supply and unit prices, or (b) broad statements of work for services and hourly labor rates that include contractor G&A and profit (often referred to as "fully burdened" or "loaded" rates). In the case of services, detailed specification of requirements can be deferred until the time at which orders are issued. Those features make such contracts readily adaptable to the various needs of different requesting agencies and analogous to shopping malls. Large numbers of such contracts have been awarded that overlap in their coverage—so many of them that the government has had to establish a website to list them. This has given rise to a paradox of choice—with so many possibilities and no readily available comparative data, requesting agencies sometimes cannot determine which vehicle offers the best value for any given requirement without undertaking considerable administrative effort.

In addition to the three types of contract vehicles, Congress has established "franchise funds"—organizations within Executive departments and independent agencies that are set up to function like commercial service providers of common administrative services and that are funded by revolving funds. The franchise funds were authorized as a pilot program by Section 403 of the Government Management Reform Act of 1994, Pub. L. No. 103-356, and have been subsequently reauthorized.

[A] Definitions

FAR 2.101 contains the following definitions relevant here:

> "Interagency acquisition" means a procedure by which an agency needing supplies or services (the requesting agency) obtains them from another agency (the servicing agency), by an assisted acquisition or a direct acquisition. The term includes—
>
> (1) Acquisitions under the Economy Act (31 U.S.C. 1535); and
>
> (2) Non-Economy Act acquisitions completed under other statutory authorities, (e.g., General Services Administration Federal Supply Schedules in subpart 8.4 and Governmentwide acquisition contracts (GWACs)).
>
> "Assisted acquisition" means a type of interagency acquisition where a servicing agency performs acquisition activities on a requesting agency's behalf, such as awarding and administering a contract, task order, or delivery order.
>
> "Direct acquisition" means a type of interagency acquisition where a requesting agency places an order directly against a servicing agency's indefinite-delivery contract. The servicing agency manages the indefinite-delivery contract but does not participate in the placement or administration of an order.
>
> "Requesting agency" means the agency that has the requirement for an interagency acquisition.
>
> "Servicing agency" means the agency that will conduct an assisted acquisition on behalf of the requesting agency.
>
> "Governmentwide acquisition contract (GWAC)" means a task-order or delivery-order contract for information technology established by one agency for Governmentwide use that is operated—
>
> (1) By an executive agent designated by the Office of Management and Budget pursuant to 40 U.S.C. 11302(e); or
>
> (2) Under a delegation of procurement authority issued by the General Services Administration (GSA) prior to August 7, 1996, under authority granted GSA by former section 40 U.S.C. 759, repealed by Pub. L. 104-106. The Economy Act does not apply to orders under a Governmentwide acquisition contract.
>
> "Multi-agency contract (MAC)" means a task-order or delivery-order contract established by one agency for use by Government agencies to obtain supplies and services, consistent with the Economy Act (see 17.502-2). Multi-agency contracts include contracts for information technology established pursuant to 40 U.S.C. 11314(a)(2).

[B] Background

[1] Controversies

Although agencies have engaged in interagency acquisitions for many years, the number of such acquisitions surged in the mid-1990s as agencies sought ways to compensate for shortages in contracting personnel, to avoid unnecessarily duplicative administrative costs, to circumvent limits on their own acquisition authority, and to extend the time available for obligating appropriated funds. The process has been referred to as "offloading." As early as 1993 GAO, agency inspectors general, and Congress expressed concerns about the ways in which agencies conducted such transactions. Those concerns were summarized by Senator William S. Cohen at a hearing conducted on July 30, 1993, by the Senate Committee on Governmental Affairs, Subcommittee on Oversight of Government Management:

> Mr. Chairman, I would like to commend you for holding this hearing to examine problems that arise when one agency of the government uses another agency's contract to buy goods and services. This practice, known as off-loading, is permitted under the Economy Act of 1932, and has created a significant loophole in the safeguards established for federal procurement. This loophole enables contracting officers to by-pass important safeguards and makes taxpayers vulnerable to waste and abuse.
>
> In 1984, Congress passed the Competition in Contracting Act (CICA) to create checks and balances in a procurement system that brought us $640 toilet seats and $435 claw hammers. It has taken almost a decade but a number of contracting offices have discovered off-loading as a way to sidestep the procurement safeguards—safeguards we included in CICA to ensure the integrity of the procurement process and protect taxpayer dollars.
>
> As commonly practiced, off-loading permits circumvention of competition and results in the unchecked expenditure of billions of taxpayer dollars. Despite the potential for abuse, agencies and contractors alike defend the off-loading loophole saying it provides a win-win situation—the contractors get the business and the government gets it's [sic] goods in a timely manner, all without having to go through the "arduous" process of competition. However, what you don't hear is that the big loser when off-loading is abused is the taxpayer. In one example of an off-load arrangement constructed specifically to avoid competition, the Army actually instructed NASA's Jet Propulsion Laboratory to award the contract to a specific vendor the Army wanted.
>
> There is also little incentive for agencies to curb offloading activity. It has become a fast way to obligate funds and receive goods and services. Another contributing factor is that agencies make money by charging fees for allowing other agencies to buy off of their existing contracts. These fees which range between one and 30 percent for each contract action, are ostensibly used to cover overhead costs. However, GAO has recently reported that off-loading fees charged by NASA's Jet Propulsion Laboratory bear little relation to the actual

cost of overhead or contract office performance. In addition, there is little or no accountability of the fees agencies charge for off-loading.

Off-loading is pervasive throughout government and is growing.

In other testimony at the same hearing, the Deputy Under Secretary of Defense (Acquisition Reform) acknowledged the problem, stating:

> I agree with the [Department of Defense Inspector General] that some program officials, in what I believe to be an earnest effort to achieve positive results and to accomplish their missions in a timely manner, have violated our regulations for placing orders under the Economy Act. Under the regulation, a DoD contracting officer must make a determination that it is in the best interest of the government to place an order under the Economy Act. I believe the main reason for this disregard of our contracting procedures is the mounting frustration of program officials with the increasing time it takes to make a contract award. Organizations such as the Library of Congress and the TVA [Tennessee Valley Authority] are able to conduct their contracting activities in a shorter period of time than DoD because they are not subject to all of the laws governing DoD. These laws have increased lead times on many non-major system awards to an average of six to eight months in DoD. The Library of Congress and the TVA were able to issue the orders in question in a few days.
>
> I am not condoning this behavior, but I understand that pressures to get the job done may lead some program officials to take short cuts in an acquisition process that must be simplified and streamlined.

[2] The MAC/GWAC Program Managers Compact

In 1997, in response to rising concerns, the Administrator of the Office of Federal Procurement Policy negotiated an agreement among agency managers of MACs and GWACs—the Multiagency/GWAC Program Managers Compact, which provided in part as follows:

> III. PRINCIPLES
>
> Judicious management of multiagency contracts and GWACs requires adherence to the following principles.
>
> [A] Structuring Multiagency Contracts and GWACs
>
> We agree to assess the potential magnitude of interagency orders to ensure that we have or will have adequate resources to properly administer the combined resultant workload. We further agree to consider, if necessary, placing limits on the size of individual orders, as well as initial limits on the amount of interagency usage, subject to periodic adjustment based on our demonstrated ability to adequately manage the contract in light of the volume of orders received.

We agree to provide electronic access to sufficient information to minimize the burden of using these contracts. We have placed or will consider placing this information on our Websites along with a link to the Acquisition Reform Network (ARNet).

We agree that the functions we perform will be limited to those that are inherently governmental. If fees are established to recover the costs of performing these functions, they shall be at the level necessary to cover actual costs for managing and administering the multiagency contract or GWAC. We agree that fees should be established so that the projected total revenue generated by the use of these contracts do not exceed projected actual costs. We further agree that fees should be adjusted so that total revenues do not exceed actual costs.

We commit to use, to the maximum extent practicable, small businesses (including small disadvantaged and women-owned businesses) at the prime or subcontract levels.

We agree to define ordering processes that are easy to understand and that emphasize streamlined procedures and electronic processes. We further agree to explain our approach for ensuring that all contractors are given a fair opportunity to be considered for individual task orders.

[B] Accepting Tasks

We agree to remind the requesting agency of its obligation to determine the economy and efficiency of using those contracts to meet its needs. We further agree to remind the requesting agency that it must follow the requirements set forth in OMB Circular A-76 when applicable.

We agree to remind the requesting agency of its obligation to perform quality reviews of work statements to ensure that tasks are within the scope of the multiagency contract or GWAC, and that they reflect specific requirements.

We agree to remind the requesting agencies of their obligation to ensure that tasks satisfy their internal requirements, such as architectural standards for information technology. We will further remind requesting agencies that their use of multiagency contracts or GWACs does not relieve them of their responsibility to comply with applicable laws, regulations, and policies governing federal procurement.

We agree to encourage the requesting agency to use performance-based work statements to the maximum extent practicable. We further agree, for services that would be in the highest demand, to develop performance based service contracting (PBSC) templates that could be used by the requesting agency to develop PBSC task orders.

We agree that contracts or GWACs should not be used for the sole purpose of obligating expiring funds at the end of a fiscal year. The requesting agency should have a bona fide need in the fiscal year to which funds are being obligated and follow all other appropriation law requirements.

[C] Processing Orders

We agree to ensure that contractors are given a fair opportunity to be considered and that the exceptions to fair opportunity recognized in FAR 16.505 are used appropriately.

We agree to incorporate a best value approach and use past performance in determining contractors for individual tasks.

We will strive to minimize contractor costs associated with preparing proposals for orders. Where appropriate, we will consider limiting the size of written proposals, or encouraging the use of oral proposals. We further agree that proposal detail should be tailored to the minimum level necessary for adequate evaluation and selection for award.

[D] Administering Orders

We agree to record information regarding contractor performance on orders and make it available to source selection officials to facilitate maximum practical consideration of past performance in awarding subsequent tasks.

[E] Recompeting or Establishing New Multiagency Contracts

We agree to recompete or establish our own multiagency contract only after we determine that such a vehicle is in the best interest of the government and the most cost effective means of satisfying our requirements. In making this decision, we will consider (1) the economies and efficiencies to be gained by establishing our own multiagency contract, in light of the existence and feasibility of having our needs met through another agency, or multiagency contracts and (2) if the requirements are generally within our mission or competency to award.

[3] The Services Acquisition Reform Act Advisory Panel

Much of the concern about interagency acquisition arose from its use in the acquisition of services. In 2003, Congress enacted the Services Acquisition Reform Act, Title XIV of the National Defense Authorization Act of 2004, Pub. L. No. 108-136. Section 1423 of the Act directed the Administrator of the Office of Federal Procurement Policy to appoint an advisory panel to review acquisition laws and regulations governing the acquisition of services. One of the topics to be investigated was "performance of acquisition functions across agency lines of responsibility and the use of Governmentwide contracts." The panel devoted Chapter 3 of its January 2007 report to interagency acquisition. See *Report of the Acquisition Advisory Panel to the Office of Federal Procurement Policy and the United States Congress*, https://www.acquisition.gov/comp/aap/24102_GSA.pdf. The panel introduced the topic as follows:

The performance of acquisition functions across agency lines is almost exclusively accomplished through the use of interagency contract vehicles described in detail in the next section. The significant increase in the use of these vehicles by agencies over the last ten years has raised a number of complex policy issues and has been the subject of extensive oversight by Congress, the Government Accountability Office ("GAO"), the inspectors general ("IGs") of various federal agencies, outside organizations, and the media. This attention has highlighted significant benefits in award efficiencies these vehicles provide to the federal government and the taxpayer. It has also uncovered past deficiencies in their creation and administration and continuing risks associated with their use.

Several critical observations have been made regarding the creation and use of interagency contract vehicles. In its January 2005 High Risk Update, GAO observed that a number of factors contribute to making these vehicles high risk in certain circumstances:

1) they are attracting rapid growth of taxpayer dollars;
2) they are being used and administered by some agencies with limited expertise in this contracting method; and
3) they contribute to a significantly more complex environment in which accountability has not always been clearly established.

After making several findings, the panel concluded:

There is little doubt that interagency contracts can and do provide significant benefits and efficiencies, but these efficiencies have been narrowly viewed primarily as transaction efficiencies such as reduced pre-award lead time and protest risk. Interagency contracts broadly defined are important to the operation of the federal acquisition process. Witnesses speaking on the subject before the Panel identified the benefits of interagency contracts and several remarked that they viewed them as essential for meeting mission needs. However, the focus on transaction-based value hides the even greater efficiencies to be gained if interagency contracts are employed toward the goal of creating strategic governmentwide efficiencies. Unfortunately, the lack of readily available, reliable and timely data on the use and management of interagency contracts has hampered the government's ability to realize the more strategic value of these contracts. This lack of data is a barrier to strategic planning as well as oversight, on both an enterprise-wide and government-wide basis.

The Panel believes that meaningful improvements to interagency contracting practices can be achieved by agencies focusing their efforts on a sound and consistent process that provides oversight during the creation and the continuation (or reauthorization) of these contracts. Many of the issues identified by GAO and agency IGs dealing with the misuse of these vehicles are related to the internal controls, management and oversight, and division of roles and responsibilities between the vehicle holder and ordering agency. These issues can best be addressed with a government-wide policy that requires agencies to specifically and deliberately address these matters at the point of creation and continuation rather than attempting to remedy these problems at the point of use. The current lack of an established process and limited transparency allows for the proliferation of these vehicles in a largely uncoordinated, bottom-up fashion, focusing attention on the short term, transaction-based benefits of reduced procurement lead time. The Panel and the Working Group received testimony from government witnesses who stated that interagency vehicles are often utilized when an agency does not have ample time to fully define its acquisition requirements. Establishing guidelines for the creation and continuation of these vehicles will help to ensure they are used as an effective tool for enterprise-wide and government-wide strategic sourcing.

See *Oversight Plan Needed to Help Implement Acquisition Advisory Panel Recommendations*, GAO-08-160 (2007).

[4] The Duncan Hunter National Defense Authorization Act

In 2009, Congress enacted the Duncan Hunter National Defense Authorization Act for Fiscal Year 2009, Pub. L. No. 110-417. Section 865 was entitled, "Preventing Abuse of Interagency Contracts" and provided as follows:

> (a) Office of Management and Budget Policy Guidance—
>
> (1) REPORT AND GUIDELINES—Not later than one year after the date of the enactment of this Act, the Director of the Office of Management and Budget shall—
>
> (A) submit to Congress a comprehensive report on interagency acquisitions, including their frequency of use, management controls, cost-effectiveness, and savings generated; and
>
> (B) issue guidelines to assist the heads of executive agencies in improving the management of interagency acquisitions.
>
> (2) MATTERS COVERED BY GUIDELINES—For purposes of paragraph (1)(B), the Director shall include guidelines on the following matters:
>
> (A) Procedures for the use of interagency acquisitions to maximize competition, deliver best value to executive agencies, and minimize waste, fraud, and abuse.
>
> (B) Categories of contracting inappropriate for interagency acquisition.
>
> (C) Requirements for training acquisition workforce personnel in the proper use of interagency acquisitions.
>
> (b) Regulations Required—
>
> (1) IN GENERAL—Not later than one year after the date of the enactment of this Act, the Federal Acquisition Regulation shall be revised to require that all interagency acquisitions—

(A) include a written agreement between the requesting agency and the servicing agency assigning responsibility for the administration and management of the contract;

(B) include a determination that an interagency acquisition is the best procurement alternative; and

(C) include sufficient documentation to ensure an adequate audit.

(2) MULTI-AGENCY CONTRACTS—Not later than one year after the date of the enactment of this Act, the Federal Acquisition Regulation shall be revised to require any multi-agency contract entered into by an executive agency after the effective date of such regulations to be supported by a business case analysis detailing the administration of such contract, including an analysis of all direct and indirect costs to the Federal Government of awarding and administering such contract and the impact such contract will have on the ability of the Federal Government to leverage its purchasing power.

(c) Agency Reporting Requirement—The senior procurement executive for each executive agency shall, as directed by the Director of the Office of Management and Budget, submit to the Director annual reports on the actions taken by the executive agency pursuant to the guidelines issued under subsection (a).

(d) Definitions—In this section:

(1) The term "executive agency" has the meaning given such term in section 4(1) of the Office of Federal Procurement Policy Act (41 U.S.C. 403(1)), except that, in the case of a military department, it means the Department of Defense.

(2) The term "head of executive agency" means the head of an executive agency except that, in the case of a military department, the term means the Secretary of Defense.

(3) The term "interagency acquisition" means a procedure by which an executive agency needing supplies or services (the requesting agency) obtains them from another executive agency (the servicing agency). The term includes acquisitions under section 1535 of title 31, United States Code (commonly referred to as the "Economy Act"), Federal Supply Schedules above $500,000, and Governmentwide acquisition contracts.

(4) The term "multi-agency contract" means a task or delivery order contract established for use by more than one executive agency to obtain supplies and services, consistent with section 1535 of title 31, United States Code (commonly referred to as the "Economy Act").

The regulations promulgated to implement the Act were added to the FAR by Federal Acquisition Circular 2005-47, Item III, 75 Fed. Reg. 77733-37, Dec. 13, 2010, which added definitions of interagency acquisition, direct acquisition, assisted acquisition, requesting agency, and servicing agency to FAR 2.101; revised FAR 8.404, Use of Federal Supply Schedules; added new Subpart 17.5, and made minor changes to several other parts. These are the core rules for interagency contracting.

Through Section 875 of the John S. McCain National Defense Authorization Act for Fiscal Year 2019, Pub. L. No. 115-232, Congress relaxed the 2008 NDAA restrictions on interagency acquisitions by eliminating the requirement for agencies to determine that use of an interagency acquisition is the "best procurement alternative." The FAR Council issued a final rule amending FAR 17.5 to reflect the same through FAR Circular 2019-02, Item II, 84 Fed. Reg. 19837, June 5, 2019.

[C] Policy and Procedure

FAR Subpart 17.5 states general policies and procedures for the conduct of interagency acquisitions, which are designed to ensure compliance with applicable laws and regulations and proper use of appropriations. FAR 17.500 applies those policies and procedures to all prospective interagency acquisitions where (1) an agency needing supplies or services obtains them using another agency's contract, or (2) an agency uses another agency to provide acquisition assistance, such as awarding and administering a contract, task order, or delivery order. FAR 17.5 does not apply to (1) orders valued at $600,000 or less that are conducted through the GSA Federal Supply Schedule program, or (2) interagency reimbursable work performed by federal employees (other than acquisition assistance) or interagency activities where contracting is incidental to the purpose of the transaction. FAR 17.501 states the general policy for interagency acquisitions as follows:

> (a) Interagency acquisitions are commonly conducted through indefinite-delivery contracts, such as task- and delivery-order contracts. The indefinite-delivery contracts used most frequently to support interagency acquisitions are Federal Supply Schedules (FSS), Governmentwide acquisition contracts (GWACs), and multiagency contracts (MACs).
>
> (b) An agency shall not use an interagency acquisition to circumvent conditions and limitations imposed on the use of funds.
>
> (c) An interagency acquisition is not exempt from the requirements of subpart 7.3, Contractor Versus Government Performance.
>
> (d) An agency shall not use an interagency acquisition to make acquisitions conflicting with any other agency's authority or responsibility (for example, that of the Administrator of General Services under title 40, United States Code, "Public Buildings, Property and Works" and 41 U.S.C. division C of subtitle 1, Procurement.)

[1] Determination of Best Procurement Approach

The initial version of FAR 17.5, reflecting the 2008 NDAA and a general skepticism toward interagency contracting, required that before proceeding with an interagency acquisition, an agency must document a determination that doing so was "the best procurement approach." Following the 2019 NDAA and subsequent FAR amendments, this "best procurement approach" determination requirement is no longer included in FAR 17.5.

The "best procurement approach" determination restricted agencies' ability to use interagency acquisitions. The best procurement approach presumably will be the one most likely to yield the best combination of price, quality, delivery, and administrative convenience. In order to make such a determination, a prospective requesting agency would likely need to conduct thorough market research of all possible alternative approaches to discover what is available under existing contracts. This market research and best approach determination was made all the more complex due to the proliferation of interagency vehicles since the mid-1990s, which has greatly complicated market research, made price comparisons for similar products and services difficult, and has caused considerable confusion. With the affirmative obligation to document "the best" approach set aside, agencies have more flexibility to commit to an interagency acquisition after a reasonable degree of market research and documentation, without necessarily having to conduct exhaustive analysis of all possible alternatives before doing so.

[2] Interagency Agreements for Assisted Acquisitions

Under the current version of FAR 17.5, the primary analysis required to undertake an inter-agency acquisition is for the servicing and requesting agencies to document an interagency agreement consistent with FAR 17.502-1(a):

> (a) Written agreement on responsibility for management and administration.
>
> (1) Assisted acquisitions.
>
> (i) Prior to the issuance of a solicitation, the servicing agency and the requesting agency shall both sign a written interagency agreement that establishes the general terms and conditions governing the relationship between the parties, including roles and responsibilities for acquisition planning, contract execution, and administration and management of the contract(s) or order(s). The requesting agency shall provide to the servicing agency any unique terms, conditions, and applicable agency-specific statutes, regulations, directives, and other applicable requirements for incorporation into the order or contract. In the event there are no agency unique requirements beyond the FAR, the requesting agency shall so inform the servicing agency contracting officer in writing. For acquisitions on behalf of the Department of Defense, also see subpart 17.7. For patent rights, see 27.304-2. In preparing interagency agreements to support assisted acquisitions, agencies should review the Office of

> Federal Procurement Policy (OFPP) guidance, Interagency Acquisitions, available at *https://www.whitehouse.gov/sites/whitehouse.gov/files/omb/assets/OMB/procurement/interagency_acq/iac_revised.pdf.*
>
> (ii) Each agency's file shall include the interagency agreement between the requesting and servicing agency, and shall include sufficient documentation to ensure an adequate audit consistent with 4.801(b).
>
> (2) Direct acquisitions. The requesting agency administers the order; therefore, no written agreement with the servicing agency is required.

For MACs and GWACs, FAR 17.502-1(b) further requires a documented business case analysis prepared in accordance with detailed OFPP guidance for *Interagency Acquisitions*. This business case analysis must:

> (1) Consider strategies for the effective participation of small businesses during acquisition planning (see 7.103(u));
>
> (2) Detail the administration of such contract, including an analysis of all direct and indirect costs to the Government of awarding and administering such contract;
>
> (3) Describe the impact such contract will have on the ability of the Government to leverage its purchasing power, e.g., will it have a negative effect because it dilutes other existing contracts;
>
> (4) Include an analysis concluding that there is a need for establishing the multi-agency contract; and
>
> (5) Document roles and responsibilities in the administration of the contract.

Several agencies have published interagency agreement guides and templates.

[3] Economy Act Determinations and Findings

If there is no specific statutory authority for an interagency acquisition, such as the statutes authorizing the Federal Supply Schedule and GWACs, agencies can conduct such acquisitions under the Economy Act, 31 U.S.C. § 1535. FAR 17.502-2 states additional prerequisites for the conduct of such interagency acquisitions. FAR 17.502-2(c) requires preparation and approval of a determination and findings (D&F) for all Economy Act acquisitions, whether assisted or direct. The D&F must state that (1) use of interagency acquisition is in the best interests of the government and (2) acquisition of the supplies or services directly from a commercial source cannot be done as conveniently or economically.

If the servicing agency must award a contract or issue an order for the requesting agency, FAR 17.502-2(c)(iii) also requires that the D&F include a statement that at least one of the following circumstances applies:

> (A) The acquisition will appropriately be made under an existing contract of the servicing agency, entered into before placement of the order, to meet the requirements of the servicing agency for the same or similar supplies or services.
>
> (B) The servicing agency has the capability or expertise to enter into a contract for such supplies or services that is not available within the requesting agency.
>
> (C) The servicing agency is specifically authorized by law or regulation to purchase such supplies or services on behalf of other agencies.

The D&F must be approved (signed) by a contracting officer of the requesting agency with authority to conduct the procurement or by another official designated by the agency head. If the servicing agency is not required to conduct its acquisitions in accordance with the FAR, e.g., the Bonneville Power Administration or the Federal Aviation Administration, the D&F must be approved by the requesting agency's Senior Procurement Executive or a higher-level official. The requesting agency must furnish a copy of the D&F to the servicing agency.

[4] Franchise Funds

In 1994 Congress authorized the establishment of six pilot "franchise funds" allowing agencies to provide services to other agencies, Section 403 of the Federal Financial Reform Act of 1994. Pub. L. No. 103-356; 31 U.S.C. § 501 note. This effort was extended several times and several of these funds have now been made permanent. See *Revolving Funds: Additional Pricing and Performance Information for FAA and Treasury Funds Could Enhance Agency Decisions on Shared Services*, GAO-16-477 (May 10, 2016) for an assessment of two of the funds.

[D] Obligation of Appropriated Funds in Assisted Acquisition

When an agency conducts a direct acquisition by issuing an order against a GSA schedule contract, a GWAC, or a MAC, the rules for obligation of funds are the same as for non-interagency acquisitions—an obligation is made and must be recorded when the agency issues the order. However, when agencies conduct assisted acquisitions, the rules become more complex. There are three key issues: first, the authority to transfer appropriated funds and the limitations on the use of funds, second, the standard for recording an obligation, and third, the bona fide needs rule.

[1] Transfer and Use of Funds

The transfer of appropriated funds within an agency or from one agency to another must be authorized by statute, such as the Economy Act, 31 U.S.C. § 1535. Unless otherwise authorized by statute, transferred funds continue to be available only for the purpose for which they were appropriated and only for the specified period of availability for obligation, 31 U.S.C. § 1532. This is true even when the funds are transferred for deposit in a revolving fund that is not subject to fiscal year limitations on availability. Thus, requesting agencies cannot "park" or "bank" funds by transferring them to servicing agencies in order to avoid restrictions on their use. This rule applies also to canceled unexpended balances of funds properly obligated within the period of availability, *United States Capitol Police—Advances to Volpe Center Working Capital Fund*, Comp. Gen. Dec. B-319349, June 4, 2010, *Unpub.*; *Implementation of the Library of Congress FEDLINK Revolving Fund*, Comp. Gen. Dec. B-288142, Sept. 6. 2001, *Unpub.*

[2] Standard for Recording Obligations

The rules that govern the obligation of funds under interagency acquisitions are in 31 U.S.C. § 1501(a)(1) and (a)(3), 2 *Principles of Federal Appropriations Law* 3d, 7-28 to 7-29. 31 U.S.C. § 1501(a)(1) applies to transactions in which the requesting agency chooses to proceed through interagency acquisition. GAO refers to such transactions as "voluntary orders." 31 U.S.C. § 1501(a)(3) applies to those transactions in which the requesting agency is required by law to place the order with the servicing agency.

31 U.S.C. § 1501(a)(1) states:

> (a) An amount shall be recorded as an obligation of the United States Government only when supported by documentary evidence of—
>
> (1) a binding agreement between an agency and another person (including an agency) that is—
>
> (A) in writing, in a way and form, and for a purpose authorized by law; and
>
> (B) executed before the end of the period of availability for obligation of the appropriation or fund used for specific goods to be delivered, real property to be bought or leased, or work or service to be provided. . . .

Thus, when a requesting agency enters into a binding agreement with a servicing agency, it must record an obligation of funds.

In order to be binding and properly recordable as an obligation under 31 U.S.C. § 1501(a)(1), an interagency agreement for a voluntary order must specify the supplies or services to be acquired in enough detail to establish the responsibilities of the servicing agency. In the absence of sufficient specificity, the agreement between the agencies is not binding and the requirement for documentary evidence of a binding agreement is not met. There is no obligation, and the recording of an obligation with the intent to complete the description of required supplies or services after the expiration of the period of funds availability would constitute improper "banking" or "parking" of funds, *Expired Funds and Interagency Agreements between Gov-Works and the Dep't of Defense*, Comp. Gen. Dec. B-308944, July 17, 2007, *Unpub.* (descriptions of supplies in Military Interdepartmental Purchase Request too vague to establish binding agreement between requesting agency and servicing agency). Any attempt by the servicing agency or the requesting agency to complete the specification and obligate the funds after the last day of availability would violate the bona fide needs rule and might violate the Antideficiency Act.

An additional condition applies to interagency acquisitions governed by the Economy Act. 31 U.S.C. § 1535(d) states:

> (d) An order placed or agreement made under this section obligates an appropriation of the ordering agency or unit. The amount obligated is deobligated to the extent that the agency or unit filling the order has not incurred obligations, before the end of the period of availability of the appropriation, in—
>
> (1) providing goods or services; or
>
> (2) making an authorized contract with another person to provide the requested goods or services.

Thus, while the requesting agency must record an obligation upon placing its order with the servicing agency, the servicing agency must subsequently obligate the funds by awarding a contract or placing an order before the period of funds availability has expired, otherwise the requesting agency must deobligate the funds, 2 *Principles of Federal Appropriations Law* 3d, 7-29 to 7-30, 12-43 to 12-46.

However, the deobligation requirement of the Economy Act does not apply to transactions carried out under other statutes. Thus, if proceeding under a different statute, and if the requesting agency validly recorded an obligation when it entered into an interagency agreement with a servicing agency, then the funds remain obligated and available for payment even if the servicing agency does not award a contract or place an order prior to the expiration of the period of funds availability. The servicing agency's contract or order must, however, fulfill a bona fide need of the requesting agency in the year for which the funds were appropriated, *2 Principles of Federal Appropriations Law* 3d, 7-30 to 7-31. This will not violate the prohibition against "banking" or "parking" of funds as long as the interagency agreement is sufficiently specific in its description of the supplies or services required so as to constitute a binding agreement with the servicing agency.

For interagency transactions that are required by law, 31 U.S.C. § 1501(a)(3) requires only documentary evidence of "an order required by law to be placed with an agency." The deobligation rule of the Economy Act does not apply in such cases. See *Comptroller General Campbell to the Administrator, General Servs. Admin.*, 34 Comp. Gen. Dec. 705 (B-184830), June 28, 1955 (obligation by agency required by law to place order with GSA for building management operations was valid even though GSA does not award contract before last day of funds availability). However, the requesting agency's order still must be for a bona fide need of the year for which the funds were appropriated. See *Chemical Safety and Hazard Investigation Board—Interagency Agreement with the Gen. Servs. Admin.*, Comp. Gen. Dec. B-318425, Dec. 8, 2009, *Unpub.*; *Natural Res. Conservation Serv.—Obligating Orders with GSA's AutoChoice Summer Program*, Comp. Gen. Dec. B-317249, July 1, 2009, *Unpub.*

[E] Fees and Revenues

Servicing agencies must recover the costs of the supplies and services acquired and their administrative expenses. As a general rule, agencies may not augment their appropriations without statutory authorization. To charge more than costs would augment the servicing agency's appropriation; to charge less would augment the requesting agency's appropriation, 2 *Principles of Federal Appropriations Law* 3d, 6-162.

[1] Reasonableness of Fees

In 2002 GAO found that servicing agencies were charging more than enough to cover their costs, in some cases substantially more. See *Contract Management: Interagency Contract Program Fees Need More Oversight*, GAO-02-734 (July 2004).

[2] Fees Under the Economy Act

The Economy Act, 31 U.S.C. § 1535(b), expressly limits the amounts to be charged by servicing agencies to "estimated or actual cost as determined by the agency or unit filling the order." The servicing agency is entitled to invoice for payment in advance without prior audit or certification of its invoice.

[3] GSA's Industrial Funding Fee

GSA's schedule program, which is carried out by its Federal Acquisition Service, is paid for through its Acquisition Services Fund, authorized by 40 U.S.C. §§ 303 and 321. Pursuant to that authority, GSA establishes an "industrial funding fee." The rate is established annually and is set to recover the direct and indirect costs of GSA's operations. The fee is included in the schedule contract prices and is collected by the contractors and then reported and paid to GSA in accordance with a clause inserted in all schedule contracts, 48 C.F.R. § 552.238-80, Industrial Funding Fee and Sales Reporting, which states:

> (a) Reporting of Federal Supply Schedule Sales. The Contractor shall report all contract sales under this contract as follows:
>
> (1) The Contractor shall accurately report the dollar value, in U.S. dollars and rounded to the nearest whole dollar, of all sales under this contract by calendar quarter (January 1-March 31, April 1-June 30, July 1-September 30, and October 1-December 31). The dollar value of a sale is the price paid by the Schedule user for products and services on a Schedule task or delivery order. The reported contract sales value shall include the Industrial Funding Fee (IFF). The Contractor shall maintain a consistent accounting method of sales reporting, based on the Contractor's established commercial accounting practice. The acceptable points at which sales may be reported include—
>
> (i) Receipt of order;
> (ii) Shipment or delivery, as applicable;
> (iii) Issuance of an invoice; or
> (iv) Payment.
>
> (2) Contract sales shall be reported to Federal Acquisition Services (FAS) within 30 calendar days following the completion of each reporting quarter. The Contractor shall continue to furnish quarterly reports, including "zero" sales, through physical completion of the last outstanding task order or delivery order of the contract.
>
> (3) Reportable sales under the contract are those resulting from sales of contract items to authorized users unless the purchase was conducted pursuant to a separate contracting authority such as a Governmentwide Acquisition Contract (GWAC); a separately awarded FAR Part 12, FAR Part 13, FAR Part 14, or FAR Part 15 procurement; or a non-FAR contract. Sales made to state and local governments under Cooperative Purchasing authority shall be counted as reportable sales for IFF purposes.
>
> (4) The Contractor shall electronically report the quarterly dollar value of sales, including "zero" sales, by utilizing the automated reporting system at an internet website designated by the General Services Administration (GSA)'s Federal Acquisition Service (FAS). Prior to using this automated system, the Contractor shall complete contract registration with the FAS Vendor Support Center (VSC). The website address, as well as registration instructions and reporting procedures, will be provided at the time of award. The Contractor shall report sales separately for each National Stock Number (NSN), Special Item Number (SIN), or sub-item.

(5) The Contractor shall convert the total value of sales made in foreign currency to U.S. dollars using the "Treasury Reporting Rates of Exchange" issued by the U.S. Department of Treasury, Financial Management Service. The Contractor shall use the issue of the Treasury report in effect on the last day of the calendar quarter. The report is available from Financial Management Service, International Funds Branch, Telephone: (202) 874-7994, internet: http://www.fms.treas.gov/intn.html.

(b) The Contractor shall remit the IFF at the rate set by GSA's FSS.

(1) The Contractor shall remit the IFF to FAS in U.S. dollars within 30 calendar days after the end of the reporting quarter; final payment shall be remitted within 30 days after physical completion of the last outstanding task order or delivery order of the contract.

(2) The IFF represents a percentage of the total quarterly sales reported. This percentage is set at the discretion of GSA's FAS. GSA's FAS has the unilateral right to change the percentage at any time, but not more than once per year. FAS will provide reasonable notice prior to the effective date of the change. The IFF reimburses FAS for the costs of operating the Federal Supply Schedules Program and recoups its operating costs from ordering activities. Offerors must include the FAS in their prices. The fee is included in the award price(s) and reflected in the total amount charged to ordering activities. FAS will post notice of the current IFF at *https://srp.fas.gsa.gov/* or successor website as appropriate.

(c) Within 60 days of award, an FAS representative will provide the Contractor with specific written procedural instructions on remitting the IFF. FAS reserves the unilateral right to change such instructions from time to time, following notification to the Contractor.(d) Failure to remit the full amount of the IFF within 30 calendar days after the end of the applicable reporting period constitutes a contract debt to the United States Government under the terms of FAR Subpart 32.6. The Government may exercise all rights under the Debt Collection Improvement Act of 1996, including withholding or setting off payments and interest on the debt (see FAR clause 52.232-17, Interest). Should the Contractor fail to submit the required sales reports, falsify them, or fail to timely pay the IFF, this is sufficient cause for the Government to terminate the contract for cause.

[4] Fees Charged by Franchise Funds and Other Revolving Funds

The amounts that may be charged by franchise funds and other revolving or working capital funds depends on their authorizing legislation. The franchise funds that provide assisted acquisition services pursuant to 31 U.S.C. § 501, note, and other authority may charge a fee of 4% above costs for acquisition of capital equipment and for the improvement and implementation of department financial management, information technology, and other support systems, and may receive payment in advance. See *Budget Issues: Franchise Fund Pilot Review*, GAO-03-1069, Aug. 2003.

[5] Interagency Agreement on Payment by Requesting Agency

The amount, method, and timing of payment of the servicing agency by the requesting agency should be agreed upon in advance and stated in the interagency agreement.

§ 11.02 GSA SCHEDULE CONTRACTING

GSA provides access by federal agencies and, in some cases, by state and local government agencies and other organizations, to contracts for a wide variety of commercial products and services through its schedules program. The program is interchangeably referred to as Federal Supply Schedules (FSS) and Multiple Award Schedules (MAS). FAR 38.101 describes the program in general terms:

> (a) The Federal Supply Schedule program, pursuant to 41 U.S.C. 152(3), provides Federal agencies with a simplified process of acquiring commercial supplies and services in varying quantities while obtaining volume discounts. Indefinite-delivery contracts are awarded using competitive procedures to firms. The firms provide supplies and services at stated prices for given periods of time, for delivery within a stated geographic area such as the 48 contiguous states, the District of Columbia, Alaska, Hawaii, and overseas. The schedule contracting office issues Federal Supply Schedule publications that contain a general overview of the Federal Supply Schedule (FSS) program and address pertinent topics.
>
> (b) Each schedule identifies agencies that are required to use the contracts as primary sources of supply.
>
> (c) Federal agencies not identified in the schedules as mandatory users may issue orders under the schedules. Contractors are encouraged to accept the orders.
>
> (d) Although GSA awards most Federal Supply Schedule contracts, it may authorize other agencies to award schedule contracts and publish schedules. For example, the Department of Veterans Affairs awards schedule contracts for certain medical and nonperishable subsistence items.
>
> (e) When establishing Federal Supply Schedules, GSA, or an agency delegated that authority, is responsible for complying with all applicable statutory and regulatory requirements (e.g., Parts 5, 6, and 19). The requirements of Parts 5, 6, and 19 apply at the acquisition planning stage prior to issuing the schedule solicitation and do not apply to orders and BPAs placed under resulting schedule contracts (except see 8.404 and 8.405-5).

A GSA schedule is a list of product and service items and of indefinite-delivery indefinite-quantity contracts for a particular class of products or services against which agencies may issue task and delivery orders. As part of a major consolidation and restricting effort, in fiscal year 2020, the 24 legacy schedules were consolidated into a single schedule, broken down into twelve large categories. The twelve categories are further subdivided into subcategories and Special Item Numbers (SINs). For example, the Office Management category consists of nine subcategories, including Mail Management and Office Supplies. Each subcategory includes numerous SINs; for example, under the Office Supplies subcategory, SIN 339940 covers Office Products, which is described as providing "a comprehensive family of paper products, general office devices, and specialty items that support the fully functional workplace." The full schedule breakdown is available online.

Schedule contracts are awarded by GSA's Federal Acquisition Service (FAS) in accordance with the FAR and with the General Services Administration Acquisition Manual (GSAM), which contains the General Services Administration Acquisition Regulation (GSAR) and non-regulatory guidance. Procedures for placing orders against GSA schedule contracts are in FAR Subpart 8.4, but GSA provides extensive additional guidance to contractors and to schedule users at its website. GSA administers its contracts, but the issuing agencies (referred to as "ordering activities") administer the orders that they place. FAS's Office of Assisted Acquisition Services provides assisted acquisition services to agencies upon request.

[A] Eligible Users

Eligibility to use GSA Schedules is established by GSA Order ADM-4800.2I, *Eligibility to Use GSA Sources of Supplies and Services*, July 19, 2016. Generally, use of the schedules is open to Executive agencies, including Executive Departments as defined by 5 U.S.C. § 101, wholly owned government corporations as defined by 31 U.S.C. § 9101(3), and independent establishments as defined by 5 U.S.C. § 104. In addition, a large number of other federal agencies, mixed-ownership government corporations, the District of Columbia, qualified nonprofit agencies, and state and local governments may use them as permitted by law. Government contractors and subcontractors may use them under some circumstances, see FAR Subpart 51.1 "Contractor Use of Government Supply Sources." The Appendices to the GSA Order provide additional details regarding which entities are eligible.

[B] Solicitation, Offer, and Award of Schedule Contracts

[1] Solicitation

GSA announces the availability of schedule contract solicitations at the Government-wide Point of Entry, www.SAM.gov, and at its own website.

Prospective offerors must identify the schedule under which they wish to offer products and services, go to GSA's webpage for that schedule, identify and read the appropriate solicitation, and then submit offers. Schedule solicitations are open-ended. There is no specific deadline for submitting offers, which may be submitted at any time while the solicitation is available. Solicitations are periodically "refreshed" to incorporate new regulations and policies and each edition describes the changes made since the last edition. See solicitation provision A-FSS-11, "Consideration of Offers Under Standing Solicitation (JAN 2016)":

> (a) This solicitation is a standing solicitation from which the Government contemplates award of contracts for supplies/services listed in the Schedule of Items. This solicitation will remain in effect unless replaced by an updated solicitation.
>
> (b) There is no closing date for receipt of offers; therefore, offers may be submitted for consideration at any time.
>
> (c) An offer may be rejected if an offeror fails to meet timeframes established by the Contracting Officer either to address deficiencies in the offer or to submit a final proposal revision. A resubmission(s) is permitted; however, it may be rejected immediately if it is still deficient in the area(s) that caused its initial rejection.
>
> (d) Contracts awarded under this solicitation will be in effect for 5 years from the date of award, unless further extended, pursuant to clause I-FSS-163, Option to Extend the Term of the Contract (Evergreen), canceled pursuant to the Cancellation clause, or terminated pursuant to the termination provisions of the contract.

The content of GSA schedule solicitations includes solicitation provisions and contract clauses that are prescribed in GSAM/GSAR 538.273. This regulation contains guidance to GSA contracting officers on when each solicitation provision or contract clause should be used.

[2] Proposal Review and Negotiation

Because solicitations are open-ended, offerors do not compete on a head-to-head basis and contract award does not entail offer-to-offer comparisons or trade-off analyses. GSA does not follow the procedures in FAR Subpart 15.3, "Source Selection."

Offeror capabilities are evaluated on the basis of nonprice factors such as experience, past performance, and others relevant to the subject matter of the contract. Offerors must propose the prices that they give to their most favored customers. GSA contracting officers analyze the prices and may then engage in price negotiations. See the instruction to GSA personnel at GSAM/GSAR 538.270-1 and 02.

Contracts are awarded to qualified offerors that propose prices that the contracting officer determines to be fair and reasonable. Once an award has been made, the contractor must publish a price list for its contract. Ordering agencies are expected to obtain the most favorable prices for schedule products or services by requesting price reductions when placing an order, FAR 8.405-4.

[C] Schedule Contracts Terms

GSA schedule contracts are indefinite-delivery indefinite-quantity contracts for commercial items, written in accordance with FAR Part 12 and other instructions in FAR and in GSAM/GSAR. Each contract is organized into two parts: Part I—Goods and Services and Part II—Contract Terms and Conditions. Part I lists and describes the special item numbers (SINs) for each contract. It also contains estimates of predicted annual sales for each SIN, which are based on historical data. Part II contains the clause at FAR 52.212-4, Contract Terms and Conditions—Commercial Items, which applies to firm-fixed-price orders and 52.212-4 Alternate I, which applies to time-and-materials orders. Part II also contains FAR 52.212-5, Contract Terms and Conditions Required to Implement Statutes or Executive Orders—Commercial Items, Alternate I, additional clauses from FAR and GSAM/GSAR, and clauses that had formerly been contained in the FSS clause manual. GSA has approved deviations from the texts of some of the standard FAR clauses. Such clauses are identified by the parenthetical "Deviation" in the clause title.

Several clauses unique to GSA schedule contracts warrant special mention. GSAM/GSAR 552.238-113, Scope of Contract (Eligible Ordering Activities) (MAY 2023), identifies the organizations authorized to place orders, as follows:

> (a) This solicitation is issued to establish contracts which may be used on a nonmandatory basis by the agencies and activities named below, as a source of supply for the supplies or services described herein, for domestic and/or overseas delivery. For Special Item Number 132-53, Wireless Services ONLY, limited geographic coverage (consistent with the Offeror's commercial practice) may be proposed.
>
> (1) Executive agencies (as defined in FAR Subpart 2.1) including nonappropriated fund activities as prescribed in 41 CFR 101-26.000;
>
> (2) Government contractors authorized in writing by a Federal agency pursuant to FAR 51.1;
>
> (3) Mixed ownership Government corporations (as defined in the Government Corporation Control Act);
>
> (4) Federal Agencies, including establishments in the legislative or judicial branch of government (except the Senate, the House of Representatives and the Architect of the Capitol and any activities under the direction of the Architect of the Capitol).
>
> (5) The District of Columbia;
>
> (6) Tribal governments when authorized under 25 USC 450j(k);
>
> (7) Tribes or tribally designated housing entities pursuant to 25 U.S.C. 4111(j);

(8) Qualified Nonprofit Agencies as authorized under 40 USC 502(b); and

(9) Organizations, other than those identified in paragraph (d) of this clause, authorized by GSA pursuant to statute or regulation to use GSA as a source of supply.

* * *

(d) The following activities may place orders against Schedule 70 contracts:

(1) State and local government may place orders against Consolidated Schedule contracts containing information technology Special Item Numbers, or security or protection, on an optional basis; provided, the Contractor accepts order(s) from such activities;

(2) The American National Red Cross may place orders against Federal Supply Schedules for products and services in furtherance of the purposes set forth in its Federal charter (36 U.S.C. 300102); provided, the Contractor accepts order(s) from the American National Red Cross; and

(3) Other qualified organizations, as defined in section 309 of the Robert T. Stafford Disaster Relief and Emergency Assistance Act (42 U.S.C. 5152), may place orders against Federal Supply Schedules for products and services determined to be appropriate to facilitate emergency preparedness and disaster relief and set forth in guidance by the Administrator of General Services, in consultation with the Administrator of the Federal Emergency Management Agency; provided, the Contractor accepts order(s) from such activities.

(4) State and local governments may place orders against Federal Supply Schedules for good or services determined by the Secretary of Homeland Security to facilitate recovery from a major disaster declared by the President under the Robert T. Stafford Disaster Relief and Emergency Assistance Act (42 U.S.C. 5121, et seq.) to facilitate disaster preparedness or response, or to facilitate recovery from terrorism or nuclear, biological, chemical, or radiological attack; provided, the Contractor accepts order(s) from such activities.

(e) Articles or services may be ordered from time to time in such quantities as may be needed to fill any requirement, subject to the Order Limitations thresholds which will be specified in resultant contracts. Overseas activities may place orders directly with schedule contractors for delivery to CONUS port or consolidation point.

(f) (1) The Contractor is obligated to accept orders received from activities within the Executive branch of the Federal Government.

(2) The Contractor is not obligated to accept orders received from activities outside the Executive branch; however, the Contractor is encouraged to accept such orders. If the Contractor elects to accept such orders, all provisions of the contract shall apply, including clause 52.232-36, Payment by Third Party. If the Contractor is unwilling to

accept such orders, and the proposed method of payment is not through the Credit Card, the Contractor shall return the order by mail or other means of delivery within 5 workdays from receipt. If the Contractor is unwilling to accept such orders, and the proposed method of payment is through the Credit Card, the Contractor must so advise the ordering activity within 24 hours of receipt of order. (Reference clause 52.232-36, Payment by Third Party.) Failure to return an order or advise the ordering activity within the time frames of this paragraph shall constitute acceptance whereupon all provisions of the contract shall apply.

(g) The Government is obligated to purchase under each resultant contract a guaranteed minimum of $2,500 (two thousand, five hundred dollars) during the contract term.

(h) All users of GSA's Federal Supply Schedules, including non-Federal users, shall use the schedules in accordance with the ordering guidance provided by the Administrator of General Services. GSA encourages non-Federal users to follow the Schedule Ordering Procedures set forth in the Federal Acquisition Regulation (FAR) 8.4, but they may use different established competitive ordering procedures if such procedures are needed to satisfy their state and local acquisition regulations and/or organizational policies.

Note that ordering eligibility notwithstanding, a schedule contractor is obligated to accept orders only from Executive branch organizations.

Clause I-FSS-106, Guaranteed Minimum (JUL 2003), states:

The minimum that the Government agrees to order during the period of this contract is $2,500. If the Contractor receives total orders for less than $2,500 during the term of the contract, the Government will pay the difference between the amount ordered and $2,500.

(a) Payment of any amount due under this clause shall be contingent upon the Contractor's timely submission of GSA Form 72A reports (see GSAR 552.238-74 "Industrial Funding Fee and Sales Reporting") during the period of the contract and receipt of the close-out sales report pursuant to GSAR 552.238-74.

(b) The guaranteed minimum applies only if the contract expires or contract cancellation is initiated by the Government. The guaranteed minimum does not apply if the contract is terminated for cause or if the contract is canceled at the request of the Contractor.

Clause I-FSS-163, Option to Extend the Term of the Contract (Evergreen) (APR 2000), provides:

(a) The Government may require continued performance of this contract for an additional 5 year period when it is determined that exercising the option is advantageous to the Government considering price and other factors. The option clause may not be exercised more than three times. When the option to extend the term of this contract is exercised the following conditions are applicable:

(1) It is determined that exercising the option is advantageous to the Government considering price and the other factors covered in (2 through 4 below).

(2) The Contractor's electronic catalog/pricelist has been received, approved, posted, and kept current on GSA Advantage!™ in accordance with clause I-FSS-600, Contract Price Lists.

(3) Performance has been acceptable under the contract.

(4) Subcontracting goals have been reviewed and approved.

(b) The Contracting Officer may exercise the option by providing a written notice to the Contractor within 30 days, unless otherwise noted, prior to the expiration of the contract or option.

(c) When the Government exercises its option to extend the term of this contract, prices in effect at the time the option is exercised will remain in effect during the option period, unless an adjustment is made in accordance with another contract clause (e.g., Economic Price Adjustment Clause or Price Reduction Clause).

In addition to the termination for convenience and termination for cause articles in FAR 52.212-4, schedule contracts include GSAM/GSAR 552.238-79, Cancellation (MAY 2019), which provides as follows:

Either party may cancel this contract in whole or in part by providing written notice. The cancellation will take effect 30 calendar days after the other party receives the notice of cancellation. If the Contractor elects to cancel this contract, the Government will not reimburse the minimum guarantee.

[D] Contract Pricing

FAR 8.404(d) describes the pricing of schedule contracts:

Supplies offered on the schedule are listed at fixed prices. Services offered on the schedule are priced either at hourly rates, or at a fixed price for performance of a specific task (e.g., installation, maintenance, and repair). GSA has already determined the prices of supplies and fixed-price services, and rates for services offered at hourly rates, under schedule contracts to be fair and reasonable. Therefore, ordering activities are not required to make a separate determination of fair and reasonable pricing, except for a price evaluation as required by 8.405-2(d). By placing an order against a schedule contract using the procedures in 8.405, the ordering activity has concluded that the order represents the best value (as defined in FAR 2.101) and results in the lowest overall cost alternative (considering price, special features, administrative costs, etc.) to meet the Government's needs. Although GSA has already negotiated fair and reasonable pricing, ordering activities may seek additional discounts before placing an order (see 8.405-4).

Although GSA maintains that it has determined that the prices in schedule contracts are fair and reasonable, FAR 8.404(d), GAO has long complained that schedule contract prices are not as advantageous as they could be if GSA made greater use of pre-award and postaward contract audits. See *Contract Management: Opportunities Continue for GSA to Improve Pricing of Multiple Award Schedules Contracts*, GAO-05-229, Feb. 2005:

> Contract negotiators at the four MAS acquisition centers that GAO reviewed use a variety of tools for obtaining most favored customer pricing—that is, the prices vendors offer their best customers. However, the GAO analysis of GSA's review of selected fiscal year 2004 MAS contract files found that nearly 60 percent lacked the documentation needed to establish clearly that the prices were effectively negotiated. Specifically, the contract documentation did not establish that negotiated prices were based on accurate, complete, and current vendor information; adequate price analyses; and reasonable price negotiations. GSA's efforts to ensure most favored customer pricing have been hindered by the significant decline in the use of pre-award and postaward audits of pre-award pricing information, two independent pricing tools that have helped GSA avoid or recover hundreds of millions of dollars in excessive pricing. In fiscal year 1995, GSA conducted 154 pre-award audits; by 2004 the number of pre-award audits fell to 40. Postaward audits—which resulted in an average annual recovery of $18 million in the early 1990s—were discontinued in 1997 when GSA revised its MAS contract audit policies to increase the use of pre-award audits—an increase that has not materialized.

Notwithstanding GSA's declaration that schedule prices are fair and reasonable, FAR 8.405-4, states that agencies may seek a price reduction whenever placing an order and must seek a price reduction when placing an order valued in excess of the simplified acquisition threshold. Contractors that agree to give a price reduction to an individual agency are not obligated to give the same reduction to other agencies. Thus, each contracting officer must bargain for better prices to the best of his or her ability.

GSA schedule contracts contain two clauses that provide for price reductions under specified circumstances. GSAM/GSAR 552.215-72, Price Adjustment—Failure to Provide Accurate Information (Aug 1997), states:

> (a) The Government, at its election, may reduce the price of this contract or contract modification if the Contracting Officer determines after award of this contract or contract modification that the price negotiated was increased by a significant amount because the Contractor failed to:
>
> (1) Provide information required by this solicitation/contract or otherwise requested by the Government; or
>
> (2) Submit information that was current, accurate, and complete; or
>
> (3) Disclose changes in the Contractor's commercial pricelist(s), discounts or discounting policies which occurred after the original submission and prior to the completion of negotiations.

(b) The Government will consider information submitted to be current, accurate and complete if the data is current, accurate and complete as of 14 calendar days prior to the date it is submitted.

(c) If any reduction in the contract price under this clause reduces the price for items for which payment was made prior to the date of the modification reflecting the price reduction, the Contractor shall be liable to and shall pay the United States—

> (1) The amount of the overpayment; and
>
> (2) Simple interest on the amount of such overpayment to be computed from the date(s) of overpayment to the Contractor to the date the Government is repaid by the Contractor at the applicable underpayment rate effective each quarter prescribed by the Secretary of Treasury under 26 U.S.C. 6621(a)(2).

(d) Failure to agree on the amount of the decrease shall be resolved as a dispute.

(e) In addition to the remedy in paragraph (a) of this clause, the Government may terminate this contract for default. The rights and remedies of the Government specified herein are not exclusive, and are in addition to any other rights and remedies provided by law or under this contract.

GSAM/GSAR 552.238-81, Price Reductions (May 2019), provides:

(a) Before award of a contract, the Contracting Officer and the Offeror will agree upon (1) the customer (or category of customers) which will be the basis of award, and (2) the Government's price or discount relationship to the identified customer (or category of customers). This relationship shall be maintained throughout the contract period. Any change in the Contractor's commercial pricing or discount arrangement applicable to the identified customer (or category of customers) which disturbs this relationship shall constitute a price reduction.

(b) During the contract period, the Contractor shall report to the Contracting Officer all price reductions to the customer (or category of customers) that was the basis of award. The Contractor's report shall include an explanation of the conditions under which the reductions were made.

(c) (1) A price reduction shall apply to purchases under this contract if, after the date negotiations conclude, the Contractor—

> (i) Revises the commercial catalog, pricelist, schedule or other document upon which contract award was predicated to reduce prices;
>
> (ii) Grants more favorable discounts or terms and conditions than those contained in the commercial catalog, pricelist, schedule or other documents upon which contract award was predicated; or
>
> (iii) Grants special discounts to the customer (or category of customers) that formed the basis of award, and the change disturbs the price/discount relationship of the Government to the customer (or category of customers) that was the basis of award.

(2) The Contractor shall offer the price reduction to the Government with the same effective date, and for the same time period, as extended to the commercial customer (or category of customers).

(d) There shall be no price reduction for sales—

(1) To commercial customers under firm, fixed-price definite quantity contracts with specified delivery in excess of the maximum order threshold specified in this contract;

(2) To Federal agencies;

(3) Made to Eligible Ordering Activities identified in GSAR Clause 552.238-113 when the order is placed under this contract (and the Eligible Ordering Activities identified in GSAR Clause 552.238-113is the agreed upon customer or category of customer that is the basis of award); or

(4) Caused by an error in quotation or billing, provided adequate documentation is furnished by the Contractor to the Contracting Officer.

(e) The Contractor may offer the Contracting Officer a voluntary Governmentwide price reduction at any time during the contract period.

(f) The Contractor shall notify the Contracting Officer of any price reduction subject to this clause as soon as possible, but not later than 15 calendar days after its effective date.

(g) The contract will be modified to reflect any price reduction which becomes applicable in accordance with this clause.

Schedule contracts also include the GSAM/GSAR 552.216-70, Economic Price Adjustment—FSS Multiple Award Schedule Contracts (Sep 1999) clause, which permits contractors to submit price decreases at any time and to request price increases under specified circumstances.

Contract prices must include the industrial funding fee that GSA charges to agencies that use schedule contracts. Contractors must report sales and remit the fees to GSA. See the GSAM/GSAR 552.238-80, Industrial Funding Fee and Sales Reporting (Jul 2020) clause:

(a) Reporting of Federal Supply Schedule Sales. The Contractor shall report all contract sales under this contract as follows:

(1) The Contractor shall accurately report the dollar value, in U.S. dollars and rounded to the nearest whole dollar, of all sales under this contract by calendar quarter (January 1-March 31, April 1-June 30, July 1-September 30, and October 1-December 31). The dollar value of a sale is the price paid by the Schedule user for products and services on a Schedule task or delivery order. The reported contract sales value shall include the Industrial Funding Fee (IFF). The Contractor shall maintain a consistent accounting method of sales reporting, based on the Contractor's established commercial accounting practice. The acceptable points at which sales may be reported include—

(i) Receipt of order;
(ii) Shipment or delivery, as applicable;
(iii) Issuance of an invoice; or
(iv) Payment.

(2) Contract sales shall be reported to Federal Acquisition Services (FAS) within 30 calendar days following the completion of each reporting quarter. The Contractor shall continue to furnish quarterly reports, including "zero" sales, through physical completion of the last outstanding task order or delivery order of the contract.

(3) Reportable sales under the contract are those resulting from sales of contract items to authorized users unless the purchase was conducted pursuant to a separate contracting authority such as a Governmentwide Acquisition Contract (GWAC); a separately awarded FAR Part 12, FAR Part 13, FAR Part 14, or FAR Part 15 procurement; or a non-FAR contract. Sales made to state and local governments under Cooperative Purchasing authority shall be counted as reportable sales for IFF purposes.

(4) The Contractor shall electronically report the quarterly dollar value of sales, including "zero" sales, by utilizing the automated reporting system at an Internet website designated by the General Services Administration (GSA)'s Federal Acquisition Service (FAS). Prior to using this automated system, the Contractor shall complete contract registration with the FAS Vendor Support Center (VSC). The website address, as well as registration instructions and reporting procedures, will be provided at the time of award. The Contractor shall report sales separately for each National Stock Number (NSN), Special Item Number (SIN), or sub-item.

(5) The Contractor shall convert the total value of sales made in foreign currency to U.S. dollars using the "Treasury Reporting Rates of Exchange" issued by the U.S. Department of Treasury, Financial Management Service. The Contractor shall use the issue of the Treasury report in effect on the last day of the calendar quarter. The report is available from Financial Management Service, International Funds Branch, Telephone: (202) 874-7994, Internet: http://www.fiscal.treasury.gov/fsreports/rpt/treasRptRateExch/treasRptRateExch_home.htm.

(b) The Contractor shall remit the IFF at the rate set by GSA's FAS.

(1) The Contractor shall remit the IFF to FAS in U.S. dollars within 30 calendar days after the end of the reporting quarter; final payment shall be remitted within 30 days after physical completion of the last outstanding task order or delivery order of the contract.

(2) The IFF represents a percentage of the total quarterly sales reported. This percentage is set at the discretion of GSA's FAS. GSA's FAS has the unilateral right to change the percentage at any time, but not more than once per year. FAS will provide reasonable notice prior to the effective date of the change. The IFF reimburses FAS for the costs

> of operating the Federal Supply Schedules Program. FAS recoups its operating costs from ordering activities as set forth in 40 U.S.C. 321. Offerors must include the IFF in their prices. The fee is included in the award price(s) and reflected in the total amount charged to ordering activities. FAS will post notice of the current IFF at *https://srp.fas.gsa.gov/* or successor website as appropriate.
>
> (c) Within 60 days of award, an FAS representative will provide the Contractor with specific written procedural instructions on remitting the IFF. FAS reserves the unilateral right to change such instructions from time to time, following notification to the Contractor.
>
> (d) Failure to remit the full amount of the IFF within 30 calendar days after the end of the applicable reporting period constitutes a contract debt to the United States Government under the terms of FAR Subpart 32.6. The Government may exercise all rights under the Debt Collection Improvement Act of 1996, including withholding or setting off payments and interest on the debt (see FAR clause 52.232-17, Interest). Should the Contractor fail to submit the required sales reports, falsify them, or fail to timely pay the IFF, this is sufficient cause for the Government to terminate the contract for cause.

After award, contractors are required to publish price lists containing the agreed upon SIN prices. See the GSAM/GSAR 552.238-77 Submission and Distribution of Authorized FSS Schedule Pricelists (MAR 2020) clause:

> (a) The Contractor shall submit its Authorized Federal Supply Schedule Price List on a common-use electronic medium as prescribed by GSA. Some structured data entry in a prescribed format may be required.
>
> (b) Eligible ordering activities will utilize GSA's online shopping and ordering system to review a Contractors' price lists.

[E] Use of GSA Schedule Contracts by Federal Agencies

[1] Requirement for Use

Agencies may use GSA schedule contracts at their discretion, unless an agency is listed in a schedule as a mandatory user or the agency has an obligation to award the contract through a means of restricted competition. Although FAR 8.002 places schedule contracts ahead of other commercial sources in the prescribed order of priorities for the acquisition of supplies and services, GAO has held that agencies that are not identified in a schedule as mandatory users are not required to order supplies or services from the schedule contract. See *Murray-Benjamin Elec. Co., LP*, Comp. Gen. Dec. B-298481, 2006 CPD ¶ 129:

> [W]hile the list of required sources found in FAR sect. 8.002 places non-mandatory FSS contracts above commercial sources in priority, it does not require an agency to order from the FSS. Further, although an agency's placement of an FSS order indicates that the agency has concluded that the order

represents the best value (FAR § 8.404(d)), the regulation does not establish a presumption that all FSS contractors represent the best value, such that the agency would be required to purchase from an FSS contractor.

In Footnote 4 of that decision, GAO reported that it sought the opinion of GSA, which confirmed that use of a schedule contract is voluntary unless a statute or regulation mandates use of the contract. Thus, an agency is not required to place an order against a schedule contract if it can obtain a better value from a nonschedule contractor. See also *ATA Defense Indus., Inc. v. United States*, 38 Fed. Cl. 489 (1997) (agency may choose competitive procedure that is best suited to the circumstances).

Consistent with the Supreme Court's holding in *Kingdomware Techs., Inc. v. United States*, 579 U.S. 162 (2016), however, Congressional mandates may restrict an agency's ability to rely on the GSA schedule in any given procurement.

[2] Applicability of Small Business Programs

Small business programs raise two similar but distinct issues with respect to GSA schedule contracts: (1) whether agencies must use a mandatory source rather than a small business set-aside before deciding to place an order against a GSA schedule contract and (2) whether agencies placing an order against schedule contracts must consider setting the order aside for competition among small business schedule contractors.

[a] Use of Mandatory Source

The first issue is addressed by FAR 8.002:

> (a) Except as required by 8.003, or as otherwise provided by law, agencies shall satisfy requirements for supplies and services from or through the sources and publications listed below in descending order of priority—
>
> (1) Supplies.
>
> (i) Agency inventories;
>
> (ii) Excess from other agencies (see Subpart 8.1);
>
> (iii) Federal Prison Industries, Inc. (see Subpart 8.6);
>
> (iv) Supplies which are on the Procurement List maintained by the Committee for Purchase From People Who Are Blind or Severely Disabled (see Subpart 8.7);
>
> (v) Wholesale supply sources, such as stock programs of the General Services Administration (GSA) (see 41 CFR 101-26.3), the Defense Logistics Agency (see 41 CFR 101-26.6), the Department of Veterans Affairs (see 41 CFR 101-26.704), and military inventory control points;

> (2) Services.
>
> > (i) Services which are on the Procurement List maintained by the Committee for Purchase From People Who Are Blind or Severely Disabled (see Subpart 8.7);
>
> (b) Sources other than those listed in paragraph (a) of this section may be used as prescribed in 41 CFR 101-26.301 and in an unusual and compelling urgency as prescribed in 6.302-2 and in 41 CFR 101-25.101-5.
>
> (c) The statutory obligation for Government agencies to satisfy their requirements for supplies or services available from the Committee for Purchase From People Who Are Blind or Severely Disabled also applies when contractors purchase the supplies or services for Government use.

See also FAR 19.502-1, which states:

> (a) The contracting officer shall set aside an individual acquisition or class of acquisitions for competition among small businesses when—
>
> > (1) It is determined to be in the interest of maintaining or mobilizing the Nation's full productive capacity, war or national defense programs; or
> >
> > (2) Assuring that a fair proportion of Government contracts in each industry is placed with small business concerns; and the circumstances described in 19.502-2 or 19.502-3(a) exist.
>
> (b) This requirement in paragraph (a) of this section does not apply to purchases at or below the micro-purchase threshold, or purchases from required sources of supply under Part 8 (e.g., Committee for Purchase From People Who are Blind or Severely Disabled).

Thus, when buying supplies or services contracting officers may use schedule contracts rather than a small business set-aside.

This issue was considered in *K-LAK Corp. v. United States*, 98 Fed. Cl. 1 (2011), where a small business which had held a contract with an agency to provide credit reports protested when, after its contract had expired, the agency decided to procure future credit services from a large business under a GSA schedule contract. The court held that the agency was not required to consider setting aside procurements before ordering under the schedules program, stating at 5 - 6:

> Much of the plaintiff's argument rests on the validity of the government's determination that K-LAK and other small businesses were incapable of supplying the credit reports the Air Force needed at a "fair market price." K-LAK argues that the Air Force did not conduct a proper study of market prices under FAR Part 19 (regarding small business set-asides) . . . This so-called "Rule of Two" requires a contracting officer to make a determination as to whether at least two small businesses could provide the relevant good

or service at a fair market price before proceeding with the procurement process with a larger business.

[The government] argues that it was not necessary for the Air Force to evaluate price under FAR Part 19 when it decided to use the FSS, because, by law, the price comparison provisions of Part 19 do not apply when an agency decides to meet its mission requirements through the FSS. In support of this contention, the government points to several FAR provisions, including FAR Part 8, which provides, "Parts 13 . . . 14, 15, and 19 [regarding small business set-asides] (except for the requirement at 19.202-1(e)(1)(iii) [regarding bundling]) do not apply to [blanket purchase agreements ("BPAs")] or orders placed against Federal Supply Schedules contracts . . . ," FAR 8.404(a); FAR Part 38, which states with regard to FSS contracting, "The requirements of parts 5, 6, and 19 apply at the acquisition planning stage prior to issuing the schedule solicitation and do not apply to orders and BPAs placed under resulting schedule contracts (see 8.404)," FAR 38.101(e); and FAR Part 19 on set-asides for small businesses, which states that requirements for setting aside acquisitions do not apply to "purchases from required sources of supply under Part 8 (e.g., . . . Federal Supply Schedule Contracts)," FAR 19.502-1(b).

The court agrees with the government and concludes . . . that because the Air Force decided to use the FSS after K-LAK's contract expired, the Air Force was not required to comply with the Rule of Two or any of the other regulations applicable to small businesses

See also *Edmond Computer Co.*, Comp. Gen. Dec. B-402863, 2010 CPD ¶ 200, stating:

Nothing in the Small Business Act suggests or requires that the Rule of Two which is set forth in the regulations that implement that Act (but is not found in the Act itself), see *Delex Sys., Inc.*, B-400403, Oct. 8, 2008, 2008 CPD ¶ 181 at 6-7-takes precedence over the FSS program. To the contrary, and as noted above, the implementing regulations for the small business set-aside program and the FSS program expressly provide that set-aside requirements for the program do not apply to FSS buys. See FAR sections 8.404(a), 19.502-1(b), 38.101(e). Accordingly, we conclude that the Small Business Act and its implementing regulations do not impose a requirement on agencies to first evaluate whether a solicitation should be set-aside for small businesses before purchasing the goods or services through the FSS program.

See also *Future Solutions, Inc.*, Comp. Gen. Dec. B-293194, 2004 CPD ¶ 39, and *Information Ventures, Inc.*, Comp. Gen. Dec. B-291952, 2003 CPD ¶ 101. Reliance on FAR 8.404(a) in those cases seems misplaced, since that paragraph appears to address the applicability of small business programs in the placement of orders *after* a decision has already been made to conduct the acquisition through the use of a schedule contract. Nevertheless, both the Court of Federal Claims and GAO have cited it as the basis for finding that contracting officers need not consider small business programs before deciding whether to use a schedule contract.

Contrast *Tolliver Grp., Inc. v. United States*, 151 Fed. Cl. 70 (2020), where the Court of Federal Claims addressed a protest challenging an agency's decision to cancel solicitations issued against the FSS and move requirements previously performed by SDVOSB contractors to a multiple-award IDIQ where only large businesses would be eligible to compete. The court found that the agency did violate its obligations under FAR Part 19, including failure to conduct a Rule of Two analysis before soliciting the work under a contract vehicle open only to large businesses, and failure to coordinate with the Small Business Administration before dissolving a pre-existing small business set aside.

[b] Set-aside Requirement

The second issue—whether small business programs apply in the issuance of orders or the establishment of BPAs—is addressed by FAR 8.404(a), which provides in part that FAR Part 19 (except for 19.102(b)(3) and 19.202-1(e)(1)(iii)) does not apply "to BPAs or orders placed against Federal Supply Schedules contracts. . . ." FAR 8.405-5 provides agencies discretion to set aside orders and BPAs for various small business categories.

Accordingly, GAO has held that agencies need not set aside competitions for the placement of orders or for the establishment of BPAs. See *Global Analytic Information Tech. Servs., Inc.*, Comp. Gen. Dec. B-297200.3, 2006 CPD ¶ 53 (agency's withdrawal of small business set aside in schedule competition unobjectionable because FAR Part 19 did not apply to schedule competitions).

Despite the inapplicability of FAR Part 19 to competitions for orders and BPAs under schedule contracts, as noted above an agency may limit competition for an order or for the establishment of a BPA to small business schedule contractors. If it does so, it may require competing contractors to certify their small business status for purposes of the particular competition, even if they previously certified their status for purposes of competing for the GSA schedule contract. See *Software Eng'g Servs. Corp.*, Comp. Gen. Dec. B-411739, 2015 CPD ¶ 215; *CMS Information Servs., Inc.*, Comp. Gen. Dec. B-290541, 2002 CPD ¶ 132.

[3] Responsibility Determinations

The requirements of FAR Subpart 9.1 regarding determinations of the responsibility of prospective contractors do not apply when agencies place orders or establish BPAs under schedule contracts. See *Advanced Tech. Sys., Inc.*, Comp. Gen. Dec. B-296493.6, 2006 CPD ¶ 151, stating:

> Responsibility is a contract formation term that refers to the ability of a prospective contractor to perform the contract for which it has submitted an offer; by law, a contracting officer must determine that an offeror is

> responsible before awarding it a contract. See 41 U.S.C. § 253b(c), (d); FAR § 9.103(a), (b). The concept of responsibility expressly applies to "prospective contractors"—not "current" or "existing" contractors—a limitation that is repeated throughout the applicable statutes and regulations, and that indicates that the requirement for a responsibility determination applies before award of a contract. See, e.g., 41 U.S.C. § 403 ("As used in this Act… the term 'responsible source' means a prospective contractor. . . ."); FAR 9.100 ("This subpart prescribes polices, standards, and procedures for determining whether prospective contractors . . . are responsible"); FAR s 9.102(a) ("This subpart applies to all proposed contracts with any prospective contractor. . . ."); and FAR s 9.103(c) ("A prospective contractor must affirmatively demonstrate its responsibility. . . .").
>
> Consistent with this statutory and regulatory framework, once an offeror is determined to be responsible and is awarded a contract, there is no requirement that an agency make additional responsibility determinations during contract performance. *E. Huttenbauer & Son, Inc.*, B-258018.3, Mar. 20, 1995, 95-1 CPD ¶ 148 at 2 (holding that a contracting officer was not required to make a new responsibility determination before deciding whether to exercise an option because the concept of responsibility has no applicability with respect to a contract once that contract has been awarded). Contrary to the protester's position, the extent of the requirement for a determination of responsibility is not tied to the type of contracting vehicle that the government elects to use for an acquisition; thus, there is no basis to conclude that the requirement for a responsibility determination is broader for orders placed under FSS contracts. In this regard, we note that FAR s 8.405 and s 8.406 set forth the ordering procedures and ordering activity's responsibilities, respectively, with regard to FSS contracts; there is no requirement in these provisions to make a responsibility determination. In sum, we conclude that the initial responsibility determination made by GSA in connection with the award of the underlying FSS contract satisfies the requirement for a responsibility determination regarding that vendor and that there is no requirement that an ordering agency perform separate responsibility determinations when placing orders under that contract. (Footnotes omitted)

While GAO holds that a contracting officer is not required to conduct a responsibility determination before placing an FSS order, where the contracting officer nevertheless chooses to do so, GAO will review the contracting officer's determination. *ESCO Marine, Inc.*, Comp. Gen. Dec. B-401438, 2009 CPD ¶ 234 ("to the extent that our decision in *Advance Tech. Sys., Inc.* can be read for the proposition that a discretionary responsibility determination such as the one at issue here cannot give rise to a valid basis of protest, that aspect of our decision will no longer be followed").

[F] Ordering

Agencies may issue individual orders and may establish a BPA under schedule contracts against which orders may be placed. Procedures for placing orders and establishing BPAs against schedule contracts are in FAR 8.405. FAR 8.405-1 states procedures for ordering supplies and for services at fixed prices for a specific task that do not require a statement of work; FAR 8.405-2 states procedures for ordering services that are priced at hourly rates and that require a statement of work; and FAR 8.405-3 states procedures for establishing BPAs. GSA provides additional procedural guidance at a webpage: Ordering Guidelines, http://www.gsa.gov/portal/category/100639 and in an online publication entitled *GSA Multiple Award Schedules Program Desk Reference*, which is available at http://www.gsa.gov/portal/content/226369.

[1] General Rules

[a] Acquisition Planning

FAR 8.404(c) states that contracting officers must engage in acquisition planning when issuing schedule orders:

> (c) *Acquisition planning*. Orders placed under a Federal Supply Schedule contract—
>
> (1) Are not exempt from the development of acquisition plans (see Subpart 7.1), and an information technology acquisition strategy (see Part 39);
>
> (2) Must comply with all FAR requirements for a consolidated or bundled contract when the order meets the definition at 2.101(b) of "consolidation" "bundling"; and
>
> (3) Must, whether placed by the requiring agency, or on behalf of the requiring agency, be consistent with the requiring agency's statutory and regulatory requirements applicable to the acquisition of the supply or service.

[b] Limiting the Number of Sources to Be Considered

[i] Circumstances Permitting Limitation of Sources

The issuance of orders against schedule contracts is not subject to the full and open competition requirement in the Competition in Contracting Act and its implementing provisions in FAR Subpart 6.1. See FAR 8.405-6:

> Orders placed or BPAs established under Federal Supply Schedules are exempt from the requirements in part 6. However, an ordering activity must

justify its action when restricting consideration in accordance with paragraphs (a) or (b) of this section[.]

Nonetheless, agencies are subject to special notice and competition requirements, 41 U.S.C. § 3302. These requirements are implemented in FAR 8.405-1, 8.405-2, and 8.405-3, as discussed below, and when these requirements are met any limitations on competition are accepted. If these requirements are not met, FAR 8.405-6(a)(1) describes other circumstances that would justify limiting sources when the order or BPA will exceed the micro-purchase threshold:

(a) *Orders or BPAs exceeding the micro-purchase threshold based on a limited sources justification.*

(1) Circumstances justifying limiting the source.

(i) For a proposed order or BPA with an estimated value exceeding the micro-purchase threshold not placed or established in accordance with the procedures in 8.405-1, 8.405-2, or 8.405-3, the only circumstances that may justify the action are—

(A) An urgent and compelling need exists, and following the procedures would result in unacceptable delays;

(B) Only one source is capable of providing the supplies or services required at the level of quality required because the supplies or services are unique or highly specialized; or

(C) In the interest of economy and efficiency, the new work is a logical follow-on to an original Federal Supply Schedule order provided that the original order was placed in accordance with the applicable Federal Supply Schedule ordering procedures. The original order or BPA must not have been previously issued under sole-source or limited-sources procedures.

(ii) See 8.405-6(c) for the content of the justification for an order or BPA exceeding the simplified acquisition threshold.

FAR 8.405-6(b)(1) states an additional restriction on the use of brand name specifications:

(b) *Items peculiar to one manufacturer.*
An item peculiar to one manufacturer can be a particular brand name, product, or a feature of a product, peculiar to one manufacturer. A brand name item, whether available on one or more schedule contracts, is an item peculiar to one manufacturer.

(1) Brand name specifications shall not be used unless the particular brand name, product, or feature is essential to the Government's requirements, and market research indicates other companies' similar products, or products lacking the particular feature, do not meet, or cannot be modified to meet, the agency's needs.

[ii] Requirement for Written Justification

FAR 8.405-6(b)(2) requires that contracting officers document the basis for using a brand name specification in an order or BPA valued at less than the simplified acquisition threshold. This document is distinct from the justification described in FAR 8.405-6(c). When using a brand name specification in an order or BPA valued in excess of the simplified acquisition threshold, contracting officers must prepare a limited sources justification and obtain its approval in accordance with FAR 8.405-6(c).

[iii] Justification Approval Levels

FAR 8.405-6(d) details the various approval requirements needed for approval of justifications for limiting sources. for orders and BPAs exceeding the simplified acquisition threshold. Contracting officers can approve such actions up to $750,000. Above that amount, approval by higher level officials is required.

[iv] Requirement to Post Justification

FAR 8.405-6(b)(3)(i) requires that when an agency uses a brand name specification in an order or BPA valued in excess of $25,000 but not exceeding the simplified acquisition threshold, the agency must post the document explaining the basis for that decision at *e-Buy* along with any RFQ. FAR 8.405-6(b)(3)(ii) establishes three exceptions to the posting requirement:

> (A) Disclosure would compromise the national security (e.g., would result in disclosure of classified information) or create other security risks. The fact that access to classified matter may be necessary to submit a proposal or perform the contract does not, in itself, justify use of this exception;
>
> (B) The nature of the file (e.g., size, format) does not make it cost-effective or practicable for contracting officers to provide access through e-Buy; or
>
> (C) The agency's senior procurement executive makes a written determination that access through e-Buy is not in the Government's interest.

Generally, FAR 5.301(a)(2)(i) and 8.405-6(a)(2) require that agencies post approved justifications for limiting sources at the Governmentwide Point of Entry, www.SAM.gov, within 14 days after placing an order or establishing a BPA unless the limitation was based on an unusual or compelling urgency, in which case the justification must be posted within 30 days. Contracting officers must screen justifications and remove proprietary information and information protected pursuant to FAR 24.202. FAR 5.301(a)(3) and 8.405-6(a)(2)(iii) state that justifications need not be posted if to do so would compromise national security or create other security risks.

In reviewing an agency's justification for limiting sources, GAO will apply "logical scrutiny," and will require supporting analyses and documentation, *NCS*

Techs., Inc., Comp. Gen. Dec. B-403435, 2010 CPD ¶ 281 (protest sustained in absence of analyses and documentation supporting restriction specifications based on need for standardization). An agency's judgment will stand as long as it is reasonable, *Systems Integration & Mgmt., Inc.*, Comp. Gen. Dec. B-402785.2, 2010 CPD ¶ 207 (mere disagreement with agency's limitation of sources based on "compelling need" does not show agency's judgment was unreasonable); *Computers Universal, Inc.*, Comp. Gen. Dec. B-296536, 2005 CPD ¶ 160 (agency reasonably extended FSS order for short period until pending protest resolved).

GAO will, however, sustain the protest of an inadequately justified brand name restriction. *Desktop Alert, Inc.*, Comp. Gen. Dec. B-408196, 2013 CPD ¶ 179.

[c] Contractor Teams

GSA allows schedule contractors to form teams to submit quotes for orders or BPAs. Contractor team arrangements (CTAs) are private relationships in which the government does not participate. A CTA is not a prime-subcontractor relationship, in which the prime remains wholly responsible for performance. Under a CTA, all team members must be schedule contractors and are to be in privity with the government under the order or BPA. GSA describes CTAs as follows at its website: *http://www.gsa.gov/portal/content/202257*:

> A GSA Schedule Contractor Team Arrangement (CTA) is an arrangement in which two or more GSA Schedule contractors team together to provide a total solution to meet a customer's needs. Under Schedule CTAs, contractors complement each other and it allows teams to compete for orders for which they may not qualify independently. GSA encourages the use of CTAs to meet buyer's requirements.
>
> NOTE: FAR 9.6, Contractor Team Arrangements, does not apply to GSA Schedules teaming. Under GSA Schedules, Teaming allows contractors to use their individual GSA Schedules to develop a solution for the government.
>
> The Schedules CTA does not create a separate legal entity, but allows Schedule contractors to meet buyer's requirements by combining the supplies and/or services from each team member's separate Schedule contract in response to a buyer's Request for Quote.

Schedule contracts include the I-FSS-40, Contractor Team Arrangements (Dec. 2019) clause, which provides as follows:

> Contractors participating in contractor team arrangements must abide by all terms and conditions of their respective contracts. This includes compliance with contract clause 552.238-80, Industrial Funding Fee and Sales

Reporting, i.e., each contractor (team member) must report sales and remit the IFF for all products and services provided under its individual contract.

[d] Protests

Unlike the award of orders against delivery order and task order contracts pursuant to FAR Subpart 16.5, which may be protested to GAO, but not to the Court of Federal Claims, when in excess of $10 million ($25 million for DoD), the award of orders and BPAs under schedule contracts may be protested to GAO and to the Court of Federal Claims regardless of dollar value. GAO has found that such protests fall within the jurisdiction granted it by the Competition in Contracting Act. See *Panacea Consulting, Inc.*, Comp. Gen. Dec. B-299307.4, 2007 CPD ¶ 141 (note 1):

> The agency, citing 41 U.S.C. § 253j(d) (2000) (which generally prohibits protests against the issuance of a task or delivery order under indefinite-delivery, indefinite-quantity contracts), asserts that our Office lacks jurisdiction to consider these protests because it is placing task orders against blanket purchase agreements entered into between the agency and vendors pursuant to the vendors' FSS contracts. The agency is incorrect. The task orders ultimately are to be placed against the successful vendor's FSS contract. The limitation on our jurisdiction to consider task/delivery order protests does not extend to orders issued under the FSS. Thus, the protests here are subject to our jurisdiction. *Severn Cos., Inc.*, B-275717.2, Apr. 28, 1997, 97-1 CPD ¶ 181 at 2-3 n.1; see also *CMS Info. Servs., Inc.*, B-290541, Aug. 7, 2002, 2002 CPD ¶ 132 at 4 n.7 (no basis to distinguish between issuance of task orders and blanket purchase agreements under the FSS since, in both cases, the acquiring activity ultimately is placing orders against a vendor's FSS contract).

See also *Savantage Financial Servs., Inc.*, Comp. Gen. Dec. B-292046, 2003 CPD ¶ 113; and *Labat-Anderson, Inc.*, Comp. Gen. Dec. B-287081, 2001 CPD ¶ 79.

The Federal Circuit has similarly confirmed that agency orders against the GSA schedules fall within the Court of Federal Claims' protest jurisdiction, as compared to orders against GWAC and IDIQ contract vehicles that are subject to the FASA task order protest bar. *Coast Pro., Inc. v. United States*, 828 F.3d 1349 (Fed. Cir. 2016). This is consistent with several prior Court of Federal Claims decisions. See *Data Mgmt. Servs. Joint Venture v. United States*, 78 Fed. Cl. 366 (2007), stating at 370-71:

> We have jurisdiction pursuant to the Tucker Act, 28 U.S.C. § 1491(b)(1) (2000), as amended by the Administrative Dispute Resolution Act of 1996, Pub.L. No. 104-320, § 12, 110 Stat. 3870, 3874-75 (1996), to consider an action by an interested party objecting to an award of a contract and any

> alleged violation of a statute or regulation in connection with a procurement. We may provide any relief, including declaratory and injunctive relief, we deem proper. 28 U.S.C. § 1491(b) (2). The court's protest jurisdiction extends to protests of task or delivery orders placed against a GSA schedule contract. See *IDEA Int'l, Inc. v. United States*, 74 Fed. Cl. 129, 135-37 (2006).

In a footnote, the court addressed what had appeared to be past inconsistencies in its reasoning about jurisdiction:

> Although the government does not question jurisdiction, it is worth clarifying a past inconsistency in the court's treatment of the issue. In *Group Seven Assocs., LLC v. United States*, 68 Fed. Cl. 28 (2005), the court suggested that "jurisdiction [was] doubtful" with respect to protests of task orders placed against a GSA schedule contract. *Id.* at 32. That conclusion was based on the fact that the court's protest jurisdiction does not extend to the issuance of all task and delivery orders. The Federal Acquisition Streamlining Act ("FASA") of 1994, Pub.L. No. 103-355, 108 Stat. 3243 (codified in scattered sections of Title 10 and 41 of the United States Code), authorized a new type of multiple award contract called either a "task order contract" or "delivery order contract," defined at 41 U.S.C. § 253k. See 41 U.S.C. § 253h(a) (2000). Under this new authority, any executive agency may issue task and delivery order contracts for the procurement of services or property. These contracts are different from GSA schedule contracts, however, even though both types of contracts utilize task or delivery orders to trigger performance or delivery. One of the ways in which FASA sought to streamline the government's acquisition of supplies and services was to prohibit protests on the issuance of task or delivery orders, except in limited circumstances. See 41 U.S.C. § 253j(d). This limitation on protests only applies to orders issued under the newly authorized "task order contracts" or "delivery order contracts" (i.e., contracts authorized under 41 U.S.C. § 253h or 253i), see 41 U.S.C. § 253f, not orders placed against GSA schedule contracts. See *IDEA Int'l*, 74 Fed.Cl. at 135-37. The court's reservations with respect to jurisdiction in *Group Seven* were therefore unfounded.

[2] Specific Ordering Procedures

[a] General

FAR 8.405-1(b) and 8.405-2(c)(1) state that agencies may place orders valued at or below the micro-purchase threshold with any contractor and prescribe no particular method of selection. Procedures for orders valued in excess of the micro-purchase threshold generally fall into two broad categories: (a) procedures in FAR 8.405-1 for ordering supplies and services at fixed prices for specific tasks that do not require a statement of work and (b) procedures in FAR 8.405-2 for ordering services priced at hourly rates that require a statement of work. The latter procedures are more demanding and time-consuming when the value of services exceeds the simplified acquisition threshold. The key procedural distinctions are: (a) how many schedule contractors an agency must consider or solicit and (b) whether the agency may make a selection simply by reviewing information or must solicit head-to-head competition by issuing an RFQ.

[b] Orders Requiring a Statement of Work

Whenever an agency seeks to buy a service that is not described in a schedule contract as a task that can be procured for a fixed price, it must describe the service that it wants to buy in sufficient detail to permit prospective contractors to prepare quotes and to establish a basis for quality assurance.

[i] Preparing the Statement of Work

If an agency's needs are generic, it might be able to describe the service that it wants in a few words or short paragraphs. However, if the agency's needs are custom, specific, and detailed, it may need to write a more extensive description. Such a detailed description is called a "statement of work." FAR does not define the term statement of work or work statement, nor does it prescribe the organization or content of statements of work in any detail except in FAR 35.005 for research and development. The term statement of work appears only once in FAR Part 37, where it is mentioned in the definition of "performance based contracting." A "performance work statement," as defined in FAR 2.101, is a type of statement of work:

> "Performance Work Statement (PWS)" means a statement of work for performance-based acquisitions that describes the required results in clear, specific and objective terms with measurable outcomes.

FAR 37.602 provides the following minimal guidance:

> (a) A Performance work statement (PWS) may be prepared by the Government or result from a Statement of objectives (SOO) prepared by the Government where the offeror proposes the PWS.
>
> (b) Agencies shall, to the maximum extent practicable—
>
> (1) Describe the work in terms of the required results rather than either "how" the work is to be accomplished or the number of hours to be provided (see 11.002(a)(2) and 11.101);
>
> (2) Enable assessment of work performance against measurable performance standards;
>
> (3) Rely on the use of measurable performance standards and financial incentives in a competitive environment to encourage competitors to develop and institute innovative and cost-effective methods of performing the work.

(c) Offerors use the SOO to develop the PWS; however, the SOO does not become part of the contract. The SOO shall, at a minimum, include—

(1) Purpose;
(2) Scope or mission;
(3) Period and place of performance;
(4) Background;
(5) Performance objectives, i.e., required results; and
(6) Any operating constraints.

Thus, it is not clear when a description of services becomes sufficiently detailed to warrant being called a statement of work. That being the case, it may not always be clear when an agency must use the more demanding ordering procedures in FAR 8.405-2. *If* an agency must use a statement of work, FAR 8.405-2(b) states:

> Statements of Work (SOWs). All Statements of Work shall include the work to be performed; location of work; period of performance; deliverable schedule; applicable performance standards; and any special requirements (e.g., security clearances, travel, special knowledge). To the maximum extent practicable, agency requirements shall be performance-based statements (see Subpart 37.6).

[ii] Ordering Procedures

The procedures in FAR 8.405-2 apply when an agency must write a statement of work to describe the services that it wants to buy. FAR 8.405-2 requires that agencies solicit head-to-head competition by issuing an RFQ. FAR 8.405-2(a) states:

> Ordering activities shall use the procedures in this subsection when ordering services priced at hourly rates as established by the schedule contracts. The applicable services will be identified in the Federal Supply Schedule publications and the contractor's pricelists.

The introductory paragraph in FAR 8.405-2(c) states:

> *Request for Quotation procedures*. The ordering activity must provide the Request for Quotation (RFQ), which includes the statement of work and evaluation criteria (e.g., experience and past performance), to schedule contractors that offer services that will meet the agency's needs. The RFQ may be posted to GSA's electronic RFQ system, e-Buy (see 8.402(d)).

FAR 8.405-2(e) requires the following minimum documentation:

> (1) The schedule contracts considered, noting the contractor from which the service was purchased;

(2) A description of the service purchased;

(3) The amount paid;

(4) The evaluation methodology used in selecting the contractor to receive the order;

(5) The rationale for any tradeoffs in making the selection;

(6) The price reasonableness determination required by paragraph (d) of this subsection;

(7) The rationale for using other than—

(i) A firm-fixed price order; or

(ii) A performance-based order; and

(8) When an order exceeds the simplified acquisition threshold, evidence of compliance with the ordering procedures at 8.405-2(c).

Following award, losing contractors must be notified and given "a brief explanation of the basis for the award decision," FAR 8.405-2(d).

(A) Orders Exceeding the Micro-purchase Threshold but not the Simplified Acquisition Threshold

When the services are valued in excess of the micro-purchase threshold, but at or below the simplified acquisition threshold, FAR 8.405-2(c)(2)(ii) requires that the agency provide its RFQ to at least three schedule contractors that offer services that will meet its needs. The agency must prepare a written explanation if it is unable to provide the RFQ to at least three contractors. The agency must specify the desired pricing arrangement—e.g., firm-fixed-price or time-and-materials.

(B) Orders Exceeding the Simplified Acquisition Threshold

When an order will exceed the simplified acquisition threshold, FAR 8.405-2(c)(3)(iii) requires that the agency either post the RFQ at the *e-Buy* website or provide it to as many schedule contractors as practicable to ensure receipt of at least three quotes from capable contractors. An agency that chooses the latter course of action and receives fewer than three quotes must prepare a written statement that, despite its efforts, no other contractors could be found, and it must describe the efforts that it undertook to find at least three schedule contractors to submit quotes. The agency must evaluate quotes received in accordance with the terms of the RFQ.

[c] Compliance with Other FAR Procedures

FAR 8.404(a) states that agencies need not comply with FAR Parts 13, 14, or 15 when placing orders or establishing BPAs:

> (a) General. Parts 13 (except 13.303-2(c)(3)), 14, 15, and 19 (except for the requirement at 19.102(b)(3) 19.202-1(e)(1)(iii)) do not apply to BPAs or orders placed against Federal Supply Schedules contracts (but see 8.405-5). BPAs and orders placed against a MAS, using the procedures in this subpart, are considered to be issued using full and open competition (see 6.102(d)(3)). Therefore, when establishing a BPA (as authorized by 13.303-2(c)(3)), or placing orders under Federal Supply Schedule contracts using the procedures of 8.405, ordering activities shall not seek competition outside of the Federal Supply Schedules or synopsize the requirement; but see paragraph (g) of this section [regarding contract actions funded by the American Recovery and Reinvestment Act of 2009].

Thus, unless otherwise stated in agency-specific rules or in the RFQ, there is no requirement to reject late quotes, conduct a public bid opening, prepare a source selection plan, establish a proposal evaluation board, establish a competitive range, conduct discussions with all offerors in the competitive range, request final proposal revisions from all offerors in the competitive range, or provide a debriefing. See *Ellsworth Assocs., Inc. v. United States*, 45 Fed. Cl. 388 (1999), stating at 395-96:

> The purpose of the FSS program is to provide federal agencies with a simplified process for obtaining certain goods and services. See FAR § 8.401, § 8.404(a). When agencies take this approach, no requirement mandates that contractors receive any advance notice of the agency's needs or the selection criteria. See FAR § 8.404(a). Because Part 8 contemplates agencies ordering off the schedule, no regulations govern the proper procedure for selecting contractors. See FAR § 8.401. This is consistent with the simplified and flexible approach Part 8 takes toward procurements. To be sure, within the FSS program an agency may choose, for any number of reasons, to engage in a more comprehensive selection process than contemplated by the scheme. When that occurs, a frustrated bidder may still challenge the agency award under the arbitrary and capricious standard articulated in 5 U.S.C. § 706(2)(A). However, the protester will not be able to prevail on the theory that the procurement procedure involved a clear and prejudicial violation of applicable statutes and regulations, because no applicable procedural regulations are contained in Part 8. A protester instead must rely on establishing that the government officials involved in the procurement process were without a rational and reasonable basis for their decision.

See also *Harmonia Holdings Grp., LLC v. United States*, 136 Fed. Cl. 298 (2018) ("Because this was a simplified procurement under FAR Subpart 8.4, Harmonia must demonstrate that FTA's decision had no rational basis.")

Following *Ellsworth*, however, the court has recognized that the FAR has been amended to require various procedural requirements for FSS orders, providing a stronger basis for review of protests challenging FSS orders. See *MVS USA, Inc. v. United States*, 111 Fed. Cl. 639 (2013), stating at 649-50:

> At the outset, the court notes that "a procurement under [S]ubpart 8.4 is different in kind from one conducted under Part 15, even if some procedures also present in Part 15 are u[s]ed." *Holloway & Co., PLLC v. United States*, 87 Fed. Cl. 381, 393 (2009) (quoting *Systems Plus, Inc. v. United States*, 68 Fed. Cl. 206, 211 (2005)) (alteration in original). In short, the rigorous competitive procedures in Part 15 do not necessarily apply. *See id.* The government argues that this distinction means that MVS cannot base its challenge on a clear and prejudicial violation of the FAR, relying on *Ellsworth Assocs., Inc. v. United States*, 45 Fed. Cl. 388 (1999)....
>
> In making this argument, however, the government fails to acknowledge that FAR Part 8 has been amended to include procedural requirements in the 14 years since *Ellsworth* was decided. Saliently, FAR 8.405–2(c)(3)(iii)(C), on which MVS relies, was established by Interim Rule, effective May 16, 2011, and as a Final Rule, effective April 2, 2012. See 76 Fed. Reg. 14541, 14548 (Mar. 16, 2011) (establishing the interim rule); 77 Fed. Reg. 12912, 12927 (Mar. 2, 2012) (establishing the final rule). Those rules implemented Section 863 of the Duncan Hunter National Defense Authorization Act for Fiscal Year 2009, Pub. L. 110–417, 122 Stat. 4356 (Oct. 14, 2008). "Section 863 mandated the development and publication of regulations in the FAR to enhance competition for the award of orders placed under multiple-award contracts." 76 Fed. Reg. 14548. As such, FAR 8.405–2(c)(3)(iii)(C) is a procedural regulation that this court may enforce and which could provide a basis for a claim that the government engaged in a clear and prejudicial violation of the FAR.

See also *Holloway & Co., PLLC v. United States*, 87 Fed. Cl. 381 (2009) (agency not required to comply with Part 15 procedures for evaluation price); *Systems Plus, Inc. v. United States*, 68 Fed. Cl. 206 (2005) (schedule ordering procedure not a "competitive proposals" requiring compliance with FAR Part 15 debriefing requirement). Accord, *Source Diversified, Inc.*, Comp. Gen. Dec. B-403437.2, 2010 CPD ¶ 297; *Digital Solutions, Inc.*, Comp. Gen. Dec. B-402067, 2010 CPD ¶ 26; *Carahsoft Tech. Corp.*, Comp. Gen. Dec. B-401169, 2009 CPD ¶ 134; *OPTIMUS Corp.*, Comp. Gen. Dec. B-400777, 2009 CPD ¶ 33.

When an agency issues an RFQ and solicits head-to-head competition based on stated evaluation criteria, it will place an extra procedural burden upon itself if it adopts procedures similar to the competitive negotiation procedures in FAR Part 15. In the event of a protest, GAO may apply its standards of review for source selections under Part 15, which otherwise would not apply. See *CourtSmart Digital Sys., Inc.*, Comp. Gen. Dec. B-292995.2, 2004 CPD ¶ 79:

> [U]nder the FSS program, FAR Subpart 8.4 anticipates that an agency will review vendors' schedules and place an order with the vendor whose goods or services represent the best value and meet the agency's needs at the lowest overall cost. *KPMG Consulting LLP*, B-290716, B-290716.2, Sept. 23, 2002, 2002 CPD ¶ 196 at 10-11; *OSI Collection Servs. Inc.; C.B. Accounts, Inc.*, B-286597.3 *et al.*, June 12, 2001, 2001 CPD ¶ 103 at 4. If,

> however, the agency issues an RFQ and thus shifts the burden to the vendors for selecting the items from their schedules, the agency must provide guidance about its needs and selection criteria sufficient to allow the vendors to compete intelligently. Where, as here, the agency intends to use the vendors' responses as the basis of a detailed technical evaluation and selection decision, the agency has elected to use an approach that is more like a competition in a negotiated procurement than a simple FSS buy, and the RFQ is therefore required to provide for a fair and equitable competition. *COMARK Fed. Sys.*, B-278343, B-278343.2, Jan. 20, 1998, 98-1 CPD ¶ 34 at 4-5. While we recognize that the FAR Part 15 procedures, for contracting by negotiation, do not govern the FSS program, *Computer Prods., Inc.*, s20 B-284702, May 24, 2000, 2000 CPD ¶ 95 at 4, where, as here, the agency has conducted such a competition and a protest is filed, we will review the record to ensure that the evaluation is reasonable and consistent with the terms of the solicitation and with standards generally applicable to negotiated procurements. *KPMG Consulting LLP*, *supra*.

See also *USCG, Inc.*, Comp. Gen. Dec. B-400184.2, 2009 CPD ¶ 9; *Advanced Tech. Sys., Inc.*, Comp. Gen. Dec. B-298854, 2007 CPD ¶ 22.

If an agency adopts a FAR Part 15 approach, the Court of Federal Claims may also assess the agency's evaluation and award consistent with FAR Part 15 principles. This issue often arises in relation to discussions, with the court finding that an agency's conduct during the procurement essentially adopted FAR Part 15 discussions standards. See *Centerra Grp., LLC v. United States*, 138 Fed. Cl. 407 (2018), stating at 415-16:

> The government and Paragon argue that the communications between Paragon and DOJ during the remand were proper because of the type of procurement at issue here, a GSA FSS task order RFQ conducted pursuant to FAR Subpart 8.4. Underlying this argument is the premise that there are fundamental differences between purchases made through the FSS, under FAR Subpart 8.4, and negotiated acquisitions under FAR Part 15. The premise is sound, in that an agency that purchases services through the FSS is not bound to follow the procedures or obey the restrictions imposed by FAR Part 15. However, an agency's exemption from FAR Part 15 is not absolute—an agency can elect to use procedures from these other parts such as FAR Part 15, although they are not presumptively applicable.
>
> Where, as here, an agency has already conducted two rounds of discussions with offerors remaining in the competition, and allowed proposal revisions after each round, the overwhelming weight of authority is that the agency must conduct any future discussions in conformance with the fairness principles enshrined in FAR Part 15, notwithstanding the fact that the procurement is otherwise governed by FAR Subpart 8.4. This is true for the simple reason that the relevant provisions of FAR Part 15 provide safeguards against communications with the agency which unfairly favor one offeror over another. The court turns first to persuasive GAO precedent on this issue.
>
> . . . .

> Thus, this court, while refusing to shoehorn FAR Subpart 8.4 procurements into the procedures outlined in FAR Part 15, will review the agency's actions to ensure that [the agency] did not violate the requirement of fundamental fairness in the procurement process by conducting discussions with only the awardee. . . .
>
> The court recognizes that the application of these fairness principles varies according to the specific facts of each protest. To the extent that there may be some disagreement as to the propriety, in general, of looking to FAR Part 15 when reviewing the fairness of discussions held in FAR Subpart 8.4 procurements, the court finds that in this case, recourse to FAR Part 15, at least for the relevant definitions of clarifications and discussions, is the only sensible approach. Further, to the extent that a rule could be discerned in any decision of this court that the fairness principles enshrined in FAR Part 15 are inapplicable to any FAR Subpart 8.4 procurement, such a rule is neither binding in this case, nor reasonable under the facts of this case. (internal citations, quotations, and alterations omitted)

Agencies should take these considerations into account before requiring the submission of detailed "technical" or "management" proposals and establishing a formal evaluation board, and before mentioning in its RFQ the establishment of a "competitive range," the conduct of "discussions," and the submission of "final proposal revisions" or using any of those procedures. Adopting the terminology and using the procedures of FAR Part 15 may diminish the advantages of the relative simplicity and informality of schedule ordering procedures.

[d] Orders Not Requiring a Statement of Work

FAR 8.405-1 prescribes procedures for ordering supplies or for ordering services that do not require a statement of work. In this situation, there is no need for a statement of work because the supplies are specifically defined in the schedule contract or the services are defined by task in the schedule contract—both at fixed prices. FAR 8.405-1(f) states that when determining best value agencies must consider price and may consider additional factors, including but not limited to the following factors:

- Past performance.
- Special features of the supply or service required for effective program performance.
- Trade-in considerations.
- Probable life of the item selected as compared with that of a comparable item.
- Warranty considerations.
- Maintenance availability.
- Environmental and energy efficiency considerations.
- Delivery terms.

Note that these factors are directed toward orders for supplies. When the agency is ordering services defined by specific tasks, it must select appropriate factors to ensure the selection of the contractor offering the best value.

[i] Orders Exceeding the Micro-Purchase Threshold but not the Simplified Acquisition Threshold

FAR 8.405-1(c) states that when placing orders valued in excess of the micro-purchase threshold, but at or below the simplified acquisition threshold, agencies need consider only "reasonably available" information at *GSA Advantage!* about the products or services of at least three schedule contractors as described in online catalogs and price lists. Agencies may request quotations instead of using *GSA Advantage!* If the agency restricts consideration to fewer than three contractors, it must document which of the circumstances listed in FAR 8.405-6 applies.

[ii] Orders Exceeding the Simplified Acquisition Threshold

FAR 8.405-1(d) states that when placing orders valued in excess of the simplified acquisition threshold agencies must seek competition among schedule contractors by issuing an RFQ. The RFQ must describe the required supplies or services and the basis for selecting the contractor to which the order will be issued. The RFQ either must be posted at GSA's *e-Buy* website or provided to as many schedule contractors as practicable to reasonably ensure receipt of quotes from at least three capable contractors. If an agency chooses the latter course of action and receives fewer than three quotes, it must make a reasonable effort to find additional sources. If it cannot find additional sources it must include in the order file a written description of its efforts to do so.

[3] Order Pricing

GSA maintains that its contracting officers have determined the fairness and reasonableness of schedule prices and that contracting officers issuing orders need not make a separate determination in that regard. However, contracting officers are required to request a price reduction on all orders and BPAs exceeding the simplified acquisition threshold. See FAR 8.405-4 stating:

> Ordering activities may request a price reduction at any time before placing an order, establishing a BPA, or in conjunction with the annual BPA review. However, the ordering activity shall seek a price reduction when the order or BPA exceeds the simplified acquisition threshold.

Seeking a price reduction is particularly desirable when the agency is ordering supplies or services at fixed prices for specified tasks following the FAR 8.405-1 procedures because the schedule price may not reflect the quantities being ordered or the conditions of the marketplace at the time the order is placed.

In addition, FAR 8.405-2(d) provides as follows concerning the evaluation of quotes for orders that require a statement of work:

> *Evaluation.* The ordering activity shall evaluate all responses received using the evaluation criteria provided to the schedule contractors. The ordering activity is responsible for considering the level of effort and the mix of labor proposed to perform a specific task being ordered, and for determining that the total price is reasonable. Place the order with the schedule contractor that represents the best value (see 8.404(d) and 8.405-4). After award, ordering activities should provide timely notification to unsuccessful offerors. If an unsuccessful offeror requests information on an award that was based on factors other than price alone, a brief explanation of the basis for the award decision shall be provided.

In short, nothing prevents an ordering agency contracting officer from bargaining for a better deal than otherwise offered under a schedule contract. GSA considers the pursuit of lower prices in all cases a "best practice." See the GSA webpage, Schedule Pricing, https://www.gsa.gov/buying-selling/purchasing-programs/gsa-schedule/schedule-features/schedule-pricing. Notwithstanding the obvious advantages of bargaining for better prices, GAO has found that contracting officers often do not do so. See *Contract Management: Not Following Procedures Undermines Best Pricing Under GSA's Schedule*, GAO-01-125.

Contractors may be deterred from offering lower prices by a misreading of the price reduction clause in schedule contracts, GSAR 552.238-81, Price Reductions (May 2019), which may lead to the perception that a discount offered to one agency will obligate the contractor to provide the same discount to other agencies. That is not the case. FAR 8.405-4 states: "Schedule contractors are not required to pass on to all schedule users a price reduction extended only to an individual ordering activity for a specific order or BPA."

[4] Content of Orders

FAR 8.406-1 provides that agencies may issue orders orally if they are for (1) supplies and services not requiring a statement of work exceeding the simplified acquisition threshold, (2) services requiring a statement of work, and (3) orders containing brand-name specifications that exceed $25,000. Otherwise, orders must be issued in writing on Optional Form 347 (FAR 53.302-347), an agency form, or in electronic format. FAR 8.406-1(d) specifies the minimum information that each order must include.

GSA allows agencies to include their own agency-specific clauses in orders and BPAs as long as they are not inconsistent with the terms and conditions of the GSA schedule contract. See GSA Multiple Award Schedule Program Desk Reference (Winter 2019) at 31:

> The GSA Schedules program is designed to assist government customers in achieving their goals. The terms and conditions, including all clauses, are available for viewing for each Schedule through GSA eLibrary. While GSA will not alter the terms and conditions of a Schedule contract in violation of CICA, nor alter the scope of a contract to meet an individual ordering activity's unique needs, an ordering activity may add terms to an order that do not conflict with the Schedule contract terms and conditions.

Agencies may include options in orders to extend the term of the order or to purchase additional quantities. See GSA Multiple Award Schedule Ordering Guide (Summer 2020) at 7:

> In accordance with the requirements of FAR 17.207, Exercise of Options, Options may be included on orders placed against Schedule contracts, provided that the options are clearly stated in the requirement and are evaluated as part of the ordering activity's best value determination.
>
> Such options may be exercised on GSA Schedule contract orders, provided that:
>
> - Funds are available;
> - The requirement covered by the option fulfills an existing government need;
> - Before exercising an option, you ensure that it is still in the government's best interest, i.e., that the option is the most advantageous method of fulfilling the government's need, price and other factors considered
> - The term for each order placed under the Schedule contract is specified in the order. Under no circumstances may an order be placed under the Schedule contract if the Schedule contract has expired or fi the government has terminated or cancelled it
> - Pricing on an order, including options, does not exceed pricing on the Schedule contract. Pricing for any order, including options, must be in place before the award of any order including those extending beyond the Schedule contract ordering period.

[5] Items Not on Schedule

Since the Court of Federal Claims' decision in *ATA Defense Indus., Inc., v. United States*, 38 Fed. Cl. 489 (1997), it has become well-established that agencies may not place orders that include non-schedule items ("open market items" or "incidental items") valued in excess of the micro-purchase threshold unless they first comply with all applicable laws and regulations. See *CourtSmart Digital Sys., Inc.*, Comp. Gen. Dec. B-292995.2, 2004 CPD ¶ 79, stating:

> The FSS program, directed and managed by the General Services Administration (GSA), gives federal agencies a simplified process for obtaining commonly used commercial supplies and services. FAR § 8.401(a). Orders placed using the procedures established for the FSS

> program satisfy the statutory and regulatory requirement for full and open competition. FAR § 6.102(d)(3), § 8.404(a). Non-FSS products and services may not be purchased using FSS procedures; instead, their purchase requires compliance with the applicable procurement laws and regulations, including those requiring the use of competitive procedures. *Symplicity Corp.*, B-291902, Apr. 29, 2003, 2003 CPD ¶ 89 at 4; see *ATA Def. Indus., Inc. v. United States*, 38 Fed. Cl. 489, 504 (1997). Therefore, where, as here, an agency solicits quotations from vendors for purchase from the FSS, the issuance of a purchase order to a vendor whose quotation includes a non-FSS item priced above the micro-purchase threshold is improper. *Symplicity Corp.*, *supra*, at 4-5; *T-L-C Sys.*, B-285687.2, Sept. 29, 2000, 2000 CPD ¶ 166 at 4.

See also *Deloitte Consulting, LLP*, Comp. Gen. Dec. B-419508, 2021 CPD ¶ 170 ("where an agency announces its intent to order from an existing FSS, all goods or services quoted must be on the vendor's schedule contract as a precondition to its receiving the order").

"The sole exception to this requirement is for items that do not exceed the micro-purchase threshold, since such items properly may be purchased outside the normal competition requirements," *AmeriGuard Security Services, Inc.*, Comp. Gen. Dec. B-411513.2, 2015 CPD ¶ 308.

See also FAR 8.402(f):

> (f) For administrative convenience, an ordering activity contracting officer may add items not on the Federal Supply Schedule (also referred to as open market items) to a Federal Supply Schedule blanket purchase agreement (BPA) or an individual task or delivery order only if—
>
> (1) All applicable acquisition regulations pertaining to the purchase of the items not on the Federal Supply Schedule have been followed (e.g., publicizing (Part 5), competition requirements (Part 6), acquisition of commercial items (Part 12), contracting methods (Parts 13, 14, and 15), and small business programs (Part 19));
>
> (2) The ordering activity contracting officer has determined the price for the items not on the Federal Supply Schedule is fair and reasonable;
>
> (3) The items are clearly labeled on the order as items not on the Federal Supply Schedule; and
>
> (4) All clauses applicable to items not on the Federal Supply Schedule are included in the order.

When an order is for services, the contract must include all labor categories and items required to perform the work. *GrantThornton, LLC*, Comp. Gen. Dec. B-416733, 2018 CPD ¶ 411; *Tarheel Specialties, Inc.*, Comp. Gen. Dec. B-298197, 2006 CPD ¶ 140 (labor needed to support operations of firearms tactical training unit not included in schedule contract for security consulting services).

However, the Court of Federal Claims has held that agencies may make "common sense identification of overlapping, related labor categories." See *HomeSource Real Estate Asset Servs., Inc. v. United States*, 94 Fed. Cl. 466 (2010), stating at 486:

> An agency that orders services against a schedule contract "shall not seek competition outside the Federal Supply Schedules." [FAR 8.404(a)]. In this case, HUD restricted competition to those vendors offering services on Schedule 520. "Where an agency announces an intention to order from an existing GSA Schedule contractor, it means that the agency intends to order all items using GSA FFS procedures and that all items are required to be within the scope of the vendor's FSS contract." *IDEA Int'l, Inc. v. United States* (IDEA Int'l), 74 Fed. Cl. 129, 139 (2006).
>
> Although the government is required to order items that fall "within the scope of the vendor's FSS contract," id., there is "no prohibition [ ] on the government's common sense identification of overlapping, related labor categories," *Career Training Concepts, Inc. v. United States* (*Career Training*), 83 Fed. Cl. 215, 227 (2008). In *Career Training* the court rejected plaintiff's protest based on its finding that the awardee's job category was "sufficiently close to the [FSS labor category] to be compliant with the solicitation." Id. at 228. Although job titles and qualifications may differ between an offeror's FSS contract and the solicitation, a government agency may find that the services offered are within the scope of an offeror's FSS contract if the function of the two job positions is "sufficiently close." *Career Training*, 83 Fed. Cl. at 228; see *Data Mgmt. Servs. Joint Venture v. United States*, 78 Fed. Cl. 366, 378 (2007).

See also *Mobile Med. Int'l Corp. v. United States*, 95 Fed. Cl. 706 (2010) (mobile trailer required by order not included in awardee's schedule contract).

[G] Blanket Purchase Agreements

Agencies may use the procedures in FAR 8.405-3 to establish BPAs with schedule contractors in order to simplify ordering and reduce administrative costs. GSA provides significant discussion of BPAs on its website.

A standard clause used in schedule contracts, I-FSS-646, Blanket Purchase Agreements (MAY 2000), stipulates the contractor's agreement to enter into BPAs:

> Blanket Purchase Agreements (BPA's) can reduce costs and save time because individual orders and invoices are not required for each procurement but can instead be documented on a consolidated basis. The Contractor agrees to enter into BPA's with ordering activities provided that:
>
> (a) The period of time covered by such agreements shall not exceed the period of the contract including option year period(s);

> (b) Orders placed under such agreements shall be issued in accordance with all applicable regulations and the terms and conditions of the contract; and
>
> (c) BPAs may be established to obtain the maximum discount (lowest net price) available in those schedule contracts containing volume or quantity discount arrangements.

BPAs against GSA schedule contracts should not be confused with the BPAs used for simplified acquisitions and described at FAR 13.303. A more apt term for schedule contract BPAs would be blanket ordering agreements. Such agreements allow agencies to select a contractor and then issue orders during an agreed-upon period of time without further consideration of other schedule contractors or further price negotiations. The contracting officer can delegate ordering under the BPA to other offices in the agency.

GAO has ruled that a BPA is not itself a contract and that orders issued against it are issued against the underlying schedule contract, *AINS, Inc.*, Comp. Gen. Dec. B-400760.2, 2009 CPD ¶ 142. The Federal Circuit has likewise confirmed that BPAs are not independent contracts, *Crewzers Fire Crew Transp., Inc. v. United States*, 741 F.3d 1390 (Fed. Cir. 2014).

Accordingly, BPAs are not stand-alone agreements and orders can no longer be issued against a BPA once the underlying schedule contract has expired. See *Canon USA, Inc.*, Comp. Gen. Dec. B-311254.2, 2008 CPD ¶ 113, stating:

> We agree with Canon that an FSS BPA is a separate agreement from its associated FSS contract. Nevertheless, we conclude that when Canon's FSS contract expired, Canon's BPA ceased to be a valid procurement vehicle for the placement of new orders because, as explained below, an FSS BPA is in effect solely a passthrough to the BPA holder's FSS contract and does not provide an independent foundation for issuing orders.

Contracts awarded under the FSS program satisfy the requirements for full and open competition, FAR 8.405-6. As relevant here, FAR § 8.405-3(a)(1) authorizes the establishment of BPAs under FSS contracts as a means to fill "repetitive needs for supplies or services." It is well-settled, however, that a BPA itself is not a contract; rather, a contract is formed by the subsequent placement of a valid order against the BPA, or by the incorporation of the basic agreement into a new contract. See *Envirosolve LLC*, B-294974.4, June 8, 2005, 2005 CPD ¶ 106 at 3 n.3, citing *Modern Sys. Tech. Corp. v. United States*, 24 Cl. Ct. 360, 363 (1991).

> As with any contract, orders placed under an FSS BPA must satisfy the applicable statutory requirements for competition.
>
> In this case, the record shows that the BPA was issued pursuant to Canon's FSS contract, the plain language of Canon's BPA states that it is established "[p]ursuant to GSA Federal Supply Schedule (FSS) Contract

> Number GS-25F-0023M," Motion to Dismiss, Tab 1, Canon BPA, at 1, and Canon itself does not dispute that the BPAs here were all "initially awarded to vendors based on their then current GSA copier schedule contracts." Protest at 5. It is therefore clear that Canon's BPA is an FSS BPA, established under FAR part 8.4.
>
> Because use of the FSS procedures constitutes full and open competition under 10 U.S.C. § 2303(2)(c), orders placed under a valid FSS contract, whether directly or via a BPA, meet the CICA competition requirements. Conversely, in the absence of a valid FSS contract, any order placed under a BPA must independently satisfy the statutory competition requirements; that is, to be a valid ordering vehicle independent from an FSS contract, the BPA itself would have to have been established using procedures that satisfy the statutory requirements for competition. That clearly is not the case here, or in any FSS BPA of this type, given that the pool of vendors that could receive a BPA was limited to FSS contract holders, as directed by FAR sect. 8.404(a) ("ordering activities shall not seek competition outside of the Federal Supply Schedules"). Consistent with this interpretation, we have stated that an FSS BPA is not established with the contractor directly, but rather is established under the contractor's FSS contract, such that FSS BPA orders "ultimately are to be placed against the successful vendor's FSS contract." *Panacea Consulting, Inc.*, B-299307.4, B-299308.4, July 27, 2007, 2007 CPD ¶ 141 at 1-2 n.1; see also *CMS Info. Servs., Inc.*, B-290541, Aug. 7, 2002, 2002 CPD ¶ 132 at 4 n.7. Thus, in our view, when, as in this case, an agency intends to place an order under an FSS BPA, the vendor must have a valid FSS contract in place because that contract is the means by which the agency satisfies the competition requirements of CICA in connection with any orders issued under the BPA.

See also *Delmock Techs., Inc.*, Comp. Gen. Dec. B-418626, 2020 CPD ¶ 220.

Pursuant to FAR 8.405-3(d)(3), however, "Contractors may be awarded BPAs that extend beyond the current term of their GSA Schedule contract, so long as there are option periods in their GSA Schedule contract that, if exercised, will cover the BPA's period of performance." GAO has held that this rule requires the underlying contract to have sufficient duration to cover the entire BPA period of performance, inclusive of all options, *GBK Partnership, LLC-Constant Assocs., Inc.*, Comp. Gen. Dec. B-417039, 2019 CPD ¶ 30.

Notwithstanding that the BPA is itself not a contract, GAO and the Court of Federal Claims tend to review protests involving the award of BPA vehicles. See *PricewaterhouseCoopers Pub. Sector, LLP v. United States*, 126 Fed. Cl. 328 (2016); *ARKRAY USA, Inc. v. United States*, 118 Fed. Cl. 129 (2014); *Noble Supply & Logistics*, Comp. Gen. Dec. B-417269, 2019 CPD ¶ 167.

§ 11.03 GOVERNMENTWIDE ACQUISITION CONTRACTS, MULTIAGENCY CONTRACTS, AND ENTERPRISE-WIDE CONTRACTS

Governmentwide Acquisition Contracts (GWACs), Multiagency Contracts (MACs), and Enterprise-wide Contracts are multiple-award IDIQ contracts awarded by agencies for use by other agencies. They differ mainly in the authority for their establishment. GWACs are authorized pursuant to 40 U.S.C. § 11302(e) (formerly ¶ 759), and are for the acquisition of information technology. Orders placed against GWACs are not subject to the Economy Act, 31 U.S.C. § 1535.

MACs are authorized for the acquisition of all kinds of supplies and services pursuant to the Economy Act, or for the acquisition of information technology by 40 U.S.C. § 11314(a)(2). All orders placed against MACs, regardless of the authority for establishment of the contract, are subject to the Economy Act. Enterprise-wide Contracts are established within an agency for its own use. However, awarding agencies may make such contracts available for other agencies to use, in which case the contracts are MACs and orders placed against them are subject to the Economy Act. GWACs, MACs, and Enterprise-wide Contracts are IDIQ contracts as discussed in Chapter 7.

[A] Establishment of GWACs and MACs

[1] Planning, Management, and Inventory

The principle issues concerning these contracts have been their proliferation and management. See Report of the Acquisition Advisory Panel to the Office of Federal Procurement Policy and the United States Congress (January 2007), 246-247:

> The pressures and incentives to create and use these vehicles, coupled with inconsistent or lacking oversight and little transparency has created an environment biased towards the uncoordinated proliferation of interagency contracts. GAO has noted that they are attracting rapid growth of taxpayer dollars with Fiscal Year 2004 FPDS-NG data showing total obligations of $142 Billion or 40 percent of the total government-wide spend for the year.
>
> * * *
>
> Certainly, uncoordinated proliferation without adequate transparency into the establishment or use of these vehicles creates serious challenges for those organizations responsible for oversight. While GWACs, franchise funds, and schedules are readily identifiable, the significant number of other interagency vehicles such as non-GWAC multi-agency contracts and the emerging trend in the proliferation of enterprise-wide contracts presents an obstacle for oversight both in terms of sheer numbers and difficulty in

identification. Lack of transparency in both the use and management of these vehicles severely hampers the government's ability to maximize their effectiveness.

In order to establish a GWAC an agency must prepare a business case and submit it to the Office of Management and Budget for approval and authorization. The Court of Federal Claims described the process in *Knowledge Connections, Inc. v. United States*, 79 Fed. Cl. 750 (2007), stating at 753:

> In February 2005, GSA sent OMB the Veterans Technology Service [VETS] business case, a proposal to establish the VETS GWAC. See GSA Determination Pursuant to Remand Order, July 25, 2007 ("Remand Determination") *754 at 10; FN8 AR 16-50 (GSA, VETS (Veterans Technology Services) Business Case For a Service-Disabled Veteran-Owned Small Business (SDVOSB) Government-Wide Acquisition Contract (GWAC) (Feb. 3, 2005)) ("Business Case"). GSA described the VETS GWAC as "a streamlined acquisition vehicle" through which GSA would "offer a pre-qualified group of SDVOSB information technology ["IT"] firms the opportunity to compete for government IT services orders from [government agencies]." AR 18 (Business Case). GSA stated that "[e]valuation criteria [would], at a minimum, focus on technical expertise, successful past performance and price." AR 21 (Business Case). GSA ascribed importance to "building brand awareness" by "forg[ing] strategic partnerships with the SBA [and] VA ["Veterans Administration"]" and noted that "frequent and consistent messaging by GSA and any strategic partners (SBA, Veterans Administration, and Department of Defense) is mandatory in order to properly explain the recent statute and Executive Order in addition to managing the expectations of both industry and federal communities." AR 33 (Business Case).
>
> OMB has the statutory obligation to direct and oversee the federal government's "acquisition and use of information technology," 44 U.S.C. § 3504(a) (1)(B)(vi), and federal agencies are required to comply with policies established by OMB in that regard. 44 U.S.C. § 3506(a)(1)(B). Correlatively, the Director of OMB is authorized by the Clinger-Cohen Act, Pub.L. No. 104-106, § 5112(e), 110 Stat. 186, 681 (Feb. 10, 1996) (codified at 40 U.S.C. § 11302(e)) (enacted as part of the National Defense Authorization Act for Fiscal Year 1996), to designate heads of executive agencies as "executive agent[s] for [g]overnment-wide acquisitions of information technology." Id. Heads of executive agencies, in turn, have authority to enter into "contract[s] that provide[ ] for multiagency acquisitions of information technology in accord[ ] with guidance issued by [OMB]." 40 U.S.C. § 11314(a)(2). "Executive agents" have "discretion on matters of procurement planning, implementation, administration, and management, subject to any terms and conditions that OMB includes in the designation." Def.'s Opp'n to Pl.'s Mot. . . . and Cross-Mot. ("Def.'s Cross-Mot."), attached Decl. of Michael Gerich, General Attorney, OFPP, OMB (Sept. 13, 2007) ("Gerich Decl.") at 2.

> OMB reviewed the Business Case submitted by GSA and designated GSA as the "executive agent" for the VETS GWAC on July 5, 2005. AR 85 (Letter from Joshua B. Bolten, Director, OMB, to Stephen A. Perry, Administrator, GSA (July 5, 2005)) ("OMB Designation"). The grant of authority embraced two primary functional areas: information systems engineering and systems operations and maintenance. AR 89 (OMB Designation, Encl. A). In designating GSA as the executive agent for the VETS GWAC, OMB stated that "[t] he GWAC would fulfill GSA's responsibilities under Executive Order 13360, which requires the agency to 'establish a Government-wide Acquisition Contract reserved for participation by service-disabled veteran businesses.'" AR 92-93 (OMB Designation, Encl. B). OMB also made the designation subject to certain terms, reporting requirements, and understandings. AR 90 (OMB Designation, Encl. B). Specifically, the designation was granted with "the expectation that contracts under this GWAC w[ould] be awarded to the most highly qualified service-disabled veteran owned small businesses. Potential contractors should not be excluded from being GWAC holders based on their lack of experience as a government contractor." AR 93 (OMB Designation, Encl. B). Thirteen months later, in August 2006, OMB extended the executive agent designation until the completion of the VETS GWAC contract period. AR 96, 99 (Letter *755 from Rob Portman, Director, OMB, to Lurita A. Doan, Administrator, GSA (Aug. 9, 2006)).

An agency awarding a GWAC contract must do so in accordance with the terms of OMB's grant of executive agent designation. *Knowledge Connections Travel, Inc. v. United States*, 76 Fed. Cl. 6 (2007) (judgment for plaintiff where record insufficient to show that agency evaluation was consistent with OMB grant of executive designation).

To date, OMB has authorized only five agencies to award GWACs: Department of Commerce, Environmental Protection Agency, General Services Administration, Department of Health and Human Services, and National Aeronautics and Space Administration.

In 1997, OMB issued Memorandum M-97-07, *Multiagency Contracts under the Information Technology Management Reform Act of 1996*. The memorandum authorized agencies to establish MACs and provided guidance for doing so. As excerpted earlier in this chapter, FAR 17.502-1(b) now requires that agencies prepare a business case analysis prior to establishing a MAC or GWAC. However, there is no requirement that the analysis be reviewed or approved outside of the agency. A number of agencies have established MACs, including Department of Commerce, Defense of Defense, Department of the Interior, Environmental Protection Agency, General Services Administration, Department of Health and Human Services, Department of the Treasury, and Department of Veterans Affairs. There is no specific authority or procedure for establishing Enterprise-wide Contracts for use only by offices of the awarding agency.

GWACs and MACs may encompass very broad scopes of work, making them virtual shopping malls for wide varieties of supplies and services.

[2] Competition and Award Controversies

As is the case in virtually all acquisitions of services under IDIQ contracts, competition is usually based on proposed labor rates that include direct costs, indirect costs, and profit. This reduces or even eliminates any chance for real price competition, which may not take place until the conduct of a competition for the award of a task order.

Perhaps the most unique feature of competitions for GWACs and MACs has been the fact that the prospect of multiple awards prompts a large response, resulting in large numbers of proposals being submitted and forcing agencies to find ways to streamline the source selection process. This can be risky if not done properly. See, for example, GAO's comments in *Kathpal Techs., Inc.*, Comp. Gen. Dec. B-283137.3, 2000 CPD ¶ 6, sustaining the protest in part because the agency did not consider price when screening proposals to select candidates for more in-depth evaluation:

> At the outset, we appreciate the difficulty faced by [Department of] Commerce in needing to evaluate more than 200 proposals, particularly given the RFP requirement for oral presentations. The agency may well have believed that the way it conducted this procurement showed that it was implementing recent reforms in the procurement system. It is true that government-wide acquisition contracts, such as the COMMITS program, are largely the creatures of recent procurement reform. See Clinger-Cohen Act of 1996, Pub. L. No. 104-106, § 5124, 110 Stat. 642, 684 (1996). It is also true that recent reforms have given contracting agencies greater discretion to more effectively and efficiently conduct procurements. For example (and of some relevance here, as discussed below), Congress has given agencies the authority to limit the number of offers included in a competitive range to the greatest number that would permit an efficient competition. See 41 U.S.C. § 253b(d)(2); FAR § 15.306(c). Our Office believes that the government procurement system can benefit substantially from the increased flexibility inherent in recent procurement reform. In this procurement, however, we are persuaded, as explained below, that the agency's conduct violated applicable law and regulations in several significant ways.
>
> [W]e disagree with the agency that it could ignore price in its initial screening evaluation. Cost or price to the government must be included in every RFP as an evaluation factor, and agencies must consider cost or price to the government in evaluating competitive proposals. 41 U.S.C. § 253a(c)(1)(B) (1994); FAR § 15-304(c)(1); *S.J. Thomas Co., Inc.*, B-283192, Oct. 20, 1999, 99-2 CPD ¶ at 3. [Footnote omitted.]

In denying the agency's request to modify this decision, Comp. Gen. Dec. B-283137.7, 2000 CPD ¶ 27, GAO did agree that oral presentations could be limited to "highly rated offerors" if that procedure was spelled out in the RFP.

One solution has been to award contracts to all competitors, as happened in the General Services Administration's 2009 award of its Alliant GWAC, where the agency awarded contracts to 59 out of 59 offerors after an initial decision to make only 29 awards was followed by a protest that was upheld by the Court of Federal Claims, *Serco, Inc. v. United States*, 81 Fed. Cl. 463 (2008). This tactic, while it may reduce the chances of a protest, may effectively neutralize the presumably beneficial effects of true competition, since all but the most incompetent firms can be expect to be successful, regardless of the prices offered. In such cases, real competition is deferred until the conduct of competition for orders, and contracting officers should negotiate aggressively for fair and reasonable prices before placing an order. Some agencies provide for "rolling admissions" to a GWAC or MAC during its term. In this way, additional contractors may be added from time to time. Agencies may also cull contractors from the pool by not exercising options to extend a contract's life.

[B] Ordering

Some interagency contracts permit only the awarding agency to place orders, necessitating an assisted acquisition. Others permit using agencies to order directly. Regardless of which agency places an order, the ordering process is governed by FAR 16.505. FAR 16.505(a) provides:

> (8) Orders placed under a task-order contract or delivery-order contract awarded by another agency (i.e., a Governmentwide acquisition contract, or multi-agency contract)—
>
> (i) Are not exempt from the development of acquisition plans (see subpart 7.1), and an information technology acquisition strategy (see part 39);
>
> (ii) May not be used to circumvent conditions and limitations imposed on the use of funds (e.g., 31 U.S.C. 1501(a)(1)); and
>
> (iii) Shall comply with all FAR requirements for a consolidated or bundled contract when the order meets the definition at 2.101(b) of "consolidation" or "bundling".).

[1] Competition

GWACs, MACs, and enterprise-wide contracts are subject to the same fair opportunity procedures for awarding orders as all other multiple award IDIQ contracts. These procedures have become more stringent as discussed in Chapter 7.

The agencies with GWACs have established websites for their contracts that provide information about ordering procedures. See, for example, the National Aeronautics and Space Administration's website for its Solutions for Enterprise-Wide Procurement (SEWP) GWAC, http://www.sewp.nasa.gov/. Agencies need not seek full and open competition when placing orders, FAR 16.505(b)(1)(ii). Instead, agencies must give contract holders a "fair opportunity" to be considered for award of an order. When placing an order valued at or below the simplified acquisition threshold, agencies need not contact each of the contract holders if the contracting officer has enough information to give each a fair opportunity to be considered. When placing orders valued in excess of the simplified acquisition threshold, agencies must give "fair notice" to all contract holders of their intention to place an order, and ensure that all proposals received are "fairly considered," FAR 16.505(b)(1)(iii). The notice must include a description of the supplier or services to be acquired and the basis on which selection of the awardee is to be made. Agencies may provide notice to fewer contractors if notice is provided to as many "as practicable." However, in such cases, an award cannot be made unless quotes or proposals are received from at least three of the contractors or the contracting officer determines no other qualified contractors could be identified.

[2] Exceptions to the Requirement for Competition

FAR 16.505(b)(2)(i) lists the exceptions to the requirement for "fair opportunity" competition:

> (A) The agency need for the supplies or services is so urgent that providing a fair opportunity would result in unacceptable delays.
>
> (B) Only one awardee is capable of providing the supplies or services required at the level of quality required because the supplies or services ordered are unique or highly specialized.
>
> (C) The order must be issued on a sole-source basis in the interest of economy and efficiency because it is a logical follow-on to an order already issued under the contract, provided that all awardees were given a fair opportunity to be considered for the original order.
>
> (D) It is necessary to place an order to satisfy a minimum guarantee.
>
> (E) For orders exceeding the simplified acquisition threshold, a statute expressly authorizes or requires that the purchase be made from a specified source.
>
> (F) In accordance with section 1331 of Public Law 111–240 (15 U.S.C. 644(r)), contracting officers may, at their discretion, set aside orders for any of the small business concerns identified in 19.000(a)(3). When setting aside orders for small business concerns, the specific small business program eligibility requirements identified in part 19 apply.
>
> (G) For DoD, NASA, and the Coast Guard, the order satisfies one of the exceptions permitting the use of other than full and open competition listed in

6.302 (10 U.S.C. 2304c(b)(5)). The public interest exception shall not be used unless Congress is notified in accordance with 10 U.S.C. 2304(c)(7).

FAR 16.505(b)(2)(ii) contains detailed rules about documenting justification for use of an exception.

[3] Competitive Procedures

Neither the statutes nor the regulations prescribe procedures for the conduct of competitions for orders. Agencies are not required to follow the source selection procedures in FAR Subpart 15.3, but contracting officers must develop fair placement procedures and may not allocate orders among contractors or permit designation of a preferred awardee. The FAR counsels contracting officers to tailor the procedures to each acquisition, FAR 16.505(b)(2)(ii)(A) through (E). Contracting officers must describe their procedures in the solicitation for the order competition and must consider proposed price or cost when selecting awardees. See Chapter 7 for more detail on these procedures.

As discussed at length in Chapter 15 regarding bid protests, the FASA task order protest bar limits the availability of protests challenging task order awards. GAO protests can be filed challenging task order awards valued above $10 million, while DoD awards cannot be protested unless valued above $25 million. For any protest of an order that falls below these values, or any protest filed at the Court of Federal Claims arising from the issuance of a task order, jurisdiction is limited to challenges alleging that the order increases the scope, period, or maximum value of the underlying contract.

CHAPTER 12

TYPES OF CONTRACTS

§12.01 INTRODUCTION

This chapter covers the types of contracts that are described in FAR Parts 16 and 17. These types of contracts fall into two broad categories—contracts that describe the pricing arrangement agreed to by the parties and contracts that call for the performance of variable quantities of the work to be determined during performance. These latter types of contracts can have one or more pricing arrangement.

There are two basic types of pricing arrangements used in government contracts—the cost-reimbursement contract, where the contractor is reimbursed for the allowable costs incurred in performance of the contract, and the fixed-price contract, where the contractor is paid a price for performing the work. In their purest form, these types of contracts are distinguished by the degree of risk of the cost of performance which is allocated to the contractor. In the firm-fixed-price contract, the contractor must complete the work to receive the price, which is preestablished and is not influenced by the cost of performance (except for price adjustments under contract clauses). Thus, if the costs are greater than the price and no price adjustments are warranted, the contractor will suffer a loss; conversely, the lower the costs the greater the profits. Further, if the work is not satisfactorily completed on time, the contractor will be liable to the government for default termination or breach. In contrast, under a cost-plus-fixed-fee contract, the contractor's profit is not affected by the cost of performance because incurred costs will be reimbursed and the amount of the fee is predetermined. Equally as important, if the costs of performance are higher than estimated, the contractor is not obligated to complete the work if the government does not continue to furnish additional funds. Further, it is extremely unlikely that the contractor would be held liable for defective or untimely work.

Fixed-price and cost-reimbursement contracts are also distinguished by the method of payment of the contractor. Under the fixed-price contract, payment is made for completed and delivered work. If this method of payment imposes financial burdens on the contractor, the government may agree to provide financing in the form of progress payments. In either case, contractors incur significant financing costs in performing most fixed-price contracts. In contrast, payment is made on cost-reimbursement contracts on the basis of costs incurred during contract performance. Under these contracts, the contractor is assured of reimbursement of costs on a regular basis and needs to provide only a minimal amount of financing.

Refinements and sophistication in contracting techniques have resulted in a variety of types of fixed-price and cost-reimbursement contracts that alter the normal risk distribution and blur the distinctions between these basic contract types. The major category of contract types that fall in this middle ground are called incentive contracts. In these contracts, the parties share the risk by negotiating arrangements that alter the contractor's profit based on the cost or quality of performance. Another means of sharing the risk is the fixed-price contract with economic price adjustment, where the costs of labor and material are adjusted if there are fluctuations in market conditions which affect the contractor's costs. In another category of contracts, the government relieves the contractor of risk by contracting for a level-of-effort or for labor-hours rather than for a completed job or task. These contracts are called time-and-materials, labor-hour, or level-of-effort contracts.

The government also uses several different types of variable quantity forms of contracts. In some of these instances, the government uses a form of contract where the contractor is bound to perform but the government is free to order some or all of the work from another party. Examples of this type of arrangement are simple options and IDIQ contracts with minimum quantities. Other forms of variable quantity contracts bind the government as firmly as the contractor. The most commonly used contracts of this type are requirements contracts and multi-year contracts. All of these types of contracts are discussed in this chapter but, due to its widespread use, the detailed aspects of the IDIQ contract are covered in Chapter 7.

§ 12.02 BASIC POLICIES

The statutory guidance on the selection of contracts is simple and direct. 10 U.S.C. § 3322(a) (formerly § 2306(a)) and 41 U.S.C. § 3901(a) and § 3905(a) give broad discretion to use any appropriate type of contract on negotiated procurements but prohibit the use of a cost-plus-a-percentage-of-cost (CPPC) system of contracts. FAR 16.102 implements these statutes by restricting the types of contracts considered appropriate to those described in Part 16, as follows:

> (a) Contracts resulting from sealed bidding shall be firm-fixed-price contracts or fixed-price contracts with economic price adjustment.
>
> (b) Contracts negotiated under Part 15 may be of any type or combination of types that will promote the Government's interest, except as restricted in this part (see 10 U.S.C. § 2306(a) and 41 U.S.C. § 3901). Contract types not described in this regulation shall not be used, except as a deviation under Subpart 1.4.
>
> (c) The cost-plus-a-percentage-of-cost system of contracting shall not be used (see 10 U.S.C. § 2306(a) and 41 U.S.C. § 3905(a)). Prime contracts (including letter contracts) other than firm-fixed-price contracts shall, by an appropriate clause, prohibit cost-plus-a-percentage-of-cost subcontracts (see clauses prescribed in Subpart 44.2 for cost-reimbursement contracts and Subparts 16.2 and 16.4 for fixed-price contracts).

This section addresses several general issues that must be considered in selecting the appropriate type of contract. The first issue is the *broad discretion* granted to contracting officers in selecting the type of contract in negotiated procurements. Second is the scope of the prohibition of CPPC systems of contracting. Finally, the section reviews the policies on undefinitized contractual actions such as letter contracts or letters of intent.

[A] Discretion

The amount of discretion afforded to agencies in selecting the type of contract depends on the procurement technique that is used. The least discretion is conferred when sealed bidding is used because in that situation the agency is required to use either firm-fixed-price contracts or fixed-price contracts with economic price adjustment, FAR 14.104; FAR 16.102(a).

Somewhat more discretion is granted in contracts for commercial products or services by allowing the use of time-and-materials or labor-hour contracts to a limited extent. See FAR 12.207 providing:

> (a) Except as provided in paragraph (b) of this section, agencies shall use firm-fixed-price contracts or fixed-price contracts with economic price adjustment for the acquisition of commercial products or commercial services.
>
> (b)(1) A time-and-materials contract or labor-hour contract (see Subpart 16.6) may be used for the acquisition of commercial services when—
>
> (i) The service is acquired under a contract awarded using—
>
> (A) Competitive procedures (e.g., the procedures in 6.102, the set-aside procedures in Subpart 19.5, or competition conducted in accordance with Part 13);
>
> (B) The procedures for other than full and open competition in 6.3 provided the agency receives offers that satisfy the Government's expressed requirement from two or more responsible offerors; or
>
> (C) The fair opportunity procedures in 16.505 (including discretionary small business set-asides under 16.505(b)(2)(i)(F)), if placing an order under a multiple award delivery-order contract; and
>
> (ii) The contracting officer—
>
> (A) Executes a determination and findings (D&F) for the contract, in accordance with paragraph (b)(2) of this section (but see paragraph (c) of this section for indefinite-delivery contracts), that no other contract type authorized by this subpart is suitable;
>
> (B) Includes a ceiling price in the contract or order that the contractor exceeds at its own risk; and
>
> (C) Prior to increasing the ceiling price of a time-and-materials or labor-hour contract or order, shall—
>
> (1) Conduct an analysis of pricing and other relevant factors to determine if the action is in the best interest of the Government:

(2) Document the decision in the contract or order file; and

(3) When making a change that modifies the general scope of—

(i) A contract, follow the procedures at 6.303;

(ii) An order issued under the Federal Supply Schedules, follow the procedures at 8.405-6; or

(iii) An order issued under multiple award task and delivery order contracts, follow the procedures at 16.505(b)(2).

FAR 12.207(b)(2) contains detailed guidance on the content of the required D&F. These stringent requirements allowing the use of time-and-materials or labor-hour contracts in procuring commercial services implement § 1432 of the National Defense Authorization Act for FY 2004, Pub. L. No. 108-136, which explicitly authorized to use of these types of contracts under limited circumstances.

The greatest discretion is granted in selecting the type of contract to be used in negotiated procurements. There FAR 16.103 balances the need to impose *reasonable risks* on the contractor with the need to use a type of contract that *motivates effective performance*, stating:

> (a) Selecting the contract type is generally a matter for negotiation and requires the exercise of sound judgment. Negotiating the contract type and negotiating prices are closely related and should be considered together. The objective is to negotiate a contract type and price (or estimated cost and fee) that will result in reasonable contractor risk and provide the contractor with the greatest incentive for efficient and economical performance.
>
> (b) A firm-fixed-price contract, which best utilizes the basic profit motive of business enterprise, shall be used when the risk involved is minimal or can be predicted with an acceptable degree of certainty. However, when a reasonable basis for firm pricing does not exist, other contract types should be considered, and negotiations should be directed toward selecting a contract type (or combination of types) that will appropriately tie profit to contractor performance.

FAR 16.104 provides a list of factors to be considered in selecting the contract type with guidance as to the application of each factor. The factors are listed as follows:

- Price competition
- Price analysis
- Cost analysis
- Type and complexity of the requirement

- Urgency of the requirement
- Period of performance or length of production run
- Contractor's technical capability and financial responsibility
- Adequacy of the contractor's accounting system
- Concurrent contracts
- Extent and nature of proposed subcontracting
- Acquisition history

The guidance in these paragraphs of the FAR makes it quite clear that the basic policy of the government is to use the type of contract that imposes sufficient risk on the contractor to motivate good performance yet relieves the contractor of unduly high risks over which it has no control and that are unpredictable.

The contracting officer has broad discretion in selecting the contract type. See, for example, *PCL Constr. Servs., Inc. v. United States*, 47 Fed. Cl. 745 (2000), *aff'd*, 96 Fed. Appx 672 (Fed. Cir. 2004), where the court denied the contractor's claim that the agency had illegally used a firm-fixed-price contract when there was substantial pricing risk, stating at 807-08:

> [T]he solicitation and contract made no secret of the variables to be encountered by the contractor selected which would require design efforts and likely modifications using the changes clause procedures. If plaintiff believed that these variables were so uncertain that it was improper to use an FFP contract, and that the scope of the contract, was, therefore, ambiguous; it had a duty to inquire as to the true nature of the contract before submitting a bid. See *Triax Pac., Inc. v. West*, 130 F.3d at 1474-75; see also *Ryan Co. v. United States*, 43 Fed. Cl. 646, 654 (1999) ("When a solicitation presents conflicting signals, a contractor is under an affirmative duty to call the ambiguity to the attention of the contracting official."). Moreover, the contractor is assumed to understand the risks inherent in the type of contract it signs at the time of execution. Among the distinguishing characteristics between the various types of contracts is the degree of risk allocated to the contractor. In addition, even if the plaintiff had an argument regarding the choice of contract type, when a statutory or regulatory restriction is designed for the protection and benefit of the government and the taxpayers, a contract made in violation of that restriction and relied on by the government is binding upon the contractor unless repudiated by the government. The plaintiff cannot gain an advantage from regulations not designed for its benefit. See *National Elec. Lab. v. United States*, 148 Ct. Cl. 308, 314, 180 F. Supp. 337, 340-41 (1960). The solicitation clearly identified the contract to be awarded as an FFP contract. PCL willingly bid on an FFP contract, and willingly signed an FFP contract, thereby assuming the risks attendant to an FFP contract.

See also *Northrop Grumman Tech. Servs., Inc.* Comp. Gen. Dec. B-406523, 2012 CPD ¶ 197, where the GAO denied a protest that the agency had required offerors to propose fixed prices per flying hour for five years, stating:

> [T]here is no legal requirement that a solicitation be drafted so as to eliminate all performance uncertainties; the mere presence of risk does not render a solicitation improper. *Aalco Forwarding, Inc., et al.*, B-277241.8, B-277241.9, Oct. 21, 1997, 97-2 CPD ¶ 110 at 22-23. Offerors have the responsibility, in offering on a fixed-price contract, to project costs and to include in their proposed fixed prices a factor covering any projected costs increase; risk is inherent in most types of contracts and offerors are expected to allow for that risk in computing their offers.

See also *Surface Techs. Corp.*, Comp. Gen. Dec. B-288317, 2001 CPD ¶ 147, and *Wartsila Defense, Inc.*, Comp. Gen. Dec. B-401224, 2009 CPD ¶ 115, where protests were denied when the contracting officer chose a cost-reimbursement contract instead of a fixed-price contract. GAO accepted the reasoning that there were sufficient unknowns to justify the use of a cost-reimbursement contract.

Historically, this broad discretion in the selection of the contract type has occasionally been used to impose very high risks on contractors undertaking major development programs. Congress reacted to this practice by limiting the use of fixed-price contracts in the § 8118 of the Omnibus Appropriations Act of 1988, Pub. L. No. 100-202. This provision was implemented in DFARS 235.006. In *American Tel. & Tel. Co. v. United States*, 177 F.3d 1368 (Fed. Cir. 1999) (en banc), the court held that violating this statute did not result in a void contract, while in *American Tel. & Tel. Co. v. United States*, 307 F.3d 1374 (Fed. Cir. 2002), *cert. denied*, 540 U.S. 937 (2003), the court held that the contractor was entitled to no relief when the government violated this statute because the statute was not intended to create a private cause of action. See also *Northrop Grumman Corp. v. United States*, 63 Fed. Cl. 38 (2004), reaching the same result.

Congress altered this policy in 2006, 2013, and 2017 restricting the use of cost-reimbursement contracts by requiring higher level approvals. These requirements are implemented in DFARS 216.301-3 as follows:

> (2) Except as provided in 235.006(b), in accordance with section 829 of the National Defense Authorization Act for Fiscal Year 2017 (Pub. L. 114–328), approval of the head of the contracting activity is required prior to awarding cost-reimbursement contracts in excess of $25 million.

See also DFARS 234.004(2) addressing the requirements for major programs as follows:

> (i) In accordance with Section 818 of the National Defense Authorization Act for Fiscal Year 2007 (Pub. L. 109-364), for major defense acquisition programs at Milestone B—

(A) The milestone decision authority shall select, with the advice of the contracting officer, the contract type for a development program at the time of Milestone B approval or, in the case of a space program, Key Decision Point B approval;

(B) The basis for the contract type selection shall be documented in the acquisition strategy. The documentation—

(1) Shall include an explanation of the level of program risk; and

(2) If program risk is determined to be high, shall outline the steps taken to reduce program risk and the reasons for proceeding with Milestone B approval despite the high level of program risk; and

(C) If a cost-reimbursement type contract is selected, the contract file shall include the milestone decision authority's written determination that—

(1) The program is so complex and technically challenging that it would not be practicable to reduce program risk to a level that would permit the use of a fixed-price type contract; and

(2) The complexity and technical challenge of the program is not the result of a failure to meet the requirements of 10 U.S.C. 2366a.

(ii) In accordance with section 811 of the National Defense Authorization Act for Fiscal Year 2013 (Pub. L. 112-239), for contracts entered into on or after October 1, 2014, the contracting officer shall—

(A) Not use cost-reimbursement line items for the acquisition of production of major defense acquisition programs, unless the Undersecretary of Defense for Acquisition and Sustainment (USD(A&S)) or the milestone decision authority when the milestone decision authority is the service acquisition executive of the military department that is managing the program, submits to the congressional defense committees—

(1) A written certification that the particular cost-reimbursement line items are needed to provide a required capability in a timely and cost-effective manner; and

(2) An explanation of the steps taken to ensure that cost-reimbursement line items are used only when to achieve the purposes of the exception; and

(B) Include a copy of such congressional certification in the contract file.

(iii) See 216.301–3 for additional contract type approval requirements for cost-reimbursement contracts.

(iv) For fixed-price incentive (firm target) contracts, contracting officers shall comply with the guidance provided at PGI 216.403–1(1)(ii)(B) and (C).

In 2017, these higher-level approval requirements in DOD were extended to FPI, CPIF and CPAF contracts. See DFARS 216.401(d).

Another provision showing the congressional attempt to limit the use of cost-reimbursement contracts is § 864 of the National Defense Authorization Act for FY 2009, Pub. L. No. 110-417, requiring the revision of the FAR on the use of cost-reimbursement contracts and calling for a review of the use of such contracts by agency Inspectors General and an annual report on use of such contracts by the Officer of Management and Budget. This resulted in a revision to FAR 16.103(c) calling for more documentation when a firm-fixed price was not used. The latest survey of agency practices shows that all of these congressional efforts to restrict the use of cost-reimbursement contracts has not stopped contracting officers from selecting a type of contract that matches the perceived risk of the effort. See *Contracting Data Analysis: Assessment of Government-wide Trends*, GAO-17-244SP (March 2017), showing relatively consistent percentages of obligations for cost-reimbursement contracts from fiscal year 2011 through 2015. In 2015 the percentages were:

	Fixed Price	**Cost-Reimbursement**	**T&M/Labor Hours**
Department of Defense	67%	32%	1%
Civilian agencies	56%	34%	10%

The broad discretion with regard to negotiated procurement has also been used, on occasion, to impose very low risks on contractors by using cost-reimbursement contracts in situations where fixed-price contracts could be used. This can occur, for example, when the following guidance in FAR 16.103 is not followed:

> (c) In the course of an acquisition program, a series of contracts, or a single long-term contract, changing circumstances may make a different contract type appropriate in later periods than that used at the outset. In particular, contracting officers should avoid protracted use of a cost-reimbursement or time-and-materials contract after experience provides a basis for firmer pricing.

One example of failure to follow this guidance was in the case of support service contracts awarded by the National Aeronautics and Space Administration (NASA) on a cost-plus-award-fee basis for many years. This policy was criticized by Congress in the early 1990s, and NASA was ordered in § 401 of the NASA Authorization Act for FY 1993, Pub. L. No. 102-588, to review its policies to allocate the risk more equitably.

Thus, the discretion conferred on the contracting officer in this area must be exercised with great care—taking into account the interests of both the government and the contractor. The number of contract types included in the regulations permit the striking of a fair balance between these interests in virtually all contracting situations.

[B] Cost-Plus-a-Percentage-of-Cost Contracts

The two major procurement statutes prohibit CPPC contracts. Both 10 U.S.C. § 3322(a) (formerly § 2306(a)) and 41 U.S.C. § 3905(a) state simply, with no further statutory guidance, that a "cost-plus-a-percentage-of-cost system of contracting shall not be used." This prohibition applies to both cost-reimbursement and fixed-price contracts. The implementation in FAR 16.102(c) repeats this language and requires that the prohibition be flowed down to subcontractors on all contracts except firm-fixed price contracts. The Supreme Court explained the basis for this statutory prohibition in *Muschany v. United States*, 324 U.S. 49 (1944), at 61-62:

> The purpose of Congress was to protect the Government against the sort of exploitation so easily accomplished under cost-plus-a-percentage-of-cost contracts under which the Government contracts and is bound to pay costs, undetermined at the time the contract is made and to be incurred in the future, plus a commission based on a percentage of these future costs. The evil of such contracts is that the profit of the other party to the contract increases in proportion to that other party's costs expended in the performance. The danger guarded against by the Congressional prohibition was the incentive to a government contractor who already had a binding contract with the Government for payment of undetermined future costs to pay liberally for reimbursable items because higher costs meant a higher fee to him, his profit being determined by a percentage of cost.

In view of the clear statutory prohibition, explicit CPPC contracts are not likely to be encountered. Since, however, the statutory language prohibits a "system of contracting" and not merely a type of contract, numerous sorts of contractual arrangements may become subject to this prohibition. Generally, any contractual arrangement where the contractor is assured of greater profits by incurring additional costs will be held illegal. GAO has enunciated general criteria for ascertaining whether a contract violates this proscription. These criteria were adopted by the Federal Circuit in *Urban Data Sys., Inc. v. United States*, 699 F.2d 1147 (Fed. Cir. 1983), at 1150:

> We accept, at the outset, the general criteria (adopted by the Board) which were developed by the Comptroller General for determining whether a contract is a cost-plus-a-percentage-of-cost contract: (1) payment is on a predetermined percentage rate; (2) the predetermined percentage rate is applied to actual performance costs; (3) the contractor's entitlement is uncertain at the time of contracting; and (4) the contractor's entitlement increases commensurately with increased performance costs. 55 Comp. Gen. 554, 562 (1975). These standards incorporate the common understanding of the "cost-plus-a-percentage-of-cost system of contracting," an understanding which was undoubtedly in Congress's mind when it enacted the prohibition.

In spite of these clear criteria, there is still some confusion as to the arrangements that will constitute such a system of contracting. See, for example, *General Eng'g & Mach. Works v. O'Keefe*, 991 F.2d 775 (Fed. Cir. 1993), where the court affirmed a board holding that the recovery of a separate material handling charge and the inclusion of material handling costs in the hourly rate of a time-and-materials contract would constitute a violation of the CPPC prohibition because it was double recovery. The board had stated in *General Eng'g & Mach. Works*, ASBCA 38788, 92-3 BCA ¶ 25,055, at 124,872:

> If [the contractor] has already received compensation for its effort in handling material as part of its general overhead, further compensation in the form of a material handling charge would constitute additional profit. The payment of that additional profit, in an amount dependent upon the amount of material costs incurred, would constitute a cost-plus-a-percentage-of-cost contractual payment, and thus be illegal.

Neither the board nor the court found that payment of material handling costs as a percentage of material costs was proscribed as long as the material handling costs were excluded from the contractor's overhead. The current contract provisions are silent on this matter. See the Payments under Time-and-Materials and Labor-Hour Contracts clause in FAR 52.232-7, which permits the inclusion of "applicable indirect costs" in charges for material without specifying whether such costs could be charged at a predetermined rate.

Similar confusion occurred in *Information Sys. & Networks Corp. v. United States*, 64 Fed. Cl. 599 (2005). There, the court correctly ruled that a contractor was not entitled to additional fee when its state taxes were increased. However, in responding to the contractor's argument that it would have negotiated a higher fee if the parties had known about the higher taxes, the court stated that awarding such fees would be a clear violation of the cost-plus-a-percentage-of-cost prohibition. In so holding, the court rejected the contractor's argument that there was no such violation because it could not have increased the state tax in order to obtain more profit.

[1] Percentage Compensation

To fall within the definition of a CPPC arrangement, the agreement must provide that some element of the contractor's compensation will be computed as a *percentage* of some of the costs of performance. Such an arrangement meets the first, second, and fourth elements of the above criteria. When the element of compensation established on a percentage basis is profit or fee, it is easy to determine that a violation has occurred. See *Alisa Corp.*, AGBCA 84-193-1, 94-2 BCA ¶ 26,952, where the board found a CPPC contract where it was stated to be an "actual cost + fixed fee" contract with the fee to be paid at 10% of actual costs. Compare *Michael Weller, Inc.*, GSBCA 10627-NHI, 94-2 BCA ¶ 26,849 (time-and-materials contract that authorized reimbursement for cost of subcontracts not a CPPC contract because the profit paid to the subcontractors was not computed as a percentage of costs); *Kellogg Brown & Root Servs., Inc.*, ASBCA 58081, 17-1 BCA ¶ 36,595 (subcontractor's markup of 21% of labor and material costs on a time-and-materials subcontract a CPPC violation because the percentage was applied to "a cost that does not vary with the performance of the contract"); and *Systems Mgmt. & Research Techs. Corp. v. Dep't of Energy*, CBCA 4068, 16-1 BCA ¶ 36,333 (no violation when an 8% fee was to be paid based on fixed labor rates (which excluded profit)—reasoning that no violation occurred because the rates were not "costs" (citing *Urban Data*)). These decisions appear to indicate that there can be no violation of the CPPC prohibition in a time-and-materials or labor-hour contract because the percentage is applied to a fixed rate or price although they allow the contractor to increase its profits by expending more hours or purchasing more material.

A violation is somewhat more difficult to see when one element of cost is paid as a percentage of another cost element. However, this is the more common form of violation. Thus, payment of indirect costs on a percentage basis has been held to violate the CPPC proscription. Such violations were found when a contract called for the payment of overhead rates at predetermined percentages of direct costs, 35 Comp. Gen. 434 (B-126794) (1956); 35 Comp. *Gen.* 63 (B-120714) (1955), and when a material handling charge was to be paid at a percentage of subcontract and material costs, *Systems Eng'g Assocs. Corp.*, ASBCA 21846, 77-2 BCA ¶ 12,740. Similarly, a contract calling for payment of overhead and profit at 15% and 10% of material costs, respectively, was held to be unenforceable, 46 Comp. Gen. 612 (B-159713) (1967). The problem created by contracts where one type of costs is paid on a percentage basis is that such compensation may be greater than the actual costs incurred by the contractor, with the result that a part of this compensation will be additional profit. Hence, these contracts contain the same improper motivation—to increase the base costs in order to increase the potential amount of profit that is derived from the cost element that is paid as a percentage of the base costs. The most unusual element of cost included under this proscription is an executive bonus. In *Air Repair, GmbH.*, ASBCA 10288, 67-1 BCA ¶ 6115, a contractor working under a cost-reimbursement contract agreed to pay its principal officer a bonus computed at a percentage of gross billings. The board found that this was a CPPC arrangement since the officer of the company had the ability to increase the amount of the bonus by increasing the costs of performing the contract.

In most cases finding this type of violation, the percentage has been applied evenly to some of the costs of performance. However, a "stepladder" compensation arrangement has also been held to be a violation. For example, in *Department of State Method of Payment Provisions*, Comp. Gen. Dec. B-196556, 80-2 CPD ¶ 87, GAO found a violation where the contractor was to be paid a management fee based on a sliding scale of actual costs incurred, as follows:

Monthly Total Actual Cost	Management Fee
$0–5,000	$250
5,001–10,000	750
10,001–15,000	1,250
15,001–20,000	1,750
Above 20,001	1,750 plus $500 for each additional $5,000 of invoiced costs

GAO rejected the argument of the agency that this formula was merely a series of fixed fees. A similar result was reached in *Marketing Consultants Int'l, Ltd.*, 55 Comp. Gen. 554 (B-183705), 75-2 CPD ¶ 384. In contrast, no violation was found in *Grey Advertising, Inc.*, 55 Comp. Gen. 1111 (B-184825), 76-1 CPD ¶ 325, where the contract provided for interim fee payments based on "costs being paid" but the total fee was fixed at the inception of the contract.

Violation can be avoided by removing the percentage basis of compensation. When fee is involved, the remedy is to use a cost-reimbursement contract with a fixed or target fee. When overhead is involved, the remedy is accomplished by compensating contractors at negotiated billing rates until the close of an accounting period, FAR 42.704, at which time final rates are negotiated on the basis of actual cost data and costs are adjusted to reflect these final rates, FAR 42.705. One statutory exception to this rule permits educational institutions to be compensated based on predetermined overhead rates, 41 U.S.C. § 4708, FAR 42.705-3. Another means of removing the percentage relationship is to include overhead and profit in fixed rates for labor. This is done in time-and-materials and labor-hour contracts where the contractor is paid a single rate for each hour of labor performed, FAR 16.601, FAR 16.602. Since this type of arrangement contains an incentive, similar to the CPPC contract, to increase costs, the regulations require close government surveillance of such contracts, FAR 16.601(c)(1).

[2] Uncertain Entitlement

To fall within the statutory proscription, a contractor's entitlement to compensation must also be uncertain *at the time of contracting*. Conversely, when the amount of entitlement is established at the time of contracting, even though it was computed on a percentage basis, the contract will not be viewed as a CPPC contract. See *Aero Spacelines, Inc. v. United States*, 530 F.2d 324 (Ct. Cl. 1976), holding that establishing profit using percentage factors in the "weighted guidelines" technique was not a violation because the amount of profit was established in the original contract. A more difficult example is found in *Muschany v. United States*, 324 U.S. 49 (1944), where the Supreme Court ruled that an arrangement permitting a broker, acquiring land on behalf of the government, to charge vendors of the land a 5% commission was not a violation of the statute. The Court reasoned that since the 5% was part of the price of the land, certain at the time of purchase, the government was fully able to determine whether it should pay that price. Thus, it concluded that the arrangement did not motivate the broker to increase its fee by increasing the cost of the land. The Court stated at 63:

> The arrangement may have been improvident from the point of view of the Government. But that question goes to the quality of management by its procurement officers. The fact that the procurement system is improvident obviously does not make it illegal. Illegality does not emerge from inadequate supervision of prices by the Real Estate Branch. Such official failures are not chargeable to a third party dealing with the Government in good faith. It may be unwise for the Government to pay its purchasing agent a commission which is figured on cost of purchases to the Government but there is no statutory prohibition.

Marketing Consultants Int'l Ltd., 55 Comp. Gen. 554 (B-183705), 75-2 CPD ¶ 384, addresses a similar situation. In that case, the contractor was buying work from subcontractors on behalf of the government, under an agreement providing for a percentage markup to compensate the contractor. For some of the purchases, where the government reviewed the subcontract prices prior to award of the subcontracts by the contractor, GAO ruled that there was no violation of the statute. For other purchases, where the contractor was authorized to award the subcontract without prior government review and approval, GAO found a violation because the amount of subcontractor compensation was uncertain "at the time of contracting." See also *United States ex rel. Becker v. Tools & Metals, Inc.*, 2011 U.S. Dist. LEXIS 76248 (N.D. Tex. July 13, 2011), denying a motion for summary judgment where the government contended that a subcontract calling for payment of vendor quoted prices plus 15% was a CPPC subcontract. The court concluded that it was not clear that this was so because the subcontract was performed by converting these quoted amounts into fixed prices for a year at a time. The case ultimately resulted in a multi-million dollar settlement. Compare *Tero Tek Int'l, Ltd.*, Comp. Gen. Dec. B-228548, 88-1 CPD ¶ 132, where a contract that provided for reimbursement of travel expenses based on actual cost plus an agreed percentage thereof subject to a regulatory guideline was held not to be a CPPC contract because the contractor's entitlement was not uncertain at the time of contracting.

[3] Ceilings

The inclusion of a ceiling price in an arrangement that otherwise violates the statute will not cure the violation, 38 Comp. Gen. 38 (B-120546) (1958); *Federal Aviation Admin.—Request for Advance Decision*, 58 Comp. Gen. 654 (B-195173), 79-2 CPD ¶ 34. In these cases, GAO reasoned that there was a violation because the contractor had the same improper motivation to increase profit by increasing the costs up to the amount of the ceiling. *Urban Data Sys., Inc. v. United States*, 699 F.2d 1147 (Fed. Cir. 1983), follows this reasoning in a more complex transaction. There the parties had agreed to a fixed-price contract that included a clause calling for a downward price adjustment computed as the difference between actual costs and anticipated costs, plus 5%. The court reasoned that this was no different from paying actual costs plus 5% profit up to a ceiling price. This holding was buttressed by the fact that the parties negotiated the fixed price using the anticipated costs plus the same 5% profit rate.

In *Department of Labor—Request for Advance Decision*, 62 Comp. Gen. 337 (B-211213), 83-1 CPD ¶ 429, GAO applied this rule on ceilings in an unusual way. The agreement provided for markups of a "maximum of . . . 7.5 percent . . . to cover overhead and profit." GAO reasoned that limiting the markup to a maximum amount was the same as providing for a ceiling price and was thus a statutory violation. This is a highly questionable decision because the contract language can be interpreted more logically as calling for a markup to be negotiated by the parties at the time of pricing new work, with a ceiling on that amount. Such an arrangement would not be a violation of the proscription since the government would not have agreed to a fixed percentage rate of compensation.

In *Fluor Enters., Inc. v. United States*, 64 Fed. Cl. 461 (2005), the court discussed the possibility that a contract permitting an A-E firm to prepare the construction cost estimate might violate the statute because that estimate would constitute the base for determining the 6% fee limitation applicable to A-E firms under 41 U.S.C. § 254(b).

[4] Pricing After Incurrence of Costs

After-the-fact pricing is quite common in government contracting and presents the appearance of CPPC contracting because the profit policy of most government agencies, adopted pursuant to FAR 15.404-4(b), computes profit largely on the basis of percentages of costs of performance. See Chapter 13. Such pricing does not violate the statute, however, when there is no agreement between the contracting parties that any fixed percentage will be applied to incurred costs in negotiating the price. Further, the policy is generally construed as calling for a lower rate of profit if substantial costs have been incurred prior to pricing, because the contractor's risk has been reduced, and contractor risk is one of the key elements considered in arriving at the government's profit position.

The courts and boards have generally agreed that after-the-fact pricing is not a statutory violation. The Court of Claims held that a contract calling for price revision after completion did not violate the CPPC prohibition; the court concluded that the contract more closely resembled a cost-plus-fixed-fee (CPFF) contract than a CPPC contract, *National Elec. Labs., Inc. v. United States*, 148 Ct. Cl. 308, 180 F. Supp. 337 (1960). In *United Food Servs., Inc.*,

64 Comp. Gen. 880 (B-217211), 85-2 CPD ¶ 326, it was held that a CPAF contract was not a CPPC contract because the amount of fee to which the contractor was entitled decreased as costs increased. In *MIG Corp.*, ASBCA 54451, 05-1 BCA ¶ 32,979, it was held that paying termination costs did not violate the statute. In *ITT Federal Servs. Int'l Corp.*, ASBCA 54001, 06-1 BCA ¶ 33,163, it was held that paying a fee on changed work was not a CPPC violation. In *Digicon Corp. v. Department of Commerce*, GSBCA 14257-COM, 98-2 BCA ¶ 29,988; *Rex Sys., Inc.*, ASBCA 49065, 98-2 BCA ¶ 29,926; *E.V. Lane Corp.*, ASBCA 9741, 65-2 BCA ¶ 5076; and *J.G. Watts Constr. Co.*, ASBCA 9454, 1964 BCA ¶ 4171, it was held that the pricing of changes following completion of work did not violate the rule. See also *Allison Div., General Motors Corp.*, ASBCA 15528, 72-1 BCA ¶ 9343, stating at 43,382-83:

> The Government also contends that to grant an increase in fixed fee for a "comparatively minor" change in the contract would transform the contract into a cost-plus-percentage-of-cost contract which is prohibited by law. 10 U.S.C. 2306. No argument or reasoning, other than the bare assertion, has been advanced by the Government in support of its contention. The change here, as we have concluded, was not minor. It substantially increased appellant's work under the contract. The fixed fee was earned when appellant had exerted the level of effort specified in the contract (i.e., 173,200 hours) in performing the work called for. ASPR 3-405.6(d)(2). In cost-plus-fixed-fee contracts, the fixed fee once negotiated does not vary with actual cost, but it may be adjusted as a result of any subsequent changes in the work or services to be performed under the contract. ASPR 3-405.6(a), cf. *Martin Marietta Corporation*, ASBCA 10062, 65-2 BCA ¶ 4973. The granting of additional profit in connection with increased work under change orders has never been considered, to our knowledge, a violation of the cost-plus-a-percentage-of-cost system of contracting.

A few questionable cases reach the opposite result. GAO has held that the conversion of a letter contract to a definitive contract, after the work was substantially completed, violated the rule, 33 Comp. Gen. 291 (B-110609) (1954). See also *Program Res., Inc.*, ASBCA 21656, 78-1 BCA ¶ 12,867, where the board concluded that allowing the contractor an additional fee for an increase in labor rates, when there was no "change" in the nature of the work, would violate the CPPC proscription. In one unusual case, the Court of Claims held that payment of any profit on government-caused delay costs would constitute a violation of the CPPC prohibition, *Laburnum Constr. Corp. v. United States*, 163 Ct. Cl. 339, 325 F.2d 451 (1963).

[5] Quantum Meruit Compensation

While contracts violating the CPPC proscription are illegal and thus unenforceable, GAO has sometimes permitted contractors to recover the fair value of goods and services provided to the government on a *quantum meruit* or *quantum valebant* basis despite the use of a CPPC contract, *Federal Aviation Admin.—Request for Advance Decision*, 58 Comp. Gen. 654 (B-195173), 79-2 CPD ¶ 34; 33 Comp. Gen. 533 (B-118109) (1954); Comp. Gen. Dec. B-167790, Apr. 12, 1973, *Unpub.* See also *Yosemite Park & Curry Co. v. United States*, 217 Ct. Cl. 360, 582 F.2d 552 (1978), where the Court of Claims granted quantum meruit relief because the agency had entered into an invalid contract when the fee exceeded the 10% statutory limitation. In *Alisa Corp.*, AGBCA 84-193-1, 94-2 BCA ¶ 26,952, the board awarded quantum meruit relief in the amount the contractor paid to a supplier for the supplies delivered to the government, stating that it was the lowest price the contractor could have negotiated.

[C] Undefinitized Contractual Actions

Government agencies sometimes encounter situations where they must issue a contract on very short notice with too little time to negotiate all of the terms and conditions or the price. In such cases, it has been common practice to issue a "letter contract" firmly binding the government to pay for the work but calling for the negotiation of a firm contract at a later date. See FAR 16.603-1, stating:

> A letter contract is a written preliminary contractual instrument that authorizes the contractor to begin immediately manufacturing supplies or performing services.

Congress has placed limitations on "undefinitized contractual actions" by the Department of Defense in 10 U.S.C. § 3372 (formerly § 2326). This statute is implemented by DFARS Subpart 217.74, which contains the following definition in DFARS 217.7401(d):

> *Undefinitized contract action* means any contract action for which the contract terms, specifications, or price are not agreed upon before performance is begun under the action. Examples are letter contracts, orders under basic ordering agreements, and provisioned item orders, for which the price has not been agreed upon before performance has begun. For policy relating to definitization of change orders, see 243.204-70 [providing similar policies to change orders exceeding $5 million].

[1] Restrictions on Use

The general policy has been to greatly restrict the use of such transactions because they are open-ended arrangements that place the risk of excessive costs largely on the government. FAR 16.603-2(a) permits the use of letter contracts when—

> (1) the Government's interests demand that the contractor be given a binding commitment so that work can start immediately and
>
> (2) negotiating a definitive contract is not possible in sufficient time to meet the requirement. However, a letter contract should be as complete and definite as feasible under the circumstances.

FAR 16.603-3 places the following limitations on the use of such contracts:

> A letter contract may be used only after the head of the contracting activity or a designee determines in writing that no other contract is suitable. Letter contracts shall not—
>
> (a) Commit the Government to a definitive contract in excess of the funds available at the time the letter contract is executed;
>
> (b) Be entered into without competition when competition is required by Part 6; or
>
> (c) Be amended to satisfy a new requirement unless that requirement is inseparable from the existing letter contract. Any such amendment is subject to the same requirements and limitations as a new letter contract.

Similar limitations are contained in 10 U.S.C. § 3372 (formerly § 2326) as implemented by DFARS 217.7404 (stating a general policy to not obligate more than 50% of a not-to-exceed price). Sole source letter contracts have been approved when properly justified in accordance with the standards discussed in Chapter 3, *Space Vector Corp.*, Comp. Gen. Dec. B-253295.2, 93-2 CPD ¶ 273 (only one company capable of meeting agency needs within time requirements); *Essex Electro Eng'rs, Inc.*, Comp. Gen. Dec. B-250437, 93-1 CPD ¶ 74 (only one firm capable of quickly supplying product needed urgently for military program); *Greenbrier Indus.*, Inc., Comp. Gen. Dec. B-241304, 91-1 CPD ¶ 92 (only one company capable of meeting urgent need); *Mil-Com Elecs. Corp. v. Aldridge*, 712 F. Supp. 232 (D.D.C. 1989). Compare *Jervis B. Webb Co.*, Comp. Gen. Dec. B-211724, 85-1 CPD ¶ 35, holding that a sole source award of a letter contract was improper because the agency had conducted inadequate acquisition planning.

[2] Terms and Conditions

A letter contract should contain the terms and conditions appropriate for the type of contract that the contracting officer believes will be used for the definitive contract, FAR 16.603-4(a). In addition, special contract clauses must be used in these contracts.

[a] Expenditure Limitations and Ceiling Prices

FAR 52.216-24 contains a mandatory standard clause limiting the government's obligations prior to definitization:

LIMITATION OF GOVERNMENT LIABILITY (APR 1984)

(a) In performing this contract, the Contractor is not authorized to make expenditures or incur obligations exceeding ________ dollars.

(b) The maximum amount for which the Government shall be liable if this contract is terminated is ________ dollars.

The amount to be inserted in this clause is the amount of costs expected to be incurred before definitization, and generally, this amount should not be greater than 50% of the estimated cost of the contract, FAR 16.603-2(d). The government is not obligated to pay more than the amount included in the clause, *Magnavox Co.*, ASBCA 17455, 74-1 BCA ¶ 10,495.

Agencies normally obligate the amount of funds set forth in these expenditure limits from current year appropriations and may not obligate any greater amount from an annual appropriation if the contract is definitized in a subsequent fiscal year. Rather, the balance of the contract amount must be obligated from the appropriations current at the time of the contract definitization, *Obligating Letter Contracts*, Comp. Gen. Dec. B-197274, 84-1 CPD ¶ 90. This rule applies even if the work called for by the letter contract is nonseverable because the only amount of work that was a bona fide need of the first fiscal year was the amount covered by the expenditure limit, with the balance of the work a bona fide need of the fiscal year in which the contract was definitized.

The Department of Defense is subject to statutory rules calling for the negotiation of a ceiling price on undefinitized contractual actions and limiting expenditures to 50% of that ceiling, 10 U.S.C. § 3372(a)(2) (formerly § 2326(b)(2)). DFARS 252.217-7027 provides a modified Contract Definitization clause to implement this requirement. FAR 16.603-4(b)(3) also requires the insertion of a ceiling price in letter contracts that are awarded on the basis of competition. This is to ensure that the contractor is held to the price that was the basis of the source selection. Such ceilings impose a significant risk on a contractor because they necessarily must be determined before all of the elements of the contract have been negotiated. See, for example, *Litton Sys., Inc.*, ASBCA 36976, 93-2 BCA ¶ 25,705, where a contractor that had agreed to a letter contract that was to become a firm-fixed-price contract was bound by the ceiling price even though its costs were substantially higher than that price. In that case, the board also ruled that the ceiling price was to be adjusted to reflect changes to the work, both additive and deductive.

The DoD procedure also permits the contracting officer to raise the level of the government's limitation of obligations to 75% of the ceiling price if the contractor has submitted a "qualifying proposal" prior to reaching the 50%

limitation, DFARS 217.7404-4. DFARS 217.7401(c) contains the following definition:

> *Qualifying proposal* means a proposal containing sufficient information for the DoD to do complete and meaningful analysis and audits of the—
>
> (1) Data in the proposal; and
>
> (2) Any other data that the contracting officer has determined DoD needs to review in connection with the contract.

[b] Definitization Schedule

FAR 52.216-25 provides the following mandatory clause setting forth the procedures for contract definitization:

> CONTRACT DEFINITIZATION (OCT 2010)
>
> (a) A [*insert specific type of contract*] definitive contract is contemplated. The Contractor agrees to begin promptly negotiating with the Contracting Officer the terms of a definitive contract that will include (1) all clauses required by the Federal Acquisition Regulation (FAR) on the date of execution of the letter contract, (2) all clauses required by law on the date of execution of the definitive contract, and (3) any other mutually agreeable clauses, terms, and conditions. The Contractor agrees to submit a _______ [*insert specific type of proposal (e.g., fixed-price or cost-and-fee)*] proposal, including data other than cost or pricing data, and certified cost or pricing data, in accordance with FAR 15.408, Table 15-2, supporting its proposal.
>
> (b) The schedule for definitizing this contract is [insert target date for definitization of the contract and dates for submission of proposal, beginning of negotiations, and, if appropriate, submission of make-or-buy and subcontracting plans and cost or pricing data]:
>
> (c) If agreement on a definitive contract to supersede this letter contract is not reached by the target date in paragraph (b) of this section, or within any extension of it granted by the Contracting Officer, the Contracting Officer may, with the approval of the head of the contracting activity, determine a reasonable price or fee in accordance with Subpart 15.4 and Part 31 of the FAR, subject to Contractor appeal as provided in the Disputes clause. In any event, the Contractor shall proceed with completion of the contract, subject to only to the Limitation of Government Liability clause.
>
> (1) After the Contracting Officer's determination or price or fee, the contract shall be governed by—
>
> (i) All clauses required by the FAR on the date of execution of this letter contract for either fixed-price or cost-reimbursement contracts, as determined by the Contracting Officer under this paragraph (c);
>
> (ii) All clauses required by law as of the date of the Contracting Officer's determination; and

(iii) Any other clauses, terms, and conditions mutually agreed upon.

(2) To the extent consistent with subparagraph (c)(1) of this section, all clauses, terms, and conditions included in this letter contract shall continue in effect, except those that by their nature apply only to a letter contract.

FAR 16.603-2(c)(3) requires that the schedule for definitization call for completion of the process "within 180 days after the date of the letter contract or before completion of 40 percent of the work to be performed, whichever occurs first." It permits the granting of additional time "in extreme cases." These provisions reflect the strong policy of the government to preclude letter contracts from running indefinitely without being firmly priced. If the parties cannot agree to the definitization, the clause permits unilateral action by the contracting officer with appeal under the Disputes clause. In *Litton Sys., Inc.*, ASBCA 36976, 93-2 BCA ¶ 25,705, the board considered such an appeal and ruled that the unilaterally definitized price should have included the costs of extra work performed by the contractor. In ASBCA 49787, 00-2 BCA ¶ 30,969, the board awarded compensation at the ceiling price of the letter contract. Earlier versions of the clause did not contain this procedure, but the Court of Claims ruled that it had jurisdiction to make a decision as to the proper definitization of a letter contract where the contractor had completed the work, but the parties had been unable to agree to a final price, *Sanders Assocs., Inc. v. United States*, 423 F.2d 291 (Ct. Cl. 1970). Section 816 of the National Defense Authorization Act for Fiscal Year 2018 (Pub. L. No. 115-91) precludes unilateral definitization of DoD letter contracts without the consent of "the service acquisition executive" of the military service.

The clause also binds the parties to the mandatory contract clauses in effect at the time the letter contract was issued and the statutory clauses in effect on the date of definitization, unless the parties agree to other clauses. Thus, a contractor must be sure to obtain agreement prior to contract execution for any variances from FAR clauses or other modifications to the language that may be desired. See *Teledyne Continental Motors*, ASBCA 22571, 85-3 BCA ¶ 18,472, where the government was bound to a clause that it had included in the modification definitizing the letter contract even though that clause increased the costs chargeable to the contract.

Paragraph (a) of the clause requires the submission of certified cost or pricing data—a requirement that will substantially increase the time necessary for definitization. FAR 16.603-4(b)(3) permits deletion of this requirement if "at the time of entering into the letter contract, the contracting officer knows that the definitive contract will be based on adequate price competition or will otherwise meet the criteria of 15.403-1 for not requiring submission of certified cost or pricing data."

[c] Payment

In letter contracts contemplating a cost-reimbursement contract, FAR 16.603-4(c) requires the use of the Payments of Allowable Costs Before Definitization clause in FAR 52.216-26. This clause is intended to motivate the contractor to definitize the contract quickly by limiting reimbursement as follows:

> (a)(1) One hundred percent of approved costs representing financing payments to subcontractors under fixed-price subcontracts; *provided*, that the Government's payments to the Contractor will not exceed 80 percent of the allowable costs of those subcontractors.
>
> (2) One hundred percent of approved costs representing cost-reimbursement subcontracts; *provided*, that the Government's payments to the Contractor shall not exceed 85 percent of the allowable costs of those subcontractors.
>
> (3) Eighty-five percent of all other approved costs.

There is no such clause to be used for letter contracts contemplating fixed-price contracts. Thus, if the contractor desires progress payments during performance of a fixed-price letter contract, one of the standard clauses should be used. See Progress Payments, FAR 52.232-16 or Performance-Based Payments, FAR 52.232-32 (fixed-price supply or service contracts) or Payment under Fixed-Price Construction Contracts, FAR 52.232-5 (fixed-price construction contracts).

§ 12.03 FIXED-PRICE CONTRACTS

One of the basic types of contract is the fixed-price contract. Such contracts can be either firm-fixed-price or fixed-price subject to adjustment by formula during or after performance. All fixed-price contracts are also subject to adjustment under a variety of contract clauses such as the Changes clause. These contracts all have the common characteristic of binding the contractor to complete the work at a fixed amount of compensation, once adjusted, regardless of the costs of performance. To obtain the benefit of the fixed price, the government must draft and administer the contract in a manner that avoids significant claims for price adjustment. If these conditions exist, the firm-fixed-price contract places the risk of incurring unforeseen costs on the contractor rather than on the government. Conversely, it provides the contractor the greatest opportunity to earn higher profits by devising ways to reduce the costs of performance.

Since there are many situations where the work can be reasonably well defined, but it is unwise to place the entire cost risk on the contractor, a number of variations on the firm-fixed-price contract are used. These variations are of three types: (i) fixed-price contracts with *formula repricing*, such as the fixed-price incentive (FPI) and the fixed-price with economic price adjustment contracts, (ii) fixed-price contracts with subjective repricing (using award fees), and

(iii) fixed-price contracts with repricing *after some costs have been incurred*, such as the fixed-price redeterminable contracts. Descriptions of the firm-fixed-price contract and its variations follow. FPI contracts and fixed-price contracts with award fees are dealt with in the section on incentive contracts.

[A] Firm-Fixed-Price Contracts

The purest form of fixed-price contract is the firm-fixed-price contract. There the bargain is stated in terms of a fixed amount of compensation with no formula or technique for varying the price in the event of unforeseen contingencies. FAR 16.202-1 describes this type of contract as follows:

> A firm-fixed-price contract provides for a price that is not subject to any adjustment on the basis of the contractor's cost experience in performing the contract. This contract type places upon the contractor maximum risk and full responsibility for all costs and resulting profit or loss. It provides maximum incentive for the contractor to control costs and perform effectively and imposes a minimum administrative burden upon the contracting parties.

The first sentence of this description is misleading in that it fails to recognize that firm-fixed-price contracts contain a number of clauses that call for price adjustments to compensate the contractor when specified events occur.

FAR 16.202-2, recognizing that the use of this type of contract might place the risk of *too high* a price on the government, contains the following guidance:

> A firm-fixed-price contract is suitable for acquiring commercial products or commercial services (see Parts 2 and 12) or for acquiring other supplies or services on the basis of reasonably definitive functional or detailed specifications (see Part 11) when the contracting officer can establish fair and reasonable prices at the outset, such as when—
>
> (a) There is adequate price competition;
>
> (b) There are reasonable price comparisons with prior purchases of the same or similar supplies or services made on a competitive basis or supported by valid certified cost or pricing data;
>
> (c) Available cost or pricing information permits realistic estimates of the probable costs of performance; or
>
> (d) Performance uncertainties can be identified and reasonable estimates of their cost impact can be made, and the contractor is willing to accept a firm fixed price representing assumption of the risks involved.

Firm-fixed-price contracts must be used with caution because both parties can be injured if the actual costs of performance are greatly at variance with the contract price. If the costs greatly exceed the price, the contractor will incur a substantial loss and may be financially unable or unwilling to complete the work at the contract price. See *Ball Bros. Research Corp.*, NASABCA 1277-6, 80-2

BCA ¶ 14,526, where the government converted a fixed-price contract to a cost-plus-fixed-fee (CPFF) contract in order to obtain completion of the work. See also *General Dynamics Corp. v. United States*, 671 F.2d 474 (Ct. Cl. 1982), where a similar "conversion" to a cost-type contract occurred after the contractor encountered great difficulties in performing a fixed-price-type contract. If the costs are far under the price, the government will have paid substantially more for the work than might have been possible under some other form of contract. When there is adequate information to assure the parties that the costs are predictable, however, the firm-fixed-price contract is the simplest form of contract to accomplish the work.

Firm-fixed-price contracts are also of questionable value if the work is not well defined and stable in nature. If the scope of the work is unclear or subject to change during performance, the contractor is likely to assert its entitlement to price adjustments during performance and contract administration will be very complex. The DoD *Guidance on Using Incentive and Other Contract Types* (DoD Guide), April 2016, contains the following explanation:

> While an FFP contract provides the maximum incentive for a contractor to control cost, it is incumbent upon the Government to ensure that the requirement is very clearly defined and that the price paid is fair and reasonable. Vague contract language may leave the requirement open to different interpretations by the contractor and the Government. In order to hold down costs, a contractor may interpret the requirement in terms resulting in a lower level of performance than the Government intended. In that instance, vague language results in ambiguities in the contract.

The claims for additional compensation that can arise under fixed-price contracts are dealt with in detail in Cibinic, Nash & Nagle, *Administration of Government Contracts* (5th ed. 2016).

The DOD Guide also cautions against the use of firm fixed-price contracts unless the government is sure that the cost estimate is accurate, stating:

> In the past, DoD has experienced a significant variation in proposed/negotiated costs based on conservative contractor estimates compared to actual cost outcomes. The estimates factor in known risks, limiting contractor risk in the sole-source, fixed-price environment. Until such time as DoD is confident actual cost outcomes will approximate estimated costs, defined as actual outcomes *within two to four percent of estimates*, use of an [fixed-price incentive] contract is preferred over a [firm fixed-price] arrangement. (Italics added)

[B] Fixed-Price Contract with Economic Price Adjustment

This type of contract provides for upward or downward adjustment of the fixed price or incentive target price if economic conditions change during contract performance. Usually, such adjustments are based on changes in material costs or labor rates (reflected by actual costs or indexes) but they can be based on changes to a contractor's prices if such prices are subject to market forces.

The use of economic price adjustment (EPA) clauses (frequently called "escalation" clauses) is a major means of risk allocation. Such clauses place on the government some or all of the risk of increases in the cost of labor or material or of the contractor's prices. Absent such a clause, these risks are allocated to the contractor by virtue of entering into a firm-fixed-price contract, *Office Automation & Training Consultants*, ASBCA 56779, 11-1 BCA ¶ 34,666 (no mutual mistake as to applicability of Service Contract Act when parties used firm-fixed-price contract); *McNamara Constr. of Manitoba, Ltd. v. United States*, 509 F.2d 1166 (Ct. Cl. 1975) (no mutual mistake as to labor rates when parties used firm-fixed-price contract); *Charles H. Siever Co.*, ASBCA 23968, 80-1 BCA ¶ 14,390, *recons. denied*, 80-2 BCA ¶ 14,589 (contractor not entitled to increase price of firm-fixed-price contract when escalation clause was not included in the contract). See *Southern Dredging Co.*, ENGBCA 5843, 92-2 BCA ¶ 24,886, denying reformation of a contract to account for increased fuel prices where the fixed-price contract did not include a price escalation clause, and stating at 124,116:

> "It is black letter law that the risk of performance costs in a firm fixed-price contract, absent a clause stating otherwise, are on the contractor." *Chevron U.S.A., Inc.*, ASBCA No. 32323, 90-1 BCA ¶ 22,602. See *Nedlog Co.*, ASBCA No. 26034, 82-1 BCA ¶ 15,519; *D.K.'s Precision and Manufacturing*, ASBCA No. 39616, 90-2 BCA ¶ 22,830. Further, neither abnormal price increases nor unusual trade conditions change this basic principle regarding a contractor's assumption of the risk of increased performance costs in a fixed-price contract. *Anthony P. Miller, Inc. v. United States* [9 CCF ¶ 72,218], 161 Ct. Cl. 455, *cert. denied,* 375 U.S. 879 (1963); *Jalaprathan Cement Co., Ltd.*, ASBCA No. 21248, 79-2 BCA ¶ 13,927.

See also *Cobra, S.A.*, ASBCA 28146, 84-3 BCA ¶ 17,535, denying reformation of a contract to include an escalation clause. These cases demonstrate the general understanding that this matter is covered by specific contract language, and absent such specific language, the risk of upward economic fluctuations is on the contractor. One exception to this rule is that upward price fluctuations that occur because of government delays can be included in the price adjustment for such delays, *ADT Constr. Group, Inc.*, ASBCA 57322, 15-1 BCA BCA ¶ 35,893.

These clauses benefit the government in the unlikely event of downward economic fluctuations. See FAR 16.203-1 describing these clauses as leading to "price adjustments [which] are based on increases or decreases" in the costs of materials and labor or in the contractor's prices.

[1] Use of Economic Price Adjustment Clauses

FAR 16.203-2 provides the following guidance on the use of this type of contract:

> A fixed-price contract with economic price adjustment may be used when (i) there is serious doubt concerning the stability of market or labor conditions that will exist during an extended period of contract performance, and (ii) contingencies that would otherwise be included in the contract price can be identified and covered separately in the contract. Price adjustments based on established prices should normally be restricted to industry-wide contingencies. Price adjustments based on labor and material costs should be limited to contingencies beyond the contractor's control. For use of economic price adjustment in sealed bid contracts, see 14.408-4.
>
> > (a) In establishing the base level from which adjustment will be made, the contracting officer shall ensure that contingency allowances are not duplicated by inclusion in both the base price and the adjustment requested by the contractor under economic price adjustment clause.
> >
> > (b) In contracts that do not require submission of certified cost or pricing data, the contracting officer shall obtain adequate data to establish the base level from which adjustment will be made and may require verification of data submitted.

FAR 16.203-3 prohibits the use of EPA clauses that do not meet certain standards:

> A fixed-price contract with economic price adjustment shall not be used unless the contracting officer determines that it is necessary either to protect the contractor and the Government against significant fluctuations in labor or material costs or to provide for contract price adjustment in the event of changes in the contractor's established prices.

This prohibition has led to considerable litigation regarding EPA clauses for petroleum products that were based on a government report of average sales prices of such products. In *Mapco Alaska Petroleum, Inc. v. United States*, 27 Fed. Cl. 405 (1992), the court held that such an EPA clause was illegal because it was not based on either the contractor's established prices or the contractor's cost of labor and material. This reasoning was accepted in *Barrett Refining Corp. v. United States*, 242 F.3d 1055 (Fed. Cir. 2001), where the court affirmed a decision that, after striking the illegal EPA clause from the contract, the contractor had an implied-in-fact contract for the fair market value of the fuel it had delivered. The court remanded the case to determine the amount that the government should recover on contracts where the illegal clause had led to overpayment for the fuel—the recovery being based on the theory that these were "unauthorized payments." Subsequently, a different panel of the court held that the clause was not illegal because the FAR did not require that EPA clauses be based on the *contractor's* established prices but, rather, it permitted such a clause to be based on any other measure of established prices, *Tesoro Hawaii Corp. v. United States*, 405 F.3d 1339 (Fed. Cir. 2005). Another panel later ruled that the compilation of sales prices used as the basis for EPA complied with the FAR requirement that such adjustments had to be based on "published or otherwise established prices." See *ConocoPhillips, Conoco, Inc. v. United States*, 501 F.3d 1374 (Fed. Cir. 2007), stating at 1378:

> The [sales price compilation's] use of an amalgamation of related products does not render [it] ineligible to serve as the basis for a price adjustment clause under the regulations. The language of FAR § 16.203-1(a), which allowed the contract price to be adjusted based on increases or decreases "in published or otherwise established prices" for particular items, gave the contracting parties substantial freedom to use "market-based references to identify 'established prices.'" *Tesoro*, 405 F.3d at 1347. Under that standard, it was permissible to use a published weighted average of multiple reference items if the reference items are sufficiently similar to the contract items that it was reasonable, at the time the parties entered into the contract, to expect the index to approximate the change in the market price of the contract item. The regulations did not require the use of particular vendors' prices, and they also did not require the use of any particular measure of the market. In such a setting, it is not surprising that the regulations gave the parties some flexibility in choosing how market-based price adjustments would be calculated. Absent some degree of flexibility, contractual agreements would constantly be subject to second-guessing through litigation over whether the method chosen in advance for price adjustment turned out after the fact to correlate sufficiently closely to what each party regards as the correct measure of market price.

The court therefore concluded that the fact that the chosen measure for determining the EPA did not reflect the amount of price variation that actually occurred in the market was not a mistake because the contractor voluntarily agreed to the measure and could have protected itself by bargaining for a better measure of price variation. The court distinguished *Beta Sys., Inc. v. United States*, 838 F.2d 1179 (Fed. Cir. 1988), which had granted reformation on the basis of mutual mistake when an index did not include the major material used on the contract. These decisions indicate that the Federal Circuit interprets the FAR as giving the contracting parties considerable leeway in selecting a measure to be used as the basis for such adjustments.

Although most EPA clauses are used in firm-fixed-price contracts, they may also be used in any fixed-price-type contract, including incentive or redeterminable contracts. On major systems contracts, EPA provisions have frequently been used in fixed-price incentive contracts. In such cases, the government bears the risk of increases in labor rates and material prices and the parties share the risk of increases in cost due to other factors.

If there is the possibility of significant economic fluctuation during contract performance, the use of an EPA clause will probably encourage more companies to participate in the competition and will permit contracting at a price free of the contingencies that would otherwise be included to compensate for such fluctuations. However, the contracting officer may conclude that there is sufficient competition to minimize contingencies in pricing and therefore use firm-fixed-price contracting. If large fluctuations in the economy are possible, it can be argued that it is not in the government's best interests to contract without EPA clauses even if it is likely that competition will limit price contingencies. In such cases, a loss contract may result with all of its inherent difficulties.

The contracting officer has substantial discretion to determine whether to use an EPA clause, and challenges to a decision to omit such a clause from a procurement will invariably fail. See, for example, *Northrop Grumman Tech. Servs., Inc.* Comp. Gen. Dec. B-406523, 2012 CPD ¶ 197 (market research indicated that commercial practice did not require an EPA clause for five years of fixed prices); *B & P Refuse Disposal, Inc.*, Comp. Gen. Dec. B-253661, 93-2 CPD ¶ 177 (contracting officer told offerors of prior increases in price and forced them to include such a contingency in bid to protect against risk); *Master Sec., Inc.*, Comp. Gen. Dec. B-232263, 88-2 CPD ¶ 449 (contracting officer determined market conditions were sufficiently stable to enable offerors to make realistic estimates of future costs); *Sentinel Elecs., Inc.*, Comp. Gen. Dec. B-212770, 84-1 CPD ¶ 5 (contracting officer determined that there were sufficient capable producers that could reasonably price work even though last delivery was 43 months after award); *Barker & Williamson*, Comp. Gen. Dec. B-208236, 82-2 CPD ¶ 454 (omission of clause in basic quantity in first year of contract upheld even though it was included in option quantities in subsequent years because contracting officer determined that pricing was sufficiently stable to permit bidders to assume risks for initial requirement); and *Tri-Wall Containers*, Comp. Gen. Dec. B-200702, 81-1 CPD ¶ 277 (omission of clause upheld because market price had been stable for eight months and three bids were received although prior-year pricing had been very volatile). See also *Argus Servs., Inc.*, Comp. Gen. Dec. B-234016.2, 89-2 CPD ¶ 227, holding that the contracting officer had the discretion not to use an EPA provision in order to have "minimum administrative burdens" even though it imposed "maximum risks" on the prospective contractor.

The government can run a competition allowing offerors to select the provisions that will mitigate long-term risk. See, for example, *American States Utils. Servs. Inc.*, Comp. Gen. Dec. B-291307.3, 2004 CPD ¶ 150, holding that it was proper to select an offeror that proposed fixed prices with economic price adjustment as posing less risk for the government than an offeror that proposed periodic price redetermination.

[2] Types of Economic Price Adjustment Provisions

FAR 16.203-1 describes three general types of EPA provisions: (1) adjustments based on established prices, (2) adjustments based on the contractor's actual costs of labor and material, and (3) adjustments based on cost indexes of labor and material.

FAR 16.203-4 provides standard clauses for use with the first two types. However, there is no standard clause for an EPA clause based on indexes—requiring each agency to draft its own clause in this area. In addition, FAR 16.203-4 permits the use of "agency prescribed" clauses with the result that great latitude is given in drafting special clauses for different contracting situations. Generally, such specially drafted EPA clauses should use some basis of measurement of the fluctuations in the contractor's prices or costs of material and labor that is not under the control of the contractor. See FAR 16.203-2 stating that such clauses should cover contingencies that are "industry-wide" or "beyond the contractor's control." This protects the government from price increases due to contractor inefficiency or intentional overspending and permits evaluation of competitive prices. For example, an EPA clause providing that the price would be adjusted in an amount equal to higher prices charged by the contractor for a component that was not being sold in substantial quantities to other customers would be improper because there would be no market constraints limiting the ability of the contractor to manipulate its prices. See *Roarda, Inc.*, Comp. Gen. Dec. B-204524.5, 82-1 CPD ¶ 438, where GAO found a clause improper because it permitted the contractor to increase the contract price if its market price increased. GAO objected that the agency had not included any mechanism in the procurement to ascertain that the contractor's price reflected "some objective standard," with the result that the price could be varied at will. In that case, consequently, there was no assurance in a sealed bid procurement that the contractor was actually the low bidder. See also *American Transparents Plastic Corp.*, Comp. Gen. Dec. B-210898, 83-2 CPD ¶ 539, stating the same "objective standard" rule.

In a sealed bid procurement, it is also important that all bidders use substantially the same basis for price adjustment so that the low price can be determined. Thus, a clause should not be used that allows the bidder to select the basis for price adjustment. See *Steuart Petroleum Co. v. United States*, 438 F. Supp. 527 (D.D.C. 1977), enjoining the performance of a contract awarded to a bidder that had selected a volatile basis for price adjustment, which cast great doubt on whether its low bid would actually lead to the low price after economic price adjustment. See also *Galaxy Custodial Servs., Inc.*, 64 Comp. Gen. 593 (B-215738), 85-1 CPD ¶ 658, criticizing an Invitation for Bids (IFB) permitting each bidder to establish a base rate because that produced an incentive to bid a base rate lower than the rate used to compute the bid. In *Amarillo Aircraft Sales & Servs., Inc.*, 63 Comp. Gen. 568 (B-214225), 84-2 CPD ¶ 269, GAO concurred in the termination of a procurement after the procuring agency determined that the contractor had used a basis for price adjustment that was not comparable to that used by other bidders and was subject to the control of the contractor. See FAR 14.408-4(b) requiring that bids that take exception to government imposed economic price adjustment clauses be found nonresponsive. In *First Am. Engineered Solutions*, Comp. Gen. Dec. B-289051, 2001 CPD ¶ 207, GAO held that it was proper to declare a bid nonresponsive when the bidder did not agree to base all option year prices on the economic price adjustment clause as required by the IFB. If the bidder inserts a price adjustment provision in a bid where the IFB does not call for a clause, an even more restrictive rule will apply. If the clause contains no ceiling, the bid will be held to be nonresponsive, *Joy Mfg. Co.*, 54 Comp. Gen. 237 (B-181136), 74-2 CPD ¶ 183. If the clause contains a ceiling, the bid will be evaluated at the ceiling price, FAR 14.408-4(a)(1). This rule removes all of the bidding advantage that would be obtained from including a clause in the bid.

In negotiated procurements, the government will be bound if it accepts an offer containing a price adjustment clause. See *United States Steel Corp.*, ASBCA 29111, 85-1 BCA ¶ 17,761, *recons. denied*, 85-1 BCA ¶ 17,921, holding the government to a provision in a letter responding to a negotiated RFP stating the price would be that "in effect at the time of shipment, subject to a 10 percent maximum escalation" from the price in effect at the time of award. The board reasoned that this type of bargain was permitted in negotiated procurement.

[a] Adjustments Based on Contractor's Established Prices

The first type of economic price adjustment provision provided for in FAR 16.203-1 uses established catalog or market prices as the basis for price adjustment. This type of adjustment is only appropriate for negotiated procurements, *Chem-Care Co.*, ASBCA 53614, 04-1 BCA ¶ 32,593. Standard contract clauses are provided for standard supplies, FAR 52.216-2, and semi-standard supplies, FAR 52.216-3. Standard supplies are those with established catalog or market prices, while semi-standard supplies are those whose "prices can be reasonably related to the prices of nearly equivalent standard supplies," FAR 16.203-4(b)(1)(ii). In the latter situation, the clause requires that the related catalog or market item be identified in the schedule of the contract. Both clauses contain the same provisions calling for upward or downward price adjustments on a pro rata basis following changes in catalog or market prices. The clause for standard supplies provides:

ECONOMIC PRICE ADJUSTMENT—STANDARD SUPPLIES
(JAN 1997)

(a) The Contractor warrants that the unit price stated in the Schedule for [*offeror insert Schedule line-item number*] is not in excess of the Contractor's applicable established price in effect on the contract date for like quantities of the same item. The term "unit price" excludes any part of the price directly resulting from requirements for preservation, packaging, or packing beyond standard commercial practice. The term "established price" means a price that—

(1) Is an established catalog or market price for a commercial item sold in substantial quantities to the general public; and

(2) Is the net price after applying any standard trade discounts offered by the Contractor.

(b) The Contractor shall promptly notify the Contracting Officer of the amount and effective date of each decrease in any applicable established price. Each corresponding contract unit price shall be decreased by the same percentage that the established price is decreased. The decrease shall apply to those items delivered on and after the effective date of the decrease in the Contractor's established price, and this contract shall be modified accordingly.

(c) If the Contractor's applicable established price is increased after the contract date, the corresponding contract unit price shall be increased, upon the Contractor's written request to the Contracting Officer, by the same percentage that the established price is increased, and the contract shall be modified accordingly, subject to the following limitations:

(1) The aggregate of the increases in any contract unit price under this clause shall not exceed 10 percent of the original contract unit price.

(2) The increased contract unit price shall be effective—

(i) On the effective date of the increase in the applicable established price if the Contracting Officer receives the Contractor's written request within 10 days thereafter; or

(ii) If the written request is received later, on the date the Contracting Officer receives the request.

(3) The increased contract unit price shall not apply to quantities scheduled under the contract for delivery before the effective date of the increased contract unit price, unless failure to deliver before that date results from causes beyond the control and without the fault or negligence of the Contractor, within the meaning of the Default clause.

(4) No modification increasing a contract unit price shall be executed under this paragraph (c) until the Contracting Officer verifies the increase in the applicable established price.

(5) Within 30 days after receipt of the Contractor's written request, the Contracting Officer may cancel, without liability to either party, any undelivered portion of the contract items affected by the requested increase.

(d) During the time allowed for the cancellation provided for in subparagraph (c)(5) above, and thereafter if there is no cancellation, the Contractor shall continue deliveries according to the contract delivery schedule, and the Government shall pay for such deliveries at the contract unit price, increased to the extent provided by paragraph (c) above.

Note that this clause addresses *the contractor's established price* not established prices of other contractors. Nonetheless, the Federal Circuit held that a clause of this nature basing adjustments on market prices in the petroleum industry were of the same nature as this clause, *Tesoro Hawaii Corp. v. United States*, 405 F.3d 1339 (Fed. Cir. 2005).

DFARS 216.203-4-70 provides two additional bases of price adjustment of this type. See the clauses at DFARS 252.216-7000 for basic steel, aluminum, brass, bronze, or copper mill products and DFARS 252.216-7001 for nonstandard steel products.

These clauses provide the necessary "objectivity" by using catalog or market prices for items that are sold by the contractor to the general public in "substantial quantities." Elaborate tests for establishing that items fall within this category were removed from FAR 15.804-3(c) in 1995 with the result that there is no current guidance on what constitutes "substantial quantities." The other terms are defined in the definition of "commercial item" in FAR 2.101 as follows:

> (i) Catalog price means a price included in a catalog, price list, schedule, or other form that is regularly maintained by the manufacturer or vendor, is either published or otherwise available for inspection by customers, and states prices at which sales are currently, or were last, made to a significant number of buyers constituting the general public; and
>
> (ii) Market prices means current prices that are established in the course of ordinary trade between buyers and sellers free to bargain and that can be substantiated through competition or from sources independent of the offerors.

The theory is that if an item meets these tests, its price will be determined by market forces and the contractor will be unable to manipulate the price to increase the amount paid under the contract containing the EPA clause.

[b] Adjustment Based on Contractor's Actual Costs

The second type of EPA provision in FAR 16.203-1 uses the actual costs of the contractor as the basis for the adjustment. The operative provisions in the standard contract clause in FAR 52.216-4 state:

> ECONOMIC PRICE ADJUSTMENT—LABOR AND MATERIAL
> (JAN 1997)
>
> (a) The Contractor shall notify the Contracting Officer if, at any time during contract performance, the rates of pay for labor (including fringe benefits) or the unit prices for material shown in the Schedule either increase or decrease. The Contractor shall furnish this notice within 60 days after the increase or decrease, or within any additional period that the Contracting Officer may approve in writing, but not later than the date of final payment under this contract. The notice shall include the Contractor's proposal for an adjustment in the contract unit prices to be negotiated under paragraph (b) below, and shall include, in the form required by the Contracting Officer, supporting data explaining the cause, effective date, and amount of the increase or decrease and the amount of the Contractor's adjustment proposal.

(b) Promptly after the Contracting Officer receives the notice and data under paragraph (a) above, the Contracting Officer and the Contractor shall negotiate a price adjustment in the contract unit prices and its effective date. However, the Contracting Officer may postpone the negotiations until an accumulation of increases and decreases in the labor rates (including fringe benefits) and unit prices of material shown in the Schedule results in an adjustment allowable under subparagraph (c)(3) below. The Contracting Officer shall modify this contract (1) to include the price adjustment and its effective date and (2) to revise the labor rates (including fringe benefits) or unit prices of material as shown in the Schedule to reflect the increases or decreases resulting from the adjustment. The Contractor shall continue performance pending agreement on, or determination of, any adjustment and its effective date.

The balance of the clause contains essentially the same provisions as the FAR 52.216-2 clause including the 10% ceiling on adjustments. The contracting officer has considerable discretion to determine not to include this clause in a contract, *Thorington Elec. & Constr. Co.*, ASBCA 56997, 12-1 BCA ¶ 34,957.

When this clause is used, FAR 16.203-4(c)(3) requires that a clause be inserted in the schedule of the contract describing the specific types of labor and material subject to price adjustment, the labor rates and material prices to be increased or decreased, and the quantities of labor and material allocable to each contract unit. In the 1980s, DFARS 216.203-4(c)(3) contained a sample provision that contained useful guidance:

The following types of labor and material are subject to price adjustment pursuant to the "Economic Price Adjustment—Labor and Material" clause of this contract.

Type of Labor and Material	Contract Item No. 1 Rates of Pay and Material Prices	Quantities and Direct Costs Per Unit of Procurement
Drill Press Operator	$3.00/hour no fringe benefits included ______ $3.00	20 min.—$1.00
Welder	$2.75/hour .05/hour—vacation pay .20/hour—pension plan ______ $3.00	10 min.—$ .50

(continues)

Type of Labor and Material	Contract Item No. 1 Rates of Pay and Material Prices	Quantities and Direct Costs Per Unit of Procurement
Copper Sheet	$ .40/lb.	2 lb.—$ .80
Purchased Parts: (1) ABC tube X5721 (2) XYZ part #9348	$1.00 each $ .50 each	3 ea.—$3.00 10 ea.—$5.00

This schedule provision is of critical importance because adjustments are made only for listed elements of the price. Thus, no adjustment will be granted for unlisted items *Tekkon Engrg. Co.*, ASBCA 56831, 10-2 BCA ¶ 34,563 (transportation costs not in any contract schedule); *Optic-Electronic Corp.*, ASBCA 24962, 83-2 BCA ¶ 16,677, *recons. denied*, 84-3 BCA ¶ 17,565 (profit-sharing plan that did not appear among the fringe benefits in the labor rates listed in the schedule). Similarly, it was held that this type of EPA clause applied only to items added to a contract by amendment rather than to all contract items, because the schedule listed only the added items, *Minowitz Mfg. Co.*, ASBCA 23784, 83-1 BCA ¶ 16,324. See also *Arcadia Mfg. Co.*, ASBCA 20764, 76-2 BCA ¶ 12,058, where the board found, in a sealed bid procurement, that the bidder's failure to include the required schedule of items covered eliminated the clause even though it was designated in the IFB. Compare *Transportes Especiales de Automoviles, S.A.*, ASBCA 43851, 93-2 BCA ¶ 25,745, ordering reformation of a negotiated contract because the contract contained the standard EPA clause but did not have the schedule required by the FAR and illustrated by the DFARS to set rates and quantities of labor. The board concluded that the parties intended to have escalation but had mistakenly omitted the schedule. In contrast, in *Tekkon Engrg. Co.*, ASBCA 56831, 10-2 BCA ¶ 34,563, the board ruled that the fact that the agency had given escalation costs without a clause in a prior contract was not proof that it intended to provide such costs in the current contract.

At first glance, this type of EPA clause appears to contain no objective basis for price increases. However, FAR 16.203-2 states that this technique should "normally be restricted to industry-wide contingencies" and "limited to contingencies beyond the contractor's control." To meet this requirement, the clause should only be used in those situations where the labor covered by the clause is used for a mix of work, some of which is not subject to economic price adjustment or reimbursement of costs, and the material covered by the clause is material bought in a competitive market. In such cases, there would be outside pressures limiting the amount of increases the contractor could pay and subsequently recover under the clause. It is clear when this clause is included that changes in quantity of items or amount of effort will not lead to escalation—only changes in labor rates or material prices, *Nuclear Components, Inc.*, ASBCA 22884, 79-2 BCA ¶ 14,006.

This clause is not well suited for use in sealed bid contracts because it requires each bidder to furnish the schedule as part of the bid. This makes evaluation rather speculative, *VBM Corp.*, Comp. Gen. Dec. B-182225, 75-1 CPD ¶ 130, and may motivate bidders to include rates in the schedule that are lower than those actually used in order to obtain greater price adjustments. See *Galaxy Custodial Servs., Inc.*, 64 Comp. Gen. 594 (B-215738), 85-1 CPD ¶ 658, suggesting that if the agency found the data inaccurate, the bid should be rejected. GAO has agreed to the use of this type of provision in two-step sealed bidding, *Norris Indus.*, Comp. Gen. Dec. B-182921, 75-2 CPD ¶ 31.

[c] Adjustments Based on Cost Indexes

The third type of EPA provision in FAR 16.203-1 uses national indexes as the basis for price adjustment. The procurement regulations contain no standard clauses for this type of price adjustment, and the FAR contains virtually no guidance on the structuring of such a clause. However, the drafting of such a clause is highly complex. GSAR 516.203-4(b) gives brief guidance on the preparation of such a clause and requires approval of the "contracting director." DoD PGI 216.203-4 contains the following elaborate guidance on drafting a clause of this type:

> (1) Do not make the clause unnecessarily complex.
>
> (2) Normally, the clause should not provide either a ceiling or a floor for adjustment unless adjustment is based on indices below the six-digit level of the Bureau of Labor Statistics—
>
> (i) Producer Price Index;
>
> (ii) Employment Cost Index for wages and salaries, benefits, and compensation costs for aerospace industries (but see paragraphs (3) and (6) of this subsection); or
>
> (iii) North American Industry Classification System (NAICS) Product Code.
>
> (3) DoD contracting officers may no longer use the BLS employment cost index for total compensation, aircraft manufacturing (NAICS Product Code 336411, formerly Standard Industrial Classification Code 3721, Aircraft) in any EPA clause in DoD contracts. This index is ineffective for use as the basis for labor cost adjustments in EPA clauses in DoD contracts.

The BLS employment cost index for wages and salaries, aircraft manufacturing may still be used in EPA clauses for labor costs. If a BLS index for benefits is desired, contracting officers should use a broader based index that will smooth the effects of any large pension contributions, such as the employment cost index for benefits, total private industry. If a total compensation index is desired, contracting officers should consider the creation of a hybrid index by combining the above referenced indices at a predetermined percentage. For example, a hybrid total compensation index could consist of 68 percent employment cost index for wages and salaries, aircraft manufacturing, and 32 percent of the employment cost index for benefits, private industry.

(4) Normally, the clause should cover potential economic fluctuations within the original contract period of performance using a trigger band. Unless the economic fluctuation exceeds the trigger value, no EPA clause adjustments are made.

(5) The clause must accurately identify the index(es) upon which adjustments will be based.

(i) It must provide for a means to adjust for appropriate economic fluctuation in the event publication of the movement of the designated index is discontinued. This might include the substitution of another index if the time remaining would justify doing so and an appropriate index is reasonably available, or some other method for repricing the remaining portion of work to be performed.

(ii) Normally, there should be no need to make an adjustment if computation of the identified index is altered. However, it may be appropriate to provide for adjustment of the economic fluctuation computations in the event there is such a substantial alteration in the method of computing the index that the original intent of the parties is negated.

(iii) When an index to be used is subject to revision (e.g., the BLS Producer Price Indexes), the EPA clause must specify that any economic price adjustment will be based on a revised index and must identify which revision to the index will be used.

(6) The basis of the index should not be so large and diverse that it is significantly affected by fluctuations not relevant to contract performance, but it must be broad enough to minimize the effect of any single company, including the anticipated contractor(s).

(7) Construction of an index is largely dependent upon three general series published by the U.S. Department of Labor, BLS. These are the—

(i) Industrial Commodities portion of the Producer Price Index

(ii) Employment Cost Index for wages and salaries, benefits, and compensation costs for aerospace industries (but see paragraphs (3) and (6) of this subsection); and

(iii) NAICS Product Code.

(8) Normally, do not use more than two indices, i.e., one for labor and one for material.

(9) The clause must establish and properly identify a base period comparable to the contract periods for which adjustments are to be made as a reference point for application of an index.

(10) The clause should not provide for an adjustment beyond the original contract performance period, including options. The start date for the

adjustment may be the beginning of the contract or a later time, as appropriate, based on the projected rate of expenditures.

(11) The expenditure profile for both labor and material should be based on a predetermined rate of expenditure (expressed as the percentage of material or labor usage as it relates to the total contract price) in lieu of actual cost incurred.

(i) If the clause is to be used in a competitive acquisition, determine the labor and material allocations, with regard to both mix of labor and material and rate of expenditure by percentage, in a manner which will, as nearly as possible, approximate the average expenditure profile of all companies to be solicited so that all companies may compete on an equal basis.

(ii) If the clause is to be used in a noncompetitive acquisition, the labor and material allocations may be subject to negotiation and agreement.

(iii) For multiyear contracts, establish predetermined expenditure profile tables for each of the annual increments in the multiyear buy. Each of the second and subsequent year tables must be cumulative to reflect the total expenditures for all increments funded through the latest multiyear funding.

(12) The clause should state that percentage of the contract price subject to price adjustment.

(i) Normally, do not apply adjustments to the profit portion of the contract.

(ii) Examine the labor and material portions of the contract to exclude any areas that do not require adjustment. For example, it may be possible to exclude—

(A) Subcontracting for short periods of time during the early life of the contract which could be covered by firm-fixed-priced subcontracting;

(B) Certain areas of overhead, e.g., depreciation charges, prepaid insurance costs, rental costs, leases, certain taxes, and utility charges;

(C) Labor costs for which a definitive union agreement exists; and

(D) Those costs not likely to be affected by fluctuation in the economy.

(iii) Allocate that portion of the contract price subject to adjustment to specific periods of time (e.g., quarterly, semiannually, etc.) based on the most probable expenditure or commitment basis (expenditure profile).

(13) The clause should provide for definite times or events that trigger price adjustments. Adjustments should be frequent enough to afford the contractor appropriate economic protection without creating a burdensome

administrative effort. The adjustment period should normally range from quarterly to annually.

(14) When the contract contains cost incentives, any sums paid to the contractor on account of EPA provisions must be subtracted from the total of the contractor's allowable costs for the purpose of establishing the total costs to which the cost incentive provisions apply. If the incentive arrangement is cited in percentage ranges, rather than dollar ranges, above and below target costs, structure the EPA clause to maintain the original contract incentive range in dollars.

(15) The EPA clause should provide that once the labor and material allocations and the portion of the contract price subject to price adjustment have been established, they remain fixed through the life of the contract and shall not be modified except in the event of significant changes in the scope of the contract. The clause should state that pricing actions pursuant to the Changes clause or other provisions of the contract will be priced as though there were no provisions for economic price adjustment. However, subsequent modifications may include a change to the delivery schedule or significantly change the amount of, or mix of, labor or material for the contract. In such cases, it may be appropriate to prospectively apply EPA coverage. This may be accomplished by—

(i) Using an EPA clause that applies only to the effort covered by the modification;

(ii) Revising the baseline data or period in the EPA clause for the basic contract to include the new work; or

(iii) Using an entirely new EPA clause for the entire contract, including the new work.

(16) Consistent with the factors in paragraphs (1) through (15) of this subsection, it may also be appropriate to provide in the prime contract for similar EPA arrangements between the prime contractor and affected subcontractors to allocate risks properly and ensure that those subcontractors are provided similar economic protection.

(17) When EPA clauses are included in contracts that do not require submission of certified cost or pricing data as provided in FAR 15.403-1, the contracting officer must obtain adequate data to establish the baseline from which adjustments will be made. The contracting officer may require verification of the data submitted to the extent necessary to permit reliance upon the data as a reasonable baseline.

This type of EPA clause is normally the most objective since it is usually based on national indexes prepared by the Bureau of Labor Statistics of the Department of Labor. When a national index is used, the effect of an EPA clause need not be evaluated in selecting the source since the index will have the same effect on all prices, *California Microwave, Inc.*, Comp. Gen. Dec. B-202317, 81-1 CPD ¶ 505.

A clause of this type is very difficult to negotiate and draft. First, the parties must agree on an index or a weighted group of indexes that match, with reasonable accuracy, the work on the contract. Second, the parties must agree on an expenditure profile that represents the expenditure of funds in performing the contract. This is to prevent the contractor from influencing the recovery under the clause by varying the incurrence of actual costs. Third, the parties must agree on those portions of the work subject to price adjustment. All of these factors require a detailed analysis of the work called for by the contract. Yet it should be anticipated that the clause finally arrived at will cover no more than a portion of the risk of fluctuations in the economy. This is especially true since the guidance suggests that no adjustments be made for deliveries beyond the scheduled delivery date. This requires the contractor to bear the risk of price fluctuations due to delays for which the government is not responsible. As a result, the contractor will seek to assure that the contract price reflects the residual pricing risk assumed by the contractor. See *American Transparents Plastic Corp.*, Comp. Gen. Dec. B-210898, 83-2 CPD ¶ 539, upholding the use of a clause based on a national index even though it did not relieve the contractor of many of the risks of fluctuations in the economy. The use of a national index was also approved in *Utah LP Gas, Inc. v. General Servs. Admin.*, GSBCA 12472, 96-1 BCA ¶ 27,960, where the contracting officer chose to use the index in the contract even though the clause permitted amendment "to substitute a more appropriate index" if the contractually specified index did not reflect market conditions. The board reviewed the contracting officer's analysis of the situation and concluded that there had been no abuse of discretion in deciding not to alter the national index.

Contracting officers in the DoD have been held bound to the DFARS guidance on the proper structuring of EPA clauses using indexes. See *Beta Sys., Inc. v. United States*, 838 F.2d 1179 (Fed. Cir. 1988), where the court ordered reformation of an index in a clause that did not match the work under the contract, and *Craft Mach. Works, Inc.*, ASBCA 35167, 90-3 BCA ¶ 23,095, where the board reformed the portion of the clause that based the price adjustment in each period on the baseline of the prior period. In both cases, it was held that the intent of the DFARS was to provide a price adjustment that fairly compensated the contractor for fluctuations in the economy and that clauses that significantly deviated from this intent were not binding on the contractor because they did not comply with regulations that had the force and effect of law. Since these decisions, the guidance (set forth above) has been moved to DFARS PGI which does not have the force and effect of law. See *Glopak Corp. v. United States*, 851 F.2d 334 (Fed. Cir. 1988), where the court refused to reform a General Services Administration contract that contained an index that did not match the contractor's costs. In that case, there was no regulation, such as the DFARS, that bound the contracting officer, and the court reasoned that reformation was only available if the resulting contract was "unconscionable." See also *Hydraulics Int'l, Inc.*, ASBCA 50325, 00-2 BCA ¶ 30,921, where the board refused to grant a contractor's motion for summary judgment that a clause did not comport with the DFARS guidance.

[3] Common Problems in Structuring Economic Price Adjustment Clauses

Most EPA clauses are tailored to the individual procurement as permitted or required by the regulations. This places a large burden on the contracting parties to analyze the situation fully and draft a contract clause that provides the intended protection from economic fluctuations. The litigated cases in this area indicate that there are numerous instances where specially drafted clauses do not achieve this goal.

[a] Clarity in Contract Language

Probably the most common problem encountered is vague or ambiguous contract language. In most cases, these ambiguities appear to result from a failure of the parties to understand fully the intricacies of the arrangement they have negotiated. For example, in *Firestone Tire & Rubber Co. v. United States*, 444 F.2d 547 (Ct. Cl. 1971), an index EPA clause called for the use of a Steel Products index without specifying any subcategories of the index. The court found that it was not reasonable to use the main index since its fluctuations did not match the fluctuations in the price of the steel components used in the contract. The court therefore "interpreted" the clause to require the use of subcategories of the index that matched the actual work. Interpretation was more appropriately used in several cases where the question was whether the cost was covered by the clause. In *Optic-Electronic Corp.*, ASBCA 24962, 83-2 BCA ¶ 16,677, *recons. denied*, 84-3 BCA ¶ 17,565, the board looked to the negotiations of the parties to determine if they might have intended to include profit-sharing as a fringe benefit even though it had been omitted from the contract schedule in a labor and material adjustment clause. The board found no evidence of such intent and therefore interpreted the contract as omitting the benefit from the price adjustment formula. Similarly, in *ITT Arctic Servs., Inc. v. United States*, 524 F.2d 680 (Ct. Cl. 1975), the contractor was denied recovery for increased "labor cost" under the EPA clause since the increases were due to currency fluctuation. In *Merritt-Chapman & Scott Corp.*, IBCA 240, 61-2 BCA ¶ 3193, the escalation clause provided for increases in wages but not subsistence payments, and the government unsuccessfully claimed that the portion of the hourly wage paid on a "remote" project in excess of the state average was actually a subsistence payment.

Interpretation was also used to determine the correct method of computing the price adjustment in *Brunswick Corp. v. United States*, 951 F.2d 334 (Fed. Cir. 1991). There the court affirmed the board decision at 91-1 BCA ¶ 23,458 that the government was correct in adjusting the base for the price adjustment by the factors included in a table in the contract. The contractor had argued that the proper adjustment was the amount it had used in computing its bid, but the court held that this was not in accord with the contract language and would give it an undue advantage over other bidders. See also *United States Steel Corp.*, ASBCA 29111, 85-1 BCA ¶7,761, *recons. denied*, 85-1 BCA ¶17,921, where the government was held bound to a contractor's brief description in the proposal of the price adjustment technique to be used even though the RFP had included one of the standard EPA clauses. Perhaps the most egregious example of lack of clarity is found in *Holland Oil Co.*, ASBCA 26603, 82-2 BCA ¶15,908, where the government was bound to a questionable price due to its inartful draftsmanship and lack of attention to detail in analyzing bids. Compare *Barry L. Miller Eng'g, Inc.*, ASBCA 20554, 75-2 BCA ¶11,567, where an unambiguous response in the contractor's proposal was held to bind the government to pay costs over the escalation ceiling in the RFP.

[b] Ceilings

One of the most troublesome elements of EPA clauses is the ceiling on the total amount of the adjustment. The three FAR clauses all contain a ceiling of 10% of the total contract price, with the provision that this ceiling may be modified when drafting the contract with the approval of the "chief of the contracting office," FAR 52.216-2, -3, and -4. The current DoD guidance on index EPA clauses provides that normally no ceiling will be used although ceilings have been used in the past in such clauses. Whenever a ceiling is used, the parties should carefully review the economic situation to ascertain whether the clause provides the necessary protection since these ceilings are enforced literally. See, for example, *Martin-Copeland Co.*, ASBCA 26551, 83-2 BCA ¶16,752, where a 10% ceiling covered only one third of the price fluctuation in the price of gold encountered by the contractor. The board held that the parties were bound to the contract agreement and that no further recovery was warranted. See also *American Transparents Plastic Corp.*, Comp. Gen. Dec. B-210898, 83-2 CPD ¶539, dismissing a protest that a 30% ceiling was inadequate to cover the risk of price fluctuations. GAO stated that there was no statutory or regulatory requirement that EPA clauses fully protect the contractor. In one curious case, the parties left the ceiling provision blank in the executed contract and the contracting officer subsequently inserted 25% in the blank, *American Optical Corp. v. United States*, 592 F.2d 1149 (Ct. Cl. 1979). The court concluded that the basic guidance in the ASPR called for the ceiling to be "reasonable" and that 25% was reasonable in a situation where the escalation provision covered the price of gold over a one-year period.

The use of ceilings creates a problem in EPA clauses where the contractor is required to warrant that the contract price does not include any contingency for items subject to escalation. See, for example, the Economic Price Adjustment—Standard Supplies clause set forth above. In *Echelon Serv. Co.*, Comp. Gen. Dec. B-208720.2, 83-2 CPD ¶86, GAO concurred with the agency's use of a ceiling and a warranty against allowances for increased costs in the original contract price and appeared to concur with the agency's view that the warranty did not prevent the inclusion of a contingency for cost elements not covered by the clause. See also *International Bus. Invs., Inc.*, Comp. Gen. Dec. B-213723, 84-1 CPD ¶ 668, reaching the same conclusion on the validity of the two provisions without discussion of whether a contingency was permitted.

[c] Pricing Elements Subject to Adjustment

The specific elements of the contractor's price that are subject to adjustment must be carefully and accurately described to avoid controversy in the application of economic price adjustment provisions. For example, in *VBM Corp.*, ASBCA 23268, 79-2 BCA ¶ 14,037, the clause called for escalation of "direct labor cost" defined as "the hours of work as of the contract date of non-supervisory employees required for the manufacture of each unit of contract supplies times the hourly rate." The board ruled that the tooling costs were within this definition since they had been treated as direct costs by the contractor in its proposal and met accounting definitions of direct costs. See also *Fermont Div., Dynamics Corp.*, ASBCA 21949, 79-1 BCA ¶ 13,774, where the board concluded that an escalation clause covering "delivered items" applied to option quantities. The board held that such escalation was warranted even though the option prices were higher than the base price for the items on the contract. Apparently, the evidence indicated that the contractor had not included a contingency in the option prices to cover higher labor or material costs. The board distinguished *F.W. Faxon Co.*, ASBCA 20925, 76-2 BCA ¶ 12,103, in which the board refused to apply an escalation clause where the government had exercised an option to extend the performance period of the contract. In that case the board concluded that the clause was clear and that it only applied to the first calendar year of performance of the work.

[d] Timing of Price Adjustments

It has been common practice to limit adjustments for economic fluctuations to price changes prior to the adjusted delivery or completion dates set forth in the contract. See the standard FAR clauses containing such a provision. Such provisions do not involve substantial risk in stable market periods but can impose unreasonable risks when markets are volatile. See, for example, *Stanwick Corp.*, ASBCA 24010, 80-1 BCA ¶ 14,252, denying any adjustment because the price increase occurred after the contract delivery date. The difficulty with this provision is that the parties are agreeing to such risks without a very clear approximation of the amount of risk that may be encountered. In instances of large inflationary increases, the resulting costs of such agreements may be greater than the contractor can sustain, while in periods of deflation, the government may pay excessive prices.

There have also been interpretation problems in contract language describing the timing of the adjustment. A contract providing for price adjustment "as of the date of delivery" was interpreted as allowing adjustment based on the scheduled delivery date rather than the actual date of late delivery, *Deloro Smelting & Refining Co. v. United States*, 317 F.2d 382 (Ct. Cl. 1963). In *Sears Petroleum & Transp. Corp.*, ASBCA 41401, 94-2 BCA ¶ 26,414, the board held that a clause in which the price was to be that in effect on the "date of delivery" meant the price was to be determined at the date on which the product was actually delivered and not the date when the contractor gave notice of readiness to deliver. Similarly, in *Ssangyong Trading Co.*, ASBCA 21614, 79-1 BCA ¶ 13,810, the board held that a clause calling for price adjustment on all items delivered "on and after" the date of a price change was to be applied literally to the specified delivery dates of items under the contract. In one case, an EPA clause provided for price increases under the contract to become effective on the date of the issuance of the trade journal in which the price increases were published rather than on the date the prices were reported to have become effective, *Sterling Oil Terminal Corp.*, ASBCA 3704, 57-1 BCA ¶ 1265. See also *St. Louis Refrigerator Car Co.*, ASBCA 10837, 65-2 BCA ¶ 5161, in which the board held that the earliest date of price adjustment was the date of delivery of the price adjustment demand to the government and not before. In *Allis-Chalmers Corp.*, Comp. Gen. Dec. B-186693, 76-2 CPD ¶ 48, GAO held that the term "latest available indices" meant published indexes rather than preliminary figures available from the Department of Labor. In *Libby Corp.*, ASBCA 40765, 96-1 BCA ¶ 28,255, the board accepted the argument that the government could not recover a price reduction based on the contract delivery date if it had been responsible for a delay but found no proof of government responsibility. See also *ECC Int'l Corp. v. United States*, 43 Fed. Cl. 359 (1999), denying cross motions for summary judgment and remanding to the contracting officer to issue a final decision on whether a contract modification permitted a price adjustment during a period of delayed performance.

[e] Effect of Changes

Changes affecting the amount or type of labor or material must be carefully analyzed to determine whether they require modifications to the EPA provisions. If such changes substantially alter the cost elements subject to price adjustment, the structure of a composite EPA formula can be significantly impacted. The ASBCA has held that because the government issues a change order that distorts or destroys the adjustment formula, it is not excused from its basic agreement to escalate, *Babcock & Wilcox Co.*, ASBCA 7531, 1962 BCA ¶ 3575. The most appropriate method of overcoming this problem would be for the parties to agree on separate price escalation provisions in any major contract amendments or supplemental agreements, Sharp, *Pricing and Contracting for Inflation*, 5 Nat. Cont. Mgt. J. 87 (1971). The parties may also agree that a change requires an EPA clause even though none had been included in the basic contract, *Minowitz Mfg. Co.*, ASBCA 23784, 83-1 BCA ¶ 16,324.

[f] Notice Requirements

Almost all EPA clauses require that the contractor notify the contracting officer, within a specified period of time, when a price adjustment is due. Such requirements have generally been held to be enforceable only when the government is prejudiced by lack of notice, and such prejudice has been difficult to demonstrate, *Chemray Coatings Corp.*, GSBCA 10117, 91-1 BCA ¶23,356; *Sky Top Plastics*, GSBCA 7000, 91-1 BCA ¶23,350; *Interlog Corp.*, ASBCA 21212, 77-1 BCA ¶12,362. However, in *Bataco Indus., Inc. v. United States*, 29 Fed. Cl. 318 (1993), *aff'd*, 31 F.3d 1176 (Fed. Cir. 1994), the court held that a notice provision was a "time-bar" provision that should be strictly enforced. The clause stated:

> (d) Price increases shall be subject to the following limitations:
>
> * * *
>
> (2) The contractor's entitlement to price increases shall be waived, unless the contractor's written request therefor is received by the contracting officer within 180 days after the date of final shipment of supplies under the contract.

The same result was reached in *Universal Dev. Corp. v. General Servs. Admin.*, GSBCA 12138, 93-3 BCA ¶26,100. This strict interpretation of the clause is completely dependent on the language setting forth the notice provision. Thus, some of these provisions may be interpreted to impose only a notice requirement (that will be waived absent prejudice to the government) while others may be interpreted to bar contractor claims for price adjustment.

[C] Fixed-Price Redeterminable

FAR 16.205 and 206 provide for two types of redeterminable contracts where the prices are established during or after performance. Contracts of this type were widely used in the past but are now infrequently used since they provide very little incentive for the contractor to control the costs of performance. Thus, the current guidance calls for their use in quite narrow circumstances.

[1] Prospective Price Redetermination

This type of redeterminable contract calls for an initial amount of work at a firm fixed price followed by subsequent amounts of work with prices to be determined prior to the beginning of each period. FAR 16.205-2 contains the following guidance:

> A fixed-price contract with prospective price redetermination may be used in acquisitions of quantity production or services for which it is possible

> to negotiate a fair and reasonable firm fixed price for an initial period, but not for subsequent periods of contract performance.
>
> (a) The initial period should be the longest period for which it is possible to negotiate a fair and reasonable firm fixed price. Each subsequent pricing period should be at twelve months.
>
> (b) The contract may provide for a ceiling price based on evaluation of the uncertainties involved in performance and their possible cost impact. This ceiling price should provide for assumption of a reasonable proportion of the risk by the contractor and, once established, may be adjusted only by operation of contract clauses providing for equitable adjustment or other revision of the contract price under stated circumstances.

FAR 16.205-3 contains the following limitations on the use of this type of contract:

> This contract type shall not be used unless—
>
> (a) Negotiations have established that—
>
> (1) The conditions for use of a firm-fixed-price contract are not present (see 16.202-2), and
>
> (2) A fixed-price incentive contract would not be more appropriate;
>
> (b) The contractor's accounting system is adequate for price redetermination;
>
> (c) The prospective pricing periods can be made to conform with operation of the contractor's accounting system; and
>
> (d) There is reasonable assurance that price redetermination actions will take place promptly at the specified times.

This is a very difficult type of contract to use because it requires great diligence on the part of both the contractor and the government agency to meet the goal of completing the annual price redetermination before the work for the next year is begun. The Price Redetermination—Prospective clause in FAR 52.216-5, which is required to be used for this type of contract, must specify the number of days before the beginning of the prospective redetermination period that the contractor must submit its proposal for the prices for that period, and Note 2 to that clause contains the following instruction:

> (2) Insert the number of days chosen so that the Contractor's submission will be late enough to reflect recent cost experience (taking into account the Contractor's accounting system), but early enough to permit review, audit (if necessary), and negotiation before the start of the prospective period.

The requirement that the pricing periods be at least 12 months in duration reflects the need for a significant amount of time to arrive at a redetermined price and attempts to ensure that such price be based on prior actual cost experience.

Yet to arrive at firm fixed prices before the beginning of each pricing period will require the agency to complete the review, audit, negotiation and internal clearance process in a period of three to six months. This is a challenging task for many agencies.

[2] Retroactive Redetermination

An infrequently used type of redetermination is the retroactive redetermination type contract with a ceiling price where the final price is negotiated after completion of the work. FAR 16.206-2 provides the following guidance:

> A fixed-ceiling-price contract with retroactive price redetermination is appropriate for research and development contracts estimated at $150,000 or less when it is established at the outset that a fair and reasonable firm fixed price cannot be negotiated and that the amount involved and short performance period make the use of any other fixed-price contract type impracticable.
>
> (a) A ceiling price shall be negotiated for the contract at a level that reflects a reasonable sharing of risk by the contractor. The established ceiling price may be adjusted only if required by the operation of contract clauses providing for equitable adjustment or other revision of the contract price under stated circumstances.
>
> (b) The contract should be awarded only after negotiation of a billing price that is as fair and reasonable as the circumstances permit.
>
> (c) Since this contract type provides the contractor no cost control incentive except the ceiling price, the contracting officer should make clear to the contractor during discussion before award that the contractor's management effectiveness and ingenuity will be considered in retroactively redetermining the price.

Because of the obvious lack of incentive in this type of contract, FAR 16.206-3 permits its use only on research and development contracts under the simplified acquisition threshold and requires the approval of the head of the contracting activity or a higher-level authority if required by agency procedures. A standard clause for this type of contract is contained in FAR 52.216-6. As discussed in § 12.02, this type of contract has been held to be a violation of the prohibition against a cost-plus-percentage-of-cost system of contracting.

§ 12.04 COST-REIMBURSEMENT CONTRACTS

When it has been decided that the nature of the work or the unreliability of the cost estimate make it necessary to use a cost-reimbursement contract, the contracting officer and the contractor have several choices. This section discusses three types of cost-reimbursement contracts. First, the basic type of cost-reimbursement contract—the cost-plus-fixed-fee (CPFF) contract—will be reviewed. The section then considers the various types of cost-sharing contracts that have been used when the parties desire to share the risks of the contract by entering into an agreement that provides for cost-sharing throughout performance of the work. The section concludes with a discussion of the cost-no-fee contract. Cost-plus-incentive-fee (CPIF), cost-plus-award-fee (CPAF), and cost-plus-award-term (CPAT) contracts are dealt with in the next section on incentive contracts. Cost-reimbursement term type contracts are covered in the section on level-of-effort contracts.

As discussed at the beginning of this chapter, in recent years Congress has enacted several provisions attempting to limit the use of cost-reimbursement contracts. As a result, FAR 16.301-2 contains the following basic guidance on the use of cost-reimbursement contracts:

> (a) The contracting officer shall use cost-reimbursement contracts only when—
>
> (1) Circumstances do not allow the agency to define its requirements sufficiently to allow for a fixed-price type contract (See 7.105); or
>
> (2) Uncertainties involved in contract performance do not permit costs to be estimated with sufficient accuracy to use any type of fixed-price contract.
>
> (b) The contracting officer shall document the rationale for selecting the contract type in the written acquisition plan and ensure that the plan is approved and signed at least one level above the contracting officer (See 7.103(j) and 7.105). See also 16.103(d).

FAR 16.301-3 provides limitations on the use of any cost-reimbursement contract as follows:

> (a) A cost-reimbursement contract may be used only when—
>
> (1) The factors in 16.104 have been considered;
>
> (2) A written acquisition plan has been approved and signed at least one level above the contracting officer;
>
> (3) The contractor's accounting system is adequate for determining costs applicable to the contract or order; and
>
> (4) Prior to award of the contract or order, adequate Government resources are available to award and manage a contract other than firm-fixed-priced (see 7.104(e)). This includes appropriate Government surveillance during performance in accordance with 1.602-2, to provide reasonable assurance that efficient methods and effective cost controls are used.
>
> (b) The use of cost-reimbursement contracts is prohibited for the acquisition of commercial items (see parts 2 and 12).

The documentation required to support the use of a cost-reimbursement contract is described in FAR 16.103(c):

(1) Each contract file shall include documentation to show why the particular contract type was selected. This shall be documented in the acquisition plan, or in the contract file if a written acquisition plan is not required by agency procedures.

(i) Explain why the contract type selected must be used to meet the agency need.

(ii) Discuss the Government's additional risks and the burden to manage the contract type selected (e.g., when a cost-reimbursement contract is selected, the Government incurs additional cost risks, and the Government has the additional burden of managing the contractor's costs). For such instances, acquisition personnel shall discuss—

(A) How the Government identified the additional risks (e.g., pre-award survey, or past performance information);

(B) The nature of the additional risks (e.g., inadequate contractor's accounting system, weaknesses in contractor's internal control, non-compliance with Cost Accounting Standards, or lack of or inadequate earned value management system); and

(C) How the Government will manage and mitigate the risks.

(iii) Discuss the Government resources necessary to properly plan for, award, and administer the contract type selected (e.g., resources needed and the additional risks to the Government if adequate resources are not provided).

(iv) For other than a firm-fixed price contract, at a minimum the documentation should include—

(A) An analysis of why the use of other than a firm-fixed-price contract (e.g., cost reimbursement, time and materials, labor hour) is appropriate;

(B) Rationale that detail the particular facts and circumstances (e.g., complexity of the requirements, uncertain duration of the work, contractor's technical capability and financial responsibility, or adequacy of the contractor's accounting system), and associated reasoning essential to support the contract type selection;

(C) An assessment regarding the adequacy of Government resources that are necessary to properly plan for, award, and administer other than firm-fixed-price contracts; and

(D) A discussion of the actions planned to minimize the use of other than firm-fixed-price contracts on future acquisitions for the same requirement and to transition to firm-fixed-price contracts to the maximum extent practicable.

In addition, FAR 16.301-2(b) requires that an acquisition plan calling for the use of a cost-reimbursement contract by approved "one level above the contracting officer" in accordance with FAR 7.103(j).

The feature that all cost-reimbursement contracts have in common is the Limitation of Cost clause, FAR 52.232-20. This clause overrides all of the contract requirements by providing that when the contractor has fully expended the funds included in the contract, there is no further obligation to continue performance or incur costs, but that when the government provides additional funds, the contractor must continue performance as long as funds are available until completion of the specified work. The clause provides, in addition, that the contractor must give notice of overruns and that the government has no obligation to provide such additional funding or to reimburse the contractor for costs incurred in excess of the contractual amount. This latter provision has been quite strictly enforced to deny contractors' reimbursement of cost overruns not approved in writing by the contracting officer, *ITT Def. Commc'ns Div.*, ASBCA 14270, 70-2 BCA ¶8370; *American Standard, Inc.*, ASBCA 15660, 71-2 BCA ¶9109. In the most liberal case on this issue, the Court of Claims found that an overrun had been funded when a contracting officer indicated approval of the funding on an internal memorandum that was not communicated to the contractor, *General Elec. Co. v. United States*, 412 F.2d 1215, *mot. for reh'g denied*, 416 F.2d 1320 (Ct. Cl. 1969). In making the decision on whether to fund the overrun, the contracting officer has great discretion. Hence, a choice can be made either to fund or not to fund the overrun after the costs have been incurred, *Eyler Assocs., Inc.*, ASBCA 16804, 75-1 BCA ¶11,320; *ARINC Research Corp.*, ASBCA 15861, 72-2 BCA ¶9721. However, a decision not to fund the overrun based entirely on the failure of the contractor to give notice of the overrun as required by the clause may lead to difficulty. It has been held to be an abuse of discretion to make such a decision in a situation where the contractor could not have known of the overrun, *General Elec. Co. v. United States*, 440 F.2d 420 (Ct. Cl. 1971). In contrast, a stringent test has been used to determine if the contractor could have learned of the overrun in such circumstances, and it has been held that it can meet this test only by showing that a fully adequate accounting system would not have revealed the overrun, *Stanwick Corp.*, ASBCA 14905, 71-1 BCA ¶8777, *recons. denied*, 71-2 BCA ¶9115. The government has also been estopped from denying overrun funding where it told the contractor funds were available and observed the occurrence of the overrun, *American Elec. Labs., Inc. v. United States*, 774 F.2d 1110 (Fed. Cir. 1985). For a complete discussion of the Limitation of Cost clause see Cibinic, Knight & Nash, *Cost-Reimbursement Contracting* 763-793 (4th ed. 2014).

It has also become quite common practice to include ceiling amounts at the inception or during performance of cost-reimbursement contracts. If such provisions are carefully drafted to provide that they establish ceiling prices and that the contractor is obligated to complete the work, they will be enforced, *LSi Serv. Corp. v. United States*, 422 F.2d 1334 (Ct. Cl. 1970); *National Civil Serv. League v. United States*, 643 F.2d 768 (Ct. Cl. 1981); *CRC Sys. Inc. v. General*

Servs. Admin., GSBCA 11173, 93-2 BCA ¶ 25,842. However, in less clearly drafted clauses, the contractor has been permitted to avoid the ceiling, *Singer—General Precision, Inc. v. United States*, 427 F.2d 1187 (Ct. Cl. 1970) (cost allocated to overhead as bidding expense); *General Dynamics Corp. v. United States*, 671 F.2d 474 (Ct. Cl. 1982) (termination clause with ceiling interpreted to permit reimbursement of costs up to ceiling after default termination but making contractor responsible for excess costs of reprocurement). Overhead rate ceilings have also been strictly enforced when clearly drafted, *Metro Mach. Corp.*, ASBCA 47005, 97-1 BCA ¶ 28,723; *General Dynamics Corp., Elec. Boat Div.*, ASBCA 21737, 83-2 BCA ¶ 16,907, 84-2 BCA ¶ 17,394. For a complete discussion of ceilings see Cibinic, Knight & Nash, *Cost-Reimbursement Contracting* 793-96 (4th ed. 2014).

[A] Cost-Plus-Fixed-Fee Contracts

In the CPFF contract, the parties negotiate an estimated cost of performance and preestablish the fee to be paid to the contractor for performing the work. This fixed fee is stated as a set amount of dollars that will vary only as the contractor is required to perform additional work not included in the original contract or less work than required by the contract. Thus, the contractor bears the risk of the adequacy of the fee while the government bears the risk of the incurrence of additional costs to permit full performance of the work. FAR 16.306(a) describes this type of contract as follows:

> A cost-plus-fixed-fee contract is a cost-reimbursement contract that provides for payment to the contractor of a negotiated fee that is fixed at the inception of the contract. The fixed fee does not vary with actual cost, but may be adjusted as a result of changes in the work to be performed under the contract. This contract type permits contracting for efforts that might otherwise present too great a risk to contractors, but it provides the contractor only a minimum incentive to control costs.

The CPFF contract is typically used for small jobs and those involving the early stages of research and development. FAR 16.306(b)(1) describes two situations where a CPFF contract is appropriate:

> (i) The contract is for the performance of research or preliminary exploration or study, and the level of effort required is unknown; or
>
> (ii) The contract is for development and test, and using a cost-plus-incentive-fee contract is not practical.

This guidance greatly restricts the use of the CPFF contract. Furthermore, the procurement regulations indicate that the government's policy is to use, whenever feasible and practical, a type of cost-reimbursement contract imposing some of the cost risk on the contractor. For example, FAR 16.306(b)(2) states:

> A cost-plus-fixed-fee contract normally should not be used in development of major systems (see Part 34) once preliminary exploration, studies, and risk reduction have indicated a high degree of probability that the development is achievable and the Government has established reasonably firm performance objectives and schedules.

In the CPFF contract, the estimated cost and the fixed fee are stated separately and, thus, must be negotiated separately. The estimated cost will, ideally, be the amount that the parties agree represents their best estimate of the amount that will be spent in accomplishing the work called for by the contract. It is not uncommon, however, for the estimated cost to be set at an amount less than the best estimate. Two factors appear to account for this practice. First, in a number of government procurements, agencies have not had sufficient funds in the budget to cover the cost estimate submitted by the contractor. In such cases, contractors have frequently been willing to agree to a lower cost estimate in order to obtain the immediate award of the contract. This will generally result in a somewhat lower fixed fee than would have been used if a higher estimated cost had been included. This lower fixed fee has been seen as a small concession compared to the risk of not being awarded the contract.

The second factor that has led to low estimated costs is the presence of competition in the contract award process. In most competitive procurements, the cost of performance is a significant evaluation factor in the source selection decision. As a result, offerors are motivated to make very optimistic estimates of the costs of performance. Although such estimates are adjusted to reflect "probable cost," through cost-realism analysis, for the purpose of selecting the winning contractor, FAR 15.404-1(d)(2), contracting officers generally award contracts based on the cost estimate submitted by the contractor in the competitive process rather than any higher probable cost that was arrived at by the cost-realism analysis. This is a questionable procedure because it results in a contract funded at too low a level to permit accomplishment of the work. A much better procedure is to include an estimated cost at a level representing the contracting officer's appraisal of the realistic cost of performance. However, it appears that only a minority of contracting officers follow this procedure, with the result that many CPFF contracts contain estimated costs that are unreasonably low.

The fixed fee in a CPFF contract is established in one of two ways. If the contract is awarded using a competitive negotiation process, the contracting officer may provide in the solicitation that each offeror propose the fixed fee that it will accept to perform the work and that this fixed fee be evaluated in the source selection process. This, of course, will induce some of the offerors to propose low fees and may result in a fixed fee that is quite low, perhaps in the range of 2% to 5% of the estimated costs. Alternatively, most often in sole source procurements, the contracting officer may provide for the fixed fee to be established using the profit formula established in the agency's regulations (see Chapter 13). In this case, the offeror will normally submit an analysis of the elements of the fee, following the agency profit formula, and the fee will be negotiated during written or oral discussions or negotiations depending on the amount of competition. In such cases, fixed fees in the range of 6% to 10% of the estimated costs can be anticipated. In addition, contractors with unique capabilities have been able in a few instances to negotiate, on a sole source basis, fee levels significantly higher than this range.

[B] Cost-Sharing Contracts

When contracting parties expect to receive mutual benefit from the performance of a contract, the most equitable arrangement may be to enter into an agreement at the outset providing for a sharing of costs. There are numerous ways to share costs of government work. One of the most common is to enter into a fixed-price contract at a price below anticipated costs. Another technique is to enter into a cooperative agreement or "other transaction" as discussed in Chapter 1. Grants also can be used as cost-sharing vehicles. This text discusses cost-sharing only in the context of procurement contracts where a cost-reimbursement contract is used with an agreement by the contractor to bear some portion of the incurred costs. FAR 16.303 describes this type of contract giving the following minimal guidance:

> (a) *Description.* A cost-sharing contract is a cost-reimbursement contract in which the contractor receives no fee and is reimbursed only for an agreed-upon portion of its allowable costs.
>
> (b) *Application.* A cost-sharing contract may be used when the contractor agrees to absorb a portion of the costs, in the expectation of substantial compensating benefits.

Some agencies have additional guidance. For example, the Environmental Protection Agency policy specifies that cost-sharing shall be used "where the principal purpose is ultimate commercialization and utilization of technologies by the private sector" and where "future economic benefits" are expected for the government as well as the contractor, EPAAR 1516.303-72(a).

FAR 35.003(b) states further that cost sharing on research and development contracts should be in accordance with agency procedures and FAR 42.707(a) provides that cost sharing may be accomplished by the negotiation of indirect cost rates lower than anticipated actual rates. FAR 31.205-23 provides that the costs of the contractor's contributed portion under cost-sharing contracts are unallowable.

Prior to issuance of the FAR in April 1984, there was considerably greater guidance on this type of contract. Both the Federal Procurement Regulation and the Defense Acquisition Regulation contained substantive provisions, and the Office of Management and Budget had issued Federal Management Circular 73-3 on this topic. The last significant policy initiative in this area occurred in December 1980 when the Office of Federal Procurement Policy circulated a proposed policy letter suggesting significant changes to the cost-sharing policy of the federal government, 45 Fed. Reg. 86952 (Dec. 1980). This policy letter would have prohibited cost-sharing on all R&D contracts. It was accompanied, however, by a policy letter suggesting recoupment of R&D costs on contracts where a clear potential for commercial sales resulted from performance of the contract, 45 Fed. Reg. 86953 (1980). Industry objection to these policies apparently resulted in a lack of further action, and no governmentwide guidance has been issued since that time.

There has also been sporadic congressional activity in this area. For many years, the Department of Labor—Health and Human Services Appropriation Act contained a provision requiring cost sharing on research grants. This provision is no longer included in the Act. But since 1970, the Department of Housing and Urban Development—Independent Agencies Appropriation Act has contained a similar provision. See the Consolidated Appropriations Act for FY 2005, Pub. L. No. 108-477, § 404:

> None of the funds provided in this Act may be used for payment, through grants or contracts, to recipients that do not share in the cost of conducting research resulting from proposals not specifically solicited by the Government: *Provided*, That the extent of cost sharing by the recipient shall reflect the mutuality of interest of the grantee or contractor and the Government in the research.

Since this provision was included in a consolidated appropriations act, it appeared to apply to all departments and agencies of the government except the Department of Homeland Security and the Department of Defense. In recent years, these appropriations have been included in Continuing Resolutions or Consolidated Appropriations Acts which have not contained such a provision.

This section discusses three aspects of cost-sharing contracts: their use on research contracts, the recovery of research and development costs through recoupment, and use of cost-sharing contracts for development of commercial products.

[1] Research Contracts

Congressional interest in cost-sharing has focused on research contracts, and prior to the FAR, the major procurement regulations gave guidance in this area. These regulations generally stated that cost sharing was appropriate when the contractor was expected to derive a significant commercial benefit from the research work. This policy has now been withdrawn, and the only significant guidance in the area is in separate agency regulations. Several agencies have broad policy guidance encouraging the use of cost-sharing contracts. See, for example, the following guidance in HHSAR 335.070-1(a):

> Contracting activities shall encourage performing organizations to contribute to the cost of performing R & D, through the use of cost-sharing contracts, where there is a probability that the contractor will receive present or future benefits from participation, such as increased technical know-how, training for employees, acquisition of equipment, and use of background knowledge in future contracts. Cost-sharing is intended to serve the mutual interests of the Government and the performing organization by helping to ensure efficient utilization of the resources available for the conduct of R & D projects and by promoting sound planning and prudent fiscal policies of the performing organization. The Contracting Officer shall use a cost-sharing contract, unless the Contracting Officer determines that a request for cost-sharing would not be appropriate because of the following circumstances:
>
> (1) The particular R & D objective or scope of effort for the project is specified by the Government rather than proposed by the performing organization. This would usually include any formal Government solicitation for a specific project.
>
> (2) The R & D effort has only minor relevance to the non-Federal activities of the performing organization, and the organization is proposing to undertake the R & D primarily as a service to the Government.
>
> (3) The organization has little or no non-Federal sources or funds from which to make a cost contribution. Organizations which are predominantly engaged in R & D and have little or no production or other service activities may not be in a favorable position to make a cost contribution. Accordingly, the Contracting Officer shall normally not request cost-sharing, if cost-sharing would require the Government to provide funds through some other means (such as fees) to enable the organization to cost-share.

This regulation provides that the amount of cost sharing should be proportional to the benefit to be derived by the contractor, HHSAR 335.070-2, and that it can be accomplished either by negotiating percentages of costs or elements of cost to be borne by the contractor, HHSAR 335.070-3.

Other agencies with policies encouraging cost sharing on research contracts include the Department of Energy, DEAR 917.7001 (primarily on projects to develop commercial technology), the Environmental Protection Agency, EPAAR 1516.303 (when purpose is commercialization of technology), and the Department of Homeland Security, HSAR 3035.003 (discretionary cost sharing and recoupment). Of these agencies, only the EPA has guidance on the implementation of the policy—including the provision in EPAAR 1516.303-73 that cost sharing may include "cash outlays, real property or interest therein, personal property or services, cost matching, or other in-kind contributions."

Some agencies have restricted their policy to contracts resulting from unsolicited proposals. For example, NASA requires cost sharing in research contracts resulting from unsolicited proposals from "for-profit organizations" unless no nongovernmental benefit will be derived from the project, NFS 1816.303-70. In contrast, no cost sharing is required if the proposal is submitted by a nonprofit organization unless there will be nongovernmental benefit. Under this policy NASA requires that the costs be shared as a minimum percentage of the total allowable costs to be determined by assessing the relative benefits of the work but not to exceed 10% in the case of contracts with nonprofit organizations. A standard clause is provided in NFS 1852.216-73 for this purpose:

> ESTIMATED COST AND COST SHARING (DEC 1991)
>
> (a) It is estimated that the total cost of performing the work under this contract will be $ ______.
>
> (b) For performance of the work under this contract, the Contractor shall be reimbursed for not more than ______ percent of the costs of performance determined to be allowable under the Allowable Cost and Payment clause. The remaining ______ percent or more of the costs of performance so determined shall constitute the Contractor's share, for which it will not be reimbursed by the Government.
>
> (c) For purposes of the ______ [insert "Limitation of Cost" or "Limitation of Funds"] clause, the total estimated cost to the Government is hereby established as $ ______ (insert estimated Government share); this amount is the maximum Government liability.
>
> (d) The Contractor shall maintain records of all contract costs claimed by the Contractor as constituting part of its share. Those records shall be subject to audit by the Government. Cost contributed by the Contractor shall not be charged to the Government under any other grant, contract, or agreement (including allocation to other grants, contracts, or agreements as part of an independent research and development program).

Several other agencies have adopted this policy of requiring cost sharing on research contracts resulting from unsolicited proposals. See DEAR 915.605(b)(5) (Department of Energy); HUDAR 2415.605-70 (Department of Housing and Urban Development); DOLAR 2915.605 (Department of Labor).

It is also possible to share costs by having the contractor agree to pay all or a part of specified costs. See, for example, *Shale Dev. Corp.*, IBCA 1256-3-79, 81-1 BCA ¶ 15,128, where the board held that a cost-sharing contract existed because the parties had agreed that the government would pay direct costs and the contractor would pay indirect costs. However, cost-sharing provisions must be carefully drafted to ensure that they carry out the parties' intent. See *Jacobs Eng'g Group, Inc. v. United States*, 434 F.3d 1378 (Fed. Cir. 2006), holding that cost sharing did not apply to costs paid as a result of a termination for convenience of the government because the termination clause called for the payment of "all cost reimbursable under this contract." A subsequent decision held that this holding did not call for the reimbursement of "foregone fee" which the parties had agreed could be counted as part of the contractor's share of costs, *Jacobs Eng'g Group, Inc. v. United States*, 75 Fed. Cl. 752 (2007), *aff'd*, 263 Fed. Appx. 875 (Fed. Cir. 2008). See also *Interstate Electronics Corp.*, ASBCA 55064, 07-2 BCA ¶ 33,643, involving a dispute over whether contract language precluded charging its share of costs as independent research and development costs, and *General Am. Research Div., Gen. Am. Transp. Corp.*, PSBCA 91, 77-1 BCA ¶ 12,732, where the board held that a CPFF contract with a special clause providing for cost sharing on overruns did not require sharing of costs incurred in a convenience termination settlement.

[2] Recoupment of Development Costs

Another method of sharing costs, after the fact, is recoupment. Recoupment is the recovery of nonrecurring costs of developing and preparing a product for manufacture from other buyers of that product. Recoupment was a standard practice of the DoD from the 1950s until 1992. However, on June 19, 1992, the White House issued a press report announcing that the President had abolished recoupment fees on all products other than "major defense equipment" (MDE) exported for military uses. As a result, recoupment is now only utilized by DoD as required by statute in contracts for foreign military sales (FMS). However, FAR 35.003(c) permits recoupment "in accordance with agency procedures." See HSAR 3035.003 setting forth the Department of Homeland Security's recoupment policy as follows:

> (c) Recoupment shall be determined on a case-by-case basis. Recoupment not otherwise required by law should be structured to address factors such as recovering the Department's fair share of its investment in nonrecurring costs related to the items acquired. Advice of legal counsel shall be obtained prior to establishing cost sharing policies and recoupment mechanisms under (FAR) 48 CFR 35.003(b) and (c).

Recoupment has been implemented by DoD in two ways. First, DoD recovers a recoupment charge directly from a foreign government if a product is sold to a foreign government under a FMS arrangement. Second, a contractor adds a recoupment charge to the contract and pays it to the government if a product is sold by the contractor directly to a foreign or domestic customer, or if a foreign company is licensed to manufacture the product.

DoD first issued a written policy on recoupment in 1967—DoD Directive 2140.2, Recovery of Nonrecurring Costs Applicable to Foreign Sales. This directive applied to sales of MDE to foreign buyers. MDE was defined as equipment that had been developed and produced with an expenditure of Research, Development, Test, and Evaluation (RDT&E) funds in excess of $25 million or a production investment in excess of $100 million. The thresholds for MDE doubled in 1972. Subsequently, in 1974, the Directive was revised to split the recoupment charge into two segments, one for nonrecurring development costs and the other for nonrecurring production costs.

Congress first adopted the recoupment policy in the Arms Export Control Act of 1976, Pub. L. No. 94-329. The Act contains a provision at 22 U.S.C. § 2761(e)(1)(B), requiring that FMS agreements include:

> a proportionate amount of any nonrecurring costs of research, development, and production of major defense equipment (except for equipment wholly paid for either from funds transferred under section 503(a)(3) of the Foreign Assistance Act of 1961 [22 U.S.C. § 2311(a)(3)] or from funds made available on a nonrepayable basis under section 23 of this Act [22 U.S.C. § 2763]).

The Office of Federal Procurement Policy subsequently determined that recoupment was not a sound policy because it had a negative impact on the competitiveness of American industry in international markets—resulting in the 1992 presidential action. In response to the new policy, DoD issued a revised Directive 2140.2, Jan. 13, 1993, which states that a "recoupment charge shall be imposed for sales of MDE only as required by Act of Congress." See 32 C.F.R. § 165.4(a). In 1996, § 4303 of the Clinger-Cohen Act, Pub. L. No. 104-106, added 22 U.S.C. § 2761(e)(2), which provides for Presidential waiver of recoupment on FMS sales to obtain standardization of military equipment by allied countries, to prevent loss of the sale or to obtain savings on procurement of equipment for the United States, and to correct prior estimates of the amount of sales. Waiver procedures are set forth in 32 C.F.R. § 165.7.

Recoupment clauses have created some difficult contractual issues. See, for example, *BMY, Div. of Harsco Corp.*, ASBCA 38172, 93-2 BCA ¶ 25,704, where the board held that the government was entitled to recoupment of nonrecurring costs only in connection with the second of two commercial sales because the government's investment in the R&D of the product at the time of the first sale was less than the $5 million required for reimbursement in the DAR clause in the contract. In *Hughes Aircraft Co.*, ASBCA 30570, 90-2 BCA ¶ 22,780, the board found the contractor liable for R&D expenditures following a commercial sale of weapons to the United Kingdom despite a subsequent international agreement between the United States and the United Kingdom that stated such costs would be paid by the United Kingdom. The board concluded the contractor was not relieved of its responsibility to pay because the agreement had not been made for the purpose of absolving the contractor of liability. In *General Elec. Co.*, ASBCA 20930, 79-2 BCA ¶ 13,956, the board held that the government was not entitled to recoupment for nonrecurring program and R&D costs because the original contractor sold the product to another contractor for use in a separate government contract. The board reasoned that no commercial sale warranting recoupment had occurred because the government would ultimately be the end user in both contracts. See also *Lockheed Martin Corp. v. United States*, 210

F.3d 1366 (Fed. Cir. 2000), holding that recoupment provisions did not divest a contractor from having "substantial rights" in the intellectual property flowing from government R&D contracts—with the result that the contractor was entitled to the research tax credit under 26 U.S.C. § 41.

[3] Support of Commercial Development

The most obvious type of agreement where cost sharing should be required is the agreement used when the government supports the work of an organization to develop a product for the commercial market. The Department of Energy (DOE) has issued the most helpful regulation dealing with this type of contract, which requires "cost participation." DEAR 917.7001(a) states:

> When DOE supports performer research, development, and/or demonstration efforts, where the principal purpose is ultimate commercialization and utilization of the technologies by the private sector, and when there are reasonable expectations that the performer will receive present or future economic benefits beyond the instant contract as a result of performance of the effort, it is DOE policy to obtain cost participation. Full funding may be provided for early phases of development programs when the technological problems are still great.

This regulation gives full discretion in establishing the type of cost sharing required on each contract. DEAR 917.7001(b) gives the following guidance on the amount of "cost participation":

> In making this determination to obtain cost participation, and evaluating present and future economic benefits to the performer, DOE will consider the technical feasibility, projected economic viability, societal and political acceptability of commercial application, as well as possible effects of other DOE-supported projects in competing technologies.

The Environmental Protection Agency has also issued a cost-sharing policy. EPAAR 1516.303-72 states:

> (a) The Agency shall use cost-sharing contracts where the principal purpose is ultimate commercialization and utilization of technologies by the private sector. There should also be a reasonable expectation of future economic benefits for the contractor and the Government beyond the Government's contract.

EPAAR 1516.303-75 gives the following guidance on the amount of cost-sharing:

> (a) Contractors should contribute a reasonable amount of the total project cost covered under the contract. The ratio of cost participation should

> correlate to the apparent advantages available to performers and the proximity of implementing commercialization, i.e., the higher the potential for future profits, the higher the contractor's share should be.
>
> * * *
>
> (c) The Contracting Officer, with the input of technical experts, may consider the following factors in determining reasonable levels of cost sharing:
>
> (1) The availability of the technology to competitors;
> (2) Improvements in the contractor's market share position;
> (3) The time and risk necessary to achieve success;
> (4) If the results of the project involve patent rights which could be sold or licensed;
> (5) If the contractor has non-Federal sources of funds to include as cost participation; and
> (6) If the contractor has the production and other capabilities to capitalize the results of the project.
>
> (d) A contractor's cost participation can be provided by other subcontractors with which it has contractual arrangements to perform the contract as long as the contractor's cost-sharing goal is met.

EPAAR 1516.303-74 also contains guidance on in-kind contributions, which can be accepted as part of a contractor's cost sharing. EPAAR 1552.216-76 contains a standard clause for cost-sharing contracts.

The Department of Defense has used similar reasoning in requiring cost sharing in contracts issued under its "manufacturing technology program" where one of the military services supports a contractor's development of improved manufacturing processes. However, § 216 of the FY 2000 National Defense Authorization Act, Pub. L. No. 106-65, adopted 10 U.S.C. § 2521(d) (now § 4841) deleting the prior requirement for mandatory cost sharing and substituting a provision calling for the amount of cost sharing proposed by competitive offerors to be used as an evaluation factor in selecting the winning contractor. This procedure has been implemented in DFARS 235.006-70(b).

[C] Cost-No-Fee Contracts

Perhaps the least used cost-reimbursement contract is the cost-no-fee contract. This contract is recognized in FAR 16.302 as a cost contract," but the only guidance given is that such contracts "may be appropriate for research and development work, particularly with nonprofit educational institutions, or other nonprofit organizations, and for facilities contracts." Since most contractors incur disallowed costs of 1% to 3%, a cost-no-fee contract is actually a loss contract.

In order to avoid losing money in the performance of a research and development contract, most nonprofit organizations are permitted to earn a fee on such contracts. See, for example, DFARS 215.404-75 stating:

> For nonprofit organizations that are [Federally Funded Research and Development Centers], the contracting officer—
>
> (a) Should consider whether any fee is appropriate. Considerations shall include the FFRDC's—
>
> (1) Proportion of retained earnings (as established under generally accepted accounting methods) that relates to DoD contracted effort;
>
> (2) Facilities capital acquisition plans;
>
> (3) Working capital funding as assessed on operating cycle cash needs; and
>
> (4) Provision for funding unreimbursed costs deemed ordinary and necessary to the FFRDC.
>
> (b) Shall, when a fee is considered appropriate, establish the fee objective in accordance with FFRDC fee policies in the DoD FFRDC Management Plan.

See also DFARS 215.404-72 providing for the use of a modified weighted guidelines approach to calculate fees for other nonprofit organizations which are "entities that have been identified by the Secretary of Defense or a Secretary of a Department as receiving sustaining support." Thus, the use of cost-no-fee contracts with nonprofit organizations is relatively rare. When such a contract is negotiated for research and development work, agencies are required to use the Cost Contract—No Fee clause in FAR 52.216-11. NASA has a special clause, Estimated Cost, NFS 1852.216-81, for such contracts.

Contracts paying a contractor to acquire facilities in order to perform government work have traditionally been cost-no-fee contracts. Prior to June 2007, FAR 45.302-2(c) required that no fee be paid on such contracts. This was implemented in the mandatory Allowable Cost and Payment—Facilities clause in FAR 52.216-13. FAR 45.302-3(c) also barred the payment of fee on any other contract calling for the furnishing of facilities. All of this guidance on facilities contracts was removed when the rewrite of FAR Part 45 was issued in 72 Fed. Reg. 27364, May 15, 2007. See *Space Gateway Support, LLC*, ASBCA 55608, 13-1 BCA ¶ 35,232, holding that FAR 45.302-3(c) barred the payment of a fee on a CPAF contract for the purchase of "government property" that was in the nature of facilities.

§ 12.05 INCENTIVE CONTRACTS

Incentive contracts are used when the pricing risk is not sufficiently large to justify the use of a cost-plus-fixed-fee contract but is too great to support the use of a firm fixed-price contract. Thus, they provide a middle alternative that the contracting parties can use to impose some risk on the contractor without requiring a full assumption of pricing risk. There are two distinct types of incentive contracts: the "objective" incentive, where the parties include a *formula* in the contract to determine the profit earned by the contractor based on the actual performance results achieved; and the "subjective" incentive, where the parties agree that the profit earned on the contract will be *determined by the government* based on an appraisal of the contractor's performance. The two objective incentive contracts are the cost-plus-incentive-fee (CPIF) contract and the fixed-price incentive (FPI) contract. The subjective incentive contracts are the cost-plus-award-fee (CPAF) contract and the cost-plus-award-term (CPAT) contract.

FAR 16.401(d) requires that the head of the contracting activity sign a determination and findings justifying that the use of every incentive and award fee contract "is in the best interest of the Government."

FAR 16.401 contains the following basic guidance on these forms of contract:

> (a) Incentive contracts as described in this subpart are appropriate when a firm-fixed-price contract is not appropriate and the required supplies or services can be acquired at lower costs and, in certain instances, with improved delivery or technical performance, by relating the amount of profit or fee payable under the contract to the contractor's performance. Incentive contracts are designed to obtain specific acquisition objectives by—
>
> (1) Establishing reasonable and attainable targets that are clearly communicated to the contractor; and
>
> (2) Including appropriate incentive arrangements designed to—
>
> (i) Motivate contractor efforts that might not otherwise be emphasized; and
>
> (ii) Discourage contractor inefficiency and waste.

Numerous kinds of incentives are included in these types of contracts. In all cases, they must include incentives or constraints on the cost of performance, FAR 16.402-1(a). Incentives on technical performance and time of performance may be included at the discretion of the procuring agency. Extensive guidance on the use of incentive contracts was contained in the 1969 DoD & NASA "Incentive Contracting Guide" (DoD/NASA Guide). More recent guidance is contained in the 2016 DoD Guide. There is also limited guidance in Chapter 16 of the Department of Energy Acquisition Guide.

This section first discusses the major types of objective incentive contract focusing on the cost incentives. It then addresses technical and delivery incentives. The section concludes with a discussion of CPAF and CPAT contracts.

[A] Cost-Plus-Incentive-Fee Contracts

The CPIF contract is an objective incentive where the parties include a formula in the contract to determine the profit earned by the contractor based on the actual performance results achieved. FAR 16.405-1(a) describes this type of contract, as follows:

> The cost-plus-incentive-fee contract is a cost-reimbursement contract that provides for the initially negotiated fee to be adjusted later by a formula based on the relationship of total allowable costs to total target costs. This contract type specifies a target cost, a target fee, minimum and maximum fees, and a fee adjustment formula. After contract performance, the fee payable to the contractor is determined in accordance with the formula. The formula provides, within limits, for increases in fee above target fee when total allowable costs are less than target costs, and decreases in fee below target fee when total allowable costs exceed target costs. This increase or decrease is intended to provide an incentive for the contractor to manage the contract effectively. When total allowable cost is greater than or less than the range of costs within which the fee-adjustment formula operates, the contractor is paid total allowable costs, plus the minimum or maximum fee.

FAR 16.405-1(b)(1) indicates that this type of contract is particularly appropriate for services or development and test programs, but it has been used in many other contracting situations as well. DoD PGI 216.104-70 suggests the use of incentive contracts on contracts for research and exploratory development and for advanced development. With regard to engineering development and operational systems development this guidance states that "the preferred contract type is cost reimbursement" without specifying when a CPIF should be used. To use CPIF contracts effectively the parties must have sufficient knowledge of the work to establish a target cost with some reasonable degree of accuracy yet not have such firm data as to make a fixed-price type contract appropriate. If the parties misjudge the problems that will be encountered in performing the contract, with the result that the target cost does not accurately reflect the costs of performance, the contractor will be paid a fee that is not commensurate with the true worth of its performance because the CPIF contract pays an incentive fee based on the relationship of actual allowable costs to target costs without regard to unforeseen problems which may have caused the discrepancy between the target and actual allowable costs.

CPIF contracts can include incentives only on the costs of performance or can include multiple incentives covering, in addition, technical performance and delivery. In this regard, DoD PGI 216.104-70(3)(iii) contains the following limitations on the use of only cost incentives on contracts for advanced development work:

> Contracting officers should not use contracts with only cost incentives where—
>
> (A) There will be a large number of major technical changes; or
>
> (B) Actions beyond the control of the contractor may influence the contractor's achievement of cost targets.

This section addresses cost incentives in the CPIF contract. Incentives on performance and delivery are addressed in a later section.

[1] Elements of the Contract Formula on Costs

There are five elements in the basic formula for CPIF contracts covering the costs of performance:

- Target Cost
- Target Fee
- Maximum Fee
- Minimum Fee
- Sharing Arrangement

The formula is expressed in contract language in the Incentive Fee clause in FAR 52.216-10, as follows:

> (e) *Fee Payable.* (1) The fee payable under this contract shall be the target fee increased by _______ [*Contracting Officer insert Contractor's participation*] cents for every dollar that the total allowable cost is less than the target cost or decreased by _______ [*Contracting Officer insert Contractor's participation*] cents for every dollar that the total allowable cost exceeds the target cost. In no event shall the fee be greater than _______ [*Contracting Officer insert percentage*] percent or less than _______ [*Contracting Officer insert percentage*] percent of the target cost.

The essence of the cost-incentive formula is that the contractor's actual fee *varies inversely* with the amount of costs incurred as long as the actual costs incurred fall within the range of sharing established by the points where the maximum and minimum fees take effect. Once these points are reached, the contract becomes a CPFF contract at either the maximum or minimum fee depending on the circumstances. The range in which the sharing arrangement is effective is commonly called the "range of incentive effectiveness" (RIE). **Figure 12-1** is a graphic illustration of the relationship of these elements of the CPIF contract where the following elements have been negotiated:

Target Cost	$100
Target Fee	$8
Maximum Fee	15% ($15)
Minimum Fee	2% ($2)
Sharing Arrangement	80/20

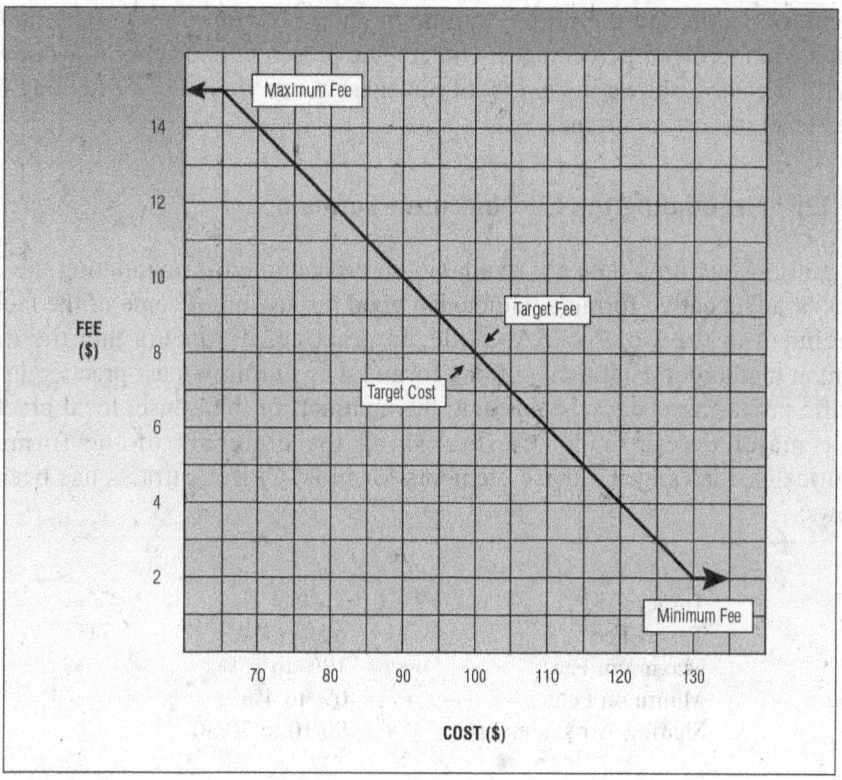

Figure 12-1

In this incentive formula, the RIE where sharing occurs is between incurred costs of $65 and $130. If the work is performed at a cost of $65 or less, the contractor is paid the maximum fee of $15, while the minimum fee of $2 is paid if the total costs of performance are $130 or more. This formula is the simplest possible with a single sharing percentage for the entire RIE. The DoD Guide illustrates this simple CPIF contract using the following elements:

Target Cost	$100
Target Fee	$9
Maximum Fee	14% ($14)
Minimum Fee	4% ($4)
Sharing Arrangement	80/20

However, it states that the incentive should be effective "over the full range of reasonably foreseeable variations from target cost."

Figure 12-1 presents the CPIF contract in terms of variations in earned fee against variations in incurred cost. This is the normal form of presentation used to depict the outcome of incentives on cost. In both this figure and in the Fee Payable clause cost and fee are expressed in terms of dollars rather than percentages, although the target, minimum and maximum fees are commonly negotiated in terms of percentages. The graphic presentation is easy to work with because it clearly shows the extent of the sharing and the outcomes at any projected level of cost incurrence.

[2] Negotiating the Cost Incentive Formula

Little general guidance is available on procedures for negotiating the elements of an incentive formula, although a good discussion of some of the factors is included in the DoD/NASA Guide. In practice, it appears that the most common method of establishing these formulas is to follow past practice in the specific procuring agency negotiating the contract. In this sense, local practice is the major determinant in establishing the elements of the formula. Historically, the range of these elements for most CPIF contracts has been as follows:

Target Cost	$100
Target Fee	6.5% to 9%
Maximum Fee	10% to 15%
Minimum Fee	0% to 4%
Sharing Arrangement	90/10 to 70/30

[a] Guidance on Cost Incentive Elements

While the incentive formula is probably best viewed as a single, unified formula for risk allocation, the formula can be established in different ways. In some instances, particularly in procurements with limited or no competition, the contracting officer will follow the guidance of FAR 16.103(a) and establish the elements of the formula through negotiation with the contractor. In such cases, the parties usually conduct negotiations using a step-by-step process beginning with the establishment of the target cost, proceeding to the negotiation of the target fee, and finally factoring in the other elements of the formula. In contrast, when the source is selected competitively, the government agency may prescribe the elements of the incentive formula in the RFP, permitting the competitors to propose the target cost but maintaining the other elements of the formula at specified percentages or amounts in order to ease the problem of evaluating the proposals. In either case, the tendency has been to arrive at a formula on a mechanical basis without regard to whether the formula is a realistic reflection of the possible outcome of the performance of a contract. For example, in the formula depicted in **Figure 12-1** the maximum fee is reached only when actual costs incurred are $65, implying that an underrun of 35% is possible. However, the facts of the procurement, including the practices used in establishing the target cost of $100, would almost always show that an underrun of this magnitude would be unlikely, if not impossible. Thus, in this formula, the maximum fee is set at an unrealistically low level of costs.

Although the elements of the incentive formula may be established in a variety of ways, the following guidance is provided on the considerations applicable to each element.

[i] Target Cost

The target cost is usually the focal point of the negotiation process since it is the baseline around which the other elements of the formula revolve. This cost is established through the competitive process or after detailed analysis of the contractor's proposal, as discussed in Chapter 13. In either case, the target cost must be subjected to cost-realism analysis to ensure that it is realistic, *Teledyne Ryan Aeronautical*, 56 Comp. Gen. 635 (B-187325, 77-1 CPD ¶ 352. If it is unrealistically low in a competitive procurement, the agency should adjust it to the probable cost of performance in order to evaluate the proposal—with a commensurate downward adjustment to the proposed target fee to reflect the incentive-sharing formula. See *Bechtel Hanford, Inc.*, Comp. Gen. Dec. B-292288, 2003 CPD ¶ 199, where this was done with the awardee but the agency did not then take into consideration the fact that this contractor had little margin between the most probable cost and the cost that would result in minimum fee. GAO granted the protest because the agency had not taken into consideration that award to that contractor would result in very little application of the incentive formula to motivate the contractor to control overrun costs (because it would reach the cost level where minimum fee applied very quickly after it exceeded the probable cost amount).

Although the CPIF contract places greater risk on the contractor than does the CPFF contract, it is generally believed that the target cost should be estimated using the same basic methodology that is used to arrive at the estimated cost in the CPFF contract. For example, the DoD Guide states that "the target fee is at the most likely cost." In competitive procurements, this would require that it be set at the probable cost of performance when cost-realism analysis indicates that the proposed target cost is unrealistically low. However, as discussed earlier with regard to CPFF contracts, most contracting officers probably do not make such adjustment with the result that numerous contracts contain a target cost level lower than probable cost—resulting in a target fee that will be unlikely to be achieved if the probable cost assessment is correct. Even in a noncompetitive environment, the target cost may be negotiated to an unduly low level because of the guidance given to contracting officers that contingencies should not be included in target costs unless they "may arise from presently known and existing conditions, the effects of which are foreseeable within reasonable limits of accuracy," FAR 31.205-7(c)(1). Another influence working to produce a low target cost is the generally optimistic view of program and technical personnel concerning the level of effort needed to accomplish R&D contracts. Such personnel may not fully recognize or anticipate the pitfalls that are frequently encountered during the course of performance; as a result, they tend to use a low estimate of labor-hours in establishing the target cost.

The same factors that may lead to a low target cost also make it difficult for the contractor and contracting officer to reach agreement on the target cost. When the contractor and contracting officer have such difficulty, the other elements of the formula provide a means of compromise. A common compromising technique is the use of a "plateau" in the sharing formula, whereby the parties agree that in a certain range of cost no sharing will take place. For example, if the contracting officer will agree to a target cost of no more than $95 and the contractor is adamant that a figure of no less than $105 is the most valid prediction of the costs of performance, the contract could provide for no sharing between these two amounts. The parties would still have to agree on an intermediate target cost for purposes of making the fee calculation, but this too is susceptible to compromise at a target cost of $100. The result would be that the middle segment of the formula would contain a CPFF plateau, which would keep either party from encountering windfall profits or losses. Another possible means of compromise is for the contracting officer to accept the contractor's position on the target cost while both parties agree that the target fee will be established using the government's anticipated target cost as the base. This reduces the target fee somewhat and gives the government some protection from excessive profits if the contractor performs the contract at a low cost. Thus, the process of establishing the target cost provides the parties with considerable flexibility in arriving at a mutually acceptable incentive formula.

[ii] Target Fee

There are two major factors that come into play in establishing the target fee—the competitive situation and the profit policy of the procuring agency, as discussed in Chapter 13. In a procurement with little or no competition, the contracting officer will generally use the agency profit formula as the starting point for negotiation of the fee. Most contractors are willing to use these profit formulas as the basis for negotiation of the target fee and many will submit their analysis in their original proposal (although FAR 15.404-4(c)(5) prohibits contracting officers from requiring such submission). However, their analysis may well result in a considerably higher fee than that arrived at by the contracting officer. In such cases, the target fee will be determined by vigorous negotiations. In contrast, in highly competitive procurements, some contractors are likely to propose lower target fees in an effort to win the competition, and contracting officers are prone to accept such fees.

Use of the agency profit formula will result in varying levels of target fee in CPIF contracts, depending primarily on the factors of performance risk and investment in facilities in DoD contracts and on contractor effort in contracts with other agencies. In addition, these formulas provide for a small increment of fee for a CPIF contract based on cost risk. The major factor determining this risk in the incentive formula is the sharing arrangement. Thus, a high contractor share should lead to a higher target fee than a low contractor share.

[iii] Maximum Fee

The maximum fee should be established at a level that provides a sufficiently wide RIE to reward the contractor for all realistic levels of cost that might be incurred to perform the contract. Thus, assuming that the parties have negotiated a target cost of $100 and have concluded that the lowest possible cost of performance is $85, the maximum fee should be established at a level so that incentive bonuses will be earned in the full range between $85 and $100. If they have agreed to a 70/30 share for underruns and a target fee of 7%, this would require a maximum fee of 11½%. Any lower maximum fee would provide no incentive for the contractor to strive to perform the contract for costs of $85.

Prior to 1997, the limiting factor in establishing the maximum fee was the statutory fee limitation on CPFF contracts—15% on R&D contracts and 10% on all other contracts. While it was generally agreed that the statutory fee limitations were not applicable to CPIF contracts, FAR 15.903(d)(2) required a deviation from the FAR before the maximum fee on a CPIF contract could exceed the CPFF level. FAC 97-02, September 30, 1997, eliminated this provision from the FAR, with the result that contracting officers are now authorized to negotiate maximum fees that provide the necessary incentive to the contractor to reduce the costs of performance. However, it is doubtful whether a contracting officers would agree to a maximum fee higher than 15% of target costs, absbent extraordinary circumstances.

[iv] Minimum Fee

The minimum fee is probably the most contentious element in the CPIF formula because in negotiating this element the parties' goals are diametrically opposed. The contracting officer generally wants a low minimum fee in order to ensure that the sharing continues over a wide range of cost overruns, while the contractor wants a high minimum fee in order to protect against the possibility of a loss contract. It is generally accepted that a minimum fee set between 2% and 3% of target cost will yield little or no profit because this amount of profit is necessary to cover *disallowed costs*. Hence, the contractor will normally argue that the minimum fee should be no less than this amount. In some cases, the government has agreed to this figure, but there have been many instances where a minimum fee under 2% has been used. There are even a few instances where the contracting parties have negotiated a minimum fee of less than 0%. As with the target fee, the negotiation of the minimum fee will depend on the competitive situation and the bargaining skills of the parties.

It has been quite common for the minimum and maximum fees to be equally distant from the target fee, and FAR 16.405-1(b)(3) requires a low minimum fee when a high maximum fee is negotiated. It is commonly believed that this is the fairest arrangement because it permits the contractor to earn as much in incentive bonuses as it risks losing in incentive penalties. However, this is not necessarily the case. If a uniform sharing arrangement is used for the entire contract, it is possible that the maximum fee will never be attainable, whereas reaching the minimum fee may be quite possible. For example, with the 80/20 sharing arrangement in **Figure 12-1** the contractor could earn $6 of additional fee by performing the work at $70 but would lose $6 of the fee by performing at $130. In most development contracting situations, where such a formula would be found, it is far more likely that the actual results will reach $130 than $70 since it is very difficult to achieve significant cost underruns. Thus, it is important that the parties analyze the true potential outcomes of minimum and maximum fees within the sharing arrangement rather than merely negotiate theoretical formulas that have the appearance of symmetry.

[v] Sharing Arrangement

The amount of motivation provided by a CPIF contract is controlled primarily by the level of sharing agreed to by the parties. Clearly, a contract where the contractor shares at a rate of 30% of costs incurred over the entire RIE is a more powerful tool than a contract where the contractor's share is only 10%. Thus, the sharing arrangement is the major element of the formula reflecting the cost risk imposed by the contract, and the contractor's share will be established, to a large extent, by the parties' appraisal of the amount of risk the procurement entails. If the work is well defined and the cost outcome relatively predictable, imposing more risk by using a higher contractor share would be expected. Conversely, if the work statement is vague and the field of technology not well defined, a lower contractor share would be appropriate. There is very little guidance on the sharing levels that are proper in varying circumstances, but it is usually agreed that a contractor share of less than 10% is relatively ineffective and a contractor share of over 30% is somewhat unusual, with the result that almost all CPIF contracts contain sharing levels within this range. Further, the great majority of the contracts in existence use shares in the middle of the range, from 15% to 25%. These practices are probably best understood and explained in terms of the traditions within procuring agencies rather than logic. Nevertheless, the establishment of the sharing level is the subject of hard negotiation in many cases and does provide the parties an opportunity to tailor the incentive formula to fit the nature and difficulty of the work called for by the contract.

Widely divergent sharing arrangements have been used in CPIF contracts. The most common is probably the single, straight-line share depicted in **Figure 12-1**, but multiple-line arrangements such as that depicted in **Figure 12-2** have also been quite common. The rationale for this arrangement is that the sharing

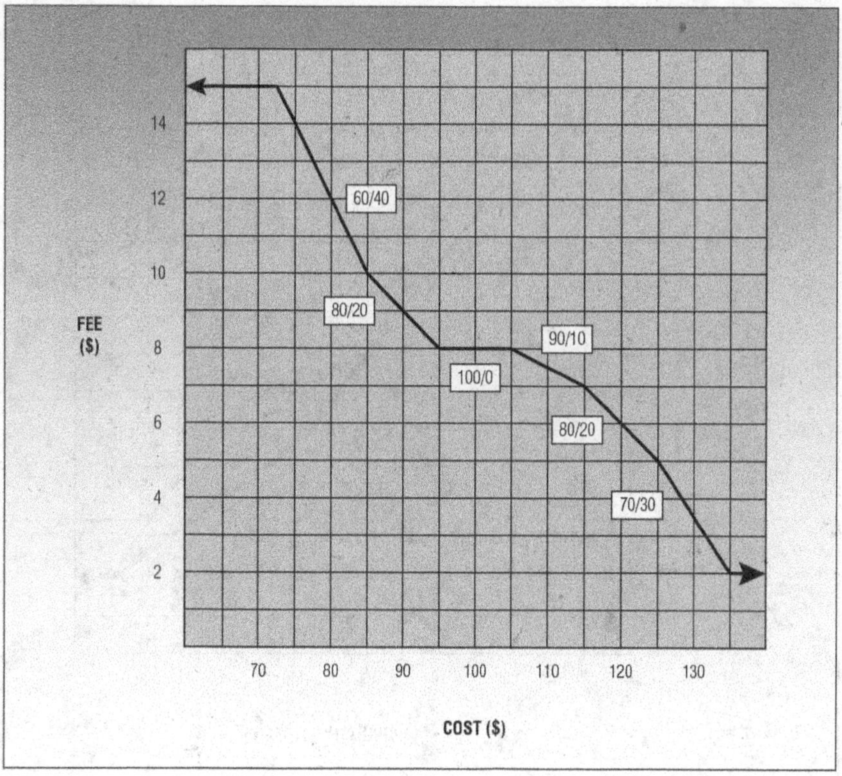

Figure 12-2

should increase, with commensurately greater rewards and penalties, as the contractor deviates from the norm of the target cost. This recognizes that the target cost estimate may not be too accurate and that deviations close to target may be desirable as the work progresses. Of course, any other sharing structure that accomplishes the objectives of the parties is equally acceptable, and the contracting officer and the contractor are expected to negotiate a sharing structure that best serves the needs of the specific procurement.

[b] Use of Range of Incentive Effectiveness

An alternate, and far more realistic, method of arriving at the elements of the CPIF contract, suggested in the DoD/NASA Guide, is to use the RIE as the major controlling element in establishing the formula. This technique is depicted in **Figure 12-3**, which reflects parties negotiating three levels of cost: the most likely cost outcome, the best foreseeable cost outcome, and the worst foreseeable cost outcome. The parties also negotiate three levels of profit, reflecting the reasonable profits that a contractor should earn at each of the three cost outcomes. They then structure the sharing arrangement as an outcome of these cost and fee amounts.

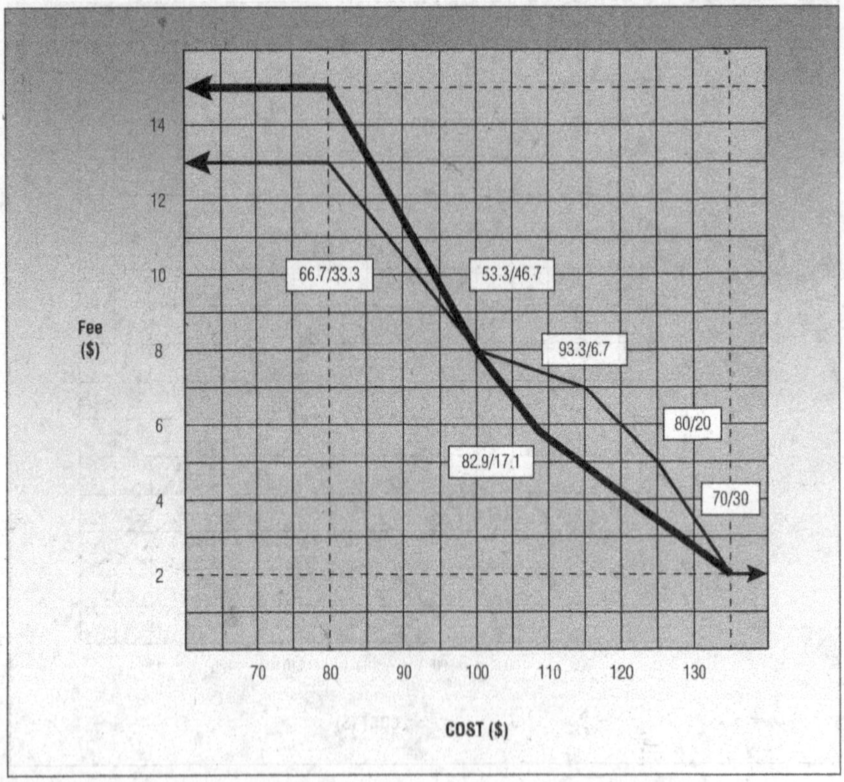

Figure 12-3

For example, in **Figure 12-3** the parties agreed on the following cost levels:

Target Cost	$100
Minimum Possible Cost	$85
Maximum Probable Cost	$135

These levels are reasonably realistic in that significant underruns are very rare, but relatively large overruns are quite common. Thus, they reflect the fact that it is difficult to reduce expenditures while accomplishing the contract goals. They also reflect the fact that target cost levels are commonly set quite optimistically. In **Figure 12-3**, the parties also agreed on the following fee levels:

Target Fee	8% ($8)
Maximum Fee	15% ($15)
Minimum Fee	2% ($2)

The 8% target fee represents the fee for a CPIF contract derived from the agency's structured profit policy. The minimum and maximum fees are set at the amount the contracting officer would be willing to agree to at maximum and minimum cost.

Figure 12-3 illustrates that when the three points derived from these numbers are connected (the bold line), they yield very disparate sharing levels on the overrun and underrun sides of target cost. The sharing arrangements are as follows:

Overrun	82.9/17.1
Underrun	53.3/46.7

While these shares may seem unusual, they reflect the fact that the government desires sharing over a wide range of potential overrun, while the parties have agreed that sharing is not realistic over nearly such a wide range of underrun. One way to reduce this disparity is to reduce the maximum fee as depicted in the alternate formula in **Figure 12-3** (the thin line). Another way to modify this formula is to reduce the overrun sharing for the first part of the overrun and to increase it as the contractor approaches minimum fee. This is also depicted in the alternate formula in **Figure 12-3**. Either of these formulas is a far more realistic reflection of the realities of the normal R&D procurement than the formula in **Figure 12-1**, and the contracting officer should not be disturbed by the higher shares for underruns, since great effort is demanded of contractors to accomplish such cost savings, and the rewards for such efforts should be substantial.

[c] Costs Subject to Incentive Sharing

Consistent with the theory of the CPIF contract that transferring a portion of the cost risk to the contractor will motivate more efficient performance, the contract language has been carefully drafted to remove certain costs not under the contractor's control from the sharing formula. See the following paragraph in the Incentive Fee clause in FAR 52.216-10:

> (e)(4) For the purpose of fee adjustment, "total allowable cost" shall not include allowable costs arising out of—
>
> (i) Any of the causes covered by the Excusable Delays clause to the extent that they are beyond the control and without the fault or negligence of the Contractor or any subcontractor;
>
> (ii) The taking effect, after negotiating the target cost, of a statute, court decision, written ruling, or regulation that results in the Contractor's being required to pay or bear the burden of any tax or duty or rate increase in a tax or duty;
>
> (iii) Any direct cost attributed to the Contractor's involvement in litigation as required by the Contracting Officer pursuant to a clause of this contract, including furnishing evidence and information requested pursuant to the Notice and Assistance Regarding Patent and Copyright Infringement clause;

(iv) The purchase and maintenance of additional insurance not in the target cost and required by the Contracting Officer, or claims for reimbursement for liabilities to third persons pursuant to the Insurance-Liability to Third Persons clause;

(v) Any claim, loss, or damage resulting from a risk for which the Contractor has been relieved of liability by the Government Property clause; or

(vi) Any claim, loss, or damage resulting from a risk defined in the contract as unusually hazardous or as a nuclear risk and against which the Government has expressly agreed to indemnify the Contractor.

The ASBCA has also held that certain costs not under the contractor's control should be removed from the incentive formula even though they are not enumerated in this clause. See *Federal Elec. Corp.*, ASBCA 9476, 65-1 BCA ¶ 4747, where the board held that the cost incentive formula in a CPIF contract did not cover the increased wages that resulted when the Canadian government disapproved a proposed wage decrease. The parties had negotiated the target cost anticipating that the Canadian government would approve a wage decrease, but the parties knew that such approval had not been granted at the time the contract was signed. The board adjusted the target cost of the contract to reflect the increased wages based on the following questionable reasoning found at 22,573:

> In arriving at these terms, the parties must have been aware of the fact that one of the cost elements—the wage rates to be paid the DEW line employees—was to some extent beyond their control, because it depended on the approval of the Canadian Department of Labour. While the witnesses for the parties at the hearing asserted that they did not doubt that the reduced wage rates would be approved, other testimony in the record leads to the conclusion that they must have been aware of the fact that such approval was not a certainty and might be denied. In any event, the record is clear that both parties negotiated on the basis of the wage rates proposed by the [contractor]. In the light of the goal inherent in incentive contracting it does not seem, therefore, likely or believable that two highly sophisticated parties, such as [the contractor] and ROAMA as representative of the Government, intended to, and did, enter into a cost-plus-incentive-fee contract, which would, upon the occurrence of a particular event beyond the control of either party and prior to commencement of the contract term deprive appellant automatically of a large portion of its proposed target fee.

[d] Relationship of Cost Incentives to Other Clauses

Cost incentives are subject to adjustment pursuant to the Changes clause of the contract if the work is altered during performance of the contract. See *Northrop Grumman Corp. v. United States*, 41 Fed. Cl. 645 (1998), where the government waived a number of the specification requirements in order to complete the work on schedule and within funding limitations. The court held that ¶(d) of the Incentive Fee clause in FAR 52.216-10 allowed the contracting officer to unilaterally restructure the incentive formula to account for the reduced work performed by the contractor. The court rejected the contractor's argument that the proper course of action for the government was to provide additional funds to complete the work (as if it were correcting defects) and to apply the original incentive formula to the higher costs.

[B] Fixed-Price Incentive Contracts

The FPI contract is very similar in concept to the CPIF contract except that it contains a ceiling price in lieu of the minimum and maximum fees. FAR 16.403(a) describes this type of contract as follows:

> A fixed-price incentive contract is a fixed-price contract that provides for adjusting profit and establishing the final contract price by application of a formula based on the relationship of total final negotiated cost to total target cost. The final price is subject to a price ceiling, negotiated at the outset. The two forms of fixed-price incentive contracts, firm target and successive targets, are further described in 16.403-1 and 16.403-2 below.

Because the ceiling price requires the contractor to complete performance no matter how high the cost, this type of contract should be used only when the contracting parties can predict the costs of performance with a reasonable degree of accuracy. The FAR provides that FPI contracts are normally used to place more cost risk on contractors in order to motivate them to control costs more vigorously than they would on cost-reimbursement contracts. Thus, these regulations discuss the use of the "profit motive" as a fundamental means of inducing lower costs of performance. However, there is another use of the FPI contract—that of protecting the government from excessive profits when a contractor will not agree to a firm-fixed-price contract at a level that the government believes represents a fair sharing of the cost risk. See *Televiso Elecs.*, 46 Comp. Gen. 631 (B-159922) (1967), where GAO upheld a contracting officer's decision to use a FPI contract when a contractor would not agree to a firm-fixed-price at a level deemed to be fair to the government. In both situations, the incentive contract gives the parties a means of sharing the cost risk so that neither will be seriously impacted by a degree of cost fluctuations from those costs projected at the outset.

The FPI contract is similar to the CPIF contract in that both provide for sharing of costs on a predetermined percentage basis. However, the FPI contract uses fixed-price clauses and contains no Limitation of Cost clause, with the result that the government is legally obligated to pay all cost up to the ceiling price without prior notification, and the contractor is obligated to complete the work and is subject to default termination which entails an assessment of excess costs of reprocurement and repayment of progress payments or other damages if it does not. The final price of the FPI contract is established by negotiation after incurrence and audit of substantially all costs of performance, while the final costs in a CPIF contract are paid through audit determination.

The FAR contains little useful guidance on when an FPI contract should be used. However, DFARS 216.403-1(b) states:

> (1) The contracting officer shall give particular consideration to the use of fixed-price incentive (firm target) contracts, especially for acquisitions moving from development to production.

DoD PGI 216.403-1(1) contains the following additional guidance:

> (i) *Not mandatory*. DFARS (b)(1) directs the contracting officer to give particular consideration to the use of fixed-price incentive (firm target) (FPIF) contracts, especially for acquisitions moving from development to production. DFARS does not mandate the use of FPIF for initial production and each acquisition situation must be evaluated in terms of the degree and nature of the risk presented in order to select the proper contract type.
>
> (ii) *Considerations*. Volume 4, chapter 1, of the Contract Pricing Reference Guide provides a detailed discussion of the considerations involved in selecting the proper contract type. For example:
>
>> (A) It is not in the Government's best interest to use FPIF when the cost risk is so great that establishing a ceiling price is unrealistic.
>>
>> (B) It is also not in the Government's best interest to use firm-fixed-price (FFP) contracts on production programs until costs have become stable. Therefore, FPIF contracts should be considered in production programs where actual costs on prior FFP contracts have varied by more than four percent from the costs considered negotiated. Contracting officers are reminded that actual costs on prior contracts for the same item, regardless of contract type or data reporting requirements of the prior contract, are cost and pricing data on the pending contract, and should be obtained from the contractor on production programs when cost or pricing data are required

Note that ¶ (b) states a preference for using an FPI contract over an FFP contract. In contrast to ¶ (a), the DoD Guide states:

> FPI is generally appropriate for programs in the early production phase at or near the end of engineering and manufacturing development (EMD) after a program has completed critical design review, built production representative prototypes, and completed some significant fraction of developmental test. DoD has experienced relatively less significant program overruns during the early production phase, indicating that FPI would provide a reasonable level of risk to share with industry.
>
> * * *

There may be instances where FPI is appropriate for mature programs in production (even if prior production lots were priced and negotiated using FFP). If, for example, the Government has reason to conclude (in retrospect) that there is a poor correlation between the price negotiated and the actual cost/price outcome realized, that should be an indicator that FPI may be appropriate.

There are two types of FPI contracts: the fixed-price incentive with a firm target price (FPIF) and the fixed-price incentive with successive targets (FPIS).

[1] Elements of the Formula

The elements of the basic formula covering the costs of performance in the FPIF contract are:

- Target Cost
- Target Profit
- Ceiling Price
- Sharing Arrangement

The formula is expressed in contract language in the Incentive Price Revision—Firm Target clause in FAR 52.216-16, as follows:

(a) *General.* The supplies or services identified in the Schedule as Items [*Contracting Officer insert Schedule line item numbers*] are subject to price revision in accordance with this clause; *provided,* that in no event shall the total final price of these items exceed the ceiling price of _______ dollars ($_______). Any supplies or services that are to be (1) ordered separately under, or otherwise added to, this contract and (2) subject to price revision in accordance with the terms of this clause shall be identified as such in a modification to this contract.

* * *

(d) Price revision. Upon the Contracting Officer's receipt of the data required by paragraph (c) above, the Contracting Officer and the Contractor shall promptly establish the total final price of the items specified in (a) above by applying to final negotiated cost an adjustment for profit or loss, as follows:

(1) On the basis of the information required by paragraph (c) above, together with any other pertinent information, the parties shall negotiate the total final cost incurred or to be incurred for supplies delivered (or services performed) and accepted by the Government and which are subject to price revision under this clause.

(2) The total final price shall be established by applying to the total final negotiated cost an adjustment for profit or loss, as follows:

(i) If the total final negotiated cost is equal to the total target cost, the adjustment is the total target profit.

(ii) If the total final negotiated cost is greater than the total target cost, the adjustment is the total target profit, less [*Contracting Officer insert percent*] percent of the amount by which the total final negotiated cost exceeds the total target cost.

(iii) If the final negotiated cost is less than the total target cost, the adjustment is the total target profit plus [*Contracting Officer insert percent*] percent of the amount by which the total final negotiated cost is less than the total target cost.

* * *

(k) *Equitable adjustment under other clauses.* If an equitable adjustment in the contract price is made under any other clause of this contract before the total final price is established, the adjustment shall be made in the total target cost and may be made in the maximum dollar limit on the total final price, the total target profit, or both. If the adjustment is made after the total final price is established, only the total final price shall be adjusted.

As in the CPIF contract, the contracting officer has significant discretion in establishing the elements of this FPIF formula. The range of these elements most commonly encountered has been:

Target Cost	$100
Target Profit	9% to 12%
Ceiling Price	$115 to $135
Sharing Arrangement	80/20 to 60/40

These common features of the FPI contract were radically altered for DoD contracts in 2011 by the issuance of DFARS 216.402-1(b) as follows:

(2) The contracting officer shall pay particular attention to share lines and ceiling prices for fixed-price incentive (firm target) contracts, with a 120 percent ceiling and a 50/50 share ratio as *the point of departure* for establishing the incentive arrangement. (Italics added)

DoD PGI 216.403-1(2) explains this guidance as follows:

While DFARS does not mandate the use of these share ratios or ceiling percentage, it is not unreasonable to expect that upon entering into production, risks have been mitigated to the point that the DFARS recommended point of departure for an FPIF incentive arrangement would be normal.

* * *

(3) *Analyzing risk.* (i) *Quantification of risk.* (A) The first step is establishing a target cost for which the probability of an underrun and overrun are considered equal and therefore, the risks and rewards are shared equally, hence the 50/50 share is the point of departure. Equally important is

> determining that the contractor has a high probability of being able to accomplish the effort within a ceiling percentage of 120 percent. In accomplishing both these steps, the analysis of risk is essential.

This guidance is followed by a long discussion of the detailed steps required to analyze the risk.

Guidance on negotiating formulas also is contained in the DoD/NASA Guide and the DoD Guide. See also Nash, *Incentive Contracting*, Government Contracts Monograph 7 (1963).

[2] Negotiation and Analysis of Formulas

The procurement regulations imply that incentive formulas are established by negotiation, and this is generally the case in noncompetitive situations. The regulations contain no guidance on the techniques that should be used in competitive procurements. Hence, contracting officers are free to allow the competitors to propose their own incentive formulas or include a required formula (specifying the target profit rate, sharing percentages, and ceiling percentage above target cost) in the RFP if they conclude that proper evaluation is not otherwise possible. This latter technique is a means of overcoming the difficulty that is encountered in comparing FPI contract proposals with different sharing formulas and ceilings. This forces all competitors to propose the same basic incentive formula and allows a valid comparison of target costs proposed by the competitors. Notwithstanding the contrary views of GAO in *Televiso Elecs.*, 46 Comp. Gen. 631 (B-159922) (1967), without such similarity, the use of target costs as the comparative number can greatly distort the comparison and lead to the selection of a contractor that is taking less cost risk than, for example, another company that has proposed a higher target cost but a lower ceiling price. In such cases where the agency permits each offeror to propose the entire incentive formula, it is more rational to evaluate the ceiling prices. See *General Elec. Co.*, Comp. Gen. Dec. B-186372, 76-2 CPD ¶ 269, for a case recognizing the validity of the agency's giving more weight in the competitive evaluation to the proposed ceiling prices than to proposed targets. See also *DRS C3 Sys., LLC*, Comp. Gen. Dec. B-310825, 2008 CPD ¶ 103, holding that it is improper for an agency to adjust the target cost for evaluation purposes if it unrealistically low (as would be done in a CPIF situation) but that it is proper to evaluate the risk that the contractor cannot perform at that cost. In *Eurest Support Servs.*, Comp. Gen. Dec. B-285813.3, 2003 CPD ¶ 139, GAO granted a protest because the agency did not assess the risk of an unrealistically low target price when the RFP called for an assessment of price realism.

Whether the contractor or the government establishes the formula independently or they establish it through negotiation, the pertinent considerations are essentially the same as those discussed above in considering CPIF contracts.

Thus, the elements of the formula should be determined by an analysis of the risk of the specific procurement on which the formula is used.

The unique element in FPIF contracts is the ceiling price, and this, of course, is the critical element. The first aspect of this ceiling that must be recognized is that it is a ceiling *price*—combining both cost and profit. Thus, except for price adjustments under contract clauses, it imposes an ultimate limitation on the amount the contractor will be paid for the work. As such, it should be established at a level commensurate with the ability of the parties to accurately estimate the costs of performance. In the past, ceiling prices have been negotiated as high as 150% of target costs in contracts where the parties had very little confidence in the accuracy of their cost estimates. However, in that situation, use of the CPIF contract is more appropriate. Thus, in normal circumstances, ceiling prices would be expected to range from 115% to 135% of the target cost. **Figure 12-4** depicts two FPI formulas—a high-risk formula with a ceiling price of $115, and a low-risk formula with a ceiling of $130.

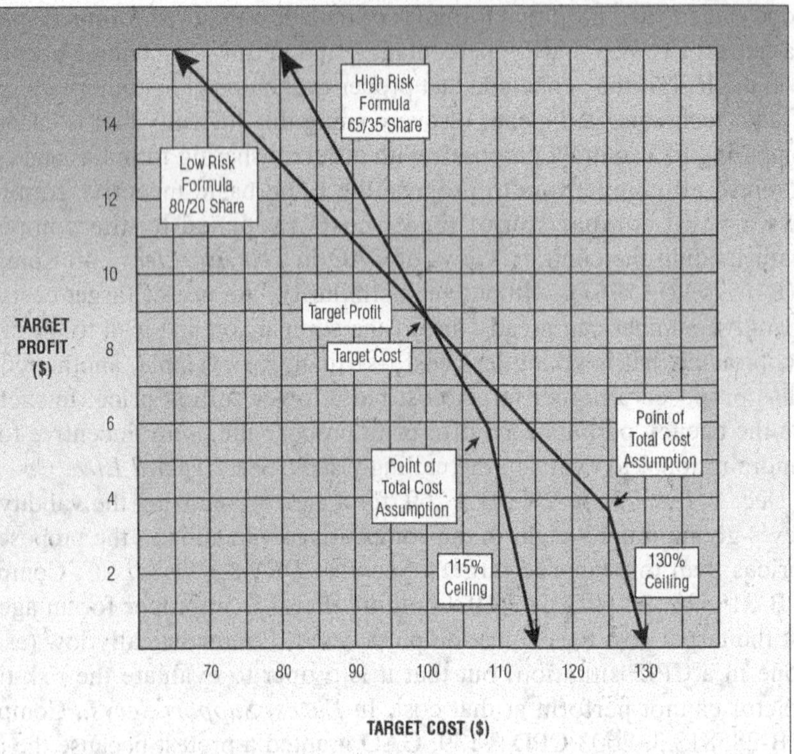

Figure 12-4

In some cases, contracts have used different ceiling prices for different elements of the work. See; for example, *Reflectone, Inc.*, ASBCA 34891, 89-3 BCA ¶21,962, *aff'd*, 891 F.2d 299 (Fed. Cir. 1989), where the board ruled that the proper interpretation of contract ceiling prices was that a ceiling on the base work and another ceiling on option work were separate ceilings that were separately enforceable. Compare *Aerojet-General Corp.*, ASBCA 13548, 70-1 BCA ¶8245, where the board found that the contract contained a single ceiling for both development and production work. See also *CTA, Inc.*, ASBCA 47062, 00-2 BCA ¶30,946, holding that the government cannot unilaterally create separate line item ceiling prices in a contract that originally contained a single ceiling and that such action is a change entitling the contractor to an equitable adjustment. When the contract contains work using two different appropriations, as in *Aerojet-General*, it is better practice to use separate ceilings for those different elements in order to avoid any possibility that work in one area might be charged to the other appropriation.

If the contractor must incur costs exceeding the target cost to complete performance of the contract, the initial overrun will be subject to the sharing arrangement—as is the case in the CPIF contract. This is clearly stated in the standard Incentive Price Revision clause which is not subject to any other interpretation. See *Southwest Marine, Inc.*, ASBCA 54550, 09-1 BCA ¶34,116, rejecting the contractor's argument that when it agreed to 0% target profit, it believed that the contracting officer was agreeing that there would be no profit (loss) sharing of overruns up to the ceiling. In that instance, the sharing formula resulted in losses even though the contractor performed the work for costs under the ceiling price.

At some point, the ceiling price will force the contractor to bear *all of the extra costs* being incurred. This point is called the *point of total cost assumption*—and it is generally at a point lower than the ceiling price. This occurs because the ceiling price is usually negotiated as a percentage of target cost, not a percentage of target price. Hence, in a FPI contract such as the high-risk contract in **Figure 12-4**, the ceiling price is 115% of target cost but only 105.5% of the target price of $109. This provides very little room for the incurrence of unanticipated costs before the contractor will bear the entire burden of overruns. In this formula, the point where the agreed sharing percentage ceases to operate and all additional costs of performance are treated as they would be in a firm-fixed-price contract is at approximately 109% of target cost. If the parties do not have the ability to predict costs within a high degree of accuracy, the use of such a formula would impose an inordinate risk on the contractor.

The point of total cost assumption is the most important feature in the FPIF contract because it identifies the point at which the contractor's risk changes from the incentive sharing that has been negotiated to a fixed-price risk—100% responsibility for costs incurred. As depicted on **Figure 12-4**, this point occurs where the share line and the ceiling line intersect, because this is the point where the ceiling overrides the sharing arrangement. Hence, the amount of ceiling is the key determinant of the point of total cost assumption. For example, in the low-risk formula in **Figure 12-4**, the point of total cost assumption occurs much further from target cost—at approximately 126% of target cost.

The DoD Guide contains some unique guidance on how contracting officers should approach the structuring of the formulas used in FPI contracts—offering higher profits for optimistic target costs. The Guide states:

> Th[e] [recommended] approach starts with the premise that the Government's objective negotiation position represents a reasonably challenging, but achievable target cost. In this context, achievable means attainable with management focus on efficient and economical performance. In return, the contractor has the opportunity to achieve rewards, through operation of higher profit rates and attractive share ratios, commensurate with the risk assumed. These reasonably higher profit rates and favorable share ratios represent the most favorable profitability profile DoD will offer during negotiations. The Government strategy is to reward the contractor for controlling cost. This should be the most favorable profitability offer from the Government made in negotiations.
>
> The reasonably challenging, but achievable target cost should form the basis of the Government offer, and is roughly analogous to the Government's optimistic cost position. The minimum or optimistic position is realistic though optimistic. It is based on a best case scenario of contract performance based on a reasonable analysis of available information. Use of an arbitrarily low position is neither appropriate nor defensible and may be counterproductive as it undermines the credibility of the Government's position. This position must reflect a cost number the Government is confident the contractor can achieve with efficient performance. This number is the Government target cost position and should be modified only if the information and data that becomes available during negotiations changes this position. The Government should not have a reasonably challenging but achievable target cost number and a higher "objective" cost that reflects a settlement position.

The DoD Guide provides considerable additional detail on establishing the elements of the incentive formula. It states that if the contractor is willing to accept the optimistic cost as the target cost, the government should give a high target profit (suggesting 13% of target cost), a large contractor share of any underruns (suggesting a 20/80 share), and a small contractor share for overruns (no suggested share). It also suggests that the ceiling price be determined by establishing the point of total cost assumption based on determining the amount of potential cost risk in the procurement. It contains several illustrative formulas—the basic formula being set forth in **Figure 12-5**. This is followed by several graphs illustrating variations to this formula if the contracting officer accepts higher target costs during negotiation of the formula.

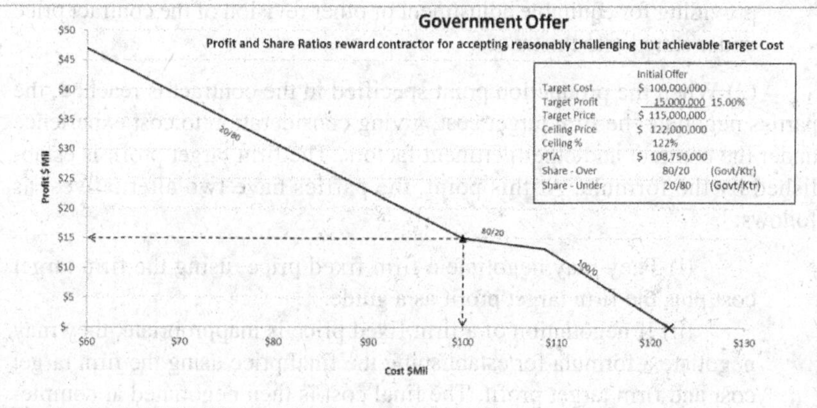

Figure 12-5

If a contractor is performing the work at costs less than target cost, ¶ (g) of the Incentive Price Revision—Firm Target clause requires it to adjust its billings if they has exceeded the costs incurred for delivered supplies or services plus the target profit attributable to those supplies or services. See *Kearfott Guidance & Navigation Corp.*, ASBCA 49271, 04-2 BCA ¶ 32,757, rejecting the contractor's arguments that this provision should not be enforced and that earned performance incentives should be included in the calculation of the adjustment and ruling on the proper allowable costs that should be included in the adjustment.

[3] Successive Targets

A less frequently used form of FPI contract is the FPIS contract. This type of contract is described in FAR 16.403-2 as follows:

> (a) *Description.* (1) A fixed-price incentive (successive targets) contract specifies the following elements, all of which are negotiated at the outset:
>
> (i) An initial target cost.
> (ii) An initial target profit.
> (iii) An initial profit adjustment formula to be used for establishing the firm target profit, including a ceiling and floor for the firm target profit. (This formula normally provides for a lesser degree of contractor cost responsibility than would a formula for establishing final profit and price.)
> (iv) The production point at which the firm target cost and firm target profit will be negotiated (usually before delivery or shop completion of the first item).
> (v) A ceiling price that is the maximum that may be paid to the contractor, except for any adjustment under other contract clauses

providing for equitable adjustment or other revision of the contract price under stated circumstances.

(2) When the production point specified in the contract is reached, the parties negotiate the firm target cost, giving consideration to cost experience under the contract and other pertinent factors. The firm target profit is established by the formula. At this point, the parties have two alternatives, as follows:

(i) They may negotiate a firm fixed price, using the firm target cost plus the firm target profit as a guide.

(ii) If negotiation of a firm fixed price is inappropriate, they may negotiate a formula for establishing the final price using the firm target cost and firm target profit. The final cost is then negotiated at completion, and the final profit is established by formula, as under the fixed-price incentive (firm target) contract (see 16.403-1 above).

This type of contract is used when the parties do not have adequate costing or pricing information to establish firm prices at the outset, but they believe that sufficiently accurate information will be available early in performance to permit the negotiation of a firm-fixed-price or a FPIF contract, FAR 16.403-2(b). The use of this type of contract is limited since it requires a significant administrative effort to conduct the two or three negotiations required. However, it does provide some flexibility in pricing long-term contracts whose performance period will extend over two or more years. The initial formula in this contract is established using the same logic as that used in negotiating the FPIF contract with a firm target but it is expected that the ceiling price would be quite high, and the initial sharing arrangement would impose a modest share on the contractor, to reflect that the parties do not have the ability to accurately predict the cost of performance at the outset.

FAR 16.406(b) calls for the use of the Incentive Price Revision—Successive Targets clause in FAR 52.216-17 in all contracts of this type.

[C] Performance and Delivery Incentives

Objective incentives have also been applied to contract performance requirements (such as the weight of an item, thrust of an engine, or speed of a vehicle) and to contract delivery requirements (such as the date of delivery or the date of meeting a contract milestone for some intermediate task). These incentives have been most frequently used on incentive contracts, which meet the requirement that a contract containing such incentives must contain an incentive or a constraint on cost, FAR 16.402-1(a). Since any fixed-price type contract contains a constraint on cost, these incentives can also be used in firm-fixed-price contracts, fixed-price contracts with economic price adjustment or redeterminable fixed price contracts. There is no guidance on whether time-and-material or labor-hour contracts provide a sufficient constraint on cost to permit the use of performance or delivery incentives on those type contracts.

Objective performance and delivery incentives were originally used by the military services and NASA on development contracts. However, their use has spread to contracts for many types of services. See FAR 37.601(b)(3) calling for the use of "performance incentives" "where appropriate." NASA uses such incentives in all hardware contracts over $25 million which are "based on performance-oriented documents" except commercial items, NFS 1816.402-270. Such incentives can be both positive and negative based on the following guidance in NFS 1816.402:

> (1) A positive incentive is generally not appropriate unless—
>
> (i) Performance above the target (or minimum, if there are no negative incentives) level is of significant value to the Government;
> (ii) The value of the higher level of performance is worth the additional cost/fee;
> (iii) The attainment of the higher level of performance is clearly within the control of the contractor; and
> (iv) An upper limit is identified, beyond which no further incentive is earned.
>
> (2) A negative incentive is generally not appropriate unless—
>
> (i) A target level of performance can be established, which the contractor can reasonably be expected to reach with a diligent effort, but a lower level of performance is also minimally acceptable;
> (ii) The value of the negative incentive is commensurate with the lower level of performance and any additional administrative costs; and
> (iii) Factors likely to prevent attainment of the target level of performance are clearly within the control of the contractor.
>
> (3) When a negative incentive is used, the contract must indicate a level below which performance is not acceptable.

Objective performance and delivery incentives of this type should be contrasted with other types of provisions used by government agencies to motivate technical or schedule performances. These other types of provisions are most frequently called "liquidated damages," requiring fixed compensation to the government for a contractor's failure to meet contract requirements—usually specified delivery or completion dates. See FAR Subpart 11.5 for guidance on the use of such clauses pertaining to the time of delivery or performance. While not termed "incentives," bonuses or rewards are also occasionally used in contracts that may or may not contain required compensation for inferior performance.

FAR 16.402-2 gives the following guidance on the use of technical performance incentives.

> (a) Performance incentives may be considered in connection with specific product characteristics (e.g., a missile range, an aircraft speed, an engine thrust, or a vehicle maneuverability) or other specific elements of the contractor's performance. These incentives should be designed to relate profit or fee to results achieved by the contractor, compared with specified targets.
>
> (b) To the maximum extent practicable, positive and negative performance incentives shall be considered in connection with service contracts for performance of objectively measurable tasks when quality of performance is critical and incentives are likely to motivate the contractor.
>
> (c) Technical performance incentives may be particularly appropriate in major systems contracts, both in development (when performance objectives are known and the fabrication of prototypes for test and evaluation is required) and in production (if improved performance is attainable and highly desirable to the Government).

FAR 16.402-3 provides guidance on the use of delivery incentives:

> (a) Delivery incentives should be considered when improvement from a required delivery schedule is a significant Government objective. It is important to determine the Government's primary objectives in a given contract (e.g., earliest possible delivery or earliest quantity production).

Performance and delivery incentives have been used in many contracts. In some instances, they have been used to balance cost incentives, attempting to ensure that the contractor does not overemphasize low costs to the detriment of performance. The FAR emphasizes the use of incentives for a different purpose: to focus attention on specific important performance and delivery objectives of the government.

[1] Enforceability of Clauses

Traditionally, liquidated damages clauses have been enforceable only if they do not assess a "penalty" for nonperformance. See *Priebe & Sons, Inc. v. United States*, 332 U.S. 407 (1947), applying this rule to a government contract and stating that such clauses would not be enforced where they were "included not to make a fair estimate of damages to be suffered but to serve only as an added spur to performance." This rule has been uniformly applied to provisions specifically termed "liquidated damages" clauses. The fundamental test that has been used to determine whether the clause provides for a "penalty" is whether the amount assessed was a reasonable forecast of damages at the time of entering into the contract, *DJ Mfg. Corp. v. United States*, 86 F.3d 1130 (Fed. Cir. 1996); *Southwest Eng'g Co. v. United States*, 341 F.2d 998 (8th Cir.), *cert. denied*, 382 U.S. 819 (1965); *International Elec. Corp. v. United States*, 646 F.2d 496 (Ct. Cl. 1981).

These principles would appear to be directly applicable to any performance or delivery incentive clause written in terms of a penalty for failure to meet the contract requirement, since in very few cases would the government be able to show that such penalties were a reasonable approximation of actual damage. No court or board decision has considered this issue concerning performance incentives. However, in *Fairchild Camera & Instrument Corp.*, ASBCA 12291, 68-2 BCA ¶ 7327, the board ruled that a delivery incentive clause has a "distinct legal identity" from a liquidated damages clause. The board stated that no reasonable forecast of damages was necessary and that the clause was enforceable as a binding agreement between the parties.

The penalty rule has been applied to contract clauses that are not termed liquidated damages clauses but that assess compensation for delinquent performance. For example, in *JMNI, Inc. v. United States*, 4 Cl. Ct. 310 (1984), the court refused to enforce a clause calling for a "payment adjustment factor" that reduced the contract payment on a pro rata basis for units of work up to 15% delinquent and provided for no payment for a unit that was more than 15% delinquent. The court found that this clause was in the nature of a liquidated damages clause and that the nonpayment for over 15% delinquency was a penalty and not a reasonable forecast of damages. The same result was reached in *Charley O. Estes*, IBCA 1198-7-78, 84-1 BCA ¶ 17,073. See also *Maintenance Eng'rs., Inc.*, VABCA 5350, 99-2 BCA ¶ 30,513, rejecting as a penalty an interpretation of a clause that would allow multiple deductions for payment for services which could result in no payment even though the contractor performed some of the work, and *Wackenhut Corp.*, IBCA 2311, 91-1 BCA ¶ 23,318, finding a clause assessing a "penalty" of 1% of the price per day unenforceable. Compare *Work Force Reforestation, Inc.*, AGBCA 90-132-3, 90-3 BCA ¶ 22,233, holding that a clause that payment on a proportional basis for reduced coverage in a tree planting contract was not a penalty; and *Double E Reforestation, Inc.*, AGBCA 85-109-1, 86-2 BCA ¶ 18,764, holding that nonpayment for coverage of less than 80% in a tree planting contract was not a penalty because the government would likely reperform the work in that circumstance.

GAO has also sustained protests of contracts which impose penalties for partially completed performance. See *Linda Vista Indus., Inc.*, Comp. Gen. Dec. B-214447, 84-2 CPD ¶ 380, applying the liquidated damages rule to a Contractor's Failure to Perform clause that called for nonpayment for an entire cleaning item if the contractor failed to perform any part of the cleaning services required for that item. See also *D. J. Findley*, Comp. Gen. Dec. B-215230, 85-1 CPD ¶ 197, and *Environmental Aseptic Servs. Admin.*, 62 Comp. Gen. 219 (B-207771), 83-1 CPD ¶ 194, finding a Performance Requirements Summary clause to be a penalty clause because it permitted nonpayment for an entire task when only part of the task was poorly performed.

[2] Structuring Practices

The procurement regulations contain no specific guidance on the structuring of performance and delivery incentives. FAR 16.402-2 contains the following general guidance on writing technical performance incentives:

> (d) Technical performance incentives may involve a variety of specific characteristics that contribute to the overall performance of the end item. Accordingly, the incentives on individual technical characteristics must be balanced so that no one of them is exaggerated to the detriment of the overall performance of the end item.
>
> (e) Performance tests and/or assessments of work are generally essential in order to determine the degree of attainment of performance targets. Therefore, the contract must be as specific as possible in establishing test criteria (such as testing conditions, instrumentation precision, and data interpretation) and performance standards (such as the quality levels of services to be provided).
>
> (f) Because performance incentives present complex problems in contract administration, the contracting officer should negotiate them in full coordination with Government engineering and pricing specialists.
>
> (g) It is essential that the Government and contractor agree explicitly on the effect that contract changes (e.g., pursuant to the Changes clause) will have on performance incentives.
>
> (h) The contracting officer must exercise care, in establishing performance criteria, to recognize that the contractor should not be rewarded or penalized for attainments of Government-furnished components.

FAR 16.402-3 contains only the following provision on delivery incentives:

> (b) Incentive arrangements on delivery should specify the application of the reward-penalty structure in the event of Government-caused delays or other delays beyond the control, and without the fault or negligence, of the contractor or subcontractor.

See also DoD PGI 216.402-2, stating that such incentives "should relate to specific performance areas or milestones, such as delivery or test schedules, quality controls, maintenance requirements, and reliability standards."

Since performance and delivery incentives are always used in conjunction with cost incentives, they are usually written in terms of dollar bonuses and penalties for deviations from contractually specified targets. Such a formula is depicted in **Figure 12-6** using the following factors:

Target Weight	100 lbs.
Maximum Bonus	$3
Maximum Penalty	$3
Sharing Arrangement	$1 for each 3 lb. Weight

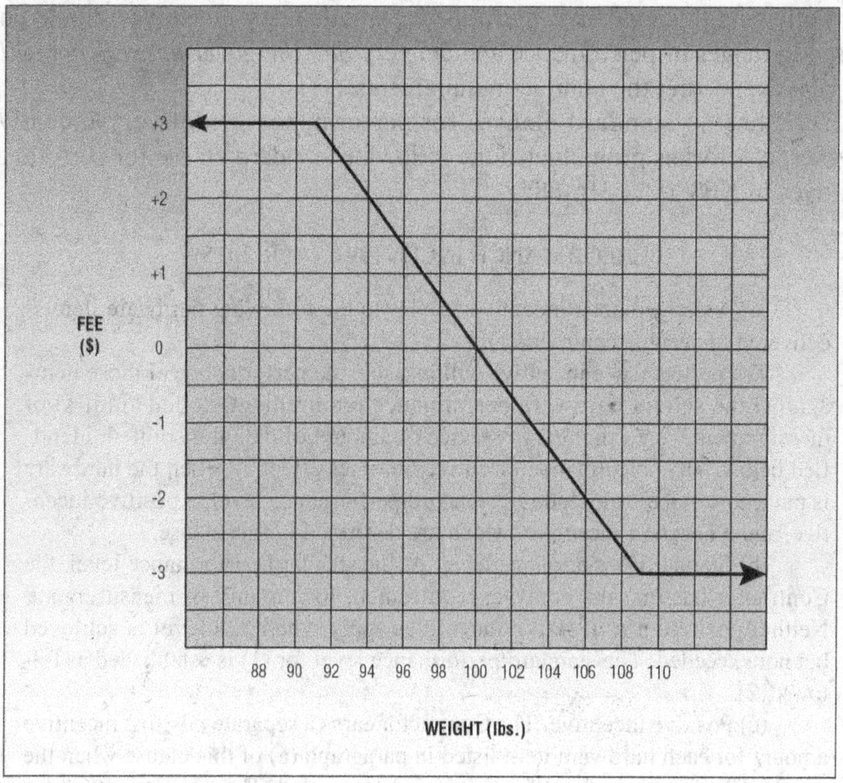

Figure 12-6

In this case, the sharing occurs over a range of 18 pounds of weight (from 91 pounds to 109 pounds), and the bonus or penalty earned is added to or deducted from the profit or fee that results from the application of the incentive formula on costs of performance.

The DFARS no longer contains any detailed guidance on the structuring of performance and delivery incentives. Prior to 1991, however, DFARS 16.402-2(S-70) contained the following guidance on the levels of performance that should be used to set the fee levels:

> "Performance," as used in this paragraph, refers not only to the performance of the article being procured, but to the performance of the contractor as well. Performance which is the minimum which the Government will accept shall be mandatory under the terms of the Completion form contract and shall warrant only the minimum profit or fee related thereto. Performance which meets the stated targets will warrant the "target" profit or fee. The incentive feature (providing for increases or decreases, as appropriate) is applied to performance targets rather than performance requirements.

Following this guidance, performance and delivery incentives should never be used in ranges of performance and delivery *that the government is not willing to accept* as meeting the contract requirements.

DoD has no standard clauses for performance or delivery incentives. However, NASA has promulgated the following standard clause for performance incentives in NFS 1852.216-88:

> PERFORMANCE INCENTIVE (APR 2015)
>
> (a) A performance incentive applies to the following hardware item(s) delivered under this contract: (1).
>
> The performance incentive will measure the performance of those items against the salient hardware performance requirement, called "unit(s) of measurement," e.g., months in service or amount of data transmitted, identified below. The performance incentive becomes effective when the hardware is put into service. It includes a standard performance level, a positive incentive, and a negative incentive, which are described in this clause.
>
> (b) Standard performance level. At the standard performance level, the Contractor has met the contract requirement for the unit of measurement. Neither positive nor negative incentives apply when this level is achieved but not exceeded. The standard performance level for (1) is established as follows: (2).
>
> (c) Positive incentive. The Contractor earns a separate positive incentive amount for each hardware item listed in paragraph (a) of this clause when the standard performance level for that item is exceeded. The amount earned for each item varies with the units of measurement achieved, up to a maximum positive performance incentive amount of $ (3) per item. The units of measurement and the incentive amounts associated with achieving each unit are shown below: (4).
>
> (d) Negative incentive. The Contractor will pay to the Government a negative incentive amount for each hardware item that fails to achieve the standard performance level. The amount to be paid for each item varies with the units of measurement achieved, up to the maximum negative incentive amount of $ (5). The units of measurement and the incentive amounts associated with achieving each unit are shown below: (6).
>
> (e) The final calculation of positive or negative performance incentive amounts shall be done when performance (as defined by the unit of measurement) ceases or when the maximum positive incentive is reached.
>
> > (1) When the Contracting Officer determines that the performance level achieved fell below the standard performance level, the Contractor will either pay the amount due the Government or credit the next payment voucher for the amount due, as directed by the Contracting Officer.
> >
> > (2) When the performance level exceeds the standard level, the Contractor may request payment of the incentive amount associated with a given level of performance, provided that such payments shall not be more frequent than monthly. When performance ceases or the

maximum positive incentive is reached, the Government shall calculate the final performance incentive earned and unpaid and promptly remit it to the contractor.

(f) If performance cannot be demonstrated, through no fault of the Contractor, within (*insert number of months or years*) after the date of hardware acceptance by the Government, the Contractor will be paid (*insert percentage*) of the maximum performance incentive.

(g) The decisions made as to the amount(s) of positive or negative incentives are subject to the Disputes clause.

(1) Insert applicable item number(s) and/or nomenclature.

(2) Insert a specific unit of measurement for each hardware item listed in (1) and each salient characteristic, if more than one.

(3) Insert the maximum positive performance incentive amount (see 1816.402-270(e)(1) and (2)).

(4) Insert all units of measurement and associated dollar amounts up to the maximum performance incentive.

(5) Insert the appropriate amount, in accordance with 1816.402-270(e).

(6) Insert all units of measurement and associated dollar amounts up to the maximum negative performance incentive.

NFS 1816.402-270 provides the following guidance on structuring such performance incentives:

(b) When a performance incentive is used, it shall be structured to be both positive and negative based on hardware performance after delivery and acceptance. In doing so, the contract shall establish a standard level of performance based on the salient hardware performance requirement. This standard performance level is normally the contract's minimum performance requirement. No incentive amount is earned at this standard performance level. Discrete units of measurement based on the same performance parameter shall be identified for performance both above and below the standard. Specific incentive amounts shall be associated with each performance level from maximum beneficial performance (maximum positive incentive) to minimal beneficial performance or total failure (maximum negative incentive). The relationship between any given incentive, both positive and negative, and its associated unit of measurement should reflect the value to the Government of that level of hardware performance. The contractor should not be rewarded for above-standard performance levels that are of no benefit to the Government.

(c) The final calculation of the performance incentive shall be done when performance, as defined in the contract, ceases or when the maximum positive incentive is reached. When the performance ceases below the standard established in the contract, the Government shall calculate the amount due and the contractor shall pay the Government that amount. Once hardware performance exceeds the standard, the contractor may request payment of the incentive amount associated with a given level of performance, provided that such payments shall not be more frequent than monthly. When hardware performance ceases above the standard level of performance, or when the maximum positive incentive is reached, the Government shall calculate the final performance incentive earned and unpaid and promptly remit it to the contractor. The exclusion at FAR 16.405 (e)(3) does not apply to decisions made as to the amount(s) of positive or negative incentive.

(d) When the deliverable hardware lends itself to multiple, meaningful measures of performance, multiple performance incentives may be established. When the contract requires the sequential delivery of several hardware items (e.g., multiple spacecraft), separate performance incentive structures may be established to parallel the sequential delivery and use of the deliverables.

(e) In determining the value of the maximum performance incentives available, the contracting officer shall follow the following rules:

(1) For a CPFF contract, the sum of the maximum positive performance incentive and fixed fee shall not exceed the limitations in FAR 15.404-4(c)(4)(i).

(2) For an award fee contract.

(i) The individual values of the maximum positive performance incentive and the total potential award fee (including any base fee) shall each be at least one-third of the total potential contract fee. The remaining one-third of the total potential contract fee may be divided between award fee and the maximum performance incentive at the discretion of the contracting officer.

(ii) The maximum negative performance incentive for research and development hardware (e.g., the first and second units) shall be equal in amount to the total earned award fee (including any base fee). The maximum negative performance incentives for production hardware (e.g., the third and all subsequent units of any hardware items) shall be equal in amount to the total potential award fee (including any base fee). Where one contract contains both cases described above, any base fee shall be allocated reasonably among the items.

(3) For cost reimbursement contracts other than award fee contracts, the maximum negative performance incentives shall not exceed the total earned fee under the contract.

It is also possible to create performance and delivery incentives in terms of a single bonus or penalty to be paid or deducted upon the meeting or missing of a target. This type of incentive is used most frequently in the case of performance milestones where the contract contains a series of bonuses to be paid upon the meeting of each milestone. Such an incentive combines both performance and delivery incentives because the bonus is paid only if the contractor performs the required work in accordance with the specifications at the time called for. There has been some criticism of this type of incentive because it gives the contractor additional profit when performance is no better than that called for by the contract. If contract requirements are demanding, however, and if the performance and delivery incentive motivates the contractor to perform well, there should be no objection to this type of incentive. The DoD Guide criticizes the use of "interim incentive payments" because they "run the risk of having paid incentives when acquisition outcomes are not met."

When performance or delivery incentives are used, the contract should include specific provisions defining conditions that must be met for the contractor to earn the bonus or suffer the loss called for by an incentive clause. One issue that should be addressed is the effect on performance incentives of government failure to fund an overrun on a CPIF contract. In such a case, for example, the contractor may not be able to conduct a test program to demonstrate that a performance incentive has been earned. See, for example, *North Am. Rockwell Corp.*, ASBCA 14329, 72-1 BCA ¶ 9207, where the board held that because the contractor submitted convincing evidence that the product met the weight requirement earning the maximum bonus on a weight incentive, a pro rata share of that bonus, commensurate with the percentage of completion of the contract, should be paid. See also *CB&I AREVA MOX Servs., LLC v. United States*, 138 Fed. Cl. 292 (2018), holding that the government had no right to take back provisional incentive payments until the end of the project even though the government contended that the contractor was so far behind schedule that it could never earn the payments.

There may also be difficulties in specifying the precise tests to be used to determine when each performance incentive has been met. This was an issue in *Western Elec. Co.*, ASBCA 16110, 73-1 BCA ¶ 10,013, where the bonus was to be paid if a missile passed through a point under guidance control. The board ruled that the contractor had earned the bonus even though the missile engine failed prior to reaching the specified point, because the missile did in fact pass through the point and the guidance system functioned sufficiently well before engine failure.

[3] Relationship of Incentive to Other Provisions

In drafting incentive contracts with performance and delivery incentives, great care must be exercised to ensure that the relationship of these incentives to other contract provisions is clearly defined. Thus, the relationship of performance incentives to the inspection and warranty clauses in the contract must be stated. Contractors failing to meet performance goals may also fail to meet specification requirements, but the penalties for these two failures are quite different. The performance incentive formula calls for a profit or fee reduction when performance goals are not met, while other provisions of the contract allow the contracting officer to reject the work, require rework until specifications are met, or even terminate the contract for default. Many contracts containing performance incentives do not spell out the rights of the parties, but in most contracting situations it is clear that the parties do not intend to provide a double remedy for the government. This issue should be addressed and resolved by specific contract language. In general, such language would state that the *sole remedy* to be assessed when the performance falls in the RIE would be the penalty under the performance incentive clause. This is logical when, as in the case of the DoD, the government does not include unacceptable ranges of performance within the incentive provision. If, as in the case of NASA, the performance incentive includes failure of an item of hardware, it is logical to conclude that the negative incentive has been calculated to include the damages that the government will suffer. See *Maintenance Eng'rs., Inc.*, VABCA 5350, 99-2 BCA ¶ 30,513, where the board discussed the parallel remedies of penalty provisions for nonperformance and the government's rights under the Inspection of Services clause in FAR 52.246-4 to reperform work and charge the cost to the contractor. The board decision is not clear as to whether these are alternate remedies or duplicative remedies.

In the case of delivery incentives, the contract should include explicit language stating the relationship of the incentive to excusable delays. FAR 16.402-3(b) requires that this issue be addressed in the contract but gives no guidance as to the preferred agreement. In many cases, contracting officers have included contract language providing that the date for calculation of the delivery incentive will be extended for excusable delays. In CPIF contracts, this is generally accomplished by keying the incentive bonus or penalty to the Excusable Delays clause in FAR 52.249-14, which is included in all cost-reimbursement contracts. This clause provides for schedule adjustments for excusable delays; and the contract language would state that such adjustments would occur prior to the computation of the incentive bonus or penalty. In FPI contracts, the incentive bonus or penalty must be keyed to ¶ (c) of the Default (Fixed-Price Supply and Service) clause in FAR 52.249-8, and the special contract clause should explicitly provide that the contractor will be granted a time extension for excusable delays (the Default clause contains no such language). Even if there is no such contract provision, it may be held that such is the proper interpretation of the total contract, *North Am. Aviation, Inc.*, ASBCA 11603, 68-1 BCA ¶ 6998 (CPIF contract); *General Precision, Inc.*, ASBCA 11071, 66-2 BCA ¶ 5904 (FPI contract). See, however, *Sosedil-Pizzarotti*, ASBCA 31135, 89-2 BCA ¶ 21,807, where the board enforced clear contract language stating that "no time extensions shall be allowed for the purpose of payment under the bonus clause provisions."

[4] Interrelationship With Cost Incentives

When performance and delivery incentives are used in incentive contracts, any increased costs incurred to achieve better performance or avoid a performance and delivery penalty will be chargeable to the contract and subject to sharing. Thus, if the contractor incurs more labor-hours or uses more expensive labor or material in attempting to enhance performance, such costs will be shared by the government to the extent that the costs are reasonable and within the RIE. In addition, the contractor has considerable latitude in selecting techniques to motivate employees. See *Celesco Indus., Inc.*, ASBCA 20569, 77-1 BCA ¶ 12,445, *sustained on other grounds*, 77-2 BCA ¶ 12,585, where the contractor established an internal incentive program to motivate its employees that used the entire performance incentive bonus for successful missile flights. After earning $70,500, which was distributed to the employees, the contractor claimed the amount as an allowable cost. The government argued that the cost was unallowable since it was a distribution of profit, but the board ruled that the employee bonuses were reasonable compensation under the Cost Principles. Compare *Petroleum Operations & Support Servs., Inc.*, EBCA 291-6-83, 85-2 BCA ¶ 18,037, denying the allowability of bonuses paid on a CPAF contract because they did not comply with the Cost Principles.

One important aspect of performance and delivery incentives is that they create a value structure, within the incentive formula, that states the value of each performance and delivery factor in the formula. For example, if the weight incentive in **Figure 12-6** is used on a contract containing the cost incentive in **Figure 12-1**, the two sharing arrangements tell the contractor the value of weight savings. The value is determined by equating each incentive to the fee bonus or penalty to be derived from the formula. Thus, the contractor will incur a fee bonus or penalty of $1 for each three pounds of weight variance and each $5 of cost variance. The result is that the incentive formula tells the contractor that the government places a value of $5 on a three-pound weight savings, as long as each expenditure or savings occurs within the RIE. From this information the contractor could be expected to make decisions on weight reduction efforts based on the cost of the reduction. If it was probable that a weight reduction of three pounds could be achieved at a cost of less than $5, the contractor would be expected to spend the funds (in an attempt to achieve the weight reduction) and increase its total fee on the contract. Thus, the formula contains an unexpressed tradeoff for each performance and delivery incentive, where fee can be maximized by spending or saving money. In some cases, this tradeoff situation is not fully thought through at the time the formula is written, with the result that the contractor may take actions during contract performance that are not desired by the government. The DoD Guide recognizes this aspect of these incentives, stating:

> Think carefully when using competing incentives. The contractor's goal will be to maximize the incentive it receives but this usually involves tradeoffs which may not be consistent with how the Government views the relative importance of the incentives. Remember that once the contract is awarded, the contractor has control over how to pursue the incentives. Examples of competing incentives:

- Cost vs. Performance: It will probably cost more to build a jet that flies at Mach 2.5 than Mach 2
- Performance vs. Schedule: It will probably take longer to build and test a missile that will travel farther and be more accurate
- Schedule vs. Cost: Can be competing but generally delivering early means less cost (shorter time for level of effort functions)

FAR 16.402-4 recognizes this issue but gives the following minimal guidance:

> A properly structured multiple-incentive arrangement should—
>
> (a) Motivate the contractor to strive for outstanding results in all incentive areas; and
>
> (b) Compel tradeoff decisions among the incentive areas, consistent with the Government's overall objectives for the acquisition. Because of the interdependency of the Government's cost, the technical performance, and the delivery goals, a contract that emphasizes only one of the goals may jeopardize control over the others. Because outstanding results may not be attainable for each of the incentive areas, all multiple-incentive contracts must include a cost incentive (or constraint) that operates to preclude rewarding a contractor for superior technical performance or delivery results when the cost of those results outweighs their value to the Government.

This requirement is generally implemented in one of two ways. First, in the ideal situation, performance and delivery incentives are structured on the basis of the government's tradeoff analysis. For example, in the weight incentive discussed above, the contracting officer determines from consultation with agency technical personnel that the value of weight savings is at least $5 for three pounds. The incentive arrangement is then structured to reflect this government tradeoff judgment. Second, special contract clauses are used to prevent incentive awards when they are not desired by the government. For example, if the contracting officer has determined that weight savings are of value only if the contractor does not overrun the target cost of the contract, a special clause will provide that no bonuses will be paid for the performance incentive on weight if there is a cost overrun. These clauses should be used judiciously, however, since they cancel out the performance and delivery incentives in the specified range of cost.

Better regulatory guidance would permit use of performance and delivery incentives only when the government can identify the specific value of enhanced performance or avoidance of performance reductions and has determined that such results are worth additional costs. If this policy were followed, the government would be assured that the contractor was not being motivated to overrun the contract in situations where the government did not desire enhanced performance.

[D] Cost-Plus-Award-Fee Contracts

The CPAF contract is used when the agency wants to include some profit motivation in the contract but does not have sufficient information to establish firm, objectively stated cost, performance, or delivery targets at the beginning of contract performance. Thus, the CPAF contract provides that the contractor's fee will be determined largely by an award given periodically by a "fee determining official" (FDO) in the procuring agency. While the basic elements to be evaluated in arriving at this award and the evaluation mechanism itself are usually disclosed to the contractor prior to performance, this type of contract is known as a "subjective" incentive because the award official has a significant amount of discretion in establishing the precise amount of award. This subjectivity has led some contractors to question the use of this type of incentive, but experience indicates that CPAF contracts are quite effective in situations where it is not possible to write a contract specification or work statement that contains a precise description of the work the contractor is expected to perform. FAR 16.405-2 describes this type of contract as follows:

> A cost-plus-award-fee contract is a cost-reimbursement contract that provides for a fee consisting of (1) a base amount fixed at inception of the contract, if applicable and at the discretion of the contracting officer, and (2) an award amount that the contractor may earn in whole or in part during performance and that is sufficient to provide motivation for excellence in the areas of cost, schedule, and technical performance.

CPAF contracts have been used primarily in service contracts and research and development contracts. Beginning in the 1960s, NASA used this type of contract in order to provide incentives for its major support service contractors, and it was NASA that provided the early guidance on CPAF contracts in the NASA Cost-Plus-Award-Fee Contracting Guide, NHB 5104.4, August 1967. Subsequently, the military services, NASA, and the Department of Energy (DOE) broadened the use of the CPAF contract to include R&D contracting. See ¶ 1.3 of the NASA Award-Fee Contracting Guide, December 1997 and DEAR 916.404-2. Note that DFARS 216.405-2(3) places limitations on use of CPAF contracts for certain types of development. Other agencies have used CPAF contracts extensively, as the advantages of CPAF contracts have become known throughout the government.

Beginning in 2005 there was considerable criticism of the use and implementation of CPAF contracts. A series of GAO reports indicated that unduly high award fees were being paid on CPAF contracts, *Defense Acquisitions: DoD Wastes Billions of Dollars Through Poorly Structured Incentives*, GAO-06-409T (Apr. 6, 2006); and *NASA Procurement: Use of Award Fees for Achieving Program Outcomes Should Be Improved*, GAO-07-58 (Jan. 2007). As a result, there has been considerable congressional activity giving guidance on when and how these contracts should be used—including language adopting GAO recommendation that award fees be based on program *outcomes* rather than subjective appraisals of the procedures followed by the contractor. The first statute adopting this GAO recommendation was § 814 of the National Defense Authorization Act for FY 2007, Pub. L. No. 109-364, requiring the issuance of regulations to "ensure that all new contracts using award fees link such fees to acquisition outcomes (which shall be defined in terms of program cost, schedule, and performance)" and providing relatively detailed criteria governing the award fees to be paid. This was followed up by provisions in the Consolidated Security, Disaster Assistance, and Continuing Appropriations Act, 2009, Pub. L. No. 110-329, which reiterates these requirements for the Department of Defense in § 8105 of the Department of Defense Appropriations Act, 2009 (Division C of the Consolidated Act), and for the Department of Homeland Security in § 533 of the Department of Homeland Security Appropriations Act, 2009 (Division D of the Consolidated Act). Finally, the National Defense Authorization Act for FY 2009, Pub. L. No. 110-417, adopted similar requirements for all civilian agencies. See 41 U.S.C. § 4711.

These statutes were implemented by Federal Acquisition Circular 2005-37, 74 Fed. Reg. 52856, Nov. 14, 2009—revising FAR 16.401. See *Defense Acquisitions: DoD Needs Better Information on Incentive Outcomes*, GAO-17-291 (July 11, 2017), indicating that these changes have led to increased use of CPIF contracts and decreased use of CPAF contracts by DoD. In contrast, the Department of Energy has continued to use CPAF contracts on almost all of their Management and Operating contracts. See *Department of Energy: Performance Evaluations Could Better Assess Management and Operating Contractor Costs*, GAO-19-5 (Feb. 2019), for a complete description of DOE's extensive use of CPAF and cost-plus-award-term contracts.

[1] Advantages and Disadvantages of CPAF Contracts

The major advantage of the CPAF contract is improved communication between the parties. In the course of making periodic awards, the government gives the contractor a detailed evaluation of performance, pointing out perceived deficiencies and weaknesses. As a result, the contractor is able to improve performance as work proceeds or persuade the government that its analysis is incorrect. In either case, the contracting parties are forced to analyze performance on a regular basis and communicate with each other regarding any problems. From the contractor's point of view, the CPAF contract has also been advantageous in that it has frequently yielded higher fees than the CPFF contract.

The major disadvantage of the CPAF contract is that substantial administrative costs are incurred through the continual evaluations and the processing of award decisions. Increasing the length of the evaluation periods can ameliorate this situation, but the CPAF contract inherently calls for a significant amount of paperwork. It has been suggested that the internal evaluation effort is not significantly greater than the work a well-staffed program management office does in its regular evaluation of a development contractor's performance, but even when the evaluation is done by a program management office, the paperwork is increased substantially. Of course, this added paperwork leads to the enhanced communication that is the strength of the CPAF contract. An agency should recognize, however, the demands that this type of contract places on its staff and limit the use of CPAF contracts to situations where the size and importance of the work justify the expenditure of such resources. NASA has recognized this issue by prohibiting the use of CPAF provisions in contracts of less $2 million per year without the approval by the procurement officer, NFS 1816.404-270.

Another disadvantage noted by some commentators is the potential for the CPAF contractor to follow government directions without challenge. Evaluators are normally the government personnel monitoring the contractor's performance, and the contractor's reaction may be to follow an evaluator's direction in order to earn a higher award fee. This disadvantage can be overcome by carefully selecting government evaluators, ensuring that they have sufficient technical and management expertise and judgment to make sound decisions. Full participation of the contractor in the award process is also helpful in ensuring that sound decisions are made in evaluating the contractor's performance.

A disadvantage identified in recent studies of CPAF contracts was the tendency of some government evaluators to give high ratings to contractors that had not met the goals of the program being implemented by the contract. In some instances, this apparently occurred on long-standing CPAF contracts where the evaluators had become accustomed to working with the contractor over a number of years. This disadvantage may result from the burdensome nature of the administrative effort demanded by this type of contract.

[2] Guidance on Use of CPAF Contracts

The regulatory guidance on the use of CPAF contracts has always emphasized that they should be used only when objectively stated criteria cannot be established. In spite of the statutory requirement that such contracts link award fees to "acquisition outcomes (which shall be defined in terms of program cost, schedule, and performance)," this regulatory guidance has not changed. See FAR 16.401(e)(1) stating that the CPAF contract is suitable for use in the following circumstances:

> (i) The work to be performed is such that it is neither feasible nor effective to devise predetermined objective incentive targets applicable to cost, technical performance, or schedule;
>
> (ii) The likelihood of meeting acquisition objectives will be enhanced by using a contract that effectively motivates the contractor toward

> exceptional performance and provides the Government with the flexibility to evaluate both actual performance and the conditions under which it was achieved; and
>
> (iii) Any additional administrative effort and cost required to monitor and evaluate performance are justified by the expected benefits as documented by a risk and cost benefit analysis to be included in the Determinations and Findings referenced in 15.401(e)(5)(iii).

See also DoD PGI 216.405-2(3) stating that the CPAF contract is suitable for level-of-effort contracts for services "where mission feasibility is established but measurement of achievement must be by subjective evaluation rather than objective measurement."

The clearest indication that "acquisition outcomes" need not be defined by using objective criteria is in DFARS 216.401-71 making it clear that when objective criteria can be established, a CPAF contract should not be used, stating:

> (1) Contracting officers shall use objective criteria to the maximum extent possible to measure contract performance. Objective criteria are associated with cost-plus-incentive-fee and fixed-price-incentive contracts.
>
> (2) When objective criteria exist but the contracting officer determines that it is in the best interest of the Government also to incentivize subjective elements of performance, the most appropriate contract type is a multiple-incentive contract containing both objective incentives and subjective award-fee criteria (*e.g.*, a cost-plus-incentive-fee/award fee or fixed-price-incentive/award fee).

The statutes contain additional guidance that appears to be resulting in greatly reduced use of CPAF contracts. They require additional regulations on when award fees can be earned including a provision to "ensure that no award fee may be paid for contractor performance that is judged to be below satisfactory performance or performance that does not meet the basic requirements of the contract." See FAR 16.401(e)(2) stating:

> Award fee shall not be earned if the contractor's overall cost, schedule, and technical performance is below satisfactory. The basis for all award-fee determinations shall be documented in the contract file to include, at a minimum, a determination that overall cost, schedule and technical performance is or is not at a satisfactory level. This determination and the methodology for determining the award fee are unilateral decisions made solely at the discretion of the Government.

It is not clear how an agency official will determine whether "overall" performance is unsatisfactory, but this requirement creates a considerable risk for a contractor that it will earn no award fee if it fails to meet one of the performance objectives of the contract.

[3] Award Fee Plan

FAR 16.401(e)(3) requires that CPAF contracts must be supported by an award fee plan as follows:

> All contracts providing for award fees shall be supported by an award-fee plan that establishes the procedures for evaluating award fee and an Award-Fee Board for conducting the award-fee evaluation. Award-fee plans shall—
>
> (i) Be approved by the FDO unless otherwise authorized by agency procedures;
>
> (ii) Identify the award-fee evaluation criteria and how they are linked to acquisition objectives which shall be defined in terms of contract cost, schedule, and technical performance. Criteria should motivate the contractor to enhance performance in the areas rated, but not at the expense of at least minimum acceptable performance in all other areas;
>
> (iii) Describe how the contractor's performance will be measured against the award-fee evaluation criteria;
>
> (iv) Utilize the adjectival rating and associated description as well as the award-fee pool earned percentages shown below in Table 16-1. Contracting officers may supplement the adjectival rating description. The method used to determine the adjectival rating must be documented in the award-fee plan;
>
> (v) Prohibit earning any award fee when a contractor's overall cost, schedule, and technical performance is below satisfactory;
>
> (vi) Provide for evaluation period(s) to be conducted at stated intervals during the contract period of performance so that the contractor will periodically be informed of the quality of its performance and the areas in which improvement is expected (e.g., six months, nine months, twelve months, or at specific milestones); and
>
> (vii) Define the total award-fee pool amount and how this amount is allocated across each evaluation period.

These mandatory elements of the plan cover most of the aspects of the CPAF contract that are discussed below (including a discussion of the application of the rating system in Table 16-1). They also require agencies to include the procedures that the agency will use to determine the amount of the award fee and to obtain high level approval of CPAF contracts before they are used.

Agencies have followed varying practices in determining whether the plan should be made part of the contract or furnished to the contractor separately. While there is no requirement that the entire award fee plan be made available to offerors or contractors, it is clear that they must be informed of the criteria and rating system. Whether or not the plan is part of the contract, it is subject to prospective revision by the government. See the clause in DFARS 252.216-7005:

AWARD FEE (FEB 2011)

The Contractor may earn award fee from a minimum of zero dollars to the maximum amount stated in the award-fee plan in this contract. In no event will award fee be paid to the Contractor for any evaluation period in which the Government rates the Contractor's overall cost, schedule, and technical performance below satisfactory. The Contracting Officer may unilaterally revise the award-fee plan prior to the beginning of any rating period in order to redirect contractor emphasis.

[4] Structuring the Award Fee

The elements of a CPAF contract are as follows:

- Estimated Cost
- Base Fee
- Award Fee Pool
- Award Periods

The amount of fee in the award fee pool is allocated to the award periods, and each award is made in accordance with the criteria provided in the contract. The estimated cost in the CPAF contract is established in the competitive process or negotiated based on a detailed analysis of the proposed costs in the same manner as the target cost in the CPIF contract. The other elements of the CPAF contract are established through negotiation, if the contract is awarded as a sole source contract, or on the basis of competitive proposals, if the contract is awarded under competitive procedures. In the latter case, some agencies have permitted offerors to propose CPAF structures and then considered the adequacy of the proposed structures in evaluating competing sources. It has been held proper for an agency to downgrade a proposal for offering a structure that does not meet the agency's needs as stated in the RFP, *Boeing Sikorsky Aircraft Support*, Comp. Gen. Dec. B-277263.2, 97-2 CPD ¶ 91 (proposed base fee too high and maximum fee too low); *Management & Tech. Servs. Co.*, Comp. Gen. Dec. B-209513, 82-2 CPD ¶ 571 (proposed base fee and maximum fee too high); *Management Servs., Inc.*, Comp. Gen. Dec. B-206364, 82-2 CPD ¶ 164 (proposed awards too high for levels of performance, and proposed employee bonuses for very high levels of performance found to be a disincentive for such performance). It has also been held proper for an agency to request assurances of "cost containment," which induced the competitors to propose cost ceilings, *Hughes Space & Commc'ns Co.*, Comp. Gen. Dec. B-266225.6, 96-1 CPD ¶ 199.

[a] Base Fee

The base fee is the minimum dollar amount of fee that a contractor can earn on a CPAF contract. By using the concept of a base fee rather than a target fee, the government has made the decision that all the incentive will be in the form of awards (no penalties). Thus, the base fee is comparable to the minimum fee in the CPIF contract. There is no guidance in the FAR on the level of base fee or its relationship to the award fees. However, DFARS 216.405-2(3)(iii) states that the base fee shall not exceed 3% of estimated cost. NASA used base fees for many years; but in 1993 NFS 1816.405-271 was issued prohibiting base fees where the award fee evaluation was "final," such as on service contracts (in effect, requiring a zero-base fee). This regulation further states that on other CPAF contracts, "such as those for hardware or software development," the base fee cannot exceed 3% and must be refunded if the final award fee evaluation is "poor/unsatisfactory." EPAAR 1516.404-271(b) provides that base fees should not exceed 3% of the estimated costs. DEAR 915.404-4-72(a)(1) permits base fees from 0% to 50% of the fee amount for a CPFF contract, arrived at by using the agency's profit policy. The regulations of other agencies contain no maximum amount for the base fee, and in the past, base fees have ranged from 0% to 5%. Many contracts have used base fees of 2% of estimated cost but a number of recent contracts have contained base fees of 0%.

Base fees in the range of 2% to 3% do little more than guarantee the contractor against loss, since such base fees are roughly equivalent to normal cost disallowances. In practice, significant awards have usually been earned on CPAF contracts, with the result that there has been only modest risk that the contractor will be required to perform the work for the base fee. However, as discussed above, there has been significant congressional pressure to ensure that no award fees would be earned for performance that is "below satisfactory." This places considerable pressure on prospective contractors to negotiated higher base fees.

[b] Award Fee Pool

Prior to 1997, the controlling requirement with regard to the award fee pool in a CPAF contract was that this fee plus the base fee could not exceed the statutory limitation on CPFF contracts. This requirement was deleted from the FAR by Federal Acquisition Circular 97-02, September 30, 1997, with the result that the contracting officer is now permitted to negotiate any amount of award fee necessary to accomplish the purpose of the contract. FAR 16.401(e)(2) contains the following minimal guidance:

> *Award-fee amount*. The amount of award fee earned shall be commensurate with the contractor's overall cost, schedule, and technical performance as measured against contract requirements in accordance with the criteria stated in the award-fee plan.

The most complete guidance is contained in DEAR 915.404-4-72(a) as follows:

> (2) The base fee plus the amount included in the award fee pool should normally not exceed the fixed fee (as subjectively determined or as developed from the fee schedule) by more than 50%. However, in the event the base fee is to be less than 50% of the fixed fee, the maximum potential award fee may be increased proportionately with the decreases in base fee amounts.
>
> (3) The following maximum potential award fees shall apply in award fee contracts: (percent is stated as percent of fee schedule amounts).

Base fee percent	Award fee percent	Maximum total percent
50	100	150
40	120	160
30	140	170
20	160	180
10	180	190
0	200	200

In *CACI, Inc.-Fed.*, 64 Comp. Gen. 439 (B-216516.2), 85-1 CPD ¶ 363, GAO ruled that the maximum fee should be computed as a percentage of contract estimated cost and not realistic cost as determined by the agency. In *CACI*, the realistic cost was lower, but the agency did not negotiate down the estimated cost to match the realistic cost.

Whether the procurement is sole source or competitive, the base fee and the award fee pool can be established by the procuring agency either specifying precise percentages in the RFP or permitting the offeror to propose the levels. For example, in *Holmes & Narver, Inc.*, Comp. Gen. Dec. B-196832, 80-1 CPD ¶ 134, GAO affirmed the propriety of an RFP provision permitting offerors to propose any base fee plus award fee pool up to 10%. The total potential fee, of course, is an important competitive factor since it places a ceiling on the government's expenditures in this part of the contract. In theory, a small award fee pool is disadvantageous to the government because, by reducing the amount of fee available for award purposes, the contractor's incentive to better its performance is also reduced; GAO did not, however, consider this aspect of the situation. In contrast, in *Boeing Sikorsky Aircraft Support*, Comp. Gen. Dec. B-277263.2, 97-2 CPD ¶ 91, and *Management & Tech. Servs. Co.*, Comp. Gen. Dec. B-209513, 82-2 CPD ¶ 571, GAO agreed with the agency's negative evaluation of proposed award fee pools, which were too small to provide sufficient incentive. Compare *CACI, Inc.-Fed.*, Comp. Gen. Dec. B-216516, 84-2 CPD ¶ 542, where the agency also permitted the offerors to propose any level of base fee and award fee pool within the regulatory maximum but stated that fee levels would not be evaluated in the source selection process. GAO affirmed this procedure even though the competitors offered different base and award fee pool levels. Not surprisingly, all of the competitors proposed a base fee plus award fee pool of 10% since the level was not to be evaluated. This gave the agency the maximum amount of incentive fee on the contract and provided significant award fees for the competing contractors.

[c] Award Periods

FAR 16.401(e)(3) contains the following guidance on the evaluation periods incorporated in the award fee plan:

> (vi) Provide for evaluation period(s) to be conducted at stated intervals during the contract period of performance so that the contractor will periodically be informed of the quality of its performance and the areas in which improvement is expected (e.g., six months, nine months, twelve months, or at specific milestones)[.]

Originally, NASA used three-month evaluation periods, but the administrative effort necessary for evaluations was too great to be performed satisfactorily in such short periods. Subsequently, agencies have normally used either four or six-month evaluation periods. See, for example, NFS 1816.405-272(a), calling for periods of at least six months but permitting shorter periods when the "additional administrative costs . . . are balanced by benefits accruing to the Government." Clearly, the period should be long enough to permit fee award well before the end of the next evaluation period. This permits the contractor to use the agency evaluation of its performance to better its performance in the following period. It is also possible to use award periods of varying length if the amount of work done in some periods of performance is substantially less than in others. For example, in an R&D contract where the initial effort is small, the contracting officer might specify a six-month award period for the initial period, followed by four-month periods thereafter. In service contracts, since the work is usually level over the life of the contract, the award periods are generally of the same duration.

Evaluation periods can also be established in terms of contractual milestones rather than calendar periods. See NFS 1816.405-272(a), suggesting this technique but stating that such periods must be no longer than 12 months. This would be appropriate in a situation where the contractor was performing critical tests or design reviews on the work under the contract and the evaluation would not be accurate until completion of the tests or reviews.

[d] Allocation of Award Fee

The award fee pool must be allocated to award periods to provide a maximum award fee for each period. See NFS 1816.405-272(b), stating:

> A portion of the total available award fee shall be allocated to each of the evaluation periods. This allocation may result in either an equal or unequal

> distribution of fee among the periods. The contracting officer should consider the nature of each contract and the incentive effects of fee distribution in determining the appropriate allocation structure.

DoD requires that a large percentage of the award fee be allocated to the final evaluation of contract performance. See DFARS 216.405-2(1) stating:

> The contracting officer shall perform an analysis of appropriate fee distribution to ensure that at least 40 percent of the award fee is available for the final evaluation so that the award fee is appropriately distributed over all evaluation periods to incentivize the contractor throughout the performance of the contract. The percentage of award fee available for the final evaluation may be set below 40 percent if the contracting officer determines that a lower percentage is appropriate, and this determination is approved by the head of the contracting activity (HCA). The HCA may not delegate this approval authority.

Several agencies have adopted clauses on this issue. See the following clause at TAR 1252.216-73:

> DISTRIBUTION OF AWARD FEE (APR 2005)
>
> (a) The total amount of award fee available under this contract is assigned according to the following evaluation periods and amounts:
>
> Evaluation Period:
>
> Available Award Fee: (insert appropriate information)
>
> (b) After the contractor has been paid 85 percent of the base fee and potential award fee, the Government may withhold further payment of the base fee and award fee until a reserve is set aside in an amount that the Government considers necessary to protect its interest. This reserve shall not exceed 15 percent of the total base fee and potential award fee or $100,000, whichever is less. Thereafter, base fee and award fee payments may continue.
>
> (c) In the event of contract termination, either in whole or in part, the amount of award fee available shall represent a prorata distribution associated with evaluation period activities or events as determined by the Government.
>
> (d) The Government will promptly make payment of any award fee upon the submission by the contractor to the contracting officer's authorized representative, of a public voucher or invoice in the amount of the total fee earned for the period evaluated. Payment may be without using a contract modification.

A similar clause, without the withholding provision, is included in HUDAR 2452.216-74 and was included in DEAR 916.405(e) until 1996.

The total award fee has generally been distributed to the award periods in rough proportion to the amount of costs to be spent in each period. However, the importance of the work in each period should also be considered in making this allocation. The NASA Guidance on Award Fee Contracting, June 1989 (NASA 1989 Guidance), suggested that a portion of the award fee pool could be allocated to specific events such as tests or demonstrations and that this portion need not be put in a specific award period:

> Tests, demonstrations, and other milestones or events are subject to possible slippage. To eliminate the need for a reallocation of award fee potential, it may be a good idea to allocate any portion of the award fee earmarked for such milestones or events to whatever evaluation periods the milestones or events ultimately occur, rather than allocating to a specific period.

This guidance has been removed from the current NASA Guide, which states, at ¶ 3.5.2, that award periods containing critical milestones should be allocated a larger portion of the award fee pool.

Some agencies have followed a practice of supplementing the award fee pool by adding award fees not earned in earlier periods to the pool available for awards in later periods. The NASA 1989 Guidance called this technique "rollover" or "rollforward" and gave the following guidance:

> The determination whether to permit a rollover of unearned award fee should be based upon an analysis of the work effort, the planned allocation of the award fee potential, and the likely effect on contractor motivation. Generally speaking, an automatic rollover of unearned award fee from one evaluation period to the next should be avoided, because it tends to reduce the effectiveness of the incentive in the current period. Instead, when rollover authority is desired, consideration should be given to providing in the evaluation plan for the exercise of that authority at the discretion of the designated Fee Determination Official.

The use of this technique in service contracts was prohibited by NASA in 1997, NFS 1816.405-273(a), and is now prohibited on all contracts by FAR 16.401(e)(4). Authority to use it was provided in the Determination of Award Fee Earned clause (used by DOT and HUD), which is discussed below. Section 814 of the National Defense Authorization Act for FY 2007, Pub. L. No. 109-364, required the issuance of regulations that "provide specific direction on the circumstances, if any, in which it may be appropriate to roll over award fees" but the FAR implemented this provision with a blanket prohibition of rollover.

When the contract calls for an "end item," NASA requires that the award fee be determined by the performance of that end item. Thus, award fees are made on an interim basis but are provisional until the final performance outcome is determined. See NFS 1816.405-273, stating:

> (b) *End item contracts.* On contracts such as those for end item deliverables where the true quality of contractor performance cannot be measured

until the end of the contract, only the last evaluation is final. At that point, the total contract award fee pool is available, and the contractor's total performance is evaluated against the award fee plan to determine total earned award fee. In addition, interim evaluations are done to monitor performance prior to contract completion, provide feedback to the contractor on the Government's assessment of the quality of its performance, and establish the basis for making interim award fee payments (see 1816.405-276(a)). These interim evaluations and associated interim payments are superseded by the fee determination made in the final evaluation at contract completion. The Government will then pay the contractor, or the contractor will refund to the Government, the difference between the final award fee determination and the cumulative interim fee payment.

These provisional award fees are implemented in the Award Fee for End Item Contracts clause in NFS 1852.216-77. Less specific guidance of this nature is given in DEAR 916.404-2 stating that the award fee "should be concentrated on the end product of the contract."

[e] Payment of Fee

No standard FAR or DFARS clauses governs the payment of base and award fees. However, FAR 16.406(e) directs agencies to use "appropriate" award fee clauses. Thus, the agencies follow different policies on the payment of these fees. The NASA Award Fee for Service Contracts clause at NFS 1852.216-76 allows the contracting officer to insert the method of award fee payment. The NASA Award Fee for End Item Contracts clause at NFS 1852.216-77 provides for payment of the base fee on a monthly (or less) basis and of award fees after each interim evaluation. The Distribution of Award Fee clause at TAR 1252.216-73 and HSAR 3052.216-73 provides for payment of the base and award fees upon receipt of an invoice from the contractor for the "total fee earned" (with potential withholding after payment of 85% of the fees). The Payment of Base and Award Fee clause at HUDAR 2452.216-71 provides for payment of the base and award fees in accordance with a schedule to be included in the contract by the contracting officer.

DFARS 216.405-2 allowed provisional payment of award fees until 2011. That provision now states:

> (2) *Award-fee evaluation and payments.* Award-fee payments other than payments resulting from the evaluation at the end of an award-fee period are prohibited. (This prohibition does not apply to base-fee payments.) The fee-determining official's rating for award-fee evaluations will be provided to the contractor within 45 calendar days of the end of the period being evaluated. The final award-fee payment will be consistent with the fee-determining official's final evaluation of the contractor's overall performance against the cost, schedule, and performance outcomes specified in the award-fee plan.

[5] Performance Evaluation Plan

Although the CPAF contract has always been intrinsically subjective, the evaluation has been done in a very methodical way. Agencies have carefully spelled out in a performance evaluation plan the areas of performance that will be evaluated, the rating system that will be used, and the way in which these ratings will be translated into fee awards. Some agencies have adopted contract clauses describing this process. See TAR 1252.216-72 prescribing the use of the following clause:

PERFORMANCE EVALUATION PLAN (OCT 1994)

(a) A Performance Evaluation Plan shall be unilaterally established by the Government based on the criteria stated in the contract and used for the determination of award fee. This plan shall include the criteria used to evaluate each area and the percentage of award fee (if any) available for each area. A copy of the plan shall be provided to the contractor ____ (insert number) calendar days prior to the start of the first evaluation period.

(b) The criteria contained within the Performance Evaluation Plan may relate to (1) Technical (including schedule) requirements if appropriate; (2) Management; and (3) Cost.

(c) The Performance Evaluation Plan may, consistent with the contract, be revised unilaterally by the Government at any time during the period of performance. Notification of such changes shall be provided to the contractor (insert number) calendar days prior to the start of the evaluation period to which the change will apply.

A similar clause is set forth in HSAR 3052.216-73 and HUDAR 2452.216-73. These clauses are explicit in giving the agency full flexibility to issue and change the evaluation plan during contract performance. This is a major advantage to both parties because, particularly in the case of R&D contracts being performed over a period of time, the parties may learn of changed circumstances, making it advisable to redirect the contractor's efforts and, thus, bringing about changes in award criteria. Of course, if such changes are made, the contractor should be fully informed of the new evaluation plan prior to the beginning of the award period. See *URS Consultants, Inc.*, IBCA 4285-2000, 02-1 BCA ¶ 31,812, *recons. denied*, 02-2 BCA ¶ 31,917, holding that ¶ (c) of the Performance Evaluation Plan clause prohibits retroactive changes to the plan.

[a] Award Criteria

The award criteria set forth elements of the contractor's performance that will be evaluated by the agency in determining the amount of award fees and the relative weight of these fees.

[i] Selecting the Criteria

A great deal of flexibility is given to contracting officers in selecting the award criteria, and it is important that the criteria be tailored to the specific procurement. See FAR 16.401(e)(3), stating that the award fee plan must:

> (ii) Identify the award-fee evaluation criteria and how they are linked to acquisition objectives which shall be defined in terms of contract cost, schedule, and technical performance. Criteria should motivate the contractor to enhance performance in the areas rated, but not at the expense of at least minimum acceptable performance in all other areas;

While, as discussed above, the statutes call for the award fees to be made on the basis of "outcomes," it seems clear from this FAR language that the criteria can be subjective as long as they are "linked to acquisition objectives." There has been a long-standing debate among the agencies as to whether award criteria should focus on *contractual results* (called "output" criteria) or *methods of performance* (called "input" criteria). See DEAR 916.404-2 stating:

> The goals and evaluation criteria should be results-oriented. The award fee should be concentrated on the end product of the contract, that is, output, be it hardware, research and development, demonstration or services, together with business management considerations. However, input criteria such as equal employment opportunity, small business programs, functional management areas, such as safety, security, etc., should not be disregarded and may be appropriate criteria upon which to base some part of the award fee.

In contrast, the NASA 1989 Guidance gave considerable discretion in this area, as follows:

> Depending upon the procurement situation, performance evaluation factors may include outputs, inputs or a combination of both. Output factors relate to the end results of contract performance, such as the quality of the end items delivered or services rendered, the actual time of their delivery or completion, and the actual costs incurred. Their use has obvious advantages, but there are potential disadvantages as well. In certain situations, end results of this type may not be discernible until it is too late for an award fee evaluation process to have any appreciable effect on the direction in which the results are heading. Also, given the uncertainties that made it necessary to use a cost reimbursement contract, an evaluation limited to output factors may not provide a true or complete picture of actual accomplishments. To illustrate, the incurrence of a cost underrun or overrun may reflect less on the contractor's cost control accomplishments than on the uncertainties existing at the time the contract cost estimate was negotiated.

For these reasons, input factors often are used instead of or as a supplement to the use of output factors. Input factors relate to those intermediate processes, procedures, actions or techniques that experience and analysis indicate will be key elements influencing successful contract performance.

Following this reasoning, output criteria call for assessment of the contractor's performance in meeting the end objectives of the contract. However, such assessment can be quite subjective in some instances. Hence, output criteria frequently do not assess only whether the contractor met an objective standard, such as an estimated cost or a scheduled completion date. See, for example, the current NASA regulation, NFS 1816.405-274, which does not contain the above guidance but rather states that in evaluating "cost control" (an input criteria), the contractor should "normally" be given "an unsatisfactory rating" if it incurs a significant overrun within its control (an output criteria). However, the regulation goes on to allow scoring using a subjective evaluation of how well the contractor-controlled costs if an overrun was "insignificant." This regulation also states that "the contractor should be rewarded for meeting the estimated cost of the contract" (calling for the input criteria to override the output criteria).

As a general rule, the better the work is defined, the more desirable it is to evaluate output criteria, and when contract objectives can be established by setting clear targets for cost, schedule or performance, a CPIF formula would be the proper type of arrangement for that element of the work. Even when the parties cannot agree on firm targets, output criteria are probably desirable because they call for less subjectivity than input criteria. Thus, output criteria would likely be used on service contracts for repetitive services. Input criteria would more likely be used on R&D contracts where the parties are not sure of the accuracy of their projections of end results and the government desires to encourage the best performance, even if the parties have originally agreed to erroneous goals.

It can be seen that the difference between output criteria and input criteria is a matter of degree not a clear distinction. See the NASA Guide at ¶ 3.4.1, giving the following specific examples of the types of output award criteria:

> a. *Technical Performance*—Accomplishment achieved in the areas of:
>
> Design: Approach in design concepts, analysis, detailed execution, and low cost design and manufacturing. Design of test specimens, models, and prototypes.
>
> Development: Conception/execution of manufacturing process, test plans, and techniques. Effectiveness of proposed hardware changes.
>
> Quality: Quality assurance, e.g., appearance, thoroughness and accuracy, inspections, customer surveys.
>
> Technical: Meeting technical requirements for design, performance and processing, e.g., weight control, quality assurance, maintainability, reliability design reviews, test procedures, equipment, performance.

Processing Documentation: Timely and efficient preparation, implementation and closeout.

Facilities/GFE: Operation and maintenance of assigned facilities and Government Furnished Equipment.

Schedule: Meeting program key milestones and contractual delivery dates; anticipating and resolving problems; recovery from delays; reaction time and appropriateness of response to changes.

Safety: Providing a safe work environment; conducting annual inspections of all facilities; maintaining accident/incident files; timely reporting of mishaps; providing safety training for all personnel.

Information Management: Ability of computer system to provide adequate, timely and cost effective support; meets security requirements; management information systems ensure accurate, relevant and timely information.

Material Management: Efficient and effective processing of requisitions, with emphasis on priority requisitions; responsiveness to changes in usage rates.

b. *Project Management*—Accomplishment achieved in the areas of:

Program Planning/Organization/Management: Assignment and utilization of personnel; recognition of critical problem areas; cooperation and effective working relationships with other contractors and Government personnel to assure integrated operation efficiency; support to interface activities; technology utilization; effective use of resources; labor relations; planning, organizing, and managing all program elements; management actions to achieve and sustain a high level of productivity; response to emergencies and other unexpected situations.

Compliance with contract provisions: Effectiveness of property and material control, Equal Employment Opportunity Program, Minority Business Enterprise Program, system and occupational safety and security. Effectiveness in meeting or exceeding small business and small disadvantaged business subcontracting goals.

Subcontracting: Subcontract direction and coordination. Purchase order and subcontractor administration.

Timely and accurate financial management reporting

c. *Cost Control*—The contractor's ability to control, adjust, and accurately project contract costs (estimating contract costs, not budget or operating plan costs) through:

Control of indirect and overtime costs. Control of direct labor costs.

Economies in use of personnel, energy, materials, computer resources, facilities, etc.

Cost reduction through use of cost saving programs, cost avoidance programs, alternate designs and process methods, etc. "Make versus buy" program decisions.

Reduced purchasing costs through increased use of competition, material inspection, etc.

The NASA Guide also contains, at ¶ 3.4.2, a few examples of commonly used input criteria:

> *Staffing*: Optimal allocation of resources; adequacy of staffing; qualified and trained personnel; identification and effective handling of employee morale problems; etc.
>
> *Planning*: Adequate, quality, innovative, self-initiated and timely planning of activities; effective utilization of personnel; quality of responses; etc.

See also Table 16-1, after DoD PGI 216.470, illustrating both output and input criteria. For example, in the cost area this table contains both "control direct charges" and "performance to cost estimate." The table does not include two mandatory criteria in DFARS 216.405-2-70 and -71 requiring "award fee reduction or denial" for "jeopardizing the health or safety of Government personnel" and "failure to comply with requirements relating to performance of private security functions" during contingency operations.

The NASA 1989 Guidance contained the following suggestion aimed at limiting the number of award criteria:

> Fragmentation of the award fee potential over a large number of performance areas and factors dilutes emphasis. Instead, broad performance areas should be selected, such as technical and business management, supplemented by a limited number of subfactors describing significant evaluation elements over which the contractor has effective management control. Project history and past performance can be helpful in identifying those key problem or improvement areas that should be subject to award fee evaluations.

There is some disagreement as to whether the award criteria should be made a part of the contract document. Prior to 1991, DFARS 216.404-2(b)(S-72)(ii) stated that this information should be set forth in the contract (there is no statement on this issue in the current DFARS), but a number of agencies reserve the right to unilaterally issue the criteria to the contractor after contract award.

[ii] Weighting the Criteria

In most CPAF contracts, the award criteria are assigned relative weights as a means of establishing the priorities of the agency in the elements of performance. Most weighting systems assign points to each evaluation criterion, generally using a total of 100 points. See Table 16-2, after DoD PGI 216.470, illustrating a comprehensive weighting system.

The NASA Guide provides, at ¶ 3.4.3, that weighting of the factors need not be done and that, when it is done, it does not control the awards, as follows:

> [T]he detailed performance evaluation plan should indicate the relative priorities assigned to the various performance areas and evaluation factors and subfactors. This may be accomplished through the use of narrative phrases such as "more important," "important," and "less important" or through the use of percentage weights. When percentages are used, the plan should state that they are for the sole purpose of communicating relative priorities, and in no way imply an arithmetical precision to the judgmental determinations of overall performance quality and the amount of award fee earned.

The NASA Guide suggests, at ¶ 3.4.3, that when weighting is done, a two-step process should be used. First, the major areas of performance are given relative weights in accordance with the agency's priorities. Thus, the agency might decide, on an R&D contract, that the weights should be as follows:

Factor	**Assigned Weight**
Technical	55
Business Management	35
Cost Control	10

The NASA Guide then suggests weighting the subfactors within each factor in the same manner. Thus, within the technical factor there might be three subfactors:

Subfactor	**Assigned Weight**
Design	55
Quality	30
Schedule	15

After the subfactors for business management and cost control are weighted in a similar manner, the agency has a complete matrix of relative weights. For most agencies other than NASA, this matrix is used for calculating the final evaluation of the award fee. See, for example, Table 16-2 after DoD PGI 216.470.

[b] Rating System

The rating system that will be used is the key determinate of whether the CPAF contract will yield a reasonable profit for the contractor. Traditionally, most agencies disclosed the grading system to the contractor but it has been held proper to use an undisclosed grading system, *Burnside-Ott Aviation Training Ctr.*, ASBCA 43184, 96-1 BCA ¶ 28,102, *aff'd*, 107 F.3d 854 (Fed. Cir. 1997). However, the FAR now prescribes a mandatory rating scheme which presumably will be used on all CPAF contracts. This rating system appears as Table 16-1 of FAR 16.401(e), and is set forth in **Figure 12-7**.

Award-Fee Adjectival Rating	Award-Fee Pool Available To Be Earned	Description
Excellent	91% — 100%	Contractor has exceeded almost all of the significant award-fee criteria and has met overall cost, schedule, and technical performance requirements of the contract in the aggregate as defined and measured against the criteria in the award-fee plan for the award-fee evaluation period.
Very Good	76% — 90%	Contractor has exceeded many of the significant award-fee criteria and has met overall cost, schedule, and technical performance requirements of the contract in the aggregate as defined and measured against the criteria in the award-fee plan for the award-fee evaluation period.
Good	51% — 75%	Contractor has exceeded some of the significant award-fee criteria and has met overall cost, schedule, and technical performance requirements of the contract in the aggregate as defined and measured against the criteria in the award-fee plan for the award-fee evaluation period.
Satisfactory	No Greater Than 50%	Contractor has met overall cost, schedule, and technical performance requirements of the contract in the aggregate as defined and measured against the criteria in the award-fee plan for the award-fee evaluation period.
Unsatisfactory	0%	Contractor has failed to meet overall cost, schedule, and technical performance requirements of the contract in the aggregate as defined and measured against the criteria in the award-fee plan for the award-fee evaluation period.

Figure 12-7

The key problem in this rating system is that it is not keyed to the base fee and the award fee but, rather, appears to be mandatory without regard to those elements of the award fee plan. Thus, it does not ensure the contractor that it yields awards commensurate with its actual performance. For example, assume that the contractor has "exceeded" a few criteria and has met almost all of the "requirements"—which the fee determination official concludes yields a score of satisfactory and a fee award of 50%. This would yield fees on two hypothetical contracts as follows:

	Contract A	Contract B
Base Fee	3%	0%
Award Fee Pool	12%	10%
Fee Earned	9%(3% + 6%)	5%(0% + 5%)

This illustrates the inequity of applying this mandatory rating system on contracts with low base fees and low award fee pools. It yields a fair result on contract A but not on contract B.

Another problem with this rating system is that it does not define the terms "criteria" and "requirements." In requiring that awards will only be made when a contractor has met the requirements, it identifies those requirements as they are "defined and measured against the criteria." As discussed above, some criteria are and have been established to match the contract requirements, such as performing within the estimated cost, while others are highly subjective evaluations of the way the contractor has performed the work. Thus, the FAR rating system creates great doubt as to how it will be applied in determining whether criteria have been "exceeded" and requirements "met." Yet the scoring system appears to yield significant awards only when the contractor has exceeded the criteria and met the "overall" requirements. This raises the possibility that a contractor performing development work could complete the work within the schedule and estimated cost yet only earn a 50% award because it has not exceeded the criteria. In addition, the scoring system calls for no award if the contractors "has failed to meet overall, cost, schedule, and performance requirements." This raises the specter of a very low fee if that language is interpreted harshly.

To be fair to contractors, CPAF contracts should be structured in a way that allows a contractor to earn the same fee on a CPAF contract that it would earn for the same level of performance on a CPFF contract. Thus, if an agency would normally negotiate a 7% fixed fee it should structure its CPAF contract to yield at least 7% for satisfactory performance. Yet in its reports on CPAF contracts, GAO appears to have disagreed with systems that gave substantial awards for average performance. This GAO criticism was based, in part, on the description of CPAF contracts in FAR 16.405-2 stating:

> A cost-plus-award-fee contract is a cost-reimbursement contract that provides for a fee consisting of (1) a base amount fixed at inception of the contract and (2) an award amount that the contractor may earn in whole or in part during performance and that is *sufficient to provide motivation for excellence* in such areas as quality, timeliness, technical ingenuity, and cost-effective management. (Emphasis added.)

GAO reports apparently interpret this language are requiring that award fees only be given for performance that is at least above average.

[c] Award Procedure

The amount of the award is usually determined by a three-step procedure within the contracting agency. The first step consists of evaluation and preliminary scoring of the contractor's performance by personnel within the procuring agency who are familiar with the contractor's performance. Generally, the personnel used for this task are the technical and business personnel who are monitoring the contractor's work on a regular basis. In cases where there is a government program manager, this function will be performed primarily by personnel in the program office. The goal of this part of the process is to obtain an evaluation by the most knowledgeable people in the agency on each aspect of the contractor's performance. Most of the guidance on CPAF contracting contains instructions calling for very detailed monitoring of contractor performance and full documentation of perceived strengths and weaknesses. Detailed documentation is essential because these evaluations form the basis of the entire award process.

The second step consists of a review of these evaluations by a board of higher-level personnel. While this step should be unnecessary on smaller procurements, FAR 16.401(e)(3) requires agencies to establish such boards on all procurements. This step ensures that the evaluations are internally consistent and that they reflect an overall view of the contractor's accomplishments. A board of this type would be expected to discern, for instance, not only that one evaluator has unreasonably downgraded a contractor, but also that the contractor's performance was marginal because of a conscious decision to devote effort to some other important task.

The third step is the award by the award official, generally called the "fee determination official." In major procurements, this official should be at the management level of the procuring agency, while in small contracts, the contracting officer might perform this task. The contract clauses generally provide that awards are purely discretionary decisions. See the following clause in TAR 1252.216-71:

> DETERMINATION OF AWARD FEE EARNED (APR 2005)
>
> (a) The Government shall evaluate contractor performance at the end of each specified evaluation period to determine the amount of award. The contractor agrees that the amount of award and the award fee methodology are unilateral decisions to be made at the sole discretion of the Government.
>
> (b) Contractor performance shall be evaluated according to a Performance Evaluation Plan. The contractor shall be periodically informed of the quality of its performance and areas in which improvements are expected.
>
> (c) The contractor shall be promptly advised, in writing, of the determination and reasons why the award fee was or was not earned. The contractor may submit a performance self-evaluation for each evaluation period. The amount of award is at the sole discretion of the Government but any self-evaluation received within (insert number) days after the end of the current evaluation period will be given such consideration, as may be deemed appropriate by the Government.
>
> (d) The amount of award fee which can be awarded in each evaluation period is limited to the amounts set forth at (identify location of award fee

> amounts). Award fee which is not earned in an evaluation period cannot be reallocated to future evaluation periods.

A similar clause is included in HSAR 3052.216-71 and HUDAR 2452.216-72. If the fee determination official is designated by a specific position within the agency, it will be an abuse of discretion for another official to dictate the amount of the award fee. See *Boeing Co. v. United States*, 75 Fed. Cl. 34 (2007), stating at 46-47:

> An agreement that "designate[s] a particular [g]overnment official to make a certain factual determination must be strictly observed." *Southern, Waldrip* [*& Harvick Co. v. United States*], 334 F.2d [245 (Ct. Cl. 1964)] at 249-50; see also *General Elec. Co. v. United States*, 412 F.2d 1215, 1220, 188 Ct. Cl. 620 (Ct. Cl. 1969) ("[T]he internal administrative scheme whereby the Boston Procurement District was to defer to the Army Weapons Command concerning funding cannot diminish . . . authority" provided by the contract to the contracting officer.); *New York Shipbuilding Corp. v. United States*, 385 F.2d 427, 433-34, 180 Ct. Cl. 446 (Ct. Cl. 1967) (Where "the parties expressly chose and named a specific official . . . as the initial decider . . . [,] the [g]overnment could not unilaterally substitute another official."); *Williams Eng'g & Contr. Co. v. United States*, 55 Ct. Cl. 349, 365, 382-83 (1920) (holding that a contract was breached when the Secretary of Navy made a decision that the contract had entrusted to the Chief of the Bureau of Yards and Docks).

The court noted that the agency could have replaced the individual holding the designated job, stating at 46:

> [T]he contract did not purport to abrogate the Secretary's authority over personnel decisions or prevent him from formally removing or replacing Mr. Twining as Manager, Albuquerque Operations. *New York Shipbuilding*, 385 F.2d at 434 (suggesting that contractual designation of the Nuclear Projects Officer "would not mean that the Maritime Administration could not change . . . the occupant of that post"). However, the Secretary was not permitted by the contract to displace the AFDO by informally "invest[ing] [AFDO] authority in himself . . . or in others of his choice," *Fischbach & Moore Int'l Corp. v. United States*, 617 F.2d 223, 226 n.7, 223 Ct. Cl. 119 (Ct. Cl. 1980) ("[W]here the contract or controlling regulations designate (without qualification) a specific officer or body as the one to render a contractual decision . . . , other persons (including higher officials) cannot displace the designated decision maker.").

A provision precluding appeal of award fee determinations under the Disputes clause is not enforceable under the Contract Disputes Act of 1978, *Burnside-Ott Aviation Training Ctr. v. Dalton*, 107 F.3d 854 (Fed. Cir. 1997). However, the review of an award decision is a very narrow one, focusing only on whether it is arbitrary or capricious. Thus, the court affirmed *Burnside-Ott*

Aviation Training Ctr., ASBCA 43184, 96-1 BCA ¶28,102, where the board ruled that the use of a conversion table was not arbitrary or capricious but was within the contracting officer's discretion even though its use was not disclosed to the contractor. The ASBCA has also taken jurisdiction over a dispute concerning the "availability" of the award fee. See *Technical Support Servs., Inc.*, ASBCA 37976, 89-2 BCA ¶21,861, where the board noted that it was not ruling that it had jurisdiction over the "amount" of the award. The sufficiency of awards was considered in *Nash Janitorial Servs., Inc.*, GSBCA 6390, 84-1 BCA ¶17,135, *recons. denied*, 84-2 BCA ¶17,355, where the board found that a contract modification agreeing to a total amount of cost and fee (including award fees) due on a services contract was void because of economic duress by the contracting officer. The conduct constituting duress was the manner in which the contracting officer administered the contract, including granting very low award fees that penalized the contractor for government actions.

The most significant review of an award fee occurred in *URS Consultants, Inc.*, IBCA 4285-2000, 02-2 BCA ¶31,812, where the contracting officer determined that a retroactive downward recalculation of award fees paid over nine years was appropriate to correct an "error" in the calculation. The board rejected this reduction in the award fees that had already been paid, holding that the unilaterally determined award fees were binding on the government because they were based on the award fee plan in place at the time of the awards and the Award Fee clause in the contract provided that the plan could only be adjusted prospectively. See also *Space Gateway Support, LLC*, ASBCA 55608, 13-1 BCA ¶35,232, where the board agreed with a contracting officer's determination that no award fee should be paid on the part of the contract that constituted the purchase of "facilities" because of a long-standing policy to not pay profit on such purchases.

One major issue in the award process is the degree of participation that should be granted to the contractor. In the past, some contracts have greatly limited the contractor's participation, giving the contractor no opportunity to submit information or see evaluations and limiting its role to a thorough debriefing after the award has been made. Earlier versions of the DFARS provided that evaluations should be furnished to the contractor for comment, but DoD PGI 216.405-2(4)(ii) now states that the agency "may . . . afford the contractor an opportunity to present information on its own behalf." The DOT/HUD clauses discussed above and the NASA Award Fee clauses in NFS 1852.216-76 and -77 also provide that the contractor is entitled to submit a self-evaluation as part of the evaluation process. Another option is to permit the contractor to make an independent presentation to the board or award official, either in writing or orally. This was included in an earlier edition of the DFARS but has been removed from the current version of the regulation. Whatever system is selected, the agency must eventually give the contractor detailed information on the basis of the award so that it can fully understand what aspects of performance were downgraded and how performance can be improved in subsequent award periods. Since the CPAF contract will function best when the contractor has a high degree of confidence in the reliability, accuracy, and fairness of the evaluations and awards, the process selected should engender such confidence.

[6] Relationship of Award Fee to Other Provisions

As with CPIF contracts, it is important that CPAF contracts state the relationship of the award fee provisions to other provisions of the contract that provide the government with remedies for less than specified performance. Since most award fee provisions call for awards only if the performance reaches the minimally acceptable level, it would be logical to state that the government could make fee adjustments under no other contract clauses as long as the award fee provisions were in effect. Similarly, clauses providing remedies other than fee adjustment, such as the Termination clause, would be applied without regard to the award fee provisions. This is a reasonable interpretation of the standard clauses, if the relationship between clauses is not well stated in the contract, since it is not reasonable to conclude that the government is providing itself a choice of remedies or overlapping remedies. The best solution, of course, is to include clear language in the contract.

Unfortunately, this issue is not adequately addressed in many CPAF contracts. A good example of the problems that can ensue is found in *Holmes & Narver Servs., Inc.*, ASBCA 33025, 88-3 BCA ¶ 20,932, where the contract contained an award fee provision on cost and technical performance and an Inspection of Services clause similar to the clause in FAR 52.246-5. The Inspection of Services clause gave the government the right to "reduce any fee payable" if the services were defective and could not be corrected. The contracting officer's attempt to reduce the base fee because of poor cost control was held to be improper because cost control was not a specified service under the contract. The board would have faced a more difficult issue if the reduction in base fee had occurred because of poor performance of the technical work called for by the contract, but it would seem that a proper interpretation would be that the award fee provisions are the stated mechanism for making such fee reductions. See also *UNC Nuclear Indus., Inc.*, EBCA 412-4-88, 90-1 BCA ¶ 22,463, interpreting a DOE contract clause stating that "in the event of contract termination . . . the amount of award fee available shall represent a pro rata distribution associated with evaluation period activities or events, and allowable costs." The board ruled that the government was wrong in using a share of the base and award fees computed by prorating (based on the number of days of performance prior to the convenience termination) the fee assigned to the evaluation period. Here the government attempted to draft a clause dealing with the possibility of convenience termination but failed to state the result with sufficient clarity. Contrast *Textron Def. Sys. v. Widnall*, 143 F.3d 1465 (Fed. Cir. 1998), where the court held that the contractor was not entitled to a pro-rata share of the award fee because the contract stated that the award fee was "not subject to" the Termination clause. The court also held that, even without the clause, the contractor would not have been entitled to a pro rata share of the entire award fee because "it had no reasonable expectation of ever receiving the total award fee." See also *Northrop Grumman Corp. v. Goldin*, 136 F.3d 1479 (Fed. Cir. 1998), where the parties omitted any contract language on the effect of a convenience termination on award fee that had been accumulated over the total period of contract performance and was to be awarded based on ultimate success. The court ruled that the contractor was entitled to an award based on the proportionate share of this fee in the pool at the time of termination.

The contract should also spell out the consequences of any plan to give employee bonuses if high levels of award fee are earned. As noted in the discussion of CPIF contracts, such bonuses are potentially allowable costs of performance, if they comply with the cost principle in FAR 31.205-6(f). See *Petroleum Operations & Support Servs., Inc.*, EBCA 291-6-83, 85-2 BCA ¶ 18,037, denying compensation of the cost of an award fee–based bonus because it was not given in accordance with a "good faith agreement" between the contractor and its employees. If the bonuses had been recognized as allowable costs, the contractor's costs would have been higher, with the possibility that its award fee would have been lower. It is this interrelationship that should be addressed in the negotiation of the contract.

[7] CPAF/CPIF Contracts

It has become quite common practice to combine CPAF and CPIF contracting techniques in a single contract. Although this practice is not covered in the FAR, it is discussed in NFS 1816.405-270(b). See also DEAR 916.405-2 stating:

> [T]he award fee arrangement shall include both technical performance (including scheduling as appropriate) and business management considerations tailored to the needs of the particular situation. In addition, in a situation where cost estimating reliability and other factors are such that the negotiation of a separate predetermined incentive sharing arrangement applicable to cost performance is determined both feasible and advantageous, cost incentives may be added. The resulting contract would then be identified as a cost-plus-incentive-fee/award-fee combination type.

As indicated, the CPAF/CPIF contract usually involves using a CPIF formula for the cost incentive and adding CPAF awards in the areas of performance and delivery. The fee is then generally divided into its constituent parts and the incentive provisions structured accordingly. For example, if it were decided to assign 40% of the fee to cost incentives and the balance to the award areas, the cost incentive would be structured at this level. Thus, if the normal

CPIF contract would have a target fee of 8%, with minimum and maximum fees of 2% and 14%, the parties would use 40% of the total fee pool (12 percentage points of fee) to structure the cost incentive in the CPAF/CPIF contract. This would yield:

Target Fee	4.4%
Minimum Fee	2.0%
Maximum Fee (on costs)	6.8%

The balance of the total fee pool (7.2 percentage points of fee) would be assigned to the award fee pool available for awards in the performance and delivery areas, and the maximum fee on the total contract would be set at 14%.

There are many variations of this structuring technique. For example, the government might decide that the above formula did not provide sufficient incentive in the cost area. In that case, it is possible to overlap the different areas using, for example, CPIF elements as follows:

Target Fee	6%
Minimum Fee	2%
Maximum Fee (on costs)	10%

The award fee pool for performance and delivery would be kept at 7.2 percentage points, and the maximum fee for the total contract would be kept at 14%. This might result in no fee being available for awards in the final periods of contract performance, but it would increase the motivation for reducing costs and would allow the cost incentive to be spread over a broader RIE.

[8] Award Fee Provisions in Fixed-Price Contracts

FAR 16.404 provides the following minimal guidance on including award fee provisions in fixed-price contracts:

> Award-fee provisions may be used in fixed-price contracts when the Government wishes to motivate a contractor and other incentives cannot be used because contractor performance cannot be measured objectively. Such contracts shall establish a fixed price (including normal profit) for the effort. This price will be paid for satisfactory contract performance. Award fee earned (if any) will be paid in addition to that fixed price.

This technique was proper prior to adoption of the FAR language. See *Diversified Contract Servs., Inc.*, Comp. Gen. Dec. B-224152, 86-2 CPD ¶ 675, where an agency used a stand-alone award fee provision to motivate the contractor to increase the quality of the services being performed. GAO ruled that this was well within the power of an agency and was a valid method of obtaining the quality of work required. For another case where an award fee provision was included in a fixed-price contract, see *Technology Applications, Inc.*, Comp. Gen. Dec. B-238259, 90-1 CPD ¶ 451.

DoD PGI 216.470 contains rather cryptic guidance on "other applications of award fees," as follows:

> The *award amount* portion of the fee may be used in other types of contracts under the following conditions—
>
> (1) The Government wishes to motivate and reward a contractor for—
>
> (i) Purchase of capital assets (including machine tools) manufactured in the united States, on major defense acquisition programs; or
>
> (ii) Management performance in areas which cannot be measured objectively and where normal incentive provisions cannot be used. For example, logistics support, quality, timeliness, ingenuity, and cost effectiveness are areas under the control of management which may be susceptible only to subjective measurement and evaluation.
>
> (2) The "base fee" (fixed amount portion) is not used.
>
> (3) The chief of the contracting office approves the use of the "award amount."
>
> (4) An award review board and procedures are established for conduct of the evaluation.
>
> (5) The administrative costs of evaluation do not exceed the expected benefits.

Although this guidance appears to permit evaluation of "cost effectiveness," the areas of evaluation for award in this situation would normally include only performance and delivery because the contractor would be motivated to control costs by the use of a fixed-price type contract.

The determination of whether a contractor had earned the bonuses attached to these types of performance and delivery incentives would be made in the same manner as described above for the CPAF contract. See *Lockheed Martin Info. Sys.*, Comp. Gen. Dec. B-292836, 2003 CPD ¶ 230, involving a procurement where the agency included the "financial incentives" that could be earned for "enhanced performance" of a fixed-price contract in a separate contract line item. In *DGR Assocs., Inc.*, Comp. Gen. Dec. B-285428, 2000 CPD ¶ 145, GAO ruled that the agency properly gave an enhanced rating to an offeror that intended to give its employees bonuses from part of its award fee for better performance.

[E] Cost-Plus-Award-Term Contracts

A type of contract that has not yet be identified in the FAR is the cost-plus-award-term (CPAT) contract. This contract is similar to the CPAF contract in that the award decision is subjectively made by the agency based on its periodic evaluation of the contractor's performance. However, the contract provides that if the contractor is evaluated as having achieved a specified level of performance, it will be awarded another period of performance. Agencies have varied in writing these contracts as to whether they (1) make a binding promise to add one or more years, subject to the availability of appropriations and a continuing requirement, or (2) merely promise to add one or more option years, which gives the contractor no *right* to additional years. This new type of contract is described in the Office of Federal Procurement Policy publication, Seven Steps to Performance-Based Services Acquisition. NASA has provided extensive guidance on the use of CPAT contracts stating that they can be used for service contracts exceeding $20 million, NFS 1816.405-277. NASA also has a standard Award Term clause at NFS 1852.216-72. See also the Defense Acquisition Guidebook providing guidance on entering into long-term life-cycle support contracts with contractors and stating at 5.1.5.1:

> Award term contracts should be used where possible to incentivize industry to provide optimal support. Incentives should be tied to metrics tailored to reflect the DoD Component's specific definitions and reporting processes. Award and incentive contracts should include tailored cost reporting to enable appropriate contract management and to facilitate future cost estimating and price analysis.

The typical CPAT contract calls for performance of services for a period of two to five years with an evaluation period after one or more years of contractually required performance. If the contractor is awarded an additional term, the contract will generally call for subsequent evaluations with the possibility of earning further periods of performance. In some cases, such contracts have made it possible for the contractor to continue working under the contract for 15 to 20 years. See, however, § 813 of the National Defense Authorization Act for Fiscal Year 2005, Pub. L. No. 108-375, applicable to DoD, NASA and the Coast Guard, placing a limitation of five years of work on task and delivery order contracts with five years of options unless the head of the agency determines that exceptional circumstances justify a longer period of time. This statute is implemented in DFARS 217.204 to provide that this statutory restriction applies to "ordering periods" not performance periods. Neither the statute nor the DFARS implementation discuss the application of these rules to award term periods.

Since only a few agencies have issued regulatory guidance on this type of contract, the process used has varied considerably. Many agencies have structured the initial period of performance with an award of a base period of one or two years followed by several years of options before the award term years go into effect. The award term periods have also varied—from one to six years. A few of these contracts have also included negative award term incentives with the agency deducting years of performance for evaluations of below average performance. Examples of the provisions from decisions litigating other issues show the wide variety of periods that have been used. See *Board of Regents of the Nev. Sys. of Higher Educ. v. United States*, 132 Fed. Cl. 435 (2017) (five-year base period and five award term years); *Olgoonik Global Sec., LLC*, Comp. Gen. Dec. B-414762, 2017 CPD ¶ 282 (one-year base period, four one-year options, and five one-year award terms); *Singhal & Co.*, Comp. Gen. Dec. B-412787, 2016 CPD ¶ 156 (blanket purchase agreements under Federal Supply Schedule with one-year base period, four one-year options, and two one-year award terms); *CACI Enter. Solutions, I*nc., Comp. Gen. Dec. B-412648, 2016 CPD ¶ 111 (two year base period, one two-year option, one one-year option, and three one-year award terms); *Jacobs Tech., Inc.*, Comp. Gen. Dec. B-411784, 2015 CPD ¶ 342 (one-year base period, a two-year option, five one-year award terms, and one seventeen-month award term); *GeoNarth, LLC*, Gen. Dec. B-411473, 2015 CPD ¶ 247 (a base year, two option years, and two award-term years); *NEIE, Inc. v. United States*, No. 3-164C (Fed. Cl. Dec. 6, 2013) (two-year base period, two-year award term and one-year award term); *Sayres & Assocs. Corp.*, Comp. Gen. Dec. B-408253, 2013 CPD ¶ 206 (task order with one-year base period, two option years, and two one-year award term options); *Northeast Military Sales, Inc.*, Comp. Gen. Dec. B-404153, 2011 CPD ¶ 2 (fixed-price award term with two-year base period, two one-year options and four one-year award term options); *Pitney Bowes Gov't Solutions, Inc. v. United States*, 93 Fed. Cl. 327 (2010) (less-than-one-year base period, four option years, and two one-year award term options); *2B Brokers*, Comp. Gen. Dec. B-298651, 2006 CPD ¶ 178 (three-year contract with four award term options); *Spherix, Inc.*, Comp. Gen. Dec. B-294572, 2005 CPD ¶ 3 (three-year requirements contract with six one-year award terms); *Bannum, Inc.*, Comp. Gen. Dec. B-298281.2, 2006 CPD ¶ 163 (three-year base period and seven one-year award terms); *Orion Int'l Tech., Inc.*, Comp. Gen. Dec. B-293256, 2004 CPD ¶ 118 (base period of three years with 12 "option" years—not specifying which were options and which were award term years); *Research Analysis & Maint., Inc.*, Comp. Gen. Dec. B-292587.4, 2004 CPD ¶ 100 (base period of three years with six two-year award terms); *Cortez, Inc.*, Comp. Gen. Dec. B-292178, 2003 CPD ¶ 184 (base period of three years with two option years and five award term years); *NLX Corp.*, Comp. Gen. Dec. B-288785, 2001 CPD ¶ 198 (base period of 39 months with two three-year award term periods).

The most difficult problem in structuring CPAT contracts is determining the pricing of award periods that are subject to unknown economic conditions years after the award of the contract. These periods have generally been included in the contract with pricing arrangements matching those used on periods with firm requirements. Thus, on a cost-plus-incentive-fee contract, the award terms would have a target cost and a target fee. On a contract with firm fixed prices for early years, later option years and award term years would usually contain fixed prices subject to economic price adjustment or price redetermination up to ceiling amounts. Some award term contracts have made the award conditional on a government determination that the price applicable to the award terms is a reasonable price. Some of these contracts have also contained provisions allowing the contractor to cancel an award term provision or an award term award with appropriate notice to the government.

When the award term is defined as an option, it is important to evaluate the costs or prices of the award periods during the initial award of the contract. Otherwise, the award option cannot be awarded without meeting the full and open competition requirement. See FAR 17.207(f). See also NFS 1816.405-277 stating:

> (h) Consistent with the Competition in Contracting Act and general procurement principles, the potential award term periods in a procurement must be priced, evaluated, and considered in the initial contract selection process in order to be valid.

A similar requirement is in EDAR 3416.47(e)(3). This Department of Education regulation also states that contractors have the right to decline the award of an award term period.

CPAT contracts have also included evaluation plans that are essentially the same as the evaluation plans used on CPAF contracts. Thus, they inform the contractor of the elements of performance that will be evaluated and the level of performance necessary to achieve high scores. See NFS 1816.405-277(i) for detailed guidance on the elements of an award term plan.

Contractor contentions regarding the proper issuance of an award term would normally be subject to the Disputes clause of the contract. See, for example, *Fluor Fed. Solutions, LLC*, ASBCA 61353, 19-1 BCA ¶ 37,237, where the board held that the agency had improperly exercised an award term option for a losing price when the contractor had not met the award criteria, and *CI<2>, Inc.*, ASBCA 56257, 14-1 BCA ¶ 35,698, where the board held that the agency had breached the contract by denying an award term year without following the procedures specified in the contract. However, in one unique case, the agency stated in the contract that the award term would be granted by issuing a new task order under specified conditions. Based, on this statement, the Federal Circuit held that the court should have treated the case as a protest not a dispute, *Coast Professional, Inc. v. United States*, 828 F.3d 1329 (Fed. Cir. 2016). Had the award term been treated in the normal way as an option, it would have been treated as a dispute. See the court's reasoning at 1356:

> The government asks us to deviate from the established rule that new Task Orders are new contracts, and instead conclude that new Task Orders resulting from award-term extensions are "akin to options." We do not agree that the award-term extension at issue in H.4, which requires a new Task Order to be issued, should be treated like an option. The FAR expressly defines an Option: "Option means the unilateral right in a contract by which, for a specified time, the Government may elect to purchase additional supplies or services called for by the contract, or may elect to extend the term of the

contract." 48 C.F.R. § 2.101 (definition of Option). Unlike an option, the award-term extensions cannot be issued unilaterally by the government. Instead, the award-term extensions can issue only if, inter alia, "[t]he contractor accepts the Government's target pricing and terms." Section H.4 specifies that the government "target prices for the current PCA Task Orders will apply to the award-term extension," so it is anticipated that the same pricing will apply; however, the contractor has the right to accept or reject the award-term extension. This is the opposite of a unilateral right.

This reasoning was used in *Continental Servs. Group, Inc. v. United States*, 130 Fed. Cl. 798 (2017), where the court interpreted *Coast Professional* to allow a dispute regarding the failure to award an award term as a protest even though the contract did not call for the issuance of new task orders (the contract used the term "award term extensions"). These decisions indicate that care must be exercised in describing the award terms; if the agency wants the decision to issue an award term (or not issue an award term) to be treated as a matter of contract administration, then the award term should be described more akin to executing an existing option than awarding a new task order.

§ 12.06 LEVEL-OF-EFFORT CONTRACTS

The standard types of contracts discussed above generally describe the work in terms of the end product to be delivered or the services to be performed. This section covers an alternate method of describing the work—in terms of the level of effort to be expended by the contractor. In this type of contract, the contractor receives the compensation called for by the contract upon expenditure of the required hours of effort or the purchase of needed material, regardless of whether the anticipated work is completed. As a result, this type of contract is used sparingly since it imposes significantly less risk on the contractor than contracts calling for completion of a specified task. In these types of contracts, the government is primarily buying hours of labor from a contractor. Hence, the most important consideration is the quality of the labor, and negotiated procurement procedures are generally used to permit the evaluation of the capabilities of each offerors' employees. See, for example, *ManTech Envtl. Research Servs. Corp.*, Comp. Gen. Dec B-292602, 2003 CPD ¶ 221, where the technical evaluation factors in a CPFF level of effort procurement were, in descending order of importance, demonstrated qualifications of assigned personnel, past performance, demonstrated corporate experience, quality of proposed program management plan, and appropriateness of the proposed quality management plan. Frequently, agencies evaluate an offeror's relative experience, *Wickman Spacecraft & Propulsion Co.*, Comp. Gen. Dec. B-219675, 85-2 CPD ¶ 690 (1985) (failure to include a small, new firm in competitive range for fixed-price level of effort contract was acceptable); *DDL Omni Eng'g*, Comp. Gen. Dec. B-220075.2, 85-2 CPD ¶ 684 (an agency was allowed to take into consideration personnel and corporate experience in evaluating the proposals). Agencies need not choose a contractor with the most specific experience but may infer that the contractor has the ability to perform the work, *U.S. Defense Sys., Inc.*, Comp. Gen. Dec. B-260702, 95-2 CPD ¶ 22 (award of a contract concerning guard services at embassies given to a contractor with comparable, but not the specific, guard experience); *Research Analysis & Maint., Inc.*, Comp. Gen. Dec. B-239223, 90-2 CPD ¶ 129 (award to contractor without experience on the specific missile at issue). An agency cannot, however, require experience to the extent that it is "unduly restrictive." See *Daniel H. Wagner, Assocs., Inc.*, 65 Comp. Gen. 305 (B-220633), 86-1 CPD ¶ 166, where the Navy had to revise its solicitation because its requirements for experience were so restrictive that competition was limited to a sole source of supply. GAO also noted that sealed bidding would be appropriate when routine services were being acquired.

There are two techniques used to contract for a level of effort. First, the parties can agree to fixed hourly rates for specified classes of labor with payment based on the number of actual hours incurred. These rates include the contractor's indirect costs and profit. If this type of contract calls for labor only, it is called a "labor-hour" contract, FAR 16.602. If it includes the purchase of materials as well as the incurrence of labor effort, it is called a "time-and-materials" contract, FAR 16.601. The second technique provides a stated amount of compensation for the incurrence of a specified number of labor-hours over a fixed period of time. This type of contract is generally called a "term" type contract and can be written as a "firm-fixed-price, level-of-effort term contract," FAR 16.207, or a cost-reimbursement term contract, FAR 16.306(d). In the former contract, the contractor is paid the price upon the incurrence of the labor-hours, while in the latter contract, the contractor is paid the fixed fee plus the costs upon the incurrence of the labor-hours. A level of effort contract that is not described in FAR Part 16 is the unit price contract for specified types of work such as excavation or backfilling. See FAR 36.207(a) permitting this type of contract for construction work.

[A] Time-and-Materials and Labor-Hour Contracts

Although time-and-materials and labor-hour contracts have been used for many years, they are not regarded as contracts that are beneficial to the government since they provide "no positive profit incentive to the contractor for cost control or labor efficiency," FAR 16.601(c)(1). This lack of incentive is due to the difficulty of monitoring or controlling the number of hours that will be expended to perform any assigned task. Thus, FAR guidance on how to use these types of contracts is minimal. However, FAR 52.301 does include these types of contracts in the matrix of contract clauses—providing guidance as to the clauses that are appropriate for these types of contract.

FAR 16.601(d) contains the following limitations on the use of T&M contracts:

> A time-and-materials contract may be used only if—
>
> (1) The contracting officer prepares a determination and findings that no other contract type is suitable. The determination and finding shall be—
>
> (i) Signed by the contracting officer prior to the execution of the base period or any option periods of the contracts; and
>
> (ii) Approved by the head of the contracting activity prior to the execution of the base period when the base period plus any option periods exceeds three years; and
>
> (2) The contract includes a ceiling price that the contractor exceeds at its own risk. The contracting officer shall document the contract file to justify the reasons for the amount of any subsequent change in the ceiling price. Also see 12.207(b) for further limitations on use of Time-and-Materials or Labor Hour contracts for acquisition of commercial items.

These same requirements are applicable to labor-hour contracts, FAR 16.602. The determination and findings supporting the use of these contracts is not required by statute but is an additional safeguard called for by the regulation.

DFARS 216.601(d)(i) contains the following additional provisions intended to limit the use of T&M and labor-hour contracts:

> (B) The determination and findings shall contain sufficient facts and rationale to justify that no other contract type is suitable. At a minimum, the determination and findings shall—
>
> (1) Include a description of the market research conducted;
>
> (2) Establish that it is not possible at the time of placing the contract or order to accurately estimate the extent or duration of the work or to anticipate costs with any reasonable degree of certainty;
>
> (3) Address why a cost-plus-fixed-fee term or other cost-reimbursement, incentive, or fixed-price contract or order is not appropriate; for contracts (including indefinite-delivery contracts) and orders for noncommercial items awarded to contractors with adequate accounting systems, a cost-plus-fixed-fee term contract type shall be preferred over a time-and-materials or labor-hour contract type;
>
> (4) Establish that the requirement has been structured to minimize the use of time-and-materials requirements (e.g., limiting the value or length of the time-and-materials portion of the contract or order; establishing fixed prices for portions of the requirement); and
>
> (5) Describe the actions planned to minimize the use of time-and-materials contracts on future acquisitions for the same requirements.

FAR 16.601(c)(1) also requires "appropriate Government surveillance" of contractor performance of these types of contract "to give reasonable assurance that efficient methods and effective cost controls are being used." See *Midwest Maint. & Constr. Co.*, GSBCA 6225, 85-1 BCA ¶ 17,716, commenting on the use of this type of contract without adequate government surveillance.

The additional limitations when these type of contracts are used to procure commercial services are prescribed in FAR 12.207(b) as follows:

> (1) A time-and-materials contract or labor-hour contract (see Subpart 16.6) may be used for the acquisition of commercial services when—
>
> (i) The service is acquired under a contract awarded using—
>
> (A) Competitive procedures (e.g., the procedures in 6.102, the set-aside procedures in Subpart 19.5, or competition conducted in accordance with Part 13);
>
> (B) The procedures for other than full and open competition in 6.3 provided the agency receives offers that satisfy the Government's expressed requirement from two or more responsible offerors; or
>
> (C) The fair opportunity procedures in 16.505, if placing an order under a multiple award delivery-order contract; and
>
> (ii) The contracting officer—
>
> (A) Executes a determination and findings (D&F) for the contract, in accordance with paragraph (b)(2) of this section (but see paragraph (c) of this section for indefinite-delivery contracts), that no other contract type authorized by this subpart is suitable;
>
> (B) Includes a ceiling price in the contract or order that the contractor exceeds at its own risk; and
>
> (C) Authorizes any subsequent change in the ceiling price only upon a determination, documented in the contract file, that it is in the best interest of the procuring agency to change the ceiling price.

DFARS 212.207 contains the following additional constraints on using these types of contracts for commercial services:

> (b) In accordance with Section 805 of the National Defense Authorization Act for Fiscal Year 2008 (Pub. L. 110-181), use of time-and-materials and labor-hour contracts for the acquisition of commercial services is authorized only for the following:
>
> (i) Services acquired for support of a commercial product, as described in paragraph (1) of the definition of commercial service at FAR 2.101 (41 U.S.C. 403(12)(E)).
>
> (ii) Emergency repair services.
>
> (iii) Any other commercial services only to the extent that the head of the agency concerned approves a written determination by the contracting officer that—

(A) The services to be acquired are commercial services as defined in paragraph (2) of the definition of commercial service at FAR 2.101 (41 U.S.C. 103);

(B) If the services to be acquired are subject to FAR 15.403-1(c)(3)(ii), the offeror of the services has submitted sufficient information in accordance with that subsection;

(C) Such services are commonly sold to the general public through use of time-and-materials or labor-hour contracts; and

(D) The use of a time-and-materials or labor-hour contract type is in the best interest of the Government.

Contractors bear very little risk in these types of contract because they will be paid for labor hours even though they are not used productively. See *CACI, Inc.-Federal v. General Servs. Admin.*, GSBCA 15588, 03-1 BCA ¶ 32,106, rejecting the government's contention that the contractor should not be paid for labor hours expended because it "failed to deliver a usable product." The board granted summary judgment for the contractor reasoning at 158,754-55:

> Appellant is correct that it was not required to deliver a usable program, and that it is entitled to be paid for services performed and goods purchased and delivered under the contract even if the contract requirements were not fully met by CACI. Respondent's allegations concerning CACI's failure to [take a step necessary to successfully perform] and complete the project are simply not germane, given the legal standard governing recovery in the context of a time and materials endeavor. In essence, these disputed facts are not material to appellant's entitlement to recover. See *Barmag Barmer Maschinenfabrik AG v. Murata Machinery, Ltd.*, 731 F.2d 831, 836 (Fed. Cir. 1984). The outcome is clear—respondent would not prevail even if we were to find these facts in its favor.

See also *E.I.L. Instruments, Inc.*, GSBCA 4459, 76-1 BCA ¶ 11,909, holding that a contractor was entitled to be paid for time spent in unsuccessfully attempting to repair government instruments.

Furthermore, the "ceiling price" in these types of contracts is not a binding contractual requirement but, rather, a limitation of cost—with the result that the contractor is no longer required to perform work when it reaches the ceiling until the government increases the ceiling. See the Payments Under Time-and-Materials and Labor-Hour Contracts clause in FAR 52.232-7, stating:

> (d) *Total cost.* It is estimated that the total cost to the Government for the performance of this contract shall not exceed the ceiling price set forth in the Schedule and the Contractor agrees to use its best efforts to perform the work specified in the Schedule and all obligations under this contract within such ceiling price.
>
> * * *

> (e) *Ceiling price*. The Government will not be obligated to pay the Contractor any amount in excess of the ceiling price in the Schedule, and the Contractor shall not be obligated to continue performance if to do so would exceed the ceiling price set forth in the Schedule, unless and until the Contracting Officer notifies the Contractor in writing that the ceiling price has been increased and specifies in the notice a revised ceiling that shall constitute the ceiling price for performance under this contract. When and to the extent that the ceiling price set forth in the Schedule has been increased, any hours expended and material costs incurred by the Contractor in excess of the ceiling price before the increase shall be allowable to the same extent as if the hours expended and material costs had been incurred after the increase in the ceiling price.

This provision contains notice requirements similar to those in the cost-reimbursement contract Limitation of Cost clause. Thus, the same legal rules barring contractor recovery for unreported overruns apply to this type of contract, *Abacus Tech. Corp. v. General Servs. Admin.*, GSBCA 16634, 06-1 BCA ¶ 33,250; *Tyrone Shanks*, ASBCA 54538, 06-1 BCA ¶ 33,155; *Corbett Tech. Co.*, ASBCA 49478, 00-1 BCA ¶ 30,801, *recons. denied*, 00-2 BCA ¶ 31.049; *Ragsdale, Beals, Hooper & Seigler v. Dep't of the Treasury*, GSBCA 13142-TD, 96-1 BCA ¶ 27,930. See also *Dawkins Gen. Contractors & Supply, Inc.*, ASBCA 48535, 03-2 BCA ¶ 32,305, stating this rule and noting that, when the ceiling is reached, the contractor is also permitted to stop work until additional funding is provided. A claim for a constructive change in the work would permit a price adjustment to the ceiling under the FAR 52.243-3 Changes clause for T&M or labor-hour contracts. See *Bendix Field Eng'g Corp.*, ASBCA 10124, 66-2 BCA ¶ 5959.

The contract clauses used in T&M and labor-hour contracts also place little risk on the contractor. The Inspection—Time-and-Material and Labor-Hour clause in FAR 52.246-6 requires in ¶ (f) that the contractor "replace or correct services or materials that at the time of delivery failed to meet contract requirements," but calls for compensation for such work under normal payment procedures except that the hourly rates are to be reduced by the amount of profit in the rate. The only limitation on this payment is in ¶ (h) which states that correction or replacement will be "without cost to the government" if due to "fraud, lack of good faith, or willful misconduct on the part of the Contractor's managerial personnel" or as a result of conduct of an employee "selected or retained" by the contractor when managerial personnel had "reasonable grounds to believe that the employee is habitually careless or unqualified. The Termination (Cost-Reimbursement), Alternate IV in FAR 52.249-6 provides that, in the event of a default termination, the contractor will be paid the hourly rate for materials and services delivered and accepted by the government. For those materials and services not delivered and accepted, the clause requires exclusion from the hourly rate of that portion "allocable to profit." Neither clause indicates how that amount of profit in the hourly rate is to be determined.

T&M and labor-hour contracts can be awarded for a single specified amount of work, but they are more frequently used as the basis for pricing tasks to be specified after contract award. In that situation, they are subject to the limitations imposed on "task order contracts"—as discussed in the following section on indefinite-delivery contracts.

The initial step required in preparing a T&M or labor-hour contract is to determine the classes or types of labor that will be required to perform the work and the qualification standards that each type of labor must meet. Agreed rates are required to be included in the contract for each category of labor provided by the contractor and its subcontractors (the term "subcontractor" is not defined). When a contract for noncommercial services is awarded after obtaining adequate price competition, the Time-and-Materials/Labor-Hour Proposal Requirements—Non-Commercial Item Acquisition With Adequate Price Competition solicitation provision in FAR 52.216-29 allows offerors to propose "blended rates" for either contractor or subcontractor employees. However, DoD does not permit blended rates. This is accomplished by requiring the use of an Alternate I to the FAR 52.216-29 provision which is set forth in DFARS 252.216-7002. When such a contract is awarded without adequate price competition, the rates must be separate rates for the contractor and its subcontractors. See FAR 16.601(c) stating:

> (2) *Fixed hourly rates*. (i) The contract shall specify separate fixed hourly rates that include wages, overhead, general and administrative expenses, and profit for each category of labor (see 16.601(e)(1)).
>
> (ii) For acquisitions of noncommercial items awarded without adequate price competition (see 15.403-1(c)(1)), the contract shall specify separate fixed hourly rates that include wages, overhead, general and administrative expenses, and profit for each category of labor to be performed by—
>
> (A) The contractor;
>
> (B) Each subcontractor; and
>
> (C) Each division, subsidiary, or affiliate of the contractor under a common control.
>
> (iii) For contract actions that are not awarded using competitive procedures, unless exempt under paragraph (c)(2)(iv) of this section, the fixed hourly rates for services transferred between divisions, subsidiaries, or affiliates of the contractor under a common control—
>
> (A) Shall not include profit for the transferring organization; but
>
> (B) May include profit for the prime contractor.
>
> (iv) For contract actions that are not awarded using competitive procedures, the fixed hourly rates for services that meet the definition of commercial item at 2.101 that are transferred between divisions, subsidiaries, or

affiliates of the contractor under a common control may be the established catalog or market rate when—

(A) It is the established practice of the transferring organization to price interorganizational transfers at other than cost for commercial work of the contractor or any division, subsidiary or affiliate of the contractor under a common control; and

(B) The contracting officer has not determined the price to be unreasonable.

If a contract does not specify subcontractor hourly rates (such as when a new subcontractor is obtained after award of the contract), the contractor must either obtain a contract amendment adding the rates or bill the subcontract costs as material costs constituting "subcontracts for . . . incidental services for which there is not a labor category specified in the contract" pursuant to ¶ (b)(1)(ii)(B) of the Payments Under Time-and-Materials and Labor-Hour Contracts clause in FAR 52.232-7. In the latter case, the contractor would be precluded from including its profit as part of the subcontractor billing.

Contractors and subcontractors must exercise great care to ensure that they only use employees that meet the labor qualifications for their category of labor that are described in the contract because the Payments Under Time-and-Materials and Labor-Hour Contracts clause provides for payment for only such labor. The clause is silent with regard to payment for labor that does not meet the labor qualifications, but ¶ (a) of the clause could be interpreted to preclude payment for such labor:

(2) The amounts shall be computed by multiplying the appropriate hourly rates prescribed in the Schedule by the number of direct labor hours performed.

(3) The hourly rates shall be paid for all labor performed on the contract that meets the labor qualifications specified in the contract. Labor hours incurred to perform tasks for which labor qualifications were specified in the contract will not be paid to the extent the work is performed by employees that do not meet the qualifications specified in the contract, unless specifically authorized by the Contracting Officer.

(4) The hourly rates shall include wages, indirect costs, general and administrative expense, and profit. Fractional parts of an hour shall be payable on a prorated basis.

* * *

(8) Unless the Schedule prescribes otherwise, the hourly rates in the Schedule shall not be varied by virtue of the Contractor having performed work on an overtime basis. If no overtime rates are provided in the Schedule and overtime work is approved in advance by the Contracting Officer, overtime rates shall be negotiated. Failure to agree upon these overtime rates shall be treated as a dispute under the Disputes clause of this contract. If the Schedule provides rates for overtime, the premium portion

of those rates will be reimbursable only to the extent the overtime is approved by the Contracting Officer.

See *Dawkins Gen. Contractors & Supply, Inc.*, ASBCA 48535, 03-2 BCA ¶ 32,305, where, although missing from the contract, this clause was included in a T&M contract by operation of law.

When competitive proposals are received for these types of contract, the contracting officer should closely analyze the elements of the proposal to determine that the price and estimated costs are fair and reasonable. However, the contracting officer need not obtain cost or pricing data and perform a detailed cost analysis if adequate competition has been obtained, *Milcom Sys. Corp.*, Comp. Gen. Dec. B-255448.2, 94-1 CPD ¶ 339; *Research Mgmt. Corp.*, 69 Comp. Gen. 368 (B-237865), 90-1 CPD ¶ 352.

Lack of clarity in the contract can lead to serious disputes over the proper billing of labor-hours. See *Software Research Assocs.*, ASBCA 33578, 88-3 BCA ¶ 21,046, where the contractor was permitted to bill the hourly rates for consultants. The government had argued that consultants were in the nature of material to be paid at actual cost, but the board reasoned that the consultants did the same work as employees of the contractor. See also *Emerson-Sack-Warner Corp.*, Comp. Gen. Dec. B-206123, 82-2 CPD ¶ 488, where the original IFB was unclear as to whether the contractor could bill the hourly rate for travel time. The procurement was canceled and readvertised under a solicitation that made it clear that such time was not to be reimbursed. On the other hand, a contractor is entitled to be paid for overtime hours worked by salaried personnel even if they are not paid for those hours, *GaN Corp.*, ASBCA 57834, 12-2 BCA ¶ 35,103. A contractor may not recover underestimated indirect costs by billing for extra hours, *Progressive Mach. Works, Inc.*, ASBCA 28785, 85-2 BCA ¶ 18,018. Contractors must also have adequate records to substantiate the hours billed, *JANA, Inc. v. United States*, 936 F.2d 1265 (Fed. Cir. 1991), *cert. denied*, 502 U.S. 1030 (1992) (government recovered payments made to contractor that could not be substantiated in subsequent audit). Compare *Lockheed Martin Integrated Sys., Inc.*, ASBCA 59508, 17-1 BCA ¶ 36,597, rejecting the government's claim for reimbursement of all subcontract labor payments because the contractor had allegedly not properly managed the subcontractors as required by FAR 42.202. The board concluded that this FAR provision did not require a contractor to "act as both CO and CAO with respect to its subcontracts."

The Payments Under Time-and-Materials and Labor-Hour Contracts clause in FAR 52.232-7 contains the following provisions on the payment for material:

> (b) Materials.
>
> (1) For the purposes of this clause—
>
> (i) *Direct materials* means those materials that enter directly into the end product, or that are used or consumed directly in connection with the furnishing of the end product or service.

(ii) *Materials* means—

(A) Direct materials, including supplies transferred between divisions, subsidiaries, or affiliates of the Contractor under a common control;

(B) Subcontracts for supplies and incidental services for which there is not a labor category specified in the contract;

(C) Other direct costs (e.g., incidental services for which there is not a labor category specified in the contract, travel, computer usage charges, etc.); and

(D) Applicable indirect costs.

(2) If the Contractor furnishes its own materials that meet the definition of a commercial item at 2.101, the price to be paid for such materials shall not exceed the Contractor's established catalog or market price, adjusted to reflect the—

(i) Quantities being acquired; and

(ii) Actual cost of any modification necessary because of contract requirements.

(3) Except as provided for in paragraph (b)(2) of this clause, the Government will reimburse the Contractor for allowable cost of materials provided the Contractor—

(i) Has made payments for materials in accordance with the terms and conditions of the agreement or invoice; or

(ii) Ordinarily makes these payments within 30 days of the submission of the Contractor's payment request to the Government and such payment is in accordance with the terms and conditions of the agreement or invoice.

(4) Payment for materials is subject to the Allowable Cost and Payment clause of this contract. The Contracting Officer will determine allowable costs of materials in accordance with Subpart 31.2 of the Federal Acquisition Regulation (FAR) in effect on the date of this contract.

(5) The Contractor may include allocable indirect costs and other direct costs to the extent they are—

(i) Comprised only of costs that are clearly excluded from the hourly rate;

(ii) Allocated in accordance with the Contractor's written or established accounting practices; and

(iii) Indirect costs are not applied to subcontracts that are paid at the hourly rates

This provision includes not only "direct materials" and subcontracts not listed in the schedule but also "other direct costs" (broadly defined). It also allows the addition of indirect costs only to the extent they are "clearly excluded from the hourly rate" to be paid for direct labor. This requirement of a clear statement in the contract has been enforced literally. See *SOS Int'l, Ltd. v. Dep't of Justice*, CBCA 3678, 14-1 BCA ¶ 35,751, holding that this clause did not allow the contractor to charge general and administration expenses to its travel costs because the contract stated that the travel costs would include the costs of "transportation, lodging, meals, and incidental expenses."

Prior to 2007 the Payments Under Time-and-Materials and Labor-Hour Contracts clause in FAR 52.232-7 clause appeared to require that subcontractor effort by treated as material costs with the result that the contractor could not include profit on such work. Two major issues arose under this clause. The first was the proper treatment of subcontracts. Some contractors argued that when the direct work on the contract was performed by subcontractors, that work should be paid for at the contractual hourly rates. This did not appear to be the correct interpretation of the clause unless the contractual schedule of rates specifically includes rates for subcontractor employees. See *Access Personnel Servs., Inc.*, ASBCA 59900, 17-1 BCA ¶ 36,845, and *Serco, Inc. v. Pension Benefit Guaranty Corp.*, CBCA 1695, 11-1 BCA ¶ 34,662, rejecting the argument that the contractor could add indirect costs and profit to subcontractor costs. See also *BearingPoint, Inc.*, ASBCA 55354, 09-2 BCA ¶ 34,289, holding that a contractor did not have to have meticulous evidence of the number of labor hours worked by subcontractor employees. Compare *U.S. ex rel. Karol v. L-3 Communs. Vertex Aero.* No. 3:10-CV-339-P, (N. Tex. 2012), holding that allegations that contractor employees were unqualified, nonproductive or working on private business were sufficient to allow a False Claims Act case to proceed to trial. *Compliance Corp.*, ASBCA 35317, 89-2 BCA ¶ 21,832, rejected the contractor's claim that it was entitled to bill for overhead on these subcontractor costs because the contract contained no provision calling for the payment of such costs.

The other major issue was the treatment of material handling costs. Since the clause permitted contractors to include such costs in labor rates or as material costs in accordance with their usual accounting practices, GAO held that an unequal bidding situation is created. See *Beta Indus., Inc.*, 60 Comp. Gen. 487 (B-200121), 81-1 CPD ¶ 391, suggesting that bidders be required to state in the bid which method they would use. There was no FAR guidance on this issue. See also *Ray Serv. Co.*, 64 Comp. Gen. 528 (B-217218), 85-1 CPD ¶ 582, holding that there is nothing intrinsically improper about including material handling costs in the hourly rate. In *General Eng'g & Mach. Works v. Sean C. O'Keefe*, 991 F.2d 775 (Fed. Cir. 1993), the court affirmed a board decision at 92-3 BCA ¶ 25,055 that the contractor was not entitled to charge a 15% material handling rate because it did not collect its material handling costs in a separate cost pool, as required by the contract. The court reasoned that this was a proper interpretation in order to avoid the possibility that the contractor could obtain double compensation for material handling in both the labor and material charges. Similarly, in *Bemol Corp. v. Dep't of the Treasury*, GSBCA 16374-TD, 05-1 BCA ¶ 32,897, the contractor's claim for material handling costs was denied because it did not collect the costs separately and did not present evidence convincing the board that the costs were not included in the indirect costs that were part of its labor rates.

Agencies are permitted to vary the compensation provisions of T&M contracts. For example, in *Systems Mgm't. & Res. Techs. Corp. v. Dep't of Energy*, CBCA 4068, 16-1 BCA ¶ 36,333, the agency issued a contract excluding profit from the labor rates in a T&M contract and calling for the payment of a fixed fee. When the agency refused to pay the entire fixed fee because the contractor had not expended the anticipated number of labor hours, the board ruled that the contract was clear in requiring the payment of the entire fixed fee and that the contract was legal, stating:

> To the extent that DOE is also claiming that SMARTECH's contract is illegal because it is a mixture of different contract types (a portion of a T&M contract and a portion of a fixed fee contract), we disagree with DOE's position. Contracts with the Government need not fall uniformly into one specific category or another, but "may be of any type *or combination of types* that will promote the Government's interest," except to the extent that a particular contract type is barred by statute. 48 CFR 16.102(b) (emphasis added). "A contract is not unenforceable merely because it does not fit neatly into a recognized category." *Ace-Federal Reporters, Inc. v. Barram*, 226 F.3d 1329, 1332 (Fed. Cir. 2000). We can see nothing inherently illegal about the type of contract that SMARTECH alleges, and that we find, was created here.

Compare *Javis Automation & Eng'g, Inc. v. Dep't of Interior*, CBCA 938, 09-2 BCA ¶ 34,309, where an IDIQ letter contract contained the T&M Payments clause and cost-reimbursement provisions. The board granted the government's claim for reimbursement of overpayments at fixed labor rates on task orders that had stated that they were CPFF in nature.

[B] Cost-Reimbursement Term Contracts

The cost-reimbursement term type contract describes the work to be performed in terms of a level of effort. FAR 16.306(d) provides the following guidance on this form of contract:

> (2) The term form describes the scope of work in general terms and obligates the contractor to devote a specified level of effort for a stated time period. Under this form, if the performance is considered satisfactory by the Government, the fixed fee is payable at the expiration of the agreed-upon period, upon contractor statement that the level of effort specified in the contract has been expended in performing the contract work. Renewal for further periods of performance is a new acquisition that involves new cost and fee arrangements.
>
> * * *

(4) The term form shall not be used unless the contractor is obligated by the contract to provide a specific level of effort within a definite time period.

When an agency adds hours of effort and extends the contract period into a new fiscal year, the appropriation for that year should be used, *Funding for Air Force Cost Plus Fixed Fee Level of Effort Contract*, Comp. Gen. Dec. B-277165, 2000 CPD ¶ 54. Conversely, when an agency states the level of effort required in a term type contract, it must fully fund that contract at the time of award from current appropriations, *Financial Crimes Enforcement Network—Obligations under a Cost-Reimbursement, Nonseverable Services Contract*, Comp. Gen. Dec. B-317139, 2009 CPD ¶ 158.

Although this FAR guidance on term type contracts pertains explicitly only to CPFF contracts, agencies have commonly used term form contracts on all types of cost-reimbursement contracts. See EPAAR 1552.211-73 prescribing a Level of Effort—Cost Reimbursement Contract clause for cost-no-fee, cost sharing, CPFF, CPIF and CPAF contracts. This clause provides for no fee adjustment if the level of effort falls within 90% and 110% of the prescribed amount.

FAR 35.005(c) provides the following guidance on work statements for level of effort research contracts:

> In reviewing work statements, contracting officers should ensure that language suitable for a level-of-effort approach, which requires the furnishing of technical effort and a report on the results, is not intermingled with language suitable for a task-completion approach, which often requires the development of a tangible end item designed to achieve specific performance characteristics. The wording of the work statement should also be consistent with the type and form of contract to be negotiated (see 16.207 and 16.306(d)). For example, the work statement for a cost-reimbursement contract promising the contractor's best efforts for a fixed term would be phrased differently than a work statement for a cost-reimbursement completion contract promising the contractor's best efforts for a defined task. Differences between work statements for fixed-price contracts and cost-reimbursement contracts should be even clearer.

Contracting agencies have a great deal of latitude in deciding how to express the required level of effort. The principal objective should be to state the desired effort in sufficient detail so as to assure that the government gets the type and amount of effort it wants while leaving contractors enough flexibility to adjust to new circumstances without the need for repeated contract amendments. The required effort can be expressed in the amount of time to be devoted to performance through the use of terms such as labor-hours, labor-days, or labor-months. In addition, different types of effort can be specified by stating that amount of effort required of different categories of personnel. However, too much detail may greatly limit the flexibility of the contractor in performing the work. Maximum flexibility is achieved under clauses that specify a range of required effort as in the following:

> Level of Effort
> Recognizing that this contract is a term form within the meaning of DAR 3-405.6(d)(2), the contractor shall devote to the research hereunder not less than 1,250,000 direct man-hours nor more than 1,360,000 direct man-hours.

The government also builds flexibility into Level of Effort clauses through provisions stating that deviations in effort up to certain limits will be acceptable and will not affect other contract provisions.

When using this type of contract, the fact that it is a term type contract should be clearly stated. See, for example, *Teledyne Brown Eng'g, Inc.*, ASBCA 58636, 14-1 BCA ¶ 35,495, where the agency issued a task order calling for a specified number of labor hours but not stating that it was a term type task order. It then issued a modification to the task order calling for a specified amount of work. When the contractor completed the work for approximately one-half the number of labor hours, it claimed that it was entitled to the full fixed fee because it was a completion type task order. The government's motion for summary judgment on the basis that it was a term type task order was denied because the board could not determine which it was without further developing the record. The issue was not resolved because the case was settled but the dispute illustrates the problem that can be caused by imprecise drafting.

Most cost type level of effort contracts are for specified work, but some of these contracts may call for work to be done as tasks are ordered up to a ceiling number of labor-hours. Such contracts are subject to the limitations on task order contracts discussed below in the section on indefinite-delivery contracts.

When a cost-reimbursement level of effort contract is awarded competitively, the contracting officer must make a cost realism analysis, as discussed in Chapter 13, to determine the probable costs of performance of the contract. See, for example, *KPMG, LLP*, Comp. Gen. Dec. B-406409, 2012 CPD ¶ 175, holding that the agency did not make a reasonable analysis of the realism of the winning offeror's low labor rates, and *SRS Techs.*, Comp. Gen. Dec. B-291618.2, 2003 CPD ¶ 70, holding that adjusting the protester's labor rates upward to account for uncompensated overtime was improper when the rates were based on average rates including uncompensated overtime. See also *Advanced Commc'n Sys., Inc.*, Comp. Gen. Dec. B-283650, 2000 CPD ¶ 3, and *Telos Corp.*, Comp. Gen. Dec. B-279493.3, 98-2 CPD ¶ 30, sustaining the contracting officer's determination that the winning offeror's labor rates were realistic, and *Delta Res. Assocs., Inc.*, Comp. Gen. Dec. B-254006.2, 94-1 CPD ¶ 47, sustaining the contracting officer's determination that the most realistic probable cost of performance was at the proposed indirect cost rates rather than at the ceiling on those rates that had been proposed by the offeror.

Since this type of level of effort contract is a cost-reimbursement contract, the contract will contain a Limitation of Cost clause providing that the contractor need not expend effort when its actual costs reach the cost estimate, and the government is not bound to compensate for costs incurred above the estimate. If the contract is incrementally funded, the contract will contain a Limitation of Funds clause. These clauses will be enforced in the same manner that they would in completion type cost-reimbursement contracts, with the contractor being denied overrun funding if the required notices are not given, *JJM Sys., Inc.*, ASBCA 51152, 03-1 BCA ¶ 32,192. However, the Level of Effort clause is controlling as to the fee to be paid and can be controlling as to the contractor's entitlement to incurred costs. See *Space Tech. Labs., Inc.*, ASBCA 7676, 1962 BCA ¶ 3609, where the board disallowed costs attributable to labor-hours in excess of the stated monthly maximum level of effort. In *Booz, Allen & Hamilton, Inc.*, EBCA 116-3-80, 80-2 BCA ¶ 14,796, the board held that the fact that the government added funds to the contract in order to permit the contractor to continue to provide labor-hours up to the stated maximum level of effort did not entitle the contractor to additional fee. In reaching this result, the board relied upon the following clause:

> In the event that during the period of this contract, the Contracting Officer shall issue Task Assignments requiring an effort of greater than *48,635* DPMH but less than *59,440* DPMH, the fixed fee of this contract shall not be adjusted. However, in the event that the contractor shall be required to furnish effort greater than *59,440* DPMH or less than *48,635* the estimated cost and fixed fee shall be adjusted.

Compare *International Space Corp.*, ASBCA 13883, 70-2 BCA ¶ 8519, where the board found that the only "practicable effect" of a generally worded level-of-effort clause was to establish the minimum effort that the contractor had to expend in order to earn the contract's fixed fee. See also *Falcon Res. & Dev. Co.*, ASBCA 26678, 83-1 BCA ¶ 16,437, where the board granted a pro rata reduction in fee when the level of effort was not attained, and *PRC Info. Scis. Co.*, EBCA 171-5-81, 82-2 BCA ¶ 15,866, where the board disagreed with the contractor's contention that the full fee was earned when the estimated costs were fully expended.

The government has been held liable when its estimate of the number of labor hours to be procured is far higher than the number of hours required. Thus, in *Sanford Cohen & Assocs., Inc.*, IBCA 4239/00, 04-2 BCA ¶ 32,738, the board held that the government was liable for a negligently prepared estimate of the number of labor hours. As a result, the board rejected the government's claim for a pro rata reduction in the fixed fee as called for by the contract's level of effort provisions and remanded the case to the parties "for a determination of damages based on an equitable adjustment in the price of hours delivered." Similarly, in *SocioTechnical Res. Applications, Inc.*, IBCA 3969, 03-1 BCA

¶ 32,214, the board awarded damages to a contractor that had retained staff anticipating that the agency would order the estimated number of labor hours. Compare *RJO Enter., Inc.*, ASBCA 50981, 03-1 BCA ¶ 32,137, holding that the government had not breached the cost-reimbursement level of effort contract by not ordering the estimated hours because the contract was for an indefinite delivery/indefinite quantity (IDIQ) term type CPFF contract under which the government had ordered far more than the minimum amount of work.

[C] Fixed-Price, Level-of-Effort Term Contract

While a fixed-price, level of effort term contract is listed as a fixed-price type contract in the FAR, it is similar to a cost-reimbursement term type contract except that, rather than paying for the costs of a specified number of labor hours, the agency pays the price upon the incurrence of the labor hours. Thus, this type of contract imposes little risk on the contractor. When a solicitation requests firm fixed-price offers or quotations, the agency can reject fixed-price level of effort offers or quotations because they do not require the pricing risk entailed by firm fixed prices, *Mangi Envtl. Group, Inc.*, Comp. Gen. Dec. B-294597, 2004 CPD ¶ 238.

FAR 16.207-2 provides the following guidance:

> A firm-fixed-price, level-of-effort term contract is suitable for investigation or study in a specific research and development area. The product of the contract is usually a report showing the results achieved through application of the required level of effort. However, payment is based on the effort expended rather than on the results achieved.

FAR 16.207-3 places the following limitations on the use of this type of contract:

> This contract type may be used only when—
>
> (a) The work required cannot otherwise be clearly defined;
> (b) The required level of effort is identified and agreed upon in advance;
> (c) There is reasonable assurance that the intended result cannot be achieved by expending less than the stipulated effort; and
> (d) The contract price is the simplified acquisition thresholds or less, unless approved by the chief of the contracting office.

Since this is a fixed-price type contract, no cost realism or price realism analysis is required although an agency can assess performance risk if it chooses to, *AllWorld Language Consultants, Inc.*, Comp. Gen. Dec. B-291409, 2003 CPD ¶ 13.

As with the cost-reimbursement term type contract, the fixed-price level of effort contract should clearly state that it is this type of contract. See *URS Fed. Support Servs. Inc.*, Comp. Gen. Dec. B-407573, 2013 CPD p 31,where the solicitation called for offerors to propose minimum staffing levels to augment the agency's maintenance mission listing various types of maintenance. The GAO denied a protest that this was an improper fixed-price level of effort contract, stating:

> [T]he PWS requires the contractor to provide augmentation labor to support the TYAD maintenance mission. In addition to certain performance metrics, the PWS includes minimum staffing levels—the minimum team complement—that the contractor is to both propose and provide during task order performance. Quite simply, the Air Force has decided to define its requirements here in both performance and staffing terms. We find this to be reasonably within the broad discretion afforded contracting agencies, and to the extent URS challenges how the Air Force has defined its needs, we find this challenge to be without merit.
>
> * * *
>
> As the required level of effort is not identified and agreed upon in advance, but left up to the discretion of each offeror, we find that the CLIN here does not represent a fixed-price, level-of-effort contract as the protester claims.

No clauses are included in the FAR for this type of contract. However, the contract should contain a schedule of the types of effort required. Failure to expend the effort should lead to a pro rata reduction in payment while complete expenditure of the required labor-hours should result in full payment without regard to the level of accomplishment of the work called for by the contract.

§ 12.07 VARIABLE QUANTITY CONTRACTS

In the previous discussion, we have addressed the types of contract in terms of the pricing arrangements that define the way that a contractor is paid for work described in the original contract. In contrast, in this section we address types of contracts in a different way – dealing with variable quantity contracts that obligate the contractor to furnish articles or services in quantities to be ordered subsequently by the government after the contract has been entered into. In these contracts, while the contractor is firmly obligated, the government's obligation is more malleable and depends upon the technique used. The techniques discussed in this section are contained in two parts of the procurement regulations. FAR 16.5 describes the requirements contract and the indefinite delivery/indefinite quantity (IDIQ) contract with stated minimum and maximum quantities. FAR 17.1 permits the use of the multi-year contract providing for firm contractual commitments over a number of years if there are both a continuing need and appropriations to cover the later years. FAR 17.2 permits the use of options by government procuring activities.

These types of contracts, permitting the government to vary the quantity of the work, can use any of the pricing arrangements previously discussed in this chapter. Thus, they can be fixed-price, cost-reimbursement, incentive, time-and-materials or labor-hours. See FAR 16.501-2(c). For a case where the distinction between the ordering arrangement and the pricing arrangement was not clear, see *Sociotechnical Res. Applications, Inc.*, IBCA 3969-98, 01-1 BCA ¶31,235.

The common characteristic of these types of contracts is that they permit government agencies to enter into binding arrangements for supplies or services that have not yet been identified as firm requirements or for which funds have not yet been appropriated. One advantage of such arrangement is that it allows the government to buy supplies or services in sufficient quantities over longer periods in order to induce contractors to introduce techniques that promote more efficient performance of the contract at reduce prices. This policy of using contracts that call for economic quantities of supplies is contained in 10 U.S.C. § 3242 (formerly § 2384a) and 41 U.S.C. § 3310(a) and implemented in FAR Subpart 7.2. The latter statute states:

> Each executive agency shall procure supplies in such quantities as (A) will result in the total cost and unit cost most advantageous to the United States, where practicable, and (B) does not exceed the quantity reasonably expected to be required by the agency.

The use of variable quantity contracts greatly increases an agency's ability to meet the objectives of these statutes when an agency has not identified current requirements supported by appropriated funds sufficient to support an immediate procurement of economic quantities yet it may be aware, from past experience, that such requirements will become available over time.

Another advantage of these types of contract is that they reduce the administrative costs of issuing numerous contracts as requirements become firm. Prior to the 1990s it was common practice to procure supplies and services annually as appropriated funds because available. However, as agencies adopted less streamlined procurement practices (see Chapter 6) and contracting offices were reduced in size, annual buying became less practicable. The result was a massive increase in the use of variable quantity contracts—often covering many years of supplies or services. While this has led to reduced administrative costs and a more stable flow of work under contracts, it has the significant disadvantage of depriving government agencies of access to new companies that might be able to fulfill their requirements more effectively or at lower prices. It also deprives the government of any benefits that might derive from regular competition for a product or a service. Contracting agencies should weigh the advantages and disadvantages of long-term variable quantity contracts in making the decision to use these types of contract.

In some of the forms of contract discussed below, the government legally binds itself to purchase the goods or services during a given period of time if the need materializes and is funded. In others, the government obligates itself to purchase an initial quantity or minimum quantity but makes no further legally binding commitment to the contractor. The basic ordering agreement, FAR

16.703, is not discussed in this section since neither party is contractually bound in this arrangement. Such agreements can constitute open offers which would form a contract upon acceptance by the government, but which have no legal effect until that time.

It can be argued that a lower price will be obtained when the government is obligated to buy a significant amount from the contractor. However, since almost all government contracts contain a Termination for the Convenience of the Government clause, giving the government the right to terminate the contract virtually at will, there is much less distinction among the actual government obligation under the various forms of variable quantity contract than would appear at first glance. Thus, any given agency will use one variable quantity form of contract in preference to another primarily because it has used that form successfully in the past and secondarily because that form may be well adapted to dealing with that agency's peculiar problems such as fiscal or administrative requirements.

[A] Statutory Requirements

Almost all variable quantity contracts state the contractor's obligation in terms of open-ended commitments to perform work in the future upon the issuance of a contract modification or a task or delivery order. When the contract calls for the issuance of a task or delivery order, it is subject to the provisions of the Federal Acquisition Streamlining Act of 1994 (FASA), Pub. L. No. 103-355, dealing with "task order contracts" and "delivery order contracts," 10 U.S.C. §§ 3401-3406 (formerly §§ 2304a-2304d) and 41 U.S.C. §§ 4101-06. These requirements were discussed in Chapter 7.

10 U.S.C. § 3404(f) (formerly § 2304a(f)) imposes limits on the length of the ordering period in task and delivery order contracts awarded by DoD, NASA and the Coast Guard. The original limit of five years was adopted in § 843 of the National Defense Authorization Act for Fiscal Year 2004, Pub. L. No. 108-136, Nov. 24, 2003. The statute was amended the following year to lengthen the ordering period to ten years with a five years limit on the initial contract, § 813 of the National Defense Authorization Act for Fiscal Year 2005, Pub. L. No. 108-375, Oct. 28, 2004. These statutes are implemented in DFARS 217.204(e). The limitations do not apply to other agencies of the government. See, however, FAR 17.204(e) containing a general five-year limitation on the length of all contracts except those for information technology. See also 10 U.S.C. § 3405(c) (formerly § 2304b(b)) and 41 U.S.C. § 4105(c) limiting the ordering period of advisory and assistance service contracts to five years with a permissible extension of six months if necessary to award a follow-on contract. See FAR 16.505(c).

[B] Requirements Contracts

A requirements contract is a contract where one party promises to buy all or a designated part of its requirements from another party. FAR 16.503(a) contains the following narrow definition:

> A requirements contract provides for filling all actual purchase requirements of designated Government activities for supplies or services during a specified contract period, with deliveries or performance to be scheduled by placing orders with the contractor. (Italics added)

This definition only contemplates requirements contracts covering *the entire government quantity* for some class of supplies or services. However, as discussed below, requirements contracts can also be used for designated parts of a government requirement.

FAR 16.506(d) instructs contracting officers to include the Requirements clause at FAR 52.216-21, or one of its four alternates, in all requirements contracts. The basic clause states:

> REQUIREMENTS (OCT 1995)
>
> (a) This is a requirements contract for the supplies or services specified, and effective for the period stated, in the Schedule. The quantities of supplies or services specified in the Schedule are estimates only and are not purchased by this contract. Except as this contract may otherwise provide, if the Government's requirements do not result in orders in the quantities described as "estimated" or "maximum" in the Schedule, that fact shall not constitute the basis for an equitable price adjustment.
>
> (b) Delivery or performance shall be made only as authorized by orders issued in accordance with the Ordering clause. Subject to any limitations in the Order Limitations clause or elsewhere in this contract, the Contractor shall furnish to the Government all supplies or services specified in the Schedule and called for by orders issued in accordance with the Ordering clause. The Government may issue orders requiring delivery to multiple destinations or performance at multiple locations.
>
> (c) Except as this contract otherwise provides, the Government shall order from the Contractor all the supplies or services specified in the Schedule that are required to be purchased by the Government activity or activities specified in the Schedule.
>
> (d) The Government is not required to purchase from the Contractor requirements in excess of any limit on total orders under this contract.
>
> (e) If the Government urgently requires delivery of any quantity of an item before the earliest date that delivery may be specified under this contract, and if the Contractor will not accept an order providing for the accelerated delivery, the Government may acquire the urgently required goods or services from another source.

> (f) Any order issued during the effective period of this contract and not completed within that period shall be completed by the Contractor within the time specified in the order. The contract shall govern the Contractor's and Government's rights and obligations with respect to the order to the same extent as if the order were completed during the contract's effective period; *provided*, that the Contractor shall not be required to make any deliveries under this contract after [insert date].

If the contract is for less than the full requirements of the government, as discussed below, the clause must be tailored to fit the precise circumstances of the procurement. The FAR contains alternate provisions for some of these circumstances.

FAR 52.216-18 provides an Ordering clause to be inserted in all requirements contracts as well as other indefinite-delivery contracts. In addition to stipulating the time period during which orders may be issued, the clause provides that the order is binding when issued:

> (c) If mailed, a delivery order or task order is considered "issued" when the Government deposits the order in the mail. Orders may be issued orally, by facsimile, or by electronic commerce methods only if authorized in the Schedule.

Boards have ruled that, in accordance with this provision, orders are binding when deposited in the mail, *Canadian Commercial Corp.*, ASBCA 20067, 75-2 BCA ¶ 11,441, and *Victory Container Corp.*, GSBCA 5596, 81-2 BCA ¶ 15,346. Note that the clause permits oral, facsimile and electronic orders only if called for by a separate schedule clause. In *General Dynamics C4 Sys., Inc.*, ASBCA 54988, 08-1 BCA ¶ 33,779, the requirement was strictly enforced by ruling that the contractor was not bound by electronically issued orders sent to the contractor on the last days of the final ordering period. This decision was reversed by *Mabus v. General Dynamics C4 Sys., Inc.*, 633 F.3d 1356 (Fed. Cir. 2011), on the grounds that the contractor was estopped from asserting that the clause was binding because it had accepted electronic orders for over four years.

[1] Nature of Requirements Contracts

A requirements contract provides the contractor with both the legal right and the legal duty to supply goods or services in an amount that is determined by *the government's need* rather than by a fixed quantity. See *Torncello v. United States*, 681 F.2d 756 (Ct. Cl. 1982); and *Mason v. United States*, 615 F.2d 1343 (Ct. Cl. 1980). The consideration of the government that makes this a legally binding contract is *its promise to satisfy its needs by buying only from the contractor or contractors with contracts.* A contract containing language that abrogates this promise is not an enforceable requirements contract, *Satellite Servs., Inc.*, Comp. Gen. Dec. B-280945, 98-2 CPD ¶ 125 (statement that agency could order from others when "in the best interests of the Government" precludes a requirements contract); *Sea-Land Serv., Inc.*, Comp. Gen. Dec. B-266238, 96-1 CPD ¶ 49 (Limitation of Government Liability clause giving government the blanket right to obtain the services from other companies overrides requirements promise).

Any contract under which an agency of the government undertakes to order all, or any specified portion, of its needs for a product or service during a designated period of time from a single contractor will be classified as a requirements contract. The key feature is that the legal obligation of the government is defined by its *needs* rather than by a fixed amount. See *East Bay Auto Supply, Inc.*, ASBCA 25542, 81-2 BCA ¶ 15,204, stating that the "good faith duty to order all requirements from the contractor renders the contract enforceable, and not illusory." Accord *A-Transport Nw. Co. v. United States*, 27 Fed. Cl. 206 (1992), *aff'd*, 36 F.3d 1576 (1994); *Hilton's Cleaners, Inc.*, ASBCA 18213, 74-1 BCA, ¶ 10,433; *Export Packing & Crating Co.*, ASBCA 16133, 73-2 BCA ¶ 10,066. Under this type of contract, the government is bound to order its requirements from the contractor but is under no obligation to have requirements as long as the absence of requirements is in good faith.

Whether a contract is in fact a requirements contract depends not upon the label attached to it by the parties but, rather, upon the nature of the rights and duties created by the contract, *Ceredo Mortuary Chapel, Inc. v. United States*, 29 Fed. Cl. 346 (1993); *Ralph Constr., Inc. v. United States*, 4 Cl. Ct. 727 (1984). See, for example, *Environmental Quality Mgmt., Inc. v. Environmental Protection* Agency, CBCA 3072, 13-1 BCA ¶ 35,300 (trial needed to determine whether contract was a requirements contract even though it did not include the Requirements clause); *ALK Servs. Inc. v. Dep't of Veterans Affairs*, CBCA 1789, 13-1 BCA ¶ 35,260 (contract was a requirements contract because it contained the Requirement clause and did not contain the IDIQ clause even though contractor agreed it was an IDIQ contract); *General Dynamics Ordnance & Tactical Sys., Inc.*, ASBCA 56870, 11-2 BCA ¶ 34,774 (trial needed to determine whether contract was a requirements contract or a basic ordering agreement because of confusing contract language); *Centurion Elecs. Serv.*, ASBCA 51956, 03-1 BCA ¶ 32,097 (contract was a requirements contract despite absence of the Requirements clause because the contract required the contractor to perform all repairs of specified equipment). In the event that the issue is litigated, the court or board will look first to the terms of the contract to determine its type. For example, in *Torncello v. United States*, 681 F.2d 756 (Ct. Cl. 1982), the court held that when the Navy contracted for an indefinite quantity of ground maintenance services, with no guaranteed minimum amount, implicit in the terms was a promise to forgo diverting work to other contractors. Accord *Myers Investigative & Sec. Servs., Inc. v. United States*, 47 Fed. Cl. 605 (2000). In *Local Communications Network, Inc.*, ASBCA 55154, 08-1 BCA ¶ 33,734, the board held that since the parties clearly intended to enter into a requirements contract, the FAR 52.216-21 clause was incorporated into the contract by operation of law. In contrast, in *Maintenance Eng'rs. v. United States*, 749 F.2d 724 (Fed. Cir. 1984), the court held that all of the language in the contract indicated that it was not a requirements contract even though it included the Requirements clause stating explicitly that it was a requirements contract. See also *Modern Sys. Tech. Corp. v. United States*, 24 Cl. Ct. 360 (1991), *aff'd*, 979 F.2d 200 (Fed. Cir. 1992), holding that a Basic Purchasing Agreement was not a requirements contract because it contained no express promise by the government to obtain its needs from the contractor. Similarly, in *Ann Riley & Assocs.*, DOTBCA 2418, 93-3 BCA ¶ 25,963, the board found that an indefinite-quantity contract was not a requirements contract because it did not include the "essential ingredient of a requirements contract, a statement that the [agency] was obligated to satisfy all of its requirements . . . from this source and no other." The board rejected government testimony that it had intended to enter into a requirements contract and had used such contracts for these services in the past.

The court or board may also consider both facts known to the parties at the time of contracting and prior course of dealing between the parties, even where these are not explicitly mentioned in the contract, *Stanley F. Horton*, DOTCAB 1231, 82-2 BCA ¶ 15,967. In *Crown Laundry & Dry Cleaners, Inc. v. United States*, 29 Fed. Cl. 506 (1993), the court looked to the intentions of the parties to determine that the contract was a requirements contract—even though the contract was labeled an indefinite-quantity contract (with no stated minimum quantity) and did not contain the Requirements clause. See also *Jez Enter., Inc.*, ASBCA 51851, 00-2 BCA ¶ 30,939, where the board ruled that it could not determine the nature of the contract from its language but was required to hold a hearing to assess the facts underlying the transaction.

Requirements contracts should be distinguished from variable quantity contracts where the amount of work may vary but can be identified by some independent criterion other than the needs of the government. In *Brawley v. United States*, 96 U.S. 168 (1877), the Supreme Court held that a requirements contract resulted when the contractor was obligated to deliver 880 cords of wood, "more or less, as shall be determined to be necessary . . . for the regular supply . . . of the troops." The Court stated at 171-72:

> Where a contract is made to sell or furnish certain goods identified by reference to independent circumstances, such as an entire lot deposited in a certain warehouse, or all that may be manufactured by the vendor in a certain establishment, or that may be shipped by his agent or correspondent in certain vessels, and the quantity is named with the qualification of "about," or "more or less," or words of like import, the contract applies to the specific lot; and the naming of the quantity is not regarded as in the nature of a warranty, but only as an estimate of the probable amount, in reference to which good faith is all that is required of the party making it. . . .
>
> If, however, the qualifying words are supplemented by other stipulations or conditions which give them a broader scope or a more extensive significancy, then the contract is to be governed by such added stipulations

> or conditions. As, if it be agreed to furnish so many bushels of wheat, more or less, according to what the party receiving it shall require for the use of his mill, then the contract is not governed by the quantity named, nor by that quantity with slight and unimportant variations, but by what the receiving party shall require for the use of his mill; and the variation from the quantity named will depend upon his discretion and requirements, so long as he acts in good faith.

The most common form of variable quantity contracts where the quantity is identified by "independent circumstances" is the construction contract with unit prices to be paid on the basis of actual work performed. See FAR 36.207 permitting the procurement of construction work on the basis of fixed-unit prices. Although both contracts obligate the government to pay only for the work that is done, the requirements contract is for needs that may arise in the future and will be ordered as they are identified, while the unit-price contract covers work that can be identified by a physical description such as excavation within specified boundaries (requiring no subsequent orders). In other respects, these contracts are quite similar. Although this section is directed to requirements contracts, it uses cases dealing with unit price contracts when the legal principles are the same.

Brawley also distinguishes another form of contract that indicates that the quantity of work may vary from a stated amount using terms such as "more or less" or "about." If the contract specifies no other criteria for determining quantity, such as requirements or a physical description, the contract will be construed to permit only slight variation. See *Brawley*, stating at 171-72:

> But when no such independent circumstances are referred to, and the engagement is to furnish goods of a certain quality or character to a certain amount, the quantity specified is material, and governs the contract. The addition of the qualifying words, "about," "more or less," and the like, in such cases, is only for the purpose of providing against accidental variations arising from slight and unimportant excesses or deficiencies in number, measure, or weight.

In determining which form of contract has been entered into, the court will look to all surrounding circumstances as well as the contract language. Thus, a contract to supply "six hundred thousand pounds, more or less, of oats . . . or such other quantity, more or less, as may be required . . . for the wants of said station" was found not to be a requirements contract because the contractor knew that another contract for oats had been awarded simultaneously, *Merriam v. United States*, 107 U.S. 437 (1883). In *Shader Contractors, Inc. v. United States*, 276 F.2d 1 (Ct. Cl. 1960), the court looked to the contract terms to find a requirements contract where the contract called for the contractor to collect the amount ordered by the contracting officers as "may be needed." The contract contained an estimated quantity of coal of 5,500 tons and an estimated quantity of refuse of

4,000 tons and contained the provision, "The quantity may vary from 75 percent to 125 percent of the figure." The court ruled that the variation provision did not override the requirements language.

[2] Use of Requirements Contracts

FAR 16.503(b) contains very general guidance stating that it is appropriate to use a requirements contract—

> for acquiring any supplies or services when the Government anticipates recurring requirements but cannot predetermine the precise quantities of supplies or services that designated Government activities will need during a definite period.

While it is clearly less burdensome for a government agency to issue a single requirements contract than to conduct a series of small, individual purchases, the requirements contract is not always preferable to a definite-quantity contract. Thus, although the regulations give no guidance on this issue, the contracting officer should carefully review the agency's needs before issuing a requirements contract. If those needs can be accumulated into an economic ordering quantity, a definite-quantity contract is usually preferable. See FAR Subpart 7.2 implementing 10 U.S.C. § 3242 (formerly § 2384a) and 41 U.S.C. § 3310(a), which require the use of economic quantities in purchasing supplies. See also *A.G. Schoonmaker, Inc.*, Comp. Gen. Dec. B-170544, 1971 CPD ¶ 3, where GAO recommended to the DoD that where appropriated funds were available and the agency's needs had been ascertained with reasonable certainty, with only the allocation of funds remaining, the regulations should express a preference for a more definite type of contract in order to achieve more realistic and reasonable bid prices.

While it is clear that a requirements contract is a task order or delivery order contract as discussed in Chapter 7, the FAR contains no general guidance on the statutory preference for multiple requirements contracts—which could be achieved by issuing two or more requirements contracts for shares of the agency's requirements. The working group that drafted the present FAR explained this omission as follows:

> The working group believes multiple awards are inconsistent with the requirements contracts which require a contractor to receive the buyer's entire requirement to establish legal consideration for the contract. See *Appeal of R.C. Swanson Printing & Typesetting Company*, GPOBCA No. 15-90, 1993 WL 668317 (1973). The working group is aware of no legal authority that recognizes the legitimacy of multiple award requirements contracts where a requirement is continuously competed. However, the working group is also aware that some individuals advocate the use of "multiple award requirements contracts."

The prior draft rule attempted to reach a compromise position by including certain elements of §§ 1004 and 1054 of FASA in FAR 16.503 while remaining silent on the issue of whether multiple awards may be made. That draft rule was criticized for its ambiguity.

As a result, FAR 16.503 was not changed. It also includes a limitation on the use of requirements contracts for advisory and assistance services in excess of 3 years and $10,000,000. This limitation is necessary to close a "loophole" so that agencies cannot escape the mandate to make multiple awards for CAAS in excess of the threshold by defining the acquisition as a requirements contract.

Although the rule does not apply the multiple award preference to requirements contracts, the rule does not preclude agencies from experimenting with a multiple award requirements contract if the agency believes it can overcome the legal problems (i.e., illusory promise) related to a multiple award requirements contract.

This intentional ambiguity in the FAR raises the possibility that issuing a single requirements contract may be a statutory violation when the multiple award preference applies. See *Nations, Inc.*, Comp. Gen. Dec. B-272455, 96-2 CPD ¶ 170, where GAO found such a violation when the agency proposed to issue a single requirements contract for simulation training services with a value of over $10 million.

The limitation in FAR 16.503 for advisory and assistance services recognizes that the task and delivery order statutes apply to requirements contracts by stating:

> (d) *Limitations on use of requirements contracts for advisory and assistance services.* (1) Except as provided in paragraph (d)(2) of this section, no solicitation for a requirements contract for advisory and assistance services in excess of three years and $13.5 million (including all options) may be issued unless the contracting officer or other official designated by the head of the agency determines in writing that the services required are so unique or highly specialized that it is not practicable to make multiple awards using the procedures in 16.504.
>
> (2) The limitation in paragraph (d)(1) of this section is not applicable to an acquisition of supplies or services that includes the acquisition of advisory and assistance services, if the contracting officer or other official designated by the head of the agency determines that the advisory and assistance services are necessarily incident to, and not a significant component of, the contract.

[3] Pricing Arrangement

FAR 16.501-2(c) provides that requirements contracts may use any "cost or pricing arrangement" permitted by the FAR. Thus, these contracts can use any fixed-price, cost-reimbursement, or incentive arrangement or can be a time-and-materials or labor-hour contract. FAR 16.501-2(c) warns:

> Cost or pricing arrangements that provide for an estimated quantity of supplies or services (e.g., estimated number of labor hours) must comply with the appropriate procedures of this subpart.

If the government's requirements are for well-defined supplies or tasks, arrangements with fixed unit prices are the most desirable. This permits the most balanced competition and assures the government that it will obtain performance of the contract at the costs that it anticipated. If the contract is for supplies that are not well defined, cost-reimbursement or incentive contracts can be used to ensure that undue risk is not being placed on the contractor. If the contract is for services that are not well defined, a time-and-materials or labor-hour contract can be used to hold the contractor to fixed labor rates while permitting flexibility as to the amount of work that needs to be done to meet the government requirement. Alternatively, a cost-reimbursement contract can be used in these circumstances. These latter types of pricing arrangements, of course, place much of the risk of increased costs on the government.

It is proper to use a pricing arrangement that requires the contractor to incur startup costs before the issuance of any orders. See *JRS Staffing Servs.*, Comp. Gen. Dec. B-408202, 2013 CPD ¶ 175, which also rejected the contention that this was a violation of the Anti-Deficiency Act.

[4] Length of Requirements Contracts

As discussed above, there are statutory limitations of ten years on task and delivery order contracts issued by DoD. FAR 17.204(e) also contains a general five-year limitation on all contracts except information technology contracts. 10 U.S.C. § 3204(c) (formerly § 2304(d)(3)) and 41 U.S.C. § 3304(c)(1)(B) contain a one-year limitation on contracts over the simplified acquisition threshold that are awarded without full and open competition based on urgency, unless the head of the agency determines that exceptional circumstances apply.

Requirements contracts may be for a single year or for multiple years. In most cases, requirements contracts for more than one year include options for a specified number of additional years where appropriations are not available at the time of contracting. See, for example, *Free State Reporting, Inc.*, Comp. Gen. Dec. B-259650, 95-1 CPD ¶ 199 (requirements for support services for base year and two option years); *Tulane Univ.*, Comp. Gen. Dec. B-259912, 95-1 CPD ¶ 210 (requirements for services for two base years and three option years). Multiple-year requirements contracts could also be issued as a single document, including later years not covered by current appropriations, if there is no possibility that the contractor could obligate the government by performing work prior to the issuance of a requirement. See 42 Comp. Gen. 272 (B-144641) (1962), where GAO ruled that a requirements contract was in violation of appropriations law because the government would be obligated to pay for work in a later year not covered under the contract. See also 67 Comp. Gen. 190 (B-224081) (1988), and 48 Comp. Gen. 494 (B-164908) (1969). In cases where a requirement contract is used in this way, an agency will normally include an "availability of funds" clause stating that the government will not be liable to pay the contractor until funds for future years have been made contractually available. See *Funding of Maint. Contract Extending Beyond Fiscal Year*, Comp. Gen. Dec. B-259274, 96-1 CPD ¶ 247, where GAO approved a requirements contract where the requirement covered two fiscal years with the second year restricted by an Availability of Funds clause, stating that "a naked contractual obligation that carries with it no financial exposure to the government does not violate the Anti-Deficiency Act." In contrast, the GAO publication *Principles of Federal Appropriations Law (Volume 1)*, Third Edition, January 2004, updated to 2015, states at 5-41 that, in order to comply with appropriations law governing contracts using "fiscal year appropriations," such contracts must contain a "renewal option" calling for the government to renew the contract at the beginning of each fiscal year. See also *Sims v. United States*, 112 Fed. Cl. 808 (2013); *JRS Staffing Servs.*, Comp. Gen. Dec. B-408202, 2013 CPD ¶ 175, holding that requiring the incurrence of startup costs before funds are available does not violate the Anti-Deficiency Act if such costs must be recovered as part of the fixed labor rates in the contract rather than as a separately priced task.

Agencies have also used multiple-year requirements contracts when multiple-year or no-year funds are being used for the procurement. This practice was explicitly permitted by FAR 17.104-4 until 1996, when the provision was deleted from the regulation. It is still legally permissible even though the FAR is silent on the subject. For examples of multiple-year requirements contracts, see *Liebert Corp.*, 70 Comp. Gen. 448 (B-232234.5), 91-1 CPD ¶ 413 (agency issued firm-fixed-price requirements contract for services and materials over a five-year period); and *CDI Marine Co.*, Comp. Gen. Dec. B-219934.2, 86-1 CPD ¶ 242 (agency issued a CPFF requirements contract for services performed over a three-year period). In *Mills Mfg. Corp.*, Comp. Gen. Dec. B-224004, 86-2 CPD ¶ 679, *recons. denied*, 87-1 CPD ¶ 393, GAO denied a protest arguing that a three-year requirements contract was improper because the protester could not obtain firm prices from its suppliers for the second and third year.

[5] Structuring the Requirement

The contracting officer has great flexibility in tailoring a requirements contract to fit the circumstances of each procurement. The government attempts to obtain the best possible price by defining the requirement in such a way that competition can be maximized and risks to the contractor minimized. The government also endeavors to structure such contracts to provide maximum assurance that its needs will be met in a timely manner and that it has the operating flexibility that it needs. The most important aspect of a requirements contract is the statement of the "requirement."

There are a number of ways in which the requirement can be stated to achieve these purposes. FAR 16.503(a) gives the following guidance on limitations on the requirement:

> (2) The contract shall state, if feasible, the maximum limit of the contractor's obligation to deliver and the Government's obligation to order. The contract may also specify maximum or minimum quantities that the Government may order under each individual order and the maximum that it may order during a specified period of time.

There is no guidance on limitations on the timing of ordering requirements, and the contractor bears the risk if the government clusters its orders in one period, *Asfaltos Panamenos, S.A.*, ASBCA 41657, 92-3 BCA ¶ 25,141, or at the end of the contract, *Victory Container Corp.*, GSBCA 5596, 81-2 BCA ¶ 15,346.

The government may also wish to obtain only a part of its overall requirements from one contractor and to obtain the balance from others either through other requirements contract or some other form of contract. In some cases, the requirement may be structured to accommodate performance by government personnel.

[a] Limiting the Requirement

Two types of limitations are commonly used in requirements contracts. First, minimum and maximum order limitations are included in almost all such contracts. Second, limitations are sometimes included to divide the work between among two or more contractors.

[i] Minimums and Maximums

The government includes minimums and maximums on individual orders and maximums for specified periods of time, FAR 16.503(a)(2). FAR 16.506(b) instructs contracting officers to insert a clause in all requirements contracts that is substantially the same as the following Order Limitations clause at FAR 52.216-19:

> (a) *Minimum order*. When the Government requires supplies or services covered by this contract in an amount of less than [*insert dollar figure or quantity*], the Government is not obligated to purchase, nor is the Contractor obligated to furnish, those supplies or services under the contract.
>
> (b) *Maximum order*. The Contractor is not obligated to honor—
>
> (1) Any order for a single item in excess of [insert dollar figure or quantity];
>
> (2) Any order for a combination of items in excess of [insert dollar figure or quantity]; or

(3) A series of orders from the same ordering office within days that together call for quantities exceeding the limitation in subparagraph (1) or (2) above.

(c) If this is a requirements contract (i.e., includes the Requirements clause at subsection 52.216-21 of the Federal Acquisition Regulation (FAR)), the Government is not required to order a part of any one requirement from the Contractor if that requirement exceeds the maximum-order limitations in paragraph (b) above.

(d) Notwithstanding paragraphs (b) and (c) above, the Contractor shall honor any order exceeding the maximum order limitations in paragraph (b), unless that order (or orders) is returned to the ordering office within days after issuance, with written notice stating the Contractor's intent not to ship the item (or items) called for and the reasons. Upon receiving this notice, the Government may acquire the supplies or services from another source.

Although inartfully drafted, this clause appears to cover only individual orders in the case of minimums, and both individual orders and a series of orders within a specified period in the case of maximums. The FAR contains no guidance on how to determine maximum or minimum order limitations. However, it is clear that the major advantage of minimum order limitations is to assure the contractor that orders will not be placed in such a manner as to be administratively burdensome. On the other hand, a high minimum order can reduce the contractor's work because it allows the government to procure quantities from other sources. These minimum order limitations should not be confused with guaranteed minimums which are used in IDIQ contracts.

Maximum order limitations are apparently intended to permit the contractor to determine the maximum resources that must be committed to the contract at any time during performance. These limitations are essential if performance is required within a short period of time after placement of orders. If more flexibility in the time of performance is granted, these limitations should be stated in terms of a maximum amount of work over a period of time rather than in terms of individual orders or a series of orders. Maximum order limitations also permit the government to avoid its requirements obligation if "one requirement" exceeds the limitations in the clause. Neither the clause nor the FAR provides any guidance as to how to determine when one requirement exists. The government has been permitted to program its requirements to issue orders within a monthly maximum order limitation. In *Victory Container Corp.*, GSBCA 5596, 81-2 BCA ¶ 15,346, the contracting officer ordered the maximum quantity permitted each month in order to build the inventory of the items called for by the contract. The board held that this practice was a good faith use of the requirements contract since the contractor was aware that the items were normally carried in inventory by the government.

While the Order Limitations clause contains no provision for total contract maximum quantities, FAR 16.503(a)(2) instructs the contracting officer to state the maximum quantity or dollar value of the entire contract. Such a contract maximum defines the scope of the original competition and assists the contractor by placing an outside limit on the resources it must commit to the contract. It also benefits the government by permitting it the freedom to seek lower prices after the maximum is reached. Such provisions must be included in the contract schedule or by separate clause. Note, however, that orders placed in excess of the maximum order limitation are not necessarily considered to be outside the scope of the contract. See *Exide Corp.*, Comp. Gen. Dec. B-276988, 97-2 CPD ¶ 51, holding that a delivery order issued under an existing requirements contract for a quantity in excess of the maximum order limitation was not beyond the scope of the contract because the contract permitted orders in excess of maximum quantity and the total quantity ordered under the contract did not significantly exceed the estimated quantity.

[ii] Dividing the Requirement

In some cases, the government can obtain more competition by dividing the requirement among two or more contractors. This technique is particularly useful when the goods or services are normally furnished by smaller contractors and the government's requirements are large. FAR 52.216-21 contains Alternate III for the Requirements clause that covers the situation where the contracting officer decides to divide the requirement between a small business set-aside contractor and a non-set-aside contractor. This provision states, in part:

> The Government may choose between the set-aside Contractor and the non-set-aside Contractor in placing any particular order. However, the Government shall allocate successive orders, in accordance with its delivery requirements, to maintain as close a ratio as is reasonably practicable between the total quantities ordered from the two Contractors.

See *Valley Forge Flag Co.*, VABCA 4667, 97-2 BCA ¶ 29,246, holding the government liable for a change outside of the scope of the contract when it ordered a larger percentage of its requirements from a contractor with a requirements contract for 60% of the government's requirements. In reaching this decision, the board stated at 145,486:

> [M]ultiple awards of separate contracts for Government requirements are not uncommon. For example, there may be awards of separate requirements contracts for certain services in separate geographical locations, or requirements for supplies may be split up based on the sizes of the orders. *Property Analysts, Inc.*, Unpub. B-259853, 95-1 CPD ¶ 270; *Pro-Mark, Inc.*, Unpub. B-247248, May 18, 1992; *City Wide Press, Inc.*, Unpub. B-231469, 88-2 CPD ¶ 127.

The FAR does not address the potential advantages of dividing requirements between contractors without using set-aside techniques. However, there is no prohibition of such practice, and it is clear that the government might benefit in some circumstances by dividing a requirement geographically, mathematically, or by prescribing the mode of competition to be used in selecting the contractor for each requirement. Dividing the requirement and issuing two or more requirements contracts would also meet the statutory preference for multiple task order or delivery order contracts. For an example of this type of requirements contract, see *Ace-Federal Reporters, Inc. v. Barram*, 226 F.3d 1329 (Fed. Cir. 2000), holding that the government had breached six mandatory Federal Supply Schedule contracts for reporting services that required designated agencies to order all of their reporting requirements for administrative hearings from one of the contractors. The decision does not restrict its reasoning to this unique type of requirements contract but would appear to be applicable to any requirements contracts awarded to multiple contractors that will share the requirement. In *Ace-Federal Reporters, Inc. v. General Servs. Admin.*, GSBCA 13298-REM, 02-2 BCA ¶ 31,913, the board awarded damages for this breach by calculating the profits lost on the work ordered from other contractors and allocating those lost profits to the six contractors based on their share of orders. See also *R&G Food Servs., Inc, v. Dep't of Agriculture*, CBCA 3487, 16-1 BCA ¶ 36,559, finding that the agency had issued multiple requirements contracts for food services.

[b] Allowing In-House Work

The government may structure the requirement by limiting it to only those requirements in excess of the quantities that the government activity may itself furnish within its own capabilities. The government is thereby obligated to obtain from the contractor only that work "required to be purchased." Alternate I of the Requirements clause at FAR 52.216-21 provides the following provision for this purpose:

> (c) The estimated quantities are not the total requirements of the Government activity specified in the Schedule, but are estimates of requirements in excess of the quantities that the activity may itself furnish within its own capabilities. Except as this contract otherwise provides, the Government shall order from the Contractor all of that activity's requirements for supplies and services specified in the Schedule that exceed the quantities that the activity may furnish within its own capabilities.

The failure to include this alternate is not dispositive as to whether the government has the right to perform some of the work with its own forces. See *Datalect Computer Servs., Ltd. v. United States*, 40 Fed. Cl. 28 (1997), *aff'd*, 215 F.3d 1344 (Fed. Cir. 1999), *cert. denied*, 529 U.S. 1037 (2000), where the court read ¶ (c) of the Requirements clause in FAR 52.216-21 to permit in-house work. That clause states, "the Government shall order from the Contractor all the supplies or services specified in the Schedule that are required to be purchased by the Government activity . . ." The court concluded that the term "required to be purchased" permitted the government to do work in-house.

The government can also structure such a contract to provide for specific situations where government employees will perform the work. For example, in *Tucson Mobilephone, Inc.*, Comp. Gen. Dec. B-247685, 92-1 CPD ¶ 487, GAO approved a requirements contract that provided for work by government employees when the contractor's personnel were not available or when the work could be done by agency personnel with the equipment on hand.

There is discord among the various courts and boards concerning both the adequacy of consideration where the government retains the right to perform work in-house and the degree of discretion that the government may exercise in performing under such contracts. The confusion stems, in part, from the language in FAR 16.503(a) which states, "A requirements contract provides for filling all actual purchase requirements of designated government activities for specific supplies or services." This occasionally leads to the incorrect conclusion that a requirements contract must obligate the government to buy all of its needs from the contractor. For example, in *Ralph Constr., Inc. v. United States*, 4 Cl. Ct. 727 (1984), the court ruled that because a requirements contract gives the contractor the right to "fill all of the government's needs," and yet the instant contract permitted the government to assign work in-house, the contract was unenforceable because of a lack of mutuality of consideration. This analysis begs the question of what the "requirements" were. The contract itself clearly stated that the supplies and services covered by the contract were not all the government needs but only those "in excess of the quantities which the activity may itself furnish within its own capabilities." Because the contract bound the government to order from the contractor if it ordered at all, there appears to have been sufficient consideration to support the contractor's promise to perform. See, however, *Jacqueline R. Sims LLC v. United States*, (2014); *Horn v. United States*, 98 Fed. Cl. 500 (2011); *Coyle's Pest Control, Inc. v. Cuomo*, 154 F.3d 1302 (Fed. Cir. 1998); and *Modern Sys. Tech. Corp. v. United States*, 24 Cl. Ct. 360 (1991), *aff'd*, 979 F.2d 200 (Fed. Cir. 1992), stating that a requirements contract is one calling for the contractor to fulfill *all* of the government's requirements. Since these contracts did not meet this requirement, the result was that the contractor was only entitled to be paid for work actually performed. GAO has followed this view in *Satellite Servs., Inc.*, Comp. Gen. Dec. B-280945, 98-2 CPD ¶ 125, finding a proposed contract illusory because it promised multiple contractors the right to compete for services unless they were "unique" or it was in "the best interest of the Government" to award sole source. See also *JRS Mgmt.*, Comp. Gen. Dec. B-4010524.2, 2010 CPD ¶ 25, where GAO repeated the holding in *Modern Systems* that a requirements contract must call for the government to buy "exclusively" from one contractor.

Some appeals boards have declined to follow the view adopted by the Claims Court in *Ralph Construction.* See *Dynamic Sci., Inc.*, ASBCA 29510, 85-1 BCA ¶ 17,710, holding that such a contract was legally binding. After noting that the government's only obligation was to procure, from the contractor alone, "such requirements as did arise during the contract term that were not to be satisfied by in-house capabilities," the board followed its holding in *Maya Transit Co.*, ASBCA 20186, 75-2 BCA ¶ 11,552, discussing that decision at 88,383:

> We characterized the contract as a "limited form" requirements type. The limitation of the requirement to that portion that the Government did not choose to meet from its own capabilities did not render the promise illusory particularly because the Government was precluded from expanding its capabilities during contract performance at the expense of the contractor.

See also *Operational Serv. Corp.*, ASBCA 37059, 93-3 BCA ¶ 26,190, where the board again reviewed a "limited form" requirements contract, stating that it did not agree with the *Ralph Construction* reasoning and did not believe that the affirmance of the Federal Circuit in the *Modern Systems* decision was an adoption of that reasoning. In *D.M. Summers, Inc.*, VABCA 2750, 89-3 BCA ¶ 22,123, the board held that the government had not breached a requirements contract by using some in-house services because the contractor was aware of this practice when it entered into the contract. See also *Missouri Dep't of Social Servs.*, ASBCA 59191, 16-1 BCA ¶ 36,563, holding that the contractor was entitled to an equitable adjustment for a partial termination for convenience under this type of contract.

After entering into such a requirements contract, the government may use its discretion in making ordering decisions, subject to a duty to act in good faith. See *Henry Angelo & Sons, Inc.*, ASBCA 15082, 72-1 BCA ¶ 9356, *recons. denied*, 72-2 BCA ¶ 9493, where the contract was for painting services beyond the capability of the Army's own forces, but because of budgetary considerations, the government decided to apply funds to other projects even though the painting was still needed. Further, the government expanded the painting work that was to be accomplished by its own forces. The board held that these actions constituted arbitrary reasons for not placing orders, did not comply with the government's duty of good faith, and constituted a partial termination. See also *Maya Transit Co.*, ASBCA 20186, 75-2 BCA ¶ 11,552, where, although the government undertook to buy only those bus services "in excess of the quantities which the activity may itself furnish within its own capabilities," it was not permitted to reduce the services ordered by reordering its budget priorities and redistributing its capabilities to assume more bus routes for its own drivers. In contrast, in *Export Packing & Crating Co.*, ASBCA 16133, 73-2 BCA ¶ 10,066, the government's decision to assign work to civilian employees, rather than order from the contract, was approved and the contract for services "which are required to be purchased by the Government" was upheld. In *Arcon-Pacific Contractors*, ASBCA 25057,

82-2 BCA ¶ 15,838, the board held that "[a]bsent bad faith, the government had discretion to determine what painting was required to be purchased." In exercising that discretion, the government was permitted to consider the most economical way of meeting its needs and to assign work in-house in a cost-effective manner.

[c] Measuring the Work Required

Another aspect of structuring the requirement is selecting the units of measure that will be used in ordering. When the government procures goods, choosing the appropriate measure is simple. When the government structures a requirements contract for services, however, it may choose to order by either unit of work actually completed or by unit of time. This choice affects the risks that each party bears.

The most common approach is to estimate, order, and pay for services on the basis of units of work supplied. The government may, for example, contract for painting services on a per-square-foot basis, *Arcon-Pacific Contractors*, ASBCA 25057, 82-2 BCA ¶ 15,838; for renovation services based on multiple descriptions of renovation work with separate prices, *MDP Constr., Inc.*, ASBCA 49527, 96-2 BCA ¶ 28,525; or for motor vehicle maintenance on a per-vehicle-serviced basis, *S & W Tire Servs., Inc.*, GSBCA 6376, 82-2 BCA ¶ 16,048. Under this type of contract, the contractor assumes the risk that each unit of work can be performed profitably at the contract unit prices without regard to variations between actual and estimated quantities. In addition, both parties assume the risk of quantity variations when such variations increase or decrease the unit costs of performance.

The government also contracts for services by unit of time. One way to do this is on an hourly basis using a labor-hour or time-and-materials pricing arrangement. For example, in *Stanley F. Horton*, DOTCAB 1231, 82-2 BCA ¶ 15,967, the government ordered snow removal services at an hourly rate. The consequences of structuring the requirement on an hourly basis are similar to those of the unit of work situation except that there is significantly less contractor risk since the contractor is paid for the hours actually incurred in performing the work. Nevertheless, this type of contract is useful in situations where the work is not easily quantifiable in other units and is also subject to fluctuation in requirements.

[6] Government Estimates

To provide equal information to all offerors as to the expected amount of supplies or services required and to provide a basis for evaluating the proposed prices, the government is required to include estimated quantities of the work in the solicitation and use these estimates to evaluate the offers. FAR 16.503(a) states:

> (1) For the information of offerors and contractors, the contracting officer shall state a realistic estimated total quantity in the solicitation and resulting contract. This estimate is not a representation to an offeror or contractor that the estimated quantity will be required or ordered, or that conditions affecting requirements will be stable or normal. The contracting officer may obtain the estimate from records of previous requirements and consumption, or by other means, and should base the estimates on the most current information available.

See *Agility Def. & Gov't Servs. v. United States*, 847 F.3d 1345 (Fed. Cir. 2017), reversing a Court of Federal Claims decision holding that the government had met this obligation by providing recent usage data rather than estimates of the required work. The court stated at 1352:

> Because DRMS anticipated increased workload, simply providing offerors with historical workload was not "the most current information available" sufficient to provide a realistic estimate under. DRMS should have based its estimate on its anticipated "surge" in workload. Although DRMS informed offerors that it "anticipate[d] an increase in property turn-ins," it did so on June 20, 2007, before it seemingly changed course on July 24, 2007 with its updated estimate in the Amendment 007 Chart, projecting stable workload for two years followed by "workload declines." DRMS was not obligated to guarantee the accuracy of its estimates or perfectly forecast its requirements, and Agility ultimately bore the risk associated with any variance in workload from a realistic estimate. *See*. But it was clearly erroneous for the Claims Court to find that DRMS complied with the requirements of by providing historical data.

GAO has ruled that it is improper merely to evaluate unit prices or fixed labor rates without the use of estimates, *R&G Food Serv., Inc.*, Comp. Gen. Dec. B-296435.4, 2005 CPD ¶ 194, *recons. denied*, 2005 CPD ¶ 201. See the discussion in Chapter 7 of evaluation of IDIQ contract prices.

Paragraph (a) of the Requirements clause in FAR 52.216-21 indicates that the government is not liable for incorrect estimates as follows:

> Except as this contract may otherwise provide, if the Government's requirements do not result in orders in the quantities described as "estimated" or "maximum" in the Schedule, that fact shall not constitute the basis for an equitable price adjustment.

[a] Liability for Incorrect Estimate

Notwithstanding the above language in the Requirements clause, the government is obligated to use care in calculating estimated quantities.

However, a variation between the estimated quantity and the actual quantity does not in itself establish a basis for contractor relief, *Bannum, Inc. v. Dep't of Justice*, DOTBCA 4450, 05-2 BCA ¶33,049; *Special Waste, Inc.*, ASBCA 36775, 90-2 BCA ¶22,935; *Standard-Southern Corp.*, ASBCA 20964, 77-1 BCA ¶12,359, *aff'd*, 223 Ct. Cl. 669 (1980). See also *Paradigm II, LLC*, ASBCA 55849, 12-2 BCA ¶35,067 (vagaries of war in Iraq excused grossly erroneous estimate); *Willamette Indus., Inc.*, Comp. Gen. Dec. B-188548, 79-2 CPD ¶338 (discrepancies between estimated and actual quantities of up to 80% insufficient to afford a legal basis for relief). The government's estimate of its needs is not generally regarded as a warranty that such amounts will be required, *Shader Contractors, Inc. v. United States*, 276 F.2d 1 (Ct. Cl. 1960).

Although early decisions required proof of government bad faith to support recovery, more recently, the government has been held to a somewhat higher degree of care. The rationale supporting these decisions is based upon *Womack v. United States*, 389 F.2d 793 (Ct. Cl. 1968), which, although not involving a requirements contract, held the government liable on a misrepresentation theory for faulty estimates furnished for bidding purposes. Following the reasoning of *Womack*, the Federal Circuit has held that the contractor is not required to prove bad faith in order to recover, *Rumsfeld v. Applied Cos.*, 325 F.3d 1328 (Fed. Cir.), *cert. denied*, 540 U.S. 981 (2003). Earlier decisions had also concluded that the government should be held to a *negligence* standard. See *Clearwater Forest Indus., Inc. v. United States*, 650 F.2d 233 (Ct. Cl. 1981) (stating that in making estimates, the government "must act in good faith and use reasonable care"); and *Integrity Mgmt. Int'l, Inc.*, ASBCA 18289, 75-1 BCA ¶11,235, *recons. denied*, 75-2 BCA ¶11,602 (reviewing prior decisions and granting relief because of government negligence in preparing estimates). For other decisions granting relief, see *Datalect Computer Servs., Ltd. v. United States*, 40 Fed. Cl. 28 (1997) (government negligent in that it knew of several facts that would likely affect estimate); *Crown Laundry & Dry Cleaners, Inc. v. United States*, 29 Fed. Cl. 506 (1993) (government negligent in not checking estimates whose accuracy had been questioned by government personnel during preparation of solicitation); *Travel Centre v. General Servs. Admin.*, GSBCA 14057, 98-1 BCA ¶29,422, *recons. denied*, 98-1 BCA ¶29,541 (GSA knew or should have known that the estimates provided were vastly overstated); *Ambulance Serv. & Transp. of Marlin*, VABCA 3485, 94-2 BCA ¶26,729 (government failed to adequately utilize available information when making estimate); *Viktoria Fit Internationale Spedition*, ASBCA 39703, 92-2 BCA ¶24,968 (contracting officer provided no convincing rationale for arriving at the estimate); *McCotter Motors, Inc.*, ASBCA 30498, 86-2 BCA ¶18,784 (government used disproportionately high prior-year quantity without determining whether that figure was an accurate forecast); *Pied Piper Ice Cream, Inc.*, ASBCA 20605, 76-2 BCA ¶12,148 (adopting reasonable care standard and finding government grossly negligent); *American Maint. & Mgmt. Servs., Inc.*, ASBCA 18756, 75-2 BCA ¶11,407, *recons. denied*, 75-2 BCA ¶11,572 (stating contractor is entitled to honest and informed estimate, but finding no negligence). In *Atlantic Garages, Inc.*, GSBCA 5891, 82-1 BCA ¶ 15,479, where the government's solicitation for large-scale engine repair was restricted to contractors in a geographical area where large-scale organizations could not be expected to be operating, the government was held to an enhanced duty to consider the potential effect of faulty estimates on smaller contractors. Compare *Medart, Inc.*, GSBCA 8939, 91-2 BCA ¶ 23,741, *aff'd*, 967 F.2d 579 (Fed. Cir. 1992), finding no liability for very inaccurate estimates because the agency had used the prior-year quantities, as suggested by FAR 16.503(a)(1), as the basis for the estimate. In affirming, the Federal Circuit stated at 582:

> The government may go beyond the requirements of the regulations, of course. And it might be well advised to do so if it wants to secure the best prices and avoid contractors raising their bids to cover the uncertainties. But we are in no position to impose such a requirement either in this case or as a general proposition in the face of the regulations promulgated by competent authority. The regulations explicitly say that estimates may be based on the most current information about previous requirements available; Medart knew this, as well as who bore the risks of variances in quantity. It should have factored the risks into its bid . . . just as the regulation was factored into the contract.

See also *MPG West, LLC*, ASBCA 61100, 20-1 BCA ¶ 37,739, finding no negligence because the agency had used past three years consumption data even though IG report had found negligence; *Apex Int'l Mgmt. Servs., Inc.*, ASBCA 37813, 94-1 BCA ¶ 26,299, finding no negligence because the agency had used historical workload figures to compile its estimates; *American Marine Decking Servs., Inc.*, ASBCA 44440, 97-1 CPD ¶ 28,821, finding no negligence where the agency had based its estimate on work in another location because it had no experience at the location covered by the contract; and *Federal Group,, Inc. v. United States*, 67 Fed. Cl. 87 (2005), finding no negligence where the agency disclosed that its estimate was subject to change because of government downsizing.

Where the government acts in good faith and without negligence but the estimate is grossly inaccurate, the contractor may be entitled to relief if the resulting contract is unconscionable. That result was reached in *Operational Serv. Corp.*, ASBCA 37059, 93-3 BCA ¶ 26,190.

The most common type of faulty estimate occurs when the agency fails to consider all relevant, available information, *Grover Contracting Corp.*, GSBCA 4115, 75-2 BCA ¶ 11,550. See *Hi-Shear Tech. Corp. v. United States*, 53 Fed. Cl. 420 (2002), *aff'd*, 356 F.3d 1372 (Fed. Cir. 2004) (estimate of quantities of spare parts did not reflect returned parts that could be repaired); *National Salvage & Serv. Corp.*, ASBCA 53750, 04-2 BCA ¶ 32,654 (estimate was not adjusted to reflect internal decisions on likelihood of ordering work); *Contract Mgmt., Inc.*, ASBCA 44885, 95-2 BCA ¶ 27,886 (estimate was not adjusted for anticipated budget shortfall); *Pruitt Energy Sources, Inc.*, ENGBCA 6134, 95-2 BCA ¶ 27,840 (estimate was not adjusted for shorter contract base period than those of prior contracts); *Fa. Kammerdiener GmbH & Co., KG*, ASBCA 45248, 94-3 BCA ¶ 27,197 (government had information rendering its estimate inaccurate well before award); and *Crown Laundry & Dry Cleaners, Inc.*, ASBCA 28889, 85-2 BCA ¶ 18,003 (government ignored available workload figures in estimating its requirements). GAO has also stated that relief in the form of contract reformation can be granted when the government has not based its estimate "on all relevant information that is reasonably available to it," *Lone Star Energy Co.*, Comp. Gen. Dec. B-199049, 80-2 CPD ¶ 98; *Union Carbide Corp.*, Comp. Gen. Dec. B-188426, 77-2 CPD ¶ 204, and that the estimates must be "reasonably accurate representations of anticipated actual needs," *CardioMetrix*, Comp. Gen. Dec. B-252758.3, 94-1 CPD ¶ 316; *Richard M. Walsh Assocs.*, Comp. Gen. Dec. B-216730, 85-1 CPD ¶ 621; *Yamas Constr. Co.*, Comp. Gen. Dec. B-217459, 85-1 CPD ¶ 599.

The Court of Claims held that, in making its estimate, the government must give consideration to all potential work, whether or not "firm" requirements exist, *Chemical Tech., Inc. v. United States*, 645 F.2d 934 (Ct. Cl. 1981). A possible way for the government to avoid this problem is to provide estimates based on firm data and to inform the offerors of additional data that may indicate greater or fewer requirements. See *International Bus. Invs., Inc.*, Comp. Gen. Dec. B-215081, 85-1 CPD ¶ 228, where GAO denied a protest alleging that workload estimates in the IFB were not based upon the best available information, reasoning, in part, that, because the information that the protester asserted to be more accurate was provided by letter to all of the bidders prior to their response to the solicitation, no prejudice had occurred to the protester.

Where the contractor fills government orders far exceeding the estimates without objecting to the validity of the estimates, the contractor will be estopped from later challenging the estimates, *Standard-Southern Corp.*, ASBCA 20964, 77-1 BCA ¶ 12,359, *aff'd*, 223 Ct. Cl. 669 (1980).

[b] Contractor Obligation to Fulfill Requirements Exceeding Government Estimate

Subject to any contract or order maximums in the schedule, the requirements contractor must supply the full requirement regardless of the extent to which it may exceed the estimate, *Kasehagen Sec. Servs., Inc.*, ASBCA 25629, 86-2 BCA ¶ 18,797; *Sponge Fishing Co.*, GSBCA 1386, 65-1 BCA ¶ 4627. Where the contractor fails to fulfill that obligation, it will be held liable for excess costs incurred by the government in reprocurement of any items that the government would have been entitled to order under the contract, irrespective of whether orders had actually been placed with the defaulted contractor, *Interroyal Corp.*, GSBCA 5439, 83-1 BCA ¶ 16,339.

This same result would not be reached under the *Uniform Commercial Code* (U.C.C.) § 2-306(1), which states that a contractor has no obligation to provide quantities "unreasonably disproportionate to any stated estimate." In *Miltex Indus., Inc.*, ASBCA 19449, 77-2 BCA ¶ 12,768, the board rejected the application of this provision, holding that federal precedent in this area consistently limited contractor liability only when the government made a bad faith estimate. Accord *Machlett Labs., Inc.*, ASBCA 16194, 73-1 BCA ¶ 9929.

Commercial impracticability has been used to avoid the contractor's obligation to supply required services. In *Selectronix Commc'ns*, ASBCA 20981, 77-1 BCA ¶ 12,547, a default termination was converted to a termination for the convenience of the government when the inventory requirements necessary for contractor compliance with an Air Force communications system repair schedule were deemed commercially impracticable.

[c] Relief for Faulty Government Overestimate

Contractors have frequently submitted claims for relief when quantity underruns were the result of faulty estimates. While the promulgation of such estimates are breaches of contract, *Atlantic Garages, Inc.*, GSBCA 5891, 82-1 BCA ¶ 15,479, the boards have sometimes dealt with such claims as terminations for convenience, *Integrity Mgmt. Int'l, Inc.*, ASBCA 18289, 75-1 BCA ¶ 11,235, *recons. denied*, 75-2 BCA ¶ 11,602; *Pied Piper Ice Cream, Inc.*, ASBCA 20605, 76-2 BCA ¶ 12,148. It has now been determined that such breaches of contract do not permit the recovery of lost profit on the incorrect estimated quantity but should be remedied by repricing the contract to pay the contractor the price that it would have offered had it known the amount of a correct estimate, *Rumsfeld v. Applied Cos.*, 325 F.3d 1328 (Fed. Cir.), *cert. denied*, 540 U.S. 981 (2003). See *Hi-Shear Tech. Corp. v. United States*, 356 F.3d 1372 (Fed. Cir. 2004), holding that a proper computation of this repricing was the award of "fixed overhead" on the lost sales plus G&A on that overhead. The court also held that reliance damages were not a proper measure of damages in this instance. See also *Admiral Elevator v. Soc. Sec. Admin.*, CBCA 470, 08-2 BCA ¶ 33,884, where the amount for a faulty estimate was determined by computing the difference between the amount the contractor was paid and the amount it would have been paid had the estimate been correct minus the cost of material not needed and the price for work not performed. Compare *Datalect Computer Servs., Ltd. v. United States*, 56 Fed. Cl. 178 (2003), *aff'd*, 97 Fed. Appx. 333 (Fed. Cir. 2004), where the court rejected a repricing claim because the contractor could not submit sufficient proof to permit computation of the amount of the repricing. *Applied Cos* also held that the situation should be treated as a termination for convenience if the government ordered no quantities as a result of the faulty estimate.

[7] Variations in Estimated Quantities Clauses

The government often uses clauses that provide for price adjustment when government requirements vary from the estimate by more than stated percentages. There is no standard variation in quantity clause prescribed for requirements contracts, but FAR 52.211-18 provides a Variations in Estimated Quantities clause for use in construction contracts. Many requirements contracts contain similar clauses calling for price adjustments for quantities varying from the estimate by more than a stated percentage. The Variations in Estimated Quantities clause is applicable to the entire contract not the delivery or task orders issued under the contract, *Emerson Constr. Co.*, ASBCA 55165, 06-2 BCA ¶ 33,382.

The government has unsuccessfully argued that these clauses protect it from liability for faulty estimates or improper actions during performance. In *Integrity Mgmt. Int'l, Inc.*, ASBCA 18289, 75-1 BCA ¶ 11,235, *recons. denied*, 75-2 BCA ¶ 11,602, the board found that the government had made a faulty estimate and reasoned that the clause did not bind the contractor to assume the burden of the first 25% of the government's negligence. In *Chemical Tech., Inc. v. United States*, 645 F.2d 934 (Ct. Cl. 1981), the court granted relief even though the deviation from the estimated quantity fell within the range of the Volume Variation clause, stating, "In its dealings with contractors, the government cannot provide inaccurate data in this manner and then be allowed to bar an equitable recovery by arguing that the resulting damages . . . fall within the 25% Volume Variation clause." It has also been held that a variation in quantity clause will not apply if the original government estimate is negligently made, *Burnham Assocs., Inc.*, ASBCA 60780, 18-1 BCA ¶ 36,934; *Marine Constr. & Dredging, Inc.*, ASBCA 38538, 95-1 BCA ¶ 27,286; *John Murphy Constr. Co.*, AGBCA 418, 79-1 BCA ¶ 13,836.

Clauses of this type will not prevent the contractor from obtaining a price adjustment under the Differing Site Conditions clause when the variation in quantity occurs because of a condition that falls within the bounds of that clause. For example, in *Continental Drilling Co.*, ENGBCA 3455, 75-2 BCA ¶ 11,541, a changed condition was found when the contractor had to use a substantially larger quantity of a drill hole casing than the estimated quantity. The board reasoned that the government estimate of a small amount of drill hole casing was an indication that a certain type of subsurface material would be encountered, whereas the need to use a large quantity of the casing indicated that a different type of material was actually present at the site. In *A.S. Horner, Inc.*, ASBCA 76-145, 79-1 BCA ¶ 13,561, a changed condition was found when the contractor had to use different methods to excavate a trench deeper than had been anticipated, and in *Brezina Constr., Inc.*, ENGBCA 3215, 75-1 BCA ¶ 10,989, a changed condition was found where the contractor was required to dispose of a large amount of material off-site although the parties had anticipated that there would be an approximate balance between the excavated material and the material used for fill. In *Brezina*, the board found a changed condition rather than a variation in quantity because the contractor had encountered an "entirely different job" than anticipated. Similarly, in *United Contractors v. United States*, 368 F.2d 585 (Ct. Cl. 1966), the court held that the Differing Site Conditions clause was applicable when unforeseen conditions were encountered, stating at 601:

> The [VEQ] clause is a ready vehicle for adjusting, with a minimum of haggling, the compensation received by contractors who are called upon in the course of performance to do, within limits, more or less work than could be estimated. But we have held that clauses of this type do not control when the cost of doing the extra work greatly differs from the stated unit-price because of factors not foreseen by either party. In that event, the [Differing Site Conditions] clause comes into play and overrides the [VEQ] clause.

This rule has been followed in *Met-Pro Corp.*, ASBCA 49694, 98-2 BCA ¶ 29,776 (very large variation from estimated quantity due to incorrect analysis of conditions at site); *Continental Drilling* Co., ENGBCA 3455, 75-2 BCA ¶ 11,541 (very large variation from estimated quantity because of cave in due to unforeseen soil condition).

The Changes clause has also been held to override the Variations in Estimated Quantities clause in situations where the government orders the contractor to perform unit priced work in excess of that contemplated when the quantity estimates were established. For example, in *Morrison-Knudsen Co. v. United States*, 397 F.2d 826 (Ct. Cl. 1968), the court found the contractor entitled to a price adjustment under the Changes clause when the government overcame unforeseen conditions by ordering the contractor to perform the work in a different manner. Similarly, in *ThermoCor, Inc. v. United States*, 35 Fed. Cl. 480 (1996), the court held that the Changes clause could override the Variations in Estimated Quantities clause but denied summary judgment in order to conduct a trial to determine whether the overrun in quantities had been caused by changes. See also *Flat Head Contractors, LLC v. Dep't of Agriculture*, CBCA 118, 07-1 BCA ¶ 33,556, where the need to construct a wall higher than indicated in the specifications was found to be a change that overrode the variation in quantity clause; and *C.H. Leavell & Co.*, ENGBCA 3492, 75-2 BCA ¶ 11,596, where a contracting officer's order to change the concrete mixtures was held to be a change rather than a variation in quantity of the contract's unit price for cement. Compare *Luedtke Eng'g Co.*, ASBCA 54226, 05-2 BCA ¶ 32,971, and *CEMS, Inc. v. United States*, 59 Fed. Cl. 168 (2003), rejecting the contractor's contention that changes had occurred which would have overridden the Variations in Quantity clause. In *Maya Transit Co.*, ASBCA 20186, 75-2 BCA ¶ 11,552, the board held that the clause was not intended to apply to a constructive change. Compare *Blaylock & Sons, Inc. v. Dep't of* Transportation, CBCA 4601, 15-1 BCA ¶ 36,039, where an Eliminated Work clause in the specifications overrode the Variation in Quantity clause when no work was ordered.

Normally, variation in quantity clauses provide that the unit prices set forth in the contract are to apply to all quantities of work within the range specified in the clause. Thus, price adjustments on overruns will be made only to that quantity above the stated percentage. In *N. Fiorito Co. v. United States*, 416 F.2d 1284 (Ct. Cl. 1969), it was held that this type of clause binds the parties to the unit prices for quantities of work up to the full extent of the variation range (110% of the estimated quantity in the clause in question) with repricing to occur only as to the quantities in excess of the range. See also *LRV Envt'l, Inc.*, ASBCA 58727, 15-1 BCA ¶ 36,042, rejecting the contractor's argument that it should be paid for estimated quantities not actual quantities.

These clauses do not provide for complete repricing of the work above or below the range. The clause in FAR 52.212-11 provides that any equitable adjustment under the clause will be based on increases or decreases in cost "due solely to the variation." In *Victory Constr. Co. v. United States*, 510 F.2d 1379 (Ct. Cl. 1975), the court held that the party demanding the adjustment had the burden of proof that the costs had varied because of the difference in quantity. The court further stated that the amount of the equitable adjustment was to be determined solely on the basis of differences in cost because of the larger or smaller quantity rather than on a complete repricing of the work based on actual incurred costs for the excess quantity. The Federal Circuit followed and more fully explained this reasoning in *Foley Co. v. United States*, 11 F.3d 1032 (Fed. Cir. 1993). See also *ThermoCor, Inc. v. United States*, 35 Fed. Cl. 480 (1996); *Clement-Mtarri Cos.*, ASBCA 38170, 92-3 BCA ¶ 25,192, *aff'd*, 11 F.3d 1072 (Fed. Cir. 1993). Compare *Burnett Constr. Co. v. United States*, 26 Cl. Ct. 296 (1992); *Bean Dredging Corp.*, ENGBCA 5507, 89-3 BCA ¶ 22,034, and *Carvel Walker*, ENGBCA 3744, 78-1 BCA ¶ 13,005, decided before *Foley* and interpreting *Victory* as calling for adjusting the price of an overrun quantity based on the total costs of the additional quantity rather than the increased costs due to the additional quantity. These cases have been effectively overruled by *Foley*.

One of the most common reasons for a price adjustment is that the increase or decrease in quantity will alter the amount of fixed costs allocable to each unit. In *Henry Angelo & Co.*, ASBCA 43669, 94-1 BCA ¶ 26,484, the board included in the adjustment for a severe underrun in estimated quantity an amount for indirect costs that would have been recovered if the estimated quantity had been ordered. Compare *P.R. Contractors, Inc. v. United States*, 76 Fed. Cl. 621 (2007), rejecting a claim for unrecovered overhead, profit, bond and taxes due to an underrun in quantities because the contractor did not prove "increased costs" of the underrun. In *Cottrell Eng'g Corp.*, ENGBCA 3038, 70-2 BCA ¶ 8462, the board found a difference in cost due to the larger quantity based on the full recovery of nonrecurring costs in the unit prices for the estimated quantity. The board therefore granted a downward equitable adjustment removing the nonrecurring costs from the unit prices for the purposes of paying for the overrun quantity. In *S & T Enters.*, AGBCA 2001-159-1, 03-2 BCA ¶ 32,282, the board denied a price increase for overrun quantities because the contractor did not prove that its increased costs were caused by the overrun. A dissenting judge argued that there should have been an adjustment because there was proof that the cost of the overrun quantity was higher than the cost of the quantity within the clause. *In KiSKA Constr. Corp.-USA and Kajima Eng'g & Constr., Inc., A Joint Venture*, ASBCA 54613, 09-1 BCA ¶ 34,089, the board granted compensation for increased quantities outside the variation range at the contract unit prices because the contractor did not claim that higher costs were incurred. In *Ronald Adams Contractor, Inc.*, AGBCA 91-155-1, 94-3 BCA ¶ 27,018, the board denied a price adjustment for either party because neither had proved that the significant overrun had altered the contractor's costs of performance.

[8] Government Failure to Order Its Requirements Under the Contract

The contractor is not entitled to compensation if the government's failure to place orders results from either risks assumed by the contractor or good faith decisions of the government to reduce its activity because of unanticipated changes in its situation. See *Technical Assistance Int'l, Inc. v. United States*, 150 F.3d 1369 (Fed. Cir. 1998), rejecting the argument that the contractor should be entitled to relief if the government's requirements changed because the facts underlying the estimate changed. In that decision, the court equated lack of good faith with bad faith, stating at 1373:

> [I]n a requirements contract case in which the seller alleges that the buyer breached the contract by reducing its requirements, the burden of proof is on the seller to prove that the buyer acted in bad faith, for example, by reducing its requirements solely in order to avoid its obligations under the contract. In the absence of such a showing, the buyer will be presumed to have varied its requirements for valid business reasons, i.e., to have acted in good faith, and will not be liable for the change in requirements.

See also *Lockheed Martin Aircraft Center*, ASBCA 55164, 08-1 BCA ¶ 33,832, requiring the contractor to prove bad faith when the government performed part of the requirement with its own forces. It is not clear whether intentional diversion of work constitutes bad faith but most of the decisions discussed below have granted relief on that basis.

[a] Obtaining Needs from Alternate Source

Relief has been granted to contractors when the government has improperly failed to order its requirements under the contract and has obtained its needs from another source or has accomplished the work in-house. In *C&S Park Serv., Inc.*, ENGBCA 3624, 78-1 BCA ¶ 13,134, the contractor was allowed to recover for losses incurred due to the reduction in work caused by government personnel performing the lawn maintenance services covered by a contract that made no allowances for in-house performance. See also *Datalect Computer Servs., Ltd. v. United States*, 56 Fed. Cl. 178 (2003), *aff'd*, 97 Fed. Appx. 333 (Fed. Cir. 2004) (agency obtained maintenance work by extending warranty of original supplier); *Vehicle Maint. Servs. v. General Servs. Admin.*, GSBCA 11663, 94-2 BCA ¶ 26,893 (work diverted to other vendors); *Erwin v. United States*, 19 Cl. Ct. 47 (1989) (work bought from other vendors); *Arcon-Pacific Contractors*, ASBCA 25057, 82-2 BCA ¶ 15,838 (government ordered another contractor to do work); *North Chicago Disposal Co.*, ASBCA 25535, 82-1 BCA ¶ 15,488 (government had no right to retroactively recoup an amount paid to a contractor where the bulk of the job was actually performed by Navy personnel ignorant of the contract); *Inland Container, Inc. v. United States*, 512 F.2d 1073 (Ct. Cl. 1975) (government requisitioned most of the goods from the GSA); *Maya Transit Co.*, ASBCA 20186, 75-2 BCA ¶ 11,552 (government performed work in-house because of budget considerations); and *Pacific Tech. Enters., Ltd.*, ASBCA 17087, 74-2 BCA ¶ 10,679 (government diverted some of its requirements to another contractor). In *MDP Constr., Inc.*, ASBCA 49527, 96-2 BCA ¶ 28,525, the government breached a requirements contract for renovation of bathrooms by including bathroom renovation in a larger contract for renovation of total buildings. Similarly, in *S & W Tire Servs., Inc.*, GSBCA 6376, 82-2 BCA ¶ 16,048, the board held that the government was in breach of a requirements contract for tire recapping when, during the contract period, it hired a new contractor to run its entire motor pool, thereby depriving the original contractor of the recapping business. But where the contractor had actual knowledge, prior to bidding, of the government's capacity for performing work in-house and of its intent to do so, the contractor was held to have bid in full realization that it would only be called upon to perform in the event that the government's capability proved inadequate to meet its requirements, *Stanley F. Horton*, DOTCAB 1231, 82-2 BCA ¶ 15,967. See also *Pegasus Aviation, Inc. v. General Servs. Admin.*, GSBCA 10112, 93-3 BCA ¶ 25,944, where the board held that the government had not diverted work where the contract provided six exceptions in which services would be sought elsewhere.

In determining whether a breach has occurred, the court or board will review the specification to ensure that the work obtained from another contract is the same work as that under the requirements contract. In *Cleek Aviation v. United States*, 19 Cl. Ct. 552 (1990), the court found no breach of a requirements contract for supplying aviation fuel directly into airplanes when the agency ordered aviation fuel for storage tanks from another contractor. The court reasoned that the two types of services were essentially different. See also *Eastern Ambulance Servs., Inc.*, VABCA 2078, 86-2 BCA ¶ 18,852, where the board found that award of a contract with a company to transport "stretcher" patients did not violate a requirements contract to provide ambulance services. The board compared the two types of services and found them dissimilar even though the "stretcher" patients could receive some medical services in transit. Compare *T&M Distributors, Inc.*, ASBCA 51279, 01-2 BCA ¶ 31,442, making numerous findings on the scope of a requirements contract and holding that supplying parts for vehicles included supplying parts for components of those vehicles.

Another factor in the interpretation of the requirements covered by the contract is the contemporaneous interpretation of the contract by the parties. In *Metropolitan Area Transit, Inc.*, VABCA 7022, 05-2 BCA ¶ 32,970, this evidence was used to deny recovery because the contractor had not contended that the contract covered services that it subsequently claimed were within its scope.

Contractors have been required to submit evidence of specific transactions that have amounted to diversions of work from the contract, *United Med. Supply Co. v. United States*, 63 Fed. Cl. 430 (2005). However, the government must preserve the evidence in its possession that will prove that work was diverted. In *United Med. Supply Co. v. United States*, 77 Fed. Cl. 257 (2007), the court sanctioned the government for destroying such evidence—by precluding the cross-examination of the contractor's expert witness that reconstructed the evidence to fill in the gaps that had been destroyed, by precluding the government from presenting expert testimony on those gaps, and by assessing the contractor's costs of this effort to the government.

[b] Government Change in Work

The contractor may also be entitled to relief on a theory that a government change in work has occurred. In *Desco Serv. Contractors*, ASBCA 21856, 77-2 BCA ¶ 12,752, a change occurred when the government decreased the frequency of vehicle maintenance inspections under the contract. See also *California Bus Lines*, ASBCA 19732, 75-2 BCA ¶ 11,601 (change in work plan reducing amount of work necessary to meet government's unchanged requirements constituted a constructive change); and *Del Rio Flying Serv.*, ASBCA 15304, 71-1 BCA ¶ 8744 (government change in definition of "students," resulting in decreased work is compensable if increased costs result).

The changes theory will not cover reductions in the government's needs that occur because of changed circumstances, *Padilla v. United States*, 58 Fed. Cl. 585 (2003) (reduced work because of Congressional moratorium on project requiring work); *East Bay Auto Supply, Inc.*, ASBCA 25542, 81-2 BCA ¶ 15,204 (reduction of fleet at base contractor was servicing caused a decline in demand for spare vehicle parts); *Solano Aircraft Serv., Inc.*, ASBCA 20677, 77-2 BCA ¶ 12,584 (military commitments in Southeast Asia reduced the number of available domestic aircraft to be serviced); *Gulf Coast Aviation Co.*, ASBCA 10189, 65-2 BCA ¶ 4928 (base closing eliminated the requirement for food services). Neither is it a change if the government cancels an order after it is issued, *California Bus Lines, Inc.*, ASBCA 42181, 91-3 BCA ¶ 24,341.

However, the contractor will be entitled to compensation for costs incurred if the cancellation order is received too late to permit it to avoid the costs, *California Bus Lines, Inc.*, ASBCA 19571, 76-1 BCA ¶ 11,655.

It is not a change to the contract when the government orders uneven quantities, *Asfaltos Panamenos, S.A.*, ASBCA 41657, 92-3 BCA ¶ 25,141. The board held that the contractor should not have relied on even ordering because there was no contract clause requiring orders to be placed uniformly. See also *Tennessee Valley Auth. v. Imperial Prof'l Coatings*, 599 F. Supp. 436 (E.D. Tenn. 1984), where construction of nuclear power plants was deferred because demand for electricity was less than anticipated. The court held that the requirements contractor for painting services had assumed the risk of a good faith decision to cancel the construction of the plant.

[c] Measuring Contractor Relief

As discussed above, the government's failure to perform its obligations under a requirements contract has been alternatively treated as a breach of contract or a constructive termination for convenience. In general, government breaches have been treated as constructive terminations for convenience when the contract contains a Termination for Convenience clause, *Nesbitt v. United States*, 345 F.2d 583 (Ct. Cl. 1965); *Inland Container, Inc. v. United States*, 512 F.2d 1073 (Ct. Cl. 1975); *Kalvar Corp. v. United States*, 543 F.2d 1298 (Ct. Cl. 1976), *cert. denied*, 434 U.S. 830 (1977). Traditionally, this rule has not been applied if the failure to order was in bad faith, *Kalvar Corp. v. United States*, 543 F.2d 1298 (Ct. Cl. 1976), *cert. denied*, 434 U.S. 830 (1977), or if it was based on circumstances known to the government at the time of award, *Torncello v. United States*, 681 F.2d 756 (Ct. Cl. 1982). In *Torncello*, the government obtained a requirement at a lower price about which it had known at the time of award of the contract. The court reasoned that the Termination for Convenience clause was not properly usable in such circumstances. See also *S & W Tire Servs., Inc.*, GSBCA 6376, 82-2 BCA ¶ 16,048, where the board found that contracting out an entire operation, of which the requirements contract was a part, was a breach and not a constructive termination, because the government knew of the decision to contract out at the time of award of the requirements contract. In *Erwin v. United States*, 19 Cl. Ct. 47 (1989), the court refused to find a constructive termination when the government ordered all of the services from other vendors because the Termination for Convenience clause limited compensation to the price of completed work. The court reasoned that use of this clause would amount to "illusory consideration" for the requirements contract. In *Viktoria Transp. GmbH & Co.*, ASBCA 30371, 88-3 BCA ¶ 20,921, the board treated a failure to order all requirements as a constructive termination for convenience rather than as a breach because there was no bad faith. This rule will also prevent the agency from issuing a termination for convenience order to avoid a requirements contract when no changed circumstances are present, *Tamp Corp.*,

ASBCA 25692, 84-2 BCA ¶ 17,460. However, termination for convenience is proper when the government finds that it had significantly underestimated the requirement, *T & M Distribs., Inc. v. United States*, 185 F.3d 1279 (Fed. Cir. 1999).

Recent cases have indicated that diversion of requirements should be treated as a breach of contract, *Rumsfeld v. Applied Cos.*, 325 F.3d 1328 (Fed. Cir.), *cert. denied*, 540 U.S. 981 (2003); *Ace-Federal Reporters, Inc. v. Barram*, 226 F.3d 1329 (Fed. Cir. 2000). This will allow the recovery of lost profits if they can be proven with some degree of certainty. See *Joe Phillips*, ASBCA 57280, 13-1 BCA ¶ 35,263, awarding profits of 30.09% after receiving extensive evidence of the costs of the diverted work. See also *T&M Distribs., Inc.*, ASBCA 51279, 01-2 BCA ¶ 31,442, awarding profits on diverted sales, and *Tamp Corp.*, ASBCA 25692, 84-2 BCA ¶ 17,460, stating that changes must be calculated to put the contractor in "as good a position as if it had been permitted to fully perform the contract." The board held that this required compensation for profits that would have been earned plus "expenses reasonably incurred as the result of the premature termination."

Alternatively, contractors may be able to assert such claims as terminations for convenience. If so, they will forego recovery of anticipated profits, but will be able to use the special cost principle in FAR 31.205-42 applicable to this type pricing. The major advantage in characterizing the claim as one for termination is the ability to recover settlement costs incurred after the termination. See *Kalvar Corp. v. United States*, 543 F.2d 1298 (Ct. Cl. 1976), *cert. denied*, 434 U.S. 830 (1977), where the prohibition of anticipated profits was broadly construed to preclude recovery for the difference between the contract price and a profitable resale price and for higher unit costs on subsequent sales of terminated items. The court also disallowed financing costs and administrative costs associated with the alleged breach on the theory that these were not recoverable under termination cost principles. The court did permit the recovery of some of the contractor's legal fees as settlement costs. Appeals boards have been somewhat more liberal in computing termination costs. See *Drain-A-Way Sys.*, GSBCA 7022, 84-1 BCA ¶ 16,929, where the board held that the unit prices should be recomputed to reflect lower volumes because of the termination. Similarly, in *Wheeler Bros.*, ASBCA 20465, 79-1 BCA ¶ 13,642, where there was a partial termination for convenience, the board permitted repricing to include the entire increase in overhead costs resulting from the reduced volume. See also *Inland Container, Inc. v. United States*, 512 F.2d 1073 (Ct. Cl. 1975), where the court permitted recovery of losses incurred in running a manufacturing plant for six months awaiting government orders under the requirements contract. The court reasoned that this loss was a reasonable approximation of initial and preparatory expenses since the plant would probably not have incurred losses had the government properly issued orders. However, profits have been limited to those earned on the completed work. See *Adams Mfg. Co.*, GSBCA 5747, 82-1 BCA ¶ 15,740, *aff'd*, 714 F.2d 161 (Fed. Cir. 1983), precluding anticipated profits where failure to order constituted a total termination for convenience, and *Arcon-Pacific Contractors*, ASBCA 25057, 82-2 BCA ¶ 15,838, where the board limited recovery to actual incurred costs plus profit on those costs in the case of a constructive partial convenience termination.

A different pricing theory applies when the government's failure to honor its requirements obligation is construed as a constructive change. There, the proper measure of the equitable adjustment is the difference between the cost of the work originally called for and the changed work. See *Desco Serv. Contractors*, ASBCA 21856, 77-2 BCA ¶ 12,752, using this technique to compute the adjustment. In *Maya Transit Co.*, ASBCA 20186, 75-2 BCA ¶ 11,552, the board stated that the unit prices of the work should be recomputed following this theory. See also *Pacific Tech. Enters., Ltd.*, ASBCA 17087, 74-2 BCA ¶ 10,679, where the equitable adjustment was computed by granting the contractor payment for work diverted to another company.

[C] Multi-year Contracts

The multi-year contract is a specialized type of requirements contract that creates a slightly different relationship between the contractor and the government. It is defined in FAR 17.103 as follows:

> *Multi-year* contract means a contract for the purchase of supplies or services for more than 1, but not more than 5, program years. A multi-year contract may provide that performance under the contract during the second and subsequent years of the contract is contingent upon the appropriation of funds, and (if it does so provide) may provide for a cancellation payment to be made to the contractor if appropriations are not made. The key distinguishing difference between multi-year contracts and multiple year contracts is that multi-year contracts, defined in [10 U.S.C. § 2306b and 41 U.S.C. § 3903], buy more than 1 year's requirement (of a product or service) without establishing and having to exercise an option for each program year after the first.

Thus, the FAR distinguishes between the multi-year contract and the other types of variable quantity contracts ("multiple year contracts" such as requirements contracts and indefinite-quantity contracts) that frequently cover multiple years as part of the basic contract requirement or by including option clauses for additional years. See *Innovative (PBX) Tel. Servs., Inc. v. Dep't of Veterans Affairs*, CBCA 122, 08-1 BCA ¶ 33,854, and *Bureau of Customs & Border Protection—Automated Commercial Env't Contract*, Comp. Gen. Dec. B-302358, 2004 U.S. Comp. Gen. LEXIS 271, holding that an IDIQ contract with option years contained no indicia of a multi-year contract.

This form of contract was devised by the DoD in the 1960s to allow its contracting activities to procure supplies for several years in spite of the fact that appropriated funds were available for such supplies for only one year. The goal was to achieve lower unit prices by permitting the contractor to spread start-up costs over more work, to introduce cost-saving methods of performing the work, and to realize the economies of continuous manufacture of goods. In 1969, the regulations were amended to include service contracts. See FAR 17.105-2, which lists the following objectives for both types of multi-year contracting:

Use of multi-year contracting is encouraged to take advantage of one or more of the following:

> (a) Lower costs.
>
> (b) Enhancement of standardization.
>
> (c) Reduction of administrative burden in the placement and administration of contracts.
>
> (d) Substantial continuity of production or performance, thus avoiding annual startup costs, preproduction testing costs, make-ready expenses, and phaseout costs.
>
> (e) Stabilization of contractor work forces.
>
> (f) Avoidance of the need for establishing quality control techniques and procedures for a new contractor each year.
>
> (g) Broadening the competitive base with opportunity for participation by firms not otherwise willing or able to compete for lesser quantities, particularly in cases involving high startup costs.
>
> (h) Providing incentives to contractors to improve productivity through investment in capital facilities, equipment, and advanced technology.

GAO has made numerous assessments of the effectiveness over the years that this technique has been in use. Its assessment, *DoD's Practices and Processes for Multiyear Procurement Should Be Improved*, GAO-08-298, February 2008, contains the following criticism:

> Multiyear contracting is big business and promises savings at some risk to the government, yet DoD's management direction and process for justifying multiyear programs to the Congress is limited, raising questions about the appropriateness of some approved multiyear programs and the cost effectiveness of investments made for the risks assumed. We identified concerns about the relative stability and savings potential of two recently approved programs, the F-22A Raptor and V-22 Osprey. We found differences in how officials interpreted and applied the statutory criteria and in the methods and data used to compute contract cost and savings. Further, few records are kept to document decisions and supporting evidence. The statutory criteria establish requirements for stable, low risk programs with realistic cost and savings estimates, but DoD has not provided sufficient guidance and a rigorous, disciplined process to ensure high quality, consistent decisions supported by strong empirical evidence.
>
> Although it is difficult to precisely determine the impact of multiyear contracting on actual procurement costs, our case studies of completed multiyear contracts for the C-17A Globemaster, F/A-18E/F Super Hornet, and Apache Longbow Helicopter identified significant unit cost growth, ranging

> from 10 to 30 percent compared to the original estimates provided to Congress. All three programs—presumably approved based on their stability—were significantly impacted during contract execution by labor and material cost increases, changes in requirements and funding, and other factors that helped drive up total contract costs much beyond original projections. Savings also do not appear to have materialized as expected in the budget justifications submitted to the Congress and ultimately more funding was needed to buy the systems. In two of the three cases, actual costs for multiyear procurement exceeded original estimates for annual contracts. While both annual and multiyear contracting are prone to the underestimation of costs and overstatement of benefits as we have noted in our prior body of work on defense acquisitions, the stakes are arguably higher for multiyear programs because of the increased up-front investment required, considerable cost increases if a program is significantly restructured, and the greater liabilities incurred if multiyear programs are cancelled.

GAO has held that multi-year contracting is not unduly prejudicial to small business, 43 Comp. Gen. 657 (B-152766) (1964). See also 46 Comp. Gen. 749 (B-160815) (1967).

In order to use multi-year procurement, an agency must comply with the Anti-Deficiency Act, 31 U.S.C. § 1341, which prohibits the making of contracts in advance of appropriations. This is accomplished by entering into a firm commitment for one year and making the government's liability for future years' quantities contingent on funds becoming available. The contractor is protected in the event the government fails to order all of the program years' quantities by the inclusion of a Cancellation under Multiyear Contracts clause in FAR 52.217-2, providing for reimbursement of unrecovered start-up costs. Since these are long term contracts, the use of economic price adjustment provisions is also permitted, FAR 17.109(b). The proper funding for these contractual commitments is discussed below.

[1] Legal Authority

There has been considerable confusion over the legal authority of agencies to use multi-year contracts. However, it seems clear that agencies have the inherent authority to use multi-year contracts because, for a number of years, Congress acquiesced to the DoD's use of multi-year contracts for the procurement of *supplies* without statutory authority when multi-year or no-year funds were being used. Ultimately, a limit was imposed on cancellation ceilings of $5 million, § 810 of the DoD Authorization Act of 1976, Pub. L. No. 94-106. This effectively precluded the use of multi-year procurements on major systems. Subsequently, in 1982, the Armed Services Committees concluded that multi-year contracts were a means of obtaining lower prices for major weapon systems. The Armed Services Procurement Act was therefore amended to encourage the DoD to use multi-year contracting under the surveillance of Congress, 10 U.S.C. § 2306(h) (pre-1994).

This provision is codified at 10 U.S.C. § 3501 (formerly § 2306b) and is applicable to DoD, NASA, and the Coast Guard. It contains a limitation on such contracts by requiring notification of Congress and a 30-day waiting period before contract award if a cancellation ceiling of more than $100 million is included in such a contract, 10 U.S.C. § 3501(g), as well as many other limitations. Thus, there is congressional oversight on the use of this technique on all major systems. This section has been amended regularly by National Defense Authorization Acts and includes some paragraphs applicable only to DoD. See DFARS 217.170 for the current requirements (including a number of Congressional notification requirements).

During this same period, Congress authorized the DoD, NASA, and the Coast Guard to enter into multi-year contracts for *services*. This was permitted for contracts outside of the United States by the enactment of 10 U.S.C. § 2306(g) in 1968. This statute was broadened in 1981 to permit such contracts within the United States. This statute is now in 10 U.S.C. § 3531 (formerly § 2306c), permitting multi-year contracts using any type of funds if they are for the following types of services:

> (1) operation, maintenance, and support of facilities and installations;
>
> (2) maintenance or modification of aircraft, ships, vehicles, and other highly complex military equipment;
>
> (3) specialized training necessitating high quality instructor skills (for example, pilot and aircrew members; foreign language training); and
>
> (4) base services (for example, ground maintenance; in-plane refueling; bus transportation; refuse collection and disposal);
>
> (5) Environmental remediation services for—
>
> (A) an active military installation;
>
> (B) a military installation being closed or realigned under a base closure law; or
>
> (C) a site formerly used by the Department of Defense.

This statute also contains limitations similar to those in 10 U.S.C. § 3501 (formerly § 2306b). It is implemented in DFARS 217.171.

The Federal Acquisition Streamlining Act of 1994, Pub. L. No. 103-355, broadened the statutory coverage of multi-year contracting. First, it moved the provision on multi-year contracting for *supplies* in 10 U.S.C. § 2306(h) to 10 U.S.C. § 2306b (now 10 U.S.C. § 3501) and brought the NASA and the Coast Guard within its coverage. In so doing, Congress imposed some of the restrictive provisions in the prior statute on these two agencies and continued to impose some special requirements on the DoD. This statute also stated that it was inapplicable to contracts under 40 U.S.C. § 759 for information resource management supplies, 10 U.S.C. § 2306b(k). This provision was deleted from the Act in 1996, Pub. L. No. 104-106, but 40 U.S.C. § 759 still provides special rules for those types of procurements. See FAR 17.102. Second, the Act added a new multi-year statute for both *supplies and services* procured by civilian agencies, 41 U.S.C.

§ 3903. This is a short statute that permits the use of multi-year contracts with any type of funds (annual, multi-year, or no-year) with fewer congressional restrictions. This statute is implemented in FAR Subpart 17.1.

These new statutes giving authority to use multi-year contracts without regard to the type of funds provide legal authority to use multiyear contracts with annual funds. The FAR is now silent on this issue.

When the FAR was issued in 1984, FAR 17.102-1 reflected the fact that multi-year contracting could be used on both supply and service contracts containing multi-year or no-year funds without statutory authority by stating:

> (a) Multiyear contracting may be used when no-year or multiyear funds are available or, in the case of 1-year funds, when multiyear contracting is specifically authorized by statute. (Specific statutory authority is needed for an agency to make financial commitments for amounts greater than those appropriated annually by the Congress. See 31 U.S.C. § 1341(a)(1).)
>
> (b) The multiyear contracting method may be used for the acquisition of services or supplies (including, but not limited to systems, subsystems, major equipment, components, parts, materials, supplies, and the advance acquisition thereof, and commercial and noncommercial items).

The perceived necessity of statutory authority for multi-year contracting using annual ("1-year") funds was based on the fear that such contracting would be construed as a procurement of more than the bona fide needs of the government for the single year for which the funds were appropriated, in violation of 31 U.S.C. § 1341, 43 Comp. Gen. 657 (B-152766) (1964). See also *Defense Logistics Agency Multiyear Contract for Storage & Rotation of Sulfadiazine Silver Cream*, 67 Comp. Gen. 190 (B-224081) (1987), and 42 Comp. Gen. 272 (B-144641) (1962), discussing this issue. In *Dep't of Health & Human Services—Multiyear Contracting and the Bona Fide Needs Rule*, Comp. Gen. Dec. B-322455, 2013 U.S. Comp. Gen. LEXIS 162, GAO made it clear that 41 U.S.C. § 3903 is a statutory exception to the bona fide needs rule which allows the obligation of current funds to cover an up to five-year multi-year period for both severable and non-severable services. In *Army's Multiple Launch Rocket Sys. Multiyear Contract*, 64 Comp. Gen. 163 (B-215825) (1984), GAO implied that the bona fide needs rule, 31 U.S.C. § 1502, also precludes multi-year contracts using multiyear funds without explaining the reasoning.

[2] Use

The statutes give agencies considerable discretion in deciding whether to use a multi-year contract or a multiple year contract, *Prisoner Transp. Servs., LLC*, Comp. Gen. Dec. B-292179, 2003 CPD ¶ 121. However, a multi-year contract can only be used when specified criteria are met. Different criteria are contained in 10 U.S.C. § 3501(a) (formerly § 2306b(a)), 41 U.S.C. § 3903, and

10 U.S.C. § 3531(a) (formerly § 2306c(a)). FAR 17.105-1 states these criteria for the first two statutes as follows:

> (a) Except for DoD, NASA and the Coast Guard, the contracting officer may enter into a multi-year contract if the head of the contracting activity determines that—
>
> (1) The need for the supplies or services is reasonably firm and continuing over the period of the contract; and
>
> (2) A multi-year contract will serve the best interests of the United States by encouraging full and open competition or promoting economy in administration, performance, an operation of the agency's programs.
>
> (b) For DoD, NASA, and the Coast Guard, the head of the agency may enter into a multi-year contract for supplies if—
>
> (1) The use of such a contract will result in significant savings of the total estimated costs of carrying out the program through annual contracts;
>
> (2) The minimum need to be purchased is expected to remain substantially unchanged during the contemplated contract period in terms of production rate, procurement rate, and total quantities;
>
> (3) There is a stable design for the supplies to be acquired, and the technical risks associated with such supplies are not excessive;
>
> (4) There is a reasonable expectation that, throughout the contemplated contract period, the head of the agency will request funding for the contract at a level to avoid contract cancellation; and
>
> (5) The estimates of both the cost of the contract and the cost avoidance through the use of a multi-year contract are realistic.

The guidance in ¶ (b) applies only to contracts for supplies—implementing 10 U.S.C. § 3501 (formerly § 2306b). The FAR contains no guidance on the criteria applicable to the separate statute for services, 10 U.S.C. § 3531 (formerly § 2306c). However, DFARS 217.171(a) contains the following guidance:

> (3) Before entering into a multiyear contract for services, the head of the agency must make a written determination that—
>
> (i) There will be a continuing requirement for the services consistent with current plans for the proposed contract period;
>
> (ii) Furnishing the services will require—
>
> (A) A substantial initial investment in plant or equipment; or
>
> (B) The incurrence of substantial contingent liabilities for the assembly, training or transportation of a specialized work force; and
>
> (iii) Using a multiyear contract will promote the best interests of the United States by encouraging effective competition and promoting economies in operations.

The FAR provisions reflect the fact that the civilian agency statute imposes very few limitations on use of multi-year contracts. For example, it contains no requirement for an estimate of savings in order to justify the use of a multiyear contract, whereas the statute applying to DoD, NASA, and the Coast Guard requires "significant" savings. Under the prior statute, GAO stated that savings should be "significant," but no fixed standard was adopted. In deciding whether projected savings were significant enough to justify multi-year procurement, cost savings were balanced against added risks. See GAO Report, GAO/NSIAD-86-1, Nov. 1985, stating at 6:

> Each proposed multiyear contract should be evaluated on its own merits, weighing the margin of savings against added risks and any other uncertainties. The savings should be high enough to offset any additional risks of entering into a multiyear contract. For example, a candidate with no risks in terms of requirement, funding, or design stability, and in which a high degree of confidence in the cost estimate does exist, may provide only a small percentage or amount of savings. If the savings are essentially ensured, they may be judged substantial enough to take advantage of them. In contrast, a candidate with high projected savings may be inappropriate for multiyear contracting if the design, funding, and/or requirement is unstable or if the cost estimate is not based on sound information and logic.

Accordingly, savings should be assessed in relation to the risk or absence of risk which is reflected in (1) the confidence in the cost estimate, (2) requirement stability, (3) funding stability, and (4) configuration or design stability.

Congress has been less than clear in enunciating the required degree of cost savings for multi-year procurement of weapons systems. The 1986 DoD Authorization Act, Pub. L. No. 99-145, declared that multi-year contracts authorized for the Army "may not be entered into unless the total anticipated cost over the period of the contract is no more than 90 percent of the total anticipated cost of carrying out the same program through annual contracts," 99 Stat. 591. The Act simultaneously authorized the Army to enter into multi-year contracts for both Bradley fighting vehicle transmissions and M1A1 tank chassis for which the estimated contract cost savings were 8.9% and 9.5% respectively, GAO Report, GAO/NSIAD-86-1, Nov. 1985. The 1986 Authorization Act contained no parallel provision for minimum cost savings for Navy multi-year contracts, 99 Stat. 594. The Act did, however, bar the use of multi-year contracting for the procurement of P-3C aircraft following GAO's report that "savings are relatively small at 5.5 percent and there is a risk that cost estimates are not sound," GAO Report, GAO/NSIAD-86-1, Nov. 1985. Both the DoD and GAO discount to present value when projecting cost savings for multi-year candidates, though different interest rates are applied in calculating present value, GAO Report, GAO/NSIAD-90-270BR, Aug. 1990, at 8.

In some cases, the savings associated with multi-year procurement are achieved by entering into multi-year subcontracts under multi-year contracts.

See discussion of "Source of Savings" in GAO Reports, GAO/NSIAD-86-1, Nov. 1985, at 13; and GAO/NSIAD-88-125, May 1988, at 42. FAR 17.106-3 encourages the use of multi-year subcontracts by contractors of DoD, NASA and the Coast Guard in order to "broaden the defense industrial base, to the maximum extent practicable."

Two of the criteria for the use of multi-year procurement deal with program stability in the areas of the government requirement and the design. Program stability has been considered to be a necessary element of multi-year procurement because significant changes during contract performance jeopardize the projected savings. Both GAO Analysis of Multiyear Candidates and the DoD Appropriations Acts have stressed that multi-year contracting should be used only for systems with stable designs. The GAO report stated that implementation of multi-year procurement should not occur until successful R&D, operational tests and evaluation, and one or two production runs have been completed. See also *Multiyear Procurement Authority for the Virginia Class Submarine Program*, GAO-03-895R, June 23, 2003, and *F/A-18E/F Aircraft Does Not Meet All Criteria for Multiyear Procurement*, GAO/NSIAD-00-158, May 2000, questioning the stability of design of weapon systems proposed for multi-year contracts. A contractor, however, has no legal right to a stable design when it enters into a multi-year contract, *Gould, Inc. v. United States*, 66 Fed. Cl. 253 (2005) (contractors not intended beneficiaries under multi-year contract statute).

The final criterion listed in FAR 17.105-1(b)(5) for the use of multi-year contracts by DoD, NASA and the Coast Guard is a measure of confidence in estimates of costs and savings. The report on 1986 Multiyear Candidates, GAO/NSIAD-86-1, stated:

> Confidence in the cost estimates may be increased by receiving firm proposals . . . on an annual and multiyear basis, and then comparing and analyzing these proposals. . . . However, this is not always practical, and DoD officials stated that the additional administrative effort and the cost to negotiate both proposals must be considered.

Cost-savings estimates are usually based on prior history, information received informally from contractors, or in-house estimates by the procuring activity, GAO Report, GAO/NSIAD-85-9, Oct. 1984, Appendix II at 5.

The use of multi-year contracts is further limited by restricting their term to a maximum of five years, absent specific statutory authority, 10 U.S.C. § 3501(k) (formerly § 2306b(k)); 41 U.S.C. § 3903(a); FAR 17.104(a). Because of the five-year limitation on multi-year contracting, the exercise of an option for advance procurement of economic order quantities to be ordered in the sixth or seventh program year has been held to be unauthorized, *Multiple Launch Rocket Sys. Multiyear Contract*, 64 Comp. Gen. 163 (B-215825) (1984). Compare *Freightliner Corp.*, ASBCA 42982, 94-1 BCA ¶ 26,538, where the board held that an option in the fifth year of a multi-year contract could be used to require the contractor to furnish items that were included in the agency's sixth budget year. Similarly, when the multi-year services statute allowed options in additional years (since repealed), options for additional services in program years six through eight were treated as proper options in *Cessna Aircraft Co.*, ASBCA 43196, 93-3 BCA ¶ 25,912.

The statutes also contain monetary restrictions on the use of multiyear contracts. 10 U.S.C. § 3501(g) (formerly § 2306b(g)) and 10 U.S.C. § 3531(g) (formerly § 2306c(d)(4)) require notification and a 30-day waiting period before award of a multi-year contract for supplies or services with a cancellation ceiling over $100 million. The civilian agency statute, 41 U.S.C. § 3903(d), contains a similar notice and waiting period requirement for any supply or service contract with a cancellation ceiling over $10 million. FAR 17.108 has adjusted these amounts for inflation to be $150 million and $15 million respectively.

GAO has upheld the use of multiple award schedule (MAS) multi-year agreements because, unlike multi-year contracts, the MAS agreement does not obligate the government to purchase the items on the schedule, *GSA—Multiple Award Schedule Multiyear Contracting*, 63 Comp. Gen. 129 (B-199079), 84-1 CPD ¶ 46. Thus, even though funds for the purchase of MAS agreement items are generally one-year appropriations, there is no violation of the Anti-Deficiency Act since each agency must make a specific determination that funds are available before issuing an order under the schedule contract.

[3] Procurement Technique

The multi-year contract is probably the most complex contract used by the government. This requires that the solicitation be carefully structured to ensure that the parties fully understand their respective rights and obligations.

[a] Sharing the Risk

In the past, almost all multi-year supply contracts have been written on a fixed-price basis. Multi-year service contracts have been written using a variety of types of pricing arrangements, including cost-reimbursement contracts. When fixed-price contracts are used, the contractor can be expected to incur costs in the first year of performance to reduce the overall contract costs but to allocate some or all of these costs to the full contract period. This means that if the contract is not carried to its full term, the contractor will have not recovered such "nonrecurring costs," defined in FAR 17.103 as follows:

> "Nonrecurring costs" means those costs which are generally incurred on a one-time basis and include such costs as plant or equipment relocation, plant rearrangement, special tooling and special test equipment, preproduction engineering, initial spoilage and rework, and specialized work force training.

See also FAR 17.106-1(c)(2), which describes nonrecurring costs to include:

> initial rework, . . . pilot runs, allocable portions of the costs of facilities to be acquired or established for the conduct of the work, costs incurred for the assembly training and transportation to and from the job site of a specialized work force, and unrealized labor learning.

This risk of nonrecovery is mitigated by the inclusion in the multi-year contract of a Cancellation Under Multiyear Contracts clause in FAR 52.217-2 which promises the contractor reimbursement, up to a cancellation ceiling, for enumerated costs if the government does not order the full quantities called for by the contract. This provision is the major distinguishing feature of the multi-year contract and is discussed in full below.

Also inherent in fixed-price multi-year contracts is the risk of changes in the cost of materials and labor over the extended period of contract performance. To mitigate this risk, FAR 17.106-1(b) suggests the use of economic price adjustment clauses. FAR 17.109(b) contains the following guidance on the clauses to be used:

> *Economic price adjustment clauses.* Economic price adjustment clauses are adaptable to multiyear contracting needs. When the period of production is likely to warrant a labor and material costs contingency in the contract price, the contracting officer should normally use an economic price adjustment clause (see 16.203). When contracting for services, the contracting officer—
>
> (1) Shall add the clause at FAR 52.222-43, Fair Labor Standards Act and Service Contract Act-Price Adjustment (Multiple Year and Option Contracts), when the contract includes the clause at FAR 52.222-41, Service Contract Labor Standards;
>
> (2) May modify the clause at FAR 52.222-43 in overseas contracts when laws, regulations, or international agreements require contractors to pay higher wage rates; or
>
> (3) May use an economic price adjustment clause authorized by FAR 16.203, when potential fluctuations require coverage and are not included in cost contingencies provided for by the clause at FAR 52.222-43.

In selecting the clause to be used in service contracts, the issue is whether the work includes a significant amount of material and whether the contractor is willing to take the risk that its labor rates will fluctuate at the same rates of fluctuation as the prevailing wages determined by the Department of Labor. The clause at FAR 52.222-43 only includes such fluctuations in prevailing wages, whereas an economic price adjustment clause can use indexes or other measures of wage fluctuation and can also include fluctuations in material prices.

The use of an economic price adjustment clause is at the contracting officer's discretion. Thus, GAO rejected a protest that the contracting officer was arbitrary in not including such a clause in a solicitation, *Kings Point Mfg. Co.*, Comp. Gen. Dec. B-220224, 85-2 CPD ¶ 680.

[b] Ensuring Government Flexibility

Although multi-year contracts are generally not used unless there is a reasonable belief that the requirements for the multi-year period will remain in effect, there is always a significant risk that program requirements will change. Reduced requirements can be implemented by use of the Termination for the Convenience of the Government clause, as discussed below. Increased requirements are frequently dealt with by the inclusion of options for additional quantities in the contract. See FAR 17.107, which states:

> Benefits may accrue by including options in a multi-year contract. In that event, contracting officers must follow both the requirements of subpart 17.2. Options should not include charges for plant and equipment already amortized, or other nonrecurring charges which were included in the basic contract.

This guidance is to ensure that the contractor does not obtain double recovery for nonrecurring costs that have already been fully included in the base prices and would be paid in cancellation charges if all of the base quantities were not ordered. Inclusion of option quantities is a discretionary decision of the contracting officer, *Kings Point Mfg. Co.*, Comp. Gen. Dec. B-220224, 85-2 CPD ¶ 680.

Options are generally included for each year of the multi-year contract. However, the fact that they are identified as an option for a designated year does not preclude the government from using an option for one year to buy quantities needed to meet the requirements of the next year, *Freightliner Corp.*, ASBCA 42982, 94-1 BCA ¶ 26,538. In that case, the board ruled that a fifth-year option could be used to buy products needed to meet the sixth year's requirements. This imposes some pricing risk on the contractor since the price of the subsequent year may be higher due to costs increases during that year. See also *Freightliner Corp.*, ASBCA 42982, 98-2 BCA ¶ 30,026, holding that fifth-year options were not limited to products that could be manufactured within the completion date of the contract. Similarly, in *Cessna Aircraft Co.*, ASBCA 43196, 93-3 BCA ¶ 25,912, the board held that the government could properly exercise an option for three additional years of services at the end of a five-year multi-year contract even though the funds for the second and third years had not been appropriated. The board reasoned that, in accordance with the legislative history of 10 U.S.C. § 2306(g) (now § 3501), this was *renewing* the multi-year contract for three years, not ordering the work for three years.

Options in multi-year contracts would normally not be evaluated as part of the initial award. Thus, the solicitation should include the Evaluation Exclusive of Options clause in FAR 52.217-3. In one unique instance the government evaluated the options and included a complex repricing clause in the contract to allow higher prices if all of the options were not exercised, *ITT Def. Commc'ns Div.*, ASBCA 44791, 98-1 BCA ¶ 29,590. When many of the option quantities were not ordered, the board resolved a dispute on the correct interpretation of the repricing clause in the contractor's favor and remanded the case to the parties to negotiate the price adjustment.

[c] Competition Requirements

Multi-year contracting may be accomplished on a competitive or noncompetitive basis, and competition may be obtained through sealed bidding, two-step sealed bidding, or negotiation, FAR 17.106-1(a). However, as in the case of any other type of procurement, the use of noncompetitive procurement must be justified. Thus, where competitive procurement would have been feasible in two to three years, a protest of a noncompetitive award of a five-year contract for telephone services was sustained, *Rolm Intermountain Corp.*, Comp. Gen. Dec. B-206327.4, 82-2 CPD ¶ 564. Similarly, in *Lear Siegler Inc.*, Comp. Gen. Dec. B-209524, 83-2 CPD ¶ 285, the fact that a limited initial quantity of F-16 fuel tanks was urgently needed and could only be obtained from a particular contractor did not justify the award of a multi-year contract for more items than were urgently needed at the time of the award. See also *Command, Control & Commc'ns Corp.*, Comp. Gen. Dec. B-210100, 83-2 CPD ¶ 448.

After submission of proposals, if a contracting officer finds that more competition is available on a multi-year procurement, it is proper to cancel the procurement and resolicit, *JRW Mgmt. Co.*, Comp. Gen. Dec. B-260396.2, 95-1 CPD ¶ 276; *Maytag Aircraft Corp.*, Comp. Gen. Dec. B-250628, 93-1 CPD ¶ 93. On reconsideration of the *Maytag* case, GAO rejected the protester's contention that the proper course of action was to have contracted for the single year's quantity and recompeted for the future years, Comp. Gen. Dec. B-250628.2, 93-1 CPD ¶ 456.

[d] Evaluation of Offers

On multi-year contracts the government solicits offers on a single-year basis as well as on a multi-year basis in order to ensure that it will obtain lower prices by buying on a multi-year basis. Administrative costs of buying annually can be included in this evaluation if they are included in the solicitation. If multi-year unit prices are not lower than single-year prices, award for a single year could be anticipated. FAR 17.106-2 provides the following general guidance on the solicitation provisions alerting offerors to these procedures:

> Solicitations for multi-year contracts shall reflect all the factors to be considered for evaluation, specifically including the following:

(a) The requirements, by item of supply or service, for the—

(1) First program year; and

(2) Multi-year contract including the requirements for each program year.

(b) Criteria for comparing the lowest evaluated submission on the first program year requirements to the lowest evaluated submission on the multi-year requirements.

(c) A provision that if the Government determines before award that only the first program year requirements are needed, the Government's evaluation of the price or estimated cost and fee shall consider only the first year.

(d) A provision specifying a separate cancellation ceiling (on a percentage or dollar basis) and dates applicable to each program year subject to a cancellation (see 17.106-1 (c) and (d)).

(e) A statement that award will not be made on less than the first program year requirements.

(f) The Government's administrative costs of annual contracting may be used as a factor in the evaluation only if they can be reasonably established and are stated in the solicitation.

(g) The cancellation ceiling shall not be an evaluation factor.

FAR 17.106-3 permits the DoD, NASA, and the Coast Guard to solicit only multi-year prices, as follows:

(f) *Annual and multi-year proposals*. Obtaining both annual and multi-year offers provides reduced lead time for making an annual award in the event that the multi-year award is not in the Government's interest. Obtaining both also provides a basis for the computation of savings and other benefits. However, the preparation and evaluation of dual offers may increase administrative costs and workload for both offerors and the Government, especially for large or complex acquisitions. The head of a contracting activity may authorize the use of a solicitation requesting only multi-year prices, provided it is found that such a solicitation is in the Government's interest, and that dual proposals are not necessary to meet the objectives in 17.105-2.

When the government selects the contractor by comparing multi-year unit prices with single-year unit prices, it has no assurance that buying single-year quantities will actually be cheaper even when the single-year price is lowest because it cannot prevent yearly price increases when buying one year at a time. Nevertheless, this evaluation procedure has been approved by GAO, *Mil-Tech Sys., Inc.*, Comp. Gen. Dec. B-212385.4, 84-1 CPD ¶632. GAO has also rejected a protest that it was irrational to evaluate the first year against a five-year price without including an inflation factor for future years if the award is made for only the single year, *Engineered Air Sys., Inc.*, Comp. Gen. Dec. B-220392.4, 86-2 CPD ¶43. In one case, the low offeror on the first-year quantity challenged the right of the government to award the contract to the low offeror on the multi-year (three-year) quantity on the grounds that to do so would be the same as evaluating option quantities. GAO held that multi-year quantities were not like options in that they did not create the same degree of uncertainty since the government was binding itself to buy the second and third-year quantities if funds were available, 43 Comp. Gen. 215 (B-152286) (1963). In another case, a disappointed offeror argued that the decision to use the multi-year alternative, based on the price comparison, was improper since some of the offerors had deliberately overpriced their single-year bids, 46 Comp. Gen. 749 (B-160815) (1967). In denying the protest, GAO noted that offerors were not precluded from submitting noncompetitive prices on the single-year part of a solicitation to ensure that they did not receive a single-year award. That decision also held that in this case, the multi-year offers were, in fact, competitive. In another case, GAO held that it was proper for a contracting officer to award on a single-year basis since the IFB permitted the government to select either the multi-year or single-year offer, *VBM Corp.*, Comp. Gen. Dec. B-182225, 75-1 CPD ¶ 130.

The evaluation process becomes even more involved if the multi-year contract is also a small business or labor-surplus area set-aside, or involves application of the Buy American Act. See 45 Comp. Gen. 735 (B-158525) (1966).

[4] Level Pricing Requirement

In the early use of multi-year contracting, the DoD adopted a policy of requiring that unit prices be the same for all program years in order to eliminate the evaluation difficulties created by unbalanced bidding, as discussed in Chapters 5 and 6. When the FAR was adopted in 1984, this requirement was included in FAR 17.103-2(e). It has been deleted from the general guidance in the FAR implementing the FASA but is discussed as follows in the special procedures applicable to the DoD, NASA, and the Coast Guard in FAR 17.106-3:

> (g) *Level unit prices.* Multi-year contract procedures provide for the amortization of certain costs over the entire contract quantity resulting in identical (level) unit prices (except when the economic price adjustment terms apply) for all items or services under the multi-year contract. If level unit pricing is not in the Government's interest, the head of a contracting activity may approve the use of variable unit prices, provided that for competitive proposals there is a valid method of evaluation.

Thus, all agencies appear to have discretion to require level unit pricing or to permit offerors to propose variable unit prices for the program years covered by the procurement. The major advantage of requiring level pricing is that it greatly simplifies the evaluation of offers by eliminating the possibility of unbalancing the prices between the program years.

There are several disadvantages to level pricing. The most serious is that a contractor must incur higher financing costs on such multi-year contracts because it cannot invoice for the high costs in early years, such as starting and learning costs, which must be spread over the entire quantity of supplies or services covered in the procurement. This may be counterbalanced by the fact that high costs of later years, such as the estimated costs of inflation in labor rates and material prices, would also be spread over the prices of all years. However, the government generally avoids this by using economic price adjustment provisions, FAR 17.109(b). Another disadvantage is that level pricing forces a large amount of costs into the cancellation cost pool, which can lead to difficulties in establishing the cancellation ceiling, as discussed below.

Under the prior mandatory level pricing requirement, contracting officers were permitted to waive the requirement where there was no prejudice to other offerors. In *Keco Indus., Inc.*, 54 Comp. Gen. 967 (B-183114), 75-1 CPD ¶ 301, variable prices were permitted in a case where the IFB contained no warning to offerors that failure to comply with the level pricing requirement would result in a nonresponsive bid. In *International Harvester Co.*, Comp. Gen. Dec. B-212341, 83-2 CPD ¶ 313, variable prices were permitted in a procurement where the IFB contained an explicit warning. See also *InterTrade Indus., Ltd.*, Comp. Gen. Dec. B-225702, 87-1 CPD ¶ 567; and *Everett Dykes Grassing Co.*, Comp. Gen. Dec. B-210223.4, 84-1 CPD ¶ 176.

Some difficulties have been encountered in determining whether the level pricing requirement applies to preproduction items. In one case where a bid was rejected because of higher prices for preproduction items, GAO ruled that the bid was responsive but that the procurement was ambiguous and should be canceled, Comp. Gen. Dec. B-169205, May 22, 1970, *Unpub.* Taking the case to the district court, the bidder obtained an order directing that it be awarded the contract, *A.G. Schoonmaker Co. v. Resor*, 319 F. Supp. 933 (D.D.C. 1970). This decision was reversed by the circuit court on the grounds that the procuring agency had not acted arbitrarily or capriciously in following the view of GAO that it should reject all bids and resolicit, *A.G. Schoonmaker Co. v. Resor*, 445 F.2d 726 (D.C. Cir. 1971). In *Keco Indus., Inc.*, 64 Comp. Gen. 48 (B-216396.2), 84-2 CPD ¶ 491, GAO ruled that the contracting officer properly waived a failure to level price a bid by submitting a lower price on two preproduction items, finding no prejudice to other bidders.

Options in multi-year contracts are not normally subject to the level pricing requirement because it is expected that they will exclude nonrecurring costs. See FAR 17.107, warning that option prices should not include "charges for plant and equipment already amortized, or other nonrecurring charges which were included in the basic contract." In *Keco Indus., Inc.*, 64 Comp. Gen. 48 (B-216396.2), 84-2 CPD ¶ 491, the IFB explicitly stated that although unit prices for base quantities in the multi-year procurement had to be level priced, varying prices could be offered for option quantities.

[5] Orders for Future Years

Since the multi-year contract is funded one year at a time, it should contain a provision establishing the procedure that will be used to order quantities of work subsequent to the first year and the limitations on the obligations of the parties. However, the FAR contains no such provision. Thus, contracting officers will have to include special provisions in each multi-year contract covering these issues. FAR 17.106-1 contains the following partial guidance:

> (g) *Payment limit*. The contracting officer shall limit the Government's payment obligation to an amount available for contract performance. The contracting officer shall insert the amount for the first program year in the contract upon award and modify it for successive program years upon availability of funds.
>
> (h) *Termination payment*. If the contract is terminated for the convenience of the Government in whole, including requirements subject to cancellation, the Government's obligation shall not exceed the amount specified in the Schedule as available for contract performance, plus the cancellation ceiling.

The prior FAR contained a Limitation of Price and Contractor Obligations clause in FAR 52.217-1 for use in this type of contract. This clause made it clear that the government was making no legal obligation for quantities not covered by firm contractual orders. It also required the contracting officer to notify the contractor, in writing, when additional funds became available for the full requirements of the next succeeding program year. Conversely, this clause provided that the contractor was only obligated to honor the contract as to future-year quantities if the government gave written notification by the contractually specified date. The Court of Claims held that the clause should be interpreted to require strict compliance, *International Tel. & Tel. v. United States*, 453 F.2d 1283 (Ct. Cl. 1972) (written order received several hours after stated cutoff date did not bind the contractor even though oral notice was given before the cutoff date). The same result obtains when the government exercises options for additional quantities, *Cessna Aircraft Co.*, ASBCA 43196, 96-1 BCA ¶ 27,966. There the board held that the option was validly exercised when the contractor received a facsimile on the last day permitted.

[6] Cancellation of Items

The major legal problems in multi-year procurements arise in formulating and administering the cancellation provisions of this type of contract.

[a] Costs Included in Ceiling

The initial use of multi-year contracts included only nonrecurring costs in the cancellation ceiling. The original DoD multi-year contracting statute, 10 U.S.C. § 2306(h)(2)(B), recognized the use of such cancellation provisions and also permitted the inclusion of recurring costs:

> [R]egulations may provide for cancellation provisions in such multiyear contracts to the extent that such provisions are necessary and in the best interests of the United States. Such cancellation provisions may include consideration of both recurring and nonrecurring costs of the contractor associated with the production of the items to be delivered under the contract.

Since there was no similar statute applicable to civilian agencies, there was some question as to whether they could include recurring costs in the ceiling. FAR 17.102-3(d)(3) (pre-1996) restricted the inclusion of recurring costs in cancellation ceilings by stating:

> The inclusion of recurring costs in cancellation ceilings is an exception to normal contract financing arrangements and requires approval by the agency head or a designee.

This provision permitted civilian agencies to include recurring costs in ceilings if the proper approvals were obtained. However, the issue was largely resolved by including a very broad definition of "nonrecurring costs" in the standard Cancellation of Items clause of FAR 52.217-2 (which only provided for the recovery of nonrecurring costs). This confusing use of terminology has been continued under the current provisions of the statutes and FAR. 10 U.S.C. § 3501(c) (formerly § 2306b(c)) continues to permit recovery of "both recurring and nonrecurring costs," while 41 U.S.C. § 3903 is silent on the subject. The Cancellation under Multiyear Contracts clause in FAR 52.217-2 resolves this issue by giving detailed guidance on the costs that may be included in the cancellation claim. Paragraphs (f) and (g) of the clause state:

> (f) The Contractor's claim may include—
>
> (1) Reasonable nonrecurring costs (see Subpart 15.4 of the Federal Acquisition Regulation) which are applicable to and normally would have been amortized in all supplies or services which are multi-year requirements;
>
> (2) Allocable portions of the costs of facilities acquired or established for the conduct of the work, to the extent that it is impracticable for the Contractor to use the facilities in its commercial work, and if the costs are not charged to the contract through overhead or otherwise depreciated;
>
> (3) Costs incurred for the assembly, training, and transportation to and from the job site of a specialized work force; and

> (4) Costs not amortized solely because the cancellation had precluded anticipated benefits of Contractor or subcontractor learning.
>
> (g) The claim shall not include—
>
> (1) Labor, material, or other expenses incurred by the Contractor or subcontractors for performance of the canceled work;
>
> (2) Any cost already paid to the Contractor;
>
> (3) Anticipated profit or unearned fee on the canceled work; or
>
> (4) For service contracts, the remaining useful commercial life of facilities. Useful commercial life means the commercial utility of the facilities rather than their physical life with due consideration given to such factors as location of facilities, their specialized nature, and obsolescence.

In spite of this broad coverage, FAR 17.106-3 contains the following special procedure applicable to DoD, NASA, and the Coast Guard:

> (e) *Recurring costs in cancellation ceilings.* The inclusion of recurring costs in cancellation ceilings is an exception to normal contract financing arrangements and requires approval by the agency head.

The ASBCA has followed the principle that costs included in cancellation ceilings should be broadly construed. For example, in *Continental Elecs. Mfg. Co.*, ASBCA 14749, 71-2 BCA ¶ 9108, the board held that cancellation costs properly included (i) higher costs of early units (computed with the use of a learning curve), (ii) costs charged to a preproduction unit above the contract unit price, and (iii) engineering costs incurred and measured after cancellation. In dealing with this issue, the board took a broad view of the matter since the contractor was forced to bid the same price for all units and had no means of recovering uneven costs other than through the cancellation charge. See also *Bermite Div. of Tasker Indus.*, ASBCA 18280, 77-1 BCA ¶ 12,349, *modified on recons.*, 77-2 BCA ¶ 12,731.

[b] Computation of Ceiling

A separate cancellation ceiling is included in the contract for each program year after the first year, FAR 17.106-1(c)(1). Thus, the ceiling decreases in amount as each year's requirement is ordered. The cancellation ceiling is estimated by the contracting officer and included in the solicitation to be applicable to all competitors, FAR 17.106-2(d). It must be established based upon a reasonable estimate of nonrecurring costs (broadly defined) of an "average" contractor, FAR 17.106-1(c)(2). The regulations permit the contracting officer to adjust the cancellation ceiling prior to award "if necessary," FAR 17.106-1(d). In a sealed bid procurement, this would be done by amendment to the solicitation, while in a negotiated procurement, it could be done during the negotiation process. Such adjustment would appear to be mandatory since the Court of Claims reformed a cancellation ceiling that was not reasonable in *Applied Devices Corp. v. United States*, 591 F.2d 635 (Ct. Cl. 1979). The court concluded that the regulations calling for inclusion of a reasonable ceiling were for the benefit of potential contractors and increased the ceiling to a reasonable amount in spite of the fact that the contractor had not protested the inadequacy of the ceiling before bid opening. A similar adjustment to the cancellation ceiling was made in *Technical & Mgmt. Servs. Corp.*, ASBCA 39999, 93-2 BCA ¶ 25,681, *aff'd*, 16 F.3d 420 (Fed. Cir. 1993).

Because the purpose of the cancellation charge is normally to reimburse the contractor for unamortized costs in the event the contract is canceled, where no such costs are involved in the procurement there is no need to include a cancellation ceiling. See FAR 17.104(b), permitting agency heads to modify cancellation terms to fit the conditions of an individual procurement. In *Big Bud Tractors, Inc.*, Comp. Gen. Dec. B-209858, 83-1 CPD ¶ 127, GAO held that the Army's RFP for the multi-year procurement of a standard commercial unit of equipment was not defective despite the fact that it did not include a cancellation ceiling where there were no unamortized nonrecurring costs.

[c] Failure to Order Full Quantity

The Cancellation Under Multiyear Contracts clause provides that cancellation may occur when *funds are not available* for "contract performance for any subsequent program year." If the government does not order the full requirement for some other reason, a termination for convenience will have occurred and the contractor will be entitled to compensation without regard to the cancellation ceiling. However, in *Varo, Inc.*, ASBCA 13739, 70-1 BCA ¶ 8099, the board construed the "funds available" provision broadly, holding that the cancellation provisions of the contract applied not only when funds were not appropriated but also when the agency decided that it no longer had a requirement for the items. The board reached this conclusion by looking to the agency's records documenting the formulation of the multi-year contracting policy. This reasoning was subsequently adopted by the Court of Claims in *Applied Devices Corp. v. United States*, 591 F.2d 635 (Ct. Cl. 1979). The court held that the Cancellation of Items clause was properly used in a situation where the agency obtained the funds necessary for the procurement from Congress but decided, based on an analysis of agency needs, that the requirement should be met by procuring different equipment. The court reasoned that in such a case, the requirement no longer existed. The court further concluded that lack of funding included a lack of requirements, stating that it "is a fallacy to suppose that requirements and funds availability exist in two separate universes of discourse." This questionable reasoning deprives the contractor of the benefits of the Termination for the Convenience of the Government clause when the government agency makes an internal decision to alter its requirements.

Contractors have been given the protection of the Termination for the Convenience of the Government clause in other circumstances. Thus, when an agency ordered the items from another contractor, a termination for convenience was found, *Maxson Elecs. Corp.*, ASBCA 12983, 72-2 BCA ¶ 9543. This result might not occur under the current clause because it also includes in the definition of "cancellation" the situation where the contracting officer "fails to notify the Contractor that funds are available for performance of the succeeding program year requirement."

A termination for convenience will also be found if work is deleted during a program year. See FAR 17.104(d), stating:

> The termination for convenience procedure may apply to any Government contract, including multiyear contracts. As contrasted with cancellation, termination can be effected at any time during the life of the contract (cancellation is effected between fiscal years) and can be for the total quantity or a partial quantity (whereas cancellation must be for all subsequent fiscal years' quantities).

See *Aeronca, Inc.*, ASBCA 13040, 70-1 BCA ¶ 8278, where the board held that a partial termination for convenience had occurred when the government funded only some of the items in the second and third program years. Similarly, the ceiling was held not to apply to a future year when the government did not completely order all prior years' quantities. In *Condec Corp.*, ASBCA 14234, 73-1 BCA ¶ 9808, the government issued a notice of convenience termination during the second year and argued that the contract price for purposes of computing the termination costs was the price for two years' quantity (with the third-year quantity being subject to the cancellation ceiling). The board disagreed, holding that the government had not proved that there was no requirement for the third year's quantity and that its action therefore constituted a termination of the total multi-year quantity. It has been suggested that this holding obligates the government agency with reduced requirements to order those requirements under the multi-year contract and to reprice as if there had been a partial termination of the year's quantity, Latham, *Multi-Year Procurement*, Federal Publications Briefing Paper 73-2 (1973).

[d] Legal Validity of Cancellation Provisions

Under normal appropriations law, agencies would be required to obligate current-year funds to cover cancellation costs within the contractual ceiling. However, 10 U.S.C. § 3501(c) (formerly § 2306b(f)) provides:

> In the event funds are not made available for the continuation of a contract made under this subsection into a subsequent fiscal year, the contract shall be canceled or terminated. The costs of cancellation or termination may be paid from—

(A) appropriations originally available for the performance of the contract concerned;

(B) appropriations currently available for procurement of the type of property concerned, and not otherwise obligated; or

(C) funds appropriated for those payments.

See also 10 U.S.C. § 3531(c) (formerly § 2306c(e)), which includes substantially the same language applying to service contracts.

These provisions were apparently written to permit DoD, NASA and the Coast Guard to incur the legal liability for paying cancellation costs without obligating funds to cover that liability. However, it appears that the statutory language was written omitting any reference to a firm obligation of the government covering cancellation costs in order to avoid any implication that Congress was granting "contract authority" pursuant to the Anti-Deficiency Act. This was in recognition that 31 U.S.C. § 1341 precludes the creation of contract authority for procurement. See House Report 97-311, the Conference Committee Report on the 1982 Defense Authorization Act (including this language in the provision giving multi-year contracting authority for major systems), stating at 126:

> The provisions agreed to by the conferees limit the authority to enter into multiyear contracts to cases where "funds are otherwise available for obligation." This language was adopted to make clear that the provision does not, by itself, provide contract authority. Rather the authority to enter into contracts is provided subject to funds being available for obligation through other actions of the Congress or other provisions of law. In adopting this language, the conferees did not intend to restrict the authority to enter into multiyear contracts solely to those cases where funds are appropriated for that purpose. On the contrary, the conferees envision that funds could be available for obligation for a multiyear contract from, for example, annually made appropriations, including funds made available through reprogramming or transfer; proceeds from sales of goods and services which under current provision of law would be available for obligation; and funds available for obligation in connection with foreign military sales.

In spite of this confusing situation, which seems to require agencies to violate the Anti-Deficiency Act, funds have not been obligated by the military services to cover cancellation ceilings. See DoD Authorization Act, 1985, Pub. L. No. 98-525, 98 Stat. 2492, directing this course of action at 2498:

> [Multiyear] contracts may include an unfunded cancellation ceiling. If funds are not made available for the continuation of such a contract in subsequent fiscal years, the contract shall be cancelled and the costs of cancellation shall be paid as provided in section 2306(h)(5) of title 10, United States Code.

Since 41 U.S.C. § 3903 contains no language similar to 10 U.S.C. § 3501(f) (formerly § 2306b(f)), it would appear that civilian agencies are required to obligate funds to cover cancellation ceilings or termination costs. See 41 U.S.C. § 3903(c), stating:

> Termination Clause—A multiyear contract entered into under the authority of this section shall include a clause that provides that the contract shall be terminated if funds are not made available for the continuation of such contract in a fiscal year covered by the contract. Funds available for paying termination costs shall remain available for that purpose until the costs associated with termination of the contract are paid.

See *Bureau of Customs and Border Protection—Automated Commercial Env't Contract*, Comp. Gen. Dec. B-302358, 2004 U.S. Comp. Gen. LEXIS 271, holding that since a multiple-year IDIQ contract was not a multi-year contract, the agency was not required to obligate funds to cover termination costs if later years' work was not procured.

FAR 17.104(c) appears to ignore the legislative history of the DoD statutes. It requires that funds covering cancellation costs be obligated at the time of contracting, as follows:

> Agency funding of multi-year contracts shall conform to the policies in OMB Circulars A-11 (Preparation and Submission of Budget Estimates) and A-34 (Instructions on Budget Execution) and other applicable guidance regarding the funding of multi-ear contracts. As provided by that guidance, the funds obligated for multi-year contracts must be sufficient to cover any potential cancellation and/or termination costs; and multi-year contracts for the acquisition of fixed assets should be fully funded or funded in stages that are economically or programmatically viable.

[7] Distinguishing Requirements Contracts

Requirements contracts are used to procure supplies or services where precise quantities are not fully known. They may be entered into for several years without following the procedures prescribed for multi-year contracts, *Mills Mfg. Corp.*, Comp. Gen. Dec. B-224004, 86-2 CPD ¶ 679, *recons. denied*, 87-1 CPD ¶ 393. The fact that a requirements contract contemplates performance over a period of years will not transform it into a multi-year contract, *Solar Turbines Int'l v. United States*, 3 Cl. Ct. 489 (1983). In *Solar Turbines*, the government used a requirements contract containing a Cancellation Ceiling Cost clause entitling the contractor to increased compensation for shortfalls in actual orders. The contractor unsuccessfully argued that Best Estimated Quantities (BEQ) were actually firm orders for minimum quantities under a multi-year contract.

Prior to the enactment of the FASA, FAR 17.104-4 (pre-1996) set forth procedures for the multi-year acquisition of supplies and services under modified requirements contracts, to be used only when anticipated annual requirements could be projected with reasonable certainty. Anticipated requirements expressed as BEQ were set forth in the contract. Nonrecurring costs were to be amortized over the BEQ, FAR 17.104-4(a)(2). If actual orders fell short of the BEQ, the contractor was to be reimbursed in accordance with the Cancellation of Items clause. In *Viktoria Transport GmbH & Co., KG*, ASBCA 30371, 88-3 BCA ¶20,921, the board held that the contractor should recover under the Termination for Convenience clause instead of the Cancellation of Items clause because the government did not order all of its requirements from the contractor.

The current FAR is silent on these issues.

[D] Indefinite-Quantity Contracts

The indefinite-quantity contract is the other form of variable quantity, indefinite-delivery contract in FAR Subpart 16.5. This type of contract is commonly called an IDIQ contract. This type of contract is so widely used that it is dealt with separately in Chapter 7.

[1] Basic Features

In the IDIQ contract, the government obligates itself to buy at least a stated minimum quantity of the goods or services, and the contract will also state a maximum quantity beyond which the contractor is not bound, FAR 16.504(a)(1). This type of contract is very similar to a contract for a firm quantity with options for additional quantities, the major difference being that the IDIQ contract can be issued initially without any firm orders being placed as long as the government is obligated to order an adequate minimum quantity. Government-wide acquisition contracts, discussed in Chapter 11, fall under the rules governing IDIQ contracts, *Chasmeleon Integrated Servs., Inc. v. United States*, 111 Fed. Cl. 564 (2013) (rejecting the contention that these rules do not apply when an agency issues hundreds of contracts).

[2] Distinguishing Requirements Contracts

There have been a number of disputes as to whether a contract is a requirements contract or an IDIQ contract. In such cases, the courts and boards have carefully analyzed the contract language to determine the type of contract intended. In *Goldwasser v. United States*, 325 F.2d 722 (Ct. Cl. 1963), the court resolved a conflict between the Indefinite Quantity clause and the specifications listing the items to be procured by concluding that the latter showed an intent to create a requirements contract. In contrast, in *Mason v. United States*, 615 F.2d 1343 (Ct. Cl. 1980), the court found that the stated minimum quantity in the contract indicated that the parties had entered into an IDIQ contract because otherwise that clause was superfluous. In *Maintenance Eng'rs v. United States*, 749 F.2d 724 (Fed. Cir. 1984), a conflict between a term in the solicitation identifying the contract as one for an indefinite quantity and a term in the General Provisions stating "this is a requirements contract" was resolved by the Order of Precedence clause giving priority to the solicitation language. In *Stanley F. Horton*, DOTCAB 1231, 82-2 BCA ¶ 15,967, the board considered both course of dealing and the knowledge of the parties at the time of contract formation and found that the contract was a requirements contract despite the absence of an explicit term barring the government from obtaining snow removal services elsewhere. In contrast, in *Ann Riley & Assocs.*, DOTBCA 2418, 93-3 BCA ¶ 25,963, the board found an IDIQ contract based on the contract language even though the government argued that it intended to create a requirements contract. Where course of dealing or other circumstances do not imply a requirements contract, the absence of a government obligation to satisfy all needs under the contract will render the contract an IDIQ contract, *Hemet Valley Flying Serv. Co. v. United States*, 7 Cl. Ct. 512 (1985). In *Hemet Valley*, the court was able to find a binding IDIQ contract despite the fact that no stated minimum quantity of flying hours was promised because the government paid a non-nominal amount for contractor's promise to maintain "availability" to fly. In *Export Packing & Crating Co.*, ASBCA 16133, 73-2 BCA ¶ 10,066, the board looked to the underlying contractual relationship to find a requirements contract and stated that there was no ambiguity despite clauses identifying the contract as both an IDIQ and requirements contract.

In *J. Cooper & Assocs., Inc. v. United States*, 53 Fed. Cl. 8 (2002), *aff'd*, 65 Fed. Appx 731 (Fed. Cir. 2003), the government issued a letter contract containing a minimum dollar amount of work and calling for the submission of a price proposal for an IDIQ contract. The court rejected the contractor's argument that when the letter contract was never converted to a firm contract, it became a requirement contract, holding that the correct interpretation of the transaction was that the parties intended to enter into an IDIQ contract.

In *Varilease Tech. Group, Inc. v. United States*, 289 F.3d 795 (Fed. Cir. 2002), the contractor argued that the options in its IDIQ contract were for all of the government's requirements because the only minimum quantity was for the base contract. The court rejected this argument holding that the clear language of the contract indicated that it was an IDIQ contract and there was "no basis in either the relevant regulations or case law for treating option periods of an IDIQ contract as separate contracts." See also *RJO Enter., Inc.*, ASBCA 50981, 03-1 BCA ¶ 32,137, where the board held that the contractor had no recourse when the government exercised its options for additional years' services on an IDIQ contract but stopped issuing orders after it had awarded a successor contract to another contractor.

Where a contract contains neither a guaranteed minimum quantity nor the Requirements clause in FAR 52.216-21, it will be held to be a requirements contract if it contains language leading to the interpretation that the government will not deal with other contractors in obtaining the work. See *Rowe, Inc. v. General Servs. Admin.*, GSBCA 15217, 03-1 BCA ¶ 32,162, *recons. denied*,

03-1 BCA ¶ 32,215 (requirements contract based on language stating agency would purchase quantities of vehicles needed "to fill any requirements determined in accordance with applicable procurement regulations and supply procedures."); and *Centurion Elecs. Serv.*, ASBCA 51956, 03-1 BCA ¶ 32,097 (requirements contract because it called for contractor to furnish "all per call repairs" of designated equipment). Compare *Coyle's Pest Control, Inc. v. Cuomo*, 154 F.3d 1302 (Fed. Cir. 1998), where the court found that such a contract was not a requirements contract because of conflicting language, stating at 1305-06:

> The contract does include terms that suggest exclusivity. For instance, the contract obligates Coyle "to furnish *all* labor, service, equipment, transportation, materials and supplies to provide subterranean termite control and related services on *assigned* properties by [HUD]." (emphasis added). While the contract states that Coyle will provide all labor and services for a given property, the clause does not require HUD to assign Coyle *all* properties in the region. Thus, this contract language falls short of the exclusivity language necessary for a requirements contract.

[E] Options

Another method of obtaining firm commitments from contractors to perform additional work is the inclusion of option clauses in contracts procuring the initial quantities. Options can be for additional quantities of work or for longer periods of performance. FAR 2.101 contains the following definition:

> "Option" means a unilateral right in a contract by which, for a specified time, the Government may elect to purchase additional supplies or services called for by the contract, or may elect to extend the term of the contract.

The major difference between options and requirements contracts or multi-year contracts is that the government makes *no binding commitment* when an option provision is used. Thus, the key characteristic of option clauses is that they give the government a unilateral right to order the additional quantities or services if that order is issued by a prescribed time. An option for additional quantities of work is very similar to an indefinite-quantity contract, but the obligation of the government is stated differently. Option clauses state that the government has the right to order specified additional quantities, while indefinite-quantity contracts state that the government has the right to purchase quantities within a specified range. It has been held that regulations pertaining to indefinite-quantity contracts are not applicable to options, *International Transducer Corp. v. United States*, 30 Fed. Cl. 522 (1994); *Schmid Labs., Inc.*, Comp. Gen. Dec. B-214333, 84-2 CPD ¶ 411.

There is no question that validly exercised options are binding on the contractor. Thus, refusal to perform an option is a proper grounds for default termination, *Specialty Transp., Inc. v. United States*, 57 Fed. Cl. 1 (2003).

Conversely, the contractor has no rights if the government fails to exercise an option, unless that failure "was a product of bad faith or so arbitrary and capricious as to be an abuse of discretion," *ALK Servs., Inc. v. Dep't of Veterans Affairs*, CBCA 1789, 13-1 BCA ¶ 354,260, and *Blackstone Consulting, Inc. v. General Servs. Admin.*, CBCA 718, 09-1 BCA ¶ 34,103, citing *Greenlee Constr., Inc. v. General Servs. Admin.*, CBCA 416, 07-1 BCA ¶ 33,514; *Nova Express*, PSBCA 5102, 08-1 BCA ¶ 33,763; and *IMS-Engineers-Architects, PC*, ASBCA 53471, 06-1 BCA ¶ 33,231, *aff'd*, 274 Fed. Appx. 898 (Fed. Cir. 2008). See also *Continental Collection & Disposal, Inc. v. United States*, 29 Fed. Cl. 644 (1993), apparently recognizing a bad faith exception to the rule giving contractors no rights to options, but finding that no bad faith was present in the situation at hand.

If circumstances change during a procurement that make it less likely that evaluated options will be exercised, the competitors must be informed of the change, *Northrop Grumman Information Tech., Inc.*, Comp. Gen. Dec. B-295526, 2005 CPD ¶ 45.

[1] Use

Options were used infrequently in the 1960s and 1970s and an effort was made by GAO in 1962 to strictly limit their use. See 41 Comp. Gen. 682 (B-148019) (1962), stating that option quantities should be limited to 25% of the contract quantity and should be exercisable no more than 90 days after award. However, as part of the acquisition streamlining efforts of the 1990s, options came into wide use in government procurement—primarily as a means of avoiding the need to issue new contracts each year for supplies and services. Thus, at the current time options for additional years' work are the norm in government procurement.

Because the government is not bound by options for additional quantities of supplies or services, there are no fiscal or legal impediments to their use. See Volume 1 of *Principles of Federal Appropriations Law*, January 2004, as updated in March 2015, stating at 5-41:

> If an agency is contracting with fiscal year appropriations and does not have multiyear contracting authority, one course of action, apart from a series of separate fiscal year contracts, is a fiscal year contract with renewal options, with each renewal option (1) contingent on the availability of future appropriations and (2) to be exercised only by affirmative action on the part of the government (as opposed to automatic renewal unless the government refuses). *Leiter v. United States*, 271 U.S. 204 (1926); 66 Comp. Gen. 556 (1987); 36 Comp. Gen. 683 (1957); 33 Comp. Gen. 90 (1953); 29 Comp. Gen. 91 (1949); 28 Comp. Gen. 553 (1949); B-88974, Nov. 10, 1949. The inclusion of a renewal option is key; with a renewal option, the government incurs a financial obligation only for the fiscal year, and incurs no financial obligation for subsequent years unless and until it exercises its right to renew. The

government records the amount of its obligation for the first fiscal year against the appropriation current at the time it awards the contract. The government also records amounts of obligations for future fiscal years against appropriations current at the time it exercises its renewal options.

FAR Subpart 17.2 prescribes general policies for the use of options, stating in FAR 17.200 that these regulations do not apply to contracts for construction, architect-engineer services, or R&D services; but that options may be used for such procurements. FAR 17.202 provides:

(a) Subject to the limitations of paragraphs (b) and (c) of this section, for both sealed bidding and contracting by negotiation, the contracting officer may include options in contracts when it is in the Government's interest. When using sealed bidding, the contracting officer shall make a written determination that there is a reasonable likelihood that the options will be exercised before including the provision at 52.217-5, Evaluation of Options, in the solicitation. (See 17.207(f) with regard to the exercise of options.)

(b) Inclusion of an option is normally not in the Government's interest when, in the judgment of the contracting officer—

(1) The foreseeable requirements involve—

(i) Minimum economic quantities (i.e., quantities large enough to permit the recovery of startup costs and the production of the required supplies at a reasonable price); and

(ii) Delivery requirements far enough into the future to permit competitive acquisition, production, and delivery.

(2) An indefinite quantity or requirements contract would be more appropriate than a contract with options. However, this does not preclude the use of an indefinite quantity contract or requirements contract with options.

(c) The contracting officer shall not employ options if—

(1) The contractor will incur undue risks; e.g., the price or availability of necessary materials or labor is not reasonably foreseeable;

(2) Market prices for the supplies or services involved are likely to change substantially; or

(3) The option represents known firm requirements for which funds are available unless—

(i) The basic quantity is a learning or testing quantity; and

(ii) Competition for the option is impracticable once the initial contract is awarded.

(d) In recognition of—

(1) The Government's need in certain service contracts for continuity of operations; and

> (2) The potential cost of disrupted support, options may be included in service contracts if there is an anticipated need for a similar service beyond the first contract period.

The regulations also provide that, unless approved in accordance with agency procedures, the total coverage of a contract with options, including the initial quantity and the option quantities, shall not exceed the requirements of the agency for five years, FAR 17.204(e). Information technology contracts are excluded from this requirement.

The guidance in FAR 17.202 is highly discretionary, with the result that there is little likelihood that offerors can successfully protest the use of options. See *Pool's Moving & Storage*, Comp. Gen. Dec. B-233563, 89-1 CPD ¶ 141, discounting contractor risks and stating:

> The regulations provide that contracting officers may include options in service contracts if there is an anticipated need for a similar service beyond the first contract period. Federal Acquisition Regulation (FAR) § 17.202(d); see *Key Air*, B-227893, Aug. 20, 1987, 87-2 CPD ¶ 188. Here, the agency made the requisite determination to include the option because it anticipated the need for services beyond the current year due to the constant relocation of military personnel at the base. We do not believe Pool's concern with unstable insurance and other operational costs is relevant to a determination to use an option in a service contract like the one involved here. The only requirement in the regulations is that the agency anticipate a need for similar services in the future. The agency did so, and protester does not dispute this. In any event, the risks cited by the protester appear to fall well within the normal type of risks associated with bidding; agencies are not obligated to eliminate these risks. See *Triple P Servs., Inc.*, B-220437.3, Apr. 3, 1986, 86-1 CPD ¶ 318.

A similar conclusion was arrived at in *Information Ventures, Inc.*, Comp. Gen. Dec. B-241441, 91-1 CPD ¶ 83; and *Canon U.S.A., Inc.*, Comp. Gen. Dec. B-232262, 88-2 CPD ¶ 538.

The most important limitation on the use of options is the provision in ¶ (b)(1)(ii) that they should not be used if adequate competition can be obtained when the future requirements are ascertained. Many agencies do not comply with this recommendation and there is no apparent means of inducing compliance. There were a few attempts by GAO to apply such a rule. See *Altron Iron Works, Inc.*, Comp. Gen. Dec. B-179212, 74-1 CPD ¶ 121, where GAO urged the procuring agency to go forward with a new procurement of standard commercial supplies rather than using option provisions. See also *Safemasters Co.*, 58 Comp. Gen. 255 (B-192941), 79-1 CPD ¶ 38, where options were found improper when realistic competition was available for subsequent procurements.

Another important limitation in ¶ (c)(3) is that options cannot be used to procure known requirements for which funds are available. In *East Wind Indus.*,

Inc., 58 Comp. Gen. 586 (B-193720), 79-1 CPD ¶ 404, GAO held that this provision precluded the testing of a currently available option by the addition of an option for the same quantity to a new procurement. GAO suggested that the proper technique was to test the option by advertising the entire new requirement as a fixed quantity.

Contractors have been unsuccessful in using ¶ (c)(1), precluding the use of options that impose undue risk on the contractor, as the basis for protests or claims. See *Madison Servs., Inc.*, Comp. Gen. Dec. B-278962, 98-1 CPD ¶ 113, holding that there was no imposition of undue risk in requiring offerors to propose variable options for from one to twelve months, and *LBM, Inc.*, 70 Comp. Gen. 493 (B-242664), 91-1 CPD ¶ 476, finding no undue risk in requiring fixed price bids for options for four years of maintenance and repair of family housing. See also *General Dynamics C4 Sys., Inc.*, ASBCA 54988, 08-1 BCA ¶ 33,779 (rejecting the argument that this provision should preclude the government from exercising an option knowing that it imposed risk on the contractor because the rule applied at the time of issuing the contract not at the time of option exercise); *Loral Fairchild Corp.*, ASBCA 45719, 97-1 BCA ¶ 28,905 (holding that technical, cost, and schedule risks were not the type of risks that precluded the use of option provisions). In *Team People, LLC*, Comp. Gen. Dec. B-414434, 2017 CPD ¶ 190, GAO rejected a protest that there was undue risk of not being able to retain qualified personnel when the awardee used the same labor rates for the base year and four option years. Compare *Tantus Techs., Inc.*, Comp. Gen. Dec. B-411608, 2014 CPD ¶ 299, granting a protest when the agency failed to consider the impact of significantly lower labor rates in option years in a cost realism analysis.

[2] Advantages and Disadvantages of Options

The major advantage of options is that they allow the government to obtain additional quantities of supplies or services if agency needs change after the contract has been awarded. Thus, options can be used to cover potential additional quantities during the year of the original contract, during subsequent years of multiple year contracts, and for additional years on a contract for a limited number of years. The latter type of options (for additional years) is probably the most frequently used at the current time.

Options for additional years' work have proved to be a major means of reducing the workload of acquisition personnel in contracting agencies. This occurs because, as a general rule, agencies tend to exercise such options rather than conduct a new procurement for the quantities covered by the options because it is almost always far easier to exercise an option than to conduct a new procurement. Thus, in a contract for one year of services with options for four additional years, the agency would not have to conduct a new procurement for five years.

A major disadvantage of options for additional years' work is that they are difficult to price accurately. If they are at fixed prices, they may impose a significant risk on the contractor or, conversely, induce the contractor to include a contingency in the price to protect against the risk. This makes them problematic for the government with the result that contracting officers may need to add economic price adjustment clauses to the contract (with the risk that they will not cover the pricing risk because of the way they are structured) and to move to a less risky type of contract such as a cost-reimbursement contract or a time-and-materials or labor-hour contract. In recent years, the use of these latter types of contract appears to have resulted from the extensive use of options for additional years' work.

Another disadvantage of options for additional years' work is that they allow agencies to avoid taking steps to conduct procurements in an efficient fashion. One of the major reasons agencies have resorted to such frequent use of such options is that conducting a new procurement takes from six months to a year or more. When an agency follows such inefficient procedures, the use of options for additional years almost becomes imperative. On the other hand, if an agency could conduct a new procurement in two to three months, options for additional years' work would be less attractive and the advantage of obtaining new prices each year more manifest. The ready availability of these options has appeared to provide many agencies with the ability to continue to use inefficient procurement procedures, whereas restrictions on the use of options might well motivate agencies to search for more efficient procedures to conduct new procurements.

[3] Standard Option Clauses

There are four standard option clauses in the FAR and two additional clauses in the DFARS. These clauses are quite narrow in their application with the result that an agency may have to tailor them to fit its needs. This is accommodated in the guidance on their use in FAR 17.208 which requires the use of clauses that are "substantially the same" as the standard FAR clauses. See *C. Martin Co.*, ASBCA 54182, 04-2 BCA ¶ 32,637, finding that a tailored clause with significant differences from the FAR 52.217-9 clause was substantially the same as that clause.

Many contracts contain option clauses that vary from the standard clauses. Government agencies must exercise care to ensure that tailored clauses accomplish their purpose. For example, in *Wackenhut Servs., Inc.*, ASBCA 55691, 08-1 BCA ¶ 33,831, the agency included the FAR 52.217-8 clause as well as a tailored option clause permitting extension of the contract for up to six years. The board held that the government could not hold the contractor to the option prices for part of the work called for by exercising an option under the tailored clause because that clause did not call for ordering "any services" as was permitted by the FAR 52.217-8 clause.

The first two standard FAR clauses are for use in contracts for supplies. The first is for use when the agency structures the option quantity as a percentage of the basic contract line(s) or as additional quantities of the basic contract line item(s). See FAR 52.217-6 providing:

> OPTION FOR INCREASED QUANTITY (MAR 1989)
>
> The Government may increase the quantity of supplies called for in the Schedule at the unit price specified. The Contracting Officer may exercise the option by written notice to the Contractor within. . . . [*insert in the clause the period of time in which the Contracting Officer has to exercise the option*]. Delivery of the added items shall continue at the same rate as the like items called for under the contract, unless the parties otherwise agree.

Note that this clause calls for delivery of additional products after delivery of the basic contract units has ended. Thus, it must be modified if an agency needs an option for additional supplies within the contract delivery period. The clause also requires the option prices to be the same as the prices of the basic contract prices. The difficulties that this requirement imposes are discussed below.

The second supply contract clause is for use when the agency structures the options as separate contract line items. See FAR 52.217-7 providing:

> OPTION FOR INCREASED QUANTITY—SEPARATELY PRICED LINE ITEM (MAR 1989)
>
> The Government may require the delivery of the numbered line item, identified in the Schedule as an option item, in the quantity and at the price stated in the Schedule. The Contracting Officer may exercise the option by written notice to the Contractor within. . . . [*insert in the clause the period of time in which the Contracting Officer has to exercise the option*]. Delivery of added items shall continue at the same rate that like items are called for under the contract, unless the parties otherwise agree.

This clause also deals only with option quantities to be delivered after completion of delivery the basic contract units. Thus, it must be modified if an agency needs an option for additional supplies within the contract delivery period. The clause does, however, allow an agency to include option prices that are different from the prices of the basic contract units.

The other two FAR clauses are for use in service contracts. The first is to allow the agency to obtain additional services for a period up to six months if the award of a follow-on contract is delayed. See FAR 37.111 stating:

> Award of contracts for recurring and continuing service requirements are often delayed due to circumstances beyond the control of contracting offices. Examples of circumstances causing such delays are bid protests and alleged mistakes in bid. In order to avoid negotiation of short extensions to

existing contracts, the contracting officer may include an option clause (see 17.208(f)) in solicitations and contracts which will enable the Government to require continued performance of any services within the limits and at the rates specified in the contract. However, these rates may be adjusted only as a result of revisions to prevailing labor rates provided by the Secretary of Labor. The option provision may be exercised more than once, but the total extension of performance thereunder shall not exceed 6 months.

The following clause is provided in FAR 52.217-8:

OPTION TO EXTEND SERVICES (NOV 1999)

The Government may require continued performance of any services within the limits and at the rates specified in the contract. These rates may be adjusted only as a result of revisions to prevailing labor rates provided by the Secretary of Labor. The option provision may be exercised more than once, but the total extension of performance hereunder shall not exceed 6 months. The Contracting Officer may exercise the option by written notice to the Contractor within [*insert the period of time within which the Contracting Officer may exercise the option*].

This clause is appropriate only when fully priced labor rates are specified in the contract. In such cases, it binds the contractor to those rates even if its costs have increased. See *JWK Int'l Corp.*, ASBCA 54153, 04-2 BCA ¶ 32,783 (barring recovery of bonuses that accrued during option period), and *Tecom, Inc.*, ASBCA 51880, 00-2 BCA ¶ 30,944 (barring recovery of payments in lieu of vacation time that could not be granted because of exercise of option). However, the clause requires the contracting officer to permit labor rate adjustments when a new wage determination applies, *Hallmark-Phoenix 3, LLC*, ASBCA 61049, 17-1 BCA ¶ 36,788. If the agency calls for pricing of this six-month option, offers without such pricing will be rejected, *REG Prods., LLC*, Comp. Gen. Dec. B-414638, 2017 CPD ¶ 213. If the agency does not call for such pricing, the agency must justify the sole source procurement if the additional services are ordered because the prices have not been evaluated in the original competition (as is frequently the case), *Major Contracting Servs., Inc.*, Comp. Gen. Dec. B-401472, 2009 CPD ¶ 170, *recons. denied*, 2009 CPD ¶ 250. See also *Walker Dev. & Trading Group, Inc.*, Comp. Gen. Dec. B-413924, 2017 CPD ¶ 21, sustaining a protest challenging the exercise of the six-month option because the agency did not submit information justifying the extension.

Although FAR 37.111 states that this clause is to be used to cover procurement delays "due to circumstances beyond the control of contracting offices," the clause contains no such limitation with the result that agencies have been permitted to use it for other purposes. See *Mission 1st Group, Inc.*, ASBCA 62461, 62646 (clause used to order three months of services after base period (in lieu of -9 clause)); *Glasgow Investigative Solutions, Inc.* ASBCA 58111, 13-1 BCA ¶ 35,286 (clause used to issue one and two-month options up to six months at end of first option year); *Petchem, Inc.*, ASBCA 53792, 05-1 BCA ¶32,870 (clause used after missing notice date in FAR 52.217-9 clause but option period limited to six months); *Griffin Servs., Inc.*, ASBCA 52280, 02-2 BCA ¶31,943 (clause properly used when agency missed the time to extend the contract under the FAR 52.217-9 clause); and *American Contract Servs., Inc.*, ASBCA 46788, 94-2 BCA ¶26,855, *recons. denied*, 94-3 BCA ¶27,025, *aff'd*, 53 F.3d 348 (Fed. Cir. 1995) (clause properly used in lieu of FAR 52.217-9 clause in order to obtain lower option prices). Compare *Overseas Leasing Group, Inc. v. United States*, 106 Fed. Cl. 644 (2012), holding that this clause did not permit short-term leases because the contract stated that all leases would be for a minimum of one year. The result is that, without limiting language, this clause can impose significant pricing risk on the contractor—particularly when it is used in conjunction with the FAR 52.217-9 clause. In that case, the requirement that the contractor accept up to six months of additional work at "the rates specified in the contract" binds the contractor to the rates paid for the last option that has been exercised under the FAR 52.217-9 clause.

There is another clause that can be used to obtain additional services from a contractor when a contract has been awarded to a follow-on contractor. The Continuity of Services clause in FAR 52.237-3 allows the agency to order the contractor to provide "phase-in training" and transition services to a new contractor for a period of up to 90 days after award. In *Arko Exec. Servs., Inc. v. United States*, 78 Fed. Cl. 420 (2007), the court held that the agency properly used the FAR 52.217-8 clause to extend the contract for two months beyond the expiration of all of the FAR 52.217-9 options, rejecting the contractor's argument that the services should have been ordered under the FAR 52.237-3 clause. The court reasoned that the FAR 52.217-8 clause had been used for the specific purpose for which it was intended, as stated in FAR 37.111. See also *APAC-Southeast, Inc.*, ASBCA 58057, 12-2 BCA ¶35,155; and *SecTek, Inc. v. Dep't of Homeland Sec.*, CBCA 1095, 09-1 BCA ¶34,137, holding that the FAR 52.217-8 clause permits the government to exercise options beyond the time limitation for options under the FAR 52.217-9 clause.

The second standard services contract clause can be used along with specific options in the contract schedule. Its use is discretionary in accordance with FAR 17.208(g) as follows:

> (g) Insert a clause substantially the same as the clause at 52.217-9, Option to Extend the Term of the Contract, in solicitations and contracts when the inclusion of an option is appropriate (see 17.200 and 17.202) and it is necessary to include in the contract any or all of the following:
>
> (1) A requirement that the Government must give the contractor a preliminary written notice of its intent to extend the contract.
>
> (2) A statement that an extension of the contract includes an extension of the option.
>
> (3) A specified limitation on the total duration of the contract.

The clause is provided in FAR 52.217-9:

OPTION TO EXTEND THE TERM OF THE CONTRACT
(MAR 2000)

(a) The Government may extend the term of this contract by written notice to the Contractor within [*insert the period of time within which the Contracting Officer may exercise the option*]; provided that the Government gives the Contractor a preliminary written notice of its intent to extend at least ______ days *[60 days unless a different number of days is inserted*] before the contract expires. The preliminary notice does not commit the Government to an extension.

(b) If the Government exercises this option, the extended contract shall be considered to include this option clause.

(c) The total duration of this contract, including the exercise of any options under this clause, shall not exceed ______ (months) (years).

This clause contains no coverage of the labor rates that will be paid in option years. Thus, it is appropriate for use in cost-reimbursement contracts but should be supplemented to state the basis of payment if it is used in contracts with fixed prices or fixed labor rates. The limitation on the duration of the contract in ¶ (c) does not preclude extensions under the FAR 52.217-8 clause, *Arko Executive Servs., Inc. v. United States*, 553 F.3d 1375 (Fed. Cir. 2009); *APAC-Southeast, Inc.*, ASBCA 58057, 12-2 BCA ¶ 35,155; *SecTek, Inc. v. Dep't of Homeland Sec.*, CBCA 1095, 09-1 BCA ¶ 34,137.

The notice of intent to extend the contract required by ¶ (a) of the clause is strictly enforced under option law. Thus, for an option to be binding on the contractor the notice must be *received* within the time specified, *White Sands Constr., Inc.*, ASBCA 51875, 04-1 BCA ¶ 32,598. See also *Cooper/Ports America, LLC*, ASBCA 61348, 19-1 BCA ¶ 37,284, finding a valid notice even though it did not state which option year was to be exercised. It is also important to insert the time when the option can be exercised in ¶ (a) properly. See *Jim Phillips Contr., Inc.*, IBCA 4319, 04-1 BCA ¶ 32,416, where the agency put "30 calendar days" in the second line of ¶ (a) of the clause. The board found that the option had not been exercised in time, commenting:

> Unfortunately, [the agency's] insertion does not make clear "within 30 days" of what? The date of the Contract? The end of the year? [The agency] doesn't say. That was [the agency's] first mistake.

The two DFARS clauses are an open-ended clause to be used to fulfill foreign military sales commitments in DFARS 252.217-7000 and a surge option clause in DFARS 252.217-7001 that allows the agency to order increased deliveries to a "maximum sustainable rate." These clauses generally call for pricing after the option is exercised although the latter clause permits prepricing if the parties have included prices in the original contract.

[4] Structuring and Evaluation of Options

Option provisions must be carefully structured to induce offerors to propose the most advantageous prices. The key considerations are the time the option can be exercised and whether the option prices will be evaluated in the selection of the winning offeror. Agencies must include a provision in the solicitation stating whether they will or will not evaluate options, *Golden N. Van Lines, Inc.*, 69 Comp. Gen. 610 (B-238874), 90-2 CPD ¶ 44. See the guidance in FAR 17.208. The absence of such a provision is a solicitation defect that must be protested before the submission of an offer, *Home Care Med., Inc.*, Comp. Gen. Dec. B-245189, 91-2 CPD ¶ 186.

The period during which an option may be exercised must be stated in the contract, FAR 17.204(b). In the case of supply contracts, it must be set "so as to provide the contractor adequate lead time to ensure continuous production," FAR 17.204(c). In *Aerojet Techsys. Co.*, Comp. Gen. Dec. B-220033, 85-2 CPD ¶ 636, GAO reasoned that because this regulation ensures the contractor's continuous production, the government erred in rejecting as nonresponsive a bid that conditioned third-year option prices on exercise of second-year options. In the case of service contracts, continuity of services should also be provided for, but the FAR is silent on this requirement. The Option to Extend Services clause in FAR 52.217-8 permits the contracting officer to select a period during which that option can be exercised, and this period should be clearly stated. See *American Contract Servs., Inc.*, ASBCA 46788, 94-2 BCA ¶ 26,855, *recons. denied*, 94-3 BCA ¶ 27,025, *aff'd*, 53 F.3d 348 (Fed. Cir. 1995), where the contracting officer used the ambiguous phrase "within 15 days," and the board held that this had to mean within 15 days of contract expiration.

FAR 17.204(d) permits the period for exercise of the option to "extend beyond the contract completion date" when funds would not be available on the completion date. This allows the contracting officer to structure the option to permit its exercise on the first day of the fiscal year (or the year when funds are available) when the period of services ends on the previous day. It should not be used to permit longer gaps in service. See *Cessna Aircraft Co.*, ASBCA 43196, 96-1 BCA ¶ 27,966, *aff'd*, 126 F.3d 1442 (Fed. Cir. 1997), *cert. denied*, 525 U.S. 818 (1998), where the board held that a clause permitting exercise of an option on the first day of the fiscal year was legally binding even though it extended beyond the contract completion date.

The other key consideration in structuring options is the determination of whether option prices will be evaluated. The goal is to give the offerors the greatest possible incentive to propose prices that are realistic and competitive. If the option quantities are included in the evaluation, the offerors will have the incentive to offer competitive prices but may be inclined to unbalance the prices between the years. This could lead to unnecessarily high prices for early years if the later years' requirements do not materialize. If the option quantities are not included in the evaluation, offerors may be inclined to inflate option prices in the hope that the agency will be forced by circumstances to exercise the options. While the FAR contains some minimal guidance on evaluation of options, it contains no guidance on structuring options to achieve the best prices. Methods of structuring and evaluation are dealt with in this section.

When options are solicited, the solicitation should state whether they will be evaluated. This can be done by incorporating one of the option clauses by reference, *Staker & Parsons Cos.*, Comp. Gen. Dec. B-402404.2, 2010 CPD ¶ 74. If there is no such statement in the solicitation, that is a patent ambiguity which must be protested before the submission of an offer, *Marine Group Boat Works, LLC*, Comp. Gen. Dec. B-404277, 2011 CPD ¶ 23.

[a] Evaluation of Option Quantities

The regulations call for the evaluation of options when the government is likely to exercise them in the course of the contract. FAR 17.206 provides:

> (a) In awarding the basic contract, the contracting officer shall, except as provided in paragraph (b) of this section, evaluate offers for any option quantities or periods contained in a solicitation when it has been determined prior to soliciting offers that the Government is likely to exercise the options. (See 17.208.)
>
> (b) The contracting officer need not evaluate offers for any option quantities when it is determined that evaluation would not be in the best interests of the Government and this determination is approved at a level above the contracting officer. An example of a circumstance that may support a determination not to evaluate offers for option quantities is when there is a reasonable certainty that funds will be unavailable to permit exercise of the option.

When the options are to be evaluated, the Evaluation of Options provision in FAR 52.217-5 is used, and GAO has upheld this method of evaluation, *S.A.F.E. Export Corp.*, Comp. Gen. Dec. B-204718, 82-1 CPD ¶ 62. This clause permits the government not to evaluate the options when it is "not . . . in the Government's best interests." GAO has stated that when this provision is used, options prices must be evaluated unless the agency determines that funds will not be available, *Verdi Consulting, Inc.*, Comp. Gen. Dec. B-41403.2, 2017 CPD ¶ 136. In contrast, option prices may not be evaluated if the agency is reasonably certain that funds will not be available, *Glen Mar Constr., Inc.*, Comp. Gen. Dec. B-410603, 2015 CPD ¶ 40. In *Foley Co.*, Comp. Gen. Dec. B-245536, 92-1 CPD ¶ 47, GAO concurred with a decision not to evaluate options when the base price of the low bidder including the options exceeded the available funding. This permitted the agency to award the contract to the bidder whose base price was within the government funding limit. GAO has affirmed the propriety of evaluating options if the contracting officer finds that funds will likely be available for their exercise, *Marshall Co.*, Comp. Gen. Dec. B-311196, 2008 CPD ¶ 78 (contracting officer found agency was assembling additional funding); *Building Constr. Enters., Inc.*, Comp. Gen. Dec. B-294784, 2004 CPD ¶ 251 (contracting officer believed that necessary funding "might be available"); *Contractors Northwest, Inc.*, Comp. Gen. Dec. B-293050, 2003 CPD ¶ 232 (contracting officer believed there was a reasonable likelihood funds would be available later); *Merlo, Inc.*, Comp. Gen. Dec. B-277384, 97-2 CPD ¶ 39 (contracting officer was advised that sufficient funding would be included in later year appropriations). See also *Thermal Combustion Innovators, Inc.*, Comp. Gen. Dec. B-279602.2, 98-2 CPD ¶ 94, where GAO rejected the protester's argument that it was unreasonable for the agency to pay higher prices in the first two years in order to obtain lower prices in later years because the agency could ensure better prices later by conducting another competition.

If the solicitation unequivocally states that options will be evaluated, the agency has no discretion to decide not to evaluate them, *Global Commc'ns Solutions, Inc.*, Comp. Gen. Dec. B-291113, 2002 CPD ¶ 194. There the solicitation stated that "the evaluation period" would be the entire period of the contract including the option periods.

If the solicitation contains options for work that can be exercised in the alternative, it is improper to add the prices of both alternates to the evaluated price, *Kruger Constr., Inc.*, Comp. Gen. Dec. B-286960, 2001 CPD ¶ 43.

When the clause calling for evaluation of options is used in an IFB, bidders must submit unequivocal offers. In *Sess Constr. Co.*, 64 Comp. Gen. 355 (B-216924), 85-1 CPD ¶ 319, a bid in which prices for option periods included the statement "plus rate of inflation, fuel, labor and gravel" was properly rejected for failure to offer a firm-fixed-price. It is also proper to refuse to evaluate a bid where the prices are conditioned upon exercise of the options. Thus, option price bids should not include separate "all or none" price discounts for option items. In *Telex Commc'ns, Inc.*, Comp. Gen. Dec. B-211236, 83-2 CPD ¶ 122, GAO concluded that where an IFB reserves the right to exercise only a portion of the options, to require evaluation of options at the bidder's "all or none" discounted price would improperly introduce uncertainty as to whether the bid was actually the lowest received.

The regulations state that the government may reject unbalanced bids if they pose an unacceptable risk to the government, FAR 14.404-2; FAR 15.404-1(g)(3), and this right of the government is stated in the standard solicitation provisions in FAR 52.214-10 and FAR 52.215-1. Guidance on determining whether an unbalanced bid poses such a risk states only that the contracting officer should consider "whether award of the contract will result in paying unreasonably high prices," FAR 15.404-1(g)(2)(ii). See Chapter 5 and Chapter 6 for a detailed discussion of unbalanced bidding.

[b] Nonevaluation of Option Quantities

Although FAR 17.206(a) states that the normal procedure is to structure options so that both the base quantity and option quantities are evaluated in making the initial award, FAR 17.206(b) states that a contracting officer may decide not to evaluate option quantities when that is "in the best interests of the Government" and is approved by a superior. GAO has also held that "[t]here is no legal or regulatory requirement that an agency evaluate options in a particular procurement," *International Bus. Invs., Inc.*, 63 Comp. Gen. 463 (B-215530), 84-1 CPD ¶ 693.

When it is decided not to evaluate options, the Evaluation Exclusive of Options clause at FAR 52.217-3 is used. The regulations give no guidance on how to deal with unusually high option prices where the option quantities are not to be evaluated, but it has been held that significantly higher unevaluated option prices, as compared to prices offered on the basic quantity, are not a sufficient reason for rejecting a bid, *R&R Inventory Serv., Inc.*, 54 Comp. Gen. 206 (B-181264), 74-2 CPD ¶ 163 (prices for second- and third-year options were 700% to 900% more than basic quantity prices, but bid was accepted as lowest on basic quantity). See also *SeaArk Marine, Inc.*, Comp. Gen. Dec. B-248755, 92-2 CPD ¶ 193, holding that the agency was not required to consider unevaluated option quantity prices when deciding whether a bid was materially unbalanced. Compare *Gracon Corp. v. United States*, 6 Cl. Ct. 497 (1984), holding that the contracting officer had discretion to accept or reject a bid containing significantly higher unevaluated option prices in accordance with a solicitation provision permitting the rejection of materially unbalanced bids. In *Gracon*, the court agreed with the contracting officer's decision to award the contract to the low bidder on the base quantity assuming that the government would not exercise the option but would meet its requirements in some other way. If a subsequent separate procurement was not possible, the proper course of action would arguably have been to reject the bid and award to the next low bidder. In solicitations calling for nonevaluation of options and containing no clause permitting rejection of materially unbalanced bids, the contracting officer would have to cancel the solicitation to avoid awarding to the low base bid with a high option price. The FAR contains no guidance on this issue.

In *Occu-Health, Inc.*, Comp. Gen. Dec. B-270228.3, 96-1 CPD ¶ 196, *recons. denied*, 96-2 CPD ¶ 80, GAO ruled that an agency was required to inform offerors that it was not going to evaluate options if it made that decision prior to the submission of best and final offers, stating:

> To read FAR 17.206(a) as broadly as [the agency] suggests—as granting an agency essentially unfettered discretion to decide not to evaluate options without advising offerors of this change under the circumstances when the agency could reasonably provide that advice—would be inconsistent with the agency's fundamental obligations to allow offerors the opportunity to respond to the government's actual needs and to obtain the offer that is most advantageous to the government.

See *ACC Constr. Co.*, Comp. Gen. Dec. B-289167, 2002 CPD ¶ 21, holding that this rule has no application to the situation where the agency finds out about a lack of funding after bid opening.

[c] Limited Evaluation

Another technique is to evaluate only those options that are exercised at the time of award. FAR 17.208(b) requires the use of the following clause at FAR 52.217-4 when this technique is used:

> Evaluation of Options Exercised at Time of Contract Award (JUN 1988)
>
> Except when it is determined in accordance with FAR 17.206(b) not to be in the Government's best interests, the Government will evaluate the total price for the basic requirement together with any option(s) exercised at the time of award.

This is the one method provided in the regulations that does not give the bidder definite information as to whether options will be evaluated. The result may be that it is the technique most likely to result in balanced bidding. In *National Council for Urban Econ. Dev., Inc.*, Comp. Gen. Dec. B-213434, 84-2 CPD ¶ 140, GAO held that where the government's RFP both provided for evaluation of option quantities and stated that options could not be exercised at the time of award, the government's decision to nevertheless exercise options at the time of award, in light of unexpected availability of funds, was valid. See also *Contractors Nw., Inc.*, Comp. Gen. Dec. B-293050, 2003 CPD ¶ 232, holding that the government was not precluded from evaluating options that would not be exercised at the time of award, as called for by the FAR 52.217-4 clause, when it also included the FAR 51.217-5 clause in the contract.

[d] Level Pricing

Another technique used to avoid unbalanced pricing is to require that option prices be the same as base prices. This technique is used in multi-year procurement, but the regulations are silent on its use in options. See, however, the Option for Increased Quantity clause in FAR 52.217-6 which requires additional items to be delivered at the original contract price. The clause appears to be open ended but the instructions on its use in FAR 17.208(d) require schedule language stating the quantity of items covered by the option—either as a percentage of the base quantity or as a specified quantity.

The FAR also permits the use of a solicitation clause preventing unbalanced pricing by low base prices. FAR 17.203 states:

> (f) Solicitations may, in unusual circumstances, require that options be offered at prices no higher than those for the initial requirement, e.g., when—
>
> (1) the option cannot be evaluated under 17.206; or
>
> (2) future competition for the option is impracticable.
>
> (g) Solicitations that require the offering of an option at prices no higher than those for the initial requirement shall—

> (1) Specify that the Government will accept an offer containing an option price higher than the base price only if the acceptance does not prejudice any other offeror; and
>
> (2) Limit option quantities for additional supplies to not more than 50 percent of the initial quantity of the same contract line item. In unusual circumstances, an authorized person at a level above the contracting officer may approve a greater percentage of quantity.

GAO has permitted award to a bidder that violated the IFB by bidding option prices higher than the base price but was the low bidder on both the base and option prices, 44 Comp. Gen. 581 (B-155847) (1965). See also Comp. Gen. Dec. B-176356, Nov. 8, 1972, *Unpub.* In cases where prejudice to other bidders has been found, however, GAO has agreed with decisions to reject the bids. See 51 Comp. Gen. 439 (B-172978) (1972), and *Bristol Elecs., Inc.*, 54 Comp. Gen. 16 (B-180247), 74-2 CPD ¶ 23, where the low bidder on the base quantity violated the solicitation instructions on level pricing, and the aggregate prices (base price plus all options) were higher than another bidder whose option prices did not exceed the base price; GAO ruled that it was improper to award to the low bidder on the base quantity. See also *Keco Indus., Inc.*, Comp. Gen. Dec. B-216396.2, 84-2 CPD ¶ 491. In *ABL Gen. Sys. Corp.*, 54 Comp. Gen. 476 (B-182066), 74-2 CPD ¶ 318, GAO ruled that a bid that was low on the base quantity, high on the option prices, but low in the aggregate should not be considered since it had violated the level bidding requirement and it was not clear that it would have been low had other bidders been permitted to submit higher option prices. Additionally, where the IFB advised prospective bidders that offers "containing an option price higher than the lowest basic price for the same item may be accepted only if such acceptance does not prejudice any other offeror," GAO upheld the rejection of a bid that was low on the base quantity but scaled option prices according to volumes ordered so that exercise of the entire option quantity would have resulted in level option pricing, but limited exercise of the option would have resulted in higher prices, *Numax Elecs. Inc.*, Comp. Gen. Dec. B-206127.2, 82-2 CPD ¶ 317.

In cases where there are significant nonrecurring costs, the contractor takes a large risk when level pricing is required. See *Contact Int'l Corp.*, ASBCA 44636, 95-2 BCA ¶ 27,887, *aff'd*, 106 F.3d 426 (Fed. Cir. 1997), where the board rejected a claim that the failure to exercise the options on a five-year requirements contract was a termination for convenience of the government. The board found that the government had full rights not to exercise the options and that the contractor "bears the attendant risks" of spreading nonrecurring costs over the five-year period. The same result was reached in *D&S Mfg. Co.*, ASBCA 32865, 87-1 BCA ¶ 19,351. See also *Metro Mach. Corp.*, ASBCA 47005, 97-1 BCA ¶ 28,723, where the contractor had agreed to overhead rate ceilings on cost-reimbursement contract with multiple options because it assumed that the options would be ordered and that it could spread its overhead costs over the large quantity of work covered by the options. When no options were ordered, the board ruled that the contractor has assumed the risk of this type of pricing and was bound by the ceilings.

[e] Prohibition of Nonrecurring Costs in Option Prices

Another method of controlling the pricing of options is to attempt to prohibit the inclusion of nonrecurring start-up costs in option prices. This forces the inclusion of all such costs in the base price. This can readily be accomplished in negotiated procurement. However, it may not be feasible in sealed bidding. See *Hitachi Denshi Am., Ltd.*, Comp. Gen. Dec. B-212925, 84-1 CPD ¶ 342, where GAO held that a bid that contained the same price for base and option quantities was responsive to such a prohibition because bidders were not required to submit cost breakdowns, and inflation during the five-year period could account for the fact that the option prices were the same as the base price.

[f] Discounting to Present Value

The most straightforward technique that could be used for evaluating options is to provide that all option-year prices be discounted to present value. This would remove most of the incentive for offerors to front-load their prices in order to obtain the free use of the money in the early years. However, the FAR is silent on the use of this technique. The government previously used a Present Value Method (PVM) of evaluation on ADPE procurements, having recognized a necessity to consider the time value of money in evaluating bids, Federal Information Resources Management Regulations, 41 C.F.R. § 201-32.205-3. However, this regulation is no longer extant. See also *Linolex Sys., Inc.*, 53 Comp. Gen. 895 (B-179047), 74-1 CPD ¶ 296. There appears to be no reason why this evaluation method could not be used in evaluating options on other types of procurement. See Chapter 5 for a discussion of the time value of money.

[5] Failure to Bid Options

If option prices are not to be evaluated, failure to bid option prices will not result in the bid being nonresponsive unless such failure deprives the government of a "substantive and valuable right," 51 Comp. Gen. 528 (B-174575) (1972). GAO reasoned that there was no such deprivation in a case where the solicitation contained no requirement limiting the amount of option prices since the bidder could have bid excessive option prices and been eligible for award if it was low bidder on the base quantity. Compare 46 Comp. Gen. 434 (B-160051) (1966), where GAO sustained the rejection of a bid omitting an unevaluated option quantity because the IFB required all options to be bid. GAO reasoned that the government was deprived of a valuable right.

If option quantities are to be evaluated, failure to bid an option will result in rejection of the bid, *Areawide Servs., Inc.*, Comp. Gen. Dec. B-240134.4, 90-2 CPD ¶ 182; *Huff & Huff Serv. Corp.*, Comp. Gen. Dec. B-233740.5, 90-1 CPD ¶ 167; *Rozier, Sidbury & Co.*, Comp. Gen. Dec. B-216741, 85-1 CPD ¶ 58; *Ainslie Corp.*, Comp. Gen. Dec. B-190878, 78-1 CPD ¶ 340. In *E.H. Morrill Co.*, 63 Comp. Gen. 348 (B-214556), 84-1 CPD ¶ 508, GAO held that a bid that did not provide prices for option work added by an amendment and whose receipt was acknowledged was nonresponsive. Subsequently, in a case that did not involve options, GAO explicitly clarified the *E.H. Morrill* decision and stated that "where an omitted item is divisible from the contract requirements, is de minimis as to total cost, and would not affect the competitive standing of the bidders, it may be waived," *Leslie & Elliott Co.*, 64 Comp. Gen. 279 (B-216676), 85-1 CPD ¶ 212.

There is another limited exception to this rule, stating that the omission of the option price can be corrected by the contracting officer if it can be determined from the face of the bid that the omission is the result of a clerical error, *Con-Chen Enters.*, Comp. Gen. Dec. B-187795, 77-2 CPD ¶ 284; 52 Comp. Gen. 604 (B-187795) (1973). In both of these cases, GAO reasoned that a clerical error was apparent because, while some options were omitted, the final option was priced in each case. Further, the pricing pattern was uniform, indicating the amount that the bidder had intended to bid. In contrast, in *Ainslie Corp.*, Comp. Gen. Dec. B-190878, 78-1 CPD ¶ 340, it was found that correction was not possible since no option prices had been bid. See also *Goldco Int'l*, Comp. Gen. Dec. B-248059, 92-2 CPD ¶ 59, where the government properly accepted a bid including a fifth option year when only four years were called for in the IFB.

[6] Exercise of Options

If the government can fulfill its needs by exercise of an option, significant savings in time and administrative costs can be realized. However, exercise of an option could be very disadvantageous to the government if the work can be obtained from another source at a lower price. Traditionally, the contracting officer has been given broad discretion in deciding whether to exercise an option, *National Cash Register Co.*, Comp. Gen. Dec. B-179045, 74-1 CPD ¶ 116; 36 Comp. Gen. 62 (B-128449) (1956) ("options . . . purely for the interest and benefit of the Government"). Thus, a bankruptcy court has refused to order a government agency to exercise an option when it was demonstrated that the decision not to exercise was not based on the fact the company was bankrupt, *In re Plum Run Serv. Corp.*, 159 B.R. 496 (S.D. Ohio 1993). Similarly, the ASBCA has held that it will not review a decision not to exercise an option unless it is demonstrated that the decision is made in bad faith or is an abuse of discretion, *Pennyrile*

Plumbing, Inc., ASBCA 44555, 96-1 BCA ¶ 28,044; *Sample Enters.*, ASBCA 44564, 94-3 BCA ¶ 27,105.

GAO will no longer consider contractor contentions that their options should be exercised, *C.G. Ashe Enters.*, 56 Comp. Gen. 387 (B-188043), 77-1 CPD ¶ 166; *Lanson Indus., Inc.*, 60 Comp. Gen. 661 (B-202942), 81-2 CPD ¶ 176; *Digital Sys. Group, Inc.*, Comp. Gen. Dec. B-252080.2, 93-1 CPD ¶ 228. In *Albert G. Gricoski Private Detective Agency*, Comp. Gen. Dec. B-214179, 84-1 CPD ¶ 157, GAO reiterated this rule and noted that the contractor's need to be reimbursed for costs not included in base prices did not require the government to exercise options. GAO will consider cases where the contracting officer is selecting among options in the contracts of competing firms, *Fjellestad, Barrett & Short*, Comp. Gen. Dec. B-248391, 92-2 CPD ¶ 118; *Mine Safety Appliance Co.*, 69 Comp. Gen. 562 (B-238597.2), 90-2 CPD ¶ 11.

It would be poor business practice to lose the opportunity of an advantageous purchase by failure to exercise an option. Thus, in all cases, the contracting officer should check market prices before failing to exercise an option. See *A.C. Elecs., Inc.*, Comp. Gen. Dec. B-185553, 76-1 CPD ¶ 295, where a decision not to exercise an option was upheld because there had been recent procurements at prices lower than the option price.

[a] Determining That Exercise Is Advantageous to the Government

Before exercising an option, the contracting officer must analyze the situation and make a number of determinations. FAR 17.207 provides:

> (b) When the contract provides for economic price adjustment and the contractor requests a revision of the price, the contracting officer shall determine the effect of the adjustment on prices under the option before the option is exercised.
>
> (c) The contracting officer may exercise options only after determining that—
>
> (1) Funds are available;
>
> (2) The requirement covered by the option fulfills an existing Government need;
>
> (3) The exercise of the option is the most advantageous method of fulfilling the Government's need, price and other factors (see paragraphs (d) and (e) below) considered;
>
> (4) The option was synopsized in accordance with Part 5 unless exempted by 5.202(a)(11) or other appropriate exemptions in 5.202; and
>
> (5) The contractor does not have an active exclusion record in the System for Award Management Exclusions (see FAR 9.405-1);
>
> (6) The contractor's past performance evaluations on other contract actions have been considered; and
>
> (7) The contractor's performance on this contract has been acceptable, e.g., received satisfactory ratings.

(d) The contracting officer, after considering price and other factors, shall make the determination on the basis of one of the following:

(1) A new solicitation fails to produce a better price or a more advantageous offer than that offered by the option. If it is anticipated that the best price available is the option price or that this is the more advantageous offer, the contracting officer should not use this method of testing the market.

(2) An informal analysis of prices or an examination of the market indicates that the option price is better than prices available in the market or that the option is the more advantageous offer.

(3) The time between the award of the contract containing the option and the exercise of the option is so short that it indicates the option price is the lowest price obtainable or the more advantageous offer. The contracting officer shall take into consideration such factors as market stability and comparison of the time since award with the usual duration of contracts for such supplies or services.

(e) The determination of other factors under (c)(3) of this section—

(1) Should take into account the Government's need for continuity of operations and potential costs of disrupting operations; and

(2) May consider the effect on small business.

(f) Before exercising an option, the contracting officer shall make a written determination for the contract file that exercise is in accordance with the terms of the option, the requirements of this section, and Part 6. To satisfy requirements of Part 6 regarding full and open competition, the option must have been evaluated as part of the initial competition and be exercisable at an amount specified in or reasonably determinable from the terms of the basic contract, e.g.—

(1) A specific dollar amount;

(2) An amount to be determined by applying provisions (or a formula) provided in the basic contract, but not including renegotiation of the price for work in a fixed-price type contract;

(3) In the case of a cost-type contract, if—

(i) The option contains a fixed or maximum fee; or

(ii) The fixed or maximum fee amount is determinable by applying a formula contained in the basic contract (but see 16.102(c));

(4) A specific price that is subject to an economic price adjustment provision; or

(5) A specific price that is subject to change as the result of changes to prevailing labor rates provided by the Secretary of Labor.

(g) The contract modification or other written document which notifies the contractor of the exercise of the option shall cite the option clause as authority.

This regulation has been regarded as an internal operating procedure which contractors cannot use to avoid the exercise of an option within the terms of the option provision in the contract, *Freightliner Corp. v. Caldera*, 225 F.3d 1361 (Fed. Cir. 2000). See, however, *Walker Development & Trading Group – Recons.*, Comp. Gen. Dec. B-411246.2, 2015 CPD ¶ 284, where GAO denied a contention that the agency had to make a "Rule of Two" analysis before exercising an option because that was not required by FAR 17.207.

The requirement for full and open competition applies to the exercise of options that have not been evaluated in the award, since such exercise can be considered to be a form of sole source contracting. See *Major Contracting Servs., Inc.*, Comp. Gen. Dec. B-401472, 2009 CPD ¶ 170, *recons. denied*, 2009 CPD ¶ 250, holding that exercising the option to extend services under the FAR 51.217-8 clause was improper because it had not been evaluated in the original competition. GAO rejected the argument that the option implicitly had been evaluated because the clause required the contractor to perform at the current contract rates. This same logic may be applicable to the FAR 52.237-3 clause. See also *Kollsman Instrument Co.*, 68 Comp. Gen. 303 (B-233759), 89-1 CPD ¶ 243, where GAO denied a protest that an option had been exercised without competition on a contract where the option prices had not been evaluated. GAO found that the agency had properly justified the lack of competition on the basis of urgency and also found that the agency had performed a sufficient check of market conditions before exercising the option.

It appears that the competition requirement does not apply to evaluated options, because they were part of the original competition. However, FAR 17.207(d) requires some analysis of the reasonableness of the price before exercising options, *Ross & McDonald Contracting, GmbH*, ASBCA 38154, 94-1 BCA ¶ 26,316 (improper to exercise option on reprocurement contract without checking validity of prices); *Banknote Corp. of Am.*, Comp. Gen. Dec. B-250151, 92-2 CPD ¶ 413 (improper to rely on original bid prices, especially when quantities were increasing); *AAA Eng'g & Drafting, Inc.*, Comp. Gen. Dec. B-236034.2, 92-1 CPD ¶ 307 (current market price must be checked to ensure that option price is reasonable). GAO has been quite lenient in enforcing this requirement. See *Sippican, Inc.*, Comp. Gen. Dec. B-257047.2, 95-2 CPD ¶ 220, where the protester, a firm that had lost the competition, had informed the agency that it could offer the option quantities at lower prices because it had reduced its costs. GAO held that the contracting officer had properly exercised his discretion in failing to conduct a competition for the option quantity, based on the following considerations:

> The record shows that the contracting officer considered (1) the prices offered in the original competition and the fact that [the contractor's] high technical score and low price had made its proposal more advantageous than the protester's proposal; (2) that only a relatively short period of time had passed since the original competition and the agency's requirements for the

> third option year remained the same as stated in the original competition; (3) that agency information showed that [the protester] had recently charged substantially more for EMATT units in a foreign procurement than [the contractor's] option price; (4) that there was no known change in the current EMATT market; (5) that since [the protester] did not provide any financial data to support its allegations of more advantageous pricing, and since prior prices known to the agency for required materials were substantial, it remained unlikely that [the protester] could reduce its material costs to the extent stated to be below those of [the contractor]; and (6) the need for continuity of operations and the cost of disruption, as well as the costs of a new competition (which would involve additional costs of proposal evaluation, start-up costs and the possible requalification of a vendor or qualification of a new contractor).

The exercise of options without testing the market has been approved in several cases. See *InGenesis, Inc.*, Comp. Gen. Dec. B-412101.2, 2016 CPD ¶ 102 (short time from original procurement and urgent need); *Nutriom, LLC*, Comp. Gen. Dec. B-402511, 2010 CPD ¶ 113 (item was critical and contractor was performing very well); *PR Newswire Ass'n, LLC*, Comp. Gen. Dec. B-401692, 2009 CPD ¶ 223 (option price was good, performance was satisfactory and administrative costs of conducting new procurement were avoided); *Antmarin, Inc.*, Comp. Gen. Dec. B-296317, 2005 CPD ¶ 149 (original price was 43% lower than competitor's price); *Alice Roofing & Sheet Metal Works, Inc.*, Comp. Gen. Dec. B-283153, 99-2 CPD ¶ 70 (original price was low, escalation rate in option was below increase in consumer price index and administrative costs of conducting new procurement were avoided); *Bulova Techs., Inc.*, Comp. Gen. Dec. B-252660, 93-2 CPD ¶ 23 (good initial price and limited competition because only competitors would be in mobilization base), and *Valentec Wells, Inc.*, Comp. Gen. Dec. B-239499, 90-2 CPD ¶ 177 (losing a mobilization base supplier).

It is proper to test the market before exercising an option by conducting a competition and evaluating the option holder's product at its option price, *Beretta USA Corp.*, Comp. Gen. Dec. B-232681, 88-2 CPD ¶ 395, *recons. denied*, 89-1 CPD ¶ 16. However, it is improper to add significant costs involved in procuring a duplicate product to the costs of the competitors, *Smith & Wesson*, Comp. Gen. Dec. B-232681.2, 89-1 CPD ¶ 134.

Even if option prices have been evaluated in the original competition, it is not proper to exercise an option unless the dollar amount can be determined from the original contract, FAR 17.207(f). In *Magnum Opus Techs., Inc. v. United States*, 94 Fed. Cl. 553 (2010), the court held that the agency had violated this requirement when it had waived the not-to-exceed labor rates in the original contract, with the result that there were no binding rates at the time the option was exercised. Compare *CFS Group, LLC—Costs*, Comp. Gen. Dec. B-403539.3, 2011 CPD ¶ 101, holding that evaluated option prices could be altered through the changes process and options exercised properly at the new prices without a new competition.

Since option prices are generally a matter of public record, they should be disclosed when examining the market or soliciting offers. GAO has held that disclosure of the option price in a solicitation is permissible, *Grant's Janitorial & Food Serv., Inc.*, Comp. Gen. Dec. B-244170, 91-1 CPD ¶512; *JL Assocs.*, Comp. Gen. Dec. B-239790, 90-2 CPD ¶261; *Milwaukee Valve Co.*, Comp. Gen. Dec. B-206249, 82-1 CPD ¶135. See, however, *Canadian Commercial Corp. v. Dep't of the Air Force*, 514 F.3d 37 (D.C. Cir. 2007), holding that it was a violation of the Freedom of Information Act 5 U.S.C. § 552(b)(4), to release option prices because they were proprietary information.

FAR 17.207(c)(5) now prohibits the exercise of an option if the contractor is on the System for Award Management list. DFARS 217.207 also requires ensuring that the contractor's Data Universal Numbering System (DUNS) number, Commercial and Government Entity (CAGE) code, name, and physical address are accurately reflected in the contract document.

Under the prior statutes and regulations, GAO held that where option prices have been evaluated in the initial award, the requirement that the exercise of options be advantageous to the government was not intended to require a new solicitation that would permit a firm that had an opportunity to compete under the original solicitation to displace the incumbent contractor by undercutting the option price, *Jaxon, Inc.*, Comp. Gen. Dec. B-213998, 84-2 CPD ¶33; *A.J. Fowler Corp.*, Comp. Gen. Dec. B-205062, 82-1 CPD ¶582. In addition, the contracting officer was permitted to consider the satisfactory performance of the incumbent contractor and administrative budget constraints that might cause lack of personnel to process a new solicitation, *Humanics, Ltd.*, Comp. Gen. Dec. B-202418.2, 82-1 CPD ¶514. Note that FAR 17.207(e) still permits consideration of continuity of operations and disruption costs. GAO has affirmed the exercise of an option where, "due to time constraints, procuring competitively would disrupt services and create substantial costs to the Government," *A. Lee Parker*, Comp. Gen. Dec. B-206735, 82-2 CPD ¶259. See also *Cerberonics, Inc.*, Comp. Gen. Dec. B-199924, 81-1 CPD ¶351, holding that a contracting officer had properly decided to exercise an option rather than conduct a new competition in a case where the option was on a cost-reimbursement basis and the agency determined that it needed the continuity of the contractor that was performing the job well. In this case, the protesting competitor had submitted an unsolicited proposal to perform the work for less than the option price. See also *Silent Hoist & Crane Co.*, Comp. Gen. Dec. B-186006, 76-1 CPD ¶392 (exercise of option upheld when repeated IFBs for additional quantity did not result in lower prices); and *Oscar Holmes & Sons, Inc.*, Comp. Gen. Dec. B-183897, 75-2 CPD ¶339 (survey of market supported exercise of option even though other firms claimed that competitive bidding would result in lower prices).

Where a contract with options has been awarded to a small business, the government may exercise options, subject to other regulatory requirements, irrespective of the fact that the company outgrows its small business status during the time of the contract, 13 CFR 121.404(g); *Vantex Serv. Corp.*, Comp. Gen. Dec. B-251102, 93-1 CPD ¶ 221; *Gallegos Research Corp.*, Comp. Gen. Dec. B-209992.2, 83-2 CPD ¶ 597. However, if the company loses its small business status through merger, sale or acquisition, it may not take advantage of this rule.

It has been held that the government may exercise an option as part of a litigation settlement, even when a minor increase in price was allowed and the agency relied on an informal market survey in its determination that exercise was in the best interests of the government, *Gulton Indus., Inc.*, Comp. Gen. Dec. B-203265, 82-2 CPD ¶ 59.

[b] Negotiation of Options

In some cases, the contracting officer has negotiated with the contractor to obtain more favorable terms on an option. GAO has held that this is permissible if it is done as part of a negotiated procurement to test the option price, *Interscience Sys., Inc.*, Comp. Gen. Dec. B-194497, 79-2 CPD ¶ 306, *recons. denied*, 81-1 CPD ¶ 61. However, an incumbent contractor may not undermine the integrity of the competitive bidding system by reducing the option price subsequent to bid opening if the option-testing competition is accomplished using sealed bid procedures, Comp. Gen. Dec. B-173504, Sept. 12, 1972, *Unpub.*

GAO has also held that negotiation to obtain a lower option is, in effect, a new procurement requiring negotiation with all competitors, *Magnavox Elec. Sys. Co.*, Comp. Gen. Dec. B-231795, 88-2 CPD ¶ 431; *Varian Assocs., Inc.*, Comp. Gen. Dec. B-208281, 83-1 CPD ¶ 160, *modified on other grounds*, 83-2 CPD ¶ 78. This rule does not apply if the original award was on a sole source basis to a mobilization base contractor, *Outdoor Venture Corp.*, Comp. Gen. Dec. B-279777, 98-2 CPD ¶ 27. It also is proper to test the market by soliciting firm prices against an option price that has to be negotiated by the agency, *Smith & Wesson*, Comp. Gen. Dec. B-232681.2, 89-1 CPD ¶ 134. In circumstances where the market included only two eligible contractors, informal negotiations on price and delivery schedules were sufficient because both eligible offerors were afforded an equal opportunity to compete, *Nuclear Metals, Inc.*, 64 Comp. Gen. 290 (B-216319), 85-1 CPD ¶ 217.

[c] Method of Exercising an Option

The government must exercise options in a timely manner and in exact compliance with the option terms, *Lockheed Martin IR Imaging Sys., Inc. v. West*, 108 F.3d 319 (Fed. Cir. 1997); *New England Tank Indus. of New Hampshire, Inc. v. United States*, 861 F.2d 685 (Fed. Cir. 1988); *Holly Corp.*, ASBCA 24975, 83-1 BCA ¶ 16,327.

[i] Strict Compliance

The strict compliance requirement governing the exercise of options has been imposed because options give the party with the right to exercise unique power over the other party. FAR 17.207 provides minimal guidance in this regard, stating:

> (a) When exercising an option, the contracting officer shall provide written notice to the contractor within the time period specified in the contract.

However, it has consistently been held that for the government's exercise of an option to be effective, the election must be positive, unambiguous, and in exact compliance with the terms of the option, 51 Comp. Gen. 119 (B-172586) (1971). Thus, exercise of an option is invalid if the option reduces the quantity of work, *Grumman Tech. Servs., Inc.*, ASBCA 46040, 95-2 BCA ¶ 27,918, unless the option contains flexible quantities, *Raven Indus., Inc.*, Comp. Gen. Dec. B-185052, 76-1 CPD ¶ 90 (clause permitting option "up to" 100% enables government to order partial quantity). Adding new contract clauses in conjunction with an option exercise will also invalidate the exercise, *Varo, Inc.*, ASBCA 47945, 96-1 BCA ¶ 28,161. An option exercise is also improper if it is sent to an official of the contractor without authority to receive such communications, *Western States Mgmt. Servs., Inc.*, ASBCA 37490, 89-2 BCA ¶ 21,803.

Exercise of an option before funds are made available, contingent of the availability of funds, is an invalid exercise, *J.E.T.S., Inc.*, ASBCA 26135, 82-2 BCA ¶ 15,986; *Lear Siegler Inc.*, ASBCA 30224, 86-3 BCA ¶ 19,155. However, exercise of an option contingent on the availability of funds is proper if that is called for in the option clause of the contract, *Western States Mgmt. Servs., Inc.*, ASBCA 37504, 92-1 BCA ¶ 24,663. Similarly, exercise of the option on the date an appropriations act is signed by the President is proper, *Cessna Aircraft Co.*, ASBCA 43196, 93-3 BCA ¶ 25,912, *aff'd*, 126 F.3d 1442 (Fed Cir. 1997). See also *Freightliner Corp.*, ASBCA 42982, 94-1 BCA ¶ 26,538, 98-2 BCA ¶ 30,026, *aff'd*, 225 F.3d 1361 (Fed. Cir. 2000), where the board held that the agency could obtain its requirements for a sixth year by exercising an option on the fifth year of a multiyear contract.

If a contractor leads the government to believe that it can exercise the option without strictly complying with the clause, it will be estopped from asserting the strict compliance rule, *Ampex Corp.*, GSBCA 5913, 82-1 BCA ¶ 15,738, *recons. denied*, 82-2 BCA ¶ 15,858 (authorized contractor employee told the government that the option notice could be sent by TWX). For another case not requiring strict compliance with the terms of the option exercise, see *Contel Page Servs., Inc.*, ASBCA 32100, 87-1 BCA ¶ 19,540, finding that an option was properly exercised when the contracting officer sent the contractor an unsigned bilateral modification exercising the option. The board reasoned that the cover letter, signed by the contracting officer, was a proper exercise of the option. In *TECOM, Inc.*, IBCA 2970 A-1, 95-2 BCA ¶ 27,607, the board required exact compliance with the option terms distinguishing *Contel Page Services* and holding that the mailing of a draft bilateral modification was not a proper option exercise. Where the period for option exercise is established by reference to the date of final delivery, amendments changing that date should specify whether the option period is also changed.

Although the strict compliance rule is generally adhered to closely, there are a few cases allowing less strict compliance when there are ambiguous option clauses. See, for example, *International Transducer Corp. v. United States*, 30 Fed. Cl. 522 (1994), where the court interpreted an option for "a part of" any line item to include an option to order parts of subline items—finding that this was a patent ambiguity for which the contractor should have sought clarification. In *Griffin Servs., Inc.*, ASBCA 52280, 04-2 BCA ¶ 32,745, where the option clause called for exercise "within the period specified in the Schedule" but the schedule contained no date, the board found that the option could be exercised at any time during the period of contract performance specified in the Schedule then in effect. See also *BMY-Combat Sys.*, ASBCA 39495, 95-2 BCA ¶ 27,809, where the board permitted exercise of an option after the full documentation of the results of the "testing process" when the contract called for exercise of the option "within 30 days after completion of initial production testing." The board used contract interpretation principles to give the government additional time to exercise the option.

There are also cases finding proper exercise of options where the language purporting to exercise the option is not completely clear. For example, in *Technical Servs. Corp.*, ASBCA 36505, 93-1 BCA ¶ 25,310, the board found a proper option exercise where a letter stated that "the Government shall exercise the second option year" and contained an incorrect line-item number and an incorrect initial date for the option work. Similarly, in *Mills Mfg. Corp.*, ASBCA 10416, 66-1 BCA ¶ 5450, the board found a proper exercise where a telegram stated that "the government proposes to exercise the option." In both cases, the board found that the total import of the communications was that the option was being exercised and that it would not require the government to be grammatically correct.

In a case where the contractor did not want to perform the untimely exercised option, the court ruled that performance was required because the contracting officer's order to perform was a constructive change, *Alliant Techsys., Inc. v. United States*, 178 F.3d 1260, *reh'g denied*, 186 F.3d 1379 (Fed. Cir. 1999).

[ii] Preliminary Notice Requirement

The FAR 52.217-9 option clause requires the government to give the contractor a "preliminary written notice of its intent to extend" the contract at least 60 days "before the contract expires" (unless the contracting officer inserts a different date). Since this date is usually before the option exercise date, it places two notice requirements on the government. This preliminary notice requirement must be strictly complied with the have a valid option exercise, *White Sands Constr., Inc.*, ASBCA 51875, 04-1 BCA ¶ 32,598. In reaching this conclusion, the board reasoned that "[t]he preliminary notice is an integral component of the process by which the government binds the contractor to another contract term."

[iii] Sequential Options

If options are sequential, failure to exercise the option properly for one year will preclude the government from exercising future year options, *Grumman Tech. Servs., Inc.*, ASBCA 46040, 95-2 BCA ¶ 27,918. There the board reasoned that the contract "came to an end" when an annual option was not exercised; in effect, no options then remained for future years. Similarly, where a contract contained several options that both parties understood were priced on a learning curve, they were required to be exercised sequentially, *Motorola, Inc.*, ASBCA 39782, 93-3 BCA ¶ 26,081 (exercise of second option improper when first option had been permitted to expire). The same reasoning was followed in *Texas Instruments, Inc.*, ASBCA 25942, 88-1 BCA ¶ 20,421 (parties understood options were based on continuous production). However, in *Loral Fairchild Corp.*, ASBCA 45719, 97-1 BCA ¶ 28,905, exercise of an option after expiration of a prior option was found proper because the FAR 52.217-7 clause permitted such exercise and there was no evidence that the parties had discussed the fact that the option prices were based on a learning curve. Prior to 1990, the FAR 52.217-7 clause calling for options for "separately priced line items" stated that such items were "independent of each other" and that the government could exercise the options independently. See *Knights' Piping, Inc.*, ASBCA 46989, 94-3 BCA ¶ 27,023, following this clause. This language has now been omitted from the FAR clause, but it appears that the contractor would be bound to "independent" options if the contract clearly gave the government this right.

[iv] Time of Effectivity

The time of exercise of an option is calculated based on the time of *receipt* of the notice not on the time of transmission. Thus, one aspect of the strict compliance rule is that, to be timely, a notice of exercise of an option must be received prior to the expiration of the contractual time for exercise. Comment f. of *Restatement, Second, Contracts* § 63, states:

> Option contracts are commonly subject to a definite time limit, and the usual understanding is that the notification that the option has been exercised must be received by the offeror before that time. Whether or not there is such a time limit, in the absence of a contrary provision in the option contract, the

> offeree takes the risk of loss or delay in the transmission of the acceptance and remains free to revoke the acceptance until it arrives. Similarly, if there is such a mistake on the part of the offeror as justifies the rescission of his unilateral obligation, the right to rescind is not lost merely because a letter of acceptance is posted.

Thus, exercise of an option is effective upon receipt unless a contrary intent is shown, *Dynamics Corp. of Am. v. United States*, 389 F.2d 424 (Ct. Cl. 1968); *Jim Phillips Contracting, Inc.*, IBCA 4319, 04-1 BCA ¶ 32,416. In *Cessna Aircraft Co.*, ASBCA 43196, 96-1 BCA ¶ 27,966, *aff'd*, 126 F.3d 1442 (Fed Cir. 1997), *cert. denied*, 525 U.S. 818 (1998), the board found receipt of a facsimile on the nonworking day it was sent, even though no contractor employee picked it up for two days. When a contract provision alters the basic rule, that provision will govern. See *USD Techs., Inc.*, ASBCA 31305, 87-2 BCA ¶ 19,680, where the contract contained a special provision stating that the option would be "considered to have been exercised at the time the Government deposits [it] in the mails." The board held that the government had the burden of proof that the option exercise was actually mailed before the option expired.

There have been a number of instances where the contract clause is rather vague as to the final date for exercising the option. In such cases, the boards have looked to the entire agreement to determine the date. For example, in *TECOM, Inc.*, IBCA 2970 A-1, 94-2 BCA ¶ 26,787, the board interpreted a clause calling for exercise of an option "within 30 calendar days of expiration date" to require exercise of the option at least 30 days *before* the final date of contract performance. See also *American Contract Servs., Inc.*, ASBCA 46788, 94-2 BCA ¶ 26,855, *recons. denied*, 94-3 BCA ¶ 27,025, *aff'd*, 53 F.3d 348 (Fed. Cir. 1995), where the board held that "within 15 days" inserted in the Option to Extend the Term of the Contract clause in FAR 52.217-9 meant within 15 days of the expiration of the contract, not within 15 days of contract award.

[v] Requirement for Written Notice

Almost all option clauses call for exercise of the option by written notice, and it has been held that oral notice will not suffice, *International Tel. & Tel. v. United States*, 197 Ct. Cl. 11, 453 F.2d 1283 (1972) (exercise of right to purchase quantities in a subsequent program year under multiyear procurement where the court decided the case using the legal principles applicable to options); *Maintenance, Inc.*, Comp. Gen. Dec. B-215619.3, 84-2 CPD ¶ 263 (oral advice that an option will be exercised is not binding on the government). See, however, *American Mach. & Foundry Co.*, ASBCA 8862, 65-1 BCA ¶ 4654, where the government was held bound to an oral agreement extending the date on which the option could be exercised. In *Diversified Marine Tech, Inc.*, DOTBCA 2455, 93-2 BCA ¶ 25,720, the board refused to compensate the contractor for work done on an option that had been orally discussed with the captain of a ship (indicating a high probability that the option would be exercised) but which had not been exercised in writing. In *System Planning Corp. v. United States*, 107 Fed. Cl. 710 (2012), the court found no exercise of an option for technical data rights through oral communications that another contractor was violating the data rights.

[vi] Performing after Improper Option Exercise

There have been a number of instances where a contractor has asserted that an option was not properly exercised but has agreed to perform the option work "under protest." In such cases, relief for the added costs of option work done pursuant to untimely exercises of options has been granted on the theory that a constructive change has occurred, *Lockheed Martin Ir Imaging Sys., Inc. v. West*, 108 F.3d 319 (Fed. Cir. 1997); *Lear Siegler Inc.*, ASBCA 12164, 69-1 BCA ¶ 7563; *Keco Indus., Inc.*, ASBCA 16645, 73-2 BCA ¶ 10,056. See also *Holly Corp.*, ASBCA 24975, 83-1 BCA ¶ 16,327, where the exercise of an option without adequate funds was held to be a constructive change order because a government employee stated funds were available and the contractor could not reasonably have known of the lack of funds. GAO has refused to consider such allegations because they are "appropriate for handling under the Disputes clause," *Murdock Mach. & Eng'g Co.*, Comp. Gen. Dec. B-183098, 75-1 CPD ¶ 98.

If the contractor honors an improper option exercise by performing without objection, it is normally estopped from later contesting the validity of the option exercise. In *E. Walters & Co. v. United States*, 576 F.2d 362 (Ct. Cl. 1978), the court held that the contractor had lost the right to an equitable adjustment for improper exercise of an option because it had performed the option work without challenge and had not raised the issue until six months after completion of performance. See also *CARAM v. General Servs. Admin.*, GSBCA 12773, 95-1 BCA ¶ 27,488, where the contractor was estopped from asserting an improper option exercise when it failed to raise the issue at any time during the option year. Similarly, in *USD Techs., Inc.*, ASBCA 31305, 87-2 BCA ¶ 19,680, the board found that the contractor was estopped from denying that an option was properly exercised when it had signed a bilateral modification "restating" the terms of the option exercise. In *TECOM, Inc.*, IBCA 2970 A-1, 95-2 BCA ¶ 27,607, the board found no estoppel where the contractor performed the option work for four and one-half months without protest but did not realize that the option had been improperly exercised until it hired an attorney.

[vii] Unconscionability

The ASBCA has considered allegations of unconscionability in the government's decision to exercise options, but these claims have been unsuccessful, *United Serv. Corp.*, ASBCA 25786, 82-2 BCA ¶ 15,985; *Mercantile Servs.*,

Ltd., ASBCA 26386, 82-1 BCA ¶ 15,767, absent evidence that the entire contract had become commercially senseless and that the government had superior knowledge regarding inflation at the time it exercised the options. In *McGrail Equip. Co.*, ASBCA 20555, 76-1 BCA ¶ 11,723, where prices had increased substantially after a government price freeze had been lifted, the exercise of an option was held not to be unconscionable. GAO has stated that the concept of unconscionability is inapplicable to the exercise of options since the exercise of an option does not constitute the making of a new contract, *Heirs of Kim Xum*, Comp. Gen. Dec. B-189121, 83-1 CPD ¶ 408.

[7] Soft Options

The traditional option used in government contracts has been on a firm-fixed-price basis with definitive specifications and a firm delivery schedule. Such options have been referred to as "hard" options. FAR 17.207(f) appears to preclude exercise of an option that does not contain firm prices and the Department of Homeland Security has prohibited the use of "unpriced options," HSAR 3017.202. See *Magnum Opus Techs., Inc. v. United States*, 94 Fed. Cl. 512 (2010), holding it improper to exercise options with no firm prices.

Nonetheless, agencies also have used options with less definite terms, referred to as "soft" options. See, for example, *Aviation Contractor Employees, Inc. v. United States*, 945 F.2d 1568 (Fed. Cir. 1991), holding that such an option to extend the contract period with no agreement on how additional work would be priced was not invalid for lack of certainty because it required the parties to negotiate in good faith to establish the price. See also *Fox Int'l, Inc.*, Comp. Gen. Dec. B-181675, 75-1 CPD ¶ 126, finding no lack of good faith when government terminated the negotiations when it found a cheaper method of fulfilling its requirements. In *North Star Steel Co. v. United States*, 477 F.3d 1324 (Fed. Cir. 2007), the court held that to prove that the government breached such a good faith obligation, the contractor would have to prove "bad faith." The decision is not clear on what conduct would constitute bad faith but it does indicate that failure to disclose vital information pertinent to the pricing would "constitute a failure to negotiate in good faith." Compare *England v. Systems Mgmt. Am. Corp.*, 38 Fed. Appx. 567 (Fed. Cir. 2002), where the court reversed a board decision holding that the government had been arbitrary and capricious in delaying finalization of option pricing until after the contractor was ineligible to receive the options (because it lost its small business status). There the court found four bases for a holding that the government had acted improperly, (1) whether the government official acted with "subjective bad faith," (2) whether the official had "no reasonable basis" supporting the decision at issue, a factor closely associated with the bad faith test stated above (3) the amount of discretion vested in the government official who rendered the decision under scrutiny and (4) whether a proven violation of the relevant statutes or regulations can alone render a decision arbitrary and capricious and thus provide a basis for recovery.

In reversing the board decision on the basis that the government action was reasonable, the court recognized that an agreement to negotiate in good faith might "actually require something more than simply not negotiating in bad faith" and made the following comment on what might constitute good faith at 573:

> "Good faith" ordinarily refers to "'that state of mind denoting honesty of purpose, freedom from intention to defraud, and, generally speaking, . . . faithfulness to one's duty or obligation.'" *Arnold M. Diamond, Inc.* [*v. Dalton*], 25 F.3d [1006 (Fed. Cir. 1994)] at 1010 (quoting *People v. Nunn*, 46 Cal. 2d 460, 296 P.2d 813, 818 (Cal. App. 1956) and discussing "good faith" as used in the Contract Disputes Act).

Thus, it is not clear what standard should be applied to determine whether a party has negotiated the price of a soft option in good faith.

Because the contractor's obligations under such soft options are uncertain, the major purpose for using options—that of protecting the government from future uncertainties—is absent. It appears that the major benefits to be gained by the government from such options are administrative convenience in the option procurement and any advantage accruing from the contractor's obligation to negotiate in good faith. In *Electronic Sys. USA, Inc.*, ASBCA 26063, 82-1 BCA ¶ 15,521, the board held that performance of work in accordance with the government's exercise of an unpriced option is compensable as a constructive change.

CHAPTER 13

CONTRACT PRICING

§13.01 INTRODUCTION

The government's policy is to purchase supplies and services at reasonable prices. In this regard, FAR 14.408-2 requires the contracting officer to determine that bid prices are reasonable before awarding the contract, and FAR 14.404-1(c)(6) permits cancellation of sealed bid solicitations if all acceptable bids are at unreasonable prices or if only one bid is received, and the reasonableness of the price cannot be established. With respect to negotiated procurement, FAR 15.402(a) requires the contracting officer to "[p]urchase supplies and services . . . at fair and reasonable prices." Reasonableness of price is also a concept applicable to contract modifications. Thus, in the vast majority of contract actions, the contracting officer is required to determine that the proposed contract price is reasonable before an award is made.

The primary focus of these requirements is to ensure that the government does not pay unreasonably high prices. However, prices that are *unreasonably low* should also be dealt with before an award is made. Such prices may place the contracting officer on notice of a possible mistake in the bid or proposal. When there is a perceived mistake in a bid received in a sealed bid procurement, the offeror must be requested to verify the price, FAR 14.407-1. The FAR contains no similar requirement for requesting verification of perceived mistakes in prices submitted in negotiated procurements, but it is good practice to follow this procedure. See *Griffy's Landscape Maint., LLC v. United States*, 46 Fed. Cl. 257 (2000) (request for verification of perceived mistake in proposal mandatory); and *C.W. Over & Sons, Inc. v. United States*, 54 Fed. Cl. 514 (2002) (no blanket rule requiring request for verification). Unreasonably low prices may also constitute evidence that the offeror is not responsible, FAR 9.103(c). In negotiated procurement, an unreasonably low price may indicate that the offeror does not understand the work, FAR 15.305(a)(1), resulting in a reduced scoring of the offeror's technical proposal. Similarly, an unreasonably low price may be perceived as creating a high risk that the offeror cannot perform the work in a satisfactory manner. Finally, proposing an unreasonably low price that is below cost may constitute "buying in," alerting the contracting officer to take precautions to prevent the contractor from obtaining improper relief from the underpricing. See FAR 3.501.

This chapter considers the process that is followed by the contracting parties in establishing the contract price or cost and fee. The first step in this process is the submission of proposed prices or estimated costs and a proposed fee by offerors. The contracting officer is then charged with the evaluation of those prices or costs and fees to determine reasonableness and/or realism. The techniques used by the government to determine reasonableness of price are price analysis and cost analysis. Price analysis looks at an offeror's proposed unit or total prices and uses data external to the offeror's anticipated costs of performance to make a judgment as to their reasonableness. In contrast, cost analysis reviews the offeror's proposed estimated costs to ascertain the reasonableness of each cost element. The first section of this chapter describes the various techniques that may have been used by offerors to arrive at their submitted prices or cost estimates. The second section deals with the contracting officer's selection of the analytical technique to be used to assess such proposals and the data necessary to use that technique. The third section considers the roles and functions of the various government personnel involved in cost analysis and price analysis. The fourth section covers the process of price analysis, while the fifth section deals with the process of cost analysis. The sixth section addresses the methods prescribed for the negotiation of profit where the parties have negotiated the costs of performance. The last section reviews the procedures to be followed in price negotiations.

§ 13.02 OFFEROR PRICE OR COST ESTIMATING TECHNIQUES

Companies use a variety of techniques to arrive at a proposed price or cost estimate. In proposing firm fixed prices where competition is expected, offerors have much greater leeway in deciding what price to propose because they generally do not have to disclose any detailed cost information in their proposals. Hence, they can factor in the impact of competition and the condition of the market as well as the expected cost of performance in arriving at a proposed fixed price. In contrast, in cost-reimbursement and incentive contracting situations, costs will have to be proposed separately, with a commensurate need to provide some detailed cost information. There, the offeror will be expected to justify the cost estimate that is submitted. Volume 1 of the DoD Contract Pricing Reference Guide (CPRG) describes two basic type of pricing used by companies—"cost-based pricing" and "market-based pricing."

In cost-based pricing, the company makes its best estimate of the cost of performing the work and then adds a profit to arrive at the price. The profit is determined by various methods—generally either by a percentage of the cost or a percentage of the investment needed to perform the prospective contract. The estimated costs are arrived at based on the amount of data that is available to the offeror from past work or industry norms that will indicate the amount of resources that will be necessary to perform the work. Thus, cost estimates for repetitive tasks will tend to be quite precise whereas cost estimates for new work will be highly judgmental. The Defense Contract Audit Manual (DCAM) describes three types of estimating techniques at 9-303:

> d. There are various methods of preparing cost estimates. The most frequently used are the detailed, comparison, and roundtable methods or a combination of the three.
>
> (1) The detailed method requires the accumulation of detailed information to arrive at estimated costs and typically uses cost data derived from the accounting system, adjunct statistical records, and other sources. The information often includes specifications; drawings; bills of material; statements of

production quantities and rates; machine and work-station workloads; manufacturing processes, including the analysis of labor efficiency, setup and rework, and material scrap, waste, and spoilage; data determining plant layout requirements; analysis of tooling and capital equipment, labor, raw material and purchased parts; special tools and dies; and composition of the indirect cost pools.

(2) The comparison method is used when specifications for the item being estimated are similar to other items already produced or currently in production and for which actual cost experience is available. Under this method, requirements for the new item are compared with those for a past or current item, the differences are isolated, and cost elements applicable to the differences are deleted from or added to experienced costs. Adjustments are also made for possible upward or downward cost trends.

(3) The roundtable method is used to estimate the cost of a new item where there is no cost experience or detailed information regarding specifications, drawings, or bills of material. Under this method, representatives of the engineering, manufacturing, purchasing, and accounting departments (among others) develop the cost estimate by exchanging views and making judgments based on knowledge and experience. This method has the advantage of speed of application and is relatively inexpensive, but may not produce readily supportable or reliable cost estimates. When this method is used, technical assistance may be required to evaluate the resultant cost estimates.

It can be seen that these descriptions relate to arriving at a cost estimate for a manufactured product. However, the same techniques are used in making estimates of the cost of construction work or other types of services. The critical issue is whether the offeror has sound information regarding the cost of performing the same or similar work. DCAM 9-303 suggests that there are a number of factors influencing the amount of detail that an offeror should consider in arriving at its cost estimate:

b. Contractors may employ uniform procedures to prepare prospective price proposals or may justifiably use a variety of method and procedures. Special problems may require a deviation from established procedures. It may be desirable in certain instances, from both the cost and time standpoints, to use overall or broad estimating procedures, rather than more precise, detailed methods; or it may be necessary to rely on the judgment of qualified personnel in design, production, or other fields. Variations in estimating procedures employed may be attributable to such factors as:

(1) the relative dollar amount of each estimate,

(2) the contractor's competitive position,

(3) the degree of firmness of specifications related to the new item, and

(4) the available cost data applicable to the same or related products/services previously furnished.

Market-based pricing is very different than cost-based pricing because it is arrived at by establishing a price in order to maximize the company's position in the market. The CPRG describes seven market-based pricing strategies at I.1.4:

I.1.4.1 Profit-Maximization Pricing
I.1.4.2 Market-Share Pricing
I.1.4.3 Market Skimming
I.1.4.4 Current-Revenue Pricing
I.1.4.5 Promotional Pricing
I.1.4.6 Demand-Differential Pricing
I.1.4.7 Market-Competition Pricing

Some of these strategies are used in open commercial markets where prices are known to competitors and are not very applicable to sealed bidding or competitive negotiation procurements where prices are not known until after an offer has been submitted. However, they might be applicable to Federal Supply Schedules or other types of procurement where prices are posted and thus available to all competitors. For example, in profit-maximization pricing the company sets the price at a level that yields the highest total profit for the quantity sold. This might be a price higher than its competitors but one that will yield sufficient sales to generate the best total profit. Similarly, in the market skimming strategy, the price is set at a high level to skim off those few customers that are willing to pay that price. The same result would occur in current-revenue pricing where the seller sets a high price on the assumption that it is unlikely that there will be long-term sales.

Strategies more applicable to sealed bidding or competitive negotiation procurements are promotional pricing and market-competition pricing. The CPRG indicates that promotional pricing may occur on task order or delivery order contracts and describes some of its implications at ¶ I.1.4.5:

> Bait-and-switch pricing can be particularly attractive to a firm preparing an offer for a delivery-order contract with multiple line items. An offeror using this strategy lures the buyer using a low-priced item (e.g., a low labor rate for a particular labor category) and then switches the buyer to a "better" item (e.g., a higher priced category of labor) during the sale.
>
> Loss-leader [pricing] can be attractive in situations where many items are commonly bought from the same source. An offeror using this strategy reduces the price of one item, or a group of items, to near cost, or even below. Customers are attracted to buy the low-priced items and buy other related items at the same time (e.g., set the price of a system low and the price of supplies for the system high).

Prestige pricing uses a high-quality, high-priced item to enhance the image of an entire product line and attract more buyers. For example, many consultants feel that buyers are reluctant to buy from firms that do not charge enough. In other words, it can be almost impossible to evaluate qualifications so high price equals high quality.

A form of loss-leader pricing that is not discussed in the CPRG is pricing of the initial quantity of a new product at a low number on the assumption that future quantities of the product will be acquired on a sole source basis from the company. This can be an effective strategy because DOD has traditionally foregone competition after a weapon system has been manufactured for several years by the developing contractor.

Perhaps the most common form of commercial pricing found in government procurement is market-competition pricing. The CPRG contains the following coverage at I.1.4.7:

> [In this strategy] different companies may set prices at a level that keeps pace with competitors' prices. When employing this strategy, the seller considers the following points:
>
> Determine competitor prices and/or anticipated prices.
>
> Set price to keep pace with competitor prices.
>
> Major strategy applications include sealed-bid and going-rate pricing.
>
> Sealed bid pricing forces the seller to:
>
> Estimate what competitors will bid.
>
> Determine what the seller can profitably bid.
>
> Submit the bid knowing that it will be accepted or rejected without further discussion.
>
> Going-rate pricing requires the seller to:
>
> Determine what competitors are charging.
>
> Establish product price within an established range of the competition.

This government guidance makes it clear that offerors factor the competitive situation into their pricing. However, it does not include any discussion of two major influences on contractor pricing decisions. The first of these influences is the relative optimism that can influence competitive pricing of work where there is no good cost experience. In this sort of "roundtable" pricing, the various experts in a company are prone to arrive at estimates of the optimal way of performing the work without sufficiently taking into account the pitfalls that may be encountered in performing a new task. Thus, their original estimates of the cost of performance may be low. Subsequently, the company's management may reduce these estimates in order to arrive at a price that will win the competition. This phenomenon is probably the explanation for the fact that many weapon system development contracts have been awarded at prices or estimated costs that could not be met during actual contract performance. See *Annual Weapon Systems Assessments*, GAO-19-336SP, May 2019, and GAO-18-360SP, Apr. 2018 as well as *Defense Acquisitions: Major Weapon Systems Continue to Experience Cost and Schedule Problems Under DoD's Revised Policy*, GAO-06-368, Apr. 13, 2006.

The second influence on pricing that is not discussed in the government guidance is below-cost pricing. In times when there is not much work being acquired, companies are tempted to propose prices that cover all of their anticipated direct costs plus only some of their indirect costs. This permits them to retain key employees that they might otherwise have to release and to cover some of the fixed costs of the business. This can be a viable short-term business strategy but imposes significant risk on the contractor if such prices cover a very long period. Some government employees might consider this a form of "buying-in" which is listed in the FAR as "an improper business practice" but is not prohibited by FAR 3.501.

§ 13.03 GOVERNMENT SELECTION OF THE ANALYTICAL TECHNIQUE

Analysis of prices by the contracting officer to determine that they are fair and reasonable is *required* in all procurement actions, FAR 14.408-2 and FAR 15.404-1(a). Thus, the contracting officer must select the analytical technique that will be used to make this determination. The major techniques are price analysis and cost analysis.

The contracting officer should obtain data to permit the use of one of these analytical techniques on all procurements. However, as discussed in § 13.05, these data need not necessarily be obtained from offerors because it may be available in the agency or obtainable through market research.

Cost analysis must be conducted when it is necessary to examine individual cost elements, such as estimated labor hours or material prices, to determine the reasonableness of price, FAR 15.404-1(a)(3). Traditionally, cost analysis was performed by obtaining cost element breakdowns and supporting factual data. This factual data is referred to by the statutes and regulations as "certified cost or pricing data" and is required to be submitted and certified by contractors and subcontractors in certain specified types of procurement actions over the statutory threshold ($2,000,000 at the current time), 10 U.S.C. §§ 3701-3708 (formerly § 2306a), and 41 U.S.C. §§ 3501-3509 (the "Truthful Cost or Pricing Data Act"—formerly the "Truth in Negotiations Act" or "TINA"). Cost analysis can also be performed by obtaining cost element breakdowns or other information regarding the estimated costs of performance of the contract with limited or no certified cost or pricing data. This type of cost analysis is frequently called *cost realism analysis*. Such analysis is required when awarding a cost-reimbursement contract, FAR 15.404-1(d)(2). Cost analysis is *never* performed on sealed bid procurements, but on negotiated procurements the contracting officer must determine whether cost analysis is necessary and, if so, what type of data are necessary to perform such analysis.

Cost analysis is *required* to be performed on all procurement actions where certified cost or pricing data are required, FAR 15.404-1(a)(3). However, GAO has made it clear that this requirement applies only when applicable statutes require obtaining certified cost or pricing data. Thus, in those instances where offerors have been required to submit certified cost or pricing data by an RFP but it is later determined that one of the statutory exceptions applies, cost analysis is not required, *Research Mgmt. Corp.*, 69 Comp. Gen. 368 (B-237865), 90-1 CPD ¶352 (adequate price competition precluded need for cost analysis). Prior to 1994, contracting officers had substantial discretion to require the submission of certified cost or pricing data and to perform detailed cost analysis using those data. However, the Federal Acquisition Streamlining Act of 1994 (FASA), Pub. L. No. 103-355, as amended by the Clinger-Cohen Act of 1996, Pub. L. No. 104-106, *prohibited* obtaining certified cost or pricing data when one of the statutory exceptions applies, 10 U.S.C. § 3703 (formerly § 2306a(b)), containing this prohibition, has been modified several times since 1996 and now states:

> (a) In General.—Submission of certified cost or pricing data shall not be required under section 3702 if this title in the case of a contract, a subcontract, or modification of a contract or subcontract—
>
> (1) for which the price agreed upon is based on—
>
> (A) adequate price competition; or
>
> (B) prices set by law or regulation.
>
> (2) for the acquisition of a commercial product or a commercial service; or
>
> (3) in an exceptional case when the head of the procuring activity, without delegation, determines that the requirements of this chapter may be waived and justifies in writing the reasons for such determination.
>
> (4) to the extent such data—
>
> (A) relates to an offset agreement in connection with a contract for the sale of a weapon system or defense-related item to a foreign country or foreign firm; and
>
> (B) does not relate to a contract or subcontract under the offset agreement for work performed in such foreign country or by such foreign firm that is directly related to the weapon system or defense-related item being purchased under the contract.

A similar provision is set forth in 41 U.S.C. § 3503 stating the same general prohibitions but omitting paragraphs (a)(4) and (c). These prohibitions are implemented in FAR 15.403-1.

Under this statutory mandate, the contracting officer must determine whether any of these exceptions applies and, if so, select the appropriate technique to be used and the data to be obtained. FAR 15.402 contains the following guidance—suggesting that contracting officers should obtain only the minimum amount of data necessary to make a determination of price reasonableness when certified cost or pricing data are not required:

Contracting officers shall—

(a) Purchase supplies and services from responsible sources at fair and reasonable prices. In establishing the reasonableness of the offered prices, the contracting officer—

(1) Shall obtain certified cost or pricing data when required by 15.403-4, along with data other than certified cost or pricing data as necessary to establish a fair and reasonable price; or

(2) When certified cost or pricing data are not required by 15.403-4, obtain data other than certified cost or pricing data as necessary to establish a fair and reasonable price, generally using the following order of preference in determining the type of data required:

(i) No additional data from the offeror, if the price is based on adequate price competition, except as provided by 15.403-3(b).

(ii) Data other than certified cost or pricing data such as—

(A) Data related to prices (e.g., established catalog or market prices, sales to non-governmental and governmental entities), relying first on data available within the Government; second, on data obtained from sources other than the offeror; and, if necessary, on data obtained from the offeror. When obtaining data from the offeror is necessary, unless an exception under 15.403-1(b)(1) or (2) applies, such data submitted by the offeror shall include, at a minimum, appropriate data on the prices at which the same or similar items have been sold previously, adequate for evaluating the reasonableness of the price.

(B) Cost data to the extent necessary for the contracting officer to determine a fair and reasonable price.

(3) Obtain the type and quantity of data necessary to establish a fair and reasonable price, but not more data than is necessary. Requesting unnecessary data can lead to increased proposal preparation costs, generally extend acquisition lead time, and consume additional contractor and Government resources. Use techniques such as, but not limited to, price analysis, cost analysis, and/or cost realism analysis to establish a fair and reasonable price. If a fair and reasonable price cannot be established by the contracting officer from the analyses of the data obtained or submitted to date, the contracting officer shall require the submission of additional data sufficient for the contracting officer to support the determination of the fair and reasonable price.

This guidance combines both price information and cost information (other than certified cost or pricing data) into a broad category of data called "data other than certified cost or pricing data." FAR 2.101 defines this category of data:

Data other than certified cost or pricing data means pricing data, cost data, and judgmental information necessary for the contracting officer to determine a fair and reasonable price or to determine cost realism. Such data may include the identical types of data as certified cost or pricing data, consistent with Table 15-2 of 15.408, but without the certification. The data may also include, for example, sales data and other information reasonably required to explain the offeror's estimating process, including, but not limited to—

(1) The judgmental factors applied and the mathematical or other methods used in the estimate, including those used in projecting from known data; and

(2) The nature and amount of any contingencies included in the proposed price.

The result of this statutory and regulatory scheme is that the contracting officer is given broad discretion to select the analytical technique to be used on a procurement but is encumbered with numerous limitations on the information that can be obtained to make the analysis. The critical first step is to determine whether TINA applies and, if so, whether the procurement falls under the monetary threshold or within one of the statutory exceptions. The contracting officer can then decide on the analytical technique that will be used and the data that will be needed to carry out the necessary analysis. This section discusses these issues separately for each of the categories of procurement described in TINA.

[A] Where Certified Cost or Pricing Data are Required

The mandatory requirement for the submission of certified cost or pricing data was placed in the Armed Services Procurement Act in 1962 by Pub. L. No. 87-653. It was later applied to civilian agencies by the Federal Procurement Regulation. Subsequently, the Competition in Contracting Act, Pub. L. No. 98-369, added the requirement to the Federal Property and Administrative Services Act in 1984. The submission requirements for certified cost or pricing data are now contained in very similar language in 10 U.S.C. § 3702 (formerly § 2306a(a)) and 41 U.S.C. § 3502.

[1] When Obtaining Certified Cost or Pricing Data Is Mandatory

Obtaining certified cost or pricing data is required and cost analysis is mandatory when the procurement action (a) is a negotiated contract or contract modification or a subcontract or subcontract modification under such a contract or contract modification; (b) is over the $2,000,000 threshold; and (c) is not within one of the statutory exceptions. Since each of the statutory exceptions is a separate class of procurement action, they will be dealt with individually in the following subsections.

[a] Type of Procurement Action

The statutes require the submission of certified cost or pricing data only on negotiated procurement actions. Thus, no cost or pricing data are submitted in the initial award of a sealed bid contract or a subcontract under such a contract. However, amendments or modifications to sealed bid contracts, as well as those to negotiated contracts, are covered because they are negotiated procurement actions, FAR 15.403-4(a)(1)(iii). This regulation provides that final negotiated pricing actions, such as termination settlements or final pricing of fixed-price incentive or redeterminable contracts, are contract modifications to which the procedures apply. Prior regulations applied this rule to final negotiated overhead rate settlements, but the current regulations are silent on this issue.

Subcontracts under negotiated contracts are covered by the statute as long as the contract and all higher-tier subcontracts are not exempted from coverage, FAR 15.403-4(a)(1)(ii). Amendments to such subcontracts are also covered, FAR 15.403-4(a)(1)(iii).

[b] Dollar Threshold

The original Truth in Negotiations Act in 1962 contained a $100,000 threshold. From 1981 to 1994 the threshold moved between $100,000 and $500,000 by various statutory changes. Then, in 1994 the Federal Acquisition Streamlining Act set the threshold at $500,000, for the entire government. 10 U.S.C. § 3702(g) (formerly § 2306a(a)(7)) and 41 U.S.C. § 3502(g) call for the adjustment of the TINA threshold every five years to account for inflation. This resulted in raising the threshold to $550,000 in 2000, FAC 97-20, 65 Fed. Reg. 60542 (effective Oct. 11, 2000); to $650,000 in 2006, FAC 2005-15, 71 Fed. Reg. 57363 (effective Sept. 28, 2006); to $700,000 in 2010, FAC 2005-45, 75 Fed. Reg. 53135 (effective Aug. 18, 2010); and to $750,000 in 2014, FAC 2005-83, 80 Fed. Reg. 38293 (effective Nov. 1, 2015). Section 811 of the National Defense Authorization Act for FY 2018 then raised the threshold to $2 million for all contracts entered into after July 1, 2018. DoD has issued Class Deviation 2022-O0005 raising the threshold to $7.5 million for contracts or subcontracts awarded to small businesses or nontraditional defense contractors pursuant to broad agency announcements, the Small Business Innovation Research program, or the Small Business Technology Transfer program.

With these numerous changes in the threshold and the accompanying delays in implementation of the statutes, it can be expected that some contracts will contain contract requirements that differ from the statutory requirements. Generally, the contract provisions dealing with contract modifications will govern over statutory provisions. However, 10 U.S.C. § 3702(f) (formerly § 2306a(a)(6)) and 41 U.S.C. § 3502(f) permit contractors to obtain contract amendments adopting the new $2 million threshold for contracts entered into before that threshold became effective. Such amendments would make the new threshold applicable to contract modifications and subcontracts for which agreement on price was reached after the date of their enactment.

For the purpose of applying the statute to contract modifications, the dollar value of a price adjustment is calculated by totaling the costs added and the costs deleted by the adjustment, FAR 15.403-4(a)(1)(iii). Thus, a $200,000 modification adding $1,200,000 and deleting $1,000,000 would be subject to the statutory requirement. The regulation notes that this rule should not be followed when "unrelated and separately priced" changes are included in the modification "for administrative convenience."

[2] Obtaining the Data

When the contracting officer determines that a procurement will be over the $2 million threshold and none of the exceptions apply, FAR 15.403-5(a) requires the contracting officer to specify that certified cost or pricing data must be submitted. However, the standard solicitation provisions allow the contractor to object to this requirement. Thus, the Requirements for Certified Cost or Pricing Data or Data Other Than Certified Cost or Pricing Data solicitation provision in FAR 52.215-20 gives the offeror the opportunity to defer the submission of cost or pricing data by claiming that either the commercial products or services exception or the prices set by law or regulation exception applies. Paragraph (a) of the provision states that if the offeror believes that it qualifies for either of these exceptions to the requirement for the submission of cost or pricing data, it may submit a written request for exception with the data pertinent to that exception. The provision is silent as to what action an offeror may take if it believes that the adequate price competition exception applies or if it wants the agency to grant a statutory waiver. However, offerors would be well advised to request either of these exceptions if they believe they are applicable. Paragraph (b) of the provision states that the offeror must submit certified cost or pricing data if it "is not granted an exception." In addition, if no exception applies—as in the case of a sole source procurement of a product or service that is not commercial—the offeror should submit the applicable cost or pricing data with the proposal (with the intention of certifying it at the conclusion of negotiations) and the provision requires that it be submitted in accordance with the instructions in Table 15-2 in FAR 15.408. FAR 52.215-20 also provides for four alternate provisions that contracting officers can use to (1) require the data to be delivered in a format other than required by Table 15-2, (2) require copies of the offeror's proposal to be submitted to the Administrative Contracting Officer and the contract auditor, (3) require the data to be submitted by electronic media, and (4) specify the type of data other than certified cost or pricing data that is required. See the instructions in FAR 15.408(l).

Similar procedures are prescribed for contract modifications. FAR 15.408(m) permits the contracting officer to insert the Requirements for Certified Cost or Pricing Data or Data Other Than Certified Cost or Pricing

Data—Modifications clause in FAR 52.215-21 in contracts "if it is reasonably certain that [such] data will be required for modifications" to the contract. This clause also permits the contractor to apply for an exception in lieu of submitting certified cost or pricing data to support a modification over the statutory threshold and contains the same alternate provisions for varied submissions of data. Since some data will be required for modifications over the statutory threshold, it is anticipated that this clause will be used in all contracts where there is any possibility that a modification over $2 million might be issued.

[B] Where Certified Cost or Pricing Data are not Required

10 U.S.C. § 3705 (formerly § 2306a(d)(1)) and 41 U.S.C. § 3505(a) state that when certified cost or pricing data are not required, "the contracting officer shall require submission of data other than certified cost or pricing data to the extent necessary to determine the reasonableness of the price" and "shall require that the data submitted include, at a minimum, appropriate information on prices at which the same or similar items have previously been sold." This is implemented in FAR 15.403-3 as follows:

> (a)(1) In those acquisitions that do not require certified cost or pricing data, the contracting officer shall—
>
> (i) Obtain whatever data are available from Government or other secondary sources and use that data in determining a fair and reasonable price;
>
> (ii) Require submission of data other than certified cost or pricing data, as defined in 2.101, from the offeror to the extent necessary to determine a fair and reasonable price (10 U.S.C. 3705(a) and 41 U.S.C. 3505(a)) if the contracting officer determines that adequate data from sources other than the offeror are not available. This includes requiring data from an offeror to support a cost realism analysis;
>
> (iii) Consider whether cost data are necessary to determine a fair and reasonable price when there is not adequate price competition;
>
> (iv) Require that the data submitted by the offeror include, at a minimum, appropriate data on the prices at which the same item or similar items have previously been sold, adequate for determining the reasonableness of the price unless an exception under 15.403-1(b)(1) or (2) applies; and
>
> (v) Consider the guidance in section 3.3, chapter 3, volume I, of the Contract Pricing Reference Guide cited at 15.404-1(a)(7) to determine the data an offeror shall be required to submit.
>
> (2) The contractor's format for submitting the data should be used (see 15.403-5(b)(2)).
>
> (3) The contracting officer shall ensure that data used to support price negotiations are sufficiently current to permit negotiation of a fair

and reasonable price. Requests for updated offeror data should be limited to data that affect the adequacy of the proposal for negotiations, such as changes in price lists.

(4) As specified in section 808 of the Strom Thurmond National Defense Authorization Act for Fiscal Year 1999 (Pub. L. 105-261), an offeror who does not comply with a requirement to submit data for a contract or subcontract in accordance with paragraph (a)(1) of this subsection is ineligible for award unless the HCA determines that it is in the best interest of the Government to make the award to that offeror, based on consideration of the following:

(i) The effort made to obtain the data.

(ii) The need for the item or service.

(iii) Increased cost or significant harm to the Government if award is not made.

Note that the definition of "data other than certified cost or pricing data" (set forth above) was rewritten by FAC 2005-45, 75 Fed. Reg. 53135 (Aug. 30, 2010) to include "identical types of data as certified cost or pricing data, consistent with Table 15-2 of 15.408, but without the certification." This was intended to make it clear to contracting officers that they have the discretion to call for the submission of uncertified cost or pricing data if they conclude that such data is needed to ensure a fair and reasonable price.

The guidance on what data to call for is followed by specific guidance on each type of procurement where certified cost or pricing data may not be required. These will be discussed separately in the material below.

[C] Actions Under the Dollar Threshold

The contracting officer has considerable discretion in selecting the analytical technique and calling for appropriate data when the procurement action is under the $2 million threshold for the submission of certified cost or pricing data. However, FAR 15.403-4(a)(2) permits heads of contracting activities, without the power of delegation, to authorize the contracting officer to obtain certified cost or pricing data on procurements under the threshold but over the simplified acquisition threshold of $250,000 when it is not prohibited by statute. In this case or when uncertified cost or pricing data were obtained, the contracting officer would perform cost analysis. In other cases, the contracting officer would be expected to use the same analytical technique for procurements in this category as would be appropriate for larger procurements of the same type. Thus, if, for example, a procurement was for a commercial product or service with a contract price of less than $2 million, it could be anticipated that the contracting officer would use the same analytical techniques that would be appropriate for procurement of commercial products or services over $2 million.

The statutes permit the obtaining of certified cost or pricing data in procurements under the threshold in *extremely limited circumstances.* See 10 U.S.C. § 3704 (formerly § 2306a(c)) and 41 U.S.C. § 3504 as follows:

> Cost or Pricing Data on Below Threshold Contracts.—
>
> (1) *Authority to Require Submission.*—Subject to paragraph (2), when certified cost or pricing data are not required to be submitted . . . for a contract, subcontract, or modification of a contract or subcontract, such data may nevertheless be required to be submitted by the head of the procuring activity, but only if the head of the procuring activity determines that such data are necessary for the evaluation by the agency of the reasonableness of the price of the contract, subcontract, or modification of a contract or subcontract. In any case in which the head of the procuring activity requires such data to be submitted under this subsection, the head of the procuring activity shall justify in writing the reason for such requirement.
>
> (2) *Exception.*—The head of the procuring activity may not require certified cost or pricing data to be submitted under this paragraph for any contract or subcontract, or modification of a contract or subcontract, covered by the exceptions [for adequate price competition, prices set by law or regulation or commercial products or services].
>
> (3) *Delegation of Authority Prohibited.*—The head of a procuring activity may not delegate the functions under this paragraph.

FAR 15.403-1(a) prohibits obtaining certified cost or pricing data on acquisitions at or below the $250,000 simplified acquisition threshold. Although FAR 15.403-4(a)(2) implements this statutory provision for acquisitions between $250,000 and $2 million, since it precludes contracting officers from obtaining certified cost or pricing data without getting the approval of the head of the contracting activity and may not be used when the major exceptions apply, it will probably be used sparingly. Its major application will be to contract modifications where there is little or no pricing information. Under the prior statute, agencies frequently required the submission of certified cost or pricing data when the price was determined to be unreasonable. See *Sperry Rand Corp. v. United States*, 548 F.2d 915 (Ct. Cl. 1977), where the court affirmed the exercise of this discretion under the Defense Acquisition Regulation (which gave considerably greater discretion to the contracting officer). In contrast, when the contracting officer did not request the data because it was determined that an exemption applied, the board held that no submission was required, *J.W. Bateson Co.*, GSBCA 4133, 76-1 BCA ¶ 11,751, *recons. denied*, 76-2 BCA ¶ 12,109.

[D] Actions Where There Is Adequate Price Competition

The statutes and the regulations prohibit the obtaining of certified cost or pricing data for this type of procurement action. Thus, when adequate price competition exists, the contracting officer is generally expected to rely heavily on the competitive prices to ascertain the reasonableness of the price. See FAR 15.404-1(a)(2) stating that "[p]rice analysis shall be used when cost or pricing data are not required."

[1] Definition of Adequate Price Competition

The statute does not define "adequate price competition," but FAR 15.403-1(c) contains the following guidance to be used in determining whether there is adequate price competition:

> (1) Adequate price competition. (i) A price is based on adequate price competition when—
>
> (A) Two or more responsible offerors, competing independently, submit priced offers that satisfy the Government's expressed requirement;
>
> (B) Award will be made to the offeror whose proposal represents the best value (see 2.101) where price is a substantial factor in source selection; and
>
> (C) There is no finding that the price of the otherwise successful offeror is unreasonable. Any finding that the price is unreasonable must be supported by a statement of the facts and approved at a level above the contracting officer;
>
> (ii) For agencies other than DoD, NASA, and the Coast Guard. A price is also based on adequate price competition when—
>
> (A) There was a reasonable expectation, based on market research or other assessment, that two or more responsible offerors, competing independently, would submit priced offers in response to the solicitation's expressed requirement, even though only one offer is received from a responsible offeror and if—
>
> (1) Based on the offer received, the contracting officer can reasonably conclude that the offer was submitted with the expectation of competition, *e.g.*, circumstances indicate that—
>
> (i) The offeror believed that at least one other offeror was capable of submitting a meaningful offer; and
>
> (ii) The offeror had no reason to believe that other potential offerors did not intend to submit an offer; and
>
> (2) The determination that the proposed price is based on adequate price competition and is reasonable, has been approved at a level above the contracting officer; or
>
> (B) Price analysis clearly demonstrates that the proposed price is reasonable in comparison with current or recent prices for the same or similar items, adjusted to reflect changes in market conditions,

> economic conditions, quantities, or terms and conditions under contracts that resulted from adequate price competition.

Prior to 2019, this regulation allowed all agencies to find adequate price competition, under limited circumstances, when *only one offer* is received by the government. Section 822 of the National Defense Authorization Act for FY 2017 prohibited such a finding by DOD, NASA or the Coast Guard with the result that those agencies will have to obtain certified cost or pricing data when only one offer is received unless another prohibition applies or the requirement is waived. See DFARS 215.371-3 for guidance on the procedures to be followed in these circumstances.

Earlier regulations required that at least two responsible offerors compete independently for the award. Under this more restrictive rule, determinations of adequate price competition were upheld even though only a small number of competitors were involved in serious consideration for award. See *Ogden Plant Maint. Co.*, Comp. Gen. Dec. B-255156.2, 94-1 CPD ¶ 275 (adequate price competition when two offerors were in competitive range; offeror downgraded on capability factors not a nonresponsible offeror); *Family Realty*, Comp. Gen. Dec. B-247772, 92-2 CPD ¶ 6 (adequate price competition where two offerors were in competitive range); and *Adrian Supply Co.*, Comp. Gen. Dec. B-241502, 91-1 CPD ¶ 138 (adequate price competition on second solicitation when two price-competitive proposals received; no adequate price competition on first solicitation when only one proposal received). In one case, the contracting officer's determination of adequate price competition was found to be reasonable, although one of two offerors thought that the government might not receive any other proposals, *ABA Electromechanical Sys., Inc.*, NASABCA 1081-13, 85-3 BCA ¶ 18,225. The other proposal and the government estimate were held to have demonstrated the reasonableness of the proposed price. However, in *Akin, Gump, Strauss, Hauer & Feld*, 53 Comp. Gen. 5 (B-177847) (1973), it was held that price competition did not exist when only one acceptable proposal was received. In *Litton Sys., Inc.*, ASBCA 35914, 96-1 BCA ¶ 28,201, the board rejected a motion for summary judgment based on the argument that the contractor had no liability for defective data because there had been adequate price competition. The board ruled that the presence of only one "responsive" offeror precluded the applicability of the exception.

In trade-off procurements, where there are multiple evaluation factors, adequate price competition will be found where price is a *substantial evaluation factor* and is so evaluated. This rule applies to both fixed-price contracts and cost-reimbursement contracts. It is derived from decisions of GAO and has now been incorporated in FAR 15.403-1(c)(1)(i)(A). See *Serv-Air, Inc.—Recons.*, 58 Comp. Gen. 362 (B-189884), 79-1 CPD ¶ 212, where cost to the government was held to be a "substantial" factor even though it was considerably less important than the other factors. The case involved the award of a fixed-price incentive contract where price was stated to be 30% of the total evaluation, with 15% for the comparative level of the price (which increased the score for prices that were low) and 15% for "cost realism" (which reduced the score for prices that were considered to be too low). GAO ruled that price was a substantial factor even though the components of the evaluation might cancel out the factor. In *Dynalectron Corp.*, 52 Comp. Gen. 346 (B-176217) (1972), cost to the government was found to be a substantial factor in a cost-plus-award-fee contract even though it was 20% of the total evaluation. In *U.S. Nuclear, Inc.*, 57 Comp. Gen. 185 (B-187716), 77-2 CPD ¶ 511, adequate price competition was found on a cost-plus-fixed-fee contract. The contracting officer also has the discretion to determine that price is not a substantial factor in these circumstances. See *Cubic Defense Sys.*, Comp. Gen. Dec. B-229884, 88-1 CPD ¶ 395, where GAO affirmed such a decision where price on a fixed-price contract was a minor factor (stating that *Serv-Air* holds that "the contracting officer has broad discretion to make that determination"). See also *United Techs. Corp.*, ASBCA 51410, 04-1 BCA ¶ 32,556, *aff'd*, 463 F.3d 1261 (Fed. Cir. 2006), holding that the contracting officer did not abuse his discretion in finding that competition was not adequate when two companies competed on a trade-off procurement and questioning the reasoning in *Serv-Air*. In spite of the *United Technologies* implication that adequate price competition could not exist in a trade-off procurement, when the final award decision is made by a trade-off analysis between the differences in price and the differences in the other factors (as is the case in almost all trade-off procurements), it would appear that price would always be a substantial factor and the contracting officer would have little discretion in this regard.

Adequate price competition also exists when the RFP provides for award on the basis of the "lowest-priced, technically acceptable offer," *D-K Assocs., Inc.*, Comp. Gen. Dec. B-213417, 84-1 CPD ¶ 396. This rule is now included in FAR 15.403-1(c)(1)(i)(A).

Adequate price competition can exist where offerors propose to furnish different products to satisfy a government performance specification. Contracting officer determinations that adequate price competition existed have been found to be reasonable in *Macro-Z Tech.*, ASBCA 56711, 12-1 BCA ¶ 35,000 (design-build competition with disparate designs and prices), *Marinette Marine Corp.*, Comp. Gen. Dec. B-400697, 2009 CPD ¶ 16 (ship design competition against performance specification); *ABA Electromechanical Sys., Inc.*, NASABCA 1081-13, 85-3 BCA ¶ 18,225 (proposals for different hardware configurations in response to the government's performance specification), and *Prudential-Maryland (J.V.) Co. v. Lehman*, 590 F. Supp. 1390 (D.D.C. 1984) (procurement of hospital ships in which the competitors were proposing different designs).

The fact that oral and written discussions are conducted does not preclude a finding of adequate price competition. See *UTL Corp.*, Comp. Gen. Dec. B-185832, 76-1 CPD ¶ 209, holding that conducting oral and written discussions and calling for "best and final offers" supported a finding of adequate price competition because competition was, in fact, enhanced. Further, adequate price competition can exist even though "full and open competition" does not occur, *International Sys. Mktg., Inc.*, GSBCA 7948-P, 85-3 BCA ¶ 18,196.

FAR 15.403-1(c)(1)(iii) allows a contracting officer to find adequate price competition by comparing the price submitted to "current or recent prices for the same or similar items." In the one litigated case on a similar statement in a prior regulation, the board held that the procurement did not meet the test, *Norris Indus., Inc.*, ASBCA 15442, 74-1 BCA ¶ 10,482. In *Norris*, the contractor argued that its prices were based on adequate price competition in view of two prior competitive procurements of the items. The board held that the two prior procurements provided too meager a basis for price comparison under the circumstances.

Adequate price competition can also be found when a split award to dual sources is contemplated. See DFARS 215.403-1(c)(1) giving the following additional guidance:

> (B) Adequate price competition normally exists when—
>
> (i) Prices are solicited across a full range of step quantities, normally including a 0-100 percent split, from at least two offerors that are individually capable of producing the full quantity; and
>
> (ii) The reasonableness of all prices awarded is clearly established on the basis of price analysis (see FAR 15.404-1(b)).

In the past the determination of whether adequate price competition existed had been held to be a discretionary decision of the contracting officer. A contracting officer's determination that adequate price competition exists was not disturbed if it was reasonably based, *Fraass Surgical Mfg. Co. v. United States*, 571 F.2d 34 (Ct. Cl. 1978). See also *Sperry Rand Corp. v. United States*, 548 F.2d 915 (Ct. Cl. 1977), recognizing that sound pricing depends upon the exercise of sound judgment. The contracting officer was required first to determine whether adequate price competition existed before the mandatory exemption would apply. However, see *Libby Welding Co.*, ASBCA 15084, 73-1 BCA ¶ 9859, holding that a contracting officer's internal notation that there was adequate price competition could have no effect when there was actually no competition at all in the procurement.

[2] Technique and Data

In most cases when there is adequate price competition, the contracting officer will be able to determine that the price is reasonable by making a price analysis. When there are two or more competitors that have submitted competitive prices, the prices submitted will frequently be sufficient to demonstrate that the award price is fair and reasonable. If the supplies or services have been procured in the past, the contracting officer will also have those prices to be used in a price analysis. Normally, such data would be sufficient in fixed-price contracting situations. In contrast, in cost-reimbursement contracts where there is adequate price competition, the contracting officer will generally need some cost data to evaluate the cost realism of the proposals. FAR 15.403-3(b) gives the following guidance on these issues:

> When adequate price competition exists (see 15.403-1(c)(1)), generally no additional information is necessary to determine the reasonableness of price. However, if there are unusual circumstances where it is concluded that additional information is necessary to determine the reasonableness of price, the contracting officer shall, to the maximum extent practicable, obtain the additional information from sources other than the offeror. In addition, the contracting officer may request information to determine the cost realism of competing offers or to evaluate competing approaches.

See *IDEAL Indus., Inc. v. United States*, 140 Fed. Cl. 328 (2018), where the court held that it was proper for an agency to terminate a contract for convenience when it had been awarded to the second low offeror after the low-priced offeror had been dropped from the competition because it did not furnish data supporting its low price. The court reasoned that the agency had reasonably corrected its mistake in requiring additional data because this regulation precluded obtaining such data when adequate price competition clearly showed that the low price was reasonable.

Obtaining pricing information from an offeror, such as the prices charged to other customers, is viewed by the statutes and regulations as a circumstance that will occur rarely. When cost data are required in order to perform a cost realism analysis in these situations, the contracting officer is *prohibited* from obtaining certified cost or pricing data.

When the contracting officer decides to obtain data in these circumstances, FAR 15.408(l)(4) calls for the use of an alternate solicitation provision to obtain "data other than certified cost or pricing data." This provision (Alternate IV in FAR 52.215-20) provides:

> (a) Submission of cost or pricing data is not required.
>
> (b) Provide information described below: [Insert description of the information and the format that are required, including access to records necessary to permit an adequate evaluation of the proposed price in accordance with 15.403-3.]

[E] Actions Where There are Prices Set by Law or Regulation

FAR 15.403-1(c)(2) contains the following brief statement on this exception:

> *Prices set by law or regulation*. Pronouncements in the form of periodic rulings, reviews, or similar actions of a governmental body, or embodied in the laws, are sufficient to set a price.

The Requirements for Cost or Pricing Data or Information Other Than Cost or Pricing Data solicitation provision in FAR 52.215-20 requires that offerors submit supporting data when this exception applies:

> (a) Exceptions from *certified* cost or pricing data. (1) In lieu of submitting certified cost or pricing data, offerors may submit a written request for exception by submitting the information described in the following subparagraphs. The Contracting Officer may require additional supporting information, but only to the extent necessary to determine whether an exception should be granted, and whether the price is fair and reasonable.
>
> (i) Identification of the law or regulation establishing the price offered. If the price is controlled under law by periodic rulings, reviews, or similar actions of a governmental body, attach a copy of the controlling document, unless it was previously submitted to the contracting office.

This guidance appears to allow the use of this exception and a determination of price reasonableness if the data submitted demonstrates that the proposed price meets the requirements of the law or regulation by which it is governed. However, FAR 15.403-3(a)(1) gives the contracting officer discretion to seek additional information to determine price reasonableness or cost realism. The contracting officer is prohibited from obtaining certified cost or pricing data in these circumstances.

[F] Actions Where There are Commercial Products or Services

The FASA added a new prohibition to obtaining cost or pricing data under the Truth in Negotiations Act to permit the government to follow commercial buying practices with a wide variety of commercial items. This created considerable confusion because there was already an exception for "catalog or market price items." The Clinger-Cohen Act of 1996 clarified this situation by deleting the "catalog or market price items" exception. Thus, there is now a single prohibition to the obtaining of cost or pricing data when procuring a commercial product or a commercial service, 10 U.S.C. § 3703(a)(2) (formerly § 2306a(b)(1)(B)); 41 U.S.C. § 3503(a)(2). Under 41 U.S.C. § 1903(c), noncommercial products or services may be treated as commercial if they are "used (1) in support of a contingency operation; or (2) to facilitate the defense against or recovery from cyber, nuclear, biological, chemical, or radiological attack against the United States." This extended authority does not apply to sole source procurements of such products or services with a price of over $19 million. See FAR 15.403-1(c)(3)(iv).

As discussed in Chapter 9, the confusing term "commercial item" was clarified in 2019 by altering the terminology to deal with "commercial products" and "commercial services." 10 U.S.C. § 3705 (formerly § 2306a(d)(1)) and 41 U.S.C. § 3505(a) contains the following mandatory requirement to obtain data to support the prices of these products and services:

(a) *Authority to Require Submission.* When certified cost or pricing data are not required to be submitted under this section for a contract, subcontract, or modification of a contract or subcontract, the contracting officer shall require submission of data other than certified cost or pricing data to the extent necessary to determine the reasonableness of the price of the contract, subcontract, or modification of the contract or subcontract. Except in the case of a contract or subcontract covered by the exceptions [for adequate price competition and prices set by law or regulation], the data submitted shall include, at a minimum, appropriate information on the prices at which the same item or similar items have previously been sold that is adequate for evaluating the reasonableness of the price for the procurement.

(b) *Limitations on authority.* The Federal Acquisition Regulation shall include the following provisions regarding the types of information that contracting officers may require under subsection (a):

(1) Reasonable limitations. Reasonable limitations on requests for sales data relating to commercial products or commercial services.

(2) Limitation on scope of request. A requirement that a contracting officer limit, to the maximum extent practicable, the scope of any request for information relating to commercial products or commercial services from an offeror to only that information that is in the form regularly maintained by the offeror in commercial operations.

(3) Information not to be disclosed. A statement that any information received relating to commercial products or commercial services that is exempt from disclosure under section 552(b) of title 5 shall not be disclosed by the Federal Government.

This requirement is implemented in FAR 15.403-3(c) as follows:

(1) At a minimum, the contracting officer must use price analysis to determine whether the price is fair and reasonable whenever the contracting officer acquires a commercial product or a commercial service (see 15.404-1(b)). The fact that a price is included in a catalog does not, in and of itself, make it fair and reasonable. If the contracting officer cannot determine whether an offered price is fair and reasonable, even after obtaining additional data from sources other than the offeror, then the contracting officer shall require the offeror to submit data other than certified cost or pricing data to support further analysis (see 15.404-1). This data may include history of sales to non-governmental and governmental entities, cost data, or any other information the contracting officer requires to determine the price is fair and reasonable. Unless an exception under 15.403-1(b)(1) or (2) applies, the contracting officer shall require that the data submitted by the offeror include, at a minimum, appropriate data on the prices at which the same or similar commercial products or commercial services have previously been sold, adequate for determining the reasonableness of the price.

FAR 15.403-3(c)(2) includes the above statutory limitations with little additional guidance.

In addition, the Requirements for Certified Cost or Pricing Data or Data Other Than Certified Cost or Pricing Data solicitation provision at FAR 52.215-20 contains the following guidance on the type of data that should be submitted to support a request for application of the commercial product or commercial service exception:

> (a)(1)(ii) *Commercial products or commercial services exception.* For a commercial product or commercial services exception, the offeror shall submit, at a minimum, information on prices at which the same or similar products or services have previously been sold in the commercial market that is adequate for evaluating the reasonableness of the price for this acquisition. Such information may include—
>
> (A) For catalog items, a copy of or identification of the catalog and its date, or the appropriate pages for the offered items, or a statement that the catalog is on file in the buying office to which the proposal is being submitted. Provide a copy or describe current discount policies and price lists (published or unpublished), e.g., wholesale, original equipment manufacturer, or reseller. Also explain the basis of each offered price and its relationship to the established catalog price, including how the proposed price relates to the price of recent sales in quantities similar to the proposed quantities.
>
> (B) For market-price items, the source and date or period of the market quotation or other basis for market price, the base amount, and applicable discounts. In addition, describe the nature of the market.
>
> (C) For items included on an active Federal Supply Service Multiple Award Schedule contract, proof that an exception has been granted for the schedule item.

Alternatively, the contracting officer can use the Alternate IV provision in FAR 52.215-20 and describe the specific data that each offeror is required to provide.

It would appear that the key issue in ascertaining the reasonableness of prices of commercial products or services is the amount of competition that will be achieved. If there will be significant competition, the competitive prices should provide sufficient information without the need for additional data. On the other hand, if the commercial product or service is sole source or the competition is very limited, the contracting officer will need additional data. FAR 15.403-1(c)(3)(ii)(A) addresses this problem by stating that the prohibition on obtaining certified cost or pricing data for commercial services only applies if the contracting officer determines in writing "that the offeror has submitted sufficient information to evaluate, through price analysis, the reasonableness of the price of such services." FAR 15.403-1(c)(3)(ii) contains the following guidance:

> (B) In order to make this determination, the contracting officer may request the offeror to submit prices paid for the same or similar commercial

services under comparable terms and conditions by both Government and commercial customers; and

(C) If the contracting officer determines that the information described in paragraph (c)(3)(ii)(B) of this section is not sufficient to determine the reasonableness of price, other relevant information regarding the basis for price or cost, including information on labor costs, material costs and overhead rates may be requested.

If such data are available through market research, there may be no need to require offerors to submit the data. If not, sales data or cost data will have to be obtained from offerors. The goal of the statutes and regulations is to obtain necessary data in the least burdensome manner possible in the circumstances of each procurement. While the guidance in the FAR is not definitive, it is sufficiently permissive to permit the contracting officer to obtain necessary information while still minimizing the data submission requirements.

The Department of Defense has issued detailed guidance on obtaining sufficient data to determine that commercial product or services prices are fair and reasonable—particularly when there is little or no competition or the product or service has not yet been sold to commercial customers. DFARS PGI 215.403-1(c)(3)(A)(2) directs contracting officers to obtain "prior non-government sales data" on the precise product or service or the predecessor product or service if the product or service being procured has not yet been sold commercially but has evolved from a commercial item. DFARS PGI 215.403-3(1) states:

> Sales data must be comparable to the quantities, capabilities, specifications, etc. of the product or service proposed. Sufficient steps must be taken to verify the integrity of the sales data, to include assistance from the Defense Contract Management Agency, the Defense Contract Audit Agency, and/or other agencies if required.

DFARS PGI 215.404-1(b)(i) points out that sometimes these types of sales data can be obtained through market research that finds data on commercial sales or in published catalogs or prices.

DFARS PGI 215.404-1(b)(ii) calls for obtaining "cost information" when sales data are not sufficient to demonstrate that the price is fair and reasonable:

> In some cases, commercial sales are not available and there is no other market information for determining fair and reasonable prices. This is especially true when buying supplies or services that have been determined to be commercial but have only been "offered for sale" or purchased on a sole source basis with no prior commercial sales upon which to rely. In such cases, the contracting must require the offeror to submit whatever cost information is needed to determine price reasonableness.

The DoD guidance then makes it clear at DFARS PGI 215.404-1(c)(iii) that such "cost information" need not be submitted in accordance with the instructions in Table 15-2 of FAR 15.408 dealing with the submission of certified cost or pricing data but can be submitted in the contractor's format.

DFARS PGI 215.403-3(4) also contains a warning about relying on prior prices paid by the government:

> Before relying on a prior price paid by the Government, the contracting officer must verify and document that sufficient analysis was performed to determine that the prior price was fair and reasonable. Sometimes, due to exigent situations, supplies and services are purchased even though an adequate price or cost analysis could not be performed. The problem is exacerbated when other contracting officers assume these prices were adequately analyzed and determined to be fair and reasonable. The contracting officer also must verify that the prices previously paid were for quantities consistent with the current solicitation. Not verifying that a previous price analysis was performed, or the consistencies in quantity, has been a recurring issue on sole source commercial items reported by oversight organizations. Sole source commercial items require extra attention to verify that previous prices paid on Government contracts were sufficiently analyzed and determined to be fair and reasonable. At a minimum, a contracting officer reviewing price history shall discuss the basis of previous prices paid with the contracting organization that previously bought the item. These discussions shall be documented in the contract file.

[G] Actions Where There are Agency Waivers

Originally, this exception permitted the waiver of the requirement for submission of certified cost or pricing data by the agency head. The FASA granted this waiver authority to "the head of the procuring activity, without delegation." The statutes require that waivers be supported by written documentation. FAR 15.403-1(c) provides the following guidance on the use of waivers:

> (4) *Waivers*. The head of the contracting activity (HCA) may, without power of delegation, waive the requirement for submission of certified cost or pricing data in exceptional cases. The authorization for the waiver and the supporting rationale shall be in writing. The HCA may consider waiving the requirement if the price can be determined to be fair and reasonable without submission of certified cost or pricing data. For example, if certified cost or pricing data were furnished on previous production buys and the contracting officer determines such data are sufficient, when combined with updated data, a waiver may be granted. If the HCA has waived the requirement for submission of certified cost or pricing data, the contractor or higher-tier subcontractor to whom the waiver relates shall be considered as having been required to provide certified cost or pricing data. Consequently, award of any lower-tier subcontract expected to exceed the certified cost or pricing data threshold requires the submission of certified cost or pricing data unless—
>
> (i) An exception otherwise applies to the subcontract; or

(ii) The waiver specifically includes that subcontract and the rationale supporting the waiver for that subcontract.

While the above waiver guidance is stated in permissive language, prior to 2010 FAR 15.402(a)(3) appeared to encourage the use of waivers by stating that contracting officers should "use every means available to ascertain whether a fair and reasonable price can be determined before requesting cost or pricing data." This guidance was deleted from the FAR by FAC 2005-45.

DoD has provided additional guidance on waivers in DFARS 215.403-1(c)(4) as follows:

> (A) The head of the contracting activity may, without power of delegation, apply the exceptional circumstances authority when a determination is made that—
>
> (1) The property or services cannot reasonably be obtained under the contract, subcontract, or modification, without the granting of the waiver;
>
> (2) The price can be determined to be fair and reasonable without the submission of certified cost or pricing data; and
>
> (3) There are demonstrated benefits to granting the waiver. Follow the procedures at PGI 215.403-1(c)(4)(A) for determining when an exceptional case waiver is appropriate, for approval of such waivers, for partial waivers, and for waivers applicable to unpriced supplies or services.
>
> * * *
>
> (C) DoD has waived the requirement for submission of certified cost or pricing data for the Canadian Commercial Corporation and its subcontractors.
>
> (D) DoD has waived certified cost or pricing data requirements for nonprofit organizations (including education institutions) on cost-reimbursement-no-fee contracts. The contracting officer shall require—
>
> (1) Submission of information other than certified cost or pricing data to the extent necessary to determine reasonableness and cost realism; and
>
> (2) Certified cost or pricing data from subcontractors that are not nonprofit organizations when the subcontractor's proposal exceeds the certified cost or pricing data threshold at FAR 15.403-4(a)(1).

Initially, GAO permitted an informal waiver, *Televiso Elecs.*, 46 Comp. Gen. 631 (B-159922) (1967), but subsequent decisions stated that this requirement must be formally complied with to justify not obtaining data, Comp. Gen. Dec. B-161448, Feb. 7, 1968, *Unpub.*; *Akin, Gump, Strauss, Hauer & Feld*, 53 Comp. Gen. 5 (B-177847) (1973). It has also been held that an agency may refuse to waive the cost or pricing data requirement and contract with another offeror on a sole source basis, *Telectro-Mek, Inc.*, Comp. Gen. Dec. B-185892, 76-2 CPD ¶ 81.

In *M-R-S Mfg. Co. v. United States*, 492 F.2d 835 (Ct. Cl. 1974), the Court of Claims held that the contracting officer could not agree to nonsubmission of data. The court stated at 841:

> Since the Government chose to ignore any data developed between March 23 and August 17, the plaintiff says the obligation to furnish accurate, complete, and current data was waived. The most basic flaw in this argument is the assumption that the obligation to furnish proper data can be waived by a Government agent. The duty to furnish accurate, complete, and current data is a duty imposed on Government contractors by a statute, and, therefore, that duty cannot be waived by a Government agent. *United States v. Stewart*, 311 U.S. 60 (1940); *Utah Power & Light Co. v. United States*, 243 U.S. 389 (1917); *see Federal Crop Ins. Corp. v. Merrill*, 332 U.S. 380 (1947); *Montilla v. United States*, 198 Ct. Cl. 48, 457 F.2d 978 (1972).

The court omitted any discussion of statutory waiver by the agency head since that was not an issue in the case. The same result was reached in *Conrac Corp. v. United States*, 558 F.2d 994 (Ct. Cl. 1977), where the court noted that a "reasonable" cutoff date for establishing the timeliness of data submissions would not have constituted an improper waiver. In *Numax Elecs., Inc.*, ASBCA 29186, 85-3 BCA ¶ 18,396, the board found that the submission of data could not be waived by the contracting officer. See also *Southwest Marine, Inc.*, DOTBCA 1577J, 95-2 ¶ 27,760, where the board held that the contracting officer's failure to request cost and pricing data did not waive the government's right to reduce the contract proceeds for defective pricing. The board stated that the contractor had a statutory duty to disclose and certify all relevant cost and pricing data regardless of whether the contracting officer asked for them.

[H] Modifications to Commercial Products or Services

10 U.S.C. § 3703(b) (formerly § 2306a(b)(2)) and 41 U.S.C. § 3503(b) prohibit the obtaining of certified cost or pricing data for modifications to contracts for commercial products or commercial services, if the modification does not change the product or service to a noncommercial product or service, and the modification is either minor or customarily available in the commercial marketplace. FAR 15.403-1(b)(3)(iii), implementing this requirement, contains no guidance on the explicit data that should be obtained to ascertain that the price for such modifications is fair and reasonable. However, FAR 52.215-21 contains a standard contract clause for modifications that permits the contractor to request an exception to the submission of cost or pricing data and submit information on prices at which the same or similar items have been sold to demonstrate that the modification is reasonably priced. This appears to assume that the prices for such modifications can be evaluated without the use of certified cost or pricing data

and that obtaining certified cost or pricing data would be done only in unusual cases.

Section 818 of the National Defense Authorization Act for FY 2005, Pub. L. No. 108-375, amended 10 U.S.C. § 2306a (now § 3703) to provide that the commercial item modification exception to the requirement for submission of cost or pricing data does not apply to modifications that are expected to cost, in the aggregate, more than $500,000 or 5% of the total price of the contract, whichever is greater, for contracts funded by the DoD, NASA, or the Coast Guard. This limitation on the exception is implemented in FAR 15.403-1(c)(3)(iii) (revising the dollar threshold) as follows:

> (B) For acquisitions funded by DoD, NASA, or Coast Guard, such modifications of a commercial product or a commercial service are exempt from the requirement for submission of certified cost or pricing data provided the total price of all such modifications under a particular contract action does not exceed the greater of the threshold for obtaining certified cost or pricing data in 15.403-4 or 5 percent of the total price of the contract at the time of contract award.
>
> (C) For acquisitions funded by DoD, NASA, or Coast Guard such modifications of a commercial product or a commercial service are not exempt from the requirement for submission of certified cost or pricing data on the basis of the exemption provided for at 15.403-1(c)(3) if the total price of all such modifications under a particular contract action exceeds the greater of the threshold for obtaining certified cost or pricing data in 15.403-4 or 5 percent of the total price of the contract at the time of contract award.

§ 13.04 ROLES OF GOVERNMENT PERSONNEL

The regulations provide that the determination of the reasonableness of the contract price is the responsibility of the contracting officer. FAR 15.402 states that the contracting officer "must . . . [p]urchase supplies and services . . . at fair and reasonable prices." See also FAR 14.408-2(a) stating that the "contracting officer shall determine . . . that prices offered are reasonable before awarding the contract." Thus, the contracting officer has the primary responsibility for performing the analysis of the contract price or estimated/target cost on all procurements. However, FAR 15.404-1(a) provides that the contracting officer may obtain assistance of "other experts."

While the contracting officer has the ultimate responsibility for the adequacy of the price analysis or cost analysis, initial analysis frequently is done by many other employees, depending on the agency and the resources available. Such assistance can be obtained from employees in other parts of the agency or employees working at locations close to the contractor's place of business or the site of the work. FAR 15.404-2(a) provides the following guidance on obtaining this "field pricing assistance":

(1) The contracting officer should request field pricing assistance when the information available at the buying activity is inadequate to determine a fair and reasonable price. Such requests shall be tailored to reflect the minimum essential supplementary information needed to conduct a technical or cost or pricing analysis.

(2) The contracting officer shall tailor the type of information and level of detail requested in accordance with the specialized resources available at the buying activity and the magnitude and complexity of the required analysis. Field pricing assistance is generally available to provide—

(i) Technical, audit, and special reports associated with the cost elements of a proposal, including subcontracts;

(ii) Information on related pricing practices and history;

(iii) Information to help contracting officers determine commerciality and a fair and reasonable price, including—

(A) Verifying sales history to source documents;

(B) Identifying special terms and conditions;

(C) Identifying customarily granted or offered discounts for the item;

(D) Verifying the item to an existing catalog or price list;

(E) Verifying historical, data for an item previously not determined commercial that the offeror is now trying to qualify as a commercial item; and

(F) Identifying general market conditions affecting determinations of commerciality and a fair and reasonable price.

(iv) Information relative to the business, technical, production, or other capabilities and practices of an offeror.

(3) When field pricing assistance is requested, contracting officers are encouraged to team with appropriate field experts throughout the acquisition process, including negotiations. Early communication with these experts will assist in determining the extent of assistance required, the specific areas for which assistance is needed, a realistic review schedule, and the information necessary to perform the review.

(4) When requesting field pricing assistance on a contractor's request for equitable adjustment, the contracting officer shall provide the information listed in 43.204(b)(5).

(5) Field pricing information and other reports may include proprietary or source selection information (see 3.104-4(j) and (k)). Such information shall be appropriately identified and protected accordingly.

DFARS PGI 215.404-2(a) gives the following additional guidance to DoD contracting officers:

(i) The contracting officer should consider requesting field pricing assistance (See PGI 215.404-2(c) for when audit assistance should be requested) for—

(A) Fixed-price proposals exceeding the certified cost or pricing data threshold;

(B) Cost-type proposals exceeding the certified cost or pricing data threshold from offerors with significant estimating system deficiencies (see DFARS 215.407-5-70(a)(4) and (c)(2)(i)); or

(C) Cost-type proposals exceeding $10 million from offerors without significant estimating system deficiencies.

(ii) The contracting officer should not request field pricing support for proposed contracts or modifications in an amount less than that specified in paragraph (a)(i) of this subsection. An exception may be made when a reasonable pricing result cannot be established because of—

(A) A lack of knowledge of the particular offeror; or

(B) Sensitive conditions (e.g., a change in, or unusual problems with, an offeror's internal systems).

The FAR guidance gives the contracting officer broad discretion on obtaining field pricing assistance but the DFARS guidance appears, in general, to limit the discretion to cases where cost analysis is necessary. Prior FAR guidance had made the obtaining of field pricing support mandatory for procurement over $500,000 when certified cost or pricing data was obtained. It also contained considerable guidance on the types of information that was generally obtained from field pricing personnel.

These provisions assume that agencies have fully staffed field offices capable of providing the type of analysis discussed in this regulation. However, most civilian agencies have no such capability, with the result that such assistance cannot be obtained. See, for example, DEAR 915.404-2(a)(1), stating that field pricing assistance is not required in the Department of Energy because "pricing support" is expected to be provided by internal DOE personnel.

[A] Field Contracting Offices

Some agencies, such as DoD and NASA, have fully staffed field offices that are available to provide field pricing support when requested. Other agencies can obtain such assistance from field personnel on only a portion of their acquisitions. These agencies can often obtain assistance from the field offices of other agencies that are familiar with the offeror. Field pricing assistance is also available from government auditors familiar with the offeror's organization, as discussed below.

FAR 15.404-2(b) encourages contracting officers to use informal means to obtain assistance from field contracting offices:

(1) Depending upon the extent and complexity of the field pricing review, results, including supporting rationale, may be reported directly to

the contracting officer orally, in writing, or by any other method acceptable to the contracting officer.

(i) Whenever circumstances permit, the contracting officer and field pricing experts are encouraged to use telephonic and/or electronic means to request and transmit pricing information.

In many cases, the factual data supporting the offeror's estimate are submitted to these personnel in the field rather than to the contracting officer negotiating the contract. Since it is expected that the data will be subsequently transmitted to the contracting officer, such submission meets the statutory requirements for the submission of certified cost or pricing data, *Singer Co. v. United States*, 576 F.2d 905 (Ct. Cl. 1978). In *Singer*, however, the court noted that submission required physical delivery of the data and disclosure of their significance to the pricing action. Thus, the furnishing of monthly reports of labor cost information to government field personnel was held not to be an adequate submission of data to support a specific pricing action. See also *Sylvania Elec. Prods., Inc. v. United States*, 479 F.2d 1342 (Ct. Cl. 1973), where the court held that submission of relevant data on another contract pricing action was not an adequate submission. In *M-R-S Mfg. Co. v. United States*, 492 F.2d 835 (Ct. Cl. 1974), the court clarified this requirement by stating that the submission requirement could be met by either physically submitting the data or making known its significance to the pricing action. In *M-R-S*, the submission requirement was not met by giving the government auditor the bill of materials and open access to all of the offeror's purchasing records. This requirement is spelled out in Table 15-2, Instructions for Submitting Cost or Pricing Data, in FAR 15.408, which states:

> Note 1: There is a clear distinction between submitting certified cost or pricing data and merely making available books, records, and other documents without identification. The requirement for submission of certified cost or pricing data is met when all accurate certified cost or pricing data reasonably available to the offeror have been submitted, either actually or by specific identification, to the Contracting Officer or an authorized representative. As later information comes into your possession, it should be submitted promptly to the Contracting Officer in a manner that clearly shows how the information relates to the offeror's proposal. The requirement for submission of certified cost or pricing data continues up to the time of agreement on price, or an earlier data agreed upon between the parties if applicable.

A proper submission was found in *Texas Instruments, Inc.*, ASBCA 30836, 89-1 BCA ¶ 21,489 (offeror submitted data correcting an error in previous data to the administrative contracting officer one day before it signed its certificate), and *FMC Corp.*, ASBCA 30069, 87-1 BCA ¶ 19,544 (offeror followed a standard practice of submitting supporting data for its incurred labor rates to the administrative contracting officer). See also *McDonnell Douglas Corp.*, ASBCA 12786, 69-2 BCA ¶ 7897, and *Boeing Co.*, ASBCA 32753, 90-1 BCA ¶ 22,270, *recons. denied*,

90-1 BCA ¶ 22,426, stating that the submission requirement would be met if government field personnel had "actual knowledge" of the data.

When the personnel providing field pricing assistance find that the offeror is unable to provide sufficient information to permit them to provide the necessary assistance to the contracting officer, they must address this problem immediately. FAR 15.404-2 states:

> (d) *Deficient proposals.* The ACO or the auditor, as appropriate, shall notify the contracting officer immediately if the data provided for review is so deficient as to preclude review or audit, or if the contractor or offeror has denied access to any records considered essential to conduct satisfactory review or audit. Oral notifications shall be confirmed promptly in writing, including a description of deficient or denied data or records. The contracting officer immediately shall take appropriate action to obtain the required data. Should the offeror/contractor again refuse to provide adequate data, or provide access to necessary data, the contracting officer shall withhold the award or price adjustment and refer the contract action to a higher authority, providing details of the attempts made to resolve the matter and a statement of the practicability of obtaining the supplies or services from another source.

[B] Auditors

All contracting agencies have access to audit services and can therefore obtain prepricing audit reviews of proposals even when they have no field contracting personnel. The contracting officer has considerable discretion in determining when to request an audit, *Del-Jen Inc.*, Comp. Gen. Dec. B-216589, 85-2 CPD ¶ 111. The major contract audit agency is the Defense Contract Audit Agency (DCAA), which performs all contract audit work for DoD, Defense Contract Audit Manual (DCAM) 1-102. Other agencies can sometimes obtain audit assistance from their Inspectors General who have this responsibility pursuant to the Inspector General Act of 1978, 5 U.S.C. App. § 1-11. When a contracting officer cannot obtain audit assistance within the agency, assistance can be obtained from another audit group under a cross-servicing arrangement. See OMB Circular A-73 and DCAM 1-303 for guidance in this area.

FAR 15.404-2 contains the following guidance on prepricing audits:

> (c) *Audit assistance for prime contracts or subcontracts.* (1) The contracting officer may contact the cognizant audit office directly, particularly when an audit is the only field pricing support required. The audit office shall send the audit report, or otherwise transmit the audit recommendations, directly to the contracting officer.
>
> > (i) The auditor shall not reveal the audit conclusions or recommendations to the offeror/contractor without obtaining the concurrence of the contracting officer. However, the auditor may discuss statements of facts with the contractor.

(ii) The contracting officer should be notified immediately of any information disclosed to the auditor after submission of a report that may significantly affect the audit findings and, if necessary, a supplemental audit report shall be issued.

(2) The contracting officer shall not request a separate preaward audit of indirect costs unless the information already available from an existing audit, completed within the preceding 12 months, is considered inadequate for determining the reasonableness of the proposed indirect costs (41 U.S.C. 4706 and 10 U.S.C. 3841).

(3) The auditor is responsible for the scope and depth of the audit. Copies of updated information that will significantly affect the audit should be provided to the auditor by the contracting officer.

(4) General access to the offeror's books and financial records is limited to the auditor. This limitation does not preclude the contracting officer or the ACO, or their representatives from requesting that the offeror provide or make available any data or records necessary to analyze the offeror's proposal.

See DCAM Chapter 9 for detailed guidance on audits evaluating pricing proposals. This manual emphasizes the need to tailor the extent of the audit in order to allow the DCAA to provide service in a timely manner. Contracting officers should take advantage of the fast service that DCAA can provide by requesting assistance on specific cost elements when that is sufficient to permit analysis of a proposal. See DCAM 9-107.1 containing the following guidance on processing such requests:

a. PCO may request specific information concerning a contractor's costs without requesting an audit or evaluation of the contractor proposal. Data to be provided should be readily available from the [field audit office] files or obtainable using a request for information (RFI) from the contractor. Examples of such information include historical incurred costs, recent costs for specific production items or lots; established pricing formulas such as for spare parts or other logistics items; established prices for standard components; and current rates for labor, indirect costs, per diem. When a PCO requests a complete audit and the auditor determines that there is sufficient information available in the [field audit office] files to meet the PCO's request, the auditor should explain the available options to the PCO and make an appropriate recommendation. (See 9-103.1d.). The PCO has the final decision in determining if a full audit is needed to determine cost reasonableness.

b. The PCO may request specific cost information by telephone, mail, fax, or electronically directly from the field auditor. Such requests should receive timely attention. Written requests are sometimes desirable for clarity, but will not be required.

FAR 15.404-2(b) requires coordination between auditors and ACOs when written audit reports are requested, stating:

(ii) When it is necessary to have written technical and audit reports, the contracting officer shall request that the audit agency concurrently forward the audit report to the requesting contracting officer and the administrative contracting officer (ACO). The completed field pricing assistance results may reference audit information, but need not reconcile the audit recommendations and technical recommendations. A copy of the information submitted to the contracting officer by field pricing personnel shall be provided to the audit agency.

FAR 15.404-3 makes the contracting officer responsible for the reasonableness of subcontract prices and provides the following guidance on the responsibility of the contractor or higher-tier subcontractor:

(a) The contracting officer is responsible for the determination of a fair and reasonable price for the prime contract, including subcontracting costs. The contracting officer should consider whether a contractor or subcontractor has an approved purchasing system, has performed cost or price analysis of proposed subcontractor prices, or has negotiated the subcontract prices before negotiation of the prime contract, in determining the reasonableness of the prime contract price. This does not relieve the contracting officer from the responsibility to analyze the contractor's submission, including subcontractor's certified cost or pricing data.

(b) The prime contractor or subcontractor shall—

(1) Conduct appropriate cost or price analyses to establish the reasonableness of proposed subcontract prices;

(2) Include the results of these analyses in the price proposal; and

(3) When required by paragraph (c) of this subsection, submit subcontractor certified cost or pricing data to the Government as part of its own certified cost or pricing data.

The FAR has no explicit statement as to when audits of subcontractor pricing should be requested. However, DFARS PGI 215.404-3 contains the following guidance:

(a) The contracting officer should consider the need for field pricing analysis and evaluation of lower-tier subcontractor proposals, and assistance to prime contractors when they are being denied access to lower-tier subcontractor records.

(i) When obtaining field pricing assistance on a prime contractor's proposal, the contracting officer should request audit or field pricing assistance to analyze and evaluate the proposal of a subcontractor at any tier (notwithstanding availability of data or analyses performed by the prime contractor) if the contracting officer believes that such assistance is necessary to ensure the reasonableness of the total proposed price. Such assistance may be appropriate when, for example—

(A) There is a business relationship between the contractor and subcontractor not conducive to independence and objectivity;

(B) The contractor is a sole source supplier and the subcontract costs represent a substantial part of the contract cost;

(C) The contractor has been denied access to the subcontractor's records; or

(D) The contracting officer determines that, because of factors such as the size of the proposed subcontract price, audit or field pricing support for a subcontract or subcontracts at any tier is critical to a fully detailed analysis of the prime contract proposal.

(E) The contractor or higher-tier subcontractor has been cited for having significant estimating system deficiencies in the area of subcontract pricing, especially the failure to perform adequate cost analyses of proposed subcontract costs or to perform subcontract analyses prior to negotiation of the prime contract with the Government; or

(F) A lower-tier subcontractor has been cited as having significant estimating system deficiencies.

(ii) It may be appropriate for the contracting officer or the ACO to provide assistance to a contractor or subcontractor at any tier, when the contractor or higher-tier subcontractor has been denied access to a subcontractor's records in carrying out the responsibilities at FAR 15.404-3 to conduct price or cost analysis to determine the reasonableness of proposed subcontract prices. Under these circumstances, the contracting officer or the ACO should consider whether providing audit or field pricing assistance will serve a valid Government interest.

(iii) When DoD performs the subcontract analysis, DoD shall furnish to the prime contractor or higher-tier subcontractor, with the consent of the subcontractor reviewed, a summary of the analysis performed in determining any unacceptable costs included in the subcontract proposal. If the subcontractor withholds consent, DoD shall furnish a range of unacceptable costs for each element in such a way as to prevent disclosure of subcontractor proprietary data.

The current FAR gives the contracting officer complete discretion as to when prepricing audits are required on major contracts. This should obviate the problem under the prior FAR where a waiver was required when certain audits were not obtained. Under such regulations, it was held that a settlement agreed to by the parties was not binding because the contracting officer did not obtain a mandatory prepricing audit and did not follow the waiver procedure, *Bromley Contracting Co.*, DOTCAB 1284, 84-2 BCA ¶ 17,233.

When government auditors work with contractors on a regular basis, they become very conversant with contractors' estimating and pricing practices. In such cases, they can be expected to know the impact of certified cost or pricing data given to them during prepricing audits, with the result that a contractor may meet the submission requirement more easily than when data are submitted to less experienced personnel. There are a number of cases where data submitted to an auditor was found to meet the submission requirement. See, for example,

Alliant Techsys., Inc., ASBCA 47626, 00-2 BCA ¶ 31,042 (contractor submitted its data to a DCAA auditor who sent it to the contracting officer); *Motorola, Inc.*, ASBCA 48841, 96-2 BCA ¶ 28,465 (subcontractor submitted its data to a DCAA auditor); *Motorola, Inc.*, ASBCA 41528, 94-2 BCA ¶ 26,596 (subcontractor disclosed data to its cognizant DCAA auditor with whom the prime contractor was conferring); *Litton Sys., Inc.*, ASBCA 34435, 93-2 BCA ¶ 25,707 (contractor submitted monthly actuals of indirect cost data to resident DCAA auditor); *Texas Instruments, Inc.*, ASBCA 23678, 87-3 BCA ¶ 20,195 (contractor submitted detailed data on the costs incurred in manufacturing parts to the DCAA auditor and to a government price analyst); *Hardie-Tynes Mfg. Co.*, ASBCA 20717, 76-2 BCA ¶ 12,121 (offeror gave the auditor the file containing the record of purchases of a part without stating which purchases were relevant to the current procurement); and *Whittaker Corp.*, ASBCA 17267, 74-2 BCA ¶ 10,938 (a purchase order was available to an auditor during a prepricing audit and the auditor specifically knew of its relevance to the audit through prior correspondence). The contractor cannot, however, mislead the auditor and escape liability. For example, in *Aerojet-General Corp.*, ASBCA 16988, 73-2 BCA ¶ 10,242, a failure of submission was found where the contractor gave the auditor all of the current factual data but incorrectly told him it would be fruitless to analyze them because they were commingled with other data. In addition, submission to an auditor may not suffice if the offeror later finds that the auditor has not included the data in the audit report, *American Mach. & Foundry Co.*, ASBCA 15037, 74-1 BCA ¶ 10,409. There, the offeror learned during contract negotiations that the contracting officer did not know of an additional quotation that had been received from a vendor and furnished to the auditor. The board held that the offeror had a duty to inform the contracting officer about the quotation even though it had been submitted to the auditor.

Auditors obtain access to a firm's books and records in several ways. If the offeror has had no previous negotiated contracts with the government, it is generally believed that the auditor has no legal right of access to the firm's books and records. See, however, *Aerospatiale Helicopter Corp.*, DOTCAB 1981, 89-1 BCA ¶ 21,559, where the board granted access to the contractor's books and records to audit data submitted to support a contract modification—based on the board's interpretation of the contract's Audit clause. Generally, offerors permit access to their records voluntarily because failure to cooperate can result in the contracting officer's refusal to negotiate with the firm. In addition, Table 15-2, Instructions for Submitting Cost or Pricing Data, in FAR 15.408 contains the following statement:

> Note 2: By submitting your proposal, you grant the Contracting Officer or an authorized representative the right to examine records that formed the basis for the pricing proposal. That examination can take place at any time before award. It may include those books, records, documents, and other types of factual information (regardless of form or whether the information is

specifically referenced or included in the proposal as the basis for pricing) that will permit an adequate evaluation of the proposed price.

The enforceability of this regulatory statement is subject to question because there is no contractual agreement at the time an offer is submitted.

Offerors that have had negotiated government contracts are generally required to give access to their books and records. While no contract clause gives the government the specific right to audit for purposes of determining reasonableness of proposed prices on a new contract, information relating to incurred costs or other data under existing contracts would frequently be subject to audit and could be useful in analyzing proposed costs. The Audit and Records—Negotiation clause in FAR 52.215-2 gives the procuring agency the right to audit costs on all but firm-fixed-price contracts, certified cost or pricing data submitted to support contract modifications, and reports as follows:

> (b) *Examination of costs.* If this is a cost-reimbursement, incentive, time-and-materials, labor-hour, or price redeterminable contract, or any combination of these, the Contractor shall maintain and the Contracting Officer, or an authorized representative of the Contracting Officer, shall have the right to examine and audit all records and other evidence sufficient to reflect properly all costs claimed to have been incurred or anticipated to be incurred directly or indirectly in performance of this contract. This right of examination shall include inspection at all reasonable times of the Contractor's plants, or parts of them, engaged in performing the contract.
>
> (c) *Certified cost or pricing data.* If the Contractor has been required to submit certified cost or pricing data in connection with any pricing action relating to this contract, the Contracting Officer, or an authorized representative of the Contracting Officer, in order to evaluate the accuracy, completeness, and currency of the certified cost or pricing data, shall have the right to examine and audit all of the Contractor's records, including computations and projections, related to—
>
> (1) The proposal for the contract, subcontract, or modifications;
>
> (2) The discussions conducted on the proposal(s), including those related to negotiating;
>
> (3) Pricing of the contract, subcontract, or modification; or
>
> (4) Performance of the contract, subcontract or modification.
>
> * * *
>
> (e) *Reports.* If the Contractor is required to furnish cost, funding, or performance reports, the Contracting Officer or an authorized representative of the Contracting Officer shall have the right to examine and audit the supporting records and materials, for the purpose of evaluating (1) the effectiveness of the Contractor's policies and procedures to produce data compatible with the objectives of these reports and (2) the data reported.

This clause implements the audit requirements of 10 U.S.C. § 3841 (formerly § 2313) and 41 U.S.C. § 3508. Note that, as amended by FAC 2005-45, it does not give the government the right to audit uncertified cost or pricing data. See *Kepa Servs., Inc. v. Dep't of Veterans Affairs*, CBCA 2727, 15-1 BCA ¶ 35,942, holding that this clause gives an agency Inspector General no audit rights to data supporting claims when no certified cost or pricing data has been submitted to support those claims.

A broad right to audit negotiated contracts is also granted to GAO in the Audit and Records—Negotiation clause in FAR 52.215-2 as follows:

> (d) *Comptroller General*—(1) The Comptroller General of the United States, or an authorized representative, shall have access to and the right to examine any of the Contractor's directly pertinent records involving transactions related to this contract or a subcontract hereunder and to interview any current employee regarding such transactions.
>
> (2) This paragraph may not be construed to require the Contractor or subcontractor to create or maintain any record that the Contractor or subcontractor does not maintain in the ordinary course of business or pursuant to a provision of law.

This clause is required to be included in all negotiated contracts by 10 U.S.C. § 3841 (formerly § 2313(c)) and 41 U.S.C. § 4706(d). However, GAO is not normally involved in prepricing audits. When using this audit authority, GAO is permitted to audit "directly pertinent records involving transactions related to this contract." In *Hewlett-Packard Co. v. United States*, 385 F.2d 1013 (9th Cir. 1967), *cert. denied*, 390 U.S. 988 (1968), the court interpreted this provision to include production costs of a catalog-priced item for which the government had not required the submission of certified cost or pricing data. In *United States v. McDonnell Douglas Corp.*, 751 F.2d 220 (8th Cir. 1984), GAO was granted access to estimates of tooling and design engineering costs. *Bowsher v. Merck & Co.*, 460 U.S. 824 (1983), held that records relating to costs of independent research and development, marketing and promotion, distribution and administration are not directly pertinent records unless the contractor "allocated these costs as attributable to the particular contract." The court was apparently distinguishing between situations where a contractor allocates these general costs of overhead to individual contracts or products, in which case they would be directly pertinent, and those cases where the costs are collected in a general pool and charged against total sales for the year. See also *Bristol Labs. Div. of Bristol-Myers Co. v. Staats*, 428 F. Supp. 1388 (S.D.N.Y. 1977), *aff'd*, 620 F.2d 17 (2d Cir. 1980), *aff'd*, 451 U.S. 400 (1981).

Inspectors General have the right to subpoena books and records necessary to carry out their functions, Inspector General Act of 1978, 5 U.S.C. App. § 6; 41 U.S.C. § 4706(c). This broad right is available in the civilian agencies to support an agency's analysis of proposed costs. Because the DoD Inspector General's duties do not include contract pricing audits (5 U.S.C. App. § 8), there is some question whether that organization's subpoena powers can be used for such purposes. See *United States v. Westinghouse Elec. Corp.*, 788 F.2d 164

(3d Cir. 1986), where the DoD Inspector General issued a subpoena to obtain records for the DCAA. The court held that the subpoena was valid based on the district court's finding that the Inspector General had an independent investigative purpose in issuing the subpoena. The court also held that this subpoena power is extremely broad, extending to documents such as a company's internal audit reports.

The DCAA has subpoena powers of its own, 10 U.S.C. § 3841 (formerly § 2313(b)). This power is granted only for books and records subject to audit under the FAR 52.215-2 Audit and Records—Negotiation clauses. In *United States v. Newport News Shipbuilding & Dry Dock Co.*, 837 F.2d 162 (4th Cir. 1988), the court denied access to reports by the company's internal auditors because they were not "cost or financial data." However, in *United States v. Newport News Shipbuilding & Dry Dock Co.*, 862 F.2d 464 (4th Cir. 1988), the court granted access to a wide variety of financial data, including state and federal income tax returns, because they were "objective factual material useful in verifying actual costs." Subsequently, access was granted for estimates, projections, and accompanying work papers on the ground that they would assist in verifying claimed costs, *United States v. Newport News Shipbuilding & Dry Dock Co.*, 737 F. Supp. 897 (E.D. Va. 1989), *aff'd*, 900 F.2d 257 (4th Cir. 1990).

§ 13.05 PRICE ANALYSIS

FAR 15.404-1(b)(1) defines "price analysis" as follows:

> Price analysis is the process of examining and evaluating a proposed price without evaluating its separate cost elements and proposed profit.

The most desirable method of determining that the price of a negotiated firm-fixed-price contract is fair and reasonable is price analysis without a detailed analysis of its cost and profit elements. This technique is faster and requires much less accumulation of detailed data by both parties. See *Gap Solutions, Inc.*, Comp. Gen. Dec. B-310564, 2008 CPD ¶ 26; and *Citywide Managing Servs. of Port Washington, Inc.*, Comp. Gen. Dec. B-281287.12, 2001 CPD ¶ 6, rejecting the contention that the agency was required to evaluate the cost elements of each offerors' proposal in order to determine that the prices were reasonable and realistic.

Price analysis is generally based on data obtained from sources other than the prospective contractor. See the preferences set forth in FAR 15.403-3. This information is gathered by the government negotiating team from as many sources as possible and should be accumulated as a product or service is repeatedly purchased. Generally, a sound price analysis will be based on several different types of data. See, for example, *Bauer Techs., Inc.*, Comp. Gen. Dec. B-415717.2, 2018 CPD ¶ 217 (agency compare price to government estimate, Federal Supply Schedule prices and competitive prices to determine that price was reasonable); *Smiths Detection, Inc.*, Comp. Gen. Dec. B-402168.4, 2011 CPD ¶ 39 (agency compare prices to prices for similar items, published price lists, and competitive prices to determine that price was realistic); and *Navistar Def., LLC*, Comp. Gen. Dec. B-401865, 2009 CPD ¶ 258 (agency used a variety of techniques to make a thorough analysis to determine that seemingly low prices were realistic). However, when strong competition is obtained, the primary element of price analysis will be the competitive prices that have been submitted to the agency.

There is a large degree of discretion when a contracting officer does a thorough price analysis and determines that a price is reasonable in spite of its being higher than other prices. See, for example, *Marinette Marine Corp.*, Comp. Gen. Dec. B-400697, 2009 CPD ¶ 16, denying a protest that the awardee's price was $245 million higher than the protester's price, stating:

> Where, as here, a fixed-price contract is contemplated, the government may use various price analysis techniques and procedures to ensure a fair and reasonable price, including the comparison of proposed prices received in response to the solicitation; adequate price competition can establish price reasonableness, as can a comparison of proposed prices with an IGCE. See Federal Acquisition Regulation (FAR) § 15.404-1(b); *MVM, Inc.*, B-290726 et al., Sept. 23, 2002, 2002 CPD ¶ 167 at 6.
>
> A price reasonableness determination is a matter of administrative discretion involving the exercise of business judgment by the contracting officer that we will question only where it is unreasonable. *Comprehensive Health Servs., Inc.*, B-310553, Dec. 27, 2007, 2008 CPD ¶ 9 at 8.

[A] Uses of Price Analysis

The major use of price analysis is to determine whether a proposed price is fair and reasonable. As discussed earlier, the determination that a price is fair and reasonable is required in sealed bidding, FAR 14.408-2(a), and in negotiated procurement, FAR 15.404-1(a). It is also required when procuring commercial items, FAR 12.209, and when using simplified acquisition procedures, FAR 13.106-3(a). Price analysis is generally used to determine that the price of the awardee is reasonable, but it can also be used to determine that no reasonable price has been offered. See *Estrategy Inc.*, Comp. Gen. Dec. B-406466, 2012 CPD ¶ 148, denying a protest where the contracting officer had cancelled a procurement because the only offeror's price was unreasonable.

Price analysis can also be used to determine price realism—whether the price is so low that it reflects a lack of understanding of the work or will impose an undue risk on the government. The only requirement in the FAR for a price realism analysis is in the Evaluation for Compensation of Professional Employees clause in FAR 52.222-46, which must be included in all contracts over $700,000 that require a "meaningful number of professional employees,"

FAR 22.1103. See *Maxim Healthcare Servs., Inc.*, Comp. Gen. Dec. B-412987.9, 2018 CPD ¶ 230, interpreting this clause as mandating a price realism analysis. No other FAR provision requires that an agency conduct a price realism analysis, *Crosstown Courier Serv., Inc.*, Comp. Gen. Dec. B-416261, 2018 CPD ¶ 300. This use of price analysis is addressed only peripherally in FAR 15.404-1(d)(3), stating that "cost realism analysis" can be used on fixed-price incentive contracts, or "in exceptional cases, on other competitive fixed-price type contracts," but that, if it is used, prices cannot be adjusted upwards as a result of the analysis. See *IBM Corp.*, Comp. Gen. Dec. B-299504, 2008 CPD ¶ 64, sustaining a protest when the agency increased a contractor's prices in the evaluation process as a result of its price realism analysis. See also *EFW, Inc.*, Comp. Gen. Dec. B-412608, 2016 CPD ¶ 304, sustaining a protest when the agency apparently confused price realism and price reasonableness and concluded that the protester's price "presented a high risk relating to realism" because its proposed target cost on a fixed-price-incentive contract contained an unduly high number of labor hours. GAO also rejected any finding of unreasonable price because the protester had proposed a 100% share above target cost.

In spite of the sparse FAR coverage, price realism analysis is a common practice with some procuring agencies. It can be performed to determine whether a fixed price for a defined quantity of work is unreasonably low or whether a fixed price for an hour of labor is unreasonably low. If the agency concludes that the "price" is unreasonably low, it can drop the offeror from the competition because it does not understand the work or because its low price constitutes a performance risk. However, this use is limited by decisions of GAO holding that price realism can only be assessed if the solicitation contains a clear statement indicating that an unrealistically low price may result in a finding of lack of understanding of the work or performance risk. See *Cognosante, LLC*, Comp. Gen. Dec. B-417111, 2019 CPD ¶ 93, stating:

> In the absence of an express price realism provision, we will only conclude that a solicitation contemplates a price realism evaluation where the solicitation expressly states that the agency will review prices to determine whether they are so low that they reflect a lack of technical understanding, and the solicitation states that a quotation can be rejected for offering low prices.

In the absence of such a statement, a low price can only be used to evaluate responsibility of the offeror, *Louis Berger Power, LLC*, Comp. Gen. Dec. B-416059, 2018 CPD ¶ 196, and *PAE Gov't Servs., Inc.*, Comp. Gen. Dec. B-407818, 2013 CPD ¶ 91. Compare *DMS All-Star Joint Venture v. United States*, 90 Fed. Cl. 653 (2010), permitting price realism analysis under a solicitation with very vague language as to whether such analysis would be conducted, and *Afghan Am. Army Servs. Corp. v. United States*, 90 Fed. Cl. 341 (2009), requiring an adequate price realism analysis when the solicitation stated that proposals that had "an unreasonable (high or low) price may be deemed to be unacceptable."

Although the contracting officer has considerable discretion in determining that a contractor's low price constitutes a performance risk, GAO will grant a protest if the risk is minimal, *Joint Venture Penauille/BMAR & Assocs., LLC*, Comp. Gen. Dec. B-311200, 2008 CPD ¶118. See also *KWR Constr., Inc. v. United States*, 124 Fed. Cl. 345 (2014), holding that rejection of the protester because its low price indicated a lack of understanding of the work was actually based on performance risk which was the equivalent of a non-responsibility determination which entitled the small business to obtain a Certificate of Competency. Compare *Team BOS/Naples—Gemmo S.p.A./DelJen*, Comp. Gen. Dec. B-298865.3, 2008 CPD ¶11, upholding a contracting officer's analysis indicating that a low price did not constitute a performance risk.

The clearest RFP statement informing that their prices will be assessed for realism is a direct statement that a price realism analysis will be conducted. Decisions finding language calling for a price realism analysis include *Macaulay-Brown, Inc*., Comp. Gen. Dec. B-417205, 2019 CPD ¶129 (agency could reject a proposal if it contained a "significant inconsistency" between proposed oral presentation, technical/management approach, and price); *ActioNet, Inc*., Comp. Gen. Dec. B-417173, 2019 CPD ¶100 ("Any quotes that are unreasonably low in price may be deemed reflective of a lack of technical understanding or indicative of failure to comprehend the complexity and risk of contract requirements, and may be grounds for rejection"); *Bisdwas Information Tech. Solutions, Inc*., Comp. Gen. Dec. B-414760.3, 2018 CPD ¶332 ("unrealistically low price . . . may be grounds for eliminating a quote from further consideration"); *SKE Italy Sri*, Comp. Gen. Dec. B-414884.3, 2018 CPD ¶37 ("artificially low unit prices" indicating a buy-in "may be rejected"); *CGI Federal, Inc*., Comp. Gen. Dec. B-410330.2, 2014 CPD ¶366 (proposals that are "unrealistically high or low in terms of price" might be "deemed to be reflective of an inherent lack of technical competence, or indicative of a failure to comprehend the complexity and risks of the proposed work"); *Rotech Healthcare, Inc*., Comp. Gen. Dec. B-410203, 2014 CPD ¶333 ("Unrealistically low proposed prices may be grounds for eliminating a proposal from competition on the basis that either the offeror does not understand the requirement or the offeror has made an unrealistic offer). Compare *STG, Inc*., Comp. Gen. Dec. B-411415, 2015 CPD ¶240, where the RFP stated that prices would be assessed to see if they were reasonable, reflected a clear understanding of the requirements, and were consistent with the methods of work proposed but the GAO rejected a protest that this language required a price realism analysis stating that "nothing in the RFP stated that the agency could reject a proposal for offering unrealistically low prices."

If the RFP states that a price realism analysis will be made, the agency must conduct the analysis. See *Esegur-Empresa de Seguranca, SA*, Comp. Gen. Dec. B-407947, 2013 CPD ¶109 (RFP statement that low prices "may" be found unacceptable does not allow agency to forego analysis); *Halfaker & Assocs.*,

LLC, Comp. Gen. Dec. B-407919, 2013 CPD ¶ 98 (RFP statement that "[u]nrealistic rates, as determined by the Contracting Officer, may also be considered in risk assessment" does not allow agency to forego analysis); *Waterfront Techs., Inc.*, Comp. Gen. Dec. B-401948.16, 2011 CPD ¶ 123 (RFP statement that "[t]he Government may reject any proposal that is evaluated to be unrealistic," required the agency to evaluate prices for realism). However, an agency may make a price realism analysis optional giving it full discretion to conduct or forego the analysis, *Bauer Techs., Inc.*, Comp. Gen. Dec. B-415717.2, 2018 CPD ¶ 217 (RFP stated agency "reserved the right" to conduct a price realism analysis); *MES Simulation & Training Corp.*, Comp. Gen. Dec. B-416210, 2018 CPD ¶ 261 (RFP stated agency "may" conduct a price realism analysis).

Price analysis is also useful in detecting mistakes. See FAR 14.407-1 requiring contracting officers to examine all bids for mistakes immediately after bid opening and requiring a request for verification of the bid if a mistake is suspected. FAR Part 15 has no similar explicit requirement when conducting a negotiated procurement but it is good practice to follow the same procedure. See, however, *University of Dayton Research Inst.*, Comp. Gen. Dec. B-296946.6, 2006 CPD ¶ 102, holding that a significant mistake could not be corrected during clarifications.

Price analysis can be done at different levels of work depending on the complexity of the procurement. In the case of procurements with multiple contract line items, prices will usually be solicited for each line item and price analysis will be performed for each line item. See, for example, *XPO Logistics Worldwide Gov't Servs., LLC v. United States*, 133 Fed. Cl. 162 (2017); *Academy Facilities Mgmt.—Advisory Opinion*, Comp. Gen. Dec. B-401094.3, 2009 CPD ¶ 139; and *Comprehensive Health Servs., Inc.*, Comp. Gen. Dec. B-310553, 2008 CPD ¶ 9, upholding the price analysis of line item prices. It is improper, however, to determine that an offeror's proposed prices are unreasonable because a single line item price is high when its total price is similar to other total prices, *R&G Food Serv., Inc.*, Comp. Gen. Dec. B-296435.4, 2005 CPD ¶ 194 (high mileage rate for delivering food not dispositive when food prices are reasonable). In procurements for complex work, prices can be required to be submitted for segments of the work—allowing price analysis for each segment. This is commonly done on construction contracts where prices are required for each element of a building, using standard construction breakdowns of the work (excavation, foundations, structure, electrical, plumbing, etc.).

Although price analysis is also done to evaluate fixed-price labor hour rates—particularly in evaluating proposals for IDIQ contracts—it is of questionable value in this area. The difficulty is that, while price analysis can indicate whether the proposed labor rate is high or low in comparison with other rates, it cannot account for the productivity of the labor that is being offered. Thus, the use of price analysis to evaluate fixed labor rates can lead to a false assessment of the costs that the government will actually pay for work that is awarded to an offeror with low labor rates on a cost-reimbursement of time-and-materials basis.

[B] Price Analysis Techniques

The price analysis techniques that are usable in this process are described in FAR 15.404-1(b)(2):

> The Government may use various price analysis techniques and procedures to ensure a fair and reasonable price. Examples of such techniques include, but are not limited to, the following:
>
> (i) Comparison of proposed prices received in response to the solicitation. Normally, adequate price competition establishes a fair and reasonable price (see 15.403-1(c)(1)(i)).
>
> (ii) Comparison of the proposed prices to historical prices paid, whether by the Government or other than the Government, for the same or similar items. This method may be used for commercial items including those "of a type" or requiring minor modifications.
>
> (A) The prior price must be a valid basis for comparison. If there has been a significant time lapse between the last acquisition and the present one, if the terms and conditions of the acquisition are significantly different, or if the reasonableness of the prior price is uncertain, then the prior price may not be a valid basis for comparison.
>
> (B) The prior price must be adjusted to account for materially differing terms and conditions, quantities and market and economic factors. For similar items, the contracting officer must also adjust the prior price to account for material differences between the similar item and the item being procured.
>
> (C) Expert technical advice should be obtained when analyzing similar items, or commercial items that are "of a type" or requiring minor modifications, to ascertain the magnitude of changes required and to assist in pricing the required changes.
>
> (iii) Use of parametric estimating methods/application of rough yardsticks (such as dollars per pound or per horsepower, or other units) to highlight significant inconsistencies that warrant additional pricing inquiry.
>
> (iv) Comparison with competitive published price lists, published market prices of commodities, similar indexes, and discount or rebate arrangements.
>
> (v) Comparison of proposed prices with independent Government cost estimates.
>
> (vi) Comparison of proposed prices with prices obtained through market research for the same or similar items.
>
> (vii) Analysis of data other than certified cost or pricing data (ad defined at 2.101) provided by the offeror.

See also FAR 13.106-3(a)(2) containing a similar list of price analysis techniques to be used when using simplified acquisition procedures. Detailed guidance on price analysis is contained in Volume 1 of the DOD Contract Pricing Reference Guides (2018) (DODCPRG).

[1] Competitive Prices

Prices proposed by competitors are the most important data used in price analysis. They are based on the identical specifications for the work and are submitted in the same time period, thus reflecting current economic conditions. Competitors' prices are particularly useful when the contract will be firm-fixed-price or fixed-price with economic price adjustment. In these cases, the competitors are motivated to estimate their costs accurately, yet are subject to competitive pressures to propose a price that is low enough to win the competition. Thus, reliance on comparison of the competitive prices to ensure reasonableness of the price may be all that is necessary. See, for example, *HSG-SKE, A MTIS-Advantage, LLC*, Comp. Gen. Dec. B-411623, 2015 CPD ¶ 360, where GAO denied a protest alleging a flawed price reasonableness determination when the protester's price and the awardee's price were within 10% of the average prices submitted and the awardee's price was 8.7% higher than the protester's price. See also *Geiler/Schrudde & Zimmerman v. United States*, 133 Fed. Cl. 578 (2017) (price analysis not "impossibly fast" when awardee's price was lowest of six competitors); *Munilla Constr. Mgmt., LLC v. United States*, 130 Fed. Cl. 635 (2017) (price analysis adequate when awardee's price was lowest of four competitors); *ManTech Security Techs. Corp.*, Comp. Gen. Dec. B-297133.3, 2006 CPD ¶ 77 (price analysis adequate when three lowest priced offerors were within 5% of each other); and *Ameriko-OMSERV*, Comp. Gen. Dec. B-252879.5, 94-2 CPD ¶ 219 (price analysis adequate where agency performed a line-item-by-line-item comparison of awardee's prices to those of its competitors). However, comparing prices is not an adequate determination of price reasonableness if it is clear that the competitors misunderstood the requirements of the contract's work statement, *Metro. Van & Storage, Inc. v. United States*, 92 Fed. Cl. 232 (2010).

While FAR 15.404-1(b)(2)(i) states that "normally, adequate price competition establishes a fair and reasonable price," this assumes that the price that is found to be reasonable is in line with the other prices. See *Cognosante, LLC*, Comp. Gen. Dec. B-417111, 2019 CPD ¶ 93, sustaining a protest where the agency found a price of $999,851,638.80 to be reasonable because there had been adequate price competition even though the protester's price was $793,914,921.11. See also *Technatomy Corp.*, Comp. Gen. Dec. B-414672.5, 2018 CPD ¶ 353, stating:

> FAR § 15.404-1(b)(2)(i) does not provide that the existence of competition, in and of itself, is sufficient to establish that all competitors' prices are

> reasonable. Rather, it is *the favorable comparison* of an awardee's price to its competitors' prices that provides the necessary assurance that a proposed price is fair and reasonable. (Italics added)

The Court of Federal Claims reached the same conclusion in *Serco Inc. v. United States*, 81 Fed. Cl. 463 (2008), holding that an agency had concluded improperly that very high fixed labor rates were fair and reasonable based on adequate price competition, and stating at 494:

> FAR § 15.404(b)(2)(i) indicates that among the techniques available for ensuring a fair and reasonable price is a "comparison of proposed prices received in response to the solicitation," adding that "[n]ormally, adequate price competition establishes price reasonableness (see 15.403-1(c)(1))." But, while this provision certainly suggests that an agency may conclude that an awardee's price is reasonable if it is ***consistent*** with the prices received from various competitors, it no way suggests that the same conclusion should obtain if that price is ***inconsistent*** with those of competitors. After all, it is not competition for competition's sake, but the favorable comparison of a given offeror's price to those of the other contestants, that provides the necessary assurance that a given price is "fair and reasonable."

Other GAO decisions have denied protests contesting the reasonableness of high prices based on the fact that there was adequate price competition. See *HP Enter. Servs., LLC*, Comp. Gen. Dec. B-43967, 2017 CPD ¶ 26 (holding that a price of $102,039,191 was fair and reasonable when the protesters' prices were $74,976,611 and $85,125,254); and *WKG & Assocs., LLC*, Comp. Gen. Dec. B-409835, 2014 CPD ¶ 250 (holding that a price of $36,000 was fair and reasonable when the protester's price was $16,000).

There are several reasons why the mere presence of competition is not always adequate to ensure that the prices proposed are fair and reasonable. For example, if the low offeror has such a decided advantage gained from past performance of the work that it is practically immune from competition, other competitive prices would not provide a valid basis for comparison. Similarly, competitive prices may be suspect when there are a very limited number of competitors. In such cases, the relative experience and sophistication of the offerors must be closely scrutinized. The contracting officer must also assess whether the market conditions are the same for the various competitors. In a period of high economic activity when the competitors are working close to their levels of capacity, competitive prices are not nearly as good an indicator of reasonable price as are prices submitted when competitors are actively seeking more work.

Competitive prices have also been used to determine that a price was unreasonable. For example, it is proper to cancel an IFB based on unreasonableness of prices (1) when the price of a nonresponsive bidder was significantly lower than the lowest responsive bid, *McCarthy Mfg. Co.*, 56 Comp. Gen. 369 (B-186550), 77-1 CPD ¶ 116; and (2) when the prices in a post-bid opening quotation were lower than the timely bids, *Mil-Base Indus.*, Comp. Gen. Dec. B-218015, 85-1 CPD ¶ 421. In *Mil-Base*, GAO recognized that such a situation could establish price unreasonableness but questioned the reliability of the quote under the facts of that case. Similarly, it is proper to cancel an RFP when only one proposal is received and there was no other information available to ensure that the price was reasonable, *Adrian Supply Co.*, Comp. Gen. Dec. B-241502, 91-1 CPD ¶ 138. Prices from small businesses have also been found unreasonable (and set-asides canceled) based on proposed prices from large business firms, *Nutech Laundry & Textiles, Inc.*, Comp. Gen. Dec. B-291739, 2003 CPD ¶ 34; *Hughes & Sons Sanitation*, Comp. Gen. Dec. B-270391, 96-1 CPD ¶ 119; *Western Filter Corp.*, Comp. Gen. Dec. B-247212, 92-1 CPD ¶ 436; *Stacor Corp.*, 57 Comp. Gen. 234 (B-189987), 78-1 CPD ¶ 68; on proposed prices from other small businesses, *Frontier Transp., Inc.*, Comp. Gen. Dec. B-400345, 2008 CPD ¶ 165 (HUBZone preference not followed in cascaded set-aside); and on prices from foreign companies, *General Metals, Inc.*, Comp. Gen. Dec. B-248446.3, 92-2 CPD ¶ 256. But see *Airborne Servs., Inc.*, Comp. Gen. Dec. B-221894, 86-1 CPD ¶ 523, holding that an informal telephone quotation from a firm was not sufficiently reliable to support a determination of unreasonable price.

Much less credence should be given to estimated costs and fees submitted in a competitive environment. While the sum of the estimated cost and fee might be considered to be a "price," the fact that offerors are not bound to the estimated cost in a cost-reimbursement contract makes such a "price" inherently unreliable. In such cases, the cost estimates of the various competitors may be established with very different goals in mind than predicting the actual costs of performance. Because the government will bear the risk of underestimates of the performance costs, competitors are not as fully motivated to predict the costs accurately. This is why cost realism analysis is required for such procurements. Comparisons of cost-reimbursement proposals are made in cost realism analysis, but they must be done very carefully, as discussed below.

[2] Historical Pricing Information

The second type of information that can be used to assess proposed prices is pricing information from prior procurements. Both contract prices and other available price information should be reviewed. See, for example, *Applied Research Solutions*, Comp. Gen. Dec. B-4149192, 2017 CPD ¶ 276 (prices unrealistic when lower than historical prices on contract with problems); *Theodor Wille Intertrade AG*, Comp. Gen. Dec. B-409976.3, 2015 CPD ¶ 65 (agency evaluated prices compared to historical, commercial and GSA prices); *CGI Federal, Inc.*, Comp. Gen. Dec. B-410330.2, 2014 CPD ¶ 366 (prices considerably lower than prior prices realistic based on different circumstances); *General*

Dynamics—Ordnance & Tactical Sys., Comp. Gen. Dec. B-401658, 2009 CPD ¶ 217 (prior prices paid by agency showed prices were realistic); *Paraclete Contracts*, Comp. Gen. Dec. B-299883, 2007 CPD ¶ 153 (prior prices paid by agency showed price was reasonable); *Crawford Labs.*, Comp. Gen. Dec. B-277069, 97-2 CPD ¶ 63 (prices double those of prior procurement unreasonable); and *TAAS Israel Indus., Ltd.*, Comp. Gen. Dec. B-260733, 95-2 CPD ¶ 23 (prior prices paid to other contractors on recent competitive procurements showed that price was reasonable). In some cases, prior prices have been used along with the government estimate to demonstrate that the price was unreasonable, *Quality Inn & Suites Conference Center*, Comp. Gen. Dec. B-283468, 99-2 CPD ¶ 72; *Western Filter Corp.*, Comp. Gen. Dec. B-247212, 92-1 CPD ¶ 436; *Freund Precision, Inc.*, Comp. Gen. Dec. B-207426, 82-2 CPD ¶ 509; *Society Brand, Inc.*, 55 Comp. Gen. 475 (B-183963), 75-2 CPD ¶ 327.

There are several variables that must be accounted for when using prior pricing information. One of the most important of these variables is changes in economic conditions between the times of the prior procurements and the current procurement. See *Honolulu Disposal Serv., Inc.—Recons.*, 60 Comp. Gen. 642 (B-200753.2), 81-2 CPD ¶ 126, finding a price unreasonable because it was 14% higher than prior years' prices, whereas the agency believed a 3% inflation adjustment was reasonable. This type of adjustment is particularly important in a period of sharply rising prices. Another important variable is differences in quantity. As a general rule, it is expected that higher quantities will yield lower prices, but this may not hold true when a company is working at full capacity. It is also important to determine the total quantities involved when the product or service is being produced or performed for other customers as well as the procuring agency. A third factor is the inclusion of nonrecurring costs in the prices. If the offeror has been forced to discontinue the work since the performance of the prior contract, startup costs may necessarily be included in the new price. This also raises the question of whether nonrecurring costs have been included in the prior prices. In order to make a fair comparison, such nonrecurring costs should be removed from both prices and assessed separately. See *General Fire Extinguisher Corp.*, 54 Comp. Gen. 416 (B-181796), 74-2 CPD ¶ 278, where prior prices from a contractor were used to demonstrate reasonableness of prices including startup costs. The source of the prior price may also be a factor. See *W.H. Compton Shear Co.*, Comp. Gen. Dec. B-208626.2, 83-2 CPD ¶ 404, where the fact that the prior price was obtained from a foreign company was validly considered in finding reasonableness of price.

If the same work has not been done in the past, comparative prices of *similar work* can be used as a rough means of price analysis. In such cases, adjustments must be made to account for the dissimilarities between the two types of work. If the differences in the work are minor, such adjustments may not be too difficult to determine. However, at a minimum, this will require a detailed analysis of the product to ascertain its specific differences from prior products. See

Resource Ltd., Comp. Gen. Dec. B-406492, 2012 CPD ¶ 195 (agency used prices paid for similar custodial services to determine that proposed price was realistic); *Family Realty*, Comp. Gen. Dec. B-247772, 92-2 CPD ¶ 6 (agency used prices received on another solicitation for similar services, along with the competitive prices on the instant procurement and the government estimate, to determine that the proposed price was reasonable).

When data is available for several years, price analysis can be very valuable. Detailed analysis will disclose pricing trends that may indicate that significant learning has occurred and should be expected to continue through the current purchase. This type of information is a valuable cross-check for the competitive pricing information discussed above.

[3] Parametric Data

Some industries compile and use very general data relating prices of products to characteristics of the product such as weight, electrical or electronic circuits, or other units of measurement. One of the oldest types of parametric information is the data compiled by the aircraft manufacturing industry relating labor hours in manufacturing to aircraft weight. Such data is a useful tool in making a price analysis—especially if the database is sufficiently large to demonstrate a consistent relationship. There is very little published guidance on the use of parametric data. However, the DCAA Contract Audit Manual contains five criteria for judging the reliability of this type of data when submitted by a contractor at DCAM 9-1003.2:

> 1. Do the procedures clearly establish guidelines for when parametric techniques would be appropriate?
> 2. Are there guidelines for the consistent application of estimating techniques?
> 3. Is there proper identification of sources of data and the estimating methods and rationale used in developing cost estimates?
> 4. Do the procedures ensure that relevant personnel have sufficient training, experience, and guidance to perform estimating tasks in accordance with the contractor's established procedures?
> 5. Is there an internal review of and accountability for the adequacy of the estimating system, including the comparison of projected results to actual results and an analysis of any differences?

If these criteria are met, parametric data submitted by contractors can provide another indication of the reasonableness of a proposed price. Such data can also be compiled and used by government agencies in analyzing prices. Supplementary guidance on parametric cost estimating is contained in the NASA *Parametric Cost Estimating Handbook* (2d ed. 2009). See also the International Society of Parametric Analysts' *Parametric Estimating Handbook* (4th ed. 2008). For a decision describing the Air Force's compilation of a parametric estimate for each offeror, based on past data, to assess cost realism, see *Boeing Co.*, Comp. Gen. Dec. B-412441, 2016 CPD ¶ 269.

Agencies have also used statistical techniques to evaluate prices. See, for example, *Croman Corp. v. United States*, 106 Fed. Cl. 198 (2012), upholding the use of a cost per pound of fire retardant in evaluating competitive helicopters; and *PWC Logistics Servs., Inc.*, Comp. Gen. Dec. B-299820, 2007 CPD ¶ 162, upholding the use of a "best case" and "worst case" analysis of material prices based on changes in prices over the past 10 years. Compare *Boeing Co.*, Comp. Gen. Dec. B-311344, 2008 CPD ¶ 114, where a protest was granted because the agency improperly used a "Monte Carlo" simulation to adjust prices for realism. The defect identified by GAO was that the agency used data on government costs of total weapon systems to determine possible variations in costs of nonrecurring engineering (only one small element of total cost variations). See also *EPW Closure Servs., LLC*, Comp. Gen. Dec. B-294910, 2006 CPD ¶ 3, criticizing an agency for accepting a contingency allowance included in a proposed price based on a "Monte Carlo" simulation performed by the offeror.

[4] Published Prices

If the product or service is sold to the public, the offeror may have published prices or standard pricing techniques that are used for these sales. Such information will frequently demonstrate that the price is reasonable—especially if the product or service is sold in a competitive market. For example, in *Logics, Inc.*, Comp. Gen. Dec. B-237412, 90-1 CPD ¶ 189, a protest was sustained where the agency failed to consider pricing information contained in a government catalog which indicated that the fair market prices of an item in question were much higher than the agency estimates. Similarly, in *Techno-Sciences, Inc.*, Comp. Gen. Dec. B-277260, 97-2 CPD ¶ 115, a protest was sustained where the agency failed to consider commercial prices in determining fair market prices. When using this type of information, care must be used in determining what discounts are given for quantity purchases and what other types of special arrangements are made for preferred customers. See *Interscience Sys., Inc.*, 59 Comp. Gen. 658 (B-195773), 80-2 CPD ¶ 106, finding that discounts were not sufficiently large to permit a determination of reasonableness based on market prices. The volume of sales to the general public will also be a factor in assessing the validity of this type of data. Thus, a large volume of sales at a published price in a competitive market would make such data highly reliable, while a low volume of sales in a narrow market would render the data less reliable.

There are a number of sites on the Internet that publish labor rates in various industries such as salary.com. The most readily available set of published fixed labor rates are the rates on Federal Supply Schedule contracts and these rates are frequently used in price analysis. See, for example, *Bauer Techs., Inc.*, Comp. Gen. Dec. B-415717.2, 2018 CPD ¶ 217; and *Oklahoma State Univ.*, Comp. Gen. Dec. B-406865, 2012 CPD ¶ 276. In the procurements protested in these decisions, the contracting officers used these rates in conjunction with other pricing information. This is necessary because Federal Supply Schedule contractors frequently provide discounts to these rates—making them somewhat unreliable in themselves to determine price reasonableness.

Published prices for similar products or services may also be useful in performing a price analysis. Of course, adjustments have to be made to reflect dissimilarities, but if the differences are minor, this may be a valid source of information. See, for example, *Eclipse Sys., Inc.*, Comp. Gen. Dec. B-216002, 85-1 CPD ¶ 267, where reasonableness of price was determined based on a "market survey" of prices of comparable products.

[5] Independent Government Cost Estimates

Although the current FAR contains no requirement that agencies prepare an independent cost estimate for each procurement, this has been very common practice. Prior to FAC 97-02, Sept. 30, 1997, FAR 15.803(b) required the development of such an estimate as follows:

> Before issuing a solicitation, the contracting officer shall (when it is feasible to do so) develop an estimate of the proper price level or value of the supplies or services to be purchased. Estimates can range from simple budgetary estimates to complex estimates based on inspection of the product itself and review of such items as drawings, specifications, and prior data.

The only mandatory requirements for the preparation of such estimates are in FAR 36.203 (construction procurements) and FAR 36.605 (architect/engineering services).

Paragraph 4.5.1 of DoD Instruction 5000.2-R, *Mandatory Procedures for Major Defense Acquisition Programs and Major Automated Information System Acquisition Programs*, March 15, 1996, also required "life-cycle cost estimates" for all major programs in the Department of Defense.

Such independent estimates can be based on all of the types of data that are discussed above plus any cost or pricing data that may be available from past procurements. They represent the agency's best estimate of the most reasonable current price for the products or services being procured. Thus, they can serve as the sole basis for finding a price reasonable, *Aluminum Specialties, Inc.*, Comp. Gen. Dec. B-281024, 98-2 CPD ¶ 116 (prices slightly below government estimate). They can also support a determination that prices are unrealistic, *First Choice, LLC*, Comp. Gen. Dec. B-417196, 2019 CPD ¶ 158.

Government estimates can also serve as a sound basis for finding a price unreasonable, *Norfolk Dredging Co.*, Comp. Gen. Dec. B-417213, 2019 CPD ¶ 127 (upholding cancellation of sealed bid procurement when protester's bid was higher than government estimate and above agency funds); *4H Constr. Corp.*, Comp. Gen. Dec. B-413558.4, 2017 CPD ¶ 54 (upholding cancellation of sealed bid procurement when all bids were more than 25% over government estimate); *Avar Consulting, Inc.*, Comp. Gen. Dec. B-410308, 2014 CPD ¶ 362 (upholding dropping protester from competitive range because its price was 20% higher than government estimate); *Division Laundry & Cleaners, Inc.*, Comp. Gen. Dec. B-311242, 2008 CPD ¶ 97 (upholding cancellation of set-aside when two small businesses were over 35% above government estimate); and *Overstreet Elec. Co.*, Comp. Gen. Dec. B-284691, 2000 CPD ¶ 79 (approving cancellation of solicitation when low bid exceeded government estimate by 32%). When offerors propose different products to meet an agency's requirements, it is reasonable for the agency to make a separate independent cost estimate for each product and determine that a higher priced product is reasonably priced based on that estimate, *Marinette Marine Corp.*, Comp. Gen. Dec. B-400697, 2009 CPD ¶ 16.

Because government estimates are made early in the procurement process, it may be necessary to update them for use in the price analysis. See, for example, *Veteran Shredding, LLC*, Comp. Gen. Dec. B-417399, 2019 CPD ¶ 210 (government estimate updated to reflect revised requirement after protest of initial procurement); *Vigor Shipyards, Inc.*, Comp. Gen. Dec. B-409635, 2014 CPD ¶ 170 (government estimate revised downward based on offeror's proposed method of performance); *Legacy Mgmt. Solutions, LLC*, Comp. Gen. Dec. B-299981.2, 2007 CPD ¶ 197 (government estimate revised downward to determine that seemingly low prices were realistic). See also *CBY Design Bldrs. v. United States*, 105 Fed. Cl. 303 (2012), where the agency properly made new government estimates for each of the competitive designs on a design build project and used those estimates along with the competitive price to determine that the proposed prices were reasonable.

The competitive prices that are proposed may also demonstrate that the government estimate is inaccurate. Even if the agency does not correct the estimate, its use cannot be successfully protested if it also used other price analysis techniques to conclude that prices were reasonable or realistic, *Dewberry Crawford Grp.*, Comp. Gen. Dec. B-415940.10, 2018 CPD ¶ 297. The agency also can ignore the government estimate, *Vion Corp. v. United States*, 122 Fed. Cl. 559 (2015), or use it carefully in conjunction with other data, *Mindleaf Techs., Inc.*, Comp. Gen. Dec. B-294242, 2004 CPD ¶ 157 (price realistic because, although it was somewhat lower than competitors' prices, it was higher than government estimate); *Synectic Solutions, Inc.*, Comp. Gen. Dec. B-299086, 2007 CPD ¶ 36 (three acceptable proposals were lower than the government estimate); *Hawkeye Glove Mfg., Inc.*, Comp. Gen. Dec. B-299237, 2007 CPD ¶ 49 (government estimate and other small business prices used to determine price reasonableness); and *Academy Facilities Mgmt.—Advisory Opinion*, Comp. Gen. Dec. B-401094.3, 2009 CPD ¶ 139 (government estimates, competitive prices and analysis of some cost data used to determine price realism). Compare *National Projects, Inc.*, Comp. Gen. Dec. B-283887, 2000 CPD ¶ 16, where all five competitive prices significantly exceeded the government estimate, but the agency still concluded that the government estimate was accurate, cancelled the IFB and conducted a negotiated procurement. In one interesting case, an agency was allowed to cancel a procurement after a specification change rendered the government estimate unreliable and left the contracting officer uncertain as to the reasonableness of the protester's price, *Adrian Supply Co.*, Comp. Gen. Dec. B-241502, 91-1 CPD ¶ 138. Verifying the price would have required an audit which could not have been completed before the end of the fiscal year, when the funds for the project expired.

[6] Market Prices

Prices of the same or similar items that are available in the commercial market provide an excellent comparison to prices proposed for government contracts. See *Tiger Truck, LLC*, Comp. Gen. Dec. B-400685, 2009 CPD ¶ 19, where GAO rejected the contention that the agency should not have used the price of foreign-made vehicles in determining whether a price was fair and reasonable. See also *SRA Int'l, Inc.*, Comp. Gen. Dec. B-413000.1, 2016 CPD ¶ 208 (upholding use of wage rates from Bureau of Labor Statistics survey to determine price realism); *Operational Support & Servs.*, Comp. Gen. Dec. B-299660.2, 2007 CPD ¶ 183 (upholding determination of fair market price based on the labor rates on Federal Supply Schedule contracts and salaries listed on websites).

Care must be exercised in using this type of information because of the large differences that may exist between commercial transactions and government procurements. In some cases, the undue complexity of government procurements may justify a significantly higher price than that being offered in the commercial market. On the other hand, there may be situations where the government is buying such large quantities of the supplies or services that it will expect to pay a lower price than the commercial market price.

[7] Information Submitted by Offeror

Occasionally, the solicitation will require offerors to submit detailed pricing information and a price can be determined unreasonable if that information demonstrates such unreasonableness. For example, in *Concepts Bldg. Sys., Inc.*, Comp. Gen. Dec. B-281995, 99-1 CPD ¶ 95, the agency solicited information on the markup that vendors would add to commercial prices. GAO agreed that the agency properly rejected a proposal calling for a markup of 13% because the agency's negotiation objective was a 7% markup.

Information in a technical proposal as to how an offeror will perform the work can also bear on the validity of a price analysis if the details of the offeror's pricing information do not match the technical proposal. See *Resource Consultants, Inc.*, Comp. Gen. Dec. B-293073.3, 2005 CPD ¶ 131, granting a protest on the basis that the winning offeror's price was not in line with its proposed method of accomplishing the work—which had unfairly earned it a high technical evaluation.

§ 13.06 COST ANALYSIS

FAR 15.404-1(c)(1) defines "cost analysis" as follows:

> Cost analysis is the review and evaluation of the separate cost elements and profit or fee in an offeror's or contractor's proposal, as needed to determine a fair and reasonable price or to determine cost realism, and the application of judgment to determine how well the proposed costs represent what the cost of the contract should be, assuming reasonable economy and efficiency.

Cost analysis differs intrinsically from price analysis in that cost analysis focuses on the reasonableness of the estimated costs of performance, not the reasonableness of the contract price. Thus, cost analysis reviews each element of cost to ascertain whether the contractor's estimate contains an accurate and reasonable prediction of the costs that will be incurred during performance of the work. The contract price is then arrived at by adding a rate of profit that is determined to be fair in accordance with the profit guidelines that will be discussed in the next section. The fundamental theory of pricing using cost analysis is that a price is fair if it includes all reasonable costs of performance plus a fair profit. This theory, of course, ignores the fact that such a price may be far out of line with the market value or intrinsic value of the work. FAR 15.404-1(f)(1) recognizes this problem, to some extent, by precluding the inclusion of costs other than manufacturing or acquisition costs in unit prices if such costs would result in unit prices greatly out of line with the "intrinsic value" of the item.

The fact that costs and profit are analyzed separately does not mean that they must be negotiated separately when the parties are agreeing on firm-fixed prices. See the basic guidance in FAR 15.405(a), which states:

> The purpose of performing cost or price analysis is to develop a negotiation position that permits the contracting officer and the offeror an opportunity to reach agreement on a fair and reasonable price. A fair and reasonable price does not require that agreement be reached on every element of cost, nor is it mandatory that the agreed price be within the contracting officer's initial negotiation position. Taking into consideration the advisory recommendations, reports of contributing specialists, and the current status of the contractor's purchasing system, the contracting officer is responsible for exercising the requisite judgment needed to reach a negotiated settlement with the offeror and is solely responsible for the final price agreement. However, when significant audit or other specialist recommendations are not adopted, the contracting officer should provide rationale that supports the negotiation result in the price negotiation documentation.

Thus, in firm-fixed-price contracts and fixed-price contracts with economic price adjustment clauses, the parties merely need to agree on a price to consummate the negotiation. In cost-reimbursement and fixed-price incentive contracts, this is not true. There, the estimated cost or target cost and the fee or profit are stated separately in the contract document and must therefore be separately negotiated. However, even in these types of contracts, there is no need for the parties to agree on each element of the costs. Compromises are frequently made among elements of cost in order to arrive at an agreement on the estimated or target cost of performing the contract. Note that FAR 15.405(a) does not reflect 10 U.S.C. § 3745 (formerly § 2324(f)(4)) and 41 U.S.C. § 4305(c)(3) which require identification of the treatment accorded specific costs included in indirect cost proposals that have been questioned by auditors, as follows:

> The Federal Acquisition Regulation shall require that all categories of costs designated in the report of the contract auditor as questioned with respect to a proposal for settlement [of indirect costs] be resolved in such a manner that the amount of the individual questioned costs that are paid will be reflected in the settlement.

See FAR 42.705-1(b)(4) implementing this requirement. While this provision requires internal documentation of the results of negotiations of indirect cost rates, it does not appear to require specific agreement on individual costs. The codified provision in 41 U.S.C. § 4305(c)(3) could be interpreted to impose this requirement on all costs not just indirect costs but this was not the interpretation of the prior statute.

Cost analysis requires a complete review of the offeror's proposed costs to ensure that they reflect an accurate projection of the costs of performance of the work to be placed under the contract. The elements of cost analysis are described in FAR 15.404-1(c) as follows:

> (2) The Government may use various cost analysis techniques and procedures to ensure a fair and reasonable price, given the circumstances of the acquisition. Such techniques and procedures include the following:
>
> (i) Verification of cost data or pricing data and evaluation of cost elements, including—
>
> (A) The necessity for, and reasonableness of, proposed costs, including allowances for contingencies;
>
> (B) Projection of the offeror's cost trends, on the basis of current and historical cost data or pricing data;
>
> (C) Reasonableness of estimates generated by appropriately calibrated and validated parametric models or cost-estimating relationships; and
>
> (D) The application of audited or negotiated indirect cost rates, labor rates, and cost of money or other factors.

(ii) Evaluating the effect of the offeror's current practices on future costs. In conducting this evaluation, the contracting officer shall ensure that the effects of inefficient or uneconomical past practices are not projected into the future. In pricing production of recently developed complex equipment, the contracting officer should perform a trend analysis of basic labor and materials, even in periods of relative price stability.

(iii) Comparison of costs proposed by the offeror for individual cost elements with—

(A) Actual costs previously incurred by the same offeror;

(B) Previous cost estimates from the offeror or from other offerors for the same or similar items;

(C) Other cost estimates received in response to the Government's request;

(D) Independent Government cost estimates by technical personnel; and

(E) Forecasts of planned expenditures.

(iv) Verification that the offeror's cost submissions are in accordance with the contract cost principles and procedures in Part 31 and, when applicable, the requirements and procedures in 48 CFR Chapter 99 (Appendix of the FAR loose-leaf edition), Cost Accounting Standards.

(v) Review to determine whether any cost data or pricing data, necessary to make the offeror's proposal suitable for negotiation, have not been either submitted or identified in writing by the contractor. If there are such data, the contracting officer shall attempt to obtain and use them in negotiations or make satisfactory allowance for the incomplete data.

(vi) Analysis of the results of any make-or-buy program reviews, in evaluating subcontract costs (see 15.407-2).

Detailed guidance on cost analysis is contained in Volume 3 of DOD CPRG.

The following material discusses three types of cost analysis: (1) analysis of the offeror's proposed costs using cost or pricing data, (2) analysis of the proposed costs without using cost or pricing data, and (3) should-cost analysis. While the above FAR guidance is primarily concerned with the first type of cost analysis, it also recognizes the other two types. Thus, ¶ (iii) reflects the analysis of the cost elements proposed by an offeror using data other than cost data or pricing data. Similarly, ¶ (ii) reflects the need for should-cost analysis.

[A] Analysis of Proposed Costs Using Cost or Pricing Data

The basic cost analysis techniques were formulated by the government (principally in DoD) when *certified* cost or pricing data was required to be submitted on many, if not most, procurements. While this requirement has been reduced by the adoption of a $2 million threshold and the prohibition of requiring such data on procurements with adequate price competition and for commercial products or services, FAC 2005-45 amended the FAR to permit contracting officers to obtain *uncertified* cost or pricing data in some instances and to follow the same procedures when calling for the submission of such data as when certified cost or pricing data are required. This section therefore addresses the analytical techniques that will be used when cost or pricing data (whether certified or uncertified) is obtained from an offeror.

The statutory requirement for the submission of certified cost or pricing data is a disclosure requirement not a use requirement. Thus, the offeror is entitled to arrive at its offered price without using the cost or pricing data that it has submitted. See *United Techs. Corp.*, ASBCA 51410, 04-1 BCA ¶ 32,556, *modified*, 05-1 BCA ¶ 32,860, *aff'd*, 463 F.3d 1261 (Fed. Cir. 2006), stating at 161,024:

> The plain language of the Act does not obligate a contractor to use any particular *cost or pricing data to put together its proposal. Indeed, TINA does not instruct a* contractor in any manner regarding the manner or method of proposal-preparation.
>
> TINA is a disclosure statute. It requires a contractor under certain circumstances to disclose and to furnish cost or pricing data to the government and to certify that the *data are accurate, current and complete. This disclosure and certification obligation is not* limited to that data actually used or relied upon by the contractor to prepare its proposal. Under the regulatory definition, the data to be provided consists of "all facts existing up to the time of agreement on price which prudent buyers and sellers would reasonably expect to have a significant effect on price negotiations. . . ." On the other hand, once a contractor has furnished accurate, current and complete data, it has fulfilled its TINA obligations. The statute does not require that all or any of that data be used to prepare the proposal. One would think that any contractor with the desire to obtain a contract award would use credible, historical cost data so as to demonstrate to the government that its proposed price is consistent therewith. However, this is a matter for the contractor to decide, and for the Government to evaluate as part of the proposal review process, and is not a mandate under TINA.

In affirming this decision, the Federal Circuit addressed the government's contention that it was entitled to recover for defective data that it had not relied on because the contractor used the defective data in arriving at its proposed price. The court ruled that proof of contractor reliance on defective cost or pricing data does not overcome lack of proof of government reliance, citing *Universal Restoration, Inc. v. United States*, 798 F.2d 1400 (Fed. Cir. 1986).

In this type of cost analysis, the contracting officer has full cost or pricing data to assist in the review the offeror's cost estimate to ensure that the proposed costs are as accurately projected as is possible under the circumstances of the procurement. Summaries of cost estimates (cost element breakdowns) are submitted in a format that depicts the manner that the offeror accumulates costs, and cost or pricing data is submitted to support this summary information. Detailed guidance on the required submission is set forth in Table 15-2 of FAR 15.408. The General Instructions in Table 15-2 call for the submission of separate cost element breakdowns for each contract line item as follows:

> D. You must show the relationship between contract line item prices and the total contract price. You must attach cost-element breakdowns for each proposed line item, using the appropriate format prescribed in the "Formats for Submission of Line Item Summaries" section of this table. You must furnish supporting breakdowns for each cost element, consistent with your cost accounting system.

These instructions also call for the submission of certified cost or pricing data as follows:

> B. In submitting your proposal, you must include an index, appropriately referenced, of all the certified cost or pricing data and information accompanying or identified in the proposal. In addition, you must annotate any future additions and/or revisions, up to the date of agreement on price, or an earlier date agreed upon by the parties, on a supplemental index.
>
> C. As part of the specific information required, you must submit, with your proposal—
>
> (1) Certified cost or pricing data (as defined at FAR 2.101). You must clearly identify on your cover sheet that certified cost or pricing data are included as part of the proposal.
>
> (2) Information reasonably required to explain your estimating process, including—
>
> (i) The judgmental factors applied and the mathematical or other methods used in the estimate, including those used in projecting from known data; and
>
> (ii) The nature and amount of any contingencies included in the proposed price.
>
> * * *
>
> F. Whenever you have incurred costs for work performed before submission of a proposal, you must identify those costs in your cost/price proposal.
>
> G. If you have reached an agreement with Government representatives on use of forward pricing rates/factors, identify the agreement, including a copy, and describe its nature.

While these instructions apply by their own terms only when certified cost or pricing data are required to be submitted, the definition of "data other than certified cost or pricing data" in FAR 2.101 states that such data "may include the identical types of data as certified cost or pricing data, consistent with

Table 15-2 of 15.408." Thus, the FAR allows contracting officers to require offerors to submit uncertified cost or pricing data following these instructions.

DOD imposes an additional submission requirement when certified cost or pricing data is to be submitted by using the Proposal Adequacy Checklist clause in DFARS 252.215-7009. This clause contains a very detailed submission requirement. NASA requires a similar clause which is located at NFS 1852.215-85.

The cost or pricing data will vary in amount depending on the element of cost being considered and the work being procured; and, typically, the parties will use this data as the basis for the negotiation of the price or estimated/target cost. However, the key issue in such negotiations will be the projections of cost submitted by the offeror and made by the government negotiators. In many cases, the government cost analysts and negotiators will explore the reasonableness of the offeror's projections, including the questioning of their validity, during negotiations. Thus, it is good practice for offerors to submit a detailed explanation of why the methodology they have used in making their projections is logical and reasonable, although there is no penalty under the Truth in Negotiations Act if the methodology is faulty or even if it is not submitted to the government since it is not cost or pricing data. (See, however, the discussion in Chapter 1 regarding the treatment of false statements about estimating methodology as fraud under the False Claims Act.) The government team will also make independent projections in most cases, and much of the ultimate price negotiation will consist of a comparison and evaluation of these different projections.

The offeror's estimate is normally broken down into categories of cost, such as labor, material, and indirect costs, which are listed in the cost element breakdowns. In accordance with Cost Accounting Standard 401, 48 C.F.R. § 9904.401, each contractor's estimating practices must be consistent with its cost accounting practices used in accumulating and reporting actual costs. Thus, while contractors have substantial freedom in establishing their cost accounting systems, the costs accumulated must be directly relatable to the cost elements in estimates. Table 15-2 reflects this freedom by prescribing no specific cost breakdown by elements of cost. The following discussion addresses the requirement for the submission of cost or pricing data, the broad types of costs that are common to almost all systems, and the requirement that certified cost or pricing data be certified at the conclusion of negotiations.

[1] Cost or Pricing Data

The statutes require that, when required, offerors must submit certified cost or pricing data that are "*accurate, complete, and current.*" There is no such explicit requirement that is attached to uncertified cost or pricing data but contractors must recognize that such a requirement would likely be applied if suit for defective data was brought under the False Claims Act, 31 U.S.C. § 3729. Thus, contractors must know what data fall within the definition of "cost or pricing data," what will constitute "complete" data, and how recent their records must be in order to comply fully with the requirement that the data be "current."

The submission requirement for certified cost or pricing data is a strict requirement. Hence, available data that are significant must be submitted even if the offeror does not use the data in arriving at the proposed price of the contract, *Rosemount, Inc.*, ASBCA 37520, 95-2 BCA ¶ 27,770; *Hardie-Tynes Mfg. Co.*, ASBCA 20717, 76-2 BCA ¶ 12,121. However, the government has the burden of proving that the data was reasonably available to the contractor before the close of negotiations, *Litton Sys., Inc.*, ASBCA 34435, 93-2 BCA ¶ 25,707.

[a] Definition of Cost or Pricing Data

The regulations contain a comprehensive definition of "cost or pricing data," emphasizing that such data are factual in nature but including some illustrations that are less than clear. See FAR 2.101, which states:

> *Cost or pricing data* (10 U.S.C. 3701(1) and 41 U.S.C. chapter 35) means all facts that, as of the date of price agreement or, if applicable, an earlier date agreed upon between the parties that is as close as practicable to the date of agreement on price, prudent buyers and sellers would reasonably expect to affect price negotiations significantly. Cost or pricing data are factual, not judgmental; and are verifiable. While they do not indicate the accuracy of the prospective contractor's judgment about estimated future costs or projections, they do include the data forming the basis for that judgment. Cost or pricing data are more than historical accounting data; they are all the facts that can be reasonably expected to contribute to the soundness of estimates of future costs and to the validity of determinations of costs already incurred. They also include such factors as—
>
> (1) Vendor quotations;
> (2) Nonrecurring costs;
> (3) Information on changes in production methods and in production or purchasing volume;
> (4) Data supporting projections of business prospects and objectives and related operations costs;
> (5) Unit-cost trends such as those associated with labor efficiency;
> (6) Make-or-buy decisions;
> (7) Estimated resources to attain business goals; and
> (8) Information on management decisions that could have a significant bearing on costs.

The statutes contain a much shorter definition at 10 U.S.C. § 3701(1) (formerly § 2306a(i)) and 41 U.S.C. § 3501(2):

> [T]he term "cost or pricing data" means all facts that, as of the date of agreement on the price of a contract (or the price of a contract modification) or, if applicable consistent with [the requirement that the data to be as close to the data of agreement on price "as is practicable"], another date agreed upon between the parties, a prudent buyer or seller would reasonably expect to affect price negotiations significantly. Such term does not include information that is judgmental, but does include the factual information from which a judgment was derived.

It has been very difficult to arrive at a precise distinction between factual data and judgmental information. However, it is very clear that recorded costs are factual—with the result that they are cost or pricing data. Thus, the term includes labor rates paid in prior periods, *Boeing Co.*, ASBCA 32753, 90-1 BCA ¶ 22,270, *recons. denied*, 90-1 BCA ¶ 22,426; *Kaiser Aerospace & Elecs. Corp.*, ASBCA 32098, 90-1 BCA ¶ 22,489, *recons. denied*, 90-2 BCA ¶ 22,695; incurred labor hours, *Grumman Aerospace Corp.*, ASBCA 35188, 90-2 BCA ¶ 22,842; and incurred indirect costs, *Norris Indus., Inc.*, ASBCA 15442, 74-1 BCA ¶ 10,482. Information in the offeror's purchasing department relating to the prices of materials is also factual in nature. Thus, the term includes purchase orders, *Grumman Aerospace Corp.*, ASBCA 35188, 90-2 BCA ¶ 22,842, and vendor quotations, *Cutler-Hammer, Inc. v. United States*, 416 F.2d 1306 (Ct. Cl. 1969). Accounting adjustments to actual cost data are also cost or pricing data, *Hughes Aircraft Co.*, ASBCA 46321, 97-1 BCA ¶ 28,972.

Accounting information on the costs of prior work on different projects may also be cost or pricing data if the information is sufficiently relevant to be usable in the analysis of proposed costs. Thus, prices paid for "similar" items were held to be cost or pricing data, *Hardie-Tynes Mfg. Co.*, ASBCA 20717, 76-2 BCA ¶ 12,121.

In some cases, a mixture of factual data and judgmental information has been held to be cost or pricing data. For example, in *Lambert Eng'g Co.*, ASBCA 13338, 69-1 BCA ¶ 7663, labor-hour estimates derived from actual information were held to be cost or pricing data even though they were not technically "actual" cost data. In *Aerojet-General Corp.*, ASBCA 12264, 69-1 BCA ¶ 7664, *modified*, 70-1 BCA ¶ 8140, the underlying factual data in an internal company report analyzing a subcontractor's pricing proposal were held to be cost or pricing data. See also *Grumman Aerospace Corp.*, ASBCA 27476, 86-3 BCA ¶ 19,091 (internal company report analyzing a subcontractor's proposal was cost or pricing data); *Texas Instruments, Inc.*, ASBCA 23678, 87-3 BCA ¶ 20,195 (computer-generated report containing an estimate of the costs of future work that was derived from actual cost data but manipulated using complex estimating formulas was cost or pricing data); and *United Techs. Corp.*, ASBCA 51410, 04-1 BCA ¶ 32,556, *modified*, 05-1 BCA ¶ 32,860, *aff'd*, 463 F.3d 1261 (Fed. Cir. 2006) (two documents summarizing the costs that "flowed into" the proposed price were cost or pricing data). All of these cases seem to find that a document is cost or pricing data because it is of material assistance in showing how the cost or pricing data relates to the proposed price. In most cases, these documents also contain some factual data. Compare *Alloy Surfaces Co.*, ASBCA 59625, 20-1 BCA ¶ 37,574, holding that "job cost reports" generated by a computerized system were not cost of pricing data because the contractor had not taken the final step of reconciling the estimated elements in the preliminary reports.

A contractor's management decisions are cost or pricing data if (1) they have a substantial relationship to a cost element and (2) they are made by an official with the authority to approve the action under consideration, *Lockheed Corp.*, ASBCA 36420, 95-2 BCA ¶ 27,722. In *Lockheed*, the board found that a decision to adopt a new strategy in collective bargaining negotiations met the first test because it would have a substantial effect on wage rates to be paid in the future. The board found, however, that this decision did not meet the second test because it had not been approved by senior corporate management as required by the policies of the company. In *Motorola, Inc.*, ASBCA 41528, 94-2 BCA ¶ 26,596, and *Motorola, Inc.*, ASBCA 48841, 96-2 BCA ¶ 28,465, a manufacturing policy memorandum directing that certain costs not be charged to government contracts was held to be cost or pricing data. In *Aerojet Ordnance Tenn.*, ASBCA 36089, 95-2 BCA ¶ 27,922, a management decision to proceed "with all possible haste" to close a waste containment pond was not cost or pricing data because the cost consequences of the decision could not be determined until the action was approved by the state of Tennessee. In contrast, *Millipore Corp.*, GSBCA 9453, 91-1 BCA ¶ 23,345, held that a decision to change the company's discount policy did constitute cost or pricing data. The board did not address the question of whether a decision to alter the discount policy had been made at a level of management with the authority to approve the decision. It would seem that, to fall within the scope of this rule, the decision would have to impact the resources expected to be used to perform the work, such as a decision to change work methods or to buy from a different vendor. Thus, it is doubtful that a management decision to project costs differently would fall within this rule since such a decision is purely judgmental.

Factual data submitted by a subcontractor on a prior contract to support the prices of "long lead" items were held to be cost or pricing data on a current contract because the items were transferred to the current contract, *General Dynamics Corp.*, ASBCA 39866, 94-1 BCA ¶ 26,339. Similarly, a cost analysis made by a subcontractor to test the validity of the price of a sub-subcontractor was cost or pricing data when it demonstrated that the subcontractor's quoted price, that had been submitted to the government, was too high, *McDonnell Aircraft Co.*, ASBCA 44504, 97-1 BCA ¶ 28,977.

Data containing only judgments are not cost or pricing data. In *Litton Sys., Inc.*, ASBCA 36509, 92-2 BCA ¶ 24,842, the board held that the estimated standard labor hours (ESLH) used by the contractor were not cost or pricing data even though there were internal reports listing these hours for parts manufactured by the contractor. The board found that the reports were not in themselves factual in nature because they contained no facts. The board distinguished these reports from documents containing mixed fact and judgment, stating at 123,944-45:

> The ESLH report is not mixed fact and judgment. In this appeal, we have no underlying document that is verifiable. The ESLH report is based on estimates made by [the contractor's] industrial engineers or test engineers and, as we have found above, no two industrial engineers or test engineers would estimate either the task or the frequency of the task the same. The ESLH report is therefore pure judgment and is, accordingly, not data and need not be disclosed.

[b] Insignificant Data

In a few cases, contractors have escaped liability for nonsubmission of cost or pricing data by demonstrating that the data were not the type that prudent buyers and sellers would have believed to have a significant effect on the pricing. For example, in *Plessey Indus., Inc.*, ASBCA 16720, 74-1 BCA ¶ 10,603, a rejected vendor quotation was found not to be significant, and in *Boeing Co.*, ASBCA 20875, 85-3 BCA ¶ 18,351, incurred labor costs at the beginning of the contract were held to be the type of information that would not have been used by prudent buyers and sellers in the pricing process. The same logic would apply to old information in the nature of cost or pricing data. For example, contractors have labor rate and overhead rate information going back many years. Only the data relating to recent years are useful in estimating future costs. Reasonable buyers and sellers might disagree over how many years' information is significant, but all would agree that obsolete information would be of no use.

The rule that all significant data must be disclosed has on occasion been interpreted very strictly. In *Sylvania Elec. Prods., Inc. v. United States*, 479 F.2d 1342 (Ct. Cl. 1973), the Court of Claims held that if there is a "logical nexus between the nondisclosed pricing data and the possibility of a lower negotiated contract price, then the data is to be considered significant and subject to disclosure." Offerors should exercise care in deciding to use this logic to withhold data that the government may believe are necessary to evaluate the proposed costs.

[c] Submission Techniques

A note in Table 15.2 provides that there are two techniques for the submission of cost or pricing data: *physical submission* or *specific identification*:

> Note 1: There is a clear distinction between submitting certified cost or pricing data and merely making available books, records, and other documents without identification. The requirement for submission of certified cost or pricing data is met when all accurate cost or pricing data reasonably available to the offeror have been submitted, either actually or by specific identification, to the Contracting Officer or an authorized representative. As later

> information comes into your possession, it should be submitted promptly to the Contracting Officer in a manner that clearly shows how the information relates to the offeror's proposal. The requirement for submission of certified cost or pricing data continues up to the time of agreement on price, or an earlier data agreed upon between the parties if applicable.

There is little guidance in the regulations or the litigated cases as to how specific identification of data is accomplished. See *M-R-S Mfg. Co. v. United States*, 492 F.2d 835 (Ct. Cl. 1974), requiring communication of the specific data that are relevant to the pricing action. It is clear, however, that merely making the data available without specific identification is insufficient. Thus, giving complete access to all contractor data does not meet the submission requirement, *Hughes Aircraft Co.*, ASBCA 46321, 97-1 BCA ¶ 28,972 (making cost ledgers available for audit); *Aerojet-General Corp.*, ASBCA 12873, 69-1 BCA ¶ 7585 (submitting data to the government plant representative); *McDonnell Douglas Corp.*, ASBCA 12786, 69-2 BCA ¶ 7897 (making data available to the government auditor and resident price analyst); *Grumman Aerospace Corp.*, ASBCA 35188, 90-2 BCA ¶ 22,842 (giving contractor complete access to subcontractor data but not identifying relevant data). However, if the government pricing personnel have actual knowledge of the data, the submission requirement is satisfied, *Texas Instruments, Inc.*, ASBCA 23678, 87-3 BCA ¶ 20,195; *Boeing Co.*, ASBCA 32753, 90-1 BCA ¶ 22,270, *recons. denied*, 90-1 BCA ¶ 22,426. In one case, *Motorola, Inc.*, ASBCA 41528, 94-2 BCA ¶ 26,596, the board inferred that current indirect cost data of a subcontractor had been submitted to a resident auditor because that auditor gave the contractor a recommendation for an overhead rate that was apparently based on knowledge of that data.

Volume 3 of DOD CPRG does not address the specific identification process but, instead, recommends that the data be submitted electronically, stating:

> Traditionally contracting officers have required offerors to submit cost or pricing data as printed documents. Most firms prepare these documents using company computers and the resulting printouts may be several inches or even several feet thick.
>
> When the contracting officer gets the paper proposal, the data usually must be entered into a Government computer for analysis. Data entry may require hours, days, or even weeks. This is an unnecessary waste of Government manpower and computer resources, because the offeror has the data in electronic files.
>
> Many activities are eliminating this wasted effort by requiring electronic data submission. Data submitted electronically are ready for immediate analysis and the cost of data entry is eliminated.
>
> You may require an offeror to submit data on a computer diskette or you may require electronic transmission (computer to computer) by Electronic Data Interchange (EDI). Whatever method you choose, make sure that the requirement does not place an unreasonable hardship on the offeror.

[d] Explaining the Significance of the Data

In a number of cases, submission of cost or pricing data without an explanation of their significance has been held to be a failure to meet the statutory requirement. Thus, a contractor must make efforts to tell the government pricing personnel how the data are relevant to the cost estimate in instances when this is not readily apparent. This obligation occurs in two distinct situations—when the data are complex or unusual in nature and when they are submitted to update previously submitted data.

Complexity of the data is determined on a case-by-case basis. For example, in *Grumman Aerospace Corp.*, ASBCA 35188, 90-2 BCA ¶ 22,842, the subcontractor had not explained the significance of labor-hour data submitted to the contractor in computerized form. The board determined that the relevance of the data was not readily apparent to the contractor's pricing personnel and that the subcontractor had failed to meet the submission requirement when it did not explain the data. See also *United Techs. Corp.*, ASBCA 51410, 04-1 BCA ¶ 32,556, *modified*, 05-1 BCA ¶ 32,860, *aff'd*, 463 F.3d 1261 (Fed. Cir. 2006), holding that two documents summarizing the costs that "flowed into" the proposed price were required to be submitted. Apparently, the board concluded that without these documents the government personnel could not fully understand the relationship of the factual cost data to the proposed price. In contrast, in *Boeing Co.*, ASBCA 32753, 90-1 BCA ¶ 22,270, *recons. denied*, 90-1 BCA ¶ 22,426, the contractor was found to have met the submission requirement when it submitted raw data on labor rates without explanation. The board found that the government personnel were fully able to use the data in their raw form and, therefore, that no further explanation of the data was required. Similarly, in *Rosemount, Inc.*, ASBCA 37520, 95-2 BCA ¶ 27,770, the contractor was found to have met the submission requirement when it gave the government its incurred labor hours for the product being procured. The board rejected the argument that the contractor was required to plot the hours on a learning curve in order to meet the submission requirement, finding that the agency's negotiators could easily have plotted the data. These latter cases illustrate the basic proposition that TINA does not require the offeror to perform routine analysis of cost or pricing data for the government.

This rule requiring explanation of the data will also apply if the data contain information that is unusual in nature. For example, in *Grumman*, the subcontractor submitted information on an interdivisional order but did not disclose that the price of the order included profit. The board ruled that this nondisclosure was a failure to meet the submission requirement because the subcontractor knew that the inclusion of profit in such orders was generally against government policy.

The rule is also applied in cases where the contractor updates prior data. For example, in *Singer Co. v. United States*, 576 F.2d 905 (Ct. Cl. 1978), the court held that the contractor's mailing of monthly labor-hour reports to government field pricing personnel and auditors did not meet the submission requirement.

The court was critical of the offeror's failure to specifically identify the relationship of this information to the cost estimate. Similarly, cost or pricing data submitted in connection with other procurements do not meet the submission requirement on a contract to which the data have not been related, *Sylvania Elec. Prods., Inc. v. United States*, 479 F.2d 1342 (Ct. Cl. 1973).

[e] Currency of the Data

Until 1995, the certificate required to be executed by the offeror before award of the contract stated that the date of currency of the data was to be the date when price negotiations were concluded. See *Arral Indus., Inc.*, ASBCA 41493, 96-1 BCA ¶ 28,030, where the board found that the date when price negotiations were concluded was best determined by the date on the certificate. This made the data used in the negotiation defective because they had not been updated. Thus, the offeror had to continually update the data until the price was agreed upon, and this requirement may not be waived by a government employee, *Singer Co. v. United States*, 576 F.2d 905 (Ct. Cl. 1978). If there is insufficient time to compile the data in a usable form, the requirement can arguably be met by submitting raw data as they exist in the contractor's records, *Conrac Corp. v. United States*, 558 F.2d 994 (Ct. Cl. 1977); *Lambert Eng'g Co.*, ASBCA 13338, 69-1 BCA ¶ 7663.

To preclude liability for not meeting the "current" requirement, offerors began to perform "sweeps" making a total review of their cost or pricing data after the conclusion of price negotiations and submitting all new data to the contracting officer. This delayed the award of the contract and led to difficult decisions as to what the government should do with the new data. This led to a FAR revision in 1995 to permit the parties to agree on variable dates of currency. This is now located in Table 15-2 as quoted above. The Certificate of Current Cost or Pricing Data, in FAR 15.406-2(a) was also revised to contain the following instruction on the date of currency of the data:

> ** Insert the day, month, and year when price negotiations were concluded and price agreement was reached or, if applicable, an earlier date agreed upon between the parties that is as close as practicable to the date of agreement on price.

In addition, FAR 15.406-2(c) contains the following guidance:

> The contracting officer and contractor are encouraged to reach a prior agreement on criteria for establishing closing or cutoff dates when appropriate in order to minimize delays associated with proposal updates. Closing or cutoff dates should be included as part of the data submitted with the proposal and, before agreement on price, data should be updated by the contractor to the latest closing or cutoff dates for which the data are available. Use of cutoff dates coinciding with reports is acceptable, as certain data may not be

> reasonably available before normal periodic closing dates (e.g., actual indirect costs). Data within the contractor's or a subcontractor's organization on matters significant to contractor management and to the Government will be treated as reasonably available. What is significant depends upon the circumstances of each acquisition.

The best way to ensure that the currency requirement is met is for the contracting officer and the offeror to reach a written agreement on the closing dates for various types of data at the conclusion of the negotiation, to reference this agreement on the face of the certificate and to attach the agreement to the certificate. In most cases, these closing dates correspond to the labor rate and indirect cost rate information already furnished to the government. The contractor should then conduct a "sweep" to check for any material cost or labor-hour information that has been accumulated during the negotiation. Such information would be furnished to the contracting officer with the signed certificate. By following this procedure, the contractor fully complies with the currency requirement of TINA.

In the absence of an agreement on cutoff dates, there is a significant question as to whether an offeror is permitted any "lag time" for the transmission of cost or pricing data within the corporate structure. In *Sylvania Elec. Prods., Inc. v. United States*, 479 F.2d 1342 (Ct. Cl. 1973), the Court of Claims established a strict rule that the data must be "current" as of the time of the price negotiation. The court held that data received by the contractor's purchasing department approximately one week prior to price negotiations were required to be furnished to the government. This decision raises the question as to whether any period of time is permitted for processing the information through a company. The original board decisions allowed such a time lag, *American Bosch Arma Corp.*, ASBCA 10305, 65-2 BCA ¶ 5280, and one later case permitted a substantial time lag (as much as six months) in a situation where the contracting officer concurred in the nonsubmission of current data, *LTV Electrosys., Inc.*, ASBCA 16802, 73-1 BCA ¶ 9957, *recons. denied*, 74-1 BCA ¶ 10,380. However, it is clear from the language in *Sylvania* that the court will not tolerate a time lag of any significant length. See, however, *Boeing Co.*, ASBCA 20875, 85-3 BCA ¶ 18,351, where the board permitted a three-week lag in the preparation of labor-cost data because this was the period required by the contractor's accounting system. In *Aerojet Ordnance Tenn.*, ASBCA 36089, 95-2 BCA ¶ 27,922, labor-hour information through the month of February was required to be submitted for a negotiation completed on March 2, 1983.

The allowance for negotiation of cutoff dates did not induce contractors to discontinue the "sweep" process with the result that the Director of Defense Pricing issued a memorandum, "Reducing Acquisition Lead Time by Eliminating Inefficiencies Associated with Cost or Pricing Data Submissions After Price Agreement (Sweep Data)," June 7, 2018. This memorandum states that "untimely submissions of 'sweep data' may be indicative of estimating system deficiencies," that the certificate should be submitted within five days of agreement on price, and that "sweep data" should not hold up award of the contract but should be addressed thereafter. The impact of this new set of requirements is yet to be determined.

[2] Types of Costs

The types of data provided and the analytical techniques available vary considerably depending on the types of cost being evaluated.

[a] Material Costs

This category encompasses all work purchased by the contractor from raw materials to major subcontracts. Table 15-2 contains guidance on the information desired for each purchased item, including the degree of competition or other information demonstrating the reasonableness of the price. In all cases, the critical information necessary to estimate the costs of any material category is the past purchases, if any, of the material, the anticipated source(s) of the material for the proposed procurement, and any pricing information that has been obtained from those sources.

[i] Vendor Data

If the work to be performed on a contract is reasonably understood, the offeror will have decided which part of that work will be purchased. Generally, the offeror also will have prepared a list of such items or services. For manufacturing contracts involving items that are fully designed, the contractor normally prepares a bill of materials that lists each material item with quantities, estimated prices, and source data. A typical bill of materials is set forth in **Figure 13-1**. See *Sylvania Elec. Prods., Inc. v. United States*, 479 F.2d 1342 (Ct. Cl. 1973), where the court held that, in spite of the fact that TINA does not normally require contractor's to create data, a bill of materials must be submitted because it is the basic factual tool necessary for estimating and analyzing the cost of materials. See also *Lockheed Aircraft Corp. v. United States*, 432 F.2d 801 (Ct. Cl. 1970), where a subcontractor had furnished raw data containing all of the purchasing records of the company but had not created a bill of materials indicating which purchased items were applicable to the contract being negotiated. The court held that this was an inadequate submission because it did not factually relate the data to the pricing action at hand. Compare *Conrac Corp. v. United States*, 558 F.2d 994 (Ct. Cl. 1977), where the contractor argued that *Lockheed* stood for the proposition that when there was insufficient time to prepare a bill of material, raw data need not be furnished. The court rejected this argument, holding that raw purchasing data must be submitted if there is no time to prepare a bill of materials, stating at 569-70:

The prices of material items frequently consists of a combination of factual data and projections. The most reliable data would be fully negotiated.

SCHEDULE A

(See Bill of Materials 1523, June 19X2)

PART NO.	NOMENCLATURE	QUANTITY PER ITEM	SCRAP FACTOR* (%)	TOTAL QUANTITY	UNIT PRICE	TOTAL
9876543	Housing casting. (Vendor — Pic Corp. PO 351522, issued 12/20 to lowest three proposals.)	1	4	468	$84.72	$39,648.96
9876542	Bearing, X design. (Vendor — Sun Co. PO 351480, issued 12/5 to only qualified source. Cost analysis performed.)	2	4	936	14.89	13,937.04
9876541	Gear, 14-tooth. (Vendor — Autoco. Two proposals. Autoco's the lower and its price used here. Bid file BB 442.)	4	4	1,872	418.00	7,824.96
9876540	Cable assembly. (Vendor — Rockaway Corp. Only proposal received. Completed 1411 attached.)	1	4	468	328.00	153,504.00
9876539	Bracket, main. (Vendor — Cee Cee Corp. Bracket is same as that used on earlier model of this system. Prior price was $22.19 each (PO 341110). 8% added in making estimate, two years since last buy.)	3	4	1,404	23.97	33,653.88
9876538	Race assembly. (Similar assembly bought 5/25 from Hup, Inc., for $150 each. Engineering estimates P/N 9876538 will cost 1/3 more to make.)	1	4	468	200.00	93,600.00
9876537	Solenoid. (Engineer estimate (estimate file — Eng-47).)	1	4	468	90.00	42,120.00
9876536	Gear, drive. (Engineer estimate, review of drawing (estimate file — Eng-487).)	1	4	468	24.00	11,232.00
	TOTAL MATERIAL					$395,520.84

Figure 13-1

> The rule in *Lockheed* is that the best price data must be furnished, not that data in less than prime form, because of time or other constraints, may handily be hidden from the Government.

Thus, the contractor is normally expected to furnish the material data in the form of a priced bill of materials referencing all of the available cost or pricing data relevant to the items listed, yet must present the raw data if the bill of materials cannot be compiled for some reason.

The quantities on a bill of materials are derived from an analysis of the detailed drawings for the item, and any mistake in the quantities will constitute defective cost or pricing data. In *Sylvania*, discussed above, a defective submission was found when an offeror duplicated the quantities of two items on the bill of materials. The court dismissed the contractor's contention that the contracting officer should have recognized the error by comparing the bill of materials with other data.

The prices of material items frequently consist of a combination of factual data and projections. The most reliable data would be fully negotiated purchase orders or subcontracts for the work under the contract. However, FAR 15.404-3(a) does not permit a determination that prices are fair and reasonable on the basis of that fact alone. Thus, contracting officers must analyze such prices before making a determination.

Normally, such prices will not be available because an offeror will not have entered into purchase orders or subcontracts with prospective vendors at the time of negotiation with the government. If there have been past purchases of an item, however, the price paid will be available and will almost always be considered to be cost or pricing data, *Grumman Aerospace Corp.*, ASBCA 35188, 90-2 BCA ¶ 22,842. Similarly, quotations from vendors for the current work are generally held to be facts that must be disclosed to the government, *Cutler-Hammer, Inc. v. United States*, 416 F.2d 1306 (Ct. Cl. 1969); *Bell & Howell Co.*, ASBCA 11999, 68-1 BCA ¶ 6993. See also *Aydin Monitor Sys.*, NASABCA 381-1, 84-2 BCA ¶ 17,297, holding that a vendor quote for a quantity greater than that to be supplied under the contract was factual data and was therefore required to be submitted. The board reasoned that the quote was significant since its total price, including the greater quantity, was less than the contractor's estimated total price for the smaller quantity actually being purchased. Similarly, the cost of items held in inventory that have a reasonable chance of being used on the contract must be disclosed, *Hardie-Tynes Mfg. Co.*, ASBCA 20367, 76-1 BCA ¶ 11,827. See also *Etowah Mfg. Co.*, ASBCA 27267, 88-3 BCA ¶ 21,054, where the board granted a price reduction when the contractor submitted vendor quotations but failed to submit subsequent purchase orders entered into with the vendors at the quoted prices. The board reasoned that there had been a violation of the submission requirement and that the purchase orders provided a more certain basis for estimating the costs of performance.

If the offeror is actively negotiating with a proposed vendor at the same time, it is negotiating the contract price with the government, any significant changes of position by the vendor are cost or pricing data and must be disclosed. See *TGS Int'l, Inc.*, ASBCA 31120, 87-2 BCA ¶ 19,683, *recons. denied*, 87-3 BCA ¶ 19,989, where the contractor failed to submit information specifying that the vendor had agreed to alter the work to be done and had failed to give the subcontractor's new proposal to the contracting officer. See also *McDonnell Aircraft Co.*, ASBCA 44504, 97-1 BCA ¶ 28,977, where nondisclosure of cost or pricing data was found when a subcontractor developed additional information about the validity of the price of a sub-subcontractor but did not disclose it to the contractor in time for it to be disclosed to the government. Changes in the offeror's negotiating position with a subcontractor may also be cost or pricing data. See *Boeing Military Airplane Co.*, ASBCA 33168, 87-2 BCA ¶ 19,714, where the company was held liable for failing to furnish all of the information relating to a dispute with a vendor on the proper price of work that had already been performed on a letter contract.

Vendor quotations and other vendor data must be included in the submission of cost or pricing data only if they would have a significant effect on the pricing action. Thus, outdated data or data not relevant to the pricing action need not be submitted or evaluated. For example, a contractor was permitted to omit data pertaining to a vendor quotation that had been rejected although the contractor subsequently decided to purchase the item from that vendor, *Chu Assocs., Inc.*, ASBCA 15004, 73-1 BCA ¶ 9906, *recons. denied*, 73-2 BCA ¶ 10,120. Similarly, in *Plessey Indus., Inc.*, ASBCA 16720, 74-1 BCA ¶ 10,603, the contractor was not required to submit a vendor quotation when the contractor had decided prior to price negotiation to manufacture the item in-house. See also *Lockheed Martin Aeronautics Co.*, ASBCA 56547, 13-1 BCA ¶ 35,220 (price of undisclosed subcontract could not have affected negotiated price); and *Boeing Co.*, ASBCA 20875, 85-3 BCA ¶ 18,351 (price of an undisclosed purchase order signed after data submission but before negotiation of the price was so close to the price of a submitted quotation from another vendor that the undisclosed data did not have a significant effect on price).

If the parties have agreed that the pricing should be based on data other than the cost or pricing data accumulated by the contractor, the requirement for submission of the data will not be enforced. See *Texas Instruments, Inc.*, ASBCA 30836, 89-1 BCA ¶ 21,489, where all of the current vendor data—purchase order prices, quotations, and subcontractor negotiations—were found not to constitute cost or pricing data because the parties had agreed that material costs would be computed using average prices of each item based on accumulated costs after the material had been used in the manufacturing process. The board found that since this pricing system made no use of the normal vendor data, the data could have no significant effect on the pricing.

The projections from the factual data are much more difficult to evaluate. If vendor quotations for the instant procurement are being used, the projection is relatively simple. There, the key issue is whether the quotation was obtained under conditions that assure that it reflects a reasonable price. Normal price analysis techniques can be used to make this judgment. In most material pricing, however, the offeror is not required to obtain vendor quotes. In such cases, the data will consist of past purchase prices and the analysis will have to consider the length of time between purchases, the number of items purchased, the economic trends, and other relevant data in order to arrive at an appraisal of the reasonableness of the projection of the estimated price. See Chapter 6 of

Volume 3 of the DOD CPRG for detailed guidance on the techniques that should be used in making this analysis.

[ii] Major Subcontracts

There is one special situation where offerors are required to submit detailed cost or pricing data relating to material purchases. FAR 15.404-3(c) requires contractors to submit certified subcontractor cost or pricing data for each subcontract cost estimate that is (1) $15 million or more or (2) both more than the certified cost or pricing data threshold ($2 million at the current time) and more than 10% of the total price. Failure to submit such data will constitute a violation of the statutory submission requirement, *Martin Marietta Corp.*, ASBCA 48223, 96-2 BCA ¶ 28,270. In addition, the contracting officer is authorized by these regulations to require the submission of subcontractor data for subcontracts of lesser amounts if it is "necessary for adequately pricing the prime contract." When such data is submitted, it becomes the offeror's data with consequent liability for price reduction if it is inaccurate, incomplete, or not current, *Lockheed Aircraft Corp. v. United States*, 432 F.2d 801 (Ct. Cl. 1970); *EDO Corp.*, ASBCA 41448, 93-3 BCA ¶ 26,135.

Because TINA applies to subcontractors as well as contractors, subcontractors are required to submit certified cost or pricing data to the contractor when the subcontract is above the $2 million threshold. The prospective contractor is then required to conduct and submit an analysis of the subcontractor's cost or pricing data to support the proposed subcontract price, FAR 15.404-3(b).

Subcontractor cost or pricing data above the thresholds need not be submitted if the subcontract falls within one of the statutory exceptions to the submission of data, FAR 15.404-3(c). The regulation contains no guidance on whether the contractor or the contracting officer is empowered to decide whether an exception applies. Prior to the issuance of FAC 97-02, September 30, 1997, FAR 15.806-2(c) appeared to state that the contracting officer had to make this determination.

When a subcontractor is a competitor of the contractor, contracting officers have permitted the subcontractor to submit required cost or pricing data directly to the government. In such cases, a government administrative contracting officer or auditor will analyze the data and, in most instances, provide the analysis to the contractor. See *Motorola, Inc.*, ASBCA 41528, 94-2 BCA ¶ 26,596, where the board found that a subcontractor had properly submitted data to a government auditor because the auditor gave the contractor up-to-date information on an indirect cost rate that was applicable to the subcontract.

[iii] New Items

When work that has not previously been performed is purchased, cost estimating, and analysis are much less precise. The specific material that will be used on the contract may not have been fully ascertained, yet the contractor will be forced to make the best possible estimate of material costs. In this situation, the most relevant data may be prices for similar work, and this information may be determined to be factual data which must be submitted to the government. See *Hardie-Tynes Mfg. Co.*, ASBCA 20717, 76-2 BCA ¶ 12,121, finding that the price of items similar to those that were to be designed for the contract were cost or pricing data. The board also held that a vendor quote for an item that the offeror was considering using on the contract had to be submitted as part of the proposal. The contractor had made its own estimate on a very broad basis without regard to prior data, but the board held, nonetheless, that the data, if available, had to be furnished to the government so that it could be used in the cost analysis. See also *Aerojet-General Corp.*, ASBCA 12264, 69-1 BCA ¶ 7664, *modified*, 70-1 BCA ¶ 8140, holding that a contractor's analysis of a subcontractor proposal was cost or pricing data.

[b] Direct Labor Costs

This category covers all of the types of labor—manufacturing, engineering, tooling, etc.—that will be directly charged to the contract. The contractor is free to group labor in any categories that assist in managing the company, as long as the costs are accumulated for the same categories that are used for estimating purposes. The instructions to Table 15-2 calls for a "time-phased breakdown" of labor-hours and labor rates, reflecting the fact that the process of estimating and analyzing labor costs normally considers hours and rates separately. See Chapter 7 of Volume 3 of the DOD CPRG for detailed guidance on the techniques that should be used in making this analysis.

[i] Labor-Hours

Labor-hours present the greatest difficulty in the analysis of costs. In cases where the contractor has performed the same or similar work in the past, the number of labor-hours incurred will be factual data which must be presented in the proposal or disclosed during the negotiations. See *McDonnell Douglas Corp.*, ASBCA 12786, 69-2 BCA ¶ 7897 (tapes containing labor-hours incurred in months prior to price negotiation); *Singer Co. v. United States*, 576 F.2d 905 (Ct. Cl. 1978) (labor-hour data adjusting standard labor-hour information to actual costs incurred in prior period); *Grumman Aerospace Corp.*, ASBCA 35188, 90-2 BCA ¶ 22,842 (reports of labor-hour lot costs containing data collected prior to conclusion of negotiations); and *Limpiezas Corona S.A.*, ASBCA 45504, 96-1 BCA ¶ 28,137 (number of employees on current janitorial services contract). When the contractor must analyze the data in order to use it for estimating purposes, it is entitled to the time necessary to make the analysis, *Litton Sys., Inc.*, ASBCA 34435, 93-2 BCA ¶ 25,707. Even if the offeror does not record labor-hours, derivative data providing approximate labor-hours must be disclosed, *Lambert Eng'g Co.*, ASBCA 13338, 69-1 BCA ¶ 7663. In *Lambert*, the board held that an offeror must disclose labor-hour information derived by dividing the recorded labor dollars by average labor rates to arrive at the approximate labor hours used by the offeror on past work. Internal company work authorizations permitting departments to incur a specified number of labor-hours of work need not be disclosed to the government because they are not factual in content, *Kaiser Aerospace & Elecs. Corp.*, ASBCA 32098, 90-1 BCA ¶ 22,489, *recons. denied*, 90-2 BCA ¶ 22,695. Similarly, pure estimates made by industrial engineers or test engineers need not be disclosed because they contain no factual element, *Litton Sys., Inc.*, ASBCA 36509, 92-2 BCA ¶ 24,842.

If an offeror uses an estimating system that factors actual labor-hours through pricing formulas, it may be necessary to disclose the entire system to the government. See *Texas Instruments, Inc.*, ASBCA 23678, 87-3 BCA ¶ 20,195, finding that such a system was cost or pricing data because disclosure was necessary for the government to fully understand the labor-hour data contained in the estimating system. However, there is no requirement to disclose a learning curve analysis of labor-hours because this technique is so well understood that any competent price analyst can plot the curve using the raw data, *Rosemount, Inc.*, ASBCA 37520, 95-2 BCA ¶ 27,770. Further, there is no requirement to present the labor-hour data in the form of a learning curve when the contractor does not use learning curve analysis, *Aerojet Ordnance Tenn.*, ASBCA 36089, 95-2 BCA ¶ 27,922.

If the contractor has begun work on the contract before the price is negotiated, incurred labor-hours would be factual data that would be expected to be disclosed, *Aerojet Ordnance Tenn.*, ASBCA 36089, 95-2 BCA ¶ 27,922; *University of California., San Francisco*, VABCA 4661, 97-1 BCA ¶ 28,642. Nondisclosure might not create contractor liability, however, if the data are so incomplete that they are not helpful in arriving at a meaningful estimate of the price. See *Boeing Co.*, ASBCA 20875, 85-3 BCA ¶ 18,351, holding that labor-hours incurred early in the performance of a development contract would not have been useful to the negotiators even if such data had been disclosed.

The projections made from labor-hours from prior contracts present far more difficult problems. In some cases, the offeror will use an accepted technique for projecting labor-hours, such as a learning curve analysis, and the government will in turn analyze this projection technique using its own calculations. In other cases, an offeror will base the projection on an estimate of the variance that can be expected from standard costs. In all cases, volume and continuity of work will be major factors affecting the projection. The most difficult situation occurs when the offeror has no previous experience in performing the work to be purchased. In such cases, the estimate of labor-hours must be made by breaking down the projected work into its constituent parts and estimating the labor-hours necessary to perform each part of the work. In most cases, each part of the work can be compared to similar work that the contractor has performed in the past, and this data can be used to support the estimate. Nevertheless, this process requires the application of a large amount of judgment, and analysis of this judgmental process is quite difficult. In such cases, parametric estimating techniques may be useful in checking the estimate.

[ii] Labor Rates

Labor rate determination is considerably easier. Even if the offeror has never performed the specific work being contracted for, there will be factual information regarding the labor rates that have been paid to the various categories of employees to be used on the contract. This information must be included as part of the offeror's cost or pricing data and must be updated as new data are accumulated, *Boeing Co.*, ASBCA 32753, 90-1 BCA ¶ 22,270, *recons. denied*, 90-1 BCA ¶ 22,426; *Kaiser Aerospace & Elecs. Corp.*, ASBCA 32098, 90-1 BCA ¶ 22,489, *recons. denied*, 90-2 BCA ¶ 22,695. Management decisions affecting labor rates must also be disclosed, *Lockheed Corp.*, ASBCA 36420, 95-2 BCA ¶ 27,722. There, the board ruled that a management decision to utilize a new bargaining strategy in collective bargaining negotiations would have been cost or pricing data if it had been made by a corporate officer with authority to adopt the policy.

Based on the historical data on labor rates and any decisions as to future plans affecting the workforce, the cost analyst can make a projection of the rates that will be paid during contract performance. This projection involves determining the rate of increase or decrease in the wages or salaries and the length of time between the date of the actual data and the time of contract performance. The estimate usually will be based on the midpoint of projected contract performance, which can be determined by analyzing the rate of usage of labor over the contract performance period. The changes in labor rate are dependent on economic conditions over the long run and may be easily determinable by reviewing the terms of the offeror's labor agreements. The other factor that must be assessed is the number of workers the contractor expects to employ during the contract performance period. If the number is increasing, average labor rates will normally decrease, while a reduction in the number of employees will normally increase the rate.

[c] Other Direct Costs

Contractors charge a variety of costs directly to contracts to obtain more accurate cost allocation. Such costs are frequently sporadic in nature varying greatly from one contract to another. They are therefore difficult to analyze based on past incurred costs. It is clear, however, that offerors must submit past data on such costs. The contracting officer will usually have to assess each type of direct cost in terms of its relationship to the work on the contract to determine if the offeror is estimating a level of cost that is reasonable under the circumstances. See Chapter 8 of Volume 3 of the DOD CPRG for a discussion of this area.

[d] Indirect Costs

Contractors maintain pools of indirect costs in a variety of categories depending on the nature of their work and the size of the organization.

Common groupings of indirect costs are manufacturing overhead, engineering overhead, and general and administrative (G&A) expense. However, any logical grouping is proper, FAR 31.203(c). A typical indirect cost pool for manufacturing overhead is set forth in **Figure 13-2**. Indirect costs are accumulated over a

EXHIBIT 1 — MANUFACTURING OVERHEAD			
ACCOUNT TITLE	YEAR ENDED DEC 31, X3	YEAR ENDED DEC 31, X4*	PROJECTED YEAR ENDING DEC 31, X5
Salaries and wages:			
Indirect labor	$1,338,330	$1,395,245	$1,472,160
Additional compensation	80,302	83,950	88,000
Overtime premium	13,214	11,296	4,500
Sick leave	63,575	67,742	72,130
Holidays	79,164	83,006	87,080
Suggestion awards	310	423	500
Vacations	140,272	147,891	154,3000
Personnel expense:			
Compensation insurance	25,545	26,304	27,500
Unemployment insurance	50,135	52,692	51,500
FICA tax	70,493	73,907	77,850
Group insurance	153,755	161,401	169,130
Travel expense	11,393	12,725	13,900
Dues and subscriptions	175	175	175
Recruiting and relocation — new employees	897	574	250
Relocation — transferees	4,290	3,562	1,825
Employees pension fund:			
Salary	25,174	26,350	27,500
Hourly	62,321	65,497	64,200
Training, conferences, and technical meetings	418	539	575
Educational loans and scholarships	400	400	400
Supplies and services:			
General operating	495,059	509,839	545,000
Maintenance	9,102	12,318	15,700
Stationary, printing, and office supplies	23,052	24,125	25,500
Material O/H on supplies	56,566	62,071	62,500
Maintenance	9,063	10,875	15,000
Rearranging	418	3,523	500
Other	3,314	2,653	2,500
Heat, light, and power	470,946	489,123	517,200
Telephone	32,382	33,874	35,000
Fixed charges:			
Depreciation	187,118	175,641	439,850
Equipment rental	7,633	7,633	7,633
Total manufacturing expense (A)	$3,416,816	$3,545,336	$3,979,858
Total manufacturing direct labor dollars (B)	$1,340,887	$1,407,931	$1,267,200
Manufacturing overhead rate (A) ÷ (B)	254.8%	251.8%	314.1%

*Includes budgetary estimate for last two months

Figure 13-2

period of time, usually the contractor's fiscal year, and are uniformly charged as a percentage of an allocation base to all of the contractor's work during that period. See Cost Accounting Standard 406, 48 C.F.R. § 9904.406, for guidance on the selection of these accounting periods. Cost Accounting Standards 410, 48 C.F.R. § 9904.410, and 418, 48 C.F.R. § 9904.418, provide guidance on the selection of allocation bases and allocation methods. Normally, allocation bases for manufacturing and engineering overhead are direct labor dollars in these categories, while the allocation base for G&A expense is total costs before G&A. However, the contractor has significant discretion to select an accounting system that most accurately allocates indirect costs to work being performed, *Ford Aerospace & Commc'ns Corp.*, ASBCA 23833, 83-2 BCA ¶ 16,813. See Chapter 9 of Volume 3 of the DOD CPRG for a discussion of this area.

Analysis of indirect costs involves analysis of the individual costs in the overhead pool and the allocation base. Except in the case of new businesses, there will always be a substantial amount of factual data on the costs in each indirect cost pool. The offeror's accounting system will contain such data for past years, and if the estimate is for work commencing during the year, there will be some data for that current year. See *Rose, Beaton & Rose*, PSBCA 459, 80-1 BCA ¶ 14,242, where incorrect inclusion of an item of cost in the indirect cost pool was held to be a violation of the obligation to disclose accurate cost or pricing data, and *Norris Indus., Inc.*, ASBCA 15442, 74-1 BCA ¶ 10,482, where failure to submit past indirect costs was a violation of the obligation to submit complete cost or pricing data. See also *PAE Int'l*, ASBCA 20595, 76-2 BCA ¶ 12,044, where inclusion of other direct costs in a G&A pool was held to be a violation of the requirement to disclose accurate data. Contractors normally collect indirect cost data on a monthly or quarterly basis, and FAR 15.406-2(c) encourages agreement on closing or cutoff dates for submission of cost or pricing data that match these periodic cost collection dates. All of this actual cost data serves as the base for evaluation of the offeror's projection of the costs in the indirect cost pool for the years of contract performance. Each cost element of the pool should be analyzed to assure that the projection is reasonable in view of the current and projected business situation of the offeror.

Analysis of the indirect cost allocation bases is considerably more difficult. These bases are estimated by forecasting the sales that the offeror will make in the accounting periods during which the contract work will be performed. Such forecasting is inherently imprecise although some of the sales will be factual, *i.e.*, in accordance with signed contracts. See *Universal Restoration, Inc. v. United States*, 798 F.2d 1400 (Fed. Cir. 1986), where newly recorded sales were held to be cost or pricing data required to be disclosed during negotiations. Current negotiation of contracts with other customers might also be thought to be factual information which must be furnished by the offeror. See *E-Sys., Inc.*, ASBCA 17557, 74-2 BCA ¶ 10,782, *recons. denied*, 74-2 BCA ¶ 10,943, holding that an offeror's study of this type of data was not cost or pricing data because the underlying factual information had been furnished to the government. In addition to the factual data on sales during the contract performance period, an estimate must be made of other sales that will be booked. Analysis of this estimate is very difficult, but information can often be obtained from other procuring activities on future contracts that will likely be awarded to the offeror.

In many instances, the prospective contracting parties will have negotiated forward pricing rate agreements and these agreements should be disclosed as part of the submission of certified cost or pricing data, FAR 15.407-3. These agreements are generally used in the negotiation of prices unless conditions have changed. See *Symetrics Indus., LLC*, ASBCA 59297, 15-1 BCA ¶ 36,070, holding that failure to disclose such an agreement was not a TINA violation because the government personnel evaluating the proposal were aware of the agreement.

[3] Certification

When certified cost or pricing data is required to be furnished by statute, the offeror is required to certify that the data is accurate, current, and complete. The certificate is furnished after completion of negotiations, *not at the time of submission of the data*. FAR 15.406-2(a) contains the following certificate to be used in such cases:

CERTIFICATE OF CURRENT COST OR PRICING DATA

This is to certify that, to the best of my knowledge and belief, the cost or pricing data (as defined in section 15.201 of the Federal Acquisition Regulation (FAR) and required under FAR subsection 15.403-4) submitted, either actually or by specific identification in writing, to the Contracting Officer or to the Contracting Officer's representative in support of ________* are accurate, complete, and current as of ________**. This certification includes the cost or pricing data supporting any advance agreements and forward pricing rate agreements between the offeror and the Government that are part of the proposal.

Firm ________________________________
Signature ____________________________
Name _______________________________
Title ________________________________
Date of Execution*** __________________

*Identify the proposal, request for price adjustment, or other submission involved, giving the appropriate identifying number (e.g., RFP No.).

**Insert the day, month, and year when price negotiations were concluded and price agreement was reached or, if applicable, an earlier date agreed upon between the parties that is as close as practicable to the date of agreement on price.

***Insert the day, month, and year of signing, which should be as close as practicable to the date when the price negotiations were concluded and the contract price was agreed to.

This certificate is to be furnished as soon as practicable after price agreement is reached. In order to avoid major updating of data after the conclusion of negotiations (with resulting delay in furnishing the certificate), FAR 15.406-2(c) encourages reaching agreement on cutoff dates for specific categories of data.

In some cases, certified cost or pricing data may be called for by an RFP, but it may be subsequently determined that there is an exception to the submission requirement, such as adequate price competition or a commercial product or service. In such cases, cost or pricing data may have already been submitted by the offeror and reviewed by the government. Under these circumstances, the question arises as to whether the data must be certified by the successful offeror. FAR 15.406-2(e) states that such data "shall not be considered certified cost or pricing data . . . and shall not be certified." This regulatory policy follows *ABA Electromechanical Sys., Inc.*, NASABCA 1081-13, 85-3 BCA ¶ 18,225, where data were submitted and audited but not certified because the contracting officer determined that adequate price competition was present, and *Intermountain Research*, Comp. Gen. Dec. B-209827, 83-2 CPD ¶ 103, where neither cost analysis nor a certificate was necessary since adequate price competition was present even though cost and pricing data were required to be submitted by the RFP.

[B] Cost Analysis Without Cost or Pricing Data

A significant amount of cost analysis can be performed on proposals submitted in negotiated procurements without obtaining full cost or pricing data. FAR 15.403-3(a)(1) recognizes that "data other than certified cost or pricing data" may be requested, but advises contracting officers to obtain cost data from "Government or other secondary sources" in preference to requiring the offeror to submit such data. See also FAR 15.402(a)(3) stating that the contracting officer should not obtain "more data than is necessary." Thus, as discussed above, in almost all negotiated procurements where competition is expected or obtained, there will be no need for cost analysis and hence no need for cost data. However, when an agency decides to conduct a cost analysis without cost or pricing data, it must be clear on the data that is to be provided. See *PMO Partnership Joint Venture*, Comp. Gen. Dec. B-403214, 2010 CPD ¶ 256, sustaining a protest where the agency called for specified data but directed DCAA to audit to see if the data conformed to FAR Table 15-2. GAO concluded that this was an improper procedure because the RFP had not contained this requirement.

The major situation where cost analysis will be required is on competitive cost-reimbursement contracts where *cost realism analysis* will be required—with the result that the contracting officer will need to have some cost data. The contracting officer can specify the type of information needed for the analysis by including in the RFP the Requirements for Certified Cost or Pricing Data or

Data Other Than Certified Cost or Pricing Data clause, FAR 52.215-20, with Alternate IV. No further guidance is provided on how the data should be used.

The most common form of cost information that will have to be obtained from offerors in order to perform a cost realism analysis will be *cost element breakdowns* for the work that is required by the contract. These breakdowns show the types of cost (material, labor, indirect costs, etc.) that the offeror anticipates will be required to perform the work. They are not cost or pricing data but are merely summary estimates that have been made by the offeror. However, they provide sufficient information to allow the contracting officer to perform a cost realism analysis—obtaining additional information (such as prior labor or indirect cost rates) from government auditors or from internal files documenting prior negotiations with the offeror. There are numerous protests holding that a cost realism analyses was properly performed using information obtained from sources other than the offeror. See, for example, *ASRC Research & Tech. Solutions, LLC*, Comp. Gen. Dec. B-400217, 2008 CPD ¶ 202 (agency used labor rates of incumbent contractor when offeror was proposing to use that work force); *NHIC Corp.*, Comp. Gen. Dec. B-310801, 2008 CPD ¶ 67 (agency obtained rate analysis from DCAA and evaluated labor hours with internal personnel); *ITT Indus. Space Sys., LLC*, Comp. Gen. Dec. B-309964, 2007 CPD ¶ 217 (agency obtained rate analysis from DCAA and evaluated labor hours and other direct costs with internal personnel); and *CIGNA Gov't Servs., LLC*, Comp. Gen. Dec. B-297915, 2006 CPD ¶ 73 (agency personnel evaluated past efficiency information on all offerors to assess labor hours used to perform tasks).

When contracting officers include a requirement for cost element breakdowns in the RFP, they should specify the level in the "work breakdown structure" that should be supported by such cost breakdowns. A work breakdown structure separates the contract work into its separate parts in a logical manner in order to ensure that all necessary tasks are considered in planning the job. See Chapter 5 of Volume 3 of the DOD CPRG containing the following guidance:

> *Work Breakdown Structure* (MIL-HDBK 881). The request for proposal (RFP) for a large complex system may require the offeror to provide cost information based on a Work Breakdown Structure (WBS) identified in the solicitation. This concept can be used in acquiring any large system, but it is most commonly used in acquiring large DoD systems.

The WBS is a product-oriented family-tree division of hardware, software, services, and other work required to complete the contract. It organizes, defines, and graphically displays contract requirements and the work required to meet those requirements. The multiple levels of the WBS "explode" the work required down to identifiable work packages. In a common WBS:

- Level 1 is the entire system;
- Level 2 identifies the major elements of Level 1;
- Level 3 identifies the major elements of Level 2;
- Level 4 and later levels provide increasingly detailed information.

The number of levels of detail that you require in the solicitation should depend on the complexity of the system and the perceived need for in-depth visibility.

The following table provides an example of a WBS structure for a missile system. For other large systems, the elements will change, but the concept will remain the same.

Missile System Work Breakdown Structure, Levels 1-3

Level 1	Level 2	Level 3
Missile System	Air Vehicle	Vehicle Integration and Assembly; Propulsion Vehicle Stages (each stage included in system design); Guidance and Control Equipment; Airborne Test Equipment; Auxiliary Equipment
	Command and Launch Equipment	Integration and Assembly Surveillance, Identification, and Tracking Sensors; Launch and Guidance Control Communications Data Processing; Launcher Equipment; Auxiliary Equipment
	Training	Equipment; Services; Facilities;
	Peculiar Support Equipment	Organizational Level; Intermediate Level; Depot Level
	System Test and Evaluation	Development of Test and Evaluation; Operational Test and Evaluation; Mock-ups; Test and Evaluation Support; Test Facilities
	Systems/Project Management	Systems Engineering; Project Management
	Data	Technical; Publications; Engineering Data; Management Data; Support Data; Data Depository
	Operational/Site Activation	Contractor Technical Support; Site Construction; Site/Ship/Vehicle Conversion; On-site System Assembly, Installation, and Checkout
	Common Support Equipment	Organizational Level; Intermediate Level; Depot Level
	Industrial Facilities	Construction; Conversion/Expansion
	Initial Spares and Repair Parts	Identified Spares Allowance List (by system grouping or element)

Cost breakdowns can be obtained for any level in the cost breakdown structure—with the understanding that the lower the level the more detailed the information that will be available to the contracting officer to use for evaluation purposes. In general, the size of the procurement will indicate which level is appropriate. Level 1—providing only a single cost element breakdown for the entire contract—will generally be sufficient for contracts with one major task. Level 2—providing cost element breakdowns for each contract line item—will be sufficient for many contracts. Levels 3 and 4—providing cost element breakdowns for parts of the work—will be called for in contracts for major systems or complex services.

[1] Cost Realism Analysis

Cost realism analysis is required on cost-reimbursement contracts to determine *the probable cost of performance* that will be used as the evaluation factor, FAR 15.404-1(d)(2). Its fundamental purpose is to ensure that an offeror has not submitted a cost estimate that is unrealistically low. See the following definition in FAR 15.404-1(d):

> (1) Cost realism analysis is the process of independently reviewing and evaluating specific *elements* of each offeror's proposed cost estimate to determine whether the estimated proposed cost elements are realistic for the work to be performed; reflect a clear understanding of the requirements; and are consistent with the unique methods of performance and materials described in the offeror's technical proposal. (Emphasis added)

While this description of cost realism analysis is somewhat cryptic, it can be seen as describing three reasons why an offeror's cost estimate might be perceived to be lower than is realistic. First, the offeror might be intentionally proposing a low cost in order to win the competition. The government is protected against this practice by adjusting the offeror's estimate to the probable cost when making the source selection decision. Second, the offeror's estimate might be low because it does not understand the work required to carry out the contract tasks. Such a low estimate is generally factored into the assessment of the offeror's management or technical capability—as well as by adjusting it to the probable cost. The third reason for a low estimate might be that the offeror has a more efficient or effective way to carry out the work. This type of seemingly low estimate should not be adjusted upward and should reflect favorably on the assessment of the offeror's management or technical capability. The difficulty faced by the contracting officer making the cost realism analysis is in determining which of these reasons explains the apparently low-cost estimate that has been submitted by an offeror. Until a sound determination in this regard is made, a successful cost realism analysis has not been conducted.

It is very clear that cost realism analysis is mandatory on cost-reimbursement contracts. See *Tidewater Constr. Corp.*, Comp. Gen. Dec. B-278360, 98-1 CPD ¶ 103, where the agency merely compared the costs proposed by the competing offerors. GAO granted the protest stating that this was a price analysis not a cost realism analysis because the agency did not analyze the individual cost elements of the offerors for realism. Neither may an agency avoid updating the cost realism analysis if the procurement is extended as a result of a sustained protest, *Futures Grp. Int'l*, Comp. Gen. Dec. B-281274.5, 2000 CPD ¶ 148, or when an offeror has altered its proposed costs in its best and final offer, *ITT Fed. Servs. Int'l Corp.*, Comp. Gen. Dec. B-283307, 99-2 CPD ¶ 76. Further, an agency risks being found to have conducted an improper cost realism analysis if the contracting officer makes an adjustment based on a guess as to the cost methodology used by the offeror and the guess proves to be incorrect, *Future-Tec Mgmt. Sys., Inc.*, Comp. Gen. Dec. B-283793.5, 2000 CPD ¶ 59. An agency must also adequately document its cost realism analysis or risk having an award overturned, *National City Bank of Indiana*, B-287608.3, 2002 CPD ¶ 190.

Cost realism analysis is accomplished by determining whether the amount of resources (labor-hours and material) that the offeror proposes for each contract task is a realistic estimate for the work that will actually be required and whether the proposed labor and indirect cost rates are those expected to be incurred. The contracting officer must specify in the solicitation the data which offerors are required to submit to permit a sound cost realism analysis, FAR 15.403-3(a)(1)(ii). See, however, FAR 15.403-5(b)(2) stating that such data "may be submitted in the offeror's own format unless the contracting officer decides that use of a specific format is essential for evaluating and determining that the price is fair and reasonable and the format has been described in the solicitation." The key information that is needed is estimated labor hours and material costs for designated elements of the work and information supporting the proposed labor and indirect cost rates. In order to compare offerors, labor hours of both the offeror and its major subcontractors should be requested (in order to account for the fact that different offerors will make different allocation of the contract tasks between their own employees and subcontractors). Generally, each offeror should be permitted to identify the labor categories to be used and the specific material to be acquired, and it is good practice to request the offerors to submit information on how they intend to perform the contract tasks with these proposed resources. Labor rate and indirect cost rate information is also needed but data supporting the accuracy of such estimates should not be obtained from the offerors if it can be readily obtained from the cognizant government auditor. It is also possible that such information will be available in the contracting agency. All available information should be used in this type of analysis.

Although virtually all cost realism adjustments result in a higher probable cost, GAO has ruled that a lower probable cost is a proper result if it is logically arrived at, *ARES Tech, Servs. Corp.*, Comp. Gen. Dec. B-415081.2, 2018 CPD

¶ 153. In that case, GAO granted the protest because the offeror had continued to propose higher rates after the agency disclosed its finding that the incumbent contractor was paying lower rates. See also *Priority One Servs., Inc.*, Comp. Gen. Dec. B-288836, 2002 CPD ¶ 79, requiring a downward adjustment where an offeror had included significant costs that were not necessary for contract performance. Compare *Indigo IT, LLC v. United States*, 143 Fed. Cl. 1 (2019), finding it proper to not adjust labor rates above one standard deviation from average rates downward because the solicitation did not call for downward adjustments, and *Concurrent Techs. Corp.*, Comp. Gen. Dec. B-412795.2, 2017 CPD ¶ 25, finding it proper to not adjust costs downward because the protester had proposed a more expensive technical approach.

The conduct of the cost realism analysis has been regularly challenged by losing offerors. In these protests, GAO and the Court of Federal Claims, in determining whether the agency has followed a rational process in arriving at the probable cost of performance, have reviewed the analytical processes used by contracting officers. The relatively relaxed standard of review was described in *Network Sec. Sys. Plus, Inc.*, Comp. Gen. Dec. B-416755, 2019 CPD ¶ 4, as follows:

> An agency's cost realism analysis requires the exercise of informed judgment, and we review an agency's judgment in this area only to see that the cost realism analysis was reasonably based and not arbitrary. *Engility Corp.*, B-413120.3 et al., Feb. 14, 2017, 2017 CPD ¶ 70 at 18. The analysis need not achieve scientific certainty; rather, the methodology employed must be reasonably adequate and provide some measure of confidence that the agency's conclusions about the most probable costs for an offeror's proposal are reasonable and realistic in view of other cost information reasonably available to the agency at the time of its evaluation. *Id.* at 18-19.

Thus, agencies are accorded substantial discretion in making a cost realism analysis but they must meet the test of rationality. See also *CSC Gov't Solutions LLC v. United States*, 129 Fed. Cl. 416 (2016), following the same standard. The result is that a cost realism analysis need not identify every adjustment that might be made to an offeror's cost of performance. See *Orbital Sciences Corp.*, Comp. Gen. Dec. B-2414603, 2017 CPD ¶ 249, stating the analysis "does not require an in-depth verification of each and every item" of proposed costs. However, an agency must follow the cost realism methodology stated in the solicitation, *Agile Defense, Inc. v. United States*, 143 Fed. Cl. 10 (2019), and must analyze the realism of each cost element identified in the solicitation, *Conley & Assocs., Inc.*, Comp. Gen. Dec. B-415458.3, 2018 CPD ¶ 161. Furthermore, when cost realism adjustments are made, offerors must be afforded equal treatment, *ENSCO, Inc.*, Comp. Gen. Dec. B-414844.4, 2018 CPD ¶ 260; *DynCorp Int'l LLC*, Comp. Gen. Dec. B-289863, 2002 CPD ¶ 83, and the adjustments that are made must be supported by sufficient data to permit analysis of the validity of the adjustments, *Day & Zimmermann Servs. v. United States*, 38 Fed. Cl. 591 (1997).

Offerors that fail to include information in their proposals supporting low proposed costs risk having their costs adjusted upward, *AECOM Mgmt. Servs., Inc.*, Comp. Gen. Dec. B-418467, 2020 CPD ¶ 172 (insufficient data to allow evaluation of subcontractor indirect costs); *TWD & Assocs., Inc.*, Comp. Gen. Dec. B-416834, 2019 CPD ¶ 13 (no proof that employees would accept lower salaries); *ORBIS Sibro, Inc.*, Comp. Gen. Dec. B-415714, 2018 CPD ¶ 100 (current salaries not proof that employees doing higher level work can be obtained at those salaries); *Science Applications Int'l Corp.*, Comp. Gen. Dec. B-408270, 2013 CPD ¶ 189 (adjustment to incumbent labor rates proper when protester failed to submit data supporting lower rates). Compare *Integral Consulting Servs., Inc.*, Comp. Gen. Dec. B-415292.2, 2018 CPD ¶ 170, where the winning offeror submitted detailed data supporting its proposed lower salaries.

In order to be rational, the cost realism analysis has to be performed on a contractor-by-contractor basis. The contracting officer must consider both the way the contractor proposes to do the work and the contractor's cost structure in order to determine whether the proposed costs are an accurate projection of the costs of that work. See *AECOM Mgmt. Servs., Inc.*, Comp. Gen. Dec. B-417506.12, 2019 CPD ¶ 342, denying a protest that the cost realism analysis should have used the agency's estimated cost. GAO found that the performance-based work statement allowed each offeror to determine the labor needed to perform each task and, after discussions, each offerors' cost estimate was a realistic reflection of its labor estimates, even though the estimates varied significantly.

Thus, a mechanical approach that applies the same factors to all offerors is likely to fail the test of rationality (generally called "normalization"). See *CFS-KBR Marianas Support Servs., LLC*, Comp. Gen. Dec. B-410486, 2015 CPD ¶ 22, sustaining a protest where the agency mechanically used an undisclosed amount of labor to adjust the offerors' labor projections rather than analyzing their particular approach to performing the work. The Court of Claims had reached the same conclusion in *Day & Zimmermann*. See also *AXIS Mgmt. Grp., LLC*, Comp. Gen. Dec. B-408575, 2013 CPD ¶ 247; *Metro Mach. Corp.*, Comp. Gen. Dec. B-297879.2, 2006 CPD ¶ 80; *Information Ventures, Inc.*, Comp. Gen. Dec. B-297276.2, 2006 CPD ¶ 45; and *Honeywell Tech. Solutions, Inc.*, B-292354, 2005 CPD ¶ 107, granting protests when the agency used its own estimate of labor hours to adjust the offered labor hours without evaluating the techniques the offerors proposed to perform the work. Similarly, in *SRS Techs.*, Comp. Gen. Dec. B-291618.2, 2003 CPD ¶ 70, GAO held that it was unreasonable to increase the rates for the protester who planned to use uncompensated overtime when the other offeror did not plan to use uncompensated overtime, reasoning that the protester was entitled to use the advantage of the lower rates since there was no prohibition on the use of uncompensated overtime and there was no indication that the protester would not use uncompensated overtime. Conversely, when there is a disparity between the offeror's technical approach and its proposed costs, the agency must address the realism of the costs, *AdvanceMed Corp.*, Comp. Gen. Dec. B-414373, 2017 CPD ¶ 160. It is not normalization to use the same methodology to analyze proposals, *Boeing Co.*, Comp. Gen. Dec. B-412441, 2016 CPD ¶ 269 (using same methodology to arrive at an independent government estimate of costs for each competitor); *Innovative Asset Solutions, LLC*, Comp. Gen. Dec. B-411687, 2016 CPD ¶ 68, and *Innovative Asset Solutions, LLC v. United States*, 125 Fed. Cl. 201 (2016) (using same "Chrystal Ball" software tool to assess proposed cost savings).

Normalization is proper if there is no logical reason to believe that the offerors' costs will be different for some element of the work. See *Univ. Research Co., LLC v. United States*, 65 Fed. Cl. 500 (2005), stating at 509:

> This Court and GAO have recognized that normalization is appropriate when there is no logical basis for differences in approach, or there is insufficient information available in the proposals. See, e.g., [*Computer Sciences Corp. v. United States*, 51 Fed. Cl. 297, 316 (2002)] at 316; *General Research Corp.*, 70 Comp. Gen. 279, B-241569 (1991). Thus, in general, the purpose of the cost realism analysis "is to segregate cost factors which are 'company unique'—depending on variables resulting from dissimilar company policies—from those which are generally applicable to all offerors and therefore subject to normalization." *Computer Sciences Corp.*, 51 Fed. Cl. at 316 (citing *SGT, Inc.*, B-281773 (1999)).

For decisions holding that normalization was proper, see *New Mexico State Univ.*, Comp. Gen. Dec. B-409566, 2014 CPD ¶ 228 (using "plug numbers" to equalize competition when one company had been doing the work for many years and asserted that workloads data was proprietary); *Data & Analytic Solutions, Inc.*, Comp. Gen. Dec. B-405278.2, 2012 CPD ¶ 103 (using the same workload assumptions when agency controlled the workload); *Energy Enter. Solutions, LLC*, Comp. Gen. Dec. B-406089, 2012 CPD ¶ 95 (using the same labor costs when offerors were using the same technical approach); *ASRC Research & Tech. Solutions, LLC*, Comp. Gen. Dec. B-400217, 2008 CPD ¶ 202 (using the same fixed labor rates for all offerors that intended to hire the incumbent workforce).

Cost realism adjustments are also improper if they alter an offeror's standard accounting practices. See *Kellogg Brown & Root Servs., Inc.*, Comp. Gen. Dec. B-298694, 2006 CPD ¶ 160, granting a protest when the agency deleted an element of cost from the offeror's indirect costs, thereby not accepting the offeror's approved accounting system. GAO reasoned that Cost Accounting Standards 401 and 402 required that the offeror to follow the allocation of costs that it proposed.

If an offeror places a contractually binding "cap" on an element of cost, that amount can be determined by a cost realism analysis to be the probable cost of performance, *BNF Techs., Inc.*, Comp. Gen. Dec. B-254953.3, 94-1 CPD ¶ 274 (contracting officer improperly adjusted capped overhead and G&A costs above the amount of the cap); *AdvanceMed Corp.*, Comp. Gen. Dec. B-404910.4, 2012 CPD ¶ 25 (contracting officer properly used cap on indirect cost rates); *Halifax Tech. Servs., Inc. v. United States*, 848 F. Supp. 240 (D.D.C. 1994) (contracting officer properly used capped labor costs in making cost realism analysis). However, if the contracting officer concludes that a realistic estimate of the rates to be incurred is below the cap, that estimate can be used in lieu of the cap, *Delta Research Assocs., Inc.*, Comp. Gen. Dec. B-254006.2, 94-1 CPD ¶ 47. Similarly, if the contracting officer reasonably concludes that the cap will only be partially effective, other costs can be adjusted to a realistic amount, *University Research Co., LLC*, Comp. Gen. Dec. B-294358.8, 2006 CPD ¶ 66. When the capped costs are used as the probable costs, the contracting officer must still consider whether the amount imposes a constraint on the offeror significant enough to hamper its ability to perform the work under contract, *MCT JV*, Comp. Gen. Dec. B-311245.2, 2008 CPD ¶ 121, *recons. denied*, 2008 CPD ¶ 167; *Cubic Field Servs., Inc.*, Comp. Gen. Dec. B-247780, 92-1 CPD ¶ 525. See *VS2, LLC v. United States*, 155 Fed. Cl. 738 (2021), agreeing with *MCT* that a cap could be analyzed as a performance risk and concluding that GAO had incorrectly concluded in *Vectrus Mission Solutions Corp.*, Comp. Gen. Dec. B-418942, 2021 CPD ¶ 87, that a cap raised only a responsibility issue.

The cost realism analysis is normally done by analyzing each major cost element: material, direct labor, indirect costs, and other direct costs.

[a] Material

This category encompasses all work to be purchased by the offeror from raw materials to major subcontracts. Most of the cost realism analysis of material costs appears to occur in reviewing the proposed subcontracts in competing offers. See, for example, *BAE Sys. Norfolk Ship Repair, Inc.*, Comp. Gen. Dec. B-297879, 2006 CPD ¶ 75, agreeing that it was reasonable to use prior labor costs rather than fixed-price quotations from subcontractors to determine the realistic costs of performance. The contracting officer had concluded that the quotations were not a good indication of the price that would ultimately be paid to the subcontractors. See also *Electronic Data Sys. Fed. Corp.*, Comp. Gen. Dec. B-207311, 83-1 CPD ¶ 264, where the offeror's proposed subcontract costs were found to be too low because they did not reflect the need for a subcontractor during the entire life of the contract. Subcontractors' labor and indirect cost rates should also be checked for cost realism when the subcontracts will be performed on a cost-reimbursement basis, *General Marine Indus. of N.Y., Inc.*, Comp. Gen. Dec. B-240059, 90-2 CPD ¶ 311; *OptiMetrics, Inc.*, 68 Comp. Gen. 714 (B-235646), 89-2 CPD ¶ 266. See also *Dayton T. Brown, Inc.*, Comp. Gen. Dec. B-229664, 88-1 CPD ¶ 321, where material costs were determined to be realistic even though they appeared low; the reasoning was that the material costs would not impact the ultimate cost to the government because they were included in indirect costs of performance. In *GEC-Marconi Elec. Sys. Corp.*, Comp. Gen.

Dec. B-276186, 97-2 CPD ¶ 23, GAO found reasonable an agency's determination that the protester's proposed material costs were unrealistically low. Similarly, in *Litton Sys., Inc., Amecom Div.*, Comp. Gen. Dec. B-275807.2, 97-1 CPD ¶ 170, GAO found it proper to add subcontract labor hours where the offeror had included no labor hours because the subcontractors had stated that they would perform the work at no cost. The agency's rationale was that the offeror had no binding agreement with the subcontractors.

[b] Direct Labor

Cost realism analysis of direct labor costs is performed by reviewing the labor-hours proposed by the offeror, as well as the labor rates that will be applied to the various categories of direct labor to be used.

Perhaps the major area where discrepancies are found in proposals is the estimated number of labor hours required for performance. One cost realism analysis technique that is commonly used is to compare the labor-hours in the cost proposal with the labor hours in the technical proposal. If they vary, the realism of the proposed costs must be addressed, *AdvanceMed Corp.*, Comp. Gen. Dec. B-414373, 2017 CPD ¶ 160. In *AdvanceMed Corp.*, Comp. Gen. Dec. B-414373.3, 2019 CPD ¶ 25, GAO denied a protest that the labor hours had not been adjusted upward because the agency had made a thorough analysis. See also *Epsilon Sys. Solutions, Inc.*, Comp. Gen. Dec. B-414410, 2017 CPD ¶ 199, denying a protest where the labor hours had not been adjusted upward even though the agency had concluded that the staffing poses a "risk." Compare *Glacier Tech. Solutions, LLC*, Comp. Gen. Dec. B-412990.3, 2017 CPD ¶ 91, where the agency properly adjusted the labor costs upward even though it had evaluated the technical approach as "good." In contrast, in *Earl Indus., LLC*, Comp. Gen. Dec. B-309996, 2007 CPD ¶ 203, a protest was granted when the agency used the hours in the cost proposal rather than adjusting them upwards to reflect the technical proposal. In *ITT Fed. Servs. Int'l Corp.*, Comp. Gen. Dec. B-289863.4, 2002 CPD ¶ 216, GAO held that the cost realism analysis was defective because the agency did not resolve the discrepancy between the effort described in the technical proposal and the quoted labor costs. See also *Frank A. Bloomer—Agency Tender Official*, Comp. Gen. Dec. B-401482.2, 2009 CPD ¶ 203, where GAO sustained a protest because the agency had accepted the offeror's estimate that it could institute a 10% reduction in the labor hours without any explanation of how that could be accomplished, and *ITT Fed. Servs. Int'l Corp.*, Comp. Gen. Dec. B-283307, 99-2 CPD ¶ 76, where GAO sustained a protest because the agency had failed to analyze the technical approach of the offeror in concluding that the labor costs were too low.

Cost realism adjustments are required if an analysis of the offeror's proposal indicates that no labor hours have been included for required elements of the work, *NV Servs.*, Comp. Gen. Dec. B-284119.2, 2000 CPD ¶ 64. Numerous cases have sustained discretionary decisions that labor-hour estimates are incorrect.

See, for example, *Smartronix, Inc.*, Comp. Gen. Dec. B-413721.2, 2017 CPD ¶ 59 (inadequate labor to meet phase-in requirements); *Innovative Test Asset Solutions LLC v. United States*, 125 Fed. Cl. 201 (2016) (innovative methods could not be done with proposed labor hours); *Lumetra v. United States*, 84 Fed. Cl. 542 (2008) (prior performance of work with substantially more hours); *Westech Int'l, Inc. v. United States*, 79 Fed. Cl. 272 (2007) (added labor hours needed to provide sufficient staff to perform required tasks); *ITT Indus. Space Sys., LLC*, Comp. Gen. Dec. B-309964, 2007 CPD ¶ 217 (proposed techniques for performing work required more labor hours); *EDO Corp.*, Comp. Gen. Dec. B-296861, 2005 CPD ¶ 196 (lack of explanation of low amounts of labor for specific tasks justified upward adjustment); *United Payors & United Providers Health Servs., Inc. v. United States*, 55 Fed. Cl. 323 (2003) (underestimate of required work led to adjusted costs); *Hernandez Eng'g, Inc.*, Comp. Gen. Dec. B-286336, 2001 CPD ¶ 89 (unsubstantiated labor hours lower than "historical" levels not realistic). See, however, *DevTech Sys., Inc.*, Comp. Gen. Dec. B-418273.3, 2021 CPD ¶ 2, finding improper adjustments when the agency added labor hours for employees that were not required by the specifications, and *Univ. Research Co., LLC v. United States*, 65 Fed. Cl. 500 (2005), finding it improper to normalize reproduction costs when offerors proposed methods for reducing these costs.

A number of cases support an agency's decision not to adjust low estimates of labor-hours because it has determined that the offeror's approach to the work will likely require fewer hours than have been used in the past, *McConnell Jones Lanier & Murphy LLP v. United States*, 128 Fed. Cl. 218 (2016); *A-T Solutions, Inc. v. United States*, 122 Fed. Cl. 170 (2015); *Honeywell Tech. Solutions, Inc.*, Comp. Gen. Dec. B-400771, 2009 CPD ¶ 49; *Palmetto GBA, LLC*, Comp. Gen. Dec. B-298962, 2007 CPD ¶ 25. See *ATA Aerospace, LLC*, Comp. Gen. Dec. B-417427.2, 2020 CPD ¶ 96 (agency properly accepted the low labor hours based on unique method proposed by offeror); *TrailBlazer Health Enters., LLC*, Comp. Gen. Dec. B-402751, 2010 CPD ¶ 183 (agency properly accepted the low labor hours based on the offeror's explanation of the innovative methods it intended to use to perform the work); *CIGNA Gov't Servs., LLC*, Comp. Gen. Dec. B-297915, 2006 CPD ¶ 73 (agency properly did not adjust seemingly low labor hours because the agency's review of past performance of the offeror indicated that it had done the work more efficiently than other contractors); and *ELS, Inc.*, Comp. Gen. Dec. B-283236, 99-2 CPD ¶ 92 (agency not required to adjust a proposal to reflect the amount of effort that the agency had included in its budget estimate).

It is improper to accept low labor hour estimates that are based on performance of the work using methods that do not meet the contract requirements, *M. Stoller Corp.*, Comp. Gen. Dec. B-400937, 2009 CPD ¶ 193. See also *Ohio KePRO, Inc.*, Comp. Gen. Dec. B-417836, 2020 CPD ¶ 47 (agency failed to analyze low level of effort for some of the work); *ATA Aerospace, LLC*, Comp.

Gen. Dec. B-417427, 2019 CPD ¶ 245 (agency failed to adjust low labor hours without any explanation of their realism).

Labor rates can also be questioned when the rates included in a proposal are not realistic. For example, in *ASRC Research & Tech. Solutions, LLC*, Comp. Gen. Dec. B-400217, 2008 CPD ¶ 202; and *Hernandez Eng'g, Inc.*, Comp. Gen. Dec. B-286336, 2001 CPD ¶ 89, the agency properly concluded that the offeror's proposed labor rates were too low because they were below the rates being paid by an incumbent service contractor. The agency assumed that the winning contractor would hire most of the incumbent employees at their current salaries. Similarly, in *TWD & Assocs., Inc.*, Comp. Gen. Dec. B-416834, 2019 CPD ¶ 13, salaries were properly adjusted upward when the protester did not submit proof that the employees had agreed to lower salaries, and in *DZSP 21, LLC*, Comp. Gen. Dec. B-410486.10, 2018 CPD ¶ 155, salaries were properly adjusted upward when the protester proposed to replace the entire staff. See also *Westech Int'l, Inc. v. United States*, 79 Fed. Cl. 272 (2007), where it was found proper to escalate Service Contract Act labor rates by 3% per year based on past experience.

Agencies can use a variety of types of data to determine that the labor rates are too low, *ICF, Inc.*, Comp. Gen. Dec. B-419049.3, 2021 CPD ¶ 117 (escalation rates developed by IHS Global Insight); *Stargates, Inc.*, Comp. Gen. Dec. B-419349, 2021 CPD ¶ 64 (salaries being paid to proposed employees); *BTAS, Inc.*, Comp. Gen. Dec. B-415810.4, 2018 CPD ¶ 346 (rates proposed by competitors); *LOGC2, Inc.*, Comp. Gen. Dec. B-416075, 2018 CPD ¶ 204 (local labor rates on salary.com); *Oak Grove Techs., LLC*, Comp. Gen. Dec. B-415772, 2018 CPD ¶ 127 (fringe benefits being paid by incumbent contractor); *Agile Defense, Inc.*, Comp. Gen. Dec. B-415774, 2018 CPD ¶ 110 (rates proposed by competitors); *Rollout Sys., LLC*, Comp. Gen. Dec. B-414145, 2017 CPD ¶ 104 (certified payroll data for current employees); *Engility Corp.*, Comp. Gen. Dec. B-413120.3, 2017 CPD ¶ 70 (rates being paid by protester at location of work); *Solera Defense Solutions, Inc.*, Comp. Gen. Dec. B-414056, 2017 CPD ¶ 46 (forward pricing rates and BLS rates); *Radian, Inc.*, Comp. Gen. Dec. B-256313.2, 94-2 CPD ¶ 104 ("rate check" furnished by the cognizant DCAA auditors); *A.T. Kearney, Inc.*, Comp. Gen. Dec. B-237731, 90-1 CPD ¶ 305 (current average rates being paid on a similar contract); *Associates in Rural Dev., Inc.*, Comp. Gen. Dec. B-238402, 90-1 CPD ¶ 495 (earlier salaries for same work).

A questionable practice is to determine that only rates below one standard deviation from the median of proposed rates are unrealistic. In *Booz Allen Hamilton, Inc.*, Comp. Gen. Dec. B-414283, 2017 CPD ¶ 159, GAO stated that it would not object to this approach in cases where the agency specified the amount of labor to be used and denied the protest because the agency also had used other comparisons to determine that the rates were realistic. However, in *Solution One Indus., Inc.*, Comp. Gen. Dec. B-417441, 2019 CPD ¶ 252, GAO concurred with the use of this approach as the sole means for adjusting the rates.

See *Noblis, Inc.*, Comp. Gen. Dec. B-414055, 2017 CPD ¶ 33, granting a protest where one offeror's data skewed the computation. Compare *Agile Defense, Inc. v. United States*, 143 Fed. Cl. 10 (2019), denying a protest when the agency adjusted rates within one standard deviation, with *Dalpar Corp.*, Comp. Gen. Dec. B-414285, 2017 CPD ¶ 135, denying a protest where no cost realism adjustment was made when the winning offeror's rates were within one standard deviation of the average rates.

When an offeror satisfactorily explains why seemingly low labor rates are an accurate prediction of the rates that will be paid, no adjustment is warranted. See *Synergy Solutions, Inc. v. United States*, 133 Fed. Cl. 716 (2017) (offeror stated it did not intend to hire all of incumbent's staff but to pay lower rates); *ITT Corp.*, Comp. Gen. Dec. B-310102.6, 2010 CPD ¶ 12 (offeror presented evidence that current employees were accepting lower rates than in the past); *Information Network Sys., Inc.*, Comp. Gen. Dec. B-284854, 2000 CPD ¶ 104 (agency concluded that the offeror could probably hire employees at labor rates that were lower than those of the incumbent contractor); *Advanced Commc'ns Sys., Inc.*, Comp. Gen. Dec. B-283650, 2000 CPD ¶ 3 (the impact of a few of the labor rates that were slightly lower than Bureau of Labor Statistics rates in the area was less than 1%). It is also proper not to adjust labor rates that are within a range specified in a reasonable government estimate, *CACI, Inc.—Federal*, Comp. Gen. Dec. B-413860.4, 2018 CPD ¶ 17. Compare *Magellan Health Servs.*, Comp. Gen. Dec. B-298912, 2007 CPD ¶ 81, and *ITT Fed. Servs. Int'l Corp.*, Comp. Gen. Dec. B-289863.4, 2002 CPD ¶ 216, where protests were granted when the agency failed to adjust very low labor rates and it was doubtful the offeror would be able to hire qualified personnel at those rates. A protest was also granted in *Ohio KePRO, Inc.*, Comp. Gen. Dec. B-417836, 2020 CPD ¶ 47, where the agency failed to analyze whether rates more than 20% under the salary.com rates were realistic.

It is proper to accept rates that appear to be low when the agency determines that they are the rates being paid by the incumbent offeror that is competing for the work, *Kalman & Co.*, Comp. Gen. Dec. B-287442.2, 2002 CPD ¶ 63, are the rates currently being paid by the offeror and its major subcontractor, *Advanced Commc'ns Sys., Inc.*, Comp. Gen. Dec. B-283650, 2000 CPD ¶ 3, are supported by commitments from personnel to work at those rates, *Telos Corp.*, Comp. Gen. Dec. B-279493.3, 98-2 CPD ¶ 30, or are the rates being currently paid to employees that will work on the contract, *ATLIS Fed. Servs., Inc.*, Comp. Gen. Dec. B-275065.2, 97-1 CPD ¶ 84. Compare *Battelle Memorial Inst.*, Comp. Gen. Dec. B-416263.5, 2020 CPD ¶ 37, where the agency properly accepted labor rates below the incumbent's rates based on commercial salary data.

When labor rates are questioned, the contracting officer must be certain that the adjustments are based on the offeror's accounting practices. For example, an adjustment of rates to reflect a 40-hour workweek was overturned in *General Research Corp.*, Comp. Gen. Dec. B-241569, 91-1 CPD ¶ 183, because the offeror had an established accounting practice (disclosed in its Cost Accounting Standards Disclosure Statement) that charged for labor based on the full hours worked by each employee. GAO stated that the contracting officer should not have relied on the incorrect advice of the Defense Contract Audit Agency (DCAA) auditor, who stated that the Disclosure Statement did not deal with this issue, but should have been familiar with the offeror's accounting practices. See also *SGT, Inc.*, Comp. Gen. Dec. B-294722.4, 2005 CPD ¶ 151, holding that the agency properly made an independent analysis of labor rates when the DCAA audit of the rates was inconclusive.

Agencies now use the Identification of Uncompensated Overtime solicitation provision in FAR 52.237-10 requiring offerors to use a lower "adjusted rate" reflecting any proposed use of uncompensated overtime and warning that these low rates will be evaluated "in a risk assessment." See *Trident Techs., LLC*, Comp. Gen. Dec. B-412020.16, 2018 CPD ¶ 65, denying a protest when the agency adjusted these adjusted rates upward because they were unrealistically low even though the provision does not call for such adjustment. Compare *Systems Integration & Research, Inc.*, Comp. Gen. Dec. B-279759.2, 99-1 CPD ¶ 54, where labor rates based on uncompensated overtime were properly accepted where the solicitation did not prohibit the use of such rates, and *SRS Techs.*, Comp. Gen. Dec. B-291618.2, 2003 CPD ¶ 70, where it was improper to adjust the rates for uncompensated overtime since the solicitation did not prohibit its use.

[c] Indirect Costs

Contracting officers also must analyze the realism of proposed indirect costs. Protests have been granted because the contracting officer did not adjust rates that were below current rates, *E.L. Hamm & Assocs., Inc.*, Comp. Gen. Dec. B-280766.3, 99-1 CPD ¶ 85 (rate substantially below the DCAA approved rate); *Futures Grp. Int'l*, Comp. Gen. Dec. B-281274.2, 2000 CPD ¶ 147 (rates were significantly below the most recent rates). Similarly, in *IT Shows, Inc.*, Comp. Gen. Dec. B-411994.5, 2017 CPD ¶ 34, a protest was granted in where the RFP called for the use of ceiling rates to evaluate realism, but the agency selected an offeror that did not propose a ceiling rate. Compare *Booz-Allen & Hamilton, Inc.*, Comp. Gen. Dec. B-275934.2, 97-1 CPD ¶ 222, where it was found proper to use the five months experienced rates to project annual rates when the offeror had revised its accounting system. In that case, the contracting officer had rejected the DCAA auditor's analysis that suggested using average rates. Similarly, in *Hanford Envtl. Health Found.*, Comp. Gen. Dec. B-292858.2, 2004 CPD ¶ 164, acceptance of a fringe benefit rate that was lower than the incumbent contractor's rate was proper when the lower rate was comparable to local rates.

Some contracting officers have avoided the detailed analysis of indirect costs by merely comparing proposed overhead rates to prior rates. While this is a rather imprecise technique, it has been affirmed as a proper basis for a cost realism analysis. See *Alphaport, Inc.*, Comp. Gen. Dec. B-414086, 2017 CPD ¶ 69, accepting an offeror's proposed rates based on the average of the past three years. Compare *CGS Adm'rs, LLC v. United States*, 110 Fed. Cl. 431 (2013), holding that it was proper to determine a probable cost using prior-year indirect cost rates when the offeror had included substantially lower rates in the proposal based on its theory that additional work would reduce its rates, with *Dellew Corp. v. United States*, 128 Fed. Cl. 187 (2016), holding that it was proper to accept lower rates when the offeror had submitted information identifying how it could lower its rates.

If an offeror agrees to place a "cap" on its indirect cost rates, it is proper to use the cap rates in determining the probable cost in making the cost realism analysis, *Tatitlek Techs., Inc.*, Comp. Gen. Dec. B-416711, 2018 CPD ¶ 410 (capped overhead rate); *IT Shows, Inc. v. United States*, 130 Fed. Cl. 204 (2016) (ceiling overhead rate); *E.L. Hamm & Assocs., Inc.*, Comp. Gen. Dec. B-280766.5, 2000 CPD ¶ 13 (capped G&A rate). It has also been held that it is improper to disregard capped rates in determining the probable cost, *Veda, Inc.*, Comp. Gen. Dec. B-278516.2, 98-1 CPD ¶ 112. However, if the contracting officer concludes that a realistic estimate of the rates to be incurred is below the cap, that estimate can be used in lieu of the cap, *Delta Research Assocs., Inc.*, Comp. Gen. Dec. B-254006.2, 94-1 CPD ¶ 47. If the capped rates are unrealistically low, the agency should consider the risk that performing at a low rate will impact the contractor's financial condition, *MCT JV*, Comp. Gen. Dec. B-311245.2, 2008 CPD ¶ 121 (protest granted because agency did not consider risk of capped rates when RFP warned of such risk).

In making the cost realism analysis of indirect costs, the contracting officer may rely entirely on the computations of the cognizant auditor, *Summit Research Corp.*, Comp. Gen. Dec. B-287523, 2001 CPD ¶ 176; *ELS, Inc.*, Comp. Gen. Dec. B-283236, 99-2 CPD ¶ 92; *SRS Techs.*, Comp. Gen. Dec. B-238403, 90-1 CPD ¶ 484. See also *Geo-Centers, Inc.*, Comp. Gen. Dec. B-276033, 97-1 CPD ¶ 182, where an agency correctly accepted a new overhead structure that had been approved by the DCAA, and *Polaris, Inc.*, Comp. Gen. Dec. B-220066, 85-2 CPD ¶ 669, where an agency was found to have correctly concluded that the offeror's projected gradual reduction in overhead rates over a five-year period led to unduly low overhead rates, based on the recommendations of the DCAA. Conversely, an auditor's recommendations may be disregarded entirely if the contracting officer believes that the information is invalid, *Electronic Warfare Integration Network*, Comp. Gen. Dec. B-235814, 89-2 CPD ¶ 356.

A cost realism adjustment generally will not be upheld if it is based on incorrect advice from the DCAA, *ASRC Research & Tech. Solutions*, Comp. Gen. Dec. B-400217, 2008 CPD ¶ 202; *LLC General Research Corp.*, Comp. Gen. Dec. B-241569, 91-1 CPD ¶ 183. In addition, reliance on unaudited information obtained from a government auditor has been found to be unjustified where the information proves to be unreliable, *L-3 Commc'ns Corp.*, Comp. Gen. Dec. B-281784.3, 99-1 CPD ¶ 81. Compare *Intermetrics, Inc.*, Comp. Gen. Dec. B-259254.2, 95-1 CPD ¶ 215, and *Radian, Inc.*, Comp. Gen. Dec. B-256313.2, 94-2 CPD ¶ 104, sustaining cost realism adjustments based on unaudited rate checks by DCAA auditors that were based on current data.

FAR 15.407-3(b) requires contracting officers to use forward pricing rates as the basis for pricing "all contracts" during the period an agreement on such rates is in effect, unless the ACO determines that a "changed condition invalidates the agreement." See FAR 42.1701 specifying the procedures for negotiation of forward pricing rates. It is proper to use such forward pricing rates in performing a cost realism analysis, *Network Sec. Sys. Plus, Inc.*, Comp. Gen. Dec. B-416755, 2019 CPD ¶ 4. In *Jonathan Corp.*, Comp. Gen. Dec. B-230971, 88-2 CPD ¶ 133, GAO agreed with the contracting officer's use of such rates in concluding that the estimated costs were too low even though the offeror attempted to demonstrate that the forward pricing rates were invalid due to changed conditions. Similarly, in *Coleman Research Corp.*, Comp. Gen. Dec. B-278793, 98-1 CPD ¶ 111, the contracting officer properly relied on recently negotiation forward pricing rates as well as rates incurred on a prior contract in rejecting low proposed rates.

[d] Other Direct Costs

Cost realism analysis has also been used to question other direct costs proposed by offerors. For example, in *Amtec Corp.*, Comp. Gen. Dec. B-240647, 90-2 CPD ¶ 482, the contracting officer properly found the estimate of travel costs too low because the discount fares proposed by an offeror would probably not be obtainable during performance. Similarly, in *CWIS, LLC*, Comp. Gen. Dec. B-287521, 2001 CPD ¶ 119, travel costs were properly adjusted upward to reflect a requirement for trips on short notice, and in *Centra Tech., Inc.*, Comp. Gen. Dec. B-274744, 97-1 CPD ¶ 35, travel costs were properly adjust upward to reflect the costs that had been incurred by the incumbent contractor. See also *Priority One Servs., Inc.*, Comp. Gen. Dec. B-288836, 2002 CPD ¶ 79, sustaining a protest where the agency failed to reduce costs of equipment which protester had included in its estimate because it misunderstood the requirements. Compare *Abt Assocs.*, Comp. Gen. Dec. B-294130.2, 2004 CPD ¶ 220, where the agency made no adjustments to travel and per diem costs because they were in line with past experience. In *Science Applications Int'l Corp.*, Comp. Gen. Dec. B-238136.2, 90-1 CPD ¶ 517, it was found proper to accept a low rate for other direct costs when the agency, after discussions, agreed with the offeror's rationale for the low rate.

[e] Use of Analysis

As discussed above, the most common use of cost realism analysis is to determine the probable cost of performance of a cost-reimbursement contract in order to use that cost in the evaluation of the proposals and the selection of the source. It is also proper to use such analysis to reduce the probable cost of performance in a cost-reimbursement contract by negotiating a cap on G&A expenses where the cost realism analysis indicates that this element of the costs is far below expected costs, *Vitro Corp.*, Comp. Gen. Dec. B-247734.3, 92-2 CPD ¶ 202.

The cost realism analysis can also be used as a negotiating tool. If the analysis indicates that the proposed price of a fixed-price contract or the estimated cost of a cost-reimbursement contract is low, the offeror can be alerted to the problem in the written or oral discussion. This provides a better understanding of the basis for the price or estimated cost and may identify problems such as mistakes or lack of understanding of the requirements of the RFP. It may also lead to a revised price or estimated cost in the offeror's final proposal revisions. See *Abt Assocs. Inc.*, Comp. Gen. Dec. B-295449, 2005 CPD ¶ 54, where the contracting officer followed this procedure with the result that the winning offeror revised its cost proposal to meet the agency's realism criteria—leading to GAO denying a protest claiming that the cost realism analysis was not reasonable.

When a cost realism analysis indicates that the probable costs of performance are significantly higher than the offeror's estimate, the agency can also downgrade the technical or management evaluation, *Fort Carson Support Servs. v. United States*, 71 Fed. Cl. 571 (2006). The low cost could signal significant risks in terms of future performance, *Cubic Field Servs., Inc.*, Comp. Gen. Dec. B-247780, 92-1 CPD ¶ 525 (proposed cap on costs of performance of cost-reimbursement contract created risk of nonperformance); *Modern Techs. Corp.*, Comp. Gen. Dec. B-236961.4, 90-1 CPD ¶ 301 (extended workweek created substantial risk offeror would be unable to hire and retain stable workforce); *Culver Health Corp.*, Comp. Gen. Dec. B-242902, 91-1 CPD ¶ 556 (low rates of compensation of proposed employees created risk of poor performance). Compare *Harris Corp. v. United States*, 628 F. Supp. 813 (D.D.C. 1986), where the court held that it was improper to downgrade a proposal merely because the offeror had made a decision to absorb some costs of performance. See also *VSE Corp.*, Comp. Gen. Dec. B-247610.2, 92-2 CPD ¶ 81, where GAO held that the contracting officer had acted properly in not downgrading an offeror's technical and management proposal; the proposed labor rates were lower than the government's estimate, but analysis indicated that they did not detract from the offeror's ability to perform the work. On the other hand, GAO granted a protest in *Serco, Inc.*, Comp. Gen. Dec. B-298266, 2006 CPD ¶ 120, because the agency had not considered whether the low number of labor hours proposed by an offeror indicated that it did not understand the work.

[2] Determining Price Reasonableness

Cost analysis using cost element breakdowns and other data on the offeror's prospective costs of performance can also be used to determine if the price of a fixed-price contract is fair and reasonable. The analysis in these circumstances is substantially the same as that made for cost realism except that the focus is on whether the price is too high. See *TAAS Israel Indus., Ltd.*, Comp. Gen. Dec. B-260733, 95-2 CPD ¶ 23, agreeing that a valid price reasonableness determination was made when the contracting officer used detailed cost element breakdowns from two competitors to perform the analysis. A similar result was reached in *Family Realty*, Comp. Gen. Dec. B-247772, 92-2 CPD ¶ 6. Cost data can also be used to make a performance risk assessment. See *General Elec. Co.*, 55 Comp. Gen. 1450 (B-186372), 76-2 CPD ¶ 269, where the source selection official concluded that there was performance risk because the contractor had not submitted detailed cost data supporting the reduced price in its BAFO, and *Systems & Processes Eng'g Corp.*, Comp. Gen. Dec. B-234142, 89-1 CPD ¶ 441, where cost data indicated a low price and, thus, a risk of inability to perform.

[C] Should-Cost Analysis

Should-cost analysis is a selective form of cost analysis used primarily on major procurements. This process is described in FAR 15.407-4(a), as follows:

> (1) Should-cost reviews are a specialized form of cost analysis. Should-cost reviews differ from traditional evaluation methods because they do not assume that a contractor's historical costs reflect efficient and economical operation. Instead, these reviews evaluate the economy and efficiency of the contractor's existing workforce, methods, materials, facilities, operating systems, and management. These reviews are accomplished by a multi-functional team of Government contracting, contract administration, pricing, audit, and engineering representatives. The objective of should-cost reviews is to promote both short and long-range improvements in the contractor's economy and efficiency in order to reduce the cost of performance of Government contracts. In addition, by providing rationale for any recommendations and quantifying their impact on cost, the Government will be better able to develop realistic objectives for negotiation.

See also DFARS PGI 215.407-4(b)(2) stating that should-cost reviews should be considered on major systems acquisitions. Should-cost analysis has been used most often on major contracts for the manufacture of high-priced equipment. Traditionally, it was performed by making a detailed industrial engineering analysis of the specific methods used by the contractor to manufacture the product and a determination of more cost-effective methods that would reduce the costs. More recently, as more work on major systems has been subcontracted, it has been used to evaluate the prices being paid to major subcontractors. In this regard, it is similar to conventional cost analysis because it challenges the profits being earned by subcontractors as well as their projections of costs. In either case, should-cost analysis basically looks for ways to decrease costs more than merely projecting current costs into the future. Congress has occasionally expressed interest in increasing the use of should-cost analysis. See § 837 of the National Defense Authorization Act for 2018, Pub. L. No. 115-91, requiring regulations providing "for the appropriate use of the should-cost review process of a major weapon system." This requirement was implemented in DFARS 215.407-4(b) providing detailed guidance on the elements of a should-cost review and requiring that the government team collaborate with the contractor during the review process.

[D] Methods for Expediting Analysis

In the case of contractors performing numerous government contracts, proposals are being submitted and analyzed on a regular basis. Since many of the elements of cost, such as labor and indirect cost rates, are the same regardless of the contract for which the costs are incurred, repetitive analysis is unnecessary. An agency's cost analysis can also be greatly expedited if the parties are in agreement on the basic estimating system used by the contractor. The regulations give guidance on these techniques for expediting cost analysis.

[1] Forward Pricing Rate Agreements

FAR 15.407-3 recognizes that major contractors frequently enter into forward pricing rate agreements with elements of DoD. These agreements are negotiated by administrative contracting officers and may cover indirect cost rates or labor rates. FAR 15.407-3(b) requires contracting officers to use the rates in these agreements "as bases for pricing all contracts, modifications, and other contractual actions" and to report conditions that would affect the agreement's validity to the administrative contracting officer. DFARS 215.407-3(b) recognizes that such agreements can be "waived" by the head of a contracting activity but requires that such waivers be reported to the cognizant administrative contracting officer.

Because the labor and indirect cost rates covered by these agreements are subject to fluctuation at any time based on the costs being incurred by the contractor, these agreements must be closely monitored to ensure that they contain valid rates. However, if the administrative contracting officer and the cognizant auditor regularly monitor them and renegotiate the rates quickly when new data call for such modification, these agreements can greatly reduce the effort needed to complete a cost analysis and negotiate a price. If the agreement covers all labor and indirect cost elements of the contractor's estimating system, only direct labor hours and material will require analysis on an individual basis. This can greatly expedite the procurement process.

[2] Business System Requirements

If a contractor has approved "business systems," the negotiation of prices is facilitated because the contracting officer can deal with the contractor's estimates with more confidence. This, of course, does not relieve the contracting officer from the necessity of analyzing the proposed costs on a specific acquisition to ensure that they are a reasonably accurate projection of actual costs.

DoD has adopted a stringent requirement that contractors subject to the Cost Accounting Standards have business systems that are in "substantial compliance" with the clauses pertaining to the six systems listed in the Contractor Business Systems clause in DFARS 252.242-7005. The penalty for not being in substantial compliance with a system is 5% withholding of payments with a maximum of 10% total withholding. See CONTRACTOR BUSINESS SYSTEMS: DOD Needs Better Information to Monitor and Assess Review Process, GAO-19-212 (Feb. 7, 2019), reporting that reviews have found substantial noncompliance with these requirements.

These requirements are not applicable to other contractors but there is FAR guidance on these six systems. The FAR and DFARS requirements are discussed in the following subsections.

[a] Accounting System

FAR Part 31 contains detailed guidance on the requirements for an acceptable accounting system when entering into almost all contracts. These requirements are particularly applicable to cost-reimbursement contracts but they also apply to repricing of fixed-price contracts, FAR 31.102. They require a logical treatment of direct and indirect costs, FAR 31.202 and .203, and the segregation of unallowable costs, FAR 31.201-6. They also impose a penalty for the inclusion of expressly unallowable costs in indirect cost proposals on major contracts, FAR 31.110.

The Accounting System Administration clause in DFARS 252.242-7006 contains a very detailed definition of an acceptable accounting system and calls for the withholding penalty if a contractor with this clause in its contract is not in substantial compliance with these requirements. DCAA is responsible for reviewing and making recommendations on whether a contractor has met these requirements.

[b] Earned Value Management System

FAR Subpart 34.2 requires contracts for "major acquisitions" to have an earned value management system to measure progress during the performance of the contract. Agencies are also permitted to require such a system for smaller contracts. The clauses Notice of Earned Value Management System—Postaward Integrated Baseline Review, FAR 52.234-3, and Earned Value Management System, FAR 52.234-4, are used to define these requirements.

The Earned Value Management System clause in DFARS 252.234-7002 contains detailed guidance on an acceptable earned value management system and calls for the withholding penalty if a contractor with this clause in its contract is not in substantial compliance with these requirements. DCMA is responsible for determining whether a contractor has met these requirements.

[c] Estimating System

FAR 15.407-5 provides that "cognizant audit activities" will establish regular programs for reviewing estimating systems used by contractors. The purpose of such a review is to identify deficiencies in contractor's estimating systems so that they can be addressed and corrected. Ultimately, this process is intended to lead to complete agreement on an estimating system with resultant reduction in the audit necessary on any proposal. Each estimating system review is to be documented by a report from the audit activity.

FAR 15.407-5(b) calls for the following procedure:

> The auditor shall send a copy of the estimating system survey report and a copy of the official notice of corrective action required to each contracting office and contract administration office having substantial business with that contractor. Significant deficiencies not corrected by the contractor shall be a consideration in subsequent proposal analyses and negotiations.

The Cost Estimating System Requirements clause in DFARS 252.215-7002 contains detailed guidance on an acceptable cost estimating system and calls for the withholding penalty if a contractor with this clause in its contract is not in substantial compliance with these requirements. DCAA is responsible for reviewing and making recommendations on whether a contractor has met these requirements.

A deficiency in an offeror's estimating system would logically require the contracting officer to make a more thorough cost realism analysis of the area where the system is found to be deficient. See *Metro Mach. Corp.*, Comp. Gen. Dec. B-402567, 2010 CPD ¶ 132, denying a protest where the agency performed a detailed review of the indirect cost rates that had been based on an estimating system that had been reported by DCAA as a failed system.

[d] Material Management and Accounting System

There is no FAR requirement that contractors with production contracts have a material management and accounting system to segregate and account for common items. However, the Material Management and Accounting System clause in DFARS 252.242-7004 requires such a system and calls for the withholding penalty if a contractor with this clause in its contract is not in substantial compliance with these requirements. DCAA is responsible for reviewing and making recommendations on whether a contractor has met these requirements.

[e] Property Management System

FAR Part 45 contains detailed guidance on the contractor's responsibility for the management of government property. The Government Property clause in FAR 52.245-1 is used to define these requirements.

The Contractor Property Management System Administration clause in DFARS 252.245-7003 requires the contractor to have a system meeting the requirements of the FAR 52.245-1 clause and calls for the withholding penalty if a contractor with this clause in its contract is not in substantial compliance with these requirements. DCMA is responsible for determining whether a contractor has met these requirements.

[f] Purchasing System

FAR 44.305-1 makes administrative contracting officers responsible for approving contractors' purchasing systems based on reviews of such systems. FAR 44.301 states the objective of purchasing system reviews as follows:

> The objective of a contractor purchasing system review (CPSR) is to evaluate the efficiency and effectiveness with which the contractor spends Government funds and complies with Government policy when subcontracting. The review provides the administrative contracting officer (ACO) a basis for granting, withholding, or withdrawing approval of the contractor's purchasing system.

The cognizant administrative contracting officer is also required to "ensure that the contractor is effectively managing its purchasing program," FAR 44.304(a).

The Contractor Purchasing System Administration clause in DFARS 252.244-7001 is used to implement this program and detailed guidance on the procedures to be followed in making purchasing system reviews is contained in DFARS 244.305-70. The clause calls for the withholding penalty if a contractor with this clause in its contract is not in substantial compliance with these requirements. DCMA is responsible for determining whether a contractor has met these requirements.

§ 13.07 NEGOTIATION OF PROFIT

In negotiated procurements where cost is negotiated separately, the parties must also negotiate the profit that will be included in the price. This occurs primarily in situations where no significant competition has been obtained. In cost-reimbursement contracts, this profit will be stated separately in the contract as a fixed fee (in a CPFF contract), a base fee (in a CPAF contract), or a target fee (in a CPIF contract). In fixed-price contracts, this profit will either be included in the price or stated as a target fee (in an FPI contract). In agencies with major procurement programs, the contracting officer is subject to specific regulatory guidance on the techniques that are to be used to determine the government's negotiation position with regard to profit.

[A] Fee Limitations

There are similar statutory limitations on the rates of fee that can be negotiated in CPFF contracts in both the Armed Services Procurement Act, 10 U.S.C. § 3322 (formerly § 2306(d)), and the Federal Property and Administrative Services Act, 41 U.S.C. § 3905(b). They prohibit fees greater than 10% of the estimated cost of all CPFF contracts except those for "experimental, developmental, or research work" where the limitation is 15%. They also contain limitations on the amount an architect-engineers can be paid as discussed in Chapter 10.

These statutes have several features. First, the statutes apply to the rate of fee *negotiated*, not the rate of fee actually *earned* by the contractor through performance of the contract. In this regard, the rate is limited in terms of a percentage of the estimated cost of the contract as determined by the "agency head" at the outset, *Fluor Enters., Inc. v. United States*, 64 Fed. Cl. 461 (2005); *CACI, Inc.—Federal*, Comp. Gen. Dec. B-216516, 85-1 CPD ¶ 363. GAO has ruled that when a settlement of an aborted cost-reimbursement contract is negotiated, the statute must be applied to limit the total fee paid in settlement, but the agency is not required to impose the percentage limitation on each part of the work performed, *National Visitors Ctr.*, Comp. Gen. Dec. B-158792, 80-1 CPD ¶ 121. Second, the statutes apply by their precise terms to only CPFF contracts and not to other types of cost-reimbursement contracts. Thus, the provisions do not apply to CPIF contracts. This rule is set forth in DoD/NASA Incentive Contracting Guide, Oct. 1969. For many years, the FAR imposed 10% and 15% limitations on the maximum fees computed as a percentage of estimated or target cost of CPAF and CPIF contracts but these limitations were deleted by FAC 97-02, Sept. 30, 1997.

In one case, the Court of Claims applied this statute in an unusual way in holding that the government was not bound by a contract containing a fee arrangement that violated the statute. In *Yosemite Park & Curry Co. v. United States*, 582 F.2d 552 (Ct. Cl. 1978), the parties had entered into a transportation contract that compensated the contractor for the cost of providing bus service plus a fee at the rate of 12% of the contractor's gross investment in equipment to perform the contract. The court held that the contract was a CPFF contract that was invalid because the fee resulted in an amount greater than 10% of the estimated costs of performance of the contract. Thus, a fee not based directly on costs of performance but yielding a rate higher than permitted by the statute may be found to be in violation of the statute. In *Yosemite Park*, the court further held that the contractor was entitled to be paid for the value of the services rendered to the government not exceeding "the entire, total, provable costs" of performance plus 10% of these costs. It is interesting to note that this judgment permitted a larger payment than is permitted by the fee limitation statute.

[B] Profit Negotiation Techniques

The techniques used to establish the government's negotiating position on profit have varied among the procuring agencies. In the 1950s and 1960s, contracting officers were given complete discretion to negotiate profits with contractors; the regulations merely contained a list of the factors that should be considered in such negotiation. In 1964, DoD adopted the "weighted guidelines" approach to profit negotiation, requiring their contracting officers to follow a prescribed formula in analyzing the profit to be negotiated and arriving at a prenegotiation position. The weighted guidelines formula was revised extensively in the 1970s to give greater recognition to facilities employed by contractors in the performance of contracts. During this period, the civilian agencies continued to give their contracting officers greater latitude. In December 1980, OFPP issued Policy Letter 80-7, 45 Fed. Reg. 82593, requiring that all agencies making noncompetitive awards over $100,000 adopt a "structured approach" to profit negotiation when these awards total $50 million or more each year. This policy letter was subsequently canceled, but the policy is now included in FAR 15.404-4. This policy requires all agencies with significant procurement functions to follow an approach similar to DoD's weighted guidelines but permit each agency to tailor its formula to the particular programs of the agency. DoD subsequently conducted another profit study, the Defense Financial and Investment Review (DFAIR), June 1985, and adopted a new weighted guidelines formula in August 1987. This newer formula departs from the FAR guidance in significant ways but has never been challenged.

[1] Goal of Structured Approach

The original weighted guidelines approach was based on a detailed study of the negotiation of profit in DoD. The study found that the rates of profit and fee negotiated were almost the same regardless of the complexity of the work, the past performance of the contractor, or variations in other elements that might be considered relevant to the amount of profit included in the contract. It was concluded that a new procedure was needed to force contracting officers to use a profit negotiation process that recognized these different aspects of procurements. A major goal was to use profit to encourage good performance and penalize bad performance. FAR 15.404-4(a) now contains the following general guidance:

> (1) Profit or fee prenegotiation objectives do not necessarily represent net income to contractors. Rather, they represent that element of the potential total remuneration that contractors may receive for contract performance over and above allowable costs. This potential remuneration element and the Government's estimate of allowable costs to be incurred in contract performance together equal the Government's total prenegotiation objective. Just as actual costs may vary from estimated costs, the contractor's actual realized profit or fee may vary from negotiated profit or fee, because of such factors as efficiency of performance, incurrence of costs the Government does not recognize as allowable, and the contract type.
>
> (2) It is in the Government's interest to offer contractors opportunities for financial rewards sufficient to stimulate efficient contract performance, attract the best capabilities of qualified large and small business concerns to Government contracts, and maintain a viable industrial base.
>
> (3) Both the Government and contractors should be concerned with profit as a motivator of efficient and effective contract performance. Negotiations aimed merely at reducing prices by reducing profit, without proper recognition of the function of profit, are not in the Government's interest. Negotiation of extremely low profits, use of historical averages, or automatic application of predetermined percentages to total estimated costs do not provide proper motivation for optimum contract performance.

Since each structured approach imposes a formula on contracting officers, their discretion is significantly limited. The goal is to make profit determination considerably more objective than it has been in the past. However, there is no indication in any of the regulations that the objective is binding on either the contractor or the government. The profit or fee to be used in the contract is subject to free bargaining and is ultimately determined in the negotiation process, where the contracting officer has a substantial amount of discretion. Some regulations require that contracting officers document their profit analysis in the contract file. See, for example, DFARS 215.404-4(c)(2)(E), NFS 1815.404-470, and DEAR 915.404-4-70-3.

Agencies also retain considerable flexibility under the FAR policy. Thus, they may accommodate different policy objectives by varying the elements of their formula and the weights given to each element.

[2] Applicability of Structured Approach

Although FAR 15.404-4(b)(1)(i) states that agencies must use a structured approach to fee determination in all procurements where cost analysis is required, agencies generally do not use such approach when the agency is conducting a competitive procurement where the only significant analysis is a cost realism analysis. See DFARS 215.404-4(b)(1) stating that the approach must be used when certified cost or pricing data is obtained, and DFARS 215.404-4(c)(1) stating that the approach should not be used when making a cost realism analysis on competitive procurements, and NFS 1815.404-4(b)(1)(i)(A)(1) stating that the structured approach should be used when the contract is "awarded on the basis of other than full and open competition."

From the outset, it has been recognized that a structured approach is not applicable to all types of procurements, and FAR 15.404-4(b)(1)(ii) permits agencies to make exceptions to their policies. DFARS 215.404-4(c)(2)(C) states that the contracting officer may use an alternate structured approach (see 215.404-73) when

> (1) The contract action is—
>
> (i) At or below the certified cost or pricing data threshold (see FAR 15.403-4(a)(1));
> (ii) For architect-engineer or construction work;
> (iii) Primarily for delivery of material from subcontractors; or
> (iv) A termination settlement; or
>
> (2) The weighted guidelines method does not produce a reasonable overall profit objective and the head of the contracting activity approves use of the alternate approach in writing.

A similar list of exceptions is included in the guidance of the other agencies.

[3] Procedure

The structured approach to profit determination is a procedure used by the contracting officer to arrive at a "prenegotiation objective" on the profit that will be used in negotiations with the contractor, FAR 15.404-4(a). The regulations require the contracting officer to calculate this objective but contain very little guidance on the procedures to be used to obtain the information necessary to make this calculation. See DEAR 915.404-4(d), which states:

> The contracting officer's analysis of these prescribed factors is based on information available prior to negotiations. Such information is furnished in proposals, audit data, performance reports, preaward surveys and the like.

See also DFARS 215.404-4(c)(5) which permits contractors to furnish specific information in proposals:

> [T]he contracting officer may encourage the contractor to—
> (1) Present the details of its proposed profit amounts in the weighted guidelines format or similar structured approach; and

(2) Use the weighted guidelines format in developing profit objectives for negotiated subcontracts.

See, however, FAR 15.404-4(c)(5), which prohibits contracting officers from *requiring* contractors to submit such information.

In all of the structured profit approaches, the profit objective is determined by separately analyzing each factor in the formula and computing the dollars of profit for that factor. The contracting officer then totals the dollars of profit for each factor to arrive at the profit objective. When these policies were implemented in the 1980s, a number of agencies adopted forms in their FAR supplements with accompanying short explanations. However, most of the forms have been taken out of the procurement regulations and placed in agency acquisition manuals. The current forms are:

AGENCY	FORM
Department of Defense	DD Form 1547
Department of Energy	DOE Form 4220.23
National Aeronautics & Space Admin.	NASA Form 634
General Services Administration	GSA Form 1766
Department of Homeland Security	DHS Form 700-17
Department of Transportation	DOT Form 4220.32

Most of the computations in the structured approaches that have been used in the past are based on the anticipated costs of performance of the work. FAR 15.404-4(c)(3) provides that the contracting officer will use the government pre-negotiation cost objective amounts as the basis for calculating the profit objective. The result is that the contracting officer's profit objective is based on the government's analysis of the costs of performance rather than the contractor's proposed costs. If the costs are changed significantly during negotiation, an adjustment in the government's negotiated profit objective is appropriate.

[4] Profit Factors

While the FAR contains no prescribed formula, FAR 15.404-4(d)(1) does require all agencies to include, at a minimum, six factors in their structured approach:

(1) contractor effort;

(2) contract cost risk;

(3) federal socioeconomic programs;

(4) capital investments;

(5) cost control and other past accomplishments; and

(6) independent development.

These were the factors in the original DOD weighted guidelines formula which were adopted by the civilian agencies that implemented the OFPP Policy Letter and the FAR in the 1980s. The civilian agencies that still prescribe the use of most of these factors are DOE, DHS, DOT, and GSA. See DEAR 915.404-4-70-2(d); the DHS Acquisition Manual (HSAM) 3015.404-4, Appendix J; the DoT Acquisition Manual (TAM) 1215.404-4; and the GSA Acquisition Manual (GSAM) 515.404-70(d). The following detailed explanation of the proper implementation of these requirements uses material from the Armed Services Pricing Manual (ASPM) that was issued in 1986 because it contains the best explanation of how these factors should be utilized. However, the policy of each civilian agency must be carefully scrutinized to determine when it has adopted some element of the current DOD weighted guidelines technique.

The current DOD profit policy, adopted in 1987, dropped a number of these techniques and substituted new techniques illustrated in DD Form 1547 (**Figure 13-3**):

This policy is set forth in DFARS 215.404-71. See DFARS 215.404-4(d)(1) explaining that the "common factors (the six FAR factors) are embodied in the DoD structured approaches and need not be further considered by the contracting officer." In late 1999, NASA adopted a new profit policy that uses the first two elements of the DOD policy and some elements of the old policy, implemented through NASA Form 634.

The following detailed explanation of the proper implementation of these requirements uses material from these regulations because they contain the best guidance on the application of the factors.

[a] Contractor Effort

The first major element in the profit computation measures the value of the work to be performed on the contract. Intrinsic to this valuation process is the concept that a contractor is entitled to a higher rate of profit on its own efforts than on the efforts of others. In addition, the formulas provide higher profits on managerial and technological effort than on other more routine types of work. FAR 15.404-4(d)(1) gives the following guidance:

> (i) *Contractor effort.* This factor measures the complexity of the work and the resources required of the prospective contractor for contract performance. Greater profit opportunity should be provided under contracts requiring a high degree of professional and managerial skill and to prospective

RECORD OF WEIGHTED GUIDELINES APPLICATION						REPORT CONTROL SYMBOL DD-A&T(Q)1751	
1. REPORT NO.	2. BASIC PROCUREMENT INSTRUMENT IDENTIFICATION NO. a. PURCHASING OFFICE	b. FY	c. TYPE PROC INST CODE	d. PRISN	3. SPIIN	4. DATE OF ACTION a. YEAR	b. MONTH

		ITEM	COST CATEGORY	OBJECTIVE
5. CONTRACTING OFFICE CODE				
6. NAME OF CONTRACTOR		13.	MATERIAL	
		14.	SUBCONTRACTS	
7. DUNS NUMBER	8. FEDERAL SUPPLY CODE	15.	DIRECT LABOR	
		16.	INDIRECT EXPENSES	
9. DOD CLAIMANT PROGRAM	10. CONTRACT TYPE CODE	17.	OTHER DIRECT CHARGES	
		18.	SUBTOTAL COSTS *(13 thru 17)*	
11. TYPE EFFORT	12. USE CODE	19.	GENERAL AND ADMINISTRATIVE	
		20.	TOTAL COSTS *(18 + 19)*	

WEIGHTED GUIDELINES PROFIT FACTORS

ITEM	CONTRACTOR RISK FACTORS	ASSIGNED WEIGHTING	ASSIGNED VALUE	BASE *(Item18)*	PROFIT OBJECTIVE
21.	TECHNICAL	%			
22.	MANAGEMENT	%			
23.	COST CONTROL	%			
24.	PERFORMANCE RISK (COMPOSITE)				
25.	CONTRACT TYPE RISK				
		COSTS FINANCED	LENGTH FACTOR	INTEREST RATE	
26.	WORKING CAPITAL			%	
	CONTRACTOR FACILITIES CAPITAL EMPLOYED		ASSIGNED VALUE	AMOUNT EMPLOYED	
27.	LAND				
28.	BUILDINGS				
29.	EQUIPMENT				
30.				TOTAL PROFIT OBJECTIVE	

NEGOTIATED SUMMARY

		PROPOSED	OBJECTIVE	NEGOTIATED
31.	TOTAL COSTS			
32.	FACILITIES CAPITAL COST OF MONEY *(DD Form 1861)*			
33.	PROFIT			
34.	TOTAL PRICE *(Line 31 + 32 + 33)*			
35.	MARKUP RATE *(Line 32 + 33 divided by 31)*	%	%	%

CONTRACTING OFFICER APPROVAL

36. TYPED/PRINTED NAME OF CONTRACTING OFFICER *(Last, First, Middle Initial)*	37. SIGNATURE OF CONTRACTING OFFICER	38. TELEPHONE NO.	39. DATE SUBMITTED *(YYYYMMDD)*

OPTIONAL USE

96.	97.	98.	99.

DD FORM 1547, APR 1998 (EG) PREVIOUS EDITION MAY BE USED. Designed using Perform Pro, WHS/DIOR, Apr 98

Figure 13-3

contractors whose skills, facilities, and technical assets can be expected to lead to efficient and economical contract performance. The subfactors in paragraphs (d)(1)(i)(A) through (D) of this subsection shall be considered in determining contractor effort, but they may be modified in specific situations to accommodate differences in the categories used by prospective contractors for listing costs—

(A) *Material acquisition.* This subfactor measures the managerial and technical effort needed to obtain the required purchased parts and material, subcontracted items, and special tooling. Considerations include the complexity of the items required, the number of purchase orders and subcontracts to be awarded and administered, whether established sources are available or new or second sources must be developed, and whether material will be obtained through routine purchase orders or through complex subcontracts requiring detailed specifications. Profit consideration should correspond to the managerial and technical effort involved.

(B) *Conversion direct labor.* This subfactor measures the contribution of direct engineering, manufacturing, and other labor to converting the raw materials, data, and subcontracted items into the contract items. Considerations include the diversity of engineering, scientific, and manufacturing labor skills required and the amount and quality of supervision and coordination needed to perform the contract task.

(C) *Conversion-related indirect costs.* This subfactor measures how much the indirect costs contribute to contract performance. The labor elements in the allocable indirect costs should be given the profit consideration they would receive if treated as direct labor. The other elements of indirect costs should be evaluated to determine whether they merit only limited profit consideration because of their routine nature, or are elements that contribute significantly to the proposed contract.

(D) *General management.* This subfactor measures the prospective contractor's other indirect costs and general and administrative (G&A) expense, their composition, and how much they contribute to contract performance. Considerations include how labor in the overhead pools would be treated if it were direct labor, whether elements within the pools are routine expenses or instead are elements that contribute significantly to the proposed contract, and whether the elements require routine as opposed to unusual managerial effort and attention.

This FAR guidance reflects the logic in the original DoD weighted guidelines. However, the 1987 DoD weighted guidelines adopted an entirely different approach to calculating this element of the formula and NASA followed suit in 1999. The other civilian agencies continue to use the old approach set forth in the DoD weighted guidelines (with variation of the ranges of profit to be applied). The following discussion reviews the approaches separately and uses the prior DoD guidance when it provides the most helpful explanation of how the computation should be made.

[i] Civilian Agency Calculation

The weighted guidelines "value added" approach is implemented in the agencies' profit formulas by assigning varying weights to the elements of cost in the government's estimate of the cost of performance. See DEAR 915.404-4-

70(d). In this procedure, purchased effort (purchased parts, subcontracted items and other material) is given a weight of 1% to 3%, 4% or 5%, and direct labor is given weights of 4% to 20% (GSAM ¶ 515.404-4(d) prescribes 4% to 12%). Each agency prescribes slightly different weights for the different types of direct labor within the following ranges:

Scientific	10% to 20%
Project management/administration	8% to 20%
Engineering	8% to 15%
Manufacturing	4% to 9%
Support services	4% to 15%

These weights reflect the higher value given technological and management effort. Indirect costs are assigned weights by analyzing the specific elements of cost in the contractor's indirect cost pools and applying a weight to each element of cost in accordance with the general value-added theory. Each agency's policy must be examined to determine the specific percentages that are prescribed. In some cases, it is necessary to look to guidance from other sources because an agency's guidance may be sparse. The most detailed explanation of the application of these weights is contained in the ASPM.

Chapter 4 of the ASPM suggested at 4-7 that indirect cost pools not be analyzed for each procurement since the weight would not change until the composition of the pool changed significantly. While the ranges of weights to be used for each cost element are prescribed by the profit formula of the agency issuing the contract, the contracting officer is given considerable discretion in selecting the weight within the range. The ASPM gave the following guidance on assigning weights to material costs at 4-4:

> Weight ranges for material are lower than the ranges for other costs because material represents the lowest investment of resources per sales dollar. Analysis of direct material costs will show variations in the managerial and technical effort needed to obtain the material. A direct material cost of $1 million could represent a single subcontract with an established source for standard material, or it could include several subcontracts that require the contractor to find suppliers to develop difficult items to complex performance specifications. Obviously, the amount of managerial and technical effort is much greater in the second case than in the first.

The contractor that obtains maximum competition in procuring direct materials exerts greater effort than the contractor that routinely places repeat orders with established vendors. Subcontracts for professional or consulting services should be assigned a weight commensurate with the management liaison involved.

The normal low weight for direct materials is 2%. A lesser weighting should be used only in unusual circumstances where the contractor makes only a minimum contribution. You might use a weighting of less than 2%, for instance, if the material represents a large part of the total contract costs, is a follow-on order with an existing vendor, and is to be shipped directly from the vendor to the Government.

The ASPM guidance on labor costs is set forth at 4-5 as follows:

> There are two basic rules in assigning weights to the labor categories. First, all labor must be rated within minimum and maximum DFARS weights. For instance, all engineering labor must carry weights within the 9-to-15 percent range, and services labor must carry weights within ranges of 5-to-15 percent for direct labor and 4 to 8 percent for overhead. Second, except for services, labor carries the same weight whether it is classified as direct or indirect.
>
> One way to arrive at an appropriate weight is to use the contractor's job designations to classify labor into the categories shown in [the following table:]

Engineering	Manufacturing	Administrative
Top scientist or engineer	Department head	Top management
Senior engineering or project manager	Supervisor	Executive assistants
Engineer	Engineer	Professional staff
Junior engineer	Skilled	Clerical
Draftsman	Semi-skilled	Support
Technical writer	Unskilled	
Clerical	Support	
Support		

> Next, [an agency] might assign weights to the classes of labor. The assigned weights remain the same whether the salary cost represented by the job designation is treated as a direct or an indirect cost. [The agency] would determine the approximate dollar amounts attributable to salaries of personnel with these job designations and would multiply the amounts by the assigned weights.
>
> Assignment by job designations is only one method of arriving at an appropriate weight assignment. Another is to find the total scale of labor rates within the labor pool of the contractor's organization, determine the average

> labor rate for the particular contract, and assign the weight that bears the same relationship to the DFARS range of weights that the average labor rate for the contract bears to the total scale of labor rates in the labor pool.
>
> For example, if the scale of labor rates within the contractor's engineering organization is from $5 to $20 per hour, and the average engineering labor in the particular contract is $12 per hour, [an agency] could determine that $12 falls within the scale of $5 to $20 as 11.8 percent falls within the 9-to-15 percent range. As a result, [an agency] might assign a weight of 11.8 percent to the direct engineering labor input.

The same technique is used for indirect costs, except that the contracting officer has the discretion to assign weights to individual items of cost outside the prescribed ranges as long as the final weight given to the total indirect cost pool falls within the range in the formula, ASPM at 4-6.

All costs of performance are included in the cost base for purposes of making this profit calculation, except that the facilities capital cost of money provided for in FAR 31.205-10(a) is specifically required to be excluded from this base, FAR 15.404-4(c)(3).

[ii] DoD and NASA Calculation

In the DoD and NASA profit calculation, the contractor effort factor is now called the "performance risk" factor. See DFARS 215.404-71-2(a), which states:

> This profit factor addresses the contractor's degree of risk in fulfilling the contract requirements. The factor consists of two parts—
>
> (1) Technical—the technical uncertainties of performance.
>
> (2) Management/cost control—the degree of management effort necessary—
>
> (i) To ensure that contract requirements are met; and
>
> (ii) To reduce and control costs.

NASA uses the same logic but it separates the management and cost control factors into two separate factors, NASA Form 634 (Instruction sheet).

This calculation is accomplished by applying gross percentages (rather than percentages by cost element) to the government's estimate of the costs of performance excluding facilities capital cost of money, DFARS 215.404-71-2(b)(4). The DFARS contains two ranges of percentages to be applied in this calculation:

Calculation	Normal Value	Designated Range
Standard Calculation	5%	3% to 7%
Alternate Calculation	9%	7% to 11%

The standard calculation is used in most types of procurements. The alternate calculation is provided for those research and development and service contracts where the contractor has made a relatively low capital investment in facilities. It provides the 4% higher profit on the technical factor in lieu of the facilities-capital-employed factor. See DFARS 215.404-71-2(c) stating:

> (2) *Technology incentive.* For the technical factor only, contracting officers may use the technology incentive range for acquisitions that include development, production, or application of innovative new technologies. The technology incentive range does not apply to efforts restricted to studies, analyses, or demonstrations that have a technical report as their primary deliverable.

See also DFARS 215.404-71-2(d)(4)(i) giving the following additional guidance on the use of this incentive:

> Use the technology incentive range only for the most innovative contract efforts. Innovation may be in the form of—
>
> (A) Development or application of new technology that fundamentally changes the characteristics of an existing product or system and that results in increased technical performance, improved reliability, or reduced costs; or
>
> (B) New products or systems that contain significant technological advances over the products or systems they are replacing.

NASA does not provide for an alternate calculation to cover technology innovations. It has adopted a normal value of 6% and a range of 4% to 8% as the sole basis for its calculation, NASA Form 634.

The DoD profit calculation is made separately on the two different criteria—technical and management/cost control. The first step in the calculation is the determination by the contracting officer of the weight to be assigned to each of these criteria. These weights are determined on the basis of the importance of the criteria to the government in the performance of the contract. For example, if the contract is for research and development work requiring the use of new technology on a CPFF contract, the following weights might be appropriate:

Technical	60%
Management/Cost Control	40%

In contrast, if the contract is for the manufacture of an item with a stable design on a fixed-price type contract, the contracting officer might assign weights as follows:

Technical	20%
Management/Cost Control	80%

The next step in the calculation is the assignment of values to each criterion. The DoD FAR Supplement contains considerable guidance on the logic of assigning these values. With regard to the technical criterion, values are assigned on the basis of the difficulty and risk of the task in the specific contract. Thus, if the contract requires the contractor to perform development work using advanced technologies that require highly skilled personnel, a value above normal would be assigned. In contrast, a contract calling for routine technical effort would be assigned a value below normal. When DoD uses the technology incentive factor, the value is assigned on the basis of the amount of innovation required by the contract in comparison with the entire contract effort. With regard to the management/cost control criterion, the focus is more on past performance of the contractor in managing and controlling costs on prior work. However, the complexity of the tasks on the contract is also taken into consideration. In the NASA formula, management and cost control are dealt with as separate criteria.

The final step in the calculation is to arrive at a composite percentage. This is done using the assigned weights and values. For example, in the research and development contract calling for use of proven technology, the calculation might be as follows:

Criterion	Weight Assigned	Value Assigned	Weighted Value
Technical	55%	5.2%	2.86%
Management/Cost Control	45%	5.6%	2.52%
Composite Value			5.38%

If it were determined that the contract called for the use of highly innovative technology, the alternate calculation would be used. Such a calculation might be as follows:

Criterion	Weight Assigned	Value Assigned	Weighted Value
Technical	60%	9.6%	5.76%
Management/Cost Control	40%	5.4%	2.16%
Composite Value			7.92%

If NASA was awarding this same contract, the calculation might be as follows:

Criterion	Weight Assigned	Value Assigned	Weighted Value
Technical	60%	7.2%	4.32%
Management	20%	6.2%	1.24%
Cost Control	20%	6.2%	1.24%
Composite Value			6.80%

[b] Contract Cost Risk

The second major factor included in structured approaches to profit is the risk assumed by the contractor in the pricing arrangement. This factor *does not measure economic risk* assumed by the contractor in undertaking the contract, but merely the pricing risk as determined by the pricing arrangement. FAR 15.404-4(d)(1) contains the following discussion of this factor:

> (ii) *Contract cost risk.* (A) This factor measures the degree of cost responsibility and associated risk that the prospective contractor will assume as a result of the contract type contemplated and considering the reliability of the cost estimate in relation to the complexity and duration of the contract task. Determination of contract type should be closely related to the risks involved in timely, cost-effective, and efficient performance. This factor should compensate contractors proportionately for assuming greater cost risks.

Since the government assumes almost all of the risk of cost overruns on cost-reimbursement contracts, this factor is insignificant on such contracts. In contrast, it is quite significant on fixed-price contracts where the contractor assumes much of this risk. However, it varies somewhat between the profit policies of the different agencies. The normal values and the designated ranges used by the DoD are set forth in DFARS 215.404-71-3(c), as follows:

Contract type	Notes	Normal value (percent)	Designated range (percent)
Firm-fixed-price, no financing	(1)	5.0	4 to 6.
Firm-fixed-price, with performance-based payments	(6)	4.0	2.5 to 5.5.
Firm-fixed-price, with progress payments	(2)	3.0	2 to 4.

(continues)

Contract type	Notes	Normal value (percent)	Designated range (percent)
Fixed-price incentive, no financing	(1)	3.0	2 to 4.
Fixed-price incentive, with performance-based payments	(6)	2.0	0.5 to 3.5.
Fixed price with redetermination provision	(3)		
Fixed-price incentive, with progress payments	(2)	1.0	0 to 2.
Cost-plus-incentive-free	(4)	1.0	0 to 2.
Cost-plus-fixed-fee	(4)	0.5	0 to 1.
Time-and-materials (including overhaul contracts priced on time-and-materials basis)	(5)	0.5	0 to 1.
Labor-hour	(5)	0.5	0 to 1.
Firm-fixed-price, level-of-effort	(5)	0.5	0 to 1.

NASA uses these same levels but adds a category for CPAF contracts with a normal value of .75% and a range of .5% to 1.5%, NASA Form 634 (Instruction sheet).

DFARS 215.404-71-3(d) provides detailed guidance on the elements of the prospective contract that should be considered when determining whether to assign a profit factor at the upper or lower end of the prescribed range. These elements are length of contract, adequacy of cost data for projections, economic environment, nature and extent of subcontracting activity, protection provided to the contractor under contract provisions (*e.g.*, economic price adjustment clauses), the ceilings and share lines contained in incentive provisions, risks associated with contracts for foreign military sales not funded by U.S. appropriations, the extent and type of performance-based payments, and the amount of costs that have been incurred on a undefinitized contract before definitization. See NASA Form 634 (Instruction sheet) for similar guidance.

Civilian agencies tend to use different weightings for this factor depending on the type of procurement but the guidance varies from agency to agency. For example, the DOE Acquisition Guide calls for higher amounts for "equipment and supply contracts," slightly lesser amounts for research and development contracts, and even lower amounts for contracts for services. These service contract amounts are quite low, as follows:

Cost-Plus-Fixed-Fee	0 to 0.5%
Cost-Plus-Incentive-Fee	1 to 2%
Fixed-Price-Incentive	2 to 3%
Firm-Fixed-Price	3 to 4%

DHS Form 700-17 and DOT Form 4220.32 follow this same logic with lower profit rates for research and development and service contracts. GSAM ¶ 515.404-4(h)(3) merely specifies a range of 0% to 7% with broad guidance that cost-reimbursement type contracts should receive 0% to 3% and fixed-price type contracts 3% to 7%—with lower rates for service contracts.

The regulations and manuals of the civilian agencies contain a varied amount of guidance on how these ranges should be applied. However, the reliability of the cost estimate, the amount of risk that has been transferred to subcontractors, and whether the pricing action has occurred after work has commenced are all relevant to establishing the profit objective within these ranges.

[c] Federal Socioeconomic Programs

This factor has been included in the weighted guidelines since its inception. FAR 15.404-4(d)(1) contains the following guidance:

> (iii) *Federal socioeconomic programs.* This factor measures the degree of support given by the prospective contractor to Federal socioeconomic programs, such as those involving small business concerns, small business concerns owned and controlled by socially and economically disadvantaged individuals, women-owned small business concerns, handicapped sheltered workshops, and energy conservation. Greater profit opportunity should be provided contractors that have displayed unusual initiative in these programs.

This factor is not considered separately in the DoD formula but is made a part of the management evaluation in the performance risk area. In NASA, the factor is not included in the performance risk evaluation but is weighted at –0.5% to 0.5% of the costs used as the base for the performance risk factor. In the formulas of the other civilian agencies, it is treated as a separate factor and handled in one of two ways. In DoE, the factor has a range of –5% to 5% of the basic profit objective derived from adding all of the other profit factors. In GSA, the factor is weighted at –0.5% to 0.5% of the costs used as the base for the contractor effort factor. In DHS, it is part of an "other" factor weighted at the same –0.5% to 0.5%. In either case, the guidance generally provides that "merely satisfactory" effort in implementing these programs is entitled to no weight, that "unusual" support is entitled to a plus weight, and that "failure or unwillingness" to support these programs should receive a minus weight. See the DOE Acquisition Guide. In either case, the regulations provide that "unusual initiative" or "extraordinary steps" in supporting these programs is entitled to positive weight and that "nonparticipation in or violation of" these programs should receive a minus weight.

[d] Capital Investments

Originally, OFPP Policy Letter 80-7 required that all structured profit approaches consider capital investment in *both facilities and working capital*. However, the DoD weighted guidelines never included investment in working capital because the DoD did not agree with this guidance. As a result, FAR 15.404-4(d)(1), issued in 1984, states this requirement in very general language, as follows:

> (iv) *Capital Investments*. This factor takes into account the contribution of contractor investments to efficient and economical contract performance.

Agencies have adopted a wide variety of techniques to calculate the amount of profit/fee under this factor. They have also adopted different approaches to the correlation of this profit factor to the allowability of the cost of facilities capital (imputed interest on the cost of facilities).

[i] Precise Measurement of Facilities Capital

In 1987, the DoD weighted guidelines adopted a rather precise mathematical method of determining the amount of profit to be given for facilities capital. This approach is now being followed by a number of agencies with significantly less guidance on its implementation.

The approach is spelled out in DFARS 215.404-71-4(f) calling for use of a factor that is computed based on the following percentages of the net book value of capital equipment employed on the contract:

Normal Value	Designated Range
17.5%	10% to 25%

Note that this computation does not include the value of land or buildings which have been capitalized.

The goal of this relatively large profit factor is to motivate the contractor to invest in labor-saving equipment. Thus, DFARS 215.404-71-4(g) provides the following guidance on selection of the percentage within the designated range:

(2) *Above normal conditions.* (i) The contracting officer may assign a higher-than-normal value if the facilities capital investment has direct, identifiable, and exceptional benefits. Indicators are—

(A) New investments in state-of-the-art technology which reduce acquisition cost or yield other tangible benefits such as improved product quality or accelerated deliveries;

(B) Investments in new equipment for research and development applications.

(ii) The contracting officer may assign a value significantly above normal when there are direct and measurable benefits in efficiency and significantly reduced acquisition costs on the effort being priced. Maximum values apply only to those cases where the benefits of the facilities capital investment are substantially above normal.

(3) *Below normal conditions.* (i) The contracting officer may assign a lower-than-normal value if the facilities capital investment has little benefit to DoD. Indicators are—

(A) Allocations of capital apply predominantly to commercial product lines;

(B) Investments are for such things as furniture and fixtures, home or group level administrative offices, corporate aircraft and hangars, gymnasiums; or

(C) Facilities are old or extensively idle.

(ii) The contracting officer may assign a value significantly below normal when a significant portion of defense manufacturing is done in an environment characterized by outdated, inefficient, and labor-intensive capital equipment.

The net book value of facilities employed on the contract is calculated using a two-step process. The first step is to compute the cost of money factors for each overhead pool of the contractor's organizations performing work on the contract. This calculation is made using Form CASB-CMF and following the procedures set forth in CAS 414, 48 C.F.R. § 9904.414. These cost-of-money factors are percentages (like overhead rates) reflecting the ratio of the imputed cost of capital (imputed interest) to the cost base (normally direct labor dollars) for the overhead pool for any fiscal period. They provide a mechanism for allocating the imputed cost of capital to any specific contract, and they are also used to calculate the net book value of assets employed in the performance of a contract. This second step of the profit calculation is made using DD Form 1861.

Here, the imputed cost of interest attributable to each overhead pool is calculated by multiplying the cost-of-money factor for each pool by the estimated expenditure of effort on the contract in that pool (direct labor dollars in most cases). The total imputed cost of capital obtained from this calculation is divided by the cost of money rate (interest rate) to provide the net book value of facilities used on the contract. This amount is then entered on DD Form 1547 (see

Figure 13-3) as the measurement base, and the weight determined to be applicable for equipment is applied to compute this profit factor.

DoE has adopted the DoD policy with regard to facilities capital, DOE Acquisition Guide ¶ 15.4-2D, using a range of 5% to 20% of facilities capital employed on contracts for manufacturing. DHS has also adopted this technique in DHS Form 700-17 using a range of 16% to 20% of the net book value of facilities capital employed on the contract. DoT also uses the range of 16% to 20% of the net book value of facilities capital employed on the contract, DOT Form 4220.32. In order to apply this factor, contracting officers in these civilian agencies may need to review DFARS 215.404-71-4 which contains the most detailed guidance on this issue.

[ii] Discretionary Determination

NASA and GSA follow discretionary approaches to this factor. GSAM ¶ 515.404-70(d). NASA provides that a weight of −1% to 1% of the cost base may be included in the profit for this factor, with minimal guidance. See also GSAM ¶ 515.404-704(d) which calls for a range of −2% to 2% with minimal guidance.

[iii] Working Capital Techniques

The DoD has adopted a "working capital adjustment" factor to compensate for the use of working capital in fixed-price type contracts with a very long period of performance and providing for progress payments, DFARS 215.404-71-3(f). This factor also compensates for unusual increases in interest rates. The factor is only applicable when cost-based progress payments are included in a fixed-price type contract and is computed by the following calculation:

$$\text{costs financed} \times \text{contract length factor} \times \text{current interest rate}$$

The costs financed are the amount of costs not paid through progress payments. Thus, if the contract contains a provision for progress payments at the rate of 75% of costs incurred, the costs financed would be 25% of the total estimated costs of performance excluding facilities capital cost of money, DFARS 215.404-71-3(e). This regulation calls for reduction of this amount "as appropriate" in the following circumstances:

(i) The contractor has little cash investment (e.g., subcontractor progress payments liquidated late in period of performance);

(ii) Some costs are covered by special financing provisions, such as advance payments; or

(iii) The contract is multiyear and there are special funding arrangements.

The contract length factor is computed using the following table:

Period to perform substantive portion (in months)	Contract length factor
21 or less	.40
22 to 27	.65
28 to 33	.90
34 to 39	1.15
40 to 45	1.40
46 to 51	1.65
52 to 57	1.90
58 to 63	2.15
64 to 69	2.40
70 to 75	2.65
76 or more	2.90

DFARS 215.404-71-3(f) provides that the contract period should exclude periods where only minimum performance is called for (usually at the beginning of the contract) and should average the end date of contract performance when multiple deliveries are required. It also provides for exclusion from the calculation of option years and multiyear contract years beyond the initial program year. The interest rate to be used is the rate established by the Secretary of the Treasury that is used to calculate the government's failure to make prompt payments.

As an example of this calculation, assume a $10 million fixed-price contract calls for progress payments of 75% and deliveries of three aircraft in months 36, 38, and 40 after award of the contract (yielding an average contract period of 38 months). This factor would be derived by the following calculation:

Costs Financed	Contract Length Factor	Interest Rate	Factor
$2,500,000	× 1.15	× 2.5%	= $71,875

NASA uses this same factor following the DoD guidance.

DoE has a much broader factor for working capital, requiring the discretionary consideration of the amount of "operating capital" needed to perform the contract under a broad factor called "other considerations"—with a profit factor of up to 4% of costs. The DOE Acquisition Guide suggests that a negative profit adjustment would be appropriate for cost-reimbursement contracts. GSAM ¶ 515.404-70(h)(4)(ii) calls for the consideration of the amount of working capital needed to finance the contract without any detailed guidance as to the amount of profit adjustment.

[e] Cost Control and Other Past Accomplishments

FAR 15.404-4(d)(1) gives the following guidance on cost control and other past accomplishments:

> (v) *Cost-control and other past accomplishments.* This factor allows additional profit opportunities to a prospective contractor that has previously demonstrated its ability to perform similar tasks effectively and economically. In addition, consideration should be given to measures taken by the prospective contractor that result in productivity improvements, and other cost-reduction accomplishments that will benefit the Government in follow-on contracts.

It can be seen that this factor covers several different aspects of the contractor's past or prospective performance. Contractor performance, in general, was a factor in the original weighted guidelines adopted by the DoD in 1964 but was deleted from the formula in 1976. The remaining elements of this factor were deleted from the DoD weighted guidelines in 1987.

The civilian agencies have adopted a broad factor called "other considerations" or "other" where a number of the FAR factors are merged and other issues are included. DoE, for example, adopted a broad factor called "other considerations" with a weight of −5% to 5% of the basic profit objective. This factor includes (1) cost control and other past accomplishments, (2) complexity of research and development or services assignment, and (3) operating capital. The DOE Acquisition Guide provides the following guidance on the cost control element of this factor:

> This subfactor benefits prospective contractors who have performed similar tasks effectively and economically, or who have taken cost-control measures that benefit Government contracts. Among other things, consideration is given to efforts to improve or develop new product, manufacturing, or performance technologies to reduce production cost.

DHS includes a similar factor on DHS Form 700-17 called "productivity" (see the discussion in Appendix J of the HSAM) and DoT includes a similar factor on DOT Form 4220.32.

GSAM ¶ 515.404-70(d) has a separate factor covering cost control and other past accomplishments with a weight of −2% to 2% of the cost base. However, the manual contains no guidance on the application of this factor.

[f] Independent Development

FAR 15.404-4(d)(1) contains the following guidance on independent development:

> (vi) *Independent development.* Under this factor, the contractor may be provided additional profit opportunities in recognition of independent development efforts relevant to the contract end item without Government assistance. The contracting officer should consider whether the development cost was recovered directly or indirectly from Government sources.

The original DoD weighted guidelines contained this factor with a weight of 1% to 4% of the cost base, but it was deleted from the DFARS in 1987. NASA has also deleted any reference to the independent development factor from its regulations.

This factor is still included in most of the civilian agency policies. DoE has a factor of 1% to 4% of costs for contractors with a "viable" independent research and development program or that develop "items with energy program applications with no direct Government assistance and little or no indirect Government assistance."

GSAM ¶ 515.404-70(d) has a factor for "independent development and additional factors" with a weight of −2% to 2% of the cost base. The manual contains no guidance on the application of this factor. DoT (DOT Form 4220.32) and DHS (DHS Form 700-17) have a factor of 1% to 4% for independent development, which is applicable to manufacturing and research and development contracts (not service contracts).

[g] Other Factors

FAR 15.404-4(d)(2) also permits agencies to include additional factors in their structured approaches to profit. Several of the civilian agencies have included such factors. See, for example, the DOE Acquisition Guide which provides for a "productivity/performance adjustment" to be added to the profit objective for follow-on contracts in cases where the contractor has taken special steps to reduce the costs of performance of an entire program. This factor is designed to overcome the reluctance of contractors to reduce costs when they anticipate follow-on contracts that would benefit from such cost reductions but would yield commensurately lower profits. DHS also discusses this factor in Appendix J of the HSAM. DoT also uses this factor in DOT Form 4220.32.

[5] Facilities Capital Cost of Money Adjustment

FAR 31.205-10(b)(3) provides that the facilities capital cost of money will be an allowable cost of performance of government contracts if it is "specifically identified or proposed in cost proposals," but FAR 15.404-4(c)(3) provides that it will not be included in the cost base for computation of the fee. FAR 15.404-4 also provides that a contractor can waive this cost, and FAR 52.215-16 provides a Waiver of Facilities Capital Cost of Money clause to be used when the contractor makes this election.

If the contractor does not waive this cost, the FAR is silent on any profit adjustment for this cost element. However, OFPP Policy Letter 80-7 (canceled in 1984 but replaced by FAR policy) addressed this issue as follows:

> (2) Agencies shall ensure that contractors are not compensated for facilities capital cost of money both as a direct or indirect cost and in profit or fee. Before the allowability of facilities capital cost of money, this cost was included in profits and fees. Therefore, profit and fee prenegotiation objectives shall be reduced if necessary to reflect this refinement in cost accounting practices. This reduction may be accomplished by means of offsets; that is, by (i) using a dollar-for-dollar offset in the Government's prenegotiation profit or fee objective or (ii) incorporating a common offset factor under an agency's structured approach. No offset is necessary when the profit rates applied to the profit analysis factors under an agency's structured approach already take into account the allowability of facilities capital cost of money.

The agencies have split on which of these two techniques to use. GSA uses the "dollar-for-dollar offset" technique by providing that any facilities capital cost of money included in the estimated cost will be deducted from the profit objective, GSAM ¶ 515.404-70(f). DoT (DOT Form 4220.32) and DHS (DHS Form 700-17) require the "dollar-for-dollar" adjustment only on research and development and service contracts.

The Departments of Defense and Energy require no such reduction because *they have incorporated the offset in the standard profit formula.* In such cases, it would be improper for the contracting officer to take any additional offset when recognizing the cost of facilities capital cost of money. Similarly, it would be unwise for the contractor to waive the recovery of such costs in these circumstances since no profit offset is required. Unfortunately, most of the agency regulations are silent on this issue. These departments do recognize the potential overlap of these treatments of the facilities capital cost of money by excluding it from the base costs used to calculate the other profit elements.

DFARS 215.404-73(b)(2) permits contracting officers to use alternate formulas in lieu of the weighted guidelines formula but requires such alternate formulas to include an offset in the amount of the facilities capital cost of money. The regulation explains the need for this adjustment as follows:

> (ii) This adjustment is needed for the following reason: The values of the profit factors used in the weighted guidelines method were adjusted to recognize the shift in facilities capital cost of money from an element of profit to an element of contract cost (FAR 31.205-10) and reductions were made directly to the profit factors for performance risk. In order to ensure that this policy is applied to all DoD contracts which allow facilities capital cost of money, similar adjustments shall be made to contracts which use alternate structured approaches.

DFARS 215.404-74(c) also requires contracting officers to apply this offset to the base fee on CPAF contracts.

[6] Application to Nonprofit Organizations

Although the structured profit approaches currently in use were devised to determine the profits negotiated with commercial organizations, a number of agency regulations provide that they will also be used to calculate the profits paid to nonprofit organizations with certain prescribed adjustments. For example, DFARS 215.404-72(b) calls for the following adjustments:

> (1) Modifications to performance risk (Blocks 21-23 of the DD Form 1547).
>
> (i) If the contracting officer assigns a value from the standard designated range (see 215.404-71-2(c)), reduce the fee objective by an amount equal to 1 percent of the costs in Block 20 of the DD Form 1547. Show the net (reduced) amount on the DD Form 1547.
>
> (ii) Do not assign a value from the technology incentive designated range.
>
> (2) Modifications to contract type risk (Block 24 of the DD Form 1547). Use a designated range of −1 percent to 0 percent instead of the values in 215.404-71-3. There is no normal value.

Since the alternate performance risk factor would be used in almost all contracts with nonprofit organizations, the net result of this policy is the use of a profit factor that is 3% (of the cost base) lower than that used with profit-making organizations. Similar guidance is contained in Appendix A of the HSAM. Similarly, NFS 1815.404-471-1 provides for the use of a structured approach for nonprofit organizations other than educational institutions. This regulation states:

> (b) For contracts with nonprofit organizations under which profit or fee is involved, an adjustment of up to 3 percent of the costs in Block 13 of NASA Form 634 must be subtracted from the total profit/fee objective. In developing this adjustment, it is necessary to consider the following factors:
>
> (1) Tax position benefits;
> (2) Granting of financing through letters of credit;
> (3) Facility requirements of the nonprofit organization; and
> (4) Other pertinent factors that may work to either the advantage or disadvantage of the contractor in its position as a nonprofit organization.

See also GSAM ¶ 515.404-70(i) containing the same guidance.

DEAR 915.404-4-70-5(c) calls for the payment of fees to nonprofit organizations other than educational institutions using the structured profit approach reduced by at least 25%.

§ 13.08 PRICE NEGOTIATION PROCEDURES

The extent of negotiation will vary from one procurement to another depending on the nature of the procurement, the type of analysis done by the government, and the past business dealings of the parties. If price analysis shows that the price of a commercial item is less than the market price, there may be little need for negotiation. In contrast, if cost analysis is done on a new item where the government agency has had little experience with the contractor, protracted negotiations may be necessary to permit the contracting officer to gain confidence in the offeror's estimating system and the price to be paid. In all cases, sufficient negotiations must be conducted to permit the contracting officer to determine that the price to be paid is fair and reasonable, FAR 15.404-1(a).

While the extent of negotiation is left to the discretion of the contracting officer, there are two procedures relating to the negotiation process that are mandatory. First, prior to entering into a price negotiation, the contracting officer must establish a prenegotiation objective. Second, after completing the negotiation, the contracting officer must prepare and circulate a price negotiation memorandum (PNM). These procedures are discussed in this section.

[A] Prenegotiation Objectives

FAR 15.406-1 requires the determination of prenegotiation objectives as follows:

> (a) The prenegotiation objectives establish the Government's initial negotiation position. They assist in the contracting officer's determination of fair and reasonable price. They should be based on the results of the contracting officer's analysis of the offeror's proposal, taking into consideration all pertinent information including field pricing assistance, audit reports and technical analysis, fact-finding results, independent Government cost estimates and price histories.
>
> (b) The contracting officer shall establish prenegotiation objectives before the negotiation of any pricing action. The scope and depth of the analysis supporting the objectives should be directly related to the dollar value, importance, and complexity of the pricing action. When cost analysis is required, the contracting officer shall document the pertinent issues to be negotiated, the cost objectives, and a profit or fee objective.

This process forces the contracting officer to assimilate all of the data prepared by the offeror, the government auditor, the administrative contracting officer, and all other specialists who have reviewed the proposed pricing action. The result should be a government negotiating position that represents the government's best estimate of a fair and reasonable price. See the DOE Acquisition Manual for a very detailed template to be used to prepare prenegotiation plans.

Some agencies require the contracting officer to obtain approval from a higher authority before the negotiation of major contracts. See, for example, NFS 1815.406-171, requiring each field center to establish a formal system for the review of prenegotiation memoranda, and NFS 1815.406-172, requiring approval of the prenegotiation position by the assistant administrator for procurement before negotiations on any procurement action selected for headquarters review.

DoD has adopted a procedure to "adjudicate" significant disagreements between the contracting officer and a DCAA auditor during preparation of the prenegotiation objectives regarding disallowed costs that have been included in contractor proposals. See DoD PGI 215.406-1.

[B] Negotiation

The contracting officer is the key government person in the negotiation process. FAR 15.404-1(a)(1) provides that the contracting officer is "responsible for evaluating the reasonableness of the offered prices," and FAR 15.306(d)(3) states "the scope and extent of discussions are a matter of contracting officer to judgment." See also FAR 15.405 providing the following guidance on price negotiation:

> (a) The purpose of performing cost or price analysis is to develop a negotiation position that permits the contracting officer and the offeror an opportunity to reach agreement on a fair and reasonable price. A fair and reasonable price does not require that agreement be reached on every element of cost, nor is it mandatory that the agreed price be within the contracting officer's initial negotiation position. Taking into consideration the advisory recommendations, reports of contributing specialists, and the current status of the contractor's purchasing system, the contracting officer is responsible for exercising the requisite judgment needed to reach a negotiated settlement with the offeror and is solely responsible for the final price agreement. However, when significant audit or other specialist recommendations are not adopted, the contracting officer should provide rationale that supports the negotiation result in the price negotiation documentation.
>
> (b) The contracting officer's primary concern is the overall price the Government will actually pay. The contracting officer's objective is to negotiate a contract of a type and with a price providing the contractor the greatest incentive for efficient and economical performance. The negotiation of a contract type and a price are related and should be considered together with the issues of risk and uncertainty to the contractor and the Government. Therefore, the contracting officer should not become preoccupied with any single element and should balance the contract type, cost, and profit or fee negotiated to achieve a total result—a price that is fair and reasonable to both the Government and the contractor.

While this guidance merely provides that the contracting officer should take "into consideration" the recommendations of other government specialists such as auditors, price analysts, technical personnel, or lawyers, FAR 15.404-2(a)(3) provides that when "field pricing assistance" is obtained, the contracting officer is "encouraged to team with appropriate field experts throughout the acquisition process, including negotiations." Auditors are required to be included in DoD negotiations involving indirect costs by 10 U.S.C. § 3745 (formerly § 2324(f)(3)), stating:

> The Federal Acquisition Regulation shall provide that, to the maximum extent practicable, the contract auditor be present at any negotiation or meeting with the contractor regarding a determination of the allowability of indirect costs of the contractor.

DoD PGI 215.404-2(c)(i) suggests obtaining audit assistance on procurements (both contractor and subcontractor) over $10 million if they are fixed-price and over $100 million if they are cost-reimbursement.

[C] Price Negotiation Memorandum

FAR 15.406-3 requires the preparation of a PNM on each negotiated procurement as follows:

> (a) The contracting officer shall document in the contract file the principal elements of the negotiated agreement. The documentation (e.g., price negotiation memorandum (PNM)) shall include the following:
>
> (1) The purpose of the negotiation.
>
> (2) A description of the acquisition, including appropriate identifying numbers (e.g., RFP No.).
>
> (3) The name, position, and organization of each person representing the contractor and the Government in the negotiation.
>
> (4) The current status of any contractor systems (e.g., purchasing, estimating, accounting, and compensation) to the extent they affected and were considered in the negotiation.
>
> (5) If cost or pricing data were not required in the case of any price negotiation exceeding the cost or pricing data threshold, the exception used and the basis for it.
>
> (6) If cost or pricing data were required, the extent to which the contracting officer—
>
> (i) Relied on the cost or pricing data submitted and used them in negotiating the price;
>
> (ii) Recognized as inaccurate, incomplete, or noncurrent any cost or pricing data submitted; the action taken by the contracting officer and the contractor as a result; and the effect of the defective data on the price negotiated; or

(iii) Determined that an exception applied after the data were submitted and, therefore, considered not to be cost or pricing data.

(7) A summary of the contractor's proposal, any field pricing assistance recommendations, including the reasons for any pertinent variances from them, the Government's negotiation objective, and the negotiated position. Where the determination of price reasonableness is based on cost analysis, the summary shall address the amount of each major cost element. When determination of price reasonableness is based on price analysis, the summary shall include the source and type of data used to support the determination.

(8) The most significant facts or considerations controlling the establishment of the prenegotiation objectives and the negotiated agreement including an explanation of any significant differences between the two positions.

(9) To the extent such direction has a significant effect on the action, a discussion and quantification of the impact of direction given by Congress, other agencies, and higher-level officials (i.e., officials who would not normally exercise authority during the award and review process for the instant contract action).

(10) The basis for the profit or fee prenegotiation objective and the profit or fee negotiated.

(11) Documentation of fair and reasonable pricing.

(b) Whenever a field pricing assistance has been obtained, the contracting officer shall forward a copy of the negotiation documentation to the office(s) providing assistance. When appropriate, information on how advisory field support can be made more effective should be provided separately.

See DoD PGI 215.406-3 altering ¶ (a)(7) above to state:

(a)(7) Include the principal factors related to the disposition of findings and recommendations contained in preaward and postaward contract audit and other advisory reports.

This provision was adopted to implement a policy memorandum from the Director, Defense Procurement and Acquisition Policy on December 4, 2009, requiring contracting officers to resolve differences with prenegotiation audit reports by the DCAA on acquisitions over $10 million. See also Air Force FAR Supplement 5315.406-3 for a very detailed checklist covering many aspects of a PNM. See also NFS 1815.406-3(a)(i) stating that no PNM is required when a contract is awarded "under competitive negotiated procedures."

Contractors should also prepare a memorandum of negotiations in at least as great detail as is required of the contracting officer. This memorandum should compare the original price or cost proposed and the price or cost agreed to with an explanation of the justification for the variations. It should also describe the results of any negotiations of the profit or fee with a similar explanation of any significant differences that were agreed to.

As stated in FAR 15.405(a), the parties to the negotiation are not required to agree on each element of cost in the ultimate negotiated price. As a result, it is very likely that the memorandum of each party will contain a different explanation of the way the final cost estimate was calculated. If there is a subsequent dispute over the adequacy of the contractor's submission of certified cost or pricing data, it would be expected that the memorandum of the contracting officer would be the best evidence of whether the price was significantly altered by the data deficiency, *McDonnell Douglas Corp.*, ASBCA 12786, 69-2 BCA ¶ 7897; and *Sperry Corp. Computer Sys., Def. Sys. Div.*, ASBCA 29525, 88-3 BCA ¶ 20,975. See, however, *Sperry Rand Corp.*, DOTCAB 1144, 82-2 BCA ¶ 15,812, *recons. denied*, 84-1 BCA ¶ 16,968, where the contractor was able to persuade the board that no price reduction should be made because its negotiation memorandum reflected the fact that it had reduced its negotiating position to reflect the undisclosed data. Compare *McDonnell Douglas Helicopter Co.*, ASBCA 41378, 92-1 BCA ¶ 24,655, where the board denied a contractor's motion for summary judgment based on its price reduction where there was no evidence that the contracting officer knew that the reduction was based on undisclosed price concessions from subcontractors. See 10 U.S.C. § 3706 (formerly § 2306a(e)(3)(C)) and 41 U.S.C. § 3506(c)(3), stating that it is not a defense to a government claim for a price reduction because of defective cost or pricing data that "the contract was based on an agreement between the contractor and the United States about the total cost of the contract and there was no agreement about the cost of each item procured under such contract." Of course, if the parties do negotiate and agree on specific costs, they will be the basis for the price adjustment for defective cost or pricing data, *Grumman Aerospace Corp.*, ASBCA 35188, 90-2 BCA ¶ 22,842.

CHAPTER 14

COLLATERAL POLICIES

§ 14.01 INTRODUCTION

The primary focus of this book is on how the federal government achieves the primary goal of any procurement: obtaining timely satisfaction of its needs at fair prices under fair terms and conditions. However, the government also uses the acquisition process to implement policies that have little or no direct relationship to, and are often in tension with, the primary goals of procurement. For example, in choosing a contractor, the government may give weight to the size of the contractor (i.e., is it a small business?); the place of performance (i.e., is work being done in an area of high unemployment?); the ownership of the contractor (i.e., is it women-owned?); and the compliance of the contractor with a variety of other federal standards (e.g., minimum wage and hour requirements). This chapter examines the major collateral policies, particularly those that have social or economic goals as their primary focus.

Implementing these collateral policies through the acquisition process sometimes conflicts with the government's policy of full and open competition and may increase the total costs of a procurement. However, the prevailing view is that these negative features are offset by the benefits that flow to many contractors that would otherwise be excluded from the process.

There are a number of ways in which collateral policies impact on the government procurement function. First, the contract price may be increased by excluding from award an offeror with a potentially lower price. For example, to implement a collateral policy, an agency may specify that award will be made only to offerors in a preferred group, even though entities outside that group may be able to offer lower prices. Contractors' administrative costs of implementing collateral programs also lead to higher overall prices. Second, agencies also incur additional costs in implementing the policies. They need to prepare, maintain, and enforce extensive regulations and may become involved in protests over whether particular awards are consistent with the rules concerning collateral policies. Some observers have also suggested that collateral policies sometimes result in awards to firms that are more likely to default, thereby seriously impeding the procurement process and ultimately causing added expense and delays to the involved agencies.

In view of these factors, there has been constant debate over whether the government should use the procurement process to implement collateral policies. Proponents of implementation argue that it is reasonable and effective to use the government's purchasing power to carry out policies aiding disadvantaged persons, reducing unemployment, reducing pollution, conserving energy, and accomplishing other beneficial purposes. These proponents also argue that the policies broaden the base of suppliers, thereby ultimately increasing competition for federal contracts.

Opponents contend that since the costs of implementing collateral policies are high and may be hidden, there rarely is any conclusive determination that the costs are justified by the benefits. They argue further that the collateral policies are often difficult to reconcile with one another and frequently become outmoded, that the acquisition process is slowed and made more complicated by the collateral policies, and that some potentially excellent contractors become discouraged by the preferences and by the complex regulations that their enforcement requires. This view has prevailed, to some extent, by the adoption in the Federal Acquisition Streamlining Act of provisions calling for the inapplicability of some of the collateral policies when the government uses simplified acquisition procedures or procures commercial items. See Chapters 8 and 9 for a discussion of this relaxation of the collateral policies.

There is a view that collateral policies can be implemented only when authorized by statute. GAO has ruled that an executive agency needs a clear grant of authority from Congress to implement a collateral policy that limits those who are eligible for award of contracts, 10 Comp. Gen. 294 (A-34106) (1931); 42 Comp. Gen. 1 (B-148930) (1962). GAO also has held that a particular executive agency's rules for collateral policies must be consistent with higher-level executive branch regulations, *Educational Servs. Grp.*, 62 Comp. Gen. 353 (B-210420), 83-1 CPD ¶ 466.

Statutory authority for collateral policies may be explicit or implicit. Examples of explicit statutory authority are the Buy American Act, 41 U.S.C. § 8301 et seq., and the Small Business Act, 15 U.S.C. § 631 et seq. Implicit authority can be found in the general language of the procurement statutes, particularly in the Federal Property and Administrative Services Act (FPASA), 40 U.S.C. § 121 (stating that "The President may prescribe policies and directives that the President considers necessary to carry out this subtitle") and § 501 (requiring procurement of goods and services in a manner "advantageous to the Federal Government in terms of economy, efficiency, or service"). See *American Fed'n of Labor & Congress of Indus. Orgs. v. Kahn*, 618 F.2d 784 (D.C. Cir.), *cert. denied*, 443 U.S. 915 (1979), where the court sustained the power of the President to deny contract awards to companies that were in violation of presidentially imposed wage and price standards; and *Contractors Ass'n of E. Pa. v. Secretary of Labor*, 442 F.2d 159 (3d Cir.), *cert. denied*, 404 U.S. 854 (1971), where the court sustained equal employment contract provisions promulgated under Executive Order 11,246. Compare *Liberty Mut. Ins. Co. v. Friedman*, 639 F.2d 164 (4th Cir. 1981), where the court held that this statutory authority did not authorize the imposition of equal employment obligations on a workers' compensation insurer. In *Chamber of Commerce v. Reich*, 74 F.3d 1322 (D.C. Cir. 1996), the court reversed the district court's finding that the President had authority under the FPASA to issue an executive order authorizing the Secretary of Labor to disqualify workers with federal contracts exceeding $100,000 who hire permanent replacement workers during a lawful economic strike. The court stated that although the broad contract management authority under the FPASA generally permits the President to draw on policy views directed beyond immediate concerns with the quality and price of purchased goods, labor relations are viewed differently because of the NLRA and its broad field of preemption.

GAO also has upheld some collateral policies where authorization was found in broad statutory language, *Fairplain Dev. Co.*, 59 Comp. Gen. 409 (B-192483), 80-1 CPD ¶ 293 (policy dealing with preference for location of federal facilities in urban areas).

§ 14.02 POLICIES ASSISTING SMALL BUSINESSES

Congress has authorized a number of programs that are designed to assist small businesses in the procurement process. These programs are under the general supervision and control of the Small Business Administration (SBA) and are promulgated by the Small Business Act, 15 U.S.C. § 631 et seq. Under this Act, the SBA establishes small business size standards, rules on size appeals, and is solely authorized to make determinations that a small business is not a responsible contractor. The Act also establishes a number of business preferences for small businesses, including "set-aside" programs and programs to assist in small business subcontracting. These various programs are discussed in this section.

[A] Size Determination

The Small Business Act defines a "small business concern" as one that is independently owned and operated and that is not dominant in its field of operation, 15 U.S.C. § 632(a)(1). The statute provides that a concern's number of employees and dollar business volume are the criteria which determine whether it qualifies as a small business. The SBA has established size criteria for numerous classes of businesses, as classified in the North American Industry Classification System (NAICS). The NAICS Manual is at *https://www.census.gov/eos/www/naics/*. See 13 C.F.R. § 121.201 for a listing of size standards by industry, NAICS code, and description. When a procurement is directed to small businesses, the contracting officer is required to identify the appropriate NAICS code in the solicitation, FAR 19.303(a). If different products or services are included in a procurement, the solicitation must state the appropriate NAICS code for each product or service, FAR 19.303(b). The contracting officer's determination of the appropriate NAICS code is "final," FAR 19.303(c), but if appealed to the SBA, the contracting officer must follow the decision of the SBA, *Eagle Home Medical Corp.*, Comp. Gen. Dec. B-402387, 2010 CPD ¶ 82. SBA decisions on the appropriate NAICS code are also binding on GAO, *DynaLantic Corp.*, Comp. Gen. Dec. B-402326, 2010 CPD ¶ 103. If an agency awards a contract based on the SBA's determination of the appropriate NAICS code, it is not required to terminate the contract if that determination is reversed by the SBA Office of Hearings and Appeals, *ONS21 Security Servs.*, Comp. Gen. Dec. B-403067, 2010 CPD ¶ 218. Similarly, if an agency terminates an award based on the SBA's determination that the awardee does not meet the size requirement, it is not required to reinstate the award if that determination is reversed by the SBA Office of Hearings and Appeals, *Trident<3>, LLC*, Comp. Gen. Dec. B-405781.3, 2012 CPD ¶ 201.

Most size determinations are based on average gross receipts or number of employees, 15 U.S.C. § 632(a)(2), 13 C.F.R. Part 121. The standards vary from one industry to another, depending on the number and sizes of firms within the industry, but they "may utilize number of employees, dollar volume of business, net worth, net income, a combination thereof, or other appropriate factors," 15 U.S.C. § 632(a)(2)(B). A company whose stock is publicly traded, as opposed to a corporation whose stock is privately held, can qualify as a small business concern if it meets the size standard designated in the solicitation, *Geo-Seis Helicopters, Inc.*, SIZ-94-3-23-32, 1994 SBA LEXIS 29.

In terms of determining annual receipts, 13 C.F.R. § 121.104(a) states:

> (1) Generally receipts are considered "total income" (or in the case of a sole proprietorship, "gross income") plus "cost of goods sold" as these terms are defined or reported on Internal Revenue Service (IRS) Federal tax return forms (such as Form 1120 for corporations; Form 1120S for S corporations; Form 1120, Form 1065 or Form 1040 for LLCs; Form 1065 for partnerships; Form 1040, Schedule F for farms; Form 1040, Schedule C for other sole proprietorships). Receipts do not include net capital gains or losses, taxes collected for and remitted to a taxing authority if included in gross or total income, such as sales or other taxes collected from customers and excluding taxes levied on the concern or its employees; proceeds from transactions between a concern and its domestic or foreign affiliates; and amounts collected for another by a travel agent, real estate agent, advertising agent, or conference management service provider, freight forwarder or customs broker. For size determination purposes, the only exclusions from receipts are those specifically provided for in this paragraph. All other items, such as subcontractor costs, reimbursements for purchases a contractor makes at a customer's request, and employee-based costs such as payroll taxes, may not be excluded from receipts.

A concern must prove that it acted as an agent if it is seeking to exclude amounts "collected for others," *Social Impact, Inc.*, SIZ-5090, 2009 SBA LEXIS 109. See also *Crown Moving & Storage Co.*, SIZ-4872, 2007 SBA LEXIS 57 (rent paid by affiliated firm is not included in computation); *Kittrell Garlock & Assocs.*, SIZ-94-10-26-142, 1995 SBA LEXIS 32 (consultants' fees of an architectural and engineering firm must be included in calculating average annual receipts).

Annual receipts for a concern that has been in business for five or more completed fiscal years means the receipts of the concern over its last five completed fiscal years divided by five, 13 C.F.R. § 121.104(c)(1). For a concern that has been in business for less than five completed fiscal years, annual receipts means the receipts for the period the concern has been in business divided by the number of weeks in business, multiplied by 52, 13 C.F.R. § 121.104(c)(2). Receipts are determined from the concern's federal tax returns and the SBA is not obligated to analyze the returns to determine whether sales have been reported for the correct year, *Mission Critical Techs., Inc.*, SIZ-5494, 2013 SBA LEXIS 102; *J.M. Waller Assocs., Inc.*, SIZ-5108, 2010 SBA LEXIS 8.

[1] Affiliates

An offeror's size is determined by considering not only the offeror itself, but by aggregating the annual receipts and number of employees of the offeror and all "affiliates," regardless of industrial classification. FAR 19.101 provides that "[b]usiness concerns are affiliates of each other if, directly or indirectly, either one controls or has the power to control the other, or another concern controls or has the power to control both." In determining affiliation, all pertinent facts may be considered, including common ownership, common management, and contractual relationships, 13 C.F.R. § 121.103; FAR 19.101. Not all affiliation factors need be considered—only those appropriate or relevant under the specific facts of the case. Moreover, equal weight need not be given to each factor; the presence of one or more of these factors may be sufficient to constitute affiliation, *Agrigold Juice Prods.*, SIZ-95-7-19-72, 1996 SBA LEXIS 7. In addition, these factors are not intended to be exhaustive. Affiliation has been a controversial issue, particularly where a finding of affiliation has the effect of disqualifying a concern that would otherwise be able to compete as a small business, *Aloha Dredging & Constr. Co. v. Heatherly*, 661 F. Supp. 738 (D.D.C. 1987). See also Reeder & Vergilio, *Small Business Set-Asides and Corporate Affiliation—A Billion Dollar Business*, 15 Pub. Cont. L.J. 279 (1985).

If an affiliation is dissolved, its sales need not be counted as long as the dissolution is completed prior to the beginning of the first year in the calculation of annual sales, *Hallmark-Phoenix 8, LLC*, SIZ-5046, 2009 SBA LEXIS 57 (sales required to be counted because dissolution not complete).

Common ownership is often considered in determining affiliation. See *ZLynx, Enters., Inc.*, SIZ-5985, 2019 SBA LEXIS 19 (father and son participated in organizations); *Eagle Support Servs. Corp.*, SIZ-5972, 2018 SBA LEXIS 104 (common investments in six concerns); *Vortec Dev. Inc.*, SIZ-4866, 2007 SBA LEXIS 58 (firms owned by a brother and sister). Similarly, where a franchiser controlled 60% of the franchisee's voting stock, the franchiser's chairman of the board was also the franchisee's chairman of the board, the franchiser provided ongoing management and assistance to the franchisee, and there were excessive restrictions on the sale of the franchisee's stock, the two firms were considered affiliates, *ERM-South, Inc.*, SIZ-95-4-12-33, 1995 SBA LEXIS 139. On the other hand, in *ROH, Inc.*, SIZ-94-11-25-156, 1995 SBA LEXIS 59, the SBA found no affiliation between firms where the challenged firm's owner had sold all its stock in a large firm and divested any interest prior to the challenged firm's self-certification as a small business, and there was no evidence to show that any ties remained between the two firms. See also *Shiloh Indus. Contractors, Inc.*, SIZ-95-9-22-90, 1996 SBA LEXIS 9 (although both firms were owned by the same family, no affiliation existed because the alleged large firm had no ownership or other interest in the other firm, and the firms did not share officers, directors, shareholders, employees, or facilities); and *Griffin Servs., Inc.*, SIZ-95-10-28-110, 1996 SBA LEXIS 4 (no affiliation where alleged affiliates no longer shared family ties, and the challenged firm's owner had given up his executive position and sold his stock in the alleged affiliate nine years prior to the challenge). See FAR 19.101(4) and (5) for guidance on the impact of stock options, convertible debentures and voting trusts in determining common ownership.

Common management is another factor often considered when examining affiliation. This occurs when a person can exercise "critical influence" over the management of two firms, *G&C Fab-Con, LLC*, SIZ-5649, 2015 SBA LEXIS 14. However, common management was not found when a person controlled one firm but was only a key employee of the other firm, *Optivision, Inc.*, SIZ-5740, 2016 SBA LEXIS 39. See *Sabre88, LLC*, SIZ-5161, 2010 SBA LEXIS 82, holding that a newly organized firm was affiliated with a firm from which the founders came and which provided most of the new firm's work.

Affiliation will be found if a large business is an "ostensible subcontractor," which "performs primary and vital requirements of a contract," or "upon which the prime contractor is unusually reliant," 13 C.F.R. § 121.103(h)(2). For this purpose, the ostensible subcontractor relationship will not be found if the small business and small business subcontractors perform the major contract requirements, *Synaptek Corp.*, SIZ-5954, 2018 SBA LEXIS 84.

Affiliation may be found based upon a contractual relationship between parties. 13 C.F.R. § 121.103(f)(2) states there is a rebuttable presumption of affiliation if the small business derives 70% of its receipts from another firm. However, receipts over past years are not determinative if the small business is deriving less than that amount at the time of self-certification as a small business, *OBXtek, Inc.*, SIZ-5451, 2013 SBA LEXIS 28. See FAR 19.101(7) for guidance on the application of this contractual relationship rule to joint ventures.

A determination of affiliation through stock ownership is provided in 13 C.F.R. § 121.103(c). This provision states that an individual, concern or other entity is an affiliate of a concern if it "owns, or has the power to control, 50 percent or more of a concern's voting stock, or a block of voting stock which is large compared to other outstanding blocks of voting stock." Similar guidance is provided in FAR 19.101(3). If a single person owns over 50% of the stock of two companies, they will be found to be affiliates even though the person does not actually exercise control, *DMS Facility Servs., LLC*, SIZ-4913, 2008 SBA LEXIS 31. See *McLane Advanced Techs., LLC*, SIZ-474, 2005 SBA LEXIS 79, for a discussion of the application of these rules to limited liability companies.

Joint venturers consisting of small businesses are not affiliates if they are awarded or solicit contracts for no more than a two-year period, starting from the date of the award of the first contract, 13 C.F.R. § 121.103(h). They can enter into subsequent joint venture agreements but, if this appears to be a "long-standing relationship," they will be considered affiliates. Similarly, subcontractor teaming agreements between small businesses to pursue bundled contract do not create an affiliation relationship, 13 C.F.R. § 121.103(b)(9).

13 C.F.R. § 121.103(b) excludes from affiliation coverage:

1. Business concerns owned in whole or substantial part by investment companies licensed, or development companies qualifying, under the Small Business Investment Act of 1958.

2. Business concerns owned and controlled by Indian Tribes.

3. Business concerns which are part of an SBA approved pool of concerns for a joint program of research and development or for defense production as authorized by the Small Business Act.

4. Business concerns which lease employees from concerns primarily engaged in leasing employees to other businesses.

5. Investors providing financial, management or technical assistance under the Small Business Investment Act of 1958.

6. Firms that are in an SBA-approved mentor/protege agreement.

7. Member shareholders of a small agricultural cooperative, as defined in the Agricultural Marketing Act (12 U.S.C. 1141j).

8. Faith based organizations.

Where a different party is involved in a later protest involving that firm, the doctrines of res judicata and collateral estoppel do not apply, and a regional office or area office may reach a contrary result as to affiliation as long as it adequately explains the legal and factual basis for that result, *Agrigold Juice Prods.*, SIZ-95-7-19-72, 1996 SBA LEXIS 7. In this case, an area office determined that Agrigold was other than a small business based on affiliation. Agrigold argued that the area office failed to give proper weight to the prior regional office determination that it was small. The SBA stated that because the regional office determination was not appealed, the Office of Hearings and Appeals had no opportunity to consider the question and, thus, the prior regional office determination did not constitute precedent.

[2] Subcontracts to Large Firms

15 U.S.C. § 644(o) limits the amount of subcontracting to large businesses by small businesses. This statute is implemented in 13 C.F.R. § 125.6, and FAR 19.505. The limitations are stated as percentages of different categories of work in accordance with the Limitations on Subcontracting clause in FAR 52.219-14, stating:

(e) Limitations on subcontracting. By submission of an offer and execution of a contract, the Contractor agrees that in performance of a contract assigned a North American Industry Classification System (NAICS) code for—

> (1) Services (except construction), it will not pay more than 50 percent of the amount paid by the Government for contract performance to subcontractors that are not similarly situated entities. Any work that a similarly situated entity further subcontracts will count towards the prime contractor's 50 percent subcontract amount that cannot be exceeded. When a contract includes both services and supplies, the 50 percent limitation shall apply only to the service portion of the contract;
>
> (2) Supplies (other than procurement from a nonmanufacturer of such supplies), it will not pay more than 50 percent of the amount paid by the Government for contract performance, excluding the cost of materials, to subcontractors that are not similarly situated entities. Any work that a similarly situated entity further subcontracts will count towards the prime contractor's 50 percent subcontract amount that cannot be exceeded. When a contract includes both supplies and services, the 50 percent limitation shall apply only to the supply portion of the contract;
>
> (3) General construction, it will not pay more than 85 percent of the amount paid by the Government for contract performance, excluding the cost of materials, to subcontractors that are not similarly situated entities. Any work that a similarly situated entity further subcontracts will count towards the prime contractor's 85 percent subcontract amount that cannot be exceeded; or
>
> (4) Construction by special trade contractors, it will not pay more than 75 percent of the amount paid by the Government for contract performance, excluding the cost of materials, to subcontractors that are not similarly situated entities. Any work that a similarly situated entity further subcontracts will count towards the prime contractor's 75 percent subcontract amount that cannot be exceeded.

This clause became effective in September 2021. Prior to that, the clause stated the limitations in terms of *costs* rather than *price*, with the result that contracts entered into before that date will contain the earlier clause and be subject to a requirement that their costs of subcontractor performance not exceed the prescribed limitation.

The contracting officer must prescribe the time when the percentage requirement will apply. See FAR 19.505(a) stating:

> (2) Compliance period. A small business contractor subject to the limitations on subcontracting is required to comply with the limitations on subcontracting—
>
> (i) For a contract that has been set aside, either by the end of the base term and then by the end of each subsequent option period, or by the end of the performance period for each order issued under the contract, at the contracting officer's discretion; and

(ii) For an order set aside under a contract as described in 19.504(a), (b), or (c)(1)(i) or an order issued in accordance with 19.504(c)(1)(ii), by the end of the performance period for the order.

When an agency uses this clause for a contract for both supplies and services, it must specify which work is the predominant work to which the clause will apply, *TFab Mfg., LLC*, Comp. Gen. Dec. B-401190, 2009 CPD ¶ 127. The result of this interpretation is that the less predominant work will not be subject to the 50% limitation. When the clause is used on a contract with option years, the contractor can perform less than 50% of the work during the early years as long as it performs 50% of the work over the entire contract, *Spectrum Security Servs., Inc.*, Comp. Gen. Dec. B-297320.2, 2005 CPD ¶ 227.

GAO will not sustain a protest that the winning offeror will not comply with this clause unless that lack of compliance is apparent on the face of the offer, *Crosstown Courier Serv., Inc.*, Comp. Gen. Dec. B-414752, 2017 CPD ¶ 269; *Chant Eng'g Co.*, Comp. Gen. Dec. B-402054, 2010 CPD ¶ 16. However, it will sustain a protest that an offeror was held unacceptable without clear evidence of noncompliance on the face of the proposal, *Leumas Residential, LLC*, Comp. Gen. Dec. B-418635, 2020 CPD ¶ 236. On the other hand, if a proposal clearly indicates that the offeror will not comply with the requirement, it is properly ruled unacceptable, *EcoAnalysts, Inc.*, Comp. Gen. Dec. B-406233, 2012 CPD ¶ 169. Compare *Hanover Ins. Co. v. Dunbar Mech. Contractors, LLC*, 964 F.3d 763 (8th Cir. 2020), reversing a decision that the clause had been violated because the awarded subcontract was for more than 50% of the contract price because the limitation relates to costs incurred not subcontract prices at the time of award.

In a total small business set-aside, service-disabled veteran-owned small business set-aside, WOSB or EDWOSB set-aside, or an 8(a) procurement for products, a small business that is not a manufacturer but is a regular dealer is permitted to offer a product that is totally manufactured by another small business, 13 C.F.R. § 121.406. This "nonmanufacturer" rule is explained in FAR 19.102(f). A nonmanufacturer must be a small business under the applicable size standard, FAR 19.001. Waivers to the requirement that the manufacturing subcontractor be a small business are issued by the SBA on an individual or class basis, FAR 19.102(f)(4). The nonmanufacturer rule is implemented by including the FAR 52.219-6(d) Notice of Small Business Set-Aside clause in solicitations, FAR 19.508(c). If a waiver has been issued, Alternate I is used. See *Walker Dev. & Trading Grp., Inc.*, Comp. Gen. Dec. B-414365, 2017 CPD ¶ 151, affirming the issuance of a contract to a nonmanufacturer obtaining the product from a large business when a class waiver had been issued. When no waiver had been issued, a bid that indicated that the end item would not be manufactured or produced by a small business was considered nonresponsive, *American Amplifier & Tel. Corp.*, 53 Comp. Gen. 463 (B-179149), 74-1 CPD ¶ 10. If a small business offers the product of a large business and no class waiver has been issued by the SBA, the contracting officer must reject the offer or seek a waiver from the SBA in accordance with FAR 19.102(f)(5), *Hydroid, LLC*, Comp. Gen. Dec. B-299072, 2007 CPD ¶ 20 (termination of contract recommended). There has been considerable controversy as to whether the nonmanufacturer rule applies to contracts that call for services along with products. See *Rotech Healthcare, Inc. v. United States*, 71 Fed. Cl. 393 (2006) (interpreting 15 U.S.C. § 637(a)(17) to require application of the rule to all contracts calling for products). The SBA regulation at 13 C.F.R. § 121.406(b) states:

> (3) The nonmanufacturer rule applies only to procurements that have been assigned a manufacturing or supply NAICS code or the Information Technology Value added resellers (ITVAR) exception to NAICS code 541519. The nonmanufacturer rule does not apply to contracts that have been assigned a service, except for the ITVAR exception to NAICS code 541519, construction, or specialty trade construction NAICS code.
>
> (4) The nonmanufacturer rule applies only to the supply component of a requirement classified as a manufacturing, or supply or ITVAR contract. If a requirement is classified as a service contract, but also has a supply component, the nonmanufacturer rule does not apply to the supply component of the requirement.

See *Eagle Home Med. Corp.*, Comp. Gen. Dec. B-402387, 2010 CPD ¶ 82, following the SBA regulation and distinguishing *Rotech* after the SBA ruled that a contract for mixed products and services should be classified as a contract for rental of equipment with the result that no manufacturing was called for by the contract (making the nonmanufacturer rule inapplicable). See also *B&B Med. Servs., Inc.*, Comp. Gen. Dec. B-404241, 2011 CPD ¶ 24, holding that the nonmanufacturer rule does not apply to procurements set aside for HUBZone concerns.

[3] Self-Certification

The initial determination of size is made by the small business, which is required to "self-certify" with its offer that it is small, 13 C.F.R. § 121.405(a). Thus, each offeror must determine whether it qualifies as a small business. In order to facilitate self-certification, federal procuring agencies are required to state the NAICS code applicable to the products and services being procured and the applicable size standard in the Small Business Program Representations solicitation provision in FAR 52.219-1, FAR 19.102(b) and FAR 19.303. The self-certification is made by checking the appropriate blank(s) in this provision, thereby representing and certifying whether the offeror is a small business concern. If a concern has made a SAM.gov certification for the same NAICS code, it can use that to meet the certification requirement, FAR 4.1201, but offerors should take care that their status has not changed at the time of submitting the offer. In sealed bid procurement, failure to self-certify at the time of bidding may not be cured after opening, *Covenant Indus., Inc.*, Comp. Gen. Dec. B-218091.2, 85-1 CPD ¶ 372; *Julie Cades*, Comp. Gen. Dec. B-248218, 92-2 CPD ¶ 18. Further, the failure of a bidder to self-certify is not cured by completion of the Place of Performance clause, which relates to responsibility of the bidder and not responsiveness of the bid, *Delta Concepts, Inc.*, 67 Comp. Gen. 522 (B-230632), 88-2 CPD ¶ 43.

FAR 19.309(c) requires the inclusion of the Post-Award Small Business Representation clause in FAR 52.219-28 in all contracts above the micro-purchase threshold. This clause requires recertification after execution of a novation agreement, the finalization of a merger of acquisition or prior to the end of a "long term" contract (a contract of more than 5 years duration, including options). With respect to multiple award contracts, SBA determines size at time of the initial offer and if the business is small at time of offer, it is small for the duration of the contract as long as it remains the same corporate entity, 13 C.F.R. § 121.404(a)(1). However, an agency has the discretion to require recertification when it issues a task or delivery order, *Oryza Grp., LLC*, Comp. Gen. Dec. B-416719, 2018 CPD ¶ 407 (task order under a GWAC); *Inuteq, LLC*, Comp. Gen. Dec. B-411781, 2015 CPD ¶ 324 (Federal Supply Schedule task order); *Enterprise Info. Servs., Inc.*, Comp. Gen. Dec. B-403028, 2010 CPD ¶ 213 (task order under a seven-year GWAC).

An offeror may represent that it is "small" if it meets the definition of a small business concern in the solicitation and the SBA has made no adverse determination regarding its size status, FAR 19.301-1(a). The certification must be current at the time the small business submits an offer including price, 13 C.F.R. § 121.404(a)(1)(iii). Thus, a self-certification at the time of a phase 1 proposal (excluding price) was not effective when the concern was not a small business at the time it submitted its phase 2 proposal which included price. See *Cox Constr. Co.*, SIZ-5070, 2009 SBA LEXIS 76, rejecting the arguments that the procedure in FAR 4.1201, calling only for annual updates, overrode the SBA regulation and that the fact that the contracting officer did not call for a new representation with the phase 2 proposal freed the offeror from the SBA requirement.

This certification must be made in accordance with a high standard of good faith because of the potential for abuse inherent in a self-certification procedure, *Bancroft Cap Co.*, 55 Comp. Gen. 469 (B-182569), 75-2 CPD ¶ 321. Lack of good faith is "not necessarily limited to an incident of intentional misrepresentation" but can also be found in a failure to exercise prudence and care in ascertaining size under prescribed guidelines, 51 Comp. Gen. 595 (B-174807) (1972). A bidder's self-certification was held to be not prepared in good faith when it certified itself as small although it knew the SBA had questioned that status, 41 Comp. Gen. 47 (B-144621) (1961). However, in 49 Comp. Gen. 369 (B-167353) (1969), GAO found no basis for imputing bad faith even though the successful bidder changed its management structure between the filing of the protest and the SBA size determination and it was held not to be a small business at the time of award. In *Mark Dunning Indus., Inc.*, Comp. Gen. Dec. B-405417.2, 2013 CPD ¶ 267, a contractor properly certified as a small business was awarded a contract two years after the initial offer when it merged becoming a large business. GAO found that the agency was not required to reexamine the contractor's size status at the time of the late award because the size determination at the time of self-certification controls.

A knowingly false certification of small business status violates 15 U.S.C. § 645(d), punishable by a fine up to $500,000 or imprisonment for up to 10 years. It can also be the basis for a civil false claims suit. See also *United States ex re. Longi v. Lithium Power Techs, Inc.*, 530 F. Supp. 2d 888 (S.D. Tex. 2008), *aff'd*, 575 F.3d 458 (5th Cir. 2009), assessing treble damages under the False Claims Act, 31 U.S.C. § 3729 et seq., requiring repayment of three times the prices of four SBIR contracts that had been obtained by falsely certifying that the firm was a small business. Compare *Ab-Tech Constr., Inc. v. United States*, 31 Fed. Cl. 429 (1994), *aff'd*, 57 F.3d 1084 (Fed. Cir. 1995), finding a false certification that the contractor was an 8(a) firm. There the court granted statutory damages under the False Claims Act of $10,000 per invoice submitted on the contract but did not grant treble damages because the contractor had fully performed the contract. The Small Business Jobs Act of 2010, Pub. L. No. 111-240, Sept. 27, 2010, added a provision to 15 U.S.C. § 632 making it a presumption that the loss to the United States for false certification is the entire contract price (establishing a right to treble damages). In addition, state law may provide a remedy for fraud, unjust enrichment, or interference with a business relationship caused by a lowest bidder that misrepresents itself as a small business, See, for example, *Tectonics, Inc. v. Castle Constr. Co.*, 753 F.2d 957 (11th Cir.), *cert. denied*, 474 U.S. 848 (1985), and *Iconco v. Jensen Constr. Co.*, 622 F.2d 1291 (8th Cir. 1980), where losing offerors recovered against contractors that falsely certified their status. Obviously, to receive such a remedy, the plaintiff must demonstrate that the firm that received the award does not qualify as a small business under the Act, *Ferguson-Williams, Inc. v. BAMSI, Inc.*, 782 F.2d 940 (11th Cir. 1986) (SBA determined that low bidder qualified as a small business; therefore, no recovery was allowed).

An offeror's self-certification is normally accepted without any further inquiry, unless it is challenged, FAR 19.301-1(b). Challenges may be made by the contracting officer, offerors in the same procurement, or other interested parties. Although such challenges are often filed with the procuring agency, the investigation and determination of whether the offeror is in fact "small" will be made by the SBA, FAR 19.302(c). An initial determination is ordinarily made by a regional office of the SBA. Any appeal must be taken to the SBA Office of Hearings and Appeals in Washington, D.C., "within the time limits and in strict accordance with the procedures contained in 13 C.F.R. Part 134," FAR 19.302(i). The procedures for protesting the self-certification of an offeror are set forth in 13 C.F.R. §§ 121.1001-1010.

Where a timely size protest is filed after a small business award, and the awardee is found by the SBA to be other than small, the agency, in the absence of legitimate countervailing reasons, should terminate the contract. In *Diagnostic Imaging Tech. Educ.*, Comp. Gen. Dec. B-257590, 94-2 CPD ¶ 148, the protester timely protested the size status of the awardee to the contracting officer, who referred the matter to the SBA. The SBA found the awardee to be other than a small business. In spite of this finding, the agency did not terminate the contract. GAO held that the agency should not have permitted the award to stand when it was apprised by the SBA that the awardee was not small, stating:

> While FAR § 19.302(j) treats post-award size protests as having no applicability to the current contract, awards under set-aside procurements to other than small businesses should be terminated if possible, and SBA's regulations provide that such timely-filed size protests "shall apply to the procurement in question even though the contracting officer may have awarded the contract prior to receipt of the protest." 13 C.F.R. § 121.1603(a)(2); *see also* FAR § 19.302(d)(1)(ii). Further, RSTI did not defend its adverse size certification by appealing SBA's determination. Thus, in the absence of countervailing reasons, it would be inconsistent with the integrity of the competitive procurement system, and the intent of the Small Business Act, to permit a large business, which under the terms of the solicitation was ineligible for award, to continue to perform the contract. *American Mobilphone Paging, Inc.*, [69 Comp. Gen. 392 (B-238027), 90-1 CPD ¶ 366].

Compare *TrustComm, Inc.*, Comp. Gen. Dec. B-408456, 2013 CPD ¶ 237, agreeing that is was proper not to terminate when the size determination was delayed and the agency needed the equipment.

GAO views the SBA as having conclusive authority to determine whether a particular business is "small" for purposes of federal procurement, *Dehler Mfg. Co.*, Comp. Gen. Dec. B-416963, 2019 CPD ¶ 7. Therefore, GAO will not make such a determination, or review SBA determinations, *TechAnax, LLC*, Comp. Gen. Dec. B-408685.22, 2019 CPD ¶ 294. Once an offeror has been found not to be small, the offeror may not, unless the SBA has issued a later decision finding the firm to be small, certify itself as small under the same or lower standards as those under which it had been found not to be small, 13 C.F.R. § 121.1009(g)(5); *Choctaw Mfg. Co. v. United States*, 761 F.2d 609 (11th Cir. 1985). See *Timothy S. Graves*, Comp. Gen. Dec. B-253813, 93-2 CPD ¶ 244, *recons. denied*, 94-1 CPD ¶ 19, where award was denied to a firm that was in fact small at the time of award. In this case, the bidder on a timber sale had been determined not to be a small business by the SBA regional office. The bidder appealed the determination to the SBA's Office of Hearings and Appeals (OHA), and while the matter was being considered by the OHA, the bidder submitted a bid on a subsequent timber sale and certified itself to be a small business. Subsequently, the OHA reversed the regional office's determination on the previous contract, and the agency proposed to award the contract to the bidder. However, the award was appealed to the OHA, which held that the bidder could not qualify as small because the regional office determination had not been reversed at the time that the bidder signed its self-certification, even though by OHA's own determination, the bidder was small at the time. GAO denied the subsequent protest on the grounds that the SBA size determination was conclusive.

Once a business is found to be other than small, it may seek recertification as small from SBA, pursuant to 13 C.F.R. § 121.1010. In *Evans Cooperage Co.*, SIZ-94-11-2-145, 1995 SBA LEXIS 55, the appellant was found to be other than small for the applicable 500-employee size standard in a particular solicitation. The appellant did not recertify but stated that it had intended to do so and that it now had fewer than 500 employees. The SBA found that this argument had no merit.

[B] Certificates of Competency

The SBA has the authority to issue certificates of competency (COCs) for all elements of responsibility of small businesses. In the original Small Business Act, Congress authorized the SBA to certify as to the "capacity and credit" of small businesses to perform particular contracts but this was changed to cover "all elements of responsibility, including, but not limited to, capability, competency, capacity, credit, integrity, perseverance, and tenacity," 15 U.S.C. § 637(b)(7)(A). Such a certificate is conclusive on a procuring agency, *Orion Tech., Inc.*, Comp. Gen. Dec. B-405970, 2012 CPD ¶ 89. The scope of the SBA's review authority is not limited to those factors specified by a contracting officer as deficient in a referral letter, but rather includes all elements of responsibility, *C & G Excavating, Inc. v. United States*, 32 Fed. Cl. 231 (1994) (contracting officer based nonresponsibility finding on capacity, whereas SBA based nonresponsibility on financial condition). Neither the SBA nor the procuring agency may create exceptions to the statutory requirement for referral to the SBA for determination regarding whether a COC should be issued, 15 U.S.C. § 637(b)(7)(C); *Sess Constr. Co.*, 64 Comp. Gen. 355 (B-216924), 85-1 CPD ¶ 319; *Small Business Admin. Request for Recons.*, Comp. Gen. Dec. B-219654.3, 86-1 CPD ¶ 420.

COCs are issued on a contract-by-contract basis. If a contracting officer determines that a small business that submitted the most favorable acceptable offer lacks responsibility, contract award must be withheld and the matter referred to the "cognizant SBA Government Contracting Area office," FAR 19.602-1(a)(2). Failure to make this referral is a protestable issue, *Competitive Range Sols., LLC*, Comp. Gen. Dec. B-413104.10, 2017 CPD ¶ 124. The SBA then offers the small business an opportunity to apply for a COC, FAR 19.602-2(a). If the small business provides the detailed information required by the application, the SBA will investigate the matter and issue or deny issuance of the COC. If the SBA has not issued a COC within 15 business days, or a longer period agreed to by the contracting officer, the agency proceeds with the acquisition, FAR 19.602-4(c). See *James F. Thomson, Jr.*, Comp. Gen. Dec. B-416918, 2019 CPD ¶ 46, holding that award was proper when the SBA failed to issue a COC within 15 days and the contracting officer was silent regarding an extension. If an agency rejects a proposal as technically unacceptable on the basis of factors not related to responsibility as well as responsibility-related ones, the agency is not required to refer the matter to the SBA under its COC procedure, *Paragon Dynamics, Inc.*, Comp. Gen. Dec. B-251280, 93-1 CPD ¶ 248.

Prior to issuance of a COC, the SBA is required to notify the contracting officer, FAR 19.602-2(d). If the contracting officer disagrees with the proposed issuance of a COC, and the controversy cannot be resolved through further communications, the procuring agency may request referral of the matter to the SBA Central Office, FAR 19.602-3. A contractor otherwise eligible for the COC program is entitled to have the involved agency notify the SBA prior to terminating negotiations, so that the contractor could have the SBA's assistance in responding to the deficiencies perceived by the agency, *CelTech, Inc. v. United States*, 24 Cl. Ct. 269 (1991).

The Court of Federal Claims will review the denial of a COC, *United Enter. & Assocs. v. United States*, 70 Fed. Cl. 1 (2006) (action of the SBA in denying COC was not arbitrary or capricious); *CSE Constr., Inc. v. United States*, 58 Fed. Cl. 230 (2003) (action of the SBA in denying COC was arbitrary and capricious because it did not consider full past performance of offeror). It will also review the granting of a COC to a competitor, *Lawson Env't Servs., LLC v. United States*, 126 Fed. Cl. 233 (2016). On the other hand, GAO will not review the denial of a COC unless the SBA decision is based on fraud or bad faith or where the SBA has disregarded its own published regulations or failed to consider vital information, *Dehler Mfg. Co.*, Comp. Gen. Dec. B-416939, 2019 CPD ¶ 55. Neither will GAO review an allegation that the contracting officer should not have referred the matter to the SBA, *Bluehorse Corp.-Reconsideration*, Comp. Gen. Dec. B-413929.2, 2017 CPD ¶ 149.

FAR 19.602-1(a)(2) provides that the COC procedure does not apply to issues of eligibility covered in FAR 9.104-1(g) or to suspended or debarred contractors. See *Aardvark Keith Moving, Inc.*, Comp. Gen. Dec. B-290565, 2002 CPD ¶ 134 (affiliated firm proposed for debarment). GAO has held that the COC procedure does not apply to an agency's determination that a proposal is technically unacceptable, *Light-Pod, Inc.*, Comp. Gen. Dec. B-401739, 2009 CPD ¶ 238, unless that determination is based on responsibility factors, *Lawson Env't Servs. LLC*, Comp. Gen. Dec. B-416892, 2019 CPD ¶ 17. Neither does it apply to a determination that a bid is nonresponsive, *Trading Atlanta Ltd.*, Comp. Gen. Dec. B-238978, 90-2 CPD ¶ 52. Nor does the COC procedure apply when an agency determines that the offer has not submitted sufficient information to demonstrate that it met the solicitation's experience requirement, *EA Eng'g, Sci., & Tech., Inc.*, Comp. Gen. Dec. B-417361, 2019 CPD ¶ 218; *MicroTechs, LLC*, Comp. Gen. Dec. B-414670, 2017 CPD ¶ 236; *Eagle Aviation Servs. & Tech., Inc.*, Comp. Gen. Dec. B-403341, 2010 CPD ¶ 242, or that the offeror's low price creates a risk of nonperformance, *Zolon Tech, Inc.*, Comp. Gen. Dec. B-299904.2, 2007 CPD ¶ 183 (price was only one element in best value determination). Compare *J2Aû JV, LLC*, Comp. Gen. Dec. B-401663.4, 2010 CPD ¶ 102, recommending that an agency allow an offeror to attempt to obtain a COC determining that it met a definitive experience requirement.

The COC procedure does not apply when an agency is evaluating proposals in a negotiated procurement if the evaluation factors are scored on a comparative basis rather than on a go/no go basis, *J. Womack Enters., Inc.*, Comp. Gen. Dec. B-299344, 2007 CPD ¶ 69; *Smith of Galeton Gloves, Inc.*, Comp. Gen. Dec. B-271686, 96-2 CPD ¶ 36. However, if there is only one non-cost evaluation factor, past performance, a determination that a contractor does not have sufficient past performance is a responsibility determination, *Phil Howry Co.*, Comp. Gen. Dec. B-291402.3, 2003 CPD ¶ 33. See *Data Monitor Sys., Inc.*, Comp. Gen. Dec. B-415761, 2018 CPD ¶ 79, agreeing with an agency decision not to evaluate past performance in a low price technically acceptable procurement because a rating of unacceptable would have required referral for a COC. Neither is the COC procedure applicable in deciding whether a small business concern comes within the "competitive range" in a negotiated procurement unless it is eliminated based solely on responsibility factors, *iAccess Techs., Inc. v. United States*, 143 Fed. Cl. 521 (2019); *C.M.P. Corp.*, Comp. Gen. Dec. B-211371, 83-2 CPD ¶ 238. However, the COC procedure does apply if an agency determines that the offeror's price is unrealistically low, *Milani Constr., LLC*, Comp. Gen. Dec. B-401942, 2010 CPD ¶ 87 (low price is a matter of responsibility).

[C] Business Preferences

It is federal policy that a "fair proportion" of government contracts and subcontracts be placed with small businesses, 15 U.S.C. § 631(a). See also 41 U.S.C. § 3104. The President is responsible for establishing annual governmentwide goals for participation by small business concerns. 15 U.S.C. § 644(g)(1) provides that these goals may not fall below the congressionally mandated minimums of 23% of the total value of all prime contract awards for small businesses, and the percentages for various classes of small businesses set forth in Figure 14-1:

Class of Small Business	Percentage
Concerns owned and controlled by socially and economically disadvantaged individuals	5%
Concerns owned and controlled by women (WOSBs)	5%
Concerns owned and controlled by service-disabled veterans (SDVOBs)	3%
HUBZone concerns	3%

Figure 14-1

Each agency is assigned goals which are to be set jointly by the head of the procuring agency and the SBA. If the procuring agency and SBA disagree, the Administrator of OFPP is empowered to resolve the dispute, 15 U.S.C. § 644(g)(2)(C).

After each fiscal year, each procuring agency must inform the SBA of the extent to which the goals have been met; and the SBA must forward to the President and Congress, and make available to the public, detailed information on these small business efforts, 15 U.S.C. § 644(h).

These goals are achieved by setting aside procurements for small businesses, directing procurements to small businesses, giving small businesses a percentage evaluation preference and encouraging subcontracting with small businesses. Each of these techniques is discussed below. Following this discussion of the basic techniques used, the unique aspects of each of the special classes of small businesses is briefly discussed.

[1] Set-Asides

The major form of preference given to small businesses in the award of federal contracts is through "set-asides," a term applied to the reservation of contracts for award only to a designated group. Congress has authorized federal agencies to restrict entire procurements ("total set-asides") or portions of procurements ("partial set-asides") for award to small businesses, 15 U.S.C. § 644(a). The primary responsibility for determining which procurements should be set aside is vested in the contracting officer, FAR 19.501(a), but SBA Procurement Center Representatives (PCRs) also review procurements not set aside to determine whether they should be set aside. See 13 C.F.R. § 125.2(b) requiring contracting officers to cooperate with PCRs in the acquisition planning process. When PCR recommendations are adopted, the set-asides are called "joint set-asides," FAR 19.501(b).

The Federal Acquisition Streamlining Act of 1994 (FASA), Pub. L. No. 103-355, § 7101, eliminated those sections of the Small Business Act that established the priority for award of partial and total set-asides. Contracting officers are required to set aside individual acquisitions or classes of acquisitions in order to assure that a fair proportion of government contracts in each NAICS category is placed with small business concerns. A contract may not be awarded under a small business set-aside if the cost of that contract exceeds a fair market price (15 U.S.C. § 644(a)(7)) as determined by the price analysis techniques set forth in FAR 15.404-1(b), FAR 19.202-6(a).

Procurements above the micro-purchase threshold and within the simplified acquisition threshold are automatically set aside for small business unless the contracting officer determines that there is no reasonable possibility of obtaining two competitive offers, FAR 19.502-2(a).

For procurements over the simplified acquisition threshold, set-asides to SDVOBs, WOSBs, HUBZone concerns and procurements reserved for disadvantaged businesses through the 8(a) program are in parity with each other but take priority over set-asides to other small businesses, FAR 19.203(c). There is very little guidance on which class of small business should be selected for a set-aside, but contracting officers need to take a balanced approach to select a class of small businesses that can meet the agency needs and that will fulfill the agency's goals for each class. See 13 C.F.R. § 125.2(f)(2) stating:

> (ii) SBA believes that Progress in fulfilling the various small business goals, as well as other factors such as the results of market research, programmatic needs specific to the procuring agency, anticipated award price, and the acquisition history, will be considered in making a decision as to which program to use for the acquisition.

[a] Total Set-Aside Procedures

Total set-asides are required if there is a reasonable expectation that offers will be made by at least two responsible small businesses, offering the products of different small business concerns, and award will be made at "fair market prices," FAR 19.502-2(b). This "rule of two" has no basis in the statutes but is a product of an agreement between the SBA and the contracting agencies. See the SBA statement of the rule in 13 C.F.R. § 125.2(f)(2). Both the FAR and the SBA regulation call for application of the "rule of two" to all "acquisitions," which has generally been interpreted to mean that it applies when an agency is awarding a new contract. The "rule of two" does not apply in awarding task or delivery orders under the Federal Supply Schedule, FAR 8.404(a); *Edmond Computer Co.*, Comp. Gen. Dec. B-402863, 2010 CPD ¶ 200, unless the procurement constitutes a bundled requirement. See *Coast to Coast Computer Prods., Inc.*, Comp. Gen. Dec. B-417500, 2019 CPD ¶ 267. GAO initially ruled that the "rule of two" applies to task and delivery orders being competed under multiple award IDIQ contracts, *Delex Sys., Inc.*, Comp. Gen. Dec. B-400403, 2008 CPD ¶ 181. GAO changed course, however, and now holds that the rule of two does not apply to task orders, a position contrary to SBA's own interpretation of the regulations. *ITility, Inc.*, Comp. Gen. Dec. B-419167, 2020 CPD ¶ 412. At least one Court of Federal Claims decision has disagreed with GAO's current position, finding that the rule of two must be applied before deciding to solicit work through a particular IDIQ vehicle. *Tolliver Grp., Inc. v. United States*, 151 Fed. Cl. 70 (2020).

The "fair market price" need not be as low as the price obtainable in full and open competition, *Society Brand, Inc.*, 55 Comp. Gen. 475 (B-183963), 75-2 CPD ¶ 327. See *Analtical Graphics, Inc.*, Comp. Gen. Dec. B-4133857, 2016 CPD ¶ 293, agreeing with a decision of a contracting officer that the prospect of price competition was a reasonable way to ensure a fair market price. GAO has ruled that receipt of only one reasonable bid is not a valid basis to challenge a set-aside because there was a reasonable expectation of at least two reasonable bids, *NJCT Corp.*, Comp. Gen. Dec. B-219455, 85-2 CPD ¶ 70. In making this determination, the past acquisition history of the item or items being procured, while important, is not the only factor to be considered. For example, in making research and development (R&D) set-asides, there must also be a reasonable expectation of obtaining from small businesses the best scientific and technical sources consistent with the requirements of the acquisition, FAR 19.502-2(b).

Contracting officers have broad discretion in determining whether particular procurements should be set aside for small businesses or whether set-asides that have been established should be withdrawn, *Analytical Graphics, Inc. v. United States*, 135 Fed. Cl. 378 (2017); *Fiskars Brands, Inc.*, Comp. Gen. Dec. B-412730, 2016 CPD ¶ 139. For decisions affirming agency conclusion that two small business competitors were not available, see *American Relocation Connections, L.L.C. v. United States*, 139 Fed. Cl. 747 (2018) (market research showed lack of two responsible small businesses); *Metasoft, LLC*, Comp. Gen. Dec. B-402800, 2010 CPD ¶ 170 (analysis of sources sought replies indicated that companies couldn't perform 50% of work with own forces); *EMMES Corp.*, Comp. Gen. Dec. B-402245, 2010 CPD ¶ 53 (analysis of sources sought replies and market research); *Information Ventures, Inc.*, Comp. Gen. Dec. B-400604, 2008 CPD ¶ 232 (analysis of sources sought replies plus prior procurement history); *Protective Grp., Inc.*, Comp. Gen. Dec. B-310018, 2007 CPD ¶ 208 (analysis of responses at industry day conference); *Marketing & Mgmt. Info., Inc.*, Comp. Gen. Dec. B-283399.4, 2000 CPD ¶ 82 (market research). For decisions affirming the agency decision to set a procurement aside, see *Guardian Moving & Storage Co.*, Comp. Gen. Dec. B-410171, 2014 CPD ¶ 334 (adequate market research and coordination with SBA); *Ceradyne, Inc.*, Comp. Gen. Dec. B-402281, 2010 CPD ¶ 70 (analysis of production capacity of two firms with IDIQ contracts); *ViroMed Labs.*, Comp. Gen. Dec. B-298931, 2007 CPD ¶ 4 (sources sought responses and contact with prospective offerors indicated at least three small businesses could submit offers).

Protests have been sustained if it is determined that an agency's decision not to set aside is unreasonable. *Tolliver Grp., Inc. v. United States*, 151 Fed. Cl. 70 (2020). In *Rhinocorps, Ltd. v. United States*, 86 Fed. Cl. 642 (2009), an injunction was granted when an agency decided not to set aside a follow-on procurement when the prior work had been performed by a small business. Similarly, in *DNO, Inc.*, Comp. Gen. Dec. B-406256, 2012 CPD ¶ 136, GAO sustained a protest when an agency failed to conduct adequate market research. See also *Information Ventures, Inc.*, Comp. Gen. Dec. B-294267, 2004 CPD ¶ 205 (agency performed inadequate market research and knew that there were three capable small businesses); *ACCU-Lab Med. Testing*, Comp. Gen. Dec. B-270259, 96-1 CPD ¶ 106 (agency improperly withdrew set-aside by relying on the prior procurement history instead of investigating the numerous small business responses to the CBD announcement and performing a current market study); *Bollinger Mach. Shop & Shipyard, Inc.*, Comp. Gen. Dec. B-258563, 95-1 CPD ¶ 56 (agency expected bids from at least two small businesses and did not have a reasonable basis for concluding that award at a fair market price could not be expected); *Thermal Sols., Inc.*, Comp. Gen. Dec. B-259501, 95-1 CPD ¶ 178 (agency received expressions of interest from five undisputed SDBs). However, GAO may object to a set-aside when the evidence strongly indicates that only one small business is likely to submit an offer, *DISA Elecs.*, 62 Comp. Gen. 271 (B-206798), 83-1 CPD ¶ 306.

[b] Partial Set-Asides

An agency may determine that small businesses cannot furnish the entire quantity that is needed but may be able to supply a portion. FAR 19.502-3 provides that a partial set-aside is appropriate when:

> (1) A total set-aside is not appropriate (see 19.502-2);
>
> (2) The requirement is severable into two or more economic production runs or reasonable lots;
>
> (3) One or more small business concerns are expected to have the technical competence and productive capacity to satisfy the set-aside portion of the requirement at a fair market price;
>
> (4) The acquisition is not subject to simplified acquisition procedures; and
>
> (5) A partial set-aside shall not be made if there is a reasonable expectation that only two concerns (one large and one small) with capability will respond with offers unless authorized by the head of a contracting activity on a case-by-case basis. Similarly, a class of acquisitions, not including construction, may be partially set aside. Under certain specified conditions, partial set-asides may be used in conjunction with multiyear contracting procedures.

A "partial set-aside" reserves for award to small businesses only a portion—called the "set-aside" portion—of the quantity being procured. Both portions must be for an economic amount of the work, FAR 19.502-3(b)(1). Both small and large offerors may submit offers on the non-set-aside portion, which is awarded first, following normal contracting procedures, FAR 19.502-3(c)(1). The set-aside portion is then awarded through negotiation with small business offerors that submitted responsive offers on the non-set-aside portion. The priority in which small business offerors will be asked to negotiate on the set-aside portion is determined by the terms of the solicitation, FAR 19.502-3(c)(2)(i). Under the standard Notice of Partial Small Business Set-Aside solicitation provision in FAR 52.219-7, negotiations are conducted first with the small business concern that submitted the lowest responsive offer on the non-set-aside portion. If the negotiations are not successful or if only part of the set-aside portion is awarded to that concern, negotiations are conducted with the concern that submitted the second low responsive offer. This process continues until a contract (or contracts) are awarded for the entire set-aside portion.

The set-aside portion is awarded at the highest unit price(s) on which the non-set-aside portion was awarded, adjusted to reflect transportation and similar factors. For example, assume that an agency needs 1 million units and believes that small businesses may be able to supply at least 400,000 units but not the entire requirement, and that 100,000 units is a reasonable production run. The agency should use a small business partial set-aside, with 600,000 units as the non-set-aside portion and 400,000 units reserved for award to small businesses. As stated above, both large and small offerors may bid on the non-set-aside portion. Assume the following simplified results of bidding:

Offeror	Size	Price	No. of Units
A	Large	$1.00	400,000 max.
B	Large	1.03	unlimited
C	Large	1.05	unlimited
D	Small	1.06	unlimited
E	Large	1.08	unlimited
F	Small	1.09	unlimited
G	Small	1.11	500,000 max.

Assume further that all offers are responsive, that all offerors are responsible. The non-set-aside portion would be awarded as follows:

A	Large	400,000 at $1.00 each
B	Large	200,000 at $1.03 each

The agency should then ask D, whose offer was the lowest small-business offer on the non-set-aside portion, whether it is willing to accept award for all or any portion of the 400,000 set-aside units at $1.03, the maximum price paid on the non-set-aside units. If D will accept award at $1.03 each, award should be made to it. If D will not take all 400,000 units, any remaining units should be offered to F, and then, if necessary, to G, at $1.03 per unit. If any of the 400,000 set-aside units cannot be awarded through this procedure, they should be awarded to B at $1.03 each without negotiation of a lower price, FAR 19.502-3(c)(2)(i).

[c] Small Business Innovation Research Set-Asides

Under the Small Business Innovation Development Act, Pub. L. No. 97-219 (1982), federal agencies with budgets over certain amounts for outside R&D must direct 3.2% of such funds to small businesses, 15 U.S.C. § 638(f). See Chapter 10 for a discussion of the procedures for such procurements.

[2] Sole Source Contracting and Evaluation Preferences

Several of the small business programs for designated classes of small businesses permit sole source contracting or call for percentage evaluation preferences. These will be discussed below in the coverage of the specific programs where they are applied.

[3] Subcontracting to Small Businesses

The government recognizes that many of its acquisitions require resources that are beyond the capability of any small business to serve as the prime contractor. However, small businesses may be able to participate as subcontractors. There are mechanisms designed to increase awards of subcontracts to small businesses.

Under procedures established in 1978 by Pub. L. No. 95-507, most federal contracts that exceed the simplified acquisition threshold must contain a clause stating that it is federal policy that small businesses have the "maximum practicable opportunity to participate in the performance of" federal contracts, 15 U.S.C. § 637(d)(1). Under ¶ (c) of the Utilization of Small Business Concerns clause in FAR 52.219-8 the contractor agrees "to carry out this policy in the awarding of subcontracts to the fullest extent consistent with efficient contract performance," and the contractor also agrees to cooperate with the contracting agency and the SBA in studies to determine the extent of compliance with the statute.

There are far more extensive requirements for contracts of $750,000 or more ($1.5 million or more for contracts for construction) awarded to any entity other than a small business, 15 U.S.C. § 637(d)(4). See FAR 19.702. The Small Business Subcontracting Plan clause in FAR 52.219-9, requiring that the contractor must provide a subcontracting plan approved by the contracting officer, is incorporated into these contracts. Paragraph (k) of the clause provides that failure to comply in good faith with the plan is a material breach. See also 15 U.S.C. § 637(d)(8). Companies can submit master subcontracting plans for "plants or divisions," FAR 19.704(b), to be incorporated in their individual plans. Contractors providing commercial products or services should submit commercial subcontracting plans, FAR 19.704(d).

The FAR 52.219-9 clause and FAR 19.704(a) provide detailed guidance on the elements of such plans including a requirement for separate treatment of each type of small business (veteran-owned small business, service-disabled veteran-owned small business, HUBZone small business, small disadvantaged business (including ANCs and Indian tribes) and women-owned small business concerns). The plans must describe the procedures the contractor will use to implement these subcontracting requirements and contain assurances that the contractor will comply with detailed reporting requirements. The plans must be included in subcontractor over the mandated thresholds.

In negotiated procurements, the successful offeror must submit a proposed plan and negotiate its terms with the contracting officer, and "[i]f the apparently successful offeror fails to negotiate a subcontracting plan acceptable to the contracting officer within the time limit prescribed by the contracting officer, the offeror will be ineligible for award," FAR 19.702(a)(1). Such negotiation is required to ensure that the plan included in the contract provides "the maximum practicable opportunity" for small businesses to participate in the performance of the contract. See *Columbia Research Corp.*, 61 Comp. Gen. 194 (B-202762), 82-1 CPD ¶ 8, where GAO approved a plan stating "zero percent of the estimated costs would be subcontracted to small business." GAO noted that the statute required only the offeror's best efforts in subcontracting to small business. Raising issues during discussions is a sufficient negotiation of the plan, *A P Logistics, LLC*, Comp. Gen. Dec. B-401600, 2010 CPD ¶ 179 (offeror that did not address issues in final proposal revisions properly rejected for unsatisfactory plan).

The acceptability of a subcontracting plan in a negotiated procurement is generally a matter of responsibility, with the result that negotiation of the plan is not a "discussion," *OGSys., LLC*, Comp. Gen. Dec. B-414672.6, 2018 CPD ¶ 352 (RFP stated that the acceptability of subcontracting plans was a responsibility matter); *Coastal Int'l Security, Inc.*, Comp. Gen. Dec. B-411756, 2015 CPD ¶ 340 (RFP required submission of subcontracting plan and provided that it was "subject to negotiations"). However, if subcontracting plans are evaluated comparatively as part of the best value decision, the negotiation of the plan is a discussion. For a detailed analysis of this issue, see *Computer Scis. Corp.*, Comp. Gen. Dec. B-298494, 2007 CPD ¶ 103. If a subcontracting plan is evaluated on a pass/fail basis, being a matter of responsibility, negotiation of an acceptable plan can continue until the time of award, *MANCON*, Comp. Gen. Dec. B-405663, 2012 CPD ¶ 68.

In sealed bid procurements, the firm selected for award must submit its plan regarding subcontract awards to small businesses, FAR 19.702(a)(2). If the plan does not meet the requirements, the contracting officer must advise the bidder of the deficiency and request a revised plan, FAR 19.705-4(b). Subcontracting plans are a matter of responsibility, not responsiveness, and thus may be submitted after bids are received and opened, *Devcon Sys. Corp.*, 59 Comp. Gen. 614 (B-197935), 80-2 CPD ¶ 46; *CH2M Hill, Ltd.*, Comp. Gen. Dec. B-259511, 95-1 CPD ¶ 203.

Agencies have authority to include in negotiated contracts the Incentive Subcontracting Program clause in FAR 52.219-10 under which the contractor may increase its profit by a percentage based upon the extent to which the actual awards to small businesses exceed the percentage negotiated and included in the clause, 15 U.S.C. § 637(d).

15 U.S.C. § 637(d)(4)(F) directs that liquidated damages shall be paid by the contractor if it does not make a good-faith effort to meet the goals in its plan. This requirement is implemented by the insertion in contracts that require

subcontracting plans of the Liquidated Damages—Subcontracting Plan clause at FAR 52.219-16. Guidance on the use of this clause is in FAR 19.705-7.

[D] Programs for Special Classes of Small Business

Congress has established a substantial number of classes of small businesses that are entitled to preferential treatment—with different rules and procedures applicable to each class. The major procedure applicable to all of the classes is the set-aside procedure. As noted earlier, for procurements over the simplified acquisition threshold, set-asides to SDVOBs, WOSBs, HUBZone concerns and procurements reserved for disadvantaged businesses through the 8(a) program are in parity with each other but take priority over set-asides to other small businesses, FAR 19.203(c). The other special procedures are discussed in this section.

[1] Small Disadvantaged Businesses

Starting in the late 1960s, the executive branch of the government began several programs to increase awards of federal contracts to "minority-owned" businesses. In 1978, most of those programs were revised and expanded by amendments to the Small Business Act, Pub. L. No. 95-507. These businesses are described as "small disadvantaged businesses" (SDBs), or "minority-owned businesses."

A 1995, Supreme Court decision cast a cloud over the entire SDB program. In *Adarand Constructors, Inc. v. Pena*, 515 U.S. 200 (1995), the Court significantly limited the federal government's authority to implement programs that favor racial minorities. In this decision, the Court held that federal affirmative action programs that use racial classifications are subject to a high level of judicial scrutiny, must serve a compelling government interest, and must be narrowly tailored to further that interest. *Adarand* has not had a significant impact on government contracting programs designed to assist SDBs. Reacting to *Adarand*, the President issued a directive to federal agencies ordering officials to review existing affirmative action programs and to eliminate or reform any program that creates a quota, creates preferences for unqualified individuals, creates reverse discrimination, or continues even after its equal opportunity purposes have been achieved, Memorandum for Heads of Executive Departments and Agencies, Evaluation of Affirmative Action Programs 1, July 19, 1995.

GAO has dismissed protest challenges to the constitutionality of the DoD's SDB set-aside program based on *Adarand*, citing a lack of clear judicial precedent, *Elrich Contracting Inc.*, Comp. Gen. Dec. B-262015, 95-2 CPD ¶71. Noting that *Adarand* set forth the standard to be applied by the federal courts in determining the constitutionality of such programs but did not actually decide whether the challenged program was unconstitutional, GAO stated that "[t]here must be clear judicial precedent before we will consider a protest based on the asserted unconstitutionality of the procuring agency's actions."

The result is that there is no set-aside program for SDBs but there are three programs that assist them: the "8(a)" program, a participation encouragement program, and a price evaluation adjustment program applicable to the Department of Defense, the National Aeronautics and Space Administration and the Coast Guard.

[a] Qualification as an SDB

15 U.S.C. § 637(a)(4) provides:

> (A) For purposes of this section, the term "socially and economically disadvantaged small business concern" means any small business concern which meets the requirements of subparagraph (B) and—
>
> (i) which is at least 51 per centum unconditionally owned by—
>
> (I) one or more socially and economically disadvantaged individuals,
>
> (II) an economically disadvantaged Indian tribe (or a wholly owned business entity of such tribe), or
>
> (III) an economically disadvantaged Native Hawaiian organization, or
>
> (ii) in the case of any publicly owned business at least 51 per centum of the stock of which is unconditionally owned by—
>
> (I) one or more socially and economically disadvantaged individuals,
>
> (II) an economically disadvantaged Indian tribe (or a wholly owned business entity of such tribe), or
>
> (III) an economically disadvantaged Native Hawaiian organization.
>
> (B) A small business concern meets the requirements of this subparagraph if the management and daily business operations of such small business concern are controlled by one or more—
>
> (i) socially and economically disadvantaged individuals described in subparagraph (A)(i)(I) or subparagraph (A)(ii)(I),
>
> (ii) members of an economically disadvantaged Indian tribe described in subparagraph (A)(i)(II) or subparagraph (A)(ii)(II), or
>
> (iii) Native Hawaiian organizations described in subparagraph (A)(i)(m) or subparagraph (A)(ii)(III).

The statute also contains separate definitions of "socially disadvantaged" and "economically disadvantaged" individuals, 15 U.S.C. § 637(a)(5) and (6). Participation requires that the individuals meet both of these tests, *Autek Sys.*

Corp. v. United States, 835 F. Supp. 13 (D.D.C. 1993), *aff'd*, 43 F.3d 712 (D.C. Cir. 1994). 13 C.F.R. § 124.103 provides the following definition of "socially disadvantaged:"

> (a) General. Socially disadvantaged individuals are those who have been subjected to racial or ethnic prejudice or cultural bias within American society because of their identities as members of groups and without regard to their individual qualities. The social disadvantage must stem from circumstances beyond their control.
>
> (b) Members of designated groups. (1) There is a rebuttable presumption that the following individuals are socially disadvantaged: Black Americans; Hispanic Americans; Native Americans (Alaska Natives, Native Hawaiians, or enrolled members of a Federally or State recognized Indian Tribe); Asian Pacific Americans (persons with origins from Burma, Thailand, Malaysia, Indonesia, Singapore, Brunei, Japan, China (including Hong Kong), Taiwan, Laos, Cambodia (Kampuchea), Vietnam, Korea, The Philippines, U.S. Trust Territory of the Pacific Islands (Republic of Palau), Republic of the Marshall Islands, Federated States of Micronesia, the Commonwealth of the Northern Mariana Islands, Guam, Samoa, Macao, Fiji, Tonga, Kiribati, Tuvalu, or Nauru); Subcontinent Asian Americans (persons with origins from India, Pakistan, Bangladesh, Sri Lanka, Bhutan, the Maldives Islands or Nepal); and members of other groups designated from time to time by SBA according to procedures set forth at paragraph (d) of this section. Being born in a country does not, by itself, suffice to make the birth country an individual's country of origin for purposes of being included within a designated group.

The regulation contains detailed guidance on the application of this definition, means of challenging the determination of social disadvantage and procedures that can be used by other individuals to demonstrate that they are socially disadvantaged.

13 C.F.R. § 124.104 provides the following definition of "economically disadvantaged:"

> (a) General. Economically disadvantaged individuals are socially disadvantaged individuals whose ability to compete in the free enterprise system has been impaired due to diminished capital and credit opportunities as compared to others in the same or similar line of business who are not socially disadvantaged.

The regulation contains detailed guidance on the information that must be submitted to meet this definition and the factors that are considered (including the key factor that the individual's net worth and adjusted gross income must each be less than $ 250,000). The size standards discussed earlier are used to determine whether these businesses qualify as small businesses, 13 C.F.R. § 124.102. There are special requirements for Indian tribes in 13 C.F.R.

§ 124.109(b), except that Alaskan Native Corporations are not subject to these requirements because they are deemed economically disadvantaged under 43 U.S.C. § 1626(e) and have special size requirements, 13 C.F.R. § 124.109(a). Special requirements for Native Hawaiian Organizations are set forth in 13 C.F.R. § 124.110(b). Key definitions are set forth in 13 C.F.R. § 124.103.

Small businesses that desire to take advantage of SDB status generally apply to the SBA to participate in the 8(a) program (discussed below) following the procedures in 13 C.F.R. §§ 124.201-124.207. Small businesses that do not want to participate in the 8(a) program can apply for separate certification as SDBs in accordance with 13 C.F.R. § 124.1003.

[b] The "8(a)" Program

The primary program designed to assist SDBs is commonly known as the "8(a)" program. The program takes its name from Section 8(a) of the Small Business Act. Section 8(a) authorizes the SBA to enter into contracts with other federal agencies and to perform such contracts by subcontracting to small businesses, 15 U.S.C. § 637(a). Beginning in the late 1960s, the SBA employed the 8(a) procedure to increase the amount of federal contract work performed by minority-owned businesses by taking contracts from procuring agencies and awarding subcontracts to minority-owned businesses. By the late 1970s, contracts valued at hundreds of millions of dollars were being awarded annually under the 8(a) program. The program has withstood challenges that it discriminated in favor of minority-owned small businesses, *Rothe Dev., Inc. v. United States Dep't of Def.*, 836 F.3d 57 (D.C. Cir. 2016), *cert. denied*, 138 S. Ct. 354 (2017). In one instance, nonminority competing contractors were granted declaratory relief because a total set-aside of all 1981 Corps of Engineers small business contracts in the Mississippi market was found to be an overly broad exercise of statutory power and, therefore, discriminatory to non-SDBs in violation of 42 U.S.C. § 2000d, *Fordice Constr. Co. v. Marsh*, 773 F. Supp. 867 (S.D. Miss. 1990).

In 1988, Congress enacted the Business Opportunity Development Reform Act, Pub. L. No. 100-656, which sought to curb abuses in the 8(a) program and make SDBs more competitive. The Act included reforms of the program which (1) require competition among 8(a) firms for manufacturing contracts exceeding $5 million and for service contracts and nonmanufacturing contracts exceeding $3 million, (2) require the SBA to establish business activity targets for businesses that have been in the program for five years, (3) authorize contracting officers to assess "liquidated damages" against prime contractors that fail to meet SDB subcontracting goals, and (4) prohibit SBA employees from holding stock in 8(a) firms for two years after leaving the SBA.

Firms participating in the 8(a) program must have an approved business plan, 15 U.S.C. § 636(j)(10)(D); 13 C.F.R. § 124.402. The maximum period of time a disadvantaged firm can remain in the program is nine years, 13 C.F.R.

§ 124.2. This is divided into a four-year developmental stage and a five-year transitional stage. See 13 C.F.R. § 124.404 for guidance on the assistance provided by SBA in each of these stages. The SBA regulations limiting the period that firms can participate in the 8(a) program were upheld in *Minority Bus. Legal Def. & Educ. Funds, Inc. v. Small Bus. Admin.*, 557 F. Supp. 37 (D.D.C. 1982). A court did not abuse its discretion by refusing to extend an 8(a) contractor's eligibility beyond nine years, even though the SBA had acted unlawfully in preventing the contractor from receiving full 8(a) benefits, *Woerner v. United States*, 934 F.2d 1277 (App. D.C. 1991).

The SBA has reasonable discretion to deny participation in the 8(a) program to clearly unqualified firms as long as applications receive thorough and careful review. See *Cognitive Prof'l Servs. Inc. v. U.S. Small Bus. Admin.*, 254 F. Supp. 3d 22 (D.D.C. 2017); *Neuma Corp. v. Abdnor*, 713 F. Supp. 1 (D.D.C. 1989).

SBA responsibility determinations for SDBs seeking contracts under the 8(a) program are covered exclusively by 15 U.S.C. § 637(a)(16) and do not involve the COC procedures required by § 637(b)(7). In *DAE Corp. v. Small Bus. Admin.*, 958 F.2d 436 (D.C. App. 1992), the court distinguished § 637(a) and § 637(b), stating at 439:

> Section 637(b)(7) no doubt does mean what it plainly says—but only where it applies. It is part of the § 8(b) program, and any small business proceeding under § 8(b) is entitled to its protections and its disadvantages. As the Comptroller General has affirmed, § 637(b)(7) is designed to help small businesses overcome the hesitance a procuring agency may have in awarding an ordinary contract to a small business. See *Custom Research, Inc.*, Comp. Gen. Dec. B-238976.2, 90-1 Comp. Gen. Dec. ¶ 567 (1990) (explaining that the COC process "is provided by law to protect small businesses from arbitrary nonresponsibility determinations made by procurement agencies.").
>
> The disadvantaged small business seeking a sole source contract under § 8(a), such as DAE, faces a vastly different situation. There, the procuring agency has asked the SBA to obtain the services of a specified disadvantaged small business —no passport is necessary because the contractor has already been admitted.

GAO will not review SBA decisions on a firm's eligibility for the 8(a) program, unless there are strong allegations of fraud, bad faith, or the SBA's violation of its own regulations, *Forway Indus.*, Comp. Gen. Dec. B-217046, 84-2 CPD ¶ 573. One court has also ruled that egregious procedural violations by SBA of its own regulations in terminating a firm's participation in the 8(a) program justify court review, *Oklahoma Aerotronics, Inc. v. United States*, 661 F.2d 976 (D.C. Cir. 1981).

[i] Obtaining Contracts

FAR 19.803 describes three ways that contracting agencies determine to award contracts under the 8(a) program:

> (a) The SBA advises an agency contracting activity of an 8(a) participant's capabilities through a search letter and asks the agency to identify acquisitions to support the firm's business plans.
>
> (b) The SBA identifies a specific requirement for a particular 8(a) firm or firms and asks the agency contracting activity to offer the acquisition to the 8(a) Program for the firm(s).
>
> (c) Agencies review other proposed acquisitions for the purpose of identifying requirements which may be offered to the SBA.

The regulation contains guidance on the information that is to be provided by the SBA when it uses either of the first two procedures. See also 13 C.F.R. § 124.501(e) urging contractors to "market their capabilities to appropriate procuring activities to increase their prospects of receiving sole source 8(a) contracts."

When an agency has determined that the 8(a) process should be used, it "offers" the procurement to the SBA with a description of the work and a recommendation of the type of procurement to be used, FAR 19.804-2. The SBA then determines whether to "accept" the requirement for the 8(a) program, FAR 19.804-3. The SBA will not accept a requirement if it has an adverse impact on a small business with a contract to perform the work, 13 C.F.R. § 124.504(c). The adverse impact rule does not apply if the requirement is changed, *Performance Value Mgmt., LLC*, Comp. Gen. Dec. B-416226, 2018 CPD ¶ 66 (agency sufficiently altered the price to be considered a new requirement); *Alpa Techs. & Servs., Inc.*, Comp. Gen. Dec. B-408762.2, 2014 CPD ¶ 66 (work changed from engineering and technology support to installation and logistics management services); *Klett Consulting Grp., Inc.*, Comp. Gen. Dec. B-404023, 2010 CPD ¶ 301 (agency had expanded the work from four states to seven states); *ANTECH, Inc.*, Comp. Gen. Dec. B-401092, 2009 CPD ¶ 91 (agency intended to use a facility in a different manner).

[ii] Competition Requirement

Procurements over specified dollar thresholds are subject to a competition requirement when possible. See FAR 19.805-1 stating:

> (a) Except as provided in paragraph (b) of this subsection, an acquisition offered to the SBA under the 8(a) Program shall be awarded on the basis of competition limited to eligible 8(a) participants when—

(1) There is a reasonable expectation that at least two eligible and responsible 8(a) firms will submit offers and that award can be made at a fair market price; and

(2) The anticipated total value of the contract, including options, will exceed $7.5 million for acquisitions assigned manufacturing North American Industry Classification System (NAICS) codes and $4.5 million for all other acquisitions.

(b) Where an acquisition exceeds the competitive threshold, the SBA may accept the requirement for a sole source 8(a) award if—

(1) There is not a reasonable expectation that at least two eligible and responsible 8(a) firms will submit offers at a fair market price; or

(2) SBA accepts the requirement on behalf of a concern owned by an Indian tribe or an Alaska Native Corporation.

Agencies may also request the SBA to approve a competitive procurement below the competitive threshold, FAR 19.805-1(d).

As noted above, the competition thresholds do not apply to Indian tribes and Alaska Native Corporations. However, 13 C.F.R. § 124.506(b) has limited this rule by stating that it will not approve such a sole source after it has agreed to a competitive procurement. See *Gov Servs., Inc.*, Comp. Gen. Dec. B-414374, 2017 CPD ¶ 143, and *JXM, Inc.*, Comp. Gen. Dec. B-402643, 2010 CPD ¶ 158, agreeing that it was proper for an agency to change a competitive 8(a) procurement to a sole source 8(a) procurement with an Alaska Native Corporation when the requirement had substantially changed. GAO's review of these sole source decisions is generally limited to allegations of fraud or bade faith, *NTELX, Inc.*, Comp. Gen. Dec. B-413837, 2017 CPD ¶ 13.

[iii] Entering Into the Contract

Although the 8(a) arrangement is technically a contract between the procuring agency and the SBA, and a subcontract between the SBA and the SDB, the procuring agency and the disadvantaged small business normally deal directly with each other. With respect to the contract with the procuring agency, 15 U.S.C. § 637(a)(3)(A) provides that, when practicable, the concern shall "participate in any negotiation of the terms and conditions of such contract."

In competitive 8(a) procurements, the contracting agency solicits offers from those firms that have been selected by the SBA, FAR 19.805-2(a). The contracting officer then conducts price negotiations with offerors, FAR 19.806. The SBA then determines the eligibility of the apparent winner, FAR 19.805-2(b)(1). See 13 C.F.R. § 124.507 for a description of the eligibility determination process.

In sole source 8(a) procurements, the agency uses standard negotiation procedures with the participation of the SBA "whenever practicable," FAR 19.808-1. Such procurements are subject to the requirements for obtaining certified cost or pricing data, FAR 19.806(a). The contracting agency is required to obtain concurrence of the SBA on the final price that is negotiated, FAR 19.806(d).

FAR 19.811-1 requires a contract between the agency and the SBA and a subcontract between the SBA and the SDB concern when the award has been made using sole source procedures. In contrast, "tripartite" contracts, where the contracting agency, the SBA and the SDB concern sign the document, are used when the award has been made using competitive procedures, FAR 19.811-2. See FAR 19.811-3 for guidance on the clauses to be used in these contracts. In either case, contract administration is normally delegated to the contracting activity, 13 C.F.R. § 124.512. The SBA does not "insure" performance of its 8(a) subcontractors, *ATC Petroleum, Inc. v. Sanders*, 860 F.2d 1104 (D.C. Cir. 1988). The subcontract between the 8(a) firm and the SBA contains a clause stating that the SBA has delegated responsibility for administering the subcontract to the procuring agency, which will act for the government, FAR 52.219-12. In such circumstances, the procuring agency may properly terminate an 8(a) contract for default and the termination need not come from the SBA, *Philadelphia Regent Builders, Inc. v. United States*, 634 F.2d 569 (Ct. Cl. 1980).

[2] HUBZone Concerns

Contractors in HUBZones are one of the types of small businesses that are given preference over other small businesses. Thus, if there are two HUBZone contractors a set-aside would be required, FAR 19.1305. However, HUBZone contractors are in parity with SDVOSBs and WOSBs—with the result that if there are also two small businesses in one or both of those categories, the contracting officer has the choice of which class of business the procurement should be set aside for. HUBZone contractors are also in parity with 8(a) concerns—giving the contracting officer a choice when there is a qualified 8(a) concern and two HUBZone contractors. However, a HUBZone set-aside is not proper if an 8(a) contractor is currently performing the requirement or the requirement has been accepted by the SBA for 8(a) participation, FAR 19.1304(d). See FAR 19.1305 for procedures to be followed when the contracting officer decides to set aside a procurement for HUBZone contractors. When this type of set-aside is made, agencies must use the Notice of Total HUBZone Set-Aside clause in FAR 52.219-3.

There are two other programs to assist HUBZone contractors—the sole source contracting program and the evaluation preference program.

[a] Certification of HUBZone Concerns

The requirements to qualify as a HUBZone concern are set forth in 13 C.F.R. § 126.200(b) as follows:

> (1) Ownership. (i) The concern must be at least 51% unconditionally and directly owned and controlled by persons who are United States citizens;
>
> (2) Size. The concern, together with its affiliates, must qualify as a small business under the size standard corresponding to its primary industry classification as defined in part 121 of this chapter.
>
> (3) Principal office. The concern's principal office must be located in a HUBZone.
>
> (4) Employees. At least 35% of the concern's employees must reside in a HUBZone. When determining the percentage of employees that reside in a HUBZone, if the percentage results in a fraction, round up to the nearest whole number;
>
> (5) Contract Performance. The concern must represent, as provided in the application, that it will "attempt to maintain" (see § 126.103) having 35% of its employees reside in a HUBZone during the performance of any HUBZone contract it receives.
>
> (6) Subcontracting. The concern must represent, as provided in the application, that it will ensure that it will comply with certain contract performance requirements in connection with contracts awarded to it as a qualified HUBZone SBC, as set forth in § 126.700.

See also FAR 19.1303. There are special requirements for Indian Tribal Governments, Alaska Native Corporations, Community Development Corporations, and small agricultural cooperatives.

A small business that wants to participate in the HUBZone program must apply to the SBA for certification and receive that certification as a prerequisite to participation, 13 C.F.R. § 126.300. The procedures followed to obtain certification are set forth in 13 C.F.R. §§ 126.301-126.309.

[b] Sole Source Contracts

When there is only one HUBZone contractor and there are not two SDVOSBs or WOSBs, the contracting agency may, in some circumstances, award a sole source HUBZone contract. See FAR 19.1306 stating:

> (a) A contracting officer shall consider a contract award to HUBZone small business concerns on a sole source basis (see 6.302-5(b)(5)) before considering a small business set-asides (see 19.203 and subpart 19.5), provided none of the exclusions at 19.1304 apply; and—
>
> > (1) The contracting officer does not have a reasonable expectation that offers would be received from two or more HUBZone small business concerns;
> >
> > (2) The anticipated price of the contract, including options, will not exceed—
> >
> > > (i) $ 7.5 million for a requirement within the North American Industry Classification System (NAICS) codes for manufacturing; or

(ii) $ 4.5 million for a requirement within all other NAICS codes;

(3) The requirement is not currently being performed by an 8(a) participant under the provisions of subpart 19.8 or has been accepted as a requirement by SBA under subpart 19.8.

(4) The acquisition is greater than the simplified acquisition threshold (see part 13);

(5) The HUBZone small business concern has been determined to be a responsible contractor with respect to performance; and

(6) Award can be made at a fair and reasonable price.

There is no guidance on the procedures to be followed when a sole source contract is awarded to a HUBZone contractor but, since the contracting officer is required to ensure that the price is fair and reasonable, normal contracting procedures should apply. This would require the submission of certified cost or pricing data when the procurement is over the $2 million threshold and the negotiation of the price before award.

[c] Price Evaluation Preference

When a procurement is open to all firms, both large and small, HUBZone contractors are given a 10% evaluation preference. FAR 19.1307 contains the following guidance:

(c) The factor of 10 percent shall be applied on a line item basis or to any group of items on which award may be made. Other evaluation factors, such as transportation costs or rent-free use of Government property, shall be added to the offer to establish the base offer before adding the factor of 10 percent.

(d) When the two highest rated offerors are a HUBZone small business concern and a large business, and the evaluated offer of the HUBZone small business concern is equal to the evaluated offer of the large business after considering the price evaluation preference, the contracting officer shall award the contract to the HUBZone small business concern.

This preference is implemented by inclusion of the Notice of Price Evaluation Preference for HUBZone Small Business Concerns clause in FAR 52.219-4.

[3] Service-Disabled Veterans-Owned Small Businesses

SDVOSBs are one of the types of small businesses that are given preference over other small businesses. Thus, if there are two SDVOSBs, the contracting officer must consider an SDVOSB set aside before a small business set aside, FAR 19.1405. However, SDVOSBs are in parity with HUBZone contractors and WOSBs—with the result that if there are also two small businesses in one or both of those categories, the contracting officer has the choice of which class of business the procurement should be set aside for. SDVOSBs are also in parity with 8(a) concerns—giving the contracting officer a choice when there is a qualified 8(a) concern and two SDVOSBs. However, an SDVOSB set-aside is not proper if an 8(a) contractor is currently performing the requirement or the requirement has been accepted by the SBA for 8(a) participation, FAR 19.1404(d). See FAR 19.1405 for procedures to be followed when the contracting officer decides to set aside a procurement for SDVOSBs. When this type of set-aside is made, agencies must use the Notice of Total Service-Disabled Veteran-Owned Set-Aside clause in FAR 52.219-27.

There is one other program to assist SDVOSBs—the sole source contracting program.

[a] Determination of SDVOSB Status

FAR. 2.101 contains the following definition:

> Service-disabled veteran-owned small business concern—
>
> (1) Means a small business concern—
>
> (i) Not less than 51 percent of which is owned by one or more service-disabled veterans or, in the case of any publicly owned business, not less than 51 percent of the stock of which is owned by one or more service-disabled veterans; and
>
> (ii) The management and daily business operations of which are controlled by one or more service-disabled veterans or, in the case of a service-disabled veteran with permanent and severe disability, the spouse or permanent caregiver of such veteran.
>
> (2) Service-disabled veteran means a veteran, as defined in 38 U.S.C. 101(2), with a disability that is service-connected, as defined in 38 U.S.C. 101(16).

FAR 19.1403 requires that a SDVOSB must represent that it is such a concern at the time it submits an offer and provides that a joint venture can qualify if one member is a SDVOSB and it meets other specified conditions.

[b] Sole Source Contracts

When there is only one SDVOSB and there are not two HUBZone contractors or WOSBs, the contracting agency may, in some circumstances, award a sole source SDVOSB contract. See FAR 19.1406 stating:

> (a) A contracting officer may award contracts to a SVDOSB concerns on a sole source basis (see 6.302-5(b)(6)), before considering small business

set-asides (see 19.203 and subpart 19.5) provided none of the exclusions of 19.1404 apply and—

(1) The contracting officer does not have a reasonable expectation that offers would be received from two or more service-disabled veteran-owned small business concerns;

(2) The anticipated award price of the contract, including options, will not exceed—

(i) $7 million for a requirement within the NAICS codes for manufacturing; or

(ii) $4 million for a requirement within any other NAICS code;

(3) The requirement is not currently being performed by an 8(a) participant under the provisions of subpart 19.8 or has been accepted as a requirement by SBA under subpart 19.8;

(4) The service-disabled veteran-owned small business concern has been determined to be a responsible contractor with respect to performance; and

(5) Award can be made at a fair and reasonable price.

[4] Women-Owned Small Businesses

WOSBs are one of the types of small businesses that are given preference over other small businesses. Thus, if there are two WOSBs, the contracting officer must consider an SDVOSB set aside before a small business set aside, FAR 19.1505. However, WOSBs are in parity with HUBZone contractors and SDVOSBs—with the result that if there are also two small businesses in one or both of those categories, the contracting officer has the choice of which class of business the procurement should be set aside for. WOSBs are also in parity with 8(a) concerns—giving the contracting officer a choice when there is a qualified 8(a) concern and two WOSBs. However, an WOSB set-aside is not proper if an 8(a) contractor is currently performing the requirement or the requirement has been accepted by the SBA for 8(a) participation, FAR 19.1504(a). There are two types of set-asides for WOSBs but no other programs to assist them.

[a] Determination of WOSB Status

There are two categories of WOSBs—economically disadvantaged WOSBs (EDWOSBs) and WOSBs. WOSBs are defined in 13 C.F.R. § 127.200 as follows:

(b) Qualification as a WOSB. To qualify as a WOSB, a concern must be:

(1) A small business as defined in part 121 of this chapter; and

(2) Not less than 51 percent unconditionally and directly owned and controlled by one or more women who are United States citizens.

To be an EDWOSB the women must be economically disadvantaged, defined in 13 C.F.R. § 127.203(a) as follows:

> A woman is economically disadvantaged if she can demonstrate that her ability to compete in the free enterprise system has been impaired due to diminished capital and credit opportunities as compared to others in the same or similar line of business. SBA does not take into consideration community property laws when determining economic disadvantage when the woman has no direct, individual or separate ownership interest in the property.

This regulation contains detailed guidance on the determination of economic disadvantage. Rules on ownership and control are contained in 13 C.F.R. § 127.201 and § 127.202.

WOSBs and EDWOSBs must be certified by the SBA. See 13 C.F.R. Part 127. FAR 19.1503 also requires that when they submit an offer they be registered in SAM.

[b] Set-Aside Procedures

Set-aside procedures are set forth in FAR 19.1505. They provide that when the SBA determines in which NAICS codes WOSBs or EDWOSBs are underrepresented and substantially underrepresented a contracting officer may set-aside acquisitions exceeding the micro-purchase threshold following standard set-aside procedures. FAR 19.1505 also provides:

> (d) The contracting officer may make an award, if only one acceptable offer is received from a qualified EDWOSB or WOSB concern.
>
> (e) The contracting officer must check whether the apparently successful offeror filed all the required eligibility documents, and file a status protest if any documents are missing. See 19.1503(d)(2).

§ 14.03 DOMESTIC PREFERENCE POLICIES

The government has a variety of policies favoring the acquisition of articles of domestic origin or acquisition from domestic sources. The major policies are the Buy American Act and the Trade Agreements Act, but there are numerous additional policies that also favor the use of domestic products or sources.

[A] Buy American Act

The Buy American Act establishes a general preference for the acquisition of domestic "articles, materials, and supplies" when they are being acquired for public use in the United States, 41 U.S.C. §§ 8301-8305. The Act was passed during the Depression of the 1930s and was designed to save and create jobs for American workers. The central consideration under the BAA has consistently been the place of manufacture; the nationality of the contractor is not relevant, *E-Systems, Inc.*, 61 Comp. Gen. 431 (B-206209), 82-1 CPD ¶ 533; *Patterson Pump Co.*, Comp. Gen. Dec. B-200165, 80-2 CPD ¶ 453. The term "acquired for public use" applies to leases as well as purchases, *National Office Equip. Co.*, Comp. Gen. Dec. B-191003, 78-1 CPD ¶ 413.

The BAA has separate provisions governing supply and construction contracts. The rules for determining whether articles, materials, or supplies are foreign or domestic are the same for both types of procurement, the differences being the terminology used and the juncture in the total manufacturing or construction process at which the test is applied. Under supply contracts, the proscriptions of the BAA fall on the articles, materials, or supplies delivered to the government; whereas, under construction contracts, they apply to the articles, materials, and supplies used by the contractor and subcontractors in constructing, altering, or repairing the building or work.

The articles, materials, and supplies covered by the BAA are discussed in the FAR using different nomenclature for supply and construction contracts. FAR 25.101 restricts the purchase of supplies that are not domestic "end products," while FAR 25.201 requires the use of only domestic "construction materials." Items delivered to the construction site simply for the use of the contractor that are not to be incorporated into the building or work, such as construction shacks and trailers, are not construction materials subject to the Buy American Act, *Mico Mobile Sales & Leasing Co.*, 51 Comp. Gen. 538 (B-174851) (1972).

The BAA applies similar distinct requirements to unmanufactured and manufactured articles, materials, or supplies.

[1] Unmanufactured Articles

For unmanufactured articles, materials, or supplies acquired by the government for use in the United States, the BAA requires that they must have been "mined" or "produced" in the United States, unless one of the exceptions discussed below applies, 41 U.S.C. § 8302(a)(1) (supply contracts) and § 8303(a)(1) (construction contracts).

[2] Manufactured Articles

The BAA requires that manufactured articles, materials, or supplies acquired by the government for public use in the United States or incorporated into domestic construction projects must have been manufactured in this country "substantially all" (more than 55% or 95% if the article consists wholly or predominantly of iron or steel) from components that have themselves been "mined, produced, or manufactured" within the United States, unless one of the exceptions discussed below is applicable, 41 U.S.C. § 8302(a)(2) (supply contracts) and § 8303(a)(2) (construction contracts). Hence, for a manufactured end product or a manufactured construction material to be domestic, it must meet two tests: it must have been manufactured in the United States, and more than 55% or 95% of its components must have been mined, produced, or manufactured in the United States. In contrast, components must meet only one test—manufacture in the United States. For example, a watch movement that was domestically manufactured (assembled) entirely from foreign-made parts is a domestic component of the watch into which it is incorporated, *Hamilton Watch Co.*, Comp. Gen. Dec. B-179939, 74-1 CPD ¶ 306.

The three major issues concerning manufactured products are (a) what constitutes manufacturing, (b) the distinction between end products and construction materials versus components, and (c) the application of the "substantially all" rule.

[a] Manufacturing

The meaning of "manufacturing" is important because it will determine whether an end product, construction material, or component is domestic. The term "manufacture" has been interpreted broadly to include the assembly of parts, *Hamilton Watch Co.*, Comp. Gen. Dec. B-179939, 74-1 CPD ¶ 306, but does not include packaging, testing, and evaluation operations, 48 Comp. Gen. 727 (B-166008) (1969). However, GAO has also held that disassembly and reassembly in the United States of a product that was manufactured outside the United States to a condition almost ready to use before the disassembly do not constitute domestic "manufacture," *Ampex Corp.*, Comp. Gen. Dec. B-203021, 82-1 CPD ¶ 163. Compare *Textron, Inc. v. Adams*, 493 F. Supp. 824 (D.D.C. 1980), where foreign disassembly and domestic reassembly was held to constitute domestic manufacture. In *DynAmerica, Inc.*, Comp. Gen. Dec. B-248237, 92-2 CPD ¶ 210, GAO held that the packing in Mexico of domestically manufactured ammunition links into feeder sleeve cartons was merely packaging that made the end product easier to use and did not constitute manufacturing. "Processing" of magnetic tape for computer use was held not to constitute manufacturing since it was a service analogous to translation, *Blodgett Keypunching Co.*, 54 Comp. Gen. 18 (B-153751), 76-2 CPD ¶ 331. Yet cold-forging foreign steel was held to be manufacturing, *United States ex rel. Kress v. Masonry Sols. Int'l, Inc.*, No. 12-2380, 2015 WL 3604760 (E.D. La. June 8, 2015).

GAO has drawn some fine distinctions in this area resulting in considerable confusion. Compare 45 Comp. Gen. 658 (B-158869) (1966), with 48 Comp. Gen. 727 (B-166008) (1969), both involving sequential manufacturing processes, from which GAO drew different conclusions. The basic test is whether the operations performed on the foreign item create a basically new material or result in a fundamental change in the item. See *A. Hirsh, Inc.*, Comp. Gen. Dec. B-237466, 90-1 CPD ¶ 247, ruling that domestic processing of foreign-bought horsehair—

including sterilization, sorting, cutting, inspecting, blending with oil, wrapping, and trimming—was not "manufacturing," because after all the processing, the horsehair was still horsehair. See also *Mechanix Wear, Inc.*, Comp. Gen. Dec. B-416704.3, 2019 CPD ¶ 171 (tanning and processing of goat/kidskins to turn them into leather is manufacturing); *City Chem. LLC*, Comp. Gen. Dec. B-296135.2, 2005 CPD ¶ 120 (sifting and selecting "contract compliant" material to select the portion of the mixture that meets the specification's particle size standard not manufacturing since it involves no changes—let alone substantial changes—to the physical character of the product); *TRS Research*, Comp. Gen. Dec. B-285514, 2000 CPD ¶ 128, ruling that ("refurbishing" foreign containers is not manufacturing because it did not "transform or alter the essential nature of the containers").

Construction cases are equally fact-sensitive. For example, where contract specifications required the construction of a water pump unit, and the complete, operable unit was delivered to the construction site, the entire unit, rather than simply its motor, was considered to be the construction material, 46 Comp. Gen. 813 (B-161061) (1967). In contrast, where circuit breakers and switchgear were brought to the site separately and installed in a building as a unit, they were each held to be construction material, *George Hyman Constr. Co.*, ASBCA 13777, 69-2 BCA ¶ 7830.

Once it is determined that an end product, construction material, or component has been "manufactured," the actual place the "manufacturing" occurred—not the relative costs of manufacturing—will control the BAA determination. Thus, if an end product is assembled (manufactured) outside of the United States from domestic components, it is not a domestic product even though substantially all of the costs of the product are incurred domestically, 52 Comp. Gen. 13 (B-175526) (1972). In this case, GAO reasoned that manufacture had occurred outside of the United States, even though only 3% of the costs were incurred for foreign work. An interesting controversy over the application of this rule occurred where a company performed final assembly and testing in the United States after 85 to 90% of the manufacture was accomplished in Mexico using American components, *Cincinnati Elecs. Corp.*, 55 Comp. Gen. 1479 (B-185842), 76-2 CPD ¶ 286. GAO denied a protest against this procedure because this issue was under consideration at a policy level in the agency. However, the regulations are still silent on whether early stages of the final assembly process can be performed outside of the United States within the requirement for domestic manufacture.

GAO has noted that the meaning of "manufacture" is difficult to ascertain and has recommended that the procurement regulations be amended to provide a precise definition, *Davis Walker Corp.*, Comp. Gen. Dec. B-184672, 76-2 CPD ¶ 182. GAO suggested that a procuring agency formulate a general definition of "manufacture." The agency replied that such a rigid approach to a fluid concept was undesirable, 654 FCR A-5 (1976). The FAR does not provide a general definition of "manufacture" for BAA purposes.

[b] End Products and Construction Materials Versus Components

FAR 25.003 contains the following definitions:

> *End product* means those articles, materials, and supplies to be acquired for public use.
>
> *Component* means an article, material, or supply incorporated directly into an end product or construction material.
>
> *Construction material* means an article, material, or supply brought to the construction site by a contractor or subcontractor for incorporation into the building or work. The term also includes an item brought to the site preassembled from articles, materials, or supplies. However, emergency life safety systems, such as emergency lighting, fire alarm, and audio evacuation systems, that are discrete systems incorporated into a public building or work and that are produced as complete systems, are evaluated as a single and distinct construction material regardless of when or how the individual parts or components of those systems are delivered to the construction site. Materials purchased directly by the Government are supplies, not construction material.

These definitions provide little guidance regarding the distinctions between supply and construction contracts. Yet this is a major issue, since the origin of parts assembled into components need not be domestic, 45 Comp. Gen. 658 (B-158869) (1966). In view of the lack of regulatory guidance, the definitions primarily rest on the exercise of procurement judgment, 48 Comp. Gen. 384 (B-165634) (1968).

There have sometimes been conflicting results. In *Bell Helicopter Textron*, 59 Comp. Gen. 158 (B-195268), 79-2 CPD ¶ 431, GAO ruled that the end product was a helicopter rather than the total work performed on the contract including furnishing the helicopter. In *Textron, Inc. v. Adams*, 493 F. Supp. 824 (D.D.C. 1980), the court disagreed, ruling that the contract end product was a helicopter system consisting of five components: a helicopter, system test and evaluation, system engineering/management, data, and integrated logistics support. The court reasoned that deference should be given to the agency's contractual statement of its need for a "system" without regard to the fact that the helicopter constituted the predominant element of the procurement. This decision concludes that an end product may be composed of various discrete products, so long as it is being procured as, and will be used as, a single unit, such as a "tool kit," *Imperial Eastman Corp.*, 53 Comp. Gen. 726 (B-177865), 74-1 CPD ¶ 153, or a modification kit, 47 Comp. Gen. 21 (B-161325) (1967). Occasionally, a solicitation will specify what items will be considered end products for BAA purposes. Compare *Ampex Corp.*, Comp. Gen. Dec. B-203021, 82-1 CPD ¶ 163, where operation and maintenance manuals were held not to be components. This follows the more prevalent GAO view that an end product is the item being manufactured, in the form in which it is required by the government, as distinguished from such things as packaging and services or tests performed after the item has been manufactured, *Patterson Pump Co.*, Comp. Gen. Dec. B-200165, 80-2 CPD ¶ 453. See also 46 Comp. Gen. 784 (B-160627) (1967), where sulfa tablets, not the bottled sulfa tablets actually delivered, were held to be the end products.

[c] "Substantially All" Rule

An end product or a manufactured construction material is considered to have been manufactured "substantially all" from components of domestic origin if the cost of all components mined, manufactured, or produced in the United States is more than 55% (or 95% for iron or steel products) of the cost of all of its components, FAR 25.101(a)(2). (For many years the test was 50%.) In applying this test, the boards and GAO have addressed two issues: what constitutes a component and what costs are included in the computation.

The term "component" is applied only to those articles, materials, and supplies directly used in the manufacture of the end product or construction material. For example, in the procurement of clothing, yarn used in the manufacture of the cloth was not considered a component because it was not directly incorporated into the clothing, 45 Comp. Gen. 658 (B-158869) (1966). See also *Ampex Corp.*, Comp. Gen. Dec. B-203021, 82-1 CPD ¶ 163 (operation and maintenance manuals were merely tools to provide instructions and not components incorporated into the end product).

In *General Kinetics, Inc.*, 70 Comp. Gen. 473 (B-242052.2), 91-1 CPD ¶ 445, the government was purchasing both "Tempest" (used for secure messages) and "non-Tempest" fax systems. The major component of each system was a commercial fax machine of foreign origin. Each of the fax machines was disassembled in the United States, certain operations were conducted, and the machines were reassembled in the United States. GAO found that the operations conducted on the Tempest fax machine, which included replacement of the programmable memory chips, addition of Tempest-required insulation, and the addition and integration of a protocol converter, were sufficient to make it a domestic component, and the "Tempest" system a domestic end product. However, the operations conducted on the non-Tempest machine, which consisted of disassembly, removal of circuit board and replacement of memory chips, and reassembly, were not sufficient to alter the essential nature of the machine, so that it remained a foreign component. Thus, the non-Tempest system was a foreign end item subject to the BAA's evaluation differential. See *Leisure-Lift, Inc.*, Comp. Gen. Dec. B-291878.3, 2003 CPD ¶ 189, holding that only the "shell" or "base unit" that cost 47.7% of the components of a motor scooter was foreign with the result that the scooter was a domestic end item. See also *City Chem. LLC*, Comp. Gen. Dec. B-296135.2, 2005 CPD ¶ 120, describing the analysis of whether a component was manufactured in the United States as follows:

> [W]here it is alleged that a foreign material has been manufactured into a component domestically and the component in turn manufactured into an

> end item domestically, we have . . . looked at whether the manufacturing process consists of two distinct phases, the first yielding a component that is distinguishable from the original material and the second yielding an end item that is distinguishable from the component.

In applying the substantially-all test, only the cost of components is considered. FAR 25.003 contains the following definition:

> Cost of components means—
>
> (1) For components purchased by the contractor, the acquisition cost, including transportation costs to the place of incorporation into the end product or construction material (whether or not such costs are paid to a domestic firm), and any applicable duty (whether or not a duty-free entry certificate is issued); or
>
> (2) For components manufactured by the contractor, all costs associated with the manufacture of the component, including transportation costs as described in paragraph (1) of this definition, plus allocable overhead costs, but excluding profit. Cost of components does not include any costs associated with the manufacture of the end product.

Domestic component costs are comprised of the purchase price of the component or the full cost of manufacture if the contractor manufactured the component, *Avantek, Inc.*, 50 Comp. Gen. 697 (B-170498) (1973). The total cost of the end product—what it would sell for, minus profit—is irrelevant, since that figure includes cost elements other than components. For example, labor, packaging, testing, and evaluation costs incurred in manufacturing the end product would not be included as part of the costs of the components of the end product. Thus, transportation costs of ready mixed concrete were not assignable as a cost of the components because the concrete was an identifiable end item at the time it was transported to the job site, *Dick Hollan, Inc.*, ASBCA 21304, 77-1 BCA ¶ 12,540. Similarly, in 53 Comp. Gen. 259 (B-179029) (1973), engineering costs were excluded from the computation because such services were not directly incorporated into the end product.

[3] Solicitation and Contract Provisions

The procuring agency is required to include BAA provisions in each solicitation and contract that is determined to be subject to the Act, FAR 25.1101 (supplies) and FAR 25.1102 (construction). For supply contracts the required clauses are the Buy American Act—Supplies clause in FAR 52.225-1, the Buy American Certificate solicitation provision in FAR 52.225-2, and the Place of Manufacture solicitation provision in FAR 52.225-18. For construction contracts valued at less than $7,032,000 the required clauses are the Buy American Act—Construction Materials clause in FAR 52.225-9 and the Notice of Buy American Act

Requirements solicitation provision in FAR 52.225-10. See DFARS 225.1101 for different clauses and solicitation provisions used in DoD contracts.

The Buy American Certificate provision requires the offeror to certify that each end product, other than those specifically identified in the certificate, is of domestic origin, and that components of unknown origin have been considered to have been mined, produced, or manufactured outside the United States. If the offeror leaves the certificate blank, the offeror will be deemed to be offering only products of domestic origin, *Consolidated Devices, Inc.*, Comp. Gen. Dec. B-214469, 84-1 CPD ¶ 383; *Lanier Bus. Prods., Inc.*, Comp. Gen. Dec. B-196736, 81-1 CPD ¶ 186. See *Designware, Inc.*, Comp. Gen. Dec. B-221423, 86-1 CPD ¶ 181, where the fact that a listed product was manufactured only in Korea was held irrelevant where the bidder left the certificate blank and the contracting officer did not know that the product was foreign. See, however, *Fitnet Purchasing All.*, Comp. Gen. Dec. B-410797, 2015 CPD ¶ 78 (quote properly rejected for failure to submit certificate); and *Airpro Equip., Inc.*, 62 Comp. Gen. 154 (B-209612), 83-1 CPD ¶ 105 (product treated as foreign when bidder left the certificate blank but identified the country of manufacture as "USA/England" in the schedule).

The standard BAA contract clauses for supply and construction require that the contractor deliver domestic end products or domestic construction materials, unless one of the specified exceptions to the Act's provisions is applicable, FAR 52.225-1 and FAR 52.225-9. If an offeror certifies that it will comply with the BAA, the contracting officer can rely on that certification unless there is reason to believe that it is not correct, *Pacific Lock Co.*, Comp. Gen. Dec. B-405800, 2011 CPD ¶ 286; *General Kinetics, Inc.*, 70 Comp. Gen. 473 (B-242052.2), 91-1 CPD ¶ 445.

If the contractor does not comply with the BAA, the contract may be terminated for default, *Sunox, Inc.*, ASBCA 30025, 85-2 BCA ¶ 18,077.

[4] Exceptions

Congress has recognized that application of the BAA might severely restrict an agency's ability to meet its needs. For example, many specific products are not manufactured, mined, or produced in the United States or, if they are available domestically, their prices might be far higher than the price of equivalent items of foreign origin. Congress has established a number of exceptions to give procuring agencies flexibility.

[a] Unreasonable Costs

The head of an agency is authorized to permit procurement of foreign items if the cost of the lowest-priced domestic item is "unreasonable," 41 U.S.C. § 8302(a)(1) and § 8303(b)(2). The President has established uniform standards for agencies to use in determining when prices of foreign supplies are considered "unreasonable," and those standards have been incorporated into the FAR, Executive Order 13881, 84 Fed. Reg. 35257 (2019); FAR 25.105.

Under these standards, agencies add a percentage to the price, inclusive of duty, of the low acceptable offer of a foreign item and then compare that increased price to the price for an item of domestic origin, FAR 25.105(a). The percentage is 20% for large businesses and 30% for small businesses, FAR 25.105(b). (For many years the percentages were 6% and 12%.) If, for example, the low responsive bid offering a foreign item is $100, the 20% differential would be $20, and the agency would, solely for evaluation purposes, treat the price of the offeror of a foreign item as $120. If the low responsive offeror of a domestic item is a small business, the differential would be 30%, and the evaluated price of the offeror of the foreign item would be treated as $130. DoD uses an evaluation factor of 50% in lieu of the above factors, DFARS 225.105(b). See *Sea Box, Inc.*, Comp. Gen. Dec. B-405711.2, 2012 CPD ¶ 116, where this factor was misapplied.

The differential is applied only to the material delivered under the contract and not necessarily to the total bid price. Thus, post-delivery services such as installation, testing, and training are exempted from the surcharge applicable to foreign end products, *Dynatest Consulting, Inc.*, Comp. Gen. Dec. B-257822.4, 95-1 CPD ¶ 167. See *STD Research Corp.*, 72 Comp. Gen. 211 (B-252073.2), 93-1 CPD ¶ 406 (agency should not apply the surcharge to an offeror's total evaluated price for a high-technology power generator, which included not only the price of foreign hardware but also post-delivery services); and *Allis-Chalmers Corp. v. Friedkin*, 635 F.2d 248 (3d Cir. 1980) (costs of installation and post-delivery services were excluded from the price of the foreign item to which the small business differential was applied).

The evaluation procedure ordinarily is applied on an item-by-item basis, or to any group of items on which award may be made as specifically provided in the solicitation, FAR 25.501(a). Absent such a provision, each item or group of closely related items will be treated separately for evaluation purposes, even though award may be made on an all-or-nothing basis, 47 Comp. Gen. 676 (B-163740) (1968); *Essex Assocs., Inc.*, 63 Comp. Gen. 503 (B-213279), 84-2 CPD ¶ 97. FAR Subpart 25.5 contains more detailed guidance on the evaluation of foreign offers on supply contracts.

This evaluation process does not apply to procurements under the Trade Agreements Act, FAR 25.105(a)(2). A separate evaluation process applies to procurements subject to the Caribbean Basin Trade Initiative, FAR 25.405 and 25.504-2, or the Israeli Trade Act, FAR 25.406 and 25.504-3.

[b] Unavailability

The requirements of the BAA do not apply to products that have been determined not to be reasonably available in commercial quantities and of a satisfactory quality, 41 U.S.C. § 8302(a)(2)(B) and § 8303(b)(1)(B); FAR 25.103(b). A list of such products is set forth in FAR 25.104(a). See *Mechanix Wear, Inc.*, Comp. Gen. Dec. B-416704, 2018 CPD ¶ 395, holding, in effect, that this list creates a mandatory exception for its products.

[c] Use Abroad

The BAA exempts articles purchased "for use outside the United States," 41 U.S.C. § 8302(a)(2)(A) and § 8303(b)(1)(A). See *Systems & Def. Servs. Int'l*, Comp. Gen. Dec. B-254254.2, 94-1 CPD ¶ 91 (contract not subject to BAA because the work was to be performed outside the United States); and *Maremont Corp.*, 55 Comp. Gen. 1362 (B-186276), 76-2 CPD ¶ 181 (BAA held not to apply to the purchase of machine guns for installation in vehicles deployed outside the United States, or to the procurement of steel towers for installation as part of a communications system in West Germany). This exception permits any foreign-made product to be offered for such procurements and does not require the furnishing of products manufactured in the country of use.

[d] Public Interest

The BAA allows the head of a procuring agency to waive application of the Act upon a determination that such application would be "inconsistent with the public interest," 41 U.S.C. § 8302(a)(1) and § 8303(b)(3). FAR 25.202(a)(1) calls for the use of this exception when an agency has an agreement with a foreign government. DoD has used this authority to grant a broad exemption from foreign acquisition restrictions for procurements of defense equipment from certain countries with which the United States has entered into Memoranda of Understanding (MOU) or other relevant agreements, DFARS Subpart 225.8. See *Self-Powered Lighting, Ltd. v. United States*, 492 F. Supp. 1267 (S.D.N.Y. 1980), where the court ruled that a MOU created a blanket exemption for all United Kingdom defense products and *American Hosp. Supply, Equipping & Consulting*, Comp. Gen. Dec. B-221357, 86-1 CPD ¶ 70, where GAO found proper use of an exemption under a MOU with Italy. Such exemptions extend to nondefense products procured by the DoD, *Allis-Chalmers Corp. v. Arnold*, 619 F.2d 44 (9th Cir. 1980). See also *Air Plastics, Inc.*, Comp. Gen. Dec. B-199307, 80-2 CPD ¶ 141 (exemption for Denmark by MOU); and *Baganoff Assocs., Inc.*, 54 Comp. Gen. 44 (B-179607), 74-2 CPD ¶ 56 (broad Canadian exemption).

The head of a procuring agency has considerable discretion in determining whether to invoke the public interest exception. However, Executive Order No. 13788, April 16, 2017, requires agencies to minimize the use of waivers. GAO has held that this exception may be invoked after bid opening, *E-Systems, Inc.*, 61 Comp. Gen. 431 (B-206209), 82-1 CPD ¶ 533. An agency has also been permitted to invoke this exception after contract award when the only domestic price is unreasonable, *John T. Brady & Co. v. United States*, 693 F.2d 1380 (Fed. Cir. 1982). In *John T. Brady & Co.*, VACAB 1300, 84-1 BCA ¶ 16,925, *recons. denied*, 84-1 BCA ¶ 17,161, the board, on remand, held that the failure of the agency to grant the exception was an abuse of discretion since the government would have incurred no additional costs by granting the exception. The board, therefore, granted the contractor a price adjustment for the difference in price between the domestic and foreign material. However, a contractor should generally request waiver of the BAA before contract award or at least before contract performance, *C. Sanchez & Son, Inc. v. United States*, 24 Cl. Ct. 14 (1991), *aff'd in part, vacated in part*, 6 F.3d 1539 (Fed. Cir. 1993). In *C. Sanchez*, a contractor sought an equitable adjustment to compensate for certain increased costs in using domestic wire and cable. Although the contractor complained during performance about the cost to a contracting officer's technical representative, it never submitted a waiver of the BAA. The Claims Court held that the contractor should have requested a waiver of the BAA before contract performance, and since it did not do so, it was not entitled to an equitable adjustment.

[e] Commercial Items

The requirements of the BAA do not apply to information technology that is a commercial item when it is an element of construction material, FAR 25.202(a)(4). This exception is derived from § 535(a) of the FY 2004 Consolidated Appropriations Act and subsequent appropriations acts. It does not apply to information technology that is an element of an end product furnished on a supply contract.

The requirements of the BAA do not apply to the components test when the agency is procuring commercial off-the-shelf items, FAR 25.101(a)(2); FAR 12.505(a). Thus, if a manufactured end item or construction material is manufactured in the United States, the components can be 100% foreign products. This rule has been adopted under the authority of 41 U.S.C. § 1907(a)(1).

[B] Trade Agreements

There have been a number of "free trade" agreements entered into over the years that apply special procedures to the procurement of foreign products and services. An early effort of this type was the "Tokyo Round" of international trade negotiations during the 1970s to reduce "nontariff barriers," such as the BAA, to international trade. The Tokyo Round resulted in a series of "international codes," one of which is known as the "Government Procurement Code." That code includes provisions designed to reduce the effect of buy-national practices of the signatory nations.

The United States joined in the agreements that resulted from the Tokyo Round, including the Government Procurement Agreement (WTO GPA). To implement those agreements, Congress enacted the Trade Agreements Act (TAA) of 1979, 19 U.S.C. § 2501 et seq. This was followed by the Uruguay Round Agreements Act, 19 U.S.C. § 3501 et seq. One provision of the TAA authorized the President to waive any otherwise applicable "law, regulation, procedure or practice regarding Government procurement" that would accord foreign products less favorable treatment than that given to domestic products, 19 U.S.C § 2511(a). That provision of the TAA was implemented by the President, Executive Order 12260, 46 Fed. Reg. 1653 (1981). Thus, the BAA and at least some other federal restrictions favoring domestic products have been superseded as to the specific products and countries covered by the President's action, FAR Subpart 25.4.

The United States has entered into a number of other "free trade" agreements that supersede the BAA to some extent. FAR 25.400(a), lists agreements with Canada, Mexico, Chile, Singapore, Australia, Morocco, the Dominican Republic-Central America, Bahrain, Oman, Peru, Israel, Korea, Columbia, and Panama. The list also includes the following special provisions:

> (3) The least developed country designation made by the U.S. Trade Representative, pursuant to the Trade Agreements Act (19 U.S.C. 2511(b)(4)), in acquisitions covered by the WTO GPA;
>
> (4) The Caribbean Basin Trade Initiative (CBTI) (determination of the U.S. Trade Representative that end products or construction material granted duty-free entry from countries designated as beneficiaries under the Caribbean Basin Economic Recovery Act (19 U.S.C. 2701, et seq.), with the exception of Panama, must be treated as eligible products in acquisitions covered by the WTO GPA);
>
> ***
>
> (6) The Agreement on Trade in Civil Aircraft (U.S. Trade Representative waiver of the Buy American Act for signatories of the Agreement on Trade in Civil Aircraft, as implemented in the Trade Agreements Act of 1979 (19 U.S.C. 2513)).

FAR 25.401(a) provides that these agreements (including the WTO GPA) do not cover:

> (1) Acquisitions set aside for small businesses;
>
> (2) Acquisitions of arms, ammunition, or war materials, or purchases indispensable for national security or for national defense purposes;
>
> (3) Acquisitions of end products for resale;
>
> (4) Acquisitions from Federal Prison Industries, Inc., under Subpart 8.6, and acquisitions under Subpart 8.7, Acquisition from Nonprofit Agencies Employing People Who Are Blind or Severely Disabled; and
>
> (5) Other acquisitions not using full and open competition, if authorized by Subpart 6.2 or 6.3, when the limitation of competition would preclude use

of the procedures of this subpart; or sole source acquisitions justified in accordance with 13.501(a).

See also DFARS 225.401-70 for a list of products subject to these trade agreements. In addition, the trade agreements do not cover specified services. FAR 25.401(b) contains a table of the services excepted from the various trade agreements.

Supplies and services covered by the trade agreements must be procured without regard to application of the BAA when they exceed specified dollar thresholds. These thresholds are revised periodically and vary for the different trade agreements. FAR 25.402(b) contains a table stating the thresholds as of Dec. 30, 2022, 87 Fed. Reg. 73890.

For protests involving these trade agreements, see *Presto Lock, Inc.*, Comp. Gen. Dec. B-218766, 85-2 CPD ¶ 183 (padlocks from Hong Kong); and *Qualimetrics, Inc.*, Comp. Gen. Dec. B-222726, 86-1 CPD ¶ 519 (use of Finnish components raises no BAA issue since Trade Agreement Act applies). See also *Tiger Truck, LLC*, Comp. Gen. Dec. B-400685, 2009 CPD ¶ 19 (agency failed to follow TAA procedure in evaluating proposals); *Olympic Container Corp.*, Comp. Gen. Dec. B-250403, 93-1 CPD ¶ 89 (no application of the BAA's differential to offers of products from non-designated countries is permitted); *Trading Atlanta Ltd.*, Comp. Gen. Dec. B-239056, 90-2 CPD ¶ 88 (since the TAA prohibits the acceptance of South African products, the protester was not prejudiced by the award to a higher-priced domestic competitor); and *Puerto Rico Marine Mgmt., Inc.*, Comp. Gen. Dec. B-247975.5, 92-2 CPD ¶ 275 (items indispensable to the national defense is not subject to the TAA; in such cases the BAA applies).

[1] Trade Agreements End Products

An article is considered to be a trade agreements country "end product" under the TAA if it is "wholly the growth, product, or manufacture of the designated country," or, "if it consists in whole or in part of materials from another country, has been substantially transformed" in the trade agreements country "into a new and different article of commerce with a name, character, or use distinct article or articles from which it was transformed." See the definitions of "WTO GPA country end product," "Free Trade Agreement country end product," and "Caribbean Basin country end product" in FAR 25.003. This means that a product will meet the test if it is either a domestic or trade agreements country product or a product that meets the substantial transformation test, *Acetris Health, LLC v. United States*, 949 F.3d 719 (Fed. Cir. 2020) (pill manufactured in the United States met test even though active ingredient, being from a non-WTO country, was not substantially transformed in United States).

There is no other guidance in the FAR as to the meaning of "substantial transformation." However, in *Klinge Corp. v. United States*, 82 Fed. Cl. 127

(2008), the court held that additional work on a refrigeration unit in the United States did not constitute substantial transformation because the unit had passed functional tests in a nonqualifying country. The court reasoned that the work in the United States did not make the unit a "new and different article." GAO had reached the opposite conclusion in *Klinge Corp.*, Comp. Gen. Dec. B-309930.2, 2008 CPD ¶ 102. In a subsequent decision, *Klinge Corp. v. United States*, 83 Fed. Cl. 773 (2008), the court apparently agreed that when a company sells spare parts, each part is subject to the substantial transformation test. See also *Pacific Lock Co.*, Comp. Gen. Dec. B-309982, 2007 CPD ¶ 191, sustaining an agency determination that padlocks that were assembled in the United States from noncompliant country components were not substantially transformed in the United States because there was no substantial content of domestic components. The agency had relied on international trade rulings that locks did not meet the substantial transformation test if the components were mainly of foreign origin. No substantial transformation was also found in *Energizer Battery, Inc. v. United States*, 190 F. Supp. 3d 1308 (Ct. Int'l Trade 2016) (assembling flashlight); *Sea Box, Inc.*, Comp. Gen. Dec. B-409963.3, 2015 CPD ¶ 72 (assembling shipping containers); *CSK Int'l, Inc.*, Comp. Gen. Dec. B-278111.2, 97-2 CPD ¶ 178 (assembling handle to tool head); *Ran-Paige Co. v. United States*, 35 Fed. Cl. 117 (1996) (attaching handles to pots); *Becton Dickinson AcuteCare*, Comp. Gen. Dec. B-238942, 90-2 CPD ¶ 55 (assembly of parts manufactured and sterilized in the United States).

The concept of substantial transformation is derived from U.S. Customs Regulations. These regulations are entitled to be given considerable deference in deciding ruling of the Customs Service, *United States v. Haggar Apparel Co.*, 526 U.S. 380 (1999). These rulings have also been relied on by contracting agencies and the GAO. However, in *Acetris Health, LLC v. United States*, 949 F.3d 719 (Fed. Cir. 2020), the court declined to elevate these rulings over the plain language of the FAR.

There are a number of Customs cases dealing with the matter. See, for example, *Crawfish Processors Alliance v. United States*, 483 F.3d 1358 (Fed. Cir. 2007) (making crawfish etouffee substantial transformation of crawfish tail meat); and *Ugine & Alz Belgium v. United States*, 551 F.3d 1339 (Fed. Cir. 2009) (cold rolling of steel did not substantially transform hot rolled steel).

[2] Procedures

FAR 25.502 provides for the following evaluation procedures for foreign supplies:

> (a) Unless otherwise specified in agency regulations, perform the following steps in the order presented:

(1) Eliminate all offers or offerors that are unacceptable for reasons other than price; e.g., nonresponsive, debarred or suspended, or a prohibited source (see Subpart 25.7).

(2) Rank the remaining offers by price.

(3) If the solicitation specifies award on the basis of factors in addition to cost or price, apply the evaluation factors as specified in this section and use the evaluated cost or price in determining the offer that represents the best value to the Government.

(b) For acquisitions covered by the WTO GPA (see Subpart 25.4)—

(1) Consider only offers of U.S.-made or designated country end products, unless no offers of such end products were received;

(2) If the agency gives the same consideration given eligible offers to offers of U.S.-made end products that are not domestic end products, award on the low offer. Otherwise, evaluate in accordance with agency procedures; and

(3) If there were no offers of U.S.-made or designated country end products, make a nonavailability determination (see 25.103(b)(2)) and award on the low offer (see 25.403(c)).

GAO has held that these procedures do not allow award to a WTO GPA foreign product unless the price is fair and reasonable, *Tiger Truck*, LLC, Comp. Gen. Dec. B-400685, 2009 CPD ¶ 19. In this decision, GAO also held that if there are no domestic products or compliant foreign products, award cannot be made to the low price non-compliant foreign product until the head of the contracting activity has made a nonavailability determination in accordance with FAR 25.502(b)(3).

In procurements subject to the WTO GPA, agencies are required to use the Trade Agreements clause in FAR 52.225-5 and the Trade Agreements Certificate solicitation provision in FAR 52.225-6. The certificate states that the products to be supplied will be from compliant countries and requires listing of products from noncompliant countries. See DFARS 225.1101 for different clauses and solicitation provisions used in DoD contracts.

In *Master Lock Co., LLC*, Comp. Gen. Dec. B-309982.2, 2009 CPD ¶ 2, GAO ruled that not listing any noncompliant products allowed the agency to award to the company, providing the following guidance on the procedure to be followed:

> When a bidder or offeror represents that it will furnish end products of designated or qualifying countries (including domestic end products) in accordance with the TAA, it is obligated under the contract to comply with that representation. That is, where a bidder or offeror leaves the certificate blank and does not exclude any end product from the certificate, and does not otherwise indicate that it is offering anything other than a TAA-compliant end product, acceptance of the offer will result in an obligation on the offeror's or bidder's part to furnish a TAA-compliant end product. *Wyse Tech., Inc.*,

B-297454, Jan. 24, 2006, 2006 CPD ¶ 23 at 6. If prior to award an agency has reason to believe that a firm will not provide compliant products, the agency should go beyond the firm's representation of compliance with the Act; however, where the agency has no information prior to award that would lead to such a conclusion, the agency may properly rely upon an offeror's representation without further investigation. *Leisure-Lift, Inc.*, B-291878.3; B-292448.2, Sept. 25, 2003, 2003 CPD ¶ 189 at 8. Where an agency is required to investigate further, we will review the evaluation and resulting determination regarding compliance with the requirements of the Act to ensure that they were reasonable. *Pacific Lock Co.*, B-309982, Oct. 25, 2007, 2007 CPD ¶ 191 at 4.

See also *Klinge Corp. v. United States*, 82 Fed. Cl. 127 (2008), holding that if a proposal contains information on its face indicating that the certificate is inaccurate, the agency must "make reasonable inquiry and satisfy itself that the product offered meets the terms of the act."

[C] Other Domestic Preferences

The government has a number of policies, besides the BAA and the trade agreements acts, favoring acquisition of articles of domestic origin. These policies either impose restrictions on the purchase of specific articles or services or require the use of price differentials in evaluating the price of foreign articles or services.

[1] Statutory Restrictions

There are a number of statutory restrictions. The oldest originated in 1941 when the military services were prohibited from using appropriated funds to procure foreign food or clothing, *A&P Surgical Co.*, 62 Comp. Gen. 256 (B-206111.2), 83-1 CPD ¶ 263. DFARS Subpart 225.70 contains detailed guidance on Appropriation or Authorization Act restrictions (commonly called "Berry Amendment requirements") applying to food, clothing, tents, fabrics, hand and or measuring tools, flags specialty metals, buses, naval air circuit breakers, anchor and mooring chain, ball and roller bearings, naval vessel components, carbon alloy and armor steel plate, supercomputers, shipyard construction or repair of vessels, overseas A/E services, photovoltaic devices, and magnets and tungsten. See also DFARS 225.7102-1 placing limitations on the various types of foreign forgings. DFARS Subpart 252.225 contains special clauses and solicitation provisions for many of these items. Agencies may accept an offeror's self-certification that it is in compliance unless it has reason to believe that the offeror will not provide compliant products. See *Inspire, Int'l*, Comp. Gen. Dec. B-413798, 2016 CPD ¶ 359; *Leisure-Lift, Inc.*, Comp. Gen. Dec. B-291878.3, 2003 CPD ¶ 18.

Additional restrictions are found in the transportation field. See FAR Subpart 47.4, implementing the statutes giving preference to U.S. flag air carriers for the transportation of freight and persons. See also FAR Subpart 47.5, implementing the numerous statutes giving preference to U.S. flag vessels for the transportation of supplies.

The provisions of such specific statutes may bar purchase of foreign materials even if the BAA would not, *Penthouse Mfg. Co.*, Comp. Gen. Dec. B-217480, 85-1 CPD ¶ 487; 49 Comp. Gen. 606 (B-168791) (1970).

[2] Balance of Payments Differentials

DoD has adopted an additional technique favoring domestic supplies and services called the Balance of Payments Program. DFARS Subpart 225.75 makes this program applicable to acquisitions of supplies, services, or construction for use outside the United States. However, DFARS 225.7501(a) contains a long list of exceptions to the application of this program. See also DFARS 225.7501(b) for guidance on the relationship of this program to trade agreements and application of a 50% evaluation factor for price reasonableness determinations. Examples of the proper evaluation of offers subject to the balance of payment procedures are set forth in DFARS PGI 225.504.

§ 14.04 POLICICS ON THE ENVIRONMENT AND ENERGY

Since the 1960s, Congress has passed a number of statutes concerning the environment and energy. These statutes and the regulations implementing them contain a variety of provisions that use federal contracts to foster the policies established for environment and energy.

[A] National Environmental Policy Act

The National Environmental Policy Act, passed in 1969, "authorizes and directs that, to the fullest extent possible . . . the policies, regulations and public laws of the United States" shall be interpreted and administered in accordance with the environmental policies set out in the Act, 42 U.S.C. § 4332. The Act also requires that an environmental impact statement be prepared in connection with all "major Federal actions significantly affecting the quality of the human environment," 42 U.S.C. § 4332(2)(C). Examples of regulations implementing this requirement include 24 C.F.R. Part 50 (Department of Housing and Urban Development) and 14 C.F.R. Part 1216.3 (National Aeronautics and Space Administration). In certain circumstances, award of a federal contract might be a "major federal action" that triggers the need for an environmental impact statement. Sometimes contract award acts as a signal that prompts opponents of a federal project (e.g., a dam or new military installation) to seek an injunction delaying the project on grounds that no environmental impact statement, or an inadequate one, has been prepared; see Nash & Linden, "Federal Procurement and the Environment, in Environmental Law Institute," Federal Environmental Law 476-87 (1974).

[B] Energy and Water Efficiency

The Energy Policy and Conservation Act, Pub. L. No. 94-163, codified at 42 U.S.C. § 6361(a)(1), passed in 1975, directs that

> [t]he President shall, to the extent of his authority under other law, establish or coordinate Federal agency actions to develop mandatory standards with respect to energy conservation and energy efficiency to govern the procurement policies and decisions of the Federal Government and all Federal agencies, and shall take such steps as are necessary to cause such standards to be implemented.

The National Energy Conservation Policy Act, Pub. L. No. 95-619, codified at 42 U.S.C. § 8201 et seq., passed in 1978, calls for a number of energy and water conservation programs with regard to federal buildings. These statutes are implemented in FAR Subpart 23.2.

FAR 23.202 contains the following broad statement of policy:

> The Government's policy is to acquire supplies and services that promote a clean energy economy that increases our Nation's energy security, safeguards the health of our environment, and reduces greenhouse gas emissions from direct and indirect Federal activities. To implement this policy, Federal acquisitions will foster markets for sustainable technologies, products, and services. This policy extends to all acquisitions, including those below the simplified acquisition threshold and those at or below the micro-purchase threshold (including those made with a Government purchase card).

[1] Energy-Efficient Products

The first technique that has been adopted to implement this policy is the requirement that agencies must procure energy-saving products unless the head of the agency determines that no product is reasonably available or cost-effective over the life of the product, FAR 23.204. Guidance is provided in FAR 23.203(a) as follows:

> (1) When acquiring energy-consuming products listed in the ENERGY STAR [REGISTERED TRADEMARK] or Federal Energy Management Program (FEMP)—
>
> (i) Agencies shall purchase ENERGY STAR or FEMP-designated products; and

(ii) For products that consume power in a standby mode and are listed on FEMP's Low Standby Power Devices product listing, agencies shall—

(A) Purchase items which meet FEMP's standby power wattage recommendation or document the reason for not purchasing such items; or

(B) If FEMP has listed a product without a corresponding wattage recommendation, purchase items which use no more than one watt in their standby power consuming mode. When it is impracticable to meet the one watt requirement, agencies shall purchase items with the lowest standby wattage practicable; and

(2) When contracting for services or construction that will include the provision of energy-consuming products, agencies shall specify products that comply with the applicable requirements in paragraph (a)(1) of this section.

When an agency is procuring products using energy or such products will be required to perform the contract, it is required to use the Energy Efficiency in Energy-Consuming Products clause in FAR 52.223-15.

[2] Energy-Savings Performance Contracts

The other technique that is called for to implement the energy-savings policy is the use of energy-savings performance contracts that are permitted by 42 U.S.C. § 8287. These contracts can turn over one or more of the energy systems in a government facility to a private company for up to 25 years in order to allow the contractor to provide an energy-savings system and to be compensated by a negotiated share of the savings. These contracts are a type of multiyear contract with cancellation ceilings allowing the recovery of capital expenditures made by the contractor in the event that the contract is not allowed to run to its full term. See 10 C.F.R. § 436.34:

(a) Subject to paragraph (b) of this section, Federal agencies may enter into a multiyear energy savings performance contract for a period not to exceed 25 years, as authorized by 42 U.S.C. 8287, without funding of cancellation charges, if:

(1) The multiyear energy savings performance contract was awarded in a competitive manner using the procedures and methods established by this subpart;

(2) Funds are available and adequate for payment of the scheduled energy cost for the first fiscal year of the multiyear energy savings performance contract;

(3) Thirty days before the award of any multiyear energy savings performance contract that contains a clause setting forth a cancellation ceiling in excess of $750,000, the head of the awarding Federal agency gives written notification of the proposed contract and the proposed

cancellation ceiling for the contract to the appropriate authorizing and appropriating committees of the Congress; and

(4) Except as otherwise provided in this section, the multiyear energy savings performance contract is subject to 48 CFR part 17, subpart 17.1, including the requirement that the contracting officer establish a cancellation ceiling.

(b) Neither this subpart nor any provision of the Act requires, prior to contract award or as a condition of a contract award, that a Federal agency have appropriated funds available and adequate to pay for the total costs of an energy savings performance contract for the term of such contract.

The Department of Energy has specified the procedures, selection method and terms and conditions that must be used in awarding energy-savings contracts. See 10 C.F.R. Part 436, Subpart B. These contracts are issued to prequalified contractors in one of two ways. First, DOE issues a list of prequalified contractors each year, 10 C.F.R. § 436.32, and other agencies have followed the same procedure. See *Strategic Resource Sols. Corp.*, Comp. Gen. Dec. B-278732, 98-1 CPD ¶ 74, holding that it was proper to exclude a contractor not on the list from the competition even though it had been added to the subsequent year's list. Second, DOE and other agencies award multiple "Super ESPCs" which are IDIQ contracts calling for the issuance of energy-savings delivery orders for work at a specific facility. When an agency conducts a competition to award a number of Super ESPCs, a protest by an offeror that is not awarded a contract is decided on the same basis as any protest of a best value negotiation procurement, *AECOM Tech. Servs., Inc.*, Comp. Gen. Dec. B-411862, 2015 CPD ¶ 353; *ABM Gov't Servs., LLC*, Comp. Gen. Dec. B-410991.2, 2015 CPD ¶ 130; *Johnson Controls, Inc.*, Comp. Gen. Dec. B-282326, 99-2 CPD ¶ 6.

The energy-savings contract or delivery order for a specific facility must be negotiated on the basis of projections of the capital expenditure the contractor will make and the savings that are anticipated over the life of the contract. The goal is to arrive at a savings share to be paid to the contractor that will permit recovery of its investment, including interest, and some reasonable profit. Guidance on analysis and negotiation of these elements of the savings formula is provided in 10 C.F.R. Part 436, Subpart A. If a contractor discloses the elements of its projected cost savings to the government during negotiations, it is not liable for submitting a false claim if it does not achieve the savings, *United States ex rel. Berg v. Honeywell Int'l, Inc.*, 740 Fed. Appx. 535 (9th Cir. 2018).

Some agencies have agreed to pay for some or all of the work to be performed by the contractor. See the delivery orders issued under a DOE Super ESPC discussed in *Honeywell Int'l, Inc.*, ASBCA 57779, 17-1 BCA ¶ 36,820, and *Ameresco Sols., Inc.*, ASBCA 56824, 11-1 BCA ¶ 34,705. The military services have been permitted to use their savings from these contracts for designated purposes, Section 736 of Pub. L. No. 100-456 and § 331 of Pub. L. No. 101-189.

An energy-savings contract or delivery order for a specific facility can include all of the energy sources being used at the facility and offerors not approved by the state or local government are entitled to compete for these contracts, *Virginia Elec. & Power Co.*, Comp. Gen. Dec. B-285209, 2000 CPD ¶ 134.

Because these contracts are generally long-term contracts, agencies must work with the contractor to ensure performance. See *Biomass One Operating Co.*, ASBCA 41972, 94-1 BCA ¶ 27,051, converting a default termination to one for convenience because the agency terminated the contract early in performance and had delayed performance.

[C] Promoting the Use of Non-Polluting Products or Processes

Several statutes require federal procuring agencies to give preference to products that are "environmentally friendly." These policies are implemented, in a general manner in FAR 23.703, requiring agencies to:

> (a) Implement cost-effective contracting preference programs promoting energy-efficiency, water conservation, and the acquisition of environmentally preferable products and services; and
>
> (b) Employ acquisition strategies that affirmatively implement the following environmental objectives:
>
> (1) Maximize the utilization of environmentally preferable products and services (based on EPA-issued guidance).
>
> (2) Promote energy-efficiency and water conservation.
>
> (3) Eliminate or reduce the generation of hazardous waste and the need for special material processing (including special handling, storage, treatment, and disposal).
>
> (4) Promote the use of nonhazardous and recovered materials.
>
> (5) Realize life-cycle cost savings.
>
> (6) Promote cost-effective waste reduction when creating plans, drawings, specifications, standards, and other product descriptions authorizing material substitutions, extensions of shelf-life, and process improvements.
>
> (7) Promote the use of biobased products.
>
> (8) Purchase only plastic ring carriers that are degradable (7 USC 8102(c)(1), 40 CFR part 238).

FAR Subpart 23.7 focuses specifically on electronic products requiring them to meet industry standards. See the Acquisition of Epeat(R)-Registered Imaging Equipment clause at FAR 52.223-13 and the Acquisition of Epeat(R)-Registered Personal Computer Products clause at FAR 52.223-16, which are used for this purpose.

The Resource Conservation and Energy Act of 1976, 42 U.S.C. § 6901 et seq., requires procuring agencies to modify their traditional policy of "buying new." Agencies are required to examine their specifications and remove requirements for "new" materials to the extent such requirements are not justified, 42 U.S.C. § 6962(c)(1). Agencies are required to procure items "composed of the highest percentage of recovered material practicable . . . consistent with maintaining a satisfactory level of competition," 42 U.S.C. § 6962. The term "recovered material" includes most material recovered from "any garbage, refuse, sludge from a waste treatment plant, water supply treatment plant, or air pollution control facility and other discarded material," 42 U.S.C. § 6903(19) and (27). Agencies must require vendors to certify that the percentage of "recovered materials" to be used in contract performance will be at least the amount required by applicable specifications or contract requirements, 42 U.S.C. § 6962(d)(2). Agencies may decide not to procure items composed of the highest percentage of recovered materials practicable consistent with maintaining a satisfactory level of competition if they determine that such items are not reasonably available in a reasonable time, or that they will not meet applicable performance standards, or are available only at an unreasonable price, 42 U.S.C. § 6962(c)(1). Similar requirements are included in the Farm Security and Rural Investment Act of 2002, 7 U.S.C. § 8102, dealing with "biobased" materials. See FAR Subpart 23.4. FAR 23.404 requires agencies to establish an "affirmative procurement program" within one year after either EPA or the Department of Agriculture has designated an item that can be made using recovered or biobased materials. Solicitation provisions and clauses to carry out these requirements are called for in FAR 23.406.

The Emergency Planning and Community Right-to-Know Act of 1986, 42 U.S.C. § 11023, and the Pollution Prevention Act of 1990, 42 U.S.C. § 13106, require owners and operators of manufacturing facilities to provide EPA and the states with information on toxic chemical releases and waste management activities. FAR 23.903 calls for the use of the Compliance With Environmental Management Systems in 52.223-19 in all solicitations and contracts for contractor operation of Government-owned or -leased facilities or vehicles, located in the United States.

Under the Noise Control Act of 1972, 42 U.S.C. § 4901 et seq., federal agencies must give preference to products that meet several prerequisites. The Environmental Protection Agency must determine through appropriate testing that the product is a "low-noise emission" product, 42 U.S.C. § 4914(b). The product must be found to be a "suitable substitute" for articles that the government is procuring. The General Services Administration must determine that the cost of the product is not more than 125% of the retail price of the least expensive article for which it is a substitute, 42 U.S.C. § 4914(c)(1). There is no implementation of this policy in the FAR.

[D] Clean Air and Water

The Clean Air Amendments of 1970, 42 U.S.C. § 7401 et seq., and the Water Pollution Control Act Amendments of 1972, 33 U.S.C. § 1251 et seq., establish a procedure to use federal contract awards to help implement the pollution control aspects of those statutes. The Environmental Protection Agency is authorized to list facilities if they are found liable for violations of air and water pollution standards. Prior to 2000, offerors on certain federal contracts were required to certify that their performance would not take place at any of these listed facilities, FAR Subpart 23.1. This requirement was deleted from the FAR by FAC 97-15, 64 Fed. Reg. 72,414, Dec. 27, 1999. The policy is now implemented by including such facilities in the SAM Excluded Parties list discussed in Chapter 4.

§ 14.05 EQUAL EMPLOYMENT OPPORTUNITY

Nondiscrimination provisions have been required in government contracts by a series of executive orders commencing with Executive Order 8802, 6 Fed. Reg. 3109 (1941). This section deals first with the current executive orders requiring equal opportunity in employment. It then reviews other sources of equal employment policies.

[A] Executive Order 11246

The major source of the equal employment opportunity requirements for federal contractors is Executive Order 11246, 30 Fed. Reg. 12319 (1965), as amended many times. This order provides that the Secretary of Labor will administer this program and promulgate regulations. This is done through the Office of Federal Contract Compliance Programs (OFCCP). See 41 C.F.R. Part 60. At the same time, Executive Order 11246, as amended, makes each contracting agency primarily responsible for ensuring that its contractors comply with the applicable regulations, rules, and orders. FAR Subpart 22.8 contains the general regulations for these procedures.

The legal authority of the President to issue Executive Order 11246, has been sustained. See *Contractors Ass'n of E. Pa. v. Secretary of Labor*, 442 F.2d 159 (3d Cir.), *cert. denied*, 404 U.S. 854 (1971). But note that the two grounds on which the court in *Contractors Association* based its decision were questioned by another court in *AFL-CIO v. Kahn*, 618 F.2d 784 (D.C. Cir.), *cert. denied*, 443 U.S. 915 (1979). See also *Regents of the Univ. of California. v. Bakke*, 438 U.S. 265 (1978), stating at 302:

> Every decision upholding the requirement of preferential hiring under the authority of Exec. Order No. 11246, . . . has emphasized the existence of

previous discrimination as a predicate for the imposition of a preferential remedy.

Other cases supporting the executive order's validity include *Farkas v. Texas Instruments, Inc.*, 375 F.2d 629 (5th Cir.), *cert. denied*, 389 U.S. 977 (1967); and *Legal Aid Soc'y of Alameda County v. Brennan*, 381 F. Supp. 125 (N.D. Cal. 1974), *aff'd in part*, 608 F.2d 1319 (9th Cir. 1979), *cert. denied*, 447 U.S. 921 (1980). For a discussion of its application to subcontractors, see *Liberty Mut. Ins. Co. v. Friedman*, 639 F.2d 164 (4th Cir. 1981). GAO has held that including nondiscrimination provisions in a federal contract does not violate the requirements of statutes requiring maximum feasible competition, 40 Comp. Gen. 592 (B-145475) (1961).

[1] Equal Opportunity Clause

Executive Order 11246, as amended, prescribes a clause that is mandatory in all contracts, absent a special exemption from the Secretary of Labor. The clause does not apply to contracts under $10,000 unless the contractor has, or reasonably can expect to have, contracts or subcontracts with the government with an aggregate value exceeding $10,000 in a 12-month period, FAR 22.807(b)(1). The required Equal Opportunity clause is set forth in FAR 52.222-26. The clause can be applicable even if it is not included in a contract. See *United States v. New Orleans Pub. Serv., Inc.*, 553 F.2d 459 (5th Cir. 1977), *vacated & remanded on other grounds*, 436 U.S. 942 (1978), where the court held that a utility supplying electricity to the government was subject to the provisions of the executive order even though the company had refused to sign a contract because of the inclusion of this clause. Compare *Liberty Mut. Ins. Co. v. Friedman*, 639 F.2d 164 (4th Cir. 1981), invalidating Labor Department regulations requiring sureties to comply with the requirements of the executive order. The court reasoned that a surety could not reasonably be construed to be a subcontractor.

Under the Equal Opportunity clause, the contractor agrees not to discriminate against any employee or applicant for employment because of race, color, religion, sex, sexual orientation, gender identity, or national origin. Paragraph (c)(2) of the clause further requires that "[t]he Contractor shall take affirmative action to ensure that applicants are employed, and that employees are treated during employment, without regard to their race, color, religion, sex, sexual orientation, gender identity, or national origin." Paragraph (b)(2) of the clause exempts religious corporations, associations, educational institutions, or societies from its application "with respect to the employment of individuals of a particular religion to perform work connected with the carrying on of the Contractor's activities." The clause also commits the contractor to furnish certain information and reports and to permit access to records by the contracting agency and the Department of Labor to ascertain compliance with the applicable requirements.

Unless an exemption applies, ¶ (c)(10) of the clause provides that a contractor must flow down the requirements of the clause in its subcontracts and purchase orders.

Affirmative action is described in detail in 41 C.F.R. Part 60-2, Subpart B. Initially the contractor must make a utilization analysis to determine if the composition of its workforce is in conformity with the composition of people living in its labor area. This requires a determination of the appropriate labor area serving the contractor, the availability of minority groups and women in categories of labor in that area, and the number of minority employees and women working in each job category. If this analysis indicates that the contractor's percentage of minority employment or women is less than those available in any labor category, "underutilization" is required to be found. In such cases, the contractor must establish a series of "placement goals" to assist in attaining percentages of minority and women employment comparable to the availability of minorities and women in the labor area. 41 C.F.R. § 60-2.16(e) states the following principles applicable to these goals:

> (1) Placement goals may not be rigid and inflexible quotas, which must be met, nor are they to be considered as either a ceiling or a floor for the employment of particular groups. Quotas are expressly forbidden.
>
> (2) In all employment decisions, the contractor must make selections in a nondiscriminatory manner. Placement goals do not provide the contractor with a justification to extend a preference to any individual, select an individual, or adversely affect an individual's employment status, on the basis of that person's race, color, religion, sex, sexual orientation, gender identity, or national origin.
>
> (3) Placement goals do not create set-asides for specific groups, nor are they intended to achieve proportional representation or equal results.
>
> (4) Placement goals may not be used to supersede merit selection principles. Affirmative action programs prescribed by the regulations in this part do not require a contractor to hire a person who lacks qualifications to perform the job successfully, or hire a less qualified person in preference to a more qualified one.

The contractor must also adopt policies for recruitment and training that will aid in achieving these goals. It is proper to consider the need to meet the goal in a hiring decision as long as the basic consideration is the qualification of the potential employees, *Sharkey v. Dixie Elec. Membership Corp.*, 262 Fed. Appx. 598 (5th Cir. 2008). The affirmative action requirement applies to promotion as well as employment. See *Legal Aid Soc'y of Alameda County v. Brennan*, 381 F. Supp. 125 (N.D. Cal. 1974), *aff'd in part*, 608 F.2d 1319 (9th Cir. 1979), *cert. denied*, 447 U.S. 921 (1980), for a decision analyzing and finding deficient an agency's efforts to ensure that its contractors are complying with the affirmative action requirement.

[2] Affirmative Action Programs

Each nonconstruction contractor or subcontractor with 50 or more employees and a contract or subcontract for $50,000 or more (or cumulatively expected to total $50,000 or more in any 12-month period) is required to develop a written affirmative action program, FAR 22.804-1. These programs are reviewed and approved by the OFCCP regional office and must be developed within 120 days from the commencement of the first contract or subcontract for $50,000 or more. The regulations require an affirmative action program for each establishment of a contractor, 41 C.F.R. § 60-2.1 (containing detailed guidance on the application of this rule). This requirement has been interpreted as applying to every establishment of a contractor regardless of whether such establishment performs work for the government. However, the Deputy Assistant Secretary of Labor may exempt a "facility" that is separate and distinct from the activities called for by the contract, FAR 22.807(b)(5), pursuant to a request from a contracting officer, FAR 22.807(c). An OFCCP Policy Interpretation issued in the 1970s contained the following statement regarding the meaning of "establishment":

> Revised Order No. 4 requires that a written affirmative action program be developed for each of the contractor's establishments. The question has arisen as to whether this means that a contractor must develop such plans for an "establishment" where it may have a few employees, such as a sales outlet. We have defined "establishment" for purposes of Revised Order No. 4 as a facility at which hiring takes place and/or personnel actions are instituted. If such authority exists at the facility, it would be required to have a written affirmative action program as specified in Revised Order No. 4. If such authority does not exist at the facility, the location that has the hiring authority and handles personnel actions for the facility would have to develop and implement an affirmative action plan. In the latter case, the personnel at the facility would be covered by the plan maintained at the hiring and personnel location.

A subsidiary not performing government work is considered an "establishment" only if the parent exercises actual control, 50 Comp. Gen. 627 (B-170536) (1971).

When the Equal Opportunity clause is required to be included in a contract, the agency must also include the Affirmative Action Compliance solicitation provision in FAR 52.222-25, requiring the offeror to represent whether it has an affirmative action program. The lack of an approved affirmative action program by a nonconstruction concern is grounds for a determination that the company is not a responsible offeror, *William Dixon Co.*, Comp. Gen. Dec. B-235241, 89-2 CPD ¶ 114. However, the OFCCP regulations do not require the contracting officer to ascertain whether such a program exists in smaller procurements. For example, the regulations provide that if "it comes to the contracting officer's attention" in the preaward period that there is no approved affirmative action program, the offeror must be declared nonresponsible unless the contracting officer "otherwise affirmatively determines that the contractor is able to comply with the equal employment obligations," 41 C.F.R. § 60-2.2(b).

Requirements become more stringent as dollar amounts increase. For instance, contracts or subcontracts over $10 million (excluding construction contracts) may not be awarded unless a compliance review of the contractor has been conducted within 24 months prior to the award and the contractor is found to be in compliance, 41 C.F.R. § 60-1.20(d). See FAR 22.805(a), providing that a "preaward clearance" should be requested from OFCCP in such circumstances and award should be withheld for as long as is feasible while the review is conducted. This procedure is intended to prevent the award of major contracts without an affirmative determination by the compliance agency that the contractor's program meets the affirmative action requirements. The procedure is not required if the contractor is listed in OFCCP's National Preaward Registry. A prospective contractor may be determined nonresponsible twice without a hearing, but is entitled to a hearing after the second determination of nonresponsibility, 41 C.F.R. § 60-2.2(b). In *Commercial Envelope Mfg. Co. v. Dunlop*, 21 Cont. Cas. Fed. (CCH) ¶ 84,097 (S.D.N.Y. 1975), the court held that this procedure did not violate any of the prospective contractor's rights and found that a contractor was properly determined nonresponsible a fifth time based on employment practices, even though the four prior determinations were based on other grounds.

Construction contractors are not required to develop affirmative action programs since many do not perform work in fixed geographic areas. However, they must comply with any "hometown plan" covering a geographic area in which they work, FAR 22.804-2(a). These hometown plans are affirmative action programs covering specific geographic areas that have been agreed to by unions, contractor associations, and governmental units in that area. See 41 C.F.R. § 60-4.5. Each contracting agency is required to maintain a list of such plans, FAR 22.804-2(b), and contracting officers are required to include the goals and timetables from such plans in solicitations for work to be performed in geographic areas with plans in effect. The Notice of Requirements for Affirmative Action to Ensure Equal Employment Opportunity for Construction solicitation provision used for this purpose is set forth in FAR 52.222-23. If the construction is to be performed in an area not covered by a plan, the contractor is not obligated to attempt to meet any goals and timetables. However, all construction contracts over $10,000 must contain the Affirmative Action Compliance Requirements for Construction clause at FAR 52.222-27, which contains 16 affirmative action steps that the contractor must take during contract performance.

All of the affirmative action program requirements are matters of responsibility not responsiveness. Thus, bidders can furnish information demonstrating that they are in compliance after bid opening, *A&C Bldg. & Indus. Maint. Corp.*, Comp. Gen. Dec. B-218035, 85-1 CPD ¶ 195.

[3] Compliance Procedures

If an individual employee has a grievance regarding a contractor's compliance with Executive Order 11246, requirements, the employee may file a complaint with OFCCP within 180 days of the violation, 41 C.F.R. § 60-1.21. Complaints filed with the contracting officer are required to be immediately forwarded to the OFCCP, FAR 22.808. That office may investigate and may, in appropriate circumstances, refer the complaint to the Equal Employment Opportunity Commission, 41 C.F.R. § 60-1.24. Procedures for consideration of complaints by OFCCP are set forth in 41 C.F.R. § 60-1.26. Executive Order 11246 gives private parties no cause of action against employers, *Utley v. Varian Assocs., Inc.*, 811 F.2d 1279 (9th Cir.), *cert. denied*, 484 U.S. 824 (1987).

The OFCCP may without any complaint by an employee or applicant review a contractor's compliance with executive order requirements. If it concludes that a violation exists, the OFCCP will ordinarily seek to resolve the matter through discussions and a "conciliation agreement" with the contractor. The OFCCP may institute administrative enforcement proceedings and may refer the matter to the Department of Justice for initiation of a lawsuit, 41 C.F.R. 60-1 Subpart B. The government may sue seeking an order barring the defendant from violating or interfering with rights of employees under the order, *United States v. Local 189, United Papermakers & Paperworkers*, 301 F. Supp. 906 (E.D. La.), *aff'd*, 416 F.2d 980 (5th Cir. 1969), *cert. denied*, 397 U.S. 919 (1970).

[4] Sanctions

Among the sanctions available for violation of the requirements of the order are cancellation of the contract and debarment of the contractor from eligibility for future government contracts, FAR 22.809. In *Timken Co. v. Vaughan*, 413 F. Supp. 1183 (N.D. Ohio 1976), the government's efforts to debar a contractor for an alleged violation of the order were unsuccessful. Upon consideration of the population surrounding the contractor's facility, the court held that the failure of the contractor's affirmative action program to include a city with a higher minority population did not violate the executive order. The court reasoned that, although the city was within a reasonable commuting distance, the population's habits indicated that residents were unlikely to seek work in the contractor's facility.

[B] Equal Opportunity for Veterans

The Vietnam Era Veterans' Readjustment Assistance Act of 1972, 38 U.S.C. § 4211 and § 4212, as amended, requires that contractors not discriminate against and take affirmative action with regard to "qualified covered veterans." Unless exempted by the Secretary of Labor, contractors awarded contracts for supplies or services, including construction, of $100,000 or more must agree to these requirements, FAR 22.1303(a). Guidance on the implementation of this policy is contained in FAR Subpart 22.13. This policy does not apply to contracts to be performed outside the United States. However, it does apply to all facilities of the contractor unless a waiver is granted, *Trinity Indus., Inc. v. Herman*, 173 F.3d 527 (4th Cir. 1999). A standard Equal Opportunity for Veterans clause on this subject is prescribed for contracts and subcontracts over $100,000, FAR 52.222-35.

The veterans covered by this policy are defined in FAR 22.1301. The clause provides that if a veteran is disabled, he or she is "qualified" if the veteran has "the ability to perform the essential functions of the employment positions with or without reasonable accommodation."

Contracts subject to the Act are also required to contain the Employment Reports on Veterans clause in FAR 52.222-37 which calls for annual reports containing data on the veterans in the contractor's workforce and its employment activity. Solicitations must contain the Compliance with Veterans' Employment Reporting Requirements provision in FAR 52.222-38 representing that the offeror has submitted the most recent report. Contracting officers are expected to verify that these reports have been filed, FAR 22.1304. Entering into a contract after failing to submit reports or submitting false reports is grounds for a false claim under 31 U.S.C. § 3729 et seq., *United States ex rel. Kirk v. Schindler Elevator Corp.*, 601 F.3d 94 (2d Cir. 2010), *rev'd on other grounds*, 563 U.S. 401 (2011).

Complaint procedures under these requirements are handled by the OFCCP in the same manner as equal opportunity complaints, FAR 22.1308. Courts will not review decisions of the OFCCP as to a company's practices under this statute because such decisions are committed to agency discretion, *Greer v. Chao*, 492 F.3d 962 (8th Cir. 2007). There is no private cause of action against a contractor under this statute, *Wikberg v. Reich*, 21 F.3d 188 (7th Cir. 1994); *Barron v. Nightingale Roofing, Inc.*, 842 F.2d 20 (1st Cir. 1988).

Contracting officers are required to implement any sanctions ordered by the Department of Labor, including withholding of progress payments and termination or suspension of a contract, FAR 22.1309; 41 C.F.R. § 60-300.66. Debarment of a contractor for noncompliance would result on its listing on the SAM Excluded Parties list.

[C] Other Sources of Equal Employment Opportunity Requirements

Most contractors and subcontractors are likely to be subject to some of the provisions of the Civil Rights Act of 1964, as amended by the Equal Employment Opportunity Act of 1972, 42 U.S.C. § 2000e-§ 2000e(17). Title VII of this Act prohibits employers with 15 or more employees and employment entities of labor organizations affecting interstate commerce from discriminating because of race, color, religion, sex, or national origin. An aggrieved employee or applicant for employment may sue the employer in a district court. The Equal Employment Opportunity Commission has power to investigate charges of discrimination under the Act and to sue if efforts to secure voluntary compliance fail.

Under Executive Order 11141, 29 Fed. Reg. 2477 (1964), federal contractors and subcontractors may not discriminate against employees or potential employees based on age, except upon the basis of a bona fide occupational qualification, retirement plan, or statutory requirement. FAR 22.901(c) provides that agencies are to bring this policy to the attention of contractors, but that no implementing contract clause is required.

All federal contracts and subcontracts over $15,000 for supplies and services, including construction, except where the Secretary of Labor grants a waiver, must include requirements barring discrimination against any employee or applicant because of physical or mental handicaps. Contractors under such contracts and subcontracts are also required to agree to take affirmative action with respect to such individuals, 29 U.S.C. § 793; Executive Order 11758, 39 Fed. Reg. 2075 (1974); 41 C.F.R. 60-741; FAR Subpart 22.14. The Affirmative Action for Workers with Disabilities clause prescribed for use is set forth at FAR 52.222-36.

§ 14.06 LABOR STANDARDS

For many years there has been extensive statutory coverage of the labor standards to be observed by federal government contractors. These statutes have imposed minimum wage levels, overtime wage restrictions, and provisions governing working conditions on various classes of work. This section considers the minimum wage provisions governing contracts for construction, supplies, and services.

[A] Davis-Bacon Act

The Davis-Bacon Act, 40 U.S.C. § 3141 et seq., establishes minimum wages, including fringe benefits, to be paid to laborers and mechanics on contracts of over $2,000 for the construction, alteration, or repair of public buildings and public works. Department of Labor regulations implementing this statute are found in 29 C.F.R. Part 5. FAR regulations are contained in Subpart 22.4.

The purpose of this Act is not to guarantee contractors that specified wage levels will be applicable, but rather to protect employees from substandard earnings by fixing a minimum wage on government projects, *United States v. Binghamton Constr. Co.*, 347 U.S. 171, *reh'g denied*, 347 U.S. 940 (1954). Therefore, the contractor has no right under the Act for recovery if the wage that must be paid to obtain employees is higher than the prevailing wage rate set forth in the contract. But see *Sunswick Corp. v. United States*, 75 F. Supp. 221 (Ct.

Cl.), *cert. denied*, 334 U.S. 827 (1948), where a contractor was allowed recovery for payment of wages higher than the wage determination when the higher payment was the result of a directive and the contract clause prohibited payment of more or less than the wage determination.

[1] Determination That Contract Is a Construction Contract

It is the procuring agency's responsibility to determine initially whether the Davis-Bacon Act is applicable to a particular contract, 29 C.F.R. § 5.5(a). GAO has held that the procuring agency's good-faith determination should not be overturned, 44 Comp. Gen. 498 (B-150828) (1965).

The Act applies only to federal contracts that essentially or substantially contemplate construction, alteration, or repair, 40 Comp. Gen. 565 (B-144901) (1961). Thus, maintenance work is not covered, *Dynalectron Corp.*, 65 Comp. Gen. 290 (B-220518), 86-1 CPD ¶ 151. Contracting officers must determine the extent of construction, alteration, or repair work that will be involved, *D.E. Clarke*, Comp. Gen. Dec. B-146824, 75-1 CPD ¶ 317. FAR 22.402 contains the following guidance:

> (a) Contracts for construction work. (1) The requirements of this subpart apply—
>
> (i) Only if the construction work is, or reasonably can be foreseen to be, performed at a particular site so that wage rates can be determined for the locality, and only to construction work that is performed by laborers and mechanics at the site of the work;
>
> (ii) To dismantling, demolition, or removal of improvements if a part of the construction contract, or if construction at that site is anticipated by another contract as provided in subpart 37.3;
>
> (iii) To the manufacture or fabrication of construction materials and components conducted in connection with the construction and on the site of the work by the contractor or a subcontractor under a contract otherwise subject to this subpart; and
>
> (iv) To painting of public buildings or public works, whether performed in connection with the original construction or as alteration or repair of an existing structure.
>
> (2) The requirements of this subpart do not apply to—
>
> (i) The manufacturing of components or materials off the site of the work or their subsequent delivery to the site by the commercial supplier or materialman;
>
> (ii) Contracts requiring construction work that is so closely related to research, experiment, and development that it cannot be performed separately, or that is itself the subject of research, experiment, or development (see paragraph (b) of this section for applicability of this subpart

to research and development contracts or portions thereof involving construction, alteration, or repair of a public building or public work);

(iii) Employees of railroads operating under collective bargaining agreements that are subject to the Railway Labor Act; or

(iv) Employees who work at contractors' or subcontractors' permanent home offices, fabrication shops, or tool yards not located at the site of the work. However, if the employees go to the site of the work and perform construction activities there, the requirements of this subpart are applicable for the actual time so spent, not including travel unless the employees transport materials or supplies to or from the site of the work.

(b) Nonconstruction contracts involving some construction work. (1) The requirements of this subpart apply to construction work to be performed as part of nonconstruction contracts (supply, service, research and development, etc.) if—

(i) The construction work is to be performed on a public building or public work;

(ii) The contract contains specific requirements for a substantial amount of construction work exceeding the monetary threshold for application of the Construction Wage Rate Requirement Statute (the word substantial relates to the type and quantity of construction work to be performed and not merely to the total value of construction work as compared to the total value of the contract); and

(iii) The construction work is physically or functionally separate from, and is capable of being performed on a segregated basis from, the other work required by the contract.

(2) The requirements of this subpart do not apply if—

(i) The construction work is incidental to the furnishing of supplies, equipment, or services (for example, the requirements do not apply to simple installation or alteration at a public building or public work that is incidental to furnishing supplies or equipment under a supply contract; however, if a substantial and segregable amount of construction, alteration, or repair is required, such as for installation of heavy generators or large refrigerator systems or for plant modification or rearrangement, the requirements of this subpart apply); or

(ii) The construction work is so merged with nonconstruction work or so fragmented in terms of the locations or time spans in which it is to be performed, that it is not capable of being segregated as a separate contractual requirement.

A contract for the furnishing and installing of a mechanized materials handling system for which 30% of the work and 40% of the dollar value of the equipment represented construction work was properly subject to the provisions of the Davis-Bacon Act, Comp. Gen. Dec. B-178159, June 6, 1973, *Unpub.*

It is sometimes difficult to ascertain whether the contract is for construction, services, or manufacturing. In one situation, the Secretary of Labor held that the construction of a mobile nuclear reactor was work covered by the Act while GAO held it was not, Opinion Letter of the Solicitor of Labor, Oct. 14, 1966, DB-52, C.C.H. Labor Law Transfer Binder, Wages, Hours and Administrative Rulings, ¶ 30,997.49; 47 Comp. Gen. 192 (B-161858) (1967). See also *American Warehouse Sys.*, Comp. Gen. Dec. B-402292, 2010 CPD ¶ 41 (free-standing mezzanine structure delivered to site and bolted to floor not construction); and *Voith Hydro, Inc.*, Comp. Gen. Dec. B-401244.2, 2009 CPD ¶ 239 (improvement of generators and excitation system in power plant construction not services).

[2] Employees Covered

The Act covers the minimum wages "to be paid various classes of laborers and mechanics." FAR 22.401 defines laborers or mechanics as workers "whose duties are manual or physical in nature (including those workers who use tools or who are performing the work of a trade), as distinguished from mental or managerial." The definition includes apprentices, trainees, and helpers, but not workers whose duties are primarily executive, supervisory, administrative, or clerical.

The Act applies to all "mechanics and laborers employed directly upon the site of the work." 29 C.F.R. § 5.2(k)(1)-(3) defines the "site of the work" as follows:

> (1) The site of the work is the physical place or places where the building or work called for in the contract will remain; and any other site where a significant portion of the building or work is constructed, provided that such site is established specifically for the performance of the contract or project;
>
> (2) Except as provided in paragraph (l)(3) of this section, job headquarters, tool yards, batch plants, borrow pits, etc., are part of the site of the work, provided they are dedicated exclusively, or nearly so, to performance of the contract or project, and provided they are adjacent or virtually adjacent to the site of the work as defined in paragraph (l)(1) of this section;
>
> (3) Not included in the site of the work are permanent home offices, branch plant establishments, fabrication plants, tool yards, etc., of a contractor or subcontractor whose location and continuance in operation are determined wholly without regard to a particular Federal or federally assisted contract or project. In addition, fabrication plants, batch plants, borrow pits, job headquarters, tool yards, etc., of a commercial or material supplier, which are established by a supplier of materials for the project before opening of bids and not on the site of the work as stated in paragraph (l)(1) of this section, are not included in the site of the work. Such permanent, previously established facilities are not part of the site of the work, even where the operations

for a period of time may be dedicated exclusively, or nearly so, to the performance of a contract.

This definition conforms to *Ball, Ball & Brosamer v. Secretary of Labor*, 24 F.3d 1447 (D.C. Cir. 1994), where the court held that a contractor was not obligated to pay Davis-Bacon Act wages to workers at a batch plant and borrow pit two miles from the construction site because those locations were not directly on the site of the work within the meaning of the Act. See also *L.P. Cavett Co. v. Dep't of Labor*, 101 F.3d 1111 (6th Cir. 1996), reversing a Department of Labor Wage Appeals Board ruling that the subcontractor's truck drivers hauling asphalt from a batch plant approximately three miles from the work site should have been paid Davis-Bacon Act wages because the plant was located on "the site of the work." In *Building & Constr. Trades Dep't, AFL-CIO v. Dep't of Labor Wage Appeals Bd.*, 932 F.2d 985 (D.C. Cir. 1991), the court held that material delivery truck drivers were not covered under the Act because the truck drivers came on to the site only to deliver materials. The court stated that the truck drivers spent 90% of their workday on the highway driving to and from commercial supply sources and stayed on the work site only long enough to drop off their loads, usually for not more than 10 minutes. In *Bechtel Constructors*, DOL-ARB, No. 95-45A, July 15, 1996, the board held that workers at sites providing concrete for a nearby federal project were subject to Davis-Bacon wage requirements. The board stated that the D.C. Circuit's ruling in *Ball, Ball & Brosamer* does not bar application of prevailing rates for all off-site plants and that "work performed in actual or virtual adjacency to one portion of a long continuous project is to be considered adjacent to the entire project."

The Federal Acquisition Streamlining Act amended the Davis-Bacon Act by waiving the application of prevailing wage-setting requirements to volunteer workers. The purpose of this waiver is to promote and provide opportunities for volunteers to provide their services in the construction, repair, or alteration of public buildings and works, 40 U.S.C. § 3161. Under 40 U.S.C. § 3162, Davis-Bacon wage-setting provisions are waived for persons who volunteer to perform services directly to a "state or local government, a public agency, or a public or private nonprofit recipient of federal assistance" as long as these persons do not work directly for a contractor, subcontractor, or government agency. Payment of expenses and nominal fees to such volunteers is authorized.

[3] Obtaining Wage Determinations

The Department of Labor is responsible for issuing wage determinations reflecting prevailing wages, including fringe benefits, FAR 22.404. There are two types of wage determinations—general and project.

A general wage determination contains prevailing wage rates for the types of construction designated in the determination and is used in contracts performed within a specified geographical area, FAR 22.404-1. General wage determinations are published on the WDOL website in SAM.gov, and are effective on the publication date of the notice or upon receipt by the contracting agency, whichever occurs first, FAR 22.404-1(a)(1). Such wage determinations contain no expiration date and are valid until modified, superseded, or canceled. If there is a general wage determination applicable to the project, the agency may use it without notifying the Department of Labor, FAR 22.404-3(a). Once incorporated into a contract, a general wage determination normally remains effective for the life of the contract unless the contract contains options to extend the period of the contract, FAR 22.404-1(a)(1). These determinations must be used whenever possible.

When no general wage determination applies, a project wage determination is issued at the specific request of a contracting agency, FAR 22.404-1(b). A contracting officer must submit requests for project wage determinations on SF 308 to the Department of Labor, FAR 22.404-3(b). The contracting officer must include a sufficiently detailed description of the work to indicate the type of construction involved, FAR 22.404-3(b). The wage determination is effective for 180 calendar days from the date of issuance and applies only to contract awards made within that time period, FAR 22.404-1(b). Once incorporated into a contract, a project wage determination is normally effective for the entire contract.

If it appears that a project wage determination may expire before award, there are different procedures for sealed bidding and negotiated procurements. With sealed bidding, the contracting officer must request a new wage determination before bid opening and extend the opening date if the original wage determination will expire prior to award, FAR 22.404-5(b)(1). If the contracting officer sees after bid opening that the wage determination will expire prior to award, the contracting officer should request that the administrator extend the expiration date, FAR 22.404-5(b)(2). If the request is granted, the contracting officer will award the contract and modify it to apply the extended expiration date to the already incorporated project wage determination, FAR 22.404-5(b)(2). If the request is denied, the administrator will issue a new project wage determination. If a new determination changes any wage rates for classifications to be used in the contract, the contracting officer may cancel the solicitation only in accordance with FAR 22.404-5(b)(2)(i). Otherwise, the contracting officer must award the contract and incorporate the new wage determination. The new determination is to be effective on the date of contract award. The contracting officer must equitably adjust the contract price for any increased or decreased cost of performance resulting from any changed wage rates, FAR 22.404-5(b)(2)(i). If the new determination does not change any wage rates, the contracting officer must award the contract and modify it to include the number and date of the new determination, FAR 22.404-5(b)(2)(ii).

With negotiated procurements, the contracting officer must request a new wage determination when it appears that the original wage determination will expire prior to award, FAR 22.404-5(c). Then the contracting officer is permitted to open and evaluate proposals and conduct necessary discussions pending the receipt of a new wage determination. The new wage determination is then given to the offerors remaining in the competition and they are allowed to revise their proposals.

[4] Procedures for Making Wage Determinations

The Act requires that the minimum wages included in wage determinations be based upon the "prevailing wages" paid to various classes of employees on projects of a similar character in the "city, town, village or other civil subdivision of the state in which the work is to be performed." The prevailing wage is the wage paid to more than 50% of the laborers or mechanics in the classification on similar projects in the area during the period in question, 29 C.F.R. § 1.2(a)(1). If the same wage is not paid to a majority in the class, the wage is calculated by taking the average wage paid to all the employees, 29 C.F.R. § 1.2(a)(1). The Labor Secretary's authority to make wage determinations in such a manner is based on the broad language employed in the Act delegating the authority, *Building & Constr. Trades Dep't, AFL-CIO v. Donovan*, 712 F.2d 611 (D.C. Cir. 1983), *cert. denied*, 464 U.S. 1069 (1984). The geographic reference point for wage determinations is normally the county in which the work is to be performed, 29 C.F.R. § 1.7(a). If there has not been sufficient similar construction in the area within the past year, the wage determination may be based upon wages paid on similar construction sites in surrounding counties, 29 C.F.R. § 1.7(b). However, the wages paid on projects in metropolitan counties may not be used as a source of data to be paid on projects in rural counties and vice versa, 29 C.F.R. § 1.7(b). In *Building & Constr. Trades Dep't*, the court upheld this regulation as furthering the intention of the statute. If no similar construction in the surrounding counties or in the state was performed within the past year, wages paid on projects completed more than one year prior to the beginning of the survey period may be considered, 29 C.F.R. § 1.7(c).

The Secretary of Labor's wage determinations are final and unreviewable by GAO, unless they are found to be arbitrary, capricious, or not supported by substantial evidence, 50 Comp. Gen. 103 (B-160778) (1970). The courts are also precluded from reviewing wage determinations, *United States v. Binghamton Constr. Co.*, 347 U.S. 171, *reh'g denied*, 347 U.S. 940 (1954). Thus, questions about the applicability or interpretation of a wage determination must be submitted to the Secretary of Labor, *North Ga. Bldg. & Constr. Trades Council v. Goldschmidt*, 621 F.2d 697 (5th Cir. 1980). However, "conformance" determinations of the Secretary of Labor that certain workers not included in an issued wage determination should or should not be classified as other workers are subject to judicial review, *Mistick PBT v. Chao*, 440 F.3d 503 (D.C. Cir. 2006).

[5] Contract Clauses

Construction contracts must include the Construction Wage Rate Requirements clause in FAR 52.222-6. This clause requires the payment of employees' wages at "rates not less than those contained in the wage determination of the Secretary of Labor which is attached hereto and made a part hereof." If the Davis-Bacon provisions are omitted from the contract but are included in the IFB, they are incorporated in the contract by reference, *International Bhd. of Elec. Workers*, Comp. Gen. Dec. B-183271, 75-1 CPD ¶ 201. The wage rate may be corrected after award if they contain clerical errors, FAR 22.404-7. In such cases, the contractor is entitled to an equitable adjustment, FAR 22.404-6(b)(5); *W.G. Yates & Sons Constr. Co. v. General Servs. Admin.*, CBCA 11-1 BCA ¶ 34,638 (Construction Wage Rate Requirements—Price Adjustment clause in FAR 52.222-32 not applicable). If a wage rate is incorrect through an error in judgment, the contract should not be corrected, *Dawson Constr. Co.*, Comp. Gen. Dec. B-189036, 78-1 CPD ¶ 108.

When a construction contract contains options, the contracting officer must ensure that the most current wage determination is applied at the time the option is exercised, FAR 22.404-12(a). One of three Construction Wage Rate Requirements—Price Adjustment clauses in FAR 52.222-30, -31, and -32 must be included in the contract depending on the method selected by the contracting officer to determine how the change in wage rates will be applied. See the guidance in FAR 22.404-12. The FAR 52.222-30 clause provides for no price adjustment because the contractor has been allowed to include higher wage rates in its prices for option years. The FAR 52.222-31 and -32 clauses provide for price adjustments on different bases but do not allow the contractor to receive profit on the increased amounts.

Construction contracts must also include nine other clauses listed in FAR 22.407. These clauses describe the procedures that must be followed by the contractor, the sanctions for noncompliance, and special dispute resolution procedures. The Withholding of Funds clause in FAR 52.222-7 permits the withholding of a reasonable amount to compensate for not paying the full amount of wages required. See *Copeland v. Veneman*, 350 F.3d 1230 (Fed. Cir. 2004), and *Overstreet Elec. Co.*, ASBCA 51653, 01-2 BCA ¶ 31,646, finding that contracting officers had acted reasonably under this clause.

[6] Enforcement

The contracting agency is responsible for enforcement of these labor requirements, including periodic review of the contractors and its subcontractors records, FAR 22.406-1(a). The Department of Labor also conducts independent investigations of compliance, 29 C.F.R. § 5.6(a)(5) and (b), and the contracting agency is required to cooperate in such investigations, FAR 22.406-12. If enforcement issues cannot be resolved by agreement with the contractor, they are subject to the Disputes Concerning Labor Standards clause in FAR 52.222-14, which calls for resolution by the Department of Labor. Such disputes are not subject to the Contract Disputes Act, *Emerald Maint., Inc. v. United States*, 925 F.2d 1425 (Fed. Cir. 1991); *Trataros Constr., Inc. v. United States*, 51 Fed. Appx. 10 (Fed. Cir. 2002).

Workers that believe that they have not been paid in accordance with the Act can file a complaint with the contracting officer or the Department of Labor. However, they have no private cause of action against the contractor, *Operating Eng'rs Health & Welfare Trust Fund v. JWJ Contracting Co.*, 135 F.3d 671 (9th Cir. 1998); *Chan v. City of New York*, 1 F.3d 96 (2d Cir. 1993); *Weber v. Heat Control Co.*, 728 F.2d 599 (3d Cir. 1984). Neither do they have a cause of action under state law, *Grochowski v. Phoenix Constr.*, 318 F.3d 80 (2d Cir. 2003). Compare *Garcia v. Skanska USA Bldg., Inc.*, 324 F. Supp. 3d 76 (D.D.C. 2018), finding a state cause of action for not paying Davis-Bacon wages. See also *United States ex rel. Wall v. Circle C Constr., LLC*, 700 F. Supp. 2d 926 (M.D. Tenn. 2010), holding that a qui tam False Claims Act suit was proper and assessing treble damages against a contractor that did not flow down the Davis-Bacon requirements to a subcontractor. Contractor employees that falsely certify compliance with the Act are also subject to criminal penalties under 18 U.S.C. § 1001, *United States v. Clark*, 787 F.3d 451 (7th Cir. 2015) (33 months prison sentence and monetary fine); *United States v. Shafer*, 23 Fed. Appx. 380 (6th Cir. 2001) (24 months prison sentence and monetary fine).

[B] Service Contract Act

The Service Contract Act of 1965, 41 U.S.C. §§ 6701-07, establishes minimum wage rates and fringe benefits based on those prevailing in the locality to be paid service employees for contracts over $2,500 which are principally for services which are furnished by service employees, 41 U.S.C. § 6703(1) and (2). It prohibits employment under hazardous or unsanitary working conditions and requires the contractor to provide notice of required compensation to all covered service employees on the first day of employment, 41 U.S.C. § 6703(3). The Act also provides remedies for noncompliance including debarment (§ 6706), contract termination ("cancellation") (§ 6705(c)), and withholding of contract funds (§ 6705(b)(1)).

The Act applies only when the services are performed in the United States, 41 U.S.C. § 6702(a)(3). Both contractors and subcontractors are subject to the Act, 41 U.S.C. § 6703.

41 U.S.C. § 6704(a) requires all contractors and subcontractors subject to the Act to pay their service employees no less than the minimum wage specified by the Fair Labor Standards Act, 29 U.S.C. § 206(a)(1). This requirement applies to contracts under $2,500 where no wage determination is required and to contracts over $2,500 where no wage determination has been issued. This

requirement is applicable even though the contract contains no applicable contract clause, Comp. Gen. Dec. B-167287, Sept. 4, 1969, *Unpub*.

The Secretary of Labor has responsibility for administering and implementing the Act, 41 U.S.C. § 6707(a). Enforcement authority is vested in both the Secretary of Labor and the head of the procuring agency, 41 U.S.C. § 6705. Pursuant to this authority, the Secretary has issued regulations governing the administration and interpretation of the Act in 29 C.F.R. Part 4. In addition, the Secretary has established the Administrative Review Board to provide administrative appellate review of Department of Labor (DOL) decisions regarding the Service Contract Act, 29 C.F.R. Part 8. FAR regulations are contained in Subpart 22.10. A supplementary regulation is provided by FAR 37.301 for the contracts involving dismantling, demolition, or removal of improvements.

[1] Scope of the Act

Rulings by the DOL on coverage of the Act are binding on the procuring agencies and GAO, 48 Comp. Gen. 22 (B-164338) (1968). See also 57 Comp. Gen. 501 (B-190505) (1978) (an agency must comply with the DOL's regulations implementing the Act unless the regulation is clearly contrary to law). However, the procuring agency makes the initial determination as to whether a contract falls within the Act; it has been held that if the contracting officer believes in good faith that the Act is not applicable, there is no duty to notify DOL or to include the Service Contract Act provisions in the contract, 53 Comp. Gen. 412 (B-178773) (1973); *Curtiss-Wright Corp. v. McLucas*, 381 F. Supp. 657 (D.N.J. 1974). GAO subsequently modified this ruling, finding that if the contracting officer is on notice that DOL may regard the procurement as subject to the Act, the matter must be referred to DOL whose decision on the question will be binding, *Hewes Eng'g Co.*, Comp. Gen. Dec. B-179501, 74-1 CPD ¶ 112. FAR 22.1003-7 requires a contracting officer that has a question as to the applicability of the Act to request advice of the "agency labor advisor" and to refer unresolved questions to DOL. A contractor cannot rely on the statement of a contracting officer that the Act does not apply when the statute is clear, *Shawview Cleaners, LLC*, ASBCA 56938, 10-2 BCA ¶ 34,550.

In general, the Service Contract Act is construed liberally by DOL. Thus, the Act has been applied to a referral service even though the service contractor had neither control over its nominal employees nor interest in the work they performed, *Menlo Serv. Corp. v. United States*, 765 F.2d 805 (9th Cir. 1985).

[a] Services Covered

The Act does not define the type of service that it covers, but DOL regulations at 29 C.F.R. § 4.130 provide examples of the types of services covered. Such services include repair and maintenance, aircraft flight services, stenographic reporting, food service, trash and garbage removal, and warehousing or storage services. See also FAR 22.1003-5. In addition, interpretations regarding the coverage of the Act are issued by the Wage and Hour Administrator of DOL. The Act's apparent legislative intent, according to 29 C.F.R. § 4.111(b), was to include "those contracts which have as their principal purpose the procurement of something other than the construction activity described in the Davis-Bacon Act or the materials, supplies, articles, and equipment described in the Walsh-Healey Act." If a contract involves both end products and services, it will be covered by the Act as long as the facts demonstrate that the contract is chiefly for services and that the furnishing of products is secondary, 29 C.F.R. § 4.131(a).

Department of Labor regulations interpret "principal purpose" to mean that the Act applies to all contracts that are primarily for services unless the contractor's use of service employees is incidental to the performance of the contract, 29 C.F.R. § 4.111(a) and § 4.113(a)(3). See 29 C.F.R. § 4.111(a) stating:

> [N]o hard and fast rule can be laid down as to the precise meaning of the term principal purpose. This remedial Act is intended to be applied to a wide variety of contracts, and the Act does not define or limit the types of services which may be contracted for under a contract the principal purpose of which is to furnish services. Further, the nomenclature, type, or particular form of contract used by procurement agencies is not determinative of coverage. Whether the principal purpose of a particular contract is the furnishing of services through the use of service employees is largely a question to be determined on the basis of all the facts in each particular case. Even where tangible items of substantial value are important elements of the subject matter of the contract, the facts may show that they are of secondary import to the furnishing of services in the particular case. This principle is illustrated by the examples set forth in § 4.131.

Although the regulation fails to define "incidental," DOL has considered the use of service employees incidental only when they have constituted less than 20% of the contract's workforce, 48 Fed. Reg. 49743 (1983). This broad interpretation of "principal purpose" has prevailed, as evidenced by DOL's rejection of a proposed change to its regulations that would have limited the scope of the Act to contracts that were principally for services and principally performed by service employees, 48 Fed. Reg. 49743 (1983).

Confusion has arisen concerning whether the Act applies to specific tasks within a contract where the contract as a whole is not principally for services. Until 1983, DOL applied the Act to any line item for services in a contract, such as maintenance and repair of automated data processing equipment. After persistent objections by the GSA and the computer industry and recommendations by GAO (Comp. Gen. Report Nos. HRD-80-102, Sept. 16, 1980, and HRD-80-102(A), Mar. 25, 1981), DOL revised its regulations to provide that the Act applies only if services are the principal part of the contract as a whole. Thus, such contracts with distinct line items should contain the appropriate labor provisions for each line item when the principal purpose it to furnish services. See 29 C.F.R. § 4.132 stating:

> If the principal purpose of a contract is to furnish services through the use of service employees within the meaning of the Act, the contract to furnish such services is not removed from the Act's coverage merely because, as a matter of convenience in procurement, the service specifications are combined in a single contract document with specifications for the procurement of different or unrelated items. In such case, the Act would apply to service specifications but would not apply to any specifications subject to the Walsh-Healey Act or to the Davis-Bacon Act. With respect to contracts which contain separate specifications for the furnishing of services and construction activity, see § 4.116(c).

FAR 22.1003-6 contains extensive guidance on the distinction between repair, which is subject to the Act, and remanufacturing, which is subject to the Walsh-Healey Act. Remanufacturing occurs when major overhaul or major modification of "an item, piece of equipment, or material" is "completely or substantially torn down," parts are replaced as needed, the item or equipment is rebuilt, and the delivered work is usable like a new item. See *Sabreliner Corp.*, Comp. Gen. Dec. B-275163, 96-2 CPD ¶ 244, holding that a contract for overhaul and repair of jet engines was properly classified as a supply contract not subject to the Service Contract Act.

[b] Service Employees

Although the Act originally applied only to blue collar workers, it was amended in 1976 to include some white-collar workers. 41 U.S.C. § 6701(3) now states:

> The term "service employee"—(A) means any individual engaged in the performance of a contract entered into by the Federal Government and not exempted under section 6702(b) of this title [41 U.S.C. § 6702(b)], whether negotiated or advertised, the principal purpose of which is to furnish services in the United States; (B) includes an individual without regard to any contractual relationship alleged to exist between the individual and a contractor or subcontractor; but (C) does not include an individual employed in a bona fide executive, administrative, or professional capacity, as those terms are defined in part 541 of title 29, Code of Federal Regulations.

The Department of Labor has found several classes of white-collar workers to be service employees. For example, 29 C.F.R. § 4.152 considers stenographers to be service employees, and wage determinations have been issued covering marine engineers, priests, ministers, librarians, and radio announcers.

The Act applies if some of the services will be performed by service employees. See 29 C.F.R. § 4.113 stating:

> (2) The coverage of the Act does not extend to contracts for services to be performed exclusively by persons who are not service employees, i.e., persons who are bona fide executive, administrative or professional personnel as defined in part 541 of this title (see paragraph (b) of this section). A contract for medical services furnished by professional personnel is an example of such a contract.

The principal issue in determining who is a "service employee" is in distinguishing such employees from "executive, administrative or professional" employees. 29 C.F.R. Part 541 contains extensive guidance on making this distinction.

[2] Wage Determinations

The principal purpose of the Act is to specify the minimum wages and benefits to be paid to service employees in accordance with prevailing rates in the locality, 41 U.S.C. § 6703. When a procuring agency determines that a prospective contract is subject to the Act, the contracting officer must obtain a wage determination, FAR 22.1007. Initially, this entails searching the WDOL website to find an applicable determination posted by DOL. This website contains a register of wage determinations for various types of services in different localities in the United States, 29 C.F.R. § 4.3. If the contract is to be performed in one of these localities, the contracting officer is authorized to select the appropriate class of service employees from the descriptions and wage rate determinations provided by DOL, *IBI Sec. Servs., Inc.*, Comp. Gen. Dec. B-218565, 85-2 CPD ¶ 7, *recons. denied*, 85-2 CPD ¶ 136. If no wage determination is found, the contracting officer must request a wage determination using DOL'S e98 electronic process—giving DOL adequate time to process the request. See the instructions in FAR 22.1008-1. Contracting officers are responsible for selecting the correct wage determination from the WDOL website but they can rely on DOL wage determinations furnished by DOL in answering specific requests, FAR 22.1008-1(d). If the wage determination does not include a class of employees to be used by a contractor, it must use "conformed" rates approximating the skill level of rates in the wage determination. See ¶ (c) of the Service Contract Labor Standards clause in FAR 52.222-41. See also *Data Monitor Sys., Inc.*, Comp. Gen. Dec. B-415761, 2018 CPD ¶ 79, holding that this procedure sufficiently meets the requirement for clarity in a solicitation to allow fair competition.

If there is a delay of over 60 days in bid opening or commencement of work under a negotiated contract, the contracting officer is required to recheck the WDOL website or obtain a new wage determination using the e98 process, FAR 22.1014. See *Office Automation & Training Consultants*, ASBCA 56779,

11-1 BCA ¶ 34,666, where the contractor was held responsible for determining the correct wage determinations when the solicitation referred to the WDOL website. See also *Beyley Constr. Grp. Corp.*, ASBCA 55692, 08-2 BCA ¶ 33,999, *aff'd*, 351 Fed. Appx. 446 (Fed. Cir. 2009), denying a claim for reformation of a contract where the contractor had not included some of the fringe benefits in its price. The board found that the agency had no reason to know of the unilateral mistake.

DOL revises wage determinations periodically and agencies are responsible for ensuring that their contracts contain current wage determinations. See 29 C.F.R. § 4.5(a)(2) requiring contracts to contain wage determination that were revised prior to award with the following exceptions:

> (i) However, revisions received by the Federal agency later than 10 days before the opening of bids, in the case of contracts entered into pursuant to competitive bidding procedures, shall not be effective if the Federal agency finds that there is not a reasonable time still available to notify bidders of the revision.
>
> (ii) In the case of procurements entered into pursuant to negotiations (or in the case of the execution of an option or an extension of the initial contract term), revisions received by the agency after award (or execution of an option or extension of term, as the case may be) of the contract shall not be effective provided that the contract start of performance is within 30 days of such award (or execution of an option or extension of term). Any notice of a revision received by the agency not less than 10 days before commencement of the contract shall be effective, if:
>
> (A) The contract does not specify a start of performance date which is within 30 days from the award; and/or
>
> (B) Performance of such procurement does not commence within this 30-day period.

See also FAR 22.1012-1. A contractor can rely on a wage determination for the life of the contract, but new wage determinations are required in the event of a modification or change to the contract or exercise of an option, 29 C.F.R. § 4.143.

There are two major issues that have to be addressed in determining the proper wage determination: (1) defining the "locality" of the work and (2) deciding between prevailing wages and higher wages under a collective bargaining agreement.

[a] Determining Locality

Wage determinations must include wages for the "locality" where the work will be performed. When a contract requires services to be performed at a government site, locality has been defined as the area in which the facility is located. However, early in the implementation of the Act there was controversy as to the meaning of "locality" when the work was to be performed at a contractor's facility. DOL defined locality as the site of the procuring activity, 41 Fed. Reg. 5388 (1976), but this was overturned in *Southern Packaging & Storage Co. v. United States*, 458 F. Supp. 726 (D.S.C. 1978), *aff'd*, 618 F.2d 1088 (4th Cir. 1980). As a result, DOL has adopted a two-step procedure for making wage determinations, 29 C.F.R. § 4.3(c) and § 4.4(a)(2).

Initially, the contracting agency attempts to identify the prospective offerors and their localities during the acquisition planning process. See FAR 22.1009-2 stating:

> The contracting officer should attempt to identify the specific places or geographical areas where the services might be performed. The following may indicate possible places of performance:
>
> (a) Locations of previous contractors and their competitors.
>
> (b) Databases available via the Internet for lists of prospective offerors and contractors.
>
> (c) Responses to a presolicitation notice (see 5.204).

A wage determination is then included in the solicitation for each locality. If the contracting officer subsequently learns that another offeror may participate in the competition, a wage determination must be obtained and included in the solicitation, FAR 22.1009-3. There is no solicitation provision informing offerors of this procedure, but an offeror that intends to compete for the work should immediately notify the contracting officer of the need for a wage determination for its locality. If the contracting officer determines initially that there may be offerors competing which are unknown, the Service Contract Act—Place of Performance Unknown solicitation provision in FAR 52.222-49 is included in the solicitation, FAR 22.1009-4. This informs offerors of the need to obtain a wage determination for their locality and places the risk of being bound by a post-contract wage determination if they do not inform the contracting officer of a need for the determination within a specified period (generally 10 to 15 days after receipt of the solicitation). In either instance, the resulting contract must contain a wage determination for the locality of the winning contractor.

[b] Collective Bargaining Agreements

The Service Contract Act originally allowed DOL to find a prevailing wage lower than the wage being paid by an incumbent contractor under a collective bargaining agreement. This provision was amended at 41 U.S.C. § 353(c) (now § 6703), making the prior collective bargaining agreement rates and fringe benefits applicable to subsequent contracts without regard to any wage determination that had been issued unless one of the statutory exceptions applies. DOL has issued procedures to implement this requirement in 29 C.F.R. § 4.1b(b). Under these procedures, the contracting officer, during acquisition planning, must determine whether there is an incumbent contractor subject to the Act that has a collective bargaining agreement with its service employees, FAR 22.1008-2. If so, the contracting officer is required to give the incumbent contractor and the collective bargaining representative of the incumbent's employees prior written notice of the proposed procurement at least 30 days before issuance of a solicitation, FAR 22.1010. If there is a new or changed agreement of which the contracting officer has not received timely notice, the procurement is allowed to proceed without regard to the terms the collective bargaining agreement, FAR 22.1012-2. Otherwise, such terms are binding on the new contractor. The procedure for incorporating the provisions of a collective bargaining agreement into the wage determination attached to the contract are set forth in FAR 22.1008-2(d). Compare *Call Henry, Inc. v. United States*, 855 F.3d 1348 (Fed. Cir. 2017), holding that the cost of withdrawing from a pension plan in a collective bargaining agreement was not covered by the SCA price adjustment provisions, with *Lear Siegler Servs., Inc. v. Rumsfeld*, 457 F.3d 1262 (Fed. Cir. 2006), holding that the increased costs of a health plan were a fringe benefit subject to price adjustment.

This "successor" contract rule does not apply if DOL makes a determination that a collective bargaining agreement was not entered into as a result of arm's-length negotiations, or the negotiated wages and benefits substantially vary from those prevailing in the locality. Determination that the predecessor contractor's collective bargaining agreement resulted from arm's-length negotiations may be made through investigation, hearing, or pursuant to the Secretary's authority, FAR 22.1002-3(a). The regulations are also quite complete in setting forth the procedures to be followed for making a determination that the rates in the collective bargaining agreement are substantially at variance with prevailing rates, 29 C.F.R. § 4.10. If a substantial variance decision is made after the contract had been awarded, the determination is made solely on a prospective basis.

This "successor" contract rule also does not apply if the incumbent contractor enters into the collective bargaining agreement for the first time and the agreement does not become binding until its contract has ended, FAR 22.1008-2(c)(1). Neither does the rule apply if the collective bargaining agreement is not implemented by the predecessor contractor and the union, *Upshaw v. Akal Security, Inc.*, No. 05 C 0-272, 2008 U.S. Dist. LEXIS 22856 (N.D. Ill. Mar. 20, 2008). In addition, the rule does not apply if the incumbent contractor enters into the collective bargaining agreement during contract performance but fails to give timely notice. See FAR 22.1008-2(c)(2) describing late notice as follows:

> (i)(A) In sealed bidding, the contracting agency receives notice of the terms of the collective bargaining agreement less than 10 days before bid opening and finds that there is not reasonable time still available to notify bidders (see 22.1012-2(a)); or
>
> (B) For contractual actions other than sealed bidding, the contracting agency receives notice of the terms of the collective bargaining agreement

after award, provided that the start of performance is within 30 days of award (see 22.1012-2(b)); and

(ii) The contracting officer has given both the incumbent contractor and its employees' collective bargaining agent timely written notification of the applicable acquisition dates (see 22.1010).

[3] Exemptions to Service Contract Act

The Secretary of Labor has authority to exempt contracts from the Service Contract Act under 41 U.S.C. § 6707(b). Statutorily exempted are contracts for transportation (§ 6702(b)(3)), communications (§ 6702(b)(4)), public utilities (§ 6702(b)(5)), individual personal services (§ 6702(b)(6)), and contracts with the Postal Service (§ 6702(b)(7)). Detailed guidance on these exemptions is in 29 C.F.R. §§ 4.118-4.122. See *Williams v. Dep't of Labor*, 697 F.2d 842 (8th Cir. 1983), where military "pack and crate" contracts were not exempted from the Act because the contracts were not primarily for carriage of freight.

Contracts covered by the Walsh-Healey Act are also exempt from the Act (§ 6702(b)(2)). See 29 C.F.R. § 4.117 exempting contracts for remanufacturing that constitute "major overhaul" or "major modification."

Similarly, contracts subject to the Davis-Bacon Act are exempt (§ 6702(b)(1)). For dismantling, demolition or removal of improvements contracts, FAR 37.301 requires the use of the Davis-Bacon Act only if "further work which will result in the construction, alteration, or repair of a public building or public work at that location is contemplated." Otherwise, the Service Contract Act applies. See also 29 C.F.R. § 4.131(f). For other contracts containing both services and construction, GAO has permitted broad discretion by contracting officers, loosely following the rule that the Davis-Bacon Act will apply if the contract contains substantial amounts of construction work, *D.E. Clarke*, Comp. Gen. Dec. B-146824, 75-1 CPD ¶ 317.

29 C.F.R. § 4.123(e)(1) exempts contracts for the maintenance and repair of automated data processing equipment and office information systems, office and business machines, and high technology scientific and medical apparatus. See also FAR 22.1003-4(c). To qualify for the exemption, the contractor is required to certify that it will maintain the same compensation plan for employees on both government and commercial equipment contracts. See *AFL-CIO v. Donovan*, 757 F.2d 330 (D.C. Cir. 1985), where the court found proper an exemption for contracts for commercial products support services of high-technology companies in view of the industry's established merit pay systems and the significant impairment of government operations which would result if computers were not available because manufacturers refused to accept service contracts. See *Savantage Fin. Servs., Inc. v. United States*, 86 Fed. Cl. 700 (2009), finding reasonable a determination that a contract for an "integrated system solution" was not subject to the Act.

Contracts with commercial contractors are also exempt. See FAR 22.1003-4(d) listing the type of services covered by this exemption and the conditions that must be met. To meet this requirement the contractor's employees must "spend only a small portion of his or her time (a monthly average of less than 20 percent of the available hours on an annualized basis, or less than 20 percent of available hours during the contract period if the contract period is less than one month) servicing the Government contract." The major conditions are that the services are sold regularly to nongovernment customers in substantial quantities and are furnished at prices at, or based on, established catalog or market prices.

DOL has declined a proposal to exempt R&D contracts from the Act after concluding that such an exemption is unnecessary and would be extremely difficult to define, 48 Fed. Reg. 49751 (1983).

[4] Contract Clauses

The Service Contract Labor Standards clause in FAR 52.222-41 is used in all contracts where the Act applies. Detailed instructions on the use of this clause are set forth in FAR 22.1006(a). The Statement of Equivalent Rates for Federal Hires clause in FAR 52.222-42 is also required to be included in these contracts. See FAR 22.1016 for instructions on the use of this clause. When service contracts cover multiple years, FAR 22.1006(c)(1) requires use of the Fair Labor Standards Act and Service Contract Labor Standards—Price Adjustment (Multiple Year and Option Contracts) clause in FAR 52.222-43. When service contracts do not cover multiple years, FAR 22.1006(c)(2) requires use of the Fair Labor Standards Act and Service Contract Labor Standards—Price Adjustment clause in FAR 52.222-44. These price adjustment clauses allow compensation for higher wages resulting from new wage determinations but do not permit the inclusion of indirect costs or profit. They require notice to the contracting officer of claimed increased amounts within 30 days of receipt of a new wage determination. See *DTS Aviation Servs., Inc.*, ASBCA 56352, 09-2 BCA ¶ 34,288, discussing the enforceability of this notice requirement. These clauses also contain a warranty that the prices in the contract do not contain any contingency for higher wages in later periods. See *JDD, Inc.*, ASBCA 55282, 06-2 BCA ¶ 33,345, granting a price adjustment under the FAR 52.222-43 clause even though the solicitation directed the offerors to include an amount in their option year prices to cover higher wages. The board concluded that the warranty in the clause precluded such a contingency. See also *Just in Time Staffing v. United States*, 143 Fed. Cl. 405 (2019), holding that the cost of negotiating a collective bargaining agreement was not a cost covered by the price adjustment provision.

[5] Enforcement

Both the contracting agency and DOL have enforcement powers. Both DOL and the contracting officer can withhold funds when it is found that a contractor has not paid the correct wages, 29 C.F.R. § 4.187. See ¶ (k) of the Service Contract Labor Standards clause and FAR 22.1022. Noncompliance with the Act is also grounds for default termination, FAR 22.1023, or "cancellation," 29 C.F.R. § 4.190. Placing a contractor in the SAM Excluded Parties list is adequate grounds for default termination, *Webco Transp. Corp.*, PSBCA 5276, 09-1 BCA ¶ 34,042.

DOL also conducts hearings and reaches decisions which are binding on "all agencies of the Government," 29 C.F.R. § 4.189, and the contracting agency is required to cooperate in all DOL investigations, FAR 22.1024. If enforcement issues cannot be resolved by agreement with the contractor, they are subject to ¶ (t) of the Service Contract Labor Standards clause, which calls for resolution by the Department of Labor.

The Act requires contractor that violate its provisions to be debarred for three years unless DOL finds that there are "unusual circumstances." See 29 C.F.R. § 4.188(b) stating:

> (3)(i) The Department of Labor has developed criteria for determining when there are unusual circumstances within the meaning of the Act. See, e.g., Washington Moving & Storage Co., Decision of the Assistant Secretary, SCA 68, August 16, 1973, Secretary, March 12, 1974; Quality Maintenance Co., Decision of the Assistant Secretary, SCA 119, January 11, 1974. Thus, where the respondent's conduct in causing or permitting violations of the Service Contract Act provisions of the contract is willful, deliberate or of an aggravated nature or where the violations are a result of culpable conduct such as culpable neglect to ascertain whether practices are in violation, culpable disregard of whether they were in violation or not, or culpable failure to comply with recordkeeping requirements (such as falsification of records), relief from the debarment sanction cannot be in order. Furthermore, relief from debarment cannot be in order where a contractor has a history of similar violations, where a contractor has repeatedly violated the provisions of the Act, or where previous violations were serious in nature.
>
> (ii) A good compliance history, cooperation in the investigation, repayment of moneys due, and sufficient assurances of future compliance are generally prerequisites to relief. Where these prerequisites are present and none of the aggravated circumstances in the preceding paragraph exist, a variety of factors must still be considered, including whether the contractor has previously been investigated for violations of the Act, whether the contractor has committed recordkeeping violations which impeded the investigation, whether liability was dependent upon resolution of a bona fide legal issue of doubtful certainty, the contractor's efforts to ensure compliance, the nature, extent, and seriousness of any past or present violations, including the impact

of violations on unpaid employees, and whether the sums due were promptly paid.

Courts give considerable deference to debarment decisions, *Karawia v. Dep't of Labor*, 627 F. Supp. 2d 137 (S.D.N.Y. 2009) (debarment proper when contractor had been subject to 57 DOL enforcement actions).

GAO will not hear challenges that a competitor will not comply with the Act, *K-Mar Indus., Inc.*, Comp. Gen. Dec. B-400487, 2009 CPD ¶ 159; *SAGE Sys. Techs., LLC*, Comp. Gen. Dec. B-310155, 2007 CPD ¶ 219.

Workers that believe that they have not been paid in accordance with the Act can file a complaint with the contracting officer or the Department of Labor, 29 C.F.R. § 4.191. However, they have no private cause of action against the contractor, *Miscellaneous Serv. Workers, Drivers & Helpers v. Philco-Ford Corp.*, 661 F.2d 776 (9th Cir. 1981). Some courts have held that there is a state cause of action for additional compensation, *Inkrote v. Protection Strategies, Inc.*, No. 3:09-CV-51, 2009 U.S. Dist. LEXIS 101070 (N.D.W. Va. Oct. 13, 2009); *Naranjo v. Spectrum Sec. Servs., Inc.*, 91 Cal. Rptr. 3d 393 (Ct. App. 2009). See also *United Gov't Sec. Officers of Am. v. Chertoff*, 587 F. Supp. 2d 209 (D.D.C. 2008), holding that the court could order an agency to incorporate a new wage DOL determination into its contract.

Aggrieved workers can file a qui tam False Claims Act suit for a contractor's false statement that it was in compliance with the Act, *United States. ex rel. Sutton v. Double Day Office Servs., Inc.*, 121 F.3d 531 (9th Cir. 1997).

[C] Contract Work Hours and Safety Standards Act

The Contract Work Hours and Safety Standards Act, 40 U.S.C. § 3701 et seq., requires that laborers and mechanics be paid overtime for all hours over 40 hours in a week. It applies to all construction contracts of $150,000 or more that are not for commercial items, transportation, the transmission of intelligence, or are not to be performed outside of the United States, FAR 22.305. See *K-Con, Inc. v. Sec'y of Army*, 908 F.3d 719, 723 (Fed. Cir. 2018), holding that inserting the clause was proper in a construction contract for work within the United States.

The Act also applies to certain service contract employees. See 29 C.F.R. § 4.181(b)(1) stating:

> The Contract Work Hours and Safety Standards Act (40 U.S.C. 327-332) applies generally to Government contracts, including service contracts in excess of $100,000, which may require or involve the employment of laborers and mechanics. Guards, watchmen, and many other classes of service employees are laborers or mechanics within the meaning of such Act. However, employees rendering only professional services, seamen, and as a

> general rule those whose work is only clerical or supervisory or nonmanual in nature, are not deemed laborers or mechanics for purposes of the Act. The wages of every laborer and mechanic for performance of work on such contracts must include compensation at a rate not less than 1 1/2 times the employees' basic rate of pay for all hours worked in any workweek in excess of 40. Exemptions are provided for certain transportation and communications contracts, contracts for the purchase of supplies ordinarily available in the open market, and work, required to be done in accordance with the provisions of the Walsh-Healey Act.

Contracts subject to the Act must contain the Contract Work Hours and Safety Standards Act—Overtime Compensation clause in FAR 52.222-4. This clause not only requires the payment of overtime to workers but also the payment of liquidated damages to the government in the event of nonpayment. These damages are assessed at the rate of $10 per day per worker. FAR 22.302(c) permits agency heads to waive or reduce liquidated damages if the violation was inadvertent. See *Myers Investigative & Sec. Servs., Inc. v. Environmental Protection Agency*, CBCA 16587-EPA, 05-2 BCA ¶ 32,983, holding that the issue of whether liquidated damages were properly assessed is a Contract Disputes Act issue not a labor standards issue (requiring resolution by the Department of Labor under the Fair Labor Standards Act and Service Contract Act—Price Adjustment clause).

The clause also calls for withholding of funds to cover insufficient payments to workers. See *Amaya v. Power Design, Inc.*, 833 F.3d 440, 443 (4th Cir. 2016), finding that the Act did not conflict with the Davis Bacon Act or the Fair Labor Standards Act and applied to federal contracts.

[D] Walsh-Healey Act

The Walsh-Healey Act, 41 U.S.C. § 6501 et seq., is the supply contract counterpart of the Davis-Bacon Act. It establishes "minimum" wages for contracts in excess of $15,000 for the manufacturing or furnishing of materials, supplies, articles, and equipment. Department of Labor regulations implementing this statute are found in 41 C.F.R. Part 50-201-1. The Walsh-Healey Act was part of a package of New Deal legislation in the 1930s. The Act sought to provide worker protection in order to alleviate two major problems faced by workers during the Depression—the number of hours worked and minimum wages. The protections of the Act have been superseded by the Fair Labor Standards Act, 29 U.S.C. § 207.

FAR 22.604-1 provides that specified supplies are statutorily exempt from the Act:

> (a) Any item in those situations where the contracting officer is authorized by the express language of a statute to purchase "in the open market"

generally (such as commercial items, see part 12); or where a specific purchase is made under the conditions described in 6.302-2 in circumstances where immediate delivery is required by the public exigency.

(b) Perishables, including dairy, livestock, and nursery products.

(c) Agricultural or farm products processed for first sale by the original producers.

(d) Agricultural commodities or the products thereof purchased under contract by the Secretary of Agriculture.

FAR 22.604-2 provides that specified supplies are exempt by regulation from the Act:

(1) Public utility services.

(2) Supplies manufactured outside the United States, Puerto Rico, and the U.S. Virgin Islands.

(3) Purchases against the account of a defaulting contractor where the stipulations of the Act statute were not included in the defaulted contract.

(4) Newspapers, magazines, or periodicals, contracted for with sales agents or publisher representatives, which are to be delivered by the publishers thereof.

Contracts subject to the Act must contain the Walsh-Healey Public Contracts Act clause in FAR 52.222-20. This clause incorporates the regulations of the Department of Labor at 41 C.F.R. Chapter 50 into the contract and requires the contractor to pay the minimum wages prescribed by the Fair Labor Standards Act.

§ 14.07 OTHER EMPLOYEE-RELATED STATUTES

Congress has enacted other statutes that have direct impact on the manner in which contractor employees are treated at the workplace. This section discusses statutes giving rights to persons with disabilities and the statute aimed at ensuring that contractors establish a drug-free workplace. Although the main purposes of these laws are not related, they share the common goals of attempting to make the contract work environment more accessible to all qualified personnel, more acceptable as a "good" place to work, and more productive.

[A] Workers with Disabilities

There are two statutes providing rights to persons with disabilities. Detailed guidance on determining whether a person has a disability and whether such a person is qualified for a job is contained in 29 C.F.R. § 1630.2 and § 1630.3.

[1] The Rehabilitation Act

The Rehabilitation Act of 1973, 29 U.S.C. § 793, requires contractors to take affirmative action with regard to hiring and promotion of "qualified individuals with disabilities." The Act is implemented by Executive Order 11758, DOL regulations in 41 C.F.R. Part 60-741; and FAR Subpart 22.14.

FAR 22.1402 requires all contracts over $15,000 to contain the Affirmative Action for Workers with Disabilities clause at FAR 52.222-36. FAR 22.1403 provides for waivers to "any or all" of the terms of this clause as follows:

> (a) The agency head, with the concurrence of the Deputy Assistant Secretary for Federal Contract Compliance of the U.S. Department of Labor (Deputy Assistant Secretary), may waive any or all of the terms of the clause at 52.222-36, Affirmative Action for Workers with Disabilities, for—
>
> (1) Any contract if a waiver is deemed to be in the national interest; or
>
> (2) Groups or categories of contracts if a waiver is in the national interest and it is—
>
> (i) Impracticable to act on each request individually; and
> (ii) Determined that the waiver will substantially contribute to convenience in administering the Act.
>
> (b)(1) The head of a civilian agency, with the concurrence of the Deputy Assistant Secretary, or, (2) the Secretary of Defense, may waive any requirement in this subpart when it is determined that the contract is essential to the national security, and that its award without complying with such requirements is necessary to the national security. Upon making such a determination, the head of a civilian agency shall notify the Deputy Assistant Secretary in writing within 30 days.

The clause was properly omitted from a solicitation to select insurance carrier to furnish contractors with Defense Base Act workers' compensation insurance coverage because the acquisition was not subject to the FAR, *Gov't Servs. Corp. v. United States*, 131 Fed. Cl. 409, 423 (2017); *Fidelity & Cas. Co. of New York*, Comp. Gen. Dec. B-281281, 99-1 CPD ¶ 16.

Complaints of violation of the clause are handled by the DOL Office of Federal Contract Compliance, 41 C.F.R. § 60-741.61, and, if received by an agency should be forwarded to that office, FAR 22.1406. DOL can impose the sanctions of withholding of payment, termination or suspension of a contract or debarment of a contractor, 41 C.F.R. § 60-741.66; FAR 22.1407.

[2] The Americans with Disabilities Act

The Americans with Disabilities Act of 1990 (ADA), 42 U.S.C. § 12101 et seq., seeks to protect "individuals with a disability" if they are qualified to perform job requirements. It defines an "individual with a disability" as someone with a physical or mental impairment that substantially limits one or more major life activities, 42 U.S.C. § 12102(2). It prohibits discrimination against such individuals and requires "reasonable accommodation" for them, 42 U.S.C. § 12112. The Act is implemented in 29 C.F.R. 1630. It is not covered in the FAR.

[a] Prohibited Discrimination

The ADA prohibits all employers (not only government contractors) from discriminating in all aspects of employment against any "qualified individual with a disability" because of that person's disability. The ADA specifically bars discrimination in job application procedures, hiring, promotion, termination, compensation, training, and other "terms, conditions, and privileges of employment," 42 U.S.C. § 12112(a).

The statute defines the term "qualified individual with a disability" to mean an "individual with a disability who, with or without reasonable accommodation, can perform the essential functions of the employment position that such individual holds," 42 U.S.C. § 12111(8). In *Minter v. D.C.*, 809 F.3d 66, 70 (D.C. Cir. 2015), the court found that—being present at work was an essential function of the job so termination was not improper when the plaintiff did not go into work for five months. Further, the court found that an individual does not count as qualified when they have been so severely injured that they cannot perform essential functions of the job.

The ADA expressly forbids any preemployment medical examination or other inquiry of a job applicant about the existence or extent of any disability, 42 U.S.C. § 12112(d). However, if all employees are subject to a medical examination, then an individual with a disability can properly be subject to the same requirement so long as the results are maintained in confidence and used only as otherwise permitted under the statute, 42 U.S.C. § 12112(d)(3). Employers are further forbidden from discriminating against an otherwise qualified individual because of the disability of another person with whom the qualified individual has a relationship, 42 U.S.C. § 12112(b)(4). Finally, the ADA requires that the job application process be accessible to people with different disabilities, and it prohibits the use of standards or tests if they tend to screen out individuals with disabilities, unless the selection criteria are job related for the position in question and consistent with business necessity, 42 U.S.C. § 12112(b)(6).

[b] Reasonable Accommodation

The ADA requires employers to make "reasonable accommodation" for the physical or mental impairments of the employee or applicant, that is, changes in the work environment or in the way things are customarily done that enable a person with a disability to enjoy equal employment opportunities, 29 C.F.R. Part 1630 App. § 1630(2)(o).

Employers are required to make only accommodations that are reasonable. An accommodation is not reasonable if the employer can demonstrate that it would impose undue hardship on the conduct of its business. This would include accommodations that are unduly costly, extensive, substantial, or disruptive, or that would fundamentally alter the nature or operation of the business, 29 C.F.R. Part 1630 App. 1630(2)(o).

[c] Defenses

Employers have several defenses available. First, accommodations need not be made if they would impose an undue hardship on the employer's business. Second, qualification standards may be used, even those that tend to screen out people with disabilities, if the standards are job-related and consistent with business necessity. Furthermore, employers are not obligated to hire anyone who poses a direct threat to the health or safety of himself or herself or to others in the workplace, 42 U.S.C. § 12113(b). Protection under the ADA does not extend to any employee or applicant who is currently engaging in the illegal use of drugs, 42 U.S.C. § 12114(a).

[d] Enforcement

The ADA is enforced by the EEOC in the same manner used to enforce Title VII of the Civil Rights Act of 1964, 42 U.S.C. § 12117(a). Any job applicant or employee who believes that discrimination has occurred can file a charge with the nearest EEOC office. The complaining party, once its administrative remedies have been exhausted, is free to file suit in federal court.

The remedies available to a successful complainant in an ADA proceeding are the same remedies available under Title VII of the Civil Rights Act of 1964, 42 U.S.C. § 12117(a). Available remedies may include hiring, reinstatement, promotion, back or front pay, reasonable accommodation, attorney fees, expert witness fees, and court costs, 42 U.S.C. § 1981a(a). Compensatory and punitive damages also may be available where intentional discrimination is found, 42 U.S.C. § 1981a(a). These damages are capped at a level corresponding to the size of the employer. For example, employers of between 15 and 100 employees will not pay damages in excess of $ 50,000, 42 U.S.C. § 1981a(b)(3)(A).

The ADA expressly prohibits retaliation against an individual who makes a charge of discrimination or who participates in any resulting investigation, proceeding, or hearing, 42 U.S.C. § 12203.

[B] Drug-Free Workplace Act of 1988

The Drug-Free Workplace Act of 1988 (DFWA), 41 U.S.C. § 701, requires most government contractors to establish and maintain a drug-free workplace as a condition of their current contracts and in order to maintain eligibility for future contracts. This Act is implemented in FAR Subpart 23.5. It is also implemented with regard to grants, cooperative agreements and other financial assistance in 29 C.F.R. Part 94.

[1] Policy

The Act prohibits award of contracts except those under the simplified acquisition threshold or for commercial items, unless the contractor has certified that it will provide a drug-free workplace and adhere to several specific practices, FAR 23.504. Contractors must:

> Publish a policy statement that prohibits any unlawful activity involving controlled substances in the workplace and specifying the actions that will be taken with respect to violations of the policy.
>
> Establish a drug-free awareness program that will inform employees about the drug-free workplace, the availability of counseling and employee assistance programs, and the sanctions that will be imposed for drug abuse violations occurring in the workplace.
>
> Notify the contracting agency in writing of any employee conviction for a drug statute violation within 10 calendar days after being made aware of the conviction.
>
> Impose sanctions (up to and including termination) on the involved employee or require the employee to participate in an approved drug abuse assistance or rehabilitation program.
>
> Make a "good faith" effort to maintain a drug-free workplace.

The Act is implemented by a Drug-Free Workplace clause at FAR 52.223-6.

[2] Drug Testing

The Act does not require drug testing of employees by contractors. However, Executive Order 12564, issued by President Reagan in 1986, did provide for random drug testing in sensitive positions. The FAR is silent on drug testing procedures. Individual agencies have issued drug testing procedures that vary depending upon the duties of the agency and the "sensitivity" of the work being performed by contractors. The DoD and NASA offer representative examples of these rules.

The drug testing protocol required of DoD contractors is found in the Drug-Free Work Force clause, DFARS 252.223-7004. This clause requires as part of a contractor's drug-free program "provisions for identifying illegal drug users on a controlled and carefully monitored basis." The clause goes on to discuss the extent of and criteria for such testing. As important considerations it lists the nature of the work being performed; the employee's duties; the efficient use of contractor resources; and the risks to health, safety, and national security that could result from the failure of employees to adequately perform their work. In addition, the clause provides that testing is appropriate (1) when there is a reasonable suspicion that an employee uses illegal drugs, (2) when an employee has been involved in an accident or unsafe practice, (3) as part of a follow-up to counseling or rehabilitation, or (4) as part of a voluntary employee drug testing program.

NASA has adopted a drug and alcohol testing program to implement the Civil Space Employee Testing Act of 1991, NFS 1823.5. This requires the use of the Drug- and Alcohol-Free Workforce clause in NFS 1852.223-74 in contracts for critical missions or contract over $5 million where employees "in a sensitive position" will perform work. Among other things, the clause requires NASA contractors to provide preemployment, reasonable suspicion, random, post-accident, and periodic follow-up testing of contractor employees "in sensitive positions."

The Department of Health and Human Services has issued "Guidelines for Federal Workplace Drug Testing Programs," 59 Fed. Reg. 29908, June 6, 1994, which, as revised, became effective in September 1994. Among other things, these Guidelines seek to establish (1) scientific and technical rules for federal agencies' workplace drug testing programs, and (2) a certification program for laboratories engaged in urine drug testing for federal agencies.

[3] Sanctions

FAR 23.504(a) provides that no offeror will be considered a responsible source in the absence of an agreement regarding a drug-free workplace. Similarly, under FAR 23.504(b), an individual will be denied award of a contract of any dollar amount unless that individual agrees that he or she "will not engage in the unlawful manufacture, distribution, dispensing, possession, or use of a controlled substance while performing the contract."

FAR 23.506 provides that the contracting officer may suspend contract payments if a contractor has failed to comply with the Drug-Free Workplace clause, or if the number of contractor employees convicted of criminal drug violations indicates that the contractor has failed to make a good-faith effort to provide a drug-free workplace. The contracting officer also has the discretion to terminate a contract for default, FAR 23.506(b), and must refer a contractor for debarment or suspension when payments are suspended or the contract is terminated, FAR 23.506(c).

CHAPTER 15

CONTRACT AWARD CONTROVERSIES

§15.01 EVOLUTION OF PROCUREMENT CONTRACT AWARD CONTROVERSIES

Contract award controversies have become a substantial part of the procurement process. Disappointed offerors often seek to challenge procurement actions. For many years, these challenges were heard without specific statutory authority. However, beginning in 1982, Congress began to take an active role in formalizing the process by adopting a number of statutes dealing with award controversies. Presently, there are three forums where procurement contract award controversies may be heard—the procuring agencies, the Government Accountability Office (GAO), and the Court of Federal Claims. In some circumstances, controversies regarding the award of government contracts, particularly nonprocurement contracts, may also be heard in the U.S. district courts.

The boards of contract appeals have not generally been involved in contract award controversies. See *Coastal Corp. v. United States*, 713 F.2d 728 (Fed. Cir. 1983), holding that the board's jurisdiction under the Contract Disputes Act of 1978, 41 U.S.C. § 601-§ 613, does not extend to implied contracts to consider bids and proposals fairly. A notable exception was the General Services Administration Board of Contract Appeals (GSBCA). In 1984 the GSBCA was granted authority to hear protests on Brooks Act automatic data processing equipment (now, information technology) procurements, 40 U.S.C. § 759(h). However, § 5101 of the Clinger-Cohen Act of 1996, Pub. L. No. 104-106, repealed this authority. During this time, the board rendered numerous decisions dealing with the award process. Those decisions and the decisions of the Court of Appeals for the Federal Circuit dealing with them can be helpful in resolving current award controversies.

Except for the time period between 1970 and 2001, the district courts have not been an available forum for procurement protests. The Supreme Court ruled in 1940 in *Perkins v. Lukens Co.*, 310 U.S. 113 (1940), that no one had a right to a government contract; as a result, it was held that disappointed bidders were not entitled to have their protests heard in court. Then, in *Scanwell Labs., Inc. v. United States*, 424 F.2d 859 (D.C. Cir. 1970), the court held that the Administrative Procedure Act (APA), 5 U.S.C. § 702, gave offerors a right to bring an action challenging agency action in the process of awarding contracts. The jurisdiction of the district courts over protests was affected by the passage of the Federal Courts Improvement Act of 1982, Pub. L. No. 97-164. This Act established the Claims Court (renamed the Court of Federal Claims by the Federal Courts Administrative Act of 1992, Pub. L. No. 102-572) and provided the court jurisdiction over preaward protests. The Act allowed the Claims Court "to afford complete relief on any contract claim brought before the contract is awarded." This Act created confusion as to whether the Claims Court possessed exclusive jurisdiction to hear preaward protests. Postaward judicial authority remained with the district courts. Section 12(d) of the Administrative Dispute Resolution Act (ADRA) of 1992, Pub. L. No. 104-320, resolved the issue by granting the Court of Federal Claims and the district courts concurrent jurisdiction to hear both preaward and postaward protests. The ADRA, however, provided that protest jurisdiction in the district courts would expire on January 1, 2001, unless extended by Congress. Congress did not renew the jurisdiction of the district courts over protests with the result that the Court of Federal Claims is now the primary judicial forum over preaward and postaward procurement protests.

Even after the ADRA sunset, there is precedent for APA review of contract award controversies in district courts in certain circumstances, particularly disputes that are not "in connection with" a procurement contract or that otherwise could not be brought in the Court of Federal Claims under ADRA. In *Resource Conservation Grp., LLC v. United States*, 597 F.3d 1238 (Fed. Cir. 2010), the Federal Circuit reasoned at 1246 in footnote 12 that: "a disappointed bidder in a nonprocurement case could also theoretically bring its bid protest challenge in a federal district court, since the ADRA only repealed jurisdiction over procurement cases." Similarly, in *SEKRI, Inc. v. United States*, 34 F.4th 1063 (Fed. Cir. 2022), at footnote 7, the Federal Circuit noted that "district courts have jurisdiction to review bid protests under the Administrative Procedures Act." In *City of Albuquerque v. Dep't of Interior*, 379 F.3d 901 (10th Cir. 2004), the Tenth Circuit acknowledged an open question as to whether the ADRA sunset eliminated district court jurisdiction to engage in APA review over procurement protests, and concluded regardless that district court APA review is available where the plaintiff did not qualify as an "interested party" with standing to pursue a protest in the Court of Federal Claims under ADRA. See also *Eco Tour Adventures, Inc. v. Jewell*, 174 F. Supp. 3d 319 (D.D.C. 2016) ("while acknowledging that the post-sunset effect of the ADRA was to repeal the express grant of district court jurisdiction over procurement actions, the Federal Circuit has indicated that the ADRA does not affect the district court's jurisdiction in the nonprocurement context"); *Goodwill Indus. Servs. Corp. v. Comm. for Purchase from People who are Blind or Severely Disabled*, 378 F. Supp. 2d 1290 (D. Colo. 2005) (finding that the ADRA sunset displaces district court jurisdiction over procurement protests, "forbidding such actions in the district courts under the APA and *Scanwell*").

Although district court litigation of contract award disputes has been rare since the 2001 ADRA sunset, such litigation may experience a renaissance as Congress and the Department of Defense encourage use of nonprocurement contract vehicles such as Other Transactions to rapidly acquire and field innovations from non-traditional contractors. Notwithstanding the potential for increased district court litigation of government contract award disputes, as noted at the outset this book is focused on procurement contracts, not all contractual vehicles available to the Federal government. Accordingly, the sections that follow are largely limited to the primary forums for procurement contract award controversies: the procuring agencies, the Court of Federal Claims, and the GAO.

This chapter first deals with the distinction between contract award controversies that may be brought by a third party and contract performance disputes. It then considers, in detail, the features of each of the three primary forums.

§ 15.02 AWARD VERSUS PERFORMANCE CONTROVERSIES

Contract award controversies must be distinguished from controversies arising during contract performance. As a general rule, performance controversies occur between the parties to a contract, and third parties cannot challenge actions that occur during the performance of a contract, *Gull Airborne Instruments, Inc. v. Weinberger*, 694 F.2d 838 (D.C. Cir. 1982). This rule has been incorporated in the protest regulations of GAO at 4 C.F.R. § 21.5(a), which identifies "contract administration" as a "protest issue[] not for consideration" and explains that: "administration of an existing contract is within the discretion of the contracting agency," and "[d]isputes between a contractor and the agency are resolved pursuant to the disputes clause of the contract and the Contract Disputes Act of 1978." The Court of Federal Claims judges tend to apply the same rule. See *Kellogg Brown & Root Servs., Inc. v. United States*, 117 Fed. Cl. 764 (2014) (acknowledging at 768 "a lengthening line of mostly persuasive precedents holding that contract awardees may not challenge agency decisions regarding their contracts by bringing bid protests"). For example, in *Davis/HRGM Joint Venture v. United States*, 50 Fed. Cl. 539 (2001), the court explained that a contractor's challenge to a termination for convenience "does not fall within the express language of [28 U.S.C.] § 1491(b) because it does not relate to an interested party's objection to a solicitation, a proposed award, or an award." See also *Outdoor Venture Corp. v. United States*, 100 Fed. Cl. 146, 152 (2011) ("Once a bidder has received a contract, it is no longer an actual or prospective bidder or offeror with regard to the particular procurement. Instead, the bidder has become an awardee, who is not an interested party.").

The Federal Circuit has generally endorsed the principle that matters of contract administration may only be resolved under the Contract Disputes Act. See *Coast Professional, Inc. v. United States*, 828 F.3d 1349 (Fed. Cir. 2016) ("If a contractor wishes to contest an agency's decision regarding exercising an option under the contract, such a challenge is a matter of contract administration governed by the CDA"); *Dalton v. Sherwood Van Lines*, 50 F.3d 1014, 1017 (Fed. Cir. 1995) ("When the Contract Disputes Act applies, it provides the exclusive mechanism for dispute resolution"). Accord *Ingersoll–Rand Co. v. United States*, 780 F.2d 74, 79 (D.C. Cir. 1985) ("[Plaintiff] is not a disappointed bidder who seeks to void the award of a contract to another; instead, it complains of wrongful termination of its own contract with the government."); *Gull Airborne Instruments, Inc. v. Weinberger*, 694 F.2d 838 (D.C. Cir. 1982) (finding no prudential standing for competitor to enforce regulations governing contract termination, holding "Gull has standing to contest the award of the contract but not its administration.").

Court of Federal Claims decisions finding the matter involved contract administration include *Acetris Health, LLC v. United States*, 137 Fed. Cl. 148 (2018), where the court dismissed plaintiff's allegations challenging the agency's finding that plaintiff's products failed to comply with the requirements of its incumbent contract and thus was not eligible for award. Similarly, in *Kellogg Brown & Root Servs., Inc. v. United States*, 117 Fed. Cl. 764, 769-70 (2014), the court dismissed the protest upon finding that the plaintiff's challenge to certain contract closeout costs was a matter of contract administration. See also *Gonzalez-McCaulley Inv. Grp., Inc. v. United States*, 93 Fed. Cl. 710 (2010) (breach of "implied contract" after agency issued notice of award but "withdrew" award); *Taylor Consultants v. United States*, 90 Fed. Cl. 531 (2009) (dismissing protest claims concerning bad faith termination of the plaintiff's contract); and *Data Monitor Sys., Inc. v. United States*, 74 Fed. Cl. 66 (2006) (no jurisdiction to enjoin termination of a contract).

GAO decisions finding the matter involved contract administration include *Lyon Shipyard, Inc.*, Comp. Gen. Dec. B-417734, 2019 CPD ¶ 365 (protest based on termination of awardee's contract); *VariQ Corp.*, Comp. Gen. Dec. B-409114.2, 2014 CPD ¶ 58 (alleged postaward performance difficulties not valid basis to support alleged evaluation errors); *Training Mgmt. Solutions, Inc.*, Comp. Gen. Dec. B-403461.2, 2010 CPD ¶ 224 (whether awardee was able to begin timely performance); *Crewzers Fire Crew Transport, Inc.*, Comp. Gen. Dec. B-402530, 2010 CPD ¶ 117 (whether agency will allow defective performance by awardees); *CES Indus., Inc.*, Comp. Gen. Dec. B-401427, 2010 CPD ¶ 43 (whether awardee will infringe a patent); *Solar Plexus, LLC*, Comp. Gen. Dec. B-402061, 2009 CPD ¶ 256 (whether awardee complies with RFP requirements); *Petro Star, Inc.*, Comp. Gen. Dec. B-401108, 2009 CPD ¶ 92 (seeking contract reformation); *Nilson Van & Storage, Inc.*, Comp. Gen. Dec. B-310485, 2007 CPD ¶ 224 (whether awardee complies with performance work statement standard to conduct background check on prospective employees); *Murray-Benjamin Elec. Co., LP*, Comp. Gen. Dec. B-298481, 2006 CPD ¶ 129 (whether agency violated its obligation to procure items under one of the contractor's existing vehicles); and *Catapult Tech., Ltd.*, Comp. Gen. Dec. B-294936, 2005 CPD ¶ 14 (exercise of an option).

[A] Actions Compromising Competition

Notwithstanding the general rule distinguishing matters of contract administration from contract award controversies, some actions that occur as a matter of contract administration sufficiently impact the contract award process to give rise to a protestable issue. Where the contract action is considered to clearly compromise the competition that led to the award, it will be considered a contract award controversy, *Webcraft Packaging, Div. of Beatrice Foods Co.*, Comp. Gen. Dec. B-194087, 79-2 CPD ¶ 120 (agency should have resolicited rather than relax specifications in contract for specialty product produced by only a few sources).

Thus, the protest process will be available where a contract modification alters the contract requirement to the extent that the modified contract is outside the scope of the original competition, *AT&T Commc'ns, Inc. v. Wiltel, Inc.*, 1 F.3d 1201 (Fed. Cir. 1993). This is determined by analyzing the entire contract to determine whether the original competitors would have anticipated that the modification would be issued under the contract. See *Ian, Evan & Alexander Corp. v. United States*, 136 Fed. Cl. 390 (2018) (modification adding substantial work and almost doubling price); *CW Gov't Travel v. United States*, 61 Fed. Cl. 559 (2004), *reh'g denied*, 63 Fed. Cl. 459 (2005), *aff'd*, 163 Fed. Appx. 853 (Fed. Cir. 2005) (new services far removed from the original requirements); *Cardinal Maint. Serv., Inc. v. United States*, 63 Fed. Cl. 98 (2004) (changes not of the type that were specifically authorized or even foreseen in original contract); and *CCL, Inc. v. United States*, 39 Fed. Cl. 780 (1997) (increasing the number of locations where computer maintenance services were to be performed).

For similar GAO decisions sustaining protests, see *Leupold Stevens, Inc.*, Comp. Gen. Dec. B-417796, 2019 CPD ¶ 397 (modification included changes prohibited by the contract and caused material increase in contract value); *Alliant Sols., LLC*, Comp. Gen. Dec. B-415994, 2018 CPD ¶ 173 (letter of technical direction directed performance of work outside of underlying contract scope); *DynCorp Int'l LLC*, Comp. Gen. Dec. B-402349, 2010 CPD ¶ 59 (training, facilities and logistics support services not related to contract for counter-narcoterrorism support services); *Poly-Pacific Techs.*, Comp. Gen. Dec. B-296029, 2005 CPD ¶ 105 (RFP did not anticipate that contractor could be relieved of the recycling requirement or that a disposal effort could be ordered in lieu of recycling); *Sprint Commc'ns Co.*, Comp. Gen. Dec. B-278407.2, 98-1 CPD ¶ 60 (modification adding transmission services were outside the scope because the initial procurement had stated that such services were not required); *MCI Telecomms. Corp.*, Comp. Gen. Dec. B-276659.2, 97-2 CPD ¶ 90 (modification permitting contractor to design, operate, and maintain customized networks beyond the scope of FTS 2000 contract for telecommunications services because this was a different type of service than those called for in original contract); and *Marvin J. Perry & Assocs.*, Comp. Gen. Dec. B-277684, 97-2 CPD ¶ 128 (modification of Federal Supply Schedule to substitute stained ash for red oak furniture beyond scope because ash was substantially cheaper).

Cases finding that the modification did not violate the competition requirements include *Navistar Def., LLC v. United States*, 146 Fed. Cl. 499 (2019) (ordering work after sole source modification within scope of modification); *Treadwell Corp. v. United States*, 142 Fed. Cl. 650 (2019) (modification extending delivery date within scope); *American Apparel, Inc. v. United States*, 108 Fed. Cl. 11 (2012) (modification adding substantial work within scope because clause stated new work could be added); *Emergent BioSolutions, Inc.*, Comp. Gen. Dec. B-402576, 2010 CPD ¶ 136 (changes in "processes and activities" in research contract did not change basic contract objectives); *Overseas Lease Grp., Inc.*, Comp. Gen. Dec. B-402111, 2010 CPD ¶ 34 (solicitation's differentiating between "non-tactical" and "up-armored" vehicles was sufficient to put protester on notice that term "non-tactical" was intended to refer to unarmored vehicles); *Lasmer Indus., Inc.*, Comp. Gen. Dec. B-400866.2, 2009 CPD ¶ 77 (part was specifically included in contract, and contract allowed the agency to order the part under a negotiated delivery schedule); *Armed Forces Hospitality*, Comp. Gen. Dec. B-298978.2, 2009 CPD ¶ 192 (lack of definitiveness in the original SOW provided the Army with additional contractual flexibility and latitude to reduce the number of rooms to be renovated and extend performance); *Chapman Law Firm Co. v. United States*, 81 Fed. Cl. 323 (2008) (geographic expansion of service and possibility of new pricing were changes clearly contemplated in the contracts); *Sallie Mae, Inc.*, Comp. Gen. Dec. B-400486, 2008 CPD ¶ 221 (statement of objective clearly placed offerors on notice that the agency intended to award contract for the management of all types of student loans); *CWT/Alexander Travel, Ltd. v. United States*, 78 Fed. Cl. 486 (2007) (given the nature of services required under the contract, price changes were viewed as inevitable); and *DOR Biodefense, Inc.*, Comp. Gen. Dec. B-296358.3, 2006 CPD ¶ 35 (RFP advised offerors that the government reserves the right to change the list of vaccine serotypes to add or delete products as need may arise).

[B] Task and Delivery Orders

As discussed in Chapter 7, a significant aspect of modern procurement is the award of IDIQ contracts where precise quantity and/or delivery needs are uncertain at the time of contract award. Technically, issuance of task and delivery orders under these contracts are matters of contract administration. Yet, each task and delivery order is also its own contract award with potential to generate contract award protests. Such protests have always been heard with regard to Federal Supply Schedule contracts and this was confirmed in *Coast Prof'l, Inc. v. United States*, 828 F.3d 1349, 1354 (Fed. Cir. 2016) ("The Supreme Court recently held that issuance of a new Task Order against a GSA Federal Supply Schedule contract constitutes an award of a contract.... It is thus a protestable event.") (citing *Kingdomware Techs., Inc. v. United States*, 136 S. Ct. 1969 (2016)). Congress has limited, however, the circumstances under which task and delivery order awards under IDIQ contracts may be protested.

The Federal Acquisition Streamlining Act of 1994 (FASA), Pub. L. No. 103-355, barred protests relating to the issuance of orders except for a protest on the ground that the order increases the scope, period, or maximum value of the contract under which the order is issued. However, § 843 of the National Defense Authorization Act of Fiscal Year 2008, Pub. L. No. 110-181, modified FASA's prior limitations on task order protests, providing that, in addition to previously permitted task order protests on the ground that the order increases the scope, period, or maximum value of the contract, a protest at GAO is also authorized to decide protests of "an order valued in excess of $10,000,000."

This still applies to agencies other than DOD, NASA, and the Coast Guard, 41 U.S.C. § 4106(f). In 2016, § 835 of the National Defense Authorization Act of Fiscal Year 2017, Pub. L. No. 114-328, raised the threshold for DOD, NASA, and the Coast Guard to $25,000,000.

The Federal Circuit has strictly interpreted the statutory provision restricting task order protests to the GAO, effectively eliminating the availability of judicial review in many cases. See *SRA Int'l, Inc. v. United States*, 766 F.3d 1409 (Fed. Cir. 2014), stating at 1413:

> The statutory language of FASA is clear and gives the court no room to exercise jurisdiction over claims made "in connection with the issuance or proposed issuance of a task or delivery order." Even if the protestor points to an alleged violation of statute or regulation, as SRA does here, the court still has no jurisdiction to hear the case if the protest is in connection with the issuance of a task order. We acknowledge that this statute is somewhat unusual in that it effectively eliminates all judicial review for protests made in connection with a procurement designated as a task order—perhaps even in the event of an agency's egregious, or even criminal, conduct. Yet Congress's intent to ban protests on the issuance of task orders is clear from FASA's unambiguous language.

The Federal Circuit recognizes, however, that the FASA bar to judicial review does not apply to task orders issued under the General Services Administration's Federal Supply Schedule authority. Moreover, even under the strict *SRA* standard, not all procurement actions relating to task orders issued under FASA will necessarily be barred, for example, where the protest challenges an agency action that is separate and independent from the solicitation of the task order. See *Tolliver Grp., Inc. v. United States*, 151 Fed. Cl. 70 (2020).

Disputes arise as to which costs associated with a protested order should be considered for jurisdictional purposes. The rule appears to be that GAO will review the compensation structure of each protested task order to calculate the value of the order. Costs of equipment and services furnished to the contractor by the government are not considered, *Quest Gov't Servs., Inc.*, Comp. Gen. Dec. B-404845, 2011 CPD ¶ 77. In *Karthik Consulting*, Comp. Gen. Dec. B-411496, 2015 CPD ¶ 164, GAO extended the rule from *Quest* to preclude jurisdiction over a task order award valued less than $10 million even though the RFQ required offerors to include a stipend payment in their price schedules. GAO found persuasive the agency explanation that the stipend amounts would be passed through from the agency to students and "do not reflect a value to be provided by the contractor under the order." In contrast, in *ESCO Marine, Inc.*, Comp. Gen. Dec. B-401438, 2009 CPD ¶ 234, for purposes of determining whether the $10 million threshold had been met, GAO held that it was not limited to consideration of the offerors' proposed prices, but properly included consideration of the estimated ship scrap values when the prospective contractors were required to sell the scrap resulting from the ship dismantling and retain the scrap sale proceeds. Essentially, the task order provided the contractor with two different forms of payment—the price and payment-in-kind (the right to keep the scrap sale proceeds). GAO will consider the value of option years where the value of the option (if exercised) is evident from the face of the solicitation, but will not include option values that are not clear from the solicitation, such as the potential value of the agency executing its option to extend services under FAR 52.217-8. See *Adams & Assocs., Inc.*, Comp. Gen. Dec. B-417534, 2019 CPD ¶ 208 (discussing distinction); *Edmund Scientific Co.*, Comp. Gen. Dec. B-410187, 2014 CPD ¶ 358 (explaining distinction); *Serco Inc.*, Comp. Gen. Dec. B-406061, 2012 CPD ¶ 61 (considering option years); *U.S. Bank*, Comp. Gen. Dec. B-404169.3, 2011 CPD ¶ 43 (considering vendor's total anticipated fees, including options).

There is a possibility that agencies might issue separate task orders in order to evade the monetary threshold and avoid protest risk. See, for example, *Armorworks Enters., LLC*, Comp. Gen. Dec. B-401671.3, 2009 CPD ¶ 225, where the agency issued three task orders totaling $21 million. GAO held that it would not aggregate separate task orders in order to take jurisdiction "absent a clear showing that the agency's decision to issue separate orders was made solely to evade our protest jurisdiction." GAO denied the protest based on the agency's reasonable explanation for issuing separate task orders.

The monetary threshold is not applicable to a blanket purchase agreement (BPA), since a BPA is not a task or delivery order contract, *C&B Constr., Inc.*, Comp. Gen. Dec. B-401988.2, 2010 CPD ¶ 1. See also *Gulfnet Comms. Co., W.L.L.*, Comp. Gen. Dec. B-417516, 2019 CPD ¶ 223; *Batelco Telecomms. Co. B.S.C.*, Comp. Gen. Dec. B-412783, 2016 CPD ¶ 155; *Envirosolve LLC*, Comp. Gen. Dec. B-294974.4, 2005 CPD ¶ 106 (sustaining protest against orders placed under multiple-award BPAs where orders were valued under $100,000).

Protests of task and delivery orders at GAO are generally decided following the same rules that apply to other protests, *Triple Canopy, Inc.*, Comp. Gen. Dec. B-310566.4, 2008 CPD ¶ 207; *Bay Area Travel, Inc.*, Comp. Gen. Dec. B-400442, 2009 CPD ¶ 65. Thus, protests objecting to the terms of the task order solicitation are subject to GAO timeliness rules, *Innovative Tech. Corp.*, Comp. Gen. Dec. B-401689, 2009 CPD ¶ 235.

Agencies are required to have a task and delivery order ombudsman to review complaints from contractors holding multiple-award task order or delivery order contracts to ensure that they are afforded a fair opportunity to be considered for task or delivery orders, 10 U.S.C. § 3406(g) (formerly § 2304c(f)) and 41 U.S.C. § 4106(g). FAR 16.505(b)(8) implements this requirement.

Task and delivery orders, regardless of the dollar value, can be challenged through the contract award controversy process if they increase the scope, period, or maximum value of the contract under which the order is issued. See *Threat Mgmt. Grp., LLC*, Comp. Gen. Dec. B-413729, 2017 CPD ¶ 9; *Tempus Nova, Inc.*, Comp. Gen. Dec. B-412821, 2016 CPD ¶ 161 (delivery order beyond scope of underlying BPA); *Global Computer Enters., Inc. v. United States*, 88 Fed. Cl.

350 (2009), *modified*, 88 Fed. Cl. 466 (2009) (provision and maintenance of audit not within scope of technical services task order); *Anteon Corp.*, Comp. Gen. Dec. B-293523, 2004 CPD ¶ 51 (physical deliverables under the task order request not reasonably within the scope of GSA's smart card contract); *Floro & Assocs.*, Comp. Gen. Dec. B-285451.3, 2000 CPD ¶ 172 (task order beyond the scope of a contract for noncomplex integration services of commercially available off-the-shelf hardware and software where it required the contractor to provide management services to assist in support of distance learning product lines); and *Ervin v. Assocs., Inc.*, Comp. Gen. Dec. B-278850, 98-1 CPD ¶ 89 (task order beyond the scope when the work was not mentioned in the original solicitation).

Task orders were found to be within the scope of the underlying contract in *People, Tech. & Processes, LLC*, Comp. Gen. Dec. B-417273, 2019 CPD ¶ 173 (general training within scope of broadly worded contract); *Outdoor Venture Corp.*, Comp. Gen. Dec. B-401628, 2009 CPD ¶ 260 (delivery order requirement for full concealment covers within scope since the SOW listed variations of Ultra Lightweight Camouflage Net Systems to be procured and noted that other versions not specifically identified could also be procured); *Morris Corp.*, Comp. Gen. Dec. B-400336, 2008 CPD ¶ 204 (logical connection between the broad scope of food service operations—the feeding of individuals housed within a specified Iraqi training camp and/or coalition base—and the food service operations required to feed detainees located within the camp); *Colliers Int'l*, Comp. Gen. Dec. B-400173, 2008 CPD ¶ 147 (task order to conduct feasibility study within scope which was broad and specifically provided for unidentified "special studies"); *Relm Wireless Corp.*, Comp. Gen. Dec. B-298715, 2006 CPD ¶ 190 (tactical radio within scope because RFP's definition of Land Mobile Radio covered similar assets designated for contingency, tactical or war ready material purposes); *Specialty Marine, Inc.*, Comp. Gen. Dec. B-293871, 2004 CPD ¶ 130 (SOW language encompassed a broad category of ships without limitation to size); *Symetrics Indus., Inc.*, Comp. Gen. Dec. B-289606, 2002 CPD ¶ 65 (retrofitting reasonably falls within definition of depot level maintenance); and *Ervin & Assocs., Inc.*, Comp. Gen. Dec. B-279083, 98-1 CPD ¶ 126 (relevant language in the solicitation's SOW sets forth the anticipated services in broad, general, and flexible terms).

§ 15.03 PROCURING AGENCIES AND OMBUDSMEN

Persons seeking to contest a procurement have always had the option of lodging a complaint with the procuring agency, and some agencies have adopted procedures to handle these protests. Until the mid-1990s, however, there were no governmentwide regulations dealing with agency protests. Executive Order 12979, 60 Fed. Reg. 55171 (Oct. 25, 1995), requires all agencies to establish administrative procedures for resolving protests. These procedures are required to:

(a) emphasize that whenever conduct of a procurement is contested, all parties should use their best efforts to resolve the matter with agency contracting officers;

(b) to the maximum extent practicable, provide for inexpensive, informal, procedurally simple, and expeditious resolution of protests, including where appropriate and as permitted by law, the use of alternative dispute resolution techniques, third party neutrals, and another agency's personnel;

(c) allow actual or prospective bidders or offerors whose direct economic interests would be affected by the award or failure to award the contract to request a review, at a level above the contracting officer, of any decision by a contracting officer that is alleged to have violated a statute or regulation and, thereby, caused prejudice to the protester.

The provisions of the executive order are implemented in FAR 33.103. This section considers the various ways in which the agencies have responded to the executive order and the FAR.

[A] Jurisdiction

Any agency of the government has inherent authority to consider a protest alleging some defect in one of its procurements. The agency protest procedures mandated by FAR Subpart 33.1 apply to all "executive agencies," as defined in FAR 2.101.

[B] Who May Protest

The FAR contains no rule limiting the parties that may file a protest with an agency. Agencies may consider protests from any party that raises legitimate concerns about the conduct of a procurement; and it is clear that some agency officials, such as the NASA ombudsman, will consider such protests. To determine the scope of an agency's protest procedures, each agency regulation must be reviewed.

FAR 33.102(e) "encourages" an "interested party" wishing to protest to seek resolution within the procuring activity. FAR 33.101 defines "interested party" as "an actual or prospective offeror whose direct economic interest would be affected by the award of a contract or by the failure to award a contract." This is the same definition as used by GAO.

[C] Time for Protest

FAR 33.103(e) states formal rules, patterned on GAO rules, on the time for submitting protests to an agency. Protests based on alleged apparent improprieties in a solicitation must be filed prior to bid opening or the closing date for receipt of proposals. In all other cases protests must be filed not later than 10 days after the basis of the protest is known or should have been known, whichever is earlier. The agency may, for good cause shown or where the protest raises issues significant to the agency's acquisition system, consider the merits of any protest that is not timely filed. In addition, there is nothing in the FAR that precludes an agency from considering untimely protests on other bases.

The FAR provides some assurance to protesters that an executive agency will not moot a protest by permitting contract performance during the consideration of the protest. FAR 33.103(f)(1) provides that if an agency protest is filed before award, award will not be made unless it is justified in writing for "urgent and compelling reasons or is determined, in writing, to be in the best interests of the Government." This decision to award in the face of a protest must be made "at a level above the contracting officer, or by another official pursuant to agency procedures." With respect to agency protests received within 10 days after award, or within 5 days after a debriefing, whichever is later, the contracting officer must immediately suspend performance unless continued performance is justified for urgent and compelling reasons or is determined to be in the best interest of the government, FAR 33.103(f)(3). Such justification or determination must be approved at a level above the contracting officer, or by another official pursuant to agency procedures, FAR 33.103(f)(3).

Pursuing an agency protest does not extend the time for obtaining a stay at GAO. Agencies may, however, include, as part of the agency protest process, a voluntary suspension period when agency protests are denied and the protester subsequently files at GAO. See, for example, DOLAR 2933.103(m):

> If the protest is denied, and contract performance has been suspended under paragraph (i) of this section, the contracting officer will not lift such suspension until five (5) days after the protest decision has been issued, to allow the protester to file a protest with the General Accounting Office, unless the HCA makes a new finding under FAR 33.103(f)(3). The contracting officer shall consider allowing such suspension to remain in effect pending the resolution of any GAO proceeding.

[D] Procedures

Protests to the contracting agency should be submitted to the person designated in the solicitation. Under the standard Service of Protest clause in FAR 52.233-2, this is generally expected to be the contracting officer, but each agency may designate the official to which protests may be sent. When the protester sends in its protest, it may "request an independent review at a level above the contracting officer," FAR 33.103(d)(4). Most agency regulations designate the official that will provide such an independent review.

Agency-level protests should include a complete statement of the complaint that the protester has with the procurement. In adopting procedures for agency-level protests, FAR 33.103(d) sets forth legalistic guidance modeled on GAO protest procedures.

Agencies are encouraged to resolve agency protests within 35 days after the protest is filed, FAR 33.103(g). Written protest decisions should be sent to the protester and should be well reasoned. One technique used to resolve an agency protest is to appoint an ombudsman. NASA has created an ombudsman program, NFS Subpart 1815.70. The contracting officer must insert a clause substantially the same as the Ombudsman clause at NFS 1852.215-84 in all solicitations (including draft solicitations) and contracts:

> (a) An ombudsman has been appointed to hear and facilitate the resolution of concerns from offerors, potential offerors, and contractors during the preaward and postaward phases of this acquisition. When requested, the ombudsman will maintain strict confidentiality as to the source of the concern. The existence of the ombudsman is not to diminish the authority of the contracting officer, the Source Evaluation Board, or the selection official. Further, the ombudsman does not participate in the evaluation of proposals, the source selection process, or the adjudication of formal contract disputes. Therefore, before consulting with an ombudsman, interested parties must first address their concerns, issues, disagreements, and/or recommendations to the contracting officer for resolution.
>
> (b) If resolution cannot be made by the contracting officer, interested parties may contact the installation ombudsman, whose name, address, telephone number, and email address may be found at: http://prod.nais.nasa/pub/pub library/Omb.html Concerns, issues, disagreements, and recommendations which cannot be resolved at the installation may be referred to the NASA ombudsman identified at the above URL. Please do not contact the ombudsman to request copies of the solicitation, verify offer due date, or clarify technical requirements. Such inquiries shall be directed to the Contracting Officer or as specified elsewhere in this document.

The scope of this ombudsman's duties extends beyond protests orders—covering all matters concerning contracts with the agency.

[E] Alternative Dispute Resolution

Another procedure for resolving a protest in lieu of either protesting with GAO or litigation is alternative dispute resolution. Alternative dispute resolution includes any procedure or combination of procedures voluntarily used to resolve issues in controversy. These techniques are now recognized and encouraged by the Administrative Dispute Resolution Act, 5 U.S.C. § 571-§ 584. FAR 33.103(c) provides:

> The agency should provide for inexpensive, informal, procedurally simple, and expeditious resolution of protests. Where appropriate, the use of

alternative dispute resolution techniques, third party neutrals, and another agency's personnel are acceptable protest resolution methods.

[F] Standards of Review

The FAR is not clear on the standards of review that will be used in dealing with agency-level protests. Its initial guidance is the broad statement that contracting officers "shall consider all protests," FAR 33.102(a). See also FAR 33.103(b), which states:

> Prior to submission of an agency protest, all parties shall use their best efforts to resolve concerns raised by an interested party at the contracting officer level through open and frank discussions.

This guidance indicates that a potential offeror can obtain the contracting officer's review of any concern regarding the procurement. In particular, this type of protest would be appropriate when a potential offeror has questions about the meaning of a solicitation or concerns that a solicitation is not properly drafted.

If the more formal "agency protest" procedure is used, FAR 33.102(b) states that the standard of review will be whether a solicitation, proposed award, or award complies with "the requirements of law and regulation." It appears that this is too narrow a statement of the standard of review that will be applied to formal agency protests, because such protests will also consider whether the actions of the contracting agency are reasonable (as that requirement is construed by GAO and the courts). In addition, agencies may adopt broader standards of review in accordance with their own internal procedures.

[G] Prejudice

As discussed below, GAO and the courts have refused to grant relief on a protest unless they find that the protester has been prejudiced by the improper agency action. There is no reason why this rule should be required in an agency protest, because agencies should correct a problem that has occurred in the procurement process as soon as they are aware of the problem, regardless of whether the particular company that raised the issue is competitively harmed by the error. That being said, if an error is truly *de minimus* and has no impact on the procurement process, an agency may rationally determine that no corrective action is warranted.

[H] Remedies

The contracting officer or an agency protest authority, such as the NASA ombudsman, has broad discretion to take any action necessary to resolve a protest that is brought to it. If a protest is brought to the head of an agency using the FAR agency protest procedures, the FAR provides that the agency can take any action that could have been recommended by GAO had the protest been filed there, including payment of certain costs associated with the protest and directing the awardee to reimburse certain government costs, FAR 33.102(b). Because this provision is permissive, there appear to be no restrictions other than the bounds of the agency's own authority preventing the contracting officer from granting other requested relief following review of an agency-level protest. This includes the authority to allow correction or withdrawal in mistake cases, *Unico Constr. Co.*, Comp. Gen. Dec. B-258862, 95-1 CPD ¶ 42; *National Heat & Power Corp.*, Comp. Gen. Dec. B-212923, 84-1 CPD ¶ 125. However, the granting of relief from mistakes in sealed bid procurements is subject to a number of restrictions within the executive agencies. Contracting officers are permitted to correct clerical mistakes apparent on the face of the bid, FAR 14.407-2, but relief for other types of mistakes must be granted by the agency heads who may delegate their authority to a limited number of central authorities, FAR 14.407-3(e). In all such mistake cases, the concurrence of legal counsel within the agency is required before a determination is made, FAR 14.407-3(f). Numerous subsidiary regulations implement the FAR and contain delegations of authority to grant relief for mistakes prior to award. See, e.g., DFARS 214.407-3, NFS 1814.407, and GSAR 514.407-3. The current FAR guidance on mistakes in negotiated procurements is unclear. See the discussion in Chapter 6.

§ 15.04 GOVERNMENT ACCOUNTABILITY OFFICE

For many years the only forum to consider contract award controversies was GAO, headed by the Comptroller General of the United States. It began to hear protests from disappointed bidders early in its existence, 10 Comp. Gen. 480 (A-36067) (1931); 11 Comp. Gen. 220 (A-39095) (1931). GAO took these protests and issued decisions under the predecessors of 31 U.S.C. § 3526 and § 3529. These statutes give GAO the authority to settle and adjust the accounts of accountable officers and the obligation to render advance decisions to certifying and disbursing officers on questions concerning the legality of payments. The procuring agencies generally acquiesced in the decisions, with the result that GAO protest procedure became firmly embedded in the procurement process.

It was not until 1984 that GAO was given specific statutory authority to hear protests, 31 U.S.C. § 3551 et seq. As originally enacted, this statute gave GAO the authority to order a stay of performance longer than the period specified in the statute, 31 U.S.C. § 3554(a)(1). This raised questions as to the constitutionality of the provision given that GAO is an office in the legislative branch and procurement is an executive function. However, this provision was deleted by § 8139 of the 1989 Department of Defense Appropriations Act, Pub. L. No. 100-463. As a result, *United States Army Corps of Eng'rs v. Ameron, Inc.*, 809 F.2d 979 (3d Cir. 1986), *cert. granted*, 485 U.S. 958 (1988), *motion denied*, 488 U.S. 809 (1988), *cert. dismissed*, 488 U.S. 918 (1988), which had been scheduled for argument to determine the constitutionality of the statute, was dismissed at the request of the Solicitor General.

[A] Jurisdiction

GAO has slightly different authority to hear protests under 31 U.S.C. § 3551 et seq. than under its prior nonstatutory authority.

[1] Statutory Authority

Jurisdiction of GAO under its statutory authority depends on the status of the agency conducting the procurement and the nature of the transaction. 31 U.S.C. § 3551 defines "protest" as a written objection to a "procurement of property or services" by a "federal agency" as defined in 40 U.S.C. § 102.

[a] Status of Agency

The term "federal agency" covers virtually all agencies of the government that operate with appropriated funds. Protests have been taken on procurements of the *Consumer Financial Protection Board, Information Experts, Inc.*, Comp. Gen. Dec. B-413887, 2017 CPD ¶ 16; the *Tennessee Valley Authority, Monarch Water Sys., Inc.*, 64 Comp. Gen. 756 (B-218441), 85-2 CPD ¶ 146, *recons. denied*, 85-2 CPD ¶ l335; the *Federal Housing Administration Fund, CoMont, Inc.*, 65 Comp. Gen. 66 (B-219730), 85-2 CPD ¶ 555; the *Bonneville Power Administration, International Line Bldrs.*, 67 Comp. Gen. 8 (B-227811), 87-2 CPD ¶ 345, *recons. denied*, 87-2 CPD ¶ 472; the *Federal Reserve Board, Computer Support Sys., Inc.*, 69 Comp. Gen. 644 (B-239034), 90-2 CPD ¶ 94; the *Overseas Private Investment Corp., MFM Lamey Grp., LLC*, Comp. Gen. Dec. B-402377, 2010 CPD ¶ 81; and *Federal Prison Industries, USA Fabrics*, Comp. Gen. Dec. B-295737, 2005 CPD ¶ 82. See, however, *Kimo Constructors, Inc.*, Comp. Gen. Dec. B-416162, 2018 CPD ¶ 148, holding that a federally recognized tribe is not a federal agency; *United Way of Nat'l Capital Area*, Comp. Gen. Dec. B-311235, 2008 CPD ¶ l 96, holding that a Local Fund Campaign Committee is not a federal agency; and *P.O.M., Inc.*, 64 Comp. Gen. 488 (B-218178), 85-1 CPD ¶ 467, holding that the District of Columbia government is not a federal agency for purposes of the statute, citing 40 U.S.C. § 472. Mixed-ownership corporations are not considered federal agencies, *Kennan Auction Co.*, Comp. Gen. Dec. B-248965, 92-1 CPD ¶ 503 (Resolution Trust Corporation); *Chas. G. Stott & Co.*, Comp. Gen. Dec. B-220302, 85-2 CPD ¶ 333 (Federal Deposit Insurance Corporation). The House of Representatives also is not considered to be a federal agency, *Court Reporting Servs., Inc.*, Comp. Gen. Dec. B-259492, 94-2 CPD ¶ 236.

Nonappropriated fund instrumentalities, as well, are not considered federal agencies, 4 C.F.R. § 21.5(g); *LDDS Worldcom*, Comp. Gen. Dec. B-270109, 96-1 CPD ¶ 45. Nevertheless, as noted above, in *Information Experts*, GAO found that the CFPB qualifies as a federal agency notwithstanding its status as a nonappropriated fund entity based on specific language in CFPB's authorizing statute indicating that it is subject to federal laws dealing with public contracts. GAO will consider a protest when a nonappropriated fund instrumentality is acting only as a mere conduit for an agency, *Premiere Vending*, Comp. Gen. Dec. B-256560, 94-2 CPD ¶ 8 (protester alleged that agency was diverting vending machine requirements to employees' association in order to avoid applicable procurement statutes and regulations). In *Americable Int'l, Inc.*, Comp. Gen. Dec. B-251614, 93-1 CPD ¶ 336, GAO dismissed a protest, holding that in awarding franchise contracts for cable television services and telephone services, a nonappropriated fund instrumentality was not acting as an agent for the Navy because there was no evidence of significant Navy participation in the procurement process.

GAO's protest jurisdiction does not depend on the intended use of the items being acquired or on the source of the funds for the acquisition, *CPT Text-Computer GmbH*, Comp. Gen. Dec. B-222037.2, 86-2 CPD ¶ 29. The key factor in determining applicability is that the procurement is conducted by a federal agency. See *Artisan Bldrs.*, 65 Comp. Gen. 240 (B-220804), 86-1 CPD ¶ 85, holding that the statutory protest authority is applicable to a procurement that the Air Force conducted for a base golf course, a nonappropriated fund activity. In *Professional Pension Termination Assocs.*, Comp. Gen. Dec. B-230007.2, 88-1 CPD ¶ 498, GAO took jurisdiction over a protest even though the procurement was partially funded with trust funds, because the Pension Benefit Guaranty Corporation, which conducted the procurement, was a federal agency. Similarly, a procurement by a federal agency for a foreign government is subject to the statute, *Cosmos Eng'rs, Inc.*, Comp. Gen. Dec. B-220000.3, 86-1 CPD ¶ 186 (procurement by Agency for International Development for foreign government); *Yoosung T&S, Ltd.*, Comp. Gen. Dec. B-291407, 2002 CPD ¶ 204 (procurement conducted by the Army, but funded by the Republic of Korea); *Ahntech-Korea Co.*, Comp. Gen. Dec. B-400145.2, 2008 CPD ¶ 169 (although Republic of Korea made the award decision, the Army conducted the procurement—it issued the solicitation, evaluated the proposals, and made the award recommendation). But see *Environmental Tectonics Corp.*, 65 Comp. Gen. 504 (B-222483), 86-1 CPD ¶ 377, denying jurisdiction although the contract was financed by a federal agency, because the solicitation was issued and award made by the government of Egypt. See also *Peter Bauwens Bauunternehmung GmbH & Co. KG*, Comp. Gen. Dec. B-277734, 97-2 CPD ¶ 98, dismissing a protest for lack of jurisdiction because the procurements were conducted by an agency of the government of Germany.

Agencies may be exempted from the protest statute by provisions in their own statutes. See *Emery Worldwide Airlines, Inc. v. United States*, 264 F.3d 1071 (Fed. Cir. 2001) (39 U.S.C. § 410(a), stating that the Postal Service is exempted from any federal law dealing with public or federal contracts except those listed). 49 U.S.C. § 106 exempts the Federal Aviation Administration from most provisions of federal acquisition law, one being the procurement protest system. Under the FAA management system, protesters should first seek informal resolution of any issues concerning protests with the contracting officer. If resolution at the contracting officer level is not desired or successful, offerors may file a protest with the FAA's Office of Dispute Resolution for Acquisition. The Presidio Trust is not subject to GAO jurisdiction because the Trust is statutorily exempt from all federal laws and regulations governing procurement by federal agencies, and CICA is not included in the list of statutes made applicable to the *Trust, Performance Excavators, Inc.*, Comp. Gen. Dec. B-291771, 2003 CPD ¶ 63.

[b] Procurement Contracts

GAO, in considering protests concerning the "procurement of property or services," will not take jurisdiction of protests over the procedures used in other types of transactions. Thus, jurisdiction will be denied over protests concerning grants or cooperative agreements, *SBMA, Inc.*, Comp. Gen. Dec. B-255780, 93-2 CPD ¶ 292; cooperative research and development agreements under 15 U.S.C. § 3710a, *Spice Corp.*, Comp. Gen. Dec. B-258267, 94-2 CPD ¶ 257; and "other transactions" under 10 U.S.C. § 2371 & 2371b, *MD Helicopters, Inc.*, Comp. Gen. Dec. B-417379, 2019 CPD ¶ 120; *Energy Conversion Devices, Inc.*, Comp. Gen. Dec. B-260514, 95-2 CPD ¶ 121. See also *Exploration Partners*, Comp. Gen. Dec. B-298804, 2006 CPD ¶ 201 (NASA's issuance of Space Act agreements pursuant to its "other transactions authority" is not tantamount to the award of contracts for the procurement of goods and services); *Fred Schreiber*, Comp. Gen. Dec. B-272181, 96-2 CPD ¶ 71 (protests against nonselection of vocational rehabilitation counselors not a procurement of goods or services); and *Michael J. O'Kane*, Comp. Gen. Dec. B-257384, 94-2 CPD ¶ 120 (nonselection of attorneys for inclusion on a list from which attorneys will be selected for appointment to represent financially eligible defendants under the Criminal Justice Act not a procurement of goods or services).

GAO will review a protest that an agency is improperly using one of these instruments instead of a procurement contract, *Rocketplane Kistler*, Comp. Gen. Dec. B-310741, 2008 CPD ¶ 22 (protest alleged that agency improperly used Space Act agreement to avoid the requirements of procurement statutes and regulations). See also *Strong Envtl., Inc.*, Comp. Gen. Dec. B-311005, 2008 CPD ¶| 57 (no basis to conclude that the Library of Congress was required to use a procurement contract, or that it was improper for the library to use a cooperative agreement); *Sprint Commc'ns Co., L. P.*, Comp. Gen. Dec. B-256586, 94-1 CPD ¶ 300 (cooperative agreement was properly used—not to avoid the requirements of procurement statutes and regulations).

While GAO will dismiss for lack of jurisdiction a protest that directly challenges the award of a nonprocurement instrument, it will assert limited "jurisdiction to review whether an agency is properly using a non-procurement instrument," *Oracle Am., Inc.*, Comp. Gen. Dec. B-416061, 2018 CPD ¶ 180. In *Oracle America*, GAO asserted jurisdiction to determine that a planned DoD award did not comply with its prototype other transactions authority at 10 U.S.C. § 2371b. Similarly, GAO asserted jurisdiction in *Air Tractor, Inc.*, Comp. Gen. Dec. B-418244, 2020 CPD ¶ 42, to hold that DoD properly exercised its experimental purchasing authority under 10 U.S.C. § 2373 to acquire supplies by contract. GAO curiously noted in the *Air Tractor* decision that: "had the agency used its authority under 10 U.S.C. § 2373 to acquire items via a non-contractual instrument, such a transaction may have fallen outside of our jurisdiction." It is not readily apparent how DoD could purchase a supply without forming some form of contract along the way. See *Kingdomware Techs, Inc. v. United States*, 136 S. Ct. 1969 (2016) (applying common law definition of contract to conclude task order is a contract).

GAO lacks jurisdiction to consider a protest challenging the award of a "pure" concession contract; that is, a no-cost contract that merely authorizes a concessionaire to provide goods or services to the public, as opposed to the government, *Crystal Cruises, Inc.*, Comp. Gen. Dec. B-238347, 90-1 CPD ¶ 141. However, GAO has recognized that some concession contracts are hybrids that require the delivery of goods and/or services to the government. Where a concession contract includes the delivery of goods or services of more than de minimis value to the government, it is a contract for the procurement of property or services subject to GAO protest jurisdiction, *DNC Parks & Resorts at Yosemite, Inc.*, Comp. Gen. Dec. B-410998, 2015 CPD ¶ 127; *Great South Bay Marina, Inc.*, Comp. Gen. Dec. B-296335, 2005 CPD ¶ 135. See also *Shields & Dean Concessions, Inc.*, Comp. Gen. Dec. B-292901.2, 2004 CPD ¶ 42, *recons. denied*, 2004 CPD ¶ 71 (concessionaire required to provide maintenance, repair and other services for government facility as well as facility improvement valued at over $800,000); *Starfleet Marine Transp., Inc.*, Comp. Gen. Dec. B-290181, 2002 CPD ¶ 113 (concessionaire for ferryboat services required to provide janitorial services for agency's docks and piers, equip ferries with public address systems for use by park rangers, and provide transportation for rangers). But see *White Sands Concessions, Inc.*, Comp. Gen. Dec. B-295932, 2005 CPD ¶ 62 (only services that concessionaire is required to furnish are those pertaining to the upkeep of the space in which it operates its business).

GAO will not exercise jurisdiction over subcontractor procurements unless specifically requested to do so by the agency, 4 C.F.R. § 21.5(h). This rule is derived from *U.S. West Commc'ns Servs., Inc. v. United States*, 940 F.2d 622 (Fed. Cir. 1991). In that case, the court of appeals, construing language similar to that applicable to GAO, held that the GSBCA did not have jurisdiction over subcontract procurements that were conducted "for" a federal agency. In light of this decision, GAO stated in *Compugen, Ltd.*, Comp. Gen. Dec. B-261769,

95-2 CPD ¶ 103, that it will not exercise jurisdiction over subcontract procurements for the government without a written request from the agency. Previously, GAO reviewed subcontractor procurements in cases where the contractor was acting "by or for the government," *St. Mary's Hosp. & Med. Ctr. of San Francisco, Cal.*, 70 Comp. Gen. 579 (B-243061), 91-1 CPD ¶ 597; *Ocean Enters., Ltd.*, 65 Comp. Gen. 585 (B-221851), 86-1 CPD ¶ 479. In *Panther Brands, LLC*, Comp. Gen. Dec. B-409073, 2014 CPD ¶ 54, GAO recounted the evolution of this jurisdictional doctrine and articulated the distinction between "for" and "by" the government, as follows:

> We continue to take jurisdiction, however, where we find that a subcontract essentially was awarded "by" the government. See *RGB Display Corp.*, B-284699, May 17, 2000, 2000 CPD ¶ 80 at 3. In this regard, we have considered a subcontract procurement to be "by" the government where the agency handled substantially all the substantive aspects of the procurement and, in effect, took over the procurement, leaving to the prime contractor only the procedural aspects of the procurement, *i.e.*, issuing the subcontract solicitation and receiving proposals.

See also *STR, LLC*, Comp. Gen. Dec. B-297421, 2006 CPD ¶ 11 (GAO would not consider a protest of an award of a subcontract as "by" the government where the contractor drafted the portion of the solicitation pertaining to evaluation of vendor responses, participated substantially in the evaluation of responses and selection of a product for award, and would be responsible for administration of the subcontract); *Baron Servs., Inc.*, Comp. Gen. Dec. B-402109, 2009 CPD ¶ 264 (DOE's approval of the issuance of the RFP does not demonstrate that DOE took over the procurement); *Alatech Healthcare, LLC*, Comp. Gen. Dec. B-400925, 2009 CPD ¶ 57 (agency review, comment, and discussion of RFP with contractor did not show that procurement was "by" the government, where the contractor was responsible for significant aspects of the procurement); and *Addison Constr., Inc.*, Comp. Gen. Dec. B-293805, 2004 CPD ¶ 105 (procurement not "by" the government where contractor drafted the sections of the solicitation pertaining to the evaluation, evaluated the bids, and selected the awardee).

[2] Nonstatutory Authority

GAO's nonstatutory protests are conducted under its advance decision statute, 31 U.S.C. § 3529. This statute authorizes GAO to issue a decision on a question involving a payment the disbursing officer or head of an agency will make or a voucher presented to a certifying official for certification. Pursuant to 4 C.F.R. § 21.13, GAO will hear procurement protests from a government agency not included in the definition of "federal agency" and protests involving sales of property from any government agency only if the agency agrees in writing to have GAO decide its protests. See, for example, *Murphy Co.*, Comp. Gen. Dec.

B-415589, 2018 CPD ¶ 39 (explaining at footnote 5 that "the Forest Service has expressly agreed to have protests concerning timber sales decided by our Office"); *Delta Timber Co.*, Comp. Gen. Dec. B-290710, 2002 CPD ¶ 161 (protest involving timber sales); *OSRAM SYLVANIA Prods., Inc.*, Comp. Gen. Dec. B-287468, 2001 CPD ¶ 158 (protest involving Defense National Stockpile Center); *Total Spectrum Mfg., Inc.*, Comp. Gen. Dec. B-225400, 86-2 CPD ¶ 673 (procurements by the Architect of the Capitol, which is not a federal agency under the definition); and *Victory Salvage Co.*, Comp. Gen. Dec. B-253006, 93-2 CPD ¶ 92 (protest involving surplus property sales).

[B] Who May Protest

GAO is required to decide protests submitted by "interested parties," 31 U.S.C. § 3553(a). 31 U.S.C. § 3551(2) states that an interested party is "an actual or prospective bidder or offeror whose direct economic interest would be affected by the award of the contract or by failure to award the contract." This definition is the same as that under the repealed GSBCA protest authority statute, 40 U.S.C. § 759(h)(9). Because the General Services Board applied the same definition and used the same rationale as that of GAO, GSBCA cases are included in this section for illustrative purposes. The key phrases in the definition are "actual or prospective bidder or offeror" and "direct economic interest." The protester must meet both tests. The protest must relate to a particular solicitation or to the proposed award or award of a particular contract, *A. Moe & Co.*, 64 Comp. Gen. 755 (B-219762), 85-2 CPD ¶ 144 (protest against the denial of its application for a master agreement for repair and alteration of vessels does not pertain to a particular solicitation or to the proposed award or award of a particular contract and, thus, does not constitute a protest within the statute).

Determining whether a protester is an interested party is a circumstantial inquiry. GAO has explained that "[d]etermining whether a party is interested involves consideration of a variety of factors, including the nature of issues raised, the benefit or relief sought by the protester, and the party's status in relation to the procurement," *Oracle Am., Inc.*, Comp. Gen. Dec. B-416061, 2018 CPD ¶ 180.

A protester of the terms of a solicitation will generally not be considered an interested party "where the protester meets the challenged requirements and, accordingly, is not prejudiced by the allegedly defective solicitation provisions," *Accenture Dec. Servs., LLC*, Comp. Gen. Dec. B-418321.4, 2021 CPD ¶ 67.

[1] Actual or Prospective Bidder or Offeror

Because *actual* bidders or offerors are determined by those who submit bids or proposals to the government, the major difficulties in this area have arisen in determining whether a party is a *prospective* bidder or offeror. The term has been taken to mean a potential competitor for the type of work being procured, *Tumpane Servs. Corp.*, Comp. Gen. Dec. B-220465, 86-1 CPD ¶ 95 (protester did not bid but would have if specifications were not defective). Parties are not potential competitors and, thus, are not interested parties, if they do not participate or do not have the capacity to participate in the market involved, *Polycon Corp.*, Comp. Gen. Dec. B-218304.2, 85-1 CPD ¶ 714 (firm's mere characterization of itself as a "prospective prime contractor" ineffective when it was a material supplier and had not bid for construction contract awards); *Julie Research Labs., Inc.*, Comp. Gen. Dec. B-219370, 85-2 CPD ¶ 185, *recons. denied*, 85-2 CPD ¶ 294 (offeror was required to do more than provide manufactured equipment, which was the only function the party contended it could perform); *Signal Corp.*, 69 Comp. Gen. 659 (B-240450), 90-2 CPD ¶ 116, *recons. denied*, 69 Comp. Gen. 725 (B-240450.2), 90-2 CPD ¶ 236 (party voluntarily released its proposed team and unequivocally asserted that it did not want to be further considered in the procurement).

Withdrawing a proposal can eliminate prospective offeror status. In *Federal Data Corp. v. United States*, 911 F.2d 699 (Fed. Cir. 1990), the court held that Federal Data was not an interested party because it knowingly removed itself from the bidding. The court also stated that the protester's desire to compete in a later solicitation if the board found the government's conduct unlawful was not sufficient to make Federal Data an interested party. See also *Robotic Sys. Tech.*, Comp. Gen. Dec. B-271760, 96-1 CPD ¶ 229, where GAO found that the protester was not an interested party where the protester during negotiations withdrew its proposed pricing with a promise to perform the contract at pricing to be provided in its BAFO but then did not submit a BAFO or otherwise confirm its earlier offer by the time specified for receipt of BAFOs.

While withdrawing a proposal may foreclose interested party status, in some cases a protester that never submitted a proposal can still quality as a prospective offeror. As GAO explained in *Oracle America, Inc.*, Comp. Gen. Dec. B-416061, 2018 CPD ¶ 180, "even a protester who did not respond to a solicitation may be an interested party if it has a direct economic interest in the competition of the procurement if its protest is sustained." Protesters have been considered interested parties if they would have submitted offers against a revised RFP. See *McRae, Indus., Inc.*, Comp. Gen. Dec. B-287609.2, 2001 CPD ¶ 127, where the protester alleged that the agency improperly waived the RFP's end-item test requirements which had deterred it from submitting a proposal. GAO reasoned that the protester would be a competitor if it sustained the protest and the agency revised the RFP to delete the requirement. Similarly, in *Poly-Pacific Techs., Inc.*, Comp. Gen. Dec. B-296029, 2005 CPD ¶ 105, the protester was found to be an interested party to protest a modification of the awarded contract that permitted the contractor to provide a product that Poly-Pacific was qualified to provide.

Prospective suppliers or subcontractors are not considered interested parties, *U.S. Polycon Corp.*, Comp. Gen. Dec. B-254655.3, 94-2 CPD ¶ 53 (protester was only a potential supplier to the ultimate awardee); *Allied Tube & Conduit*, Comp. Gen. Dec. B-252371, 93-1 CPD ¶ 345 (prospective supplier of pipe); *Control Techs., Inc.*, Comp. Gen. Dec. B-251335, 93-1 CPD ¶ 16 (mechanical and electrical subcontractor). GAO extended this general rule to conclude that "a supplier or subcontractor for a contract is generally not an interested party to file a protest arguing that a modification of the contract is outside the scope of the contract." *Team Wendy, LLC*, Comp. Gen. Dec. B-417700, 2019 CPD ¶ 2019.

Associations or organizations that do not perform contracts are not interested parties and cannot bring protests in their own name, *American Fed'n of Gov. Employees*, Comp. Gen. Dec. B-219590.3, 86-1 CPD ¶ 436 (government employees' union, protesting contracting-out cost comparison); *Northwest Forest Workers Assocs.*, Comp. Gen. Dec. B-218891.2, 85-1 CPD ¶ 685 (association representing organizations, some of which submitted bids); *Don Strickland's Consultant & Advisory Serv.*, Comp. Gen. Dec. B-217178, 85-1 CPD ¶ 141 (consultant who refused to identify prospective bidders it was representing).

An agent may represent an interested party in a protest where it files the protest on behalf of a specified party and has been authorized to act for that party, *E&R, Inc.*, Comp. Gen. Dec. B-255868, 94-1 CPD ¶ 218. However, the agent is not itself a prospective bidder or offeror and, thus, is not an interested party to protest on its own behalf, *Bulloch Int'l*, Comp. Gen. Dec. B-265982, 96-1 CPD ¶ 5; *Priscidon Enters., Inc.*, Comp. Gen. Dec. B-220278, 85-2 CPD ¶ 549. Persons acting as private attorneys general are not interested parties, *Julie Research Labs., Inc.*, GSBCA 8070-P-R, 86-2 BCA ¶ 18,881.

Federal employees and/or their representatives qualify as "interested parties" for the purpose of protesting public-private competitions conducted pursuant to OMB Circular A-76, 4 C.F.R. § 21.0(a)(2). 31 U.S.C. § 3551 provides:

> (2) The term "interested party"—
>
> * * *
>
> (B) with respect to a public-private competition conducted under Office of Management and Budget Circular A-76 with respect to the performance of an activity or function of a Federal agency, or a decision to convert a function performed by Federal employees to private sector performance without a competition under Office of Management and Budget Circular A-76, includes—
>
> (i) any official who is responsible for submitting the agency tender in such competition; and
>
> (ii) any one individual who, for the purpose of representing the Federal employees engaged in the performance of the activity or function for which the public-private competition is conducted in a

> protest under this subchapter that relates to such public-private competition, has been designated as the agent of the Federal employees by a majority of such employees.

[2] Direct Economic Interest

In order to have a direct economic interest, an actual or prospective offeror must be in line for award or be able to compete for award if its position in the protest is upheld. In reversing a holding of the General Services Board that the fourth lowest bidder in a sealed bid procurement had a sufficient economic interest to protest, the Federal Circuit held in *United States v. International Bus. Machs. Corp.*, 892 F.2d 1006 (Fed. Cir. 1989), that "Congress intended the phrase 'interested party' to be a meaningful limitation on the authority of the board to entertain" a protest. The court stated at 1011:

> The board was troubled by the "logic" that would allow the award of a questionable procurement to go unchallenged if the second-lowest bidder did not file a protest. It believed this result would be "contrary to the notions of full and open and fair and equal competition and would significantly undermine the integrity of the procurement and protest processes." *Id.* But, as the Supreme Court has said in an analogous context, the requirement that a party seeking review must allege facts showing that he is himself adversely affected does not insulate executive action from judicial review, nor does it prevent any public interests from being protected through the judicial process. It does serve as at least a rough attempt to put the decision as to whether review will be sought in the hands of those who have a direct stake in the outcome. *Sierra Club*, 405 U.S. at 740. Congress has decided that the coincidence of a disappointed bidder's "direct economic" interest with the public interest adequately accommodates both. By striking a different balance more solicitous of the latter, the board has upset this congressional scheme. Congress simply did not intend for the board to entertain the protests of innumerable disappointed bidders who have little or no chance of receiving the contract.

In negotiated procurement it is much more difficult to determine whether the protester has a direct economic interest in the award. GAO defined the problem in *Meridian Mgmt. Corp.*, Comp. Gen. Dec. B-271557, 96-2 CPD ¶ 64, as follows:

> A protester must be an actual or prospective offeror whose direct economic interest would be affected by the award of a contract or the failure to award a contract. 4 C.F.R. sec. 21.0(a). Determining whether a party is interested involves consideration of a variety of factors, including the nature of the issue raised, the benefit of relief sought by the protester, and the party's status in relation to the procurement. *Black Hills Refuse Serv.*, 67 Comp. Gen. 261 (1988), 88-1 CPD ¶ 151. A protester is not an interested party where it

would not be in line for contract award were its protest to be sustained. *ECS Composites, Inc.*, B-235849.2, Jan. 3, 1990, 90-1 CPD ¶ 7.

It is often easy to establish that a protester is an interested party with a direct economic interest if the relief being requested is to permit all the offerors to submit revised proposals. For example, in *Meridian*, the protester was held to be an interested party because it was arguing that the agency had improperly waived a mandatory contract requirement in selecting the winner. GAO reasoned that because the proper relief was notifying all offerors of the waiver and permitting them to submit revised proposals, all offerors were interested parties. Similarly, in *Loral Infrared & Imaging Sys., Inc.*, Comp. Gen. Dec. B-247127.3, 92-2 CPD ¶ 52, the protester was found to be an interested party because it claimed that the agency should have established a competitive range and conducted discussions instead of awarding without discussions, and GAO found that Loral's proposal would have been in the competitive range.

A protester will also be found to be an interested party with a direct economic interest if it claims that its proposal was improperly evaluated and that proper evaluation would have put it in line for award, *International Data Prods. Corp.*, Comp. Gen. Dec. B-274654, 97-1 CPD ¶ 34. See *Northwest EnviroService, Inc.*, 71 Comp. Gen. 453 (B-247380.2), 92-2 CPD ¶ 38 (contention that had its past performance been properly assessed, protester would have been the best value for the agency); *Rome Research Corp.*, Comp. Gen. Dec. B-245797.4, 92-2 CPD ¶ 194 (contention that proper evaluation of management experience and technical qualifications would have made protester the best value because it was the lowest-cost offeror); *A. G. Personnel Leasing, Inc.*, Comp. Gen. Dec. B-238289, 90-1 CPD ¶ 416 (contention that proper evaluation of its proposal would have placed protester in competitive range); and *SAMCA*, Comp. Gen. Dec. B-237981.3, 90-1 CPD ¶ 413 (contention that protester should have been placed in competitive range because deficiencies in its proposal were easily correctable).

If an offeror is challenging the evaluation of the winning offeror and not claiming that its proposal was improperly evaluated, it must challenge all higher-ranked offerors to be an interested party. See *Ruchman & Assocs., Inc.*, Comp. Gen. Dec. B-415400, 2018 CPD ¶ 1, where GAO found that the protester was not an interested party because "even if Ruchman's quotation were rated acceptable for the technical and past performance factors, it would not be in line for selection here as it submitted the third-highest price in an LPTA competition." See also *Technical LLC*, Comp. Gen. Dec. B-417177, 2019 CPD ¶ 125 ("even if the protester were correct about the agency's evaluation of the ASM proposal, Offeror A, rather than Technica, would be in line for award, should ASM's proposal be eliminated from consideration"); *PAE Gov't Servs., Inc.*, Comp. Gen. Dec. B-407818, 2013 CPD ¶ 92 (dismissing arguments where "PAE is the third-lowest priced offeror, and the protester does not challenge the evaluation of second-lowest priced offeror."); and *Joint Mgmt. & Tech. Servs.*, Comp. Gen. Dec. B-294229.2, 2004 CPD ¶ 208 (protester lacks interested party status where it failed to challenge evaluation of competitor that would be higher rated than protester even if protest grounds were sustained). Compare *Verdi Consulting, Inc.*, Comp. Gen. Dec. B-414103.2, 2017 CPD ¶ 136 (finding interested party status where protester challenged evaluation in best value procurement that would impact trade-off decision, notwithstanding post hoc agency argument that protester would not be in line for award); and *J2A*^{2}*JV, LLC*, Comp. Gen. Dec. B-401663.4, 2010 CPD ¶ 102 (submitter of the tenth lowest price proposal in a low price, technically acceptable procurement an interested party to challenge the finding that a lower priced proposal was technically acceptable because the agency had not determined the technical acceptability or the eligibility of the intervening lower priced proposals).

If a protester is challenging the evaluation of the winning offeror and also claiming that its proposal was improperly evaluated, but loses on the latter challenge, it must challenge all higher-ranked offerors to be an interested party. See *EMS Ice, Inc.*, Comp. Gen. Dec. B-401688.3, 2009 CPD ¶ 211, where, after finding that the agency had properly determined that the protester's price was unreasonable, the protester was not an interested party to challenge the winning offeror's evaluation because there were intervening offerors in line for award. See also *DynCorp Int'l LLC*, Comp. Gen. Dec. B-294232, 2004 CPD ¶ 187, concluding that the agency reasonably decided that DynCorp's proposal was ineligible for award as written, and since there was another technically acceptable proposal in line for award, even if it were to sustain DynCorps challenges, Offeror A would be in line for award, not DynCorp.

If an offeror not only challenges the award but also claims that evaluation of other proposals was inconsistent with stated evaluation factors and that its proposal represented the best value to the government, it will be found to be an interested party, *Wyle Labs., Inc.*, 69 Comp. Gen. 648 (B-239113), 90-2 CPD ¶ 107. See *Native Am. Indus. Distribs., Inc.*, Comp. Gen. Dec. B-310737.3, 2008 CPD ¶ 76 (offeror in a best value procurement whose price was low is an interested party even though another offeror had a higher technical score); *Arora Grp., Inc.*, Comp. Gen. Dec. B-288127, 2001 CPD ¶ 154 (recognizing an offeror whose proposal was ranked fifth as an interested party only because its protest challenged the agency's application of the evaluation criteria in general, and, if successful, could have placed the contractor in line for the award).

Parties that are ineligible for award do not have a direct economic interest in the award. See *CAE USA, Inc.*, Comp. Gen. Dec. B-414259, 2017 CPD ¶ 386; *Bunzl Dist. California, LLC*, Comp. Gen. Dec. B-412475.4, 2016 CPD ¶ 314. Thus, they will normally not be interested parties unless they are contesting their ineligibility, *Philis Healthcare Informatics*, Comp. Gen. Dec. B-400733.8, 2009 CPD ¶ 246 (firm did not submit firm fixed price proposal as required by RFP); *Para Scientific Co.*, Comp. Gen. Dec. B-310976, 2008 CPD ¶ 54 (firm did not qualify as a small business concern under the appropriate NAICS code identified for the procurement); *ECI Def. Grp.*, Comp. Gen. Dec. B-400177, 2008 CPD ¶ 141 (protester had not acknowledged material amendment); *Boehringer*

Ingelheim Pharm., Inc., Comp. Gen. Dec. B-294944.3, 2005 CPD ¶ 32 (protester's drug had not been shown to be effective in the treatment of either of the two medical conditions identified in the solicitations); and *Qwest Commc'ns Int'l, Inc.*, Comp. Gen. Dec. B-287459, 2001 CPD ¶ 117 (protester was subject to restrictions imposed by Communications Act and therefore was unable to offer service). But see *Designer Assocs., Inc.*, Comp. Gen. Dec. B-293226, 2004 CPD ¶ 114, where GAO found the protester to be an interested party despite fact that the protester was not an 8(a) contractor, and the procurement was conducted under the 8(a) program, because the protester challenged the decision to place the procurement under the 8(a) program. See also *Am. Relocation Connections*, Comp. Gen. Dec. B-416035, 2018 CPD ¶ 174 (protester interested party to challenge accuracy of SAM profile which showed protester was ineligible under applicable NAICS code); and *Allied Tech. Grp., Inc.*, Comp. Gen. Dec. B-402135, 2010 CPD ¶ 152 (protester that had submitted an "unacceptable" quotation found to be an interested party to challenge the acceptability of the only vendor to submit an acceptable quotation).

Ineligibility for a procurement may result from the offeror's suspension or debarment, *Inchcape Shipping Servs. Holdings, Ltd.*, Comp. Gen. Dec. B-412687, 2013 CPD ¶ 286; *Triton Elec. Enters, Inc.*, Comp. Gen. Dec. B-294221, 2004 CPD ¶ 139 (protester was proposed for debarment). Ineligibility may also result from the restrictive nature of the procurement, *Sales Res. Consultants, Inc.*, Comp. Gen. Dec. B-284943, 2000 CPD ¶ 102 (protester not an FSS vendor); *Air Transport Ass'n*, Comp. Gen. Dec. B-278621, 98-1 CPD ¶ 56 (protester not a small business concern and RFP properly set aside for small business); *Precision Kinetics*, Comp. Gen. Dec. B-249975.2, 93-1 CPD ¶ 226 (protester not an approved source); *S. A. SABER*, Comp. Gen. Dec. B-249874, 92-2 CPD ¶ 403 (protester not a small disadvantaged business (SDB) in procurement properly set aside for SDBs); and *Cable Antenna Sys.*, 65 Comp. Gen. 313 (B-220752), 86-1 CPD ¶ 168, *recons. denied*, 86-1 CPD ¶ 298 (incumbent not permitted to participate in a procurement intended to establish a second source for future competition).

At GAO, winners of multiple-award IDIQ contracts are not interested parties because their economic interest is too speculative. GAO bases this rule on the proposition that the protester's status as an awardee precludes the award of an additional contract. See *AAR Airlift Grp. Inc.*, Comp. Gen. Dec. B-414690, 2017 CPD ¶ 273, stating:

> By definition, an IDIQ contract awardee, such as [the protester], cannot be an actual or prospective offeror with respect to another IDIQ contract awarded under the same solicitation. *Aegis Def. Services, LLC* [Comp. Gen. Dec. B-412755, 2016 CPD ¶ 98], at 3-4. This conclusion stems from the simple fact that a contractor that has already been awarded an IDIQ contract cannot be awarded additional IDIQ contracts, even if it could show flaws in the agency's award of those contracts. Indeed, if [the protester] were to

successfully challenge the IDIQ awards to [the other two companies], it would not result in further IDIQ contract awards to [the protester].

The Court of Federal Claims judges, however, are divided on this issue. Compare *Aero Spray, Inc. v. United States*, 156 Fed. Cl. 548 (2021), with *National Air Cargo Grp., Inc. v. United States*, 126 Fed. Cl. 281 (2016).

A potential competitor is an interested party in challenging the propriety of a sole source procurement, but generally the protester must have responded to any market research announcement seeking statements of capability from prospective offerors, *Technology Advancement Grp., Inc.*, Comp. Gen. Dec. B-417609, 2019 CPD ¶ 290, and must also establish that the protester could meet the terms of the RFP as written. *Israel Aerospace Indus.*, Comp. Gen. Dec. B-417681, 2019 CPD ¶ 292 (compiling cases). However, once the sole source procurement has been held to be proper, the potential competitor is no longer an interested party, *Boeing Co.*, Comp. Gen. Dec. B-414706, 2017 CPD ¶ 274. See also *International Training, Inc.*, Comp. Gen. Dec. B-272699, 96-2 CPD ¶ 132 (protester not an interested party to protest the failure of a contracting agency to follow sole source acquisition procedures because the solicitation contained restrictive requirements that made the protester ineligible for award, and the protester did not challenge these restrictive provisions).

[C] Time for Protest

Prior to the enactment of the statutory protest authority, GAO had adopted very restrictive time limitations on the filing of protests in order to ensure that the impact of protests on the procurement process was minimized. Although these time limitations remain in effect under the statutory protest authority, the statutes also contain additional protections when protests are timely filed—providing for limitations on contract award when a protest is filed before award and a stay of performance if the protest is filed quickly after award.

Neither a protester's unfamiliarity with GAO regulations, *Optical Energy Techs., Inc.*, Comp. Gen. Dec. B-401520, 2009 CPD ¶ 153, nor its decision to wait for a response to a congressional inquiry, provides a basis for suspending GAO timeliness regulations, *Professional Office Ctr.*, Comp. Gen. Dec. B-229704, 87-2 CPD ¶ 607. GAO Bid Protest Regulations are published in the Federal Register and the Code of Federal Regulations; protesters are charged with constructive notice of their contents.

[1] Protests of Solicitation Improprieties

Protests of improprieties in solicitations are required to be filed before the closing date for receipt of proposals, 4 C.F.R. § 21.2(a)(1). The basis for this strict rule was explained in *Caddell Constr. Co.*, Comp. Gen. Dec. B-401281, 2009 CPD ¶ 130, as follows:

> Underlying our timeliness rules regarding solicitation improprieties is the principle that challenges which go to the heart of the underlying ground rules by which a competition is conducted, should be resolved as early as practicable during the solicitation process, but certainly in advance of an award decision if possible, not afterwards.

In *ASRC Fed. Data Solutions, LLC*, Comp. Gen. Dec. B-417655, 2019 CPD ¶ 325, GAO reiterated: "It is well-settled that a party who has the opportunity to object to allegedly improper or patently ambiguous terms in a solicitation, but fails to do so prior to the time set for receipt of quotations, waives its ability to raise the same objection later." GAO emphasized that the "rule prevents an offeror from taking advantage of the government, as well as other offerors, by waiting silently during the procurement process, only to spring forward after award with an alleged defect in an effort to restart the procurement."

There are numerous protests that are dismissed because they concern solicitation improprieties. See, for example, *AlliantCorps, LLC*, Comp. Gen. Dec. B-415744.2, 2018 CPD ¶ 136 (argument that agency should have permitted offerors to substitute contract references during performance where solicitation prohibited such substitution); *Ball Aerospace & Techs. Corp.*, Comp. Gen. Dec. B-402148, 2010 CPD ¶ 37 (allegation that evaluation scheme would not determine likely costs to the government); *CES Indus., Inc.*, Comp. Gen. Dec. B-401427, 2010 CPD ¶ 43 (allegation that agency improperly conducted the procurement on an unrestricted basis); *Sea Box, Inc.*, Comp. Gen. Dec. B-401523, 2009 CPD ¶ 190 (conflict between the closing date listed on the GSA e-Buy system and the closing date listed on the RFQ); *General Dynamics—Ordnance & Tactical Sys.*, Comp. Gen. Dec. B-401658, 2009 CPD ¶ 217 (postaward challenge to evaluation scheme that could produce a misleading result); *Armorworks Enters., LLC*, Comp. Gen. Dec. B-400394, 2008 CPD ¶ 176 (allegation that RFP procedures and testing methods were inherently unreliable and deviated from industry practice); and *Hart Sec. Ltd.*, Comp. Gen. Dec. B-400796.2, 2008 CPD ¶ 229 (challenge to agency's amendment requiring successful offeror to hold a facility security clearance).

Alleged solicitation improprieties that did not exist in the initial solicitation but which are subsequently incorporated into the solicitation by amendment must be filed prior to the next closing time for receipt of proposals, 4 C.F.R. § 21.2(a)(1). GAO has recognized an exception, however, where a protester does not have a reasonable opportunity to file its protest before the due date because there was an extremely limited time within which to challenge the solicitation provisions at issue. See *Eastern Forestry*, Comp. Gen. Dec. B-411848, 2015 CPD ¶ 348 (protester learned basis for protest from an amendment posted at 7:00 p.m. the night before bid opening at 10:00 a.m. the following day); *Dube Travel Agency & Tours, Inc.*, Comp. Gen. Dec. B-270438, 96-1 CPD ¶ 141 (amendment not received until one day before proposals due); and *Skyline*

Indus., Inc., Comp. Gen. Dec. B-257340, 94-2 CPD ¶ 111 (time for receipt of proposals was "practically simultaneous with solicitation itself"). However, where there is a reasonable opportunity to file a protest, GAO will not waive the timeliness rule. See *Warrior Service Co.*, Comp. Gen. Dec. B-417491, 2019 CPD ¶ 178 (protester had five calendar days before quotations due); *WareOnEarth Commc'ns, Inc.*, Comp. Gen. Dec. B-298408, 2006 CPD ¶ 107 (protester received the amendments four days—or, as the protester describes them, two working days—before revised proposals were due and was able to prepare and timely submit the revised pricing information required by the agency); and *Concepts to Operations, Inc.*, Comp. Gen. Dec. B-248606, 92-2 CPD ¶ 164 (three calendar days, one business day, was sufficient time to file protest).

Protests of the ground rules of how a procurement will be conducted will be treated as challenges to the terms of a solicitation. See *Domain Name Alliance Registry*, Comp. Gen. Dec. B-310803.2, 2008 CPD ¶ 168, finding the post-closing argument that agency should have held discussions with protester untimely where the agency unequivocally indicated prior to closing that agency did not contemplate holding discussions as part of corrective action. In *Caddell Constr. Co.*, Comp. Gen. Dec. B-401281, 2009 CPD ¶ 130, the agency structured the procurement to allow for the prequalification of firms' eligibility as United States persons and publicly identified prequalified firms. This specifically provided offerors with an opportunity to challenge the eligibility of other potential offerors before the submission of proposals and would have allowed for the early resolution of any eligibility questions. GAO denied the protest stating:

> Although, as a general rule, a protester is not required to protest that another firm should be excluded from the competition until after the firm has been selected for award, see, e.g., *REEP, Inc.*, B-290688, Sept. 20, 2002, 2002 CPD ¶ 158 at 1-2 (protest that awardee had impermissible organizational conflict of interest), we have applied a different rule where a protester is aware of the facts giving rise to its allegation that another firm should be ineligible to compete and where the protester has been expressly advised that the agency has determined that the firm in question is eligible. See *Abt Assocs., Inc.*, B-294130, Aug. 11, 2004, 2004 CPD ¶ 174 at 2; *International Sci. & Tech. Inst., Inc.*, B-259648, Jan. 12, 1995, 95-1 CPD ¶ 16 at 3-4. In such cases, we have found that the protester cannot wait until an award has been made to file its protest, but instead must protest before the closing time for receipt of proposals.

There are varying timing requirements to protest the scope of an agency's corrective action. If a protester is challenging an agency decision to take corrective action in the first instance, such a challenge must generally be raised within 10 days after the agency announces the corrective action. *Enhanced Veterans Sols.*, Comp. Gen. Dec. B-414189.2, 2017 CPD ¶ 246. More often, protesters challenge the scope of the corrective action. As a general rule, where the agency makes clear that it will or will not take a certain action during corrective action (*e.g.*, opening discussions or accepting revised proposals), a protest challenging that act or omission is considered a challenge to the ground rules of the competition and must be raised prior to the proposal submission deadline. See *Delta Risk, LLC*, Comp. Gen. Dec. B-416420, 2018 CPD ¶ 305, stating:

> A protest allegation that challenges the ground rules that the agency has announced for performing corrective action and recompetition is analogous to a challenge to the terms of the solicitation and must be filed prior to the deadline for submitting revised proposals. Where, as here, no further submissions are anticipated, such challenges must be raised within 10 days of when the scope of the agency's corrective action was known or should have been known.

See also *Veterans Evaluation Servs., Inc.*, Comp. Gen. Dec. B-412940, 2017 CPD ¶ 17 (challenge to the agency's failure to conduct a technical evaluation during corrective action untimely because protester was put on notice prior to submitting a revised proposal); *Domain Name Alliance Registry*, Comp. Gen. Dec. B-310803, 2008 CPD ¶ 168 (argument that agency should have held discussions with protester during corrective action untimely where agency unequivocally indicated that agency did not contemplate holding discussions as part of corrective action). But see *American K-9 Detection Servs., Inc.*, Comp. Gen. Dec. B-400464, 2009 CPD ¶ 10 (protest of failure to open discussions during corrective action not untimely where the agency "did not clearly announce the ground rules of the corrective action and did not specifically indicate that no further discussions would be conducted.").

A protest challenging the scope of corrective action will be dismissed as premature if the agency has not yet committed to the challenged scope, *Leidos, Inc.*, Comp. Gen. Dec. B-418242.5, 2020 CPD ¶ 93 (challenge to scope of corrective action dismissed as premature where agency communications were ambiguous as to whether discussions would be opened).

Generally where a solicitation for an IDIQ contract gives clear notice of an agency's intention to procure particular requirements under an IDIQ contract, any protest to those terms of the solicitation must be filed before the closing date for receipt of proposals. However, where the work statement is broad or vague and it is unclear what work will be placed under the task order a different rule has emerged. In *LBM, Inc.*, Comp. Gen. Dec. B-290682, 2002 CPD ¶ 157, the Army argued that LBM's protest of the transfer of the Fort Polk motor pool services to the LOGJAMSS contract should be dismissed as untimely. The Army believed that LBM should have been on notice from the LOGJAMSS solicitation that the Fort Polk motor pool services "could" be ordered under the LOGJAMSS contracts. GAO disagreed, stating:

> We have recognized that the increasing use of IDIQ contracts with very broad and often vague statements of work may place an unreasonable burden upon potential offerors, who may be required to guess as to whether particular work, for which they are interested in competing, will be acquired under a particular IDIQ contract. *See Valenzuela Eng'g, Inc.*, B-277979, Dec. 9, 1997, 98-1 CPD ¶ 51 (Letter to the Acting Sec'y of the Army, Jan. 26, 1998, at 2). This burden may be particularly problematic for small businesses. *Id.* In our view, it is unreasonable to require a small business that believes that one specific acquisition should continue to be set aside for small businesses to identify the possibility, at the time proposals for IDIQ contracts to perform a broad and undefined scope of work are solicited, that the specific, and relatively small, acquisition it is interested in may ultimately be transferred to the IDIQ contracts.
>
> The breadth and vagueness of the LOGJAMSS scope of work illustrate this, since it encompassed a "wide range of logistical functions and supporting tasks" and was undefinitized at the time the LOGJAMSS contracts were solicited. Accordingly, we conclude that LBM could not reasonably be aware, and required to protest, at the time the LOGJAMSS contracts were being competed (and apparently years before the Army considered using those contracts for the Fort Polk motor pool services), that the broad and nonspecific scope of work in the LOGJAMSS solicitation could be improperly used as a vehicle for the agency to perform the motor pool services at Fort Polk without first taking the steps legally required regarding a possible further acquisition of that work under a small business set-aside.

See also *Ocuto Blacktop & Paving Co.*, Comp. Gen. Dec. B-284165, 2000 CPD ¶ 32 (protest filed at time of task order for landfill capping is timely where solicitations for IDIQ contracts "do not provide clear notice that the [agency] will use these contracts to procure environmental remediation work at [particular] sites"). However, where the solicitation for the IDIQ contract is not broad and vague, but rather gives clear notice of the agency's intention to procure particular requirements under an IDIQ contract, any protest to those terms of the solicitation must be filed before the solicitation closing date, *Datamaxx Grp., Inc.*, Comp. Gen. Dec. B-400582, 2008 CPD ¶ 231 (protest untimely where EAGLE solicitation provided clear notice that software development services would be acquired); and *MadahCom, Inc.*, Comp. Gen. Dec. B-297261.2, 2005 CPD ¶ 209 (protest that a solicitation improperly restricts competition to multiple-award task order contract holders, and that the task orders will exceed the scope of the underlying contracts timely when filed before the closing date for receipt of proposals).

[2] Protests Not Apparent in Solicitation

Protests on any other ground are required to be filed at GAO within 10 calendar days after the basis of the protest is known or should have been known, whichever is earlier, 4 C.F.R. § 21.2(a)(2). This rule primarily applies to competitive range protests and postaward protests, but can also apply in numerous scenarios including challenges to solicitation amendments and the evaluation process where no future proposal submission deadline is available. See, for example, *Armorworks Enters., LLC*, Comp. Gen. Dec. B-400394, 2008 CPD ¶ 176 (challenge to solicitation amendment, issued after initial proposals had been submitted, and which did not provide offerors with an opportunity to submit revised proposals, should have been filed within 10 days of issuance of the amendment).

On its face, the rule would require all postaward protests to be filed within 10 days after the notice of award is issued. There is an important exception, however, for protests challenging a procurement conducted on the basis of competitive proposals where a debriefing is requested and, when requested, is required. In this case, with respect to any protest basis that is known or should have been known either before or as a result of the debriefing, the initial protest cannot be filed before the debriefing date offered to the protester but must be filed not later than 10 calendar days after the date on which the debriefing is held, 4 C.F.R. § 21.2(a)(2). In other words, a post-debriefing protest will be considered timely if filed as late as 10 days after the debriefing, even as to issues that should have been known before the debriefing, if that debriefing is "required." See *Dominion Aviation, Inc.—Recons.*, Comp. Gen. Dec. B-275419.4, 98-1 CPD ¶ 62 (challenge to protester's evaluation of its performance history as marginal untimely where not filed within 10 days of debriefing); *Black & Veatch Special Projects Corp.*, Comp. Gen. Dec. B-279492.2, 98-1 CPD ¶ 173 (protester had 10 days from date of debriefing to file protest concerning issues it first learned at debriefing); and *WP Photographic Servs.*, Comp. Gen. Dec. B-278897.4, 98-1 CPD ¶ 151 (protester had 10 days to raise particular objections concerning the evaluation of its proposal after debriefing).

"Requested and required" debriefings also preclude protests submitted prior to the debriefing, 4 C.F.R. § 21.2(a)(2); *VAS Realty, LLC—Recons.*, Comp. Gen. Dec. B-417142, 2019 CPD ¶ 147; *Real Estate Ctr.*, Comp. Gen. Dec. B-274081, 96-2 CPD ¶ 74. This rule is designed to encourage early and meaningful debriefings but to preclude strategic or defensive protests. See also *Minotaur Eng'g*, Comp. Gen. Dec. B-276843, 97-1 CPD ¶ 194.

The rule giving protesters 10 days to file a protest after a "requested and required" debriefing is inapplicable where a protester's proposal is eliminated from a competition prior to award, and the protester chooses to delay receipt of a debriefing regarding elimination until after award. See 10 U.S.C. § 3305(a); 41 U.S.C. § 3705(a); FAR 15.505(a)(2); *Loc Performance Prods., Inc.*, Comp. Gen. Dec. B-417431, 2019 CPD ¶ 149; *United Int'l Investigative Servs., Inc.*, Comp. Gen. Dec. B-286327, 2000 CPD ¶ 173. In this situation, a protester may not passively await information providing a basis for protest; rather, a protester has an affirmative obligation to diligently pursue such information, *Automated Med. Prods. Corp.*, Comp. Gen. Dec. B-275835, 97-1 CPD ¶ 52. See *University of Massachusetts Donahue Inst.*, Comp. Gen. Dec. B-400870.3, 2009 CPD ¶ 173, where the protester delayed debriefing regarding the elimination of its proposal until after award. GAO held that challenging the agency's elimination of the proposal, filed more than three months after the protester received notice of the proposal's elimination, was untimely where the protester received all of the information on which the protest was based at the time the proposal was eliminated from the competition.

Protests originally filed with an agency must be filed at GAO within 10 days of actual or constructive knowledge of initial adverse agency action, 4 C.F.R. § 21.2(a)(3); *MLS-Multinational Logistic Servs., Ltd.*, Comp. Gen. Dec. B-415782, 2018 CPD ¶ 105; *International Garment Processors*, Comp. Gen. Dec. B-299743, 2007 CPD ¶ 130; and *Lifecare Mgmt. Partners*, Comp. Gen. Dec. B-297078, 2006 CPD ¶ 8. In *Timothy J. Penny*, Comp. Gen. Dec. B-221710, Feb. 20, 1986, *Unpub.*, GAO held that these time limitations could not be avoided by having the protest filed through a member of Congress.

A requested debriefing does not toll the requirement that a protest be filed within 10 days of adverse action on an agency-level protest, *RTI Techs., LLC*, Comp. Gen. Dec. B-401075, 2009 CPD ¶ 86; *M2 Global Tech., Ltd.*, Comp. Gen. Dec. B-400946, 2009 CPD ¶ 13.

For the purposes of timeliness rules, the mechanical receipt of e-mail during a firm's regular business hours constitutes notice of an agency's award. In *Golight, Inc.*, Comp. Gen. Dec. B-401866, 2009 CPD ¶ 184, the protest was untimely because it was not filed within 10 calendar days of the Friday that it was received during business hours. GAO rejected the protester's argument that its employee (to whom the e-mail was directed) had left for the day and did not open the e-mail until the following Monday. See also *American Office Servs., Inc.*, Comp. Gen. Dec. B-290511, 2002 CPD ¶ 122 (protester on notice of protest basis as of date of receipt of agency e-mail containing proposal deficiency information). Compare *Supreme Edgelight Devices, Inc.*, Comp. Gen. Dec. B-295574, 2005 CPD ¶ 58 (receipt of an agency-level protest decision on a non-business day did not constitute actual or constructive knowledge of initial adverse agency action). Where an e-mail notification of exclusion from the competitive range enters an offeror's computer system after close of business on a weekday or on a weekend or holiday and is not opened before the following business day, receipt of the notice is considered to have occurred on that business day, *International Res. Grp.*, Comp. Gen. Dec. B-286663, 2001 CPD ¶ 35. GAO stated that to construe receipt of an e-mail notification as occurring when the notification enters the offeror's computer system outside of normal business hours would lead to a reduction of the three-day period for requesting a debriefing granted by the FAR to a single day when the notification is transmitted after close of business on Friday or on Saturday of a weekend followed by a Monday holiday. See also *Tribologik Corp.*, Comp. Gen. Dec. B-417532, 2019 CPD ¶ 284 (notice received outside of protester's business hours did not provide constructive notice of award). Constructive notice of award, starting the running of the 10-day period, will be found where posting of the notice is made to the designated government point of entry (GPE), previously FedBizOpps, *CBMC, Inc.*, Comp. Gen. Dec. B-295586, 2005 CPD ¶ 2; *Boswell & Dunlap, LLP*, Comp. Gen. Dec. B-416623, 2018 CPD ¶ 351 (discussing rule). But see *Worldwide Language Res., Inc.*, Comp. Gen. Dec. B-296984, 2005 CPD ¶ 206 (announcement of award on DoD's official website, *www.DefenseLink.mil*, did not place protesters on constructive notice of award and thus require protesters to file within 10 days of the announcement because DefenseLink has not been designated by statute or regulation as the public medium for announcement of procurement actions).

GAO regulations permit consideration of late protests for "good cause" or if the protest raises "issues significant to the procurement system," 4 C.F.R. § 21.2(c). GAO, in order to maintain the value of the time limitations, has construed these exceptions strictly. The good cause exception is available only for a compelling reason beyond the protester's control, *Oracle Corp.*, Comp. Gen. Dec. B-260963, 95-1 CPD ¶ 231 (argument that dismissal of protest would be "particularly unfair" did not meet good cause exception); *John Cuneo, Inc.*, Comp. Gen. Dec. B-227983.2, 87-2 CPD ¶ 147 (protester's lack of awareness of the bid protest timeliness requirements not a good cause); *Arian Fashions, Inc.*, Comp. Gen. Dec. B-247314.3, 92-1 CPD ¶ 223 (fact that basis of protest arose during a holiday was not a good cause).

The "significant issue" exception is also applied strictly. See, for example, *Merck & Co.*, Comp. Gen. Dec. B-248655, 92-1 CPD ¶ 454, refusing to decide a protest issue raised late and stating that "we strictly construe and seldom use the exception, limiting it to protests that raise issues of widespread interest to the procurement community." Other decisions finding no significant issue include *Goel Servs., Inc.*, Comp. Gen. Dec. B-310822.2, 2008 CPD ¶ 99 (argument that HUBZone price evaluation preference should have been included in solicitation); *Ervin & Assocs., Inc.*, Comp. Gen. Dec. B-279083, 98-1 CPD ¶ 126 (alleged over-breadth of the statement of work for an indefinite-quantity task order contract); *International Sci. & Tech. Inst., Inc.*, Comp. Gen. Dec. B-259648, 95-1 CPD ¶ 16 (organizational conflict of interest of awardee); and *American Material Handling, Inc.*, Comp. Gen. Dec. B-255467.2, 94-1 CPD ¶ 158 (propriety of solicitation specifications).

GAO is most likely to find a significant issue when it has not ruled on an issue and believes that its decision will be of value to the procurement community. See, for example, *DRS Tech. Servs., Inc.*, Comp. Gen. Dec. B-411573.2, 2015 CPD ¶ 363 (untimely challenge to solicitation evaluation scheme which failed to account for differences in offerors' transition plans); *Tiger Truck, LLC*, Comp. Gen. Dec. B-400685, 2009 CPD ¶ 19 (the interplay between the obligation to conduct meaningful discussions and the rules governing TAA procurements); *Celadon Labs., Inc.*, Comp. Gen. Dec. B-298533, 2006 CPD ¶ 158 (the application of conflict of interest regulations to peer review evaluators in Small Business Innovation Research procurements); *Gene Quigley, Jr.*, 70 Comp. Gen. 273 (B-241565), 91-1 CPD ¶ 182 (newly promulgated regulations on individual sureties); *Discount Mach. & Equip., Inc.*, 70 Comp. Gen. 108 (B-240525), 90-2 CPD ¶ 420 (failure of an agency to refer an adverse agency nonresponsibility determination on a small business to Small Business Administration); *Golden N. Van Lines, Inc.*, 69 Comp. Gen. 610 (B-238874), 90-2 CPD ¶ 44 (failure to specify whether option prices would be evaluated); *Baszile Metal Serv.*, Comp. Gen. Dec. B-237925, 90-1 CPD ¶ 378 (DoD's regulatory requirements that SDB regular dealers provide a product manufactured by a small business concern when there is no SDB manufacturer in order to be eligible for an SDB evaluation preference in unrestricted procurements); *Cincinnati Milacron Mktg. Co.*, Comp. Gen. Dec. B-237619, 90-1 CPD ¶ 241 (interpretation of a congressional restriction on the use of appropriated funds); and *F. J. O'Hara & Sons, Inc.*, 69 Comp. Gen. 274 (B-237410), 90-1 CPD ¶ 197 (statutory restriction on the purchase of food).

[3] Statutory Stay

Although the statutes do not limit the filing times for jurisdictional purposes, they do contain provisions that delay award or suspend contract performance pending the decision on a protest. These provisions were enacted to ensure that effective relief could be obtained by successful protesters. If a protest is filed before award, 31 U.S.C. § 3553(c) provides that while a protest is pending, "a contract may not be awarded in any procurement after the federal agency has received notice of the protest" from GAO. If a protest is filed after award but within specified time limitations, 31 U.S.C. § 3553(d) provides that the federal agency shall, on receipt of notice of the protest from GAO, "immediately direct the contractor to cease performance under the contract." Both of these stay provisions have exceptions based on urgency or compelling circumstances, 31 U.S.C. § 3553(c)(2) and (d)(3)(C). In addition, performance of a contract awarded prior to receipt of a protest may be continued during a protest based on a finding that it is "in the best interests of the United States," 31 U.S.C. § 3553(d)(3)(C). These findings must be made by "the head of the procuring activity," and the authority to make such findings may not be delegated, 31 U.S.C. § 3553(e).

The period for notice of the protest begins "on the date of contract award and ends on the later of (A) the date that is 10 [calendar] days after the date of the contract award; or (B) the date that is 5 [calendar] days after the debriefing date offered to an unsuccessful offeror for any debriefing that is requested and, when requested, is required." Thus, the general rule is that an agency must suspend contract performance if it receives notice of a protest by the tenth calendar day following contract award or the fifth calendar day following a timely requested debriefing, whichever is later, 31 U.S.C. § 3553.

The enhanced postaward debriefing rights for DoD procurement created by the National Defense Authorization Act for Fiscal Year 2018 creates an important exception to the standard timing rules for obtaining a stay. Congress amended Title 10 to provide that once DoD provides an unsuccessful offeror a debriefing,

DoD must allow the offeror an "enhanced debriefing" by submitting, within two business days, additional questions, which DoD must respond to within five business days after receipt of the questions. Only after DoD answers the offeror's follow-up questions may the agency consider the debriefing concluded. Then DoD must implement the stay if it receives notice of a protest filed within five days after responding to the follow-up questions. However, if the offeror does not take advantage of the enhanced debriefing by submitting questions, the stay will not be required if the protest is filed later than five days after the original debriefing (and 10 days after notice of the grounds for the protest), *NIKA Techs., Inc. v. United States*, 987 F.3d 1025 (Fed. Cir. 2021).

Under 31 U.S.C. § 3553, an agency is required to suspend performance of a contract only if the agency receives notice *from the Comptroller General* within 10 days of contract award. Prior to implementing GAO's Electronic Protest Docketing System (EPDS), discussed below, this created a practical difficulty for protesters to ensure a protest was filed early enough to ensure GAO could give the agency notice of protest prior to the deadline. See *BDM Mgmt. Servs. Co.*, Comp. Gen. Dec. B-228287, 88-1 CPD ¶ 93, holding that there was no duty to suspend contract performance where a protest was filed on the eighth day after award (a Friday) and the agency was notified by GAO within one working day, on the eleventh day after award (a Monday). There is no recourse if GAO fails to notify the agency of the protest, *Florida Professional Review Org.*, Comp. Gen. Dec. B-253908.2, 94-1 CPD ¶ 17. Notice by the protester to the agency is insufficient to trigger suspension of contract performance, *Technology for Commc'ns Int'l v. Garrett*, 783 F. Supp. 1446 (D.D.C. 1992) (although protester notified Navy of protest, GAO did not notify the agency until the fourteenth day after contract award). This problem is largely resolved now as, upon filing, EPDS will automatically generate an e-mail, copying the protester, notifying the procuring agency that a new protest has been filed: "Filing a document in EPDS constitutes notice to all parties of that filing," 21 C.F.R. § 21.0(g).

An agency can override a stay on a finding of urgent and compelling circumstances or, in the case of postaward protests, on a finding of urgent and compelling circumstances *or* if the override is in the government's best interests, 31 U.S.C. § 3553(c)(2) and (d)(3)(C). If an agency decides to award a contract or to proceed with performance in spite of the statutory stay, GAO has no authority to challenge this action. However, a protester can challenge the agency's decision to override the stay requirement by filing a suit in the Court of Federal Claims under 28 U.S.C. § 1491(b). In *RAMCOR Servs. Grp., Inc. v. United States*, 185 F.3d 1286 (Fed. Cir. 1999), the Federal Circuit held that the Court of Federal Claims had jurisdiction to rule on the validity of an agency's decision to override the automatic stay of an award when a timely protest was filed in GAO. This extends both to 31 U.S.C. § 3553(d)(3)(C) determinations premised upon asserted "best interests of the United States" as well as those based upon asserted "urgent and compelling circumstances that significantly affect interests of the United States," *PGBA, LLC v. United States*, 57 Fed. Cl. 655 (2003). Review of override decisions are guided by the standards as set forth in the Administrative Procedure Act, 28 U.S.C. § 1491(b)(4); 5 U.S.C. § 706(2)(a) (see discussion below regarding standard of review in Court of Federal Claims procurement protests).

In *Reilly's Wholesale Produce, Inc. v. United States*, 73 Fed. Cl. 705 (2006), the court identified the relevant factors an agency must consider and address when considering both "best interest" and "urgent and compelling circumstances" overrides at 711:

> (i) whether significant adverse consequences will necessarily occur if the stay is not overridden; (ii) conversely, whether reasonable alternatives to the override exist that would adequately address the circumstances presented; (iii) how the potential cost of proceeding with the override, including the costs associated with the potential that the GAO might sustain the protest, compare to the benefits associated with the approach being considered for addressing the agency's needs; and (iv) the impact of the override on competition and the integrity of the procurement system, as reflected in the Competition in Contracting Act. (Citations omitted)

In addition to these factors, the Court of Federal Claims judges have identified issues that the agency should not consider in exercising its override rights. For example, the government's decision to override a stay may not be based simply on its view that the new contract is better than the old one or that the agency simply prefers to override the stay rather than await GAO's decision, *Safeguard Base Operations, LLC v. United States*, 140 Fed. Cl. 670 (2018); *Advanced Sys. Dev., Inc. v. United States*, 72 Fed. Cl. 25 (2006) ("The allegation that the new contract is better than the old one in terms of cost or performance is not enough to justify a best interests determination."); *Superior Helicopter LLC v. United States*, 78 Fed. Cl. 181 (2007) (Forest Service's conclusion that exclusive-use contracts were more "advantageous" than the CWN contracts is an invalid justification for overriding automatic stay).

The court has stated that the "payment of significantly higher costs under an incumbent or bridge contract could be the sort of significant adverse consequence to justify an override when these are shown to be prohibitive," *Supreme Foodservice GmbH v. United States*, 109 Fed. Cl. 369 (2013). Yet, justifications based on agency claims of cost savings have proven not likely to withstand judicial review, *Nortel Gov't Solutions, Inc. v. United States*, 84 Fed. Cl. 243 (2008) (rejecting government cost saving arguments on grounds that "similar amounts have been found insufficient to support a best interests override"). In *Automation Techs., Inc. v. United States*, 72 Fed. Cl. 723 (2006), the court held that the estimated $103,196.27 per month cost saving during an expected delay of almost three months in the context of an anticipated five-year $49,500,000 contract with options was insufficient to support an override. In *E-Management Consultants, Inc. v. United States*, 84 Fed. Cl. 1 (2008), the National Highway Traffic Safety Administration reasoned that the benefits of overriding the stay included avoiding termination costs of any replacement contract and maintaining uninterrupted performance beyond the calendar year. The court, however, stated "these are not the sorts of benefits envisioned in the cost-benefit calculation." If the agency will lose a significant amount of money without a stay, it may be able to justify the override, *Chapman Law Firm Co. v. United States*, 67 Fed. Cl. 188 (2005) (without the override the agency estimated it would lose $3 million per month and that government properties would be unmanaged and subject to vandalism).

When several offerors are available to perform the work or mechanisms like bridge contracts are available, the court is likely to sustain a challenge to the override, *Nortel Gov't Solutions, Inc. v. United States*, 84 Fed. Cl. 243 (2008) (agency override was arbitrary and capricious, in part, because the bridge contract provided a reasonable alternative); *Keeton Corrections, Inc. v. United States*, 59 Fed. Cl. 753 (2004) (agency override lacked a rational basis where the agency could have continued awarding short term sole source contracts to incumbent). But see *Alion Science & Tech. Corp. v. United States*, 69 Fed. Cl. 14 (2005) (upholding override noting the time-critical nature of the contract and the lack of multiple vendors).

In considering the effect of the override on the integrity of the procurement system, the court will not permit an agency to point to its likelihood of ultimately winning the contract. In *E-Management Consultants, Inc. v. United States*, 84 Fed. Cl. 1 (2008), the court held that the agency failed to consider the impact of its override on the procurement system and that the override memorandum failed to meet even the deferential standards of APA review, stating at 10:

> [T]he OM [override memorandum] failed to offer any reasoning that shows that it actually considered the integrity of the procurement system Congress created in CICA. . . . The text of the paragraphs in which the consideration is mentioned reads in full as follows:
>
> I considered the impact on competition and on the integrity of the procurement process, should the agency decline to suspend performance.
>
> In my view, the competition process is best served by allowing the awardee to proceed. As noted above, I conclude from discussions with the relevant agency officials that the agency has a reasonable chance of prevailing. Moreover, the protester is not next in line for award. Taken together, these two points lead me to conclude that allowing the awardee to proceed is the fairest approach. As an extra safeguard, however, the awardee's performance will be limited to essential efforts during the pendency of the protest. *Id.*
>
> The claimed consideration of the impact on the procurement system do not recognize or vindicate the purpose of the automatic stay. NHTSA first states that it "has a reasonable chance of prevailing." . . . This observation does not relate to the integrity of the procurement system. It relates to the merits of the protest, not to the automatic stay in CICA. NHTSA also states that the protestor is not "next in line." . . . Again, this is not an appropriate evaluation of the impact of the override on the procurement system. The purpose of the procurement system as envisioned in CICA is a fair process in which

> disappointed bidders can seek review at GAO. GAO was given the automatic stay in CICA to promote these policies. *See* H.R. Rep. No. 98-861 at 1435-36 (Conf. Rep.). NHTSA then states that it has "limited [Centech's performance] to essential efforts during the pendency of the protest." . . . Again, this statement has nothing to do with the integrity of the procurement process. The CICA stay was meant to prevent the "fait accompli" of a contractor establishing a relationship in a new contract with an agency long before GAO issued its decision. *See* H.R. Rep. No. 99-138, at 4-5. Limiting the contractor to "essential efforts," . . . does not address Congress' concerns.

The Court of Federal Claims judges approach the *Reilly's* factors differently. Some judges treat the *Reilly's* factors as the substantive standard against which an override decision must be judged; accordingly, an agency's failure to consider even one of the *Reilly's* factors can be fatal. See *Nortel Gov't Sols., Inc. v. United States*, 84 Fed. Cl. 243 (2008). Some judges reject *Reilly's* altogether, finding that the only appropriate standard is the APA's general arbitrary and capricious standard of review and declining to require agencies to address any specific element in the override. See *DynCorp Int'l LLC v. United States*, 113 Fed. Cl. 298 (2013); *PlanetSpace Inc. v. United States*, 86 Fed. Cl. 566 (2009). Others engage with the *Reilly's* analysis but decide the case more broadly in terms of the general APA arbitrary and capricious standard. See *Analysis Grp., LLC v. United States*, No. 09-542C, 2009 WL 3747171 (Fed. Cl. Nov. 5, 2009). The decisions are further divided as to whether the *Reilly's* factors are limited to overrides invoking "urgent and compelling" circumstances or whether they extend to overrides that invoke a "best interests" justification. See *PMTech, Inc. v. United States*, 95 Fed. Cl. 330, 344-45 (2010). In addition, the judges disagree as to whether a plaintiff must separately prove entitlement to injunctive relief in order to overturn the stay, or whether defeating the override under the *Reilly's* test is adequate to restore the stay. See *Supreme Foodservice GmbH v. United States*, 109 Fed. Cl. 369 (2013); *Superior Helicopter LLC v. United States*, 78 Fed. Cl. 181 (2007); *Reilly's Wholesale Produce v. United States*, 73 Fed. Cl. 705 (2006).

This conflicting body of Court of Federal Claims decisions leaves agencies, contractors, and their counsel in a difficult position. It is often impossible to anticipate what standards will apply in an override challenge, at least until a Court of Federal Claims judge is assigned to the case. Even then, not every judge will have published a definitive position on each issue relevant to an override challenge. This creates the practical reality that agencies and protesters must draft override decisions and override challenges against multiple alternative standards.

In the non-precedential yet significant decision in *Safeguard Base Operations, LLC v. United States*, 792 Fed. Appx. 945 (Fed. Cir. 2019), the Federal Circuit dismissed as moot an appeal seeking clarification as to the correct standard applicable to CICA override challenges. The panel agreed with the government and the awardee that "Safeguard's appeal is now moot because the GAO has denied its bid protest, and that decision would have terminated the CICA stay even in the absence of DHS's override." In doing so, *SBO* implicitly suggests that the Federal Circuit may never decide the merits of an appeal from a Court of Federal Claims' override decision. It is difficult to conceive of a realistic circumstance where the Federal Circuit could receive full briefing and decide an appeal of a Court of Federal Claims' decision in an override challenge before the 100-day GAO protest deadline expires. Notwithstanding dismissal as moot, the *SBO* panel decision includes language that seems to cast doubt on the idea that agencies must address the *Reilly's* factors to justify an override, or that the Court of Federal Claims must apply the *Reilly's* framework, suggesting instead that the general APA standard of review is the relevant legal standard, stating at 948-49:

> We note that the Reilly's factors do not even bind the Claims Court, *AINS, Inc. v. United States*, 365 F.3d 1333, 1336 n.1 (Fed. Cir. 2004), *abrogated on other grounds by Slattery v. United States*, 635 F.3d 1298 (Fed. Cir. 2011), let alone comprise an indispensable aspect of an agency rational basis. *Cf. Dell Fed. Sys., L.P. v. United States*, 906 F.3d 982, 992 (Fed. Cir. 2018) (holding that "highly deferential" rational basis test governed Claims Court review of agency action for purposes of deciding injunctive relief in protest of bid reopening).

Regardless of the assigned judge, consistent with the Court of Federal Claims' jurisdictional statute, 28 U.S.C. § 1491(b)(3), overrides related to procurements involving national defense and security are more likely to withstand challenge, *Maden Tech Consulting Inc. v. United States*, 74 Fed. Cl. 786 (2006) (procurement of electromagnetic spectrum engineering services to support war fighters in Iraq and Afghanistan); *Kropp Holdings, Inc. v. United States*, 63 Fed. Cl. 537 (2005) ("where legitimate 'interests of national defense and national security' are raised and established to the court's satisfaction, the circumstances under which the court should find it 'necessary' to reach the merits of an override decision should be the exception, rather than the rule"); and *SDS Int'l, Inc. v. United States*, 55 Fed. Cl. 363 (2003) (absolutely essential to the success of the Weapons School and to the quality of our warriors that courseware development, production and presentation, as well as the contractor aircrew training not receive further interruption).

[D] Intervenors

4 C.F.R. § 21.0 defines an "intervenor" as:

> an awardee if the award has been made or, if no award has been made, all bidders or offerors who appear to have a substantial prospect of receiving an award if the protest is denied.

Potential intervenors become aware of a protest by the fact that the contracting agency must immediately give notice of a protest to the awardee, if award has been made or, if award has not been made, to all bidders or offerors who appear to have a reasonable prospect of receiving an award, 4 C.F.R. § 21.3(a). Most often, it is the awardee that files as an intervenor. See, for example, *Boeing Co.*, Comp. Gen. Dec. B-414706, 2017 CPD ¶ 274 (awardee of sole source award intervened to defend challenge to sole source award); *B. L. Harbert-Brasfield & Gorrie, JV*, Comp. Gen. Dec. B-402229, 2010 CPD ¶ 89 (awardee filed as intervenor when protester challenged award on basis of organizational conflict of interest); and *Boeing Co.*, Comp. Gen. Dec. B-311344, 2008 CPD ¶ 114 (awardee filed as intervenor when protester challenged technical and cost evaluations of proposals). However, offerors that are likely to win an award may also file as intervenors. See, for example, *Government Tech. Servs., Inc.*, Comp. Gen. Dec. B-258082.2, 94-2 CPD ¶ 93 (intervenor next offeror in line).

Upon receiving notification of a protest, any intervenor may file a request for dismissal, if it believes that a protest or specific protest allegations should be dismissed before submission of an agency report, 4 C.F.R. § 21.3(b). If the protest is not dismissed, the agency must prepare the agency report and, subject to any protective order, simultaneously furnish a copy to the protester and any intervenors, 4 C.F.R. § 21.3(e). As with protesters, intervenors have 10 days after receipt of the agency report to provide comments, 4 C.F.R. § 21.3(i). These comments must be given to the contracting agency and all other participating parties, 4 C.F.R. § 21.3(i).

Sometimes a party will find itself in the position of filing as an intervenor after having been a protester on the procurement. In *Executive Conference Ctr., Inc.*, Comp. Gen. Dec. B-275882.2, 97-1 CPD ¶ 138, the contracting officer, in response to a protest after award, terminated the award and awarded the contract to the protester, waiving its failure to acknowledge an amendment because the amendment was immaterial. The original awardee then protested and the original protester intervened to preserve its award. GAO sustained the protest holding that the amendment was material. Similarly, in *Alice Roofing & Sheet Metal Works, Inc.*, Comp. Gen. Dec. B-275477, 97-1 CPD ¶ 86, a protester persuaded a contracting officer to reverse the agency's award and was awarded the contract. When the original awardee protested, the original protester intervened and assisted the agency in persuading GAO to deny the protest.

[E] Procedures

Protests at GAO are governed by its protest procedures, 4 C.F.R. Part 21. GAO also publishes guidance for the bid protest process, available online at *www.gao.gov*.

[1] Filing a Protest

Protests are filed directly with GAO, not with the contracting agency. A copy of the protest, however, should be sent to the contracting agency at the time the protest is filed. Solicitations generally contain the provision at FAR 52.233-2 designating an individual (usually the contracting officer) for service of a protest.

[a] Manner of Protest

Historically, all protests were filed with GAO in writing by hand delivery, mail, commercial carrier, facsimile, or other electronic means. In 2018, GAO launched the Electronic Protest Docketing System (EPDS), an automated case management system that allows parties to file and access documents over the Internet. GAO updated its protest regulations and issued guidance requiring all new protest to be filed via EPDS except those containing classified material, 4 C.F.R. § 21.2(b). Upon filing, EPDS will automatically generate an e-mail, copying the protester, notifying the procuring agency that a new protest has been filed. "Filing a document in EPDS constitutes notice to all parties of that filing," 21 C.F.R. § 21.0(g).

Protests are properly filed on a day if they are received in EPDS by 5:30 p.m., eastern time, 4 C.F.R. § 21.0(g). Where a protest is transmitted to GAO outside of business hours, GAO will consider the protest to have been filed at the time GAO next opens for business following receipt of the submissions, *FitNet Purchasing Alliance*, Comp. Gen. Dec. B-400553, 2008 CPD ¶ 177; *Guam Shipyard*, Comp. Gen. Dec. B-294287, 2004 CPD ¶ 181.

4 C.F.R. § 21.1(c) provides that the protest must:

> (1) Include the name, street address, email address, and telephone and facsimile numbers of the protester,
> (2) Be signed by the protester or its representative,
> (3) Identify the contracting agency and the solicitation and/or contract number,
> (4) Set forth a detailed statement of the legal and factual grounds of protest including copies of relevant documents,
> (5) Set forth all information establishing that the protester is an interested party for the purpose of filing a protest,
> (6) Set forth all information establishing the timeliness of the protest,
> (7) Specifically request a ruling by the Comptroller General of the United States, and
> (8) State the form of relief requested.

In addition, ¶ (d) provides that a protest may:

> (1) Request a protective order,

(2) Request specific documents, explaining the relevancy of the documents to the protest grounds, and

(3) Request a hearing, explaining the reasons that a hearing is needed to resolve the protest.

Failure to specifically request a ruling by GAO or to state the form of relief requested has not been considered a fatal defect to the consideration of the protest on the merits, *Air Shunt Instruments*, Comp. Gen. Dec. B-293766, 2004 CPD ¶ 125; *Carolina Auto Processing*, Comp. Gen. Dec. B-226841, 87-2 CPD ¶ 8; *Container Prods. Corp.*, 64 Comp. Gen. 641 (B-218556), 85-1 CPD ¶ 727.

[b] Detailed Statement

The protest must include a detailed statement of its legal and factual grounds, 4 C.F.R. § 21.1(c). In *Mercer Prods. & Mfg. Co.*, Comp. Gen. Dec. B-251126, 92-2 CPD ¶ 385, GAO dismissed a request for reconsideration because the protester did not provide a detailed statement as to why it believed the awards to be improper. In *Image Contracting, Inc.*, Comp. Gen. Dec. B-245599, 91-2 CPD ¶ 588, GAO found that a detailed statement of the protest was insufficient because it merely stated that the technical specifications for the project were inadequate. In discussing the importance of the detailed statement, GAO stated:

> This requirement is intended to provide us and the agency with a sufficient understanding of the grounds for the protest and with an opportunity to consider and resolve the matter without disrupting the orderly process of government procurement.

In *Coffman Specialists, Inc.*, Comp. Gen. Dec. B-400706.2, 2008 CPD ¶ 211, GAO held that the protester failed to state sufficient legal and factual grounds for it to consider the protest, stating, "by [the protester's] own admission, in filing its protest 'prematurely,' it made 'certain assumptions . . . on the basis of belief,' acknowledging that it 'still does not have knowledge that the bases it makes [in its] protest are true and accurate,' and that it 'makes the allegations based on its good faith belief.'"

Protests will be denied if the legal or factual grounds are unconvincing on their face. See *FPM Remediations, Inc.*, Comp. Gen. Dec. B-401017.2, 2009 CPD ¶ 88 (protester's failure to receive a small business award resulted from its inaccurate representation that it was eligible for a HUBZone award, not from any violation of procurement law or regulation by the agency); *Med-South, Inc.*, Comp. Gen. Dec. B-401214, 2009 CPD ¶ 112 (no evidence to support contentions that the three offerors that responded to the solicitation cannot meet a solicitation requirement to be "established" in the state of Alabama and cannot comply with the "non-manufacturing rule" requirement); *View One, Inc.*, Comp.

Gen. Dec. B-400346, 2008 CPD ¶ 142 (bare allegations that the agency "failed to perform a proper price/technical tradeoff" with neither evidence nor explanation to support it theory); *Siebe Envtl. Controls*, Comp. Gen. Dec. B-275999.2, 97-1 CPD ¶ 70 (protester's belief that it has been and would be a good contractor and that it submitted a proposal that met all necessary criteria so that it should not have been excluded from competitive range); and *TAAS Israel Indus., Inc.*, Comp. Gen. Dec. B-251789, 94-1 CPD ¶ 197 (mere allegation that the agency's determination was wrong).

[2] Actions Following Receipt of Protest

Upon receipt of a protest, an agency has two courses of action. It can either take corrective action or defend against the protest.

[a] Solving the Problem

Prior to GAO resolving a protest, an agency may, on its own initiative, take corrective action. In such cases, GAO will dismiss the protest, *Adams & Assocs., Inc.*, Comp. Gen. Dec. B-417120, 2019 CPD ¶ 21.

[i] Discretion to Take Corrective Action

Contracting officials in negotiated procurements have broad discretion to take corrective action, before or after a protest has been decided, when the agency determines that such action is necessary to ensure fair and impartial competition, *Leidos, Inc.*, Comp. Gen. Dec. B-418242, 2020 CPD ¶ 93; *MayaTech Corp.*, Comp. Gen. Dec. B-400491.4, 2009 CPD ¶ 55. The principal constraint on this authority is that the corrective action must be appropriate to remedy the impropriety, *Computing Devices Int'l*, Comp. Gen. Dec. B-258554.3, 94-2 CPD ¶ 162. As long as the agency acts in good faith, GAO will find that the agency's corrective action is appropriate. Compare *ZAFER Constr. Co.*, Comp. Gen. Dec. B-401871.4, 2010 CPD ¶ 88 (rejecting argument that corrective action was overbroad where Army invited entirely new proposal submissions and explained that due to the time lapse between proposal submission and the corrective action, the agency was concerned that the original price proposals submitted by the offerors would no longer accurately reflect the offerors' costs for the project and that the need to take corrective action also provided an opportunity to allow offerors to improve the quality of their technical submissions to account for any changed circumstances between the original proposal submission and the time of corrective action), with *Honeywell Tech. Solutions, Inc.*, Comp. Gen. Dec. B-400771.6, 2009 CPD ¶ 49 (rejecting argument that corrective action is over-restrictive for not permitting complete proposals revisions where NASA's decision to update the past performance information from each offeror was a reasonable way to remedy the identified procurement impropriety while not affecting other portions of offerors' proposals and the evaluation thereof). See also *Pemco Aeroplex, Inc.*, Comp. Gen. Dec. B-310372.3, 2008 CPD ¶ 126 (since prior GAO decision was based on an informational deficiency in the agency's evaluation record, it was not unreasonable for the agency to correct that deficiency by performing and documenting the required analyses based on the information that was already available; protester's assertion that the agency was obligated to reopen discussions with all offerors was without merit); *ICON Consulting Grp., Inc.*, Comp. Gen. Dec. B-310431.2, 2008 CPD ¶ 38 (reasonable to allow protester opportunity to compete for an award with remaining unsuccessful offerors, but not permitting protester to compete for one of the two 8(a) contracts already awarded); *CMKC & Maint., Inc.*, Comp. Gen. Dec. B-293803.2, 2004 CPD ¶ 243 (within the agency's discretion to reevaluate the quotations and make a new award determination based on a fully documented evaluation record); *Hyperbaric Techs., Inc.*, Comp. Gen. Dec. B-293047.2, 2004 CPD ¶ 87 (reasonable to solicit and evaluate revised proposals and make new best value determination); *PCA Aerospace, Inc.*, Comp. Gen. Dec. B-293042.3, 2004 CPD ¶ 65 (rescinding contract reasonable where dramatic price differentials may reasonably be interpreted to suggest that offerors had dissimilar understandings of the requirements); *Strand Hunt Constr., Inc.*, Comp. Gen. Dec. B-292415, 2003 CPD ¶ 167 (terminating contract reasonable); *Computer Assocs. Int'l, Inc.*, Comp. Gen. Dec. B-292077.2, 2003 CPD ¶ 157 (limited request for price information from each vendor reasonable way to remedy the suspected procurement impropriety while not affecting other portions of vendor's quotes and the evaluation thereof); *Johnson Controls World Servs., Inc.*, Comp. Gen. Dec. B-286714.3, 2001 CPD ¶ 145 (reasonable in organizational conflict of interest protest to require party to terminate its teaming relationship with conflicted organization and make the contents of a database available to mitigate prior awardee's potential competitive advantage and potential impaired objectivity). It is not necessary for an agency to conclude that the protest is certain to be sustained before it may take corrective action. Even if the protest could be denied, the agency still has the prerogative to take corrective action, *Main Bldg. Maint., Inc.*, Comp. Gen. Dec. B-279191.3, 98-2 CPD ¶ 47.

Cases where GAO found the corrective action taken by the agency to have been unreasonable include *NavQSys, LLC*, Comp. Gen. Dec. B-417028, 2019 CPD ¶ 130 (agency failed to adequately document basis for corrective action); *Deloitte Consulting, LLP*, Comp. Gen. Dec. B-412125, 2016 CPD ¶ 355 (agency unreasonably limited scope of proposal revisions permitted during corrective action); *Ewing Constr. Co.*, Comp. Gen. Dec. B-401887.3, 2010 CPD ¶ 108 (agency downgraded rating from "significant weakness" to "deficiency" without reopening discussions to inform protester of downgrading); *American K-9 Detection Servs., Inc.*, Comp. Gen. Dec. B-400464.6, 2009 CPD ¶ 107 (disclosure of one offeror's price does not justify agency limiting of discussions to single issue which allowed one offeror to submit acceptable proposal but did not allow protester to improve its proposal); *Cooperativa Muratori Riuniti*,

Comp. Gen. Dec. B-294980.5, 2005 CPD ¶ 144 (where agency amends request for proposals after closing and permits offerors to submit revised proposals, it should permit offerors to revise aspects of their proposals that were not the subject of the amendment absent evidence that the amendment could not reasonably have any effect on other aspects of proposals, or that allowing such revisions would have a detrimental impact on the competitive process); and *Saltwater, Inc.—Recons.*, Comp. Gen. Dec. B-294121.3, 2005 CPD ¶ 33 (agency did not correct the issue that was raised in the original protest); *Rockwell Elec. Commerce Corp.*, Comp. Gen. Dec. B-286201.6, 2001 CPD ¶ 162 (agency did not correct original problems and only reopened discussions with one offeror in competitive range).

The Federal Circuit and Court of Federal Claims similarly recognize contracting officials' broad discretion to take corrective action where the agency determines that such action is necessary to ensure fair and impartial competition. See *Dell Fed. Sys., L.P. v. United States*, 906 F.3d 982 (Fed. Cir. 2018); *SP Sys., Inc. & DB Consulting Grp., Inc. v. United States*, 86 Fed. Cl. 1 (2009) (agency decision to follow GAO recommendation to correct mistake in evaluation of proposals without reopening competition reasonable even though it resulted in selecting a different contractor); *Carahsoft Tech. Corp. v. United States*, 86 Fed. Cl. 325 (2009) (agency made reasonable decision to allow another round of price proposals but no revised technical proposals except permitting original protester to withdraw an unacceptable indemnification clause); and *Consolidated Eng'g Servs., Inc. v. United States*, 64 Fed. Cl. 617 (2005) (agency decision to expand the scope of the corrective action to permit revisions to key personnel and subcontactors reasonable, as was its decision to limit revisions to those areas). Compare *Sheridan Corp. v. United States*, 94 Fed. Cl. 663 (2010), where the court found that reopening the competition after award based on initial proposals when the protest issue was unfair evaluation of proposals, was totally unnecessary and unfairly allowed the losing competitors to submit new prices knowing the winning offeror's price.

[ii] Types of Corrective Action

An agency may take any corrective action that GAO recommends, such as amending the solicitation and requesting proposal revisions, *Computing Devices Int'l*, Comp. Gen. Dec. B-258554.3, 94-2 CPD ¶ 162; *Federal Sec. Sys., Inc.*, Comp. Gen. Dec. B-281745.2, 99-1 CPD ¶ 86; *International Res. Grp.*, Comp. Gen. Dec. B-286683, 2001 CPD ¶ 35; canceling the solicitation and resoliciting, *Noelke GmbH*, Comp. Gen. Dec. B-278324.2, 98-1 CPD ¶ 46; reopening negotiations, *Rockville Mailing Serv., Inc.*, Comp. Gen. Dec. B-270161.2, 96-1 CPD ¶ 184; terminating the contract and reevaluating proposals, *Strand Hunt Constr., Inc.*, Comp. Gen. Dec. B-292415, 2003 CPD ¶ 167; *Aquidneck Sys. Int'l, Inc.*, Comp. Gen. Dec. B-257170.2, 94-2 CPD ¶ 122; or payment of the protester's proposal preparation costs, *Southern Techs., Inc.*, Comp. Gen. Dec.

B-278030, 97-2 CPD ¶ 167. In addition, subsequent to an ADR "outcome prediction," an agency may re-open a solicitation and allow offerors to make only limited revisions to their proposals, *Consolidated Eng'g Servs., Inc. v. United States*, 64 Fed. Cl. 617 (2005).

[b] Conducting the Protest

GAO is required to decide a protest in 100 calendar days, 31 U.S.C. § 3554(a). To comply with this requirement, GAO protest procedures specify the precise times when the parties must take actions or deliver documents. These times are set to permit the parties adequate time to prepare documents while giving GAO time to decide the protest.

[i] Notification

GAO has one day to notify the contracting agency of GAO's receipt of the protest, 31 U.S.C. § 3553(b)(1); 4 C.F.R. § 21.3(a). As discussed above, the time for invoking a suspension of contract performance under 31 U.S.C. § 3553(d) continues to run until the agency receives notice of the protest from GAO, and there is no recourse if GAO fails to comply with this one-day notification requirement. This practical problem is largely resolved by the automatic notice generated by the EPDS system.

[ii] Requests for Dismissal

GAO may summarily dismiss a protest because the protest is untimely, the protester does not qualify as an interested party, or the protest fails to meet the requirement of specificity, 4 C.F.R. § 21.5. In addition, this GAO rule lists the substantive issues it will not consider in a protest, effectively identifying the most common basis for dismissal, including matters of contract administration, issues within the purview of the SBA, suspensions and debarments, protests by other than federal agencies, and subcontract protests.

[iii] Early Request for Documents

A protest may include a request for the early release of documents relevant to the protest, 4 C.F.R. § 21.1(d)(2). In such cases, the agency should send the documents to the protester as quickly as possible or arrange for an on-site review of documents. When such a request is made, the contracting agency must provide to all parties and GAO a list of the documents released and the documents that the agency intends to withhold from the protester, as well as the reasons for such withholding, 4 C.F.R. § 21.3(c). Objections to any proposed withholdings must be submitted to GAO within two days of the receipt of the list.

This procedure is intended to facilitate the resolution of disputes about the release of documents and to enable the protester to more easily meet the time limitations imposed after receipt of the agency report, 61 Fed. Reg. 39041 (July 26, 1996). However, the procedure is required only when the protester submits a specific request for release of documents at the time the protest is filed.

[iv] Agency Report

31 U.S.C. § 3553(f) requires that a protest file be made available to the parties to the protest. The contracting agency must file its report within 30 calendar days from the date it receives notification from GAO of receipt of protest, 4 C.F.R. § 21.3(c). The agency must simultaneously send a copy of the report to the protester and any intervenors, 4 C.F.R. § 21.3(e). If a protective order has been issued, parties under the protective order will receive the entire file. Those not under the protective order will receive only a redacted version. If no protective order has been issued, only GAO will receive protected documents.

4 C.F.R. § 21.3(d) provides that the agency report should include:

> the contracting officer's statement of the relevant facts, including a best estimate of the contract value, a memorandum of law, and a list and a copy of all relevant documents, or portions of documents, not previously produced, including, as appropriate: the protest; the bid or proposal submitted by the protester; the bid or proposal of the firm which is being considered for award, or whose bid or proposal is being protested; all evaluation documents; the solicitation, including the specifications; the abstract of bids or offers; and any other relevant documents. In appropriate cases, the contracting agency may request that the protester produce relevant documents, or portions of documents, that are not in the agency's possession.

The procuring agency may request an extension of time for submission of the agency report, 4 C.F.R. § 21.3(f). GAO will grant an extension of time on a case-by-case basis, *Blue Rock Structures, Inc.*, Comp. Gen. Dec. B-400811, 2009 CPD ¶ 26; *Military Agency Servs. Pty., Ltd.*, Comp. Gen. Dec. B-290414, 2002 CPD ¶ 130.

[v] Reverse Discovery

"In appropriate cases, the contracting agency may request that the protester produce relevant documents, or portions of documents, that are not in the agency's possession," 4 C.F.R. § 21.3(d). This is known as the reverse discovery rule. This rule is narrowly construed. In *Boeing Co.*, Comp. Gen. Dec. B-311344, 2008 CPD ¶ 114, Boeing objected to the Air Force request to produce broad categories of documents bearing upon, among other things, Boeing's interpretation of the solicitation and several of its protest allegations. The agency responded that its request was reasonable and limited, and sought relevant documents, which would be "necessary to allow GAO to perform a complete and accurate review of the issues in Boeing's protests." GAO denied the Air Force request, stating that its regulations do not provide for wide-open discovery requests by the agency.

[vi] Additional Documents

If a protester becomes aware of the existence of relevant documents after submission of the initial protest, it has two days from the time it first knew or should have known of the existence of additional documents to submit a written request for them to GAO and the agency, 4 C.F.R. § 21.3(g). This provision further provides that the agency must then respond within two days either with the documents, or a portion of the documents, and a list or with an explanation for why it is not required to produce the documents. GAO has stated that this procedure may not be used "to obtain information that will give rise to, or otherwise perfect a basis of protest," *Highland Eng'g, Inc.*, Comp. Gen. Dec. B-402634, 2010 CPD ¶ 137; *Quimba Software*, Comp. Gen. Dec. B-299000, 2007 CPD ¶ 14.

GAO will decide any dispute that arises concerning the release of withheld documents and whether this should be done under a protective order, 4 C.F.R. § 21.3(h). When withheld documents are provided, the protester's comments on the agency report must be filed within the original comment filing period unless GAO determines that an extension is appropriate, 4 C.F.R. § 21.3(h).

[vii] Comments on Agency Report

Comments on the agency report must be filed with GAO within 10 calendar days after receipt of the report, with a copy provided to the contracting agency and other participating parties, 4 C.F.R. § 21.3(i). Under this provision, if the protester fails to file comments or a written statement expressing continuing interest within the deadline, GAO will dismiss the protest, *Keymiaee Aero-Tech, Inc.—Recons.*, Comp. Gen. Dec. B-274803.3, 97-1 CPD ¶ 163; *Carmon Constr., Inc.*, Comp. Gen. Dec. B-271316.2, 96-2 CPD ¶ 3. In addition, if the protester fails to respond to the rebuttal of any protest issue, GAO will consider that the protester has abandoned that issue, *Dynamic Instruments, Inc.*, Comp. Gen. Dec. B-291071, 2002 CPD ¶ 183; *Strategic Resources, Inc.*, Comp. Gen. Dec. B-287398, 2001 CPD ¶ 131; *O. Ames Co.*, Comp. Gen. Dec. B-283943, 2000 CPD ¶ 20.

Protests are rarely sustained where the protester does not file substantive comments on the report. See, for example, *DUCOM, Inc.*, Comp. Gen. Dec. B-285485, 2000 CPD ¶ 144, where GAO noted that the Army provided a detailed response to each evaluation challenge raised in DUCOM's protest. DUCOM's comments on the agency report specifically addressed just two issues, which involved only six of 20 disadvantages noted by the SSEB. In the absence of any argument from DUCOM to the contrary, GAO held it had no basis to find the Army's evaluation unreasonable.

[viii] Supplemental Issues

A protester may raise new grounds for protest if the new grounds were first discovered upon receipt of the agency report and the protester raises these supplemental issues within 10 days of its receipt of the agency report, *Anteon Corp.*, Comp. Gen. Dec. B-293523, 2004 CPD ¶ 51. Typically, the 10-day deadline to file comments on the agency report and 10-day deadline for supplemental protest issues coincide to provide a single filing deadline in response to the agency report. The timeliness deadline for supplemental protest issues, however, is more strictly enforced. While GAO occasionally exercises its discretion to extend the deadline for comments on the agency report, GAO has held that such an extension does not and cannot serve to extend the 10-day deadline for supplemental protests. See *InGenesis, Inc.*, Comp. Gen. Dec. B-416564.3, 2020 CPD ¶ 120; *Planning & Dev. Collaborative Int'l*, Comp. Gen. Dec. B-299041, 2007 CPD ¶ 28; *ATA Def. Indus., Inc.*, Comp. Gen. Dec. B-282511.8, 2000 CPD ¶ 81.

[ix] Further Submissions

Although no further submissions are specifically provided for in the rules, GAO may permit or request further submissions by the parties, 4 C.F.R. § 21.3(j). In practice, particularly in postaward protests, the administrative record often reveals supplemental bases of protest filed simultaneously with the protester's comments. Once the supplemental protest grounds are filed, GAO will require the agency to promptly file a supplemental report, followed by comments on the supplemental report and the potential for further rounds of supplemental protest.

[3] Protective Orders

GAO is authorized by statute to issue protective orders, 31 U.S.C. § 3553(f)(2). 4 C.F.R. § 21.4(a) provides:

> At the request of a party or on its own initiative, GAO may issue a protective order controlling the treatment of protected information. Such information may include proprietary, confidential, or source-selection-sensitive material, as well as other information the release of which could result in a competitive advantage to one or more firms. The protective order shall establish procedures for application for access to protected information, identification and safeguarding of that information, and submission of redacted copies of documents omitting protective information. Because a protective order serves to facilitate the pursuit of a protest by a protester through counsel, it is the responsibility of protester's counsel to request that a protective order be issued and to submit timely applications for admission under that order.

If there is no protective order, proprietary and procurement-sensitive documents must be furnished to GAO but not to nongovernmental parties, 4 C.F.R. § 21.4(b).

[a] Admissible Parties

Three kinds of parties may be admitted under the protective order: (1) outside counsel, (2) in-house counsel, and (3) experts or consultants. The result is that if a protester is not represented by counsel, it will be denied access to proprietary and procurement-sensitive documents, *PPG-CMS-PSI JV*, Comp. Gen. Dec. B-298239, 2006 CPD ¶ 111; *JoaQuin Mfg. Corp.*, Comp. Gen. Dec. B-275185, 97-1 CPD ¶ 48. In such cases, a GAO attorney will review the withheld documents to determine if they support the protester's arguments, *Encompass Group LLC*, Comp. Gen. Dec. B-310940.3, 2009 CPD ¶ 60; *TEAM Support Servs., Inc.*, Comp. Gen. Dec. B-279379.2, 98-1 CPD ¶ 167. See also *Dominion Aviation, Inc.,—Recons.*; Comp. Gen. Dec. B-275419.4, 98-1 CPD ¶ 62, denying a motion to reconsider issues found in the redacted GAO decision that was based on its review of proprietary materials that had not been released to the protester because it had no counsel. GAO stated that the protester had made a business decision not to retain counsel and obtain access to information under the protective order and could not later raise protest grounds based on information it essentially opted not to receive earlier.

In determining whether counsel should be admitted under a protective order, GAO will look to whether the attorney is involved in the competitive decision-making process and whether there is otherwise an unacceptable risk of inadvertent disclosure of protected information, *WellPoint Military Care Corp.*, Comp. Gen. Dec. B-415222.5, 2019 CPD ¶ 168. Where an attorney is involved in competitive decision-making, the attorney will not be granted access to proprietary data of another company because there is an unacceptable risk of inadvertent disclosure of protected material, *U.S. Steel Corp. v. United States*, 730 F.2d 1465 (Fed. Cir. 1984).

Although it is often easier to establish that outside counsel is not involved in the decision-making process, GAO will determine the admission of counsel on a case-by-case basis. See *AirTrak Travel*, Comp. Gen. Dec. B-292101, 2003 CPD ¶ 117, where GAO admitted outside counsel based on evidence that the agency had competent in-house counsel to participate in competitive decision-making and the counsel was hired on a case-by-case basis. Compare *Allied-Signal Aerospace Co.*, Comp. Gen. Dec. B-250822, 93-1 CPD ¶ 201, where GAO excluded outside counsel because they were also officials involved in competitive decision-making for the firms they represented. See also *Colonial Storage Co.*, Comp. Gen. Dec. B-253501.5, 93-2 CPD ¶ 234, where GAO did not admit an interested party's counsel under a protective order because the counsel had represented the interested party at a presolicitation conference and had also participated in price discussions between the interested party and the agency. Although an individual outside counsel may be excluded from admission under the protective order, other attorneys from the same law firm may be admitted if adequate procedures are in place to guarantee access by only those attorneys admitted, *Mine Safety Appliances Co.*, Comp. Gen. Dec. B-242379.2, 91-2 CPD ¶ 506.

In-house counsel who are not involved in competitive decision-making may be admitted under a protective order when the risk of inadvertent disclosure of proprietary or procurement-sensitive information is small, *Robbins-Gioia, Inc.*, Comp. Gen. Dec. B-274318, 96-2 CPD ¶ 222. In *Earle Palmer Brown Cos.*, Comp. Gen. Dec. B-243544, 91-2 CPD ¶ 134, GAO stated:

> In determining whether to grant access to protected material, we consider such factors as whether counsel primarily advises on litigation matters or also advises on pricing and production decisions, including the review of bids and proposals, the degree of physical separation and security with respect to those who participate in competitive decision-making and level of supervision to which in-house counsel is subject.

Here, GAO denied admittance under the protective order, stating that the direct relationship between the chief executive officer of the company and in-house counsel made the risk of inadvertent disclosure too high. Similarly in *McDonnell Douglas Corp.*, Comp. Gen. Dec. B-259694.2, 95-2 CPD ¶ 51, GAO denied admittance under the protective order because the in-house counsel were in the position of advising the firm's competitive strategists. See also *TRW, Inc.*, Comp. Gen. Dec. B-243450.2, 91-2 CPD ¶ 160, where, in denying admittance under the protective order, GAO stated that there were only two attorneys in the office and, thus, the general legal counsel would likely be relied on to render legal advice on many subjects, including business-related decisions.

Similarly, with regard to experts or consultants, if the risk of inadvertent disclosure is too high, GAO will not admit such individuals under a protective order. In *Harmonia Holdings Grp., LLC*, Comp. Gen. Dec. B-417475, 2019 CPD ¶ 333, GAO rejected a technical consultant's application based on representations that he provided marketing and proposal support, among other concerns. In *Systems Research & Applications Corp.*, Comp. Gen. Dec. B-299818, 2008 CPD ¶ 28, GAO held that admission of a consultant to a GAO protective order was appropriate, over the objection that the consultant once held a position with the protester and that the consultant's daughter was currently employed by the protester. GAO stated that the record showed that the consultant had no continuing interest in the protester and the consultant's daughter held a relatively low-level position with the protester in a division that was unrelated to the work to be performed under the protested contract. In *Restoration & Closure Servs., LLC*, Comp. Gen. Dec. B-295663.12, 2005 CPD ¶ 92, GAO denied the consultants' applications for admission to the protective order. The applications agreed to restrict the consultants' activities only with regard to the particular site for the procurement being protested and thus permitted the consultants to engage or assist in the preparation of proposals for the same type of work at other sites where a party to the protest could be a competitor. *Bendix Field Eng'g Corp.*, Comp. Gen. Dec. B-246236, 92-1 CPD ¶ 227, is an interesting case where the agency requested that admission of experts to a protective order be made contingent upon a promise to avoid participation in future procurements for prepositioning for a period of five years. GAO found this to be reasonable given the large dollar value of the contract and the competition-sensitive nature of the information to be made available to the experts.

Even if there is little risk of inadvertent disclosure, if the information is highly sensitive, GAO may decline to admit experts or consultants, *EER Sys. Corp.*, Comp. Gen. Dec. B-256383, 94-1 CPD ¶ 354 (information contained proprietary engineering approaches and solutions that would be invaluable to any practicing engineer).

If the terms of the protective order are violated, both counsel and client are subject to a variety of sanctions, including dismissal of the protect. See *PWC Logistics Servs. Co. KSC(c)*, Comp. Gen. Dec. B-310559, 2008 CPD ¶ 25 (GAO dismissed protest after protester's attorney, who had been admitted under protective order, revealed protected information to protester); *Network Secs. Tech., Inc.*, Comp. Gen. Dec. B-290741.2, 2002 CPD ¶ 193 (GAO provides notice that, in a future case, it might impose the sanction of dismissal where protester's attorney discloses protected information to client).

[b] Procedure

An individual seeking admission under a protective order must submit an application to GAO with copies furnished to all other parties, 4 C.F.R. § 21.4(c). See Guide to GAO Protective Orders, GAO-09-770SP (June 2009) for sample forms. Although there is no time limit for filing an application, it should be done as soon as possible. Parties have two days to object to the applicant's admission, 4 C.F.R. § 21.4(c). GAO may, however, consider objections raised after that time.

[4] Alternative Dispute Resolution

GAO has also adopted alternative dispute resolution (ADR) procedures to more efficiently resolve protests. 4 C.F.R. § 21.0(h) provides:

> Alternative dispute resolution encompasses various means of resolving cases expeditiously, without a written decision, including techniques such as outcome prediction and negotiation assistance.

GAO may use alternative dispute resolution procedures at the request of one or more of the parties, or where GAO deems appropriate. This may take the form of negotiation assistance either before or after a protest is filed, or outcome prediction, where GAO will advise the parties of the likely outcome of the protest in order to allow the party likely to be unsuccessful to take appropriate action to resolve the protest without a written decision.

With negotiation assistance ADR, a GAO attorney acts as a facilitator. If settlement is reached, the protest is withdrawn or rendered academic. If no settlement is reached, GAO will issue a written decision.

With outcome prediction ADR, a GAO attorney concludes, based on precedent and/or facts, and with the concurrence of supervising attorneys, that one party is likely to prevail. It is initiated either by a party's request or by the GAO attorney. The purpose is to share the view of GAO regarding the likely outcome, therein saving the parties' time and resources. These predictions have proven to be highly reliable—with the result that when a party is advised that it is likely to lose the protest, it should proceed in accordance with the prediction.

[5] Hearings

A hearing on the protest is permitted at the request of one of the parties or on GAO's initiative, 4 C.F.R. § 21.7(a). A hearing is not automatic but, rather, is held at the discretion of GAO, *Jack Faucett Assocs.*, Comp. Gen. Dec. B-254421, 94-2 CPD ¶ 72. Requests for hearings must set forth the reasons why a hearing is necessary, 4 C.F.R. § 21.7(a). See *Spectrum Sys., Inc.*, Comp. Gen. Dec. B-401130, 2009 CPD ¶ 110, denying a request for a hearing because the protester provided no reasonable basis for the necessity of a hearing and no legitimate reason for a hearing was apparent. GAO stated:

> As a general rule, we conduct hearings where there is a factual dispute between the parties which cannot be resolved without oral examination or without assessing witness credibility, or where an issue is so complex that developing the protest record through a hearing is more efficient and less burdensome than proceeding with written pleadings only. Absent evidence that a protest record is questionable or incomplete, this Office will not hold a bid protest hearing merely to permit the protester to orally reiterate its protest allegations or otherwise search for additional grounds of protest since such action would undermine our ability to resolve protests expeditiously and without undue disruption of the procurement process.

A prehearing conference (usually by telephone) is generally conducted prior to the hearing to decide on the timing, the procedures to be followed, the issues to be considered, and the witnesses who will be called to testify, 4 C.F.R. § 21.7(b).

Generally, hearings are conducted as soon as practicable after receipt by the parties of the agency report and relevant documents, 4 C.F.R. § 21.7(c). Hearings are usually limited to one day and are conducted at GAO in Washington, D.C., or, at the discretion of GAO, at other locations, 4 C.F.R. § 21.7(c).

Witnesses are not sworn but are reminded that false testimony may subject them to criminal penalties. If a witness fails to appear or to answer a question,

GAO may draw inferences unfavorable to the party for whom the witness would have testified, 4 C.F.R. § 21.7(f). In *HEROS, Inc.*, Comp. Gen. Dec. B-292043, 2003 CPD ¶ 111, GAO concluded that the sole source contractor did not have proprietary data blocking a competitive procurement, based partly on the fact the company refused to permit any cross-examination of its key witnesses. See also *Network Sec. Techs., Inc.*, Comp. Gen. Dec. B-290741.2, 2002 CPD ¶ 193 (GAO drew unfavorable inference regarding a violation of a protective order because of former counsel's failure to appear at GAO hearing); *Du & Assocs., Inc.*, Comp. Gen. Dec. B-280283.3, 98-2 CPD ¶ 156 (GAO inferred that a CO did not give a purported instruction to the protester because neither a witness nor a document alleged to prove the instruction were produced).

Post-hearing comments are to be submitted within five days of the hearing unless GAO sets a different time, 4 C.F.R. § 21.7(g).

[6] Time for Decision

GAO has 100 calendar days to render a decision on a protest.

[a] Statutory Deadline

The 100 calendar days deadline begins the day the protest is submitted to GAO, 31 U.S.C. § 3554(a)(1). Although there is no specific exception authorizing an extension of time, where supplemental protests have been filed, GAO may "roll over" a protest—that is, dismiss the earlier protest and incorporate it into the last supplemental protest, 31 U.S.C. § 3554(a)(2). This, in effect, can extend the time taken to have the protest decided well beyond the 100-calendar-day period.

[b] Express Option

In cases that can be decided on an expeditious basis, GAO may decide to use the "express option procedures," calling for a decision within 65 calendar days. A request for use of the express option may be submitted by any party in writing and must be received by GAO within five days after the protest or supplemental protest is filed, 4 C.F.R. § 21.10(c). When the express option is used, the following schedule applies, as set forth in 4 C.F.R. § 21.10(d):

> (1) The contracting agency shall file a complete report with GAO and the parties within 20 days after it receives notice from GAO that the express option will be used.
>
> (2) Comments on the agency report shall be filed with GAO and the other parties within 5 days after receipt of the report.
>
> (3) If a hearing is held, no separate comments on the agency report under paragraph (d)(2) of this section should be submitted unless specifically

> requested by GAO. Consolidated comments on the agency report and hearing shall be filed within 5 days after the hearing was held or as specified by GAO.
>
> (4) Where circumstances demonstrate that a case is no longer suitable for resolution using the express option, GAO shall establish a new schedule for submissions by the parties.

For cases using the express option procedures, see *B&S Transp., Inc.*, Comp. Gen. Dec. B-299144, 2007 CPD ¶ 16 (granted agency's request to use the express option where agency contended that fast-tracking would allow it to meet its deadlines in the Army's Base Realignment and Closure plan); *AshBritt Inc.*, Comp. Gen. Dec. B-297889, 2006 CPD ¶ 48 (express option used pursuant to agency request); *Integrated Support Sys. Inc.*, Comp. Gen. Dec. B-283137.2, 99-2 CPD ¶ 51; *Aalco Forwarding, Inc.*, Comp. Gen. Dec. B-277241.20, 98-2 CPD ¶ 1 (express option utilized in procurement with 99 protesters); and *Possehn Consulting*, Comp. Gen. Dec. B-278579, 98-1 CPD ¶ 10.

[c] Summary Decision and Accelerated Schedule

At the request of a party or on its own initiative, GAO may set up an accelerated schedule for deciding a protest and may issue a summary decision on a protest, 4 C.F.R. § 21.10(e).

[d] Decision Distribution

Decisions are distributed to the parties through the EPDS. If the decision is protected, only the parties under the protective order and the contracting agency will receive copies. Protected decisions are redacted and then made available to the public. Protest decisions are available electronically, per 4 C.F.R. § 21.12.

[7] Reconsiderations

GAO will reconsider a protest decision at the request of a protester, an intervenor, or a federal agency involved in the protest, 4 C.F.R. § 21.14. Copies of the request must be sent to all parties that participated in the protest.

The request for reconsideration must be filed within 10 calendar days of the date the basis for the request for reconsideration was or should have been known, 4 C.F.R. § 21.14(b). Normally, that is 10 days after receipt of the decision, but if the protester learns of the decision in some other way, the 10-day rule will be enforced strictly. See *Speedy Food Serv., Inc.*, Comp. Gen. Dec. B-274406.2, 97-1 CPD ¶ 5, where the request for reconsideration was dismissed as untimely because it was not filed within 10 days of the time the protester saw the decision on the Internet. In *Sodexho Mgmt., Inc.—Costs*, Comp. Gen. Dec. B-289605.3, 2003 CPD ¶ 136, GAO found an untimely request when the agency did not file within 10 days of learning of the basis for its request for reconsideration when the protester submitted its initial cost claim with supporting documentation.

The request for reconsideration must do more than restate the arguments in the initial protest. 4 C.F.R. § 21.14(a) provides:

> GAO will not consider a request for reconsideration that does not contain a detailed statement of the factual and legal grounds upon which reversal or modification is deemed warranted, specifying any errors of law made or information not previously considered.

In *Tri-Star Indus.*, Comp. Gen. Dec. B-254767.3, 94-1 CPD ¶388, GAO stated that the request for reconsideration must be based on (1) the failure to consider evidence that should have been considered, (2) newly discovered evidence that the party could not reasonably have furnished for the initial consideration, or (3) errors of law. See *MadahCom, Inc.—Recons.*, Comp. Gen. Dec. B-297261.2, 2005 CPD ¶209 (wrong timeliness standard applied); *Dep't of the Navy*, Comp. Gen. Dec. B-237342.2, 90-2 CPD ¶39 (GAO misread agency record); and *Gracon Corp.*, Comp. Gen. Dec. B-236603.2, 90-1 CPD ¶496 (labor hours for electrical work considered in prior protest were in error). More often, the party seeking reconsideration fails to provide a basis for reconsideration. See *U.S. Marine Corps—Recons.*, Comp. Gen. Dec. B-415171, 2019 CPD ¶5 (request failed to demonstrate that prior decision contained errors of fact or law to present information not previously considered); *Small Business Admin.—Recons.*, Comp. Gen. Dec. B-401057.2, 2009 CPD ¶148 (SBA's request primarily states its disagreement with GAO legal analysis regarding the statutory requirements for HUBZone set-asides); *Metro Machine Corp.—Recons. & Modification of Recommendation*, Comp. Gen. Dec. B-311245.5, 2008 CPD ¶167 (awardee/requester showed no error in, but simply disagreed with, GAO recommendation that the agency conduct meaningful discussions); *Shields & Dean Concessions, Inc.—Recons.*, Comp. Gen. Dec. B-292901.4, 2004 CPD ¶71 (request did not show that decision contained no errors of fact or law, or present information not previously considered); *Social Security Administration; MCI WorldCom Commc'ns, Inc.—Recons.*, Comp. Gen. Dec. B-2086201.4, 2001 CPD ¶157 (GAO decision did not err in identifying the approximate potential value of Rockwell's price reduction under a fair and proper competition); and *RGII Techs., Inc.—Recons. & Protest*, B-278352.2, 98-1 CPD ¶130 (repetition of arguments made during consideration of the original protest and mere disagreement with GAO decision do not meet standard for reconsideration).

GAO rarely finds that the protester is offering newly discovered evidence that could not possibly have been furnished during the initial consideration, *Dep't of the Navy—Request for Modification of Remedy*, Comp. Gen. Dec. B-401102.3, 2009 CPD ¶162 (information not new where Navy failed to mention the DoD memoranda during the protest; it cannot now proffer this information and the associated arguments for the first time on reconsideration);

Allstate Van & Storage, Inc., Comp. Gen. Dec. B-270744.2, 96-2 CPD ¶ 72 (information proffered seven months after the protester had learned of the evidence not new).

There is no statutory deadline for issuing a decision on reconsideration. In addition, there is no requirement to withhold award or suspend performance during the pendency of the reconsideration, 4 C.F.R. § 21.14(c).

[F] Standards of Review

31 U.S.C. § 3554(b)(1) provides that GAO will review an agency action to determine if it "complies with statute or regulation." Under this standard, a protester must establish that the contracting agency has prejudicially violated a statute or regulation or has taken a discretionary action without a rational basis. GAO has given agencies considerable latitude in applying this rational basis standard to discretionary actions. The Federal Circuit has made clear that administrative protest authorities are not permitted to substitute their judgment for that of the agency, *Unisys Corp. v. Dep't of the Air Force*, GSBCA 13129-P, 95-2 BCA ¶ 27,622, *rev'd*, 98 F.3d 1325 (Fed. Cir. 1996).

GAO traditionally acted in accordance with this guidance of the court, as shown by standard language in GAO decisions in protests challenging the rationality of discretionary decisions of contracting agencies. See, for example, *North South Consulting Grp., LLC*, Comp. Gen. Dec. B-416849, 2019 CPD ¶ 3, stating:

> In reviewing an agency's evaluation of proposals and source selection decision, we examine the supporting record to determine whether the decision was reasonable, consistent with the stated evaluation criteria, and adequately documented. *Johnson Controls World Servs., Inc.*, B-289942, B-289942.2, May 24, 2002, 2002 CPD ¶ 88 at 6. The source selection official has broad discretion in determining the manner and extent to which he or she will make use of proposal evaluation results, and this judgment is governed only by the tests of rationality and consistency with the stated evaluation criteria. *Pacific-Gulf Marine, Inc.*, B-415375, B-415375.2, Jan. 2, 2018, 2018 CPD ¶ 124 at 7.

See also *Enterprise Servs., LLC*, Comp. Gen. Dec. B-415368.2, 2018 CPD ¶ 44, stating:

> It is not our role to independently evaluate proposals and substitute our judgment for that of the contracting activity. *Analytic Servs., Inc.*, B-405737, Dec. 28, 2011, 2012 CPD ¶ 16 at 8. Rather, we will review an evaluation to ensure that it was reasonable and consistent with the evaluation criteria in the solicitation and applicable procurement statutes and regulations; a protester's disagreement with the evaluation, without more, does not show that it lacked a reasonable basis. *Id.*

Similarly, in *Raytheon Co.*, Comp. Gen. Dec. B-416211, 2018 CPD ¶ 262, GAO stated:

> A protester's disagreement with the agency's judgment in its determination of the relative merit of competing proposals, without more, does not establish that the evaluation was unreasonable.

Nonetheless, there are numerous GAO decisions finding agency actions unreasonable. For example, the GAO Bid Protest Annual Report to Congress for Fiscal Year 2019, GAO-20-220SP (Nov. 05, 2019) identifies the five most prevalent reasons for sustaining protests during the 2019 fiscal year as (1) unreasonable technical evaluation; (2) inadequate documentation of the record; (3) flawed selection decision; (4) unequal treatment; and (5) unreasonable cost or price evaluation. Reports for prior and subsequent years contain similar information.

[G] Prejudice

Competitive prejudice is an essential element of every viable protest, 51 Comp. Gen. 678 (B-174367) (1972); *Lithos Restoration Ltd.*, 71 Comp. Gen. Dec. 367 (B-247003.2), 92-1 CPD ¶ 379. The protester must establish that but for the agency's actions, it would have had a substantial chance of receiving the award, *Armorworks Enters., LLC*, Comp. Gen. Dec. B-400394.3, 2009 CPD ¶ 79. Essentially the same standard is applied by the courts, *Statistica, Inc. v. United States*, 102 F.3d 1577 (Fed. Cir. 1996); *Bannum, Inc. v. United States*, 404 F.3d 1346 (Fed. Cir. 2005); *Galen Med. Assocs., Inc. v. United States*, 369 F.3d 1324 (Fed. Cir. 2004); *Information Tech. & Applications Corp. v. United States*, 316 F.3d 1312 (Fed. Cir. 2003). In some instances, GAO states the test as a "reasonable possibility that the protester would have otherwise been the successful offeror as a sufficient basis for sustaining a protest," *CDA Inv. Techs., Inc.*, Comp. Gen. Dec. B-272093.3, 97-1 CPD ¶ 103; *Truetech, Inc.*, Comp. Gen. Dec. B-402536.2, 2010 CPD ¶ 129. The Federal Circuit in *Statistica* stated that "reasonable likelihood" should be interpreted to be the same as "substantial chance."

General allegations of prejudice will not suffice. See *MCI Constructors, Inc.*, Comp. Gen. Dec. B-274347, 96-2 CPD ¶ 210, where GAO found a failure to show prejudice when the protester failed to present information showing how it could reduce its price by the nearly $7 million margin with the low offeror. See also *Labrador Airways Ltd.*, Comp. Gen. Dec. B-241608, 91-1 CPD ¶ 167, where the protester did not demonstrate to GAO that it was prejudiced because the agency relaxed specifications for commercial flight services for one offeror. The protester alleged in general terms that on past contracts this requirement resulted in a net cost to the protester, but failed to provide any information showing how it calculated this cost or how much of this cost was included in its offer.

Protesters have readily demonstrated prejudice when they have been denied the opportunity to revise their proposals in the same manner as a competitor. For example, in *Global Assocs. Ltd.*, Comp. Gen. Dec. B-271693, 96-2 CPD ¶ 100, GAO found that the protester was prejudiced when the agency conducted discussions with only the awardee after the submission of best and final offers.

Where GAO finds an agency failed to hold meaningful discussions, GAO "will resolve any doubts concerning the prejudicial effect of the agency's action in favor of the protester; a reasonably possibility of prejudice is a sufficient basis for sustaining the protest," *Delfasco, LLC*, B-409514, 2016 CPD ¶ 192. See also *Cotton & Co., LLP*, Comp. Gen. Dec. B-282808, 99-2 CPD ¶ 48 (finding prejudice based on misleading discussions of weakness where awardee was higher priced and protester could have revised proposal to resolve agency concerns); *Ogden Support Servs., Inc.*, Comp. Gen. Dec. B-270354, 96-1 CPD ¶ 175 (sustaining protest where agency engaged in misleading discussions and did not inform the protester of the evaluated weaknesses and deficiencies in its proposal because it would have had an opportunity to improve its score to a level approaching the awardee's score and its proposal may well have remained low in cost). But see *McDonald-Bradley*, Comp. Gen. Dec. B-270126, 96-1 CPD ¶ 54, where an allegation that the protester was misled during discussions was denied because the protester did not demonstrate a reasonable possibility that it was prejudiced. The protester argued that the agency misled the firm during discussions into believing that its proposed wages had to be consistent with the Service Contract Act requirements, but GAO found no proof that the protester would have lowered its wages further in its BAFO or that an adjustment to the protester's price would have made its pricecompetitive. Similarly, in *Alliance Tech. Servs., Inc.*, Comp. Gen. Dec. B-311329, 2008 CPD ¶ 108, GAO found no prejudice by lack of meaningful discussions because even with a perfect score under the particular subfactor where the discussions were allegedly not meaningful, the total evaluated score would have remained lower technically than the other two awardees' proposals, and its price would remain higher than both awardees' prices. See also *D.N. Am., Inc.*, Comp. Gen. Dec. B-292557, 2003 CPD ¶ 188 (protester had not shown that it would have or could have identified contracts of a larger size or that its subcontractor's references would have included other than contracts for hardware support had these issues been raised during discussions).

Prejudice has also been demonstrated when the agency makes errors in initiating the procurement. In *Comint Sys. Corp.*, Comp. Gen. Dec. B-274853, 97-1 CPD ¶ 14, the agency's letter offering a requirement to the SBA for acceptance into the 8(a) program failed to give complete and accurate information regarding the proposed offering. GAO found prejudice because the failure to provide the information deprived the SBA of the opportunity to make a fully informed decision with respect to the acquisition and deprived the protester of a potential opportunity to participate in the procurement.

Prejudice has been found where an agency materially relaxes its requirements for one offeror. See *George Hyman Constr. Co.*, Comp. Gen. Dec. B-265798, 95-2 CPD ¶ 173, where the agency relaxed a go/no-go key personnel experience evaluation criterion. GAO noted that the key personnel experience requirements were very restrictive and that a prospective offeror had requested that the requirements be amended to be less restrictive, which the agency declined to do. Additionally, one offeror was rejected as technically unacceptable for failing to meet these requirements. Thus, GAO held that there was a reasonable possibility of prejudice by relaxing these requirements for the awardee. In *Lockheed Martin Corp.*, Comp. Gen. Dec. B-295402, 2005 CPD ¶ 24, prejudice was found where a senior procurement official, who was involved in discussions that culminated in the deletion of a performance requirement that favored the protester, acknowledged bias in favor of the ultimate awardee. However, where a proposal deviates from a specification by a negligible amount, prejudice is unlikely to be found. See *First Federal Corp.—Costs*, Comp. Gen. Dec. B-293373.2, 2004 CPD ¶ 94 (one-half mile deviation from the 25-mile requirement appears minor on its face and protester did not show how it would have altered its proposal to improve its competitive standing had it been given an opportunity to respond to the relaxed requirement); *Gulf Copper Ship Repair, Inc.*, Comp. Gen. Dec. B-292431, 2003 CPD ¶ 155 (deviation of one inch water depth specification).

When the procurement defect is a failure to evaluate proposals properly, the protester must show that proper evaluation would have given it a chance to win the competition. This test was met in *Labat-Anderson, Inc.*, 71 Comp. Gen. 252 (B-246071), 92-1 CPD ¶ 193, where the agency had so significantly deviated from its evaluation scheme that it was not clear how a reevaluation would have scored the competitors. Prejudice will not be found where the outcome of the evaluation is unchanged. In *Calnet, Inc.*, Comp. Gen. Dec. B-402558.2, 2010 CPD ¶ 130, GAO held that even if the protester were correct that the agency improperly failed to consider the protester's third past performance questionnaire, there was no prejudice. Including the scores of the third questionnaire in the calculation would have given the protester and awardee the same overall score but the awardee offered a lower price and therefore remained in line for award ahead of the protester. See also *Alsalam Aircraft Co.*, Comp. Gen. Dec. B-401298.4, 2010 CPD ¶ 23 (even if awardee failed to include the fringe benefit costs, a cost realism adjustment would not overcome its $11.4 million advantage over the protester's overall price); *PM Servs. Co.*, Comp. Gen. Dec. B-310762, 2008 CPD ¶ 42 (even agreeing with protester regarding the agency's evaluation of its proposal, awardee's proposal remained technically superior and was offered at a 4.4% lower cost); *American Cybernetic Corp.*, Comp. Gen. Dec. B-310551.2, 2008 CPD ¶ 40 (even assuming that protester's technical proposal should have been assigned the highest possible rating, no reasonable possibly that the contracting officer would have concluded that protester's proposal was worth paying more than twice the price); *Med Optical*, Comp. Gen. Dec. B-296231.2, 2005 CPD ¶ 169 (even if protester received perfect scores in both areas where it challenged the agency's evaluation, its proposal would still be lower rated technically and substantially higher priced than the awardee's); *Restoration & Closure Servs., LLC*, Comp. Gen. Dec. B-295663.6, 2005 CPD ¶ 92 (protester's evaluated cost was $47 million higher than awardee's, and the protester made no claim that it would have been able to reduce its proposed costs); and *AVCARD*, Comp. Gen. Dec. B-293775.2, 2004 CPD ¶ 9 (given that protester's proposal was significantly higher priced than the awardee's, in order to prevail in its protest, protester would have had to demonstrate that agency should have rated proposal higher than awardee's proposal in at least one of the non-price evaluation areas to demonstrate prejudice).

When the evaluation errors are minor, prejudice is difficult to prove. See *SWR, Inc.*, Comp. Gen. Dec. B-294835, 2005 CPD ¶ 7 (although agency improperly failed to take into account the relative weights of the evaluation factors in scoring proposals, there was no basis for finding that correctly weighted scoring would have had any significant impact on the award decision); *Wadsworth Builders, Inc.*, Comp. Gen. Dec. B-291633, 2003 CPD ¶ 43 (even assuming the agency should have regarded the combat arms range project as relevant and considered it in evaluating the protester's past performance, there was no basis to conclude that this would have resulted in an increase in protester's past performance rating); *Innovative Mgmt., Inc.*, Comp. Gen. Dec. B-291375, 2003 CPD ¶ 11 (no prejudice by the agency's alleged error in not having protester's original transparencies available for use during its oral presentation); *SBC Fed. Sys.*, Comp. Gen. Dec. B-283693, 2000 CPD ¶ 5 (although agency may have improperly performed a price/technical trade-off in violation of the solicitation's evaluation scheme, protester not prejudiced because proposal was technically unacceptable).

Prejudice will not be found in circumstances where the protester does not demonstrate that it at least could have won the competition. See *SERAPH, Inc.*, Comp. Gen. Dec. B-297452, 2006 CPD ¶ 18 (no prejudice for alleged improper evaluation of key personnel because proposal was not selected for award due to the agency's evaluation conclusion that the proposal represented a moderate risk under the understanding of work evaluation factor, and not because of lack of experience); *Information Ventures, Inc.*, Comp. Gen. Dec. B-297225, 2005 CPD ¶ 216 (protester made no attempt to show that it could have met the agency's requirement, regardless of the time provided); *United Valve Co.*, Comp. Gen. Dec. B-295879, 2005 CPD ¶ 85 (agency had waived schedule specified in the solicitation for both competitors, and protester's own requested schedule was already longer than schedule granted to awardee, and protester's proposal offered a higher price); *United Enter. & Assocs.*, Comp. Gen. Dec. B-295742, 2005 CPD ¶ 67 (although SBA did not follow applicable certificate of competency procedures, the SBA agreed with the procuring agency that the 8(a) vendor was not responsible for this requirement, and thus SBA would not have exercised its right to appeal the agency's determination not to contract with that vendor, which was the only action under applicable regulations that SBA could take to contest the procuring agency's determination); *CourtSmart Digital Sys., Inc.*, Comp. Gen. Dec. B-292995.8, 2005 CPD ¶ 28 (protester did not show that it could or would have modified its quotation had it known of the agency's interpretation of the "field tested" requirement); *Kloppenburg Enters., Inc.*, Comp. Gen. Dec. B-294709, 2004 CPD ¶ 246 (although GAO recognizes that an agency is obligated to ensure that prospective contractors are registered in the CCR database before award, no prejudice where agency made award only after confirming that awardee would promptly register in the CCR database); *Cross Match Techs., Inc.*, Comp. Gen. Dec. B-293024.3, 2004 CPD ¶ 193 (solicitation provision that provides for incorporating into a BPA additional, unevaluated items, in quantities for which no estimates are provided in the solicitation, and at prices that are subsequently to be negotiated was improper, but record showed that the amount involved could have accounted for no more than small portion of awardee's overall price advantage); *Frasca Int'l, Inc.*, Comp. Gen. Dec. B-293299, 2004 CPD ¶ 38 (to the extent that protester was unable to compete, it was due to breakdown of teaming discussions caused by protester's untimely proposals submission, not to bundling); *Bath Iron Works Corp.*, Comp. Gen. Dec. B-290470, 2002 CPD ¶ 133 (agency's denial of protester's use of a decommissioned destroyer for testing while allowing the awardee to use such constituted unequal treatment but was not prejudicial because record showed protester would have obtained no material technical benefit or evaluation advantage had it been allowed to use of the destroyer).

Prejudice has also been found where an agency materially changes its requirements but does not issue an amendment to the solicitation and the protester could have improved its competitive position if given an opportunity to respond to the changed requirements through a revised proposal. See *Symetrics Indus., Inc.*, Comp. Gen. Dec. B-274246.3, 97-2 CPD ¶ 59, sustaining the protest, finding that the agency was required to amend the solicitation upon receiving information that funds were unavailable for the purchase of a significant portion of an estimated quantity included in the RFP for an indefinite-quantity, indefinite-delivery contract. GAO stated that the change in quantity was material and there was a reasonable possibility that the protester would have changed its price. See also *Mgmt. Sys. Designers, Inc.*, Comp. Gen. Dec. B-244383, 91-2 CPD ¶ 518 (finding prejudice where agency failed to amend solicitation "since offerors might have revised their technical cost proposals if they had been aware of the substantial change in requirements."). But see *M. K. Taylor Contractors, Inc.*, Comp. Gen. Dec. B-291730.2, 2003 CPD ¶ 97 (although agency improperly failed to issue amendment of the changed requirements, no prejudice found since, by protester's own calculations, increased quantities would not have led protester to reduce its price sufficiently to give it a substantial chance of receiving the award).

Prejudice generally cannot be proved if the protester is ineligible for award. See *Wyeth-Lederle Vaccines & Pediatrics*, Comp. Gen. Dec. B-274490, 96-2 CPD ¶ 229, holding that the protester suffered no prejudice as a result of the agency's inclusion of the single-award clause in the solicitation because even if the single-award clause were removed, the protester would still be ineligible for award because it did not possess the required license.

Prejudice will not be found where the agency accepts an expired offer if no changes are permitted to be made to the proposal, *Scot, Inc.*, Comp. Gen. Dec. B-295569, 2005 CPD ¶ 66.

[H] Remedies

GAO can make recommendations to the agency but does not have the authority to direct the agency to take action or to refrain from doing so. Only in rare cases, however, do agencies fail to follow these recommendations. GAO is required to report annually to Congress all cases in which procuring agencies do not fully implement GAO's recommendations, 31 U.S.C. § 3554(e)(2). There are only two instances in the last 11 years where GAO's recommendations were not fully implemented by the respective agencies. See *Caddell Constr. Co.*, Comp. Gen. Dec. B-411005.1, 2015 CPD ¶ 132, and *Mission Critical Solutions*, Comp. Gen. Dec. B-401057, 2009 CPD ¶ 93. See GAO Bid Protest Annual Reports to the Congress (Fiscal Years 2009-2019).

[1] Nonmonetary Remedies

GAO can recommend a variety of nonmonetary remedies. 31 U.S.C. § 3554(b)(1) states:

> If the Comptroller General determines that the solicitation, proposed award, or award does not comply with a statute or regulation, the Comptroller General shall recommend that the Federal agency—
>
> (A) refrain from exercising any of his options under the contract;
> (B) recompete the contract immediately;
> (C) issue a new solicitation;
> (D) terminate the contract;
> (E) award a contract consistent with the requirements of such statute and regulation;
> (F) implement any combination of recommendations under clauses (A), (B), (C), (D), and (E); or
> (G) implement such other recommendations as the Comptroller General determines to be necessary in order to promote compliance with procurement statutes and regulations.

If award has already been made, GAO, in making recommendations, is prohibited from considering any cost or disruption resulting from the termination, recompetition, or reaward of the contract, 31 U.S.C. § 3554(b)(2). In *Price Waterhouse*, Comp. Gen. Dec. B-220049, 86-1 CPD ¶ 333, an agency requested reconsideration of a decision that sustained a protest and recommended possible contract termination. GAO held that its decision would not be reconsidered based upon the estimated costs of termination where the agency proceeded with performance of the contract upon a finding that to do so would be in the best interests of the government. See also *Spherix, Inc.*, Comp. Gen. Dec. B-294572, 2005 CPD ¶ 3; and *Dep't of the Navy*, Comp. Gen. Dec. B-274944.4, 97-2 CPD ¶ 16.

GAO has recommended that the agency amend the solicitation, *FC Bus. Sys., Inc.*, Comp. Gen. Dec. B-278730, 98-2 CPD ¶ 9 (where RFP did not provide a common definition of a staff year, agency should amend solicitation to explain how it will take into consideration the differences in the number of hours per staff year proposed by the offerors or otherwise establish a uniform basis for preparing and evaluating offers); *Hoescht Marion Roussel, Inc.*, Comp. Gen. Dec. B-279073, 98-1 CPD ¶ 127 (where solicitation fails to realistically state agency's estimated requirements for various drug dosages, agency should amend RFP); *Comark Fed. Sys.*, Comp. Gen. Dec. B-278343.2, 98-1 CPD ¶ 34 (where agency failed to advise vendors of the basis for the source selection, agency should amend RFQ to advise firms holding basic purchasing agreements of agency's needs, including whether agency is willing to conduct a cost/technical trade-off).

GAO has also recommended that the agency make a new competitive range determination, *Trifax Corp.*, Comp. Gen. Dec. B-279561, 98-2 CPD ¶ 24, reinstate a wrongfully disqualified offeror to the competitive range, *KPMG Peat Marwick*, Comp. Gen. Dec. B-251902.3, 93-2 CPD ¶ 272, or conduct new oral presentations, *e-LYNXX Corp.*, Comp. Gen. Dec. B-292761, 2003 CPD ¶ 219. See *Kathpal Techs., Inc.*, Comp. Gen. Dec. B-283137.3, 2000 CPD ¶ 6 (GAO recommended agency either afford all technically acceptable offerors an opportunity to make oral presentations or amend the solicitation to properly inform offerors that oral presentations would not be considered as part of offerors' proposals and obtain revised proposals).

A common remedy in negotiated procurement is to reopen discussions, request new revised proposals and reevaluate proposals, *Haworth, Inc.*, Comp. Gen. Dec. B-297077, 2005 CPD ¶ 215 (agency erroneously concluded that awardee's quotation met the stated requirements and erroneously downgraded protester's under the "environmental factors" evaluation factor); *Technical Support Servs., Inc.*, Comp. Gen. Dec. B-279665.2, 98-2 CPD ¶ 26 (agency had disregarded the solicitation's stated best value evaluation scheme); *Century Envtl. Hygiene, Inc.*, Comp. Gen. Dec. B-279378, 98-1 CPD ¶ 164 (evaluation of protester's proposal was inconsistent with the solicitation evaluation criteria); *Biosperics, Inc.*, Comp. Gen. Dec. B-278278, 98-1 CPD ¶ 161 (agency failed to inform firm that its cost/pricing was considered unrealistically low but instead twice encouraged the firm to reduce its proposed price); *Hughes STX Corp.*, Comp. Gen. Dec. B-278466, 98-1 CPD ¶ 52 (cost evaluation was unreasonable and discussions with the protester concerning its proposed direct labor rates were not meaningful); *CitiWest Props., Inc.*, Comp. Gen. Dec. B-274689.4, 98-1 CPD ¶ 3 (agency failed to conduct meaningful discussions). In some cases, GAO recommends that discussions be reopened but that they be of limited nature, *Boeing Sikorsky Aircraft Support*, Comp. Gen. Dec. B-277263.2, 97-2 CPD ¶ 91. Here, GAO recommended that the agency reopen negotiations regarding costs and fees with offerors in the competitive range and allow them to submit revised cost proposals.

In some instances, GAO may recommend termination of the task order or contract. See *Tarheel Specialties, Inc.*, Comp. Gen. Dec. B-298197, 2006 CPD ¶ 140 (recommended that DHS/ICE terminate the task order to USIS, assess its requirements, and determine whether it is appropriate to obtain these services under the FSS program, and then either resolicit under the FSS program or by full and open competition).

In cases where the integrity of the procurement process appears threatened, GAO may recommend that the agency exclude a bidder from the competition. Specifically, GAO "has held that exclusion of an offeror from a competition is warranted where it made a material misrepresentation in its proposal and where the agency's reliance on the misrepresentation had a material effect on the evaluation results," *Patricio Enters., Inc.*, Comp. Gen. Dec. B-412738, 2016 CPD ¶ 145 (compiling citations).

In rare cases GAO recommends that award be made to the protester. See *Spectrum Sec. Servs., Inc.*, Comp. Gen. Dec. B-297320.2, 2005 CPD ¶ 227 (recommended that contract be terminated and that the agency consider award to protester or the other small business offeror); *Dismas Charities, Inc.*, Comp. Gen. Dec. B-292091, 2003 CPD ¶ 125 (in the event proposal is selected for award, the agency should terminate awardee's contract, and award a contract to the protester); *R. & W. Flammann GmbH*, Comp. Gen. Dec. B-278486, 98-1 CPD ¶ 40 (where agency improperly canceled procurement, GAO recommended that award be made to protester on the basis of its low offer); *For Your Information, Inc.*, Comp. Gen. Dec. B-278352, 97-2 CPD ¶ 164 (where agency had improperly awarded contract to technically unacceptable offeror, GAO recommended that the agency terminate the contract and make award to the protester, which was the only offeror that submitted a technically acceptable proposal); *Tri-State Gov't Servs., Inc.*, Comp. Gen. Dec. B-277315.2, 97-2 CPD ¶ 143 (where agency improperly accepted nonconforming offer, GAO recommended that contract be terminated and award be made to protester).

[2] Monetary Remedies

The monetary remedies that protesters have been able to recover are the costs of pursuing the protest, including attorneys' fees, and the costs of preparing the bid or proposal. Recovery of anticipated profits has been uniformly denied, *Baker Support Servs., Inc.*, Comp. Gen. Dec. B-256192.3, 95-1 CPD ¶ 75.

When GAO recommends payment of protest costs and/or bid or proposal preparation costs, it leaves it to the parties to agree on the amount. The protester is required to submit to the procuring agency a detailed and certified claim within 60 calendar days after receipt of GAO recommendation that the costs be paid, 4 C.F.R. § 21.8(f)(1).

The procuring agency must decide the claim "as soon as practicable after the claim is filed" and notify GAO within 60 calendar days after GAO decision recommending the payment of costs, 4 C.F.R. § 21.8(f)(3). If the parties cannot reach agreement on the amount within a reasonable time, the protester may refer the matter to GAO for decision, 4 C.F.R. § 21.8(f)(2). A protester must diligently pursue a claim for protest costs, *Aalco Forwarding, Inc.—Costs*, Comp. Gen. Dec. B-277241.30, 99-2 CPD ¶ 36. Failure to timely pursue a claim may result in forfeiture of the right to recover protest costs, *Holloway & Co., PLLC—Costs*, Comp. Gen. Dec. B-311342.5, 2009 CPD ¶ 146 (request for recommendation for reimbursement of protest costs not diligently pursued where protester delayed filing at GAO until more than eight months had passed without receiving a response from the contracting agency); *L-3 Commc'ns Corp., Ocean Sys. Div.—Costs*, Comp. Gen. Dec. B-281784.5, 2004 CPD ¶ 40 (although protester filed its claim with the agency in a timely fashion, the protester failed to continue pursuit of the claim for an extended period of time, nearly three years).

GAO will not ordinarily recommend the amount of costs to be paid for pursuing the claim, *Princeton Gamma-Tech, Inc.*, 68 Comp. Gen. 401 (B-228052.5), 89-1 CPD ¶ 401, except where the parties cannot agree on the amount, 4 C.F.R. § 21.8(f)(3). GAO, if determining the amount of costs to be paid, may also recommend that the agency pay the costs of pursuing this claim for costs before GAO, 4 C.F.R. § 21.8(f)(5). However, it will only recommend payment of claims costs if it is shown that the agency unreasonably delayed consideration of the claim, or otherwise failed to give it reasonable consideration, *Voith Hydro, Inc.*—Costs, Comp. Gen. Dec. B-416243.4, 2019 CPD ¶ 272, *modified on recons.*, 2020 CPD ¶ 41.

[a] Bid or Proposal Preparation Costs

31 U.S.C. § 3554(c)(1)(B) permits GAO to award the costs of preparing a bid or proposal to a successful protester. However, bid or proposal costs are not awarded merely if a protest is sustained; rather, recovery is appropriate only when a protester is unreasonably excluded from the competition and no other remedy is appropriate. This is often the case when performance of the contract is complete or when it is impractical to terminate the contract because performance has reached its latter stages, *Savannah Cleaning Sys., Inc.*, Comp. Gen. Dec. B-415817, 2018 CPD ¶ 119 (delivery completed—GAO recommended reimbursement of costs of quotation preparation and of filing and pursuing the

protest); *Data Integrators, Inc.*, Comp. Gen. Dec. B-310928, 2008 CPD ¶ 27 (delivery completed—GAO recommended reimbursement of costs of quotation preparation and of filing and pursuing the protest, including reasonable attorneys' fees); *International Program Grp., Inc.*, Comp. Gen. Dec. B-400278, 2008 CPD ¶ 172 (order completely performed—GAO recommended reimbursement of costs of filing and pursuing the protest); *Information Ventures, Inc.*, Comp. Gen. Dec. B-293518, 2004 CPD ¶ 76 (sole source contract was completed—protester had no proposal costs but GAO recommended reimbursement of costs of filing and pursuing the protest, including reasonable attorneys' fees); *Mechanical Contractors, S.A.*, Comp. Gen. Dec. B-277916.2, 98-1 CPD ¶ 68 (25% of the work completed and the agency had determined that urgent and compelling circumstances existed requiring several additional weeks to conduct discussions and reevaluate proposals—GAO recommended reimbursement of proposal preparation costs); and *Aerospace Design & Fabrication, Inc.*, Comp. Gen. Dec. B-278896.2, 98-1 CPD ¶ 139 (unique circumstances created a situation where reevaluation and reconsideration of the selection decision could not return the parties to their respective positions prior to the agency error—GAO recommended reimbursement of proposal preparation costs).

GAO will not award proposal costs if the protester would not have been in line for the award, *Temps & Co.*, 65 Comp. Gen. 819 (B-221846.2), 86-2 CPD ¶ 236. But see *EHE Nat'l Health Servs., Inc.*, 65 Comp. Gen. 1 (B-219361.2), 85-2 CPD ¶ 362, where GAO found that a protester had a substantial chance of receiving the award when the protester was one of three firms in line for award.

If a solicitation is canceled for valid reasons not related to the protest, no bid or proposal preparation costs will be awarded, *Veterans Electric, LLC*, Comp. Gen. Dec. B-415064.3, 2018 CPD ¶ 228. See also *QuanTech, Inc.*, Comp. Gen. Dec. B-278380.3, 98-1 CPD ¶ 165 (no proposal preparation costs awarded where agency reasonably canceled procurement in order to take corrective action); and *Fischer & Porter Co.*, Comp. Gen. Dec. B-227941.3, 88-1 CPD ¶ 327 (no bid preparation costs awarded where legislation passed subsequent to a GAO decision sustaining a protest had the effect of rendering the decision moot).

A protester is generally not entitled to the award of bid or proposal preparation costs if it will have an opportunity to compete for award of the contract under a resolicitation conducted as a result of its protest, *Lockheed Martin Corp.—Costs*, Comp. Gen. Dec. B-295402.2, 2005 CPD ¶ 192; *KIME Enters.*, Comp. Gen. Dec. B-241996.5, 91-2 CPD ¶ 523. However, GAO may recommend reimbursement where changed circumstances render no longer relevant a proposal that was previously submitted. In *COBRO Corp.*, Comp. Gen. Dec. B-287578.2, 2001 CPD ¶ 181, GAO recommended the award of bid and proposal costs where the protester had expended substantial cost and effort on a proposal which was likely to have virtually no value under a recompetition for a fundamentally different requirement. See also *Rockwell Elec. Commerce Corp.—Modification of Recommendation*, Comp. Gen. Dec. B-286201.8, 2002 CPD ¶ 47, recommending the reimbursement of proposal preparation costs since the agency stated it would not follow GAO's recommendation to cure the improprieties in the competition. GAO held that since the agency would not take appropriate corrective action, Rockwell would not have a meaningful opportunity to compete based on the proposal submitted. See *Aberdeen Tech. Servs.—Modification of Recommendation*, Comp. Gen. Dec. B-283727.3, 2001 CPD ¶ 146, recommending the reimbursement of protester's costs of preparing its proposal where the agency canceled the solicitation and acknowledged it would be unable to issue a new solicitation for "some 2 years" after GAO's original decision.

GAO has awarded bid preparation costs where a protester bid was improperly rejected even though the agency's subsequent review of the bid determined that it was not eligible for award, *Industrial Storage Equip.—Pac.*, Comp. Gen. Dec. B-228123.2, 88-1 CPD ¶ 328.

[b] Protest Costs

GAO has the authority to grant protest costs, including reasonable attorney fees, 31 U.S.C. § 3554(c). Protest costs can be granted even when other corrective action is taken in a sustained protest, *Norse Inc.*, Comp. Gen. Dec. B-233534, 89-1 CPD ¶ 293 (protester was both reinstated into the contract competition and granted protest costs).

GAO has consistently rejected assertions that its cost reimbursement authority is properly applied to litigation costs incurred in connection with matters brought in another forum, since GAO does not view those costs as having been incurred in filing and pursuing a protest with GAO, *Sodexho Mgmt., Inc.—Costs*, Comp. Gen. Dec. B-289605.3, 2003 CPD ¶ 136 (GAO statutory authority to recommend reimbursement of costs does not extend to the costs associated with Sodexho's administrative appeal of the initial A-76 cost comparison). See also *Rice Servs., Ltd.—Costs*, Comp. Gen. Dec. B-284997.2, 2001 CPD ¶ 88; *Diverco, Inc.,—Claim for Costs*, Comp. Gen. Dec. B-240639.5, 92-1 CPD ¶ 460.

[i] Grounds for Protest Costs

Generally, no protest costs will be granted if GAO has not made a decision on the merits, *Signal Corp.*, 69 Comp. Gen. 659 (B-240450), 90-2 CPD ¶ 116; *Moody Bros.*, Comp. Gen. Dec. B-237278.3, 89-2 CPD ¶ 590. For instance, if an agency cancels a solicitation for a valid reason unrelated to the protest, the protester will not be entitled to recover the costs of filing and pursuing its protest, *AECOM-Inquip Joint Venture—Costs*, Comp. Gen. Dec. B-415907.3, 2019 CPD ¶ 26 (agency needs changed); *Watt & Scott Gen. Contractors, Inc.*, Comp. Gen. Dec. B-257776.3, 95-1 CPD ¶ 183 (inability to proceed with work due to weather conditions); *Digital Sys. Grp., Inc.*, Comp. Gen. Dec. B-257835.2, 95-1 CPD ¶ 173 (agency did not receive any proposals that satisfied requirement); *Red River Serv. Corp.*, Comp. Gen. Dec. B-259462.2, 95-2 CPD ¶ 106 (bid acceptance period had expired). However, if the cancellation occurs after the date for the submission of the agency report, it may not be considered prompt corrective action with the result that protest costs may be allowed. See *KAES Enters., LLC—Protest & Costs*, Comp. Gen. Dec. B-402050.4, 2010 CPD ¶ 49, granting the protest costs incurred with regard to the single issue that was deemed meritorious in an outcome prediction conference—followed by cancellation of the procurement because the agency's requirements had changed.

Protest costs will not be awarded unless the grounds for the protest are clearly meritorious. See *Odle Mgmt. Grp., LLC*, Comp. Gen. Dec. B-414952.4, 2019 CPD ¶ 37, stating:

> We will recommend reimbursement only where the underlying protest is clearly meritorious, i.e., not a close question. *InfraMap Corp.—Costs*, B-405167.3, Mar. 26, 2012, 2012 CPD ¶ 123 at 3. A protest is clearly meritorious where a reasonable agency inquiry into the protester's allegations would reveal facts showing the absence of a defensible legal position. *First Fed. Corp.—Costs*, B-293373.2, Apr. 21, 2004, 2004 CPD ¶ 94 at 2.

Clearly meritorious protests include *CSRA LLC—Costs*, Comp. Gen. Dec. B-415171, 2018 CPD ¶ 307 (agency unduly limited scope of proposal revisions); *Facility Servs. Mgmt., Inc.—Costs*, Comp. Gen. Dec. B-402757.5, 2010 CPD ¶ 236 (agency selected offeror when its key personnel did not meet RFP requirements); *ManTech Sys. Eng'g Corp.*, Comp. Gen. Dec. B-401542.6, 2010 CPD ¶ 14 (notwithstanding clear misevaluation of cost proposal, agency elected to defend protest); *Commercial Design Grp., Inc.—Costs*, Comp. Gen. Dec. B-400923.3, 2009 CPD ¶ 126 (had agency conducted a reasonable review of the allegations in initial protest, it would have discovered that awardee's proposed computer-aided design manager's resume did not provide a sufficient basis to conclude that he met RFP requirements); *Pond Sec. Grp. Italia JV—Costs*, Comp. Gen. Dec. B-400149.2, 2009 CPD ¶ 61 (alleged defect affected protester's ability to compete at the time the protest was pending); *Salvation Army Cmty. Corrs. Program—Costs*, Comp. Gen. Dec. B-298866.3, 2007 CPD ¶ 165 (no reasonable explanation in the record for the agency's evaluation in a number of areas); *Shindong-A Express Tour Co., Ltd.—Costs*, Comp. Gen. Dec. B-292459.3, 2004 CPD ¶ 75 (initial protest provided ample information to permit the Army to conclude that the awardee's proposal was unacceptable under the solicitation's stated evaluation scheme); *Martin Elecs., Inc.—Costs*, Comp. Gen. Dec. B-291732.2, 2003 CPD ¶ 84 (agency's selection of one awardee was unreasonable and unsupported and agency's evaluation of another awardee's proposal was inconsistent with the solicitation's stated evaluation criteria); and *Georgia Power Co.*, Comp. Gen. Dec. B-289211.5, 2002 CPD ¶ 81 (agency did not reasonably evaluate whether awardee's past performance was for services similar in size, magnitude, and complexity to the solicitation requirement).

If GAO informs the parties through outcome prediction ADR that a protest is likely to be sustained, it is generally an indication that the protest is viewed as clearly meritorious, *National Opinion Research Ctr.—Costs*, Comp. Gen. Dec. B-289044.3, 2002 CPD ¶ 55. See *EG Mgmt. Servs., Inc.—Costs*, Comp. Gen. Dec. B-415797.3, 2019 CPD ¶ 39 (ADR found award made without consideration of price); *KAES Enters., LLC—Protest & Costs*, Comp. Gen. Dec. B-402050.4, 2010 CPD ¶ 49 (ADR found exclusion of KAES's proposal from the competitive range without consideration of its price); *Panacea Consulting, Inc.—Costs*, Comp. Gen. Dec. B-299307.3, 2007 CPD ¶ 133 (ADR found that the record showed that the agency had weighted the evaluation criteria differently during the evaluations than the manner stated in the solicitation); and *TyeCom, Inc.*, Comp. Gen. Dec. B-287321.3, 2002 CPD ¶ 101 (during ADR conference GAO attorney handling the protest explained that protest was likely to be sustained because the agency had made an award to an offer which had submitted a substantially lower-rated technical proposal, on the basis of low proposed cost under a cost-reimbursement contract, without performing any meaningful cost realism analysis).

Cases where GAO found the protest to be not clearly meritorious include *MLT Mgmt. Servs., LLC—Costs*, Comp. Gen. Dec. B-415936.7, 2019 CPD ¶ 122 (evaluation errors may not have changed selection decision); *ARP Sciences, LLC*, Comp. Gen. Dec. B-415318.4, 2019 CPD ¶ 77 (reasonable for source selection official to change decision after peer review); *Contrack Int'l, Inc.—Costs*, Comp. Gen. Dec. B-401871.3, 2010 CPD ¶ 122 (although agency was unreasonable on two issues, it was reasonable on another protest issue with result that protest was not clearly meritorious); *AGFA HealthCare Corp.—Costs*, Comp. Gen. Dec. B-400733.6, 2009 CPD ¶ 90 (although agency's failure to evaluate alleged noncompliance with mandatory standards in RFP was a serious issue, GAO did not agree that the issue was so clearly meritorious as to reveal the absence of any defensible legal position); *Triple Canopy, Inc.—Costs*, Comp. Gen. Dec. B-310566.9, 2009 CPD ¶ 62 (while acknowledging that the issues presented were "close questions," protests not clearly meritorious); *New England Radiation Therapy Mgmt. Servs., Inc.—Costs*, Comp. Gen. Dec. B-297397.3, 2006 CPD ¶ 30 (whether or not solicitation was ambiguous and whether awardee's price was or was not in accordance with the RFP schedule was not apparent from the record); and *J.F. Taylor, Inc.*, Comp. Gen. Dec. B-266039.3, 96-2 CPD ¶ 5 (interpretation of the solicitation's requirements and the awardee's compliance with the requirements not clearly meritorious).

[ii] Severability of Issues

As a general rule, GAO recommends reimbursement of costs incurred with respect to all issues pursued, not merely those upon which the protester prevails, *Voith Hydro, Inc.—Costs*, Comp. Gen. Dec. B-416243.4, 2019 CPD ¶ 272; *AAR Aircraft Servs.—Costs*, Comp. Gen. Dec. B-291670.6, 2003 CPD ¶ 100. However, in appropriate cases GAO will limit its recommendation for the award of protest costs where a part of their costs is allocable to a protest issue that is so clearly severable as to essentially constitute a separate protest. See *CSRA LLC—Costs*, Comp. Gen. Dec. B-415171, 2018 CPD ¶ 307 (limiting protest costs to one of two protest grounds); *KAES Enters., LLC—Protest & Costs*, Comp. Gen. Dec. B-402050.4, 2010 CPD ¶ 49 (costs limited to specific ground on which protester was likely to prevail—agency's failure to consider price when excluding the firm's proposal from the competitive range); *Facility Servs. Mgmt., Inc.—Costs*, Comp. Gen. Dec. B-402757.5, 2010 CPD ¶ 236 (challenge of evaluation of awardee's key personnel clearly severable from issues concerning evaluation of protester's proposal); *Core Tech Int'l Corp.—Costs*, Comp. Gen. Dec. B-310600.3, 2009 CPD ¶ 58 (challenge to use of HUBZone price evaluation credit clearly severable from meritorious challenges of technical evaluation and adequate discussions); and *Al Qabandi United Co.*, Comp. Gen. Dec. B-400047.2, 2008 CPD ¶ 112 (challenges of affirmative responsibility determination and relaxation of specification requirements severable from meritorious challenge of price evaluation).

In determining whether protest issues are so clearly severable as to essentially constitute separate protests, GAO considers, among other things, the extent to which the claims are interrelated or intertwined—*i.e.*, the successful and unsuccessful claims share a common core set of facts, are based on related legal theories, or are otherwise not readily severable, *Sodexho Mgmt., Inc.—Costs*, Comp. Gen. Dec. B-289605.3, 2003 CPD ¶ 136. In *BAE Tech. Servs., Inc.—Costs*, Comp. Gen. Dec. B-296699.3, 2006 CPD ¶ 122, GAO held that the protester was entitled to recover costs attributed to almost all of the issues raised as they are "largely intertwined parts of [its] basic objection that the [agency] misevaluated proposals and treated offerors unequally." See also *Burns & Roe Servs. Corp.—Costs*, Comp. Gen. Dec. B-310828.2, 2008 CPD ¶ 81 (misevaluation of proposals, failure to hold meaningful discussions and treating offerors unequally involve the same core facts); *T Square Logistics Servs. Corp., Inc.—Costs*, Comp. Gen. Dec. B-297790.6, 2007 CPD ¶ 108 (reasonableness of the evaluation of proposals under the past performance factor and the failure to conduct meaningful discussions based on this evaluation were interconnected and based on common factual underpinnings); *Blue Rock Structures, Inc.—Costs*, Comp. Gen. Dec. B-293134.2, 2005 CPD ¶ 190 (all of protester's arguments pertained to the reasonableness of the agency's evaluation of proposals and source selection determination). But see *Honeywell Tech. Solutions, Inc.—Costs*, Comp. Gen. Dec. B-296860.3, 2005 CPD ¶ 226, where GAO did not recommend reimbursement of costs associated with the unresolved issues, which were severable from the organizational conflict of interest issue addressed during ADR.

In the case where issues are severable and information submitted to support a claim is not detailed enough to establish how much of the claimed amount was incurred in pursuit of the successful protest issues, GAO has recognized a "page count" method—that is, an estimate based on the number of pages in the protester's submissions to GAO that were devoted to a particular issue—is a reasonable means of determining this amount, *Ace Info Solutions, Inc.—Costs*, Comp. Gen. Dec. B-414650.27, 2019 CPD ¶ 179; *ViON Corp.—Costs*, Comp. Gen. Dec. B-256363.3, 95-1 CPD ¶ 219. In *Intercon Assocs., Inc.—Costs*, Comp. Gen. Dec. B-296697.2, 2006 CPD ¶ 95, GAO held that, given the absence of more probative evidence from Intercon, it was reasonable for the agency to use a page count of Intercon's comments to segregate the costs attributable to a valid protest issue from the costs attributable to a mooted protest issue. See also *BAE Tech. Servs., Inc.—Costs*, Comp. Gen. Dec. B-296699.3, 2006 CPD ¶ 122, finding that the contemporaneous records documenting the time spent on the protest by BAE's attorneys and other legal staff were not sufficiently detailed to permit an allocation of hours to two severable issues where the protest was not sustained. GAO found it appropriate to reduce the claimed protest costs by 5.5% using a page count of the total number of pages in its submissions to GAO that were devoted to the two severable issues.

[iii] Corrective Action

Where the contracting agency decides to take corrective action in response to a protest, GAO may recommend that the protester be reimbursed the reasonable costs of filing and pursuing the protest, including attorneys' fees and consultant and expert witness fees, 4 C.F.R. § 21.8(e). GAO will not, however, award bid and proposal costs, *Mapp Bldg. Servs.—Costs*, Comp. Gen. Dec. B-289160.2, 2002 CPD ¶ 60 ("[O]ur regulations do not provide for recovery of such costs where an agency has taken corrective action").

GAO will not recommend reimbursement of protest costs if an agency takes timely corrective action; rather, a protester should be reimbursed its costs where an agency *unduly delayed* its decision to take corrective action in the face of a *clearly meritorious* protest, *CSRA LLC—Costs*, Comp. Gen. Dec. B-415171, 2018 CPD ¶ 307. Undue delay in taking corrective action is generally not found if the agency takes the action before the filing of the agency report, *Aircraft & Turbine Support Corp.—Costs*, Comp. Gen. Dec. B-417145.2, 2019 CPD ¶ 78. Undue delay was found in *Core Tech Int'l Corp.—Costs*, Comp. Gen. Dec. B-400047.2, 2009 CPD ¶ 59 (corrective action occurring only after the agency report and ADR); *World Commc'ns Ctr., Inc.—Costs*, Comp. Gen. Dec. B-310398.4, 2008 CPD ¶ 19 (agency did not terminate the award and cancel the solicitation until after the agency had produced its report, the protester had filed its comments on the report, and GAO attorney assigned to the protest had requested additional information); *Salvation Army Cmty. Corrs. Program*, Comp. Gen. Dec. B-298866.3, 2007 CPD ¶ 165 (corrective action after the protester filed its comments on the agency report and GAO informed the parties that a hearing would be conducted); *Johnson Controls World Servs., Inc.—Costs*, Comp. Gen. Dec. B-295529.4, 2005 CPD ¶ 162 (agency did not investigate the protest allegations and withheld relevant protest documents until more than 70 days after the initial protest filing); and *Miller Elevator Serv. Co.—*

Costs, Comp. Gen. Dec. B-284870.3, 2000 CPD ¶ 126 (corrective action well after the agency had submitted its report and the protester had responded to it).

For cases finding that the protester was not entitled to award of protest costs because the agency took prompt corrective action, see *BAI, Inc.—Costs*, Comp. Gen. Dec. B-416681.7, 2019 CPD ¶ 309; *Apptis, Inc.—Costs*, Comp. Gen. Dec. B-402146.3, 2010 CPD ¶ 123; and *Metalcraft, Inc.—Costs*, Comp. Gen. Dec. B-402181.3, 2010 CPD ¶ 116 (agency's corrective action took place prior to the submission of its supplemental agency report); *AGFA HealthCare Corp.—Costs*, Comp. Gen. Dec. B-400733.6, 2009 CPD ¶ 90 (agency took corrective action on the date comments were due on the second supplemental report); *Intercontinental Constr. Contracting, Inc.—Costs*, Comp. Gen. Dec. B-400729.3, 2009 CPD ¶ 44 (agency promptly determined its evaluation was flawed and took corrective action within 18 days after the protester submitted its comments on the agency report); *Coronet Mach. Corp.—Costs*, Comp. Gen. Dec. B-400197.2, 2008 CPD ¶ 213 (Army initiated corrective action 10 days prior to the report due date); *Alaska Structures, Inc.—Costs*, Comp. Gen. Dec. B-298156.2, 2006 CPD ¶ 109 (decision to cancel the solicitation occurred prior to the date set for the filing of the agency's report); and *Security Consultants Grp., Inc.—Costs*, Comp. Gen. Dec. B-293344.6, 2004 CPD ¶ 228 (agency took prompt corrective action in cancelling the solicitation and notifying GAO of intent to reinstate protester's contract prior to the due date for the agency's report).

As a prerequisite to GAO recommending that costs be reimbursed where a protest has been settled by corrective action, not only must the protest have been meritorious, it must have been clearly meritorious, *i.e.*, not a close question, *CSRA LLC—Costs*, Comp. Gen. Dec. B-415171, 2018 CPD ¶ 307 (finding one protest ground clearly meritorious and one not); *PADCO, Inc.*, Comp. Gen. Dec. B-289096.3, 2002 CPD ¶ 135 (even if protest ground clearly meritorious, corrective action was timely). The mere fact that an agency decides to take corrective action does not establish that a statute or regulation clearly has been violated, *Sun Chem. Corp.—Cost*, Comp. Gen. Dec. B-288466.4, 2001 CPD ¶ 199; *Spar Applied Sys.—Declaration of Entitlement*, Comp. Gen. Dec. B-276030.2, 97-2 CPD ¶ 70. There are a number of cases where GAO has found a protest not clearly meritorious because corrective action has forestalled the assembly of the record on which the protest could be resolved. See *Yardney Tech. Prods., Inc.*, Comp. Gen. Dec. B-297648.3, 2006 CPD ¶ 65 (protest grounds not clearly meritorious where agency cancelled solicitation prior to final reports and GAO had not fully analyzed the parties' positions); *LENS, JV—Costs*, Comp. Gen. Dec. B-295952.4, 2006 CPD ¶ 9 (protest not clearly meritorious where resolution of the protest required further record development such as a hearing to complete and clarify the record); *Sandi-Sterling Consortium—Costs*, Comp. Gen. Dec. B-296246.2, 2005 CPD ¶ 173 (merits of protest would have required development of the protest record—including a complete agency report and the protester's comments on the report—and GAO would have had to conduct substantial further legal analysis); and *East Penn Mfg. Co.—Costs*, Comp. Gen. Dec. B-291503.4, 2003 CPD ¶ 83 (protest not clearly meritorious where decision would have required further steps to complete and clarify the record).

To be eligible for protest costs when the agency takes corrective action, the protester is required to file with GAO within 15 calendar days after being advised of the procuring agency's decision to take corrective action, 4 C.F.R. § 21.8(e). The protester must also file a copy with the procuring agency, which then has 15 calendar days to respond.

[c] Amount Recoverable

GAO will award proposal preparation costs that are reasonable and sufficiently documented. See *Sodexho Mgmt., Inc.—Costs*, Comp. Gen. Dec. B-289605.3, 2003 CPD ¶ 136, stating:

> A protester seeking to recover its proposal preparation costs must submit evidence sufficient to support its claim that those costs were incurred and are properly attributable to proposal preparation. *Stocker & Yale, Inc.—Claim for Costs*, B-242568.3, May 18, 1993, 93-1 CPD ¶ 387 at 4; *Patio Pools of Sierra Vista, Inc.—Claim for Costs*, B-228187.4, B-228188.3, Apr. 12, 1989, 89-1 CPD ¶ 374 at 3. The amount claimed may be recovered to the extent that it is adequately documented and is shown to be reasonable; a cost is reasonable if, in its nature and amount, it does not exceed that which would be incurred by a prudent person in the preparation of his or her proposal. *Patio Pools of Sierra Vista, Inc.—Claim for Costs, supra*; see also FAR § 31.201-3(a). Where a protester has aggregated allowable and unallowable costs in a single claim, such that our Office cannot tell from the record what portion is unallowable, we will recommend that the entire amount be disallowed even though some portion of the claim may be properly payable. *TRESP Assocs., Inc.—Costs*, B-258322.8, Nov. 3, 1998, 98-2 CPD ¶ 108 at 4. Although we recognize that the requirement for documentation may sometimes entail certain practical difficulties, we do not consider it unreasonable to require a protester to document in some detail the amount and purposes of its employees' claimed efforts and to establish that the claimed hourly rates reflect the employees' actual rates of compensation plus reasonable overhead and fringe benefits. *W. S. Spotswood & Sons, Inc.—Claim for Costs*, B-236713.3, July 19, 1990, 90-2 CPD ¶ 50 at 3. The mere submission of voluminous documentation in support of a claim is not enough to meet these standards.

GAO will award protest costs only if they are related to the protest. The costs incurred in protesting to the agency are not reimbursable, *Galen Med. Assocs., Inc.—Costs*, Comp. Gen. Dec. B-288661.6, 2002 CPD ¶ 114. Similarly, time spent attending a debriefing or in settlement discussions is not reimbursable, *Blue Rock Structures, Inc.—Costs*, Comp. Gen. Dec. B-293134.2, 2005 CPD 190, and a protester's time spent soliciting help from members of Congress is not recoverable, *Omni Analysis*, 69 Comp. Gen. 433 (B-233372.4), 90-1 CPD ¶ 436. However, costs of challenging an agency's corrective action have been found to be related costs, *T Square Logistics Servs. Corp., Inc.—Costs*, Comp. Gen. Dec. B-297790.6, 2007 CPD ¶ 108. Related costs have included the salaries of the protester's president and other employees for the time they worked on the protest, *Ultraviolet Purification Sys., Inc.*, Comp. Gen. Dec. B-226941.3, 89-1 CPD ¶ 376. See, however, *Berkshire Computer Prods.*, Comp. Gen. Dec. B-240327.3, 95-1 CPD ¶ 6, denying the award of protest costs because the protester did not establish that the costs claimed to have been paid to an unsalaried consultant and an attorney were related to the protest.

GAO will not allow the recovery of costs that may be related to the protest but are not properly documented, *W.S. Spotswood & Sons*, 69 Comp. Gen. 622 (B-236713.3), 90-2 CPD ¶ 50. The burden is on the protester to adequately document the costs incurred, and the protester cannot rely on standard rates to substantiate its claim. See *John Peeples*, 70 Comp. Gen. 661 (B-233167.2), 91-2 CPD ¶ 125. GAO will also disallow legal expenses or fees that are not adequately documented by the law firm, *Diverco, Inc.*, Comp. Gen. Dec. B-240639.5, 92-2 CPD ¶ 460. In *Solutions Lucid Grp., LLC—Costs*, Comp. Gen. Dec. B-400967.2, 2009 CPD ¶ 198, GAO denied the protester's request for recommendation that it be reimbursed $52,800 in protest costs where the protester failed to furnish sufficient evidence to establish the number of hours worked and rates of compensation for the individuals who worked on the protest. See also *DTV Transition Grp., Inc.—Costs*, Comp. Gen. Dec. B-401466.2, 2010 CPD ¶ 84 (claim not adequately documented where protester did not submit requested additional documentation—*i.e.*, copies of the analysis performed by experts, documentation of attorneys' fees, and supporting records such as timesheets, calendars, expense reports, billing statements, and receipts); *Al Long Ford—Costs*, Comp. Gen. Dec. B-297807.2, 2007 CPD ¶ 189 (claim did not identify the dates on which the hours were worked or the nature of the tasks performed, nor did it include documentation supporting the claimed rates of compensation or establishing protester's obligation to compensate the consultant); and *TRS Research—Costs*, Comp. Gen. Dec. B-290644.2, 2003 CPD ¶ 112 (disallowed costs where the protester does not demonstrate adequate documentation demonstrating the reasonableness of outside counsel's hourly rates).

[i] Attorneys' Fees

Attorneys' fees usually are the primary component of a claim for protest costs and may be part of proposal preparation costs. GAO generally accepts the number of attorney hours claimed, unless the agency identifies specific hours as excessive and articulates a reasonable analysis as to why payment for those hours should be disallowed, *Voith Hydro, Inc.—Costs*, Comp. Gen. Dec. B-416243.4, 2019 CPD ¶ 272. Simply concluding that the hours claimed are excessive or suggest duplication of effort is inadequate to justify denying a claim for protest costs, *Princeton Gamma-Tech, Inc.—Claim for Costs*, Comp. Gen. Dec. B-228052.5, 89-1 CPD ¶401; *Omni Analysis*, 69 Comp. Gen. 433 (B-233372.4), 90-1 CPD ¶436. In *BAE Tech. Servs., Inc.—Costs*, Comp. Gen. Dec. B-296699.3, 2006 CPD ¶122, GAO held that the agency's unsupported view that the hours claimed were excessive was insufficient to justify denying or reducing a claim when it had annotated each time charge by each BAE attorney for each day. However, GAO will examine the reasonableness of the attorney hours claimed to determine whether they exceed, in nature and amount, what a prudent person would incur in pursuit of his or her protest, *SKJ & Assocs., Inc.*, Comp. Gen. Dec. B-291533.3, 2003 CPD ¶130; *Price Waterhouse—Claim for Costs*, Comp. Gen. Dec. B-254492.3, 95-2 CPD ¶38. In *Pulau Elecs. Corp.—Costs*, Comp. Gen. Dec. B-280048.11, 2000 CPD ¶122, GAO held that Pulau's use of a five-person team was not unreasonable in the context of substantively and procedurally demanding protests. In *Galen Med. Assocs., Inc.—Costs*, Comp. Gen. Dec. B-288661.6, 2002 CPD ¶114, Galen's claim included a request that it be reimbursed for a total of 938.5 hours for various individuals at various hourly rates: 346.25 hours for an outside attorney, 220 hours for a consultant and 363 hours for Galen's president. GAO held that these claimed hours were far beyond what should have been necessary to reasonably pursue a protest that was relatively limited and straightforward in nature. GAO stated its file in this case was only open for approximately nine weeks, and yet these hours amount to 8.6 full-time (40-hour) workweeks for the attorney, nine full-time workweeks for Galen's president and 5.5 full-time workweeks for Galen's consultant. There was no hearing in the matter and the documents involved were not voluminous. The core government exhibit amounted to only 39 pages and the protester's submissions to GAO amounted to only 22 pages. The hours claimed equate to approximately 42 hours per page, and the cost amounts to approximately $7,154 per page. GAO stated that in its view, this amount was excessive and went well beyond what a prudent person would have expended in pursuit of the protest. See also *Armour of Am., Inc.*, Comp. Gen. Dec. B-237690.2, 92-1 CPD ¶257, where GAO determined that legal fees were excessive even though well documented. There, GAO disallowed all 36 hours of the attorneys' billed time for pursuit of issues that were clearly untimely, disallowed one-fourth of Armour's attorneys' hours attributable to legal research and writing, and disallowed one-third of the total time claimed by Armour's attorneys for travel to and from the informal bid protest conference held at GAO offices. In *Price Waterhouse*, Comp. Gen. Dec. B-254492.3, 95-2 CPD ¶38, GAO reviewed each hour billed to determine the reasonableness of the attorney hours claimed. GAO found that although 13.5 hours seemed to be high in preparing a protective order, it was not excessive. However, 4.5 hours to review the agency's notice to authorize contract performance pursuant to the statutory best interest clause was considered excessive by GAO.

There is a statutory cap on attorneys' fees, except where the protester is a small business concern. The top rate reimbursable to large businesses for attorneys' fees is $150 per hour, 31 U.S.C. § 3554(c)(2)(B). However, the attorneys' fee cap may be increased where "the agency determines, based on the recommendation of GAO on a case-by-case basis, that an increase in the cost of living or a special factor, such as the limited availability of qualified attorneys for the proceedings involved, justifies a higher fee," 31 U.S.C. § 3554(c)(2)(B).

GAO routinely recommends an upward departure from the $150 cap to reflect the fact that the cost of living has increased, as measured by the Department of Labor's (DOL) Consumer Price Index (CPI). See *Sodexho Mgmt., Inc.—Costs*, Comp. Gen. Dec. B-289605.3, 2003 CPD ¶ 136, discussing the § 3554 ceiling on attorneys' fees and the cost-of-living adjustment, and concluding that the statute contemplates an increase in the specified $150 per hour rate in order to offset any decrease in the value of the rate due to increases in the cost of living. Since *Sodexho*, GAO has found that the justification for an upward departure from the $150 cap is self-evident if the claimant asserts that the cost of living has increased, as measured by DOL's CPI. See, for example, *Transportation Sec. Admin.—Costs*, Comp. Gen. Dec. B-400340.8, 2010 CPD ¶ 119 (protester calculated fees at $210.77 to $211.12 per hour (depending on the month of billing) using DOL's CPI—All Urban Consumers); *Core Tech Int'l Corp.—Costs*, Comp. Gen. Dec. B-400047.3, 2009 CPD ¶ 121 (protester provided a detailed explanation of its calculation of the rates using DOL's CPI—All Urban Consumers); *EBSCO Publ'g, Inc.—Costs*, Comp. Gen. Dec. B-298918.4, 2007 CPD ¶ 90 (upward adjustment of attorney fees to reflect increase in cost of living as measured by the applicable CPI); *Dep't of the Army; ITT Fed. Servs. Int'l Corp.—Costs*, B-296783.4, 2006 CPD ¶ 72 (upward adjustment of attorneys' fees to a rate of $238 per hour using DOI's CPI for All Urban Consumers, U.S. City Average for Legal Services); and *Dep't of State—Costs*, Comp. Gen. Dec. B-295352.5, 2005 CPD ¶ 145 (Inter-Con's requested fees properly supported and reasonable).

Notwithstanding the lack of a fee cap for small business concern's attorneys' fees, GAO will only recommend rates charged by an attorney that are consistent with customary rates for similar work in the community, as well as the experience, reputation and ability of the practitioner, *Public Commc'ns Servs., Inc.—Costs*, Comp. Gen. Dec. B-400058.4, 2009 CPD ¶ 131 (finding reasonable an hourly rate of $705 per hour). GAO will also look to surveys of area law firms' hourly rates to determine the reasonableness of rates, *CourtSmart Digital Sys., Inc.—Costs*, Comp. Gen. Dec. B-292995.7, 2005 CPD ¶ 47 (hourly rate of $475 reasonable for an attorney experienced in government procurement law who was a partner in a Washington, D.C. firm; noting that according to an article published in the January 2003 edition of Legal Times, the hourly rates for partners from 19 Washington, D.C. area law firms surveyed ranged from $185 to $750). But see *TRS Research—Costs*, Comp. Gen. Dec. B-290644.2, 2003 CPD ¶ 112 (despite numerous requests by the agency, protester did not submit any documentation to show that the $425 hourly rate claimed by TRS counsel was representative of that charged for similar services in the Philadelphia area where he practices). GAO will also consider, where relevant and appropriate, the fee rates found allowable by it in other similarly complex proceedings, *Blue Rock Structures, Inc.—Costs*, Comp. Gen. Dec. B-293134.2, 2005 CPD ¶ 190 ("Given our approval of $475 as a reasonable hourly rate for a partner in a Washington firm in *CourtSmart*, we see no basis to object to the lower rate billed by Blue Rock's attorney, who is also a partner in a Washington firm.").

GAO will permit a protester to recover the work of support staff such as paralegals, but not library services, which GAO deems more appropriately to overhead, *Public Commc'ns Servs., Inc.—Costs*, Comp. Gen. Dec. B-400058.4, 2009 CPD ¶ 131; *Pulau Elecs. Corp.—Costs*, Comp. Gen. Dec. B-280048.11, 2000 CPD ¶ 122.

[ii] Labor Costs

A protester's internal labor costs for preparing a bid or proposal or a protest may be recovered where the rates reflect "actual rates of compensation plus reasonable overhead and fringe benefits," *Sodexho Mgmt., Inc.—Costs*, Comp. Gen. Dec. B-289605.3, 2003 CPD ¶ 136. However, a protester may not recover profit, *Celadon Labs, Inc.*, Comp. Gen. Dec. B-298533.2, 2008 CPD ¶ 208; *Blue Rock Structures, Inc.—Costs*, Comp. Gen. Dec. B-293134.2, 2005 CPD ¶ 190; *SKJ & Assocs., Inc.*, Comp. Gen. Dec. B-291533.3, 2003 CPD ¶ 130. If a protester aggregates allowable and unallowable costs, the entire amount is disallowed even though some of the costs are reasonable, *TRESP Assocs., Inc.—Costs*, Comp. Gen. Dec. B-258322.8, 98-2 CPD ¶ 108. A protester may reasonably show the hours spent by employees through a general explanation of the tasks conducted and estimate of the time spent by those employees, *Data Based Decisions, Inc.—Costs*, Comp. Gen. Dec. B-232663.3, 89-2 CPD ¶ 538. There Data Based successfully supported the costs of its president salary for 133.75 hours and its out-of-pocket expenses by providing a document that listed by date a brief description of the work performed by the president and the amount of time spent. See, however, *AeroSage, LLC—Costs*, Comp. Gen. Dec. B-416381.6, 2019 CPD ¶ 107 (denying claim for the president's salary because the rate was not adequately documented); and *Eastern Forestry & Tree Serv. Inc.—Costs*, Comp. Gen. Dec. B-411848.3, 2017 CPD ¶ 229 (denying claim for 307.5 hours of labor to prepare 10 pages of protest as excessive). See also *International Program Grp., Inc.—Costs*, Comp. Gen. Dec. B-400278.4, 2009 CPD ¶ 128, rejecting a claim for costs of a legal assistant at $80 per hour when the only evidence submitted was a lump-sum quarterly payment. GAO concluded this was not evidence of actual costs.

[iii] Outside Consultants & Expert Witnesses

There is a statutory cap on fees for consultants and expert witnesses for large businesses. See 31 U.S.C. § 3554(c)(2)(A) limiting the rate to the "highest rate of compensation for expert witnesses paid by the Federal Government." FAR 33.104(h)(5)(i) provides that this will be the rate established under 5 U.S.C. § 3109 and 5 C.F.R. § 304.105. This is the rate of pay for a federal employee (GS-15, step 10), even where the consultant billed at a higher rate, *Dep't of the Army*, Comp. Gen. Dec. B-296783.4, 2006 CPD ¶ 72. In *Eastern Forestry & Tree Serv., Inc.—Costs*, Comp. Gen. Dec. B-411848.3, 2017 CPD ¶ 229, GAO denied consultant costs because the protester submitted conflicting evidence on his pay rate. In *Solutions Lucid Grp., LLC—Costs*, Comp. Gen. Dec. B-400967.2, 2009 CPD ¶ 198, GAO denied consultant costs because the evidence submitted did not show that the protester was obligated to reimburse the consultant even though it lost the protest or that the protester had actually paid the consultant.

[3] Revision of Remedies

31 U.S.C. § 3554(e)(1) requires that GAO report promptly to the Senate's Committee on Governmental Affairs and Committee on Appropriations and the House's Committee on Government Reform and Oversight and the Committee on Appropriations any case in which a federal agency fails to implement fully a recommendation of the Comptroller General. The report is required to include "a comprehensive review of the pertinent procurement including the circumstances of the failure of the Federal agency to implement a recommendation of the Comptroller General," 31 U.S.C. § 3554(e)(1)(A). The report must also include a recommendation regarding whether "in order to correct an inequity or to preserve the integrity of the procurement process," Congress should consider (1) private relief legislation, (2) legislative rescission or cancellation of funds, (3) further investigation by Congress, or (4) other action, 31 U.S.C. § 3554(e)(1)(B).

The details of implementing GAO recommendations for corrective action are within the sound discretion and judgment of the contracting agency, *Rel-Tek Sys. & Design, Inc.—Modification of Remedy*, Comp. Gen. Dec. B-280463.7, 99-2 CPD ¶ 1. Such discretion must be exercised reasonably and in a fashion that remedies the procurement impropriety that was the basis for GAO protest recommendation. In *Futures Grp. Int'l*, Comp. Gen. Dec. B-281274.5, 2000 CPD ¶ 148, GAO had sustained the protest because the contemporaneous record did not evidence that USAID reasonably found the awardee's proposed rates realistic. In response to this decision the agency took corrective action by determining that the awardee's probable costs were the lowest and confirming award to that firm. GAO held this to be unreasonable because the agency was advised by the DCAA that the awardee's proposed uncapped indirect rates were understated by an amount that would have affected the outcome of the competition. See also *Rockwell Elec. Commerce Corp.*, Comp. Gen. Dec. B-286201.6, 2001 CPD ¶ 162, finding the agency did not act reasonably in its response to an earlier sustained decision by reopening discussions and requesting proposal revisions from only one offeror in the competitive range.

In some circumstances, it may not be feasible or practicable for an agency to follow GAO's recommendation. In such cases, the agency may request that GAO modify its recommendation for corrective action. See *Dep't of Commerce—Recons.*, Comp. Gen. Dec. B-277260.4, 98-2 CPD ¶ 35 (recommendation modified because agency established, through a site visit by GAO, that a significant portion of the contract work had been completed and that it would be impracticable to disturb award); *Dep't of Transp.; Computer Sci. Corp.—Recons. & Modification of Remedy*, Comp. Gen. Dec. B-278466.2, 98-1 CPD ¶ 140 (recommendation modified where original remedy would endanger agency's ability to address Year 2000 problem); and *National Aeronautics & Space Admin.—Recons. & Modification*, Comp. Gen. Dec. B-274748.3, 97-1 CPD ¶ 159 (recommendation modified where it was not practicable to return the items because they had already been delivered and paid for).

GAO may modify its recommendation if it finds the agency's request to be reasonable. See *Dep't of the Treasury, Bureau of Engraving & Printing—Request for Modification Remedy*, Comp. Gen. Dec. B-296490.6, 2007 CPD ¶ 101 (modification request on recommendation to reevaluate proposals and make new source selection decision granted where agency determined that its needs would be best met by splitting original requirements and competing under two new solicitations); *Dep't of State; Wackenhut Int'l, Inc.—Reconsideration & Modification of Recommendation*, Comp. Gen. Dec. B-295352.3, 2005 CPD ¶ 81 (modification request on recommendation to terminate reasonable in view of security concerns at the embassy as well as significant change in the agency's needs for guard service); *SMF Sys. Tech. Corp.*, Comp. Gen. Dec. B-292419.3, 2003 CPD ¶ 203 (disruption to agency's mission to provide medical services was considered in fashioning recommendation); and *J & J/BMAR Joint Venture, LLP—Costs*, Comp. Gen. Dec. B-290316.7, 2003 CPD ¶ 129 (wartime exigencies provide reasonable basis for delay in implementing corrective action).

The agency also may decide to perform the work in-house, rather than take corrective action, *Pemco Aeroplex, Inc.*, Comp. Gen. Dec. B-275587.9, 98-2 CPD ¶ 17.

In an unusual case, the Air Force defied a GAO recommendation. In *Pemco Aeroplex, Inc.*, Comp. Gen. Dec. B-280397, 98-2 CPD ¶ 79, GAO sustained a protest challenging the Air Force's decision to consolidate its depot workload requirements into a single solicitation. GAO recommended that the Air Force cancel the current solicitation and resolicit its requirements without bundling the workloads. The Air Force subsequently announced that it had gone ahead with the consolidated procurement, stating that awarding the depot work to one contractor will save up to $638 million during the nine-year life of the contract.

Another interesting case is *Mission Critical Solutions*, Comp. Gen. Dec. B-401057, 2009 CPD ¶ 93, *recons. denied*, 2009 CPD ¶ 148, where GAO held that HUBZone set-asides take precedence over the 8(a) program. Following GAO decision, on July 10, 2009 the Office of Management and Budget issued a memorandum directing executive branch agencies to disregard GAO's ruling pending legal review by the executive branch. On August 21, 2009, the Office of Legal Counsel (OLC) of the U.S. Department of Justice issued an opinion disagreeing with GAO's analysis, agreeing with the SBA's view that the HUBZone statute establishes "parity" with the 8(a) program. OLC stated further that its opinion was binding on the executive branch while GAO's decision was not, and directed agencies to disregard GAO decisions that are inconsistent with its opinion. Subsequently, the Court of Federal Claims agreed with GAO position, *Mission Critical Solutions v. United States*, 91 Fed. Cl. 386 (2010); *DGR Assocs., Inc. v. United States*, 94 Fed. Cl. 189 (2010), and GAO continued to grant protests when the HUBZone priority was not honored, *DGR Assocs., Inc.*, Comp. Gen. Dec. B-402494, 2010 CPD ¶ 115; *Rice Servs., Inc.*, Comp. Gen. Dec. B-402966.2, 2010 CPD ¶ 217. The matter was resolved by a statutory amendment providing for parity among the programs.

§ 15.05 COURT OF FEDERAL CLAIMS

The Court of Federal Claims and its predecessors initially relied upon the Tucker Act, 28 U.S.C. § 1491(a)(1), to take jurisdiction over contract award controversies. This statute gives the court jurisdiction over claims "founded either upon the Constitution, or any Act of Congress, or any regulation of an executive department, or upon any express or implied contract with the United States." As early as 1956, the Court of Claims used the government's "implied contract to consider bids fairly" in holding that a disappointed bidder would be entitled to bid preparation costs if it could show that its bid had not been evaluated in good faith, *Heyer Prods. Co. v. United States*, 140 F. Supp. 409 (Ct. Cl. 1956). The court again held that its jurisdiction extended to implied contracts to consider bids and proposals fairly and honestly in *Keco Indus., Inc. v. United States*, 492 F.2d 1200 (Ct. Cl. 1974). However, lacking general equitable powers, the court could not grant injunctive relief but could only award damages.

Injunctive relief became available in 1982 when 28 U.S.C. § 1491(b)(3) was added to the statute. However, the court held that this grant of jurisdiction also was limited to the implied contract to consider bids and proposals fairly and honestly. See *United States v. John C. Grimberg Co.*, 702 F.2d 1362 (Fed. Cir. 1983).

The Administrative Dispute Resolution Act of 1996 (ADRA), Pub. L. No. 104-320, repealed this provision but gave new "bid protest" jurisdiction to the court by enacting 28 U.S.C. § 1491(b), which states:

> (1) [T]he United States Court of Federal Claims ... shall have jurisdiction to render judgment on any action by an interested party objecting to a solicitation by a Federal agency for bids or proposals for a proposed contract or to a proposed award or the award of a contract or any alleged violation of statute or regulation in connection with a procurement or a proposed procurement. ... [T]he United States Court of Federal Claims ... shall have jurisdiction to entertain such an action without regard to whether suit is instituted before or after award.
>
> (2) To afford relief in such an action, the courts may award any relief that the court considers proper, including declaratory and injunctive relief except that any monetary relief shall be limited to bid preparation and proposal costs.

Some Court of Federal Claims judges subsequently decided that the court had protest jurisdiction under both 28 U.S.C. § 1491(a)(1) (damages) and 28 U.S.C. § 1491(b)(1) (injunction and/or damages). The Federal Circuit in *Resource Conservation Grp., LLC v. Dep't of the Navy*, 597 F.3d 1238 (Fed. Cir. 2010), raised questions about this dual jurisdiction, holding that relief in the "procurement" context is exclusive under 28 U.S.C. § 1491(b)(1), while relief under 28 U.S.C. § 1491(a)(1) is still available when a claim arises from a federal solicitation which is not a procurement such as a lease of real property. Following *Resource Conservation*, the Court of Federal Claims judges were divided as to what remained of their § 1491(a) jurisdiction in a bid protest involving a procurement contract properly filed under § 1491(b)(1); in other words—when a procurement protest is raised under § 1491(b)(1), may the protester raise a separate claim alleging breach of the implied contract to consider proposals fairly? This was resolved in *Safeguard Base Operations, LLC v. United States*, 989 F.3d 1326 (Fed. Cir. 2021), holding that the Court of Federal Claims "has jurisdiction over implied-in-fact contract claims in the procurement context under § 1491(b)(1), and only § 1491(b)(1)." This essentially collapses the breach of implied duty action into a claim of arbitrary and capricious action under § 1491(b).

[A] Jurisdiction

Several legal issues are relevant to determining whether a protest properly falls within the Court of Federal Claims 28 U.S.C. § 1491(b) jurisdiction.

[1] Procurement Protests

28 U.S.C. § 1491(b)(1) gives the court jurisdiction to hear protests "in connection with" a procurement or a proposed procurement of a "federal agency."

[a] Federal Agency

While the protest statute does not define the term "federal agency," it is defined in 40 U.S.C. § 472 as:

> any executive agency or any establishment in the legislative or judicial branch of the Government, including any wholly owned Government corporation.

The term "federal agency" is defined in other statutes, as well. Some definitions seem to be very broad. For example, 22 U.S.C. § 4802 states that "federal agency" "includes any department or agency of the United States Government." Some definitions do not include the legislative or judicial branches of the government within the definition. For example, 40 U.S.C. § 304e defines "federal agency" as "any executive department, independent establishment, commission, board, bureau, or office in the executive branch, or other agency of the United States." See also 5 U.S.C. § 804, which states that "federal agency" means any agency as is defined in § 551(1). This section defines "agency" as "each authority of the Government of the United States, whether or not it is within or subject to review by another agency, but does not include such entities as Congress, the courts, territories or possessions of the United States, the government of the District of Columbia, and courts martial and military commissions." Other statutory definitions include the legislative and judicial branches of the government. For example, 5 U.S.C. § 7901 defines "federal agency" as "an Executive agency as defined under Section 105 of title 5, United States Code, and shall include any agency of the legislative or judicial branch of Government." 40 U.S.C. § 612 is similar but excludes the Senate, the House of Representatives, and the Architect of the Capitol and any activities under his direction. 40 U.S.C. § 762, and 41 U.S.C. § 423 state that "federal agency" "has the meaning given such term by Section 3(b) of the Federal Property and Administrative Services Act of 1949" (40 U.S.C. § 472).

28 U.S.C. § 451 defines "agency" as "any department, independent establishment, commission, administration, authority, board or bureau of the United States or any corporation in which the United States has a proprietary interest, unless the context shows that such term was intended to be used in a more limited sense." This definition has been used in protest cases. See *Emery Worldwide Airlines, Inc. v. United States*, 264 F.3d 1071 (Fed. Cir. 2001) (USPS is a "federal agency" within the meaning of the Tucker Act and the definition of "agency" in 28 U.S.C. § 451 governs that determination); *Hewlett-Packard Co. v. United States*, 41 Fed. Cl. 99 (1998) (Tucker Act as amended by the Administrative Disputes Resolution Act confers jurisdiction on court to hear protests challenging procurement decisions of the Postal Service).

[b] In Connection with a Procurement

The Federal Circuit has explained that "the operative phrase 'in connection with' is very sweeping in scope," and "covers a broad range of potential disputes arising during the course of the procurement process," *RAMCOR Servs. Grp., Inc. v. United States*, 185 F.3d 1286 (Fed. Cir. 1999).

Beyond the operative phrase "in connection with," the breadth of § 1491(b) also derives from the broad definition of the term "procurement," which the Federal Circuit has confirmed must be read in relation to its definition within the Office of Federal Procurement Policy Act, *Distributed Sols., Inc. v. United States*, 539 F.3d 1340, 1345-46 (Fed. Cir. 2008). Accordingly, "Procurement" means: "All stages of the process of acquiring property or services, beginning with the process for determining a need for property or services and ending with contract completion or closeout," 41 U.S.C. § 111 (formerly 41 U.S.C. § 403(2)). Applying that broad standard in *Distributed Solutions*, the Federal Circuit concluded that § 1491(b) encompassed a challenge of the rationality of agency market research decisions that resulted in a determination to forego a direct procurement and instead acquire services through subcontracts under an existing prime contractor. In *Systems Application & Techs, Inc. v. United States*, 691 F.3d 1374 (Fed. Cir. 2012), the Federal Circuit likewise applied this broad test to conclude that an agency decision to take corrective action (clearly not a procurement in itself) was nevertheless protestable.

The breadth of the procurement process subject to protest is further illustrated by the unique facts of the Federal Circuit decision finding that an agency decision was not part of the procurement process, *AgustaWestland N. Am., Inc. v. United States*, 880 F.3d 1326 (Fed. Cir. 2018). In *AgustaWestland*, the court held that an Army Executive Order designating the UH-72 as its Institutional Training Helicopter was not a protestable agency action because: "The initiative did not, however, direct or even discuss the procurement of UH-72A Lakota helicopters" and "in fact, the initiative only contemplated using existing Army assets." Based on those facts, the Federal Circuit concluded that the challenged Army order "was not a procurement decision subject to Tucker Act jurisdiction because it did not begin 'the process for determining a need for property or services.'"

Notwithstanding the broad definition of "in connection with a procurement" set forth in *Distributed Solutions*, the Court of Federal Claims judges continue to maintain a distinction between protests made in connection with a procurement and disguised breach of contract disputes that must be raised under the Contract Disputes Act. See *Timberline Helicopter, Inc. v. United States*, 140 Fed. Cl. 614 (2018); *Gov't Tech Servs., LLC v. United States*, 90 Fed. Cl. 522 (2009).

In a curious decision that reveals at least one limit to the scope of § 1491(b) jurisdiction, in *Cleveland Assets, LLC v. United States*, 883 F.3d 1378 (Fed. Cir. 2018), the Federal Circuit held that appropriation legislation conditioning GAO's solicitation of certain leases on obtaining congressional approval could not be the basis of protest because the legislation invoked was a mere "appropriation" statute and not "in connection with a procurement." The court stated at 1381-82:

> The only statute alleged to be violated by Cleveland Assets in Count II is 40 U.S.C. § 3307, an *appropriation*, not a procurement, statute. The plain text of § 3307 demonstrates that the statute is directed to "appropriations [being] made only" pursuant to approval by the specified congressional committees. 40 U.S.C. § 3307(a) (emphasis added). While the word "procurement" is nowhere to be found in the statute, "appropriation" is used eight times.
>
> The statutory structure confirms our plain language reading of the statute. The structure of 40 U.S.C. § 3307 directs GSA how to apply for an appropriation, but it says nothing of how GSA must run its procurement once the appropriation is made. For instance, the statute explains what material must be included in the "prospectus of a proposed project," § 3307(b), the extent to which the estimated maximum cost may be increased, § 3307(c), when approval of a project may be rescinded, § 3307(d), and limitations on leasing certain types of spaces, § 3307(g). Moreover, Chapter 33 of title 40, under which § 3307 exists, generally dictates requirements for GSA's construction, alteration, and lease of government buildings, such as ensuring compliance with building codes and zoning laws. See, e.g., 40 U.S.C. § 3312. But none of the surrounding statutory sections dictate GSA's procurement procedures for any such construction, alteration, or lease.
>
> If we were to read § 3307 as a procurement statute, every appropriations bill and rider would become a potential source of challenge for any interested party under 28 U.S.C. § 1491(b)(1). We therefore affirm the Claims Court's dismissal of Count II of Cleveland Assets' complaint.

The idea that a protester must allege a violation of a procurement statute, as opposed to a violation of a statute that occurs in connection with a procurement would seem inconsistent with *RAMCOR*, which stated at 185 F.3d at 1289: "As long as a statute has a connection to a procurement proposal, an alleged violation suffices to supply jurisdiction." See also *Systems Application & Techs.*, 691 F.3d at 1382 (stating that the court has jurisdiction over "objections related to a statutory or regulatory violation so long as those objections are in connection with a procurement or proposed procurement"). While *Cleveland Assets* should be largely irrelevant to most protests asserting violations of the procurement statutes or the FAR, etc., the decision may in some cases require difficult determinations as to whether a particular statute qualifies as a "procurement statute."

See also *LABAT-Anderson, Inc. v. United States*, 65 Fed. Cl. 570 (2005) (even though the protest did not involve review of a solicitation or award, it involved a government decision not to conduct a solicitation and thus was "in connection with a procurement"); and *Knowledge Connections, Inc. v. United States*, 79 Fed. Cl. 750 (2007) (court does not lose jurisdiction over a protest "because [an agency] allegedly only violated the APA, not a procurement statute"); *Savantage Fin. Servs. v. United States*, 81 Fed. Cl. 300 (2008) (DHS's decision to migrate to the Oracle and SAP constituted a procurement because it reflected DHS's determination of a need to consolidate its financial management software systems, and its selection of the Oracle and SAP systems to meet that need); and *K-LAK Corp. v. United States*, 93 Fed. Cl. 749 (2010) (claims challenging the decision to exit the 8(a) program and use the FSS concerned an alleged violation of statutes and regulations in connection with a procurement). But see *R&D Dynamics Corp. v. United States*, 80 Fed. Cl. 715 (2007) (declining to assume jurisdiction over a postaward protest related to the Army's Small Business Innovation Research Program because the claim did not arise "in connection with a procurement or proposed procurement" despite plaintiff's argument that GAO has routinely held that it has jurisdiction over protest actions related to the SBIR program).

[2] Implied-in-Fact Jurisdiction

28 U.S.C. § 1491(a)(1) confers jurisdiction over "any express or implied contract with the United States."

[a] Contract of the United States

The language of 28 U.S.C. § 1491(a)(1) permitting monetary relief is extremely broad, extending to "any contract of the United States." The following nonappropriated fund activities are explicitly included within the definition of the United States:

- Army and Air Force Exchange Service
- Navy Exchanges
- Marine Corps Exchanges
- Coast Guard Exchanges
- Exchange Councils of the National Aeronautics and Space Administration

The only government agency excluded from coverage is the Tennessee Valley Authority, 28 U.S.C. § 1491(c). In *Slattery v. United States*, 635 F.3d 1298 (Fed. Cir. 2011), the court ruled in an en banc decision that this contract jurisdiction covered any entity that was acting on behalf of the government even though it had been given no appropriated funds. Earlier decisions had interpreted the statute as barring jurisdiction when an agency was receiving no appropriated funds and was not a listed agency. See *McDonald's Corp. v. United States*, 926 F.2d 1126 (Fed. Cir. 1991) (Navy resale and services support office covered even though it was not specifically listed in the statute because the legislative history showed that Congress intended to waive sovereign immunity for military organizations funded by resale activities); *Wolverine Supply, Inc. v. United States*, 17

Cl. Ct. 190 (1989) (Eielson AFB central base fund not covered because it was not included in the NAFI military exchanges set forth in the statute); *Eubanks v. United States*, 25 Cl. Ct. 131 (1992) (United States was not a party to the contract between housing authority and property owner, and its funding and regulating program did not establish any contractual obligation).

[b] Nonprocurement Contracts

Relief under 28 U.S.C. § 1491(a)(1) is available where an issue arises from a federal solicitation which is not a "procurement," *i.e.*, where the federal solicitation concerns a sale, not an acquisition, or where a federal solicitation concerns the lease of federal real property, and not a federal "procurement" of property or services, *Resource Conservation Grp., LLC v. Dep't of Navy*, 597 F.3d 1238 (Fed. Cir. 2010). As discussed above, the judges in the Court of Claims have reached different conclusions as to whether relief under this statute can be obtained on procurement contracts.

[B] Standing—Who May Protest

Like all federal courts, every case before the Court of Federal Claims must satisfy the Article III standing and other justiciability requirements imposed by the U.S. Constitution and Supreme Court. See *Weeks Marine, Inc. v. United States*, 575 F.3d 1352 (Fed. Cir. 2009). In addition to the Article III standing requirements, more stringent "statutory standing" requirements apply to a plaintiff invoking the Court of Federal Claims protest jurisdiction at 28 U.S.C. § 1491(b). "Standing is a threshold jurisdictional issue, which . . . may be decided without addressing the merits of a determination," *Castle v. United States*, 301 F.3d 1328 (Fed. Cir. 2002).

[1] Interested Parties—§ 1491(b)(1)

The threshold issue in determining whether a party has standing under § 1491(b)(1) is whether a protester qualifies as an "interested party." That section states that the Court of Federal Claims has jurisdiction "to render judgment on an action by an interested party objecting to a solicitation. . . ." Following the ADRA, the Federal Circuit was faced with the choice of interpreting § 1491(b) to convey standing to any party that would have had standing to bring an action under the APA in district court or to limit standing to those plaintiffs that satisfy the definition of "interested party" in 31 U.S.C. § 3551(2)(A). The Federal Circuit chose the latter, more restrictive approach, *American Fed. of Gov. Employees AFL-CIO v. United States*, 258 F.3d 1294 (Fed. Cir. 2001). A two-part test is applied to determine whether a protester is an "interested party": (1) the protester must show that it was an actual or prospective offeror; and (2) the protester must have a direct economic interest in the procurement. There is an open question among Court of Federal Claims judges as to whether an additional "prudential standing" requirement applies to protesters invoking § 1491(b).

[a] Actual or Prospective Offeror

As before GAO, the protester must be an actual or prospective offeror. Identifying an actual offeror is straight forward: If the protester actually submitted a proposal, it is an actual offeror. Identifying a prospective offeror is considerably more involved.

A series of Federal Circuit decisions impose fairly strict rules. A subcontractor that fails to submit a proposal or protest prior to the proposal submission deadline is not a prospective offeror, *MCI Telecommunications Corp. v. United States*, 878 F.2d 362 (Fed. Cir. 1989). An offeror that withdraws its proposal prior to submitting a protest is not a prospective offeror. See *Fed. Data Corp. v. United States*, 911 F.2d 699 (Fed. Cir. 1990). While filing a protest prior to the proposal submission deadline is necessary to preserve prospective offeror status, just because a company files an agency protest prior to proposal submission does not necessarily mean the offeror retains prospective offeror status to bring a separate postaward protest months later despite having not submitted a proposal, *Rex Serv. Corp. v. United States*, 448 F.3d 1305 (Fed. Cir. 2006). And, a protester does not qualify as a prospective offeror to protest a sole source award where the protester failed to respond to the agency's request for a statement of capability. *Digitalis Educ. Sols. v. United States*, 664 F.3d 1380 (Fed. Cir. 2012).

The general theme in these cases is that prospective offeror status must be preserved by pursuing protest rights prior to the proposal submission deadline. The exception that proves the rule was addressed by the Federal Circuit, *CGI Fed. Inc. v. United States*, 779 F.3d 1346 (Fed. Cir. 2015), which confirmed that where a protester timely filed a preaward protest at GAO and thereby preserved its prospective offeror status, the protester retained that prospective offeror status by promptly pursuing a second round of protest litigation in the Court of Federal Claims after GAO denied the initial protest, even though the proposal submission deadline lapsed unanswered while the GAO protest was pending.

[b] Direct Economic Interest

To establish interested party status and thus statutory standing under 28 U.S.C. § 1491(b), the protester must establish a direct economic interest in the procurement. The direct economic interest requirement embodies the notion that "prejudice (or injury) is a necessary element of standing," *Myers Investigative & Sec. Servs., Inc. v. United States*, 275 F.3d 1366 (Fed. Cir. 2002). This inquiry is similar to but distinct from the requirement that to succeed a protester must show that it was prejudiced by a significant error in the procurement process. "Although the inquiries may be similar, prejudice must be shown either as part of, or in addition to, showing a direct economic interest," *CliniComp Int'l, Inc. v. United States*, 904 F.3d 1353 (Fed. Cir. 2018). See also *American Relocation Connections, L.L.C. v. United States*, 789 Fed. Appx. 221, 228 (Fed. Cir. 2019) ("For standing, we presume the party bringing a bid protest will succeed on the merits of its claim and ask whether it has alleged an injury (or prejudice) caused by the procuring agency's actions.... But once we find that a party has standing, we must turn to the merits of the party's claim and determine whether it can prove it was prejudiced based on the record evidence."). Prejudice for standing is something less than prejudice on the merits because it is determined on the basis of the protester's allegations not the court's ruling on the validity of those allegations, *Linc Gov't Servs., LLC v. United States*, 95 Fed. Cl. 155 (2010) (calling this concept "allegational prejudice"). It can be demonstrated by cumulating the alleged errors, *USFalcon, Inc. v. United States*, 92 Fed. Cl. 436 (2010).

As with standing generally, the direct economic interest standard depends on the circumstances of the litigation. See *DaimlerChrysler Corp. v. Cuno*, 547 U.S. 332, 352 (2006) ("The standing inquiry requires careful judicial examination of a complaint's allegations to ascertain whether the particular plaintiff is entitled to adjudication of the particular claims asserted."); *Digitalis Educ. Sols. v. United States*, 664 F.3d 1380, 1386 (Fed. Cir. 2012) ("We cannot analyze standing in a vacuum, but rather must take into account the circumstances of the litigant.").

"Generally, to prove the existence of a direct economic interest, a party must show that it had a 'substantial chance' of winning the contract," *Orion Tech., Inc. v. United States*, 704 F.3d 1344, 1348 (Fed. Cir. 2013). In preaward protests challenging the terms of a solicitation, a more lenient standard applies and the protester must show only a "non-trivial competitive injury which can be addressed by judicial relief," *Weeks Marine Inc. v. United States*, 575 F.3d 1352 (Fed. Cir. 2009). In *Weeks Marine*, the court observed that in a preaward protest it is difficult for a prospective offeror to make the showing of prejudice because "there is no factual foundation for a 'but for' prejudice analysis." In some preaward protests, however, the more demanding "substantial chance" standard applies where a protester initiates the action after the agency has evaluated the proposals. See *Orion Tech.*, 704 F.3d at 1348-49 (distinguishing preaward protest challenging terms of a solicitation that may benefit from the lenient *Weeks Marine* standard from preaward protests filed after proposals submission and agency evaluation to which courts must apply the more demanding substantial chance standard); *Omran Holding Grp. v. United States*, 128 Fed. Cl. 273 (2016) (finding substantial chance test appropriate in a preaward challenge to non-responsiveness finding).

In a challenge to the use of a sole source contract, a slightly different standard applies, and the protester "need only establish that it could compete for the contract if the bid process were made competitive." *Myers*, 275 F.3d at 1370 (internal citation and quotation omitted); *CliniComp*, 904 F.3d at 1360 (plaintiff challenging sole source award must show that it is "at least qualified to compete for the contract it seeks").

In some cases, the direct economic interest at issue must be considered in relation to a future, reopened competition. This exception was addressed by the Federal Circuit in *Impresa Construzioni Geom. Domenico Garufi v. United States*, 238 F.3d 1324 (Fed. Cir. 2001), stating at 1334:

> This case is unlike other cases where we have found that (1) a contractor that did not submit a proposal did not have an economic interest, see, e.g., *MCI Telecommunications Corp. v. United States*, 878 F.2d 362 (Fed. Cir. 1989), (2) a bidder who withdrew from the procurement did not have an economic interest, see, e.g., *Fed. Data Corp. v. United States*, 911 F.2d 699 (Fed. Cir. 1990), or (3) a bidder rated below second lacked the required "direct economic interest in the award of the contract," see, e.g., *United States v. International Business Machines Corp.*, 892 F.2d at 1010–12. In those cases, the bid protester had no economic interest in the outcome since, if the protest were successful, the award would go to another party. In this case, as the government has conceded at oral argument, if appellant's bid protest were allowed because of an arbitrary and capricious responsibility determination by the contracting officer, the government would be obligated to rebid the contract, and appellant could compete for the contract once again. Under these circumstances, the appellant has a "substantial chance" of receiving the award and an economic interest and has standing to challenge the award. *Alfa Laval Separation, Inc. v. United States*, 175 F.3d 1365, 1367 (Fed. Cir. 1999).

See also *Magnum Opus Techs., Inc. v. United States*, 94 Fed. Cl. 512 (2010) (discussing case law, recognizing that if protester prevailed, "it will be able to compete in any re-solicitation for the services it alleges should have been subject to competition.").

Cases finding prejudice for standing purposes include *Coastal Int'l Sec., Inc. v. United States*, 93 Fed. Cl. 502 (2010) (plaintiff was in competitive range and record indicated that the competition between the two proposals was very close); *Hunt Bldg. Co. v. United States*, 61 Fed. Cl. 243 (2004) (protester was one of two offerors in the competitive range, with both deemed by the agency to be outstanding); *PGBA, LLC, v. United States*, 60 Fed. Cl. 196 (2004) (proposal was fully within the zone of consideration for a contractual award, and agency's handling of the data—access element showed unequal and unfair treatment). In *Systems Plus, Inc. v. United States*, 69 Fed. Cl. 757 (2006), the court held that the protester would have had a substantial chance of winning the contract. The protester was a qualified small business, and its proposal was found to be technically acceptable. Also, as the incumbent supplier on many deliverables under the agreement, the protester demonstrated it was capable of performing the contract. But see *Homesource Real Estate Asset Servs., Inc. v. United States*, 94 Fed. Cl. 466 (2010), where the court held that even if plaintiff's protest grounds were sustained, there were eight vendors that did not receive any award and had higher technical ratings than plaintiff. Any of these eight vendors would have provided a better choice to the government. Therefore, even if plaintiff were to succeed in its protest on the merits, there was not a substantial chance it would be awarded the contract.

[c] Prudential Standing

The doctrine of "prudential standing" is a function of APA litigation. The Supreme Court explained in *Bennett v. Spear*, 520 U.S. 154 (1997), at 162:

> The question of standing "involves both constitutional limitations on federal-court jurisdiction and prudential limitations on its exercise... [U]nlike their constitutional counterparts," prudential limitations "can be modified or abrogated by Congress. Numbered among these prudential requirements is the doctrine... that a plaintiff's grievance must arguably fall within the zone of interest protected or regulated by the statutory provision or constitutional guarantee invoked in the suit... [T]he breadth of the zone of interests varies according to the provisions of law at issue... Congress legislates against the background of our prudential standing doctrine, which applies unless it is expressly negated. (Citations omitted)

The Court of Federal Claims judges are divided as to whether the "zone of interests" prudential standing test applies to protesters invoking § 1491(b) jurisdiction. Compare *Hallmark-Phoenix 3, LLC v. United States*, 99 Fed. Cl. 65, 69-71 (2011) (prudential standing *does* apply), with *Santa Barbara Applied Research, Inc. v. United States*, 98 Fed. Cl. 536, 544 (2011) (prudential standing *does not* apply), and *MORI Assocs., Inc. v. United States*, 102 Fed. Cl. 503, 542 (2011) (same); see also *Springfield Parcel C, LLC v. United States*, 124 Fed. Cl. 163, 190 (2015) (While "Subsection 3307(a), might not provide an independent basis for a private cause of action, it could... supply a basis for a claim of a contravention of law in a bid protest."). The Federal Circuit was presented with an opportunity to resolve this divide, but declined the invitation in *Cleveland Assets, LLC v. United States*, 883 F.3d 1378 (Fed. Cir. 2018).

That the "zone of interests" requirement does not provide an additional standing hurdle for protests filed under § 1491(b) seems to follow directly from the Supreme Court's analysis in *Bennett* and its conclusion that prudential standing did not apply in that case. *Bennett* involved an environmental statute with a "citizen-suit" provision under which "any person" was authorized to sue to enjoin any alleged violation of the statute. The Supreme Court found that the citizen suit provision "negates the zone-of-interests test (or, perhaps more accurately, expands the zone of interests)." The Court recognized that Congress had identified a class of plaintiffs (*i.e.*, "any person") and given them standing to act as private attorneys general to enforce the public interest in the environment protected by the statute, noting at 165 that: "the obvious purpose of the particular provision in question is to encourage enforcement by so-called 'private attorneys general.'"

The entire point of protest jurisdiction under § 1491(b) is to authorize prospective contractors to act as private attorneys general to ensure the public's interest in a lawful procurement process. Congress enacted § 1491(b) through the Administrative Disputes Resolution Act of 1996 (ADRA), Pub. L. No. 104-320, in order to vest the Court of Federal Claims with the same protest jurisdiction previously exercised by district courts pursuant to *Scanwell Labs., Inc. v. Shaffer*, 424 F.2d 859 (D.C. Cir. 1970). See *American Fed'n of Gov't Employees, AFL-CIO v. United States*, 258 F.3d 1294 (Fed. Cir. 2001) ("Congress intended to confer on the [COFC] jurisdiction previously exercised only by district courts under *Scanwell*."). And *Scanwell* made it clear that the very reason a disappointed contractor has standing under the Administrative Procedure Act to challenge the propriety of an agency's procurement process was in the capacity as a private attorney general serving the public interest. Thus, there should be no question that protests brought under § 1491(b) need not satisfy any additional requirement of prudential standing, because Congress has already stated in § 1491(b) that any interested party may protest the lawfulness of an agency procurement. The aim of "prudential standing," to narrow the class of potential plaintiffs, is achieved through the "interested party" requirement, which limits standing under § 1491(b)(1) to actual or prospective offerors whose direct economic interest would be affected by the award of the contract or by failure to award the contract. There is no additional "zone of interests" requirement. Nor is it necessary for any allegedly contravened statute to itself contain a citizen-suit provision, as "Congress's use of the modifier 'any' in the ADRA, so that [Court of Federal Claims has] jurisdiction over interested parties' objections to 'any alleged violation of statute or regulation in connection with a procurement,' ... expands standing beyond the zone-of-interests test." *MORI Assocs., Inc. v. United States*, 102 Fed. Cl. 503, 542 (2011). Accordingly, even where a statute does not itself provide independent basis for a private cause of action, "it could ... supply a basis for a claim of a contravention of law in a bid protest," *Springfield Parcel C, LLC v. United States*, 124 Fed. Cl. 163 (2015).

[2] Disappointed Offerors—§ 1491(a)(1)

As noted above, this jurisdiction applies only to nonprocurement contracts. The most common form of implied contract in contract award cases under § 1491(a)(1) arose when the government issued a solicitation, thereby making an offer to honestly and fairly consider responses, and the prospective contractor accepted this offer by submitting a bid or proposal, *Keco Indus., Inc. v. United States*, 428 F.2d 1233 (Ct. Cl. 1970); *United States v. John C. Grimberg Co.*, 702 F.2d 1362 (Fed. Cir. 1983); *National Forge Co. v. United States*, 779 F.2d 665 (Fed. Cir. 1985). Such cases were usually characterized as "disappointed bidder" cases. In order to obtain jurisdiction on the basis of such implied contracts, the "disappointed bidder" had to plead that it had accepted the government's offer contained in the solicitation. Thus, a party that did not submit a bid or proposal had no contract claim because it did not furnish the government the consideration requested for its promise, *Hero, Inc. v. United States*, 3 Cl. Ct. 413 (1983). In that case, the plaintiff expended effort in preparing a bid but did not submit the bid, contending that the specifications were defective. The court refused to grant an injunction preventing award under the solicitation, reasoning that the mere expenditure of effort and money in preparing a bid without actually submitting it is not sufficient consideration for the government's implied promise. In *Harris Sys. Int'l, Inc. v. United States*, 5 Cl. Ct. 253 (1984), the court found no jurisdiction in an action by a small-business minority firm that had not submitted a proposal because the procuring agency had demanded that the SBA nominate another firm under the 8(a) set-aside. The court also held that the fact that the SBA had originally nominated the plaintiff to the Air Force did not establish an implied contract. In *Eagle Constr. Corp. v. United States*, 4 Cl. Ct. 470 (1984), the court found that the government's cancellation of a solicitation after technical proposals were received was not improper under the circumstances. Thus, the plaintiff who submitted a proposal under that solicitation but failed to submit one under the new solicitation for the same work had no disappointed bidder status under the new solicitation. See also *Control Data Sys., Inc. v. United States*, 32 Fed. Cl. 520 (1994) (incumbent contractor did not submit a proposal for follow-on contract, and the plaintiff's claim was therefore not a preaward protest within the jurisdiction of the court); *Durable Metals Prods., Inc. v. United States*, 27 Fed. Cl. 472 (1993) (no jurisdiction because offeror withdrew from procurement); *Howard v. United States*, 21 Cl. Ct. 475 (1990) (proposal submitted after closing date for receipt of proposals; thus, no valid offer that the government could accept); and *Data Transformation Corp. v. United States*, 13 Cl. Ct. 165 (1987) (informal presentation made to an agency of the plaintiff's technical ability to perform the work called for under the planned program was not the same as a response to a solicitation and did not create an implied-in-fact contract). While the court's rationale in nonbidder cases is clearly supportable where the plaintiff has not expended effort in reliance on the solicitation or decides to forgo the procurement, it is questionable where expenditures have been made in reliance on a solicitation that contains defective specifications or is otherwise improper.

The mere submission of a bid did not establish the necessary contractual relationship; the submission had to be responsive to the invitation for bids. In *Yachts Am., Inc. v. United States*, 3 Cl. Ct. 447 (1983), *aff'd*, 779 F.2d 656 (Fed. Cir. 1985), the documents and letter submitted to the agency were found to be wholly nonresponsive and, thus, failed to give the plaintiff the status of a disappointed bidder. However, the court would review the bid and the solicitation to determine whether it was responsive and, if it so found, would exercise its jurisdiction, *Olympia USA, Inc. v. United States*, 6 Cl. Ct. 550 (1984). See also *Blount, Inc. v. United States*, 22 Cl. Ct. 221 (1990) (court exercised jurisdiction to determine whether a clause in the IFB not addressed by the bid related to bidder responsiveness or responsibility). The disappointed bidder also had to be able to show actual or threatened injury. In *Caddell Constr. Co. v. United States*, 9 Cl. Ct. 610 (1986), the court held that an offeror ranked sixth had no substantial chance for award and, thus, had no standing to sue. In addition, the firm submitting the offer had to be eligible to receive the award, *ATL, Inc. v. United States*, 735 F.2d 1343 (Fed. Cir. 1984) (bids following a firm's suspension or debarment could not create implied contract because such firms are ineligible for award); *Gibraltar Indus., Inc. v. United States*, 2 Cl. Ct. 589 (1983), *vacated as moot*, 726 F.2d 747 (Fed. Cir. 1984) (bidder determined not to be a small business could not create implied contract by bidding on small business set-aside). However, a suspension or debarment issued after a bid or proposal has been submitted does not deprive the disappointed offeror of jurisdiction over such a previous bid or proposal, *Sterlingwear of Boston, Inc. v. United States*, 11 Cl. Ct. 517 (1987); *Electro-Methods, Inc. v. United States*, 728 F.2d 1471 (Fed. Cir. 1984). The court would take jurisdiction over claims alleging that the agency has improperly applied responsibility standards to an offeror, *Hayes Int'l Corp. v. United States*, 7 Cl. Ct. 681 (1985). See also *Skytech Aero, Inc. v. United States*, 26 Cl. Ct. 251 (1992), where an unsuccessful bidder alleged that the Army acted arbitrarily and capriciously by awarding a contract to a bidder that was not responsible and whose bid was nonresponsive. The court exercised jurisdiction and held that a preaward survey conducted by the Army allowed a reasonable conclusion that the bidder was responsible. The Court of Federal Claims has jurisdiction to review certificate of competency determinations by the SBA, *Cavalier Clothes, Inc. v. United States*, 810 F.2d 1108 (Fed. Cir. 1987); *Stapp Towing, Inc. v. United States*, 34 Fed. Cl. 300 (1995); *Related Indus., Inc. v. United States*, 2 Cl. Ct. 517 (1983).

In several rare cases, the court found preaward implied contracts to exist in situations other than disappointed bidder cases. See *Western Pioneer, Inc. v. United States*, 8 Cl. Ct. 291 (1985), where the court held that a letter requesting that the plaintiff submit its proposed operating plan constituted "a sufficient request . . . such as to form an implied contract to fairly and honestly consider [the] responding proposal." See also *Standard Mfg. Co. v. United States*, 7 Cl. Ct. 54 (1984), where the plaintiff alleged that it responded to a *Commerce Business Daily* (CBD) notice in which the Air Force stated its intention to award a sole source contract and invited interested parties to identify interests in the procurement or to submit proposals for the work. The court held that such facts are sufficient to create an implied promise for the Air Force to give fair and impartial consideration to the response. Similarly, in *Magnavox Elec. Sys. Co. v. United States*, 26 Cl. Ct. 1373 (1992), the court held that a CBD notice of intent to conduct a sole source procurement and plaintiff's response that it could perform the work resulted in an implied contract to give plaintiff's response fair and impartial consideration. However, in *Motorola, Inc. v. United States*, 988 F.2d 113 (Fed. Cir. 1993), the court affirmed a decision of the Court of Federal

Claims denying jurisdiction over a suit filed by a company that assisted the government in drafting the procurement specification but did not submit an offer because a bid sample was required. The Federal Circuit adopted the Court of Federal Claims decision, which disagreed with the rationale in *Standard Manufacturing*, stating that government requests for information and responses from prospective bidders are not the equivalents of offer and acceptance. See also *Garchik v. United States*, 37 Fed. Cl. 52 (1996), where the court denied jurisdiction over a proposal submitted in response to a CBD announcement that the agency proposed to enter into a sole source lease. In *American Hoist & Derrick, Inc. v. United States*, 3 Cl. Ct. 198 (1983), the plaintiff was a large business that was precluded from bidding on a solicitation because the procurement was set-aside for small businesses. However, the court took jurisdiction on the basis of an implied contract alleged to have been formed when the plaintiff released its proprietary data to the government in exchange for an agreement that it would be permitted to bid on the procurement. See also *Yachts Am., Inc. v. United States*, 3 Cl. Ct. 447 (1983), *aff'd*, 779 F.2d 656 (Fed. Cir. 1985). In *Airborne Data, Inc. v. United States*, 702 F.2d 1350 (Fed. Cir. 1983), the court held that an implied contract was formed when an unsolicited proposal was received in response to regulations inviting the submittal of such proposals. In *Pressman v. United States*, 33 Fed. Cl. 438 (1995), the court held that the agency's regulations prohibiting the release of confidential information did not give rise to an implied contract not to disclose confidential information contained in unsolicited proposals. The court distinguished *Airborne Data*, stating that in that case the text of the regulations contained an explicit promise of confidentiality, whereas in *Pressman* the regulations, although binding on the agency, could not be construed as suggesting that the agency was directing an offer to the general public to confidentially consider unsolicited proposals.

[C] Time for Protest

There are three legal frameworks relevant to protest timing: the Tucker Act's six-year statute of limitations, the judicially crafted *Blue & Gold* rule, and the common law doctrine of laches.

All actions filed at the Court of Federal Claims are subject to a strict six-year statute of limitations, although some actions within the court's jurisdiction are subject to a shorter time bar. See 28 U.S.C. § 2501 and 28 U.S.C. § 1498(b) (providing three-year limitation period for copyright actions). Notwithstanding a consistent line of Supreme Court precedent finding that statutes of limitation are generally not jurisdictional and are therefore subject to equitable tolling, the Supreme Court has distinguished the Tucker Act's six-year statute of limitations as jurisdictional, *John R. Sand & Gravel Co. v. United States*, 552 U.S. 130 (2008).

There is no express statutory deadline unique to protests filed under 28 U.S.C. § 1491(b), and neither the FAR nor agency supplemental regulations impose any mandatory administrative exhaustion obligation that would require an agency level or GAO protest prior to seeking judicial review before the court. See *Darby v. Cisneros*, 509 U.S. 137, 154 (1993) (discussing relationship between administrative exhaustion requirements and judicial review of agency action). Section 1491(b)(3) does, however, urge the court to "give due regard to the interest of national defense and national security and the need for expeditions resolution" of protests. The Federal Circuit has interpreted this language to impose a prudential timeliness requirement, known as the *Blue & Gold* rule, that a party who has the opportunity to object to the terms of a government solicitation containing a patent error and fails to do so "prior to the close of the bidding process" waives its ability to raise the same objection afterwards in a § 1491(b) action in the Court of Federal Claims," *Blue & Gold Fleet, L.P. v. United States*, 492 F.3d 1308 (Fed. Cir. 2007). There have been numerous decisions following this rule. See, for example, *Peraton Inc. v. United States*, 146 Fed. Cl. 94 (2019) (denying protester's postaward attempt to amend a prior protest mooted by corrective action and request for stay pending award when it was contesting the corrective action); *Land Shark Shredding, LLC v. United States*, 145 Fed. Cl. 338 (2019) (rejecting postaward arguments that cascading set-aside scheme in solicitation was improper); *Telos Identity Mgmt. Sols., LLC v. United States*, 143 Fed. Cl. 787 (2019) (rejecting postaward argument that solicitation statement that agency intended to award single IDIQ contract was improper); *Voith Hydro, Inc. v. United States*, 142 Fed. Cl. 233 (2019) (rejecting postaward argument that evaluation criteria were improper); and *Unisys Corp. v. United States*, 89 Fed. Cl. 126 (2009) (propriety of a price evaluation methodology that was explicitly described in the RFQ). In *MLS-Multinational Logistic Servs. v. United States*, 143 Fed. Cl. 341 (2019), the court did not apply the rule because the protester had filed a protest with the agency contesting solicitation terms before submitting its proposal and had continuing discussions with agency until months award before filing its suit in the court. See *Bannum, Inc. v. United States*, 779 F.3d 1376 (Fed. Cir. 2015), assuming that filing a formal, agency-level protest or a GAO protest before proposal submission would preserve a protestor's postaward challenge to a solicitation in the court. Compare *Per Aarsleff A/S v. United States*, 829 F.3d 1303 (Fed. Cir. 2016) (postaward protest of solicitation defect untimely where protester knew of solicitation defect prior to award, asked agency for clarification, received non-answer, and did not pursue preaward protest).

In *COMINT Sys. Corp. v. United States*, 700 F.3d 1377 (Fed. Cir. 2012), the Federal Circuit expanded the *Blue & Gold* rule to apply where the protester failed to file a preaward protest concerning a solicitation amendment issued after the initial proposal submission deadline. The Federal Circuit applied the *COMINT* logic in *Inserso Corp. v. United States*, 961 F.3d 1343 (Fed. Cir. 2020), ruling that Inserso had forfeited its right to protest an unfair competitive advantage given to some of its competitors by the disclosure of pricing information during the period when the agency was conducting discussions. A dissent argued that the entire *Blue & Gold* rule is wrong because of the reasoning of the Supreme

Court in *SCA Hygiene Products Aktiebolag v. First Quality Baby Prods., LLC*, 137 S. Ct. 954 (2017), holding that the court could not impose a shorter timeliness rule (through laches) when Congress had adopted a statutory statute of limitations.

Some Court of Federal Claims decisions interpret *Blue & Gold* and *COMINT* to broadly require protest of any concerns that are known or should have been known prior to award. See *RMGS, Inc. v. United States*, 140 Fed. Cl. 728 (2018) (protest of restrictive OCI clause after signing contract containing clause and protesting on barred contract); *MSC Indus. Direct Co. v. United States*, 140 Fed. Cl. 632 (2018) (protest contending that agency policy changes required new RFQ known before award); *Synergy Sols., Inc. v. United States*, 133 Fed. Cl. 716, 740 (2017) (protest of known lack of discussions not asserted prior to award); *QTC Med. Servs., Inc. v. United States*, 132 Fed. Cl. 610, 621-22 (2017) (protest of misleading discussions not asserted prior to submission of final proposal revisions); *Jacobs Tech., Inc. v. United States*, 100 Fed. Cl. 179, 182 n.4 (2011) (preaward protest proper). Others are less willing to find waiver of a postaward protest argument that involves concerns originating before award. See *ATSC Aviation, LLC v. United States*, 141 Fed. Cl. 670, 693-96 (2019) (allowing timely postaward protest of exclusion from competitive range on grounds that allegedly were only known after award and only relief requested was being added to pool of IDIQ contractors). See also *iAccess Techs., Inc. v. United States*, 143 Fed. Cl. 521 (2019), refusing to apply the GAO rule requiring filing within 10 days of notice of the protest grounds when iAccess filed its preaward protest over three months after learning of its exclusion from the competitive range.

In addition to *Blue & Gold*, the common law doctrine of laches may serve as an independent timeliness requirement, particularly in the context of a significantly delayed postaward protest where *Blue & Gold* may not apply but the delay is prejudicial to the agency and awardee. The Court of Federal Claims judges are divided as to whether laches applies to protests filed under § 1491(b). The court applied laches to bar a protest in *Global Dynamics, LLC v. United States*, 137 Fed. Cl. 105 (2018). In doing so, the *Global Dynamics* decision relied on the *Blue & Gold* decision itself, which acknowledged the doctrine of laches in support of its holding, as well as *Nat'l Telecommuting Inst., Inc. v. United States*, 123 Fed. Cl. 595 (2015). Subsequently, and without acknowledging *Global Dynamics*, the Court of Federal Claims held in *ATSC Aviation, LLC v. United States*, 141 Fed. Cl. 670 (2019), that the doctrine of laches is not available in the context of a bid protest. The *ATSC* analysis relied on a pair of Supreme Court rulings that where the common law doctrine of laches cannot apply where Congress has already legislated a statute of limitations. *SCA Hygiene Prods. Aktiebolag v. First Quality Baby Prods.*, 137 S. Ct. 954 (2017); and *Petrella v. Metro-Goldwyn-Mayer, Inc.*, 572 U.S. 663 (2014). In light of these Supreme Court directives, the *ATSC* decision reasons that the Tucker Act's six-year statute of limitations precludes application of laches.

There are a few older decisions holding postaward protests untimely on the basis of laches, *National Telecommuting Inst., Inc. v. United States*, 123 Fed. Cl. 595 (2015) (six-month delay); *Reilly v. United States*, 104 Fed. Cl. 69 (2012) (nine-month delay). In one case, the court deemed timely a protest filed 14 months after the protester knew or should have known of the basis of the protest, *CW Gov't Travel, Inc. v. United States*, 61 Fed. Cl. 559 (2004).

[D] Intervenors

Intervenors are permitted under the Rules of the United States Court of Federal Claims (RCFC) 24, which states:

> (a) Intervention of Right. On timely motion, the court must permit anyone to intervene who:
>
> (1) is given an unconditional right to intervene by a federal statute; or
>
> (2) claims an interest relating to the property or transaction that is the subject of the action, and is so situated that disposing of the action may as a practical matter impair or impede the movant's ability to protect its interest, unless the existing parties adequately represent that interest.
>
> (b) Permissive Intervention.
>
> (1) *In General.* On timely motion, the court may permit anyone to intervene who:
>
> (A) is given a conditional right to intervene by a federal statute; or
>
> (B) has a claim or defense that shares with the main action a question of law or fact.
>
> (2) By a Government Officer or Agency.
> [Not used.]
> (3) *Delay or Prejudice.* In exercising its discretion, the court must consider whether the intervention will unduly delay or prejudice the adjudication of the original parties' rights.

The court has held that the requirements for intervention are to be construed in favor of intervention, *Cherokee Nation of Oklahoma v. United States*, 69 Fed. Cl. 148 (2005). Consistent with other circuit courts, the Federal Circuit has articulated a four-part test for intervention as a matter of right in *Wolfsen Land & Cattle Co. v. Pacific Coast Fed'n of Fishermen's Ass'ns*, 695 F.3d 1310 (Fed. Cir. 2012), at 1315:

> First, the motion must be timely. Second, the movant must claim some interest in the property affected by the case. This interest must be "legally

> protectable"—merely economic interest will not suffice. Third, that interest's relationship to the litigation must be "of such a direct and immediate character that the intervenor will either gain or lose by the direct legal operation and effect of the judgment." Fourth, . . . the movant must demonstrate that said interest is not adequately addressed by the government's participation. (Citations omitted)

These requirements are to be "construed in favor of intervention," but failure to demonstrate any element of the test may be fatal.

First, although there are no strict deadlines associated with a motion, the circumstantial analysis generally considers: (1) the length of time during which the would-be intervenors actually knew or reasonably should have known of their rights; (2) whether the prejudice to the rights of existing parties by allowing intervention outweighs the prejudice to the would-be intervenors by denying intervention; and (3) the existence of unusual circumstances militating either for or against a determination that the application is timely. See *Fairholme Funds, Inc. v. United States*, 681 Fed. Appx. 945, 949 (Fed. Cir. 2017); *Belton Indus., Inc. v. United States*, 6 F.3d 756 (Fed. Cir. 1993). See also *Wackenhut Servs., Inc. v. United States*, 85 Fed. Cl. 273 (2008) (motion submitted two days after complaint, no party opposed motion and the court was unaware of any prejudice to the existing parties or any unusual circumstances); and *Information Scis. Corp. v. United States*, 73 Fed. Cl. 70 (2006) (submitted seven days after complaint, neither party opposed intervention, and court was unaware of any prejudice to existing parties or any unusual circumstances militating against intervention). However, in *TRW Envtl. Safety Sys., Inc. v. United States*, 16 Cl. Ct. 516 (1989), the Claims Court held that an unsuccessful bidder's motion to intervene in another unsuccessful bidder's suit for injunctive relief was untimely: the bidder waited 84 days from knowing of the suit before moving to intervene.

Second, with respect to the intervenor's "interest," RCFC Rule 24(a)(2) requires that an intervenor "claim[] an interest relating to the property transaction that is the subject of the action," and the Supreme Court has characterized the adequate interest requirement as requiring that the applicant have an interest 'relating to the property or transaction which is the subject of the action' that is 'significantly protectable,'" *American Renovation & Constr. Co. v. United States*, 65 Fed. Cl. 254 (2005) (quoting *Donaldson v. United States*, 400 U.S. 517 (1971)). The Federal Circuit has emphasized that "[i]ntervention is proper only to protect those interests which are 'of such a direct and immediate character that the intervenor will either gain or lose by the direct legal operation and effect of the judgment'" and that the "interest thus may not be either indirect or contingent," *American Mar. Transp., Inc. v. United States*, 870 F.2d 1559 (Fed. Cir. 1989). See also *Klamath Irrigation Dist. v. United States*, 64 Fed. Cl. 328 (2005). A "merely economic" interest will not suffice; rather, the interest must be "legally protectable," *Wolfsen*, 695 F.3d at 1315.

Third, "[i]ntervention is proper only to protect those interests which are of such a direct and immediate character that the intervenor will either gain or lose by the direct legal operations and effect of the judgment." *American Mar. Transp.*, 870 F.2d at 1561. The Court of Federal Claims has framed the issue as whether "the disposition of this case may as a practical matter impair or impede the applicant's ability to protect its interests." *Klamath*, 64 Fed. Cl. at 332. In most protests, the intervenor will be the awardee of the protested procurement and thus the awardee and its evaluation are directly at issue in the protest. In addition, to the extent the protester seeks access to the intervenor's proprietary proposal and evaluation materials, the intervenor's interest in protecting those materials is likewise at issue. See *Northrop Grumman Info. Tech. v. United States*, 74 Fed. Cl. 407 (2006) (permitting intervention in bid protest, noting "trade secrets and proprietary information are the very type of interest the protection of which justifies intervention under Rule 24(a)"); *Armour of Am. v. United States*, 70 Fed. Cl. 240 (2006) (permitting intervention and recognizing cognizable interest in protecting propriety information at issue in litigation).

Fourth, the "burden of demonstrating inadequacy of representation is not heavy: according to the Supreme Court, this requirement 'is satisfied if the applicant shows that representation of his interests "may be" inadequate; and the burden of making that showing should be treated as minimal,'" *Klamath*, 64 Fed. Cl. at 335-36 (quoting *Trbovich v. United Mine Workers of Am.*, 404 U.S. 528 (1972)). See also *Wolfsen*, 695 F.3d at 1315. In the context of a protest where the awardee seeks to intervene, while the government and intervenor may both initially share the goal of defeating the protest, it does not necessarily follow that the government and intervenor share the same interests much less that the government can adequately represent the intervenor's interests throughout the litigation. See *CHE Consulting*, 71 Fed. Cl. at 634-35 (finding intervenor's interests were not adequately represented by a competitor or the government in a protest where the competitor challenged solicitation provisions that the intervenor had an interest in preserving); *Armour of Am.*, 70 Fed. Cl. at 245 (finding inadequate representation of interests to protect intervenor's proprietary information); *Coastal Int'l Sec. Inc. v. United States*, 93 Fed. Cl. 502, 526 (2010); *Mgmt. Sols. & Sys., Inc. v. United States*, 75 Fed. Cl. 820, 827 (2007).

The standard for permissive intervention is much more discretionary. "The Court's decision regarding permissive intervention is discretionary, and the absence of an abuse of discretion, the trial court's ruling will be upheld." *Choctaw Nation of Okla. v. United States*, 69 Fed. Cl. 148 (2005) (citing *Chapman v. Manbeck*, 931 F.2d 46 (Fed. Cir. 1991)). Permissive intervention is appropriate when the movant's claims or defenses share a common question of law or fact with the main action, and the intervention will not unduly delay the action or prejudice the rights of existing parties. See *ACME Worldwide Enters., Inc. v. United States*, 137 Fed. Cl. 469 (2018) (granting permissive intervention where there was doubt as to whether the elements of intervention as of right were satisfied). Although a motion to intervene permissively must be timely, the timeliness requirement for permissive intervention is often applied less strictly. See *ACME Worldwide* (citing *R&G Mortg. Corp. v. Fed. Home Loan Mortg. Corp.*, 584 F.3d 1 (1st Cir. 2009)). Similarly, for permissive intervention, the intervenor need not necessarily demonstrate the legal interest necessary to support intervention as of right, but "need only show that it has an interest sufficient to support a legal claim or defense which is founded upon that interest and which satisfies the Rule's commonality requirement." *ACME Worldwide* (quoting *Diamond v. Charles*, 476 U.S. 54 (1986)).

[E] Procedures

28 U.S.C. § 1491(b)(4) directs the Court of Federal Claims to review procurement protests applying the APA standard of review at 5 U.S.C. § 706. This in effect means that protest litigation under § 1491(b) is subject to the body of procedural law developed under the APA. This primarily impacts the scope of record materials upon which the court must make its decision as well as the standard of review that the court applies when reviewing that record.

The Court of Federal Claims follows the rules set forth in the Rules of the United States Court of Federal Claims (RCFC). These rules are based upon the Federal Rules of Civil Procedure. To implement APA review of protest cases, RCFC Rule 52.1 addresses the administrative record and "Motions for Judgment on the Administrative Record," the primary procedural mechanism through which protests are resolved. Appendix C to the RCFC, which is entitled "Procedures in Procurement Protest Cases Pursuant to 28 U.S.C. § 1491(b)" describes standard practices in Court of Federal Claims protest cases.

[1] Administrative Record

As dictated by § 1491(b), the Court of Federal Claims reviews protests "under the standards set forth in the [Administrative Procedure Act]," *Impresa Construzioni Geom. Domenico Garufi v. United States*, 238 F.3d 1324, 1332 (Fed. Cir. 2001). "The task of the reviewing court is to apply the appropriate APA standard of review, 5 U.S.C. § 706, to the agency decision based on the record the agency presents to the reviewing court," *Axiom Res. Mgmt., Inc. v. United States*, 564 F.3d 1374 (Fed. Cir. 2009) (quoting *Florida Power & Light Co. v. Lorion*, 470 U.S. 729 (1985)).

Courts have developed an important and complex body of law to resolve the many disputes that arise regarding what materials are included in the administrative record and the circumstances under which the administrative record may be supplemented. Before engaging the contents of the administrative record, however, two issues should be considered. First, while the merits of a legal challenge to agency action will generally be confined to the administrative record, courts must make some findings in the first instance that are not tied to the administrative record before the agency. The most common examples are factual findings regarding the court's own jurisdiction, the parties' standing, entitlement to injunctive relief, and prejudice. See *Navistar Def., LLC v. United States*, 146 Fed. Cl. 499 (2019); *MSC Indus. Direct Co., Inv. v. United States*, 140 Fed. Cl. 632 (2018) (citing *Cedars Sinai Med. Ctr. v. Watkins*, 11 F.3d 1573, 1584 (Fed. Cir. 1993)); *CW Gov't Travel, Inc. v. United States*, 110 Fed. Cl. 462 (2013); *PlanetSpace, Inc. v. United States*, 90 Fed. Cl. 1 (2009); *AshBritt, Inc. v. United States*, 87 Fed. Cl. 344, 367 (2009). The court may consider evidence relevant to these issues in the first instance without engaging in record supplementation.

Second, many disputes over the contents of the administrative record can be avoided through the court's authority to take judicial notice over certain facts, particularly the contents of official government documents that are often at issue in protests but not necessarily included in the agency record. See *Harkon, Inc. v. United States*, 132 Fed. Cl. 697, 701 (2017); *Alabama Aircraft Indus., Inc.-Birmingham v. United States*, 82 Fed. Cl. 757 (2008).

With respect to the contents of the administrative record, there is an important distinction between the compilation of documents that the government provides a court in response to a protest and the body of information that constitutes the administrative record required for APA review. The APA directs a court evaluating agency action to "review the whole record or other parts of it cited by a party," 5 U.S.C. § 706. The "whole record" includes "all documents and materials that the agency directly or indirectly considered," *Bar MK Ranches v. Yuetter*, 994 F.3d 735 (10th Cir. 1993); *MG Altus Apache Co. v. United States*, 102 Fed. Cl. 744 (2012) (the record should contain "all relevant information on which the agency relied or allegedly should have relied in making the challenged decision."). In other words, when conducting APA review a court "should have before it neither more nor less than did the agency when it made its decision," *IMS, P.C. v. Alvarez*, 129 F.3d 618 (D.C. Cir. 1997).

As a starting point for gathering the "whole record," RCFC Appendix C provides a detailed list as guidance regarding the type of documents that may be appropriate for the United States to include as "core documents" in the administrative record pertaining to protests:

(a) the agency's procurement request, purchase request, or statement of requirements;

(b) the agency's source selection plan;

(c) the bid abstract or prospectus of bid;

(d) the Commerce Business Daily or other public announcement of the procurement;

(e) the solicitation, including any instructions to offerors, evaluation factors, solicitation amendments, and requests for best and final offers;

(f) documents and information provided to bidders during any pre-bid or pre-proposal conference;

(g) the agency's responses to any questions about or requests for clarification of the solicitation;

(h) the agency's estimates of the cost of performance;

(i) correspondence between the agency and the protester, awardee, or other interested parties relating to the procurement;

(j) records of any discussions, meetings, or telephone conferences between the agency and the protester, awardee, or other interested parties relating to the procurement;

(k) records of the results of any bid opening or oral motion auction in which the protester, awardee, or other interested parties participated;

(l) the protester's, awardee's, or other interested parties' offers, proposals, or other responses to the solicitation;

(m) the agency's competitive range determination, including supporting documentation;

(n) the agency's evaluations of the protester's, awardee's, or other interested parties' offers, proposals, or other responses to the solicitation, including supporting documentation;

(o) the agency's source selection decision including supporting documentation;

(p) preaward audits, if any, or surveys of the offerors;

(q) notification of contract award and the executed contract;

(r) documents relating to any pre- or post-award debriefing;

(s) documents relating to any stay, suspension, or termination of award or performance pending resolution of the bid protest;

(t) justifications, approvals, determinations, and findings, if any, prepared for the procurement by the agency pursuant to statute or regulation; and

(u) the record of any previous administrative or judicial proceedings relating to the procurement, including the record of any other protest of the procurement.

Where a party seeks to have the government add evidence to the record generated or considered by the agency during the procurement and decision-making process, the court considers such a request as one to complete the record. This is based on the premise that a "complete administrative record is the predicate to meaningful and effective judicial review of agency action," *Joint Venture of Comint Sys. Corp. v. United States*, 100 Fed. Cl. 159 (2011) (noting that a court "certainly cannot engage in effective judicial review in the absence of a complete agency record"); *Tauri Grp., LLC v. United States*, 99 Fed. Cl. 475 (2011) (ordering agency to complete record with documents agency relied on during evaluation, individual evaluation worksheets, documents referenced in agency declarations filed in support of decision); *Kerr Contractors, Inc. v. United States*, 89 Fed. Cl. 312 (2009), *aff'd*, 374 Fed. Appx. 979 (Fed. Cir. 2010) (granting motion to include agency's responses to questions about solicitation in record); *Alabama Aircraft Indus., Inc.-Birmingham v. United States*, 82 Fed. Cl. 757 (2008) (granting motion to include civil and criminal settlement agreements between awardee and government in record because documents "were available to agency at time it made its decision and underpinned a part of its consideration of [the awardee's] past performance").

Supplementing the administrative record is distinct from directing the government to complete the administrative record by providing all of the materials actually considered by the agency. *Joint Venture of Comint Sys. Corp.*, 100 Fed. Cl. at 167 ("Admission of new evidence into an agency-assembled record is a separate and distinct issue from completing the record through incorporation of materials generated or considered by the agency itself during the procurement process"). Motions to supplement the administrative record are governed by *Axiom Resource Mgmt., Inc. v. United States*, 564 F.3d 1374 (Fed. Cir. 2009). In *Axiom*, the Federal Circuit directed that: "supplementation of the record should be limited to cases in which 'the omission of extra-record evidence precludes effective judicial review'" (quoting *Murakami v. United States*, 46 Fed. Cl. 731 (2000), *aff'd*, 398 F.3d 1342 (Fed. Cir. 2005)). The court stated that determination of whether to order supplementation of the administrative record depends on whether supplementation is "necessary in order not 'to frustrate effective judicial review'" (quoting *Camp v. Pitts*, 411 U.S. 138 (1973)). "Evidentiary determinations by the Court of Federal Claims, including motions to supplement the administrative record, are reviewed for abuse of discretion," but a decision to supplement must be accompanied by an explanation of the reason why supplementation is necessary for effective judicial review, *AgustaWestland N. Am., Inc. v. United States*, 880 F.3d 1326 (Fed. Cir. 2018) (quoting *Axiom*, 564 F.3d at 1378) (finding abuse of discretion where the Court of Federal Claims "provided nothing more than conclusory statements that it could not conduct effective judicial review without the supplemented material.").

Notwithstanding that supplementation is the exception rather than the rule, it is a necessary and established aspect of judicial review of agency action. To perform an effective review pursuant to the APA, the court must have a record containing the information upon which the agency relied when it made its decision as well as any documentation revealing the agency's decision-making process. See *Citizens to Preserve Overton Park v. Volpe*, 401 U.S. 402, 420 (1971) ("[S]ince the bare record may not disclose the factors that were considered or the Secretary's construction of the evidence[,] it may be necessary for the [d]istrict [c]ourt to require some explanation in order to determine if the Secretary acted within the scope of his authority and if the Secretary's action was justifiable under the applicable standard.").

"Although the Federal Circuit's holding in *Axiom* makes clear that supplementation of the administrative record should occur rarely, it is not prohibited and may be used when it is necessary for the Court to gain a complete understanding of the issues before it," *Palantir USG, Inc. v. United States*, 129 Fed. Cl. 218 (2016), *affd*, 904 F.3d 980 (Fed. Cir. 2018) (internal citation, quotation, and alteration omitted). "Effective judicial review is not possible when the administrative record is missing relevant information that by its very nature would not be found in an agency record—such as evidence of bad faith, information relied upon but omitted from the paper record, or the content of conversations," *Starry Assocs., Inc. v. United States*, 125 Fed. Cl. 613 (2015); *Pitney Bowes Gov't Solutions, Inc. v. United States*, 93 Fed. Cl. 327 (2010).

Supplementation can also "encompass[] materials that were never considered by the agency in reaching the challenged procurement decision" if such "documents may illuminate the proprietary of that decision or the procurement process," *L-3 Commc'ns Integrated Sys., L.P. v. United States*, 91 Fed. Cl. 347 (2010), *amended on recons. in part*, 98 Fed. Cl. 45 (2011) (permitting supplementation of documents with "extra agency record material," "not material that was generated in furtherance of the procurement decision at issue and which should have been included in the AR in the first place"); *Contracting Consulting Engrg., LLC v. United States*, 104 Fed. Cl. 36 (2012) (granting motion to supplement "when necessary to prove that evidence not in the record is evidence without which the court cannot fully understand the issues"); *East West, Inc. v. United States*, 100 Fed. Cl. 53 (2011) ("the record may be supplemented with relevant information contained in the procurement files or generally known in an industry or discipline, which was inappropriately ignored by an agency.").

The court may permit supplementation of the record with information that the protester argues the agency either did consider or should have considered in making the protested decision. See *Montana Fish, Wildlife, & Parks Found., Inc. v. United States*, 91 Fed. Cl. 434 (2010) (Inspector General file when the agency decision was based, in part, on report); *Allied Tech. Grp., Inc. v. United States*, 92 Fed. Cl. 226 (2010) (Internet materials such as memoranda from the Office of Personnel Management and the Office of Management and Budget, Internet articles, and a screen short of an agency website); *PlanetSpace, Inc. v. United States*, 90 Fed. Cl. 1 (2009) (146 pages of documents received in response to a Freedom of Information Act request); and *Kerr Contractors, Inc. v. United States*, 89 Fed. Cl. 312 (2009) (agency's responses to questions regarding clarification of the solicitation).

Supplementation of the record may warrant that the protester conduct limited discovery to obtain relevant information from the government and third parties. The Supreme Court itself acknowledged the potential need to depose government officials in *Citizens to Preserve Overton Park v. Volpe*, 401 U.S. 402 (1971), and the Federal Circuit directed deposition of a contracting officer in *Impresa Construzioni Geom. Domenico Garufi v. United States*, 238 F.3d 1324 (Fed. Cir. 2001). That being said, in *Information Tech. & Applications Corp. v. United States*, 316 F.3d 1312 (Fed. Cir. 2003) that Federal Circuit made clear that "discovery of the contracting officer's reasoning is not lightly to be ordered and should not be ordered unless record evidence raises serious questions as to the rationality of the contracting officer's [decision]." For cases permitting supplementation by discovery, see *Palantir USG*, 129 Fed. Cl. at 235-243 (permitting discovery through deposition and document request); *Starry Assocs.*, 125 Fed. Cl. at 621-24 (permitting supplementation through discovery by means of deposing multiple agency officials); *Diversified Maintenance*, 93 Fed. Cl. at 804-06 (granting plaintiff's motion for discovery in a bid protest, allowing plaintiff to depose and seek production from third parties); *Orion*, 60 Fed. Cl. at 343 (discovery warranted for "relevant information that by its very nature would not be found in an agency record—such as evidence of bad faith, information relied upon but omitted from the paper record, or the content of conversations").

"While Government officials are presumed to operate in good faith, a protester is entitled to investigate bias if it can make a threshold showing of motivation for the Government employees in question to have acted in bad faith or conduct that is hard to explain absent bad faith, and that discovery could lead to evidence which would provide a level of proof required to overcome the presumption of regularity," *Starry Assocs.*, 125 Fed. Cl. at 622 (internal citation and quotations omitted). "[B]efore authorizing discovery into alleged bias on the part of agency officials in a protest, trial courts have required a plaintiff to assert a reasonable factual predicate for such allegations," *L-3 Commc'ns*, 91 Fed. Cl. at 355 ("In other words, while a protester must establish clear and convincing evidence of bad faith or bias to prevail on the merits, a lesser showing suffices—that the allegations 'appear to be sufficiently well grounded'—to warrant supplementation of the administrative record."). The allegation of bias or bad faith must have an evidentiary foundation and not rest merely on counsel's argument, suspicion, or conjecture, *Madison Servs., Inc. v. United States*, 92 Fed. Cl. 120 (2010). "A party may rely on extra-record evidence to support its claim that discovery regarding bad faith conduct is necessary," *Beta Analytics Intern., Inc. v. United States*, 61 Fed. Cl. 223, 226 (2004).

In cases where the Court of Federal Claims reviews a protest that was previously reviewed before GAO, the parties may dispute the extent to which the entire record from GAO should be considered by the court. The majority of documents in the GAO record will be the administrative record documents produced by the agency. Parties before GAO often, however, introduce additional materials including declarations by the protester to demonstrate prejudice and by the contracting officer or other agency officials to explain the procurement decisions. The Court of Federal Claims judges express varying degrees of willingness to automatically consider documents produced before GAO. In *Bannum v. United States*, 89 Fed. Cl. 184 (2009), the court determined that documents related to contract performance should be supplements to the administrative record because without the documents, the court would not be able to assess whether the contracting agency provided a coherent and reasonable explanation of its exercise of discretion. In its reasoning the court cited RCFC Appendix C, provision 22(u), which explicitly anticipated the inclusion of the agency report submitted to GAO in the record in a subsequent protest filed at the Court of Federal Claims that involves the same procurement. See also *Holloway & Co., PLLC v.*

United States, 87 Fed. Cl. 381 (2009), noting that the purpose of RCFC Appendix C, provision 22(u) is to ensure that the full record of all proceedings related to the procurement is before the court for review. The court allowed supplementation of the record with six documents generated before GAO because provision 22(u) indicates that core documents include the record of the previous protest. But see *Allied Tech. Grp., Inc. v. United States*, 92 Fed. Cl. 226 (2010), stating that inclusion of documents in the record of a GAO protest is not automatic. The court denied the admission of declarations of a number of witnesses because they were opinion testimony proclaiming or denying the alleged superiority of the competing products, were not before the contracting officer at the time of the award decision, and were not necessary to organize or understand the administrative record. As noted at the outset of this section, in many cases these disputes can be resolved by parsing between materials that can be considered by the court as relevant to standing, prejudice, injunctive relief, etc.; documents that the court can consider by judicial notice; documents that are part of the administrative record as a matter of law regardless of whether the government includes them in the record filed with the court; and materials that truly supplement the record.

[2] Protective Orders

The vast majority of protest litigation is subject to strict protective orders that keep most of the record and pleadings hidden from the public. This is justified in most cases because the record is replete with competition sensitive and proprietary information. It is important, however, to keep in mind that protective orders are an exception to the presumption of public access to judicial records. As the Supreme Court has explained in *Nixon v. Warner Comms., Inc.*, 435 U.S. 589 (1978), stating at 597-98:

> It is clear that the courts of this country recognize a general right to inspect and copy public records and documents, including judicial record and documents. . . . American decisions generally do not condition enforcement of this right in a proprietary interest in the document or upon a need for it as evidence in a lawsuit. The Interest necessary to support the issuance of a writ compelling access has been found, for example, in the citizen's desire to keep a watchful eye on the workings of public agencies . . . and in a newspaper publisher's intentions to publish information concerning the operation of government. . . .

See also *Bond v. Utreras*, 585 F.3d 1061 (7th Cir. 2009) ("It is beyond dispute that most documents filed in court are presumptively open to the public; members of the media and the public may bring third-party challenges to protective orders that shield court records and court proceedings from public view"); *Phillips v. G.M. Corp.*, 307 F.3d 1206 (9th Cir. 2002) ("Not only can the public generally gain access to unprotected information produced during discovery, but it also has a federal common law right of access to all information filed with the court. This common law right of access is well settled in the law of the Supreme Court and this circuit.").

The Supreme Court has also recognized a trial court's discretion to limit public access to judicial records and files. See *Nixon*, 435 U.S. at 598-99:

> It is uncontested, however, that the right to inspect and copy judicial records is not absolute. Every court has supervisory power over its own records and files, and access has been denied where court files might have become a vehicle for improper purposes. For example, the common-law right of inspection has bowed before the power of a court to insure that its records are not "used to gratify private spite or propose public scandal" through the publication of the "the painful and sometimes disgusting details of a divorce case." . . . Similarly, courts have refused to permit their files to serve as reservoirs of libelous statements for press consumption, . . . or as sources of business information that might harm a litigant's competitive standing.
>
> It is difficult to distill from the relatively few decisions a comprehensive definition of what is referred to as the common-law right of access or to identify all the factors to be weighed in determining whether access is appropriate. The few cases that have recognized such a right do agree that the decision as to access is one best left to the sound discretion of the trial court, a discretion to be exercised in light of the relevant facts and circumstances of the particular case.

Not only do judges have great discretion to determine where good cause for a protective order exists, several circuit courts have held that where documents are produced under a pre-existing protective order, the presumption of public access to court records is inherently rebutted by the trial court's initial decision to institute the protective order, shifting the burden to the movant to justify why documents filed under seal should not be protected. See *Phillips*, 307 F.3d at 1213:

> [O]ther courts have determined that the federal common law right of access does not apply to documents filed under seal. . . . We [the 9th Circuit] agree with these courts. When a court grants a protective order for information produced during discovery, it already has determined that "good cause" exists to protect this information from being disclosed to the public by balancing the needs for discovery against the need for confidentiality. Applying a strong presumption of access to documents a court has already decided should be shielded from the public would surely undermine, and possibly eviscerate, the broad power of the district court to fashion protective orders.

Protests filed at the Court of Federal Claims are typically accompanied by a motion to file under seal and motion for protective order, which are routinely granted. RCFC 26(c) governs protective orders, and RCFC Form 8 is a standard form protective order to be used in protest cases. This form specifies that the only persons allowed access to protected information are "counsel for a party and independent consultants and experts assisting such counsel in connection with this litigation" as well as paralegal, clerical and administrative support personnel assisting counsel. RFCF Form 9 provides the protective order application for outside or inside counsel, and RCFC Form 10 provides the protective order application for expert consultants and witnesses.

As with GAO protective orders, the baseline standard is that an applicant for access to a protective order must certify that they are not involved in competitive decision making. See *Zeidman Techs., Inc. v. United States*, 136 Fed. Cl. 50 (2018), stating at 52:

> The Federal Circuit has recognized that protected information is made particularly vulnerable when accessed by individuals involved with competitive-decision making. *See U.S. Steel Corp. v. United States*, 730 F.2d 1465, 1468 (Fed. Cir. 1984). Competitive-decision making involves "advice and participation in any or all of the [company's] decisions (pricing, product design, etc.) made in light of similar or corresponding information about a competitor." *See id.* at 1468 n.3.

Objections to outside counsel are rare; more often, disputes arise when inside counsel or expert witnesses and consultants seek access. The standard protective order provides a process for parties to object to a protective order application. In reviewing an objection to an application for access to protected information, the court considers: (1) "the nature and sensitivity of the information at issue"; (2) "the party's needs for access to the information in order to effectively represent its position"; (3) "the overall number of applications received"; and (4) "any other concerns that may affect the risk of inadvertent disclosure." RCFC Appendix C, ¶ 18(c). With respect to the need for access, as the court recognized in *Zeidman*, a protester "does not necessarily need to conduct an expert evaluation of all competing proposals in order to challenge the alleged errors in the procurement process." "After all, when evaluating a protest, the court's review is highly deferential to the agency's award decision . . . [and] the court looks only to whether the decision had a rational basis and considered relevant factors." Most of the decisions are decided on the issue of risk of inadvertent disclosure, closely related to the concept of competitive decision-making. The decisions recognize that it is inherently difficult for the human mind to isolate knowledge of competitively valuable information obtained under protective order from other aspects of the individual's life. See *Hitkansut LLC v. United States*, 111 Fed. Cl. 228, 239 (2013) ("Even accepting that [the applicant] would make a conscious and sustained effort to comply with the terms of the protective order, the fallibility of the human brain is paramount. It is simply impossible for a human being to segregate, or 'unlearn,' certain pieces of knowledge. Furthermore, [the party] has not made a sufficient showing of need in connection with its request for access by [the applicant].").

The form protective order does not contemplate third-party objections to protective order applications or challenges to protest filings made under seal. As in other circuits, the appropriate mechanism to do so is by motion for limited intervention. "Intervention is the proper means for a non-party to challenge a protective order," *Baystate Techs., Inc. v. Bowers*, 283 Fed. Appx. 808 (Fed. Cir. 2008) (reversing and remanding district court denial of non-party motion to intervene to challenge protective order). The courts of appeal uniformly agree that Rule 24(b) permissive intervention is the appropriate vehicle for a third party to object to protective order issues.

The Court of Federal Claims can impose sanctions on attorneys who violate a protective order, *Pacific Gas & Elec. Co. v. United States*, 82 Fed. Cl. 474 (2008) (ordering attorney to pay costs incurred by government).

[F] Standard of Review

The proper standard to be applied in protest cases is provided by 5 U.S.C. § 706(2)(A), which provides a reviewing court shall set aside the agency action if it is arbitrary, capricious, an abuse of discretion, or otherwise not in accordance with law, *Banknote Corp. of Am. v. United States*, 365 F.3d 1345 (Fed. Cir. 2004). In *Impresa Construzioni Geom. Domenico Garufy v. United States*, 238 F.3d 1324 (Fed. Cir. 2001), the court held that 28 U.S.C. § 1491(b), by its plain terms and according to its legislative history, "applies the Administrative Dispute Resolution Act standard of review previously applied by the district courts." Thus, the standards outlined in *Scanwell Labs., Inc. v. Shaffer*, 424 F.2d 859 (D.C. Cir. 1970), and the line of cases following that decision apply. Under the APA standard as applied in the *Scanwell* line of cases, and now in ADRA cases, an award may be set aside if either (1) the procurement official's decision lacked a rational basis, making it arbitrary or capricious, or (2) the procurement procedure involved a violation of statute or regulation.

Agency action is arbitrary and capricious when the "agency 'entirely failed to consider an important aspect of the problem, offered an explanation for its decision that runs counter to the evidence before the agency, or [the decision] is so implausible that it could not be ascribed to a difference in view or the product of agency expertise,'" *Alabama Aircraft Indus., Inc.-Birmingham v. United States*, 586 F.3d 1372 (Fed. Cir. 2009) (quoting *Motor Vehicle Mfrs. Ass'n v. State Farm Mut. Auto. Ins. Co.*, 463 U.S. 29 (1983)).

> To satisfy the APA standard, an "agency must examine the relevant data and articulate a satisfactory explanation for its action including a 'rational connection between the facts found and the choice made.'" *Motor Vehicle Mfrs.*, 463 U.S. 43 (quoting *Burlington Truck Lines v. United States*, 371 U.S. 156 (1962)). The arbitrary and capricious standard is highly deferential, *Advanced Data Concepts, Inc. v. United States*, 216 F.3d 1054 (Fed. Cir. 2000). When the court finds a reasonable basis for an agency's action, the

> court "should stay its hand even though it might, as an original proposition, have reached a different conclusion . . ." *Honeywell, Inc. v. United States*, 870 F.2d 644, 648 (Fed. Cir. 1989) (internal quotation and citation omitted).

"The higher the degree of discretion allotted the contracting officer, the more difficult it is for a protester to prove that the procurement decision was arbitrary or capricious," *Office Depot, Inc. v. United States*, 95 Fed. Cl. 517 (2010). The court will not involve itself in the "minutiae of the procurement process in such matters as technical ratings," *E.W. Bliss Co. v. United States*, 77 F.3d 445 (Fed. Cir. 1996). "[W]here the court must 'review technical matters that are within the agency's expertise, the highest degree of deference is warranted,'" *Bean Stuyvesant, L.L.C. v. United States*, 48 Fed. Cl. 303 (2000) (quoting *G.E. Gov't Servs., Inc. v. United States*, 788 F. Supp. 581, 590 (D.D.C. 1992)).

There are, however, limits to the discretion afforded to agency decision-making. First, "[i]t is rudimentary in administrative law that discretion as to the substance of the ultimate decision does not confer discretion to ignore the required procedures of decisionmaking," *Bennett v. Spear*, 520 U.S. 154, 172 (1997). Accordingly, agencies have no discretion to reach a decision without following the decision-making procedures required by law. And, while agency officials are "entitled to [a] presumption of regularity," that does not "shield [their] action from a thorough, probing, in-depth review," during which a court's "inquiry into the facts is to be searching and careful," *Citizens to Preserve Overton Park, Inc. v. Volpe*, 401 U.S. 402 (1971). The presumption of regularity is an important tool to prevent protesters and courts from second guessing the propriety of routine but undocumented agency decisions, but the presumption is properly rebutted where the record draws into question the agency's actions. In *Impresa Construzioni*, the Federal Circuit Court found the presumption of regularity an insufficient explanation for the contracting officer's actions and ordered extra-record testimony from the contracting officer, 238 F.3d at 1337-40. In *Palantir USG, Inc. v. United States*, 904 F.3d 980 (Fed. Cir. 2018), where the record indicated the Army had only marginally considered potential commercial solutions during the procurement planning process, the Federal Circuit affirmed the Court of Federal Claims' finding that the presumption of regularity could not be used to infer full compliance with the Army's statutory obligation to prioritize commercial solutions.

Courts need not defer to "an explanation for agency action that is incongruent with what the record reveals about the agency's priorities and decisionmaking process," *Dep't of Commerce v. New York*, 139 S. Ct. 2551 (2019) ("[W]e cannot ignore the disconnect between the decision made and the explanation given. . . . The reasoned explanation requirement of administrative law, after all, is meant to ensure that agencies offer genuine justifications for important decisions, reasons that can be scrutinized by courts and the interested public. Accepting contrived reasons would defeat the purpose of the enterprise.").

Deference is perhaps at its highest when a protester alleges that the agency acted with bad faith or bias. In considering whether the government acted in bad faith, the court requires the protester to prove that the government acted with specific intent to injure it. See *Galen Med. Assocs., Inc. v. United States*, 369 F.3d 1324 (Fed. Cir. 2004), stating at 1330:

> [W]hen a bidder alleges bad faith, "in order to overcome the presumption of good faith [on behalf of the government], the proof must be almost irrefragable." *Info. Tech. Applications Corp. v. United States*, 316 F.3d 1312, 1323 n.2 (Fed. Cir. 2003). "Almost irrefragable proof" amounts to "clear and convincing evidence." *Am-Pro Protective Agency, Inc. v. United States*, 281 F.3d 1234, 1239-40 (Fed. Cir. 2002). "In the cases where the court has considered allegations of bad faith, the necessary 'irrefragable proof' has been equated with evidence of some specific intent to injure the plaintiff." *Torncello v. United States*, 231 Ct. Cl. 20, 681 F.2d 756, 770 (Ct. Cl. 1982).

See also *Aviation Enters., Inc. v. United States*, 8 Cl. Ct. 1 (1985) (refusing to find bad faith on the basis of "speculation and innuendo"); and *Shields Enters., Inc. v. United States*, 28 Fed. Cl. 615 (1993) (no evidence that the government specifically intended to injure the plaintiff or that the government operated with any prejudice toward the plaintiff). See, however, *Parcel 49C Ltd. P'ship v. United States*, 31 F.3d 1147 (Fed. Cir. 1994), affirming a decision that the General Services Administration abused its discretion when it canceled a solicitation for the lease of office space allegedly based on changes in the needs of the using agency. The court found that the using agency's needs did not change until five years into the future and concluded that the GSA had relied upon this interpretation merely as a pretext for ridding itself of the procurement. In a fact pattern similar to *Parcel 49C*, the court in *126 Northpoint Plaza L.P. v. United States*, 34 Fed. Cl. 105 (1995), found bad faith when GSA officials canceled a solicitation in an effort to accommodate the Immigration and Naturalization Service, which was trying to avoid contracting with a particular offeror.

In negotiated procurement the court often takes a more deferential view of whether an agency's actions were rational or reasonable than it does in sealed bidding, *Logicon, Inc. v. United States*, 22 Cl. Ct. 776 (1991). There, the court found that the government had a rational basis for reopening negotiations on a contract after having initially decided to award the contract to the plaintiff. In *Overstreet Elec. Co. v. United States*, 59 Fed. Cl. 99 (2003), the court characterized the standard of review as "near draconian." Further, in *Galen Med. Assocs., Inc. v. United States*, 369 F.3d 1324 (Fed. Cir. 2004), the court stated at 1330:

> Because the bid protest at issue here involved a "negotiated procurement," the protestor's burden of proving that the award was arbitrary, capricious, an abuse of discretion, or otherwise not in accordance with law is greater than in other types of bid protests. *LeBarge Prods., Inc. v. West*, 46 F.3d 1547, 1555 (Fed. Cir. 1995) (citing *Burroughs Corp. v. United States*,

> 617 F.2d 590, 597-98 (Ct. Cl. 1980)). "The higher burden exists because the contracting officer engages in what is 'inherently a judgmental process.'" *Omega World Travel v. United States*, 54 Fed. Cl. 570, 578 (2002) (citing *Burroughs*, 617 F.2d at 598). "[T]he greater the discretion granted to a contracting officer, the more difficult it will be to prove the decision was arbitrary and capricious." *Burroughs*, 617 F.2d at 597. "In formally advertised bidding the pertinent statutes and regulations are far more strict about the conduct of the procurement than in a negotiated one, consequently in negotiated procurement the contracting officer is entrusted with a relatively high degree of discretion." *Id.*

See *Blackwater Lodge & Training Ctr. v. United States*, 86 Fed. Cl. 488 (2009) (government reasonably determined awardee had instituted policies and procedures to resolve safety problems and there was no reason to disturb this judgment); *Medical Dev. Int'l, Inc. v. United States*, 89 Fed. Cl. 691 (2009) (government did not act arbitrary or capricious in conducting competitive range determination three months after the firm prices had expired because the contracting officer reasonably viewed the offers as definite enough to become binding upon the government's acceptance); *Dyonyx, L.P. v. United States*, 83 Fed. Cl. 460 (2008) (rational basis to exclude plaintiff from competitive range); *PHT Supply Corp. v. United States*, 71 Fed. Cl. 1 (2006) (risk rating based on past performance upheld because the solicitation did not limit the government's review to technically relevant contracts and assessment of the awardee's risk had a rational basis); *Avtel Servs., Inc. v. United States*, 70 Fed. Cl. 173 (2005) (contracting officer's decision not to disqualify the eventual awardee from competition not arbitrary and capricious); and *Gulf Grp., Inc. v. United States*, 61 Fed. Cl. 338 (2004) (risk rating based on past performance not arbitrary or capricious).

[G] Prejudice

In order for a protester to prevail, it must show not only that there was a significant error in the procurement process, but also that the error was prejudicial. The prejudice inquiry is related to but distinct from the requirement to demonstrate a direct economic interest in order to establish interested party status. "Although the inquiries may be similar, prejudice must be shown either as part of, or in addition to, showing a direct economic interest," *CliniComp Int'l, Inc. v. United States*, 904 F.3d 1353 (Fed. Cir. 2018). The distinction was most notably addressed by the Federal Circuit in *Labatt Food Serv., Inc. v. United States*, 577 F.3d 1375 (Fed. Cir. 2009), warning that "conflating the standing requirements of prejudicial error and economic interest . . . would create a rule that, to an unsuccessful but economically interested offeror in a bid protest, any error is harmful." The Federal Circuit rejected a melding of the standards under which "there would be no such thing as an error non-prejudicial to an economically interested offeror in a bid context" and instead reiterated "the established law in this circuit that non-prejudicial errors in a bid process do not automatically invalidate a procurement."

To establish prejudice, a protester need not prove that, but for any given error, the protester would have received the contract, *Alfa Laval Separation, Inc. v. United States*, 175 F.3d 1365 (Fed. Cir. 1999). It need only show that "it would have had a substantial chance of securing the contract," *CliniComp Int'l, Inc. v. United States*, 904 F.3d 1353, 1358 (Fed. Cir. 2018) (quoting *Labatt*, 577 F.3d at 1378). The rationale for the substantial chance test was established in *Morgan Business Assocs. v. United States*, 619 F.2d 892 (Ct. Cl. 1980).

Although subsequent opinions from different judges and different tribunals later employed different formulations of the substantial chance test, the Federal Circuit confirmed that all of these variations ultimately require that "a protester must demonstrate that but for the alleged error, there was a 'substantial chance that [it] would receive an award—that it was within the zone of active consideration.'" *Statistica, Inc. v. Christopher*, 102 F.3d 1577, 1581-81 (Fed. Cir. 1996) (emphasis and alteration in original) (quoting *Morgan*, 619 F.2d at 896; *CACI, Inc.-Fed. v. United States*, 719 F.2d 1567 (Fed. Cir. 1983)).

While the prejudice requirement and substantial chance standard were applied to protests well before the ADRA, the prejudice requirement is not unique to protest litigation and is expressly incorporated into the general APA standard of review. Pursuant to 5 U.S.C. § 706, courts engaging in APA review are directed that "due account shall be taken of the rule of prejudicial error." See *Shinseki v. Sanders*, 556 U.S. 396 (2009); *System Studies & Simulation, Inc. v. United* States, 22 F. 4th 994 (Fed. Cir. 2021); *American Relocation Connections, L.L.C. v. United States*, 789 Fed. Appx. 221 (Fed. Cir. 2019) (no prejudice from incorrect NAICS code where protester could not meet allegedly correct NAICS code).

In many cases, prejudice is clearly lacking. De minimis errors by the agency are not sufficient grounds for overturning a contract award, *Andersen Consulting Co. v. United States*, 959 F.2d 929 (Fed. Cir. 1992) ("Any good lawyer can pick lint off any Government procurement, pundits say. We will not set aside an award, even if violations of law are found, unless those violations have some significance," quoting the GSBCA decision, 91-1 BCA ¶23,474). In *Office Design Grp. v. United States*, 951 F.3d 1366 (Fed. Cir. 2020), the Federal Circuit found that a single instance of unequal evaluation was non-prejudicial where: "Even if the VA awarded ODG the additional 6 points it afforded to the awardee, ODG's technical score would only increase to 18 points, well below the acceptable 40-point threshold for award." In *Labatt*, the Federal Circuit agreed the agency improperly accepted proposal revisions from all offerors by an unauthorized transmission method, but found no prejudice because that error affected all offerors the same (Labatt did not "suffer disparate treatment or particularized harm") and that error was not the reason Labatt was excluded from the competition. 577 F.3d at 1379-81. Labatt was ineligible for award because it missed a proposal submission deadline. See also *Grumman Data Sys. Corp. v. Widnall*, 15 F.3d 1044 (Fed. Cir. 1994) (Air Force departure from standard accounting principles in conducting its best value analysis may have violated some technical accounting principles but was de minimis).

In many cases, courts will find that errors in the technical evaluation are not prejudicial due to the awardee's significant price advantage. In *Electronic Data Sys., LLC v. United States*, 93 Fed. Cl. 416 (2010), the court found the large price differential to preclude a finding of prejudice, stating at 436:

> The difficulty for plaintiff in this regard is the sheer size of the differential between its price and that of BAE—in raw terms, slightly more than $50 million, representing nearly a 29 percent spread. This differential is the proverbial elephant in the parlor—and, strive as it might, plaintiff cannot squeeze that pachyderm out the door. That price variance weighed heavily on Treasury's best value determination because the two offerors had nearly identical merit ratings—ratings, to be sure, that plaintiff has challenged before this court, albeit unsuccessfully. While plaintiff correctly notes that prejudice may be found despite the existence of a price differential, it cannot be gainsaid that a significant difference in price, when accompanied by nearly identical technical ratings, can and often does preclude such a finding. And the cases so indicate. *See, e.g., Axiom Res. Mgmt., Inc. v. United States*, 78 Fed. Cl. 576, 590 (2007) (no prejudice where significant differences in price); *see also Data Gen.*, 78 F.3d at 1563 (indicating that price differential is a factor that may be considered in assessing prejudice).

See also *Allied Tech. Grp., Inc. v. United States*, 92 Fed. Cl. 226 (2010) (assigning higher technical rating would not have affected award as evaluated price was at least 218% higher than awardee's); and *Axiom Res. Mgmt., Inc. v. United States*, 78 Fed. Cl. 576 (2007) (despite apparent errors in the plaintiff's technical approach and past performance ratings, the awardee's lower price still trumped plaintiff's price). See, however, *Alfa Laval Separation, Inc. v. United States*, 175 F.3d 1365 (Fed. Cir. 1999), reversing a Court of Federal Claims decision that waiver of a mandatory specification was not prejudicial because there was a $5 million price difference between proposals. The appellate court concluded that the plaintiff had established prejudice because "[t]he only bid competing with Alfa Laval was unacceptable under the standards set out in the RFP," adding that because the plaintiff "submitted the only bid meeting all of the government's requirements, . . . it must have had a substantial chance to receive the contract award." As to the large differential in pricing, the court stated that "while price differential may be taken into account, it is not solely dispositive; we must consider all the surrounding circumstances in determining whether there was a substantial chance that a protester would have received an award but for a significant error in the procurement process."

While prejudice or lack thereof will be relatively clear in most cases; some, particularly postaward protests challenging a procurement that calls for a best value trade-off, the administrative record will not answer the question of whether any given error in the procurement would, if corrected, result in the protester having a substantial chance of receiving award. When in doubt, the established precedent that a protester need not prove that but for the error it would have received the contract, *Alfa Laval Separation, Inc. v. United States*, 175 F.3d 1365 (Fed. Cir. 1999), would seem to caution against the court concluding in the first instance that the protester would necessarily lose in a new source selection decision made against a corrected evaluation record. As stated in *Centerra Grp., LLC v. United States*, 138 Fed. Cl. 407 (2018), "substantial chance of award to the protester exists even if the precise contours of the but-for world cannot be discerned." See also *Patricio Enters., Inc.*, Comp. Gen. Dec. B-412740, 2016 CPD ¶ 152 ("we have no basis—and we decline the agency's invitation—to speculate about how the SSA would have viewed the relative merits of . . . proposals in light of a new, reasonable . . . evaluation").

That a court should not attempt to divine in the first instance how a source selection official's award decision may be impacted by corrections in the underlying procurement process is consistent with basic principles of administrative law governing the APA standard of review. In the context of APA review, the prejudice or "harmless error" rule is counterbalanced by the *Chenery* doctrine, established by the Supreme Court in *SEC v. Chenery Corp.*, 318 U.S. 80 (1943) ("[A] reviewing court . . . must judge the propriety of such action solely by the grounds invoked by the agency."). Under *Chenery*, reviewing courts "may not supply a reasoned basis for the agency's action that the agency itself has not given" and "must judge the propriety of such action solely by the grounds invoked by the agency," *Bowman Transp., Inc. v. Ark.-Best Freight Sys., Inc.*, 419 U.S. 281 (1974); see also *Braniff Airways, Inc. v. Civil Aeronautics Bd.*, 379 F.2d 453 (D.C. Cir. 1967) ("Of course an error cannot be dismissed as 'harmless' without taking into account the limited ability of a court to assume as a judicial function, even for the purpose of affirmance, the distinctive discretion assigned to the agency."); *OMV Med., Inc. v. United States*, 219 F.3d 1337 (Fed. Cir. 2000) (rejecting rationale for agency procurement decision not present in the administrative record). But see *Oracle Am. Inc. v. United States*, 975 F.3d 1279 (Fed. Cir. 2020) (upholding prejudice finding as consistent with *Chenery*).

[H] Remedies

The ultimate remedy sought by a protester is to receive award of the contract. However, such relief is granted in only the rarest of cases. More often, the protester asks the court to enjoin the procurement from moving forward until the agency cures a defect in the procurement, or to remand the procurement to the agency for further consideration. In some cases, the remedy may involve declarations of the rights of the parties or directions to recompete the contract. Monetary relief also may be granted. See 28 U.S.C. § 1491(b)(2) stating:

> [T]he courts may award any relief that the court considers proper, including declaratory and injunctive relief except that any monetary relief shall be limited to bid and proposal costs.

The court has discretion to award *both* injunctive relief and bid or proposal preparation costs, *CNA Corp. v. United States*, 83 Fed. Cl. 1 (2008), *aff'd*, 332 Fed. Appx. 638 (Fed. Cir. 2009). In *Alabama Aircraft Indus., Inc.—Birmingham v. United States*, 85 Fed. Cl. 558 (2009), *rev'd on other grounds*, 586 F.3d 1372 (Fed. Cir. 2009), in addition to the prior decision enjoining the Air Force from proceeding with a contract and requiring a resolicitation, the court awarded proposal preparation costs in order to place Alabama Aircraft in the position it would have been but for the errors. Due to those errors, Alabama Aircraft was required to pay for and submit another proposal in a continuing effort to obtain an award of the contract. In *Geo-Seis Helicopters, Inc. v. United States*, 77 Fed. Cl. 633 (2007), when an injunction issued by the court was partial and only set aside part of the contract in question, the court found it appropriate to include proposal preparation costs as part of the award. Other cases also have awarded complete, permanent injunctive relief along with proposal preparation costs. See *United Payors & United Providers Health Servs., Inc. v. United States*, 55 Fed. Cl. 323 (2002) (ordered termination of the contract and allowed resolicitation of proposals); *MVM, Inc. v. United States*, 47 Fed. Cl. 361 (2000) (injunction ordered previously); *Seattle Sec. Servs. v. United States*, 45 Fed. Cl. 560 (2000) (awarded injunctive relief). But see *Ashbritt, Inc. v. United States*, 87 Fed. Cl. 344 (2009), where the court declined to award both injunctive and monetary relief because Ashbritt had achieved the goal of its protest—to secure, through injunctive relief, the chance to compete for further awards under the procurement on an even playing field. Likewise, in *KWR Constr., Inc. v. United States*, 124 Fed. Cl. 345 (2015), the court found the protester was entitled to an injunction and opportunity to compete for the award but declined to grant proposal costs.

[1] Nonmonetary Remedies

The types of nonmonetary remedies that a protester may obtain in the Court of Federal Claims are either provisional (temporary restraining order (TRO) or preliminary injunction) or final relief (declaratory relief or permanent injunction).

The rules for granting a TRO or preliminary injunction are identical to those followed by the district courts. See RCFC 65. The four factors the court examines when determining whether a preliminary injunction should be granted are the same as in the district courts: (1) reasonable likelihood of success on the merits, (2) irreparable harm if the injunction is not granted, (3) substantial harm to the other parties if the stay is granted, and (4) consideration of the public interest, *Hydro Eng'g, Inc. v. United States*, 37 Fed. Cl. 448 (1997). The court seldom grants either a TRO or a preliminary injunction. As a general rule, courts interfere with the government procurement process "only in extremely limited circumstances," *Banknote Corp. of Am., Inc. v. United States*, 56 Fed. Cl. 377 (2003) (quoting *United States v. John C. Grimberg Co.*, 702 F.2d 1362, 1372 (Fed. Cir. 1983)), *aff'd*, 365 F.3d 1345 (Fed. Cir. 2004). In *Magellan Corp. v. United States*, 27 Fed. Cl. 446 (1993), the court denied a request for preliminary injunction, stating that the disruption to the ongoing procurement process would not be justified in view of the unlikelihood of success on the merits. In discussing its review of requests for preliminary injunctions, the court stated at 447:

> The court has the authority to enter an injunction blocking the award to any bidder other than Magellan. 28 U.S.C. § 1491(a)(3). The limited question is whether the status quo ante should be maintained while the plaintiff undertakes discovery and proofs on its request for permanent relief. Prior decisions of this court and of the United States Court of Appeals for the Federal Circuit, however, make it clear that such authority should not be routinely exercised. As the Federal Circuit wrote in *United States v. John C. Grimberg Co.*, 702 F.2d 1362 (Fed. Cir. 1983), equitable powers "should be exercised in a way which best limits judicial interference in contract procurement." *Id.* at 1372.

The decision on whether or not to grant an injunction is within the sound discretion of the trial court, *FMC Corp. v. United States*, 3 F.3d 424 (Fed. Cir. 1993); *Asociacion Colombiana de Exportadores de Flores v. United States*, 916 F.2d 1571 (Fed. Cir. 1990). Confirming the difficult nature of obtaining injunctive relief in a protest case, the Federal Circuit has stated that even if a trial court finds that the government's actions in soliciting and awarding a contract were arbitrary, capricious, or not in accordance with law, the trial court retains discretion on whether to issue an injunction, *PGBA, LLC v. United States*, 389 F.3d 1219 (Fed. Cir. 2004). In *PGBA*, the court reasoned that the statutory scheme for reviewing procurement decision "does not deprive a court of its equitable discretion in deciding whether injunctive relief is appropriate," and that 28 U.S.C. § 1491(b)(4) "does not automatically require a court to set aside an arbitrary, capricious, or otherwise unlawful contract award." Once the trial court denies injunctive relief, on appeal "the movant faces a heavy burden of showing that the trial court abused its discretion, committed an error of law, or seriously misjudged the evidence," *FMC Corp. v. United States*, 3 F.3d 424 (Fed. Cir. 1993).

The court will examine whether a plaintiff can establish likely success on the merits before looking at the other factors for preliminary injunctive relief. As the Federal Circuit noted in *Dell Fed. Sys., L.P. v. United States*, 906 F.3d 982 (Fed. Cir. 2018), "proving success on the merits is a necessary element for a permanent injunction." In *iAccess Techs., Inc. v. United States*, 143 Fed. Cl. 521 (2019), the court explained that "because plaintiff has not succeeded on the merits of its protest, the court need not examine the factors required to support an award of injunctive relief." While a protester must establish likelihood of success on the merits, the protester does not necessarily have to demonstrate success on every argument raised; assuming the remaining factors militate toward injunctive relief, a likelihood of success on just one of many arguments can support enjoining an entire procurement. See *Amazon Web Servs., Inc. v. United States*, 147 Fed. Cl. 146 (2020).

When assessing irreparable injury, "[t]he relevant inquiry in weighing this factor is whether the plaintiff has an adequate remedy in the absence of an injunction," *Magellan Corp. v. United States*, 27 Fed. Cl. 446, 447 (1993). "The Court of Federal Claims has repeatedly held that a protester suffers irreparable harm if it is deprived of the opportunity to compete fairly for a contract," *Palantir USG, Inc. v. United States*, 129 Fed. Cl. 218 (2016) (compiling cases). This applies in preaward challenges to solicitation defects and postaward challenges to the evaluation process. In *Palantir*, the court found irreparable harm where the government had failed to conduct sufficient market research to determine whether a non-developmental solution could meet its needs, and Palantir was harmed because it could not compete under a solicitation calling for developmental solutions. In *Serco, Inc. v. United States*, 81 Fed. Cl. 463 (2008), the government was enjoined from proceeding with awards made under a government-wide acquisition contract because it conducted an improper and flawed evaluation. The protesters demonstrated they would suffer irreparable injury if an injunction were not granted because the only other available relief—the potential for recovery of proposal preparation costs—would not compensate them for the loss of valuable business over a contract term of potentially a decade.

The public interest must weigh in favor of injunctive relief, *Klinge Corp. v. United States*, 82 Fed. Cl. 127 (2008) (public interest weighs in favor of preventing the government from awarding a contract in contravention of the Trade Agreements Act and in preventing the government from failing to make proper inquiry into compliance when it had a duty to do so). The public interest is served by ensuring that the government conduct fair and legal procurement procedures, giving honest and fair consideration to all bids, *Aeroplate Corp. v. United States*, 67 Fed. Cl. 4 (2005). Preserving the integrity of the public procurement system is in the public interest, *MVM, Inc. v. United States*, 46 Fed. Cl. 137 (2000); *Day & Zimmerman Servs. v. United States*, 38 Fed. Cl. 591 (1997). The integrity of the procurement process includes the requirement that government officials follow applicable procurement law and regulation, *Rotech Healthcare, Inc. v. United States*, 71 Fed. Cl. 393 (2006) (procurement approach adopted by the VA violated the letter and the spirit of the nonmanufacturer rule and the Small Business Act as a whole). In *Palantir USG, Inc. v. United States*, 129 Fed. Cl. 218 (2016), the court found that the public interest in the Army's compliance with statute overrode the government's asserted national security concerns. In *Serco, Inc. v. United States*, 81 Fed. Cl. 463 (2008), the court found the public interest would be served by granting the injunction, particularly in the context of a massive procurement that will impact the public potentially for a decade.

When an appeal is taken to the Court of Appeals for the Federal Circuit, an appellant may request a stay of contract award pending appeal under RCFC 62(c). However, the court follows a stringent test in determining whether to issue a stay pending appeal. This test mirrors the TRO test: "(1) a strong likelihood that the movant will prevail on the merits of the appeal; (2) irreparable injury to the movant unless the stay is granted; (3) no substantial harm to the other parties if the stay is granted; and (4) consideration of the public interest," *Aerolease Long Beach v. United States*, 31 Fed. Cl. 342 (1994). In *Telos Corp. v. United States*, 129 Fed. Cl. 573 (2016), the court stated that it was "not aware of a single instance in which an RCFC 62(c) injunction has been issued." One year later, the court granted a motion for stay pending appeal in *PDS Consultants, Inc. v. United States*, 133 Fed. Cl. 810 (2017), where the case involved "an issue of first impression involving important contracting preferences" and the court was "persuaded that the loss of these contracts would have a severe impact on not only [the intervenor/incumbent's] business but also [its] mission as a nonprofit to provide employment, training, and services to persons who are blind."

The final relief by the Court of Federal Claims may take the form of a declaratory judgment or a permanent injunction. The test for a permanent injunction is almost identical to that for a temporary restraining order or preliminary injunction, but rather than the likelihood of success on the merits, a permanent injunction requires actual success on the merits, *Amoco Prod. Co. v. Village of Gambill, Alaska*, 480 U.S. 531 (1987). In *PGBA, LLC v. United States*, 389 F.3d 1219 (Fed. Cir. 2004), the court set out the test for a permanent injunction, stating at 1228-29, that a court must consider:

> (1) whether, as it must, the plaintiff has succeeded on the merits of the case; (2) whether the plaintiff will suffer irreparable harm if the court withholds injunctive relief; (3) whether the balance of hardships to the respective parties favors the grant of injunctive relief; and (4) whether it is in the public interest to grant injunctive relief.

The injunction may prohibit the agency from undertaking some activity or it may be mandatory, directing that certain actions be taken. See *Klinge Corp. v. United States*, 82 Fed. Cl. 127 (2008) (direction to terminate the contract); *Informatics Corp. v. United States*, 40 Fed. Cl. 508 (1998) (award of contract enjoined and reevaluation of plaintiff's proposal ordered); *ATA Def. Indus., Inc. v. United States*, 38 Fed. Cl. 489 (1997) (permanent injunction prohibiting continued performance of legally defective procurement); *Day & Zimmermann, Inc. v. United States*, 38 Fed. Cl. 591 (1997) (contract award enjoined unless and until discussions were held and resulting BAFOs were considered); and *126 Northpoint Plaza L.P. v. United States*, 34 Fed. Cl. 105 (1995) (original solicitation reinstated).

Although the Court of Federal Claims judges have developed a robust body of law applying the injunction factors to procurement-specific circumstances, in general the court applies the same standards for injunctive relief that apply to all federal courts. The primary exception is that in passing ADRA Congress directed that the court "shall give due regard to the interests of national defense and national security and the need for expeditious resolution of the action." 28

U.S.C. § 1491(b)(3). This is often invoked as the basis for denying or limiting the scope of injunctive relief. As the court explained in *Linc Gov't Servs., LLC v. United States*, 96 Fed. Cl. 672 (2010) "when military and national security interests are implicated, the public interest factor gains 'inflated' importance to the court's balancing of the equities" (injunction denied based on testimony that it would impede effort in Iraq). See also *Geo-Seis Helicopters v. United States*, 77 Fed. Cl. 633 (2007) (national security considerations caused injunction to be limited in scope); *Filtration Dev. Co. v. United States*, 60 Fed. Cl. 371 (2004) (limited injunctive relief in light of national defense considerations); *Gentex Corp. v. United States*, 58 Fed. Cl. 634 (2003) (plaintiff found not to have met burden of demonstrating that injunctive relief is warranted, given urgency of procurement for the nation's military); and *Cincom Sys. v. United States*, 37 Fed. Cl. 266 (1997) (application for TRO and motion for preliminary injunction denied for national security reasons). Nevertheless, claims of national security concern are not given automatic deference, but instead are analyzed carefully in conjunction with the injunction factors. See *Systems Application & Techs., Inc. v. United States*, 100 Fed. Cl. 687 (2011), *aff'd*, 691 F.3d 1374 (Fed. Cir. 2012), quoting *Gentex Corp. v. United States*, 58 Fed. Cl. 634 (2003), stating at 722:

> The Tucker Act requires that the Court consider the interest of national defense in its bid protest decisions. Nonetheless, "claims of national security . . . are often advance by the Government in challenges to procurement decisions. The Court will not blindly accede to such claims but is bound to give them most careful consideration." While the Court certainly must give serious consideration to national defense concerns and arguably should err on the side of caution when such vital interests are at stake, allegations involving national security must be evaluated with the same analytical rigor as other allegations of potential harm to parties or to the public.

[2] Monetary Remedies

The monetary remedies that protesters have been able to recover are generally limited to the costs of preparing the bid or proposal. In some instances, the protester may receive attorneys' fees and expenses under the Equal Access to Justice Act (EAJA). Recovery of anticipated profits (or lost profits) has been uniformly denied. See *Keco Indus., Inc. v. United States*, 492 F.2d 1200 (Ct. Cl. 1974) (improper to award lost profits in the absence of a contract and no certainty that protester would have received award); *Rockwell Int'l Corp. v. United States*, 8 Cl. Ct. 662 (1985) (prior precedent flatly precludes such an award); *La Strada Inn, Inc. v. United States*, 12 Cl. Ct. 110 (1987) (disappointed bidder may not recover anticipated profits on a contract improperly awarded to another); *Finley v. United States*, 31 Fed. Cl. 704 (1994) (lost profits are speculative in nature and have consistently been denied); and *Gentex Corp. v. United States*, 61 Fed. Cl. 49 (2004) (protester's attempt to recover a 15% "markup" on its bid and preparation costs was unsuccessful because profit is not an allowable cost).

[a] Bid or Proposal Preparation Costs

The Court of Federal Claims may award bid or proposal preparation costs in a protest action, 28 U.S.C. § 1491(a)(1); 28 U.S.C. § 1491(b)(2). The Federal Circuit has held that "a losing competitor may recover the costs of preparing its unsuccessful proposal if it can establish that the Government's consideration of the proposals submitted was arbitrary or capricious," *E. W. Bliss Co. v. United States*, 77 F.3d 445 (Fed. Cir. 1996) (quoting *Lincoln Servs., Ltd. v. United States*, 678 F.2d 157 (Ct. Cl. 1982)). See also *Gentex Corp. v. United States*, 58 Fed. Cl. 634 (2003) ("[A] losing competitor may recover the costs of preparing its unsuccessful proposal if it can establish that the Government's consideration of the proposal submitted was arbitrary or capricious or in violation of applicable statute or regulation.").

Bid or proposal cost may not be awarded if the protester has a reasonable chance of winning the competition when the corrective action is taken. Thus, if the court issues an injunction providing the protester with a fair opportunity to win the competition, the costs may be denied. See *AshBritt, Inc. v. United States*, 87 Fed. Cl. 344 (2009), *clarified*, 87 Fed. Cl. 654 (2009), stating at 379-80:

> Under the Tucker Act, this Court "may award any relief that the court considers proper," including declaratory and injunctive relief and bid and proposal preparation costs. 28 U.S.C. § 1491(b)(2). This provision of the Tucker Act, "through use of the permissive 'may,' provides the Court of Federal Claims with discretion in fashioning relief." *PGBA, L. L. C. v. United States*, 389 F.3d 1219, 1226 (Fed. Cir. 2004). Because the Court grants AshBritt's request for injunctive relief, and AshBritt will have the opportunity to re-compete for additional awards, the Court declines to award bid and proposal preparation costs. While the Tucker Act does not preclude monetary damages if injunctive relief has been granted, the Court takes into account "the facts and circumstances of the particular case" in exercising its discretion whether to award both injunctive relief and bid and proposal preparation costs. *See CNA Corp. v. United States*, 83 Fed. Cl. 1, 11 (2008).
>
> Bid and proposal preparation costs are a form of reliance damages which are properly awarded when the costs have been wasted. *See Centech Group, Inc. v. United States*, 79 Fed. Cl. 562, 564 (2007) (finding that the protester may be entitled to bid and proposal preparation costs "if it can demonstrate that such costs were wasted."). Here, AshBritt has achieved the goal of its protest—to secure, through injunctive relief, the chance to compete for further awards under this procurement on a level playing field. If AshBritt succeeds in winning additional awards, its bid and proposal preparation costs will not have been "wasted" in this procurement. Furthermore, AshBritt has

> already received both a primary award and a reach back assignment under this procurement which were not displaced by the Court's injunction here, demonstrating that its bid and proposal preparation costs were not wasted. As such, the Court declines to award the additional relief of bid and proposal preparation costs.

However, such costs will be awarded if the protester has no chance to win the competition. See *Klinge Corp. v. United States*, 83 Fed. Cl. 773 (2008), *recons. denied*, 86 Fed. Cl. 713 (2009) (agency responded to injunction by recompeting using Federal Supply Schedule and protester had no Schedule contract); *L-3 Commc'ns Integrated Sys, L.P. v. United States*, 79 Fed. Cl. 453 (2007) (protester learned well after award that agency official had tilted award to competitor); *IDEA Int'l, Inc. v. United States*, 74 Fed. Cl. 129 (2006) (contract award based on defective procedures allowed to proceed because of urgency); *Morgan Bus. Assocs. v. United States*, 619 F.2d 892 (Ct. Cl. 1980) (agency lost proposal). Costs have also been awarded when the court concludes that a losing protester has been required to expend excessive proposal costs because of a badly written RFP, *Centech Grp., Inc. v. United States*, 79 Fed. Cl. 562 (2007), *aff'd*, 554 F.3d 1029 (Fed. Cir. 2009).

To be awarded bid or proposal preparation costs in a successful protest action, the protester must show those costs to be allocable and reasonable, *Coflexip & Servs., Inc. v. United States*, 961 F.2d 951 (Fed. Cir. 1992). Expenses compensable as bid preparation costs are those in the nature of researching specifications, reviewing bid forms, examining cost factors, and preparing draft and actual bids, *Finley v. United States*, 31 Fed. Cl. 704 (1994). Costs incurred in anticipation of or to qualify for a contract award are not recoverable bid preparation expenses, *Lion Raisins, Inc. v. United States*, 52 Fed. Cl. 115 (2002). In *Lion Raisins*, the costs of litigating a Small Business Administration size protest and obtaining a Certificate of Competency were not reimbursable bid and proposal preparation costs, because they were not incurred specifically for the bid. Here, the solicitation did not reference a set-aside for small business, eligibility to bid was not predicated on size, and the resolution of the size protest was irrelevant to contract award. However, although costs must support an initial or revised proposal, there is no requirement that a solicitation must be issued before such costs may be recovered, *Naplesyacht.com, Inc. v. United States*, 49 CCF ¶ 78,366 (2005). In *Naplesyacht*, the government had contested the costs as appearing to be related to procurements conducted under the GSA supply schedule and otherwise unrelated to the disputed solicitation. The court found, however, that the record sufficiently detailed that the protester began to prepare its proposal when it responded to requests for sources from the government. In addition, other correspondence established the government conducted pre-solicitation activities, including site visits to the protester's facilities. E-mail correspondence described the government's need for a specified foot length and other requirements that it later included in the boat manufacturing solicitation.

The court found the costs allocable as related to research and preparation of the protester's initial and final proposals. If the parties cannot agree on the costs after the court has held the protester entitled to recover, the court can reopen the case and rule on the proper amount to be paid, *CNA Corp. v. United States*, 83 Fed. Cl. 1 (2008).

[b] Protest Costs

The costs of pursuing a protest in the Court of Federal Claims are not recoverable except under the Equal Access to Justice Act (EAJA), 28 U.S.C. § 2412, *Grumman Data Sys. Corp. v. United States*, 28 Fed. Cl. 803 (1993). See also *Coflexip & Servs., Inc. v. United States*, 20 Cl. Ct. 412 (1990) (court is without jurisdiction to award protest costs in the absence of a waiver of sovereign immunity); and *AT&T Techs., Inc. v. United States*, 18 Cl. Ct. 315 (1989) (damages for breach of the implied contract to fairly and honestly consider offers are limited exclusively to bid and proposal preparation costs).

Under the EAJA, an award of reasonable attorneys' fees may be made to a qualifying "party" who prevails in an action by or against the United States, provided that certain criteria are met, 28 U.S.C. § 2412(d)(1)(A). A qualifying "party" is a corporation or other organization with a net worth of less than $7 million and 500 or fewer employees, 28 U.S.C. § 2412(d)(2)(B). In *Lion Raisins, Inc. v. United States*, 57 Fed. Cl. 505 (2003), the court held that the net worth of two other business related to an entity that requested attorneys' fees and costs under the EAJA was irrelevant for purposes of determining whether the EAJA claimant was eligible to collect the fees. The government had asserted that Lion Raisins was an affiliate of two other business entities and that the net worth of these entities should be aggregated in determining Lion Raisin's net worth. The court explained that the plain language of EAJA counseled against aggregation, stating at 510:

> The jurisprudence makes clear that aggregation, if required at all, is necessary only when the underlying litigation pursued by the . . . claimant substantially benefitted another party, or if the claimant was not the real party in interest to the underlying litigation. This is not the situation in the case at bar. . . . Most important to the issue of aggregation, only plaintiff had a direct interest in the underlying lawsuit. While . . . [the other entities] may profit from plaintiff's ability to perform government contracts, even the more restrictive formulations of EAJA eligibility would not require aggregation for this type of attenuated benefit from the underlying litigation.

See also *Information Scis. Corp. v. United States*, 78 Fed. Cl. 673 (2007), where the government contended that the intervenor's net worth should include the assets and liabilities of its "working partners" and perhaps its principles. The court found that the intervenor did not have a formal legal or contractual relationship with any entity, and even if it had an implicit contractual relationship with its working partners, mere affiliation did not justify aggregating the net worth of affiliated companies under the EAJA. An applicant must present evidence showing its net worth was less than $7 million at the time the action is filed, *Al Ghanim Combined Grp. Co. v. United States*, 67 Fed. Cl. 494 (2005) (applicant's self-serving, nonprobative affidavit claiming a net worth below the threshold was inadequate to establish that its net worth did not exceed $7 million for purposes of EAJA).

Eligibility for such an award requires that: (1) the claimant be a "prevailing party"; (2) the government's position was not "substantially justified"; (3) no "special circumstances make an award unjust"; and (4) any fee application be submitted to the court within 30 days of final judgment in the action and be supported by an itemized statement, *Commissioner, INS v. Jean*, 496 U.S. 154 (1990); *Loomis v. United States*, 74 Fed. Cl. 350 (2006); *Lion Raisins, Inc. v. United States*, 57 Fed. Cl. 505 (2003).

The burden of establishing substantial justification rests upon the government, *White v. Nicholson*, 412 F.3d 1314 (Fed. Cir. 2005). In determining substantial justification, the court must "look at the entirety of the government's conduct [both prior to and during litigation] and make a judgment call whether the government's overall position had a reasonable basis in both law and fact," *Chiu v. United States*, 948 F.2d 711 (Fed. Cir. 1991). See also *Doty v. United States*, 71 F.3d 384 (Fed. Cir. 1995) ("[T]he term 'position of the United States' [in the EAJA] refers to the government's position throughout the dispute, including not only its litigating position but also the agency's administrative position."). See *Savantage Fin. Servs., Inc. v. United States*, 52 CCF ¶ 79,007 (Fed. Cl. 2008) (government's defense, which essentially argued its actions amounted to a software standardization decision that was not a procurement within the Court of Federal Claims' protest jurisdiction, was based on an unreasonable application of the Federal Acquisition Streamlining Act and a recent court decision); *Universal Fid. LP v. United States*, 70 Fed. Cl. 310 (2006) (restrictions were unreasonable and the government took corrective action late in the proceedings); and *Dubinsky v. United States*, 44 Fed. Cl. 360 (1999) (government assertion that procurement was conducted in accordance with simplified acquisition procedures was not reasonable because the protester successfully showed that the solicitation was conducted as a standard procurement, consequently making the government's discussions with the awardee improper). But see *Klinge Corp. v. United States*, 53 CCF ¶ 79,183 (2009), where an application for attorneys' fees and expenses under the EAJA was denied because the government's overall litigation position in the protest was substantially justified. In its EAJA application, the protester argued the government's decision to cancel the solicitation was based on its unreasonable conclusion that the protester did not comply with the Trade Agreements Act. Even though the government was mistaken in fact and law, the court found no government bad faith or animus toward the protester and no government desire to help the awardee. The government's position will not be found to be reasonable or substantially justified when explicit, unambiguous regulations directly contradict that position, *Information Scis. Corp. v. United States*, 78 Fed. Cl. 673 (2007), 86 Fed. Cl. 269 (2009), 88 Fed. Cl. 626 (2009) (even though court resolved most of the protest challenges in the government's favor and did not rule the contracting officer's and SSA's decisions were unreasonable, violations of the FAR were ipso facto unreasonable in law); *Hillensbeck v. United States*, 74 Fed. Cl. 477 (2006) (government's position conflicted with unambiguous statutory definition and regulations); *Loomis v. United States*, 74 Fed. Cl. 350 (2006) (military failed to comply with its own regulations); *Filtration Dev., Co. v. United States*, 63 Fed. Cl. 612 (2005) (government position contradicted unambiguous regulatory requirements relating to organizational conflicts of interest). In *Geo-Seis Helicopters, Inc. v. United States*, 79 Fed. Cl. 74 (2007), the government argued that its position in the underlying litigation was justified because there was significant GAO precedent supporting the contracting officer's position. The court determined that the plain language of the FAR precluded the government's position. The court held that the FAR and not GAO or the court establish the parameters for the contracting officer's position.

The government's position may be found to be substantially justified even though the court previously overturned the government's actions. See *RAMCOR Servs. Grp., Inc. v. United States*, 185 F.3d 1286 (Fed. Cir. 1999) ("Although INS had lost the underlying action, that outcome does not alone show that its position had no substantial justification.").

The court follows the Supreme Court's decision in *Buckhannon Board & Care Home, Inc. v. West Virginia Dep't of Health & Human Res.*, 532 U.S. 598 (2001), in deciding prevailing party status under EAJA, *Brickwood Contractors, Inc. v. United States*, 288 F.3d 1371 (Fed. Cir. 2002). In *Buckhannon*, the Supreme Court rejected the catalyst theory and set forth standards for a party to prevail under attorney fees statutes. Under the catalyst theory, a party "prevails" because the lawsuit brought about a voluntary change in the defendant's conduct. The Court found the catalyst theory insufficient because "[i]t allows an award where there is no judicially sanctioned change in the legal relationship of the parties." The Court then proceeded to construe the phrase "prevailing party" as requiring some judicial action that changes the legal relationship between the parties on the merits of the claim. In other words, to prevail, a party must have received a judicial imprimatur tantamount to a judgment in favor of that party on the merits of the original claim. That judicial action could take the form of a consent decree settling the claim in favor of the plaintiff, a judgment on the merits, or an award of damages. A party may qualify as a prevailing party where it succeeds on a jurisdictional issue that resolves the case without reaching the merits, *Raniere v. Microsoft Corp.*, 887 F.3d 1298 (Fed. Cir. 2018). As a practical matter, in most cases, the prevailing party rule will preclude recovery of protest costs where the agency takes voluntary corrective action. In *Dellew Corp. v. United States*, 855 F.3d 1375 (Fed. Cir. 2017), the Federal Circuit reversed an award of protest fees under EAJA where the Court of Federal Claims made several comments during oral argument indicating that it intended to rule in the protester's favor and the government took corrective action before the court issued a formal decision, concluding that even in those circumstances the corrective action was voluntary and the protester could not qualify as a prevailing party. See also *Rice Servs., LTD v. United States*, 405 F.3d 1017 (Fed. Cir. 2005) (reversing an award of legal fees because the protester did not achieve prevailing party status as a result of the government's voluntary decision to withdraw a solicitation); *Universal Fid. LP v. United States*, 70 Fed. Cl. 310 (2006) (contractor was a "prevailing party" because the court's order advised the parties the solicitation would be enjoined, the matter had been fully briefed, and the court and the parties agreed no hearing was necessary; the court's conclusions were legal in nature, exhibited an essence of finality and were made late in the proceedings, and an opinion granting injunctive relief would have been issued had the government declined curative action); *Filtration Dev. Co., LLC v. United States*, 63 Fed. Cl. 612 (2005) (protester was a prevailing party because a permanent injunction granted in its favor altered the legal relationship between the parties); *Knowledge Connections, Inc. v. United*, 76 Fed. Cl. 612 (2007) (court order remanding a bid protester's claim to the government procuring agency for further consideration was not sufficient to establish "prevailing party" status because the order did not provide any resolution to the key question on the merits, did not grant any relief, and the Court of Federal Claims retained jurisdiction over the appeal); and *Advanced Sys. Tech., Inc. v. United States*, 74 Fed. Cl. 171 (2006) (when a preliminary injunction only grants temporary relief preserving the status quo, "prevailing party" status is not conferred, because such a preliminary injunction is not a judicially sanctioned material alteration of the parties' legal relationship.").

Attorneys' fees are capped at $125 per hour unless the court makes special findings justifying a higher fee. See *Geo-Seis Helicopters, Inc. v. United States*, 79 Fed. Cl. 74 (2007) (entitled to cost of living adjusted allowing rate of $167.27). "[E]gregious agency misconduct is not a 'special factor'" that warrants an increased rate, *Starry Assocs., Inc. v. United States*, 892 F.3d 1372 (Fed. Cir. 2018). The fee application with supporting documentation must be submitted to the court within 30 days of final judgment.

§ 15.06 FEDERAL TORT CLAIMS ACT

Unsuccessful offerors and bidders may seek relief in district court under the Federal Tort Claims Act (FTCA), 28 U.S.C. § 1346(b), but such actions have generally not been successful. In *Scanwell Labs., Inc. v. Thomas*, 521 F.2d 941 (D.C. Cir. 1975), *cert. denied*, 425 U.S. 910 (1976), an unsuccessful bidder bought an FTCA action in district court while its claim for recovery of bid preparation costs was pending in the Court of Claims, alleging in both actions that the government had violated its procurement regulations by awarding the contract to a nonresponsive bidder. The court first concluded that it need not decide the question of whether the plaintiff would be limited to proceeding under "one theory or the other," but stated that its "solution" would be "merely to prevent a double recovery." Turning then to the merits of the tort action, the court held that the plaintiff's claim was based upon alleged negligent misrepresentation and was therefore barred by the FTCA exceptions under 28 U.S.C. § 2680(h). The court in Scanwell also held that the government's action in evaluating the bids fell within the discretionary function exception to the Act, 28 U.S.C. § 2680(a), even though it had held in prior litigation that there was "no discretion to ignore the regulations regarding responsiveness of bids," 521 F.2d at 948.

In *Edelman v. Federal Hous. Admin.*, 382 F.2d 594 (2d Cir. 1967), the Second Circuit found that a claim by a disappointed bidder alleging that the government had failed to fairly consider its bid was barred by the misrepresentation exception. In *Covington v. United States*, 303 F. Supp. 1145 (N.D. Miss. 1969), a claim alleging that the Government had fraudulently misrepresented the amount of funds available for the solicited work, causing the bid to be rejected as nonresponsive for exceeding the funding limitation, was held to fall within this same exception. See also *Armstrong & Armstrong, Inc. v. United States*, 356 F. Supp. 514 (E.D. Wash. 1973), *aff'd*, 514 F.2d 402 (9th Cir. 1975), where the court held that a claim by an unsuccessful bidder that the Bureau of Reclamation had acted "negligently, arbitrarily, and capriciously" in denying it award of a contract was a claim based upon interference with contract rights and was thus barred under 28 U.S.C. § 2680(h), which expressly excepts claims based upon interference with contract rights from the waiver of sovereign immunity under 28 U.S.C. § 1336(b). It is evident from these decisions that even where disappointed bidders have succeeded in convincing a court that claims arising out of contract award decisions sound in tort, the breadth of the exceptions to the waiver of immunity set forth in 28 U.S.C. § 2680(a)-(m) has effectively precluded that class of plaintiffs from obtaining relief under the FTCA. See, however, *Myers & Myers, Inc. v. United States Postal Serv.*, 527 F.2d 1252 (2d Cir. 1975), where the Second Circuit held that refusal to renew a contract based upon a nonresponsibility determination might be a de facto debarment requiring a hearing and remanded the case to the district court for decision under the FTCA, with instructions that the discretionary function exception to the Act would not apply if it was found that the procurement official had "behave[d] unconstitutionally or outside the scope of . . . authority." In *Cecile Indus., Inc. v. United States*, 793 F.2d 97 (3d Cir. 1986), the court held that the government's failure to follow debarment regulations did not constitute actionable fraud.

§ 15.07 CHOICE OF FORUM

The current system gives protesters more than one available forum to hear protests; thus, protesters are able to select the forum best suited to their needs. This freedom of choice is recognized in the GAO protest statute, 31 U.S.C. § 3556, which states that it "does not give the Comptroller General exclusive jurisdiction over protests" and that nothing "shall affect the right of any interested party" to bring suit in the Court of Federal Claims. However, care must be taken in selecting the forum because the filing of a protest may be held to be a binding election of that forum by the protester. There are a number of statutory provisions dealing with this issue.

GAO protest regulations provide that GAO will dismiss any protest where "the matter involved" is before a court of competent jurisdiction or where the matter has been decided on the merits by a court, unless the court requests a decision by GAO, 4 C.F.R. § 21.11(b). This rule applies to both initial protests and requests for reconsideration. 4 C.F.R. § 21.11(a) requires a protester to notify GAO immediately of any court proceedings that involve the subject matter of a protest and to file all relevant documents with GAO.

When the subject matter is before a court of competent jurisdiction, GAO will dismiss the protest. In *Oahu Tree Experts*, Comp. Gen. Dec. B-282247, 99-1 CPD ¶ 69, the matter involved whether the contracting agency knew the "marginal" CPAR ratings to be motivated by bias, instead of an impartial assessment of the protester's performance. To answer this question, GAO stated that it must first determine whether bias did, in fact, taint the ratings—the same question posed in Oahu's federal complaint. GAO held that while Oahu correctly observed that its federal complaint does not mention the instant procurement and seeks different relief (*i.e.*, the correction of the CPAR rather than the termination of the awardee's contract), these differences do not overcome the fact that Oahu has placed the same facts in issue before both the federal court.

A later-filed court action will also divest GAO of jurisdiction. In *Prince George's Contractors, Inc.*, 64 Comp. Gen. 786 (B-218640.2), 85-2 CPD ¶ 195, the protest was dismissed because the protester filed suit in the district court after filing a protest with GAO. In addition, GAO will not consider a request for costs and attorneys' fees for an action that was adjudicated in a court decision, *Pitney Bowes, Inc.*, 64 Comp. Gen. 623 (B-218241), 85-1 CPD ¶ 696. In that case, the protest was first filed at GAO; but when the agency refused to suspend contract performance, the protester went to court and obtained an injunction. GAO ruled that its authority to award such remedies was ancillary to its jurisdiction to rule on the protest and that the district court injunction ousted it from jurisdiction in the case.

In determining whether the matter involved is before a court, GAO has ruled that it will not consider a protest where the court proceeding pertains to a matter that "might have been decided" by the court, even though it was not decided, *Santa Fe Corp.*, 64 Comp. Gen. 429 (B-218234.2), 85-1 CPD ¶ 361, *recons. denied*, 85-1 CPD ¶ 499; *Affiliated Textiles, Inc.*, Comp. Gen. Dec. B-242970.2, 91-2 CPD ¶ 127; *Techniarts Eng'g—Recons.*, Comp. Gen. Dec. B-238520.7, 92-1 CPD ¶ 504. Thus, GAO will not rule on a protest if any factual issue related to the protest is being litigated in a court. In *Meisel Rohrbau GmbH & Co.*, 67 Comp. Gen. 380 (B-228152.3), 88-1 CPD ¶ 371, GAO concluded that a pending court case requesting reinstatement of a prior solicitation was relevant to the current protest contesting the cancellation of the replacement solicitation. See also *North Shore Strapping Co.*, Comp. Gen. Dec. B-248003, 92-1 CPD ¶ 532, where GAO dismissed a protest alleging the use of restrictive specifications because it was within the scope of a pending court suit alleging unfair treatment of the protester by the procuring agency. But if the matter before the court is not relevant to the protest, GAO will not dismiss the protest. See *Rix Indus., Inc.*, Comp. Gen. Dec. B-241498, 91-1 CPD ¶ 165, finding that a pending litigation involving an offeror's alleged theft of trade secrets concerning the product to be manufactured under the contract was not relevant to the issue of whether that offeror could perform the pending contract. In *Sprint Commc'ns Co. LP*, Comp. Gen. Dec. B-288413.11, 2002 CPD ¶ 171, GAO dismissed a protest and request for reconsideration where the protester alleged that the agency had relied on misrepresented facts in determining that the awardee was responsible. GAO concluded that, although the award of the contract being protested was not being litigated, it could not reasonable rule of the protest because the misrepresentations of the awardee were the subject of a suit filed by the Securities Exchange Commission as well as grand jury indictments of officials of the company.

GAO dismisses protests when there is a case pending in court even if a party other than the protester files the court suit. See, for example, *Arbinger Co.—Advisory Opinion*, Comp. Gen. Dec. B-413156.4, *Unpub.* (discussed at Comp. Gen. Dec. B-413156.21, 2017 CPD ¶ 100). This can result in a protest being dismissed because another party filed a subsequent suit in a court. *Test Sys. Assocs.*, Comp. Gen. Dec. B-256813.6, 96-2 CPD ¶ 161, is a good example of the peculiar nature of these cases. There, an unsuccessful offeror filed a protest at GAO and shortly thereafter in district court challenging the award to TSAI. On its own initiative, the agency took corrective action and terminated TSAI's contract and notified TSAI of its intention to award to Dixon. TSAI filed its first protest with GAO (B-256813.3) on the basis of an ambiguous clause and for terminating its contract and rejecting its offer. In the meantime, Dixon choose not to withdraw its civil action in district court. TAO advised TSAI to intervene in Dixon's court action, but it did not. GEO then dismissed TSAI's protest, stating that the dispositive issue was before the district court. See also *Geronimo Serv. Co.*, Comp. Gen. Dec. B-242331.3, 91-1 CPD ¶ 321, where GAO refused to hear a protest of the award of a contract that was being litigated in district court in a suit filed by another protester. GAO noted that although the court had requested an advisory opinion from GAO, that opinion could not rule on Geronimo's protest because it had not intervened in the district court action An action filed in court will also deprive the government of the ability to obtain reconsideration by GAO if the protester files a suit in court after winning the protest, *Dep't of the Navy—Recons.*, Comp. Gen. Dec. B-253129.4, 96-1 CPD ¶ 175.

A court may specifically request that GAO provide an advisory opinion on the merits of a protest, *PAE-Parsons Global Log. Servs., LLC—Advisory Opinion*, Comp. Gen. Dec. B-417506.13, 2019 CPD ¶ 364; *Fluor Intercontinental, Inc.—Advisory Opinion*, Comp. Gen. Dec. B-417506.14, 2019

CPD ¶ 46; *Facility Servs. Mgmt., Inc.—Advisory Opinion*, Comp. Gen. Dec. B-414857.9, 2018 U.S. Comp. Gen. LEXIS 452; *Arbinger Co.—Advisory Opinion*, Comp. Gen. Dec. B-413156.21, 2017 CPD ¶ 100; and *Planning & Learning Techs., Inc.—Advisory Opinion*, Comp. Gen. Dec. B-413156.23, 2017 CPD ¶ 102. Once GAO gives a decision to the court, it will not reconsider that decision unless the court requests such action, *Ace Fed. Reporters, Inc.*, Comp. Gen. Dec. B-241309.3, 91-1 CPD ¶ 54.

§ 15.08 APPELLATE REVIEW OF GAO DECISIONS

There is no specified appeals procedure for GAO decisions because they are not in the nature of judicial decisions. If a protester is dissatisfied with a GAO decision, an action may be brought in the Court of Federal Claims, assuming that all requirements for jurisdiction are met, 31 U.S.C. § 3556. It is the agency's procurement award decision, not GAO's recommendation, that is subject to review by the court, *Advanced Constr. Servs., Inc. v. United States*, 51 Fed. Cl. 362 (2002) ("Construing § 1491(b)(1) in the expansive manner advocated by [the protester] would violate the well-established principle that it is the agency's decision, not the decision of GAO that is the subject of judicial review when a bid protester protests an award previously reviewed by GAO."); *Cubic Applications, Inc. v. United States*, 37 Fed. Cl. 339 (1997). Although the court is conducting its review of the agency's award decision under the APA, GAO recommendation is considered to be part of the agency record, 31 U.S.C. § 3556.

The Court of Federal Claims will not make a de novo review but, rather, will determine whether GAO's recommendation was rational, *Honeywell, Inc. v. United States*, 870 F.2d 644 (Fed. Cir. 1989). There, the contracting officer held that a competitor's bid was not responsive, but GAO ruled to the contrary and recommended that the Army award the contract to the competitor. When the Army stated that it would follow that recommendation, Honeywell, Inc., the second low bidder on the contract, filed suit in the Claims Court to enjoin the award. The Claims Court held that GAO did not have a rational basis for its recommendation and enjoined the award. The Court of Appeals for the Federal Circuit reversed because the court had retried the issue of whether the contracting officer's decision was correct rather than determining whether GAO decision was rational, stating at 647:

> The question before the Claims Court was whether the Army justifiably followed the GAO's recommendation that the bid identified Haz-Tad as the bidder and therefore was responsive to the solicitation. The Claims Court recognized that the controlling inquiry in deciding that question was whether the GAO's decision was a rational one. After paying lip service to that standard, however, the Claims Court impermissibly undertook what can fairly be characterized only as its own independent de novo determination of whether the bid documents identified Haz-Tad as the bidder.

Carothers Constr., Inc. v. United States, 18 Cl. Ct. 745 (1989), further articulated the scope of review at 751:

> Although Carothers Construction Inc. (Carothers) was not required to file a protest with the GAO, it elected to do so. This election precludes the Claims Court from conducting its own independent de novo determination. *Honeywell*, 870 F.2d at 647.
>
> Even if the court would come to a different conclusion, the procurement agency's decision to follow the Comptroller General's recommendation is proper, unless the Comptroller General's decision itself was irrational. *Honeywell*, 870 F.2d at 648. "If the court finds a reasonable basis for the agency's action, the court should stay its hand even though it might, as an original proposition, have reached a different conclusion as to the proper administration and application of the procurement regulations." *Id.* at 648 (citing *M. Steinthal & Co. v. Seamans*, 147 U.S. App. D.C. 221, 455 F.2d 1289, 1301 (D.C. Cir. 1971)).

In *Centech Grp., Inc. v. United States*, 79 Fed. Cl. 562 (2007), *aff'd*, 554 F.3d 1029 (2009), Centech argued that the Air Force irrationally ignored the responsibility determination of the SBA and followed GAO's independent finding of unacceptability. The court found GAO determination rational because Centech's proposal did not provide the information the RFP requested, making it unacceptable. The court found an agency decision to follow an irrational GAO decision itself irrational in *Turner Constr. Co. v. United States*, 94 Fed. Cl. 561 (2010), *motion to stay injunction denied*, 94 Fed. Cl. 586 (2010). There, the court concluded that GAO conducted an improper de novo review of the contracting officer's OCI determination without giving the agency the deference it was due. GAO had overturned the contracting officer's determination without highlighting any hard facts to base its OCI determination. The court held that the Army was arbitrary and capricious in implementing GAO's decision, stripping Turner of the contract.

There have been instances where the court has overturned agency actions that were validated by GAO, *Latecoere Int'l Inc. v. Dep't of the Navy*, 19 F.3d 1342 (11th Cir. 1994). There, the court disagreed with GAO's finding that the arbitrary rating of a proposal did not prejudice Latecoere. The court stated that GAO based its conclusion that "Latecoere was not prejudiced by the arbitrary elevation of [the other offeror's] ratings on two assumptions, one of which has no support in the record, and the other of which is flatly contradicted by the record." In *E.W. Bliss Co. v. United States*, 33 Fed. Cl. 123 (1995), *aff'd*, 77 F.3d 445 (Fed. Cir. 1996), the court, although acknowledging that GAO decisions should be given a high degree of deference, stated: "The Court of Claims is not bound by the views of the Comptroller General nor do they operate as a legal or judicial determination of the rights of the parties," quoting *Burroughs Corp. v. United States*, 617 F.2d 590, 597 (Ct. Cl. 1980) (citing *Font v. United States*, 593 F.2d 388 (Ct. Cl. 1979)). In distinguishing *Honeywell*, the *Bliss* court stated that the Federal Circuit decision focused on the fact that the Claims Court did not give deference to either GAO or the contracting officer's decision but, rather, engaged in an independent de novo analysis. Thus, *Honeywell* should not be read as conferring on GAO a degree of deference beyond that set forth in *Burroughs.* The court stated at 135:

> The weight of precedent instructs that, although the review is not de novo and the GAO's decision is accorded deference, the court is to answer the question whether the agency's procurement decision or the GAO's decision on the protest was reasonable based on the record before the contracting officer or the GAO.

Although the court went to great lengths in analyzing the scope of its review, it in fact agreed with GAO's decision. Similarly, in *SP Sys., Inc. v. United States*, 86 Fed. Cl. 1 (2009), SP Systems originally won a NASA award, but, after GAO sustained a protest against the evaluations of cost realism, management approach, and past performance that led to that award, the agency followed GAO's specific recommendations for corrective action and (after re-evaluation) awarded the contract to a competitor. SP Systems then filed suit in the Court of Federal Claims, which found both GAO's decision and the agency's decision to follow it, reasonable, even though there were other ways the agency might have re-evaluated proposals.

If GAO's recommendation is plainly contrary to a statutory or regulatory requirement, that decision is irrational and an agency is not justified in following it. In *Firth Constr. Co. v. United States*, 36 Fed. Cl. 268 (1996), an offeror was the apparent low bidder but had failed to submit a completed Standard Form (SF) 1442. After bid opening, the offeror faxed a completed SF 1442 to the agency and was awarded the contract. Following a protest, the Office of Counsel of the agency advised the contracting division that the award was improper because the bid was nonresponsive due to the lack of an original signature on the SF 1442. Given this advice, the contracting officer canceled the award. The offeror protested to GAO, and GAO sustained the protest. The agency announced its intention to follow GAO's recommendation and award the contract to the offeror, and Firth Construction filed suit in the Court of Federal Claims. The court determined that the bid was nonresponsive because it lacked an original signature. Thus, the court held that GAO's decision was irrational and that the agency would be arbitrary and capricious to follow it. Similarly in *Grunley Walsh Int'l, LLC v. United States*, 78 Fed. Cl. 35 (2007), the Department of State disqualified plaintiff's prequalification based upon GAO's recommended interpretation of a statutory business-volume requirement. In holding that GAO's recommended interpretation is afforded no deference because it plainly lacked a reasonable basis and thus was arbitrary and capricious, the court stated at 43-44:

> Although the court does not specifically reach the question of whether the GAO afforded proper deference to the DOS's original interpretation under

> *Chevron, U.S.A., Inc. v. Natural Res. Def. Council, Inc.*, 467 U.S. 837 (1984), the court must address defendant's argument for affording deference to the DOS's new interpretation. Adoption of defendant's position would effectively strip this court of any real review in any case where the agency followed a recommendation of the GAO on an interpretation of a statute or regulation. The court declines to play that shell game. In entrusting this court with bid protest jurisdiction under APA standards, Congress necessarily meant for the court to undertake a meaningful review of agency action.
>
> Defendant cites *Honeywell, Inc. v. United States*, 870 F.2d 644 (Fed. Cir. 1989), in support of its argument. *Honeywell* stands for the rule that "a procurement agency's decision to follow the [GAO]'s recommendation . . . was proper unless the [GAO]'s decision itself was irrational." 870 F.2d at 648. In order to review an agency's action when it is based upon the recommendation of the GAO, it is necessary to examine the underlying decision of the GAO. *See Firth Constr. Co. v. United States*, 36 Fed. Cl. 268, 271-72 (1996) (citing and applying *Honeywell* to overturn agency action that was based on a decision of the GAO). The GAO decision constitutes the very reason(s) for the agency action. Put another way, an agency action is not insulated from meaningful review simply because the GAO recommended it.

See also *Geo-Seis Helicopters, Inc. v. United States*, 77 Fed. Cl. 633 (2007), where the agency accepted amendments to the winning bid after the bid closing date in reliance on GAO precedent allowing agencies to issue amendments that extend the closing date after the closing date has passed. GAO denied a protest based on this precedent and Geo-Seis filed suit in the Court of Federal Claims. The court held that the agency violated the APA by relying on GAO precedent, stating that the refusal of the contracting officer to "adhere to the categorical reality of the 'late is late' rule renders arbitrary her decision to accept [the winning bidder's] first and second revised proposals."

§ 15.09 APPELLATE REVIEW OF COURT OF FEDERAL CLAIMS PROTEST DECISIONS

The Federal Circuit has jurisdiction over appeals from the Court of Federal Claims, 28 U.S.C. § 1295(a)(3). An appeal must be filed within 60 days from the date of entry of the judgment or order, Fed. R. App. P. 4(a)(1); R.C.F.C. 72. The Federal Circuit reviews legal decision of the Court of Federal Claims de novo, and applies the same standard of review as the Court of Federal Claims, *Dysart v. United States*, 369 F.3d 1303 (Fed. Cir. 2004).

The Court of Federal Claims is bound by the decisions of the United States Supreme Court, the precedential decisions of the Federal Circuit, and the published decisions of the Federal Circuit's predecessor courts, the Court of Claims and the Court of Customs and Patent Appeals, *South Corp. v. United States*, 690 F.2d 1368 (Fed. Cir. 1982) (adopting as precedent the decisions of the predecessor Court of Claims and Court of Customs and Patent Appeals). Court of

Federal Claims judges are not bound by the decisions of other Court of Federal Claims judges, *Casa De Cambio Comdiv S. A., de C. V. v. United States*, 291 F.3d 1356 (Fed. Cir. 2002).

Chapter 16

U.S. FEDERAL PROCUREMENT: AN INTERNATIONAL PERSPECTIVE

§ 16.01 INTRODUCTION

This chapter, a new addition to *Formation of Government Contracts*, will offer a comparative perspective on U.S. federal procurement. As Duke University's Professor Ralf Michaels has noted, a comparative approach improves the law; it "should inform national lawmaking, assist judges in the resolution of difficult questions, provide a basis for legal unification or harmonization, or simply increase knowledge and extend awareness, especially in legal education." Ralf Michaels, *Comparative Law*, in *Oxford Handbook of European Private Law* (Basedow, Hopt, Zimmermann eds., Oxford University Press), available at *https://scholarship.law.duke.edu/faculty_scholarship/2388/*. At the same time, a comparative approach also helps build bridges of understanding between nations, which is critically important to those who will work internationally—both those who are interested in the U.S. procurement system, and those from the United States who want to understand how the U.S. systems compares to others abroad. See, e.g., Christopher R. Yukins, *The U.S. Federal Procurement System: An Introduction,* 2017 Upphandlingsrattslig Tidskrift (UrT) 69, *https://ssrn.com/abstract=3063559.*

Those bridges of understanding are especially important because, despite a rapidly globalizing economy, public procurement markets tend to be uniquely isolated. See, e.g., Guy I. Seidman & Eran Ifargan, *Public and International Procurement: A Comparative Approach*, in *Transnational Law of Public Contracts,* at 44, 49-51 (Mathias Audit & Stephan Schill, eds.) (Bruylant, Brussels 2015). Cross-border trade in public procurement typically amounts to only a few percentage points in markets that total trillions of dollars. See id. Compared to mainstream commercial markets, there is far less cross-border trade in procurement markets; to the extent the private and public markets run in parallel (and they often do), this suggests that public purchasers may be receiving, on balance, more costly and lower-quality goods and services than their commercial counterparts. The balkanization of the world's procurement markets is due in part to purchasing officials' "home preference," often in response to legal and political pressures to buy from local vendors first.

But another, perhaps equally important, cause of balkanized world procurement markets may be the procurement rules themselves. When procurement rules differ from nation to nation, or even from town to town, vendors find it more difficult to penetrate new markets, and cross-border trade in procurement tends to break down. See, e.g., Albert Sanchez Graells, *Public Procurement and the EU Competition Rules* 11 (Hart 2011) ("Public procurement rules can themselves generate significant distortions of competitive market dynamics—and, in so doing, can be largely self-defeating, as they can restrict the effective chances for the public buyer to obtain best value.").

Since World War II, enormous efforts have been made to break down these artificial, rules-based barriers to procurement trade. The United States helped launch what eventually became the World Trade Organization (WTO) and its Agreement on Government Procurement (GPA) shortly after the war. See generally Gabrielle Marceau and Annet Blank, *History of The Government Procurement Negotiations Since 1945*, 5 Pub. Proc. L. Rev. 77, 79 (1996). The GPA, as part of a broader effort to reduce non-tariff barriers to trade, encourages common approaches to procurement rules. Similarly, the United Nations Commission on International Trade Law (UNCITRAL) has published a Model Law on Public Procurement. The UNCITRAL model law offers model provisions, shaped by international best practices, which many governments around the world have incorporated into their own laws. These efforts at harmonization and sharing best practices, and others led by the World Bank and its fellow multilateral development banks, the Organization for Economic Cooperation and Development (OECD), and national agencies such as the U.S. Agency for International Development (USAID), have helped drive a remarkable convergence of procurement laws around the world. As nations' procurement systems mature, their laws typically look more and more alike.

Probably the most important work to reduce rules-based barriers to procurement trade has come in the European Union (EU), as part of a much more expansive effort to draw European Union member states together by using common rules in a common market. See, e.g., *EU Public Procurement Law: An Introduction* 16 (Sue Arrowsmith ed. 2010), *https://www.nottingham.ac.uk/pprg/documentsarchive/asialinkmaterials/eupublicprocurementlawintroduction.pdf*. Under the Treaty for the Functioning of the European Union (TFEU), the EU's procurement directives frame the member states' procurement laws, which must conform to the directives. *See, e.g.,* Sue Arrowsmith, *The Law of Public and Utilities Procurement*, chs. 3 & 4 (Sweet & Maxwell-Thomson 2005); Peter Trepte, *Regulating Public Procurement* 342-67 (Oxford U. Press 2004). Because the EU procurement directives have had such a broad impact internationally, and the EU member states are among the most important public procurement markets in the world, this chapter will look often to the European Union (and its former member state, the United Kingdom) in making comparative assessments of U.S. federal procurement law. See generally Daniel Schoeni, *Public Procurement in the U.S. Federal Government and The European Union: Hidden Non-Tariff Barriers* (PhD thesis submitted May 2022, University of Nottingham) (considering trade barriers created by U.S. and European "embedded legal cultures").

There are two basic approaches to comparative law, as Professor Michaels has noted—"functional and cultural." See Ralf Michaels, *Comparative Law, supra*. A "functional" approach "starts from the premise that the function of law lies in responding to social problems and that all societies face in essence the same problems. This makes it possible to compare legal institutions, even if they display different doctrinal structures, as long as they fulfil the same function, because in this case they are functionally equivalent." *Id.* A "cultural" approach, in contrast, "rejects the reduction of law to its function and instead understands national law as an expression and development of the general culture of a society," which means that ostensibly similar legal functions may, in fact, perform very differently because they are lodged in societies which differ markedly in culture, history, politics and economics. *Id.* While Professor Michaels argues that the "discrepancies between the approaches are smaller than the sometimes-fierce debate suggests," mindful that it is easy to misconstrue the norms and influences that inform foreign law, this chapter will offer cautious cross-border comparisons, rooted first in the U.S. experience.

This chapter will track the preceding chapters of this book, providing in each instance a comparison to illuminate, from a global perspective, critical facets of the U.S. federal procurement regime. As with the rest of this volume, the focus will be on U.S. federal procurement, which for reasons of federalism stands apart from state and local procurement in the United States. *See, e.g.*, Danielle Conway, *State and Local Government Procurement* (American Bar Ass'n (ABA) 2015); *Guide to State Procurement: A 50-State Primer on Purchasing Laws, Processes, and Procedures* (Melissa Javon Copeland, ed.) (ABA 3d ed. 2022). For some chapters, such as those on competitive methods and contractor qualification, the (generally unintended) parallels between U.S. practices and those abroad are startling and revealing. In other cases—such as cost principles—though there are few points of comparison abroad, the unique advances in U.S. practice tell us a great deal about the U.S. system itself over the centuries of the republic's history. See, e.g., James F. Nagle, *A History of Government Contracting* (2d ed. 2012) (detailed history of U.S. government procurement), *available on* www.publicprocurementinternational.com; Joshua I. Schwartz, *The Centrality of Military Procurement: Explaining the Exceptionalist Character of United States Federal Public Procurement Law*, in *Public Procurement: Global Revolution III—An International Conference for the Procurement Community* (University of Nottingham 2006).

§16.02 BASIC PRINCIPLES OF FEDERAL PROCUREMENT

From a foreign perspective, perhaps the most striking thing about U.S. procurement law is its practicality—that rather than being driven by abstract principle, the U.S. system is built around experimentation and change, constantly evolving to harvest success and abandon failure. While procurement law on the European continent tends to echo the approach of French philosopher René Descartes (a "Cartesian" approach) and flow from first principles, such as the equal treatment of bidders, the United States procurement system takes a different approach, one less tied to abstract principle. As Alexis de Tocqueville, an extraordinarily insightful observer of U.S. culture, wrote in the 1830s:

> In America, the purely practical part of the sciences is admirably cultivated, and care is taken with those theoretical aspects of science that are immediately necessary for the application at hand. In this respect the American mind has invariably shown itself to be clear, free, original, and fertile. But almost no one in the United States devotes himself to the essentially theoretical and abstract aspects of human knowledge. In this the

> Americans carry to excess a tendency that can, I think, be found in all democratic peoples, though to a lesser degree.

Alexis de Tocqueville, *Democracy in America*, at 523 (1835) (Library of America ed., 2012).

In the nineteenth century the United States was the birthplace of "Pragmatism"—a philosophical approach, popularized by Williams James and other leading thinkers of his day, which holds that something is true only insofar as it succeeds. See, e.g., "Pragmatism," *Stanford Encyclopedia of Philosophy* (2008), *https://plato.stanford.edu/entries/pragmatism/*. As the discussion below will reflect, this indelibly American philosophical approach helps explain both success and failure in the U.S. procurement system.

Chapter 1, which describes the basic principles of federal procurement, reflects the system's bedrock pragmatism precisely because it makes almost no mention at all of principles—instead, it describes the constitutional, legislative and regulatory structures on which the U.S. system is built, and then turns to the anti-corruption measures used to maintain the integrity of U.S. procurement.

This is not to suggest that the U.S. system is unprincipled—as Professor Steven Schooner has noted, there are recognized "desiderata" in the U.S. system, as in any other system, see Steven L. Schooner, *Desiderata: Objectives for a System of Government Contract Law,* 2011 Pub. Proc. L. Rev. 103, available at *https://ssrn.com/abstract=304620*, and other regulatory regimes echo those same goals, see, e.g., *UNCITRAL Model Law on Public Procurement* preamble (2011). The *desiderata* identified by Professor Schooner are more goals than principles, though, and these "desiderata" may rise and fall in importance as the system evolves.

What does set the U.S. system apart, though, is an abiding and pragmatic suspicion of abstract principles. This is in contrast to other regimes, such as the European Union's *acquis communautaire* (gathered law and guidance). The European Union, for example, places first priority on principles of European integration, and therefore may give short shrift to the core goal of U.S. procurement: "best value" (or, as the term is used internationally, "value for money"). See, e.g., FAR 1.102 ("The vision for the Federal Acquisition System is to deliver on a timely basis the best value product or service to the customer, while maintaining the public's trust and fulfilling public policy objectives."); World Bank, *Procurement for Projects and Programs* ("Value for Money is a core procurement principle in all procurements financed by the World Bank. This means the focus is on bids that provide the best overall value for money, taking into account quality, cost, and other factors as needed, rather than a focus on the lowest evaluated compliant bid."); Sue Arrowsmith, *The Past and Future Evolution of EC Procurement Law: From Framework to Common Code?*, 35 Pub. Cont. L.J. 337 (2006) (role of European principles in shaping EU procurement regime); Martin Trybus, *European Union Law and Public Procurement*, at 6 (Institute of European Law Working Papers No. 05/2017) ("all public procurement related laws and actions have to satisfy the requirements of the [Treaty on the Functioning of the European Union] regime on the free movement goods"); Abigail Semple, *Reform of EU Public Procurement Law: Intergovernmental or Supranational Policy-making?* (July 15, 2018), available at *https://ssrn.com/abstract=3377984*.

[A] Structure and Goals of the U.S. System

To fully appreciate the "desiderata" or systemic goals that Professor Schooner identified in the U.S. procurement system, as Chapter 1 suggests it is useful to compare the federal government's grants system. While the U.S. government typically spends over $600 billion per year on procurement, the parallel grants system—federal assistance to states, local governments, non-profit entities and others—is consistently larger, year by year. (Readily accessible data on both federal contracts and grants awards are available at *www.usaspending.gov*, and grants opportunities and awards are at www.grants.gov.) While the federal government generally requires structured competitions for the award of federal contracts, and transparency before and after award, awards of federal grants are typically less rigorously competitive, and (unlike procurement contracts) are infrequently subject to the accountability of bid challenges ("bid protests" in the U.S. system, discussed in Chapter 15 and below).

The laxer rules applied to federal grants, compared to federal procurement contracts, help illuminate a central assumption in U.S. administrative practice—a perceived need to control and direct the actions of an administrative agent, which can vary with the depth of moral hazard faced by the agent and the strength of the agent's relative informational advantage. "Principal-agent" theory, put forward by economists in the 1970's, holds that an agent has a natural, selfish tendency to deviate from the goals of the principal—an inherent conflict-of-interest, which is exacerbated where the agent holds an informational advantage. See, e.g., Jon D. Michaels, *Privatization's Pretensions*, 77 U. Chi. L. Rev. 717 (2010) (application of principal-agent theory in procurement). To check the agents' natural tendency to stray from the principal's ends, the principal (in procurement, the government) may *monitor* or *sanction* the agent (the intermediary contracting official, and the contractor itself). See Christopher Yukins, *A Versatile Prism: Assessing Procurement Law Through the Principal-Agent Model*, 40 Pub. Cont. L.J. 63 (2010), available at *https://ssrn.com/abstract=1776295*. Because of a popular assumption that those receiving grants (philanthropic organizations, for example) share goals more closely aligned with those of the granting government, with grants there is less of a perceived need for the government/principal to oversee and control its grantees/agents. This may explain why the administrative tools normally used to ensure that a perhaps indifferent contracting official will purchase best value—enforced competition and transparency, for example—are given smaller roles in the grants process.

Thus, understanding that the U.S. system views competition and transparency in an *instrumental* manner, as tools to help ensure procuring officials will purchase best value, helps explain why in other contexts the federal procurement system demands so much less. In other quarters, for example in the case of "other transactions" (procurements which are specially exempt from normal FAR requirements, by statute), Congress has proved willing to forfeit open competition, transparency and uniformity (another of Professor Schooner's "desiderata") in return for speed and efficiency (a competing "desideratum"). See U.S. Office of the Under Secretary of Defense for Acquisition and Sustainment, *Other Transactions Guide* (2018). To allow federal purchasers to achieve those other ends, such as the very rapid acquisition of cutting-edge weapons technology, Congress has essentially afforded "other transactions" a sweeping exemption from the FAR. The "other transaction" model reflects a pragmatic frustration with the bureaucratic slowness of FAR-based procurements; it also reflects, though, an abiding faith that certain contracting officials (such as the "agreement officers" who negotiate and run "other transactions" agreements) can be trusted to act appropriately, even without regulatory restraints, because of a shared commitment to a common national good.

The sprawling U.S. procurement system is rife with contradictions, though, and other doctrines—such as the "personal services" bar discussed in Chapter 1—reflect not a trust in government officials, but an abiding suspicion of bureaucracy. The "personal services" bar generally prohibits agency officials from directly supervising contractor employees. See, e.g., Kenneth J. Allen, *The Obsolete Services Restrictions of the Antideficiency Act—Still the Law*, 17-12 Briefing Papers 1 (2017). While the personal services bar seems, on its face, an effort to protect the lower tiers of the civil service from being replaced by contract workers, in practice the personal services bar also serves as a protection against a shadow bureaucracy, unseen and unaccountable, made up of contractor employees under civil servants' direction. The personal services bar, though awkward in practice because it fractures lines of authority between civil servants and contractor employees, thus offers a durable reminder of a libertarian, pragmatic streak in U.S. society.

To knit together this complex and often contradictory system, there are four sources of law in the U.S. procurement system. See Daniel E. Schoeni & Christopher R. Yukins, *Common Principles of Public Contracts in the United States of America*, 1-2021 Ius Publicum Network Review (Nov. 2021), *http://www.ius-publicum.com/repository/uploads/02_11_2021_18_01-D.Schoeni_C.Yukins_IUSPUB_publication_note.pdf*. When a constitutional provision applies, that is the highest level of authority and controls all else. The next source of law is the U.S. government's procurement statutes, which are typically revised and updated through what has for decades been an annual tradition: Title VIII of each year's National Defense Authorization Act, which addresses procurement reform. Then come the regulations—dominated by the Federal Acquisition Regulation (FAR), a regulatory behemoth which applies uniformly across the government, but is supplemented by agency-specific (and generally consistent) procurement regulations. Finally comes the "federal common law" of government contracts, including decisions issued by the U.S. Supreme Court, the federal circuit courts of appeals (especially the U.S. Court of Appeals for the Federal Circuit), the trial courts (especially the U.S. Court of Federal Claims), the Civilian and Armed Services Boards of Contract Appeals, the Government Accountability Office, and the potentially hundreds of federal trial courts and agencies that issue decisions bearing on federal procurement. Because of the common law tradition inherited from the British, the U.S. decisions can be legion, dense and conflicting.

To make sense of this confusing welter of law, it helps to identify the key *structural* elements that do so much to shape the federal procurement system. See Daniel E. Schoeni & Christopher Yukins, *supra*. The first structural element is the Constitution's careful balance of powers between the executive and legislative branches. Congress, the legislative branch, retains the "power of the purse"—the power to control spending and thus, however mechanically, control the levers of government. To preserve the democratic authority of Congress, different legal doctrines in federal procurement law—fiscal law principles barring contracting without an underlying appropriation, for example, or the *Christian* doctrine which reads missing clauses into contracts if those clauses reflect important policies enacted by Congress, see *G. L. Christian & Assocs. v. the United States,* 312 F.2d 418 (Ct. Cl. 1963)—confirm Congress' ultimate control, as the democratic voice of the popular will.

For these same structural reasons, federal procurement law protects the constitutional prerogative of the executive branch. Authority flows from the President to the heads of the agencies, and then down, ultimately, to the contracting officer. Unlike procuring entities in some foreign jurisdictions, which can spread responsibility (and accountability) across an entire agency or office, in the U.S. system authority devolves to a highly accountable *individual* contracting officer. The generally hostile doctrines of apparent and implied authority mean that the contractor bears risk that the contracting official lacks actual authority; by shifting risk to the contractor, the legal framework confirms that the constitutional imperative come first, even if it causes economic harm to the unwary contractor.

At the same time, the U.S. legal regime lends at least some potential relief to the injured contractor, for example under the doctrine of equitable estoppel if a contractor has reasonably relied, to its costly detriment, on a rogue contracting official. Constitutional concerns are thus counterbalanced by economic realities—by the need to treat vendors fairly so that they remain engaged in (so that they compete in) the federal marketplace.

What emerges from all this is more than just a confusing mash of commercial, constitutional and common law—instead, it is a system pragmatically built on a principled structure of institutions and markets (rather than abstract principles), informed by a cautious unease with government and bound together by a stubborn hope that officials will procure best value for a broader common good. See FAR 1.102(d) (buyers are "to exercise personal initiative and sound business judgment in providing the best value . . . to meet the customer's needs"); Steven L. Schooner, *Fear of Oversight: The Fundamental Failure of Businesslike Government*, 2001 Am. U.L. Rev., 627, 714–17 (arguing that procurement is not an administrative function which can be improved simply by modeling businesses practices from the private sector); Mark Cancian, *Acquisition Reform: It's Not as Easy as It Seems*, 1995 Acquisition Rev. Q. 189, 191–92 (noting the popular belief that "without explicit guidance and close scrutiny the [Department of Defense] will waste money").

[B] Anti-Corruption Measures

Two observations help explain the anti-corruption measures in U.S. federal procurement. The first involves the sheer large number of anti-corruption measures, in statutes, regulations and practice, which have been developing and multiplying since the early days of the republic. As a result, the U.S. anti-corruption systems provide important lessons for other governments, though the U.S. system itself often borrows useful lessons from other legal regimes. Second, those anti-corruption measures stand in a sort of ring-fence around the U.S. procurement system, and reinforce both the *internal* strength of the system *and* the *external legitimacy* of the system. Thus, for example, bid protests may unearth both spectacular corruption and everyday procedural failures. Understanding that dual nature of anti-corruption devices—they both protect and reinforce the U.S. procurement system—makes it easier to understand the pragmatic compromises the system sometimes draws in order to balance those two goals.

The standards of conduct that U.S. officials must follow are a good example of that pragmatic approach, and its increasingly global context. Like most employees of the federal government, contracting officials in the executive branch must follow the *Standards of Ethical Conduct for Employees of the Executive Branch*, published at 5 C.F.R. Part 2635 by the U.S. Office of Government Ethics. The standards meet an international expectation: the United States, like almost every nation in the world, has joined the United Nations Convention Against Corruption (UNCAC), which in Article 8 calls for codes of conduct for public officials.

Article 9 of UNCAC, which covers procurement, goes beyond and calls for special protective "measures to regulate matters regarding personnel responsible for procurement," such as a "declaration of interest in particular public procurements [and] screening procedures." These stronger ethical requirements for procurement officials reflect the higher corruption risks that surround public procurement. See OECD, *Preventing Corruption in Public Procurement* 6 (2016) ("Public procurement is one of the government activities most vulnerable to corruption. In addition to the volume of transactions and the financial interests at stake, corruption risks are exacerbated by the complexity of the process, the close interaction between public officials and businesses, and the multitude of stakeholders."). Rules issued under the Procurement Integrity Act, set forth at Sections 3.104-1 et seq. of the FAR, implement these stronger ethical requirements for U.S. procurement officials. These rules followed the "Illwind" series of prosecutions in the 1980s, a scandal which grew out of illicit trading for bid details and sensitive government information ("source selection" information), and which engulfed much of the U.S. defense industry. See U.S. Federal Bureau of Investigation, *Operation Illwind*, *https://www.fbi.gov/history/famous-cases/operation-illwind*. The U.S. procurement integrity laws now, for example, require senior procurement officials to disclose contacts regarding employment from contractors, and can make disclosure of bidding or source selection information a crime. See FAR 3.104-3 & 3.104-5; see also Jessica Tillipman & Vijaya Surampudi, *The Compliance Mentorship Program: Improving Ethics and Compliance in Small Government Contractors*, 49 Pub. Cont. L.J. 217 (2020), available at *ssrn.com/abstract=3559458*.

In keeping with international best practices, as Chapter 1 notes the U.S. procurement rules now requires many contractors to erect "corporate compliance" systems (what are sometimes called "self-cleaning" or "selbstreinigung" remedial efforts in the European Union). See FAR 3.1004 & 52.203-13. The FAR's requirements were modeled on the corporate compliance guidelines issued by the U.S. Sentencing Commission in the 1990's, which themselves can be traced back to corporate anti-corruption systems implemented by major U.S. corporations (including defense contractors) from the 1960's. See, e.g., Christopher R. Yukins, *Mandatory Disclosure: A Case Study in How Anti-Corruption Measures Can Affect Competition in Defense Markets* (2016), available at *https://ssrn.com/abstract=2600676*.

As compliance requirements have proliferated internationally, to a remarkable extent those requirements have evolved in parallel. The basic required elements of a compliance system—a corporate code of conduct, for example, and an informed leadership, training, and regular reassessment of the system and surrounding compliance risks—are the same in countries all over the world. As a result, as the U.S. Justice Department and the U.S. Securities & Exchange Commission suggest in their guidance, *A Resource Guide to the U.S. Foreign Corrupt Practices Act* (2d ed. 2020), businesses (including contractors) typically design compliance systems "focused on anti-corruption compliance more broadly," *id.* & n.326 (listing similar compliance requirements internationally). In practice, this means that a contractor which establishes a compliance system in the U.S. federal procurement system should be able to use the same compliance system (adapted for peculiarities of local law) in foreign procurement markets as well. By the same token, a commercial company in the United States which has installed a corporate compliance system under the U.S. Sentencing Guidelines can, with appropriate adjustments, use the same compliance system to meet the requirements of the federal procurement rules.

The way that compliance rules have developed in parallel internationally has brought comparative issues to the fore. While (as Chapter 1 explains) the U.S. imposes *mandatory disclosure* obligations on contractors that have concluded, after due investigation, that their employees have engaged in serious violations such as bribery or fraud, see American Bar Association, *Guide to the Mandatory Disclosure Rule: Issues, Guidelines, and Best Practices* (2009), other regimes (such as the United Kingdom's Bribery Act of 2010) do *not* require mandatory disclosure, or (as in the case of the World Bank) contemplate *voluntary* disclosure by a contractor which discovers corruption in its ranks.

For the same reasons, important elements that emerge in one of these parallel rules systems may reemerge in other systems abroad. Thus, for example, the European Union's requirement that a contractor guilty of wrongdoing "shall prove that it has paid or undertaken to pay compensation in respect of any damage caused by the criminal offence or misconduct" in order to be readmitted to public procurement under Article 57 of the EU Procurement Directive 2014/24/EU, in time may bring questions of victim compensation into clearer focus in the U.S. regime. Although the FAR does not explicitly require contractors to reimburse victims of their corruption, the U.S. rules governing debarment, see FAR 9.406, do ask whether a contractor facing potential debarment has "made or agreed to make full restitution." Chapter 8 of the U.S. Sentencing Commission's *Sentencing Guidelines* (as noted, the source of the FAR requirements) says that an organization guilty of criminal conduct "should take reasonable steps, as warranted under the circumstances, to remedy the harm resulting from the criminal conduct," and those steps "may include, where appropriate, providing restitution to identifiable victims, as well as other forms of remediation." *Id.* § 8B2.1 application notes.

Because contractors caught in corruption may face enforcement actions from many different quarters, nationally and internationally, these converging anti-corruption requirements are both a boon and a burden. Parallel standards reduce compliance costs for contractors, but multiple lines of enforcement exposure—enforcement demands from different nations when corruption occurs, for example—can sharply increase costs and risks for contractors working internationally.

Those cross-border difficulties can be amplified in the U.S. system because federal officials have enormous discretion in applying anti-corruption standards. Thus, for example, although the U.S. standards for contractor qualification (called "responsibility" in the U.S. system), see FAR Subpart 9.1, closely parallel the UNCITRAL standards for contractor qualification, see UNCITRAL Model Law on Public Procurement, Art. 9, in application U.S. contracting officers have substantial discretion in making responsibility determinations. Similarly, U.S. debarring officials have great discretion when they decide more broadly that vendors are not "presently responsible," and so should be barred from federal procurement in general. See FAR Subpart 9.4; John Pachter, Christopher Yukins & Jessica

Tillipman, *U.S. Debarment: An Introduction, in The Cambridge Handbook of Compliance* 288 (Benjamin van Rooij & D. Daniel Sokol eds., 2021).

There is a pragmatic logic to the discretion that the U.S. system lends contracting officers and debarring officials, because they are in the best position to assess whether their agency (in the case of a responsibility determination for a given contract) or the government as a whole (for a government-wide debarment) can handle the performance and reputational risks presented by a particular contractor. Different agencies (and governments) tolerate those risk differently. But in practice the deference afforded responsibility and debarment decisions means that anti-corruption efforts in the U.S. government can seem uneven and even unfair, from an international perspective.

One way to mitigate that unevenness of enforcement would be to make the information underlying corruption and enforcement more broadly available, both domestically and internationally. Outside the U.S. system, tools have already been developed to gather qualification and debarment information from procurement systems around the globe. The World Bank, for example, makes at least part of its investigative information available to borrower nations affected by corruption in World Bank projects. See, e.g., Pascale Hélène Dubois, J. David Fielder, Robert Delonis, Frank Fariello & Kathleen Peters, *The World Bank's Sanctions System: Using Debarment to Combat Fraud and Corruption in International Development, in Good Governance and Modern International Financial Institutions* (Brill 2018). Here, however, the U.S. lags behind, because not all of its information regarding contractor qualification (in the System for Award Management, www.sam.gov) is available to users outside the U.S. government, and most contractor performance information is not available at all outside the government. This checkered transparency may be due to stakeholders in the U.S. system—for example, to vendors that resist disclosure of information that they consider proprietary, or to agency gatekeepers which have little incentive to make more qualification information publicly available.

That said, the U.S. qualification and exclusion (debarment) system does have important lessons to offer. The U.S. government uses system-wide debarment, not merely contract-by-contract exclusion as contemplated by the European Union directives—although the EU directives allow member states to develop more expansive exclusion systems, and some are. See Christopher Yukins & Michal Kania, *Suspension and Debarment in the U.S. Government: Comparative Lessons for the EU's Next Steps in Procurement*, 19-2 UrT 47 (2019), available at *http://ssrn.com/abstract=3422499*; Albert Sanchez Graells, *Public Procurement and Competition: Some Challenges Arising from Recent Developments in EU Public Procurement Law*, in *Research Handbook on EU Public Procurement Law*, at 434 (C. Bovis, ed.) (Edward Elgar Publishing 2016) ("Given the optional terms in which Article 57 [of the EU Directive] is drafted, such open regulation at [the] EU level can give rise to different regimes across different Member States and, consequently, might facilitate strategic behaviour by infringing undertakings—thereby reducing deterrence. A stricter and uniform system of suspension and debarment . . . would contribute to . . . limiting privately-created distortions of competition."). Because the U.S. debarment system is explicitly focused on the government's interests and *not* on punishment, see FAR 9.402(b) ("The serious nature of debarment and suspension requires that these sanctions be imposed only in the public interest for the Government's protection and not for purposes of punishment."), debarring officials can (and do) engage directly with accused contractors to demand assurance that the contractors are undertaking appropriate remedial measures. See American Bar Association, *The Practitioner's Guide to Suspension and Debarment* (4th ed. 2018, eds. Frederic Mark Levy & Michael T. Wagner). Under FAR 9.406-3, a debarring official and the accused contractor may enter into an administrative agreement (akin to Brazil's "leniency agreements," see generally Christopher R. Yukins & Cristiana Fortini Silva, *A Comparative View of Debarment and Suspension of Contractors in Brazil and in the USA*, 66 Admin. & Constit. L. Rev. 61 (Brazil 2016), available at *https://ssrn.com/abstract=3080396*). Those administrative agreements in the U.S. system are to be publicly available, FAR 9.406-3, and they may explain, for example, what remedial measures the contractor must take in order to avoid debarment.

Another important anti-corruption device in the U.S. system is its approach to politics in procurement. In many systems around the world, efforts have been made to erect practical and legal barriers between politics and procurement, because of the acute risk that corrupt politicians will attempt to distort procurement outcomes to serve their own interests, or the interests of their personal or political allies. In some systems, for example, procurement officials will insist on memorializing their exchanges with politicians, to discourage interference. In others, legal barriers have gone up. In Trinidad & Tobago, for example, Section 59 of the Procurement and Disposal of Public Property Act (2015) makes it unlawful for any person "with intent to gaining an advantage or concession for himself or any other person," to "approach . . . any member or an associate of a member of procuring entity," or any consultant or service provider for that procuring agency, "with respect to any matter that is before that procuring entity or that is expected to come before that procuring entity."

The U.S. system, recognizing the practical need for open communications and planning in procurement, see, e.g., FAR 15.201 (allowing free interactions between government officials and the public at least until a solicitation is issued), does not bar all contact between procurement officials and politicians. Interactions that distort the outcome of a procurement are, however, barred. The covenant against contingent fees, for example, discourages influence-peddling by former politicians by sharply limiting those who can recover percentage fees when a vendor is awarded a contract. FAR Subpart 3.4. And if a politician interferes directly with an award decision, that award—shaped now by that interference, and not by the criteria in the solicitation—is subject to challenge in a bid protest.

That is not to say, however, that the U.S. system has completely insulated procurement from politics. Although U.S. law bars contracting firms from making political contributions to federal campaigns, 52 U.S.C. § 30119, U.S. campaign finance laws still allow contractors' executives and employees to contribute directly to federal campaigns, see 11 C.F.R. § 115.6 (Federal Election Commission implementing regulation), and those elected officials necessarily play an important role in planning procurement, and in directing and overseeing the procurement system. Here again, the U.S. legal regime reflects practical compromises between procurement integrity and the constitutional rights of free speech which protect campaign contributions.

Another area which reflects pragmatic compromises—here, between procurement integrity and market dynamics—involves payments between prime contractors and subcontractors which may violate the Anti-Kickback Act of 1986. The Anti-Kickback Act, like the United Kingdom's Bribery Act, bans "commercial bribery," i.e., payments between private parties to gain an illicit advantage. The practical problem is that payments between private parties to award an advantage (a percentage commission paid a reseller, for example, or a tip a head waiter for a coveted table) are a regular part of commerce, and in the United States' highly dynamic economy, Congress and the state legislatures have been reluctant to ban such payments outright. See, e.g., Jeffrey Boles, *Examining the Lax Treatment of Commercial Bribery in the United States: A Prescription for Reform*, 51 Am. Bus. L.J. 119 (2014). The relatively aggressive approach taken against commercial bribery in procurement by the Anti-Kickback Act may be due to the government's inherent difficulties in discerning, and mitigating, incentive payments passing between the government's contractors and subcontractors. To resolve this tension between commercial imperative and the distorting effects of kick-backs (discussed in Chapter 1), the Anti-Kickback Act bars only payments for *improperly* obtaining or rewarding favorable treatment, see, e.g., U.S. Department of Justice, *Criminal Resource Manual* § 927, Anti-Kickback Act of 1986, and" "payments specifically authorized by a contract or behavior that would be commonly recognized as incidental business accommodations" are typically excluded. E.g., *Morse Diesel Int'l, Inc. v. United States,* 66 Fed. Cl. 788, 800 (2005).

A final example of a U.S. anti-corruption measure with potentially important comparative lessons is the False Claims Act. See, e.g., John Boese & Douglas Baruch, *Civil False Claims and Qui Tam Actions* (5th ed. 2021). This statute, enacted in 1863 to address contractor fraud during the Civil War, is an important example for other procurement systems because it presents a unique combination of elements that, taken together, make this a powerful weapon against fraud in public procurement:

- *Penalties*: While the False Claims Act also carries criminal penalties, it is more commonly the subject of civil actions. Because the Act allows for treble damages and minimum civil penalties of more than $11,000 for every "claim"—an invoice, for example—the government's recovery in a case can amount to millions of dollars, and in fiscal year 2020 the Justice Department recovered more than $2 billion in settlements and judgments under the Act. See U.S. Department of Justice, *The False Claims Act, https://www.justice.gov/civil/false-claims-act.*

- *Whistleblowers:* An individual may bring a False Claims Act action in the name of the government. These are known as "qui tam" actions, after the Latin—"qui tam pro domino rege quam pro se ipso in hac parte sequitur," meaning "who sues in this matter for the king as well as for himself." This old English practice, largely abolished in the United Kingdom after the Common Informers Act of 1951, see J. Ll. J. Edwards, *Common Informers Act, 1951*,14 Mod. L. Rev. 462 (Oct. 1951), remains a vital part of False Claims Act enforcement in the United States. As Chapter 1 explains, the person who brings the action, colloquially known as a "qui tam relator," can share in the government's recovery. This creates a strong incentive for disclosure by an "insider" (an employee of a contractor, for example) to bring suit as a relator. This is important because the complex nature of modern federal procurement often makes it difficult for "outsiders"—members of civil society, for example—to discern and act upon frauds in federal procurement.
- *Intent requirement*: As Chapter 1 explains, civil recovery is available under the False Claims Act for "reckless" fraud. While the Act does not define that term, the Model Penal Code, which was broadly relied upon in drafting state criminal laws across the United States, does define recklessness in Section 2.02: a defendant acts "recklessly" when he "disregards a substantial and unjustifiable risk that the [act] exists or will result from his conduct." The Model Penal Code stressed that the "risk must be of such a nature and degree that, considering the nature and purpose of the actor's conduct and the circumstances known to him, its disregard involves a gross deviation from the standard of conduct that a law-abiding person would observe in the actor's situation." While the Model Penal Code's definition is of course not binding under the False Claims Act, the central elements of recklessness under the model code—acting in the face of a known risk, contrary to commonly recognized standards—help explain the standard as applied by the courts, as discussed in Chapter 1. *See United States ex rel. Schutte v. Supervalue Inc.*, No. 21-1326 (U.S. Sup. Ct. June 1, 2023) (discussing "recklessness" standard under FCA).

The False Claims Act, like the other U.S. anti-corruption measures discussed above, offers important lessons to other procurement systems around the world. As with the other measures, the False Claims Act both checks misconduct from without and reinforces sound processes from within the procurement system. From a comparative perspective, the anti-corruption measures illustrate the highly pragmatic way that U.S. law integrates commercial and governmental interests. Finally, because they are constantly evolving and advancing, with extensive experimentation, successes and failures, the U.S. measures leave open the door to future improvements, perhaps taken from abroad, such as the use of anti-money laundering systems to capture corruption in procurement. See, e.g., Eastern and Southern Africa Anti-Money Laundering Group, *Procurement Corruption in the Public Sector and Associated Money Laundering in the ESAAMLG Region* (Oct. 2019).

§ 16.03 CONTRACT FORMATION PRINCIPLES

The contract formation principles reviewed in Chapter 2 are, in the main, really common law principles that have carried into federal procurement. The United States, a former colony, inherited the British common law which has continued to evolve in the over two centuries since independence.

Chapter 2's rules of federal contracts formations stand out from a comparative perspective because they reflect a system built up from the basics of contracting—drawing on common law traditions, and building each step of the legal structure, beginning with common law rules of offer and acceptance. By constructing a system of rules grounded in the common law and shaped by the government's contracting realities, federal procurement law was able to evolve more organically than many of its counterparts abroad. In the European Union, in contrast, the legal structure is built on a latticework of rules and principles meant to reinforce an integrated European economy, not to achieve best value in procurement. See, e.g., Sue Arrowsmith, *The Purpose of the EU Procurement Directives: Ends, Means and the Implications for National Regulatory Space for Commercial and Horizontal Procurement Policies*, 14 Cambridge Yearbook of European Legal Studies 1 (2012) (EU procurement directives "seek to promote the internal market . . . solely by three means—prohibiting discrimination, implementing transparency, and removing barriers to access," and they do not "promote a single market by standardising procedures, [or] replicate in the public market the competitive process of the private market [or] seek value for taxpayers' money").

Because the U.S. rules are flexibly grounded in the common law and can be adapted pragmatically to meet the government's special needs in a very unique public procurement market, U.S. law can (for example) accommodate implied-in-fact contracts—something much less likely under the European Union's rules, which demand procedural formality to advance the EU's economic integration. As one European scholar put it:

> [In] public procurement law the contract is the result of a complex procedure with rules and terms strictly established by national and European legislation. In civil law, for a promise to become an enforceable contract,

> parties must agree on the essential terms of the contract [and] manifestation of the will may be expressed in either oral or written words . . . or by conduct or some combination of conduct and word (implied contract). [But under the EU legislation] the public procurement contract is defined as a written contract, incompatible with a conduct manifestation.

Vrancianu Adelina, *The Specificities of a Public Procurement Contract Formation* (IAFOR Int'l Conf. on Global Studies 2016).

From a U.S. perspective, what is most striking about the common law rules outlined in Chapter 2 is how often federal procurement law *deviates* from that U.S. common law tradition. These distinct differences in federal contracting hint at an important divide in U.S. law: public procurement law, at both the formations stage and in contract administration, is in many ways markedly different from commercial law. The differences are not merely textual; there are separate courts, boards and other forums for disputes in public contracts, and public procurement's legal and contracting communities tend to stand apart from their commercial counterparts as well. At the formations stage, as is discussed below, those differences can be traced to the very different fiscal, political and administrative pressures that shape the public contracting process. Those same pressures divide public contract administration from the commercial world, but equally important is the very different risk allocation that public contracting demands. The normal allocations of risk in the private sector, driven by efficiency and economic leverage, too often simply cannot work in the public sector because of the very unique demands of the public marketplace. (The discussion here focuses on the differing principles in the formations stage; public-private differences in the law of contract administration can be assessed in the sister volume, *Administration of Government Contracts*.)

The divergence between U.S. commercial law and federal government contracts law can be traced, at least in part, to the broader evolution of U.S. law in the twentieth century, the time when U.S. procurement law came of age. During the first half of the twentieth century, legal realism—a school of thought which holds that the law should be built upon the existing norms and realities of its surrounding society—played a prominent role. See, e.g., L.L. Fuller, *American Legal Realism,* 82 U. Penn. L. Rev. (1934). Professor Karl Llewelyn, one of the leading proponents of legal realism, was a central figure in the drafting of Article 2 of the Uniform Commercial Code, on the law of sales. Llewelyn's approach was profoundly pragmatic, and because of the realities of the marketplace he crafted Article 2 with separate rules to accommodate "merchants" and "nonmerchants." As one commentator later noted, Llewelyn "believed the policies and considerations involved in a mercantile situation differed from those in a nonmercantile situation, and that a unitary approach to sales rules would inevitably muddle policies and rationales." Ingrid Michelsen Hillinger, *The Article 2 Merchant Rules: Karl Llewellyn's Attempt to Achieve the Good, the True and the Beautiful in Commercial Law,* 73 Geo. L.J. 1141, 1147 (1985).

Much as legal realism helped mold Article 2 to the realities of the marketplace, that same spirit of pragmatic flexibility allowed U.S. procurement law in the twentieth century to evolve *away* from mainstream commercial law, again because of the very different demands of the public procurement marketplace. A unitary approach to the law of contracts formations, one that rigidly bound public procurement into commercial contract law, only would have muddled U.S. procurement law.

This pragmatic approach means that federal procurement law, to meet the government's special ends, can accommodate very disparate approaches, sometimes at odds with commercial law, and sometimes at odds with federal procurement's own bedrock norms. For example, as Chapter 2 explains, although federal procurement law normally disfavors open-ended contracts because of the government's need for certainty and accountability, federal law specifically accommodates letter contracts, a form of contract born of urgency which "authorizes the contractor to begin immediately manufacturing supplies or performing services." FAR 16.603-1. In describing letter contracts, the FAR uses a language of practicality that echoes the Uniform Commercial Code: a letter contract can be used if time demands it, but the letter contract should be "as complete and definite as feasible under the circumstances."

In that same spirit of pragmatic flexibility, federal procurement law can remain *un*prescriptive in order to accommodate rapidly evolving technologies. Chapter 2 notes, for example, that federal procurement law continues to evolve in its approach to electronic commerce, and does not demand advanced digital signatures for authentication and signature. That flexibility in U.S. law contrasts sharply with many nations which impose specific demands for signature technology in public contracting. See, e.g., CMS, *E-public procurement* (2019) (30-nation survey of e-signature requirements), *https://cms.law/en/int/publication/e-public-procurement.*

In many ways, while Chapter 2 is strictly speaking about the formal rules of contract formation—of offer and acceptance, for example, and reliance and consideration—the chapter frames the rest of this volume, because it confirms the pragmatic flexibility that allowed federal procurement to develop its own unique form of contract law.

§ 16.04 ACQUISITION PLANNING

Chapter 3 describes the acquisition planning required under the FAR, and called for by related agency-specific guidance. For those coming to the U.S. system from abroad, there are three key distinctive aspects to planning in the U.S. acquisition system: planning is integrated into the procurement rules (unlike some other systems), the standard planning process can be slow and cumbersome (which helps explain alternative acquisition channels which have emerged), and planning under the federal rules integrates contract formation and administration.

[A] Planning as An Integrated Part of Rules

The U.S. federal procurement regime, unlike many other major rules systems around the world, integrates extensive planning guidance directly into the rules which govern contract formation. As Chapter 3 explains, federal policymakers clearly understood that planning works hand-in-hand with effective competitive, to produce effective results in procurement. In contrast, Article 40 of the European Union's procurement directive 2014/24/EU, for example, makes only a brief reference to planning—"Before launching a procurement procedure, contracting authorities may conduct market consultations with a view to preparing the procurement and informing economic operators of their procurement plans and requirements." Even there, the EU directive is focused on the distortions that planning might cause, such as the conflicts of interest that vendors involved in the planning might have; again, the focus is on an efficient European marketplace, not on achieving best value.

Unsurprisingly, the EU Member States often follow the same approach as they have implemented the EU directive in their own laws. For example, the United Kingdom's Procurement Regulations 2015 (the UK's pre-Brexit law, which transposed the 2014 EU directive) copied the directive almost verbatim.

Perhaps the most useful comparison to the U.S. planning requirements is in the World Bank's Procurement Framework (2016). Much as in the U.S. system, the World Bank's *Procurement Regulations for IPF Borrowers* note that the acquisition "process . . . starts with the identification of a need and continues through planning, preparation of specifications/requirements, budget considerations, selection, contract award, and contract management"—for those accustomed to the U.S. system, a familiar and holistic approach.

But the World Bank's approach also points up a recurring source of delay in the U.S. acquisition system—the need to coordinate acquisition planning with technical personnel (who help generate the statement of requirements) and fiscal personnel (who coordinate the agency's budgetary matters). In part as a result of this need for coordination, and more broadly because of the sheer complexity of the system, acquisitions can stretch out for many years. Procurement officials and policy makers have sought to shorten the time needed to complete an acquisition. Part of that period is known as "PALT," or "Procurement Acquisition Lead Time," and that PALT period (commonly understood as the time between initial solicitation and contract award, see 85 Fed. Reg. 3428 (Jan. 21, 2021)) can extend into years for a larger procurement.

As the Office of Federal Procurement Policy (OFPP) has noted, closer measurement of the delays in the acquisition process will drive the "pursuit of more innovative procurement practices, especially when the data are used in combination with other inputs for evaluating the overall effectiveness of the acquisition process in delivering value to the taxpayer, such as cost and the quality of the contractor's performance." 85 Fed. Reg. at 3429. With the pragmatism and innovation characteristic of American society, U.S. procurement policy makers will continue to look for faster, better ways to achieve best value. See, e.g., GAO, *Senior Leaders Should Use Leading Companies Key Practices to Improve Performance* (Rep. No. GAO-21-491, July 2021). That drive to speed the process and to deliver better value has helped spawn new procurement methods, such as "other transactions" (discussed elsewhere in this volume) and the General Services Administration's "commercial platforms" initiative (which opened online marketplaces such as Amazon to direct purchases by government employees), see Christopher Yukins, Abraham Young, Kristen Ittig & Eric Valle, *GSA's Commercial Marketplaces Initiative: Opening Amazon and Other Private Marketplaces To Direct Purchases By Government Users*, Briefing Papers (Thomson Reuters), No. 20-13 (December 2020).

This desire for speed in acquisitions, coupled with an abiding concern for lowering barriers to small businesses (what would be known abroad as "Small- and Medium-sized Enterprises," or "SMEs") has opened the door to the "simplified acquisition procedures" discussed in Chapter 3. These procedures can be used for purchases of commercial products and services (which are broadly defined) up to $7.5 million, see FAR 13.000. As is discussed below, the rules are relaxed for commercial products and services on the assumption that commercial market pressures, rather than strict procurement rules, will suffice to ensure fair prices and good quality.

[B] Planning and the Competitive Process

While the U.S. system is unique in the sheer complexity of the planning process laid out by regulation, it parallels systems abroad in the ways that planning is integrated into the competitive process. The U.S. rules that apply when market research and government requirements demand specific approaches to competition—"sole-source" procurements, for example, or procurements for architects and engineers' services—in many ways parallel similar rules in other systems internationally.

There is a striking similarity between U.S. and foreign rules which apply when, due to planning and market research, the government decides to narrow competition (known as "other than full and open competition" in the U.S. system). As Chapter 3 explains, Congress mandated under the Competition in Contracting Act that "full and open competition" be the norm in U.S. competition, i.e., that all responsible sources be afforded an opportunity to compete.

In the U.S. system, as abroad, that open competition can be narrowed for efficiency's sake. For example a contracting officer may narrow the number of offerors in a competitive negotiation (i.e., may reduce the number of offerors in the "competitive range") in order to keep the negotiations workable. FAR 15.306. Similarly, under the European Union's procurement directives, the number of offerors can be reduced through restricted tendering, under which the number of offerors can be narrowed based upon short statements of qualification submitted by the offerors. EU Directive 2014/24/EU, Art. 28; Martin Trybus,

European Law and Public Procurement, supra, at 11-12; UNCITRAL *Model Law on Public Procurement*, Art. 45.

The rules for narrowing competition even further—for restricting competition to only a small handful of competitors, or even only one—are also strikingly similar in the U.S. and foreign systems. Under the U.S. rules, as in the European Union and under the UNCITRAL model law, competition can be narrowed to a single vendor if (for example) only one competitor is available to meet the government's special requirements, a catastrophe makes broader competition impossible, the vendor's intellectual property rights in the article at issue mean that no other sources are available, or national security interests make broader competition unworkable. See FAR Subpart 6.3; EU Directive 2014/24/EU Art. 28; UNCITRAL Model Law on Public Procurement, Art. 34.

These parallels extend to the U.S. and EU treatment of a material modification to an existing contract. As Chapter 3 explains, this is, in practical terms, a form of sole-source procurement which is sometimes known as a "cardinal change" in the U.S. system. Under both U.S. and EU law, if the modification does not open the door to a new field of potential competitors—if the change was (in U.S. terms) "within the scope of the competition which was initially conducted"—then the modification is not "out of scope" or a "cardinal change" requiring a new competition. *American Air Filter Co.*, 57 Comp. Gen. 567 (B-188408), 78-1 CPD ¶ 443.

The Court of Justice for the European Union's treatment of this issue in its 2008 decision in *Pressetext Nachtrichtenagentur,* Case C-454/06 [2008] ECR I-4401 (the foundation for Article 72 of the current Directive 2014/24/EU) was striking, both because the court's analysis began in such a different place compared to the U.S. procurement regime (focusing on procurement law as an instrument of European Union integration rather than a means for best value) and because the court concluded with a rule roughly identical to the U.S. rule on cardinal change:

> It is clear from the case-law that the principal objective of the [European] Community rules in the field of public procurement is to ensure the free movement of services and the opening-up to undistorted competition in all the Member States. . . .
>
> In order to pursue that two-fold objective, Community law applies inter alia the principle of non-discrimination on grounds of nationality, the principle of equal treatment of tenderers and the obligation of transparency resulting therefrom. . . .
>
> [The EU] Directive . . . implements those principles and that obligation of transparency in respect of contracts coming within its ambit . . . by requiring inter alia certain award procedures. . . .
>
> In order to ensure transparency of procedures and equal treatment of tenderers, amendments to the provisions of a public contract during the

> currency of the contract constitute a new award of a contract within the meaning of [the] Directive . . . when they are materially different in character from the original contract and, therefore, such as to demonstrate the intention of the parties to renegotiate the essential terms of that contract. . . .
>
> An amendment to a public contract during its currency may be regarded as being material when it introduces conditions which, had they been part of the initial award procedure, would have allowed for the admission of tenderers other than those initially admitted or would have allowed for the acceptance of a tender other than the one initially accepted.
>
> Likewise, an amendment to the initial contract may be regarded as being material when it extends the scope of the contract considerably to encompass services not initially covered. . . .

Id., paras. 31-36; see Christopher Bovis, *Public Contracts in Public Procurement Regulation*, in *Research Handbook on EU Public Procurement Law*, at 117-18 (C. Bovis, ed.) (Edward Elgar Publishing 2016) (discussing further authority in Court of Justice for the European Union); *EU Public Procurement Law: An Introduction, supra,* at 127; Sune Troels Poulsen, *The Possibilities of Amending a Public Contract Without a New Competitive Tendering Procedure Under EU Law*, 2012 Pub. Proc. L. Rev. 167, 170 (under *Pressetext* and related authorities, an "amendment will only be 'material' if it can be assumed there would have been a different tender or group of tenderers if the amendment had been known at the time of the competitive tendering procedure for the contract, so the competition for the contract possibly could have had a different winner").

[C] Planning and Contract Administration

In comparative terms, *Pressetext* and the doctrine of material changes may mark a high point in parallels between the U.S. and EU laws of public contract formation, because while the European Union's procurement directives remain focused on market integration of European markets through public contracting, the U.S. rules are shaped in important ways by the demands of contract administration—the activities which follow contract award.

As Chapter 3 explains, the U.S. has its own rules, for example, regarding very limited recompetition after a contract is terminated for default. Those rules are an integral part of competition and planning, and there is no parallel rule under the EU procurement directives, because termination—an aspect of administration, not formation—lies outside the EU directives' ambit. See, e.g., Albert Sanchez-Graells, *The Emergence of Trans-EU Collaborative Procurement: A "Living Lab" for European Public Law*, 2020 Pub. Proc. L. Rev. 16, 23-24 (EU directive's limited cross-reference to contract administration issues). One of the few substantive references in the main EU directive (2014/24/EU) to termination are to situations where competition has been distorted (Art. 73)—not to termination in the ordinary course, due to default.

This is not to suggest that the European Union's Member States do not have sophisticated means of contract administration—they do. See, e.g., David O. Cox *et al.*, *Contract Administration: Technology and Practice in Europe* (2002) (U.S. researchers visited EU Member States to investigate contract administration procedures, and concluded that European agencies "appear to be better exploiting the efficiencies and resources that the private sector offers, through the use of innovative financing, alternative contracting techniques, design-build, concessions, performance contracting, and active asset management," and through "contracts that focus on the users, while seeking to allocate risk appropriately," using techniques that "the United States can directly and immediately employ"). What is different, however, is that because the sources of law regarding public contract formation in the European Union—the EU directives and the decisions of the Court of Justice for the European Union—are focused first on using public contracts' formation to advance European economic integration, the EU procurement rules are not directly shaped by concerns of contract administration.

§ 16.05 CONTRACTOR QUALIFICATION

Chapter 4 of the text examines contractor qualification—what is called "contractor responsibility" in the U.S. system—which is a vitally important topic from a global perspective, one that raises several points of comparison. The first and perhaps most obvious point stems from *when* in the contracting process vendors' qualifications are typically assessed, and what that tells us about different award systems. The second comparative analysis goes to the *what* question, i.e., elements of qualification, and how they are assessed. Qualification standards are remarkably similar from one system to another, and this opens opportunities for cooperative information-sharing among nations and institutions. There are important efforts underway around the world to gather qualification information from different nations and institutions, to use qualification information from abroad when assessing firms and individuals that work across borders. As a result, sharing common approaches to qualification has become increasingly important in an interconnected, global economy. The third comparative analysis focuses on *who*—on which vendors should be disqualified, either from a specific procurement (on a finding of "non-responsibility" or "non-qualification") or more generally from an entire procurement system (through suspension or debarment). On this third point, because suspension and debarment were addressed in detail in an earlier section of this chapter on anti-corruption measures, and because Chapter 3 focuses on *organizational conflicts of interest* (OCIs) as a ground for exclusion, this chapter will focus on OCIs as well.

[A] Timing and Standards for Qualification

Qualification (or "responsibility") stands apart from the other elements of an award decision. In the U.S. system, for example, price, past performance and technical elements of a vendor's proposal are typically evaluated and scored by subject-matter experts; the vendor's qualification (or responsibility) is assessed separately by the contracting officer, and is a "binary" decision, yes or no.

In the U.S. system, that responsibility determination can be reserved until the very end of the competitive process; indeed, the contracting officer's signature on the contract may be the only written confirmation that she has found the awardee responsible. See FAR 9.105-2. Under the European Union's procurement directives, in contrast, qualification decisions are routinely made much earlier in the award process, often (as was discussed above) as part of a "restricted tender" in which the field of competitors is narrowed based upon vendors' brief statements of qualifications.

The comparative question, then, is why the timing is so different under the two regimes—why does the EU system encourage early qualification decisions, while the U.S. system postpones that decision? The answer may lie in the dramatically different competitive methods favored in the two systems. In a 2017 study, the European Commission determined that, of the procurements studied, over 150,000 involved restricted tenders while only 0.2% (roughly 5,000 of 2.5 million) used multilateral negotiations, called "competitive dialogue" in the European Union. See European Commission, *Measurement of Impact of Cross-Border Penetration in Public Procurement*, at 70 (2017). In the U.S. federal system, in contrast, roughly 60 percent of procurements use some form of multilateral negotiation, either through competitive negotiations under FAR Part 15 or through second-stage competitions under standing catalogue ("framework" or "indefinite-delivery/indefinite-quantity") contracts, discussed below. Multilateral negotiations are thus much more prevalent in the U.S. federal system, which may explain why responsibility determinations are deferred: as the agency accumulates information on the contractor through negotiations, the agency's view of the vendor's dependability may evolve. Deciding qualification too early could, in this U.S. context, be both imprudent and anti-competitive, and this may explain why the responsibility determination is made so much later in the U.S. process.

The difference in timing—the early qualification decision common in the EU—also may be due in part to how *past performance* was until recently handled under the EU system of rules, in a way very different from the U.S. approach.

In the U.S. system, reforms driven forward in the 1990s by then-Administrator of the Office of Federal Procurement Policy Steven Kelman (a long-time professor at Harvard's John F. Kennedy School of Government) helped ensure that the FAR now treats past work both as an element of responsibility (qualification) under FAR Part 9, and as an evaluation factor (FAR Subpart 42.15). See Steven Kelman, *Procurement and Public Management: The Fear of*

Discretion and the Quality of Government Performance (1990); Juan-Carlos Guerrero and Christopher J. Kirkpatrick, *Evaluating Contractor Past Performance in the United States*, 2001 Pub. Proc. L. Rev. 243, 246-47. By making past performance a scored evaluation criterion, rather than merely an element of a broader (and binary yes/no) qualification determination, the federal government in effect pushed contractors to deliver better performance. In other words, in a market filled with contractors that return to compete again and again over the years, treating past performance as a variable for award on the *next* contract helps to reduce performance risk on a *current* contract.

While the U.S. system thus established a clear means of reducing performance risk by assessing past performance, the EU system did not—which may help explain why it is more common in the EU system to see earlier qualification decisions that narrow the field of competitors. The Court of Justice for the European Union has played an activist role in shaping EU law on procurement, see Christopher Bovis, *Judicial Activism and Public Procurement*, in *Research Handbook on EU Public Procurement Law*, at 325 ("The current reform agenda of public procurement is guided by doctrines developed by the Court which attempt to fuse the underlying principles of public procurement regulation with the fundamental principles enshrined in the EU Treaties by supplementing the deficiencies of the public procurement Directives with primary EU law."), and until the 2014 revision to the European Union directives, the court (and the European Commission) helped steer the EU Member States *away* from treating past performance as an award criterion. As Norwegian Professor Kai Krüger observed, regarding the court's pivotal 2008 decision in *Emm G Lianakis AE v Alexandroupolis*, C-532/06, 2008 E.C.R. I-251 (1st Chamber) (known as the "*Lianakis*" decision):

> [The European] Commission's . . . worries over Member States' disregard of the procurement regime's distinction between qualification and award criteria were victoriously and fully endorsed in the obiter [dictum] of *Lianakis* . . . a quasi-preliminary ruling with a condensed but perhaps not unambiguous message from the Court to the European procurement environment:
>
> > Consequently, it must be held that, in a tendering procedure, a contracting authority is precluded by . . . [prior] Directive . . . from taking into account as "award criteria" rather than as "qualitative selection criteria" the tenderers' experience, manpower and equipment, or their ability to perform the contract by the anticipated deadline.
> >
> > . . . In the public procurement setting, experience, manpower and equipment offered to qualify for the performance of a public contract can only be assessed in a binary context. This is because the qualification test under [the 2004] Directive . . . only allows for acceptance or non-acceptance of operators' technical capability to perform according to criteria set through pre-qualification, a restricted tender procedure

> or selection of relevant candidates in the negotiated procedure or the competitive dialogue. . . .
>
> The [prior Directive thus] could be understood so as to exclude any qualification/selection criteria per se from the subsequent . . . award stage.
>
> A literal interpretation would mean an extremely Calvinistic approach—not very welcome in the public contract world, whether seen from the private operators' or from the contracting authorities' position. The assessment of competence, professional skills and experience by comparative parameters makes sense when it is apparent that the contract candidates seeking the award vary in their qualities and abilities to meet the public requirement.
>
> The *Lianakis* rationale is to underpin the principle of transparency in EU regulated public procurement, avoiding broad discretionary assessments by requiring step-by-step decision-making subject to effective judicial review by courts, surveillance authorities or complaint boards. . . .

Kai Krüger, *Superiority in Experience and Skills May Distinguish a Better Tender Bid! Critical Reflections from Norway on the* Lianakis *Ruling*, 2009 Pub. Proc. L. Rev. 138. Professor Krüger thus explained why the European Commission and the Court of Justice for the European Union resisted making past performance an independent award criterion, arguably at the cost of increased performance risk.

While the EU rules regarding past performance have loosened with the 2014 EU procurement directives, the language of the directive was muddied through extensive debates and compromises during the drafting process, see Roberto Caranta, *Public Procurement and Award Criteria*, in *Research Handbook on EU Public Procurement Law*, at 149, 165, and (unlike FAR Subpart 42.15 in the U.S. system) Article 67 of Directive 2014/24/EU is not definitive as to whether past performance can and should be independently scored. *Cf.* UK Crown Commercial Service, *A Brief Guide to the 2014 EU Public Procurement Directives* 12 (Oct. 2016) (pre-Brexit UK government guide to implementing the 2014 directives, which noted that suppliers "may also be assessed on their technical capacity and ability e.g., that they will be adequately equipped to do the job and that their track record is satisfactory").

To the extent this uncertainty about scoring past performance leaves residual performance risk, it may help explain the continuing reliance on earlier qualification decisions as EU purchasing agencies seek to mitigate performance risk by narrowing the competition to only the most apparently qualified vendors. This is akin to the risk-mitigation done by U.S. procuring officials when they narrow the number of architects or engineers who will be engaged in negotiations under the Brooks Act (discussed in Chapter 4), and by borrower nations procuring under the World Bank Procurement Framework when they narrow the number of consultants (who can be critical to performance success) competing under a World Bank-funded project (see World Bank *Procurement Regulations for Investment Project Financing Borrowers* §§ 7.34-7.39 (Nov. 2020); see generally Christopher Yukins & Sope Williams-Elegbe, *The World Bank's Procurement Framework: An Assessment of Aid Effectiveness*, in *Public Procurement and Aid Effectiveness: A Roadmap Under Construction* (Annamaria La Chimia & Peter Trepte, eds.) (Hart Publishing 2019)).

While the *timing* of qualification decisions may vary dramatically between the U.S. federal system and the European Union's Member States, the *grounds* for qualification are very similar in the two systems—and in other systems around the world. Like the grounds for responsibility set out in FAR 9.104, the qualification grounds in Articles 56-64 of EU Directive 2014/24/EU and Article 9 of the UNCITRAL model law look to (among other things) whether bidders have adequate financial and technical resources, appropriate facilities and licensing, and a demonstrated history of integrity.

Where differences in qualification standards arise, they are often traceable to differences in process. Under Article 57 of EU Directive 2014/24/EU, for example, vendors are subject to *mandatory* exclusion by contracting agencies ("procuring entities") if they have been found to have participated in certain types of criminal, terrorist, human trafficking or fraudulent activities. Because these exclusion grounds apply throughout the European Union, presumably a vendor would in effect be barred (i.e., not qualified) across the entire EU, though on a procurement-by-procurement basis. In the U.S. system, in contrast, while FAR Subpart 9.1's responsibility grounds do not *mandate* non-qualification on these grounds, as a practical matter a vendor guilty of offenses of this type might be debarred (excluded for a term of years) on a system-wide basis under FAR Subpart 9.4.

Importantly, both the U.S. and EU systems are moving to aggregate contractor qualification data online, to make that information easier for agencies and contractors to compile and update, and to make that information more readily available for contracting officials making qualification decisions. The U.S. government has gathered disparate sources of information together in the "System for Award Management," available at *www.sam.gov*. The System for Award Management includes contract opportunities, contract award data, and contractor-specific qualification data (though not all of that is public). Contractor performance assessment reports (CPARs) are posted separately, at *www.cpars.gov*; while U.S. government officials may see that data, outside government only contractors may view their own data. See generally FAR 42.1503 (procedures).

The European Union has erected its own system of certification, in an effort to integrate and streamline contractor qualification. This system is described in Articles 59-62 of EU Directive 2014/24/EU, the main directive on public procurement. The directive calls for a "European Single Procurement Document," or "ESPD." The European Commission is charged with designing this electronic form, and with overseeing its practical implementation, including "solutions optimising the cross-border access to . . . databases and the use of certificates in the internal market." Although they can request supporting documentation (if not otherwise available from national databases) from bidders, contracting authorities must accept the ESPD, which the bidder self-updates, as "preliminary evidence . . . of certificates issued by public authorities or third parties" confirming that the bidder is not to be excluded and meets relevant selection criteria. If the necessary information can be accessed through a third-party database, the ESPD is to explain how to effect that access. Bidding firms ("economic operators") may reuse an ESPD from a previous procurement, so long as they confirm that the information remains correct. Bidders may confirm that they are *not* excludable (i.e., not mandatorily non-responsible, in U.S. terms) by "declaration on oath . . . before a competent judicial or administrative authority, a notary or a competent professional or trade body, in the Member State or country of origin . . . where the economic operator [bidder] is established."

Article 61 of the Directive calls for an online repository of vendor certificates, "e-Certis." A guide and further information on the e-Certis system, published by the European Commission, are available at *https://ec.europa.eu/tools/ecertis/*. See Roger Bickerstaff, *E-procurement Under the New EU Procurement Directives*, 2014 Pub. Proc. L. Rev. 134, 145.

When solicitations require certificates that a bidder complies with certain quality assurance standards the EU Member States must honor such certificates from other Member States. These quality assurance standards can include those covering accessibility for persons with disabilities, akin to the requirements under Section 508 of the Rehabilitation Act in the United States. See U.S. General Services Administration, *Section 508* (implementation of U.S. Access Board accessibility standards), *www.section508.gov*; Christopher R. Yukins, *Making Federal Information Technology Accessible: A Case Study in Social Policy and Procurement*, 34 Pub. Cont. L. J. 667 (2004).

When a bidder (an "economic operator") in the EU system has no reasonable possibility of obtaining a required certificate regarding quality assurance measures "within the relevant time limits . . . the economic operator [must prove] that the proposed quality assurance measures comply with the required quality assurance standards"—a potentially important alternative channel should (for example) contractor cybersecurity certifications become common requirements in public marketplaces. *Cf.* Defense Federal Acquisition Regulation Supplement (DFARS) 252.204-7008, *Compliance with Safeguarding Covered Defense Information Controls* (if an offeror proposes to vary from cybersecurity requirements set by the National Institute of Standards and Technology (NIST), the offeror "shall submit to the Contracting Officer, for consideration by the [Department of Defense] Chief Information Officer (CIO), a written explanation of . . . [why] a particular security requirement is not applicable; or . . . [how] an alternative but equally effective, security measure is used to . . . achieve equivalent protection"); see also William T. Kirkwood, *Protecting Controlled Unclassified Information: An Evaluation of Approaches to Protecting Sensitive Information in Public Procurement in the EU and the US*, 2019 Pub. Proc. L. Rev. 121.

In the long term, the critical question is whether the model contemplated by the EU Directive—cross-border sharing of qualification information—can be extended internationally. There have been experiments in aggregating contractor qualification information from different nations, and the ProAct initiative, *https://www.procurementintegrity.org/*, which gathers debarment information from multiple jurisdictions. The challenge will be extending these initial efforts to allow efficient sharing of qualification information between nations and governments, to reduce the reputational and performance risks that are the focus of contractor qualification.

In this regard, the multilateral development banks' agreement on cross-debarment may prove a useful model for transnational efforts to address contractor qualification. Under the cross-debarment agreement, many of the leading multilateral development banks (such as the World Bank and the African Development Bank) agreed that, when one of the banks debars a contractor for sanctionable conduct, presumptively all of the other banks would similarly debar the contractor. See *www.crossdebarment.org* (information on the 2010 Agreement for Mutual Enforcement of Debarment Decisions Among Multilateral Development Banks); Pascale Hélène Dubois, *Domestic and International Administrative Tools to Combat Fraud & Corruption: A Comparison of US Suspension and Debarment with the World Bank's Sanctions System*, 2012 U. Chi. Legal F. 195 (2012); Frank A. Fariello, Jr. & Conrad C. Daly, *Coordinating the Fight Against Corruption Among MDBs: The Past, Present, and Future of Sanctions*, 45 Geo. Wash. Int'l L. Rev. 253 (2013); Christopher R. Yukins, *Cross-Debarment: A Stakeholder Analysis*, 45 Geo. Wash. Int'l L. Rev. 219 (2013); William A Roberts, III, Tracye Winfrey Howard & Samantha S. Lee, *Two Systems, Two Types of Risk: How the World Bank Sanctions Regime Differs from US Suspension and Debarment*, Proc. Law (ABA), Fall 2015. The banks employ generally similar *standards* and *procedures* for debarment, and the bases for debarment are largely (though not completely) transparent. *Cf.* Hans-Joachim Priess, *Questionable Assumptions: The Case for Updating the Suspension and Debarment Regimes at the Multilateral Development Banks*, 45 Geo. Wash. Int'l L. Rev. 271 (2013) (arguing that multilateral development banks do not fairly afford equal treatment in sanctions systems).

The banks' cross-debarment initiative may offer an important formula for sharing qualification information across borders: (1) similar (but not necessarily identical) qualification standards (which, as explained above, already exist in the EU and U.S. systems, and around the world); and (2) procedures and information which are reasonably transparent and which fairly allow vendors to challenge false information. See also Sati Harutyunyan, *Risk and Expectation in Exclusion from Public Procurement: Understanding Market Access and Harmonization Between the European Union and the United States*, 45 Pub. Cont. L.J. 449 (2016) (discussing cross-border challenges in meeting EU's requirement for equal treatment of vendors); Nathaniel E. Castellano, *Suspensions, Debarments, and Sanctions: A Comparative Guide to United States and World Bank Exclusion Mechanisms*, 45 Pub. Cont. L.J. 403 (2016).

[B] Organizational Conflicts Of Interest

While organizational conflicts of interest (OCIs) present an issue of contractor qualification—if a contractor has a conflict of an interest, it should not be found "qualified" or "responsible," see, e.g., FAR Subpart 9.5—unlike the other types of qualification information discussed above, it will be difficult to share meaningful information regarding organizational conflicts across borders. This is because the three types of organizational conflicts commonly recognized internationally (conflicts that arise when (1) a contractor helps draft specifications against which it will bid, (2) a contractor's competing commitments means it may provide biased advise to a government, and (3) a contractor's access to information gives it an unfair competitive advantage, see FAR Subpart 9.5; UNCITRAL *Model Law on Public Procurement* Art. 21; EU Directive 2014/24/EU), are necessarily highly *contextual*. This in turn is because a government's ability to monitor and check conflicts of interest can vary based on market forces, informational asymmetries, social and political structures, and many other factors. See, e.g., Peter Trepte, *Regulating Procurement* 84-85 (Oxford U. Press 2004); Christopher Yukins, *A Versatile Prism: Assessing Procurement Law Through the Principal-Agent Model,* 40 Pub. Cont. L.J. 63 (2010); see also WTO Agreement on Government Procurement, Art. X.5 (as is common in trade agreements related to procurement, the Agreement on Government Procurement (GPA) says that a party to the agreement "shall not seek or accept, in a manner that would have the effect of precluding competition, advice that may be used in the preparation or adoption of any technical specification for a specific procurement from a person that may have a commercial interest in the procurement"). As was noted in conjunction with a proposed U.S. rule on OCIs published in 2011, 76 Fed. Reg. 23236 (and abandoned in 2021, 86 Fed. Reg. 14863 (March 19, 2021)) in some cases OCIs should be alleviated because the government lacks sufficient information to counteract any contractor bias, while in others (such as when a contractor helps write specifications for its own competition) an OCI may undermine the critical integrity of a procurement process itself.

From a comparative perspective, perhaps the most interesting decision on organizational conflict of interests came in Joined Cases C-21/03 & C-34/03, *Fabricom SA v. Belgium*, 2005 E.C.R. I-1577, I-1593 (2005), a decision by the Court of Justice for the European Union. By comparing that decision to contemporaneous developments in the U.S. system, as commentators have noted, one can see the two systems, U.S. and EU, approaching one another—with no apparent coordination, and yet still meeting on common ground. See, e.g., Gregory S. Hayken, *Comparative Study: The Evolution of Organisational Conflicts of Interest Law in Europe and the United States*, 15 Pub. Proc. L. Rev. 137

(2006); James Jurich, *International Approaches to Conflicts of Interest in Public Procurement: A Comparative Review*, 7 Eur. Proc. & Pub. Priv. Part. L. Rev. 242 (2012).

The facts of the Fabricom decision were summarized in William T. Kirkwood, *Inherently Governmental Functions, Organizational Conflicts of Interest, and the Outsourcing of the United Kingdom's MoD Defense Acquisition Function: Lessons Learned from the U.S. Experience*, 44 Pub. Cont. L.J. 443 (2015):

> Fabricom SA . . . was excluded from a tender for which it had done preparatory work. The authority for Fabricom's exclusion was found in two substantially similar provisions of Belgian law that mandated a blanket exclusion of firms that had done preparatory work for tenders. The basis for Fabricom's exclusion was an irrebuttable presumption that such firms would have a de facto unfair competitive advantage.
>
> Fabricom sought annulment of these two statutes before the Conseil d'État based on claims that the statutes violated principles of equal treatment of all tenderers. The Belgian State disputed these claims, asserting that the statutes were intended to promote free competition by restricting unfair competitive advantage by firms involved in work preparatory to a tender. The Conseil d'État stayed the proceedings to obtain a ruling from the ECJ [European Court of Justice] on the application of EU directives. [The first question] presented by the Conseil d'État to the ECJ . . . can be summarized as follows:
>
>> . . . Do the directives permit an absolute exclusion from tendering of firms participating in preparatory works for a tender, without affording the firm an opportunity to prove that such participation is not capable of distorting competition?

The Court of Justice responded that the EU directives "do not permit an absolute exclusion from tendering of firms participating in preparatory works for a tender, without affording the firm an opportunity to prove that such participation is not capable of distorting competition." The court's conclusion was subsequently codified by Article 41 of EU Directive 2014/24/EU. See id. at 454-56; Christopher Vajda, *Law As A Tool to Build Cross-Border Markets: The Experience of the Court of Justice of the EU in Opening Up Government Contracts*, 47 Pub. Cont. L.J. 357, 368 (2018) (analysis by former judge of the Court of Justice, discussing how *Fabricom* fit into the fabric of EU principles upheld by the court).

What is striking about the *Fabricom* decision is that during the same period that U.S. policymakers were concerned that organizational conflicts of interest posed a risk to the integrity of the U.S. procurement system and needed to be curbed, see, e.g., Daniel I. Gordon, *Organizational Conflicts of Interest: A Growing Integrity Challenge*, 35 Pub. Cont. L.J. 25, 26-28 (2005), the Court of Justice in *Fabricom* approached the same problem from the opposite direction to say that contracting officials should not automatically exclude firms that might be burdened by a conflict of interest. The common ground between the two approaches was that a contracting official must carefully assess a potential conflict, and work with the vendor potentially to mitigate the conflict of interest—the rule that *Fabricom* yielded, which was already in FAR Subpart 9.5, which was included in Article 21 of the UNCITRAL model law, and which is now codified in Article 41 of EU Directive 2014/24/EU. See, e.g., Michael D. Pangia, *Developing an Organizational Conflicts of Interest Framework: The U.S. System as a Starting Point,* 47 Pub. Cont. L.J. 539 (2018).

§ 16.06 SEALED BIDDING

Because sealed bidding is rare in a modern federal procurement, policy discussions in the U.S. system tend to center on competitive negotiations. This means in practice that developments in the federal system tend to be slightly out of the international mainstream, because most nations (and state and local governments in the United States) are only now slowly turning to multilateral negotiations ("competitive dialogues" in many systems) as an alternative to sealed bidding ("open tendering" in most nations outside the United States). As was discussed above, the shift to competitive negotiations has been possible only because of the robust anti-corruption measures in place in the federal system, including a well-established bid protest (bid challenge) system. One likely explanation for the decline in sealed bidding has been the advance in technology: the more difficult it is for the U.S. government to define its needs with precision against a rapidly evolving market for high technology (in aerospace and information technology, for example), the less relevant sealed bidding (which requires rigidly defined specifications) has become.

As a comparative matter, sealed bidding in the U.S. system offers relatively few insights to foreign observers, probably because (as Chapter 5 explains) by the early twenty-first century sealed bidding had receded into the backwater of federal procurement. A study of 2014 data showed that sealed bidding constituted *only roughly 2 percent* of federal procurement:

Solicitation Procedures Fiscal Year 2014: U.S. Government Procurement

Methods
Negotiated Proposals: 38.64% [A]
Single Source Solicited: 28.68%
Subject to Multiple Award Fair Opportunity: 21.42% [B]
Simplified Acquisition: 4.27%
None: 2.27%
Sealed Bid: 2.06% [C]
Two Step: 1.14%
Basic Research: 0.88%
Architect—Engineer: 0.42%
No Solicitation Procedure Reported—

Alternative Sources: 0.13%
Program Solicitation: 0.09%
Broad Agency Announcement: 0.00%
Simplified Acquisition Procedures-Non-Competitive: 0.00%

Christopher Yukins, *The U.S. Federal Procurement System: An Introduction*, 2017 UrT 69, 89 (citing study prepared using data from the Federal Procurement Data System by Umer Chaudhry), available at *https://ssrn.com/abstract=3063559*. The survey results, prepared by Umer Chaudhry, showed that [C] sealed bidding represented only roughly 2% of federal awards, while [A] negotiated proposals (competitive negotiations) and [B] multiple-award "fair opportunity" awards (second-stage competitions commonly using competitive negotiation methods) together amounted to roughly 60% of the reported awards. As a practical matter, because sealed bidding is so rare, a U.S. federal procurement practitioner (especially one working outside the construction (or "works") sector) may go years or even decades without encountering sealed bidding. Instead, as the table above reflects, multilateral competitive negotiations (discussed in Chapter 6, and assessed comparatively in Section VI below) are far more common in the U.S. procurement system.

In the European Union, in contrast, sealed bidding (open tendering) has continued to dominate Member States' procurement systems. A 2021 study of reported procurements in the EU-wide *Tenders Electronic Daily* (TED) database (the central EU repository for opportunity and award data for contracts above the threshold for EU regulation) by the European Commission found that competitive dialogues (rough analogues to U.S. competitive negotiations) and competitive procedures with negotiation (also roughly analogous to U.S. competitive negotiations) amounted respectively to .2 and 6.0% percent of the total number of awards, while open tendering (analogous to sealed bidding in the U.S. system) amounted to 83.4% of Member States' reported procurements.

Number and value of awards and cross-border procurement by type of procedure, 2016-2019 average

Type of Procedure	**Distribution of Total Awards**	
	Number	**Value**
Open	83.4%	65.8%
Competitive with Negotiation	6.0%	16.6%
Restricted	4.4%	9.5%
Negotiated without Prior Publication	6.1%	6.6%
Competitive Dialogue	0.2%	1.6%

European Commission, *Study on the Measurement of Cross-Border Penetration in the EU Public Procurement Market*, at 68 (Mar. 2021) (from Table 2-24).

These 2021 data did suggest a broader use of multilateral negotiations compared to a parallel study published a decade earlier (before competitive procedures with negotiations were introduced by the 2014 directives). The 2011 study showed that competitive dialogues represented only .1% of the total number of reported awards in the EU's TED system, while 83% of awards (the same proportion as in 2021, ten years later) were done by open tendering (the analogue to sealed bidding) under the "classical directive," the main public procurement directive from 2004 and the predecessor to EU Directive 2014/24/EU. See European Commission, *Cross-Border Procurement Above EU Thresholds,* at 73 (Mar. 2011).

As is discussed below, multilateral competitive negotiations with vendors provide substantial benefits to public buyers. Unlike traditional sealed bids/open tenders, these types of procurements are typically launched through a request for proposals with broadly stated performance goals, which allows firms in a highly competitive marketplace—not the government purchaser, as in traditional bidding—to proffer the best solution, based on their knowledge of solutions emerging in the market. Awards using competitive negotiations are typically made on a best-value basis, balancing cost and quality, which means that the government can assess its available resources against the best technologies presented by active market participants.

Given these advantages, the question posed by the award data described above—and still not answered—is *why*: why have EU public agencies not used multilateral competitive negotiations more often, following an historical trajectory similar to that of the U.S. system? The obvious answers might be a fear of corruption (which is harder to control in multilateral negotiations, compared to traditional open tendering) or a lack of capacity (training, experience and manpower) in EU public agencies. A study of competitive dialogues conducted in the European Union before 2010 suggested, however, that neither corruption nor capacity was the driving reason for EU agencies' reluctance to use multilateral negotiations. The study found that Germany, which has robust legal and social guards against corruption, was a relatively "light" user of competitive dialogue, and that *local* governments, which are likely to have *less* capacity than national governments, were leading users of competitive dialogue. The study concluded:

> [W]e can draw out some general trends in the use of competitive dialogue prior to 2010. In terms of number of contracts placed using this procedure, local government was the most regular competitive dialogue user, with the health sector following closely behind. Furthermore, the infrastructure and ICT [information and communications technologies] categories together represented the majority of regular purchases being made using

> competitive dialogue; this is unsurprising as complex infrastructure and IT systems were used as examples of 'particularly complex contracts' that would warrant use of competitive dialogue. It is quite difficult to generalise findings beyond this, however, as the "other" categories proved to be substantial in many of the subject Member States; this demonstrates that many interesting non-regular purchases are also made using competitive dialogue—some of which are country specific, and some of which only occurred once in the entire EU during the time investigated.

Sylvia de Mars & Richard Craven, *An Analysis of Use of Competitive Dialogue in the EU*, in *Competitive Dialogue in EU Procurement*, at 144, 177 (Sue Arrowsmith & Steen Treumer, eds.) (Cambridge U. Press 2012).

While the study (and the EU data surveyed above) thus leave unanswered why multilateral negotiations are not used more widely, they do suggest that over time sealed bidding/open tendering may recede in the European Union and elsewhere (as they have in the U.S. system), as governments turn to multilateral negotiations to purchase emerging technologies for ever more complex problems.

§ 16.07 BASIC NEGOTIATION PROCEDURES

Chapter 6 addresses competitive negotiations in the U.S. system under FAR Part 15, which are analogous to competitive dialogues under EU Directive 2014/24/EU. The EU Defense Procurement Directive, No. 2009/81/EC, issued in 2009, also allows for competitive dialogue in Article 27. See generally Martin Trybus, *The New EU Defence Procurement Regime*, in *Research Handbook on EU Public Procurement Law, supra,* at 523; Christopher Yukins, *Feature Comment—The European Defense Procurement Directive: An American Perspective*, 51 Gov't Contractor ¶ 383 (2009). After a long and contentious debate, the UNCITRAL model law (which was finalized in 2011, and is intended primarily for use in developing nations) was expanded to include multilateral competitive negotiations (called "requests for proposals with dialogue" under Article 49), and the World Bank has included the competitive dialogue method in its revamped Procurement Framework, launched in 2016, see World Bank, *How to Undertake a Competitive Dialogue Procurement Process* (Oct. 2017). Multilateral competitive negotiations have thus gained broad acceptance around the world, and a comparative assessment of the different implementations yields important lessons. This section will examine some of the key issues in implementation, including conditions for use, planning, confidentiality, publicity, selection, dialogue, and actions in the final tender phase, including with the preferred bidder. For a detailed review of these issues in the EU context, see the summary prepared by Professor Emerita Sue Arrowsmith (University of Nottingham) and the late Professor Steen Treumer (University of Copenhagen) in *Competitive Dialogue in EU Procurement, supra,* ch.1.

At the outset, it is important to stress the different conceptual approaches taken to implementation in the U.S. system and the European Union. As the cited text by Sue Arrowsmith and Steen Treumer describes, although there were precursors in the EU Member States, in the European Union competitive dialogue devolved in a more Cartesian way from accepted principles (or "propositions," in their analysis). In the U.S. system, in contrast, competitive negotiations have evolved in a more pragmatic way, through a tolerance for experimentation, success and failure, and (as Chapter 6 reflects) the law in the U.S. system has not always kept pace with evolving practices in the field.

[A] Lowest Price Technically Acceptable

An example of this pull-and-tug between practice and the law in the U.S. system is a competitive method known as "Low Priced Technically Acceptable," or "LPTA." While the LPTA method is technically a form of competitive negotiation under FAR Part 15, as Chapter 6 points out in practice LPTA works much more like traditional sealed bidding, though with the possibility of exchanges between offerors and the agency. See FAR 15.101-2. In a procurement run using the LPTA method, offerors present combined technical and price proposals against a minimum set of technical requirements. Among those offers that pass the minimum technical requirements, the lowest-price offer wins.

Many have argued that the LPTA procurement method is a throwback to procurement based on low price. Contracting officials, however, have embraced this simpler procurement method, and GAO estimated that perhaps 25 percent of U.S. Department of Defense competitively awarded contracts and orders valued at or above $5 million may be made using the LPTA method. GAO, *Information on Agencies' Use of the Lowest Price Technically Acceptable Process*, GAO-19-691 (Sept. 26, 2019). As Chapter 6 suggests, this may be because low-price awards are easier to implement and explain, they reduce the nominal prices paid by the government, and awards based on low price allow contracting officials to avoid bid protests based on technical and past performance evaluations. Focusing on low price reduces administrative costs and protest risks for contracting officials, even if the award does not necessarily result in the best value for users.

After long debate and numerous studies noting industry's opposition to low-priced awards, see, e.g., GAO, *DOD Should Clarify Criteria for Using Lowest Price Technically Acceptable Process* (GAO-19-54) (Nov. 2018), as Chapter 6 notes Congress passed a series of laws intended to curb the use of the LPTA method. Defense Department regulators took several years to publish a final rule implementing those statutory restrictions. 84 Fed. Reg. 50785 (Oct. 1, 2019); see GAO Report GAO-19-691, *supra*.

The debate over the LPTA method highlights both the strengths and weaknesses of competitive negotiations in the U.S. system. While LPTA awards may reduce administrative costs and bid challenges—both by-products of more complex competitive negotiations/competitive dialogues—as industry has argued, see, e.g., National Defense Industrial Association (NDIA), *Source*

Selection, https://www.ndia.org/policy/acquisition-reform/source-selection, low-priced awards are less likely to encourage vendors to put their best technical solutions forward, and so may reduce the government's access to cutting-edge solutions in the marketplace.

[B] Elements Of Competitive Negotiations/Competitive Dialogues

In assessing the elements of a competitive negotiation or competitive dialogue (and a "competitive procedure with negotiation," a similar competitive method added in Article 29 of the 2014 EU directive), the central point—the lodestar for analysis—is the need for governments to access complex emerging technologies. See, e.g., EU Directive 2014/24/EU, Art. 26 ("Member States shall provide that contracting authorities may apply a competitive procedure with negotiation or a competitive dialogue . . . with regard to works, supplies or services fulfilling one or more of the following criteria . . . (i) the needs of the contracting authority cannot be met without adaptation of readily available solutions; (ii) they include design or innovative solutions; (iii) the contract cannot be awarded without prior negotiations because of specific circumstances related to the nature, the complexity or the legal and financial make-up or because of the risks attaching to them"); UNCITRAL Model Law Art. 30 ("a procuring entity may engage in procurement by means of request for proposals with dialogue in accordance with article 49 . . . where: . . . [i]t is not feasible for the procuring entity to formulate a detailed description of the subject matter of the procurement . . . and the procuring entity assesses that dialogue with suppliers or contractors is needed to obtain the most satisfactory solution to its procurement needs").

As the European Commission explained in a 1998 report, it was necessary to accommodate competitive dialogues in order to access new and emerging technologies:

> Many contributions confirmed the Commission's finding that, especially in the case of particularly complex contracts in areas that are constantly changing, such as high technology, purchasers are well aware of their needs but do not know in advance what is the best technical solution for satisfying those needs. Discussion of the contract and dialogue between purchasers and suppliers are therefore necessary in such cases. But the standard procedures laid down by the 'traditional' Directives leave very little scope for discussion during the award of contracts and are therefore regarded as lacking in flexibility in situations of this type.

European Commission, *Public Procurement in the European Union,* COM (1998) 143, at 7 (Mar. 11, 1998); see Sue Arrowsmith & Steen Treumer, *supra*, at 26-27.

To succeed with competitive dialogues, as with competitive negotiations, procurement officials must engage in careful planning. See, e.g., Sue

Arrowsmith & Steen Treumer, *supra*, at 63. The EU and U.S. systems take very different approaches to that planning, however. While Professors Arrowsmith and Treumer concluded that this planning should honor classic principles of equal treatment and transparency—keys to economic integration across the European single market—the U.S. rules are much more aggressive in encouraging agencies to engage with the market.

While the U.S. rules point to the need to preserve procurement integrity (i.e., to protect competitively sensitive government plans), FAR 15.201 explicitly encourages exchanges "of information among all interested parties, from the earliest identification of a requirement through receipt of proposals." The rule makes clear that the purpose of these exchanges is "to improve the understanding of Government requirements and industry capabilities," both in the government and in industry, thereby "enhancing the Government's ability to obtain quality supplies and services . . . and increase efficiency in proposal preparation, proposal evaluation, negotiation, and contract award." The rule encourages early exchanges through public conferences, hearings, market research, draft solicitations, public requests for information (RFIs), and even "[o]ne-on-one meetings with potential offerors," though the rule cautions that any meetings "that are substantially involved with potential contract terms and conditions should include the contracting officer." The rule clearly states that general information "about agency mission needs and future requirements may be disclosed at any time," though after "release of the solicitation, the contracting officer must be the focal point of any exchange with potential offerors." Furthermore, if "specific information about a proposed acquisition . . . is disclosed to one or more potential offerors, that information must be made available to the public" in order "to avoid creating an unfair competitive advantage."

In order to encourage vendors to put their best technical solutions forward in a multilateral competitive negotiation, a government must ensure the *confidentiality* of offerors' information. The World Bank's guidance for competitive dialogue explained why this confidentiality is so critical:

> Confidentiality is fundamental to ensuring fairness and integrity in the Procurement Process. In addition to the confidentiality of the Proposal evaluation, as required by the Procurement Regulations, Borrowers shall not disclose information marked by an Applicant or Proposer as confidential to another Applicant or Proposer. Confidential information may include proprietary information, trade secrets and commercially or financially sensitive information. In a Competitive Dialogue, this includes a Proposer's design and proposed solution, new ideas, and innovation. Ensuring confidentiality gives Proposers reassurance that their commercially sensitive information will be protected.

World Bank, *How to Undertake a Competitive Dialogue Procurement Process* 14 (Oct. 2017). The EU Directive 2014/24/EU ensures this same confidentiality in competitive dialogues (Article 29) and competitive procedures with negotiation (Article 30) by cross-referencing the confidentiality guarantees of Article 21.

Once vendors have put forward their proprietary solutions, the challenge for a procuring agency is how to assimilate innovative approaches into the multilateral negotiations without disclosing the individual offerors' trade secrets. Professors Arrowsmith and Treumer, in reviewing approaches taken in the EU Member States, noted that some nations took a "patchwork" approach and gathered vendors' best solutions into a revised statement of needs. *Id.* at 75. In the U.S. system, however, as Chapter 6 notes, the rules strongly disfavor "technical transfusion" among offerors, FAR 15.306(e). Creating a patchwork of different vendors' solutions would raise risks of technical transfusion.

Both the EU and the U.S. systems call for procuring agencies to disclose the *relative weighting of evaluation factors*. See, e.g., EU Directive 2014/24/EU, Art. 67 ("The contracting authority shall specify, in the procurement documents, the relative weighting which it gives to each of the criteria chosen to determine the most economically advantageous tender.... Those weightings may be expressed by providing for a range with an appropriate maximum spread."); 41 U.S. Code § 3306(c)(1)(C) ("In prescribing the evaluation factors to be included in each solicitation for competitive proposals, an executive agency shall ... establish clearly the relative importance assigned to the evaluation factors and subfactors, including the quality of the product or services to be provided (including technical capability, management capability, prior experience, and past performance of the offeror)").

The U.S. laws, however, caution that agencies may not rigidly define the relative importance of selection criteria "as specific numeric weights that would be applied uniformly." E.g., 41 U.S. Code § 3306(c)(1)(C)(2). This *requirement for flexibility in evaluation factors* plays two roles in the U.S. approach. First, a more flexible approach allows agencies leeway to accommodate new information on capabilities in the market, as the competitive process unfolds. Second, the more flexible approach leaves the ultimate deciding official (the "source selection authority," who is the contracting officer in smaller procurements) the discretionary space to make an *independent best-value award decision*. As Chapter 6 explains, GAO has held that a source selection official may not simply rely on a calculated evaluation score in making an award decision. Instead, the source selection official, who is accountable for her decision, must make an independent and almost always subjective best-value award decision. See, e.g., FAR 15.303; Under Secretary of Defense for Acquisition, Technology & Logistics, *Department of Defense Source Selection Procedures* (Apr. 1, 2016) (describing roles of members of source selection team). In order to accommodate rapid advances in technology and the government's own evolving understanding of its requirements and market capabilities, the U.S. rules by design afford the awarding official with substantial discretion, and center that award decision in one person (not the agency) to ensure accountability. In comparison to many other rules systems which *resist* giving procuring officials discretion and insist on objective decision making—including the UN Convention Against Corruption, in Article 9—the U.S. system's support for discretionary and subjective decision making in procurement is quite striking.

As Chapter 6 reflects, an enormous body of U.S. caselaw has developed around the *dialogues* (or in U.S. terms, the "exchanges") that form an essential part of multilateral negotiations. While both the U.S. and EU systems insist that offerors be *treated fairly* in those exchanges, the EU traces that obligation for fairness to the general principles which inform the EU's integration, such as equal treatment and non-discrimination, see, e.g., Roberto Caranta, *Public Procurement and Award Criteria, supra*, at 150, while the U.S. rules are much more instrumental and tie the concept of "fairness" to public legitimacy and a healthy public market. See FAR 15.306(e) ("Government personnel involved in the acquisition shall not engage in conduct that . . . [f]avors one offeror over another"). FAR 1.102-2 states, for example, that federal procurement officials shall conduct "business with integrity, fairness, and openness," as an "essential consideration in every aspect of the System is maintaining the public's trust." With regard to contractors, "[f]airness and openness require open communication among team members, internal and external customers, and the public." While the rule says that all "contractors and prospective contractors shall be treated fairly and impartially," the rule explicitly states that contractors "need not be treated the same." See, e.g., Ralph C. Nash Jr., *Fair Treatment of Contractors: Do FAR Provisions Confer Rights?*, 27 Nash & Cibinic Rep. ¶ 35 (2013) (discussing authorities); Omer Dekel, *The Legal Theory of Competitive Bidding for Government Contracts*, 37 Pub. Cont. L.J. 237, 246 (2008) (discussing rationales for equal treatment of bidders). The extensive U.S. caselaw in this area can be traced to that central tension—the need to treat all bidders fairly in order to maintain public trust and a robust market, although effective negotiations mean that ultimately not all bidders can be treated the same. *Office Design Group v. United States*, 951 F.3d 1366 (Fed. Cir. 2020).

Chapter 6 addresses debriefings after award and stays during the pendency of a bid protest; those issues are addressed below.

§16.08 INDEFINITE-DELIVERY/INDEFINITE QUANTITY CONTRACTS ("FRAMEWORK AGREEMENTS")

This volume's Chapter 7 addresses what are known in the U.S. system as "indefinite-delivery/indefinite quantity" (IDIQ) contracts. These types of contract structures, which operate like ordering catalogues and are commonly used around the world, are known as "framework agreements" outside the U.S. system. This section will review the history of IDIQ contracts and framework agreements, noting how this contracting strategy emerged, in parallel developments, in the U.S. and EU systems in the 1990s and early 2000s. The discussion will then address similar issues that have arisen in the two systems, including contract types, award procedures, transparency and protests (challenges). As the discussion below reflects, material differences between the U.S. and EU systems often seem to turn on happenstance, on chance dissimilarities in terminology. But as Professor Michaels noted (see the beginning of this chapter) in his summary of comparative law study, divergences between similar functions in different legal systems may be explained by differences in the surrounding social, economic or political contexts—in this case, perhaps by stakeholder interests that shape framework agreements in the U.S. federal market.

There are at least two common kinds of "framework agreements" in the U.S. federal procurement system: multiple award schedule (MAS) contracts awarded by the U.S. General Services Administration (GSA) under FAR Subpart 8.1 and GSA's special statutory authority, and IDIQ contracts awarded by various agencies (including GSA) under FAR Subpart 16.5 and separate statutory authority. As Chapter 7 reflects, the two types of agreements (GSA MAS vs. IDIQ) are sometimes subject to dramatically different rules. In terms of practical structure, however, the GSA schedule contracts and IDIQs are very similar, and both types of U.S. contract are in turn (at least in broad terms) very similar to framework agreements recognized internationally. *Cf.* World Bank, *Framework Agreements: An Overview of How to Design, Establish and Operate a Framework Agreement in Investment Project Financing* (2018); UNCITRAL *Model Law on Public Procurement,* Ch. 7 (framework agreement procedures).

Under this construct, an agreement—a sort of catalogue—is originally entered between a public agency and one or more contractors. Generally, this master agreement (generally a "framework agreement" outside the United States, or "IDIQ contract" or "GSA MAS contract" in the U.S. system) which each contractor enters into lists of goods or services, with prices. When a requirement arises (either in the original agency or in another entity which is authorized to use the agreement), the requiring entity can launch a second-stage "mini-competition" among the contractors holding framework agreements to fulfill the requirement. In this "mini-competition" (also sometimes called a "call-off" or "second-stage competition"), the prices of the original agreements typically serve as ceiling prices, but the requiring entity can typically seek lower prices from the competing contractors. As a result of the "mini-competition" (or "call-off"), the selected contractor is awarded a task or delivery order (in the U.S. system) or a "framework contract" (in the EU system). See generally Gian Luigi Albano & Caroline Nicholas, *The Law and Economics of Framework Agreements* 4-5 (Cambridge U. Press 2016).

Framework agreements and IDIQ contracts came to the fore in the U.S. and EU systems in the 1990s. This contracting strategy may be seen as the successor to qualified supplier lists, which survive in the U.S. system. See 10 U.S.C. § 2319, *Encouragement of New Competitors,* 41 U.S.C. § 3311 (administrative requirements before qualification requirements can be established) & FAR Subpart 9.2 (implementing regulations). While supplier lists historically had been useful tools to identify qualified suppliers quickly and efficiently, framework agreements/IDIQs provided much more information on the goods and services offered by contractors found eligible for master agreements, and so a more efficient way to meet public agencies' sometimes unpredictable demands. See generally Christopher Yukins, *Are IDIQs Inefficient? Sharing Lessons with European Framework Contracting*, 37 Pub. Cont. L.J. 545, 556-67 (2008).

Although the European Commission raised early objections to framework agreements in the United Kingdom in the mid-1990s, see Christopher R. Yukins, *supra* at 552-53, framework agreements were fully endorsed by the 2004 EU public procurement directive which included a provision specifically addressed to framework agreements. The 2004 directive, EC/2004/18, Art. 32, allowed for two different types of framework agreements: those from which purchases could be made directly, and those which would require a second-stage competition for award. The current EU Directive 2014/24/EU addresses framework agreements in Article 33, and the closely related "dynamic purchasing agreements" (analogous to online catalogues) in Article 34.

Article 33 of the EU Directive 2014/24/EU imposes a number of important requirements on framework agreements. Framework agreements are generally limited to four years in duration, and user agencies must be clearly identified at the outset of the agreement. Framework agreements can be "closed" (with no new contractors allowed) or "open" (allowing contractors to join the contract after initial award). For every contract to be awarded under a standing framework agreement, "contracting authorities shall consult in writing the economic operators capable of performing the contract."

Article 34 of the EU directive addresses dynamic purchasing systems, which are closely akin to framework agreements and work much like online catalogues. Under Article 34, dynamic purchasing systems are online listing of goods and services. After a call for competition, candidates may be admitted to a dynamic purchasing system through a liberalized version of "restricted tendering," a competitive method which restricts the number of bidders through pre-qualification (discussed above).

The 2011 UNCITRAL model law's provisions on frameworks were developed after a series of serious scandals due to misuse of IDIQ agreements in the U.S. system, see, e.g., Steven Schooner, *Contractor Atrocities at Abu Ghraib: Compromised Accountability in a Streamlined, Outsourced Government,* 16 Stan. L. & Pol'y Rev. 549 (2005); GAO, *Interagency Contracting: Problems with DOD's and Interior's Orders to Support Military,* GAO-05-201 (Apr. 2005), and during the time the 2014 EU directives were first being formulated. The UNCITRAL model law therefore took a more cautious approach, discussed in brief below, to ensure that framework agreements are not abused.

As the discussion above reflects, there is enormous variance across procurement systems in their implementations of framework agreements. That variance is amplified in application; in the European Union, for example, different Member States have employed different strategies for framework agreements under the 2014 directive. That variance is itself a useful comparative tool, however, for it highlights key differences and potential policy concerns:

- *"Open" vs. "Closed" Frameworks:* By setting up an analytical divide between "open" frameworks (which can be joined at any time) versus "closed" frameworks (which are awarded to a limited number of participant vendors), the UNCITRAL model law highlighted the competitive differences between the two models. Closed framework agreements (such as the IDIQ contracts typically awarded under FAR Part 16) raise issues of competition, because they "effectively close off full competition in the procurement market concerned for the period of their duration." UNCITRAL, *Guide to Enactment of the UNCITRAL Model Law on Public Procurement* 256 (2012). "In addition," the UNCITRAL guide to enactment noted, "the parties to closed framework agreements will be known to each other, raising the risk of collusion at the second stage," though the Guide also noted that the "risks concerned will vary from market to market—some markets are inherently more competitive than others." *Id.*
- *Mandatory Use:* Agencies which sponsor framework agreements have a strong incentive to *require* that customer agencies purchase *only* from the standing agreements; mandatory use may create efficiencies and potential revenues (in the form of user fees) for the sponsoring agencies. The European Commission has encouraged centralized purchasing agencies to consider making their framework agreements mandatory-use. European Commission, *Make Better Use of Framework Agreements, https://ec.europa.eu/regional_policy/sources/good_practices/GP_fiche_16.pdf* (sponsoring contracting authorities "should make the use of central purchasing as broadly mandatory as possible, while allowing limited exceptions paired with rigorous oversight where necessary"). In the U.S. system, however, mandatory-use IDIQ contracts suffered a setback when in 2000 the U.S. Court of Appeals for the Federal Circuit ruled that, if users bypass a mandatory-use contract, the injured contractor may recover lost profits from the sponsoring agency. *Ace-Federal Reporters., Inc. v. Barram*, 226 F.3d 1329 (Fed. Cir. 2000). Today, mandatory-use framework agreements (IDIQ or GSA MAS contracts, for example) are relatively uncommon in the federal marketplace.
- *Transparency:* In implementation, framework agreements can be highly non-transparent. Incumbent contractors, purchasing agencies and the sponsoring agency itself all have incentives to avoid transparency so as to reduce transaction costs, and to avoid disruptive and potentially embarrassing inquiries and challenges. A lack of transparency reduces competition, but that itself may be an incentive for vendors to join a "closed" marketplace. The U.S. system offers starkly different models of transparency. GSA's "eBuy" portal, www.gsa.gov/ebuy, is closed to outsiders (open only to agencies and GSA contractors), and is the designated portal for potentially billions of dollars in annual framework

contracting. FAR 8.402(d); FAR 8.405-2(c). GSA opened portions of the eBuy portal to the public in a pilot initiative in transparency, the "Open GSA First Pilot," but ended the pilot in 2019. *https://www.gsa.gov/tools-overview/buying-and-selling-tools/ebuy/ebuy-open-gsa-first-pilot*. In contrast, when the Obama administration launched billions of dollars in fiscal-stimulus spending under the American Recovery and Reinvestment Act of 2009 (ARRA), the implementing regulations required that all orders (framework contracts) using ARRA funds be published at opportunity and award. FAR 16.505(a)(11).

- *Pricing:* While "closed" framework agreements typically present straightforward pricing issues—competitive ceiling prices negotiated at award of the master agreement, and then same-or-lower prices in a second-stage award—"open" frameworks can be more complicated. Since vendors can join an open framework agreement at any time (weeks or years after a competitor), there is normally no pressure of price competition at award. In the U.S. system, GSA addresses this problem through the Price Reductions clause, GSAM 552.238-81, a most-favored-customer clause under which contractors agree to keep their GSA MAS prices below agreed-upon commercial benchmark prices. That approach, however, burdens others in the market who must bear the indirect costs of prices artificially buoyed by the most-favored-customer requirement, see, e.g., Aaron Woodward, *The Perverse Effect of the Multiple Award Schedules' Price Reductions Clause*, 41 Pub. Cont. L.J. 527, 550-51 (2012), and enforcing the most-favored-customer commitment creates substantial audit and compliance costs. Congress has offered a new approach: "no-price" master agreements for services. For example, under Section 876 of the National Defense Authorization Act for Fiscal Year 2019, GSA may award major IDIQ contracts for services on a "no-price" basis: the master agreements will be awarded without any reference to price, and prices will be negotiated in the "call-off" stage, when contractors compete for awards. 85 Fed. Reg. 50989 (Aug. 19, 2020).

- *Bid Challenges:* As the discussion above reflects, in the U.S. system the rules regarding bid protests (bid challenges) of orders under framework agreements are markedly uneven. For example, while bid protests involving GSA multiple award schedule orders under FAR Part 8 can be brought at GAO, only larger IDIQ orders under FAR Part 16 (and the thresholds have changed over time) can be protested there. Under the UNCITRAL model law, in contrast, because the UNCITRAL model law adopted the EU taxonomy of "framework agreements" leading to second-stage "framework contracts," the legal protections that adhere to *contracts* apply to what would be termed mere "orders" under U.S. IDIQ agreements. The UNCITRAL guide to enactment explains that, although "the framework agreement may be a binding contract, the definition of the 'procurement contract' under . . . the Model Law does not include a framework agreement. The procurement contract for the purposes of . . . the Model Law is concluded at the second stage of the procedure, when the procuring entity awards a procurement contract under the framework agreement. . . . This means that the safeguards and procedures under the Model Law apply throughout the framework agreement procedure." With regard to bid challenges, the UNCITRAL guide to enactment was explicit: "[B]oth stages of the framework agreement procedures are subject to [bid] challenge under chapter VIII of the Model Law."

- *Alternatives:* The EU's embrace of "dynamic purchasing systems" signals that EU policymakers, like other observers, may believe that the framework agreements which replaced traditional supplier lists are themselves merely transient solutions which could be supplanted by more flexible, Internet-based approaches. *Cf.* UK Cabinet Office, *Transforming Public Procurement: Government Response to Consultation* 46-47 (Dec. 2021) (as part of post-Brexit revamp, UK government proposes "Dynamic Market" which will allow suppliers to join at any time). Indeed, the U.S. Congress endorsed the use of popular online marketplaces, such as Amazon, as new purchasing channels for federal users buying directly. The "micro-purchase" authority used for this initiative is discussed in more detail in the following section.

Globally, framework agreements—IDIQ contracts, as they are known in the United States—are clearly an important, evolving experiment in public contracting. As the preceding discussion shows, because framework agreements are evolving in parallel in different national and regional procurement systems, a comparative assessment is quite useful, for it opens a window on potential future advances and reforms.

§ 16.09 SIMPLIFIED ACQUISITIONS

Chapter 8 reviews the simplified procedures for smaller purchases which are largely gathered in Part 13 of the FAR. From a comparative perspective, those laxer rules for smaller purchases reflect a simple, common principle in procurement: for lower-value procurements, fewer processes and less oversight are needed because fewer public resources are at stake. A closer look at the U.S. rules for simplified purchases, viewed through the prism of similar rules in the European Union, shows however that the way the U.S. rules are shaped, when compared to analogous rules in other systems, reveals core elements of the U.S.

system: a pragmatic flexibility and an abiding confidence that the commercial market will help ensure that the government receives fair prices and sound quality.

The starting point for this comparative analysis are the "below-threshold" purchases by the Member States of the EU—purchases which fall below the threshold for applying the EU-wide procurement directives. As the European Commission explains:

> EU law sets minimum harmonised rules for tenders whose monetary value exceeds a certain amount and which are presumed to be of cross-border interest. The European rules ensure that the award of contracts of higher value for the provision of public goods and services must be fair, equitable, transparent and non-discriminatory. For tenders of lower value however, national rules apply, which nevertheless have to respect general principles of EU law.

European Commission, Internal Market, Industry, Entrepreneurship and SMEs, *Thresholds*. The thresholds vary, and are for example generally higher for the EU defense directive, 2009/81/EC. Pursuant to Commission Delegated Regulation (EU) 2021/1952 of November 10, 2021, the thresholds for supplies are generally €140,000 (roughly $160,000), and for works (construction) €5,382,000 (roughly $6 million).

The U.S. thresholds for simplified purchases are roughly the same, though with some important differences. The simplified acquisition threshold is $250,000, FAR 2.101, though that threshold generally increases to $7.5 million for commercial products and services, FAR 13.003(c)(1) (discussed further below). Like the EU thresholds, the U.S. thresholds very roughly align with the thresholds for application of the WTO Agreement on Government Procurement (GPA), the leading free trade agreement governing procurement. See FAR 25.402 (thresholds for GPA and other international trade agreements applicable to U.S. procurement).

In a 2011 report, *Understanding the EU Financial Thresholds,* SIGMA (an EU-focused research unit within the Organization for Economic Co-operation and Development (OECD)) noted that below-threshold contracts "comprise the vast majority of contracts awarded by contracting authorities and are therefore of great importance in all EU member states," because below-threshold contracts "represent significant expenditure by contracting authorities and major business opportunities for economic operators, not least for small and medium enterprises (SMEs)." The large share of EU public contracts that fall below threshold means in practice that the "majority of contracts awarded by contracting authorities are awarded using national rules, policies and procedures." *Id.;* see, e.g., Dacian C. Dragos & Roxana Vornicu, *Public Procurement Below Thresholds in the European Union*, 10 Eur. Proc. & Pub. Priv. Partn. L. Rev. 187, 187 (2015) ("less than 20% of public procurement procedures are subject to the provisions of EU Public Procurement Directives . . . [and with regard to] the value of the works, goods or services is concerned, 80% of the tender procedures are conducted below the thresholds").

Despite the Member States' relative autonomy in handling below-threshold procurements, the Member States do need to honor the *principles* reflected in the EU laws, and must adhere to the EU's governing treaties. See European Commission, *Commission Interpretative Communication on the Community Law Applicable to Contract Awards Not or Not Fully Subject to the Provisions of the Public Procurement Directives*, 2006/C 179/02 (reviewing applicable principles and their practical application in procurement). In accordance with those principles, the SIGMA study, at pages 2-3, noted that Member States' rules for below-threshold procurement should:

- Be efficient and effective and therefore use processes, timescales and documents which reflect the needs and outcomes of the particular procurement.
- Be proportionate and avoid unnecessary bureaucracy so as to avoid imposing over complex or disproportionate bureaucratic and administrative burdens or costs on the contracting authority or the economic operator relative to the size, value and complexity of the contract being procured.
- Ensure appropriate competition since open, fair competition should help to attract a broader range of potential bidders, including SMEs and startup companies which may be attracted to lower value contracts in particular.
- Be transparent since transparency of process assists open and fair competition and also assists in safeguarding against corruption and favoritism.
- Comply with Treaty rules and principles and, where relevant to a particular contract, comply with basic standards developed by the Court of Justice of the European Union (CJEU).
- Make the most efficient use of public money ensuring the optimal allocation of resources to achieve the intended outcomes.

Romanian procurement experts Dacian Dragos and Roxana Vornicu noted that the "ultimate test for the application of EU law principles to below thresholds public procurement is the 'cross border interest' assessment [which] entails an evaluation performed by each contracting authority in order to determine whether the projected contract would be of interest for tenderers outside the Member State in which the procedure is conducted." Dacian Dragos & Roxana Vornicu, *supra*, at 197. In other words, these principles provide a framework—a sort of litmus test—for assessing whether procurement rules align with the EU's core goal of integrating procurement with the broader European single market. Placing that observation into the U.S. context, these European principles could help an assessment of whether the rules for simplified acquisition integrate the U.S. government's simplified purchases into the broader commercial market.

Assessed against those benchmarks for commercial integration, the U.S. rules for simplified acquisitions fare quite well—in fact, the purpose statement of FAR Part 13 aligns almost precisely with the European principles set forth above:

> The purpose of this part is to prescribe simplified acquisition procedures in order to—
>
> (a) Reduce administrative costs;
>
> (b) Improve opportunities for small, small disadvantaged, women-owned, veteran-owned, HUBZone, and service-disabled veteran-owned small business concerns to obtain a fair proportion of Government contracts;
>
> (c) Promote efficiency and economy in contracting; and
>
> (d) Avoid unnecessary burdens for agencies and contractors.

FAR 13.002.

Turning to detail and applying the EU benchmarks, the U.S. simplified acquisition rules do indeed use processes "which reflect the needs and outcomes of the particular procurement" by calling for purchasing officials to "promote competition to the maximum extent practicable." To ensure "appropriate competition" across a "broader range of potential bidders," as the EU principles suggest, contracting officers under the U.S. rules are not to solicit based on personal preference, or to restrict solicitations only to well-known brands, and should seek "quotations or offers from two sources not included in the previous solicitation." FAR 13.104. In line with the European benchmark suggestions that officials use "open, fair competition" to "help attract a broader range of potential bidders, including SMEs and start up companies," FAR 13.003(b) says that "acquisitions of supplies or services that have an anticipated dollar value . . . below the simplified acquisition threshold . . . shall be set aside for small business concerns." To ensure transparency of process, as suggested by the EU benchmarks, to assist "open and fair competition and . . . in safeguarding against corruption and favouritism," FAR 13.106-1 encourages U.S. contracting officials to solicit through an "electronic commerce method that employs widespread electronic public notice"—though the rule also allows much less transparency, so long as the contracting official solicits the requisite number of sources. Finally, in keeping with the EU benchmarks which call for officials to make "the most efficient use of public money ensuring the optimal allocation of resources to achieve the intended outcomes"—"fit for purpose," in the language of the World Bank Procurement Framework—under FAR 13.104 a "contracting officer must promote competition to the maximum extent practicable to obtain supplies and services from the source whose offer is the most advantageous to the Government, considering the administrative cost of the purchase."

The FAR's simplified acquisition procedures thus generally align quite neatly with the European benchmarks for rules that integrate smoothly in the broader market. In one critical aspect, however, the U.S. rules go farther than the European model, and suggest that beyond *integrating* with the commercial marketplace, the U.S. system relies on it.

As noted, while normally the upper threshold for simplified acquisitions is $250,000, for commercial products and services the threshold goes to $7.5 million—30 times as high. The purpose of this special exception is to "vest contracting officers with additional procedural discretion and flexibility," to allow commercial acquisitions in this dollar range in a "simplified manner that maximizes efficiency and economy and minimizes burden and administrative costs." FAR 13.500. This provision, originally included as a pilot in Section 4202 of the Clinger-Cohen Act of 1996 (Division D of Public Law 104-106, 10 U.S.C. § 2304 note) and continued over many years, was made permanent by Section 815 of the National Defense Authorization Act for FY 2015, Public Law No. 113-291.

Looking back, the conference report which accompanied the original 1996 legislation provided little insight on this substantial exception for commercial goods and services. H.R. Conf. Rep. No. 104-450, 104th Cong., 2d Sess. 966-67 (Jan. 22, 1996). Looking forward, however, it is possible to see a potential broadening of this exception in the future—a doubling of the threshold to $15 million, for "readily available items," as proposed by the Advisory Panel on Streamlining and Codifying Acquisition Regulations (the "Section 809 Panel"), a panel of senior procurement experts which was created by Section 809 of the FY 2016 National Defense Authorization Act (Public Law 114-92).

The Section 809 panel noted that a House report which preceded the 1996 legislation said that the "purchase of a commercial item logically lends itself to simplified procedures because there exists a yardstick in the commercial marketplace against which to measure price and product quality and to serve a surrogate for Government-unique procedures." *Report of the Advisory Panel on Streamlining and Codifying Acquisition Regulations*, Vol. 2, Recomm. 28 (quoting H. Rep. 104-222 & 61 Fed. Reg. 47384, 47385 (Sept. 6, 1996)). The Section 809 panel recommended legislative changes to ease use of the existing exception, *id.*, and went beyond to recommend a much higher threshold—up to $15 million—for much simpler purchasing of "readily available items," i.e., products or services that require "no customization by the vendor and can be put on order by customers," which were "developed and paid for by private investment (not the government) and have established supply chains." *Id.* Vol. 2, Recomm. 35.

Tracing the historical arc of the U.S. simplified acquisition procedures helps clarify an important assumption underlying the U.S. rules—that the commercial marketplace will provide a "yardstick" to ensure the government receives good prices and sound quality—and sheds light on the possible future trajectory of those rules. A comparative assessment drawing on the EU principles for below-threshold contracts suggests that the U.S. rules for simplified acquisitions are already integrated with the broader commercial marketplace; the more recent proposals for reform suggest how heavily the U.S. system may come to rely on that marketplace.

§ 16.10 COMMERCIAL PRODUCTS AND SERVICES

Chapter 9 of the text reviews the special rules applicable to commercial products and services under Part 12 of the FAR. The previous section drew on a comparison to EU contracting to explain simplified purchasing rules for commercial items. A traditional comparative assessment of that type is difficult for commercial-item contracting, however, because systems around the world do exactly the same thing—in fact, the United States is unique in how often it is *not* simply contracting for commercial goods and services. To help clarify the U.S. rules regarding commercial products and services, therefore, this section will explore this type of contracting from the perspective of a foreign vendor entering the U.S. federal marketplace. This example assumes the vendor would have access to the U.S. market via the Government Procurement Agreement, a reciprocal defense procurement agreement, or other free trade agreement. See, e.g., Christopher Yukins & Allen Green, *International Trade Agreements and U.S. Procurement Law*, in *The Contractor's Guide to International Procurement* (Erin Loraine Felix & Marques Peterson, eds.) (ABA 2018).

To understand commercial products and services purchased under FAR Part 12, it is not enough simply to review a standard-form (SF 1449) contract. The standard U.S. commercial-item contract does not look altogether different from a standard contract in Europe, such as the UK Ministry of Defense's SC1, *MOD Terms and Conditions for Less Complex Requirements (Supply of Goods)*, which is in fact a largely standard commercial contract with additional protections and provisions specially written for the government. Focusing on the contract itself, however, would overlook the important changes that the "commercial item revolution" brought to U.S. procurement.

The "revolution" was born of the end of the Cold War, when the U.S. government sought to reduce defense expenditures and streamline operations. It was also clear by the end of the 20th century that the U.S. government was no longer a main player in developing new technologies, and that the government therefore needed better access to new solutions emerging in industry. Therefore, as part of a broader procurement reform effort in the mid-1990s, Congress passed legislation to liberalize commercial-item acquisition—a "revolution" which continues to play out today, as vendors and government seek new ways to use simpler, more commercially oriented rules for procurement. See Christopher Yukins, *U.S. Government Contracting in the Context of Global Public Procurement*, at 271, in *The Internationalization of Government Procurement*

Regulation (Aris Georgopoulos, Bernard Hoekman & Petros C. Mavroidis, eds.) (Oxford U. Press 2017). It is worthwhile stressing, though, that in the United States (unlike the European Union), it was not Congress' intent to use commercial-item contracting to better integrate federal procurement (which represents roughly three percent of the U.S. economy) into the broader U.S. market. Although the United States was founded on principles of economic integration, and nearly three centuries of policy and law bend towards the nation's economic integration, the federal government's purchasing still stands largely apart. The goal of the "commercial item revolution," in other words, was not to integrate federal purchasing into the broader market, but to make it easier to access emerging technologies in the federal sphere.

To return to our example, a foreign vendor entering the U.S. market might follow one of the newest pathways for commercial-item procurement, the "commercial marketplaces" (including Amazon.com) which (as Chapter 9 notes) were opened for micro-purchases (generally up to $10,000) by federal users. Besides the practical limitations of the low dollar threshold, the foreign vendor would encounter many open problems with those platforms—issues such as fees, platform owners' access to vendors' sales data, cybersecurity requirements, government socioeconomic requirements, and a weak initial market response to the platforms. See, e.g., GAO, *GSA Online Marketplaces: Plans to Measure Progress and Monitor Data Protection Efforts Need Further Development* (Nov. 2021) (noting only $5.9 million in first year of sales, despite earlier projects of $6 billion); Christopher Yukins, Abraham Young, Kristen Ittig & Eric Valle, *GSA's Commercial Marketplaces Initiative: Opening Amazon & Other Private Marketplaces To Direct Purchases By Government Use*, 20-13 Briefing Papers 1 (2020).

The foreign vendor also might access the federal marketplace as a subcontractor. The federal rules call for prime contractors, when subcontracting, to purchase commercial goods and services whenever possible, and the rules say that these subcontracts contain a minimal number of special government requirements. See FAR Subpart 44.2. In fact, however, relatively few statutes are *not* applicable to commercial-item subcontracts, see FAR 12.504, and prime contractors often seek to "flow down" as many requirements as possible from the prime contract, whether appropriate or not, in an effort to shift legal risk. Subcontracts thus are not automatic safe harbors from the federal regulatory burden, even for commercial products and services.

The vendor, entering the federal market as a prime contractor, could join one of the "framework agreements" (IDIQ or multiple award schedule contracts) discussed above, though they would present more special government requirements. These arrangements grew rapidly in the wake of the reforms to commercial-item contracting, in part because the preference for standard commercial products and services meant that it was easier to sell them as "catalogue" items on standing framework agreements. Despite Congress' admonition that commercial item prime contracts contain as few special government requirements as possible, the

GSA multiple award schedule contract (one of the most popular "framework" vehicles) lists hundreds of special requirements, and many special requirements are still included as part of the standard commercial-item clauses under FAR 52.212-5. Despite FAR Part 12's assurance that commercial goods and services should be subject to minimal government-standard clauses, many non-commercial requirements have been added by GSA, such as the: Technical Data clause (which reserves intellectual property rights in excess of most commercial licenses); the Price Reductions clause (the most favored customer provision discussed above, which imposes price compliance requirements well in excess of a commercial norm); and, the Price Adjustment clause (a sweeping non-commercial requirement to disclose discounts at the initial negotiation). Thus, although the GSA multiple award schedule contract is a commercial item contract—indeed, one of the largest single vehicles in the federal market for commercial goods and services—GSA's contract, burdened with hundreds of special government requirements, reflects the limited progress made by the "commercial item revolution" nearly three decades later. That partial failure in turn helps explain the other federal initiatives, discussed below, to open procurement channels to emerging commercial technologies.

§ 16.11 SPECIAL NEGOTIATION PROCEDURES

Chapter 10 reviews a number of special negotiation procedures that federal agencies are authorized to use: "Other Transaction Authority" (OTA), broad agency announcements (BAA), procurement under the Small Business Innovation Research (SBIR) program, procurement of architect and engineering services under the Brooks Act, two-step design/build contracts, special procedures for information technology (IT) procurement, and various agency-unique procedures. These special negotiation procedures in the U.S. system have analogues abroad, and a comparative assessment offers useful insights on both the U.S. and foreign approaches.

This Section addresses each of the special procedures (and their analogues abroad) in turn. The discussion below compares OTA contracting to the United Kingdom's Ministry of Defense, and assesses whether the United Kingdom's program may have lessons regarding the use of standardized contractual terms in OTA contracts. The discussion then turns to broad agency announcements in the U.S. system which, like the European Union's Defense Industry Initiative encourage innovation, but which do not raise the trade frictions that the EU's initiative has triggered. The discussion assesses similar trade frictions that may arise regarding the SBIR program in the U.S. system, an initiative which "locks" development and production with a U.S. business, and which may be expanded to secure domestic sources of critical supplies. The discussion reviews two-step design/build contracts, but more to assess how those contracts have been used abroad—in public-private partnerships driven by private capital—and why similar vehicles have *not* been used in the U.S. federal government. The discussion reviews how the complexity of information technology procurement has helped expand the use of multilateral competitive negotiations (discussed above) in systems around the world. Finally, the discussion notes how anomalous special agency procedures are in the largely uniform U.S. system, and how foreign systems reflect the costs and benefits of uniformity.

[A] Other Transaction Authority—UK Comparison

As Chapter 10 notes, the government's use of OTA contracting has expanded rapidly in recent years, especially in the U.S. Department of Defense. A 2019 report from the Government Accountability Office explained why: while historically the U.S. government has "helped commercial companies pioneer innovative technologies that, in turn, have supported U.S. technological superiority on the battlefield and spurred the development of new commercial products," the Defense Department's "influence on the type of technologies developed by U.S. companies has diminished over the past several decades as companies significantly increased the amount of their own funds they invested in research and development." The Defense Department has found it difficult to capture those commercial advances, due to commercial firms' "concerns about intellectual property, the length of time it takes [the Defense Department] to award a contract, and the need to establish a government-unique cost accounting system," among other concerns. GAO, *Defense Acquisitions: DOD's Use of Other Transactions for Prototype Projects Has Increased*, at 1, GAO-20-84, Nov. 22, 2019).

Two aspects of the Defense Department's use of OTA contracts bear special comparative assessment: the Defense Department's use of private consortia to distribute opportunities for development and awards among consortium members, and that the Defense Department is not required to use standard FAR contract clauses in OTA agreements. On these issues the United Kingdom's parallel initiative for accelerating innovation offers useful points of comparison.

With regard to consortia and the award of OTA agreements, a 2021 report from the U.S. Department of Defense Office of the Inspector General explained:

> DoD can award OTs through a consortium (two or more individuals, companies, or organizations), to allow the DoD and industry to communicate in one forum. A Consortium Management Organization (CMO) acts as the consortium's single point of contact and manages its membership. Usually, the DoD awards a base OT agreement to a CMO, selects a member to perform a project, and awards the project to the CMO. The CMO enters into a separate agreement with the member selected to perform the project.

DoD IG, *Audit of Other Transactions Awarded Through Consortiums*, DODIG-2021-077 (Nov. 2021); see also U.S. Air Force, *Other Transaction Authority (OTA) Overview* (the "OT Consortium model provides tremendous flexibility, speed, and access to the broadest possible pool of prospective vendors"); *DoD Other Transactions Guide*, at 39 (OTA contracts need not be awarded through a consortium). The DoD IG report described some of the problems that had emerged through the use of consortia:

> DoD contracting personnel did not always plan and execute OTs awarded through consortiums in accordance with OT laws and regulations. Specifically, of the 13 base OT awards we reviewed, valued at $24.6 billion, DoD contracting personnel did not[:] . . . properly track OTs awarded through consortiums and did not have an accurate count of OTs and associated dollar values . . . because [in part] there was no guidance on how to award the projects to a consortium; consistently award OTs in accordance with applicable laws and regulations because there is little guidance or training on awarding consortium OTs; or . . . have a consistent basis to negotiate CMO fees because there was no guidance in place for establishing these fees. . . . In addition, DoD contracting personnel did not ensure the security of controlled or restricted information being sent to the consortium because DoD contracting personnel relied on the CMOs to vet consortium members and ensure proper safeguarding of controlled and restricted data. Further, the DoD did not require consortium members to register in the [central vendor qualification information database, the] System for Award Management (SAM). . . . As a result, DoD officials do not have access to important information associated with OTs awarded through consortiums, such as which contractor received the OT award and the specific costs associated with funded OT projects. Without this information, the DoD does not have the necessary oversight of the projects it is funding. . . .

Id. at 1, 3-5 (citing DOD, *Other Transactions Guide* (Nov. 2018)). Congress, responding to concerns of this type, in the National Defense Authorization Act for Fiscal Year 2022, Public Law 117-81 (Dec. 27, 2021), directed a number of actions regarding OTA procurements, including (in Section 824) a comprehensive Defense Department report on the use of Other Transaction Authority.

In assessing issues in OTA contracts, the UK government's Defence and Security Accelerator (DASA) (part of the UK Ministry of Defence) offers a useful comparison. The purpose of the DASA program is very similar to that of OTA contracts. The DASA program "finds and funds exploitable innovation to support UK defence and security quickly and effectively, and support UK prosperity." The program's vision "is for the UK to have strategic advantage through the most innovative defence and security capabilities in the world." *https://www.gov.uk/government/organisations/defence-and-security-accelerator/about*. The DASA initiative achieves this "by welcoming ideas from innovators small and large," so long as those funded "have not previously worked with Government"—a requirement much like the OTA objective that "nontraditional contractors" play an integral part in a funded project (see Chapter 16).

Rather than using consortia to make awards (as with OTA contracts in the United States), the UK DASA program works directly with firms but relies on regional "Innovation Partners" to identify and encourage innovators. See *Defence and Security Accelerator (DASA) Annual Review 2020/2021*. DASA's strategy does not rely on consortia to gather and present solutions, but instead provides support for innovators as they develop new technologies and seek out new partners, in government, industry and academia:

> DASA acknowledges that business readiness, including commercialisation, is as important as technology readiness in the development of an idea into a solution fit for purpose. Through our refreshed strategy we will focus effort on increasing the pull through of innovative ideas supporting the exploitation and commercialisation of solutions into capability. Businesses that show technical promise will be given the opportunity, support and guidance to develop their business and systems readiness, through access to defence and security business support schemes, such as defence innovation loans, and by developing an innovation ideas marketplace for ideas to be brokered with larger organisations in a position to develop and commercialise them.

Innovation for a Safer Future: DASA Strategy 2021-2024 (May 2021). While the scale of DASA projects is much smaller than that of OTA transactions, DASA's focus—on connecting innovators with many points of support across the private sector—stands in contrast to the Defense Department's use of private consortia to put solutions forward.

The UK DASA program also contrasts with OTA contracts because DASA contracts rely on standard terms. The *DOD Other Transactions Guide* emphasizes that, unlike "FAR-based contracts, the terms and conditions for the award of an OT may take considerable time to negotiate as the proposed solutions, schedules, terms and conditions, and price are likely to vary significantly amongst competitors." *Id.* at 17. The UK DASA program, in contrast, relies on a standardized contract, *MOD Terms and Conditions for Contracting for Innovation—Core Terms,* MOD Innovation SC (Nov. 2020), which includes mandatory terms, such as those addressing payment and disputes. The UK Ministry of Defence's standard contract leaves it to the parties to negotiate certain conditions, including which standard Ministry of Defence contracting clauses (DEFCONS) will be incorporated into the contract. Rather than taking the path available to Defense Department OTA contracts—bypassing traditional standardized contracting terms which can reduce transaction costs and reflect experience in risk allocation between the government and its contractors—the UK DASA program uses standard contract clauses as building blocks within a standardized contract with innovators. Granted, while the Defense Department is not required to use standard FAR and DFARS clauses in its OTA contracts, it is not prohibited from doing so, and it is not uncommon to see those standard clauses in OTA contracts. In some cases, it may well make sense to rely on well-established contract language that both parties may have context for, rather than re-inventing the wheel by drafting clauses from scratch. In other cases, however, the reliance on FAR and

DFARS clauses in OTA contracts may be more attributable to reflexive habit than reasoned decision making.

[B] Broad Area Announcements—Research & Development

Compared to many issues relating to "other transactions," broad agency announcements (BAAs) are firmly grounded in traditional FAR approaches. As Chapter 10 explains, FAR Part 35 governs research and development contracting, and under FAR 35.016 an agency may publish a BAA "for the acquisition of basic and applied research and that part of development not related to the development of a specific system or hardware procurement." The FAR explains that BAAs "may be used by agencies to fulfill their requirements for scientific study and experimentation directed toward advancing the state-of-the-art or increasing knowledge or understanding rather than focusing on a specific system or hardware solution," and are to be used "only be used when meaningful proposals with varying technical/scientific approaches can be reasonably anticipated." *Id.*

The European Union's primary procurement directive, 2014/24/EU, contains a limited exception for research and development contracts. Under Article 14 of the Directive, the normal procedural requirements apply if, under a covered public service contract for research and development services, (a) the benefits accrue exclusively to the contracting authority for its use in the conduct of its own affairs, and (b) the service provided is wholly remunerated by the contracting authority. Only if *both* conditions apply "is there an obligation [to] hold a procurement procedure"—in other words, if "one of the conditions is not fulfilled, there will be no such obligation." Michael Steinicke & Peter L. Vesterdorf, *EU Public Procurement Law: Brussels Commentary* 280 (C.H. Beck—Hart—Nomos 2018).

The European Union's directive thus creates an incentive for procuring agencies to co-fund research and development with the private sector, in order to avoid traditional procurement procedures. Recital 35 to the Directive (a prefatory, explanatory comment on the directive) makes it clear that this was precisely the drafters' goal—to nudge agencies to co-finance research and development with industry:

> The co-financing of research and development (R&D) programmes by industry sources should be encouraged. It should consequently be clarified that this Directive applies only where there is no such co-financing and where the outcome of the R&D activities go to the contracting authority concerned. This should not exclude the possibility that the service provider, having carried out those activities, could publish an account thereof as long as the contracting authority retains the exclusive right to use the outcome of the R&D in the conduct of its own affairs . . .

This bias in the exception for research and development contracts—in essence, using the threat of cumbersome procurement rules to encourage public agencies to seek private co-financing for research and development, and to share the fruits of that research and development beyond the agency—dates back to earlier versions of the procurement directives, which noted that "the encouragement of research and development is a means of strengthening the scientific and technological basis of European industry and the opening-up of public contracts will contribute to this end." See Martin Dischendorfer, *Consolidated Version of Directive 93/28/EEC*, 1999 Pub. Proc. L. Rev. 80, 83. The EU directives thus reflect the contrasting perspective of EU regulators—rather than curbing traditional contracting rules to bring cutting-edge research into the government (as "other transactions" and BAAs do in the U.S. system), the EU directives have used the *threat* of those cumbersome contracting rules to encourage agencies to bridge into private research and development efforts.

[C] SBIR Program—Innovation Partnerships

The parallels between the EU and U.S. regulatory regimes regarding research and development extend to the U.S. "Small Business Innovative Research" (SBIR) program, which was the precursor to the European Union's special rules regarding "innovation partnerships" under Article 31 of EU Directive 2014/24/EU. Dr. Anca Ramona Apostol described how the European Union developed special rules regarding "innovation partnerships" in response, in part, to disappointing outcomes in direct European Commission funding for research and development; instead, the EU decided to encourage agencies to fund new technologies through procurement, using the special procedural rules for innovation partnerships. See Anca Ramona Apostol, *Pre-Commercial Procurement in Support of Innovation: Regulatory Effectiveness?*, 2012 Pub. Proc. L. Rev. 213. She wrote:

> [T]he European Commission started in 2005–2006 to investigate the possibilities to use public procurement of R&D services in the field of ICT [information and communications technology] in order to enhance the innovation capability of Europe. This initiative was triggered by the observation that the United States succeeds more often to pull technological R&D into the commercialisation phase and that this is partly due to the use of public procurement of R&D and of the subsequently developed solutions within the Small Business Innovation Research (SBIR) program. The United States uses this instrument to provide a home market to its innovative domestic firms in specifically identified areas in which the United States aspires to become global leader.

Id. at 214-15 (citing National IST Research Directors Forum Working Group on Public Procurement Support of ICT Research and Innovation (March 2006), *Pre-commercial Procurement of Innovation: A Missing Link in the European Innovation Cycle*, 9-11 (Mar. 2006)).

Professor Marta Andhov (née Andrecka) described how innovation partnerships under Article 16 of the EU directive drive new technologies; her description showed that, as with SBIR arrangements, the purchasing agency supports development and then purchases the product of that innovation:

> The innovation partnership must aim at the development of an innovative product, service or works and the subsequent purchase of the resulting supplies, services or works. On the one hand, the innovation partnership combines both a pre-commercial and a commercial stage of procurement, as its subject matter is both: an innovation development (pre-commercial stage) and a subsequent purchase of the innovation (commercial stage). The latter is under the condition that the innovation corresponds to the performance levels and maximum costs agreed between the contracting authorities and the bidders. . . . [T]he establishment of the innovation partnership may be seen not only as an answer to existing challenges, but also as a new way of realising the objective of a smart, sustainable and inclusive growth that characterises the Europe 2020 strategy.

Marta Andrecka, *Innovation Partnership in the New Public Procurement Regime—A Shift of Focus from Procedural to Contractual Issues?*, 2015 Pub. Proc. L. Rev. 48, 54. Innovation partnerships are thus part of a broader strategy of advancing growth and technology in the European Union.

The European Union takes a similar approach, though with different ends, under the European Defense Fund (EDF), a multi-year, multi-billion-Euro initiative handled under EU Regulation 2021/697 (Apr. 29, 2021). The recitals to the Regulation explain that, given increasing geopolitical risks to the European Union's Member States, the purpose of the EDF is to strengthen the European defense technological and industrial base (EDTIB). Defense development efforts supported by the Fund therefore must be "carried out by legal entities cooperating within a consortium of at least three eligible legal entities which are established in at least three different Member States or associated countries." Development of common prototypes will be funded only where Member States intend to buy the final product or use the technology in a coordinated manner. European Commission, *Fact Sheet: The European Defence Fund* (June 2021). Although the results of research actions supported by the Fund "shall not be subject to any control or restriction by a . . . third country," the United States and other countries have been invited to participate in Fund-supported individual efforts under the EU's Permanent Structured Cooperation (PESCO) defense initiative. See European Commission, *PESCO: Canada, Norway and the United States will be invited to participate in the project Military Mobility* (May 6, 2021). This limited opening to U.S. firms resolves, at least in part, concerns that excluding U.S. firms would violate the United States' many reciprocal defense procurement agreements with its European allies, which are intended to open bilateral defense trade in materiel, services and research and development. See Christopher Yukins, *European Commission Proposes Expanding the European Defence*

Fund—A Major Potential Barrier to Transatlantic Defense Procurement, 60 Gov. Contr. ¶ 196 (June 27, 2018).

Viewed more broadly, these various initiatives—the U.S. SBIR program, and the "innovation partnerships" and the European Defense Fund in Europe—are of a piece, because they tie publicly subsidized technological development to preferred follow-on procurement. From a comparative perspective, these initiatives which have developed in parallel (indeed, sometimes borrowing from one another) reflect common functions which, though they arose in different contexts with very different goals, share many common features.

[D] Architect-Engineer Contracts—Consultant Services

In the U.S. federal procurement system (as Chapter 10 explains), special procedures are used to procure architectural and engineering (A&E) services under the Brooks Act. Unlike normal procurements, A&E services are purchased using a two-step system: competing firms are ranked, and then the purchasing agency attempts to negotiate an agreement with only the top-ranked firm. The logic behind this special approach is straightforward: that "the quality of these services is basic and essential to the quality of construction," and because the costs of these architectural and engineering services "represents but a smaller part of the total cost of construction . . . [i]t was thought important to be less cost conscious in the selection" of architects and engineers services. Noel Keyes, *Government Contracting Under the Federal Acquisition Regulation* § 36.51 (3d ed.); *Ass'n of Soil & Found. Eng'rs,* B-209196, Apr. 5, 1983, 83-1 CPD ¶ 362 n.1. A comparative example from the World Bank suggests, however, that this same logic might be extended to other, similarly critical services.

Under the World Bank's Procurement Framework, consulting services include any advisory or professional services provided by a consultant. See World Bank, *Procurement Regulations for IPF Borrowers: Procurement in Investment Project Financing—Goods, Non-Consulting and Consulting Services* (4th ed. 2020). While consulting services can be purchased using a number of different competitive methods, a *quality based selection* (QBS) method, which evaluates without using cost as an evaluation criterion, is to be used for "complex or highly specialized assignments" for which it is difficult to define a precise statement of work (terms of reference (TOR)), assignments for which innovative products will be expected for the consultant, assignments "that have a high downstream impact," and assignments "that can be carried out in substantially different ways," so that proposals will not be comparable. *Id.* § 7.9. For those types of consultancies, proposal quality "is evaluated without using cost as an evaluation criterion," unless the "request for proposals requests both technical and financial Proposals"; if so, the financial proposal "of only the highest technically qualified firm is opened and evaluated to determine the Most Advantageous Proposal." *Id.*

Rather than segregating consulting services by category (as the Brooks Act does for architectural and engineering services), the World Bank takes a broader approach which sweeps up all consulting services, and then isolates those which pose special risks—for example, services that, if inferior, could severely impact a project, or which demand innovation from the consultant—and reserves for those a special competitive method which works much like the Brooks Act. From this comparative perspective, limiting Brooks Act procedures to architectural and engineering services alone may be somewhat arbitrary, as other services could pose similar challenges and risks. In the same vein, the comparison suggests that "traditional" competitive methods (sealed bidding, for example) themselves may raise performance risks, which may in turn help explain why new procurement methods regularly emerge to allow buyers to bypass more traditional competitive methods.

[E] Other Agency Procedures—Benefits Of Uniformity

Chapter 10 closes by discussing disparate agency rules at those agencies which have legal authority to write their own procurement rules, such as the Federal Aviation Administration. As Professor Schooner pointed out in his *Desiderata* piece, *supra,* a core goal (a "desideratum") of many successful procurement systems is to have *uniformity* across a government. Indeed, the Federal Acquisition Regulation itself is built on a principle of government-wide uniformity in procurement rules—a uniformity which took roughly 200 years to achieve. The occasional "balkanization" of the U.S. government's procurement system into separate rules for different agencies stands in sharp contrast with that principle of uniformity, and runs contrary to global lessons learned about the benefits of uniformity. See, e.g., Attila Kovacs, *The Global Procurement Harmonisation Initiative*, 2005 Pub. Proc. L. Rev. 15.

Internationally, there have been various paths to uniformity, largely because the different systems can have radically different goals. The European Union's core goal in public procurement is to use government purchasing as a tool for integrating markets across Europe. The European Union's procurement directives are an extension of competition rules applied in private markets, and, as Albert Sanchez Graells has noted, under EU law "the traditional division between public and private aspects of internal market law and competition rules has become increasingly blurry." A. Sanchez Graells, *Public Procurement and the EU Competition Rules* 4 (Hart Publishing 2011). To encourage market integration, EU member states must shape their procurement laws to meet EU directives. See European Commission, *Public Procurement, https://ec.europa.eu/growth/single-market/public-procurement_en.*

Like the European Union, the UN Commission on International Trade Law (UNCITRAL) has a distinct goal: to encourage cross-border trade by "developing and maintaining a robust cross-border legal framework for the facilitation of international trade and investment" through the "progressive harmonization and modernization of the law of international trade" by "preparing and promoting the use and adoption of" model legal texts. UNCITRAL, *https://uncitral.un.org/*

en. UNCITRAL's model public procurement law, however, is focused less on trade than on building capacity, especially in developing nations, by offering model "procedures and principles aimed at achieving value for money and avoiding abuses in the procurement process." UNCITRAL, *UNCITRAL Model Law on Public Procurement* (2011), *https://uncitral.un.org/en/texts/procurement/modellaw/public_procurement*. Because the UNCITRAL model law is focused on procurement outcomes—on achieving "best value" in procurement—instead of imposing a uniform set of legal rules, the UNCITRAL model law offers a flexible "toolbox" which can be adapted to a government's special circumstances. E.g., Caroline Nicholas, *Recent Development in the Context of the UNCITRAL Model Law on Public Procurement* 5 (OECD Meeting of Leading Practitioners in Public Procurement, Feb. 2013).

International trade agreements offer a third model for uniformity among procurement systems. Trade agreements such as the World Trade Organization's Agreement on Government Procurement set minimum requirements for member states, requirements which are intended to eliminate non-tariff barriers to trade in procurement (such as non-transparent procurements, or procurements which impose technical requirements which only local vendors can meet). *E.g.*, Sue Arrowsmith, *Government Procurement in the WTO* (Kluwer Law Int'l 2003). While the trade agreements are nominally only about trade, by defining efficient practices, the trade agreements have helped foster an extraordinary convergence in public procurement laws around the world. The following chart illustrates some of the common elements of procurement regimes:

	U.S. Federal Acquisition Regulation (FAR)	European Union Procurement Directives	UNCITRAL Model Law
Acquisition Planning	Yes	Yes	Yes
Publication of Opportunities	Yes	Yes	Yes
Exclusion of Non-Qualified Vendors	Yes	Yes	Yes
Electronic Reverse Auctions	Yes	Yes	Yes
Open Tendering (Sealed Bidding)	Yes	Yes	Yes
Competitive Dialogue (Multilateral Negotiations)	Yes	Yes	Yes
Framework Agreements (Catalogue Contracts)	Yes	Yes	Yes
Publication of Awards	Yes	Yes	Yes
Bid Challenges	Yes	Yes	Yes
Contract Administration	Yes	No	No

As the table above reflects, this *convergence* between procurement regimes between procurement regimes has been most pronounced regarding issues of contract *formation*, and the most notable gap has been in rules regarding *contract administration*—a potential area of convergence in the coming years.

§ 16.12 INTERAGENCY ACQUISITIONS

Chapter 11 of the text reviews interagency acquisitions in the U.S. federal government, the process through which one agency acquires goods or services by placing an order against a contract awarded by another agency, or an agency asks another to award a contract or place an order on its behalf. As Chapter 11 notes, much of this type of interagency procurement in the U.S. government is done through indefinite-delivery/indefinite-quantity (IDIQ) contracts, which were discussed in detail above with regard to Chapter 7. Following the requirements of FAR Subpart 17.5, a federal agency may also purchase through another agency's contract under the Economy Act, as Chapter 11 describes. This section describes similar arrangements between public agencies outside the United States; in the European Union, for example, these arrangements are known as "joint procurement." See, e.g., *Joint Public Procurement and Innovation: Lessons Across Borders* (Gabriella Racca & Christopher Yukins, eds., Bruylant (Brussels) 2019), available at *www.publicprocurementinternational.com.*

As Chapter 11 notes, the Economy Act's requirements implemented under FAR Subpart 17.5 do not apply to interagency agreements for reimbursable work performed by federal employees. FAR 17.500(c). This is loosely analogous to the exception for "public/public co-operation" under Article 12 of the European Union's primary procurement directive, Directive 2014/24/EU. See SIGMA, *In-house Procurement and Public/Public Co-operation* 2-3 (OECD, Sept. 2016), *https://www.sigmaweb.org/publications/Public-Procurement-Policy-Brief-39-200117.pdf*; see also Rhodri Williams, *Public-Public Cooperation-Teckal in Practice*, 2012 Pub. Proc. L. Rev. NA1. Under Article 12, contracts between two public agencies fall outside the EU directive when the contracting agency exercises control over the combined initiative, and those providing private capital to support the initiative do not control it.

Chapter 11 describes the coordination required between federal agencies when undertaking interagency procurement. Among other things, the agencies must enter into a detailed agreement regarding the allocation of roles and responsibilities between the agencies. FAR 17.502-1. This is analogous to the European Union's Directive 2014/24/EU, which in Recital 73 called for rules to clarify agencies' respective obligations in order to facilitate joint procurement between EU member states' public agencies, as a means of advancing economic integration in the European Union:

> [N]ew rules on cross-border joint procurement should be established in order to facilitate cooperation between contracting authorities and enhancing

> the benefits of the internal market by creating cross-border business opportunities for suppliers and service providers. Those rules should determine the conditions for cross-border utilisation of central purchasing bodies and designate the applicable public procurement legislation, including the applicable legislation on remedies [bid protests], in cases of cross-border joint procedures. . . .

See also Dorthe Kristensen Balshøj, *Can Intermediary Central Purchasing Bodies Be Subject to Competition Law?*, 2019 Pub. Proc. L. Rev. 59 (arguing for the extension of normal EU competition rules to public central purchasing bodies); *Centralising Public Procurement* (Carina Risvig Hamer & Mario Comba, eds.) (Edward Elgar Publishing 2021).

In an echo from the U.S. experience (see Chapter 11), the Directive's recitals also warned that joint procurement (interagency procurement in the U.S. system) should not be used "for the purpose of circumventing mandatory public law rules, in conformity with Union law. . . . Such rules might include, for example, provisions on transparency and access to documents or specific requirements for the traceability of sensitive supplies." *Id.* Recital 73. Specific requirements for EU joint procurements between agencies from different member states are set forth in Article 39 of Directive 2014/24/EU. See, e.g., Ivo Locatelli, *Process Innovation Under the New Public Procurement Directives*, in *Joint Public Procurement and Innovation: Lessons Across Borders, supra;* Albert Sanchez-Graells, *The Emergence of Trans-EU Collaborative Procurement: A "Living Lab" for European Public Law*, 2020 Pub. Proc. L. Rev. 16, 21-24. Notably—and presumably because of the promise that joint procurement holds for European integration—under Article 39 an EU member state may "not prohibit its contracting authorities from using centralised purchasing activities offered by central purchasing bodies located in another Member State." Unlike some analogous joint procurements (known as "cooperative purchasing") among state and local governments in the United States, which can defer to the *buyer* agency's procurement rules, see, e.g., Justin Kaufman, *Cooperative Purchasing: A US Perspective*, in *Joint Public Procurement and Innovation: Lessons Across Borders, supra*, under Article 39 of the EU Directive the joint procurement is to be conducted "in accordance with the national provisions of the Member State where the central purchasing body is located."

As was described above with regard to Chapter 7, on IDIQ arrangements in the U.S. government, a key difference between the U.S. rules and others (including the EU requirements described here, and the UNCITRAL model procurement law at Article 62), is that the U.S. federal rules treat IDIQ agreements as *contracts*, and the follow-on awards as *orders* which are not entitled to the same procedural protections as *contracts*. See generally Carina Risvig Hamer, *Regular Purchases and Aggregated Procurement: The Changes in the Public Procurement Directives Regarding Framework Agreements, Dynamic Purchasing Systems and Central Purchasing Bodies*, 2014 Pub. Proc. L. Rev.

201. Note that while the regulations and practice distinguish between "orders" and their overarching "contracts," the United States Supreme Court has confirmed that orders are contracts. *Kingdomware Technologies, Inc. v. United States*, 579 U.S. 162 (2016); *Coast Professional Inc. v. United States*, 828 F.3d 1349 (Fed. Cir. 2016).

This helps explain why, while in the U.S. system orders under IDIQ contracts are generally subject to much lower competition, transparency and accountability requirements, in the EU and UNCITRAL rules the "framework contracts" which are awarded in a second competitive stage under master "framework agreements" are subject to much more stringent requirements. As the *Guide to Enactment* for the UNCITRAL model law explains, the "rules and procedures are designed to ensure effective competition at the second stage." *Id.* at 279.

This fundamental difference between the U.S. system and its international counterparts—the common U.S. assumption that orders under IDIQ and GSA Multiple Award Schedule contracts (potentially worth up to billions of dollars) are not true "contracts"—means, in practice, that interagency awards in the U.S. system may be far less transparent. Thus, for example, while interagency orders through the GSA eBuy system (discussed above with regard to Chapter 7) may be largely invisible to members of the general public, under the EU directives a second-stage competition in a joint procurement must follow normal transparency principles. See, e.g., *Autorità Garante della Concorrenza e del Mercato - Antitrust and Coopservice*, C-216/17 (Court of Justice for the European Union, Dec. 19, 2018) ("a contracting authority may act on its own behalf and on behalf of other contracting authorities that are specifically indicated but are not direct parties to a framework agreement, provided that the requirements as to advertising and legal certainty and, consequently, those relating to transparency are complied with"). Similarly, while U.S. interagency orders under IDIQ contracts may not be challengeable under the complex patchwork of U.S. rules governing bid protests (see Chapters 7 and 11), analogous framework contracts are subject to normal bid challenge requirements under the EU Remedies (bid protest) directive, see, e.g., *Centralising Public Procurement: The Approach of EU Member States* 94 (Carina Risvig Hamer & Mario Comba, eds.) (Edgar Elgar 2021), and under the UNCITRAL model law, see *Guide to Enactment of the UNCITRAL Model Law on Public Procurement*, *supra*, at 293.

§ 16.13 TYPES OF CONTRACTS: FIXED-PRICE AND COST-REIMBURSEMENT

As Chapter 12 explains, there are two basic forms of contract in the U.S. federal procurement system: *fixed-price* and *cost-reimbursement* contracts. In a firm-fixed-price contract, the contractor must complete the work to receive a pre-established price. In contrast, under a standard cost-reimbursement contract, the contractor will be reimbursed for the costs it incurs, and the government bears most of the risks of increased costs. Outside the United States, however, cost-reimbursable contracts (and rules governing such contracts) are relatively rare. *Cf.* Sam Jack & Jun Jin, *Harnessing Innovation in Procurement: Perspective from a Bilateral Development Agency,* 2020 Pub. Proc. L. Rev. 103, 112 (USAID almost never uses fixed-price contracts in its work abroad). While some public agencies outside the United States engage in cost-reimbursement contracting, see, e.g., *Advanced Technology Projects and International Procurement: The Case of the European Space Agency,* 1993 Pub. Proc. L. Rev. 13, 21; W.A. Peeters, *Incentives in Government Procurement Contracts,* 1993 Pub. Proc. L. Rev. 197 (reviewing different forms of incentive-based contracts), fixed-price contracting is much more common globally. Even in cases where a major rules regime, such as the European Union's, call for an assessment of contracting costs—such as EU Directive 2014/24/EU, which in Article 69 endorses life-cycle cost analysis as a means of calculating the full costs of an award—the rules regimes offer little guidance on how costs should be assessed. More by default than by design, therefore, procurement rules outside the United States focus on fixed-price contracting, and offer fewer comparative lessons for cost-reimbursement contracting.

The United Kingdom's Single Source Contract Regulations 2014 are among the most prominent examples of cost-reimbursement contracting outside the U.S. system. Regulation 10 defines six different means of calculating costs in covered Ministry of Defence contracts:

- Firm pricing method: Under the firm pricing method, the allowable costs are the allowable costs as estimated at the time of agreement.
- Fixed pricing method: Under the fixed pricing method, the allowable costs are the allowable costs as (a) estimated at the time of agreement; and (b) adjusted in accordance with changes in specified indices or rates between the time of agreement and a specified time (and different times, indices or rates may be specified in relation to different allowable costs).
- Cost-plus pricing method: Under the cost-plus pricing method, the allowable costs are the actual allowable costs determined during the contract or after the contract completion date.
- Estimate-based fee pricing method: Under the estimate-based fee pricing method, the allowable costs by which the CPR [contractor profit rate] is multiplied are the allowable costs as estimated at the time of agreement.
- Volume-driven pricing method: Under the volume-driven pricing method, the allowable costs are the allowable costs per unit of volume multiplied by the actual volume of output of the contract. The allowable costs (a) must be estimated at the time of agreement; and (b) may be

adjusted in accordance with changes in specified indices or rates between the time of agreement and a specified time.

- Target pricing method: Under the target pricing method, the allowable costs are the allowable costs as estimated at the time of agreement.

In accordance with the UK Defence Reform Act 2014, Regulation 20 calls for guidance from the UK Single Source Regulatory Office (SSRO) on allowable costs. That guidance, which is regularly updated, is available through the SSRO at *www.gov.uk/government/organisations/single-source-regulations-office*.

The World Bank, in contrast, offers relatively little guidance regarding "reimbursable-cost contracts" under its *Procurement Regulations* (4th ed. Nov. 2020). Section 3.12 states only that that under "reimbursable-cost contracts, payments cover all actual costs, plus an agreed fee to cover overhead and profit." Section 3.13 suggests that these "types of contracts may be appropriate for circumstances such as emergency repairs and maintenance work"—a notably narrow band of possible application. "To minimize risk to the Borrower," the contractor must make "all records and accounts available for inspection," either by the borrower government or an agreed neutral third party, and the contract must include "appropriate incentives to limit costs." *Id.*

§ 16.14 CONTRACT PRICING

Chapter 13 describes in detail the means the U.S. government uses to assess a vendor's proposed pricing and costs, and if necessary to renegotiate pricing. "Price analysis" in the U.S. system, as the chapter explains, assesses an offeror's proposed prices by using data external to the offeror's anticipated costs of performance to make a judgment as to the reasonableness of the proposed prices. In contrast, as the chapter notes, "cost analysis" reviews the offeror's proposed estimated costs to ascertain the reasonableness of each cost element.

The U.S. processes for price and cost analyses are sometimes more mature than those found in other nations. As noted above, few nations engage in cost-based contracting, and many nations simply rely on competitive forces to ensure that prices paid are reasonable. *Cf.* U.K. Government, Government Commercial Function, *Bid Evaluation: Guidance Note*, at 18-20 (May 2021) (describing price analysis techniques). Other governments, to avoid overpriced purchasing, may set "indicative" prices that will (if exceeded) trigger greater scrutiny of purchases, see, e.g., Alex Nelson Malanga, *PPRA to Set Indicative Prices in Public Procurement,* The Citizen, July 15, 2022 (Tanzanian Public Procurement Regulatory Authority to announce indicative prices of key supplies), including ceiling prices; *cf.* Geo Quinot, Sope Williams-Elegbe & Kingsley Tochi Udeh, *Emergency Procurement and Responses to COVID-19 in Africa: The Contrasting Cases of South Africa and Nigeria,* at 529-30 (South African authorities unsuccessfully attempted to cap prices paid by local authorities for critical supplies during the pandemic), *in Public Procurement Regulation in (a) Crisis?* (Sue Arrowsmith, Luke R.A. Butler, Annamaria La Chimia & Christopher Yukins, eds., Hart Publishing 2021).

One of the thornier issues in pricing analysis internationally is *abnormally low tenders*, which are known as "unrealistically" low pricing in the U.S. federal system. As Chapter 13 notes, while in the U.S. system the contracting officer must verify apparently unrealistically low pricing in a *sealed bid* (an "open tender," to use the international term), there is no such default legal requirement for verification of perceived mistakes in pricing in competitive negotiation under FAR Part 15 (which, as noted, make up the substantial majority of federal procurements). Unrealistically low pricing—pricing below cost—can create serious performance and cost risks for the government. While the FAR does not deal with these performance and cost risks in detail in procurements under negotiated procurements, other systems do call for procuring entities to make a close analysis of "abnormally low" tenders. See, e.g., World Bank, *Guide to the Identifications and Treatment of Abnormally Low Bids and Proposals* (July 2016); UNCITRAL *Model Law on Public Procurement* Art. 20; SIGMA/OECD, *Public Procurement Brief 35: Abnormally Low Tenders* (2016) (discussing treatment of abnormally low tenders under EU procurement directives); Sue Arrowsmith, *The Law of Public and Utilities Procurement* § 7.139 (Sweet & Maxwell-Thomson, 2005) (discussing EU directives and caselaw of the Court of Justice for the European Union regarding abnormally low tenders).

§ 16.15 COLLATERAL POLICIES

The tension in U.S. procurement described at the opening of Chapter 14—the debate between those who argue that the procurement system should focus only on best value, not "collateral" socioeconomic policies, and those who believe that socioeconomic goals are an integral part of the procurement process—is a conflict which splits the broader international procurement community, as well.

[A] The Debate Over Socioeconomic Policies

Professor Christopher McCrudden (now of Queen's University, Belfast) published a landmark study of socioeconomic initiatives in procurement, *Buying Social Justice* (Oxford Univ. Press 2006). McCrudden drew on many examples of socioeconomic policies in procurement from around the world—what he called "linkages" between procurement and social goals—and argued that although "whether one considers procurement linkages beneficial or not depends on how procurement linkages work out in practice," in fact "the potential for benefits to accrue from such linkages is worth experimentation and engagement." *Id.* at 115. He described the longstanding debate between two camps:

those who favor incorporating public (social and economic) goals into public procurement versus those who believe that procurement should be focused solely on achieving best value:

> The relationship between the movements for status equality and economically-driven public procurement regulation aiming at achieving greater economic efficiency is complex and multi-faceted. Almost inevitably, the relationship is often characterized as involving two "sides," antagonistic and suspicious of each other. Reconciliation has not been helped by the relative degree of ignorance of many on each side of the histories, concerns, and aspirations of the other. Often, debates between the two seem more like two cultures talking past each other rather than real engagement. This is as true of those coming from an economically-driven procurement perspective, who are often skeptical (at best) of social movements seeking to use public procurement to further their ends, as it is of those coming from an equality perspective, who frequently view public procurement professionals as barriers to the use of a legitimate public policy tool to help achieve important political (even moral) ends. Too often, one side characterizes the other in ways that bear little relationship to its own perception of itself. So, public procurement professionals are stereotyped as unreconstructed free-market liberals, whilst equality movements are seen either as closet protectionists, or their "useful fools."

Id. at 15.

Professor McCrudden chronicled the most common arguments against linking public procurement to "exogenous" social and political goals—arguments taken from experiences around the world but which, as Chapter 14 reflects, often echo equally well in the U.S. debate. Socioeconomic goals are said to be irrelevant to public procurement's core goal—to achieve best value. Opponents of "linkages" to social and economic goals also point to higher costs of procurement, reduced competition and economic atrophy in protected sectors. Socioeconomic requirements can also impose special burdens on those *not* favored—a form of unfairness and discrimination, they might argue. Opponents will also argue, McCrudden noted, that social problems are better dealt with directly, rather than through procurement, because "policy problems cannot be resolved through the medium of public procurement because . . . only some sectors of the economy, which happen to be particularly dependent on government contracts and can therefore be subjected to particular burdens, will be affected." Separately, and applying principles of public choice theory, McCrudden said, opponents may also argue that socioeconomic "linkages" in procurement "can be seen as creating rents for those groups that have persuaded politicians to favor them." Opponents also point out that socioeconomic requirements amplify the principal-agent problems that can clog procurement; the "more policies extraneous to the main purpose of the contract are taken into account, the more the process of awarding the public sector contract will have to become bureaucratized in order to deal with this problem," and the less likely the best-value outcome. Socioeconomic requirements can also, McCrudden noted, effect an abuse of power, because if "different levels of government adopt different values on particular issues, or significantly differ on the means of delivering these values," then procurement may be used "as a tool for the implementation of the contested value." *Id.* at 121-22.

McCrudden also noted, though, the arguments *for* socioeconomic preferences, arguments which also resonate with the U.S. experience. The first is that socioeconomic preferences in procurement can drive genuine change in society; their "power lies in the firm's economic interest in obtaining orders from public authorities and linkage seeks to use this economic interest for the promotion of social policy objectives, usually in addition to the use of other regulatory approaches." The second argument in favor of socioeconomic preferences, McCrudden noted, is that they help "mainstream" public goals, at a time when "government and public bodies are increasingly required to weave equality into the fabric of decision-making across all spheres of government." Third, the line between corporate and government spending has grown increasingly blurred, and (proponents of socioeconomic preferences claim) arguing that government should follow a purely "commercial" model seems futile. Many argue, McCrudden noted, that "award of public contracts is not simply an economic activity by the administration, in which the administration can consider itself simply as equivalent to a private sector organization," and this in turn "makes it difficult for a public purchaser to appear as an entirely neutral actor in the market place." Fourth, he said, preferences allow government to "internalize" externalities, such as the costs of pollution, as the "use of government contracting is more likely to produce reductions in status equality than other methods of delivering public services," and so "procurement linkage may operate as a method of government intervention to internalize unacceptable externalities." Next, McCrudden noted, proponents may argue that preferences allow government to increase competition, often by counteracting the social, political and economic impulses in procurement which favor market concentration. Finally, he said, socioeconomic goals in procurement allow governments to afford equality, arguably a necessary step insofar as "status equality [is] a public good that will not be adequately supplied in the absence of government intervention." *Id.* at 122-28.

While Professor McCrudden's taxonomy of arguments regarding socioeconomic policies in procurement, pro and con, is reflected in many ways in the U.S. procurement system, perhaps the debate echoes most simply in a rule that the U.S. system holds in common with others around the world: as Chapter 14 explains, in the U.S. system a procuring agency may not impose a socioeconomic preference unilaterally, but instead must have established authority (a statute, for example) for that preference. The UNCITRAL model law takes the same approach, and the model law's *Guide to Enactment* explains: "the policies concerned can be pursued through procurement only insofar as they are set out in other provisions of the law of the enacting State, or in the procurement regulations: they cannot be policies of the procuring entity alone." *Id.* at 7. In the U.S. system, this requirement for independent authority in law—a requirement that a socioeconomic preference be grounded in an open, democratic process—lends authority and consensus to socioeconomic policies that can otherwise be badly divisive in U.S. society.

The U.S. system's approach to socioeconomic policies differs from other nations' in *how* those policies are couched. Although Chapter 14 addresses the U.S. policies under one mantle, in practice the U.S. system tends to approach socioeconomic issues in a more fragmented, balkanized way—procurement policies meant to advance U.S. industry, for example, are viewed as radically different from preferences based on gender or ethnic identity. "Sustainability" in the U.S. procurement system typically means only *environmental* (or "green procurement") policies. In the European Union and elsewhere, in contrast, socioeconomic policies are treated generally as "sustainability" measures, which can be aimed at economic, social justice and environmental goals. See, e.g., World Bank, *Sustainable Procurement: An Introduction for Practitioners to Sustainable Procurement in World Bank IPF projects* 2 (Apr. 2019) ("The concept of sustainability is based on three pillars, namely: economic, environmental and social. Effective sustainable procurement supports sustainable development."). Though the difference may seem merely semantic, sharp contrast manifests in practice—the United States may narrowly address carbon gas emissions in procurement, for example, while a more comprehensive policy initiative abroad may simultaneously address issues of "green" procurement (as a matter of environmental sustainability), local production of environmentally sustainable technologies (economic sustainability), and the asymmetrical impacts of rising sea levels (social justice).

All that said, there are remarkably strong parallels between U.S. socioeconomic policies and those in foreign procurement systems. For reasons of space, the discussion below can address these similarities only briefly, with regard to small- and medium-sized businesses, domestic preferences in international trade, environmentally sound procurement, and employment practices.

[B] Small Business

While the United States, like many countries around the world, affords small businesses (typically called "small and medium-sized enterprises" or "SME's" in other nations) special treatment in procurement, the U.S. approach is often more complex and comprehensive. As Chapter 14 reflects, the U.S. generally covers a very broad range of small businesses, in a mature system with extensive preferences, with measures that have been conditioned by constitutional concerns (such as those involving race-based preferences) and administrative developments over more years. In contrast, SME preferences (long resisted in many systems) are just now coming of age in procurement systems around the world.

One of the most obvious differences between U.S. procurement system and others internationally is how the United States defines "small" business. Under the U.S. standards, while special measures are not extended to "medium" businesses (despite longstanding pressure from many in the business community), "small" businesses are defined to include firms which are far larger than their SME counterparts abroad. The U.S. standards define "small" businesses in the semiconductor manufacturing sector, for example, to include those with up to 1500 employees. 13 CFR § 121.201. Internationally, in contrast, as the Organization for Economic Cooperation and Development (OECD) notes, the "most frequent upper limit designating an SME is 250 employees, as in the European Union," while generally small firms are considered "those with fewer than 50 employees." OECD, Glossary of Statistical Terms, *Small and Medium-Sized Firms, https://stats.oecd.org/glossary/.*

Another important difference is in the U.S. approach, which both seeks to broaden small businesses' ability to compete in the procurement market and to extend procurement preferences to small businesses. Small business measures in procurement can be divided into two categories: "facilitative" measures intended to improve small businesses' access to public procurement markets, and preferences, typically intended to steer procurement contracts to preferred persons or firms. As author William Kirkwood noted, the U.S. system has evolved since the Small Business Act was originally passed a few years after World War II, in a steady march from "facilitation" to outright preferences, driven by new political, economic and social imperatives:

> The United States' active interest in supporting small businesses began in earnest in World War II, based on the need to shore up the industrial supply base through loan and other support to small business. This interest culminated in the passage of The Small Business Act in 1953 and the Small Business Investment Act of 1958. These acts were concerned with protecting small businesses and facilitating the creation and expansion of new businesses, with an overall intent of protecting the vibrancy of the defense industrial supply base.
>
> This may be seen in Section 202 of the original Small Business Act which established that among the purposes of the Small Business Act was the goal to aid, counsel, assist, and protect, insofar as is possible, the interests of small-business concerns in order to preserve free competitive enterprise. . . .
>
> Similarly, the Small Business Investment Act's original statement of policy was
>
> > [to] improve and stimulate the national economy in general and the small-business segment . . . by establishing a program to stimulate and supplement the flow of . . . funds which small-business concerns need for the sound financing of their business operations and for their growth, expansion, and modernization. . . .
>
> Sixty years later, the Small Business Act has evolved, and has expanded beyond its facilitative roots, and grown to include a wide array of targeted small business preference programs.

William Kirkwood, *The Evolution of Small Business Preferences in the United States and Selected Lessons Learned for the European Union*, 4 Eur. Proc. & Public-Priv. Part. L. Rev. 311, 311-12 (2016).

In the European Union, traditionally the focus was on facilitating SMEs' involvement in public procurement, rather than encouraging preferences that some feared could foster divisions in the European common market. See, e.g., Martin Burgi, *Small and Medium-Sized Enterprises and Procurement Law—European Legal Framework and German Experiences*, 2007 Pub. Proc. L. Rev. 284, 287 ("Some preferment measures of SME-promotion are, in fact, the instruments of local promotion."). Perhaps the best-known example of "facilitative" EU policy instruments was the European Commission's 2008 Small Business Act—apparently an *homage* to the U.S. legislation—which has evolved into a collection of best practices intended to make it easier for small businesses to compete. See European Commission, *Small Business Act: Database of Good Practices* (2015); see also Bernard Hoekman & Bedri Kamil Onur Tas, *Procurement Policy and SME Participation in Public Purchasing*, 58 Small Bus. Econ. 383 (2022) (finding, in European survey, that "governments seeking to enhance participation by SMEs in public procurement without explicitly favoring SMEs can do so by improving the overall quality of procurement processes"). In recent years, moreover, EU policymakers' opposition to preferences has eased. See, e.g., Max V. Kidalov, *Small Business Contracting in the United States and Europe: A Comparative Assessment*, 40 Pub. Cont. L.J. 443, 455-56 (2011).

A final difference between the U.S. procurement system and those abroad—the relatively strong enforcement mechanisms in the U.S. system, discussed in Chapter 14—stems, in part, from the comparative maturity of the U.S. system. Competitors and U.S. agencies closely monitor firms claiming to be "small" (or small businesses claiming to fall into a preferenced subcategory, such as women-owned small businesses). If it appears that an allegedly small business has grown beyond the applicable size standards, for example, or a large firm exercises control over a small firm (and thus is "affiliated" so the two firms' resources must be considered together), that question can be assessed against exacting standards in a well-developed adjudicative process coordinated through the U.S. Small Business Administration. Although other procurement systems internationally are embracing measures for SME's, often as a means of reducing income disparities in society, see, e.g., Asian Development Bank, *SME Development: Government Procurement and Inclusive Growth* (2012) (SME initiatives in southeast Asia); John Linarelli, *The Limited Case for Permitting SME Procurement Preferences in the WTO Agreement on Government Procurement* (discussing preferences in South Africa, Malaysia and Japan), *in The WTO Regime on Government Procurement: Challenge and Reform* (Sue Arrowsmith & Robert D. Anderson, eds., Cambridge U. Press 2011); European Bank for Reconstruction and Development, *Public Procurement: Is Open Competition Good for Small and Medium-Sized Enterprises?* (2017) (discussing SME initiatives in Italy, Cyprus and Ukraine); T. Mphela & J.P.W. Shunda,

Can Small, Medium and Micro Enterprises Survive in Public Procurement? Lessons from Botswana, 18 J. Pub. Proc. 90 (2018), new measures to facilitate or preference SME's are sometimes put into place with few, if any, corresponding enforcement systems to ensure that firms which call themselves "small" or "medium-sized" in fact qualify for SME protections. This may be due to the relative newness of the SME-related measures, or because of broader circumstances in a given country (the pressing need to entice the smallest enterprises into the "visible" economy, for example, or the large gulf between a nation's small businesses and its dominant large firms).

[C] Domestic Preferences

With regard to domestic preferences in procurement, the United States stands in an ambivalent position: while the United States has been a leader in instituting its own domestic preferences, since World War II the United States has also been a leading proponent of opening procurement markets internationally. See generally Christopher R. Yukins & Allen B. Green, International Trade Agreements and U.S. Procurement Law, *in The Contractor's Guide to International Procurement* (Marques Peterson & Erin Loraine Felix, eds., American Bar Assoc. 2018). That "push-and-pull" has created a Byzantine regulatory structure, outlined in Chapter 14, for extensive U.S. domestic preferences must accommodate a complex web of U.S. promises to open procurement markets under an expanding range of international trade agreements.

The Buy American Act of 1933 is perhaps the leading example of these conflicting currents in U.S. policy. Enacted in the midst of the Great Depression in a effort to preserve U.S. jobs (and in response to an earlier "Buy Britain" initiative there), see, e.g., William A. Reinsch, *A World in Crisis: Will Buying American Help or Hurt?* (Apr. 10, 2020), www.csis.org, the Buy American Act marked a watershed in domestic preferences internationally—it is repeatedly cited by those around the world who favor protecting domestic procurement markets. In fact, however, the Buy American Act's sweeping requirements to buy only domestic materials and manufactured goods, see 41 U.S.C. § 8303, were confined to a price preference by President Eisenhower in 1953, and then were effectively confined to only smaller procurements (generally capped at roughly $200,000 for supplies, depending on currency fluctuations) by the Trade Agreements Act and the many bilateral, regional and plurilateral trade agreements entered into by the United States. Although the Buy American Act price preferences were increased substantially by President Trump on his last full day in office in 2017, the *cap* on those preferences was not. As a result, the Buy American Act applies to only a relatively small portion of federal procurement (roughly $10 billion of annual procurement spending of approximately $600 billion). See, e.g., U.S. Government Accountability Office, *Buy American Act: Actions Needed to Improve Exception and Waiver Reporting and Selected Agency Guidance*, GAO-19-17, at 15 (Dec. 18, 2018).

Though the Buy American Act has been circumscribed *practically*, it continues to play an outsized role *politically* in helping to inspire "buy national" domestic preferences, both in the United States and abroad. See, e.g., E.O. 13881, 84 Fed. Reg. 34257 (July 15, 2019) (Trump administration policy to "enforce the Buy American Act to the greatest extent permitted by law"); E.O. 14005, *Ensuring the Future Is Made in All of America by All of America's Workers* (Jan. 25, 2021) (Biden administration policy "that the United States Government should, consistent with applicable law, use terms and conditions of Federal financial assistance awards and Federal procurements to maximize the use of goods, products, and materials produced in, and services offered in, the United States."); Build America, Buy America Act, Pub. L. 117–58, Div. G, Title IX, Subtitle A, 135 Stat. 1294 (2021) (extending domestic preferences to infrastructure funded with federal grants); Andrea Shalal, *China Quietly Sets New 'Buy Chinese' Targets for State Companies—U.S. Sources*, Reuters, Aug. 2, 2021; Andrea Novais, *Introduction to the Buy Brazilian Act*, The Brazil Business (Sept. 10, 2012) (drawing historical links from Buy American Act to Brazilian legislation).

The legal measure which circumscribed the Buy American Act was the Trade Agreements Act of 1979, which authorized the President (and through him, the U.S. Trade Representative), in implementing trade agreements, to waive the Buy American Act for purchases above the thresholds set by those agreements. See, e.g., Jean Heilman Grier, *Trade Agreements Act of 1979: Broad Authority, Narrow Application* (2014), *https://trade.djaghe.com/*. The Trade Agreements Act followed decades of efforts by the United States to open procurement markets after World War II, partly in response to the worldwide protectionism which had helped aggravate the global tensions which in turn led to the war—market-opening efforts which ultimately culminated in the WTO Government Procurement Agreement (GPA) and a wide range of similar agreements worldwide. See, e.g., Sue Arrowsmith, *Government Procurement in the WTO*, ch. 1 (Kluwers 2003); Bernard Hoekman & Petros C. Mavroidis, *The World Trade Organization's Agreement on Government Procurement: Expanding Disciplines, Declining Membership?*, World Bank Policy Research Working Group Paper No. WPS1429 (1995); Annet Blank & Gabrielle Marceau, *The History of the Government Procurement Negotiations Since 1945* (1996), *reprinted in* Simon J. Evenett & Bernard Hoekman, *The WTO and Government Procurement* (2006); Office of the U.S. Trade Representative, *Government Procurement* (list of U.S. trade agreements related to procurement), *https://ustr.gov/issue-areas/government-procurement*.

The Trade Agreements Act imposed a reciprocal *constraint* on trade as well, by requiring that the U.S. government procure only from those nations which have a free trade agreement with the United States, are Caribbean Basin nations, or are least-developed nations. See, e.g., FAR 25.502. This "walled garden" serves as an incentive for other nations to join free trade agreements with the United States, as only by doing so can other nations access the federal procurement market. See, e.g., Christopher R. Yukins & Steven L. Schooner, *Incrementalism: Eroding the Impediments to a Global Public Procurement Market*, 38 Geo. J. Int'l L. 529, 569 (2007) (citing statutory authorities).

This "walled garden" strategy—of blocking vendors from non-signatory nations—is not the norm internationally, as most nations entering into trade agreements regarding procurement agree not to discriminate against vendors from other signatory nations, but do not block third-country vendors. Nevertheless, some nations, such as Hungary, see Act CXLIII of 2015 on Public Procurement, Art. 74 ("The contracting authority may exclude from the procedure . . . the tenderers or candidates who are not eligible for national treatment [under international agreements, per Article 2(5)]"), *do* allow their contracting agencies to block goods or services from nations that have not entered into free-trade agreements involving procurement, and the European Commission has issued non-binding guidance allowing its member states to exclude vendors from nations without relevant free-trade arrangements with the European Union. See European Commission, *Guidance on the Participation of Third Country Bidders and Goods in the EU Procurement Market*, OJ C 271, pp. 43-66 (2019), *https://ec.europa.eu/docsroom/documents/36601*; Pascal Friton, *The EU's Drive for Market Disclosure—Protectionism or Just a Means to a (Justified) End?*, 2020 Gov't Contracts Year in Review Br. 6 (the "European Commission especially argues that non-EU companies do not have secured access to procurement procedures in the EU").

A vitally important element of the United States' international trade arrangements involving procurement are *reciprocal defense procurement agreements* which the United States has entered into with its allies. These agreements are entered into between the U.S. Department of Defense and the ministries of defense in allied nations ("qualifying countries" under the Defense Federal Acquisition Regulation Supplement), and these agreements generally ensure that trade in defense materiel, services and research and development will be done without barriers. See 19 U.S.C. § 2512(b)(3); FAR 25.403(c)(2); DFARS 225.003(1); DFARS 225.403; see also Luke Butler, *Transatlantic Defence Procurement: EU and US Defence Procurement Regulation in the Transatlantic Defence Market* (Cambridge U. Press 2017). While the primary purpose of a reciprocal defense procurement agreement is to encourage "rationalization, standardization, and interoperability of conventional defense equipment with allies and other friendly governments," 86 Fed. Reg. 62155 (2021), these agreements also play an important role in opening U.S. defense export markets.

The more protectionist elements of U.S. policy, outlined above, have paralleled more protectionist initiatives in other countries. The European Union, for example, has long debated the "International Procurement Instrument," which would impose price penalties on vendors from countries which refused to enter into free trade agreements with the EU. See, e.g., European Parliament, *International Procurement Instrument* (Mar. 2020). In a separate initiative, if adopted in final form, member states in the European Union could exclude vendors that received government subsidies from their home countries. See European Commission, *Commission proposes new Regulation to address distortions caused by foreign subsidies in the Single Market* (May 5, 2021). These types of initiatives reflect a growing EU willingness to engage in protectionist measures, and an echo of the shift towards protectionism in the U.S. system.

[D] Environmental Measures

As Chapter 14 reflects, the U.S. government's procurement system uses a broad variety of measures to address environmental concerns, from debarring contractors that violate the Clean Air Act or the Clean Water Act, see 2 C.F.R. Part 1532; Environmental Protection Agency, *Information Regarding the Suspension and Debarment Process, Clean Water Act and Clean Air Act Ineligibilities, How to Contest a Notice, and How to Seek Reinstatement, https://www.epa.gov/grants/information-regarding-suspension-and-debarment-process-clean-water-act-and-clean-air-act*, to environmental requirements embedded in the procurement planning process, see FAR 7.105(b)(17). See generally Michael Bowsher, Pascal Friton, Paul Lalonde, Andrea Sundstrand & Christopher Yukins, *International Procurement Developments in 2022: New Perspectives in Global Procurement*, part V, 2022 Gov. Contr. Year in Rev. 59 (Thomson Reuters 2023) (building upon the discussion in this section); Christopher Yukins & Nathaniel Green, Feature Comment: *The Inflation Reduction Act: A New Role For Green Procurement?*, 64 Gov. Contractor ¶ 260 (2022). Perhaps the most pressing environmental measures in U.S. public procurement, though, are those that would address global warming, by reducing carbon gas emissions in the goods and services purchased by the federal government. Because of the uniquely global nature of this problem, there is a unique urgency to understanding how the emerging U.S. measures compare to similar efforts abroad. See, e.g., UN Environmental Program, *Sustainable Public Procurement, https://www.unep.org/explore-topics/resource-efficiency/what-we-do/sustainable-public-procurement* (gathering reports and data on efforts around the world to improve sustainability in procurement).

The U.S. government's efforts to improve environmental sustainability in procurement stretch back many years. In January 2007, President George W. Bush signed Executive Order (EO) 13423, "Strengthening Federal Environmental, Energy, and Transportation Management," 72 Fed. Reg. 3919 (2007). President Bush's executive order instructed federal agencies to conduct activities in an "environmentally, economically and fiscally sound, integrated, continuously improving, efficient, and sustainable manner."

President Barack Obama issued a much more ambitious executive order in 2009, EO 13514, Federal Leadership in Environmental, Energy, and Economic Performance, 74 Fed. Reg. 52117 (Oct. 5, 2009). The 2009 executive order helped chart a future path for environmental sustainability in federal procurement because it called for the General Services Administration, in coordination with the other agencies, to provide recommendations "regarding the feasibility of working with the Federal vendor and contractor community to provide information that will assist Federal agencies in tracking and reducing . . . greenhouse gas emissions related to the supply of products and services to the Government." These recommendations were to "consider the potential impacts on the procurement process, and the Federal vendor and contractor community including small businesses and other socioeconomic procurement programs," and to explore the feasibility of: (a) requiring contractors to register in a database tracking greenhouse gas emissions; (b) requiring contractors to make information available on their greenhouse gas emissions, and on their efforts to mitigate greenhouse gas emissions; (c) using federal purchasing preferences for products manufactured using processes that minimized greenhouse gas emissions. The resulting report, U.S. General Services Administration, *Executive Order 13514 Section 13: Recommendations for Vendor and Contractor Emissions* (Apr. 2010), in many ways foresaw the environmental sustainability measures that would unfold over the subsequent years, both in the United States and abroad.

The 2010 report from the General Services Administration stressed that reporting and curbing greenhouse gas emissions in the federal supply chain "should be done with the recognition that it is an emerging management concept, and any initiative should be flexible enough to work with changing practices." The report urged measures that would be easy to implement, transparent, would apply with parity across industry sectors and regions, and would leverage existing systems for tracking and reducing greenhouse gas emissions, including those being built in the private sector. The report ultimately recommended using greenhouse gas emissions as a favorable *evaluation factor* in federal contract awards, rather than simply preferring those contractors that track greenhouse gas emissions (as a matter of qualification) or making sustainability a rigid mandatory requirement. "The reasoning behind recommending an evaluation factor instead of a purchasing preference or mandatory contracting goal," the report concluded, "is an evaluation factor allows agencies the discretion to trade the price of a given procurement against the [greenhouse gas] emissions associated with that procurement and thereby enable reductions in . . . [greenhouse gas] GHG emissions through the acquisition system."

President Obama's 2009 executive order and the 2010 GSA report marked, for many years, high points in federal efforts to reduce greenhouse gas emissions in federal procurement. President Obama issued a superseding executive order in 2015, EO 13693, Planning for Federal Sustainability in the Next Decade, 80 Fed. Reg. 15869 (2015), which called for more modest pilot programs to reduce greenhouse gas emissions in federal procurement. After President Donald Trump took office in 2017, his administration took a much less ambitious approach to environmental sustainability in procurement. President Trump issued an executive order, EO 13834, Efficient Federal Operations, 83 Fed. Reg. 23771 (2018), which superseded the Obama order, and which shifted the focus to energy and water sustainability—not a reduction in greenhouse gas emissions. It was not until the Biden administration took office in early 2021 that the focus returned to reducing greenhouse gas emissions, see, e.g., EO 14008, Tackling the Climate Crisis at Home and Abroad, 86 Fed. Reg. 7619 (January 27, 2021), in line with parallel efforts around the world to address the crisis of global warming, see, e.g., Denise Lu & Christopher Flavelle, *Rising Seas Will Erase More Cities by 2050, New Research Shows*, N.Y. Times, Oct. 29, 2019; see also EO 14057, Catalyzing Clean Energy Industries and Jobs Through Federal Sustainability, 86 FR 70935 (2021) (President Biden's order called for federal agencies to reorient procurement to achieve "climate-resilient" infrastructure, train federal workers in climate issues and sustainability, prioritize the purchase of sustainable products, and advance partnerships (domestically and internationally) to improve environmental sustainability).

In a December 2021 article, *No Time to Waste: Embracing Sustainable Procurement to Mitigate the Accelerating Climate Crisis*, 61 Contract Management, Issue 12, page 24 (Dec. 2021), available at *https://ssrn.com/abstract=3980915*, Professor Steven Schooner described some of the options policymakers in public procurement might use to reduce greenhouse gas emissions in the supply chain. Policymakers' options in addressing global warming broadened with the 2012 revision of the WTO Government Procurement Agreement, which in now Article X(7) now specifically reserves the right of parties to shape specifications in order "to promote the conservation of natural resources or protect the environment." Some of the leading measures being used in the United States and around the world:

- *Strengthen Planning*: Professor Schooner argued that environmental sustainability should be made a more central part of the procurement planning process. Brazil, for example, revised its procurement laws to require that environmental considerations play a much more prominent role in the procurement planning process. See, e.g., Gabriel Cozendey & Joana Chiavari, *The New Bidding Law Offers Opportunities to Improve Infrastructure Projects and Prevent Socio-Environmental Impacts* (Rio de Janeiro, Climate Policy Initiative, 2021), *https://www.climatepolicyinitiative.org/wp-content/uploads/2021/05/NT-The-New-Bidding-Law.pdf*.
- *Eco-Labels*: In an interesting example of parallel regulation, both the European Union and the United States have endorsed the use of "eco-labels" in procurement. "Eco-labels" are certificates which confirm that a given good or service meets a certain environmental standard; they are often affixed to a product as a label, for consumer recognition. See, e.g., European Commission, *Environment: Eco-Labels*, *https://ec.europa.eu/environment/gpp/eco_labels.htm*. As a common first step in environmental sustainability, eco-labels have gained broader use in countries across the world, according to a 2017 survey by the United Nations. See

UN Environment, *Factsheets on Sustainable Public Procurement in National Governments—Supplement to the Global Review of Sustainable Public Procurement*, at IX (2017); see also UN Environment Programme, *Comparative Analysis of Green Public Procurement and Ecolabelling Programmes in China, Japan, Thailand and the Republic of Korea: Lessons Learned and Common Success Factors* (2017), *https://www.oneplanetnetwork.org/sites/default/files/from-crm/comparative_analysis_gpp_180917_web.pdf*. In the U.S. procurement system, FAR 23.103 calls for agencies to "advance sustainable acquisition by ensuring that 95 percent of new contract actions for the supply of products and for the acquisition of services (including construction)" must require that the products provided meet certain "eco-label" standards, such as those that are energy-efficient, i.e., ENERGY STAR® or Federal Energy Management Program (FEMP)-designated. Although environmental preferences can in practice raise trade barriers, in the European Union extensive caselaw in the Court of Justice for the European Union and provisions in the European procurement directives allow for the use of eco-labels. See, e.g., Vilhelmiina Ihamäki, Eva van Ooij & Stefan van der Panne, *Green Public Procurement in the European Union and the Use of Eco-Labels, https://www.maastrichtuniversity.nl/sites/default/files/2014/Green_Public_Procurement_in_the_European_Union_and_the_Use_of_Eco-Labels.pdf.;* Bogdana Neamtu & Dacian C. Dragos, *Sustainable Public Procurement: The Use of Eco-Labels*, 2015 EPPPL 92.

- *Favoring Suppliers That Assess Their Products and Services:* Another strategy is to create a preference for those suppliers that assess, for example, the greenhouse gas emissions attributable to their own goods and services. Because of the costs and burdens of assessing greenhouse gas emissions, at least initially, this strategy risks creating a procurement bias against small and medium-sized enterprises. See, e.g., Working Group 3C of the 10YFP Sustainable Public Procurement Programme, *Promoting the Participation of Small and Medium Size Enterprises (SMEs) in Green Public Procurement*, at 27 (Sylvia Aguilar, coordinator, Dec. 2016). Nevertheless, President Biden's May 2021 executive order called for amendments to the FAR that would require major Federal suppliers to publicly disclose greenhouse gas emissions and climate-related financial risks, and to set science-based greenhouse gas reduction targets. See 87 Fed. Reg. 68312 (2022) (proposed rule).
- *Favoring Products and Services That Carry Fewer Greenhouse Gas Emissions:* Perhaps the most powerful strategy is to make greenhouse gases an evaluation factor in award; as Professor Schooner suggested, to call for solicitations to "require at least some consideration of the

social cost of greenhouse gas emissions and, where appropriate and feasible, give preference to offeror projecting a lower social cost" greenhouse gas emissions. Steven L. Schooner, No Time to Waste, *supra*, at 27. President Biden's May 2021 executive order said that federal agency procurements should, "where appropriate and feasible, give preference to bids and proposals from suppliers with a lower social cost of greenhouse gas emissions." For a case study of Japan's successful efforts to build environmental evaluation factors into the purchase of fire extinguishers, within the framework of national laws and policies calling for "green" procurement, see Green Purchasing Center Malaysia, *A Sampling of Successes in Green Public Procurement—Case Studies of Green Public Procurement Implementation in Asia-Pacific Countries*, at 20-26 (2017), *https://www.oneplanetnetwork.org/sites/default/files/from-crm/case_studies_140317_web.pdf*; see also Organization for Economic Cooperation & Development, *Smart Procurement: Going Green—Best Practice for Green Procurement*, at 24-34 (2015) (lessons learned from Estonia, Netherlands, Austria and Denmark in using environmental sustainability as a evaluation factor for award).

As the discussion above reflects, environmentally sustainable ("green") public procurement is advancing around the world, under a common imperative to address global warming. Environmentally sustainable procurement provides an interesting comparative example, because the lessons and strategies are being rapidly shared, so the law—in principle at least—should be advancing in parallel in nations around the world. The fact that progress is *not* uniform, but instead at different stages in different nations, depending on resources, capacity, and popular and political will, makes "green procurement" a compelling example of "contextual" comparative law—an example of an area of law that is shaped in large part by its political, social and economic contexts.

§ 16.16 CONTRACT AWARD CONTROVERSIES

As Chapter 15 reflects, the U.S. government has a highly evolved bid challenge system, which has developed for over a century. As in many other nations, bid challenges (called "bid protests") can be brought before the procuring agency itself, an independent administrative body (the Government Accountability Office), or a court (the U.S. Court of Federal Claims). See, e.g., Andrew E Shipley and Daniel Chudd, *Bid Protests: A Guide to Challenging Federal Procurements* (American Bar Association 2021); Christopher R. Yukins, *Stepping Stones to Reform: Making Agency-Level Bid Protests Effective for Agencies and Bidders by Building on Best Practices from Across the Federal Government*, 50 Pub. Cont. L.J. 197, 203-206 (2021).

The basic structure of the U.S. system—the alternative channels for review, the likely parties, and the available relief—corresponds to bid challenge systems around the world. See, e.g., United Nations Commission on International Trade Law (UNCITRAL), *Model Law on Public Procurement* Ch. VIII (2011) (allowing for challenges before court, independent administrative or procuring agency). These parallels are not surprising, because international instruments that the United States has joined, such as the United Nations Convention Against Corruption (which includes almost all nations), and the WTO's Government Procurement Agreement (which includes many industrialized nations), also call for parties to have effective bid challenge processes in place. See WTO, *Overview of the Agreement on Government Procurement, https://www.wto.org/english/tratop_e/gproc_e/gpa_overview_e.htm* (discussing Article XX's requirements for an effective bid challenge system). Based in part on the experience in the U.S. government, bid challenges are now commonly available in public procurement systems around the world. See, e.g., International Bank for Reconstruction & Development, World Bank Group, *Benchmarking Public Procurement 2017: Assessing Public Procurement Regulatory Systems in 180 Economies,* at 38-43 (2016), *http://documents.worldbank.org/curated/en/121001523554026106/Benchmarking-Public-Procurement-2017-Assessing-Public-Procurement-Regulatory-Systems-in-180-Economies.pdf.*

That is not to say, however, that bid challenge systems are the same the world over. Some nations (and some states in the United States) have no bid challenge system at all; in others, the bid challenge systems have developed in highly distinct ways. To make sense of these differences from a comparative perspective, in this part we will review common elements of bid challenge system, using the conceptual model developed by Daniel Gordon, a former associate dean and professor at GW Law School, who headed the bid protest unit at the Government Accountability Office and also served as the Administrator of the Office of Federal Procurement Policy in the Obama White House. See Daniel I. Gordon, *Constructing a Bid Protest Process: Choices Every Procurement Challenge System Must Make*, 35 Pub. Cont. L.J. 427 (2006), available at *https://www.jstor.org/stable/25755368.* The core elements of any bid challenge system, wrote Gordon, must resolve a number of key questions, including the following.

- *Where in the Government Is the Protest Forum Located?* As noted, the United States government, as in many nations around the world, bid challenges can be brought in one of three different forums: the procuring agency, an independent administrative agency, or the courts. As with, for example, the UNCITRAL model law, if a challenge in the U.S. federal system fails at the agency level, a protest can then be brought successively at GAO and the Court of Federal Claims (what some have described as a "climbing a ladder"). But while there are *functional* parallels between systems, there are sharp *institutional* differences which confirm the importance of context in any comparative assessment. In the U.S. system, for example, the independent agency which hears the largest number of bid protests is the Government Accountability Office, an arm of Congress, the U.S. government's supreme audit authority. GAO's institutional posture is markedly different, for example, from that of the Canadian government's bid challenge forum, the Canadian International Trade Tribunal (CITT). The jurisdiction of the CITT is grounded in trade agreements, both with other nations and among the Canadian provinces. See Government Of Canada, *Canadian International Trade Tribunal, https://www.citt-tcce.gc.ca/en/collections/procurement-inquiries/procurement-inquiries.html* (with links to trade agreements, including Canada's agreement on internal trade); see also European Commission, *Practical Guide on Remedies* 5-7 (2007) (explaining how remedies (bid challenges) are an integral part of the EU's efforts to ensure open competition between member states in procurement). This commitment to open competition across borders is a useful rubric for bid challenges, for ultimately it means that the decisions of the CITT, like those of the GAO in the U.S. system, help promote healthy competition in the procurement system. The differences in institutional posture also mean, however, that other goals that fall neatly into the GAO's purview, such as highlighting institutional failures as a "watchdog" for the legislature, may not be as readily achieved in other bid challenge forums in other countries.

- *What Is the Jurisdiction of the Bid Challenge Forum?* In assessing the importance of subject matter jurisdiction in bid challenge forums, a useful example is to compare the 1994 and 2011 versions of the UNCITRAL model procurement law. The 1994 version exempted many categories of procurement decisions from review; the 2011 version, in contrast, made most procurement decisions under the model law presumptively subject to challenge. The shift reflected a view held by many: unless officials who violate the law are subject to potential challenge, a law on public procurement ultimately may prove just hortatory—a collection of quaint admonitions which can be ignored to further selfish interests. See UNCITRAL *Model Law on Public Procurement - Guide to Enactment*, Part 3, para. 159 (many of the "exceptions from review found in . . . the . . . 1994 Model Law were deleted. . . . This list of exceptions had raised criticism from practitioners and the donor community alike, in that it invited abusive practices and did not promote accountability in the procurement process. . . . The deletion of the exceptions was also considered necessary in order to align the Model Law with the United Nations Convention against Corruption . . . and other international and regional instruments regulating public procurement.")

- *Who Has Standing to Protest*? In a comprehensive article (which drew in part on the World Bank's "Global Public Procurement" database, *https://www.worldbank.org/en/topic/governance/brief/global-public-procurement-database*), Ian Hargreaves surveyed the bid challenge standing requirements in nearly a hundred jurisdictions around the world. See Ian Hargreaves, *Understanding the Standards of Bid Protest Standing: A Comparative Analysis of Bid Protest Standing Rights and Requirements Across Ninety-Eight Countries and the European Union*, 51 Pub. Cont. L.J. 227 (2022). This question of standing—i.e., which persons or entities have the legal authority to bring a bid challenge—plays a critical role, because to the extent a bid challenge system is a whistleblower system, expanding the field of potential whistleblowers can enhance accountability in the procurement system. In his article, Hargreaves pointed out that some nations allow a broader range of interested persons—beyond actual bidders—to bring bid challenges. "[M]ore developed countries," he observed, "generally confer standing to a broader range of parties, while developing countries generally confer standing to a narrower range of parties." *Id.* at 238. Broadening the range of potential challengers thus would (as Hargreaves noted) align the U.S. federal system "more closely with the European Union (EU) and United Kingdom (U.K.) standards" for standing. That expansion also would more closely align the federal system with those U.S. states which allow citizens (often under principles of "taxpayer" standing) to bring suit to challenge state governments' procurement decisions. See Zachary Jacobson, *The Features of Bid Protest Systems and Their Adoption Across the United States* (surveying 50 states' bid protest requirements), *https://publicprocurementinternational.com/wp-content/uploads/2022/07/Zach-Jacobson-Research-Paper-Survey-State-Bid-Protests-Final.pdf.*
- *What Evidence Does the Forum Have Before It in Reaching Its Decision?* This question goes to the administrative record made available to the protester, because that is typically the only evidence the protester can bring before the forum in presenting its challenge. In the U.S. system, FAR 33.103 does not require that the protester be afforded access to the agency record in an agency level protest, but says only that, to "the extent permitted by law and regulation, the parties may exchange relevant information." At GAO (the independent administrative forum), agencies responding to a bid challenge need only produce "relevant" materials—a standard which agencies can abuse, to produce very limited records in an effort to prevail in the challenge. At the Court of Federal Claims, under Appendix C to the Court's rules, in contrast the government must produce a much broader administrative record.

- *What Are the Time Limits at the Forum*? As Daniel Gordon stressed, there are two key questions about timeliness in a bid protest process: (1) how soon the protest must be filed and (2) how soon the protest must be resolved. The time limits for filing a protest vary from country to country, and are often strictly drawn. See, e.g., SIGMA/OECD, *Public Procurement Review and Remedies Systems in the European Union* (Report No. GOV/SIGMA(2007)5, at 27 (Apr. 6, 2007) (surveying timeliness requirements in EU member states). Bid challenges are part of a broader procurement system, and challenges must be not only promptly brought but also quickly resolved to minimize any disruptive effect on the procurement. *Id.* at 27-28 ("A related issue are the time limits within which the courts of law and review bodies have to render a judgement or decision. In many [EU] Member States the time limits for contracting authorities and entities to deal with a complaint against one of their procurement decisions are very tight."); see, e.g., SIGMA/OECD, *Public Procurement - Brief 12: Remedies,* at 6 (2016) (for a bid challenge system to meet minimum standards for "effectiveness," the "review must be as rapid as possible. . . . [and] . . . legal . . . procedures and the conduct of review bodies must ensure rapid consideration and resolution"), *https://www.sigmaweb.org/publications/Public-Procurement-Policy-Brief-12-200117.pdf.*

- *Is the Procurement "Put on Hold" During the Protest?* The next element in Gordon's analysis looks to whether a procurement under protest will be stayed during the protest proceedings. As Chapter 15 explains, in the U.S. system, a timely agency-level protest should stay the procurement, a timely challenge at the GAO should trigger a statutory stay of the procurement during the protest, and at the Court of Federal Claims the government may accede to a voluntary stay during a bid challenge. Holding the contract in abeyance is essential in the U.S. system because damages are generally not available and, as Gordon confirmed through empirical research, a vendor that brings a challenge often does not want to "win" the protest so much as the vendor wants a chance to compete fairly for the contract. These same practical considerations may apply with special force in the other nations, where due to principles of *pacta sunt servanda* a contract cannot be undone once it has been signed. See, e.g., Richard Hyland, *Pacta Sunt Servanda: A Meditation*, 34 Va. J. Int'l L. 405 (1994). While in the U.S. federal system a contract that has been wrongfully awarded can simply be terminated for the government's convenience, the European Union takes a different approach. The European Union's Remedies Directive, EU Directive 2007/66/EC, which governs bid challenges in the EU member states, provides in Article 2a that presumptively a "contract may not be concluded following the decision to award a contract . . . before the expiry of a period of at least 10 calendar days . . . following the date on which the contract award decision is sent to the tenderers and candidates concerned." This "standstill" period means, in effect, that every contract covered by the directive must be held in abeyance for 10 days to allow time for a bid challenge—while in the U.S. system, only those contracts that are actually challenged (a very small percentage of the total) must be "held up."

- *How Difficult Is It for the Protester to Win?* Daniel Gordon's groundbreaking 2006 article was written in part for an international readership, and so he duly noted that the standard of review is an important element of any challenge system and may well vary between systems. Even in the U.S. system, the standard of review can, in practice, vary by case and issue, and the related statistic—how likely a bid challenge is to succeed—can be very difficult to calculate, because of (sometimes controversial) uncertainties in the data. See, e.g., Will Dawson, Note, *Data Scarcity in Bid Protests: Problems and Proposed Solution*, 51 Pub. Cont. L. Rev. 131 (2022).

Probably more than any other area of public contract formations, bid challenges show strong areas of overlap—and comparative lessons—between U.S. procurement and parallel systems abroad.